AN ENGLISH DICTIONARY

ETYMOLOGICAL, PRONOUNCING
AND EXPLANATORY

WITH LISTS OF AFFIXES AND PREFIXES
ABBREVIATIONS, LATIN, FRENCH, AND
ITALIAN PHRASES, AND A SUPPLEMENT
OF WORDS OF RECENT INTRODUCTION

BY

JOHN OGILVIE, LL.D.

EDITOR OF THE "IMPERIAL" "COMPREHENSIVE"
AND "STUDENT'S" DICTIONARIES

LONDON
BLACKIE & SON, Limited, 50 OLD BAILEY, E.C.
GLASGOW DUBLIN BOMBAY
1908

KEY TO THE PRONUNCIATION

In showing the pronunciation the simplest and most easily understood method has been adopted, that of *re-writing* the word in a different form. In doing so, the same letter is made use of for the same *sound*, no matter by what letter the sound may be expressed in the principal word. The *key* by this means is greatly simplified, the reader having only to bear in mind one mark for each sound, or refer to the foot of the page, where the key is printed in full.

The pronunciation of foreign words, as French, German, and Italian, can be only approximately represented by this system. The key, however, is applicable to the Latin, Greek, and Hebrew words, as those languages are pronounced in England.

Accent.—The accented syllable is denoted in this Dictionary by the mark ′. This mark, called an accent, is placed above and beyond the syllable which receives the accent, as in the words *la′bour, delay′,* and *comprehen′sion.* Monosyllabic words are not marked with an accent.

Many polysyllabic words are pronounced with two accents, the true or primary and the secondary or euphonic accent. Where both accents are marked in a word, the true accent is thus marked ″, and the secondary, or inferior one, by this mark ′, as in the word *excommu′-nica″tion.*

ABBREVIATIONS AND SIGNS EMPLOYED IN THIS DICTIONARY

a.	adjective.		Ch.	Chaldee.
adv.	adverb.		Sans.	Sanscrit.
conj.	conjunction.		Hind.	Hindoostanee.
interj.	interjection.		Pers.	Persian.
n.	noun.		W.	Welsh.
p.a.	participial adjective.		Armor.	Armoric.
p.n.	participial noun.		Gael.	Gaelic.
pp.	participle passive, and perfect.		Ir.	Irish.
ppr.	participle of the present tense.		Sp.	Spanish.
prep.	preposition.		Fr.	French.
pret.	preterite.		It.	Italian.
pron.	pronoun.		Gr.	Greek.
sing.	singular.		L.	Latin.
pl.	plural.		G.	German.
vi.	verb intransitive.		Old G.	Old German.
vt.	verb transitive.		Goth.	Gothic.
†	obsolete or not used.		Sax.	Saxon.
=	the sign of equality.		D.	Dutch.
			Dan.	Danish.
Ar.	Arabic.		Sw.	Swedish.
Heb.	Hebrew.		Icel.	Icelandic.

Preterites and Participles.—The preterites and participles of verbs are given at full length, unless where the preterites and past participles are formed by the addition of *ed*, and the present participles by the addition of *ing* to the verb.

PREFACE.

THIS DICTIONARY has been prepared with great care, both with a view to general utility and suitableness, and for the purpose of satisfying a demand for a Dictionary of handy size and moderate price. Its contents, as well as the plan of its compilation, besides fitting it for most purposes for which a dictionary is required, make it specially adapted to meet the requirements of Junior Pupils; and although brevity had necessarily to be studied, yet clearness and simplicity of language in regard to the significations have been aimed at throughout. But its distinctive features will be best understood by pointing them out in detail.

Pronunciation.—The pronunciation given represents the usage of cultivated society, and the method of showing the different sounds is very simple and clear to the eye.

Etymology.—The etymologies, though necessarily brief, are intended to give a distinct idea of the radical or primary significations of the words. The proximate root of each word is first given, then the word from which this is derived, with its meaning. If the ultimate root is doubtful a word etymologically akin can often be given. For example: Legible, *a.* [L. *legibilis—lego*, to read]. Heaven, *n.* [Sax. *heofen—hebban*, to raise]. Right, *a.* [Sax. *riht*—Goth. *raihts*, straight]. When the proximate root has a prefix, the prefix is not usually given separately, but the proximate root is immediately followed by the simple word from which it is derived. Thus, **Aggregate**, *a.* [L. *aggrego, aggregatus—grex, gregis*, a flock or herd]. In such cases it is presumed that the person using the book is sufficiently acquainted with the prefixes, their forms, and meanings, to enable him to supply at once the prefix in each particular instance (in this case *ag*, for *ad*), and to understand its import, especially when aided by the primary signification. When, however, a word occurs having a prefix differing in origin from that of the words preceding or following after, such prefix is given separately and explained. For example, the prefix in *Above* must not be confounded with that in *Abound, Abuse*, and therefore it is put thus: **Above**, *prep.* [Sax. *abufan—a* for *on, be*, by, and *ufan*, high, upwards].

Primary Significations.—The primary signification of each word precedes the other significations, and is printed in italics in order to distinguish it. The primary significations of words should be strongly impressed on the mind, as they form the basis of the other significations, or the source from which they spring, with less or greater degrees of divergence.

Fulness of Words.—All English words in general use are given; at least, none are omitted which are likely to occur in the common run of literature, or in ordinary school-books,

Fulness of Significations.—The different significations of words are explained with sufficient fulness to meet all the requirements of a general school and family dictionary, and care has been taken to render their number proportionate to the importance of the word.

Preterites and Participles.—The preterites and participles of verbs are given at full length when the conjugation is irregular, or when there is any peculiarity in the spelling (as doubled letters or the omission of *e*); but they are not given where the preterites and past participles are formed merely by the addition of *ed*, and the present participles by the addition of *ing* to the verb.

Participial Adjectives and Nouns.—In all cases where participial adjectives and nouns are in general use, or are of importance, they are given and explained in their alphabetical places.

Arrangement.—In order that the significations of words may be readily got at—as it is for this that the Dictionary is most frequently consulted—the preterites and participles of verbs are placed after the significations, and are followed by the etymologies.

Shakespearian Words.—As the plays of Shakespeare are so generally read, and are frequently used as school-books, the principal words and significations occurring in that author, but which are not in modern use, have been introduced. Such words and significations are distinguished by daggers.

Prefixes and Affixes, &c.—A list of prefixes and affixes, with their meanings and their derivations, so far as the latter can be ascertained, is added to the work. Also a list of such Latin, French, and Italian words and phrases as occur most frequently in English books.

ENGLISH DICTIONARY.

A.

A, the indefinite article, is a contraction of Sax. *an, ane*, one. It is used before nouns singular, beginning with a consonant. [See AN.]

Aaronic, Aaronical, ā-ron'ik, ā-ron'ik-al, *a.* Pertaining to Aaron, or to his priesthood.

Aback, a-bak', *adv.* On back, toward the back; backwards; by surprise; unexpectedly. [Sax. *on-bæc.*]

Abacus, ab'a-kus, *n.* A board for reckoning on; a table forming the crowning of a column and its capital. [L.]

Abaft, a-bäft', *adv.* or *prep.* On or towards the aft or hinder part of a ship. [Sax. *on-be-æftan.*]

Abandon, a-ban'dun, *vt.* To forsake entirely; to renounce; to desert; to yield up. [Fr. *abandonner.*]

Abandoned, a-ban'dund, *p.a.* Depraved; extremely wicked.

Abandonment, a-ban'dun-ment, *n.* A total desertion; a state of being forsaken.

Abase, a-bās', *vt.* To bring low; to cast down; to depress, humble, degrade, or disgrace. *ppr.* abasing, *pret. & pp.* abased. [Fr. *abaisser.*]

Abasement, a-bās'ment, *n.* State of being abased; degradation.

Abash, a-bash', *vt.* To put to confusion; to make ashamed; to confound; to disconcert. [O. Fr. *esbahir, esbahissant.*]

Abate, a-bāt', *vt.* To beat down; to lessen; to mitigate.—*vi.* To become less; to fail. *ppr.* abating, *pret. & pp.* abated. [Fr. *abattre*; L. *batuo*, to strike.]

Abatement, a-bāt'ment, *n.* Act of abating; a mitigation; deduction.

Abba, ab'a, *n.* In the Chaldee and Syriac, a father; a superior.

Abbacy, ab'ba-si, *n.* The dignity, rights, and privileges of an abbot. [Low L. *abbatia.*]

Abbess, ab'bes, *n.* A female superior of a nunnery.

Abbey, ab'bē, *n.* Abbeys, *pl.* A monastery; a society of monks, governed by an abbot; or of nuns, by an abbess. [Fr. *abbaye.*]

Abbot, ab'but, *n.* The male superior of an abbey. [Low L. *abbas.*]

Abbreviate, ab-brē'vi-āt, *vt.* To shorten; to cut short. *ppr.* abbreviating, *pret. & pp.* abbreviated. [Low L. *abbrevio, abbreviatus*—L. *brevis*, short.]

Abbreviation, ab-brē-vi-ā"shon, *n.* A shortening; a letter, or a few letters, used for a word.

Abbreviator, ab-brē'vi-ā-tėr, *n.* One who abbreviates or abridges.

Abdicate, ab'di-kāt, *vt.* To go from, as a legal right; to resign voluntarily, as supreme power; to relinquish.—*vi.* To resign power. *ppr.* abdicating, *pret. & pp.* abdicated. [L. *abd.co, abdicatus*—*dico*, to say.]

Abdication, ab-di-kā'shon, *n.* Act of abdicating an office.

Abdomen, ab-dō'men, *n.* The lower belly. [L. from *abdo*, to hide.]

Abdominal, ab-dom'in-al, *a.* Pertaining to the lower belly.

Abduction, ab-duk'shon, *n.* A leading away; the felonious carrying off a man's daughter, wife, &c. [Low L. *abductio.*]

Abed, a-bed', *adv.* On or in bed.

Aberrant, ab-e'rant, *a.* Wandering from; deviating from an established rule. [L. *errans—erro*, to wander.]

Aberration, ab-e-rā'shon, *n.* A wandering from; alienation of the mind; a small apparent motion of the fixed stars. [L. *aberratio—erro*, to wander.]

Abet, a-bet', *vt.* To urge on; to encourage. *ppr.* abetting, *pret. & pp.* abetted. (Chiefly in a bad sense.) [O. Fr. *abetter.*]

Abetment, a-bet'ment, *n.* Act of abetting.

Abettor, a-bet'ėr, *n.* One who abets.

Abeyance, a-bā'ans, *n.* Contemplation of law; temporary extinction. (With *in* before it.) [Norm. *abbaiaunce.*]

Abhor, ab-hor', *vt.* To shrink from with horror; to hate; to loathe. *ppr.* abhorring, *pret. & pp.* abhorred. [L. *abhorreo—horreo*, to shudder.]

Abhorred, ab-hord', *p.a.* Hated extremely; detested.

Abhorrence, ab-hor'rens, *n.* Act of abhorring; extreme detestation.

Abhorrent, ab-hor'rent, *a.* Hating; inconsistent with. (With *to*.)

Abib, ā'bib, *n.* The first month of the Jewish ecclesiastical year. [Heb. *ab*, swelling.]

Abide, a-bīd', *vi.* To stay in a place; to dwell; to tarry; to continue.—*vt.* To wait for; to endure; to bear without aversion. *ppr.* abiding, *pret. & pp.* abode. [Sax. *abidan.*]

Abiding, a-bīd'ing, *p.a.* Permanent.

Ability, a-bil'li-ti, *n.* State of being able; power to do anything; talent; skill; in *pl.* the powers of the mind. [Fr. *habilité*; L. *habeo*, to have or hold.]

Abject, ab'jekt, *a.* Cast away; mean; despicable. [L. *abjectus—jacio*, to cast.]

Abject!, ab'jekt, *n.* A person in the lowest condition.

Abjuration, ab-jū-rā'shon, *n.* Act of abjuring; oath taken for that end.

Abjure, ab-jūr', *vt.* To renounce upon oath; to reject with solemnity. *ppr.* abjuring, *pret. & pp.* abjured. [L. *abjuro—juro*, to swear.]

Ablative, ab'lat-iv, *a.* That takes away; the term applied to the case in Lat. grammar whose usual sign in Eng. is *from.*—*n.* The sixth case in Lat. nouns. [L. *ablativus—fero, latum*, to carry.]

Ablaze, a-blāz', *adv.* On fire; in a blaze.

Able, ā'bl, *a.* Having strong or active faculties of mind or body; having power sufficient; capable; skilful [Norm. *hable*—L. *habeo*, t have.]

Abluent, ab'lū-ent, *a.* Washing away; cleansing by liquids. [L. *abluo, abluens*—*luo*, to wash.]

Ablution, ab-lū'shon, *n.* A washing away from; a purification by water [L. *ablutio.*]

Ably, ā'bli, *adv.* With ability.

Abnegate, ab'nē-gāt, *vt.* To deny wholly; to deny and reject. *ppr.* abnegating, *pret. & pp.* abnegated. [L. *abnego, abnegatus—nego*, to deny.]

Abnegation, ab-nē-gā'shon, *n.* A denial; a renunciation.

Abnormal, ab-norm'al, *a.* Away from rule; deviating from a fixed rule; departing from a type or standard. [L. *abnormis—norma*, a rule.]

Aboard, a-bōrd', *adv.* or *prep.* On board; in a ship or vessel; in; with.

Abode, a-bōd', *n.* Stay; continuance; residence; habitation. [from *abide.*]

Abode!, a-bōd', *vt.* To foretoken.

Abolish, a-bol'ish, *vt.* To destroy; te abrogate. [Fr. *abolir, abolissant*; L. *alo*, to nourish.]

Abolition, ab-ō-li'shon, *n.* Act of abolishing; state of being abolished.

Abolitionist, ab-ō-li'shon-i-t, *n.* One who seeks to abolish anything, especially slavery.

Abominable, a-bom'in-a-bl, *a.* That is to be abominated; loathsome.

Abominableness, a-bom'in-a-bl-nes, *n.* Quality of being abominable.

Abominably, a-bom'in-a-bli, *adv.* Very odiously; detestably; sinfully.

Abominate, a-bom'in-āt, *vt.* To turn from, as a thing of evil omen; to hate extremely; to abhor. *ppr.* abominating, *pret. & pp.* abominated. [L. *abominor, abominatus—omen*, an omen.]

Abomination, a-bom'in-ā"shon, *n.* Ha-

tred; detestation; pollution; loathsomeness.
Aboriginal, ab-ŏ-rij′in-al, *a. From the first origin;* primitive; simple. [L. *ab,* and *origo, originis,* origin—*orior,* to arise.]
Aborigines, ab-ŏ-rij′in-ēz, *n. pl. The original* inhabitants of a country. [L.]
Abortion, a-bor′shon, *n. That which springs from its source out of season;* a miscarriage; a coming to nought. [L. *abortio—orior* to arise.]
Abortive, a-bort′iv, *a. Pertaining to abortion;* immature; causing abortion. *n.† An abortion.*
Abortively, a-bort′iv-li, *adv.* Immaturely; in an untimely manner.
Abortiveness, a-bort′iv-nes, *n. State of being abortive;* abortion.
Abound, a-bound′, *vi. To flow over, as waves after wave;* to be in great plenty; to have in great plenty. (With *in* or *with.*) [L. *abundo—unda,* a wave.]
Abounding, a-bound′ing, *p.a.* Having or being in great plenty; being very prevalent.
About, a-bout′, *prep. Around;* near to; relating to; engaged in.—*adv. Around;* round; nearly; here and there. [Sax. *abutan—utan,* without.]
Above, a-buv′, *prep. T over in a higher place;* superior to; more; beyond; before.—*adv.* To or in a higher place; overhead; chief; chiefly. [Sax. *abufan—ufan,* high.]
Above-board, a-buv′bōrd, *adv. Above the board* or table; without concealment or deception.
Abrade, a-brād′, *vt. To scrape off;* to waste by friction. *ppr.* abrading, *pret.* & *pp.* abraded. [L. *abrado—rado,* to scrape.]
Abrahamic, a-bra-ham′ik, *a. Pertaining to Abraham.*
Abrasion, ab-rā′zhon, *n. A rubbing off;* substance worn off by rubbing.
Abreast, a-brest′, *adv. With the breasts in a line;* side by side.
Abridge, a-brij′, *vt. To shorten;* to epitomize; to condense. *ppr.* abridging, *pret.* & *pp.* abridged. [Fr. *abréger;* L. *brevis,* short.]
Abridged, a-brijd′, *p.a. Made shorter;* epitomised; deprived of.
Abridgment, a-brij′ment, *n.* An epitome; a summary.
Abroach, a-brōch′, *adv.* In a posture to flow out; set afloat; in a state to be diffused.
Abroad, a-brąd′, *adv.* At large; in the open air; away from home; in a foreign country; widely. [Sax. *on,* and *bred,* a surface.]
Abrogate, ab′rō-gāt, *vt.* To take *away* its force, as from a law; to repeal; to make void. *ppr.* abrogating, *pret.* and *pp.* abrogated. [L. *abrogo, abrogatus—rogo,* to ask.]
Abrogation, ab-rō-gā′shon, *n. Act of abrogating;* a repeal; annulment.
Abrupt, ab-rupt′, *a. Broken off;* severed; steep; rugged; sudden; unceremonious.—*n. An abrupt place.* [L. *abruptus—rumpo,* to break.]
Abruptly, ab-rupt′li, *adv.* Suddenly; unceremoniously.
Abruptness, ab-rupt′nes, *n.* Suddenness; unceremonious haste.
Abscess, ab′ses, *n. A going away* of humours into one mass; a gathering of purulent matter in some part of the body. [L. *abscessus—cedo,* to go.]
Abscond, ab-skond′, *vi. To hide;* to hide one's self. (Generally used of persons eluding legal arrest.) [L. *abscondo—condo,* to hide.]

Absence, ab′sens, *n. State of being absent,* opposed to presence; inattention to things present. [Fr.; L. *absentia.*]
Absent, ab′sent, *a. Being away from;* not present; at a distance; wanting in attention; lost in thought. [L. *absens—Old* L. *ens,* being.]
Absent, ab-sent′, *vt. To keep away from.* (Used with the recipr. pron.)
Absentee, ab-sen-tē′, *n. One who absents himself* from his country, property, post, or duty.
Absenteeism, ab-sen-tē′izm, *n. State or habit of an absentee.*
Absolute, ab′sō-lūt, *a. Loosened from;* completed; unlimited; certain; despotic. [L. *absolutus—solvo, solutum,* to loose.]
Absolutely, ab′sō-lūt-li, *adv.* Unconditionally; peremptorily.
Absoluteness, ab′sō-lūt-nes, *n. State or quality of being absolute.*
Absolution, ab-sō-lū′shon, *n. A loosing from guilt,* or its punishment.
Absolutism, ab′sō-lūt-ism, *n.* The principles of *absolute* government.
Absolve, ab-solv′, *vt. To loose from;* to free from, as from guilt or punishment. *ppr.* absolving, *pret.* & *pp.* absolved. [L. *absolvo—solvo,* to loose.]
Absorb, ab-sorb′, *vt. To drink in;* to *swallow up;* to waste wholly. [L. *absorbeo—sorbeo,* to drink in.]
Absorbable, ab-sorb′a-bl, *a. That may be absorbed* or swallowed up.
Absorbent, ab-sorb′ent, *a. Imbibing;* swallowing.—*n. That which absorbs.* [L. *absorbens.*]
Absorption, ab-sorp′shon, *n. Act or process of imbibing* or swallowing up. [Fr.]
Absorptive, ab-sorp′tiv, *a.* Having power to absorb or imbibe.
Abstain, ab-stān′, *vi. To keep back from;* to refrain; to forbear. [L. *abstineo—teneo,* to hold.]
Abstemious, ab-stē′mi-us, *a. Keeping one's self from wine;* sparing in the use of food or drink; temperate; sober. [L. *abstemius—temetum,* wine.]
Abstemiousness, ab-stē′mi-us-nes, *n. Quality of being abstemious.*
Abstergent, ab-stērj′ent, *a. Serving to cleanse.* [L. *tergeo,* to wipe off.]
Abstinence, ab′sti-nens, *n. A keeping from* the indulgence of the appetites; forbearance of necessary food; a fasting. [Lat. *abstinentia—teneo,* to hold.]
Abstinent, ab′sti-nent, *a. Abstaining from;* refraining from indulgence. [Fr.]
Abstinently, ab′sti-nent-li, *adv. With abstinence.*
Abstract, ab-strakt′, *vt. To draw from;* to separate and consider by itself; to epitomize; to purloin. [L. *abstraho, abstractus—traho,* to draw.]
Abstract, ab′strakt, *a. That is drawn away from;* existing in the mind only; that is general in language or in reasoning.—*n.* A summary; the state of being abstracted; a smaller quantity containing the power of a greater. [L. *abstractus.*]
Abstractedly, ab-strakt′ed-li, *adv.* In a separate state.
Abstraction, ab-strak′shon, *n. Act of abstracting,* or state of being separated; deep thought; absence of mind.
Abstractive, ab-strakt′iv, *a.* Having *the power* or *quality of abstracting.*
Abstractly, ab-strakt′li, *adv.* Separately; absolutely.
Abstractness, ab′strakt-nes, *n. State of being abstract;* abstraction.
Abstruse, ab-strūs′, *a. Thrust away*

from; difficult of comprehension; obscure; concealed. [L. *abstrusus—trudo,* to thrust.]
Abstrusely, ab-strūs′li, *adv. In an abstruse manner;* obscurely.
Abstruseness, ab-strūs′nes, *n. State or quality of being abstruse.*
Absurd, ab-sérd′, *a. That comes,* as an improper answer, *from one deaf;* contrary to reason; opposed to manifest truth; deaf to reason. [L. *absurdus—surdus,* deaf.]
Absurdity, ab-sérd′i-ti, *n. Quality of being absurd;* that which is absurd.
Absurdly, ab-sérd′li, *adv. In an absurd manner;* inconsistently.
Absurdness, ab-sérd′nes, *n. Absurdity.*
Abundance, a-bun′dans, *n. An overflowing;* plenteousness; copiousness; wealth. [L. *abundantia—unda,* a wave.]
Abundant, a-bun′dant, *a. Overflowing;* abounding; plentiful; ample. [L. *ab undans.*]
Abundantly, a-bun′dant-li, *adv.* Fully; amply; plentifully.
Abuse, a-būz′, *vt. To turn from the proper use;* to misapply; to waste away; to impose upon; to vilify; to violate. *ppr.* abusing, *pret.* & *pp.* abused. [Fr. *abuser*—L. *utor, usus,* to use.]
Abuse, a-būs′, *n. Misuse;* reproach; violation; perversion of meaning.
Abused, a-būzd′, *p.a.* Perverted; reproached.
Abusive, a-būs′iv, *a. Practising abuse;* containing abuse.
Abusiveness, a-būs′iv-nes, *n. Quality of being abusive.*
Abut, a-but′, *vi. To approach to;* to border; to meet. (With *upon.*) *ppr.* abutting, *pret.* & *pp.* abutted. [Fr. *aboutir—bout,* end.]
Abutment, a-but′ment, *n. That which abuts;* solid support for the extremity of a bridge, arch, &c.
Abuttal, a-but′al, *n.* A boundary of land at the end; a headland.
Abyss, a-bis′, *n.* A *bottomless* gulf; a deep pit or mass of waters; hell. [Gr. *abussos—a,* priv. and *bussos,* bottom.]
Acacia, a-kā′shi-a, *n.* Egyptian *thorn,* a plant. [L. a thorn.]
Academic, Academical, ak-a-dem′ik, ak-a-dem′ik-al, *a.* Belonging to an *academy* or university.
Academic, ak-a-dem′ik, *n.* A student in a university or *academy.*
Academically, ak-a-dem′ik-al-li, *adv. In an academical manner.*
Academician, ak′a-dē-mi′′shi-an, *n.* A member of an academy for promoting arts and sciences; a member of the French academy. [Fr. *académicien.*]
Academy, a-kad′ē-mi, *n.* The school of Plato; a place of education; a seminary of arts or sciences; a society of persons for the cultivation of arts and sciences. [Gr. *Akadēmia,* from *Akadēmos,* the owner of a grove near Athens, where Plato taught.]
Acanthus, a-kan′thus, *n.* A prickly plant, the model of the foliage of the Corinthian order. [L.]
Accede, ak-sēd′, *vi. To come to;* to assent to; to comply with. *ppr.* acceding, *pret.* & *pp.* acceded. [L. *accedo—cedo,* to come.]
Accelerate, ak-sel′lē-rāt, *vt. To hasten;* to quicken the speed of; to further. *ppr.* accelerating, *pret.* & *pp.* accelerated. [L. *accelero, acceleratus—celer,* swift.]
Accelerated, ak-sel′lē-rāt-ed, *p.a. Quickened* in motion.
Accelerating, ak-sel′lē-rāt-ing, *p.a.* Increasing the *velocity* of.

Fāte, fär, fat, fąll; mē, met, hėr; pīne, pin; nōte, not, mōve; tūbe, tub, bųll; oil, pound.

Acceleration, ak-sel'lē-rā"shon, *n. Act of accelerating*; state of being accelerated.
Accelerative, ak-sel'lē-rāt-iv, *a. Adding to the velocity of.*
Accent, ak'sent, *n.* A tone or modulation of the voice; stress of the voice on a syllable or word; the mark which indicates this stress; manner of speaking; in poetry, expressions in general (pl.) [L. *accentus—cantus*, tone.]
Accent, ak-sent', *vt.* To express or note the *accent* of.
Accented, ak-sent'ed, *p.a. Uttered or marked with accent.*
Accentual, ak-sent'ū-al, *a. Pertaining to accent.*
Accentuate, ak-sent'ū-āt, *vt. To mark the proper accents of in writing. ppr.* accentuating, *pret. & pp.* accentuated.
Accentuation, ak-sent'ū-ā"shon, *n.* Act of marking with the proper *accents.*
Accept, ak-sept', *vt. To take;* to receive with pleasure; to admit with approbation; to receive as obligatory, and promise to pay; to consent to, as terms of a treaty. [L. *accepto—capio*, to take.]
Acceptable, ak-sept'a-bl, *a. That is likely to be accepted;* pleasing; gratifying.
Acceptableness, Acceptability, ak-sept'a-bl-nes, ak-sept'a-bil"li-ti, *n. Quality of being acceptable.*
Acceptably, ak-sept'a-bli, *adv. In an acceptable manner.*
Acceptance, ak-sept'ans, *n. Reception* with approbation; a bill of exchange accepted.
Acceptation, ak-sep-tā'shon, *n.* Kind reception; meaning in which a word is understood.
Accepted, ak-sept'ed, *p.a.* Kindly received; received with a pledge to pay.
Accepter, Acceptor, ak-sept'er, ak-sept'or, *n. A person who accepts.*
Access, ak'ses, *n. A going to*; approach; means of approach; liberty to approach; increase. [L. *accessus—cedo, cessum*, to go, move.]
Accessary, ak'ses-a-ri. See ACCESSORY.
Accessibility, ak-ses'i-bil"li-ti, *n. Quality of being accessible.*
Accessible, ak-ses'i-bl, *a. That may be approached*; easy of approach; affable.
Accessibly, ak-ses'i-bli, *adv. So as to be accessible.*
Accession, ak-se'shon, *n. A coming to;* augmentation. [L. *accessio*.]
Accessorial, ak-ses-sō'ri-al, *a. Pertaining to an accessory.*
Accessory, ak'ses-sō-ri, *a.* Joined to; additional, contributing to; aiding.—*n.* An accomplice; something which promotes a design. [Low L. *accessorius*.]
Accidence, ak'si-dens, *n. Things falling to words;* the changes which the declinable parts of speech severally undergo; a work exhibiting such changes briefly. [L. *accidens*, pl. *accidentia*, things falling to—*cado*, to fall.]
Accident, ak'si-dent, *n. That which falls to* a subject; quality of a being not essential to it; an event proceeding from an unforeseen cause; an unfortunate event occurring casually. [L. *accidens*.]
Accidental, ak-si-dent'al, *a. Incidental;* happening by chance; contingent; not necessarily belonging to.—*n.* A property or thing not essential.
Accidentally, ak-si-dent'al-li, *adv. By accident* or chance; casually.
Acclaim, ak-klām', *n. Acclamation.*
Acclamation, ak-kla-mā'shon, *n.* A shout of applause; unanimous election, expressed by word of mouth, and at once. [L. *acclamatio—clamo*, to cry out.]
Acclimatise, ak-kli'mat-iz, *vt. To habituate* to a climate different from the native one.—*vi.* To become habituated to a new climate. *ppr.* acclimatizing, *pret. & pp.* acclimatized.
Acclimatized, ak-kli'mat-izd, *p.a. Inured to a new climate.*
Acclivity, ak-kliv'i-ti, *n. A bending upwards;* a rise, as of a hill, viewed from below. [L. *acclivitas—clivus*, a slope.]
Accommodate, ak-kom'mō-dāt, *vt. To make suitable*; to adjust; to furnish with; to reconcile; to lend to. *ppr.* accommodating, *pret. & pp.* accommodated. [L. *accommodo, accommodatus—commodum*, a convenience.]
Accommodating, ak-kom'mō-dāt-ing, *p.a.* Obliging; complying.
Accommodation, ak-kom'mō-dā"shon, *n. Act of accommodating*; state of being accommodated.
Accompaniment, ak-kum'pa-ni-ment, *n. That which accompanies;* the subordinate part or parts, in music. [Fr. *accompagnement*.]
Accompany, ak-kum'pa-ni, *vt. To go with as a companion;* to wait upon; to associate with; to perform in unison with.—*vi.* To be a companion; to perform the accompanying part in music. *ppr.* accompanying, *pret. & pp.* accompanied. [Fr. *accompagner—compagnie*, company.]
Accompanying, ak-kum'pa-ni-ing, *p.a.* Attending.
Accomplice, ak-kom'plis, *n. One united with another;* an associate in a crime; an accessory. (Used in a bad sense.) [Fr. *complice;* L. *plico*, to fold.]
Accomplish, ak-kom'plish, *vt. To fulfil;* to execute fully; to perfect. [Fr. *accomplir, accomplissant;* L. *pleo*, to fill.]
Accomplishable, ak-kom'plish-a-bl, *a. That may be accomplished.*
Accomplished, ak-kom'plisht, *p.a.* Elegant; polished; having a finished education.
Accomplishment, ak-kom'plish-ment, *n. Fulfilment;* entire performance; acquirement; embellishment.
Accord, ak-kord', *n. Union of hearts;* harmony; will; consent.—*vt.* To give cordially; to bring to an agreement, as persons, or to settle, as things.—*vi.* To agree; to be in correspondence. (With *with*, and sometimes *to*.) [Fr. *accord;* L. *cor, cordis*, the heart.]
Accordance, ak-kord'ans, *n. Cordial agreement with;* conformity to; harmony; unison; coincidence.
Accordant, ak-kord'ant, *a.* Corresponding; consonant; agreeable.
According, ak-kord'ing, *p.a.* Agreeing; harmonizing.
Accordingly, ak-kord'ing-li, *adv. Agreeably;* suitably; conformably.
According-to, ak-kord'ing-tö, *prep.* In a manner suitable to; agreeably to; in proportion to.
Accordion, ak-kord'i-on, *n.* A small, melodious, keyed wind-instrument.
Accost, ak-kost', *vt. To go up to the side of;* to speak to first; to address. [Fr. *accoster;* L. *costa*, a rib, the side.]
Accouchement, ak-kösh'mong, *n.* Delivery in child-bed. [Fr. *couche*, a bed.]
Accoucheur, ak-kö-sher', *n.* A man who assists women in child-birth. [Fr.]
Account, ak-kount', *n. A reckoning up* of debts or expenses; a register of facts relating to money; narration; advantage; end; importance.—*a. † Accounted.* —*vt. To reckon;* to consider; to deem; to value.—*vi. To render an account;* to give or render reasons; to explain (with *for*). [Fr. *compte*, number; L. *computo*, to sum up.]
Accountability, ak-kount'a-bil"li-ti, *n. State of being accountable;* liability.
Accountable, ak-kount'a-bl, *a. Liable to be called to account;* amenable.
Accountableness, ak-kount'a-bl-nes, *n. State of being accountable.*
Accountably, ak-kount'a-bli, *adv. In an accountable manner.*
Accountant, ak-kount'ant, *n. One skilled* or employed in *accounts.*
Accountantship, ak-kount'ant-ship, *n. The office* or duties of an *accountant.*
Accoutre, ak-kö'ter, *vt. To equip with care;* to furnish with a military dress and arms. *ppr.* accoutring, *pret.* and *pp.* accoutred. [Fr. *accoutrer;* L. *cultura*, care—*colo*, to tend.]
Accoutrements, ak-kö'ter-ments, *n. pl.* Military dress and arms; dress (in a ludicrous sense).
Accredit, ak-kred'it, *vt. To invest with credit;* to give authority to; to receive, as an envoy; to bring into vogue, as a word. [Fr. *accrediter;* L. *credo, creditum*, to give faith to.]
Accredited, ak-kred'it-ed, *p.a.* Authorized; sanctioned.
Accretion, ak-krē'shon, *n. A growing to*, or increase by natural growth. [L. *accretio—cresco, cretus*, to grow.]
Accretive, ak-krēt'iv, *a.* Increasing by growth.
Accrue, ak-krö', *vi. To arise* or come; to be added. *ppr.* accruing, *pret. & pp.* accrued. [Fr. *accrotre, accru;* L. *cresco*, to grow.]
Accumulate, ak-kū'mū-lāt, *vt. To augment by heaping up;* to gather together; to amass.—*vi. To increase greatly. ppr.* accumulating, *pret. & pp.* accumulated. [L. *accumulo, accumulatus—cumulus*, a heap.]
Accumulated, ak-kū'mū-lāt-ed, *p.a. Collected into a heap.*
Accumulation, ak-kū'mū-lā"shon, *n. Act of accumulating;* state of being accumulated; a heap; a collection.
Accumulative, ak-kū'mū-lāt-iv, *a. That accumulates*, or is accumulated.
Accuracy, ak'kū-ra-si, *n. State of being accurate;* precision which results from care. [L. *accuratio.*]
Accurate, ak'kū-rat, *a. Done with care;* exact, without defect or failure; exact, without negligence or ignorance. [L. *accuratus—curo, curatum*, to take care of.]
Accurately, ak'kū-rāt-li, *adv.* Exactly.
Accurateness, ak'kū-rāt-nes, *n.* Accuracy.
Accursed, ak-kērs'ed, *a. Devoted to execration;* doomed; wicked. [Sax. *cursian*, to curse.]
Accusable, ak-kūz'a-bl, *a. That may b' accused.*
Accusation, ak-kū-zā'shon, *n. Act of accusing;* impeachment; that of which one is accused.
Accusative, ak-kūz'at-iv, *a. Accusing;* a term of grammar, signifying the relation of the noun on which the action implied in the verb terminates. [L. *accusativus*.]
Accuse, ak-kūz', *vt. To charge* with a crime; to impeach; to censure. *ppr.* accusing, *pret.* and *pp.* accused.—*n.† Accusation.* [L. *accuso—causa*, cause.]
Accused, ak-kūzd', *p.a. Charged* with a crime or offence; blamed.
Accuser, ak-kūz'er, *n. One who accuses.*
Accusing, ak-kūz'ing, *p.a. Charging* with a crime; blaming.
Accustom, ak-kus'tum, *vt. To inure to*

ch, chain; j, job; g, go; ng, sing; TH, then; th, thin; w, wig; wh, whig; zh, azure; † obsolete.

a custom; to make familiar with by use; to familiarise. [Fr. *accoutumer—coutume*, custom.]
Accustomed, ak-kus'tumd, *p.a.* According to custom; usual; often practised.
Ace, as, *n.* A *unit*; a single point; a particle; an atom. [Fr. *as*; L. *assus*, simple.]
Aceldama, a-sel'da-ma, *n.* A *field of blood*, sometimes used figuratively. [Ch. *akeldama—akel*, a field, and *da'ma*, blood.]
Acephalous, a-sef'al-us, *a. Without a head*; deprived of its first syllable, as a line of poetry. [Gr. *kephalē*, a head.]
Acerbity, a-serb'i-ti, *n. Sharpness*; a sourness; bitterness or severity of language. [L. *acerbitas*.]
Acescence, a-ses'ens, *n. A turning sour.*
Acescent, a-ses'ent, *a. Turning sour*; tending to sourness. [L. *acescens*.]
Acetic, a-set'ik, *a.* Relating to pure acid of *vinegar*. [from L. *acetum*, vinegar.]
Acetify, as-e'ti-fi, *vt.* or *i. To turn into acid or vinegar. ppr.* acetifying, *pret. & pp.* acetified. [L. *acetum*, and *facio*, to make.]
Acetous, as-et'us, *a. Having the quality of vinegar*; sour; acid.
Ache, āk, *vi. To be in pain*, or in continued pain; to suffer grief or distress. *ppr.* aching, *pret. & pp.* ached.—*n. Pain*, or continued pain. [Sax. *acan*.]
Acheron, ak'e-ron, *n. The river of pain*; fabled river of hell. [Gr. *achos*, pain, and *roos*, a river.]
Achieve, a-chēv', *vt. To bring to a head*; to accomplish; to obtain, as the result of exertion. *ppr.* achieving, *pret. & pp.* achieved. [Fr. *achever—chef*, the head.]
Achievement, a-chēv'ment, *n. Act of achieving*; exploit; an escutcheon.
Aching, āk'ing, *p.a. Being* in continued *pain*.—*n.* Pain.
Achromatic, a-krō-mat'ik, *a. Free from colour*; preventing the effect of colours. (Gr. *chrōma*, colour.]
Acid, as'id, *a. Sharp*; sour to the taste, like vinegar.—*n. A sour substance*; a substance capable of uniting with certain other substances, and forming salts. [L. *acidus*.]
Acidifiable, as-id'i-fi-a-bl, *a. Capable of being acidified.*
Acidification, as-id'i-fi-kā"shon, *n.* The *a*ct or process of *acidifying.*
Acidifier, as-id'i-fi-er, *n.* A principle whose presence is necessary for acidity.
Acidify, as-id'i-fi, *vt. To make acid*; to convert into an acid. *ppr.* acidifying, *pret. & pp.* acidified. [L. *acidus*, and *facio*, to make.]
Acidity, as-id'i-ti, *n. Quality of being acid*; sourness. [Fr. *acidité*.]
Acidulate, as-id'ū-lat, *vt. To make acid in a moderate degree. ppr.* acidulating, *pret. & pp.* acidulated. [from L. *acidulus*, somewhat acid.]
Acidulous, as-id'ū-lus, *a. Slightly acid* or sour. [L. *acidulus.*]
Acknowledge, ak-nol'lej, *vt. To lay down that one knows*; to own the knowledge of; to avow; to own or confess. *ppr.* acknowledging, *pret. & pp.* acknowledged. [Sax. *ac*, but, *cnawan*, to know, and *lecgan*, to lay.]
Acknowledged, ak-nol'lejd, *p.a.* Owned; confessed.
Acknowledgment, ak-nol'lej-ment, *n. Act of acknowledging*; recognition; return for a benefit received.
Acme, ak'mē, *n. The top or highest point.* [Gr. *akmē*.]
Acolyte, ak'ol-it, *n.* One of the lowest

order in the Romish church. [from Gr. *akolouthos*, to follow.]
Aconite, ak'on-it, *n.* The herb wolfs-bane. [Gr. *akoniton*.]
Acorn, ā'korn, *n. Oak-corn*; the fruit of the oak. [Sax. *acern—ac*, oak.]
Acerned, ā'kornd, *p.a. Fed with acorns.*
Acoustic, a-kous'tik, *a. Pertaining to the sense of hearing*, or to the doctrine of sounds. [Gr. *akoustikos*.]
Acoustics, a-kous'tiks, *n.* The science *of sounds.*
Acquaint, ak-kwānt', *vt. To make fully known to*; to make familiar; to inform; to apprise. [O. Fr. *accointer*; L. *cognitus*, known—*nosco*, to know.]
Acquaintance, ak-kwānt'ans, *n.* Familiar knowledge; slight knowledge, short of friendship; a person or persons well known.
Acquaintanceship, ak-kwānt'ans-ship, *n. State of being acquainted.*
Acquiesce, ak-kwi-es', *vi. To rest satisfied*; to admit without opposition; to comply; to submit. *ppr.* acquiescing, *pret. & pp.* acquiesced. [L. *acquiesco —quies*, rest.]
Acquiescence, ak-kwi-es'ens, *n. State of acquiescing*; quiet assent.
Acquiescent, ak-kwi-es'ent, *a. Resting satisfied with*; easy; submitting.
Acquiescing, ak-kwi-es'ing, *p.a.* Quietly submitting to; resting content in.
Acquirable, ak-kwir'a-bl, *a. That may be acquired.*
Acquire, ak-kwir', *vt.* To obtain; to procure. *ppr.* acquiring, *pret.* and *pp.* acquired. [L. *acquiro—quero*, to seek.]
Acquirement, ak-kwir'ment, *n. Act of acquiring*; that which is acquired; attainment.
Acquisition, ak-kwi-zi'shon, *n. Act of acquiring*; the thing acquired. [L. *acquisitio*.]
Acquisitive, ak-kwiz'it-iv, *a. Prone or eager to acquire.*
Acquit, ak-kwit', *vt. To give quiet to*; to set free; to absolve. *ppr.* acquitting, *pret. & pp.* acquitted. [Fr. *acquitter*; L. *quietus*, quiet.]
Acquittal, ak-kwit'al, *n.* A setting free from a charge; a judicial discharge.
Acquittance, ak-kwit'ans, *n.* Discharge or release from a debt; a writing which is evidence of a discharge; a receipt in full!
Acre, ā'kėr, *n.* Primarily, a *field*; a quantity of land, containing 4840 square yards. [Sax. *acer.*]
Acreage, ā'kėr-āj, *n. The number of acres* in a piece of land.
Acred, ā'kėrd, *p.a. Possessing acres* or landed property.
Acrid, ak'rid, *a. Sharp*; hot or biting to the taste; corroding; harsh. [L. *acer*, acris.]
Acridity, ak-rid'i-ti, *n. Acridness.*
Acridness, ak'rid-nes, *n. A sharp*, bitter, pungent quality.
Acrimonious, ak-ri-mō'ni-us, *a. Full of acrimony*; severe; sarcastic.
Acrimoniously, ak-ri-mō'ni-us-li, *adv. With sharpness* or bitterness.
Acrimony, ak'ri-mo-ni, *n. Sharpness*; harshness; severity. [L. *acrimonia— acer*, sharp.]
Acropolis, a-krop'o-lis, *n. The highest part of a city*; the citadel of Athens. [Gr. *akros*, highest, and *polis*, a city.]
Across, a-kros', *prep.* or *adv.* From side to side; transversely; crosswise.
Acrostic, a-kros'tik, *n.* A composition in verse, in which the first or the last letters of the lines, taken in order, form the name of a person, &c. [Gr. *akra*, extremity, and *stichos*, a row.]

Act, akt, *vi. To be in action*; to exert power; to conduct one's self.—*vt. To do*; to perform, as an assumed part; to counterfeit.—*n. A deed*; power, or the effect of power, put forth; a state of reality; a state of readiness; a part of a play; law, as an act of parliament. [L. *ago*, *actus*, to do.]
Acted, akt'ed, *p.a. Done*; performed.
Acting, akt'ing, *p.n. Action*; act of performing a part of a play.
Action, ak'shon, *n. A deed*; operation; a series of events; gesture; a suit or process; an engagement. [Fr.—L. *actio.*]
Actionable, ak'shon-a-bl, *a. Liable to an action* at law.
Active, ak'tiv, *a. That acts or is in action*; busy; quick; industrious; requiring action; denoting action. [Fr. *actif*; L. *activus.*]
Actively, ak'tiv-li, *adv. In an active manner.*
Activity, ak-tiv'i-ti, *n. Quality of being active*; agility; nimbleness.
Actor, akt'er, *n. He that acts*; an active agent; a stage-player.
Actress, akt'res, *n.* A female stage-player.
Actual, ak'tū-al, *a. Existing in act*; real; certain; positive. [Fr. *actuel*; L. *actualis.*]
Actuality, ak-tū-al'li-ti, *n. State of being actual*; reality.
Actually, ak'tū-al-li, *adv.* In fact; really; in truth.
Actuary, ak'tū-a-ri, *n.* A registrar or clerk; the manager of a joint-stock company; accountant; calculator. [L. *actuarius.*]
Actuate, ak'tū-āt, *vt. To put into action*; to incite; to animate. *ppr.* actuating. *pret. & pp.* actuated.
Acumen, a-kū'men, *n. Sharpness*; keenness; sagacity. [L.]
Acuminate, a-kū'min-āt, *vt.* To render sharp or keen. *ppr.* acuminating, *pret. & pp.* acuminated.
Acute, a-kūt', *a. Sharpened*; sharp; ending in a sharp point; penetrating; having nice sensibility; sharp in sound. [L. *acutus.*]
Acutely, a-kūt'li, *adv. Sharply.*
Acuteness, a-kūt'nes, *n. Sharpness*; shrewdness; faculty of nice perception; sharpness of sound.
Adage, ad'āj, *n.* A saying expressive of something *proper to be done*; a proverb; a maxim. [L. *adagium*, from *ago*, to act.]
Adamant, ad'a-mant, *n. That which is untamable*; the diamond; anything extremely hard; the loadstone. [Gr. *adamas—damaō*, to tame.]
Adamantine, ad-a-mant'in, *a. Made of adamant*; very hard.
Adamic, ad'am-ik, *a. Pertaining to Adam.*
Adamite, ad'am-it, *a. Of the time of Adam.*
Adapt, a-dapt', *vt. To fit to*; to adjust; to proportion. [L. *apto.*]
Adaptability, a-dapt'a-bil"li-ti, *n. Capability of being adapted.*
Adaptable, a-dapt'a-bl, *a. That may be adapted.*
Adaptation, a-dap-tā'shon, *n.* Act of making suitable: suitableness.
Add, ad, *vt. To set to*; to join to; to augment; to annex. [L. *addo—do*, to place.]
Adder, ad'ėr, *n. A venomous serpent* of several species. [Sax. *aetter.*]
Addict, ad-dikt', *vt.* To give up or attach to; to dedicate (generally in a bad sense), with the recipr. pron. [L. *addico*, *addictum—dico*, to declare.]

Fāte, fär, fat, fall; mē, met. hėr; pine, pin; nōte, not, move; tūbe, tub, bull; oil, pound.

Addictedness, ad-dikt'ed-nes, n. *Quality or state of being addicted.*
Addiction†, ad-dik'shon, n. *The state of being addicted.*
Addition, ad-di'shon, n. *Act of adding;* the thing added; increase; a title given to a man over and above his Christian name; appendage. [L. *additio.*]
Additional, ad-di'shon-al, a. *That is added.*
Additive, ad'it-iv, a. *That is to be or may be added.*
Addle, ad'l, a. *Diseased;* putrid; empty. —*vt.* To make corrupt or barren. *ppr.* addling, *pret. & pp.* addled. [Sax. *adl.*]
Addle-headed, ad'l-hed-ed, a. Having barren brains; of weak intellect.
Address, ad-dres', *vt.* To direct *in writing;* to speak to; to apply to by words or writing; to court; to consign to; to apply (with recipr. pron.)—*n.* Verbal or written application; tact; adroitness; courtship (generally in the plural); direction of a letter. [Fr. *adresser;* L. *dirigo,* to make straight.]
Adduce, ad-dūs', *vt.* To *lead to;* to bring forward; to urge; to cite. *ppr.* adducing, *pret. & pp.* adduced. [L. *adduco* —*duco,* to lead.]
Adducible, ad-dūs'i-bl, a. *That may be adduced.*
Adept, a-dept', n. *One who reaches or attains to;* one fully skilled in any art.—a. Well skilled; completely versed or acquainted. [L. *adeptus,* having obtained—*apiscor,* to reach after.]
Adequacy, ad'ē-kwa-si, n. *State or quality of being adequate.*
Adequate, ad'ē-kwāt, a. *Equal to;* proportionate: fully sufficient. [L. *adæquatus—æquus,* equal.]
Adequately, ad'ē-kwāt-li, *adv. In an adequate manner.*
Adhere, ad-hēr', *vi. To stick;* to be joined or held in contact; to cling; to remain firm. *ppr.* adhering, *pret. & pp.* adhered. [L. *adhæreo—hæreo,* to stick to.]
Adherence, ad-hēr'ens, n. *State of adhering;* attachment; fidelity.
Adherent, ad-hēr'ent, a. *Sticking to;* united with.—**n.** A follower; a partizan. [L. *adhærens.*]
Adhesion, ad-hē'shon, n. *Act or state of sticking* to; sticking, or being attached to; adherence. [L. *adhæsio—hæreo,* to stick.]
Adhesive, ad-hē'siv, a. *Apt or tending to adhere;* sticky; tenacious.
Adhesiveness, ad-hē'siv-nes, n. *Stickiness;* tenacity.
Adhortatory, ad-hor'ta-tō-ri, a. Containing *counsel or warning.* [from L. *adhortor,* to exhort.]
Adieu, a-dū', *adv.* Form of parting; farewell.—*n.* A farewell. [Fr. *à Dieu,* to God.]
Adipose, ad'i-pōs, a. Pertaining to or *consisting of fat;* fat. [L. *adiposus,* from *adeps,* fat.]
Adit, ad'it, n. *A going to;* an approach; the horizontal opening into a mine. [L. *aditus—eo, itum,* to go.]
Adjacency, ad-jā'sen-si, n. *State of lying contiguous to.*
Adjacent, ad-jā'sent, a. *Lying near to;* contiguous. [L. *adjacens—jaceo,* to lie.]
Adjectival, ad'jek-tiv-al, a. *Belonging to or like an adjective.*
Adjective, ad'jek-tiv, n. A word *put to* or used with a noun, to express some quality or circumstance respecting it. [L. *adjectivus,* added—*jacio,* to throw, set.]
Adjoin, ad-join', *vt. To join to;* to fasten; to unite; to connect. (In these transi-

tive senses it is rarely used.)—*vi. To lie* or be next; to be contiguous. [L. *adjungo—jungo,* to join.]
Adjoining, ad-join'ing, p.a. Adjacent; contiguous.
Adjourn, ad-jèrn', *vt.* To continue *from day to day;* to put off *to a future day.* —*vi.* To leave off for a time; to stop; to give over. [Fr. *ajourner—jour,* a day.]
Adjourned, ad-jèrnd', p.a. Put off or deferred.
Adjournment, ad-jèrn'ment, n. Putting off *till* another *day* or time; interval during which a public body defers business.
Adjudge, ad-juj', *vt.* To decree judicially; to determine; to decide. *ppr.* adjudging, *pret. & pp.* adjudged. [Fr. *adjuger;* L. *judico,* to judge.]
Adjudicate, ad-jū'di-kāt, *vt.* To *adjudge;* to try and determine, as a court. *ppr.* adjudicating, *pret. & pp.* adjudicated. [L. *adjudico, adjudicatus—judico,* to judge.]
Adjudication, ad-jū'di-kā"shon, n. *Judicial sentence;* judgment or decision of a court.
Adjudicator, ad-jū'di-kāt-or, n. *One who adjudicates* or adjudges.
Adjunct, ad'jungkt, n. *Something joined to* another; a person joined to another. a. United with. [L. *adjunctum—jungo,* to join.]
Adjuration, ad-jū-rā'shon, n. *Act of adjuring;* an oath or solemn charge. [L. *adjuratio.*]
Adjure, ad-jūr', *vt.* To *charge on oath;* to charge earnestly and solemnly. *ppr.* adjuring, *pret. & pp.* adjured. [L. *adjuro—juro,* to swear.]
Adjust, ad-just', *vt. To rectify;* to *make exact;* to regulate; to adapt; to settle. [Fr. *ajuster;* L. *justus,* just.]
Adjustable, ad-just'a-bl, a. *That may or can be adjusted.*
Adjustment, ad-just'ment, n. *Act of adjusting;* arrangement; settlement. [Old Fr. *adjustement.*]
Adjutancy, ad'jū-tan-si, n. Skilful arrangement in aid; *the office of an adjutant.*
Adjutant, ad'jū-tant, n. An officer who assists the superior officers, conducts correspondence, &c. [L. *adjutans,* assisting.]
Admeasurement, ad-me'zhūr-ment, n. *Act of measuring according to rule;* dimensions; adjustment of proportion.
Adminicle, ad-min'i-kl, n. *Support;* aid; furtherance. [L. *adminiculum—manus,* the hand.]
Administer, ad-min'is-tér, *vt. To minister;* to dispense; to manage; to distribute.—*vi.* To add something. [L. *administro—minister,* a servant.]
Administration, ad-min'is-trā"shon, n. *Act of administering;* management; distribution; the executive part of a government.
Administrative, ad-min'is-trāt-iv, a. *That administers.*
Administrator, ad-min-is-trāt'or, n. *One who administers;* one who manages an intestate estate.
Admirable, ad'mi-ra-bl, a. *Worthy of admiration;* wonderful; excellent; surprising. [Fr.—L. *admirabilis.*]
Admirableness, ad'mi-ra-bl-nes, n. *Quality of being admirable.*
Admirably, ad'mi-ra-bli, *adv. In an admirable manner.*
Admiral, ad'mi-ral, n. *The chief commander* of a fleet or navy. [Fr. *amiral* —Ar. *amir,* a lord.]
Admiralty, ad'mi-ral-ti, n. A board of

officers for the administration of naval affairs; the place where this board transacts business.
Admiration, ad-mi-rā'shon, n. Wonder mingled with pleasing emotions; amazement; surprise. [L. *admiratio.*]
Admire, ad-mīr', *vt. To wonder at;* to regard with wonder, surprise, or affection; to delight in. *ppr.* admiring, *pret. & pp.* admired. [L. *admiror—miror,* to wonder.]
Admired, ad-mīrd', p.a. Regarded with admiration.
Admirer, ad-mīr'ėr, n. *One who admires;* a lover.
Admiringly, ad-mīr'ing-li, *adv. With admiration.*
Admissibility, ad-mis'i-bil"li-ti, n. *Quality of being admissible.*
Admissible, ad-mis'i-bl, a. *That may be admitted.*
Admissibly, ad-mis'i-bli, *adv. So as to be admitted.*
Admission, ad-mi'shon, n. *Admittance;* access; introduction; concession. [L. *admissio.*]
Admit, ad-mit', *vt.* To suffer to enter; to allow; to grant; to concede. *ppr.* admitting, *pret. & pp.* admitted. [L. *admitto—mitto,* to send.]
Admittance, ad-mit'ans, n. Allowance; permission to enter; the right of entrance.
Admixture, ad-miks'tūr, n. That which *is mixed* with something else; a mixing. [L. *mistura—misceo,* to mingle.]
Admonish, ad-mon'ish, *vt.* To *put one in mind of,* as of a fault; to caution; to reprove solemnly. [L. *admoneo—moneo,* to advise.]
Admonisher, ad-mon'ish-ėr, n. *One who admonishes.*
Admonishment†, ad-mon'ish-ment, n. *Admonition.*
Admonition, ad-mō-ni'shon, n. *Act of admonishing;* gentle or solemn reproof; instruction; direction.
Admonitory, ad-mon'i-tō-ri, a. *Containing admonition.*
Adnascent, ad-nas'ent, a. *Growing to or on* something else. [L. *adnascens—nascor,* to grow.]
Ado, a-dö', n. [Sax. pref. *a,* and *don,* to do.] *A doing;* a stir; difficulty.
Adolescence, ad-ō-les'ens, n. *A growing up to manhood;* the age of youth; the period of life between childhood and manhood. [Fr.; L. *adolescentia—oleo,* to nourish.]
Adolescent, ad-ō-les'ent, a. *Growing;* advancing to manhood. [L. *adolescens.*]
Adopt, a-dopt', *vt.* To take by *choice;* to take and treat as a child, giving a title to the rights of a child; to embrace. [L. *adopto—opto,* to choose.]
Adopted, a-dopt'ed, p.a. Received as son and heir; embraced.
Adoption, a-dop'shon, n. *Act of adopting;* state of being adopted. [L. *adoptio.*]
Adoptive, a-dopt'iv, a. *That adopts;* or that is adopted. [L. *adoptivus.*]
Adorable, a-dōr'a-bl, a. *Deserving to be adored.*
Adorableness, a-dōr'a-bl-nes, n. *Quality of being adorable.*
Adorably, a-dōr'a-bli, *adv.* In a *manner* worthy of *adoration.*
Adoration, a-dōr-ā'shon, n. *Act of adoring;* the worship paid to God; homage; profound reverence.
Adore, a-dōr', *vt. To speak to* with reverence; to address in prayer; to worship with reverence and awe; to love intensely. *ppr.* adoring, *pret. & pp.* adored. [L. *adoro—oro,* to speak.]

ch, chain; j, job; g, go; ng, sing; TH, then; th, thin; w, wig; wh, whig; zh, azure; † obsolete.

Adorer, a-dōr'ėr, n. *One who adores.*
Adoring, a-dōr'ing, p.a. Honouring or addressing as divine.
Adoringly, a-dōr'ing-li, adv. *With adoration.*
Adorn, a-dorn', vt. *To deck with ornaments; to embellish; to beautify.* [L. *adorno—orno*, to fit out.]
Adorning, a-dorn'ing, n. *Ornament; decoration.*
Adown, a-doun', prep. *Towards the ground.—adv. Down; on the ground; at the bottom.*
Adrift, a-drift', adv. *Floating at random; at the mercy of any impulse.* [from Sax. *adrifan*, to drive.]
Adroit, a-droit', a. *Going direct to the mark; dexterous; ready.* [Fr. from *droit*—L. *directus*, straight.]
Adroitly, a-droit'li, adv. *With dexterity; in a ready, skilful manner.*
Adroitness, a-droit'nes, n. *Dexterity; skill; readiness.*
Adscititious, ad'si-ti"shus, a. *Added or assumed; additional.* [from L. *adscisco*, to take knowingly—*scio*, to know.]
Adstriction, ad-strik'shon, n. *A binding to; a binding fast.* [L. *adstrictio—stringo*, to bind.]
Adulation, ad-ū-lā'shon, n. *A fawning like that of a dog to his master; high compliment.* [Fr.; L. *adulatio—ululo*, to howl like a dog.]
Adulatory, ad'ū-lā-tō-ri, a. *Flattering; praising excessively or servilely.*
Adult, a-dult', a. *Grown up to maturity or manhood.—n. A person grown to maturity or manhood.* [L. *adultus—olesco*, to grow.]
Adulterate, a-dul'tėr-āt, vt. *To change to another, but a worse state; to contaminate. ppr. adulterating, pret. & pp. adulterated.* [L. *adultero, adulteratus—alter*, other.]
Adulterate, a-dul'tėr-āt, a. *Adulterated.*
Adulterated, a-dul'tėr-āt-ed, p.a. *Corrupted; debased by mixture.*
Adulteration, a-dul'tėr-ā"shon, n. *Act of adulterating, or the state of being adulterated.*
Adulterer, a-dul'tėr-ėr, n. *A man who is guilty of adultery.* [L. *adulter.*]
Adulteress, a-dul'tėr-es, n. *A woman guilty of adultery.*
Adulterine, a-dul'tėr-in, a. *Proceeding from adulterous commerce; spurious; illegal.*
Adulterous, a-dul'tėr-us, a. *Guilty of adultery; pertaining to adultery.*
Adulterously, a-dul'tėr-us-li, adv. *In an adulterous manner.*
Adultery, a-dul'tėr-i, n. *Going to the marriage-bed of another; unfaithfulness to the marriage-bed.* [L. *adulterium—alter*, other.]
Adumbrate, ad-um'brāt, vt. *To give a faint shadow of; to shadow out; to describe. ppr. adumbrating, pret. & pp. adumbrated.* [L. *adumbro, adumbratus—umbra*, a shadow.]
Adumbration, ad-um-brā'shon, n. *Act of making a faint resemblance; a faint sketch.*
Adust, a-dust', a. *Burnt; looking as if burnt.* [L. *uro, ustum*, to burn.]
Advance, ad-vans', vt. *To forward; to put forward; to improve; (in commerce) to pay beforehand; to supply.—vi. To go forward; to be promoted. ppr. advancing, pret. & pp. advanced.—n. A going forward; preferment; first hint or step; rise in value; a giving beforehand.* [Fr. *avancer*—L. *ab*, and *ante*, before.]
Advanced, ad-vanst', p.a. *In the van of intellectual or religious progress.*

Advancement, ad-vans'ment, n. *Act of moving forward; improvement; elevation.*
Advantage, ad-van'tāj, n. *A state of advance; superiority; gain; opportunity; increase.—vt. To forward; to promote. ppr. advantaging, pret. & pp. advantaged.* [Fr. *avantage—avant*, before.]
Advantageous, ad-van-tāj'us, a. *Profitable; beneficial; useful.*
Advantageously, ad-van-tāj'us-li, adv. *In an advantageous manner.*
Advantageousness, ad-van-tāj'us-nes, n. *Quality or state of being advantageous.*
Advent, ad'vent, n. *A coming to; arrival; the coming of our Saviour.* [L. *adventus—venio*, to come.]
Adventitious, ad-ven-ti'shi-us, a. *That comes to; accidental; casual; accessory; foreign.* [L. *adventitius—venio*, to come.]
Adventure, ad-ven'tūr, n. *A coming to a place; an accident; occurrence; a bold undertaking.—vt. To put into the power of chance; to risk or hazard. vi. To dare; to try the chance. ppr. adventuring, pret. & pp. adventured.* [Fr. *aventure*—L. *venio*, to come.]
Adventurer, ad-ven'tūr-ėr, n. *One who risks, hazards, or braves.*
Adventuress, ad-ven'tūr-es, n. *A female adventurer.*
Adventurous, ad-ven'tūr-us, a. *Prone to incur hazard; daring; full of hazard.* [Fr. *aventureux.*]
Adventurously, ad-ven'tūr-us-li, adv. *In a manner to incur hazard.*
Adverb, ad'vėrb, n. *A word used to modify the sense of a verb, participle, adjective, or another adverb.* [L. *adverbium—verbum*, a word.]
Adverbial, ad-vėrb'i-al, a. *Pertaining to an adverb.*
Adverbially, ad-vėrb'i-al-li, adv. *In the manner of an adverb.*
Adversary, ad'vėr-sa-ri, n. *One who turns against; one who fronts another; an antagonist; in Scrip. by way of eminence, Satan, the great enemy of mankind.* [L. *adversarius—verto*, to turn.]
Adversative, ad-vėrs'at-iv, a. *Noting or causing opposition.—n. A word denoting opposition.*
Adverse, ad'vėrs, a. *Turned against; fronting; hostile; unprosperous.* [L. *adversus—verto*, to turn.]
Adversely, ad-vėrs'li, adv. *In an adverse manner.*
Adverseness, ad-vėrs'nes, n. *State of being adverse; unprosperousness.*
Adversity, ad-vėrs'i-ti, n. *That which is turned against, or opposes success, desire, or happiness; calamity; distress.* [L. *adversitas.*]
Advert, ad-vėrt', vi. *To turn to; to regard; to attend; to refer. (With to.)* [L. *adverto—verto*, to turn.]
Advertence, ad-vėrt'ens, n. *A turning of the mind to; consideration; heedfulness.*
Advertent, ad-vėrt'ent, a. *Turning the mind to; attentive; heedful.*
Advertise, ad-vėr-tīs', vt. *To turn the attention of others to; to inform; to announce; to publish a notice of. ppr. advertising, pret. & pp. advertised.* [Fr. *avertir, avertissant*—L. *verto*, to turn.]
Advertisement, ad-vėr'tiz-ment, n. *Act of advertising; information; intelligence; public notice.*
Advertiser, ad-vėr-tīs'ėr, n. *One who advertises.*
Advertising, ad-vėr-tīs'ing, p.a. *Containing or furnishing advertisements.*

Advice, ad-vīs', n. *A giving one's views to; opinion offered; counsel; reflection; intelligence; consultation.* [O. Fr. *advis*—L. *viso*, to view attentively.]
Advisable, ad-vīz'a-bl, a. *Proper to be advised or done; prudent; fit.*
Advisableness, ad-vīz'a-bl-nes, n. *Quality of being advisable.*
Advisably, ad-vīz'a-bli, adv. *With advice.*
Advise, ad-vīz', vt. *To impart one's views to; to counsel; to warn; to inform.—vi. To deliberate or consider. ppr. advising, pret. & pp. advised.* [Fr. *aviser*—L. *viso*, to view.]
Advised, ad-vīzd', p.a. *Cautious; done with advice.*
Advisedly, ad-vīz'ed-li, adv. *With deliberation or advice.*
Advisedness, ad-vīz'ed-nes, n. *Deliberate consideration.*
Adviser, ad-vīz'ėr, n. *One who advises.*
Advising, ad-vīs'ing, p.n. *Counsel; advice.*
Advocacy, ad'vō-ka-si, n. *Act of pleading for; defence; vindication.*
Advocate, ad'vō-kāt, n. *One called upon to give advice or aid; one who pleads; an intercessor.—vt. To plead in favour of, to vindicate. ppr. advocating, pret. & pp. advocated.* [L. *advocatus—voco*, to call.]
Advocateship, ad'vō-kāt-ship, n. *The office or duty of an advocate.*
Advocation, ad-vō-kā'shon, n. *The act of pleading; plea; apology.*
Advowson, ad-vou'zn, n. *Right of perpetual presentation to a benefice.* [O. Fr. *advoeson*—L. *advocatio*, a calling to.]
Adze, adz, n. *A kind of axe.* [Sax. *adese.*]
Ædile, ē'dīl, n. *See* **Edile**.
Ægis, ē'jis, n. *A shield.* [L.]
Æneid, ē-nē'id, n. *See* **Eneid**.
Aerate, ā'ėr-āt, vt. *To put air into; to combine with carbonic acid; to saturate, as a liquid with air. ppr. aerating, pret. & pp. aerated.* [from L. *aer*, air.]
Aeration, ā-ėr-ā'shon, n. *The impregnation of a liquid with carbonic acid gas.*
Aerial, ā-ē'ri-al, a. *Belonging to the air; produced by air; inhabiting the air; high; lofty.* [L. *aerius*, from *aer*, air.]
Aerie, ē'rē, n. *The nest, containing the eggs, of a bird of prey; a brood of such birds; an eyry.* [Sax. *æg*, an egg.]
Aeriform, ā'ėr-i-form, a. *Having the form or nature of air.* [L. *aer*, and *forma*, form.]
Aerify, ā'ėr-i-fī, vt. *To infuse air into. ppr. aerifying, pret. & pp. aerified.* [L. *aer*, and *facio*, to make.]
Aerolite, ā'ėr-ō-līt, n. *A stone falling from the air; a meteoric stone.* [Gr. *aėr*, and *lithos*, a stone.]
Aerology, ā-ėr-ol'o-ji, n. *A treatise on the air.* [Gr. *aėr*, and *logos*, a discourse.]
Aerometer, ā-ėr-om'et-ėr, n. *An airmeasurer.* [Gr. *aėr*, and *metron*, measure.]
Aeronaut, ā'ėr-ō-nat, n. *One who sails or floats in the air.* [Gr. *aėr*, and *nautēs*, a sailor.]
Aeronautic, ā'ėr-ō-nat"ik, a. *Pertaining to aerial sailing.*
Aeronautics, ā'ėr-ō-nat"iks, n. *The science or art of sailing in the air.*
Aerostatic, ā'ėr-ō-stat"ik, a. *Pertaining to aerostatics.* [Gr. *aėr*, and *statos*, standing.]
Aerostatics, ā'ėr-ō-stat"iks, n. *The science which treats of air in a state of rest.*

Fāte, fär, fat, fall; mē, met, hėr; pīne, pin; nōte, not, mōve; tūbe, tub, bull; oil, pound.

Æsthetic, Æsthetical, ĕs-thet'ĭk, ĕs-thet'ĭk-al, *a*. Pertaining to æsthetics. [Gr. *aisthetikos*, perceptive.]
Æsthetics, ĕs-thet'ĭks, *n*. The science of *perceptions*; the philosophy of taste; the science of the beautiful in nature and art.
Afar, a-fär', *adv*. At, to, or from a great distance.
Afeard†, a-fērd', *a*. Frighted; terrified.
Affability, af-fa-bil'i-ti, *n*. Courteousness; civility; urbanity.
Affable, af'fa-bl, *a*. Easy *to be spoken to;* courteous; accessible. [L. *affabilis* — *for, fari,* to speak.]
Affably, af'fa-bli, *adv*. In an *affable manner.*
Affair, af-fār', *n*. That which is *to do,* or which is *done;* business; rencounter; in pl. transactions in general; public concerns. [Fr. *affaire* — L. *facio,* to do.]
Affect, af-fekt', *vt*. To *act upon;* to move the feelings of; to aim at; to pretend to; to be fond of. [L. *afficio, affectum* — *facio,* to do.]
Affectation, af-fek-tā'shon, *n*. False pretence; an elaborate appearance; self-sufficiency. [L. *affectatio.*]
Affected, af-fekt'ed, *p.a*. Inclined to; full of affectation; assumed artificially, not naturally.
Affectedly, af-fekt'ed-li, *adv*. In an *affected manner;* feignedly.
Affectedness, af-fekt'ed-nes, *n*. Quality *of being affected.*
Affecting, af-fekt'ing, *p.a*. Pathetic; tender; exciting; moving the sensibility.
Affectingly, af-fekt'ing-li, *adv*. In an *affecting manner.*
Affection, af-fek'shon, *n*. The state of *being affected;* fondness; love; propensity; affectation†.
Affectionate, af-fek'shon-āt, *a*. Full of *affection;* tender; loving; fond. [Fr. *affectionné.*]
Affectionately, af-fek'shon-āt-li, *adv*. With *affection;* fondly.
Affectioned, af-fek'shond, *p.a*. Inclined.
Affeer†, af-fēr', *vt*. To confirm; to give a sanction to.
Affiance, af-fī'ans, *n*. Faith pledged to; reliance (used chiefly in reference to God).—*vt*. To pledge one's *faith to;* to promise marriage to; to trust. *ppr.* affiancing, *pret. & pp.* affianced. [Norm. *affiaunce*; L. *fides,* faith.]
Affianced, af-fī'anst, *p.a*. Pledged as to *one's faith;* betrothed.
Affidavit, af-fi-dā'vit, *n*. A declaration upon oath. (Law L. *affidavit,* he pledged his faith.]
Affiliate, af-fil'li-āt, *vt*. To assign by law a *child,* as a bastard, to its father. *ppr.* affiliating, *pret.* and *pp.* affiliated. [Fr. *affilier*—L. *filius,* a son.]
Affiliated, af-fil'li-āt-ed, *p.a*. Associated; auxiliary.
Affiliation, af-fil'li-ā'shon, *n*. The legal assignment of a *child,* as illegitimate, to its father.
Affined, af-find', *a*. Joined in affinity. [Old Fr. *affiner,* to join—L. *finis,* a boundary.]
Affinity, af-fin'i-ti, *n*. Relation constituted by marriage; resemblance; chemical attraction. [L. *affinitas—finis,* a boundary.]
Affirm, af-ferm', *vt*. To confirm; to assure; to declare; to ratify.—*vi*. To declare solemnly. [L. *affirmo—firmus,* strong.]
Affirmable, af-ferm'a-bl, *a*. That may *be affirmed.*
Affirmation, af-ferm-ā'shon, *n*. Act of *affirming;* declaration; ratification. [L. *affirmatio.*]
Affirmative, af-ferm'at-iv, *a*. That *affirms;* positive.—*n*. That which *contains an affirmation.* [Fr. *affirmatif.*]
Affirmatively, af-ferm'at-iv-li, *adv*. In *an affirmative manner.*
Affix, af-fiks', *vt*. To *fasten to;* to add at the close; to subjoin. [L. *affigo, affixum—figo,* to fix.]
Affix, af'fiks, *n*. A syllable or letter *added to* the end of a word.
Afflatus, af-flā'tus, *n*. A *breathing on;* divine inspiration. [L. *flo,* to breathe, *flatus,* a breathing.]
Afflict, af-flikt', *vt*. To *dash against;* to distress; to grieve; to harass (in the passive with *at* or *by*). [L. *affflicto—figo,* to strike.]
Afflicted, af-flikt'ed, *p.a*. Suffering grief or distress of any kind.
Afflicting, af-flikt'ing, *p.a*. Grievous; distressing.
Affliction, af-flik'shon, *n*. State *of being afflicted;* distress; grief; pain; trouble; adversity. [L. *afflictio.*]
Afflictive, af-flikt'iv, *a*. Containing *affliction;* painful; calamitous. [Fr. *afflictif.*]
Affluence, af'flū-ens, *n*. A *flowing to;* abundance; opulence. [Fr.—L. *affluentia—fluo,* to flow.]
Affluent, af'flū-ent, *a*. Flowing *to;* abounding in goods or riches; abundant.—*n*. A river that flows into another river. [L. *affluens.*]
Afflux, af'fluks, *n*. A *flowing to;* that which flows to. [L. *affluxum—fluo,* to flow.]
Afford, af-fōrd', *vt*. To *bring to market*†; to supply; to grant; to be able to give, grant, buy, or expend. [O. Fr. *affeurer* — L. *forum,* a market-place.]
Affray, af-frā', *n*. An encounter; a tumult. [Fr. *effrayer,* to scare.]
Affright, af-frīt', *vt*. To *frighten;* to terrify; to alarm.—*n*. Sudden and great fear; terror.
Affront, af-frunt', *vt*. To meet *face to facet;* to *insult to the face;* to offend by disrespect.—*n*. Open defiance; outrage, whether by word or by deed. [Fr. *affronter*—L. *frons,* front, face.]
Affronting, af-frunt'ing, *p.a*. Contumelious; abusive; insulting.
Affusion, af-fū'shon, *n*. The act *of pouring upon,* or sprinkling with a liquid substance. [Fr.—L. *fundo,* to pour.]
Affy†, af-fī', *vt*. To betroth in order to marriage.
Afield, a-fēld', *adv*. To or in the *field.*
Afloat, a-flōt', *adv.* or *a*. Floating; passing from place to place.
Afoot, a-fut', *adv*. In motion; in action.
Aforehand, a-fōr'hand, *adv*. Beforehand; before.
Aforementioned, a-fōr'men-shond, *a*. Mentioned *before.*
Aforesaid, a-fōr'sād, *a*. Said or recited *before.*
Aforetime, a-fōr'tīm, *adv*. In *time past;* in a former time.
Afraid, a-frād', *a*. Struck *with fear;* fearful. [the *pp.* of *affray.*]
Afresh, a-fresh', *adv*. Anew; again.
African, af'rik-an, *a*. Belonging to *Africa.*—*n*. A native of *Africa.*
Aft, aft, *a.* or *adv*. Hind; back; abaft; astern. [Sax. *æft.*]
After, aft'er, *a*. More *aft;* later in time; future.—*prep.* Following in place; later in time; according to; about; in imitation of.—*adv.* Posterior; later in time. [compar. of *aft.*]
After-ages, aft'er-āj-es, *n. pl*. Later ages; succeeding times; posterity.
After-all, aft-er-al', *adv*. When all has been weighed, said, or done.
Aftermost, aft'er-mōst, *a. superl.* Most *aft,* or most towards the hind part; hindmost.
Afternoon, aft'er-nōn, *n*. The part of the day which *follows noon.*
After-piece, aft'er-pēs, *n*. A piece performed after a play; a farce.
After-thought, aft'er-that, *n*. Reflection after an act; later thought or expedient.
Afterward, Afterwards, aft'er-wērd, aft'er-wērds, *adv*. In *later* or subsequent *time.* [Sax. *after* and *weard.*]
Again, a-gen', *adv*. Moreover; a second time; once more; in return. [Sax. *on,* and *gen,* besides.]
Against, a-genst', *prep*. In *opposition to;* contrary to; bearing upon; in expectation of. [Sax. *togeanes.*]
Agape, a-gāp', *a*. Gaping; having the mouth wide open.
Agate, ag'āt, *n*. A precious stone, so called from a river in Sicily, where it was first found. [Fr.]
Agazed†, a-gāzd', *p.a.* Struck *with amazement.*
Age, āj, *n*. The *whole duration* of a being; a generation of men; a hundred years; number of years during which a person has lived; decline of life; a certain part of human life; maturity; a particular period of time as distinguished from others; the period marked by law for certain functions of civil life. [Fr. *âge.*]
Aged, āj'ed, *a*. Old; having lived or existed long; having a certain age.
Agency, ā'jen-si, *n*. State *of being in action;* instrumentality; management; office or business of an agent. [Fr. *agence*—L. *ago,* to act.]
Agent, ā'jent, *n*. One *who acts;* a deputy; an active cause or power. [Fr.]
Agglomerate, ag-glom'me-rāt, *vt*. To *roll up into a ball* or mass.—*vi*. To gather *into a ball* or mass. *ppr.* agglomerating, *pret. & pp.* agglomerated. [Lat. *agglomero, agglomeratus — glomus, glomeris,* a ball of yarn.]
Agglomeration, ag-glom'me-rā'shon, *n*. Act *of winding into a ball;* state of being gathered into a ball.
Agglutinant, ag-glū'tin-ant, *a*. Uniting, as *glue;* causing adhesion.
Agglutinate, ag-glū'tin-āt, *vt*. To glue *to;* to cause to adhere. *ppr.* agglutinating, *pret. & pp.* agglutinated. [L. *agglutino, agglutinatus — gluten,* glue.]
Agglutination, ag-glū'tin-ā'shon, *n*. Act *of agglutinating;* state of being agglutinated.
Agglutinative, ag-glū'tin-āt-iv, *a*. That tends to unite.
Aggrandize, ag'gran-dīz, *vt*. To make *great;* to make greater in power or rank; to magnify. *ppr.* aggrandising, *pret. & pp.* aggrandized. [Fr. *agrandir, agrandissant*—L. *grandis,* great.]
Aggrandizement, ag'gran-dīz-ment, *n*. Act *of aggrandising;* augmentation. [Fr. *agrandissement.*]
Aggravate, ag'gra-vāt, *vt*. To add to the *weight of;* to heighten; to exasperate. *ppr.* aggravating, *pret. & pp.* aggravated. [L. *aggravo, aggravatus—gravis,* heavy.]
Aggravating, ag'gra-vāt-ing, *p.a*. Making worse; heightening.
Aggravation, ag-gra-vā'shon, *n*. Act *of aggravating;* state of being aggravated; provocation.
Aggregate, ag'gre-gāt, *vt*. To *bring together,* as a *herd;* to heap up. *ppr.* aggregating, *pret. & pp.* aggregated.— *a*. Formed of parts *collected into a mass*

ch, *chain*; j, *job*; g, *go*; ng, *sing*; ᴛʜ, *then*; th, *thin*; w, *wig*; ᴡʜ, *whig*; zh, *azure*; † obsolete.

or sum.—n. A sum, mass, or assemblage of particulars. [L. *aggrego, aggregatus—grex, gregis,* a herd.]
Aggregately, ag-grē-gāt-li, *adv.* Collectively.
Aggregation, ag-grē-gā'shon, *n. Act of aggregating;* state of being aggregated; an aggregate.
Aggression, ag-gre'shon, *n.* The first act of hostility; attack; encroachment; injury. [L. *aggressio—gradior, gressus,* to step, to go.]
Aggressive, ag-gres'iv, *a. Taking the first step against;* making an invasion; prone to encroachment.
Aggressiveness, ag-gres'iv-nes, *n. Quality of being aggressive.*
Aggressor, ag-gres'or, *n.* The person who commences hostilities.
Aggrieve, ag-grēv', *vt.* To bear heavily upon; to pain, oppress, or injure. *ppr.* aggrieving, *pret. & pp.* aggrieved. [O. Fr. *agrever;* L. *gravis,* heavy.]
Aggrieved, ag-grēvd', *p.a.* Pained; oppressed.
Aghast, a-gast', *a.* or *adv. Deprived of breath;* caused to hold the *breath;* paralyzed with sudden fright. [Sax. *a,* priv. and *gast,* breath.]
Agile, aj'il, *a. Ready to act;* nimble. [Fr.—L. *ago,* to act.]
Agility, a-jil'i-ti, *n.* Power of moving quickly; nimbleness; activity; briskness. [Fr. *agilité.*]
Agio, ā'ji-ō, *n.* The difference between the value of bank-notes and the current money. [It. *aggio.*]
Agitate, aj'it-āt, *vt.* To put in violent motion; to shake briskly; to distract; to excite; to consider on all sides; to revolve in the mind. *ppr.* agitating, *pret. & pp.* agitated. [L. *agito, agitatum—ago,* to act.]
Agitated, aj'it-āt-ed, *p.a.* Disturbed; discussed.
Agitation, aj-it-ā'shon, *n.* Excitement; emotion; discussion.
Agitator, aj'it-āt-or, *n.* One who excites discontent, sedition, or revolt.
Aglet†, ag'let, *n. A point* or *tag* at the ends of fringes or of lace. [Fr. *aiguillette.*]
Agnate, ag'nāt, *a.* Connected with by birth; related by the father's side. [L. *agnatus—nascor,* to be born.]
Ago, a-gō', *adv.* or *a. Passed by;* past; gone away; in time past. [Sax. *agongen,* passed, from *gan,* to go.]
Agog, a-gog', *adv. In a state of desire;* highly excited by eagerness after an object. [Fr. *à gogo.*]
Agoing, a-gō'ing, *adv.* In the act of going; in motion.
Agonize, ag'ō-nīz, *vi.* To strive for a prize; to struggle; to writhe with extreme pain.—*vt.* To distress with extreme pain; to torture. *ppr.* agonizing, *pret. & pp.* agonized. [Gr. *agōnizomai—agōn,* a struggle.]
Agonizing, ag'ō-nīz-ing, *p.a.* Giving extreme pain.
Agonizingly, ag'ō-nīz-ing-li, *adv.* With extreme anguish.
Agony, ag'ō-ni, *n. Contest;* extreme pain of body or mind, so as to cause writhing; anguish; throe; the pangs of death (in this sense generally in the plural). [Gr. *agōnia.*]
Agrarian, a-grā'ri-an, *a. Relating to fields;* pertaining to an equal division of lands. [L. *agrarius—ager,* a field.]
Agrarianism, a-grā'ri-an-izm, *n.* The principles of those who favour an equal division of lands.
Agree, a-grē', *vi.* To be in concord; to become friends; to correspond; to suit.

ppr. agreeing, *pret. & pp.* agreed. [Fr. *agréer*—L. *gratia,* favour.]
Agreeable, a-grē'a-bl, *a.* Suitable to; pleasing; grateful.
Agreeableness, a-grē'a-bl-nes, *n. Quality of being agreeable;* suitableness; quality of pleasing.
Agreeably, a-grē'a-bli, *adv.* In an agreeable manner; conformably.
Agreement, a-grē'ment, *n.* Harmony; conformity; stipulation.
Agrestic, a-gres'tik, *a. Rural;* rustic. [L. *agrestis—ager,* a field.]
Agricultural, ag-ri-kul'tūr-al, *a. Pertaining to agriculture.*
Agriculture, ag'ri-kul-tūr, *n.* The art or science of *cultivating the ground;* husbandry. [L. *ager,* a field, and *cultura,* culture—*colo,* to till.]
Agriculturist, ag-ri-kul'tūr-ist, *n. One skilled in agriculture.*
Aground, a-ground', *adv.* Stranded; impeded by insuperable obstacles.
Ague, ā'gū, *n.* An intermittent fever, accompanied with cold fits and shivering. [Fr. *aigu,* acute.]
Agued, ā'gūd, *p.a. Having a fit of ague;* shivering with cold or fear.
Aguish, ā'gū-ish, *a. Having the qualities of an ague.*
Ah, ä, *interj.* An exclamation expressive of surprise, pity, complaint, contempt, dislike, joy, exultation, &c.
Aha, ä-hä', *interj.* An exclamation expressing triumph or contempt.
Ahead, a-hed', *adv. With the head foremost;* further on; onward.
Ahold†, a-hōld', *adv.* A sea-term, meaning as near the wind as may be.
Ahoy, a-hoi', *exclam. Hold!* a sea-term used in hailing.
Ahungry†, a-hung'gri, *a. Hungry;* in want of meat.
Aid, ād, *vt.* To *help;* to relieve.—*n. Help;* assistance; a helper. [Fr. *aider*—L. *adjutare—juvo,* to help.]
Aid-de-camp, ād'de-kong, *n.* An officer attendant on a general, to convey his orders. [Fr.]
Aidless, ād'les, *a.* Without aid.
Ail, āl, *vt.* To *pain;* to affect with uneasiness.—*vi.* To be in pain or trouble. [Sax. *elan.*]
Ailing, āl'ing, *p.a.* Indisposed; full of complaints.
Ailment, āl'ment, *n.* Pain; disease.
Aim, ām, *vi.* To determine; to intend; to point with a missive weapon; to attempt to reach; to endeavour after.—*vt.* To level, as a firearm.—*n. That which is aimed at;* direction; purpose; drift. [Old Fr. *esmer;* L. *œstimare,* to appraise.]
Aimless, ām'les, *a. Without aim.*
Air, ār, *n. That which blows;* the fluid which we breathe; a light breeze; publication; a tune; mien; gesture; (pl.) affected manner.—*vt.* To *expose to the air;* to ventilate; to dry. [Fr.; L. *aër.*]
Air-bladder, ār'blad-dėr, *n.* The *bladder* of a fish containing *air.*
Air-built, ār'bilt, *a. Erected in the air;* chimerical.
Air-cushion, ār'kush-on, *n.* A bag of air-tight cloth, expanded by blowing air into it.
Air-drawn†, ār'drän, *a. Drawn* or painted in *air.*
Air-gun, ār'gun, *n.* A *gun* to discharge bullets by means of condensed *air.*
Airily, ār'i-li, *adv. In an airy manner.*
Airiness, ār'i-nes, *n. Exposure to the air;* gaiety; liveliness; openness.
Airing, ār'ing, *n. An exposure to the air* or to a fire; a short excursion in the open air.

Airless, ār'les, *a. Destitute of free* or fresh *air.*
Air-plant, ār'plant, *n. A plant* which derives its nutriment almost entirely from the *atmosphere.*
Air-pump, ār'pump, *n.* A machine for *pumping* the *air* out of a vessel.
Air-shaft, ār'shaft, *n.* A passage for *air* into a mine.
Air-tight, ār'tīt, *a. So tight* or compact as to be impermeable to *air.*
Air-vessel, ār'ves-sel, *n.* A spiral duct, or a vesicle, in plants, containing air.
Airy, ār'i, *a. Open to the free air;* high in air; light; thin; unsubstantial; vain; gay.
Aisle, īl, *n. A wing* or side of a church; a passage in a church. [Old Fr.; L. *ala,* a wing.]
Ajar, a-jär', *adv. On the turn;* partly open, as a door. [Sax. *acerran,* to return.]
Akin, a-kin', *a. Of kin;* related to; partaking of the same properties.
Alabaster, al'a-bas-tėr, *n.* A kind of soft marble from which boxes *without handles,* for holding ointments, were made.—*a. Made of alabaster;* of the colour of alabaster. [L. *alabastrum*—Gr. *a,* priv. and *labē,* a handle.]
Alack, a-lak', *interj.* An exclamation expressive of sorrow. [probably a corruption of *alas.*]
Alacrity, a-lak'ri-ti, *n. Liveliness;* cheerful readiness; promptitude. [L. *alacritas—alacer,* lively.]
Alamode, ä-lä-mōd', *adv. According to the fashion.* [Fr. *à la mode.*]
Alarm, a-lärm', *n. A call to arms;* sudden surprise; fright; a contrivance as a signal of danger, or for rousing from sleep.—*vt.* To *call to arms;* to disturb. [Fr. *alarme;* L. *ad,* and *arma,* arms.]
Alarm-bell, a-lärm'bel, *n. A bell* that gives notice of danger.
Alarm-gun, a-lärm'gun, *n. A gun* fired as a signal of *alarm.*
Alarming, a-lärm'ing, *p.a.* Exciting apprehension; terrifying.
Alarmingly, a-lärm'ing-li, *adv.* So as to excite apprehension.
Alarmist, a-lärm'ist, *n.* One who from timidity is prone to excite *alarm.*
Alarum, a-lär'um, *n.* The same as *alarm,* but now disused except in poetry.
Alas, a-las', *interj.* An exclamation expressive of *weariness,* sorrow, grief, pity, concern, or apprehension of evil. [Fr. *helas!*]
Albeit, al-bē'it, *adv. Be it all;* be it so; admit all that; notwithstanding. [*all, be,* and *it.*]
Albino, al-bī'nō, *n.* A person whose skin and hair are preternaturally *white.* [Sp.; L. *albus,* white.]
Albugineous, al-bū-jin'ē-us, *a.* Resembling the *white of an eye* or of an egg. [L. *albūgo,* the white of the eye.]
Album, al'bum, *n.* Among the Romans, a *white* table; a book, originally *blank,* for the insertion of autographs, portraits in miniature, sketches, short pieces of poetry, prose, &c. [L. from *albus,* white.]
Albumen, al-bū'men, *n. The white of an egg;* a substance of the same kind, largely found in animals and vegetables. [L. from *albus,* white.]
Albuminous, al-bū'min-us, *a. Pertaining to* or having the properties of *albumen.*
Alchemist, al'kem-ist, *n. One who practises alchemy.*
Alchemy, al'ke-mi, *n. The occult art;* a pretended science, aiming at the trans-

Fāte, fär, fat, fall; mē, met, hėr; pīne, pin; nōte, not, mōve; tūbe, tub, bull; oil, pound.

mutation of metals into gold, &c. [It. *alchimia*—Ar. *al*, the, and *kimia*, from *kama*, to hide.]
Alcohol, al'kŏ-hol, n. Anything reduced to impalpable powder!; pure spirit of a highly intoxicating nature, obtained from fermented liquors by distillation. [Ar. *al kohol*, antimony.]
Alcoholic, al-kō-hol'ik, a. *Pertaining to alcohol*
Alcove, al'kōv, n. *A vaulted apartment;* a recess in a chamber or room for holding a bed, &c.; any shady recess. [Sp. *alcoba;* Ar. *qobbah*, a vault.]
Alder, ạl'dẽr, n. A tree generally growing in *moist* land. [Sax. *ælr;* Sw. *al*, water.]
Alderlievest†, ạl'dẽr-lēv'est, a. Most beloved; most dear.
Alderman, ạl'dẽr-man, n. **Aldermen**, pl. A senior: a magistrate or officer of a town corporate in England and Ireland. [Sax. *eald*, old, comp. *alder*, and *man*.]
Aldermanly, ạl'dẽr-man-li, a. *Pertaining to* or like an *alderman.*
Ale, āl, n. *Beverage* made by infusing malt in hot water, fermenting the infusion, and adding hops. [Sax. *eala*.]
Alee, a-lē', adv. *On the lee;* on the side opposite to the wind.
Alembic, a-lem'bik, n. *A chemical vessel* used in distillation. [Ar. *al anbikon*, a chemical vessel.]
Alert, a-lẽrt', a. *Erect;* being on one's guard; quick; prompt. [Fr. *alerte;* It. *erto*, straight.]
Alertness, a-lẽrt'nes, n. Briskness; nimbleness; sprightliness; levity.
Alexandrine, al'legs-an'drin, a. Relating to a verse of twelve syllables.
Algebra, al'je-bra, n. The science of quantity in general; the science of computing by symbols. [Ar. *al geber*.]
Algebraic, **Algebraical**, al-jē-brā'ik, al-jē-brā'ik-al, a. *Pertaining to algebra.*
Algebraically, al'jē-brā'ik-al-li, adv. By *algebraic process.*
Algebraist, al'jē-brā-ist, n. *One versed in the science of algebra.*
Alias, ā'li-as, adv. *Otherwise*. [L. from *alius*, another, other.]
Alibi, al'i-bi, n. *Elsewhere;* the plea of a person who, charged with a crime, alleges that he was *elsewhere* when the crime was committed. [L.]
Alien, āl'yen, a. *Pertaining to another* person, place, or thing; foreign; estranged from.—n. A foreigner; a stranger. [L. *alienus*—*alius*, another.]
Alienable, āl'yen-a-bl, a. *That may be alienated* or transferred to another.
Alienate, āl'yen-āt, vt. To transfer or give away *to another*, as property or right; to estrange. *ppr.* alienating, *pret. & pp.* alienated. [L. *alieno, alien-atum—alius*, other.]
Alienation, āl-yen-ā'shon, n. *Act of alienating;* estrangement. [L. *alienatio*.]
Alight, a-līt', vi. To get down; to dismount; to descend; to settle upon. [Sax. *alihtan*.]
Alike, a-līk', a. *Like;* similar.—adv. In the same manner, form, or degree. [Sax. *gelic*.]
Aliment, al'i-ment, n. *Nourishment;* food. [L. *alimentum—alo*, to nourish.]
Alimental, al-i-ment'al, a. *Nourishing;* nutritious.
Alimentary, al-i-ment'a-ri, a. *Pertaining to aliment* or food; nourishing.
Alimony, al'i-mo-ni, n. Allowance to a woman legally separated from her husband. [L. *alimonia*.]
Aliquot, al'i-kwot, a. An aliquot part of a number or quantity is *some certain*

part. [L.—*alius*, another, and *quot*, how many.]
Alive, a-līv', a. *On or in life;* living; unextinguished; cheerful; susceptible. [*on* and *life*.]
Alkalescent, al-ka-les'ent, a. *Slightly alkaline.*
Alkali, al'ka-li, n. **Alkalies**, pl. The plant *kali;* a substance which, when combined with an acid, produces a neutral salt, as potash, soda, and ammonia. [Ar. *al kali*.]
Alkaline, al'ka-lin, a. *Having the properties of an alkali.*
Alkoran, al'kō-ran, n. *The book* which contains the Mahometan doctrines of faith and practice. [Ar. *al*, the, and *koran*, book.]
All, ạl, a. *Whole;* every part; the whole of; every one.—n. *The whole* number; the whole; the aggregate amount. *adv.* Wholly; entirely. [Sax. *eal*.]
Allah, al'la, n. The Arabic name of the Supreme Being.
Allay, al-lā', vt. *To lay down;* to assuage; to pacify; to soothe; to repress. [Sax. *alecgan*.]
Allayment, al-lā'ment, n. *Act of allaying;* that which allays.
Allegation, al-lē-gā'shon, n. Primarily, *a sending to;* affirmation; a plea; a declaration. [L. *allegatio—lego*, to send.]
Allege, al-lej', vt. *To bring forward;* to adduce; to assert; to plead in excuse. *ppr.* alleging, *pret. & pp.* alleged. [L. *allego—lego*, to send.]
Allegiance, al-lē'ji-ans, n. *The obligation* of a subject to his prince or government; loyalty. [Old Fr.; L. *ligo*, to bind.]
Allegiant, al-lē'ji-ant, a. Loyal.
Allegorical, al-lē-gor'ik-al, a. *Pertaining to* or resembling *an allegory;* figurative.
Allegorically, al-lē-gor'ik-al-li, adv. By *way of allegory.*
Allegorist, al'lē-gō-rist, n. *One who uses allegory*, or allegorizes.
Allegorize, al'lē-gō-rīz, vi. *To turn into allegory.—vi.* To use allegory. *ppr.* allegorising, *pret. & pp.* allegorised.
Allegory, al'lē-gō-ri, n. *A speech or discourse* which conveys a meaning *different* from the literal one. [Gr. *allēgoria—allos*, other, and *agora*, oration.]
Allegro, al-lē'grō. A word denoting a brisk sprightly movement. [It.; Fr. *leger*, light.]
Alleluiah, Allelujah, al-lē-lū'ya, al-lē-lū'ya, n. *Praise ye Jehovah;* a word used to express pious joy. [Heb.]
Alleviate, al-lē'vi-āt, vt. *To make light* or *lighter;* to assuage; to mitigate. *ppr.* alleviating, *pret. & pp.* alleviated. [Low L. *allevio, alleviatus*—L. *levis*, light.]
Alleviating, al-lē'vi-āt-ing, p.a. *Making lighter;* mitigating.
Alleviation, al-lē-vi-ā'shon, n. *That which alleviates;* a lessening or mitigation.
Alley, al'lē, n. *A walk* in a garden; a passage or *way* in a city narrower than a street. [Fr. *allée—aller*, to go.]
All-fools'-Day, ạl'fōlz-dā, n. The first of April.
All-hail, ạl-hāl', *interj. All health;* a phrase of salutation. [*all*, and Sax. *hæl*, health.]
All-Hallow, All-Hallows, ạl-hal'lō, ạl-hal'lōz, n. *All-Saints'* Day.
All-Hallowmas or -tide, ạl-hal'lō-mas, -tid, n. The time near *All-Saints.*
Alliance, al-lī'ans, n. *State of being allied;* affinity; confederacy; league. [Fr.; L. *ligo*, to bind.]

Allied, al-līd', p.a. United by treaty.
Allies, al-līz', n. pl. Princes or states which have entered into *league* for their mutual defence; confederates.
Alligation, al-li-gā'shon, n. *Act of tying together;* a rule of arithmetic.
Alligator, al'li-gā-tor, n. *The lizard;* the American crocodile. [Sp. *lagarto;* L. *lacerta*, a lizard.]
Alliteration, al-lit-ẽr-ā'shon, n. The repetition of the same *letter* at the beginning of two or more words in close succession. [L. *litera*, a letter.]
Alliterative, al-lit'ẽr-āt-iv, a. *Pertaining to alliteration.*
Allocate, al'lō-kāt, vt. *To place near;* to distribute; to assign to each his share. *ppr.* allocating, *pret. & pp.* allocated. [L. *ad*, and *loco, locatus*, to place.]
Allocation, al-lō-kā'shon, n. Distribution; assignment.
Allocution, al-lō-kū'shon, n. *An address;* a formal address (especially of the Pope). [L. *allocutio—loquor*, to speak.]
Allodial, al-lō'di-al, a. Held independent of a lord paramount.
Allodium, al-lō'di-um, n. Every man's own land; freehold estate. [Low L.]
Allopathic, al-lō-path'ik, a. *Pertaining to allopathy.*
Allopathy, al-lop'a-thi, n. A mode of curing diseases, by using medicines which produce in the system a condition *contrary* to that of the *disease.* [Gr. *allos*, another, and *pathos*, affection.]
Allot, al-lot', vt. To give *or* distribute *by lot;* to apportion. *ppr.* allotting, *pret. & pp.* allotted. [Fr. *allotir*.]
Allotment, al-lot'ment, n. *Act of allotting;* a share assigned by lot.
Allow, al-lou', vt. To give *place* or leave *to;* to admit; to abate; to bestow, as compensation. [Fr. *allouer;* L. *ad*, and *loco*, to place.]
Allowable, al-lou'a-bl, a. *That may be allowed.*
Allowableness, al-lou'a-bl-nes, n. *Quality of being allowable.*
Allowably, al-lou'a-bli, adv. *In an allowable manner.*
Allowance, al-lou'ans, n. *Act of allowing;* that which is allowed; a stated sum or quantity; permission; abatement.
Alloy, al-loi', vt. *To unite*, as gold or silver with baser metals; to mix, as one metal with another; to reduce or abate by mixture.—n. A baser metal mixed with a finer; a metallic compound; evil mixed with good. [Fr. *allier*—L. *ligo*, to bind.]
All-saints' Day, ạl'sānts-dā, n. The first of November.
All-souls' Day, ạl'sōlz-dā, n. The second of November.
Allude, al-lūd', vi. *To hint playfully;* to refer; to make some reference. *ppr.* alluding, *pret. & pp.* alluded. [L. *alludo—ludo*, to play.]
Allure, al-lūr', vt. To draw to, *by some lure;* to lure; to entice; to decoy. *ppr.* alluring, *pret. & pp.* allured. [Fr. *leurrer*, from *leurre*, a lure.]
Allurement, al-lūr'ment, n. *That which allures;* temptation; enticement.
Alluring, al-lūr'ing, p.a. Inviting; attractive.
Alluringly, al-lūr'ing-li, adv. In an alluring manner.
Allusion, al-lū'zhon, n. *A playing with;* a hint; a reference to something previously known. [Fr.; L. *ludo*, to play.]
Allusive, al-lū'siv, a. *Containing allusion.*
Alluvial, al-lū'vi-al, a. *Pertaining to*

ch, chain; j, job; g, go; ng, sing; ᴛʜ, then; th, thin; w, wig; wh, whig; sh, azure; † obsolete.

alluvium; formed by or deposited from water.
Alluvion, al-lū'vi-on, *n*. The gradual washing of earth and other substances to a shore; that which is thus washed. [L. *alluvio*.]
Alluvium, al-lū'vi-um, *n*. **Alluvia**, *pl*. That which is added by the *wash* or flow of water; deposit of matter brought from a higher to a lower level, by water. [Low L. from L. *alluo*—*luo*, to wash.]
Ally, al-lī', *vt*. To *bind to*; to unite by affinity, friendship, or treaty. *ppr.* allying, *pret. & pp.* allied.—*n*. One related by marriage or other tie; an associate; a prince or state united by treaty. [Fr. *allier*—L. *ligo*, to bind.]
Almanac, al'ma-nak, *n*. The *calendar*; a book containing *a calendar of days*, weeks, and months, &c. [Ar. *al*, and *manack*, a calendar.]
Almightiness, al-mī'ti-nes, *n*. *Omnipotence*; an attribute of God only.
Almighty, al-mī'ti, *a*. *Possessing all power*; omnipotent.—*n*. The *omnipotent* God.
Almond, ä'mund, *n*. The nut of the almond-tree, either sweet or bitter. [Fr. *amande*; L. *amygdalus*.]
Almond-oil, ä'mund-oil, *n*. A bland fixed *oil*, obtained from *almonds*.
Almonds, ä'munds, *n.pl*. The tonsils of the throat.
Almond-tree, ä'mund-trē, *n*. A fruittree which produces the *almond*.
Almoner, al'mon-ėr, *n*. [Fr. *aumonier*.] An officer, whose duty is to distribute *alms*.
Almonry, al'mon-ri, *n*. The place where *alms* are distributed.
Almost, al'most, *adv*. Nearly; well nigh; for the greatest part.
Alms, ämz, *n. pl*. Primarily, *pity*; a charitable gift. [Sax. *almes*; Gr. *eleëmosinē*, pity.]
Alms-deed, ämz'dēd, *n*. An act of charity; a charitable gift.
Alms-house, ämz'hous, *n*. A house where poor persons are lodged and supported.
Alms-man, ämz'man, *n*. A person supported by alms.
Aloe, al'ō, *n*. A succulent plant, with broad prickly leaves, which yields a very bitter medicinal gum, called by the same name. [L. *aloē*.]
Aloetic, al-ō-et'ik, *a*. *Pertaining to* or partaking of the qualities of aloes.
Aloft, a-loft', *adv*. In the sky; on high; high above the ground. [Sax. *lyft*, the air.]
Alone, a-lōn', *a*. *All-one*; solitary.—*adv*. By himself; by itself. [*all* and *one*.]
Along, a-long', *adv*. *Lengthwise*; in a line with the length; throughout; forward.—*prep*. By the side of; near to. [Sax. *and-lang*.]
Aloof, a-lōf', *adv*. *All-off*; at a distance; separate; apart.
Aloud, a-loud', *adv*. *On loud*; loudly; with a loud voice.
Alp, alp, *n*. **Alps**, alps, *pl*. A high mountain. [Celt. *alp*, a height.]
Alpaca, al-pak'a, *n*. The Peruvian sheep, a native of the Andes, having long, soft, and woolly hair; cloth made of its hair.
Alpha, al'fa, *n*. The first letter in the Greek alphabet; the first or beginning.
Alphabet, al'fa-bet, *n*. The letters of a language arranged in the customary order. [Gr. *alpha* and *beta*, the first and second letters of the Gr. alphabet.]
Alphabetical, al-fa-bet'ik-al, *a*. *Relating to an alphabet; in the order of an alphabet*.
Alphabetically, al-fa-bet'ik-al-li, *adv*. In an *alphabetical* manner or order.
Alpine, al'pin, *a*. *Relating to the Alps* or high mountains; mountainous; growing on high mountains. [L. *alpinus*.]
Already, al-red'i, *adv*. *All-ready*; now; at this time; early; at some time past.
Also, al'sō, *adv*. *All-so*; likewise; in like or the same manner. [Sax. *eal* and *swa*.]
Altar, al'tėr, *n*. *A place raised up*; an elevated place, on which sacrifices were offered; the communion table; a church. [L. *altare—altus*, high.]
Altar-cloth, al'tėr-kloth, *n*. A *cloth* to lay upon an *altar* in churches.
Altar-piece, al'tėr-pēs, *n*. A painting placed over the altar in a church.
Alter, al'tėr, *vt*. *To make other*; to make some change in; to vary.—*vi*. To vary. [Fr. *altérer*—L. *alter*, other.]
Alterable, al'tėr-a-bl, *a*. *That may alter, or be altered*.
Alteration, al-tėr-ā'shon, *n*. Partial change or variation. [L. *alteratio*.]
Alterative, al'tėr-at-iv, *a*. *Causing alteration*.—*n*. A medicine which gradually induces a salutary *change* in the constitution.
Altercate, al'tėr-kāt, *vi*. *To say different*; to dispute; to wrangle. *ppr.* altercating, *pret. & pp.* altercated. [L. *altercor, altercatus—alter*, other.]
Altercation, al-tėr-kā'shon, *n*. Debate; contention; dispute. [L. *altercatio*.]
Alternate, al-tėrn'āt, *a*. *Being by turns*; interchangeable.—*vt*. *To cause to follow by turns*; to interchange.—*vi*. *To happen or act by turns*; to follow reciprocally. *ppr.* alternating, *pret. & pp.* alternated. [L. *alternatus—alter*, other.]
Alternately, al-tėrn'āt-li, *adv*. *By turns*; in reciprocal succession.
Alternation, al-tėrn-ā'shon, *n*. Reciprocal succession; interchange.
Alternative, al-tėrn'at-iv, *n*. A choice given of two things, so that if one is taken the other must be rejected. [Fr. *alternatif*.]
Alternatively, al-tėrn'at-iv-li, *adv*. In the manner of alternatives.
Although, al-THŌ', *conj*. *All-though*: all be it; be it so; allow all; notwithstanding; however. [*all* and *though*.]
Altitude, al'ti-tūd, *n*. *Height*: highest point; eminence; high degree. [L. *altitudo—altus*, high.]
Altogether, al-tō-geTH'ėr, *adv*. *Allgathered*; wholly; entirely; completely; without exception. [Sax. *eal-geador*.]
Alto-rilievo, al'tō-rē-lē'vō, *n*. *High relief*; a term in sculpture. [It. *alto*, high, *rilievo*, prominence.]
Alum, al'um, *n*. A mineral *salt*, of great use in medicine and the arts. [L. *alūmen*; Gr. *hals, halos*, salt.]
Alumina, al-ū'min-a, *n*. The base of *alum*; the characteristic ingredient of common clay. [from L. *alumen*, alum.]
Aluminous, al-ū'min-us, *a*. *Pertaining to or containing alumina*; clayey.
Alumish, al'um-ish, *a*. *Having the nature of alum*.
Alumnus, a-lum'nus, *n*. *A nursling*; a graduate of a university. [L. from *alo*, to nourish.]
Alvine, al'vin, *a*. *Belonging to the lower belly*. [from *alvus*, the belly.]
Always, al'wāz, *adv*. In all ways or goings; at all times; continually. [Sax. *ealle-waega*.]
Am, am. The first person singular, present tense, indicative mood, of the verb *to be*. [Sax. *eom*.]

Amain, a-mān', *adv*. *With strength*; vigorously; violently. [Sax. *a*, and *maegn*, strength.]
Amalgam, a-mal'gam, *n*. A pasty compound; a compound of quicksilver with another metal; a compound of different things. [Gr. *malagma—malasso*, to soften.]
Amalgamate, a-mal'gam-āt, *vt*. To mix, as quicksilver with another metal; to mix.—*vi*. To unite in an amalgam; to blend. *ppr.* amalgamating, *pret. & pp.* amalgamated.
Amalgamation, a-mal'gam-ā'shon, *n*. *The act or operation of amalgamating*.
Amanuensis, a-man'ū-en"sis, *n*. *One whose hand only is used in writing*; one who writes what another dictates, or copies what another writes. [L. *a manibus esse*, to be by the hand.]
Amaranth, am'a-ranth, *n*. *The unfading flower*; a colour inclining to purple. [Gr. *amarantos*, unfading—*a*, priv. and *maraino*, to die away.]
Amaranthine, am-a-ran'thin, *a*. *Belonging to amaranth*; unfading.
Amaryllis, am-a-ril'lis, *n*. Lily-asphodel, a genus of beautiful plants. [L.]
Amass, a-mas', *vt*. *To form into a mass*; to accumulate; to heap up. [Fr. *amasser*—L. *massa*, a mass.]
Amateur, am-a-tūr', *n*. *A lover of any art or science*, as distinguished from a professor. [Fr.—L. *amo*, to love.]
Amatory, am'a-tō-ri, *a*. *Relating to love*; causing love; amorous. [L. *amatorius*.]
Amaze, a-māz', *vt*. To put *into a maze*; to astonish; to bewilder. *ppr.* amazing, *pret. & pp.* amazed. [from *maze*.]
Amazedly, a-māz'ed-li, *adv*. *With amazement*.
Amazedness, a-māz'ed-nes, *n*. *State of being amazed*; astonishment.
Amazement, a-māz'ment, *n*. *State of being amazed*; perplexity.
Amazing, a-māz'ing, *p.a*. Very wonderful; exciting astonishment.
Amazingly, a-māz'ing-li, *adv*. In an astonishing degree.
Amazon, am'a-zon, *n*. One of a race of female warriors, who *cut off the right breast* to enable them to use their weapons better; a masculine woman; a virago. [Gr. *a*, priv. and *mazos*, a breast.]
Amazonian, am-a-zō'ni-an, *a*. *Relating to the Amazons*; warlike; bold.
Ambassade, am'bas-sād, *n*. Embassy.
Ambassador, am-bas'sa-dor, *n*. A representative of a sovereign power at the court of another. [Fr. *ambassadeur*; Sans. *ambyht*, a message.]
Ambassadress, am-bas'sa-dres, *n*. *The wife of an ambassador*.
Amber, am'bėr, *n*. A yellow substance, highly electric, and when pounded or heated, of a *fragrant* odour.—*a*. Consisting of amber. [Fr. *ambre*—Ar. *ambar*, perfume.]
Ambergris, am'bėr-grēs, *n*. *Gray amber*; a fragrant, solid, opaque, ash-coloured, inflammable substance. [Fr. *ambre*, and *gris*, gray.]
Ambidexter, am-bi-deks'tėr, *n*. One whose *hands are both right*; one ready to act on either side in party disputes. [L. *ambo*, both, and *dexter*, the right hand.]
Ambidextrous, am-bi-deks'trus, *a*. *Using both hands alike*.
Ambient, am'bi-ent, *a*. *Going round about; surrounding*. [L. *ambiens—ambi*, round about, and *eo*, to go.]
Ambiguity, am-bi-gū'i-ti, *n*. *A driving round about*; doubtfulness of signification. [L. *ambiguitas—ago*, to drive.]

Fāte, fär, fat, fall; mē, met, hėr; pīne, pin; nōte, not, mōve; tūbe, tub, bull; oil, pound.

Ambiguous, am-big'ū-us, *a. Driving about;* having two or more uncertain significations; doubtful. [L. *ambiguus* —*ago,* to drive.]
Ambiguously, am-big'ū-us-li, *adv. In an ambiguous manner.*
Ambition, am-bi'shon, *n.* Primarily, a *going round;* an inordinate desire of power or eminence. [L. *ambitio,* from *ambio,* to go about—*eo,* to go.]
Ambitious, am-bi'shus, *a. Full of ambition;* aspiring. [L. *ambitiosus.*]
Ambitiously, am-bi'shus-li, *adv. In an ambitious manner.*
Amble, am'bl, *vi. To pace;* to go between a walk and a trot; to walk daintily†. *ppr.* ambling, *pret. & pp.* ambled.—*n.* A pace of a horse between a walk and a trot. [Fr. *ambler*—L. *ambulo,* to walk.]
Ambler, am'bl-ėr, *n.* A horse *which ambles.*
Ambling, am'bl-ing, *p.n. The motion of a horse that ambles.*
Ambrosia, am-brō'zhi-a, *n.* The imaginary food of the heathen gods, which was supposed to confer *immortality* upon them. [Gr. *a,* priv. and *brotos,* mortal.]
Ambrosial, am-brō'zhi-al, *a. Of the nature of ambrosia;* fragrant; delicious.
Ambulance, am'bū-lans, *n. An itinerant* hospital for the wounded in battle. [Fr.]
Ambulatory, am'bū-la-tō-ri,a. Movable. *n. A place to walk in.* [L. *ambulatorius.*]
Ambuscade, am-bus-kād', *n.* A going *into a bush,* as for concealment; an ambush; the troops lying in wait. [Fr. *embuscade*—It. *bosco,* a wood.]
Ambush, am'bush, *n. A lying hid in a bush or wood;* station where troops lie in wait; troops lying in wait. [Fr. *embuche*—*bois,* a wood.]
Ameliorate, a-mēl'yėr-āt, *vt. To make better. ppr.* ameliorating, *pret. & pp.* ameliorated. [Fr. *ameliorer*—L. *melior,* better.]
Amelioration, a-mēl'yėr-ā"shon, *n. A making better;* improvement.
Amen, ā-men', *adv. Be it established. n. Stability;* truth; a title of Christ. [Heb. from *āman,* to establish.]
Amenable, a-mēn'a-bl, *a.* Liable *to be brought* into court; accountable; responsible. [O. Fr. *amener,* to bring to; L. *manus,* the hand.]
Amend, a-mend', *vt. To free from stain;* to correct; to reform; to improve.—*vi.* To grow better. [Fr. *amender*—L. *a,* from, and *menda,* a stain.]
Amendment, a-mend'ment, *n.* A change for the better; correction; reformation.
Amends, a-mendz', *n.pl.* Compensation; satisfaction; recompense. [Old Fr. *amendes.*]
Amenity, a-men'i-ti, *n. Pleasantness;* agreeableness of situation. [Fr. *aménité* —L. *amœnus,* pleasant.]
Amerce, a-mėrs', *vt.* To inflict a penalty upon *at mercy;* to punish by fine. *ppr.* amercing, *pret. & pp.* amerced. [a, and Fr. *merci,* mercy.]
Amerceable, a-mėrs'a-bl, *a.* Liable *to* amercement.
Amercement, a-mėrs'ment, *n.* A pecuniary penalty inflicted on an offender.
America, a-me'ri-ka, *n.* One of the great continents, lying west of the Atlantic ocean. [from *Amerigo Vespucci.*]
American, a-me'ri-kan, *n. A native of America.*—*a. Pertaining to America.*
Amethyst, am'ē-thist, *n.* A jewel supposed to *drive away intoxication;* a variety of quartz, precious stone of a bluish violet or purple colour. [L.

amethystus—Gr. *a,* priv. and *methuo,* to make drunk.]
Amethystine, a-mē-thist'in, *a. Pertaining to or resembling amethyst.*
Amiability, ā'mi-a-bil"li-ti, *n. Lovebleness;* power of pleasing.
Amiable, ā'mi-a-bl, *a. Lovable;* deserving of love; charming; pleasing. [Fr. *aimable*—L. *amo,* to love.]
Amiableness, ā'mi-a-bl-nes, *n. Quality of being amiable.*
Amiably, ā'mi-a-bli, *adv. In an amiable manner.*
Amianth, am'i-anth, *n. See* AMIANTHUS.
Amianthus, am-i-an'thus, *n.* Mountainflax, a mineral *incorruptible* by fire. [Gr. *amiantos,* incorruptible—*a,* priv. and *miaino,* to vitiate.]
Amicable, am'ik-a-bl,*a. Friendly;* kind; obliging; peaceable. [Low L. *amicabilis* —L. *amo,* to love.]
Amicableness, am'ik-a-bl-nes, *n. Quality of being amicable.*
Amicably, am'ik-a-bli, *adv. In a friendly manner.*
Amid, Amidst, a-mid', a-midst', *prep. In the midst of;* encompassed or enveloped with. *Amid* is used mostly in poetry. [a, and Sax. *midd.*]
Amiss, a-mis', *a. In error; in the wrong;* out of order; improper.—*n.* Culpability. *adv.* In a faulty manner; improperly. [a, and Sax. *missian,* to err.]
Amity, am'i-ti, *n. Friendship;* harmony; good-will. [Fr. *amitié*—L. *amo,* to love.]
Ammonia, am-mō'ni-a, *n.* Volatile alkali; a substance which, in its uncombined form, exists in a state of gas. [from the Egyptian name of the god Jupiter *Ammon.*]
Ammoniac, Ammoniacal, am-mō'ni-ak, am-mō-nī'ak-al, *a. Pertaining to ammonia.*
Ammoniac, am-mō'ni-ak, *n.* A gum obtained from a plant.
Ammonite, am'mon-īt, *n.* Serpentstone, a fossil shell, of many species, now extinct. [*cornu Ammonis,* the horn of Ammon.]
Ammunition, am-mū-ni'shon, *n.* That which is used *for defence or attack;* military stores; materials for charging firearms. [L. *munitio*—*munio,* to defend.]
Amnesty, am'nes-ti, *n.* An act *of oblivion;* a general pardon of the offences of subjects against the government. [Gr. *amnēstia*—*a,* priv. and *mnaomai,* to remember.]
Among, Amongst, a-mung', a-mungst', *prep. Mixed with;* conjoined with; amidst; throughout; of the number. [Sax. *onmang*—*mengan,* to mingle.]
Amorous, am'or-us, *a. Inclined to love;* enamoured; fond; relating to love. [Fr. *amoureux*—L. *amo,* to love.]
Amorously, am'or-us-li, *adv. In an amorous manner.*
Amorousness, am'or-us-nes, *n. Quality of being amorous;* fondness.
Amorphous, a-mor'fus, *a. Without shape;* of irregular shape. [Gr. *a,* priv. and *morphē,* shape.]
Amount, a-mount', *vi. To mount up to;* to rise to; to result in.—*n.* What the whole *mounts up to;* the sum total; the effect or result. [Fr. *à* and *monter.*]
Amphibian, am-fib'i-an, *n.* **Amphibia,** am-fib'i-a, *pl.* An animal capable of living *both* under *water and on land.* [Gr. *amphi,* both or about, and *bios,* life.]
Amphibious, am-fib'i-us, *a.* Being of *double life or nature;* having the power of living in air and water.

Amphibrach, am'fi-brak, *n.* A poetical foot of three syllables, having *a short* syllable *on each side* of the middle one, which is long. [Gr. *amphi,* on both sides, and *brachus,* short.]
Amphiscii, am-fis'i-ī, *n.pl.* The inhabitants between the tropics, whose *shadows* in one part of the year are cast *to the north,* and in the other *to the south.* [Gr. *amphi,* on both sides, and *skia,* a shadow.]
Amphitheatre, am-fi-thē'a-tėr, *n. A double theatre;* an edifice in an oval or circular form, with rows of seats all round, rising higher as they recede from the area. [Gr. *amphitheatron* —*amphi,* and *theatron,* theatre.]
Amphitheatrical, am'fi-thē-at"rik-al, *a. Pertaining to* or exhibited in *an amphitheatre.*
Ample, am'pl, *a. Filled up;* spacious; copious; rich; diffusive. [Fr.—L. *amplus,* large, wide—*pleo,* to fill.]
Ampleness, am'pl-nes, *n.* Largeness; spaciousness; abundance; liberality.
Amplification, am'pli-fi-kā"shon, *n. Act of amplifying; enlargement;* discussion. [L. *amplificatio.*]
Amplifier, am'pli-fī-ėr, *n. He or that which amplifies* or enlarges.
Amplify, am'pli-fī, *vt. To make ample; to enlarge;* to treat copiously.—*vi.* To speak copiously; to be diffuse. *ppr.* amplifying, *pret. & pp.* amplified. [Fr. *amplifier;* L. *amplus,* large, and *facio,* to make.]
Amplitude, am'pli-tūd, *n. Ampleness;* extent; wideness; abundance. [L. *amplitudo.*]
Amply, am'pli, *adv. In an ample manner;* largely; liberally; fully; copiously.
Amputate, am'pū-tāt, *vt. To cut off round* about; to cut off, as a limb. *ppr.* amputating, *pret. & pp.* amputated. [L. *amputo*—*am,* round about, and *peto,* to prune.]
Amputation, am-pū-tā'shon, *n. Act of amputating.* [L. *amputatio.*]
Amulet, am'ū-let, *n.* That which *drives away;* a charm against evils or witchcraft. [L. *amuletum*—*amolior,* to drive away.]
Amuse, a-mūz', *vt. To entertain with the Muses;* to entertain; to beguile. *ppr.* amusing, *pret. & pp.* amused. [Fr. *amuser*—L. *Musa,* a Muse.]
Amusement, a-mūz'ment, *n. That which amuses;* diversion; entertainment.
Amusing, a-mūz'ing, *p.a.* Giving moderate pleasure; pleasing.
Amusingly, a-mūz'ing-li, *adv. In an amusing manner.*
An, an, *a. One;* the form of the indefinite article, used before words beginning with a vowel-sound. [Sax. *an, ane,* one.]
Anabaptist, an-a-bap'tist, *n.* One who *rebaptises;* one who maintains that adults only should be baptized. [Late Gr. *anabaptistes*—*baptiso,* to baptise.]
Anachronism, an-ak'ron-ism, *n.* A turning *back* in the order of *time;* error in chronology by which an event is placed too early, and sometimes too late. [Gr. *ana,* back, and *chronos,* time.]
Anacreontic, a-nak're-on"tik, *a. Pertaining to Anacreon;* noting a kind of verse or measure; amatory.
Anagram, an'a-gram, *n. A transposition of the letters of a name* or sentence, by which a new word or sentence is formed. [Gr. *ana,* backward, and *gramma,* a letter.]
Anal, ā'nal, *a. Pertaining to* or lying near the *anus* or vent. [L. *anus,* the fundament.]

ch, chain; j, job; g, go; ng, sing; ᴛʜ, *then;* th, *thin;* w, *wig;* wh, *whig;* zh, *azure;* † obsolete.

Analogical, an-a-loj'ik-al, *a. Having analogy;* according to analogy.
Analogically, an-a-loj'ik-al-li, *adv. In an analogical manner.*
Analogous, an-al'og-us, *a. Having analogy;* proportional; corresponding.
Analogously, an-al'og-us-li, *adv. In an analogous manner.*
Analogy, an-al'o-ji, *n. Equality of ratios;* proportion; the *likeness* in some circumstances between things in other respects different; similarity. [Gr. *analogia—ana,* up to, and *logos,* ratio.]
Analysis, an-al'i-sis, *n. A loosening up;* a resolution of a thing into its elements; a resolving; consideration of anything in its separate parts; synopsis. [Gr. *analusis—ana,* and *luō,* to loosen.]
Analyst, an'a-list, *n. One who analyzes.*
Analytical, an-a-lit'ik-al, *a. Pertaining to analysis.*
Analytically, an-a-lit'ik-al-li, *adv. In the manner of analysis.*
Analytics, an-a-lit'iks, *n. The science of analysis.*
Analyzable, an'a-liz-a-bl, *a. That can be analyzed.*
Analyze, an'a-liz, *vt. To loose;* to resolve, as a thing into its first principles. *ppr.* analysing, *pret.* and *pp.* analyzed. [Gr. *ana,* again, and *luō, lusō,* to loose.]
Anapest, an'a-pest, *n. A dactyl struck back;* a poetical foot consisting of three syllables, the first two short, the last long. [Gr. *anapaistos—paiō,* to strike.]
Anapestic, an-a-pes'tik, *a. Pertaining to an anapest;* consisting of anapests.
Anarchical, an-ärk'ik-al, *a. Pertaining to anarchy;* without rule or government.
Anarchist, an'ärk-ist, *n. An author or promoter of anarchy.*
Anarchy, an'är-ki, *n.* State of being *without rule;* want of law, order, or government; political confusion. [Gr. *anarchia—a,* priv. and *archē,* rule.]
Anathema, a-nath'e-ma, *n.* Primarily, an offering *put* up in a temple; any person or thing devoted; a curse or ecclesiastical denunciation. [Gr. *ana,* and *tithēmi,* to place.]
Anathematize, a-nath'e-mat-iz, *vt. To pronounce an anathema* against. *ppr.* anathematizing, *pret.* & *pp.* anathematized.
Anatomical, an-a-tom'ik-al, *a. Relating to anatomy* or dissection.
Anatomically, an-a-tom'ik-al-li, *adv. In an anatomical manner.*
Anatomist, a-nat'ō-mist, *n. One skilled in anatomy,* or in the art of dissection.
Anatomize, a-nat'ō-miz, *vt. To cut up;* to open up by cutting; to lay open; to search into. *ppr.* anatomizing, *pret.* & *pp.* anatomized.
Anatomy, a-nat'ō-mi, *n. A cutting up;* doctrine of the structure of the body learned by dissection; dissection; a skeleton†. [Gr. *anatomē—ana,* and *temnō,* to cut.]
Ancestor, an'ses-tér, *n. One who goes before;* a progenitor; a forefather. [L. *antecessor—cedo,* to go.]
Ancestral, an-ses'tral, *a. Relating to* or claimed from *ancestors.*
Ancestry, an'ses-tri, *n. A series of progenitors;* lineage; descent; the honour of descent.
Anchor, angk'ér, *n. That which hooks;* an iron instrument for holding a ship at rest in water; that which gives safety or security.—*vt. To hook or hold fast* by an anchor; to place at anchor; to fix securely.—*vi.* To cast anchor; to fix or rest on. [L. *ancora;* Gr. *angkas,* a bend.]

Anchorage, angk'ér-aj, *n. A place where a ship can anchor;* the anchor and all the necessary tackle for anchoring.
Anchorite, angk'ō-rit, *n.* One who *retreats from the world;* a hermit. [Gr. *anachōrētēs—ana,* and *chōreō,* to go.]
Anchovy, an-chō'vi, *n. A small fish of the herring kind,* used as a sauce. [Sp. *anchova.*]
Ancient, an'shi-ent, *a.* Having *existed formerly;* old; that happened in former times; of long duration; known for a long period; antique. [Fr. *ancien;* L. *antiquus—ante,* before.]
Ancient†, an'shi-ent, *n. A flag;* the bearer of a flag. [corrupted from *ensign;* Fr. *enseigne.*]
Anciently, an'shi-ent-li, *adv.* In old times; in times long since passed.
Ancientness, an'shi-ent-nes, *n. State of being ancient;* antiquity.
Ancients, an'shi-ents, *n. pl.* Those who lived in old times; very old men.
Ancillary, an'sil-la-ri, *a.* Pertaining to *a maid-servant;* subservient or subordinate. [L. *ancilla,* a maid-servant.]
And, and, *conj.* A particle which connects words and sentences together, and signifies that a word or part of a complete sentence is to be added to what precedes. [Sax.]
Anecdote, an'ek-dōt, *n.* History *not yet made known;* a biographical incident; a short story. [Gr. *a,* priv. and *ekdotos,* given out—*didōmi,* to publish.]
Anecdotical, an-ek-dot'ik-al, *a. Pertaining to an anecdote.*
Anemone, a-nem'ō-nē, *n. Wind-flower,* a genus of plants. [Gr. *anemōnē,* from *anemos,* wind.]
Aneroid, an'ē-roid, *a.* Dispensing with the use of quicksilver, as a certain kind of barometer. [Gr. *a,* priv. *nēros,* wet, and *eidos,* form.]
Aneurism, an'ū-rizm, *n. A soft, pulsating tumour,* caused by the *dilatation* of an artery. [Gr. *aneurisma—ana,* up, and *euros,* wide.]
Aneurismal, an-ū-riz'mal, *a. Pertaining to an aneurism.*
Anew, a-nū', *adv. On new;* afresh.
Angel, an'jel, *n.* Primarily, a *messenger;* a spirit employed by God in human affairs; an inhabitant of heaven; a very beautiful person.—*a.* Resembling angels; angelic. [L. *angelus;* Gr. *anggellō,* to tell.]
Angelic, Angelical, an-jel'ik, an-jel'ik-al, *a. Belonging to* or *resembling an angel* or *angels.* [L. *angelicus.*]
Angelically, an-jel'ik-al-li, *adv. Like an angel.*
Angel-like, an'jel-lik, *a. Resembling an angel.*
Anger, ang'gér, *n. Trouble;* vexation; a violent passion of the mind, excited by a real or supposed injury; resentment; indignation.—*vt. To excite anger in;* to irritate. [Sax. *ange,* trouble.]
Angerly†, ang'gér-li, *adv. In an angry manner.*
Angle, ang'gl, *n. A corner;* the inclination of two lines which meet in a point but have different directions; the point where two lines meet. [Fr.; L. *angulus.*]
Angle, ang'gl, *n. A hook;* a fishing-rod, with its line and book.—*vi. To fish with an angle,* or with rod, line, and hook. *ppr.* angling, *pret.* & *pp.* angled. [Sax. *angel.*]
Angler, ang'gl-ér, *n. One that fishes with an angle.*
Anglican, ang'glik-an, *a. English;* pertaining to England, or to the English Church. [from *Angles.*]

Anglicism, ang'gli-sizm, *n. An English idiom.*
Anglicize, ang'gli-siz, *vt. To make English;* to convert into English. *ppr.* anglicizing, *pret.* & *pp.* anglicized.
Anglo-Saxon, ang-glō-saks'on, *n. An English Saxon;* the language of the English Saxons.—*a.* Pertaining to the *Anglo-Saxons,* or their language.
Angrily, ang'gri-li, *adv. In an angry manner;* peevishly.
Angry, ang'gri, *a. Affected with anger;* provoked; wrathful; resentful.
Anguish, ang'gwish, *n. Extreme pain,* either of body or mind; agony; grief. *vt.* To distress with extreme pain. [Fr. *angoisse—*L. *ango,* to cause pain.]
Angular, ang'gū-lér, *a. Having an angle,* angles, or corners; pointed.
Angularity, ang-gū-la'ri-ti, *n. Quality of being angular.*
Anight, a-nit', *adv. In the night-time.*
Anile, an'il, *a. Relating to an old woman;* aged; imbecile. [L. *anilis,* from *anus,* an old woman.]
Anility, a-nil'i-ti, *n. State of being an old woman.* [L. *anilitas.*]
Animadversion, an'i-mad-vér''shon, *n. A turning of the mind to something;* remark by way of censure or criticism; stricture; censure. [L. *animadversio.*]
Animadvert, an'i-mad-vért'', *vi. To turn the mind to;* to criticize; to censure (with *upon*). [L. *animadverto—animus,* the mind, and *verto,* to turn.]
Animal, an'i-mal, *n. A breathing being;* an organized being endowed with life, sensation, and the power of voluntary motion.—*a. That belongs to animals;* gross. [L. *anima,* breath.]
Animalcular, an-i-mal'kūl-ér, *a. Pertaining to animalcules.*
Animalcule, an-i-mal'kūl, *n. A little animal;* an animal so minute that it cannot be distinctly seen without a microscope. [L. *animalculum,* dimin. from *animal.*]
Animate, an'i-māt, *vt. To quicken;* to give natural life to; to enliven; to encourage. *ppr.* animating, *pret.* & *pp.* animated.—*a.* Alive; possessing animal life. [L. *animo, animatus.*]
Animated, an'i-māt-ed, *p.a.* Lively; vigorous; full of spirit.
Animating, an'i-māt-ing, *p.a.* Enlivening; encouraging.
Animation, an-i-mā'shon, *n. Vivacity;* sprightliness; vigour. [L. *animatio.*]
Animosity, an-i-mos'i-ti, *n.* Violent hatred; active enmity; malignity. [L. *animositas.*]
Animus, an'i-mus, *n. Mind;* intention; purpose. [L.]
Anise, an'is, *n.* An aromatic plant, the seeds of which are used in making cordials. [L. *anisum.*]
Anker, ang'kér, *n.* A liquid measure of eight and a half imperial gallons. [D.]
Ankle, ang'kl, *n.* The joint which connects the foot with the leg. [Sax. *ancleow;* Gr. *angkos,* a bend.]
Ankled, ang'kld, *a. Relating to the ankles;* having ankles.
Annalist, an'nal-ist, *n. A writer of annals.*
Annals, an'nalz, *n. pl.* A relation of events in chronological order, each event being recorded under *the year* in which it happened. [L. *annales—annus,* a year.]
Anneal, an-nēl', *vt. To burn;* to heat, as glass or metals, and then cool very slowly, to render them less brittle, or to fix colours laid on glass. [Sax. *ancelan—ælan,* to kindle.]
Annealing, an-nēl'ing, *p.a.* The pro-

Fāte, fär, fat, fall; mē, met, hėr; pine, pin; nōte, not, mōve; tūbe, tub, bull; oil, pound.

cess of applying heat to remove brittleness from metals, glass, &c.
Annex, an-neks′, *vt.* To unite at the end; to subjoin.—*vi.* To join; to be united. [L. *annecto, annexus—necto,* to tie.]
Annexation, an-neks-ā′shon, *n. Act of annexing;* conjunction; union.
Annexment, an-neks′ment, *n. The thing annexed.*
Annihilable, an-nī′hil-a-bl, *a. That may be annihilated.*
Annihilate, an-nī′hil-āt, *vt.* To reduce to nothing; to destroy the existence of. *ppr.* annihilating, *pret. & pp.* annihilated. [L. *annihilo, annihilatus—nihilum,* nothing.]
Annihilation, an-nī′hil-ā″shon, *n. Act of reducing to nothing;* state of being reduced to nothing.
Anniversary, an-ni-vėrs′a-ri, *a. That returns every year.*—*n.* A day on which some remarkable event is *annually* celebrated. [L. *anniversarius.*]
Annotate, an′nō-tāt, *vi. To write notes;* to make remarks on a writing. *ppr.* annotating, *pret. & pp.* annotated. [L. *annoto, annotatus—nōto,* to mark.]
Annotation, an-nō-tā′shon, *n.* A remark on some passage of a book. [L. *annotatio.*]
Annotator, an′nō-tāt-ėr, *n. A writer of notes;* a commentator.
Announce, an-nouns′, *vt.* To make known; to publish; to declare; to proclaim. *ppr.* announcing, *pret. & pp.* announced. [Fr. *annoncer;* L. *nuntius,* a messenger.]
Announcement, an-nouns′ment, *n. Act of announcing;* proclamation.
Annoy, an-noi′, *vt.* To hurt; to molest; to vex. *n.* Molestation. [Norm. *annoyer*—L. *noceo,* to hurt.]
Annoyance, an-noi′ans, *n. Act of annoying;* state of being annoyed.
Annual, an′nū-al, *a. Yearly;* lasting a year.—*n.* A plant whose root dies yearly; a book published yearly. [Fr. *annuel;* L. *annus,* a year.]
Annually, an′nū-al-li, *adv. Yearly.*
Annuitant, an-nū′it-ant, *n. One who receives an annuity.*
Annuity, an-nū′i-ti, *n. A yearly allowance;* a sum of money, payable yearly, &c. [Fr. *annuité;* L. *annus,* a year.]
Annul, an-nul′, *vt.* To reduce to nothing; to make void or of no effect; to repeal. *ppr.* annulling, *pret. & pp.* annulled. [Fr. *annuller*—L. *nullus,* no one.]
Annular, an′nū-lėr, *a. Having the form of a ring;* pertaining to a ring. [L. *annularis—anus,* a rounding.]
Annulment, an-nul′ment, *n. Act of annulling.*
Annunciation, an-nun′si-ā″shon, *n. An announcing;* anniversary of the angel's salutation to the Virgin Mary, being the 25th of March. [from *announce.*]
Anodyne, an′ō-dīn, *n. That which frees from pain;* any medicine which allays or mitigates pain.—*a.* Assuaging pain. [Gr. *a,* priv. and *odúnē,* pain.]
Anoint, a-noint′, *vt.* To rub over with oil; to consecrate by unction. [Fr. *oindre, oint;* L. *ungo,* to smear.]
Anointed, a-noint′ed, *p.a.* Consecrated with oil.—*n.* The Messiah, or Son of God.
Anomalous, a-nom′a-lus, *a. Uneven;* deviating from a general rule. [Gr. *anómalos.*]
Anomaly, a-nom′a-li, *n. Irregularity;* deviation from established rule. [Gr. *anomalēs—a,* priv. and *omalos,* even.]
Anon, a-non′, *adv.* Immediately. [Sax. *on an.*]

Anonymous, a-non′im-us, *a. Nameless;* without the real name of the author. [L. *anonymus*—Gr. *a,* priv. and *onóma,* a name.]
Anonymously, a-non′im-us-li, *adv. Without a name.*
Another, an-uṯẖ′ėr, *a. One other;* not the same; different; any other. [*an,* or *one,* and *other.*]
Anserine, an′sėr-in, *a. Relating to the goose or goose tribe.* [L. *anserinus,* from *anser,* a goose.]
Answer, an′sėr, *vt. To speak in return to;* to reply to; to correspond to; to satisfy; to serve; to suit: to solve; to obey.—*vi.* To reply; to be accountable; to correspond; to succeed; to have a good effect.—*n.* A reply; a solution. [Sax. *andswarian—and,* against, and *swarian,* to speak.]
Answerable, an′sėr-a-bl, *a. That may be answered;* accountable; proportionate; suitable.
Answerably, an′sėr-a-bli, *adv.* In due proportion; suitably.
Answering, an′sėr-ing, *p a.* Replying; corresponding to.
Ant, ant, *n. An emmet;* a pismire. [from Sax. *æmet.*]
Antagonism, an-tag′ōn-izm, *n.* Opposition of action; contest.
Antagonist, an-tag′ōn-ist, *n.* One who struggles with another in combat; an opponent; that which acts in opposition.—*a.* Acting in opposition. [Gr. *antagonistēs — anti,* and *agōn,* a struggle.]
Antagonistic, an-tag′ōn-ist″ik, *a. Opposing in combat;* contending against.
Antarctic, ant-ärk′tik, *a. Opposite to the Great Bear;* relating to the southern pole, or to the region near it. [Gr. *anti,* and *arktos,* the bear.]
Antecedent, an-tē-sē′dent, *a. Going before;* prior; foregoing.—*n. That which goes before;* the noun to which a relative refers; the first of the two terms of a ratio; (pl.) a man's previous history and fortunes. [L. *antecedens—cedo,* to go.]
Antecedently, an-tē-sē′dent-li, *adv.* Previously; at a time preceding.
Ante-chamber, an′tē-chām-bėr, *n.* An apartment *before the chief apartment,* to which it leads.
Antedate, an′tē-dāt, *n. Prior date:* a date antecedent to another.—*vt.* To date before the true time. *ppr.* antedating, *pret. & pp.* antedated. [L. *ante,* and *do, datus,* to give.]
Antediluvian, an′tē-di-lū″vi-an, *a. Before the flood.*—*n.* One who lived before the flood. [L. *ante,* and *diluvium,* a flood.]
Antelope, an′tē-lōp, *n. The beautiful eye;* a sort of quadrupeds, intermediate between the deer and goat. [Gr. *anthos,* beautiful, and *ops,* an eye.]
Antemeridian, an′tē-mē-rid″i-an, *a.* Being *before mid-day;* pertaining to the forenoon. [L. *ante,* and *meridies,* mid-day.]
Antemundane, an-tē-mun′dān, *a.* Being *before the creation of the world.* [L. *ante,* and *mundus,* the world.]
Antenna, an-ten′nē, *n.pl.* The feelers of an insect. [L. *antenna,* a sailyard.]
Antenuptial, an-tē-nup′shi-al, *a.* Being *before nuptials* or marriage. [*ante* and *nuptial.*]
Antepenult, an′tē-pē-nult″, *n.* That which is *before the penultimate;* the last syllable of a word except two. [L. *ante, pene,* almost, and *ultimus,* last.]
Antepenultimate, an′tē-pē-nul″ti-māt,

a. Pertaining to the antepenult, or last syllable but two.—*n.* Same as *antepenult.*
Anterior, an-tē′ri-ėr, *a. Before; prior;* previous; in front. [L. comp. of *ante.*]
Anteroom, an′tē-rōm, *n.* Room through which the passage is to a principal apartment.
Anthem, an′them, *n.* A sacred song sung by *two opposite choirs,* or sung in alternate parts; a sacred song or hymn set to music. [Gr. *antiphonia—anti,* and *phōnē,* voice.]
Anther, an′thėr, *n.* The summit of the stamen in a *flower.* [Gr. *anthēros,* flowery.]
Anthological, an-tho-loj′ik-al, *a. Pertaining to anthology.*
Anthology, an-thol′o-ji, *n. A co'lection of flowers,* or of beautiful pieces of poetry; a discourse on flowers. [Gr. *anthos,* a flower, and *lego,* to gather.]
Anthracite, an′thra-sīt, *n. Burning-coal stone;* a hard, compact, mineral coal. [Gr. *anthrax,* a burning c al, and *lithos,* a stone.]
Anthropology, an-thrō-pol′o-ji, *n. A discourse upon man;* the doctrine of the human mind and body. [Gr. *anthrōpos,* man, and *logos,* discourse.]
Antic, an′tik, *a. Antique!;* grotesque; fantastic.—*n. That which is antique;* a grotesque figure; a buffoon; buffoonery. [Fr. *antique;* L. *antiquus.*]
Antichrist, an′ti-krist, *n.* The great adversary of Christ. [Gr. *anti,* and *Christ.*]
Antichristian, an-ti-kris′ti-an, *a. Pertaining to Antichrist.*
Anticipate, an-tis′i-pāt, *vt. To take beforehand;* to pre-occupy; to forestall; to enjoy or suffer prospectively; to foretaste; to preclude. *ppr.* anticipating, *pret. & pp.* anticipated. [L. *anticipo, anticipatus—capio,* to take.]
Anticipation, an-tis′i-pā″shon, *n. Act of anticipating;* foretaste.
Anti-climax, an-ti-klī′maks, *n.* That which is *opposed to climax;* a sentence in which the ideas become less striking at the close. [Gr. *anti-klimax.*]
Anti-constitutional, an-ti-kon′sti-tū″-shon-al, *a. Opposed to or against the constitution.*
Antidotal, an′ti-dōt-al, *a.* Acting as an *antidote;* counteracting poison.
Antidote, an′ti-dōt, *n.* That which is *given against* something evil; a remedy for poison or any evil. [Gr. *antidōtos — anti,* and *didōmi,* to give.]
Anti-evangelical, an-ti-ē′van-jel″ik-al, *a. Opposed to what is evangelical.*
Anti-ministerial, an-ti-min′is-tē″ri-al, *a. Opposed to the ministry,* or administration of government.
Antimonial, an-ti-mō′ni-al, *a. Pertaining to antimony.*
Antimony, an′ti-mo-ni, *n.* A metal, brittle, of a silver-white colour, used in the arts and in medicine. [Fr. *antimoine.*]
Antinomian, an-ti-nō′mi-an, *a. Against* the moral *law.*—*n.* One who opposes the moral *law.* [Gr. *anti,* and *nomos,* a law.]
Antipathy, an-tip′a-thi, *n. A feeling against;* instinctive aversion; dislike; opposition. [Gr. *anti,* and *pathos,* feeling.]
Antiphrasis, an-tif′ra-sis, *n.* The use of *words* in a sense *opposite* to their proper meaning. [Gr. *anti,* and *phrasō,* to speak.]
Antipodal, an-tip′od-al, *a. Pertaining to the antipodes.*
Antipodes, an-tip′o-dez, *n.pl.* Those

who live on the opposite side of the globe, and whose *feet* are directly *opposite* to ours. [Gr. *anti*, and *pous, podos*, a foot.]

Antiquarian, an-ti-kwā'ri-an, *a*. Pertaining to antiquaries, or to antiquity. *n*. One versed in *antiquities*.

Antiquarianism, an-ti-kwā'ri-an-ism, *n. Love or knowledge of antiquities.*

Antiquary, an'ti-kwa-ri, *n*. One devoted to the study of *ancient things;* one versed in antiquities.—*a Old!.* [L. *antiquarius—ante*, before.]

Antiquate, an'ti-kwāt, *vt*. To put out of use, from *age;* to abrogate. *ppr.* antiquating, *pret. & pp.* antiquated. [L. *antiquo, antiquatus*.]

Antiquated, an'ti-kwāt-ed, *p.a. Grown old;* obsolete; out of use.

Antique, an-tēk', *a. Old;* of genuine antiquity; old-fashioned.—*n.* Anything *very old;* busts, statues, paintings, and vases, the works of Grecian and Roman antiquity. [Fr.; L. *antiquus*.]

Antiqueness, an-tēk'nes, *n. Quality of being antique.*

Antiquity, an-tik'wi-ti, *n. Ancient times;* people of ancient times; great age; (pl.) the remains of ancient times, as statues, paintings, coins, books, manuscripts, &c. [L. *antiquitas*.]

Antiscii, an-ti'shi-ī, *n. pl.* The people who live on different sides of the equator, whose *shadows* at noon are cast in *contrary directions.* [Gr. *anti*, and *skia*, a shadow.]

Anti-scriptural, an-ti-skrip'tūr-al, *a. Opposed or contrary to Scripture.*

Antiseptic, an-ti-sep'tik, *a.* Counteracting *putrefaction.* [Gr. *antiseptos—sepō*, to make putrid.]

Anti-slavery, an-ti-slā'vė-ri, *a. Hostility to slavery.*

Antistrophe, an-tis'tro-fi, *n. A turning again;* the stanza of a chorus or ode, succeeding the *strophe.* [Gr. *anti*, and *strephō*, to turn.]

Antithesis, an-tith'e-sis, *n. A placing against;* an opposition of thoughts or words; contrast. [Gr. *anti*, and *tithēmi*, to place.]

Antithetical, an-ti-thet'ik-al, *a.* Pertaining *to antithesis.*

Anti-trinitarian, an-ti-trin'i-tā'ri-an, *n.* One who *denies the Trinity.*

Antitype, an'ti-tip, *n. That which is shadowed out by a type;* that of which the type is the pattern. [Gr. *antitupos—tupos*, a type.]

Antitypical, an-ti-tip'ik-al, *a.* Pertaining *to an antitype;* explaining the type.

Antler, ant'lėr, *n.* A start or branch of a stag's horn. [Fr. *andouiller;* L. *ante*, before.]

Antlered, ant'lėrd, *p.a. Furnished with antlers.*

Antoeci, an-tē'sī, *n. pl. People who dwell opposite to each other;* those who live under the same latitude and longitude, but on different sides of the equator. [Gr. *anti*, and *oikeō*, to dwell.]

Anus, ā'nus, *n.* The opening of the body by which excrement is expelled. [L.]

Anvil, an'vil, *n. That on which anything is formed;* an iron block on which smiths hammer and shape their work. [Sax. *anfilt—an*, in, on, and G. *bilden*, to form.]

Anxiety, ang-zī'e-ti, *n. State of being anxious;* trouble of mind, arising from doubt or uncertainty; restlessness. [L. *anxietas*.]

Anxious, angk'shi-us, *a. Suffering mental pressure; solicitous;* greatly concerned; uneasy. [L. *anxius—ango*, to press.]

Anxiously, angk'shi-us-li, *adv. In an anxious manner.*

Anxiousness, angk'shi-us-nes, *n. Quality or state of being anxious.*

Any, en'ni, *a. Every;* whatever; one; some; either.—*adv.* At all; in any degree. [Sax. *anig*.]

Anywise, en'ni-wiz, *adv. In any manner.*

Aorist, ā'ėr-ist, *n.* An *indefinite past tense* in the Greek verb. [Gr. *aoristos*, indefinite—*a*, priv. and *horizō*, to bound.

Aorta, ā-ort'a, *n.* The great artery which *rises up* from the left ventricle of the heart. [Gr. *aortē—aeirō*, to raise up.]

Aortal, Aortic, ā-ort'al, ā-ort'ik, *a. Pertaining to the aorta* or great artery.

Apace, a-pās', *adv. On pace;* with a quick pace; quick; fast; speedily; hastily.

Apart, a-pärt', *adv. In part; separately;* aside; exclusive of. [Fr. *aparté*, words spoken aside; L. *pars*, a part.]

Apartment, a-pärt'ment, *n. A part of a house* separated from other parts; a room; (pl.) a suite of rooms; lodgings. [Fr. *appartement*.]

Apathetic, ap-a-thet'ik, *a. Void of feeling;* free from passion; insensible; indifferent.

Apathy, ap'a-thi, *n. Want of feeling;* insensibility; stoicism. [Gr. *a*, priv. and *pathos*, feeling.]

Ape, āp, *n.* A tailless monkey; a servile imitator; a simpleton!.—*vt.* To imitate servilely; to mimic, as an ape. *ppr.* aping, *prep. & pp.* aped. [Sax. *apa*.]

Aperient, a-pē'ri-ent, *a. Opening;* mildly purgative—*n. A laxative;* a mild purgative. [L. *aperiens—pario*, to bring forth.]

Aperture, ap'ėr-tūr, *n. An opening;* a hole; a passage; a gap. [L. *apertura*.]

Apex, ā'peks, *n. Apexes, Apices*, ā'peks-ez, ap'i-sēz, *pl. The extreme end of a thing;* the tip or summit of anything. [L.]

Aphaeresis, Apheresis, a-fē'rē-sis, a-fē'rē-sis, *n. The taking away* of a letter or syllable from the beginning of a word. [Gr. *aphairesis*, a taking away —*apo*, from, and *haireō*, to take.)

Aphelion, a-fē'li-on, *n.* The point of a planet's orbit *most distant from the sun.* [Gr. *apo*, and *helios*, the sun.]

Aphorism, af'or-ism, *n. A precise* and pithy saying expressed in few words; a maxim; a precept. [Gr. *aphorismos* —*apo*, and *horos*, a limit.]

Apiarist, ā'pi-a-rist, *n. One who keeps an apiary.*

Apiary, ā'pi-a-ri, *n. The place where bees are kept.* [L. *apiarium—apis*, a bee.]

Apiece, a-pēs', *adv.* In a separate share; to each; noting the share of each.

Apish, āp'ish, *a. Resembling an ape.*

Apishness, āp'ish-nes, *n. Quality of being apish.*

Apocalypse, a-pok'a-lips, *n. An uncovering;* revelation; the last book of the New Testament. [Gr. *apokalupsis* —*apo*, and *kaluptō*, to cover.]

Apocalyptic, a-pok'a-lip'tik, *a.* Pertaining *to the Apocalypse.*

Apocope, a-pok'ō-pē, *n. The cutting off* of the last letter or syllable of a word. [Gr. *apo*, and *koptō*, to cut.]

Apocrypha, a-pok'ri-fa, *n. pl. Things hidden from;* books whose authenticity as inspired writings is not generally admitted. [Gr. *apo*, and *kruptō*, to hide.]

Apocryphal, a-pok'ri-fal, *a.* Pertaining *to the Apocrypha;* not canonical.

Apogee, ap'ō-jē, *n.* The point in the moon's orbit *most remote* from the *earth.* [Gr. *apo*, and *gē*, the earth.]

Apologetic, a-pol'ō-jet'ik, *a. Containing apology;* defending; excusing. [Gr. *apologētikos—apo*, and *logos*, an account.]

Apologetics, a-pol'ō-jet'iks, *n. pl.* That branch of theology which defends the Holy Scriptures.

Apologist, a-pol'ō-jist, *n. One who apologizes;* one who speaks or writes in *defence* of.

Apologize, a-pol'ō-jīz, *vi. To make an apology;* to write or speak in favour, or to make excuse. *ppr.* apologizing, *pret.* and *pp.* apologized.

Apologue, ap'o-log. *n.* A story; tale; a moral fable. [Gr. *apologos—logos*, an account.]

Apology, a-pol'ō-ji, *n. That which is said in defence;* a vindication; a justification; excuse. [Gr. *apologia—apo*, and *lego*, to speak.]

Apophthegm, ap'o-them, *n. That which is spoken out;* a terse pointed saying. [Gr. *apophthegma—phthengomai*, to speak.]

Apoplectic, ap-ō-plek'tik, *a. Pertaining to or consisting in apoplexy.*

Apoplexed, ap'ō-plekst, *p.a. Seized with apoplexy.*

Apoplexy, ap'ō-plek-si, *n. A violent stroke or shock;* a sudden privation of sense and voluntary motion. [Gr. *apoplēxia—plessō*, to strike.]

Apostasy, a-pos'ta-si, *n. A standing away from;* a total departure from one's faith; desertion of a party. [Gr. *apostasis—stasis*, a standing.]

Apostate, a-pos'tāt, *n.* One who renounces his religion or his party. *a.* False; traitorous. [Gr. *apostatēs*.)

Apostatize, a-pos'ta-tīz, *vi. To depart from;* to abandon one's religion or party. *ppr.* apostatising, *pret. & pp.* apostatized.

Apostle, a-pos'l, *n. One sent forth;* person sent with mandates by another (particularly applied to those whom our Saviour commissioned to preach the gospel). [Gr. *apostolos—apo*, and *stellō*, to send off.]

Apostleship, a-pos'l-ship, *n. The office of an apostle.*

Apostolic, Apostolical, ap-os-tol'ik, ap-os-tol'ik-al, *a. Pertaining to the apostles*, or to their doctrines.

Apostrophe, a-pos'tro-fē, *n. A turning from;* a turning from the audience, and addressing the absent or the dead, as if present; a mark (') indicating that a word is contracted. [Gr. *strephō*, to turn.]

Apostrophize, a-pos'trof-īz, *vt. To make an apostrophe. vt. To address by apostrophe. ppr.* apostrophizing, *pret. & pp.* apostrophised.

Apothecary, a-poth'e-ka-ri, *n.* One who prepares and sells drugs or medicines. [Fr. *apothicaire*—Gr. *apo*, and *thēkē*, a chest.]

Apothegm, ap'o-them, *n.* See **APOPHTHEGM**.

Apotheosis, ap-o-thē'ō-sis, *n. A deification;* a placing among the gods. [Gr. *apotheosis—apo*, and *Theos*, God.]

Appal, ap-pal', *vi. To cause to grow pale;* to depress with fear; to dismay.—*vi.* To grow faint; to be dismayed. *ppr.* appalling, *pret.* and *pp.* appalled. [L. *palleo*, to grow pale.]

Appalling, ap-pal'ing, *p.a.* Adapted to depress courage.

Appanage, ap'pan-āj, *n. Provision;* lands appropriated by a prince to the

Fāte, fār, fat, fall; mē, met, hėr; pīne, pin; nōte, not, mōve; tūbe, tub, bull; oil, pound.

maintenance of his younger children. [Fr. *apanage*—L. *panis*, bread.]
Apparatus, ap-pa-rā'tus, *n.* **Apparatus** or **Apparatuses,** *pl. A preparation;* instruments; a complete set of instruments for performing any operation. [L. *ad*, and *paro*, to prepare.]
Apparel, ap-pa'rel, *n.* Equipment; clothing; decorations; furniture of a ship.—*vt. To dress;* to array. *ppr.* apparelling, *pret. & pp.* apparelled. [Fr. *appareil;* L. *paro*, to prepare.]
Apparent, ap-pā'rent, *a. Appearing;* that may be seen; certain. [L. *apparens—pāreo*, to appear.]
Apparently, ap-pā'rent-li, *adv.* Openly.
Apparition, ap-pa-ri'shon, *n. An appearance;* a form; a spectre. [Fr.— L. *pareo*, to appear.]
Appeal, ap-pēl', *vi. To call;* to refer to a superior judge or court; to refer to another, as judge; to address one's self to the feelings, &c., of an audience; to have recourse.—*vt.* To remove, as a cause, from an inferior to a superior court.—*n.* The removal of a cause from a lower to a higher tribunal; a reference to another; an address to the feelings of an audience. [Fr. *appeler;* Old L. *pello,* to speak.]
Appealant, ap-pēl'ant, *n. He that appeals.*
Appear, ap-pēr', *vi. To come or be in sight;* to be or become visible; to come before; to be obvious; to seem. [L. *appareo*—*ad*, and *pareo*, to appear.]
Appearance, ap-pēr'ans, *n. Act of coming into sight;* the thing seen; semblance; likelihood; presence; air; aspect.
Appeasable, ap-pēz'a-bl, *a. That may be appeased.*
Appease, ap-pēz', *vt. To pacify;* to tranquillize. *ppr.* appeasing, *pret. & pp.* appeased. [Fr. *appaiser*—L. *pax*, peace.]
Appellant, ap-pel'ant, *n. One who appeals;* a challenger. [from L. *appellans.*]
Appellate, ap-pel'āt, *a. Pertaining to appeals.*
Appellation, ap-pel-ā'shon, *n.* The word by which a person or thing is called; name; title. [L. *appellatio*—Old L. *pello,* to speak.]
Appellative, ap-pel'at-iv, *a. Pertaining to a common name;* general.—*n.* A common name; a name which stands for a whole class of beings.
Append, ap-pend', *vt. To hang or attach to;* to add; to annex. [L. *ad*, and *pendo,* to cause to hang down.]
Appendage, ap-pend'āj, *n. Something added;* a subordinate part.
Appendant, ap-pend'ant, *a. Hanging to;* annexed.—*n. That which belongs to another thing,* as subordinate to it.
Appendix, ap-pen'diks, *n.* **Appendixes, Appendices,** ap-pen'diks-ez, ap-pen'di-sez, *pl.* An adjunct or appendage; a supplement. [L. *pendo*, to cause to hang down.]
Appertain, ap-pér-tān', *vi. To pertain;* to belong; to relate. [Fr. *appartenir;* L. *pertineo*, to pertain.]
Appertainment, ap-pér-tān'ment, *n. That which belongs.*
Appetence, Appetency, ap'pē-tens, ap'pē-ten-si, *n. A seeking after;* desire; sensual appetite. [L. *appetentia—peto*, to seek.]
Appetite, ap'pē-tit, *n. A longing after;* natural desire; a craving for food or other sensual gratifications; relish for food; hunger. [L. *appettius—peto,* to seek.]

Applaud, ap-plạd', *vt. To clap with the hands at;* to praise by clapping the hands, beating with the feet, &c.; to commend. [L. *applaudo*—*plaudo,* to clap.]
Applause, ap-plạs', *n. Plaudit;* commendation; approbation. [L. *applausus—plausus,* a clapping.]
Apple, ap'l, *n. That which is round;* the fruit of the apple-tree; the apple of the eye is the pupil. [Sax. *apl.*]
Appliance, ap-pli'ans, *n. Act of applying,* or thing applied; aid. [L. *plico,* to fold.]
Applicability, ap'pli-ka-bil''li-ti, *n. Quality of being applicable.*
Applicable, ap'pli-ka-bl, *a. That may be applied;* fit to be applied; suitable.
Applicably, ap'pli-ka-bli, *adv. In an applicable manner.*
Applicant, ap'pli-kant, *n. One who applies.* [L. *applicans.*]
Application, ap-pli-kā'shon, *n. Act of applying;* close study; great industry; the transferring of something to something else; a referring of something to a particular case; the thing applied; a request; entreaty. [L. *applicatio.*]
Apply, ap-pli', *vt. To fasten to;* to suit to; to use; to put; to fix the mind upon; to have recourse by entreaty; to solicit; to fit.—*vi.* To suit; to agree. *ppr.* applying, *pret. & pp.* applied. [L. *applico—plico,* to lay together.]
Appoint, ap-point', *vt. To bring to a point;* to furnish; to equip; to establish; to constitute; to allot; to determine. *vi.* To ordain; to determine. [Old Fr. *appointer;* L. *punctum,* a point.]
Appointment, ap-point'ment, *n. Act of appointing;* decree; stipulation; establishment; (pl.) salary; office of emolument.
Apportion, ap-pōr'shon, *vt. To portion out;* to divide and assign in just proportion. [L. *ad*, and *portio*, portion.]
Apportioner, ap-pōr'shon-ėr, *n. One who apportions.*
Apportionment, ap-pōr'shon-ment, *n. Act of apportioning.*
Apposite, ap'pō-zit, *a. Put or set to;* very applicable; well adapted. [from L. *appositus—ad,* and *pono, positus,* to put.]
Appositely, ap'pō-zit-li, *adv.* Suitably.
Appositeness, ap'pō-zit-nes, *n.* Fitness; propriety.
Apposition, ap-pō-zi'shon, *n.* In grammar, one noun is in apposition with another, when, being in the same case, it explains, adds to, or modifies its meaning in any way. [L. *appositio.*]
Appraise, ap-prāz', *vt. To fix a price on;* to set a value on. *ppr.* appraising, *pret. & pp.* appraised. [Fr. *apprecier* —L. *pretium,* price.]
Appraisement, ap-prāz'ment, *n. Act of setting the value;* a valuation.
Appraiser, ap-prāz'ėr, *n. One who appraises* or values.
Appreciable, ap-prē'shi-a-bl, *a. That may be appreciated.*
Appreciate, ap-prē'shi-āt, *vt. To set a price on;* to value; to estimate justly. *ppr.* appreciating, *pret. & pp.* appreciated. [Fr. *apprecier*—L. *pretium,* price.]
Appreciated, ap-prē'shi-āt-ed, *p.a. Valued;* prized; estimated.
Appreciation, ap-prē'shi-ā''shon, *n. Act of appreciating;* a just valuation of merit, weight, or any moral consideration.
Apprehend, ap-prē-hend', *vt. To take hold of;* to seize in order for trial; to take hold of by the mind; to conceive;

to imagine; to fear.—*vi.* To think; to suppose; to imagine. [L. *apprehendo —prehendo,* to seize.]
Apprehensible, ap-prē-hen'si-bl, *a. That may be apprehended* or conceived.
Apprehension, ap-prē-hen'shon, *n.* Seizing or *taking hold of;* opinion; faculty of conceiving ideas; suspicion; dread. [L. *apprehensio.*]
Apprehensive, ap-prē-hen'siv, *a.* Fearful; inclined to believe; sensible.
Apprehensiveness, ap-prē-hen'siv-nes, *n. Quality of being apprehensive.*
Apprentice, ap-pren'tis, *n. A learner;* one who is indentured to a master to *learn a trade,* an art, &c.—*vt.* To bind as an apprentice. *ppr.* apprenticing, *pret. & pp.* apprenticed. [Norm. *apprentise,* a student of the law; L. *prehendo,* to take.]
Apprenticeship, ap-pren'tis-ship, *n.* The term during which an *apprentice* serves; condition of an apprentice.
Apprise, ap-prīs', *vt. To instruct;* to inform; to make known to. *ppr.* apprising, *pret. & pp.* apprised. [Fr. *appris,* taught; L. *prehendo,* to take.]
Approach, ap-prōch', *vi. To come or draw near;* to approximate.—*vt. To come near to;* to come near by natural affinity.—*n. Act of drawing near;* an avenue to a house; progress towards. [Fr. *approcher*—L. *prope,* near.]
Approachable, ap-prōch'a-bl, *a. That may be approached.*
Approbation, ap-prō-bā'shon, *n. Approval;* attestation; a liking. [L. *approbatio—probo,* to approve.]
Appropriable, ap-prō'pri-a-bl, *a.* That may be appropriated.
Appropriate, ap-prō'pri-āt, *vt.* To take to one's self as one's own; to set apart for. *ppr.* appropriating, *pret. & pp.* appropriated.—*a.* Set apart for a particular use or person; suitable; adapted. [Fr. *approprier*—L. *proprius,* one's own.]
Appropriately, ap-prō'pri-āt-li, *adv. In an appropriate manner.*
Appropriateness, ap-prō'pri-āt-nes, *n.* Peculiar fitness.
Appropriation, ap-prō'pri-ā''shon, *n. Act of appropriating;* application to a special use or purpose.
Approvable, ap-prōv'a-bl, *a. That may be approved.*
Approval, ap-prōv'al, *n. Approbation.*
Approve, ap-prōv', *vi. To deem good;* to like; to be pleased with; to sanction (with *of*). *ppr.* approving, *pret. & pp.* approved. [Fr. *approuver*—L. *probus,* proper.]
Approver, ap-prōv'ėr, *n. One who approves.*
Approving, ap-prōv'ing, *p.a. Yielding approbation.*
Approximate, ap-prok'si-māt, *a. Next;* approaching to; nearly true.—*vt. To carry near to;* to cause to approach. *vi. To come near;* to approach. *ppr.* approximating, *pret. & pp.* approximated. [L. *ad,* and *proximus,* next.]
Approximately, ap-prok'si-māt-li, *adv. By approximation.*
Approximation, ap-prok'si-mā''shon, *n. Act of approximating;* approach; a drawing, moving, or advancing near.
Appurtenance, ap-pér'ten-ans, *n.* That which *pertains* to something else; an appendage. [Fr. *appartenance*—L. *pertineo,* to pertain.]
Apricot, ā'pri-kot, *n. The early fruit;* a delicious kind of stone-fruit, resembling the peach. [Fr. *abricot;* L. *præ,* and *coquo,* to ripen.]
April, ā'pril, *n.* The fourth month of

the year, in which buds begin to *open*. [L. *Apritis—aperio*, to open.]
Apron, ā'prun, *n. A cloth*, or piece of leather, worn on the fore part of the body, as a protection to the clothes; a cover for the vent of a cannon; a piece of leather spread before a person's legs in a gig, &c. [Old Fr. *naperon—nappe*, a table-cloth.]
Aproned, ā'prund, *p.a. Wearing an apron.*
Apropos, ap'rō-pō, *adv. To the purpose; opportunely;* by the way. [Fr. from *à*, and *propos*, purpose.]
Apsis, ap'sis, *n.* **Apsides, Apses**, ap'si-dēz, ap'sēz, *pl.* The apsides are the two points in a planet's orbit which are at the greatest and least distance from the sun or the earth, and which are *connected* by an imaginary line drawn from the one to the other. [Gr. *hapsis*, connection, from *haptō*, to connect.]
Apt, apt, *a. Joined;* suitable; inclined; liable; ready; dexterous. [L. *aptus*—Gr. *haptō*, to join.]
Apteryx, ap'tē-riks, *n.* A genus of birds found in New Zealand, with only short rudiments of wings, and without a tail. [Gr. *a*, priv. and *pterux* a wing.]
Aptitude, ap'ti-tūd, *n. Fitness;* disposition; suitableness; readiness. [Fr.; L. *aptus*, fit.]
Aptly, apt'li, *adv. In an apt manner.*
Aptness, ap'nes, *n. Aptitude.*
Aquarius, a-kwā'ri-us, *n. The water-bearer;* a sign in the zodiac, which the sun enters about the 21st of January. [L. from *aqua*, water.]
Aquatic, a-kwat'ik, *a. Watery;* living or growing in water.—*n.* A plant which grows in water. [L. *aquaticus*.]
Aqueduct, ak'wē-dukt, *n.* A conduit made for *conveying water* from one place to another, either above or under the surface of the ground. [L. *aqua*, and *duco*, to lead.]
Aqueous, ā'kwē-us, *a. Watery.*
Aquiline, ak'wil-in, *a. Belonging to the eagle;* curved and hooked like the beak of an eagle. [L. *aquilinus*, from *aquila*, an eagle.]
Arab, a'rab, *n.* A *native of Arabia.*
Arabesque, a'rab-esk, *a.* In the *manner of the Arabian* architecture, sculpture, &c. [Fr.]
Arabian, a-rā'bi-an, *a. Pertaining to Arabia.*—*n. A native of Arabia.*
Arabic, a'rab-ik, *a. Belonging to Arabia*, or the language of the Arabians.—*n. The language of the Arabians.*
Arable, a'ra-bl, *a. Fit for ploughing* or tillage. [L. *arabilis—aro*, to plough.]
Aramean, a-ra-mē'an, *a.* Pertaining to the Syrians and Chaldeans, or to their language.
Arbiter, är'bit-ėr, *n. One who goes to;* a person appointed by parties in controversy to decide their differences; an umpire; a ruler or governor. [L. *ad*, to, and *beto*, to go.]
Arbitrarily, är'bi-tra-ri-li, *adv. By will only;* despotically; absolutely.
Arbitrariness, är'bi-tra-ri-nes, *n. Quality of being arbitrary.*
Arbitrary, är'bi-tra-ri, *a. Done by an arbiter;* despotic; uncontrolled. [L. *arbitrarius*.]
Arbitrate, är'bi-trāt, *vi. To act as an arbiter;* to hear and decide; to determine. *ppr.* arbitrating, *pret. & pp.* arbitrated. [L. *arbitror, arbitratus*.]
Arbitration, är-bi-trā'shon, *n.* The hearing and determination of a cause by a person or persons chosen by the parties.

Arbitrator, är'bi-trāt-ėr, *n.* A person chosen to decide a dispute; an umpire.
Arborescence, är-bor-es'sens, *n. The state of being arborescent;* the resemblance of a tree.
Arborescent, är-bor-es'sent, *a. Resembling a tree;* becoming woody. [L. *arborescens—arbor*, a tree.]
Arboriculture, är-bo'ri-kul''tūr, *n. The art of cultivating trees* and shrubs. [L. *arbor*, and *colo*, to cultivate.]
Arbour, är'bėr, *n.* A bower; a place of retirement and shelter in a garden, &c., formed of *trees* or shrubs. [perhaps from L. *arbor*, a tree.]
Arc, ärk, *n.* Any part of the circumference of a circle or other *curved* line. [L. *arcus*, a bow.]
Arcade, är-kād', *n. A series of arches;* a walk arched above; an arched building or gallery. [Fr.]
Arcadian, är-kā'di-an, *a. Pertaining to Arcadia.*
Arcanum, är-kān'um, *n. That which is inclosed;* generally used in the pl. *arcana*, mysteries. [L. from *arceo*, to inclose.]
Arch, ärch, *a. Cunning;* sly; mirthful. [G. *arg*, crafty.]
Arch, ärch, priv. *n. A bow;* a portion of the circumference of a circle or other curve; a concave structure supported by its own curve; a vault; the vault of heaven.—*vt. To cover with an arch;* to form with a curve.—*vi.* To build or make arches. [L. *arcus*.]
Archæological, är-kē-ō-loj''ik-al, *a. Relating to archæology.*
Archæologist, är-kē-ol'o-jist, *n.* One versed in *archæology.*
Archæology, är-kē-ol'o-ji, *n.* The scientific study of *antiquities;* knowledge of ancient art. [Gr. *archaios*, ancient, and *logos*, discourse.]
Archangel, ärk-ān'jel, *n. A chief angel;* an angel of the highest order. [Gr. *archos*, chief, *arche*, the first place, and *angel*.]
Archangelic, ärk-an-jel'ik, *a. Belonging to archangels.*
Archbishop, ärch-bish'up, *n. A chief bishop;* a bishop who superintends the bishops, his suffragans, in his province.
Archbishopric, ärch-bish'up-rik, *n. The province of an archbishop.*
Archdeacon, ärch-dē'kn, *n.* A church dignitary next in rank below a bishop.
Archdeaconry, ärch-dē'kn-ri, *n. The office or residence of an archdeacon.*
Archdeaconship, ärch-dē'kn-ship, *n. The office of an archdeacon.*
Archduchess, ärch-duch'es, *n.* A title given to the females of the House of Austria.
Archduke, ärch-dūk', *n.* A title given to princes of the House of Austria.
Arched, ärcht, *p.a. Covered with an arch;* in the form of an arch.
Archer, ärch'ėr, *n. A bowman;* one who shoots with a bow and arrow. [Fr. —L. *arcus*, a bow.]
Archery, ärch'ė-ri, *n. The practice, art, or skill of archers.*
Archetype, är'kē-tīp, *n. The original type* or model from which a thing is made; an authentic draught. [Gr. *archetupos—tupos*, a type.]
Arching, ärch'ing, *p.a. Curving like an arch.*
Archipelago, är-ki-pel'a-gō, *n. The Ægean Sea;* a sea abounding in small islands. [Gr.; a corruption of *Aigaios*, Ægean, and *pelagos*, sea.]
Architect, är'ki-tekt, *n. The chief workman;* one who plans buildings, &c.;

a contriver, a former or maker. [Gr. *archos*, and *tektōn*, a worker.]
Architectural, är-ki-tek'tūr-al, *a. Pertaining to* or according to the rules of *architecture.*
Architecture, är'ki-tek-tūr, *n.* The art of planning and constructing houses, bridges, &c.; frame, structure, or workmanship. [L. *architectūra*—Gr. *archos*, and *teuchō*, to make.]
Archives, är'kīvz, *n. pl.* Registers; public papers preserved as records of facts. [Fr.; Gr. *archaios*, old.]
Archly, ärch'li, *adv.* Shrewdly; wittily; roguishly; jestingly.
Archness, ärch'nes, *n. Quality of being arch;* cunning; wagishness.
Archway, ärch'wā, *n. A way* or passage *under an arch.*
Arctic, ärk'tik, *a. Pertaining to the northern* constellation called the *Great Bear*, or to the northern regions; northern. [Gr. *arktikos—arktos*, a bear.]
Ardency, är'den-si, *n. Ardour;* eagerness.
Ardent, är'dent, *a. Burning;* fervent; violent; vehement; passionate; eager. [L. *ardens*.]
Ardently, är'dent-li, *adv. With ardour.*
Ardour, är'dėr, *n. A flame*; warmth; fervency; vehemence; affection. [L. *ardor—ardeo*, to take fire.]
Arduous, är'dū-us, *a. High;* difficult; laborious; hard to attain. [L. *arduus*, Celt. *ard*, high.]
Arduously, är'dū-us-li, *adv. In an arduous manner.*
Arduousness, är'dū-us-nes, *n. State of being arduous;* difficulty of execution.
Are, är. The plural pres. indic. of the substantive verb *to be*. [Sw. *vara*, to be.]
Area, ā'rē-a, *n.* Any open surface; superficial contents; any inclosed space. [L. *areo*, to dry.]
Arena, a-rē'na, *n.* Primarily, *sand;* an open space of ground, strewed with *sand* or sawdust, for combatants; any place of public contest. [L. *sand—areo*, to dry.]
Argent, är'jent, *a. Silvery; like silver*. [from L. *argentum*, silver.]
Argillaceous, är-jil-lā'shē-us, *a. Of the nature of clay;* clayey. [L. *argillaceus*, from *argilla*, white clay.]
Argue, är'gū, *vi.* To offer reasons to make something *clear;* to dispute; to reason.—*vt. To make clear;* to show reasons for; to persuade by reasons; to discuss. *ppr.* arguing, *pret. & pp.* argued. [L. *arguo*—Gr. *argos*, bright.]
Argument, är'gū-ment, *n.* The means by which an assertion may be made *clear* and *shown* to be true; a proof; a plea; subject of any discourse; heads of contents; controversy. [L. *argumentum*.]
Argumentation, är'gū-ment-ā''shon, *n. Act, art*, or *process of arguing* or reasoning; a using of arguments.
Argumentative, är-gū-ment'at-iv, *a. Consisting of argument*; containing argument; addicted to argument.
Argumentatively, är-gū-ment'at-iv-li, *adv. In an argumentative manner.*
Arian, ā'ri-an, *a. Pertaining to Arius*, who denied the divinity of Christ and of the Holy Spirit.—*n.* One who adheres to the doctrines of *Arius.*
Arid, a'rid, *a. Dry;* dried; parched. [L. *aridus*, from *areo*, to be dry.]
Aridity, a-rid'i-ti, *n. Dryness;* a state of being without moisture.
Aries, ā'ri-ēz, *n. The Ram*, the first of the twelve signs in the zodiac. [L. a ram.]

Fāte, fär, fat, fall; mē, met, hėr; pīne, pin; nōte, not, mōve; tūbe, tub, bull; oil, pound.

Aright, a-rīt', *adv.* On right; rightly; justly. [Sax. a for *on*, and *riht*, right.]
Arise, a-rīz', *vi.* To rise up; to get up; to come into view; to spring upwards; to proceed from; to revive from death. *pret.* arose, *ppr.* arising, *pp.* arisen. [Sax. *arisan.*]
Aristocracy, a-ris-tok'ra-si, *n.* A form of government in which the *nobility* have *supreme power*; the chief persons in a state. [Gr. *aristos*, best, and *kratos*, strength.]
Aristocrat, a'ris-to-krat, *n.* One who favours *aristocracy*; a haughty overbearing person. [Fr. *aristocrate.*]
Aristocratic, a-ris-to-krat'ik, *a.* Pertaining to aristocracy; haughty.
Aristocratically, a-ris-to-krat'ik-al-li, *adv.* In an *aristocratical manner.*
Aristotelian, a-ris-to-tē'li-an, *a.* Pertaining to *Aristotle*, or to his philosophy.—*n.* A follower of *Aristotle.*
Arithmetic, a-rith'met-ik, *n.* The art or science of *numbering*; that branch of mathematics which treats of numbers, and teaches the art of computation. [from Gr. *arithmos*, number.]
Arithmetical, a-rith-met'ik-al, *a.* Pertaining to arithmetic.
Arithmetically, a-rith-met'ik-al-li, *adv.* By means of arithmetic.
Arithmetician, a-rith'me-ti''shi-an, *n.* One skilled in arithmetic.
Ark, ärk, *n.* A chest; the vessel which contained the tables of the covenant among the Jews; the large floating vessel in which Noah was preserved during the deluge; a depository. [L. *arca,* from *arceo,* to inclose.]
Arm, ärm, *n.* The limb of the human body from the shoulder to the hand; anything extending from the main body, as an inlet of the sea, branch of a tree, &c.; power; might.—*vt.* To furnish *with arms;* to strengthen; to fortify (in a moral sense).—*vi.* To provide one's self *with arms;* to take or put on arms. [Sax.—Gr. *arō*, to join to.]
Armada, är-mā'da, *n.* A *fleet of armed ships;* a squadron. [Sp.; L. *arma,* armour.]
Armadillo, är-ma-dil'lō, *n.* A quadruped covered with a *hard bony shell.* [Sp. from L. *arma,* armour.]
Armament, ärm'a-ment, *n.* A land or naval force equipped for war. [L. *armamenta—arma*, arms.]
Armed, ärmd, *p.a.* Furnished with the means of security; fortified (in a moral sense).
Armenian, är-mē'ni-an, *a.* Pertaining to *Armenia.*—*n.* A native of Armenia; the language of the country.
Armiger, ärm'ij-ėr, *n.* An esquire. [L. *arma*, arms, and *gero*, to bear.]
Arminian, är-min'i-an, *a.* Pertaining to *Arminius.*—*n.* One of a party of Christians who deny the doctrine of predestination.
Arminianism, är-min'i-an-izm, *n.* The peculiar doctrines of the *Arminians.*
Armipotent, är-mip'ō-tent, *a.* Powerful in *arms.* [L. *arma,* arms, and *potens,* powerful.]
Armistice, ärm'is-tis, *n.* A cessation of hostilities for a short time; a truce. [Fr.—L. *arma,* arms, and *sisto,* to stop.]
Armorial, är-mō'ri-al, *a.* Belonging to *armour,* or to the arms of a family.
Armoric, är-mo'rik, *a.* Designating the north-western part of France, now Bretagne.—*n.* The language of Bretagne, one of the Celtic dialects.
Armour, ärm'ėr, *n.* Defensive arms. [L. *arma,* arms.]

Armourer, ärm'ėr-ėr, *n.* A maker o arms; one who has the care of arms.
Armoury, ärm'é-ri, *n.* A repository of arms and instruments of war.
Armpit, ärm'pit, *n.* The hollow place under the shoulder.
Arms, ärms, *n. pl.* Weapons of offence or *defence;* hostility; ensigns armorial. [L. *arma.*]
Army, är'mi, *n.* A host; a great number; a vast multitude. [Fr. *armée.*]
Aroma, a-rō'ma, *n.* Strong perfume; the fragrant principle in plants, &c.; a pleasant odour. [Gr. *aroma—ari,* greatly, and *osō,* to smell.]
Aromatic, a-rō-mat'ik, *a.* Fragrant; spicy; having an agreeable odour.—*n.* A fragrant plant or drug; a perfume.
Aromatise, a-rō'mat-īz, *vt.* To impregnate *with aroma* or fragrant odours.
Around, a-round', *prep.* About; on all sides of; encircling.—*adv.* On every side.
Arouse, a-rouz', *vt.* To rouse; to stir up. *ppr.* arousing, *pret. & pp.* arou-ed.
Arrack, a'rak, *n.* In India, a spirituous liquor. [Hind.]
Arraign, a-rān', *vt.* To call to account; to indict; to censure. [Old Fr. *arraigner*—L. *ratio,* account.]
Arraigner, a-rān'ėr, *n.* One who arraigns.
Arraignment, a-rān'ment, *n.* Act of *arraigning*; accusation; charge.
Arrange, a-rānj', *vt.* To place in a *line*; to put in proper order; to adjust; to classify. *ppr.* arranging, *pret. & pp.* arranged. [Fr. *arranger—rang,* a rank.]
Arranged, a-rānjd', *p.a.* Put in order; adjusted.
Arrangement, a-rānj'ment, *n.* Orderly disposition; adjustment; classification.
Arrant, a'rant, *a.* Primarily, *vagabond;* downright; thorough; mere. [L. *errans—erro,* to wander.]
Arras, a'ras, *n.* Tapestry; hangings woven with figures. [from *Arras,* in Artois.]
Array, a-rā', *n.* Order; order of battle: posture of defence; equipment.—*vt.* To *set in order;* to draw up; to adorn. [Norm. *araies,* array; Sw. *reda,* to prepare.]
Arrear, a-rēr', *n.* That which remains *behind;* that which is due or unpaid. (Generally in the plural.) [Fr. *arrière*—L. *retro,* backward.]
Arrest, a-rest', *vt.* To stop; to seize; to apprehend.—*n.* A stopping; a seizure by warrant; obstruction; delay. [Old Fr. *arrester*—L. *resto,* to stand back.]
Arrival, a-rīv'al, *n.* Act of coming to a *place;* persons or things arriving.
Arrive, a-rīv', *vi.* To come; to reach; to attain. *ppr.* arriving, *pret. & pp.* arrived. [Fr. *arriver*—L. *ripa,* the bank of a river.]
Arrogance, a'rō-gans, *n.* Act of taking much *upon one's self;* assumption; haughtiness; insolent bearing. [Fr.]
Arrogant, a'rō-gant, *a.* Assuming; haughty; overbearing. [L. *arrogans.*]
Arrogantly, a'rō-gant-li, *adv.* In a rogant manner.
Arrogate, a'rō-gāt, *vt.* To ask more than is proper; to assume from pride or vanity. *ppr.* arrogating, *pret. & pp.* arrogated. [L. *rogo, rogatus,* to ask.]
Arrow, a'rō, *n.* A straight-pointed weapon, to be discharged from a bow. [Sax. *arewa.*]
Arrow-headed, a'rō-hed-ed, *a.* Shaped *like the head of an arrow;* wedge-like, as characters.
Arrowroot, a'rō-röt, *n.* A plant, a native of South America; the starch of the plant, a nutritive medicinal food.
Arrowy, a'rō-i, *a.* Consisting of, formed, or moving like arrows.
Arsenal, är'sē-nal, *n.* A public establishment where naval and military engines are manufactured or stored. [Fr.; Armor. *ar sanal,* the granary.]
Arsenic, är'sen-ik, *n.* A strong virulent mineral poison; an oxide of a brittle metal, called also arsenic. [Gr. *arsenikon,* male.]
Arsenical, är-sen'ik-al, *a.* Consisting of or containing arsenic.
Arson, är'son, *n.* A burning; the malicious setting on fire of a house. [O. Fr. —L. *ardeo, arsum,* to burn.]
Art, ärt. The second person, indicative mood, present tense, of the substantive verb am. [Sax. *eart.*]
Art, ärt, *n.* Practical knowledge or *skill;* a system of rules to facilitate the performance of certain actions; contrivance; adroitness; cunning; profession, business, or trade. [L. *ars, artis;* Gr. *arétē,* skill.]
Arterial, är-tē'ri-al, *a.* Pertaining to an artery or the arteries.
Artery, är'tė-ri, *n.* Primarily, the *windpipe;* a tube which conveys the blood from the heart to all parts of the body. [Gr. *artēria—aēr,* air, and *tereō,* to contain.]
Artesian, är-tē'zi-an, *a.* Designating a well made by boring into the earth till water is reached. [from *Artois,* in France.]
Artful, ärt'fŭl, *a.* Performed with art; skilful; full of stratagems.
Artfully, ärt fŭl-li, *adv.* With art.
Artfulness, ärt'fŭl-nes, *n.* Quality of being artful; craft; address.
Artichoke, är'ti-chōk, *n.* An esculent plant somewhat resembling a thistle. [Fr. *artichaut.*]
Article, är'ti-kl, *n.* A small joint; a member; a separate item; stipulation; a point of faith; a particular commodity; a part of speech.—*vt.* To bind by *articles.*—*vi.* To stipulate. *ppr.* articling, *pret. & pp.* articled. [L. *articulus* —Gr. *arthros,* a joint, from *arō,* to fit.]
Articulate, är-tik'ū-lāt, *a.* Jointed; uttered distinctly, as sounds; clear. *vi.* To utter distinct sounds, syllables, or words.—*vt.* To joint; to form into distinct elementary sounds, syllables, or words. *ppr.* articulating, *pret. & pp.* articulated. [L. *articulatus.*]
Articulately, är-tik'ū-lāt-li, *adv.* Distinctly; clearly.
Articulation, är-tik'ū-lā''shon, *n.* The juncture of the *bones,* or the parts of a plant; distinct utterance.
Artifice, ärt'i-fis, *n.* An artful device; fraud; stratagem. [Fr.—L. *ars, artis,* art, and *facio,* to make.]
Artificer, är-tif'is-ėr, *n.* One who contrives by *art;* a mechanic.
Artificial, ärt-i-fi'shi-al, *a.* Made by art; not natural; not indigenous.
Artificially, ärt-i-fi'shi-al-li, *adv.* In an *arti : tal manner.*
Artillery, är-til'lė-ri, *n.* Weapons of war; cannon; great ordnance; the troops for the management of artillery; gunnery. [Fr. *artillerie*—L. *ars,* art.]
Artisan, ärt'i-zan, *n.* One trained to manual dexterity; a mechanic. [Fr.]
Artist, ärt'ist, *n.* One skilled in the practice of *some art;* specially, a person who practises one of the fine arts. [Fr. *artiste.*]
Artistic, är-tist'ik, *a.* Pertaining to or artist; conformed to art.

ch, *chain*; j, *job*; g, *go*; ng, *sing*; ᴛʜ, *then*; th, *thin*; w, *wig*; wh, *whig*; zh, *azure*; † obsolete.

2

Artistically, är-tist'ik-al-li, *adv*. In an *artistic manner*.
Artless, ärt'les, *a*. *Wanting art*; simple; unaffected; without guile.
Artlessly, ärt'les-li, *adv*. *In an artless manner*.
Artlessness, ärt'les-nes, *n*. *Quality of being artless*.
As, as, *adv*. *Also*; like; even; similarly; equally; in respect of it, that, or which; while; for example.—*conj*. In the same or like manner; in the manner that; in respect that; that. [Sax. *ase*; old G. *also*.]
Asbestos, as-bes'tos, *n*. A mineral fibrous substance, which is *incombustible*. [Gr. *a*, priv. and *sbennumi*, to put out.]
Ascend, as-send', *vi*. *To climb*; to go or come up; to rise; to soar; to become higher; to become superior; to go backward in the order of time.—*vt*. To go or move upward upon; to climb. [L. *ascendo—scando*, to climb.]
Ascendant, as-send'ant, *a*. Superior; predominant; overpowering.—*n*. Superiority or commanding power or influence.
Ascendency, as-send'en-si, *n*. Governing or controlling influence or power; authority; sway.
Ascending, as-send'ing, *p.a*. Climbing; proceeding from the less to the greater.
Ascension, as-sen'shon, *n*. *Act of ascending*; a rising or mounting upwards. [L. *ascensio*.]
Ascension Day, as-sen'shon dā, *n*. A festival held on Holy Thursday, in commemoration of our Saviour's *ascension* into heaven.
Ascent, as-sent', *n*. *Rise*; a mounting upward; the means of ascending; the rise of a hill; an eminence. [L. *ascensus—scando*, to climb.]
Ascertain, as-sér-tān', *vt*. *To make certain*; to make to be certainly known; to establish; to become cognizant of. [Fr. *certain*, true; L. *certus*, certain.]
Ascertainable, as-sér-tān'a-bl, *a*. *That may be ascertained*.
Ascetic, as-set'ik, *a*. Unduly rigid in devotional *exercises*; rigid.—*n*. One who *exercises* devotion and mortification. [from Gr. *askētos—askeō*, to exercise.]
Asceticism, as-set'i-sizm, *n*. *State or practice of ascetics*.
Ascii, a'shi-i, *n.pl*. Persons who at certain times of the year have *no shadow* at noon, as the inhabitants of the torrid zone. [L. *ascii*—Gr. *a*, priv. and *skia*, a shadow.]
Ascribable, as-krīb'a-bl, *a*. *That may be ascribed*.
Ascribe, as-krīb', *vt*. *To write to* the account; to charge against; to attribute; to assign. *ppr*. ascribing, *pret*. & *pp*. ascribed. [L. *ascribo—scribo*, to write.]
Ascription, as-krip'shon, *n*. *Act of ascribing*; the thing ascribed.
Ash, ash, *n*. A large hardy tree, the wood of which is extensively used where strength and elasticity are required.—*a*. *Pertaining to the ash*; made of ash. [Sax. *œsc*.]
Ashamed, a-shāmd', *a*. *Affected by shame*; abashed, or confused by guilt. [*a* and *shame*.]
Ashen, ash'en, *a*. *Pertaining to ash*; made of ash.
Ashes, ash'es, *n.pl*. The dust or loose earthy particles produced by combustion; the remains of a dead body. [Sax. *asca*.]
Ashlar, Ashler, ash'lēr, ash'lēr, *n*. A facing of *dressed* and squared *stones*, to cover walls of brick or rubble. [It. *acciare*, to hew smooth—*asce*, an axe.]

Ashore, a-shōr', *adv*. *On shore*; on the land; to or at the shore.
Ash-Wednesday, ash-wenz'dā, *n*. The first day of Lent, supposed to be so called from a custom of sprinkling *ashes* on the head.
Ashy, ash'i, *a*. *Belonging to* or composed of *ashes*; having the colour of ashes; pale.
Asiatic, ā-shi-at'ik, *a*. *Belonging to Asia*.—*n*. *A native of Asia*.
Aside, a-sīd', *adv*. *To or on one side*; not straight or perpendicular; out of the right way; apart; at a small distance.
Asinine, as'i-nīn, *a*. *Belonging to* or *resembling the ass*. [L. *asininus—asinus*, an ass.]
Ask, ask, *vt*. *To petition*; to beg; to demand; to inquire; to require; to solicit. *vi*. To request or petition; to make inquiry (with *for*). [Sax. *ascian*.]
Askance, Askant, a-skans', a-skant', *adv*. Awry; obliquely; toward one corner of the eye. [D. *schuins*, sideways.]
Aslant, a-slant', *a*. or *adv*. *On slant*; on one side; obliquely; not perpendicularly.
Asleep, a-slēp', *a*. or *adv*. *On or to sleep*; sleeping; at rest; dead.
Aslope, a-slōp', *a*. or *adv*. With leaning or inclination; obliquely.
Asp, asp, *n*. A small poisonous serpent of Egypt and Libya, whose bite is supposed to cause inevitable and painless death. [L. and Gr. *aspis*.]
Asparagus, as-pa'ra-gus, *n*. A well-known esculent plant. [Gr. *asparagos—an, ana*, up, and *spargaō*, to swell.]
Aspect, as'pekt, *n*. That which is *looked at*; look; appearance; point of view; situation. [L. *aspectus—specio*, to look.]
Aspen, asp'en, *n*. A species of the poplar, with *trembling* leaves.—*a*. *Pertaining to* or *resembling the aspen*. [Sax. *æsp*.]
Asperity, as-pe'ri-ti, *n*. *Roughness* of surface; harshness; sharpness; moroseness. [L. *asperitas—asper*, rough.]
Asperse, as-pérs', *vt*. *To scatter* calumny *upon*; to slander. *ppr*. aspersing, *pret*. & *pp*. aspersed. [L. *aspergo—spargo*, to scatter.]
Aspersion, as-pér'shon, *n*. Calumny; defamation.
Asphalt, as-falt', *n*. Jews' pitch; a bituminous, hard, *firm* substance, used for pavement, &c. [Gr. *asphaltos—a*, priv. and *sphallō*, to slip.]
Asphaltic, as-falt'ik, *a*. *Pertaining to asphalt*, or containing it.
Asphodel, as'fō-del, *n*. The day-lily, a *perennial* plant. [Gr. *aspho*·*elos—a*, priv. and *sphallō*, to be made to fall.]
Asphyxia, as-fik'si-a, *n*. *A cessation of the pulse*; suspended animation, particularly from suffocation, &c. [Gr. *asphuxia—a*, priv. and *sphuzō*, to throb.]
Aspirant, as-pīr'ant, *n*. *One who aspires*; a candidate.
Aspirate, as'pi-rāt, *vt*. To pronounce with an audible *breathing*. *ppr*. aspirating, *pret*. & *pp*. aspirated.—*n*. The mark of such breathing, particularly in Greek (').—*a*. *Pronounced with a full breath*. [L. *aspiro, aspiratus—spiro*, to breathe.]
Aspiration, as-pi-rā'shon, *n*. *A breathing after*; eager pursuit of; ardent desire for; pronunciation of a letter with an audible emission of breath. [L. *aspiratio—spiro*, to breathe.]
Aspire, as-pīr', *vi*. *To breathe toward or after*; to aim at what is elevated, great, noble, or difficult; to soar. (With *to* or *after*.) *ppr*. aspiring, *pret*. & *pp*. aspired. [L. *aspiro—spiro*, to breathe.]

Aspiring, as-pīr'ing, *p.a*. Ambitious; having an ardent desire to rise to eminence.
Aspiringly, as-pīr'ing-li, *adv*. In an aspiring manner.
Asquint, a-skwint', *adv*. To the corner or angle of the eye; obliquely. [D. *schuinte*, wryness.]
Ass, as, *n*. A well-known animal, dull and *slow*, but patient, hardy, and sure-footed; a dolt. [Sax. *assa*; L. *asinus*.]
Assail, as-sāl', *vt*. *To leap against*; to fall upon; to assault. [Fr. *assaillir*—L. *salio*, to leap.]
Assailable, as-sāl'a-bl, *a*. *That may be assailed*.
Assailant, as-sāl'ant, *n*. *One who assails*. [Fr.]
Assassin, as-sas'sin, *n*. One who kills, or attempts to kill, by surprise or secret assault. [Fr.]
Assassinate, as-sas'sin-āt, *vt*. To murder by surprise or secret assault. *ppr*. assassinating, *pret*. & *pp*. assassinated.
Assassination, as-sas'sin-ā'shon, *n*. Act of murdering by surprise.
Assault, as-salt', *n*. *A leaping against*; an attack; a storming.—*vt*. *To assail*; to fall upon by violence; to storm. [O. Fr.—L. *salio*, to leap.]
Assaulter, as-salt'ér, *n*. *One who assaults*.
Assay, as-sā', *n*. *Proof*; trial; endeavour; determination of the quantity of gold or silver in coin or bullion; substance to be assayed. [Fr. *essai*.]—*vt*. *To weigh accurately*; to try; to ascertain the purity or alloy of, as of a metal.—*vi*. To try or endeavour. [Fr. *essayer*; L. *exigo*, to examine—*ago*, to deal with.]
Assayer, as-sā'ér, *n*. *One who assays*.
Assaying, as-sā'ing, *pn*. Act of ascertaining the purity of the precious metals.
Assemblage, as-sem'blāj, *n*. *An assembly*; a collection of individuals, or of particular things. [Fr.]
Assemble, as-sem'bl, *vt*. *To bring together*.—*vi*. *To come together*. *ppr*. assembling, *pret*. & *pp*. assembled. [Fr. *assembler*—L. *simul*, together.]
Assembling, as-sem'bl-ing, *p.n*. A bringing together; a meeting together.
Assembly, as-sem'bli, *n*. *An assemblage*; a convocation. [Fr. *assemblée*.]
Assent, as-sent', *n*. *Act of agreeing* to anything; consent.—*vi*. *To agree*; to yield; to admit a thing as true. [O Fr. —L. *sentio*, to think, to feel.]
Assert, as-sért', *vt*. Primarily, *to fasten to*; to maintain; to declare positively; to vindicate. [L. *assero, assertum—sero*, to join.]
Assertion, as-sér'shon, *n*. *Act of asserting*; positive declaration or averment.
Assess, as-ses', *vt*. To determine at a *sitting* a charge to be paid upon; to rate. [L. *assideo, assessum—sedeo*, to sit.]
Assessable, as-ses'a-bl, *a*. *That may be assessed*.
Assessed, as-sest', *p.a*. Valued; set; fixed.
Assessment, as-ses'ment, *n*. *Act of assessing*; the sum levied; a tax.
Assessor, as-ses'ér, *n*. A legal adviser who *sits beside* the magistrate or judge to assist him. [L.]
Assets, as'sets, *n.pl*. Goods *sufficient* for the discharge of all legal claims; goods answerable for payment. [Fr. *assez*—L. *ad*, and *satis*, enough.]
Asseverate, as-sev'é-rāt, *vt*. *To declare with great seriousness*; to protest. *ppr*. asseverating, *pret*. & *pp*. asseverated. [L. *assevēro, asseveratus—asserus*, serious.]

Fāte, fär, fat, fall; mē, met, hér; pīne, pin; nōtes, not, mōve; tūbe, tub, bull; oil, pound.

ASSEVERATION — 19 — ATMOSPHERE

Asseveration, as-sev'ē-rā"shon, n. Positive and solemn declaration.
Assiduity, as-si-dū'i-ti, n. A sitting close to; close application; diligence; watchful care. [L. assiduitas—sedeo, to sit.]
Assiduous, as-sid'ū-us, a. Sitting close to; unceasingly diligent; unwearied. [L. assiduus.]
Assign, as-sīn', vt. To mark out; to designate; to allot; to make over, as a right; to set forth.—n. A person to whom property or any right is or may be transferred. [Fr. assigner—L. signo, to mark.]
Assignable, as-sīn'a-bl, a. That may be assigned.
Assignation, as-sig-nā'shon, n. An appointment to meet, as lovers; a making over by transfer of title.
Assigned, as-sīnd', p.a. Allotted; designated.
Assignee, as-si-nē', n. One to whom an assignment is made.
Assigner, as-sīn'ėr, n. One who assigns.
Assignment, as-sīn'ment, n. Act of assigning; thing assigned; a writ of transfer.
Assimilate, as-sim'il-āt, vt. To make like to; to cause to resemble; to turn to its own substance by digestion.—vi. To become similar; to become of the same substance. ppr. assimilating, pret. & pp. assimilated. [L. assimulo, assimulatus—similis, like.]
Assimilation, as-sim'il-ā"shon, n. Act of assimilating; process of being assimilated; a state of resemblance.
Assist, as-sist', vt. To place one's self beside; to help; to succour; to sustain. vi. To lend aid; to contribute. [L. assisto—sisto, to stand.]
Assistance, as-sist'ans, n. Help; aid; succour. [Fr.]
Assistant, as-sist'ant, a. Helping; aiding.—n. One who assists or aids; a supporter; an auxiliary.
Assize, as-sīz', n. Assizes, as-sīz'es, pl. In England a court of judicature held twice a year in every county (generally pl.); a statute regulating weights, measures, or prices; weight, &c., thus regulated. [Fr. and O. Fr. assises—L. sedeo, to sit.]
Associable, as-sō'shi-a-bl, a. That may be associated with; companionable.
Associate, as-sō'shi-āt, vt. To join in company with; to combine.—vi. To unite one's self; to keep company. ppr. associating, pret. & pp. associated. p.a. Joined to or with; confederate.—n. A companion; a friend; a coadjutor. [L. associo, associatum—socius, a companion.]
Association, as-sō'si-ā"shon, n. Act of associating; union; confederacy; a body of persons joined together for the support or furtherance of some object. [Fr.]
Assonance, as'sō-nans, n. A sounding to; resemblance of sounds. [Fr.—L. sono, to sound.]
Assort, as-sort', vt. To sort; to distribute into classes or kinds; to arrange.—vi. To suit; to agree; to consort. [Fr. assortir—L. sors, sortis, a lot.]
Assortment, as-sort'ment, n. Act of assorting; a quantity of things assorted.
Assuage, as-swāj', vt. Primarily, to sweeten; to soften; to calm.—vi. To abate or subside. ppr. assuaging, pret. & pp. assuaged. [Norm. assoager, to comfort—L. suavis, sweet.]
Assuagement, as-swāj'ment, n. That which mitigates; mitigation.

Assuasive, as-swā'siv, a. Softening; tranquillising. [L. ad and suavis.]
Assume, as-sūm', vt. To take to; to take for granted; to usurp.—vi. To claim more than is due; to be arrogant. ppr. assuming, pret. & pp. assumed. [L. assumo—sūmo, to take.]
Assuming, as-sūm'ing, p.a. Taking upon one's self more than is just; arrogant.
Assumption, as-sum'shon, n. Act of assuming; the thing assumed; the taking up of any person into heaven. [L. assumptio.]
Assurance, ash-shūr'ans, n. Act of assuring; certain knowledge; secure confidence; certainty; ground of confidence; impudence; security; positive declaration; insurance. [Fr.]
Assure, ash-shūr', vt. To make sure or secure; to give confidence by promise; to confirm; to insure. ppr. assuring, pret. & pp. assured. [Fr. assurer—L. securus, secure.]
Assured, ash-shūrd', p.a. Certain; indubitable.
Assuredly, ash-shūr'ed-li, adv. Certainly; indubitably.
Assuredness, ash-shūr'ed-nes, n. State of being assured.
Assurer, ash-shūr'ėr, n. One who assures or insures.
Aster, as'tėr, n. A genus of plants, with compound flowers, resembling little stars. [Gr. astēr, a star.]
Asterisk, as'tė-risk, n. A little star; the figure of a star, thus *, used in printing and writing. [Gr. asteriskos.]
Astern, a-stėrn', adv. On the stern; in or at the hinder part of a ship.
Asteroid, as'tėr-oid, n. A small planet. [Gr. astēr, a star, and eidos, form, species.]
Asthma, ast'ma, n. Short-drawn breath; a frequent, difficult, and short respiration, with cough and wheezing. [Gr.—aō, to blow or breathe.]
Asthmatic, ast-mat'ik, a. Pertaining to asthma; affected by asthma.
Astir, a-stėr', a. On stir; stirring; active. [Sax. on, and stir.]
Astonish, as-ton'ish, vt. To stun, as with a sudden clap of thunder; to strike dumb; to amaze. [Old Fr. estonner, estonnissant—L. attono, to thunder at.]
Astonishing, as-ton'ish-ing, p.a. Tending to astonish; marvellous.
Astonishment, as-ton'ish-ment, n. State of being astonished; amazement.
Astound, as-tound', vt. To stun; to strike dumb with amazement. [Sax. astundian.]
Astounding, as-tound'ing, p.a. Adapted to astonish.
Astraddle, a-strad'l, adv. On straddle; astride with the legs across a thing.
Astral, as'tral, a. Belonging to the stars; starry. [Fr.—L. astrum, a star.]
Astray, a-strā', adv. On stray; out of the right way or proper place.
Astriction, as-trik'shon, n. Act of binding close together; contraction. [L. astrictio.]
Astride, a-strīd', adv. On stride; with the legs apart or across a thing.
Astringency, as-trinj'en-si, n. Power of contracting, or of giving firmness.
Astringent, as-trinj'ent, a. Binding; contracting; strengthening.—n. A medicine which contracts and strengthens. [L. astringens—stringo, to bind.]
Astrologer, as-trol'o-jėr, n. One versed in astrology. [Gr. astrologos.]
Astrological, as-trō-loj'ik-al, a. Pertaining to astrology.
Astrology, as-trol'o-ji, n. The pretended art of foretelling future events by the

situation and different aspects of the stars. [Gr. astron, mostly in pl. astra, a star, the stars, and logos, discourse.]
Astronomer, as-tron'ō-mėr, n. One versed in astronomy.
Astronomical, as-trō-nom'ik-al, a. Pertaining to astronomy.
Astronomically, as-trō-nom'ik-al-li, adv. In an astronomical manner.
Astronomy, as-tron'ō-mi, n. The laws of the stars; the science which teaches the knowledge of the heavenly bodies. [Gr. astronomia—astron, a star, and nomos, a law.]
Astrut, a-strut', adv. On strut; in a strutting manner.
Astute, as-tūt', a. Primarily, city-bred; shrewd; crafty; penetrating. [L. astutus—Gr. astu, a city.]
Astutely, as-tūt'li, adv. Shrewdly.
Astuteness, as-tūt'nes, n. Quality of being astute; shrewdness; cunning.
Asunder, a-sun'dėr, adv. Separately; apart; into parts; in a divided state. [Sax. asundran—sunder, separate.]
Asylum, a-sī'lum, n. A place where one is safe from seizure; a sanctuary; an institution for the care or relief of the unfortunate. [L. a, priv. and sulē, the right of seizure.]
Asyndeton, a-sin'de-ton, n. The dispensing with conjunctions in speech. [Gr. a, priv. sun, and deō, to bind.]
At, at, prep. A word which denotes presence, nearness, or direction towards; near or close to; by; in; on; with; in a state of; engaged or employed in, on, or with. [Sax. æt.]
Athanasian, ath-a-nā'si-an, a. Pertaining to Athanasius, or to his creed.
Atheism, ā'thē-izm, n. Godlessness; the disbelief of the existence of a God.
Atheist, ā'thē-ist, n. One who is godless; one who disbelieves the existence of a God. [Gr. atheos—a, priv. and Theos, God.]
Atheistic, Atheistical, ā-thē-ist'ik, ā-thē-ist'ik-al, a. Pertaining to atheism or atheists; impious; godless.
Atheneum, Athenæum, ath-ē-nē'um, ath-ē-nē'um, n. A public reading-room; an establishment connected with literature, science, or art. [Gr. athēnaion, the temple of Athēna, the tutelary goddess of Athens.]
Athenian, a-thēn'i-an, a. Pertaining to Athens.—n. A native or inhabitant of Athens.
Athirst, a-thėrst', a. On or in thirst; thirsty; wanting drink.
Athlete, ath-lēt', n. A prize-fighter; a contender for victory. [Gr. athlētēs.]
Athletic, ath-let'ik, a. Pertaining to a wrestler or to wrestling; strong; robust; vigorous. [Gr. athlētikos—athlos, a contest.]
Athwart, a-thwart', prep. Across; from side to side.—adv. Crossly; wrong; wrongfully.
Atlantean, at-lan-tē'an, a. Resembling Atlas; gigantic. [L. Atlanteus.]
Atlantic, at-lan'tik, a. Pertaining to the Atlantic Ocean.—n. The ocean between Europe, Africa, and America. [from Atlas, a mountain in the western part of Africa, the shores of which this ocean washes.]
Atlas, at'las, n. A collection of maps, so called from having originally on the title-page a figure of Atlas supporting the world. [Gr.—tlēnai, to bear.]
Atmosphere, at'mos-fėr, n. The air, sphere; the whole mass of air sur, rounding the earth; air; pervading influence. [Gr. atmos, smoke or steam, and sphaira, sphere.]

ch, chain j, job; g, go; ng, sing; VH, then; th, thin; w, wig; wh, whig; zh, azure; † obsolete.

Atmospheric, at-mos-fe′rik, *a.* Pertaining to the atmosphere.
Atom, at′om, *n.* A particle of matter that *cannot be divided;* the smallest component part of a body; anything extremely small. [Gr. *atomos—a*, priv. and *temnō*, to cut.]
Atomic, a-tom′ik, *a.* Pertaining to or consisting of *atoms;* extremely minute.
Atone, a-tōn′, *vi.* To be or to become at one; to make reconciliation; to stand as a substitute. *ppr.* atoning, *pret. & pp.* atoned. [*at* and *one*.]
Atonement, a-tōn′ment, *n.* A bringing into *unity;* reconciliation; satisfaction.
Atoning, a - tōn′ing, *p.a.* Reconciling; making amends or satisfaction.
Atrip, a-trip′, *adv.* Drawn out of the ground in a perpendicular direction, as an anchor.
Atrocious, a-trō′shi-us, *a.* Extremely cruel; wicked in a high degree; enormous; flagitious. [L. *atrox*, *atrōcis*, savage.]
Atrociously, a-trō′shi-us-li, *adv.* In an atrocious manner.
Atrociousness, a-trō′shi-us-nes, *n.* Quality of being atrocious.
Atrocity, a-tros′i-ti, *n.* Horrible cruelty; enormous wickedness; enormity.
Atrophy, at′rō-fi, *n.* Want of *nourishment;* a consumption; a wasting away. [Gr. *a*, priv. and *trophē*, nourishment.]
Attach, at-tach′, *vt.* To affix; to cause to adhere to; to connect; to arrest; to gain over; to win.—*vi.* To be *attached;* to adhere. [Fr. *attacher*—L. *tango*, to touch.]
Attache, at-ta-shā′, *n.* One attached to the suite of an ambassador. [Fr.]
Attached, at-tacht′, *p.a.* Bound to; united.
Attachment, at-tach′ment, *n.* State of being *attached;* fidelity; tender regard; a seizing or apprehending.
Attack, at-tak′, *vt.* To assault; to assail; to make an onset upon; to invade. *n.* An assault; invasion; charge. [Fr. *attaquer;* L. *tango*, to touch.]
Attain, at-tān′, *vi.* To come to a certain state.—*vt.* To *reach;* to come to; to gain; to obtain. [Old Fr. *attaindre;* L. *ango*, to touch.]
Attainable, at-tān′a-bl, *a.* That may be attained.
Attainableness, at-tān′a-bl-nes, *n.* Quality of being attainable.
Attainder, at-tān′dėr, *n.* Act of *attainting;* extinction of civil rights, in consequence of being convicted of a capital crime. [from Old Fr. *attaindre*, to attaint—L. *tango*, to touch.]
Attainment, at-tān′ment, *n.* Act of attaining; acquirement; accomplishment.
Attaint, at-tānt′, *vt.* To *taint;* to find guilty of high treason or felony, and thereby subject to forfeiture of civil rights, and corruption of blood. [L. *tango*, to touch.]
Attar, at′tär, *n.* A highly *fragrant*, concrete oil, obtained in India from the petals of the rose. [Hindost. *utr*, essence, scent.]
Attemper, at-tem′pėr, *vt.* To temper; to mix in just proportions; to modify; to soften. [L. *attempero—tempero*, to mix in due proportion.]
Attempt, at-temt′, *vt.* To *put to the trial;* make an effort upon.—*n.* An essay; enterprise. [Fr. *attenter*—L. *tento*, to try.]
Attend, at-tend′, *vt.* To *stretch to;* to wait on; to accompany; to be present at; to watch; to follow; to mind. *vi.* To *stretch to something;* to hearken;

to be diligent; to wait; to accompany or be present; to serve. [L. *attendo—tendo*, to stretch.]
Attendance, at-tend′ans, *n.* Act of *attending;* service; retinue; close application of mind. [Fr.]
Attendant, at-tend′ant, *a.* Accompanying, as subordinate.—*n.* One who *attends* or waits on; one who is present; that which accompanies.
Attending, at-tend′ing, *p.a.* Accompanying.
Attention, at-ten′shon, *n.* Act of *attending;* heed; close mental application; civility; courtesy.
Attentive, at-tent′iv, *a. Regarding with attention;* heedful. [Fr. *attentif*.]
Attentively, at-tent′iv-li, *adv.* With attention.
Attentiveness, at-tent′iv-nes, *n.* State of *being attentive;* heedfulness; attention.
Attenuate, at-ten′ū-āt, *vt.* To *make thin* or slender; to diminish; to make small or slender. *ppr.* attenuating, *pret. & pp.* attenuated. [L. *attenuo*, *attenuatus—tenuis*, thin.]
Attenuated, at-ten′ū-āt-ed, *p.a.* Made *thin;* emaciated.
Attenuation, at-ten′ū-ā″shon, *n. Act of attenuating;* thinness; slenderness.
Attest, at-test′, *vt.* To *bear witness to;* to certify; to call to witness. [Fr. *attester;* L. *testis*, a witness.]
Attestation, at-test-ā′shon, *n.* Act of *attesting;* testimony; witness.
Attested, at-test′ed, *p.a.* Proved by testimony; witnessed to.
Attic, at′tik, *a.* Pertaining to *Attica* or to Athens; pure; classical; characterized by keenness of intellect, with judgment, wit, elegance, and brevity; designating an order of small square pillars at the uppermost extremity of a building, as originally used in *Athens*. *n.* The uppermost room or story of a building. [Gr. *Attikos*.]
Attire, at-tīr′, *vt.* To dress; to array; to deck. *ppr.* attiring, *pret. & pp.* attired.—*n.* Dress; head-dress; ornamental dress. [O. Fr. *atour*, an attire.]
Attitude, at′ti-tūd, *n.* Posture *adapted to some purpose;* posture; gesture. [Fr.; L. *apto*, to fit.]
Attitudinize, at-ti-tūd′in-īz, *vi.* To assume affected *attitudes*, airs, or postures. *ppr.* attitudinizing, *pret. & pp.* attitudinized.
Attorney, at-tėr′ni, *n.* **Attorneys**, at-tėr′niz, *pl.* One who *takes the turn*, or acts in the stead of another, especially in matters of law; one who practises in the courts of common law, called properly an attorney-at-law. [Norm. *attournon*, also *torne;* O. Fr. *tour*, a turn, work.]
Attorneyship, at-tėr′ni-ship, *n.* The *office of an attorney*.
Attract, at-trakt′, *vt.* To *draw to;* to entice; to allure. [L. *attraho*, *attractus—traho*, to draw.]
Attractability, at-trakt′a-bil″li-ti, *n. Quality of being attractable.*
Attractable, at-trakt′a-bl, *a.* That may be attracted.
Attractingly, at-trakt′ing-li, *adv.* In an attracting manner.
Attraction, at-trak′shon, *n.* Act of *attracting;* the force which *draws* bodies toward each other; allurement; charm. [L. *attractio*.]
Attractive, at-trakt′iv, *a.* Having the *quality or power of attracting;* alluring; inviting; engaging. [Fr. *attractif*.]
Attractively, at-trakt′iv-li, *adv.* With the power of attracting.

Attractiveness, at-trakt′iv-nes, *n.* Quality of being attractive.
Attributable, at-trib′ūt-a-bl, *a.* That may be attributed.
Attribute, at-trib′ūt, *vt.* To *give to;* to ascribe; to impute. *ppr.* attributing, *pret. & pp.* attributed. [L. *attribuo—tribuo*, *tributus*, to give.]
Attribute, at′tri-būt, *n.* That which is *attributed;* quality; property; a perfection of the Deity.
Attribution, at-tri-bū′shon, *n. Act of attributing*, or the quality ascribed.
Attributive, at-trib′ūt-iv, *a.* That *attributes;* attributing.—*n.* That which is attributed.
Attrition, at-tri′shon, *n.* A *rubbing against;* act of wearing, or state of being worn by rubbing; grief for sin arising only from fear. [Fr.; L. *terotritum*, to rub.]
Attune, at-tūn′, *vt.* To *put in tune;* to adjust to another sound; to make musical. *ppr.* attuning, *pret. & pp.* attuned. [*ad* and *tune*.]
Auburn, ạ′bėrn, *a.* Of the colour produced by *burning;* reddish brown; of a tan colour. [Sax. *a*, and *brun*, from *byrnan*, to burn.]
Auction, ạk′shon, *n.* A public sale of property, in which one person bids after another, each succeeding bidder *increasing* the price offered by the preceding, and the property falling to the last bidder; things sold at an auction. [L. *auctio—augeo*, to increase.]
Auctioneer, ạk-shon-ēr′, *n.* The *person who sells at auction.* [L. *auctionarius*, pertaining to an auction.]
Audacious, ạ-dā′shi-us, *a. Daring* (in a bad sense); impudent; having effrontery; courageous. [L. *audax—audeo*, to dare.]
Audaciousness, ạ-dā′shi-us-nes, *n. Quality of being audacious;* audacity.
Audacity, ạ-das′i-ti, *n. Daring;* boldness; confidence; impudence; effrontery.
Audible, ạ′di-bl, *a. That may be heard.* [L. *audibilis—audio*, to hear.]
Audibleness, ạ′di-bl-nes, *n. Quality of being audible.*
Audibly, ạ′di-bli, *adv.* In an *audible* manner.
Audience, ạ′di-ens, *n.* A *hearing;* an auditory; admittance to a hearing; the ceremonial hearing of ambassadors or ministers by a sovereign. [Fr.; L. *audio*, to hear.]
Audit, ạ′dit, *n.* The settling of accounts by examining documents, with a *hearing* of the parties concerned; a final account.—*vt.* To examine and adjust, as accounts. [L. *audit*, he hears.]
Auditor, ạ′dit-ėr, *n.* A *hearer;* one who examines and adjusts accounts. [L.]
Auditorship, ạ′dit-ėr-ship, *n. The office o auditor.*
Auditory, ạ′di-tō-ri, *a.* Pertaining to the sense or organs *of hearing.*—*n. An audience;* an assembly of *hearers;* the place where hearers assemble. [L. *auditorius.*]
Auger, ạ′gėr, *n.* The *nave-borer;* an instrument for boring large holes, used by carpenters, &c. [Sax. *nafe-gar-nafu*, nave, and *gar*, a borer.]
Aught, ạt, *n.* Anything; any part; a whit. [Sax. *awiht*, from *wiht*, a creature.]
Augment, ạg-ment′, *vt. To make larger; to increase;* to add to; to swell.—*vi.* To grow larger. [Fr. *augmenter;* L. *augeo*, to increase.]
Augment, ạg′ment, *n. Increase;* state of increase; a prefix to a word.

Fate, fär, fat, fạll; mē, met, hėr; pīne, pin; nōte, not, mōve; tūbe, tub, bụll; ọil, pound.

Augmentable, ąg-ment'a-bl, *a. Capable of augmentation.*
Augmentation, ąg-ment-ā'shon, *n. Act of augmenting;* increase; addition.
Augmentative, ąg-ment'at-iv, *a. Having the quality of augmenting.—n.* A derivative word denoting an *increase* of that which is expressed by its primitive.
Augur, ą'gėr, *n.* One who foretold the future by observing the flight and motions of *birds;* a soothsayer.—*vi.* To predict by signs; to conjecture.—*vt.* To predict or foretell. [L.—*avis*, a bird, and *gero*, to bear.]
Augural, ą'gū-ral, *a. Pertaining to an augur or augury.* [L. *auguralis.*]
Augurer, ą'gėr-ėr, *n. One who augurs.*
Augury, ą'gū-ri, *n.* An omen; prediction. [L. *augurium.*]
August, ą-gust', *a. Sacred; grand;* solemn; awful; majestic. [L. *augustus*—*augeo*, to increase.]
August, ą'gust, *n.* The eighth month of the year, named in honour of the Roman emperor Octavius *Augustus.*
Augustan, ą-gust'an, *a. Pertaining to Augustus,* or to his reign; classic.
Augustness, ą-gust'nes, *n. Quality of being august;* elevation of look; dignity.
Aulic, ą'lik, *a. Pertaining to a royal court.* [L. *aulicus—aula,* a palace.]
Aunt, änt, *n.* The sister of one's father or mother. [O. Fr. *ante*—L. *amita.*]
Aureate, ą-rē'āt, *a. Golden.* [L. *aurum,* gold.]
Aurelia, ą-rē'li-a, *n.* The chrysalis of an insect which is *gold-coloured.* [L. *aurum,* gold.]
Auricle, ą'ri-kl, *n. A little ear;* the external ear; one of two appendages to the heart, which cover the ventricles, and resemble ears. [L. *auricula*—*auris,* an ear.]
Auricula, ą-rik'ū-la, *n.* Species of primrose. [L. an auricle—*auris,* an ear.]
Auricular, ą-rik'ū-lėr, *a. Pertaining to the ear;* secret, as conveyed only to the ear. [Fr. *auriculaire.*]
Auriferous, ą-rif'ėr-us, *a. That yields or produces* gold. [L. *aurum,* gold, and *fero,* to produce.]
Aurist, ą'rist, *n. One skilled in disorders of the ear.* [from L. *auris,* the ear.]
Aurora, ą-rō'ra, *n. The morning hour;* the morning twilight; in poetry, the goddess of the morning. [Gr. *ēōs,* daybreak, and *hōra,* hour.]
Aurora Borealis, ą-rō'ra bō-rē-ā'lis, *n.* The *northern aurora;* a meteor appearing at night in the northern sky, and resembling the dawn of day. [L.]
Auscultation, ąs-kul-tā'shon, *n. Act of listening;* a method of discovering diseases of the lungs, &c., by applying the ear to a tube in contact with the chest. [L. *auscultatio—auris,* the ear, and *colo, cultum,* to use.]
Auscultator, ąs'kul-tāt-ėr, *n. One who practises auscultation.*
Auspices, ą'spis-ez, *n. pl. Omens drawn from observing birds;* favourable appearance; protection; influence. [L. *auspicium—avis,* a bird, and *specio,* to observe.]
Auspicious, ą-spi'shi-us, *a. Having or bringing good auspices;* fortunate; propitious; happy.
Auspiciously, ą-spi'shi-us-li, *adv. Happily;* prosperously; favourably.
Auspiciousness, ą-spi'shi-us-nes, *n. State or quality of being auspicious.*
Austere, ą-stēr', *a. Stiffened;* rigid; sour with astringency; stern; severe. [L. *austerus;* Gr. *auō,* to parch up.]

Austerely, ą-stēr'li, *adv. In an austere manner.*
Austereness, ą-stēr'nes, *n. Quality of being austere;* severity of manners.
Austerity, ą-ste'ri-ti, *n. Austereness;* severity of manners or life; rigour. [L. *austeritas.*]
Austral, ąs'tral, *a. Southern;* lying or being in the south. [L. *australis—auster,* the south.]
Authentic, ą-then'tik, *a.* Literally, *done with one's own hand;* having a genuine authority; true; correct; warranted. [Fr. *authentique;* Gr. *autoentēs,* one who does anything with his own hand.]
Authentically, ą-then'tik-al-li, *adv. In an authentic manner.*
Authenticate, ą-then'ti-kāt, *vt.* To establish by ascertaining the original author or authority. *ppr.* authenticating, *pret. & pp.* authenticated.
Authentication, ą-then'ti-kā'shon, *n. Act of authenticating;* confirmation.
Authenticity, ą-then-tis'i-ti, *n. Quality or state of being authentic,* or of resting upon proper authority; genuineness.
Author, ą'thėr, *n. One who enlarges;* one who creates, or brings into being; an originator; the writer of an original work. [Fr. *auteur;* L. *augeo,* to increase.]
Authoress, ą'thėr-es, *n. A female author.*
Authoritative, ą-tho'ri-tā-tiv, *a. Having due authority;* positive; peremptory.
Authoritatively, ą-tho'ri-tā-tiv-li, *adv. In an authoritative manner.*
Authority, ą-tho'ri-ti, *n.* Legal or genuine power; sway; right; influence; testimony; credibility; precedent; an originator; (pl.) precedents; respectable opinions; body of men in power. [L. *auctoritas—augeo,* to increase.]
Authorize, ą'thor-iz, *vt. To give authority to;* to make legal; to accredit; to countenance. *ppr.* authorizing, *pret. & pp.* authorised. [Fr. *autoriser.*]
Authorized, ą'thor-izd, *p.a.* Supported by or derived from *authority.*
Authorship, ą'thėr-ship, *n. Quality or state of being an author.*
Autobiographer, ą'tō-bī-og'ra-fėr, *n.* One who writes *his own life.*
Autobiographical, ą-tō-bī'ō-graf'ik-al, *a. Pertaining to or containing autobiography.*
Autobiography, ą'tō-bī-og'ra-fi, *n.* Memoirs of *one's life written by one's self.* [Gr. *autos,* one's self, *bios,* life, and *graphō,* to write.]
Autocracy, ą-tok'ra-si, *n. Self-derived power;* absolute power residing in and exercised by a single person. [Gr. *autos,* self, and *kratos,* power.]
Autocrat, ą'tō-krat, *n.* An absolute prince or sovereign. [Gr. *autos,* self, and *kratos,* power.]
Autograph, ą'tō-graf, *n. A person's own handwriting.* [Gr. *autos,* one's self, and *graphē,* writing.]
Autography, ą-tog'ra-fi, *n. An autograph;* a process in lithography, by which drawing is transferred from paper to stone.
Automaton, ą-tom'a-ton, *n. Automata,* ą-tom'a-ta, *pl. A selfmoving machine,* or one which moves by invisible machinery. [Gr. *autos,* self, and *maō,* to move.]
Autopsy, ą'top-si, *n. A seeing with one's own eyes;* examination or dissection of a body after death. [Gr. *autopsia—autos,* one's self, and *opsis,* sight.]
Autumn, ą'tum, *n. The season of increase;* the third season of the year, in

which the fruits of the earth, having *grown* to maturity, are cut down and gathered in. [L. *autumnus—augeo,* to increase.]
Autumnal, ą-tum'nal, *a. Belonging or peculiar to autumn.*
Auxiliary, ąg-zil'i-a-ri, *a. Strengthening;* aiding; subsidiary.—*n. One who strengthens or aids;* a confederate; (pl.) foreign troops employed in war; a verb which helps to form the moods and tenses of other verbs. [L. *auxiliaris—augeo,* to increase.]
Avail, a-vāl', *vt. To advantage;* to profit; to promote.—*vi. To have efficacy;* to be of use; to answer the purpose. *n. Advantage;* use; service. [Norm. *avails,* advantage—L. *valeo,* to be strong.]
Available, a-vāl'a-bl, *a. That one may avail one's self of;* advantageous; having efficacy; able to effect the object; valid.
Availableness, a-vāl'a-bl-nes, *n. State or quality of being available;* validity.
Avalanche, av'a-lansh, *n.* A large body of snow or ice *sliding down* a mountain; a snow-slip. [Fr.—L. *vallis,* a valley.]
Avarice, av'a-ris, *n. An eager panting after;* covetousness; inordinate desire of procuring and hoarding up wealth. [Fr.—L. *aveo,* to strive after.]
Avaricious, av-a-ri'shi-us, *a. Covetous;* greedy of gain; niggardly; sordid.
Avariciously, av-a-ri'shi-us-li, *adv. In an avaricious manner.*
Avast, a-vąst', *exclam. Enough! hold! stop! stay!* (A seaman's term.) [Ger. *basta,* enough.]
Avaunt, a-vąnt', *interj.* Hence! begone! [Fr. *avant,* L. *ante,* before.]
Ave, ā'vē, *n. Hail;* an abbreviation of the *Ave-Maria,* or *Hail-Mary.* [L.]
Avenge, a-venj', *vt. To take vengeance for,* without malice; to punish; to vindicate. *ppr.* avenging, *pret. & pp.* avenged. [Fr. *venger—*L. *vindico,* to punish.]
Avenger, a-venj'ėr, *n. One who avenges.*
Avenue, av'ē-nū, *n. A way or approach to;* an alley of trees leading to a house, gate, wood, &c. [Fr.—L. *venio,* to come.]
Aver, a-vėr', *vt.* To declare to *be true;* to declare positively; to assert. *ppr.* averring, *pret. & pp.* averred. [Fr. *avérer;* L. *vērus,* true.]
Average, av'ėr-āj, *n.* Primarily, the duty which the tenant paid his lord by the service of *beasts and carriages;* medium; mean proportion.—*a.* Medial; containing a mean proportion.—*vt.* To find the mean of, as of unequal quantities.—*vi.* To form a mean or medial sum or quantity. *ppr.* averaging, *pret. & pp.* averaged. [Low L. *averagium;* Norm. *avers.*]
Averment, a-vėr'ment, *n. That which is averred;* affirmation; declaration.
Averse, a-vėrs', *a.* Turned *from;* disinclined to; not favourable. [L. *aversus—verto,* to turn.]
Averseness, a-vėrs'nes, *n. Quality of being averse;* repugnance; dislike.
Aversion, a-vėr'shon, *n. A turning away from;* dislike; antipathy. [Fr.]
Avert, a-vėrt', *vt.* To *turn* aside or away *from;* to keep off or prevent. [L. *averto—verto,* to turn.]
Aviary, ā'vi-a-ri, *n.* A building or inclosure for keeping *birds.* [L. *aviarium,* from *avis,* a bird.]
Avidity, a-vid'i-ti, *n. An eager desire for something; greediness;* strong appetite; eagerness. [L. *aviditas—aveo,* to covet.]

ch, *chain;* j, *job;* g, *go;* ng, *sing;* TH, *then;* th, *thin;* w, *wig;* wh, *whig;* zh, *azure;* † *obsolete.*

Avocation, av-ō-kā′shon, *n.* A calling from; (pl.) employments which call one *aside*, or which demand time and attention. [L. *avocatio—voco*, to call.]
Avoid, a-void′, *vt.* To shun; to escape from; to endeavour to shun. [Fr. *vuider*; L. *vito*, to shun.]
Avoidable, a-void′a-bl, *a.* That may be avoided.
Avoidance, a-void′ans, *n.* Act of avoiding; the state of being vacant.
Avoirdupois, av′ėr-dū-poiz″, *n.* or *a.* That which has a fixed *weight*; a weight, of which a pound contains sixteen ounces, or 7000 grains troy. [Fr. *avoir du pois*, to have weight.]
Avouch, a-vouch′, *vt.* To avow; to vouch; to affirm; to maintain; to vindicate. [Norm. *voucher*, to call; L. *advocare—voco*, to call.]
Avow, a-vou′, *vt.* To declare with confidence; to justify; not to dissemble; to confess frankly. [Fr. *avouer—*L. *voco*, to call.]
Avowable, a-vou′a-bl, *a.* That may be avowed.
Avowal, a-vou′al, *n.* An open declaration; frank acknowledgment.
Avowed, a-voud′, *p.a.* Openly declared.
Avowedly, a-vou′ed-li, *adv.* In an open manner; with frank acknowledgment.
Await, a-wāt′, *vt.* To *wait for;* to look for or expect; to attend upon; to be in store for. [*a* and *wait.*]
Awake, a-wāk′, *vt.* To rouse out of *sleep;* to *wake;* to rouse from a state of torpor or death.—*vi.* To break from *sleep;* to *wake;* to be in a state of vigilance; to revive from a state of stupor or death. *pret.* awoke, awaked, *ppr.* awaking, *pp.* awaked.—*a.* Not sleeping; in a state of vigilance or action. [Sax. *awacian.*]
Awaken, a-wāk′n, *vt.* and *i.* To awake.
Awakening, a-wāk′n-ing, *p.a. Awaking. p.n.* Act of awaking.
Award, a-wạrd′, *vt.* Primarily, to look at; to adjudge; to assign by sentence. *vi.* To judge; to determine; to make an award.—*n.* A judgment; the decision of an arbitrator or of arbitrators. [Fr. *regarder*, to look at.]
Aware, a-wār′, *a.* Put on *guard;* vigilant; apprised; made acquainted. [Sax. *gewarian*, to take care.]
Away, a-wā′, *adv. Out of the way;* absent; at a distance; in motion from; to another place; by degrees; in continuance.—*exclam.* Begone! [Sax. *aweg—a*, from, and *wæg*, way.]
Awe, ạ, *n. Fear; terror;* fear mingled with reverence or submission.—*vt.* To strike with *fear* and reverence. *ppr.* awing, *pret.* & *pp.* awed. [Sax. *oga.*]
Aweigh, a-wā′, *adv. On weigh;* a trip.
Awe-struck, ạ′struk, *a. Impressed* or *struck with awe.*
Awful, ạ′fụl, *a. Full of awe;* that strikes with terror; dreadful; solemn.
Awfully, ạ′fụl-li, *adv. In* an *awful manner.*
Awfulness, ạ′fụl-nes, *n. Quality* or *state of being awful.*
Awhile, a-hwīl′, *adv. A* time; for some time. [*a* and *while.*]
Awkward, ạk′wėrd, *a. Clumsy;* inexpert; inelegant; ungraceful in manners. [Old Eng. *awk*, clumsy, and Sax. *weard*, towards.]
Awkwardly, ạk′wėrd-li, *adv. In a* rude or bungling manner; inelegantly; badly.
Awkwardness, ạk′wėrd-nes, *n. State* or *quality of being awkward.*
Awl, ạl, *n.* A pointed iron instrument for piercing small holes in leather. [Sax. *œl.*]
Awn, ạn, *n.* A scale or husk; the beard of corn or grass. [Dan. *avne.*]
Awned, ạnd, *a. Furnished with an awn.*
Awning, ạn′ing, *n.* A cover of canvas spread over the deck of a vessel to *shelter* from the sun, &c. [Low D. *haveninmg*, from *haven*, a shelter.]

Awny, ạn′i, *a.* Full of beard.
Awry, a-rī′, *a.* or *adv. Writhed;* turned or twisted toward one side; distorted; asquint. [Sax. *writhan*, to writhe.]
Axe, aks, *n. That which breaks;* an instrument, usually of iron, with .steel edge, for hewing timber and chopping wood. [Sax. *eax;* Gr. *axinē.*]
Axial, aks′i-al, *a. Pertaining to an axis.*
Axiom, aks′i-om, *n. That which is assumed* as the basis of demonstration; a self-evident truth; an established principle; a maxim. [Gr. *axiōma—axioō*, to deem worthy.]
Axiomatic, aks′i-ō-mat″ik, *a. Pertaining to an axiom.*
Axiomatically, aks′i-ō-mat″ik-al-li,*adv.* By the use of *axioms.*
Axis, aks′is, *n. Axes*, aks′ēz, *pl.* The straight line, real or imaginary, that passes through anything, and on which it may be supposed to revolve; something like an axle. [L.—Gr. *axōn*, an axle.]
Axle, Axle-tree, aks′l, aks′l-trē, *n.* The *pole* on which a wheel turns, or which *impels* the wheels of a vehicle. [Sax. *œx*, and *tree.*]
Ay, Aye, āē, ēā, *adv. Yea; yes;* indeed. [Sax. *ja.*]
Aye, āē, *n.* **Ayes,** āēz, *pl.* An affirmative; one who votes in the affirmative.
Aye, ā, *adv. Always;* ever; continually. [Sax. *aa.*]
Azimuth, az′i-muth, *n.* An arc of the horizon between the meridian of place and the vertical circle. [Ar. *asimuth.*]
Azote, az′ōt, *n.* Nitrogen gas, which is *destructive to animal life.* [Gr. *a*, priv. and *sōtikos*, from *saō*, to live.]
Azure, a′zhūr, *a.* Of a *light cœsar blue;* sky-coloured.—*n.* The fine *blue colour of the sky;* the sky. [Fr. *asur—*Pers. *azruk*, blue.]
Azured, a′zhōrd, *p.a. Coloured azure;* being of an *azure* colour.

B.

Baa, bä, *n. The cry of a sheep.—v.i.* To cry like a sheep.
Baal, bā′al, *n.* An idol among the ancient Chaldeans and Syrians, representing the sun. [Heb. *baghal*, lord.]
Babble, bab′bl, *vi.* To talk *confusedly;* to prate idly; to talk much; to tell secrets; to murmur.—*vt.* To prate; to utter. *ppr.* babbling, *pret.* and *pp.* babbled.—*n.* Idle talk; senseless prattle. [Fr. *babiller.*]
Babbler, bab′bl-ėr, *n. One who babbles.*
Babbling, bab′bl-ing, *p.a.* Telling secrets; blabbing.—*p.n.* Foolish talk; loquacity.
Babe, bab, *n.* An infant; a young child of either sex, who is able to say *ba-ba*, or *pa-pa*, father. [Sw. Goth.]
Babel, bā′bel, *n. Confusion;* disorder. [Heb.]
Baboon, ba-bōn′, *n.* A monkey of the largest kind. [Fr. *babouin.*]
Baby, bā′bi, *n. A little babe;* an infant of either sex.—*a. Like a baby;* pertaining to a baby.
Babylonian, Babyloniah, ba-bi-lōn′i-an, ba-bi-lōn′ish, *a. Pertaining to Babylon.*
Babylonian, ba-bi-lōn′i-an, *n. An inhabitant of Babylon.*
Bacchanal, Bacchanalian, bak′ka-nal, bak-ka-nā′li-an, *n. A devotee to Bacchus;* a drunkard.—*a.* Revelling in intemperate drinking; riotous; noisy. [from L. *Bacchus*, the god of wine.]
Bacchanals, bak′ka-nalz, *n. pl.* Drunken feasts or revels.
Bachelor, bach′el-ėr, *n. A young man;* a young man who has taken the first degree in the liberal arts and sciences; an unmarried man. [Fr. *bachelier*, a young man.]
Bachelorship, bach′el-ėr-ship, *n. State of being a bachelor.*
Back, bak, *n.* The part of the body which is *behind* in man; in animals, the upper part, which in quadrupeds is a ridge; the outer part of the hand; the hinder part of a thing.—*vt.* To get upon *the back of;* to mount; to support; to cause to recede; to indorse. *vi.* To move or go back.—*adv.* To the place left; behind; in return to a former state. [Sax. *bac.*]
Backbite, bak′bīt, *vt.* To bite at the *back;* to speak evil of privily; to calumniate secretly. *ppr.* backbiting, *pp.* backbitten.
Backbiter, bak′bīt-ėr, *n. One who backbites.*
Backbiting, bak′bīt-ing, *p.n.* Secret calumny.
Backbone, bak′bōn, *n. The bone of the back*, or the spine.
Back-door, bak′dōr, *n. A door on the back* part of a building; a private passage; an indirect way.
Backer, bak′ėr, *n. One who backs* or supports another in a contest.
Backgammon, bak-gam′mon,*n.* A game played by two persons, upon a table, with box and dice. [W. *bach*, little, and *cammawn*, combat.]
Back-ground, bak′ground, *n. A place of obscurity* or shade.
Backslide, bak-slīd′, *vi.* To *apostatise;* to relapse. *pret.* backslid, *ppr.* backsliding, *pp.* backslidden.

Fāte, fär, fat, fạll; mē, met, hėr; pīne, pin; nōte, not, mōve; tūbe, tub, bull; oil, pound.

Backslider, bak-slīd'ėr, n. An apostate.
Backsliding, bak-slīd'ing, p.n. Act of apostatizing.
Backward, Backwards, bak'wėrd, bak'wėrds, adv. Toward the back, or the past; with the back forwards; back; from better to worse.
Backward, bak'wėrd, a. That loiters behind others; late; slow; averse; dull; behind in progress.—n. The state behind or past.
Backwardly, bak'wėrd-li, adv. Unwillingly; reluctantly; aversely; perversely.
Backwardness, bak'wėrd-nes, n. Unwillingness; reluctance; dilatoriness.
Bacon, bā'kn, n. Swine's flesh salted or pickled, and baked by heat. [from Sax. bacan, to cook.]
Bad, bad, a. Hurtful; destructive; injurious; vicious; not good; ill. [Pers. bad.]
Badge, baj, n. Some ornament bestowed as a prize in games, &c.; a mark or cognizance worn. [Sax. beag, a crown.]
Badger, baj'ėr, n. A burrowing animal, which is very eagerly hunted and baited by dogs.—vt. To worry, as in a badger hunt. [W. badd, a boar, and daiar, the earth.]
Badinage, bā'di-nāzh, n. Light or playful discourse; raillery; banter. [Fr.]
Badly, bad'li, adv. In a bad manner.
Badness, bad'nes, n. The state of being bad; evil; want of good qualities.
Baffle, baf'fl, vt. To mock; to frustrate; to defeat. ppr. baffling, pret. & pp. baffled.—n. A defeat by artifice, shifts, and turns. [Old Fr. baffer, to deceive, mock.]
Bag, bag, n. That which bulges out; a sack; a purse; a certain quantity of a commodity, put into a sack.—vt. To put into a bag; to make to swell out; to load with bags.—vi. To swell like a full bag. ppr. bagging, pret. & pp. bagged. [Sax. balg.]
Bagatelle, bag-a-tel', n. A trifle; a kind of game. [Fr.—L. bacca, a berry.]
Baggage, bag'āj, n. The whole goods of an army, that is, the tents, clothing, utensils, and other necessaries; luggage; lumber. [Fr. bagage.]
Bagging, bag'ing, p.n. The cloth for bags; the act of putting into bags.
Bagpipe, bag'pīp, n. A musical wind-instrument, consisting of a bag for a bellows, and pipes.
Bail, bāl, vt. To deliver to another; to liberate from custody, as an offender, on security for his reappearance; to give security for the reappearance of; to deliver goods in charge. ppr. -ing, pret. & pp. -ed.—n. A delivering over to another; release from custody on security being given; the security thus given; the person or persons who give such security. [Norm. bailler, to let forth, to deliver.]
Bailable, bāl'a-bl, a. That may be bailed; that admits of bail.
Bailiff, bā'lif, n. A subordinate officer to whom authority is delegated by the sheriff; a steward. [Norm. balhif.]
Bailiwick, bā'li-wik, n. The extent or limit of a bailiff's jurisdiction. [baitif and Sax. wic.]
Bait, bāt, n. A bit of food put on a hook to allure fish; an enticement; a hasty refreshment taken on a journey.—vt. To put meat on a hook, as a lure; to give a portion of food and drink to, as to a beast upon the road.—vi. To take a hasty refreshment on a journey. [Sax. batan, to put meat upon a hook.]

Bait, bāt, vt. To harass by inciting dogs to attack; to harass; to attack with violence. [Goth. beitan, to bite, to incite.]
Baize, bāz, n. A coarse woollen stuff, with a long nap. [Sp. bajeta.]
Bake, bāk, vt. To prepare by fire; to harden by fire or the sun's rays; to dress and prepare for food, in an oven.—vi. To do the work of baking; to be baked. ppr. baking, pret. & pp. baked. [Sax. bacan; Sans. pach, to cook.]
Baker, bāk'ėr, n. One whose occupation is to bake.
Bakery, bāk'ė-ri, n. A place for baking; a bakehouse.
Baking, bāk'ing, p.n. The hardening of anything by heat; the quantity baked at once.
Balance, bal'ans, n. A pair of scales for weighing; equilibrium; equality; difference between the debtor and creditor side of an account; overplus; that which makes equal in weight, &c.; part of a watch; a sign of the zodiac. vt. To weigh in a balance; to bring to an equilibrium; to weigh, as reasons; to regulate; to counterpoise; to settle, as an account.—vi. To be in equilibrium; to have equal weight, power, influence, &c.; to hesitate; to fluctuate. ppr. balancing, pret. & pp. balanced. [Fr.—L. bis, twice, and lanx, a platter.]
Balcony, bal'kō-ni, n. A platform on the outside of a window, supported on beams projecting from the wall, or by columns. [It. balcone.]
Bald, bald, a. Wanting hair; destitute of a natural covering; unadorned; worthless; mean. [Sp. peldo, featherless, hairless.]
Baldly, bald'li, adv. Nakedly; meanly.
Baldness, bald'nes, n. State of being bald; loss of hair; inelegance of style; want of ornament.
Baldrick, Baldric, bald'rik, bald'rik, n. The belt of a warrior strong in arms; a war-girdle. [Low L. baldringus.]
Bale, bāl, n. A ball; a round mass; a bundle or package of goods.—vt. To make up in a bale. ppr. baling, pret. & pp. baled. [Norm. bale, ball.]
Bale, bāl, vt. To free from water with a pail; to lave out water, as from a boat. [Dan. balle, a tub; Gael. ballam, a pail or tub.]
Baleful, bāl'ful, a. Calamitous; deadly; pernicious. [Sax. beal, ruin.]
Balefully, bāl'ful-li, adv. Perniciously.
Baling, bāl'ing, p.n. Act or operation of making up into a bale, as cotton, &c.; act of freeing from water, as a boat.
Balk, bak, n. A ridge of land left unploughed; a great beam; a disappointment.—vt. To baffle; to disappoint; to frustrate. [Sax. balc, a ridge.]
Ball, bal, n. A round body; a globe; a bullet; anything round or rounded. vt. To form, as snow, into balls, as on horses' hoofs or feet. [G.]
Ball, bal, n. An entertainment of dancing. [Fr. bal.]
Ballad, bal'lad, n. A song, originally adapted to a dance; a popular song; a short narrative poem of the lyric kind; a short air. [It. ballata, from ballare, to dance.]
Ballast, bal'last, n. The load of sand, &c., which a ship carries when there is no cargo; heavy matter laid in the hold of a ship to keep it steady; that which is used to make a thing steady. vt. To load with ballast; to make or keep steady. [Sax. bat, a boat, and hlæst, a burden.]
Ball-cartridge, bal'kär-trij, n. A cartridge furnished with a ball.

Ballet, bal'lā, n. A kind of dramatic dance; a kind of dramatic poem. [Fr.]
Balloon, bal-lön', n. Any spherical hollow body; a round chemical vessel; a ball on the top of a pillar, &c.; a large bag, generally of silk, filled with a gas which makes it rise and float in the atmosphere. [Fr. ballon.]
Ballot, bal'lot, n. A little ball; a written vote put privately into a box or urn; act of voting by ballot.—vi. To vote by ballot. [Fr. ballotte.]
Balm, bäm, n. Balsam; the name of several aromatic plants.—vt. To anoint with balm; to soothe; to assuage. [Fr. baume.]
Balmy, bäm'i, a. Aromatic; odoriferous; soft; soothing; mitigating.
Balsam, bal'sam, n. An oily, aromatic substance, flowing from certain trees; a soothing and fragrant ointment; that which soothes or gives ease. [Gr. balsamon.]
Balsamic, bal-sam'ik, a. Unctuous; soft; mitigating; mild.
Baluster, bal'us-tėr, n. A small column, one of the supporters of the rail to a flight of stairs, and so named from being originally adorned with flowers. [Fr. balustre—L. balaustium, the flower of the pomegranate.]
Balustrade, bal-us-trād', n. A row of balusters joined by a rail. [Fr.]
Bamboo, bam-bö', n. A plant of the reed kind. [Sans. venu.]
Ban, ban, n. A public proclamation issued by one in authority; interdiction; curse; excommunication; (pl.) notice of a marriage proposed.—vt. To curse; to execrate. ppr. banning, pret. & pp. banned. [Sax. bannan, to publish; old G. ban, an anathema.]
Band, band, n. That which binds; a bond; a fillet; any means of connection; a company of soldiers; a body of musicians or of persons united.—vt. To bind together; to tie; to unite in a troop or confederacy.—vi. To unite in a band; to confederate. [Sax. banda.]
Bandage, band'āj, n. That which binds; a fillet, roller, or swath for a wound, &c.; something bound over another. vt. To bind with a bandage or fillet. ppr. bandaging, pret. & pp. bandaged. [Fr.]
Bandbox, band'boks, n. A slight paper box for bands, caps, bonnets, &c.
Banded, band'ed, p.a. United in a band.
Bandit, band'dit, n. Banditti, Bandits, ban-dit'ti, ban'dits, pl. One proclaimed as banished; an outlaw; a robber; a highwayman. [It. bandito—bandire, to banish.]
Bandrol, band'rōl, n. A little banner; a little flag. [Fr. banderole.]
Bandy, ban'di, n. A club bent at the lower part for striking a ball; a play at ball with such a club.—vt. To beat to and fro, as with a bandy; to give and receive reciprocally; to toss about. vt. To contend, as at some game. ppr. bandying, pret. & pp. bandied. [Fr. bander, to bend.]
Bandy-legged, ban'di-legd, a. Having crooked legs.
Bane, bān, n. That which causes hurt or death; destruction; ruin; poison; mischief. [Sax. bana, a killer]
Baneful, bān'ful, a. Full of bane; pernicious; poisonous; destructive.
Banefulness, bān'ful-nes, n. Quality of being baneful.
Banefully, bān'ful-li, adv. Perniciously; destructively.
Bang, bang, vt. To thump; to handle roughly; to treat with violence.—n. A

ch, chain; j, job; g, go; ng, sing; ᴛʜ, then; th, thin; w, wig; wh, whig; zh, azure; † obsolete.

blow with a club; a heavy blow. [Icel. *banga*, to knock.]

Banish, ban'ish, *vt.* To declare to be exiled; to condemn to leave one's country; to drive away; to exile. [Fr. *bannir, bannissant.*]

Banished, ban'isht, *p.a.* Compelled to leave one's country; driven away.

Banishment, ban'ish-ment, *n.* Act of banishing; expulsion from one's native country; exile. [Fr. *bannissement.*]

Bank, bangk, *n.* A bench; the ground rising from the side of a river, lake, &c.; any heap piled up; a bench of rowers; a stock of money; place where money is deposited; a banking company.—*vt.* To raise, as a bank; to fortify with a bank.—*vi.* To keep an account with a banker. [Fr. *banc*, Sax. *bænce*, a bench.]

Banker, bangk'ér, *n.* One who keeps a bank.

Banking, bangk'ing, *n.* *p.a.* Pertaining to a bank.—*p.n.* The business of a banker.

Bank-note, bangk'nōt, *n.* A promissory note, payable on demand, issued by a banking company.

Bankrupt, bangk'rupt, *n.* A trader whose *bench is broken*; one who is declared in debt beyond the power of payment; a trader who fails.—*a.* Unable to pay just debts; failing in trade. [*bank*, and L. *ruptus*, broken—*rumpo*, to break.]

Bankruptcy, bangk'rupt-si, *n.* Act of becoming a bankrupt; failure in trade.

Bank-stock, bangk'stok, *n.* A share or shares in the capital *stock of a bank*.

Banner, ban'nér, *n.* A military *sign of union*; the principal standard of a prince or state; a streamer borne at the end of a lance or elsewhere. [Fr. *bannière*.]

Bannered, ban'nérd, *p.a.* Furnished with or bearing banners.

Banneret, ban'nér-et, *n.* A little banner; the person who bore it; a rank between that of knight and baron, now extinct. [Fr.]

Banquet, bangk'wet, *n.* A feast; a sumptuous feast; anything delightful.—*vt.* To treat with a feast.—*vi.* To feast; to fare sumptuously. [Fr.]

Banqueting, bang'kwet-ing, *p.n.* A feast; luxurious living.

Banter, ban'tér, *vt.* To joke or jest with; to play upon; to rally.—*n.* A joking or jesting; raillery; pleasantry. [Fr. *badiner*, to rally.]

Bantling, bant'ling, *n.* An image-pledge; a young child; an infant. [Sw. Goth. *pant*, a pledge, and *ling*, an image.]

Baptism, bap'tizm, *n.* An *immersing* in water; a sprinkling with water; one of the two Christian sacraments, by which a person is initiated into the visible church. [Late Gr. *baptisma*—Gr. *baptō*, to dip in water.]

Baptismal, bap-tiz'mal, *a.* Pertaining to baptism.

Baptist, bap'tist, *n.* John, the forerunner of Christ; one of a denomination of Christians who deny the validity of infant baptism.

Baptistery, bap'tis-te ri, *n.* A place where the sacrament of baptism is administered. [Late Gr. *baptistērion*.]

Baptize, bap-tīz', *vt.* To immerse; to dip under water; to sprinkle with water; to administer the sacrament of baptism to. *ppr.* baptizing, *pret. & pp.* baptized. [Gr. *baptizō*.]

Baptized, bap-tīzd', *p.a.* Having received baptism.

Bar, bär, *n.* That which secures; a bolt; obstacle; a long piece of wood or metal; inclosed place in an inn or court; any tribunal; body of barristers; an exception in pleading; sandbank at the mouth of a river.—*vt.* To secure with a *bar or bars*; to hinder or prevent; to prohibit; to except. *ppr.* barring, *pret. & pp.* barred. [Sax. *beorgan*, to secure.]

Barb, bärb, *n.* Beard, or that which resembles it; the jags or points which stand backward in an arrow, fish-hook, &c.; a spine.—*vt.* To furnish with *barbs*; to put armour on, as on a horse. [L. *barba*, a beard.]

Barb, barb, *n.* A Barbary horse. [Fr. *barbe.*]

Barbarian, bär-bā'ri-an, *a.* Belonging to savages; rude; uncivilized.—*n.* A foreigner; a savage; one who is rude and uncivilized. [L. *barbarus*—Gr. *barbaros*, strange to Greek blood.]

Barbarism, bär'bär-izm, *n.* Rudeness; ignorance; cruelty; an impropriety of speech. [Gr. *barbarismos*.]

Barbarity, bär-ba'ri-ti, *n.* The state or manners *of a barbarian*; ferociousness; impurity of speech.

Barbarize, bär'bär-iz, *vt.* To make barbarous. *ppr.* barbarizing, *pret. & pp.* barbarized.

Barbarous, bär'bär-us, *a.* In a state of barbarism; cruel; inhuman; contrary to the rules of speech.

Barbarously, bär'bär-us-li, *adv.* In a savage, cruel, or inhuman manner.

Barbed, bärbd, *p.a.* Bearded; jagged with hooks or points; armed, as a war-horse.

Barbel, bär'bel, *n.* A fish having on its upper jaw four *beard-like* appendages. [D. *barbeel*.]

Barber, bär'bér, *n.* One who shaves beards, and dresses hair. [Fr. *barbier*—L. *barba*, a beard.]

Barberry, bär'be-ri, *n.* A thorny shrub bearing red berries. [L. *berbēris*.]

Bard, bärd, *n.* One who composed and sung warlike songs and heroic achievements, among the ancient Celts; a poet. [Gael.; W. *bardd*, a priest, a poet.]

Bardic, bärd'ik, *a.* Pertaining to bards.

Bare, bär, *a.* Open; uncovered; plain; simple; lean; mere.—*vt.* To lay open; to make naked. *ppr.* baring, *pret. & pp.* bared. [Sax. *bar.*]

Barefaced, bär'fāst, *a.* With the face bare; shameless; glaring.

Barefoot, bär'fụt, *a.* or *adv.* With the feet bare.

Barely, bär'li, *adv.* Nakedly; poorly; merely; scarcely.

Bareness, bär'nes, *n.* State of being bare; nakedness; leanness; poverty.

Bargain, bär'gin, *n.* A *contest* between buyer and seller; a contract; a gainful transaction; a thing bought or sold; stipulation.—*vi.* To *higgle*; to make a contract. [It. *barpagnare*, to cavil.]

Bargainer, bär'gin-ér, *n.* One who makes a bargain.

Bargaining, bär'gin-ing, *p.n.* The act of making bargains.

Barge, bärj, *n.* A boat or vessel of pleasure or state; a flat-bottomed boat of burden; the boat used by the commander of a ship of war. [D. *bargie*.]

Bargeman, bärj'man, *n.* The man who manages a barge.

Barilla, ba-ril'la, *n.* A plant, from the ashes of which the best kind of mineral alkali is obtained; the alkali procured from this plant. [Sp. *barrilla*, impure soda.]

Bar-iron, bär'l-ėrn, *n.* Iron wrought into malleable *bars*.

Bark, bärk, *n.* The exterior covering of a tree *which protects* it; the rind; Peruvian bark; tanner's bark.—*vt.* To strip of bark, as trees. [Dan.]

Bark, bärk, *n.* A small ship. [Fr. *barque*.]

Bark, bärk, *vi.* To make the *noise of dogs*, when they threaten or pursue; to clamour at.—*n.* The peculiar *noise made by a dog*, wolf, &c. [Sax. *beorcan*.]

Barley, bär'lē, *n.* Bread-plant; a species of grain, now used especially for making malt. [W. *bara*, bread, and *llys*, a plant.]

Barley-corn, bär'lē-korn, *n.* A grain *of barley*; the third part of an inch.

Barley-sugar, bär-lē-shug'ér, *n.* Sugar boiled till it is brittle, formerly with a decoction of *barley*, and candied.

Barm, bärm, *n.* Yeast; the ferment put into drink to make it work, and into bread to lighten and swell it. [Sax. *beorma*.]

Barmaid, bär'mād, *n.* A maid or woman who tends a bar.

Barmy, bärm'i, *a.* Containing barm.

Barn, bärn, *n.* A repository for barley or corn; a covered building for securing grain, hay, &c. [Sax. *bere*, barley, and *ern*, place.]

Barnacle, bär'na-kl, *n.* A shell-fish, often found on the bottoms of ships; a species of goose. [Fr. *barnache*—L. *perna*, a sea-muscle.]

Barometer, ba-rom'et-ėr, *n.* An instrument for *measuring the weight* of the atmosphere, and hence determining the probable changes of weather, or the height of any ascent. [Gr. *baros*, weight, and *metron*, measure.]

Barometric, ba-rō-met'rik, *a.* Pertaining or relating to the barometer.

Barometrically, ba-rō-met'rik-al-li, *adv.* By means of a barometer.

Baron, ba'ron, *n.* A title or rank of nobility next in degree to a viscount; a title of certain judges, &c. [Fr.—L. *vir*, a man.]

Baronage, ba'ron-āj, *n.* The whole *body of barons*; the dignity or estate of a baron.

Baroness, ba'ron-es, *n.* A *baron's wife*.

Baronet, ba'ron-et, *n.* A little baron; a dignity or degree of honour next below a baron. [Fr.]

Baronetage, ba'ron-et-āj, *n.* The collective body of baronets.

Baronetcy, ba'ron-et-si, *n.* The condition or rank of a baronet.

Baronial, ba-rō'ni-al, *a.* Pertaining to a baron.

Barony, ba'ron-i, *n.* The lordship, honour, or *fee of a baron*.

Barouche, ba-rösh', *n.* Originally, a *two-wheeled* carriage, now a four-wheeled carriage, with a falling top and seats, as in a coach. [G. *barutsche*—L. *bis*, twice, and *rota*, a wheel.]

Barque, bärk, *n.* A ship which carries three masts without a mizzen-topsail. [Fr. from Low L. *barca*.]

Barrack, ba'rak, *n.* A building for lodging soldiers, especially in garrison. (Chiefly used in the plural.) [Fr. *baraque*.]

Barrel, ba'rel, *n.* A round wooden cask secured by *hoops*; the quantity which a barrel holds; anything long and hollow; a cylinder.—*vt.* To *put in a barrel*; to pack in a barrel. *ppr.* barrelling, *pret. & pp.* barrelled. [Fr. *baril*—W. *bar*, a rail.]

Barrel-bulk, ba'rel-bulk, *n.* In shipping, a measure of capacity for freight, equal to five cubic feet.

Barrelled, ba'reld, *p.a.* Having a barrel or tube.

Barren, ba'ren, *a.* Not bearing; unfruit-

Fāte, fär, fat, fạll; mē, met, hėr; pīne, pin; nōte, not. mōve; tūbe, tub, bụll; oil, pound.

ful; not inventive; dull; unmeaning. [Goth. *obairan.*]

Barrenness, ba'ren-nes, *n. The state or quality of being barren.*

Barricade, ba-ri-kād', *n. That which obstructs;* a fortification made in haste, of trees, earth, &c., in order to *obstruct* the progress of an enemy.—*vt.* To fortify; to secure. *ppr.* barricading, *pret. & pp.* barricaded. [Fr.]

Barrier, ba'ri-èr, *n. That which defends;* defence; impediment. [Fr. *barrière.*]

Barrister, ba'ris-tėr, *n. One who pleads at the bar;* a counsellor at law. [from *bar.*]

Barrow, ba'rō, *n. A small vehicle which carries* a load; a small hand or wheel carriage. [Sax. *berewe—beran,* to bear.]

Barrow, ba'rō, *n. A hill; a place of defence;* a heap; a sepulchral mound. [Sax. *beorg.*]

Barter, bar'tėr, *vi.* To exchange.—*vt.* To give, as one thing for another, in commerce.—*n.* Traffic by exchange of commodities; a trucking. [Old Fr. *barater.*]

Baryta, Barytes, ba-rī'ta, ba-rī'tēz, *n. The heaviest* of the alkaline earths. [Gr. *barus,* heavy.]

Barytone, ba'ri-tōn, *a. Pertaining to or noting a grave deep sound,* or male voice.—*n. A deep grave sound;* a male voice. [Gr. *barus,* heavy, and *tōnos,* tone.]

Basalt, ba-zalt', *n. An iron-*coloured stone or igneous rock, occurring in columnar and regular masses. [L. *basaltes;* Ethiopic, *basal,* iron.]

Basaltic, ba-zalt'ik, *a. Pertaining to basalt;* formed of or containing basalt.

Base, bās, *a. Low* in place, value, or station; despicable; disingenuous; without dignity of sentiment. [Fr. *bas,* low.]

Base, bās, *n. That on which one steps;* that on which anything rests; foundation; lower side; support; chief ingredient of a compound; the gravest part in music.—*vt. To place on a basis;* to found; to establish on a base. *ppr.* basing, *pret. & pp.* based. [L. *basis;* Gr. *bainō,* to step.]

Base-born, bās'born, *a.* Born out of wedlock; born of low parentage; vile.

Baseless, bās'les, *a. Without a base;* having no foundation or support.

Base-line, bās'lin, *n. A main line* taken as a *base* of operations.

Basely, bās'li, *adv. In a base manner.*

Basement, bās'ment, *n.* The ground floor or *lowest* story of a building.

Base-minded, bās'mind-ed, *a. Of a low spirit or mind;* mean.

Baseness, bās'nes, *n. Lowness;* meanness; vileness; worthlessness; disingenuousness.

Bashful, bash'fụl, *a.* Having a *downcast* look; modest; wanting confidence. [Fr. *baisser,* to lower.]

Bashfully, bash'fụl-li, *adv.* Modestly; in a shy or timorous manner.

Bashfulness, bash'fụl-nes, *n. Quality of being bashful;* extreme modesty.

Basilisk, baz'il-isk, *n. A little king;* the cockatrice, a fabulous serpent with a white spot on its head resembling a royal diadem; a genus of crested lizards. [Gr. *basiliskos.*]

Basin, bā'sn, *n. A hollow* dish; a reservoir; anything resembling a basin; a pond; a bay; a dock; tract of country drained by a river. [Fr. *bassin—*G. *biegen,* to bend.]

Basis, bā'sis, *n.* Bases, bā'ēz, *pl. A stepping;* that with which one steps; a foot; that whereon one steps; foundation; that on which anything rests; groundwork. [Gr.—*bainō,* to step.]

Bask, bask, *vi.* To lie in *warmth,* or in the sun; to enjoy ease and prosperity. *vt.* To *warm* by continued exposure to heat, or to the sun's rays; to warm with genial heat. [from the root of *bake.*]

Basket, bas'ket, *n.* A domestic vessel made of *twigs,* &c., *interwoven;* the contents of a basket.—*vt. To put in a basket.* [W. *basged—basg,* a plaiting.]

Bass, bās, *n.* A hassock or mat made of the *inner bark* of the linden tree, rushes, sedges, flags, &c., *interwoven.* [Sax. *bæst.*]

Bass, bās, *n. The base* in music; the *lowest part* in the harmony of a musical composition.—*a. Low; deep; grave.* [It. *basso.*]

Bassoon, bas-sōn', *n. A* musical wind-instrument which serves for a *bass.* [Fr. *basson.*]

Bass-relief, bā'rē-lēf, *n. Low-relief;* sculpture, whose figures do not stand out far from the ground on which they are formed. [It. *basso,* low, and *rilievo,* relief.]

Bastard, bas'tėrd, *n.* A child begotten and born out of wedlock; an illegitimate child.—*a.* Illegitimate; spurious; not genuine; false. [Old Fr.]

Bastardise, bas'tėrd-īz, *vt. To make or prove to be a bastard. ppr.* bastardizing, *pret. & pp.* bastardized.

Bastardy, bas'tėrd-i, *n. The state of being a bastard.*

Baste, bāst, *vt.* To rub, as meat; to drip fat or butter on, as on meat while roasting. *ppr.* basting, *pret. & pp.* basted. [Old Fr. *bastonner.*]

Baste, bāst, *vt. To put together,* as the pieces of a garment by slight preparatory stitching; to sew slightly. *ppr.* basting, *pret. & pp.* basted. [Old Fr. *bastir,* to put together.]

Bastinado, bas-ti-nā'dō, *n. A sound beating with a stick;* the blows given with a stick.—*vi. To beat with a stick* or cudgel. [Fr. *bastonnade—*Old Fr. *baston,* a stick.]

Basting, bāst'ing, *p.n.* A moistening with dripping; a sewing together slightly with long stitches.

Bastion, bas'ti-on, *n.* A large mass of earth or masonry *raised up* before or standing out from a rampart; a bulwark. [Fr.—Old Fr. *bastir,* to build.]

Bat, bat, *n.* A heavy *stick;* a stick used *to strike* the ball in the game of cricket.—*vi.* To manage a *bat,* or play with one. *ppr.* batting, *pret. & pp.* batted. [Sax.]

Bat, bat, *n.* An animal having the body of a mouse, but with wings attached to the fore-feet, by which it flies by *night.* [Scot. *bak.*]

Batch, bach, *n. A baking;* the quantity of bread baked at one time. [D. *baksel.*]

Bate, bāt, *vt. To beat down;* to abate. *ppr.* bating, *pret. & pp.* bated. [Fr. *battre—*L. *batuo,* to beat.]

Bath, bäth, *n.* Place to *bathe* in; immersion in water, hot air, vapour, &c.; ablution with water; a Jewish measure. [Sax. *bæth.*]

Bathe, bāᴛʜ, *vt.* To wash *in a bath;* to wash or moisten with water or other liquid.—*vi. To lave* one's body in water; to be immersed in a fluid. *ppr.* bathing, *pret. & pp.* bathed. [Sax. *bathian;* Old G. *badōn,* to wash one's self.]

Bathing, bāᴛʜ'ing, *p.n. The act of bathing* or washing the body in water.

Bathos, bā'thos, *n.* A ludicrous *sinking* in poetry. [Gr. depth.]

Batlet, bat'let, *n. A small bat* or square or round piece of wood with a handle for beating linen.

Baton, bā-tong', *n. A truncheon;* a marshall's staff; a badge of honour or office. [Fr. *bâton.*]

Battalion, bat-ta'li-on, *n.* A body of infantry, consisting of from 500 to 800 men. [Fr. *bataillon—*L. *batuo,* to beat.]

Batten, bat'n, *n. A piece of wood* from 1 to 7 inches broad, and from 1 to 2½ thick.—*vt. To form or fasten with battens.* [from Ft. *bâton,* a stick.]

Batter, bat'tėr, *vt. To beat down;* to beat with violence; to injure or impair with beating or by hard usage; to attack with engines of war. [Fr. *battre.*]

Batter, bat'tėr, *n.* A mixture of several ingredients *beaten* together with some liquid. [from Fr. *battre,* to beat.]

Battering-ram, bat'tėr-ing-ram, *n.* An ancient military engine for *battering* down walls.

Battery, bat'tė-ri, *n. Act of battering;* a number of cannon ranged in order for battering; a parapet or raised work on which they are mounted; in law, a violent assault. [Fr. *batterie.*]

Batting, bat'ing, *p.n. The management of a bat* at play.

Battle, bat'l, *n.* Encounter of two armies; an engagement; a combat.—*vi. To join battle;* to contend in fight. *ppr.* battling, *pret. & pp.* battled. [Fr. *bataille—*L. *batuo,* to strike.]

Battle-axe, bat'l-aks, *n. An axe* anciently used as a weapon *of war.*

Battledoor, bat'l-dōr, *n.* An instrument used *to strike* a ball or shuttlecock. [Sp. *batallador,* combatant.]

Battlement, bat'l-ment, *n.* A wall raised on a building with openings to look through, or to *discharge missile weapons* through. [from *battle,* and the suffix *ment.*]

Battlemented, bat'l-ment-ed, *p.a. Having battlements.*

Battling, bat'l-ing, *p.n.* Conflict; battle.

Battue, bat'tụ, *n. A beating; a beating up* of game; the game beaten up. [Fr.]

Bauble, bạ'bl, *n. A baby's plaything;* a trifling piece of finery; a gewgaw. [Fr. *babiole.*]

Bawd, bạd, *n.* A procurer or procuress; a pimp. [Old Fr. *baud,* bold.]

Bawdy, bạ'di, *a.* Obscene; filthy.

Bawl, bạl, *vi. To bellow;* to shout; to clamour. [Sax. *bellan.*]

Bawling, bạl'ing, *p.n.* The act of crying with a loud sound.

Bay, bā, *a. Red* or *reddish;* reddish-brown; inclining to a chestnut colour. [Fr. *bai.*]

Bay, bā, *n. A bending or curving of the shore;* an arm of the sea. [Sax. *bige,* a turning.]

Bay, bā, *n.* The laurel tree, which bears *red berries;* (pl.) an honorary garland originally made of *laurel branches.* [Fr. *baie—*L. *bacca,* a berry.]

Bay, bā, *n. A barking at;* the bark of a dog when his prey has made a stand. *vi. To bark,* as a dog at his game.—*vt. To bark at;* to follow with barking. [Old Fr. *abbayer,* to bark at.]

Baying, bā'ing, *p.n. The barking of a dog.*

Bayonet, bā'on-et, *n.* A dagger-like weapon, for fixing on the end of a musket.—*vt. To stab with a bayonet. ppr.* bayonetting, *pret. & pp.* bayonetted. [Fr. *baïonnette,* so called because first made at Bayonne.]

Bay-window, bā'win-dō, *n.* A window

---

ch, *chain;* j, *job;* g, *go;* ng, *sing;* ᴛʜ, *then;* th, *thin;* w, *wig;* wh, *whig;* zh, *azure;* † obsolete.

which projects outwards, so as to form a kind of *bay* within.

Bazaar, ba-zär', *n.* A *market-place*; a spacious hall or suite of rooms for the sale of goods. [Ar. *bāzār*.]

Bdellium, del'li-um, *n.* An *aromatic* gum-resin, produced by a tree in the East Indies. [L. from Gr. *bdellion*.]

Be, bē, *vi. substantive.* To have *life* or *existence*; to exist; to be made to be; to become; to remain. (Used as an auxiliary.) *ppr.* being, *pret.* was, *pp.* been. [Sax. *beon*, to be.]

Beach, bēch, *n.* The *shore* of the sea; the strand.

Beached, bēcht, *p.a.* Exposed to the waves; stranded.

Beachy, bēch'i, *a.* Having a *beach* or *beaches.*

Beacon, bē'kn, *n.* Something on an eminence to be *fired* as a signal; a light to direct seamen; that which gives notice of danger.—*vt. To afford light to*, as a beacon; to light up. [Sax. *beacen*.]

Bead, bēd, *n.* That which is used in *praying* in the Roman Catholic church; a little perforated ball, to be strung with others on a thread; any small globular body; a small moulding. [from Sax. *bead*, a prayer.]

Beadle, bē'dl, *n.* A messenger or crier of a court, who *bids* or cites persons to appear and answer; a petty officer in a parish, church, university, &c. [Sax. *bydel*.]

Beadleship, bē'dl-ship, *n.* The *office* of a *beadle.*

Bead-roll, bēd'rōl, *n.* Among Roman Catholics, a list or catalogue of persons *to be prayed for.*

Beagle, bē'gl, *n.* A *small* hound or hunting dog. [Ir. *beag*, little.]

Beak, bēk, *n.* The bill or nib of a bird; anything ending in a point like a bird's beak. [Fr. *bec.*]

Beaked, bēkt, *p.a. Having a beak*; ending in a point like a beak.

Beaker, bēk'ėr, *n.* A cup or glass. [G. *becher.*]

Beam, bēm, *n.* The *firm, fixed* part of a tree; the main timber in a building; part of a balance which sustains the scales; pole of a carriage; a ray of light; probably so named, because when admitted through an orifice, into a darkened room, it represents the figure of a *beam* of wood.—*vt. To send forth*, as *beams*; to emit (followed ordinarily by *forth*).—*vi.* To emit *beams* or rays of light; to shine. [Sax. a tree.]

Beaming, bēm'ing, *p.a. Emitting beams* or rays of light.

Beamy, bēm'i, *a. Emitting beams* or *rays*; radiant; shining.

Bean, bēn, *n.* A name given to several kinds of pulse. [Sax.]

Bear, bār, *vt. To carry*; to uphold; to suffer; to bring; to produce; to cherish; to permit; to have; to show; to behave (with recipr. pronoun).—*vi.* To suffer; to be patient; to be fruitful; to take effect; to act in any character; to be situated as to the point of the compass; to refer to. *pret.* bore, *ppr.* bearing, *pp.* born, borne. [Sax. *beran*.]

Bear, bār, *n. A wild rough* quadruped, of several species; one of two northern constellations, the *Greater* and *Lesser Bear.* [Sax. *bera*.]

Bear, Bere, bār, bēr, *n. A kind of barley.* [Sax. *bere*.]

Bearable, bār'a-bl, *a. That can be borne.*

Beard, bērd, *n.* The hair that is produced on the chin, lips, and adjacent parts of the face; the barb of an arrow; the awn of corn; anything resembling a beard.—*vt. To take by the beard*; to defy to the face; to furnish with a beard. [Sax.]

Bearded, bērd'ed, *p.a. Having a beard.*

Beardless, bērd'les, *a. Without a beard*; not having arrived to manhood.

Bearer, bār'ėr, *n. The person or thing that bears*; one who carries a letter, &c.; a tree or plant that yields its fruit; that which supports anything.

Bearing, bār'ing, *p.n. A carrying*; carriage; deportment; mien; relation; tendency; influence; situation of an object with respect to another object.

Bearish, bār'ish, *a. Partaking of the qualities of a bear.*

Beast, bēst, *n.* An *animal* that is wild and savage; any four-footed animal; a brutal man. [D. *beest*; L. *bestia.*]

Beastliness, bēst'li-nes, *n. State or quality of being beastly*; brutality.

Beastly, bēst'li, *a. Brutal*; *brutish*; filthy; bestial; obscene.

Beat, bēt, *vt. To strike with repeated blows*; to punish with stripes; to overcome; to crush; to harass.—*vi.* To move in a *pulsatory manner*; to throb. *pret.* beat, *ppr.* beating, *pp.* beat, beaten.—*n. A stroke*; a pulsation; a succession of strokes; a round or course frequently trodden. [Sax. *beatan*.]

Beaten, bēt'n, *p.a.* Worn by use.

Beater, bēt'ėr, *n. He or that which beats* or strikes.

Beatific, bē-a-tif'ik, *a. That has the power to make happy or blessed.* [L. *beatus*, happy or blessed, and *facio*, to make.]

Beatification, bē-at'i-fi-kā″shon, *n. A making happy or blessed.*

Beatify, bē-at'i-fi, *vt. To make happy*; *to bless*; to declare a person blessed after death. *ppr.* beatifying, *pret.* & *pp.* beatified. [L. *beatus* and *facio.*]

Beating, bēt'ing, *p.n. Act of striking*; chastisement by blows; a conquering.

Beatitude, bē-at'i-tūd, *n. Blessedness*; a declaration of blessedness made by Christ. [L. *beatitūdo—beo*, to bless.]

Beau, bō, *n. Beaux,* bō, *pl.* One who is fond of *fine dress*; a gallant; a lover. [Fr. from *bel*—L. *bellus*, fine.]

Beau-ideal, bō-i-dē'al, *n.* An *imaginary* standard of *perfection.* [Fr.]

Beauteous, bū'tē-us, *a. Beautiful*; fair.

Beautiful, bū'ti-ful, *a. Full of beauty*; lovely; fair; elegant; handsome.—*n. That which possesses beauty.*

Beautifully, bū'ti-ful-li, *adv. In a beautiful manner.*

Beautify, bū'ti-fi, *vt. To make beautiful*; to adorn; to grace; to deck.—*vi.* To become *beautiful*; to advance in beauty. *ppr.* beautifying, *pret.* & *pp.* beautified. [*beauty*, and L. *facio.*]

Beauty, bū'ti, *n.* The quality of loveliness; an assemblage of graces, which pleases the senses, particularly the eye or the ear; a particular grace or excellence; symmetry of parts; elegance; grace; gracefulness; a beautiful person. [Fr. *beauté*—L. *bellus*, handsome.]

Beaver, bē'vėr, *n.* An amphibious quadruped valuable for its fur; the fur of the beaver, or a hat made of it.—*a. Made of beaver*, or of the fur of the beaver. [Sax. *beofer*—L. *fiber.*]

Beaver, bē'vėr, *n.* The part of a helmet that covers the lower part of the face, and which, raised up or let down, enables the wearer to drink. [Fr. *bevere*—L. *bibo, bibere,* to drink.]

Beavered, bē'vėrd, *p.a. Covered with or wearing a beaver.*

Becalm, bē-käm', *vt. To make calm or quiet*; to still.

Becalmed, bē-kämd', *p.a. Quieted.*

Because, bē-kaz'. *By cause*; for this cause that; for the cause or reason next explained. [Sax. *be* for *by*, and *cause.*]

Beck, bek, *n. A nod*; *a sign* with the hand or head.—*vi.* To make a *sign* with the head or hand; to nod.—*vt.* To notify by a motion of the head or hand. [Sax. *bicnian*, to nod.]

Beckon, bek'n, *vi. To make a sign* by nodding, &c.—*vt.* To nod or make a significant sign to. [Sax. *bicnian.*]

Become, bē-kum', *vi. To come to*, or *come to be*; to enter into some state or condition; to be changed to.—*vt.* To go *or enter into*; to be suitable to; to accord with; to add grace to; to be worthy of. *pret.* became, *ppr.* becoming, *pp.* become. [Sax. *becuman.*]

Becoming, bē-kum'ing, *p.a.* Fit; suitable; graceful.

Becomingly, bē-kum'ing-li, *adv. After a becoming* or proper *manner.*

Bed, bed, *n.* Something to sleep or rest on; the channel of a river; a hollow place, in which anything rests; place where anything is deposited; a layer; a seam of strata.—*vt.* To lay in a place of rest; to sow; to lay in any hollow place; to stratify.—*vi To go to bed*; to cohabit. *ppr.* bedding, *pp.* bedded. [Sax.]

Bedaub, bē-dab', *vt. To daub over*; to besmear; to soil with anything dirty.

Bedchamber, bed'chām-bėr, *n.* An apartment or chamber for a *bed.*

Bedded, bed'ed, *p.a.* Inclosed, as in a bed; stratified.

Bedding, bed'ing, *p.n.* A bed and its furniture; the materials of a bed, whether for man or beast.

Bedeck, bē-dek', *vt. To deck*; to adorn.

Bedew, bē-dū, *vt. To moisten*, as *with dew*; to moisten gently.

Bedim, bē-dim', *vt. To make dim*; to obscure or darken. *ppr.* bedimming, *pret.* & *pp.* bedimmed.

Bedizen, bē-di'zn, *vt.* To dress overmuch; to adorn gaudily; to deck showily. [*be* and *dizen.*]

Bedlam, bed'lam, *n.* A madhouse; an hospital for lunatics; a place of uproar. *a.* Belonging to a mad-house. [corrupted from *Bethlehem*, a religious house in London, opened in 1545 for the reception of lunatics.]

Bedrid, Bedridden, bed'rid, bed'rid-n, *a. Confined* to bed by age or infirmity.

Bedroom, bed'röm, *n.* A sleeping apartment.

Bedrop, bē-drop', *vt. To sprinkle*, as *with drops. ppr.* bedropping, *pret.* & *pp.* bedropped.

Bedstead, bed'sted, *n.* A frame for supporting a bed.

Bee, bē, *n.* The insect that makes honey, remarkable for its *industry* and art. [Sax. *beo.*]

Beech, bēch, *n.* A tree which produces mast or nuts, formerly *eaten* by man. [Sax. *bece*, akin to Gr. *phagó*, to eat.]

Beechen, bēch'en, *a. Pertaining to the beech*; consisting of the wood or bark of the beech.

Beef, bēf, *n.* The flesh of an *ox*, bull, or cow.—*a.* Consisting of the flesh of the *ox* or bovine kind. [Fr. *bœuf*; L. *bos, bovis*, an ox or cow.]

Beef-eater, bēf'ēt-ėr, *n.* A yeoman of the guard, who attends at the sideboard. [Old Fr. *buffetier*, from *buffet*, a side-board.]

Fāte, fär, fat, fall; mē, met, hėr; pīne, pin; nōte, not, mōve; tūbe, tub, bull; oil, pound.

Beef-wood, bēf'wŭd, n. The wood of an Australian tree, resembling beef.
Beer, bēr, n. A liquor made generally from malted barley and hops. [Sax. bere, barley, beer.]
Bees-wax, bēs'waks, n. The wax collected by bees, and of which their cells are constructed.
Beet, bēt, n. A sweet, succulent root, much used as a vegetable, and in making sugar. [Ger. beete—L. beta.]
Beetle, bē'tl, n. An instrument to beat with; a heavy wooden mallet.—vi. To jut; to be prominent; to hang over. ppr. beetling, pret. & pp. beetled. [Sax. bitl, from beatan, to beat.]
Beetle, bē'tl, n. An insect having a hard or shelly wing-case. [Sax. bitel, probably from bitan, to bite.]
Beetle-browed, bē'tl-broud, a. Having prominent brows.
Beetling, bē'tl-ing, p.a. Jutting; being prominent.
Beeves, bēvz, n. pl. of beef. Cattle; black-cattle.
Befall, bē-fal', vi. To fall to; to happen to; to occur to.—vi. To happen. pret. befell, ppr. befalling, pp. befallen. [Sax. befeallan.]
Befit, bē-fit', vt. To fit; to suit; to be suitable to; to become. ppr. befitting, pret. & pp. befitted.
Befitting, bē-fit'ing, p.a. Suitable; becoming; appropriate.
Befool, bē-föl', vt. To fool; to delude.
Before, bē-fōr', prep. Near the fore part; in front of; in presence of; in advance of; sooner than; in preference to; prior to.—adv. In time preceding; sooner than; hitherto; further onward; in front. [Sax.]
Beforehand, bē-för'hand, adv. In a state of anticipation; previously.
Befoul, bē-foul', vt. To make foul; to soil. [Sax. befylan.]
Befriend, bē-frend', vt. To act as a friend to.
Beg, beg, vt. To ask in charity; to ask earnestly; to supplicate; to entreat for; to take for granted.—vi. To ask alms or charity; to live upon alms. ppr. begging, pret. & pp. begged. [Sw. begara, to ask.]
Beget, bē-get', vt. To get; to obtain; to produce; to generate. pret. begot, ppr. begetting, pp. begot, begotten. [Sax. begetan—be, and getan, to get.]
Begetter, bē-get'er, n. One who begets.
Beggar, beg'gėr, n. One who begs; a suppliant.—vt. To reduce to beggary; to impoverish.
Beggarliness, beg'gėr-li-nes, n. Meanness; extreme poverty.
Beggarly, beg'gėr-li, a. Like a beggar; contemptible; poor.—adv. Meanly; indigently; despicably.
Beggary, beg-gē'ri, n. State of a beggar; state of extreme indigence.
Begging, beg'ing, p.n. The act of soliciting alms; the practice of asking alms.
Begin, bē-gin', vi. To be or become; to come into existence; to do the first act; to commence any action or state.—vt. To enter upon; to originate. pret. began, ppr. beginning, pp. begun. [Sax. beginnan.]
Beginner, bē-gin'ėr, n. The person who begins; one in his rudiments.
Beginning, bē-gin'ing, p.n. Entrance into being; the first cause, act, or state; origin; commencement; first ground or materials.
Begird, bē-gėrd', vt. To gird round about; to bind. pret. begirt, begirded, ppr. begirding, pp. begirt. [Sax. begyrdan.]

Begone, bē-gon', interj. Be thou or ye gone! go away! depart!
Begrudge, bē-gruj', vt. To grudge; to envy the possession of. ppr. begrudging, pret. & pp. begrudged.
Beguile, bē-gīl', vt. To impose on by guile; to ensnare; to wile away; to pass pleasantly. ppr. beguiling, pret. & pp. beguiled.
Beguilement, bē-gīl'ment, n. Act of beguiling or deceiving.
Beguiler, bē-gīl'ėr, n. He or that which beguiles or deceives.
Beguiling, bē-gīl'ing, p.a. Deluding; deceiving.
Behalf, bē-haf', n. Need; convenience; advantage; favour; support; part; side. [Sax. behefe.]
Behave, bē-hāv', vt. To carry or bear; to conduct. (With the reciprocal pronoun.)—vi. To act; to conduct one's self. ppr. behaving, pret. & pp. behaved. [Sax. behabban—habban, to have.]
Behaviour, bē-hāv'i-ėr, n. Manner of behaving; conduct; carriage; deportment.
Behead, bē-hed', vt. To cut off the head of; to decapitate.
Behemoth, bē'hē-moth, n. Supposed to be the river-horse, or hippopotamus. [Heb. beasts.]
Behest, bē-hest', n. Declared will; mandate. [be, and Sax. hǣse, from hatan, to command.]
Behind, bē-hīnd', prep. On or at the hinder part; in the rear of; posterior to; remaining after; inferior to.—adv. In the rear; backwards; remaining; past. [Sax. behindan.]
Behindhand, bē-hīnd'hand, adv. Backwards; in arrears.
Behold, bē-hōld', vt. To look upon; to consider; to regard with attention. vi. To look; to direct or fix the mind. ppr. beholding, pret. & pp. beheld. interj. See! lo! observe! [Sax. behealdan.]
Beholden, bē-hōld'n, p.a. Holden or bound; obliged; indebted.
Behoof, bē-höf', n. Need; necessity; advantage; profit; benefit. [from Sax. behoflan.]
Behoove, bē-höv', vt. To be fit for; to be needful, or necessary for. ppr. behooving, pret. & pp. behooved. [Sax. behaflan, to be fit, to have need of.]
Being, bē'ing, p.n. Existence; a particular state; a person existing; an intelligent existence or spirit; any living creature.
Belabour, bē-lā'bėr, vt. To beat soundly; to thump.
Belated, bē-lāt'ed, p.a. Benighted.
Belay, bē-lā', vt. To lay round about; to fasten, as a cable, by laying it round the bits. [be and lay.]
Belch, belsh, vt. To throw out; to eject, as wind from the stomach; to utter vehemently.—vi. To eject wind from the stomach; to issue out, as by eructation.—n. Eructation. [Sax. bealcan.]
Beldam, hel'dam, n. An old woman; an old witch or hag.
Beleaguer, bē-lē'gėr, vt. To surround with an army; to blockade; to besiege. [G. belagern—lagern, to lay.]
Beleaguerer, bē-lē'gėr-ėr, n. One who beleaguers.
Belfry, bel'fri, n. Primarily, a watchtower; that part of a steeple or other building in which a bell or bells are hung. [Fr. beffroy, a tower.]
Belial, bē'li-al, n. An evil spirit. [Heb.]
Belie, bē-lī', vt. To lie to; to represent falsely; to convict of falsehood. ppr.

belying, pret. & pp. belied. [be and lie.]
Belief, bē-lēf', n. Assent; a firm persuasion of; credit given to testimony; creed; opinion. [Sax. geleaf.]
Believe, bē-lēv', vt. To give belief to; to trust in; to credit; to be firmly persuaded of; to deem to be true; to put confidence in.—vi. To exercise belief to have a firm persuasion; to confide; to think. ppr. believing, pret. & pp. believed. [Sax. geleafan.]
Believer, bē-lēv'ėr, n. One who believes; a professor of Christianity.
Bell, bel, n. That which peals; a hollow body of cast metal, used for giving sounds by being struck; anything in the form of a bell. [Sax.]
Belladonna, bel-la-don'na, n. A plant; the deadly nightshade. [It. a fair lady.]
Belle, bel, n. A fine young lady; a lady of superior beauty, and much admired. [Fr.—L. bellus, fine.]
Belles-lettres, bel-let'ėr, n.pl. The fine or elegant departments of learning; polite literature. [Fr. from belle, fine, and lettre, a letter, pl. lettres, learning.]
Bell-founder, bel'found-ėr, n. A man whose occupation is to found bells.
Bellied, bel'lid, p.a. Swelled out in the middle.
Belligerent, bel-lij'ėr-ent, a. Waging war; carrying on war.—n. A nation or state carrying on war. [L. belligerens—bellum, war, and gero, to wage.]
Bell-metal, bel'me-tal, n. A mixture of copper and tin, and usually a small portion of brass or zinc.
Bellow, bel'lō, vi. To make a hollow loud noise, as a bull; to roar.—n. A loud outcry; roar. [Sax. bellan.]
Bellows, bel'lōs, n. sing. and pl. An instrument for blowing fires, supplying wind to organ-pipes, &c. [Sax. bælg or bylig.]
Bell-ringer, bel'ring-ėr, n. One whose business is to ring a church or other bell.
Belly, bel'li, n. That which swells out; that part of the body which contains the bowels; the corresponding part in animals; the womb; any hollow inclosed place.—vi. To become protuberant, like the belly. ppr. bellying, pret. & pp. bellied. [Sax. bælig.]
Belong, bē-long', vi. To pertain; to be the property; to be the business; to relate; to adhere; to be the quality of. [D. belangen, to concern—langen, to reach to.]
Belonging, bē-long'ing, p.n. That which pertains to one.
Beloved, bē-luvd', p.a. Loved; greatly loved.
Below, bē-lō', prep. Under in place; beneath; unworthy of.—adv. In a lower place; beneath; on earth; in hell.
Belt, belt, n. A leathern girdle; a bandage; anything resembling a belt.—vt. To gird, as with a belt; to encircle. [Sax.]
Belted, belt'ed, p.a. Wearing a belt; having a belt or belts.
Bemire, bē-mīr', vt. To drag in the mire; to cover with mire. ppr. bemiring, pret. & pp. bemired.
Bemoan, bē-mōn', vt. To moan for; to lament; to bewail.
Bench, bensh, n. A bank; a long seat; seat of justice; body of judges.—vt. To furnish with benches; to seat on a bench. [Sax. benco.]
Bencher, bensh'ėr, n. A senior member in the inns of court.
Bend, bend, vt. To crook by straining,

as a bow; to turn out of a straight line; to crook; to curve; to direct to a certain point; to apply closely; to subdue.—*vi.* To become crooked; to lean or turn; to yield. *pret.* bended or bent, *ppr.* bending, *pp.* bended or bent—bended in solemn style.—*n.* A curve; a flexure. [Sax. *bendan.*]

Beneath, bē-nēth', *prep.* Below; lower in place, rank, dignity, &c.; than; unworthy of; not equal to.—*adv.* In a lower place below. [Sax. *beneoth-nythan*, downwards]

Benediction, ben-ē-dik'shon, *n. Act of speaking well of;* act of blessing; expression of good wishes; thanks. [L. *benedictio—bene*, well, and *dico*, to speak.]

Benefaction, ben-ē-fak'shon, *n. The doing of a good office; a benefit conferred.* [L. *benefactio—bene,* well, and *facio*, to do.]

Benefactor, ben-ē-fak'tėr, *n. He who confers a benefaction* or a benefit.

Benefactress, ben-ē-fak'tres, *n.* A female who confers a benefit.

Benefice, ben'ē-fis, *n.* An ecclesiastical living conferred by a patron, but which is inferior to that of a bishop. [L. *beneficium—bene*, well, and *facio*, to do.]

Beneficed, ben'ē-fist, *p.a. Possessed of a benefice* or church preferment.

Beneficence, bē-nef'i-sens, *n. The practice of doing good;* active goodness, kindness, or charity. [L. *beneficentia*.]

Beneficent, be-nef'i-sent, *a. Doing good;* kind; bountiful; liberal.

Beneficently, be-nef'i-sent-li, *adv. In a beneficent manner.*

Beneficial, ben-ē-fi'shi-al, *a. Conferring benefits;* advantageous; helpful.

Beneficially, ben-ē-fi'shi-al-li, *adv.* Advantageously; profitably; helpfully.

Beneficiary, ben-ē-fi'shi-a-ri, *n.* A person who is benefited or assisted.

Benefit, ben'ē-fit, *n. A good deed;* service; performance in a theatre for the behoof of some person or persons.—*vt. To do good to;* to do a service to.—*vi.* To gain advantage. [Fr. *bienfait*—L. *benefactum—bene,* and *facio,* to do.]

Benevolence, bē-nev'ō-lens, *n. Goodwill;* kindness of heart; love to mankind; good done. [L. *benevolentia—bene,* well, and *volo*, to wish.]

Benevolent, bē-nev'ō-lent, *a.* Kind; affectionate. [L. *benevolens.*]

Benevolently, bē-nev'ō-lent-li, *adv.* In a kind manner; with good-will.

Benight, bē-nit', *vt. To involve in night;* to overwhelm in darkness, gloom, or ignorance.

Benighted, bē-nit'ed, *p.a. Involved in darkness* or *in ignorance.*

Benign, bē-nin', *a. Of a good kind;* beneficent; gracious; generous; propitious. [L. *benignus—bene,* well, and *genus,* kind.]

Benignant, bē-nig'nant, *a.* Kind; gracious; favourable.

Benignantly, bē-nig'nant-li, *adv. In a benignant manner.*

Benignity, bē-nig'ni-ti, *n.* Goodness of heart; kindness of nature; graciousness; actual goodness. [L. *benignitas.*]

Benignly, bē-nin'li, *adv.* Graciously.

Bent, bent, *p.a. Inclined;* prone to, or having a fixed propensity towards; determined.—*n. Flexure* or *flexion;* a bias of mind; inclination; fixed purpose.

Bent, bent, *n.* A kind of grass which creeps, and roots by its wiry stems, and thus binds the soil. [from *bind.*]

Benumb, bē-num', *vt. To deprive of* sensation; to make torpid; to stupify. [Sax. *beniman—niman,* to seize.]

Bepraise, bē-prās', *vt. To praise greatly* or extravagantly. *ppr.* bepraising, *pret. & pp.* bepraised.

Bequeath, bē-kwēth', *vt.* To leave by declaration of one's will; to hand down to posterity. [Sax. *becwæthan—cwæthan,* to say.]

Bequest, bē-kwest', *n. That which is bequeathed;* a legacy.

Bere, bėr, *n.* The name of a species of barley in Scotland. [Sax. *ber.*]

Bereave, bē-rēv', *vt. To deprive of;* to strip; to make destitute. *pret.* bereaved, bereft, *ppr.* bereaving, *pp.* bereaved, bereft. [Sax. *bereafian—reafian,* to rob.]

Bereaved, bē-rēvd', *p.a. Deprived;* made destitute.

Bereavement, bē-rēv'ment, *n. Act of bereaving;* state of being bereft; deprivation.

Bereft, bē-reft', *p.a.* Made destitute.

Bergamot, bėrg'a-mot, *n.* A species of pear or citron; perfume yielded by the citron. [Fr. *bergamotte.*]

Berried, be'rid, *p.a. Furnished with* or *having berries.*

Berry, be'ri, *n.* The fruit borne by certain plants; a pulpy fruit, containing naked seeds. [Sax. *beria—beran,* to bear.]

Berth, bėrth, *n.* A station in which a ship rides at anchor; a place in a ship to sleep in.—*vt. To allot berths to,* on shipboard. [from *bear.*]

Beryl, be'ril, *n.* A brilliant mineral of great hardness. [Gr. *berallion.*]

Beseech, bē-sēch', *vt. To seek from;* to ask or pray with urgency; to entreat; to solicit. *ppr.* beseeching, *pret. & pp.* besought. [Sax. *be,* and *secan,* to seek.]

Beseechingly, bē-sēch'ing-li, *adv. In a beseeching manner.*

Beseem, bē-sēm', *vt.* To become; to be fit for or worthy of; to be decent for. [G. *geziemen,* to be suited.]

Beseeming, bē-sēm'ing, *p.a. Becoming;* fit; worthy of.

Beset, bē-set', *vt. To set upon;* to surround; to blockade; to press on all sides. *ppr.* besetting, *pret. & pp.* beset. [Sax. *besettan—settan,* to set.]

Besetting, bē-set'ing, *p.a.* Entangling without probable means of escape.

Beside, bē-sid', *prep. By the side of;* near; in addition to; distinct from; out of the straight course; out of; not according to.

Beside, Besides, bē-sid', bē-sidz', *adv. By the side of;* over and above; not included in the number.

Besiege, bē-sēj', *vt. To lay siege to;* to beset; to invest; to hem in. *ppr.* besieging, *pret. & pp.* besieged.

Besieger, bē-sēj'ėr, *n. One who lays siege to;* one employed in a siege.

Besieging, bē-sēj'ing, *p.a. Employed in a siege;* surrounding in a hostile manner.

Besmear, bē-smēr', *vt. To smear over;* to bedaub; to soil.

Besmearer, bē-smēr'ėr, *n.* One who besmears.

Besom, bē'zum, *n. A bundle of twigs* for sweeping; a broom.—*vt.* To sweep, as with a besom. [Sax. *besm,* pl. *besman,* twigs.]

Besot, bē-sot', *vt.* To infatuate; to stupify. *ppr.* besotting, *pret. & pp.* besotted.

Besotted, bē-sot'ed, *p.a. Made sottish* or stupid.

Bespangle, bē-spang'gl, *vt.* To adorn with spangles; to sprinkle with something brilliant. *ppr.* bespangling, *pret. & pp.* bespangled.

Bespatter, bē-spat'tėr, *vt.* To soil with mud, filth, &c.; to asperse.

Bespeak, bē-spēk', *vt. To speak for beforehand;* to forebode; to indicate; to address. *pret.* bespoke, *ppr.* bespeaking, *pp.* bespoke, bespoken.

Bespread, bē-spred', *vt. To spread over;* to cover over. *ppr.* bespreading, *pret. & pp.* bespread.

Besprinkle, bē-spring'kl, *vt. To sprinkle over;* to scatter over. *ppr.* besprinkling, *pret. & pp.* besprinkled.

Best, best, *a. superl.* First in regard to usefulness; having good qualities in the highest degree; exceeding all.—*n.* The utmost; highest endeavour.—*adv.* In the highest degree; beyond all others. [Sax. *betest,* from *bet,* better.]

Bestead, bē-sted', *vt. To stead,* or fill the place of; to assist; to serve. *ppr.* besteading, *pret. & pp.* bestead.

Bestial, bes'ti-al, *a. Belonging to a beast,* or to the class of beasts; brutish; vile; sensual. [L. *bestialis.*]

Bestiality, bes-ti-al'i-ti, *n. The quality* or *nature of beasts;* beastliness.

Bestially, bes'ti-al-li, *adv.* Brutally.

Bestir, bē-stėr', *vt. To stir up;* to put into brisk or vigorous action. (Usually with recip. pron.) *ppr.* bestirring, *pret. & pp.* bestirred.

Bestow, bē-stō', *vt.* To place; to lay up; to give; to confer; to dispose of; to apply. [Sax. *be,* and *stow,* a place.]

Bestowal, bē-stō'al, *n. Act of bestowing;* disposal.

Bestower, bē-stō'ėr, *n. One who bestows;* a giver; a disposer.

Bestraddle, bē-strad'dl, *vt. To bestride.* *ppr.* bestraddling, *pret. & pp.* bestraddled.

Bestrew, bē-strō', *vt. To strew over;* to scatter over; to besprinkle. *pret.* bestrewed, *ppr.* bestrewing, *pp.* bestrewed, bestrown.

Bestride, bē-strid', *vt. To stride* or *step over;* to place a leg on each side of; to ride upon. *pret.* bestrid or bestrode, *ppr.* bestriding, *pp.* bestrid, bestridden.

Bestud, bē-stud', *vt. To set with studs;* to adorn with bosses. *ppr.* bestudding, *pret. & pp.* bestudded.

Bet, bet, *n. A pledge;* a wager; that which is pledged in a contest.—*vt.* To wager; to stake at a wager. *ppr.* betting, *pret. & pp.* betted. [Sax. *bad,* a pledge—*badian,* to pledge.]

Betake, bē-tāk', *vt. To take to;* to commit to; to have recourse to. (With recipr. pron.) *pret.* betook, *ppr.* betaking, *pp.* betaken.

Bethink, bē-thingk' *vt. To think upon;* to call to mind; to recollect. (Generally with recipr. pron.) *ppr.* bethinking, *pret. & pp.* bethought.

Betide, bē-tid', *vt. To come to in time;* to happen to; to befall.—*vi.* To come to pass; to happen. *pret.* betid or betided, *ppr.* betiding, *pp.* betid. [Sax. *tid,* time.]

Betimes, bē-tīmz', *adv. By the time;* seasonably; early.

Betoken, bē-tō'kn, *vt.* To show by a token; to foreshew; to portend. [Sax. *betacan.*]

Betray, bē-trā', *vt. To deliver* up by treachery; to entrap; to disclose treacherously or in breach of trust. [F. *betriegen,* to deceive.]

Betrayal, bē-trā'al, *n. Act of betraying;* treachery.

Betrayed, bē-trād', *p.a.* Disclosed in breach of confidence or trust.

Fāte, fär, fat, fạll; mē, met, hėr; pīne, pin; nōte, not, mōve; tūbe, tub, bu̦ll: oil, pound.

BETRAYER 29 BINOCULAR

Betrayer, bē-trā'ėr, n. *One who betrays.*
Betroth, bē-trōth', vt. *To pledge the troth or truth to; to affiance; to pledge to marriage.*
Betrothed, bē-trōtht', p.a. *Contracted for future marriage; affianced.*
Betrothment, bē-trōth'ment, n. *Mutual promise or contract of marriage.*
Better, bet'ėr, a. comp. *Useful in a higher degree than another; further advanced; superior; improved.*—*adv.* *More; in a more excellent manner; in a higher degree.*—*vt.* *To make better; to ameliorate; to advance.*—*n.* A superior. (Almost always used in the plural.) [Sax. *betere*, better—*beterian*, to better.]
Betting, bet'ing, p.n. *The laying of a wager.*
Bettor, bet'ėr, n. *One who bets or lays a wager.*
Between, bē-twēn' prep. *In the middle of two; dividing so as to be shared by two; in the middle of; from one to another; belonging to two; noting difference of one from the other.* [Sax. *bè*, and *tweġen*, two.]
Betwixt, bē-twikst', prep. *Between; in the midst of two; passing between.* [Sax. *betwyxt.*]
Bevel, be'vel, n. *An instrument for taking angles; an angle that is not a right angle.*—*a.* *Slant; awry; oblique.*—*vt.* *To cut or form to a bevel angle.* ppr. bevelling, pret. & pp. bevelled. [Fr. *beveau.*]
Bevelled, be'veld, p.a. *Formed to a bevel angle.*
Beverage, bev'ėr-aj, n. *Drink; any pleasant mixed liquor.* [It. *beveraggio*—L. *bibo, bibere,* to drink.]
Bevy, be'vi, n. *A flock of birds, particularly of quails; a company, especially of females.*
Bewail, bē-wāl', vt. *To utter a wail of distress for; to lament.*—*vi.* *To express or utter deep grief.*
Beware, bē-wār', vi. *To guard one's self; to avoid; to take care of.* (With *of.*) [Sax. *bewerian.*]
Bewilder, bē-wil'dėr, vt. *To bring into the state of one in a wild, who knows not his way; to confuse; to perplex.* [G. *verwildern.*]
Bewildering, bē-wil'dėr-ing, p.a. *Perplexing with intricacy.*
Bewilderment, bē-wil'dėr-ment, n. *State of being bewildered.*
Bewitch, bē-wich', vt. *To enchant; to fascinate; to charm; to overpower by charms.*
Bewitchery, bē-wich'ėr-i, n. *The resistless power of anything that pleases.*
Bewitching, bē-wich'ing, p.a. *That has power to bewitch; that has power to control by the arts of pleasing.*
Bewitchingly, bē-wich'ing-li, adv. *In a fascinating manner.*
Bewitchment, bē-wich'ment, n. *Power of charming; fascination.*
Bewray, bē-rā', vt. *To discover; to reveal.* [Sax. *be,* and *wregan,* to accuse.]
Beyond, bē-yond', prep. *On the further side of; farther onward than; out of the reach of; before; above.*—*adv.* *At a distance; yonder.* [Sax. *begeond*—*Fris. ond,* over against.]
Biangular, bi-ang'gū-lėr, a. *Having two angles.* [L. *bi, bis,* and Eng. *angular.*]
Bias, bī'as, n. *A sloping; a leaning of the mind; bent; anything which influences one.*—*vt.* *To cause to slope; to give a particular direction to, as to the mind; to prejudice.* [Fr. *biais,* a slope.]
Biased, bī'ast, p.a. *Prejudiced.*

Bib, bib, n. *A small piece of cloth worn by infants over the breast to drink in the liquid flowing from the mouth.* [from L. *bibo,* to drink.]
Bibber, bib'ėr, n. *A drinker; a tippler.* [from L. *bibo,* to drink.]
Bible, bī'bl, n. THE BOOK, *by way of eminence; the Holy Scriptures.* [Gr. *biblion*—*bublos,* the papyrus.]
Bible-oath, bī'bl-ōth, n. *An oath on the Bible; a sacred obligation.*
Biblical, bib'lik-al, a. *Pertaining to the Bible.*
Biblically, bib'lik-al-li, adv. *In accordance with the Bible.*
Biblicist, bib'li-sist, n. *One skilled in biblical knowledge.*
Bibliological, bib'li-ō-loj'ik-al, a. *Pertaining to bibliology.*
Bibliology, bib-li-ol'o-ji, n. *A treatise on books; biblical literature.* [Gr. *biblion,* and *logos,* discourse.]
Bibliomania, bib'li-ō-mā"ni-a, n. *Book-madness; a rage for possessing rare and curious books.* [Gr. *biblion,* and *mania,* madness.]
Bibliopolist, bib-li-op'ol-ist, n. *A book-seller.* [Gr. *biblion,* and *pōleō,* to sell.]
Bicipital, bī-sip'it-al, a. *Having two heads or origins.* [L. *bis,* and *caput, capitis,* the head.]
Bicker, bik'ėr, vi. *To fight off and on; to quarrel; to scold.* [Scot.]
Bid, bid, vt. *To ask; to request; to invite; to solicit; to demand;* [Sax. *beodan*] *to offer; to propose to give.* pret. bid or bade, ppr. bidding, pp. bid, bidden. [Sax. *biddan.*]
Bidding, bid'ing, p.n. *Invitation; order; offer.*
Bide, bid, vi. *To dwell; to remain.*—*vt.* *To endure; to abide; to wait for.* [Sax. *bidan,* to tarry, remain.]
Bidental, bī-dent'al, a. *Having two teeth.* [L. *bidens*—*bis,* and *dens, dentis,* a tooth.]
Biennial, bī-en'ni-al, a. *Continuing for two years; taking place once in two years.*—*n.* *A plant which endures two years.* [L. *bis,* and *annus,* a year.]
Biennially, bī-en'ni-al-li, adv. *Once in two years; at the return of two years.*
Bier, bēr, n. *That which bears; a frame of wood for conveying dead human bodies to the grave.* [Sax. *bær.*]
Big, big, a. *Heaped up; large; bulky; protuberant; pregnant; full; arrogant.* (Old G. *pigo* or *piga,* a heap.]
Bigamist, big'am-ist, n. *One who has two wives or husbands at once.*
Bigamy, big'a-mi, n. *A two-fold marriage; the crime of having two wives or husbands at a time.* [L. *bis,* and Gr. *gamos,* marriage.]
Bigg, big, n. *A variety of winter barley, having six rows of grains.* (Dan. *byg.*]
Bight, bit, n. *A bend or small bay; the double part of a rope when folded.* [Icel. *bugt,* a bending.]
Bigly, big'li, adv. *In a tumid manner.*
Bigness, big'nes, n. *Quality of being big; bulk; size; largeness; dimensions.*
Bigot, big'ot, n. *A person who is obstinately wedded to a particular creed.* (Sp. *bigote,* a mustache, a symbol of firmness.]
Bigoted, big'ot-ed, p.a. *Obstinately attached to some creed.*
Bigotry, big'ot-ri, n. *Blind zeal in favour of a creed, party, sect, or opinion.*
Bijou, bē-zhö', n. *Bijoux,* bē-zhö', pl. *A trinket or a little box; a jewel.* [Fr.]
Bilateral, bī-lat'ėr-al, a. *Having two sides.* [L. *bis,* and *latus, lateris,* side.]
Bilberry, bil'be-ri, n. *A shrub and its fruit; the whortleberry.* [Sax. *bleo,* blue, and *berry.*]
Bile, bil, n. *A yellow bitter liquid secreted in the liver; that which was supposed to cause melancholy; wrath; anger.* [L. *bilis.*]
Bilge, bilj, n. *The protuberant part of a cask at the middle; the breadth of a ship's bottom.*—*vi.* *To suffer a fracture in the bilge or bottom, as a ship.* ppr. bilging, pret. & pp. bilged. [a different orthography of *bulge.*]
Bilged, biljd, p.a. *Having a fracture in the bilge.*
Biliary, bil'i-a-ri, a. *Belonging to the bile; conveying the bile.* [Fr. *biliaire.*]
Bilingual, bi-lin'gwal, a. *In two languages.* [L. *bis,* and *lingua,* tongue.]
Bilious, bil'i-us, a. *Pertaining to bile; affected by bile.* [L. *biliosus.*]
Biliteral, bī-lit'ėr-al, a. *Consisting of two letters* [L. *bis,* and *litera,* a letter.]
Bilk, bilk, vt. *To frustrate; to defraud.* [probably a corrupt form of *balk.*]
Bill, bil, n. *The beak of a bird; anything resembling a bird's beak; a cutting instrument with a hook for pulling; a hatchet.*—*vi.* *To join bills, as doves; to fondle.* [Sax. *bile.*]
Bill, bil, n. *Primarily, a sealed document; an account of money due, of goods purchased, &c.; security given for money; draught of a proposed new law; an advertisement posted up; written declaration of some wrong.* [Norm. *bille*—Low L. *bulla,* a seal.]
Billet, bil'let, n. *A little bill; a small paper or note in writing; a ticket directing soldiers where to lodge.*—*vt.* *To direct, as a soldier by a billet,* where to lodge.—*vi.* *To be quartered, as soldiers; to lodge.* [Fr.]
Billet, bil'let, n. *A small log of wood for firewood.* [Fr. *billot.*]
Billiard, bil'i-ėrd, a. *Pertaining to the game of billiards.*
Billiards, bil'i-ėrdz, n. pl. *A game played on a table with small ivory balls and maces or sticks.* [Fr. *billard.*]
Billion, bil'li-on, n. *A million of millions.* [L. *bis,* from *bis,* two; and Eng. *million.*]
Billow, bil'lō, n. *A great wave of the sea swelling and raging.*—*vi.* *To swell; to rise and roll in large waves.* [Old G. *belgan,* to swell, to rage.]
Billowy, bil'lō-i, a. *Full of billows; swelling or swelled into large waves.*
Bimanous, bī-mān'us, a. *Having two hands.* [L. *bis,* and *manus,* a hand.]
Bin, bin, n. *A wooden chest, used as a repository of corn or other commodities.* [Sax. *bin,* a manger.]
Binary, bī'na-ri, a. *Compounded of two; twofold.* [L. *binus,* from *bis,* two.]
Bind, bind, vt. *To tie or fasten; to gird; to oblige; to cover or wrap up; to render costive; to make firm; to form a border round.*—*vt.* *To be bound; to be obligatory.* pret. bound, ppr. binding, pp. bound.—*n.* *That which is bound; a stalk of hops which is bound to a pole by winding round it.* [Sax. *bindan.*]
Binder, bind'ėr, n. *He or that which binds; one who binds books or sheaves.*
Binding, bind'ing, p.a. *That binds; that obliges; obligatory.*—*p.n.* *Act of binding; a bandage; the cover and sewing, &c., of a book; act of obliging.*
Bind-weed, bind'wēd, n. *A plant with bending twining stems; convolvulus.*
Binnacle, bin'a-kl, n. *A case in which a ship's compass is kept.* [formerly *bittacle,* from Fr. *habitacle,* a little lodge.]
Binocular, bi-nok'ū-lėr, a. *Having two*

ch, chain; j, job; n. oo; ng, sing; vn, then; th, thin; w, wig; wh, whig; zh, azure; † obsolete.

eyes; adapted for both eyes. [L. *binus*, two, and *oculus*, the eye.]
Binomial, bi-nō'mi-al, *a.* or *n.* An algebraic expression consisting of *two terms*. [L. *bis*, and *nomen*, a term.]
Biographer, bi-og'ra-fėr, *n. A writer of biography* or of lives.
Biographical, bi-ō-graf'ik-al, *a. Pertaining to biography.*
Biographically, bi-ō-graf'ik-al-li, *adv. In the manner of a biography.*
Biography, bi-og'ra-fi, *n. A delineation of the life* and character of a particular person. [Gr. *bios*, life, and *graphō*, to delineate.]
Biology, bi-ol'o-ji, *n. A discourse of or concerning life*; the science of life. [Gr. *bios*, life, and *logos*, discourse.]
Bipartite, bi-pärt'it, *a. Divided into two parts*; having *two* correspondent *parts*. [L. *bis*, and *partītus*, divided.]
Biped, bī'ped, *n.* An animal having *two feet*, as man. [L. *bipes—bis*, and *pes*, *pedis*, a foot.]
Birch, bėrch, *n.* A tree having white bark and a fragrant odour. [Sax. *birce*.]
Birch, Birchen, bėrch, bėrch'en, *a. Made of birch*; consisting of birch. [Sax. *birces*, *beorcen*.]
Bird, bėrd, *n.* An animal *brooded over* when young by the mother; a general name for the feathered race.—*vi.* To *catch birds*. [Sax.—*bredan*, to nourish.]
Birdlime, bėrd'līm, *n.* A viscous substance, used to catch birds.
Bird's-eye, bėrds'ī, *a.* Seen from above, as if by a flying bird.
Birth, bėrth, *n. A bearing, or a being born*; that which is *born*; act of coming into life; extraction. [Sax. *beorth—beran*, to bear.]
Birth-day, bėrth'dā, *n. The day on which a person is born*, or its anniversary; day of origin.—*a.* Pertaining to the *day of birth.*
Birth-place, bėrth'plās, *n. The place where a person is born*; place of origin.
Birthright, bėrth'rīt, *n. Any right to which a person is entitled by birth.*
Biscuit, bis'ket, *n. Bread twice baked*; a kind of hard dry bread made into cakes. [Fr.—L. *bis*, and *coquo*, to cook.]
Bisect, bi-sekt', *vt. To cut or divide into two equal parts*. [L. *bis*, and *seco*, *sectus*, to cut.]
Bisection, bi-sek'shon, *n. Act of bisecting*; division of any line or quantity into two equal parts.
Bishop, bish'up, *n. An overseer*; a spiritual superintendent; a prelate; head of a diocese. [Gr. *episcopos—epi*, over, and *skopeō*, to look at or after, to view.]
Bishopric, bish'up-rik, *n. Jurisdiction of a bishop*; a diocese. [*bishop*, and Sax. *ric*, dominion.]
Bismuth, bis'muth, *n.* A metal of a yellowish or reddish-*white* colour. [G. *wismuth—weiss*, white, and *muth*, mettle.]
Bison, bī'son, *n.* A quadruped of the bovine genus. [L.]
Bissextile, bis-seks'til, *n.* Leap-year; every fourth year, so called by the Romans, because on that year the *sixth* of the calends of March was repeated *twice*. [L. *bissextilis—bis*, and *sextus*, sixth.]
Bit, bit, *n. That which bites*; the iron part of a bridle which is inserted in the mouth of a horse.—*vt. To put a bit* in the mouth of. *ppr.* bitting, *pret. & pp.* bitted. [Sax. *bita*, a morsel.]
Bitch, bich, *n.* The female of the dog kind; a name of reproach for a woman. [Sax. *bicca*.]
Bite, bit, *vt. To crush or sever with the teeth*; to pinch; to cause to smart; to wound by reproach, sarcasm, &c.; to hold fast; to corrode. *pret.* bit, *ppr.* biting, *pp.* bit, bitten.—*n. Act of biting*; wound made by biting; a morsel or mouthful. [Sax. *bitan*.]
Biter, bīt'ėr, *n. He or that which bites.*
Biting, bīt'ing, *p.a.* Sharp; severe; sarcastic.
Bitingly, bīt'ing-li, *adv.* In a sarcastic or jeering manner.
Bitter, bit'tėr, *a. Biting* to the tongue or taste; sharp; cruel; severe; painful; calamitous; distressing. [Sax. *biter—bitan*, to bite.]
Bitterish, bit'tėr-ish, *a. Somewhat bitter.*
Bitterly, bit'tėr-li, *adv. In a bitter manner*; sharply; cruelly; severely.
Bittern, bit'tėrn, *n.* A bird that utters a sound like the *lowing of a bull*; a bird of the heron kind. [D. *butoor*; L. *bos-taurus*, a bull.]
Bitterness, bit'tėr-nes, *n. Quality of being bitter*; sharpness; malice; sorrow; deep distress.
Bitters, bit'tėrz, *n. pl.* A liquor in which *bitter* herbs or roots are steeped.
Bitumen, bi-tū'men, *n.* A mineral, pitchy, inflammable substance. [L.]
Bituminous, bi-tū'min-us, *a. Having the qualities of or containing bitumen.*
Bivalve, bī'valv, *n.* A crustaceous animal having *two valves*, or shells, which open and shut.
Bivalve, Bivalvular, bī'valv, bi-valv'ū-lėr, *a. Having two shells* which open and shut, as the oyster. [L. *bis*, and *valvæ*, leaves, folds.]
Bivouac, bi'vō-ak, *n.* The encamping of soldiers for the night, without covering or tents.—*vi.* To encamp during the night, without tent or covering. *ppr.* bivouacking, *pret. & pp.* bivouacked. [Fr.—G. *bei*, by, near, and *wachen*, to watch.]
Bizarre, bi-zär', *a. Odd; fantastical; extravagant.* [Fr.—L. *bis*, and *varius*, different.]
Blab, blab, *vt.* To chatter about; to utter thoughtlessly; to tell indiscreetly.—*vi. To talk much*; to talk confusedly; to tell tales. *ppr.* blabbing, *pret. & pp.* blabbed. [D. *labben*.]
Blabbing, blab'ing, *p.a.* Tattling.
Black, blak, *a.* Destitute of light; of the colour of night; dark; gloomy; overclouded; sullen; atrocious.—*n.* The darkest colour; a stain; a negro; a mourning dress.—*vt. To make black*; to blacken; to soil. [Sax. *blæ*.]
Black-ball, blak'bal, *n.* A composition of tallow, &c., for *blacking* shoes; a ball of a black colour, used as a negative in voting.—*vt.* To reject by putting *black balls* into a ballot-box.
Blackberry, blak'be-ri, *n.* A plant of the bramble kind, and its *fruit*, which is of a *black* colour. [Sax. *blaceīrian*.]
Blackbird, blak'bėrd, *n.* A species of thrush, of a *black* colour.
Black-cattle, blak'kat-l, *n. pl.* Cattle of the bovine genus, as bulls, oxen, and cows.
Blackcock, blak'kok, *n.* A species of grouse.
Blacken, blak'n, *vt. To make black*; to darken; to soil; to defame.—*vi. To grow black* or dark. [Sax. *blæcan*.]
Black-flag, blak'flag, *n.* A pirate's flag, so named from its colour.
Blackfriar, blak'frī-ėr, *n.* A friar of the Dominican order, so named from the colour of his garments.
Blackguard, blak'gärd, *n.* A mean, vile, scurrilous fellow.—*a.* Mean; contemptible.
Blackguardism, blak'gärd-izm, *n. The conduct or language of a blackguard.*
Blacking, blak'ing, *p.a.* A substance used for *blacking* shoes.
Black-iron, blak'ī-ėrn, *n.* Malleable iron.
Blackish, blak'ish, *a. Somewhat black.*
Black-lead, blak'led, *n.* A mineral substance of a *dark* colour used for pencils; plumbago.
Black-letter, blak'let-tėr, *n.* The old English, or modern Gothic letter or character.—*a.* Printed in black letter.
Black-list, blak'list, *n.* A list of parties to be punished.
Blackness, blak'nes, *n. Black colour*; darkness; enormity in wickedness.
Black-rod, blak'rod, *n.* The usher belonging to the order of the Garter. [*black and rod.*]
Blacksmith, blak'smith, *n.* A smith who works in iron.
Blackthorn, blak'thorn, *n.* A species of *dark-coloured* thorn; the sloe.
Bladder, blad'dėr, *n.* A thin sac or bag in animals, which contains the urine, bile, &c.; a blister; a pustule; anything resembling the animal bladder. [Sax. *blædr—*Old G. *blæan*, to blow.]
Blade, blād, *n.* The *leaf* or spire of grass; a leaf; cutting part of a sword, knife, &c., shaped like a grass leaf; a broad bone of the shoulder; flat part of an oar. [Sax. *blæd*, a leaf.]
Blain, blān, *n. A tumour* of the skin; a pustule; a blister. [Sax. *blegen—blawan*, to blow.]
Blamable, blām'a-bl, *a. Deserving of blame* or censure.
Blamableness, blām'a-bl-nes, *n.* State of being *worthy of blame.*
Blamably, blām'a-bli, *adv.* Culpably.
Blame, blām, *vt.* To censure; to condemn; to reprimand; to pass an unfavourable judgment upon. *ppr.* blaming, *pret. & pp.* blamed.—*n. Expression of disapprobation*; censure; fault; crime. [Fr. *blâmer—*Gr. *blaptō*, to hurt, and *phēmi*, to speak.]
Blameless, blām'les, *a. Free from blame.*
Blamelessly, blām'les-li, *adv.* Innocently; without fault.
Blamelessness, blām'les-nes, *n.* Innocence; a state of being not worthy of censure.
Blanch, blansh, *vt.* To make *white* by taking out the colour; to change to white.—*vi. To grow white.* [Fr. *blanchir*.]
Blanched, blansht, *pp. Whitened.*
Blanching, blansh'ing, *p.n. The act of whitening.*
Bland, bland, *a. Soft*; smooth; soothing; gentle; mild. [L. *blandus*.]
Blandish, bland'ish, *vt. To soften*; to soothe; to caress; to flatter. [Old Fr. *blandir*, *blandissant—*L. *blandus*, soft.]
Blandishment, bland'ish-ment, *n. Act of blandishing*; soft words; kind speeches; caresses; flattery.
Blandness, bland'nes, *n. State of being bland.*
Blank, blangk, *a. Of a white colour*; pale from fear, &c.; confused; void; void of writing; not having rhyme.—*n. A white* unwritten paper; a lot by which nothing is gained; the white mark which a shot is to hit. [Fr. *blanc*.]
Blanket, blangk'et, *n. A white* woollen covering for a bed; a covering for horses, &c. [Fr. *blanchet*.]
Blanketing, blangk'et-ing, *p.n.* Cloth for blankets.
Blankly, blangk'li, *adv.* In a *blank* manner; with paleness or confusion.

Fāte, fär, fat, fall; mē, met, hėr; pīne, pin; nōte, not, mōve; tūbe, tub, bull; oil, pound.

Blankness, blangk'nes, n. State of being blank.

Blank-verse, blangk'vėrs, n. Verse which is void of rhyme; applied particularly to the English heroic verse of five feet without rhyme.

Blaspheme, blas-fēm', vt. To speak irreverently of, as of the Supreme Being; to speak or write reproachfully of, as of God or of sacred things; to speak evil of.—vi. To utter blasphemy. ppr. blaspheming, pret. & pp. blasphemed. [Gr. blasphēmeō.]

Blasphemer, blas-fēm'ėr, n. One who blasphemes.

Blasphemous, blas'fēm-us, a. Impiously irreverent in regard to God or sacred things.

Blasphemously, blas'fēm-us-li, adv. In a blasphemous manner.

Blasphemy, blas'fēm-i, n. Profane speaking; an indignity offered to God. [Gr. blasphēmia.]

Blast, blast, n. A gust of wind; a gale; a storm; sound of a wind-instrument; forcible stream of air, &c.; violent explosion of gunpowder; pernicious influence, as of wind; blight.—vt. To strike as with a blast; to blight; to strike with some sudden plague, &c.; to destroy; to make infamous; to blow up by gunpowder.—vi. To be struck as with a blast; to be blighted. [Sax. blǽst, a blast; Old G. blâsan, to blow.]

Blasted, blast'ed, p.a. blighted; injured.

Blasting, blast'ing, p.n. The act of splitting by an explosion of gunpowder.

Blaze, blāz, n. The stream of light and heat from any body when burning; wide diffusion of a report; that which shines and spreads widely.—vi. To flame; to send forth or show a bright and expanded light; to be conspicuous.—vt. To make public far and wide. ppr. blazing, pret. & pp. blazed. [Sax. blase, a torch.)

Blazing, blāz'ing, p.a. Flaming; emitting flame or light.

Blazon, blāz'on, vt. To display or set forth conspicuously; to adorn; to explain, as the figures on ensigns armorial.—n. Show; the act of drawing or explaining coats of arms. [Fr. blasonner.]

Blazoned, blāz'ond, p.a. Displayed pompously; explained; deciphered in the manner of heralds.

Blazoner, blāz'on-ėr, n. One who blazons; a herald.

Blazonry, blāz'on-ri, n. The art of explaining coats of arms in proper terms.

Bleach, blēch, vt. To make white or whiter.—vi. To grow white in any manner. [Sax. blǽcan.]

Bleached, blēcht, p.a. Whitened; made white.

Bleacher, blēch'ėr, n. One whose occupation is to whiten cloth.

Bleachery, blēch'ėr-i, n. A place for bleaching.

Bleaching, blēch'ing, p.n. The act or art of whitening, especially cloth.

Bleak, blēk, a. Blackened by piercing cold; exposed; chill; cold; dreary. [Sax. blac.]

Bleakness, blēk'nes, n. State or quality of being bleak; exposure to the wind; coldness.

Blear, blēr, a. Sore, as with blisters; dimmed or impaired, as the eyes.—vt. To dim or impair with soreness, as the eyes. [Dan. blære, a blister.]

Blear-eyed, blēr'īd, a. Having sore eyes; having the eyes dim with rheum.

Bleat, blēt, vi. To make the noise of a sheep; to cry as a sheep.—n. The cry of a sheep. [Sax. blǽtan.]

Bleating, blēt'ing, p.a. Crying as a sheep.—p.n. The cry of a sheep.

Bleed, blēd, vi. To emit blood; to lose blood; to die by slaughter; to feel agony, as from bleeding; to issue forth or drop, as blood.—vt. To take blood from. ppr. bleeding, pret. & pp. bled. [Sax. bledan.]

Bleeding, blēd'ing, p.a. Suffering extreme pain from sympathy or pity. p.n. A discharge of blood; the operation of letting blood; the drawing of sap from a tree.

Blemish, blem'ish, vt. To break; to mark with any deformity; to mar; to tarnish; to sully.—n. A mark of deformity; reproach; fault; dishonour. [Norm. broken.]

Blemished, blem'isht, p.a. Tarnished; soiled.

Blench, blensh, vi. To shrink; to start back; to flinch.

Blend, blend, vt. To mix together; to confound.—vi. To be mixed; to be united. [Sax. blendan.]

Bless, bles, vt. To make joyous or glad; to make happy or prosperous; to wish happiness to; to consecrate; to praise. ppr. blessing, pret. & pp. blessed or blest. [Sax. bledsian.]

Blessed, bles'ed, p.a. Happy; prosperous; holy and happy; happy in heaven.

Blessedness, bles'ed-nes, n. Beatitude; sanctity, joy.

Blessing, bles'ing, p.n. Benediction; a prayer imploring happiness upon; any means of happiness.

Blest, blest, a. Made happy; making happy; cheering.

Blight, blīt, n. That which renders pale; that which withers up; mildew; anything blasting.—vt. To wither up; to corrupt with mildew; to frustrate. [Old G. bleih, pale.]

Blighted, blīt'ed, p.a. Disappointed; frustrated.

Blighting, blīt'ing, p.a. Blasting.

Blind, blīnd, vt. To make blind; to darken; to obscure; to eclipse.—a. Darkened; destitute of sight; unable to discern or understand; ignorant; depraved; heedless.—n. A screen; a cover; something to mislead the eye or the understanding. [Sax.]

Blinded, blīnd'ed, p.a. Deprived of intellectual or moral discernment.

Blindfold, blīnd'fōld, a. Having the eyes covered; having the mental eye darkened.—vt. To cover the eyes of; to hinder from seeing.

Blinding, blīnd'ing, p.a. Depriving of sight or of understanding.

Blindly, blīnd'li, adv. Implicitly; heedlessly; inconsiderately.

Blindness, blīnd'nes, n. Want of bodily sight; want of intellectual or moral discernment; ignorance.

Blind-worm, blīnd'wėrm, n. A small reptile without feet, like a snake.

Blink, blingk, vi. To twinkle; to see obscurely, or with the eyes partially closed.—vt. To shut the eyes upon; to shut out of sight; to avoid.—n. A twinkle; a glimpse or glance; a wink. [G. blinken.]

Blinking, blingk'ing, p.a. Winking; twinkling.

Bliss, blis, n. Blessedness; supreme felicity; heavenly joys. [Sax.]

Blissful, blis'ful, a. Full of bliss.

Blissfully, blis'ful-li, adv. In a blissful manner.

Blissfulness, blis'ful-nes, n. Exalted happiness; felicity; fulness of joy.

Blister, blis'tėr, n. A thin bladder on the skin; a pustule; that which raises blisters.—vi. To rise in blisters.—vt. To raise a blister or blisters on. [G. blatter, a vesicle.]

Blister-fly, blis'tėr-flī, n. The Spanish fly, used in raising a blister.

Blistery, blis'tėr-i, a. Full of blisters.

Blithe, blīvн, a. Joyful; gay; mirthful. [Sax.]

Blithely, blīvн'li, adv. In a gay, joyful manner.

Blitheness, blīvн'nes, n. The quality of being blithe; gaiety; sprightliness.

Blithesome, blīvн'som, a. Gay; merry.

Bloat, blōt, vt. To blow up; to swell up or make turgid.—vi. To grow turgid; to dilate. [Old G. blât, a blowing, from blasan, to blow.]

Bloated, blōt'ed, p.a. Grown turgid; inflated.

Bloater, blōt'ėr, n. A herring dried in smoke.

Block, blok, n. A log; a heavy piece of wood or stone; a lump of solid matter; that on which anything is formed; piece of wood in which one or more wheels of a pulley are placed; a pulley; an obstacle; a blockhead.—vt. To inclose or shut up, as with a block or blocks; to stop up; to obstruct; to form into blocks (often with up). [D. blok.]

Blockade, blok-ād', n. The blocking up of a place, by surrounding it with hostile troops or ships.—vt. To block up, as a town by troops or ships; to besiege closely. ppr. blockading, pret. & pp. blockaded. [It. bloccato, blocked up.]

Blockhead, blok'hed, n. A stupid fellow; a dolt.

Blockish, blok'ish, a. Like a block; stupid; dull.

Blockishness, blok'ish-nes, n. Stupidity; dulness.

Block-tin, blok'tin, n. Pure tin, as it comes in blocks from the foundry.

Blonde, blond, a. Of a fair complexion. n. A person of fair complexion.

Blood, blud, n. The red fluid which circulates through the arteries and veins of men and animals; family; kindred; high birth; royal lineage; murder; the juice of anything.—a. Pertaining to blood; of the colour of blood; of a superior or particular breed. vt. To bleed; to stain with blood; to inure to blood. [Sax. blôd.]

Blood-heat, blud'hēt, n. A degree of heat equal to that of human blood, which is about 98° Fah.

Blood-horse, blud'hors, n. A horse of the purest breed.

Blood-hound, blud'hound, n. A hound of remarkably acute smell.

Bloodiness, blud'i-nes, n. State of being bloody; disposition to shed blood.

Bloodshed, blud'shed, n. The shedding or spilling of blood; slaughter.

Blood-shot, blud'shot, a. Red and inflamed by a turgid state of the blood-vessels.

Blood-sucker, blud'suk-ėr, n. Any animal that sucks blood; a cruel man.

Bloodthirsty, blud'thėrs-ti, a. Eager to shed blood.

Blood-vessel, blud'ves-sel, n. An artery or a vein.

Bloody, blud'i, a. Stained with blood; cruel; given to the shedding of blood.

Bloody-flux, blud'i-fluks, n. The dysentery.

Bloody-sweat, blud'i-swet, n. A sweat accompanied by a discharge of blood; the sweating-sickness.

Bloom, blöm, n. A blossom; a flower;

an expanded bud; state of youth; native flush on the cheek; blue colour upon plums, &c.—*vi. To shine; to glow;* to put forth flowers or blossoms; to resemble flowers newly blown; to show the beauty and freshness of youth. [Sax. *bloma.*]

Blooming, blōm'ing, *p.a.* Showing the freshness and beauty of youth.

Bloomy, blōm'i, *a. Full of bloom or blossoms;* flowery; flourishing.

Blossom, blos'som, *n. A blowing;* the flower of a plant.—*vi. To bloom;* to blow; to flower; to flourish. [Sax. *blosma.*]

Blot, blot, *vt. To remove;* to cancel (with *out*); to stain; to disgrace.—*n.* An obliteration; a spot or stain on paper; a disgrace; reproach. [Goth. *blauthjan,* to remove.]

Blotch, bloch, *n. Spot or pustule* upon the skin; an eruption. [from the root of *bloat.*]

Blotchy, bloch'i, *a. Having blotches.*

Blotter, blot'ėr, *n.* A waste-book.

Blotting-paper, blot'ing-pā-pėr, *n.* Unsized paper, serving to imbibe ink.

Blow, blō, *n. A stroke;* stroke of death; a sudden or calamitous event; egg of a fly, or act of depositing it. [Old G. *bliuwan,* to strike.]

Blow, blō, *vi.* To make a current of air; to emit air or breath; to be in motion, as air; to pant; to sound by being blown.—*vt. To impel by wind;* to swell up with wind; to warm by the breath; to sound, as a wind-instrument; to spread by report; to infect with the eggs of flies. *pret.* blew, *ppr.* blowing, *pp.* blown. [Sax. *blawan.*]

Blow, blō, *vi.* To put forth buds or flowers; to bloom; to blossom; to flourish.—*n. A blossoming.* [Sax. *blowan.*]

Blower, blō'ėr, *n. One who blows;* a contrivance to increase the draught of a chimney; a species of whale.

Blown, blōn, *p.a.* Expanded, as a blossom.

Blowpipe, blō'pīp, *n.* A tube used by jewellers and other artificers.

Blowze, blouz, *n. A ruddy, fat-faced* woman. [from D. *blozen,* to blush.]

Blowsy, blouz'i, *a. Ruddy-faced;* fat and ruddy.

Blubber, blub'bėr, *n. A bubble;* the fat of whales and other large sea-animals; the sea-nettle. [D. *bobbel.*]

Blubber, blub'bėr, *vi.* To weep in a noisy manner, so as *to swell* the cheeks.

Bludgeon, blud'jon, *n.* A short stick, with one end loaded (used to *strike*). [Goth. *bliggvan,* to strike.]

Blue, blū, *n.* The colour which the sky exhibits; one of the seven primary colours.—*a. Of a blue colour;* sky-coloured.—*vt. To dye of a blue colour.* *ppr.* bluing, *pret. & pp.* blued. [Sax. *bleow;* Norm. *bloie.*]

Bluebell, blū'el, *n.* A beautiful flowering plant, with *blue bell*-shaped flowers.

Blue-bottle, blū'bot-l, *n.* A fly with a large *blue* belly.

Blueness, blū'nes, *n. The quality of being blue;* a blue colour.

Bluff, bluf, *a. Swollen out;* blustering; big; burly.—*n.* A high steep bank, *projecting* into the sea or into a river. [Old Eng. *bloughty,* swelled.]

Bluffness, bluf'nes, *n. A swelling* or bloatedness; surliness.

Bluish, blū'ish, *a. Blue in a small degree.*

Bluishness, blū'ish-nes, *n. A small degree of blue* colour.

Blunder, blun'dėr, *vi. To be confused;* to err stupidly; to stumble.—*vt.* To *mix* foolishly.—*n.* A gross mistake; a stupid error; inadvertence. [allied to Sax. *blendan,* to mix.]

Blunderbuss, blun'dėr-bus, *n.* A short *gun,* with a large bore, which *blunders* in its aim. [*blunder,* and D. *bus,* tube.]

Blundering, blun'dėr-ing, *p.a.* Mistaking grossly.

Blunt, blunt, *a. Dull* on the edge or point; not sharp; dull in understanding; unceremonious; rude; plain.—*vt. To dull* the edge or point of; to repress, weaken, or impair. [Sw. Goth. *plump,* dull.]

Bluntly, blunt'li, *adv. In a blunt manner;* unceremoniously.

Bluntness, blunt'nes, *n. Dulness* of edge or point; rude sincerity or plainness.

Blur, blėr, *n. A pustule; a spot;* a stain; a blot.—*vt. To spot;* to obscure; to soil; to stain. *ppr.* blurring, *pret. & pp.* blurred. [D. *blaar,* blister.]

Blurt, blėrt, *vt. To throw out with a sudden blast of wind;* to utter suddenly or rudely (with *out*). [Icel. *blaer,* a blast.]

Blush, blush, *vi. To redden* with shame or confusion; to bear a blooming red colour.—*n. A red colour* on the cheeks or face, caused by shame or confusion; sudden appearance or glance. [Sax. *ablisian;* D. *bloosen,* from *blos,* a blush, redness.]

Blushing, blush'ing, *p.a. Reddening* in the cheeks or face.

Blushingly, blush'ing-li, *adv. In a blushing manner.*

Bluster, blus'tėr, *vi. To roar like the loud wind;* to boast; to swagger.—*n.* Loud noise; boast; swagger. [Sax. *blastan.*]

Blusterer, blus'tėr-ėr, *n. One who blusters;* a swaggerer.

Blustering, blus'tėr-ing, *p.a.* Noisy; windy.

Boa, bō'a, *n.* A kind of serpent, comprising several species; a long serpent-like piece of fur worn round the neck by ladies. [L. *boa, bova.*]

Boar, bōr, *n.* The male of swine, whether wild or tame. [Sax. *bar.*]

Board, bōrd, *n. A piece of timber broad and thin;* a table; food; persons seated round a table; a council; a court; the deck of a ship.—*vt. To cover with boards;* to supply with food; to place as a boarder; to enter, as a ship by force. *vi.* To live in a house at a certain rate for meals. [Sax. *bord,* a table.]

Boarder, bōrd'ėr, *n.* One who receives *board;* one who boards a ship in action.

Boarding, bōrd'ing, *p.n.* Act of *covering with boards,* and also the covering itself; food; act of entering a ship forcibly.

Boarish, bōr'ish, *a. Like a boar;* swinish.

Boast, bōst, *vi. To brag;* to talk ostentatiously; to enlarge or magnify.—*vt. To brag;* to magnify (with recipr. pron.).—*n.* A vaunting; the cause of boasting. [W. *bostiaw,* to brag.]

Boaster, bōst'ėr, *n. One who boasts.*

Boastful, bōst'ful, *a. Given to boasting.*

Boasting, bōst'ing, *p.n. Act of boasting.*

Boastingly, bōst'ing-li, *adv.* In an ostentatious manner; with boasting.

Boat, bōt, *n.* A small open vessel, usually impelled by oars; a small ship; a steamer.—*vt. To transport in a boat.* *vi.* To go in a boat. [Sax. *bat.*]

Boatman, bōt'man, *n. A man who manages a boat.*

Boatswain, bōt'swān, *n. A boat-servant;* one who has charge of a ship's boats, sails, rigging, &c. [Sax. *batswan.*]

Bob, bob, *n.* A pendant; something that plays up and down, or backwards and forwards; a short jerking motion; something curtailed or short.—*vt. to* move with a short jerking motion. *vi.* To play backward and forward, or up and down; to angle or fish for eels. *ppr.* bobbing, *pret. & pp.* bobbed. [Icel. *bobbi,* a knot.]

Bobbin, bob'in, *n. A small pin* of wood, with a notch, to wind the thread about in weaving lace. [Fr. *bobine.*]

Bobbinet, bob-in-et', *n.* A kind of lace.

Bode, bōd, *vt. To utter;* to portend; to be the omen of.—*vi.* To foreshow; to presage. *ppr.* boding, *pret. & pp.* boded. [Sax. *bodian,* to command, to tell.]

Bodice, bod'is, *n. Something worn round the body* or waist; a kind of stays.

Bodied, bo'did, *p.a. Having a body.*

Bodiless, bo'di-les, *a. Having no body.*

Bodily, bo'di-li, *a. Relating to the body;* actual.—*adv. In the form of a body;* corporeally; entirely.

Boding, bōd'ing, *p.a.* Foreshowing.

Bodkin, bod'kin, *n.* An instrument for *piercing* holes; a kind of large needle. [Icel. *broddr.*]

Body, bo'di, *n.* The trunk of an animal; the material substance of an animal; the main stem of a tree; matter; a person; main part; main army; the bulk; a system; strength; reality; any solid figure.—*vt. To give a body to;* to produce in some form; to embody (with *forth*). *ppr.* bodying, *pret. & pp.* bodied. [Sax. *bodig.*]

Body-guard, bo'di-gärd, *n.* The *guard* that protects or defends the *person.*

Bog, bog, *n. Soft* ground; a quagmire; a morass.—*vt.* To whelm or plunge, as in mud and mire. *ppr.* bogging, *pret. & pp.* bogged. [Gael. *bog,* soft.]

Boggle, bog'l, *vi.* To stop or stick, like one in a *bog;* to hesitate; to doubt. *ppr.* boggling, *pret. & pp.* boggled. [from *bog.*]

Boggling, bog'l-ing, *p.a.* Hesitating.

Boggy, bog'i, *a. Containing bogs.*

Boil, boil, *vi. To be agitated* by the action of heat; *to rise in bubbles* from the surface; to be hot; to be cooked by boiling; to move like boiling water; to be in a state of agitation.—*vt. To heat to a boiling state;* to dress or cook in boiling water. [Fr. *bouillir*—L. *bulla,* a bubble.]

Boil, boil, *n. A sore, angry swelling* upon the flesh. [Sax. *byl,* a bubble.]

Boiled, boild, *p.a. Dressed or cooked by boiling.*

Boiler, boil'ėr, *n. A person who boils;* a vessel in which anything is boiled; or steam generated.

Boiling, boil'ing, *p.n. Act or state of boiling.*

Boisterous, bois'tėr-us, *a. Raging;* tempestuous; stormy; noisy. [Dan. *bister,* raging.]

Boisterously, bois'tėr-us-li, *adv. In a boisterous manner.*

Boisterousness, bois'tėr-us-nes, *n. State or quality of being boisterous.*

Bold, bōld, *a. Daring;* courageous; intrepid; confident; impudent; executed with spirit; steep and abrupt. [Sax. *bald.*]

Boldly, bōld'li, *adv. In a bold manner.*

Boldness, bōld'nes, *n. Quality of being bold;* intrepidity; assurance.

Bole, bōl, *n.* The body or stem of a tree. [Sw. Goth. *bol,* the trunk of a tree.]

Bole, bōl, *n.* A kind of fine clay, often highly coloured by iron, and formed into cakes or flat *masses,* as a drug. [Gr. *bōlos,* a mass.]

Boll, bōl, *n. A round pod or pericarp.* *vi.* To form into a pericarp. [Sax. *bolla,* a bowl.]

BOLSTER — BOULDER

Bolster, bōl'stėr, n. A roll of straw, &c.; a long pillow used to support the head of persons lying on a bed; a pad.—vt. To support with a bolster or pad; to hold up; to maintain. [Sax.]

Bolt, bōlt, n. An arrow; a dart; a pointed shaft; that which darts like a bolt; a thunderbolt; that which shuts or fastens a door, as a bar; anything which fastens or secures.—vi. To start forth like a bolt.—vt. To throw or blurt out precipitately; to swallow at a gulp; to fasten or secure with a bolt, &c. [Sax.]

Bolt, bōlt, vt. To sift, as ground wheat, so as to separate the bran from it, and leave the flour. [Old Fr. beluter—L. epluda, chaff.]

Bolted, bōlt'ed, p.a. Sifted.

Bolter, bōlt'ėr, n. A machine for separating bran from flour.

Boltsprit, bōlt'sprit, n. See Bowsprit.

Bolt-upright, bōlt'up-rit, a. Perfectly upright, as a bolt placed on its head.

Bomb, bum, n. A loud humming sound; a large round hollow shell of cast-iron, filled with gunpowder, to be thrown from a mortar, so that it may explode where it falls. [L. bombus.]

Bombard, bum-bärd', vt. To attack with shells or shot thrown from mortars or guns. [Fr. bombarder.]

Bombardier, bum-bärd-ėr, n. One who attends the loading and firing of mortars.

Bombardment, bum-bärd'ment, n. The act of throwing shells and shot into a town, fort, or ship.

Bombasin, Bombasine, bum-ba-zēn', bum-ba-zēn', n. A twilled fabric, ordinarily black, of which the warp is silk and the weft worsted. [Fr. bombasin —L. bombyx, the silkworm.]

Bombast, bum'bast, n. Originally, a stuff of soft loose texture, used to swell garments; high-sounding words. [It. bombagia, cotton.]

Bombastic, bum-bast'ik, a. Swelled; inflated; turgid; high-sounding.

Bombaset, Bombasette, bum-ba-zet', n. A sort of thin woollen cloth.

Bond, bond, n. That which binds; a band; a connection; union; obligation; a writing by which a person binds himself to perform some act; in pl. chains; imprisonment.—a. Bound; captive.—vt. To place in bond, as goods. [Sax.]

Bondage, bond'āj, n. State of being bound; slavery; thraldom.

Bonded, bond'ed, p.a. That lies under a bond to pay duty, as goods.

Bondsman, bondz'man, n. One who is in bonds; a surety.

Bone, bōn, n. A firm, hard substance, composing the skeleton of an animal body; a piece of this substance; something made of bone.—vt. To take out bones from the flesh of, as in cookery. ppr. boning, pret. & pp. boned. [Sax. ban.]

Boned, bōnd, p.a. Having bones.

Bonfire, bon'fīr, n. A beacon-fire; a large fire lighted up in the open air, as an expression of public joy and exultation. [Dan. baun, a beacon, and fire.]

Bonnet, bon'net, n. A kind of hat or cap; a dress for the head worn by women. [Fr.]

Bonny, bon'ni, a. Good!; beautiful; gay; blithe. [Fr. bon, bonne—L. bonus, good.]

Bonus, bō'nus, n. A premium in addition to interest; an extra dividend to shareholders. [L. good.]

Bony, bōn'i, a. Pertaining to or consisting of bones; full of bones; stout; strong.

Booby, bō'bi, n. A blockhead; a water-bird, so named from its apparent stupidity.—a. Stupid; dull. [Sp. bobo.]

Book, buk, n. Any printed or written literary composition; a volume; division of a volume; volume of sheets for writing.—vt. To enter in a book. [Sax. boc.]

Bookish, buk'ish, a. Given to books or reading; fond of study.

Bookseller, buk'sel-ėr, n. One who sells books.

Bookworm, buk'wėrm, n. A worm that eats holes in books; a student closely attached to books.

Boom, böm, n. A beam; a long pole to extend the bottom of a sail; a chain or bar across a river or mouth of a harbour. [D.]

Boom, böm, vi. To make the sound of a trumpet; to make a sound like the bittern; to swell; to rush with violence, as a ship sailing fast.—n. A hollow roar, as of waves, cannon, &c. [Sax. byme, a trumpet.]

Booming, böm'ing, p.a. Rushing with violence; roaring like waves.—p.n. A deep hollow sound.

Boon, bön, n. A prayer; answer to a prayer; a favour granted; a gift, grant, or benefaction. [Dan. bon.]

Boon, bön, a. Gay; merry; pleasant; jolly. [Fr. bon—L. bonus, good.]

Boor, bör, n. A farmer; a tiller of the ground; a rustic; a clown. [D. boer.]

Boorish, bör'ish, a. Clownish; rustic.

Boorishness, bör'ish-nes, n. Quality of being boorish; coarseness of manners.

Boot, böt, vt. To profit; to benefit; to enrich (generally with it).—n. Profit; gain; advantage. [Sax. bot, compensation.]

Boot, böt, n. A leather covering for the leg, united with a shoe; a receptacle or box in a coach.—vt. To put boots on. [Fr. botte.]

Booted, böt'ed, p.a. Having boots on.

Booth, böth, n. A shed erected with boughs, branches, boards, &c. for a temporary residence. [Gael. both, a cottage.]

Bootless, böt'les, a. Destitute of boot; unavailing; unprofitable; useless.

Bootlessness, böt'les-nes, n. State of being bootless or useless, or without avail.

Booty, bö'ti, n. That which is captured by violence or in war; spoil; plunder; pillage. [Icel. býti.]

Boracic, bō-ras'ik, a. Relating to borax; containing borax.

Borax, bō'raks, n. A mineral salt, containing small shining crystals, used by workers in metal as a flux. [Ar. borak, from baraka, to shine.]

Border, bor'dėr, n. The outer edge of anything; boundary; margin; verge; rim.—vi. To approach near; to touch at the confines; to be contiguous (with on or upon).—vt. To surround or adorn with a border. [Sax. bord.]

Borderer, bor'dėr-ėr, n. One who dwells on a border, or near to a place.

Bordering, bor'dėr-ing, p.a. Lying adjacent to.

Bore, bōr, vt. To pierce through; to make a hole in or through; to pester.—vi. To be pierced. ppr. boring, pret. & pp. bored.—n. The hole made by boring; the diameter of a round hole; a person or thing that wearies or annoys. [Sax. borian.]

Bore, bōr, n. A sudden rise of the tide in certain estuaries, accompanied with a loud noise. [Icel. byîr, a whirlwind.]

Boreal, bō'rē-al, a. Northern; pertaining to the north or the north wind. [L. borealis.]

Boreas, bō'rē-as, n. A bellowing wind; the northern wind; a cold, northerly wind. [Gr.]

Borer, bōr'ėr, n. He or that which bores.

Boring, bōr'ing, p.a. Piercing.—p.n. The act of making a hole with an instrument; the hole made.

Borough, bu'ro, n. Primarily, a fortified town; a town with a corporation; a town that sends members to parliament. [Sax. burh, a hill.]

Borrow, bo'ro, vt. To receive from another for a time on credit; to receive as a loan; to appropriate, as that which belongs to another. [Sax. borgian.]

Borrowed, bo'rōd, p.a. Copied; assumed.

Borrower, bo'rō-ėr, n. One who borrows.

Bosky, bosk'i, a. Woody or bushy. [Low L. boscum, a wood.]

Bosom, bō'sum, n. The breast; figuratively, the seat of tenderness; the heart; the receptacle of secrets; inclosure; retreat; asylum.—vt. To inclose in the bosom; to conceal.—a. Intimate; much beloved; confidential. [Sax. bosm—bugan, to bend.]

Boss, bos, n. A protuberant ornament or part; a stud; a knob. [Fr. bosse.]

Bossy, bos'i, a. Containing a boss; ornamented with bosses.

Botanic, Botanical, bō-tan'ik, bō-tan'ik-al, a. Pertaining to botany.

Botanically, bō-tan'ik-al-li, adv. According to the system of botany.

Botanist, bot'an-ist, n. One skilled in botany.

Botanize, bot'an-iz, vi. To study botany; to search for and collect plants, as a botanist. ppr. botanizing, pret. & pp. botanized.

Botanizing, bot'an-iz-ing, p.n. The seeking of plants for botanical purposes.

Botany, bot'a-ni, n. The science which treats of plants. [Gr. botanē, fodder.]

Botch, boch, n. A swelling on the skin; that which resembles a botch; a patch added clumsily; ill-finished work in mending.—vt. To mark with botches; to mend clumsily. [It. bozza.]

Botcher, boch'ėr, n. One who botches.

Botchy, boch'i, a. Marked with botches; full of botches.

Both, bōth, a. The two, taken by themselves; the one and the other.—conj As well; on the one side and on the other side. [Sax. butu.]

Bottle, bot'l, n. A hollow round vessel of glass, leather, &c., with a narrow mouth, for holding liquors; the contents of a bottle.—vt. To put into bottles. ppr. bottling, pret. & pp. bottled. [Fr. bouteille; Low L. butta, a cask.]

Bottom, bot'tom, n. The lowest part; the base; the deepest part; the ground under the water; extremity of the trunk of an animal; seat of the body; native strength; a ship; dregs or grounds.—vt. To furnish with a bottom; to found or build upon.—vi. To rest upon as its ultimate support. [Sax. botm.]

Bottomless, bot'tom-les, a. Without a bottom; fathomless.

Bottomry, bot'tom-ri, n. The act of borrowing money on a ship's bottom, or the ship itself.

Boudoir, bö-dwąr', n. A lady's private room. [Fr.]

Bough, bou, n. The large branch of a tree that bends outward from the trunk. [Sax. boga—bugan, to bend.]

Boulder, bōl'dėr, n. See Bowlder.

---

ch, chain; j, job; g, go; ng, sing; TH, then; th, thin; w, wig; wh, whig; zh, azure; † obsolete.

Bounce, bouns, *vi.* To thump so as to make a sudden noise; to fly or rush out suddenly; to spring or leap against anything so as to rebound; to boast or bully; to be bold or strong. *ppr.* bouncing, *pret. & pp.* bounced.—*n.* A strong sudden thump; a boast; a bold lie. [D. *bonsen.*]

Bouncer, bouns'er, *n.* One who bounces; a boaster; a liar; a bold lie.

Bouncing, bouns'ing, *p.a.* Stout; strong; large and heavy.

Bound, bound, *n.* That which limits; a boundary.—*vt.* To limit; to confine; to circumscribe. [Old Fr. *bouns.*]

Bound, bound, *vi.* To leap; to jump; to spring; to move forward by leaps; to rebound.—*n.* A leap; a spring; a jump; a rebound. [Fr. *bondir.*]

Bound, bound, *a.* Ready to set out; going or intending to go (with *to* or *for*). [Icel. *boen.*]

Boundary, bound'a-ri, *n.* A visible mark designating a bound or limit; a limit; confines.

Bounden, bound'en, *a.* Appointed; indispensable; obligatory. [from *bind.*]

Boundless, bound'les, *a.* Without bound or limit; unlimited; unconfined.

Boundlessly, bound'les-li, *adv.* Without bound or limit.

Boundlessness, bound'les-nes, *n.* Quality of being boundless or without limits.

Bounteous, boun'te-us, *a.* Liberal; kind; bountiful.

Bounteously, boun'te-us-li, *adv.* Liberally; generously; largely.

Bountiful, boun'ti-ful, *a.* Free to give; liberal; munificent; generous.

Bountifully, boun'ti-ful-li, *adv.* In a bountiful manner.

Bounty, boun'ti, *n.* Goodness; liberality; munificence; generosity. [Fr. *bonté*—L. *bonitas.*]

Bouquet, bö-kā', *n.* A bunch of flowers; a nosegay. [Fr.—Low L. *boscum*, a wood.]

Bourn, Bourne, börn, börn, *n.* A bound; a limit. [Fr. *borne.*]

Bout, bout, *n.* A bending; as much of an action as is performed at one time; trial; attempt. [Sax. *bogeht*, bent.]

Bovine, bō'vin, *a.* Pertaining to oxen and cows. [Low L. *bovinus*—L. *bos, bovis,* an ox or cow.]

Bow, bou, *vt.* To bend; to arch; to bend, as one's body, in token of respect; to depress.—*vi.* To bend; to make a reverence; to yield.—*n.* A bending of the head or body, in token of reverence; the curving part of a ship's side, towards the stem. [Sax. *bugan,* to bend.]

Bow, bō, *n.* A curved instrument to shoot arrows; the rainbow; an instrument with which stringed instruments are played on; a curve.

Bowed, bōd, *p.a.* Bent like a bow.

Bowels, bou'els, *n. pl.* The intestines; the vital parts; interior part of anything; the seat of pity or kindness; tenderness; compassion. [Old Fr. *boel.*]

Bower, bou'ér, *n.* An anchor carried at the bow of a ship.

Bower, bou'ér, *n.* A covered place in a garden, formed of boughs or branches; a shady recess or sheltered retreat. [Sax. *bur.*]

Bowl, bōl, *n.* A round mass or ball, used for play by rolling it on a level plat of ground; a round concave vessel to hold liquors, rather wide than deep; the hollow part of anything.—*vi.* To play with bowls, or at bowling; to move rapidly, like a ball; to roll.—*vt.* To roll as a bowl. [Sax. *bolla,* a cup.]

Bowlder, bōl'dér, *n.* A smooth round stone, such as is found on the seashore; a rounded piece of rock. [from *bowl.*]

Bowler, bōl'er, *n.* One who bowls.

Bowling, bōl'ing, *p.n.* The act or art of throwing the ball at cricket.

Bowling-green, bōl'ing-grēn, *n.* A level piece of ground kept smooth for bowling.

Bowman, bō'man, *n.* An archer.

Bowshot, bō'shot, *n.* The space which an arrow may pass when shot from a bow.

Bowsprit, bō'sprit, *n.* A large spar which projects over the bow of a ship, to carry a sail forward. [D. *boegspriet.*]

Box, boks, *n.* A tree, the wood of which is very dense; a case made of the wood of such tree; a case of wood, metal, &c.; quantity that a box contains; a seat in a play-house; driver's seat on a coach. *vt.* To inclose in a box; to furnish with boxes. [L. *buxus,* the box-tree.]

Box, boks, *n.* A blow with the fist; a blow with the open hand on the ear. *vi.* or *t.* To strike with the hand or fist. [Gr. *pux,* with clenched fist.]

Boxer, boks'ér, *n.* One who boxes.

Boxing, boks'ing, *p.n.* The act or art of fighting with the fist.

Boxwood, boks'wud, *n.* The wood of the box-tree; also the plant itself.

Boy, boi, *n.* A male child; a male beyond the period of infancy, and under that of manhood; a lad. [L. *puer.*]

Boyhood, boi'hud, *n.* The state of a boy.

Boyish, boi'ish, *a.* Belonging to a boy.

Boyishly, boi'ish-li, *adv.* Childishly; in a trifling manner.

Boyishness, boi'ish-nes, *n.* The manners or behaviour of a boy; childishness.

Brace, brās, *n.* That which binds; that which strengthens; a bandage; two things tied together; a couple; a pair. *vt.* To draw tight; to make tight and firm; to strain up; to strengthen. *ppr.* bracing, *pret. & pp.* braced. [Fr. *bras,* arm, strength—L. *brachium,* the arm.]

Bracelet, brās'let, *n.* An ornament for the wrist, worn by ladies. [Fr.—L. *brachium,* the arm.]

Bracing, brās'ing, *p.a.* Having the quality of giving strength or tone. *p.n.* Act of bracing, or state of being braced.

Bracket, brak'et, *n.* A contrivance for holding things together; a support for something fixed to a wall; (pl.) crooked lines used in printing, to inclose one or more words.—*vt.* To place within brackets.

Bracketing, brak'et-ing. *p.n.* A series of brackets, for the support of something.

Brackish, brak'ish, *a.* Damaged or rendered unfit for use: salt in a moderate degree, as water. [G. *brack,* refuse or damaged matter.]

Brackishness, brak'ish-nes, *n.* Quality of being brackish.

Brad, brad, *n.* A small pointed nail, without a head. [Dan. *braad,* a goad or sting.]

Brag, brag, *vi.* To crack; to bluster; to vaunt; to talk big. *ppr.* bragging, *pret. & pp.* bragged.—*n.* A boast or boasting; the thing boasted. [Dan. *brag,* a crack.]

Braggart, brag'ärt, *a.* Boastful.—*n.* A boaster.

Braid, brād, *vt.* To weave, knit, or wreathe; to intertwine.—*n.* A texture formed by weaving together different strands; something braided; a knot. [Sax. *bredan.*]

Braided, brād'ed, *p.a.* Edged with braid.

Brain, brān, *n.* The mass of nervous matter occupying the cavity of the skull; seat of sensation and of the intellect; the understanding. (Often used in the plural.)—*vt.* To dash out the brains of; to put an end to. [Sax. *bragen.*]

Brain-fever, brān'fē-vér, *n.* An inflammation of the brain.

Brainless, brān'les, *a.* Without understanding; silly; thoughtless; witless.

Brain-sick, brān'sik, *a.* Disordered in the understanding; giddy.

Brake, brāk, *n.* A fern; a place overgrown with brakes, briars, or brambles. [Dan. *bregne,* fern.]

Brake, brāk, *n.* That which breaks; an instrument to break flax; a large heavy harrow for breaking clods; a contrivance for retarding the motion of carriage-wheels. [from *break.*]

Braky, brāk'i, *a.* Full of brakes; rough; thorny.

Bramble, bram'bl, *n.* A prickly plant or shrub. [Sax. *brembel.*]

Brambly, bram'bli, *a.* Full of brambles.

Bran, bran, *n.* The refuse or worthless part of corn; the husks of ground corn. [Fr.]

Branch, bransh, *n.* The shoot of a tree or plant; the offshoot of anything, as of a river, family, &c.; part; a limb; any distinct article; offspring.—*vi.* To shoot or spread in branches; to shoot out. *vt.* To divide or form into branches. [Fr. *branche.*]

Branching, bransh'ing, *p.a.* Furnished with branches; shooting out branches.

Branchy, bransh'i, *a.* Full of branches.

Brand, brand, *n.* A burning piece of wood; a sword, resembling a brand when waved; a mark made with a hot iron; any note of infamy.—*vt.* To burn with a hot iron; to stigmatize as infamous. [Sax.—*brennan,* to burn.]

Brandish, brand'ish, *vt.* To shake, as a weapon; to vibrate or flourish.—*n.* A shaking or waving; a flourish. [Fr. *brandir, brandissant.*]

Brandy, bran'di, *n.* Distilled wine; an ardent spirit distilled from wine. [G. *brant-wein,* from *brennen,* to burn, to distil, and *wein,* wine.]

Brasier, brā'zhér, *n.* One who works in brass; a pan for holding coals.

Brass, bras, *n.* A metal of the colour of live-coals; a yellow alloy of copper and zinc; impudence; a brazen face. [Sax. *bræs.*]

Brassy, bras'i, *a.* Made of brass; hard as brass; like brass.

Brat, brat, *n.* A child, so called in contempt. [G. *brut,* brood.]

Bravado, bra-vā'dō, *n.* A boast or brag; an arrogant menace. [Sp. *bravdda.*]

Brave, brāv, *a.* Daring; bold; gallant; dauntless; valiant; noble.—*n.* A blusterer.—*vt.* To set boastfully at defiance; to encounter with courage and fortitude. *ppr.* braving, *pret. & pp.* braved. [Dan. *brav.*]

Bravely, brāv'li, *adv.* Courageously.

Bravery, brāv'é-ri, *n.* Courage; heroism; valour; dauntlessness.

Bravo, brā'vō, *n.* A daring villain; a bandit; an assassin.—*interj.* brā'vo, Bravely, or well done. [It.]

Brawl, bral, *vi.* To quarrel noisily; to wrangle; to squabble; to rail.—*n.* A noisy quarrel; a squabble. [Fr. *brailler.*]

Brawler, bral'ér, *n.* One who brawls; a noisy fellow; a wrangler.

Brawling, bral'ing, *p.a.* Quarrelling.

Brawn, bran, *n.* The flesh of a boar; the fleshy muscular part of the body; bulk; muscular strength. [Sax. *bár,* a boar, *pl. báren.*]

Fāte, fär, fat, fall; mē, met, hér; pīne, pin; nōte, not, mōve; tūbe, tub, bull; oil, pound.

Brawny, brạn'i, *a.* Muscular; fleshy.
Bray, brā, *vt.* To break into small pieces; to pound, beat, or grind small. [Sax. *bracan*, to break.]
Bray, brā, *vi.* To roar; to make a loud harsh sound, as an ass.—*n.* The harsh sound or roar of an ass; a harsh grating sound. [Fr. *braire*.]
Brayer, brā'ėr, *n.* One who brays like an ass; an instrument to temper ink in printing-offices.
Braze, brāz, *vt.* To cover with brass; to solder with brass, or an alloy of brass and zinc. *ppr.* brazing, *pret. & pp.* brazed. [Fr. *braser*.]
Brazen, brāz'n, *a.* Made of brass; pertaining to brass; impudent.
Brazen-faced, brāz'n-fāst, *a.* Impudent; bold to excess; shameless.
Breach, brēch, *n.* The act of breaking, or state of being broken; a break; infringement; quarrel; injury.—*vt.* To make a breach or opening in the walls of. [Fr. *brèche*; G. *brechen*, to break.]
Bread, bred, *n.* That which nourishes; food made of flour or meal baked; anything which supports life. [Sax. *breod—bredan*, to nourish.]
Bread-corn, bred'korn, *n.* Corn of which bread is made.
Breadfruit-tree, bred'frōt-trē, *n.* A tree which grows in the South Sea Islands, to the height of forty feet, and produces a globular *fruit*, which forms an excellent substitute for bread.
Breadth, bredth, *n.* The broad dimension of anything; the measure across any plane surface, from side to side; width. [Sax. *brœd*, broad.]
Break, brāk, *vt.* To sever by fracture; to rend; to burst open; to crush; to tame; to make bankrupt; to discard; to open; to interrupt; to intercept; to dissolve, as any union.—*vi.* To come to pieces with violence; to burst; to burst forth; to dawn; to become bankrupt; to decline in vigour; to fall out. *ppr.* breaking, *pret.* broke, *pp.* broke or broken.—*n.* An opening made by fracture; a breach; an open place; a pause; a line in printing, noting suspension of the sense; the dawn. [Sax. *brœcan*.]
Breakage, brāk'āj, *n.* A breaking; allowance for things broken.
Break-down, brāk'doun, *n.* An accident; a downfall.
Breaker, brāk'ėr, *n.* He or that which breaks; (pl.) waves breaking into foam.
Breakfast, brek'fast, *n.* The first meal in the day.—*vi.* To eat the first meal in the day.—*vt.* To furnish with breakfast.
Breaking, brāk'ing, *p.a.* Rending asunder.
Break-neck, brāk'nek, *a.* Endangering the neck; steep and dangerous.
Breakwater, brāk'wạ-tėr, *n.* A mole at the entrance of a harbour, estuary, &c., to break the force of the waves.
Breast, brest, *n.* The fore part of the body, between the neck and the belly; the part of a beast which answers to the breast in man; the heart; the conscience; the affections.—*vt.* To bear the breast against; to meet in front; to oppose breast to breast. [Sax.]
Breast-bone, brest'bōn, *n.* The bone of the breast.
Breasted, brest'ed, *p.a.* Having a breast.
Breast-knot, brest'not, *n.* A knot of ribbons worn on the breast.
Breastplate, brest'plāt, *n.* Armour for the breast.
Breath, breth, *n.* Vapour; smell; the air drawn into and expelled from the lungs in respiration; life; a single respiration; respite; pause; a gentle breeze; an instant. [Sax. *brœth—œthm*, breath.]
Breathe, brēth, *vi.* To draw into and eject *air* from the lungs; to live; to take breath; to rest.—*vt.* To inspire and exhale, as air in breathing; to infuse; to utter softly or in private; to suffer to take breath. *ppr.* breathing, *pret. & pp.* breathed.
Breathing, brēth'ing, *p.a.* Exhibiting to the life.—*p.n.* Respiration; secret prayer; breathing-place; vent; accent.
Breathless, breth'les, *a.* Being out of breath; spent with labour; dead.
Breathlessness, breth'les-nes, *n.* State of being breathless.
Bred, bred, *p.a.* Educated.
Breech, brēch, *n.* That part where the body divides into two legs; the lower part of the body behind; the hinder part of a gun, or anything else.—*vt.* To put into *breeches*. [from *break*.]
Breeches, brēch'ez, *n. pl.* A garment worn by men, covering the hips and thighs. [Sax. *broc*, pl. *brœc*.]
Breed, brēd, *vt.* To nourish; to educate; to engender; to bring forth; to give birth to; to contrive; to occasion.—*vi.* To produce offspring; to be with young; to be produced. *ppr.* breeding, *pret. & pp.* bred.—*n.* That which is bred; race; progeny; kind; a number produced at once; a brood. [Sax. *bredan*.]
Breeder, brēd'ėr, *n.* One that breeds; one that is prolific; a producer.
Breeding, brēd'ing, *p.a.* Bearing and nourishing; educating.—*p.n.* The raising of a breed or breeds; education; deportment.
Breeze, brēz, *n.* A light wind; a gentle gale. [Fr. *brise*.]
Breezy, brēz'i, *a.* Fanned with gentle winds; subject to frequent breezes.
Brethren, bre᷄H'ren, *n. pl.* of *brother*; used in the solemn or scriptural style.
Breve, brēv, *n.* A short note; a note in music equal to two semibreves. [It.—L. *brevis*, short.]
Brevet, bre-vet', *n.* A short document; a commission to an officer, entitling him to take rank above his actual rank or pay. [Fr.—L. *brevis*.]
Brevetcy, bre-vet'si, *n.* The rank or condition of a brevet.
Breviary, brē'vi-a-ri, *n.* A book containing the daily service of the Roman Catholic and the Greek Church. [Fr. *breviaire*.]
Brevity, brē'vi-ti, *n.* Shortness; conciseness. [L. *brevitas*.]
Brew, brō, *vt.* To prepare, as ale or beer, from an infusion of malt, &c.; to mingle; to concoct; to plot.—*vi.* To perform the business of brewing; to be in a state of mixing or collecting. [Sax. *briwan*.]
Brewer, brō'ėr, *n.* One who brews.
Brewery, brō'è-ri, *n.* A house where brewing is carried on.
Brewing, brō'ing, *p.n.* The quantity brewed at once.
Bribe, brīb, *n.* A reward given to pervert the judgment or corrupt the conduct.—*vt.* To give a bribe to; to gain over by bribes. *ppr.* bribing, *pret. & pp.* bribed. [Fr.]
Briber, brīb'ėr, *n.* One who gives bribes.
Bribery, brīb'è-ri, *n.* The act or practice of giving or taking bribes.
Brick, brik, *n.* A square mass of burned clay, used in building, &c.; a loaf shaped like a brick.—*a.* Made of brick; relating to bricks.—*vt.* To lay with bricks; to fashion in imitation of bricks. [Fr. *brique*—Armor. *prt*, clay.]
Brickbat, brik'bat, *n.* A piece or fragment of a brick.
Brick-kiln, brik'kiln, *n.* A kiln or furnace in which bricks are burned.
Bricklayer, brik'lā-ėr, *n.* One who builds with bricks.
Bridal, brīd'al, *n.* A bride or wedding-feast; a wedding.—*a.* Belonging to a bride or to a wedding; nuptial; connubial. [Sax. *bryd-eals*, bride-ale.]
Bride, brīd, *n.* A woman espoused or contracted to be married. [Sax. *bryd*.]
Bride-cake, brīd'kāk, *n.* The cake which is made for a wedding.
Bridegroom, brīd'grōm, *n.* The bride's-man; a man about to be married. [Sax. *brydguma*—*bryd*, bride, and *guma*, a man.]
Bridemaid, Bride's-maid, brīd'mād, brīds'mād, *n.* A woman who attends on a bride at her wedding.
Bridewell, brīd'wel, *n.* A house of hard labour for offenders. [from St. Bride's well in London.]
Bridge, brij, *n.* Any structure across a river, &c., to furnish a passage; the upper part of the nose; the part of a stringed instrument that supports the strings.—*vt.* To build a *bridge* over. *ppr.* bridging, *pret. & pp.* bridged. [Sax. *bricge*.]
Bridle, brī'dl, *n.* The strap or instrument with which a horse is governed by a rider; something resembling a bridle in form or use; a restraint; a curb; a check.—*vt.* To check; to restrain; to curb.—*vi.* To hold up the head and draw in the chin. *ppr.* bridling, *pret. & pp.* bridled. [Sax. *bridl*.]
Brief, brēf, *a.* Short; concise.—*n.* A short writing; a writ or precept; an abridgment of a client's case. [Fr. *bref*—L. *brevis*, short.]
Briefless, brēf'les, *a.* Having no brief.
Briefly, brēf'li, *adv.* Concisely.
Brier, brī'ėr, *n.* A prickly shrub; the sweet-brier and the wild brier, species of the rose. [Sax. *brœr*.]
Briery, brī'ėr-i, *a.* Full of briers; rough.
Brig, brig, *n.* A vessel with two masts, square-rigged, or rigged nearly like a ship's mainmast and foremast. [from *brigantine*.]
Brigade, bri-gād', *n.* A division of troops under a brigadier.—*vt.* To form into a brigade or brigades. *ppr.* brigading, *pret. & pp.* brigaded. [Fr.]
Brigadier, bri-ga-dēr', *n.* The officer who commands a brigade. [Fr. from *brigade*.]
Brigand, bri'gand, *n.* Primarily, a mountaineer; a freebooter. [Fr.; W. *brig*, summit.]
Brigandage, bri'gand-āj, *n.* The employment of a brigand; robbery; plunder.
Brigantine, brig'an-tīn, *n.* A light swift-sailing vessel, which was used by brigands or pirates; a brig. [Fr. *brigantin*.]
Bright, brīt, *a.* Clear; shining; full of light and splendour; glittering; sparkling; manifest; illustrious; acute; witty. [Sax. *briht*.]
Brighten, brīt'n, *vt.* To make bright or brighter; to increase the lustre of; to make gay or witty; to make illustrious.—*vi.* To grow bright or more bright; to clear up.
Brightly, brīt'li, *adv.* Splendidly; with lustre.
Brightness, brīt'nes, *n.* Quality of being bright; splendour; acuteness.
Brill, bril, *n.* A fish allied to the turbot.
Brilliancy, Iril'i-an-si, *n.* Quality or state of being brilliant; splendour.
Brilliant, bril'i-ant, *a.* Shining; sparkling; twinkling; splendid.—*n.* A diamond of the finest cut. [Fr. *brillant*.]

Brilliantly, bril'i-ant-li, *adv.* Splendidly.
Brim, brim, *n.* *The rim* or brink of anything; the upper edge of the mouth of a vessel; the top.—*vi.* *To be full to the brim.* *ppr.* brimming, *pret. & pp.* brimmed. [Sax. *brymm.*]
Brimful, brim'ful, *a.* *Full to the brim.*
Brimmer, brim'èr, *n.* *A bowl full to the top.*
Brimstone, brim'stōn, *n.* *Burning-stone;* sulphur; an inflammable substance of a lemon-yellow colour. [Sax. *bryne*, a burning, and *stone.*]
Brindled, brind'ld, *a.* Marked with *brown* streaks, as if *burned* in; variegated. [from Sax. *brennan*, to burn.]
Brine, brīn, *n.* *The sea; salt water;* water strongly impregnated with salt. [Sax. *bryne.*]
Bring, bring, *vt.* To lead or cause to come; to fetch from; to carry to; to conduct; to produce; to attract; to lead by degrees; to prevail upon. *ppr.* bringing, *pret. & pp.* brought. [Sax. *bringan.*]
Bringer, bring'èr, *n.* *One who brings.*
Brink, bringk, *n.* The border of a steep place, as of a precipice, cliff, or river; verge; border. [Dan.]
Briny, brīn'i, *a.* *Pertaining to brine* or to the sea.
Brisk, brisk, *a.* *Lively;* full of life and spirit; gay; bright; sharp and smart to the taste; effervescing. [W. *brysg.*]
Brisket, brisk'et, *n.* The breast of an animal, which is very *gristly*; that part of the breast that lies next to the ribs. [Icel. *briosk*, a gristle.]
Briskly, brisk'li, *adv.* Actively; vigorously; with life and spirit.
Briskness, brisk'nes, *n.* *Liveliness;* gaiety; vivacity; effervescence.
Bristle, bris'l, *n.* The stiff hair of swine; stiff hair resembling bristles.—*vt.* To erect the *bristles* of.—*vi.* To rise or stand erect as bristles. *ppr.* bristling, *pret. & pp.* bristled. [Sax. *bristl.*]
Bristliness, bris'li-nes, *n.* *Quality of being bristly.*
Bristly, bris'li, *a.* *Thick set with bristles,* or with hairs like bristles; rough.
Britannic, bri-tan'ik, *a.* *Pertaining to Great Britain.*
British, brit'ish, *a.* *Pertaining to Great Britain* or its inhabitants.
Briton, brit'on, *n.* *A native of Britain.* [Sax. *Bryt*—W. *brit*, spotted.]
Brittle, brit'l, *a.* *Apt to break;* easily breaking short; not tough or tenacious. [from Sax. *bryttian*, to break.]
Brittleness, brit'l-nes, *n.* Fragility; opposed to toughness and tenacity.
Broach, brōch, *n.* *A spit*; a brooch. *vt.* *To pierce,* as with a *spit*; to tap; to let out; to utter; to open up; to publish first. [Fr. *broche*, a spit.]
Broacher, brōch'èr, *n.* *One who broaches; a spit.*
Broad, brąd, *a.* *Extended in breadth;* wide; extensive; open; unrestricted; indelicate. [Sax. *brad.*]
Broaden, brąd'n, *vi.* *To grow broad. vt. To make broad.*
Broadside, brąd'sīd, *n.* A discharge of all the guns on one side of a ship at the same time; a sheet of paper printed on one side only.
Broadsword, brąd'sōrd, *n.* *A sword with a broad blade* and a cutting edge.
Brocade, brō-kād', *n.* A silk or satin stuff, variegated with gold and silver, or enriched with flowers, &c. [Sp. *brocddo.*]
Brocaded, brō-kād'ed, *a.* *Worked like brocade;* dressed in brocade.

Broccoli, brok'ko-li, *n.* A variety of cauliflower. [It.]
Brochure, brō-shōr', *n.* *A stitched book;* a pamphlet. [Fr.]
Broider, broid'èr, *vt.* To ornament with *needle-work.* [Fr. *broder.*]
Broil, broil, *n.* *A brawl; a disturbance;* a noisy quarrel; a confused tumult. [Fr. *brouille.*]
Broil, broil, *vt.* To dress or cook over *coals,* or before the fire.—*vi.* To be subjected to heat; to be greatly heated. [Fr. *brûler.*]
Broken, brōk'n, *p.a.* Subdued; made bankrupt.
Broker, brō'kèr, *n.* An agent who transacts business for merchants; a dealer in old goods or pawns. [Sax. *brucan*, to profit.]
Brokerage, brō'kèr-āj, *n.* *The business of a broker;* the pay or gain of a broker.
Bronchial, brong'ki-al, *a.* Belonging to tne ramifications *of the windpipe* in the lungs. [from Gr. *bronchos*, the windpipe.]
Bronchitis, brong-kī'tis, *n.* An *inflammation* of the smaller ramifications of *the windpipe.*
Bronze, bronz, *n.* A compound metal of a brown colour; a colour to imitate bronze; a figure made of bronze; a copper medal.—*vt.* To colour, harden, or make appear on the surface like *bronze.* *ppr.* bronzing, *pret. & pp.* bronzed. [Fr.]
Bronzed, bronzd, *p.a.* *Made* to resemble *bronze;* browned.
Brooch, brōch, *n.* *A broach;* an ornamental *pin* or buckle used to fasten dress; a jewel. [Fr. *broche*, a spit.]
Brood, brōd, *vi.* To sit, as on eggs; to regard or think with long anxiety; to ponder anxiously and constantly. (With *over* or *on.*)—*n.* *That which is bred,* or the number bred at once; a hatch; offspring. [Sax. *brod—bredan,* to nourish.]
Brook, bruk, *n.* A small natural stream of water which *breaks forth* from a source, and struggles through obstacles with babbling noise. [Sax. *broc—brecan,* to burst forth.]
Brook, bruk, *vt.* To use†; to enjoy†; to bear; to endure. [Sax. *brucan.*]
Brooklet, bruk'let, *n.* *A small brook.*
Broom, brōm, *n.* A shrub having leafless pointed branches and yellow flowers; a besom, so named because frequently made of broom twigs. [Sax. *brom.*]
Broomy, brōm'i, *a.* *Full of broom;* containing broom.
Broth, broth, *n.* That which is *brewed* or boiled; liquor in which flesh is boiled and macerated. [Sax.]
Brothel, broth'el, *n.* A house of lewdness. [Fr. *bordel.*]
Brother, bruᴛʜ'èr, *n.* **Brothers**, or **Brethren**, bruᴛʜ'èrz, or breᴛʜ'ren, *pl.* A male born of the same parents with another; any one closely united with another or others; one who resembles another in manners; an associate; one of the same society; a fellow-creature. [Sax. *brothor.*]
Brotherhood, bruᴛʜ'èr-hud, *n.* *The state or quality of being a brother;* an association; a fraternity.
Brotherly, bruᴛʜ'èr-li, *a.* *Like a brother;* becoming brothers; kind.—*adv.* Like a brother.
Brougham, brǫm, *n.* A kind of fourwheeled carriage for general use.
Brow, brou, *n.* The prominent ridge over the eye; the arch of hair on it; the forehead; the general air of the

countenance; the edge of a precipice, hill, or any high place. [Sax. *bruwa.*]
Browbeat, brou'bēt, *vt.* *To bear down with a stern brow,* or with arrogant speech. *ppr.* browbeating, *pret.* browbeat, *pp.* browbeaten.
Brown, broun, *a.* *Of a burned colour;* of a dusky colour, inclining to red and black.—*n.* A colour resulting from the mixture of red, black, and yellow.—*vt. To make brown* or dusky; to give a bright brown colour to. [Sax. *brun—byrnan*, to burn.]
Brownish, broun'ish, *a.* *Somewhat brown.*
Brown-study, broun'stu-di, *n.* Gloomy study; dull thoughtfulness.
Browse, brouz, *vt.* To eat or nibble off, as the ends of shrubs, &c.—*vi.* To feed on the tender branches or shoots of shrubs and trees. *ppr.* browsing, *pret. & pp.* browsed.—*n.* The tender branches or twigs of trees and shrubs, fit for the food of goats, &c. [Fr. *brouser.*]
Bruin, brö'in, *n.* *The brown animal;* a familiar name given to a bear. [Old G. *brün.*]
Bruise, brōz, *vt.* *To crush;* to dash together, so as to *break* or reduce to small fragments; to make a contusion upon the flesh of. *ppr.* bruising, *pret. & pp.* bruised.—*n.* A contusion; a hurt from a blow with something blunt or heavy. [Sax. *brysan.*]
Bruised, brōzd, *p.a.* *Crushed;* broken.
Bruiser, brōz'èr, *n.* A boxer.
Bruit, brōt, *n.* *A noise spread abroad;* report; rumour; fame.—*vt.* To noise abroad. [Fr.]
Bruited, brōt'ed, *pp. Noised* or rumoured abroad; reported.
Brumal, brō'mal, *a.* Belonging to the winter. [L. *bruma*, winter.]
Brunette, brō-net', *n.* A woman with a *brownish* or dark complexion. [Fr.]
Brunt, brunt, *n.* *The heat* of battle; the onset when it *burns* most fiercely; shock; force of a blow; a sudden effort. [Old G. *brant*, a burning.]
Brush, brush, *n.* *A bundle of shoots, twigs, or bristles;* an instrument to clean by sweeping; a painter's large pencil; an assault†; a skirmish†; a thicket; the tail of a fox.—*vt.* To sweep with *a brush;* to paint with a brush; to touch lightly in passing; to remove by brushing.—*vi.* To move nimbly in haste; to move lightly; to move or skim over. [Fr. *brosse*, a bush.]
Brushwood, brush'wud, *n.* A thicket of small trees and shrubs; small branches of trees cut off. [from Fr. *brosse,* a bush, and *wood.*]
Brushy, brush'i, *a.* Rough; shaggy.
Brusque, brōsk, *a.* *Brisk;* sharp; rude; rough. [Fr.]
Brutal, brōt'al, *a.* Unfeeling. *like a brute;* inhuman; savage; ferocious.
Brutality, brōt-al'i-ti, *n.* *Quality of being brutal;* inhumanity; savageness; cruelty; insensibility to pity or shame.
Brutalize, brōt'al-īz, *vt.* *To make brutal. vi.* *To become brutal. ppr.* brutalizing, *pret. & pp.* brutalized.
Brutally, brōt'al-li, *adv. In a brutal manner.*
Brute, brōt, *a.* Senseless; irrational; bestial; rough; uncivilized.—*n.* A beast; a brutal person; a savage; a low-breed, unfeeling man. [Fr. *brut*; L. *brutus,* heavy, dull.]
Brutish, brōt'ish, *a.* *Brutal;* beastly; ferocious; grossly sensual. [Old G. *bruttisc,* terrible of aspect.]
Brutishness, brōt'ish-nes, *n.* *Quality of being brutish;* brutality.

Fāte, fär, fat, fąll; mē, met, hèr; pīne, pin; nōte, not, mȯve; tūbe, tub, bųll; oil, pound.

Bubble, bub'bl, n. A small *bladder* of water or other fluid, inflated with air; that which will burst easily; a vain project; a fraud.—vi. To *rise* in *bubbles;* to run with a gurgling noise.—vt. To cheat. ppr. bubbling, pret. & pp. bubbled. [D. *bobbel.*]
Bubbling, bub'bl-ing, p.a. Running with a gurgling sound.
Buccaneer, buk-a-nēr', n. A pirate; a freebooter. [Fr. *boucanier.*]
Buccaneering, buk-a-nēr'ing, p.n. The *employment of buccaneers.*
Buck, buk, n. The male of certain animals, as deer, goats, &c.; a gay young fellow. [Sax. *buc,* a he-goat.]
Bucket, buk'et, n. A small vessel in which water is drawn or carried; a cavity on the rim of a water-wheel. [Sax. *buc.*]
Buckle, buk'l, n. A link of metal, with a tongue or catch, made to fasten one thing to another.—vt. To *fasten with a buckle* or *buckles;* to prepare for action (with recip. pron.); to join in battle (with *with*). ppr. buckling, pret. & pp. buckled. [G. *buckel,* a knob, a boss.]
Buckler, buk'lėr, n. A kind of shield. vt. To support; to defend. [Fr. *bouclier* —L. *buccula,* the handle of a shield.]
Buckram, buk'ram, n. A coarse linen cloth stiffened with glue, and originally having open *holes* or interstices. a. Stiff; precise. [Fr. *bougran*—*buco,* a hole.]
Bucolic, bū-kol'ik, a. *Pertaining to the ears of cattle;* pastoral.—n. A pastoral poem. [Gr. *boukolikos*—*bous,* an ox, and *koleō,* to take care of.]
Bud, bud, n. The first *shoot* or opening of a plant or flower; a germ; a gem. vi. To *put forth* buds or germs; to begin to grow or shoot forth.—vt. To insert the bud of, as of a plant, under the bark of another tree. ppr. budding, pret. & pp. budded. [Fr. *bouton*—*bouter,* to push out.]
Budding, bud'ing, p.a. Putting forth *buds.*—p.n. The *act of inserting buds.*
Budge, buj, vi. To *move off;* to stir; to wag. ppr. budging, pret. & pp. budged. [Fr. *bouger.*]
Budget, buj'et, n. A *bag;* a little sack with its contents; a stock or store; the papers respecting the finances of the British nation. [Fr. *bougette.*]
Buff, buf, n. Leather prepared from the skin of the *buffalo,* elk, &c.; the colour of the leather; a very light yellow.—a. Of the colour of buff leather; light yellow; made of buff leather. [from *bufalo.*]
Buffalo, buf'fa-lō, n. A species of the *wild ox,* larger than the common ox; the bison. [It. *bufalo;* L. *bos, bovis,* an ox.]
Buffer, buf'ėr, n. Any apparatus for deadening concussion between a moving body and one on which it strikes, as the ends of a railway-carriage.
Buffet, bu-fet', n. A kind of cupboard for holding *wine, glasses,* plates, &c. [Fr.]
Buffet, buf'fet, n. A thump; a box; a slap.—vt. To thump; to box; to contend against. [It. *buffetto.*]
Buffeting, buf'fet-ing, p.n. A succession of blows; attack.
Buffoon, buf-fön', n. One who makes sport by low jests and antic gestures; a droll; a mimic. [Fr. *bouffon*—*boufer,* to puff.]
Buffoonery, buf-fön'é-ri, n. The *arts and practices of a buffoon.*
Buffy, buf'i, a. Of the colour of *buff;* light yellow; applied to the *blood.*

Bug, bug, n. A disgusting insect that infests houses, beds, &c.
Bugbear, Bug, bug'bār, bug, n. A *frightful object;* anything imaginary that is considered frightful. [W. *bwg,* a hobgoblin.]
Bugle, Bugle-horn, bū'gl, bū'gl-horn, n. A *hunting-horn;* a military instrument of music; an elongated glass bead, commonly black. [Old Fr. *bugle,* an ox.]
Build, bild, vt. To construct and raise, as an edifice; to raise on a foundation; to establish; to consolidate.—vi. To exercise the art or practise the business of *building;* to construct, rest, or depend, as on a foundation.—n. Construction; make; form. pret. built, ppr. building, pp. built. [Sax. *byldan,* to confirm.]
Builder, bild'ėr, n. One *who builds.*
Building, bild'ing, p.n. The art of constructing edifices, &c.; an edifice; a house.
Bulb, bulb, n. A *round body;* a round scaly root, either above or below ground (usually the latter). [L. *bulbus.*]
Bulbous, bulb'us, a. *Containing bulbs* or a *bulb;* growing from bulbs; round or roundish.
Bulbul, bul'bul, n. The Persian nightingale. [Pers.]
Bulge, bulj, n. A *swelling out;* the bilge or protuberant part of a cask.—vi. To *swell out;* to be protuberant; to bilge. ppr. bulging, pret. & pp. bulged. [G. a swelling wave.]
Bulk, bulk, n. That which *swells out;* carcass; the whole magnitude of anything; the gross; the majority; extent. [of the same origin as *bulge.*]
Bulkiness, bulk'i-nes, n. *Quality of being bulky;* greatness in bulk.
Bulky, bulk'i, a. Large; of great size or *bulk;* of great dimensions.
Bull, bul, n. The *animal that bellows;* the male of cattle, of which cow is the female; a sign of the zodiac. [G. *bulle.*]
Bull, bul, n. A seal of a *round shape;* an edict issued by the pope, and having his seal affixed to it; a verbal blunder or contradiction. [L. *bulla,* a bubble.]
Bull-dog, bul'dog, n. A species of *dog* of remarkable courage.
Bullet, bul'let, n. *Something rounded;* a *small ball;* a ball of iron or lead, used to load muskets, rifles, pistols, &c., with. [Fr. *boulet*—*boule,* a bowl.]
Bulletin, bul'le-tin, n. An official statement or report of facts, events, &c.; an official report respecting the health of some great personage. [Fr.]
Bull-fight, bul'fit, n. A Spanish amusement, of a barbarous nature.
Bullfinch, bul'finsh, n. A *finch* with a *thick* neck, having the breast, cheeks, and neck of a crimson colour.
Bullion, bul'li-on, n. Gold or silver in the lump, unwrought, uncoined; gold and silver, both coined and uncoined, when reckoned by weight. [Fr. *billon.*]
Bullock, bul'lok, n. An ox or castrated bull. [Sax. *bulluca.*]
Bull-trout, bul'trout, n. A large species of trout.
Bully, bul'li, n. A *noisy, blustering, quarrelsome fellow.*—vt. To insult and overbear *with noise.*—vi. To *bluster;* to be noisy and quarrelsome. ppr. bullying, pret. & pp. bullied. [Sax. *bulgian,* to bellow.]
Bulrush, bul'rush, n. A *large, strong* kind of rush.
Bulwark, bul'wėrk, n. A bastion or a rampart, &c.; an outwork; a fortification; any means of defence or safety. [Sw. *bolwarck.*]
Bum-boat, bum'bōt, n. A small boat for carrying provisions to a ship at a distance from shore. [D. *boom,* a tree, and *boat,* a canoe.]
Bump, bump, n. A heavy blow, or the noise of it; a lump produced by a blow. vi. To make a loud, heavy, or hollow noise, as the bittern.—vt. To knock; to thump. [Goth. and Icel. *bomps,* a blow.]
Bumper, bump'ėr, n. A cup or glass filled to the brim; a crowded house at a theatre, &c.
Bumpkin, bump'kin, n. A *clumsy,* awkward rustic; a clown. [*boom,* log, and *kin,* kind.]
Bunch, bunsh, n. A knob or lump; a cluster; a collection; a knot.—vi. To swell out in a *bunch* or protuberance. [Icel. *bunki,* a heap.]
Bunchy, bunsh'i, a. *Growing in bunches;* like a *bunch;* having tufts.
Bundle, bun'dl, n. A number of things bound together; a package made up loosely; a roll.—vt. To *tie* or *bind in a bundle* or roll. ppr. bundling, pret. & pp. bundled. [Sax. *byndel*—root of *bind.*]
Bung, bung, n. The stopple of the orifice in the bilge of a cask.—vt. To stop; to close up. [Sax. *pyngan,* to prick; to pack in or up.]
Bungle, bung'gl, vi. To perform in a clumsy manner.—vt. To make or mend clumsily; to manage awkwardly. ppr. bungling, pret. & pp. bungled.—n. A botch; inaccuracy; clumsy performance. [W. *bon y gler,* the lowest class of minstrels.]
Bungler, bung'gl-ėr, n. A clumsy, awkward workman.
Bungling, bung'gl-ing, p.a. Clumsy; awkwardly done.
Bunion, bun'i-on, n. An excrescence on the great toe. [Fr. *bigne.*]
Bunn, Bun, bun, bun, n. A small cake, or a kind of sweet bread. [Ir. *bunna,* a cake.]
Bunting, bunt'ing, n. A bird having a knob in the roof of the mouth. [Sw. *bunt.*]
Bunting, bunt'ing, n. A thin woollen stuff *of different colours,* of which the flags and signals of ships are made. [G. *bunt,* parti-coloured.]
Buoy, boi, n. A floating mark (as a large cask, &c.) to point out shoals, rocks, an anchor, &c.—vt. To keep afloat; to bear up; to keep from sinking (with *up*). — vi. To float. [Fr. *bouée.*]
Buoyancy, boi'an-si, n. The *quality of being buoyant;* lightness of spirits; vivacity.
Buoyant, boi'ant, a. Floating; light; elastic. [from *buoy.*]
Bur, bėr, n. The rough prickly *head* of the burdock, chestnut, &c. [Fr. *bourre,* down.]
Burden, bėr'dn, n. written also Burther. That *which is borne;* load; freight; that which is oppressive; [Fr. *bourdon*] the drum of a bagpipe; chorus of a song; that which is often repeated. vt. To load; to impose a weight upon; to oppress. [Sax. *byrthen*—*beran,* to bear.]
Burdensome, bėr'dn-sum, a. *Grievous to be borne;* heavy; oppressive.
Burdock, bėr'dok, n. A plant with a rough prickly *head.* [*bur* and *dock.*]
Bureau, bū-rō', n. An office or court; place where the duties of a public office are transacted; a chest of drawers,

having a writing-table which folds up. [Fr.]

Burgage, bėrg'āj, n. A species of tenure in *boroughs*, by which the citizens hold their lands or tenements.

Burgess, bėr'jes, n. A freeman of a *borough*; representative of a borough in parliament. [Fr. *bourgeois.*]

Burglar, bėrg'lėr, n. One who *robs a house* by night. [*burg,* and Armor. *laer,* a thief.

Burglarious, bėrg-lā'ri-us, a. Constituting the *crime of burglary.*

Burglary, bėrg'la-ri, n. Act of nocturnal house-breaking, with an intent to commit a felony. [Norm. *burgerie.*]

Burgundy, bėr'gun-di, n. A kind of wine, so called from *Burgundy.*

Burial, be'ri-al, n. *Act of burying*; interment; a funeral.

Burier, be'ri-ėr, n. One who buries a deceased person.

Burin, bū'rin, n. *A graver*; an instrument for engraving. [Fr.]

Burlesque, bėr-lesk', a. Jocular; tending to excite laughter by *ludicrous images.*—n. *Ludicrous representation;* a composition tending to excite laughter.—*vt.* To turn into *ridicule*; or to make ludicrous by representation. ppr. burlesquing, pret. & pp. burlesqued. [Fr.]

Burly, bėr'li, a. *Like a boor*; great in size; clumsy; boisterous. [G. *bauer,* a boor.]

Burn, bėrn, *vt.* To *set on fire*; to consume with fire; to scorch; to inflame; to harden by fire.—*vi.* To *be on fire;* to be inflamed with desire; to act as fire; to rage fiercely; to glow. ppr. burning, pret. & pp. burned or burnt.—n. A hurt caused by fire. [Sax. *bernan.*]

Burner, bėrn'ėr, n. That which gives out light or flame.

Burning, bėrn'ing, p.a. Much heated; scorching; vehement.

Burning-glass, bėrn'ing-glas, n. A glass which collects the rays of the sun into a focus, producing an intense heat.

Burnish, bėr'nish, *vt.* To *make brown,* or *of flame colour,* as brass; to polish. *vi.* To grow bright or glossy.—n. Gloss; brightness; lustre. [Fr. *brunir, brunissant.*]

Burnt-offering, bėrnt'of-fėr-ing, n. Something *offered,* and *burned* on an altar.

Burr, bėr, n. The down of several plants, seed-vessels, fruits, and flowers (see Bur]; a roughness in sounding the letter *r*; the lobe or lap of the ear. [Fr. *bourre.*]

Burrow, bu'rō, n. A hollow place in the earth, made by small animals, as rabbits, where they lodge for shelter. [Sax. *beorh,* refuge.]—*vi.* To excavate a hole under ground; to lodge in any deep or concealed place. [Sax. *beorgan,* to protect.]

Bursar, bėrs'ėr, n. A treasurer of a college; a student in a Scottish university maintained either in whole or in part by funds derived from endowments. [Fr. *boursier—bourse,* a purse.]

Bursary, bėrs'a-ri, n. *Allowance paid to a bursar* or student; an exhibition.

Burst, bėrst, *vi.* To *fly* or *break open;* to rush forth; to break away; to come with violence.—*vt.* To *break* by force; to rend; to rupture; to open suddenly. ppr. bursting, pret. & pp. burst.—n. A violent disruption; a rupture. [Sax. *burstan.*]

Burthen, bėr'vнn. See BURDEN.

Bury, be'ri, *vt.* To put into a grave; to inter; to entomb; to overwhelm; to conceal; to hide. ppr. burying, pret. & pp. buried. [Sax. *byrian.*]

Bush, bush, n. A cluster of trees or shrubs; a shrub with branches; a foxtail.—*vi.* To grow thick or bushy. [G. *busch.*]

Bush, bush, n. A hollow cylinder of metal which lines the *box* or hollow of the nave of a wheel in which the axle works; a similar circle let into other holes. [D. *bus,* a box.]

Bushel, bush'el, n. A dry measure containing eight gallons or four pecks. [Fr. *boisseau.*]

Bushiness, bush'i-nes, n. *Quality of being bushy.*

Bushy, bush'i, a. *Full of bushes*; thick and spreading, like a bush.

Busily, bi'zi-li, adv. *In a busy manner.*

Business, bi'zi-nes, n. That which occupies the time and labour of men; concern; affair; trade; office.

Busk, busk, n. A piece of steel or whalebone, or wood, worn by women on the breast. [Fr. *busc.*]

Buskin, bus'kin, n. A kind of half boot or high shoe, covering the foot and leg to the middle, worn by the ancient actors of tragedy; tragedy. [Old Fr. *brossequin.*]

Buskined, bus'kind, p.a. *Dressed in buskins.*

Buss, bus, n. *A kiss;* a salute with the lips.—*vt.* To kiss; to salute with the lips. [Gael. *bus,* a mouth.]

Bust, bust, n. The chest and thorax; the figure of a person in relief, showing only the head, shoulders, and stomach. [It. *busto.*]

Bustard, bus'tėrd, n. A large *heavy flying* bird, with feathery ears. [Old Fr. *bistarde*—L. *bis,* twice, and *tardus,* slow.]

Bustle, bus'l, *vi.* To be very active; to be very quick in motion. ppr. bustling, pret. & pp. bustled.—n. Rapid motion with noise and agitation; tumult. (from Sax. *brastlian,* to crackle.]

Busy, bi'zi, a. Occupied; actively engaged; meddling; troublesome.—*vt.* To *make or keep busy;* to employ with constant attention; to keep engaged. (With the recipr. pron.) ppr. busying, pret. & pp. busied. [Sax. *bysig.*]

Busy-body, bi'zi-bo-di, n. An officious meddling person.

But, but, conj. or prep. *Without*; except; unless; only; however; nevertheless. [from Sax. *butan.*]

Butcher, buch'ėr, n. One who slaughters animals for market; one who delights in bloody deeds.—*vt.* To kill or slaughter, as animals for food; to slaughter cruelly. [Fr. *boucher*—*bouche,* the mouth.]

Butchery, buch'ėr-i, n. Great slaughter; massacre.

But-end, but'end, n. The largest or blunt end of a thing.

Butler, but'lėr, n. A *bottler*; one who has the care of wines in great houses. [Old Fr. *bouteillier*—*bouteille,* a bottle.]

Butlership, but'lėr-ship, n. *The office of a butler.*

Butt, but, n. The striking end of a thing; a mark to be shot at; the point to which a purpose is directed; a push given by the head of an animal; the person at whom ridicule, jests, or contempt is directed. [It. *botto,* a blow.] *vi.* To *thrust the head forward.*—*vt.* To strike by thrusting the head or horns against, as a ram does. [It. *buttare.*]

Butt, but, n. A vessel or cask of large capacity, holding 126 gallons of wine. [Sax. *byt, butte.*]

Butter, but'tėr, n. An oily substance obtained from cream or milk by churning; any substance resembling butter. *vt.* To smear or spread with *butter.* [Sax. *buter;* L. *butyrum.*]

Butter-cup, but'tėr-kup, n. A wild flower which has the colour of *butter.*

Butterfly, but'tėr-flī, n. The name of a very extensive group of beautiful winged insects, so named probably from the colour of one of the species.

Buttery, but'tėr-i, a. *Having the qualities of butter.*—n. An apartment in a house where *butter,* milk, provisions, and utensils were formerly kept.

Buttock, but'tok, n. *The protuberant termination* of the body behind; the rump.

Button, but'n, n. A *knob*; a catch used to fasten together the different parts of dress.—*vt.* To *fasten with a button* or *buttons.* [Fr. *bouton.*]

Buttress, but'tres, n. That which *abuts,* or serves as an abutment; a projection from a wall to impart additional strength; any prop.—*vt.* To support by a *buttress*; to prop. [Fr. *abouter,* to border on.]

Buxom, buks'um, a. Gay; lively; brisk; wanton; jolly. [Sax. *bocsum.*]

Buy, bī, *vt.* To *acquire by payment*; to purchase; to acquire by paying a price for; to bribe.—*vi.* To negotiate or treat about a purchase. ppr. buying, pret. & pp. bought. [Sax. *bygan.*]

Buyer, bī'ėr, n. *One who buys.*

Buzz, buz, *vi.* To *hum,* as bees; to whisper.—*vt.* To whisper; to spread, as report, by whispers.—n. *The noise of bees;* a whisper. (formed from the sound.]

Buzzard, buz'ėrd, n. A species of hawk; a blockhead. [Fr. *busard.*]

By, bī, prep. Used to denote the instrument, agent, cause, manner, or means; at; near; beside; close to; through or with; in; for.—adv. Near; beside; passing; in presence; in comp. something out of the direct way. [Sax. *big.*]

Bye, By, bī, bī, n. Primarily a *village*; a dwelling; a way. [Dan. *bye.*]

By-end, bī'end, n. *Private end*; secret purpose or advantage.

By-gone, bī'gon, a. *Past; gone by.*

By-lane, bī'lān, n. A *private lane,* or one out of the usual road.

By-law, bī'la, n. *A private law*; one of the local laws of a city, town, or private corporation.

By-path, bī'path, n. *A private path*; an obscure way.

By-stander, bī'stand-ėr, n. *One who stands by or near*; a spectator; a mere looker-on. [Sax. *bigstandan,* to stand by.]

By-view, bī'vū, n. *Private view*; self-interested purpose.

By-way, bī'wā, n. *A private,* secluded, or obscure *way.*

By-word, bī'wėrd, n. *A passing or current word*; a common saying; a proverb. [Sax. *big,* and *word.*]

Fāte, fär, fat, fall; mē, met, hėr; pīne, pin; nōte, not, mōve; tūbe, tub, bull; oil, pound.

C.

Cab, kab, n. A covered carriage with two or four wheels, drawn usually by one horse. [from *cabriolet*.]

Cabal, ka-bal', n. A number of persons united in some secret intrigue; intrigue; secret artifice.—vi. To form secret plots; to plot or conspire. ppr. caballing, pret. & pp. caballed. [Fr. *cabale*.]

Caballer, ka-bal'ėr, n. One who cabals; an intriguer.

Cabbage, kab'aj, n. A culinary vegetable which grows into a head. [Fr. *caboche*—L. *caput*, the head.]

Cabbage, kab'aj, vt. To purloin, as pieces of cloth in cutting out clothes. ppr. cabbaging, pret. & pp. cabbaged. [D. *kabassen*, to hide as in a basket.]

Cabbage-rose, kab'aj-rōz, n. A species of rose; called also Provence rose.

Cabin, kab'in, n. A hut; a small room; an apartment in a ship for officers and passengers.—vt. To confine in a cabin. [Fr. *cabane*.]

Cabinet, kab'in-et, n. A casket for jewels, &c.; a closet; a small room; a set of drawers for curiosities; a private room in which consultations are held; the collective body of ministers of state. [Fr.]

Cabinet-council, kab'in-et-koun-sil, n. A council of state or of cabinet ministers, held with privacy.

Cabinet-maker, kab'in-et-māk-ėr, n. A man who makes articles of fine wooden furniture.

Cable, kā'bl, n. The strong rope or chain by which the ship is tied to the anchor; a large rope or chain.—vt. To furnish with a cable. ppr. cabling, pret. & pp. cabled. [Fr.]

Cabman, kab'man, n. The driver of a cab.

Cabriolet, kab'ri-ō-lā", n. An open two-wheeled carriage, with an occasional cover for the head. [Fr.]

Cackle, kak'l, vi. To make the noise of a goose or hen; to chatter; to prate. ppr. cackling, pret. & pp. cackled.—n. Idle talk; silly prattle. [D. *kakelen*.]

Cackling, kak'l-ing, p.n. The broken noise of a goose or hen.

Cadaverous, ka-dav'ėr-us, a. Resembling a dead human body; pale; ghastly. [L. *cadaverosus*—*cado*, to fall.]

Caddy, kad'di, n. A small box for keeping tea. [dimin. of *cade*, a barrel.]

Cade, kād, n. A barrel or cask. [L. *cadus*.]

Cadence, kā'dens, n. A falling; a state of sinking; a fall of the voice at the end of a sentence; the close of a musical passage or phrase. [Fr.; L. *cado*, to fall.]

Cadenced, kā'denst, p.a. Having a particular cadence.

Cadet, ka-det', n. A younger member of a family; a gentleman who carries arms in a regiment as a private, in order to obtain a commission; a young man in a military school. [Fr.]

Cadetship, ka-det'ship, n. The commission given to a cadet to enter the East India service; the rank of a cadet.

Cæsura, sē-zū'ra, n. A section of a verse; a pause in verse, to aid the recital, and render the versification more melodious. [L.—*cædo*, *cæsum*, to cut.]

Cæsural, sē-zū'ral, a. Pertaining to the cæsura.

Cag, kag, n. A small cask or barrel. [See Keg.]

Cage, kāj, n. An inclosure formed of wire, twigs, &c., for confining birds and beasts; a prison for petty malefactors.—vt. To confine in a cage; to confine. ppr. caging, pret. & pp. caged. [Fr. *cage*.]

Cairn, kārn, n. A rounded heap of stones erected as a sepulchral monument. [W. *carn*.]

Caitiff, kā'tif, n. A captive; a mean villain; a despicable knave. [It. *cattivo*—L. *capio*, to take.]

Cajole, ka-jōl', vt. To coax; to court; to wheedle; to deceive by flattery. ppr. cajoling, pret. & pp. cajoled. [Fr. *cajoler*.]

Cajolery, ka-jōl'e-ri, n. Flattery; a wheedling to delude.

Cake, kāk, n. A small round flat mass of dough baked; a composition of flour, butter, sugar, &c., baked into a small round mass; anything in the form of a cake.—vt. To form into a cake or mass.—vi. To concrete, or grow into a hard mass. ppr. caking, pret. & pp. caked. [D. *koek*.]

Calamitous, ka-lam'it-us, a. Full of calamity, misery, or distress; miserable; adverse; afflictive. [Fr. *calamiteux*.]

Calamity, ka-lam'i-ti, n. That which falls upon and beats down; disaster; distress; misery. [Fr. *calamité*—L. *calamitas*—*cado*, to fall.]

Calash, ka-lash', n. A light carriage with very low wheels; a hooded carriage; a sort of stiffened hood for protecting a lady's head-dress. [Fr. *calèche*.]

Calcareous, kal-kā'rē-us, a. Partaking of the nature of lime or chalk; containing lime. [L. *calcarius*—*calx*, *calcis*, limestone.]

Calcination, kal-sin-ā'shon, n. Reduction of substances to cinders, or to a friable state. [Fr.]

Calcine, kal-sin', vt. To reduce, as a substance to a calx or powder.—vi. To be converted by heat into a friable substance. ppr. calcining, pret. & pp. calcined. [Fr. *calciner*.]

Calculable, kal'kū-la-bl, a. That may be calculated.

Calculary, kal'kū-la-ri, a. Relating to the disease of the stone in the bladder. [from L. *calculus*, a small stone.]

Calculate, kal'kū-lāt, vt. To compute; to reckon; to rate; to adjust.—vi. To make a computation. ppr. calculating, pret. & pp. calculated. [L. *calculo*, *calculatus*—*calculus*, a small stone.]

Calculated, kal'kū-lāt-ed, p.a. Suited; adapted by design.

Calculation, kal-kū-lā'shon, n. The art or process of calculating; estimate.

Calculator, kal'kū-lāt-ėr, n. One who calculates, computes, or reckons.

Calculus, kal'kū-lus, n. Calculi, pl. A small pebble; the stone in the bladder, kidneys, &c.; a method of calculation employed in mathematics. [L.]

Caldron, kal'dron, n. A large kettle or boiler for heating or boiling liquids. [Old Fr. *chauderon*—L. *caleo*, to be warm.]

Calendar, ka'len-dėr, n. A register of the months, weeks, and days of the year, with the feasts or festivals of the church, &c.; an almanac; a list of criminal causes which stand for trial. [L. *calendarium*—Gr. *kaleō*, to call.]

Calender, ka'len-dėr, vt. To pass under or over a heated roller; to press between rollers, for the purpose of making smooth, glossy, and wavy.—n. A machine or hot press, used to press cloths and make them smooth or glossy. [Old Fr. *calendrer*—L. *caleo*, to be hot.]

Calends, ka'lends, n. pl. Among the Romans, the first day of each month, on which the holidays, &c., were called or proclaimed. [L. *calenda*—Gr. *kaleō*, to call.]

Calf, käf, n. Calves, kävz, pl. The young of the cow and of some other animals; a dolt; the fleshy protuberant part of the leg behind. [Sax. *ceulf*; Sans. *kalabha*, an elephant's calf.]

Calibre, ka'li-bėr, n. Capacity of the bore of a gun, or concave diameter of it; the extent of mental or intellectual qualities; a sort or kind. [Fr.]

Calico, ka'li-kō, n. A stuff made of cotton, first imported from Calicut in India.

Caligraphy, ka-lig'ra-fi, n. Fair or elegant writing or penmanship. [Gr. *kalos*, beautiful, and *graphē*, writing.]

Calipers, Caliper-compasses, ka'li-pėrs, ka'li-pėr-kum-pas-sez, n. pl. Compasses with curved legs for measuring the diameter of round bodies. [from *calibres*.]

Calisthenic, ka-lis-then'ik, a. Pertaining to calisthenics.

Calisthenics, ka-lis-then'iks, n. pl. Exercises designed to promote grace of movement and strength of body. [Gr. *kalos*, beautiful, and *sthenos*, strength.]

Calk, kak, vt. To press or drive oakum into the seams of, as of a ship, to make them water-tight. [L. *calco*, to press in.]

Calker, kak'ėr, n. A man who calks a ship.

Calking-iron, kak'ing-ī-ėrn, n. An instrument like a chisel used in calking ships.

Call, kal, vt. To name; to style; to summon; to convoke; to ask, or command to come; to appoint; to appeal to; to utter aloud.—vi. To utter a loud sound, or to address by name; to stop at a place without intention of staying; to make a short visit.—n. A vocal address, of summons or invitation; demand; divine vocation; invitation; impulse; a short visit; something used to call together; an inquiry. [Icel. *kalla*.]

Calling, kal'ing, p.n. Act of one who calls; that which a person is called upon, or required to direct his attention to; employment; business; profession.

Callosity, kal-los'i-ti, n. Hardness of skin or horny hardness. [Fr. *callosité*—L. *callus*, hard.]

Callous, kal'lus, a. In a state of hardness; hardened; unfeeling; obdurate. [L. *callus*, hard.]

Callousness, kal'lus-nes, n. Hardness (applied to the body); insensibility (applied to the mind or heart); obduracy.

ch, chain; j, job; g, go; ng, sing; ᴢʜ, then; th, thin; w, wig; wh, whig; sh, azure; † obsolete.

Callow, kal'lō, *a.* Bald; destitute of feathers; naked; unfledged. [Sax. *calo.*]
Calm, käm, *a.* Still; free from wind; peaceable; in a state of rest; serene; composed.—*n.* Absence of wind; tranquillity; freedom from agitation.—*vt.* To reduce to a state of *calmness*; to still; to quiet; to tranquillize; to assuage. [Fr. *calme.*]
Calmly, käm'li, *adv.* In a calm or quiet manner.
Calmness, käm'nes, *n.* State of being calm; quietness; tranquillity.
Calomel, ka'lō-mel, *n.* A *good* remedy for the *black* bile; a preparation of mercury, much used in medicine. [Gr. *kalos*, good, and *melas*, black.]
Caloric, ka-lo'rik, *n. Heat*; the principle or matter of heat, or the simple element of heat. [Fr. *calorique*—L. *calor*, heat.]
Calorific, ka-lo-rif'ik, *a. Causing heat*; heating. [L. *calor*, heat, and *facio*, to make.]
Calotype, ka'lō-tip, *n. A beautiful image*; an invention for making pictures on paper or other surfaces by the agency of light. [Gr. *kalos*, beautiful, and *tupos*, type.]
Caltrop, kal'trop, *n.* An instrument with iron points to wound horses' feet. [Sax. *coltræppe*, a species of thistle.]
Calumniate, ka-lum'ni-āt, *vt. To defame falsely* and maliciously; to slander; to asperse.—*vi.* To utter calumnies. *ppr.* calumniating, *pret. & pp.* calumniated. [L. *calumnior, calumniatus.*]
Calumniated, ka-lum'ni-āt-ed, *p.a.* Falsely and maliciously accused.
Calumniation, ka-lum'ni-ā"shon, *n.* False and malicio s accusation.
Calumniator, ka-lum'ni-āt-ėr, *n.* One who *calumniates.*
Calumnious, ka-lum'ni-us, *a. Partaking of calumny*; injurious to reputation.
Calumniously, ka-lum'ni-us-li, *adv.* Slanderously.
Calumny, ka'lum-ni, *n. Artifices!*; false and malicious defamation; backbiting; evil-speaking. [L. *calumnia.*]
Calvary, kal'va-ri, *n. A place of skulls,* particularly the place where Christ was crucified. [L. *calvaria,* the skull.]
Calve, käv, *vi.* To bring or cast forth a *calf*, as a cow. *ppr.* calving, *pret. & pp.* calved. [Sax. *calfian*, from *cealf.*]
Calvinism, kal'vin-izm, *n. The theological tenets* or doctrines of *Calvin.*
Calvinist, kal'vin-ist, *n. One who embraces the doctrines of Calvin.*
Calvinistic, kal-vin-ist'ik, *a. Pertaining to Calvin*, or to his *tenets.*
Calx, kalks, *n.* **Calxes,** or **Calces,** kalk'sèz, or kal'sēz, *plur. A small stone*; lime or chalk. [L. *calx, calcis.*]
Calyx, kā'liks, *n.* **Calyxes,** kā'liks-ez, *pl. A covering;* the outer *covering* of a flower; the flower-cup. [L. *calyx.*]
Cambrian, käm'bri-an, *a. Pertaining to Cambria*, or Wales; applied to a system of geology.
Cambric, käm'brik, *n.* A species of fine white linen, for which *Cambray* was famous.
Camel, kam'el, *n. The animal which toils*; a large quadruped used in Asia and Africa for carrying burdens, and for riders. [L. *camelus*—Heb. *ghamal*, to toil.]
Camellia, ka-mel'i-a, *n.* A genus of beautiful green-house shrubs. [from Jos. *Camellus.*]
Camelopard, kam-el'ō-pärd, *n. The camel panther;* the giraffe. [L. *camelus,* and *pardalis*, the female panther.]
Cameo, kam'ē-ō, *n. Any precious stone* (originally the onyx) carved in bas-relief. [It. *cammeo.*]
Camera Obscura, kam'ē-ra ob-skū'ra, *n.* An optical instrument for exhibiting in a *dark chamber* the images of external objects. [L. a dark chamber.]
Camlet, kam'let, *n.* A stuff originally made of camel's hair, now made chiefly of wool or goat's hair. [Fr. *camelot.*]
Camomile, kam'ō-mil, *n. The ground-apple;* a bitter medicinal plant. [Gr. *chamai-melon—chamai*, on the ground, and *melon*, apple.]
Camp, kamp, *n.* The ground on which an army pitch their tents; place of fighting†; disposition of an army for rest; an army encamped on the same field.—*vi. To pitch a camp; to encamp.* [Sax.]
Campaign, kam-pān', *n.* The time during which an army keeps the *field* every year, during a war.—*vi. To serve in a campaign.* [Fr. *campagne,* an open field.]
Campaigner, kam-pān'èr, *n.* An old soldier; a veteran.
Camphor, kam'fėr, *n.* A solid, concrete, fragrant substance, from the *kupuru,* a tree in Borneo, and from the Indian laurel. [Low L. *camphora.*]
Camphorated, kam'fėr-āt-ed, *p.a. Impregnated with camphor.*
Can, kan, *n.* A cup or vessel for liquors. [D. *kan.*]
Can, kan, *vi. To be able;* to have sufficient moral or physical power. *pret.* could.
Canal, ka-nal', *n.* A channel; a water-course made by art for boats to sail along; a duct of the body. [L. *canalis—canna,* a pipe or reed.]
Canary, ka-nā'ri, *n.* Wine made in the *Canary Isles;* a bird from the *Canary Isles.*
Cancel, kan'sel, *vt. To cross the lines of,* as of a writing; to obliterate; to revoke; to set aside. *ppr.* cancelling, *pret. & pp.* cancelled.—*n. Act of cancelling*; in printing, the suppression and reprinting of a leaf or more of a work; the part thus altered. [Fr. *canceller*—L. *cancelli,* a lattice.]
Cancer, kan'sėr, *n.* One of the signs of the zodiac; a hard tumour, supposed to have a resemblance to a *cancer* or crab. [L. a crab.]
Cancerous, kan'sėr-us, *a. Like a cancer;* having the qualities of a cancer.
Candid, kan'did, *a. Fair;* open; sincere; ingenuous. [L. *candidus—canso,* to be hoary.]
Candidate, kan'di-dāt, *n.* One who proposes himself, or is proposed, for some office; one who aspires after preferment, or some high attainment. In Rome, such a one wore a *white* gown. [L. *candidatus—candidus,* white.]
Candidateship, kan'di-dāt-ship, *n. The state of a candidate.*
Candidly, kan'did-li, *adv. In a candid manner.*
Candidness, kan'did-nes, *n. Candour.*
Candied, kan'did, *a. Preserved with sugar,* or incrusted with it; made to resemble sugar-candy.
Candle, kan'dl, *n. That which shines;* a torch; a light; tallow, wax, &c., of a cylindrical form, surrounding a wick, and used for giving light. [Sax. *candel*—L. *candela.*]
Candlemas, kan'dl-mas, *n. The candle-feast;* the feast observed on the second day of February, in honour of the purification of the Virgin Mary. [*candle* and *mass.*]
Candlestick, kan'dl-stik, *n. A stick,* or an instrument, to hold a *candle.* [Sax. *candel-sticca.*]
Candour, kan'dėr, *n. Fairness;* frankness; sincerity; ingenuousness. [L. *candor.*]
Candy, kan'di, *vt.* To conserve with *sugar;* to form into congelations or crystals.—*vi.* To take on the form of candied sugar; to become congealed. *ppr.* candying, *pret. & pp.* candied. *n. Sugar* or molasses congealed or crystallized; a sweetmeat. [It. *candire.*]
Cane, kān, *n. A reed;* a walking-stick. *vt.* To beat with a *cane* or walking-stick. *ppr.* caning, *pret. & pp.* caned. [L. *canna.*]
Canine, ka-nin', *a. Pertaining to dogs;* having the properties or qualities of a dog. [L. *caninus—canis,* a dog.]
Caning, kān'ing, *p.n.* A beating with a *stick* or *cane.*
Canister, kan'is-tėr, *n.* A *wicker-basket;* a small box or case for tea, coffee, &c. [L. *canistra, -orum.*]
Canker, kang'kėr, *n.* Something resembling the disease *cancer;* a malignant ulcer; anything that corrodes; a disease of trees; a disease in horses' feet.—*vt.* To corrode; to infect or pollute.—*vi.* To grow corrupt; to decay by corrosion. [Sax. *cancre.*]
Cankered, kang'kėrd, *p.a.* Eaten, corroded, or corrupted.
Cankerous, kang'kėr-us, *a.* Corroding like a *canker.*
Canker-worm, kang'kėr-wėrm, *n.* A *worm destructive* to trees or plants.
Cannel-coal, Candle-coal, kan'nel-kōl, kan'dl-kōl, *n.* A kind of coal which *burns* readily and brightly, and is used as a substitute for *candles.*
Cannibal, kan'ni-bal, *n.* A savage who eats human flesh.—*a. Relating to cannibalism.* [a corruption of *Caribales,* a name given by Columbus to the *Caribs,* who ate human flesh.]
Cannibalism, kan'ni-bal-izm, *n.* The act or practice of eating human flesh by mankind.
Cannon, kan'nun, *n.* A large piece of ordnance; a great gun. [Fr. *canon*—L. *canna,* a reed.]
Cannonade, kan-nun-ād', *n. An attack with cannon.*—*vt. To attack with cannon* or heavy artillery; to batter with cannon-shot. *ppr.* cannonading, *pret. & pp.* cannonaded.
Cannonading, kan-nun-ād'ing, *p.n. Act of battering with cannon-shot.*
Cannoneer, kan-nun-nēr', *n. An engineer* who *manages* cannon.
Cannot, kan'not, an auxiliary verb implying *to be unable.* [*can* and *not.*]
Canoe, ka-nō', *n.* A small boat hollowed out of the trunk of a tree, or made of bark or skins. [of West Indian origin.]
Canon, kan'on, *n.* A *reed* used as a *measure!;* a rule of doctrine or discipline; a law in general; the genuine books of the Holy Scriptures; a regular dignitary of the church; a catalogue of saints canonized; a formula; a large kind of printing type. [Gr. *kanōn—kanna,* a reed.]
Canonical, kan-on'ik-al, *a. According to the canon* or rule; regular; spiritual; ecclesiastical. [L. *canonicus.*]
Canonically, kan-on'ik-al-li, *adv. In a manner agreeable to the canon.*
Canonicals, kan-on'ik-alz, *n. pl.* The full dress of the clergy worn when they officiate.
Canonist, kan'on-ist, *n. One versed in canon law.*
Canonization, kan'on-iz-ā"shon, *n. Act of canonising;* state of being canonized.

Fāte, fär, fat, fạll; mē, met, hėr; pīne, pin; nōte, not, mōve; tūbe, tub, bụll; oil, pound.

Canonize, kan'on-īz, vt. To enrol in the canon as a saint. ppr. canonizing, pret. & pp. canonized.
Canonry, Canonship, kan'on-ri, kan'on-ship, n. The office of a canon; an ecclesiastical benefice in a cathedral or collegiate church.
Canopied, kan'ō-pid, p.a. Covered with a canopy.
Canopy, kan'ō-pi, n. A bed curtain to keep off gnats or mosquitoes; a covering over the head or a bed; a decorated covering over a throne, altar, pulpit, &c.—vt. To cover with a canopy. ppr. canopying, pret. & pp. canopied. [Fr. canapé; Gr. kōnōps, a gnat.]
Cant, kant, vi. To speak in a sing-song or whining tone; to use the particular tone or phraseology of a sect or party. n. A whining manner of speech, either in conversation or preaching; barbarous jargon peculiar to thieves, rogues, and beggars; slang.—a. Vulgar; inelegant; affected. [L. canto, to sing.]
Cant, kant, vt. To raise on the edge or corner; to turn over or round; to toss; to jerk.—n. A toss; a jerk; a throw. [Ger. kanten.]
Canteen, kan-tēn', n. A tin or wooden vessel used by soldiers for carrying liquor; a place in barracks where provisions, liquors, coffee, &c., are sold. [Fr. cantine.]
Canter, kan'tėr, n. A moderate gallop, said to be named from the pilgrims riding to Canterbury at this pace.—vi. To move in a canter.—vt. To ride upon a canter.
Cantharides, kan-tha'ri-dēz, n. pl. Spanish flies, used to raise a blister. (Gr. kanthāris, a blistering fly; pl. kantharidēs.]
Canticle, kan'ti-kl, n. A little song; a song; in the pl. the Song of Solomon. [It. cantico.]
Cantlet, kant'let, n. A little corner; a piece; a fragment. [from Old Fr. chantel; It. canto, a corner.]
Canto, kan'tō, n. A part or division of a poem; the treble part of a musical composition. [It.—L. cano, cantum, to sing, sound, play.]
Canton, kan'ton, n. A small division of territory or its inhabitants.—vt. To divide into cantons; to allot, as separate quarters to different parts of an army. (In milit. lan. pron. kan-tōn'.) [It. cantone.]
Cantonal, kan'ton-al, a. Pertaining to a canton; divided into cantons. [In milit. lan. pron. kan-tōn'al.]
Cantoament, kan-tōn'ment, n. A part of a town assigned to a particular body of troops; separate quarters.
Canvas, kan'vas, n. A coarse cloth made of hemp or flax; sail-cloth; sails of ships; cloth for sieves or sifting; cloth for painting on, &c. [Fr. canevas; L. cannabis, hemp.]
Canvass, kan'vas, vt. To sift something as if through canvas; to scrutinize; to solicit the votes of.—vi. To solicit votes or interest; to use efforts to obtain.—n. A sifting; scrutiny; solicitation. [Old Fr. canabasser—L. cannabis, hemp.]
Canvasser, kan'vas-ėr, n. One who canvasses.
Cany, kān'i, a. Full of canes; made of cane.
Canzonet, kan-zō-net', n. A little or short song. [It. canzonetta.]
Caoutchouc, kou'chŏk, n. India-rubber, a very elastic gum, formed of the juice of various plants, natives of South America and Asia. [Indian, cachucu.]

Cap, kap, n. A covering for the head; something used as a cover; an ensign of some dignity; the top; a reverence made by moving or removing the cap. vt. To cover; to cover the top or end of; to furnish with a cap. ppr. capping, pret. & pp. capped. (Sax. cæppe.]
Capability, kā-pa-bil'li-ti, n. Quality of being capable.
Capable, kā'pa-bl, a. Having sufficient ability, power, or fitness to perform; sufficiently able to know; equal to; qualified for. [Fr.]
Capacious, ka-pā'shi-us, a. Holding or embracing much; wide; large; comprehensive. [L. capax, capacis—capio, to hold.]
Capaciousness, ka-pā'shi-us-nes, n. State or quality of being capacious.
Capacity, ka-pas'i-ti, n. State of being capable or capacious; power of holding; extent of space; ability; faculty; state; profession. [Fr. capacité; L. capio, to hold.]
Caparison, ka-pa'ri-son, n. The ornamental covering laid over the saddle or furniture of a horse.—vt. To cover with a cloth, as a horse. [Fr. caparaçon, a cover.]
Caparisoned, ka-pa'ri-sond, p.a. Covered with a cloth.
Cape, kāp, n. The head or termination of a neck of land, extending into the sea; a head-land; the neck piece of a cloak or coat that covers the shoulders. [It. capo—L. caput, the head.]
Caper, kā'pėr, vi. To skip like a she-goat; to prance; to spring.—n. A skip; a spring; a jump. [Fr. cabrer—L. capra, a she-goat.]
Caper, kā'pėr, n. The flower-bud of a prickly plant, the caper-bush, much used for pickling. [Fr. capre.]
Caperer, kā'pėr-ėr, n. One who capers.
Capillary, kap'il-la-ri, a. Long and slender, like a hair; having a bore of very small diameter, like that of a hair, as a tube.—n. A tube with a very small bore; a fine vessel or canal. [L. capillaris.]
Capital, kap'it-al, a. Affecting the head or life; first in importance; chief; metropolitan; of great size. [L. capitalis, from caput, head.]—n. The head or uppermost part of a column; the upper part; the chief city; the stock of a bank, company, tradesman, &c.; a large letter or type. [L. capitellum.]
Capitalist, kap'it-al-ist, n. A man who has a capital fund or stock; one who has surplus pecuniary means which he may invest at pleasure.
Capitalize, kap'it-al-īz, vt. To convert into capital, as money; to print in capital letters. ppr. capitalizing, pret. & pp. capitalized.
Capitally, kap'it-al-i, adv. In a capital or excellent manner; chiefly; by capital punishment.
Capitation, kap-it-ā'shon, n. A tax upon each individual; a poll-tax. [L. capitatio.]
Capitol, kap'it-ol, n. The temple of Jupiter in Rome, built on the summit of Mount Saturnius. [L. Capitolium.]
Capitular, Capitulary, ka-pit'ū-lėr, ka-pit'ū-la-ri, n. An act passed in an ecclesiastical chapter; body of laws or statutes of a chapter; the member of a chapter. [L. capitulum, a little head.]
Capitular, ka-pit'ū-lėr, a. Belonging to a chapter or capitulary.
Capitulate, ka-pit'ū-lāt, vi. To yield on certain heads; to surrender by treaty. vt. To surrender on conditions. ppr. capitulating, pret. & pp. capitulated. [from L. capitulum, a little head.]
Capitulation, ka-pit'ū-lā'shon, n. Surrender on certain heads or conditions.
Capon, kā'pon, n. A young cock cut or castrated. [Sax. capun.]
Capped, kapt, p.a. Furnished with a cap or cover.
Caprice, ka-prēs', n. A freak; a fancy, a sudden change of opinion or humour, with no apparent reason. [Fr. caprice—capra, a she-goat.)
Capricious, ka-pri'shi-us, a. Full of caprice; changeable; fanciful.
Capriciously, ka-pri'shi-us-li, adv. In a capricious manner; whimsically.
Capriciousness, ka-pri'shi-us-nes, n. Quality of being capricious; caprice.
Capricorn, kā'pri-korn, n. The Goat's Horn, one of the twelve signs of the zodiac. [L. Capricornus—caper, a he-goat, and cornu, a horn.]
Capsize, kap-sīz', vt. To upset or overturn. ppr. capsizing, pret. & pp. capsized. [from cap and seize.]
Capstan, kap'stan, n. A machine employed in ships to raise great weights, or to weigh anchors. [Fr. cabestan.]
Capsular, kap'sū-lėr, a. Pertaining to a capsule; hollow like a chest.
Capsule, kap'sūl, n. A little chest; a dry, many-seeded seed-vessel, which opens by valves. [Fr.—L. capsula.]
Captain, kap'tān, n. A head officer; the commander of a ship; the commander of a troop of horse, or of a company of infantry; a chief; a warrior. [Fr. capitaine—L. caput, the head.]
Captaincy, kap'tān-si, n. The rank, post, or commission of a captain.
Captainship, kap'tān-ship, n. Skill in military affairs.
Caption, kap'shon, n. Seizure; arrest. [L. captio.]
Captious, kap'shi-us, a. Ready to catch at faults, or to find fault; ready to take offence; censorious; insnaring. [L. captiosus—capio, to take.]
Captiously, kap'shi-us-li, adv. In a captious manner.
Captivate, kap'ti-vāt, vt. To take captive; to charm; to fascinate. ppr. captivating, pret. & pp. captivated. [L. captivo, captivatus.]
Captivating, kap'ti-vāt-ing, p.a. Having power to engage the affections.
Captive, kap'tiv, n. One taken in war; one charmed by beauty or excellence; one insnared by love or wiles.—a. Made prisoner; kept in bondage. [Fr. captif—L. capio, to take.]
Captivity, kap-tiv'i-ti, n. State or condition of being a captive; slavery. [Fr. captivité.]
Captor, kap'tėr, n. One who takes, as a prisoner or a prize. [L.]
Capture, kap'tūr, n. Act of taking; the thing taken; a prize; arrest.—vt. To take or seize by force or stratagem. ppr. capturing, pret. & pp. captured. [Fr.—L. capio, to take.]
Capuchin, ka-pū-shēn', n. A hooded friar; a garment for females, consisting of a cloak and hood. [Fr. capucin, from capuce, a cowl.]
Car, kār, n. A small vehicle that runs on wheels; a carriage; a chariot of war or of triumph. [W.]
Carabine, Carbine, ka'ra-bin, kār'bin, n. A kind of short gun or firearm. [Fr. carabine.]
Carabineer, ka'ra-bi-nēr', n. One who carries a carabine; a sort of light horseman.
Caracole, ka'ra-kōl, n. A half-turn, which a horseman makes.—vi. To move

in a *caracole;* to wheel. *ppr.* caracoling, *pret. & pp.* caracoled. [Fr.]
Carafe, ka'raf, n. A glass water-bottle or decanter. [Fr.]
Carat, ka'rat, n. *A weight of four grains,* for weighing diamonds and other precious stones; a word employed to denote the proportion of pure gold in a mass of metal; a twenty-fourth part of a metallic mass. [Fr.]
Caravan, ka'ra-van, n. *A company of travellers associated together* for mutual security in traversing various unsafe parts of Asia and Africa; a large close carriage. [Fr. *caravane.*]
Caravansary, ka-ra-van'sa-ri, n. A kind of *inn* or building in the East, where *caravans* and travellers rest at night. [Ar. *karavansera.*]
Caraway, ka'ra-wā, n. A plant, said to be originally from *Caria,* in Asia Minor, whose seeds form an aromatic stimulant and condiment. [Gr. *karos.*]
Carbine, kär'bin, n. See CARABINE.
Carbon, kär'bon, n. *Pure charcoal;* an elementary substance, bright, brittle, and inodorous. [L. *carbo, carbonis,* a piece of burning wood.]
Carbonaceous, kär-bon-ā'shē-us, a. *Pertaining to or containing carbon.*
Carbonate, kär'bon-āt, n. A salt formed by the union of *carbonic* acid with a base. [Fr.]
Carbonic, kär-bon'ik, a. *Pertaining to carbon,* or obtained from it.
Carboniferous, kär-bon-if'ér-us, a. *Producing carbon.* [L. *carbo, carbonis,* and *fero,* to produce.]
Carbonize, kär'bon-iz, vt. *To convert into carbon.* ppr. carbonizing, *pret. & pp.* carbonized.
Carbuncle, kär'bung-kl, n. *A precious stone* of a fiery red colour; an inflammatory tumour. [L. *carbunculus.*]
Carbuncled, kär'bung-kld, p.a. *Set with carbuncles;* spotted.
Carburetted, kär'bū-ret-ed, p.a. Combined with carbon, or holding carbon in solution.
Carcanet, kär'ka-net, n. *A chain or collar* of jewels for the *neck.* [Fr. *carcan.*]
Carcass, kär'kas, n. Skeleton; a dead body; body of an animal; anything decayed or in a ruinous state; shell of a building; a kind of bomb or shell. [Fr. *carcasse.*]
Card, kärd, n. *A paper* or piece of pasteboard with figures, used in games; a piece of pasteboard containing a person's name, &c., used for invitations, &c.: a paper on which the points of the compass are marked; a note. [Fr. *carte*—L. *charta,* paper.]
Card, kärd, n. An instrument for combing and breaking wool or flax.—*vt.* To comb, as wool, flax, hemp, &c., with a *card.* [D. *kaards.*]
Carder, kärd'ér, n. *One who cards* wool.
Cardiac, kär'di-ak, a. *Pertaining to the heart;* cordial; strengthening. [L. *cardiacus.*]
Cardinal, kär'din-al, a. That serves as a *hinge;* chief; fundamental.—n. An ecclesiastical prince in the Roman Catholic Church; a woman's short cloak. [L. *cardinalis—cardo,* a hinge.]
Cardinalate, Cardinalship, kär'din-al-āt, kär'din-al-ship, n. *The office, rank, or dignity of a cardinal.*
Care, kār, n. Solicitude; concern; mindfulness; attention; oversight; object of watchful regard.—*vi.* To be *solicitous;* to be concerned; to be inclined; to have regard. *ppr.* caring, *pret. & pp.* cared. [Sax. *caru;* Goth. *kara.*]
Careen, ka-rēn', vt. To lay, as a ship so that her *keel* may be on one *side,* for the purpose of repairing.—*vi.* To incline to one side, as a ship under a press of sail. [Fr. *caréner*—L. *carina,* a keel.]
Career, ka-rēr', n. *A course;* a race; a rapid running; general course of action; procedure.—*vi.* To move or *run* rapidly. [Fr. *carrière*—L. *carrus,* a car.]
Careful, kār'ful, a. *Solicitous;* anxious; watchful; cautious. (With *of* or *for.*)
Carefully, kār'ful-li, adv. *In a careful manner.*
Carefulness, kār'ful-nes, n. *Quality of being careful.*
Careless, kār'les, a. Heedless; incautious; negligent.
Carelessly, kār'les-li, adv. *In a careless manner* or way.
Carelessness, kār'les-nes, n. *Quality of being careless.*
Caress, ka-res', vt. To treat with *fondness;* to fondle; to embrace with tender affection.—n. An act of endearment; any expression of affection. [Fr. *caresser*—L. *carus,* dear.]
Caressingly, ka-res'ing-li, adv. *In a caressing manner.*
Caret, kā'ret, n. In writing, this mark, Λ, which shows that something *awanting* in the line is mentioned above, or inserted in the margin. [L. there is wanting.]
Care-worn, kār'wōrn, a. *Worn* or vexed with *care.*
Cargo, kär'gō, n. The goods, merchandise, or whatever is conveyed in a ship. [Sp.]
Caricature, ka-ri-ka-tūr', n. A painting or description so *overcharged* as to excite ridicule.—*vt.* To represent by *caricature;* to ridicule. *ppr.* caricaturing, *pret. & pp.* caricatured. [It. *caricatura*—L. *carrus,* a car.]
Carious, kā'ri-us, a. *Rotten;* decayed, as a bone. [L. *cariōsus,* from *caries,* rottenness.]
Carman, kär'man, n. *A man* who drives *a cart* or car.
Carminative, kär-min'at-iv, n. A medicine which acts like a *charm,* and frees the stomach and bowels from flatulence and from pain. [from L. *carmen,* a song, a magic formula.]
Carmine, kär'min, n. A bright crimson colour used by painters. [Fr. *carmin.*]
Carnage, kär'nāj, n. Great slaughter in war; massacre; butchery. [Fr.—L. *caro, carnis,* flesh.]
Carnal, kär'nal, a. *Pertaining to flesh;* fleshly; sensual. [L. *carnalis*—*caro,* flesh.]
Carnality, kär-nal'i-ti, n. *Quality or state of being carnal;* fleshly lust.
Carnally, kär'nal-i, adv. *In a carnal manner;* according to the flesh.
Carnation, kär-nā'shon, n. A sweet-scented plant with *flesh-coloured* flowers. [Fr.—L. *caro,* flesh.]
Carnationed, kär-nā'shond, p.a. Made like *carnation* colour.
Carnelian, kär-nē'li-an, n. *A flesh-coloured* stone, a variety of chalcedony. [Fr. *cornaline;* L. *caro,* flesh.]
Carnival, kär'ni-val, n. A festival celebrated in Roman Catholic countries during the week before Lent; time of luxury. [It. *carnovale*—L. *caro,* flesh, and *vale,* farewell.]
Carnivorous, kär-niv'ō-rus, a. *Feeding on flesh;* an epithet applied to animals which naturally seek flesh for food. [L. *caro,* flesh, and *voro,* to eat.]
Carol, ka'rol, n. *A song* of joy and exultation; a song of devotion; a warble.—*vi.* To sing; to warble; to sing in joy or festivity.—*vt.* To celebrate in song. *ppr.* carolling, *pret. & pp.* carolled. [It. *carola*—L. *chorus,* a choral dance.]
Carolling, ka'rol-ing, p.a. A singing or warbling.
Carotid, ka-rot'id, a. A large artery conveying the blood from the neck to the head. [Fr. *carotide.*]
Carousal, ka-rouz'al, n. A noisy drinking bout or revelling; festivity. [Fr. *carrousel.*]
Carouse, ka-rouz', vi. *To drink hard* with noisy jollity; to guzzle. *ppr.* carousing, *pret. & pp.* caroused.—*n.* A *drinking* match; carousal. [Old Fr. *carrousser.*]
Carouser, ka-rouz'ér, n. *One who carouses.*
Carp, kärp, vi. *To snap or catch; to pick;* to find fault (with *at*). [L. *carpo,* to pick.]
Carp, kärp, n. *A voracious* fish, found in rivers and ponds, and good for food. [Fr. *carpe*—L. *carpo,* to pick.]
Carpenter, kär'pen-tér, n. One who works in timber; a framer and builder of houses and of ships. [Fr. *charpentier*—L. *carpentum,* a waggon.]
Carpentry, kär'pen-tri, n. *The trade, art, or work of a carpenter.*
Carpet, kär'pet, n. A kind of stuff embroidered with figures of various fruits; a covering for floors, tables, stairs, &c.; level ground covered as with grass. *vt. To cover with a carpet.* [It. *carpetta.*]
Carpeting, kär'pet-ing, p.n. *Cloth for carpets;* carpets in general.
Carping, kärp'ing, p.a. Cavilling.
Carriage, ka'rij, n. *Act of carrying;* that which carries; a vehicle; conveyance; price of carrying; behaviour; demeanour. [Fr. *charriage*—L. *currus,* a car.]
Carrier, ka'ri-ér, n. *One who,* or that which *carries;* a messenger.
Carrion, ka'ri-on, n. The dead and putrefying *flesh* of animals.—*a.* Relating to dead and putrefying *carcasses;* feeding on carrion. [Fr. *carogne*—L. *caro, carnis,* flesh.]
Carronade, ka'ron-ād, n. A short piece of ordnance, having a large calibre, first made at *Carron* in Scotland.
Carrot, ka'rot, n. A yellowish or *reddish* esculent root of a tapering form. [Fr. *carotte.*]
Carroty, ka'rot-i, a. *Like a carrot* in colour; fiery red.
Carry, ka'ri, vt. To bear, convey, or transport; to accomplish; to gain; to conquer.—*vi.* To convey, to propel, in military language; to bear the head in a particular manner, as a horse (with recip. pron.) *ppr.* carrying, *pret. & pp.* carried.—*n.* Onward motion, as of the clouds. [Fr. *charrier.*]
Carrying, ka'ri-ing, p.a. Bearing; conveying; removing, &c.
Cart, kärt, n. *A carriage* of burden with two wheels.—*vt.* To carry or convey on *a cart;* to place on a cart. [W.]
Cartage, kärt'āj, n. *Act of carrying in a cart,* or the price paid for carting.
Carte, kärt, n. *A card;* a bill of fare at a tavern, eating-house, &c. [Fr.]
Cartel, kär'tel, n. *A paper* of agreement between enemies for the exchange of prisoners; a ship commissioned to exchange the prisoners. [Fr. —L. *charta,* paper.]
Carter, kärt'ér, n. *One who owns or drives a cart* or team.
Cartilage, kär'ti-lāj, n. *Gristle;* a white elastic substance, half fleshy, half bony. [Fr.—L. *cartilago.*]
Cartilaginous, kär-ti-laj'in-us, a. *Pertaining to or resembling a cartilage.*

Cartoon, kär-tön', n. The large thick paper on which designs are drawn for fresco subjects; the design itself; a painting in fresco; a design drawn as a pattern for tapestry, mosaics, &c. [It. *cartone*—L. *charta*, paper.]

Cartouch, kär-töch', n. A paper case for holding musket-balls and powder; a wooden bomb. [Fr. *cartouche*—L. *charta*, paper.]

Cartridge, kär'trij, n. A charge of gunpowder and ball put up in paper. [Fr. *cartouche*.]

Cartridge-box, kär'trij-boks, n. A case with cells *for cartridges*.

Cartridge-paper, kär'trij-pā-pėr, n. Thick stout paper, of which *cartridges* are made.

Cartulary, kär'tū-la-ri, n. A registerbook or record, as of a monastery or church. [Fr. *cartulaire*.]

Carve, kärv, vt. To *cut; to engrave;* to cut into small pieces; to shape by cutting; to distribute; to plan.—vi. To cut up meat; to sculpture; to engrave. ppr. carving, pret. & pp. carved. [Sax. *ceorfan*.]

Carved, kärvd, p.a. Formed by carving.

Carver, kärv'ėr, n. *One who carves;* a large table-knife for carving.

Carving, kärv'ing, p.n. *Act of cutting*, as meat; the act or art of cutting figures in wood or ivory; figures carved.

Cascade, kas'kād, n. *A waterfall;* a small cataract. [Fr.—L. *cado*, to fall.]

Case, kās, n. *That which contains;* a box; a receptacle; outer part of a building.—vi. To cover with a *case;* to put in a case or box. ppr. casing, pret. & pp. cased. [Fr. *caisse*—L. *capio*, to hold.]

Case, kās, n. *That which falls;* an event; the particular state or circumstances that *befall* a person; condition; a suit in court; a change of termination in nouns. [L. *casus—cado*, to fall.]

Case-harden, kās'härd-n, vt. To harden *on the outside*, as iron, by converting it into steel.

Casemate, kās'māt, n. A bomb-proof vault in a fortress. [Fr.]

Casemated, kās'māt-ed, p.a. *Furnished with a casemate*.

Casement, kās'ment, n. A case for a window; a portion of a window-sash made to open or turn on hinges; a hollow moulding. [It. *casamento*—L. *casa*, a cottage.]

Caseous, kā'sē-us, a. *Pertaining to cheese;* having the qualities of cheese. [L. *caseus*, cheese.]

Case-shot, kās'shot, n. Musket-balls, stones, old iron, &c., put in *cases* to be discharged from cannon.

Cash, kash, n. *Money in a case;* ready money; coin; gold and silver.—vt. To *turn into money*, or to exchange for money. [Fr. *caisse*, a money-chest—L. *capsa*, a box.]

Cashier, kash-ēr', n. *A keeper of a cashchest;* one who superintends the books, payments, &c., of a bank or moneyed institution. [Fr. *caissier*.]

Cashier, kash-ēr', vt. To *deprive of office;* to discard; to break. [Fr. *casser*, to break—L. *cassus*, empty.]

Cashmere, kash'mēr, n. A rich and costly kind of shawl; so called from *Cashmere* in India, the country where first made.

Casing, kās'ing, p.n. Act of plastering a house with mortar on the outside; a covering; a case.

Cask, kask, n. A vessel for *containing liquors;* the quantity which a cask contains. [Fr. *casque*.]

Casket, kask'et, n. *A little cask;* a small chest or box for jewels or other small articles. [dimin. of *cask*.]

Casque, kask, n. A head-piece; a helmet. [Fr. *casque*.]

Cassia, ka'shi-a, n. A sweet spice extracted from the *bark* of a species of the laurel-tree; wild cinnamon; a tree which yields senna. [L.]

Cassimere, kas'si-mėr, n. A twilled woollen cloth. (Also spelled *kerseymere*.) [Sp. *casimiro*.]

Cassock, kas'sok, n. A close garment, resembling a long frockcoat, worn by clergyman. [Sp. *casaca*—L. *casa*, a cottage.]

Cassocked, kas'sokt, p.a. *Clothed with a cassock*.

Cast, kast, vt. To *throw;* to drive from by force; to impel by violence; to throw off; to defeat; to condemn; to compute; to model; to found; to throw down; to sow; to bring forth immaturely.—vi. To revolve in the mind; to contrive (with *about*); to be capable of receiving form; to warp. ppr. casting, pret. & pp. cast.—n. *A throw;* the thing thrown; manner of throwing; distance passed by a thing thrown; a squinting; state of chance; form; a tinge; air; mien; that which is formed from a mould; a small statue of bronze, &c. [Dan. *kaste*.]

Castanet, kas'ta-net, n. A small piece of wood or ivory, two of which are struck together in dancing in order to mark the time. [Sp. *castañeta*—L. *castanea*, the chestnut-tree.]

Castaway, kast'a-wā, n. *He or that which is thrown away;* a person abandoned by God.—a. Of no value.

Caste, kast, n. *A tribe;* a distinct order in society; a distinct hereditary order of people among the Hindoos, the number being four. [Fr.]

Castellated, kas'tel-lāt-ed, a. Adorned with turrets and battlements.

Caster, kast'ėr, n. A small phial for the table, out of which something is shaken; a small wheel on a swivel on which a table, &c., is *cast* or rolled on the floor.

Casters, kast'erz, n. pl. A stand with bottles for oil, vinegar, &c. [See **Caster**.]

Castigate, kas'ti-gāt, vt. To set right by word or deed; to punish by stripes; to chasten; to check. ppr. castigating, pret. & pp. castigated. [L. *castigo*—*castus*, chaste, and *ago*, to make.]

Castigation, kas-ti-gā'shon, n. *Chastisement;* punishment; correction.

Castigator, kas'ti-gāt-ėr, n. One who corrects.

Casting, kast'ing, p.n. *Act of casting* or *throwing;* founding; that *which is cast in a mould;* something formed of castmetal.

Cast-iron, kast'ī-ėrn, n. *Iron* which has been *cast* into pigs or moulds.

Castle, kas'l, n. *A fort;* a house with towers, usually encompassed with walls and moats, and having a donjon or keep in the centre; a fortress; the mansion of a nobleman or prince. [L. *castellum*—*castrum*, a fort.]

Castle-building, kas'l-bild-ing, n. The act of forming visionary schemes having no foundation.

Castled, kas'ld, p.a. *Furnished with castles*.

Cast-off, kast'of, a. Laid aside; rejected.

Castor, kas'tėr, n. The beaver. [L.]

Castor-oil, kas'tėr-oil, n. A medicinal oil obtained from a plant, a native of the tropics.

Castrate, kas'trāt, vt. To geld; to mutilate; to render imperfect. ppr. castrating, pret. & pp. castrated. [L. *castro*, *castratus*.]

Castrated, kas'trāt-ed, p.a. Purified from obscene expressions.

Castration, kas-trā'shon, n. *Act of castrating*.

Cast-steel, kast'stēl, n. Blistered *steel* melted, *cast* into ingots, and again rolled out into bars.

Casual, ka'zhū-al, a. *Falling out;* happening by chance; occasional; contingent. [Fr. *casuel*—L. *cado*, to fall.]

Casually, ka'zhū-al-li, adv. *In a casual manner;* without design; by chance.

Casualty, ka'zhū-al-ti, n. *Accident;* occurrence; contingency; misfortune.

Casuist, ka'zū-ist, n. One who studies and resolves *cases* of conscience. [Fr. *casuiste*—L. *cado*, to fall.]

Casuistic, ka-zū-ist'ik, a. Relating to cases of conscience.

Casuistry, ka'zū-is-tri, n. The science of determining *cases* of conscience.

Cat, kat, n. A domestic animal of the feline tribe, that catches mice; a sort of ship; a double tripod with six feet; an instrument for flogging. [Sax.]

Catacomb, ka'ta-kōm, n. *A cavity below ground;* a subterranean place for the burial of the dead. (Gr. *kata*, down, and *kumbos*, a cavity.)

Catalepsy, ka'ta-leps-i, n. A disease which suddenly *takes hold of* body and mind, suspending both motion and sensation. [Gr. *katalēpsis—lambanō*, to take.]

Cataleptic, ka-ta-lep'tik, a. *Pertaining to catalepsy*.

Catalogue, ka'ta-log, n. An *enumeration* of the names of men or things disposed *in order;* a list; a roll; a register.—vt. To *form into a catalogue;* to make a list of. ppr. cataloguing, pret. & pp. catalogued. [Gr. *kata*, and *logos*, computation.]

Cataplasm, ka'ta-plazm, n. That which is *spread over;* a plaster; a poultice. [Gr. *kataplasma*.]

Cataract, ka'ta-rakt, n. *The dashing* and *tumbling down* of water over a precipice; a waterfall; a disease of the eye by which vision is *confounded* or *destroyed*. [Gr. *katarraktēs—rēgnūō*, to break.]

Catarrh, ka-tärh', n. *A flowing down* of mucus from the nose, &c.; a cold; influenza. [L. *catarrhus*—Gr. *rheō*, to flow.]

Catarrhal, ka-tärh'al, a. *Pertaining to* or produced by *catarrh*.

Catastrophe, ka-tas'trō-fē, n. *An overturning;* the change which produces the final event; calamity or disaster. [Gr. *strephō*, to turn.]

Catch, kach, vt. To *lay hold on;* to take and hold fast; to seize; to stop the falling of; to snatch; to grasp; to gripe; to entangle; to receive by contagion; to be seized with; to get.—vi. To *lay hold;* to be contagious; to spread by infecting. ppr. catching, pret. & pp. catched or caught.—n. *Seizure;* act of seizing; anything that seizes or takes hold, as a hook; a sudden advantage taken; a snatch; a song, the parts of which are *caught up* by different singers. [Sax. *gelæccan*.]

Catching, kach'ing, p.a. That *catches* or seizes; infectious; contagious.

Catch-penny, kach'pen-ni, n. A thing of little value intended to gain money in market.

Catchup, Catsup, kach'up, kat'sup, n. A liquor extracted from salted mushrooms, used as a sauce. [Chinese *kitjap*.]

Catch-word, kach'wėrd, n. A word under the last line of a page, which

is repeated at the top of the next page.
Cate, kāt. *See* CATES.
Catechetic, ka-tē-ket'ik, *a. Relating to a catechism or catechisms;* relating to or consisting in asking questions and receiving answers.
Catechetically, ka-tē-ket'ik-al-li, *adv. In a catechetic manner;* in the way of question and answer.
Catechise, ka'tē-kiz, *vt. To sound into one's ears;* to instruct orally, or by question and answer, especially in the doctrines of the Christian religion; to question; to examine. *ppr.* catechising, *pret. & pp.* catechised. [Gr. *katēchizō—kata,* and *ēcheō,* to sound.]
Catechism, ka'tē-kizm, *n.* A form of elementary instruction by questions and answers; a summary of principles in any science or art, but appropriately in religion, in the form of questions and answers. [Low L. *catechismus.*]
Catechist, ka'tē-kist, *n. One who catechises.* [Gr. *katēchistēs.*]
Catechumen, ka-tē-kū'men, *n.* One who is in the first rudiments of Christianity; one who is receiving instruction and preparing himself for baptism. [Gr. *katēchoumenos.*]
Categorical, ka-tē-go'ri-kal, *a. Pertaining to a category;* absolute; positive.
Categorically, ka-tē-go'ri-kal-li, *adv.* Absolutely; directly; positively.
Category, ka'tē-go-ri, *n.* One of the highest classes to which the objects of knowledge can be reduced; class; rank; condition. [Gr. *katēgoria—agora,* an assembly.]
Cater, ka'tėr, *vi. To buy or procure provisions,* food, entertainment, &c. [Fr. *acheter,* to buy.]
Caterer, ka'tėr-ėr, *n. One who caters;* a provider or purveyor of provisions.
Cateress, ka'tėr-es, *n. A woman who caters;* a female provider of food.
Caterpillar, kat'ėr-pil-lėr, *n.* An insect; a grub that devours leaves. [probably from Fr. *chaton,* a catkin, and *piller,* to strip.]
Caterwaul, kat'ėr-wal, *vi. To wawl* or *cry,* as *cats* in rutting time. [probably from *cat,* and *wawl,* wail.]
Caterwauling, kat'ėr-wal-ing, *p.n.* The *cry of cats;* a harsh noise or cry.
Cates, kāts, *n. pl.* Delicious food or viands *purchased;* dainties. [Fr. *acheter,* to buy.]
Catgut, kat'gut, *n.* The *intestines of a cat;* the intestines of sheep and other animals dried and twisted, used as strings for musical instruments, &c.; a kind of linen or canvas.
Cathartic, ka-thär'tik, *a. Purging; cleansing* the bowels.—*n. A medicine that purges,* and thus *cleanses* the stomach and bowels. [Gr. *kathartikos—kathēros,* clean.]
Cathedral, ka-thē'dral, *n. A chair or seat;* the see or seat of a bishop; the principal church in a diocese.—*a. Pertaining to a cathedral,* or to a bishop's seat or see. [Gr. *kathedra—hedra,* a seat.]
Catholic, ka'thol-ik, *a. All; whole; universal;* liberal; generally useful; pertaining or relating to the *Catholic* or universal Church; pertaining or relating to the Roman Catholic Church or to its adherents.—*n.* A member of the Catholic Church; an adherent of the Roman Catholic Church. [Gr. *katholikos—kata,* and *holos,* whole.]
Catholicism, ka-thol'i-sizm, *n.* Adherence to the Catholic church; adherence to the Roman Catholic church; the Roman Catholic religion; liberality of sentiments.
Catholicity, ka-thol-is'i-ti, *n.* The religion of the Catholic church; liberality.
Catholicon, ka-thol'i-kon, *n.* A remedy for *all* diseases; a panacea. [Gr. *katholikon—holos,* whole, perfect.]
Catkin, kat'kin, *n.* The blossom of the willow, birch, &c., which resembles a *kitten* or cat's tail. [dimin. of *cat.*]
Catmint, Catnip, kat'mint, kat'nip, *n.* A strong-scented plant, which *cats* are fond of.
Catoptric, kat-op'trik, *a. Relating to catoptrics,* or vision by reflection. [Gr. *katoptrikos.*]
Catoptrics, kat-op'triks, *n.* That part of optics which treats of vision by *reflected light.* [from Gr. *katoptrikos—optomai,* to see.]
Cat's-paw, kats'pa, *n. The paw of a cat;* a light air of wind; a dupe; a tool.
Cattle, kat'tl, *n. sing.* or *plur.* Beasts of pasture, especially oxen, bulls, and cows; also, horses, sheep, and goats. [D. *kateel,* cattle.]
Cattle-plague, kat'tl-plāg, *n.* Murrain.
Cattle-show, kat'tl-shō, *n.* An exhibition of domestic animals for prizes, or for the encouragement of agriculture.
Caudle, ka'dl, *n.* A kind of *warm drink,* mixed with wine, &c., for the sick. [Fr. *chaudeau—*L. *calidus,* hot.]
Caul, kal, *n.* A membrane in the abdomen, *covering* the greatest part of the lower intestines; a kind of net for inclosing the hair. [Sax. *cuhle,* a cowl.]
Cauliflower, ka'li-flou-ėr, *n. Cabbage flower;* a variety of *cabbage,* having numerous and compact *flowers,* forming a large white head. [L. *caulis,* cabbage, and *flower.*]
Causal, kaz'al, *a. Relating* to or *implying a cause or causes.*
Causality, kaz-al'i-ti, *n. The agency of a cause.*
Causally, kaz'al-li, *adv.* According to the order or series of *causes.*
Causation, kaz-ā'shon, *n. The act* or *agency of a cause* in producing an effect.
Causative, kaz'a-tiv, *a. That expresses a cause* or reason; that effects a cause.
Cause, kaz, *n.* That which produces an effect; an efficient agent; reason; incitement; origin; a suit in court; sake; account; design; that which a person or party espouses.—*vt.* To effect by agency, power, or influence. *ppr.* causing, *pret. & pp.* caused. [Fr., L. *causa.*]
Causeless, kaz'les, *a. Having no cause;* without just ground, reason, or motive.
Causelessly, kaz'les-li, *adv. Without cause* or reason.
Causelessness, kaz'les-nes, *n.* State *of being* causeless.
Causeway, Causey, kaz'wā, kaz'ē, *n. A way* paved with stones, &c.; a raised way or path. [Norm. *calsay—*L. *calx,* the heel.]
Caustic, kas'tik, *a. Burning; corroding;* severe; pungent; cutting.—*n.* A substance which *burns* the flesh of animal bodies. [Gr. *kaustikos—kaiō,* to burn.]
Caustically, kas'tik-al-li, *adv. In a caustic manner;* severely.
Causticity, kas-tis'i-ti, *n. Quality of being caustic;* severity; cutting remarks.
Cauterization, ka'tėr-iz-ā'shon, *n.* Act *of cauterising.*
Cauterize, ka'tėr-iz, *vt. To burn* with *caustics,* or a hot iron, as morbid flesh. *ppr.* cauterizing, *pret. & pp.* cauterized. [Fr. *cautériser—*Gr. *kaiō,* to burn.]

Cautery, ka'tė-ri, *n. A burning* or searing by a hot iron, or by caustic medicines. [Fr. *cautère.*]
Caution, ka'shon, *n. Care;* wariness; counsel; precept.—*vt.* To warn to be *cautious;* to warn; to exhort; to take heed of. [Fr.—L. *caveo,* to take care.]
Cautionary, ka'shon-a-ri, *a. Containing caution;* given as a pledge.
Cautious, ka'shi-us, *a. Using caution;* wary; circumspect; prudent. [L. *cautus.*]
Cautiously, ka'shi-us-li, *adv. With caution.*
Cautiousness, ka'shi-us-nes, *n. Quality of being cautious.*
Cavalcade, ka'val-kād, *n.* A procession of persons on *horseback.* [Fr.—L. *caballus,* a nag.]
Cavalier, ka-va-lēr', *n. A horse-soldier;* a knight; a gay military man; (pl.) the appellation of the party of Charles I.—*a. Like a cavalier;* gay; warlike; disdainful. [Fr.—L. *caballus,* a nag.]
Cavalierly, ka-va-lēr'li, *adv.* Haughtily; arrogantly; disdainfully.
Cavalry, ka'val-ri, *n.* A body of *horse-soldiers,* or of military troops *mounted.* [Fr. *cavalerie—cheval,* a horse.]
Cave, kāv, *n. A hollow place* in the earth; a cavern; a den. [Fr.—L. *cavus,* hollow.]
Caveat, kā'vē-at, *n.* A notice *to beware;* a warning; a process to stop proceedings in a court. [L. let him beware, from *caveo,* to take care.]
Cavern, ka'vėrn, *n. A deep hollow place* in the earth. [L. *caverna—cavus,* hollow.]
Caverned, ka'vėrnd, *p.a. Full of caverns;* having caverns; inhabiting a cavern.
Cavernous, ka'vėrn-us, *a. Hollow;* full of caverns. [L. *cavernosus.*]
Caviare, Caviar, ka-vi-är', ka-vi-är', *n.* An article of food, prepared from the roes of some large fish, as the sturgeon. [Fr. *caviar.*]
Cavil, ka'vil, *vi.* To carp; to censure; to wrangle; to make use of sophisms. *ppr.* cavilling, *pret. & pp.* cavilled. *n. Hollow* or frivolous objections; sophism; subtlety. [Old Fr. *caviller,* to wrangle—L. *cavus,* hollow.]
Caviller, ka'vil-ėr, *n. One who cavils.*
Cavity, ka'vi-ti, *n. A hollow place;* hollowness; an opening or aperture. [L. *cavitas.*]
Caw, ka, *vi.* To cry like a crow, rook, or raven—*n.* The cry of the rook or crow. [Sax. *caw.*]
Cayenne Pepper, kā-en' pep'pėr, *n.* A very pungent *pepper,* so named from having originally been brought from *Cayenne.*
Cease, sēs, *vi. To leave off; to give over;* to desist; to fail; to stop; to be at an end; to abstain.—*vt.* To put a stop to; to put an end to. *ppr.* ceasing, *pret. & pp.* ceased. [Fr. *cesser—*L. *cedo,* to go.]
Ceaseless, sēs'les, *a. Without a stop* or pause; incessant; perpetual.
Ceaselessly, sēs'les-li, *adv. Incessantly.*
Cedar, sē'dėr, *n.* A large evergreen tree valued for its timber, which is remarkable for its durability and its odour.—*a. Made of cedar;* belonging to cedar. [L. *cedrus;* Gr. *kedros.*]
Cede, sēd, *vt. To go away from;* to give up; to surrender; to resign. *ppr.* ceding, *pret. & pp.* ceded. [Fr. *céder—*L. *cedo,* to go from.]
Ceil, sēl, *vt. To cover, as the inner roof* of a building; or to cover, as the top or roof of a room. [Fr. *ciel,* heaven, a canopy—L. *cælum,* the heavens.]
Ceiling, sēl'ing, *p.n.* The upper horizon-

tal or curved surface of a room opposite the floor.
Celebrate, se'lē-brāt, vt. To make famous; to praise; to honour with public ceremony and solemn rites. ppr. celebrating, pret. & pp. celebrated. [L. celebro, celebratus—creber, frequent.]
Celebrated, se'lē-brāt-ed, p.a. Famous; renowned; illustrious.
Celebration, se-lē-brā'shon, n. Honour or distinction bestowed; solemn performance.
Celebrity, se-leb'ri-ti, n. Fame; renown; distinction; eminence. [L. celebritas.]
Celerity, sē-le'ri-ti, n. Speed; quickness or rapidity of motion. [L. celeritas—celer, quick.]
Celery, se'lo-ri, n. An evergreen plant of the parsley family, cultivated for use as a salad. [Fr. céleri.]
Celestial, sē-les'ti-al, a. Heavenly; belonging or relating to heaven; belonging to the visible heaven.—n. An inhabitant of heaven. [L. cœlestis—cœlum, heaven.]
Celiac, sē'li-ak, a. Pertaining to the lower belly or intestines. [L. caliacus; Gr. koilia, the belly.]
Celibacy, se'li-ba-si, n. An unmarried state; a single life. [L. cœlibatus, state of being single—cœlebs, single.]
Celibate, se'li-bat, a. Pertaining to a single life.
Cell, sel, n. A secluded place; a small room; a cave; a hut; a small cavity. [L. cella.]
Cellar, sel'ler, n. An apartment under ground, where provisions, liquors, &c., are deposited; a pantry. [L. cellarium.]
Cellarage, sel'ler-āj, n. Space for cellars; cellars; charge for cellar-room.
Cellaret, sel-la-ret', n. A case of cabinet-work, for holding bottles of liquors.
Cellular, sel'ū-lėr, a. Consisting of little cells or cavities. [L. cellula, a small store-room—cella, a store-room.]
Celt, selt, n. One of the primitive inhabitants of the south of Europe.
Celtic, selt'ik, a. Pertaining to the primitive inhabitants of the south and west of Europe, or to the early inhabitants of Italy, Gaul, Spain, and Britain.—n. The language of the Celts. [W. celt, a covert, celtiad, one who dwells in a covert.]
Cement, sē-ment', n. Any glutinous substance which serves to unite bodies; mortar; bond of union; that which unites firmly.—vt. To unite by the use of cement; to unite firmly or closely. vi. To become solid; to unite and cohere. [L. cœmentum, a rough stone.]
Cementation, sē-ment-ā'shon, n. Act of cementing; cohesion.
Cemented, sē-ment'ed, p.a. Firmly united; consolidated.
Cemetery, sem'e-te-ri, n. A resting-place; a place where the dead are buried. [Gr. koimētērion—koimaō, to put to sleep.]
Cenobite, sē'nō-bit, n. One of a religious order living in common. [Gr. koinobiotēs—koinos, common, and biotēs, same as bios, life.]
Cenotaph, se'nō-taf, n. An empty tomb; a monument erected to one who is buried elsewhere. [Fr. cénotaphe—Gr. kenos, empty, and taphos, a tomb.]
Censer, sens'ėr, n. A vase or pan in which incense is burned. [Fr. encensoir—L. candeo, to glow.]
Censor, sen'sėr, n. One who scrutinizes; a censurer; one who is given to censure. [L.—censeo, to value.]

Censorial, sen-sō'ri-al, a. Belonging to a censor.
Censorious, sen-sō'ri-us, a. Addicted to censure; prone to find fault; severe.
Censoriously, sen-sō'ri-us-li, adv. In a censorious manner.
Censoriousness, sen-sō'ri-us-nes, n. Quality of being censorious.
Censorship, sen'sėr-ship, n. The office or dignity of a censor.
Censurable, sen'shūr-a-bl, a. Blamable; culpable.
Censurableness, sen'shūr-a-bl-nes, n. Quality of being censurable.
Censurably, sen'shūr-a-bli, adv. In a manner worthy of blame.
Censure, sen'shūr, n. Severe judgment; act of blaming; reproof; condemnation; reproach; judicial sentence.—vt. To form an opinion of; to blame; to reprehend. ppr. censuring, pret. & pp. censured. [Fr.—L. censūra.]
Census, sen'sus, n. An enumeration of the inhabitants of a country, taken by order of the legislature. [L.]
Cent, sent, n. An American copper coin, the hundredth part of a dollar.—Per cent., a certain rate by the hundred. [Fr.—L. centum, a hundred.]
Centage, sent'āj, n. Rate by the cent or hundred.
Centaur, sen'tar, n. A fabulous being, half man and half horse. [L. centaurus.]
Centenarian, sen-ten-ā'ri-an, n. A person a hundred years old.
Centenary, sen'ten-a-ri, a. Relating to or consisting of a hundred.—n. The number of a hundred; the period of a hundred years. [L. centenarius.]
Centennial, sen-ten'ni-al, a. Consisting of a hundred years; happening every hundred years. [from L. centum, a hundred, and annus, a year.]
Centesimal, sen-tes'i-mal, a. The hundredth.—n. The hundredth part of anything. [L. centesimus.]
Centigrade, sen'ti-grād, a. Having or divided into a hundred degrees. [L. centum, and gradus, a degree.]
Centiped, sen'ti-ped, n. That which has a hundred feet; an insect having a great number of feet. [L. centipēda—pes, pedis, a foot.]
Central, sen'tral, a. Placed in the centre or middle. [L. centrālis.]
Centralization, sen'tral-iz-ā'shon, n. Act of centralising.
Centralize, sen'tral-iz, vt. To render central; to bring within a small compass; to concentrate in some particular part. ppr. centralizing, pret. & pp. centralized.
Centrally, sen'tral-li, adv. In a central manner.
Centre, sen'tėr, n. The middle point of anything; the middle point of a sphere, globe, or circle; the middle.—vt. To place or fix on a centre; to collect to a point.—vi. To be collected to a point; to rest on; to be placed in the middle. ppr. centring, pret. & pp. centred. [L. centrum—Gr. kenteō, to prick.]
Centric, Centrical, sen'trik, sen'trik-al, a. Placed in the centre; central; middle.
Centrically, sen'trik-al-li, adv. In a central position.
Centrifugal, sen-trif'ū-gal, a. Flying, or tending to fly, from the centre. [L. centrum, and fugio, to fly.]
Centripetal, sen-trip'et-al, a. Seeking the centre; tending toward the centre. [L. centrum, and peto, to seek.]
Centuple, sen'tū-pl, a. A hundredfold. [Fr.—L. plico, to fold.]

Centurion, sen-tū'ri-on, n. Among the Romans the captain of a hundred men. [L. centurio.]
Century, sen'tū-ri, n. A hundred; the period of a hundred years. [L. centuria.]
Cephalic, sē-fal'ik, a. Pertaining to, or good for, the head. [Gr. kephalikos—kephalē, the head.]
Cerate, sē'rāt, n. A thick ointment, composed of wax and oil. [L. cerātum.]
Cere, sēr, n. The naked wax-like skin that covers the base of the bill in some birds.—vt. To wax or cover with wax. ppr. cering, pret. & pp. cered. [L. cera, wax.]
Cereal, sē'rē-al, a. Pertaining to corn or edible grain, as wheat, rye, &c.—n. pl. Cereals. The edible grains. [L. cerealis—Ceres, the goddess of corn.]
Cerebral, se-rē'bral, a. Pertaining to the brain. [from L. cerebrum.]
Cerecloth, sēr'kloth, n. A cloth smeared with melted wax, or with some glutinous matter. [L. cera, wax, and cloth.]
Cerement, sēr'ment, n. Cloths dipped in melted wax, for infolding dead bodies. [from L. cera.]
Ceremonial, se-rē-mō'ni-al, a. Relating to religious rites; ritual.—n. Sacred rite; a system of established rules and ceremonies; outward form.
Ceremonially, se-rē-mō'ni-al-li, adv. In a ceremonial or formal manner.
Ceremonious, se-rē-mō'ni-us, a. Formally civil; formal; too observant of forms.
Ceremoniously, se-rē-mō'ni-us-li, adv. In a ceremonious manner.
Ceremoniousness, se-rē-mō'ni-us-nes, n. Addictedness to ceremony.
Ceremony, se'rē-mō-ni, n. Outward rite or observance in religion; form; observance. [L. cæremonia—curo, to attend to.]
Certain, sėr'tān, a. Ascertained; undeniable; decided; particular; some; one. [Fr.—L. certus.]
Certainly, sėr'tān-li, adv. Without doubt or question; without failure.
Certainty, sėr'tān-ti, n. A fixed or real state; truth; fact; regularity.
Certificate, sėr-tif'i-kāt, n. A written testimony properly authenticated; a credential. [Fr. certificat—L. certus, and facio, to make.]
Certified, sėr'ti-fid, p.a. Assured; informed.
Certifier, sėr'ti-fi-ėr, n. One who certifies.
Certify, sėr'ti-fi, vt. To give certain information to, or of; to assure; to attest; to testify to in writing. ppr. certifying, pret. & pp. certified. [Fr. certifier—L. certus, and facio, to make.]
Cerulean, sē-rū'lē-an, a. Azure; sky-coloured; blue. [L. cœruleus.]
Cerumen, sē-rū'men, n. The wax or yellow matter secreted by the ear. [Fr.]
Ceruse, sē'rūs, n. White-lead; a kind of paint resembling wax, for the female face. [Fr.]
Cess, ses, n. A rate or tax.—vt. To rate, or impose a tax on.
Cessation, ses-ā'shon, n. A staying; a discontinuing; stop; vacation; a truce. [L. cessatio—cedo, to withdraw.]
Cession, se'shon, n. A quitting; surrender; resignation. [L. cessio—cedo, to withdraw.]
Cesspool, ses'pöl, n. A sunk cavity for the reception of sewage; any foul receptacle. [from L. sedeo, to settle.]
Cestus, ses'tus, n. The girdle of Venus. [L.]
Cetaceous, sē-tā'shē-us, a. Pertaining to fishes of the whale kind. [from L. cetē, a whale.]

---

ch, chain; j, job; g, go; ng, sing; ᴛʜ, then; th, thin; w, wig; wh, whig; zh, azure; † obsolete.

Chafe, chaf, *vt.* To make warm by rubbing; to fret by rubbing; to cause to fume or rage; to inflame.—*vi.* To be fretted, galled, or worn by friction; to fret; to rage. *ppr.* chafing, *pret. & pp.* chafed.—*n.* A heat; a fretting. [Fr. *schauffer*—L. *calidus*, hot, and *facio*, to make.]

Chafed, chaft, *p.a.* Excited; enraged.

Chafer, chāf′er, *n.* A beetle that devours roots, leaves, and young shoots. [Sax. *ceafor*.]

Chaff, chaf, *n.* The husk of corn and grasses; refuse; worthless matter. [Sax. *ceaf*.]

Chaffer, chaf′fer, *vi.* To cheapen; to haggle. [Sax. *ceapian*.]

Chafferer, chaf′fer-er, *n.* One who chaffers.

Chaffinch, chaf′finsh, *n.* A *finch* or songbird, said to be fond of *chaff*.

Chaffy, chaf′i, *a. Like chaff*; full of chaff; light.

Chagrin, sha-grēn′, *n.* Ill-humour; vexation; fretfulness.—*vt.* To fret; to excite ill-humour in; to vex; to mortify. [Fr.]

Chain, chān, *n.* A series of links, usually of metal, fitted into one another; a series of things linked together; a line of things connected; that which binds; a line formed of links, 66 feet long, for measuring land; (pl.) bondage; slavery.—*vt.* To bind with a *chain;* to confine; to unite. [Fr. *chaine*—L. *catena*.]

Chain-cable, chān′kā-bl, *n.* A *cable* composed of *iron links*.

Chained, chānd, *p.a.* Bound; enslaved.

Chain-pump, chān′pump, *n.* A powerful *pump*, used in large ships.

Chain-shot, chān′shot, *n.* Two balls connected by a *chain*.

Chair, chār, *n.* A movable seat; a professor's seat; a seat of justice; a sedan; a sort of chaise.—*vt.* To place or carry in a *chair*. [Fr. *chaire*—L. *cathedra*.]

Chairman, chār′man, *n.* The presiding officer of an assembly; a president; one who carries a sedan.

Chairmanship, chār′man-ship, *n. The office of a chairman*.

Chaise, shās, *n.* A two-wheeled carriage drawn by one horse. [Fr.]

Chalcedony, kal-sed′ō-ni, *n.* A precious stone; a variety of quartz, having a whitish colour. [from *Chalcedon*.]

Chaldee, kal′dē, *a. Pertaining to Chaldea.*—*n.* The language of the Chaldeans.

Chaldron, chāl′dron, *n.* A measure of coals, consisting of 36 bushels. [Fr. *chaudron*.]

Chalice, chal′is, *n.* A communion *cup*. [Fr. *calice;* L. *calyx*.]

Chalk, chak, *n.* A well-known white calcareous earth or carbonate of lime. *vt.* To rub or mark with chalk; to trace a course or plan, as if with chalk (with *out*). [Sax. *cealc*.]

Chalkiness, chak′i-nes, *n. The state of being chalky*.

Chalky, chak′i, *a. Resembling chalk;* consisting of or containing chalk.

Challenge, chal′lenj, *n.* A call; a summons to fight; a calling in question; an exception taken. *vt.* To summon to a fight or contest; to defy; to dare; to call in question or to account; to object to. *ppr.* challenging, *pret. & pp.* challenged. [Norm. *calenge*.]

Challengeable, chal′lenj-a-bl, *a. That may be challenged*.

Challenger, chal′lenj-er, *n.* One *who challenges*.

Chalybeate, ka-lib′ē-āt, *a.* Impregnated with particles *of iron*.—*n.* A well or medicine into which *iron* or *steel* enters. [from L. *chalybs*, steel.]

Chamber, chām′ber, *n.* An apartment in an upper story of a dwelling-house; any private apartment; a bedroom; an office; a hall of justice or legislation; a legislative body. [Fr. *chambre*—L. *camera*, an arched roof.]

Chambered, chām′bėrd, *p.a. Having chambers* or cells; shut up, as in a chamber.

Chamberlain, chām′ber-lān, *n.* One who has charge of the private apartments of a monarch or noble; an officer of state; a city officer, who keeps the public accounts. [Fr. *chambellan*.]

Chamberlainship, chām′ber-lān-ship, *n. The office of a chamberlain*.

Chamber-maid, chām′ber-mād, *n.* A *female* servant who has the care of *chambers* or bedrooms.

Chameleon, ka-mē′lē-on, *n. The ground-lion*, so called from its high back; a species of lizard, distinguished for its sudden and great changes of colour. [L. *chamæleon*—Gr. *chamai*, on the ground, and *leōn*, a lion.]

Chamois, sha′mwa, *n.* A species of antelope, whose skin is made into soft leather. [Fr.]

Chamomile, ka′mō-mīl, *n. The ground-apple;* a bitter plant, whose flowers are much used in medicine. [Gr. *chamai*, on the ground, and *melon*, an apple.]

Champ, champ, *vt.* To devour, with violent action of the teeth; to bite, as the bit, spoken of a horse.—*vi.* To bite repeatedly, and with violence (with *upon*). [Icel. *kampa*, to chew.]

Champagne, sham-pān′, *n.* A kind of brisk sparkling wine, from *Champagne* in France.

Champaign, sham′pān, *a. Open; level; plain*. [from L. *campus*, a plain.]

Champion, cham′pi-on, *n.* One who undertakes a *combat* in his own cause, or in that of another; a hero; one bold in contest.—*vt.* To furnish with a champion. [Fr.—L. *campus*, a plain.]

Championship, cham′pi-on-ship, *n. State of being a champion*.

Chance, chans, *n. That which falls out;* accident; fortune; an event, good or evil; risk; possibility of an occurrence; opportunity.—*vi. To fall out;* to come without design. *ppr.* chancing, *pret. & pp.* chanced.—*a. Happening by chance;* casual; fortuitous. [Fr.—L. *cado*, to fall.]

Chancel, chan′sel, *n.* That part of a church where the altar or communion-table is placed, formerly inclosed with *lattices*. [Fr.—L. *cancelli*, a lattice.]

Chancellor, chan′sel-ler, *n.* A high judicial officer who presides over a court of chancery or other court. [Fr. *chancelier*—Low L. *cancellarius*.]

Chancellorship, chan′sel-ler-ship, *n. The office of a chancellor;* the time during which one is chancellor.

Chancery, chan′se-ri, *n.* The highest court of justice in England, next to the parliament, presided over by the lord-*chancellor*. [Fr. *chancellerie*.]

Chandelier, shan-de-lēr′, *n.* A frame with branches to hold a number of *candles* or lights. [Fr.—L. *candeo*, to shine.]

Chandler, chand′ler, *n. A maker and seller of candles;* a dealer, as *tallow-chandler, ship-chandler*, &c. [Fr. *chandelier*.]

Chandlery, chand′lē-ri, *n.* The commodities sold by a *chandler*.

Change, chānj, *vt.* To barter!; to cause to turn from one state to another; to put, as one thing in the place of another; to turn; to give, as one kind of money for another; to quit one thing or state for another.—*vi.* To be altered; to undergo variation. *ppr.* changing, *pret. & pp.* changed.—*n.* Any variation in form or essence; revolution; dissolution; exchange of money for money; small money. [Fr. *changer*—L. *cambire*, to barter.]

Changeable, chānj′a-bl, *a.* Subject to alteration; fickle; wavering.

Changeableness, chānj′a-bl-nes, *n. Quality of being changeable*.

Changeably, chānj′a-bli, *adv.* Inconstantly.

Changed, chānjd, *p.a.* Altered.

Changeful, chānj′ful, *a. Full of change;* inconstant; mutable; fickle; uncertain.

Changefully, chānj′ful-li, *adv. In a changeful manner*.

Changefulness, chānj′ful-nes, *n. Quality of being changeful*.

Changeling, chānj′ling, *n.* A child left or taken in the place of another; an idiot; one apt to change. [*change*, and *ling*, offspring.]

Changer, chānj′er, *n. One who changes*.

Changing, chānj′ing, *p.a.* Altering; shifting.

Channel, chan′nel, *n. A canal;* a pipe for the conveyance of water; a gutter; the hollow bed of running water; a narrow sea; deeper part of a strait, bay, or harbour; means of passing or transmitting.—*vt. To form into a channel;* to groove. *ppr.* channelling, *pret. & pp.* channelled. [Fr. *canal*—L. *candida*—*canna*, a pipe.]

Channelled, chan′neld, *p.a.* Grooved longitudinally.

Chant, chant, *vt. To sing;* to sing after the manner of a chant.—*vi. To sing;* to repeat after the manner of a chant. *n. Song;* melody; a peculiar kind of sacred music; a part of church service. [Fr. *chanter*—L. *canto*, to sing.]

Chanter, chant′er, *n. A singer;* the chief singer or priest of the chantry.

Chanticleer, chan′ti-klēr, *n.* The bird that *sings* or crows *clearly;* a cock. [*chant* and *clear*.]

Chanting, chant′ing, *p.n. Act of singing* or performing, as a chant.

Chantry, chant′ri, *n.* An endowed chapel where priests daily *sing* or say mass for the souls of the donors or others. [Fr. *chantrerie*.]

Chaos, kā′os, *n. A vast gap;* a vast shapeless heap; the state of matter before the Creator reduced it to order; disorder. [L.—Gr. *chao*, to gape.]

Chaotic, kā-ot′ik, *a. Relating to or resembling chaos;* confused.

Chap, chop, *vt. To open;* to crack or open longitudinally.—*vt.* To crack; to open in long slits. *ppr.* chapping, *pret. & pp.* chapped.—*n.* A longitudinal cleft or chink. [Sax. *yppan, pp. yeypped*.]

Chap, chop, *n.* That part of the mouth by which an animal chews; the jaw (generally in the pl.) [Sax. *ceaplas*.]

Chapel, chap′el, *n.* A place of worship containing one altar, attached to a church; a place of worship; a church. [Fr. *chapelle*—Low L. *capella*.]

Chaperon, sha′pe-rōn, *n.* A married lady who accompanies an unmarried one in public places.—*vt. To act as chaperon to.* [Fr.]

Chapiter, chap′i-ter, *n.* The *head* or capital of a column (Bible). [from L. *caput*, the head.]

Chaplain, chap′lān, *n.* A clergyman who belongs to a ship of war, to a regi-

ment of land forces, &c.; a clergyman retained to perform divine service in a family. [Fr. *chapelain*.]
Chaplaincy, chap'lān-si, *n*. *The office or station of a chaplain*.
Chaplainship, chap'lān-ship, *n*. *The office or business of a chaplain*.
Chaplet, chap'let, *n*. *A garland to be worn on the head;* the circle of a crown; a rosary. [Fr. *chapelet*—L. *caput*, the head.]
Chapman, chap'man, *n*. *Chapmen*, *pl*. *A market-man;* a merchant. [Sax. *ceapman*—*ceap*, saleable commodities, and *man*.]
Chaps, chops, *n.pl.* The mouth or jaws; the jaws of a vice.
Chapter, chap'tėr, *n*. *Head* of a subject; division of a book; a society of clergymen belonging to a cathedral or collegiate church; an organised branch of some fraternity. [Fr. *chapitre*—L. *caput*, the head.]
Char, char, *n*. A delicious fish of the salmon kind.
Char, **Chare**, chār, *n*. *A turn* by the day; a single job or task.—*vi.* To do little *turns* or jobs; to work by the day. *ppr.* charring, *pret. & pp.* charred, chared. [Sax. *cerran*, to turn.]
Char, chār, *vt.* To *reduce* to coal or carbon by burning. *ppr.* charring, *pret. & pp.* charred. [from L. *carbo*, a coal.]
Character, ka'rak-tėr, *n*. *A mark engraved;* a letter or figure; manner of writing; distinctive qualities by which a person or thing is separated from another or others; representation of personal qualities; the person with his assemblage of qualities; reputation. [Fr. *caractère;* Gr. *charasso*, to cut.]
Characteristic, ka'rak-tėr-is'tik,*a*. *That constitutes character;* that marks distinctive qualities.—*n*. *That which constitutes character;* distinctive quality. [Gr. *charaktēristikos*.]
Characteristically, ka'rak-tėr-is'tik-al-li,*adv. In a manner that distinguishes character*.
Characterise, ka'rak-tėr-iz,*vt.* *To mark;* to give a character to; to designate. *ppr.* characterising, *pret. & pp.* characterised. [Gr. *charaktērisō*.]
Charade, sha-rād', *n*. A species of riddle upon the syllables of a word. [Fr.]
Charcoal, chär'kōl, *n*. *Coal* made by *charring* wood; the residue of animal, vegetable, and many mineral substances, when heated to redness in close vessels.
Charge, chärj, *vt. To load;* to lay on; to put a price on; to intrust; to impute, as a debt or crime; to command; to confide; to rush on; to attack.—*vi.* To make a *charge*, or an onset. *ppr.* charging, *pret. & pp.* charged.—*n*. *That which is laid on;* that which loads a musket, &c.; order given; person or thing committed to another's care; trust; office; accusation; cost; management; imposition; tax; duty; signal to attack; an assault or onset. [Fr. *charger*—L. *carrus*, a waggon.]
Chargeable, chärj'a-bl, *a*. *Subject to be charged;* expensive; imputable; censurable.
Charger, chärj'ėr, *a*. A large dish that holds a heavy *charge;* a horse on which the rider *charges* the enemy.
Charily, chā'ri-li,*adv.* Carefully; warily.
Chariness, chā'ri-nes, *n*. *Quality of being chary;* caution; frugality.
Chariot, chā'ri-ot, *n*. A carriage with four wheels, used for convenience and pleasure; a car used formerly in war. [Fr.—L. *carrus*, a car.]

Charioteer, chā'ri-ot-ėr'', *n*. *The person who drives* or conducts *a chariot*.
Charitable, chā'rit-a-bl, *a*. Liberal to the poor; pertaining to or partaking of charity; indulgent; kind in judging of others; disposed to tenderness. [Fr.]
Charitableness, chā'rit-a-bl-nes,*n*. *Quality of being charitable*.
Charitably, chā'rit-a-bli, *adv. In a charitable manner;* kindly; liberally.
Charity, cha'ri-ti, *n*. A disposition to relieve the wants of others; tenderness; love; benevolence; almsgiving; disposition to think well of others; love to God; good-will to man. [Fr. *charité*—L. *carus*, dear.]
Charlatan, shär'la-tan, *n*. A quack; an empiric; a mountebank. [Fr.]
Charm, chärm, *n*. *Enchantment;* a spell; that which gives exquisite pleasure and gains the affections.—*vt.* To enthral by some secret influence; to bewitch; to enrapture; to summon by incantations. [Fr. *charme*—L. *carmen*, a song, an incantation.]
Charmed, chärmd, *p.a*. Delighted; enchanted.
Charmer, chärm'ėr, *n*. *One who charms*.
Charming, chärm'ing,*p.a.* Enchanting; captivating; fascinating.
Charmingly, chärm'ing-li, *adv. In a charming manner*.
Charnel-house, chär'nel-hous,*n*. A place under or near churches where the bones of the dead are reposited; a seat of corruption. [Fr. *charnel*, fleshly—L. *caro*, flesh.]
Chart, chärt, *n*. *A card;* a marine map, or a delineation of coasts, islands, shoals, rocks, &c. [L. *charta*, paper.]
Charter, chär'tėr, *n*. A writing, given as evidence of a grant, contract, &c.; a writing conferring powers or privileges; privilege.—*vt.* To establish by *charter;* to hire or to let a ship by charter or contract. [Fr. *chartre*—L. *charta*, paper.]
Chartered, chär'tėrd, *p.a. Privileged by charter;* granted by charter.
Char-woman,chär'wum-un,*n*. A woman hired for odd work, or for single days. [from *char*, a turn.]
Chary, chā'ri, *a*. *Careful;* wary; frugal. [Sax. *cearig*.]
Chase, chās, *vt.* To pursue, as an enemy or as game; to hunt; to follow with eagerness; to emboss. *ppr.* chasing, *pret. & pp.* chased.—*n.* A hunting or hunt; game hunted; ground where game is preserved or hunted; earnest seeking. [Fr. *chasser*—L. *capio*, to take.]
Chased, chāst, *p.a. Enchased*.
Chaser, chās'ėr, *n*. *One who chases;* a gun at the head or stern of a ship; an enchaser.
Chasm, kazm, *n*. *A gap or wide opening;* a fissure; a void space; a vacuity. [Gr. *chasma—chainō*, to yawn.]
Chaste, chāst. *a*. *Clean;* unpolluted; modest; free from impure desires; free from illicit intercourse; free from barbarisms; pure in taste and style. [Fr. —L. *castus*.]
Chastely, chāst'li, *adv. In a chaste manner;* purely.
Chasten, chās'n, *vt.* *To cleanse;* to free from spot or error; to afflict in order to reclaim. [Old Fr. *chastier*—L. *castigo*, to chasten.]
Chastened, chās'nd, *p.a*. Afflicted for correction.
Chasteness, chāst'nes, *n*. Purity.
Chastise, chas-tiz', *vt.* To correct; to punish; to reduce to obedience; to re-

press. *ppr.* chastising, *pret. & pp.* chastised. [Old Fr. *chastier*.]
Chastisement, chas'tiz-ment, *n*. Correction. [Fr. *châtiment*.]
Chastity, chas'ti-ti, *n*. *Purity* of the body; purity of language or style, and of the mind. [Fr. *chasteté;* L. *castitas*.]
Chat, chat, *vi. To chatter;* to talk in a familiar manner. *ppr.* chatting, *pret. & pp.* chatted.—*n*. *Free*, familiar talk; idle talk. [Old G. *chatan*, to speak.]
Chateau, shä'tō, *n. A castle;* a seat in the country. [Fr. *châteaux*—L. *castellum*.]
Chattel, chat'tel, *n*. The word *chattels* now comprehends all goods, movable or immovable, except such as have the nature of freehold. [Flem. *kateyl*, movable property.]
Chatter, chat'tėr, *vi.* To sound like the teeth when one shivers; to talk carelessly; to jabber.—*n*. Sounds like those of a magpie or monkey; idle talk. [dimin. of *chat*.]
Chatterer, chat'tėr-ėr, *n*. *One who chatters;* a prater; an idle talker; a bird that makes a chattering sound.
Chattering, chat'tėr-ing, *p.a.* Talking idly; moving rapidly and clashing, as the teeth.
Chatty, chat'i, *a*. Talkative.
Chaw, cha, *vt. To crush with the jaws;* to chew; to ruminate. [Sax. *ceowan*.]
Cheap, chep, *a.* To be had at a low rate; bearing a low price; common; not respected. [An ellipsis for *good cheap*, that is a good bargain.]
Cheapen, chēp'n, *vt.* To ask the price of, as of a commodity; to beat down in price. [Sax. *ceapian*, to bargain.]
Cheaply, chēp'li, *adv.* At a small price.
Cheapness, chēp'nes, *n. State or quality of being cheap;* lowness in price.
Cheat, chēt, *vt*. To defraud; to obtain by trick, artifice, or low cunning; to beguile.—*n*. A deceitful act; a fraud; a person who cheats. [from *escheat*.]
Check, chek, *vt. To stop;* to curb; to chide; to compare with corresponding evidence; to control by a counter-reckoning.—*vi. To stop;* to make a stop; to clash or interfere.—*n*. An attack made on the king by a piece or pawn in chess, by which he is brought to a sudden *stop;* a stop; control; he or that which stops; a token; corresponding cipher of a draft; an order for money. [Fr. *échec*, check.]
Check, chek,*a. Checkered*.—*n. Checkered* cloth.
Checker, chek'ėr, *vt.* To form into little squares, like *a chess-board;* to variegate with different qualities, scenes, or events. [Fr. *échiquier*, a chess-board.]
Checker, chek'ėr, *n. One who checks* or restrains; a chess-board.
Checker, **Checker-work**, chek'ėr, chek'-ėr-werk, *n*. Work varied alternately; work consisting of cross-lines or stripes.
Checkered, chek'ėrd, *p.a.* Diversified.
Checkers, chek'ėrz, *n. pl*. Draughts.
Checkmate, chek'māt, *n*. A movement in the game of chess, when the *king is* attacked and cannot come out of *check*, so that the game is finished; defeat; overthrow.—*vt.* To place, as the adversary's king, in irretrievable *check;* to arrest and defeat. *ppr.* checkmating, *pret. & pp.* checkmated. [Ar. *shâhmât*, the shah or king is dead.]
Cheek, chēk, *n*. The side of the face below the eyes on each side. [Sax. *cheos*.]
Cheer, chēr, *n.* That which affects the *countenance* with gladness; entertainment; fare; a shout of joy; mirth;

jollity; a state of gladness, joy, or animation.—*vt.* To brighten the countenance of; to gladden; to console; to salute with shouts; to applaud.—*vi.* To grow cheerful; to become gladsome or joyous. [Old Fr. *chere*, visage, countenance.]
Cheerer, chēr'ėr, *n.* One who cheers.
Cheerful, chēr'fųl, *a.* Having good spirits; moderately joyful; causing joy; lively; gay; sprightly; willing.
Cheerfully, chēr'fųl-li, *adv.* In a cheerful manner.
Cheerfulness, chēr'fųl-nes, *n.* Good spirits; a state of moderate joy or gaiety; alacrity.
Cheerily, chēr'i-li, *adv.* With cheerfulness; with spirit.
Cheeriness, chēr'i-nes, *n.* Cheerfulness.
Cheering, chēr'ing, *p.a.* Enlivening.
Cheerless, chēr'les, *a.* Without joy, gladness, or comfort; gloomy; dejected.
Cheerlessness, chēr'les-nes, *n.* Destitution of comfort or enjoyment.
Cheery, chēr'i, *a.* Cheerful; gay; sprightly; having power to make gay.
Cheese, chēz, *n.* Curd pressed into a firm cake or mass, and used as food; anything in the form of cheese. [Sax. *cyse*; L. *caseus*.]
Cheese-cake, chēz'kāk, *n.* A cake made of soft curds, sugar, and butter.
Cheesemonger, chēz'mung-gėr, *n.* One who deals in or sells cheese.
Cheese-press, chēz'pres, *n.* A press or engine for making cheese.
Cheesy, chēz'i, *a.* Having the nature, qualities, taste, or form of cheese.
Chemical, kem'ik-al, *a.* Pertaining to chemistry.
Chemically, kem'ik-al-li, *adv.* By chemical process or operation.
Chemise, she-mēz', *n.* A shift or under garment worn by females. [Fr.]
Chemist, kem'ist, *n.* A person versed in chemistry; a professor of chemistry.
Chemistry, kem'ist-ri, *n.* The science which treats of the composition of substances, and of the changes which they undergo. [Fr. *chimie*—Gr. *cheō*, to pour.]
Cheque, chek, *n.* An order for money.
Cherish, che'rish, *vt.* To cheer; to treat with tenderness; to nurse; to encourage. [Fr. *chérir*, *chérissant*.]
Cherished, che'risht, *p.a.* Treated with tenderness; fostered.
Cherishing, che'rish-ing, *p.n.* Support; encouragement.
Cherry, che'ri, *n.* A well-known tree and its fruit.—*a.* Like a red cherry in colour; red; ruddy; blooming. [Fr. *cerise*—L. *cerasus*.]
Cherry-cheeked, che'ri-chēkt, *a.* Having ruddy cheeks.
Cherub, che'rub, *n.* Cherubs, che'rubs, *pl.* A celestial spirit; an angel of the second order; a figure representing a cherub; a beautiful child. [Heb. *kerub*; *pl. kerubim*; etymol. uncertain.]
Cherubic, che-rū'bik, *a.* Pertaining to cherubs; angelic.
Cherubin, che'rub-in, *n.* Properly, cherubs. [Fr. *chérubin*, a cherub.]
Chess, ches, *n.* An ingenious game played by two parties, with thirty-two pieces of different forms on a checkered board. [Fr. *échec*.]
Chess-board, ches'bōrd, *n.* The checkered board used in the game of chess.
Chess-man, ches'man, *n.* A piece used in the game of chess.
Chess-player, ches'plā-ėr, *n.* One who plays chess, or is skilled in that game.
Chest, chest, *n.* A box of wood or other material in which things are laid up;

the cavity of the body which contains the heart, lungs, &c.; the trunk; a certain quantity by measure.—*vt.* To reposit in a chest; to hoard. [Sax. *cest*.]
Chested, chest'ed, *p.a.* Having a chest.
Chestnut, ches'nut, *n.* A tree and its edible fruit or nuts, said to have been originally found in Castana in Pontus.—*a.* Being of the colour of a chestnut; of a brown colour. [Old Fr. *chastaigne*—L. *castanea*.]
Chevalier, she'va-lēr, *n.* A horseman; a knight or cavalier; a gallant man. [Fr.—*cheval*, a horse.]
Chew, chō, *vt.* To chaw; to grind with teeth; to champ; to bite.—*vi.* To ruminate; to meditate (with *on*). [Sax. *ceowan*.]
Chicane, shi-kān', *n.* Shift; artifice; sophistry. [Fr. *chicanerie*.]—*vi.* To invent or use subterfuges, cavils, or artifices. *ppr.* chicaning, *pret. & pp.* chicaned. [Fr. *chicaner*.]
Chicaner, shi-kān'ėr, *n.* One who uses chicane or chicanery. [Fr. *chicaneur*.]
Chicanery, shi-kān'ė-ri, *n.* Mean or unfair artifices of wrangling; trick; quibble. [Fr. *chicanerie*.]
Chiccory, chik'o-ri, *n.* An herb, also called succory. [L. *cichorium*.]
Chick, Chicken, chik, chik'en, *n.* The young of various birds, especially of the domestic hen; a young child. [Sax. *cicen*.]
Chicken-hearted, chik'en-härt-ed, *a.* Timid; fearful; cowardly.
Chicken-pox, chik'en-poks, *n.* An eruptive disease, generally appearing in children.
Chickweed, chik'wēd, *n.* A weed of which chickens and birds are fond.
Chide, chid, *vt.* To rebuke sharply; to reproach; to quarrel with.—*vi.* To scold; to contend in angry words. *ppr.* chiding, *pret.* chid, *pp.* chid, chidden. [Sax. *cidan*.]
Chief, chēf, *a.* Being at the head; highest; first; leading.—*n.* A head or principal person; a leader; principal part; upper part. [Fr. *chef*—Gr. *kephalē*, the head.]
Chiefly, chēf'li, *adv.* Mostly; principally; mainly; especially; eminently.
Chieftain, chēf'tān, *n.* A captain; a chief; the head of a troop, army, or clan. [from *chief*.]
Chieftaincy, Chieftainship, chēf'tān-si, chēf'tān-ship, *n.* Headship; captaincy; the government over a clan.
Chiffonier, shif'fon-ēr, *n.* A receptacle for rags; a movable cupboard. [Fr. —*chiffon*, a rag.]
Chilblain, chil'blān, *n.* A blain or sore produced by a chill, or by cold.—*vt.* To produce chilblains upon.
Child, child, *n.* Children, chil'dren, *pl.* That which is born of woman; an infant; one very young; a son or a daughter; offspring; issue; one having the qualities of a child; one chosen and adopted by God; one whose principles and morals are the product of another; anything the effect of another; (pl.) descendants whether near or remote; the inhabitants of a country. [Sax. *cild*—*cennan*, to bring forth.]
Child-bearing, child'bār-ing, *n.* The act of bringing forth children.
Childbed, child'bed, *n.* The state of a woman in labour.
Childbirth, child'bėrth, *n.* The act of bringing forth a child; travail; labour.
Childe, child, *n.* Formerly, a noble youth; a cognomen prefixed to the family name by the eldest son.
Childhood, child'hụd, *n.* The state of a

child, or the time in which persons are children. [Sax. *cildhad*.]
Childish, child'ish, *a.* Belonging to or like a child; puerile; trifling.
Childishly, child'ish-li, *adv.* In a childish manner.
Childishness, child'ish-nes, *n.* Quality or state of being childish.
Childless, child'les, *a.* Destitute of children or offspring.
Childlike, child'līk, *a.* Like a child; becoming a child; docile; innocent; dutiful; without art or guile.
Chill, chil, *n.* A shivering with cold; a cold fit; that which checks or disheartens.—*a.* Shivering with cold; tending to cause shivering; distant; dispirited.—*vt.* To make cold; to cause to shiver; to discourage. [Sax. *cyl*, a very great coldness.]
Chilliness, chil'i-nes, *n.* State of being chilly; a sensation of shivering; rigours.
Chilling, chil'ing, *p.a.* Cooling; causing to shiver.
Chillness, chil'nes, *n.* State of being chill; coolness; coldness; a shivering.
Chilly, chil'i, *a.* Moderately chill.
Chime, chim, *n.* The sound of bells in harmony; a set of bells tuned to each other; correspondence of relation.—*vi.* To sound in consonance; to correspond or agree; to coincide.—*vt.* To cause to sound in harmony; to strike or cause to sound, as a set of bells. *ppr.* chiming, *pret. & pp.* chimed. (Chaucer, *chimbe*; L. *campana*, a bell.)
Chimera, ki-mē'ra, *n.* A fabulous monster vomiting flames, with the head of a lion, the body of a goat, and the tail of a serpent; any wild imagination. [Gr. *chimaira*, a she-goat.]
Chimerical, ki-me'rik-al, *a.* Wildly or vainly conceived; fanciful; unfounded.
Chimney, chim'nē, *n.* Chimneys, *pl.* The funnel through which the smoke is conveyed; a flue; a glass funnel for a lamp, &c. [Fr. *cheminée*—Gr. *kaiō*, to burn.]
Chimney-piece, chim'nē-pēs, *n.* An ornamental piece of wood or stone, set round a fireplace.
Chin, chin, *n.* The part of the face beneath the under lip; the point of the under jaw. [Sax. *cyn*.]
China, chī'na, *n.* A species of fine porcelain, originally made in China.
Chincough, chin'kof, *n.* A cough which seizes children; the hooping-cough. [G. *kind*, a child, Old Belg. *kugh*, a cough.]
Chine, chin, *n.* The ridge of the back; a piece of the backbone of an animal, with the adjoining parts, cut for cooking. [Fr. *échine*—L. *spina*, the backbone.]
Chinese, chi-nēz', *n. sing.* and *pl.* A native or natives of China; also, (sing.) the language of China.
Chink, chingk, *n.* A gap; a crack or fissure; a cleft.—*vi.* To gape; to crack; to part and form a fissure. [Sax. *cina*, a fissure.]
Chink, chingk, *vt.* To shake, as coins, so as to make a sound.—*vi.* To make a small sharp sound, as by the collision of little pieces of money. [from the root of *jingle*.]
Chinky, chingk'i, *a.* Full of fissures.
Chinned, chind, *a.* Having a long chin.
Chintz, chints, *n.* Cotton cloth spotted, or printed with flowers and other devices in a number of different colours. [Pers. *chins*, spotted.]
Chip, chip, *n.* A fragment; a small piece.—*vt.* To hew into chips; to diminish, by cutting away a little at a time.—*vi.* To fly off in small pieces.

Fāte, fär, fat, fall; mē, met, hėr; pīne, pin; nōte, not, mōve; tūbe, tub, bụll; oil, poụṛ

CHIROPODIST — 49 — CHUCKLING

ppr. chipping, pret. & pp. chipped. [Fr. couper, to cut.]
Chiropodist, kir-op'od-ist, n. One who extracts corns, removes bunions, &c. [Gr. cheir, the hand, and pous, podos, the foot.]
Chirp, chėrp, vi. To make the lively cheerful noise of certain small birds, or of certain insects.—n. A particular voice of certain birds or insects. [G. sirpen.]
Chirper, chėrp'ėr, n. One that chirps or is cheerful; a chirping bird.
Chirping, chėrp'ing, p.a. Making the noise of certain small birds.
Chirrup, chi'rup, vi. To chirp.
Chisel, chiz'el, n. A cutting tool, used in wood-work, masonry, sculpture, &c. vt. To cut, gouge, or engrave with a chisel. [Fr. ciseau, a graver; L. cœdo, to cut.]
Chiseled, chiz'eld, p.a. Cut or engraved with or as with a chisel.
Chit, chit, n. A sprout; a lively pert child. [Sax. cith, a young twig or shoot.]
Chivalric, shi'val-rik, a. Partaking of the character o chivalry.
Chivalrous, shi'val-rus, a. Pertaining to chivalry; warlike; bold; gallant.
Chivalrously, shi'val-rus-li, adv. In a chivalrous spirit.
Chivalry, shi'val-ri, n. That which becomes cavaliers; the customs pertaining to the order of knighthood; system of knighthood; heroic defence of life and honour. [Fr. chevalerie.]
Chloric, klō'rik, a. Pertaining to chlorine, or obtained from it.
Chloride, klō'rid, n. A compound of chlorine and some other substance, as potash, soda, lime, &c.
Chlorine, klō'rin, n. A greenish yellow gas, of intolerably suffocating properties. [Gr. chlōros, green.]
Chloroform, klō'rō-form, n. A volatile thin liquid, which produces temporary insensibility to pain when its vapour is inhaled, and is therefore employed in surgical operations. This use was discovered by Sir James Simpson of Edinburgh. [chlor, and form, from formic, the name of an acid obtained from ants, L. formica.]
Chocolate, cho'kō-lāt, n. A preparation from the seeds of the cacao-tree; liquor or beverage made from it. [Mex. chocolatl.]
Choice, chois, n. Act of choosing; option; the thing chosen; best part of anything; the object of choice.—a. Worthy of being chosen; select; precious; rare. [from choose.]
Choir, kwir, n. A body of singers in a church; that part of a church appropriated for the singers. [Old Fr. chœur; Gr. choros, a dance in a ring.]
Choke, chōk, vt. To strangle by compressing the throat of; to stop or block up; to extinguish; to stifle.—vi. To be suffocated; to be blocked up. ppr. choking, pret. & pp. choked. [Sax. acocan.]
Choke-damp, chōk'damp, n. Carbonic acid gas; a suffocating vapour in coal-mines, &c.
Choking, chōk'ing, p.a. Suffocating.
Choky, chōk'i, a. That tends to or has power to choke or suffocate.
Choler, kol'ėr, n. Anger; wrath; irritation of the passions. [L. cholera, bile.]
Cholera, kol'e-ra, n. A disease accompanied by purging and vomiting, with great pain and debility, and very fatal in some of its forms. [Gr. cholē, bile, and rheō, to flow.]

Choleric, ko'lė-rik, a. Abounding with choler; irascible; petulant; peevish.
Choose, chōz, vt. To pick out; to take, as one thing in preference to another; to adopt. — vi. To have the power of choice; to prefer. ppr. choosing, pret. chose, pp. chosen. [Sax. ceosan.]
Chooser, chōz'ėr, n. One who chooses.
Chop, chop, vt. To cut with a quick blow; to cut into small pieces; to divide (with off).—vi. To open into chinks; to chap. ppr. chopping, pret. & pp. chopped.—n. A piece chopped off; a small piece of meat; a crack or cleft. [D. kappen.]
Chop, chop, n. The chap; the jaw; (pl.) the jaws; the mouth.
Chop-fallen, chop'fal-en, a. Dejected; dispirited.
Chopping, chop'ing, a. Chubby; stout; changing suddenly.
Choppy, chop'i, a. Chappy; full of clefts or cracks.
Choral, kō'ral, a. Belonging to a choir or concert. [from chorus.]
Choralist, kō'ral-ist, n. A member of a choir; a musician.
Chord, kord, n. A string of gut; string of a musical instrument; the harmonious combination of three or more musical sounds heard together; a straight line joining the ends of the arc of a circle or curve.—vt. To string. [L. chorda.]
Chorister, ko'rist-ėr, n. A singer in a choir or concert; the leader of a choir in churches. [Fr. choriste.]
Chorus, kō'rus, n. A dance in a ring; a company of persons singing in concert; a piece performed by a whole company in concert; in the Gr. drama, the persons who are supposed to behold what passes in the acts of a tragedy, and sing their sentiments between the acts; verses of a song in which the company join the singer; any union of voices in general. [L.—Gr. choros.]
Chosen, chōz'n, p.a. Select; distinguished by preference; eminent.
Chough, chuf, n. A kind of daw, so called from the sound it utters. [Sax. ceo.]
Chouse, chous, vt. To cheat; to impose upon; to trick or defraud. ppr. chousing, pret. & pp. choused.—n. A trick; imposition.
Chrism, krizm, n. An ointment; consecrated oil used by Roman Catholics in sacred ceremonies. [Gr. chrisma.]
CHRIST, krist, n. The Anointed; the Messiah; the Saviour. [Gr. Christos, from chriō, chriso, to anoint.]
Christen, kris'n, vt. To initiate into the Christian Church; to baptize; to name. [Sax. cristnian.]
Christendom, kris'n-dum, n. That portion of the globe which is subject to Christian rule; the countries inhabited by Christians; the whole body of Christians. [Sax. Cristendom.]
Christening, kris'n-ing, p.n. Initiation into the Christian religion; act or ceremony of baptizing.
Christian, kris'ti-an, n. A professed follower of Christ; one united to Christ; an inhabitant of Christendom.—a. Relating to Christ or Christianity; professing the religion of Christ; ecclesiastical. [L. Christianus.]
Christianity, kris-ti-an'i-ti, n. The religion of Christians. [Low L. Christianitas.]
Christianize, kris'ti-an-īz, vt. To convert to Christianity. ppr. christianizing, pret. & pp. christianized.
Christian-like, kris'ti-an-līk, a. Becoming a Christian.

Christmas, kris'mas, n. The festival of Christ's nativity, observed annually on the 25th day of December.—a. Belonging to the time of Christ's nativity. [Christ and mass.]
Christ's-thorn, krists'thorn, n. A deciduous shrub, said to be that which furnished the crown of thorns.
Chromatic, krō-mat'ik, a. Relating to colour; proceeding by semitones. [Gr. chrōmatikos.]
Chrome, Chromium, krōm, krō'mi-um, n. A grayish white, brittle, hard metal, from which coloured preparations are made. [Gr. chrōma, colour.]
Chromic, krōm'ik, a. Pertaining to chrome, or obtained from it.
Chronic, kron'ik, a. Relating to time; continuing a long time, as a disease. [Fr. chronique—Gr. chronos, time.]
Chronicle, kron'i-kl, n. An historical account of events disposed in the order of time; a history.—vt. To record, as events in the order of time; to register. ppr. chronicling, pret. & pp. chronicled. [from Gr. chronos, time.]
Chronicler, kron'i-kl-ėr, n. A writer of a chronicle or chronicles; an historian.
Chronological, kron-ō-loj'ik-al, a. Relating to chronology.
Chronologically, kron-ō-loj'ik-al-li, adv. In a chronological manner.
Chronologist, kro-nol'o-jist, n. One who studies or is versed in chronology.
Chronology, kro-nol'o-ji, n. The doctrine of time or of dates; the method of ascertaining the true periods when past events took place, and arranging them in their proper order. [Gr. chronos, time, and logos, doctrine.]
Chronometer, kro-nom'et-ėr, n. An instrument that measures time with greater exactness than an ordinary clock or watch. [Gr. chronos, and metron, measure.]
Chronometric, Chronometrical, kron-ō-met'rik, kron-ō-met'rik-al, a. Pertaining to a chronometer; measured by a chronometer.
Chrysalis, kri'sa-lis, n. Chrysalides, kri-sal'i-dēz, pl. A grub of a golden colour; the form which certain insects assume before they arrive at their winged state. [L.—Gr. chrūsos, gold.]
Chrysolite, kri'sō-līt, n. Golden stone; a mineral of a yellowish or greenish colour. [Gr. chrusos, and lithos, a stone.]
Chrysoprase, kri'so-prāz, n. A golden-green or yellowish-green mineral, a variety of quartz. [Gr. chrusoprasos—chrūsos, and prason, a leek.]
Chub, chub, n. A small river-fish with a thick head. [Sax. copp.]
Chubby, chub'i, a. Round or full-cheeked; plump; having a large fat face. [Fr. jouffu, from joue, the cheek, the jaw.]
Chuck, chuk, vi. To make the noise of a hen when she calls her chickens.—vt. To call, as a hen her chickens.
Chuck, chuk, vt. To strike or hit gently; to tap under the chin; to pat; to throw with quick motion; to pitch.—n. A sudden, small noise; a slight blow under the chin. [Fr. choquer, to strike.]
Chuckle, chuk'l, vt. To call, as a hen her chickens; to fondle. ppr. chuckling, pret. & pp. chuckled.
Chuckle, chuk'l, vi. To laugh in the throat; to feel inward triumph or exultation. ppr. chuckling, pret. & pp. chuckled.—n. A short and suppressed laugh in the throat. [from Icel. kok, the throat.]
Chuckling, chuk'l-ing, p.n. Suppressed

ch, chain; j, job; g, go; ng, sing; ᴛʜ, then; th, thin; w, wig; wh, whig; sh, asure; † obsolete.

4

laughter; inward triumph or exultation.
Chuffy, chuf'i, a. Surly; angry. [Fr. *jouffu.*]
Chum, chum, n. A *chamber-fellow*, especially in a college; one who resides in the same room. [Sax. *cuma*, a guest.]
Church, chėrch, n. *The Lord's house*; a house consecrated to the worship of God among Christians; the collective body of Christians; the body of clergy; ecclesiastical authority.—*vt*. To perform with any one the office of returning thanks in the *church* after any signal deliverance, as from the dangers of childbirth. [Late Gr. *to kuriakon*, from *Kurios*, the Lord.]
Church-going, chėrch'gō-ing, a. *Going to church* regularly.
Churching, chėrch'ing, p.n. The act or form of offering thanks in *church* after childbirth.
Churchman, chėrch'man, n. *An ecclesiastic*; an adherent of the Church of England.
Church-militant, chėrch'mi-li-tant, n. *The church as warring* against spiritual evil of all kinds.
Church-music, chėrch'mū-zik, n. *Music* suited to *church*-service.
Church-rate, chėrch'rāt, n. *A tax levied on parishes* in England for repairing, maintaining, &c., *churches.*
Churchwarden, chėrch'war-den, n. *A keeper or guardian of the church*, and a representative of the parish.
Churchyard, chėrch'yärd, n. *The yard or inclosed ground adjoining to a church*, in which the dead are buried.
Churl, chėrl, n. A rude, ill-bred man; a robust fellow; a rustic labourer; a miser. [Sax. *ceorl.*]
Churlish, chėrl'ish, a. Surly; sullen; avaricious.
Churlishly, chėrl'ish-li, adv. *In a churlish manner.*
Churlishness, chėrl'ish-nes, n. *Quality of being churlish.*
Churn, chėrn, n. A vessel in which cream is *turned* or agitated, in order to produce butter.—*vt*. To agitate, as cream for making butter; to shake with violence or continued motion. [Sax. *cerene—cyran*, to turn.]
Churning, chėrn'ing, p.n. *The act of one who churns*; the quantity of butter made at one time.
Chyle, kīl, n. A milky fluid in animals, prepared from the chyme, and passing into the blood as the means of nutrition. [Gr. *chulos—cheō*, to pour.]
Chylifaction, kīl-i-fak'shon, n. The process by which *chyle is formed from food.* [*chyle*, and L. *facio*, to make.]
Chyme, kīm, n. The pulp formed by the food after it has undergone the action of the stomach. [Gr. *chumos—from cheō*, to pour.]
Cibarious, si-bā'ri-us, a. *Pertaining to food*; useful for food; edible. [L. *cibarius*, from *cibus*, food.]
Cicatrize, si'ka-trīz, vt. *To induce the formation of a scar* in, as in wounded flesh.—*vi*. To heal or be healed; to form a skin; to skin over. ppr. cicatrizing, pret. & pp. cicatrized. [Fr. *cicatriser*—L. *cicātrix*, a scar.]
Cicerone, chi-che-rō'ne, n. A guide; one who shows strangers the curiosities of a place, and is eloquent, like *Cicero*, in his descriptions of them. [It. from L. *Cicero.*]
Ciceronian, si-se-rō'ni-an, a. *Relating to or resembling Cicero.*
Cider, sī'dėr, n. The juice of apples ex-
pressed, a liquor used for drink. [Fr. *cidre.*]
Ciderkin, sī'dėr-kin, n. The liquor made of the gross matter of apples after the *cider* is pressed out.
Cigar, si-gär', n. *A small roll of tobacco*, used for smoking. [Fr. *cigare.*]
Ciliary, si'li-a-ri, a. *Belonging to the eye-lashes*, or to processes resembling them in animals or vegetables. [L. *cilium*, an eye-lid.]
Cimbric, sim'brik, a. *Pertaining to the Cimbri*, the inhabitants of the modern Jutland.—n. *The language of the Cimbri.*
Cimmerian, sim-mē'ri-an, a. Pertaining to the *Cimmerians*, who dwelt in perpetual darkness; extremely dark.
Cincture, singk'tūr, n. *That which girds*; a girdle, or something worn round the head or body. [Fr. *ceinture*—L. *cingo*, to gird.]
Cinctured, singk'tūrd, p.a. *Having a cincture* or girdle.
Cinder, sin'dėr, n. (chiefly used in the pl.) The dross of *burned coals*, &c.; ashes; a hot coal that has ceased to flame. [Fr. *cendre*—L. *cinis*, ashes.]
Cindery, sin'dėr-i, a. *Resembling cinders*, or composed of them.
Cinerary, si'ne-ra-ri, a. *Pertaining to ashes.* [L. *cinerarius*, from *cinis*, *cineris*, ashes.]
Cinnabar, sin'na-bär, n. Dragon's-blood; native red sulphuret of mercury; vermilion. [L. *cinnābaris.*]
Cinnamon, sin'na-mon, n. The spicy bark of a tree of Ceylon. [L. *cinnamōmum*—Heb. *kinnāmōn.*]
Cipher, sī'fėr, n. Any mark used in *numberings*; a character (0) which, standing by itself, expresses nothing, but when placed at the right hand of a whole number increases its value tenfold; an intertexture of letters, as the initials of a name; a device; disguised manner of writing; a person of no character.—*vi*. To compute by figures; to practise arithmetic. [Low L. *ciphra*, numeral marks.]
Ciphering, sī'fėr-ing, p.n. The art of computing by numbers.
Circle, sėr'kl, n. *That which goes round about*; a ring, a plane figure contained by a curved line, every point of which is equally distant from a point within the figure, called the centre; the curved line itself; a series ending where it begins; an inconclusive form of argument; circuit; inclosure; a class or society.—*vt*. *To move round*; to encircle; to inclose.—*vi*. *To move circularly*. ppr. circling, pret. & pp. circled. [Fr. *cercle*—L. *circulus.*]
Circled, sėr'kld, p.a. *Having the form of a circle*; round.
Circlet, sėr'klet, n. *A little circle*; a circle; an orb.
Circling, sėr'kl-ing, p.a. *Going round*; encompassing; inclosing.
Circuit, sėr'kit, n. *Act of going round*; the space inclosed in a circle; space measured by travelling round; the journey of judges through several counties to hold courts; the district visited by judges. [Fr.—L. *circum*, and *eo*, to go.]
Circuitous, sėr-kū'it-us, a. *Going in a circuit*; round about; not direct.
Circuitously, sėr-kū'it-us-li, adv. *In a circuit.*
Circular, sėr'kū-lėr, a. Round; successive in order; always returning; addressed to a number of persons.—n. A paper addressed to a number of individuals. [L. *circulāris.*]
Circulate, sėr'kū-lāt, vi. *To move round*, and return to the same point; to spread; to have currency.—*vt*. To spread; to give currency to. ppr. circulating, pret. & pp. circulated.—n. *A circulating decimal.* [L. *circulo, circulātus*—Syr. *karak*, to surround.]
Circulating, sėr'kū-lāt-ing, p.a. Having two or more figures which are constantly repeated in the same order; as, a *circulating* decimal.
Circulation, sėr-kū-lā'shon, n. *Act of circulating*; state of being circulated; diffusion; currency.
Circulatory, sėr'kū-la-tō-ri, a. *Circular; circulating.*
Circumambient, sėr-kum-am'bi-ent, a. *Surrounding*; encompassing. [L. *circum*, and *ambiens*, going round.]
Circumcise, sėr'kum-sīz, vt. *To cut around*; to cut off, as the foreskin, according to the Jewish law. ppr. circumcising, pret. & pp. circumcised. [L. *circumcido, circumcisus*—*caedo*, to cut.]
Circumcision, sėr-kum-si'zhon, n. The initiatory rite of the Jewish church.
Circumference, sėr-kum'fe-rens, n. The line that *is carried round a figure*; the bounding line of a circle's sphere, or round body. [L. *circumferentia*—*fero*, to bear, to carry.]
Circumflex, sėr'kum-fleks, n. A line which is *turned about*; an accent denoting a rise and fall of the voice on the same long syllable, marked in Greek thus ˜, and in Latin thus ˆ; a wavering or undulation of the voice.—*vt*. To mark or pronounce with a circumflex. [L. *circumflexus*—*flecto*, to band.]
Circumflexion, sėr-kum-flek'shon, n. The act of giving anything *a circular* direction or figure.
Circumfluent, sėr-kum'flū-ent, a. *Flowing round*; surrounding, as a fluid. [L. *circumfluens*—*fluo*, to flow.]
Circumfuse, sėr-kum-fūs', vt. *To pour round*, as a fluid; to spread round; to surround. ppr. circumfusing, pret. & pp. circumfused. [L. *circumfundo, circumfūsus*—*fundo*, to pour.]
Circumfusion, sėr-kum-fū'zhon, n. *Act of pouring or spreading round.* [L. *circumfusio.*]
Circumjacent, sėr-kum-jā'sent, a. *Lying round about.* [L. *circumjacens*—*jaceo*, to lie.]
Circumlocution, sėr-kum-lō-kū'shon, n. *A circuitous speech*; the use of a number of words to express an idea instead of a single term. [L. *circumlocutio*—*loquor*, to speak.]
Circumlocutory, sėr-kum-lok'ū-tō-ri, a. *Pertaining to circumlocution.*
Circumnavigate, sėr-kum-na'vi-gāt, vt. *To sail round*; to pass round by water. ppr. circumnavigating, pret. & pp. circumnavigated. [L. *circumnavigo*—*navis*, a ship.]
Circumnavigation, sėr-kum-na'vi-gā'shon, n. *Act of circumnavigating.*
Circumnavigator, sėr-kum-na'vi-gāt-ėr, n. *One who sails round.*
Circumpolar, sėr-kum-pōl'ėr, a. *Situated about* or near the pole. [L. *circum* and Eng. *polar.*]
Circumrotary, sėr-kum-rō'ta-ri, a. *Turning or whirling round, as a wheel.*
Circumrotation, sėr-kum'rō-tā'shon, n. *Act of turning round, as a wheel*; the state of being whirled round. [L. *circum* and *rotatio.*]
Circumscribe, sėr'kum-skrīb, vt. *To write around*; to limit; to restrict. ppr. circumscribing, pret. & pp. cir-

Fāte, fär, fat, fall; mē, met, hėr; pīne, pin; nōte, not, mōve; tūbe, tub, bull; oil, pound.

cumscribed. [L. *circumscribo—scribo*, to write.]
Circumscribed, sĕr'kum-skrībd, *p.a.* Limited; confined.
Circumspect, sĕr'kum-spekt, *a.* *Watchful on all sides*; wary; thoughtful. [L. *circumspectus—specio*, to view.]
Circumspection, sĕr-kum-spek'shon, *n.* Watchfulness; deliberation; wariness. [L. *circumspectio*.]
Circumspectly, sĕr'kum-spekt-li, *adv.* With circumspection.
Circumspectness, sĕr'kum-spekt-nes, *n.* Caution; vigilance.
Circumstance, sĕr'kum-stans, *n.* A surrounding; something attending, or relative to a main fact or case; accident; event; (pl.) state of affairs; one's state or condition in life; station. [L. *circumstantia—sto*, to stand.]
Circumstantial, sĕr-kum-stan'shi-al, *a.* Consisting in or pertaining to circumstances; attending; incidental; particular.—*n. pl.* Circumstantials are things only incidental to the main subject.
Circumstantially, sĕr-kum-stan'shi-al-li, *adv.* According to circumstances; accidentally; minutely; exactly.
Circumstantiate, sĕr-kum-stan'shi-āt, *vt.* To confirm by circumstances; to describe minutely. *ppr.* circumstantiating, *pret. & pp.* circumstantiated.
Circumvallation, sĕr-kum'val-lā"shon, *n. A surrounding with a wall or trench*, as a camp or besieged place; the wall or trench which thus surrounds. [L. *vallum*, a palisaded rampart.]
Circumvent, sĕr-kum-vent', *vt. To come round about;* to ensnare; to impose on; to cheat. [L. *venio*, *ventum*, to come.]
Circumvention, sĕr-kum-ven'shon, *n.* Fraud; imposture; delusion.
Circus, sĕr'kus, *n.* *Circuses*, *pl.* A circlet; a round building for the exhibition of shows and feats of horsemanship; the open space inclosed, in which were exhibited games and shows. [L.]
Cirrus, si'rus, *n.* A lock or curl; a form of high cloud composed of thin filaments; a tendril. [L.]
Cistern, sis'tern, *n.* An artificial receptacle for holding water or other liquids; a natural reservoir; a hollow place containing water. [L. *cisterna*.]
Citable, sīt'a-bl, *a.* That may be cited.
Citadel, si'ta-del, *n.* A fortress in or near a city, intended for its defence; a place of arms. [Fr. *citadelle*.]
Citation, sī-tā'shon, *n.* Act of *citing*; quotation; mention; a summons to appear in court, or before a judge. [L. *citatio—cito*, to call.]
Cite, sīt, *vt.* To summon to appear in a court; to call authoritatively; to quote; to bring forward or produce. *ppr.* citing, *pret. & pp.* cited. [L. *cito*, to call.]
Citizen, si'ti-zen, *n.* A native or inhabitant of a city; a freeman of a city; a dweller in any place.—*a.* Having the qualities of a citizen. [Fr. *citoyen*.]
Citizenship, si'ti-zen-ship, *n.* State of being vested with the rights and privileges of a citizen.
Citric, sit'rik, *a.* Belonging to citrons, or to lemons or limes.
Citron, sit'ron, *n.* The fruit of the citron tree, a large species of lemon. [Fr.]
City, si'ti, *n.* Citizenship; a large town; a borough or town corporate; properly one which is or has been the seat of a bishop or the capital of his see; the inhabitants of a city. [Fr. *cité*; L. *civitas*.]
Cives, sīvz, *n.* A species of garlic growing in tufts. [Fr. *cive*.]

Civet, si'vet, *n.* A semifluid substance taken from a bag under the tail of the civet-cat, and used as a perfume. [Fr. *civette*.]
Civet-cat, si'vet-kat, *n.* The animal that produces *civet*.
Civic, si'vik, *a.* Pertaining to a city or citizen; civil; relating to civil affairs or honours. [L. *civicus*.]
Civil, si'vil, *a.* Relating to the policy and government of a city or state; having refinement of manners; courteous; affable; political; lay; legislative, not military; intestine, not foreign. [L. *civilis—civis*, a citizen.]
Civilian, si-vil'i-an, *n.* One skilled in the civil law; one versed in law and government; one engaged in civil, not military or clerical pursuits.
Civility, si-vil'i-ti, *n.* Quality of being civil; good breeding; urbanity; courtesy; (pl.) acts of politeness. [L. *civilitas*, politeness.]
Civilization, si'vil-iz-ā"shon, *n.* Act of *civilizing*, or the state of being civilized.
Civilize, si'vil-īz, *vt.* To reclaim from a savage state; to instruct in the arts of regular life. *ppr.* civilizing, *pret. & pp.* civilized. [Fr. *civiliser*.]
Civilized, si'vil-īzd, *p.a.* Instructed in arts, learning, and civil manners.
Civilizer, si'vil-īz-ėr, *n.* He or that which *civilizes*.
Civilizing, si'vil-īz-ing, *p.a.* Instructing in arts and civility of manners.
Civilly, si'vil-li, *adv.* In a civil manner.
Clack, klak, *n.* A click; continual or excessive talk; the instrument that clacks.—*vt.* To make a sudden, sharp noise; to talk incessantly. [Fr. *claquet*, the clapper of a mill.]
Claim, klām, *vt.* To call for; to demand as due; to maintain as a right; to ask.—*n.* A demand as of right; a title to something in the possession of another; a pretension. [Old Fr. *clamer*—L. *clamo*, to cry out.]
Claimable, klām'a-bl, *a.* That may be claimed.
Claimant, klām'ant, *n.* One who claims.
Clam, klam, *vt.* To lime; to glue. *ppr.* clamming, *pret. & pp.* clammed. [Sax. *clæmian*, from *geliman*, to glue.]
Clam, klam, *n.* A bivalve shell-fish, of different kinds.
Clamant, klam'ant, *a.* Crying aloud; beseeching. [L. *clamans*.]
Clamber, klam'bėr, *vi.* To climb with difficulty, or with hands and feet. [G. *klammern*, to cling to.]
Clamminess, klam'i-nes, *n.* State of being clammy or viscous; stickiness.
Clammy, klam'i, *a.* Sticky; adhesive; glutinous. [from *clam*, to glue.]
Clamorous, klam'ėr-us, *a.* Noisy; vociferous; turbulent; boisterous.
Clamorously, klam'ėr-us-li, *adv.* With loud noise or words.
Clamour, klam'ėr, *n.* A shout or cry; outcry; loud and continued noise; uproar.—*vi.* To call aloud; to utter loud voices repeatedly; to make importunate demands. [L. *clamor*.]
Clamourer, klam'ėr-ėr, *n.* One who clamours.
Clamp, klamp, *n.* A piece of timber or of iron, used to strengthen anything, or to fasten work together.—*vt.* To fasten or strengthen with clamps. [Sax. *clam*, a bandage.]
Clan, klan, *n.* The children of a common ancestor; a race; a family; a tribe; a collection of families united under a chieftain. [Gael. *clann*, offspring, a family.]
Clandestine, klan-des'tin, *a.* Secret;

underhand; done secretly and wrongfully. [L. *clandestinus—clam*, secretly.]
Clandestinely, klan-des'tin-li, *adv.* Secretly; privately.
Clang, klang, *vi.* To make a sharp shrill sound, as by striking metallic substances.—*vt.* To strike with a sharp sound.—*n.* A sharp shrill sound, made by striking together metallic bodies; any like sound. [L. *clango*.]
Clangour, klang'gėr, *n.* A clang; a sharp, shrill, harsh sound. [L. *clangor*.]
Clank, klangk, *n.* The loud, shrill, sharp sound made by the collision of metallic bodies.—*vi.* To make a sharp shrill sound.—*vt.* To strike with a sharp sound. [L. *clangor*.]
Clannish, klan'ish, *a.* Disposed to adhere closely, as the members of a clan.
Clansman, klanz'man, *n.* One belonging to the same clan.
Clap, klap, *vt.* To strike together with a quick motion, so as to make a noise; to drive together; to strike with something broad; to shut hastily; to applaud by striking the hands together; to pat.—*vi.* To move together suddenly with noise; to strike the hands together in applause. *ppr.* clapping, *pret. & pp.* clapped or clapt.—*n.* A noise made by sudden collision; a burst of sound; a sudden explosion; act of applause. [Sax. *clappan*.]
Clapper, klap'ėr, *n.* He or that which *claps*; the tongue of a bell.
Clap-trap, klap'trap, *n.* A trick to gain applause.—*a.* Deceitful; artful.
Clare-obscure, klār'ob-skūr, *n.* Light and shade in painting. [Fr. *clair-obscur*—L. *clarus*, clear, and *obscūrus*, dark.]
Claret, kla'ret, *n.* A species of light French wine of a clear pale red colour. [Fr. *clairet*—L. *clarus*, clear.]
Clarification, kla'ri-fi-kā"shon, *n.* The clearing of liquid substances by chemical means. [L. *clarificatio*.]
Clarifier, kla'ri-fī-ėr, *n.* That which clarifies or purifies.
Clarify, kla'ri-fī, *vt.* To purify from feculent matter; to fine.—*vi.* To become clear, pure, or fine. *ppr.* clarifying, *pret. & pp.* clarified. [Fr. *clarifier*—L. *clarus*, and *facio*, to make.]
Clarion, kla'ri-on, *n.* A kind of trumpet whose tube is narrower than that of the common trumpet. [Fr. *clairon*.]
Clarionet, Clarinet, kla'ri-on-et, kla'rin-et, *n.* A small clarion; a kind of hautboy. [Fr. *clarinette*.]
Clash, klash, *vi.* To strike against with force; to meet in opposition; to interfere.—*vt.* To strike, as noisily against.—*n.* A striking together with noise; opposition. [G. *klatschen*, to clack.]
Clashing, klash'ing, *p.n.* A striking against with noise; interference.
Clasp, klasp, *n.* That which fastens; a hook for fastening; a catch; a close embrace; a throwing of the arms round.—*vt.* To shut or fasten together with a clasp; to catch and hold by twining; to inclose and hold in the hand; to embrace closely; to hug. [Gael. *clasp*, to tie.]
Clasper, klasp'ėr, *n.* He or that which *clasps*; the tendril of a vine.
Class, klas, *n.* A rank of persons or things; a division; a number of pupils of the same standing at the same school; a set of things ranged under a common denomination.—*vt.* To arrange in or into a class or classes; to arrange in sets or ranks; to classify. [Fr. *classe*—L. *classis*.]

ch, *chain*; j, *job*; g, *go*. ng, *sing*; ᴛʜ, *then*: th, *thin*: w, *wig*; wh, *whig*; zh, *azure*; †obsolete.

Class-fellow, klas'fel-lō, *n. One of the same class.*
Classic, Classical, klas'ik, klas'ik-al, *a.* Relating to ancient Greek and Roman authors of the first rank; pertaining to writers of the first rank among the moderns; of the first rank; pure; chaste; refined. [L. *classicus.*]
Classic, klas'ik, *n.* A writer whose style is pure and refined; a Greek or Roman author of this character; a book written by an author of the first class; one versed in classical authors.
Classicism, klas'i-sizm, *n.* A *classic* idiom or expression.
Classification, klas'i-fi-kā''shon, *n. Act of forming into a class or classes.* [Fr.]
Classify, klas'i-fī, *vt.* To distribute into *classes*; to arrange in sets according to some common properties. *ppr.* classifying, *pret. & pp.* classified. [Fr. *classifier*—L. *facio*, to make.]
Classman, klas'man, *n.* An Oxford scholar examined and passed for his degree, according to his merit.
Clatter, klat'tėr, *vi.* To utter repeated sharp or *rattling* sounds, by being struck together; to talk fast and idly. *vt. To strike*, so as to *make a rattling noise.—n.* A repetition of abrupt sharp sounds; tumultuous and confused noise. [D. *klateren.*]
Clause, klaz, *n.* A member of a sentence; a distinct part of a contract, will, &c. [Fr.—L. *claudo, clausum*, to shut.]
Clavicle, klā'vi-kl, *n.* The collar-bone, resembling an *ancient key*. [L. *clavicula—clavis*, a key.]
Claw, klā, *n.* The sharp hooked nail of a beast, bird, or other animal; the whole foot of an animal, armed with talons; that which resembles a claw. *vt. To scrape;* to scratch or tear in general; to tickle. [Sax.]
Clay, klā, *n. That which sticks;* a tenacious and unctuous kind of earth; earth in general.—*vt. To cover with clay;* to purify and whiten with clay, as sugar. [Sax. *claeg.*]
Clayed, klād, *p.a.* Purified and whitened with *clay.*
Clayey, klā'ē, *a.* Partaking of *clay;* like clay.
Clayish, klā'ish, *a. Partaking of the nature of clay.*
Clean, klēn, *a. Polished; pure; purified;* chaste; innocent; guiltless; clever. *adv.* Quite; perfectly.—*vt. To purify;* to cleanse. [Sax. *clan.*]
Cleanliness, klen'li-nes, *n.* Freedom from dirt, filth, or any foul matter; neatness of person or dress; purity.
Cleanly, klen'li, *a. Clean-like;* free from any foul matter; neat; carefully avoiding filth. [Sax. *clænlic.*]—*adv. In a clean manner;* neatly; without filth. [Sax. *clænlice.*]
Cleanness, klēn'nes, *n.* Freedom from dirt and foreign matter; neatness; purity; innocence.
Cleanse, klenz, *vt. To purify;* to make *clean* or pure; to remove filth from; to free from guilt or crime. *ppr.* cleansing, *pret. & pp.* cleansed. [Sax. *clansian.*]
Cleanser, klenz'ėr, *n. He or that which cleanses.*
Cleansing, klens'ing, *p.n. Act of purifying;* purging.
Clear, klēr, *a. Bright; shining;* open; fair; luminous; pure; indisputable; plain; shrill; cheerful; serene; acute; free from debt; free from guilt; innocent; freed; free from deductions. *adv.* Manifestly; quite; indicating entire separation.—*vt. To make clear;* to free from obstructions; to remove embarrassment from; to cleanse; to free from obscurity (with up); to justify; to make gain beyond all expenses and charges; to prepare, as waste land for tillage or pasture; to leap over without touching.—*vi. To become clear;* to become fair; to be disengaged. [Fr. *clair*—L. *clarus.*]
Clearance, klēr'ans, *n. Act of clearing;* a certificate that a ship or vessel has been *cleared* at the custom-house.
Clearer, klēr'ėr, *n.* One who or *that which clears* or enlightens.
Clear-headed, klēr'hed-ed, *a. Having a clear head* or understanding.
Clearing, klēr'ing, *p.n. Act of making clear;* vindication.
Clearly, klēr'li, *adv. In a clear manner.*
Clearness, klēr'nes, *n. State of being clear;* brightness; sincerity; distinctness; acuteness.
Clear-sighted, klēr'sīt-ed, *a. Seeing with clearness;* having acuteness of sight; discerning; perspicacious.
Clear-sightedness, klēr'sīt-ed-nes, *n. State of being clear-sighted.*
Cleavable, klēv'a-bl, *a. That may be cleft* or divided.
Cleavage, klēv'āj, *n. The act or manner of cleaving* or splitting. [Fr. *clivage.*]
Cleave, klēv, *vi. To stick;* to adhere with strong attachment; to be shaped or adapted. *ppr.* cleaving, *pret.* cleaved and clave, *pp.* cleaved. [Sax. *cleofian.*]
Cleave, klēv, *vt. To split;* to *rive;* to open or sever.—*vi.* To part asunder; to separate. *ppr.* cleaving, *pret.* clove or cleft, *pp.* cloven or cleft. [Sax. *cleafan.*]
Cleaver, klēv'ėr, *n. One who cleaves;* that which cleaves; a butcher's axe.
Clef, klef, *n. A key;* a character prefixed to a staff in music. [Fr.]
Cleft, kleft, *p.a.* Divided; split; parted asunder.—*n.* A space or opening made by splitting; a crevice; a fissure; a chink.
Clemency, kle'men-si, *n.* Calmness; placidness; tenderness; indulgence; a readiness to pardon or spare. [L. *clementia.*]
Clement, kle'ment, *a.* Calm; gentle; ready to pardon, forgive, or spare. [L. *clemens.*]
Clemently, kle'ment-li, *adv. With clemency.*
Clepsydra, klep'si-dra, *n.* A water-clock among the ancients. [L.]
Clergy, klėr'ji, *n.pl.* The body or order of men *chosen* or *set apart* to the service of God, in the Christian church. [Fr. *c ergé*—Gr. *kleros*, lot.]
Clergyman, klėr'ji-man, *n.* A man in holy orders; a man regularly authorized to preach the gospel and administer its ordinances.
Cleric, Clerical, kle'rik, kle'rik-al, *a.* Befitting the *clergy* or a clergyman; pertaining to a clerk or writer. [L. *c ericus.*]
Clerk, klärk, *n.* A clergyman; one who reads the responses in church; one who is employed under another as a writer. [Sax. *clerc*, from L. *clericus.*]
Clerkship, klärk'ship, *n. The office or business of a clerk.*
Clever, kle'vėr, *a. Sapacious; skilful;* adroit; acute; ready; talented; executed with ability. [Sax. *gleaw/erhth.*]
Cleverly, kle'vėr-li, *adv. In a clever manner.*
Cleverness, kle'vėr-nes, *n. Quality of being clever;* dexterity; adroitness; skill.
Clew, klū, *n. A ball;* a ball of thread; the thread that guides a person in a labyrinth; anything that directs one in an intricate case; the corner of a sail. (This word is also written *clue.*) *vt.* To truss up to the yard, as sails, in order to furling. [Sax. *cleow.*]
Click, klik, *vi. To make a small sharp noise,* or rather a succession of such sounds, as by a gentle striking.—*n.* A small sharp sound. [formed from the sound.]
Clicking, klik'ing, *p.n.* A small sharp noise.
Client, klī'ent, *n.* One who consults and employs a counsellor or lawyer. [Fr.—L. *cliens;* Sans. *sru*, to hear.]
Clientship, klī'ent-ship, *n. The condition of a client.*
Cliff, klif, *n. A cleft;* the precipitous side of a rocky mountain; a steep bank; any precipice. [Sax. *clif—cliftan*, to cleave.]
Cliffy, klif'i, *a. Having cliffs;* craggy.
Climacteric, klī-mak-te'rik, *n. A gradation* in the years of a person's life; a dangerous pause or stop in a man's life, generally determined by multiples of 7, as 35, 49, 63. [Gr. *klimaktērikos—klimax*, a ladder.]
Climacteric, klī-mak-te'rik, *a.* Noting a *scale or gradation;* denoting a critical period of human life.
Climate, klī'māt, *n.* That which *inclines* towards the poles*;* a region differing from another in respect of the seasons, dryness, wind, &c.; all those modifications of the atmosphere by which our organs are sensibly affected. [Fr. *climat*—Gr. *klinō*, to bend.]
Climatic, klī-mat'ik, *a.* Pertaining to a *climate;* limited by a climate.
Climax, klī'maks, *n. A scale or ladder;* ascent; gradation; a figure of rhetoric, in which a sentence, or series of sentences, rises in strength as it were step by step. [Gr.]
Climb, klīm, *vi. To creep up step by step;* to ascend with labour; to ascend by means of tendrils.—*vt.* To mount or ascend with labour, or a slow motion. [Sax. *climan.*]
Climber, klīm'ėr, *n.* A plant that rises on some support; a bird that climbs.
Clime, klīm, *n. A climate;* a tract or region of the earth. [L. *clima.*]
Clinch, klinsh, *vt. To rivet;* to gripe with the hand; to bend inward to the palm, as the fingers; to fasten; to make firm. *n.* Act of holding fast; a word used in a double meaning. [D. *klinken.*]
Clincher, klinsh'ėr, *n.* A cramp or holdfast; a smart reply, or the person who makes it.
Cling, kling, *vi.* To hang by twining round; to adhere closely; to stick; to infold; to embrace. *ppr.* clinging, *pret. & pp.* clung. [Sw. Goth. *klanga*, to lay hold on.]
Clinic, Clinical, klin'ik, klin'ik-al, *a. Pertaining to a bed;* relating to a sickbed; confined to bed. [Gr. *klinikos—klinō*, to lie down.]
Clink, klingk, *vt. To cause to ring;* to strike so as to make a small sharp sound, or a succession of such sounds. *vi. To ring;* to clank.—*n. A sharp sound* made by the collision of small sonorous bodies. [G. *klingen.*]
Clip, klip, *vt.* To nip, *shear*, or *divide;* to cut off with shears or scissors; to separate by a sudden stroke; to cut short.—*n.* Act or product of sheepshearing. *ppr.* clipping, *pret. & pp.* clipped. [Dan. *klippe*, to shear, to shave.]
Clipper, klip'ėr, *n. One who clips;* a sharp fast-sailing vessel.

Fāte, fär, fat, fạll; mē, met, her; pine, pin; pōte, not, mōve; tūbe, tub, bull; oil, pound.

CLIPPING   63   COADJUTOR

Clipping, klip'ing, p.n. The act of cutting off; a piece separated by clipping.
Clique, klēk, n. A party; a coterie; a faction; a cabal. [Fr.]
Cloak, klōk, n. A mantle; that which conceals; a pretext.—vt. To cover with a cloak; to hide; to veil. [Flem. klocke.]
Clock, klok, n. A machine which measures time and its divisions. [D. klok.]
Clock-work, klok'wėrk, n. The machinery and movements of a clock; well-adjusted work.
Clod, klod, n. A concreted mass; a hard lump of earth of any kind; a mass of earth cohering; a stupid fellow.—vi. To collect into a thick mass; to clot. vt. To pelt with clods. ppr. clodding, pret. & pp. clodded. [Sax. clud.]
Cloddy, klod'i, a. Consisting of clods; earthy; mean; gross.
Clodhopper, klod'hop-ėr, n. A clown.
Clog, klog, vt. To load with something that hinders motion; to hinder; to restrain.—vi. To be loaded. ppr. clogging, pret. & pp. clogged.—n. Anything laid on which retards motion; hindrance; encumbrance; a kind of shoe. [Sax. gelogian, to place upon.]
Clogged, klogd, p.a. Shackled; obstructed.
Cloggy, klog'i, a. That clogs or has power to clog; thick; gross.
Cloister, klois'tėr, n. A place inclosed; a monastery or nunnery; a square shut up within a monastery; an arcade. vt. To shut up in a cloister; to confine closely within walls; to immure. [Fr. cloître—L. claudo, clausum, to shut.]
Cloistered, klois'tėrd, p.a. Retired from the world.
Close, klōz, vt. To shut; to make fast by pressing together; to finish; to bring to a period; to cover; to overwhelm. vi. To come close together; to end. ppr. closing, pret. & pp. closed.—n. A closing; final end; a pause; a grapple in wrestling. [from a. which see.]
Close, klōs, a. Shut; tight; made fast, so as to have no opening; firm; tenacious; having no vent; confined; private; brief; near to; stingy; trusty; attentive; intense; disposed to keep secrets; wary; pressed home; warm; oppressive; strictly adhering to the original—n. A place shut up; a small field surrounded by a fence; a narrow passage.—adv. Closely; densely; pressingly. [L. clausus, shut—claudo, to shut.]
Closed, klōzd, p.a. Ended.
Close-fisted, klōs'fist-ed, a. Griping; covetous; niggardly.
Closely, klōs'li, adv. In a close manner.
Closeness, klōs'nes, n. State or quality of being close.
Closer, klōz'ėr, n. A finisher; a piece used to close in the end of a course of brickwork.
Closet, kloz'et, n. A small private apartment; any room for privacy; a cabinet. vt. To conceal; to take into a private apartment for consultation. (dimin. of the n. close.)
Closing, klōz'ing, p.a. That ends or concludes.—p.n. End; conclusion.
Closure, klō'zūr, n. That which closes or shuts; that by which separate parts are made to adhere. [L. clausūra.]
Clot, klot, n. A clod; a mass of soft or fluid matter concreted.—vi. To form into clots; to become thick; to coagulate. ppr. clotting, pret. & pp. clotted. [D. klut.]
Cloth, kloth, n. A texture formed by weaving threads of wool, linen, cotton, silk, &c., used for garments; the covering of a table; any texture or covering;

the clerical profession, as distinguished by the dress. [Sax. clath.]
Clothe, klōᴛʜ, vt. To put clothes on; to cover with dress; to furnish with raiment; to put on; to cover or spread over. ppr. clothing, pret. & pp. clothed or clad. [from the n. cloth.]
Clothes, klōᴛʜz, n.pl. of cloth. Whatever covering is worn, or made to be worn, for decency or comfort; attire; dress; blankets, &c., put upon a bed.
Clothier, klōᴛʜ'i-ėr, n. A maker or seller of cloths or clothes.
Clothing, klōᴛʜ'ing, p.n. Garments in general; raiment.
Clotted, klot'ed, p.a. Concreted into a mass.
Clotty, klot'i, a. Full of clots, or small hard masses.
Cloud, kloud, n. That which covers; a collection of watery particles, in the state of visible vapour, suspended in the air at some height, obscuring the sun, and throwing the earth into shade; a collection of smoke or dust floating in the air; anything resembling a cloud; state of obscurity; a great multitude; a crowd.—vt. To obscure; to darken; to variegate with colours resembling clouds; to give the appearance of sullenness to; to tarnish.—vi. To grow cloudy; to become obscure with clouds. [Sax. klid—hlidan, to cover.]
Cloud-capt, kloud'kapt, a. Capped with clouds; lofty.
Cloudiness, kloud'i-nes, n. Obscurity; gloom.
Cloudless, kloud'les, a. Being without a cloud; unclouded; clear; bright.
Cloudlet, kloud'let, n. A little cloud.
Cloudy, kloud'i, a. Consisting of a cloud or clouds; dark; not easily understood; indicating gloom or ill-nature; marked with veins or spots, as marble.
Clout, klout, n. A patch of cloth, leather, &c.; a rag; a piece of cloth for mean purposes.—vt. To patch; to cover with a piece of cloth or leather; to join clumsily. [Sax. clut.]
Clouted, klout'ed, p.a. Patched; mended clumsily.
Clove, klōv, n. The dried spicy bud of an East Indian tree, so called from its resemblance to a nail. [Sp. clavo—L. clavus, a nail.]
Clove, klōv, n. Cloves of garlic are the parts into which the bulb separates or divides. [Sax. clufe—cleafan, to cleave.]
Cloven-footed, Cloven-hoofed, klōv'n-fut-ed, klōv'n-höft, a. Having the foot or hoof divided into two parts, as the ox.
Clove-pink, klōv'pingk, n. The carnation pink, having an odour resembling that of the East Indian cloves.
Clover, klō'vėr, n. Trefoil, a grass of which the leaf appears as if cleft into three lobes or divisions. [Sax. clafer—cleafan, to cleave.]
Clovered, klō'vėrd, p.a. Covered with clover.
Clown, kloun, n. A clod; a coarse, ignorant, ill-bred man; a country fellow; a fool. [Sw. Goth. kluns, a clod.]
Clownish, kloun'ish, a. Resembling a clown; coarse; uncultivated.
Clownishly, kloun'ish-li, adv. In the manner of clowns.
Clownishness, kloun'ish-nes, n. Quality of being clownish.
Cloy, kloi, vt. To stop or choke up; to glut; to fill to loathing. [Old Fr. encloyer—L. clavus, a nail.]
Cloying, kloi'ing, p.a. Filling to satiety or disgust.
Club, klub, n. A cudgel; a bludgeon;

one of the four suits of cards, marked with a club or rather a clover-leaf. [G. klopfen, to strike.]
Club, klub, vi. To join and contribute a certain proportion to a common expense, and for some common end.—vt. To unite for the accomplishment of a common end.—n. An association for promoting some common object, literary, &c.; the dividing of expense at a club or social meeting. ppr. clubbing, pret. & pp. clubbed. [Sax. cloftan, to cleave, to adhere.]
Club-footed, klub'fut-ed, a. Having short, crooked, or deformed feet.
Club-house, klub'hous, n. A house where a club meets.
Club-law, klub'la, n. Government by violence; the law of brute force.
Club-moss, klub'mos, n. A kind of moss, whose minute seeds are burned in theatres to imitate lightning.
Club-room, klub röm, n. The apartment in which a club meets.
Cluck, kluk, vi. To make the noise of the domestic hen when calling her chickens. [Sax. cloccan; formed from the sound.]
Clue, klū, n. See CLEW.
Clump, klump, n. A lump; a thick, short piece of wood, or other solid substance; a cluster of trees or shrubs. [G. klump.]
Clumsily, klum'zi-li, adv. In a clumsy manner.
Clumsiness, klum'zi-nes, n. Quality of being clumsy.
Clumsy, klum'zi, a. Lumpish; unwieldy; ungainly; uncouth; ill-made; badly executed.
Cluster, klus'tėr, n. A sticking together; a bunch, as of grapes; a number of things of the same kind growing together; a knot; a number of individuals collected into a close body.—vi. To be or to keep close together; to grow in clusters or bunches; to collect together in masses.—vt. To collect into a cluster or close body. [Sax.—D. klissen, to adhere.]
Clustery, klus'tėr-i, a. Growing in clusters; full of clusters.
Clutch, kluch, vt. To catch or seize hold of; to grasp; to gripe; to close tightly. n. A grip; something that holds fast; (pl.) the claws of a rapacious animal; the hands, used as instruments of rapacity, cruelty, or power. [from Sax. gelæccan—læccan, to seize.]
Clutter, klut'tėr, n. A clatter; a bustle; disorder.—vt. To crowd together in disorder; to fill with things in confusion.—vi. To make a bustle.
Clyster, klis'tėr, n. That which cleanses; an injection; a liquid substance injected into the lower intestines, to cleanse the bowels, &c. [Gr. klustēr—kluzō, to cleanse.]
Coach, kōch, n. A carriage of pleasure or state, distinguished from a chariot by having seats fronting each other; a close four-wheeled vehicle, for commodious travelling.—vt. To convey in a coach.—vi. To ride in a coach. [Fr. coche.]
Coach-box, kōch'boks, n. The seat on which the driver of a coach sits.
Coachman, kōch'man, n. The person who drives a coach.
Coachmanship, kōch'man-ship, n. Skill in driving coaches.
Co-adaptation, kō-ad-ap-tā'shon, n. Mutual adaptation.
Co-adjust, kō-ad-just', vt. To adjust by mutual adaptation.
Coadjutor, kō-ad-jū'tėr, n. A fellow-

ch, chain; j, job; g, go; ng, sing; ᴛʜ, then; th, thin; w, wig; wh, whig; zh, azure; † obsolete.

COADJUTORSHIP 54 **COETANEOUS**

helper or assistant; an ally; an associate; a colleague.
Coadjutorship, kō-ad-jū'tėr-ship, n. Joint assistance.
Coadjutrix, kō-ad-jū'triks, n. *A female assistant.*
Coagent, kō-ā'jent, n. *A fellow-agent;* an assistant or associate in an act.
Coagulable, kō-ag'ū-la-bl, a. Capable of being concreted or curdled.
Coagulate, kō-ag'ū-lāt, vt. To curdle; to congeal.—vi. To turn from a fluid into a fixed state; to congeal. *ppr.* coagulating, *pret. & pp.* coagulated. [L. *coagulo, coagulatus—ago,* to drive.]
Coagulation, kō-ag-ū-lā'shon, n. *Act of coagulating;* state of being coagulated; the body formed by coagulating. [L. *coagulatio.*]
Coal, kōl, n. *That which burns,* giving out *heat* and *flame;* any combustible substance in a state of ignition; charcoal; a solid, black, inflammable substance dug out of the earth and used as fuel.—vt. To burn to charcoal; to char; to supply with coals.—vi. To take in coals. [Sax. *col*—Old G. *kol,* fire.]
Coal-black, kōl'blak, a. *Black as coal.*
Coalesce, kō-al-es', vi. *To grow together;* to unite and adhere in one body. *ppr.* coalescing, *pret. & pp.* coalesced. [L. *coalesco—alo,* to nourish.]
Coalescence, kō-al-es'ens, n. *Act of coalescing;* state of being united; union.
Coalescent, kō-al-es'ent, a. *Coalescing;* joined; united.
Coaling, kōl'ing, p.n. Act of supplying with or taking in *coals.*
Coalition kō-al-i'shon, n. *Act of coalescing;* union of persons, parties, &c., into one body or party; alliance; confederation. [Fr.]
Coalitionist, kō-al-i'shon-ist, n. *One who joins or promotes a coalition.*
Coal-mine, kōl'mīn, n. *A mine* or pit containing mineral *coal.*
Coal-pit, kōl'pit, n. *A pit where coal* is dug.
Coal-tar, kōl'tär, n. *Tar* made from *coal.*
Coal-work, kōl'wėrk, n. *A colliery.*
Coaly, kōl'i, a. *Like coal;* containing coal.
Coarse, kōrs, a. *Crass;* rude; not fine; not refined; crude; inelegant; indelicate. [L. *crassus,* thick, dense.]
Coarsely, kōrs'li, adv. *In a coarse manner.*
Coarseness, kōrs'nes, n. *Quality or state of being coarse;* grossness; rudeness; roughness.
Coast, kōst, n. *The side;* the border of a country; the sea-shore; the country near the sea-shore.—vi. To sail by or near a *coast* or shore; to sail from port to port in the same country. [Old Fr. *coste*—L. *costa,* a side.]
Coaster, kōst'ėr, n. A trading vessel, steamer, &c., which sails along *a coast.*
Coast-guard, kōst'gärd, n. A government force employed along the *coast,* to prevent smuggling.
Coasting, kōst'ing, p.a. Sailing along or near *a coast.*
Coastwise, kōst'wīz, adv. *By way of or along the coast.*
Coat, kōt, n. *That which covers the body* or a part of it; an upper or outside garment; vesture, as indicating office; hair or fur covering of animals; a membrane; a layer; a covering for defence; that on which ensigns armorial are portrayed.—vt. *To cover with a coat;* to spread over with a layer of any substance. [Fr. *cotte.*]
Coating, kōt'ing, p.n. *A covering,* or the act of covering; cloth for coats.

Coax, kōks, vt. *To wheedle;* to soothe; to persuade by fondling and flattering. [from *cosen.*]
Coaxer, kōks'ėr, n. *A wheedler.*
Coaxingly, kōks'ing-li, adv. *By coaxing.*
Cob, kob, n. *A thump;* a top or tuft; the top or head; anything round; a knob; anything round and bulky; a strong pony; a spider; a sea-mew. [W. *cob.*]
Cobalt, kō'balt, n. A mineral of grayish colour, and a metal obtained from it, which in the state of oxide yields a permanent blue. [G.]
Cobble, kob'l, vt. *To mend,* as *shoes;* to mend coarsely, as shoes; to do clumsily. *ppr.* cobbling, *pret. & pp.* cobbled. [Dan. *kobler,* to mend shoes.]
Cobbler, kob'l-ėr, n. *A mender of shoes;* a clumsy workman.
Co-bishop, kō-bish'up, n. *A joint* or co-adjutant *bishop.*
Cobnut, kob'nut, n. A large nut.
Cobweb, kob'web, n. *A spider's net or web;* any snare.—a. Fine; slight; flimsy.
Cobwebbed, kob'webd, p.a. *Covered with cobwebs.*
Cochineal, ko'chi-nēl, n. A kind of wood-louse, which forms a red or *scarlet dye;* a Mexican insect; a valuable red or scarlet dye, produced by forming these insects into a dried mass. [Sp. *cochinilla.*]
Cock, kok, n. The male of the domestic fowl, so named from his *call;* the male of other birds; a vane in the shape of a cock; a person or thing having any resemblance to a cock, in any respect; a chief man; a spout for drawing off liquids; the projecting corner of a hat; the style of a dial; the needle of a balance; part of the lock of a gun.—vt. To set erect, as a *cock* holds his head; to set, as the brim of a hat so as to make sharp corners; to set, as the hat on the head with an air of defiance; to set or draw back, as the cock of a gun in order to fire. [Sax. *cocc.*]
Cock, kok, n. *A small conical pile of hay.*—vt. To make up in *conical piles,* as hay. [from *cog.*]
Cockade, kok-ād', n. *A badge for the head,* originally a plume of *cock's* feathers; a knot of ribbon worn on the hat, usually by officers of the army or navy. [Fr. *cocarde,* from *coq,* a cock.]
Cockaded, kok-ād'ed, p.a. *Wearing a cockade.*
Cockatoo, kok-a-tö', n. *The prattler;* a bird of the parrot kind. [Fr. *caqueteur.*]
Cockatrice, kok'a-tris, n. *The cock's adder;* a serpent imagined to proceed from a cock's egg. [Sax. *cocc,* a cock, and *attr, atter,* an adder.]
Cock-boat, kok'bōt, n. A small boat.
Cockchafer, kok'chāf-ėr, n. *The beetle-chafer;* the May-bug, an insect most destructive to vegetation. [Scot. *clock,* a beetle, and *chafer.*]
Cock-crowing, kok'krō-ing, n. The time at which cocks *crow;* early morning.
Cocked, kokt, p.a. Turned up at the side.
Cocker, kok'ėr, vt. *To indulge;* to pamper (with *up*). [W. *cocru,* to indulge.]
Cockle, kok'l, n. A weed that chokes growing corn; the corn-rose. [Sax. *coccel.*]
Cockle, kok'l, n. A small *shell-fish,* having a double and *wrinkled* shell; the body or fireplace of an air-stove. [Fr. *coque, coquille*—L. *cochlea,* a snail.]
Cock-loft, kok'loft, n. *The top loft;* the upper room over the garret.

Cockney, kok'nē, n. An effeminate citizen; a native of the city London, by way of contempt.—a. Pertaining to or resembling a Cockney. [L. *coquina,* a kitchen.]
Cockneyism, kok'nē-izm, n. The peculiar dialect, &c., of a *Cockney.*
Cockpit, kok'pit, n. *A pit where game-cocks* fight; an apartment in a ship of war, where wounds are dressed.
Cockroach, kok'rōch, n. The *black beetle;* a troublesome insect infesting pantries, &c.
Cock's-comb, koks'kōm, n. *The comb of a cock;* a plant, lousewort; the plant yellow-rattle. [See COXCOMB.]
Cockswain, kok'swān, n. The *petty officer* of a small boat; an officer on board of a ship who has the care of a boat and its crew. [*Cog,* a small boat, and *swain,* a boy, a servant.]
Cocoa, kō'kō, n. A species of palm-tree and its large shelly nut; corrupted from *cacao,* a preparation made from the ground nuts of the chocolate-tree, used as a beverage. [Sp. *cóco.*]
Cocoon, kō-kön', n. The silky oblong *ball* in which the silkworm involves itself during the period of its change; the envelope of other larvæ. [Fr. *cocon.*]
Cod, Codfish, kod, kod'fish, n. A species of sea fish, much used for food, allied to the haddock. [Low L. *gadus;* Gr. *gados,* a kind of fish—the hake.]
Cod, kod, n. Any husk or case containing the seeds of a plant; a pod. [Sax. *codd.*]
Coddle, kod'l, vt. To make soft by heat of water; to fondle; to make delicate by over-nursing. *ppr.* coddling, *pret. & pp.* coddled. [from *caudle.*]
Code, kōd, n. Originally, a collection of the laws and constitutions of the Roman emperors; a digest of laws. [Fr.—L. *codex,* a book.]
Codicil, kod'i-sil, n. A writing by way of supplement to a will. [Late L. *codicillus*—L. *codex,* a book.]
Codification, kōd'i-fi-kā''shon, n. *Act or process of reducing laws to a code.* [Fr.]
Codify, kōd'i-fi, vt. *To reduce to a code.* *ppr.* codifying, *pret. & pp.* codified. [Fr. *codifier.*]
Codling, Codlin, kod'ling, kod'lin, n. An apple *coddled;* an apple not quite ripe; a cooking apple.
Codling, kod'ling, n. *A young codfish.*
Cod-liver oil, kod'li-vėr oil, n. A medicinal *oil* obtained from the *livers* of the common cod.
Coefficient, kō-ef-fi'shi-ent, a. *Jointly efficient;* acting in union to the same end.—n. *That which* unites in action with something else to produce the same effect. [L. *efficiens—facio,* to make.]
Coequal, kō-ē'kwal, a. *Jointly equal; equal to another* person or thing; of the same rank, dignity, or power.—n. One who is *equal* to another. [L. *æqualis.*]
Coerce, kō-ėrs', vt. To restrain by force; to repress; to compel. *ppr.* coercing, *pret. & pp.* coerced. [L. *coerceo—arceo,* to shut up.]
Coercion, kō-ėr'shon, n. *Act of coercing;* restraint; check; compulsion; force.
Coercive, kō-ėrs'iv, a. *That has power to coerce;* constraining; forcing.
Coercively, kō-ėrs'iv-li, adv. By constraint.
Coessential, kō-es-sen'shi-al, a. *Jointly essential;* partaking of the same essence.
Coetaneous, kō-ē-tā'nē-us, a. Contem-

Fāte, fär, fat, fąll; mē, met, hėr; pīne, pin; nōte, not, mōve; tūbe, tub, bu̧ll; oil, pound.

porary in origin. [L. *coætaneus—ætas*, age.]
Coeternal, kō-ē-tér'nal, *a. Equally eternal* with another.
Coeval, kō-ē'val, *a. Of the same age*; contemporary.—*n. One of the same age*; one who begins to exist at the same time. [L. *coævus—ævum*, age.]
Coexecutor, kō-eks-ek'ū-tér, *n. A joint executor.*
Coexist, kō-egz-ist', *vi.* To live at the same time with another.
Coexistence, kō-egz-ist'ens, *n. Existence at the same time with another.*
Coexistent, kō-egz-ist'ent, *a. Existing at the same time with another.*
Coexisting, kō-egz-ist'ing, *p.a. Existing at the same time with another* (with *with*).
Coextend, kō-eks-tend', *vt.* To extend through the same space or duration with another.
Coextension, kō-eks-ten'shon, *n.* The act of extending equally, or the state of being equally extended.
Coextensive, kō-eks-ten'siv, *a. Equally extensive.*
Coffee, kof'fē, *n.* A tree and its fruit or berries; a favourite beverage made from the seeds by decoction. [Fr. *café*; Ar. *cahwa.*]
Coffee-house, kof'fē-hous, *n. A house* where *coffee* and other refreshments are supplied.
Coffee-room, kof'fē-röm, *n.* A room in which *coffee* was dispensed; a public room, often divided into boxes, in which meals or refreshments are taken.
Coffer, kof'fér, *n.* A chest for holding gold, silver, jewels, &c.; a treasure. [Fr. *coffre*—Armor. *kof*, the belly.]
Coffer-dam, kof'fér-dam, *n. A case of* piling, water-tight, serving as a barrier to exclude water in laying the foundation of piers, bridges, &c.
Coffin, kof'in, *n.* The chest in which a dead human body is buried or entombed; something hollow, or which incloses in the manner of a *coffin*.—*vi.* To inclose in a *coffin*; to confine; to cover. [Old Fr. *cofin*, a basket—L. *cophinus.*]
Cog, kog, *vt.* To deceive; to delude; to falsify; to defraud —*vi.* To deceive; to cheat; to lie; to wheedle. *ppr.* cogging, *pret. & pp.* cogged. [W. *coegiaw.*]
Cog, kog, *n.* The tooth of a wheel.—*vt.* To fix a *cog* into, as into the rim of a wheel; to furnish with cogs. *ppr.* cogging, *pret. & pp.* cogged. [Sw. *kugge*, the cog of a wheel.]
Cog, kog, *n.* A yawl or fishing-boat. [Sw. Goth. *kogg*, a kind of boat.]
Cogency, kō'jen-si, *n. Urgency*; united force; compelling power; strength. [from L. *cogens*, driving—*ago*, to impel.]
Cogent, kō'jent, *a. Having and exercising united force*; powerful; urgent; irresistible. [L. *cogens, cogentis.*]
Cogently, kō'jent-li, *adv. In a cogent manner.*
Cogitate, koj'it-at, *vi.* To engage in continuous *thought*; to reflect; to meditate. *ppr.* cogitating, *pret. & pp.* cogitated. [L. *cogito, cogitatus—agito*, to put in motion—*ago*, to rouse.]
Cogitation, koj-it-ā'shon, *n.* Act of thinking much or deeply; thought; contemplation; purpose. [L. *cogitatio.*]
Cogitative, koj'it-āt-iv, *a. Thinking* much; having the power of thinking.
Cognate, kog'nat, *a. Born of the same* stock; akin; of the same nature. [L. *cognatus—natus*, born.]
Cogniac, Cognac, kō'ni-ak, kō'ni-ak, *n.*

The best kind of brandy, so named from a town in France.
Cognition, kog-ni'shon, *n.* Certain *knowledge*, as from personal view or experience. [L. *cognitio—nosco*, to know.]
Cognizable, kog'niz-a-bl, *a.* That may be *known*; that falls or may fall under notice; that may be tried and determined. [Fr. *connaissable.*]
Cognizance, kog'niz-ans, *n. Judicial knowledge*; trial, or right to try and determine; knowledge; that by which a person is known; a badge. [Fr. *connaissance.*]
Cognizant, kog'niz-ant, *a. Having knowledge of.* [Old Fr.]
Cognomen, kog-nō'men, *n.* A name added to a family name; a surname. [L. *nomen*, name.]
Cognominal, kog-nō'min-al, *a. Pertaining to a cognomen* or surname. [L. *nominalis*, from *nomen*.]
Cohabit, kō-hab'it, *vi. To dwell together*; to dwell or live together as husband and wife, though not legally married. [L. *habito*, to dwell—*habeo*, to have.]
Cohabitation, kō-hab-it-ā'shon, *n. Act or state of cohabiting.*
Cohabiting, kō-hab'it-ing, *p.a. Dwelling together.*
Coheir, kō-ār', *n. A joint heir.* [L. *cohæres—hæres*, an heir.]
Coheiress, kō-ār'es, *n. A joint heiress.*
Cohere, kō-hēr', *vi. To stick together*; to adhere; to remain in contact; to be suitable (with *with*). *ppr.* cohering, *pret. & pp.* cohered. [L. *cohæreo—hæreo*, to stick.]
Coherence, kō-hēr'ens, *n. A sticking together*; union of parts of the same body, or a cleaving together of two bodies, by means of attraction; connection; consistency; logical dependence.
Coherent, kō-hēr'ent, *a. Sticking together*; suitable or suited; regularly adapted; consistent.
Coherently, kō-hēr'ent-li, *adv.* In a coherent manner.
Cohesion, kō-hē'zhon, *n. Act of sticking together*; the attraction by which the particles of bodies of the same kind are kept together, and form into masses; connection; coherence. [Fr. *cohésion.*]
Cohesive, kō-hē'siv, *a. That has the* power of *cohering*; tending to unite in a mass.
Cohesiveness, kō-hē'siv-nes, *n. Quality of being cohesive.*
Cohort, kō'hort, *n.* A company of soldiers, among the Romans, being the tenth part of a legion; a body of warriors in general. [L. *cohors, cohortis.*]
Coif, koif, *n. A kind of caul or cap worn* on the head.—*vt. To cover or dress with a coif.* [Fr. *coife*—L. *caput*, the head.]
Coignet, koin, *n.* A corner or external angle; a jutting point, as of a wall.
Coil, koil, *vt. To gather*, as a line or cord, into a circular form; to wind into a ring, as a serpent or a rope.—*n.* A rope *gathered* into a ring; a noise; tumult. [Fr. *cueillir*—L. *colligo*, to collect—*lego*, to gather.]
Coin, koin, *n. A wedge*; a piece of metal, as gold, &c., legally stamped, and made current as money; that which serves for payment.—*vt.* To *stamp* legally, as a metal, and convert it into *money*; to mint; to form by stamping; to invent; to forge; to fabricate. [Fr.; L. *cuneus*, a wedge.]
Coinage, koin'āj, *n.* The act or art of stamping metallic money; metal legally stamped and rendered current

as money; coin; coins of a particular stamp; expense of coining; new production; fabrication.
Coincide, kō-in-sīd', *vi.* To fall in together, as two things; to fall upon and agree with the same point, line, or surface; to concur; to be consistent; to agree (with *with*). *ppr.* coinciding, *pret. & pp.* coincided. [L. *coincido—cado*, to fall.]
Coincidence, kō-in'si-dens, *n. Concurrence*; consistency; agreement.
Coincident, kō-in'si-dent, *a.* Meeting and agreeing, as lines, surfaces, or bodies; consistent; accordant.
Coincidently, kō-in'si-dent-li, *adv. In a coincident manner.*
Coiner, koin'ér, *n. One who coins*; a minter; a forger; an inventor.
Coining, koin'ing, *p.a.* The act, art, or practice of stamping metallic money.
Coition, kō-i'shon, *n. A going together*; sexual intercourse. [L. *coitio—eo, itum*, to go.]
Cojuror, kō-jū'rér, *n. A fellow-juror*; one who swears to another's credibility.
Coke, kōk, *n.* Pitcoal *burned to charcoal*, or fossil coal charred.—*vt.* To convert into *coke*. *ppr.* coking, *pret. & pp.* coked. [from L. *coquo*, to bake, to burn.]
Colander, kol'an-dér, *n.* A *strainer*; a sieve. [L. *colo, colatus*, to strain.]
Cold, kōld, *a.* Not hot; chill; shivering; frigid; indifferent; reserved; without heat or affection; stoical; unaffecting; exciting no interest or feeling.—*n.* Absence of heat; sensation produced by the escape of heat; cause of the sensation; coldness; chilliness; a shivering; a disease occasioned by cold; catarrh. [Sax. *ceald*—G. *kalt.*]
Cold-blooded, kōld'blud-ed, *a. Having cold blood*; without sensibility or feeling.
Coldish, kōld'ish, *a. Somewhat cold.*
Coldly, kōld'li, *adv. In a cold manner.*
Coldness, kōld'nes, *n.* Want of heat; unconcern; frigidity of temper; disregard; reserve.
Cole, kōl, *n.* A kind of cabbage. [Sax. *cawl.*]
Colewort, kōl'wért, *n. A plant* which has a *stalk*; a species of cabbage. [Sax. *cawlwyrt.*]
Colic, kol'ik, *n.* A painful flatulence in the stomach or bowels. [L. *colicus*, pertaining to the colic.]
Collaborator, kol-lab'ō-rāt-ér, *n. An associate in labour*, particularly literary or scientific. [Fr. *collaborateur*; L. *laboro, laboratus*, to labour.]
Collapse, kol-laps', *n. A closing by falling together*; a wasting of the body; extreme depression of the bodily energies.—*vi. To fall together*, as the two sides of a vessel; to shrink up; to waste away. *ppr.* collapsing, *pret. & pp.* collapsed. [from L. *collapsus—labor, lapsus*, to fall.]
Collar, kol'lér, *n. Something round the neck*; part of the dress that surrounds the neck; a badge worn round the neck by knights; something in the form of a collar; part of a horse's harness that goes round the neck.—*vt. To seize by the collar*; to put a collar on. [L. *collaris—collum*, the neck.]
Collar-bone, kol'lér-bōn, *n. A bone*, or rather two bones, of the *neck*.
Collared, kol'lérd, *p.a.* Rolled up and bound close with a string.
Collate, kol-lāt', *vt. To lay together* and compare, as manuscripts, books, &c.; to confer; to place in a benefice.—*vi.* To place in a benefice. *ppr.* collating,

ch, *chain*; j, *job*; g, *go*; ng, *sing*; ᴛʜ, *then*; th, *thin*; w, *wig*; wh, *whig*; zh, *azure*; † obsolete.

pret. & pp. collated. [L. *confero, collatus—fero,* to bear or bring.]
Collateral, kol-lat'ér-al, *a. Placed side by side;* running parallel or together; not direct; descending from the same stock, but not one from the other; connected.—*n. A collateral* relation or kinsman. [L. *collateralis—latus, lateris,* a side.]
Collaterally, kol-lat'ér-al-li, *adv.* In a *collateral manner or relation.*
Collation, kol-lā'shon, *n. Act of collating;* that which is *collated;* comparison of manuscripts, books, &c.; act of placing in a benefice; a collection of several kinds of food for a repast; a repast between full meals. [L. *collatio—fero, latum,* to bring.]
Collative, kol-lāt'iv, *a.* Relating to church livings, where the bishop and patron are one and the same person.
Collator, kol-lāt'ér, *n. One who collates.*
Colleague, kol'lēg, *n.* A partner or associate in office, employment, &c.; a coadjutor. [L. *collēga—lego,* to choose.]
Collect, kol-lekt', *vt. To bring together;* to bring into one body, place, or sum; to muster; to gain by information; to infer or deduce; to bring into united action.—*vi.* To run together; to accumulate. [L. *colligo, collectum—lēgo,* to gather.]
Collect, kol'lekt, *n.* A short comprehensive prayer in the services of the Churches of England and of Rome, *collected* out of the epistle and gospel of the day; a short prayer adapted to a particular day or occasion.
Collected, kol-lekt'ed, *p.a.* Cool; firm; prepared.
Collectedly, kol-lekt'ed-li, *adv. In a collected* state or *manner.*
Collectedness, kol-lekt'ed-nes, *n. A collected state* of the mind; recovery from surprise.
Collection, kol-lek'shon, *n. Act of collecting;* that which is collected; a gathering together; a group; a compilation. [L. *collectio.*]
Collective, kol-lekt'iv, *a. Tending to collect;* gathered into a mass; congregated; united; reasoning; inferring; expressing a multitude united. [L. *collectivus.*]
Collectively, kol-lekt'iv-li, *adv. In a collected state;* in a mass or body.
Collector, kol-lekt'ér, *n.* A compiler; one who collects customs or taxes.
Collectorship, kol-lekt'ér-ship, *n. The office or district of a collector.*
College, kol'lej, *n. A community;* a number of persons living by some common rules; a society of men set apart for the promotion of learning or religion; a seminary of learning, established by authority, endowed with revenues, and possessing certain rights and privileges; an establishment or edifice for students who are acquiring languages, philosophy, &c. [L. *collegium—lego,* to choose.]
Collegian, kol-lē'ji-an, *n. A member of a college;* an inhabitant of a college.
Collegiate, kol-lē'ji-at, *a. Pertaining to* or containing *a college;* instituted after the manner of a college.
Collier, kol'li-ér, *n. One who works in a coal-mine;* a coal-merchant; a ship that carries coals. [from *coal.*]
Colliery, kol'li-é-ri, *n. A coal-mine;* the coal-trade.
Collision, kol-li'zhon, *n. Act of striking together;* state of being struck together; state of contrariety; conflict; clashing; encounter. [L. *collisio—lædo,* to strike.]
Collocate, kol'lō-kāt, *vt. To place to-*

gether; to set; to station. *ppr.* collocating, *prest. & pp.* collocated. [L. *colloco, collocatus—loco,* to place.]
Collocation, kol-lō-kā'shon, *n. Act of collocating;* a setting together; the state of being placed with something else. [L. *collocatio.*]
Collodion, kol-lō'di-on, *n. That which resembles glue;* a solution of gun-cotton in ether, used in surgery and photography. [Gr. *kollōdēs—kolla,* glue, and *eidos,* resemblance.]
Collop, kol'lop, *n.* A small slice of meat, made tender by *beating,* and to be dressed on the coals. [G. *klopps—klopfen,* to beat.]
Colloquial, kol-lō'kwi-al, *a. Pertaining* to common *conversation,* or to mutual discourse.
Colloquialism, kol-lō'kwi-al-izm, *n. A colloquial* form of expression.
Colloquy, kol'lō-kwē, *n. A speaking together; mutual discourse* of two or more; dialogue. [L. *colloquium—loquor,* to speak.]
Collude, kol-lūd', *vi. To play into the* hand of each other; to conspire in a fraud; to act in concert. *ppr.* colluding, *pret. & pp.* colluded. [L. *colludo—lūdo,* to play.]
Collusion, kol-lū'zhon, *n. Act of colluding;* fraud by concert. [L. *collusio.*]
Collusive, kol-lū'siv, *a.* Fraudulently concerted between two or more.
Collusively, kol-lū'siv-li, *adv. By collusion.*
Colocynth, kol'ō-sinth, *n.* A violent purgative. [Gr. *kolokunthis.*]
Colon, kō'lon, *n. A member;* a member of a sentence; a pause less than that of a period; the point (:) used to mark this pause; the largest of the intestines. [Gr. *kōlon.*]
Colonel, kér'nel, *n.* The chief commander of a regiment of troops. [Fr.—L. *columna,* a column.]
Colonelcy, kér'nel-si, *n. The office, rank, or commission of a colonel.*
Colonial, ko-lō'ni-al, *a. Pertaining to a colony.*
Colonist, ko'lon-ist, *n. An inhabitant of a colony.*
Colonization, ko'lon-iz-ā"shon, *n. Act of colonising,* or state of being colonized.
Colonize, ko'lon-iz, *vt. To establish a colony* in; to migrate to and settle in as inhabitants. *ppr.* colonizing, *pret. & pp.* colonized.
Colonnade, ko-lon-ād', *n. A range of columns* placed at regular intervals. [It. *colonnata.*]
Colony, ko'lō-ni, *n.* A body of people transplanted from their mother country to inhabit some distant place; the country colonized; the body of inhabitants in a territory colonized. [L. *colonia—colo,* to cultivate.]
Colophon, ko'lo-fōn, *n.* Conclusion of a book, generally containing the place or the year, or both, of its publication. [Gr. *kolophōn,* a summit, top.]
Colossal, kō-los'al, *a. Like a colossus;* very large; huge; gigantic.
Colossus, kō-los'us, *n.* A statue of a gigantic size at Rhodes. [L.]
Colour, kul'ér, *n.* Hue; tint; the appearance which bodies present to the eye, or a sensation caused by the rays of light reflected from bodies; a red colour, as of the cheeks; appearance to the mind; pretence; semblance; (pl.) a flag; substances used for colouring by painters.—*vt. To give* some kind of *colour to;* to tinge; to give a specious appearance to; to set in a fair light; to make plausible; to exaggerate in

representation.—*vi. To show colour;* to turn red; to blush. [L. *color.*]
Colourable, kul'ér-a-bl, *a.* Designed to cover or conceal; specious; plausible.
Colourably, kul'ér-a-bli, *adv.* Speciously; plausibly.
Colour-blindness, kul'ér-blind-nes, *n.* Inability to distinguish *colours.*
Coloured, kul'érd, *p.a.* Tinged; having a specious appearance.
Colouring, kul'ér-ing, *p.n. Act of giving a colour to;* the state of being coloured; fair artificial representation.
Colourist, kul'ér-ist, *n. One who colours;* a painter who excels in giving the proper colours to his designs.
Colourless, kul'ér-les, *a. Destitute of colour;* transparent.
Colportage, kol'pōr-tāj, *n.* The system of distributing tracts, &c., by *colporteurs.*
Colporteur, Colporter, kol'pōr-tér, kol'-pōr-tér, *n.* One who travels for the sale and distribution of religious tracts. [Fr. *colporteur*—L. *collum,* the neck, and *porto,* to carry.]
Colt, kōlt, *n.* A young male of the horse kind; a young foolish fellow. [Sax. *colt.*]
Colter, kōl'tér, *n. The cutter;* the fore *cutting-iron* of a plough. (Written also *coulter.*) [L. *culter,* a ploughshare.]
Coltish, kōlt'ish, *a. Like a colt;* wanton; frisky; gay.
Colt's-tooth, kōlts'tōth, *n.* A superfluous *tooth* in young horses.
Columbine, ko'lum-bīn, *a. Like or pertaining to a dove;* of a dove-colour, or like the neck of a dove.—*n.* A plant whose flowers resemble *doves* in form. [L. *columbinus—columba,* a dove.]
Columbium, kō-lum'bi-um, *n.* A rare metal.
Column, ko'lum, *n.* A round pillar; any body pressing perpendicularly on its base; anything having a columnar character. [L. *columna.*]
Columnar, ko-lum'nér, *a. Formed in columns;* having the form of columns.
Colure, kō-lūr', *n. Colures,* kō-lūrz', *pl.* Two great circles supposed to intersect each other at right angles in the poles of the world, one passing through the solstitial and the other through the equinoctial points of the ecliptic. [Gr. *kolouros—kolos,* mutilated, and *ouros,* tail.]
Coma, kō'ma, *n. Deep sleep;* stupor; a preternatural propensity to sleep. [Gr. *kōma—koimaō,* to lull to sleep.]
Comatose, kō'ma-tōs, *a. Preternaturally disposed to sleep;* lethargic; affected with stupor.
Comb, kōm, *n.* An instrument with teeth for separating, cleansing, and adjusting hair, wool, or flax; the crest of a cock; any instrument resembling a comb.—*vt.* To separate and adjust with a comb. [Sax. *camb.*]
Comb, kōm, *n.* One of the cells in which bees lodge their honey; an assemblage of such cells. [Sax. *comb.*]
Combat, kom'bat, *vi.* To fight; to contend; to contest; to act in opposition. *vt.* To oppose by force; to resist; to contend against.—*n.* A fighting; an engagement; a duel. [Fr. *combattre—battre,* to beat.]
Combatable, kom-bat'a-bl, *a. That may be combated,* disputed, or opposed.
Combatant, kom'bat-ant, *a.* Contending; disposed to contend; fit to contend.—*n. One who combats;* a fighter; a champion.
Combative, kom'bat-iv, *a. Disposed or inclined to combat;* pugnacious.
Comber, kōm'ér, *n. One who combs.*

Fāte, fär, fat, fall; mē, met, hér; pine, pin; nōte, not, move; tūbe, tub, bull; oil, pound.

Combinable, kom-bīn'a-bl, *a. Capable of combining.*
Combination, kom-bin-ā'shon, *n. Act of combining;* state of being combined: union of two or more persons or things to accomplish some object; union of numbers, quantities, or sounds; chemical union; confederacy; conspiracy. [Low L. *combinatio.*]
Combine, kom-bīn', *vt.* To cause to unite; to bring into union or confederacy.—*vi.* To come into close union; to unite; to league together; to unite chemically, and form a new compound. *ppr.* combining, *pret. & pp.* combined. [Fr. *combiner*—L. *bini*, two and two.]
Combined, kom-bīnd', *p.a.* Associated; confederated.
Combustibility, kom-bus'ti-bil″li-ti, *n. The quality of being combustible.*
Combustible, kom-bust'i-bl, *a.* Capable of catching *fire*; inflammable.—*n.* A substance easily *set on fire.* [Fr.—L. *uro*, to burn.]
Combustion, kom-bust'shon, *n. A burning*; the operation of fire on inflammable substances; chemical combination, attended with heat and light; conflagration. [Low L. *combustio.*]
Come, kum, *vi.* To move toward; to advance nearer from any distance, as opposed to *go*; to draw nigh; to reach; to happen; to appear in sight; to rise; to spring up. *ppr.* coming, *pret.* came, *pp.* come. [Sax. *cuman.*]
Comedian, ko-mē'di-an, *n. An actor or writer of comedies*; a comic actor.
Comedy, ko'mē-di, *n.* A dramatic representation of the lighter passions and actions of mankind. [L. *comœdia.*]
Comeliness, kum'li-nes, *n. The quality of being comely*; suitableness; gracefulness.
Comely, kum'li, *a. Becoming*; graceful; handsome; decent; agreeable.—*adv.* In a comely manner. [from *come* or *become.*]
Comestible, kom'es-ti-bl, *a. Suitable to be eaten.*—*n. pl. Eatables.* [L. *edo, esum*, to eat.]
Comet, kom'et, *n.* A heavenly body belonging to the solar system, having a luminous tail resembling a *long beard.* [L. *cometa*—Gr. *komē*, hair.]
Comfit, kum'fit, *n.* A dry sweetmeat; any kind of fruit or root preserved with sugar and dried. [Fr. *confiture*—L. *facio*, to make.]
Comfort, kum'fėrt, *vt. To strengthen*; to encourage; to console; to gladden. *n. That which gives strength*; support; consolation; countenance; relief; that which gives consolation; moderate enjoyment. [Fr. *conforter*—L. *fortis*, strong.]
Comfortable, kum'fėrt-a-bl, *a. Possessing comfort*; being in a state of moderate enjoyment; that affords comfort, ease, or enjoyment.
Comfortably, kum'fėrt-a-bli, *adv. In a comfortable manner.*
Comforter, kum'fėrt-ėr, *n. One who comforts*; that which gives comfort; a title given to the Holy Spirit.
Comforting, kum'fėrt-ing, *p.a.* Encouraging; consoling.
Comfortless, kum'fėrt-les, *a. Destitute of comfort*; forlorn; wretched.
Comic, kom'ik, **Comical**, kom'ik-al, *a. Relating to comedy*; raising mirth; diverting; ludicrous. [L. *comicus.*]
Comically, kom'ik-al-li, *adv. In a comical manner.*
Coming, kum'ing, *p.a. Future*; yet to come.

Comity, ko'mi-ti, *n. Courtesy*; mildness; civility; in international law, the obligation of nations to give effect to foreign laws when not injurious to their own rights. [Fr. *comité*—L. *comis*, kind.]
Comma, kom'ma, *n.* A *segment*; the point marked thus (,), noting the subordinate clauses of a sentence. [Gr. *komma—koptō*, to cut off.]
Command, kom-mand', *vt.* To enjoin authoritatively; to charge; to dictate to; to govern; to lead, as a general; to subject to the eye; to claim; to secure. *vi.* To have supreme authority.—*n. Mandate*; supreme power; control; injunction; power of overlooking; power of defending or protecting. [Fr. *commander*—L. *manus*, the hand, and *do*, to give.]
Commandant, kom-man-dant', *n. A commander*; a commanding officer of a place or of a body of forces. [Fr.]
Commander, kom-mand'ėr, *n. One who commands*; a leader; an officer in the navy, between a lieutenant and captain.
Commandery, kom-mand'ė-ri, *n.* A manor belonging to an order of knights.
Commanding, kom-mand'ing, *p.a.* Controlling by influence, authority, or dignity; imperious.
Commandingly, kom-mand'ing-li, *adv. In a commanding manner.*
Commandment, kom-mand'ment, *n.* A *command*; authority; a precept of the moral law; a law.
Commemorable, kom-mem'o-ra-bl, *a.* Worthy to be *commemorated.*
Commemorate, kom-mem'o-rāt, *vt.* To call to *remembrance* by a solemn act; to celebrate with honour and solemnity. *ppr.* commemorating, *pret. & pp.* commemorated. [L. *commemoro, commemoratus—memor*, mindful.]
Commemoration, kom-mem'o-rā″shon, *n.* Solemn celebration in honour of some person or event. [L. *commemoratio.*]
Commemorative, kom-mem'o-rāt-iv, *a. Tending to preserve in remembrance.*
Commence, kom-mens', *vi.* To take the *first step*; to begin to be.—*vt. To begin*; to enter upon; to perform the first act of. *ppr.* commencing, *pret. & pp.* commenced. [Fr. *commencer*—L. *initio*, to begin—eo, *itum*, to go.]
Commencement, kom-mens'ment, *n. Beginning*; rise; origin; first existence.
Commend, kom-mend', *vt.* To *commit to the care of*; to recommend; to represent as worthy of notice, regard, or kindness; to praise; to make acceptable or more acceptable. [L. *commendo—mando*, to put into one's hand.]
Commendable, kom-mend'a-bl, *a.* Worthy of approbation or praise.
Commendation, kom-men-dā'shon, *n.* Praise; recommendation; approval; (pl.) regards; compliments. [L. *commendatio.*]
Commendatory, kom-mend'a-tō-ri, *a.* Presenting to favourable notice or reception; containing praise.
Commensurability, kom-men'sūr-a-bil″li-ti, *n. The capacity of being measured* by another, or of having a common measure. [Fr. *commensurabilité*—L. *mensūra*, measure.]
Commensurable, kom-men'sūr-a-bl, *a.* That may be *measured* by the same number or quantity. [Fr.]
Commensurably, kom-men'sūr-a-bli, *adv. In a commensurable manner.*
Commensurate, kom-men'sūr-āt, *a.* Proportional; *having equal measure* or extent. [Low L. *commensuratus.*]
Commensurately, kom-men'sūr-āt-li, *adv. With equal measure* or extent.
Commensurateness, kom-men'sūr-āt-nes, *n. Quality of being commensurate.*
Comment, kom-ment', *vi.* To write notes on an author; to make remarks or criticisms (with *upon*). [L. *commentor—mens*, the mind.]
Comment, kom'ment, *n.* An explanatory note; observation; criticism.
Commentary, kom'ment-a-ri, *n.* Exposition; illustration; book of annotations.
Commentator, kom'ment-āt-ėr, *n. One who comments*; one who writes annotations; an expositor; an annotator.
Commerce, kom'mėrs, *n. An interchange of goods, &c., between* nations or individuals, either by barter or by purchase and sale; trade; intercourse; fellowship. [Fr.—L. *merx, mercis*, wares.]
Commercial, kom-mėr'shi-al, *a. Pertaining to commerce*; trading.
Commercially, kom-mėr'shi-al-li, *adv. In a commercial manner* or view.
Commination, kom-mi-nā'shon, *n. A threatening*; recital of God's threatenings on stated days. [L. *comminatio—minor, minatus*, to threaten.]
Comminatory, kom-mi'na-tō-ri, *a. Threatening*; denouncing punishment.
Commingle, kom-ming'gl, *vt. To mingle together*; to blend.—*vi. To unite together. ppr.* commingling, *pret. & pp.* commingled. [*con* and *mingle.*]
Comminute, kom'mi-nūt, *vt. To make small or fine*; to pulverize. *ppr.* comminuting, *pret. & pp.* comminuted. [L. *comminuo, comminutus—minuo*, to lessen—*minor*, less.]
Comminuted, kom'mi-nūt-ed, *a. Broken small* or ground down, as bone.
Comminution, kom-mi-nū'shon, *n. Act of comminuting*; pulverization.
Commiserate, kom-mis'ė-rāt, *vt. To pity*; to compassionate; to feel for; to condole with. *ppr.* commiserating, *pret. & pp.* commiserated. [L. *commiseror, commiseratus—miser*, pity—*miser*, wretched.]
Commiseration, kom-mis'ė-rā″shon, *n. Act of commiserating*; pity. [L. *commiseratio.*]
Commissariat, kom-mis-sā'ri-at, *n.* That department of the service which is charged with the supply of provisions for the soldiers; the whole body of officers in the *commissary's* department. [Fr.]
Commissary, kom'mis-sa-ri, *n.* A delegate; a deputy; an officer of the bishop; an officer who has the charge of furnishing provisions, clothing, &c., for an army. [Fr. *commissaire*—L. *mitto, missum*, to send.]
Commissaryship, kom'mis-sa-ri-ship, *n. The office of a commissary.*
Commission, kom-mi'shon, *n.* Trust; charge; warrant; mandate; employment; a written document, investing one with an office; allowance made to an agent, &c., for transacting business; a body of men joined in an office or trust, or their appointment; perpetration.—*vt. To commit to*; to appoint; to empower. [Fr.—L. *mitto*, to send.]
Commissioned, kom-mi'shond, *p.a. Furnished with a commission*; authorized.
Commissioner, kom-mi'shon-ėr, *n. One who has a commission* from proper authority to perform some office.
Commit, kom-mit', *vt.* To put into the

hands of; to intrust; to deposit; to send to prison; to perpetrate; to endanger (with recip. pron.); to pledge by some act or step; to refer to a committee for consideration. *ppr.* committing, *pret. & pp.* committed. [L. *committo—mitto*, to send.]

Commitment, kom-mit'ment, *n.* An order for confining in prison; commission; act of pledging or endangering.

Committal, kom-mit'al, *n.* State of being *committed* to custody; a pledge, actual or implied.

Committee, kom-mit'tē, *n.* A body of persons appointed to manage any matter.

Committer, kom-mit'ėr, *n. One who commits*; one who does or perpetrates.

Commix, kom-miks', *vt.* To *mingle together*; to blend; to mix, as different substances. [L. *commisceo—misceo*, to mix.]

Commixture, kom-miks'tūr, *n. Act of mixing together*; the state of being mingled; compound.

Commode, kom-mōd', *n.* A kind of small sideboard, with drawers, shelves, &c. [Fr.]

Commodious, kom-mō'di-us, *a. Of a suitable measure*; adapted to its use or purpose; suitable; fit; comfortable. [L. *commodus—mōdus*, a measure.]

Commodiously, kom-mō'di-us-li, *adv. In a commodious manner*; suitably.

Commodiousness, kom-mō'di-us-nes, *n.* Convenience; fitness.

Commodity, kom-mo'di-ti, *n.* That which affords convenience; any article of commerce; (pl.) goods; merchandise; produce of land and manufactures. [Fr. *commodité*—L. *commoditas.*]

Commodore, kom'mo-dōr, *n.* A flag-officer next in rank and command below a rear-admiral. [It. *comandatore*—L. *mando*, to place in one's hands.]

Common, kom'mon, *a.* Having no separate owner; general; free to all; popular; usual; of no rank; not noble; of little value; prostitute; both active and passive, as a verb; both masculine and feminine, as a noun.—*n.* An open tract of ground, the use of which is not appropriated to an individual, but belongs to the public or to a number. *vi.* To have a joint right with others in common ground. [L. *communis—munus*, a gift.]

Commonable, kom'mon-a-bl, *a. Held in common*; that may be pastured on common land.

Commonage, kom'mon-aj, *n.* The right of pasturing on a *common.*

Commonalty, kom'mon-al-ti, *n. The common people*; all who are below the rank of nobility; the bulk of mankind. [Fr. *communauté.*]

Common-council, kom'mon-koun-sil, *n. The council of a city or corporate town.*

Commoner, kom'mon-ėr, *n. One of the common people*; a member of the House of Commons; a student of the second rank in the university of Oxford.

Common-law, kom'mon-la, *n.* The unwritten law, which has been established by immemorial usage.

Commonly, kom'mon-li, *adv.* Usually.

Commonness, kom'mon-nes, *n. State or quality of being common or usual*; frequent occurrence.

Commonplace, kom'mon-plas, *n.* A source of argument; a usual topic on any subject; a memorandum.—*a.* Ordinary; common; trite.

Common-prayer, kom'mon-prā-ėr, *n.* A formulary of public worship; the liturgy of the Church of England.

Commons, kom'monz, *n.pl. The common people*, who possess no honours or titles; the lower House of Parliament; food provided at a common table.

Common-sense, kom'mon-sens, *n.* That plain intelligence which is *common* to mankind in general; good sense in relation to common things.

Commonwealth, kom'mon-welth, *n. The public good*; the state; body politic; a form of government; a free state; a republic. [*common* and *weal.*]

Commotion, kom-mō'shon, *n. A moving together*; violent agitation of the elements or of human passions; excitement; tumultuous disorder. [L. *commotio—moveo*, *motum*, to move.]

Commune, kom-mūn', *vi.* To converse; to confer; to meditate. *ppr.* communing, *pret. & pp.* communed. [Fr. *communier.*]

Communicability, kom-mū'ni-ka-bil''i-ti, *n. The quality of being communicable.*

Communicable, kom-mū'ni-ka-bl, *a.* Capable of being imparted from one to another. [Fr.]

Communicably, kom-mū'ni-ka-bli, *adv. With communication.*

Communicant, kom-mū'ni-kant, *n. One who communicates*; a partaker with others at the Lord's table; one who is entitled to partake of the sacrament of the Lord's supper. [L. *communicans.*]

Communicate, kom-mū'ni-kāt, *vt. To make common*; to bestow; to reveal; to publish; to give or deliver.—*vi. To share with others*; to partake of the Lord's supper; to have a passage from one to another; to have intercourse (with *with*). *ppr.* communicating, *pret. & pp.* communicated. [L. *communico, communicatus—communis*, common.]

Communicated, kom-mū'ni-kāt-ed, *p.a.* Bestowed; delivered.

Communication, kom-mū'ni-kā''shon, *n. Act of communicating*; that which is communicated; intercourse; a letter or despatch received; conference; a passage from one place to another. [L. *communicatio.*]

Communicative, kom-mū'ni-kāt-iv, *a. Ready to communicate*; not reserved; open; free. [Fr. *communicatif.*]

Communicativeness, kom-mū'ni-kāt-iv-nes, *n. The quality of being communicative.*

Communion, kom-mū'ni-on, *n.* A mutual participation in anything; mutual intercourse; interchange of offices; union; concord; union in religious worship; body of Christians having one common faith and discipline; celebration of the Lord's supper; the Lord's supper. [Fr.]

Community, kom-mū'ni-ti, *n. Fellowship*; mutual participation; the commonwealth; a society of persons living under the same regulations. [L. *communitas.*]

Commutability, kom-mūt'a-bil''li-ti, *n. Quality of being commutable.*

Commutable, kom-mūt'a-bl, *a. That may be exchanged*; that may be given for another. [L. *commutabilis.*]

Commutation, kom-mū-tā'shon, *n. Exchange*; equivalent; change; the substitution of a less for a greater penalty. [L. *commutatio.*]

Commutative, kom-mūt'āt-iv, *a. Relative to exchange*; interchangeable. [Fr. *commutatif.*]

Commute, kom-mūt', *vt.* To put in the place of another; to give or receive for another; to exchange; to exchange, as one punishment for another of less severity. *ppr.* commuting, *pret. & pp.* commuted. [L. *commuto—muto*, to change.]

Compact, kom-pakt', *a. Fastened together*; firm; solid; pithy; not diffuse. *vt.* To *fasten together*; to consolidate; to unite firmly. [L. *compactus—pango, pactum*, to fasten.]

Compact, kom'pakt, *n. An agreement made with any one*; a contract. [L. *compactum—paciscor*, to make a bargain—*pango*, to fasten.]

Compacted, kom-pakt'ed, *p.a.* Firmly united.

Compactly, kom-pakt'li, *adv.* Closely; densely; with close union of parts.

Compactness, kom-pakt'nes, *n.* Close union of parts; closeness; density.

Companion, kom-pa'ni-on, *n. One of the same village*; one who keeps company with another; an associate; an accomplice. [Fr. *compagnon*—L. *pagus*, a village.]

Companionable, kom-pa'ni-on-a-bl, *a. Qualified to be agreeable in company*; fit for good fellowship; sociable.

Companionless, kom-pa'ni-on-les, *a.* Having no companion.

Companionship, kom-pa'ni-on-ship, *n.* Fellowship; association.

Company, kum'pa-ni, *n.* A number of persons assembled together; an assembly; a group; a circle; a society; a corporation; partners in a firm; the soldiers united under the command of a captain; the crew of a ship, including the officers; also, a fleet.—*vi.* To associate (with *with*). *ppr.* companying, *pret. & pp.* companied. [Fr. *compagnie.*]

Comparable, kom'pa-ra-bl, *a. That may be compared*; worthy of comparison; being of equal regard. [L. *comparabilis.*]

Comparably, kom'pa-ra-bli, *adv. In a manner worthy to be compared.*

Comparative, kom-pa'ra-tiv, *a. Estimated by comparison*; not positive; having the power of comparing different things; expressing more or less, as distinguished from positive and superlative. [L. *comparativus.*]

Comparatively, kom-pa'ra-tiv-li, *adv. By comparison.*

Compare, kom-pār', *vt.* To set or bring together, as things, and to examine the relations they bear to each other; to estimate, as one thing by another; to represent as similar; to form in its several degrees of signification, as an adjective.—*vi. To hold comparison*; to be like or equal. *ppr.* comparing, *pret. & pp.* compared. [L. *comparo—păro*, to make equal.]

Comparison, kom-pa'ri-son, *n. Act of comparing*; state of being compared; proportion; the formation of an adjective in its several degrees of signification; a simile. [Fr. *comparaison.*]

Compartment, kom-pärt'ment, *n.* One of the portions into which anything is divided; a design composed of several different figures, disposed with symmetry, for ornament. [Fr. *compartiment*—L. *pars, partis*, a part.]

Compass, kum'pas, *n.* A round; a circular course; stretch; grasp; the limit of a space, and the space included; circumference; moderate bounds; limit of the voice or of sound; range of notes in a musical instrument; an instrument for directing the course of ships; an instrument for describing circles. *vt.* To pass round; to inclose or encircle; to besiege; to obtain; to procure; to purpose; to contrive. [Fr. *compas*—L. *passus*, a step.]

Fāte, fär, fat, fạll; mē, met, hėr; pīne, pin; nōte, not, mōve; tūbe, tub, bụll; oil, pound.

Compassable, kum'pas-a-bl, a. Capable of being accomplished.
Compasses, kum'pas-ez, n.pl. An instrument for describing circles, measuring figures, &c.
Compassion, kom-pa'shon, n. Fellow-suffering; fellow-feeling; pity; sympathy; commiseration. [Fr.—L. patior, passus, to suffer.]
Compassionate, kom-pa'shon-āt, a. Ready to pity; merciful; tenderhearted.—vt. To pity; to commiserate. ppr. compassionating, pret. & pp. compassionated.
Compassionately, kom-pa'shon-āt-li, adv. With compassion; mercifully.
Compatibility, kom-pat'i-bil"i-ti, n. Quality of being compatible.
Compatible, kom-pat'i-bl, a. That may bear or endure with; that may exist with; consistent; suitable; agreeable. [Fr.—L. patior, to bear.]
Compatibly, kom-pat'i-bli, adv. Fitly.
Compatriot, kom-pā'tri-ot, n. One of the same country, and having like interests and feelings. [con and patria.]
Compeer, kom-pēr', n. One who is like another; an equal; an associate. [L. compar—par, equal.]
Compel, kom-pel', vt. To drive together; to urge with force; to constrain; to necessitate. ppr. compelling, pret. & pp. compelled. [L. compello—pello, to drive.]
Compellable, kom-pel'a-bl, a. That may be driven, forced, or constrained.
Compellation, kom-pel-lā'shon, n. An addressing; a ceremonious appellation, as sire, &c. [L. compellatio—pello, to accost.]
Compend, **Compendium**, kom'pend, kom-pen'di-um, n. A hanging together; an abridgment; a summary; an epitome; a brief compilation. [L. compendium—pendo, to cause to hang down, to weigh.]
Compendious, kom-pen'di-us, a. Short; comprehensive; concise; not circuitous.
Compendiously, kom-pen'di-us-li, adv. In a short or brief manner; summarily.
Compendiousness, kom-pen'di-us-nes, n. Shortness; brevity.
Compensate, kom-pens'āt, vt. To counterbalance; to make good; to give equal value to; to make amends for; to remunerate; to requite.—vi. To make amends; to supply an equivalent (with for). ppr. compensating, pret. & pp. compensated. [L. compenso, compensatum—pendo, to weigh.]
Compensated, kom-pens'āt-ed, p.a. Recompensed; rewarded.
Compensation, kom-pens-ā'shon, n. Act of compensating; equilibrium; remuneration; amends.
Compensatory, kom-pens'ā-tō-ri, a. Serving for compensation; amends.
Compete, kom-pēt', vi. To seek for the same thing as another; to carry on competition; to strive; to contend; to claim to be equal; to come into competition (with with). ppr. competing, pret. & pp. competed. [L. competo—pēto, to seek.]
Competence, **Competency**, kom'pē-tens, kom'pē-ten-si, n. Suitableness; fitness; sufficiency without superfluity; legal capacity or right. [L. competentia.]
Competent, kom'pē-tent, a. Suitable; fit; sufficient; qualified; belonging; having adequate power or right. [L. competens.]
Competently, kom'pē-tent-li, adv. Sufficiently; adequately.
Competition, kom-pē-ti'shon, n. Mutual contest for the same object; rivalry; struggle; emulation; double claim. [Low L. competitio.]
Competitive, kom-pet'it-iv, a. Relating to competition; emulous; rival.
Competitor, kom-pet'it-ėr, n. One who competes; a rival; an opponent.
Compilation, kom-pil-ā'shon, n. Act of compiling; that which is compiled; a literary work made up of parts collected from various authors. [L. compilatio.]
Compile, kom-pīl', vt. To gather from various sources, in order to form an aggregate; to form, as a literary work by collecting parts from the same or from different authors; to arrange; to compose. ppr. compiling, pret. & pp. compiled. [L. compilo—pilo, to pillage.]
Compiler, kom-pīl'ėr, n. One who compiles.
Complacence, **Complacency**, kom-plā'sens, kom-plā'sen-si, n. State of being pleased; a feeling of quiet pleasure; the cause of pleasure; complaisance; softness of manners. [Low L. complacentia—L. placeo, to please.]
Complacent, kom-plā'sent, a. Pleasing; civil; affable; mild; complaisant. [L. complacens.]
Complacently, kom-plā'sent-li, adv. In a complacent manner; softly.
Complain, kom-plān', vi. To express grief, sorrow, or distress; to lament; to repine; to murmur; to express a sense of injury or wrong; to charge; to inform against (with of). [Fr. complaindre—L. plango, to lament aloud.]
Complainant, kom-plān'ant, n. One who complains; one who urges a suit; a plaintiff. [Fr. complaignant.]
Complainer, kom-plān'ėr, n. One who complains.
Complaining, kom-plān'ing, p.a. Querulous; finding fault.
Complaint, kom-plānt', n. Expression of grief, regret, pain, censure, or resentment; lamentation; murmuring; accusation; information against; a malady. [Fr. complainte.]
Complaisance, kom'plā-zans, n. A pleasing deportment; courtesy; urbanity. [Fr.—L. placeo, to please.]
Complaisant, kom'plā-zant, a. Pleasing in manners; desirous to please; courteous; affable. [Fr.]
Complaisantly, kom'plā-zant-li, adv. With complaisance.
Complement, kom'plē-ment, n. That which fills up; completion; full quantity or number. [L. complementum—pleo, to fill.]
Complementary, kom-plē-ment'a-ri, a. Completing; supplying a deficiency.
Complete, kom-plēt', a. Filled full; having no deficiency; brought to an end; finished; total; absolute.—vt. To fill full; to fill up; to finish; to accomplish; to perform; to fulfil; to execute. ppr. completing, pret. & pp. completed. [L. completus—pleo, to fill.]
Completely, kom-plēt'li, adv. Fully.
Completeness, kom-plēt'nes, n. State of being complete; perfection.
Completion, kom-plē'shon, n. Act of completing; state of being complete; fulfilment; accomplishment.
Complex, kom'pleks, a. Connected together; interwoven; involved; made up of two or more particulars or parts; composite; not simple. [L. complexus—plecto, to braid.]
Complexion, kom-plek'shon, n. The hue of the skin, particularly of the face; the colour of the external parts of a body or thing; the temperament of the body; general appearance.
Complexional, kom-plek'shon-al, a. Depending on or pertaining to complexion.
Complexioned, kom-plek'shond, p.a. Having a complexion.
Complexity, kom-pleks'i-ti, n. State of being complex; complexness; intricacy.
Complexly, kom'pleks-li, adv. In a complex manner; not simply.
Compliance, kom-plī'ans, n. Submission; concession; assent or consent; obedience.
Compliant, kom-plī'ant, a. Yielding; bending; submissive; obliging.
Compliantly, kom-plī'ant-li, adv. In a yielding manner.
Complicacy, kom'pli-ka-si, n. A state of being complex or intricate.
Complicate, kom'pli-kāt, vt. To foll and twist together; to make complex; to unite mutually or intimately; to make intricate. ppr. complicating, pret. & pp. complicated. [L. complico, complicatus—plico, to fold.]
Complicated, kom'pli-kāt-ed, p.a. Involved; composed of two or more things or parts united.
Complication, kom-pli-kā'shon, n. That which consists of many things mutually united; entanglement; intricacy. [Fr.]
Complicity, kom-plis'i-ti, n. Complication; state or condition of being an accomplice. [Fr. complicité.]
Complier, kom-plī'ėr, n. One who complies, yields, or obeys.
Compliment, kom'pli-ment, n. A courteous compliance with the wishes of another; an expression that pleases; act of civility; delicate flattery; a favour bestowed.—vt. To pay a compliment to; to bestow a favour upon; to flatter; to praise.—vt. To pass compliments. [Fr.]
Complimentary, kom-pli-ment'a-ri, a. Containing compliment; flattering.
Complot, kom'plot, n. A plotting together; a joint plot; a conspiracy. [Fr. con and plot.]
Comply, kom-plī', vi. To bend to the wishes of another; to yield or assent; to fulfil; to accord; to be obsequious (with with). ppr. complying, pret. & pp. complied. [L. plico, to fold.]
Complying, kom-plī'ing, p.a. Yielding compliance.
Component, kom-pōn'ent, a. Composing; forming one of the elements of a compound.—n. A constituent part. [L. componens—pōno, to place.]
Comport, kom-pōrt', vi. To agree with; to suit; to accord.—vt. With the reciprocal pronoun, to bear or carry one's self; to behave. [Fr. comporter—L. porto, to carry.]
Compose, kom-pōz', vt. To place together; to form, as a compound, or one entire body; to constitute; to invent and put together in order, as words, sentences, &c.; to make, as a discourse; to write, as an author; to calm; to adjust; to regulate. ppr. composing, pret. & pp. composed. [Fr. composer—L. pono, positum, to place.]
Composed, kom-pōzd', p.a. Calm; sedate; quiet; tranquil.
Composedly, kom-pōz'ed-li, adv. Calmly; seriously; sedately.
Composedness, kom-pōz'ed-nes, n. State of being composed; calmness.
Composer, kom-pōz'ėr, n. An author, especially a musical author.
Composing, kom-pōz'ing, p.a. Quieting; soothing; adjusting.

ch, chain; j, job; g, go; ng, sing; ᴛʜ, then; th, thin; w, wig; wh, whig; zh, azure; † obsolete

Composite, kom'pōz-it, *a.* Compounded; noting the last of the five orders of architecture, which is richer than the Corinthian, but less light and delicate. *n.* That which is made up of parts. [L. *compositus—pono, positum,* to place.]

Composition, kom-pō-zi'shon, *n. Act of composing* or compounding; that which is composed; the whole body or mass formed of different ingredients; a mixture; a literary or musical work; invention and arrangement of the parts of a discourse, &c.; adjustment; regulation; orderly disposition; mutual agreement to terms; agreement to receive or pay part of a debt in place of the whole; the part paid; act of setting types. [L. *compositio.*]

Compositor, kom-poz'it-ér, *n.* One who composes, or sets in order; one who sets types and makes up pages and forms. [L.]

Compost, kom'pōst, *n.* A mixture for manure, or for plastering houses. [It. *composta*—L. *pono,* to set.]

Composure, kom-pō'zhūr, *n.* A settled frame of mind; calmness; tranquillity. [from *compose.*]

Compound, kom-pound', *vt.* To put together; to mix; to adjust; to adjust or pay by agreement; to discharge, as a debt by paying a part; to unite, as two or more words so as to form one.—*vi.* To come to terms; to agree; to come to terms by granting something on each side; to discharge a debt by paying a part (with *for* or *with*). [L. *compono—pono,* to set.]

Compound, kom'pound, *a.* Composed of two or more ingredients, words, divisions, or parts.—*n.* A mass *composed* of two or more elements; the result of composition.

Compounder, kom-pound'ér, *n.* One who compounds.

Comprehend, kom-prē-hend', *vt.* To hold *in the grasp;* to embrace within limits; to contain; to imply; to conceive; to understand. [L. *comprehendo*—obsolete *hendo,* to hold.]

Comprehensible, kom-prē-hens'i-bl, *a.* That may be comprehended; intelligible. [L. *comprehensibilis.*]

Comprehension, kom-prē-hen'shon, *n. Act of comprehending;* power of comprehending; mental power to understand; quality of containing within a narrow compass. [L. *comprehensio.*]

Comprehensive, kom-prē-hens'iv, *a. Having the quality of* comprising much; capacious; large; compendious. [Fr. *compréhensif.*]

Comprehensively, kom-prē-hens'iv-li, *adv. In a comprehensive manner.*

Comprehensiveness, kom-prē-hens'iv-nes, *n. Quality of being comprehensive.*

Compress, kom-pres', *vt.* To press together by force; to squeeze; to condense; to crowd. [L. *comprimo, compressus—premo,* to press.]

Compress, kom'pres, *n.* A bolster of soft linen cloth, used in surgery to make due *pressure* upon any part.

Compressed, kom-prest', *p.a.* Forced into a narrower compass; condensed.

Compressibility, kom-pres'i-bil"li-ti, *n. The quality of being compressible.*

Compressible, kom-pres'i-bl, *a. Capable of being compressed.*

Compression, kom-pre'shon, *n. Act of compressing;* state of being compressed. [L. *compressio.*]

Comprisal, kom-priz'al, *n. Act of comprising* or comprehending.

Comprise, kom-priz', *vt.* To *comprehend;* to embrace; to contain; to inclose. *ppr.* comprising, *pret. & pp.* comprised. [Fr. *compris,* pp. of *comprendre*—L. *prehendo,* to seize.]

Compromise, kom'prō-miz, *n.* An amicable *agreement* to settle differences by mutual concessions; mutual agreement; adjustment. [Fr. *compromis.*] *vt.* To settle, as differences by mutual concessions; to commit; to pledge by some act or declaration; to accord†. *ppr.* compromising, *pret. & pp.* compromised. [L. *con,* and *promitto,* to promise.]

Compulsatory†, kom-pul'sa-tō-ri, *a.* Forcing; constraining.

Compulsion, kom-pul'shon, *n.* A *driving* or urging by *force;* state of being compelled; force; forcible constraint. [Low L. *compulsio*—L. *pello,* to drive.]

Compulsive, kom-pul'siv, *a. Having power to compel;* driving.

Compulsively, kom-pul'siv-li, *adv. By compulsion;* by force.

Compulsory, kom-pul'sō-ri, *a. Driving by violence;* constraining; forcible.

Compunction, kom-pungk'shon, *n.* A *pricking of heart;* remorse; contrition; penitential sorrow. [L. *compunctio—pungo,* to prick.]

Compunctious, kom-pungk'shi-us, *a. Pricking* the conscience; giving pain for offences committed.

Compurgation, kom-pèr-ga'shon, *n.* Act of justifying a man by the oath of others. [from L. *compurgo—purgo, purgatus,* to purge.]

Compurgator, kom-pér'gāt-ér, *n.* One who swears to the veracity or innocence of another.

Computable, kom-pūt'a-bl, *a. Capable of being computed.*

Computation, kom-pū-tā'shon, *n.* Act or process *of computing;* reckoning; estimate; sum; amount. [L. *computatio.*]

Compute, kom-pūt', *vt.* To count: to number; to estimate; to rate. *ppr.* computing, *pret. & pp.* computed. [L. *computo—puto,* to reckon.]

Computer, kom-pūt'ér, *n. One who computes;* a reckoner; a calculator.

Comrade, kom'rad, *n.* A *chamber-fellow;* a companion; an associate. [Fr. *camarade*—L. *camera,* a chamber.

Comradeship, kom'rad-ship, *n.* State of being a comrade or comrades.

Con, kon, *vt.* To *know*†; to learn; to make one's self master of; to fix in the mind or commit to memory. *ppr.* conning, *pret. & pp.* conned. [Sax. *cunnan,* to know.]

Concatenate, kon-ka'tē-nāt, *vt.* To link together; to unite in a successive series or chain. *ppr.* concatenating, *pret. & pp.* concatenated. [Low L. *concateno, concatenatus*—L. *catena,* a chain.]

Concatenation, kon-ka'tē-na"shon, *n.* A series of links united; a successive order of things depending on each other. [Low L. *concatenatio.*]

Concave, kon'kāv, *a. Hollow,* as the inner surface of a sphere; opposed to convex; vaulted; arched.—*n. A hollow;* a cavity; an arch or vault. [L. *concavus—cavus,* hollow.]

Concavity, kon-kav'i-ti, *n. Hollowness;* the internal surface of a hollow spherical body. [Low L. *concavitas.*]

Conceal, kon-sēl', *vt.* To *hide completely;* to secrete; to cover; to disguise. [Low L. *concelo—celo,* to hide.]

Concealable, kon-sēl'a-bl, *a. That may be concealed,* hid, or kept close.

Concealed, kon-sēld', *p.a.* Withdrawn from sight; covered.

Concealment, kon-sēl'ment, *n. Act of concealing;* state of being concealed; privacy; retreat; a hiding-place.

Concede, kon-sēd', *vt. To go from;* to yield; to grant, allow, or admit.—*vi.* To admit; to grant. *ppr.* conceding, *pret. & pp.* conceded. [L. *concedo—cēdo,* to go.]

Conceded, kon-sēd'ed, *p.a.* Granted.

Conceit, kon-sēt', *n.* That which the mind *takes hold* of; *conception;* fancy; fantastical notion; sentiment; self-flattering opinion; vanity. [Old Fr. *concept*—L. *capio, captum,* to take.]

Conceited, kou-sēt'ed, *p.a. Having conceit;* vain; boastful; egotistical.

Conceitedly, kon-sēt'ed-li, *adv. In a conceited manner.*

Conceitedness, kon-sēt'ed-nes, *n. State or quality of being conceited;* conceit.

Conceitless†, kon-sēt'les, *a. Without conceit;* stupid.

Conceivable, kon-sēv'a-bl, *a.* That may be imagined or thought; that may be understood or believed. [Fr. *concevable.*]

Conceivably, kon-sēv'a-bli, *adv.* In a *conceivable* or intelligible manner.

Conceive, kon-sēv', *vt.* To admit into the womb and breed; to take within the mind; to comprehend; to understand; to believe.—*vi.* To become pregnant; to understand; to think; to have a complete idea (with *of*). *ppr.* conceiving, *pret. & pp.* conceived. [Fr. *concevoir*—L. *capio,* to take.]

Concentrate, kon-sen'trāt, *vt.* To *cause to move to a common centre;* to bring nearer to each other; to combine; to condense. *ppr.* concentrating, *pret. & pp.* concentrated. [Fr. *concentrer*—L. *centrum,* a centre.]

Concentrated, kon-sen'trāt-ed, *p.a.* Reduced to narrow compass; condensed.

Concentration, kon-sen-trā'shon, *n. Act of concentrating;* state of being concentrated; condensation. [Fr.]

Concentrative, kon-sen'trāt-iv, *a. Tending to concentrate.*

Concentric, kon-sen'trik, *a. Having a common c. ntre.* [Fr. *concentrique.*]

Conception, kon-sep'shon, *n. Act of conceiving;* state of being conceived; thing conceived; image in the mind; mental faculty by which ideas are originated in the mind. [L. *conceptio—capio,* to take.]

Conceptious†, kon-sep'shi-us, *a. Apt to conceive;* pregnant.

Concern, kon-sérn', *vt.* To *separate* to one's self†; to belong to; to affect the interest of; to touch nearly; to awaken interest in; to make anxious.—*n.* That which relates or belongs to one; affair; moment; care; persons connected in business, or their affairs in general. [Fr. *concerner*—L. *cerno,* to separate.]

Concerned, kon-sérnd', *p.a.* Interested; solicitous; anxious.

Concerning, kon-sérn'ing, *prep.* Having relation to; respecting.—*n.*† Concern.

Concernment, kon-sérn'ment, *n.* Affair, importance; meddling; emotion of mind.

Concert, kon-sért', *vt. To plan together;* to contrive or adjust.—*vi.* To consult with; to contrive. [Fr. *concerter*—L. *sero, sertum,* to join together.]

Concert, kon'sért, *n.* Agreement in a design; union formed by mutual communication of views; harmony; a company of musicians playing or singing the same piece of music at the same time; or the performance of a company of performers; a singing in company.

Fāte, fär, fat, fạll; mē, met, hėr; pīne, pin; nōte, not, move; tūbe, tub, bụll; oil, pound.

Concerted, kon-sért'ed, p.a. *Mutually contrived or planned.*
Concertina, kon-sért-ē'na, n. A new musical instrument, of the accordion species.
Concerto, kon-sért'ō, n. A piece of music composed for a particular instrument to show off its power. [It.]
Concession, kon-se'shon, n. *Act of conceding;* act of granting or yielding; the thing yielded; a grant. [L. *concessio—cedo*, to go, to go away.]
Concessive, kon-ses'iv, a. *Implying concession.*
Conch, kongk, n. *A marine shell.* [L. *concha.*]
Conchology, kong-kol'o-ji, n. *The doctrine or science of shells*, and the animals that inhabit them. [Gr. *kongchē*, a shell, and *logos*, doctrine.]
Conciliate, kon-si'li-āt, vt. *To bring together;* to win, as the favour or consent; to bring to a state of friendship; to reconcile; to pacify. ppr. conciliating, pret. & pp. conciliated. [L. *concilio, conciliatus—cieo*, to bring together.]
Conciliating, kon-si'li-āt-ing, p.a. Winning; having the quality of gaining favour.
Conciliation, kon-si'li-ā"shon, n. Act of gaining favour or affection; reconciliation.
Conciliator, kon-si'li-āt-ėr, n. *One who conciliates* or reconciles.
Conciliatory, kon-si'li-a-tō-ri, a. Kind; winning; persuasive.
Concise, kon-sis', a. *Cut short;* shortened; brief; abridged; comprehensive. [L. *concisus—cœdo*, to cut.]
Concisely, kon-sis'li, adv. Briefly.
Conciseness, kon-sis'nes, n. Brevity in speaking or writing.
Concision, kon-si'shon, n. *A cutting off or separating.* [L. *concisio.*]
Conclave, kon'klāv, n. *A private apartment*, particularly the room in which the cardinals at Rome are *locked up* in privacy for the election of a pope; the assembly of cardinals thus shut up; a close assembly. [L. *conclave—clavis*, a key.]
Conclude, kon-klūd', vt. *To shut up*; to end; to determine; to decide; to deduce.—vi. To end; to determine; to settle opinion; to form a final judgment. ppr. concluding, pret. & pp. concluded. [L. *concludo—claudo*, to shut.]
Conclusion, kon-klū'zhon, n. *Act of concluding;* that which is concluded; inference; consequence; final decision; end; close. [L. *conclusio.*]
Conclusive, kon-klū'siv, a. *That concludes* or determines; final; convincing; consequential. [Fr. *conclusif.*]
Conclusively, kon-klū'siv-li, adv. Decisively; with final determination.
Conclusiveness, kon-klū'siv-nes, n. *Quality of being conclusive* or decisive.
Concoct, kon-kokt', vt. To digest; to devise; to plot; to plan. [L. *concoquo, concoctum—cōquo*, to cook.]
Concocted, kon-kokt'ed, p.a. Devised.
Concoction, kon-kok'shon, n. *Act of concocting;* digestion; act of devising anything. [L. *concoctio.*]
Concomitance, kon-kom'it-ans, n. *Accompaniment;* a going or being together, or in connection with another thing. [Low L. *concomitantia—L. comes, comitis*, a companion.]
Concomitant, kon-kom'it-ant, a. *Accompanying;* concurrent; attending. n. That which is conjoined with; a thing that accompanies another. [L. *comitor, comitans*, to accompany.]

Concomitantly, kon-kom'it-ant-li, adv. In company with others.
Concord, kong'kord, n. *Union of hearts;* union in feelings, opinions, &c.; harmony between persons or things; harmony; agreement of words in construction. [Fr. *concorde—*L. *cor, cordis*, the heart.]
Concordance, kon-kord'ans, n. Agreement; index for the investigation of the meanings of words. [Fr.]
Concordant, kon-kord'ant, a. *Agreeing together;* correspondent; harmonious. [Fr.]
Concordantly, kon-kord'ant-li, adv. *In conjunction.*
Concordat, kon-kord'at, n. An *agreement* made by a temporal sovereign with the pope relative to ecclesiastical matters. [Fr.]
Concourse, kong'kōrs, n. *A running together;* confluence; an assembly of men; an assemblage of things; the junction of two bodies†. [Fr. *concours*—L. *curro, cursum*, to run.]
Concrete, kon'krēt, a. *Grown together;* composed of particles united in one mass; congealed; existing in a subject; expressing a particular subject. n. A compound; a hard mass, formed by mixing lime, sand, pebbles, &c., together; a term which includes both the quality and the subject in which it exists. [L. *concretus—cresco, crētum*, to grow.]
Concrete, kon-krēt', vi. *To grow together;* to coalesce, as separate particles, into a mass or solid body. ppr. concreting, pret. & pp. concreted.
Concreted, kon-krēt'ed, p.a. United into a solid mass; congealed.
Concretely, kon-krēt'li, adv. *In a concrete manner.*
Concreteness, kon-krēt'nes, n. State of *being concrete.*
Concretion, kon-krē'shon, n. *Act of concreting;* state of being concreted; a mass concreted. [L. *concretio.*]
Concubinage, kon-kū'bin-āj, n. The state of living together as husband and wife without being married. [Fr.]
Concubine, kong'kū-bin, n. *A woman who cohabits with a man*, but who is not his wife; a mistress. [Fr.—L. *cubo*, to lie.]
Concupiscence, kon-kū'pis-ens, n. Irregular *desire of sexual pleasure;* inclination for unlawful enjoyments. [Low L. *concupiscentia—*L. *cupio*, to desire.]
Concupiscent†, kon-kū'pis-ent, a. Lustful; libidinous.
Concur, kon-kėr', vi. *To run together;* to unite, as in one action or opinion; to combine; to assent. ppr. concurring, pret. & pp. concurred. [L. *concurro—curro*, to run.]
Concurrence, kon-ku'rens, n. *Act of concurring;* union; joint action; joint or equal claims or rights.
Concurrent, kon-ku'rent, a. *Concurring;* acting in conjunction; accompanying; associated.—n. *That which concurs;* joint cause. [L. *concurrens.*]
Concurrently, kon-ku'rent-li, adv. With *concurrence;* unitedly.
Concurring, kon-kėr'ing, p.a. Agreeing; meeting in the same point.
Concussion, kon-ku'shon, n. *Act of shaking violently* by the impulse of another body; state of being shaken; a shock. [L. *concussio—quatio*, to shake.]
Concussive, kon-kus'iv, a. *Having the power or quality of shaking;* agitating.
Condemn, kon-dem', vt. To pronounce to be wrong; to declare to be utterly

guilty; to censure; to reprove; to reject; to declare to be forfeited; to doom to punishment; to sentence. [L. *condemno—damno*, to doom.]
Condemnation, kon-dem-nā'shon, n. *Act of condemning;* state of being condemned; sentence of punishment; cause of blame. [L. *condemnatio.*]
Condemnatory, kon-dem'na-tō-ri, a. *Condemning;* bearing condemnation.
Condemned, kon-demd', p.a. Relating to one who is sentenced to punishment.
Condemning, kon-dem'ing, p.a. Pronouncing to be wrong or guilty.
Condensable, kon-dens'a-bl, a. *Capable of being condensed.*
Condensation, kon-dens-ā'shon, a. *Act of making more dense;* state of being condensed. [Low L. *condensatio—*L. *densus*, thick.]
Condensative, kon-dens'āt-iv, a. *Having a power or tendency to condense.*
Condense, kon-dens', vt. *To make dense or compact;* to reduce into a smaller compass; to thicken; to contract.—vi. To become dense; to grow thick. ppr. condensing, pret. & pp. condensed. [L. *condenso—densus*, thick, close.]
Condensed, kon-denst', p.a. Compressed into a narrower compass.
Condenser, kon-dens'ėr, n *He or that which condenses.*
Condensing, kon-dens'ing, p.a. *Making dense;* growing dense or more dense.
Condescend, kon-dē-send', vi. *To come down to the level of another;* to descend from the privileges of superior rank; to stoop; to yield; to submit; to deign. [Fr. *condescendre—*L. *descendo—descend—scando*, to climb.]
Condescending, kon-dē-send'ing, p.a. Yielding to inferiors; courteous; obliging; kind.
Condescendingly, kon-dē-send'ing-li, adv. By way of kind concession; courteously.
Condescension, kon-dē-sen'shon, n. *Act of condescending;* courtesy; complaisance.
Condign, kon-din', a. *Wholly deserving or deserved;* well merited; suitable. [L. *condignus—dignus*, worthy.]
Condignly, kon-din'li, adv. *According to merit.*
Condiment, kon'di-ment, n. *Seasoning;* that which is used to give relish to meat, and to gratify the taste. [L. *condimentum—condio*, to make savoury.]
Condition, kon-di'shon, n. *A putting together*†; state in which things are put together; state; quality; property; a particular mode of being; external circumstances; station; case; temper; stipulation; article of agreement. [L. *conditio—do, datum*, to give.]
Conditional, kon-di'shon-al, a. Made with limitations; not absolute; made or granted on certain terms.
Conditionally, kon-di'shon-al-li, adv. With certain limitations.
Conditioned, kon-di'shond, p.a. Having a certain *condition*, state, or qualities.
Condolatory, kon-dōl'a-tō-ri, a. *Expressing condolence.*
Condole, kon-dōl', vi. *To grieve with another;* to feel and express pain at the distress of another; to sympathize. (With *with.*) ppr. condoling, pret. & pp. condoled. [L. *condoleo—doleo*, to grieve.]
Condolement, kon-dōl'ment, n. Sympathetic grief; sorrow with others.
Condolence, kon-dōl'ens, n. *Act of condoling;* grief felt and expressed for the sorrows of another; sympathy.

---
*r*b, chain; j, job; g, go; ng, sing; ᴛʜ, then; th, thin; w, wig; wh, whig; zh, asure; † obsolete.

Condone, kon-dōn', *vt.* To pardon; to overlook the offence of; said of either the husband or the wife. *ppr.* condoning, *pret. & pp.* condoned. [L. *dōno*, to remit, forgive as a debt.]

Conduce, kon-dūs', *vi.* To lead to the same end; to contribute. (With *to* or *toward*.) *ppr.* conducing, *pret. & pp.* conduced. [L. *conduco—duco*, to lead.]

Conducible, kon-dūs'i-bl, *a. Leading* or tending to; promoting; conducive. [L. *conducibilis.*]

Conducive, kon-dūs'iv, *a.* Having a tendency to promote.

Conduct, kon'dukt, *n. Guidance* of one's self; personal behaviour; deportment; life; management; escort. [L. *conductus—duco, ductum*, to lead.]

Conduct, kon-dukt', *vt.* To lead or guide; to guard on the way; to manage; to command; to behave (with recipr. pron.); to afford a passage to. [L. *conduco, conductus—duco*, to lead.]

Conductibility, kon-dukt'i-bil''i-ti, *n.* Quality of being *conductible.*

Conductible, kon-dukt'i-bl, *a.* That may be conducted or conveyed.

Conducting, kon-dukt'ing, *p.a.* Transmitting; conveying.

Conduction, kon-duk'shon, *n. Transmission by a conductor;* property by which certain bodies transmit heat or electricity through their substance. [L. *conductio.*]

Conductive, kon-dukt'iv, *a. That conducts;* directing; leading; managing.

Conductivity, kon-duk-tiv'i-ti, *n.* Power of transmitting electricity.

Conductor, kon-dukt'ėr, *n. A leader;* a director; something that conducts or guides; a body that transmits readily certain fluids.

Conductress, kon-duk'tres, *n. A female who leads* or directs; a directress.

Conduit, kon'dit, *n.* A channel or pipe to *convey* water, &c., or to drain off filth. [Fr.—L. *duco*, to lead.]

Cone, kōn, *n.* A solid body having a circle for its base, and its top *terminated in a point;* the conical fruit of several evergreen trees, as of the pine, fir, &c. [L. *conus.*]

Confabulate, kon-fab'ū-lāt, *vi.* To *talk* familiarly together. *ppr.* confabulating, *pret. & pp.* confabulated. [L. *fabulor*, to speak.]

Confabulation, kon-fab'ū-lā''shon, *n.* Easy conversation; familiar talk. [L. *confabulatio.*]

Confection, kon-fek'shon, *n.* A mixture; a sweetmeat; a preserve. [L. *confectio—facio*, to make.]

Confectionary, kon-fek'shon-a-ri, *n.* A place where sweetmeats are *made* or sold; sweetmeats in general.

Confectioner, kon-fek'shon-ėr, *n.* One whose occupation is to *make* or to sell sweetmeats, &c.

Confederacy, kon-fe'de-ra-si, *n. A league* between two or more persons or states; an alliance; a confederation; the persons or parties united by a league. [Low L. *confoederatio*—L. *foedus, foederis*, a league.]

Confederate, kon-fe'de-rāt, *a. Allied by* treaty; engaged in a confederacy.—*n. One who is united with others in a league. vi.* To *unite in a league.—vt.* To *unite in a league. ppr.* confederating, *pret. & pp.* confederated. [Low L. *confoederatus.*]

Confederated, kon-fe'de-rāt-ed, *p.a.* United in a league.

Confederation, kon-fe'de-rā''shon, *n.* A league; alliance, particularly of princes, nations, or states. [Fr. *confédération*—L. *foedus*, a league.]

Confer, kon-fėr', *vi.* To converse together; to counsel or advise with.—*vt.* To bring together, *as an offering;* to give or bestow; to grant. *ppr.* conferring, *pret. & pp.* conferred. [L. *confero—fero*, to bring.]

Conference, kon'fėr-ens, *n.* Serious discourse between two or more; conversation; a meeting for consultation, or for the adjustment of differences. [Fr. *conférence.*]

Confess, kon-fes', *vt.* To acknowledge, as a crime; to own; to admit; to avow; to assent; publicly to declare a belief in and adherence to; to declare to be true; to hear a confession, as a priest. *vi.* To make *confession,* as to a priest; to disclose. [Fr. *confesser*—L. *fateor, fassus*, to confess.]

Confessed, kon-fest', *p.a.* Owned; avowed.

Confessedly, kon-fes'ed-li, *adv.* Avowedly; undeniably.

Confession, kon-fe'shon, *n. Act of confessing;* that which is confessed; disclosure of sins or faults to a priest; a formulary of articles of faith; a creed; profession. [L. *confessio.*]

Confessional, kon-fe'shon-al, *n. The seat* where a priest sits to hear *confessums.*

Confessor, kon-fes'ėr, *n. One who confesses;* one who makes a profession of his faith in the Christian religion; a priest who hears the confessions of others (pron. kon'fes-ėr). [Fr. *confesseur.*]

Confidant, kon'fi-dant, *n. m.* **Confidante**, kon'fi-dant, *n.f. One in whom another confides;* a confidential or bosom friend. [Fr. *confident, confidente.*]

Confide, kon-fīd', *vi.* To *trust wholly;* to have a firm faith; to credit. (With *in.*)—*vt.* To *intrust;* to commit to the charge of, with a belief in the fidelity of. *ppr.* confiding, *pret. & pp.* confided. [L. *confido—fido*, to trust.]

Confidence, kon'fi-dens, *n.* Firm belief in the integrity and veracity of another, or in the truth of a fact; self-reliance; audacity; excessive boldness; ground of trust; he or that which supports; assurance of safety. [Fr.—L. *confidentia.*]

Confident, kon'fi-dent. *a. Having confidence;* trusting; positive; dogmatical; having an excess of assurance. [L. *confidens.*]

Confidential, kon-fi-den'shi-al, *a.* Admitted to *special confidence;* that is to be treated or kept in confidence; private.

Confidentially, kon-fi-den'shi-al-li, *adv. In confidence.*

Confidently, kon'fi-dent-li, *adv. In a confident manner;* positively.

Confider, kon-fīd'ėr, *n. One who confides;* one who intrusts to another.

Confiding, kon-fīd'ing, *p.a. Trusting;* reposing confidence.

Configuration, kon-fig'ūr-ā''shon, *n.* External *form;* the figure which bounds a body; relative position of the planets. [Fr.—L. *figura*, shape.]

Confinable, kon-fīn'a-bl, *a.* That may be *confined* or limited.

Confine, kon'fīn, *n. A common boundary;* limit; edge; exterior part. (Generally used in the pl.) [L. *confinis.*]

Confine, kon-fīn', *vt.* To *bound;* to shut up; to imprison; to restrain; to fasten in. *ppr.* confining, *pret. & pp.* confined. [Fr. *confiner*—L. *finis*, a boundary.]

Confined, kon-fīnd', *p.a.* Limited; secluded; close.

Confineless, kon-fīn'les, *a. Without limitation;* endless.

Confinement, kon-fīn'ment, *n. Act of confining;* state of being confined; imprisonment; seclusion.

Confiner, kon-fīn'ėr, *n.* He who or that which *confines.*

Confirm, kon-fėrm', *vt.* To *make firm* or more *firm;* to fix more firmly; to establish; to make certain by additional evidence; to put past doubt; to strengthen; to admit to the full privileges of a Christian by the imposition of a bishop's hands. [L. *confirmo—firmus*, strong.]

Confirmable, kon-fėrm'a-bl, *a. That may be confirmed*, established, or ratified.

Confirmation, kon-fėrm-ā'shon, *n. Act of confirming;* that which confirms; additional evidence; establishment; ratification; church rite by which any one is confirmed. [L. *confirmatio.*]

Confirmatory, kon-fėrm'a-tō-ri, *a. That serves to confirm;* giving additional strength, force, or stability.

Confirmed, kon-fėrmd', *p.a.* Established; admitted to the full privileges of the church.

Confirmer, kon-fėrm'ėr, *n.* He or that which *confirms.*

Confiscable, kon-fis'ka-bl, *a. That may be confiscated;* liable to forfeiture.

Confiscate, kon-fis'kāt, *vt.* To seize as forfeited to the *public treasury. ppr.* confiscating, *pret. & pp.* confiscated. [L. *confisco, confiscatus—fiscus*, a money bag, the state treasury.]

Confiscated, kon-fis'kāt-ed, *p.a.* Adjudged to the *public treasury.*

Confiscation, kon-fis-kā'shon, *n. Act of confiscating.* [L. *confiscatio.*]

Confiscator, kon-fis'kāt-ėr, *n. One who confiscates.*

Confiscatory, kon-fis'ka-tō-ri, *a.* Consigning to forfeiture.

Conflagration, kon-fla-grā'shon, *n. A burning up;* a great burning, as of many houses or a forest. [L. *conflagratio—flagro*, to burn.]

Conflict, kon'flikt, *n.* A violent collision; a combat; struggle; a striving to overcome; agony; antagonism. [L. *conflictus—fligo*, to strike.]

Conflict, kon-flikt', *vi.* To meet in violent collision; to fight; to engage in strife. [L. *confligo, conflictus—fligo*, to strike.]

Conflicting, kon-flikt'ing, *p.a. Contrary;* contradictory.

Confluence, kon'flū-ens, *n. A flowing together;* the meeting or place of meeting of two or more streams or rivers; a concourse. [L. *confluentia—fluo*, to flow.]

Confluent, kon'flū-ent, *a. Flowing together;* running into each other; united. [L. *confluens.*]

Conflux, kon'fluks, *n. A flowing together;* a concourse; a crowd; a small stream which flows into a large one. [L. *confluxio.*]

Conform, kon-form', *vt.* To *cause to be of the same form* as another; to make suitable; to make to be in uniformity with. (With *to* or *unto.*)—*vi.* To *be of the same form* as another; to comply or yield; to live or act according. (With *to.*) [L. *conformo—forma*, form.]

Conformable, kon-form'a-bl, *a. Having the same form* as another; like; resembling; in accordance or uniformity; agreeable; compliant. (Usually with *to.*)

Conformably, kon-form'a-bli, *adv.* With or in conformity; suitably.

Conformation, kon-form-ā'shon, *n.* The manner in which a body is *formed*; structure; particular make; act of conforming or of producing suitableness. [L. *conformatio*.]

Conformist, kon-form'ist, *n.* One who *conforms*; one who complies with the worship of the established church.

Conformity, kon-form'i-ti, *n.* State of being *conformed*; resemblance; agreement; compliance with. (With *to*, *with*, or *between*.)

Confound, kon-found', *vt.* To pour together; to confuse; to disorder; to perplex; to dismay; to astonish; to overthrow; to mistake by error. [Fr. *confondre*—L. *fundo*, to pour.]

Confounder, kon-found'er, *n.* One who *confounds*.

Confraternity, kon-fra-tėr'ni-ti, *n.* A brotherhood; a society or body of men united in some profession. [Fr. *confraternité*—L. *frater*, a brother.]

Confront, kon-frunt', *vt.* To stand front to front, in presence of; to face; to oppose; to bring into the presence of; to set together for comparison; to compare. [Fr. *confronter*—L. *frons*, *frontis*, the forehead.]

Confuse, kon-fūz', *vt.* To pour together; to mix, as things, so that they cannot be distinguished; to derange; to confound; to disconcert; to stupify. *ppr.* confusing, *pret. & pp.* confused. [L. *confundo*, *confūsus*—*fundo*, to pour.]

Confused, kon-fūsd', *p.a.* Perplexed; put to shame; disconcerted.

Confusedly, kon-fūz'ed-li, *adv.* In a confused manner.

Confusion, kon-fū'zhon, *n.* State of being confused; disorder; shame; agitation; overthrow; ruin.

Confutable, kon-fūt'a-bl, *a.* That may be confuted.

Confutation, kon-fūt-ā'shon, *n.* Act of confuting; refutation; overthrow.

Confute, kon-fūt', *vt.* To pour, as cold water upon hott; to prove to be false; to convict of error; to overthrow; to refute. *ppr.* confuting, *pret. & pp.* confuted. [L. *confuto*—*fundo*, to pour.]

Congé, kon'jē, *n.* Leave; farewell; act of reverence or civility; parting bow. *vi.* To take leave with the customary civilities; to bow or courtesy. [Fr. *congé*.]

Congeal, kon-jēl', *vt.* To cause to freeze wholly; to turn into ice; to bind or fix as with cold.—*vi.* To freeze wholly; to be turned into ice; to pass from a fluid to a solid state. [L. *congelo*—*gelu*, frost.]

Congealable, kon-jēl'a-bl, *a.* That may be congealed.

Congealed, kon-jēld', *p.a.* Frozen; concreted.

Congealment, kon-jēl'ment, *n.* Congelation; a clot or concretion; that which is formed by congelation.

Congelation, kon-jel-ā'shon, *n.* Act or process of congealing; state of being congealed. [L. *congelatio*.]

Congener, kon-jen'ėr, *n.* One of the same origin or kind. [L. *genus*, *generis*, kind.]

Congenial, kon-jē'ni-al, *a.* Partaking of the same nature with another; similar; kindred; natural; adapted. [L. *genialis—genius*, inclination.]

Congeniality, kon-jē-ni-al'i-ti, *n.* Participation of the same nature; natural affinity; suitableness.

Congenital, kon-jen'it-al, *a.* Of the same birth; pertaining to an individual from his birth. [L. *congenitus—gigno*, *genitum*, to beget.]

Conger, kong'gėr, *n.* The sea-eel. [L.]

Congeries, kon-jē'ri-ēz, *n.* A heap or mass; a collection of several particles or bodies in one aggregate. [L. *gero*, to bear or carry.]

Congestion, kon-jest'shon, *n.* A heaping up; undue fulness of blood-vessels; stagnation of the blood. [L. *congestio—gero*, to bear or carry.]

Congestive, kon-jest'iv, *a.* Indicating congestion, or an accumulation of blood.

Conglobate, kon-glōb'āt, *a.* Formed into a globe.—*vt.* To form into a globe or ball. *ppr.* conglobating, *pret. & pp.* conglobated. [L. *conglobatus—globus*, a ball.]

Conglobation, kon-glōb-ā'shon, *n.* Act of forming into a ball; a round body.

Conglobulate, kon-glob'ū-lāt, *vi.* To gather into a little round mass. [L. *globulus*, dimin. of *globus*.]

Conglomerate, kon-glom'ėr-āt, *a.* Rolled into a ball; formed of a collection of small glands; composed of stones or fragments of rocks cemented together.—*n.* A stone or rock composed of rounded pebbles cemented together. *vt.* To gather into a ball; to collect into a round mass. *ppr.* conglomerating, *pret. & pp.* conglomerated. [L. *conglomeratus—glomus*, *glomeris*, a ball or clue.]

Conglomerated, kon-glom'ėr-āt-ed, *p.a.* Gathered or rolled into a ball.

Conglomeration, kon-glom-ėr-ā'shon, *n.* Act of conglomerating; state of being conglomerated; collection.

Conglutinate, kon-glū'tin-āt, *vt.* To glue together; to heal by uniting. *ppr.* conglutinating, *pret. & pp.* conglutinated. [L. *conglutino*, *conglutinatus—glūten*, *glūtinis*, glue.]

Conglutination, kon-glū'tin-ā"shon, *n.* Act of gluing together; a healing by uniting the parts of a wound; union.

Conglutinative, kon-glū'tin-āt-iv, *a.* Having the power of uniting by glue or other substance of like nature.

Congratulate, kon-grat'ū-lāt, *vt.* To wish joy warmly to; to felicitate.—*vt.* To express sympathetic joy. (With *with*.) *ppr.* congratulating, *pret. & pp.* congratulated. [L. *congratulor*, *congratulatus—gratus*, pleasing.]

Congratulation, kon-grat'ū-lā"shon, *n.* Act of congratulating; an expression of sympathetic joy at the happiness or good fortune of another; the form in which joy is expressed.

Congratulator, kon-grat'ū-lāt-ėr, *n.* One who offers congratulations.

Congratulatory, kon-grat'ū-la-tō-ri, *a.* Expressing congratulation.

Congree†, kon-grē', *vi.* To agree.

Congreet†, kon-grēt', *vt.* To salute mutually.

Congregate, kong'grē-gāt, *vt.* To collect together; to assemble.—*vi.* To come together; to assemble; to meet. *ppr.* congregating, *pret. & pp.* congregated. [L. *congrego*, *congregatus—grex*, *gregis*, a flock.]

Congregated, kong'grē-gāt-ed, *p.a.* Clustered together.

Congregation, kong-grē-gā'shon, *n.* Act of congregating; an assembly; an assembly met for divine worship. [L. *congregatio*.]

Congregational, kong-grē-gā'shon-al, *a.* Pertaining to a congregation, or to the Congregationalists.

Congregationalist, kong-grē-gā'shon-al-ist, *n.* One who adheres to a mode of church government, in which each separate congregation or church forms an independent body.

Congress, kong'gres, *n.* An assembly; a meeting of ambassadors, &c., for the settlement of affairs between different nations; the legislature of the United States. [L. *congressus—gradior*, to go.]

Congruence, kong'grū-ens, *n.* A rushing together; fitness; suitableness of one thing to another; consistency. [L. *congruentia—ruo*, to rush.]

Congruent, kong'grū-ent, *a.* Suitable.

Congruity, kon-grū'i-ti, *n.* Suitableness; the relation of agreement between things; pertinence; consistency. [Fr. *congruité*.]

Congruous, kong'grū-us, *a.* Accordant; suitable; consistent; agreeable to; fit. [L. *congruus*.]

Congruously, kong'grū-us-li, *adv.* Suitably; pertinently; consistently.

Conic, Conical, kon'ik, kon'ik-al, *a.* Having the form of a cone; pertaining to a cone, or to the sections of a cone. [L. *conicus*.]

Conically, kon'ik-al-li, *adv.* In the form of a cone.

Conics, kon'iks, *n.* That part of geometry which treats of the cone and the curves which arise from its sections.

Coniferous, kōn-if'ėr-us, *a.* Bearing seed-vessels of a conical figure, as the pine, fir, &c. [L. *coniferus—conus*, and *fero*, to bear.]

Conjecturable, kon-jek'tūr-a-bl, *a.* That may be conjectured or guessed.

Conjectural, kon-jek'tūr-al, *a.* Depending on conjecture. [L. *conjecturalis*.]

Conjecturally, kon-jek'tūr-al-li, *adv.* By conjecture; by guess.

Conjecture, kon-jek'tūr, *n.* A throwing together; a casting about in the mind for something unknown; a guess; opinion without proof; surmise; notion.—*vt.* To judge of by guess, or on slight evidence; to surmise; to imagine. *vi.* To form conjectures. *ppr.* conjecturing, *pret. & pp.* conjectured. [L. *conjectūra—jacio*, *jactum*, to throw.]

Conjecturer, kon-jek'tūr-ėr, *n.* One who conjectures.

Conjoin, kon-join', *vt.* To join together; to unite in close connection; to associate.—*vi.* To meet; to join.

Conjoint, kon-joint', *p.a.* United; connected; associated.

Conjointly, kon-joint'li, *adv.* Jointly.

Conjugal, kon'jū-gal, *a.* Pertaining to the marriage-bond; belonging to marriage; connubial. [L. *conjugalis—jugum*, a yoke.]

Conjugally, kon'jū-gal-li, *adv.* Matrimonially; connubially.

Conjugate, kon'jū-gāt, *vt.* To join together; to distribute, as the inflections of a verb into the several voices, moods, tenses, numbers, and persons. *ppr.* conjugating, *pret. & pp.* conjugated. [L. *conjugo*, *conjugatus—jugum*, a yoke, a band.]

Conjugation, kon-jū-gā'shon, *n.* A joining together; the inflection of verbs, or a connected scheme of all the derivative forms of a verb. [L. *conjugatio*.]

Conjunct, kon-jungkt', *a.* United; concurrent. [L. *conjunctus*.]

Conjunction, kon-jungk'shon, *n.* Act of joining together; state of being joined; connection; a connecting word used to join sentences, parts of sentences, and words. [L. *conjunctio—jungo*, to join.]

Conjunctive, kon-jungk'tiv, *a.* Closely united; connecting together; subjunctive; serving to unite.

Conjunctively, kon-jungk'tiv-li, *adv.* In conjunction or union; together.

Conjunctly, kon-jungkt'li, *adv. Jointly*; in union; together.

Conjuncture, kon-jungk'tūr, *n. A joining together*; a combination of critical circumstances; a critical time; an occasion; concurrence. [Fr. *conjoncture*.]

Conjuration, kon-jūr-ā'shon, *n.* An invoking of supernatural aid by prayers, spells, and incantations; act of summoning in a sacred name; enchantment. [L. *conjuratio*.]

Conjure, kon-jūr', *vt.* To call upon by a sacred name; to enjoin solemnly. *ppr.* conjuring, *pret. & pp.* conjured. [L. *conjuro—juro*, to swear.]

Conjure, kun'jėr, *vt.* To bewitch; to charm; to enchant; to summon up by enchantments; to raise up needlessly. *vi.* To practise the arts of a conjurer; to use charms, magic, or sorcery. *ppr.* conjuring, *pret. & pp.* conjured. [L. *conjuro—juro*, to swear.]

Conjurer, kun'jėr-ėr, *n. One who practises conjuration*; an enchanter; a man of sagacity.

Conjuror, kon-jūr'ėr, *n. One bound by oath with others.*

Connascence, kon-nas'ens, *n.* State of being born at the same time with another; a growing together. [Low L. *nascentia—L. nascor*, to be born.]

Connate, kon'nāt, *a. Born with another*; being of the same birth; united in origin. [L. *nascor, nātus*, to be born.]

Connatural, kon-na'tūr-al, *a. Of the same nature with another*; connected by nature; united in nature.

Connect, kon-nekt', *vt. To knit together*; to conjoin; to combine; to associate. *vi.* To unite or cohere together; to have a close relation. [L. *connecto—necto*, to bind.]

Connected, kon-nekt'ed, *p.a. Linked together*; consistent; united; related.

Connectedly, kon-nekt'ed-li, *adv. In a connected manner.*

Connecting, kon-nekt'ing, *p.a.* Uniting; conjoining.

Connection, kon-nek'shon, *n. Act of connecting*; state of being connected; a relation by blood or marriage; relationship. [L. *connexio*.]

Connective, kon-nekt'iv, *a. Having the power of connecting*; tending to connect.—*n.* A word that connects other words and sentences; a conjunction.

Connector, kon-nekt'ėr, *n. He or that which connects.*

Connexion, kon-nek'shon, *n. Connection.*

Connivance, kon-niv'ans, *n. Act of winking at*; voluntary blindness to an act; intentional forbearance to see, generally implying consent. [Low L. *conniventia*.]

Connive, kon-nīv', *vi. To wink*; to pretend ignorance or blindness; to forbear to see (with *at*). *ppr.* conniving, *pret. & pp.* connived. [L. *conniveo*, akin to *nicto*, to wink.]

Connoisseur, kon'nä-sūr, *n.* A critical judge or master of any art, particularly of painting and sculpture. [Fr.—L. *nosco*, to know.]

Connoisseurship, kon'nä-sūr-ship, *n. The skill of a connoisseur.*

Connubial, kon-nū'bi-al, *a. Pertaining to marriage*; conjugal; matrimonial. [L. *connubialis—nubo*, to be married to.]

Conquer, kong'kėr, *vt.* To gain, *acquire*, or take by force; to vanquish; to subjugate; to surmount.—*vi.* To overcome; to gain the victory. [Fr. *conquerir—*L. *quæro*, to seek.]

Conquerable, kong'kėr-a-bl, *a. That may be conquered* or subdued.

Conquered, kong'kėrd, *p.a.* Gained; won.

Conquering, kong'kėr-ing, *p.a.* Vanquishing; subjugating.

Conqueror, kong'kėr-ėr, *n. One who conquers.*

Conquest, kong'kwest, *n. Act of conquering*; that which is conquered; a gaining by struggle; subjugation. [Old Fr. *conqueste*.]

Consanguineous, kon-san-gwin'ē-us, *a. Of the same blood*; descended from the same parent or ancestor. [L. *consanguineus—sanguis*, blood.]

Consanguinity, kon-san-gwin'i-ti, *n. Relationship by blood*; relationship by descent from a common ancestor. [Fr. *consanguinité*.]

Conscience, kon'shi-ens, *n. A knowing of a thing along with another*; internal knowledge of right and wrong; the moral sense; the faculty within us by which our actions are judged; the determination of conscience; justice; honesty; private thoughts; truth. [Fr.—L. *scio*, to know.]

Conscientious, kon-shi-en'shi-us, *a. Regulated by conscience*; scrupulous; just; exact.

Conscientiously, kon-shi-en'shi-us-li, *adv. According to the dictates of conscience.*

Conscientiousness, kon-shi-en'shi-us-nes, *n. Quality of being conscientious.*

Conscionable†, kon'shon-a-bl, *a.* Reasonable; just.

Conscious, kon'shi-us, *a.* Possessing the power of *knowing* one's own thoughts; knowing from memory; knowing by internal perception; made the object of consciousness; aware; sensible. [L. *conscius—scio*, to know.]

Consciously, kon'shi-us-li, *adv. In a conscious manner.*

Consciousness, kon'shi-us-nes, *n.* State of being conscious; perception of what passes in one's own mind.

Conscript, kon'skript, *a. Written down together*; enrolled.—*n.* One enrolled to serve as a soldier in the army. [L. *conscriptus—scribo, scriptum*, to write.]

Conscription, kon-skrip'shon, *n.* A compulsory enrolment of individuals for military or naval service. [L. *conscriptio*.]

Consecrate, kon'sē-krāt, *vt.* To appropriate to *sacred* uses; to devote to the service of God; to canonize; to dignify. *ppr.* consecrating, *pret. & pp.* consecrated. [L. *consecro, consecratus—sacer*, sacred.]

Consecrated, kon'sē-krāt-ed, *p.a. Made sacred*; dedicated to the service of God.

Consecration, kon-sē-krā'shon, *n.* Act of separating from a common to a *sacred* use, or of devoting a person or thing to the service of God; dedication.

Consecutive, kon-sek'ūt-iv, *a. Following in a train*; succeeding one another in a regular order. [Fr. *consécutif—*L. *sequor, secūtus*, to follow.]

Consecutively, kon-sek'ūt-iv-li, *adv.* By way of consequence or succession.

Consent, kon-sent', *n. A sense in unison with that of another*; yielding of the mind to what is proposed; accord of minds; harmony; concord; concurrence; joint operation. [L. *consensus*.] *vi.* To be of the same mind; to harmonize; to yield; to assent; to comply; to concede. [Fr. *consentir—*L. *sentio*, to feel.]

Consentient, kon-sen'shi-ent, *a.* Agreeing in mind; accordant in opinion. [L. *consentiens*.]

Consequence, kon'sē-kwens, *n.* That which *follows* something on which it depends; an effect produced by some preceding cause; a result; end; inference; influence; importance; distinction. [L. *consequentia—sequor*, to follow.]

Consequent, kon'sē-kwent, *a. Following*, as the natural effect; following by necessary inference.—*n. That which follows* a cause; effect; deduction. [L. *consequens*.]

Consequential, kon-sē-kwen'shi-al, *a. Following* as the effect; conclusive; assuming the air of a person of consequence; pompous.

Consequentially, kon-sē-kwen'shi-al-li, *adv. With just deduction of consequences*; by consequence; with conceit.

Consequently, kon'sē-kwent-li, *adv. By consequence*; therefore.

Conservancy, kon-sėrv'an-si, *n. Conservation*; preservation. [Low L. *conservantia—*L. *servo*, to keep.]

Conservation, kon-sėrv-ā'shon, *n. Preservation*; the keeping of a thing in a safe or entire state. [L. *conservatio*.]

Conservatism, kon-sėrv'at-izm, *n.* The tendency to *preserve* what is established.

Conservative, kon-sėrv'at-iv, *a. Preservative*; adhering to existing institutions; opposed to political changes. *n. One who aims to preserve* from injury or radical change; one opposed to political changes in the state.

Conservator, kon'sėrv-āt-ėr, *n. A preserver*; one who preserves from injury.

Conservatory, kon-sėrv'a-tō-ri, *n.* A greenhouse for exotics.

Conserve, kon-sėrv', *vt.* To keep together; to *save*; to candy or pickle for preservation. *ppr.* conserving, *pret. & pp.* conserved. [L. *conservo—servo*, to save.]

Conserve, kon'sėrv, *n. That which is conserved*, particularly fruits, by means of sugar, &c.

Consider, kon-si'dėr, *vt.* To look at carefully; to view with attention; to fix the mind on; to weigh; to contemplate; to have respect to; to think; to regard; to take into account.—*vi.* To think seriously; to revolve in the mind; to ponder. [Fr. *considérer—*L. *considero*.]

Considerable, kon-si'dėr-a-bl, *a. Worthy of consideration*; deserving of notice; valuable; moderately large. [Fr. *considérable*.]

Considerably, kon-si'dėr-a-bli, *adv.* In a degree not trifling or unimportant.

Considerance†, kon-si'dėr-ans, *n. Act of considering.*

Considerate, kon-si'dėr-āt, *a.* Given to sober reflection; careful; serious; deliberate; mindful of the rights of others. [L. *consideratus*.]

Considerately, kon-si'dėr-āt-li, *adv. In a considerate manner.*

Considerateness, kon-si'dėr-āt-nes, *n. Quality of being considerate.*

Consideration, kon-si'dėr-ā"shon, *n.* Mental view; serious deliberation; contemplation; importance; a moderate degree of respectability; motive of action; an equivalent. [L. *consideratio*.]

Considered, kon-si'dėrd, *p.a.* Viewed attentively; examined.

Considering, kon-si'dėr-ing, *prep.* Taking into account or *consideration*; making allowance for.

Consign, kon-sīn', *vt.* To deliver over to another by a *sealed* or formal agreement; to give in trust; to give, grant, or deliver; to commit; to deposit.—*vt.* To submit; to give one's self up; to

yield consent. [L. *consigno—signum*, a seal.]
Consignee, kon-sin-ē', *n.* The person to whom goods are delivered in trust for sale.
Consignment, kon-sīn'ment, *n. Act of consigning;* the thing consigned; the goods sent to a factor for sale.
Consignor, kon-sīn-or', *n. One who consigns.*
Consist, kon-sist', *vi. To stand together;* to be in a fixed state, as a body composed of parts in union; to subsist; to be comprised; to lie; to be made up; to be compatible; to agree. [L. *consisto—sisto*, to cause to stand.]
Consistence, Consistency, kon-sist'ens, kon-sist en-si, *n. A standing together;* that state of a body in which component parts remain fixed; a degree of density; make; firmness of constitution; harmony of parts; agreement with one's self; accordancy. [Fr. *consistance*.]
Consistent, kon-sist'ent, *a. Standing together;* fixed; firm; not contradictory; compatible; suitable; uniform; conformable (with *with*). [L. *consistens*.]
Consistently, kon-sist'ent-li, *adv. In a consistent manner.*
Consistorial, kon-sis-tō'ri-al, *a. Pertaining or relating to a consistory.*
Consistory, kon'sis-tō-ri, *n.* A place of justice in a spiritual court, or the court itself; the court of a diocesan bishop; college of cardinals; a solemn assembly. [L. *consistorium*.]
Consociation, kon-sō'shi-ā"shon, *n. Association;* alliance; companionship. [L. *consociatio—socius*, a companion.]
Consolable, kon-sōl'a-bl, *a. That may be consoled* or comforted. [Fr.]
Consolation, kon-sōl-ā'shon, *n. A solace;* alleviation of misery; refreshment of mind or spirits; the cause of comfort. [L. *consolatio—solor, solatus*, to console.]
Consolatory, kon-sol'a-tō-ri, *a. Tending to give solace* or comfort; refreshing to the mind; assuaging grief. [L. *consolatorius*.]
Console, kon-sōl', *vt. To give solace to;* to comfort; to soothe; to support. *ppr.* consoling, *pret. & pp.* consoled. [L. *consolor—solor*, to comfort.]
Consolidate, kon-sol'id-āt, *vt. To make wholly solid;* to harden or make dense and firm; to unite into one; to unite, as parts that have been separated; to compress.—*vi. To grow solid;* to grow firm and hard. *ppr.* consolidating, *pret. & pp.* consolidated. [L. *consolido, consolidatus—solidus*, solid.]
Consolidated, kon-sol'id-āt-ed, *p.a. Made solid;* united.
Consolidation, kon-sol'id-ā"shon, *n. Act of consolidating;* state of being consolidated.
Consoling, kon-sōl'ing, *p.a. Giving consolation;* comforting.
Consols, kon'sols, *n.pl.* The three per cent. *consolidated* annuities; a sort of transferable government stock. [from *consolidated*.]
Consonance, kon'sō-nans, *n. Agreement of simultaneous sounds;* concord; consistency; congruity; suitableness. [Fr.—L. *sono*, to sound.]
Consonant, kon'sō-nant, *a. Having agreement;* accordant; consistent.—*n.* A letter sounded along with a vowel, and which cannot be sounded by itself. [L. *consonans*.]
Consonantal, kon-sō-nant'al, *a. Partaking of the nature of a consonant.*
Consonantly, kon'sō-nant-li, *adv. By consonance;* consistently; in agreement.
Consort, kon'sort, *n.* One who *shares the lot* of another; a partner; a wife or husband; a ship keeping company with another. [L. *consors—sors, sortis*, a lot.]
Consort, kon-sort', *vi. To partake of the same lot;* to keep company; to associate (with *with*).
Conspectuity†, kon-spek-tū'i-ti, *n. Faculty of seeing.*
Conspicuous, kon-spik'ū-us, *a. That is in view;* open to the view; manifest; distinguished; celebrated. [L. *conspicuus—specio*, to see.]
Conspicuously, kon-spik'ū-us-li, *adv. In a conspicuous manner.*
Conspicuousness, kon-spik'ū-us-nes, *n. Openness to the view;* state of being visible at a distance; fame; renown.
Conspiracy, kon-spi'ra-si, *n. A breathing together;* a plot; a cabal; a confederacy; a combination of men for an evil purpose; a treasonable combination. [L. *conspiratio—spiro*, to breathe.]
Conspirant†, kon-spir'ant, *a. Conspiring.*
Conspirator, kon-spi'rāt-ėr, *n.* One who engages in a plot or *conspiracy.*
Conspire, kon-spīr', *vi. To breathe together;* to plot; to combine for some evil purpose; to hatch sedition; to tend to one end. *ppr.* conspiring, *pret. & pp.* conspired. [L. *conspiro—spiro*, to breathe.]
Conspirer†, kon-spir'ėr, *n. One who conspires.*
Constable, kun'sta-bl, *n The count of the stable*†; an officer of the peace; a petty officer appointed to keep the sovereign's peace in a parish or district. [Old Fr. *connestable;* Low L. *comes stabuli*—L. *stabulum*, a stall.]
Constableship, kun'sta-bl-ship, *n. The office of a constable.*
Constabulary, kon-stab'ū-la-ri, *a. Pertaining to constables;* consisting of constables.—*n. The body of constables.*
Constancy, kon'stan-si, *n. A standing firmly;* unalterable continuance; stability; persevering resolution; lasting affection. [L. *constantia—sto, stans*, to stand.]
Constant, kon'stant, *a. Standing firm;* permanent; unalterable; perpetual; assiduous; resolute; d termined; unshaken.—*n.* That which remains unchanged; a quantity which remains the same throughout a problem. [L. *constans*.]
Constantly, kon'stant-li, *adv. In a constant manner.*
Constellation, kon-stel-lā'shon, *n. A group of fixed stars,* expressed and represented under the name and figure of an animal or other emblem; an assemblage of splendours or excellences. [L. *constellatio—stella*, a star.]
Consternation, kon-stėr-nā'shon, *n. A throwing down* or prostration of the mind; horror; amazement; astonishment; perturbation. [L. *consternatio—sterno*, to throw down.]
Constipate, kon'sti-pāt, *vt. To stop,* as a passage, by filling it; to make costive. *ppr.* constipating, *pret. & pp.* constipated. [L. *constipo, constipatus—stipo*, to compress, to fill with.]
Constipation, kon-sti-pā'shon, *n. A filling* to hardness of the intestinal canal; costiveness.
Constituency, kon-stit'ū-en-si, *n.* The body of *constituents.*
Constituent, kon-stit'ū-ent, *a. Constituting;* forming; composing or making, as an essential part; having the power of constituting.—*n. He or that which constitutes;* one who constitutes or elects, as a representative; an essential part. [L. *constituens*.]
Constitute, kon'sti-tūt, *vt. To set up;* to fix; to give formal existence to; to compose; to appoint; to make and empower. *ppr.* constituting, *pret. & pp.* constituted. [L. *constituo, constitūtus—statuo*, to set—*sto*, to stand.]
Constitution, kon-sti-tū'shon, *n. Act of constituting;* that which is constituted; natural qualities; the particular temperament of the human body; the frame of mind, affections, or passions; the established form of government in a state; a system of fundamental laws for the government of a state; a particular law or ordinance.
Constitutional, kon-sti-tū'shon-al, *a. Bred in the constitution;* consistent with the civil constitution; legal; relating to a constitution.
Constitutionalist, kon-sti-tū'shon-al-ist, *n. An adherent to the constitution.*
Constitutionally, kon-sti-tū'shon-al-li, *adv.* In consistency with the *constitution* or frame of government.
Constitutionist, kon-sti-tū'shon-ist, *n. One who adheres to the constitution* of the country.
Constitutive, kon'sti-tūt-iv, *a. That constitutes;* elemental; essential; having power to enact, establish, or create.
Constrain, kon-strān', *vt. To secure by bonds;* to urge by force; to necessitate; to press. [Fr. *contraindre*—L. *stringo*, to bind.]
Constrainable, kon-strān'a-bl, *a. That may be constrained.*
Constrained, kon-strānd', *p.a.* Compelled; forced.
Constraining, kon-strān'ing, *p.a.* Compelling; forcing.
Constraint, kon-strānt', *n. Irresistible force* or its effect; necessity; obligation; urgency; restraint. [Fr. *contrainte*.]
Constricted, kon-strikt'ed, *p.a. Drawn together;* bound; contracted.
Constriction, kon-strik'shon, *n. A drawing together* or contraction; compression. [L. *constrictio—stringo*, to bind.]
Constrictor, kon-strikt'ėr, *n. That which draws together;* a muscle that closes an orifice; a large serpent which crushes its prey in its folds.
Construct, kon-strukt', *vt. To build;* to frame with contrivance; to put together, as the parts of a thing in their proper place and order; to devise; to make. [L. *construo, constructum—struo*, to build.]
Construction, kon-struk'shon, *n. Act or mode of constructing;* structure; fabrication; proper arrangement of words in a sentence, according to the rules of syntax; sense; interpretation. [L. *constructio*.]
Constructional, kon-struk'shon-al, *a. Pertaining to construction.*
Constructive, kon-strukt'iv, *a. Having ability to construct;* created or deduced by construction; not directly expressed but inferred.
Constructively, kon-strukt'iv-li, *adv. In a constructive manner.*
Construe, kon'strū, *vt. To put together;* to place in a regular order; to arrange, as words in their natural order, so as to discover the sense of a sentence; to interpret; to render; to explain. *ppr.* construing, *pret. & pp.* construed. [L. *construo—struo*, to build.]
Consubstantial, kon-sub-stan'shi-al, *a.*

Having the same substance; co-essential. [Late L. *consubstantialis*—L. *substantia*, substance.]

Consubstantiality, kon-sub-stan′shi-al″li-ti, n. *Quality of being consubstantial;* participation of the same nature.

Consubstantiation, kon-sub-stan′shi-ā″shon, n. The doctrine of the *substantial union* of the body and blood of Christ in the sacramental elements.

Consul, kon′sul, n. One of the two chief magistrates of the ancient Roman republic; a person commissioned by a king or state to reside in a foreign country, and protect the commercial interests of his own country. [L.—*consulo,* to consult.]

Consular, kon′sūl-ėr, a. Pertaining to a consul.

Consulate, kon′sūl-āt, n. The office or jurisdiction of a consul; the residence of a consul. [L. *consulatus*.]

Consulship, kon′sul-ship, n. The office of a consul, or the term of his office.

Consult, kon-sult′, vi. To seek the opinion or advice of another; to deliberate in common; to consider with deliberation. (With *with*.)—vt. To ask counsel of; to refer to for information; to have regard to; to plan. [L. *consulto—salio,* to leap.]

Consultation, kon-sult-ā′shon, n. Act of *consulting;* a meeting or a council for deliberation. [L. *consultatio*.]

Consulter, kon-sult′ėr, n. One who consults.

Consulting, kon-sult′ing, p.a. Giving or receiving advice.

Consumable, kon-sūm′a-bl, a. That may be consumed.

Consume, kon-sūm′, vt. To destroy; to use up; to waste; to burn up; to swallow up; to squander.—vi. To waste away slowly; to be exhausted. (With *away*.) ppr. consuming, pret. & pp. consumed. [L. *consumo—sumo,* to take.]

Consumer, kon-sūm′ėr, n. One who consumes; that which consumes.

Consuming, kon-sūm′ing, p.a. That destroys.

Consummate, kon′sum-āt, vt. To sum up!; to finish; to complete; to perfect; to bring or carry to the utmost point or degree.—a. Complete; perfect; carried to the utmost extent or degree. ppr. consummating, pret. & pp. consummated. [L. *consummo, consummatus—summa,* the sum.]

Consummately, kon-sum′āt-li, adv. Completely; perfectly.

Consummation, kon-sum-ā′shon, n. Act of *consummating;* end; termination; perfection. [L. *consummatio*.]

Consumption, kon-sum′shon, n. Act of *consuming;* state of being consumed; decline; a gradual wasting away, particularly through a diseased state of the lungs. [L. *consumptio*.]

Consumptive, kon-sum′tiv, a. Wasting; exhausting; affected with or inclined to a consumption.

Consumptiveness, kon-sum′tiv-nes, n. State of being consumptive, or a tendency to consumption.

Contact, kon′takt, n. A touching together; close union or juncture of bodies. [L. *contactus—tango,* to touch.]

Contagion, kon-tā′jon, n. Communication of a disease by *contact;* poisonous emanation; infection; that which propagates mischief; pestilence. [L. *contagio—tango,* to touch.]

Contagious, kon-tā′ji-us, a. Caught or communicated by *contact;* poisonous; pestilential; spreading from one to another. [Low L. *contagiosus*.]

Contagiously, kon-tā′ji-us-li, adv. By contagion.

Contagiousness, kon-tā′ji-us-nes, n. Quality of being contagious.

Contain, kon-tān′, vt. To hold together; to be able to hold; to comprise; to embrace; to restrain.—vi. To live in continence or chastity. [L. *contineo—teneo,* to hold.]

Containable, kon-tān′a-bl, a. That may be contained or comprised.

Contaminate, kon-tam′in-āt, vt. To stain by *touching;* to corrupt the purity or excellence of; to defile; to pollute; to taint; to vitiate. ppr. contaminating, pret. & pp. contaminated. [L. *contamino, contaminatus—tango,* to touch.]

Contaminating, kon-tam′in-āt-ing, p.a. Polluting; defiling.

Contamination, kon-tam′in-ā″shon, n. Pollution; defilement; taint.

Contemn, kon-tem′, vt. To treat lightly; to consider and treat as despicable; to despise; to scorn; to spurn; to overlook. [L. *contemno—temno,* to slight.]

Contemner, kon-tem′ėr, n. One who contemns; a despiser; a scorner.

Contemplate, kon-tem′plāt, vt. To view carefully on all sides, and with reference to an object; to survey; to muse on; to meditate on; to design; to purpose.—vi. To look around carefully; to study; to muse; to meditate. ppr. contemplating, pret. & pp. contemplated. [L. *contemplor, contemplatus*.]

Contemplated, kon-tem′plāt-ed, p.a. Meditated on; intended.

Contemplation, kon-tem-plā′shon, n. Act of *contemplating;* meditation; continued attention of the mind to a particular subject. [L. *contemplatio*.]

Contemplative, kon-tem′plāt-iv, a. Given to contemplation; thoughtful; having the power of thought or meditation; employed in study.

Contemplatively, kon-tem′plāt-iv-li, adv. With contemplation.

Contemporaneous, kon-tem′pō-rā″nē-us, a. Living or being at the same time. [L. *tempus, temporis,* time.]

Contemporaneously, kon-tem′pō-rā″nē-us-li, adv. At the same time with some other event.

Contemporary, kon-tem′pō-ra-ri, a. See **Cotemporary,** the preferable word.

Contempt, kon-tem′, n. Act of *contemning;* state of being despised; scorn; derision; contumely; disgrace; disobedience to the rules, &c., of a court. [L. *contemptus—temno,* to despise.]

Contemptible, kon-tem′ti-bl, a. Worthy of contempt; despicable; vile; mean; base; worthless. [Low L. *contemptibilis*.]

Contemptibleness, kon-tem′ti-bl-nes, n. The state or quality of being contemptible; baseness; meanness.

Contemptibly, kon-tem′ti-bli, adv. In a contemptible manner.

Contemptuous, kon-tem′tū-us, a. Manifesting contempt; apt to despise; insolent; supercilious.

Contemptuously, kon-tem′tū-us-li, adv. In a contemptuous manner.

Contemptuousness, kon-tem′tū-us-nes, n. Quality of being contemptuous.

Contend, kon-tend′, vi. To strive in opposition; to vie; to oppose; to dispute, to wrangle; to argue. (With *with*.) [L. *contendo—tendo,* to stretch.]

Contender, kon-tend′ėr, n. One who contends.

Contending, kon-tend′ing, p.a. Clashing; opposing; rival.

Content, kon-tent′, a. Having a mind at peace; easy; satisfied; having enough; pleased or gratified with what one has.—vt. To satisfy the mind of; to make quiet; to make easy in any situation; to please or gratify.—n. That which is contained (usually pl.); rest of the mind in the present condition; acquiescence; moderate happiness. [See **Contents**.] [L. *contentus—teneo,* to hold.]

Contented, kon-tent′ed, p.a. Satisfied; quiet; easy in mind; not complaining, opposing, or demanding more.

Contentedly, kon-tent′ed-li, adv. In a contented manner.

Contentedness, kon-tent′ed-nes, n. State of being contented.

Contention, kon-ten′shon, n. Act of *contending;* a violent effort to obtain something, or to resist a person, claim, or injury; conflict; debate. [L. *contentio*.]

Contentious, kon-ten′shi-us, a. Provoking or relating to contention; litigious; quarrelsome. [Fr. *contentieux*.]

Contentiousness, kon-ten′shi-us-nes, n. Quality or state of being contentious.

Contentment, kon-tent′ment, n. State of being contented; satisfaction; content. [Fr. *contentement*.]

Contents, kon′tents, n. pl. The thing or things held or comprehended within a limit; area or solidity; capacity; heads of a book; index.

Conterminous, kon-tėr′min-us, a. Bordering upon; touching at the boundary; contiguous. [L. *conterminus—terminus,* a boundary.]

Contest, kon-test′, vt. To bring an action regarding by calling witnesses; to debate; to controvert; to oppose.—vi. To strive; to contend; to emulate. (With *with*.) [Fr. *contester*—L. *testis,* a witness.]

Contest, kon′test, n. Struggle for victory; encounter; debate; controversy; competition.

Contestable, kon-test′a-bl, a. That may be disputed or debated; disputable. [Fr.]

Context, kon′tekst, n. That which is woven together with; connection; the parts of a discourse which precede or follow the sentence quoted. [L. *contextus—texo, textum,* to weave.]

Contexture, kon-teks′tūr, n. The interweaving of several parts into one body; system; constitution; texture. [Fr.]

Contiguity, kon-ti-gū′i-ti, n. Actual contact of bodies; nearness of situation or place. [Fr. *contiguité*.]

Contiguous, kon-tig′ū-us, a. Touching one another; meeting at the surface or border; adjacent. [L. *contiguus—tango,* to touch.]

Contiguously, kon-tig′ū-us-li, adv. In a manner to touch.

Contiguousness, kon-tig′ū-us-nes, n. State of being contiguous.

Continence, kon′ti-nens, n. A keeping or holding within due bounds; self-command; restraint of the desires and passions; chastity; forbearance. [L. *continentia—teneo,* to hold.]

Continent, kon′ti-nent, a. Keeping within due bounds; restraining; moderate in the indulgence of lawful pleasure; chaste.—n. A great extent of land not disjoined by a sea; a connected tract of land of great extent; the mainland of Europe as distinguished from England. [L. *continens,* holding together—*teneo,* to hold.]

Continental, kon-ti-nent′al, a. Pertaining or relating to a continent, particularly to the continent of Europe.

Continently, kon'ti-nent-li, *adv. In a continent manner*; chastely.
Contingence, Contingency, kon-tin'jens, kon-tin'jen-si, *n. Quality of being contingent*; an event which may occur; chance; incident. [Fr. *contingence*.]
Contingent, kon-tin'jent, *a. Touching each other*; falling or coming by chance; not fixed; uncertain; fortuitous; incidental; dependent upon that which is unknown.—*n*. That which may happen; a quota; a suitable share; just proportion. [L. *contingens—tango*, to touch.]
Contingently, kon-tin'jent-li, *adv*. Accidentally; dependently.
Continual, kon-tin'ū-al, *a. That continues*; not intermitting; uninterrupted; frequently recurring. [Fr. *continuel*.]
Continually, kon-tin'ū-al-li, *adv*. Without pause or cessation; unceasingly.
Continuance, kon-tin'ū-ans, *n*. Permanence in one state; duration; prolongation.
Continuate, kon-tin'ū-āt, *a*. Unbroken.
Continuation, kon-tin'ū-ā'shon, *n*. Uninterrupted succession in space or in time; prolongation; production. [L. *continuatio*.]
Continue, kon-tin'ū, *vi. To keep together*; to remain in a state or place; to be durable; to persevere; to be steadfast.—*vt*. To draw out; to protract; to prolong; to extend in space or duration; to persevere in. *ppr.* continuing, *pret. & pp.* continued. [Fr. *continuer*—L. *teneo*, to hold.]
Continued, kon-tin'ūd, *p.a*. Uninterrupted; unceasing.
Continuer, kon-tin'ū-ėr, *n. One who continues*; a continuator.
Continuing, kon-tin'ū-ing, *p.a*. Permanent.
Continuity, kon-ti-nū'i-ti, *n. State of being continuous*; close union of parts; unbroken texture; cohesion. [L. *continuitas*.]
Continuous, kon-tin'ū-us, *a. Joined together closely*; conjoined; continued. [L. *continuus—teneo*, to hold.]
Continuously, kon-tin'ū-us-li, *adv. In continuation* without interruption.
Contortion, kon-tor'shon, *n. A twisting together*; a writhing; wry motion; distortion. [Fr. *contorsion*—L. *torqueo, tortum*, to twist.]
Contour, kon-tör', *n*. The line that bounds a rounded body; the line that defines or terminates a figure; outline. [Fr.—L. *tornus*, a turner's wheel.]
Contraband, kon'tra-band, *n. Illegal traffic*; prohibition of trading in goods contrary to the laws of a state or of nations.—*a*. Prohibited; forbidden. [It. *contrabbando*; Low L. *bannum*, a public edict.]
Contrabandist, kon'tra-band-ist, *n. One who traffics illegally*; a smuggler.
Contract, kon-trakt', *vt. To draw together*; to cause to shrink; to wrinkle; to shorten; to narrow; to reduce; to bargain for; to betroth; to bring on; to get; to incur.—*vi*. To shrink up; to become shorter or narrower; to bargain; to make a mutual agreement. *p.a.* Affianced. [L. *contraho, contractus—traho*, to draw.]
Contract, kon'trakt, *n. A drawing together*; a covenant; a compact; formal bargain; bond; the writing which contains stipulations.
Contracted, kon-trakt'ed, *p.a. Drawn together*; narrow; mean; selfish.
Contractedly, kon-trakt'ed-li, *adv. In a contracted manner*.

Contractedness, kon-trakt'ed-nes, *n. State of being contracted*; narrowness.
Contractibility, kon-trakt'i-bil'li-ti, *n. Capability of being contracted*.
Contractible, kon-trakt'i-bl, *a. Capable of contraction*.
Contractile, kon-trakt'il, *a. Having the power of contracting*, as living fibres. [Fr.]
Contractility, kon-trakt-il'i-ti, *n. Quality of being contractile*.
Contracting, kon-trakt'ing, *p.a. Making* or having made a *contract or treaty*; stipulating.
Contraction, kon-trak'shon, *n. Act of contracting*; state of being contracted; abridgment; a marriage contract. [L. *contractio*.]
Contractor, kon-trakt'ėr, *n. One who contracts*.
Contradict, kon-tra-dikt', *vt. To speak against*; to oppose by words; to deny; to be contrary to; to impugn; to resist. [L. *contradico, contradictus—dico*, to speak.]
Contradicter, kon-tra-dikt'ėr, *n*. One who *contradicts*.
Contradiction, kon-tra-dik'shon, *n*. Opposition by words; a contrary assertion; inconsistency with itself; repugnancy. [L. *contradictio*.]
Contradictorily, kon-tra-dik'tō-ri-li, *adv. In a contradictory manner*.
Contradictory, kon-tra-dik'tō-ri, *a. Implying contradiction*; affirming the contrary; inconsistent; contrary.
Contradistinction, kon'tra-dis-tingk''-shon, *n. Distinction by opposites*.
Contradistinctive, kon'tra-dis-tingkt''-iv, *a. Distinguishing by contrast*.
Contradistinguish, kon'tra-dis-ting''-gwish, *vt. To distinguish by contrast*.
Contralto, kon-tral'tō, *n*. In music, the part immediately below the treble; the voice performing this part. [It.]
Contraposition, kon'tra-pō-zi''shon, *n. A placing over against*; opposite position.
Contrariety, kon-tra-rī'e-ti, *n. State of being contrary*; opposition; repugnance; inconsistency. [L. *contrarietas*.]
Contrarily, kon'tra-ri-li, *adv. In a contrary* or opposite *manner*.
Contrariwise, kon'tra-ri-wiz, *adv. On the contrary*; on the other hand.
Contrary, kon'tra-ri, *a. Opposite*; repugnant; discordant; inconsistent.—*n. A thing that is contrary* (chiefly pl.); a proposition contrary to another, or a fact contrary to what is alleged.—*vt*. To contradict; to thwart. [L. *contrarius—contra*, against.]
Contrast, kon-trast', *vt*. To set in opposition, to show the difference; to place so as to heighten the effect.—*vi*. To stand in contrast or opposition to. [Fr. *contraster*—L. *sto*, to stand.]
Contrast, kon'trast, *n. Opposition*; the placing of opposite things in view, to exhibit the superior excellence of one to more advantage.
Contrasted, kon-trast'ed, *p.a*. Examined in opposition.
Contravene, kon-tra-vēn', *vt. To come against*; to hinder; to set aside. *ppr.* contravening, *pret. & pp.* contravened. [L. *contravenio—venio*, to come.]
Contravention, kon-tra-ven'shon, *n*. Opposition; obstruction.
Contribute, kon-trib'ūt, *vt. To give in common with others*; to impart, as a portion or share to a common purpose.—*vi*. To give a part; to conduce; to have a share in any act or effect (with *to*). *ppr*. contributing, *pret. &*

pp. contributed. [L. *contribuo, contributus—tribuo*, to give.]
Contribution, kon-tri-bū'shon, *n. Act of contributing*; that which is contributed; a share; a tax; a charitable collection; bestowal of aid to a common purpose.
Contributive, kon-trib'ūt-iv, *a. Tending to contribute*; lending aid to promote, in concurrence with others.
Contributor, kon-trib'ūt-ėr, *n. One who contributes*.
Contributory, kon-trib'ū-tō-ri, *a. Contributing to*, or promoting the same end; bringing assistance to some joint design.—*n*. One who brings assistance to some joint design.
Contrite, kon'trit, *a. Bruised*; worn; deeply affected with grief and sorrow for having offended God; penitent; repentant. [L. *contritus—tero*, to bruise.]
Contritely, kon'trit-li, *adv. In a contrite manner*; with penitence.
Contrition, kon-tri'shon, *n*. Deep sorrow for sin; repentance; compunction; remorse. [L. *contritio*.]
Contrivable, kon-triv'a-bl, *a. That may be contrived*, invented, or devised.
Contrivance, kon-triv'ans, *n. Act of contriving*; thing contrived; invention; shift; ingenious performance.
Contrive, kon-triv', *vt*. To invent; to devise; to plan; to plot; to hatch; [L. *tero*] to wear out or away!.—*vi*. To form or design; to plan; to scheme. *ppr.* contriving, *pret. & pp.* contrived. [Fr. *controuver—trouver*, to find.]
Contrived, kon-trivd', *p.a*. Planned; devised.
Contriver, kon-triv'ėr, *n*. An inventor.
Control, kon-trōl', *n. A counter roll*; check; restraint; superintendence; command. [Fr. *contrôle*—L. *rotula*, a little wheel.]—*vt*. To keep under check by a *counter roll*; to superintend; to restrain; to regulate; to overpower. *ppr.* controlling, *pret. & pp.* controlled. [Fr. *contrôler*.]
Controllable, kon-trōl'a-bl, *a. That may be controlled*.
Controller, kon-trōl'ėr, *n*. An officer who checks the accounts of collectors of public monies.
Controllership, kon-trōl'ėr-ship, *n. The office of a controller*.
Controlling, kon-trōl'ing, *p.a*. Checking; governing.
Controlment, kon-trōl'ment, *n. Power or act of controlling*; the state of being controlled; control; restraint.
Controversial, kon-trō-vėr'shi-al, *a. Relating to controversy*.
Controversialist, kon-trō-vėr'shi-al-ist, *n. One who carries on a controversy*.
Controversy, kon'trō-vėr-si, *n. A turning against*; a disputation between parties, particularly in writing; a debate; strife; litigation; a state of resistance. [L. *controversia*.]
Controvert, kon'trō-vėrt, *vt. To turn against*; to deny, and attempt to disprove or confute; to agitate contrary opinions against. [L. *verto*, to turn.]
Controverted, kon'trō-vėrt-ed, *p.a*. Disputed.
Controvertible, kon-trō-vėrt'i-bl, *a. That may be controverted*.
Controvertibly, kon-trō-vėrt'i-bli, *adv. In a controvertible manner*.
Contumacious, kon-tū-mā'shi-us, *a. Swelling up against*; opposing rightful authority with pride and stubbornness; headstrong. [L. *contumax, contumacis—tumeo*, to swell up.]
Contumaciously, kon-tū-mā'shi-us-li, *adv*. Obstinately; stubbornly.

Contumaciousness, kon-tū-mā'shi-us-nes, n. *Quality of being contumacious.*
Contumacy, kon'tū-ma-si, n. A swelling up *against;* unyielding resistance to rightful authority. [L. *contumacia.*]
Contumelious, kon-tū-mē'li-us, a. Contemptuous; rude and sarcastic; insolent; proudly rude; ignominious. [L. *contumeliosus.*]
Contumeliously, kon-tū-mē'li-us-li, adv. *In a contumelious manner.*
Contumely, kon'tū-me-li, n. Rudeness compounded of haughtiness and contempt; insolence; contemptuous language. [L. *contumelia — tumeo*, to swell.]
Contuse, kon-tūz', vt. *To beat small;* to bruise; to injure by a blow, or by pressure, without breaking the skin or substance. ppr. *contusing*, pret. & pp. *contused*. [L. *tundo*, *tusum*, to beat.]
Contusion, kon-tū'zhon, n. *Act of bruising*, or the state of being bruised; a bruise. [L. *contusio.*]
Convalescence, kon-va-les'ens, n. *A becoming sound;* the insensible recovery of health and strength after disease; state of a body renewing its vigour after sickness. [L. *convalescentia — valesco*, to grow strong.]
Convalescent, kon-va-les'ent, a. *Recovering health after sickness.* — n. *One recovering from sickness.*
Convenable, kon-vēn'a-bl, a. *That may be convened* or assembled.
Convene, kon-vēn', vi. *'Io come together;* to assemble. — vt. *To cause to come together;* to summon to meet or appear. ppr. *convening*, pret. & pp. *convened*. [L. *convenio — venio*, to come.]
Convener, kon-vēn'ėr, n. *One who convenes* or calls an assembly together.
Convenience, kon-vē'ni-ens, n. Fitness; propriety; commodiousness; ease. [L. *convenientia.*]
Convenient, kon-vē'ni-ent, a. Fit; suitable; adapted; commodious; promotive of comfort. [L. *conveniens.*]
Conveniently, kon-vē'ni-ent-li, adv. *In a convenient manner;* fitly; suitably.
Convent, kon'vent, n. A body of monks or nuns; an abbey; a monastery; a nunnery. [Old Fr. — L. *conventus.*]
Convent†, kon-vent', vt. *To summon;* to call before a judge.
Conventicle, kon-ven'ti-kl, n. *A minor assembly;* a meeting of dissenters from the Established Church of England for religious worship, or the place where they meet. [L. *conventiculum.*]
Convention, kon-ven'shon, n. *A meeting;* an assembly for civil or ecclesiastical purposes; an agreement. [L. *conventio.*]
Conventional, kon-ven'shon-al, a. Formed by agreement; arising out of custom or tacit agreement. [Fr. *conventionnel.*]
Conventionalism, kon-ven'shon-al-izm, n. That which is received by tacit agreement, as a phrase, &c.
Conventionally, kon-ven'shon-al-li, adv. *In a conventional manner.*
Conventual, kon-ven'tū-al, a. *Belonging to a convent;* monastic. — n. *One who lives in a convent.* [Fr. *conventuel.*]
Converge, kon-vėrj', vi. *To tend* to one and the same point or object; to *incline* and approach nearer together. ppr. *converging*, pret. & pp. *converged*. [L. *vergo*, to incline.]
Convergence, kon-vėrj'ens, n. *Tendency to one point or object.*
Convergent, kon-vėrj'ent, a. *Tending* to one point or object; approaching each other as they proceed, as lines.

Converging, kon-vėrj'ing, p.a. *Tending* to one point, mark, or object; approaching each other, as lines extended.
Conversable, kon-vėrs'a-bl, a. *Disposed to converse;* fluent in conversation; communicative; sociable.
Conversably, kon-vėrs'a-bli, adv. *In a conversable manner.*
Conversant, kon'vėrs-ant, a. *Having much converse*, intercourse, or familiarity with; versed in; skilful; proficient (with *in* or *with*); having concern (with *about*). [It. *conversante.*]
Conversation, kon-vėr-sā'shon, n. Familiar intercourse; intimate fellowship; interchange of ideas; easy talk; behaviour; conduct. [L. *conversatio.*]
Conversational, kon-vėr-sā'shon-al, a. *Pertaining to conversation.*
Conversationist, kon-vėr-sā'shon-ist, n. *An adept in conversation.*
Conversazione, kon-vėr-sä'tsi-ō"nā, n. *A meeting for conversation*, generally on literary topics. [It.]
Converse, kon-vėrs', vi. To hold intercourse and be intimately acquainted; to talk familiarly; to convey thoughts reciprocally; to speak; to talk; to commune. (With *with*.) ppr. *conversing*, pret. & pp. *conversed*. [L. *conversor — versor*, to move about in a place — *verto*, *versum*, to turn.]
Converse, kon'vėrs, n. Familiar discourse or talk; acquaintance by customary intercourse; transposition of the terms of a proposition. — a. *Turned round;* opposite or reciprocal.
Conversely, kon'vėrs-li, adv. With change of order; reciprocally.
Conversion, kon-vėr'shon, n. *A turning* from one state to another; a change of heart; change from one sect or party to another; interchange of terms in logic. [L. *conversio.*]
Convert, kon-vėrt', vt. *To turn* into another substance or form; to change from one state to another; to change from one religion or party to another; to turn from a bad life to a good; to turn from one use to another; to change, as a proposition into a reciprocal one. — vi. *To turn round;* to undergo a change. [L. *converto — verto*, to turn.]
Convert, kon'vėrt, n. One who is *turned* from sin to holiness; a person who renounces one creed or party for another.
Converted, kon-vėrt'ed, p.a. Changed from a state of sin to a state of holiness.
Convertibility, kon-vėrt'i-bil''li-ti, n. *Capability of being changed* from one form or state to another. [Fr. *convertibilité.*]
Convertible, kon-vėrt'i-bl, a. *Susceptible of change;* transformable; that may be used the one for the other. [Fr.]
Convertibly, kon-vėrt'i-bli, adv. Reciprocally; with interchange of terms.
Converting, kon-vėrt'ing, p.a. Changing from a state of sin to a state of holiness.
Convertite†, kon'vėrt-it, n. *A convert.*
Convex, kon'veks, a. Vaulted; rounded; rising on the exterior surface into a round form; spherical; opposed to concave. [L. *convexus — veho*, to carry.]
Convexity, kon-veks'i-ti, n. Protuberance in a circular form; roundness. [Fr. *convexité.*]
Convexly, kon'veks-li, adv. *In a convex form.*
Convey, kon-vā', vt. To transport by carriage, ships, &c.; to transfer; to remove secretly; to deliver; to impart;

to manage with privacy†. — vi. To steal†. [L. *conveho — veho*, to carry.]
Conveyable, kon-vā'a-bl, a. *That may be conveyed* or transferred.
Conveyance, kon-vā'ans, n. *Act of conveying;* the thing conveyed; a means of conveying; a carriage; transference; a deed which conveys or transfers property; artifice†.
Conveyancer, kon-vā'ans-ėr, n. One who draws deeds or writings by which property is *conveyed* or transferred.
Conveyancing, kon-vā'ans-ing, n. *The business of a conveyancer;* the act or practice of drawing deeds, &c., for transferring the title to property.
Conveyer, kon-vā'ėr, n. *He or that which conveys;* one given to artifices†.
Convict, kon-vikt', vt. To prove or decide to be guilty; to show by evidence; to prove manifestly†. — p.a. Proved or found guilty†. [L. *convinco*, *convictus — vinco*, to conquer.]
Convict, kon'vikt, n. A person proved or found guilty of a crime alleged against him; a felon.
Conviction, kon-vik'shon, n. *Act of convicting;* state of being convicted; state of being sensible of guilt.
Convictive, kon-vikt'iv, a. *Having the power to convince* or *convict.*
Convince, kon-vins', vt. To conquer or persuade by argument; to satisfy by evidence or proof, as the mind; to force to acknowledge or assent to. ppr. *convincing*, pret. & pp. *convinced*. [L. *convinco — vinco*, to conquer.]
Convinced, kon-vinst', p.a. Persuaded in mind; satisfied with evidence.
Convincing, kon-vins'ing, p.a. *Working conviction;* calculated to persuade.
Convive†, kon-viv', vt. To entertain.
Convivial, kon-vi'vi-al, a. Festive; festal; jovial; social. [L. *convivalis — vivo*, to live.]
Conviviality, kon-vi'vi-al''li-ti, n. The good humour or mirth indulged in at an entertainment.
Convocate, kon'vō-kāt, vt. To *call* or summon to meet; to assemble by summons. [L. *convoco*, *convocatus.*]
Convocation, kon-vō-kā'shon, n. An assembly, particularly of clergy or heads of a university; a synod; a congress; a council. [L. *convocatio.*]
Convoke, kon-vōk', vt. To *call together;* to assemble by summons. ppr. *convoking*, pret. & pp. *convoked*. [L. *convoco — voco*, to call.]
Convolution, kon-vō-lū'shon, n. *Act of rolling* anything upon itself; the state of being rolled together; a winding or twisting; a winding motion. [L. *convolutio — volvo*, *volutum*, to roll.]
Convolvulus, kon-volv'ū-lus, n. Bindweed. [L.]
Convoy, kon-voi', vt. To attend on the way, for protection or defence, either by sea or land; to escort. [Fr. *convoyer* — L. *via*, a way.]
Convoy, kon'voi, n. *Act of convoying;* escort for defence; a ship or ships of war accompanying a fleet of merchantmen, &c., for protection; the fleet thus protected; conveyance†.
Convulse, kon-vuls', vt. To contract violently, as the muscles; to affect by irregular spasms; to shake; to disturb; to put into commotion; to rend. ppr. *convulsing*, pret. & pp. *convulsed*. [L. *convello*, *convulsus — vello*, to pluck.]
Convulsion, kon-vul'shon, n. A violent involuntary contraction of the muscles, with alternate relaxations; any violent and irregular motion; disturbance. [L. *convulsio.*]

Fāte, fär, fat, fall; mē, met, hėr: pīne, pin; nōte, not, mōve; tūbe, tub, bull; oil, pound.

Convulsive, kon-vuls'iv, a. Tending to convulse; spasmodic; agitating.
Convulsively, kon-vuls'iv-li, adv. In a convulsive manner.
Cony, kō'ni, n. A rabbit. [D. konijn.]
Cony-catch, kō'ni-kach, vt. To deceive; to trick.
Coo, kö, vi. To cry, or make a low sound, as pigeons or doves. [from the sound.]
Cooing, kö'ing, p.n. Invitation, as the note of the dove.
Cook, kuk, vt. To prepare, as victuals for the table, by fire or heat; to prepare as food for eating; to prepare for any purpose; to concoct; to tamper with.—n. One who prepares victuals for the table; a man or woman who dresses meat or vegetables for eating. [Sax. cōc, a cook; L. coquo, to cook.]
Cookery, kuk'è-ri, n. The art of preparing victuals for the table.
Cook-room, kuk'röm, n. A room for cookery in a ship; a galley.
Cool, köl, a. Moderately cold; producing coolness; calm; dispassionate; self-possessed; frigid; impudent.—n. A moderate degree or state of cold.—vt. To make cool; to allay the heat of; to moderate, as excitement, &c.; to calm; to assuage; to render indifferent.—vi. To grow cool; to become less hot; to lose ardour, zeal, affection, &c. [Sax. cōl; D. koel.]
Cooler, köl'ėr, n. That which cools; anything which abates excitement.
Cool-headed, köl'hed-ed, a. Having a temper not easily excited; free from passion.
Cooling, köl'ing, p.a. Making or becoming cool.
Coolly, köl'li, adv. In a cool or indifferent manner; without heat or ardour.
Coolness, köl'nes, n. Moderate degree of cold; indifference.
Coop, köp, n. A barrel or cask; a box for confining poultry; a pen for small animals.—vt. To confine in a coop; to shut up or confine in a narrow compass; to imprison. [D. kuip.]
Cooper, kö'pėr, n. One who makes barrels, tubs, and casks of various kinds.
Cooperage, kö'pėr-āj, n. The work or pay of a cooper; workshop of a cooper.
Co-operate, kō-op'ėr-āt, vi. To act with another; to use mutual efforts to promote the same object; to concur in producing the same effect. ppr. co-operating, pret. & pp. co-operated. [L. operor, operatus, to work—opus, operis, work.]
Co-operation, kō-op'ėr-ā''shon, n. Act of co-operating; joint operation.
Co-operative, kō-op'ėr-āt-iv, a. Operating jointly to the same end.
Co-operator, kō-op'ėr-āt-ėr, n. One who co-operates.
Co-ordinate, kō-or'din-āt, a. Holding the same order; equal; not subordinate. [L. con, and ordino, ordinatus, to set in order—ordo, order.]
Co-ordinately, kō-or'din-āt-li, adv. In the same order or rank.
Co-ordination, kō-or'din-ā''shon, n. The state of being co-ordinate.
Coot, köt, n. A wading bird with a short tail. [W. cwt, a short tail.]
Copal, kō'pal, n. A resin; the concrete juice of certain trees used as a varnish. [Sp. copal.]
Copartner, kō-pärt'nėr, n. A joint-partner; an associate.
Copartnership, kō-pärt'nėr-ship, n. Joint-partnership.
Copatain, kō'pa-tān, a. Having a high crown.

Cope, kōp, n. A cover for the head; a sacerdotal cloak, worn in sacred ministrations; the arch or concave of the sky; the roof or covering of a house; the arch over a door, &c.—vt. To co er, as with a cope. ppr. coping, pret. & pp. coped. [Sax. cappa, a cap, cope.]
Cope, kōp, vi. To contend; to strive or struggle; to compete; to encounter; to interchange kindness!.—vt.! To match one's self against. ppr. coping, pret. & pp. coped. [Icel. kapp, fervour of spirit, contention.]
Copernican, kō-pėr'ni-kan, a. Pertaining to Copernicus, or to his astronomical system.
Copestone, kōp'stōn, n. Head or top stone.
Copier, **Copyist**, kō'pi-ėr, kō'pi-ist, n. One who copies; a transcriber; an imitator.
Coping, kōp'ing, p.n. The top or cover of a wall.
Copious, kō'pi-us, a. Abundant; furnishing full supplies; plentiful; exuberant; overflowing; abounding in words or images; diffuse. [L. copiosus—copia, plenty.]
Copiousness, kō'pi-us-nes, n. Exuberance; diffusiveness of style.
Copper, kop'pėr, n. A valuable metal, of a pale red colour, tinged with yellow; a vessel made of copper, particularly a large boiler; a copper coin.—a. Resembling copper.—vt. To cover with sheets of copper. [G. kupfer.]
Copperas, kop'pėr-as, n. Copper-rust; green vitriol or sulphate of iron. [Fr. couperose.]
Copper-fastened, kop'pėr-fas-nd, a. Fastened with copper bolts, as the planks of ships.
Copperish, kop'pėr-ish, a. Containing copper; like copper, or partaking of it.
Copperplate, kop'pėr-plāt, n. A plate of polished copper, on which designs are engraved; a print from a copperplate.
Coppersmith, kop'pėr-smith, n. One who works in copper.
Coppery, kop'pėr-i, a. Made of copper; like copper in taste or smell.
Copse, kops, n. A wood of small growth. [Old Fr. coupeis, wood newly cut.]
Coptic, kop'tik, a. Pertaining to the descendants of the ancient Egyptians, called Copts.—n. The language of the Copts.
Copula, kop'ū-la, n. A band; the word which unites the subject and predicate of a proposition. [L.]
Copulate, kop'ū-lāt, vi. To couple; to come together, as different sexes. ppr. copulating, pret. & pp. copulated. [L. copulo, copulatus.]
Copulation, kop-ū-lā'shon, n. Coition. [L. copulatio.]
Copulative, kop'ū-lāt-iv, a. That unites; noting a conjunction that connects two or more subjects or predicates.—n. A copulative conjunction.
Copy, ko'pi, n. A likeness; a transcript of an original; the imitation or likeness of any figure, &c.; an original work; an example for imitation.—vt. To make a likeness of; to write, print, or engrave according to an original; to transcribe; to follow or imitate as a pattern in manners or life.—vi. To endeavour to be like; to do anything in imitation of something else. ppr. copying, pret. & pp. copied. [Fr. copie.]
Copyhold, ko'pi-hōld, n. A tenure for which the tenant has nothing to show except the rolls made by the steward of the lord's court; land held in copyhold.

Copyholder, ko'pi-hōld-ėr, n. One who is possessed of land in copyhold.
Copyist, ko'pi-ist, n. A transcriber.
Copyright, ko'pi-rit, n. The exclusive right of an author or his representatives to print, publish, and vend a literary work. This right extends also to engravings, sculptures, &c., and to designs for useful and ornamental articles.
Coquet, kō-ket', vt. To trifle in love; to endeavour to attract admiration out of vanity. ppr. coquetting, pret.& pp coquetted. [Fr. coqueter—coq, a cock.]
Coquetry, kō'ket-ri, n. Attempts to attract admiration, or love, from vanity; trifling in love. [Fr. coquetterie.]
Coquette, kō-ket', n. A gay airy girl; a woman who endeavours to win a man's heart, and having won it, rejects it; a jilt. [Fr.]
Coquettish, kō-ket'ish, a. Practising coquetry.
Coral, ko'ral, n. A hard calcareous substance, red, white, or black, found in the ocean; a piece of coral, used as a child's toy.—a. Made of coral; resembling coral. [Gr. korallion.]
Coralled, ko'rald, p.a. Furnished with coral.
Coralliferous, ko-ral-lif'ėr-us, a. Producing or containing coral. [L. fero, to produce.]
Coralline, ko'ral-in, a. Consisting of coral; like coral; containing coral.—n. A submarine calcareous plant, consisting of many jointed branches, and often resembling moss. [L. corallinus.]
Coralloid, ko'ral-oid, a. Having the form of coral; branching like coral. [Gr. eidos, form.]
Cord, kord, n. A small rope, composed of several strands twisted together; a rope; a band; a sinew.—vt. To bind with a cord; to fasten with cords. [Fr. corde—L. chorda.]
Cordage, kord'āj, n. Term applied to all sorts of cords or ropes used in the running rigging of a ship. [Fr.]
Cord-grass, kord'gras, n. A tough stiff sort of marine grass.
Cordial, kord'i-al, a. Hearty; proceeding from the heart; heartfelt; invigorating.—n. A medicine which increases the action of the heart; a medicine which increases strength; a beverage; anything that gladdens or exhilarates. [Fr.—L. cor, cordis, the heart.]
Cordiality, kor-di-al'li-ti, n. Heartiness; sincerity; sincere affection and kindness.
Cordially, kor'di-al-li, adv. Heartily.
Cordon, kor'don, n. A ribbon bestowed as a badge of honour; a series of military posts; a row of projecting stones in fortification. [Fr.]
Cordovan, kor'dō-van, n. Spanish leather, originally from Cordova.
Corduroy, kor-dū-roi', n. The king's cord; a thick cotton stuff corded or ribbed. [Fr. corde du roi.]
Core, kōr, n. The heart or inner part of a thing; the central part of fruit containing the kernels or seeds. [Norm.—L. cor, the heart.]
Coriander, ko-ri-an'dėr, n. A plant which produces aromatic seeds; also the seeds of the plant. [L. coriandrum—Gr. koriannon.]
Corinthian, ko-rin'thi-an, a. Pertaining to Corinth; noting an order in architecture, the most delicate of all the orders, and enriched with a profusion of ornaments.—n.† A debauched man.
Corival†, kō-ri'val, n. A rival.—vt. To rival; to pretend to equal.

ch, chain; j, job; g, go; ng, sing; ᴡʜ, then; th, thin; w, wig; wh, whig; zh, azure; † obsolete.

Cork, kork, n. The bark of a tree, a species of oak, of which stopples for bottles and casks are made; the tree itself; a stopple made of cork.—vt. To stop with corks, as bottles or casks. [G. kork—L. cortex, bark.]
Corky, kork'i, a. Consisting of cork; resembling cork.
Cormorant, kor'mo-rant, n. The seacrow, or water-raven, distinguished for its voracity; a glutton. [Fr. cormoran.]
Corn, korn, n. A kernel; the seeds of plants which grow in ears, and which are made into bread, as the seeds of wheat, rye, barley, and oats.—vt. To sprinkle with salt in grains, as meat; to form into small grains; to feed with corn, as a horse. [Sax.]
Corn, korn, n. A hard horny excrescence on the toe or foot. [L. cornu.]
Cornea, kor'nē-a, n. The strong, horny, transparent membrane in the fore part of the eye, through which the rays of light pass. [from L. cornu, a horn.]
Corned, kornd, p.a. Cured by salting.
Corncrake, korn'krāk, n. A bird which frequents cornfields; the land-rail.
Corneous, kor'nē-us, a. Horny; consisting of a horny substance; hard. [L. corneus—cornu, a horn.]
Corner, kor'nėr, n. The outer or inner angle of a building, &c.; inner angle of a room, &c.; angle; a secret or retired place; a narrow place; utmost limit. [Old Fr. corniere—L. cornu, a horn.]
Corner-cap, kor'ner-kap, n. The chief ornament.
Corner-stone, kor'ner-stōn, n. The stone which lies at the corner of two walls, and unites them; the principal stone.
Cornet, kor'net, n. A sort of trumpet, shaped like a horn; an officer of a troop of cavalry who bears the standard. [Fr.—L. cornu, a horn.]
Cornetcy, kor'net-si, n. The commission or rank of a cornet.
Corneter, kor'net-ėr, n. One who blows a cornet.
Cornice, kor'nis, n. The projection at the top of the wall of a building; uppermost moulding of a pediment, room, &c. [It.—L. corōna, a crown.]
Cornish, korn'ish, a. Pertaining to Cornwall.—n. The language of Cornwall.
Cornist, korn'ist, n. A performer on the cornet or horn.
Cornopean, kor-nō'pē-an, n. A kind of horn; a musical instrument of modern invention. [from L. cornu.]
Corn-pipe, korn'pip, n. A pipe made by slitting the joint of a green stalk of corn.
Cornucopia, kor-nū-kō'pi-a, n. Cornucopiæ, kor-nū-kō'pi-ē, pl. The horn of plenty, an emblem of abundance of fruits. [L. cornu, and copia, plenty.]
Corny, kor'ni, a. Horny; strong, stiff, or hard like horn. [from L. cornu.]
Corny, korn'i, a. Producing corn; containing corn.
Corolla, ko-rol'la, n. A little crown; the inner covering of a flower. [L.—corōna, a crown.]
Corollary, ko'rol-la-ri, n. Something added, as a garland of flowers; surplus; something added to a proposition demonstrated; an inference; a deduction. [L. corollarium.]
Coronal, ko-rō'nal, a. Belonging to the crown of the head.—n. The first seam of the skull; the frontal bone. [L. coronālis.]
Coronation, ko-rō-nā'shon, n. Solemnity of crowning a sovereign; the pomp or assembly attending a coronation! [Low L. coronatio.]
Coroner, ko'rō-nėr, n. An officer in England whose chief duty is to hold a court of inquiry, to ascertain the cause of sudden or violent death. [Law L. coronator.]
Coronet, ko'rō-net, n. An inferior crown worn by noblemen; an ornamental head-dress; something that surmounts. [It. coronetta—L. corōna, a crown.]
Coroneted, ko'rō-net-ed, p.a. Wearing or entitled to wear a coronet.
Corporal, kor'po-ral, n. The lowest officer of a company of infantry; a naval officer under the master-at-arms. [Fr. caporal—L. caput, the head.]
Corporal, kor'po-ral, a. Belonging or relating to the body; material; corporeal. [L. corporalis.].
Corporally, kor'po-ral-li, adv. Bodily.
Corporalship, kor'po-ral-ship, n. A corporal's office or command.
Corporate, kor'po-rāt, a. Formed into a legal body, and empowered to act in legal processes as an individual; united. [L. corporātus—corpus, a body.]
Corporately, kor'po-rāt-li, adv. In a corporate capacity.
Corporation, kor-po-rā'shon, n. A body politic, formed and authorized by law to act as a single person; a society empowered to transact business as an individual. [L. corporatio.]
Corporeal, kor-pō'rē-al, a. Consisting of a material body; material; opposed to spiritual. [L. corporeus.]
Corporeally, kor-pō're-al-li, adv. In body; in a bodily form or manner.
Corps, kōr, pl. kōr, n. sing. and pl. A body of troops; any division of an army. [Fr.—L. corpus.]
Corpse, korps, n. The dead body of a human being; a carcass; remains. [L. corpus, a body, substance.]
Corpulence, kor'pū-lens, n. Grossness of body; excessive fleshiness or fatness. [L. corpulentia.]
Corpulent, kor'pū-lent, a. Having a gross or fleshy body; very fat; stout; lusty.
Corpuscle, kor'pus-l, n. A little body; a minute particle or physical atom. [L. corpusculum.]
Corpuscular, kor-pus'kū-lėr, a. Pertaining to small particles, supposed to be the constituent materials of all large bodies.
Correct, ko-rekt', a. Set right; conformable to a just standard; accurate; precise; exact; punctual.—vt. To make right; to bring to the standard of truth; to remove faults from; to reform; to chastise; to chasten. [L. correctus, from corrigo—rego, to keep right.]
Corrected, ko-rekt'ed, p.a. Amended.
Correction, ko-rek'shon, n. Act of correcting; state of being corrected; emendation of faults; discipline; chastisement; counteraction of what is inconvenient or hurtful. [L. correctio—rego, rectum, to keep in a straight line.]
Correctional, ko-rek'shon-al, a. Tending to or intended for correction. [Fr. correctionnel.]
Correctioner, ko-rek'shon-ėr, n. One who is, or who has been, in the house of correction.
Corrective, ko-rekt'iv, a. Having the power to correct; tending to rectify.—n. That which corrects; restrictiont.
Correctly, ko-rekt'li, adv. In a correct manner; exactly; accurately.
Correctness, ko-rekt'nes, n. Freedom from faults or errors; accuracy; exactness; regularity; precision.
Corrector, ko-rekt'ėr, n. He or that which corrects.
Correlation, ko-rē-lā'shon, n. Mutual or reciprocal relation. [Fr. corrélation.]
Correlative, ko-rel'āt-iv, a. Having a mutual relation; thus father and son, husband and wife, are correlative terms; reciprocal.—n. He or that which stands in reciprocal relation. [L. relativus—refero, to carry back.]
Correspond, ko-rē-spond', vi. To answer one to another; to be congruous; to be adapted to; to hold intercourse by sending and receiving letters. [Fr. correspondre—L. respondeo, to answer.]
Correspondence, ko-rē-spond'ens, n. Relation; mutual adaptation of one thing to another; intercourse by interchange of letters; the letters interchanged; friendly intercourse; reciprocal exchange of civilities. [Fr. correspondance.]
Correspondent, ko-rē-spond'ent, a. Suitable; congruous; answerable; adapted. n. One with whom an intercourse is carried on by letters or messages. [Fr. correspondant.]
Correspondently, ko-rē-spond'ent-li, adv. In a corresponding manner.
Corresponding, ko-rē-spond'ing. p.a. Answering; agreeing; suiting.
Correspondingly, ko-rē-spond'ing-li, adv. In a corresponding manner.
Corresponsive, ko-rē-spons'iv, a. Answerable; adapted.
Corridor, ko'ri-dōr, n. A gallery running round a building, leading to several chambers at a distance from each other. [Fr.—L. curro, to run.]
Corrigible, ko'ri-ji-bl, a. That may be set right; that may be reformed; punishable. [Fr.]
Corrigibleness, ko'ri-ji-bl-nes, n. Quality of being corrigible.
Corrival, ko-ri'val, n. A fellow-rival; a competitor.
Corroborant, ko-rob'ō-rant, a. Having the power or quality of giving strength. [L. corroborans.]
Corroborate, ko-rob'ō-rāt, vt. To strengthen greatly; to confirm; to make more certain. ppr. corroborating, pret. & pp. corroborated. [L. corroboro, corroboratus—robur, roboris, strength.]
Corroborated, ko-rob'ō-rāt-ed, p.a. Confirmed; rendered more certain; strengthened; established.
Corroborating, ko-rob'ō-rāt-ing, p.a. Strengthening; giving firmness.
Corroboration, ko-rob'ō-rā'shon, n. Act of strengthening; addition of strength, assurance, or security; confirmation.
Corroborative, ko-rob'ō-rāt-iv, a. Having the power of giving strength, or additional strength; tending to confirm.
Corrode, ko-rōd', vt. To eat or wear away by degrees; to consume by slow degrees; to prey upon; to waste away. ppr. corroding, pret. & pp. corroded. [L. corrodo—rodo, to gnaw.]
Corrodible, ko-rōd'i-bl, a. That may be corroded.
Corroding, ko-rōd'ing, p.a. Eating away gradually; impairing; wasting.
Corrosion, ko-rō'zhon, n. Action of eating or wearing away by slow degrees; state of being eaten or worn away. [from corrode.]
Corrosive, ko-rōs'iv, a. Corroding; eating away; having the quality of fretting or vexing; consuming; vexing.—n. That which eats or wears away gradually. [Fr. corrosif.]

Corrosiveness, ko-rōs'iv-nes, n. *Quality of corroding.*
Corrugate, ko'rū-gāt, vt. *To make full of wrinkles; to wrinkle; to contract into folds or furrows. ppr. corrugating, pret. & pp. corrugated.* [L. *corrugo, corrugatus*—*ruga*, a wrinkle.]
Corrugation, ko-rū-gā'shon, n. *A wrinkling;* contraction into wrinkles.
Corrupt, ko-rupt', vt. *To break to pieces; to change from a sound to a putrid state; to vitiate; to defile; to taint; to pervert; to bribe; to falsify.*—vi. *To become putrid; to rot; to become vitiated; to lose purity.*—a. *Changed from a sound to a putrid state; tainted; depraved; rendered impure; changed to a worse state.* [L. *corrumpo, corruptus*—*rumpo*, to break.]
Corrupted, ko-rupt'ed, p.a. Depraved; marred; bribed.
Corrupter, ko-rupt'ėr, n. *One who corrupts;* one who vitiates or taints.
Corruptibility, ko-rupt'i-bil'i-ti, n. *The possibility of being corrupted.*
Corruptible, ko-rupt'i-bl, a. *That may become putrid; subject to decay and destruction.*—n. *That which may decay and perish;* the human body. [Fr. *corruptible.*]
Corruptibly, ko-rupt'i-bli, adv. In such a manner as to be corrupted.
Corrupting, ko-rupt'ing, p.a. Depraving; vitiating.
Corruption, ko-rup'shon, n. *Act of corrupting;* the destruction of the natural form or mode of existence of bodies by putrefaction; putrid matter; pus; perversion of moral principles; loss of purity or integrity; pollution; taint of blood; bribe-taking; bribery. [L. *corruptio.*]
Corruptive, ko-rupt'iv, a. *Having the quality of corrupting* or vitiating.
Corruptly, ko-rupt'li, adv. *In a corrupt manner;* with corruption; viciously.
Corruptness, ko-rupt'nes, n. Putrid state; state of moral impurity.
Corsair, kor'sār, n. A cruiser; a rover; a pirate; a piratical vessel. [Fr. *corsaire*—L. *curro*, to run.]
Corse, kors, n. *A corpse;* the dead body of a human being. (A poetical word.) [Fr. *corps*—L. *corpus*, a body.]
Corselet, kors'let, n. *A little cuirass,* or an armour to cover the *body* for protection, worn formerly by pikemen. [Fr. *corselet.*]
Corset, kor'set, n. An article of dress laced closely round the female *body;* stays. [Fr.]
Cortege, kor'tāzh, n. *A court retinue;* a train of attendants. [Fr. *cortége*—*cour,* a court.]
Cortical, kor'tik-al, a. *Belonging to,* consisting of, or resembling *bark;* belonging to the external covering. [from L. *cortex, corticis,* bark.]
Coruscant, ko-rus'kant, a. Flashing; glittering by flashes. [L. *coruscans.*]
Coruscate, ko-rus'kit, vi. To throw off flashes of light, as a bright *helmet;* to tremble; to glitter; to gleam; to flash. ppr. coruscating, pret. & pp. coruscated. [L. *corusco, coruscatus.*]
Coruscation, ko-rus-kā'shon, n. A glittering or flashing; a quick vibration of light; a flash of intellectual brilliancy. [L. *coruscatio.*]
Corvette, kor-vet', n. A sloop of war, ranking next below a frigate. [Fr.— L. *curvus,* crooked.]
Corvine, kor'vin, a. *Pertaining to the crow.* [from L. *corvus,* a crow.]
Coryphæus, ko-ri-fē'us, n. *The chief* or leader of the ancient chorus; the chief

of a company. [L.—Gr. *koruphē,* the top of the head.]
Cosier, kō'zhi-ėr, n. A tailor who botches his work.
Cosmetic, koz-met'ik, a. *Adorning;* improving beauty, particularly that of the skin.—n. A wash or any external application that helps to improve the complexion. [Gr. *kosmetikos*—*kosmos,* order, an ornament, the world.]
Cosmic, Cosmical, koz'mik, koz'mik-al, a. *Relating to* the whole frame of the *universe;* rising or setting with the sun. [Gr. *kosmikos* — *kosmos,* the world.]
Cosmically, koz'mik-al-li, adv. With the sun at rising or setting.
Cosmogony, kos-mog'on-i, n. *The origin or creation of the world or universe.* [Gr. *kosmogonia*—*kosmos,* order, the world, and *gonē,* generation.]
Cosmography, koz-mog'ra-fi, n. *A description of the* system of the material *world* or universe. [Gr. *kosmographia*—*kosmos,* and *graphō,* to describe.]
Cosmologist, kos-mol'o-jist, n. *One* versed *in cosmology.*
Cosmology, koz-mol'o-ji, n. *The science* of the *world* or universe. [Gr. *kosmologia*—*kosmos,* and *logos,* doctrine.]
Cosmopolitan, kos-mo-pol'i-tan, a. *Free from local* attachments or prejudices; capable of living in any part of the world. [Gr. *kosmos,* world, and *politēs,* citizen.]
Cosmopolite, kos-mop'o-lit, n. *A citizen of the world;* one who is at home in every place.
Cosmorama, kos-mo-rä'ma, n. A picturesque *view of the world* or parts of it. [Gr. *kosmos,* and *horama,* a view.]
Cost, kost, vi. To be bought for; to be had at the price of; to require to be laid out; to require to be borne or suffered. *ppr.* costing, *pret. & pp.* cost. n. *That which anything stands at;* that which is paid for anything; charge; expenditure; loss; suffering; luxury; great expense; (pl.) expenses of a lawsuit. [G. *kosten,* to bear a price.]
Costard, kos'tärd, n. A large apple; the head.
Costermonger, kos'tėr-mung-gėr, n. A hawker who sells any kind of fruit, &c.
Costive, kos'tiv, a. *Constipated; stuffed,* as the intestines; bound in the body or bowels. [from It. *costipato*—L. *stipo,* to cram.]
Costively, kos'tiv-li, adv. *With costiveness.*
Costiveness, kos'tiv-nes, n. *State of being costive.*
Costliness, kost'li-nes, n. *State of being costly;* expensiveness; sumptuousness.
Costly, kost'li, a. Of a high price; valuable; precious; dear; sumptuous.
Costmary, kost'ma-ri, n. A species of tansy, dedicated to the *Virgin Mary.* [L. *costum,* an aromatic plant, and *Maria.*]
Costume, kos'tūm, n. An *established* mode of dress, particularly that which is appropriate to a given age, place, person, &c.; the accessories of a painting, &c. [Old Fr. *coustume*—L. *consuetudo,* habit.]
Costumer, kos'tūm-ėr, n. *One who deals in costumes.*
Co-supreme, kō-sū-prēm', n. *A partaker of supremacy.*
Co-surety, kō-shūr'ti, n. *A joint surety;* one who is surety with another.
Cot, Cote, kot, kōt, n. A small house; a cottage; a shed or inclosure for beasts. [Sax. *cota.*]
Cot, Cott, kot, kot, n. *A small bed;* a

kind of suspended hammock on board of ships. [Old Fr. *coste, cotte.*]
Cotet, kōt, vi. To go side by side with; to pass by.
Cotemporaneous, kō-tem'pō-rā"nē-us,a. Living or being *at the same time with another.* [L. *contemporaneus*—*tempus, temporis,* time.]
Cotemporaneously, kō-tem'pō-rā"nē-us-li, adv. *At the same time with some other event.*
Cotemporary, kō-tem'pō-ra-ri, a. Living or being *at the same time with another.* n. *One* who lives *at the same time with another.* [Fr. *contemporaire.*]
Coterie, kō'te-rē, n. A circle of familiar friends; a meeting for social or literary intercourse; an exclusive society. [Fr.]
Cotidal, kō-tid'al, a. Marking places where the *tide,* or high water, takes place *at the same time,* as cotidal lines.
Co-trustee, kō-trus-tē', n. *A joint trustee.*
Cott, kot, n. A small bed. [See *Cot.*]
Cottage, kot'tāj, n. *A cot;* a hut; a small habitation for poor persons; a small but neat and tasteful house. [Old Fr. *cotage.*]
Cottager, kot'tāj-ėr, n. *One who lives in a hut or cottage.*
Cotton, kot'tn, n. A soft, downy substance, resembling fine wool, growing in the pods of several species of plants; cloth made of cotton.—a. *Pertaining to,* made of, or consisting of *cotton.* [Ar. *kotn.*]
Cotton-thistle, kot'tn-this-l, n. A kind of *woolly thistle.*
Cotton-wood, kot'tn-wud, n. A large tree of the poplar kind.
Cotton-wool, kot'tn-wul, n. *Cotton* in the raw state.
Cottony, kot'tn-i, a. Covered with hairs *like cotton.*
Couch, kouch, vi. *To lie down,* as on a bed or place of repose; to stoop; to bend down; to lie down in secret; to lie close and concealed.—vt. *To lay down;* to place upon a bed; to comprise; to express; to phrase; to fix, as a spear in the rest; to depress, as a cataract in the eye. [Fr. *coucher*—L. *loco,* to place or lay.]—n. *A bed;* a place for rest or sleep; a seat of repose; a place for rest and ease. [Fr. *couche.*]
Couching, kouch'ing, p.n. Act of stooping or bowing; act of removing a cataract.
Cough, kof, n. A violent convulsive effort of the lungs to throw off offending matter; a violent sonorous expulsion of air from the lungs.—vi. To make a violent effort with noise to expel the air from the lungs, and throw off any offensive matter.—vt. To expel from the lungs by a violent effort with noise; to expectorate (with *up*). [D. *kuch.*]
Coughing, kof'ing, p.n. A violent effort with noise to expel the air from the lungs.
Could, kud. Had sufficient physical or moral power. [Sax. *cuthe,* was able.]
Coulter, kōl'tėr, n. *A plough-knife;* the fore iron of a plough, with a sharp edge, that cuts the earth or sod. [Old Fr. *coultre*—L. *culter,* a knife.]
Council, koun'sil, n. Men *called together* for deliberation and advice; a body of men specially designated to advise a sovereign in the administration of the government; an assembly of divines convened for regulating matters of doctrine and discipline; a convocation. [Fr. *concile*—L. *cieo,* to put in motion.]
Council-board, koun'sil-bōrd, n. *Coun-*

cil-table; the table round which a council holds consultation.

Councillor, koun'sil-ėr, *n. A member of a council.*

Counsel, koun'sel, *n. A considering together;* advice; direction; interchange of opinions; design; prudence; secrecy; a counsellor or counsellors, who plead causes; a barrister; an advocate.—*vt. To give counsel* or deliberate opinion to; to advise; to warn or instruct. *ppr.* counselling, *pret. & pp.* counselled. [Fr. *conseil*—L. *consilio*, to consult.]

Counsellable, koun'sel-a-bl, *a. That may be counselled;* willing to receive counsel.

Counsellor, koun'sel-ėr, *n. Any person who gives,* or is authorized to give, *counsel;* a member of a council; a councillor; a person retained by a client to plead his cause in a court of judicature; a barrister.

Count, kount, *vt. To compute;* to calculate; to rate; to estimate; to consider; to judge; to impute.—*vi.* To found an account or reckoning; to depend; to rely (with *on* or *upon*); to add to the number.—*n. Reckoning;* a particular charge in an indictment. [Fr. *compter*—L. *computo*—*puto*, to clear up.]

Count, kount, *n. A companion of* a prince; a title of nobility on the continent of Europe, equivalent to the English earl, and whose domain is a county. [Fr. *comte*—L. *comes*, a companion.]

Countable, kount'a-bl, *a. That may be numbered.*

Countenance, koun'ten-ans, *n. The whole form* of the human face, or system of features; visage; air; aspect; favour; good-will; encouragement.—*vt.* To favour; to encourage; to vindicate by any means. *ppr.* countenancing, *pret. & pp.* countenanced. [Fr. *contenance*—L. *teneo*, to hold.]

Counter, kount'ėr, *n. He or that which counts;* that which is used as a means of *counting;* an imitation of a piece of money, used in games; a table on which money is counted, or on which goods are laid for examination. [from *count.*]

Counter, kount'ėr, *adv. Contrary;* in an opposite direction.—*a. Contrary;* in opposition. [Fr. *contre*—L. *contra.*]

Counteract, koun-tėr-akt', *vt. To act in opposition to;* to hinder; to defeat; to prevent. [L. *ago, actus,* to act.]

Counteracting, koun-tėr-akt'ing, *p.a.* Hindering; frustrating.

Counteraction, koun'tėr-ak-shon, *n. Action in opposition;* hindrance.

Counter-attraction, kount'ėr-at-trak-shon, *n. Opposite attraction.*

Counterbalance, koun-tėr-bal'ans, *vt. To weigh against* with an equal weight; to act against with equal power.—*n.* Equal *weight,* power, or agency, acting in opposition to anything. *ppr.* counter*b*alancing, *pret. & pp.* counterbalanced.

Counterbalancing, koun-tėr-bal'ans-ing, *p.a.* Opposing by equal *weight,* power, or operation.

Countercharge, koun'tėr-chärj, *n.* An *opposing charge.*

Countercharm, koun'tėr-chärm, *n.* That which has the power of *opposing* the effect of a *charm.* [*counter* and *charm.*]

Countercheck, koun-tėr-chek', *vt. To check in opposition;* to stop by some obstacle; to check.—*n. Check;* rebuke; a censure to check a reprover.

Counter-evidence, koun'tėr-ev-i-dens,

n. Evidence which *opposes* other evidence.

Counterfeit, koun'tėr-fit, *vt. To make in opposition* to the reality; to forge; to copy without right, and with a view to defraud; to feign; to imitate.—*vi.* To feign; to dissemble.—*a. Made* in imitation of something else with a view to defraud; fictitious; dissembled; fraudulent.—*n.* An impostor; one who pretends to be what he is not; a copy intended to be passed off as an original; a forgery. [Fr. *contrefait,* pp. of *contrefaire*—L. *facio,* to make.]

Counterfeited, koun'tėr-fit-ed, *p.a.* Copied; imitated; feigned.

Counterfeiter, koun'tėr-fit-ėr, *n. One who counterfeits;* a forger.

Counterfeiting, koun'tėr-fit-ing, *p.n.* Act of forging or imitating.

Counter-irritant, koun'tėr-i-rit-ant, *n.* A substance employed to produce an artificial *disease,* in order to relieve another one.

Counter-irritation, koun'tėr-i-ri-tā"-shon, *n.* The production of a secondary disease, in order to relieve a primary one.

Countermand, koun-tėr-mand', *vt.* To revoke, as a former *command;* to oppose; to contradict, as the orders of another.—*n. A contrary order;* revocation of a former order. [Fr. *contremander*—L. *mando,* to command.]

Countermarch, koun'tėr-märch, *vt.* To march back.—*n. A marching back;* a returning.

Countermark, koun'tėr-märk, *n. A mark set over against* some other mark; a second or third mark put on a bale of goods belonging to several merchants; the mark of the London goldsmiths' company, added to that of the artificer; a second mark on a coin or medal.

Countermine, koun'tėr-min, *n. A mine* formed to defeat the purpose of one made by an enemy; means of counteraction; a counterplot. [L. *contra,* and Eng. *mine.*]

Countermine, koun-tėr-min', *vt. To defeat by a countermine;* to frustrate by secret and opposite measures. *ppr.* countermining, *pret. & pp.* countermined.

Countermotion, koun'tėr-mō-shon, *n. An opposing motion.*

Counterpane, koun'tėr-pān, *n.* Uppermost bed-cover; coverlet; quilt.

Counterpart, kount'tėr-pärt, *n. The part* that answers to another; a person or thing having qualities lacking in another; a copy; a duplicate of an indenture or deed.

Counterplot, koun-tėr-plot', *vi. To oppose one plot* to another.—*vt.* To plot *against* in order to defeat another plot; to baffle by an opposite plot. *ppr.* counterplotting, *pret. & pp.* counterplotted.

Counterplot, koun'tėr-plot, *n. A plot or artifice opposed to another.*

Counterpoint, koun'tėr-point, *n.* Written harmony, originally consisting of *points* placed *opposite* to each other. [Fr. *contrepointe*—L. *punctum,* a point.]

Counterpoise, koun'tėr-poiz, *vt. To counterbalance;* to act against with equal power or effect. *ppr.* counterpoising, *pret. & pp.* counterpoised.—*n.* A *weight* which balances another weight in the *opposite* scale; equivalence of power or force; equilibrium. [Fr. *contrepeser*—L. *penso,* to weigh.]

Counterpressure, koun'tėr-pre-shūr, *n. Opposing pressure.*

Counterscarp, koun'tėr-skärp, *n.* The exterior slope of the ditch of a fortified place *facing* the *scarp;* a covered way. [Fr. *contrescarpe.*]

Counterseal, koun-tėr-sēl', *vt. To affix a seal* to *against* another; to seal with another.

Countersign, koun-tėr-sin', *vt. To sign,* as a writing, *over against* the signature of another; to sign, as what has already been signed by a superior, to render it more authentic.

Countersign, koun'tėr-sin, *n.* A military watchword.

Counter-signature, koun'tėr-sig-na-tūr, *n.* The name of a secretary *countersigned* to a writing.

Counterstroke, koun'tėr-strōk, *n. A stroke returned.*

Countersway, koun'tėr-swā, *n.* Opposite influence.

Countervail, koun-tėr-vāl', *vt. To act against* with equal power or effect. [L. *contra,* and *valeo,* to be strong.]

Countervailing, koun-tėr-vāl'ing, *p.a. Opposing* with equal *strength* or value; balancing; obviating an effect.

Counterwork, koun-tėr-wėrk', *vt. To work in opposition to;* to counteract.

Countess, kount'es, *n.* The consort of an earl or *count.*

Counting, kount'ing, *p.n. The art of computing* or reckoning.

Countless, kount'les, *a.* That cannot be *counted;* innumerable.

Country, kun'tri, *n.* The *land* lying about or near a city or town; a region; a territory; a kingdom; the land of one's birth or residence; the inhabitants of a region; rural parts, as opposed to town.—*a. Pertaining to the country;* rural; ignorant; peculiar to one's own country. [Fr. *contrée*—L. *terra,* the earth, land.]

Country-dance, kun'tri-dans, *n. A dance* in which the partners are arranged *opposite to each other* in lines. [Fr. *contre danse.*]

Countryman, kun'tri-man, *n.* One born in the same *country* with another; one who dwells in the country; a rustic; a husbandman.

County, koun'ti, *n.* A circuit or particular portion of a state or kingdom in which courts are held; a shire; a *count.*—*a. Pertaining to a county.* [Fr. *comté*—L. *comes,* a companion.]

County-town, koun'ti-toun, *n. That town* where the various courts of a *county* are held.

Couple, ku'pl, *n. That which joins together;* a band; a chain, &c.; two of the same kind, and near in place, or considered together; a pair; a brace; two things of any kind linked together; a man and his wife; a male and a female betrothed, or united in affection.—*vt. To join* together; to join in wedlock; to marry.—*vi. To join* in embraces; to unite. *ppr.* coupling, *pret. & pp.* coupled. [Fr.—L. *copula,* a band, tie.]

Coupled, ku'pld, *p.a.* Linked together; married.

Coupler, ku'pl-ėr, *n. He or that which couples.*

Couplet, kup'let, *n. Two verses;* two lines that rhyme; a division of a hymn or ode. [Fr.]

Coupling, ku'pl-ing, *p.n. Act of joining together;* a hook, chain, or bar.

Courage, ku'rij, *n. Strength of heart;* intrepidity; dauntlessness; active fortitude; hardihood. [Fr.—L. *cor,* the heart, and *ago,* to move.]

Courageous, ku-rā'je-us, *a.* Bold to em-counter difficulties and dangers; brave; heroic; fearless.

Courageously, ku-rā'jē-us-li, *adv.* With courage; bravely; boldly; stoutly.

Courier, kö'rē-ér, *n.* A running messenger; a messenger sent express for conveying despatches, usually on public business; a travelling attendant. [Fr. *courrier*—L. *curro*, to run.]

Course, kōrs, *n.* A *running*; flight; a passage; journey; voyage; route; a moving forward; line of motion; point of compass on which a ship sails; ground on which a race is run; gradual advance; order of succession; stated and orderly method; methodical procedure through any science, art, or branch of learning; whole range of subjects taught in a university, &c.; a continuous range or layer of stones in masonry; way of life; line of conduct; natural bent; orderly structure; dishes set on table at one time; ceremony.—*vi.* To run after; to hunt; to cause to run; to run through or over. *vi.* To run; to move with speed. *ppr.* coursing, *pret. & pp.* coursed. [Fr.—L. *cursus*, a running—*curro*, to run.]

Courser, kōrs'ér, *n.* A *runner*; a swift horse; a war-horse; a hunter.

Coursing, kōrs'ing, *p.n.* The act or sport of chasing and hunting hares, foxes, or deer.

Court, kōrt, *n.* A *place shut in* by the wings or parts of a building; a place forming a kind of recess from a public street; a palace; the place of residence of a king; the family and retinue of a sovereign; the judge or judges assembled for deciding causes; the place where judges assemble; a seat of justice; any jurisdiction; the art of pleasing; flattery; the parliament, consisting of the sovereign, lords, and commons, being the supreme court of the kingdom.—*vt.* To pay court to; to endeavour to please by civilities; to woo; to attempt to gain by address; to seek. [Old Fr.—L. *cohors, cohortis.*]

Court-cupboard, kōrt'kup-bōrd, *n.* A movable closet in which plate was displayed on special occasions.

Court-day, kōrt'dā, *n.* A day in which a court sits to administer justice.

Courted, kōrt'ed, *p.a.* Flattered; sought.

Courteous, kōrt'ē-us, *a.* Exhibiting the polished manners of a court; complaisant; affable; respectful. [Fr. *courtois.*]

Courteously, kōrt'ē-us-li, *adv.* In a courteous manner.

Courteousness, kōrt'ē-us-nes, *n.* Quality of being courteous.

Courter, kōrt'ér, *n.* One who courts.

Courtesy, kōrt'e-si, *n.* Urbanity; complaisance; condescending affability; good breeding; act of kindness; a favour graciously conferred; the act of civility or reverence performed by a woman, as by gently bending the knee. *vi.* To make a courtesy; to perform an act of civility or reverence, as a woman. *ppr.* courtesying, *pret. & pp.* courtesied. [Fr. *courtoisie.*]

Courtezan, kōrt'ē-zan, *n.* A prostitute. [Fr. *courtisane.*]

Courthand, kōrt'hand, *n.* The hand or manner of writing used in records and judicial proceedings.

Courthouse, kōrt'hous, *n.* A house appropriated to courts and public meetings.

Courtier, kōrt'i-ér, *n.* A man who attends courts; a person of courtly manners; a refined flatterer.

Courting, kōrt'ing, *p.n.* Act of paying court.

Courtliness, kōrt'li-nes, *n.* Quality of being courtly; elegance of manners; grace of mien; civility.

Courtly, kōrt'li, *a.* Relating to a court; elegant; polite; with dignity; flattering.

Court-martial, kōrt-mär'shal, *n.* Court-martial, *pl.* A court consisting of military or naval officers for the trial of offences of a military or naval character.

Court-plaster, kōrt'plas-tér, *n.* Sticking plaster made of black silk.

Court-roll, kōrt'rōl, *n.* The records of a court.

Courtship, kōrt'ship, *n.* Act of courting or soliciting favour; act of wooing in love.

Courtyard, kōrt'yärd, *n.* A court or inclosure round a house.

Cousin, kuz'n, *n.* One who springs from the same blood; the son or daughter of an uncle or aunt; a kinsman or blood relation; (pl.) the children of brothers and sisters. [Fr.—L. *con*, and *sanguis*, blood.]

Cove, kōv, *n.* An inlet, bending and sheltered; a small inlet, creek, or bay; a sheltered recess in the seashore. [Sax. *cof, cofe*—Heb. *kāfaf*, to bend.]

Coved, kōvd, *p.a.* Formed with a cove; arched over.

Covenant, kuv'en-ant, *n.* A coming together; a contract; compact; bargain; a bond of union; a writing containing the terms of an agreement.—*vi.* To enter into a formal agreement; to agree; bargain; stipulate. [Fr. *convenant*, agreeing—L. *venio*, to come.]

Covenanted, kuv'en-ant-ed, *p.a.* Pledged or promised by covenant.

Covenanter, kuv'en-ant-ér, *n.* One who makes a covenant; a subscriber to the Scottish national Covenant in the reign of Charles I.

Cover, kuv'ér, *vt.* To overspread, so as to hide; to conceal by some intervening object; to cloak; to secrete; to defend; to clothe; to wrap up; to brood on; to be sufficient for; to include.—*n.* Anything which veils or conceals; disguise; shelter; defence; protection; retreat, as of a fox or hare; the table furniture for the use of one person at a meal. [Fr. *couvrir*—L. *con*, and *operio*, to cover.]

Covered, kuv'érd, *p.a.* Hid; concealed; used for concealment.

Covering, kuv'ér-ing. *p.n.* Envelope; integument; clothing; dress; bed-clothes.

Coverlet, kuv'ér-let, *n.* The cover of a bed; a piece of furniture designed to be spread over all the other covering of a bed. [Fr. *lit*—L. *lectus*, a bed.]

Covert, kuv'ért, *a.* Covered; concealed; disguised; sheltered; under authority or protection.—*n.* A place which covers and shelters; a thicket; a shady place, or a hiding-place. [Fr. *couvert.*]

Covertly, kuv'ért-li, *adv.* Secretly; closely; in private; insidiously.

Coverture, kuv'ért-ūr, *n.* Shelter; defence; the legal state of a married woman. [Fr. *couverture.*]

Covet, kuv'et, *vt.* To wish for; to long for (in a good sense); to desire unlawfully; to hanker after; to desire to obtain by unlawful means.—*vi.* To have an earnest desire (with *after*). [Fr. *convoiter*—L. *voveo, votum*, to wish for.]

Covetable, kuv'et-a-bl, *a.* That may be coveted.

Coveted, kuv'et-ed, *p.a.* Greatly wished or longed for.

Covetous, kuv'et-us, *a.* Eager to obtain; excessively eager to obtain and possess; avaricious; eager for gain. [Fr. *convoiteux.*]

Covetously, kuv'et-us-li, *adv.* In a covetous manner.

Covetousness, kuv'et-us-nes, *n.* An inordinate desire of obtaining; avarice; eagerness for gain; eagerness.

Covey, kuv'ē, *n.* A hatch of birds; a small flock or number of birds together; a brood of partridges; a company; a set. [Fr. *couvée*—L. *cubo*, to lie down.]

Cow, kou, *n.* Cows, *pl.* Kine, old pl. The female of the bull, or of the bovine genus of animals. [Sax. *cu.*]

Cow, kou, *vt.* To sink the spirits or courage of; to oppress with habitual timidity; to dishearten. [Dan. *kue.*]

Coward, kou'érd, *n.* One who turns tail; a person who wants courage to meet danger; a craven; a dastard.—*a.* Destitute of courage; dastardly; timid; base. [Old Fr. *couard*—L. *cauda*, the tail.]

Cowardice, kou'érd-is, *n.* Want of courage to face danger. [Old Fr. *couardise.*]

Cowardliness, kou'érd-li-nes, *n.* Want of courage; timidity; cowardice.

Cowardly, kou'érd-li, *a.* Wanting courage to face danger; faint-hearted; mean; base.—*adv.* In the manner of a coward; meanly; basely.

Cowed, koud, *p.a.* Dispirited; crushed.

Cower, kou'ér, *vi.* To crouch; to sink by bending the knees; to shrink through fear. [G. *kauern.*]

Cowering, kou'ér-ing, *p.a.* Timorous.

Cowherd, kou'hérd, *n.* One who tends cows.

Cowhide, kou'hīd, *n.* The hide of a cow, made or to be made into leather.

Cowish, kou'ish, *a.* Timorous; fearful.

Cowl, koul, *n.* A monk's hood; a cover for a chimney which turns with the wind. [Sax. *cuhle.*]

Cowled, kould, *a.* Hooded; in shape of a cowl.

Cow-pox, kou'poks, *n.* The vaccine disease, which appears on the teats of the cow.

Cowslip, kou'slip, *n.* A plant of the genus primrose, of several varieties, appearing early in the spring. [Sax. *cuslippa*—*cu*, a cow, and *lippa*, a lip.]

Coxcomb, koks'kōm, *n.* The capt; a fop; a superficial pretender to knowledge or accomplishments.

Coxcombry, koks'kōm-ri, *n.* The manners of a coxcomb; foppishness.

Coxswain. See COCKSWAIN.

Coy, koi, *a.* Quiet; gentle; reserved; shrinking; modest; bashful.—*vt.* To allure.—*vi.* To make difficulty. [Fr. *coi*—L. *quietus—quies*, rest.]

Coyish, koi'ish, *a.* Somewhat coy.

Coyly, koi'li, *adv.* With reserve; with disinclination to familiarity.

Coyness, koi'nes, *n.* Quality of being coy; shyness; bashfulness.

Coz, koz, *n.* A familiar contraction of cousin.

Cozen, kuz'n, *vt.* To flatter; to fawn upon; to cheat; to defraud; to beguile. [Middle High G. *kōsen*, to flatter.]

Cozenage, kuz'n-āj, *n.* Cheat; trick; artifice; the practice of cheating.

Cozener, kuz'n-ér, *n.* One who cheats or defrauds.

Crab, krab, *n.* That which gripes; a crustaceous fish with strong claws for griping; a wild apple; a morose person; an engine with claws for launching ships, &c.; a portable crane for raising materials; Cancer, a sign of

the zodiac.—*a.* Sour; rough; austere. [Sax. *crabba.*]
Crabbed, krab'ed, *a.* Rough; peevish; cynical; perplexing.
Crabbedly, krab'ed-li, *adv.* Peevishly.
Crabbedness, krab'ed-nes, *n. Quality of being crabbed;* peevishness; perplexity.
Crack, krak, *n.* A disruption; a chink or fissure; a crevice; any sudden or sharp sound; a sharp sound uttered suddenly; a violent report.—*vt.* To rend, break, or burst into chinks; to cause to sound sharply; to snap; to thrust out, or utter with smartness; to make crazy.—*vi.* To burst partially; to split; to open in chinks; to utter a loud or sharp sudden sound. [Fr. *crac.*]
Crack-brained, krak'brānd, *a.* Having the intellect impaired; crazy.
Cracked, krakt, *p.a.* Partially severed; impaired; crazy.
Cracker, krak'ėr, *n. He or that which cracks;* a quantity of gunpowder confined so as to explode with noise.
Crackle, krak'l, *vi.* To make small abrupt noises, rapidly or frequently repeated. *ppr.* crackling, *pret. & pp.* crackled. [dimin. of *crack.*]
Crackling, krak'l-ing, *p.n. The making of small abrupt cracks;* the rind of roasted pork.
Cracknel, krak'nel, *n.* A hard brittle cake or biscuit. [Fr. *craquelin.*]
Cradle, krā'dl, *n. A small car;* a movable bed in which infants are rocked; state of infancy; something resembling a cradle; a case or frame to hold or keep together.—*vt.* To lay or rock *in a cradle;* to quiet; to nurse in infancy.—*vi.* To lie or lodge *in a cradle.* *ppr.* cradling, *pret. & pp.* cradled. [Sax. *cradel.*—L. *crates,* wicker-work.]
Craft, kraft, *n.* Ability; art; skill; cunning; artifice; guile; manual art; a vessel or ship.—*vi.*† To indulge in deceit. [Sax. *cræft.*]
Craftily, kraf'ti-li, *adv.* In *a crafty manner;* artfully; cunningly.
Craftiness, kraf'ti-nes, *n.* Artfulness; cunning; stratagem.
Craftsman, krafts'man, *n.* One skilled in a manual occupation; an artificer.
Crafty, kraf'ti, *a.* Skilful in devising and pursuing a scheme; cunning; artful; sly; deceitful.
Crag, krag, *n. A steep rugged rock;* a rough broken rock, or point of a rock; gravel or sand mixed with shells. [Gael. *creag.*]
Cragged, krag'ed, *a. Full of crags* or broken rocks; rough; rugged.
Craggy, krag'i, *a. Full of crags;* abounding with broken rocks.
Crake, krāk, *n.* The corn-crake or landrail, so named from its singular cry.
Cram, kram, *vt.* To thrust in by force; to stuff; to crowd; to fill with food beyond satiety.—*vi.* To stuff; to eat greedily or beyond satiety. *ppr.* cramming, *pret. & pp.* crammed. [Sax. *crammian.*]
Cramp, kramp, *n. That which contracts;* a spasmodic *contraction* of a limb or some muscle; restriction; impediment; piece of iron bent at the ends, serving to hold together pieces of timber, stones, &c.—*vt.* To pain or *affect with spasms;* to restrain; to hinder from action or expansion. [D. *kramp;* Dan. *krampe.*]
Cramped, krampt, *p.a.* Confined; restrained.
Cranberry, kran'be-ri, *n.* A red, sour berry much used for making sauce, &c. [G. *kranbeere.*]
Crane, krān, *n.* A migratory bird with *long legs,* a long neck, and a long beak; a machine used for raising and removing great weights; a crooked pipe for drawing liquors out of a cask. [Sax. *cran.*]
Crane's-bill, krānz'bil, *n.* The plant *Geranium,* of many species.
Cranial, krā'ni-al, *a. Relating to or like a cranium* or skull.
Craniologist, krā-ni-ol'o-jist, *n.* One versed in craniology.
Craniology, krā-ni-ol'o-ji, *n. A discourse on the cranium* or skull. [Gr. *kranion,* and *logos,* discourse.]
Cranium, krā'ni-um, *n. The skull* of an animal; the assemblage of bones which inclose the brain. [L.—Gr. *kranion,* a skull.]
Crank, krangk, *n.* A winding; anything bent or turned; an iron axis with a part bent like an elbow, for producing a horizontal or perpendicular motion. [D. *krinkel,* a curve.]
Crank, krangk, *a.* Weak†; liable to be overset, as a ship that wants steadiness. [Old G. *krank,* weak.]
Crankle, krangk'l, *vt.* To crinkle.—*n.* A crinkle.
Crankness, krangk'nes, *n. State* or quality of being *crank;* liability to be overset, as a ship.
Cranny, kran'ni, *n. A notch;* any small narrow opening, or chink, as in a wall or other substance; a secret, retired place.—*vi.* To make crannies. *ppr.* crannying, *pret. & pp.* crannied. [Fr. *cran,* a notch, mark.]
Crape, krāp, *n.* A thin, transparent stuff of a *crisp texture,* usually black, made of raw silk, and much used in mourning. [Fr. *crêpe.*]
Crare†, krār, *n.* A slow, unwieldy trading vessel.
Crash, krash, *vi.* To make the sound caused by the act of *crushing;* to make *the loud sound of many things falling* and breaking at once.—*n.* The sound produced by the act of *crushing.*
Crashing, krash'ing, *p.n.* The sound of many things falling and breaking at once.
Crasis, krā'sis, *n.* A contraction of two syllables into one. [Gr. a mixing.]
Crass, kras, *a.* Gross; thick; coarse. [L. *crassus,* thick.]
Crate, krāt, *n.* Wicker-work; a kind of basket of wicker-work, used for the transportation of china, crockery, &c. [L. *crates.*]
Crater, krā'tėr, *n. A bowl;* a cup-shaped cavity; the circular cavity or mouth of a volcano. [L.—Gr. *kratēr,* a bowl.]
Craunch, kranch, *vt. See* CRUNCH.
Cravat, kra-vat', *n.* A kind of neckcloth, said to have been first introduced into France from the *Cravates,* or Croatians. [Fr. *cravate.*]
Crave, krāv, *vt.* To ask; to ask with earnestness; to ask submissively; to beseech; to long for; to call for, as a gratification. *ppr.* craving, *pret. & pp.* craved. [Sax. *crafian.*]
Craven, krā'vn, *n.* A coward; a weakhearted, spiritless fellow; a vanquished, dispirited cock.—*a.* Cowardly; with meanness; base.—*vt.*† *To make cowardly.* [Old Fr. *cravanter,* to foil.]
Craver, krāv'ėr, *n. One who craves.*
Craving, krāv'ing, *p.a.* Demanding gratification.—*p.n.* Vehement or urgent desire or calling for; a longing for.
Craw, kra, *n. The crop* or first stomach of fowls. [Dan. *kros.*]
Crawfish, Crayfish, krā'fish, krā'fish, *n.* A species of crab or lobster found in fresh-water streams. [Fr. *écrevisse.*]
Crawl, kral, *vi. To creep;* to move slowly by drawing the body along the ground, as a worm; to move slowly on the hands and knees; to advance slowly, slily, or weakly; to move about stealthily; to move about despised; to insinuate one's self. [D. *krielen.*]
Crawler, kral'ėr, *n. He or that which crawls;* a creeper; a reptile.
Crawling, kral'ing, *p.a. Creeping;* insinuating.
Crawlingly, kral'ing-li, *adv. In a crawling manner.*
Crayon, krā'on, *n. A piece of drawing chalk;* a sort of pencil; the name of small cylinders of colouring substances used for drawing on paper; a drawing made with crayons.—*vt.* To sketch with *a crayon;* to sketch. [Fr.—L. *creta,* chalk.]
Craze, krāz, *vt. To crush;* to break or impair the natural force of; to shatter; to impair the intellect of. *ppr.* crazing, *pret. & pp.* crazed.—*n.* A strong habitual desire. [Fr. *écraser,* to crush.]
Crazed, krāzd, *p.a.* Deranged in intellect.
Crazedness, krāz'ed-nes, *n.* An impaired state of the intellect.
Crazily, krāz'i-li, *adv.* In a broken or *crazy manner.*
Craziness, krāz'i-nes, *n. State of being crazy;* weakness of intellect; derangement.
Crazy, krāz'i, *a. Crushed;* broken; deranged. [Fr. *écrasé.*]
Creak, krēk, *vi. To make a sharp, grating sound,* of some continuance, as by the friction of hard substances.—*vi. To produce a creaking sound with.* [Old Fr. *criquer.*]
Creaking, krēk'ing, *p.n.* A harsh, grating sound.
Cream, krēm, *n.* That part of a liquor that separates from the rest, and collects on the surface; the oily part of milk, which rises and forms a scum on the surface; the best part of a thing. *vt.* To skim; to take off cream from; to take off, as the best part of a thing. *vi. To gather cream;* to flower or mantle. [Fr. *crême*—L. *cremor.*]
Cream-faced, krēm'fāst, *a.* White; pale; having a coward look.
Creamy, krēm'i, *a. Like cream;* having the nature of cream; luscious.
Crease, krēs, *n. A line or mark* made by folding or doubling anything; a hollow streak like a groove.—*vt.* To make a *crease* or mark in by compressing, folding, or doubling. *ppr.* creasing, *pret. & pp.* creased. [Icel. *kreisti,* to press.]
Create, krē-āt', *vt. To bring into being from nothing;* to cause to be; to shape; to beget; to bring forth; to produce by new combinations; to form anew; to invest with a new character. *ppr.* creating, *pret. & pp.* created.—*p.a.*† Begotten; created. [L. *creo, creatus*—Sans. *kri,* to do, make, effect.]
Created, krē-āt'ed, *p.a. Formed out of nothing;* caused to exist.
Creating, krē-āt'ing, *p.a. Forming out of nothing;* originating.
Creation, krē-ā'shon, *n. Act of creating;* creatures; the world; the universe; act of investing with a new character; any part of the things created; anything caused to exist. [Fr. *création.*]
Creative, krē-āt'iv, *a. Having the power to create,* or exerting the act of creation.
Creator, krē-āt'ėr, *n. The being that creates;* a producer; distinctively, the

Supreme Being; that which creates. [L.]
Creature, krē'tūr, n. *A created being; everything not self-existent; a living being; a beast; man; a human being; that which is formed or imagined; a person who owes his rise and fortune to another; a dependant.* [Fr. *créatures.*]
Credence, krē'dens, n. *Reliance of the mind on evidence of facts derived from the testimony of others; trust; that which gives a claim to credit or confidence.* [Low L. *credentia*—L. *credo*, to believe.]
Credent, krē'dent, a. *Believing; not to be questioned.* [L. *credens*.]
Credential, krē-den'shi-al, a. *Giving a title to credit.*—n. *That which gives a title to credit;* the warrant upon which belief is claimed; (pl.) writings or letters showing that one is entitled to credit, or is invested with authority; the letters of power given to envoys.
Credibility, kred-i-bil'i-ti, n. *State or quality of being credible.* [Fr. *crédibilité.*]
Credible, kred'i-bl, a. *Worthy of credit or of belief; having a claim to credit.* [L. *credibilis.*]
Credibleness, kred'i-bl-nes, n. *State or quality of being credible; just claim to credit or belief.*
Credibly, kred'i-bli, adv. *In a credible manner.*
Credit, kred'it, n. *Trust; reliance on testimony; faith; confidence; honour; influence; character; reputed integrity; trust in commerce; transfer of goods, &c., in confidence of future payment; reputation for pecuniary worth; the side of an account in which payment is entered; money possessed or due.*—vt. *To trust; to believe; to confide in the truth of; to sell or lend to, in confidence of future payment; to procure credit or honour to; to enter upon the credit side of an account; to set to the credit of.* [Fr. *crédit*—L. *credo, creditum,* to trust.]
Creditable, kred'it-a-bl, a. *Reputable; estimable.*
Creditableness, kred'it-a-bl-nes, n. *Quality of being creditable.*
Creditably, kred'it-a-bli, adv. *Reputably; with credit; without disgrace.*
Creditor, kred'it-ėr, n. *One who gives credit in commerce; one to whom a sum of money is due.* [L.]
Credulity, kre-dū'li-ti, n. *A disposition to believe on slight evidence, or no evidence at all.* [Fr. *crédulité.*]
Credulous, kred'ū-lus, a. *Apt to believe on slight evidence; unsuspecting; easily deceived.* [L. *credulus.*]
Credulously, kred'ū-lus-li, adv. *With credulity.*
Credulousness, kred'ū-lus-nes, n. *Quality of being credulous; easiness of belief.*
Creed, krēd, n. *That which is believed; any system of principles believed or professed; a brief summary of the articles of Christian faith; a symbol.* [Fr. *credo,* belief.]
Creek, krēk, n. *A corner; a small inlet or cove; a recess in the shore of the sea or of a river.* [D. *kreek.*]
Creeky, krēk'i, a. *Containing creeks.*
Creep, krēp, vi. *To move with a slow and low pace; to move as a reptile; to crawl; to move along the ground, or on the surface of any other body, in growth, as a vine; to move feebly or timorously; to move insensibly, as time; to move secretly; to steal in; to be servile; to fawn.* ppr. *creeping,* pret. & pp. *crept.* [Sax. *creópan.*]
Creeper, krēp'ėr, n. *A reptile; a creeping plant; a small bird that runs along the branches of trees; a kind of grapnel used for dragging the bottom of a river, harbour, &c., to recover things lost.*
Creeping, krēp'ing, p.a. *Crawling; stealing along.*
Creosote, krē'ō-sōt, n. *A flesh-preserver; an antiseptic oily liquid obtained from tar.* [Gr. *kreas, kreōs,* flesh, and *sōtēr,* a preserver.]
Crepitation, krep-it-ā'shon, n. *Act of bursting with a frequent repetition of small sharp sounds,* as salt in fire; a small *crackling* noise. [Fr. *crépitation*—L. *crepo, crepitum,* to crack.]
Crepuscular, krē-pus'kūl-ėr, a. *Pertaining to twilight.* [from L. *crepusculum,* twilight.]
Crescent, kres'ent, n. *That which increases; the moon in her state of increase, until one half of her face is enlightened; anything resembling the shape of the new moon;* a likeness of the new moon, as that borne in the Turkish flag; the standard itself, and figuratively the Turkish power; a range of buildings in the form of a crescent. [L. *crescens,* growing.]
Crescive, kres'iv, a. *Increasing.*
Cress, kres, n. A plant of several species, used as a salad. [G. *kresse.*]
Crest, krest, n. *A tuft on the head of certain birds;* any tuft worn on the head; the plume of feathers or tuft of horse-hair on the top of the ancient helmet; the helmet itself; the top; a lofty mien; pride; spirit; in heraldry, the ornament of the helmet.—vt. *To furnish with a crest.* [Old Fr. *creste;* L. *crista,* a cock's comb.]
Crested, krest'ed, p.a. *Wearing a crest;* having a comb; having a tuft on the head, like a crest.
Crest-fallen, krest'fal-en, a. *Dejected;* dispirited; heartless; spiritless.
Cretaceous, krē-tā'shē-us, a. *Chalky;* having the qualities of chalk. [L. *cretaceus*—*creta,* chalk.]
Crevice, krev'is, n. *A crack;* a cleft; a fissure; a cranny. [Fr. *crevasse*—L. *crepo,* to crack.]
Crew, krö, n. *A crowd;* a company, in contempt; a gang; the company of sailors belonging to any vessel. [Sax. *cruth.*]
Crib, krib, n. *A small bed or couch;* a small habitation; a hut; a manger; a rack; a stall for oxen; a cage.—vt. *To shut up in a narrow habitation;* to cage. ppr. *cribbing,* pret. & pp. *cribbed.* [Sax. *cryb.*]
Cribbage, krib'āj, n. *A game at cards,* in which the dealer makes up a third hand for himself, partly from the hand of his opponent.
Crick, krik, n. *A local spasm or cramp;* a stiffness of the neck.
Cricket, krik'et, n. *An insect which makes a sharp creaking or chirping sound,* and which burrows in the ground floor of houses, near the fire. [Fr. *criquet.*]
Cricket, krik'et, n. *A play in which balls are struck with a bat.* [Sax. *cricc,* a staff.]
Cricketer, krik'et-ėr, n. *One who plays cricket.*
Crier, krī'ėr, n. *One who cries;* one who makes proclamation.
Crime, krīm, n. *An act which violates a law or rule of right, divine or human,* and *subjects to judgment;* a violation of public law, of a deep and atrocious nature; any great wickedness; iniquity; a great fault; a heavy offence; vice. [L. *crimen*—Gr. *krinō,* to judge.]
Crimeful, krīm'ful, a. *Criminal; wicked.*
Criminal, krim'in-al, a. *Guilty; wicked; abandoned; atrocious; partaking of a crime; relating to crimes.*—n. *A malefactor;* a culprit; a convict; a felon.
Criminality, krim-in-al'i-ti, n. *The quality of being criminal;* guiltiness.
Criminally, krim'in-al-li, adv. *In a criminal manner; wickedly.*
Criminate, krim'in-āt, vt. *To allege to be guilty of a crime, offence, or wrong.* ppr. *criminating,* pret. & pp. *criminated.* [L. *criminor, criminatus.*]
Crimination, krim-in-ā'shon, n. *Accusation;* charge of having been guilty of a criminal act, offence, or wrong. [L. *criminatio.*]
Criminative, krim'in-āt-iv, a. *Charging with crime;* criminatory.
Criminatory, krim'in-ā-tō-ri, a. *Relating to accusation;* accusing.
Crimp, krimp, a. *Easily crumbled;* friable, brittle. [Sax. *acrymman,* to crumble.]
Crimp, krimp, vt. *To wrinkle;* to pinch up in ridges; to plait; to curl or crisp the hair; to decoy for the army or navy. [G. *krimpen,* to shrink.]
Crimson, krim'zn, n. *The colour produced by the cochineal insect;* a deep red colour; a red tinged with blue; also, a red colour in general.—a. *Of a beautiful deep red.*—vt. *To dye with crimson.*—vi. *To become of a deep red colour;* to be tinged with red; to blush. [It. *cremisi,* from Ar. *kirmist,* the name of the insect which produces the dye.]
Cringe, krinj, vi. *To bend;* to bend with servility; to fawn; to make court by mean compliances. ppr. *cringing,* pret. & pp. *cringed.*—n. *A bow;* servile civility. [Sax. *crangan,* to submit.]
Cringe, krinj, vt. *To cause to shrink or wrinkle.*
Cringing, krinj'ing, p.a. *Bowing servilely.*
Cringingly, krinj'ing-li, adv. *In a cringing manner.*
Crinkle, kring'kl, vi. *To wrinkle;* to run in and out in little or short bends or turns.—vt. *To form with short turns or wrinkles.* ppr. *crinkling,* pret. & pp. *crinkled.*—n. *A winding or turn;* a wrinkle. [D. *krinkelen.*]
Crinoline, krin'ō-lin, n. *A texture of which the warp is of flax,* and the woof of *horse-hair;* a lady's stiff petticoat, expanded by hoops. [Fr.—L. *crinis,* hair, and *linum,* flax.]
Cripple, krip'l, n. *A lame person;* one who has lost or never enjoyed the use of his limbs.—a. *Lame.*—vt. *To cause to creep or halt;* to lame; to disable; to deprive of the power of exertion. ppr. *crippling,* pret. & pp. *crippled.* [G. *krüppel.*]
Crippled, krip'ld, p.a. *Disabled.*
Crisis, krī'sis, n. *Crises,* pl. *A deciding, turning-point of a disease;* a critical time; time when anything is at its height; juncture; conjuncture. [Gr. *krisis*—*krinō,* to separate.]
Crisp, krisp, a. *Formed into stiff curls or ringlets;* brittle; easily broken or crumbled; winding.—vt. *To curl;* to form into ringlets, as the hair; to wreathe or interweave; to make wavy. vt. *To form little curls,* as ripples. [Old G.]
Crisped, krispt, p.a. *Frizzled;* made brittle.
Crisper, krisp'ėr, n. *He or that which*

ch, chain; j, job; g, go; ng, sing; ᴛʜ, then; th, thin; w, wig; wh, whig; zh, azure; † obsolete.

crisps or curls; an instrument for crisping cloth.

Crisply, krisp′li, *adv.* With crispness.

Crispness, krisp′nes, *n.* A state of being *crisped* or curled; brittleness.

Crispy, krisp′i, *a.* Curled; brittle; dried, so as to break short.

Criterion, kri-tē′ri-un, *n.* Criteria, *pl.* Standard of judging; a rule; a measure; a test. [Gr. *kritērion—krinō*, to separate, to judge.]

Critic, krit′ik, *n.* One who judges; one skilled in judging of the merit of literary works; a judge of excellence in the fine arts generally; a careful observer; a close or severe examiner or judge.—*a.* Critical; relating to criticism. [Gr. *kritikos*, judging—*krinō*, to judge.]

Critical, kri′tik-al, *a.* Relating to or containing criticism; capable of judging; able to decide; nicely judicious; inclined to find fault; relating to a crisis; decisive; fraught with weighty consequences; momentous. [Gr. *kritikos*.]

Critically, kri′tik-al-li, *adv.* In a critical manner; exactly.

Criticism, krit′i-sizm, *n.* Act or art of criticising; critical examination; critical exhibition of the merits and defects of a literary work, or a work of art; stricture; critique.

Criticizable, krit′i-siz-a-bl, *a.* That may be criticised.

Criticize, krit′i-siz, *vi.* To examine and judge critically; to make remarks on the merits and demerits of a literary performance or a work of art; to animadvert.—*vt.* To examine carefully with reference to beauties and faults; to pass judgment on with respect to merit or blame. *ppr.* criticizing, *pret. & pp.* criticized.

Critique, kri-tēk′, *n.* A critical examination; remarks or animadversions on beauties and faults; a review. [Fr.]

Croak, krōk, *vi.* To make a low hoarse noise in the throat, as a frog or other animal; to cry, as a raven or crow; to speak with a low hollow voice; to forebode evil without much cause; to murmur.—*n.* The low harsh sound uttered by a frog or a raven, or a like sound. [Old Fr. *crodquer*, to croak as a raven—L. *crocio*.]

Croaker, krōk′ėr, *n.* A discontented murmurer.

Croaking, krōk′ing, *p.n.* A low harsh sound, as of a raven; act of foreboding evil; grumbling.

Crochet, krō′shā, *n.* A species of knitting performed by means of a small hook, called a crochet-needle, the material being fancy worsted, cotton, or silk. [Fr.]

Crockery, krok′ė-ri, *n.* Earthenware; vessels formed of clay, glazed and baked. [Sax. *crock*, a pitcher.]

Crocodile, krok′ō-dil, *n.* A large amphibious animal of the lizard kind, said to have a *dread of the crocus* or saffron. *a.* Pertaining to or like a crocodile. [Gr. *krokodeilos—krokos*, saffron, and *deilos*, fearful.]

Crocus, krō′kus, *n.* A plant which produces flowers of a *yellow colour*, from which saffron is made. [Gr. *krokos*.]

Croft, kroft, *n.* A close or a little field inclosed, adjoining or near to a rural dwelling-house; a little farm. [Sax.]

Crone, krōn, *n.* A decrepit, crafty, murmuring old woman. [Gael. *cronan*; Scot. *croon*.]

Crony, krō′ni, *n.* Old acquaintance; a familiar friend. [from *crone*.]

Crook, krōk, *n.* A *hook*; a curving instrument; a shepherd's staff, curving at the end; a pastoral staff; an artifice; a trick.—*vt.* To bend; to curve; to turn from a straight line; to turn from rectitude; to pervert.—*vi.* To bend or be bent. [Sw. *krok.*]

Crooked, krōk′ed, *p.a.* Bowed; awry; winding in moral conduct; without rectitude; deceitful; untoward.

Crookedly, krōk′ed-li, *adv.* In a crooked manner.

Crookedness, krōk′ed-nes, *n.* State of being crooked; perverseness; obliquity of conduct; depravity.

Crook-shouldered, krōk′shōl-dėrd, *a.* Having bent shoulders.

Crop, krop, *n.* That which is cut off or gathered; a cluster; ears of corn; the corn or fruits of the earth while growing or when collected; harvest; the craw of a bird, into which the food is collected; hair cut close or short.—*vt.* To cut off, as the top or the ends of; to eat off; to pull off; to pluck; to reap; to cut off prematurely; to gather before it falls; to cultivate or take crops from.—*vi.*† To yield harvest. *ppr.* cropping, *pret. & pp.* cropped or cropt. [Sax.—a berry, an ear of corn.]

Crop-eared, krop′ērd, *a.* Having the ears cropped or cut short.

Cropful, krop′ful, *a.* Having a full crop or belly; satiated.

Cropping, krop′ing, *p.n.* Act of cutting off; the raising of crops.

Croquet, krō-kā′, *n.* A kind of game.

Crosier, krō′zhi-ėr, *n.* A bishop's crook or pastoral staff, a symbol of pastoral authority and care. [Low L. *crocia—L. crux, crucis,* a cross.]

Crosiered, krō′zhi-ėrd, *p.a.* Bearing a crosier.

Cross, kros, *n.* A gibbet, consisting of two pieces of timber placed across each other, either in form of a T or of an X; the instrument by which the Saviour suffered; the ensign of the Christian religion; the religion itself; the sufferings of Christ by crucifixion; the doctrine of Christ's sufferings; anything in the form of a cross; a line drawn through another; anything that perplexes; trial of patience; a mixing of breeds in producing animals; the mark of a cross instead of a signature; a piece of money stamped with the figure of a cross.—*a.* Passing from side to side; opposite; perverse; fretful; contradictory; perplexing.—*vt.* To put across or athwart; to mark with a cross; to cancel; to pass from side to side of; to thwart; to perplex; to clash with; to stop.—*vi.* To lie or be athwart; to move or pass from one side toward the other.—*prep.* Transversely; over; from side to side, so as to intersect. [Norm. *croisse*; L. *crux*.]

Cross-barred, kros′bärd, *a.* Secured by transverse bars.

Crossbow, kros′bō, *n.* A weapon for shooting, formed by placing a bow athwart a stock.

Cross-breed, kros′brēd, *n.* A breed produced from the male and female of different breeds.

Cross-examination, kros′egz-am-in-ā-shon, *n.* The examination or interrogation of a witness called by one party by the opposite party or his counsel.

Cross-examine, kros′egz-am-in, *vt.* To examine, as a witness of the opposite party, in order to test evidence. *ppr.* cross-examining, *pret. & pp.* cross-examined.

Cross-grained, kros′grānd, *a.* Perverse; untractable.

Crossing, kros′ing, *p.n.* A thwarting; a passing across; path across.

Crossly, kros′li, *adv.* Peevishly; fretfully.

Crossness, kros′nes, *n.* Peevishness; fretfulness; perverseness.

Cross-purpose, kros′pėr-pus, *n.* A contrary purpose; contradictory system; an enigma; a riddle.

Cross-question, kros′kwes-chon, *vt.* To cross-examine.

Cross-road, kros′rōd, *n.* A road which crosses the country or other roads.

Cross-wind, kros′wind, *n.* A side wind; an unfavourable wind.

Crosswise, kros′wiz, *adv.* Across; in the form of a cross.

Crotchet, kroch′et, *n.* A note in music, half the length of a minim; a peculiar turn of the mind; a fancy; a perverse conceit; (*pl.*) hooks or brackets in printing, inclosing words; a sentence or passage distinguished from the rest [Fr. *crochet*, dim. of *croc*, a hook.]

Crotchety, kroch′et-i, *a.* Having crotchets in the brain; whimsical.

Croton-oil, krō′ton-oil, *n.* Oil obtained from the seeds of a plant. The oil is a violent purgative. [Gr. *krotōn*, a tick, a thorn bearing the castor-berry.

Crouch, krouch, *vi.* To creep; to lie close to the ground, as an animal; to cringe; to stoop meanly; to fawn. [Old G. *kriuchan*, to creep.]

Crouching, krouch′ing, *p.a.* Cringing.

Croup, krōp, *n.* A disease of the windpipe in children, accompanied by a hoarse cough and difficulty of breathing. [Goth. *hropjan*, to cry out.]

Croup, krōp, *n.* The rump of a fowl; the buttocks of a horse. [Fr. *croupe*.]

Crow, krō, *n.* A large black carnivorous bird, so called from the *croaking sound* it utters; a bar of iron with a beak, or two claws, used in raising and moving heavy weights, &c.; the sound which a cock utters; a boast.—*vi.* To cry as a cock in joy, gaiety, or defiance; to utter a sound expressive of joy, as an infant; to boast in triumph; to swagger. *ppr.* crowing, *pret.* crew or crowed, *pp.* crowed or crown. [Sax. *craw*.]

Crowd, kroud, *n.* A number of persons collected into a close body without order; a throng; a great multitude; a swarm; the populace; the vulgar.—*vt.* To fill by pressing together; to encumber by multitudes.—*vi.* To press in numbers; to press; to be numerous. [Sax. *cruth*.]

Crowded, kroud′ed, *p.a.* Filled by a promiscuous multitude.

Crow-flower, krō′flou-ėr, *n.* A plant and flower.

Crowfoot, krō′fut, *n.* A plant, whose flower has a resemblance to the *foot of a crow.*

Crow-keeper, krō′kēp-ėr, *n.* A person employed to scare off crows; a scarecrow.

Crown, kroun, *n.* A *garland*; a wreath; that which encircles the head; a diadem worn on the head by kings as a badge of regal authority; regal power; dignity; honorary distinction; glory; perfection; a coin five shillings in value.—*vt.* To invest with a crown; to invest with regal dignity and power; to cover, as with a crown; to honour; to adorn; to bestow an honorary reward on; to recompense; to finish; to perfect. [Fr. *couronne*—L. *corōna*.]

Crowned, kround, *p.a.* Invested with a crown, or with regal power; rewarded

with a crown, wreath, garland, or distinction; perfected.
Crowner, kroun'ėr, n. He or that which crowns.
Crownet, kroun'et, n. A chief end.
Crown-glass, kroun'glas, n. The finest sort of window-glass.
Crowning, kroun'ing, p.a. Highest; greatest.
Crow-quill, krō'kwil, n. The quill of the crow, used in fine writing.
Crow's-feet, krōs'fēt, n. pl. The wrinkles under the eyes, the effects of age.
Crucial, krō'shi-al, a. Passing across; severe; searching, as if bringing to the cross. [Fr.—L. crux, a cross.]
Crucible, krō'si-bl, n. An earthen melting pot, used by chemists and goldsmiths. [Low L. crucibulum.]
Cruciferous, krō-sif'ėr-us, a. Having four petals in the form of a cross, as certain flowers. [L. crucifer—fero, to bear.]
Crucified, krō'si-fīd, p.a. Put to death on the cross.
Crucifier, krō'si-fī-ėr, n. One who puts another to death on a cross.
Crucifix, krō'si-fiks, n. A representation, in painting or statuary, of our Lord fastened to the cross. [Fr.—L. crux, a cross, and figo, fixum, to fix.]
Crucifixion, krō-si-fik'shon, n. The act or mode of putting to death by nailing to a cross; the death of Christ on the cross.
Cruciform, krō'si-form, a. Cross-shaped; consisting of four equal petals, disposed in the form of a cross. [L. crux, and forma, form.]
Crucify, krō'si-fī, vt. To put to death by nailing the hands and feet of to a cross; to mortify; to destroy the power of; to torment. ppr. crucifying, pret. & pp. crucified. [Fr. crucifier.]
Crude, krōd, a. Bloody'; raw; not prepared by fire or heat; unripe; in its natural state; undressed; indigested; harsh; unrefined; not brought to perfection. [L. crudus—cruor, blood.]
Crudely, krōd'li, adv. In a crude manner.
Crudeness, krōd'nes, n. State or quality of being crude; crudity.
Crudity, krōd'i-ti, n. State of being crude; rawness; unripeness; that which is in a crude state. [L. cruditas.]
Crudy, krōd'i, a. Concreted; curdled.
Cruel, krō'el, a. Eager for blood; unmerciful; barbarous; ferocious; brutal; severe. [Fr.—L. cruor, blood.]
Cruelly, krō'el-li, adv. With cruelty.
Cruelty, krō'el-ti, n. Blood-thirstiness; a savage temper; inhumanity; barbarity; a cruel act; barbarous treatment. [Fr. cruauté.]
Cruet, krō'et, n. A vial or small glass bottle for holding vinegar, oil, &c. [Fr. cruchette.]
Cruise, krōs, vi. To sail hither and thither in directions which cross each other; to rove on the sea, in search of an enemy's ships, or for protecting commerce; to rove for plunder. ppr. cruising, pret. & pp. cruised.—n. A voyage made in courses that cross each other; a sailing to and fro in search of an enemy's ships, or by a pirate in search of plunder. [G. kreusen.]
Cruiser, krōs'ėr, n. A person or a ship that cruises.
Crumb, krum, n. A fragment; usually a small piece of bread or other food, broken or cut off; the soft part of bread which is easily crumbled. [Sax. cruma.]

Crumble, krum'bl, vt. To divide into minute parts.—vi. To part into small pieces or fragments; to perish. ppr. crumbling, pret. & pp. crumbled. [D. kruimelen.]
Crumbled, krum'bld, p.a. Broken into small pieces.
Crumbling, krum'bl-ing, p.a. Falling into small pieces; decaying.
Crummy, krum'i, a. Full of crumbs; soft.
Crump, krump, a. Crooked; bent. [Sax.]
Crumple, krum'pl, vt. To press into wrinkles; to rumple or crook.—vi. To contract; to shrink. ppr. crumpling, pret. & pp. crumpled. [from crump.]
Crumpled, krum'pld, p.a. Drawn or pressed into wrinkles.
Crunch, krunch, vt. To crush between the teeth; to craunch. [formed from the sound.]
Crupper, krup'ėr, n. A strap of leather which is buckled to a saddle, and, passing under a horse's tail, prevents the saddle from shifting forward. [Fr. croupière.]
Crural, krōr'al, a. Belonging to the leg; shaped like a leg or root. [L. cruralis—crus, cruris, a leg.]
Crusade, krō-sād', n. A military expedition under the banner of the cross, as that against the infidels of the Holy Land; any war undertaken on pretence of defending the cause of religion; a romantic enterprise. [Fr. croisade—L. crux, a cross.]
Crusader, krō-sād'ėr, n. A person engaged in a crusade.
Crusado, krō-sā'dō, n. A Portuguese coin.
Cruse, krōs, n. A small cup; a bottle or cruet. [D. kroes.]
Crush, krush, vt. To bruise; to pound; to squeeze so as to bruise; to break; to beat down by power; to prostrate; to oppress.—vi. To be pressed into a smaller compass by external weight or force.—n. A violent collision or rushing together, which breaks or bruises the bodies; a fall that bruises into a confused mass. [Sw. krossa—Sans. krish, to attenuate.]
Crushed, krusht, p.a. Squeezed so as to break; oppressed by power.
Crushing, krush'ing, p.a. Overwhelming; oppressing.
Crust, krust, n. A shelly covering; an incrustation; a piece of bread hardened by baking or long keeping; a piece of hard bread.—vt. To cover with a crust; to spread over the surface of, as a substance harder than the matter covered.—vi. To gather into a hard covering; to concrete or freeze, as superficial matter. [L. crusta.]
Crustaceous, krus-tā'shē-us, a. Pertaining to crust; of the nature of crust; shelly; belonging to shell-fish. [Fr. crustacée.]
Crustated, krust'āt-ed, p.a. Covered with a crust.
Crustily, krust'i-li, adv. In a crusty manner; peevishly; harshly; morosely.
Crustiness, krust'i-nes, n. Hardness; moroseness; surliness.
Crusty, krust'i, a. Having a crust; pertaining to a hard covering; abrupt in speech or manner; snappish.
Crutch, kruch, n. A staff with a cross-piece at the head used by cripples; a support.—vt. To support on crutches; to prop or sustain, with miserable helps, that which is feeble. [Sax. cryc—L. crux, a cross.]
Crutched, krucht, p.a. Supported with crutches.

Cry, krī, vi. To utter a loud voice; to utter the loud shrill sounds of weeping, joy or gladness, prayer or entreaty, &c.; to clamour.—vt. To proclaim; to name loudly and publicly for giving notice. ppr. crying, pret. & pp. cried.—n. Cries, pl. A loud sound uttered by the mouth, whether of man or of beast; a shriek or scream; acclamation; weeping; loud voice in distress, prayer, supplication, terror, alarm, joy, &c.; noise; fame; outcry; yell; a pack of hounds!. [Fr. crier.]
Crying, krī'ing, p.a. Notorious; calling for vengeance and punishment.
Crypt, kript, n. A subterranean cell or cave under a church, for the interment of persons. [Fr. crypte—Gr. krupto, to hide.]
Cryptogamic, Cryptogamous, krip-tō-gam'ik, krip-tog'a-mus, a. Having the fructification concealed, as certain plants. [Gr. kruptos, concealed, and gamos, marriage.]
Cryptogamy, krip-tog'a-mi, n. Concealed fructification.
Crystal, kris'tal, n. A regularly shaped transparent mass of quartz; a superior kind of glass; anything having the form of a crystal.—a. Consisting of or like crystal; clear; pellucid. [L. crystallus—Gr. kruos, ice, and stello, to set.]
Crystalline, kris'tal-in, a. Clear; pellucid; pure. [L. crystallinus.]
Crystallizable, kris'tal-iz-a-bl, a. That may be crystallised.
Crystallisation, kris'tal-iz-ā'shon, n. Act or process of crystallising.
Crystallise, kris'tal-iz, vt. To form into crystals; to cause to form crystals.—vi. To be converted into crystals; to unite, as the separate particles of a substance, and form a regular solid. ppr. crystallizing, pret. & pp. crystallized.
Cub, kub, n. The young of certain quadrupeds, as of the bear and the fox; a puppy; a whelp; a young boy or girl (in contempt).—vi. To bring forth a cub or cubs. ppr. cubbing, pret. & pp. cubbed. [probably akin to Icel. kobbi, a seal.]
Cube, kūb, n. A solid square; a die; a body, having the shape of a die; a regular solid body, with six equal square sides, and containing equal angles; the product of a number obtained by taking that number three times as a factor.—vt. To raise to the third power, by multiplying a number into itself twice. ppr. cubing, pret. & pp. cubed. [Fr.—L. cubus.]
Cubic, Cubical, kūb'ik, kūb'ik-al, a. Relating to or having the form or properties of a cube; that may be or is contained within a cube. [L. cubicus.]
Cubit, kū'bit, n. The bone of the arm from the elbow to the wrist; the length of the arm from the elbow to the extremity of the middle finger, used as a measure of length. [L. cubitum, the elbow—cubo, cubitum, to lie down.]
Cuckold, kuk'old, n. A man whose wife is false to his bed; the husband of an adulteress.—vt. To make a cuckold of. [from It. cucolo—L. cuculus, a cuckoo.]
Cuckoldom, kuk'old-um, n. State of a cuckold; the act of adultery.
Cuckoo, kụ'kō, n. A well-known bird, so named from the sound of its note. [Fr. coucou.]
Cuckoo-bud, kụ'kō-bud, n. Buttercup.
Cucumber, kū'kum-bėr, n. A plant whose fruit is of a crooked or twisted shape. [Fr. concombre—L. cucumis.]

---

ch, chain; j, job; g, go; ng, sing; ᴠʜ, then; th, thin; w, wig; wh, whig; zh, asure; † obsolete.

Cud, kud, n. The food which ruminating animals bring up in portions from the first stomach to be thoroughly chewed. [Sax. *ceowan*, to chew.]

Cuddle, kud'dl, vi. To cower; to squat; to lie close and snug.—vt. To hug; to embrace; to fondle. ppr. cuddling, pret. & pp. cuddled. [Old Fr. *cadeler*, to pamper.]

Cudgel, kuj'el, n. A short thick stick to beat with; a club.—vt. To beat with a cudgel; to beat in general. ppr. cudgelling, pret. & pp. cudgelled. [W. *cogel.*]

Cue, kū, n. The tail; a long roll of hair; a catch-word; a hint; the part which any man is to play in his turn; humour; the straight rod used in playing billiards. [Fr. *queue*—L. *cauda*, the tail.]

Cuff, kuf, n. A buffet; a stroke; a box. vt. To beat; to strike with talons or wings, as a fowl.—vi. To fight; to scuffle. [Sw. Goth. *kuffa*, to insult with stripes.]

Cuff, kuf, n. The part of a sleeve turned or folded back from the hand. [Fr. *coiffe*, a lining, as applied to the sleeve.]

Cuirass, kwi-ras', n. A breastplate; a piece of defensive armour. [Fr. *cuirasse*—L. *corium*, leather.]

Cuirassier, kwi-ras-sēr', n. A soldier armed with a cuirass or breastplate.

Cuish, kwis, n. Defensive armour for the thighs.

Culinary, kū'lin-a-ri, a. Relating to the kitchen, or to the art of cookery; used in kitchens. [L. *culinarius—culina*, a kitchen.]

Cull, kul, vt. To pick out; to separate, as one or more things from others; to select from many. [Fr. *cueillir*—L. *colligo*, to collect—*lego*, to gather.]

Cullender, kul'en-dėr, n. A strainer.

Culler, kul'ėr, n. One who culls.

Cullion, kul'i-un, n. A mean wretch; a cully. [Old Fr. *couille, couillon.*]

Cully, kul'li, n. The companion of a courtezan; a mean dupe. [Old Fr. *couillon.*]

Culm, kulm, n. The straw or dry stalks of corn and grasses. [L. *culmus.*]

Culminate, kul'min-āt, vi. To reach the summit; to be vertical; to come or be in the meridian; to be in the highest point of altitude, as a planet. ppr. culminating, pret. & pp. culminated. [Low L. *culmino, culminatum*—L. *culmen*, the top.]

Culmination, kul-min-ā'shon, n. The transit of a heavenly body over the meridian; top; highest point.

Culpability, kulp-a-bil'i-ti, n. Blamableness; culpableness.

Culpable, kulp'a-bl, a. Faulty; blameworthy; censurable; criminal; immoral; sinful. [Low L. *culpabilis*—L. *culpa*, a fault.]

Culpably, kulp'a-bli, adv. In a culpable manner; blamably.

Culprit, kul'prit, n. The condition of one charged with an offence; a person arraigned in court for a crime; any person convicted of a crime; a criminal. [L. *culpa redtus*—*reus*, the defendant.]

Cultivable, kul'ti-va-bl, a. Capable of being tilled or cultivated.

Cultivate, kul'ti-vāt, vt. To till; to raise by tillage; to manure, plough, dress, sow, and reap; to improve by care or study; to refine by correction of faults and enlargement of powers or good qualities; to study; to strive to make better; to foster; to improve; to civilise. ppr. cultivating, pret. & pp. cultivated. [Low L. *cultivo, cultivatum*—L. *colo, cultum*, to till.]

Cultivated, kul'ti-vāt-ed, p.a. Tilled; effected by cultivation; cherished.

Cultivation, kul-ti-vā'shon, n. The raising or improvement by tillage; practice directed to improvement or increase; culture; refinement; advancement.

Cultivator, kul'ti-vāt-ėr, n. One who cultivates.

Culture, kul'tūr, n. Act of preparing the earth for crops; cultivation; application of labour or other means to correct, to improve, to refine, to strengthen, to advance. [L. *cultūra—colo*, to till.]

Culverin, kul'vėr-in, n. A long slender piece of ordinance, so named from being ornamented with sculptured serpents. [Fr. *couleurines.*]

Culvert, kul'vėrt, n. A passage under a road or canal, covered with a bridge; an arched drain for the passage of water. [Old Fr.]

Cumber, kum'bėr, vt. To trouble; to embarrass; to entangle; to obstruct; to distract, as with cares. [Sw. *bekymra*, to trouble.]

Cumbersome, kum'bėr-sum, a. Troublesome; unwieldy; unmanageable.

Cumbrous, kum'brus, a. Burdensome; troublesome; oppressive.

Cumbrously, kum'brus-li, adv. In a cumbrous manner.

Cumbrousness, kum'brus-nes, n. State of being cumbrous.

Cumin, Cummin, kum'in, kum'in, n. An annual plant, whose seeds have a bitterish warm taste, with an aromatic flavour, and are used for seasoning. [L. *cuminum*—Heb. *kammon.*]

Cumulate, kū'mū-lāt, vt. To gather into a heap; to heap together. ppr. cumulating, pret. & pp. cumulated. [L. *cumulo, cumulatus*—*cumulus*, a heap.]

Cumulative, kū'mū-lāt-iv, a. Forming a mass or heap; that augments by addition; that is added to something else. [Fr. *cumulatif.*]

Cunning, kun'ing, a. Knowing; astute; subtle; artful; full of stratagems.—n. Knowledge; faculty or act of using stratagem to accomplish a purpose; fraudulent skill; craftiness; artifice. [Sax. *cunnan*, to know.]

Cunningly, kun'ing-li, adv. In a cunning manner; with artful deceit; craftily.

Cup, kup, n. A small vessel to drink out of; anything hollow, like a cup; a glass cup used for drawing blood; the liquor contained in a cup; a draught; afflictions; good received; blessings and favours; (pl.) social entertainment in drinking; a drinking bout.—vt. To apply a cupping-glass to, as to a scarified part of the body; to procure a discharge of blood; to supply with cups. ppr. cupping, pret. & pp. cupped. [Sax. *cop.*]

Cup-bearer, kup'bār-ėr, n. An attendant of a prince or at a feast, who conveys wine or other liquors to the guests; an officer of state.

Cupboard, kup'bōrd, n. A small case or inclosure in a room, with shelves, destined to receive cups, plates, dishes, and the like. [*cup*, and Sax. *bur*, a room.]

Cupel, kū'pel, n. A small cup or vessel used in refining precious metals. [Fr.—L. *cupella*, a small cask.]

Cupellation, kū-pel-lā'shon, n. The process of refining gold, silver, and some other metals, in a cupel.

Cupid, kū'pid, n. The god of love. [L. *Cupido.*]

Cupidity, kū-pid'i-ti, n. A longing to possess something; an inordinate desire of wealth or power; covetousness. [Fr. *cupidité*; L. *cupiditas*—*cupio*, to desire.]

Cupola, kū'pō-la, n. A hemispherical vault on the top of a building, adorning the round top of a structure. [It.]

Cupping, kup'ing, p.n. A drawing of blood with a cupping-glass.

Cupping-glass, kup'ing-glas, n. A glass vessel like a cup, to be applied to the skin after scarification, for drawing blood.

Cur, kėr, n. A dog that snarls, but wants courage to bite; a worthless dog; a surly snarling person (used in contempt). [Belg. *korre*, a country-house dog.]

Curability, kūr-a-bil'i-ti, n. State of being curable.

Curable, kūr'a-bl, a. That may be healed or cured; admitting a remedy. [Fr.]

Curacy, Curateship, kū'ra-si, kū'rāt-ship, n. The office of a curate; a benefice held by license from the bishop.

Curate, kū'rāt, n. One to whom the cure or care of souls is committed; generally, a clergyman employed to perform the duties of a rector or vicar. [L. *curator*—*curo*, to care for.]

Curative, kū'rāt-iv, a. Relating to the cure of diseases; tending to cure.

Curator, kū-rāt'ėr, n. One who has the care and superintendence of anything; a guardian appointed by law. [L.]

Curb, kėrb, vt. To curve or make crooked; to control; to check; to hold back; to restrain with a curb, as a horse.—n. That which keeps in check; restraint; part of a bridle which serves to manage a horse. [Fr. *courber*—L. *curvo*, to curve.]

Curd, kėrd, n. The thickened part of milk, which is formed into cheese.—vt. To curdle; to congeal.—vi. To become thickened. [Ir. *cruth*, curdled milk.]

Curdiness, kėrd'i-nes, n. State of being curdy.

Curdle, kėrd'l, vi. To change into curds; to congeal; to coagulate.—vt. To change into curds, as milk; to cause to thicken or coagulate. ppr. curdling, pret. & pp. curdled.

Curdy, kėrd'i, a. Like curd; full of curd; coagulated.

Cure, kūr, n. Care; act of healing; restoration to health from disease; a remedy; the care of souls; spiritual charge.—vt. To heal; to remove or destroy, as a disease; to prepare for preservation; to pickle.—vi. To be healed. ppr. curing, pret. & pp. cured. [Fr.—L. *cūra*, care.]

Cured, kūrd, p.a. Prepared for preservation.

Cureless, kūr'les, a. That cannot be cured or healed; incurable.

Curer, kūr'ėr, n.) e who cures; a healer.

Curfew, kėr'fū, n. Formerly, the ringing of a bell or bells at night, as a signal to the inhabitants to put out their fires and retire to rest. [Fr. *couvre-feu*—*couvrir*, to cover, and *feu*, fire.]

Curiosity, kū-ri-os'i-ti, n. A strong desire to see something novel, or to discover something unknown; a disposition to pry into; scrupulousness; nice performance; a thing unusual; an object of curiosity; a rarity. [Fr. *curiosité*—L. *curiositas*—*cura*, care.]

Curious, kū'ri-us, a. Strongly desirous to see what is novel, or to discover what is unknown; addicted to re-

search or inquiry; prying; accurate; careful; difficult to please; exciting inquiry; singular; artfully constructed; what could hardly be expected. [Fr. *curieux*—L. *cura*, care.]
Curiously, kū'ri-us-li, *adv. In a curious manner.*
Curl, kėrl, *vt. To form into ringlets;* to raise in waves; to ripple.—*vi.* To take a twisted or coiled form; to shrink into ringlets; to rise in undulations; to ripple; to writhe; to shrink.—*n. A ringlet* of hair, or anything of a like form; a waving; a winding; a twist. [D. *krullen*, to curl.]
Curlew, kėr'lū, *n.* A wading water-bird, so named from its cry. [Fr. *corlieu*.]
Curling, kėrl'ing, *p.a. Forming into ringlets.*
Curly, kėrl'i, *a. Having curls;* tending to curl; full of ripples.
Currant, ku'rant, *n.* The fruit of several well-known shrubs, as the red-currant, the white-currant, and the black-currant; a small kind of dried grape, from the Levant. [from *Corinth* in Greece.]
Currency, ku'ren-si, *n. A running;* a flowing; a constant flow; circulating medium; the aggregate of coin, notes, &c., in circulation in a country; general estimation; a passing from person to person, or from age to age.
Current, ku'rent, *a. Running;* passing from hand to hand; circulating, general, or popular; established by common estimation; generally received; present in its course.—*n. A running;* a stream; progressive motion of the water in the sea or a lake, &c., at certain places; tide; successive course. [L. *currens*—*curro*, Heb. *kārar*, to run.]
Currently, ku'rent-li, *adv. In a current manner;* generally.
Curricle, ku'ri-kl, *n.* A chaise or carriage, with two wheels, drawn by two horses abreast. [L. *curriculum*—*curro*, to run.]
Carried, ku'rid, *p.a. Dressed as leather;* prepared with curry.
Currier, ku'ri-ėr, *n. A man who dresses and colours leather* after it is tanned. [Fr. *corroyeur*—L. *corium*, skin.]
Currish, kėr'ish, *a. Like a cur;* brutal; snappish; snarling; churlish.
Curry, ku'ri, *n.* A stew, variously made, and highly seasoned with curry-powder, &c.; a highly spiced Indian mixture, called also curry-powder. [from Hind. *gormu*, *quliyu*, to stew.]
Curry, ku'ri, *vt. To dress, as leather* after it is tanned; to rub and clean, as the *skin* of a horse with a comb; to scratch or claw; to rub or stroke; to make smooth; to seek, as favour by flattery (with *with*). *ppr.* currying, *pret. & pp.* curried. [Fr. *corroyer*.]
Curry-comb, ku'ri-kōm, *n. A comb for rubbing* and cleaning horses.
Currying, ku'ri-ing, *p.n.* Act of rubbing down a horse; the art of dressing skins after they are tanned.
Curse, kėrs, *vt.* To utter a wish of evil against; to imprecate evil upon; to injure; to torment with great calamities. *vi.* To utter imprecations; to use profane language; to swear.—*n.* Imprecation of evil; malediction; execration; divine condemnation; torment; vexation; a great affliction. *ppr.* cursing, *pret. & pp.* cursed or curst. [Sax. *cursian*, to curse.]
Cursed, kėrs'ed, *p.a. Deserving a curse;* execrable; detestable; abominable.
Cursing, kėrs'ing, *p.n. The uttering of a curse;* execration.

Cursive, kėr'siv, *a. Running;* rapid; flowing. [It. *corsivo*—L. *curro*, to run.]
Cursorary, kėr'sō-ra-ri, *a. Cursory;* hasty.
Cursorily, kėr'sō-ri-li, *adv. In a running* or hasty manner; slightly; hastily.
Cursory, kėr'sō-ri, *a. Running;* superficial; careless; desultory. [L. *cursorius*.]
Curst, kėrst, *a.* Vexatious; malignant.
Curt, kėrt, *a. Cut short;* curtailed. [L. *curtus*—Sans. *krit*, to cut.]
Curtail, kėr-tāl', *vt. To cut short;* to shorten; to cut off the end or a part of; to diminish; to abridge. [Fr. *court*, L. *curtus*, short, and *tailler*, to cut.]
Curtain, kėr'tan, *n.* A cloth hanging round a bed, at a window, or in a theatre, which may be contracted or expanded at pleasure.—*vt. To inclose with curtains;* to furnish with curtains. [It. *cortina*, a bed-curtain.]
Curtain-lecture, kėr'tan-lek-tūr, *n. Lecture* given *in bed* by a wife to her husband.
Curtly, kėrt'li, *adv.* Shortly; briefly.
Curtness, kėrt'nes, *n. Shortness.*
Curtsy, kėrt'si. *See* COURTESY.
Curvature, kėrv'a-tūr, *n.* The continual *bending* of a line from a straight direction. [L. *curvatūra—curvo*, to curve.]
Curve, kėrv, *a. Curved;* inflected in a regular form, and forming part of a circle.—*n. A bending* without angles; that which is bent; a bow.—*vt. To bend;* to form into an arch. *ppr.* curving, *pret. & pp.* curved. [L. *curvus*.]
Curvet, kėr-vet', *n.* A particular leap of a horse, in which he *bends* his body, and springs out, raising his fore-legs together.—*vi.* To leap; to bound; to spring and form a *curvet;* to leap and frisk.—*vt.* To cause to move briskly. *ppr.* curvetting, *pret. & pp.* curvetted. [It. *corvetta*—L. *curvo*, *curvatum*, to bend.]
Curvilinear, Curvilineal, kėrv-i-lin'ē-ėr, kėrv-i-lin'ē-al, *a. Consisting of curve lines;* bounded by curve lines. [L. *curvus*, and *linea*, a line.]
Curvirostral, kėrv-i-ros'tral, *a. Having a crooked beak.* [L. *curvus*, and *rostrum*, a bill or beak.]
Cushion, kush'on, *n.* A pillow for a seat; a soft pad placed on a chair, sofa, &c.; a stuffed bag; something resembling a pillow.—*vt. To seat on a cushion;* to furnish with cushions. [Fr. *coussin*.]
Cusp, kusp, *n. A point;* the point or horn of the moon, or other luminary; a point formed by the meeting of two curves. [L. *cuspis*.]
Custard, kus'tėrd, *n.* A curdy kind of composition, of milk and eggs, sweetened, and baked or boiled. [W. *cwstard*.]
Custard-apple, kus'tėrd-ap-pl, *n.* An *apple* having a soft pulp like a *custard.*
Custodial, kus-tō'di-al, *a. Relating to custody* or guardianship.
Custodian, kus-tō'di-an, *n. A keeper;* one who has care or custody, as of some public building.
Custody, kus'tō-di, *n. A keeping;* guardianship; care; watch; penal safe-keeping; imprisonment; security. [L. *custodia—custos*, a keeper.]
Custom, kus'tum, *n. Old use;* habit; way; long established practice; established mode; fashion; a buying of goods; practice of frequenting a shop to make purchases; a tax or impost on goods, exported or imported. [Old Fr. *coustume*.]

Customable, kus'tum-a-bl, *a. Subject* to the payment of the duties called *customs.* [Old Fr. *coustumable*.]
Customarily, kus'tum-a-ri-li, *adv.* Habitually; commonly.
Customary, kus'tum-a-ri, *a. According to custom;* habitual; usual; accustomed; holding or held by custom. [Low L. *coustumarius*.]
Customer, kus'tum-ėr, *n. One who is in the habit* of purchasing at a shop, &c.; one who buys goods or wares.
Custom-house, kus'tum-hous, *n.* The *house* where vessels enter and clear, and where the *customs* are paid.
Customs, kus'tumz, *n. pl.* Duties charged on certain commodities, on their being brought into, or sent from, a country.
Cut, kut, *vt.* To divide or sever into pieces, by an *edged* instrument; to hew; to lop off; to carve, as meat; to engrave; to divide; to pierce; to affect deeply; to intersect; to castrate; to divide, as cards.—*vi.* To enter and divide the parts; to be severed by a cutting instrument; to divide by passing; to use a cutting instrument or edge-tool.—*p.a.* Deeply affected.—*n.* The action of an *edged* instrument; a wound; a stroke with a whip; a severe remark; a channel; a part cut off; any small piece; a lot; a near passage by which an angle is cut off; a carving or engraving; an engraved picture; act of dividing a pack of cards; manner in which a thing is cut; form; fashion. *ppr.* cutting, *pret. & pp.* cut. [Icel. *kuta*, to cut with a knife.]
Cutaneous, kū-tā'nē-us, *a. Belonging to the skin;* existing on or affecting the skin. [from L. *cutis*, the skin.]
Cuticle, kū'ti-kl, *n.* The *thin*, pellucid exterior coat of the *skin*, which rises in a blister; the thin vesicular membrane that covers the surface of vegetables. [L. *cuticula—cutis*, the skin.]
Cuticular, kū-tik'ū-lėr, *a. Pertaining to the cuticle.*
Cutlass, kut'las, *n.* A broad, curving sword; a hanger, used by soldiers in the cavalry, by seamen, &c. [Fr. *coutelas*—L. *culter*, a knife.]
Cutler, kut'lėr, *n.* One who makes, sells, or sharpens *knives* and other cutting instruments. [Fr. *coutelier*—L. *culter*, a knife.]
Cutlery, kut'lė-ri, *n. Hardware made* or sold by cutlers.
Cutlet, kut'let, *n. A small piece of veal* for broiling. [Fr. *côtelette*—L. *costa*, a rib.]
Cutter, kut'ėr, *n. He or that which cuts;* a fore-tooth that cuts meat; a small boat used by ships of war; a vessel with one mast and a straight running bow-sprit.
Cut-throat, kut'thrōt, *n. One who cuts throats;* a murderer; an assassin.—*a.* Murderous.
Cutting, kut'ing, *p.a.* Piercing the heart; sharp; severe; pungent; satirical.—*p.n. A piece cut off;* an incision; an excavation made through earth or rock, in making a road, canal, &c.; a twig or scion, cut off for the purpose of grafting or planting it.
Cuttingly, kut'ing-li, *adv. In a cutting manner.*
Cuttle, Cuttle-fish, kut'tl, kut'tl-fish, *n.* A soft-bodied marine animal, which *hides itself*, when pursued, by discharging a black liquor from a small bladder. [Sax. *cudele*—W. *cudd*, gloom.]
Cutwater, kut'wa-tėr, *n.* The fore part of a ship's prow, which *cuts the water.*

ch, *chain*; j, *job*; g, *go*: ng, *sing*; ᴛʜ, *then*; th, *thin*; w, *wig*; wh, *whig*; zh, *azure*; † obsolete.

Cycle, sī'kl, n. A *circle;* a round of years, or period of time, in which the same course begins again; an imaginary orb or circle in the heavens. [Fr.—Gr. *kuklos,* a circle.]
Cyclic, Cyclical, sī'klik, sī'klik-al, a. *Pertaining to,* or containing, *a cycle.*
Cycloid, sī'kloid, n. A geometrical curve, on which depends the doctrine of pendulums. [Gr. *kuklos,* a circle, and *eidos,* form.]
Cycloidal, sī-kloid'al, a. *Pertaining or relating to a cycloid.*
Cyclone, sī'klōn, n. A *rotatory storm* or whirlwind of extended circuit. [Gr. *kuklos,* a circle.]
Cyclopean, sī-klō-pē'an, a. Pertaining to the *Cyclops,* fabulous giants of antiquity, which are said to have had but *one eye of a circular form in the middle of the forehead;* gigantic; barbarous; vast; terrific. [from Gr. *kuklōps,* round-eyed.]
Cyclopedia, Cyclopædia, sī-klō-pē'di-a, sī-klō-pē'di-a, n. *A circle of learning;* the circle of the arts and sciences; a book or books that contain treatises on every branch of the arts and sciences, arranged in alphabetical order. [Gr. *kuklos,* and *paideia,* learning—*pais,* a boy or girl.]
Cyclopedic, sī-klō-pēd'ik, a. *Belonging to a cyclopedia.*
Cygnet, sig'net, n. *A swan;* a young swan. [Fr. *cygne*—L. *cygnus,* a swan.
Cylinder, si'lin-dẽr, n. A long round *body which is easily rolled;* a long circular body of uniform diameter, whose ends form equal and parallel circles. [Gr. *kulindros*—*kulindō,* to roll.]
Cylindric, Cylindrical, si-lin'drik, si-lin'drik-al, a. *Having the form of a cylinder,* or partaking of its properties.
Cymbal, sim'bal, n. *A basin-shaped* musical instrument of brass. In playing, two of them are struck together, producing a sharp ringing sound. [L. *cymbalum.*]
Cynic, Cynical, sin'ik, sin'ik-al, a. *Having the qualities of a surly dog;* snarling; captious; surly; currish; austere. n. A surly ill-natured man; a misanthrope. [Gr. *kunikos—kuōn,* a dog.]
Cynicism, sin'i-sizm, n. Austerity.
Cynics, sin'iks, n.pl. An ancient sect of *snarling* philosophers, who valued themselves on their contempt of riches, of arts, sciences, and amusements. The followers of Antisthenes were so called. [Gr. *Kunikos—kuōn,* a dog.)
Cynosure, si'nō-shōr, n. *The dog's tail;* the constellation of the Little Bear, to which, as containing the north star, the eyes of mariners and travellers were, in former times, continually turned; anything to which attention is strongly directed. [Gr. *kunosoura—kuōn,* a dog, and *oura,* tail.]
Cypress, si'pres, n. A tree valued for the durability of its wood; the emblem of mourning for the dead. [Fr. *cyprès*—L. *cupressus.*]
Cyst, sist, n. *A bag which includes* morbid matter in animal bodies. [Sax.]
Czar, zär, n. *A king; a chief;* a title of the Emperor of Russia. [Sclav.]
Czarina, zä-rē'na, n. A title of the Empress of Russia.
Czarowitz, zär'ō-vits, n. The title of the eldest son of the Czar of Russia. [Rus. *csarovics.*]

D.

Dab, dab, vt. To cuff; to strike gently with the hand; to strike gently with some soft or moist substance. ppr. dabbing, pret. & pp. dabbed.—n. A gentle blow with the hand; a small mass of anything soft or moist; a small flat fish. [Fr. *dauber.*]
Dabble, dab'bl, vt. *To dip a little or often;* to wet; to moisten; to sprinkle. vi. To dip the hands, throw water, and splash about; to play in mud and water; to do anything in a superficial manner; to meddle. ppr. dabbling, pret. & pp. dabbled. [Belgic, *dabbelen.*]
Dabbler, dab'bl-ẽr, n. *One who dabbles;* a superficial meddler.
Dabbling, dab'bl-ing, p.n. Act of *dipping* superficially into anything.
Dace, dās, n. A small river fish of a bright silvery colour. [D. *daas.*]
Dactyl, dak'til, n. *A finger;* a poetical foot of three syllables, one long, followed by two short. [Gr. *dactulos,* a finger.]
Dactylic, dak-til'ik, a. *Pertaining to,* or consisting chiefly or wholly of, *dactyls.—*n. A line consisting of *dactyls.*
Dad, Daddy dad, dad'di, n. *Father,* a child's word. [W. *tad;* Hindoo, *dada;* formed from the sound.]
Daff¹, daf, vt. To put off.
Daffodil, daf'fō-dil, n. A plant, the yellow narcissus, or king's spear. [Fr. *asphodèle*—Gr. *asphodēlos.*]
Dagger, dag'gẽr, n. *A dirk;* a poniard; a blunt blade of iron, used in fencing; a mark of reference in printing, in the form of a dagger, thus †. [Ir. *daigear* —Heb. *dākar,* to pierce, to stab.]
Daggle, dag'gl, vt. *To trail in mud or wet grass;* to befoul; to dirty, as the lower end of a garment.—vi. To run through mud and water. ppr. daggling, pret. & pp. daggled. [from Sw. Goth. *dagg,* dew.]
Daggled, dag'gld, pp. *Dipped or trailed in mud* or foul water; befouled.
Dahlia, dā'li-a, n. A beautiful flowering plant, having many varieties. [from *Dahl,* a Swedish botanist.]
Daily, dā'li, a. Happening or being *every day;* done day by day; enjoyed every day; diurnal.—adv. Day by day. [Sax. *dœglic.*]
Daintily, dān'ti-li, adv. *In a dainty manner;* nicely; delicately; deliciously.
Daintiness, dān'ti-nes, n. Delicacy; deliciousness; fastidiousness.
Dainty, dān'ti, a. *Toothsome;* nice; scrupulous; squeamish; luxurious; delicious; fine; pleasing to the palate. n. Something nice; that which is exquisitely delicious; a delicacy; a term of fondness'. [Old G. *zant,* a tooth.]
Dairy, dā'ri, n. *The place where milk is* set for cream, managed, and converted into butter or cheese; the occupation of making butter and cheese.—a. Pertaining to the keeping of cows, managing of milk, and making of butter and cheese. [Low L. *dayeria,* a place for keeping milk.]
Dairy-maid, dā'ri-mād, n. A female servant who manages a dairy.
Dais, dā'is, n. A raised floor at the upper end of the dining-hall, where the high *table* stood; a canopy, with its seat, at the high table; the high table itself. [Old Fr—Low L. *discus,* a table.]
Daisied, dā'sid, p.a. *Full of daisies;* adorned with daisies.
Daisy, dā'zi, n. *The day's eye;* a well-known plant, bearing a white flower, with a tinge of red, and a yellow centre. [Sax. *dœges-eye.*]
Dale, dāl, n. *A vale* or valley; a low place between hills. [Sax. *dœl.*]
Dalliance, dal'li-ans, n. Acts of fondness; interchange of caresses; delay'; procrastination.
Dally, dal'li, vi. To amuse one's self with idle play; to wanton; to linger; to loiter. ppr. dallying, pret. & pp. dallied. [Icel. *dœlleiki,* familiarity.]
Dam, dam, n. *A female parent* (used chiefly of beasts). [from *dame.*]
Dam, dam, vt. *To stop up;* to shut in; to stop, as a stream of water by a bank of earth, or by any other work (with *in* or *up*). ppr. damming, pret. & pp. dammed.—n. *That which stops;* a mole, or mound of earth, or any wall raised *to obstruct* a current of water. [Sax. *demman,* to stop.]
Damage, dam'āj, n. *Hurt;* harm; any permanent injury; loss; mischief; (pl.) compensation for injury or loss.—vt. *To hurt;* to *injure;* to lessen the soundness or value of. ppr. damaging, pret. & pp. damaged. [Old Fr.—L. *damnum,* loss.]
Damageable, dam'āj-a-bl, a. *That may be damaged,* injured, or impaired.
Damaged, dam'ājd, p.a. *Hurt;* impaired; injured.
Damask, dam'ask, n. Cloth woven with flowers and figures, originally made of silk, or silk and flax, and brought from *Damascus;* but now, of a mixture of flax and cotton, or of cotton and wool; a red colour.—a. Of the colour of *damask,* or of the rose so called.—vt. To form flowers on; to variegate; to diversify. [It. *dommasco.*]
Damasked, dam'askt, p.a. Variegated with flowers; having the colour of the damask rose.
Dame, dām, n. *A mistress;* a matron; a lady; a title of honour to a woman; the wife of a knight or baronet. [Fr. —L. *domina—domus,* a house.]
Damn, dam, vt. *To sentence to punishment;* to doom to punishment in hell; to decide to be wrong; to censure; to decide to be bad, by hissing, &c. [Fr. *damner*—L. *damno.*]
Damnable, dam'na-bl, a. *Deserving damnation;* odious; detestable; pernicious.
Damnableness, dam'na-bl-nes, n. *The state or quality of deserving damnation.*

Fāte, fär, fat, fall; mē, met, hẽr; pīne, pin; nōte, not, mōve; tūbe, tub, bṳll; oil, pound.

Damnably, dam'na-bli, *adv.* In a damnable manner.

Damnation, dam-nā'shon, *n.* Condemnation; sentence to everlasting punishment in the future state. [L. *damnatio.*]

Damnatory, dam'na-tō-ri, *a.* Containing a sentence of condemnation.

Damned, dam'ned, colloquially pronounced damd, *a.* Hateful; detestable.

Damning, dam'ning, *p.a.* That condemns or exposes to damnation.

Damp, damp, *a.* Steamy; moist; humid; being in a state between dry and wet.—*n.* Vapour; moisture; fog; depression of spirits; chill; (pl.) noxious exhalations issuing from the earth. *vt.* To moisten; to chill; to dispirit; to restrain. [Old G. *damf,* vapour.]

Damper, damp'ėr, *n.* He or that which damps or checks.

Dampish, damp'ish, *a.* Moderately damp or moist.

Dampishly, damp'ish-li, *adv.* In a dampish manner.

Dampishness, damp'ish-nes, *n.* State of being dampish.

Dampness, damp'nes, *n.* Moisture; fogginess; moistness; moderate humidity.

Damsel, dam'zel, *n.* A young lady; a young woman; a girl. [Old Fr. *damoisel*—L. *domina.*]

Damson, dam'zn, *n.* A small black plum, originally from *Damascus.* [contracted from *damascene.*]

Dance, dans, *vi.* To leap or spring; to move with measured steps, regulated by a tune.—*vt.* To make to dance; to move up and down, or back and forth; to dandle. *ppr.* dancing, *pret. & pp.* danced.—*n.* A leaping and frisking about; a leaping or stepping with motions of the body adjusted to the measure of a tune; a tune by which dancing is regulated. [Fr. *danser.*]

Dancer, dans'ėr, *n.* One who dances.

Dancing, dans'ing, *p.n.* The act of moving in measured steps; the act of frisking.

Dancing-master, dans'ing-mas-tėr, *n.* One who teaches the art of dancing.

Dandelion, dan'di-li-un, *n.* The lion's tooth; a well-known plant bearing a bright yellow compound flower. [Fr. *dent de lion.*]

Dandle, dan'dl, *vt.* To shake on the knee, as an infant; to move up and down in the hand; to fondle; to trifle with. *ppr.* dandling, *pret. & pp.* dandled. [G. *tandeln.*]

Dandruff, dan'druf, *n.* A filthy tetter or scab; a scurf which forms on the head. [Sax. *tan,* a tetter, and *drof,* dirty.]

Dandy, dan'di, *n.* A fop; a coxcomb. [Fr. *dandin,* ninny.]

Dandyish, dan'di-ish, *a.* Like a dandy.

Dandyism, dan'di-ism, *n.* The manners and dress of a dandy.

Danger, dān'jėr, *n.* Exposure to injury; jeopardy; loss; pain, or other evil; domain'.—*vt.* To put in hazard. [Fr.—L. *damnum,* loss.]

Dangerous, dān'jėr-us, *a.* Perilous; hazardous; causing risk of harm; unsafe; insecure. [Norm. *dangerous,* dubious.]

Dangerously, dān'jėr-us-li, *adv.* With danger; perilously.

Dangle, dang'gl, *vi.* To hang loose; to hang and swing; to hang on any one; to follow officiously.—*vt.* To carry suspended loosely. *ppr.* dangling, *pret. & pp.* dangled. [Icel. *dingla.*]

Dangler, dang'gl-ėr, *n.* One who dangles; a man who hangs about women.

Dapper, dap'pėr, *a.* Active; nimble; brisk; little and active; neat; lively. [D. brave.]

Dapple, dap'pl, *a.* Marked with little clouds or spots; spotted; variegated with spots of different colours.—*vt.* To spot; to variegate with spots. *ppr.* dappling, *pret. & pp.* dappled. [Icel. *depill,* a little cloud.]

Dappled, dap'pld, *p.a.* Spotted.

Dare, dār, *vi.* To have boldness; to be ready to face danger; to be bold enough; to venture. *ppr.* daring, *pret. & pp.* durst.—*vt.* To challenge; to provoke; to defy; to brave; to venture on. *ppr.* daring, *pret. & pp.* dared.—*n.* Boldness; defiancet. [Sax. *dyrran.*]

Dareful†, dār'ful, *a.* Full of daring.

Daring, dār'ing, *p.a.* Bold; intrepid; fearless; audacious; impudently bold and defying.—*p.n.* A bold act; a hazardous attempt.

Daringly, dār'ing-li, *adv.* Boldly; courageously; fearlessly; imprudently.

Dark, därk, *a.* Destitute of light; clouded; black or blackish; disheartening; involved in mystery; unenlightened; suspicious; keeping designs in concealment.—*n.* Darkness; obscurity; absence of light; secrecy; a state unknown; a state of ignorance. [Sax. *deorc.*]

Darken, därk'n, *vt.* To render dark; to deprive of light; to make black or obscure; to deprive of bodily or mental vision; to render stupid; to perplex; to make less clear; to sully.—*vi.* To grow dark or darker; to grow less white or clear. [Sax. *adeorcian.*]

Darkened, därk'nd, *p.a.* Deprived of light; made ignorant.

Dark-house†, därk'hous, *n.* A madhouse.

Darkish, därk'ish, *a.* Somewhat dark; dusky.

Darkling, därk'ling, *a.* Being in the dark, or without light. (A poetical word.)

Darkly, därk'li, *adv.* Obscurely; dimly.

Darkness, därk'nes, *n.* Absence of light; blackness; gloom; want of clearness; ignorance; privacy; infernal gloom; hell; perplexities.

Darksome, därk'sum, *a.* Dark; gloomy.

Darling, där'ling, *a.* Dearly beloved; regarded with great kindness and tenderness. — *n.* One much beloved; a favourite. [Sax. *deorling.*]

Darn, därn, *vt.* To patch; to mend a rent or hole by imitating the texture of the stuff with yarn or thread and a needle; to sew together with yarn or thread. [W. *darn,* a patch.]

Darnel, där'nel, *n.* A plant injurious to corn. [from Sax. *deriam,* to hurt.]

Darning, därn'ing, *p.n.* Act of mending, as a hole in a garment.

Dart, därt, *n.* That which pierces and wounds; a pointed missile weapon to be thrown by the hand; a short lance. *vt.* To throw, as a pointed instrument, with a sudden thrust; to throw suddenly; to shoot.—*vi.* To fly or shoot, as a dart; to fly rapidly; to start suddenly and run. [Fr. *dard*—Armor. *dared,* a dart.]

Darter, därt'ėr, *n.* One who throws a dart; a bird that darts into the water after fish.

Dash, dash, *vt.* To strike suddenly or violently; to break by collision; to throw, as water suddenly, in separate portions; to sprinkle; to mix and adulterate; to sketch out hastily; to erase at a stroke; to destroy; to frustrate; to strike with shame or fear; to daunt; to abash.—*vi.* To break and fly off; to rush or scatter; to rush with violence, and break through.—*n.* A sudden stroke; a violent striking of two bodies; infusion; a rushing or onset with violence; an act; a flourish; a mark in writing or printing (—), noting a pause in the sentence. [Icel. *daska,* to strike through.]

Dashing, dash'ing, *p.a.* Rushing; blustering; precipitate.

Dastard, das'tėrd, *n.* One easily dismayed; a coward; one who meanly shrinks from danger.—*a.* Cowardly. [Sax. *adastrigan,* to discourage.]

Dastardly, das'tėrd-li, *a.* Cowardly; meanly timid; base.

Data, dā'ta, *n. pl.* Things given; principles or facts admitted, by which to find things unknown. [L. pl. from *datum,* a thing given—*do,* to give.]

Date, dāt, *n.* Any given time; that addition to a writing which specifies the year, month, and day when it was given; the time when any event happened; the number which marks the time when any writing, coin, &c., was executed; period; age; duration.—*vt.* To fix the date of.—*vi.* To reckon; to begin; to have origin (with *from*). *ppr.* dating, *pret. & pp.* dated. [Fr.—L. *do, datum,* to give.]

Date, dāt, *n.* The fruit of the great palm-tree or date-tree, the husk of which has some resemblance to a finger. [Fr. *datte*—Gr. *daktulos,* a finger.]

Date-palm, Date-tree, dāt'päm, dāt'trē, *n.* The kind of palms which bear dates.

Dative, dāt'iv, *a.* That is given or appointed; that pertains to giving, as the third case of nouns in Greek and Latin. *n.* The third case of nouns in grammar, whose sign in Eng. is *to.* [L. *dativus*—*do,* to give.]

Daub, däb, *vt.* To smear; to cover with mud or other soft substance; to paint coarsely; to disguise; to flatter grossly. *vi.* To play the hypocrite.—*n.* A coarse painting. [W. *dwbaw,* to daub.]

Dauber, däb'ėr, *n.* One who daubs; a coarse painter; a low and gross flatterer.

Daubery†, däb'ė-ri, *n.* A daubing; imposition.

Dauby, däb'i, *a.* Viscous; glutinous.

Daughter, dä'tėr, *n.* The female offspring of a man or woman; a female child of any age; a female descendant; a daughter-in-law; a term of kindness or compassion; a woman; a female inhabitant. [Sax. *dohter.*]

Daughter-in-law, dä'tėr-in-la, *n.* A son's wife.

Daughterly, dä'tėr-li, *a.* Becoming a daughter; dutiful.

Daunt, dänt, *vt.* To tame; to subdue the courage of; to intimidate; to discourage; to damp; to depress. [Fr. *dompter*—L. *domo, domitum,* to subdue.]

Dauntless, dänt'les, *a.* Undaunted; bold; fearless; intrepid.

Dauntlessly, dänt'les-li, *adv.* In a dauntless manner.

Dauntlessness, dänt'les-nes, *n.* Fearlessness; intrepidity.

Daw, da, *n.* A bird of the crow kind, so named from its chattering. [Old G. *tāha.*]

Dawdle, da'dl, *vi.* To waste time in trifling employment. *ppr.* dawdling, *pret. & pp.* dawdled.

Dawn, dan, *vi.* To become day; to begin to grow light in the morning; to glimmer obscurely; to begin to open

DAWNING 82 **DEBITOR**

or appear.—*n. The daying;* the break of day; the first appearance of light in the morning; first opening; beginning. [Sax. *dagian—dag,* day.]

Dawning, dan'ing, *p.a.* Opening; expanding; beginning to show intellectual light; beginning.—*p.n.* The first appearance of light in the morning; the first opening or appearance of the intellectual powers; beginning.

Day, dā, *n. The time of light;* the time between the rising and setting of the sun; the time from noon to noon, or from midnight to midnight; light; time specified; age; time, with reference to the existence of a person or thing; the contest of a day; battle; an appointed time; anniversary; the same day of the month in any future year. [Sax. *daeg*—Sans. *div,* to shine.]

Day-bed†, dā'bed, *n.* A couch or sofa.

Day-book, dā'buk, *n.* A *book* in which merchants, &c., make entries of their *daily* transactions; a journal of accounts.

Daybreak, dā'brāk, *n.* The *dawn,* or first appearance of light in the morning.

Day-dream, dā'drēm, *n.* A vision to the waking senses.

Daylight, dā'lit, *n. The light of the day.*

Day-lily, dā'li-li, *n.* A *lily* distinguished for the beauty of its flowers.

Daysman, dāz'man, *n.* One who sits as judge on a *day* fixed or appointed; an umpire or arbiter; a mediator.

Dayspring, dā'spring, *n. The dawn;* the beginning of the day.

Day-star, dā'stär, *n. The star that ushers in the day;* the morning-star, Lucifer.

Daywork, dā'werk, *n. Work* done or imposed *by the day.*

Daze†, dāz, *vt.* To stupify; to stun; to benumb. *ppr.* dazing, *pret. & pp.* dazed. [Sax. *dwaes,* dull.]

Dazzle, daz'zl, *vt.* To overpower with excess of light; to strike with a bright light; to dim or blind by a glare of light; to excite to surprise; to strike with terror.—*vi.* To be intensely bright; to be overpowered by light. *ppr.* dazzling, *pret. & pp.* dazzled. [as if *dwaesle,* from Sax. *dwaes.*]

Deacon, dē'kon, *n.* A *servant;* a person in the lowest degree of holy orders; the master of an incorporated company. [Gr. *diakonos—diakō,* to run, to hasten; or perhaps *dia,* and *konis,* dust.]

Deaconship, dē'kon-ship, *n. The office of a deacon.*

Dead, ded, *a.* Deprived of life; without life; deceased; without vegetable life; deep or sound; perfectly still; motionless; breathless; vacant; useless; dull; not lively; heavy; cold; tasteless; spiritless; perfect; unerring; wanting in religious spirit.—*n.* The *dead* signifies dead men, the state of the dead, or death; the time when there is a *death*-like stillness, or a deep gloom; depth, as in the midst of winter. [Sax.]

Deaden, ded'n, *vt.* To deprive of a portion of vigour, force, or sensation; to blunt; to retard; to make vapid; to give a dead appearance to; to darken; to dim. [Sax. *adeadam.*]

Dead-letter, ded'let-tèr, *n.* A *letter* which lies for a certain period uncalled for at the post-office, and is then sent to the general post-office to be opened.

Dead-level, ded'le-vel, *n.* Perfect or complete *level.*

Dead-light, ded'lit, *n.* A strong wooden shutter, with a ball of glass in the centre, made to suit a cabin-window.

Deadliness, ded'li-nes, *n. The quality of being deadly.*

Dead-lock, ded'lok, *n.* A *lock* which has no spring-catch; a complete standstill.

Deadly, ded'li, *a. That may cause death;* mortal; destructive; murderous; implacable.—*adv.* In a *deadly manner;* in a manner resembling death.

Dead-march, ded'märch, *n.* A *piece of solemn military music* for the funeral of soldiers.

Deadness, ded'nes, *n.* Want of natural life; want of animation; coldness, vapidness, indifference; mortification of the natural desires.

Dead-wall, ded'wal, *n.* A blank *wall;* a wall in which there is no opening.

Dead-weight, ded'wāt, *n.* A great *weight;* a heavy or oppressive burden.

Deaf, def, *a.* Deprived of or wanting the sense of hearing; not listening; not regarding; rejecting; deafened; stifled. [Sax. *deaf.*]

Deafen, def'n, *vt. To make deaf;* to deprive of the power of hearing; to render impervious to sound, as a floor or wall.

Deafening, def'n-ing, *p.a. Making deaf;* rendering impervious to sound.

Deaf-mute, def'mūt, *n.* A *deaf and dumb person.*

Deafness, def'nes, *n.* Incapacity of perceiving sounds; unwillingness to hear and regard.

Deal, dēl, *n.* A *part;* an indefinite quantity, degree, or extent; the art or practice of dealing cards; the division of a piece of timber made by sawing. [Sax. *dæl,* a part.]—*vt. To part;* to portion out; to distribute; to throw about; to give out in succession; to distribute, as the cards of a pack to the players. *vi.* To traffic; to trade; to behave well or ill; to distribute cards. *ppr.* dealing, *pret. & pp.* dealt. [Sax. *bedælen.*]

Dealer, dēl'èr, *n.* A trader; a trafficker; a merchant.

Dealing, dēl'ing, *p.n.* Conduct in relation to others; behaviour; intercourse in buying and selling; traffic; action.

Dean, dēn, *n.* A *head of ten men*†; an ecclesiastical dignitary in cathedral and collegiate churches, and the head of a chapter; an officer in a university or college. [Fr. *doyen;* Low L. *decanus*—L. *decem,* ten.]

Deanery, dēn'é-ri, *n.* The revenue, jurisdiction, or house of *a dean.*

Deanship, dēn'ship, *n. The office of a dean.*

Dear, dēr, *a. Regarded; beloved;* scarce; rare; narrow; costly; bearing a high price in comparison of the usual price; valuable; in a bad sense, grievous†. *n.* A *darling,* a word denoting tender affection or endearment.—*adv.*† *Dearly.* [Sax. *dyre,* beloved.]

Dear-bought, dēr'bat, *a.* Purchased at a high price.

Dearly, dēr'li, *adv.* At a high price; with great fondness.

Dearn†, dèrn, *a.* Lonely; solitary.

Dearness, dēr'nes, *n.* Fondness; nearness to the heart or affections; preciousness; tender love; scarcity; high price.

Dearth, dèrth, *n.* Scarcity, which renders food dear; want; need; famine; sterility; barrenness.

Death, deth, *n.* Extinction of life; entire loss of vitality; decease; departure; separation of the soul from the body; cause of death; mode of dying; murder; state of being under

the power of sin or its consequences; damnation. [Sax.—*deadian,* to die.]

Death-bed, deth'bed, *n.* The *bed* on which a person *dies,* or to which he is confined in his last sickness.

Deathful, deth'ful, *a. Causing death;* full of slaughter; murderous.

Deathless, deth'les, *a. Not subject to death* or extinction.

Deathlike, deth'lik, *a. Resembling death;* gloomy; quiet; motionless.

Deathliness, deth'li-nes, *n. The quality of being deathly.*

Deathly, deth'li, *a. Deadly;* fatal.

Debar, dē-bär', *vt.* To hinder from approach, entry, or enjoyment; to prevent; to exclude; to refuse. *ppr.* debarring, *pret. & pp.* debarred. [*de* and *bar.*]

Debark, dē-bärk', *vt. To land from a ship or boat;* to disembark. [Fr. *débarquer—barque,* a vessel.]

Debase, dē-bās', *vt.* To bring low; to lower; to sink; to reduce; to abase; to degrade; to vitiate. *ppr.* debasing, *pret. & pp.* debased.

Debased, dē-bāst', *p.a.* Adulterated; rendered mean.

Debasement, dē-bās'ment, *n. Act of debasing;* state of being debased.

Debasing, dē-bās'ing, *p.a.* Lowering; tending to debase or degrade.

Debatable, dē-bāt's-bl, *a. That may be debated;* disputable.

Debate, dē-bāt', *n.* Contention in words or arguments; disputation; discussion; dispute; controversy; quarrel. [Fr. *débat.*]—*vt. To beat down by words;* to contend for in arguments; to strive to maintain by reasoning, as a cause; to dispute; to argue; to contest.—*vi.* To examine different arguments in the mind; to dispute (with *upon*). *ppr.* debating, *pret. & pp.* debated. [Fr. *battre*—L. *batuo,* to beat.]

Debated, dē-bāt'ed, *p.a.* Disputed.

Debater, dē-bāt'èr, *n. One who debates.*

Debating, dē-bāt'ing, *p.a.* Disputing; discussing.

Debauch, dē-bach', *vt. To put out of order;* to seduce; to corrupt; to pollute; to pervert; to mislead.—*vt.* To riot; to revel.—*n.* Excess in eating or drinking; lewdness. [Fr. *débaucher—bauche,* a course.]

Debauched, dē-bacht', *p.a.* Vitiated in morals.

Debauchee, dē-ba-shē', *n. One addicted to debauchery;* one habitually lewd; a libertine; a rake. [Fr. *débauché.*]

Debaucher, dē-bach'èr, *n. One who debauches* or corrupts others.

Debauchery, dē-bach'é-ri, *n.* Seduction from duty or allegiance; corruption of fidelity; gluttony; intemperance; habitual lewdness.

Debenture, dē-ben'tūr, *n.* A certificate given to an exporter of goods, showing that he is entitled to a certain bounty or drawback. [Fr. *débenture*—L. *debentur,* they are owing—*debeo,* to owe.]

Debilitate, dē-bil'i-tāt, *vt. To weaken;* to enfeeble; to enervate. *ppr.* debilitating, *pret. & pp.* debilitated. [Fr. *débiliter*—L. *debilito—debilis,* weak.]

Debilitating, dē-bil'i-tāt-ing, *p.a. Weakening;* enfeebling.

Debility, dē-bil'i-ti, *n. Weakness;* feebleness; imbecility. [Fr. *débilité.*]

Debit, deb'it, *n. Debt;* money due for what is sold on credit; the left-hand page of a ledger.—*vt. To charge with debt;* to enter as an account on the debtor side of a book or ledger. [L. *debitum—debeo,* to owe.]

Debitor†, deb'it-èr, *n.* A *debtor.*

Fāte, fär, fat, fall; mē, met, hèr; pine, pin; nōte, not, move: tūbe, tub, bull; oil, pound.

Debonair, de-bō-nār', a. Gentle; gracious. [Fr. *débonnaire*.]
Debris, dā-brē', n. Wreck; fragments of rock and other substances, detached from the summit and sides of a mountain, and piled up below; rubbish; remains. [Fr.—*briser*, to break.]
Debt, det, n. That which is due from one person to another; due; obligation; that which any one is obliged to do or to suffer; sin; guilt; crime. [L. *debitum*—*debeo*, to owe.]
Debted, det'ed, a. Indebted.
Debtor, det'er, n. One who owes; one who is indebted; one who is under obligation to do something; the side of an account in which debts are charged. [L. *debitor*.]
Debut, dē-bō', n. A starting-point; first appearance before the public, as of an actor or public speaker, &c. [Fr.—*but*, an aim.]
Decade, de'kād, n. The number of ten; an aggregate consisting of ten. [Fr. *décade*—L. *decem*, ten.]
Decadence, dē-kā'dens, n. A falling down; decay. [Fr. *décadence*—L. *cado*, to fall.]
Decagon, de'ka-gon, n. A figure having ten angles and ten sides. [Gr. *deka*, and *gōnia*, an angle.]
Decahedron, de-ka-hē'dron, n. A solid figure or body having ten sides. [Gr. *deka*, and *hedra*, a side.]
Decalogue, de'ka-log, n. The ten commandments given by God to Moses. [Gr. *deka*, and *logos*, discourse.]
Decamp, dē-kamp', vi. To break up a camp; to march off; to take one's self off. [Fr. *décamper*.]
Decampment, dē-kamp'ment, n. Departure from a camp; a marching off.
Decant, dē-kant', vt. To pour from a tankard; to pour off gently from a vessel, as liquor; to pour from one vessel into another. [Fr. *décanter*—L. *canthārus*, a tankard.]
Decanter, dē-kant'ėr, n. A glass bottle used for holding wine or other liquors.
Decapitate, dē-kap'it-āt, vt. To behead. ppr. decapitating, pret. & pp. decapitated. [L. *decapito*, *decapitatum*—*caput*, the head.]
Decapitation, dē-kap'it-ā''shon, n. Act of beheading.
Decarbonise, dē-kār'bon-īz, vt. To deprive of carbonic acid. ppr. decarbonising, pret. & pp. decarbonised. [*de* and *carbon*.]
Decay, dē-kā', vi. To fall down or off; to become weaker; to waste; to wither; to fade; to fail.—vt. To cause to fail; to impair.—n. A falling down; gradual failure; gradual loss of strength, &c.; corruption; putrefaction. [Fr. *déchoir*—L. *cado*, *cadere*, to fall.]
Decayed, dē-kād', p.a. Fallen off; impaired; wasted; corrupted.
Decaying, dē-kā'ing, p.a. Falling off; declining; perishing.
Decease, dē-sēs', n. A going away; departure from this life; death.—vi. To depart from this life; to die. ppr. deceasing. pret. & pp. deceased. [L. *decessus*—*cedo*, *cessum*, to go.]
Deceased, dē-sēst', p.a. Dead.
Deceit, dē-sēt', n. A catching away or up; fraud; a stratagem; guile; art; cunning. [Old Fr. *decepte*—L. *capio*, *captum*, to catch.]
Deceitful, dē-sēt'fůl, a. Fraudulent; insidious; false; hollow.
Deceitfully, dē-sēt'fůl-li, adv. In a deceitful manner.
Deceitfulness, dē-sēt'fůl-nes, n. Quality of being deceitful.

Deceivable, dē-sēv'a-bl, a. Subject to deceit; exposed to imposture.
Deceivableness, dē-sēv'a-bl-nes, n. Liability to be deceived; liability to deceive.
Deceivably, dē-sēv'a-bli, adv. In a deceivable manner.
Deceive, dē-sēv', vt. To lead into error; to defraud; to delude; to circumvent; to fail. ppr. deceiving. pret. & pp. deceived. [Fr. *décevoir*—L. *capio*, *capēre*, to catch.]
Deceived, dē-sēvd', p.a. Led into error; misled; deluded.
Deceiver, dē-sēv'ėr, n. One who deceives.
December, dē-sem'bėr, n. The tenth month of the year, among the early Romans, but now the twelfth month. [L.—*decem*, ten.]
Decemvir, dē-sem'vėr, n. Decemviri, or Decemvirs, dē-sem'vi-ri, or dē-sem'vėrs, pl. One of ten magistrates, who had absolute authority for a short period in ancient Rome. [L. *decem*, and *vir*, a man.]
Decency, dē'sen-si, n. That which is becoming in words or behaviour; decorum; becoming ceremony; suitableness to character; propriety in speech; modesty. [Fr. *décence*—L. *decet*, it becomes.]
Decennial, dē-sen'ni-al, a. Consisting of ten years; happening every ten years. [L. *decennalis*.]
Decent, dē'sent, a. Becoming; seemly; not gaudy or ostentatious; proper; not immodest; graceful. [Fr. *décent*—L. *decens*.]
Decently, dē'sent-li, adv. In a decent or becoming manner.
Deception, dē-sep'shon, n. Act of deceiving; state of being deceived; artifice practised; fraud; double-dealing. [Fr. *déception*—L. *deceptio*.]
Deceptious, dē-sep'shi-us, a. Tending to deceive.
Deceptive, dē-sep'tiv, a. Tending to deceive; misleading; false; delusive. [Old Fr. *deceptif*.]
Deceptively, dē-sep'tiv-li, adv. In a manner to deceive.
Decidable, dē-sīd'a-bl, a. That may be decided.
Decide, dē-sīd', vt. To cut short; to end; to determine; to settle; to fix the event of; to resolve.—vi. To determine; to form a definite opinion. ppr. deciding, pret. & pp. decided. [L. *decido*—*cado*, to cut.]
Decided, dē-sīd'ed, p.a. That implies decision; clear; resolute.
Decidedly, dē-sīd'ed-li, adv. Clearly; indisputably.
Deciduous, dē-sid'ū-us, a. Falling off every year, as leaves; fading; having a temporary existence. [L. *deciduus*—*cado*, to fall.]
Decimal, de'si-mal, a. Tenth; reckoned by ten; increasing or diminishing by tens.—n. A tenth; a fraction having ten or some power of ten for its denominator. [Fr. *décimal*; L. *decimus*.]
Decimate, de'si-māt, vt. To select by lot and punish with death, as every tenth man; to tithe; to take every tenth. ppr. decimating, pret. & pp. decimated. [L. *decimo*, *decimatus*.]
Decimation, de-si-mā'shon, n. A selection of every tenth man by lot, as for punishment.
Decipher, dē-sī'fėr, vt. To explain, as what is written in ciphers, or secret characters; to read, as what is obscurely written or partially obliterated; to unravel; to interpret. [Fr. *déchiffrer*—*chiffrer*, to number.]

Decipherable, dē-sī'fėr-a-bl, a. That may be deciphered.
Decipherer, dē-sī'fėr-ėr, n. One who explains what is written in ciphers.
Deciphering, dē-sī'fėr-ing, p.n. Act of explaining or unfolding.
Decision, dē-si'zhon, n. A cutting short; determination of a difference, doubt, or event; conclusion; final judgment; firmness of purpose; putting an end to controversy. [L. *decisio*—*cado*, to cut.]
Decisive, dē-sī'siv, a. Having the power of deciding; conclusive; absolute.
Decisively, dē-sī'siv-li, adv. In a decisive or conclusive manner.
Decisiveness, dē-sī'siv-nes, n. Quality or state of being decisive.
Deck, dek, vt. To cover; to clothe; to dress elegantly; to adorn; to decorate. n. The covering of a ship, which constitutes a floor. [Sax. *decan*, to cover.]
Decker, dek'ėr, n. One who decks; a ship having decks, as a three-decker.
Decking, dek'ing, p.n. Ornament; embellishment.
Declaim, dē-klām', vi. To speak or plead loudly, or earnestly, to a public body; to make a formal speech; to harangue; to inveigh. [L. *declamo*—*clamo*, to cry out.]
Declaimer, dē-klām'ėr, n. One who declaims; a speaker in public.
Declaiming, dē-klām'ing, p.n. Act of speaking in public; a harangue.
Declamation, de-kla-mā'shon, n. A harangue; a speech made in public, in the tone and manner of an oration; exercise in speaking or oratory. [L. *declamatio*.]
Declamatory, dē-klam'a-tō-ri, a. Treated in the manner of a rhetorician; appealing to the passions; noisy; rhetorical, without solid sense or argument. [L. *declamatorius*.]
Declarable, dē-klār'a-bl, a. That may be declared or proved.
Declaration, de-kla-rā'shon, n. Act of declaring; that which is declared; verbal utterance; an explicit and open statement; a solemn affirmation. [L. *declaratio*.]
Declarative, dē-klār'at-iv, a. Explanatory; making proclamation. [Fr. *déclaratif*.]
Declaratory, dē-kla'ra-tō-ri, a. Making declaration, clear manifestation, or exhibition; expressive. [Fr. *déclaratoire*.]
Declare, dē-klār', vt. To show clearly; to make clearly known by words; to tell explicitly; to publish; to assert; to testify; to reveal.—vi. To announce clearly some purpose; to make a statement; to protest. ppr. declaring, pret. & pp. declared. [Fr. *déclarer*—L. *clarus*, clear.]
Declared, dē-klārd', p.a. Made known; manifested.
Declension, dē-klen'shon, n. A bending from; an oblique direction; a declining toward a worse state; the inflection of the terminations of nouns, adjectives, and pronouns to form the oblique cases. [Fr. *déclinaison*—L. *declinatio*—Gr. *klīnō*, to bend.]
Declinable, dē-klīn'a-bl, a. That may be declined.
Declination, de-klin-ā'shon, n. A bending aside; descent; decay; deviation from a straight line; angular distance of a heavenly body, north or south from the celestial equator. [L. *declinatio*.]
Decline, dē-klīn', vi. To bend downwards; to deviate from a right line, or from rectitude; to swerve; to fail; not

ch, chain; j, job; g, go; ng, sing; ᴛʜ, then; th, thin; w, wig; wh, whig; zh, azure: † obsolete.

to comply.—*vt. To bend downward*; to move from a fixed point or right line; to refuse; to be cautious not to do or interfere with; to inflect; to change, as the termination of a noun, &c., for forming the oblique cases. *ppr.* declining, *pret. & pp.* declined.—*n.* A falling off; a tendency to a worse state; a gradual decay of health or vigour; consumption. [L. *declino*—Gr. *klinō*, to make to bend.]

Declining, dē-klīn'ing, *p.a.* Failing; decaying.

Declivity, dē-klī'vi-ti, *n. Inclination downward*; a downward slope; a gradual descent. [L. *declivitas—clivus*, a slope.]

Decoct, dē-kokt', *vt. To boil down*; to prepare by boiling; to digest by heat; to strengthen. [L. *docoquo, decoctum—coquo*, to boil.]

Decoction, dē-kok'shon, *n. A boiling down*; a solution of the active principles of vegetables, obtained by boiling them in water. [Fr. *décoction*.]

Decomposable, dē-kom-pōz'a-bl, *a. That may be decomposed*.

Decompose, dē-kom-pōz', *vt. To separate* the constituent parts of; to disunite, as elementary particles combined by chemical attraction; to resolve into original elements.—*vi.* To become resolved from existing combinations. *ppr.* decomposing, *pret. & pp.* decomposed. [Fr. *décomposer*—L. *pono, positum*, to place, set.]

Decomposition, dē-kom-pō-zi'shon, *n.* Resolution of a compound body into its original elements; chemical analysis; decay.

Decompound, dē-kom-pound', *vt. To decompose*. [L. *de, com* for *con*, and *pono*, to place.]

Decorate, de'kō-rāt, *vt. To render graceful*; to adorn; to beautify; to deck; to embellish. *ppr.* decorating, *pret. & pp.* decorated. [L. *decōro, decoratus—decus*, grace.]

Decoration, de-kō-rā'shon, *n. Act of decorating*; that which adorns; ornament; embellishment; trappings.

Decorative, de'kō-rāt-iv, *a.* Adorning; suited to embellish.

Decorous, dē-kō'rus, *a. Seemly*; becoming; proper; befitting. [L. *decōrus*.]

Decorously, dē-kō'rus-li, *adv. In a becoming manner*.

Decorum, dē-kō'rum, *n. Seemliness*; fitness; propriety of speech or behaviour; suitableness; becoming formality. [L.]

Decoy, dē-koi', *n. A cage* or inclosure for catching ducks or wild fowls; any allurement that misleads into evil, danger, or the power of an enemy. *vt.* To catch, as wild *ducks* by means of a *cage* or other contrivance; to lure into a net or snare; to entice; to seduce. [*duck*, and D. *kooi*, a cage.]

Decrease, dē-krēs', *vi. To grow or become less*; to lessen; to diminish.—*vt. To cause to become less*; to diminish gradually. *ppr.* decreasing, *pret. & pp.* decreased.—*n.* Gradual diminution; decay; the wane of the moon. [L. *decresco—cresco*, to grow.]

Decreasing, dē-krēs'ing, *p.a.* Becoming less; diminishing; waning.

Decree, dē-krē', *n. A decision*; an edict; an order or law; established rule; predetermined purpose; judicial decision. *vt.* To enact; to order; to award; to fix; to determine judicially.—*vi.* To make an edict; to appoint by edict. *ppr.* decreeing, *pret. & pp.* decreed. [Fr. *décret*—L. *cerno, cretum*, to decide.]

Decrement, de'krē-ment, *n. Decrease*; the quantity lost by gradual diminution or waste. [L. *decrementum*.]

Decrepit, dē-krep'it, *a. That can only creep about quietly*; broken down with age; being in the last stage of decay. [L. *decrepitus—crepo*, to crack.]

Decrepitate, dē-krep'it-āt, *vt. To calcine* in a strong heat, with a continual *crackling* of the substance. — *vi. To crack much* or frequently; *to crackle*, as salts when roasting. *ppr.* decrepitating, *pp.* decrepitated. [L. *crepito, crepitatus—crepo*, to crack.]

Decrepitation, dē-krep'it-ā''shon, *n.* The separation of parts with a *crackling* noise, occasioned by heat, as in certain salts.

Decrepitude, dē-krep'it-ūd, *n.* The broken, crazy state of the body, produced by decay and the infirmities of age.

Decretal, dē-krēt'al, *a. Containing a decree*. [L. *decretalis—cerno, crētum*, to discern.]

Decretal, dē-krēt-al, *n.* An authoritative *decree*; a decree of the pope; a collection of papal decrees.

Decretive, dē-krēt'iv, *a. Having the force of a decree*; making a decree.

Decretory, dē'krē-tō-ri, *a.* Definitive; established by a decree. [L. *decretorius.*]

Decrial, dē-krī'al, *n.* A clamorous censure; condemnation by censure.

Decry, dē-krī', *vt. To cry down*; to rail or clamour against; to disparage; to detract from; to depreciate. *ppr.* decrying, *pret. & pp.* decried. [Fr. *décrier—crier*, to cry.]

Decumbent, dē-kum'bent, *p.a. Lying down*; recumbent; prostrate. [L. *decumbens*.]

Decuple, de'kū-pl, *a. Tenfold*; containing ten times as many.—*n. A number ten* times repeated. [Fr. *décuple*—L. *decem*, ten.]

Dedicate, de'di-kāt, *vt. To consecrate* to the Divine Being or to a sacred purpose; to give wholly to; to allot; to inscribe to a patron or friend. *ppr.* dedicating, *pret. & pp.* dedicated.—*a.†* Set apart; devoted. [L. *dedico, dedicatus—dico*, to proclaim.]

Dedicated, de'di-kāt-ed, *p.a.* Consecrated; inscribed to; given wholly to.

Dedication, de-di-kā'shon, *n.* Consecration; act of devoting to some person, use, or thing; inscription or address, as to a patron or friend. [L. *dedicatio*.]

Dedicator, de'di-kāt-er, *n. One who dedicates*.

Dedicatory, de'di-ka-tō-ri, *a. Composing a dedication*.

Deduce, dē-dūs', *vt. To lead down*; to draw or bring from; to gather, as a truth, from premises; to infer from what precedes; to trace; to collect; to derive. *ppr.* deducing, *pret. & pp.* deduced. [L. *deduco—duco*, to lead.]

Deducible, dē-dūs'i-bl, *a. That may be deduced*; derivable, as a result.

Deduct, dē-dukt', *vt. To draw or take from*; to subtract; to remove in numbering, estimating, or calculating. [L. *deduco, deductum—duco*, to lead.]

Deduction, dē-duk'shon, *n. Act of deducting*; that which is deducted; an inference; abatement; discount. [L. *deductio*.]

Deductive, dē-dukt'iv, *a. Deducible*; that is or may be deduced from premises.

Deductively, dē-dukt'iv-li, *adv. By regular deduction*; by way of inference.

Deed, dēd, *n. That which is done*; an act; performance; a fact; feat; illustrious act; reality; a written instrument. [Sax. *dæd—dón*, to do.]

Deedless, dēd'les, *a. Not having performed deeds* or exploits; inactive.

Deem, dēm, *vt. To judge*; to think; to consider; to suppose.—*vi. To judge*; to think; to be of opinion; to estimate. *n.†* Opinion. [Sax. *deman*, to think.]

Deep, dēp, *a. Sunk low*; being far below the surface; descending far downward; profound; low in situation; far from the outer part; not superficial; not easily fathomed; sagacious; designing; grave in sound; very still or solemn; thick; black; strongly coloured; mysterious; heartfelt; affecting greatly; absorbed; swallowed up.—*n.* The sea; the abyss of waters; the ocean; any great collection of water; that which is profound or incomprehensible; the most still or solemn part; the midst. *adv.* Deeply; to a great depth. [Sax. *deóp—dyppan*, to immerge.]

Deep-drawing, dēp'drā-ing, *a. Of deep draught*.

Deepen, dēp'n, *vt. To make deep or deeper*; to darken; to increase; to strengthen; to make more profound; to make more sad, grave, or gloomy. *vi.* To become more deep.

Deep-fet, dēp'fet, *a.* Deeply fetched or drawn.

Deep-laid, dēp'lād, *a. Laid deep*; formed with profound skill or artifice.

Deeply, dēp'li, *adv. At or to a great depth*; profoundly; with great sorrow.

Deepness, dēp'nes, *n. State or quality of being deep*; depth; profundity.

Deer, dēr, *n. sing. & pl.* A quadruped of several species, as the stag, the fallow-deer, the roebuck, the rein-deer, &c. [Sax. *deór*.]

Deer-stalking, dēr'stak-ing, *n.* The hunting of deer on foot, by stealing upon them unawares.

Deface, dē-fās', *vt. To unmake*; to destroy or mar, as the surface of a thing; to disfigure; to erase. *ppr.* defacing, *pret. & pp.* defaced. [Old Fr. *desfacer*.]

Defaced, dē-fāst', *p.a.* Destroyed; disfigured; erased.

Defacement, dē-fās'ment, *n.* Injury to the *surface* or beauty; obliteration; that which mars beauty or disfigures.

Defalcate, dē-fal'kāt, *vt. To cut off*, as with a *pruning-hook*. *ppr.* defalcating, *pret. & pp.* defalcated. [Fr. *défalquer*—L. *falx, falcis*, a pruning-hook.]

Defalcation, dē-fal-kā'shon, *n. A lopping off*; a deficit; a withdrawment of funds intrusted to the care of some one; that which is cut off or withdrawn. [Fr. *défalcation*.]

Defalcator, dē-fal'kāt-er, *n.* One who is guilty of a breach of trust, or of embezzlement in money matters.

Defamation, de-fa-mā'shon, *n.* Slander; calumny; aspersion; reproach. [Low L. *defamatio*.]

Defamatory, dē-fam'a-tō-ri, *a.* Calumnious; slanderous; false and injurious to reputation. [Fr. *diffamatoire*.]

Defame, dē-fām', *vt. To speak against* the *fame* or reputation of; to calumniate; to asperse; to detract from. *ppr.* defaming, *pret. & pp.* defamed. [Fr. *diffamer*—L. *fama*, fame.]

Defamer, dē-fām'er, *n.* A slanderer; a detractor; a calumniator.

Default, dē-falt', *n. A failing or failure*; an omission of that which ought to be done; neglect to do what duty or law requires; offence. [Old Fr.—L. *fallo*, to make to fall, to deceive.]

Fāte, fär, fat, fall; mē, met, hėr; pīne, pin; nōte, not, mōve; tūbe, tub, bull; oil, pound.

Defaulter, dē-fảlt'ėr, n. One who fails to perform a public duty; one who fails to account for public money intrusted to his care; a delinquent.

Defeat, de-fēt', n. An undoing; frustration; overthrow; loss of battle.—vt. To undo; to ruin; to frustrate; to foil; to overthrow; to conquer; to discomfit. [Fr. défaite—L. facio, factum, to do.]

Defeated, dē-fēt'ed, p.a. Effectually resisted; overthrown; rendered null.

Defecate, de-fē-kāt, vt. To clear from lees; to purify; to purge of extraneous matter. ppr. defecating, pret. & pp. defecated. [L. defæco, defæcatus—fæx, fæcis, lees.]

Defecation, de-fe-kā'shon, n. Act of separating from lees; a cleansing from impurities or foreign matter.

Defect, dē-fekt', n. Something not done which ought to have been done; a falling short in moral conduct or in judgment; a blemish; fault; mistake; flaw; anything unnatural or misplaced. [L. defectus—facio, to make, to do.]

Defection, dē-fek'shon, n. Want or failure of duty; a falling away; apostasy; revolt from duty or allegiance; a falling off from a cause, party, or principle. [Fr. défection.]

Defective, dē-fekt'iv, a. Having a defect or defects; wanting either in substance, quantity, or quality; deficient; faulty; blamable. [Fr. défectif.]

Defectively, dē-fekt'iv-li, adv. In a defective manner; imperfectly.

Defence, dē-fens', n. A guarding against danger; guard; protection; security; fortification; vindication, apology; plea; opposition; denial of a charge, accusation, &c.; skill in fencing, &c. [Fr. défense—L. defendo, to defend.]

Defenceless, dē-fens'les, a. Unarmed; unguarded; weak; unsheltered.

Defencelessly, dē-fens'les-li, adv. In an unprotected manner.

Defencelessness, dē-fens'les-nes, n. State of being defenceless.

Defend, dē-fend', vt. To ward off; to prohibit; to secure against attacks or injury; to repel, as a demand, charge, or accusation; to resist; to support; to justify; to vindicate; to protect. [L. defendo—obsol. fendo, to strike.]

Defendant, dē-fend'ant, n. A defender; he who defends against an assailant; the person that opposes a complaint, demand, or charge.—at. Proper or serving for defence. [Old Fr.]

Defender, dē-fend'ėr, n. One who defends; one who maintains, supports, protects, or vindicates; a champion; a pleader.

Defensible, dē-fens'i-bl, a. That may be vindicated, maintained, or justified; justifiable.

Defensive, dē-fens'iv, a. Proper for defence; carried on in resisting attack; in a state or posture to defend.—n. That which defends. [Fr. défensif.]

Defensively, dē-fens'iv-li, adv. In a defensive manner.

Defensory, dē-fens'ō-ri, a. Tending to defend. [Low L. defensorius.]

Defer, dē-fėr', vt. To carry or put to a distance; to put off to a future time; to postpone; to adjourn. ppr. deferring, pret. & pp. deferred. [L. differo—fero, to carry.]

Defer, dē-fėr', vi. To bring down; to yield to another's opinion; to submit in opinion. ppr. deferring, pret. & pp. deferred. [L. defero—fero, to carry.]

Deference, de'fėr-ens, n. A deferring or yielding in opinion; regard; respect; submission. [Fr. déférence.]

Deferential, de-fėr-en'shi-al, a. Expressing deference; respectful.

Deferentially, de-fėr-en'shi-al-li, adv. With deference.

Defiance, dē-fi'ans, n. Act of defying; a daring; a challenge to fight; a call upon one to make good any assertion or charge, or to maintain any cause or point; contempt of opposition or danger; a contemptuous daring or resistance. [Fr. défiance.]

Deficiency, de-fi'shi-en-si, n. Defect; want; failing; any want of perfection; something less than is necessary. [from L. deficiens.]

Deficient, de-fi'shi-ent, a. Defective; imperfect; falling short; not adequate; not having a full supply. [L. deficiens, being wanting—facio, to make.]

Deficit, de'fi-sit, n. Want; deficiency; lack. [L. it wants.]

Defier, dē-fi'ėr, n. One who defies.

Defile, dē-fil', vt. To make foul; to pollute; to make unclean; to dirty; to tarnish; to violate the chastity of. ppr. defiling, pret. & pp. defiled. [Sax. afylan.]

Defile, dē-fil', vi. To march off in a line, or file by file; to file off.—n. A narrow way in which troops may march only in a line or file, or with a narrow front; a long narrow pass, as between hills, &c. ppr. defiling, pret. & pp. defiled. [Fr. défiler—L. filum, a thread.]

Defiled, dē-fild', p.a. Polluted; violated; vitiated.

Defilement, dē-fil'ment, n. Act of defiling or state of being defiled.

Defiler, dē-fil'ėr, n. One who defiles.

Definable, dē-fin'a-bl, a. That may be defined.

Definably, dē-fin'a-bli, adv. In a definable manner.

Define, dē-fin', vt. To bound off; to limit; to determine with precision; to ascertain; to express precisely; to ascertain and explain clearly and exactly, as the signification of a word. ppr. defining, pret. & pp. defined. [Fr. définir—L. finis, end, limit.]

Definement, dē-fin'ment, n. The act of defining.

Definer, dē-fin'ėr, n. He who defines.

Definite, de'fin-it, a. Limited; determinate; precise; exact; fixed and settled with precision; serving to define. [L. definitus.]

Definitely, de'fin-it-li, adv. Precisely.

Definition, de-fi-ni'shon, n. A bounding off; a limiting; the description of the essence of a thing by its kind and difference; an explanation in words, which distinguishes the thing explained from other things. [Fr. définition.]

Definitive, dē-fin'it-iv, a. Limiting the extent; positive; express; determining; final.—n. That which defines; a word used to define the extent of the signification of a common noun. [Fr. définitif.]

Definitively, dē-fin'it-iv-li, adv. In a definitive manner.

Deflagrate, de'fla-grāt, vi. To burn down with a sudden and sparkling combustion, as nitre. [L. deflagro—flagro, to burn.]

Deflagration, de-fla-grā'shon, n. A sudden and sparkling combustion. [Fr. deflagration.]

Deflagrator, de'fla-grāt-ėr, n. A galvanic instrument for producing rapid and powerful combustion.

Deflect, dē-flekt', vi. To turn down; to deviate from a true course or right line; to swerve.—vt. To turn down or aside; to turn or bend from a right line. [L. deflecto—flecto, to bend.]

Deflection, dē-flek'shon, n. A bending downward or turning aside; deviation; inflection.

Defloration, dē-flōr-ā'shon, n. Act of deflouring; rape. [Fr. défloration—L. flos, floris, a flower.]

Deflour, dē-flour', vt. To deprive of the bloom, the prime grace, or beauty; to ravish. [L. defloro—flos, a flower.]

Defloured, dē-flourd', p.a. Ravished; robbed of prime beauty.

Defluxion, dē-fluk'shon, n. A flowing down; a flowing of humours or fluid matter from a superior to an inferior part of the body; a discharge of fluid matter from a mucous membrane. [L. defluxio—fluo, fluxus, to flow.]

Deforce, dē-fōrs', vt. To keep out of possession, as the right owner, by deforcement. ppr. deforcing, pret. & pp. deforced. [Old Fr. deforcer.]

Deforcement, dē-fōrs'ment, n. The holding by force of lands or tenements to which another person has a right.

Deform, dē-form', vt. To mar or alter in form; to disfigure; to render disgusting; to disgrace morally; to dishonour; to make ungraceful. [L. deformo—forma, form.]

Deformation, dē-form-ā'shon, n. A deforming; a disfiguring or defacing.

Deformed, dē-formd', p.a. Disfigured; misshapen; base; disgraceful.

Deformity, dē-form'i-ti, n. Want of proper form; irregularity of shape or features; distortion; disfigurement; gross deviation from order or the established laws of propriety. [Fr. difformité.]

Defraud, dē-frad', vt. To take away from by fraud; to deprive of or withhold from wrongfully; to beguile; to deceive. [Old Fr. defrauder—L. fraus, fraudis, fraud.]

Defrauder, dē-frad'ėr, n. One who defrauds.

Defray, dē-frā', vt. To discharge or pay, as the expenses of anything; to provide for, as a charge. [Fr. défrayer—frais, expenses.]

Defrayment, dē-frā'ment, n. Act of defraying; payment.

Deft, deft, a. Apt; fit; convenient. [Sax. dæfe, fit.]

Deftly, deft'li, adv. Aptly; fitly; neatly.

Defunct, dē-fungkt', a. Having finished the course of life; dead; deceased.—n. A dead person; one deceased. [L. defunctus—fungor, to discharge.]

Defunction, dē-fungk'shon, n. State of being defunct; death.

Defy, dē-fi', vt. To distrust; to challenge; to provoke to combat; to brave with contempt of opposition; to treat with contempt; to despise. ppr. defying, pret. & pp. defied. [Fr. défier—L. fido, to trust.]

Degeneracy, dē-jen'e-ra-si, n. A growing worse or inferior; a decline in good qualities; a departure from the virtue of ancestors; meanness.

Degenerate, dē-jen'e-rāt, vi. To become worse than one's kind; to decay in good qualities; to suffer a diminution of valuable qualities, either naturally or morally. ppr. degenerating, pret. & pp. degenerated.—a. Having lost the good qualities of the race; fallen from the virtue or excellence of ancestors or of kind; mean; corrupt. [L. degenero, degeneratus—genus, generis, race, birth.]

Degenerately, dē-jen'e-rāt-li, adv. In a degenerate manner.

ch, chain; j, job; g, go; ng, sing; ᴠʜ, then; th, thin; w, wig; wh, whig; zh, azure; † obsolete.

Degenerateness, dĕ-jen′ĕ-rāt-nes, n. State of being degenerate; degeneracy.
Degenerative, dĕ-jen′ĕ-rāt-iv, a. Tending to degenerate.
Deglutition, dĕ-glū-ti′shon, n. Act of swallowing down food; the power of swallowing. [L.—glutio, to swallow.]
Degradation, de-gra-dā′shon, n. Act of degrading; state of being degraded; debasement; disgrace; dishonour; diminution; a gradual wasting away. [Fr. dégradation.]
Degrade, dē-grād′, vt. To reduce from a higher to a lower rank; to strip of honours; to reduce in estimation; to lessen the value of; to lower; to debase; to depose; to dishonour. ppr. degrading, pret. & pp. degraded. [Fr. dégrader—L. gradus, a step, degree.]
Degraded, dē-grād′ed, p.a. Lowered in rank, dignity, or intellect.
Degrading, dē-grād′ing, p.a. Dishonouring; disgracing the character.
Degree, dē-grē′, n. A step; a portion of space of indefinite extent; step in relationship, rank, order, class, quality, dignity; step in elevation or descent; measure; extent; the 360th part of the circumference of a circle; 60 geographical miles; a mark of distinction conferred by universities on students and men eminent for learning; (pl.) comparative steps in the signification of adjectives; divisions marked on a scale, quadrant, &c. [Fr. degré—L. gradus, a step.]
Deification, dē′if-ik-ā″shon, n. The act of exalting to the rank of or enrolling among the heathen deities. [L. deus, a god, and facio, to make.]
Deiform, dē′i-form, a. Of a god-like form; like a god. [L. deus, and forma, form.]
Deify, dē′i-fī, vt. To make into a god; to exalt to the rank of a heathen deity; to extol and adore as an object of supreme regard. ppr. deifying, pret. & pp. deified. [L. deus, and facio, to make.]
Deign, dān, vi. To deem worthy; to vouchsafe; to condescend.—vt. To think worthy of notice or regard; to grant or allow; to condescend to give to [Fr. daigner—L. dignus, worthy.]
Deism, dē′ism, n. The doctrine or creed of a deist. [Fr. déisme.]
Deist, dē′ist, n. One who believes in the existence of a God; one who acknowledges the existence of a God, but denies revealed religion; a freethinker. [Fr. déiste, from L. deus, a god.]
Deistic, Deistical, dē-ist′ik, dē-ist′ik-al, a. Pertaining to deism or to deists.
Deity, dē′i-ti, n. The source of light, both natural and spiritual; the Supreme Being; a fabulous god or goddess; a superior being. [Fr. déité—L. deus, a god—Sans. div, to shine.]
Deject, de-jekt′, vt. To throw down; to dispirit; to cast down the spirits of; to dishearten; to sink; to debase; to humble. [L. deficio, dejectus—jacio, to throw.]
Dejected, dē-jekt′ed, p.a. Cast down; depressed; grieved; discouraged.
Dejectedly, dē-jekt′ed-li, adv. In a dejected manner.
Dejection, dē-jek′shon, n. A casting down; depression of mind; melancholy; lowness of spirits occasioned by grief or misfortune.
Delay, dē-lā′, vt. To defer; to put off; to retard; to stop; to protract.—vi. To stop; to linger; to move slow, or to stop for a time; to procrastinate—n. A deferring or putting off; a lingering; stay; procrastination; hindrance. [Fr. délai—L. fero, latum, to carry.]

Dele, dē′le, vt. Blot out; erase. [L. imperative of deleo, to blot out.]
Deleble, dē′lē-bl, a. That may be blotted out. [L. delebilis.]
Delectable, dē-lekt′a-bl, a. Delightful; highly pleasing; that gives great joy or pleasure. [L. delectabilis.]
Delectably, dē-lekt′a-bli, adv. Delightfully.
Delectation, dē-lek-tā′shon, n. Great pleasure; delight. [Fr. délectation.]
Delegate, de′lē-gāt, vt. To send with power to transact business, as a representative; to commit; to deliver to another's care and exercise. ppr. delegating, pret. & pp. delegated.—n. One sent to act for another; a representative; a deputy; a substitute. [L. delēgo, delegatus—lego, to send as an ambassador.]
Delegated, de′lē-gāt-ed, p.a. Committed to another's power, as authority.
Delegation, de-lē-gā′shon, n. Act of delegating; persons delegated.
Delete, dē-let′, vt. To blot out; to erase. ppr. deleting, pret. & pp. deleted. [L. deleo, deletum—lino, to rub over.]
Deleterious, de-lē-tē′ri-us, a. Hurtful; noxious; poisonous; pernicious. [Gr. dēlētērios.]
Deletion, dē-lē′shon, n. Act of deleting; destruction.
Deliberate, dē-lib′ē-rāt, vi. To weigh well in one's mind; to consider; to consider which is best or preferable; to hesitate; to pause.—vt. To balance well in the mind; to weigh; to consider. ppr. deliberating, pret. & pp. deliberated.—a. As applied to persons, weighing carefully facts and arguments; slow in determining; discreet; as applied to things, formed with deliberation; well advised; slow. [L. delibero, deliberatus—libro, to weigh.]
Deliberately, dē-lib′ē-rāt-li, adv. In a deliberate manner; slowly; cautiously.
Deliberateness, dē-lib′ē-rāt-nes, n. Calm consideration; due attention to the arguments for and against a measure; caution.
Deliberation, dē-lib′ē-rā″shon, n. Thoughtful consideration in order to a choice; circumspection; prudence; mutual discussion and examination of the reasons for and against a measure; mature reflection. [Fr. délibération.]
Deliberative, dē-lib′ē-rāt-iv, a. Proceeding or acting by deliberation; having a right to deliberate; apt or disposed to consider. [Fr. délibératif.]
Deliberatively, dē-lib′ē-rāt-iv-li, adv. By or with deliberation.
Delicacy, de′li-ka-si, n. That which captivates; that which delights the senses, particularly the taste; daintiness; fineness of texture; tenderness; feminine beauty; minute accuracy; elegance; politeness; gentle treatment; a nice perception of beauty and deformity; weakness of constitution; slenderness; nice susceptibility of impression. [Fr. délicatesse—Obs. L. lacio, to entice.]
Delicate, de′li-kāt, a. Attracting; pleasing to the taste or senses; choice; fine; soft; clear or fair; nice in forms; nice; critical; easily hurt; minute; nicely interwoven; soft and smooth to the touch; tender; not able to endure hardship; not robust. [Fr. délicat—L. delicatus.]
Delicately, de′li-kāt-li, adv. In a delicate manner; finely.
Delicateness, de′li-kāt-nes, n. State of quality of being delicate; delicacy.
Delicious, dē-li′shi-us, a. Highly pleasing to the taste; most sweet or grateful to the senses; affording exquisite pleasure; charming; delightful. [Fr. délicieux.]
Deliciously, dē-li′shi-us-li, adv. In a delicious manner.
Deliciousness, dē-li′shi-us-nes, n. Quality of being delicious; delight.
Delight, dē-līt′, n. That which entices; that which yields great pleasure; a high degree of pleasure; rapture; charm; joy.—vt. To entice; to affect with great pleasure; to give or afford high satisfaction or joy to.—vi. To take great pleasure; to be greatly pleased or rejoiced. (With in.) [Fr. délecter—L. delecto—lacio, to entice.]
Delighted, dē-līt′ed, p.a. Filled with delight.
Delightful, dē-līt′ful, a. Affording great pleasure and satisfaction; charming; gratifying; beautiful.
Delightfully, dē-līt′ful-li, adv. In a delightful manner.
Delightfulness, dē-līt′ful-nes, n. Quality of being delightful.
Delineate, dē-lin′ē-āt, vt. To draw the lines which exhibit the form of; to make a draught of; to paint; to portray; to design; to sketch; to describe; to exhibit a likeness of in words. ppr. delineating, pret. & pp. delineated. [L. delineo, delineatus—linea, a line.]
Delineation, dē-lin′ē-ā″shon, n. Act of delineating; outline; sketch; representation in words; description. [Fr. délinéation—L. delineatio.]
Delineator, dē-lin′ē-āt-ėr, n. One who delineates.
Delinquency, dē-lin′kwen-si, n. A leaving or omission of duty; a fault; an offence; a crime. [Low L. delinquentia—L. linquo, to leave.]
Delinquent, dē-lin′kwent, a. Leaving or neglecting duty.—n. One who fails to perform his duty; a public officer who neglects his duty; one who commits a fault or crime. [L. delinquens.]
Deliquesce, de-li-kwes′, vi. To melt down gradually and become liquid by attracting and absorbing moisture from the air. ppr. deliquescing, pret. & pp. deliquesced. [L. deliquesco—liqueo, to be fluid.]
Deliquescence, de-li-kwes′ens, n. Act or process of deliquescing.
Deliquescent, dē-li-kwes′ent, a. That deliquesces; liquefying in the air.
Delirious, dē-li′ri-us, a. Going out of the furrow in ploughing; roving in mind; disordered in intellect; light-headed; raving; frenzied; insane. [L. deliruslira, a furrow.]
Deliriously, dē-li′ri-us-li, adv. In a delirious manner.
Delirium, dē-li′ri-um, n. State of being delirious; a wandering of the mind connected with fever; disorder of the intellect. [L.]
Delitescence, dē-li-tes′ens, n. A hiding closely; retirement; obscurity. [Low L. delitescentia—L. lateo, to lurk.]
Deliver, dē-liv′ėr, vt. To free from, as danger or bondage; to disburden, as a woman of a child; to liberate; to save; to extricate; to surrender; to commit; to yield up; to transfer; to pronounce; to give forth in words or in action. [Fr. délivrer—L. libero, to free.]
Deliverance, dē-liv′ėr-ans, n. Release, as from captivity; state of being delivered; redemption; escape. [Fr. délivrance.]
Deliverer, dē-liv′ėr-ėr, n. One who delivers.
Delivery, dē-liv′ėr-i, n. Act of delivering; childbirth; rescue; surrender; a

Fāte, fär, fat, fall; mē, met, hėr; pīne, pin; nōte, not, mōve; tūbe, tub, bųll; oil, pound.

giving up; a passing from one to another; style of utterance; pronunciation, or manner of speaking.
Dell, del, n. *A dale;* a hollow place; a small, narrow valley between two hills. [from *dale.*]
Delta, del'ta, n. The Greek letter Δ; the space between two mouths of a river, as the Delta of the Nile.
Delude, dē-lūd', vt. *To play upon;* to impose on; to deceive; to lead astray; to cheat; to circumvent. ppr. deluding, pret. & pp. deluded. [L. *deludo—ludo,* to play.]
Deluded, dē-lūd'ed, p.a. Deceived; misled; led into error.
Deluder, dē-lūd'ėr, n. *One who deludes.*
Deluding, dē-lūd'ing, p.a. Deceiving; leading astray.
Deluge, del'ūj, n. A general *inundation;* any overflowing of water; a flood; a swell of water over the natural banks of a river or shore or of the ocean; the great flood in the days of Noah; a sweeping or overwhelming calamity. vt. To cover with *water;* to inundate; to drown; to overwhelm with any flowing spreading body; to cause to sink under the weight of a general calamity. ppr. deluging, pret. & pp. deluged. [Fr. *déluge*—L. *luo,* to wash.]
Delusion, dē-lū'zhon, n. *Act of deluding;* state of being deluded; a false belief; illusion; fallacy; error. [L. *delusio—ludo,* to play.]
Delusive, dē-lū'siv, a. *Apt to delude* or deceive; tending to mislead the mind.
Delusively, dē-lū'siv-li, adv. In a delusive manner.
Delusiveness, dē-lū'siv-nes, n. Quality of being *delusive;* tendency to deceive.
Delusory, dē-lū'sō-ri, a. *Delusive.*
Delve, delv, vt. To dig; to open with a spade, as the ground; to fathom; to trace out.—vi. To labour with the spade. ppr. delving, pret. & pp. delved. [Sax. *delfan.*]
Delver, delv'ėr, n. *One who delves.*
Demagnetise, dē-mag'net-īz, vt. *To deprive of magnetic polarity.* ppr. demagnetising, pret. & pp. demagnetized.
Demagogue, dem'a-gog, n. *A leader of the people;* a popular and factious orator; a seditious leader. [Gr. *dēmagōgos—dēmos,* the people, and *agō,* to lead.]
Demain†, **Demesne**, dē-mān', dē-mēn', n. *A manor house,* and the land adjacent or near, which a *lord* keeps in his own hands. [Old Fr. *demaine*—L. *dominus,* a lord—*domus,* a house.]
Demand, dē-mand', vt. To seek *at the hands of,* as due by right; to require; to call for; to exact; to interrogate (with *of*).—n. An asking for by virtue of a right, real or supposed; an asking with authority; the asking of a price for goods offered for sale; that which is or may be claimed as due; debt; the calling for in order to purchase; desire to purchase or possess; manifested want. [Fr. *demander*—L. *manus,* the hand, and *do,* to give.]
Demandable, dē-mand'a-bl, a. *That may be demanded.*
Demandant, dē-mand'ant, n. *One who demands;* the plaintiff in a real action.
Demarkation, dē-märk-ā'shon, n. *Act of marking off,* or of ascertaining and setting a limit; a limit fixed; line of separation marked or determined. [Fr. *démarcation.*]
Demean, dē-mēn', vt. *To lead by the hand;* to conduct; to behave; to behave meanly; to debase; to lessen.

(With the recipr. pron.) [Fr. *démener*—L. *manus,* the hand.]
Demeanour, dē-mēn'ėr, n. Manner of conducting or behaving one's self; behaviour; carriage; deportment.
Demented, dē-ment'ed, a. *Deprived of the mind* or senses; insane. [from L. *mens, mentis,* the mind.]
Demerit, dē-me'rit, n. *Absence of merit;* that which deserves punishment or blame; vice or crime. [Fr. *démérite*—L. *mereo, meritum,* to deserve.]
Demi-god, de'mi-god, n. *Half a god;* one partaking of the divine nature.
Demisable, dē-mīz'a-bl, a. *That may be demised* or leased.
Demise, dē-mīz', n. *A sending or bringing down;* a laying down, as of the crown or royal authority; the death of the reigning monarch, or of any distinguished individual; a conveyance of an estate by lease or will.—vt. *To send down* to a successor; to transfer or convey; to lease; to bequeath; to grant by will. ppr. demising, pret. & pp. demised. [L. *demissio—mitto, missum,* to send.]
Demission, dē-mi'shon, n. *A lowering;* depression; transfer; resignation. [L. *demissio.*]
Demit, dē-mit', vt. *To let fall;* to lay down formally, as an office. ppr. demitting, pret. & pp. demitted. [L. *mitto,* to send.]
Demi-tint, de'mi-tint, n. A gradation of colour between positive light and positive shade.
Democracy, dē-mok'ra-si, n. A form of *government* in which the supreme power is lodged in the hands of the *people* collectively. [Gr. *dēmokratia—dēmos,* the people, and *kratos,* strength, power, rule.]
Democrat, dem'ō-krat, n. *One who adheres to democracy.* [Fr. *démocrate.*]
Democratic, Democratical, dem-ō-krat'ik, dem-ō-krat'ik-al, a. *Pertaining to democracy.* [Fr. *démocratique.*]
Democratically, dem-ō-krat'ik-al-li, adv. In a *democratical manner.*
Demolish, dē-mol'ish, vt. *To pull down,* as a *heap* or structure; to separate, as any collected mass, or as the connected parts of a thing; to destroy. [Fr. *démolir,* (pp.) *démolis*—L. *molior,* to cast, to throw.]
Demolition, dē-mō-li'shon, n. *Act of pulling down,* or destroying a pile or structure; ruin; destruction. [Fr. *démolition.*]
Demon, de'mon, n. *A spirit,* holding a middle place between men and the celestial deities of the pagans; an evil spirit or genius; a devil; a fiend-like man. [L. *dæmon*—Gr. *daimōn,* a god.]
Demoniac, Demoniacal, dē-mō'ni-ak, dē-mō-nī'ak-al, a. Influenced or produced by *demons* or evil spirits.
Demoniac, dē-mō'ni-ak, n. *A human being possessed by a demon.*
Demoniacally, dē-mō-nī'ak-al-li, adv. *In a demoniacal manner.*
Demonological, dē'mon-o-loj''ik-al, a. *Pertaining to demonology.*
Demonology, dē-mon-ol'o-ji, n. A *treatise* on *demons* or evil spirits. [Gr. *daimōn,* and *logos,* discourse.]
Demonstrable, dē-mon'stra-bl, a. That may be *proved* beyond doubt; capable of being shown by certain evidence.
Demonstrably, dē-mon'stra-bli, adv. In a manner to preclude doubt.
Demonstrate, dē-mon'strāt, vt. *To show* or prove to be certain; to prove beyond the possibility of doubt; to evince; to manifest; to exhibit. ppr. demon-

strating, pret. & pp. demonstrated. [L. *demonstro, demonstratus—monstro,* to point out—*moneo,* to teach.]
Demonstration, de-mon-strā'shon, n. *A pointing out;* act or process of *demonstrating;* the highest degree of evidence; evidence which satisfies the mind of the certainty of a fact or proposition; show; exhibition; a military manœuvre. [L. *demonstratio.*]
Demonstrative, dē-mon'strāt-iv, a. Proving by certain evidence; invincibly conclusive. [L. *demonstrativus.*]
Demonstratively, dē-mon'strāt-iv-li, adv. In a *demonstrative manner.*
Demonstrativeness, dē-mon'strāt-iv-nes, n. *Quality of being demonstrative.*
Demonstrator, de'mon-strāt-ėr, n. *One who demonstrates.*
Demoralisation, dē-mo'ral-iz-ā''shon, n. *Act of demoralising.*
Demoralise, dē-mo'ral-īz, vt. To *corrupt* the *manners* or *morals* of; to destroy or lessen the effect of moral principles on; to deprave; to vitiate. ppr. demoralising, pret. & pp. demoralised. [Fr. *démoraliser*—L. *mos, moris,* manner, custom, way.]
Demoralising, dē-mo'ral-īz-ing, p.a. Tending to destroy *morals* or moral principles.
Demulcent, dē-mul'sent, a. *Softening;* mollifying; lenient. [L. *demulceno—mulceo,* to soften.]
Demur, dē-mėr', vi. To doubt; to pause; to hesitate; to object (with *to*). ppr. demurring, pret. & pp. demurred.—n. Stop; pause; hesitation as to the propriety of proceeding; suspense of decision. [Fr. *demeurer*—L. *mora,* a delay.]
Demure, dē-mūr', a. *Of good manners;* staid; sober; grave; affectedly modest. vi. To look demurely. [Fr. *des mœurs,* having manners.]
Demurely, dē-mūr'li, adv. *In a demure manner;* gravely; solemnly.
Demureness, dē-mūr'nes, n. Gravity of countenance; affected modesty.
Demurrer, dē-mėr'ėr, n. *One who demurs;* a stop at some point in law pleadings; an issue on matter of law.
Demy, dē-mī', n. A particular size of paper; a kind of paper of small size, a degree smaller than medium, and two degrees smaller than royal. [Fr. *demi,* half—L. *medius,* middle.]
Den, den, n. *A narrow vale;* a cave in the earth; a pit, or subterranean recess, used for concealment or security; a haunt; a retreat. [Sax. *dens.*]
Denary, de'na-ri, a. *Containing ten.—n. The number ten.* [L. *denarius,* from *deni,* ten each.]
Denationalise, dē-na'shon-al-īz, vt. *To divest of national character* or *rights,* by transference to the service of another nation. ppr. denationalising, pret. & pp. denationalized.
Denaturalize, dē-na'tūr-al-īz, vt. To render *unnatural;* to alienate from nature. ppr. denaturalizing, pret. & pp. denaturalized.
Denay†, dē-nā', n. *Denial.*
Deniable, dē-nī'a-bl, a. *That may be denied* or contradicted.
Denial, dē-nī'al, n. *Act of denying;* negation; contradiction; an assertion that a declaration is not true; refusal to grant; a refusing to acknowledge; a disowning.
Denier, dē-nī'ėr, n. *One who denies.*
Denier, de'ni-ėr, n. *A small French coin;* a small copper coin.
Denizen, de'ni-zn, n. *A citizen;* an inhabitant; an alien who is made a sub-

ch, *chain;* j, *job;* g, *go;* ng, *sing;* ᴡʜ, *then;* th, *thin;* w, *wig;* wh, *whig;* zh, *azure;* † obsolete.

ject by the king's letters-patent; a stranger admitted to residence in a foreign country.—*vt.* To make a denizen of; to provide with denizens. [Norm. *deinsseins,* denizens—*deins,* within, and *né,* born.]

Denizenship, dē'ni-zn-ship, *n.* State of being a denizen.

Denominate, dē-nom'in-āt, *vt.* To give a name to; to name; to call; to style; to designate. *ppr.* denominating, *pret. & pp.* denominated. [L. *denomino, denominatus—nomen,* a name.]

Denomination, dē-nom-in-ā'shon, *n.* A naming; a society of individuals called by the same name; a class; a sect.

Denominational, dē-nom-in-ā'shon-al, *a.* Pertaining to a denomination.

Denominative, dē-nom'in-āt-iv, *a.* That confers a distinct appellation; derived from a substantive or adjective, as a verb.

Denominator, dē-nom'in-āt-er, *n.* He who or that which gives a name; that number placed below the line in vulgar fractions which shows into how many equal parts the unit is divided.

Denotable, dē-nōt'a-bl, *a.* That may be denoted or marked.

Denote, dē-nōt', *vt.* To mark or point out; to indicate or imply. *ppr.* denoting, *pret. & pp.* denoted. [L. *denoto—nota,* a mark.]

Denotement†, dē-nōt'ment, *n.* Sign; indication.

Denouement, dē-nö'mäng, *n.* The unravelling of the plot of a play or novel; the development of any series of events. [Fr.—L. *nodus,* a knot.]

Denounce, dē-nouns', *vt.* To declare, as a threat; to threaten by some outward sign; to stigmatize; to censure. *ppr.* denouncing, *pret. & pp.* denounced. [Fr. *dénoncer*—L. *nuncio,* to declare.]

Denouncement, dē-nouns'ment, *n.* Act of denouncing; denunciation.

Denouncer, dē-nouns'er, *n.* One who denounces or declares a menace.

Dense, dens, *a.* Thick; close; compact; having its constituent parts closely united. [Fr.—L. *densus,* thick.]

Densely, dens'li, *adv.* In a dense manner; with great compactness.

Density, dens'i-ti, *n.* Thickness; closeness of constituent parts; compactness. [Fr. *densité.*]

Dent, dent, *n.* A tooth†; a notch made by the pressure of a harder body on a softer; an indentation.—*vt.* To make a dent or small hollow upon. [Fr.; L. *dens, dentis.*]

Dental, den'tal, *a.* Pertaining to the teeth; formed or pronounced by the teeth, with the aid of the tongue.—*n.* An articulation formed by placing the end of the tongue against the upper teeth. [Fr. *dentale.*]

Dentated, den'tāt-ed, *a.* Toothed; notched. [L. *dentatus.*]

Dented, dent'ed, *a.* Indented; impressed with little hollows.

Denticle, den'ti-kl, *n.* A small tooth or projecting point. [L. *denticulus.*]

Dentiform, den'ti-form, *a.* Having the form of a tooth, or of teeth. [L. *dens* and *forma.*]

Dentifrice, den'ti-fris, *n.* A powder or other substance to be used in rubbing or cleaning the teeth. [Fr.—L. *dens,* and *frico,* to rub.]

Dentist, den'tist, *n.* A tooth surgeon; one whose occupation is to clean and extract teeth, or repair or replace them when decayed.

Dentition, den-ti'shon, *n.* The breeding or cutting of teeth in infancy; the system of teeth peculiar to an animal. [L. *dentitio.*]

Denudation, dē-nūd-ā'shon, *n.* Act of stripping off covering; a making bare.

Denude, dē-nūd', *vt.* To make bare or naked; to divest; to lay bare; to uncover. *ppr.* denuding, *pret. & pp.* denuded. [L. *denudo—nudo,* to make bare.]

Denunciation, dē-nun-si-ā''shon, *n.* Solemn or formal declaration, accompanied with a menace; a public menace; arraignment. [L. *denunciatio.*]

Denunciator, dē-nun'si-āt-er, *n.* He who denounces. [L.]

Denunciatory, dē-nun'si-a-tō-ri, *a.* Characterised by denunciation.

Deny, dē-nī', *vt.* To say no to, or in regard to; to declare not to be true; to contradict; to disavow; to renounce; to refuse to grant; to withhold; to disown; to refuse to acknowledge; not to confess; not to afford or yield. *ppr.* denying, *pret. & pp.* denied. [Fr. *denier*—L. *nego,* to deny—*ne,* not, and *aio,* to say.]

Deodorize, dē-ō'dėr-īz, *vt.* To deprive of odour. *ppr.* deodorizing, *pret. & pp.* deodorized. [L. *odor,* smell.]

Deodorizing, dē-ō'dėr-īz-ing, *p.a.* Depriving of odour or smell.

Deoxidation, dē-ok'sid-ā''shon, *n.* The act or process of reducing from the state of an oxide.

Deoxidize, dē-ok'sid-īz, *vt.* To deprive of oxygen. *ppr.* deoxidizing, *pret. & pp.* deoxidized.

Depart, dē-pärt', *vi.* To go forth or away; to disappear; to desist; to abandon; to apostatize; to vary; to leave the world; to die; to deviate. (With *from.*)—*n.* The act of departing. [Fr. *départir—partir,* to set out.]

Departed, dē-pärt'ed, *p.a.* Gone; vanished; dead.

Departing, dē-pärt'ing, *p.a.* Going; dying.

Department, dē-pärt'ment, *n.* A separate part; a division of territory; a separate allotment or part of business; a distinct province, in which a class of duties are allotted to a particular person; a separate station. [Fr. *département.*]

Departmental, dē-pärt'ment-al, *a.* Pertaining to a department.

Departure, dē-pärt'ūr, *n.* Act of going away; a moving from or leaving a place; withdrawal; abandonment; death.

Depasture, dē-pas'tūr, *vt.* To eat up; to consume.—*vi.* To feed; to graze. *ppr.* depasturing, *pret. & pp.* depastured. [L. *pasco, pastum,* to feed.]

Depend, dē-pend', *vi.* To hang from or on something; to be sustained by being attached to something above; to be closely connected with anything; to rest or rely solely; to have a support; to be subservient; to adhere; to hold; to be retained; to trust; to confide; to be in suspense; to be undetermined. (With *on* or *upon.*) [L. *dependeo—pendeo,* to hang.]

Dependant, dē-pend'ant, *n.* One who depends on another; one who is sustained by, or who relies on, another; a retainer. [L. *dependens.*]

Dependence, Dependency, dē-pend'ens, dē-pend'en-si, *n.* A state of hanging down from a supporter; anything hanging down; a series of things hanging to another; state of deriving support from; confidence; state of being related to a cause or antecedent; connection; state of being subject to; that which is subordinate; a subject province remote from the kingdom to which it belongs. [Fr. *dépendance.*]

Dependent, dē-pend'ent, *a.* Hanging down; subject to the power of; relying solely on for support or favour. (Often with *on* or *upon.*)—*n.* One who depends on another; one who is at the disposal of another. [L. *dependens.*]

Dependantly, dē-pend'ent-li, *adv.* In a dependent manner.

Depending, dē-pend'ing, *p.a.* Pending; undecided.

Depict, dē-pikt', *vt.* To paint; to portray; to form a likeness of in colours; to represent in words; to delineate; to describe; to represent. [L. *depingo, depictum—pingo,* to paint.]

Depilatory, dē-pil'a-tō-ri, *a.* Any application which is used to take off the hair of an animal body, such as lime, &c. [L. *depilo,* to pluck out the hair—*pilus,* a hair.]

Depletion, dē-plē'shon, *n.* Act of emptying out or drawing off; act of diminishing the quantity of blood in the vessels by venesection; blood-letting. [Low L. *depletio*—L. *pleo,* to fill.]

Depletory, dē-plē'tō-ri, *a.* Calculated to obviate fulness of habit.

Deplorable, dē-plōr'a-bl, *a.* Worthy of being deplored; that demands lamentation; lamentable; sad; dismal; grievous; miserable; pitiable.

Deplorableness, dē-plōr'a-bl-nes, *n.* State of being deplorable; misery.

Deplorably, dē-plōr'a-bli, *adv.* In a manner to be deplored.

Deplore, dē-plōr', *vt.* To weep bitterly for; to feel or express deep and poignant grief for; to bewail. *ppr.* deploring, *pret. & pp.* deplored. [L. *deploro—ploro,* to cry out.]

Deploy, dē-ploi', *vt.* To unfold; to display; to extend, as a body of troops. *vi.* To open; to extend; to form a more extended front or line.—*n.* The expansion of a body of troops, previously compacted into a column, so as to present a large front. [Fr. *déployer*—L. *plico,* to fold.]

Deployment, dē-ploi'ment. Same as DEPLOY.

Depolarization, dē-pō'lär-īz-ā''shon, *n.* Act of depriving of polarity, as the rays of light.

Depolarize, dē-pō'lär-īz, *vt.* To deprive of polarity. *ppr.* depolarizing, *pret. & pp.* depolarized.

Deponent, dē-pōn'ent, *a.* Laying down; that has a passive form, but which lays aside its proper passive, and assumes an active signification.—*n.* One who gives a deposition under oath; one who gives written testimony to be used as evidence in a court of justice; a deponent verb. [L. *deponens—pono,* to place or lay.]

Depopulate, dē-pop'ū-lāt, *vt.* To unpeople; to deprive of inhabitants.—*vi.* To become dispeopled. *ppr.* depopulating, *pret. & pp.* depopulated. [L. *depopulor, depopulatus—populus,* the people.]

Depopulation, dē-pop-ū-lā'shon, *n.* Act of depriving of people; havoc; destruction or expulsion of inhabitants; waste of people.

Depopulator, dē-pop'ū-lāt-er, *n.* One who depopulates. [L.]

Deport, dē-pōrt', *vt.* To carry off or away†; to transport†; to demean; to behave; to conduct (with the recipr. pron). [Fr. *déporter*—L. *porto,* to carry.]

Deportation, dē-pōrt-ā'shon, *n.* A carrying away; a removal from one

country to another; exile; banishment. [L. *deportatio*.]
Deportment, dē-pōrt'ment, *n*. Carriage; demeanour; manner of acting in relation to the duties of life. [Fr. *déportement*.]
Deposable, dē-pōz'a-bl, *a*. That may be deposed or deprived of office.
Deposal, dē-pōz'al, *n*. Act of deposing or divesting of office.
Depose, dē-pōz', *vt*. To put down; to degrade from a throne or other high station; to divest of office.—*vi*. To bear witness; to give testimony in writing, according to due form of law. *ppr*. deposing, *pret. & pp*. deposed. [Fr. *déposer*—L. *pono*, to place.]
Deposit, dē-poz'it, *vt*. To lay down; to lay aside; to drop; to throw down; to lay up; to lay in a place for preservation; to lodge in the hands of a person for safe-keeping; to intrust to; to commit to one as a pledge.—*n*. Any matter laid down or lodged; anything intrusted to the care of another; a sum of money left with a bank; a pawn; a thing given as security; a place where things are deposited. [L. *depono, depositus—pono*, to place.]
Depositary, dē-poz'it-a-ri, *n*. One to whom a thing is committed for safe-keeping, or to be used for the benefit of the owner; a trustee; a guardian. [Fr. *dépositaire*.]
Deposited, dē-poz'it-ed, *p.a*. Put away; laid up or aside.
Deposition, dē-pō-zi'shon, *n*. Act of laying down; that which is thrown down, laid, or lodged; act of giving written testimony under oath; act of dethroning a king; the degrading of a person from an office. [L. *depositio*.]
Depositor, dē-poz'it-ėr, *n*. One who makes a deposit.
Depository, dē-poz'it-ri, *n*. A place where anything is deposited or lodged for safe-keeping. [Low L. *depositorium*.]
Depot, dē-pō', *n*. A deposit; a place of deposit; a place where stores and provisions are kept, and where recruits are trained; a railway station. [Fr. *dépôt*—L. *depositum*.]
Depravation, dē-pra-vā'shon, *n*. Act of depraving; state of being made bad or worse; degeneracy; contamination. [L. *depravatio*.]
Deprave, dē-prāv', *vt*. To distort; to make bad or worse; to impair the good qualities of; to corrupt; to vitiate; to pollute. *ppr*. depraving, *pret. & pp*. depraved. [L. *depravo—pravus*, crooked.]
Depraved, dē-prāvd', *p.a*. Destitute of holiness or good principles; vicious; profligate.
Depravity, dē-prav'i-ti, *n*. State of being depraved; a corruption of moral principles; destitution of holiness; corruption; wickedness; contamination. [L. *pravitas*, crookedness.]
Deprecate, dep'rē-kāt, *vt*. To beg off; to pray against; to pray deliverance from; to seek to avert by prayer. *ppr*. deprecating, *pret. & pp*. deprecated. [L. *deprecor, deprecatus—precor*, to pray.]
Deprecatingly, dep'rē-kāt-ing-li, *adv*. By deprecation.
Deprecation, dep-rē-kā'shon, *n*. Act of deprecating; a praying that an evil may be prevented; entreaty. [L. *deprecatio*.]
Deprecatory, dep'rē-kā-tō-ri, *a*. That serves to deprecate; tending to remove or avert evil by prayer; having the form of prayer. [Low L. *deprecatorius*.]
Depreciate, dē-prē'shi-āt, *vt*. To cry down the price or value of; to undervalue; to disparage; to detract from; to traduce.—*vi*. To fall in value; to become of less worth. *ppr*. depreciating, *pret. & pp*. depreciated. [Low L. *deprecio, depreciatus*—L. *pretium*, price.]
Depreciated, dē-prē'shi-āt-ed, *p.a*. Lessened in value or price; undervalued.
Depreciation, dē-prē'shi-ā"shon, *n*. Act of depreciating, or of lessening or crying down price or value; the falling of value; reduction of worth.
Depreciatory, dē-prē'shi-a-tō-ri, *a*. Tending to depreciate.
Depredation, de-prē-dā'shon, *n*. Act of plundering; waste; a taking away by any act of violence. [Low L. *depradatio*—L. *prada*, plunder.]
Depredator, de'prē-dāt-ėr, *n*. One who plunders or pillages; a spoiler; a waster. [Low L. *depradator*.]
Depress, dē-pres', *vt*. To press down; to let fall; to bring down; to sink; to lower; to abase; to cast down; to humble; to deject; to dispirit. [L. *deprimo, depressus—premo*, to press.]
Depressed, dē-prest', *p.a*. Dejected; dispirited; humbled; sunk; rendered languid.
Depressing, dē-pres'ing, *p.a*. Abasing; impoverishing; rendering languid.
Depressingly, dē-pres'ing-li, *adv*. In a depressing manner.
Depression, dē-pre'shon, *n*. Act of pressing down; state of being pressed down; a low state; a sinking of a surface; a hollow; act of humbling; abasement; a sinking of the spirits; dejection; a low state of strength, business, or property. [L. *depressio—premo*, to press.]
Depressive, dē-pres'iv, *a*. Able or tending to depress or cast down.
Deprivation, de-pri-vā'shon, *n*. Act of depriving; state of being deprived; loss; want; bereavement; deposition. [L. *privatio—privo*, to deprive.]
Deprive, dē-prīv', *vt*. To take away; to strip; to bereave; to hinder from possessing or enjoying; to divest of an ecclesiastical preferment, dignity, or office. *ppr*. depriving, *pret. & pp*. deprived. [L. *privo*.]
Depth, depth, *n*. Deepness; the distance of a thing from the surface to the bottom, or to the extreme part downward or inward; the middle of a season, as of winter; the darkest or stillest part, as of the night; the inner part; abstruseness; unsearchableness; extent of penetration, or of the capacity of penetrating.
Deputation, de-pū-tā'shon, *n*. Act of deputing; a special commission to act as the substitute of another; the person or persons authorized and sent to act or transact business for another. [Fr. *députation*.]
Depute, dē-pūt', *vt*. To send as a representative; to appoint and send with a special commission to transact business in another's name; to appoint to an office. *ppr*. deputing, *pret. & pp*. deputed. [Fr. *députer*—Low L. *deputo*—L. *puto*, to clear up, settle.]
Deputy, dep'ū-ti, *n*. A representative; a person appointed to act for another, especially a person sent with a special commission to act in the place of another; a lieutenant; a viceroy; a substitute; a delegate; an agent. [Fr. *député*.]
Deracinate, dē-ras'in-āt, *vt*. To pluck
up by the roots. [L. *radix, radicis*, a root.]
Derange, dē-rānj', *vt*. To disturb the regular order of; to throw into disorder; to displace; to discompose; to disconcert; to disorder the intellect of. *ppr*. deranging, *pret. & pp*. deranged. [Fr. *déranger—rang*, a rank.]
Deranged, dē-rānjd', *p.a*. Disordered in mind; delirious; distracted.
Derangement, dē-rānj'ment, *n*. A putting out of order; disorder; irregularity; disorder of the intellect; insanity.
Derelict, de'rē-likt, *a*. Wholly forsaken; left; abandoned.—*n*. Anything forsaken, or intentionally cast away. [L. *derelinquo, derelictus—linquo*, to leave.]
Dereliction, de-rē-lik'shon, *n*. Act of forsaking; abandonment; relinquishment; state of being left or forsaken. [L. *derelictio*.]
Deride, dē-rīd', *vt*. To laugh to scorn; to laugh at in contempt; to turn to ridicule; to make sport of; to ridicule; to mock; to jeer. *ppr*. deriding, *pret. & pp*. derided. [L. *derideo—rideo*, to laugh.]
Derider, dē-rīd'ėr, *n*. One who derides.
Deridingly, dē-rīd'ing-li, *adv*. By way of derision or mockery.
Derision, dē-ri'zhon, *n*. Act of deriding; scorn; ridicule; a laughing-stock. [L. *derisio*.]
Derisive, dē-rīs'iv, *a*. Containing derision; mocking; ridiculing.
Derivable, dē-rīv'a-bl, *a*. That may be drawn, as from a source or origin, or from ancestors; deducible; that may be traced from a radical word, from a cause, or from a principle.
Derivably, dē-rīv'a-bli, *adv*. By derivation.
Derivation, de-ri-vā'shon, *n*. Act of deriving; the drawing or tracing of a word from its root; transmission; deduction; that which is derived or deduced. [L. *derivatio*.]
Derivative, dē-riv'āt-iv, *a*. Derived; taken or having proceeded from another; secondary.—*n*. That which is derived; a word which takes its origin in another word, or is formed from it. [L. *derivativus*.]
Derivatively, dē-riv'āt-iv-li, *adv*. In a derivative manner; by derivation.
Derive, dē-rīv', *vt*. To draw off, as a stream from its regular course; to draw or receive, as from a source or origin; to deduce, as from a root; to trace; to infer.—*vi*. To come or proceed from. *ppr*. deriving, *pret. & pp*. derived. [L. *derivo—rivus*, a stream.]
Derived, dē-rīvd', *p.a*. Received; descended; transmitted.
Dernier, der'ni-ėr, *a*. Last; final; ultimate. [Fr.—L. *retro*, backwards.]
Derogate, de'rō-gāt, *vi*. To detract; to lessen by taking away a part. (With *from*.) *ppr*. derogating, *pret. & pp*. derogated. [L. *derogo, derogatus—rogo*, to ask.]
Derogation, de-rō-gā'shon, *n*. Act of derogating, or of taking from anything established by law or otherwise; a lessening or diminishing; detraction; disparagement. (With *of, from*, or *to*.) [L. *derogatio*.]
Derogatory, dē-rog'a-tō-ri, *a*. Tending to lessen by taking something from; that lessens the extent, effect, or value. (With *from, to*, or *unto*.) [Low L. *derogatorius*.]
Descant, des'kant, *n*. A song; a discourse; discussion; disputation; animadversion, or a series of comments. [Old Fr. *deschant*.]

Descant, des-kant', *vi.* *To sing;* to discourse at large; to make a variety of remarks; to animadvert freely. (With *on* or *upon.*) [Old Fr. *deschanter*—L. *canto*, from *cano*, to sing.]

Descend, dē-send', *vi. To pass from a higher to a lower place;* to rush; to come or fall suddenly; to invade, as an enemy; to proceed from a source; to proceed, as from father to son; to pass from general to particular considerations; to come down from an elevated station; to fall in sound.—*vt. To go down* upon or along. [Fr. *descendre*—L. *scando*, to climb.]

Descendant, dē-send'ant, *n. Any person descending* from an ancestor in any degree; issue; offspring, in the line of generation. [Fr. *descendant*.]

Descendent, dē-send'ent, *a. Descending;* proceeding from an original or ancestor. [L. *descendens*.]

Descendibility, dē-send'i-bil''li-ti, *n. Quality of being descendible.*

Descendible, dē-send'i-bl, *a. That may be descended* or passed down; that may descend from an ancestor to an heir.

Descending, dē-send'ing, *p.a. Moving downward;* proceeding from an ancestor.

Descent, dē-sent', *n. Act of descending;* inclination downward; slope; fall from a higher to a lower state; invasion of troops from the sea; a passing from an ancestor to an heir; birth; lineage; a generation; distance from the common ancestor; issue; descendants; a rank in the scale of subordination; lowest place. [Fr. *descente*.]

Describable, dē-skrīb'a-bl, *a. That may be described;* capable of description.

Describe, dē-skrīb', *vt. To copy off;* to mark or trace out; to show to others in words; to set forth; to represent; to define; to portray; to relate; to represent by lines and other marks on paper; to give a clear and vivid exhibition of in language. *ppr.* describing, *pret. & pp.* described. [L. *describo*—*scribo*, to write.]

Description, dē-skrip'shon, *n. Act of describing;* the appearance of anything delineated; delineation; act of representing a thing by words or by signs, or the passage containing such representation; recital; explanation; a representation of names, nature, or properties; a definition; the qualities expressed in a representation; sort; stamp. [L. *descriptio*—*scribo*, to write.]

Descriptive, dē-skrip'tiv, *a. Containing description;* tending to describe; having the quality of representing. [Fr. *descripti*.]

Descry, dē-skrī', *vt. To discover,* as anything concealed; to find out; to have a sight of from a distance; to see; to behold; to espy; to discern. *ppr.* descrying, *pret. & pp.* descried. [Norm. *descrie*, discovered.]

Desecrate, de'sē-krāt, *vt. To divert from a sacred purpose;* to divest of a sacred character or office; to render unhallowed. *ppr.* desecrating, *pret. & pp.* desecrated. [L. *desecro*, *desecratus*—*sacer*, sacred.]

Desecrated, de'sē-krāt-ed, *p.a.* Treated sacrilegiously.

Desecration, de-sē-krā'shon, *n. Act of diverting from a sacred purpose or use;* profanation.

Desert, de'zėrt, *a. Forsaken;* wild; waste; empty; unoccupied. [L. *desertus*.]—*n.* A place *deserted;* an uninhabited tract of land; a solitude; a vast sandy plain. [L. *desertum*.]

Desert, dē-zėrt', *vt. To disjoin one's self from;* to quit with a view not to return to; to forsake or leave, as service; to abandon; to relinquish; to quit.—*vi.* To run away; to quit a service without permission. [Fr. *déserter*—L. *sero*, *sertum*, to join together.]

Desert, dē-zėrt', *n. Diligent service;* due; excellence; that which is deserved; merit or demerit; claim to reward or liability to punishment. [Old Fr. *deserte*, merit—L. *servio*, to serve.]

Deserted, dē-zėrt'ed, *p.a.* Wholly forsaken; left.

Deserter, dē-zėrt'ėr, *n. One who deserts;* a soldier or seaman who quits the service without permission.

Desertion, dē-zėr'shon, *n. Act of deserting;* act of forsaking, as a party, a friend, a country, an army, or a ship; act of quitting with an intention not to return; state of being deserted.

Deserve, dē-zėrv', *vt.* To merit; to have a just claim to, as an equivalent for labour or services; to be worthy of, whether of good or evil.—*vi.* To merit; to be worthy of recompence (with *ill* or *well.*) *ppr.* deserving, *pret. & pp.* deserved. [Old Fr. *deservir*—L. *servio*, to serve—*servus*, a slave.]

Deservedly, dē-zėrv'ed-li, *adv.* Justly; according to desert.

Deserving, dē-zėrv'ing, *p.a.* Worthy of reward or praise; meritorious; possessed of good qualities that entitle to approbation.—*n.* Act of meriting; desert.

Desiccative, dē-sik'at-iv, *a. Drying;* that has the power to dry.—*n.* An application which tends to dry up secretions. [Fr. *desiccatif*—L. *sicco*, to dry.]

Desiderate, dē-sid'ėr-āt, *vt. To long or greatly wish for;* to desire; to want; to miss. *ppr.* desiderating, *pret. & pp.* desiderated. [L. *desidero*, *desideratus.*]

Desideratum, dē-sid'ėr-ā''tum, *n.* Desiderata, *pl. That which is desired;* that which is not possessed, but which is desirable; any perfection which is wanted. [L.]

Design, dē-sīn', *vt. To mark or trace out;* to delineate by drawing the outline of; to form an outline of in the mind; to form, as a plan, purpose, or intention; to set apart for some end; to intend; to propose; to mean. *vi.* To intend. [Fr. *dessiner*, to draw—L. *signum*, a mark.]—*n. Something traced out;* a representation of a thing by an outline; first idea represented by visible lines; a plan drawn out in the mind; purpose; aim; project. [Fr. *dessin.*]

Designable, dē-sīn'a-bl, *a. Capable of being designed* or marked out.

Designate, de'sig-nāt, *vt. To trace out;* to point out; to distinguish from others by indication; to characterize; to describe; to allot. *ppr.* designating, *pret. & pp.* designated. [L. *designo*, *designatus*—*signum*, a sign.]

Designation, de-sig-nā'shon, *n. Act of marking out by signs;* a showing; a distinguishing from others; appointment; direction; a selecting and appointing; import. [L. *designatio*.]

Designed, dē-sīnd', *p.a.* Planned; intended.

Designedly, dē-sīn'ed-li, *adv. By design;* purposely; intentionally.

Designer, dē-sīn'ėr, *n. One who designs;* one who frames a scheme; a contriver.

Designing, dē-sīn'ing, *p.a.* Artful; intriguing; deceitful; treacherous.

Desirable, dē-zīr'a-bl, *a. Worthy of being desired;* that is to be wished for with earnestness; agreeable.

Desirableness, dē-zīr'a-bl-nes, *n. The quality of being desirable.*

Desirably, dē-zīr'a-bli, *adv. In a desirable manner.*

Desire, dē-zīr', *n. A longing ardent wish for something not possessed;* a passion excited by the love of an object, and directed to its attainment; eagerness to enjoy; aspiration; longing; a prayer; the object of desire; love; affection; appetite; lust. [Fr. *désir*—L. *desiderium*.]—*vt. To long for, as for something not possessed;* to wish for the possession or enjoyment of; to covet; to express a wish for in the way of petition; to express a wish for in the way of direction; to ask; to request; to entreat. *ppr.* desiring, *pret. & pp.* desired. [Fr. *désirer.*]

Desired, dē-zīrd', *p.a.* Coveted; entreated.

Desirous, dē-zīr'us, *a. Full of desire;* solicitous to possess and enjoy; anxious; covetous. [Fr. *désireux*.]

Desist, dē-sist', *vi. To remove one's self away from anything;* to cease to act or proceed; to forbear; to leave off. (With *from.*) [L. *desisto*—*sisto*, to place one's self—*sto*, to stand.]

Desk, desk, *n. A table;* an inclining table to write upon; the pulpit in a church; the clerical profession. [Sax. *disc*, a plate—D. *disch*, a table.]

Desolate, de'sō-lāt, *a. Left alone;* forsaken; waste; laid waste; in a ruinous condition; afflicted; deprived of comfort.—*vt. To leave alone;* to deprive of inhabitants; to make desert; to lay waste; to ravage; to destroy, as improvements or works of art. *ppr.* desolating, *pret. & pp.* desolated. [L. *desolo*, *desolatus*—*solus*, alone.]

Desolately, de'sō-lāt-li, *adv. In a desolate manner.*

Desolateness, de'sō-lāt-nes, *n. State of being desolate.*

Desolating, de'sō-lāt-ing, *p.a.* Wasting; ravaging.

Desolation, de-sō-lā'shon, *n. Act of desolating;* waste; ravage; a place wasted; a desolate state or place; melancholy; sadness. [Low L. *desolatio.*]

Despair, dē-spār', *n. A hopeless state;* despondency; that which causes despair; that of which there is no hope; loss of hope in the mercy of God. [Fr. *désespoir*—L. *spēro*, to hope.]—*vi. To be hopeless;* to give up all hope or expectation; to despond. [Fr.*désespérer.*]

Despairing, dē-spār'ing, *p.a. Giving up all hope* or expectation.

Despairingly, dē-spār'ing-li, *adv. In a despairing manner.*

Despatch, des-pach', *vt.* To send away *in haste,* as a messenger, letters, &c.; to accelerate; to send out of the world; to execute speedily; to finish.—*n.* Message on public business, sent with expedition; a message sent in haste; transaction of business with due diligence; due diligence; management. [Fr. *dépêcher*—L. *spatior*, to go.]

Desperado, des-pē-rā'dō, *n. A desperate fellow;* a furious man; one regardless of safety. [Sp. from *desperār*, to despair.]

Desperate, des'pē-rāt, *a. Without hope;* despairing; without care of safety; fearless of danger; furious, as a man in despair; lost beyond hope of recovery. [L. *desperatus*.]

Desperately, des'pē-rāt-li, *adv. In a desperate manner.*

Fāte, fär, fat, fąll; mē, met, hėr; pīne, pin; nōte, not, mōve; tūbe, tub, bųll; oil, pound.

Desperateness, dĕs′pĕ-rāt-nes, n. State of being desperate.
Desperation, des-pĕ-rā′shon, n. A despairing; a giving up of hope; fury; disregard of safety or danger. [L. desperatio.]
Despicable, des′pik-a-bl, a. That deserves to be despised; contemptible; vile; worthless; degrading. [Low L. despicabilis.]
Despicably, des′pik-a-bli, adv. Meanly.
Despisable, dĕ-spīz′a-bl, a. That may be despised; despicable; contemptible.
Despise, dĕ-spīz′, vt. To look down upon; to have the lowest opinion of; to scorn; to disdain; to undervalue. ppr. despising, pret. & pp despised. [L. despicio—specio, to look at.]
Despised, dĕ-spizd′, p.a. Disdained; abhorred.
Despiser, dĕ-spīz′ėr, n. A contemner.
Despite, dĕ-spīt′, n. A looking down upon; malice enraged; active malignity; defiance with contempt; an act of malice or contempt.—vt. To vex. ppr. despiting, pret. & pp. despited. prep. In spite of; notwithstanding. [Old Fr.—L. despectus—specio, to view.]
Despiteful, dĕ-spīt′ful, a. Full of spite; malicious; malignant.
Despitefully, dĕ-spīt′ful-li, adv. With despite; maliciously; contemptuously.
Despitefulness, dĕ-spīt′ful-nes, n. Quality of being despiteful; malice.
Despoil, dĕ-spoil′, vt. To take from by force; to rob; to bereave; to rifle. [L. despolio—spolium, spoil.]
Despond, dĕ-spond′, vi. To depart from one's promise; to lose hope; to be cast down; to be dejected in mind; to lose all courage, spirit, or resolution; to sink by loss of hope. [L. despondeo—spondeo, to promise.]
Despondence, Despondency, dĕ-spond′ens, dĕ-spond′en-si, n. Hopelessness; despair; permanent depression.
Despondent, dĕ-spond′ent, a. Depressed and inactive in despair.
Despondently, dĕ-spond′ent-li, adv. Without hope.
Desponding, dĕ-spond′ing, p.a. Yielding to discouragement; depressed in spirit.
Despondingly, dĕ-spond′ing-li, adv. In a desponding manner.
Despot, des′pot, n. An absolute ruler (generally in a bad sense); a tyrant. [Gr. despotēs—a master, lord.]
Despotic, des-pot′ik, a. Absolute in power; tyrannical; arbitrary. [Gr. despotikos.]
Despotically, des′pot′ik-al-li, adv. With unlimited power; arbitrarily.
Despotism, des′pot-izm, n. The power or spirit of a despot; authority uncontrolled by men, constitution, or laws, and depending alone on the will of the prince; an arbitrary government. [Fr. despotisme.]
Dessert, dĕ-zėrt′, n. That which is served when the substantial part of a meal is removed, consisting of fruits, &c. [Fr.—L. servio, to serve.]
Destination, des-tin-ā′shon, n. Act of destining; the purpose for which anything is intended; ultimate design; appointment; purpose; destiny; place to which a thing is appointed. [L. destinatio.]
Destine, des′tin, vt. To set or appoint to a purpose; to design; to doom; to ordain; to fix unalterably, as by a divine decree. ppr. destining, pret. & pp. destined. [L. destino—Gr. histēmi, to set.]
Destined, des′tind, p.a. Ordained; fixed unalterably.

Destiny, des′ti-ni, n. State appointed or predetermined; ultimate fate; invincible necessity; a fixed order of things established by a divine decree. [Fr. destin, destinée.]
Destitute, des′ti-tūt, a. Set away; left weak or helpless; forsaken; not having; needy; comfortless; friendless; forlorn. [L. destitutus—statuo, to set.]
Destitution, des-ti-tū′shon, n. Want; a state in which something is wanted or not possessed; poverty. [L. destitutio.]
Destroy, dĕ-stroi′, vt. To pull down, as a structure; to rase; to overthrow; to dismantle; to devastate; to kill; to devour; to extinguish; to put an end to. [L. destruo—struo, to build.]
Destroyer, dĕ-stroi′ėr, n. One who destroys.
Destroying, dĕ-stroi′ing, p.a. Laying waste; killing; putting an end to.
Destructibility, dĕ-strukt′i-bil″i-ti, n. The quality of being destructible.
Destructible, dĕ-strukt′i-bl, a. Liable to destruction. [Low L. destructibilis.]
Destruction, dĕ-struk′shon, n. A pulling down; demolition; overthrow; death; massacre; cause of destruction; a destroyer. [L. destructio.]
Destructive, dĕ-strukt′iv, a. Having the quality of destroying; deadly; fatal; pernicious; mischievous. [Low L. destructivus.]
Destructively, dĕ-strukt′iv-li, adv. With destruction; ruinously.
Destructiveness, dĕ-strukt′iv-nes, n. Quality of destroying or ruining.
Desuetude, des′wĕ-tūd, n. The cessation of use; disuse; discontinuance of practice, custom, or fashion. [L. desuetudo—suesco, to become used.]
Desultorily, de′sul-tō-ri-li, adv. In a desultory manner; without method.
Desultoriness, de′sul-tō-ri-nes, n. The quality of being desultory.
Desultory, de′sul-tō-ri, a. Leaping; passing from one subject to another, without order or natural connection; coming suddenly; started at the moment; cursory; hasty. [L. desultorius—salio, saltum, to leap.]
Detach, dĕ-tach′, vt. To separate; to disengage; to disjoin; to withdraw; to separate and send away, as a part of a military force, or of a fleet. [Fr. détacher.]
Detached, dĕ-tacht′, p.a. Separate.
Detachment, dĕ-tach′ment, n. Act of detaching; state of being detached; a body of troops, or number of ships, selected from the main army or fleet, and employed on some special service.
Detail, dĕ-tāl′, vt. To cut off into parts; to select for a particular service, as an officer or body of troops; to particularize; to specify; to relate minutely and distinctly. [Fr. détailler—L. talea, a cutting.)—n. A cutting off into parts or portions; the parts or portions themselves; a selecting of certain individuals for a particular service; a minute and particular narration; narrative; explanation. [Fr. détail.]
Detailed, dĕ-tāld′, p.a. Minutely recited.
Detain, dĕ-tān′ vt. To keep back or from; to withhold; to arrest; to check; to retard. [L. detineo—teneo, to hold.]
Detainer, dĕ-tān′ėr, n. One who detains or withholds; a holding or keeping possession of what belongs to another.
Detainment, dĕ-tān′ment, n. Act of detaining; detention.
Detect, dĕ-tekt′, vt. To uncover; to bring to light, as something hidden; to lay

open; to find out, as a crime or criminal. [L. detego, detectus—tego, to cover.]
Detecter, dĕ-tekt′ėr, n. One who detects.
Detection, dĕ-tek′shon, n. Act of detecting; discovery of a person or thing attempted to be concealed. [L. detectio.]
Detective, dĕ-tekt′iv, a. Skilled or employed in detecting.—n. A policeman whose business is to detect rogues.
Detention, dĕ-ten′shon, n. Act of detaining; a keeping what belongs to another; confinement; delay from necessity. [L. detentio.]
Deter, dĕ-tėr′, vt. To frighten from; to prevent by prohibition or danger. ppr. deterring, pret. & pp. deterred. [L. deterreo—terreo, to frighten.]
Detergent, dĕ-tėrj′ent, a. Cleansing; purging.—n. That which cleanses or purges away. [L. detergens—tergeo, to wipe.]
Deterging, dĕ-tėrj′ing, p.a. Cleansing; carrying off obstructions or foul matter.
Deteriorate, dĕ-tē′ri-ō-rāt, vi. To grow downwards; to grow worse; to degenerate—vt. To cause to grow downwards; to make worse; to reduce in quality. ppr. deteriorating, pret. & pp. deteriorated. [Fr. détériorer—L. deterior, worse—de, down from.]
Deterioration, dĕ-tē′ri-ō-rā″shon, n. A growing or making worse; the state of growing worse.
Determent, dĕ-tėr′ment, n. Act of deterring; that which deters.
Determinable, dĕ-tėr′min-a-bl, a. That may be decided with certainty; that may end or be determined.
Determinate, dĕ-tėr′min-at, a. Fixed; positive; decisive. [L. determinatus—terminus, a limit.]
Determinately, dĕ-tėr′min-āt-li, adv. With certainty; resolutely.
Determination, dĕ-tėr′min-ā″shon, n. Act of determining; decision of a question in the mind; firm resolution; purpose; judgment; award; strong direction to a given point; absolute direction to a certain end. [Fr. détermination.]
Determine, dĕ-tėr′min, vt. To bound; to limit; to fix permanently; to conclude; to decide; to fix on; to establish; to give a direction to; to resolve on; to cause to cease; to bring to an end.—vi. To come to a determination; to resolve; to come to an end. ppr. determining, pret. & pp. determined. [L. determino—terminus, a bound—Heb. tėrėm, a cutting off.]
Determined, dĕ-tėr′mind, p.a. Having a firm or fixed purpose; resolute; definite.
Determinedly, dĕ-tėr′mind-li, adv. In a determined manner.
Deterring, dĕ-tėr′ing, p.a. Discouraging; frightening.
Detest, dĕ-test′, vt. To hate extremely; to abhor; to loathe; to abominate. [L. detestor—testor, to bear witness.]
Detestable, dĕ-test′a-bl, a. Extremely hateful; abominable; execrable; abhorred. [L. detestabilis.]
Detestableness, dĕ-test′a-bl-nes, n. Extreme hatefulness.
Detestably, dĕ-test′a-bli, adv. Very hatefully; abominably.
Detestation, dĕ-test-ā′shon, n. Extreme hatred; abhorrence; loathing. [Fr. détestation.]
Detested, dĕ-test′ed, p.a. Hated extremely; abhorred.

Dethrone, dē-thrōn', *vt.* To remove from a throne; to depose; to divest of royal authority and dignity, or of supreme power. *ppr.* dethroning, *pret. & pp.* dethroned. [Fr. *detrôner*—L. *thronus*—Gr. *thronos*, a throne.]

Dethroned, dē-thrōnd', *p.a.* Deposed.

Dethronement, dē-thrōn'ment, *n.* Deposition of a king, emperor, or prince.

Detonate, de'tō-nāt, *vt.* To cause to explode; to cause to burn with a sudden report.—*vi.* To explode; to burn with a sudden report. *ppr.* detonating, *pret. & pp.* detonated. [L. *detono*, *detonatus—tōno*, to thunder.]

Detonating, de'tō-nāt-ing, *p.a.* Exploding.

Detonation, de-tō-nā'shon, *n.* A sudden report made by the inflammation of certain combustible bodies. [Fr. *détonation*.]

Detract, dē-trakt', *vt.* To draw away from; to disparage; to depreciate; to calumniate; to derogate from. (With *from.*) [L. *detraho*, *detractus—traho*, to draw.]

Detraction, dē-trak'shon, *n.* Act of detracting; depreciation; slander; defamation; derogation. [Fr. *détraction*.]

Detractor, dē-trakt'ėr, *n.* One who detracts; a slanderer. [L.]

Detriment, de'tri-ment, *n.* A rubbing off; loss; damage; injury; prejudice; mischief; harm. [L. *detrimentum—tėro*, *tritum*, to rub.]

Detrimental, de-tri-ment'al, *a.* Causing detriment; injurious; hurtful.

Detritus, dē-trīt'us, *n.* That which is rubbed away or worn off; a mass of substances worn off from solid bodies by attrition, and reduced to small portions. [from L.—rubbed away.]

Detruncate, dē-trung'kāt, *vt.* To cut off, as boughs from the trunk; to lop; to shorten by cutting. *ppr.* detruncating, *pret. & pp.* detruncated. [L. *detrunco*, *detruncatus—trunco*, to cut shorter.]

Detruncation, dē-trung-kā'shon, *n.* Act of cutting off. [L. *detruncatio*.]

Deuce, dūs, *n.* Two; a card with two spots; a die with two spots. [Fr. *deux*.]

Deuce, Deuse, dūs, *n.* An evil spirit; a demon; the devil. [Armor. *teus*, a phantom, a spectre.]

Deuterogamist, dū-tėr-og'a-mist, *n.* One who marries the second time.

Deuterogamy, dū-tėr-og'a-mi. *n.* A second marriage after the death of the first husband or wife. [Gr. *deuteros*, second, and *gamos*, marriage.]

Deuteronomy, dū-tėr-on'ō-mi, *n.* The second law; the name given to the fifth book of the Pentateuch. [Gr. *deuteros*, second, and *nomos*, law.]

Devastate, de'vas-tāt, *vt.* To desolate; to destroy; to demolish; to plunder. *ppr.* devastating, *pret. & pp.* devastated. [L. *devasto*, *devastatus—vasto*, to waste.]

Devastation, de-vas-tā'shon, *n.* Act of devastating; state of being devastated. [Fr. *dévastation*.]

Develop, dē-vel'up, *vt.* To unroll; to disclose or make known, as something concealed or withheld from notice; to lay open; to unravel. [Fr. *développer*—L. *volvo*, to roll.]

Developed, dē-vel'upt, *p.a.* Unfolded; laid open.

Development, dē-vel'up-ment. *n.* An unfolding; an unravelling; disentanglement; expansion; growth; gradual change from an embryo state to full maturity; full exhibition. [Fr. *développement*.]

Deviate, dē'vi-āt, *vi.* To go out of the way; to stray from the path of duty; to wander; to swerve; to err. *ppr.* deviating, *pret. & pp.* deviated. [L. *devio*, *deviātum—via*, a way.]

Deviation, dē-vi-ā'shon, *n.* A turning aside from the right way, course, or line; want of conformity to the rules prescribed by God; sin. [Fr. *déviation*.]

Device, dē-vīs', *n.* That which is devised or invented with care and art; contrivance; scheme; stratagem; an emblem; emblem on a shield. [Fr. *devis*.]

Devil, de'vil, *n.* The Accuser; an evil spirit; Satan; the chief of the apostate angels; a very wicked person; an idol or false god.—*vt.* To pepper excessively in cooking. [Gr. *diabolos—ballo*, to throw at.]

Devilish, de'vil-ish, *a.* Partaking of the qualities of the devil; diabolical; infernal; hellish.

Devilishly, de'vil-ish-li, *adv.* In a manner suiting the devil; diabolically.

Devilishness, de'vil-ish-nes, *n.* The qualities of the devil.

Devilry, de'vil-ri, *n.* Communication with the devil; extreme wickedness.

Devious, dē'vi-us, *a.* Out of the common way or track; wandering; rambling; excursive. [L. *devius—via*, a way.]

Deviously, dē'vi-us-li, *adv.* In a devious manner.

Deviousness, dē'vi-us-nes, *n.* Departure from a regular course; wandering.

Devisable, dē-vīz'a-bl, *a.* That may be devised; that may be bequeathed.

Devise, dē-vīz', *vt.* To strike out by viewing in the mind; to contrive; to invent; to discover; to scheme; to strike out [Old Fr. *deviser*—L. *viso*, to look at often]; to give or bequeath by will.—*ppr.* devising, *pret. & pp.* devised. [L. *divido*, *divisus*, to divide.] *n.* Act of giving or bequeathing by will. [Low L. *divisa*.]

Deviser, de-vīz'ėr, *n.* One who contrives or invents; a contriver.

Devisor, de-vīz'ėr, *n.* One who bequeaths lands or tenements.

Devoid, dē-void', *a.* Void; empty; vacant; destitute; not possessing; free from.

Devoir, de-vwa', *n.* That which is due; service or duty; an act of civility; respectful notice due to another. [Fr.—L. *debeo*, *debēre*, to owe.]

Devolution, de-vō-lū'shon, *n.* Act of rolling down; a passing or falling upon a successor. [Low L. *devolutio*.]

Devolve, dē-volv', *vt.* To roll down; to deliver over, or from one possessor to a successor.—*vi.* To roll down; to fall by succession from one possessor to his successor. *ppr.* devolving, *pret. & pp.* devolved. [L. *devolvo—volvo*, to roll.]

Devote, dē-vōt', *vt.* To set apart by vow; to consecrate; to doom; to yield to; to apply closely to (with recipr. pron.) *ppr.* devoting, *pret. & pp.* devoted. [L. *devoveo*, *devōtus—voveo*, to vow.]

Devoted, dē-vōt'ed, *p.a.* Ardent; zealous; strongly attached.

Devotedness, dē-vōt'ed-nes, *n.* State of being devoted or given up wholly; consecration.

Devotee, de-vō-tē', *n.* One given wholly to religion; one who is superstitiously given to religious ceremonies. [Fr. *dévot*, fem. *dévote*, the old Eng. spelling.]

Devotion, dē-vō'shon, *n.* Act of devoting; state of being solemnly set apart for a particular purpose; consecration; a solemn attention to the Supreme Being in worship; acts of religion; prayer; an act of reverence, respect, or ceremony; ardent love or affection; earnestness. [Fr. *dévotion*.]

Devotional, dē-vō'shon-al, *a.* Pertaining to devotion; used in devotion.

Devotionally, dē-vō'shon-al-li, *adv.* In a devotional manner.

Devour, dē-vour', *vt.* To swallow or gulp down; to eat ravenously; to swallow up; to enter upon and pursue with great eagerness; to waste; to slay; to spend in dissipation and riot. [Fr. *dévorer*—L. *vōro*, to swallow whole.]

Devourer, dē-vour'ėr, *n.* One who devours.

Devouring, dē-vour'ing, *p.a.* Destroying; consuming.

Devout, dē-vout', *a.* Devoted to religion; expressing devotion; holy; pure; religious; earnest; solemn. [L. *devōtus—voveo*, to vow.]

Devoutly, dē-vout'li, *adv.* In a devout manner; piously.

Devoutness, dē-vout'nes, *n.* Quality of being devout.

Dew, dū, *n.* Moisture from the atmosphere condensed into drops on the surface of cold bodies, as leaves, grass, &c.; wetness; damp.—*vt.* To wet with dew; to moisten; to damp. [Sax. *deaw*; Old G. *tau*.]

Dewdrop, dū'drop, *n.* A drop of dew, which sparkles at sunrise.

Dewiness, dū'i-nes, *n.* State of being dewy.

Dew-lap, dū'lap, *n.* The flesh that hangs from the throat of oxen, which laps or licks the dew in grazing.

Dew-point, dū'point, *n.* The temperature at which dew begins to form.

Dewy, dū'i, *a.* Partaking of dew; like dew; moist with dew.

Dexter, deks'tėr, *a.* Right, as opposed to left. [L.]

Dexterity, deks-te'ri-ti *n.* Right-handedness; adroitness; cleverness; tact; aptitude. [Fr. *dextérité*.]

Dexterous, deks'tėr-us, *a.* Right-handed; skilful and active in manual employment; adroit; ready; prompt in contrivance; done with dexterity.

Dexterously, deks'tėr-us-li, *adv.* With dexterity; expertly; skilfully; artfully.

Diabetes, di-a-bē'tēs, *n.* A passing through; a morbid discharge of saccharine urine. [Gr. *diabētēs—bainō*, to go.]

Diabolical, di-a-bol'ik-al, *a.* Devilish; partaking of any quality ascribed to the devil. [Late Gr. *diabolikos*.]

Diabolically, di-a-bol'ik-al-li, *adv.* In a diabolical manner; very wickedly.

Diaconal, di-ak'on-al, *a.* Pertaining to a deacon. [Fr. from L. *diaconus*.]

Diaconate, di-ak'on-āt, *n.* The office of a deacon. [Fr. *diaconal*.]

Diadem, di'a-dem, *n.* A head-band or fillet worn by kings as a badge of royalty; a crown; supreme power; a distinguished or principal ornament. [Gr. *diadēma—deō*, to bind.]

Diademed, di'a-demd, *p.a.* Adorned with a diadem; crowned; ornamented.

Diaeresis, Dieresis, di-ē're-sis, *n.* A division; the dissolution of a diphthong; the mark (¨) placed over two vowels, denoting that they are to be pronounced as distinct letters; as *aër*. [Gr. *—dia*, asunder, and *haireō*, to take.]

Diagnostic, di-ag-nos'tik, *a.* Distinguishing; characteristic; indicating the nature of a disease. [Gr. *gnōstikos—ginōskō*, to know.]

Diagonal, di-ag'on-al, *a.* Passing from

corner to corner; extending from one angle to another of a quadrilateral or multilateral figure.—*n.* A right line drawn from angle to angle of a quadrilateral or multilateral figure, and dividing it into two parts. [Gr. *diagōnios—gōnia,* a corner.]
Diagonally, dī-ag'on-al-li, *adv. In a diagonal direction.*
Diagram, dī'a-gram, *n. That which is marked out by lines;* a figure, draught, or scheme, delineated for the purpose of demonstrating the properties of any figure, as a square, circle, &c. [Gr. *diagramma—graphō,* to write.]
Dial, dī'al, *n.* An instrument for showing the time *of the day* by the sun's shadow. [L. *diālis,* aerial—*dies,* a day.]
Dialect, dī'a-lekt, *n. Speech;* the idiom of a language peculiar to a province or to a kingdom; language; manner of speaking. [Gr. *dialectos—legō,* to pick out, to speak.]
Dialectic, dī-a-lek'tik, *a. Pertaining to a dialect or dialects;* relating to logic; logical; argumentative; not radical. [Gr. *dialektikos.*]
Dialectician, dī'a-lek-ti"shi-an, *n.* A logician; a reasoner.
Dialectics, dī-a-lek'tiks, *n.* Argumentation *in dialogue;* that branch of logic which teaches the rules and modes of *discussion or of reasoning.*
Dialling, dī'al-ing, *n.* The art of *constructing dials.*
Dialogue, dī'a-log, *n.* A conversation between two or more persons, either real or imaginary; a conference.—*vi.*† To discourse together.—*vt.'* To express, as in a dialogue. [Fr.—Gr. *legō,* to speak.]
Dial-plate, dī'al-plāt, *n. The plate of a dial,* and also of a clock or watch, on which the lines are drawn to show the time of the day.
Diameter, dī-am'et-ėr, *n. That which measures through* the middle; a right line passing through the centre of a circle, and terminated by the circumference; a right line passing through the centre of a sphere, from one side to the other; the distance through the centre of any object. [Gr. *diametros—metron,* measure.]
Diametrical, dī-a-met'rik-al, *a.* Being in the direction *of a diameter;* direct. [Gr. *dia* and *metrikos.*]
Diametrically, dī-a-met'rik-al-li, *adv.* In a *diametrical* direction; directly.
Diamond, dī'a-mond, *n. Adamant;* a gem of the most valuable kind, remarkable for its hardness; a very small printing letter.—*a. Resembling a diamond;* consisting of diamonds. [Fr. *diamant*—Gr. *a,* priv. and *damaō,* to subdue.]
Diamonded, Diamond-shaped, dī'a-mond-ed, dī'a-mond-shāpt, *a.* In squares, like *a diamond;* shaped like a diamond.
Diaper, dī'a-pėr, *n.* A cloth woven in flowers or figures, much used for towels or napkins; a towel or napkin.—*vt.* To variegate or diversify, as cloth, with figures; to flower.—*vi.* To draw flowers or figures, as upon cloth. [Fr. *diapré.*]
Diapered, dī'a-pėrd, *p.a.* Flowered; variegated.
Diaphanous, dī-af'an-us, *a. Seen through;* having power to transmit rays of light, as glass; pellucid; transparent; clear. [Gr. *diaphanēs—phainō,* to show.]
Diaphragm, dī'a-fram, *n.* The midriff, a muscle *separating* the chest from the abdomen; a circular ring used in optical instruments. [Gr. *diaphragma—phrassō,* to fence in.]
Diarrhœa, dī-a-rē'a, *n. A flowing through;* a morbidly frequent evacuation of the intestines; a lax. [Gr. *diarrhoia—rheō,* to flow.]
Diarrhœtic, dī-a-ret'ik, *a. Producing diarrhœa* or lax.
Diary, dī'a-ri, *n.* An account *of daily events* or transactions; a journal. [L. *diarium—dies,* a day.]
Diatonic, dī-a-ton'ik, *a.* A term applied to the natural scale of music. [Gr. *diatonikos—tonos,* tone.]
Diatribe, dī'a-trib, *n.* A continued discourse, which *wastes away* much time; a strain of reproach. [Gr. *diatribē—tribō,* to rub.]
Diatribist, dī'a-trib-ist, *n.* One who prolongs his discourse or discussion.
Dibble, dib'bl, *n.* A pointed instrument which is *dipped* or thrust into the earth, to make holes for planting seeds, &c.—*vt.* To plant with a *dibble,* or to make holes for planting seeds, &c. *ppr.* dibbling, *pret. & pp.* dibbled. [dimin. from *dip.*]
Dice, dīs, *n. pl.* of *die;* also, a game with dice.—*vi.*† To play with dice.
Dicer, dīs'ėr, *n. A player at dice.*
Dicing, dīs'ing, *p.n. The practice of playing at dice.*
Dictate, dik'tāt, *vt.* To deliver, as an order or direction; to prescribe; to tell what to say or to write; to suggest; to point out. *ppr.* dictating, *pret. & pp.* dictated.—*n. That which is dictated;* an order delivered; an authoritative precept or maxim; an impulse. [L. *dicto, dictatus—dico, dictum,* to say.]
Dictation, dik-tā'shon, *n. Act of dictating;* words dictated; the act or practice of prescribing. [Low L. *dictatio.*]
Dictator, dik'tāt-ėr, *n. One who dictates;* one who prescribes rules for the direction of others; one invested with absolute authority. [L.]
Dictatorial, dik-ta-tō'ri-al, *a. Pertaining to a dictator;* absolute; authoritative; overbearing. [Fr.]
Dictatorially, dik-ta-tō'ri-al-li, *adv. In a dictatorial manner.*
Dictatorship, dik-tāt'ėr-ship, *n. The office of a dictator;* the term of a dictator's office.
Diction, dik'shon, *n. A speaking;* expression of ideas by *words;* manner of expression; language; style; phraseology. [L. *dictio—dico,* to speak.]
Dictionary, dik'shon-a-ri, *n. A book of words;* a book containing the words of a language arranged in alphabetical order, with their etymologies, explanations of their meanings, and usages; a lexicon; a work explanatory of the terms, &c., of any science or subject under words or heads alphabetically arranged. [Fr. *dictionnaire.*]
Dictum, dik'tum, *n.* Dicta, dik'ta, *pl. An authoritative saying* or assertion. [L.—*dico, dictum,* to speak.]
Did, did, *pret.* of *do.* [Sax. *dyde,* from *dón, gedón,* to do.]
Didactic, di-dak'tik, *a. Adapted to teach; instructive;* preceptive; containing doctrines, principles, or rules. [Gr. *didaktikos—didaskō,* to teach.]
Didactically, di-dak'tik-al-li, *adv. In a didactic manner.*
Didactics, di-dak'tiks, *n. pl. The art or science of teaching.*
Didst, didst. The second person sing. of the pret. of *do.*
Die, dī, *vi. To fail; to dissolve;* to be deprived of life, either animal or vegetable; to expire; to sink gradually; to languish (often with *out* or *away*); to come to nothing; to cease; to vanish; to be lost; to be insensible; to cease to be under the power (with *to*). [Sax. *dydan*—Heb. *dāva,* to be sick, to languish.]
Die, dī, *n.* Dice, dīs, *pl.* A small cube marked on its faces with numbers, from one to six, used in gaming; any cubic body; a flat tablet; the cubical part of a pedestal; hazard; chance. [Fr. *dé.*]
Die, dī, *n.* Dies, dīz, *pl.* A stamp used in coining money, in foundries, &c. [from the preceding.]
Diet, dī'et, *n. Food;* food prescribed for the prevention or cure of disease; allowance of provision; board or boarding.—*vt. To feed;* to board; to furnish provisions for.—*vi. To feed;* to eat according to rules prescribed; to eat. [Fr. *diète;* Gr. *diaita,* life, food.]
Diet, dī'et, *n.* An appointed *day* of assembling; the assembly itself; a convention of princes, &c., to deliberate on the affairs of the Germanic empire. [from L. *dies,* a day.]
Dietary, dī'et-a-ri, *a. Pertaining to the rules of diet.*—*n. Rule of diet;* allowance of food, especially among the inmates of an almshouse.
Dieter, dī'et-ėr, *n. One who diets;* one who prescribes rules for eating.
Dietetic, di-et-et'ik, *a. Pertaining to diet,* or to the rules for regulating the kind and quantity of food to be eaten. [Gr. *diaitētikē—technē,* art.]
Dietetics, di-et-et'iks, *n. Principles for regulating the diet.*
Differ, dif'fėr, *vi. To come apart;* to be unlike or distinct; not to accord; to disagree; to contend; to be at variance. [L. *differo—fero,* to bear.]
Difference, dif'fėr-ens, *n. State of being different;* dissimilarity; unlikeness; that which distinguishes one thing from another; dispute; contest; point in dispute; a logical distinction; remainder of a sum after a lesser sum is subtracted; distinction. [Fr. *différence*—L. *fero,* to bear, carry.]
Different, dif'fėr-ent, *a. Differing;* not the same; various; unlike; dissimilar. (With *from.*) [Fr. *différent.*]
Differential, dif-fėr-en'shi-al, *a. Creating a difference;* making discrimination; discriminating.—*n.* An increment, usually an indefinitely small one, which is given to a variable quantity. [Fr. *différentiel.*]
Differently, dif'fėr-ent-li, *adv. In a different manner;* variously.
Difficult, dif'fi-kult, *a. Not easy to be made, done, or borne;* hard; painful; perplexed; hard to be pleased; unyielding; rigid. [Sp. *dificultóso*—L. *dis,* and *facio, factum,* to make.]
Difficulty, dif'fi-kul-ti, *n. Hardness to be done;* that which is hard to be performed or surmounted; obstacle; perplexity; trouble; objection; cavil. [Fr. *difficulté.*]
Diffidence, dif'fi-dens, *n. Mistrust;* timidity; modest reserve; excessive modesty; bashfulness. [Low L. *diffidentia*—L. *fido,* to trust.]
Diffident, dif'fi-dent, *a. Distrustful;* distrustful of one's self; doubtful of one's own power or competency; bashful; reserved. [L. *diffidens.*]
Diffidently, dif'fi-dent-li, *adv.* In a self-distrusting manner; modestly.
Diffuse, dif-fūz', *vt. To pour out and spread,* as a fluid; to circulate; to expand; to publish; to proclaim. *ppr.* diffusing, *pret. & pp.* diffused.—*a.*

Widely spread; dispersed; using many words; expansive. [L. *diffundo, diffusus—fundo*, to pour.]
Diffusely, dif-fūs'li, *adv.* Widely; extensively; copiously; with many words.
Diffuseness, dif-fūs'nes, *n.* Quality of being diffuse, or of lacking conciseness.
Diffusible, dif-fūz'i-bl, *a.* That may be diffused; that may flow or be spread in all directions; that may be dispersed.
Diffusion, dif-fū'zhon, *n. Act of diffusing*; a spreading or scattering; state of being spread or scattered; dispersion; spread; propagation; circulation. [Fr.]
Diffusive, dif-fūs'iv, *a. Having the quality of diffusing* or dispersing.
Diffusively, dif-fūs'iv-li, *adv.* Widely.
Diffusiveness, dif-fūs'iv-nes, *n.* Quality or state of being *diffuse*; extensiveness; verboseness.
Dig, dig, *vt.* To open and break up, as the earth with a spade or other sharp instrument; to form an opening in, as in the earth by piercing and removing the loose earth; to pierce; to penetrate. *vi.* To work with a spade or other piercing instrument; to do servile work; to work in search of; to search. *ppr.* digging, *pret.* digged or dug. *pp.* digged or dug. [Sax. *dician*, to trench.]
Digest, di'jest, *n. That which is digested*; an orderly distribution; a body of laws arranged under proper titles. [L. *digestum*, neut. of *digestus*.]
Digest, di-jest', *vt. To dissolve and concoct* in the stomach, as food; to soften and prepare by heat; to dispose methodically; to dispose and nourish in the mind, so as to improve the understanding and heart; to brook; to receive without open resentment. [L. *digero, digestus—gero, gestum*, to bear about with one.]
Digested, di-jest'ed, *p.a.* Reduced to method; arranged in due order; borne.
Digester, di-jest'er, *n. He or that which digests.*
Digestibility, di-jest'i-bil'li-ti, *n.* Quality of being digestible.
Digestible, di-jest'i-bl, *a. Capable of being digested.*
Digestion, di-jest'shon, *n. Act of digesting*; the process of dissolving aliment in the stomach; the operation of gently heating a substance with some solvent; orderly arrangement. [Fr.]
Digestive, di-jest'iv, *a. Having the power to cause digestion*; capable of preparing by heat; methodising; reducing to order.—*n. That which increases or aids digestion.* [Fr. *digestif*.]
Digger, dig'er, *n. One who digs.*
Digging, dig'ing, *p.n. The act or place of digging.*
Dight, dīt, *vt.* To put in order; to dress.
Digit, di'jit, *n. The pointer*; a finger; the measure of three-fourths of an inch; the twelfth part of the diameter of the sun or moon; any integer under 10, so called from counting on the fingers. [L. *digitus*; Sans. *dish*, to point out, to show.]
Digital, di'jit-al, *a. Pertaining to the fingers or to digits.* [L. *digitalis*.]
Digitated, di'jit-ā-ted, *a. Having fingers or toes*; branching into several distinct leaflets like fingers, as a leaf. [L. *digitatus*.]
Dignified, dig'ni-fīd, *p.a. Marked with dignity*; noble; stately; grave.
Dignify, dig'ni-fī, *vt. To make worthy*; to invest with dignity; to exalt in rank or office; to make illustrious; to adorn;

to ennoble. *ppr.* dignifying, *pret. & pp.* dignified. [Fr. *dignifier*—L. *dignus*, worthy, and *facio*, to make.]
Dignitary, dig'ni-ta-ri, *n.* An ecclesiastic who holds a *dignity*, or a benefice which gives him some pre-eminence over mere priests and canons. [Fr. *dignitaire.*]
Dignity, dig'ni-ti, *n. Worth*; nobleness or elevation of mind; honourable place; degree of excellence; grandeur of mien; an elevated office, giving a high rank in society; the rank or title of a nobleman. [Fr. *dignité*—L. *dignitas*.]
Digress, di-gres', *vi. To go apart*; to go from the way; to wander; to depart from the main subject of a discourse or narration. [L. *digredior, digressus—gradior*, to step.]
Digression, di-gre'shon, *n. Act of digressing*; a departure from the main subject under consideration; the part of a discourse which deviates from the main subject, but which may have some relation to it. [L. *digressio*.]
Digressional, di-gre'shon-al, *a. Departing from the main purpose or subject.*
Digressive, di-gres'iv, *a. Departing from the main subject*; partaking of the nature of digression.
Digressively, di-gres'iv-li, *adv. By way of digression.*
Dike, dīk, *n. A mound*; a mound of earth, of stones, or of other materials, forming an embankment; a vein of basalt, green-stone, or other stony substance.—*vt. To surround or protect with a dike*; to secure by a bank. *ppr.* diking, *pret. & pp.* diked. [Sax. *dic*, a mound, bank.]
Dilacerate, di-la'sē-rāt, *vt. To rend asunder*; to separate by force. *ppr.* dilacerating, *pret. & pp.* dilacerated. [L. *dilacero, dilaceratus—lacero*, to tear.]
Dilaceration, di-la'sē-rā''shon, *n. Act of rending asunder*; a tearing. [Fr. *dilacération.*]
Dilapidate, di-la'pi-dāt, *vt.* To pull down; to squander.—*vi.* To go to ruin; to fall by decay. *ppr.* dilapidating, *pret. & pp.* dilapidated. [L. *dilapido, dilapidatus—lapis*, a stone.]
Dilapidated, di-la'pi-dāt-ed, *p.a.* Wasted; ruined; pulled down.
Dilapidation, di-la'pi-dā''shon, *n.* Decay; ruin; destruction; ecclesiastical waste; a voluntary wasting or suffering to go to decay any building in possession of an incumbent. [Fr.]
Dilatability, di-lāt'a-bil''li-ti, *n.* Quality of being dilatable.
Dilatable, di-lāt'a-bl, *a. Capable of being dilated*; capable of expansion; possessing elasticity; elastic. [Fr.]
Dilatation, di-lat-ā'shon, *n.* The expanding of a body into greater bulk by its own elastic power; the state of being expanded. [Fr.]
Dilate, di-lāt', *vt.* To expand; to swell. *vi.* To widen; to swell or extend in all directions; to speak largely and copiously; to dwell on in narration (with *on* or *upon*). *ppr.* dilating, *pret. & pp.* dilated. [Fr. *dilater*—L. *fero, latum*, to carry.]
Dilated, di-lāt'ed, *p.a.* Expanded; distended.
Dilatorily, di'la-tō-ri-li, *adv. With delay*; tardily.
Dilatoriness, di'la-tō-ri-nes, *n. Quality of being dilatory* or late; lateness.
Dilatory, di'la-tō-ri, *a.* Slow; late; tardy; given to procrastination; making de-

lay; sluggish; loitering. [Fr. *dilatoire.*]
Dilemma, di-lem'ma, *n. Something taken twice*; a difficult or doubtful choice; a vexatious alternative; a state of things in which evils present themselves on every side. [Gr. *dilemma—lambano*, to take.]
Diligence, di'li-jens, *n.* Carefulness; steady application in business of any kind; assiduity; watchful attention; constancy; heedfulness. [L. *diligentia—lego*, to choose.]
Diligent, di'li-jent, *a.* Careful of or about; constant in effort to accomplish what is undertaken; industrious; persevering; prosecuted with care and constant effort. [L. *diligens*.]
Diligently, di'li-jent-li, *adv. In a diligent manner.*
Diluent, di'lū-ent, *a. Diluting*; weakening the strength of, by mixture with water.—*n.* That which thins; that which weakens the strength of. [L. *diluens—luo*, to wash.]
Dilute, di-lūt', *vt.* To render liquid or more liquid; to make thin or more fluid; to make weak or weaker, as colour, by mixture.—*vi.* To become attenuated or diluted. *ppr.* diluting, *pret. & pp.* diluted.—*a.* Thin; reduced in strength, as spirit or colour. [L. *diluo, dilutus—luo*, to wash.]
Dilution, di-lū'shon, *n. Act of diluting*, or of making thin, weak, or more liquid. [Low L. *dilutio*.]
Diluvial, Diluvian, di-lū'vi-al, di-lū'vi-an, *a. Pertaining to a flood or deluge*, more especially to the deluge in Noah's days; effected or produced by a deluge. [L. *diluvialis—diluo*, to wash away.]
Diluvialist, di-lū'vi-al-ist, *n. One who explains geological phenomena by the deluge.*
Dim, dim, *a. Fading*; obscured; shut up from the sight; dusky; not seeing clearly; not clearly seen; mysterious; tarnished.—*vt. To dull*; to cloud; to obscure; to render dull, as the powers of conception; to sully. *ppr.* dimming, *pret. & pp.* dimmed. [Sax.—Heb. *tāman*, to conceal.]
Dimension, di-men'shon, *n. A measuring*; the measure of a thing; the extent of a body, or length, breadth, and thickness, or depth (usually in the plural); the definite bulk or size of a thing. [Fr.—L. *metior, mensus*, to measure.]
Dimensioned, di-men'shond, *a. Having dimensions.*
Diminish, di-min'ish, *vt. To lessen*; to take from; to abate; to degrade.—*vi. To become less*; to decrease. [Fr. *diminuer*—L. *minuo*, to lessen.]
Diminished, di-min'isht, *p.a. Lessened*; made smaller; contracted.
Diminution, di-min-ū'shon, *n. Act of diminishing*; state of becoming less. [Fr.—L. *diminutio.*]
Diminutive, di-min'ūt-iv, *a. Small*; little.—*n.* A word formed from another word, usually an appellative or generic term, to express a *little thing* of the kind; something very small. [Fr. *diminutif.*]
Diminutively, di-min'ūt-iv-li, *adv. In a diminutive manner.*
Diminutiveness, di-min'ūt-iv-nes, *n.* Want of bulk; want of dignity.
Dimissory, di-mis'sō-ri, *a. Sending away*; dismissing from the diocese of one bishop into that of another; granting leave to depart. [Low L. *dimissorius*—L. *mitto, missum*, to send.]
Dimity, di'mi-ti, *n. Cloth woven with a*

Fāte, fär, fat, fall; mē, met, hėr; pīne, pin; nōte, not, mōve; tūbe, tub bull; oil, pound.

double thread. [Gr. *dis*, twice, and *mitos*, a thread of the warp.]

Dimly, dim′li, *adv.* In a *dim* or obscure manner; darkly; darkishly; with a faint light.

Dimmish, dim′ish, *a. Somewhat dim*; obscure.

Dimness, dim′nes, *n. State of being dim*; dulness of sight; want of brightness; stupidity.

Dimple, dim′pl, *n.* A small natural cavity or depression in the cheek or other part of the face.—*vi.* To sink into *depressions* or little inequalities. *ppr.* dimpling, *pret. & pp.* dimpled. [seemingly corrupted from *dintle*, a little hole, dimin. of *dint*, a hole.]

Dimpled, dim′pld, *p.a. Set with dimples.*

Din, din, *n. Thunder!*; a loud sound; a rattling or rumbling sound, long continued.—*vt. To thunder!*; to stun with noise; to harass with clamour. *ppr.* dinning, *pret. & pp.* dinned. [Sax. *dyne*, noise—Sans. *stan*, to thunder.]

Dine, dīn, *vi. To feed*; to eat the chief meal of the day.—*vt. To feed!*; to give *a dinner to*; to furnish with the principal meal. *ppr.* dining, *pret. & pp.* dined. [Sax. *dynan*, to feed.]

Ding, ding, *vt. To beat*; to thrust or dash with violence. [Sax. *dencgan*.]

Dingdong, ding′dong. A term used to express the sound of bells.

Dinginess, din′ji-nes, *n.* A dusky or dark hue; brownness.

Dingle, ding′gl, *n.* A narrow dale or valley between hills. [dimin. from *den*.]

Dingy, din′ji, *a. Dung-coloured*; of a dark colour; brown; soiled; sullied. [from Sax. *dyngan*, to manure.]

Dining, dīn′ing, *p.a. Pertaining to dinner.*

Dinner, din′nèr, *n.* The meal taken about the middle of the day; the principal meal of the day, eaten between noon and evening; an entertainment; a feast. [Fr. *dîner*.]

Dint, dint, *n.* The mark made by a blow; a cavity made by a *blow*; force; power exerted.—*vt.* To make a mark or cavity on by a *blow* or by pressure. [Sax. *dynt*, a blow.]

Diocesan, di-os′es-an, *a. Pertaining to a diocese.*—*n.* A bishop; one in possession of a diocese. [Low L. *diocesanus*.]

Diocese, di′ō-sēs, *n. Housekeeping*†; a province; an ecclesiastical division of a kingdom or state, subject to the authority of a bishop. [Gr. *dioikēsis*—*oikos*, a house.]

Dioptric, di-op′trik, *a.* Assisting the sight in the view of distant objects; pertaining to dioptrics. [Gr. *dioptrikos—optomai*, to see.]

Dioptrics, di-op′triks, *n.* The science of refracted light, or of light passing through different mediums, as through air, water, or glass.

Diorama, di-ō-rä′ma, *n. A seeing through*; a contrivance for giving a high degree of optical illusion to paintings exhibited in a building prepared for the purpose, the spectator looking through a large aperture. [Gr. *horama*, a sight —*horaō*, to see.]

Dioramic, di-ō-ram′ik, *a. Pertaining to a diorama.*

Dip, dip, *vt. To plunge* for a short time in water, or other liquid substance; to put into a fluid and withdraw; to baptize by immersion; to take concern in. —*vi.* To be *immersed* in a liquid; to enter; to pierce; to engage; to look cursorily (with *on* or *into*); to choose

by chance; to incline downward. *ppr.* dipping, *pret. & pp.* dipped or dipt. *n. Act of dipping* in any liquid; a sloping; depression. [Sax. *dyppan*.]

Diphtheria, dif-thē′ri-a, *n.* An inflammatory disease of the throat, which is accompanied by the formation of a false *membrane*. [Gr.*diphthēra*, leather —*dephō*, to soften, to prepare.]

Diphthong, dif′thong, *n. A double vowel* sound; a union of two vowels pronounced in one syllable. [Gr. *diphthongos—phthongos*, sound.]

Diphthongal, dif-thong′gal, *a. Belonging to a diphthong.*

Diploma, di-plō′ma, *n. Anything folded double*, as a letter; a letter or writing conferring some power, authority, privilege, or honour. [Gr. *diplōma*—*diploō*, to double.]

Diplomacy, di-plō′ma-si, *n.* The science of conducting negotiations, and making treaties *between nations or states*; forms of negotiation; a diplomatic body; the agency or management of ministers at a foreign court; skill in securing advantages. [Fr. *diplomatie*.]

Diplomatic, dip-lō-mat′ik, *a. Relating to diplomacy* or to a body of ministers at a foreign court; relating to diplomatics.

Diplomatically, dip-lō-mat′ik-al-li, *adv.* According to the rules of *diplomacy*.

Diplomatics, dip-lō-mat′iks, *n.* The science of deciphering ancient writings, as *diplomas*, charters, &c., and of ascertaining their authenticity, date, &c.

Diplomatist, di-plō′mat-ist, *n. One skilled* or engaged in *diplomacy*.

Dipper, dip′ėr, *n. He or that which dips*; a ladle; a bird, the water-ousel.

Dire, dīr, *a. Fearful*; dismal; terrible; gloomy; destructive; evil in a great degree. [L. *dirus*.]

Direct, di-rekt′, *a. Made straight*; right; appearing to move forward from west to east, as a heavenly body; in the line of father and son; leading or tending to an end by a straight course; open; not ambiguous; plain; express. *vt. To set straight*; to point or aim in a straight line, toward a place or object; to show the right course to; to conduct; to lead; to dispose; to prescribe; to point out; to instruct. [L. *directus—rego, rectum*, to make straight.]

Directed, di-rekt′ed, *p.a.* Regulated; governed; instructed.

Direction, di-rek′shon, *n. Act of directing*; aim at a certain point; a pointing toward, in a straight line or course; course; guidance; instruction in what manner to proceed; a putting into the right path; prescription; command; the address of a letter; promptness!. [Fr.]

Directive, di-rekt′iv, *a. Having the power of direction*; informing; instructing. [Low L. *directivus*.]

Directly, di-rekt′li, *adv.* In a *straight line* or course; rectilineally; expressly; without ambiguity.

Directness, di-rekt′nes, *n. State or quality of being direct*; straightness; a straight course; nearness of way.

Director, di-rekt′ėr, *n. One who directs*; one who prescribes to others, by virtue of authority; an instructor; a counsellor; one appointed to transact the affairs of a company; a rule; that which controls by influence.

Directorate, di-rekt′ėr-āt, *n. Office* or *body of directors*. [Fr. *directorat*.]

Directorial, di-rek-tō′ri-al, *a. Containing direction* or command. [Low L. *directorius*.]

Directorship, di-rek′tėr-ship, *n. The condition* or *office of a director*.

Directory, di-rek′tō-ri, *a. Containing directions*; enjoining; instructing.—*n. A rule to direct*; a book containing directions for public worship; a book containing an alphabetical list of the inhabitants of a city, with their places of abode; a board of directors. [Fr. *directoire*.]

Directress, Directrix, di-rekt′res, di-rekt′riks, *n. A female who directs.*

Direful, dīr′ful, *a. Dire*; dreadful; terrible; calamitous.

Direfully, dir′ful-li, *adv.* Dreadfully.

Direfulness, dir′ful-nes, *n. Dreadfulness*; calamitousness.

Dirge, dėrj, *n.* A funeral service in Latin, beginning with *Dirige Domine nos—direct or guide us, O Lord*; a hymn intended to express grief, sorrow, and mourning. [L. *dirige—rego*, to rule.]

Dirk, dėrk, *n.* A kind of *dagger* or poniard. [Ir. *duirc*.]

Dirt, dėrt, *n. Excrement*; earth; mire; whatever, adhering to anything, renders it foul or unclean.—*vt.* To make foul; to soil; to bedaub; to defile. [Sax. *gedritan*, to go to stool.]

Dirtily, dėrt′i-li, *adv.* In a *dirty manner*; foully; nastily; filthily.

Dirtiness, dėrt′i-nes, *n. State of being dirty*; filthiness; foulness; nastiness.

Dirty, dėrt′i, *a. Soiled with dirt*; foul; not clean; not pure; cloudy; dark; mean; despicable; grovelling.—*vt. To soil with dirt*; to make filthy; to tarnish. *ppr.* dirtying, *pret. & pp.* dirtied.

Disability, dis-a-bil′i-ti, *n. Want of ability*; want of competent intellectual power; want of qualification; incapacity to do a legal act.

Disable, dis-ā′bl, *vt. To render unable*; to deprive of competent natural or mental strength; to disqualify; to incapacitate. *ppr.* disabling, *pret. & pp.* disabled. [*dis* and *able*.]

Disabled, dis-ā′bld, *p.a.* Rendered incapable; deprived of means.

Disabuse, dis-a-būz′, *vt.* To undeceive; to disengage from fallacy or deception; to set right. *ppr.* disabusing, *pret. & pp.* disabused. [Fr. *désabuser*.]

Disadvantage, dis-ad-van′tāj, *n. Want of advantage*; that which prevents success, or renders it difficult; injury; damage. [Fr. *désavantage*.]

Disadvantageous, dis-ad′van-tāj″ē-us, *p.a.* Unfavourable to success or prosperity; not adapted to promote interest, reputation, or other good.

Disadvantageously, dis-ad′van-tāj″ē-us-li, *adv. In a disadvantageous manner.*

Disaffect, dis-af-fekt′, *vt.* To alienate the *affections* of; to make less faithful to a person, party, or cause; to make discontented.

Disaffected, dis-af-fekt′ed, *p.a.* Indisposed to favour or support; unfriendly.

Disaffection, dis-af-fek′shon, *n.* Alienation of *affection*; positive enmity, or opposition of feeling; dislike; disloyalty; hostility.

Disagree, dis-a-grē′, *vi. Not to agree*; to be not the same; to be of a different opinion; to dissent; to be in a state of opposition; to be unsuitable or unfitted. (With *with*.) *ppr.* disagreeing, *pret. & pp.* disagreed.

Disagreeable, dis-a-grē′a-bl, *a. Not agreeable*; offensive; displeasing.

ph, *chain*; j, *job*; g, *go*; ng, *sing*; ᴛʜ, *then*; th, *thin*; w, *wig*; wh, *whig*; zh, *azure*; † obsolete.

Disagreeableness, dis-a-grē'a-bl-nes, n. Unsuitableness; unpleasantness; offensiveness to the mind or to the senses.
Disagreeably, dis-a-grē'a-bli, adv. Unsuitably; unpleasantly; offensively.
Disagreement, dis-a-grē'ment, n. Difference; unsuitableness; unlikeness; discrepancy; dissension; discord.
Disallow, dis-al-lou', vt. To refuse to allow; not to grant; not to make or suppose lawful; to disapprove; to prohibit; to condemn; to reject.—vi. To refuse permission; not to grant. (With of.)
Disallowable, dis-al-lou'a-bl, a. Not allowable; not to be suffered.
Disallowance, dis-al-lou'ans, n. Refusal to allow; disapprobation; condemnation; censure; rejection.
Disannex, dis-an-neks', vt. To separate, as that which has been annexed.
Disannul, dis-an-nul', vt. To annul; to make void; to deprive of authority or force. ppr. disannulling, pret. & pp. disannulled. [dis, augment. and annul.]
Disappear, dis-ap-pēr', vi. To vanish from the sight; to cease; to withdraw from observation; to cease to be.
Disappearance, dis-ap-pēr'ans, n. A removal from sight.
Disappoint, dis-ap-point', vt. To defeat of expectation or intention; to hinder from the enjoyment of that which was intended or expected; to frustrate; to foil; to defeat.
Disappointed, dis-ap-point'ed, p.a. Frustrated; unprepared.
Disappointment, dis-ap-point'ment, n. Defeat or failure of expectation, hope, wish, or intention; frustration; miscarriage.
Disapprobation, dis-ap'prō-bā"shon, n. A disapproving; dislike; the act of the mind which condemns what is supposed to be wrong.
Disapproval, dis-ap-pröv'al, n. Disapprobation; dislike.
Disapprove, dis-ap-pröv', vt. To condemn in opinion or judgment; to censure as wrong; to manifest dislike of; to reject as disliked. (Sometimes with of.) ppr. disapproving, pret. & pp. disapproved. [Fr. désapprouver.]
Disapprovingly, dis-ap-pröv'ing-li, adv. By disapprobation.
Disarm, dis-ärm', vt. To take the arms or weapons from; to deprive of force or means of annoyance; to render harmless; to quell; to divest of anything injurious. [Fr. désarmer.]
Disarmament, dis-ärm'a-ment, n. Act of disarming.
Disarmed, dis-ärmd', p.a. Deprived of arms; rendered harmless; subdued.
Disarming, dis-ärm'ing, p.n. The act of depriving of arms.
Disarrange, dis-a-rānj', vt. To put out of arrangement; to derange. ppr. disarranging, pret. & pp. disarranged.
Disarrangement, dis-a-rānj'ment, n. Act of disarranging, or of disturbing order or method; disorder.
Disarray, dis-a-rā', vt. To strip of array; to undress; to throw into disorder; to rout, as troops.—n. Disorder; confusion; loss or want of array or regular order; undress.
Disaster, diz-as'tėr, n. Any unfortunate event, especially a sudden misfortune; mishap; calamity; mischance; unhappiness; grief; catastrophe; fatal end. vt. To blast by the influence of a baleful star. [Fr. désastre—Gr. astēr, a star.]
Disastrous, diz-as'trus, a. Ill-starred;

unlucky; occasioning loss or injury; gloomy; threatening a fatal result.
Disastrously, dis-as'trus-li, adv. Unfortunately; in a dismal manner.
Disavouch, dis-a-vouch', vt. To disavow.
Disavow, dis-a-vou', vt. To annul, as a vow; to deny; to disown; to deny to be true, as a fact or charge respecting one's self; to reject; to dissent from. [dis and avow.]
Disavowal, dis-a-vou'al, n. A disowning; denial; rejection.
Disband, dis-band', vt. To dismiss from military service; to scatter; to disperse.—vi. To retire from military service; to break up; to separate; to dissolve connection.
Disbanded, dis-band'ed, p.a. Dismissed from military service; separated.
Disbar, dis-bär', vt. To expel, as a barrister from the bar. ppr. disbarring, pret. & pp. disbarred. [dis and bar.]
Disbelief, dis-bē-lēf', n. Refusal of credit or faith; denial of belief; distrust; unbelief; scepticism.
Disbelieve, dis-bē-lēv', vt. Not to believe; to hold not to be true or not to exist; to refuse to credit. ppr. disbelieving, pret. & pp. disbelieved.
Disbench, dis-bensh', vt. To drive from a bench.
Disburden, dis-bėr'dn, vt. To remove a burden from; to throw off, as a burden; to discharge; to relieve.—vi. To ease the mind; to be relieved.
Disburse, dis-bėrs', vt. To pay out, as money; to spend or lay out. ppr. disbursing, pret. & pp. disbursed. [Fr. débourser—L. bursa, a purse.]
Disbursement, dis-bėrs'ment, n. Act of disbursing, or of paying out; the money or sum paid out. [Fr. déboursement.]
Disburthen, dis-bėr'THen, vt. and i. A different orthography of disburden.
Disc, disk, n. A round flat body; the face of a celestial body; the face of a circular plate; the width of the aperture of a telescope. [L. discus.]
Discard, dis-kärd', vt. To turn out from service or employment, or from society; to cast off; to dismiss; to displace; to discharge.
Discase, dis-kās', vt. To take off a covering from; to strip.
Discern, dis-sėrn', vt. To distinguish; to discriminate; to discover; to see; to discover by the intellect; to have knowledge of; to judge.—vi. To see or understand the difference; to make distinction; to judge. [L. discerno—cerno, to distinguish.]
Discerner, dis-sėrn'ėr, n. One who discerns; that which distinguishes or causes to understand.
Discernible, dis-sėrn'i-bl, a. That may be discerned.
Discernibly, dis-sėrn'i-bli, adv. In a manner to be discerned.
Discerning, dis-sėrn'ing, p.a. Having power to discern; capable of seeing, knowing, and judging; sharp-sighted; penetrating; acute.
Discerningly, dis-sėrn'ing-li, adv. With discernment; acutely; with judgment.
Discernment, dis-sėrn'ment, n. Act or power of discerning; judgment; discrimination; sagacity.
Discharge, dis-chärj', vt. To unload or remove the cargo of; to free from; to release; to let go the charge of; to let fly or go, as a missile; to fire off; to give vent to; to pay; to clear off by payment; to send away, as a creditor by payment; to acquit; to relieve; to clear; to put away; to expel; to execute; to dismiss; to set at liberty;

to disclose; to cancel; to put an end to; to relieve, as of incumbent weight. vi. To throw off or deliver a load. ppr. discharging, pret. & pp. discharged.—n. Act of discharging; an unloading, as of a ship; a throwing out; matter emitted; dismission from office or service; writing which evidences the dismission; release from obligation, debt, or penalty; absolution from a crime; price paid for deliverance; execution; release from imprisonment; escape; payment, as of a debt. [Fr. décharger.]
Discharged, dis-chärjd', p.a. Let off; shot; dismissed from service; paid; freed from debt or penalty; liberated; performed; executed.
Discharger, dis-chärj'ėr, n. He or that which discharges.
Disciple, dis-sī'pl, n. A learner; one who receives instruction from another; an adherent to the doctrines of another; a pupil; a follower; a partizan.—vt. To teach; to punish. [L. discipulus—disco, to learn.]
Discipleship, dis-sī'pl-ship, n. The state of a disciple.
Disciplinable, dis'si-plin-a-bl, a. Capable of discipline, or of instruction; that may be subjected to discipline. [Fr.]
Disciplinarian, dis'si-plin-ā"ri-an, a. Pertaining to discipline.—n. One who enforces discipline or adherence to stated rules; a martinet.
Disciplinary, dis'si-plin-a-ri, a. Pertaining to discipline; intended for instruction. [Fr. disciplinaire.]
Discipline, dis'si-plin, n. Instruction; training; culture; instruction and government; order; rule; subjection to laws; punishment; correction; execution of ecclesiastical laws.—vt. To subject to discipline; to train up in good order, method, good conduct, and habits; to direct; to chastise; to punish. ppr. disciplining, pret. & pp. disciplined. [Fr.—L. disciplina.]
Disciplined, dis'si-plind, p.a. Instructed; educated; corrected; chastised; punished.
Disclaim, dis-klām', vt. To deny all claim to; to reject as not belonging to one's self; openly to reject any union or connection with; to disown; to renounce.—vi. To disavow all part or share.
Disclaimer, dis-klām'ėr, n. One who disclaims; a formal disavowal; renunciation.
Disclose, dis-klōz', vt. To open; to uncover; to unveil; to discover; to reveal; to divulge. ppr. disclosing, pret. & pp. disclosed. [L. claudo, clausum, to shut.]
Disclosure, dis-klō'zhėr, n. Act of disclosing; an uncovering and opening to view; utterance of what was secret; that which is disclosed or made known. [Low L. clausūra, a shutting.]
Discoloration, dis-kul'ėr-ā"shon, n. Act of altering the colour; a staining; alteration of colour; alteration of complexion or appearance; a stain.
Discolour, dis-kul'ėr, vt. To alter the natural hue or colour of; to stain; to alter the complexion of; to change the appearance of. [L. discoloro—color, colour.]
Discoloured, dis-kul'ėrd, p.a. Altered in colour; stained.
Discomfit, dis-kom'fit, vt. To unfasten; to defeat; to scatter in fight; to cause to flee; to vanquish.—n. Rout; disper-

sion; defeat; overthrow. [Fr. *déconfire*, *déconfit*—L. *Apo*, to fix.]
Discomfited, dis-kom'fit-ed, *p.a.* Routed; defeated; overthrown.
Discomfiture, dis-kom'fit-ūr, *n.* Rout; overthrow; frustration; disappointment. [Old Fr. *desconfiture*.]
Discomfort, dis-kum'fert, *n.* Want of comfort; uneasiness; disturbance of peace; pain; grief; inquietude.
Discomfortable, dis-kum'fért-a-bl, *a. Uncomfortable.*
Discommend, dis-kom-mend', *vt.* To blame; to censure; to mention with disapprobation.
Discompose, dis-kom-pōz', *vt.* To derange; to throw into confusion, as affairs; to disturb the peace and quietness of, as of the mind or temper; to disconcert; to vex. *ppr.* discomposing, *pret. & pp.* discomposed.
Discomposed, dis-kom-pōzd', *p.a.* Disordered; ruffled; agitated.
Discomposure, dis-kom-pō'zhūr, *n. State of being discomposed;* disorder; agitation; disturbance; perturbation.
Disconcert, dis-kon-sért', *vt.* To discompose; to break or interrupt, as a plan or harmonious scheme; to unsettle, as the mind; to ruffle; to frustrate.
Disconcerted, dis-kon-sért'ed, *p.a.* Broken; disordered; defeated.
Disconnect, dis-kon-nekt', *vt.* To dissolve, as a pre-existing *connection;* to separate; to disunite.
Disconnected, dis-kon-nekt'ed, *p.a.* Separated; disunited.
Disconnection, dis-kon-nek'shon, *n. Act of disconnecting* or separating; state of being disunited; separation.
Disconsolate, dis-kon'sō-lāt, *a. Comfortless;* hopeless, or not expecting comfort; sad; gloomy; cheerless. [L. *consolor*, *consolatus*, to console.]
Disconsolately, dis-kon'sō-lāt-li, *adv. In a disconsolate manner.*
Discontent, dis-kon-tent', *n. Want of content;* uneasiness of mind; dissatisfaction.
Discontented, dis-kon-tent'ed, *p.a.* Uneasy in mind; dissatisfied; unquiet.
Discontentedly, dis-kon-tent'ed-li, *adv. In a discontented manner* or mood.
Discontentedness, dis-kon-tent'ed-nes, *n. State of being discontented;* uneasiness of mind; dissatisfaction.
Discontenting, dis-kon-tent'ing, *p.a. Feeling discontent.*
Discontentment, dis-kon-tent'ment, *n. Discontent;* uneasiness; inquietude.
Discontinuance, dis-kon-tin'ū-ans, *n. Interruption of continuance;* want of union; separation.
Discontinuation, dis-kon-tin'ū-ā"shon, *n.* Disruption of parts; separation of parts; intermission. [Fr.]
Discontinue, dis-kon-tin'ū, *vt.* To leave off; to cause to cease; to break off; to cease to take or receive.—*vi.* To cease; to leave the possession or lose an established or long-enjoyed right. *ppr.* discontinuing, *pret. & pp.* discontinued.
Discontinuity, dis-kon'tin-ū"i-ti, *n. Want of continuity;* disunion of parts.
Discontinuous, dis-kon-tin'ū-us, *a. Not continuous;* broken off; interrupted.
Discord, dis'kord, *n. Want of concord;* disagreement; want of order or harmony; variance; dissension; strife; disagreement of sounds. [L. *discordia*—*cor, cordis,* the heart.]
Discordance, dis-kord'ans, *n. Want of concord;* discord; disagreement; inconsistency. [Fr.]
Discordant, dis-kord'ant, *a. Wanting agreement;* being at variance; disagreeing; incongruous; contrary; dissonant; inharmonious; jarring. [L. *discordans.*]
Discordantly, dis-kord'ant-li, *adv. In a discordant manner.*
Discount, dis'kount, *n. A counting apart;* a sum deducted for prompt payment; an allowance, according to the rate of interest, for money advanced before it is due; a lending; the act of discounting.
Discount, dis-kount', *vt. To count back;* to pay back again; to advance the amount of, as of a bill, deducting the interest or other rate.
Discountable, dis-kount'a-bl, *a. That may be discounted.*
Discountenance, dis-koun'ten-ans, *vt. To abash;* to dishearten; to restrain by frowns, censure, or cold treatment. *n.* Cold treatment; disapprobation; whatever tends to check or discourage. *ppr.* discountenancing, *pret. & pp.* discountenanced.
Discounter, dis'kount-er, *n. One who advances money on discounts.*
Discounting, dis-kount'ing, *p.n.* The act or practice of advancing money on discounts.
Discourage, dis-ku'rāj, *vt. To dishearten;* to attempt to repress or prevent: to dissuade. *ppr.* discouraging, *pret. & pp.* discouraged.
Discouraged, dis-ku'rājd, *p.a. Disheartened;* dejected; checked.
Discouragement, dis-ku'rāj-ment, *n. Act of disheartening;* act of deterring from an undertaking; that which destroys or abates courage; that which deters from an undertaking. [Fr. *découragement.*]
Discouraging, dis-ku'rāj-ing, *p.a. Tending to dishearten.*
Discouragingly, dis-ku'rāj-ing-li, *adv. In a discouraging manner.*
Discourse, dis-kōrs', *n. A running over a subject in speech;* speech; a treatise; a speech; a sermon; mutual intercourse by spoken language; talk; the power of the mind to reason; act of this power.—*vi.* To treat of in a solemn set manner; to pass from premises to consequences.—*vt.* To utter or give forth. *ppr.* discoursing, *pret. & pp.* discoursed. [Fr. *discours*—L. *curro, cursum,* to run.]
Discourteous, dis-kōr'tē-us, *a. Void of courtesy;* rude; wanting in good manners.
Discourteously, dis-kōr'tē-us-li, *adv. In a rude or uncivil manner.*
Discourteousness, dis-kōr'tē-us-nes, *n.* Incivility; discourtesy.
Discourtesy, dis-kōr'tē-si, *n.* Incivility; rudeness; act of disrespect.
Discover, dis-kuv'er, *vt. To uncover;* to find out, as something not known before; to have the first sight of; to disclose; to bring out; to reveal; to tell; t detect.
Discoverable, dis-kuv'er-a-bl, *a. That may be discovered.*
Discovered, dis-kuv'erd, *p.a.* Disclosed to view; laid open; found out; detected.
Discoverer, dis-kuv'er-er, *n. One who discovers;* an explorer; a scout; a spy.
Discovery, dis-kuv'ē-ri, *n. Act of discovering;* a making known; action of finding something hidden; act of coming to the knowledge of; act of espying; first sight of; that which is first brought to light, seen, or known.
Discredit, dis-kred'it, *n. Want of credit;* some degree of disgrace; disrepute; dishonour; disbelief; distrust.—*vt.* To give no credit to; to disbelieve; to deprive of credit; to make less reputable; to bring into disesteem; to deprive of credibility. [Fr. *discrédit.*]
Discreditable, dis-kred'it-a-bl, *a. Tending to injure credit;* injurious to reputation; disgraceful; disreputable.
Discreditably, dis-kred'it-a-bli, *adv. In a discreditable manner.*
Discreet, dis-krēt', *a. Discerning;* prudent; wise in avoiding errors or evil, and in selecting the best means to accomplish a purpose; wary; not rash. [Fr. *discret*—L. *cerno, cretum,* to separate, to see distinctly.]
Discreetly, dis-krēt'li, *adv. In a discreet manner;* with discretion.
Discrepancy, dis'krep-an-si, *n.* Discordance; difference; disagreement; contrariety. [L. *discrepantia*—*crepo,* to crack.]
Discretion, dis-kre'shon, *n. Quality of being discreet;* knowledge and prudence; true discernment, united with caution; knowledge to govern one's self properly; capacity for wise management; exercise of judgment and prudence; liberty of acting according to one's own judgment. [Fr. *discretion*—L. *cerno, cretum,* to separate.]
Discretionarily, dis-kre'shon-a-ri-li, *adv. At discretion;* according to discretion.
Discretionary, dis-kre'shon-a-ri, *a.* Unrestrained except by *discretion* or judgment; that is to be directed by discretion only. [Fr. *discrétionnaire.*]
Discretive, dis-krēt'iv, *a. Disjunctive;* separating.
Discretively, dis-krēt'iv-li, *adv. In a discretive manner.*
Discriminate, dis-krim'in-āt, *vt. To separate;* to distinguish; to observe the difference between; to select from others; to make a distinction between; to distinguish by some note or mark. *vi. To make a difference* or distinction; to distinguish. (With *between.*) *ppr.* discriminating, *pret. & pp.* discriminated.—*a.* Distinguished; having the difference marked+. [L. *discrimino, discriminatus*—*cerno,* to separate.]
Discriminately, dis-krim'in-āt-li, *adv.* Distinctly; with minute distinction.
Discriminating, dis-krim'in-āt-ing, *p.a.* Distinguishing; able to make nice distinctions.
Discrimination, dis-krim'in-ā"shon, *n.* Act of observing a difference; discernment; clearness; acuteness; judgment; distinction. [Low L. *discriminatio.*]
Discriminative, dis-krim'in-āt-iv, *a.* That distinguishes; that makes the mark of distinction; characteristic; that observes distinction.
Discriminatively, dis-krim'in-āt-iv-li, *adv. With discrimination.*
Discrown, dis-kroun', *vt. To deprive of a crown.*
Discursive, dis-kérs'iv, *a. Running about+;* reasoning; capable of knowing and inferring by discourse; proceeding regularly from premises to consequences; roving; rambling. [Fr. *discursif*—L. *curro, cursum,* to run.]
Discursively, dis-kērs'iv-li, *adv. In a discursive manner.*
Discus, dis'kus, *n. A round, flat piece of iron, copper, or stone,* to be thrown in play; a quoit; the face of the sun or moon. [L.]
Discuss, dis-kus', *vt. To shake asunder;* to disperse; to debate; to agitate by argument; to clear of objections and difficulties; to sift; to examine by disputation; to ventilate; to reason on.

[L. *discutio, discussum—quatio, quassum,* to shake.]
Discussing, dis-kus'ing, p.n. *Discussion;* examination.
Discussion, dis-ku'shon n. Act of discussing; debate; the agitation of a subject with a view to elicit truth; the treating of a subject by argument. [Fr.]
Disdain, dis-dān', vt. *To think unworthy;* to deem worthless; to consider to be unworthy of notice, or unworthy of one's character; to scorn; to contemn.—n. Contempt; scorn; arrogance; haughtiness; pride. [Old Fr. *desdaigner*—L. *dignus,* worthy.]
Disdained, dis-dānd', pp. Despised; contemned; disdainful.
Disdainful, dis-dān'ful, a. *Full of disdain;* expressing disdain; contemptuous; scornful; haughty; indignant.
Disdainfully, dis-dān'ful-li, adv. Contemptuously; with scorn.
Disdainfulness, dis-dān'ful-nes, n. *Quality of being disdainful;* contempt.
Disease, diz-ēz', n. *Want of ease;* the cause of *uneasiness;* any state of a living body in which the natural functions of the organs are disturbed; illness; mental disorder; corrupt state of morals; civil disorder.—vt. *To afflict with disease;* to infect; to derange the vital functions of. ppr. diseasing, pret. & pp. diseased.
Diseased, diz-ēzd', p.a. Disordered; distempered; sick.
Disembark, dis-em-bärk', vt. *To remove from a bark or vessel to the land;* to put on shore.—vi. *To go out of a bark or ship to the land;* to land; to go ashore.
Disembarkation, dis-em-bärk-ā"shon, n. *Act of disembarking.*
Disembarrass, dis-em-ba'ras, vt. *To free from perplexity;* to clear; to extricate.
Disembarrassment, dis-em-ba'rasment, n. *Act of disembarrassing,* or of extricating from perplexity.
Disembitter, dis-em-bit'tėr, vt. *To free from bitterness;* to render pleasant.
Disembodied, dis-em-bo'did, p.a. *Divested of the body;* separated.
Disembody, dis-em-bo'di, vt. *To divest of body;* to free from flesh; to discharge from military array. ppr. disembodying, pret. & pp. disembodied.
Disembogue, dis-em-bōg', vt. *To pour out at the mouth of,* as a stream; to vent; to discharge into the ocean, a river, or a lake.—vi. To become discharged. ppr. disemboguing, pret. & pp. disembogued. [Sp. *desembocar,* to flow into the sea—Fr. *bouche,* a mouth.]
Disembowel, dis-em-bou'el, vt. *To take out the bowels of;* to take or draw from the bowels. ppr. disembowelling, pret. & pp. disembowelled.
Disembroil, dis-em-broil', vt. *To free from broil;* to disentangle; to free from perplexity.
Disenchant, dis-en-chant', vt. *To free from enchantment;* to deliver from the power of charms or spells.
Disenchantment, dis-en-chant'ment, n. *Act of disenchanting.*
Disencumber, dis-en-kum'bėr, vt. *To deliver from clogs and impediments;* to disburden.
Disencumbered, dis-en-kum'bėrd, p.a. *Freed from encumbrance.*
Disencumbrance, dis-en-kum'brans, n. *Deliverance from encumbrance,* or anything burdensome.
Disengage, dis-en-gāj', vt. *To set free;* to release; to extricate; to set free from any obligation or pursuit; to withdraw; to wean.—vt. *To set one's self free;* to withdraw one's affections. (With *from.*) ppr. disengaging, pret. & pp. disengaged.
Disengaged, dis-en-gājd', p.a. Vacant; not particularly occupied.
Disengagement, dis-en-gāj'ment, n. *Act of disengaging; state of being disengaged;* act of separating; release from obligation; freedom from attention; leisure.
Disengaging, dis-en-gāj'ing, p.a. Separating; loosing.
Disennoble, dis-en-nō'bl, vt. *To deprive of that which ennobles;* to deprive of title; to degrade. ppr. disennobling, pret. & pp. disennobled.
Disentangle, dis-en-tang'gl, vt. *To free from entanglement;* to free from perplexity; to set free from difficulties; to unravel; to clear; to disengage. ppr. disentangling, pret. & pp. disentangled.
Disentanglement, dis-en-tang'gl-ment, n. *Act of disentangling.*
Disenthrall, dis-en-thral', vt. To give freedom to.
Disentitle, dis-en-tī'tl, vt. *To deprive of title.* ppr. disentitling, pret. & pp. disentitled.
Disesteem, dis-es-tēm', n. *Want of esteem;* slight dislike; disregard.—vt. To dislike in a moderate degree; to consider with slight contempt; to slight.
Disfavour, dis-fā'vėr, n. Dislike; discountenance; unfavourable regard. vt. *To withhold or withdraw favour from;* to discountenance.
Disfiguration, dis-fi'gūr-ā"shon, n. *Act of disfiguring;* state of being disfigured.
Disfigure, dis-fi'gūr, vt. *To mar the figure of;* to change to a worse form; to impair the beauty, symmetry, or excellence of. ppr. disfiguring, pret. & pp. disfigured.
Disfigured, dis-fi'gūrd, p.a. Impaired in form or appearance.
Disfigurement, dis-fi'gūr-ment, n. Change of external form to the worse; defacement of beauty.
Disfranchise, dis-fran'chīz, vt. *To deprive of the rights and privileges of a free citizen;* to deprive of chartered rights. ppr. disfranchising, pret. & pp. disfranchised.
Disfranchised, dis-fran'chīzd, p.a. Deprived of some particular *franchise.*
Disfranchisement, dis-fran'chīz'ment, n. *Act of disfranchising;* state of being disfranchised.
Disfurnish, dis-fėr'nish, vt. *To strip of furniture;* to strip.
Disgorge, dis-gorj', vt. *To discharge from the gorge;* to vomit; to discharge violently from a confined place; to yield up what had been obtained wrongfully; to surrender. ppr. disgorging, pret. & pp. disgorged. [Old Fr. *desgorger—gorge,* the throat.]
Disgorgement, dis-gorj'ment, n. *Act of disgorging;* a vomiting.
Disgrace, dis-grās' n. *State of being deprived of grace or favour;* cause of shame; disfavour; opprobrium; reproach; dishonour; infamy.—vt. *To put out of grace;* to bring to shame; to degrade; to dishonour; to defame. ppr. disgracing, pret. & pp. disgraced.
Disgraced, dis-grāst' p.a. *Put out of favour;* brought under reproach.
Disgraceful, dis-grās'ful, a. Shameful; procuring shame; sinking reputation.
Disgracefully, dis-grās'ful-li, adv. *In a disgraceful manner.*
Disgracefulness, dis-grās'ful-nes, n. *Quality of being disgraceful;* ignominy.

Disguise, dis-gīz', vt. *To hide by a counterfeit appearance;* to cloak by a false show; to dissemble; to alter the form of and cause to exhibit an unusual appearance. ppr. disguising, pret. & pp. disguised.—n. *A counterfeit habit;* a false appearance; an assumed appearance, intended to deceive the beholder. [Old Fr. *desguiser—guise,* way.]
Disguised, dis-gīzd', p.a. Concealed by a *counterfeit habit* or appearance.
Disgust, dis-gust', n. *Distaste;* loathing; an unpleasant sensation in the mind, excited by something offensive.—vt. *To cause distaste in;* to offend the mind or moral taste of. [Old Fr. *desgoust*—L. *gustus,* taste.]
Disgustful, dis-gust'ful, a. Exciting aversion in the natural or moral taste.
Disgusting, dis-gust'ing, p.a. Provoking dislike; odious; hateful.
Disgustingly, dis-gust'ing-li, adv. *In a manner to give disgust.*
Dish, dish, n. A broad, round, open vessel, used for serving up meat at table; something in shape of a dish; the meat served in a dish; any particular kind of food.—vt. *To put in a dish;* to make hollow or concave. [Sax. *disc.*]
Dishabille, dis'a-bil, n. *An undress;* a loose, negligent dress for the morning. [Fr. *déshabillé.*]
Dishabit, dis-hab'it, vt. To drive from *a habitation.*
Dishearten, dis-härt'n, vt. *To deprive of heart;* to discourage; to impress with fear; to deject; to deter.
Disheartened, dis-härt'nd, p.a. *Discouraged;* cast down.
Disheartening, dis-härt'n-ing, p.a. *Discouraging;* depressing the spirits.
Dishevel, di-she'vel, vt. *To put out of order, as the hair;* to spread loosely, as the hair. ppr. dishevelling, pret. & pp. dishevelled. [Fr. *décheveler*—L. *capillus,* hair.]
Dishevelled, di-she'veld, p.a. Hanging loosely; flowing in disorder.
Dishonest, dis-on'est, a. *Void of honesty;* destitute of probity or good faith; having or exercising a disposition to deceive and defraud; proceeding from fraud or marked by it; knavish; perfidious; lewd.
Dishonestly, dis-on'est-li, adv. *In a dishonest manner.*
Dishonesty, dis-on'est-i, n. *Want of honesty,* or integrity in principle; faithlessness; disgrace; unchastity.
Dishonour, dis-on'ėr, n. *Want of honour;* disgrace; ignominy; reproach; opprobrium.—vt. *To deprive of honour;* to disgrace; to treat with indignity; to violate the chastity of; to decline to accept or pay, as a draft.
Dishonourable, dis-on'ėr-a-bl, a. *Destitute of honour;* base; vile; staining the character; in a state of neglect.
Dishonourably, dis-on'ėr-a-bli, adv. In a *dishonourable manner.*
Dishonoured, dis-on'ėrd, p.a. Disgraced; brought into disrepute.
Disinclination, dis-in'klin-ā"shon, n. Want of propensity; unwillingness; dislike; slight aversion.
Disincline, dis-in-klīn', vt. *To take away inclination from;* to make disaffected; to alienate from. ppr. disinclining, pret. & pp. disinclined.
Disinclined, dis-in-klīnd', p.a. *Not inclined;* averse.
Disinfect, dis-in-fekt', vt. *To cleanse from infection;* to purify from contagious matter.
Disinfectant, dis-in-fekt'ant, n. An

Disinfected dis-in-fekt'ed, p.a. *Cleansed from infection.*
Disinfecting, dis-in-fekt'ing, p.a. *Purifying from infection.*
Disinfection, dis-in-fek'shon, n. *Purification from infecting matter.*
Disingenuous, dis-in-jen'ū-us, a. *Not ingenuous;* not open, frank, and candid; unbecoming true honour; crafty; sly; cunning.
Disingenuously, dis-in-jen'ū-us-li, adv. *In a disingenuous manner;* unfairly.
Disingenuousness, dis-in-jen'ū-us-nes, n. *Low craft;* conduct or practices characterized by unfairness.
Disinherit, dis-in-he'rit, vt. *To deprive of an inheritance;* to prevent, as an heir, from coming into possession of any property or right.
Disinheritance, dis-in-he'rit-ans, n. *Act of disinheriting.*
Disinherited, dis-in-he'rit-ed, p.a. *Cut off from an inheritance.*
Disintegrable, dis-in'tē-gra-bl, a. *That may be disintegrated.*
Disintegrate, dis-in'tē-grāt, vt. *To separate,* as *the integrant parts* of a body by mechanical division. ppr. disintegrating, pret. & pp. disintegrated. [L. *integro, integratus—integer*, whole.]
Disintegrated, dis-in'tē-grāt-ed, p.a. *Separated into integrant parts* without chemical action.
Disintegration, dis-in'tē-grā"shon, n. *Act of separating integrant parts of a substance.* [L. *integratio.*]
Disinter, dis-in-tēr', vt. *To take out of a grave or out of the earth;* to bring from obscurity into view. ppr. disinterring, pret. & pp. disinterred.
Disinterested, dis-in'tēr-est-ed, a. *Not interested;* free from self-interest; not dictated by private advantage; impartial.
Disinterestedly, dis-in'tēr-est-ed-li, adv. *In a disinterested manner.*
Disinterestedness, dis-in'tēr-est-ed-nes, n. *Freedom from bias or prejudice on account of private interest;* indifference.
Disinterment, dis-in-tēr'ment, n. *Act of disinterring* or taking out of the earth.
Disinthral, dis-in-thral', vt. *To liberate from thrall;* to rescue from oppression. ppr. disinthralling, pret. & pp. disinthralled.
Disinthralment, dis-in-thral'ment, n. *Liberation from bondage.*
Disjoin, dis-join', vt. *To part asunder;* to disunite; to sever; to detach.—vi. To be separated; to part.
Disjoint, dis-joint', vt. *To separate, as parts united by joints;* to put out of joint; to separate, as united parts; to break, as the natural relations of a thing; to make incoherent.—vi. To fall in pieces.
Disjointed, dis-joint'ed, p.a. *Not coherent;* disconnected.
Disjointedness, dis-joint'ed-nes, n. *State of being disjointed.*
Disjunction, dis-jungk'shon, n. *Act of disjoining;* disunion. [L. *disjunctio.*]
Disjunctive, dis-jungk'tiv, a. *Separating;* uniting words or sentences in construction, but *disjoining* the sense. n. *A word that disjoins.* [L. *disjunctivus.*]
Disjunctively, dis-jungk'tiv-li, adv. *In a disjunctive manner;* separately.
Disk, disk, n. *A quoit;* the face of a celestial body, as of the sun, moon, or planets. [L. *discus.*]

Dislike, dis-līk', n. *Disrelish;* a moderate degree of hatred; aversion; antipathy; repugnance.—vt. *Not to like;* to regard with some aversion; to regard with some disgust, as food; to displease‡. ppr. disliking, pret. & pp. disliked.
Disliked, dis-līkt', p.a. *Regarded with dislike.*
Disliken‡, dis-līk'n, vt. *To make unlike.*
Dislimn‡, dis-lim', vt. To strike out of a picture.
Dislocate, dis'lō-kāt, vt. *To displace;* to put out of joint; to disjoint. ppr. dislocating, pret. & pp. dislocated. [L. *loco, locatus,* to place.]
Dislocation, dis-lō-kā'shon, n. *Act of dislocating;* state of being dislocated; displacement. [Fr.—L. *loco,* to place.]
Dislodge, dis-loj', vt. *To remove from a place of rest;* to drive from a place of rest, or from any station; to remove, as an army to other quarters.—vi. To go from a place of rest. ppr. dislodging, pret. & pp. dislodged.
Dislodgment, dis-loj'ment, n. *Act of dislodging;* displacement.
Disloyal, dis-loi'al, a. *Void of loyalty;* not true to allegiance; false to a sovereign; faithless; treacherous.
Disloyally, dis-loi'al-li, adv. *In a disloyal manner;* perfidiously.
Disloyalty, dis-loi'al-ti, n. *Want of loyalty* to a sovereign; violation of allegiance to a prince. [Old Fr. *desloyauté.*]
Dismal, diz'mal, a. *Dreary;* gloomy; dark; doleful; horrid; direful; calamitous; sorrowful; melancholy. [L. *dies malus,* an evil day.]
Dismally, diz'mal-li, adv. *Gloomily.*
Dismantle, dis-man'tl, vt. *To deprive,* as of dress; to strip; to throw open or off; to unrig; to deprive or strip, as of military furniture; to deprive, as of outworks or forts; to break down. ppr. dismantling, pret. & pp. dismantled.
Dismantled, dis-man'tld, p.a. *Divested.*
Dismask, dis-mask', vt. *To divest of a mask.*
Dismast, dis-mast', vt. *To break and carry away the masts* from.
Dismasted, dis-mast'ed, p.a. *Deprived of a mast* or masts.
Dismay, dis-mā', vt. *To produce fright* or terror in, as by *witchcraft;* to frighten; to appal; to dishearten; to depress.—n. A sinking of the spirits; dejection; fear; fright; terror.—vi. To be disheartened. [Sp. *desmaydr*—L. *maga,* a witch—Heb. *magor,* fear.]
Dismayed, dis-mād', p.a. Disheartened; terrified.
Dism‡, dem, n. The number ten.
Dismember, dis-mem'bēr, vt. *To separate, as member from member;* to tear or cut in pieces; to separate, as a part from the main body; to mutilate.
Dismembered, dis-mem'bērd, p.a. *Divided member from member.*
Dismemberment, dis-mem'bēr-ment, n. *The act of dismembering;* mutilation; division; separation.
Dismiss, dis-mis', vt. *To send away;* to permit to depart; to remove from office or employment; to despatch. [L. *dimitto, dimissus—mitto,* to send.]
Dismissal, dis-mis'al, n. *Dismission.*
Dismissed, dis-mist', p.a. *Sent away;* permitted to depart.
Dismission, dis-mi'shon, n. *Act of sending away;* removal from office; discharge. [L. *dimissio.*]
Dismount, dis-mount', vi. *To descend from a horse;* to descend from an elevation.—vt. To cause *to descend;* to unhorse; to throw or remove, as cannon from their carriages, or to render them unfit for service.
Dismounted, dis-mount'ed, p.a. *Thrown from carriages.*
Disobedience, dis-ō-bē'di-ens, n. *Neglect or refusal to obey;* the omission of that which is commanded to be done, or the doing of that which is forbid; breach of duty prescribed by authority.
Disobedient, dis-ō-bē'di-ent, a. *Omitting to do what is commanded,* or doing what is prohibited; not observant of duty or rules prescribed by authority.
Disobediently, dis-ō-bē'di-ent-li, adv. *In a disobedient manner.*
Disobey, dis-ō-bā', vt. *To omit or refuse to do what is commanded,* or to do what is forbid; to transgress, as an order or injunction.
Disoblige, dis-ō-blīj', vt. *To withhold a kindness or a service from;* to offend by an act of incivility; to injure in a slight degree. ppr. disobliging, pret. & pp. disobliged.
Disobligement, dis-ō-blīj'ment, n. *Act of disobliging.*
Disobliging, dis-ō-blīj'ing, p.a. *Not obliging;* not disposed to gratify the wishes of another; unkind; unaccommodating; discourteous.
Disobligingly, dis-ō-blīj'ing-li, adv. *In a disobliging manner;* offensively.
Disorbed, dis-orbd', a. *Thrown out of the proper orbit.*
Disorder, dis-or'dēr, n. *Want of order;* disarrangement; turbulence; bustle; malady; disease.—vt. *To put out of order;* to disturb, as any regular disposition or arrangement of things; to discompose; to produce indisposition in.
Disordered, dis-or'dērd, p.a. *Irregular;* unrestrained in behaviour; deranged.
Disorderly, dis-or'dēr-li, a. *Being without proper order;* confused; turbulent; contrary to law or good order.—adv. *In a disorderly manner.*
Disorganization, dis-or'gan-iz-ā"shon, n. *Act of disorganising;* state of being disorganized.
Disorganize, dis-or'gan-īz, vt. *To break or destroy the organic structure of;* to dissolve the regular system or union of parts in; to disarrange; to break up. ppr. disorganizing, pret. & pp. disorganized.
Disorganized, dis-or'gan-īzd, p.a. *Reduced to disorder.*
Disorganizing, dis-or'gan-īz-ing, p.a. *Disposed or tending to disorganise.*
Disown, dis-ōn', vt. *To refuse to acknowledge as belonging to one's self;* to disavow; to renounce; to disallow.
Disowned, dis-ōnd', p.a. *Not owned;* disallowed.
Disownment, dis-ōn'ment, n. *Act of disowning.*
Disparage, dis-pa'rāj, vt. *To dishonour by a comparison with something of less value or excellence;* to depreciate; to undervalue; to reproach; to derogate from; to degrade. ppr. disparaging, pret. & pp. disparaged. [Norm. *desparagier*—L. *dispar,* unequal.]
Disparagement, dis-pa'rāj-ment, n. *Injury by union or comparison with something of inferior excellence;* indignity; detraction; reproach; dishonour. [Norm.—L. *par,* equal.]
Disparaging, dis-pa'rāj-ing, p.a. *Disgracing;* dishonouring.
Disparagingly, dis-pa'rāj-ing-li, adv. *In a manner to disparage* or dishonour.
Disparity, dis-pa'ri-ti, n. *Inequality;*

ch, *chain;* j, *job;* g, *go;* ng, *sing;* ᴛʜ, *then;* th, *thin;* w, *wig;* wh, *whig;* zh, *asure;* † obsolete.

Dispark, dis-pärk', *vt.* To throw open, as a park; to lay open.

Dispassionate, dis-pa'shon-āt, *a.* Free from passion; unmoved by feelings; not dictated by passion; cool; serene; temperate; moderate.

Dispassionately, dis-pa'shon-āt-li, *adv.* Without passion; calmly; coolly.

Dispel, dis-pel', *vt.* To drive asunder; to scatter by driving or force; to banish.—*vi.* To fly different ways; to disappear, as clouds. *ppr.* dispelling, *pret. & pp.* dispelled. [L. *dispello—pello*, to drive.]

Dispensable, dis-pens'a-bl, *a.* That may be dispensed with.

Dispensary, dis-pens'a-ri, *n.* A shop in which medicines are dispensed to the poor, and medical advice given gratis; a shop in which medicines are compounded.

Dispensation, dis-pens-ā'shon, *n.* Act of dispensing; act of dealing out to different persons or places; exemption; that which is dispensed; the distribution of good and evil, natural or moral, in the divine government; a system of principles and rites enjoined. [Fr.—L. *dispensatio*.]

Dispensatory, dis-pens'a-tō-ri, *a.* Having power to grant dispensations.—*n.* A book containing the method of preparing the various kinds of medicines. [Low L. *dispensatorius*.]

Dispense, dis-pens', *vt.* To weigh out; to deal out in portions; to distribute; to administer; to apply; to distribute, as justice; to allow; to exempt; to excuse; to grant dispensation for. (With *with* in the last three senses.) *ppr.* dispensing, *pret & pp.* dispensed. [Fr. *dispenser*—L. *penso*, to weigh out.]

Dispenser, dis-pens'ėr, *n.* One who dispenses; one who distributes.

Dispensing, dis-pens'ing, *p.a.* That may dispense with; granting dispensation.

Dispeople, dis-pē'pl, *vt.* To depopulate. *ppr.* dispeopling, *pret. & pp.* dispeopled.

Disperse, dis-pėrs', *vt.* To scatter on all sides; to drive asunder; to dispel; to distribute; to deal out.—*vi.* To be scattered; to vanish, as fog or vapours. *ppr.* dispersing, *pret. & pp.* dispersed. [L. *dispergo, dispersus—spargo*, to scatter.]

Dispersed, dis-pėrst', *p.a.* Scattered.

Dispersion, dis-pėr'shon, *n.* Act of dispersing; state of being scattered; dissipation. [Fr.]

Dispirit, dis-pi'rit, *vt.* To deprive of spirit; to dishearten; to discourage; to cast down; to intimidate.

Dispirited, dis-pi'rit-ed, *p.a.* Dejected; intimidated; wanting energy.

Dispiriting, dis-pi'rit-ing, *p.a.* Dejecting; intimidating.

Displace, dis-plās', *vt.* To remove from its place; to remove from any state, condition, office, or dignity; to derange; to dismiss. *ppr.* displacing, *pret. & pp.* displaced.

Displacement, dis-plās'ment, *n.* The act of removing from the usual or proper place.

Display, dis-plā', *vt.* To unfold; to spread before the eyes or mind; to make manifest; to show; to show off; to parade. *vi.* To lay anything open; to talk without restraint; to make a great show of words.—*n.* An opening or unfolding; an exhibition of anything to the view, or to the thoughts; ostentatious show; pomp; exhibition. [Old Fr. *desployer*—L. *plico*, to fold.]

Displease, dis-plēz', *vt.* To offend; to dissatisfy; to provoke; to irritate; to be disagreeable to; to raise aversion in.—*vi.* To disgust; to raise aversion. *ppr.* displeasing, *pret. & pp.* displeased.

Displeasing, dis-plēz'ing, *p.a.* Disgusting; disagreeable.

Displeasure, dis-ple'zhūr, *n.* Dissatisfaction; offence; anger; resentment; that which displeases.

Displume, dis-plūm', *vt.* To strip of plumes; to strip of badges of honour.

Disponge†, dis'punj, *vt.* To sprinkle, as with water from a sponge.

Disport, dis-pōrt', *n.* Play; sport; pastime.—*vi.* To sport; to move lightly and without restraint; to move in gaiety.—*vt.* To divert or amuse (with recipr. pron.). [*dis*, augment. and *sport*.]

Disposable, dis-pōz'a-bl, *a.* Subject to disposal; not previously engaged or employed; free to be used or employed.

Disposal, dis-pōz'al, *n.* Act of disposing; disposition; government; conduct; power or right of bestowing.

Dispose, dis-pōz', *vt.* To place here and there; to set in right order; to range; to adjust; to set right; to apply to a particular purpose; to form for any purpose; to set in a particular frame, as the mind.—*vi.*† To bargain; to make terms. *ppr.* disposing, *pret. & pp.* disposed.—*n.*† Cast of mind. [Fr. *disposer*—L. *pono, positum*, to place.]

Disposed, dis-pōzd', *p.a.* Inclined; minded.

Disposer, dis-pōz'ėr, *n.* He who or that which disposes; a bestower; one who directs or regulates.

Disposing, dis-pōz'ing, *p.n.* Act of arranging; direction.

Disposition, dis-pō-zi'shon, *n.* Act of disposing, or state of being disposed; disposal; arrangement; order; natural fitness; natural constitution of the mind; the temper or frame of mind; affection of kindness or ill-will; inclination. [Fr.—L. *dispositio*.]

Dispossess, dis-poz-zes', *vt.* To put out of possession; to deprive of the actual occupancy of a thing.

Dispossession, dis-poz-ze'shon, *n.* Act of putting out of possession.

Dispraise, dis-prāz', *n.* The opposite of praise; blame; censure; reproach. *vt.* To blame; to censure; to mention with disapprobation, or some degree of reproach. *ppr.* dispraising, *pret. & pp.* dispraised.

Disproof, dis-prōf', *n.* A removal of proof adduced; confutation.

Disproperty†, dis-pro'pėr-ti, *vt.* To cause to be no longer property; to plunder.

Disproportion, dis-prō-pōr'shon, *n.* Want of proportion of one thing to another; want of suitableness; inequality.—*vt.* To deprive of proportion; to make unsuitable in form or quantity; to join unfitly.

Disproportional, dis-prō-pōr'shon-al, *a.* Not having due proportion to something else; unsuitable in form or quantity; inadequate.

Disproportionally, dis-prō-pōr'shon-al-li, *adv.* Without proportion.

Disproportionate, dis-prō-pōr'shon-āt, *a.* Not proportioned; unsymmetrical; inadequate.

Disproportionately, dis-prō-pōr'shon-āt-li, *adv.* In a disproportionate degree; unsuitably; inadequately.

Disproportioned, dis-prō-pōr'shond, *p.a.* Not proportioned.

Disproval, dis-prōv'al, *n.* Act of disproving; disproof.

Disprove, dis-prōv', *vt.* To divest of proof which has been adduced; to prove to be false; to confute. *ppr.* disproving, *pret. & pp.* disproved.

Dispurse†, dis-pėrs', *vt.* To disburse.

Disputable, dis-pūt'a-bl, *a.* Liable to be called in question or contested; contentious†. [Fr.]

Disputant, dis'pūt-ant, *n.* One who argues in opposition to another. [L. *disputans*.]

Disputation, dis-pūt-ā'shon, *n.* Act of disputing; controversy in words; an exercise in colleges, in which parties reason in opposition to each other on some question proposed. [L. *disputatio*.]

Disputatious, dis-pūt-ā'shi-us, *a.* Inclined to dispute; apt to controvert.

Disputative, dis-pūt'at-iv, *a.* Disposed to dispute; disputatious.

Dispute, dis-pūt', *vi.* To discuss; to contend in argument; to reason or argue in opposition; to debate; to altercate.—*vt.* To attempt to prove to be false; to call in question; to impugn; to argue; to discuss; to strive or contend for; to strive to maintain; to struggle against†.—*n.* Strife or contest in words or by arguments; disputation; controversy; difference. *ppr.* disputing, *pret. & pp.* disputed. [Fr. *disputer*—L. *puto*, to reckon.]

Disputer, dis-pūt'ėr, *n.* One who disputes; one who is given to disputes.

Disqualification, dis-kwo'li-fi-kā'shon, *n.* Act of disqualifying; that which disqualifies; disability.

Disqualify, dis-kwo'li-fī, *vt.* To divest of the qualities necessary for any purpose; to make unfit; to deprive of legal capacity. *ppr.* disqualifying, *pret. & pp.* disqualified.

Disquantity†, dis-kwon'ti-ti, *vt.* To diminish the quantity of.

Disquiet, dis-kwī'et, *n.* Want of quiet; want of tranquillity in body or mind; anxiety.—*a.*† Deprived of quiet.—*vt.* To deprive of peace or tranquillity; to make restless.

Disquieted, dis-kwī'et-ed, *p.a.* Made uneasy or restless; disturbed.

Disquieting, dis-kwī'et-ing, *p.a.* Tending to disturb the mind.

Disquietude, dis-kwī'et-ūd, *n.* Want of peace or tranquillity; uneasiness; anxiety.

Disquisition, dis-kwi-zi'shon, *n.* A systematic inquiry into any subject, by arguments; a treatise; elaborate essay. [Fr.—L. *disquisitio—quaero, quaesitum*, to seek.]

Disregard, dis-re-gärd', *n.* A withholding of regard; neglect; slight.—*vt.* To omit to take notice of; to neglect to observe; to slight as unworthy of notice.

Disregardful, dis-re-gärd'ful, *a.* Neglectful; negligent; heedless.

Disrelish, dis-rel'ish, *n.* Distaste; nauseousness; distaste or dislike, in a figurative sense.—*vt.* To have no relish for; to dislike; to feel some disgust at; to deprive of relish.

Disrepair, dis-rē-pār', *n.* A state of being not in repair.

Disreputable, dis-re'pūt-a-bl, *a.* Not reputable; not honourable; low; mean; tending to bring into disesteem; shameful.

Disreputably, dis-re'pūt-a-bli, *adv.* In a disreputable manner.

Disrepute, dis-rē-pūt', *n.* Loss of repute; disesteem; disgrace.

Disrespect, dis-rē-spekt′, n. *Want of respect;* disesteem; rudeness.—*vt.* To show disrespect to.
Disrespectful, dis-rē-spekt′fṳl, a. *Wanting in respect;* irreverent; uncivil; discourteous; unpolite; rude.
Disrespectfully, dis-rē-spekt′fṳl-li, adv. *In a disrespectful manner.*
Disrobe, dis-rōb′, vt. To divest of robes or garments; to strip of covering; to divest of any surrounding appendage. ppr. disrobing, pret. & pp. disrobed.
Disroot, dis-rōt′, vt. *To tear up the roots of or by the roots.*
Disruption, dis-rup′shon, n. *Act of rending asunder;* breach; rent; dilaceration. [L. *disruptio*—L. *rumpo, ruptum,* to break.]
Dissatisfaction, dis-sa′tis-fak″shon, n. *Want of satisfaction;* discontent; disapprobation; dislike.
Dissatisfactory, dis-sa′tis-fak″tō-ri, a. *Unable to give satisfaction;* giving discontent; displeasing.
Dissatisfied, dis-sa′tis-fid, p.a. Discontented; not pleased.
Dissatisfy, dis-sa′tis-fi, vt. *Not to satisfy;* to displease; to excite uneasiness in by frustrating expectations. ppr. dissatisfying, pret. & pp. dissatisfied.
Disseat, dis-sēt′, vt. *To remove from a seat.*
Dissect, dis-sekt′, vt. *To cut asunder;* to cut up; to anatomize; to divide and examine minutely or carefully. [L. *disseco, dissectus*—*seco,* to cut.]
Dissected, dis-sekt′ed, p.a. Opened and examined.
Dissectible, dis-sekt′i-bl, a. *That may be dissected.*
Dissecting, dis-sekt′ing, p.a. *Used in dissection.*
Dissection, dis-sek′shon, n. *Act of dissecting* an animal or vegetable for examination; anatomy; act of separating into constituent parts for the purpose of critical examination. [Fr.—L. *dissectio.*]
Dissector, dis-sekt′ér, n. *One who dissects;* an anatomist.
Disseize, dis-sēz′, vt. *To deprive of actual possession;* to dispossess wrongfully. ppr. disseizing, pret. & pp. disseized.
Dissemble, dis-sem′bl, vt. *To put on the semblance of;* to hide under a false appearance; to disguise; to conceal; to cloak.—vi. To assume a false appearance; to conceal the real fact or sentiments under some pretence. ppr. dissembling, pret. & pp. dissembled. [Fr. *dissembler*—L. *simulo,* to make like.]
Dissembler, dis-sem′bl-ér, n. *One who dissembles.*
Disseminate, dis-se′min-āt, vt. *To scatter* for growth and propagation, *like seed;* to propagate; to circulate; to diffuse. ppr. disseminating, pret. & pp. disseminated. [L. *dissemino, disseminatus*—*semino,* to sow.]
Dissemination, dis-se′min-ā″shon, n. *Act of disseminating;* state of being disseminated. [Fr. *dissémination.*]
Disseminator, dis-se′min-āt-ér, n. *One who disseminates.*
Dissension, dis-sen′shon, n. *Difference of sentiment;* disagreement in opinion; breach of friendship and union; strife; quarrel. [L. *dissensio.*]
Dissent, dis-sent′, vi. *To differ in sentiment;* to disagree in opinion; to separate from an established church, in regard to doctrines, rites, or government.—n. *Difference of opinion or sentiment;* a separation from an established church. [L. *dissentio*—*sentio,* to think.]

Dissenter, dis-sent′ér, n. One who separates from the service and worship of an established church.
Dissentient, dis-sen′shi-ent, a. *Declaring dissent;* disagreeing.—n. One who declares his dissent. [L. *dissentiens.*]
Dissenting, dis-sent′ing, p.a. Separating from the communion of an established church.
Dissertation, dis-sér-tā′shon, n. A formal discourse, intended to illustrate a subject; a written essay, treatise, or disquisition. [Fr.—L. *dissertatio*—*sero, sertum,* to set or plant.]
Dissertator, dis′sér-tāt-ér, n. *One who writes a dissertation.* [Low L.]
Disserve, dis-sérv′, vt. *To do a bad office to;* to injure; to hurt; to harm. ppr. disserving, pret. & pp. disserved.
Disservice, dis-sér′vis, n. *An ill-service;* an injury; harm; mischief.
Dissever, dis-sev′ér, vt. *To separate;* to part *in two;* to divide asunder; to disunite. [Old Fr. *desseverer.*]
Dissimilar, dis-si′mi-lér, a. *Unlike;* not similar; not having the resemblance of; heterogeneous. [L. *dissimilis*—*similis,* like.]
Dissimilarity, dis-si′mi-la″ri-ti, n. *Unlikeness;* want of resemblance; dissimilitude.
Dissimilarly, dis-si′mi-lér-li, adv. *In a dissimilar manner.*
Dissimulation, dis-si′mū-lā″shon, n. *Act of dissembling;* a hiding under a false appearance; a feigning; false pretension; a pretending that to be which is not. [Fr.—L. *dissimulatio*—*similo,* to make like.]
Dissipate, dis′si-pāt, vt. *To scatter* in wasteful extravagance; to scatter, as the attention; to spend; to squander; to consume.—vi. *To scatter;* to disperse; to separate into parts and disappear; to vanish. ppr. dissipating, pret. & pp. dissipated. [L. *dissipo, dissipatus*—Old L. *supo,* to throw.]
Dissipated, dis′si-pāt-ed, p.a. Loose; dissolute; devoted to pleasure and vice.
Dissipation, dis-si-pā′shon, n. *Act of dissipating;* state of being dispersed; a dissolute, irregular course of life; a trifle which distracts attention. [Fr.—L. *dissipatio.*]
Dissociate, dis-sō′shi-āt, vt. *To separate, as from society;* to separate; to disunite; to part. ppr. dissociating, pret. & pp. dissociated. [L. *dissocio, dissociatus*—*socio,* to unite.]
Dissociation, dis-sō′shi-ā″shon, n. *Act of disuniting;* a state of separation; disunion. [L. *dissociatio.*]
Dissolubility, dis-so′lū-bil″li-ti, n. *Capacity of being dissolved* by heat or moisture, and converted into a fluid.
Dissoluble, dis′sō-lū-bl, a. *Capable of being dissolved;* that may be melted; convertible into a fluid; that may be disunited. [Fr.—L. *solvo,* to loose.]
Dissolubleness, dis′sō-lū-bl-nes, n. *Quality of being dissoluble.*
Dissolute, dis′sō-lūt, a. *Loosed; loose;* loose in behaviour and morals; licentious; luxurious; debauched. [L. *dissolutus*—*solvo,* to loose.]
Dissolutely, dis′sō-lūt-li, adv. *In a dissolute manner.*
Dissoluteness, dis′sō-lūt-nes, n. *Quality of being dissolute;* looseness of manners and morals; dissipation.
Dissolution, dis-sō-lū′shon, n. *Act of dissolving;* state of being dissolved; a melting; a thawing; separation of parts; decomposition; death; separation of the soul and body; separation of the parts which compose a system;

destruction; the breaking up of an assembly, or the putting an end to its existence. [Fr.—L. *dissolutio.*]
Dissolvable, diz-zolv′a-bl, a. *That may be dissolved;* capable of being melted.
Dissolve, diz-zolv′, vt. *To loosen asunder;* to separate; to melt; to relax; to break up; to cause to separate; to put an end to; to clear; to resolve; to cause to vanish; to rescind.—vi. *To be loosened asunder;* to ɪ e melted; to sink away; to melt away in pleasure; to crumble; to be broken; to waste away; to perish; to languish away; to die; to break up; to be dismissed, as a meeting. ppr. dissolving, pret. & pp. dissolved. [L. *dissolvo*—*solvo,* to loose.]
Dissolvent, diz-zolv′ent, a. *Having power to dissolve.*—n. *That which has the power of disuniting* the parts, by heat, moisture, or other agency; a solvent. [L. *dissolvens.*]
Dissolver, diz-zolv′ér, n. *He or that which dissolves.*
Dissonance, dis′sō-nans, n. *Disagreement in sound;* discord; disagreement. [Fr.—L. *sono,* to sound.]
Dissonant, dis′sō-nant, a. *Discordant in sound;* harsh; unharmonious; unpleasant to the ear; incongruous (usually with *from* or *to*). [Fr.]
Dissuade, dis-swād′, vt. *To exhort against;* to attempt to draw from a measure, by reason or importunity; to render averse. ppr. dissuading, pret. & pp. dissuaded. [Fr. *dissuader*—L. *suadeo,* to advise.]
Dissuasion, dis-swā′zhon, n. *Act of dissuading;* exhortation in opposition to something. [Fr.]
Dissuasive, dis-swā′siv, a. *Tending to dissuade.*—n. *That which dissuades,* or tends to dissuade.
Dissuasively, dis-swā′siv-li, adv. *In a way to dissuade.*
Dissyllabic, dis-sil-lab′ik, a. *Consisting of two syllables only.*
Dissyllable, dis′sil-la-bl, n. A word consisting of *two syllables* only. [Fr. *dissyllabe.*]
Distaff, dis′taf, n. The *staff* to which a bunch of flax or *tow* is tied, and from which the thread is drawn in spinning. [Sax. *distæf,* corrupted from *tow,* and *staf,* a staff.]
Distain, dis-tān′, vt. *To take out the colour of;* to sully; to tarnish; to blot; to discolour. [Old Fr. *desteindre*—L. *tingo,* to dye.]
Distance, dis′tans, n. *A standing apart;* extent of space between two objects; length of time; ideal space; a space marked on the course where horses run; the remoteness which respect requires; reserve; alienation of heart; remoteness in succession; the interval between two notes in music.—vt. *To stand apart from;* to throw off from the view; to leave behind in a race; to leave at a great distance behind; greatly to surpass. ppr. distancing, pret. & pp. distanced. [Fr.—L. *sto,* to stand.]
Distant, dis′tant, a. *Standing apart;* separate; remote in place or in time; far; remote in natural connection; not allied; remote in view; not easily seen; indirect; faint; implying haughtiness; cool; shy. [Fr.—L. *distans.*]
Distantly, dis′tant-li, adv. Remotely; at a distance; with reserve.
Distaste, dis-tāst′, n. *Aversion of the taste;* disrelish; aversion of mind; alienation of affection; disgust.
Distasteful, dis-tāst′fṳl, a. *Disgusting to the taste;* loathsome; proceeding from

ch, *chain*; j, *job*; g, *go*; ng, *sing*; ᴛʜ, *then*; th, *thin*; w, *wig*; wh, *whig*; zh, *azure*; † obsolete.

or attended with disgust or opposition; offensive; manifesting distaste.
Distastefully, dis-tāst'fụl-li, *adv. In a distasteful manner.*
Distastefulness, dis-tāst'fụl-nes, *n. Quality of being distasteful.*
Distemper, dis-tem'pėr, *n.* Any morbid state of an animal body, or of any part of it; disorder; disease; sickness; bad constitution of the mind; bad temper.—*vt.* To disease; to disorder; to derange, as the functions of the body or mind; to deprive of temper; to disturb.
Distemperature, dis-tem'pėr-a-tūr, *n. Intemperateness;* outrageousness; slight illness; mental uneasiness; perturbation of mind; loss of regularity; disorder.
Distempered, dis-tem'pėrd, *p.a.* Diseased in body, or disordered in mind.
Distend, dis-tend', *vt. To stretch asunder;* to stretch out; to swell; to stretch in all directions.—*vi.* To dilate; to spread in all directions. [L. *distendo*—*tendo*, to stretch.]
Distention, dis-ten'shon, *n. Act of distending;* state of being distended. [L. *distentio*.]
Distich, dis'tik, *n.* A *couple* of *verses* or poetic lines, making complete sense. (Gr. *distichos*—*stichos*, a row.]
Distil, dis-til', *vi. To drop down; to fall in drops;* to flow gently, or in a small stream; to practise distillation.—*vt. To let fall in drops;* to extract spirit from, by evaporation and condensation. *ppr.* distilling, *pret. & pp.* distilled. [Fr. *distiller*—L. *stilio*, to drop.]
Distillation, dis-til-ā'shon, *n. Act of distilling;* the operation of extracting spirit from a substance by evaporation and condensation. [Fr.]
Distillatory, dis-til'a-to-ri, *a. Belonging to distillation;* used for distilling. [Fr. *distillatoire*.]
Distilled, dis-tild', *p.a.* Extracted by evaporation.
Distiller, dis-til'ėr, *n. One who distils.*
Distillery, dis-til'ė-ri, *n. The building and works where distilling is carried on.* [Fr. *distillerie*.]
Distilling, dis-til'ing, *p.n.* Act or process of extracting spirit by distillation.
Distinct, dis-tingkt', *a. Separated by points;* having the difference marked; not the same in number or kind; separate in place; different; clear; definite. [Fr.—L. *distinctus*—*distinguo*.]
Distinction, dis-tingk'shon, *n. Act of distinguishing;* difference made; discernment; substantial difference; separation; difference in treatment; elevation of rank in society; preference; eminence. [Fr.—L. *distinctio*.]
Distinctive, dis-tingkt'iv, *a. That marks distinction or difference;* having the power to distinguish and discern. [Fr. *distinctif*.]
Distinctively, dis-tingkt'iv-li, *adv. With distinction;* plainly.
Distinctly, dis-tingkt'li, *adv. In a distinct manner;* clearly; plainly; obviously; with meaning.
Distinctness, dis-tingkt'nes, *n. Quality or state of being distinct;* plainness; clearness; precision; nice discrimination in marking differences.
Distinguish, dis-ting'gwish, *vt. To separate by visible marks;* to mark out by some peculiarity; to separate by any quality which constitutes difference; to discern critically; to judge; to perceive; to separate from others by some mark of honour; to make eminent; to signalise.—*vi. To make a distinction;* to find or show the difference. [L. *dis-*

tinguo—Gr. *stiso*, to mark with a pointed instrument.]
Distinguishable, dis-ting'gwish-a-bl, *a. Capable of being distinguished;* remarkable.
Distinguishably, dis-ting'gwish-a-bli, *adv. So as to be distinguished.*
Distinguished, dis-ting'gwisht, *p.a. Separated* from others by being superior in some respect; made eminent or known.
Distinguishing, dis-ting'gwish-ing, *p.a. Constituting distinction* from everything else; peculiar.
Distort, dis-tort', *vt. To turn different ways;* to twist; to force or put out of the true posture or direction; to turn aside from the true meaning; to wrest. [L. *distorqueo*, *distortus*—*torqueo*, to twist.]
Distorted, dis-tort'ed, *p.a.* Wrested, perverted.
Distortion, dis-tor'shon, *n. Act of distorting;* a twisting out of regular shape; a writhing motion; crookedness; a perversion of the true meaning of words. [Fr. *distorsion*—L. *distortio*.]
Distract, dis-trakt', *vt. To draw away; to separate forcibly;* to pull in different directions; to throw into confusion; to perplex; to disorder the reason of; to render raving or furious. [L. *distraho*, *distractus*—*traho*, to draw.]
Distracted, dis-trakt'ed, *p.a.* Disordered in intellect; mad; furious; insane.
Distractedly, dis-trakt'ed-li, *adv.* Madly; furiously; wildly.
Distracting, dis-trakt'ing, *p.a.* Perplexing; harassing.
Distraction, dis-trak'shon, *n. Act of distracting;* state of being distracted; a diversity of direction; derangement. [Fr.—L. *distractio*.]
Distrain, dis-trān', *vt. To draw tight*; to seize, as goods, for debt.—*vi.* To make seizure of goods. [Old Fr. *destraindre* —L. *stringo*, to draw tight.]
Distrainable, dis-trān'a-bl, *a.* Liable to be taken for distress.
Distress, dis-tres', *n. A drawing asunder;* act of distraining; the thing taken by distraining; anguish of body or mind; general affliction, as of a nation; calamity, a state of danger.—*vt. To draw asunder;* to distrain; to afflict with pain or anguish; to perplex. [Old Fr. *destresse*—L. *districtio*—*stringo*, *strictum*, to draw tight.]
Distressed, dis-trest', *p.a.* Severely afflicted; oppressed with calamity or misfortune.
Distressful, dis-tres'fụl, *a. Full of distress;* proceeding from pain or anguish; calamitous; indicating distress.
Distressfully, dis-tres'fụl-li, *adv. In a distressful or painful manner.*
Distressing, dis-tres'ing, *p.a.* Very afflicting.
Distributable, dis-tri'būt-a-bl, *a. That may be distributed.*
Distribute, dis-tri'būt, *vt. To give* in portions; to apportion; to deal out; to give in charity; to administer, as justice; to classify.—*vi.* To give in charity. *ppr.* distributing, *pret. & pp.* distributed. [L. *distribuo*, *distributus*—*tribuo*, to give.]
Distributer, dis-tri'būt-ėr, *n. One who distributes* or deals out in parts.
Distribution, dis-tri-bū'shon, *n. Act of distributing;* apportionment; division and disposition of the parts of anything. [Fr.—L. *distributio*.]
Distributive, dis-tri'būt-iv, *a. That distributes;* that deals to each his proper

share; that separates or divides.—*n.* A word that divides or *distributes*, as *each*, *every*, *either*, *neither*. [Fr. *distributif*.]
Distributively, dis-tri'būt-iv-li, *adv. By distribution;* singly; not collectively.
District, dis'trikt, *n.* A limited extent of country; a circuit within which power may be exercised, and to which it is restrained; a province; a country. [Fr.—Low L. *districtus*.]
Distrust, dis-trust', *vt. To have no trust in;* to discredit; to doubt the truth or sincerity of; not to confide in; to suspect of evil.—*n. Want of trust;* doubt of reality or sincerity; suspicion of evil designs; discredit; loss of confidence on the part of others.
Distrustful, dis-trust'fụl, *a.* Apt to distrust; suspicious; not confident.
Distrustfully, dis-trust'fụl-li, *adv. In a distrustful manner.*
Distrustfulness, dis-trust'fụl-nes, *n. State of being distrustful.*
Distrustingly, dis-trust'ing-li, *adv. In a distrustful manner.*
Disturb, dis-tėrb', *vt. To throw into disorder;* to disarrange; to disquiet; to agitate; to molest; to hinder; to ruffle; to move. [L. *disturbo*—*turba*, turmoil—Gr. *thorubos*, a noise.]
Disturbance, dis-tėrb'ans, *n. State of being disturbed;* tumult; derangement; commotion; excitement of passion; interruption of a right.
Disturbed, dis-tėrbd', *p.a.* Uneasy; disarranged; disordered.
Disturber, dis-tėrb'ėr, *n. He or that which disturbs or disquiets.*
Disturbing, dis-tėrb'ing, *p.a.* Moving; making a tumult; incommoding the quiet enjoyment of.
Disunion, dis-ū'ni-un, *n. A severing of union;* disjunction; breach of concord.
Disunite, dis-ū-nīt', *vt. To destroy the unity of;* to disjoin; to part.—*vi.* To part; to become separate. *ppr.* disuniting, *pret. & pp.* disunited.
Disuse, dis-ūs', *n. Cessation of use, practice, or exercise;* cessation of custom; desuetude.
Disuse, dis-ūz', *vt. To cease to use;* to neglect or omit to practise. *ppr.* disusing, *pret. & pp.* disused.
Disused, dis-ūzd', *p.a.* No longer used; obsolete, as words, &c.
Disvalue, dis-va'lū, *vt. To undervalue.*
Disvouch, dis-vouch', *vt.* To discredit; to contradict.
Ditch, dich, *n. That which is digged;* a trench in the earth made by digging; any long, hollow receptacle of water.—*vt. To dig or make a ditch or ditches.*—*vi. To dig a ditch or ditches in;* to drain by a ditch; to surround with a ditch. [Sax. *dic*.]
Ditcher, dich'ėr, *n. One who digs ditches.*
Dittied, dit'ti-ed, *p.a.* Sung; adapted to music.
Ditto, dit'tō, contracted into *do.*, *adv.* or *n. Said;* as said; aforesaid, or the same thing. [It. *detto*—L. *dictum*—*dico*, to say.]
Ditty, dit'ti, *n. Something said or sung;* a song; a sonnet, or a little poem to be sung. [Old Fr. *dict*, *dicté*—L. *dico*, *dictum*, to say.]
Diuretic, dī-ū-ret'ik, *a. Tending to produce discharges of urine.*—*n. A medicine that provokes urine.* [Fr. *diurétique*—Gr. *ouron*, urine.]
Diurnal, di-ėrn'al, *a. Relating to a day;* daily; performed in a day, or in twenty-four hours.—*n.* In the Roman Catholic church, a book containing the office of each day. [L. *diurnus*—*dies*, a day.]

Fāte, fär, fat, fạll; mē, met, hėr; pīne, pin; nōte, not, mōve; tūbe, tub, bụll; oil, pound.

Diurnally, di-ėrn'al-li, *adv. Daily.*
Divan, di-van', *n. A council of state;* the great council of the Turkish empire; a movable sofa; a smoking room or establishment. [Ar. *diwān.*]
Divaricate, di-va'ri-kāt, *vi.* To open; to fork; to part into two branches.—*vt.* To cause to branch apart. *ppr.* divaricating, *pret. & pp.* divaricated. [L. *divarico, divaricatus—ed rus*, grown apart.]
Divarication, di-va'ri-kā''shon, *n.* A forking; a separation into two branches; a crossing of fibres at different angles. [Low L. *divaricatio.*]
Dive, dīv, *vi.* To plunge into water, as an animal head foremost; to go deep into any subject; to plunge into any business, so as to be thoroughly engaged in it; to penetrate. *ppr.* diving, *pret. & pp.* dived. [Sax. *dufian.*]
Diver, dīv'ėr, *n. One who dives;* a bird which dives.
Diverge, di-vėrj', *vi.* To *shoot,* extend, or proceed from a point in *different* directions, or not in parallel lines. *ppr.* diverging, *pret. & pp.* diverged. [Low L. *divergo—L. vergo*, to incline.]
Divergence, Divergency, di-vėrj'ens, di-vėr'jen-si, *n. Act of diverging;* a receding from each other. [Fr.]
Divergent, di-vėrj'ent, *a.* Receding from each other, as lines or rays which proceed from the same point. [Fr.]
Diverging, di-vėrj'ing, *p.a.* Receding from each other as they proceed.
Divers, di'vėrs, *a. Different;* diverse; several; more than one, but not a great number. [Fr.—L. *diversus.*]
Diverse, di'vėrs', *a. Turned different ways;* different; various. [L. *diversus—verto,* to turn.]
Diversely, di-vėrs'li, *adv. In a diverse manner;* variously.
Diversifiable, di-vėrs'i-fī-a-bl, *a. Capable of being diversified.*
Diversification, di-vėrs'i-fi-kā''shon, *n. Act of diversifying;* state of being diversified.
Diversified, di-vėrs'i-fīd, *p.a.* Distinguished by various forms, or by a variety of aspects.
Diversify, di-vėrs'i-fī, *vt. To make various* in form or qualities; to variegate; to give diversity to; to distinguish by different things. *ppr.* diversifying, *pret. & pp.* diversified. [Fr. *diversifier*—L. *verto, versum,* to turn, and *facio,* to make.]
Diversion, di-vėr'shon, *n. Act of turning aside from any course;* that which *diverts;* amusement; sport; act of drawing the attention and force of an enemy from the point where the principal attack is to be made; the feint which diverts. [Fr.—Low L. *diversio.*]
Diversity, di-vėrs'i-ti, *n. State of being diverse;* contrariety; variety; distinct being, as opposed to identity; variegation. [Fr. *diversité*—L. *diversitas.*]
Divert, di-vėrt', *vt. To turn aside;* to turn, as the mind from business or study; to gratify; to amuse; to exhilarate; to draw, as the forces of an enemy to a different point; to subvert†. [L. *diverto—verto,* to turn.]
Diverting, di-vėrt'ing, *p.a.* Pleasing; amusing; entertaining.
Divest, di-vest', *vt. To strip of clothes;* to strip of anything that covers, surrounds, or attends. (Old Fr. *desvestir*—L. *vestio,* to clothe.]
Dividable, di-vīd'a-bl, *a. That may be divided;* divided; parted.
Dividant, di-vīd'ant, *a.* Different; separate.
Divide, di-vīd', *vt. To part asunder;* to part, as an entire thing; to part, as a thing into two or more *pieces;* to interpose a barrier between; to distribute; to apportion, as dividends, &c.; to set at variance; to separate into two parts, for ascertaining opinions for and against a measure.—*vi. To part;* to open; to separate; to break friendship; to vote by the division of a legislative house into two parts. *ppr.* dividing, *pret. & pp.* divided. [L. *divido*—Etruscan, *idwo,* to part—Ch. *ḥadam,* a piece.]
Divided, di-vīd'ed, *p.a. Parted.*
Dividend, di'vi-dend, *n. That which is to be divided;* the number which is to be divided; the share of the profit of stock in trade which belongs to each proprietor according to his proportion of the stock; a share divided to creditors out of the estate of a bankrupt. [Fr. *dividende*—L. *dividendum—divido,* to divide.]
Divider, di-vīd'ėr, *n. He or that which divides;* a distributor; one who, or that which, disunites.
Dividing, di-vīd'ing, *p.a.* That indicates separation or difference.
Divination, di-vin-ā'shon, *n. Act of divining;* conjectural presage; prediction. [Fr.—L. *divinatio.*]
Divine, di-vīn', *a. Of or belonging to the Deity;* appropriated to God; excellent in the highest degree; apparently above what is human; godlike; holy; spiritual.—*n. One versed in divine things or divinity;* a minister of the gospel.—*vt.* To foretell, as if by *divine* inspiration; to know beforehand; to presage; to conjecture; to guess.—*vi. To practise divination;* to have or utter presages; to guess or conjecture. *ppr.* divining, *pret. & pp.* divined. [Fr. *divin*—L. *divinus—divus,* a god.]
Divinely, di-vin'li, *adv. In a divine manner;* by the influence of God; excellently.
Divineness, di-vin'nes, *n. The quality of being divine.*
Diviner, di-vin'ėr, *n.* One who pretends to predict events, or to reveal hidden things, by the aid of supernatural means; one who guesses; a conjecturer.
Diving-bell, dīv'ing-bel, *n.* A machine, originally *bell*-shaped, by means of which persons may *descend below the surface of the water,* and remain for some time without injury.
Divinity, di-vin'i-ti, *n. The state of being divine;* Deity; the essence of God; the Supreme Being; a pretended deity of pagans; the science of divine things; theology; supernatural power†; loftiness†. [Fr. *divinité*—L. *divinitas—divus,* a god.]
Divisibility, di-viz'i-bil''li-ti, *n. Quality of being divisible.* [Fr. *divisibilité.*]
Divisible, di-viz'i-bl, *a. Capable of division;* that may be separated or disunited; separable. [L. *divisibilis—divido,* to divide.]
Divisibly, di-viz'i-bli, *adv. In a divisible manner.*
Division, di-vi'shon, *n. Act of dividing;* state of being divided; that which divides; separation; the part separated; a portion; a separate body of men; disunion; difference; a distinguishing mark; the process of finding how many times one number is contained in another; the rule by which this is effected; part of a discourse. [Fr.—L. *divisio.*]
Divisive, di-viz'iv, *a. Forming division;* creating division or discord.
Divisor, di-viz'or, *n.* In arith. and algebra the number by which the dividend is *divided.* [L.]
Divorce, di-vōrs', *n. A turning away; a separation;* a legal dissolution of the bonds of matrimony; the sentence by which marriage is dissolved: disunion of things closely united.—*vt. To turn away;* to separate, as the husband or wife, from the other; to separate, as things closely connected; to force asunder; to take away. *ppr.* divorcing, *pret. & pp.* divorced. [Fr.—L. *divortium—verto,* to turn.]
Divorced, di-vōrst', *p.a. Separated;* parted; forced asunder.
Divorcement, di-vōrs'ment, *n. Divorce,* dissolution of the marriage tie.
Divulge, di-vulj', *vt. To make public;* to tell or make known, as something before secret; to publish; to disclose; to spread.—*vi.*† To become publicly known. *ppr.* divulging, *pret. & pp.* divulged. [Fr. *divulguer*—L. *vulgus,* the common people.]
Dizziness, diz'zi-nes, *n. State of being dizzy;* giddiness; a whirling in the head.
Dizzy, diz'zi, *a. Confused;* giddy; having a sensation of whirling in the head, with proneness to fall; causing giddiness.—*vt.* To whirl round; to make giddy; to confuse. *ppr.* dizzying, *pret. & pp.* dizzied. [Sax. *dysi.*]
Do, dö, *vt.* or *auxiliary. To effect by the agency of the hand;* to perform; to bring to pass; to discharge; to exert; to put forth; to finish; to achieve; to bring to an end by action; to make; to take, as a step or measure; to answer the purpose; to confer; to bestow.—*vi. To act or behave in any manner,* well or ill; to be in a state with regard to sickness or health; to succeed; to fit; to answer the design. *ppr.* doing, *pret.* did, *pp.* done.—*n.*† *A deed;* a feat; bustle; ado. [Sax. *dón.*]
Dobbin, dob'bin, *n.* An old jaded horse.
Docile, dō'sil, *a. Easily taught;* ready to learn; easily managed; tractable; pliant; yielding. [L. *docilis—doceo,* to teach.]
Docility, dō-si'li-ti, *n. Teachableness;* readiness to learn; aptness to be taught. [Fr. *docilité.*]
Dock, dok, *n.* A plant with broad leaves, exhaustive of the soil, and injurious to crops. [Sax. *docce.*]
Dock, dok, *vt. To cut or lop off,* as *the tail;* to curtail; to cut short; to cut off, as a part; to deduct from; to cut off or defeat; to bar.—*n.* The tail of a beast *cut short;* the stump of a tail; the solid part of the tail. [Icel. *dockr,* the tail.]
Dock, dok, *n.* A *dike;* a broad deep trench on the side of a harbour, or bank of a river, in which ships are built or repaired; [Flem. *docke,* a cage] the place where a criminal stands in court.—*vt.* To place, as a ship in a *dock.* [D. *dok.*]
Docket, dok'et, *n. A small piece* of paper containing the heads of a writing; a bill, tied to goods, containing some direction; an alphabetical list of cases in a court.—*vt.* To make, as an abstract of the heads of a writing; to abstract and enter in a book; to mark with a docket. [dimin. of *dock,* to curtail.]
Dockyard, dok'yärd, *n.* A *yard* or magazine, near a harbour, for containing all kinds of naval stores and timber.
Doctor, dok'tėr, *n. A teacher;* one who has passed all the degrees of a faculty,

and is empowered to practise and teach it; a person who has received the highest degree in a faculty; a learned man; a physician. [L.—from *doceo, doctum*, to teach.]
Doctrinal, dok'trin-al, *a. Pertaining to doctrine*; containing a doctrine; pertaining to the act or means of teaching.
Doctrinally, dok'trin-al-li, *adv.* In the form of *doctrine* or instruction.
Doctrine, dok'trin, *n. Instruction;* whatever is taught; a principle in any science; whatever is laid down as true by a master; tenet; act of teaching; knowledge; the truths of the gospel in general; instruction and confirmation in the truths of the gospel. [Fr.—L. *doctrina—doceo*, to teach.]
Document, do'kū-ment, *n.* Written *evidence* or proof; any authoritative paper containing instructions or proof for the establishment of facts. [Fr.—L. *documentum*.]
Documentary, do-kū-ment'a-ri, *a.* Pertaining to written *evidence*; consisting in documents.
Documented, do'kū-ment-ed, *p.a. Furnished* with *documents* necessary to establish facts.
Dodge, doj, *vi.* To start suddenly aside; to be evasive; to play fast and loose; to raise expectations and disappoint them; to quibble.—*vt.* To evade by a sudden shift of place.—*ppr.* dodging, *pret. & pp.* dodged.—*n.* A trick; an artifice; an evasion.
Doe, dō, *n. A she-deer;* the female of the fallow-deer. [Sax. *da*.]
Doer, dō'ėr, *n. One who does;* one who performs or executes; an actor.
Doeskin, dō'skin, *n. The skin of a doe;* a compact twilled cloth for trouserings.
Doff, dof, *vt. To put off,* as dress; to put or thrust away; to shift off with a view to delay†. [from *do* and *off*.]
Dog, dog, *n. The animal that bites;* a well-known domestic animal of many varieties; a term of reproach; something which fastens or holds fast.—*vt.* To hunt; to follow insidiously; to follow close; to worry with importunity. *ppr.* dogging, *pret. & pp.* dogged. [D.; Sans. *daksh*, to bite.]
Dog-briar, dog'brī-ėr, *n. The brier* that bears the hip.
Dog-cart, dog'kärt, *n. A carriage* with a box for holding sportsmen's *dogs;* also, a sort of double-seated gig for four persons.
Dog-cheap, dog'chēp, *a. Cheap as dog's* meat or offal; very cheap.
Dog-day, dog'dā, *n.* One of the days when Sirius, or the Dog-star, rises and sets with the sun.
Dog-eared, dog'ėrd, *a.* Having the corners of the leaves turned down and soiled (said of a book).
Dog-fish, dog'fish, *n.* A species of shark.
Dogged, dogd, *p.a. Like a surly obstinate dog;* sullen; severe.
Doggedly, dog'ed-li, *adv.* Sullenly; with obstinate resolution.
Doggedness, dog'ed-nes, *n.* Sullenness; moroseness; obstinate resolve.
Doggerel, dog'ge-rel, *n.* A loose irregular kind of poetry.—*a.* An epithet given to a kind of loose, irregular measure in burlesque poetry. [from *dog.*]
Doggish, dog'ish, *a. Like a dog;* churlish; growling; snappish; brutal.
Doggishness, dog'ish-nes, *n. Quality of being doggish.*
Dog-grass, dog'gras, *n.* Couch-grass.

Dog-head, dog'hed, *n.* Part of a gunlock.
Dogma, dog'ma, *n. That which seems true;* a settled opinion; a doctrinal point, particularly in matters of faith and philosophy. [Gr. — *dokeo*, to think.]
Dogmatic, Dogmatical, dog-mat'ik, dog-mat'ik-al, *a. Pertaining to a dogma;* asserting with authority or with arrogance; overbearing in assertion; asserted with authority. [Fr. *dogmatique—*Gr. *dogmatikos*.]
Dogmatically, dog-mat'ik-al-li, *adv.* Positively; in a magisterial manner; arrogantly.
Dogmatism, dog'mat-ixm, *n.* Positive assertion; arrogance; positiveness in opinion. [Fr. *dogmatisme.*]
Dogmatist, dog'mat-ist, *n.* A positive asserter; a bold or arrogant advancer of principles. [Fr. *dogmatiste.*]
Dogmatize, dog'mat-z, *vi.* To teach with bold and undue confidence; to advance principles with arrogance. *ppr.* dogmatizing, *pret. & pp.* dogmatized. [Fr. *dogmatiser.*]
Dog-rose, dog'rōz, *n.* The wild brier that bears the hip†; the flower of the same.
Dog-star, dog'stär, *n.* Sirius, *a star* of the first magnitude, whose rising and setting with the sun give name to the *dog-days.*
Dog-tooth, dog'tōth, *n.* **Dog-teeth**, dog'tēth, *plur.* A sharp-pointed human *tooth* growing between the fore teeth and grinders; an eye-tooth.
Doings, dö'ingz, *n. pl. Things done;* transactions; feats; behaviour; conduct; bustle.
Doit, doit, *n.* A small Dutch copper coin worth about half a farthing; any small piece of money. [Fr. *doigt*, a finger—L. *digitus*, a finger.]
Dole, dōl, *n. A part or portion;* that which is dealt out; that which is given in charity; gratuity.—*vt. To deal out;* to part; to portion out; to distribute. *ppr.* doling, *pret. & pp.* doled. [Sax. *dal*—Sans. *dal*, to be cut.]
Doleful, dōl'fųl, *a. Full of pain, grief, sorrow,* &c.; expressing grief; feeling grief; producing sorrow; sorrowful; sad; gloomy. [Old Fr. *dueil*, mourning; L. *doleo*, to suffer pain.]
Dolefully, dōl'fųl-li, *adv. In a doleful manner;* sorrowfully; dismally; sadly.
Dolefulness, dōl'fųl-nes, *n. State of being doleful;* sorrow; melancholy.
Dolesome, dōl'sum, *a. Doleful.*
Doll, dol, *n. A baby image or idol;* a puppet or baby for a child. [probably from *idol.*]
Dollar, dol'lėr, *n.* A silver coin of Spain and of the United States, of the value of about 4s. 4d. sterling. [Low Sax. *dahler*.]
Dolorous, dō'lėr-us, *a. Full of dolour;* impressing sorrow or grief; painful; giving pain. [L. *dolorosus.*]
Dolorously, dō'lėr-us-li, *adv.* Sorrowfully; in a manner to express pain.
Dolour, dō'lėr, *n. Pain; grief; sorrow;* lamentation. [L. *dolor.*]
Dolphin, dol'fin, *n.* A small species of whale which played or tumbled before storms, as if to warn seamen, and so was counted the friend of men; a fish celebrated for its changes of colour when dying. [L. *delphin.*]
Dolt, dōlt, *n. One who is dulled* or dull; a blockhead.
Doltish, dōlt'ish, *a. Dull* in intellect.
Doltishness, dōlt'ish-nes, *n.* Stupidity.
Domain, dō-mān', *n.* Territory governed

by a sovereign; estate; the land about the mansion-house of a lord, and in his immediate occupancy. [Fr. *domaine*—L. *dominium*—*domus*, a house.]
Dome, dōm, *n. A house!;* a concave ceiling raised over a circular or polygonal building; a cupola; something resembling a dome. [Fr.—L. *domus*, a house—Gr. *dēmō*, to build.]
Domed, dōmd, *p.a. Furnished with a dome.*
Domestic, dō-mes'tik, *a. Belonging to the house;* living in retirement; tame; pertaining to a nation considered as a family; not foreign; made in one's own house, nation, or country.—*n.* One who lives in the *house* or family of another, as an assistant for hire. [Fr. *domestique*—L. *domesticus.*]
Domesticate, dō-mes'tik-āt, *vt.* To cause to retire from the public; to make familiar, as if at home; to tame. *ppr.* domesticating, *pret. & pp.* domesticated. [Low L. *domesticor, domesticatus.*]
Domesticated, dō-mes'tik-āt-ed, *p.a. Made domestic.*
Domestication, dō-mes'tik-ā'shon, *n. Act of domesticating;* act of taming or reclaiming wild animals. [Low L. *domesticatio.*]
Domicile, do'mi-sil, *n. A dwelling; an abode* or mansion; the place where a person has his home, or where he has his family residence. [Fr.—L. *domicilium*—*domus*, a house.]
Domicile, do'mi-sil, *vt.* To establish in a fixed residence. *ppr.* domiciling, *pret. & pp.* domiciled. [Fr. *domicilier.*]
Domiciled, do'mi-sild, *p.a.* Having gained a permanent residence or inhabitancy.
Domiciliary, do-mi-si'li-a-ri, *a. Pertaining to a domicile,* or the residence of a person or family. [Fr. *domiciliaire.*]
Domiciliation, do-mi-si'li-ā'shon, *n.* Permanent residence; inhabitancy.
Dominant, dom'in-ant, *a. Ruling;* having the rule; governing; predominant; ascendant. [L. *dominans—dominans,* a lord.]
Dominate, dom'in-āt, *vt. To be lord or master over;* to rule; to predominate over. *ppr.* dominating, *pret. & pp.* dominated. [L. *dominor, dominatus—domus,* a house.]
Domination, dom-in-ā'shon, *n. Rule;* the exercise of power in ruling; government; tyranny. [Fr.—L. *dominatio.*]
Domineer, dom-in-ēr', *vi. To rule* with insolence; to bluster; to swell with conscious superiority. (With *over.*) [Fr. *dominer.*]
Domineering, dom-in-ēr'ing, *p.a.* Overbearing; insolent.
Dominical, dō-min'ik-al, *a. That notes the Lord's day;* pertaining to the Lord's day or the Lord's prayer. [Fr.]
Dominion, dō-min'i-on, *n. Lordship;* sovereignty; right of possession and use without being accountable; district governed; country; region; persons governed; a ruling power of very high rank. [L. *dominium.*]
Don, don, *n.* A Spanish title, corresponding to Eng. Mr.; a grand personage. [from L. *dominus*, a lord.]
Don, don, *vt. To do on;* to put on; to invest one's self with. *ppr.* donning. *pret. & pp.* donned. [*do, on.*]
Donation, dō-nā'shon, *n. Act of giving,* act by which a thing is transferred; a free gift; that which is given; a gift; a present. [L. *donatio—dono,* to give.]
Donative, don'at-iv, *n.* A *gift;* a gra-

Fāte, fär, fat, fall; mē, met, hėr; pine, pin; nōte, not, mōve; tūbe, tub, bųll; oil, pound.

tuity; a present; a benefice given to a person by the founder or patron, without either presentation, institution, or introduction by the ordinary. *a. Vested or vesting by donation.* [Fr. *donatif.*]

Donjon, don'jon, *n. A dungeon*; *a turret*; the central building or keep of an ancient castle, to which the garrison could retreat in case of necessity. [Fr.]

Donkey, dong'kē, *n.* A nickname said to be applied to an ass from his *colour*; an ass of any kind. [probably from *dun*, and dimin. *kin*.]

Donor, dō'nėr, *n. One who gives*; one who confers anything gratuitously; one who grants an estate. [Fr. *donneur*.]

Doom, dōm, *vt. To pronounce judgment on*; to condemn to any punishment; to destine; to fix irrevocably the fate of; to punish by a penalty.—*n. Judicial sentence*; sentence; condemnation; decree; fate; destiny; destruction. [Sax. *déman*, to judge.]

Doomed, dōmd, *p.a.* Condemned; destined; fated.

Doomsday, dōmz'dā, *n. A day of sentence; the day of the final doom or judgment.* [*doom* and *day*.]

Door, dōr, *n. An opening* into a house, or into any room or closet, by which persons *enter*; the frame of boards that shuts the opening of a house; a house; often in the plural, *doors*—entrance; avenue; means of approach. [Sax. *duru*—Sans. *dvāra*.]

Doorway, dōr'wā, *n. The passage of a door*; the entrance to a building.

Dor, **Dorr**, dor, *n.* The name of the black beetle or the hedge-chafer, so called from its droning or *humming* sound. [Sax. *dora*, a drone, a locust.]

Dorian, dō'ri-an, *a. Pertaining to Doris* in Greece.

Doric, dor'ik, *a. Pertaining to Doris in Greece*; denoting one of the orders in architecture—the earliest and plainest of the Grecian orders. [Fr. *dorique*.]

Dormancy, dor'man-si, *n. State of being dormant*; quiescence; sleep; abeyance.

Dormant, dor'mant, *a. Sleeping*; not used; suspended; inactive; not in exercise. [Fr.—L. *dormio*, to sleep.]

Dormer, **Dormer-window**, dor'mėr, dor'mėr-win-dō, *n.* A window pierced through a sloping roof, the frame being placed vertically on the rafters.

Dormitory, dor'mi-tō-ri, *n. A place to sleep in*; a gallery in convents, divided into several cells, where the religious sleep. [L. *dormitorium*.]

Dormouse, dor'mous, *n. Dormice*, *pl. The sleeping mouse*; an animal allied to the mouse. [L. *dormiens mus*.]

Dorsal, dor'sal, *a. Pertaining to the back.* [Low L. *dorsualis*—L. *dorsum*, the back.]

Dose, dōs, *n. That which is given*; the quantity of medicine given at one time; anything given to be swallowed; anything nauseous that one is obliged to take; a quantity; a portion; as much as a man can swallow. [Fr.—Gr. *didōmi*, *dōsō*, to give.]—*vt.* To proportion, as a medicine properly to the patient or disease; to give medicine to; to give anything nauseous to. *ppr*. dosing, *pret. & pp.* dosed. [Fr. *doser*.]

Dot, dot, *n. That which stops up*; a small point made with a pen or other pointed instrument; a speck, used in marking a writing or other thing. *vt. To mark with a dot or dots*; to diversify with small objects.—*vt. To make dots* or spots. *ppr.* dotting, *pret. & pp.* dotted. [from Sax. *dyttan*, to stop up.]

Dotage, dōt'āj, *n. A doting*; feebleness of understanding, particularly in old age; childishness of old age; excessive fondness. [from *dote*.]

Dotal, dōt'al, *a. Pertaining to dower*, or a woman's marriage portion; constituting dower or comprised in it. [Fr.]

Dotant†, dōt'ant, *n.* A dotard.

Dotard, dōt'ėrd, *n.* A man whose intellect is impaired by age; one in his second childhood. [from *dote*.]

Dotation, dō-tā'shon, *n. Act of bestowing a marriage portion* on a woman; endowment; establishment of funds for support, as of an hospital. [Fr. —Low L. *dotatio*—L. *dōs*, *dōtis*, a dowry.]

Dote, dōt, *vi. To ha e the intellect impaired* by age, so that the mind wanders or wavers; to be silly or insane; to be foolishly fond (with *on* or *upon*). *ppr.* doting, *pret. & pp.* doted. [Belg. *doten*.]

Doter, dōt'ėr, *n. One who dotes*.

Doting, dōt'ing, *p.a. Having the mind impaired by age*; regarding with excessive fondness.

Dotingly, dōt'ing-li, *adv.* By excessive fondness.

Dotted, dot'ed, *p.a. Marked with dots* or small spots; diversified with small detached objects.

Dotterel, **Dottrel**, dot'tėr-el, dot'trel, *n.* A bird proverbial, perhaps unjustly, *for stupidity* and silliness. [from *dote*.]

Double, du'bl, *a. Twofold*; two of a sort together, containing the same quantity or length repeated; having one added to another; of two kinds; two in number; deceitful; acting two parts, one openly, the other in secret.—*vt. To fold over*; to fold, as paper; to increase or extend by adding an equal sum, value, quantity, or length; to contain twice as much; to add, as one to another in the same order; to sail round, as a cape, point, &c.—*vi. To increase twofold*; to wind in running, as a hare; to play tricks; to use sleights. *ppr.* doubling, *pret. & pp.* doubled. *n. Twice as much*; a turn in running to escape pursuers; a shift; an artifice to deceive; strong beer†.—*adv. Twice*; twofold. [Fr.—L. *duo*, two, and *plico*, to fold.]

Double-bass, du'bl-bās, *n.* The lowest-toned instrument of music of the violin class.

Double-charge, du'bl-chärj, *vt.* To *charge* or intrust with a *double* portion.

Double-dealer, du'bl-dēl-ėr, *n. One who practises double-dealing.*

Double-dealing, du'bl-dēl-ing, *n.* Deceitful practice; the profession of one thing and the practice of another.

Double-entry, du'bl-en-tri, *n.* A mode of book-keeping in which every transaction *is entered in two different books* and forms, to guard against error.

Double-hearted, du'bl-härt-ed, *a. Having a false heart*; deceitful.

Double-minded, du'bl-mind-ed, *a. Having different minds* at different times; unsettled; wavering; unstable.

Doubleness, du'bl-nes, *n. State of being doubled* or double; duplicity.

Doubler, du'bl-ėr, *n. He or that which doubles*.

Double-star, du'bl-stär, *n.* A star which usually appears single, but in the telescope is resolved into *two stars*.

Doublet, dub'let, *n.* A garment made *doubly thick*; a wadded garment for defence; two; a pair. [Fr.]

Double-tongued, du'bl-tungd, *a. Making contrary declarations* on the same subject at different times; deceitful.

Doubling, du'bl-ing, *n. Act of making double*; a fold; an artifice; a shift; act of sailing round a cape, &c.; the turning of a hare to deceive the hounds.

Doubloon, dųb-lōn', *n.* A Sp anish and Portuguese coin, being *double* the value of the pistole. [Fr. *doublon*.]

Doubly, du'bli, *adv.* In twice the quantity; to twice the degree.

Doubt, dout, *vi. To go from one side to the other*; to waver in judgment; to be uncertain; to hesitate; to question; to be apprehensive; to suspect. *vt. To hold in doubt*; to deem uncertain; to question; to hesitate to believe; to fear; to distrust; to withhold confidence from.—*n.* A wavering in opinion or judgment; suspense; uncertainty of condition; fear; difficulty objected. [Fr. *douter*—L. *dubito*—*duo*, two, and obsol. *bito*, to go.]

Doubter, dout'ėr, *n. One who doubts*.

Doubtful, dout'fųl, *a. Full of doubt or doubts*; hesitating; not clear in its meaning; obsc re; admitting of doubt; of uncertain issue; not secure; not confident; not without fear.

Doubtfully, dout'fųl-li, *adv. In a doubtful manner*; dubiously.

Doubtfulness, dout'fųl-nes, *n. A state of doubt*; uncertainty of meaning; uncertainty of condition; uncertainty of issue.

Doubting, dout'ing, *p.a.* Wavering in mind; hesitating.

Doubtingly, dout'ing-li, *adv. In a doubting manner*; dubiously.

Doubtless, dout'les, *adv. Without doubt* or question; unquestionably.

Doubtlessly, dout'les-li, *adv.* Unquestionably.

Douceur, dö'sėr, *n. That which sweetens*; a present or gift; a bribe; sweetness of manner. [Fr.—L. *dulcis*, sweet.]

Douche, dösh, *n. A jet or current of water* or vapour *directed* with considerable force upon some diseased part of the body, with a view to strengthen it. [Fr.—L. *duco*, to lead.]

Dough, dō, *n.* A mass composed of flour or meal moistened and kneaded, but not baked; paste of bread. [Sax. *dah*.]

Doughtily, dou'ti-li, *adv. With doughtiness*.

Doughtiness, dou'ti-nes, *n. Quality of being doughty*; valour; bravery.

Doughty, dou'ti, *a. Noble*; stout; brave; valiant. (Often used ironically.) [Sax. *dohtig*.]

Doughy, dō'i, *a. Like dough*; soft; yielding to pressure; pale.

Dove, duv, *n.* A pigeon; a word of endearment, or an emblem of innocence. [Icel. *dúfa*—Heb. *tūb*, goodness of appearance, beauty.]

Dove-eyed, duv'īd, *a.* Having *eyes* like those of a *dove*.

Dovelet, duv'let, *n. A young or small dove.*

Dovetail, duv'tāl, *n.* A mode of fastening boards and timbers together by letting one piece into another in the form of a *dove's tail* spread, or wedge reversed.—*vt.* To unite by a tenon; to connect strongly.

Dowager, dou'ā-jėr, *n. A widow with a dowry* or jointure; a title particularly given to the widows of princes and persons of rank. [Fr. *douairière*—*douaire*, a dower.]

Dowdy, dou'di, *n.* An awkward, ill-

ch, *chain*; j. *job*; g, *go*; ng, *sing*; ᴛʜ, *then*; th, *thin*; w, *wig*; wh, *whig*; zh, *asure*; † obsolete.

dressed, inelegant woman.—*a.* Awkward; ill-dressed; vulgar-looking.

Dower, dou'ér, *n. Anything given; an endowment;* that portion of the lands or tenements of a man which his widow enjoys during her life, after the death of her husband; the property which a woman brings to her husband in marriage; dowry. [Fr. *douaire*—Gr. *didōmi*, to give.]

Dowered, dou'érd, *p.a. Furnished with dower,* or a portion.

Dowerless, dou'ér-les, *a. Destitute of dower.*

Dowery, Dowry, dou'é-ri, dou'ri, *n.* A different spelling of *dower,* but less used.

Dowlas, dou'las, *n.* A kind of coarse linen cloth.

Down, doun, *n.* The fine soft feathers of fowls, particularly of the duck kind; fine hair; the pubescence of plants; the little crown of certain seeds of plants; anything that soothes or mollifies. [G. *dune.*]

Down, doun, *n. A hill; a mount;* a bank of sand thrown up by the sea; a tract of poor, naked, hilly land, used only for pasturing sheep; (pl.) a well-known road for shipping in the English Channel. [Sax. *dun*—Armor. *tūn.*]

Down, doun, *adv. From a hill;* tending from a higher to a lower place; on the ground; below the horizon, as the sun; in the direction from a higher to a lower condition; into disgrace; into subjection; into a due consistence; at length; prostrate on the ground, or on any flat surface.—*prep.* Along a descent; from a higher to a lower place; toward the mouth of a river, or toward the place where water is discharged into the ocean or a lake.—*n.* Downcast; dejected. [Sax. *adūn*; Armor. *doun*, deep.]

Downcast, doun'kast, *a. Cast downward;* directed to the ground; dejected.

Downfal, doun'fal, *n. A falling down,* or body of things falling; ruin; a sudden fall by violence, in distinction from slow decay; a depression of reputation or estate.

Downfallen, doun'fal-en, *a. Fallen down;* ruined.

Downgyved, doun'jīvd, *a.* Hanging down, like the loose cincture of fetters.

Down-hearted, doun'härt-ed, *a. Dejected in spirits.*

Downhill, doun'hil, *a.* -Descending; sloping; figuratively, easy.

Dowiness, doun'i-nes, *n. State of being downy.*

Downlooked, doun'lukt, *a. Having a downcast countenance;* dejected; gloomy; sullen.

Downright, doun'rit, *a. Straight down;* directly to the point; plain; unceremonious; blunt.—*adv. Right down;* in plain terms; without ceremony; completely; without stopping short.

Down-sitting, doun'sit-ing, *n. The act of sitting down;* repose; a resting.

Down-stairs, doun'stárs, *a.* or *adv. Descending the stairs;* below.

Down-train, doun'trān, *n.* A departing railway *train;* that is, one proceeding from the chief terminus.

Downtrod, Downtrodden, doun'trod, doun'trod-n, *a. Trodden down;* trampled down.

Downward, Downwards, doun'wérd, doun'wérds, *adv.* From a higher place to a lower; in a direction from a head or source; in a course of lineal descent from an ancestor; in the course of falling from distinction.—*a.* Moving from a higher to a lower place, as on a slope, or in the open air; tending toward the earth or its centre; bending; descending from a head or source; tending to a lower condition or state; depressed. [Sax. *dunewerd.*]

Downy, doun'i, *a. Covered with down* or nap; made of down; soft; soothing.

Dowry, dou'ri, *n.* The money, goods, or estate, which a woman brings to her husband in marriage; the portion given with a wife; the reward paid for a wife; a gift; a fortune given. [Norm. *douer,* gift.]

Doxological, doks-o-loj'ik-al, *a. Pertaining to doxology.*

Doxology, doks-ol'o-ji, *n.* A *hymn* in praise of the Almighty; a particular form of giving glory to God. [Late Gr. *doxologia*—*doxa,* glory (late), and *lego,* to utter.]

Doze, dōz, *vi. To languish from fatigue;* to sleep lightly; to live in a state of drowsiness; to be half asleep.—*vt.* To pass or spend in drowsiness. *ppr.* dozing, *pret. & pp.* dozed.—*n.* A slight sleep; a slumber. [Dan. *döse,* to make dull.]

Dozen, du'zn, *a. Two and ten;* twelve in number.—*n.* The number twelve of things of a like kind. [Fr. *douzaine*—L. *duodecim*—*duo,* two, and *decem,*ten.]

Doziness, dōz'i-nes, *n. Drowsiness.*

Dozing, dōz'ing, *p.n.* A slumbering.

Dozy, dōz'i, *a. Drowsy;* heavy; inclined to sleep; sleepy; sluggish.

Drab, drab, *n.* A low, dirty woman; a strumpet. [Sax. *drabbe.*]

Drab, drab, *n. Cloth;* a kind of thick woollen cloth of a dull brown colour, resembling fuller's earth.—*a.* Being of a dun colour, like the cloth so called. [Fr. *drap.*]

Drachm, dram, *n.* A Greek silver coin, averaging in value 9½d.; a Greek weight, the eighth part of an ounce. [Gr. *drachmē.*]

Draff, draf, *n. Refuse;* the wash given to swine, or grains to cows; waste matter. [D. *draf,* hog's wash.]

Draft, draft, *n. A drawing;* a drawing of men from an army; an order directing the payment of money; a bill of exchange; a drawing of lines for a plan; sketch; depth of water necessary to float a ship; a writing composed; an allowance for waste on goods sold by weight. *vt. To draw;* to draw the outline of; to compose and write; to draw, as men from a military band or post; to detach. [corrupted from *draught.*]

Drafted, draft'ed, *p.a. Drawn.*

Draftsman, drafts'man, *n. One who draws* plans or designs.

Drag, drag, *vt. To draw;* to *haul;* to draw along the ground by main force; to draw along in contempt; to haul about roughly and forcibly; to explore with a drag.—*vi. To be drawn along;* to hang so low as to trail on the ground; to fish with a drag; to be moved slowly; to proceed heavily. *ppr.* dragging, *pret. & pp.* dragged. *n.* A net drawn along the bottom of the water; a low cart; an instrument with hooks to catch hold of things under water; a machine for dredging docks, &c.; a contrivance for stopping the rotation of one wheel of a carriage, in descending hills, &c.; whatever is drawn; a boat in tow; whatever serves to retard a ship's way; a person or thing that is an obstacle to progress or prosperity. [Sax. *dragan;* Dan. *drage.*]

Draggle, drag'gl, *vt.* To wet and dirty by *drawing* on the ground or mud, or on wet grass.—*vi.* To become wet or dirty by being *drawn* on the mud or wet grass. *ppr.* draggling. *pret. & pp.* draggled. [dimin. of *drag.*]

Drag-net, drag'net, *n. A net to be drawn* along the bottom of a river or pond for taking fish.

Dragon, dra'gon, *n.* A fabulous kind of winged *keen-sighted,* scaly lizard or serpent; a fiery shooting; a meteor; a luminous exhalation from marshy grounds; a fierce, violent person, male or female; a kind of small lizard, having an expansion of the skin on each side, which forms a kind of wing, serving to sustain the animal when it leaps from branch to branch. [L. *draco*—Gr. *derkomai,* to see.]

Dragonish, dra'gon-ish, *a. In the form of a dragon;* dragon-like.

Dragon's-blood, dra'gonz-blud, *n.* The red thickened juice of certain tropical plants, used for colouring varnishes, staining marble, &c.

Dragoon, dra-gön', *n.* One of a class of soldiers, who originally carried a carbine, called a *dragon;* a soldier who serves on horseback or on foot as occasion may require.—*vt.* To enslave by *soldiers;* to harass; to compel to submit by violent measures; to force. [Fr. *dragon.*]

Drain, drān, *vt. To draw off* by degrees: to filter; to make dry; to exhaust of water by causing it to flow off in channels.—*vi.* To flow off gradually. *n.* A channel through which water or other liquid flows off; a trench to convey water from wet land; a watercourse; a sewer; (pl.) the grain from the mash-tub. [Dan. *draine.*]

Drainage, drān'āj, *n. A draining;* the mode in which the waters of a country pass off by its rivers; the act or art of draining; the system of drains; that which flows out of drains.

Drainer, drān'ér, *n. A utensil* on which articles are placed to drain.

Draining, drān'ing, *p.n. The process of drawing off* the water from wet lands, and lands liable to be flooded by excessive rains, by means of drains or trenches.

Drake, drāk, *n. The head or leader of the duck* kind; the male of ducks. [G. *enterich;* Dan. *andrik.*]

Dram, dram, *n. A small portion;* a weight of the eighth part of an ounce troy, or sixty grains; the sixteenth part of an ounce avoirdupois; as much spirituous liquor as is drunk at once. [contracted from L. *drachma.*]

Drama, dra'ma, *n. A deed or action;* representation of an act or actions; an action as represented on the stage; a poem or composition representing a picture of human life, and accommodated to action; dramatic literature. [Gr. *drama*—*drao,* to act.]

Dramatic, Dramatical, dra-mat'ik, dra-mat'ik-al, *a. Pertaining to the drama;* represented by action; theatrical. [Gr. *dramatikos.*]

Dramatically, dra-mat'ik-al-li, *adv. In the manner of the drama.*

Dramatist, dra'mat-ist, *n. The author of a dramatic composition.*

Dramatize, dra'mat-īz, *vt. To compose in the form of the drama. ppr.* dramatizing, *pret. & pp.* dramatized. [Gr. *dramatiso.*]

Drape, drāp, *vt. To cover with cloth* or drapery. *ppr.* draping, *pret. & pp.* draped. [Old Fr. *drap,* cloth.]

Fāte, fär, fat, fạll; mē, met, hėr; pīne, pin; nōte, not, mōve; tūbe, tub, bụll; oil, pound.

Draped, drāpt, *p.a.* Having on drapery.
Draper, drāp'ėr, *n.* One who sells cloths. [Fr. *drapier*.]
Draperied, drā'pė-rid, *p.a.* Furnished with drapery.
Drapery, drāp'ė-ri, *n.* Cloth-work; the trade of making cloth; cloth; stuffs of wool; hangings, tapestry, &c.; the representation of the clothing or dress of human figures, &c., in sculpture and painting. [Fr. *draperie*.]
Drastic, dras'tik, *a.* Active; powerful; acting with strength or violence. (Generally applied to purgatives.) [Fr. *drastique*—Gr. *draō*, to act.]
Draught, draft, *n.* Act of drawing; capacity of being drawn; force necessary to draw anything; the drawing of liquor into the mouth; the quantity of liquor drunk at once; act of delineating; that which is delineated; a written sketch; that which is taken by sweeping with a net; a drawing of men; a sink; an order for the payment of money; a bill of exchange; the depth of water necessary to float a ship; a current of air; the rate of motion of the ascending current of heated air in a chimney.—*a.* Used for drawing; drawn from the barrel.—*vt.* To draw out; to call forth. [Sax. *dragan*, to draw; Dan. *dragt*, burden.]
Draughts, drafts, *n. pl.* A game played on a checkered board.
Draughtsman, drafts'man, *n.* See DRAFTSMAN.
Draw, drą, *vt.* To pull along; to haul; to pull towards one; to pull out; to cause to come; to raise from any depth; to suck; to cause to move towards itself; to engage; to take out; to let out, as a liquid; to get; to produce; to bear; to receive, procure, or take; to lead, as a motive; to lengthen; to represent by lines drawn upon a surface; to describe; to represent by words; to infer; to derive; to entice; to compose according to a given form; to draft; to require, as a certain depth of water for floating; to inhale.—*vi.* To pull; to exert strength in drawing; to shrink; to advance; to unsheathe a sword; to practise the art of delineating figures; to collect the matter of an ulcer; to make a written demand for payment of money due (with *on*). *ppr.* drawing, *pret.* drew, *pp.* drawn.—*n.* Act of drawing; the lot or chance drawn. [Sax. *dragan*.]
Drawable, drą'a-bl, *a.* That may be drawn.
Drawback, drą'bak, *n.* Any deduction from profit; money paid back or remitted to an importer on the exportation of goods.
Drawbridge, drą'brij, *n.* A bridge which may be raised up, let down, or drawn aside to admit or hinder communication at pleasure.
Drawer, drą'ėr, *n.* He or that which draws or pulls; he who draws a bill of exchange; a sliding box in a case or table, which is drawn out at pleasure; (pl.) a close under-garment made to draw over the lower limbs.
Drawing, drą'ing, *p.n.* Act of pulling; delineation; representation; likeness; the distribution of prizes and blanks in a lottery.
Drawing-master, drą'ing-mas-tėr, *n.* One who teaches the art of drawing.
Drawing-room, drą'ing-röm, *n.* A withdrawing-room, a room appropriated for the reception of company; the formal reception of company at a court, or by persons in high station;

the company assembled in a drawing-room.
Drawl, drąl, *vi.* To loiter; to speak with slow, prolonged utterance.—*vt.* To utter, as words in a slow, lengthened tone.—*n.* A lengthened utterance of the voice. [D. *draalen*, to linger.]
Drawling, drąl'ing, *p.a.* Uttering words slowly.
Drawn, drąn, *p.a.* Pulled; hauled; induced, as by a motive; having equal advantage, and neither party a victory.
Draw-well, drą'wel, *n.* A deep well, from which water is drawn.
Dray, drā, *n.* That which is dragged along; a low carriage on wheels, drawn by a horse. [Sax. *dræge*—*dragan*, to draw.]
Dread, dred, *n.* A shaking with fear; fear, united with respect; terror; cause of fear; the person or the thing dreaded.—*a.* Exciting great fear; terrible; awful; venerable in the highest degree.—*vt.* To fear in a great degree.—*vi.* To be in great fear. [Sax. *drǽd*, fear.]
Dread-bolted, dred'bōlt-ed, *a.* Having bolts to be dreaded, as thunder.
Dreadful, dred'ful, *a.* Full of dread; awful; tremendous; inspiring awe or veneration.
Dreadfully, dred'ful-li, *adv.* Terribly.
Dreadfulness, dred'ful-nes, *n.* Quality of being dreadful; terribleness.
Dreadless, dred'les, *a.* Free from dread; secure.
Dream, drēm, *n.* The representation of something in sleep, accompanied by thoughts more or less disjointed; a vain fancy; a visionary scheme; an unfounded suspicion.—*vi.* To have ideas or images in the mind, in the state of sleep; to think; to imagine; to think idly.—*vt.* To see in a dream; to spend idly or vainly; to waste or while away (with *away*, &c.) *ppr.* dreaming, *pret.* & *pp.* dreamed or dreamt. [D. *droom*, a dream—Old Sax. *drōm*, sleep.]
Dreamer, drēm'ėr, *n.* One who dreams; a fanciful man; a visionary.
Dreaminess, drēm'i-nes, *n.* State of being dreamy.
Dreamy, drēm'i, *a.* Full of dreams; relating to dreams.
Drear, drēr, *a.* Repentant with sadness; sad; mournful; dismal; gloomy with solitude. [Sax. *dreórig*.]
Drearily, drē'ri-li, *adv.* Gloomily.
Dreariness, drē'ri-nes, *n.* Dismalness.
Dreary, drē'ri, *a.* Repentant with sadness; distressing; gloomy; solitary. [Sax. *dreórig*.]
Dredge, drej, *n.* A net or drag for taking oysters, &c.; a dredging-machine. *vt.* To take with a dredge; to deepen with a dredging-machine. *ppr.* dredging, *pret.* & *pp.* dredged. [Sax. *drœpe*—*dragan*, to drag.]
Dredge, drej, *vt.* To sprinkle; to sprinkle flour on, as on meat while roasting. *ppr.* dredging, *pret.* & *pp.* dredged. [Dan. *drysse*.]
Dredger, drej'ėr, *n.* One who fishes with a dredge; a utensil for scattering flour on meat while roasting; a dredging-machine.
Dredging, drej'ing, *p.n.* Act of catching with a dredge, deepening with a dredging-machine, or sprinkling with flour.
Dreggy, dreg'i, *a.* Containing dregs or lees; consisting of dregs; foul; muddy; feculent. [Icel. *dreggiadr*.]
Dregs, dregz, *n.pl.* Lees; grounds; any foreign matter of liquors that subsides to the bottom of a vessel; sweepings;

the most vile and despicable part. [Icel. *dregg*, sediment.]
Drench, drensh, *vt.* To cause to drink; to plunge; to soak; to steep; to saturate with drink; to purge violently. *n.* A soaking; a swill; a large portion of liquid medicine given to an animal by pouring down the throat; a dose of physic to be forced down the throat. [Sax. *drencan*, to give to drink.]
Drenched, drensht, *p.a.* Soaked; thoroughly wet; purged with a dose.
Drenching, drensh'ing, *p.a.* Wetting thoroughly; soaking.
Dress, dres, *vt.* To put in proper order; to cleanse, as a wound, and to apply medicaments; to make suitable; to curry, rub, and comb; to put clothes on; to attire; to apparel; to clothe; to array; to adorn; to embellish.—*vi.* To put on clothes; to be clothed; to pay particular regard to dress or raiment. *ppr.* dressing, *pret.* & *pp.* dressed or drest.—*n.* Array; elegant attire; clothing; garments; habit; a suit of clothes; a lady's gown; splendid clothes; habit of ceremony; skill in adjusting dress, or the practice of wearing elegant clothing. [Fr. *dresser*—L. *dirigo*, to set straight—*rego*, to guide.]
Dresser, dres'ėr, *n.* One who dresses; a table or bench on which meat and other things are dressed or prepared for use.
Dressing, dres'ing, *p.n.* Act of one who dresses; manure spread over land; that which is applied to a sore; the stuffing of fowls, pigs, &c.; a term applied to starch, &c., used in stiffening or preparing silk, linen, and other fabrics; (pl.) mouldings round doors, windows, &c.
Dressing-case, dres'ing-kās, *n.* A box containing articles necessary for the toilet.
Dressing-room, dres'ing-röm, *n.* An apartment for dressing the person.
Dressy, dres'i, *a.* Showy in dress.
Dribble, drib'bl, *vi.* To fall in a quick succession of drops; to slaver; to fall weakly and slowly.—*vt.* To throw down in drops. *ppr.* dribbling, *pret.* & *pp.* dribbled. [dimin. of *drip*.]
Dribblet, drib'let, *n.* A very small drop; a small piece or part; a small sum; odd money in a sum.
Dried, drid, *p.a.* Freed from moisture. [from *dry*.]
Drift, drift, *n.* That which is driven; a driving; a force urging forward; impulse; overbearing power; course of anything; scope; design; anything driven by force; a number of things driven at once; the velocity of a current.—*vi.* To move along like anything driven; to accumulate in heaps by the force of wind; to be driven into heaps; to be driven along; to float or be driven along by a current of water.—*vt.* To drive into heaps. [from Sax. *drifan*, to drive.]
Drifted, drift'ed, *p.a.* Driven along; driven into heaps.
Drifting, drift'ing, *p.n.* The act of drifting; a drift.
Drill, dril, *vt.* To bore or perforate by a vibratory motion; to pierce with a drill; to teach, as soldiers their proper movements; to form into drills or rows like soldiers arranged in lines; to teach by repeated exercise; to sow, as grain in rows.—*vi.* To sow in drills; to muster for exercise.—*n.* That which bores; a pointed instrument, used for boring holes; act of training soldiers;

ch, *chain*; j, *job*; g, *go*; ng, *sing*; ᴛʜ, *then*; th, *thin*; w, *wig*; wh, *whig*; zh, *azure*; † obsolete.

a row of grain; the channel in which the grain is deposited. [Sax. *thirlian*.]
Drilling, dril'ing, *p.n.* Act of piercing with a *drill*; that mode of sowing in which the seed is deposited in regular rows.
Drill-sergeant, dril'sär-jent, *n.* A non-commissioned officer, who teaches and trains soldiers to their duty.
Drink, dringk, *vi.* To swallow liquor for quenching *thirst*; to take spirituous liquors to excess; to be a habitual drunkard; to feast; to be entertained with liquors.—*vt.* To swallow, as liquids; to receive, as a fluid, into the stomach; to absorb; to see. *ppr.* drinking, *pret.* drank, and *pp.* drunk or drunken, the latter used adjectively.—*n.* Liquor to be swallowed; any fluid to be taken into the stomach; beverage; potion. [Sax. *drincan*; Sans. *trish*, to thirst.]
Drinkable, dringk'a-bl, *a. That may be drunk*; fit or suitable for drink.
Drinker, dringk'ėr, *n. One who drinks;* one who practises drinking spirituous liquors to excess; a drunkard.
Drinking, dringk'ing, *p.a.* Connected with the use of ardent spirits; making a free use of liquor.—*p.n. Act of one who drinks;* act of swallowing liquors; the practice of drinking to excess.
Drink-offering, dringk'of-fėr-ing, *n.* A Jewish *offering of wine*, &c.
Drip, drip, *vi. To fall in drops;* to have any liquid falling from it in drops. *vt. To let fall in drops. ppr.* dripping, *pret. & pp.* dripped.—*n. A falling in drops*, or that which falls in drops; the melted fat which *drips* from meat while roasting; the eaves. [Sax. *drypan*.]
Dripping, drip'ing, *p.n. A falling in drops;* the fat which falls from meat in roasting; that which falls in drops.
Drive, driv, *vt. To cause to run forward by force;* to force; to force along; to hunt; to impel, as a team of horses, and to direct their course; to take on a drive; to hurry on inconsiderately; to distress; to urge; to impel by moral influence; to carry on; to keep in motion.—*vi. To be caused to run along;* to be moved by any physical force or agent; to rush and press with violence; to pass in a carriage; to aim at; to make an effort to reach, as an object or end; to aim a blow; to strike at with force. *ppr.* driving, *pret.* drove, *pp.* driven.—*n.* Force; an excursion in a carriage for exercise; a course on which carriages are driven. [Sax. *drifan*, G. *treiben*, to drive.]
Drivel, dri'vel, *vi. To drawl;* to mutter indistinctly; to dote; to let the spittle fall in drops, like a child, an idiot, or a dotard. *ppr.* drivelling, *pret. & pp.* drivelled.—*n.* Slaver; saliva flowing from the mouth; nonsense. [Icel. *drafla*.]
Driveller, dri'vel-ėr, *n.* An idiot; a fool; a slaverer; a slabberer.
Drivelling, dri'vel-ing, *p.a.* Foolish; slavering.—*p.n.* A course of weak contemptible action or conduct.
Driver, driv'ėr, *n. He or that which drives.*
Driving, driv'ing, *p a.* Having great force of impulse.—*p.n.* The act of impelling; tendency.
Drizzle, driz'l, *vi. To fall as water from the clouds in very fine particles;* to rain in small drops.—*vt.* To shed in small drops or particles. *ppr.* drizzling, *pret. & pp.* drizzled.—*n.* A small rain. [Sax. *dreósan*, to fall.]

Drizzling, driz'l-ing, *p.n. The falling of rain* or sleet in small drops.
Drizzly, driz'l-i, *a.* Shedding small rain, or small particles of snow.
Droll, drōl, *a. Causing mirth or laughter;* comic; waggish; queer; facetious; laughable; ludicrous.—*n.* One whose occupation is *to raise mirth* by odd tricks; a jester; a farce; something exhibited to raise mirth or sport. [Fr. *drôle,* facetious.]
Drollery, drōl'ė-ri, *n. Sportive tricks;* gestures or tales adapted to raise mirth; a puppet-show. [Fr. *drôlerie.*]
Dromedary, drum'ē-da-ri, *n. The swift goer or runner;* the Arabian camel, with one bunch on the back, in distinction from the Bactrian camel, which has two bunches; any quick-travelling camel. [Fr. *dromadaire*—Old Gr. *dramō*, to run.]
Drone, drōn, *n.* The male or non-working bee; one who earns nothing by industry; a humming or low sound; the largest tube of the bagpipe, which emits a continued deep note.—*vi.* To live in idleness; to give a low, heavy, dull sound. *ppr.* droning, *pret. & pp.* droned. [Sax. *dran*.]
Droning, drōn'ing, *p.n.* Dull, drivelling utterance.
Dronish, drōn'ish, *a.* Idle; sluggish.
Droop, dröp, *vi.* To lean downward, as a body that is weak; to languish from grief or other cause; to grow weak; to be dispirited; to draw toward a close. *vt.* To let sink or *hang down.* [Icel. *drūipa*, to hang the head.]
Drooping, dröp'ing, *p. a.* Declining; languishing; failing.
Droopingly, dröp'ing-li, *adv. In a drooping manner.*
Drop, drop, *n. A small globule* of any liquid; a small portion of water falling in rain; a diamond hanging from the ear; an earring; something hanging in the form of a drop; a very small quantity of liquor; the part of a gallows which sustains the criminal before he is executed, and which is suddenly dropped.—*vt. To cause to flow in small globules,* as a fluid; to cover with drops; to let fall, as any substance; to lay aside; to quit; to utter slightly; to insert indirectly; to leave; to set down and leave, as a passenger; to suffer to come to nothing; to lower.—*vi. To flow in small globules,* as a liquid; to distil; to fall; to descend suddenly; to die, or to die suddenly; to cease; to come to nothing; to come unexpectedly; to lower. *ppr.* dropping, *pret. & pp.* dropped. [Sax. *dropa*, G. *tropfen*, a drop.]
Dropping, drop'ing, *p.n.* Act of *dropping;* a distilling; a falling; that which drops.
Dropsical, drop'sik-al, *a. Diseased with dropsy;* inclined to dropsy; partaking of the nature of dropsy.
Dropsy, drop'si, *n. A watery aspect;* an unnatural collection of water in any part of the body; a disease in succulent plants, from an excess of water. [Fr *hydropisie*—Gr. *hudōr*, water, and *ops*, the countenance.]
Drosky, dros'ki, *n.* A low, four-wheeled vehicle, among the Russians, without a top. [Rus. *droitsschka*.]
Dross, dros, *n. That which falls;* the scum of metals thrown off in the process of melting; crust of metals; waste matter; refuse; impure matter. [Sax. *dros*, filth, dregs.]
Drossiness, dros'i-nes, *n. A state of being drossy;* foulness; rust; impurity.

Drossy, dros'i, *a. Like dross;* pertaining to dross; full of dross; worthless.
Drought, drout, *n. Dryness;* want of rain or of water; dryness of the weather; aridness; dryness of the throat and mouth; thirst; lack. [contracted from Sax. *drugothe*—*drigan,* to dry.]
Droughtiness, drout'i-nes, *n. A state of dryness* of the weather; want of rain.
Droughty, drout'i, *a. Dry,* as the weather; thirsty.
Drove, drōv, *n.* A collection of cattle *driven;* any collection of irrational animals, moving or driving forward; a road for driving cattle; a crowd of people in motion. [Sax. *draf.*]
Drover, drōv'ėr, *n.* One who makes it his business to purchase fat cattle, and *drive* them to market.
Drown, droun, *vt. To immerge in water;* to immerse; to extinguish the life of by immersion in water or other fluid; to overflow; to inundate, as the earth; to overwhelm; to extinguish.—*vi.* To be suffocated in water or other fluid; to perish in water. [Sax. *adrencan*.]
Drowned, dround, *p.a.* Having life put out by immersion in water; inundated; overwhelmed.
Drowning, droun'ing, *p.a.* Perishing in water.—*p.n.* Act of suffocating by immersion under water.
Drowse, drouz, *vi.* To nod in slumber; to sleep imperfectly; to be heavy or dull.—*vt.* To make heavy with sleep; to make dull or stupid. *ppr.* drowsing, *pret. & pp.* drowsed. [Belgic, *droosen*.]
Drowsily, drou'zi-li, *adv.* Sleepily.
Drowsiness, drou'zi-nes, *n. Sleepiness;* heaviness with sleep.
Drowsy, drou'zi, *a. Inclined to sleep;* heavy with sleepiness; disposing to sleep; lulling; stupid.
Drub, drub, *vt.* To cudgel; to thrash. *ppr.* drubbing, *pret & pp.* drubbed.—*n.* A blow with a cudgel; a thump; a knock. [Sax. *drepan*.]
Drubber, drub'ėr, *n. One who drubs.*
Drubbing, drub'ing, *p.n.* A cudgelling; a sound beating.
Drudge, druj, *vi.* To do *laborious work;* to work hard; to labour in mean offices. *ppr.* drudging, *pret. & pp.* drudged.—*n. One who labours* hard in servile employments; a slave. [from Sax. *dreogan,* to work.]
Drudgery, druj'ė-ri, *n. Hard labour;* toilsome work; ignoble toil.
Drudgingly, druj'ing-li, *adv. With labour* and fatigue; laboriously.
Drug, drug, *n. That which is dried,* as an herb, &c.; the general name of substances used in medicine, tanning, &c.; an article of slow sale; a drudget. *vt. To season with drugs;* to tincture with something offensive; to dose to excess with drugs. *ppr.* drugging, *pret. & pp.* drugged. [Sax. *drig,* D. *droog,* dry.]
Drugget, drug'get, *n.* A coarse woollen cloth, thick and strong, stamped on one side with figures, and used as a covering for carpets. [Fr. *droguet.*]
Druggist, drug'ist, *n. One who deals in drugs;* one whose occupation is merely to buy and sell drugs, without compounding or preparation. [Fr. *droguiste.*]
Druid, drö'id, *n.* A priest or minister of religion, among the ancient Celtic nations, in Gaul, Britain, and Germany, who performed religious rites in groves of oak. [Gael. *druidh*—Gr. *drus*, an oak, any timber tree.]
Druidic, Druidical, drö-id'ik, drö-id'ik-al, *a. Pertaining to the Druids.*

Fāte, fär, fat, fall; mē, met, hėr; pīne, pin; nōte, not, mōve; tūbe, tub, bųll; oil, pound.

Druidism, drū'id-izm, *n.* The doctrines, rites, and ceremonies of *the Druids.*
Drum, drum, *n.* A martial instrument of music; something in the form of a drum; the tympanum of the ear; the hollow part of the ear behind the tympanum; a revolving cylinder or barrel.—*vi.* To beat or play a tune on a drum; to beat with the fingers, as with drum-sticks; to beat, as the heart.—*vt.* To expel with *beal of drum. ppr.* drumming, *pret. & pp.* drummed. [Dan. *tromme,* a drum.]
Drumble, drum'bl, *vi.* To be confused; to be sluggish.
Drumhead, drum'hed, *n. The head of a drum;* the top part of a capstan.
Drum-major, drum'mā-jėr, *n. The chief or first drummer* of a regiment.
Drummer, drum'ėr, *n. One whose office is to beat the drum* in military exercises.
Drunk, drungk, *p.a.* Stupified or inflamed by the action of spirit on the stomach and brain; drunken.
Drunkard, drungk'ėrd, *n.* One given to an excessive use of strong *drink;* a person who is habitually or frequently drunk.
Drunken, drungk'en, *p.a.* Inebriated with strong liquor; given to drunkenness; proceeding from intoxication; done in a state of drunkenness. [Sax. *druncen.*]
Drunkenness, drungk'en-nes, *n.* Intoxication; inebriety; intemperance in drinking; disorder of the faculties.
Dry, drī, *a. Without moisture;* thirsty; arid; free from rain or mist; free from juice; not green; without tears; not giving milk; barren; uninteresting; sarcastic; keen; harsh; cold.—*vt.* To free from water or from *moisture;* to deprive of natural juice or greenness; to parch with thirst; to deprive of water by draining; to drain; to exhaust.—*vi. To grow thirsty* or *dry;* to lose moisture; to become free from moisture or juice; to evaporate wholly; to be exhaled (with *up*). *ppr.* drying, *pret. & pp.* dried. (Sax. *dri;* Sans. *drakh,* to be dry; *trish,* to thirst.]
Dryad, drī'ad, *n.* A nymph supposed to preside over woods. [Gr. *Druades,* pl. from *drus,* a tree.]
Dryer, drī'ėr, *n. He or that which dries;* that which exhausts of moisture.
Dry-foot†, drī'fut, *n.* A dog that pursues game by the scent of the foot.
Drying, drī'ing, *p.a.* Adapted to exhaust *moisture;* becoming quickly dry.—*p.n.* The act or process of depriving of *moisture* or greenness.
Dryly, drī'li, *adv.* Without moisture; frigidly; sarcastically.
Dryness, drī'nes, *n. State of being dry;* destitution of water or moisture; want of water or other fluid; aridness; want of juice; want of greenness; barrenness; want of ornament; want of that which enlivens; formality of style in painting.
Dry-nurse, drī'nėrs, *n.* A *nurse* who attends and feeds a child by hand.
Dry-rot, drī'rot, *n.* A rapid decay of timber, by which its substance is converted into *a dry powder.*
Drysalter, drī'salt-ėr, *n.* A *dealer* in *salted or dry meats,* pickles, sauces, &c.
Drysaltery, drī'salt-ė-ri, *n. The articles kept by a drysalter;* the business of a drysalter.
Dual, dū'al, *a. Expressing the number two;* as, the dual number in Greek. [L. *dualis—duo,* two.]
Dualism, dū'al-izm, *n.* A dividing into two; the doctrine of two gods, a good and an evil one.
Dualist, dū'al-ist, *n.* One who holds the doctrine of *dualism.*
Duality, dū-al'i-ti, *n. That which expresses two in number;* division; separation; the state of being two.
Dub, dub, *vt. To furnish with arms†;* to tap with a sword; to confer the title of knighthood upon by a tap with a sword; to confer any dignity or new character upon. *ppr.* dubbing, *pret. & pp.* dubbed. [Old Fr. *adouber.*]
Dubious, dū'bi-us, *a. Moving in two directions;* wavering in opinion; undetermined; not clear; equivocal; uncertain. [L. *dubius—duo,* two, and *via,* a way.]
Dubiously, dū'bi-us-li, *adv.* Doubtfully.
Dubiousness, dū'bi-us-nes, *n. Doubtfulness;* a state of wavering and indecision of mind; uncertainty.
Ducal, dūk'al, *a. Pertaining to a duke.* [Fr.]
Ducally, dūk'al-li, *adv. After the manner of a duke.*
Ducat, duk'at, *n.* A coin of several countries in Europe, struck in the dominions of *a duke.* [Fr.]
Duchess, duch'es, *n. The consort or widow of a duke;* a lady who has the sovereignty of a duchy. [Fr. *duchesse.*]
Duchy, duch'i, *n. A dukedom;* the dominions of a duke. [Fr. *duché.*]
Duck, duk, *n.* A species of coarse cloth or light canvas, used for small sails, sacking of beds, &c. [Sw. *duk,* cloth.]
Duck, duk, *n. The diver;* a well-known water-bird, which *dives* with its head under water; an inclination of the head, resembling the motion of a duck in water.—*vt. To plunge,* as the head in water and immediately withdraw it.—*vi. To dip;* to plunge into water, and immediately withdraw; to plunge the head in water or other liquid; to drop the head suddenly; to bow; to cringe (in the two last senses with to). [G. *ducken,* to dip or dive.]
Ducking, duk'ing, *p.n.* Act of *plunging* in water and withdrawing.
Duckling, duk'ling, *n. A young duck.*
Duct, dukt, *n.* Any tube or canal by which a fluid or other substance is con¦lucted, especially in the internal structure of animals and plants. [L. *ductus—duco,* to lead.]
Ductile, duk'til, *a. That may be drawn out;* that may be drawn out into wire or threads, as a metal; docile; tractable; complying. [Fr.—L. *ductilis.*]
Ductility, duk-til'i-ti, *n. Property of being ductile;* the property of metals, which renders them capable of being extended by drawing without breaking; obsequiousness; ready compliance. [Fr. *ductilité.*]
Dudgeon, du'jon, *n. Something sharp or pointed;* a small dagger, or the handle of a dagger. [G. *degen,* a sword.]
Dudgeon, du'jon, *n. Malice;* inward anger or resentment; sullenness; ill-will; discord. [W. *dygen.*]
Due, dū, *a. Owed;* owing; that ought to be paid or done to another; suitable; becoming; exact; that ought to have arrived, or to be present, before the time specified.—*adv.* Directly; exactly.—*n. That which is owed or owing;* that which law or justice requires to be paid or done; that which office or rank requires to be given, paid, or done; that which law or custom requires; right; just title.—*vt.*†
To pay as due; to endue. [Fr. *dû, pp.* of *devoir*—L. *debeo, debere,* to owe.]
Duel, dū'el, *n.* A premeditated *combat between two persons;* a single combat; any contention or contest. [Fr.—L. *duo,* two.]
Duelling, dū'el-ing, *p.a. Pertaining to or employed in duelling.*—*n.* Act or practice of fighting in single combat.
Duellist, dū'el-ist, *n.* One who fights in single combat.
Duello†, dū-el'lō, *n.* The practice of *duelling.*
Duenna, dū-en'na, *n. The chief lady* in waiting on the Queen of Spain; an old widow, or an old woman who is kept to guard a younger; a governess. [Sp. *dueña*—L. *domina.*]
Duet, dū'et, *n.* A piece of music composed for *two performers,* vocal or instrumental. [It. *duetto.*]
Dug, dug, *n. The pap or nipple;* now applied only to a cow or other beast, unless in contempt. [Mid. High G. *degen,* to suckle.]
Duke, dūk, *n. A leader;* a title of nobility next below the princes; in some countries on the Continent, a sovereign prince. [Fr. *duc*—L. *dux,* a leader, —*duco,* to lead.]
Dukedom, dūk'dum, *n. The jurisdiction or possessions of a duke;* the title or quality of a duke.
Dulcet, dul'set, *a. Sweet* to the ear; melodious; harmonious. [It. *dolciato* —L. *dulcis,* sweet.]
Dulcimer, dul'si-mėr, *n.* An instrument of music, so called from the *sweetness* of its *sounds.* [Sp. *dulcémele*—L. *dulcis,* sweet, and *melos,* an air.]
Dull, dul, *a. Stupid; blockish;* without life or spirit; slow of hearing or seeing; slow to learn or comprehend; awkward; drowsy; sad; gross; cheerless; not bright or clear; tarnished; not briskly burning; obscure; blunt; cloudy; overcast; not lively or animated.—*vt. To make dull;* to stupify; to blunt, as edge-tools; to make sad; to make insensible; to render lifeless, as the attention; to make slow of motion; to sully; to tarnish or cloud.—*vi. To become dull* or blunt; to become stupid. [Sax. *dol,* Old G. *tol,* foolish.]
Dullard, dul'ėrd, *n. A stupid person;* a blockhead; a dunce.
Dull-brained, dul'brānd, *a. Stupid;* doltish; of dull intellect.
Dully, dul'li, *adv. Stupidly;* sluggishly.
Dulness, dul'nes, *n. Stupidity;* slowness of comprehension; weakness or intellect; heaviness; slowness; dimness; bluntness; want of brightness.
Duly, dū'li, *adv.* Properly; fitly; in a suitable or becoming manner. [from *due.*]
Dumb, dum, *a.* Destitute of the power of speech; unable to utter articulate sounds; mute; silent; not using or accompanied with speech.—*vt.*† To silence. [Sax.]
Dumbly, dum'li, *adv.* Mutely.
Dumbness, dum'nes, *n.* Inability to utter articulate sounds; muteness; silence, or holding the peace.
Dumb-show, dun'shō, *n. Gesture without words;* pantomime.
Dummy, dum'mi, *n. One who is dumb;* the fourth or exposed hand when three persons play at whist.
Dump, dump, *n.* A *dull* state of the mind; sadness; melancholy; absence of mind (pl.) low spirits; melancholy; gloom. [D. *dom,* dull.]
Dumpish, dump'ish, *a. Dull;* stupid; sad; melancholy; depressed in spirits.

ch, *chain;* j, *job;* g, *go;* ng, *sing;* ᴛʜ, *then*: th, *thin:* w, *wig;* wh, *whig;* zh, *azure;* † obsolete.

Dumpishness, dump'ish-nes, n. State of being dull, heavy, and moping.
Dumpling, dump'ling, n. A kind of thick pudding or mass of paste in cookery; a cover of paste inclosing an apple and boiled, called *apple-dumpling*. [from *dumpy*.]
Dumpy, dump'i, a. *Short and thick.* [Icel. *doomp*, a short and stout servant maid.]
Dun, dun, a. *Of a dark dull colour;* of a colour partaking of a brown and black; of a dull brown colour; swarthy; gloomy. [Sax.]
Dun, dun, vt. To demand a debt from in a *clamorous* manner; to call upon for payment; to urge importunately for anything.—n. A clamorous importunate creditor; an urgent demand of payment in writing. ppr. dunning, pret. & pp. dunned. [Sax. *dynan*, to din, to make a noise.]
Dunce, duns, n. One slow at learning; a person of weak intellect; a dullard; a dolt; a thick-skull. [from *Duns Scotus*, the great leader of the schoolmen.]
Dung, dung, n. The excrement of animals.—vt. To manure with dung; to immerse in a bath of cow-dung and warm water, as calico.—vi. To void excrement. [Sax.]
Dungeon, dun'jon, n. A strong tower in the middle of a castle or fort; a close prison, or a deep, dark place of confinement; a subterraneous place of close confinement. [Fr. *donjon*.]
Dunghill, dung'hil, n. *A heap of dung;* any mean abode; a man meanly born†. a. Sprung from the dunghill; mean; low.
Dunging, dung'ing, p.n. The application of a bath of cow-dung, diffused through hot water, to cotton goods.
Dungy, dung'i, a. *Full of dung.*
Dunnish, dun'ish, a. *Inclined to a dun colour;* somewhat dun.
Duo, dū'ō, n. The number *two;* a song in two parts. [L.]
Duodecimal, dū-ō-de'si-mal, a. Proceeding in computation *by twelves;* twelfth. [L. *duodecim*, twelve.]
Duodecimals, dū-ō-de'si-malz, n. pl. A system of numbers, the scale of which is *twelve.*
Duodecimo, dū-ō-de'si-mō, a. Consisting of *twelve leaves* to a sheet.—n. A book in which a sheet is folded into *twelve leaves.* [L. *duodecim*.]
Dupe, dup, vt. To open.
Dupe, dūp, n. A person who is cheated or *deceived,* or one easily led astray by his credulity.—vt. To deceive; to cheat; to trick. ppr. duping, pret. & pp. duped. [Fr.—L. *decipere*, to deceive—*capio*, to take.]
Duplex, dū'pleks, a. *Double;* twofold. [L. *duo*, and *plico*, to fold.]
Duplicate, dū'pli-kāt, a. *Double; twofold.*—n. A *double or second copy;* a copy; a transcript. [L. *duplicatus—plico*, to fold.]
Duplication, dū-pli-kā'shon, n. Act of doubling; a doubling; a fold; the multiplication of a number by 2. [Fr. —L. *duplicatio*.]
Duplicity, dū-pli'si-ti, n. *Doubleness of heart or speech;* act of dissembling one's real opinions, with a design to mislead; guile; deception. [Fr. *duplicité*—Low L. *duplicitas.*]

Durability, dūr-a-bil'i-ti, n. Power of *continuing in any given state, without perishing.*
Durable, dūr'a-bl, a. *Lasting; continuing;* having the quality of lasting long without perishing; permanent; firm; stable; constant. [Fr.—L. *durabilis—duro*, to last—*dūrus*, hard.]
Durableness, dūr'a-bl-nes, n. *Power of lasting;* durability; permanence.
Durably, dūr'a-bli, adv. In a lasting manner; with long continuance.
Durance, dūr'ans, n. *Continuance;* imprisonment; custody of the jailer. [Old It. *duransa*—L. *diu*, long, *dies*, a day.]
Duration, dūr-ā'shon, n. *Continuance* in time; power of continuance; permanency. [L. *duratio*.]
Dure†, dūr, vi. *To last;* to endure; to continue. [L. *duro*.]
Duress, dūr'es, n. *Hardship;* imprisonment. [Old Fr. *duresse*.]
During, dūr'ing, prep. For the time of the *continuance* of.
Dusk, dusk, a. *Darkened†;* tending to darkness, or moderately dark; moderately black.—n. A tending to *darkness;* a middle degree between light and darkness; twilight; tendency to a black colour. [Sax. *thiostrig*, dark.]
Duskily, dusk'i-li, adv. With a tendency to blackness or *darkness.*
Duskiness, dusk'i-nes, n. Incipient or partial *darkness.*
Duskish, dusk'ish, a. *Moderately dusk;* partially obscure; slightly dark or black.
Dusky, dusk'i, a. Partially *dark* or obscure; tending to blackness in colour; not bright; sad; intellectually clouded; gloomy.
Dust, dust, n. Powder; fine dry particles of earth; fine earth; anything finely pulverized; earth; unorganized earthy matter; state of dissolution; the grave; a mean and dejected state; the pollen of the anther in flowers.—vt. To free *from dust;* to brush, wipe, or sweep away dust from; to sprinkle, as with dust. [Sax.—Sans. *tusta*.]
Duster, dust'ėr, n. *A utensil to clear from dust;* a sieve.
Dustiness, dust'i-nes, n. State of being *dusty.*
Dusting, dust'ing, p.n. Act of removing *dust.*
Dusty, dust'i, a. *Covered or sprinkled with dust;* clouded with dust; like dust; of the colour of dust. [Sax. *dystig*.]
Dutch, duch, a. Pertaining to Holland, or to its inhabitants. [G. *Deutsch*, German.]
Duteous, dū'tē-us, a. *Performing that which is due;* dutiful; respectful to superiors; obsequious. [from *duty.*]
Duteously, dū'tē-us-li, adv. *In a duteous manner.*
Dutiful, dū'ti-fu̧l, a. *Duteous;* obedient; submissive to superiors; respectful; expressive of respect; required by duty.
Dutifully, dū'ti-fu̧l-li, adv. In a dutiful manner.
Dutifulness, dū'ti-fu̧l-nes, n. Obedience; habitual performance of duty; reverence; respect.
Duty, dū'ti, n. *That which is due;* that which a person owes to another; obligation; obedience; submission; act of reverence; any service, particularly that of a soldier on guard; military or naval service; tax; impost or customs.
Dwarf, dwarf, n. Anything stunted in growth; an animal or plant which is much below the ordinary size of the species; a man that never grows beyond two or three feet in height.—vt. To stunt; to make or keep small.—a. Being below the common size; stunted; dwarfish. [Low G.]
Dwarfish, dwarf'ish, a. *Like a dwarf;* below the common stature or size; very small; low; petty; despicable.
Dwarfishness, dwarf'ish-nes, n. Smallness of stature; littleness of size.
Dwell, dwel, vi. *To tarry;* to live in a place; to reside; to be domiciled; to stay; to be fixed in attention; to hang upon with fondness; to continue long. ppr. dwelling, pret. & pp. dwelled. usually contracted into dwelt. [Icel. *dvel,* to abide.]
Dweller, dwel'ėr, n. An inhabitant.
Dwelling, dwel'ing, p.n. Habitation; place of residence; abode; domicile; residence.
Dwindle, dwin'dl, vi. *To decay;* to become less; to shrink; to fall away. vt. To make less; to bring low; to break; to disperse. ppr. dwindling, pret. & pp. dwindled. [Sax. *devinan,* to pine.]
Dye, dī, vt. *To stain;* to give a new and permanent colour to. ppr. dyeing, pret. & pp. dyed.—n. Tinge; a colouring liquid or matter. [Sax. *deagan.*]
Dyeing, dī'ing, p.n. Art of giving new and permanent colours.
Dyer, dī'ėr, n. One whose occupation is to dye cloth and the like.
Dye-stuffs, dī'stufs, n. pl. *Materials* used in *dyeing.*
Dying, dī'ing, p.a. Mortal; destined to death; uttered just before death; pertaining to death.—p.n. Death.
Dyke, dīk. See Dike.
Dynamic, Dynamical, di-nam'ik, di-nam'ik-al, a. *Pertaining to strength or power,* or to dynamics. [Gr. *dunamikos—dunamai*, to be able.]
Dynamically, di-nam'ik-al-li, adv. *In a dynamical manner.*
Dynamics, di-nam'iks, n. *The science of forces* producing motion, or of the motion of bodies acted on by forces which are not in equilibrium.
Dynastic, di-nas'tik, a. *Relating to a dynasty.*
Dynasty, dī'nas-ti, n. Power†; a succession of kings of the same line or family, who *govern* a particular country. [Gr. *dunasteia—dunamai*, to be able —Heb. *din,* to rule.]
Dysenteric, dis-en-te'rik, a. *Accompanied with dysentery;* proceeding from dysentery.
Dysentery, dis'en-te-ri, n. A *disorder of the intestines;* a flux in which the stools consist chiefly of blood and mucus. [Fr. *dyssenterie*—Gr. *dus,* bad, and *entron,* intestines.]
Dyspepsy, dis-pep'si, n. *Bad digestion;* indigestion or difficulty of digestion. [Fr. *dyspepsie*—Gr. *dus,* and *peptō,* to digest.]
Dyspeptic, dis-pep'tik, a. *Pertaining to* or *consisting in dyspepsy;* afflicted with bad digestion.—n. A person afflicted with bad digestion. [Gr. *dus,* and *peptikos,* conducive to digestion.]

Fāte, fär, fat, fa̧ll; mē, met, hėr; pīne, pin; nōte, not, mōve; tūbe, tub, bu̧ll; oil, pound.

E.

Each, ēch, *a. Every one* of any number separately considered or treated. [Sax. *ælc*—Sans. *ēka*, one.]

Eager, ē'gėr, *a. Sharp*†; sour†; biting†; ardent to pursue, perform, or obtain; inflamed by desire; impetuous; earnest; intense. [Fr. *aigre*—L. *acer.*]

Eagerly, ē'gėr-li, *adv.* With great ardour of desire; ardently; earnestly.

Eagerness, ē'gėr-nes, *n.* Ardent desire to do, pursue, or obtain anything; vehemence; impetuosity; fervour; avidity.

Eagle, ē'gl, *n.* A rapacious bird with a *crooked beak,* often called the king of birds; a military standard having the figure of an eagle on it, denoting power. [Fr. *aigle*—L. *aquila*—Sans. *ak,* to go crookedly.]

Eagle-eyed, ē'gl-īd, *a. Sharp-sighted as an eagle;* having acute intellectual vision.

Eaglet, ē'gl-et, *n. A young eagle.*

Eagle-wood, ē'gl-wụd, *n.* A fragrant wood, used by the Asiatics for burning as incense.

Ean, ēn, *vt.* To bring forth, as young.

Eanling†, ēn'ling, *n.* A lamb newly dropped.

Ear, ėr, *n.* One of the two organs of *hearing;* the power of distinguishing sounds and judging of harmony; a favourable hearing; heed; regard; opinion; taste; anything resembling an ear or ears. [Sax. *eare*—Sans. *sru,* to hear.]

Ear, ėr, *n. A spike,* as of corn.—*vi.* To *shoot as an ear;* to form ears, as corn. [Sax.]

Ear,† ėr, *vt. To plough* or till. [Sax. *erian*—L. *aro,* to plough.]

Ear-drum, ėr'drum, *n.* A membrane of the internal ear.

Eared†, ėrd, *p.a. Having ears;* having spikes formed, as corn; ploughed.

Earing, ėr'ing, *ppr. Shooting out,* as ears *of corn;* ploughing†; tilling†. *p.n.* A ploughing of land†.

Earl, ėrl, *n.* A British title of nobility, the third in rank, being next below a marquis, and next above a viscount. [Sax. *eorl,* a chief.]

Earldom, ėrl'dum, *n. The seignory, jurisdiction, or dignity of an earl.*

Earless, ėrles, *a. Destitute of ears;* disinclined to hear or listen.

Earliness, ėr'li-nes, *n.* State of advance or forwardness; promptness.

Earl-marshal, ėrl-mär'shal, *n.* One of the great officers of state in England, whose business it is to take cognizance of all matters relating to honour, pedigree, and military solemnities.

Early, ėr'li, *a. Being at the beginning of the day;* prior in time; being in good season; timely; seasonable; before the usual time.—*adv.* Soon; in good season; betimes. [Sax. *arĭtce;* Icel. *âr,* the morning.]

Earn, ėrn, *vt.* To gain by labour, service, or performance; to win by labour; to deserve. [Sax. *earnian.*]

Earnest, ėrn'est, *a.* Ardent and constant in the pursuit of an object; eager; zealous; fervent; springing from strong desire; intent; serious.—*n.* Seriousness; a reality; first-fruits; a part paid or delivered beforehand as a pledge and security for the whole; a pledge of something more to come. [Sax. *eornest.*]

Earnestly, ėrn'est-li, *adv.* Warmly; zealously; importunately; eagerly.

Earnestness, ėrn'est-nes, *n.* Ardour in the pursuit of anything; eagerness; vehemence; importunity; solicitude; intenseness of desire; seriousness.

Earnings, ėrn'ingz, *p.n. pl. That which is earned;* that which is gained or merited by labour or performance; wages; reward.

Ear-ring, ėr'ring, *n.* A jewel or ornament worn in the *ear;* a pendant.

Ear-shot, ėr'shot, *n.* The distance at which words may be heard.

Earth, ėrth, *n. That which may be* ploughed, *and which bears or yields increase;* the loose particles of inorganic matter on the surface of the globe; the terraqueous globe which we inhabit; the world, as opposed to other scenes of existence; the inhabitants of the globe; dry land, opposed to the sea; a distinct part of the globe; the ground; the surface of the globe.—*vt. To hide, or cause to hide in the earth;* to cover with earth or mould.—*vi.* To retire under ground; to burrow. [Sax. *eorthe*—Sans. *dhara*—*dhri,* to bear.]

Earth-born, ėrth'born, *a.* Springing originally *from the earth;* earthly; produced by earthly things.

Earth-bound, ėrth'bound, *a. Bound to the earth.*

Earthen, ėrth'en, *a. Made of earth.*

Earthenware, ėrth'en-wār, *n. Ware made of earth* or clay; crockery.

Earthiness, ėrth'i-nes, *n. Quality of being earthy;* grossness.

Earthliness, ėrth'li-nes, *n. Worldliness;* strong attachment to worldly things.

Earthling, ėrth'ling, *n. An inhabitant of the earth;* a mortal; a frail creature.

Earthly, ėrth'li, *a. Pertaining to the earth;* carnal; sordid; worldly; sensual; of anything on earth.

Earthly-minded, ėrth'li-mīnd-ed, *a.* Having a *mind* devoted to *earthly* things.

Earthquake, ėrth'kwāk, *n. A shaking of the earth;* sometimes a slight tremor; at other times a violent shaking or convulsion; at other times a rocking or heaving of the earth.

Earthward, ėrth'wėrd, *adv. Toward the earth.*

Earth-work, ėrth'wėrk, *n.* The displacement of *earth* by cuttings, &c., in the formation of railways; a fortification of *earth.*

Earth-worm, ėrth'wėrm, *n.* The *dewworm;* a worm that lives underground; a mean, sordid wretch.

Earthy, ėrth'i, *a.* Resembling or partaking *of earth;* relating to earth; gross; not refined.

Ear-trumpet, ėr'trum-pet, *n.* A *tube* applied to the *ear* to aid in hearing.

Ear-wax, ėr'waks, *n.* A *thick viscous substance,* secreted by the glands of the *ear.*

Earwig, ėr'wig, *n. The ear-worm,* a well-known insect, supposed to creep into the human brain through the ear; one who gains the ear of another by stealth and insinuations. [Sax. *earwigga*—*wigga,* a kind of fly.]

Ear-witness, ėr'wit-nes, *n.* One who is able to give *testimony* to a fact from his own *hearing.*

Ease, ēz, *n.* State of repose; freedom from pain or annoyance; freedom from mental pain; rest from labour; freedom from difficulty; freedom from stiffness, as ease of style; freedom from formality; unaffectedness.—*vt.* To *give ease* to; to free from pain; to relieve; to free from anxiety; to tranquillise; to alleviate; to appease; to release from pressure. *ppr.* easing, *pret. & pp.* eased. [Fr. *aise*—L. *otium.*]

Easel, ēz'el, *n. The frame which bears* the painter's canvas. [G. *esel,* an ass.]

Easement, ēz'ment, *n. That which gives ease;* relief from any evil; accommodation.

Easily, ēz'i-li, *adv. In an easy manner.*

Easiness, ēz'i-nes, *n. State of being easy; ease;* freedom from difficulty; a yielding without reluctance; freedom from stiffness or formality; tranquillity; freedom from pain.

East, ēst, *n. That part of the heavens where the morning light appears;* one of the four cardinal points; the eastern parts of the earth; the regions lying east of Europe, or other country.—*a.* Toward the rising sun; or toward the point where the sun rises when in the equinoctial.—*adv.* Toward the rising sun. [Sax.—Gr. *ēos,* the morning light.]

Easter, ēs'tėr, *n.* A festival of the Christian church, observed in commemoration of our Saviour's resurrection, and occurring on Sunday, the third day after Good Friday. [Sax.]

Easter-day, ēs'tėr-dā, *n. The festival of Easter.*

Easterling, ēst'ėr-ling, *n.* A native of some country *eastward* of another; a piece of money coined in the East by Richard II. of England.—*a.* Relating to the money of the *Easterlings* or Baltic traders.

Easterly, ēst'ėr-li, *a. Coming from the east,* as wind; toward the east; looking toward the east.—*adv. On the east;* in the direction of east.

Eastern, ēst'ėrn, *a. Oriental;* dwelling in the east; situated toward the east; in an easterly direction. [Sax.]

Easter-term, ēs'tėr-tėrm, *n.* One of the four terms during which the superior courts at Westminster are open. It begins on the 15th April, and ends on the 8th May.

Eastward, ēst'wėrd, *adv.* In the direction *of east* from some point or place.

Easy, ēz'i, *a. Being at ease* or rest; free from pain; free from anxiety; not difficult; that presents no great obstacles; smooth; gentle; complying; not unwilling; satisfied; affluent; not stiff; not harsh; not burdensome.

Eat, ēt, *vt. To bite* or chew *and swallow,* as food; to wear away; to gnaw; to consume; to devour. (With *up* in the last two senses.)—*vi.* To take food; to be maintained in food; to taste or relish; to corrode (chiefly with *into*). *ppr.* eating, *pret.* ēat or āte; *pp.* eaten. [Sax. *etan*—Sans. *ad,* to eat.]

Eatable, ēt'a-bl, *a. That may be eaten;* proper for food.—*n.* That which is fit for food; that which is used as food.

---

ch, *ch*ain; j, *j*ob; g, *g*o; ng, si*ng*; ᴛʜ, *th*en; th, *th*in; w, *w*ig; wh, *wh*ig; zh, a*z*ure; † obsolete.

Eater, ēt'ėr, n. *One who eats*; that which eats or corrodes; a corrosive.

Eating, ēt'ing, p.n. The act of chewing and swallowing food.

Eaves, ēvz, n. pl. *The lower border of the roof of a building*, which overhangs the walls, and casts off the water that falls on the roof. [Sax. *efese*.]

Eavesdrop, ēvz'drop, n. The water which falls in drops from the *eaves* of a house.—*vi*. To stand under the *eaves* or near the windows of a house, to listen and learn what is said within doors; to watch for opportunities of hearing the private conversation of others. *ppr.* eavesdropping, *pret. & pp.* eavesdropped.

Eavesdropper, ēvz'drop-ėr, n. One who skulks about a house to listen.

Ebb, eb, n. *A going away from*; the reflux of the tide; the return of tidewater toward the sea; a falling from a better to a worse state.—*vi*. To go away; to flow back, as the water of a tide toward the ocean; to decay; to decrease; to lower. [Sax. *ebbe*—Gr. *apo*, from.]

Ebbing, eb'ing, p.n. The reflux of the tide.

Ebon, eb'on, a. *Consisting of ebony*; like ebony; black.

Ebony, eb'on-i, n. *Stonewood*; a hard, heavy, and durable wood, which admits of a fine polish or gloss. [L. *ebēnus*—Heb. *eben*, a stone.]

Ebriety, ē-brī'e-ti, n. *Act of draining a goblet*; *drunkenness*; intoxication by spirituous liquors. [L. *ebrietas*—*ebrius*, drunk.]

Ebullition, ē-bul-li'shon, n. *A boiling up*; the operation of boiling; effervescence; a sudden burst, as of passion; a pouring forth; an overflowing; outbreak; effort. [Fr.—L. *bullio*, to boil.]

Eccentric, ek-sen'trik, a. *Deviating from the centre*; not having its axis in the centre; not having the same centre; deviating from stated methods, usual practice, or established forms or laws; departing from the usual course; singular; odd; strange. n. A circle *not having the same centre as another*; a wheel or disk having its axis placed out of the centre; that which is irregular. [Fr. *exoentrique*—L. *centrum*, the centre.]

Eccentrically, ek-sen'trik-al-li, adv. *In an eccentric manner*.

Eccentricity, ek-sen-tris'i-ti, n. *Deviation from a centre*; state of having a centre different from that of another circle; the distance of the centre of a planet's orbit from the centre of the sun; departure from that which is usual; singularity; oddness. [Fr. *excentricité*.]

Ecclesiastes, ek-klē'zi-as''tēz, n. *A preacher*; a canonical book of the Old Testament. [Gr. *ekklēsiastēs*.]

Ecclesiastic, Ecclesiastical, ek-klē'zi-as''tik, ek-klē'zi-as''tik-al, a. *Pertaining or relating to the church*; not civil or secular. [Gr. *ekklēsiastikos*—*ekklēsia*, a meeting—*kaleō*, to call.]

Ecclesiastic, ek-klē'zi-as''tik, n. *A person consecrated to the service of the church*; a person in orders; a clergyman.

Ecclesiastically, ek-klē'zi-as''tik-al-li, adv. *In an ecclesiastical manner*.

Ecclesiasticus, ek-klē'zi-as''tik-us, n. A book of the Apocrypha.

Echo, e'kō, n. *A sound*; a sound repeated; a sound reverberated from a solid body; repercussion of sound.—*vi*. To sound; to resound; to reflect sound; to give the repercussion of a sound; to be sounded back.—*vt*. To send back, as sound; to return what has been uttered. [Gr. *ēchō, ēchē*, a sound of any sort.]

Echoing, e'kō-ing, p.a. *Reverberating*; sending back sound.

Eclat, e-klä', n. *A bursting forth*, as of light; a burst of applause; applause; renown; splendour; pomp. [Fr. *éclat*—Gr. *klaō*, to break.]

Eclectic, ek-lek'tik, a. *Selecting*; relating to the *Eclectics*.—n. One of a class of ancient philosophers who *selected* from the various systems such principles as they judged to be sound; a Christian who adhered to the doctrines of the Eclectics; one of a sect of physicians. [Gr. *eklektikos*—*legō*, to choose.]

Eclectically, ek-lek'tik-al-li, adv. By way of choosing or *selecting*.

Eclecticism, ek-lek'ti-sizm, n. *The practice of selecting* from different systems; the doctrine of the Eclectics.

Eclipse, ē-klips', n. *A defect or failure*; an interception of the light of the sun, moon, or other luminary, by some opaque body; darkness; obscuration. *vt*. To darken or hide, as a luminous body, in whole or in part, and intercept its rays; to obscure; to cloud; to darken; to veil; to put out. *ppr.* eclipsing, *pret. & pp.* eclipsed. [Gr. *ekleipsis*—*leipō*, to leave.]

Ecliptic, ē-klip'tik, a. *Pertaining to the ecliptic*; suffering an eclipse; pertaining to an eclipse.—n. *The line in which eclipses take place*; the apparent path of the sun round the earth; a great circle on the terrestrial globe, answering to and falling within the plane of the celestial ecliptic. [Gr. *ekleiptikos*—*leipō*, to fail.]

Eclogue, ek'log, n. *A picking out*; that which is *chosen out*; a pastoral poem, in which shepherds are introduced conversing with each other. [Gr. *eklogē*—*legō*, to choose.]

Economic, Economical, ē-kon-om'ik, ē-kon-om'ik-al, a. *Pertaining to economy*; managing domestic or public pecuniary concerns with frugality; frugal; sparing; careful. [Fr. *économique*.]

Economically, ē-kon-om'ik-al-li, adv. *With economy*; with frugality.

Economics, ē-kon-om'iks, n. *The science of household affairs*.

Economist, ē-kon'om-ist, n. One who practises economy; one who is conversant with political economy. [Fr. *économiste*.]

Economize, ē-kon'om-īz, *vi*. To manage with frugality.—*vt*. To use with prudence; to expend with frugality. *ppr.* economizing, *pret. & pp.* economized. [Fr. *économiser*.]

Economy, ē-kon'o-mi, n. *The management of household affairs*; a frugal and judicious use of money; a system of rules; the regular operations of nature in the generation, nutrition, and preservation of animals or plants; due order of things; judicious management of public affairs; system of management. [Fr. *économie*—Gr. *oikos*, a house, and *nomos*, law.]

Ecstasied, ek'sta-si-ed, p.a. Ravished; transported; delighted.

Ecstasy, ek'sta-si, n. *A standing aside or out of*; a trance; a state in which the mind is fixed or lost; excessive joy; rapture; a degree of delight that arrests the whole mind; enthusiasm; excessive elevation and absorption of mind; madness'; distraction'. [Fr. *extase*—Gr. *histēmi*, to stand.]

Ecstatic, ek-stat'ik, a. *Causing ecstasy*; suspending the senses; entrancing; ravishing; delightful beyond measure. [Fr. *extatique*.]

Ecstatically, ek-stat'ik-al-li, adv. *In an ecstatic manner*.

Ecumenic, Ecumenical, e-ku-men'ik, e-ku-men'ik-al, a. *General; universal*. (Applied to general councils of the church.) [Fr. *œcuménique*.]

Eddy, ed'di, n. *A current of water running back*; a whirlpool; a current of water or air in a circular direction. a. Whirling; moving circularly.—*vi*. To move circularly, or as an eddy. *ppr.* eddying, *pret. & pp.* eddied. [Sax. *ed*, backward, and *ed*, running water.]

Eddying, ed'di-ing, p.a. Moving circularly, as an eddy.

Eden, ē'den, n. *A place of pleasure*; the country and garden in which Adam and Eve were placed by God himself; paradise. [Heb. pleasure.]

Edge, ej, n. *The extreme border of anything*; margin; brim; the thin cutting side of an instrument; that which cuts; that which injures; a narrow part rising from a broader; sharpness of mind or appetite; keenness; intenseness of desire; fitness for action; acrimony.—a. *Having an edge*; edged. *vt*. To bring to an edge; to furnish with an edge; to sharpen; to fringe; to exasperate; to instigate; to move, as with the edge turned forward; to move by little and little.—*vi*. To move sideways; to move gradually; to sail close to the wind. *ppr.* edging, *pret. & pp.* edged. [Sax. *ecg*.]

Edged, ejd, p.a. Sharp; keen.

Edge-tool, ej'töl, n. *An instrument having a sharp edge*.

Edgewise, ej'wīz, adv. *With the edge turned forward*; in the direction of the edge; sideways; with the side foremost.

Edging, ej'ing, p.n. That which is added on the *edge*, or which forms the edge; a border; a fringe; trimming; a narrow lace.

Edible, ed'i-bl, a. *Eatable*; fit to be eaten as food. [from L. *edo*, to eat.]

Edict, ē'dikt, n. *That which is proclaimed* by authority as a rule of action; an order issued by a prince to his subjects; a decree; manifesto; ordinance. [L. *edictum*—*dico*, to speak.]

Edictal, ē-dikt'al, a. *Pertaining to an edict*.

Edification, ed'i-fi-kā''shon, n. *A building*; a building up, in a moral and religious sense; improvement of the mind in any species of useful knowledge. [Fr.—L. *œdificatio*.]

Edifice, ed'i-fis, n. *A structure*; a fabric; a large or splendid building.

Edified, ed'i-fid, p.a. *Built up*; instructed.

Edify, ed'i-fī, *vt*. *To build up*, in a moral sense; to instruct and improve in knowledge generally, and particularly in religious knowledge. *ppr.* edifying, *pret. & pp.* edified. [Fr. *édifier*—L. *œdes*, a building and *facio*, to make.]

Edifying, ed'i-fī-ing, p.a. *Improving*; adapted to instruct.

Edifyingly, ed'i-fī-ing-li, adv. *In an edifying manner*.

Edile, ē'dil, n. A Roman magistrate who had the charge of *public buildings*. [L. *œdilis*, from *œdes*, a building.]

Edit, ed'it, *vt*. *To give out*; to put forth; to publish; to superintend, as a publication; to conduct, as a literary publication. [L. *edo, editum*—*do*, to give.]

Fate, fär, fat, fall; mē, met, hėr; pīne, pin; nōte, not, mōve; tūbe, tub, bull; oil, pound.

Edition, ē-di'shon, n. *A putting forth; the publication of any book or writing; any publication of a book before published; one impression or the whole number of copies published at once.* [Fr.—L. *editio.*]

Editor, ed'it-ėr, n. *One who gives forth; a publisher; a person who prepares a book for publication; one who superintends the publication of a newspaper, &c.* [L.]

Editorial, ed-i-tō'ri-al, a. *Pertaining to an editor; written by an editor.*

Editorially, ed-i-tō'ri-al-li, adv. *In the manner of an editor.*

Editorship, ed'it-ėr-ship, n. *The business of an editor.*

Educate, ed'ū-kāt, vt. *To bring up, as a child; to teach; to discipline; to enlighten, as the understanding; to instil principles of arts, science, morals, religion, and behaviour into. ppr. educating, pret. & pp. educated.* [L. *edūco, educatus—dūco*, to lead.]

Educated, ed'ū-kāt-ed, p.a. *Trained; disciplined.*

Education, ed-ū-kā'shon, n. *The bringing up, as of a child; instruction; the art of developing and cultivating the physical, intellectual, and moral faculties; formation of manners and improvement of the mind, especially in youth.* [Fr.]

Educational, ed-ū-kā'shon-al, a. *Pertaining to education.*

Educationist, ed-ū-kā'shon-ist, n. *One who is versed in or promotes education.*

Educator, ed'ū-kāt-ėr, n. *One who educates.* [L.]

Educe, ē-dūs', vt. *To draw out; to elicit; to extract. ppr. educing, pret. & pp. educed.* [L. *edūco—dūco*, to lead.]

Educible, ē-dūs'i-bl, a. *That may be educed.*

Eductor, ē-dukt'ėr, n. *He or that which brings forth, elicits, or extracts.*

Eel, ēl, n. *A serpent-like fish, covered with a thick slimy skin, and living much in mud.* [Sax. *ǣl*—Sans. *ali*, a scorpion.]

Eel-pout, ēl'pout, n. *A fresh-water fish somewhat resembling the eel.*

Efface, ef-fās', vt. *To remove from the face of anything; to render illegible; to blot out; to expunge; to destroy, as any impression on the mind; to wear away. ppr. effacing, pret. & pp. effaced.* [Fr. *effacer*—L. *facies*, a face.]

Effaceable, ef-fās'a-bl, a. *Capable of being effaced.*

Effacement, ef-fās'ment, n. *Act of effacing.*

Effect, ef-fekt', n. *That which is done or produced by an agent or cause; result; event; purpose; consequence intended; advantage; validity; completion; reality; not mere appearance; striking appearance; first impression produced by a work of art; result of all the peculiar excellences of the true master;—(pl.) goods; movables; personal estate.—vt. To make out; to produce, as a cause or agent; to cause to be; to fulfil; to execute.* [Old Fr.—L. *facio, factum*, to make.]

Effective, ef-fekt'iv, a. *Having the power to produce; efficacious; efficient; effectual; powerful; energetic.* [Fr. *effectif.*]

Effectively, ef-fekt'iv-li, adv. *With effect; powerfully; with real operation.*

Effectiveness, ef-fekt'iv-nes, n. *Quality of being effective.*

Effectless, ef-fekt'les, a. *Without effect; without advantage.*

Effector, ef-fekt'ėr, n. *One who effects; one who produces or causes.* [L.]

Effectual, ef-fek'tū-al, a. *Producing an effect, or the effect desired or intended; having power to produce the effect; veracious.†*

Effectually, ef-fek'tū-al-li, adv. *With effect; efficaciously; thoroughly.*

Effectuate, ef-fek'tū-āt, vt. *To carry into effect; to bring to pass. ppr. effectuating, pret. & pp. effectuated.* [Low L. *effectuo, effectuatus.*]

Effeminacy, ef-fem'in-a-si, n. *Womanish softness or weakness; delicacy and weakness unbecoming a man; unmanly delicacy; voluptuousness; indulgence in unmanly pleasures.*

Effeminate, ef-fem'in-at, a. *Made a woman of; womanish; soft or delicate in an unmanly degree; weak; resembling the practice or qualities of the female sex; voluptuous; cowardly. vt. To unman; to weaken.—vi. To grow womanish or weak; to melt into weakness. ppr. effeminating, pret. & pp. effeminated.* [L. *effeminatus—femina*, a woman.]

Effeminately, ef-fem'in-āt-li, adv. *In an effeminate manner; womanishly.*

Effervesce, ef-fėr-ves', vi. *To boil up or over; to bubble and hiss, as fermenting liquors, or any fluid; to work, as new wine. ppr. effervescing, pret. & pp. effervesced.* [L. *effervesco—ferveo*, to boil.]

Effervescence, ef-fėr-ves'ens, n. *Act of boiling up; that commotion of a fluid which takes place when some part of the mass flies off in the form of gas, producing innumerable small bubbles.* [Fr.]

Effervescent, ef-fėr-ves'ent, a. *Boiling up; gently bubbling, by means of the disengagement of gas.* [Fr.]

Effervescing, ef-fėr-ves'ing, p.a. *Bubbling by means of an elastic fluid extricated in the dissolution of bodies.*

Effete, ef-fēt', a. *No longer capable of producing young; worn out with age or excessive indulgence; barren.* [L. *effetus—fētus*, offspring.]

Efficacious, ef-fi-kā'shi-us, a. *Producing the effect intended; having power adequate to the purpose intended; powerful.* [L. *efficax, efficacis.*]

Efficaciously, ef-fi-kā'shi-us-li, adv. *Effectually.*

Efficacy, ef'fi-ka-si, n. *Power to produce effects; production of the effect intended; virtue; force; energy.* [Fr. *efficace*—L. *facio*, to make.]

Efficiency, ef-fi'shi-en-si, n. *Effectual agency; power of producing the effect intended.* [Low L. *efficientia.*]

Efficient, ef-fi'shi-ent, a. *Effecting; capable; producing; that causes anything to be what it is; characterized by energy.* [L. *efficiens—facio*, to do.]

Efficiently, ef-fi'shi-ent-li, adv. *With effect; effectively.*

Effigy, ef'fi-ji, n. *The image or likeness of a person; representation; any substance fashioned into the shape of a person; portrait; figure, in sculpture or painting.* [L. *effigies—fingo*, to form.]

Effloresce, ef-flo-res', vi. *To bloom; to form a mealy powder on the surface; to form saline vegetation on the surface. ppr. efflorescing, pret. & pp. effloresced.* [L. *effloresco—flos, floris*, a flower.]

Efflorescence, ef-flo-res'ens, n. *The time of flowering; a redness of the skin; the formation of a mealy powder on the surface of bodies; the powder thus formed.* [Fr.]

Efflorescent, ef-flo-res'ent, a. *Shooting out in the form of flowers.* [Fr.]

Effluent, ef'flū-ent, a. *Flowing out. n. A stream that flows out of another stream, or out of a lake.* [Fr.—L. *fluo, fluens*, to flow.]

Effluvial, ef-flū'vi-al, a. *Pertaining to effluvia; containing effluvia.*

Effluvium, ef-flū'vi-um, n. *Effluvia*, ef-flū'vi-a, pl. *That which flows out; the minute particles which exhale from terrestrial bodies, such as the odour or smell of plants; the exhalations from diseased bodies, &c.* [L.—*effluo—fluo*, to flow.]

Efflux, ef'fluks, n. *Act of flowing out or issuing in a stream; flow; emanation.* [L. *fluxus*, a flowing.]

Effluxion ef-fluk'shon, n. *Act of flowing out; that which flows out; effluvium; emanation.* [L. *fluxio*, a flowing—*fluo*, to flow.]

Effort, ef'fōrt, n. *An exertion of strength; exertion; struggle; strenuous endeavour; essay.* [Fr.—L. *fortis*, strong.]

Effrontery, ef-frun'te-ri, n. *Boldness of front; boldness transgressing the bounds of modesty and decorum; audacity.* [Fr. *effronterie*—L. *frons, frontis*, the forehead.]

Effulgence, ef-fulj'ens, n. *A shining forth; a flood of light; great lustre or brightness; splendour.* [Low L. *effulgentia*—L. *fulgeo*, to shine.]

Effulgent, ef-fulj'ent, a. *Shining; gleaming; bright; splendid.* [L. *fulgens.*]

Effulgently, ef-fulj'ent-li, adv. *With effulgence.*

Effuse, ef-fūs', vt. *To pour out, as a fluid; to shed. ppr. effusing, pret. & pp. effused.* [L. *effundo, effusus—fundo*, to pour.]

Effusion, ef-fū'shon, n. *Act of pouring out, as a liquid; waste; the pouring out, as of water, of blood, of grace, of words, and the like; that which is poured out.* [Fr. —L. *effusio.*]

Effusive, ef-fūs'iv, a. *Pouring out; that pours forth largely.*

Effusively, ef-fūs'iv-li, adv. *In an effusive manner.*

Eft, eft, n. *A newt; the common lizard.* [Sax. *efete.*]

Eftest†, eft'est, a. *Soonest; first.*

Egg, eg, n. *A roundish body produced by the females of birds and certain other animals, containing the substance from which a like animal is produced; anything shaped like an egg.* [Sax. *aeg;* Dan. *egge.*]

Eglantine, eg'lan-tin, n. *A species of rose, whose branches are beset with prickles and thorns like a hedgehog; the sweet-brier.* [Fr. *églantine*—D. *egel*, a hedgehog.]

Egotism, ē'got-izm, n. *The practice of too frequently using the word I; an exaggerated love of self, leading to self-exaltation.* [Fr. *egoisme*, from L. *ego*, I.]

Egotist, ē'got-ist, n. *One who repeats the word I very often in conversation or writing; one who magnifies his own achievements.*

Egotistic, Egotistical, ē-got-ist'ik, ē-got-ist'ik-al, a. *Addicted to egotism; conceited; containing egotism.*

Egotistically, ē-got-ist'ik-al-li, adv. *In an egotistic manner.*

Egotize, ē'got-iz, vi. *To talk or write much of one's self; to make pretensions to self-importance. ppr. egotizing, pret. & pp. egotized.*

Egregious, ē-grē'ji-us, a. *Chosen from the herd; eminent; standing out with remarkable prominence; extraordinary; monstrous; enormous.* [L. *egregius—grex, gregis*, a flock.]

ch, *chain;* j, *job;* g, *go;* ng, *sing;* ᴛʜ, *then;* th, *thin;* w, *wig;* wh, *whig;* zh, *azure;* † *obsolete.*

Egregiously, e-grē′ji-us-li, *adv*. Greatly; enormously; shamefully.
Egress, ē′gres, *n*. *Act of going out*, or the power of departing from any confined place; exit; departure; issue. [L. *egressus—gradior*, to go.]
Egyptian, ē-jip′shan, *a*. *Pertaining to Egypt* in Africa.—*n*. *A native of Egypt*; also, a gipsy.
Eh, eh, *interj*. Denoting inquiry or slight surprise.
Eider, **Eider-duck**, ī′dėr, ī′dėr-duk, *n*. A species of sea-duck, producing down of the finest and softest kind. [Icel. *ædur*.]
Eider-down, ī′dėr-doun, *n*. *Down* or soft feathers of the eider-duck. (G. *eider-dune*.]
Eight, āt, *a*. Twice four; expressing the number twice four. [Sax. *eahta*.]
Eighteen, āt′ēn, *a*. *Eight and ten* united. [Sax. *eahta*, and *tyn*, ten.]
Eighteenmo, āt′en-mō, *n*. A book in which a sheet is folded into *eighteen* leaves. [*eighteen* and last syllable of L. *decimo*.]
Eighteenth, āt′ēnth, *a*. Next in order after the seventeenth; noting one of *eighteen* parts into which anything is divided.
Eightfold, āt′fōld, *a*. *Eight* times the number or quantity.
Eighth, ātth, *a*. *Noting the number eight*; the ordinal of eight.
Eighthly, ātth′li, *adv*. *In the eighth place*.
Eightieth, āt′i-eth, *a*. The ordinal of *eighty*.
Eighty, āt′i, *a*. *Eight times ten*; fourscore. [Sax. *eahta-tig*.]
Either, ī′ṻėr, *pron*. *One or another* of any number; one of two; each; every one, separately considered.—*conj*. Correlative to *or*, indicating the first of certain things. [Sax. *ægther*.]
Ejaculate, ē-jak′ū-lāt, *vt*. *To throw out*; to utter, as a short prayer. *ppr*. ejaculating, *pret*. & *pp*. ejaculated. [L. *ejaculor, ejaculatus—jacio*, to throw.]
Ejaculation, ē-jak′ū-lā″shon, *n*. The uttering of a short prayer, or a short occasional prayer uttered. [Fr.—Low L. *ejaculatio*.]
Ejaculatory, ē-jak′ū-la-tō-ri, *a*. Uttered in short sentences, as prayer. [Fr. *ejaculatoire*.]
Eject, ē-jekt′, *vt*. *To throw out*; to thrust out, as from a place inclosed; to dismiss from an office; to turn out; to dispossess of land or estate; to drive away; to banish. [L. *ejicio, ejectum—jacio*, to throw.]
Ejection, ē-jek′shon, *n*. *Act of casting out*; expulsion; dismission from office; dispossession; vomiting, &c. [L. *ejectio*.]
Ejectment, ē-jekt′ment, *n*. *A casting out*; a writ or action which lies for the recovery of possession of land from which the owner has been ejected, and for trial of title.
Ejector, ē-jekt′or, *n*. *One who ejects*. [Low L.]
Eke, ēk, *vt*. *To increase*; to add to; to supply, as what is wanted; to lengthen; to prolong. *ppr*. eking, *pret*. & *pp*. eked. [Sax. *ecan*.]—*adv*. *In addition*; also; likewise. [Sax. *eac*.]
Elaborate, ē-lab′o-rāt, *vt*. *To labour on*; to produce with labour; to refine by successive operations. *ppr*. elaborating, *pret*. & *pp*. elaborated—*a*. *Wrought with labour*; finished with great diligence; studied; high-wrought. [L. *elaboro, elaboratus—labor*, toil.]
Elaborately, ē-lab′o-rāt-li, *adv*. *In an elaborate manner*.

Elaboration, ē-lab′o-rā″shon, *n*. Refinement by successive operations; the various changes which substances undergo in the acts of assimilation in animals and vegetables. [Fr.]
Elapse, ē-laps′, *vi*. *To slide away*; to slip or glide away; to pass away silently, as time. *ppr*. elapsing, *pret*. & *pp*. elapsed. [L. *elabor, elapsus—labor, lapsus*, to glide.]
Elastic, ē-las′tik, *a*. *Springing back* when forced out of its position; having the power of returning to the form from which it is bent or distorted. [Fr. *élastique*—Ar. *lastik*, springy.]
Elastically, ē-las′tik-al-li, *adv*. *In an elastic manner*.
Elasticity, ē-las-tis′i-ti, *n*. The inherent property in certain bodies, by which they recover their former figure or state, after external pressure, tension, or distortion. [Fr. *elasticité*.]
Elate, ē-lāt′, *a*. *Exalted*; elevated in mind; flushed, as with success; haughty; swelling.—*vt*. *To carry up*; to exalt; to raise, as the mind or spirits; to puff up; to make proud. *ppr*. elating, *pret*. & *pp*. elated. [L. *elatus—fero, latum*, to bear.]
Elated, ē-lāt′ed, *p.a*. *Elevated* in mind or spirits; puffed up.
Elation, ē-lā′shon, *n*. *A lifting up*; an inflation of mind proceeding from self-approbation; haughtiness; pride of prosperity. [L. *elatio*.]
Elbow, el′bō, *n*. *The bend of the arm*, or the outer angle made by the bend of the arm; any angle; the obtuse angle of a wall.—*vt*. *To push with the elbow*; to push or drive to a distance; to encroach on.—*vi*. To jut into an angle; to project; to bend. [Sax. *elboga—elne*, an ell, and *boga*, anything curved.]
Elbow-room, el′bō-rōm, *n*. *Room to extend the elbows* on each side; room for motion or action.
Eld', eld, *n*. *Old times*; antiquity.
Elder, eld′ėr, *a*. *Older*; having lived a longer time; prior in origin; preceding in the date of a commission.—*n*. *One who is older*; a person advanced in life, and who, on account of his age, experience, and wisdom, is selected for office; an office-bearer in the Presbyterian church. [Sax. *ealdor*.]
Elder, eld′ėr, *n*. *The hollow tree*; a small tree having a spongy pith, and bearing dark purple berries, which are used for making a kind of wine. [Old G. *holuntur—hol*, a concave.]
Elderly, eld′ėr-li, *a*. *Somewhat old*; advanced beyond middle age.
Eldership, eld′ėr-ship, *n*. *Seniority*; the office of an elder in the Presbyterian church; order of elders.
Eldest, eld′est, *a*. *Oldest*; most advanced in age; that was born before others. [Sax. *ealdest*.]
Elect, ē-lekt′, *vt*. *To choose out*, from among two or more; to take for an office; to manifest preference for by vote; to select as an object of mercy.—*a*. *Chosen*; taken by preference from among two or more; chosen as the object of mercy; chosen to an office, but not yet in office.—*n*. *One chosen out*; persons who are chosen by God to salvation; a nation or body set apart as a peculiar church and people. [L. *eligo, electus—lego*, to choose.]
Election, ē-lek′shon, *n*. *Act of choosing*; choice; act of selecting one or more from others; act of choosing a person to fill an office or employment; voluntary preference; free will; divine choice; predetermination; the public choice of officers, particularly members of parliament; those who are elected. [Fr.—L. *electio*.]

Electioneer, ē-lek′shon-ēr″, *vi*. To make interest for a candidate at *an election*.
Electioneering, ē-lek′shon-ēr″ing, *p.n*. The arts used for securing the choice of one to office.
Elective, ē-lekt′iv, *a*. *Dependent on choice*; bestowed by election; pertaining to or consisting in choice; exerting the power of choice. [Fr. *électif*.]
Elector, ē-lekt′ėr, *n*. *One who elects*; a person who has the right of voting for a public officer. [Low L.]
Electoral, ē-lekt′ėr-al, *a*. *Pertaining to election or electors*. [Fr.]
Electorial, ē-lek-tō′ri-al, *a*. *Relating to an elector* or an election.
Electorship, ē-lekt′ėr-ship, *n*. *The office of an elector*.
Electric, Electrical, ē-lek′trik, ē-lek′trik′al, *a*. Pertaining to, containing, or exhibiting *electricity*; derived from electricity. [Fr. *électrique*.]
Electric, ē-lek′trik, *n*. A body capable of exhibiting *electricity*, and of resisting the passage of it from one body to another; a non-conductor of electricity, employed to excite or accumulate the electric fluid; as glass, amber, &c.
Electrically, ē-lek′trik-al-li, *adv*. In the *manner of electricity*.
Electrician, ē-lek-tri′shi-an, *n*. *A person who is versed in the science of electricity*.
Electricity, ē-lek-tris′i-ti, *n*. *The attractive property* which amber acquires when rubbed; the subtile agent called the *electric fluid*, usually excited by the friction of glass; the science which unfolds the phenomena and laws of the electric fluid. [Fr. *electricité*—Gr. *electron*, amber.]
Electric Machine, ē-lek′trik ma-shēn′, *n*. *A machine for exciting electricity*, and exhibiting its effects.
Electrifiable, ē-lek′tri-fī-a-bl, *a*. *That may be electrified*.
Electrified, ē-lek′tri-fīd, *p.a*. *Charged with electricity*; suddenly roused or excited.
Electrify, ē-lek′tri-fī, *vt*. *To charge with electricity*; to give an electric shock to; to excite or rouse suddenly; to give a sudden impulse to; to charm; to enchant.—*vi*. *To become electric*. *ppr*. electrifying, *pret*. & *pp*. electrified.
Electrifying, ē-lek′tri-fī-ing, *p.a*. Producing a sudden impulse or excitement.
Eleemosynary, el-ē-mos′i-na-ri, *a*. *Given in charity*; given to support the poor; relating to charitable donations; founded by charitable donations, for the purpose of dispensing some gratuity or benefit.—*n*. *One who subsists on charity*; a dependant. [from Gr. *éleemosiné*, alms—*eleos*, pity.]
Elegance, Elegancy, el′ē-gans, el′ē-gan-si, *n*. *A choosing* with judgment; fastidiousness; that which pleases by its grace or beauty; gracefulness; refinement; purity; neatness. [Fr. *élégance*—L. *lego*, to choose.]
Elegant, el′ē-gant, *a*. *Choosing* with judgment; fastidious; luxurious; pleasing to good taste; pleasing by beauty or propriety; handsome; symmetrical; sensible to beauty; rich; costly and ornamental. [Fr. *élégant*.]
Elegantly, el′ē-gant-li, *adv*. *In an elegant manner*.
Elegiac, el-ē′ji-ak, *a*. *Belonging to elegy*; expressing sorrow; used in *elegies*.—*n*. *Elegiac verse*. [Low L. *elegiacus*.]

Fāte, fär, fat, fall; mē, met, hėr; pīne, pin; nōte, not, mōve; tūbe, tub, bull; oil, pound.

Elegist, el'ē-jist, n. *A writer of elegies.*
Elegy, el'ē-ji, n. A poem or a song expressive of sorrow; a poetical composition, in Greek or Latin, composed of distichs, each consisting of a hexameter and a pentameter. [L.—Gr. *elegeia—elegos*, a lament.]
Element, el'ē-ment, n. *A first principle;* an ingredient; that which cannot be divided by chemical analysis; the substance which forms the natural habitation of an animal; the proper state of anything; the state of things suited to one's temper; the outline; moving principle; that which excites action; the atmosphere'; (pl.) the letters of the alphabet; the first principles of an art or science; data employed in a calculation; the bread and wine used in the Lord's supper. [Fr. *élément*—L. *elementum*.]
Elemental, el-ē-ment'al, a. *Pertaining to or produced by elements.*
Elementally, el-ē-ment'al-li, adv. *According to elements;* literally.
Elementary, el-ē-ment'a-ri, a. *Relating to or explaining elements;* primary; uncombined; rudimental; collecting, digesting, or explaining principles. [Fr. *élémentaire*.]
Elephant, el'ē-fant, n. A thick-skinned quadruped, having a long trunk and tusks, and famous for its sagacity and docility. [Fr. *éléphant*—Gr. *elephas*.]
Elephantine, el-ē-fant'in, a. *Pertaining to the elephant;* huge; resembling an elephant. [Fr. *éléphantin*.]
Elevate, el'ē-vāt, vt. *To lift up;* to raise from a low or deep place to a higher; to promote; to refine or dignify; to raise above low conceptions; to cheer; to animate; to make louder; to swell. *ppr.* elevating, *pret. & pp.* elevated. [L. *elevo, elevatus—levo,* to lift up.]
Elevated, el'ē-vāt-ed, *p.a. Elated;* excited.
Elevating, el'ē-vāt-ing, *p.a.* Dignifying; cheering.
Elevation, el-ē-vā'shon, n. *Act of raising* from a lower place to a higher; act of exalting in rank; state of being elevated; dignity; height; an elevated station; a rising ground; a hill; a passing of the voice from any note to one more acute; a swelling of voice. [Fr. *élévation*—L. *elevatio*.]
Elevator, el'ē-vāt-ėr, n. *He or that which raises or elevates.* [Fr. *élévatoire*.]
Eleven, ē-lev'n, a. One *left* after ten; one over the number of the fingers; ten and one added. [Sax. *aendlefene—aen,* one, and *lęfan,* to leave.]
Eleventh, ē-lev'nth, a. Next in order to the tenth. [Sax. *andlyfta*.]
Elf, elf, n. **Elves,** elvz, pl. A diminutive wandering spirit; *a fairy*; a hobgoblin; an evil spirit; a diminutive person; a dwarf.—vt. To entangle in an intricate manner. [Sax.]
Elfin, elf'in, a. *Relating to elves.—n. An elf;* a little urchin.
Elfish, elf'ish, a. *Resembling elves;* clad in disguise.
Elflock, elf'lok, n. Hair twisted in a lock, so denominated as if the work of fairies.
Elicit, ē-lis'it, vt. *To draw out;* to bring to light; to deduce by reason or argument. [L. *elicio, elicitus—lacio,* to entice.]
Elide, ē-līd', vt. *To strike or dash out;* to cut off, as a syllable. *ppr.* eliding, *pret. & pp.* elided. [L. *elido—laedo,* to strike.]
Eligibility, el'i-ji-bil'li-ti, n. *Worthiness or fitness to be chosen;* the quality

of a thing which renders it preferable to another. [Fr. *éligibilité*.]
Eligible, el'i-ji-bl, a. *Fit to be chosen;* worthy of choice; preferable; suitable; proper; desirable. [Fr. *éligible*—L. *lego,* to choose.]
Eligibly, el'i-ji-bli, adv. In a *manner* to be worthy of *choice;* suitably.
Eliminate, ē-lim'in-āt, vt. *To turn out of doors;* to disengage; to separate; to leave out of consideration. *ppr.* eliminating, *pret. & pp.* eliminated. [L. *elimino, eliminatus—limen,* threshold.]
Elimination, ē-lim'in-ā'shon, n. *Act of eliminating;* the act of discharging by the pores; separation. [Fr. *élimination*.]
Elision, ē-li'zhon, n. *A striking out;* the cutting off of a vowel or syllable, particularly at the end of a word, for the sake of euphony. [Fr. *élision*.]
Elite, ē-lēt', n. *A choice or select body;* the chosen part, particularly of an army; the flower of an army; the best part. [Fr. *élite*—L. *lego,* to choose.]
Elixir, ē-liks'ėr, n. *That which is extracted by boiling,* &c.; refined spirit; a compound tincture; any cordial. [Fr. *élixir*—L. *elixus,* boiled thoroughly.]
Elizabethan, ē-liz'a-bēth"an, a. Pertaining to Queen Elizabeth or her times.
Elk, elk, n. A species of deer, so called from its *strength.* [Sax. *elch*—Gr. *alkē,* strength.]
Ell, el, n. A measure of length, said to have been originally the length between the ends of the extended *arms,* or a fathom. The English ell is 45 inches. [Sax. *elle*—L. *ulna*.]
Ellipse, el-lips', n. *A deficiency;* one of the conic sections, produced by cutting a cone by a plane passing obliquely through its opposite sides; a figure of an oval shape. [Gr. *elleipsis—leipo,* to leave.]
Ellipsis, el-lips'is, n. **Ellipses,** pl. *Omission;* a figure of syntax, by which one or more words are omitted. [Gr. *elleipsis*.]
Elliptic, Elliptical, el-lip'tik, el-lip'tik-al, a. *Pertaining to an ellipse;* having the form of an ellipse; having a part omitted. [Gr. *elleiptikos*.]
Elliptically, el-lip'tik-al-li, adv. *According to* the figure called *an ellipse;* with a part omitted.
Ellipticity, el-lip-tis'i-ti, n. *Quality of being elliptical;* deviation from the form of a sphere or circle. (Applied to the figure of the earth.)
Elm, elm, n. A well-known tree, several species of which are valuable for their timber. [Sax. *ellm*—L. *ulmus*.]
Elmy, elm'i, a. *Abounding with elms.*
Elocution, el-ō-kū'shon, n. *A speaking out; distinct utterance;* manner of speaking; management of the voice in speaking; pronunciation; delivery. [Fr. *élocution*—L. *loquor, locutus,* to speak.]
Elocutionary, e-lō-kū'shon-a-ri, a. *Pertaining to elocution,* or containing it.
Elocutionist, e-lō-kū'shon-ist, n. *One who is versed in,* or teaches, *elocution.*
Elogium, ē-lō'ji-um, n. *An utterance;* a short saying or maxim; the praise bestowed on a person or thing; panegyric. [L.—Gr. *logos,* a word.]
Elongate, ē-long'gāt, vt. *To lengthen;* to extend; to remove further off. *ppr.* elongating, *pret. & pp.* elongated. [Low L. *elongo, elongatus—longus,* long.]
Elongation, ē-long-gā'shon, n. *Act of*

lengthening; state of being extended; extension; continuation; the distance of a planet from the sun, as it appears to the eye of a spectator on the earth. [Fr.]
Elope, ē-lōp', vi. *To run away;* to escape privately; to run away from a husband with another man, or to quit a father's or guardian's house privately with a lover. *ppr.* eloping, *pret. & pp.* eloped. [Sax. *hleápan,* to leap.]
Elopement, ē-lōp'ment, n. *Act of eloping;* private departure from the station to which one is assigned by duty, particularly of a wife from her husband, or a daughter or ward with a lover.
Eloquence, e'lō-kwens, n. *A speaking out;* power, beauty, and appropriateness of language; the expression of strong emotion in a manner adapted to excite similar emotion in the minds of others; oratory, the power of expressing just thoughts and strong emotions with fluency and force. [Fr. *éloquence*—L. *eloquentia*.]
Eloquent, e'lō-kwent, a. Having the power of fluent and elegant *speech;* having the power of expressing truth or strong emotions in a vivid and appropriate manner; adapted to express truth or strong emotion with elegance and power. [Fr. *éloquent*—L. *loquor,* to speak.]
Eloquently, e'lō-kwent-li, adv. *With eloquence;* in an eloquent manner.
Else, els, *a. or pron. Other;* one or something besides.—*adv. Otherwise;* in the other case; if the fact were different; besides; except that mentioned. [Sax. *elles.*]
Elsewhere, els'hwār, adv. In some *other* place.
Elucidate, ē-lū'sid-āt, vt. *To make clear;* to free from obscurity; to clear up; to explain. *ppr.* elucidating, *pret. & pp.* elucidated. [Low L. *elucido, elucidatus*—L. *lux, lucis,* light.]
Elucidation, ē-lū'sid-ā"shon, n. Act of throwing *light* on any obscure subject; illustration; comment. [Fr. *élucidation*.]
Elucidator, ē-lū'sid-āt-ėr, n. One who explains; an expositor.
Elucidatory, ē-lū'sid-a-tō-ri, *a. Tending to elucidate.*
Elude, ē-lūd', vt. *To play upon'; to mock;* to avoid by artifice or dexterity; to baffle; to foil; to evade; to escape; to shun. *ppr.* eluding, *pret. & pp.* eluded. [Fr. *éluder*—L. *ludo,* to play.]
Eludible, ē-lūd'i-bl, a. *That may be eluded* or escaped.
Elusory, ē-lū'sō-ri, a. *Tending to elude* or deceive; deceitful; deceptive.
Elysian, ē-li'zhi-an, a. *Pertaining to Elysium;* yielding the highest pleasures; deliciously soothing; exceedingly delightful. [L. *elysius*.]
Elysium, ē-li'zhi-um, n. A place assigned, in ancient mythology, to happy souls after death; the seat of happiness *to come;* any delightful place. [L. *Elysium*—Gr. *eluth,* to come.]
Emaciate, ē-mā'shi-āt, vt. *To'cause to waste away* or lose flesh gradually; to waste the flesh of and reduce to leanness. *ppr.* emaciating, *pret. & pp.* emaciated. [Low L. *emacio, emaciatus*—L. *macer,* lean.]
Emaciated, ē-mā'shi-āt-ed, *p.a.* Thin; lean.
Emaciation, ē-mā'shi-ā"shon, n. *Act of making lean* or thin in flesh; a becoming lean by a gradual waste of flesh; leanness.
Emanate, em'a-nāt, vi. *To flow out;* to

ch, *chain;* j, *job;* g, *go;* ng, *sing;* ᴛʜ, *then;* th, *thin;* w, *wig;* wh, *whig;* zh, *azure;* †obsolete.

flow from; to proceed from a source or fountain; to issue; to spring. *ppr.* emanating, *pret. & pp.* emanated. [L. *emano, emanatus—mano,* to flow.]
Emanation, em-a-nā'shon, *n. Act of flowing from* a fountain-head or origin; that which issues or proceeds from any source, substance, or body; effluvium. [Fr. *émanation.*]
Emancipate, ē-man'si-pāt, *vt.* To *set free from slavery*; to liberate; to free from bondage or restraint of any kind. *ppr.* emancipating, *pret. & pp.* emancipated. [L. *emancipo, emancipātum—mancipium,* a slave.]
Emancipated, ē-man'si-pāt-ed, *p.a. Set free from slavery*; liberated.
Emancipation, ē-man'si-pā"shon, *n. Deliverance* from *slavery,* or from civil, or any other restraint; liberation; freedom; enfranchisement. [Fr. *emancipation.*]
Emancipator, ē-man'si-pāt-ėr, *n.* One *who emancipates* or liberates from bondage or restraint. [Low L.]
Emasculate, ē-mas'kū-lāt, *vt.* To *unman;* to deprive of masculine strength or vigour; to weaken; to vitiate by unmanly softness. *ppr.* emasculating, *pret. & pp.* emasculated. [Low L. *emasculo—*L. *mas,* a male.]
Emasculated, ē-mas'kū-lāt-ed, *p.a. Castrated;* weakened.
Emasculation, ē-mas'kū-lā"shon, *n. Act of emasculating;* castration; effeminacy; unmanly weakness. [Fr. *émasculation.*]
Emball', em-bal', *vt.* To encircle; to embrace.
Embalm, em-bām', *vt.* To *anoint with balm*; to preserve from decay by means of balm or other aromatic oils or spices; to fill with sweet scent, as the air; to cherish tenderly the memory of. [Fr. *embaumer.*]
Embalmer, em-bām'ėr, *n.* One *who embalms* bodies for preservation.
Embalming, em-bām'ing, *p.n.* Act or art of filling a dead body with spices for preservation.
Embank, em-bangk', *vt.* To *inclose with a bank;* to defend with a bank, mounds, or dikes.
Embankment, em-bangk'ment, *n.* A mound or *bank* raised for various purposes, as for protecting against inundation or for the passage of a railway.
Embargo, em-bär'gō, *n.* A *barring in*; a restraint on ships, or prohibition of sailing for a limited time.—*vt.* To bar *in*; to prevent, as ships from sailing for a limited time. [Fr.]
Embark, em-bärk', *vt.* To *put on board a ship*; to engage; to put to risk or venture; to engage as a person in any affair.—*vi.* To *go on board of a ship;* to engage in any business, or to undertake it; to take a share. [Fr. *embarquer—barque,* a ship.]
Embarkation, em-bärk-ā'shon, *n. Act of putting* or *going on board of a ship*; that which is embarked. [Fr.]
Embarrass, em-ba'ras, *vt.* To *put a bar in the way of*; to involve in difficulties; to perplex; to disconcert; to embroil; to render intricate or entangled. [Fr. *embarrasser—barre,* a bar.]
Embarrassed, em-ba'rast, *p.a.* Confused; confounded.
Embarrassing, em-ba'ras-ing, *p.a.* Confusing; confounding; abashing.
Embarrassment, em-ba'ras-ment, *n.* Perplexity; intricacy; entanglement; trouble; distress; anxiety; abashment.
Embassad', em'bas-säd, *n.* An *embassy.*

Embassy, em'bas-si, *n.* The public function of an *ambassador;* the person or persons intrusted with a public or solemn message; any solemn message. [Fr. *ambassade.*]
Embattle, em-bat'tl, *vt.* To *arrange in order of battle*; to furnish with battlements.—*vi.* To be ranged in order of battle. *ppr.* embattling, *pret. & pp.* embattled. [*en* and *battle.*]
Embattlement, em-bat'tl-ment, *n.* An indented parapet, belonging originally to *military* works, but now used in decorative architecture.
Embay, em-bā', *vt.* To *inclose in a bay*; to landlock; to inclose between capes or promontories.
Embellish, em-bel'lish, *vt.* To *make beautiful or elegant*; to make graceful or elegant, as manners; to adorn, to ornament; to beautify; to illustrate. [Fr. *embellir, embellissant—*L. *bellus,* pretty—*bonus,* good.]
Embellisher, em-bel'lish-ėr, *n.* One *who embellishes.*
Embellishment, em-bel'lish-ment, *n. Act of embellishing*; anything that adds beauty or elegance; grace. [Fr. *embellissement.*]
Ember-days, em'bėr-dāz, *n. pl.* Days observed in the church, which return at certain seasons in the *course* or *circuit* of the year. [Sax. *ymb-ren.*]
Embers, em'bėrz, *n. pl. Hot ashes* or *cinders*; the residuum of wood, coal, or other combustibles not extinguished. [Sax. *æmyrian.*]
Ember-weeks, em'bėr-wēks, *n. pl.* The *weeks* on which the *ember-days* fall.
Embezzle, em-bez'zl, *vt.* To *purloin*; to appropriate fraudulently, as that which is intrusted to one's care and management; to waste. *ppr.* embezzling, *pret. & pp.* embezzled. [Norm. *embeasiler,* to filch.]
Embezzlement, em-bez'zl-ment, *n.* Act of fraudulently appropriating the money or goods intrusted to one's care and management; the thing appropriated; larceny by clerks, servants, or agents.
Embezzler, em-bez'zl-ėr, *n.* One *who embezzles.*
Emblaze, em-blāz', *vt.* To *set in a blaze*; to adorn with glittering embellishments.
Emblazon, em-blā'zon, *vt.* To *adorn with figures of heraldry*; to deck in glaring colours; to display pompously. [Fr. *blasonner.*]
Emblazoner, em-blā'zon-ėr, *n.* A *blazoner*; one who emblazons; one who publishes and displays with pomp.
Emblazoning, em-blā'zon-ing, *n.* Act or art of adorning with ensigns armorial.
Emblazonment, em-blā'zon-ment, *n.* An *emblazoning.*
Emblazonry, em-blā'zon-ri, *n.* Pictures on shields; display of figures.
Emblem, em'blem, *n.* That *which* is *put or thrown in*; a picture representing one thing to the eye and suggesting another to the understanding; a painted enigma; an allusive picture; a typical designation; a figure; a type. [Fr. *emblême—*Gr. *ballo,* to throw or cast.]
Emblematic, Emblematical, em-blem-at'ik, em-blem-at'ik-al, *a. Pertaining to an emblem*; representing by some allusion or customary connection, or by similar qualities; using emblems. [Fr. *emblématique.*]
Emblematically, em-blem-at'ik-al-li, *adv. By way or means of emblems.*
Embloom, em-blöm', *vt.* To *cover* or enrich *with bloom.* [*en* and *bloom.*]

Embodier, em-bo'di-ėr, *n. He that embodies.*
Embodiment, em-bo'di-ment, *n. Act of embodying*; the state of being embodied.
Embody, em-bo'di, *vt.* To *clothe with a body*; to form into a body; to invest with matter; to form into a system; to bring into a band, company, army, or other regular assemblage; to collect. *ppr.* embodying, *pret. & pp.* embodied.
Embolden, em-bōld'en, *vt.* To *give boldness* or courage to; to encourage.
Emboldened, em-bōld'end, *p.a.* Encouraged.
Emborder, em-bor'dėr, *vt.* To *adorn with a border.* [Old Fr.]
Emboss, em-bos', *vt.* To *form bosses* on; to fashion in raised work; to cut or form with prominent figures; to cover, as with bosses.
Embossing, em-bos'ing, *p.n.* The formation of ornamental figures in relief; the figures thus formed.
Embossment, em-bos'ment, *n.* A *prominence like a boss*; a jut; relief; raised work.
Embouchure, em'bö-shör, *n.* A *mouth* or *aperture,* as of a river, cannon, &c. [Fr.]
Embowel, em-bou'el, *vt.* To *take out the bowels* or entrails of; to eviscerate; to take out the internal parts of; to sink or inclose in another substance. *ppr.* embowelling, *pret. & pp.* embowelled.
Embower, em-bou'er, *vt.* To *inclose in or cover with a bower*; to shelter with trees.
Embowered, em-bou'ėrd, *p.a. Covered with a bower*; sheltered with trees.
Embrace, em-brās', *vt.* To *take within the arms*; to press to the bosom in token of affection; to seize ardently; to lay hold on; to comprehend; to encircle; to include; to accept.—*vi.* To *join in an embrace. ppr.* embracing, *pret. & pp.* embraced.—*n.* Pressure to the bosom with the *arms*; a hug; reception of one thing into another; conjugal endearment. [Fr. *embrasser—*L. *brachium,* the arm.]
Embrasure, em-brā'zhör, *n.* An opening in a wall or parapet to hold or receive cannon, through which they are pointed and *fired.* [Norm. *embreaser,* to burn; Fr. *braise,* burning charcoal.]
Embrocate, em-brō-kāt, *vt.* To *foment* and rub, as a diseased part of the body with a liquid substance. [Low L. *embroco, embrocatum.*]
Embrocation, em-brō-kā'shon, *n. Act of moistening* and rubbing a diseased part with a cloth or sponge dipped in some liquid; the liquid with which an affected part is washed. [Fr.]
Embroider, em-broi'dėr, *vt.* To *border* with ornamental needle-work or figures; to adorn with raised figures of needle-work. [Fr. *broder.*]
Embroidered, em-broi'dėrd, *p.a.* Adorned with figures of needle-work.
Embroiderer, em-broi'dėr-ėr, *n.* One *who embroiders.*
Embroidery, em-broi'de-ri, *n.* Work in gold, silver, silk, or other thread, formed by the needle on cloth, stuffs, and muslin, into various figures; variegated needle-work; artificial ornaments. [Fr. *broderie.*]
Embroil, em-broil', *vt.* To *mingle*; to intermix in confusion; to involve in troubles or perplexities; to encumber; to disorder; to trouble. [Fr. *embrouiller—brouiller,* to jumble.]

Fāte, fär, fat, fall; mē, met, hėr; pīne, pin; nōte, not, move; tūbe, tub, bull; oil, pound.

Embroilment, em-broil′ment, n. A state of contention, perplexity, or confusion; disturbance.
Embryo, em′bri-ō, n. The first rudiments of an animal in the womb; the rudimentary plant engendered within the seed; the beginning or first state of anything.—a. Pertaining to or noting anything in its first rudiments or unfinished state. [Fr. *embryon*—Gr. *bruō*, to be full of anything.]
Embryonic, em-bri-on′ik, a. Pertaining to an *embryo*, or in the state of one.
Emendation, ē-mend-ā′shon, n. A correcting of what is erroneous or faulty; an alteration for the better; correction of an error or fault. [L. *emendatio*—*mendum*, a fault, an error.]
Emendator, ē-mend′āt-ėr, n. A corrector of faults in writings; one who corrects or improves. [L.]
Emendatory, ē-mend′ā-tō-ri, a. Contributing to emendation. [Low L. *emendatorius*.]
Emerald, e′me-rald, n. A bright, shining precious stone of a green colour, and identical, except in colour, with beryl; a printing type, in size between minion and nonpareil. [Sp. *esmeralda*—L. *smaragdus*.]
Emerge, ē-merj′, vi. To come forth or up; to rise out of a fluid or other covering substance; to proceed from; to reappear, after being eclipsed; to leave, as the sphere of the obscuring object; to rise out of a state of obscurity; to rise into view. ppr. emerging, pret. & pp. emerged. [L. *emergo*—*mergo*, to dip.]
Emergence, Emergency, ē-merj′ens, ē-merj′en-si, n. Act of emerging; act of rising or starting into view; act of issuing from or quitting; a sudden occasion; unforeseen casualty; pressing necessity; exigency. [Low L. *emergentia*.]
Emergent, ē-merj′ent, a. Rising out of a fluid, or anything that covers or surrounds; issuing from; rising out of a depressed state; coming suddenly; casual; urgent; pressing. [Fr.—L. *emergens*.]
Emerods, ē′me-rods, n. with a plural termination. Hemorrhoids; livid, painful, and bleeding tubercles about the anus; piles. [Gr. *haima*, blood, and *rheō*, to flow.]
Emersion, ē-mėr′shon, n. Act of rising out of a fluid or other surrounding substance; the reappearance of a heavenly body after an eclipse; the reappearance of a star which has been hid by the effulgence of the sun's light. [Fr.]
Emery, e′me-ri, n. A variety of sapphire, distinguished for its extreme hardness, and used in cutting gems, and for polishing steel, marble, &c. [Fr. *emeri*.]
Emetic, ē-met′ik, a. Inducing to vomit; causing vomiting.—n. A medicine that provokes vomiting. [Gr. *emetikos*—*emeō*, to vomit.]
Emigrant, em′i-grant, a. Removing or having removed from one place or country to another distant place, with a view to reside.—n. One who changes his habitation, or quits one country to settle in another.
Emigrate, em′i-grāt, vi. To depart; to remove from one country or state to another for the purpose of residence. ppr. emigrating, pret. & pp. emigrated. [L. *emigro*, *emigratus*—*migro*, to remove from one place to another.]
Emigration, em-i-grā′shon, n. Act of emigrating; a removal of inhabitants from one country or state to another, for the purpose of residence. [Fr. *émigration*.]
Eminence, em′in-ens, n. A rising up or above; elevation; height; a hill; top; a conspicuous place or position; distinction; fame; a title of honour given to cardinals and others. [Fr. *éminence*—L. *eminentia*.]
Eminent, em′in-ent, a. Rising up or above others; elevated; exalted in rank; high in office; distinguished; illustrious. [Fr. *éminent*—L. *mineo*, *minens*, to jut.]
Eminently, em′in-ent-li, adv. In a degree to attract observation.
Emissary, em′is-sa-ri, n. One sent forth or out; a person sent on a private message or business; a secret agent; a spy. [Fr. *émissaire*—L. *mitto*, to send.]
Emission, ē-mi′shon, n. Act of sending or throwing out; an issuing out; that which is sent out or issued. [Fr. *émission*—L. *mitto*, *missum*, to send.]
Emissive, ē-mis′iv, a. Sending out; emitting.
Emit, ē-mit′, vt. To send forth or out; to let fly; to discharge; to dart or shoot; to send. ppr. emitting, pret. & pp. emitted. [L. *emitto*—*mitto*, to send.]
Emmet, em′met, n. An ant, so named from its industrious habits. [Sax. *āmet*—Heb. *amets*, to be active.]
Emmew†, em-mū′, vt. To confine, as in a cage.
Emollient, ē-mol′li-ent, a. Softening; making supple.—n. An external application which softens or allays irritation, and alleviates inflammatory soreness, swelling, and pain. [L. *emolliens*—*mollio*, to soften.]
Emolument, ē-mol′ū-ment, n. The result of effort; gain; advantage; the profit arising from office or employment; that which is received as a compensation for services. [L. *emolumentum*—*molior*, to exert one's self.]
Emotion, ē-mō′shon, n. A moving of the mind; any agitation of mind, or excitement of sensibility; feeling; agitation; perturbation; tremor. [L. *emotio*—*moveo*, *motum*, to move.]
Emotional, ē-mō′shon-al, a. Pertaining to emotion.
Empale, em-pāl′, vt. To put to death by fixing on a stake. ppr. empaling, pret. & pp. empaled. [Fr. *empaler*—L. *palus*, a stake.]
Empalement, em-pāl′ment, n. A putting to death by thrusting a stake into the body. [Fr.]
Emperor, em′pėr-ėr, n. The sovereign or supreme monarch of an empire; a title of dignity superior to that of king. [Fr. *empereur*—L. *impero*, to command.]
Emphasis, em′fa-sis, n. A stress or force of voice laid on a word or clause of a sentence, in order to enforce a meaning; impressiveness; weight; the marked attention which a writer or speaker bestows on a topic, by which it is brought into prominent notice. [Gr.—*phāsis*, a saying—*phēmi*, to speak.]
Emphasize, em′fa-sīz, vt. To place emphasis on; to utter or pronounce with a particular stress of voice. ppr. emphasizing, pret. & pp. emphasized.
Emphatic, Emphatical, em-fat′ik, em-fat′ik-al, a. Requiring emphasis; characterized by peculiar force or expressiveness; expressive; strong; energetic. [Fr. *emphatique*.]
Emphatically, em-fat′ik-al-li, adv. With emphasis; strongly; forcibly.
Empire, em′pīr, n. Command; supreme power in governing; imperial power; the territory under the dominion of an emperor; supreme control; governing influence; sway; any region, land, or water, over which dominion is extended. [Fr.—L. *impero*, to command.]
Empiric, em-pi′rik, n. One who makes trial; one whose knowledge is founded exclusively on experience; a quack; a charlatan. [Fr. *empirique*—Gr. *peirāō*, to try.]
Empiric, Empirical, em-pi′rik, em-pi′rik-al, a. Versed in experiments; following or relying upon experience; derived from experiment; used and applied without science.
Empirically, em-pi′rik-al-li, adv. By experiment; in the manner of quacks.
Empiricism, em-pi′ri-sizm, n. The method or practice of an empiric; the practice of medicine without a medical education; quackery. [Fr. *empirisme*.]
Employ, em-ploi′, vt. To infold†; to engage; to occupy; to keep at work; to exercise; to make use of; to engage as an agent, substitute, instrument, or means; to devote to an object; to fill up with occupation.—n. That which engages the mind or occupies the labour of a person; business; object of study or industry; employment; duty; public office; agency; service for another. [Fr. *employer*—L. *plico*, to fold.]
Employer, em-ploi′ėr, n. One who employs; one who engages or keeps in service.
Employment, em-ploi′ment, n. Act of employing; that which engages the head or hands; vocation; agency; office; trade; profession; function.
Empoison, em-poi′zn, vt. To poison; to administer poison to. [Fr. *empoisonner*.]
Empoisoned, em-poi′znd, p.a. Poisoned; imbittered.
Emporium, em-pō′ri-um, n. A place to pass through for trading; a town or city of trade; a city or town of extensive commerce. [L.—Gr. *peraō*, to pass through.]
Empower, em-pou′ėr, vt. To give legal or moral power to; to confer authority upon; to authorize; to enable.
Empress, em′pres, n. The consort of an emperor; a female invested with imperial power or sovereignty. [Fr. *impératrice*.]
Emptiness, em′ti-nes, n. A state of being empty; a state of containing nothing except air; absence of matter; void space; want of solidity; inability to satisfy desire; want of intellect or knowledge.
Empty, em′ti, a. Vacant; containing nothing, or nothing but air; void; destitute of solid matter; unsatisfactory; unburdened; hungry; vacant of head; wanting solidity; waste; desolate [Sax. *æmti*.]—vt. To make empty; t. deprive of the contents; to make desolate.—vi. To become empty; to pour out or discharge its contents. ppr. emptying, pret. & pp. emptied. [Sax. *æmtian*, to be vacant.]
Empty-hearted, em′ti-härt-ed, a. Destitute of feeling.
Emptying, em′ti-ing, p.n. The act of making empty.
Empurple, em-pėr′pl, vt. To tinge or dye of a purple colour. ppr. empurpling, pret. & pp. empurpled.
Empyreal, em-pi-rē′al, a. Formed of pure fire or light; refined beyond aerial substance; pertaining to the highest and purest region of heaven. [Fr. *empyrée*—Gr. *pur*, *puros*, fire.]

Empyrean, em-pi-rē'an, *a. Empyreal.*—*n.* The highest heaven, where the pure element of fire has been supposed to subsist.

Emu, ē'mū, *n.* A bird of very large size, found in Australia. It is related to the ostrich.

Emulate, em'ū-lāt, *vt.* To strive to equal or excel, in qualities or actions; to imitate, with a view to equal or excel; to rival; to be equal to.—*a.!* Striving to excel. *ppr.* emulating, *pret. & pp.* emulated. [L. *æmulor, æmulatus*—*æmilus,* that strives after another.]

Emulation, em-ū-lā'shon, *n. Act of emulating;* desire of superiority; rivalry; desire of excellence, attended with effort to attain to it; contest; strife. [Fr. *émulation*—L. *æmulatio.*]

Emulative, em'ū-lāt-iv, *a. Inclined to emulation;* rivalling.

Emulator, em'ū-lāt-ėr, *n. One who emulates;* a rival; a competitor. [L. *æmulator.*]

Emulous, em'ū-lus, *a. Eager to emulate,* or to imitate, equal, or excel; desirous of like excellence with another; rivalling; engaged in competition. [L. *æmulus.*]

Emulously, em'ū-lus-li, *adv.* With desire of equalling or excelling another.

Emulsion, ē-mul'shon, *n. A milky medicinal substance produced by uniting oil and water through the intervention of some substance capable of combining with both.* [Fr. *émulsion*—L. *mulgeo, mulsum,* to milk.]

Emulsive, ē-muls'iv, *a.* Producing or yielding a *milk-like* substance.

Enable, en-ā'bl, *vt.* To *make able;* to furnish with sufficient power; to empower; to strengthen. *ppr.* enabling, *pret. & pp.* enabled.

Enact, en-akt', *vt.* To *put in act;* to establish by law; to institute; to perform; to order; to act; to represent.

Enacting, en-akt'ing, *p.a.* Giving legislative forms and sanction.

Enactment, en-akt'ment, *n.* The passing of a bill into a law; the act of giving validity to a law.

Enactor, en-akt'ėr, *n. One who enacts* or passes a law.

Enamel, en-am'el, *n.* A substance imperfectly *melted;* a substance of the nature of glass, rendered opaque by an admixture of oxides of metals with a flux; that which is enamelled; a smooth glossy surface of various colours, resembling enamel; the smooth hard substance which covers the visible part of a tooth.—*vt.* To lay enamel on, *as a metal;* to paint in enamel; to form a glossy surface on, like enamel. *vi.* To practise the art of enamelling. *ppr.* enamelling, *pret. & pp.* enamelled. [*en,* and Fr. *émail*—G. *schmelzen,* to melt.]

Enameller, en-am'el-ėr, *n. One who enamels.*

Enamelling, en-am'el-ing, *p.n. Act or art of laying on enamel.*

Enamour, en-am'ėr, *vt.* To *inspire with love;* to charm; to fill with delight. [Old Fr. *enamourer*—L. *amor,* love.]

Enamoured, en-am'ėrd, *p.a.* Charmed; delighted.

Encage, en-kāj', *vt.* To shut up or confine *in a cage;* to coop. *ppr.* encaging, *pret. & pp.* encaged.

Encamp, en-kamp', *vi.* To *pitch a camp;* to halt on a march, spread tents, and remain for a night or for a longer time; to lodge in a camp.—*vt.* To form *into a camp;* to place, as a marching army in temporary quarters.

Encampment, en-kamp'ment, *n.* The place where an army or company is *encamped;* a camp. [Fr.]

Encaustic, en-kas'tik, *a. Burnt in;* pertaining to the art of painting in heated or burned wax; pertaining to painting on glass or porcelain.—*n.* The method of painting in heated or burned wax. [Gr. *kaustikos,* burning—*kaio,* to burn.]

Encave, en-kāv', *vt.* To *put into a cave;* to hide in a cave or recess. *ppr.* encaving, *pret. & pp.* encaved.

Enchain, en-chān', *vt.* To *fasten with a chain;* to hold in bondage; to enthral; to confine. [Fr. *enchainer*—L. *catena,* a chain.]

Enchainment, en-chān'ment, *n. Act of enchaining,* or state of being enchained.

Enchant, en-chant', *vt.* To *influence by songs* of fascination; to practise sorcery on; to charm; to enrapture; to bewitch. [Fr. *enchanter*—L. *canto,* from *cano, cantum,* to sing.]

Enchanted, en-chant'ed, *p.a.* Fascinated; delighted beyond measure; inhabited by witches, &c.

Enchanter, en-chant'ėr, *n.* A sorcerer; one who charms or delights. [Fr. *enchanteur.*]

Enchanting, en-chant'ing, *p.a.* Charming; delighting; ravishing.

Enchantingly, en-chant'ing-li, *adv.* In a manner to delight or charm.

Enchantment, en-chant'ment, *n. Act of enchanting;* incantation; magic; overpowering influence of delight; fascination. [Fr. *enchantement.*]

Enchantress, en-chant'res, *n.* A sorceress; a woman whose beauty or excellences give irresistible influence.

Enchase, en-chās', *vt.* To *incase;* to enrich or beautify, as any work in metal by some design; to adorn by being fixed on the surface. *ppr.* enchasing, *pret. & pp.* enchased. [Fr. *enchâsser*—L. *capsa,* a box or case.]

Encircle, en-sėr'kl, *vt.* To *inclose with a circle;* to encompass; to embrace; to go or come round. *ppr.* encircling, *pret. & pp.* encircled.

Enclasp, en-klasp', *vt.* To *clasp;* to fasten with a clasp.

Enclitic, en-klit'ik, *a. Inclining or inclined;* noting a particle or word so closely united to another as to seem to be a part of it; throwing back the accent upon the foregoing syllable.—*n.* A particle or word that throws the accent or emphasis back upon the former syllable. [Gr. *engklitikos*—*klino,* to make to bend.]

Enclitically, en-klit'ik-al-li, *adv.* In an *enclitic* manner.

Enclose, en-klōz', *vt.* To *inclose.* [*en* and *close.*]

Enclosure, en-klō'zhur, *n. Inclosure.*

Encoffin, en-kof'fin, *vt.* To *put in a coffin.*

Encomiast, en-kō'mi-ast, *n. One who praises another;* a panegyrist. [Gr. *engkōmiastes*—*komos,* a festal ode.]

Encomiastic, en-kō'mi-ast'ik, *a. Containing encomium;* bestowing praise; laudatory. [Gr. *engkōmiastikos.*]

Encomiastically, en-kō'mi-ast'ik-al-li, *adv.* In an encomiastic manner.

Encomium, en-kō'mi-um, *n.* Encomiums, *pl.* A *laudatory oration;* panegyric; applause; eulogium; praise. [Gr. *engkōmion.*]

Encompass, en-kum'pas, *vt.* To bring within a given circuit or *compass;* to inclose; to environ; to hem in.

Encompassment, en-kum'pas-ment, *n.* A surrounding; a going round.

Encore, äng-kōr'. *Yet; once more;* a word used by the auditors and spectators of plays and other sports when they call for a repetition of a particular part.—*vt.* To call for a repetition of. *ppr.* encoring, *pret. & pp.* encored. [Fr.]

Encounter, en-koun'tėr, *n. A running against;* a meeting in contest or in kindness; a conflict; a battle; onset; a meeting; accidental meeting of two or more; eager and warm conversation. *vt.* To *run against;* to meet suddenly; to rush against in conflict; to engage with; to meet and oppose; to attack; to strive against.—*vi.* To meet unexpectedly; to rush together in combat; to meet in opposition or debate. [Fr. *encontre*—L. *contra,* against.]

Encounterer, en-koun'tėr-ėr, *n. One who encounters.*

Encourage, en-ku'rāj, *vt.* To *give courage to;* to hearten; to inspire with spirit or strength of mind; to embolden; to countenance; to foster. *ppr.* encouraging, *pret. & pp.* encouraged. [Fr. *encourager*—L. *cor,* the heart.]

Encouraged, en-ku'rājd, *p.a.* Inspirited; animated; incited.

Encouragement, en-ku'rāj-ment, *n. Act of giving courage;* incentive; countenance; reward; profit. [Fr.]

Encourager, en-ku'rāj-ėr, *n. One who encourages.*

Encouraging, en-ku'rāj-ing, *p.a.* Furnishing ground to hope for success.

Encouragingly, en-ku'rāj-ing-li, *adv.* In a manner to give courage.

Encrimson, en-krim'zn, *vt.* To *cover with a crimson colour.*

Encroach, en-krōch', *vi.* To *draw away as by a hook;* to make invasion, as upon the rights and possessions of another; to advance by stealth; to pass the proper bounds; to intrude; to invade. (With *on* or *upon.*) [Old Fr. *encrocher*—*croc,* a hook.]

Encroacher, en-krōch'ėr, *n. One who encroaches.*

Encroaching, en-krōch'ing, *p.a. Tending or apt to encroach.*

Encroachingly, en-krōch'ing-li, *adv.* By way of *encroachment.*

Encroachment, en-krōch'ment, *n. Act of encroaching;* invasion; inroad; that which is taken by encroaching on another. [Fr. *accrochement.*]

Encrust, en-krust', *vt.* To *cover with a crust.*

Encumber, en-kum'bėr, *vt.* To *trouble;* to load; to embarrass; to obstruct; to perplex; to entangle; to load with debts or legal claims. [Fr. *encombrer;* Sw. *bekymra,* to trouble.]

Encumbered, en-kum'bėrd, *p.a.* Loaded; loaded with debts.

Encumbrance, en-kum'brans, *n. That which encumbers;* burden; hindrance; legal claims or liabilities.

Encurtain, en-kėr'tān, *vt.* To *inclose with curtains.*

Encyclical, en-sī'klik-al, *a. Circular;* sent to many persons or places. [Gr. *engkuklikos*—*kuklos,* a circle.]

Encyclopedia, Encyclopædia, en-sī'klō-pē'di-a, en-sī'klō-pē'di-a, *n. The circle of learning,* or of the sciences; a collection of the principal facts, principles, and discoveries in all branches of science and the arts, digested under proper titles, and arranged in alphabetical order. [Fr. *encyclopédie*—Gr. *kuklos,* a circle, and *paideia,* instruction—*pais, paidos,* a boy, a girl.]

Encyclopedic, en-sī'klō-ped'ik, *a. Pertaining to an encyclopedia.* [Fr. *encyclopédique.*]

Encyclopedist, en-sī'klō-ped-ist, *n. The*

Fāte, fär, fat, fall; mē, met, hėr; pīne, pin; nōte, not, mōve; tūbe, tub, bull; oil, pound.

compiler of an encyclopædia, or one who .... in such compilation. [Fr. *en-cyclopédiste*.]

End, end, *n*. *Final point of space or time; the extreme point of a line, or the extremity of anything that has more length than breadth; the last part; conclusion; final state; extreme limit; final determination; completion; close of life; death; consequence; issue; conclusive event; a broken piece; the ultimate point at which one aims; aim; drift.—vt. To bring to an end; to conclude; to close; to put to death.—vi. To come to an end; to be finished; to close; to cease; to come to a close.* [Sax. *ende*—Sans. *anta*.]

End-all, end'al, *n*. Final close.

Endanger, en-dānj'ėr, *vt*. *To bring into danger or peril; to put in hazard; to expose to loss or injury.*

Endear, en-dēr', *vt*. *To make dear; to make more beloved.*

Endeared, en-dērd', *p.a*. *Rendered dear; beloved, or more beloved.*

Endearing, en-dēr'ing, *p.a*. *Making dear or more beloved; having a tendency to make dear or beloved.*

Endearment, en-dēr'ment, *n*. *That which endears; ground of affection; that which increases affection; the state of being beloved; tender affection.*

Endeavour, en-dev'ėr, *n*. *Effort put forth in the performance of duty; an exertion of physical strength or of the intellectual powers toward the attainment of an object or the accomplishment of a purpose; aim; object.—vi. To put forth efforts in the performance of duty; to exert physical strength or intellectual power for the accomplishment of an object; to try; to strive; to struggle; to aim (with* after*).—vt. To attempt to gain; to use efforts to effect.* [Norm. *devoyer*—L. *debeo*, to owe.]

Endeavourer, en-dev'ėr-ėr, *n*. *One who makes an effort or attempt.*

Endemic, en-dem'ik, *a*. *Peculiar to a people or nation, as a disease.—n. A disease of an endemic nature.* [Fr. *endémique*—Gr. *dēmos*, people.]

Ending, end'ing, *p.n*. *Termination; conclusion; the terminating syllable or letter of a word.*

Endless, end'les, *a*. *Without end; everlasting; infinite; incessant; perpetually recurring; seemingly without end.*

Endlessly, end'les-li, *adv*. *Without end or termination: incessantly.*

Endlessness, end'les-nes, *n*. *Quality or state of being endless.*

Endlong, end'long, *adv*. *Along; in a line; with the end forward.* [Sax. *andlang*.]

Endogen, en'dō-jen, *n*. *A plant whose stem or trunk grows by internal increase. Such are palms, grasses, rushes, &c.* [Gr. *endon*, within, and *ginomai*, to grow.]

Endogenous, en-do'jen-us, *a*. *Increasing by internal growth.*

Endow, en-dou', *vt*. *To settle a dower on; to settle on as a permanent provision; to enrich or furnish, as with any gift, quality, or faculty; to induo; to invest.* [... and Fr. *douer*, to endow—L. *dos, dotis*, a marriage portion.]

Endowed, en-doud', *p.a*. *Supplied with a permanent fund; indued; furnished with any gift.*

Endower, en-dou'ėr, *n*. *One who enriches with a portion.*

Endowment, en-dou'ment, *n*. *Act of endowing, or revenue permanently* appropriated to any object; any quality or faculty bestowed by the *Creator; talent.*

Endurable, en-dūr'a-bl, *a*. *That can be endured; that can be borne or suffered.*

Endurance, en-dūr'ans, *n*. *State of enduring; state of lasting; a bearing up against hardships; patience; fortitude.*

Endure, en-dūr', *vi*. *To become or remain hard; to continue in the same state without perishing; to last; to suffer without resistance or without yielding; to submit.—vt. To support without breaking; to sustain; to bear, as hardships; to bear with patience; to bear without opposition or sinking under; to undergo; to tolerate. ppr. enduring, pret. & pp. endured.* [Fr. *endurer*—L. *durus*, hard.]

Enduring, en-dūr'ing, *p.a*. *Lasting long; permanent.*

Endwise, end'wīz, *adv*. *On the end; in an upright position; with the end forward.*

Enemy, en'e-mi, *n*. *One who is unfriendly; a foe; an antagonist; one who hates or dislikes; a hostile army; the great adversary of mankind.* [Fr. *ennemi*—L. *in*, priv. and *amicus*, a friend—*amo*, to love.]

Energetic, en-ėr-jet'ik, *a*. *Having energy; working; operating with force, vigour, and effect; vigorous; moving.* [Gr. *energētikos*.]

Energetically, en-ėr-jet'ik-al-li, *adv*. *With energy and effect.*

Energize, en'ėr-jīz, *vi*. *To act with energy.—vt. To give energy or force to. ppr. energizing, pret. & pp. energized.*

Energy, en'ėr-ji, *n*. *Inherent power to operate or act; power exerted; vigorous power in action; effectual operation; strength or force producing the effect; strength of expression; force of utterance.* [Gr. *energeia—ergon*, work.]

Enervate, e-nėrv'āt, *vt*. *To deprive of nerve, strength, or force; to unnerve; to debilitate. ppr. enervating, pret. & pp. enervated.* [L. *enervo, enervatus—nervus*, a nerve.]

Enervated, e-nėrv'āt-ed, *p.a*. *Deprived of vigour or force.*

Enervating, e-nėrv'āt-ing, *p.a*. *Depriving of strength, force, or vigour.*

Enfeeble, en-fē'bl, *vt*. *To make feeble; to reduce the strength or force of; to enervate. ppr. enfeebling, pret. & pp. enfeebled.*

Enfeebled, en-fē'bld, *p.a*. *Deprived of strength.*

Enfeeblement, en-fē'bl-ment, *n*. The act of weakening; enervation.

Enfeebling, en-fē'bl-ing, *p.a*. *Weakening; enervating.*

Enfeoff, en-fef', *vt*. *To give a fief to; to invest with a fee; to give up†.* [Low L. *feoffare*.]

Enfeoffment, en-fef'ment, *n*. *Act of giving the fee simple of an estate; the deed by which one is invested with the fee of an estate.* [Low L. *feoffamentum*.]

Enfetter†, en-fet'tėr, *vt*. *To fetter.*

Enfilade, en-fi-lād', *n*. *A line; a range; a fire of artillery, raking the whole length of a fortification or body of troops.—vt. To rake with shot, in the direction of a line, or through the whole length of a line. ppr. enfilading, pret. & pp. enfiladed.* [Fr.—L. *filum*, a thread.]

Enforce, en-fōrs', *vt*. *To give force to; to gain by force; to strengthen; to impel; to urge on; to urge with energy; to impress on the mind; to compel; to* constrain; to put in force or in execution; to urge or press, as with a charge. *ppr. enforcing, pret. & pp. enforced.*

Enforcement, en-fōrs'ment, *n*. *Act of enforcing; force applied; that which gives force, energy, or effect; sanction; that which constrains; a putting in execution, as law.*

Enfranchise, en-fran'chiz, *vt*. *To endow with a franchise; to set free; to admit to the privileges of a freeman or citizen. ppr. enfranchising, pret. & pp. enfranchised.*

Enfranchised, en-fran'chīzd, *p.a*. *Admitted to the rights and privileges of freemen.*

Enfranchisement, en-fran'chīz-ment, *n*. *Act of enfranchising; release from slavery; the admission of persons to the freedom of a corporation or state; investiture with the privileges of free citizens.*

Enfreet, en-frē', *vt*. *To set free.*

Engage, en-gāj', *vt*. *To bind by pledge or contract, to attach; to undertake to do (with recipr. pron.); to win; to attract; to encounter, to attack in conflict.—vi. To pledge one's word; to bind one's self; to embark in any business; to undertake. ppr. engaging, pret. & pp. engaged.* [Fr. *engager—gage*, a pledge.]

Engaged, en-gājd', *p.a*. *Pledged; promised; affianced; betrothed.*

Engagement, en-gāj'ment, *n*. *Act of engaging; obligation by contract; promise; adherence to a party or cause; employment of one's time; avocation; business; the conflict of armies or fleets; battle; a general action.*

Engaging, en-gāj'ing, *p.a*. *Winning; attractive; pleasing.*

Engaol, en-jāl', *vt*. *To imprison.*

Engender, en-jen'dėr, *vt*. *To breed; to produce; to cause to bring forth; to occasion; to call forth; to create.—vi. To be caused or produced.* [Fr. *engendrer*—L. *genus*, birth, descent.]

Engine, en'jin, *n*. *An ingenious contrivance; a compound machine, by which any physical power is applied to produce any given effect; a military machine; any instrument; anything used to effect a purpose; an agent for another.* [Fr. *engin*—L. *gigno*, to produce.]

Engineer, en-jin-ēr', *n*. *One who constructs or manages engines; one who forms plans of works for offence or defence; one who constructs roads, railways, &c.* [Fr. *ingénieur*.]

Engineering, en-jin-ēr'ing, *p.n*. *The business of an engineer.*

Engird, en-gėrd', *vt*. *To gird round; to surround; to encircle.*

Engirded, Engirt, en-gėrd'ed, en-gėrt', *p.a*. *Surrounded; encompassed.*

English, ing'glish, *a*. *Belonging to England, or to its inhabitants.—n. The people or language of England.—vt. To translate into English.* [Sax. *Englisc*.]

Englut†, en-glut', *vt*. *To gulp down.*

Engrain, en-grān', *vt*. *To dye in grain, or in the raw material; to dye deep.*

Engrave, en-grāv', *vt*. *To cut, as metals, stones, or other hard substances, with a chisel or graver; to cut, as figures, letters, or devices on stone or metal; to represent by incisions; to impress deeply; to infix, as in the memory. ppr. engraving, pret. engraved, pp. engraved or engraven.*

Engraved, Engraven, en-grāvd', en-grāv'en, *p.a*. *Imprinted; deeply impressed.*

Engraver, en-grāv'ėr, *n*. *One who engraves; a sculptor; a carver.*

Engraving, en-grāv'ing, *p.n. Act or art of engraving;* a print; an impression from an engraved plate.
Engross, en-grōs', *vt. To seize in the gross;* to take the whole of; to swallow up; to occupy; to engage; to copy in a large hand; to take in undue quantities or degrees. [Fr. *grosser*, to enlarge—*gros*, big.]
Engrossed, en-grōst', *p.a.* Absorbed; deeply engaged.
Engrosser, en-grōs'èr, *n. One who engrosses.*
Engrossing, en-grōs'ing, *p.n. Act of engrossing;* the copying of a writing in fair and legible characters.
Engrossment, en-grōs'ment, *n. Act of engrossing;* act of taking the whole; a copy of a written instrument in a large fair hand.
Enguard†, en-gärd', *vt. To guard;* to defend.
Engulf, en-gulf', *vt. To ingulf;* to swallow up.
Enhance, en-hans', *vt. To raise* to a *higher* point; to heighten; to increase; to aggravate.—*vi. To be raised;* to swell; to grow larger. *ppr.* enhancing, *pret. & pp.* enhanced. [Fr. *hausser*, to raise —L. *altus*, high.]
Enhanced, en-hanst', *p.a.* Raised.
Enhancement, en-hans'ment, *n. Act of enhancing;* rise; augmentation.
Enigma, ē-nig'ma, *n. A dark saying,* in which some known thing is concealed under obscure language; an obscure question; a riddle. [Gr. *ainigmaainos*, a tale.]
Enigmatic, Enigmatical, ē-nig-mat'ik, ē-nig-mat'ik-al, *a. Relating to or containing an enigma;* obscure; darkly expressed; obscurely conceived. [Fr. *énigmatique*.]
Enigmatically, ē-nig-mat'ik-al-li, *adv.* In an obscure manner.
Enigmatist, ē-nig'mat-ist, *n. A maker of enigmas.* [Late Gr. *ainigmatistēs*.]
Enjoin, en-join', *vt. To join or attach to'*; to lay upon; to order or direct with urgency; to admonish with authority; to prescribe. [Fr. *enjoindre*—L. *jungo, jungere*, to join.]
Enjoy, en-joi', *vt. To have or feel gladness* or delight in; to perceive with pleasure; to take pleasure in the possession of; to have and use with satisfaction, or as a good or desirable thing. [Fr. *jouir*, to enjoy—L. *gaudeo, gaudēre*, to be glad.]
Enjoyable, en-joi'a-bl, *a. Capable of being enjoyed.*
Enjoyment, en-joi'ment, *n. State of enjoying;* pleasure; satisfaction in the possession of what is good or desirable; fruition; happiness. [Fr. *enjouement*.]
Enkindle, en-kin'dl, *vt. To kindle;* to inflame; to rouse into action. *ppr.* enkindling, *pret. & pp.* enkindled.
Enlard, en-lärd', *vt. To cover with lard* or grease.
Enlarge, en-lärj', *vt. To make large or larger;* to extend in limits, breadth, or size; to dilate; to increase; to set at large.—*vi. To grow large or larger;* to extend; to be diffuse; to exaggerate. *ppr.* enlarging, *pret. & pp.* enlarged. [Fr. *élargir*—L. *largus*, large.]
Enlarged, en-lärjd', *p.a.* Augmented; released from confinement or straits.
Enlargement, en-lärj'ment, *n. Act of enlarging;* state of being enlarged; increase; expansion.
Enlighten, en-lit'en, *vt. To shed light on;* to supply with light; to make clear; to enable to see more clearly; to instruct; to illuminate with divine knowledge. [Sax. *enlihtan*.]
Enlightened, en-lit'end, *p.a.* Instructed; informed; furnished with clear views.
Enlightener, en-lit'en-èr, *n. One who enlightens* or illuminates.
Enlightening, en-lit'en-ing, *p.a. Giving light to;* instructing.
Enlightenment, en-lit'en-ment, *n. Act of enlightening;* state of being enlightened.
Enlist, en-list', *vt. To enter on a list;* to engage in public service, by entering the name of in a register; to employ in advancing some object.—*vi.* To engage voluntarily in public service by *enrolling* one's name; to enter heartily into a cause, as one devoted to its interests.
Enlistment, en-list'ment, *n. Act of enlisting;* voluntary engagement to serve as a soldier or sailor; voluntary enrolment.
Enliven, en-liv'en, *vt. To give life or heart to;* to quicken; to give vivacity or sprightliness to; to exhilarate; to gladden; to invigorate. [Sax. *liban*, to live—Heb. *libba*, the heart.]
Enlivener, en-liv'en-èr, *n. He or that which enlivens* or animates.
Enlivening, en-liv'en-ing, *p.a. Giving life,* spirit, or animation.
Enmesh, en-mesh', *vt.* To catch, as with the meshes of a net; to entrap.
Enmity, en'mi-ti, *n. Quality of being an enemy;* hostility; hatred; ill-will; a state of opposition. [Fr. *inimitié*—L. *in*, priv. and *amicus*, a friend.]
Ennoble, en-nō'bl, *vt. To make noble;* to elevate in degree, qualities, or excellence; to dignify. *ppr.* ennobling, *pret. & pp.* ennobled. [Fr. *ennoblir*—L. *nobilis*, noble.]
Ennobling, en-nō'bl-ing, *p.a.* Exalting; dignifying.
Ennui, än-nwē', *n.* Dulness of spirit, connected with a feeling of disgust; weariness; heaviness; listlessness. [Fr.]
Enormity, ē-nor'mi-ti, *n. That which is out of rule;* any wrong or sinful act; depravity; atrocious crime; excessive degree of crime or guilt. [Fr. *enormité*—L. *enormitas*—*norma*, a rule.]
Enormous, ē-nor'mus, *a. Out of rule;* irregular; great beyond the common measure; exceeding in bulk or height the common measure; huge; outrageous; flagitious; extremely wicked. [L. *enormis*—*norma*, a rule.]
Enormously, ē-nor'mus-li, *adv.* Excessively; beyond measure.
Enough, ē-nuf', *a.* That *satisfies* desire; that may answer the purpose.—*n. A sufficiency;* that which is equal to the powers or abilities.—*adv. Sufficiently;* fully; quite; an exclamation denoting sufficiency. [Sax. *genoh*.]
Enrage, en-rāj', *vt. To excite rage in;* to make furious; to incense; to provoke. *ppr.* enraging, *pret. & pp.* enraged. [Fr. *faire enrager*.]
Enraged, en-rājd', *p.a.* Provoked to madness.
Enrapt, en-rap', *vt.* To bear away in ecstasy.
Enrapture, en-rap'tūr, *vt. To carry away* with pleasure; to delight beyond measure. *ppr.* enrapturing, *pret. & pp.* enraptured. [L. *rapio*, to snatch away.]
Enraptured, en-rap'tūrd, *p.a. Transported* with pleasure.
Enrapturing, en-rap'tūr-ing, *p.a. Transporting* with pleasure.
Enrich, en-rich', *vt. To make rich;* to supply with abundant property; to fertilize; to store; to supply with an abundance of anything desirable, splendid, or ornamental. [Fr. *enrichir*—*riche*, rich.]
Enrichment, en-rich'ment, *n. Act of enriching;* improvement.
Enrol, en-rōl', *vt. To write in a roll;* to insert, as a name, or enter in a list or catalogue; to record; to leave in writing. *ppr.* enrolling, *pret. & pp.* enrolled. [Fr. *enrôler*—*rôle*, a roll.]
Enrolment, en-rōl'ment, *n. Act of enrolling;* a register; a record; a writing in which anything is recorded.
Enroot†, en-röt', *vt. To fix by the root;* to fix fast.
Ensample, en-sam'pl, *n. An example.* [L. *exemplum*.]
Ensanguined, en-san'gwind, *p.a. Suffused or stained with blood.* [L. *sanguis, sanguinis*, blood.]
Ensconce, en-skons', *vt. To cover,* as *with a sconce;* to protect; to secure or hide. *ppr.* ensconcing, *pret. & pp.* ensconced.
Enseam†, en-sēm', *vt.* To cover with grease.
Enshield†, en-shēld', *a.* Defended, as with a *shield.*
Enshrine, en-shrīn', *vt. To inclose in a shrine;* to deposit for safe-keeping in a cabinet; to preserve as sacred. *ppr.* enshrining, *pret. & pp.* enshrined.
Enshrined, en-shrīnd', *p.a.* Placed, as in a shrine.
Enshroud, en-shroud', *vt. To cover with a shroud.*
Ensign, en'sīn, *n. A mark or badge;* any mark of distinction; the flag of a military band or of a vessel; a commissioned officer next below the lieutenant. [Fr. *enseigne*—L. *signum*, a mark.]
Ensigncy, en'sīn-si, *n. The rank, office, or commission of an ensign.*
Enskied†, en-skīd', *p.a. Placed in the sky.*
Enslave, en-slāv', *vt. To reduce to slavery;* to reduce to subjection, as to habits or passions. *ppr.* enslaving, *pret. & pp.* enslaved.
Enslavement, en-slāv'ment, *n. Act of enslaving;* state of being enslaved.
Enslaver, en-slāv'èr, *n. One who enslaves.*
Ensue, en-sū', *vt. To follow* as a consequence of premises; to follow in a train of events or course of time; to come after.—*vt.† To follow;* to pursue. *ppr.* ensuing, *pret. & pp.* ensued. [Fr. *ensuivre*—L. *sequor*, to follow.]
Ensuing, en-sū'ing, *p.a.* Coming next after; succeeding.
Entablature, en-tab'la-tūr, *n.* That part of an architectural order which lies upon the capitals of the columns, comprehending the architrave, frieze, and cornice. [Old Fr.—L. *tabula*, a board.]
Entail, en'tāl, *n.* An estate or fee entailed, or limited in descent to a particular heir or heirs; rule of descent settled for an estate. [Fr. *entailler*, to notch—*tailler*, to cut.]
Entail, en-tāl', *vt. To cut off,* as an estate from the heirs general; to settle or fix unalienably, as the descent of lands and tenements by gift to a man and to certain heirs specified. [Fr. *entailler*.]
Entailed, en-tāld', *p.a. Settled or fixed by entail.*
Entangle, en-tang'gl, *vt. To knit or interweave* in such a manner as not to be easily separated; to perplex; to embarrass; to ensnare; to catch. *ppr.* entangling, *pret. & pp.* entangled.
Entangled, en-tang'gld, *p.a.* Involved; embarrassed; insnared.

Fate, fär, fat, fall; mē, met, hèr; pine, pin; nōte, not, mōve; tūbe, tub, bull; oil, pound.

Entanglement, en-tang'gl-ment, n. Act of entangling; state of being entangled.
Enter, en'tėr, vt. To go into; to pierce; to advance into; to set down in writing; to register; to enrol; to insert.—vi. To go or come in; to pass into; to pierce; to penetrate mentally; to go into minutely; to engage in, as a business or project; to begin; to be an ingredient. [Fr. entrer—L. intro, to the inside.]
Entered, en'tėrd, p.a. Set down in writing.
Entering, en'tėr-ing, p.a. Beginning; preparing the way.—p.n. Entrance; a passing in.
Enterprise, en'tėr-priz, n. That which is taken hold of; that which is undertaken; a bold or hazardous undertaking; attempt; an adventurous spirit; hardihood.—vt. To take in hand; to undertake. ppr. enterprising, pret. & pp. enterprised. [Fr.—L. prehendo, prenson, to seize.]
Enterprising, en'tėr-priz-ing, p.a. Bold or forward to undertake; prompt to attempt great or untried schemes.
Entertain, en-tėr-tān', vt. To hold together; to receive, as a guest; to treat hospitably; to sustain in one's service; to cherish in the mind; to hold; to cherish; to treat with conversation; to please; to admit, with a view to consider and decide. [Fr. entretenir—L. inter, and teneo, to hold.]
Entertainer, en-tėr-tān'ėr, n. One who entertains.
Entertaining, en-tėr-tān'ing, p.a. Pleasing; amusing; diverting.
Entertainment, en-tėr-tān'ment, n. Act of entertaining; hospitable treatment at table; a festival; amusement; recreation; sport.
Entertissued', en-tėr-ti'shūd, a. Having various colours intermixed.
Enthrone, en-thrōn', vt. To place on a throne; to exalt to an elevated place or seat; to induct or instal, as a bishop into a vacant see. ppr. enthroning, pret. & pp. enthroned.
Enthusiasm, en-thū'zi-azm, n. A heat or ardour of mind caused by a belief of divine and private revelations; fanaticism; heat of imagination; heat of imagination, tempered by reason or experience. [Fr. enthousiasme—Gr. entheos, inspired—theos, a god.]
Enthusiast, en-thū'zi-ast, n. A fanatic; a zealot; one whose mind is highly excited with the love or in the pursuit of an object; a person of ardent zeal; one of elevated fancy or exalted ideas. [Fr. enthousiaste.]
Enthusiastic, en-thū'zi-as''tik, a. Filled with enthusiasm; warm; ardent; devoted; visionary; fanatical. [Gr. enthousiastikos.]
Enthusiastically, en-thū'si-as''tik-al-li, adv. With enthusiasm.
Entice, en-tīs', vt. To set on fire; to incite or instigate, by exciting hope or desire; to decoy; to seduce; to coax; to urge or lead astray. ppr. enticing, pret. & pp. enticed. [Fr. attiser—L. titio, a firebrand.]
Enticeable, en-tīs'a-bl, a. Capable of being enticed.
Enticement, en-tīs'ment, n. Act of enticing; blandishment; seduction; wile.
Enticer, en-tīs'ėr, n. One who entices.
Enticing, en-tīs'ing, p.a. Having the qualities that entice or allure.
Enticingly, en-tīs'ing-li, adv. Charmingly; in a winning manner.
Entire, en-tīr', a. Untouched; whole; undivided; unbroken; complete in its parts; not participated with others; full; comprising all requisites in itself; sincere; hearty; solid; fixed; undisputed; wholly devoted; faithful; in full strength. [Fr. entier—L. integer, whole—tango, to touch.]
Entirely, en-tīr'li, adv. In the whole; wholly; completely; fully.
Entireness, en-tīr'nes, n. Fulness; totality; unbroken form or state.
Entitle, en-ti'tl, vt. To give a title to; to style; to characterise; to give a claim to; to dignify by a title or honourable appellation; to give a right to demand or receive; to qualify. ppr. entitling, pret. & pp. entitled. [Fr. intituler—L. titulus, a title.]
Entity, en'ti-ti, n. Being; essence; existence. [Fr. entité—Low L. entitas—L. sum, esse (obsol. ens), to be.]
Entomb, en-tōm', vt. To deposit in a tomb, as a dead body; to bury in a grave; to inter.
Entombment, en-tōm'ment, n. Burial.
Entomologic, en'tom-o-loj''ik, a. Pertaining to entomology, or to the science of insects. [Fr. entomologique.]
Entomologist, en-tom-ol'o-jist, n. One versed in the science of insects. [Fr. entomologiste.]
Entomology, en-tom-ol'o-ji, n. A discourse or treatises on insects; the science or natural history of insects. [Fr. entomologie—Gr. entoma, insects (temnō, to cut), and logos, discourse.]
Entrail, en'trāl, n. Entrails, en'trālz, pl. The internal parts of animal bodies; the bowels; the internal parts, as of the earth. [Fr. entrailles—Gr. entos, within.]
Entrance, en'trans, n. Act of entering into a place; ingress; the door or avenue by which a place may be entered; commencement; beginning; act of taking possession. [from L. intrans, going into—intro, to go into.]
Entrance, en-trans', vt. To put in a trance; to put in an ecstasy; to ravish with delight or wonder. ppr. entrancing, pret. & pp. entranced. [Old Fr. transe, a trance—L. transeo, to go beyond.]
Entranced, en-transt', p.a. Enraptured; ravished.
Entrancement, en-trans'ment, n. A state of trance or ecstasy.
Entrap, en-trap', vt. To catch, as in a trap; to inveigle; to decoy; to embarrass. ppr. entrapping, pret. & pp. entrapped. [Fr. attraper.]
Entreat, en-trēt', vt. To seek to obtain by treaty, engagement, or promise; to pray with urgency; to beg; to supplicate.—vi. To make an earnest petition or request; to supplicate; to pray. [Fr. traiter—L. tracto, to handle.]
Entreated, en-trēt'ed, p.a. Handled; dealt with.
Entreatingly, en-trēt'ing-li, adv. In an entreating manner.
Entreaty, en-trēt'i, n. Urgent prayer; earnest petition; solicitation; suit.
Entry, en'tri, n. Act of entering; way in or into; entrance; the passage by which persons enter a house; act of entering and taking possession of lands or other estate; act of committing to writing. [Fr. entrée.]
Entwine, en-twīn', vt. To twine; to twist round; to intwine. ppr. entwining, pret. & pp. entwined.
Entwist, en-twist', vt. To twist or wreathe round.
Enumerate, ē-nū'me-rāt, vt. To count or tell, number by number; to reckon or mention, as a number of things, each separately. ppr. enumerating, pret. & pp. enumerated. [L. enumero, enumeratus—numerus, number—Gr. nemō, to distribute.]
Enumeration, ē-nū'me-rā''shon, n. Act of enumerating; an account of a number of things, in which mention is made of every particular article. [Fr. enumération—L. enumeratio.]
Enunciate, ē-nun'si-āt, vt. To utter; to make a formal statement of; to pronounce; to proclaim. ppr. enunciating, pret. & pp. enunciated. [L. enuncio, enunciatus—nuncio, to tell.]
Enunciation, ē-nun'si-ā''shon, n. Act of enunciating; expression; manner of uttering articulate sounds; declaration; public attestation; intelligence; the words in which a proposition is expressed. [L. enunciatio.]
Enunciator, ē-nun'si-āt-ėr, n. He who enunciates or declares. [Low L.]
Enunciatory, ē-nun'si-ā-tō-ri, a. Containing enunciation; declarative.
Envelop, en-vel'op, vt. To roll or fold in; to cover by folding; to inwrap; to cover on all sides; to hide. [Fr. envelopper—L. volvo, to roll.]
Envelope, Envelop, en'vel-ōp, n. That which infolds; a wrapper; a cover; a covering for a letter, parcel, &c.; an investing integument.
Envelopment, en-vel'ōp-ment, n. A wrapping; an inclosing or covering on all sides.
Envenom, en-ven'om, vt. To taint with poison, or any substance noxious to life; to taint with malice; to make odious; to exasperate. [Fr. envenimer—L. venenum, poison—Sans. van, to strike, to wound.]
Envenomed, en-ven'omd, p.a. Imbittered; exasperated.
Enviable, en'vi-a-bl, a. That may excite envy; very desirable.
Enviably, en'vi-a-bli, adv. In an enviable manner.
Envious, en'vi-us, a. Feeling or harbouring envy; feeling uneasiness at a view of the excellence, prosperity, or happiness of another; tinctured with envy, as feelings; excited by envy, as remarks. [Fr. envieux—L. invidiosus.]
Enviously, en'vi-us-li, adv. In an envious manner; with envy.
Enviousness, en'vi-us-nes, n. Quality or state of being envious.
Environ, en-vī'ron, vt. To encompass; to encircle; to besiege; to invest. [Fr. environner—L. gyro, to turn round.]
Environment, en-vī'ron-ment, n. A surrounding, or being surrounded. [Old Fr. environnement.]
Environs, en'vi-rons, n. pl. The places which surround another place; neighbourhood; vicinity. [Fr.]
Envoy, en'voi, n. One sent on his way; a person next in rank to an ambassador, deputed by a prince to negotiate a treaty, or transact other business, with a foreign prince or government. [Fr. envoyé, sent—L. via, a way.]
Envoyship, en'voi-ship, n. The office of an envoy.
Envy, en'vi, vt. To look with an evil eye upon; to hate on account of happiness; to repine at, as at another's prosperity; to grudge; to withhold maliciously. ppr. envying, pret. & pp. envied. [Fr. envier—L. video, to look at.]—n. Pain or discontent excited by the sight of another's superiority or success, accompanied with some degree of hatred; malice; ill-will; spite. [Fr. envie—L. invidia.]
Envying, en'vi-ing, p.n. Ill-will at

others on account of some supposed superiority.

Eolian, ē-ō′li-an, *a.* Pertaining to *Æolia*, or to the dialect of Æolia, in Asia Minor, inhabited by Greeks; relating to *Æolius*, the fabled deity of the winds; played upon by the wind.

Eolic, ē-ol′ik, *a. Relating to Æolia*, or to the Greek dialect of Æolia.

Epact, ē′pakt, *n.* Days added to find the age of the moon; the number of days by which the last new moon has preceded the beginning of the year. [Gr. *epaktos—epi*, and *agō*, to lead.]

Epaulet, e′pal-et, *n. A shoulder knot or piece*; an ornamental badge worn on the shoulder by military men. [Fr. *épaulette*—L. *scapulæ*, the shoulderblades.]

Epauletted, e′pal-et-ed, *p.a. Furnished with epaulets.*

Epergne, e-pārn′, *n.* An ornamental stand for a large dish in the centre of a table. [Fr.]

Epha, ē′fä, *n.* A Hebrew measure, containing about of 4-9th English bushel. [Heb. *eypha*, rarely *epha*, very probably of Egyptian origin.]

Ephemera, e-fē′me-ra, *n.* The day-fly or May-fly; a fly that lives *one day* only; a short-lived insect. [Fr. *éphémère*—Gr. *epi*, and *hēmēra*, a day.]

Ephemeral, e-fē′me-ral, *a.* Continuing *one day* only; beginning and ending in a day; short-lived; existing for a short time only. [from Gr. *ephēmeron*.]

Ephemeris, e-fē′me-ris, *n.* A diary.

Ephod, ē′fod, *n. That which is girded on*; a girdle, a part of the priestly habit among the Jews. [Heb. from *aphad*, to gird on.]

Epic, e′pik, *a. Narrative*; rehearsing; heroic; relating to heroic poetry or poems.—*n.* An epic or a heroic poem. [Fr. *épique*—Gr. *epos*, a word, a song.]

Epicure, e′pi-kūr, *n.* A follower of the doctrines unjustly ascribed to *Epicurus*; a man devoted to sensual enjoyments; a voluptuary; a sensualist. [from L. *Epicūrus*.]

Epicurean, e′pi-kū-rē′an, *a. Pertaining to Epicurus*; given to luxury; contributing to the luxuries of the table.—*n. A follower of Epicurus*; one given to the luxuries of the table. [L. *Epicurēus.*]

Epicurism, e′pi-kūr-izm, *n.* The *doctrines of Epicurus*; luxury; indulgence in gross pleasure. [Fr. *épicurisme*.]

Epicycle, e′pi-sī-kl, *n. A little circle revolving while its centre moves round in the circumference of a greater circle.* [Gr. *epi*, and *kuklos*, a circle.]

Epidemic, Epidemical, e-pi-dem′ik, e-pi-dem′ik-al, *a. That falls at once upon the people*, as a plague; generally prevailing; affecting great numbers. [Gr. *epidemios—demos*, the people.]

Epidemic, e-pi-dem′ik, *n.* A disease generally prevailing, but not dependent on any local cause.

Epiglottis, e-pi-glot′is, *n.* The cartilage at the root of the *tongue* that falls upon the *glottis*, or superior opening of the larynx. [Gr. *epiglōttis—glōtta*, the tongue.]

Epigram, e′pi-gram, *n. That which is written upon a statue, &c.;* an inscription; a short poem treating only of one thing, and ending with some lively and natural thought. [Fr. *épigramme*—Gr. *gramma*, a writing.]

Epigrammatic, Epigrammatical, e′pi-gram-mat′′ik, e′pi-gram-mat′′ik-al, *a. Writing epigrams*; dealing in epigrams; suitable to epigrams; concise; pointed; poignant. [Fr. *épigrammatique.*]

Epigrammatically, e′pi-gram-mat′′ik-al-li, *adv. In an epigrammatic manner.*

Epigrammatist, e-pi-gram′mat-ist, *n. One who composes epigrams*, or deals in them. [Fr. *épigrammatiste.*]

Epilepsy, e′pi-lep-si, *n.* A disease which *lays hold of* the patient suddenly, causing him to fall to the ground; the falling-sickness; a disease characterized by spasms and loss of sense. [Gr. *epilēpsia—lambanō*, to seize.]

Epileptic, e-pi-lep′tik, *a. Pertaining to*, affected with, or consisting *of epilepsy.—n. One affected with epilepsy.* [Gr. *epilēptikos*.]

Epilogical, e-pi-loj′ik-al, *a. Relating to or like an epilogue.* [Gr. *epilogikos*.]

Epilogue, e′pi-log, *n. A conclusion*; peroration; a short poem addressed to the spectators by one of the actors in a drama after the conclusion of the play. [Gr. *epilogos—epi*, and *lego*, to speak.]

Epiphany, ē-pif′a-ni, *n. A manifestation*; a church-festival celebrated on the 6th day of January, in commemoration of *the appearance* of our Saviour to the wise men of the East. [Gr. *epiphaneia—phainō*, to bring to light.]

Episcopacy, e′pis-kō-pā-si, *n. Oversight*; applied particularly to the government of the church by *bishops* or prelates. [Low L. *episcopatus—*Gr. *epi*, and *skopeō*, to see.]

Episcopal, ē-pis′kō-pal, *a. Belonging to* or vested in *bishops*; governed by bishops. [Low L. *episcopalis.*]

Episcopalian, ē-pis′kō-pā′′li-an, *a. Pertaining to bishops, or government by bishops.—n. One who belongs to an episcopal church.*

Episcopalianism, ē-pis′kō-pā′′li-an-izm, *n. The system of episcopal religion*; Episcopacy.

Episcopate, ē-pis′kō-pāt, *n.* The office and dignity *of a bishop*; the order of bishops. [Fr. *épiscopal*.]

Episode, e′pi-sōd, *n. A coming in upon*; that which is superadded; a separate story introduced for the purpose of giving a greater variety to the events related in a poem; an incidental narrative. [Gr. *epeisodion—epi, eis*, into, and *hodos*, an entrance.]

Episodic, Episodical, e-pi-sōd′ik, e-pi-sōd′ik-al, *a. Pertaining to an episode*; contained in an episode. [Gr. *epeisodios*.]

Episodically, e-pi-sōd′ik-al-li, *adv. By way of episode.*

Epistle, ē-pis′l, *n. Anything sent to;* a writing sent, communicating intelligence to a distant person; a letter. [L. *epistŏla*—Gr. *epi*, and *stellō*, to send.]

Epistolary, ē-pis′tō-la-ri, *a. Pertaining to epistles*; suitable to correspondence; contained in letters. [Late L. *epistolaris.*]

Epitaph, e′pi-taf, *n.* That which is written *on a tomb*; an inscription on a monument in honour of the dead; a eulogy in prose or verse, composed without any intent to be engraven on a monument. [Fr. *épitaphe*—Gr. *epi*, and *taphos*, a burial.]

Epithet, e′pi-thet, *n.* Anything *put upon* or *added*; an adjective expressing some real quality of the thing to which it is applied. [Gr. *epithetos—tithēmi*, to place.]

Epitome, e-pi′tō-mi, *n. That which is cut short*; a brief summary of any book; a compendium. [Gr. *epitōmē—temnō*, to cut.]

Epitomist, e-pi′tom-ist, *n. An epitomiser.*

Epitomize, e-pi′tom-īz, *vt. To shorten*, as a writing or discourse; to abstract; to reduce into smaller compass; to condense. *ppr.* epitomising, *pret. & pp.* epitomized.

Epitomized, e-pi′tom-īzd, *p.a.* Abridged; shortened.

Epitomiser, e-pi′tom-īz-ėr, *n. One who epitomises* or abridges.

Epoch, ē′pok, *n. A holding* in!; a *fixed* point of time, from which succeeding years are numbered; any fixed time or period; the period when anything begins; era; date. [Gr. *epochē—epi*, and *echō*, to hold.]

Epode, ē′pōd, *n. A song to* or *over* something; that which is subjoined to the strophe and antistrophe in lyric poetry; any little verse or verses that follow one or more great ones. [Gr. *epodē*—*epi*, and *ōdē*, a song.]

Epsom-salt, ep′sum-salt, *n.* The sulphate of magnesia, a cathartic. [from *Epsom*, a town in England.]

Equability, ē-kwa-bil′i-ti, *n. State* or *quality of being equable*; continued equality at all times; uniformity; evenness. [L. *æquabilitas*.]

Equable, ē′kwa-bl, *a. Equal* and uniform at all times; even; smooth; undisturbed; unruffled. [L. *æquabilis—æquus*, equal.]

Equableness, ē′kwa-bl-nes, *n. State of being equable.*

Equably, ē′kwa-bli, *adv.* In an *equable* or uniform manner.

Equal, ē′kwal, *a. Even; uniform; same as one in regard to essence or attributes; alike*; of the same extent, magnitude, measure, or degree, when compared; the same in motion, space, or time; being in just proportion; adequate; fair; just; being on the same terms.—*n.* One not inferior or superior to another.—*vt. To make equal to*; to equalize; to rise to the same state, rank, or estimation with; to become or be equal to; to recompense fully; to answer in full proportion; to be of like excellence or beauty as. *ppr.* equalling, *pret. & pp.* equalled. [L. *æqualis—æquus*, level—Sans. *eka*, one.]

Equality, ē-kwal′i-ti, *n. State or quality of being equal*; likeness; evenness; plainness; sameness in state, condition, or course. [L. *æqualitas.*]

Equalization, ē′kwal-iz-ā′′shon, *n. Act of equalising*; state of being equalised. [Fr. *égalisation*.]

Equalize, ē′kwal-iz, *vt. To make equal*; to bring or reduce to an equality; to make even. *ppr.* equalising, *pret. & pp.* equalised. [Fr. *égaliser*.]

Equally, ē′kwal-li, *adv. In an equal manner*; evenly; uniformly.

Equalness, ē′kwal-nes, *n. Equality.*

Equanimity, ē-kwa-nim′i-ti, *n. Evenness of mind*; that calm temper or firmness of mind which is not easily elated or depressed. [L. *æquanimitas—æquus*, and *animus*, mind.]

Equate, ē-kwāt′, *vt. To make equal*; to reduce to an equation; to reduce to mean time or motion. *ppr.* equating, *pret. & pp.* equated. [L. *æquo, æquatus.*]

Equation, ē-kwā′shon, *n. A making equal*; the statement in algebra of the equality of two quantities; difference between mean and apparent time. [Fr. *équation*.]

Equator, ē-kwā′tėr, *n. That which makes equal*; a great circle of the heavens, which, when the sun enters it, makes

EQUATORIAL 123 **ERRATUM**

the days and nights *equal*. It is equally distant from the two poles of the world, or has the same poles as the world. [Fr. *équateur*.]
Equatorial, ē-kwa-tō'ri-al, *a*. *Pertaining to the equator*. [Fr. *équatorial*.]
Equerry, e'kwe-ri, *n*. *One who has the charge of horses; an officer of princes or nobles, who has the care of their horses*. [Low L. *equarius*—L. *equus*, a horse.]
Equestrian, ē-kwes'tri-an, *a*. *Pertaining to horses or horsemanship; being on horseback; skilled in horsemanship; celebrated by horse-races, as games*.—*n*. *A horseman*. [Fr. *équestre* —L. *eques*, a horseman.]
Equiangular, ē'kwi-ang'gū-lėr, *a*. *Consisting of or having equal angles*. [Fr. *equiangle*—L. *angulus*, an angle.]
Equidifferent, ē-kwi-dif'fėr-ent, *a*. *Having equal differences*; arithmetically proportional. [L. *æquus*, and *differens*, differing—*fero*, to bear.]
Equidistant, ē-kwi-dis'tant, *a*. *Being at an equal distance from some point or thing*. [L. *æquus*, and *distans*, standing apart—*sto*, to stand.]
Equilateral, ē-kwi-lat'ėr-al, *a*. *Having all the sides equal*. [L. *æquus*, and *lateralis*—*latus*, a side.]
Equilibrium, ē-kwi-li'bri-um, *n*. *Equality of weight or force; a state of rest produced by the mutual counteraction of two or more forces; equal balancing of the mind between motives or reasons; equal distribution*. [Fr. *équilibre* —L. *libra*, a balance.]
Equimultiple, ē-kwi-mul'ti-pl, *a*. *Multiplied by the same number or quantity*. *n*. *Any number or quantity multiplied by the same number or quantity as another*. [Fr. *équimultiple*—L. *multiplico*, to multiply—*plico*, to fold.]
Equine, ē-kwin', *a*. *Pertaining to a horse; denoting the horse kind*. [L. *equinus*—*equus*, a horse.]
Equinoctial, ē-kwi-nok'shi-al, *a*. *Having the nights equal to the days; pertaining to the equinoxes.*—*n*. *The equator*. [Fr. *équinoxial*—L. *æquus*, and *nox, noctis*, night.]
Equinox, ē'kwi-noks, *n*. *The precise time when the sun enters one of the equinoctial points, making the day and the night of equal length*. [L. *æquus*, and *nox, noctis*, night.]
Equip, ē-kwip', *vt*. *To fit, as a ship for sea; to furnish with men, artillery, and munitions of war, a ship; to furnish with arms for military service; to dress out; to decorate*. *ppr*. *equipping, pret. & pp. equipped*. [Fr. *équiper*—Goth. *skapan*, to form.]
Equipage, e'kwi-pāj, *n*. *An equipment; attendance; retinue; carriage of state; accoutrements; habiliments; ornamental furniture*. [Fr. *équipage*.]
Equipaged, e'kwi-pājd, *p.a*. *Furnished with an equipage*.
Equipment, ē-kwip'ment, *n*. *Act of equipping; anything that is used in equipping; furniture; habiliments; warlike apparatus; necessaries for an expedition or for a voyage*.
Equipoise, ē'kwi-poiz, *n*. *Equality of weight or force; equilibrium; a state in which the two ends or sides of a thing are balanced*. [L. *æquus*, and *pondus*, weight.]
Equipollence, Equipollency, ē-kwi-pol'lens, ē-kwi-pol'len-si, *n*. *Equality of power or force; ability, power, or force in the same degree*. [Fr. *équipollence* —L. *polleo*, to be able.]
Equipollent, ē-kwi-pol'lent, *a*. *Having*

equal power, strength, or force; equivalent; having equivalent signification. [Fr. *équipollent*.]
Equiponderance, ē-kwi-pon'dėr-ans, *n*. *Equality of weight;* equipose. [Fr. *équiponderance* — L. *pondus, ponderis*, weight.]
Equiponderant, ē-kwi-pon'dėr-ant, *a*. *Being of the same weight*.
Equipped, ē-kwipt', *p.a*. *Furnished with habiliments, &c*.
Equitable, e'kwit-a-bl, *a*. *Distributing equal justice; just; upright; impartial; honest; due to justice; reasonable; fair; held or exercised in equity*. [Fr. *équitable*—L. *æquus*, equal.]
Equitableness, e'kwit-a-bl-nes, *n*. *Quality of being equitable or just; equity*.
Equitably, e'kwit-a-bli, *adv*. *In an equitable manner; justly; impartially*.
Equity, e'kwi-ti, *n*. *Equality;* uniformity; right, as contemplated by the law of nature; impartial distribution of justice; a just regard to right or claim; fairness; uprightness. [Fr. *équité*—L. *æquus*, even.]
Equivalent, ē-kwiv'a-lent, *a*. *Equal in value, excellence, worth, or weight; of the same import or meaning*.—*n*. *That which is equal in value*, weight, or dignity, with something else; compensation. [Fr. *équivalent*—L. *valeo, valens*, to be strong.]
Equivalently, ē-kwiv'a-lent-li, *adv*. *In an equal manner*.
Equivalve, ē'kwi-valv, *a*. *Having the valves or shells equal in size and form, as certain shell-fish*. [L. *æquus*, and *valva*, a valve.]
Equivocal, ē-kwiv'ō-kal, *a*. *Equally significant of one meaning or of another; capable of a double interpretation; doubtful; indeterminate*. [L. *æquus*, and *vocālis*—*vox, vocis*, a word.]
Equivocally, ē-kwiv'ō-kal-li, *adv*. *Ambiguously; in a doubtful sense*.
Equivocate, ē-kwiv'ō-kāt, *vi*. *To use words of a doubtful signification; to use ambiguous expressions with a view to mislead; to shuffle; to quibble*. *ppr*. *equivocating, pret. & pp. equivocated*. [Low L. *æquivoco, æquivocatus*—L. *voco*, to call.]
Equivocation, ē-kwiv'ō-kā"shon, *n*. *Act of equivocating; ambiguity of speech; evasion*. [Low L. *æquivocatio*—L. *voco*, to call.]
Equivocator, ē-kwiv'ō-kāt-ėr, *n*. *One who equivocates; one who is not plain and open in speech*.
Era, ē'ra, *n*. *A fixed point of time, from which any number of years is begun to be counted; an epoch; a period; point; date; age*. [Fr. *ère*—Low L. *aera*.]
Eradicate, ē-rad'i-kāt, *vt*. *To pull up by the roots; to root out; to destroy; to extirpate; to exterminate*. [L. *eradico, eradicatum*—L. *radix, radicis*, a root.]
Eradication, ē-rad'i-kā"shon, *n*. *Act of plucking up by the roots; state of being plucked up by the roots; total destruction*. [Low L. *eradicatio*.]
Erasable, ē-rās'a-bl, *a*. *That may or can be erased*.
Erase, ē-rās', *vt*. *To scrape out; to efface; to expunge; to blot out; to destroy; to raze*. *ppr*. *erasing, pret. & pp. erased*. [L. *erado, erasum*—*rado*, to scrape.]
Erasement, ē-rās'ment, *n*. *A rubbing out; obliteration*.
Eraser, ē-rās'ėr, *n*. *One who erases; a kind of knife used to erase writing, &c*.
Erastian, ē-ras'ti-an, *n*. *A follower of*

Thomas *Erastus*, a German physician, who maintained that the church is wholly dependent on the state for its government and discipline.—*a*. *Relating to the Erastians or their principles*.
Erastianism, ē-ras'ti-an-izm, *n*. *The principles of the Erastians*.
Erasure, ē-rā'zhėr, *n*. *Act of erasing;* obliteration; place where a word or letter has been erased. [Low L. *rasūra*, a scraping—L. *rado, rāsum*, to scrape.]
Ere, ār, *adv*. *Before; sooner than*. *prep*. Before. [Sax. *aer*.]
Erect, ē-rekt', *a*. *Upright; directed upward; upright and firm; bold; undismayed; stretched; intent; extended*. *vt*. *To raise and set in an upright direction; to set up; to build; to set up anew; to found; to raise; to encourage; to cheer*. [L. *erigo, erectus—rego*, to make straight.]
Erecter, ē-rekt'ėr, *n*. *One who erects*.
Erectile, ē-rekt'il, *a*. *That which may be erected*.
Erection, ē-rek'shon, *n*. *Act of erecting;* act of building; state of being raised, built, or elevated; settlement; formation; elevation; anything erected; a building of any kind; distension and extension. [Fr. *érection*—L. *rego, rectum*, to make straight.]
Erectly, ē-rekt'li, *adv*. *In an erect posture*.
Erectness, ē-rekt'nes, *n*. *Uprightness of posture or form*.
Erelong, ār'long, *adv*. *Before a long time had elapsed;* before a long time shall elapse; before long.
Eremite, e'rē-mit, *n*. *One who lives in a desert or wilderness; a hermit*. [L. *eremita*.]
Erenow, ār'nou, *adv*. *Before this time*.
Erewhile, ār'hwil, *adv*. *Some time ago*.
Ergo, ėr'gō, *adv*. Therefore. [L.]
Ermine, ėr'min, *n*. *The mouse of Armenia, improperly so called; an animal of the weasel kind, a native of Northern Europe and America, valued for its fur; the fur of the ermine; an emblem of the purity of judges, and also of their dignity*. [Fr. *hermine*.]
Ermined, ėr'mind, *p.a*. *Clothed with ermine; adorned with the fur of the ermine*.
Erode, ē-rōd', *vt*. *To gnaw off or away; to corrode*. *ppr*. *eroding, pret. & pp. eroded*. [L. *erodo*—*rodo*, to gnaw.]
Erosion, ē-rō'zhon. *n*. *Act of gnawing off; eating away; state of being eaten away;* corrosion. [L. *erosio*.]
Err, er, *vi*. *To wander from the right way; to stray; to deviate from the true course or purpose; to depart from rectitude; to mistake; to blunder*. [Fr. *errer*—L. *erro*, to stray.]
Errand, e'rand, *n*. *A message;* a mandate; something to be told or done; any special business to be transacted by a messenger. [Sax. *aerend*.]
Errant, e'rant, *a*. *Wandering;* wandering about in search of adventures, as a knight-errant; wild; vile; wicked. [Fr. *errant*—L. *errans, erro*, to stray.]
Errantry, e'rant-ri, *n*. *A wandering state;* a roving or rambling about; the employment of a knight-errant.
Erratic, e-rat'ik, *a*. *Wandering; not fixed or stationary; irregular*. [Fr. *erratique*—L. *erraticus*.]
Erratically, e-rat'ik-al-li, *adv*. *Without rule; irregularly*.
Erratum, e-rā'tum, *n*. *Errata, pl. An error or mistake in writing or printing*. [L.—*erro*, to wander up and down, to mistake.]

---

ch, *chain*; j, *job*; g, *go*; ng, *sing*; ᴛʜ, *then*; th, *thin*; w, *wig*; wh, *whig*; zh, *azure*; † obsolete.

Erring, ėr'ing, *p.a.* Wandering from the truth or the right way.

Erroneous, e-rō'nē-us, *a.* Wandering; mistaking; deviating, by mistake, from the truth; not conformable to truth; erring from truth or justice. [Low L. *erroneus*.]

Erroneously, e-rō'nē-us-li, *adv.* By mistake; not rightly.

Error, e'rėr, *n.* A *wandering* from the truth; a mistake in judgment; a mistake made in writing or other performance; a blunder; deviation from law, justice, or right; sin; iniquity. [L.]

Erse, ėrs, *n.* The language of the descendants of the Gaels or Celts, in the Highlands of Scotland. [Ir.]

Erst, ėrst, *adv. Earliest*; at first; at the beginning; long ago; before; till then or now; hitherto. [Sax. *ærest*.]

Erubescence, e-rū-bes'ens, *n.* A *becoming red*; redness of the skin or surface of anything; a blushing. [Low L. *erubescentia*—L. *ruber*, red.]

Erubescent, e-rū-bes'ent, *a.* Red or reddish; blushing. [L. *erubescens*.]

Eructate, ē-rukt'āt, *vt.* To belch *up*; to eject from the stomach, as wind. [L. *eructo, eructatum—ructo*, to belch.]

Eructation, ē-ruk-tā'shon, *n.* Act of *belching*; a violent ejection of wind or other matter from the earth. [Fr. *éructation*.]

Erudite, e'rū-dīt, *a. Freed from roughness or rudeness*; well polished; taught; learned; conversant with books. [L. *eruditus—rūdis*, rough, rude.]

Eruditely, e'rū-dīt-li, *adv.* With *erudition* or learning.

Erudition, e-rū-di'shon, *n.* Learning; knowledge gained by study, or from books and instruction. [Fr. *érudition*—L. *eruditio.*]

Erupted, ē-rupt'ed, *p.a.* Forcibly thrown out, as lava from a volcano. [L. *eruptus—rumpo*, to break.]

Eruption, ē-rup'shon, *n.* A *breaking forth*; explosion; sudden rushing or sallying forth; a sudden hostile excursion; a breaking out of pimples upon the skin; pustules. [Fr. *éruption*—L. *rumpo, ruptum*, to break.]

Eruptive, ē-rupt'iv, *a. Bursting out or forth*; produced by eruption. [Sp. *eruptivo*.]

Erysipelas, e-ri-si'pe-las, *n.* Red *skin*; a disease called *St. Anthony's fire*; a peculiar form of inflammation which occurs chiefly in the skin, generally accompanied with pustules on the affected part, and with symptomatic fever. [Gr.—*eruthros*, red, and *pella*, skin.]

Erysipelatous, e'ri-si-pel"at-us, *a. Resembling erysipelas.*

Escalade, es-ka-lād', *n.* The assault of a fortress by *scaling* the walls; a furious attack made by troops on a fortified place, in which ladders are used to pass a ditch or mount a rampart.—*vt. To scale*; to mount and pass or enter by means of ladders. *ppr.* escalading, *pret. & pp.* escaladed. [Fr.—L. *scala*, a ladder.]

Escallop, es-kol'lop, *n.* A bivalve shell; *a scallop.* [D. *schulp*, a shell.]

Escapade, es-ka-pād', *n. Fling* of a horse; an impropriety of speech or behaviour of which an individual is unconscious; a vagary; a prank; a frolic. [Fr.—L. *pes, pedis*, a foot.]

Escape, es-kāp', *vt.* To get out of the way of; to obtain security from; to pass without harm; to pass unobserved; to avoid the danger of.—*vi.* To flee, shun, and ⊃e secure from danger; to avoid an evil; to be passed without harm. *ppr.* escaping, *pret. & pp.* escaped.—*n.* Flight, to shun danger or injury; state of being freed from danger without harm; an evasion of legal restraint or the custody of the sheriff, without due course of law. [Fr. *échapper.*]

Escapement, es-kāp'ment, *n.* The contrivance in a timepiece which connects the train of wheel-work with the pendulum or balance, giving to the latter the impulse by which it is kept in vibration. [Fr. *échappement.*]

Escarp, es-kärp', *vt. To form into a scarp*; to make to slope suddenly.—*n. A sudden slope*; the side of the ditch next the rampart. [Fr. *escarper.*]

Escarpment, es-kärp'ment, *n.* A precipitous side of any hill or rock; ground cut away nearly vertically about a position, in order to prevent an enemy from arriving at the latter. [Fr. *escarpement.*]

Escheat, es-chēt', *n.* That which *falls* to the original proprietor, or to the state, as lands or other property through failure of heirs, or by forfeiture.—*vi.* To revert, as land, to the lord of a manor, by means of the extinction of the blood of the tenant. [Old Fr. *eschoëite*—L. *ex*, and *cado*, to fall.]

Escheatable, es-chēt'a-bl, *a.* Liable to escheat.

Eschew, es-chö', *vt. To shun; to avoid*; to fly from. [Old Fr. *eschever*; Sax. *scunian*, to shun.]

Escort, es'kort, *n.* A *guard*; a body of armed men which attends an officer or baggage conveyed by land from place to place, to protect them; protection on a journey. [Fr. *escorte*—L. *cohors*, a place walled round, a company of soldiers.]

Escort, es-kort', *vt. To attend and guard* on a journey or excursion.

Escot†, es-kot', *vt.* To pay the reckoning for.

Escritoire, es-kri-twor', *n.* A box with instruments and conveniences *for writing*; a scrutoire. [Old Fr. *escriptoire*—L. *scribo, scriptum*, to write.]

Esculapian, es-kū-lā'pi-an, *a.* Medical. [from *Æsculapius*.]

Esculent, es'kū-lent, *a. Eatable;* that is or may be used by man for food *n. Something that is eatable.* [L. *esculentus—edo, esum*, to eat.]

Escutcheon, es-kuch'on, *n.* A *shield*; the shield on which a coat of arms is represented; that part of a vessel's stern where her name is written. [Old Fr. *escusson*—L. *scutum*, a shield.]

Escutcheoned, es-kuch'ond, *p.a.* Having a coat of arms or ensign.

Esophagus, ē-so'fa-gus, *n.* The canal through which *food* and drink *are conveyed* to the stomach; the gullet. [Gr. *oisophagos*—root *oiō*, to convey, and *phagō*, to eat.]

Esoteric, es-ō-te'rik, *a. Inner*; mysterious; taught to a select few, as certain doctrines of the ancient philosophers. [Fr. *ésotérique*—Gr. *esōterikos*—*eis*, into.]

Esoterics, es-ō-te'riks, *n.pl.* Doctrines mysterious or hidden; instructions or doctrines taught privately.

Espalier, es-pa'li-ėr, *n.* A row of trees in a garden, having the branches trained and spread out like a fan, and held in with *stakes* or *poles*; one such tree; a lattice-work of wood, on which to train fruit-trees and ornamental shrubs.—*vt.* To form, as an espalier. [Fr.—L. *palus*, a stake.]

Especial, es-pe'shi-al, *a.* Peculiar; chief: special. [Fr. *spécial.*]

Especially, es-pe'shi-al-li, *adv.* In an uncommon degree; specially.

Esperance†, es'pe-rans, *n.* Hope. [L. *spes*, hope.]

Espial, es-pī'al, *n. Act of espying.*

Espionage, es-pi-on-āj, *n. Practice or employment of spies*; practice of watching others without being suspected. [Fr. *espionnage.*]

Esplanade, es-pla-nād', *n. A level ground* within a fortified place; void space between the glacis of a citadel and the first houses of the town; a grass-plot in a garden. [Fr.—L. *planus*, plain.]

Espousal, es-pouz'al, *a. Relating to the act of espousing.*—*n. Act of espousing*; adoption; protection; (pl.) *act of betrothing* a man and woman to each other; a contract or mutual promise of marriage. [Fr. *espousailles.*]

Espouse, es-pous', *vt. To give as spouse*; to promise in marriage, by contract in writing, or by some pledge; to marry; to wed; to embrace; to adopt; to support; to take to one's self, with a view to maintain. *ppr.* espousing, *pret. & pp.* espoused. [Fr *épouser*—L. *spondeo, sponsum*, to promise solemnly.]

Espouser, es-pouz'ėr, *n. One who espouses.*

Espy, es-pī', *vt. To see at a distance;* to descry; to discover; to discover or see unexpectedly; to examine; to survey. *vi.* To look narrowly; to look about; to watch. *ppr.* espying, *pret. & pp.* espied. [Old Fr. *espier*—L. *specio*, to see.]

Esquire, es-kwīr', *n.* A *shield-bearer*; a title of dignity next in degree below a knight; a title of justices of the peace and other magistrates; a title of courtesy.—*vt.* To attend; to wait on. *ppr.* esquiring, *pret. & pp.* esquired. [Old Fr. *escuyer*—L. *scutum*, a shield.]

Essay, es-sā', *vt. To try;* to make experiment of. [Fr. *essayer.*]

Essay, es'sā, *n. A trial or experiment*; an endeavour; an effort made for the performance of anything; a composition intended to prove or illustrate a particular subject; a short treatise. [Fr. *essai*.]

Essayist, es'sā-ist, *n. A writer of an essay or of essays.*

Essence, es'ens, *n. Being;* the nature or being of anything; formal existence; that which makes a thing to be what it is; the very substance; constituent substance; the predominant virtues of any plant separated from grosser matter; perfume; odour; scent.—*vt.* To perfume; to scent. *ppr.* essencing. *pret. & pp.* essenced. [Fr.—L. *essentia*—*sum, esse*, to be.]

Essenced, es'senst, *p.a.* Perfumed.

Essential, es-sen'shi-al, *a. Relating to or containing the essence*; necessary to the existence of a thing; pure; volatile. *n.* Something that is *essential ;* the chief point; the most prominent characteristic; nature. [Fr. *essentiel.*]

Essentiality, es-sen'shi-al"li-ti, *n. The quality of being essential.*

Essentially, es-sen'shi-al-li, *adv. In essence*; by the constitution of nature.

Establish, es-tab'lish, *vt.* To make to stand firmly or unalterably; to found permanently; to institute; to form; to enact; to ordain; to sanction; to make firm; to confirm; to make good; to verify; to fulfil. [Old Fr. *establir—establissant*—L. *stabilio—sto*, to stand.]

Established, es-tab'lisht, *p.a.* Ratified;

confirmed, set up and supported by the state.
Establisher, es-tab'lish-ėr, n. He who establishes or confirms.
Establishment, es-tab'lish-ment, n. Act of establishing; state of being established; confirmation; sanction; fundamental principle; ground; ordinance; system of laws; constitution of government; stated allowance; income; vages; that which is established; a place of residence or of transacting business; that form of religious worship which is established and supported by the state; settlement or final rest. [Old Fr. establissement.]
Estate, es-tāt', n. State; condition; fixedness; circumstances of any person or thing; rank; landed property; possessions; fortune; the title or interest which a man has in lands, tenements, &c.; an order or class of men in the body politic; (pl.) dominions; possessions of a prince; classes or divisions of the people of a country.—vt.† To settle, as a fortune. [Old Fr. estat—L. status, a standing—sto, to stand.]
Esteem, es-tēm', vt. To value in money†; to appreciate; to set a high value on; to regard with reverence, respect, or friendship; to hold in opinion; to think; to compare in value; to estimate by proportion.—n. Estimation; judgment of merit or demerit; high value or estimation; great regard; favourable opinion. [Fr. estimer—L. æstimo—æs, money.]
Esteemed, es-tēmd', p.a. Valued; highly valued.
Estimable, es'tim-a-bl, a. Worthy of esteem or respect; deserving our good opinion or regard. [Fr.]
Estimably, es'tim-a-bli, adv. In an estimable manner.
Estimate, es'tim-āt, vt. To judge and form an opinion of the value of; to calculate; to reckon; to rate; to appraise; to appreciate; to prize; to esteem. ppr. estimating, pret. & pp. estimated.—n. A judgment or opinion of the value, degree, extent, or quantity of anything; valuation; approximate calculation of the probable cost of any undertaking. [L. æstimo, æstimatus—æs, money.]
Estimation, es-tim-ā'shon, n. Act of estimating; valuation; appreciation; computation; a reckoning; notion; esteem; honour. [Fr.]
Estrange, es-trānj', vt. To alienate; to divert from its original use or possessor; to alienate the affections of. ppr. estranging, pret. & pp. estranged. [Old Fr. estranger; Low L. extraneus—L. extra, without.]
Estrangement, es-trānj'ment, n. Alienation; a keeping at a distance; removal.
Estuary, es'tū-a-ri, n. A place where the sea advances and retires; a frith; a narrow passage, or the mouth of a river or lake, where the tide meets the current or flows and ebbs. [L. æstuarium—æstuo, to boil up.]
Et cetera, et sē'te-ra, and the contraction &c. or &c., denote and the rest, or others of the kind; and so forth. [L.]
Etch, ech vt. To eat into; to produce figures or designs, as on copper or other metallic plates by means of lines or strokes first drawn, and then eaten into by aquafortis.—vi. To practise etching. [D. etsen.]
Etching, ech'ing, p.n. The act or art of etching; a mode of engraving; the impression taken from an etched plate.

Eternal, ē-tėrn'al, a. Everlasting; that has always been and always shall be; without beginning of existence; without end of existence; endless; immortal; unchangeable.—n. An appellation of God. [Fr. éternel—L. æternus—Gr. aei, always, aiōn, eternity.]
Eternally, ē-tėrn'al-li, adv. Without beginning or end of duration, or without end only; for ever; unchangeably; endlessly.
Eternity, ē-tėrn'i-ti, n. Continuance without beginning or end; duration without end; the state or time after death. [Fr. éternité.]
Eternize, ē-tėrn'īz, vt. To make eternal or endless; to immortalize. ppr. eternizing, pret. & pp. eternized. [Fr. éterniser.]
Ether, ē'thėr, n. Pure refined air; a thin, subtile matter, much finer and rarer than air, which, as some philosophers suppose, begins from the limits of the atmosphere, and occupies the heavenly space; a very light, volatile, and inflammable fluid, produced from spirit of wine with an acid. [Fr. éther—Gr. aithō, to light up.]
Ethereal, ē-thē're-al, a. Formed of ether; heavenly; relating to or existing in the air. [L. ætherius.]
Etherealism, ē-thē'rē-al-izm, n. Quality of being ethereal.
Etherealize, ē-thē'rē-al-īz, vt. To convert into ether; to render ethereal. ppr. etherealising, pret. & pp. etherealised.
Ethereally, ē-thē're-al-li, adv. In an ethereal or heavenly manner.
Ethic, Ethical, eth'ik, eth'ik-al, a. Relating to manners or morals; treating of morality; delivering precepts of morality. [Fr. éthique—Gr. ethos, custom, manners.]
Ethically, eth'ik-al-li, adv. According to the doctrines of morality.
Ethics, eth'iks, n. The science of moral duty; a system of rules for regulating the actions of men.
Ethiopian, ē-thi-ōp'i-an, a. Pertaining to Ethiopia.—n. A native of Ethiopia. [Gr. Aithiops, Aithiōpos, an Ethiopian.]
Ethiopic, ē-thi-op'ik, n. The language of Ethiopia.—a. Relating to Ethiopia.
Ethnic, Ethnical, eth'nik, eth'nik-al, a. Relating to a nation or people; relating to the races of mankind; heathen; pagan. [Gr. ethnikos.]
Ethnography, eth-nog'ra-fi, n. A description of the different races of men, their manners, customs, institutions, and languages; a work on that subject. [Gr. ethnos, a nation, and graphō, to describe.]
Ethnological, eth-no-loj'ik-al, a. Relating to ethnology.
Ethnology, eth-nol'o-ji, n. That branch of science which treats of the different races of men. [Gr. ethnos, a nation, and logos, a discourse.]
Ethology, eth-ol'o-ji, n. A treatise on ethics; the science of ethics; a treatise on morality. [Gr. ethos, custom, and logos, a discourse.]
Etiquette, et-i-ket', n. A ticket†; forms of ceremony or decorum; the forms which are observed toward particular persons or in particular places; ceremony. [Fr. étiquette.]
Etymological, et'i-mo-loj''ik-al. a. Pertaining to etymology; according to or by means of etymology. [Fr. étymologique.]
Etymologically, et'i-mo-loj''ik-al-li, adv. According to etymology.

Etymologist, et-i-mol'o-jist, n. One versed in etymology. [Fr. étymologiste.]
Etymology, et-i-mol'o-ji, n. An account of the true origin of words; that part of philology which traces and explains the origin of words; that part of grammar which comprehends the various inflections and modifications of words. [Gr. etymos, true, and logos, account.]
Etymon, e'ti-mon, n. An original root or primitive word. [Gr. etumon.]
Eucharist, ū'ka-rist, n. A giving of thanks; the sacrament of the Lord's Supper. [Gr. eucharistia—eu, well, and charis, grace, thanks.]
Eucharistic, Eucharistical, ū-ka-rist'ik, ū-ka-rist'ik-al, a. Containing expressions of thanks; pertaining to the Lord's Supper. [Fr. eucharistique.]
Eulogist, ū'lo-jist, n. One who praises and commends another.
Eulogistic, ū-lo-jis'tik, a. Commendatory; full of praise.
Eulogistically, ū-lo-jis'tik-al-li, adv. With commendation.
Eulogium, ū-lō'ji-um, n. Eulogy; praise; encomium. [Low L.—Gr. eulogia.]
Eulogize, ū'lo-jīz, vt. To speak well of; to praise; to extol. ppr. eulogizing, pret. & pp. eulogized. [Gr. eulogeō.]
Eulogy, ū'lo-ji, n. A speaking well of; a speech or writing in commendation of a person; praise. [Gr. eulogia—eu, and logos, a speaking—legō, to speak.]
Eunuch, ū'nuk, n. A chamberlain†; a male of the human species castrated, to whom the guardianship of wives and daughters is intrusted in some eastern countries. [Gr. eunouchos—eunē, a bed, and echō, to have charge of.]
Eupepsy, ū-pep'si, n. Good digestion or concoction in the stomach. [Gr. eupepsia—peptō, to digest.]
Eupeptic, ū-pep'tik, a. Having good digestion.
Euphemism, ū'fem-izm, n. A speaking delicately; a figure by which a delicate word is substituted for one which is offensive. [Fr. euphémisme—Gr. phēmi, to speak.]
Euphemistic, ū-fem-ist'ik, a. Rendering more decent or delicate in expression.
Euphemize, ū'fem-īz, vt. To express one's self in delicate language.
Euphonic, Euphonical, ū-fon'ik, ū-fon'ik-al, a. Having euphony; agreeable in sound. [Fr. euphonique.]
Euphonious, ū-fō'ni-us, a. Having euphony; agreeable in sound. [Gr. euphōnos, sweet-voiced.]
Euphoniously, ū-fō'ni-us-li, adv. With euphony; harmoniously.
Euphony, ū'fo-ni, n. An agreeable or harmonious sound; an easy, smooth enunciation of sounds. [Fr. euphonie—Gr. phōnē, sound.]
Euroclydon, ū-rok'li-don, n. A tempestuous wind raising great waves of the sea, such as drove ashore, on Malta, the ship in which St. Paul was sailing to Italy. [Gr. euros, a south-east wind, and kludōn, a wave.]
European, ū-rō-pē'an, a. Pertaining to Europe.—n. A native of Europe.
Evacuate, ē-vak'ū-āt, vt. To empty out; to eject; to void; to discharge; to withdraw, as from a place. ppr. evacuating, pret & pp. evacuated. [L. evacuo, evacuatus—vacuo, to empty.]
Evacuated, ē-vak'ū-āt-ed, p.a. Ejected; discharged; vacated.
Evacuation, ē-vak'ū-ā''shon, n. Act o' emptying; act of quitting; discharge of any matter by the natural passages of

ch, chain; j, job; g, go; ng, sing; ᴛʜ, then; th, thin; w, wig; wh, whig; zh, azure; † obsolete.

Evacuator — **Exact**

the body, or by an artificial opening. [Low L. *evacuatio*.]

Evacuator, ē-vak'ū-āt-ėr, n. One who evacuates. [Low L.]

Evade, ē-vād', vi. To go out hastily; to escape; to practise artifice for the purpose of eluding; to prevaricate; to shuffle.—vt. To avoid by dexterity; to avoid or escape by stratagem; to slip away from; to elude by subterfuge or ingenuity. ppr. evading, pret. & pp. evaded. [L. *evado—vado*, to walk hastily.]

Evanescence, ē-van-es'sens, n. A vanishing away; a disappearing; a gradual departure from sight or possession; state of being liable to vanish. [from L. *evanescens—vanus*, void.]

Evanescent, ē-van-es'sent, a. Vanishing away; decaying; subject to vanishing; fleeting; imperceptible. [L. *evanescens*.]

Evanescently, ē-van-es'sent-li, adv. In a vanishing manner.

Evangelic, Evangelical, ē-van-jel'ik, ē-van-jel'ik-al, a. Pertaining to good tidings; according to the gospel; consonant to the doctrines and precepts of the gospel; contained in the gospel; sound in the doctrines of the gospel; orthodox. [Fr. *évangélique*—Gr. *eu*, and *anggellō*, to proclaim.]

Evangelically, ē-van-jel'ik-al-li, adv. In a manner according to the gospel.

Evangelicism, ē-van-jel'i-sizm, n. Evangelical principles.

Evangelist, ē-van'jel-ist, n. A bringer of good tidings; one of the four writers of the history of our blessed Saviour Jesus Christ; a preacher of the gospel; a missionary. [Fr. *évangéliste*.]

Evangelization, ē-van'jel-iz-ā"shon, n. Act of evangelizing.

Evangelize, ē-van'jel-iz, vt. To announce good news to; to teach or preach the gospel to and convert to a belief of the gospel. ppr. evangelising, pret. & pp. evangelized. [Fr. *évangéliser*.]

Evanish, ē-van'ish, vi. To vanish away; to disappear. [Fr. *évanouir*, ppr. *évanouissant*—L. *vanus*, empty.]

Evaporable, ē-vā'pėr-a-bl, a. That may evaporate or be evaporated.

Evaporate, ē-vā'pėr-āt, vi. To pass off in vapour; to escape and be dissipated; to exhale; to pass off without effect; to be wasted.—vt. To convert into vapour; to disperse in vapours. ppr. evaporating, pret. & pp. evaporated. [L. *evapóro*, *evaporatus*—*vapor*, steam.]

Evaporated, ē-vā'pėr-āt-ed, p.a. Converted into vapour; dissipated.

Evaporation, ē-vā'pėr-ā"shon, n. Act of evaporating; the conversion of a fluid into vapour; discharge. [Fr. *évaporation*.]

Evasion, ē-vā'shon, n. Act of evading; artifice to elude; shift; subterfuge. [Fr. *évasion*—L. *vado*, to walk hastily.]

Evasive, ē-vā'siv, a. That evades; shuffling; equivocating; artfully contrived to elude a question or argument. [Fr. *évasif*.]

Evasively, ē-vā'siv-li, adv. By evasion.

Eve, ēv, n. The consort of Adam and mother of the human race; so called by Adam because she was the mother of all living. [Heb. *chavva*, life—obs. *chaia*, to live.]

Eve, Even, ēv, ē'vn, n. The departure of day; the latter part or close of the day, and beginning of the night; the evening before a holiday; the period just preceding some important event. [Sax. *aefen, aefnung*; G. *abend*.]

Even, ē'vn, a. Having a surface one and the same; level; of an equal surface; flat; not rough or waving; equal; calm; level with; equal on both sides; fair; just; owing nothing on either side; capable of being divided into two equal parts, without a remainder.—vt. To make even or level; to equalize; to place in an equal state, as to obligation, or in a state in which nothing is due on either side.—adv. Equally; likewise; in like manner; exactly; verily; so much as; at the very time; in the very case; as was not to be expected. [Sax. *efen*—Sans. *eka*, one and the same.]

Even-handed, ē'vn-hand-ed, a. Impartial; equitable; just.

Evening, ē'vn-ing, n. The parting of the day; the latter part and close of the day, and the beginning of darkness or night; the decline or latter part of life; the decline of anything. a. Being at the close of day; appearing at the close of day.

Evenly, ē'vn-li, adv. In an even manner.

Even-minded, ē'vn-mind-ed, a. Having equanimity.

Evenness, ē'vn-nes, n. State of being even; equality of surface; impartiality between parties; equanimity.

Event, ē-vent', n. That which comes; an incident; an adventure; the consequence of anything; that in which an action terminates; issue; result; conclusion. [L *eventus—venio*, to come.]

Eventful, ē-vent'ful, a. Full of events; producing numerous or great changes, either in public or private affairs.

Eventide, ē'vn-tīd, n. The time of evening; evening. [*even*, and Sax. *tid*, time.]

Eventual, ē-vent'ū-al, a. Coming forth as a consequence; consequential; ultimate. [Fr. *éventuel*.]

Eventually, ē-vent'ū-al-li, adv. In the event; in the final issue.

Ever, ev'ėr, adv. Through the period of life; always; everlastingly; at any period or point of time, past or future; in any degree. [Sax. *aefer*.]

Evergreen, ev'ėr-grēn, n. A plant that retains its greenness through all the seasons.—a. Always green; verdant throughout the year.

Everlasting, ev-ėr-last'ing, a. Age-lasting; enduring for ever; eternal; immortal; continuing during the present state of things.—n. Eternity; the Eternal Being; something which endures for a long time.

Everlastingly, ev-ėr-last'ing-li, adv. Eternally; perpetually; continually.

Ever-living, ev'ėr-liv-ing, a. Living without end; eternal; immortal.

Evermore, ev'ėr-mōr, adv. At all times; eternally.

Every, ev'ė-ri, a. Ever each; each individual of a whole collection; all taken separately. [Sax. *aefre*, ever, and *aelc*, each.]

Everyday, ev'ė-ri-dā, a. Used or being every day; common; usual.

Everywhere, ev'ė-ri-hwār, adv. In every place; in all places.

Evict, ē-vikt', vt. To dispossess by a course of legal proceedings; to recover, as lands or tenements by law; to take away by sentence of law. [L. *evinco, evictum—vinco*, to overcome.]

Eviction, ē-vik'shon, n. Dispossession by judicial sentence. [Low L. *evictio*.]

Evidence, ev'i-dens, n. That which elucidates, and enables the mind to see truth; conclusive testimony; any writing which contains proof; a witness. vt. To make clear; to elucidate; to evince; to show. ppr. evidencing, pret. & pp. evidenced. [Fr. *évidence*—L. *video*, to see.]

Evident, ev'i-dent, a. Clear; obvious; plain; open to be seen; clear to the mental eye. [Fr. *évident*.]

Evidently, ev'i-dent-li, adv. In an evident manner; plainly; clearly.

Evil, ē'vil, a. Not well; not good; having bad qualities of a natural or moral kind; bad; ill; mischievous; pernicious; destructive; wrong; vicious; sinful; unhappy; calamitous.—n. That which is not well or not good: anything which produces pain, suffering, distress, loss, or calamity; misfortune; injury; wrong; depravity; malignity; sin; malady.—adv. Not well; ill; not with justice or propriety; not virtuously; not innocently; not happily; not kindly. [Sax. *yfel*.]

Evil-eyed, ē'vil-īd, a. Looking with an evil eye, or with envy or bad design.

Evil-minded, ē'vil-mind-ed, a. Having evil dispositions; disposed to mischief or sin; malicious; malignant; wicked.

Evil-speaking, ē'vil-spēk-ing, n. Slander; defamation; calumny.

Evince, ē-vins', vi. To show in a clear manner; to prove beyond any reasonable doubt; to manifest; to argue. ppr. evincing, pret. & pp. evinced. [L. *evinco—vinco*, to overcome.]

Evincible, ē-vins'i-bl, a. That may be evinced or proved; capable of proof.

Eviscerate, ē-vis'sė-rāt, vt. To take out the entrails of; to disembowel. ppr. eviscerating, pret. & pp. eviscerated. [L. *eviscero, evisceratus—viscera*, the entrails.]

Evisceration, ē-vis'sė-rā"shon, n. Act of eviscerating. [Low L. *evisceratio*.]

Evitate, ev'it-āt, vt. To shun; to avoid. [L. *vito*, to shun.]

Evoke, ē-vōk', vt. To call forth or out; to summon forth. ppr. evoking, pret. & pp. evoked. [L. *evoco—voco*, to call.]

Evolution, ē-vō-lū'shon, n. An unfolding; a development; a series of things unfolded; the extraction of roots in arithmetic and algebra; (pl.) the movements of troops or ships of war in changing their positions for attack or defence. [Fr. *évolution*.]

Evolutionary, ē-vō-lū'shon-a-ri, a. Pertaining to evolution.

Evolutionist, ē-vō-lū'shon-ist, n. One skilled in the military movements.

Evolve, ē-volv', vt. To unfold; to develop; to open and expand; to follow out and detect through intricacies; to unravel.—vi. To open itself; to disclose itself. ppr. evolving, pret. & pp. evolved. [L. *evolvo—volvo, volutum*, to roll.]

Evolvement, ē-volv'ment, n. Act of evolving; the state of being evolved.

Evulsion, ē-vul'shon, n. Act of plucking or pulling out by force. [L. *evulsio—vello*, to pluck.]

Ewe, ū, n. A female sheep. [Sax. *eowu*.]

Ewer, ū'ėr, n. A kind of pitcher for holding water, which accompanies a wash-hand basin. [Sax. *Awer*, a ewer.]

Exacerbate, eks-as'ėr-bāt, vt. To make harsh, sharp, or sour; to exasperate; to increase the violence of, as of a disease. ppr. exacerbating, pret. & pp. exacerbated. [L. *exacerbo, exacerbatus—acerbus*, harsh, sharp.]

Exacerbation, eks-as'ėr-bā"shon, n. The irritation of angry or malignant passions or qualities; a periodical increase of violence in a disease. [Fr.]

Exact, egz-akt', a. Done thoroughly; strictly accurate; methodical; strict; punctual; accurate; true. [Fr.—L. *ex*-

---

Fāte, fär, fat, fall; mē, met, hėr; pīne, pin; nōte, not, mōve; tūbe, tub, bull; oil, pound.

actus.]—*vt.* To drive out; to enforce; to force to pay or yield; to extort by means of authority; to demand of right; to enjoin with pressing urgency. [L. *exigo, exactum—ago,* to drive.]
Exacting, egz-akt'ing, *p.a.* Oppressive and unreasonably severe in making demands.
Exaction, egz-ak'shon, *n. Act of exacting;* authoritative demand; extortion; that which is exacted; tribute demanded or levied with severity. [Fr.]
Exactly, egz-akt'li, *adv. In an exact manner;* precisely; nicely; accurately.
Exactness, egz-akt'nes, *n. Quality of being exact;* accuracy; nicety; precision.
Exactor, egz-akt'ėr, *n. One who exacts;* an extortioner; one who is unreasonably severe in his demands. [L.]
Exaggerate, egz-aj'ė-rāt, *vt. To heap on or up;* to accumulate; to enlarge beyond the truth; to amplify; to depict or delineate extravagantly. *ppr.* exaggerating, *pret. & pp.* exaggerated. [L. *exaggero, exaggeratus—agger,* a heap.]
Exaggerated, egz-aj'ė-rāt-ed, *p.a.* Enlarged beyond the truth.
Exaggeration, egz-aj'ė-rā"shon, *n. A heaping up;* accumulation; a representation of things beyond the truth. [L. *exaggeratio.*]
Exalt, egz-ạlt', *vt. To raise high;* to raise to power or dignity; to fill with joy or confidence; to raise with pride; to magnify; to glorify. [Fr. *exalter—*L. *altus—*Heb. *ghāl,* high, lofty.]
Exaltation, egz-ạlt-ā'shon, *n. Act of exalting;* elevation to power, office, or excellence; state of greatness or dignity. [Fr.]
Exalted, egz-ạlt'ed, *p.a.* Honoured with office or rank; refined; dignified; sublime.
Examinable, egz-am'in-a-bl, *a.* That *may be examined;* proper for judicial examination or inquiry.
Examination, egz-am'in-ā"shon, *n. Act of examining;* close inquiry into facts, &c., by interrogation; scrutiny by study; search; research; inquisition. [Low L. *examinatio.*]
Examine, egz-am'in, *vt. To try by a balance;* to weigh; to balance; to try by experiments or by a rule or law; to search into; to interrogate, as a witness, a student, &c.; to search; to explore. *ppr.* examining, *pret. & pp.* examined. [Fr. *examiner—*L. *examimen,* the tongue of a balance.]
Examiner, egz-am'in-ėr, *n. One who examines,* tries, or inspects; one who interrogates a witness or an offender.
Examining, egz-am'in-ing, *p.a.* Having power to examine; appointed to examine.
Example, egz-am'pl, *n. A sample;* a pattern; a model; he or that which is proposed to be imitated; a precedent to be followed or avoided; a warning; precedent which disposes to imitation; a particular case illustrating a general rule; an instance; an illustration; *vt.* ↑ To set an example. [L. *exemplum —eximo,* to take out or away.]
Exasperate, egz-as'pė-rāt, *vt. To make rough or harsh;* to irritate; to enrage; to incense; to increase the malignity of; to make worse. *ppr.* exasperating, *pret. & pp.* exasperated. [L. *exaspero, exasperatus—asper,* rough.]
Exasperated, egz-as'pė-rāt-ed, *p.a.* Angry; irritated.
Exasperating, egz-as'pė-rāt-ing, *p.a.* Irritating; increasing violence.

Exasperation, egz-as'pė-rā"shon, *n. Act of exasperating;* extreme degree of anger; increase of malignity. [Low L. *exasperatio.*]
Excavate, eks'ka-vāt, *vt. To hollow out;* to form a cavity or hole in; to form by hollowing. *ppr.* excavating, *pret. & pp.* excavated. [L. *excavo, excavatus—cavus,* hollow.]
Excavation, eks-ka-vā'shon, *n. Act of hollowing out,* or making hollow; a hollow or a cavity formed by removing the interior substance. [L. *excavatio.*]
Excavator, eks'ka-vāt-ėr, *n. One who excavates;* a machine for excavating.
Exceed, ek-sēd', *vt. To go out from;* to go beyond; to proceed beyond, as any limit, measure, or quantity; to surpass; to outdo.—*vi. To go too far;* to pass the proper bounds; to bear the greater proportion; to be more or larger. [L. *excedo—cedo,* to go.]
Exceeding, ek-sēd'ing, *a.* Great in extent, quantity, or duration; very large.—*adv.* In a very great degree; unusually.
Exceedingly, ek-sēd'ing-li, *adv.* To a very great degree; in a degree beyond what is usual; greatly; very much.
Excel, ek-sel', *vt. To rise high above;* to surpass; to go beyond; to transcend; to outdo.—*vi.* To have good qualities in an unusual degree; to be eminent or distinguished. *ppr.* excelling, *pret. & pp.* excelled. [L. *excello—celsus,* raised high—obs. Heb. *heikal,* to be high.]
Excellence, Excellency, ek'sel-lens, ek'-sel-len-si, *n. State of excelling;* superiority in dignity; pre-eminence; greatness; any good or valuable quality in persons or things; worth; virtue; a title of honour given to certain persons in high official situations, now restricted to *excellency.* [Fr.]
Excellent, ek'sel-lent, *a. Rising above* in dignity, value, or virtues; being of great value; distinguished for superior attainments; choice; exquisite. [Fr. —L. *excellens.*]
Excellently, ek'sel-lent-li, *adv. In an excellent manner.*
Except, ek-sept', *vt. To take out of any* number specified; to take out, as any particular, from a general description. *vi.* To object; to make objection. (With *to* and *against.*)—*prep.* Exclusively of; without.—*conj.* Unless; if not. [Fr. *excepter—*L. *capio,* to take.]
Excepting, ek-sept'ing, *prep. With exception of;* excluding; except.
Exception, ek-sep'shon, *n. Act of excepting;* state of being excepted; exclusion; that which is excepted; the person or thing specified as distinct; an objection; offence. [Fr.]
Exceptionable, ek-sep'shon-a-bl, *a.* Liable to objection; objectionable.
Exceptional, ek-sep'shon-al, *a.* Forming or making an exception.
Exceptionless, ek-sept'les, *a.* Usual.
Exceptor, ek-sept'ėr, *n.* One who *makes exceptions,* or who objects. [Low L.]
Excerpt, ek-sėrpt', *n. That which is picked out;* an extract; a passage selected from an author. [L. *excerptum —carpo, carptum,* to pick.]
Excess, ek-ses', *n. State of exceeding; that which exceeds;* more than enough; that which is beyond the common measure; intemperate conduct; riotousness; that by which one number or magnitude exceeds another. [Fr. *excès—*L. *excessus—cedo, cessum,* to go.]
Excessive, ek-ses'iv, *a. That exceeds;* beyond any given degree, measure, or limit; beyond due bounds; intemper-

ate; extreme; vehement; exceeding. [Fr. *excessif.*]
Excessively, ek-ses'iv-li, *adv.* In an extreme degree; beyond measure; exceedingly; vehemently; violently.
Exchange, eks-chānj', *vt. To change,* as one thing for another; to barter; to commute; to interchange; to bargain. *ppr.* exchanging, *pret. & pp.* exchanged.—*n. Act of exchanging;* interchange; barter; act of giving up one thing or state for another; act of giving and receiving reciprocally; the form of exchanging one debt or credit for another; the place where the merchants, &c., of a city meet to transact business at certain hours; a method of finding how much of the money of one country is equivalent to a given sum of the money of another. [Fr. *échanger.*]
Exchangeability, eks-chānj'a-bil"li-ti, *n. Quality of being exchangeable.*
Exchangeable, eks-chānj'a-bl, *a. Capable, fit,* or proper to be exchanged.
Exchanger, eks-chānj'ėr, *n. One who exchanges;* one who practises exchange.
Exchequer, eks-chek'ėr, *n.* A court of record in London, consisting of two divisions, a court of revenue, and a court of common law; so called from a *checkered* cloth which formerly covered the table. [Fr. *échiquier,* a chessboard.]
Excisable, ek-sīz'a-bl, *a. Liable or subject to excise.*
Excise, ek-sīz', *n. A part cut off* from certain goods; an inland tax on articles produced and consumed within the kingdom, and also on licenses to deal in certain commodities.—*vi.* To lay or impose an *excise* upon, as on articles produced and consumed at home. *ppr.* excising, *pret. & pp.* excised. [Fr. from L. *excido, excisum—cedo,* to cut.]
Exciseman, ek-sīz'man, *n.* An officer of inland revenue.
Excision, ek-si'zhon, *n. A cutting out* any part, as of the body; amputation; the cutting off of a person or nation, as a judgment; destruction. [Fr.—Low L. *excisio—*L. *cædo, cæsum,* to cut.]
Excitability, ek-sīt'a-bil"li-ti, *n. Quality of being easily excited;* susceptibility of increased vital action. [Fr. *excitabilité.*]
Excitable, ek-sīt'a-bl, *a. Capable of being excited.* [Low L. *excitabilis.*]
Excite, ek-sīt', *vt. To call out or forth;* to call into action; to awaken; to incite; to stimulate; to inspirit; to irritate. *ppr.* exciting, *pret. & pp.* excited. [Fr. *exciter—*L. *cito,* to put in rapid motion—*cieo,* to move.]
Excited, ek-sīt'ed, *p.a.* Roused; stimulated; inflamed.
Excitement, ek-sīt'ment, *n. Act of exciting;* state of being roused into action; commotion; that which rouses, or induces to action. [Fr.]
Exciter, ek-sīt'ėr, *n. He or that which excites.*
Exciting, ek-sīt'ing, *p.a.* Stimulating.
Excitingly, ek-sīt'ing-li, *adv. In an exciting manner.*
Exclaim, eks-klām', *vi. To call or cry out;* to utter the voice with vehemence; to declare with loud vociferation.—*n.*† Outcry. [L. *exclamo—clamo,* to cry out.]
Exclamation, eks-klam-ā'shon, *n. Act of exclaiming;* a vehement exertion of voice; a sentence of passionate import, or passionately uttered; a note by which emphatical utterance is marked,

ch, *chain*; j, *job*; g, *go*; ng, *sing*; ᴛʜ, *then*; th, *thin*; w, *wig*; wh, *whig*; zh, *azure*; † obsolete.

thus, !; a word expressing outcry; an interjection. [Fr.]
Exclamatory, eks-klam'a-tō-ri, a. Containing or expressing exclamation.
Exclude, eks-klūd', vt. To shut out; to thrust out; to debar; to prohibit; to emit; to except. ppr. excluding, pret. & pp. excluded. [L. excludo—claudo, to shut.]
Exclusion, eks-klū'shon, n. Act of excluding; state of being excluded; prohibition; ejection or emission. [Fr.—Low L. exclusio.]
Exclusionist, eks-klū'zh n-ist, n. One who would preclude another from s me privilege.
Exclusive, eks-klū'siv, a. Excluding; debarring from participation; not including; debarring from fellowship; illiberal.—n. One of a coterie who exclude others from their fellowship. [Fr. exclusif.]
Exclusively, eks-klū'siv-li, adv. In an exclusive manner.
Exclusiveness, eks-klū'siv-nes, n. State or quality of being exclusive.
Excogitate, eks-ko'jit-āt, vt. To strike out by thinking; to invent or devise by serious thinking. ppr. excogitating, pret. & pp. excogitated. [L. excogito, excogitatus—cogito, to think.]
Excogitation, eks-ko'jit-ā"shon, n. Invention or contrivance by serious and earnest thinking. [L. excogitatio.]
Excommunicate, eks-kom-mū'ni-kāt, vt. To eject or interdict from the communion of the church by an ecclesiastical censure. ppr. excommunicating, pret. & pp. excommunicated. [L. communico, communicatus, to make common—communis, common—munus, a service.]
Excommunicated, eks-kom-mū'ni-kāt-ed, p.a. Expelled from communion with a church.
Excommunication, eks-kom-mū'ni-kā"-shon, n. Expulsion from the communion of a church, and deprivation of its rights, privileges, and advantages. [Fr.]
Excommunicator, eks-kom-mū'ni-kāt-ėr, n. One who excommunicates. [Low L.]
Excommunicatory, eks-kom-mū'ni-kā-tō-ri, a. Relating to or causing excommunication.
Excrement, eks'krē-ment, n. That which is separated from the nutriment by digestion, and discharged from the animal body as being superfluous; ordure; dung. [L. excrementum—cerno, crētum, to separate.]
Excremental, eks-krē-ment'al, a. Pertaining to, or of the nature of, excrement. [Fr. excrémentiel.]
Excrementitious, eks'krē-men-ti"shi-us, a. Pertaining to, consisting of, or containing excrement. [Fr. excrémenteux.]
Excrescence, eks-kres'ens, n. That which grows out; a preternatural protuberance growing on any part of the body; any preternatural enlargement of a plant; a preternatural production. [Fr. excroissance—L. cresco, to grow.]
Excrescent, eks-kres'ent, a. Growing out of something else, in a preternatural manner; superfluous. [L. excrescens.]
Excrete, eks-krēt', vt. To separate and throw off, as ly natural passages; to evacuate; to discharge. ppr. excreting, pret. & pp. excreted. [L. excerno, excretus—cerno, to separate.]
Excretion, eks-krē'shon, n. Ejection of excrementitious matter from the ani-

mal system; that which is excreted. [Fr. excrétion.]
Excretive, eks-krēt'iv, a. Having the power of separating and ejecting excrementitious matter from the body.
Excretory, eks'krē-tō-ri, a. Having the quality of excreting or throwing off excrementitious matter by the glands. n. A little duct or vessel destined to receive secreted fluids, and to excrete them. [Fr. excrétoire.]
Excruciate, eks-krō'shi-āt, vt. To torture, as if on a cross; to rack. ppr. excruciating, pret. & pp. excruciated. [L. excrucio, excruciatus—crux, crūcis, a cross.]
Excruciating, eks-krō'shi-āt-ing, p.a. Extremely painful; agonizing; distressing.
Exculpate, eks-kul'pāt, vt. To clear by words from a charge or imputation of fault or guilt; to absolve; to excuse; to justify; to vindicate. ppr. exculpating, pret. & pp. exculpated. [Low L. exculpo, exculpatus—L. culpa, a fault.]
Exculpation, eks-kul-pā'shon, n. Act of exculpating; excuse; vindication. [Low L. exculpatio.]
Exculpatory, eks-kul'pa-tō-ri, a. That clears from the charge of fault or guilt; clearing from imputation.
Excursion, eks-kėr'shon, n. A running out or forth; any rambling from a point or place, and return to the same point or place; a ramble; a trip or jaunt for pleasure; a wandering from a subject or main design. [Fr.—L. curro, cursum, to run.]
Excursionist, eks-kėr'shon-ist, n. One who goes on an excursion.
Excursive, eks-kėr'siv, a. Rambling; wandering; deviating.
Excursively, eks-kėr'siv-li, adv. In a wandering manner.
Excusable, eks-kūz'a-bl, a. Admitting of excuse or justification; pardonable. [Fr.]
Excusably, eks-kūz'a-bli, adv. In an excusable manner; pardonably.
Excuse, eks-kūz', vt. To release from a charge; to acquit of guilt; to pardon, as a fault; to forgive entirely; to free from a duty; to release; to admit an apology for; to absolve; to pardon; to vindicate. ppr. excusing, pret. & pp. excused. [L. excūso—causa, a cause, a suit.]
Excuse, eks-kūs', n. A plea offered in extenuation of a fault; apology.
Excuser, eks-kūz'ėr, n. One who offers excuses, or pleads for another.
Execrable, ek'sē-kra-bl, a. That ought to be execrated; abominable; accursed. [Fr. exécrable—L. execrabilis.]
Execrably, ek'sē-kra-bli, adv. Cursedly; detestably.
Execrate, ek'sē-krāt, vt. To exclude from sacred things; to curse; to detest utterly; to abominate. ppr. execrating, pret. & pp. execrated. [L. exsecror, exsecratus—sācer, accursed.]
Execrated, ek'sē-krāt-ed, p.a. Cursed; denounced; imprecated.
Execration, ek-sē-krā'shon, n. A curse pronounced; detestation expressed; object execrated; an abomination. [Fr. exécration.]
Execute, ek'sē-kūt, vt. To follow out, or up; to carry out; to effect; to achieve; to inflict capital punishment on.—vi. To perform the proper office. ppr. executing, pret. & pp. executed. [Fr. exécuter—L. sequor, secūtus, to follow.]
Executer, ek-sē-kūt-ėr, n. One who executes; one who carries into effect.
Execution, ek-sē-kū'shon, n. Act of

executing; performance; that which is executed; the carrying into effect a sentence or judgment of court; act of signing and sealing a legal instrument; capital punishment; the mode of performing a work of art, and the dexterity with which it is accomplished; a facility of voice or finger in music. [Fr. exécution—L. exsecūtio.]
Executioner, ek-sē-kū'shon-ėr, n. One who executes; one who puts to death criminals condemned by law.
Executive, egz-ek'ūt-iv, a. That executes; carrying the laws into effect, or superintending the enforcement of the laws. n. Executive authority in government; the person or persons who administer the government. [Fr. exécutif.]
Executively, egz-ek'ūt-iv-li, adv. In the way of executing or performing.
Executor, egz-ek'ūt-ėr, n. One who executes; the person appointed by a testator to execute his will; an executioner. [L.]
Executorship, egz-ek'ūt-ėr-ship, n. The office of an executor.
Executory, egz-ek'ū-tō-ri, a. That executes; that is to be executed or carried into effect in future. [Fr. exécutoire.]
Executrix, egz-ek'ū-triks, n. A woman appointed by a testator to execute his will. [Low L.]
Exegetic, Exegetical, eks-ē-jet'ik, eks-ē-jet'ik-al, a. Explanatory; tending to unfold or illustrate; expository. [Fr. exégétique—Gr. égeomai, to lead the way, from ago, to lead.]
Exegetically, eks-ē-jet'ik-al-li, adv. By way of explanation.
Exegetics, eks-ē-jet'iks, n. pl. A branch of theology which comprehends apologetic divinity, the history of the sacred canon, sacred philology, and interpretation.
Exemplar, egz-em'plėr, n. A pattern to be copied or imitated; the idea or image of a thing, formed in the mind of an artist, by which he conducts his work. [L.]
Exemplarily, egz'em-pla-ri-li, adv. In an exemplary manner.
Exemplary, egz'em-pla-ri, a. Acting as an exemplar; worthy of imitation; such as may deter from crimes; such as may attract notice and imitation; explanatory. [Fr. exemplaire—L. exemplum, an example.]
Exemplification, egz-em'pli-fi-kā"shon, n. A showing or illustrating by example; a transcript.
Exemplify, egz-em'pli-fi, vt. To show or illustrate by example; to copy. ppr. exemplifying, pret. & pp. exemplified. [Low L. exemplifico, exemplificare.]
Exempt, egz-emt', vt. To take out; to free from; to relieve; to privilege; to grant immunity from.—a. Taken or left out; free by privilege; not liable; clear. [Fr. exempter—L. eximo, exemptus—ēmo, to take, to buy.]
Exemption, egz-em'shon, n. Act of exempting; the state of being exempt; immunity; privilege. [Fr.—L. exemptio.]
Exequies, eks'ē-kwis, n. pl. The following out of a corpse; funeral rites. [L. exsequiæ—sequor, to follow.]
Exercise, eks'ėr-sis, n. Act of exercising; a keeping in practice, in use, or in constant and regular employment; use; practice; bodily exertion for health or amusement; exertion of the mind for improvement; practice to acquire skill; application of the mental powers; that which is appointed for one to perform; a lesson or ex-

Fāte, fär, fat, fall; mē, met, hėr; pīne, pin; nōte, not, mōve; tūbe, tub, bull; oil, pound.

ample for practice. [Fr. *exercice*.]
vt. To bring out of an inactive state; to busy; to keep busy in action; to exert; to use; to use for improvement in skill; to practise habitually; to train to use; to use, as efforts; to perform the duties of; to pain or afflict. *ppr.* exercising, *pret. & pp.* exercised. [L. *exerceo—arceo*, to ward off.]
Exert, egz-ert', *vt.* To put out; to bring out; to put or thrust forth, as strength, force, or ability; to strain; to urge to effort (with recipr. pron.); to do or perform. [L. *exsero, exsertum—sero*, to plant, to produce.]
Exertion, egz-er'shon, *n.* Act of exerting; act of putting into motion or action; endeavour.
Exhalation, eks-hal-a'shon, *n.* Act or process of exhaling or sending forth fluids in the form of steam or vapour; that which is exhaled; vapour; steam; effluvia. [Fr.]
Exhale, egz-hal', *vt.* To breathe out; to cause to be emitted in vapour or minute particles; to evaporate.—*vi.* To fly off or vanish, as vapour. *ppr.* exhaling, *pret. & pp.* exhaled. [L. *exhalo—halo*, to breathe.]
Exhaust, egz-hast', *vt.* To empty by drawing out; to use the whole of; to consume; to use or expend entirely; to call into exercise†. [L. *exhaurio, exhaustum—haurio*, to draw up.]
Exhausted, egz-hast'ed, *p.a.* Wholly used or expended; consumed.
Exhauster, egz-hast'er, *n.* He or that which exhausts.
Exhaustible, egz-hast'i-bl, *a.* That may be exhausted.
Exhausting, egz-hast'ing, *p.a.* Tending to exhaust.
Exhaustion, egz-hast'shon, *n.* Act of exhausting; state of being exhausted. [Fr.]
Exhaustive, egz-hast'iv, *a.* That exhausts.
Exhaustless, egz-hast'les, *a.* Not to be exhausted; inexhaustible.
Exhibit, egz-hib'it, *vt.* To hold or reach out; to offer to view; to show; to offer publicly or officially; to administer, as a remedy. [L. *exhibeo, exhibitum—habeo*, to hold.]
Exhibiter, egz-hib'it-er, *n.* One who exhibits.
Exhibition, eks-hi-bi'shon, *n.* Act of exhibiting; representation of feats or actions in public; display of oratory in public; any public show; pension, as to indigent students in the English universities. [Fr.]
Exhibitioner, eks-hi-bi'shon-er, *n.* One who is maintained at an English university by an exhibition.
Exhibitor, egz-hib'it-er, *n.* One who exhibits.
Exhibitory, egz-hib'it-to-ri, *a.* Exhibiting; showing; displaying.
Exhilarate, egz-hil'a-rat, *vt.* To make cheerful; to cheer; to enliven; to gladden. *ppr.* exhilarating, *pret.&pp.* exhilarated. [L. *exhilaro, exhilaratus—hilaris*, Gr. *hilaros*, cheerful.]
Exhilarating, egz-hil'a-rat-ing, *p.a.* Cheering; gladdening.
Exhilaration, egz-hil'a-ra''shon, *n.* Act of exhilarating; act of making glad or cheerful; state of being enlivened; joyousness; gaiety. [Low L. *exhilaratio*.]
Exhort, egz-hort', *vt.* To incite by advice; to stimulate to exertion; to urge by arguments to a good deed; to encourage to do well; to warn. [Fr. *exhorter*—L. *hortor, hortatus*, to incite.]

Exhortation, eks-hort-a'shon, *n.* Act of exhorting; the form of words intended to incite and encourage; advice; counsel. [Fr.—L. *exhortatio*.]
Exhortatory, egz-hort'a-to-ri, *a.* That exhorts. [Low L. *exhortatorius*.]
Exhorter, egz-hort'er, *n.* One who exhorts or encourages.
Exhumation, eks-hum-a'shon, *n.* Act of exhuming; the disinterring of a corpse; the digging up of anything buried. [Fr.]
Exhume, eks-hum', *vt.* To take out of the ground; to unbury; to disinter. *ppr.* exhuming, *pret. & pp.* exhumed. [Fr. *exhumer*—L. *humus*, earth.]
Exigence, Exigency, eks'i-jens, eks'i-jen-si, *n.* That which drives forth; pressing necessity; urgency; distress; necessity. [Fr. *exigence*—L. *ex*, and *ago*, to drive.]
Exigent, eks'i-jent, *n.* A state of pressing need†.
Exile, eks'il, *n.* State of being expelled from one's native soil; banishment; an abandonment of one's country; the person banished. [Fr. *exil*—L. *solum*, soil, land.]
Exile, egz-il', *vt.* To banish from one's country; to drive from one's country by misfortune, necessity, or distress. *ppr.* exiling, *pret. & pp.* exiled. [Fr. *exiler*.]
Exiled, egz-ild', *p.a.* Banished.
Exist, egz-ist', *vi.* To stand out or forth; to be; to have an essence or real being; to live; to have life or animation; to endure. [Fr. *exister*—L. *sisto*, to stand.]
Existence, egz-ist'ens, *n.* State of being; life; continued being; continuation; anything that exists, a being. [Fr.]
Existent, egz-ist'ent, *a.* Being; having being or existence. [L. *exsistens*.]
Existing, egz-ist'ing, *p.a.* Having existence, being, or life.
Exit, eks'it, *n.* A going out; the departure of a player from the stage; the act of quitting the stage of life; death; a way of departure; passage out of a place. [L. *exitus*, a going out—*eo, itum*, to go.]
Exodus, eks'o-dus, *n.* Way or passage out; the departure of the Israelites from Egypt under the conduct of Moses; the second book of the Old Testament. [Gr. *hodos*, way.]
Exogen, eks'o-jen, *n.* In botany, a plant whose stem is formed by successive additions to the outside of the wood. [Gr. *exo*, outward, and *genos*, race.]
Exogenous, eks-oj'en-us, *a.* Pertaining to the *class* of plants that grow on the outside.
Exonerate, egz-on'e-rat, *vt.* To disburden; to exculpate; to acquit; to justify; to discharge. *ppr.* exonerating, *pret. & pp.* exonerated. [L. *exonero, exoneratus—onus, oneris*, a burden.]
Exonerative, egz-on'e-rat-iv, *a.* That exonerates; freeing from an obligation.
Exorable, eks'or-a-bl, *a.* Easy to be entreated; that can be persuaded; placable. [L. *exorabilis—oro*, to pray.]
Exorbitance, egz-or'bit-ans, *n.* A going beyond the usual limit; enormity; extravagance; a deviation from rule or the ordinary limits of right or propriety. [Low L. *exorbitantia*—L. *orbis*, a circle, routine.]
Exorbitant, egz-or'bit-ant, *a.* Departing from the usual track; extravagant; enormous. [Fr.]
Exorbitantly, egz-or'bit-ant-li, *adv.* Enormously; excessively.
Exorcise, eks'or-siz, *vi.* To drive away in consequence of adjuring by some

holy name; to deliver from the influence of malignant spirits. *ppr.* exorcising, *pret. & pp.* exorcised. [Fr. *exorciser*—Gr. *orkizo*, to bind by oath.]
Exorcism, eks'or-sizm, *n.* The expulsion of evil spirits from persons or places by certain *adjurations* and ceremonies. [Fr. *exorcisme*.]
Exorcist, eks'or-sist, *n.* One who pretends to expel evil spirits by *conjuration*, prayers, and ceremonies. [Fr. *exorciste*.]
Exordium, egz-or'di-um, *n.* **Exordiums**, *pl.* The laying of the warp of a web†; the introductory part of a discourse; the preface of a composition. [L.—*ordior*, to begin—Gr. *erion*, wool, and *deō*, to bind.]
Exoteric, Exoterical, eks-o-te'rik, eks-o-te'rik-al, *a.* External; public; opposed to esoteric or secret. [Fr. *exoterique*—Gr. *exō*, outward.]
Exotic, egz-ot'ik, *a.* External; introduced from a foreign country; not native.—*n.* A plant, shrub, or tree not native; a word of foreign origin introduced into a language. [Fr. *exotique*—Gr. *exō*, outward.]
Expand, ek-spand', *vt.* To spread out; to open; to dilate; to enlarge in bulk; to distend; to extend.—*vi.* To open or spread out; to spread. [L. *expando—pando*, to spread out.]
Expanded, ek-spand'ed, *p.a.* Opened; enlarged; diffused.
Expanding, ek-spand'ing, *p.a.* Opening; dilating.
Expanse, ek-spans', *n.* That which is spread out; a surface widely extended; a wide extent of space or body. [L. *expansum—pando*, to spread.]
Expansibility, ek-spans'i-bil''li-ti, *n.* The capacity of being expanded. [Fr. *expansibilité*.]
Expansible, ek-spans'i-bl, *a.* Capable of being expanded. [Fr.]
Expansibly, ek-spans'i-bli, *adv.* In an expansible manner.
Expansion, ek-span'shon, *n.* Act of expanding; state of being expanded; dilatation; distance between remote bodies; enlargement; increase. [Fr.—L. *expansio*.]
Expansive, ek-spans'iv, *a.* Having the power to expand; having the capacity of being expanded. [Fr. *expansif*.]
Expansively, ek-spans'iv-li, *adv.* In an expansive manner.
Expansiveness, ek-spans'iv-nes, *n.* Quality of being expansive.
Expatiate, ek-spa'shi-at, *vi.* To step out; to move at large; to wander in space without restraint; to enlarge in discourse or writing. *ppr.* expatiating, *pret. & pp.* expatiated. [L. *expatior, exspatiatus—spatium*, space, a walk.]
Expatriate, eks-pa'tri-at, *vt.* To expel from one's country; to banish; to exile. *ppr.* expatriating, *pret. & pp.* expatriated. [Fr. *expatrier*—L. *patria*, one's fatherland—*pater*, a father.]
Expatriation, eks-pa'tri-a''shon, *n.* Act of expatriating; banishment; the forsaking of one's own country. [Fr.]
Expect, ek-spekt', *vt.* To look or wait for; to hope for long for; to apprehend; to look forward to, as to something that is believed to be about to happen or come. [L. *exspecto*—*specto*, to look at—*specio*, to behold.]
Expectancy, ek-spekt'an-si, *n.* Act or state of expecting; something expected; hope. [Low L. *exspectantia*.]
Expectant, ek-spekt'ant, *a.* Looking earnestly for; depending upon something; suspended.—*n.* One who expects;

one held in dependence by his belief or hope of receiving some good. [L. *exspectans*.]

Expectation, ek-spekt-ā'shon, *n*. *Act of expecting*; anticipation of something future, whether good or evil; the object of expectation; a state or qualities which promise future excellence; the value of any prospect of prize or property which depends on the happening of some uncertain event. [Fr.—L. *exspectatio—specio*, to behold.]

Expected, ek-spekt'ed, *p.a. Looked for*; waited for; anticipated.

Expecter, ek-spekt'er, *n. One who expects.*

Expectorant, eks-pek'tō-rant, *a*. Having the quality of promoting discharges *from the lungs.*—*n.* A medicine which promotes discharges from the lungs. [L. *expectorans*.]

Expectorate, eks-pek'tō-rāt, *vt.* To expel, as phlegm *from the breast* or lungs. *ppr.* expectorating, *pret. & pp.* expectorated. [L. *expectoro, expectoratus—pectus, pectŏris*, the breast.]

Expectorated, eks-pek'tō-rāt-ed, *p.a.* Discharged *from the breast* or lungs.

Expectoration, eks-pek'tō-rā'shon, *n.* Act of expectorating; the matter thus discharged. [Fr.]

Expedience, Expediency, eks-pē'di-ens, eks-pē'di-en-si, *n. Quality of being expedient*; propriety under the particular circumstances of a case; advantage; adventure; expedition. [Low L. *expedientia*.]

Expedient, eks-pē'di-ent, *a. Hastening*; tending to promote the object proposed; proper under the circumstances; advantageous; quick†; expeditious†. *n.* A *quick* or ready way or means; any means which may be employed to accomplish an end; means devised in an exigency; shift; contrivance. [L. *expediens—pes, pedis*, the foot.]

Expediently, eks-pē'di-ent-li, *adv.* Fitly; suitably; conveniently; hastily†.

Expedite, eks'pē-dit, *vt. To hasten*; to quicken; to accelerate the motion or progress of; to despatch; to send from; to hasten by rendering easy. *ppr.* expediting, *pret. & pp.* expedited. [L. *expedio, expeditus—pes, pedis*, a foot.]

Expedition, eks-pē-di'shon, *n. State of being unimpeded*; haste; despatch; the march of an army, or the voyage of a fleet, to a distant place, for hostile purposes; any enterprise by a number of persons; the collective body which undertakes; execution†. [Fr. *expédition*.]

Expeditious, eks-pē-di'shi-us, *a. Quick*; hasty; speedy; prompt; nimble; active; swift; acting with celerity.

Expeditiously, eks-pē-di'shi-us-li, *adv.* Hastily; with celerity.

Expel, eks-pel', *vt. To drive out*; to eject; to throw out; to banish; to exclude; to keep out or off. *ppr.* expelling, *pret. & pp.* expelled. [L. *expello—pello*, to drive.]

Expelled, eks-peld', *p.a.* Forced to leave; banished.

Expend, ek-spend', *vt. To weigh out*, as money in payment; to lay out; to deliver or distribute, either in payment or in donations; to consume, as time or labour; to waste. [L. *expendo—pendo, pensum*, to weigh.]

Expenditure, ek-spend'i-tūr, *n. Act of expending*; a laying out, as of money; money expended; expense.

Expense, ek-spens', *n. A laying out or expending*; the employment of time or labour; money expended; cost;

charge; that which is disbursed in payment or in charity. [L. *expensum*.]

Expensive, ek-spens'iv, *a. Requiring much expense*; dear; given to expense; lavish.

Expensively, ek-spens'iv-li, *adv. With great expense*; at great cost or charge.

Expensiveness, ek-spens'iv-nes, *n. Quality of being expensive*; quality of being addicted to expense.

Experience, eks-pē'ri-ens, *n. Trial*; experiment; a series of trials or experiments; observation of a fact, or of the same facts or events happening under like circumstances; trial from suffering or enjoyment; suffering itself; the use of the senses; knowledge derived from trials, use, practice, or from a series of observations.—*vt. To try*; to make trial of; to know by trial or frequent practice or observation. *ppr.* experiencing, *pret. & pp.* experienced. [Fr. *expérience*—L. *experientia*—Old L. *perior*, to try.]

Experienced, eks-pē'ri-enst, *p.a.* Taught by practice or by repeated observations; skilful by means of use or observation.

Experiment, eks-pe'ri-ment, *n. A trial*; an operation designed to discover something unknown, or to establish it when discovered.—*vi. To make trial*; to try; to operate on a body in such a manner as to discover some unknown fact, or to establish it when known. [L. *experimentum*.]

Experimental, eks-pe'ri-ment"al, *a. Pertaining to experiment*; derived from experiment; built on experiments; taught by experience; having personal experience. [Fr. *expérimental*.]

Experimentally, eks-pe'ri-ment"al-li, *adv.* By experiment or experience.

Experimenter, eks-pe'ri-ment-ėr, *n. One who makes* or is skilled in *experiments*.

Expert, eks-pėrt', *a. Tried*; experienced; well instructed; dexterous; adroit; clever; having a facility of performance from practice.—*n.* An expert person; a scientific witness. [Fr.]

Expertly, eks-pėrt'li, *adv.* In a skilful or dexterous manner; adroitly.

Expertness, eks-pėrt'nes, *n. Quality of being expert*; dexterity; adroitness.

Expiable, eks'pi-a-bl, *a. That may be expiated*; that may be atoned for and done away. [Low L. *expiabilis*.]

Expiate, eks'pi-āt, *vt. To atone for*; to make reparation for. *ppr.* expiating, *pret. & pp.* expiated. [L. *expio, expiatus—pius*, dutiful.]

Expiated, eks'pi-āt-ed, *p.a. Atoned for.*

Expiation, eks-pi-ā'shon, *n. Act of expiating*; the act of making satisfaction for an offence; atonement; the means by which atonement for crimes is made. [Fr. from L. *expiatio*.]

Expiator, eks'pi-āt-ėr, *n. One who expiates.* [Low L.]

Expiatory, eks'pi-a-tō-ri, *a. Having the power to make atonement or expiation.* [Fr. *expiatoire*.]

Expiration, eks-pir-ā'shon, *n. Act of breathing out* vapour; the last emission of breath; death; cessation; close; termination of a limited time. [Fr.]

Expiratory, eks-pir'a-tō-ri, *a.* Pertaining to the *expiration* of breath from the lungs.

Expire, eks-pīr', *vt. To breathe out*; to throw out, as the breath from the lungs; to exhale; to bring to a close†. *vi.* To emit the last *breath*, as an animal; to die; to come to nothing; to come to an end; to close or conclude, as a given period. *ppr.* expiring, *pret.*

& pp. expired. [L. *exspiro—spiro*, to breathe.]

Expiring, eks-pīr'ing, *p.a.* Dying; pertaining to, or uttered at, the time of dying.

Explain, eks-plān', *vt.* To make *plain* or intelligible; to clear of obscurity; to elucidate; to clear up.—*vi. To give explanations.* [L. *explano—planus*, even.]

Explanation, eks-plan-ā'shon, *n. Act of explaining*; act of clearing from obscurity; the sense given by an interpreter; exposition; interpretation; a mutual exposition of terms, meaning, or motives, with a view to adjust a misunderstanding. [L. *explanatio*.]

Explanatory, eks-plan'a-tō-ri, *a. Serving to explain.* [Low L. *explanatorius*.]

Expletive, eks'plēt-iv, *a. Serving to fill out*; added for supply or ornament. *n.* A word or syllable not necessary to the sense, but inserted to *fill* a vacancy. [Fr. *explétif*—L. *pleo*, to fill.]

Expletory, eks'plē-tō-ri, *a. Serving to fill out*; expletive.

Explicable, eks'pli-ka-bl, *a. That may be unfolded* to the mind; that may be made intelligible; that may be accounted for. [Fr.]

Explication, eks-pli-kā'shon, *n. Act of unfolding*; explanation; interpretation; the sense given by an expositor or interpreter. [Fr.—L. *explicatio—plico, plicitum*, to fold.]

Explicit, eks-plis'it, *a. Unfolded*; plain in language; express, not merely implied; unreserved; having no disguised meaning or reservation. [Fr. *explicite*—L. *plico*, to fold.]

Explicitly, eks-plis'it-li, *adv. In an explicit manner*; plainly; expressly.

Explicitness, eks-plis'it-nes, *n. Quality of being explicit*; plainness of language or expression; clearness; direct expression.

Explode, eks-plōd', *vt. To hoot out†*; to drive out of use; to drive out or cause to burst with violence and noise.—*vi.* To utter a *report with sudden violence*; to burst and expand with force and a violent report. *ppr.* exploding, *pret. & pp.* exploded. [L. *explodo—plaudo*, to clap.]

Exploded, eks-plōd'ed, *p.a. Condemned*; cried down.

Exploit, eks-ploit', *n. That which is developed*; a deed or act; a heroic act; a deed of renown; a great or noble feat or achievement. [Fr.—L. *plico*, to fold.]

Exploration, eks-plōr-ā'shon, *n. Act of exploring*; strict or careful examination. [Fr.]

Explore, eks-plōr', *vt. To search for*, as *with tears*; to seek to discover; to examine closely by the eye; to search by any means; to try, as the sea with a plummet; to search or pry into; to examine closely with a view to discover truth. *ppr.* exploring, *pret. & pp.* explored. [L. *exploro—ploro*, to cry out, to weep aloud.]

Explorer, eks-plōr'ėr, *n. One who explores.*

Explosion, eks-plō'shon, *n. Act of exploding*; a bursting with noise; a sudden expansion of any elastic fluid, with force and a loud report; the discharge of a piece of ordinance; the sudden burst of sound in a volcano; a violent manifestation of feeling. [Fr.]

Explosive, eks-plō'siv, *a. That explodes*; driving or bursting out with violence and noise; causing explosion.

Exponent, eks-pō'nent, n. That which sets forth; that which points out; an index; the index of a power in algebra; one who, or that which, stands as an index or representative. [L. *exponens—pono*, to set.]

Export, eks-pōrt', vt. To carry out; to convey or transport, in traffic, as produce and goods from one country to another. [Fr. *exporter*—L. *porto*, to carry.]

Export, eks'pōrt, n. Act of exporting; a commodity actually conveyed from one country to another in traffic (chiefly pl.)

Exportable, eks-pōrt'a-bl, a. That may be exported.

Exportation, eks-port-ā'shon, n. Act of exporting, or of conveying goods and productions from one country to another. [Fr.—L. *exportatio*.]

Exported, eks-pōrt'ed, p.a. Carried out of a country or state in traffic.

Exporter, eks-pōrt'ėr, n. The person who exports.

Expose, eks-pōz', vt. To put or set out; to set to public view; to disclose; to uncover or draw from concealment; to remove from shelter; to lay open to attack, censure, &c.; to make liable; to put in danger; to cast out to chance; to exhibit; to offer for sale. ppr. exposing, pret. & pp. exposed. [Fr. *exposer*—L. *pono*, *positum*, to set.]

Exposed, eks-pōzd', p.a. Open to the wind or cold; unprotected.

Exposer, eks-pōz'ėr, n. One who exposes.

Exposition, eks-pō-zi'shon, n. Act of exposing; explanation, interpretation; a work containing explanations or interpretations; display; show. [Fr.]

Expositor, eks-poz'it-ėr, n. One who expounds; an interpreter; a book which expounds and explains. [Low L.]

Expository, eks-poz'i-tō-ri, a. Containing exposition; explanatory.

Expostulate, eks-pos'tū-lāt, vi. To make urgent demands; to find fault; to remonstrate; to debate; to reason earnestly with a person on some impropriety of his conduct (with *with*).—vt. To discuss; to examine. ppr. expostulating, pret. & pp. expostulated. [L. *expostello, expostulatus—posco*, to ask for urgently.]

Expostulation, eks-pos'tū-lā"shon, n. Act of expostulating; reasoning with a person in opposition to his conduct; remonstrance; earnest and kindly protest. [L. *expostulatio*.]

Expostulatory, eks-pos'tū-lā-tō-ri, a. Containing expostulation. [Low L. *expostulatorius*.]

Exposture, eks-pos'tūr, n. Exposure.

Exposure, eks-pō'zhur, n. Act of exposing or laying open; state of being laid open to view, to danger, or to any inconvenience; the situation of a place in regard to the points of the compass, or to a free access of air and light.

Expound, eks-pound', vt. To put or set out; to lay open the meaning of; to clear of obscurity; to explain; to interpret; to unfold. [L. *expono—pono*, to put.]

Expounder, eks-pound'ėr, n. One who expounds; one who interprets.

Express, eks-pres', vt. To press out; to set forth in words; to represent in language; to utter; to declare; to exhibit by copy or resemblance; to form a likeness of; to describe; to show or make known; to signify; to designate; to make known the feelings of (with recipr. pron.) [L. *exprimo, expressum—premo*, to press.]—a. Clearly exhibited;

distinct; clear; plain; not ambiguous; given in direct terms; resembling; bearing an exact representation; intended or sent for a particular purpose, or on a particular errand; employed for regular and speedy conveyance.—n. A messenger or vehicle sent on a particular occasion; a message sent; a regular conveyance for messages, packages, &c. [Fr. *exprès*.]

Expressed, eks-prest', p.a. Squeezed or forced out, as juice or liquor.

Expressible, eks-pres'i-bl, a. That may be expressed.

Expression, eks-pre'shon, n. Act of expressing; act of forcing out by pressure; act of uttering, declaring, or representing; declaration; a phrase or mode of speech; elocution; the peculiar manner of utterance, suited to the subject and sentiment; a natural and lively representation of the subject in painting and sculpture; the tone, grace, or modulation of voice or sound in music, suited to any particular subject; that manner which gives life and reality to ideas and sentiments; the outward signs that make known internal feeling. [Fr.—L. *expressio—premo*, to press.]

Expressionless, eks-pre'shon-les, a. Destitute of expression.

Expressive, eks-pres'iv, a. Serving to express; representing with force; emphatical. [Fr. *expressif*.]

Expressively, eks-pres'iv-li, adv. In an expressive manner; clearly.

Expressiveness, eks-pres'iv-nes, n. Quality of being expressive; power or force of representation; the quality of presenting a subject strongly to the senses or to the mind.

Expressly, eks-pres'li, adv. In direct terms; plainly.

Expressure, eks-pre'shūr, n. The act of expressing.

Expugn, eks-pūn', vt. To take by assault; to storm; to reduce; to subdue. [L. *expugno*—L. *pugno*, to fight.]

Expulse, eks-puls', vt. To drive out.

Expulsion, eks-pul'shon, n. Act of driving out; a driving away by violence; state of being driven out or away. [Fr.—L. *expulsio*.]

Expulsive, eks-puls'iv, a. Having the power of driving out or away; serving to expel. [Fr. *expulsif*.]

Expunge, eks-punj', vt. To prick out; to blot out, as with a pen; to r b out, as words; to erase; to do away or wipe out. ppr. expunging, pret. & pp. expunged. [L. *expungo—pungo*, to prick.]

Expurgate, eks-pėr'gāt, vt. To render pure; to cleanse; to purify from anything noxious, offensive, or erroneous. ppr. expurgating, pret. & pp. expurgated. [L. *expurgo,expurgatus—purus*, pure, and *ago*, to drive.]

Expurgated, eks-pėr'gāt-ed, p.a. *Purged*; cleansed; purified.

Expurgation, eks-pėr-gā'shon, n. Act of purging or cleansing; purification. [L. *expurgatio*.]

Expurgator, eks-pėr'gāt-ėr, n. One who expurgates or purifies. [L.]

Expurgatory, eks-pėr'ga-tō-ri, a. Cleansing; serving to purify from anything noxious or erroneous. [Fr. *expurgatoire*.]

Exquisite, eks'kwi-zit, a. Sought out with care; exact; highly finished; ripely considered; very excellent; capable of great delicacy of perception; refined; existing in the highest degree; matchless, as pain or pleasure; very sensibly felt.—n. One dressed with

extreme care; a fop; a dandy. [L. *exquisitus—quæro*, to seek.]

Exquisitely, eks'kwi-zit-li, adv. Nicely; accurately; with great perfection.

Exsufflicate, ek suf li-kāt,a. Contemptible.

Extant, eks'tant, a. Standing out; standing above any surface; in being; not suppressed, destroyed, or lost. [L. *extans—sto*, to stand.]

Extemporaneous, eks-tem'pō-rā"nē-us, a. Arising out of the time or occasion; on the spur of the moment; uttered at the time the subject occurs, without previous study; unpremeditated. [L. *tempus, temporis*, time.]

Extemporaneously, eks-tem'pō-rā"nē-us-li, adv. Without previous study or premeditation.

Extempore, eks-tem'pō-rē, adv. In an extemporaneous manner.—a. Without previous study. [L. *ex tempore*, on the spur of the moment.]

Extemporize, eks-tem'pō-rīz, vi. To speak on the spur of the moment; to discourse without notes or written composition. ppr. extemporizing, pret. & pp. extemporized.

Extemporizer,eks-tem'pō-rīz-ėr, n. One who speaks without previous study or without written composition.

Extend, eks-tend', vt. To stretch out; to continue in length; to spread in breadth; to dilate in size; to reach out; to spread over; to diffuse; to prolong; to bestow on; to impart.—vi. To stretch; to be continued in length or breadth. [L. *extendo—tendo*, to stretch.]

Extended, eks-tend'ed, p.a. Prolonged; spread; enlarged; communicated.

Extender, eks-tend'ėr, n. He or that which extends or stretches.

Extensibility, eks-tens'i-bil"li-ti, n. The capacity of being extended, or of suffering extension. [Fr. *extensibilité*.]

Extensible, eks-tens'i-bl, a. That may be extended; susceptible of enlargement. [Fr.]

Extension, eks-ten'shon, n. Act of extending; state of being extended; that property of a body by which it occupies a portion of space. [Fr.]

Extensive, eks-tens'iv, a. Having great extent or enlargement; large; comprehensive; widely diffused. [Low L. *extensivus*.]

Extensively,eks-tens'iv-li, adv. Widely; to a great extent.

Extensiveness, eks-tens'iv-nes, n. Quality of being extensive; wideness.

Extent, eks-tent'. n. A stretching out; compass; bulk; size; length. [Low L. *extentus*, a stretching out.]

Extenuate, eks-ten'ū-āt, vt. To make thin or fine; to lessen; to weaken the force of; to palliate. ppr. extenuating, pret. & pp. extenuated. [L. *extenuo, extenuatus—tenuis*, thin.]

Extenuating, eks-ten'ū-āt-ing, p.a. Diminishing; palliating.

Extenuation, eks-ten'ū-ā"shon, n. Act of making thin; act of representing anything as less wrong than it is in fact; palliation; mitigation. [Fr. *extenuation*.]

Extenuator,eks-ten'ū-āt-ėr, n. One who extenuates. [L.]

Exterior, eks-tē'ri-ėr, a. External; outer; on the outside; extrinsic; foreign.—n. The outward surface; outward or visible deportment; appearance; (pl.) outward forms and ceremonies. [L.]

Exteriorly, eks-tē'ri-ėr-li, adv. Outwardly; externally.

Exterminate, eks-tėr'min-āt, vt. To drive beyond the limits; to drive away;

ch, *chain*; j, *job*; g, *go*; ng, *sing*; ᴛʜ, *then*; th, *thin*; w, *wig*; wh, *whig*; zh, *azure*; † obsolete.

to extirpate; to root out; to take away; to cause to disappear. *ppr.* **exterminating.** *pret. & pp.* **exterminated.** [L. *termino, terminatus—terminus*, a limit— Heb. *térem*, a cutting off.]
Exterminating, eks-tėr'min-āt-ing, *p.a.* Eradicating.
Extermination, eks-tėr'min-ā″shon; *n.* Act of exterminating; eradication; a taking away or causing to disappear. [Fr.]
Exterminator, eks-tėr'min-āt-ėr, *n.* He or that which exterminates. [Low L.]
Exterminatory, eks-tėr'min-ā-tō-ri, *a.* Serving to exterminate.
Exterminet, eks-tėr'min, *vt.* To exterminate.
Extern†, eks-tėrn', *a., External.*
External, eks-tėrn'al, *a. Outward;* not internal; not being within, as causes or effects derived from, or related to, the body; visible; foreign. [L. *externus—extra*, on the outside.]
Externally, eks-tėrn'al-li, *adv. Outwardly;* in appearance; visibly.
Externals, eks-tėrn'als, *n.pl. The outward parts;* exterior form; outward rites and ceremonies; visible forms.
Extinct, ek-stingkt', *a. Put out;* quenched; being at an end; annihilated; destroyed.—*vt.*† To put out. [L. *extinctus*, from *extinguo*.]
Extinction, ek-stingk'shon, *n. Act of putting out;* act of putting out light or fire; state of being put out; destruction; extermination; suppression; a putting an end to, as of hopes. [Fr.]
Extinguish, ek-sting'gwish, *vt. To put out;* to quench; to suffocate; to abolish; to destroy; to put an end to; to suppress; to cloud or obscure by superior splendour. [L. *extinguo—stinguo*, to scratch out.]
Extinguishable, ek-sting'gwish-a-bl, *a.* That may be quenched or destroyed.
Extinguished, ek-sting'gwisht, *p.a. Put out;* suppressed; destroyed.
Extinguisher, ek-sting'gwish-ėr, *n. He or that which extinguishes;* a hollow, conical utensil to be put on a candle or lamp to extinguish it.
Extinguishment, ek-sting'gwish-ment, *n. Act of extinguishing;* extinction; abolition; a putting an end to or a coming to an end.
Extirp†, ek-stėrp', *vt. To extirpate.*
Extirpate, ek-stėrp'āt, *vt. To root out;* to eradicate; to destroy totally; to cut out; to remove completely. *ppr.* **extirpating,** *pret. & pp.* **extirpated.** [L. *exstirpo, exstirpatus—stirps*, stock, root.]
Extirpated, ek-stėrp'āt-ed, *p.a. Plucked up by the roots;* rooted out; eradicated; totally destroyed.
Extirpation, ek-stėrp-ā'shon, *n. Act of rooting out;* eradication; total destruction; complete removal. [Low L. *extirpatio*.]
Extirpator, ek-stėrp'āt-ėr, *n. One who roots out.* [L.—Fr. *extirpateur*.]
Extol, eks-tol', *vt. To lift out or up;* to elevate; to praise; to magnify; to commend highly; to glorify. *ppr.* **extolling,** *pret. & pp.* **extolled.** [L. *extollo—tollo*, to lift up.]
Extolment†, eks-tol'ment, *n. The act of extolling;* state of being extolled.
Extort, eks-tort', *vt. To twist out;* to draw from by force; to wrest or wring from; to gain by oppression; to exact violently. [L. *extorqueo, extortus—torqueo*, to twist.]
Extorted, eks-tort'ed, *p.a. Drawn or wrung from* by compulsion.
Extortion, eks-tor'shon, *n. Act of ex-*torting; illegal exaction or compulsion; rapacity; oppressive exaction. [Fr. *extorsion*.]
Extortioner, eks-tor'shon-ėr, *n. One who practises extortion.*
Extra, eks'tra, *a. Noting something beyond, or more than, what is usual or agreed upon;* extraordinary; additional. [L.]
Extract, eks-trakt', *vt. To draw out or forth;* to bring out; to take out or from; to take out or select, as a part; to draw, write, or copy out. [L. *extrāho, extractus—traho*, to draw.]
Extract, eks'trakt, *n. That which is drawn out;* a passage taken from a book; an essence; tincture.
Extraction, eks-trak'shon, *n. Act of drawing out;* descent; lineage; birth; the operation of drawing essences, tinctures, &c., from a substance; operation of finding the roots of numbers or quantities. [Fr.]
Extractive, eks-trakt'iv, *a. That is or may be extracted.* [Fr. *extractif*.]
Extractor, eks-trakt'ėr, *n. He or that which extracts or draws out.*
Extradition, eks-tra-di'shon, *n. A giving up* or surrender *from;* the delivery, under a treaty, of a criminal by one government to another, to which he naturally belongs, with a view to trial and punishment. [Fr.—L. *trado, traditus*, to deliver up.]
Extra-judicial, eks'tra-jṳ-di″shi-al, *a. Out of the ordinary course of legal procedure;* out of the proper court.
Extra-mundane, eks-tra-mun'dān, *a. Beyond the limit of the material world.* [L. *extra*, and *mundānus—mundus*, the world.]
Extra-mural, eks-tra-mūr'al, *a. Without or beyond the walls,* as of a fortified city. [L. *extra*, and *murālis—murus*, a wall.]
Extraneous, eks-trā'nē-us, *a. That is without;* foreign; not belonging to a thing; not intrinsic; irrelevant. [L. *extraneus—extra*, without.]
Extraneously, eks-trā'nē-us-li, *adv. In an extraneous manner.*
Extraordinarily, eks-tra-or'din-a-ri-li, *adv.* In an *extraordinary manner.*
Extraordinary, eks-tra-or'din-a-ri, *a. Beyond that which is ordinary;* beyond or out of the common order; not in the usual or regular course; unwonted; exceeding the common degree; remarkable; eminent; rare; wonderful; particular. [Fr. *extraordinaire*—L. *ordo, ordinis*, order.]
Extraught†, eks-trạt', *obs. pp.* of *extract.*
Extravagance, Extravagancy, eks-trav'a-gans, eks-trav'a-gan-si, *n. A wandering beyond limits;* a going beyond the limits of strict truth or probability; excess of affection, passion, or appetite; wildness; prodigality; dissipation; lavish expenditure. [Fr.— L. *vagor*, to wander.]
Extravagant, eks-trav'a-gant, *a. Wandering beyond limits;* exceeding due bounds; irregular; wild; not within the ordinary limits of truth; prodigal; profuse in expenses. [Fr.]
Extravagantly, eks-trav'a-gant-li, *adv. In an extravagant manner.*
Extreme, eks-trēm', *a. Outermost;* furthest; at the utmost point, edge, or border; far out of the ordinary course; most violent; last; worst or best that can exist; most pressing.—*n. That which is outermost;* the utmost point or verge of a thing; end; furthest or highest degree; (pl.) points at the greatest distance from each other; predicate and subject of a conclusion; first and last terms of a proportion. [Fr. *extrême*—L. *extremus*.]
Extremely, eks-trēm'li, *adv.* In the utmost degree; to the utmost point.
Extremity, eks-trem'i-ti, *n. That which is extreme;* the utmost point, part, or side; termination; the highest or furthest degree; the utmost distress; the utmost violence; the most aggravated state; (pl.) the utmost or terminating parts, as the limbs, &c. [Fr. *extrémité*—L. *extremitas*.]
Extricable, eks'tri-ka-bl, *a. That can be e*x*tricated.* [L.]
Extricate, eks'tri-kāt, *vt. To free from perplexities;* to disentangle; to set free; to send out. *ppr.* **extricating,** *pret. & pp.* **extricated.** [L. *extrīco, extricatus—trica*, perplexities.]
Extrication, eks-tri-kā'shon, *n. Act of extricating;* disentanglement; act of evolving. [Low L. *extricatio*.]
Extrinsic, Extrinsical, eks-trin'sik, eks-trin'sik-al, *a. Being on the outside;* external; not contained in or belonging to a body; extraneous; foreign. [Fr. *extrinsèque*—L. *secus*, beside.]
Extrinsically, eks-trin'sik-al-li, *adv. From without;* externally.
Extrude, eks-trōōd', *vt. To thrust out;* to urge, force, or press out; to expel. *ppr.* **extruding,** *pret. & pp.* **extruded.** [L. *extrudo—trūdo*, to thrust.]
Extrusion, eks-trō'zhon, *n. Act of extruding;* a driving out; expulsion. [It. *estrusione*.]
Exuberance, Exuberancy, eks-ū'bė-rans, eks-ū'bė-ran-si, *n. An overflowing quantity;* richness, as of imagination; overflow; rankness; luxuriance. [Fr. *exubérance*—L. *uber*, rich—*über*, a teat.]
Exuberant, eks-ū'bė-rant, *a. Overflowing;* luxuriant; rich; pouring forth abundance; producing in plenty. [L. *exuberans*.]
Exuberantly, eks-ū'bė-rant-li, *adv. In an exuberant manner.*
Exudation, eks-ūd-ā'shon, *n. A sweating out;* a discharge of moisture from animal bodies; the discharge of the juices of a plant, moisture from the earth, &c. [Low L. *exsudatio*—L. *sūdo*, to sweat.]
Exude, eks-ūd', *vt. To sweat out;* to discharge, as the juices of a living body through the pores; to discharge, as the liquid matter of a plant by incisions.—*vi. To come out by sweating.* *ppr.* **exuding,** *pret. & pp.* **exuded.** [L. *exsudo—sudo*, to sweat.]
Exult, egz-ult', *vi. To spring up vigorously;* to rejoice exceedingly at success or victory. [L. *exulto—salio, saltum*, to leap.]
Exultation, eks-ult-ā'shon, *n. Act of exulting;* lively joy at success or victory, or at any advantage gained; triumph; rapture; ecstacy. [L. *exsultatio*.]
Exulting, egz-ult'ing, *p.a. Rejoicing* greatly or in triumph.
Exultingly, egz-ult'ing-li, *adv. In an exulting manner.*
Eyas, ī'as, *n. A nestling;* a young hawk just taken from *the nest*, not able to prey for itself. [Fr. *niais*, probably from L. *nidus*, a nest.]
Eyas-musket, ī'as-mus-ket, *n. A young hawk;* a small child.
Eye, ī, *n. That which sees;* that which *enables us to see;* the organ of sight or vision; sight; face; aspect; regard; notice; vigilance; view of the mind; sight or view, either in a literal or

figurative sense; power of perception; inspection; something resembling an eye in form; a small hole; a loop or ring for fastening.—*vt.* To *fix the eye on;* to look on; to observe or watch narrowly.—*vi.*† To have an appearance. *ppr.* eying, *pret. & pp.* eyed. [Sax. *eage*—Old G. *auga*—Heb. *ain.*]
Eyeball, i'bạl, *n. The ball*, globe, or apple *of the eye.*
Eye-beam, i'bēm, *n. A glance of the eye.*
Eyebrow, i'brou, *n. The brow* or hairy arch *above the eye.*
Eyed, id, *p.a. Having eyes.*
Eye-drop, i'drop, *n. A* tear.
Eye-glass, i'glas, *n. A glass to assist the sight.*
Eyelash, i'lash, *n.* The line of hair that edges the eyelid.

Eyeless, i'les, *a. Wanting eyes;* destitute of sight.
Eyelet, Eyelet-hole, i'let, i'let-hōl, *n. A small eye or hole* to receive a lace or small rope of cord. [Fr. *œillet.*]
Eyeliad|, i'li-ad, *n. A glance of the eye.* [Fr. *œillade.*]
Eyelid, i'lid, *n. The cover of the eye;* that portion of movable skin with which an animal covers the eyeball, or uncovers it, at pleasure.
Eye-piece, i'pēs, *n.* In a telescope, the lens or combination of lenses with which the image is viewed and magnified.
Eye-salve, i'sāv, *n. Ointment for the eye.*
Eye-service, i'sėr-vis, *n. Service* performed only under a master's *eye.*
Eyesight, i'sit, *n. The sight of the eye;* view; observation; the sense of seeing.

Eyesore, i'sōr, *n. Something offensive* to the *eye* or sight.
Eye-string, i'string, *n.* The tendon by which the eye is moved.
Eye-tooth, i'tōth, *n. A tooth under the eye;* a pointed tooth in the upper jaw next to the grinders, called also a canine tooth; a fang.
Eye-wink, i'wink, *n.* A motion of the eyelid; a hint.
Eye-witness, i'wit-nes, *n.* One who *sees* a thing done; one who has ocular view of anything.
Eying, i'ing, *ppr.* Viewing; watching; observing.
Eyry, i'ri, *n. An eggery;* the place where birds of prey construct their nests and hatch their young; an aerie. [G. *ei*, an egg. Old G. pl. *eigir*, eggs, genitive *eiers.*]

F.

Fable, fā'bl, *n. Something spoken;* a fictitious *narrative*, intended to instruct or amuse; an apologue; fiction; falsehood; an idle story; vulgar fictions; the plot in an epic or dramatic poem. *vi.* To feign; to write fiction; to tell falsehoods.—*vt.* To feign; to invent; to devise and speak of as true or real. [Fr.—L. *fabula—fāri, fatus,* to speak.]
Fabled, fā'bld, *p.a. Told* or celebrated in *fables.*
Fabler, fā'bl-ėr, *n. A writer of fables* or fictions; a fabulist.
Fabric, fab'rik, *n. Any work made of wood, stone, or metal;* workmanship; texture; frame or structure of a building; construction; the building itself; a house; a church, &c.; any system composed of connected parts; cloth manufactured. [Fr. *fabrique*—L. *faber,* a worker in hard materials.]
Fabricate, fab'rik-āt, *vt. To make;* to *fashion;* to build; to devise; to form by art and labour; to form or devise falsely, as a story or lie. *ppr.* fabricating, *pret. & pp.* fabricated. [L. *fabrico, fabricatus—faber,* a workman.]
Fabrication, fab-rik-ā'shon, *n. Act of fabricating;* construction; the act of devising falsely; forgery; that which is fabricated; a falsehood. [Fr.]
Fabricator, fab'rik-āt-ėr, *n.* One who constructs. [L.]
Fabulist, fa'bū-list, *n. The inventor or writer of fables.* [Fr. *fabuliste.*]
Fabulous, fa'bū-lus, *a. Containing or abounding in fable;* feigned, as a story devised; related in fable; invented; not real. [L. *fabulōsus.*]
Fabulously, fa'bū-lus-li, *adv. In a fabulous manner.*
Facade, fa-sād', *n. Face or front;* front view of an edifice; the front which a building of considerable size presents to a *street,* court, garden, &c. [Fr. *façade*—L. *facies,* the face.]
Face, fās, *n.* The *make* of a body; external appearance; the surface of the fore part of an animal's head, particularly of the human head; the countenance; look; air of the face; front of a thing; the flat surface that presents itself first to view; appearance; boldness; a bold front; presence; sight; the person.—*vt. To meet in front;* to stand opposite to; to oppose with firmness; to cover with additional superficies.—*vi.* To turn the face. *ppr.* facing, *pret. & pp.* faced. [Fr.—L. *facies—facio,* to make.]
Facet, fas'et, *n. A little face;* a small surface. [Fr. *facette.*]
Facetious, fa-sē'shi-us, *a. Well made|;* fine; witty; humorous; jocose; sprightly; abounding with wit and good humour; exciting laughter. [Fr. *facétieux*—L. *facētus—facio,* to make.]
Facetiously, fa-sē'shi-us-li, *adv.* Merrily; gaily; wittily; with pleasantry.
Facetiousness, fa-sē'shi-us-nes, *n. Quality of being facetious;* sportive humour; pleasantry; jocoseness.
Facial, fā'shi-al, *a. Pertaining to the face.* [from L. *facies.*]
Facile, fa'sil, *a. That may be made or done;* easy; flexible; easily persuaded to good or bad; ready in performing; dexterous. [Fr. *facile*—L. *facio,* to make.]
Facilitate, fa-sil'it-āt, *vt. To make easy;* to free from difficulty or to diminish it; to lessen the labour of. *ppr.* facilitating, *pret. & pp.* facilitated. [Fr. *faciliter*—L. *facilis,* easy.]
Facility, fa-sil'i-ti, *n. Easiness* to be performed; readiness proceeding from skill or use; dexterity; easiness to be persuaded; readiness of compliance; (pl.) means by which anything is *rendered easy;* convenient advantages. [Fr. *facilité*—L. *facilitas.*]
Facing, fās'ing, *p.n.* A thin covering of better material, placed over anything, to improve its appearance or increase its strength.
Facinorous, fa-sin'o-rus, *a.* Atrociously wicked. [L. *facinus,* a bad deed.]
Facsimile, fak-si'mi-lē, *n. That which is made exactly like;* an exact copy or likeness, as of handwriting. [L. *facio,* and *similis,* like.]
Fact, fakt, *n. Anything done;* a deed; an event; a circumstance; reality; truth. [L. *factum—facio,* to make.]
Faction, fak'shon, *n. A doing;* a *taking part with any one;* a party, in political society, acting in union, in opposition to the prince, government, or state; discord; dissension. [Fr.—L. *factio.*]
Factionary|, fak'shon-a-ri, *n.* A partyman.
Factious, fak'shi-us, *a. Given to faction;* turbulent; prone to clamour against public measures or men; pertaining to, or proceeding from, faction. [L. *factiōsus.*]
Factiously, fak'shi-us-li, *adv. In a factious manner;* by means of faction.
Factiousness, fak'shi-us-nes, *n. Quality of being factious.*
Factitious, fak-ti'shi-us, *a. Made by art,* in distinction from what is produced by nature; artificial. [L. *factitius—facio,* to make.]
Factitiously, fak-ti'shi-us-li, *adv. In a factitious* or unnatural *manner.*
Factor, fak'tėr, *n. A doer;* an agent or substitute, particularly a mercantile agent; a commission merchant; one of two or more numbers or quantities, which, when multiplied together, form a product. [L. *facio,* to do.]
Factorage, fak'tėr-āj, *n. Agency of a factor;* the allowance given to a factor by his employer; a commission.
Factorship, fak'tėr-ship, *n. The business of a factor;* a factory.
Factory, fak'tō-ri, *n. A house or place where factors reside* to transact business for their employers; the body of factors in any place; a manufactory.
Factotum, fak-tō'tum, *n. A person employed to do all kinds of work.* [L. *facio,* to make, and *totus,* all, whole.]
Faculty, fa'kul-ti, *n. The power of doing anything;* the peculiar skill derived from practice; dexterity; that power of the mind which enables it to receive, revive, or modify perceptions; talent; gift; privilege; a right or power granted to a person; the individuals constituting a scientific profession, or a branch of one, taken collectively; the professors of medicine; the masters and professors of the several sciences in a college or university; one of the departments of a university. [Fr. *faculté*—L. *facultas—facilis,* easy.]
Fade, fād, *vi.* To disappear gradually,

FADED   134   **FALLOW**

as one going on his way; to grow dim; to perish gradually; to languish; to become poor and miserable; to be transient; to lose colour. — *vt.* To cause to wither. *ppr.* fading, *pret. & pp.* faded. [Fr.—L. *vado*, to go.]

Faded, fād'ed, *p.a.* Withered; decayed.

Fading, fād'ing, *p.a.* Subject to decay; liable to lose freshness and vigour; liable to perish; transient.

Fag, fag, *vi.* To fail; to become weary; to flag; to drudge; to labour to weariness. *vt.* To work almost to death; to compel to drudge. *ppr.* fagging, *pret. & pp.* fagged.—*n.* A laborious drudge; one who labours to weariness; a public schoolboy in England who acts as a drudge for another. [Sax. *fæge*, dying.]

Fag-end, fag'end, *n.* The end of a web of cloth; the untwisted end of a rope; the refuse or meaner part of anything.

Fagging, fag'ing, *p.n.* Laborious drudgery; the acting as drudge for another at an English public school.

Fagot, Faggot, fag'ot, *n.* A bundle of sticks used for fuel, or for raising batteries, filling ditches, &c., in fortification.—*vt.* To tie together; to bind in a bundle; to collect promiscuously. [Fr. *fagod*; Gr. *phakelos*, a bundle.]

Fahrenheit, fah'ren-hīt, *a.* Pertaining to or measured by means of a thermometer, so called from the inventor of the scale—a French chemist. In this scale the freezing-point is marked 32 deg., and the boiling-point 212 deg.

Fail, fāl, *vi.* To fall down; to sink; to decay; to decline; to wane; to cease to be abundant for supply; to be entirely wanting; to cease; to be entirely exhausted; to be lost; to die; not to produce the effect; to be deficient in duty; to be frustrated; to fall short; to become bankrupt.—*vt.* To forsake; to abandon; to cease or to neglect or omit to afford aid, supply, or strength to; to omit; to be wanting to.—*n.* Omission; non-performance; failure; death†. [G. *fehlen*; W. *faelu*, to fail.]

Failing, fāl'ing, *p.a.* Becoming deficient or insufficient; decaying; declining.—*p.n.* Act of failing; imperfection; weakness; miscarriage; the act of becoming bankrupt.

Failure, fāl'ūr, *n.* A failing; cessation of supply or total defect; non-performance; decay; a breaking, or becoming bankrupt.

Fain, fān, *a.* Glad; joyful; pleased; rejoiced; inclined; apt; content to accept.—*adv.* Gladly; with joy or pleasure (with *would*). [Sax. *faegen*, glad.]

Faint, fānt, *vi.* To become feeble; to lose strength and colour, and become senseless and motionless; to swoon; to be weak; to lose spirit; to vanish.—*vt.*† To cause to faint; to depress.—*a.* Enfeebled so as to be inclined to swoon; not strong, as colour; not loud, as sound; not striking, as a resemblance; not vigorous; done in a feeble manner; depressed. [Armor. *gwaned*, weakened.]

Faint-hearted, fānt'härt-ed, *a.* Cowardly; timorous; dejected.

Fainting, fānt'ing, *p.a.* Swooning; growing faint.—*p.n.* A temporary loss of strength, colour, and respiration; a swoon.

Faintish, fānt'ish, *a.* Slightly faint.

Faintishness, fānt'ish-nes, *n.* A slight degree of faintness.

Faintly, fānt'li, *adv.* With faintness.

Faintness, fānt'nes, *n.* State of being faint; feebleness; want of brightness;

weakness, as of sound; feebleness of mind; timorousness.

Fair, fār, *a.* Shining; free from a dark hue; white; beautiful; pleasing to the eye; pure; not cloudy; prosperous; unobstructed; frank; just; peaceful; not violent; not effected by insidious methods; not foul; candid; honourable; mild; merited; not narrow; legible; untarnished; middling.—*n.* Elliptically, a fair woman; a handsome female; the *fair*, the female sex; beauty'. *adv.* Openly; frankly; honestly; happily; successfully; on good terms. [Sax. *faeger*—Icel. *fagr*, splendid.]

Fair, fār, *n.* A stated market in a particular town or city; a stated meeting of buyers and sellers for trade. [Fr. *foire*—L. *forum*, a market-place.]

Fairily, fā'ri-li, *adv.* In the manner of a fairy.

Fairing, fār'ing, *n.* A present given at a fair.

Fairish, fār'ish, *a.* Moderately fair.

Fairly, fār'li, *adv.* In a fair manner; openly; ingenuously; plainly; legibly; gently.

Fairness, fār'nes, *n.* Quality of being fair; clearness; whiteness; purity; beauty; elegance; ingenuousness; openness; equality of terms; freedom from obscurity.

Fair-spoken, fār'spōk-en, *a.* Using fair speech; courteous; plausible.

Fairy, fā'ri, *n.* A fay; an imaginary being supposed to assume a human form, dance in meadows, steal infants, and play a variety of pranks; an enchantress†.—*a.* Belonging to fairies; given by fairies. [G. *fee*; Obsol. L. *for*—L. *fari, fatus*, to speak.]

Faith, fāth, *n.* Belief; trust; reliance; fidelity; truthfulness; credit given; the assent of the mind to the truth of what is declared by another; trust in the honesty or veracity of another; belief on probable evidence; trust and belief in God and in his revealed will; trust and belief in Christ as a Saviour; a system of doctrines believed; a system of revealed truths received by Christians; creed; a strict adherence to duty and fulfilment of promises; word or honour pledged; promise given. [Armor. *fiz*, faith=L. *fides—fido*, to trust.]

Faith-breach, fāth'brēch, *n.* Breach of fidelity.

Faithed†, fāth't, *a.* Honest; sincere.

Faithful, fāth'ful, *a.* Full of faith; firm in adherence to the truth and to the duties of religion; of true fidelity; loyal; trusty; observant of compacts, vows, &c.; true to one's word; true to the marriage-covenant; constant; worthy of belief.

Faithfully, fāth'ful-li, *adv.* In a faithful manner; with good faith.

Faithfulness, fāth'ful-nes, *n.* Fidelity; loyalty; firm adherence to allegiance and duty; veracity; strict performance of promises, vows, or covenants; constancy in affection.

Faithless, fāth'les, *a.* Without belief in the revealed truths of religion; disloyal; perfidious; neglectful; false; not observant of promises.

Faithlessly, fāth'les-li, *adv.* In a faithless manner.

Faithlessness, fāth'les-nes, *n.* Unbelief as to revealed religion; treachery; disloyalty; inconstancy.

Falchion, fal'shon, *n.* A short, broad, crooked sword; a scymitar. [It. *falsione*, a scymitar—L. *falx, falcis*, a reaping-hook.]

Falcon, fa'kn, *n.* A hawk, so called from its *hooked* talons and beak; a hawk trained to sport, as in falconry. [Fr. *faucon*—L. *falco—falx*, a reaping-hook.]

Falconer, fa'kn-ėr, *n.* A person who breeds and trains hawks for taking wild fowls. [Fr. *fauconnier*.]

Falconry, fa'kn-ri, *n.* The art of training hawks to the exercise of hawking; the practice of taking wild fowls by means of hawks. [Fr. *fauconnerie*.]

Faldstool, fald'stöl, *n.* A folding stool or portable seat made to fold up in the manner of a camp-stool; a stool for the king to kneel on at his coronation; the chair within the altar, formerly used by the bishops.

Fall, fal, *vi.* To drop from a higher to a lower place; to tumble down or over; to flow out of its channel into a pond, lake, or sea, as a river; to sin; to depart from the faith; to die, particularly by violence; to vanish; to be plunged into misery; to sink into weakness; to be given up; to pass into a worse state than the former; to decline from violence to calmness, as the wind; to pass into a new state of body or mind; to become; to happen; to come, as fortune; to light on; to rush on; to assail, as fear; to begin with vehemence; to rush or hurry to; to pass by lot or otherwise; to be uttered carelessly; to languish; to issue; to terminate.—*vt.*† To let fall; to drop; to bring forth. *ppr.* falling, *pret.* fell, *pp.* fallen.—*n.* Act of falling from a higher to a lower place; descent; overthrow; diminution; decrease of price; a sinking of tone; cadence; a slope; descent of water; a cascade; outlet of a river into the ocean, or into a lake or pond; the distance which anything falls; departure from goodness or innocence, from faith or duty; the apostasy; the act of our first parents in eating the forbidden fruit; the apostasy of the rebellious angels. [Sax. *feallan*—Gr. *sphallō*, to make to fall.]

Fallacious, fal-lā'shi-us, *a.* Deceitful; misleading; sophistical; mocking expectation; delusive; false. [Fr. *fallacieux*—L. *fallo*, to deceive.]

Fallaciously, fal-lā'shi-us-li, *adv.* In a fallacious manner; deceitfully.

Fallaciousness, fal-lā'shi-us-nes, *n.* Quality of being fallacious.

Fallacy, fal'la-si, *n.* Deceptive or false appearance; that which misleads the eye or the mind; a sophism. [L. *fallacia—fallax*, deceitful.]

Fallen, fal'en, *p.a.* Degraded; ruined.

Fallibility, fal-i-bil'i-ti, *n.* Quality of being fallible; liableness to deceive or to be deceived. [Fr. *faillibilité*—L. *fallo*, to deceive.]

Fallible, fal'i-bl, *a.* Liable to fail or mistake; that may err in judgment; that may deceive. [Fr. *faillible*—Low L. *fallibilis*.]

Fallibly, fal'i-bli, *adv.* In a fallible manner.

Falling, fal'ing, *p.a.* Declining; sinking.—*p.n.* An indenting or hollow.

Falling-sickness, fal'ing-sik-nes, *n.* The epilepsy.

Fallow, fal'lō, *a.* Reddish yellow; yellowish; left unsowed after ploughing; uncultivated.—*n.* Land left unsown for a season, after being ploughed, so called from its *yellowish* colour.—*vt.* To plough, harrow, and break, as land without seeding it. [Sax. *fealo*—L. *fulvus*, reddish yellow.]

Fāte, fär, fat, fall; mē, met, hėr; pīne, pin; nōte, not, mōve; tūbe, tub, bull; oil, pound.

Fallow-deer, fal'lō-dėr, n. A kind of deer smaller than the stag, and most common in England, where it is often domesticated in the parks. It is of a brownish bay colour. [Sax. *falewe*, pale yellow.]

Fallowing, fal'lō-ing, p.n. The operation of ploughing and harrowing land without sowing it.

Fallowness, fal'lō-nes, n. A fallow state; barrenness.

False, fals, a. *Deceptive*; deceitful; perfidious; unfaithful; not genuine or real; assumed for the purpose of deception; not true; expressing what is contrary to that which exists; forged; not genuine; not solid or sound; not agreeable to rule; not honest or just; not fair; not faithful or loyal.—*vt.*† To mislead by want of truth; to deceive; to make untruthful.—*adv.* Not truly; not honestly; falsely. [Icel. *falskr*—L. *falsus—fallo*, to deceive.]

False-hearted, fals'härt-ed, a. *Deceitful*; hollow; treacherous; perfidious.

False-heartedness, fals'härt-ed-nes, n. Perfidiousness; treachery.

Falsehood, fals'hod, n. *Quality of being false;* contrariety to fact; want of truth; untruth; fiction; a lie; want of honesty; deceitfulness; imposture.

Falsely, fals'li, adv. In a *false manner.*

Falseness, fals'nes, n. *Quality of being false;* want of integrity or veracity; duplicity; treachery; perfidy.

Falsifiable, fals'i-fi-a-bl, a. *That may be falsified*, counterfeited, or corrupted.

Falsification, fals'i-fi-kā"shon, n. *Act of making false;* a counterfeiting; the giving to a thing an appearance of something which it is not; wilful misstatement. [Fr.]

Falsified, fals'i-fid, p.a. *Made false.*

Falsifier, fals'i-fī-ėr, n. *One who falsifies.*

Falsify, fals'i-fi, vt. To *make false;* to forge; to prove to be false; to break by falsehood.—vi. To tell lies; to violate the truth. *ppr.* falsifying *pret. & pp.* falsified. [Fr. *falsifier*—L. *falsus,* and *facio*, to make.]

Falsity, fals'i-ti, n. Quality of being false; a lie; contrariety to truth. [Low L. *falsitas*.]

Falter, fal'tėr, vi. To *fail or break in the utterance of words;* to stammer; to fail in exertion; to fall in the regular exercise of the understanding. [Icel. *valtr*, inclined to fall, frail.]

Faltering, fal'tėr-ing, p.a. Hesitating; failing.—p.n. Feebleness; deficiency.

Falteringly, fal'tėr-ing-li, adv. In a *faltering manner;* hesitatingly.

Fame, fām, n. Common talk; report of good or great actions; report that exalts the character; celebrity; renown; notoriety. [Fr.—L. *fama;* Gr. *phēmi*, to speak—Sans. *bhā*, to shine.]

Famed, fāmd, p.a. *Much talked of;* renowned; celebrated.

Fameless, fām'les, a. Without renown.

Familiar, fa-mil'i-ėr, a. *Pertaining to a family;* domestic; well acquainted with; intimate; affable; well known; easy; common; intimate in an unlawful degree.—n. An intimate; one long acquainted; a demon or evil spirit supposed to attend at call. [L. *familiaris—familus,* a servant.]

Familiarity, fa-mil'i-a"ri-ti, n. *State of being familiar;* frequent converse; affability; freedom from ceremony; intimacy. [Fr. *familiarité.*]

Familiarise, fa-mil'i-ėr-īz, vt. To *make familiar;* to accustom; to make well known or easy by practice or converse; to bring down from a state of distant superiority. *ppr.* familiarising, *pret. & pp.* familiarised. [Fr. *familiariser.*]

Familiarly, fa-mil'i-ėr-li, adv. In a *familiar manner.*

Family, fa'mi-li, n. The collective body of *slaves* in a man's house; a household, including parents, children, and servants; a tribe or race; kindred; course of descent; line of ancestors; honourable descent; a group of animals or plants of the same value as a natural order; a collection of genera which are nearly allied to each other. [L. *familia—*Oscan, *famel*, a slave.]

Famine, fa'min, n. *Hunger;* scarcity of food; dearth; a general want of provisions sufficient for the inhabitants of a country or besieged place; destitution. [Fr.—L. *fames*, hunger.]

Famish, fa'mish, vt. To *destroy with hunger;* to starve; to exhaust the strength of, by hunger or thirst; to kill by denial of anything necessary; to force by famine.—vi. To *die of hunger;* to be exhausted in strength, or to come near to perish, for want of food or drink; to be distressed with want. [Fr. *afamer.*]

Famishing, fa'mish-ing, p.a. Perishing by want of food.

Famous, fām'us, a. *Much talked of* and praised; renowned; distinguished or notorious, in a bad sense. (With *for.*) [Fr. *fameux—*L. *fama*, fame.]

Famously, fām'us-li, adv. With great renown or celebration.

Fan, fan, n. An instrument for *winnowing grain* by agitating the air; an instrument used by ladies to agitate the air, and cool the face, in warm weather; something by which the air is moved; a wing; an instrument to raise the fire or flame.—*vt.* To *winnow;* to cool and refresh the face of, by moving the air with a fan; to blow on; to move as with a fan. *ppr.* fanning, *pret. & pp.* fanned. [Sax *fann;* Fr. *van.*]

Fanatic, Fanatical, fa-nat'ik, fa-nat'ik-al, a. *Seized with a divine fury,* as certain priests who officiated in heathen *temples;* furious; wild in opinions, particularly in religious opinions; excessively enthusiastic. [Fr. *fanatique*—L. *fanum,* a temple—Sans. *van,* to worship.]

Fanatic, fa-nat'ik, n. A person affected by excessive enthusiasm; an enthusiast; a visionary.

Fanatically, fa-nat'ik-al-li, adv. *With wild enthusiasm.*

Fanaticism, fa-nat'i-sizm, n. *Quality of a fanatic;* excessive enthusiasm; religious frenzy.

Fancied, fan'si-ed, p.a. Imagined; liked.

Fancier, fan'si-ėr, n. *One who fancies.*

Fanciful, fan'si-ful, a. *Full of fancy;* guided by the imagination rather than by reason and experience; imaginative; visionary; whimsical; wild.

Fancifully, fan'si-ful-li, adv. In a *fanciful manner;* wildly; whimsically.

Fancy, fan'si, n. An *appearance presented* to the mind; image; idea; an opinion; the faculty by which the mind forms images of things at pleasure; taste; liking; caprice; false notion; something that pleases without real use or value.—*vi.* To imagine; to suppose without proof.—*vt.* To form a conception of; to portray in the mind; to like. *ppr.* fancying, *pret. & pp.* fancied.—*a.* Fine; elegant; adapted to please the taste or fancy. [Gr. *phantasia—phainō,* to bring to light.]

Fancy-free, fan'si-frē, a. Free from the power of love.

Fancy-sick, fan'si-sik, a. Distempered in mind.

Fane, fān, n. A *place dedicated to some deity by forms of consecration;* a temple; a church. (Used in poetry.) [L. *fanum*—Sans. *van,* to worship.]

Fanfaronade, fan'fa-ron-ād, n. A swaggering; vain boasting; ostentation; a bluster. [Fr. *fanfaronnade.*]

Fang, fang, n. *That which takes or catches hold of;* a claw or talon; a pointed tooth; the tusk of a boar or other animal, by which the prey is seized and held.—*vt.*† To *catch;* to seize. [Sax. *fang*, a taking.]

Fanged, fangd, p.a. *Furnished with fangs.*

Fangled†, fang'gld, a. New made; showy.

Fanner, fan'ėr, n. *One who fans;* a ventilator; (pl.) a machine for winnowing grain.

Fanning, fan'ing, p.a. Light; gentle.

Fan-palm, fan'päm, n. The taliput-tree, a native of Ceylon and the East Indies. Its leaves are used for umbrellas, &c., and its pith is made into a kind of bread.

Fantail, fan'tāl, n. A kind of bird; a variety of the domestic pigeon.

Fantasied†, fan'ta-zid, a. *Filled with fancies.*

Fantastic, Fantastical, fan-tas'tik, fan-tas'tik-al, a. *Fanciful;* existing only in imagination; not real; having the nature of a phantom†; capricious; indulging the vagaries of imagination; odd. [Fr. *fantastique—*Gr. *phainō,* to bring to light.]

Fantastically, fan-tas'tik-al-li, adv. In *a fantastic manner;* fancifully.

Fantasy†, fan'ta-si, n. The same as *fancy.*

Fap†, fap, a. Fuddled.

Far, fär, a. *Gone to a distance;* remote; remote from purpose; contrary to design or wishes; remote in affection; at enmity with; more or most distant of the two.—*adv.* To a great extent or *distance* in space or in time; remotely; in great part; by many degrees; very much; to a certain point. [Sax. *feor—*Goth. *faran,* to go.]

Farce, färs, n. A mixture of various viands; a short play, in which ridiculous qualities and actions are greatly exaggerated, for the purpose of exciting laughter; ridiculous parade; mere show.—*vt.*† To swell out or render pompous. [Fr.—L. *farcio*, to stuff.]

Farcical, färs'ik-al, a. *Belonging to a farce;* appropriated to farce; droll; ludicrous; ridiculous.

Fardel†, fär'del, n. A burden or little pack. [Old Fr.]

Fare, fār, vi. To *go;* to be in any state, good or bad; to be attended with any circumstances fortunate or not; to feed; to be entertained; to happen well or ill.—n. The price of *passage or going;* the sum paid or due for conveying a person by land or water; food; provisions of the table. *ppr.* faring, *pret. & pp.* fared. [Sax. and Goth. *faran,* to go—Heb. *pāra,* to run.]

Farewell, fär'wel, adv. *interj.* or v. *imper.* used interjectionally. *Go well;* be well; be happy.—n. A wish of happiness or welfare at parting; the parting compliment.—a. Valedictory; taking leave.

Far-fetched, fär'fecht, a. *Brought from a remote place;* not naturally deduced; forced.

Farina, fa-rī'na, *n. Ground corn; meal; flour.* [L.—*far, farris*, a sort of grain.]
Farinaceous, fa-rin-ā'shē-us, *a. Made of farina*, as food; containing meal; yielding farina or flour; like meal; mealy; pertaining to meal. [Low L. *farinaceus.*]
Farm, färm, *n. Food*¹; place where food is produced; a portion of land under cultivation, taken on lease or rented; ground let to a tenant for tillage, pasture, &c., on condition of his paying a certain sum, annually or otherwise, for the use of it.—*vt.* To let out, as lands, to tenants at a certain rent; to take on lease at a certain rent; to lease, as taxes, imposts, or other duties, at a certain sum or rate per cent.—*vi.* To till the soil. [Sax. *farma—feormian,* to procure food.]
Farmer, färm'ėr, *n. One who farms;* one who leases and cultivates a farm. [Sax. *feormere.*]
Farming, färm'ing, *p.a.* Carrying on the business of agriculture; belonging to a farm.—*p.n. The business of a farmer;* agriculture; tillage of land.
Farrago, fa-rā'gō, *n.* A mass composed of various materials confusedly mixed; a medley. [L.—*far,* grits.]
Farrier, fa'ri-ėr, *n. A worker in iron;* a smith who shoes horses; one who professes to cure the diseases of horses. [L. *ferrarius—ferrum,* iron—*firmus,* strong, solid.]
Farriery, fa'ri-e-ri, *n.* The art of curing the diseases of horses and cattle; the veterinary art.
Farrow, fa'rō, *n. A little pig;* a litter of pigs.—*vt.* or *i. To bring forth pigs.* [Sax. *fearh*—L. *verres,* a boar pig.]
Farther, fär'THėr, *a. comp. More remote;* tending to a greater distance.—*adv.* At or to a greater *distance;* more remotely; moreover. [Sax. *forther.*]
Farthermost, fär'THėr-mōst, *a. superl. Being at the greatest distance.*
Farthest, fär'THest, *a. superl. Most distant* or remote.—*adv.* At or to the greatest *distance.* [Sax. *feorrœst.*]
Farthing, fär'THing, *n. The fourth* of a penny; very small price or value. [Sax. *feorthung—feorth,* the fourth.]
Fascicle, fas'si-kl, *n. A small bundle;* a collection. [Fr. *fascicule;* L. *fasciculus—fascis,* a bundle.]
Fascinate, fas'si-nāt, *vt. To bewitch;* to charm; to captivate; to operate on by some powerful or irresistible influence. *ppr.* fascinating, *pret. & pp.* fascinated. [L. *fascino, fascinatus.*]
Fascinated, fas'si-nāt-ed, *p.a. Bewitched; enchanted;* charmed.
Fascinating, fas'si-nāt-ing, *p.a. Bewitching; enchanting;* charming.
Fascination, fas-si-nā'shon, *n. Act of bewitching;* enchantment; a powerful or irresistible influence on the affections; unseen, inexplicable influence; a spell. [Fr.]
Fashion, fa'shon, *n. The make or form of anything;* the state of anything with regard to its external appearance; form; pattern; form of a garment; prevailing mode of dress; manner; mode; custom; prevailing mode; genteel life; workmanship.—*vt. To make or form;* to mould; to shape; to adapt; to make according to the rule prescribed by custom; to counterfeit. [Fr. *façon*—L. *facio,* to make.]
Fashionable, fa'shon-a-bl, *a. Made according to the prevailing form or mode;* established by custom; prevailing at a particular time; observant of the fashion; dressing or behaving ac-

cording to the prevailing fashion; genteel; modish; stylish.
Fashionably, fa'shon-a-bli, *adv.* In a *manner* according to *fashion.*
Fashion-mongering, fa'shon-mung-gėr-ing, *a. Behaving like one who studies the fashions.*
Fast, fast, *a. Bound;* tight; immovable; strong; fortified; firmly fixed; closely adhering; deep; sound; profound; firm in adherence.—*adv.* Firmly; immovably. [Sax. *fœst*—Sans. *pash,* to bind.]
Fast, fast, *a. Borne swiftly;* moving rapidly; going on in a rapid heedless course; dissipated; wild.—*adv.* Swiftly; rapidly. [W. *ffest,* speedy; L. *festino,* to hasten—*fero,* to bear.]
Fast, fast, *vi. To abstain from eating and drinking;* to omit to take the usual meals for a time; to abstain from food partially, or from particular kinds of food.—*n.* Abstinence from food; an abstinence from particular kinds of food for a certain time; a religious mortification by abstinence; the time of fasting, whether a day, week, or longer. [Sax. *fœstan,* Goth. *fastan,* to fast.]
Fasten, fas'n, *vt. To bind;* to make *fast* or close; to lock, bolt, or bar; to secure; to hold together; to cement or to link; to unite closely in any way; to affix; to annex.—*vi. To become fast;* to fix one's self; to seize and hold on. [Sax. *fœstnian*—Sans. *pash,* to bind.]
Fastener, fas'n-ėr, *n. One who makes fast or firm.*
Fastening, fas'n-ing, *p.n.* Anything that binds *and makes fast;* that which is intended for that purpose.
Faster, fast'ėr, *n. One who fasts* or abstains from food.
Fastidious, fas-tid'i-us, *a. Squeamish;* disdainful; delicate to a fault; over nice; difficult to please; critical; suited with difficulty; dainty. [Fr. *fastidieux*—L. *fastus,* scornful contempt.]
Fastidiously, fas-tid'i-us-li, *adv.* Disdainfully; contemptuously.
Fastidiousness, fas-tid'i-us-nes, *n. Squeamishness* of mind, taste, or appetite; disdainfulness.
Fasting, fast'ing, *p.n.* Act of abstaining from food.
Fastly, fast'li, *adv.* Firmly; surely.
Fastness, fast'nes, *n. State of being fast;* firm adherence; security; a stronghold; a fortress or fort; a castle. [Sax. *fœstennes,* a walled town.]
Fat, fat, *a. Full-fed;* plump; unctuous; coarse; heavy; stupid; rich; producing a large income; fertile; fruitful; nourishing.—*n.* The unctuous, concrete part of animal flesh; solid animal oil; the best or richest part of anything.—*vt. To fatten;* to make plump and fleshy with abundant food. *ppr.* fatting, *pret. & pp.* fatted. [Sax. *fœtt—fedan,* to nourish.]
Fat, fat, *n.* A vat. [*See* VAT.]
Fatal, fāt'al, *a. Proceeding from fate;* appointed by fate or destiny; causing death; deadly; calamitous, as an event. [Fr.—L. *fatalis—fari, fatus,* to speak.]
Fatalism, fāt'al-izm, *n.* The *doctrine* that all things are subject to *fate.* [Fr. *fatalisme.*]
Fatalist, fāt'al-ist, *n.* One who maintains that all things happen by *fate* or inevitable necessity. [Fr. *fataliste.*]
Fatality, fāt-al'i-ti, *n. Invincible necessity;* an invincible necessity existing in things themselves; decree of fate; tendency to danger; mortality. [Fr. *fatalité.*]

Fatally, fāt'al-li, *adv. By a decree of fate* or destiny; mortally.
Fate, fāt, *n. That which is spoken* with resistless power; destiny; inevitable necessity; event pre-determined; final event; death; doom; lot; fortune. [L. *fatum—fari, fatus,* to speak.]
Fated, fāt'ed, *a. Decreed by fate;* destined; invested with the power of fatal determination.
Fateful, fāt'ful, *a. Bearing fatal power;* producing fatal events.
Fates, fāts, *n. pl.* The *fabled* Destinies; goddesses supposed to preside over the birth and life of men. They were three in number, Clotho, Lachesis, and Atropos.
Father, fä'THėr, *n. The natural guardian of a child;* he by whom the son or daughter is begotten; the first ancestor; a term of respect given to reverend men; the oldest member of any profession, in respect of that profession; one who acts with paternal kindness or care; a creator, a name given to God as Creator; the appellation of the first person in the Trinity; the title given to dignitaries of the church, superiors of convents, and to Roman Catholic priests; the appellation of the ecclesiastical writers of the first centuries.—*vt. To become a father to;* to adopt; to adopt as one's own; to profess to be the author of; to ascribe to one as his offspring or production; to give a father to. [Sax. *fœder*—Sans. *pā,* to guard.]
Fatherhood, fä'THėr-hud, *n. State of being a father,* or the character or authority of a father.
Father-in-law, fä'THėr-in-lā, *n.* The *father* of one's husband or wife.
Fatherless, fä'THėr-les, *a. Destitute* of a living *father;* without a known author.
Fatherliness, fä'THėr-li-nes, *n. Quality of being fatherly;* parental kindness.
Fatherly, fä'THėr-li, *a. Like a father,* in affection and care; tender; paternal.
Fathom, faTH'um, *n. The bosom;* the space between the extremities of *both* arms extended; a measure of length, containing six feet; reach; depth of thought or contrivance.—*vt. To encompass with the arms;* to reach; to master; to reach in depth; to sound; to penetrate; to find the bottom or extent of. [Sax. *fœthem;* Old G. *fadam.*]
Fathomable, faTH'um-a-bl, *a. Capable of being fathomed.*
Fathomless, faTH'um-les, *a. That cannot be fathomed;* bottomless.
Fatigate, fa'tēg-āt, *a. Wearied;* tired.
Fatigue, fa-tēg', *n. State of being employed to weariness;* weariness with bodily labour or mental exertion; labour; toil; the labours of military men; extra duty, distinct from the use of arms.—*vt. To employ to weariness;* to tire; to exhaust the strength of by severe or long-continued exertion, bodily or mental; to harass. *ppr.* fatiguing, *pret. & pp.* fatigued. [Fr.—L. *fatigo,* to tire.]
Fatiguing, fa-tēg'ing, *p.a.* Inducing *weariness* or lassitude.
Fatling, fat'ling, *n. A young animal,* as a lamb, kid, &c., *fattened* for slaughter; a fat animal.
Fatness, fat'nes, *n. Quality* or *state* of *being fat;* unctuous or greasy matter; richness; that which gives fertility.
Fatten, fat'n, *vt. To make fat;* to feed for slaughter; to make fertile; to enrich.—*vi. To grow fat* or corpulent; to be pampered. [Sax. *fœttian.*]

Fāte, fär, fạt, fạll; mē, met, hėr; pine, pin; nōte, not, mōve; tūbe, tub, bụll; oil, pound.

Fattener, fat'n-ėr, n. *He or that which fattens.*

Fattening, fat'n-ing, p.n. *The process of making fat;* the state of becoming fat.

Fatty, fat'i, a. *Having the qualities of fat;* greasy; unctuous; oleaginous.

Fatuity, fa-tū'i-ti, n. *State or quality of being fatuous;* weakness or imbecility of mind; feebleness of intellect. [Fr. *fatuité*—L. *fatuitas.*]

Fatuous, fa'tū-us, a. *Babbling;* foolish; silly; feeble in mind; weak; imbecile; impotent; without force or fire. [L. *fatuus*—*fari, fatus,* to speak.]

Fat-witted†, fat'wit-ed, a. Heavy; dull; stupid.

Fauces, fę'sēz, n. pl. *A cleft;* the upper part of the throat, from the root of the tongue to the entrance of the gullet. [L.—obsol. *faux, faucis,* the throat.]

Faugh, fą, interj. An exclamation of contempt or abhorrence.

Fault, falt, n. *That which a person is deceived into;* a failing; an error; a defect; a blemish; any deviation from propriety; a neglect of duty or propriety; an offence; trespass; puzzle; difficulty. [Old Fr. *faulte*—L. *fallo,* to deceive.]

Faultily, falt'i-li, adv. *In a faulty manner;* defectively; erroneously.

Faultiness, falt'i-nes, n. *State or quality of being faulty;* viciousness; evil disposition; actual offences.

Faultless, falt'les, a. *Without fault;* free from blemish; free from incorrectness; perfect.

Faultlessly, falt'les-li, adv. *Without being guilty of a fault.*

Faultlessness, falt'les-nes, n. *Freedom from faults or defects.*

Faulty, falt'i, a. *Containing faults;* defective; guilty of a fault; blamable; wrong; bad.

Faun, fan, n. Among the Romans, a kind of demigod or rural deity who was the *protector* of agriculture and of shepherds; called also a sylvan deity. [L. *faunus,* from *faveo,* to protect.]

Favour, fā'vėr, n. *A shining graciously upon;* propitious aspect; good-will; kindness; grace; defence; a kind act; leave; a yielding to another; pardon; the person or thing favoured; something bestowed as an evidence of goodwill; a token of love; a knot of ribbons; *appearance*†; advantage; benefit; prejudice.—*vt. To shine* graciously upon; to regard with good-will or kindness; to be propitious to; to befriend; to palliate; to represent favourably. [L. *favor*—*faveo,* to be well disposed toward—Sans. *bhā,* to shine.]

Favourable, fā'vėr-a-bl, a. *Shining upon;* kind; propitious; tender; averse to censure; conducive to; suitable; beneficial. [Fr. *favorable.*]

Favourableness, fā'vėr-a-bl-nes, n. *The quality of being favourable.*

Favourably, fā'vėr-a-bli, adv. *In a favourable manner.*

Favoured, fā'vėrd, p.a. *Regarded with good-will* or kindness; featured.

Favourer, fā'vėr-ėr, n. *One who favours.*

Favouring, fā'vėr-ing, p.a. Countenancing; wishing well to; facilitating.

Favourite, fā'vėr-it, n. *A person or thing regarded with peculiar favour;* a darling; a minion; one unduly loved. a. *Regarded with particular favour,* kindness, affection, or esteem. [Fr. *favori, favorite.*]

Favouritism, fā'vėr-it-izm, n. *Disposition to favour* one or more persons or classes, to the neglect of others having equal claims; exercise of power by favourites.

Fawn, fan, n. *A young* deer; a buck or doe of the first year; a colour resembling that of a fawn.—*vi. To bring forth a fawn.* [Fr. *faon.*]

Fawn, fan, vi. *To be joyful int;* to court favour by frisking about one, as a dog; to cringe and bow to gain favour; to flatter meanly. (With *upon.*)—n. A servile cringe or bow; mean flattery. [Sax. *faegnian,* to rejoice.]

Fawner, fan'ėr, n. *One who fawns;* one who cringes and flatters meanly.

Fawning, fan'ing, p.a. Courting servilely; flattering by cringing and meanness.

Fawningly, fan'ing-li, adv. In a cringing servile way; with mean flattery.

Fay, fā, n. *A fairy;* an elf. [Fr. *fée.*]

Fealty, fē'al-ti, n. *Fidelity* to a lord; a faithful adherence of a tenant or vassal to the superior of whom he holds his lands; loyalty. [Old Fr. *feaulté*—L. *fidelitas*—*fido,* to trust.]

Fear, fēr, n. *Fright;* a painful emotion excited by an expectation of evil or the apprehension of impending danger; dread; the object of fear; slavish dread; filial regard mingled with awe; the worship of God; the law and word of God; reverence; due regard.—*vt. To be apprehensive of,* as of pain or death; to be afraid of; to dread; to reverence; to venerate; *to be anxious fort; to terrify*†.—*vi.* To be in *apprehension* of evil; to be afraid. [Sax. *faer*—L. *vereor,* to be afraid of.]

Fearful, fēr'ful, a. *Filled with fear;* apprehensive; timid; impressing fear; dreadful; frightful; to be reverenced.

Fearfully, fēr'ful-li, adv. *In a fearful manner.*

Fearfulness, fēr'ful-nes, n. Timorousness; timidity; awe; dread; terror.

Fearless, fēr'les, a. *Free from fear;* undaunted; courageous; bold; intrepid.

Fearlessly, fēr'les-li, adv. *Without fear.*

Fearlessness, fēr'les-nes, n. *Freedom from fear;* courage; intrepidity.

Feasibility, fēz-i-bil'i-ti, n *Quality of being feasible,* or capable of execution.

Feasible, fēz'i-bl, a. *That may be done;* practicable. [Fr. *faisable*—L. *facio,* to do.]

Feasibly, fēz'i-bli, adv. *Practicably.*

Feast, fēst, n. *A bright* or *festal* day; a sumptuous entertainment; a banquet; a stated celebration of some event; a festival; something delicious to the mind or soul; that which delights and entertains.—*vi. To partake of a feast;* to eat sumptuously; to be highly gratified.—*vt.* To entertain with sumptuous provisions; to gratify luxuriously. [Old Fr. *feste*—L. *festum*—Sans. *bhā,* to shine.]

Feasting, fēst'ing, p.n. The act of eating luxuriously; a feast.

Feast-won, fēst'wun, a. *Won* or procured by giving a *feast.*

Feat, fēt, n. *Anything done;* a deed; any extraordinary act of strength, skill, or cunning.—a.† Skilful; neat. *vt.†* To form; to fashion. [Fr. *fait*—L. *factum*—*facio,* to do.]

Feather, feth'ėr, n. *That which enables a bird to fly;* a plume of a bird; a general name of the covering of birds; nature; an ornament; an empty title; something resembling a feather.—*vt. To dress in feathers;* to cover with foliage in a feathery manner; to enrich; to exalt. [Sax. *faether*—Gr. *petómai,* Sans. *pat,* to fly.]

Feathered, feth'ėrd, p.a. Covered or fitted with *feathers;* winged; clothed.

Feathery, feth'ėr-i, a. *Feathered;* clothed or covered with feathers.

Featly†, fēt'li, adv. Neatly.

Feature, fē'tūr, n. *The make of any part of the face;* any single lineament; the fashion; the make; the whole turn of the body; the make of any part of the surface of a thing; outline; prominent parts, as of a bill or law. [Norm. *faiture*—L. *factūra*—*facio,* to make.]

Featured, fē'tūrd, a. *Having features,* or good features.

Febrifuge, fē'bri-fūj, n. *Any medicine that drives away* or mitigates *fever.*—a. *Having the quality of dispelling* or mitigating fever. [Fr. *fébrifuge*—L. *febris,* a fever, and *fugo,* to put to flight.]

Febrile, fē'bril, a. *Pertaining to fever;* indicating fever, or derived from it. [Fr. *fébrile.*]

February, feb'rū-a-ri, n. *The month of purification* among the ancient Romans; the second month in the year [L. *Februarius*—Sabine *februum,* a purgation.]

Feculence, fe'kū-lens, n. *State or quality of being feculent;* foulness; impurity; sediment; dregs. [Fr. *féculence.*]

Feculent, fe'kū-lent, a. *Abounding with sediment;* foul or filthy; impure; abounding with extraneous substances [Fr. *féculent*—L. *fæx,* sediment.]

Fecund, fē'kund, a. *Fruitful,* said of plants and animals; prolific; fertile; productive. [Fr. *fécond.*]

Fecundate, fē'kund-āt, vt. *To make fruitful* or prolific; to impregnate. ppr. fecundating, pret. & pp. fecundated. [L. *fecundo, fecundatus*—*fecundus,* fruitful.]

Fecundation, fē-kund-ā'shon, n. *Act of making fruitful* or prolific. [Fr. *fécondation.*]

Fecundity, fē-kund'i-ti, n. *Fruitfulness;* the quality in female animals of producing young in great numbers; fertility; richness of invention. [Fr. *fécondité.*]

Federal, fē'dėr-al, a. *Pertaining to a league or contract:* derived from an agreement; consisting in a compact between parties, chiefly between states or nations. [Fr. *fédéral*—L. *fœdus, fœderis,* a league.]

Federation, fē-dėr-ā'shon, n. *Act of uniting in a league;* a league; a confederacy. [Low L. *federatio.*]

Fee, fē, n. *That which is acquired, as cattle, goods, money;* hire; reward; recompense for professional services; an estate in trust, granted by a prince or lord, to be held on condition of personal service.—*vt. To pay a fee to;* to hire; to engage in one's service by advancing a fee or sum of money to, as a lawyer. ppr. feeing, pret. & pp. feed. [Sax. *feoh,* cattle—Goth. *faihu,* goods, silver.]

Feeble, fē'bl, a. *Weak;* infirm; sickly; impotent; deficient in vigour, as mental powers, sound, light, &c.—*vt.* To make *feeble;* to weaken. [Fr. *faible*—L. *debilis,* weak—*de,* and *habeo,* to have.]

Feeble-minded, fē'bl-mind-ed, a. *Weak in mind;* wanting firmness or constancy.

Feebleness, fē'bl-nes, n. *Weakness* of body or mind; want of vigour, firmness, or stability.

Feebly, fē'bli, adv. *Weakly.*

Feed, fēd, vt. *To give food to;* to furnish with anything of which there is constant consumption; to consume, as grass by cattle; to glut; to satiate; to

fatten.—*vi.* To take food; to eat; to subsist by eating; to prey (with *on* or *upon*); to pasture; to graze; to grow fat. *ppr.* feeding, *pret. & pp.* fed.—*n.* That which is eaten; fodder; pasture; pasture ground; a certain portion of provender given to a horse, cow, &c. [Sax. *fédan.*]

Feeder, fēd'ėr, *n.* One who feeds; one who eats or subsists; an encourager; a stream that supplies a main canal with water; a branch railway.

Feeding, fēd'ing, *p.n.* Act of giving food to; a fattening; act of eating; that which is eaten; pasture.

Feel, fēl, *vt.* To touch; to perceive by the touch; to have the sense of; to suffer or enjoy; to be affected by; to perceive mentally; to know; to have a real and just view of; to sound; to search for; to explore.—*vi.* To have perception by the touch; to have the sensibility moved; to know with feeling; to excite sensation; to have perception mentally. *ppr.* feeling, *pret. & pp.* felt.—*n.* The sense of feeling; the perception caused by the touch. [Sax. *gefélan*, to feel, to perceive.]

Feeler, fēl'ėr, *n.* One who feels; an observation put forth in order to ascertain the views of others; (pl.) the horns of insects.

Feeling, fēl'ing, *p.a.* Expressive of great sensibility; affecting; possessing great sensibility.—*p.n.* The sense of touch; one of the five senses; nice sensibility; emotion; tenderness of heart; consciousness; any state of emotion.

Feelingly, fēl'ing-li, *adv.* In a feeling manner; tenderly.

Feere†, fēr, *n.* A consort, husband or wife.

Fee-simple, fē'sim-pl, *n.* An absolute fee.

Feign, fān, *vt.* To form; to invent or imagine; to form an idea of, as of something not real; to make a show of; to represent falsely; to forge. [Fr. *feindre*—L. *fingo, fingere*, to feign.]

Feigned, fānd, *p.a.* Invented; imagined.

Feignedly, fān'ed-li, *adv.* In fiction; in pretence; not really.

Feigning, fān'ing, *p.n.* A false appearance; artful contrivance; deception.

Feint, fānt, *n.* A pretence; a pretence of doing something not intended to be done; an appearance of aiming at one part when another is intended to be struck. [Fr. *feinte*—L. *fingo*, to feign.]

Feldspar, Feldspath, feld'spär, feld'spath, *n.* Fieldspar; a mineral. [G. *feld* and *spath*.]

Felicitate, fē-lis'it-āt, *vt.* To wish joy or happiness to; to congratulate. *ppr.* felicitating, *pret. & pp.* felicitated. *a.† Made very happy.* [Low L. *felicito, felicitatus*—L. *felix*, happy.]

Felicitation, fē-lis'it-ā″shon, *n.* Congratulation. [Fr. *félicitation.*]

Felicitous, fē-lis'it-us, *a.* Prosperous; delightful; appropriate.

Felicitously, fē-lis'it-us-li, *adv.* Happily.

Felicity, fē-lis'i-ti, *n.* Great happiness; the joys of heaven; bliss; blissfulness; prosperity; enjoyment of good. [Fr. *félicité*—L. *felicitas.*]

Feline, fē'lin, *a.* Pertaining to cats, or to their species; like a cat; deceitful. [L. *felinus*—*felis*, a cat.]

Fell, fel, *a.* Cruel; barbarous; fierce; savage; bloody. [Sax.]

Fell, fel, *n.* A covering; a skin of a beast. [Sax.—L. *pellis*, a skin.]

Fell, fel, *vt.* To cause to fall; to knock down; to bring to the ground by cutting or striking. [Sax. *fyllan.*]

Feller, fel'ėr, *n.* One who hews or knocks down.

Fellow, fel'lō, *n.* A partner; a companion; one of the same kind; one of a pair; one equal to or like another; an appellation of contempt; a member of a college, or of any incorporated society.—*vt.*† To pair with. [Icel. *félagi*, a partner.]

Fellow-like†, Fellowly†, fel'lō-līk, fel'lō-li, *a.* Like a companion.

Fellowship, fel'lō-ship, *n.* Partnership; familiar intercourse; companionship; joint interest; intimate familiarity; company; an establishment in colleges for the maintenance of a fellow.

Felly, fel'i, *n.* That which goes round; one of the circular pieces of wood which being joined together form the circular rim of a cart or carriage wheel. [Sax. *faelga*—Old G. *felga*, a bending.]

Felon, fe'lon, *n.* A cruel person; a person who has committed a capital crime; a culprit; a whitlow.—*a.* Cruel; felonious; malignant; malicious; proceeding from a depraved heart; disloyal. [Fr.—Low L. *felo.*]

Felonious, fe-lō'ni-us, *a.* Cruel; malicious; villainous; done with the deliberate purpose to commit a crime.

Feloniously, fe-lō'ni-us-li, *adv.* In a felonious manner.

Felony, fe'lon-i, *n.* Cruelty; any crime which incurs the forfeiture of lands or goods; any offence punishable with death; a heinous crime. [Fr. *félonie.*]

Felt, felt, *n.* A cloth made of wool, or wool and fur, fulled or wrought into a compact substance by rolling and pressure with lees or size.—*vt.* To make into felt; to cover with felt. [Sax.]

Felted, felt'ed, *p.a.* Worked into felt.

Felting, felt'ing, *p.n.* The process of making felt.

Female, fē'māl, *n.* One of that sex which conceives and brings forth young; a girl; a woman.—*a.* Noting the sex which produces young; not male; pertaining to females; feminine; soft; delicate; weak. [Fr. *femelle*—L. *femina*; Sans. *bhā*, to be; in one form, to nourish.]

Feminine, fem'in-in, *a.* Pertaining to females; soft; tender; destitute of manly qualities; denoting the gender, or words which signify females, or the terminations of such words. [Fr. *féminin*—L. *femininus.*]

Femininely, fem'in-in-li, *adv.* In a feminine manner.

Femoral, fem'o-ral, *a.* Belonging to the thigh. [Fr. *fémoral*—L. *femur, femoris*, the thigh.]

Fen, fen, *n.* Muddy land; a moor or marsh; a bog; a swamp where water stagnates. [Sax.]

Fence, fens, *n.* That which defends or guards; a wall, hedge, ditch, bank, &c., intended to confine beasts from straying; defence; skill in fencing or defence.—*vt.* To defend; to guard; to secure by an inclosure.—*vi.* To practise the art of fencing; to fight and defend by giving and avoiding blows and thrusts; to raise a fence; to guard. *ppr.* fencing, *pret. & pp.* fenced. [from *fend.*]

Fenced, fenst, *p.a.* Inclosed with a fence; guarded.

Fencer, fens'ėr, *n.* One who fences; one who teaches or practises the art of fencing with sword or foil.

Fencibles, fens'i-blz, *n. pl.* Soldiers enlisted for the defence of the country, but not liable to be sent abroad.

Fencing, fens'ing, *p.n.* The art of using skilfully a sword or foil in attack or defence.

Fend†, fend, *vt.* To defend; to ward off. [Obsol. L. *fendo.*]

Fender, fend'ėr, *n.* That which defends; a utensil employed to prevent coals of fire from rolling forward to the floor.

Fennel, fen'nel, *n.* A plant much cultivated for the agreeable aromatic flavour of its seeds and finely-divided leaves. [Sax. *finol.*]

Fenny, fen'i, *a.* Growing in fens; boggy; marshy; moorish.

Fen-sucked†, fen'sukt, *a.* Sucked out of marshes.

Feoff, fef, *vt.* To invest with a fee or feud; to give or grant to one, as any corporeal hereditament.—*n.* A fief. [Low L. *feoffare.*]

Feoffee, fef-fē', *n.* The person enfeoffed.

Feoffment, fef'ment, *n.* The gift or grant of a fee. [Low L. *feoffamentum.*]

Feoffor, Feoffer, fef'ėr, *n.* One who infeoffs or grants a fee.

Ferment, fėr'ment, *n.* That which causes fermentation, as yeast, leaven, &c.; intestine motion; tumult; agitation. [L. *fermentum*—*ferveo*, to boil up.]

Ferment, fėr-ment', *vt.* To cause to boil up or swell, by exciting into motion; to set in motion; to heat.—*vi.* To rise and swell by internal commotion; to work; to effervesce. [L. *fermento.*]

Fermentable, fėr-ment'a-bl, *a.* Capable of fermentation. [Fr.]

Fermentation, fėr-ment-ā'shon, *n.* Act or process of fermenting. [Low L. *fermentatio.*]

Fermented, fėr-ment'ed, *p.a.* Having undergone the process of fermentation.

Fern, fėrn, *n.* A well-known plant, of many species, having leaves resembling feathers. [Sax. *fearn*—Gr. *pteron*, a feather.]

Ferny, fėrn'i, *a.* Abounding or overgrown with fern.

Ferocious, fe-rō'shi-us, *a.* Wild; fierce; savage; indicating cruelty; rapacious; barbarous; cruel. [L. *ferox, ferocis.*]

Ferociously, fe-rō'shi-us-li, *adv.* Fiercely; with savage cruelty.

Ferocity, fē-ros'i-ti, *n.* Fierceness; savage wildness; fury; fierceness indicating a savage heart. [Old Fr. *ferocité.*]

Ferret, fe'ret, *n.* A kind of weasel employed in unearthing rabbits; [Fr. *furet*, coarse silk] a kind of narrow tape made of coarse spun silk.—*vt.* To search or hunt out like a ferret; to drive out of a lurking-place. [Fr. *furet.*]

Ferriferous, fe-rif'ėr-us, *a.* Producing or yielding iron. [L. *ferrum*, iron, and *fero*, to produce.]

Ferruginous, fe-rö'jin-us, *a.* Of the colour of the rust or oxide of iron; partaking of iron; containing particles of iron. [Fr. *ferrugineux.*]

Ferrule, fe'rūl, *n.* A ring of metal put round the end of a cane, staff, or other thing, to strengthen it. [Fr. *virole*—L. *viriola*, a little bracelet.]

Ferry, fe'ri, *vt.* To carry over a river, strait, or other water, in a boat. *ppr.* ferrying, *pret. & pp.* ferried.—*n.* A passage; a ford; the place of passage where boats pass over water to convey passengers; right of transporting passengers over a lake or stream; a ferry-boat; a wherry. [Sax. *ferian*—L. *fero*, to carry.]

Fertile, fer'til, *a. Fruitful*; rich; prolific; inventive; able to produce abundantly. [Fr.—L. *fertilis*.]
Fertilely, fer'til-li, *adv. Fruitfully*.
Fertility, fer-til'i-ti, *n. Fruitfulness*; richness; abundant resources; fertile invention. [Fr. *fertilité*—L. *fertilitas*.]
Fertilise, fer'til-īz, *vt*. To make fertile or fruitful; to enrich. *ppr.* fertilizing, *pret. & pp.* fertilized. [Fr. *fertiliser*.]
Fertilizing, fer'til-iz-ing, *p.a.* Enriching; furnishing the nutriment of plants.
Ferule, fe'rūl, *n.* A little wooden pallet or slice, used to punish children in school; a rod used for the same purpose. [L. *ferula*, a twig—*ferio*, to smite.]
Fervency, fer'ven-si, *n. Heat of mind;* ardour; eagerness; pious ardour; warmth of devotion.
Fervent, fer'vent, *a. Boiling hot;* hot in temper; vehement; ardent; earnest; animated. [L. *fervens—ferveo*, to boil.]
Fervently, fer'vent-li, *adv. In a fervent manner*.
Fervid, fer'vid, *a. Very hot; boiling;* very warm in zeal; vehement; eager; earnest. [L. *fervidus—ferveo*, to boil.]
Fervidly, fer'vid-li, *adv. Very hotly*.
Fervidness, fer'vid-nes, *n. Quality or state of being fervid*; glowing heat.
Fervour, fer'ver, *n. State of being boiling hot*; heat of mind; ardour; warm or animated zeal and earnestness. [L. *fervor*.]
Festal, fest'al, *a. Pertaining to a feast*; joyous; gay; mirthful. [Low L. *festalis*—L. *festus*, festive.]
Festally, fest'al-li, *adv. In a joyous or festive manner*.
Fester, fes'tėr, *vi.* To rankle; to putrefy; to become malignant.—*n*. A small inflammatory tumour. [perhaps from L. *pus*, the matter of a sore.]
Festering, fes'tėr-ing, *p.a.* Rankling; growing virulent.
Festinate†, fes'tin-āt, *a. Hasty;* hurried. [L. *festinatus*.]
Festival, fes'tiv-al, *a. Festive;* joyous; mirthful.—*n. The time of feasting;* a feast; an anniversary day of joy, civil or religious. [Old Fr.—L. *festum*, a feast.]
Festive, fes'tiv, *a. Pertaining to or becoming a feast;* mirthful. [L. *festivus*.]
Festively, fes'tiv-li, *adv. In a festive manner*.
Festivity, fes-tiv'i-ti, *n. Festive gaiety;* social joy or exhilaration of spirits at an entertainment. [L. *festivitas*.]
Festoon, fes-tön', *n*. Something in imitation of a *festive garland or wreath;* an ornament of carved work in the form of a wreath of flowers, fruits, and leaves, intermixed or twisted together. *vt*. To form in festoons, or to adorn with festoons. [Fr. *feston*.]
Festooned, fes-tönd', *p.a. Made into festoons*, or adorned with them.
Fetch, fech, *vt*. To bring or draw; to make; to heave, as a sigh; to reach; to arrive at; to obtain as its price.—*vi*. To move or turn; to reach or attain.—*n*. A trick; an artifice. [Sax. *feccan*.]
Fetid, fē'tid, *a. Stinking;* having a strong or rancid scent. [L. *fœtidus—fœteo*, to stink.]
Fetidness, fē'tid-nes, *n. The quality of smelling offensively;* a fetid quality.
Fetlock, fet'lok, *n. The tuft of hair that grows behind on a horse's feet;* the joint on which this hair grows. [*feet, lock*.]
Fetter, fet'ėr, *n.* A *chain for the feet;* anything that confines or restrains

from motion. (Generally used in the plural.)—*vt. To put fetters upon;* to bind; to impose restraints on. [Sax. *fueter—fot*, a foot.]
Fettered, fet'ėrd, *p.a.* Confined; restrained from motion.
Fetus, fē'tus, *n. Fœtus*, fē'tus-es, *pl. The young* of an animal in the womb after being perfectly formed. [L.]
Feud, fūd, *n. A deadly quarrel;* an inveterate quarrel between families or parties in a state; an affray; strife. [Sax. *fæhthe—fian*, to hate.]
Feud, fūd, *n. A fee; a fief;* a right to lands or hereditaments held in trust, or on the terms of performing certain conditions, as military service, &c. [from Low L. *feudum*.]
Feudal, fūd'al, *a. Pertaining to feuds, fiefs*, or fees; embracing tenures by military services. [Old Fr.]
Feudalism, fūd'al-izm, *n. The feudal system;* the principles and constitution of feuds, or lands held by military services.
Feudalist, fūd'al-ist, *n. One versed in feudal law*.
Feudality, fūd-al'i-ti, *n. State or quality of being feudal*. [Old Fr. *feudalité*.]
Feudatory, fūd'a-tō-ri, *n. The tenant of a feud or fief;* a tenant or vassal who holds his lands of a superior on condition of military service.—*a.* Held from another on some conditional tenure. [Old Fr. *feudataire*.]
Fever, fē'vėr, *n. A hot distemper* affecting the whole body; heat; agitation; excitement by anything that strongly affects the passions.—*vt. To put in a fever.—vi.* To be seized with fever. [Fr. *fièvre*—L. *febris—ferveo*, to boil.]
Feverish, fē'vėr-ish, *a. Having a slight fever;* diseased with fever or heat; uncertain.
Feverishly, fē'vėr-ish-li, *adv. In a feverish manner*.
Feverishness, fē'vėr-ish-nes, *n. The state of being feverish;* a slight febrile affection.
Few, fū, *a. Not many;* small in number. [Sax. *feawa*.]
Fewness, fū'nes, *n. Quality of being few;* smallness of number; paucity.
Fiat, fī'at. A decree; a command to do something. [L. let it be done, from *fio*, to become.]
Fibre, fī'bėr, *n. A thread;* a fine, slender body which constitutes a part of the frame of animals; a filament of slender thread in plants or minerals; any fine, slender thread. [Fr.—L. *fibra*, a thread.]
Fibred, fī'bėrd, *p.a. Having fibres*.
Fibril, fī'bril, *n. A small fibre*. [Fr. *fibrille*.]
Fibrous, fī'brus, *a. Composed or consisting of fibres;* containing fibres. [Fr. *fibreux*.]
Fickle, fik'l, *a. Moving to and fro; wavering;* of a changeable mind; unsteady; vacillating; capricious. [Sax. *ficol*.]
Fickleness, fik'l-nes, *n. Quality of being fickle;* inconstancy; unsteadiness in opinion or purpose; changeableness, as of fortune.
Fico, fē'kō, *n. A fig;* an act of contempt.
Fictile, fik'til, *a. Moulded into form* by art; made of clay; manufactured by the potter. [L. *fictilis—fingo*, to form.]
Fiction, fik'shon, *n. A making or feigning;* act of feigning; that which is feigned; a falsehood; a lie; a fabrication; fictitious or feigned writings. [L. *fictio—fingo*, to form.]

Fictitious, fik-ti'shi-us, *a. Containing fiction;* imaginary; counterfeit; not genuine. [Low L. *fictitius*.]
Fictitiously, fik-ti'shi-us-li, *adv. By fiction;* falsely; counterfeitly.
Fiddle, fid'l, *n. A stringed instrument of music;* a violin.—*vi. To play on a fiddle;* to trifle; to shift the hands often and do nothing, like one that plays on a fiddle.—*vt.* To play, as a tune on a fiddle. *ppr.* fiddling, *pret. & pp.* fiddled [Sax. *fithele*—L. *fides*.]
Fiddler, fid'lėr, *n. One who plays on a fiddle* or violin.
Fiddling, fid'l-ing, *p.a. Act of playing on a fiddle*.
Fidelity, fi-del'i-ti, *n. Faithfulness;* trustiness; exact observance of duty; firm adherence to a person or party with which one is united; loyalty; integrity. [Fr. *Fidélité*—L. *fidelitas*.]
Fie, fī. An exclamation denoting contempt or dislike. [from Sax. *fian*, to hate.]
Fief, fēf, *n. A fee; a feud;* an estate held of a superior on condition of military service. [Fr. *fief*.]
Field, fēld, *n. An open level tract of land easy to walk in;* a piece of land inclosed for tillage or pasture; ground not inclosed, fitted for tillage; the ground where a battle is fought; a battle; a wide expanse; open space for action; compass; the ground or blank space on which figures are drawn. [Sax. *feld*—L. *pes, pedis*, the foot.]
Field-book, fēld'būk, *n. A book* used in surveying fields, &c., in which are set down the angles, stations, distances, &c.
Field-day, fēld'dā, *n. A day* when troops are drawn out for instruction in field exercises and evolutions.
Fielded†, fēld'ed, *p.a. Being in the field of battle*.
Field-marshal, fēld-mär'shal, *n.* The commander of an army; a military officer of the highest rank.
Field-sports, fēld'spōrts, *n. pl. Diversions of the field*, as shooting and hunting.
Field-works, fēld'wėrks, *n. pl. Works* thrown up in besieging or defending a place.
Fiend, fēnd, *n. A hater;* a foe; an implacable foe; the devil; an infernal being. [Sax. *feond—fian*, to hate.]
Fiendish, fēnd'ish, *a. Like a fiend;* malicious.
Fiendishness, fēnd'ish-nes, *n. Quality of being fiendish;* maliciousness.
Fierce, fėrs, *a. Wild; ferocious;* savage; ravenous; easily enraged; outrageous; not to be restrained; angry; ardent. [L. *ferox, ferocis*.]
Fiercely, fėrs'li, *adv. In a fierce manner;* violently; with rage.
Fierceness, fėrs'nes, *n. Ferocity;* impetuosity; savageness; quickness to attack; violence; outrageous passion.
Fierily, fī'ėr-i-li, *adv. In a hot or fiery manner*.
Fieriness, fī'ėr-i-nes, *n. Heat;* heat of temper; irritability.
Fiery, fī'ėr-i, *a. Consisting of fire;* hot like fire; ardent; impetuous; easily provoked; fierce. [from *fire*.]
Fiery-footed, fī'ėr-i-fut-ed, *a.* Swift in motion.
Fife, fīf, *n. A small pipe*, used as a wind-instrument, chiefly in martial music with drums.—*vi. To play on a fife. ppr.* fifing, *pret & pp.* fifed. [G. *pfeife*.]
Fifer, fīf'ėr, *n. One who plays on a fife*.

Fifteen, fif'ten, a. Five and ten. [Sax. *fíftyne*.]
Fifteenth, fif'tenth, a. The fifth after the tenth; the ordinal of fifteen; containing one part in fifteen.—n. A fifteenth part. [Sax. *fífteotha*.]
Fifth, fifth, a. The ordinal of five.—n. A fifth part. [Sax. *fífta*.]
Fifthly, fifth'li, adv. In the fifth place.
Fiftieth, fif'ti-eth, a. The ordinal of fifty.—n. A fiftieth part. [Sax. *fífteotha*.]
Fifty, fif'ti, a. Five tens; five times ten. [Sax. *fíftig*.]
Fig, fig, n. The fruit of the fig-tree; the tree itself, growing in warm climates; a worthless thing.—vt.† To insult with motions of the fingers. [Sax. *fic*—L. *ficus*.]
Fight, fit, vi. To strike or beat with the fist; to contend in arms for victory; to struggle.—vt. To maintain, as a struggle for victory over enemies; to contend with in battle or single combat; to war against; to cause to fight. ppr. fighting, pret. & pp. fought.—n. A struggle for victory; a battle; an encounter; a duel. [Sax. *feohtan*—G. *fechten*.]
Fighter, fit'er, n. One who fights; a combatant; a warrior.
Fighting, fit'ing, p.a. Qualified for war; fit for battle.—p.n. Contention; strife; quarrel.
Figment, fig'ment, n. A fiction; something feigned or imagined; a fabrication. [L. *figmentum—fingo*, to form.]
Figurate, fig'ūr-āt, a. Formed; of a certain determinate form; resembling anything of a determinate form. [L. *figuratus—fingo*, to form.]
Figurately, fig'ūr-āt-li, adv. In a figurate manner.
Figuration, fig-ūr-ā'shon, n. Act of forming, or of giving figure; determination to a certain form. [L. *figuratio*.]
Figurative, fig'ūr-āt-iv, a. Containing a figure or figures; representing by resemblance; not literal or direct; abounding in figures of speech. [Fr. *figuratif*—L. *figurativus*.]
Figuratively, fig'ūr-āt-iv-li, adv. In a figurative manner; not literally.
Figure, fig'ūr, n. The form of anything as expressed by the outline; person; distinguished appearance; appearance of any kind; a statue; representation in painting; design on cloth; a character denoting a number; a diagram; a horoscope; type; emblem; symbol; a mode of speaking or writing, in which words are turned from their ordinary signification; price.—vt. To form or mould into any determinate shape; to show by a corporeal resemblance, as in a picture or statuary; to make a drawing of; to cover with figures; to mark with figures; to represent by a typical resemblance; to image in the mind; to conceive; to note by characters.—vi. To make a figure; to be distinguished. ppr. figuring, pret. & pp. figured. [Fr.—L. *figura*—fingo, to form.]
Figured, fig'ūrd, p.a. Adorned with figures; free and florid.
Figuring, fig'ūr-ing, p.n. Act of making figures.
Filament, fil'a-ment, n. A slender thread; a substance resembling a thread. [Fr.—L. *filum*, a thread.]
Filamentous, fil-a-ment'us, a. Like a thread; consisting of fine filaments.
Filbert, fil'bėrt, n. The fruit of the cultivated hazel. [etymol. uncertain.]

Filch, filsh, vt. To pilfer; to steal; to pillage; to take wrongfully. [etymol. uncertain.]
Filcher, filsh'ėr, n. A thief; one guilty of petty theft.
File, fil, n. A thread or line; a line or wire on which papers are strung; the whole number of papers strung on a line or wire; a row of soldiers ranged one behind another, from front to rear; a roll or list.—vt. To string; to arrange or insert in a bundle, as papers, indorsing the article on each paper; to present or exhibit officially, or for trial.—vi. To march in a file or line, as soldiers, not abreast, but one after another. ppr. filing, pret. & pp. filed. [Fr.—L. *filum*, a thread.]
File, fil, n. An instrument used in polishing metals, and also in cutting them; anything to smooth.—vt. To rub and smooth with a file; to polish; to cut as with a file; to wear off or away. ppr. filing, pret. & pp. filed. [Sax. *feol*—L. *polio, politum*, to polish—Heb. *palat*, to be smooth.]
Filet, fil, vt. To defile.
Filer, fil'ėr, n. One who uses a file.
Filial, fil'i-al, a. Pertaining to a son or daughter; becoming a child in relation to his parents; bearing the relation of a son. [Fr.—L. *filius*, a son; *filia*, a daughter.]
Filially, fil'i-al-li, adv. In a filial manner.
Filiform, fil'i-form, a. Having the form of a thread or filament; slender. [L. *filum*, and *forma*, form.]
Filigree, fil'i-grē, n. A kind of enrichment on gold and silver, wrought delicately in the manner of little threads or grains, or of both intermixed.—a. Relating to work in filigree. [L. *filum*, a thread, and *granum*, a grain.]
Filigreed, fil'i-grēd, p.a. Ornamented with filigree.
Filings, fil'ingz, p.n. pl. Fragments or particles rubbed off by the act of filing.
Fill, fil, vt. To occupy, as empty space; to pour into; to put or pour in, till the thing will hold no more; to cause to abound; to satisfy; to surfeit; to make plump; to press and dilate on all sides or to the extremities; to supply, as a vacant office; to hold; to possess and perform the duties of; to officiate in, as an incumbent.—vi. To fill a cup or glass for drinking; to give to drink; to grow or become full.—n. Fulness; as much as supplies want. [Sax. *fyllan*, L. *pleo*, to fill.]
Filler, fil'ėr, n. He or that which fills.
Fillet, fil'let, n. A little band to tie about the hair of the head; the fleshy part of the thigh in veal; meat rolled together and tied round; something resembling a fillet.—vt. To bind with a fillet or little band. ppr. filletting, pret. & pp. filletted. [Fr. *filet*—L. *filum*, a thread.]
Filling, fil'ing, p.n. A making full; supply.
Fillip, fil'ip, vt. To strike with the nail of the finger, forced from the thumb with a sudden spring.—n. A jerk of the finger forced suddenly from the thumb. [probably formed from the sound.]
Filly, fil'li, n. A female or mare colt; a wanton girl. [Sax. *fola*.]
Film, film, n. A thin skin; a pellicle, as on the eye.—vt. To cover with a thin skin or pellicle. [Sax. a skin.]
Filminess, film'i-nes, n. State of being filmy.

Filmy, film'i, a. Composed of thin membranes or pellicles.
Filter, fil'tėr, n. A strainer; a piece of woollen cloth, paper, or other substance, through which liquors are passed.—vt. To purify as liquor, by passing it through a filter, or a porous substance.—vi. To percolate; to pass through a filter. [Fr. *filtre*—It. *feitro*, felt.]
Filtering, fil'tėr-ing, p.n. Act of passing through a filter.
Filth, filth, n. That which defiles; foulness; dirt; any foul matter; waste matter; nastiness; anything that sullies the moral character. [Sax. *fylth*—*fúl*, foul.]
Filthily, filth'i-li, adv. In a filthy manner; foully; grossly.
Filthiness, filth'i-nes, n. State of being filthy; foulness; dirtiness; filth; defilement by sin; impurity.
Filthy, filth'i, a. Abounding in filth; unclean; squalid; defiled by sinful practices; morally impure; obtained by base and dishonest means.
Filtrate, fil'trāt, vt. To filter; to strain; to purify, as liquor, by straining. ppr. filtrating, pret. & pp. filtrated. [Low L. *filtro, filtratus*.]
Filtration, fil-trā'shon, n. Act or process of filtering; the mechanical separation of a liquid from the undissolved particles floating in it. [Fr.]
Fin, fin, n. A feather; one of the projecting wing-like organs which enable fishes to balance themselves in an upright position, and assist in regulating their movements in the water; anything resembling a fin. [Sax.—L. *pinna*, a feather.]
Fin, fin, n. A native of Finland.
Finable, fin'a-bl, a. That admits a fine; subject to a fine or penalty.
Final, fin'al, a. Pertaining to the end; last; ultimate; conclusive; decisive. [Fr.—L. *finis*, the end.]
Finale, fē-nä'lā, n. Close; end; the last note or end of a piece of music; that which closes a concert, &c. [It.]
Finality, fi-nal'i-ti, n. Final state; the state of being final.
Finally, fi'nal-li, adv. At the end or conclusion; ultimately; lastly; completely; beyond recovery.
Finance, fi-nans', n. Revenue; income of a king or state; (pl.) funds in the public treasury, or accruing to it; the income or resources of individuals. [Fr.—Low L. *financia*, a money payment.]
Financial, fi-nan'shi-al, a. Pertaining to finance, or to public revenue.
Financially, fi-nan'shi-al-li, adv. In relation to finances.
Financier, fi-nan'sėr, n. A manager of the public revenues; one skilled in matters of finance. [Fr.]
Finch, finsh, n. A small singing bird, so called from the sound of its note. [Sax. *finc*.]
Find, find, vt. To come upon; to discover by the eye; to recover; to obtain by searching or by accident; to light upon; to get; to obtain; to invent; to perceive; to learn; to supply; to furnish; to procure.—vi. To come to a determination or conclusion; to be informed; to discover. ppr. finding, pret. & pp. found. [Sax. *findan*—Sans. *vid*, to come upon.]
Finder, find'ėr, n. One who finds or discovers; that which finds or discovers.
Finding, find'ing, p.n. Discovery; act of discovering; a verdict.
Fine, fin, a. Thin; of very small diameter; keen; made of fine materials; clear; refined; exquisite; beautiful in

thought; very handsome; elegant in manners; excellent; brilliant or acute; amiable; showy; splendid; [Old G. *fehan*] artful; fraudulent.—*vt.* To make *fine*; to refine; to purify; to purify, as a metal; to decorate'. *ppr.* fining, *pret. & pp.* fined. [G. *fein.*]

Fine, fīn, *n.* A sum of money paid by way of penalty for an offence, as a *final* settlement; a mulct; amercement; forfeiture; end.—*vt.* To impose a pecuniary penalty upon for an offence; to set a fine on by judgment of a court; to punish by fine. *ppr.* fining, *pret. & pp.* fined. [L. *finis*, an end.]

Fineless, fīn'les, *a. Endless;* boundless.

Finely, fīn'li, *adv.* In a *fine* manner; in minute parts; gaily; handsomely; nicely; delicately.

Fineness, fīn'nes, *n.* Thinness; smallness; slenderness; clearness; purity; delicacy; keenness; elegance; capacity for delicate or refined conceptions; splendour.

Finer, fīn'ėr, *n. One who refines.*

Finery, fīn'ė-ri, *n. Fine things;* showy articles of dress; gay clothes; jewels, trinkets, &c.; show; splendour; gaiety of colours or appearance; a furnace where cast-iron is converted into malleable iron.

Finesse, fi-nes', *n. Artifice;* stratagem; subtlety of contrivance to gain a point. *vi.* To use *artifice* or stratagem. *ppr.* finessing, *pret. & pp.* finessed. [Fr.]

Finessing, fi-nes'ing, *p.n. The practice of artifice.*

Fin-footed, fin'fut-ed, *a.* Having feet with toes connected by a membrane.

Finger, fing'gėr, *n.* That which is adapted for *seizing;* one of the extreme parts of the hand; a small member shooting to a point; a certain measure; the hand; ability; skill in playing on a keyed instrument.—*vt.* To *handle with the fingers;* to touch lightly; to handle without violence; to toy with; to pilfer; to touch, as an instrument of music; to perform with the fingers, as work; to execute, as delicate work. *vi.* To dispose the fingers aptly in playing on an instrument. [Sax.—G. *fangen,* to catch.]

Finger-board, fing'gėr-bōrd, *n.* The board of a stringed musical instrument, where the *fingers* act on the strings; the range of keys of a pianoforte, organ, &c.

Fingered, fing'gėrd, *p.a. Having fingers,* or parts like fingers.

Fingering, fing'gėr-ing, *p.n.* Act of touching lightly or handling; manner of touching an instrument of music.

Finical, fin'ik-al, *a. Very fine;* pretending to superfluous elegance. [from *fine.*]

Finically, fin'ik-al-li, *adv.* With great nicety or spruceness; foppishly.

Fining, fīn'ing, *p.n. The process of refining* or purifying, as liquors; that which is used to refine.

Finish, fin'ish, *vt. To terminate;* to arrive at the end of, in performance; to put an end to; to close; to perfect; to polish to the degree of excellence intended.—*vi. To terminate.*—*n.* Completion; that which gives perfection to a work of art. [Fr. *finir*, *ppr. finissant*—L. *finis*, end.]

Finished, fin'isht, *p.a.* Complete; perfect; polished to the highest degree of excellence.

Finisher, fin'ish-ėr, *n. One who finishes;* one who puts an end to; one who completes or perfects.

Finishing, fin'ish-ing, *p.a.* Perfecting.

bringing to an end.—*p.n.* Completion; last polish; finish.

Finite, fī'nit, *a. Limited; bounded;* circumscribed; not infinite. [L. *finio, finitus,* to end.]

Finitely, fī'nit-li, *adv. Within limits;* to a certain degree only.

Finless, fin'les, *a. Destitute of fins.*

Finnish, fin'ish, *a.* Pertaining to Finland, or to its language.

Finny, fin'i, *a. Furnished with fins.*

Fir, fėr. *n.* A resinous tree, the wood of which *readily takes fire,* is much used as fuel, and applied to a great variety of purposes. [Sax. *furh*—Gr. *pur,* fire.]

Fire, fīr, *n. That which purifies;* that which burns; caloric; the burning of fuel on a hearth, or in any other place; light; splendour; torture by burning; violence of passion; vigour of fancy; intellectual activity; the passion of love; ardent affection; rage; contention; affliction.—*vt. To set on fire;* to irritate, as the passions; to animate; to give life or spirit to; to discharge; to drive by fire!.—*vi. To take fire;* to be irritated; to discharge artillery or fire-arms. *ppr.* firing, *pret. & pp.* tired. [Sax. *fyr*—Gr. *pur,* fire—Sans. *pā,* to purify.]

Fire-arms, fīr'ärmz, *n.pl. Arms* or weapons which expel their charge by the *combustion* or explosion of powder.

Fire-brand, fīr'brand, *n.* A piece of *wood* kindled or on *fire;* an incendiary; one who inflames factions.

Fire-brigade, fīr'bri-gād, *n. A body of men* managing an engine or engines to extinguish *fires.*

Fire-cock, fīr'kok, *n.* A *cock* or spout to let out water for extinguishing *fire.*

Fire-damp, fīr'damp, *n.* The explosive carburetted hydrogen of coal-mines.

Fire-engine, fīr'en-jīn, *n.* An *engine* for throwing water to extinguish *fire.*

Fire-escape, fīr'es-kāp, *n.* A machine to facilitate *escape* from the upper part of a building when on fire.

Fire-fly, fīr'flī, *n.* A winged insect which emits a brilliant light at night.

Fire-new, fīr'nū, *a.* Fresh from the forge; bright.

Fire-ship, fīr'ship, *n.* A *vessel* filled with combustibles and furnished with grappling-irons, to hook and set *fire* to an enemy's ships.

Fire-side, fīr'sīd, *n. A place near the fire* or hearth; home; domestic life.

Fire-works, fīr'wėrks, *n. pl.* Preparations of gunpowder, sulphur, &c., used for making explosions in the air on occasions of public rejoicing, or for the purposes of war.

Fire-worship, fīr'wėr-ship, *n. The worship of fire,* which prevailed chiefly in Persia.

Firing, fīr'ing, *n. Act of one who fires;* fire-wood or coal.

Firkin, fėr'kin, *n.* An old measure of capacity, being the *fourth part* of a barrel, or seven and a half imp. gallons. [Sax. *feower,* four, and dimin. *kin.*]

Firm, fėrm, *a. Strong;* dense; hard; solid; not fluid; not easily moved; fixed; unshaken; resolute; stanch; not giving way.—*n.* A partnership or house; the name or title under which a company transact business.—*vt. To make firm* or fast; to strengthen; to fix; to establish. [Fr. *ferme*—L. *firmus,* strong—Sans. *dhri,* to hold.]

Firmament, fėrm'a-ment, *n.* The sky seemingly *fixed* above the earth; the apparently solid vault or concave of

the heavens, in which the stars appear to be *fixed;* the sky or heavens; an expanse; a wide extent. [Fr.—L. *firmamentum.*]

Firmamental, fėrm-a-ment'al, *a. Pertaining to the firmament;* celestial.

Firmly, fėrm'li, *adv. In a firm manner;* with unshaken resolution.

Firmness, fėrm'nes, *n. Quality of being firm;* stability; steadfastness; fixedness; certainty; compactness; hardness; solidity.

First, fėrst, *a. Foremost* in time, place, or progression; preceding all others in rank or estimation; chief; highest; the ordinal of *one.*—*adv. Before* anything else in the order of time, or in order of proceeding or consideration; before all others in place or progression, or in rank. [Sax. *fyrst*—*fore,* before.]

First-born, fėrst'born, *a. First brought forth;* eldest.—*n. The first in the order* of birth; the eldest child; most exalted.

First-floor, fėrst'flōr, *n.* The floor next above the ground-floor.

Firstling, fėrst'ling, *n. The first* produce, as of sheep or cattle; the thing first thought or done!. [*first,* and termin. *ling.*]

First-rate, fėrst'rāt, *a.* Of the highest excellence; pre-eminent; being of the largest size, as a ship of war.

Firth, fėrth, *n. See* FRITH.

Fiscal, fis'kal, *a.* Pertaining to the public *treasury* or revenue.—*n. Exchequer;* revenue; a treasurer. [Fr. *fisc,* exchequer—L. *fiscus,* a money-basket.]

Fish, fish, *n. An animal that inhabits the water;* the flesh of such animals used as food. *Fish,* in the singular, is used for fishes in general, or the whole race.—*vi. To attempt to catch fish;* to attempt to obtain by artifice, or indirectly to seek to draw forth.—*vt.* To search by raking or sweeping; to catch; to draw out or up. [Sax. *fisc*—L. *piscis,* a fish—Sans. *vāsi,* water.]

Fisher, fish'ėr. *n. One who is employed in catching fish.*

Fisherman, fish'ėr-man, *n. One whose occupation is to catch fish.*

Fishery, fish'ė-ri, *n. The business of catching fish;* a place for catching fish.

Fish-hook, fish'hök, *n. A hook to catch fishes;* part of a fish-tackle.

Fishify†, fish'i-fī, *vt.* To change to fish.

Fishing, fish'ing, *p.a. Used or employed in fishing,* or by fishermen.—*p.n. Art or practice of catching fish.*

Fishmonger, fish'mung-gėr, *n. A dealer in fish.*

Fishwoman, fish-wu'man, *n. A woman who sells fish.*

Fishy, fish'i, *a. Consisting of fish;* inhabited by fish; having the qualities of fish; like fish.

Fissile, fis'sil, *a. That may be split* or divided in the direction of the grain, or of natural joints. [L. *fissilis*—*findo,* Sans. *bhid,* to cleave.]

Fissure, fī'shūr, *n. A cleft;* a narrow chasm made by the parting of any substance; a longitudinal opening; a slit; a deep narrow groove. [Fr.—L. *fissura*—*findo,* to cleave.]

Fist, fist, *n. The hand fast closed* or clenched; the band with the fingers doubled into the palm.—*vt. To strike with the fist;* to gripe with the fist. [Sax. *fyst*—G. *fügen,* to join.]

Fistula, fis'tū-la, *n. A shepherd's pipe;* a deep, narrow, sinuous ulcer. [L.—Gr. *phusaō,* to blow.]

Fistular, fis′tū-lėr, *a.* Hollow, like a pipe or reed. [L. *fistularis*.]

Fit, fit, *n.* A sudden and violent attack of disorder, in which the body is often convulsed, and sometimes senseless; a convulsion; a turn; a period or interval; a temporary affection or attack; a passing humour. [It. *fitta*, a pricking pain—L. *figo, fixum*, to fix, pierce.]

Fit, fit, *a.* Made so as to suit a particular purpose; adapted; meet; becoming suited to the nature and propriety of things; qualified; adequate.—*vt.* To adapt; to accommodate, as a person with anything; to prepare; to qualify; to furnish duly; to be suitable to.—*vi.* To be proper or becoming; to suit or be suitable; to be adapted. *ppr.* fitting, *pret. & pp.* fitted.—*n.* The close and easy *fitting* of an article of dress; adjustment of dress to the body. [Fr. *fait*—L. *facio, factum*, to make—Goth. *fetjan*, to arrange.]

Fitch, fich, *n.* A vetch; a chick-pea. [It. *veccia*—L. *vicia*.]

Fitful, fit′ful, *a.* Full of *fits*; varied by sudden impulses.

Fitfully, fit′ful-li, *adv.* By *fits*; at intervals.

Fitfulness, fit′ful-nes, *n.* State of being *fitful*.

Fitly, fit′li, *adv.* Suitably; properly.

Fitment, fit′ment, *n.* The act of fitting; that which fits.

Fitness, fit′nes, *n.* Propriety; justness; qualification; convenience.

Fitted, fit′ed, *p.a.* Made *suitable*; adapted; prepared; qualified.

Fitter, fit′ėr, *n.* He or that which makes *fit*, or confers fitness; one who puts the parts of machinery together.

Fitting, fit′ing, *p.a.* Fit or appropriate. *p.n.* Anything used in fitting up.

Fittingly, fit′ing-li, *adv.* Suitably.

Five, fiv, *a.* Four and one added; the half of ten. [Sax. *fif*.]

Fivefold, fiv′fōld, *a.* In *fives*; consisting of five in one; five times repeated.

Fix, fiks, *vt.* To make fast, firm, or stable; to settle; to define; to appoint; to set, settle, or direct steadily; to deprive of volatility; to withhold from motion.—*vi.* To become fast; to settle or remain permanently; to cease to flow or be fluid; to congeal. [Fr. *fixer*—L. *figo, fixus*, Sans. *pash*, to bind, to fix.]

Fixation, fiks-ā′shon, *n.* Act of *fixing*; state of being *fixed*; stability; firmness.

Fixed, fikst, *p.a.* Firm; fast; fastened; intently directed; deprived of volatility.

Fixedly, fiks′ed-li, *adv.* Steadfastly.

Fixedness, fiks′ed-nes, *n.* State of being *fixed*; state of a body which resists volatilization by heat; firm coherence of parts.

Fixture, fiks′tūr, *n.* That which is *fixed* or made *fast*; that which is permanently attached to something as an appendage; something fixed or immovable; fixedness.

Fixure†, fiks′ūr, *n.* Position; firmness.

Flabbiness, flab′bi-nes, *n.* State or quality of being *flabby*; flaccidity.

Flabby, flab′bi, *a.* Soft; yielding to the touch; easily shaking; hanging loose by its own weight. [from *flap*.]

Flaccid, flak′sid, *a.* Flabby; soft and weak; hanging down by its own weight; yielding to pressure. [L. *flaccidus*—*flaccus*, flabby.]

Flaccidity, flak-sid′i-ti, *n.* State or quality of being *flaccid*; want of firmness or stiffness.

Flag, flag, *vi.* To slacken; to be loose and yielding; to grow faint, languid, weak, or dejected.—*vt.* To let fall into feebleness; to suffer to droop; to enervate. *ppr.* flagging, *pret. & pp.* flagged. [G. *flacken*, to become slow.]

Flag, flag, *n.* A broad *flat stone* used for paving, or a pavement of flat stones.—*vt.* To lay *with* broad *flat stones*. *ppr.* flagging, *pret. & pp.* flagged. [Icel. *flaki*, anything level or flat and broad.]

Flag, flag, *n.* An aquatic plant with a bladed leaf. [Fr. *lis*.]

Flag, flag, *n.* That which *floats in the air*; an ensign or colour; a cloth on which are usually painted or wrought certain figures, and borne on a staff. [G. *flagge*, a naval banner—Sax. *fleogan*, to fly.]

Flagellation, fla-jel-lā′shon, *n.* A *beating or whipping*; a flogging; the discipline of the scourge. [Low L. *flagellatio*—L. *flagellum*, a whip.]

Flageolet, fla′jel-et, *n.* A cross *flute*; a small wind-instrument of music, with a mouth-piece. It has a sharp but pleasant sound. [Fr.]

Flagginess, flag′i-nes, *n.* State or quality of being *flaggy*; want of tension.

Flagging, flag′ing, *p.n.* Act of *laying with flag-stones*; a pavement or sidewalk of flag-stones.

Flagging, flag′ing, *p.a.* Growing weak; drooping.

Flaggy, flag′i, *a.* Weak; limber; abounding with the plant called flag.

Flagitious, fla-ji′shi-us, *a.* Shameful; deeply criminal; atrocious; guilty of enormous crimes; corrupt; abandoned. [L. *flagitiosus*—*flagito*, to demand hotly.]

Flagitiously, fla-ji′shi-us-li, *adv.* With extreme wickedness.

Flagitiousness, fla-ji′shi-us-nes, *n.* State or quality of being *flagitious*.

Flagon, fla′gon, *n.* A vessel with a narrow mouth, used for *holding* and conveying liquors. [Fr. *flacon*—L. *lagena*.]

Flagrancy, flā′gran-si, *n.* Notoriousness; excess; enormity.

Flagrant, flā′grant, *a.* Ardent; flaming in notice; glaring; notorious; enormous. [L. *flagrans*—*flagro*, to flame.]

Flagrantly, flā′grant-li, *adv.* In a flagrant manner; glaringly; notoriously.

Flail, flāl, *n.* A wooden instrument for thrashing or beating grain from the ear by hand. [G. *flegel*.]

Flake, flāk, *n.* A layer of *snowy* particles; a small scale-like collection of snow, as it falls from the clouds or from the air; a collection of little scaly particles of fire, separated and flying off; any scaly matter in layers; any mass cleaving off in scales.—*vt.* To form *into flakes*.—*vi.* To break or separate in layers; to peel or scale off. *ppr.* flaking, *pret. & pp.* flaked. [Sax. *flacea*, flakes of snow.]

Flakiness, flāk′i-nes, *n.* The state of being *flaky*.

Flaky, flāk′i, *a.* Consisting of *flakes* or locks; lying in flakes; consisting of layers, or cleaving off in layers.

Flambeau, flam′bō, *n.* A *li* āt made of thick wicks covered with wax. [Fr. —L. *flamma*, a blaze.]

Flame, flām, *n.* Light emitted from *fire*; a *blaze*; burning vapour; fire in general; heat of passion; ardour of temper or imagination; brightness of fancy; vigour of thought; ardent love; rage; one beloved.—*vi.* To *blaze*; to burn in vapour or in a current; to shine like burning gas; to break out in violence of passion; to rage. *ppr.* flaming, *pret. & pp.* flamed. [Fr. *flamme*—L. *flamma* for *fagma*—Sans. *bhrāj*, to shine.]

Flaming, flām′ing, *p.a.* Bright; red; violent.—*p.n.* A *bursting out in a flame*.

Flamingly, flām′ing-li, *adv.* Most brightly; with great show or vehemence.

Flange, flanj, *n.* A projecting rim or rib on any substance, such as the rims by which cast-iron pipes are connected together; or a raised edge on the rim of a wheel, and also on the rails of a certain kind of railway. [Old Fr. *flanchere*, a side piece.]

Flanged, flanjd, *p.a.* Having a flange.

Flank, flangk, *n.* One of the two parts of the body which enable it to *bend*; the part of the side of an animal, between the ribs and the hip; the side of an army; the extreme right or left; that part of a bastion which reaches from the curtain to the face; the side of any building.—*vt.* To attack, as the side or *flank* of an army or body of troops; to place, as troops, so as to attack the flank; to secure on the side; to turn, as the flank; to pass round the side of.—*vi.* To border; to touch; to be posted on the side. (G. *flanken*, to bend.]

Flannel, flan′nel, *n.* A soft, nappy, woollen cloth, of loose texture. [Fr. *flanelle*—L. *lana*, wool.]

Flannelled, flan′neld, *p.a.* Covered or wrapped in flannel.

Flap, flap, *n.* Anything broad and limber that hangs loose or is easily moved; the motion or sound of anything broad and loose, or a stroke with it; the loose part of a coat behind from the hip downward.—*vt.* To beat *with a flap*; to move, as something broad; to let fall, as the brim of a hat.—*vi.* To move and sound, as wings; to fall, as the brim of a hat or other broad thing. *ppr.* flapping, *pret. & pp.* flapped. [D.]

Flap-dragon, flap′dra-gon, *n.* A game in which the players catch raisins out of burning brandy.—*vt.†* To swallow whole, like a flap-dragon.

Flap-eared, flap′ērd, *a.* Having broad loose ears.

Flap-jack, flap′jak, *n.* A sort of broad pancake; also, an apple-puff.

Flapper, flap′ėr, *n.* He or that which *flaps*.

Flapping, flap′ing, *p.a.* Striking; beating.

Flare, flār, *vi.* To burn with an unsteady light; to flutter with splendid show; to glitter with transient lustre; to be exposed to too much light.—*n.* An unsteady, broad, offensive light. *ppr.* flaring, *pret. & pp.* flared. [probably a corruption of *glare*—which see.]

Flaring, flār′ing, *p.a.* Burning with a wavering light; glittering; showy.

Flaringly, flār′ing-li, *adv.* In a *flaring* manner.

Flash, flash, *n.* A sudden burst of *flame*; a sudden burst, as of wit; a short transient state.—*a.* Vile; low; vulgar.—*vi.* To break forth, as a sudden flood of *flame and light*; to burst or break forth with a flood of flame and light; to break out, as a sudden expression of wit, merriment, or bright thought. *vt.* To strike or to throw *like a burst of light*. (Sans. *ush*, to burn, to shine, second pret. *uvash*.]

Flashily, flash′i-li, *adv.* With empty show; with a sudden glare.

Flashing, flash′ing, *p.a.* Bursting forth, as a *flood of* flame and *light*, or as

FLASHY 143 FLIGHTILY

wit, mirth, or joy.—*p.a.* Act of blazing; a sudden burst of light, &c.
Flashy, flash'i, *a.* Dazzling for a moment, but not solid; showy but empty; insipid.
Flask, flask, *n.* A kind of bottle; a vessel for powder. [Dan. *flaske*.]
Flat, flat, *a.* Having an even extended surface; level; lying the whole length on the ground; not erect; totally fallen; tasteless; dead; without relief or prominence; low; spiritless; absolute; downright, as a refusal; not sharp or acute, as a sound.—*n.* A level or extended plain; a level ground lying at a small depth under the surface of water; a shallow; the broad side of a blade; depression of thought or language; a surface without relief or prominences; a flat note in music, and also the sign ♭ to express it. [Sw.—Gr. *platus*, flat—Heb. *palat*, to be smooth.]
Flatlong, flat'long, *a.* With the flat side downward.
Flatly, flat'li, *adv.* Horizontally; evenly; without spirit; positively.
Flatness, flat'nes, *n.* State or quality of being flat.
Flatten, flat'n, *vt.* To make or lay flat; to reduce to an equal or even surface; to level; to make vapid; to depress; to render less acute or sharp, as a sound. *vi.* To grow or become flat; to become stale, vapid, or tasteless; to become dull or spiritless; to become as a sound less sharp or acute.
Flatter, flat'ér, *vt.* To inflate with exaggerated praises; to deceive with fair words; to praise falsely; to gratify by praise; to please a person by favourable notice; to compliment; to raise false hopes in. [Fr.—L. *flo, flatum*, to blow.]
Flatterer, flat'tér-ér, *n.* One who flatters; a fawner; a wheedler.
Flattering, flat'tér-ing, *p.a.* Pleasing; favourable; encouraging hope.
Flatteringly, flat'tér-ing-li, *adv.* In a flattering manner.
Flattery, flat'tér-i, *n.* False praise; obsequiousness; sycophancy; improper commendation. [Fr. *flatterie*.]
Flattish, flat'ish, *a.* Somewhat flat.
Flatulence, Flatulency, flat'ū-lens, flat'ū-len-si, *n.* Windiness in the stomach; air generated in a weak stomach and intestines; emptiness.
Flatulent, flat'ū-lent, *a.* Windy; affected with air in the stomach and intestines; generating wind; empty; puffy. [Low L. *flatulentus*—L. *flo, flatum*, to blow.]
Flatulently, flat'ū-lent-li, *adv.* In a flatulent manner.
Flatwise, flat'wīs, *a.* or *adv.* With the flat side downward or next to another object; not edgewise. [*flat* and *wise*.]
Flaunt, flant, *vi.* To flutter; to display oneself ostentatiously or saucily.—*n.* Anything displayed for show. [G. *flattern*, to flirt.]
Flaunting, flant'ing, *p.a.* Making an ostentatious display.
Flauntingly, flant'ing-li, *adv.* In a flaunting way.
Flavour, flā'vér, *n.* Odour; taste; the quality of a substance which affects the smell or taste in any manner.—*vt.* To give flavour to. [Fr. *flaireur*, to smell.]
Flavoured, flā'vérd, *p.a.* Having flavour.
Flavourless, flā'vér-les, *a.* Without flavour; tasteless.
Flaw, fla, *n.* A piece rent off; a crack; a defect made by breaking or splitting; a fault; a speck; a sudden and short burst of wind; a tumult; commotion. *vt.* To break. [W. *flaw*, a splinter.]
Flawy, fla'i, *a.* Full of flaws or cracks; broken; defective; faulty.
Flax, flaks, *n.* That which is fit for weaving; a plant, the fibres of which are formed into threads; the fibres of the plant prepared, and spun into threads for cloth. [Sax. *fleax*—D. *flechten*, to plait—Sans. *prich*, to join together.]
Flax-dresser, flaks'dres-ér, *n.* One who combs and prepares flax for the spinner.
Flaxen, flaks'n, *a.* Made of flax; of the colour of flax; fair, long, and flowing.
Flax-wench, flaks'wensh, *n.* A prostitute.
Flaxy, flaks'i, *a.* Like flax; flaxen.
Flay, flā, *vt.* To take off the skin or rind of; to skin; to strip off. [Sax. *flean*.]
Flea, flē, *n.* A well-known insect, that escapes by leaping with great agility, and whose bite is very troublesome. [Sax.—*fleon*, to flee.]
Flea-bite, flē'bīt, *n.* The bite of a flea, or the red spot caused by the bite; a trifling wound or pain.
Fleam, flēm, *n.* A sharp instrument used for opening the veins of animals for letting blood. [D. *vlym*, a lancet.]
Flecked, flekt, *p.a.* Spotted; variegated with divers colours. [G. *fleck*, a spot.]
Flection, flek'shon, *n.* See FLEXION.
Fledge, flej, *a.* Furnished with feathers or wings; able to fly.—*vt.* To supply with the feathers necessary for flight; to furnish with any soft covering. *ppr.* fledging, *pret.* & *pp.* fledged. [G. *flügen*, to furnish with wings.]
Fledgeling, flej'ling, *n.* A young bird just fledged.
Flee, flē, *vi.* To run away; to run with rapidity, as from danger; to hasten from expected evil; to hasten away. *vt.* To shun; to run from; to keep at a distance from. *ppr.* fleeing, *pret.* & *pp.* fled. [Sax. *fleon*.]
Fleece, flēs, *n.* The coat of wool shorn from a sheep at one time.—*vt.* To shear off, as a growth of wool; to strip of money or property; to take from, by severe exactions; to spread over, as with wool; to make white. *ppr.* fleecing, *pret.* & *pp.* fleeced. [Sax. *flys*—L. *vellus*—Syr. *gasa*, to shear, to cut off.]
Fleeced, flēst, *p.a.* Furnished with a fleece.
Fleecer, flēs'ér, *n.* One who strips or takes by heartless exactions.
Fleecy, flēs'i, *a.* Resembling wool or a fleece; covered with wool; woolly; soft; complicated.
Fleer, flēr, *vi.* To leer; to grin with an air of civility; to mock; to make a wry face in contempt.—*n.* A leer; derision or mockery, expressed by words or looks. [formed from *leer*.]
Fleering, flēr'ing, *p.a.* Deriding; counterfeiting an air of civility.
Fleet, flēt, *n.* That which floats; a navy or squadron of ships; a number of ships in company. [Sax. *fliet*, a ship—*fleotan*, to float.]
Fleet, flēt, *a.* Swift of pace; moving with lightness and celerity; moving with velocity, as the wind.—*vt.* To fly swiftly; to flit as a light substance; to be in a transient state.—*vt.* To cause to pass lightly. [Icel. *fliotr*, quick.]
Fleeting, flēt'ing, *p.a.* Not durable; transient; momentary.
Fleetly, flēt'li, *adv.* Rapidly; swiftly.
Fleetness, flēt'nes, *n.* Swiftness; rapidity; speed; quickness.
Flesh, flesh, *n.* The muscular part of an animal; animal food, in distinction from vegetable; the body of beasts and birds used as food; the soft, pulpy substance of fruit; that part of a root, fruit, &c., which is fit to be eaten; the body, as distinguished from the soul; animal nature; mankind; human nature; corporeal appetites; a corrupt nature; kindred; family.—*vt.* To feed with flesh, as an incitement; to initiate. [Sax. *flæsc*.]
Flesh-brush, flesh'brush, *n.* A brush for exciting action in the skin by friction.
Flesh-coloured, flesh'kul-érd, *a.* Being of the colour of flesh.
Flesh-fly, flesh'fli, *n.* A fly that feeds on flesh, and deposits her eggs in it.
Flesh-hook, flesh'hōk, *n.* A hook to draw flesh from a pot.
Fleshiness, flesh'i-nes, *n.* Abundance of flesh or fat; plumpness; corpulence; grossness.
Fleshless, flesh'les, *a.* Destitute of flesh.
Fleshliness, flesh'li-nes, *n.* Carnal passions and appetites.
Fleshly, flesh'li, *a.* Carnal; worldly; lascivious; animal; human; not celestial.
Fleshment, flesh'ment, *n.* The act of fleshing.
Flesh-monger, flesh'mung-gér, *n.* One who deals in flesh; a pander.
Flesh-tints, flesh'tints, *n. pl.* The colours which best represent the human body in painting.
Flesh-wound, flesh'wönd, *n.* A wound which affects the flesh only.
Fleshy, flesh'i, *a.* Muscular; fat; gross; full of pulp; plump, as fruit.
Flewed, flūd, *a.* Having large chaps.
Flexibility, fleks-i-bil'i-ti, *n.* Flexibleness; pliancy; ductility of mind; readiness to comply; facility. [Fr. *flexibilité*.]
Flexible, fleks'i-bl, *a.* That may be bent; pliant; supple; capable of yielding to entreaties, arguments, or other moral force; easily managed or turned; not firm; obsequious; wavering. [Fr.—L. *flecto, flexum*, to bend.]
Flexibleness, fleks'i-bl-nes, *n.* Quality of being flexible; flexibility.
Flexibly, fleks'i-bli, *adv.* In a flexible manner.
Flexion, flek'shon, *n.* Act of bending; a bend; a flexure; a part bent; a fold. [L. *flexio—flecto, flexum*, to bend.]
Flexor, fleks'ér, *n.* The muscle that bends.
Flexuous, fleks'ū-us, *a.* Winding; wavering; not steady. [L. *flexuosus*.]
Flexure, fleks'ūr, *n.* A bending; the form of bending; act of bending; the part bent; a joint; the bending of the body; obsequious cringe. [L. *flexura*.]
Flicker, flik'ér, *vi.* To flutter; to waver or twinkle, as an unsteady flame. [Sax. *flicorian*, to move the wings.]
Flickering, flik'ér-ing, *p.a.* Wavering; having a fluttering motion.
Flier, flī'ér, *n.* One who flies or flees; a part of a machine which, by moving rapidly, equalises and regulates the motion of the whole.
Flight, flīt, *n.* Act of fleeing or flying; act of running away, to escape danger; a passing through the air by the help of wings; manner of flying; a flock of birds or a number of beings flying in company; a volley, as of arrows; the birds produced in the same season; space passed by flying; a soaring; lofty elevation, as of fancy; wandering; extravagant sally; a series of steps or stairs. [Sax. *fliht—fleogan*, to flee.]
Flightily, flīt'i-li, *adv.* In a flighty manner.

ch, *chain*; j, *job*; g, *go*; ng, *sing*; ᴛʜ, *then*; th, *thin*; w, *wig*; wh, *whig*; zh, *azure*; † obsolete.

Flightiness, flīt'i-nes, n. Levity; giddiness; wildness; volatility.
Flighty, flīt'i, a. *Flestinḡt; full of flights;* wild; unsettled; disordered in mind; somewhat delirious.
Flimsily, flim'zi-li, adv. *In a flimsy manner.*
Flimsiness, flim'zi-nes, n. Thin, weak texture; weakness; want of solidity.
Flimsy, flim'zi, a. *Filmy;* thin; slight; weak; without force; spiritless; shallow. [from the root of *flm.*]
Flinch, flinsh, vi. *To shrink;* to withdraw; to fail of proceeding, or of performing anything; to fail. [Old G. *wenkjan*, to shrink.]
Flincher, flinsh'ér, n. *One who flinches.*
Flinching flinsh'ing, p.n. *A shrinking* or drawing back under pain or difficulty.
Fling, fling, vt. *To cause to fly* from the hand; to hurl; to cast with violence; to scatter; to drive by violence; to throw to the ground; to baffle.—vi. *To fly* into violent and irregular motions; to cast in the teeth; to sneer; to rush away angrily. *ppr.* flinging, *pret. & pp.* flung.—n. A throw; a cast from the hand; a sneer; a contemptuous remark. [Sax. *fligan*, to cause to fly.]
Flint, flint, n. *A very hard silicious stone,* which strikes fire with steel; a piece of this stone formerly used in firearms, to strike fire; anything proverbially hard. [Sax.]
Flintiness, flint'i-nes. n. *Quality of being flinty* or hard.
Flinty, flint'i, a. *Consisting of, composed of, or like flint;* full of flint stones; very hard; cruel; inexorable.
Flippancy, flip'an-si, n. *Quality of being flippant;* fluency of speech; heedless pertness.
Flippant, flip'ant, a. *Nimble;* of smooth, fluent, and rapid speech; talkative; pert; petulant. [Sax. *Aleapan*, to jump.]
Flippantly, flip'ant-li, adv. *In a flippant manner.*
Flirt, flért, vt. *To toss or throw;* to move suddenly.—vi. To throw out bantering or sarcastic words; to jeer; to act with giddiness, or from a desire to attract notice; to coquet with men; to be unsteady or fluttering.—n. A sudden jerk; a young girl who acts with giddiness, or plays at courtship; a coquette.—a.† Pert; wanton. [probably formed from *fleer.*]
Flirtation, flért-ā'shon, n. *A quick, sprightly motion;* playing at courtship; coquetry.
Flirt-gill†, flért'jil, n. *A woman of light behaviour.*
Flirting, flért'ing, p.a. *Giddy;* coquettish.
Flit, flit, vi. *To move with celerity through the air;* to flutter; to pass rapidly, as a light substance, from one place to another; to be unstable; to be easily or often moved. *ppr.* flitting, *pret. & pp.* flitted. [Dan. *flytte,* to move, to remove.]
Flitch, flich, n. *The side of a hog salted and cured.* [Sax. *flicce.*]
Flitting, flit'ing, p.a. *Flying rapidly;* moving by starts; fluttering.—p.n. *A flying with celerity;* a fluttering.
Float, flōt, n. *That which swims;* a raft; anything that floats on the surface of a fluid, as the water-gauge of a steam-engine; a wave†. [Sax. *fiota.*]—vi. *To be borne on the surface of a fluid;* to swim; to be buoyed up; not to be aground; to move or be conveyed on water; to be buoyed up and moved in a fluid, as in air; to move with a light, irregular course.—vt. To cause to be conveyed on water; to flood; to cover with water. [Sax. *flcotan*—Sans. *plu*, to swim.]
Floatable, flōt'a-bl, a. *That may be floated.*
Floatage, flōt'aj, n. *Anything that floats on the water.*
Float-board, flōt'bōrd, n. *A board* of an under-shot water-wheel, on which the water strikes.
Floating, flōt'ing, p.a. Circulating; passing; not fixed.—p.n. *Act of swimming* on the surface of water; the watering of meadow-lands.
Flock, flok, n. *A lock or flock of wool;* a kind of woolly paper. [Icel. *floki.*]
Flock, flok, n. *A company,* as of sheep, goats, birds, &c.; a Christian congregation in relation to their pastor. vi. To gather in *companies* or crowds; to crowd together; to move in crowds. [Sax. *flocc,* a company.]
Flocky, flok'i, a. *Abounding with flocks* or little tufts, like wool.
Flog, flog, vt. *To whip;* to chastise with repeated blows. *ppr.* flogging, *pret. & pp.* flogged. [L. *flagello*, to whip.]
Flogging, flog'ing, p.n. *A whipping* for punishment.
Flood, flud, n. *A great flow of water;* a body of moving water; a deluge; the general deluge in the days of Noah; a river; the flowing of the tide; a great quantity; abundance; a great body or stream of any fluid substance; the flowing in of the tide.—vt. *To overflow;* to deluge; to overwhelm. [Sax. *flod.*]
Flood-gate, flud'gāt, n. *A gate* to be opened for letting water *flow* through an opening or passage; an avenue for a flood or great body.
Flood-mark, flud'mårk, n. *The mark* or line to which the *tide* rises; highwater mark.
Floor, flōr, n. *A pavement;* that part of a building or room on which we walk; a platform of boards laid on timbers; a story in a building; a flat, hard surface, made of loam, lime, &c., used in some kinds of business, as in malting; the bottom of a vessel on each side of the keelson.—vt. *To lay a floor upon;* to furnish with a floor; to strike down; to put down by some decisive argument, retort, &c. [Sax. *flór.*]
Floored, flōrd, p.a. *Struck down;* vanquished.
Flooring, flōr'ing, p.n. *A pavement;* the bottom of a room or building; materials for floors; act of laying a floor.
Flora, flō'ra, n. *The goddess of flowers,* a catalogue of flowers or plants; the plants of a particular country. [L. from *flos, floris,* a flower—Sans. *phull,* to blossom.]
Floral, flō'ral, a. *Pertaining to or containing the flower;* immediately attending the flower. [L. *floralis.*]
Florescence, flō-res'ens, n. *A flowering;* the season when plants expand their flowers. [from L. *florescens—flos,* a flower.]
Floret, flō'ret, n. *A floweret;* the partial or separate little flower of an aggregate flower. [Fr. *fleurette.*]
Floricultural, flō-ri-kul'tūr-al, a. *Relating to floriculture.*
Floriculture, flō'ri-kul-tūr, n. *The culture or cultivation of flowers* or flowering plants. [L. *flos, floris,* and *cultūra*—*colo*, to till.]
Floricu'turist, flō'ri-kul-tūr-ist, n. *One skilled in the cultivation of flowers.*
Florid, flo'rid, a. *Flowery;* bright in colour; flushed with red; of a lively red colour; embellished with flowers of rhetoric; enriched with lively figures; highly decorated. [L. *floridus.*]
Floridly, flo'rid-li, adv. *In a showy and imposing way.*
Floridness, flo'rid-nes, n. *Quality of being florid;* freshness of complexion; ambitious elegance.
Florin, flo'rin, n. *A coin,* originally made at *Florence,* in value from 1s. to 2s. 4d.; a new British silver coin, value 2s. [Fr.]
Florist, flo'rist, n. *A cultivator of flowers;* one who writes an account of plants. [Fr. *fleuriste.*]
Floss, flos, n. *A downy or silky substance* in certain plants; untwisted filaments of the finest silk, used in embroidery on satin, &c. [Icel. *flos,* the nap of cloth.]
Flotation, flōt-ā'shon, n. *Act of floating;* the doctrine of floating bodies. [from *float.*]
Flotilla, flō-til'la, n. *A little fleet,* or fleet of small vessels. [Sp. from *flota,* a fleet.]
Flounce, flouns, vi. *To plunge;* to flounder; to spring, turn, or twist with sudden effort or violence; to struggle, as a horse in mire.—vt. *To deck or trim* with a flounce or flounces, as a dress. *ppr.* flouncing, *pret. & pp.* flounced. n. A sudden jerking motion of the body; a frill or ruffle sewed to the skirt of a dress, with the lower border loose, spreading, and *waving.* [Sw. *flunsa.*]
Flounder, floun'dér, n. *A flat-fish found* in the sea, and near the mouths of rivers, generally swimming near the *bottom.* [Dan. *flynder*—L. *fundus,* the bottom.]
Flounder, floun'dér, vi. *To fling the limbs and body,* as in making efforts to move; to struggle, as a horse in mire; to roll, toss, and tumble. [allied to *flounce.*]
Flour, flour, n. *The flower* or finest part of wheat-corn; meal.—vt. *To convert into flour;* to sprinkle with flour. [Fr. *fleur de farine*—L. *flos, floris,* a flower.]
Flourish, flu'rish, vi. *To begin to blossom or flower;* to come out in blossom; to prosper; to grow in grace and in goodness; to use florid language; to be copious and flowery; to make ornamental strokes in writing; to move or play in bold and irregular figures; to boast.—vt. *To adorn with flowers;* to cause to move in circles or vibrations; to brandish, as a sword; to set off; to grace; to mark; to set with a flourish or irregular stroke.—n. Beauty; showy splendour; ambitious copiousness; parade of words and figures; show; fanciful strokes of the pen or graver; the decorative notes which a singer or musical performer adds to a passage for the sake of effect. [Fr. *fleurir*, *ppr.* *fleurissant*—L. *flos,* a flower.]
Flourishing, flu'rish-ing, p.a. *Prosperous;* increasing.
Floury, flour'i, a. *Resembling flour.*
Flout, flout, vt. *To act proudly towards;* to mock or insult.—vi. To practise mocking; to sneer; to behave with contempt (often with *at*).—n. A mock; an insult. [Goth. *flautan,* to act wrongly, to boast.]
Flow, flō, vi. *To move or run,* as water from its spring or source; to become liquid; to issue; to abound; to be full; to glide along smoothly; to be smooth, as composition or utterance; to hang loose and waving; to rise, as the tide; to circulate, as blood; to move in a

Fāte, får, fat, fall; mē, met, her; pine, pin; nōte, not, move; tūbe, tub, bull; oil, pound.

stream, as air.—*vt.* To *flow* over; to cover with water; to inundate.—*n.* A *moving along, as of water*; a stream of water or other fluid; the rise of water; fulness; copiousness; free expression of generous feelings. [Sax. *flowan*—Sans. *plu*, to swim, to fly.]

Flower, flou'ér, *n. Bloom;* a blossom or flower is the flower-bud of a plant, when the petals are expanded; the early part of life; the prime; youth; the finest part; the essence; he or that which is most distinguished for anything valuable; an ornamental expression.—*vi.* To *blossom; to bloom;* to be in the prime and spring of life; to flourish; to be youthful, fresh, and vigorous.—*vt.* To *embellish with figures of flowers;* to cause to blossom. [Fr. *fleur*—L. *flos, floris*—Sans. *phull,* to expand, to flower.]

Floweret, flou'ér-et, *n. A small flower;* a floret. [Fr. *fleurette,* dimin. of *fleur.*]

Flowerinees, flou'ér-i-nes, *n.* State of being *flowery; floridness* of speech; abundance of figures.

Flowering, flou'ér-ing, *p.a. Blossoming; blooming.*—*p.n. Act of blossoming;* the season when plants blossom; act of adorning with flowers.

Flowery, flou'ér-i, *a. Full of flowers;* adorned with artificial flowers; highly embellished with figurative language.

Flowing, flō'ing, *p.a.* Abounding; fluent or smooth, as style.—*p.n. Act of moving along, as a fluid;* an issuing; rise or great abundance of water.

Flowingly, flō'ing-li, *adv. With volubility;* with abundance.

Flown, flōn, *p.a.* Flushed; inflated.

Fluctuate, fluk'tū-āt, *vi. To wave;* to roll hither and thither; to waver; to hesitate; to be in an unsettled state; to experience sudden vicissitudes. *ppr.* fluctuating, *pret. & pp.* fluctuated. [L. *fluctuo, fluctuatus—fluo,* to flow—Sans. *plu,* to swim.]

Fluctuating, fluk'tū-āt-ing, *p.a.* Unsteady; wavering; changeable.

Fluctuation, fluk-tū-ā'shon, *n. A motion like that of waves;* a wavering; a rising and falling suddenly. [L. *fluctuatio.*]

Flue, flō, *n. A passage for the escape of smoke in a chimney;* a pipe for conveying heat to water in certain kinds of steam-boilers; a passage in a wall for conducting heat from one part of a building to the other. [Icel. *flug,* escape.]

Flue, flō, *n. Light down,* such as rises from beds, cotton, &c.; soft down, fur, or hair. [G. *flaum,* allied to *fliegen,* to fly.]

Fluency, flō'en-si, *n. Quality of being fluent;* freedom from harshness; readiness of utterance; volubility. [Low L. *fluentia*—L. *fluo,* to flow.]

Fluent, flō'ent, *a. Flowing;* ready in the use of words; copious; having words at command, and uttering them with facility and smoothness. [L. *fluens.*]

Fluently, flō'ent-li, *adv. With ready flow;* volubly.

Fluid, flō'id, *a. Flowing;* that may flow; liquid, as water, spirit, air.—*n. That which flows;* a liquid; opposed to solid. [Fr. *fluide*—L. *fluidus.*]

Fluidity, flō-id'i-ti, *n. Quality or state of being fluid;* that quality of bodies which renders them impressible to the slightest force; particles; a liquid state; opposed to solidity. [Fr. *fluidité*—L. *fluo,* to flow.]

Fluke, flōk, *n.* That part of an anchor which fastens in the ground. [G. *flunk,* the fluke of an anchor.]

Flummery, flum'mé-ri, *n.* A sort of jelly made of *flour or meal;* pap; anything insipid or nothing to the purpose; flattery. [W. *llymry.*]

Fluor, flō'or, *n.* A beautiful mineral, often crystallized, and usually called *fluor-spar.* [Low L.]

Fluoric, flō-or'ik, *a. Pertaining to fluor;* obtained from fluor.

Flurry, flu'ri, *n.* A sudden blast or gust, or a light temporary breeze; commotion; bustle; hurry.—*vt.* To put in agitation; to excite or alarm. *ppr.* flurrying, *pret. & pp.* flurried. [probably a corruption of *flutter.*]

Flush, flush, *vi. To flow* and spread suddenly; to appear suddenly, as redness or a blush; to become suddenly red; to glow.—*vt.* To cause the blood to *rush* suddenly into the *face of;* to elevate; to excite the spirits of; to animate with joy.—*a. Flowing;* abounding; fresh; full of vigour; glowing; bright; level in respect to surface.—*n. A sudden flow* of blood to the face; the redness of face which proceeds from such an afflux of blood; sudden excitement; bloom; growth. *adv.* In a manner so as to be even or level with. [G. *fliessen,* to flow.]

Flushed, flusht, *p.a.* Overspread with a red colour, as the face; animated.

Flushing, flush'ing, *p.n. A flowing* of blood into the face; a glow of red in the face.

Fluster, flus'tér, *vt.* To make hot and rosy with drink; to make half drunk. *vi.* To be in a heat or bustle.—*n.* Heat; glow from drinking. [from *flush.*]

Fluster, flus'tér, *vt. To hurry on;* to agitate; to confuse.—*vi. To hurry;* to be in a heat or bustle; to be agitated. *n. Precipitancy;* agitation; confusion; disorder. [Icel. *flaustra.*]

Flute, flōt, *n.* A small wind-instrument with holes and keys in the side; a channel cut along the shaft of a column; a similar channel in the muslin of a lady's ruffle.—*vi. To play on a flute.*—*vt.* To play or sing in a clear soft note; to form *flutes* or channels in, as in a column; to form, as corresponding channels in the muslin of a lady's ruffle. *ppr.* fluting, *pret. & pp.* fluted. [Fr. *flûte*—L. *flo, flatum,* to blow.]

Fluted, flōt'ed, *p.a.* Channelled; furrowed.

Fluting, flōt'ing, *p.n.* A channel or furrow in a column, or in the muslin of a lady's ruffle; fluted work.

Flutist, flōt'ist, *n. A performer on the flute.*

Flutter, flut'ér, *vi.* To *move* or *flap* the wings rapidly, without flying; to hover; to fluctuate; to be in uncertainty. *vt.* To hurry the mind of; to disorder; to throw into confusion.—*n. Vibration;* quick and irregular motion; agitation of the mind; disorder. [D. *flodderen,* to flap.]

Fluttering, flut'tér-ing, *p.a.* Hovering; agitating.—*p.n.* Act of *flipping* the wings without flight; a wavering; agitation.

Fluty, flōt'i, *a.* Soft and clear in tone, like a *flute.*

Fluvial, flō'vi-al, *a. Belonging to rivers;* growing or living in streams or ponds. [Fr.—L. *fluo,* to flow.]

Fluviatile, flō'vi-a-til, *a. Belonging to rivers;* existing in rivers. [Fr.]

Flux, fluks, *n. Act of flowing;* the motion or passing of a fluid; the passing of anything in continued succession; any flow of matter; dysentery; the flow of the tide, opposed to reflux; any mixture used to promote the fusion of metals or minerals; fusion; a liquid state from the operation of heat.—*vt. To bring into a flowing* or liquid state; to melt; to fuse; to make fluid. [Fr.—L. *fluo, fluxum,* to flow.]

Fluxion, fluk'shon, *n. Act of flowing;* the matter that flows; an infinitely small quantity; a differential quantity. [L. *fluxio.*]

Fluxional, Fluxionary, fluk'shon-al, fluk'shon-a-ri, *a. Pertaining to mathematical fluxions;* variable.

Fly, flī, *vi. To move* or sail *through air by the aid of wings,* as a bird; to pass or move in air by the force of wind or other impulse; to move rapidly, in any manner; to pass away; to pass rapidly, as time; to break suddenly; to flee; to run away; to vibrate or play, as a flag in the wind.—*vt. To flee from;* to shun; to cause to float in the air. *ppr.* flying, *pret.* flew, *pp.* flown.—*n. An insect that flies;* a winged insect common in houses; a contrivance which, by revolving, serves to equalize and regulate the motion of machines; a light carriage. [Sax. *fleógan*—Sans. *plu,* to fly.]

Fly-blown, flī'blōn, *p.a.* Tainted with maggots.

Flying, flī'ing, *p.a. Floating;* waving; light, and suited for prompt motion. *p.n. Act of moving in the air with wings;* flight.

Flying-fish, flī'ing-fish, *n.* A species of *fish* of the pike tribe, which has the power of *sustaining itself in the air* for a time by means of its long pectoral fins.

Fly-leaf, flī'lēf, *n.* A *leaf* of blank paper at the beginning and end of a book.

Fly-slow, flī'slō, *a.* Moving as slowly as a fly sometimes does.

Fly-wheel, flī'wēl, *n.* A *wheel* in machinery that equalizes its movements.

Foal, fōl, *n. A young animal;* the offspring or young of a mare, she-ass, &c.; a colt or filly.—*vt. To bring forth,* as a *colt* or *filly.*—*vi. To bring forth young,* as a mare and certain other beasts. [Sax. *fole*—L. *pullus,* a young animal.]

Foam, fōm, *n. Froth; spume.*—*vi. To froth;* to gather foam; to be in a rage; to fume.—*vt. To cause to froth or give out foam;* to throw out with rage or violence. (With *out.*) [Sax. *fam.*]

Foaming, fōm'ing, *p.a.* Gathering froth; mantling.

Foamy, fōm'i, *a. Covered with foam;* frothy.

Fob, fob, *n. A little pocket* for a watch; a tap or slight blow. [Teut. *fuppe.*]

Focal, fō'kal, *a. Belonging to a focus.* [from L. *focus.*]

Focus, fō'kus, *n.* Focuses or Foci, *pl.* A point in which rays of light meet and produce *great heat,* after being reflected or refracted; a central point; point of concentration. [L.—*foveo,* to warm.]

Fodder, fod'dér, *n. Food* or dry food for cattle, horses, and sheep, as hay, straw, and other kinds of vegetables.—*vt. To feed* with dry food or cut grass, &c.; to furnish with hay, straw, oats, &c. [Sax.—*fedan,* to feed.]

Foe, fō, *n. One hating and hated;* one *inspiring fear and hate;* an enemy; an opposing army or nation at war; an antagonist; one who opposes anything in principle; an ill-wisher. [Sax. *fah*—*fian,* to hate.]

Foeman, fō'man, *n. An enemy* in war.

Fog, fog, n. A dense *watery* vapour near the surface of the land or water; a cloud of dust or smoke.—*vt.* To envelop, as with a fog. [Sax. *fuht*, moist.]

Fog, fog, n. *Long dry grass;* after-grass; long grass that remains in pastures till winter. [W. *fog.*]

Foggage, fog'āj, n. *Fog;* rank or coarse grass not mowed or eaten down in summer or autumn. [Low L. *fogagium.*]

Fogginess, fog'i-nes, n. *State of being foggy;* a state of the air filled with watery exhalations.

Foggy, fog'i, a. *Filled with fog;* cloudy; misty; producing frequent fogs.

Foh, fō. An exclamation of *abhorrence* or contempt; the same as *poh* and *fy.* [from Sax. *feon*, to hate.]

Foible, foi'bl, n. *A weakness;* a weak point in character; a particular moral weakness; a frailty; a defect; (pl.) moral failings or defects. [Fr. *faible*—L. *debilis*, weak.]

Foil, foil, *vt.* To *befool;* to frustrate; to disappoint; to render vain or nugatory.—n. Defeat; the failure of success when on the point of being secured; miscarriage. [Fr. *affoler—fol*, a fool.]

Foil, foil, n. *A blunt sword*, or one that has a button at the end, covered with leather. [from Old Fr. *refouls*, dulled —*fouler*, to trample on.]

Foil, foil, n. *A leaf* or thin plate of metal; a thin leaf of metal placed under precious stones, to increase their brilliancy; anything of different qualities, which serves to set off a thing to advantage; something resembling a leaf. [Fr. *feuille*—L. *folium*, a leaf.]

Foiler, foil'ér, n. One who *foils.*

Foison†, foi'son, n. Plenty; abundance. [L. *fusio*, a pouring—*fundo*, to pour.]

Foist, foist, *vt.* To introduce *fallaciously;* to insert surreptitiously, wrongfully, or without warrant. (With *in.*) [Fr. *fausser*—L. *fallo, falsum*, to deceive.]

Fold, fōld, n. A pen or *inclosure* for sheep; a place where a flock of sheep is kept, whether in the field or under shelter; a flock of sheep; hence figuratively, the Church.—*vt.* To shut up or confine, as sheep in a fold. [Sax. *fald*—Old G. *waltjan*, to protect.]

Fold, fōld, n. *A doubling;* the doubling of any flexible substance, as cloth; a plait; one part turned or bent and laid on another.—*vt.* To *double;* to lap or lay in plaits; to double and insert one part in another, as a letter; to double, as the arms.—*vi.* To close over another of the same kind. [Sax. *feald.*]

Folder, fōld'ér, n. *One who folds;* an instrument used in folding paper.

Folding, fōld'ing, *p.a.* Doubling; that may close over another.—*p.n.* A *fold;* a doubling; the keeping of sheep in inclosures.

Foliage, fō'li-āj, n. *Leaves in general;* a cluster of leaves, flowers, and branches. [Fr. *feuillage*—L. *folium*, a leaf.]

Foliated, fō'li-āt-ed, *p.a. Leaved;* consisting of plates or thin layers; in the form of a plate; being in laminæ or leaves. [L. *foliatus.*]

Foliation, fō-li-ā'shon, n. *The leafing of plants;* act of beating a metal into a thin plate, leaf, or foil. [Low L. *foliatio.*]

Folio, fō'li-ō, n. *A leaf;* a leaf of a book; a whole sheet folded into two leaves; a book of the largest size, formed by sheets of paper once doubled; a page, or rather both the right and left hand pages of an account book, expressed by the same figure; a certain number of words in conveyances, &c.—a. Pertaining to paper folded but once, or to a volume of the largest size. [Fr.—L. *folium*, a leaf.]

Folk, fōk, n. *The crowd:* people in general, or any part of them without distinction; persons; certain people, discriminated from others. [Sax. *folc* —L. *vulgus*, a crowd.]

Follow, fol'lō, *vt.* To go or come *after;* to walk, ride, or move behind, but in the same direction; to chase; to accompany; to attend, for any purpose; to succeed in order of time; to result from, as an effect from a cause; to pursue with the eye; to copy; to practise; to seek or pursue after; to walk in, as a road; to use; to be occupied with; to adhere to; to honour; to serve; to be led or guided by.—*vi.* To come after another; to accompany; to be posterior in time; to be consequential, as effect to cause; to result, as an inference. [Sax. *fylgean.*]

Follower, fol'lō-ér, n. *One who comes after* another in the same course; an imitator; one who obeys, worships, and honours; one who embraces the same system; a disciple; a dependant; a companion or associate; one of the same faction or party.

Following, fol'lō-ing, *p.a.* Being next after; succeeding; subsequent.—*p.n.* A collecti n of followers.

Folly, fol'li, n. *Foolishness;* want of understanding; a weak or absurd act, not highly criminal; an absurd act which is highly sinful; any conduct contrary to the laws of God or man; sin; depravity of mind. [Fr. *folie*—*fol*, mad.]

Foment, fō-ment', *vt.* To apply *warm lotions to;* to bathe with warm medicated liquors; to abet; to cherish and promote by excitements (in a bad sense). [Low L. *fomento*—L. *foveo*, to warm.]

Fomentation, fō-ment-ā'shon, n. *Act of fomenting;* the lotion applied to a diseased part; instigation; encouragement. [Low L. *fomentatio.*]

Fomenter, fō-ment'ér, n. *One who foments;* one who encourages.

Fond, fond, a. *Foolish;* foolishly tender and loving; doting; much pleased; delighted with; relishing highly.—*vi.† To be fond of.* [Icel. *fana*, to play the fool.]

Fondle, fon'dl, *vt.* To treat *with fondness;* to dote on; to treat with tenderness; to caress. *ppr.* fondling, *pret. & pp.* fondled. [from *fond.*]

Fondly, fond'li, *adv. Foolishly;* weakly.

Fondness, fond'nes, n. Weakness; tender interest, feeling, or passion; love; strong inclination; strong appetite or relish.

Font, font, n. A large basin or stone vessel, in which *water* is contained for baptizing children or other persons in the church. [Fr. *fonte*—L. *fons, fontis*, a fountain.]

Font, font, n. *A casting;* a complete assortment of printing types of one size. [Fr. *fonte*—L. *fundo*, to melt.]

Food, fōd, n. *That which feeds* or is fed upon; aliment; nutriment; meat; whatever supplies nourishment and growth to plants; something that sustains, nourishes, and augments. [Sax. *foda—fedan*, to feed.]

Fool, fōl, n. One destitute of reason or the common powers of understanding; a person who acts absurdly; a simpleton; a silly person; a wicked person; a term of reproach; a buffoon.—*vi.* To *play the fool;* to spend time in idleness, sport, or mirth.—*vt.* To *make foolish;* to *befool;* to disappoint; to defeat; to deceive; to impose on. [Fr. *fol.*]

Foolery, fōl'é-ri, n. *Habitual folly;* attention to trifles; any act of folly or weakness; object of folly; absurdity.

Fool-hardiness, fōl'här-di-nes, n. Courage without sense or judgment.

Fool-hardy, fōl'här-di, a. Daring without judgment; madly rash and adventurous; foolishly bold; venturesome.

Fooling, fōl'ing, *p.n. Act of playing the fool.*

Foolish, fōl'ish, a. Void of understanding; acting without judgment or discretion in particular things; proceeding from or marked with folly; silly; ridiculous; wicked; proceeding from depravity; sinful.

Foolishly, fōl'ish-li, *adv. In a foolish manner;* unwisely; absurdly.

Foolishness, fōl'ish-nes, n. *Folly;* want of understanding; want of wisdom or good judgment; an absurdity.

Foolscap, fōlz'kap, n. *The cap of a fool;* a kind of paper about 17 inches by 14.

Foot, fut, n. Feet, fēt, *pl. The part of the body by which we tread and on which we stand;* the lower extremity of the leg; the lower end of anything; the base; foundation; condition; state; footing; soldiers who march and fight on foot; a measure consisting of twelve lineal inches; a certain number of syllables, constituting part of a verse.—*vi.* To dance; to tread to measure or music; to skip; to walk.—*vt.* To tread; to dance; to kick; to spurn; to set on foot; to hold with the foot; to trip; to add a foot to, as to a stocking. [Sax. *fot*—L. *pes, pedis*—Sans. *pad*, to go.]

Foot-ball, fut'bal, n. *A ball to be driven by the foot;* the sport of kicking the foot-ball.

Foot-boy, fut'boi, n. A menial; an attendant in livery.

Foot-cloth, fut'kloth, n. *The covering* of a horse, reaching down to his heels.

Footed, fut'ed, *p.a.* Shaped in the foot; established.

Footfall, fut'fal, n. A *footstep;* tread of the foot; a trip or stumble.

Footing, fut'ing, *p.n. Ground for the foot;* firm foundation to stand on; basis; place; tread; state; condition; settlement.

Footman, fut'man, n. A menial servant; a runner; a servant in livery.

Footmark, fut'märk, n. *Mark of a foot.*

Foot - soldier, fut'sōl-jér, n. A soldier that serves on foot.

Foot-stalk, fut'stak, n. The *stalk of a leaf;* a partial stem supporting the leaf.

Footstep, fut'step, n. A track; the mark or impression of the foot; vestige; (pl.) example; course.

Footstool, fut'stōl, n. A *stool for the feet.*

Footway, fut'wā, n. *A path for passengers on foot.*

Fop, fop, n. One whose ambition is to gain admiration by showy dress and pertness; a gay, trifling man; a coxcomb. [L. *vappa*, a spoiled or worthless fellow.]

Fopling, fop'ling, n. A *petty fop.*

Foppery, fop'é-ri, n. Showy folly; foolery; idle affectation; impertinence.

Foppish, fop'ish, a. Vain of dress; finical; dressing in the extreme of fashion; affected in manners.

Foppishly, fop'ish-li, *adv. In a foppish*

Fāte, fär, fat, fall; mē, met, hér; pīne, pin; nōte, not, mōve; tūbe, tub, bull; oil, pound.

manner; with vain ostentation of dress; in a trifling or affected manner.
Foppishness, fop'ish-nes, *n.* Vanity and extravagance in dress; showy vanity.
For, for, *prep.* In the place of; because of; as equivalent to; in the character of; toward; in advantage of; on account of; in favour of; leading to, as a motive; toward the obtaining of; in opposition to; by reason of; with respect to; on the part of; through a certain space; during; in quest of; according to; as far as; of tendency to; notwithstanding; in recompense of; in proportion to; regarding; by means of; as being.—*conj.* The word by which a reason is introduced of something before advanced; because; on this account that; properly, *for that.* [Sax.]
Forage, fo'rāj, *n.* Food of any kind for horses and cattle; act of providing forage.—*vi.* To collect food for horses and cattle, by wandering about and stripping the country; to feed on spoil; to rove in search of food.—*vt.* To strip of provisions for horses, &c.; to supply with forage or fodder. *ppr.* foraging, *pret. & pp.* foraged. [Fr. *fourrage*—Low L. *foragium.*]
Forager, fo'rāj-ėr, *n.* One who forages.
Foraging, fo'rāj-ing, *p. a.* Ravaging; stripping.—*p. n.* An incursion for forage or plunder.
Forasmuch, for-az-much', *conj.* In consideration of; because that. [*for, as, and much.*]
Forbear, for-bār', *vt.* To bear off or away; to keep away; to cease; to delay; to refrain; to decline.—*vt.* To bear, keep, or hold away from; to avoid doing; to treat with indulgence and patience; to withhold. *ppr.* forbearing, *pret.* forbore, *pp.* forborne. [Sax. *forberan.*]
Forbearance, for-bār'ans, *n.* Act of forbearing; act of ceasing from; restraint of passions; long-suffering; mildness.
Forbearing, for-bār'ing, *p. a.* Patient; long-suffering.
Forbearingly, for-bār'ing-li, *adv.* In a forbearing manner; with forbearance.
Forbid, for-bid', *vt.* To bid away from; to prohibit; to oppose; to obstruct. *vi.* To utter a prohibition. *ppr.* forbidding, *pret.* forbade, *pp.* forbid, forbidden. [*for* and *bid.*]
Forbidden, for-bid'n, *p. a.* Prohibited; obstructed.
Forbidding, for-bid'ing, *p. a.* Repelling approach; offensive; odious; abhorrent.
Force, fōrs, *n. Strength;* might; energy; the quantity of power produced by motion, or the action of one body on another; violence; coercion; moral power to convince the mind; virtue; power for war; troops; an army or navy; destiny; internal power; any unlawful violence; anything that moves or tends to move a body.—*vt.* To exert strength upon or against; to compel; to overpower; to impel; to enforce; to press; to lay stress upon; to compel by strength of evidence; to storm; to take by violence; to ravish; to distort; to hasten the growth of, as of plants, fruits, &c., by artificial means.—*vi.* To use force or violence; to make a difficult matter of a thing. *ppr.* forcing, *pret. & pp.* forced. [Fr.—L. *fortis*, strong—*fero*, to bear.]
Force', fōrs, *vt.* To stuff; to lard. [See **Farce**.]
Forced, fōrst, *p. a.* Affected; overstrained.
Forceful, fōrs'ful, *a. Impelled by force;*

driven with force; acting with power; impetuous.
Forcefully, fōrs'ful-li, *adv.* Violently; impetuously.
Forceless, fōrs'les, *a.* Having little or no force; feeble; impotent.
Forceps, for'seps, *n.* A pair of pincers or tongs for seizing hot iron, &c.; a surgical instrument. [L. *capio*, to take.]
Forcer, fōrs'ėr, *n.* He or that which forces; the solid piston of a force-pump.
Forcible, fōrs'i-bl, *a.* Having force; driving forward with force; efficacious; impressive; weighty; strong; acting by violence; done by force; suffered by force.
Forcibly, fōrs'i-bli, *adv.* In a forcible manner; powerfully.
Forcing, fōrs'ing, *p. a.* Urging by force; using force; compelling.—*p. n.* Act of one who forces; art of raising plants, flowers, and fruits, at an earlier season than the natural one, by artificial heat.
Ford, fōrd, *n.* A shallow place in a river or other water, where it may be passed on foot, or by wading.—*vt.* To pass or cross, as a river or other water by walking on the bottom; to pass as through water by wading; to wade through. [Sax.—*faran*, to go, to pass.]
Fordable, fōrd'a-bl, *a.* That may be forded.
Fordo, fōr-dō', *vt.* To destroy; to ruin; to exhaust.
Fore, fōr, *a.* In front of; being in front, or toward the face; prior or anterior in place, time, order, or importance; coming first; preceding.—*adv.* In the part that precedes or goes first. [Sax.]
Fore-arm, fōr'ärm, *n.* That part of the arm which is farthest advanced; the part between the elbow and the wrist.
Forearm, fōr-ärm', *vt.* To arm for attack or resistance before the time of need.
Forebode, fōr-bōd', *vt.* To foretell; to prognosticate; to have a secret sense of, as of something future. *ppr.* foreboding, *pret. & pp.* foreboded.
Foreboder, fōr-bōd'ėr, *n.* One who forebodes; a prognosticator.
Foreboding, fōr-bōd'ing, *p. n.* Prognostication.
Forecast, fōr-kast', *vt.* To cast in the mind beforehand; to contrive beforehand; to provide against.—*vi.* To form a scheme previously; to contrive beforehand.
Forecast, fōr'kast, *n.* Contrivance beforehand; antecedent policy; foresight.
Forecastle, fōr'kas-l, *n.* That part of the upper deck of a vessel forward of the foremast; the forward part of a merchant vessel, under the deck, where the sailors live. [*fore* and *castle.*]
Foreclose, fōr-klōz', *vt.* To close or shut out thoroughly; to shut up; to preclude; to stop; to prevent. *ppr.* foreclosing, *pret. & pp.* foreclosed. [*fore* and *close.*]
Foreclosure, fōr-klōz'ūr, *n.* Act of foreclosing; prevention.
Fore-deck, fōr'dek, *n.* The fore-part of a deck, or of a ship.
Foredoom, fōr-dōm', *vt.* To doom beforehand; to predestinate.
Forefather, fōr'fä-THėr, *n.* A progenitor; one who precedes another in the line of genealogy, in any, usually in a remote degree.
Forefend, fōr-fend', *vt.* To fend off; to keep off; to hinder; to avert; to forbid or prohibit; to guard; to secure. [*for* and *fend.*]

Forefinger, fōr'fing-gėr, *n.* The finger before the others, which is next to the thumb.
Fore-foot, fōr'fut, *n.* One of the anterior feet of a quadruped; the hand.
Forefront, fōr'frunt, *n.* The foremost part.
Forego, fōr-gō', *vt.* To go away from; to resign; voluntarily to avoid, as the enjoyment of good; to go before. *ppr.* foregoing, *pret.* forewent, *pp.* foregone.
Foregoing, fōr-gō'ing, *p. a.* Going before in time or place; antecedent.
Foregone, fōr-gon', *p. a.* Predetermined; made up or decided beforehand; gone by.
Foreground, fōr'ground, *n.* The part of the field or expanse of a picture which seems to lie before the figures.
Forehand, fōr'hand, *a.* Done early; done sooner than is regular.—*n.* The chief part; prudence.
Forehanded, fōr'hand-ed, *a.* Early; timely; seasonable.
Forehead, fōr'hed, *n.* The front part of the head; the part of the face which extends from the hair on the top of the head to the eyes; confidence; assurance; impudence.
Foreign, fo'rin, *a.* That is out of doors or abroad; belonging to another nation or country; alien; strange; produced in a distant country; coming from another country; not belonging; not to the purpose; excluded; held at a distance; not native or natural. [Fr. *forain*—L. *foris*, out of doors.]
Foreigner, fo'rin-ėr, *n.* A person born in a foreign country.
Forejudge, fōr-juj', *vt.* To judge beforehand, or before hearing the facts and proof; to prejudge. *ppr.* forejudging, *pret. & pp.* forejudged.
Forejudgment, fōr-juj'ment, *n.* Judgment previously formed.
Foreknow, fōr-nō', *vt.* To know beforehand; to foresee. *ppr.* foreknowing, *pret.* foreknew, *pp.* foreknown.
Foreknowledge, fōr-nol'ej, *n.* Knowledge of a thing before it happens.
Foreland, fōr'land, *n.* Land which projects forward; a headland.
Foreman, fōr'man, *n.* The first or chief man; the chief man of a jury, who acts as their speaker; a chief workman; an overseer.
Foremast, fōr'mast, *n.* The forward mast in any vessel.
Foremost, fōr'mōst, *a.* First in place, rank, or dignity; most advanced; first in time.
Forenoon, fōr'nōn, *n.* The part of the day before noon; the former part of the day, from the morning to noon.
Forensic, fō-ren'sik, *a.* Belonging to the forum or market-place, where public courts were held; belonging to courts of judicature; used in courts or legal proceedings. [L. *forensis*—*forum*, a market-place.]
Fore-ordain, fōr-or-dān', *vt.* To ordain or appoint beforehand.
Fore-part, fōr'pärt, *n.* The anterior part; the part first in time; the part most advanced in place; the beginning.
Forepass, fōr-pas', *vt.* To pass by or along.
Forerider, fōr'rīd-ėr, *n.* One who rides before.
Forerun, fōr-run', *vt.* To run or advance before; to come before as an earnest of something to follow.
Forerunner, fōr'run-ėr, *n.* One who runs before; a harbinger; a precursor; a sign

---

ch, *chain;* j, *job;* g, *go;* ng, *sing;* ᴛʜ, *then;* th, *thin;* w, *wig;* wh, *whig;* zh, *azure;* † obsolete.

foreshowing something to follow; an ancestor†.

Foresaid, för-sād', *p.a.* Said or spoken before; aforesaid.

Foresee, för-sē', *vt.* To see beforehand; to foreknow. *ppr.* foreseeing, *pret.* foresaw, *pp.* foreseen.

Foreshadow, för-sha'dō, *vt.* To shadow or typify beforehand.

Foreshadowing, för-sha'dō-ing, *p.n.* Act of shadowing beforehand; anticipation.

Foreshorten, för-short'n, *vt.* To shorten in drawing and painting, the parts of figures that stand forwar l.

Foreshortening, för-short'n-ing, *p.n.* The shortening of the projecting parts of figures.

Foreshow, för-shō', *vt.* To show beforehand; to foretell; to represent beforehand. *ppr.* foreshowing, *pret.* foreshowed, *pp.* foreshown.

Foreside, för'sid, *n.* The front side; also, a spacious outside.

Foresight, för'sit, *n.* Foreknowledge; provident care of futurity; forethought.

Foreskirt, för'skėrt, *n.* The loose part of a coat before.

Foreslow†, för-slō', *vi.* To be dilatory.

Forespeak, för-spēk', *vt.* To speak beforehand; to foreshow; to forbid†.

Fore-spent†, för-spent', *a.* Tired; exhausted.

Forespoken, för-spōk'n, *a.* Previously spoken.

Forest, fo'rest, *n.* An extensive wood, or a large tract of land covered with trees; a certain territory privileged for wild beasts of the chase to rest and abide in under the protection of the sovereign for his pleasure in hunting. *a.* Relating to a forest; sylvan; rustic. [Old Fr.—Fr. *forêt*.]

Forestall, för-stạl', *vt.* To take beforehand; to anticipate; to hinder by preoccupation or prevention; to deprive† (with *of*).

Forester, fo'rest-ėr, *n.* An officer appointed to watch a forest and preserve the game; an inhabitant of a forest.

Forestry, fo'rest-ri, *n.* The art of cultivating or of forming forests.

Foretaste, för'tāst, *n.* A taste beforehand; anticipation.—*vt.* To taste before possession; to have previous enjoyment or experience of. *ppr.* foretasting, *pret. & pp.* foretasted.

Foretell, för-tel', *vt.* To tell beforehand; to predict.—*vi* To utter prediction or prophecy. *ppr.* foretelling, *pret. & pp.* foretold.

Foreteller, för-tel'ėr, *n.* One who predicts or prophesies; a foreshower.

Forethink, för-thingk', *vi.* To think beforehand; to anticipate in the mind†.

Forethought, för'thạt, *n.* A thinking beforehand; foresight; provident care.

Foretooth, för'töth, *n.* Fore-teeth, *pl.* One of the teeth in the fore-part of the mouth; an incisor.

Forever, for-ev'ėr, *adv.* At all times; through endless ages; continually; eternally.

Fore-vouched, för-voucht', *a.* Affirmed before.

Fore-ward†, för'werd, *n.* The van; the front.

Fore-wind, för'wind, *n.* A favourable wind.

Forewarn, för-warn', *vt.* To warn beforehand; to give previous notice to; to caution beforehand.

Forfeit, for'fit, *vt.* To misdo; to lose by misdoing; to alienate, as the right to possess, by some neglect or crime. [Fr. *forfaire, forfait*—L. *foris*, without, and *facio*, to do.]—*n.* That which is forfeited or lost, or the right to which is alienated by a crime,offence,neglect of duty, or breach of contract; a fine; a penalty. *a.* Lost for a crime; liable to penal seizure. [Fr. *forfait*.]

Forfeitable, for'fit-a-bl, *a. Liable to be forfeited*; subject to forfeiture.

Forfeited, for'fit-ed, *p.a.* Lost or alienated by an offence, crime, or breach of condition.

Forfeiture, for'fit-ūr, *n. Act of forfeiting;* that which is forfeited; a fine; a penalty. [Fr. *forfaiture*.]

Forge, förj, *n.* A place where iron is wrought by heating and hammering; a furnace for heating iron; any place where anything is made; act of beating or working iron or steel.—*vt.* To fabricate; to form by heating and hammering; to make by any means; to make falsely; to feign; to make in the likeness of something else. *ppr.* forging, *pret. & pp.* forged. [Fr.—L. *faber*, a worker in hard materials.]

Forged, förjd, *p.a.* Beaten into shape; counterfeited.

Forger, förj'ėr, *n. One who forges;* one who counterfeits.

Forgery, förj'ė-ri, *n.* The crime of counterfeiting; that which is forged or counterfeited.

Forget, for-get', *vt.* To let away what had once been gotten; to let go from the memory; not to remember; to slight; to neglect. *ppr.* forgetting, *pret.* forgot, *pp.* forgot, forgotten. [Sax. *forgitan—getan*, to obtain.]

Forgetful, for-get'fụl, *a. Apt to forget*; unmindful; heedless; neglectful; causing to forget; oblivious.

Forgetfully, for-get'fụl-li, *adv. In a forgetful manner*.

Forgetfulness, for-get'fụl-nes, *n.* Quality of being apt to forget; loss of remembrance ; obliviousness; negligence; heedlessness.

Forgive†, förj'et-iv, *a.* Forging; inventive.

Forging, förj'ing, *p.n.* Act of beating into shape; the act of counterfeiting; a piece of forged work in metal.

Forgive, for-giv', *vt. To give away or up;* to remit, as a debt or penalty; to pardon, as an offence; to overlook, as an offence, and treat the offender as not guilty. *ppr.* forgiving, *pret.* forgave, *pp.* forgiven. [Sax. *forgifan—gifan*, to give.]

Forgiveness, for-giv'nes, *n.* The pardon of an offender; the remission of an offence; willingness to forgive; remission of a debt or fine.

Forgiving, for-giv'ing, *p.a. Disposed to forgive*; mild; merciful; compassionate.

Fork, fork, *n.* An instrument for *lifting* and *carrying* various substances; an instrument divided at the end into two or more points or prongs, and used for lifting or pitching anything; something resembling a fork; a branch or division; (pl.) the point where two roads meet, or where two rivers meet and unite.—*vi.* To shoot into blades, as corn; to divide into two.—*vt.* To raise or pitch *with a fork*, as hay, &c. [Sax. *forc*—L. *furca—fero*, to carry.]

Forked, forkt, *p.a.* Opening into two or more parts, points, or shoots.

Forky, fork'i, *a. Forked;* opening into two or more parts, shoots, or points.

Forlorn, for-lorn', *a. Deserted;* left without resource; destitute; abandoned; solitary; friendless; miserable.

n. A lost or solitary person. [Sax. *for loren—leoran*, to go away.]

Form, form, *n. Make; shape;* contour; external appearance of a body; manner of arranging particulars; pattern; beauty; elegance; dignity; order; empty show; semblance; stated method; established practice; ritual or prescribed mode; ceremony; likeness; manner; system; disposition of component parts; a long seat without a back; a class; the seat or bed of a hare.—*vt. To shape or mould;* to plan; to modify; to arrange; to contrive; to invent; to make up; to model by instruction and discipline, as one's character; to combine; to compile; to enact; to ordain.—*vi. To take a form.* [Fr. *forme*—L. *forma*—Heb. *bara*, to cut out, to form, to produce.]

Formal, form'al, *a. Relating to outward form;* according to form; regular; precise; exact to affectation; done in due form; express; having the form without the substance; proper. [Low L. *formalis*.]

Formalist, form'al-ist, *n. One who observes forms;* one who rests in external religious forms. [Fr. *formaliste*.]

Formality, form-al i-ti, *n. Quality of being formal;* ceremony; established order; mode; decorum to be observed; conventional rule. [Fr. *formalité*.]

Formally, form'al-li, *adv. In a formal manner.*

Formation, form-ā'shon, *n.* Act of forming; act of creating; the operation of collecting things together; production; manner in which a thing is formed; any assemblage of rocks or strata, referred to a common origin. [Fr.]

Formative, form'āt-iv, *a. Having the power of giving form;* plastic; serving to form; derivative.—*n. That which serves merely to give form,* and is no part of the radical (grammar).

Formed, formd, *p.a.* Arranged; combined; constituted.

Former, form'ėr, *n. He who forms.*

Former, form'ėr, *a. comp. deg. Anterior;* previous; before in time; past, and frequently ancient; near the beginning; mentioned before another. [Sax. *form*, first.]

Formerly, form'ėr-li, *adv.* In time past; heretofore; in days of yore.

Formidable, for'mid-a-bl, *a.* Adapted to *excite fear*, and deter from approach, encounter or undertaking; dreadful; fearful; frightful. [Fr.—L. *formido*, to fear, to dread.]

Formidably, for'mid-a-bli, *adv. In a manner to impress fear.*

Formless, form'les, *a. Without a determinate form;* shapeless.

Formula, form'ō-la, *n.* **Formulæ**, *pl. A small form;* a prescribed form; a rule; a prescription in medicine; a confession of faith; a general expression for resolving certain problems in mathematics; an expression by means of symbols of the composition of chemical substances. [L.]

Formulary, form'ū-la-ri, *n. A book containing stated and prescribed forms,* as of oaths, declarations, prayers, and the like; a book of precedents. [Fr. *formulaire*.]

Fornication, for-ni-kā'shon, *n.* The incontinence of unmarried persons, male or female; also, the criminal conversation of a married man with an unmarried woman; adultery, incest, or idolatry (scriptural). [L. *fornicatio—fornix*, a vault.]

Fornicator, for'ni-kāt-ėr, *n. One guilty*

Fāte, fär, fat, fạll; mē, met, hėr; pīne, pin; nōte, not, mōve; tūbe, tub, bụll; oil, pound.

of fornication; a lewd person; an idolater. [Low L.]

Forsake, for-sāk', *vt.* Not to ask for or go to; to abandon; to depart from; to leave; to withdraw from; to fail. *ppr.* forsaking, *pret.* forsook, *pp.* forsaken. [Sax. *forsacan—secan*, to seek.]

Forsaken, for-sāk'n, *p.a.* Forlorn; destitute.

Forsaking, for-sāk'ing, *p.n.* Act of deserting; dereliction.

Forsooth, for-söth', *adv.* In very truth; in fact; certainly; very well. (Chiefly used in contempt or irony.) [Sax. *forsoth—soth,* truth.]

Forswear, for-swār', *vt.* To renounce upon oath; to abjure; to deny upon oath; to swear falsely; to perjure one's self (with recipr. pron. in the last two significations).—*vi.* To swear falsely; to commit perjury. *ppr.* forswearing, *pret.* forswore, *pp.* forsworn. [Sax. *forswerian—swerian,* to swear.]

Forswearer, for-swār'ėr, *n.* One who swears a false oath.

Fort, fört, *n. A fortified* place; a place surrounded with means of defence; a castle. [Fr.—L. *fortis,* strong.]

Forte, för'tā, *adv.* A direction to sing or play with *force.* [It.—L. *fortis,* strong.]

Forte, fört, *n. The strong point;* a peculiar talent or faculty; that in which one excels. [Fr.—L. *fortis,* strong.]

Forted, fört'ed, *p.a. Furnished with forts;* guarded by forts.

Forth, förth, *adv. Out from;* forward in place or order; beyond the boundary of a place; out into public view; abroad; onward in time.—*prep.* Forth from. [Sax. *fore,* before.]

Forthcoming, fōrth-kum'ing, *a. Coming forth;* making appearance.

Forthright', fōrth'rīt, *n. A straight path.*

Forthwith, fōrth-with', *adv. Without delay;* directly. [*forth* and *with.*]

Fortieth, for'ti-eth, *a.* The ordinal of *forty.*

Fortification, for'ti-fi-kā"shon, *n.* The art or science of *fortifying* places; the works erected to defend a place; a fortified place; a castle; additional strength. [Fr.]

Fortified, for'ti-fīd, *p.a.* Made strong against attacks.

Fortifier, for'ti-fī-ėr, *n. One who fortifies.*

Fortify, for'ti-fī, *vt.* To make strong; to strengthen by forts, batteries, and other works of art; to invigorate; to furnish with strength or means of resisting force. *ppr.* fortifying, *pret. & pp.* fortified. [Fr. *fortifier*—L. *fortis,* strong, and *facio,* to make.]

Fortini, fört'in, *n. A little fort.*

Fortitude, for'ti-tūd, *n. Strength;* resoluteness; that firmness of mind which enables a person to encounter danger with coolness and courage, or to bear pain or adversity without murmuring. [L. *fortitudo—fortis,* strong.]

Fortnight, fort'nīt, *n.* The space of *fourteen* days; two weeks. [contracted from *fourteen nights.*]

Fortnightly, fort'nīt-li, *adv.* Once a *fortnight.*

Fortress, fort'res, *n. A stronghold;* a place of defence or security; security. *vt.*† *To fortify.* [Fr. *forteresse.*]

Fortuitous, for-tū'it-us, *a. A Happening by chance;* accidental; casual. [L. *fortuitus—fors, fortis,* chance.]

Fortuitously, for-tū'it-us-li, *adv. Accidentally;* casually.

Fortunate, for'tū-nāt, *a.* Made prosperous; successful; coming by good luck;

receiving some unforeseen good. [L. *fortunatus—fortūna,* fortune.]

Fortunately, for'tū-nāt-li, *adv.* By good *fortune;* happily.

Fortune, for'tūn, *n. Whatever brings itself; chance;* the deified power of chance; the arrival of something in a sudden or unexpected manner; the good or ill that befalls man; event; means of living; estate; great wealth; the portion of a man or woman, generally of a woman; futurity; destiny. *vt.*† To dispose of.—*vi.*† To fall out; to happen. [L. *fortūna—fors,* chance—*fero,* to bring.]

Fortune-teller, for'tūn-tel-ėr, *n.* One who pretends to fore*tell* the *fortunes* or events of the lives of others.

Forty, for'ti, *a. Four times ten.* [Sax. *feowertig.*]

Forum, fō'rum, *n. An outside place;* a public or market place; a public place in ancient Rome, where causes were judicially tried; a tribunal; a court; jurisdiction. [L.—*foris,* out of doors.]

Forward, for'wėrd, *adv. Toward a place in front;* onward; progressively.—*a. Near or towards the fore-part;* ready; prompt; violent; immodest; advanced beyond the usual degree; advanced for the season; quick; hasty; too ready.—*vt. To place or move towards the front;* to help onward; to quicken; to hasten; to send forward; to transmit, as a letter. [Sax. *fore* and *ward.*]

Forwarder, for'wėrd-ėr, *n.* He that promotes or advances in progress.

Forwardly, for'wėrd-li, *adv.* Eagerly; hastily; quickly.

Forwardness, for'wėrd-nes, *n.* Promptness; eagerness; want of due reserve or modesty; confidence; a state of advance beyond the usual degree; earliness.

Forwards, for'wėrdz, *adv.* Same as *forward.*

Fosse, fos, *n. A ditch* or moat; a trench; a kind of cavity in a bone, with a large aperture. [Fr. *fossé*—L. *fossa,* a ditch—*fodio, fossum,* to dig.]

Fosset, fos'et, *n.* A faucet.

Fossil, fos'sil, *a. Dug out* of the earth. *n.* A substance *dug out* of the earth; a petrified animal or vegetable substance found in the strata composing the surface of our globe. [Fr. *fossile*—L. *fodio,* to dig.]

Fossiliferous, fos-sil-if'ėr-us, *a. Containing fossils,* or the petrified remains of animal or vegetable substances. [L. *fossilis,* and *fero,* to bear.]

Fossilist, fos'sil-ist, *n. One versed* in the science of *fossils.*

Fossilize, fos'sil-īz, *vt. To convert into a fossil* or petrified state.—*vi. To be changed into a fossil state. ppr.* fossilizing, *pret. & pp.* fossilized.

Foster, fos'tėr, *vt. To nourish;* to support; to bring up; to promote the growth of; to encourage; to sustain and promote. [Sax. *fostrian—foster,* a nurse.]

Foster-brother, fos'tėr-bruth-ėr, *n.* A male *nursed* at the same breast, or fed by the same *nurse,* but not the offspring of the same parents.

Foster-child, fos'tėr-child, *n. A child nursed* by a woman not the mother, or bred by a man not the father.

Fosterer, fos'tėr-ėr, *n. One who feeds and nourishes* in the place of parents.

Fostering, fos'tėr-ing, *p.a. Nourishing;* cherishing.

Foul, foul, *a. Stinking;* filthy; impure; covered with or containing extraneous matter which is offensive; turbid; ob-

scene or profane; cloudy and stormy; rainy or tempestuous; wicked; abominable; unfair; loathsome; shameful; coarse; full of weeds; entangled; covered with weeds or barnacles, as a ship's bottom; contrary, as wind; dangerous.—*vt. To defile;* to daub; to dirty; to bemire; to soil; to entangle with something that impedes motion. [Sax. *ful*—Icel.*fúll,*putrid—Sans.*puy,*to rot.]

Foul-faced, foul'fāst, *a.* Ugly.

Foully, foul'li, *adv. Filthily;* scandalously; shamefully; not honestly.

Foul-mouthed, foul'mouтнd, *a.* Using language scurrilous, obscene, or profane.

Foulness, foul'nes, *n. Quality or state of being foul;* filthiness; quality or state of containing or being covered with anything extraneous which is offensive; pollution; atrociousness; wickedness; unfairness; want of candour.

Foumart, fö'märt, *n. The foul marten* or pole-cat. [Old Fr. *ful,* fetid, and *merder,* a marten.]

Found, found, *vt. To lay, as the bottom* of anything; to begin to build; to raise; to construct; to establish, as on something solid; to institute; to give birth to; to establish on a base. [Fr. *fonder*—L. *fundus,* the bottom.]

Found, found, *vt. To cause to flow;* to cast; to form by melting a metal and pouring it into a mould. [Fr. *fondre*—L. *fundo,* to pour.]

Foundation, found-ā'shon, *n. Act of founding;* the base of an edifice; the base of anything; rise; endowment; an established revenue, particularly for a charity; settlement; institution. [Late L. *fundatio.*]

Foundationer, found-ā'shon-ėr, *n.* One who derives support from the funds or *foundation* of a college or great school.

Founder, found'ėr, *n. One who lays a foundation;* an author; an originator; an endower. [Fr. *fondeur*] one who casts metals.

Founder, found'ėr, *vi. To sink;* to trip; to fill or be filled with water, *and sink,* as a ship; to miscarry.—*vt.* To cause internal inflammation in the feet of, as of a horse, so that he is ready to *stumble or fall.* [Fr. *fondre,* to sink.]

Foundered, found'ėrd, *p.a. Sunk* in the sea, as a ship.

Foundery, found'ė-ri, *n. The art of founding,* or of casting metals into various forms for use; the casting of statues; the house and works occupied in casting metals. [Fr. *fonderie.*]

Founding, found'ing, *p.n.* The art of casting or forming of *melted* meta any article, according to a given design.

Foundling, found'ling, *n.* A child *found* without a parent or owner; a deserted or exposed infant.

Fount, Fountain, fount, fount'ān, *n. A perennial spring of water from the earth;* a spring or source of water; a spouting of water; an artificial spring; the head or source of a river; original; the source of anything. [Fr. *fontaine*—L. *fons, fontis—fundo,* to pour.]

Fountainhead, fount'ān-hed, *n. The head or source of a fountain;* primary source; original; first principle.

Four, fōr, *a.* Twice two. [Sax. *feower.*]

Fourfold, fōr'fōld, *a. Quadruple;* four times told.—*n. Four times as much.*

Fourscore, fōr'skōr, *a. Four times twenty;* eighty.

Foursquare, fōr'skwār, *a.* Having *four sides and four angles equal;* quadrangular.

Fourteen, fōr'tēn, a. *Four and ten; twice seven.*
Fourteenth, fōr'tēnth, a. *The ordinal of fourteen; the fourth after the tenth.*
Fourth, fōrth, a. *The ordinal of four.*
Fourthly, fōrth'li, adv. *In the fourth place.*
Fowl, foul, n. *A flying or winged animal; a bird; a domestic or barn-door bird.—vi.* To catch wild *fowls* for game or food. [Sax. *fugel—fleógan*, to fly.]
Fowler, foul'ėr, n. *A sportsman who pursues and takes wild fowls.*
Fowling, foul'ing, p.a. *The art or practice of catching or shooting fowls or birds;* falconry.
Fowling-piece, foul'ing-pēs, n. *A light gun for shooting fowls or birds.*
Fox, foks, n. *A well-known animal, remarkable for rapacity and cunning; a sly cunning fellow; a sword'.* [Sax. —Goth. *fahan*, to seize.]
Fox-brush, foks'brush, n. *The tail of a fox.*
Foxglove, foks'gluv, n. *A handsome herb, whose leaves are used as a powerful medicine, both sedative and diuretic.*
Fox-hound, foks'hound, n. *A hound for chasing foxes.*
Foxship, foks'ship, n. *Artfulness; cunning.*
Foxy, foks'i, a. *Having too much the colour of a fox in the shading, &c., as a painting.*
Fracas, fra-kä', n. *A repeated and violent shaking; an uproar; a disturbance; a brawl.* [Fr.—L. *quassare*, to shake violently.]
Fract†, frakt, vt. *To break.* [L. *frango.*]
Fraction, frak'shon, n. *A breaking; state of being broken, especially by violence; a broken part; a fragment; one or more parts of something considered as a unit or whole.* [Fr.—L. *fractio—frango, fractus*, to break.]
Fractional, frak'shon-al, a. *Belonging to a fraction or broken number.*
Fracture, frak'tūr, n. *A breach in any body, especially a breach caused by violence; a rupture of a solid body; the rupture of a bone; the manner in which a mineral breaks, and by which its texture is displayed.—vt. To break; to burst asunder; to separate, as continuous parts. ppr. fracturing, pret. & pp. fractured.* [Fr.—L. *fractūra—frango*, Heb. *parak*, to break.]
Fragile, fra'jil, a. *Easily broken; frail; liable to fail; infirm; weak.* [Fr.—L. *fragilis—frango*, to break.]
Fragility, fra-jil'i-ti, n. *Easiness to be broken; liability to fail; frailty; liability to fault.* [Fr. *fragilité.*]
Fragment, frag'ment, n. *A piece separated from anything by breaking; an imperfect part; a small detached portion.* [Fr.—L. *frango*, to break.]
Fragmentary, frag'ment-a-ri, a. *Composed of fragments.*
Fragrance, frā'grans, n. *Quality of being fragrant; sweetness of smell; grateful odour or perfume.* [Sp. *fragrāncia—* L. *fragro*, to emit a scent.]
Fragrant, frā'grant, a. *Throwing out an agreeable odour; sweet-smelling; sweet-scented; balmy; spicy; aromatic.* [L. *fragrans.*]
Fragrantly, frā'grant-li, adv. *With sweet scent or odour.*
Frail, frāl, a. *Fragile: weak; liable to fail and decay; perishable; weak in mind or resolution; liable to error or deception.* [Fr. *frêle—*L. *fragilis—frango*, to break.]
Frailty, frāl'ti, n. *State or quality of being frail; infirmity; liableness to be deceived or seduced; weakness or infirmity of body; fault proceeding from weakness; failing; foible.* [Norm. *frealte—*L. *fragilitas.*]
Frame, frām, vt. *To make; to construct; to fabricate by orderly construction and union of various parts; to adjust; to make suitable; to make or compose, as laws; to shape; to form and digest by thought, as ideas; to plan; to invent; to place in a frame; to surround with a frame.—vi.† To proceed; to go. n. Anything framed; the bodily structure; the skeleton of a building; regularity; form; scheme; structure; constitution; adjusted state; contrivance; particular state, as of the mind.* [Sax. *fremman—*L. *formo*, to shape.]
Framed, frāmd, p.a. *Composed; devised; adjusted.*
Framer, frām'ėr, n. *One who frames.*
Framework, frām'wėrk, n. *That which supports or incloses anything else; work done in a kind of loom, called a frame.*
Framing, frām'ing, p.n. *Act of constructing a frame; the frame thus constructed.*
Franc, frangk, n. *A silver coin of France, of the value of about 9½d.* [Fr.]
Franchise, fran'chiz, n. *Freedom; a particular privilege or right granted by a prince or sovereign to an individual, or to a number of persons; the right of voting in an election for a member of parliament.* [Fr.—*franc*, free.]
Franciscan, fran-sis'kan, n. *A monk of the order of St. Francis.*
Frangibility, fran-ji-bil'i-ti, n. *The state or quality of being frangible.* [Low L. *frangibilitas.*]
Frangible, fran'ji-bl, a. *That may be broken; easily broken.* [Low L. *frangibilis—*L. *frango*, to break.]
Frank, frangk, a. *Free; free in uttering real sentiments; not reserved; ingenuous; leading to the utterance of one's sentiments without reserve, as a disposition; without conditions, as a gift.—n.† A sty for swine.—vt.† To shut up in a sty.* [Old G. *franko*, free.]
Frankincense, frangk'in-sens, n. *Incense freely offered; an odoriferous gum-resin used as a perfume.*
Frankly, frangk'li, adv. *In a frank manner;* openly; freely; unreservedly.
Frankness, frangk'nes, n. *Freedom in communication; openness; ingenuousness; fairness.*
Frantic, fran'tik, a. *Frenzied; raving; furious; outrageous; wild and disorderly; distracted; characterized by violence, fury, and disorder; noisy; turbulent.* [Fr. *phrénetique—*Gr. *phrenitikos.*]
Frantically, Frantickly, fran'tik-li, fran'tik-al-li, adv. *Madly; distractedly; outrageously.*
Fraternal, fra-tėr'nal, a. *Brotherly; becoming brothers.* [Fr. *fraternel—*L. *frater*, a brother.]
Fraternally, fra-tėr'nal-li, adv. *In a brotherly manner.*
Fraternity, fra-tėr'ni-ti, n. *Brotherhood; a body of men associated for their common interest, business, or pleasure; men of the same class or character.* [Fr. *fraternité—*L. *frater*, a brother.]
Fraternization, fra'tėr-niz-ā''shon, n. *Act of holding fellowship as brethren.*
Fraternise, fra'tėr-niz, vi. *To associate as brethren*, or as men of like occupation or disposition. *ppr.* fraternizing, *pret. & pp.* fraternized. [Fr. *fraterniser.*]
Fraterniser, fra'tėr-niz-ėr, n. *One who fraternises.*
Fratricidal, fra-tri-sid'al, a. *Pertaining to fratricide.*
Fratricide, fra'tri-sid, n. *The crime of murdering a brother; one who murders a brother.* [L. *fratricidium—frater*, and *cado*, to kill.]
Fraud, frad, n. *A cheating; deceit; artifice by which the right or interest of another is injured; guile; craft; wile; stratagem.* [Fr. *fraude—*L. *fraus, fraudis.*]
Fraudful, frad'ful, a. *Full of fraud; deceitful in making bargains; trickish; treacherous; containing fraud or deceit.*
Fraudfully, frad'ful-li, adv. *Deceitfully; treacherously; by stratagem.*
Fraudulence, frad'ū-lens, n. *Deceitfulness; trickishness in making bargains or in social concerns.* [L. *fraudulentia.*]
Fraudulent, frad'ū-lent, a. *Deceitful; treacherous; dishonest; practising deceit in making contracts; containing fraud; founded on fraud; proceeding from fraud.* [L. *fraudulentus.*]
Fraudulently, frad'ū-lent-li, adv. *By fraud;* by artifice or imposition.
Fraught, frat, p.a. *A freighted; laden; stored; full.—n.† A freight.* [D. *vracht*, a load.]
Fraughtage†, frat'āj, n. *Cargo.*
Pray, frā, n. *An affray; a combat; a fight; a contest; altercation; feud.—vt. To frighten;* to terrify. [See AFFRAY.]
Fray, frā, vt. *To rub; to fret, as cloth, by wearing; to ruffle; to grate upon. n. A rub; a fret or chafe in cloth.* [Fr. *frayer—*L. *frico, fricāre*, to rub.]
Freak, frēk, n. *A sudden starting or change of place; a sudden causeless change or turn of the mind; a fancy; caprice; sport.* [Icel. *frakkr*, quick, agile.]
Freakish, frēk'ish, a. *Apt to change the mind suddenly; capricious.*
Freakishly, frēk'ish-li, adv. *Capriciously; with sudden change of mind.*
Freakishness, frēk'ish-nes, n. *Capriciousness; whimsicalness.*
Freckle, frek'l, n. *A spot of a yellowish clour in the skin; any small spot or discoloration.—vt. or i. To give freckles to, or acquire freckles. ppr. freckling, pret. & pp. freckled.* [Dan. *fregne*, a freckle.]
Freckled, frek'ld, p.a. *Spotted; having small yellowish spots on the skin or surface.*
Freckly, frek'l-i, a. *Full of freckles; sprinkled with spots.*
Free, frē, a. *Delivered; being at liberty; not being under restraint, physical or moral; not enslaved; not in a state of vassalage; subject only to fixed laws, made by consent; instituted by a free people; not arbitrary or despotic; not imprisoned or under arrest; allowed; open; not obstructed; licentious; candid; ingenuous; generous; gratuitous; guiltless; clear; not encumbered with; open to all; without restriction or without expense; enjoying certain immunities; admitted to special rights; possessing without slavish conditions; disjoined.—vt. To deliver; to release from bondage; to rescue or release from slavery, captivity, or confinement; to disentangle; to exempt; to release from obligation or duty; to remove, as any encumbrance. ppr. freeing, pret. & pp. freed.* [Sax. *frio—*Old G. *fri.*]

Fāte, fär, fat, fall; mē, met, hėr; pine, pin; nōte, not, move; tūbe, tub, bull; oil, pound.

Freebooter, frē'boot-ėr, n. A robber; a pillager; a plunderer. [G. freibeuter.]
Freedman, frēd'man, n. A man who has been a slave and is manumitted.
Freedom, frē'dum, n. State of being free; a state of exemption from the control of another; liberty; particular privileges; franchise; exemption from any constraint, in consequence of predetermination or otherwise; facility of doing anything; frankness; license; violation of the rules of decorum. [Sax. freodóm.]
Free-footed†, frē'fųt-ed, a. Not restrained in the march.
Free-hearted, frē'härt-ed, a. Open or liberal hearted; frank.
Freehold, frē'hōld, n. A right in land or tenement which is held by a free-tenure for ever, or descends to certain heirs, or is held for term of life.
Freeholder, frē'hōld-ėr, n. The possessor of a freehold.
Free-liver, frē'liv-ėr, n. One who gives great license to his appetites.
Freely, frē'li, adv. In a free manner.
Freeman, frē'man, n. One who is free; one who is not subject to the will of another; one not a slave; one who enjoys or is entitled to a franchise or peculiar privilege.
Freeness, frē'nes, n. State or quality of being free; openness; unreservedness; frankness; ingenuousness; liberality.
Free-school, frē'skōl, n. A school open to admit pupils without restriction.
Free-spoken, frē'spōk-n, a. Accustomed to speak without reserve.
Freestone, frē'stōn, n. Any species of stone composed of sand or grit, so called because it is easily cut or wrought.
Free-thinker, frē'think-ėr, n. One who indulges thoughts or opinions without control; an unbeliever; one who discards revelation.
Free-trade, frē'trād, n. Trade or commerce free from restrictions.
Free-will, frē'wil, n. Unrestrained will; the power of directing our own actions, without restraint by necessity or fate. a. Spontaneous.
Freezable, frēz'a-bl, a. That may be frozen.
Freeze, frēz, vi. To be congealed by cold; to be hardened into ice or a like solid body; to be of that degree of cold at which water congeals; to stagnate, as the blood; to shiver or stiffen with cold. vt. To congeal; to harden into ice; to kill by cold; to chill; to give the sensation of cold and shivering to. ppr. freezing, pret. froze, pp. frozen. [Sax. fryzan—L. frigeo, to be stiff with cold.]
Freezing, frēz'ing, p.n. The process or state of congelation.
Freight, frāt, n. That which is conveyed by water; the cargo, or any part of the cargo, of a ship; lading; the hire of a ship, or money charged or paid for the transportation of goods.—vt. To load with goods, as a ship or vessel of any kind, for transporting them from one place to another; to load or burden. [G. fracht, from fahren, to convey.]
Freightage, frāt'āj, n. Money paid for freight.
Freighter, frāt'ėr, n. One who charters and loads a ship.
French, frensh, a. Pertaining to France or its inhabitants.—n. The language spoken by the people of France.
Frenzied, fren'zi-ed, p.a. Affected with frenzy or madness.
Frenzy, fren'zi, n. Disorder of the mind; madness; distraction; any violent agitation of the mind, approaching to distraction; insanity. [Fr. phrénésie—Gr. phrēn, the mind.]
Frequency, frē'kwen-si, n. A return or occurrence of a thing often repeated at short intervals. [Fr. fréquence—L. frequens, frequent.]
Frequent, frē'kwent, a. That takes place repeatedly or often; often seen or done; often happening at short intervals; often occurring; used often to practise anything. [Fr. fréquent.]
Frequent, frē-kwent', vt. To visit often; to resort to often or habitually. [L. frequento, from frequens.]
Frequentative, frē-kwent'āt-iv, a. Denoting the frequent repetition of an action, as a verb.—n. A verb which denotes the frequent repetition of an action. [It. frequentativo.]
Frequented, frē-kwent'ed, p.a. Often visited.
Frequently, frē'kwent-li, adv. Often; many times; at short intervals; commonly.
Fresco, fres'kō, n. Freshness; shade; a method of painting on walls, performed with water-colours on fresh plaster. [It. fresco, fresh.]
Fresh, fresh, a. Cooled by rain; having the colour and appearance of young thriving plants; having the appearance of a healthy youth; ruddy; recently grown, made, or obtained; vigorous; brisk; not forgotten; not salt; pure and cool; unfaded; sweet; not stale; unpractised; unused.—n. A spring or pool of fresh water. [Sax. fersc—Sans. vrish, to rain.]
Freshen, fresh'n, vt. To make fresh; to sweeten; to separate, as water from saline particles; to take saltness from. vi. To grow fresh; to lose salt or saltness; to grow brisk or strong.
Freshly, fresh'li, adv. With freshness; briskly.
Freshman, fresh'man, n. A novice; a student during his first year's residence at an English university.
Freshness, fresh'nes, n. State or quality of being fresh; vigour; spirit; liveliness; renewed vigour; coolness; invigorating quality or state; ruddiness; freedom from saltness; rawness; briskness, as of wind.
Fret, fret, vt. To eat away; to gnaw; to wear away; to tease; to vex; to make angry; to agitate violently by external impulse or action; to diversify.—vi. To eat or wear on; to be vexed; to utter peevish expressions; to be agitated or in violent commotion. ppr. fretting, pret. & pp. fretted.—n. Agitation of the mind; irritation; ill-humour; peevishness; vexation. [Sax. fretan, to gnaw, eat up.]
Fret, fret, vt. To variegate; to make rough or uneven the surface of; to furnish with frets, as an instrument of music. ppr. fretting, pret. & pp. fretted.—n. A short piece of wire fixed on the finger-board of a guitar, &c., which, being pressed against the strings, varies the tone; a rippling on the surface of water. [Sax. fraetwan, to adorn.]
Fretful, fret'ful, a. Disposed to fret; peevish; irritable; petulant; angry.
Fretfully, fret'ful-li, adv. Peevishly.
Fretfulness, fret'ful-nes, n. Peevishness; ill-humour; disposition to complain.
Fretted, fret'ed, p.a. Agitated; vexed; variegated; furnished with frets.
Fretting, fret'ing, p.a. Corroding; making rough on the surface; variegating. p.n. A state of chafing; vexation; peevishness.

Fretwork, fret'wėrk, n. Raised work; work adorned with frets.
Friability, Friableness, fri-a-bil'i-ti, fri'a-bl-nes, n. Quality of being friable.
Friable, fri'a-bl, a. Easily rubbed down, crumbled, or pulverized; easily reduced to powder. [Fr.—L. frio, friatus, to crumble down.]
Friar, fri'ėr, n. A brother or member of any religious order; a monk. [Fr. frère—L. frater, a brother.]
Fribble, frib'bl, a. Frivolous; trifling; silly.—n. A frivolous, contemptible fellow.—vi. To trifle. ppr. fribbling, pret. & pp. fribbled. [Fr. frivole—L. frivolus, silly.]
Fribbler, frib'bl-ėr, n. A trifler.
Fricassee, fri-kas-sē', n. That which is fried; a dish made by cutting chickens, rabbits, or other small animals, into pieces, and dressing them in a frying-pan, or a like utensil, with strong sauce. [Fr. fricassée—L. frigo, to roast or fry.]
Fricasseed, fri-kas-sēd', p.a. Fried; dressed in fricassee.
Friction, frik'shon, n. A rubbing; act of rubbing the surface of one body against that of another; the effect of rubbing, or the resistance which a moving body meets with from the surface on which it moves. [Fr.—L. frico, frictum, to rub.]
Friday, fri'dā, n. Friga's day; the sixth day of the week, formerly consecrated to Friga, the Venus of the North. [Sax. frig-dœg—Friga and dœg.]
Fried, frid, p.a. Dressed in a frying-pan; heated.
Friend, frend, n. One who loves, or is attached to another by affection; a companion; a favourer; one who is propitious; a favourite; a term of salutation; one of the religious sect called Quakers. [Sax. freond, ppr. of freon, to love.]
Friended†, frend'ed, a. Inclined to love; well-disposed.
Friending†, frend'ing, p.n. Friendliness.
Friendless, frend'les, a. Destitute of friends; wanting support; forlorn.
Friendliness, frend'li-nes, n. Friendly disposition; good-will.
Friendly, frend'li, a. Like or becoming a friend; kind; favourable; benevolent; disposed to peace; social; not hostile; favourable; promoting the good of; amicable. — adv.† In the manner of friends.
Friendship, frend'ship, n. Intimacy resting on mutual respect and esteem; minds united by mutual benevolence; personal kindness; friendly aid; help; assistance.
Frieze, frēz, n. The nap on woollen cloth; a kind of coarse woollen cloth or stuff, with a nap on one side.—vt. To form a nap on, as on cloth; to frizzle; to curl. ppr. friezing, pret. & pp. friezed. [Belg. vries, a winter garment napped on both sides.]
Frieze, frēz, n. That part of the entablature of a column which is between the architrave and cornice, often ornamented. [Fr. frise.]
Friezed, frēzd, p.a. Napped; shaggy with nap or frieze.
Frigate, fri'gāt, n. A ship of war, less than a ship of the line, usually having two decks. [Fr. frégate.]
Fright, frit, n. Sudden and violent fear; a passion excited by the sudden appearance of danger; affright; dismay. [Sax. fyrhto—Old G. forht.]
Fright, Frighten, frit, frit'n, vt. To alarm suddenly with danger; to af-

---

ch, chain; j, job; g, go; ng, sing; ᴡʜ, then; th, thin; w, wig; wh, whig; zh, azure; † obsolete.

fright; to terrify; to intimidate. [Sax. *frihtan*.]
Frighted, Frightened, frīt'ed, frīt'nd, *p.a.* *Terrified*; suddenly alarmed with danger.
Frightful, frīt'fu̇l, *a.* *Full of fright*; *full of something which causes fright*; impressing terror; dreadful; awful; horrible.
Frightfully, frīt'fu̇l-li, *adv.* *In a frightful manner*; dreadfully.
Frightfulness, frīt'fu̇l-nes, *n.* *The quality of being frightful.*
Frigid, frī'jid, *a.* *Cold*; wanting heat; wanting warmth of affection; wanting vigour; unanimated; wanting spirit; wanting the fire of genius or fancy; stiff; wanting zeal; formal; lifeless. [L. *frigidus — frigeo*, to stiffen with cold.]
Frigidity, fri-jid'i-ti, *n.* *Coldness*; want of warmth; impotency; coldness of affection; want of animation or intellectual fire. [Fr. *frigidité.*]
Frigidly, frī'jid-li, *adv.* *Coldly*; dully.
Frigidness, frī'jid-nes, *n.* *Frigidity.*
Frigorific, fri-gō-rif'ik, *a.* *Causing cold*; cooling. [Fr. *frigorifique* — L. *frigus, frigoris*, cold, and *facio*, to make.]
Frill, fril, *n.* *A crisped edging of fine linen on the bosom of a shirt or other similar thing*; a ruffle. — *vt.* *To decorate with frills or ruffles.* [from *frizzle*, to crisp.]
Frilled, frild, *p.a.* *Decorated with frills or ruffles*; having frills.
Frilling, fril'ing, *p.n.* Ruffles; gathers, &c.
Fringe, frinj, *n.* *A border*; an ornamental appendage to the borders of garments, consisting of loose threads; something resembling fringe; margin; extremity. — *vt.* *To adorn or border with fringe or a loose edging. ppr.* fringing, *pret. & pp.* fringed. [Fr. *frange* — L. *fimbriæ*, fibres.]
Fringed, frinjd, *p.a.* *Bordered with fringe.*
Fringy, frinj'i, *a.* *Adorned with fringes.*
Frippery, frip'ė-ri, *n.* *Old worn-out clothes*; waste matter; trumpery; the trade or traffic in old clothes; the place where old clothes are sold. — *a.* Trifling; contemptible. [Fr. *friperie* — *friper*, to wear to rags.]
Frisk, frisk, *vi.* To leap about briskly; to skip; to spring suddenly one way and the other; to dance, skip, and gambol in frolic and gaiety. — *n.* A frolic; a fit of wanton gaiety. [G. *frisch*, fresh.]
Frisking, frisk'ing, *p.a.* Leaping; skipping; dancing about.
Frisky, fris'ki, *a.* Jumping with gaiety; gay; frolicsome; lively.
Frith, frith, *n.* *A narrow channel*; a narrow passage of the sea; a strait; the opening of a river into the sea. [L. *fretum*, a strait.]
Fritter, frit'tėr, *n.* A kind of small pancake *fried*; a small piece of meat fried; a small piece. — *vt.* To cut into *small pieces to be fried*, as meat; to break into small pieces; to take away or waste by degrees (with *away*). [It. *frittella* — L. *frigo, frictus*, to fry.]
Frivolity, fri-vol'i-ti, *n.* Acts or habits of trifling. [Fr. *frivolité.*]
Frivolous, fri'vol-us, *a.* Overflowing with words; *silly; empty*; worthless; of little weight, worth, or importance; not worth notice. [L. *frivolus*, silly, pitiful, worthless.]
Frivolously, fri'vol-us-li, *adv.* *In a frivolous* or trifling *manner.*

Frivolousness, fri'vol-us-nes, *n.* Trifling, or of very little worth or importance.
Frizz, friz, *vt.* To form into small curls with a *crisping*-pin; to form into little hard burs, as the nap of cloth. [Fr. *friser*, to curl.]
Frizzle, friz'l, *vi.* *To curl; to crisp*, as hair. *ppr.* frizzling, *pret. & pp.* frizzled. — *n.* *A curl*; a lock of hair crisped. [Old Fris. *frislen.*]
Fro, frō, *adv.* *From*; away; back or backward. [Sax. *fra.*]
Frock, frok, *n.* An upper coat, or an outer garment made of wool; a loose garment or shirt worn by men over their other clothes, and for a kind of gown worn by females. [Fr. *froc*, a monk's habit — L. *floccus*, a lock of wool.]
Frog, frog, *n.* An amphibious animal, remarkable for its activity in swimming and leaping, and for the transformation it undergoes before arriving at maturity; [Port. *froco*, tuff of wool or silk] a kind of button or tassel on a coat or vestment. [Sax. *froga.*]
Frolic, Frolick, fro'lik, *a.* *Glad*; *joyous*; *merry*; dancing, playing, or frisking about. — *n.* A wild prank; a gambol; a freak; a scene of gaiety and mirth, as in dancing or play. — *vi.* To play wild pranks; to play tricks of levity, mirth, and gaiety. [G. *fröhlich*, joyous.]
Frolicsome, fro'lik-sum, *a.* *Full of frolics*, or of gaiety and mirth; given to pranks.
Frolicsomely, fro'lik-sum-li, *adv.* With wild gaiety.
Frolicsomeness, fro'lik-sum-nes, *n.* Quality of being frolicsome; gaiety.
From, from, *prep.* The sense of *from*, which expresses the idea of distance in relation to a source, is literal or figurative, but it is uniformly the same. In certain phrases, generally or always elliptical, *from* is followed by certain adverbs, denoting place, region, or position indefinitely, no precise point being expressed; as, *from above, from beneath, from before, from behind*, &c. It sometimes signifies, *remote from*, forth from, and out from. *From* precedes another preposition, followed by its proper object or case; as, *from amid, from among, from beneath, from beyond, from afar.* [Sax. *fram.*]
Front, frunt, *n.* *The forehead* or part of the face above the eyes; the whole face; the fore part of anything; the van; the part or place before the face; the most conspicuous part; impudence. — *a.* *Relating to the front* or face. *vt.* To stand with the *front* opposed to; to oppose face to face; to stand over against. — *vi.* To have *the face or front* toward any point of the compass; to be opposite; to stand foremost. [Fr. — L. *frons, frontis*, the forehead.]
Frontage, frunt'āj, *n.* *The front part* of an edifice, structure, quay, &c.
Frontal, front'al, *a.* *Belonging to the forehead.* — *n.* An ornament for the *forehead*; a frontlet; a front piece over a small door or window. [Fr.]
Fronted, frunt'ed, *p.a.* *Formed with a front.*
Frontier, fron'tėr, *n.* *That part of a country which fronts* another country; the extreme part of a country, bordering on another country. — *a.* Lying on the exterior part; bordering; conterminous. [Fr. *frontière.*]
Frontiered, fron'tėrd, *p.a.* *Guarded on the frontiers.*
Fronting, frunt'ing, *p.a.* *Standing with*

the front toward; front to front, or opposite.
Frontispiece, fron'tis-pēs, *n.* *A front view*; the face that directly presents itself to the eye; an engraving *fronting* the first page of a book, or at the beginning. [Old Fr. *frontispice* — L. *frons*, and *specio*, to view.]
Frontless, frunt'les, *a.* Wanting shame or modesty; not diffident.
Frontlet, frunt'let, *n.* A fillet or band worn *on the forehead.* [dimin. from *front.*]
Front-view, frunt'vū. *n.* *A view of the front part* of an edifice or other object.
Frost, frost, *n.* *Act of freezing*; congelation of water; frozen dew; hoar frost; that state of the air which occasions freezing; the appearance of plants sparkling with icy crystals; coldness of temperament. — *vt.* To cover with anything resembling *hoar-frost.* [Sax. *forst* — Old G. *friusan*, to freeze.]
Frost-bitten, frost'bit-n, *p.a.* *Nipped*, withered, or affected *by frost.*
Frosted, frost'ed, *p.a.* *Covered* with a composition like white *frost*; having the hair changed to a gray or white colour, as if covered with hoar-frost.
Frostily, frost'i-li, *adv.* *With frost* or excessive cold; coldly.
Frostiness, frost'i-nes, *n.* *State or quality of being frosty*; freezing cold.
Frosting, frost'ing, *p.n.* The composition resembling *hoar-frost*, used to cover cake, &c.
Frost-work, frost'wėrk, *n.* *Work resembling hoar-frost* on shrubs.
Frosty, frost'i, *a.* *Producing frost*; containing frost; chill in affection or courage; resembling hoar-frost; white; gray-haired. [G. *frostig.*]
Froth, froth, *n.* *Foam; spume;* the bubbles caused in liquors by fermentation; any empty show of wit or eloquence; light unsubstantial matter. *vt. To cause to foam.* — *vi.* *To foam*; to throw up spume; to throw out foam or bubbles. [Icel. *froda.*]
Frothily, froth'i-li, *adv.* *With foam* or spume; in an empty trifling manner.
Frothiness, froth'i-nes, *n.* Emptiness; senseless matter.
Frothy, froth'i, *a.* *Full of foam or froth*, or consisting of froth or light bubbles; soft; not solid; vain; unsubstantial.
Frounce, frouns, *vt.* To curl or frizzle, as the hair about *the forehead* or face; to gather into plaits. *ppr.* frouncing, *pret. & pp.* frounced. — *n.* A curl; an ornament of dress. [Fr. *froncer*, to pucker.]
Froward, frō'wėrd, *a.* Averse; unyielding; ungovernable; disobedient; wayward. [*from* and *ward.*]
Frowardly, frō'wėrd-li, *adv.* Perversely.
Frowardness, frō'wėrd-nes, *n.* Perverseness; reluctance to yield or comply; disobedience; peevishness.
Frown, froun, *vi.* *To knit the forehead*; to express displeasure by contracting the brow and looking grim or surly; to look stern; to scowl (with *on* or *at*); to lower; to look threatening. — *vt.* To repel by expressing displeasure; to rebuke. — *n.* *A wrinkling of the brow;* a sour or stern look, expressive of displeasure; any expression of displeasure. [Old Fr. *refrongner* — L. *frons*, the forehead.]
Frowning, froun'ing, *p.a.* Lowering; threatening.
Frowningly, froun'ing-li, *adv.* Sternly.
Frozen, frōz'n, *p.a.* *Congealed by cold*;

Fāte, fär, fat, fa̯ll; mē, met, hėr; pīne, pin; nōte, not, mōve; tūbe, tub, bu̯ll; oil, pound.

Fructification, fruk'ti-fi-kā"shon, n. *Act of fructifying;* fecundation; the distribution and arrangement of the organs of reproduction in plants. [Low L. *fructificatio*—L. *fructus*, fruit, and *facio*, to make.]
Fructify, fruk'ti-fī, vt. To make fruitful; to fertilise.—vi. To bear fruit. ppr. fructifying, pret. & pp. fructified. [Fr. *fructifier*—L. *fructus*, and *facio*, to make.]
Fructifying, fruk'ti-fī-ing, p.a. Rendering fruitful or productive.
Frugal, frū'gal, a. Pertaining to produce; economical in the use of money, goods, or provisions of any kind; careful; thrifty; saving unnecessary expense; not profuse or lavish. [Fr.—L. *frux, frugis*, produce of the fields.]
Frugality, frū-gal'i-ti, n. Prudent economy; thrift; good husbandry or housewifery; a prudent and sparing use or appropriation of anything. [Fr. *frugalité*.]
Frugally, frū'gal-li, adv. In a frugal manner; with economy.
Frugivorous, frū-jiv'er-us, a. Feeding on fruits, seeds, or corn, as birds. [L. *fruges*, fruits, and *voro*, to eat.]
Fruit, frōt, n. Whatever is produced for the enjoyment of man or animals; produce; whatever the earth produces for the nourishment of animals, or for clothing or profit; the produce of a tree or other plant; offspring; young; consequence; result; profit; good derived.—vi. To produce fruit. [Fr.—L. *fructus—fruor*, to enjoy.]
Fruiterer, frōt'ėr-ėr, n. One who deals in fruit.
Fruitery, frōt'é-ri, n. A repository for fruit. [Fr. *fruiterie*.]
Fruitful, frōt'ful, a. Very productive; fertile; not barren; abounding in anything; plenteous; prolific.
Fruitfully, frōt'ful-li, adv. In a fruitful manner; plenteously; abundantly.
Fruitfulness, frōt'ful-nes, n. Quality of producing fruit in abundance; fertility; quality of being prolific; productiveness of the intellect; exuberant abundance.
Fruition, frū-i'shon, n. A using or enjoying; enjoyment; the pleasure derived from use or possession. [from L. *fruor*, to enjoy.]
Fruitless, frōt'les, a. Destitute of fruit; unprofitable; abortive; ineffectual; destitute of offspring.
Fruitlessly, frōt'les-li, adv. Without any valuable effect; idly; vainly.
Fruitlessness, frōt'les-nes, n. Unfruitfulness; unprofitableness.
Frush, frush, vt. To dash violently to pieces.
Frustrate, frus'trāt, vt. To disappoint; to balk; to foil; to bring to nothing; to render of no effect. ppr. frustrating, pret. & pp. frustrated.—a.† Vain; useless; null; void. [L. *frustror, frustratus—frustra*, in error, in vain.]
Frustration, frus-trā'shon, n. Disappointment; defeat. [L. *frustratio*.]
Frustum, frus'tum, n. A piece; a piece or part of a solid body separated from the rest. [L.—*frango*, to break.]
Fry, frī, vt. To parch; to dress with fat by heating or roasting in a pan over a fire.—vi. To suffer the action of fire or extreme heat; to be agitated; to boil. ppr. frying, pret. & pp. fried.—n. A dish of anything fried. [Fr. *frire*, to fry—L. *frigo, frigere*, to roast, fry.]

Fry, frī, n. A swarm of little fish; a swarm of little animals, &c. [Fr. *frai*, spawn of fish.]
Fub, fub, vt. To puff up; to put off or delay.
Fuchsia, fū'shi-a, n. A well-known beautiful flowering shrub, so called from *Fuchs*, a German botanist.
Fudge, fuj, interj. Stuff; nonsense; an exclamation of contempt.
Fuel, fū'el, n. Any matter which serves as aliment to fire; combustible matter; anything that serves to feed or increase flame, heat, or excitement. [Low L. *focale*—L. *focus*, a hearth.]
Fugacious, fū-gā'shi-us, a. Flying or fleeing away; volatile. [Fr. *fugace*—L. *fugax—fugio*, to flee away.]
Fugacity, fū-gas'i-ti, n. Quality of flying away; volatility; uncertainty; instability. [Fr. *fugacité*.]
Fugitive, fū'jit-iv, a. Apt to flee away; readily wafted by the wind; volatile; readily escaping; fleeting; not fixed; eloping; wandering; vagabond; temporary.—n. One who flees from his station or duty; a deserter; one who flees from danger; one who has fled and taken refuge under another power; one who has fled from punishment. [Fr. *fugitif*—L. *fugio*, to flee away.]
Fugleman, fū'gl-man, n. A file leader; one who stands in front of a line of soldiers when under drill, and whose movements, in the manual exercise, they are all simultaneously to follow; an example. [G. *flügelmann—flügel*, a wing.]
Fulcrum, ful'krum, n. Fulcra or Fulcrums, pl. A support; the foot of a couch; that on which anything rests; that by which a lever is sustained, or the point about which it moves. [L. *fulcio*, to prop up.]
Fulfil, ful-fil', vt. To complete; to perform; to answer in execution what has been foretold; to answer, as any desire by compliance or gratification; to answer, as a law by obedience; to bring to pass; to carry into effect. ppr. fulfilling, pret. & pp. fulfilled. [*full* and *fill*.]
Fulfilment, Fulfilling, ful-fil'ment, ful-fil'ing, n. Accomplishment; execution; performance.
Fulham, ful'ham, n. A false die.
Full, ful, a. Filled completely, or to the utmost extent of capacity; abounding with; plump; fat; crowded; having the mind or memory filled; entire; that fills, as a meal; strong; loud; clear; mature; denoting the completion of a sentence, as a stop; spread to view in all dimensions; adequate; equal, as pay for work; copious; ample. n. Complete measure; the highest state or degree, as of the tide; the whole; the total; state of satiety; the moon's time of being full.—adv. Quite; to the same degree; with the whole effect; exactly. [Sax.—*fyllan*, Goth. *fulljan, gafulljan*, to fill.]
Full, ful, vt. To thicken, as cloth in a mill; to scour, cleanse, and thicken in a mill. [Sax. *fullian*, to full—L. *fullo*, a fuller.]
Full-blown, ful'blōn, a. Fully expanded, as a blossom.
Full-dress, ful'dres, n. A complete dress or costume; evening dress.
Full-dressed, ful'drest, a. Dressed in form or for company.
Fuller, ful'er, n. One who fulls cloth.
Fuller's-earth, ful'erz-erth, n. A soft friable clay, which absorbs grease, and is much used in fulling cloth.

Full-fraught, ful'frat, a. Laden or stored to fulness.
Full-hot, ful'hot, a. Heated to the utmost.
Fulling, ful'ing, p.n. The art or practice of thickening cloth, and making it compact and firm, in a mill.
Full-length, ful'length, a. Extending the whole length.
Full-manned, ful'mand, a. Completely furnished with men.
Full-orbed, ful'orbd, a. Having the orb complete, as the moon.
Full-pay, ful pā, n. Allowance given to officers and non-commissioned officers, without any deduction whatever.
Fully, ful'li, adv. With fulness; completely; amply; perfectly.
Fulminate, ful'min-āt, vi. To lighten and thunder; to detonate; to issue forth ecclesiastical censures, as if with the force of a thunder-bolt.—vt. To utter or send out, as a denunciation or censure; to cause to explode.—n. A compound substance which explodes by percussion, friction, or heat. ppr. fulminating. pret. & pp. fulminated. [L. *fulmino, fulminatus—fulgeo*, to flash.]
Fulminating, ful'min-āt-ing, p.a. Exploding; detonating; hurling menaces.
Fulmination, ful-min-ā'shon, n. A thundering; denunciation of censure, as by papal authority; excommunication; the explosion of certain chemical preparations; detonation. [L. *fulminatio*.]
Fulness, ful'nes, n. State of being full or filled, so as to leave no part vacant; copiousness; completeness; satiety; wealth; swelling, as of the soul; extent; loudness; force of sound, such as fills the ear.
Fulsome, ful'sum, a. Foul; gross; disgusting; nauseous. [Sax. *fúl*, foul, and term. *some*.]
Fulsomely, ful'sum-li, adv. Rankly; nauseously; grossly.
Fulsomeness, ful'sum-nes, n. Nauseousness; offensive grossness.
Fumble, fum'bl, vi. To seek or grope about awkwardly or in perplexity; to play childishly; to turn over and over. vt. To manage awkwardly. ppr. fumbling, pret. & pp. fumbled. [D. *fommelen*.]
Fume, fūm, n. Smoke; vapour from combustion, as from burning wood or tobacco; exhalation from the stomach, as of liquor; heat, as of passion. [L. *fumus*, smoke.]—vi. To smoke; to yield vapour or visible exhalations; to be in a rage; to be hot with anger.—vt. To smoke; to fumigate; to perfume; to disperse or drive away in vapours. ppr. fuming, pret. & pp. fumed. [Fr. *fumer*—L. *fumus*, smoke.]
Fumigate, fūm'i-gāt, vt. To smoke; to expose to smoke or gas to purify from infection, &c. ppr. fumigating, pret. & pp. fumigated. [L. *fumigo, fumigatus—fumus*, smoke, and *ago*, to drive.]
Fumigation, fūm-i-gā'shon, n. Act of applying smoke or gas, to purify from infection, &c.; vapours; scent raised by fire. [Low L. *fumigatio*.]
Fuming, fūm'ing, p.a. Raging.
Fumous, Fumy, fūm'us, fūm'i, a. Producing fume or smoke; full of vapour.
Fun, fun, n. Sport; the perception or enjoyment of drollery and oddity; frolic; mirthful drollery; merriment. [allied to Sax. *faegen*, glad, joyful.]
Function, fungk'shon, n. The doing of anything; performance; office; the activity appropriate to any business;

duty; charge; place; the office of any particular part of animal bodies; faculty, animal or intellectual; the proper office of any organ in vegetable economy. [L. *junctio—fungor*, to perform.]

Functional, fungk'shon-al, *a. Relating to some office or function;* official; performed by the functions, as of animal or vegetable bodies.

Functionally, fungk'shon-al-li, *adv.* By means of the functions.

Functionary, fungk'shon-a-ri, *n.* One who discharges any function; one who holds an office or trust. [Fr. *fonctionnaire*.]

Fund, fund, *n. A stock or capital;* (pl.) money lent to government, constituting the stock of a national debt, for which interest is paid; money or income destined to the payment of the interest of a debt, or for the support of some permanent object; abundance; ample stock or store.—*vt.* To provide and appropriate a *fund* for paying the interest of, as a debt; to place in a fund, as money. [Old Fr. *fond*—L. *funda*, a money-bag.]

Fundament, fun'da-ment, *n. A foundation; the seat;* the lower part of the body, or its aperture. [L. *fundamentum—fundo*, to found.]

Fundamental, fun-da-ment'al, *a. Pertaining to the foundation;* essential; necessary; leading.—*n.* A leading principle which serves as the *ground-work* of a system; an essential.

Fundamentally, fun-da-ment'al-li, *adv.* Essentially; at the foundation.

Funded, fund'ed, *p.a. Placed in the public funds;* furnished with funds for regular payment of the interest of.

Funeral, fū'nė-ral, *n.* Burial; interment; the ceremony of burying a dead body; obsequies.—*a.* Used at the interment of the dead. [Fr. *funérailles*—L. *funus, funeris*, a funeral.]

Funereal, fū-nē'rē-al, *a. Suiting a funeral;* dark; dismal; mournful. [L. *funereus*.]

Fungous, fung'gus, *a. Like a mushroom;* growing suddenly, but not substantial or durable. [from L. *fungus*.]

Fungus, fung'gus, *n.* **Fungi** or **Funguses,** fun'jī or fung'gus-es, *pl. A mushroom;* a toadstool; a plant which forms mould, mildew, &c.; a spongy excrescence in animal bodies, as proud flesh formed in wounds. [L.]

Funicular, fū-nik'ū-lėr, *a. Consisting of a small cord or fibre,* or an assemblage of ropes. [from L. *funiculus*, a small cord.]

Funnel, fun'nel, *n. That through which anything is poured in;* a utensil for conveying liquids into close vessels; a tunnel; the shaft of a chimney through which smoke ascends. [L. *infundibulum—fundo, fusum,* to pour.]

Funnily, fun'i-li, *adv.* In a droll or comical manner.

Funny, fun'i, *a.* Droll; comical; ridiculous. [from *fun*.]

Fur, fėr, *n. That which serves for a covering;* the woolly skins of wild beasts used to line garments; the short, fine, soft hair of certain animals, growing thick on the skin; strips of skin with fur, used on garments for lining; a coat of morbid matter collected on the tongue in persons affected with fever; a coating on the interior of tea-kettles, &c., deposited by hard water.—*a. Pertaining to or made of fur.—vt.* To line *with fur;* to cover with morbid matter, as the tongue. *ppr.* furring, *pret.* & *pp.* furred. [Fr. *fourrure—fourrer,* to put on.]

Furbish, fėr'bish, *vt. To rub or scour to brightness;* to burnish; to restore to original purity. [Fr. *fourbir, ppr. fourbissant.*]

Furbisher, fėr'bish-ėr, *n.* One who polishes or makes bright by rubbing.

Furious, fū'ri-us, *a. Full of madness or rage;* violent; impetuous; frenzied; frantic. [Fr. *furieux*—L. *furo, furere,* to rave.]

Furiously, fū'ri-us-li, *adv.* With impetuous motion or agitation; violently.

Furiousness, fū'ri-us-nes, *n. State of being furious;* violent agitation; madness; frenzy.

Furl, fėrl, *vt.* To draw up; to wrap close to the yard, stay, or mast, and fasten by cord, as a sail. [Fr. *ferler*.]

Furlong, fėr'long, *n. The length of a furrow;* a measure of length; the eighth part of a mile; forty rods, poles, or perches. [Sax. *furlang*.]

Furlough, fėr'lō, *n. Leave or permission to go away;* leave of absence to a soldier for a limited time.—*vt.* To furnish *with a furlough;* to grant leave of absence to, as to an officer or soldier. [Dan. *forlof*—Sax. *lyfan*, to allow.]

Furnace, fėr'nas, *n. An oven for heating, melting, baking,* &c.; a place where a vehement fire and heat may be made and maintained, for melting ores, metals, &c.; a smaller apparatus in which fuel is burned for culinary purposes; grievous afflictions.—*vt.* To throw out, as sparks from a furnace. [Fr. *fournaise*—L. *fornax*, an oven.]

Furnish, fėr'nish, *vt.* To supply with anything necessary, as bread from the *oven;* to store, as with knowledge; to fit up; to fit for an expedition. [Fr. *fournir, fournissant*—L. *furnus* or *fornax*, an oven.]

Furnished, fėr'nisht, *p.a.* Supplied; garnished; fitted with necessaries.

Furniture, fėr'ni-tūr, *n. That which is furnished;* goods, vessels, utensils, and other appendages, necessary or convenient for housekeeping; appendages; decorations. [Fr. *fourniture*.]

Furred, fėrd, *p.a.* Lined *with fur;* covered with fur.

Furrier, fu'ri-ėr, *n. A dealer in furs;* one who dresses furs.

Furriery, fu'ri-ėr-i, *n. Furs in general;* the trade in furs; dressing of furs.

Furrow, fu'rō, *n. A trench in the earth made by a plough;* a long, narrow channel in wood or metal; a groove; a hollow made by wrinkles in the face.—*vt.* To cut or cleave with the plough; to make furrows in; to make long, narrow channels in; to wrinkle. [Sax. *fur, furh*—Sans. *bark,* to cut.]

Furrowed, fu'rōd, *p.a. Marked with furrows;* cut in furrows.

Furrow-weed, fu'rō-wēd, *n.* A weed growing on ploughed land.

Furrowy, fu'rō-i, *a. Full of furrows.*

Furry, fėr'i, *a. Covered with fur;* dressed in fur; consisting of fur or skins.

Further, fėr'тнėr, *a. Forth to a greater distance;* more or most distant; farther; additional.—*adv. To a greater distance.—vt.* To cause to move *forth to a greater distance;* to help forward; to promote; to forward; to help or assist; to countenance. [Sax. *furthra,* compar. of *forth.*]

Furtherance, fėr'тнėr-ans, *n.* A helping *forward;* promotion; advancement.

Furtherer, fėr'тнėr-ėr, *n. One who helps to advance;* a promoter.

Furthermore, fėr'тнėr-mōr, *adv. More in addition;* moreover; besides; in addition to what has been said.

Furthermost, fėr'тнėr-mōst, *a.* Most remote.

Furthest, fėr'тнest, *a. Most advanced,* either in time or place.—*adv.* At the greatest distance.

Furtive, fėr'tiv, *a. Obtained by theft;* stolen; sly; stealthy. [Fr. *furtif*—L. *fur, furis,* a thief—Gr. *phōr—pherō,* to bear, to bear away.]

Furtively, fėr'tiv-li, *adv. In a furtive manner;* by stealth.

Fury, fū'ri, *n. A raging;* a violent rushing; madness; frenzy; enthusiasm; a goddess of vengeance, in mythology; a stormy, violent woman. [L. *furor,* a raging—*furo,* to rage.]

Furze, fėrz, *n.* A prickly evergreen shrub; whin; gorse. [Sax. *fyrs*.]

Furzy, fėrz'i, *a. Overgrown with furze.*

Fuse, fūz, *vt. To pour;* to liquefy by heat; to dissolve.—*vi.* To be *melted;* to be reduced from a solid to a fluid state by heat. *ppr.* fusing, *pret.* & *pp.* fused. [L. *fundo, fusum.*]

Fuse, fūz, *n.* A tube filled with combustible matter, used in blasting or discharging a shell; a sky-rocket; a squib.

Fusee, fū-zē', *n. A spindle;* the cone or conical part of a watch or clock, round which is wound the chain or cord. [Fr. *fusée*—L. *fusus,* a spindle.]

Fusibility, fūz-i-bil'i-ti, *n. Quality of being fusible.* [Fr. *fusibilité.*]

Fusible, fūz'i-bl, *a. That may be fused,* melted, or liquefied. [Fr.—L. *fundo, fusus,* to pour.]

Fusil, fū'sil, *n.* A light musket or firelock. [Fr.—*feu,* fire.]

Fusileer, fū-sil-ēr', *n. A soldier armed with a fusil;* an infantry soldier, distinguished by wearing a cap nearly like that of a grenadier. [Fr. *fusilier.*]

Fusion, fū'zhon, *n. Act or operation of fusing* or of melting by heat, without the aid of a solvent; state of being melted; a uniting two or more things into one; state of being blended or united. [Fr.—L. *fusio,* a pouring.]

Fuss, fus, *n. Hurry;* undue importance; tumult; much ado about trifles. [Sax. *fus,* ready, nimble.]

Fussily, fus'i-li, *adv.* In a bustling manner.

Fussy, fus'i, *a. Making a fuss;* moving and acting with fuss; bustling.

Fustian, fus'ti-an, *n.* A kind of coarse, thick twilled cotton cloth; bombast; a swelling style.—*a. Made of fustian;* swelling in style above the dignity of the thoughts or subject. [Old Fr. *fustaine.*]

Fustiness, fus'ti-nes, *n. A fusty state* or *quality;* an ill smell from mouldiness, or mouldiness itself.

Fusty, fus'ti, *a. Tasting or smelling of a foul or mouldy cask;* mouldy; ill-smelling; rank; rancid. [Old Fr. *fuste,* a cask.]

Futile, fū'til, *a. That easily lets out;* silly; trifling; trivial; useless; worthless. [Fr.—L. *fundo,* to pour, to spread out, to display.]

Futility, fū-til'i-ti, *n. Quality of being futile;* emptiness; worthlessness; uselessness. [Fr. *futilité.*]

Future, fū'tūr, *a. That is to be;* noting the tense of a verb which expresses a future act or event.—*n. Time to come;* a time subsequent to the present. [Fr. *futur*—L. *futurus*—Sans. *bhū,* to be.]

Fāte, fär, fat, fall; mē, mē', hėr; pine, pin; nōte, not, mōve; tūbe, tub, bull; oil, pound.

G.

Gabardine, ga-bär-dēn, n. A coarse frock or loose upper garment; a mean dress. [Sp. *gabardina*.]
Gabble, gab'l, vi. To prate; to talk fast, or to talk without meaning. ppr. gabbling, pret. & pp. gabbled.—n. Rapid talk without meaning; inarticulate sounds rapidly uttered, as of fowls. [D. *gabberen*.]
Gabbler, gab'l-ėr, n. A prater; a noisy talker.
Gabbling, gab'l-ing, p.n. The making of a confused noise; rapid, indistinct utterance.
Gable, gā'bl, n. The pointed end of a house; the triangular end of a house, from the cornice or eaves to the top. [G. *giebel*, Old G. *gibil*, the tip or point of a thing.]
Gad, gad, n. A sting; a goad; a wedge or ingot of steel or iron. [Sax.]
Gad, gad, vi. To go or walk about; to rove or ramble idly or without any fixed purpose. ppr. gadding, pret. & pp. gadded. [from *pat*, third pers. sing. pres. indic. of Old G. *ga*, to go.]
Gadder, gad'ėr, n. A rambler; one who roves about idly.
Gadfly, gad'flī, n. An insect which stings cattle, and incites them to run about wildly. [Sax. *gad*, a sting, and *fly*.]
Gaelic, gā'lik, a. Pertaining to the Gaels, tribes of Celtic origin, inhabiting the Highlands of Scotland.—n. The language of the Highlanders of Scotland. [Gael. *Gaelig*.]
Gag, gag, vt. To lock or shut up; to stop the mouth of by thrusting something into the throat, so as to hinder speaking; to silence. ppr. gagging, pret. & pp. gagged.—n. Something thrust into the mouth and throat to hinder speaking. [Sax. *cæggian*, to lock—*cæg*, a key.]
Gage, gāj, n. A pledge; something laid down as a security; something thrown down as a challenge to combat, to be taken up by the one who accepts the challenge.—vt. To pledge; to bind by pledge, caution, or security; to engage. ppr. gaging, pret. & pp. gaged. [Fr.]
Gage, gāj. See GAUGE.
Gaiety, gā'e-ti. See GAYETY.
Gaily, gā'li, adv. In a gay manner; joyfully; merrily. [from *gay*.]
Gain, gān, vt. To win; to acquire; to get, as profit or advantage; to receive, as honour; to draw into any interest or party; to conciliate.—vi. To have advantage or profit; to grow rich; to encroach; to come forward by degrees; to get ground; to prevail against, or have the advantage; to obtain influence with. (With *on* or *upon*.)—n. Something obtained, as an advantage; profit; benefit; overplus in computation: anything opposed to loss. [Sax. *gynan*, to win.]
Gainer, gān'ėr, n. One who gains.
Gainful, gān'fụl, a. Full of gain; profitable; advantageous; advancing interest or happiness; lucrative.

Gainfully, gān'fụl-li, adv. With increase of wealth; profitably.
Gainfulness, gān'fụl-nes, n. State of being gainful; profit; advantage.
Gaingiving†, gān'giv-ing, n. A misgiving.
Gainings, gān'ings, n. pl. Acquisitions made by labour or successful enterprise.
Gainless, gān'les, a. Not producing gain; unprofitable.
Gainsay, gān'sā, vt. To speak against; to oppose in words; to controvert; to dispute. ppr. gainsaying, pret. & pp. gainsaid. [Sax. *ongean*, against, and *say*.]
Gainsayer, gān'sā-ėr, n. One who contradicts; an opposer.
'Gainst, gānst. See AGAINST.
Gairish, gār'ish, a. Furnished†; tawdry; extravagantly gay; flighty. [Sax. *gedro*, ready.]
Gairishly, gār'ish-li, adv. Gaudily.
Gairishness, gār'ish-nes, n. Gaudiness; finery; ostentatious show.
Gait, gāt, n. A going; manner of walking or stepping. [from Sax. *gan*, to go.]
Gaiter, gā'tėr, n. A kind of high shoe; a covering of cloth for the leg.—vt. To dress with gaiters. [Old Fr. *guestres*, high shoes.]
Gala, gā'la, n. A show; festivity; mirth. A *gala* day is a day of pomp, show, or festivity. [Fr. feast.]
Galaxy, ga'lak-si, n. The Milky Way; that long, white, luminous track, occasioned by a multitude of stars, which seems to encompass the heavens like a girdle; an assemblage of splendid persons or things. [Fr. *galaxie*—Gr. *gala*, *galaktos*, milk.]
Gale, gāl, n. A sounding wind; a blast; a breeze; a gust; a vehement wind; a storm. [Sax. *gyllan*, to roar.]
Galiot, gā'li-ot, n. A small galley or sort of brigantine, built for chase. [Fr. *galiote*.]
Gall, gal, n. A bitter yellowish-green fluid, secreted by the gall-bladder beneath the liver; the bile; rancour; malignity; bitterness of mind. [Sax. *gealla—gealew*, yellow.]
Gall, gal, n. The oak-apple; a hard round excrescence produced by a small insect, on a kind of oak-tree. [L. *galla*.]
Gall, gal, vt. To scratch; to fret and wear away by friction; to break the surface of by rubbing; to vex; to chagrin; to injure; to annoy.—vi. To fret; to be teased.—n. A wound in the skin by rubbing. [Fr. *se galer*, to scratch one's self.]
Gallant, gal'lant, a. Gay; splendid; noble-minded; brave; daring; frank; showing politeness and attention to ladies.—n. A gay sprightly man; a courtly or fashionable man; a man who is polite and attentive to ladies; a lover; a suitor; a seducer. [Fr. *galant—gala*, show.]

Gallant, gal-lant', a. Courtly; civil; polite and attentive to ladies; courteous.—vt. To attend or wait on, as a lady. [Fr. *galant*.]
Gallantly, gal'lant-li, adv. Gaily; splendidly; bravely; nobly; in the manner of a wooer or gallant.
Gallantry, gal'lant-ri, n. Show; finery; bravery; intrepidity; boldness; daring; courage; nobleness; civility or polite attentions to ladies; vicious love or pretensions to love; lewdness; debauchery; gallant persons†. [Fr. *galanterie*.]
Galled, gald, p.a. Fretted; teased; vexed.
Gallery, gal'le-ri, n. A kind of walk along the floor of a house, into which the doors of the apartments open; the upper floor of a church, theatre, &c.; a long portico, with columns on one side; a frame like a balcony in large ships; a collection of works in painting or sculpture. [Fr. *galerie*.]
Galley, gal'le, n. Galleys, pl. A low, flat-built vessel, with one deck, and navigated with sails and oars; the cook-room of a ship of war, or other large ship. [Fr. *galée*.]
Galley-slave, gal'le-slāv, n. A person condemned for a crime to work at the oar on board of a *galley*.
Gallic, gal'ik, a. Pertaining to Gaul, or France. [L. *Gallicus—Gallia*, Gaul.]
Gallic, gal'ik, a. Belonging to or derived from *galls*, or oak-apples. [from *gall*, no. 2.]
Gallicism, gal'i-sism, n. A French idiom; a mode of speech peculiar to the French nation. [Fr. *gallicisme*.]
Gallinaceous, gal-le-nā'she-us, a. Designating or pertaining to that order of birds which includes the pheasant, turkey, &c. [L. *gallinaceus—gallus*, a cock.]
Galling, gal'ing, p.a. Adapted to fret or chagrin; vexing.—p.n. A fretting or wearing of the skin by friction.
Gallipot, gal'li-pot, n. A small pot or vessel, of potter's clay, painted and glazed, used for containing medicines. [D. *klei*, clay, and *pot*, pot.]
Gallon, gal'lun, n. A liquid measure of four quarts or eight pints. [Sp. *galon*.]
Gallop, gal'lup, vi. To move or run with leaps or bounds, as a horse; to ride with a galloping pace; to move very fast (with *over*).—n. The pace of a quadruped, particularly of a horse, by springs or leaps. [Fr. *galoper*.]
Gallopade, gal-lup-kd', n. A sidelong or curvetting kind of *gallop*; a kind of dance; a kind of music appropriate to the dance.—vi. To *gallop*; to move about briskly. ppr. gallopading, pret. & pp. gallopaded. [Fr. *galopade*.]
Gallopading, gal-lup-kd'ing, p.a. Galloping; dancing a gallopade.
Galloper, gal'lup-ėr, n. A horse that gallops; a man that gallops or makes haste.
Gallow†, gal'lō, vt. To fright or terrify.

ch, chain; j, job; g, go; ng, sing; ᴡʜ, then; th, thin; w, wig; wh, whig; zh, azure; † obsolete.

Gallows, gal'lŏz, n. **Gallowses,** pl. A cross; a gibbet. [Sax. galga.]
Galls, galz, n. pl. Excoriations produced by the friction of harness.
Galoche, ga-lōsh', n. A shoe to be worn over another shoe to keep the foot dry. [Fr.]
Galvanic, gal-van'ik, a. Pertaining to galvanism; containing or exhibiting it.
Galvanism, gal'van-izm n. A species of electricity, usually developed by the mutual action of various metals and chemical agents upon each other. [from Galvani, of Bologna, the discoverer.]
Galvanist, gal'van-ist, n. One versed in galvanism.
Galvanize, gal'van-iz, vt. To affect with galvanism. ppr. galvanizing, pret. & pp. galvanized.
Galvanized, gal'van-izd, p.a. Affected with galvanism; plated, as with gold, silver, &c., by means of galvanism.
Gambadoes, gam-bā'dōz, n. pl. Leather coverings for the legs in riding on horseback. [It. gamba, a leg.]
Gamble, gam'bl, vi. To play or game for money. ppr. gambling, pret. & pp. gambled. [from game.]
Gambler, gam'bl-ėr, n. One who games.
Gambling, gam'bl-ing, p.n. The act or practice of gaming for money.
Gamboge, gam-bōj', n. A concrete vegetable juice, brought from Cambodja, or Cambodia, in Asia, and employed as a pigment and as an active cathartic.
Gambol, gam'bol, vi. To dance and skip about in sport; to frisk; to leap; to play in frolic; to start.—n. A skipping or leaping about in frolic; a skip; a sportive prank. ppr. gambolling, pret. & pp. gambolled. [Fr. gambiller.]
Game, gām, n. Joy; pleasure; sport of any kind; an exercise or play for amusement or winning a stake; a match for trial of skill; a single match at play; advantage in play; scheme pursued; field-sports; the chase, falconry, &c.; animals pursued or taken in the chase, or in the sports of the field.—vi. To play at any sport or diversion; to play for a stake or prize; to practise gaming. ppr. gaming, pret. & pp. gamed. [Sax. gamen, joy; Old G. gaman, jest, play.]
Game-cock, gām'kok, n. A cock bred or used to fight.
Gameful, gām'ful, a. Full of game or games.
Gamekeeper, gām'kēp-ėr, n. One who has the care of game.
Gamesome, gām'sum, a. Gay; sportive; playful; frolicsome.
Gamesomely, gām'sum-li, adv. Merrily; playfully.
Gamester, gām'stėr, n. A person addicted to gaming; a gambler.
Gaming, gām'ing, p.n. The act or art of playing any game in a contest for a victory, or for a prize or stake; the practice of gamesters.
Gaming-house, gām'ing-hous, n. A house where gaming is practised.
Gaming-table, gām'ing-tā-bl, n. A table appropriated to gaming.
Gammon, gam'mun, n. The leg or thigh of a hog, pickled and smoked or dried; a smoked ham; an imposition or hoax. vt. To pickle and dry in smoke; to impose on by making believe improbable stories. [It. gambone—gamba, the leg.]
Gamut, gam'ut, n. The lowest note in the musical scale of Guido, or the diatonic scale; the musical scale itself. [Gr. gamma, and syllable ut.]

Gander, gan'dėr, n. The male of the goose. [Sax. gandra.]
Gang, gang, n. A number going together; a crew or band; a select number of a ship's crew, appointed on a particular service, under a suitable officer; a course or vein in mining. (Except at sea, mostly used in abhorrence or contempt.) [Sax. gangan, to go.]
Gangliated, gang'gli-āt-ed, a. Having ganglions; intermixed or intertwined.
Ganglion, gang'gli-on, n. Ganglia, gang'gli-a, pl. A nerve-knot; a collection of nerve-cells, from which nerve-fibres are given off in one or more directions; a morbid enlargement in the course of a tendon. [Gr.—a tumour under the skin.]
Ganglionic, gang-gli-on'ik, a. Pertaining to a ganglion.
Gangrene, gang'grēn, n. An eating away of the flesh; the first stage of mortification.—vt. To mortify.—vi. To become mortified. ppr. gangrening, pret. & pp. gangrened. [Fr. gangrène—Gr. ganggraina—grao, to eat.]
Gangrenous, gang'grēn-us, a. Mortified; indicating mortification of living flesh.
Gangway, gang'wā, n. A way or avenue into or out of any inclosed place; the part of a vessel on the spar-deck, forming a passage along each side.
Gannet, gan'et, n. The solan goose, an aquatic bird of the pelican tribe. [Sax. ganot, a sea-fowl.]
Gantlet, gant'let, n. See GAUNTLET.
Gantlet, Gantlope, gant'let, gant'lŏp, n. Originally a kind of military punishment, in which the culprit was compelled to run between two files or ranks, armed with rods, &c., receiving a blow from each man; a mode of punishment said to have been invented at Ghent; a similar mode of punishment on board ships. [Gant for Ghent, and D. loopen, to run.]
Gaol, jāl, n. A little cage or cave; a cell; a prison; a place for the confinement of debtors and criminals.—vt. To imprison; to confine in prison. [Fr. geôle—L. cavus, hollow.]
Gaoler, jāl'ėr, n. The keeper of a jail.
Gap, gap, n. An opening; a cleft or break; a breach; way of entrance or departure; a flaw; an interstice or vacuity; a chasm. [Icel.]
Gape, gāp, vi. To open the mouth wide; to yawn; to open the mouth for food, as young birds; to open in fissures; to open the mouth in wonder, surprise, eager longing, hope, or expectation, or with a desire to injure or devour; to desire earnestly; to crave. ppr. gaping, pret. & pp. gaped.—n. A gaping; the width of the mouth when opened, as of a bird, fish, &c. [Sax. geapan.]
Gaping, gāp'ing, p.a. Yawning; opening in fissures; craving.
Garb, gärb, n. Comeliness; dress; clothes; habit; fashion or mode of dress. [Old Fr. garbe, a garb.]
Garbage, gärb'āj, n. Waste or refuse matter; the bowels of an animal; refuse parts of flesh; offal. [etym. uncertain.]
Garbed, gärbd, p.a. Dressed; habited.
Garble, gär'bl, vt. To sift; to pick out or separate from a whole such parts as may serve a purpose; to destroy or mutilate by picking out. ppr. garbling, pret. & pp. garbled. [Old Fr. grabeller, to sift.]
Garbled, gär'bld, p.a. Separated; culled out to serve a purpose.
Garbler, gär'bl-ėr, n. One who picks

out to serve a purpose, as in making quotations.
Garden, gär'dn, n. A piece of ground inclosed and appropriated to the cultivation of herbs or plants, fruits and flowers; a rich, well-cultivated spot or tract of country; a delightful spot.—a. Pertaining to or produced in a garden. vi. To lay out and to cultivate a garden. [G. garten—Old G. gartjan, to surround.]
Gardener, gärdn-ėr, n. One who gardens; one whose occupation is to make, tend, and dress a garden.
Gardening, gär'dn-ing, p.n. The act or art of laying out and cultivating gardens; horticulture, including also floriculture, arboriculture, and landscape-gardening.
Gargle, gär'gl, vt. To wash, as the throat and mouth with a liquid preparation, which is kept from descending into the stomach by a gentle expiration of air.—n. Any liquid preparation for washing the mouth and throat. ppr. gargling, pret. & pp. gargled. [Fr. gargouiller, to dabble—L. gurgulio, the windpipe.]
Garish, gār'ish, a. Showy; dazzling.
Garland, gär'land, n. A circle or chaplet made of branches or flowers; an ornament of flowers, fruits, and leaves intermixed; a sculptured representation of a wreath; a collection of little printed pieces of prose or verse.—vt. To deck with a garland. [Fr. guirlande, a crown of flowers.]
Garlic, gär'lik, n. A plant so named because its leaves are like lances or javelins. [Sax. garlec—gar, a dart.]
Garlicky, gär'lik-i, a. Like or containing garlic.
Garment, gär'ment, n. That which is prepared for clothing; any article of clothing, as a coat, a gown, &c.; (pl.) clothing in general; dress. [Norm. garnement—Fr. garnir, to furnish.]
Garner, gär'nėr, n. A granary; a place where grain is stored for preservation. vt. To store in a granary. [Fr. grenier—L. granum, a grain.]
Garnet, gär'net, n. A precious stone, having a resemblance in colour and form to the seeds of the pomegranate; a sort of tackle in ships. [Fr. grenat.]
Garnish, gär'nish, vt. To adorn; to set off; to embellish with something laid round a dish.—n. Ornament; something added for embellishment; something round a dish as an embellishment. [Fr. garnir, ppr. garnissant.]
Garnishing, gär'nish-ing, p.n. That which garnishes; ornament.
Garniture, gär'ni-tūr, n. Ornamental appendages; embellishment; furniture; dress. [Fr.]
Garret, ga'ret, n. That part of a house which is on the upper floor, immediately under the roof; an apartment in the highest story of a house. [Old Fr. garite, a place of refuge built on high.]
Garreteer, ga-ret-ēr', n. An inhabitant of a garret; a poor author.
Garrison, ga'ri-sn, n. A body of troops furnished for defence; a fort, castle, or fortified town, furnished with troops to defend it.—vt. To place troops for defence, as in a fortress; to furnish with soldiers; to secure or defend by fortresses manned with troops. [Fr. garnison—garnir, to supply with.]
Garrisoned, ga'ri-snd, p.a. Furnished with troops in a fort for defence.
Garrote, ga-rōt', n. A mode of capital punishment in Spain, by seating the criminal on a stool, with his back to

Fāte, fär, fat, fall; mē, met, hėr; pine, pin; nōte, not, mōve; tūbe, tub, bull; oil, pound.

a *stake*, placing an iron collar about his neck, and tightening it with a screw until life is extinct.—*vt.* To strangle with the garrote; to strangle. *ppr.* garroting, *pret. & pp.* garroted. [Sp. *garrote*, a cudgel.]
Garrulity, ga-rū'li-ti, *n. A chattering;* talkativeness; loquacity; the practice or habit of talking much. [L. *garrulitas—garrio*, to chatter.]
Garrulous, ga'rū-lus, *a. Chattering; babbling; prating;* talkative. [L. *garrulus*.]
Garrulously, ga'rū-lus-li, *adv.* In a talkative manner.
Garter, gär'tėr, *n.* A string or band used to tie a stocking to *the leg;* the badge of the highest order of knighthood in Great Britain, called the Order of the Garter; the order itself.—*vt.* To *bind with a garter;* to invest with the order of the Garter. [Fr. *jarretière—jarret,* hough.]
Gas, *gas, n. Breath;* a kind of air differing from common air; any permanently elastic aeriform fluid, especially that obtained from coal. [Fr. *gaz.*]
Gasalier, gas-a-lēr', *n. A gas-lamp.*
Gascon, gas'kon, *n. A native of Gascony* in France.
Gasconade, gas-kon-ād', *n.* A boast or boasting; a vaunt; a bravado; a bragging.—*vi.* To boast; to brag; to vaunt; to bluster. *ppr.* gasconading, *pret. & pp.* gasconaded. [Fr. *gasconnade.*]
Gasconading, gas-kon-ād'ing, *p.a.* Boasting; bragging.
Gaseous, ga'ze-us, *a. In the form of gas* or an aeriform fluid.
Gas-fitter, gas'fit-ėr, *n. One who fits* up the pipes, brackets, &c., for *gas*-lighting.
Gash, gash, *vt.* To *make a gash* or long deep *incision* in; to cut.—*n.* A deep and long *cut;* an incision of considerable length, particularly in flesh. [Heb. *gusar,* to cut.]
Gasification, gas'i-fi-kā''shon, *n. Act or process of converting into gas.*
Gasify, gas'i-fi, *vt.* To convert *into gas,* or an aeriform fluid by combination with caloric. *ppr.* gasifying, *pret. & pp.* gasified. [*gas*, and L. *facio.*]
Gas-lamp, gas'lamp, *n. A lamp lighted by gas.*
Gasometer, gaz-om'et-ėr, *n.* An instrument intended *to measure,* collect, preserve, or mix different *gases.* Also, the reservoir or storehouse for the gas produced in gas-manufactories. [*gas*, and Gr. *metron*, a measure.]
Gasp, gasp, *vi.* To *open the mouth wide* in catching the breath or in laborious respiration, particularly in dying.—*vt.* To emit, as breath by opening wide the mouth convulsively.—*n.* Act of opening the mouth to catch the breath; the short catch of the breath in the agonies of death. [Dan. *gispe,* to gasp.]
Gasping, gasp'ing, *p.n.* The opening of the mouth to catch breath.
Gas-tight, gas'tit, *a.* Sufficiently *close* to prevent the escape of *gas.*
Gastric, gas'trik, *a. Belonging to the belly,* or rather to the stomach. [Gr. *gaster,* the belly.]
Gastronomy, gas-tron'o-mi, *n. The art or science of good eating;* epicurism; good living. [Gr. *gaster,* the belly, and *nomos,* a law or rule.]
Gate, gāt, *n. A way; passage;* a large door which gives entrance into a walled city or large edifice; a frame of timber iron, &c., which opens or closes a passage into any inclosure; also the passage; the frame which shuts or stops the passage of water through a dam, lock, &c.; an avenue. [Sax. *geat;* Goth. *gaggan,* to go.]
Gate-house, gāt'hous, *n. A structure* forming a park-entrance; a house forming an entrance to a private mansion, to any public building, palace, &c.
Gateway, gāt'wā, *n. A way* under an arch, or through the *gate* of some inclosure; the gate or entrance itself.
Gather, gaᴛʜ'ėr, *vt. To bring together;* to congregate; to muster; to pick up; to glean; to collect by cropping, picking, or plucking, as fruit; to cull; to bring into one body or interest; to gain; to pucker; to deduce by inference; to collect by reasoning.—*vi.* To assemble; to increase; to grow larger by accretion of like matter.—*n.* A fold in cloth, made by drawing; a wrinkle; a pucker. [Sax. *gaderian.*]
Gatherer, gaᴛʜ'ėr-ėr, *n. One who gathers* or collects.
Gathering, gaᴛʜ'ėr-ing, *p.n.* The act of *collecting* or assembling; an assembly; a collection of pus; an abscess.
Gaud, gad, *n. An ornament.* [L. *gaudium,* joy, the object which produces joy.]
Gauded†, gad'ed, *p.a. Adorned* with trinkets.
Gaudily, gad'i-li, *adv. Showily;* with ostentation of fine dress.
Gaudiness, gad'i-nes, *n. Showiness;* tinsel appearance; ostentatious finery.
Gaudy, gad'i, *a. Showy;* splendid; gay; ostentatiously fine; gay beyond the simplicity of nature or good taste. [from Old Eng. *gaud.*]
Gauge, gāj, *vt.* To ascertain the contents of, as of a cask; to estimate; to measure. *ppr.* gauging, *pret. & pp.* gauged.—*n.* A measuring-rod; a measure; an instrument for indicating the state of a phenomenon; the number of feet which a ship sinks in the water; the distance between the rails in a railway; the calibre of a gun; size or dimensions of metal wire. [Fr *jauger.*]
Gauger, gāj'ėr, *n. One who gauges;* an officer whose business is to ascertain the contents of casks; a surveying officer under the board of excise.
Gauging, gāj'ing, *p.n.* The art of measuring the contents or capacities of vessels of any form.
Gaul, gal, *n. A name of ancient France;* also an inhabitant of Gaul. [L. *Gallia.*]
Gaunt, gant, *a. Attenuated; lean;* thin; slender; hollow; empty, as an animal after long fasting. [Sax. *gewaned—gewanian,* to wane.]
Gauntlet, gant'let, *n. A large iron glove* with fingers covered with small plates, formerly worn by cavaliers armed at all points. [Old Fr. *gantelet—gant,* a glove.]
Gauntleted, gant'let-ed, *p.a. Wearing a gauntlet.*
Gauntly, gant'li, *adv. Leanly;* meagrely.
Gauze, gaz, *n.* A very thin, slight, transparent stuff, of silk or linen, perhaps first introduced from *Gaza* in Palestine. [Fr. *gaze.*]
Gauzy, gaz'i, *a. Like gauze;* thin as gauze.
Gawk, gak, *n. A cuckoo;* a fool; a simpleton. [Sax. *gvec.*]
Gawky, gak'i, *a. Awkward;* clumsy; clownish; foolish.
Gay, gā, *a. Gaudy; showy;* in high spirits; merry; joyous; sprightly; frolicsome; jolly; jovial. [Fr. *gai.*]
Gayety, gā'e-ti, *n. Finery; show;* mirth; airiness; act of juvenile pleasure. (This word is frequently spelled *gaiety.*) [Fr. *gaieté.*]
Gayly, gā'li, *adv. Splendidly;* with mirth and frolic; finely; pompously.
Gaze, gāz, *vi.* To fix the eyes and *look steadily* and earnestly; to look with eagerness or curiosity; to stare; to gape. *ppr.* gazing, *pret. & pp.* gazed. *n. A fixed look;* a look of eagerness, wonder, or admiration; a continued look of attention; the object gazed on; that which causes one to gaze. [Sax. *gaseon—seon,* to look.]
Gazelle, ga-zel', *n.* A small, swift, elegantly formed species of antelope, celebrated for the lustre and soft expression of its eyes. [Fr.]
Gazer, gāz'ėr, *n. One who gazes.*
Gazette, ga-zet', *n.* A bill or paper of news, or a short relation of the general occurrences of the time; a newspaper; appropriately, the official newspaper. *vt. To insert in a gazette;* to announce or publish in a gazette. *ppr.* gazetting, *pret. & pp.* gazetted. [Fr.]
Gazetteer, ga-zet-tēr', *n. A writer or publisher of news;* the title of a newspaper; a book containing a brief description of empires and kingdoms, also of cities, towns, and rivers, in a country, or in the whole world, alphabetically arranged.
Gazing-stock, gāz'ing-stok, *n.* A person *gazed at* with scorn or abhorrence; an object of curiosity or contempt.
Gean, gēn, *n.* The wild cherry. [Fr. *guigne.*]
Gear, gēr, *n. Preparation;* furniture; harness; tackle; habit; dress; ornaments; a train of toothed wheels. [Sax. *gearwa,* clothing—*gyrian,* to prepare.]
Gearing, gēr'ing, *p.n.* Harness; a train of toothed wheels working into each other, for transmitting motion in machinery.
Geese, gēs, *n. plural of goose.*
Gelatine, jel'a-tin, *n.* A substance which coagulates into a viscous substance, as *if congealed;* a concrete transparent substance, obtained by boiling in water the soft and the solid parts of animals; the principle of jelly, glue. [Fr. *gelatine—*L. *gelo,* to freeze.]
Gelatinous, je-lat'in-us, *a. Of the nature* or consistence of *gelatine;* resembling or containing jelly; viscous or moderately stiff. [Fr. *gélatineux.*]
Geld, geld, *vt.* To *castrate;* to deprive of any essential part; to free from any thing immodest; to purify; to purge. *ppr.* gelding, *pret. & pp.* gelded or gelt. [G. *gelten.*]
Gelded, Gelt, geld'ed, gelt, *p.a.* Castrated; emasculated. [Sax. *gylte.*]
Gelding, geld'ing, *p.n. Act of castrating;* a castrated animal, but chiefly a horse.
Gelid, je'lid, *a. Icy cold; very cold.* [L. *gelidus—gelo,* to cause to freeze.]
Gem, jem, *n. A bud;* a precious stone of any kind; a jewel; probably so named from the notion of the swelling brightness of buds.—*vt. To adorn, as with gems;* to bespangle; to embellish, as with detached beauties.—*vi.* To bud; to germinate. *ppr.* gemming, *pret. & pp.* gemmed. [L. *gemma—germen,* a bud.]
Gemini, je'mi-ni, *n. pl. The Twins;* a constellation or sign of the zodiac, containing the two bright stars Castor and Pollux. [L. twins.]
Gemmed, jemd, *p.a. Adorned* with *jewels or buds.*

ch, *chain;* j, *job;* g, *go;* ng, *sing;* ᴛʜ, *then;* th, *thin;* w, *wig;* wh, *whig;* zh, *azure;* † obsolete.

Gemmeous, jem'ē-us, *a.* Pertaining to gems; of the nature of gems; resembling gems. [L. *gemmeus*.]

Gemmy, jem'i, *a.* Full of gems; bright; glittering; neat; spruce; smart.

Gender, jen'dėr, *n.* A kind; a sex, male or female; a difference in words to express distinction of sex.—*vt.* To beget; to procreate.—*vi.* To copulate; to breed. [Fr. *genre*—L. *genus*, *generis*.]

Genealogical, jē-nē-a-loj"ik-al, *a.* Pertaining to genealogy; pertaining to the descent of persons from an ancestor; according to the descent of a person or family from an ancestor. [Fr. *généalogique*.]

Genealogically, jē-nē-a-loj"ik-al-li, *adv.* In a genealogical manner.

Genealogist, jē-nē-al'o-jist, *n.* He who traces genealogies, or descents of persons or families. [Fr. *généalogiste*.]

Genealogy, jē-nē-al'o-ji, *n.* An account of the descent of a person or family from an ancestor; pedigree; lineage; regular descent of a person or family from a progenitor. [Fr. *généalogie*—Gr. *genos*, race, and *logos*, account.]

Genera, jen'ė-ra, *n. pl.* See GENUS.

Generable, jen'ė-ra-bl, *a.* That may be engendered. [Sp. *generable*.]

General jen'ė-ral, *a.* Of or belonging to a genus; generic; not special; not limited to a particular import; public; common to many, or the greatest number; not directed to a single object; extensive, though not universal; usual.—*n.* The whole; that which comprehends all, or the chief part; the common or chief commander of the different regiments which compose an army; the chief commander of a division of an army; [Fr. *générale*] a beat of drum, serving as a signal to a whole army; the chief of an order of monks; the public†. [Fr. *général*—L. *genus*, race, kind—Sans. *jan*, to be born.]

Generalissimo, jen'ė-ral-is'si-mō, *n.* The supreme commander; the chief commander of an army or military force. [It.]

Generality, jen-ė-ral'i-ti, *n.* State of being general; the bulk; the greatest part. [Fr. *généralité*.]

Generalization, jen'ė-ral-iz-a"shon, *n.* Act of making general; act of reducing particulars to generals, or to their genera. [Fr. *généralisation*.]

Generalize, jen'ė-ral-iz, *vt.* To make general, or common to a number; to extend from particulars or species to genera. *ppr.* generalizing, *pret. & pp.* generalized. [Fr. *généraliser*.]

Generally, jen'ė-ral-li, *adv.* In general; extensively, though not universally; usually; in the main; without detail; in the whole taken together.

Generalship, jen'ė-ral-ship, *n.* The office, skill, or conduct of a general officer; military skill in a commander.

Generate, jen'ė-rāt, *vt.* To beget; to bear; to bring forth; to cause to be; to bring into life; to cause; to form. *ppr.* generating, *pret. & pp.* generated. [L. *genero*, *generatus*—*genus*, kind—Sans. *jan*, to beget.]

Generating, jen'ė-rat-ing, *p.a.* Producing.

Generation, jen-ė-rā'shon, *n.* Procreation; production; a single succession in natural descent; an age; the people of the same period; a series of descendants from the same stock; progeny; a family; a race; breed. [Fr. *génération*.]

Generative, jen'ė-rāt-iv, *a.* Having the power of generating or propagating its own species; having the power of producing. [Fr. *génératif*.]

Generator, jen'ė-rāt-ėr, *n.* He or that which generates; the principal sound or sounds in music by which others are produced. [L.]

Generic, Generical, jē-ne'rik, jē-ne'rik-al, *a.* Pertaining to a genus or kind; comprehending the genus. [Fr. *générique*.]

Generically, jē-ne'rik-al-li, *adv.* regard to a genus.

Generosity, jen-ė-ros'i-ti, *n.* Quality of being generous; nobleness of soul; liberality; munificence; bounty. [Fr. *générosité*.]

Generous, jen'ė-rus, *a.* Noble; honourable; bountiful; free to give; strong; full of spirit, as wine; sprightly; courageous, as a steed. [Fr. *généreux*—L. *genus*, race.]

Generously, jen'ė-rus-li, *adv.* Nobly; honourably; not meanly; magnanimously; liberally; munificently.

Genesis, jen'ė-sis, *n.* Act of producing; creation; the first book of the Old Testament. [Gr. *gennaō*, to produce.]

Genetic, jen-et'ik, *a.* Pertaining to the origin of a thing, or its mode of production. [Gr. *gennētikos*, fit for begetting.]

Geneva, jė-nē'va, *n.* A spirit distilled from grain or malt, with the addition of *juniper-berries*, or often of oil of turpentine; gin. [Fr. *genièvre*, a juniper-tree, from L. *juniperus*.]

Genial, jē'ni-al, *a.* Of or belonging to birth; gay; joyous; festive; enlivening; contributing to life and cheerfulness; supporting life. [Old Fr.—L. *genius*, a tutelar deity.]

Geniality, jē-ni-al'i-ti, *n.* Gaiety; cheerfulness. [Low L. *genialitas*.]

Genially, jē'ni-al-li, *adv.* Gaily; cheerfully.

Genital, jen'it-al, *a.* Pertaining to generation; causing generation or birth. [Fr. *génital*—L. *gigno*, to beget.]

Genitals, jen'it-alz, *n. pl.* The parts of an animal which are the immediate instruments of generation.

Genitive, jen'it-iv, *a.* Pertaining to a case in the declension of nouns, expressing primarily the thing from which something else proceeds, but which has been extended to signify property, possession, &c.; the possessive case.—*n.* The genitive case of nouns. [L. *genitivus*—*gigno*, to beget.]

Genitor, jen'it-ėr, *n.* One who procreates; a sire; a father. [L.]

Genius, jē'ni-us, *n.* Geniuses, *pl.* A good or evil spirit; a tutelary deity; the peculiar structure of mind which is given by nature to an individual; a particular aptitude of mind for a particular study or course of life; strength of mind; uncommon powers of intellect, particularly the power of invention; a man endowed with uncommon vigour of mind; mental powers or faculties; nature; disposition; peculiar character. [L. *gigno*, to beget.]

Genteel, jen-tēl', *a.* Having the manners that indicate good birth; polite; well-bred; refined; having the manners of well-bred people; graceful in mien or form; elegant; free from anything low or vulgar. [Fr. *gentil*—L. *gens*, *gentis*, a race.]

Genteelish, jen-tēl'ish, *a.* Somewhat genteel.

Genteelly, jen-tēl'li, *adv.* In a genteel manner; politely; gracefully.

Genteelness, jen-tēl'nes, *n.* Quality of being genteel; gentility.

Gentian, jen'shi-an, *n.* A medicinal plant. [L. *gentiana*.]

Gentile, jen'til, *a.* Pertaining to a family, race, or nation; pertaining to pagans or heathens; denoting one's race or country.—*n.* Any person not a Jew or a Christian a heathen; a pagan; a worshipper of false gods. [L. *gentilis*.]

Gentilism, jen'til-izm, *n.* Heathenism.

Gentility, jen-til'i-ti, *n.* Good extraction; dignity of birth; politeness of manners; easy graceful behaviour; the manners of well-bred people; gracefulness of mien. [Fr. *gentilité*.]

Gentle, jen'tl, *a.* Well-born; free from coarseness or vulgarity; affable; mild; meek; placid; tame; not rough or severe; not wild, turbulent, or refractory; soothing, as music; treating with mildness; not violent.—*n.*† One well born.—*vt.*† To make genteel. [L. *gentilis*—*gens*, *gentis*, a race.]

Gentlefolk, jen'tl-fōk, *n.* Persons of good breeding and family. It is more generally used in the plural, gentlefolks.

Gentleman, jen'tl-man, *n.* A person well-born, or of a good family; every man above the rank of yeoman, comprehending noblemen; a man who, without a title, bears a coat of arms; every man whose education or occupation raises him above menial service or an ordinary trade; a man of good breeding, politeness, and civil manners; a term of complaisance; one who serves a man of rank and attends upon his person; in the highest sense a man of strict integrity and honour, of self-respect, and intellectual refinement, as well as refined manners and good breeding. [Fr. *gentilhomme*.]

Gentlemanlike, Gentlemanly, jen'tl-man-lik, jen'tl-man-li, *a.* Pertaining to or becoming a gentleman; polite; complaisant; like a man of birth and good breeding.

Gentleness, jen'tl-nes, *n.* Quality of being gentle; softness of manners; sweetness of disposition; courteousness; meekness; tenderness; mild treatment.

Gentlewoman, jen'tl-wu-man, *n.* A woman of good family or of good breeding; a woman above the vulgar; a woman who waits about the person of a lady of high rank.

Gently, jen'tl-i, *adv.* Softly; meekly; mildly; with tenderness.

Gentry, jen'tri, *n.* Birth; people of education and good breeding; the classes of people between the nobility and the vulgar; courtesy†. [corrupted from *gentlery*.]

Genuflection, je-nū-flek'shon, *n.* Act of bending the knee, particularly in worship. [Fr. *génuflexion*—L. *genu*, the knee, and *flecto*, *flexum*, to bend.]

Genuine, jen'ū-in, *a.* Native; natural; belonging to the original stock; real; pure; true; unalloyed. [L. *genuinus*—*gigno*, to beget.]

Genuinely, jen'ū-in-li, *adv.* Without adulteration or foreign admixture.

Genuineness, jen'ū-in-nes, *n.* State or quality of being genuine, or of the true original; freedom from adulteration; freedom from anything false; p rity; reality.

Genus, jē'nus, *n.* Genera, jen'ė-ra, *pl.* A race; kind; that which has several species under it; a class of a greater extent than species; an assemblage of species possessing certain characters in common, by which they are dis-

tinguished from all others. [L. *genus*—*gyno*, Sans. *jan*, to beget.]
Geocentric, Geocentrical, jē-o-sen'trik, jē-o-sen'trik-al, *a.* Having the same centre with the *earth*, applied to the position of a celestial object as seen from the earth. [Gr. *gē*, the earth, and *kentron*, a centre.]
Geocentrically, jē-o-sen'trik-al-li, *adv. In a geocentric manner.*
Geodesic, Geodesical, jē-o-des'ik, jē-o-des'ik-al, *a.* Geodetic.
Geodesy, jē-od'ē-si, *n. A division or distribution of the earth*; the geometry of the earth. [Fr. *géodésie*—Gr. *gē*, the earth, and *daiō*, to divide.]
Geographer, jē-og'ra-fėr, *n. One who is versed in geography*, or one who compiles a treatise on the subject.
Geographical, jē-o-graf'ik-al, *a. Pertaining to geography*; relating to or containing a description of the terraqueous globe. [Fr. *géographique*.]
Geographically, jē-o-graf'ik-al-li, *adv. In a geographical manner.*
Geography, jē-og'ra-fi, *n. A description of the earth*, and of its several countries, kingdoms, states, cities, &c.; a book containing a description of the earth. [Fr. *géographie*—Gr. *gē*, the earth, and *graphō*, to describe.]
Geological, jē-o-loj'ik-al, *a. Pertaining to geology.* [Fr. *géologique*.]
Geologically, jē-o-loj'ik-al-li, *adv. In a geological manner.*
Geologist, jē-ol'o-jist, *n. One versed in the science of geology.*
Geology, jē-ol'o-ji, *n. The science of the formation and structure of the earth beneath its surface*, as to its rocks, strata, soil, minerals, organic remains, the changes which it has undergone, and the causes of those changes. [Fr. *géologie*—Gr. *gē*, the earth (Heb. *gagab*, to till), and *logos*, an account.]
Geometer, jē-om'et-ėr, *n. One skilled in geometry*; a geometrician. [Fr. *géomètre*.]
Geometrical, jē-o-met'rik-al, *a. Pertaining to geometry*; done by geometry; disposed according to geometry. [Fr. *géométrique*.]
Geometrically, jē-o-met'rik-al-li, *adv. According to the laws of geometry.*
Geometrician, jē-om'e-tri'shi-an, *n. One skilled in geometry.*
Geometry, jē-om'e-tri, *n. The measurement of the earth*; the science which treats of the properties of figured space, and which unfolds the doctrines, proportions, relations, and measurement of lines, surfaces, solids, velocity, weight, &c. [Gr. *geōmetria*—*gē*, the earth, and *metron*, a measure.]
Georama, jē-o-rā'ma, *n. An instrument or machine which exhibits a very complete view of the earth.* [Gr. *gē*, and *horama*, a sight—*horaō*, to see.]
George, jorj, *n. A figure of St. George on horseback*, worn by knights of the Garter.
Georgian, jorj'i-an, *a. Relating to the reigns of the four Georges, kings of Great Britain.*
Georgic, jorj'ik, *n. A rural poem*; a poetical composition on the *tillage* or cultivation *of the earth*, &c.—*a.* Relating to the doctrine of *agriculture* and rural affairs. [Gr. *geōrgikos*, belonging to tillage—*gē*, the earth (Heb. *gagab*, to till), and *ergō*, to work.]
Geranium, jē-rā'ni-um, *n. Crane's-bill*, a plant cultivated for its fragrance and beautiful flowers. [L.—Gr. *geranos*, a crane.]
Germ, jėrm, *n. A bud; a twig or offshoot;* origin; first principle; that from which anything springs. [Fr. *germe*—L. *germen*, a sprig.]
German, jėr'man, *a. Come of the same germ* or stock; *being brothers or sisters* that have the same father or mother; closely allied. Cousins *german* are the sons or daughters of brothers or sisters, first cousins. [L. *germānus—germen*, a bud.]
German, jėr'man, *a. Belonging to Germany.*—*n. A native of Germany*; the German language.
Germane, jėr mān', *a.* Closely allied; appropriate.
Germanic, jėr-man'ik, *a. Pertaining to Germany.* [L. *Germanicus*.]
Germanism, jėr'man-izm, *n. An idiom of the German language.*
Germinal, jėrm'in-al, *a. Pertaining to a germ.* [Low L. *germinalis*.]
Germinate, jėrm'in-āt, *vi. To sprout;* to bud; to begin to vegetate or grow, as seeds. *ppr.* germinating, *pret. & pp.* germinated. [L. *germino, germinatum*—*germen*, a bud—*gero*, to bear.]
Germination, jėrm-in-ā'shon, *n. Act of sprouting or budding*; the first beginning of vegetation in a seed or plant; the time in which seeds vegetate. [Fr.—L. *germinatio*.]
Gerund, je'rund, *n. A part of a Latin verb, which declares the doing or carrying on of that which the verb signifies.* [Late L. *gerundium*—L. *gero*, to bear, to carry on.]
Gerundial, je-run'di-al, *a. Pertaining to or like a gerund.*
Gest, jest, *n. A roll of the several days, &c., in a royal progress.*
Gestation, jest-ā'shon, *n. A bearing;* act of carrying young in the womb from conception to delivery; pregnancy. [L. *gestatio*—*gero, gestus*, to bear.]
Gesticulate, jes-tik'ū-lāt, *vi.* To make *gestures* or motions, as in speaking; to use postures.—*vt. To represent by gesture*; to act. *ppr.* gesticulating, *pret. & pp.* gesticulated. [L. *gesticulor, gesticulatus*—*gero*, to bear.]
Gesticulation, jes-tik'ū-lā''shon, *n. Act of making gestures* to express passion, or enforce sentiments; gesture; antic tricks or motions. [Fr.—L. *gesticulatio*.]
Gesticulator, jes-tik'ū-lāt-ėr, *n. One who gesticulates.* [Late L.]
Gesticulatory, jes-tik'ū-lā-tō-ri, *a. Representing in gestures.*
Gesture, jes'tūr, *n. The carriage of the body;* any action or posture intended to express an idea or a passion, or to enforce an argument or opinion; general action or motion of the body. [Low L. *gestūra*—L. *gero*, to carry.]
Get, get, *vt. To obtain;* to gain possession of; to attain; to reach; to win; to induce; to have; to beget; to learn; to con, as a lesson.—*vi. To arrive at any place*, state, or condition by degrees, followed by some modifying word; to become, followed by an adjective; to gain; to be increased. *ppr.* getting, *pret.* got (gat. obs.), *pp.* got, gotten. [Sax. *getan*—Old G. *gezan*, to acquire, *fargezan*, to forget.]
Getting, get'ing, *p.n. Act of obtaining;* acquisition.
Gewgaw, gū'ga, *n. A showy trifle;* a toy; a splendid plaything.—*a.* Showy without value. [probably from Old Eng. *gaud*, a pleasing trifle, a toy.]
Ghast! gast, *vt.* To affright.
Ghastliness, gast'li-nes, *n. State of being ghastly*; horror of countenance; a deathlike look; resemblance of a ghost; paleness.
Ghastly, gast'li, *a. Like a ghost in appearance*; hideous; frightful, as wounds.—*adv. In a ghastly manner.* [Sax. *gastlic*.]
Ghost, gōst, *n. Spirit;* the soul of man; the soul of a deceased person; the soul or spirit separate from the body; a spectre.—*vt.* To haunt with an apparition. [Sax. *gast*.]
Ghostly, gōst'li, *a. Relating to the soul or spirit;* spiritual; not carnal or secular.
Giant, jī'ant, *n.* Originally, an *earth-born* monster; a man of extraordinary bulk and stature; a person of extraordinary strength or powers, bodily or intellectual.—*a. Like a giant.* [Fr. *géant*—L. *gigas, gigantis*, a giant—Gr. *gnia, gē*, the earth.]
Giantess, jī'ant-es, *n. A female giant.*
Giantlike, jī'ant-līk, *a. Resembling a giant* in stature; of unusual size.
Gibberish, gib'bėr-ish, *n.* Unintelligible language; unmeaning words. [from *jabber*.]
Gibbet, jib'bet, *n. Gallows;* a machine in form of a gallows, on which notorious malefactors are hanged in chains; the projecting beam of a crane, on which the pulley is fixed.—*vt.* To *hang and expose on a gibbet* or gallows. [Fr. *gibet*—L. *gabalus*.]
Gibbosity, gib-os'i-ti, *n. Protuberance;* a round or swelling prominence; convexity. [Fr. *gibbosité*.]
Gibbous, gib'us, *a. Hunched; humped;* protuberant; convex; applied to the shape of the moon during the week before and after the full moon. [L. *gibbus*.]
Gibe, jīb, *vi. To scoff;* to utter taunting, sarcastic words; to flout; to fleer; to sneer.—*vt. To scoff at;* to treat with sarcastic reflections; to taunt; to mock. *ppr.* gibing, *pret. & pp.* gibed.—*n. A scoff;* an expression of censure mingled with contempt; a taunt; a reproach. [Sax. *gabban*, to scoff.]
Giber, jīb'ėr, *n. One who gibes.*
Gibingly, jīb'ing-li, *adv.* With censorious contemptuous expressions; scornfully.
Giblet, jib'let, *a. Made of giblets.*
Giblets, jib'lets, *n. pl.* Those parts of poultry which are usually excluded in roasting, as the head, feet, pinions, heart, gizzard, liver, &c. [Goth. *gibla*, Chal. *gaph*, a wing.]
Giddily, gid'i-li, *adv. In a giddy manner.*
Giddiness, gid'i-nes, *n. State of being giddy;* dizziness; inconstancy; frolic; wantonness; levity.
Giddy, gid'i, *a. Reeling;* dizzy; having in the head a sensation of a circular motion or swimming; that induces giddiness; unstable; fickle; rendered wild by excitement or joy. [Sax. *gidig*.]
Giddy-paced, gid'i-pāst, *a. Moving irregularly.*
Gier-eagle, jēr'ē-gl, *n. The vulture-eagle;* a bird of the eagle kind. [G. *geier*, a vulture.]
Gift, gift, *n. Anything given;* act of *giving* or conferring; power of giving; an offering; a bribe; gratuity; power; some quality conferred by the Author of our nature; endowment; faculty. *vt.* To endow with any power or faculty. [Sax.—*gifan*, to give.]
Gifted, gift'ed, *p.a* Furnished with any particular talent; talented.
Gig, gig, *n. A top or whirligig;* any

little thing that is whirled round in play; a light carriage with one pair of wheels, drawn by one horse; a ship's light boat, designed for rapid motion; also, a long narrow rowing-boat, adapted for racing; an active, playful person; a giglet. [Low L. *giga*.]

Gigantic, ji-gan'tik, *a*. *Like a giant*; of extraordinary size; huge; colossal; immense. [L. *giganticus*.]

Gigantically, ji-gan'tik-al-li, *adv*. In a *gigantic manner*.

Giggle, gig'l, *n*. *A kind of laugh*, with short catches of the voice or breath. *vi*. *To titter*; to laugh with short catches of the breath or voice; to laugh in a silly, puerile manner. *ppr*. giggling, *pret. & pp*. giggled. [Sax. *geagl*, a jaw, a laugh.]

Giggler, gig'l-ėr, *n*. *One who giggles*.

Giggling, gig'l-ing, *p.n*. The act of *laughing* with short catches; a tittering.

Giglet, gig'let, *n*. *A giggler*; *a lascivious girl*. — *a*. Giddy; inconstant; wanton. [Sax. *peagl*, a laugh.]

Gigot, zhi'gō, *n*. *The hip joint*†; a leg of mutton†. [Fr. — Gr. *ischion*, the hip-joint.]

Gild, gild, *vt*. *To overlay with gold* in leaf or powder; to adorn with lustre; to illuminate; to give a fair and agreeable external appearance to.—*vt*.† To make drunk. *ppr*. gilding, *pret. & pp*. gilded or gilt. [Sax. *gildan—gold*, gold.]

Gilded, gild'ed, *p.a*. Illuminated.

Gilder, gild'ėr, *n*. *One who gilds*.

Gilding, gild'ing, *p.n*. The art or practice of overlaying things with *gold-leaf* or a thin coating of gold; that which is laid on in overlaying with *gold*.

Gill, gil, *n*. The organ of respiration in fishes; the flap that hangs below the beak of a fowl. [Sax. *ciolon*, the throat.]

Gill, jil, *n*. A measure of capacity, containing the fourth part of a pint. [Sax. *waegel*, a gill.]

Gillyflower, jil'li-flou-ėr, *n*. A plant with beautiful *flowers*, having a clove-like odour. [Fr. *giroflée*, from Late L. *caryophyllum*, the clove-tree.]

Gilt, gilt, *p.a*. Illuminated; adorned. *n. Gilding*; gold laid on the surface of a thing. [from *gild*.]

Gimblet, gim'let, *n*. See GIMLET.

Gimlet, gim'let, *n*. *A small wimble*; a small instrument with a pointed screw at the end, for boring holes in wood. [Old Fr. *gimbelet*.]

Gimmal†, gim'al, *n*. Joined work whose parts move within each other; a quaint piece of machinery.

Gimp, gimp, *n*. A kind of silk twist or edging. [Old Fr. *guimpe*.]

Gin, jin, *n*. A distilled spirit flavoured with *juniper* berries. [D. *jenever*, gin — L. *juniperus*, the juniper.]

Gin, jin, *n*. *A machine* for driving piles, raising great weights, &c.; a contrivance for catching animals; a trap; a snare.—*vt*. To clear, as cotton of its seeds by *a machine*; to catch in a trap. *ppr*. ginning, *pret. & pp*. ginned. [a contraction of *engine*.]

Ging†, ging, *n*. Same as *gang*.

Ginger, jin'jėr, *n*. A plant, the root of which is much used for culinary and other purposes, on account of its hot, spicy quality. [Fr. *gingembre* — L. *zingiberi*.]

Gingerly, jin'jėr-li, *adv*. In the manner *of a young* person; cautiously; timidly; delicately; gently. [from Sax. *geongra*, comp. of *geong*, young.]

Gingle, jing'gl. See JINGLE.

Gipsy, jip'si, *n*. One of an oriental vagabond race, scattered over Europe and parts of both Asia and Africa, having, it is believed, come originally from India; a name of slight reproach to a woman; the language of the gipsies.—*a*. *Pertaining to or resembling the gipsies*. [a corruption of *Egyptian*.]

Giraffe, ji-raf', *n*. The camelopard. [Sp. *girafa*.]

Gird, gėrd, *vt*. To bind by *surrounding* with any flexible substance; to make fast by binding; to put on; to invest; to dress; to encircle; to encompass, as with a river; to give a blow to†.—*vi*. To gibe; to sneer. *ppr*. girding, *pret. & pp*. girded or girt.—*n*. A sarcasm. [Sax. *gyrdan*—Old G. *gurtjan*, to surround.]

Girdle, gėr'dl, *n*. *That which girds*; a band; something drawn round the waist of a person, and tied or buckled. *vt*. *To bind with a girdle*, or with a belt or sash; to gird; to shut in. *ppr*. girdling, *pret. & pp*. girdled. [Sax. *gyrdel*.]

Girl, gėrl, *n*. A female child, or young woman; sometimes applied to any unmarried woman. [Sans. *gauri*, as if *gaurilā*, a girl eight years old.]

Girlhood, gėrl'hud, *n*. *The state of a girl*.

Girlish, gėrl'ish, *a. Like a girl*, or a young woman or child; befitting a girl; pertaining to the youth of a female.

Girlishly, gėrl'ish-li, *adv*. *In the manner of a girl*.

Girlishness, gėrl'ish-nes, *n. Quality of being girlish*.

Girt, gėrt, *vt*. *To gird*; to surround.

Girth, gėrth, *n*. *That which girds*; the band or strap by which a saddle or any burden on a horse's back is made fast, by passing under his belly; a circular bandage; the compass measured by a girth; the circumference of a tree, an animal, &c. [from Sax. *gyrdan*.]

Gist, jist, *n*. *That on which anything rests* or lies; the main point of a question; the point on which an action at law rests. [Old Fr. *giste*, a bed—L. *jaceo, jacitum*, to lie.]

Give, giv, *vt*. To bestow; to grant without requiring a recompense; to deliver; to impart; to pay; to yield; to lend; to expose; to yield to the power of; to allow; to afford; to empower; to pay or render, as thanks; to utter; to show; to send forth; to emit, as heat; to devote one's self (with recipr. pron.); to pledge; to allow or admit—*vi*. To yield to pressure; to begin to melt; to _____ to recede; to shed tears†. *ppr*. giving, *pret*. gave, *pp*. given. [Sax. *gifan*—Old G. *geban*, Goth. *giban*.]

Given, giv'n, *p.a*. Granted; admitted or supposed.

Giver, giv'ėr, *n*. *One who gives*; a donor.

Giving, giv'ing, *p.n*. Act of conferring.

Gizzard, giz'ėrd, *n*. The strong, muscular stomach of a bird. [Fr. *gésier*.]

Glacial, glā'shi-al, *a. Icy*; consisting of ice; frozen; relating to glaciers. [Fr. — L. *glacies*, ice.]

Glacier, gla'shi-ėr, *n*. A field or immense *mass of ice*, formed in deep but elevated valleys, or on the sides of the Alps or other mountains. [Fr. *glacière*—L. *glacies*, ice.]

Glacis, glā'sis, *n*. A place rendered *slippery* by wet falling on it, and being *frozen* over; an easy, insensible slope; in fortification, a sloping bank. [Fr.]

Glad, glad, *a. Rejoicing*; affected with pleasure; pleased; exhilarated; rendered cheerful; wearing the appearance of joy; bright; imparting pleasure; exhilarating; pleasing; expressing gladness or joy; exciting joy. *vt. To make glad*; to gladden; to exhilarate. *ppr*. gladding, *pret. & pp*. gladded. [Sax.—Sans. *hlād*, to rejoice.]

Gladden, glad'n, *vt. To make glad*; to exhilarate; to enliven; to gratify.—*vi*. To become glad; to rejoice. [Sax. *gladian*, to be glad.]

Gladdening, glad'n-ing, *p.a*. Cheering; exhilarating.

Glade, glād, *n*. An opening in a wood through which *light may shine*; any green clear space or opening in a wood. [Old G. *glat*, clear — Icel. *glaedda*, to light up.]

Gladiator, glā'di-āt-ėr, *n. A swordplayer*; a prize-fighter. [L.—*gladius*, a sword.]

Gladiatorial, glā'di-a-tō''ri-al, *a. Pertaining to gladiators*. [L. *gladiatorius*.]

Gladly, glad'li, *adv*. With pleasure; joyfully.

Gladness, glad'nes, *n. State of being glad*; joy, or a moderate degree of joy; pleasure of mind; cheerfulness.

Gladsome, glad'sum, *a. Joyful*; pleased; cheerful; pleasing. [*glad* and *some*.]

Gladsomely, glad'sum-li, *adv*. With joy; with pleasure.

Gladsomeness, glad'sum-nes, *n*. Joy, or moderate joy; pleasure of mind.

Glair, glār, *n. Anything clear*; the white of an egg, used as a varnish for paintings; any viscous, transparent substance resembling the white of an egg.—*vt*. To smear with the white of an egg; to varnish. [Old Fr. *glaire*—L. *clarus*, clear.]

Glance, glans, *n*. A sudden shoot of light or *splendour*; a glimpse or sudden look; a rapid or momentary view or cast; a snatch of sight.—*vi*. To shine; to gleam; to glisten; to shoot or dart a ray of light or splendour; to dart aside; to look with a sudden rapid cast of the eye; to move quickly; to hint; to censure by oblique hints. *vt*. To shoot or dart suddenly or obliquely; to cast for a moment. *ppr*. glancing, *pret. & pp*. glanced. [Old G. *glanz*, splendid, clear.]

Glancingly, glans'ing-li, *adv. By glancing*; in a glancing manner; transiently.

Gland, gland, *n*. A soft granular organ, resembling an *acorn*, occurring in many parts of the body, and consisting of a congeries of blood-vessels, nerves, and a peculiar tissue; an excretory or secretory duct or vessel in a plant. [L. *glans, glandis*, an acorn.]

Glanders, glan'dėrz, *n*. A disease of the mucous membrane in horses in which the *glands* beneath and within the lower jaw are enlarged. [from *gland*.]

Glandular, gland'ū-lėr, *a. Containing glands*; consisting of glands; pertaining to glands; covered with hairs bearing glands on their tips, as certain plants.

Glare, glār, *n. A bright dazzling light*; a fierce piercing look.—*vi. To shine with a clear, bright, dazzling light*; to look with fierce piercing eyes, to be ostentatiously splendid. *ppr*. glaring, *pret. & pp*. glared. [Dan. *glar*—*l. clarus*, clear.]

Glaring, glār'ing, *p.a. Clear*; notorious; barefaced.

Glaringly, glār'ing-li, *adv*. *Clearly*; openly; notoriously.

Glass, glas, *n. That which glistens*; a

Fāte, fär, fat, fąll; mē, met, her; pine, pin; nōte, not, mōve; tūbe, tub, bųll; oil, pound.

hard, brittle, transparent substance, a compound of silica and an alkali; a small drinking vessel of glass; a mirror; a vessel to be filled with sand for measuring time; the quantity of liquor that a glass vessel contains; a lens; a telescope; the time which a glass runs. *a. Made of glass*; vitreous. [Sax. *glæs—glinan*, to glisten.]
Glass-blower, glas'blō-ėr, *n.* One whose business is to blow and fashion glass vessels.
Glass-faced†, glas'fāst, *a.* Mirror-faced.
Glass-gazing†, glas'gāz-ing, *a.* Addicted to viewing one's self in a glass.
Glass-house, glas'hous, *n.* A house where glass is made; also a house made of glass.
Glassiness, glas'i-nes, *n.* Quality of being glassy; a vitreous appearance.
Glass-work, glas'wėrk, *n.* The manufacture of glass; also a place where glass is made.
Glassy, glas'i, *a.* Made of glass; vitreous; resembling glass in its properties.
Glaze, glāz, *vt.* To furnish with glass; to incrust with a vitreous substance, as earthenware; to polish; to make smooth and glossy, as the surface. *ppr.* glazing, *pret. & pp.* glazed.—*n.* The vitreous coating or glazing of potter's ware. [from *glass.*]
Glazed, glāzd, *p.a.* Rendered smooth; shining.
Glazier, glā'zhėr, *n.* One whose business is to set window-glass.
Glazing, glāz'ing, *p.n.* Act or art of setting glass; the art of crusting with a vitreous substance; the act of giving a smooth shining surface to; the vitreous substance with which potter's ware is incrusted; any factitious shining exterior; act of furnishing or covering with glass, as houses, &c.
Gleam, glēm, *n.* A shoot of light; a ray; a small stream of light; brightness; splendour.—*vi.* To shoot or dart, as rays of light; to shine; to flash; to spread a flood of light. [Sax.]
Gleaming, glēm'ing, *p.n.* A shoot or shooting of light.
Gleamy, glēm'i, *a.* Darting beams of light; casting light in rays.
Glean, glēn, *vt.* To clean, as a field; to gather, as the stalks and ears of grain which reapers leave behind them; to collect, as things thinly scattered.—*vi.* To gather stalks or ears of grain left by reapers.—*n.* A collection made by gleaning, or by gathering here and there a little. [Fr. *glaner*—Armor. *glan*, clean.]
Gleaner, glēn'ėr, *n.* One who gathers after reapers; one who collects detached parts or numbers, or who gathers slowly with labour.
Gleaning, glēn'ing, *p.n.* Act of one who gleans; that which is collected by gleaning.
Glebe, glēb, *n.* A clod; turf; soil; ground; the land belonging to a parish church or ecclesiastical benefice. [Fr. *glèbe*—L. *gleba,* a clod.]
Gleby, glēb'i, *a.* Turfy; cloddy.
Glee, glē, *n.* Joy; mirth, particularly the mirth enjoyed at a feast; a composition for voices in three or more parts. [Sax. *gleo*, music, sport.]
Gleeful, glē'fųl, *a.* Full of glee; joyous.
Gleek†, glēk, *n.* A jest; a trick.—*vi.* To make sport; to sneer.
Glen, glen, *n.* A deep narrow vale through which a river or stream flows; a dale; a depression or space between hills. [Ir. *gleaṅṅ,* a glen.]
Glib, glib, *a.* Slippery; admitting a body to slide easily on the surface; voluble; flippant, as a tongue.—*vt.†* To castrate. [D. *glibberen,* to slide.]
Glibly, glib'li, *adv.* Smoothly; volubly.
Glibness, glib'nes, *n.* Smoothness; slipperiness; volubility of the tongue.
Glide, glīd, *vi.* To flow gently; to move without noise or violence, as a river; to move or slip along with ease, as on a smooth surface. *ppr.* gliding, *pret. & pp.* glided.—*n.* Act or manner of moving smoothly, swiftly, and without labour or obstruction. [Sax. *glīdan.*]
Glidingly, glīd'ing-li, *adv.* In a gliding manner.
Glimmer, glim'mėr, *vi.* To gleam or shine faintly, and with frequent intermissions; to give a feeble light.—*n.* A faint light; feeble scattered rays of light. [G. *glimmern.*]
Glimmering, glim'mėr-ing, *p.a.* Shining faintly; shooting feeble scattered rays of light.—*p.n.* A faint beaming of light; a faint view.
Glimpse, glimps, *n.* A quick gleam or flash of light; a transient glance; a short transitory view; short fleeting enjoyment. [Dan. *glimt.*]
Glisten, glis'n, *vi.* To shine; to glitter; to sparkle with light. [Sax. *glisnian.*]
Glistening, glis'n-ing, *p.a.* Sparkling; emitting rays of light.
Glister, glis'tėr, *vi.* To glisten; to shine; to be bright; to sparkle; to be brilliant. *n. Glitter;* lustre. [D. *glinsteren.*]
Glitter, glit'tėr, *vi.* To shine; to sparkle with light; to be showy, specious, or striking, and hence attractive.—*n. Brightness;* lustre. [Icel. *glyttir,* to shine.]
Glittering, glit'tėr-ing, *p.a.* Shining; sparkling; splendid; brilliant.
Gloaming, glōm'ing, *n.* The time of the day when the light shines obscurely; the fall of the evening; the twilight. [Sax. *glomung.*]
Gloat, glōt, *vi.* To stare; to gaze earnestly; to stare with admiration or desire (usually in a bad sense). [G. *glotsen,* to stare.]
Gloating, glōt'ing, *p.a.* Gazing with earnestness.
Globate, glōb'āt, *a.* Having the form of a globe. [L. *globatus—globus,* a globe.]
Globe, glōb, *n.* A round solid body; a ball; a sphere; the earth; an artificial sphere of metal, paper, or other matter, on whose convex surface is drawn a map of the earth or of the heavens; anything in the form of a globe or circle. [Fr.—L. *globus*, a globe.]
Globe-fish, glōb'fish, *n.* A fish of a globular shape.
Globular, glob'ū-lėr, *a.* Having the form of a ball or sphere; spherical.
Globularity, glob-ū-la'ri-ti, *n.* State of being globular; sphericity.
Globule, glob'ūl, *n.* A little globe; a small particle of matter of a spherical form; one of the red particles of the blood. [Fr.—L. *globulus.*]
Gloom, glöm, *n.* Fading light; obscurity; thick shade; cloudiness or heaviness of mind; sadness; aspect of sorrow; darkness of prospect or aspect. *vi.* To shine obscurely; to be cloudy, dark, or obscure; to be sullen, sad, or melancholy. [Sax. *glomung,* the faint light of evening.]
Gloomily, glöm'i-li, *adv.* Obscurely; dimly; darkly; dismally; sullenly.
Gloominess, glöm'i-nes, *n.* Want of light; obscurity; dismalness; sullenness; melancholy; moroseness.
Gloomy, glöm'i, *a.* Obscure; imperfectly illuminated, or destitute of

light; cloudy; melancholy; downcast; sad; wearing the aspect of sorrow; heavy of heart.
Glorification, glō'ri-fi-kā''shon, *n.* Act of giving glory, or of ascribing honours to; elevation to glory. [Fr.]
Glorified, glō'ri-fīd, *p.a. Made glorious;* exalted to glory.
Glorify, glō'ri-fī, *vt.* To make glorious; to ascribe glory or honour to; to magnify and honour in worship; to extol. *ppr.* glorifying, *pret. & pp.* glorified. [Fr. *glorifier*—L. *gloria,* glory, and *facio,* to make.]
Glorious, glō'ri-us, *a.* Full of glory; of exalted excellence and splendour; renowned; celebrated; grand; brilliant; splendid. [Fr. *glorieux*—L. *gloriosus.*]
Gloriously, glō'ri-us-li, *adv.* In a glorious manner; splendidly; illustriously.
Glory, glō'ri, *n. Brightness;* splendour, as of the sun; praise ascribed in adoration; celestial bliss; the divine presence; the divine perfections or excellence; that which honours or makes renowned; that of which one may boast.—*vi.* To exult with joy; to rejoice; to be proud with regard to something. *ppr.* glorying, *pret. & pp.* gloried. [Fr. *gloire*—L. *gloria—clarus,* clear.]
Glorying, glō'ri-ing, *p.n.* Act of exulting; exultation; boasting; display of pride.
Gloss, glos, *n. Brightness* proceeding from a smooth surface; a specious appearance; an interpretation artfully specious; comment; remark intended to illustrate a subject.—*vt.* To give a superficial lustre to; to give a specious appearance to; to palliate; to cover; to varnish (with over).—*vi.* To comment; to write or make explanatory remarks. [Icel. *glossi,* brightness.]
Glossarial, glos-sā'ri-sl, *a.* Containing explanation.
Glossarist, glos'a-rist, *n.* A writer of glosses or comments.
Glossary, glos'a-ri, *n.* A dictionary or vocabulary, explaining words which are obscure, antiquated, local, &c.; a dictionary of difficult words and phrases in any language or writer. [Fr. *glossaire*—Gr. *glōssa,* a language.]
Glossily, glos'i-li, *adv.* In a glossy manner.
Glossiness, glos'i-nes, *n. Quality of being glossy.*
Glossology, glos-ol'o-ji, *n.* The science which investigates the agreement and differences of the various languages spoken or written by different nations. [Gr. *glōssa,* a tongue, and *logos,* discourse.]
Glossy, glos'i, *a. Smooth and shining;* reflecting lustre from a smooth surface; highly polished.
Glottal, glot'al, *a.* Pertaining to the glottis.
Glottis, glot'is, *n.* The narrow opening at the root of the tongue, or at the upper part of the trachea or windpipe. [Gr. *glōttis—glōtta,* the tongue.]
Glove, gluv, *n.* A cover for the hand, or for the hand and arm, with a separate sheath for each finger.—*vt.* To cover with a glove. *ppr.* gloving, *pret. & pp.* gloved. [Sax. *glof—cliofan,* to divide.]
Glover, gluv'ėr, *n.* One who makes or sells gloves.
Glow, glō, *vi.* To shine with a white heat; to burn with vehement heat; to feel great heat of body; to be bright or red with heat or animation, or with blushes; to be ardent; to rage, as passion.—*vi.†* To make hot, so as to shine. *n.* White heat; brightness of colour;

redness; vehemence of passion. [Sax. glowan—Gr. agláos, splendid.]
Glowing, glō'ing, p.a. Exhibiting a bright colour; vehement; inflamed.
Glowingly, glō'ing-li, adv. With great brightness; with ardent heat or passion.
Glowworm, glō'wĕrm, n. An insect which emits a light of a lambent, electric, greenish colour.
Gloze, glōz, vi. To flatter; to wheedle; to fawn; to talk smoothly.—vt. To palliate by specious exposition. (With over.) ppr. glozing, pret. & pp. glozed. n. Flattery; adulation. [Sax. glesan, to flatter.]
Glozer, glōz'ĕr, n. A flatterer.
Glozing, glōz'ing, p.a. Specious representation.
Glue, glū, n. That which causes to adhere; a tenacious, viscid matter, which serves as a cement to unite other substances.—vt. To join with glue or a viscous substance; to unite; to hold together. ppr. gluing, pret. & pp. glued. [Old Fr. glu—Obsol L. gluo, to draw together.]
Gluey, glū'i, a. Viscous; glutinous.
Glueyness, glū'i-nes, n. Quality of being gluey.
Glut, glut, vt. To swallow greedily†; to cloy; to fill beyond sufficiency; to satiate; to feast or delight even to satiety. ppr. glutting, pret. & pp. glutted.—n. Plenty, even to loathing; more than enough; anything that fills or obstructs the passage; the supply of any article in the market beyond the demand. [L. glutio—Sans. gri, to devour.]
Gluten, glū'ten, n. Glue; a tough, elastic substance found in the flour of wheat and other grain. [L.]
Glutinous, glū'tin-us, a. Gluey; viscous; viscid; tenacious; resembling glue; besmeared with a slippery moisture. [L. glutinōsus—gluten, glue.]
Glutton, glut'n, n. One who swallows food to excess; one eager of anything to excess; a voracious carnivorous animal. [Fr. glouton—L. glutio, to glut.]
Gluttonous, glut'n-us, a. Given to excessive eating; consisting in excessive eating.
Gluttonously, glut'n-us-li, adv. With the voracity of a glutton.
Gluttony, glut'n-i, n. Excess in eating; luxury of the table; voracity.
Gnarl, närl, vi. To growl; to murmur.
Gnarled, närld, a. Knotty; full of knots. [G. knorrlein, dimin. of knorren, a knot.]
Gnarly, närl'i, a. Full of knots; knotty.
Gnash, nash, vt. To strike or bring together with force, as the teeth or jaws. vi. To grind the teeth; to strike or dash the teeth together, as in rage, pain, or anguish; to growl. [Dan. knasker, to crush between the teeth.]
Gnashing, nash'ing, p.n. A grinding or striking of the teeth in rage or anguish.
Gnashingly, nash'ing-li, adv. With gnashing.
Gnat, nat, n. A small winged insect, which causes itching of the skin by its sting; anything proverbially small. [Sax. gnæt—Low Sax. gniden, to rub.]
Gnaw, na, vt. To bite or scrape off with the fore-teeth; to wear away by biting; to eat by biting off small portions of with the fore-teeth; to bite in agony or rage; to fret; to corrode.—vi. To use the teeth in biting. [Sax. gnagan.]
Gnawing, na'ing, p.a. Corroding; eating by slow degrees.

Gneiss, nīs, n. A species of granite, composed of quarts, feldspar, and mica, and having a slaty structure. [G.]
Gnome, nōm, n. One that knows; an imaginary being, formerly supposed to inhabit the inner parts of the earth; a dwarf. [Fr.—Gr. gignosko, to know.]
Gnomon, nō'mon, n. The stile or pin of a dial, which by its shadow shows the hour of the day; the index of the hourcircle of a globe; the part of a parallelogram which remains when one of the parallelograms about its diagonal is removed. [Gr. gnomon—gi, nosko, to know.]
Go, gō, vi. To move step by step; to pass; to proceed from one place, state, or station to another; to travel; to depart; to advance; to penetrate; to apply; to be applicable; to apply one's self; to be about to do; to be accounted in value; to circulate; to flow; to have a tendency or direction; to share; to be guided; to be pregnant; to be alienated in payment; to be loosed; to be wasted; to reach; to avail; to be of force or value; to have a currency or use; to conduce; to be carried on; to terminate; to die; to proceed in a train; to fare; to be in a good or ill state; to operate. ppr. going, pret. went, pp. gone. [Sax. gan; Sans. gá, gam, to go.]
Goad, gōd, n. A prick; a pointed instrument used to stimulate a beast to move faster.—vt. To prick; to urge forward; to instigate. [Sax. gad.]
Goal, gōl, n. The pole set to bound a race, and to which racers run; the mark; any starting-post; the end or final purpose; the end aimed at. [Fr. gaule, a pole—L. vallus, a pole.]
Goat, gōt, n. A well-known quadruped, with long hair and horns. [Sax. gat.]
Goatherd, gōt'hĕrd, n. One whose occupation is to tend goats.
Goatish, gōt'ish, a. Resembling a goat in any quality; of a rank smell.
Goatishness, gōt'ish-nes, n. Quality of being goatish; lustfulness.
Goat-sucker, gōt'suk-ĕr, n. A bird, so called from the opinion that it would suck goats; the night-jar.
Gobble, gob'l, vt. To swallow with open mouth; to swallow in large pieces; to swallow hastily.—vi. To make a noise in the throat, as a turkey. ppr gobbling, pret. & pp. gobbled. [Fr. gober—Gæl. gob, the mouth.]
Gobbler, gob'l-ĕr, n. One who swallows in haste; a gormandiser.
Goblet, gob'let. n. A kind of cup or drinking-vessel, containing as much as may be taken at one large draught or swallow. [Fr. gobelet, from gob.]
Goblin, gob'lin, n. A demon; an evil spirit; a walking spirit; a frightful phantom; a fairy; an elf. [Fr. gobelin.]
God, god, n. The Good; the Author of all goodness; the Supreme Being; Jehovah; the Eternal and Infinite Spirit, the Creator, and the Sovereign of the universe; a false god; a heathen deity; an idol; a ruler; a judge; any person or thing deified and honoured as the chief good. [Sax.—Goth. guth.]
Godchild, god'child, n. A child in a godly or spiritual sense; one for whom a person becomes sponsor at baptism, and promises to see educated as a Christian.
Goddess, god'es, n. A heathen deity of the female sex; a woman of superior charms or excellence, in the language of love.
Godfather, god'fä-ᴛнĕr, n. A father in

a godly or spiritual sense; a man who becomes sponsor for a child at baptism. [Sax. god and feder.]
Godhead, god'hed, n. Godship; divinity; divine nature or essence; a deity in person; a god or goddess. [god, and Sax. had.]
Godless, god'les, a. Having or acknowledging no God; ungodly; atheistical.
Godlessly, god'les-li, adv. Atheistically; in an impious manner; impiously.
Godlessness, god'les-nes, n. State of being godless or impious.
Godlike, god'līk, a. Resembling God; divine; resembling a deity or heathen divinity; of superior excellence.
Godliness, god'li-nes, n. Quality of being godly; piety; belief in God, and reverence for his character and laws; a religious life; the system of Christianity.
Godly, god'li, a. Reverencing God, and his character and laws; pious; devout; holy; religious; righteous.
Godmother, god'muᴛн-ĕr, n. A mother in a godly sense; a woman who becomes sponsor for a child at baptism.
Godsend, god'send, n. An unexpected acquisition or good fortune, received as coming from God.
God-speed, god'spēd, n. Good-speed, that is, success.
Godward, god'wĕrd, adv. Toward God.
God-yield†, god'yēld, adv. A term of thanks.
Goer, gō'ĕr, n. One who goes; one who transacts business between parties; a term applied to a horse, as, a good goer.
Goggle, gog'l, vi. To roll the eyes; to strain the eyes. ppr. goggling, pret. & pp. goggled.—a. Having full eyes; staring with rolling eyes. — n. A strained or affected rolling of the eye; (pl.) a kind of spectacles to cure squinting. [Old Eng. goggle-eyed, one-eyed.]
Goggle-eyed, gog'l-īd, a. Having prominent, distorted, or rolling eyes.
Going, gō'ing, p.n. Act of moving; act of walking; way; course of life; deportment; course of providential agency or government.
Gold, gōld, n. A precious metal of a bright yellow colour, the most ductile and malleable of all the metals, and the heaviest except platina; money; wealth; something pleasing or valuable; a bright yellow colour.—a. Made of gold; consisting of gold. [Sax.—gelew, Sans. gaura, yellow.]
Gold-beater, gōld'bet-ĕr, n. One who beats gold into thin leaves for gilding.
Gold-dust, gōld'dust, n. Gold in very fine particles.
Golden, gōld'n, a. Made of gold; bright; shining; splendid; of a gold colour; most valuable; happy; pure; innocent, as the golden age; pre-eminently auspicious, as opportunity.
Goldenly, gōld'n-li, adv. Splendidly.
Golden-rule, gōld'n-röl, n. The most excellent rule; the rule of doing as we would he done by.
Gold-field, gōld'fēld, n. District or region where gold is found.
Goldfinch, gōld'finsh, n. A beautiful singing bird, so called from the yellow colour of its wings. [Sax. goldfinc.]
Gold-fish, gōld'fish, n. A fresh-water fish having the upper part of the body of a bright orange colour.
Gold-lace, gōld'lās, n. A lace wrought with gold.
Gold-leaf, gōld'lēf, n. Gold beaten into a thin leaf.
Goldsmith, gōld'smith, n. One who

Fāte, fär, fat, fall; mē, met, hĕr; pīne, pin; nōte, not, move; tūbe, tub, bull; oil, pound.

manufactures vessels and ornaments *of gold* and silver.
Golf, golf, *n.* A game with a small ball and a *bat* or *club*. [D. *kolf*—a club or bat.]
Golfing, golf'ing, *p.n.* The act of playing at the game *of golf*.
Gondola, gon'dō-la, *n.* A long and narrow pleasure-boat, used at Venice on the canals. [It.]
Gondolier, gon-dō-lēr', *n. A man who rows a gondola*. [Fr.]
Gong, gong, *n.* A kind of metallic drum, resembling the lid of a caldron, which the Chinese strike with a wooden mallet. [probably named from the sound.]
Good, gụd, *a. Benevolent;* merciful; gracious; worthy; virtuous; religious; conformable to the moral law; beneficial; fit; expedient; well adapted to the end; conducive to happiness; valid; firm; complete in its kind; perfect; uncorrupted; suitable to the taste or to health; wholesome; medicinal; suited to strengthen the healthful functions; full; useful; valuable; equal; sufficient; convenient for any purpose; suitable; safe; able; skilful; pleasant; cheering; prosperous; fair; unblemished; cheerful; elegant; polite; serious; seasonable; festive; companionable; merry; comely; well-formed; mild; pleasant; calm; friendly.—*n.* That which contributes to diminish or remove pain, or to increase happiness or prosperity; benefit; welfare; advancement of happiness; spiritual improvement; earnest; a piece of property; moral works; moral qualities; virtue; righteousness.—*interj.* Well! right! [Sax. *gōd*—Goth. *god.*]
Good-breeding, gụd-brēd'ing, *n.* Polite manners, formed by *a good education*.
Good-bye, gụd-bī'. A salutation at parting, equivalent to, *A good way* or journey be to you; farewell.
Good-day, gụd-dā', *n.* or *interj.* A term of salutation at meeting or parting, equivalent to, I wish you a *prosperous day*; farewell.
Good-dent, gụd-den', *interj.* Good-evening.
Good-Friday, gụd-frī'dā, *n.* A fast in memory of our Saviour's crucifixion, being the *Friday* before Easter.
Good-humour, gụd-hū'mēr, *n. A cheerful temper* or state of mind.
Good-humoured, gụd-hū'mẽrd, *a. Being of a cheerful temper*.
Good-humouredly, gụd-hū'mẽrd-li, *adv. In a cheerful way*.
Goodliness, gụd'li-nes, *n. Quality of being goodly*; beauty of form; grace.
Goodly, gụd'li, *a. Good-looking*; being of a handsome form; graceful; desirable.
Good-man, gụd-man', *n.* A familiar appellation of civility; a rustic term of compliment; a familiar appellation of a husband; also, the master of a family.
Good-manners, gụd-man'nẽrz, *n. pl. Propriety of behaviour*; politeness.
Good-morning, gụd-morn'ing, *n.* or *exclam.* A f rm of morning salutation, equivalent to, I wish the *morning* may be favourable to you.
Good-nature, gụd-nā'tūr, *n. Natural mildness* and kindness of disposition.
Good-natured, gụd-nā'tūrd, *a. Naturally mild in temper*; not easily provoked.
Goodness, gụd'nes, *n. State or quality of being good* in any of its various senses; acts of kindness; mercy; acts of compassion; moral virtue; religion; the physical qualities which constitute value or perfection.

Good-night, gụd-nīt', *n.* or *interj.* A form of salutation in parting for the night, equivalent to, I wish you a *good* or agreeable *night*.
Goodnow†, gụd'nou, *interj.* An exclamation of wonder or entreaty.
Goods, gụdz, *n. pl. Good things;* household furniture; personal or movable estate; wares; commodities.
Good-sense, gụd-sens', *n. Sound judgment*.
Good-speed, gụd-spēd', *n. Good success*.
Good-tempered, gụd-tem'pẽrd, *a. Having a good temper*; good-natured.
Good-wife, gụd-wīf', *n.* The mistress of a family in rural life.
Good-will, gụd-wil', *n. Benevolence;* kind feeling; entire willingness; facilities for business or trade; custom.
Goodwoman, gụd-wụ'man, *n.* The mistress of a family in humble life.
Goose, gös, *n. Geese, pl.* A large, well-known web-footed water-fowl, proverbially noted for foolishness; a tailor's smoothing-iron, the handle of which resembles the neck of *a goose;* a silly person; a simpleton. [Sax. *gōs.*]
Gooseberry, gös'be-ri, *n.* The fruit of *a prickly shrub*, and the shrub itself. [*gorseberry—gorse,* furze.]
Goose-quill, gös'kwil, *n.* The large feather or *quill of a goose,* or a pen made with it.
Goosery, gös'e-ri, *n. A place for geese;* the qualities of a goose; folly.
Gor-cock, gor'kok, *n.* The moorcock or red grouse. [probably *gor* is from the sound uttered by the bird.]
Gordian, gor'di-an, *a.* Intricate; difficult. [from *Gordius,* a Phrygian king, who formed a knot so intricate that no one could unloose it.]
Gore, gōr, *n. Blood flowing from a wound;* blood; but generally thick or clotted blood. [Sax. *gor.*]
Gore, gōr, *n.* A wedge-shaped or triangular piece of cloth sewed into a garment to widen it in any part.—*vt.* To *piece with a gore. ppr.* goring, *pret. & pp.* gored. [Icel. *geiri.*]
Gore, gōr, *vt. To stab or pierce with* a pointed instrument, as a spear; to pierce with the point of a horn. *ppr.* goring, *pret. & pp.* gored. [from Sax. *gar,* a dart.]
Gorge, gorj, *n. The throat;* the canal of the neck by which food passes to the stomach; a narrow passage between hills or mountains; the entrance into a bastion; that which is gorged or swallowed.—*vt. To swallow* with greediness; to glut; to fill, as the throat or stomach; to satiate. *ppr.* gorging, *pret. & pp.* gorged. [Fr.—L. *gurges*, a whirlpool.]
Gorged, gorjd, *a. Having a gorge* or throat.
Gorgeous, gor'jē-us, *a.* Originally relating to *an ornament for the throat* or neck of females; showy; fine; glittering with gay colours; magnificent. [Old Fr. *gorgias*, gaudy.]
Gorgeously, gor'jē-us-li, *adv.* With *showy* magnificence; splendidly; finely.
Gorget, gor'jet, *n.* A piece of armour for defending *the throat or neck;* a kind of breast-plate like a half-moon; a pendant metallic ornament worn by officers when on duty. [Fr. *gorgette.*]
Gorgon, gor'gon, *n.* A fabled monster *of terrific aspect*, the sight of which turned the beholder to stone; anything very ugly or horrid.—*a. Like a gorgon;* very ugly or terrific. [Gr. *gorgōn—gorgos,* fierce.]
Gorilla, gor-il'la, *n.* The largest animal of the ape kind found in Africa, called also the great chimpanzee.
Gormand, gor'mand, *n.* A glutton.—*a.* Gluttonous; voracious. [Fr. *gourmand.*]
Gormandize, gor'mand-īz, *vi. To eat greedily* or *to excess. ppr.* gormandizing, *pret. & pp.* gormandized.
Gormandizer, gor'mand-īz-ẽr, *n. A greedy,* voracious eater.
Gormandizing, gor'mand-īz-ing, *p.n.* Act or habit of *eating greedily* and voraciously.
Gorse, gors, *n. Furze or whin;* a thick, prickly shrub with yellow flowers, which grows on *waste, uncultivated* places. [Sax. *gorst*, furze.]
Gorsy, gors'i, *a. Abounding in* or *resembling gorse*.
Gory, gō'ri, *a. Covered with gore,* or with clotted blood; bloody; murderous.
Goshawk, gos'hak, *n. A goose-hawk;* a voracious bird of the *hawk* family, which was flown at *geese*, cranes, partridges, &c. [Sax. *goshafoc.*]
Gosling, gos'ling, *n. A young goose;* a goose not full grown. [Sax. *gos* and *ling.*]
Gospel, gos'pel, *n. Good news; glad tidings;* a revelation of the grace of God to fallen man through a Mediator; a history of the life and doctrines of Jesus Christ; divinity; any general doctrine.—*a. Relating to the gospel;* accordant with the gospel.—*vt.*† *To instruct in the gospel.* [Sax. *godspell—god,* good, and *spell,* tidings.]
Gospeller, gos'pel-ẽr, *n. He who reads the gospel at the altar*.
Gossamer, gos'a-mēr, *n.* A fine, filmy substance, like cobwebs, floating in the air in calm, clear, sunny weather, especially in autumn; the morning dew that covers the fields like a spider's web. [etymol. uncertain.]
Gossip, gos'sip, *n.* Originally one who is *of kin* in a *godly* sense; a sponsor; an idle tattler; mere tattle; idle talk. *vi.* To prate; to run about and tattle; to tell idle tales. [*godsibb—sib,* alliance.]
Gossiper, gos'sip-ẽr, *n. One who gossips*.
Gossiping, gos'sip-ing, *p.a.* Running from place to place and tattling; containing gossip.—*p.n.* A prating; a running about to collect tales and tattle.
Goth, goth, *n.* One of an ancient and distinguished tribe which inhabited Central Europe; one rude or uncivilized; a barbarian. [G. *Gothen,* the Goths.]
Gothic, goth'ik, *a. Pertaining to the Goths;* denoting a style of architecture with high and sharply pointed arches, clustered columns, &c.; rude; ancient; barbarous.—*n. The language of the Goths*.
Gothicism, goth'i-sizm, *n. Gothic idiom;* rudeness of manners; barbarousness; conformity to the Gothic style of building.
Gouge, gouj, *n. A semicircular* chisel used to cut holes, channels, or grooves in wood or stone.—*vt. To scoop out with a gouge,* or as with a gouge. *ppr.* gouging, *pret. & pp.* gouged. [Fr.]
Gourd, gōrd, *n.* A plant which produces fruit of a large size, in some species *bottle-shaped;* the fruit of the plant, which is much prized in hot countries; a false diet. [Fr. *gourde—* L. *cucurbita.*]
Gourmand, gōr'mänd, *n. See* **Gormand**. [Fr.]

ch, *chain;* j, *job;* g, *go;* ng, *sing;* ᴛʜ, *then;* th, *thin;* w, *wig;* wh, *whig;* zh, *azure;* † obsolete.

Gout, gout, *n.* A painful disease, affecting generally the small joints; and so called because it was supposed to be produced by a humour which distilled *drop by drop* on the diseased part; a clot. [Fr. *goutte*—L. *gutta*, a drop.]
Gout, gö, *n. Taste; relish.* [Fr.—L. *gustus,* taste.]
Goutiness, gout'i-nes, *n. State of being subject to the gout;* gouty affections.
Gouty, gout'i, *a. Diseased with the gout;* pertaining to the gout.
Govern, gu'vern, *vt.* To steer, *as a ship;* to rule; to regulate by authority; to keep within the limits prescribed; to control; to command, as the feelings; to affect so as to determine the case, mood, &c., in grammar.—*vi.* To exercise authority; to administer the laws; to have the control. [Fr. *gouverner*—L. *guberno*—Gr. *kūbē*, head, and *naus*, a ship.]
Governable, gu'vern-a-bl, *a.* That may *be governed* or subjected to authority.
Governance, gu'vern-ans, *n.* Direction; control.
Governess, gu'vern-es, *n.* An instructress; an educated woman who has the care of instructing and directing young ladies.
Governing, gu'vern-ing, *p.a.* Holding the superiority; directing; controlling.
Government, gu'vern-ment, *n. Rule;* control; restraint; exercise of authority; administration of public affairs; system of polity in a state; any territory over which the right of sovereignty is extended; right of governing; the council or persons who administer the laws of a kingdom or state; executive power; the influence of a word in grammar in regard to construction; limberness! [Fr. *gouvernement.*]
Governmental, gu-vern-ment'al, *a. Pertaining to government;* sanctioned by government.
Governor, gu'vern-ėr, *n. He who governs;* one invested with supreme authority; a tutor; one possessing delegated authority; a contrivance in mills, machinery, &c., for maintaining a uniform velocity. [Fr. *gouverneur.*]
Governorship, gu'vern-ėr-ship, *n. The office of a governor.*
Gown, goun, *n.* A woman's upper garment; a long, loose, upper garment worn by professional men, as divines, &c.; a long, loose, upper garment, worn in sickness, &c.; the dress of peace; any sort of dress. [W. *gwn.*]
Gowned, gound, *p.a. Dressed in a gown.*
Gownsman, gounz'man, *n.* One whose professional habit *is a gown,* as a divine or a lawyer, and particularly a member of an English university.
Grace, grās, *n. Favour;* kindness; disposition to oblige another; appropriately, the free, unmerited love and favour of God in Christ; a state of reconciliation to God; religious affection; spiritual instruction; eternal life; that, in manner or language, which renders it agreeable; natural or acquired excellence; beauty; a single beauty; beauty deified; a shake in music by way of embellishment; the title of a duke or an archbishop; a short prayer before or after meat.—*vt.* To favour; to dignify and raise, by an act of favour; to decorate; to embellish. *ppr. gracing, pret. & pp.* graced. [Fr. *grâce*—L. *gratus,* kind, dear—Gr. *charis, charitos,* favour, grace.]
Grace-cup, grās'kup, *n.* The *cup* or health drunk after *grace* is said.

Graced, grāst, *pp.* Exalted; dignified; honoured; graceful; virtuous!
Graceful, grās'ful, *a. Full of grace;* beautiful with dignity; agreeable in appearance, with an expression of dignity or elevation of mind or manner.
Gracefully, grās'ful-li, *adv. In a graceful manner;* elegantly.
Gracefulness, grās'ful-nes, *n.* Elegance of manner or deportment; beauty with dignity in manner, motion, or countenance.
Graceless, grās'les, *a. Void of grace;* unregenerate; unsanctified; corrupt.
Gracelessly, grās'les-li, *adv. Without grace.*
Gracelessness, grās'les-nes, *n. Want of grace;* profligacy.
Graces, grās'ez, *n. pl.* Three beautiful fabled sisters, who attended Venus, and were supposed to confer beauty.
Gracious, grā'shi-us, *a. Full of grace;* favourable; disposed to forgive offences and impart unmerited blessings; benignant; proceeding from divine grace; renewed by grace; winning regard; beautiful. [Fr. *gracieux.*]
Graciously, grā'shi-us-li, *adv. Kindly;* favourably; in a pleasing manner.
Graciousness, grā'shi-us-nes, *n.* Possession of *graces* or good qualities; pleasing manner; mercifulness.
Gradation, gra-dā'shon, *n.* A series of ascending *steps* or degrees; progress from one degree or state to another; a degree in any series; order. [Fr.—L. *gradus,* a step.]
Grade, grād, *n. A step;* a degree or rank in order or dignity; a step in any ascending series; the degree of ascent or descent in a road or railway.—*vt.* To reduce to a level, as the line of a road. *ppr.* grading, *pret. & pp.* graded. [Fr.—L. *gradus,* a step.]
Gradient, grā'di-ent, *a.* Rising or descending by regular steps or degrees of inclination.—*n.* The degree of ascent or descent in a railway. [L. *gradiens,* going—*gradus,* a step.]
Gradual, grad'ū-al, *a. Advancing step by step;* regular and slow; proceeding by degrees in a descending or ascending line or progress.—*n. An order of steps.* [Fr. *graduel.*]
Gradually, grad'ū-al-li, *adv. By degrees;* step by step; regularly; slowly.
Graduate, grad'ū-āt, *vt. To raise a step;* to honour with a degree in a college or university; to confer a degree on; to divide, as any space into small regular intervals; to form, as shades or nice differences; to improve, as colours; to prepare; to mark, as degrees or differences of any kind.—*vi. To receive a degree* from a university; to pass by degrees; to change gradually. *ppr.* graduating, *pret. & pp.* graduated.—*n.* One who has received a *degree* in a college or university, or from some professional incorporated society. [Low L. *graduo, graduatus*—L. *gradus,* a step.]
Graduated, grad'ū-āt-ed, *p.a.* Marked with *degrees* or regular intervals; tempered.
Graduation, grad-ū-ā'shon, *n.* Act of conferring or receiving academical *degrees;* act of dividing any space into small regular intervals. [Low L. *graduatio.*]
Graft, graft, *n.* A small scion of a tree, inserted in another tree by making an *incision* in it, the tree serving as the stock which is to support and nourish the scion.—*vt.* To insert, as a scion into another tree; to propagate by insertion or inoculation; to insert, as something in a body to which it did not originally belong.—*vi.* To practise the insertion of foreign scions on a stock. [Sax. *græft,* cut—*grafan,* to cut.]
Grafted, graft'ed, *p.a.* Inserted on a foreign stock.
Grafter, graft'ėr, *n. One who grafts.*
Grafting, graft'ing, *p.n.* Act *of inserting grafts* or scions.
Grain, grān, *n.* A *single seed* of any cereal plant; corn in general, as wheat, rye, barley, oats; any small hard mass, as of sand; a minute particle; a small weight; a component part of stones and metals; state of the grit of any body composed of grains; the fibres of wood; the direction of the fibres; the substance of wood as modified by the fibres; a rough texture on the outside of the skin of animals; the body or substance of a thing, considered with respect to the size, form, or direction of the constituent particles; dye; the heart or temper.—*vt.* To paint in imitation of the *grain* or fibres of wood; to form into grains, as powder. [Fr.—L. *granum,* a kernel.]
Grained, grānd, *p.a. Painted in* imitation *of the grain* of wood; roughened.
Graining, grān'ing, *p.n.* A kind of painting in imitation of the *grain* of wood.
Grainy, grān'i, *a. Full of grains* or corn; full of kernels.
Graminivorous, gra-min-iv'ō-rus, *a. Feeding on grass.* [L. *gramen,* grass, and *voro,* to devour.]
Grammar, gram'mär, *n.* That which relates to *letters;* the art of speaking or writing a language with propriety; a system of general principles and of particular rules for speaking or writing a language; propriety of speech; a book containing the elements of any science. [Fr. *grammaire*—Gr. *gramma,* a letter—*graphō,* to write.]
Grammarian, gram-mā'ri-an, *n.* One who is versed in or who teaches *grammar;* a philologist. [Fr. *grammatirien.*]
Grammar-school, gram'mär-skōl, *n.* A *school* in which the learned languages, as Latin and Greek, are taught grammatically.
Grammatical, gram-mat'ik-al, *a. Belonging to grammar;* according to the rules of grammar. [Fr.—L. *grammaticus.*]
Grammatically, gram-mat'ik-al-li, *adv.* According to the principles and rules *of grammar.*
Grampus, gram'pus, *n. A large fish of* the whale tribe, very active and voracious. [Fr. *grandpoisson,* great fish.]
Granary, gra'na-ri, *n. A storehouse for grain* after it is thrashed. [L. *granaria*—*granum,* a grain.]
Grand, grand, *a. Big; great;* great, figuratively; majestic; high in power or dignity; magnificent; chief; noble; elevated; expressed with great dignity; advanced in age; old. [Fr.—L. *grandis,* great—*cresco,* to grow.]
Grandam, gran'dam, *n. An old woman;* a grandmother. [*grand* and *dame.*]
Grand-child, grand'child, *n.* A son's or daughter's child.
Grand-daughter, grand'da-tėr, *n.* The daughter of a son or daughter.
Grand-duke, grand'dūk, *n. An arch-duke;* a reigning duke.
Grandee, gran-dē', *n.* A man of *great* or elevated rank; a nobleman. [Sp. *grande.*]
Grandeur, grand'yėr, *n. Greatness;*

Fāte, fär, fat, fall; mē, met, hėr; pīne, pin; nōte, not, mōve; tūbe, tub, bull; oil, pound.

sublimity; splendour of appearance; magnificence; elevation of thought, sentiment, or expression; elevation of mien. [Fr.]
Grandfather, grand'fä-ᴛнėr, n. An old father; a father's or mother's father.
Grandiloquence, grand-il'ō-kwens, n. Lofty speaking; pompous language. [Low L. grandiloquentia—L. loquor, to speak.]
Grandly, grand'li, adv. In a grand or lofty manner; splendidly; sublimely.
Grandmother, grand'muᴛн-ėr, n. The mother of one's father or mother.
Grandness, grand'nes, n. State of being grand; grandeur; greatness with beauty.
Grand-piano, grand'pi-a-nō, n. A large kind of piano, having great compass and strength.
Grandsire, grand'sīr, n. An old sire; a grandfather; any ancestor.
Grandson, grand'sun, n. The son of a son or daughter.
Grange, grānj, n. A barn; a farm, with the buildings, stables, &c. [Fr.—L. granum, a grain.]
Granite, gran'it, n. An aggregate rock, composed of grains of quartz, feldspar, and mica, or at least of two of them, confusedly crystallized together. [Fr. —L. granum, a grain.]
Granitic, gran-it'ik, a. Like granite; having the nature of granite; consisting of granite.
Granivorous, gran-iv'ō-rus, a. Eating or subsisting on grain or seeds. [L. granum, grain, and voro, to eat up.]
Grant, grant, vt. To gratify with; to promise; to bestow, as a gift; to confer on, without compensation, in answer to request; to admit as true what is not proved; to transfer, as the title of a thing, to another for a consideration; to convey by deed or writing; to cede.—n. A bestowing; the thing granted; a gift; an allowance; a conveyance in writing of such things as cannot pass or be transferred by word only, as land, &c.; the thing conveyed by deed or patent; admission of something as true. [Low L. grantare —L. gratus, pleasing.]
Granting, grant'ing, p.a. Conceding; bestowing.
Grantor, grant-or', n. The person who grants; one who conveys lands, &c.
Granular, gran'ū-lėr, a. Consisting of grains; resembling grains. [from L. granum.]
Granulate, gran'ū-lāt, vt. To form into grains; to make rough on the surface. vi. To be formed into grains. ppr. granulating, pret. & pp. granulated. [Fr. granuler.]
Granulated, gran'ū-lāt-ed, p.a. Consisting of grains; having the form of grains.
Granulation, gran-ū-lā'shon, n. Act of forming into grains; a process by which minute grain-like fleshy bodies are formed on the surface of wounds during their healing; the fleshy grains themselves. [Fr.]
Grape, grāp, n. A single berry of the vine; the fruit from which wine is made; grape-shot. [Fr. grappe—Low L. grappus.]
Grapery, grāp'ė-ri, n. A building or inclosure used for the rearing of grapes.
Grapeshot, grāp'shot, n. A cluster of small shot, confined in a canvas bag, forming a kind of cylinder.
Grapestone, grāp'stōn, n. The stone or seed of the grape.

Graphic, graf'ik, a. Pertaining to the art of writing; well delineated; describing with force and accuracy. [Fr. graphique—Gr. graphō, to write.]
Graphically, graf'ik-al-li, adv. In a picturesque manner.
Grapnel, grap'nel, n. A small anchor fitted with four or five flukes or claws, used to hold boats or small vessels. [Fr. grappin—G. greifen, to gripe.]
Grapple, grap'l, vt. To seize; to gripe; to lay fast hold on, either with the hands or with hooks; to hold fast in affection.—vi. To seize; to contend or struggle in close fight, as wrestlers. ppr. grappling, pret. & pp. grappled. n. A seizing; the wrestler's hold; close fight; a hook by which one ship fastens on another. [Belg. grabbelen.]
Grappling, grap'l-ing, p.n. A laying fast hold of.
Grapy, grāp'i, a. Like grapes; full of clusters of grapes; made of grapes.
Grasp, grasp, vt. To gripe; to seize and hold by clasping with the fingers or arms; to seize; to take possession of. vi. To gripe; to grapple; to seize; to encroach. (With at.)—n. The gripe of the hand; hold; reach of the arms; and figuratively, the power of seizing. [High G. gripsen, to seize.]
Grasping, grasp'ing, p.a. Avaricious; greedy of gain.
Grass, gras, n. Herbage; the plants which constitute the food of cattle and other beasts; an order of plants in botany.—vt. To cover with grass or with turf; to furnish with grass; to bleach, as flax on the grass or ground. [Sax. græs—Old G. gras—Sans. gras, to devour.]
Grasshopper, gras'hop-ėr, n. An insect that lives and hops among grass. [grass and hop.]
Grassiness, gras'i-nes, n. State of abounding with grass. [from grassy.]
Grassy, gras'i, a. Abounding with grass; resembling grass; green.
Grate, grāt, n. A work or frame, composed of parallel or cross bars, with interstices; a kind of lattice-work, used for doors, windows, &c.; the iron frame and bars for holding coals used as fuel.—vt. To furnish with grates; to make fast with cross-bars. ppr. grating, pret. & pp. grated. [It. grata— L. crates, a hurdle.]
Grate, grāt, vt. To rub; to wear away in small particles, by rubbing with anything rough; to rub, so as to cause a harsh or discordant sound; to offend; to irritate.—vi. To rub hard, so as to offend; to offend by oppression or importunity; to make a harsh sound by the friction of rough bodies. ppr. grating, pret. & pp. grated. [Fr. gratter—L. rado, to rub.]
Grated, grāt'ed, p.a. Furnished with a grate.
Grateful, grāt'fụl, a. Pleasing; acceptable; gratifying; delicious; having a due sense of benefits; willing to acknowledge and repay acts of kindness. [from L. gratus.]
Gratefully, grāt'fụl-li, adv. With a due sense of benefits or favours.
Gratefulness, grāt'fụl-nes, n. Gratitude; quality of being agreeable or pleasant to the mind or to the taste.
Grater, grāt'ėr, n. An instrument with a rough indented surface for grating, or rubbing off small particles of a body.
Gratification, gra-ti-fi-kā'shon, n. Act of gratifying; that which affords pleasure; delight; recompense. [Fr.—L. gratificatio.]

Gratified, gra'ti-fīd, p.a. Pleased; indulged according to desire; glad.
Gratify, gra'ti-fī, vt. To do a favour to; to please; to delight; to humour; to satisfy; to recompense. ppr. gratifying, pret. & pp. gratified. [Fr. gratifier —L. gratus, and facio, to make.]
Gratifying, gra'ti-fī-ing, p.a. Giving pleasure; affording satisfaction.
Grating, grāt'ing, p.a. Fretting; irritating.—p.n. A harsh sound or rubbing; [from n. grate] a partition of bars or lattice-work of wood or iron; a grate.
Gratis, grā'tis, adv. Out of favour or kindness; without recompense; freely; without a return. [L.]
Gratitude, gra'ti-tūd, n. Quality of being grateful; an emotion of the heart, excited by a favour or benefit received; a sentiment of kindness toward a benefactor; thankfulness. [Fr.—L. gratus, thankful.]
Gratuitous, gra-tū'it-us, a. That is done out of favour; free; not required by justice; granted without claim or merit; not called for; taken without proof. [L. gratuitus—gratia, favour.]
Gratuitously, gra-tū'it-us-li, adv. Freely; without proof.
Gratuity, gra-tū'i-ti, n. That which is given out of kindness; a free gift; a donation; something given in return for a favour; an acknowledgment. [Fr. gratuité—L. gratus, agreeable.]
Gratulate, grat'ū-lāt, vt. To manifest one's joy to; to congratulate.—a.† Worthy of joy. [L. gratulor, gratulatus, from gratus.]
Gratulation, grat-ū-lā'shon, n. A manifestation of joy; congratulation. [L. gratulatio.]
Gratulatory, grat'ū-la-tō-ri, a. Expressing gratulation; congratulatory. [Sp. gratulatório.]
Grave, grāv, vt. To cut into; to dig; to carve on stone or other hard substance with a chisel, as letters or figures; [G. griebe, pl. grieben, the dregs of melted tallow] to clean, as a ship's bottom and cover with pitch, which was formerly done with the dregs of melted tallow or fat.—vi. To make incisions; to carve; to practise engraving. ppr. graving, pret. graved, pp. graven or graved. [Sax. grafan— Heb. gârab, to scratch.]—n. The pit in which a dead human body is deposited; a tomb; any place where the dead are reposited; a place of great slaughter or mortality; death. [Sax. græf.]
Grave, grāv, a. Heavy; momentous; serious; sage; staid; thoughtful; sedate; not gay; not tawdry; low, in music; opposed to sharp. [Fr.—L. gravis, heavy.]
Grave-clothes, grāv'klōᴛнz, n. pl. The clothes in which the dead are interred.
Grave-digger, grāv'dig-ėr, n. One whose occupation is to dig graves.
Gravel, gra'vel, n. Very small pebbles, larger than the particles of sand, but often intermixed with them; a disease produced by small calculous concretions in the kidneys and bladder.—vt. To cover with gravel; to puzzle; to hurt the foot of, as of a horse, by gravel lodged under the shoe. ppr. gravelling, pret. & pp. gravelled. [Fr. gravelle.]
Gravelled, gra'veld, p.a. Stopped; embarrassed.
Gravelling, gra'vel-ing, p.n. Act of covering with gravel.
Gravelly, gra'vel-i, a. Abounding with gravel; consisting of gravel.

ch, chain; j, job; g, go; ng, sing; ᴛн, then; th, thin; w, wig; wh, whig; zh, azure; † obsolete.

Gravely, gräv'li, *adv.* In a grave, solemn manner; soberly; seriously.

Graveness, gräv'nes, *n.* Seriousness; solemnity.

Graver, gräv'er, *n.* One who engraves; a sculptor; an engraving tool.

Grave-stone, gräv'stōn, *n.* A stone laid over a grave, or erected near it, as a monument.

Graving, gräv'ing, *p.n.* Act of cutting figures in hard substances; carved work; the act of cleaning a ship's bottom, and covering it with pitch.

Gravitate, gra'vi-tāt, *vi.* To be affected by gravity; to obey the law of gravitation; to tend towards the centre. *ppr.* gravitating, *pret. & pp.* gravitated. [Low L. *gravito, gravitatum*—L. *gravis*, heavy.]

Gravitation, gra-vi-tā'shon, *n.* The force by which bodies are drawn towards the centre of the earth, or towards any other centre; the tendency of all matter in the universe toward all other matter. [Fr.]

Gravity, gra'vi-ti, *n.* Weight; the tendency of a body toward the centre of the earth; the force of attraction; seriousness; solemnity of deportment; relative importance; lowness of sound, in music. [Fr. *gravité.*]

Gravy, grā'vi, *n.* The fat and other liquid matter that drips from flesh in roasting. [Gr. *griebe*, a piece remaining of melted fat.]

Gray, grā, *a.* Having the colour of the hair of an old person; white, with a mixture of black; of a mixed colour; of the colour of ashes; old; mature. *n.* A gray colour; an animal of a gray colour, as a horse. [Sax. *graeg.*]

Gray-beard, grā'bērd, *n.* An old man.

Grayish, grā'ish, *a.* Somewhat gray.

Grayling, grā'ling, *n.* A fish of the salmon tribe, much esteemed for its flavour.

Grayness, grā'nes, *n.* Quality of being gray.

Gray-wacke, grā-wa'kē, *n.* A grit rock, consisting of pebbles and sand firmly united together.

Graze, grāz, *vt.* To brush lightly, as the surface of a thing in passing; to lacerate slightly by rubbing. *ppr.* grazing, *pret. & pp.* grazed. [Fr. *raser*—L. *rado*, to rub off.]

Graze, grāz, *vt.* To feed with grass, as cattle; to feed on; to tend, as grazing cattle.—*vi.* To eat grass; to feed on growing herbage; to supply grass. *ppr.* grazing, *pret. & pp.* grazed. [Sax. *grasian.*]

Grazier, grā'zhėr, *n.* One who pastures cattle, and who rears them for market.

Grazing, grā'ing, *p.a.* Supplying pasture.—*p.n.* A pasture; the act of feeding on grass; the raising or feeding of cattle.

Grease, grēs, *n.* Animal fat in a soft state; oily matter of any kind, as lard. *vt.* To smear with grease. *ppr.* greasing, *pret. & pp.* greased. [Fr. *graisse*—L. *crassus*, fat.]

Greasily, grēs'i-li, *adv.* With grease, or an appearance of it; grossly.

Greasiness, grēs'i-nes, *n.* State of being greasy; oiliness; unctuousness.

Greasy, grēs'i, *a.* Smeared with grease; unctuous; like grease; gross; fat of body; indelicate.

Great, grāt, *a.* Large in bulk; large in number; expressing a large or unusual degree of anything; long-continued; weighty; chief; of vast power and excellence; illustrious; admirable; eminent; noble; dignified; majestic;

generous; of elevated sentiments; rich; swelling; proud; difficult; distant by one more generation, in the ascending or descending line, as great-grandfather, &c.—*n.* The whole; the gross; the lump or mass; people of rank or distinction. [Sax.—L. *grandis*, large.]

Great-hearted, grāt'härt-ed, *a.* High-spirited; undejected; noble.

Greatly, grāt'li, *adv.* In a great degree; much; nobly; illustriously; bravely.

Greatness, grāt'nes, *n.* Quality of being great; largeness of bulk, dimensions, number, or quantity; high rank; eminence; power; swelling pride; elevation of sentiment; nobleness; strength of intellectual faculties; grandeur; pomp; intensity.

Greaves, grēvz, *n. pl.* Armour for the legs; a sort of boots. [Fr. *grèves.*]

Grecian, grē'shan, *a.* Pertaining to Greece.—*n.* A native or inhabitant of Greece; a Jew who knew Greek; one well versed in the Greek language.

Grecism, grēs'izm, *n.* An idiom of the Greek language. [Fr. *grécisme.*]

Greedily, grēd'i-li, *adv.* Voraciously; ravenously; with keen or ardent desire.

Greediness, grēd'i-nes, *n.* Voracity; ardent desire; eagerness; avidity.

Greedy, grēd'i, *a.* Clamorous for food, &c.; having a keen appetite for food or drink; having a keen desire of anything; rapacious. [Sax. *graedig—graedan*, to cry for.]

Greek, grēk, *a.* Pertaining to Greece. *n.* A native of Greece; the language of Greece.

Green, grēn, *a.* Having the colour of herbage and plants when growing; verdant; fresh; containing its natural juices; not roasted; half raw; unripe; young; raw; wan; of a greenish pale colour.—*n.* The colour of growing plants; a colour composed of blue and yellow; a piece of ground covered with verdant herbage, (pl.) fresh leaves or branches of trees or other plants; the leaves and stems of young plants, used in cookery.—*vt.* To make green. [Sax. *grene—grovan*, to germinate.]

Green-eyed, grēn'īd, *a.* Having green eyes; jealous.

Greengrocer, grēn'grō-sėr, *n.* A retailer of fresh vegetables or fruit.

Green-hand, grēn'hand, *n.* One who is raw and inexperienced.

Greenhouse, grēn'hous, *n.* A house in which tender plants are sheltered from the weather.

Greenish, grēn'ish, *a.* Somewhat green.

Greenishness, grēn'ish-nes, *n.* Quality of being greenish.

Greenness, grēn'nes, *n.* Quality of being green; viridity; unripeness; vigour; newness.

Green-sward, grēn'swärd, *n.* Turf green with grass.

Green-wood, grēn'wud, *n.* A wood when green, as in summer.—*a.* Pertaining to a green wood.

Greet, grēt, *vt.* To wish peace to; to salute in kindness and respect; to hail; to send kind wishes to; to meet and address with kindness.—*vi.* To meet and salute. [Sax. *gretan—grith*, peace.]

Greeting, grēt'ing, *p.n.* Salutation at meeting; compliment addressed from one absent.

Gregarious, grē-gā'ri-us, *a.* Having the habit of assembling or living in a flock or herd; not habitually solitary. [L. *gregarius—grex, gregis*, a flock.]

Gregariously, grē-gā'ri-us-li, *adv.* In a flock or herd; in a company.

Gregorian, grē-gō'ri-an, *a.* Denoting what belongs to Gregory; as, the Gregorian calendar of Pope Gregory.

Grenade, grē-nād', *n.* A small bombshell, resembling a pomegranate, which is to be fired by means of a fusee, and thrown by hand among enemies. [Fr.—L. *granatum*, a pomegranate.]

Grenadier, gren-a-dēr', *n.* A tall foot-soldier, wearing a high cap. [from Fr. *grenade.*]

Greyhound, grā'hound, *n.* A hunting-dog; a tall, fleet dog kept for the chase. [Sax. *grighund*—Icel. grey, a dog, and hound.]

Griddle, grid'l, *n.* A circular plate of iron, or a pan broad and shallow, for baking cakes. [W. *greidell.*]

Gridiron, grid'ī-ėrn, *n.* A grated utensil for broiling flesh and fish over coals; the frame upon which a ship rests, for inspection or repair, at low water. [Sw. Goth. *gradda*, to bake, and *iron.*]

Grief, grēf, *n.* That which weighs down, grievance; the pain of mind produced by loss, misfortune, in'ury, or evils of any kind; sorrow; regret that we have done wrong; pain accompanying repentance; cause of sorrow; trouble. [Fr.—L. *gravis*, Sans. *guru*, heavy.]

Grievance, grēv'ans, *n.* That which causes grief; that which burdens, implying a sense of wrong done; burden; hardship; trouble; affliction.

Grieve, grēv, *vt.* To weigh down; to burden; to afflict; to wound the feelings of; to excite regret in; to offend.—*vi.* To feel grief; to sorrow; to mourn; to lament. (With *at* or *for.*) *ppr.* grieving, *pret. & pp.* grieved. [Fr. *grever*—L. *gravis*, heavy.]

Grieving, grēv'ing, *p.a.* Sorrowing; exercised with grief; mourning.

Grievingly, grēv'ing-li, *adv.* In sorrow; sorrowfully.

Grievous, grēv'us, *a.* Causing grief; heavy; hard to be borne; atrocious, as an offence; tending to irritate; destructive; causing mischief.

Grievously, grēv'us-li, *adv.* In a grievous manner.

Grievousness, grēv'us-nes, *n.* Weight that gives pain or distress; pain; affliction; calamity; enormity; atrociousness.

Griffin, Griffon, grif'fin, grif'fon, *n.* A fabled monster, having four legs, wings, and a crooked beak like that of an eagle. [Fr. *griffon*—Gr. *grupos*, having a crooked beak.]

Grill, gril, *vt.* To broil, as on a grate or gridiron; to torment, as if by broiling. [Fr. *griller*—L. *crates*, a grate.]

Grilse, grils, *n.* A young salmon on its first return to fresh-water.

Grim, grim, *a.* Enraged; ferocious; frightful; hideous; ugly; stern; surly. [Sax.—*grama*, anger.]

Grimace, gri-mās', *n.* A distortion of the countenance from habit, affectation, or insolence; an air of affectation. [Fr.]

Grimaced, gri-māst', *p.a.* Distorted; having a crabbed look.

Grime, grīm, *n.* Foul matter; sullying blackness, deeply insinuated.—*vt.* To sully or soil deeply. *ppr.* griming, *pret. & pp.* grimed. [Icel. *grīma.*]

Grimly, grim'li, *adv.* Fiercely; ferociously; sourly; sullenly.

Grimness, grim'nes, *n.* Fierceness of look; sternness; crabbedness.

Grimy, grīm'i, *a.* Full of grime; foul.

Grin, grin, *vi.* To open the lips so as to show the teeth; to set the teeth together and open the lips; to fix the teeth, as in anguish.—*vt.* To express by grin-

Fāte, fär, fat, fall; mē, met, hėr; pīne, pin; nōte, not, mōve; tūbe, tub, bull; oil, pound.

-ning, ppr. grinning, pret. & pp. grinned.—n. Act of closing the teeth and showing them, or of withdrawing the lips and showing the teeth. [Sax. *grinnian*—L. *ringor*, to open the mouth wide.]

Grind, grind, vt. To bruise; to crush; to break and reduce to fine particles by friction; to break and reduce to small pieces by the teeth; to sharpen by friction; to polish by friction, as glass; to rub, as one against another; to oppress by severe exactions; to crush in pieces; to ruin.—vi. To perform the operation of grinding; to move a mill; to be moved or rubbed together; to be pulverised by friction; to be polished by friction; to be sharpened by grinding. ppr. grinding, pret. & pp. ground. [Sax. *grindan—rendan*, to rend.]

Grinder, grind'er, n. One who grinds; a tooth that grinds or chews food; a jaw-tooth; (pl.) the teeth in general.

Grinding, grind'ing, p.a. Oppressing; crushing.—p.n. Act of reducing to powder; sharpening or polishing; oppressing.

Grinner, grin'er, n. One who grins.

Gripe, grīp, vt. To seize with the hand; to catch with the hand, and to clasp closely with the fingers; to squeeze; to clutch; to pinch; to compress; to give pain to, as to the bowels; to straiten. vi. To seize or catch by pinching; to get money by hard bargains or mean exactions; to feel the colic. ppr. griping, pret. & pp. griped.—n. Grasp; fast hold with the hand or paw, or with the arms; squeeze; oppression; pinching distress; something which grasps or holds fast; (pl.) pinching pain in the bowels. [Sax. *gripan—gana grah*, to seize.]

Griping, grīp'ing, p.a. Oppressing; tyrannical.—n. A peculiar pain of the bowels.

Gripingly, grīp'ing-li, adv. In a griping manner.

Grisly, gris'li, a. Dreadful; fearful; ghastly; frightful. [Sax. *grislic*.]

Grist, grist, n. That which is ground; corn for grinding; supply; profit; gain. [Sax. —*grindan*, to grind.]

Gristle, gris'l, n. A cartilage; a smooth, elastic substance in animal bodies. [Sax.]

Gristliness, gris'li-nes, n. State of being gristly.

Gristly, gris'li, a. Consisting of gristle; like gristle; cartilaginous.

Grit, grit, n. That which is crushed; sand; the coarse part of meal; oats hulled or coarsely ground; rough, hard particles; a hard sandstone. [Sax. *greot*, sand, dust—*grindan*, to grind.]

Grittiness, grit'i-nes, n. Quality of containing grit, or consisting of grit.

Gritty, grit'i, a. Containing sand or grit; consisting of grit; sandy.

Grizzle, griz'l, n. Gray; a gray colour; a mixture of white and black. [Fr. *gris*.]

Grizzled, griz'ld, a. Gray; of a mixed colour.

Grizzly, griz'li, a. Somewhat gray; gray with age.

Groan, grōn, vi. To breathe with a deep, murmuring sound; to utter a mournful voice, as in pain or sorrow; to moan; to be afflicted.—n. A deep, mournful sound, uttered in pain, sorrow, or anguish; any low rumbling sound. [Sax. *granian*.]

Groaning, grōn'ing, p.n. Lamentation; a deep sound uttered in pain or sorrow.

Groat, grat, n. A great piece or coin, of copper or brass, as distinguished from the small copper coin, of which there were five in the groat; an English money of account, equal to fourpence; a proverbial name for a small sum. [D. *groot*—Old G. *grôs*, great.]

Grocer, grō'sér, n. Originally one who sold goods in the gross; a merchant who deals in tea, sugar, &c. [Old Fr. *grossier—gros*, great.]

Grocery, grō'sé-ri, n. The commodities sold by grocers.

Grog, grog, n. A mixture of spirit and cold water not sweetened.

Grogram, Grogran, grog'ram, grog'ran, n. A kind of stuff made of silk and mohair, and having a coarse grain or texture. [Old Fr. *grosgrain*.]

Groin, groin, n. The part of the human body where there is a division between the belly and thighs in front; the line or angular curve made by the intersection of simple vaults crossing each other at any angle.—vt. To fashion into groins. [Icel. *grein*, a branch.]

Groined, groind, p.a. Having a groin or groins.

Groom, gröm, n. A boy; a servant; a man or boy who has the charge of horses; an officer in the royal household.—vt. To feed and take care of, as a groom does horses. [Belg. *grom*.]

Groom, gröm, n. A man recently married, or one who is attending his proposed spouse in order to be married. [Sax. *guma*, Old G. *gomo*, a man.]

Grooming, gröm'ing, p.n. The care and feeding of horses.

Groove, gröv, n. A furrow, channel, or long hollow cut by a tool; a channel in the edge of a moulding, stile, or rail. vt. To cut a channel with an edged tool in; to furrow. ppr. grooving, pret. & pp. grooved. [Sax. *graef—grafan*, to grave.]

Grope, grōp, vi. To feel along with the hand; to search in the dark, or as a blind person, by feeling; to seek blindly in intellectual darkness.—vt. To search by feeling in the dark. ppr. groping, pret. & pp. groped. [Sax. *gropian*—Heb. *gáraph*, to gripe.]

Gropingly, grōp'ing-li, adv. In a groping manner.

Gross, grōs, a. Thick; fat; coarse; rude; not delicate; obscene; large; palpable; dense; not refined or pure; enormous; shameful; dull; whole.—n. The bulk; the mass; the bulk or the whole undivided; all parts taken together; the sum total; the number of twelve dozen. [Fr. *gros*—L. *crassus*, thick.]

Grossly, grōs'li, adv. In a gross manner.

Grossness, grōs'nes, n. Thickness; bulkiness; fatness; density; rudeness; vulgarity; enormity.

Grot, Grotto, grot, grot'tō, n. A concealed cavity; a natural cave or rent in the earth; an artificial ornamented cave, for coolness and refreshment. [Fr. *grotte*—Gr. *kruptō*, to conceal.]

Grotesque, grō-tesk', a. That is in the style of a grotto; wildly formed; ludicrous; antic.—n. Whimsical figures or scenery; artificial grotto-work. [Fr. —*grotte*, a grotto.]

Grotesquely, grō-tesk'li, adv. In a fantastical manner.

Grotesqueness, grō-tesk'nes, n. State of being grotesque.

Grotto-work, grot'tō-wérk, n. Ornamental work or shell-work in a garden.

Ground, ground, n. That which we go upon; the upper part of the earth, without reference to the materials which compose it; territory; land; a floor or pavement; foundation; fundamental cause; first principles; that which is first put on the surface on which a figure is represented, in painting; field or place of action; (pl.) dregs; lees.—vt. To lay or set on the ground; to found; to fix or set, as on a foundation or principle; to fix firmly.—vi. To run aground; to strike the bottom and remain fixed, as a ship. [Sax. *grund*—L. *gradior*, to step, to go.]

Grounded, ground'ed, p.a. Settled in first principles.

Ground-floor, ground'flōr, n. That floor of a house which is at the base, or that which is on a level with the exterior ground.

Ground-form, ground'form, n. The basis of a word in grammar, to which the other parts are added in declension and conjugation; the root.

Ground-ivy, ground'ī-vi, n. A well-known plant which creeps along the ground.

Groundless, ground'les, a. Wanting ground or foundation; wanting cause or reason for support; false.

Groundlessly, ground'les-li, adv. Without reason or cause.

Groundlessness, ground'les-nes, n. Want of just cause, reason, or authority for support.

Groundling, ground'ling, n. A fish that keeps at the bottom of the water; a spectator in the pit of the theatre.

Ground-plot, ground'plot, n. The ground on which a building is placed.

Ground-rent, ground'rent, n. Rent paid for ground, especially for the ground on which a building stands.

Ground-swell, ground'swel, n. A swell and heaving of the ocean with great power from beneath.

Groundwork, ground'werk, n. The basis; that to which the rest are additional; first principle; original reason.

Group, gröp, n. A cluster; an assemblage; a number collected without any regular form; an assemblage of two or more figures of men, beasts, or other things, in painting and sculpture, which have some relation to each other.—vt. To form into a group or an assemblage. [Fr. *groupe*—Sax. *crop*, a group.]

Grouped, gröpt, p.a. Formed or placed in a cluster or crowd.

Grouping, gröp'ing, p.n. The art of combining the objects of a picture or piece of sculpture.

Grouse, grous, n. A heathcock, or cock of the wood, highly prized for food. [Pers. *khuroos*, a cock.]

Grout, grout, n. Dregs; lees; coarse meal; a thin, coarse mortar for pouring into the joints of masonry; a finer material for finishing the best ceilings. vt. To fill up, as the joints or spaces between stones, with coarse mortar. [Gael. *grud*, lees, grounds.]

Grove, grōv, n. A recess or hollow space, natural or artificial, in the interior of a thick wood; the trees surrounding such a recess; a small wood, with a shaded avenue. [Sax. *graf—grafan*, to grave.]

Grovel, gro'vel, vi. To move with the body prostrate on the earth; to act in a prostrate posture; to be low or mean. ppr. grovelling, pret. & pp. grovelled. [Icel. *grufa*, a lying flat on the belly.]

Groveller, gro'vel-ér, n. One who grovels; an abject wretch.

Grovelling, gro'vel-ing, p.a. Mean; without dignity or elevation.

---

ch, chain; j, job; g, go; ng, sing; vs, then; th, thin; w, wig; wh, whig; zh, azure; † obsolete.

Grow, grō, vi. To *vegetate*, as *plants*, or to be augmented by natural process, as animals; to be gradually produced; to increase; to wax; to improve; to make progress; to become; to be changed from one state to another; to proceed, as from a cause or reason; to accrue; to swell.—*vt. To cause to grow*; to raise. *ppr*. growing, *pret*. grew, *pp*. grown. [Sax. *growan*—Old G. *gruojan*—Sans. *hari*, green.]

Grower, grō'ėr, n. *One who grows*; that which increases; one who raises or produces.

Growing, grō'ing, *p.a*. Advancing in size or extent; thriving.

Growl, groul, vi. *To murmur or snarl*, as a dog; to utter an angry, grumbling sound.—*vt. To express by growling*. n. A deep snarl; an angry murmur. [G. *grollen*, to roar.]

Growler, groul'ėr, n. A snarling cur.

Growling, groul'ing, *p.a*. Grumbling. *p.n*. Act of grumbling or snarling.

Grown, grōn, *p.a*. *Increased in growth*; having arrived at full size or stature.

Growth, grōth, n. *Act of growing*; the gradual increase of vegetable and animal bodies; product; increase in extent; advancement; influence.

Grub, grub, vi. *To dig*; to be employed meanly.—*vt. To dig*; to root out by digging. (With *up*.) *ppr*. grubbing, *pret. & pp*. grubbed.—n. An insect which crows *dig up* and devour; an insect in the larva state. [Goth. *graban*, to dig.]

Grubber, grub'ėr, n. *One who grubs*; an instrument for digging up the roots of trees, &c.

Grubbing, grub'ing, *p.n*. Act of digging up by the roots.

Grudge, gruj, vi. *To grumble*; to complain; to be unwilling or reluctant; to be envious.—*vt. To grumble at*; to be discontented at, as at another's enjoyments; to permit or grant with reluctance; to give or take unwillingly. *ppr*. grudging, *pret. & pp*. grudged. n. Sullen malice; unwillingness to benefit; aversion; spite; pique. [Icel. *graedska*, hatred.]

Grudging, gruj'ing, *p.n*. Uneasiness at the possession of something by another; reluctance.

Grudgingly, gruj'ing-li, *adv*. Unwillingly; with reluctance or discontent.

Gruel, grü'el, n. A kind of light food made by boiling *groats* or meal in water. [Fr. *gruau*, water-gruel; Sax. *grut*, meal of wheat or barley.]

Gruff, gruf, a. Of a *rough* or stern manner or voice; sour; surly; severe; rugged; harsh. [D. *grof*, coarse.]

Gruffly, gruf'li, *adv*. Roughly; harshly.

Gruffness, gruf'nes, n. *Roughness* of voice or manner; sternness.

Grumble, grum'bl, vi. To growl; to murmur with discontent; to utter a low voice by way of complaint; to snarl; to roar. *ppr*. grumbling, *pret. & pp*. grumbled. [Fr. *grommeler*, to mutter.]

Grumbler, grum'bl-ėr, n. *One who grumbles*; a discontented man.

Grumbling, grum'bl-ing, *p.a*. Murmuring through discontent.—*p.n*. A murmuring through discontent.

Grumblingly, grum'bl-ing-li, *adv*. With *grumbling* or complaint.

Grunt, grunt, vi. *To murmur like a hog*; to utter a deep guttural sound. n. *A deep guttural sound*, as of a hog. [Dan. *grynte*.]

Grunter, grunt'ėr, n. *One who grunts*; a hog; a pig.

Grunting, grunt'ing, *p.n*. The guttural sound of swine or other animals.

Guano, gwä'nō, n. A rich manure, composed chiefly of the *excrements* of seafowls, and brought from the South American and African coasts. [Peruv. *huano*, dung.]

Guarantee, ga-ran-tē', n. *A warrant*; an undertaking by a third person that the stipulations of a covenant shall be observed by the contracting parties or by one of them; one who binds himself to see the stipulations of another performed.—*vt. To warrant*; to engage for, as for the performance of a duty, or the payment of a debt; to undertake to secure to another, at all events; to save harmless. *ppr*. guaranteeing, *pret. & pp*. guaranteed. [Fr. *garantie*—Sax. *warian*, to guard.]

Guard, gärd, vt. *To ward*; to keep watch over; to protect the edge of; to defend; to secure against injury, loss, or attack; to secure against the attacks of malevolence.—vi. To *watch*, by way of caution or defence; to be in a state of defence or safety.—n. *Ward*; *watch*; security against injury, loss, or attack; that which secures against attack or injury; a man or body of men occupied in preserving a person or place from attack or injury; a sentinel; an escort; care; heed; that which secures against censure; caution of expression; part of the hilt of a sword; a posture of defence. [Fr. *garder*—Sax. *weardian*, to watch.]

Guardage†, gärd'āj, n. *Wardship*.

Guardant, gärd'ant, a. *Acting as guardian*.—n. *A guardian*.

Guarded, gärd'ed, *p.a*. Circumspect; framed or uttered with caution.

Guardedly, gärd'ed-li, *adv*. With circumspection.

Guardedness, gärd'ed-nes, n. Caution; circumspection.

Guardian, gärd'i-an, n. *One who guards*, preserves, or secures; one appointed to take charge of the estate and education of an orphan or ward.—a. Protecting. [Fr. *gardien*.]

Guardianship, gärd'i-an-ship, n. The *office of a guardian*; protection; care.

Guardless, gärd'les, a. Without guard.

Guard-room, gärd'röm, n. *A room for the accommodation of guards*.

Guardsman, gärds'man, n. An officer or a private in a body of troops whose duty it is to *guard* the person of a sovereign, a prince, &c.

Gudgeon, gu'jon, n. A small freshwater fish, easily caught; a person easily cheated; a bait. [Fr. *goujon*—L. *gobius*.]

Guerdon, gėr'don, n. A reward; requital; recompense.—*vt. To give guerdon to*; to reward. [Old Fr.]

Guess, ges, vt. *To conjecture*; to divine; to form, as an opinion without certain means of knowledge; to surmise; to form, as an opinion from some reasons that render a thing probable.—vi. *To conjecture*; to judge at random.—n. *Conjecture*; judgment without any certain evidence or grounds. [D. *gissen*.]

Guessing, ges'ing, *p.n*. *The forming of conjectures*.

Guessingly, ges'ing-li, *adv*. By way of conjecture.

Guess-work, ges'wėrk, n. Work performed at hazard.

Guest, gest, n. *A stranger*; a stranger or friend received into the house of another, and treated with hospitality. [Sax. *gest*.]

Guest-rope†, gest'rōp, n. A rope to tow with.

Guidance, gid'ans, n. *The act of guiding*; direction; government; a leading.

Guide, gid, vt. To *conduct* in a *course or path*; to direct; to influence; to regulate; to superintend. *ppr*. guiding, *pret. & pp*. guided.—n. *A person who leads or directs*; one who directs another in his conduct or course of life; a director; that which leads or conducts. [Fr. *guider*.]

Guide-book, gid'buk, n. A book for the *guidance* of travellers.

Guild, gild, n. *A payment*; a tax; those who paid the tax; a fraternity; a corporation; a company associated for some purpose, particularly for carrying on commerce. [Sax. *geld*—*gildan*, to pay.]

Guildhall, gild-hal', n. *The hall where a guild* usually assembles, particularly that of the city of London.

Guile, gil, n. *Wile*; *fraud*; craft; artifice; duplicity.—*vi.†* To deceive. [Old Fr. *guile*.]

Guileful, gil'ful, a. *Full of guile*; wily; cunning; crafty; fraudulent; treacherous.

Guilefully, gil'ful-li, *adv*. Artfully.

Guilefulness, gil'ful-nes, n. *Quality of being guileful*; deceit; secret treachery.

Guileless, gil'les, a. *Free from guile* or deceit; artless; frank; sincere; honest.

Guilelessly, gil'les-li, *adv*. *In a guileless manner*.

Guilelessness, gil'les-nes, n. *Quality of being guileless*; simplicity.

Guillotine, gil-lō-tēn', n. A machine for beheading persons at a stroke.—*vt. To behead with the guillotine*. [Fr.]

Guilt, gilt, n. Moral *debt contracted by an offence*; sin; that state of a moral agent which results from his actual commission of a crime or offence, knowing it to be a violation of law; criminality, in a political or civil view. [Sax. *gylt*—*gildan*, to pay.]

Guiltily, gilt'i-li, *adv*. *In a guilty manner*.

Guiltiness, gilt'i-nes, n. *State of being guilty*; wickedness; criminality; guilt.

Guiltless, gilt'les, a. *Free from guilt*.

Guiltlessly, gilt'les-li, *adv*. *Without guilt*; innocently.

Guiltlessness, gilt'les-nes, n. Innocence; freedom from guilt or crime.

Guilty, gilt'i, a. *Justly chargeable with guilt*; criminal; having knowingly committed a crime or offence; corrupt; sinful. [Sax. *gyltig*.]

Guinea, gi'nē, n. Formerly, a gold coin of Great Britain, of the value of twenty-one shillings sterling. [from *Guinea*, in Africa.]

Guise, giz, n. *Habit*; external appearance; dress; mien; cast of behaviour. [Fr. *guise*.]

Guiser, giz'ėr, n. *A person in disguise*; a mummer who goes about at Christmas.

Guitar, gi-tär', n. *A kind of harp or lyre*; a stringed instrument of music. [Sp. *guitarra*; Gr. *kithára*, a harp.]

Gulf, gulf, n. A *bay*; an arm or part of the sea extending into the land; a large bay; a deep place in the earth; a whirlpool; an absorbing eddy; anything insatiable. [Fr. *golfe*—Gr. *kolpos*, a bay of the sea.]

Gulfy, gulf'i, a. Full of whirlpools or gulfs.

Gull, gul, vt. *To beguile*; to deceive; to cheat; to trick; to defraud.—n. A cheating; trick; fraud; one easily cheated. [D. *kullen*, to fool.]

Gull, gul, n. A web-footed sea-bird with

Fäte, fär, fat, fall; mē, met, hėr; pine, pin; nōte, not, mōve; tübe, tub, bull; oil, pound.

GULLET — HACK

long wings, so named from its *wailing* cry. [W. *gwylan*, to weep.]
Gullet, gul'let, *n.* The throat; the passage in the neck of an animal by which food and liquor are taken into the stomach. [Fr. *gueule*—L. *gula*, the throat.]
Gully, gul'li, *n.* A channel or hollow worn in the earth by a current of water. [Fr. *goulet*.]
Gulp, gulp, *vt.* To swallow eagerly, or in large draughts.—*n.* A large *swallow*, or as much as is swallowed at once. [D. *gulpen*.]
Gum, gum, *n.* The palate, as the seat of *taste*; the hard fleshy substance of the jaws which invests the teeth. [Sax. *goma*—Icel. *gomr*, the palate.]
Gum, gum, *n.* A concrete *juice* which exudes through the bark of many different plants.—*vt.* To smear with *gum*; to unite by a viscous substance. *ppr.* gumming, *pret. & pp.* gummed. [L. *gummi*, Gr. *kommi*.]
Gum-boil, gum'boil, *n.* A *boil on the gum*.
Gumminess, gum'i-nes, *n.* Viscousness; accumulation of gum.
Gummy, gum'i, *a.* Consisting of *gum*; viscous; productive of gum; covered with gum or viscous matter.
Gumption, gum'shon, *n.* Shrewdness.
Gun, gun, *n.* A firearm; a musket; a rifle; a cannon, &c. [probably corrupted from *engine*, according to Selden.]
Gun-boat, gun'bōt, *n.* A boat or small vessel fitted to carry *cannon*.
Gun-carriage, gun'ka-rij, *n.* A wheel-*carriage* for moving *cannon*.
Gunner, gun'ér, *n.* A cannonier; an officer appointed to manage artillery.
Gunnery, gun'é-ri, *n.* The science of artillery.
Gunpowder, gun'pou-dér, *n.* An explosive composition used in *guns*, &c.
Gunshot, gun'shot, *n.* The distance of the point-blank range of a *cannon-shot*.—*a.* Made by the shot of a *gun*, as a wound.
Gunstone, gun'stōn, *n.* A stone used for the shot of cannon.
Gunwale, gun'wāl, *n.* The lower part of any *gun*-port of a ship; the upper edge of a ship's side.

Gargle, gėr'gl, *vi.* To run, as liquor, with a purling noise; to run or flow *in* a broken *noisy current*.—*n.* A gush or flow of liquid, or the sound produced by it. *ppr.* gurgling, *pret. & pp.* gurgled. [It. *gorgogliare*—L. *gurges*, a whirlpool.]
Gurgling, gėr'gl-ing, *p.a.* Running or flowing with a purling sound.—*p.n.* A running with a broken noisy *current*.
Gurnard, Gurnet, gėr'nård, gėr'net, *n.* A fish remarkable for the *bony* plates which cover the head. [Ir. *guirnead*.]
Gush, gush, *vi.* To pour; to pour out *violently*; to issue with violence and rapidity, as a fluid.—*vt.* To emit in copious effusion.—*n.* A sudden and violent issue of a fluid; the fluid thus emitted. [G. *guss*, a torrent.]
Gushing, gush'ing, *p.a.* Flowing copiously.—*p.n.* A rushing forth with violence.
Gusset, gus'set, *n.* A small piece of cloth inserted in a garment, for the purpose of strengthening some part. [Fr. *pousset*, the armpit.]
Gust, gust, *n.* Taste; *tasting*, or the *sense of tasting*; relish; pleasure; gratification; turn of fancy; intellectual taste.—*vt.?* To have a relish of. [L. *gustus*—Gr. *geuō*, to give one a taste of.]
Gust, gust, *n.* A *sudden gush* of wind; a violent blast of wind; a sudden, violent burst of passion. [Icel. *gustr*, a cold blast.]
Gusto, gust'ō, *n.* Relish; nice appreciation. [It.—L. *gustus*, taste.]
Gusty, gust'i, *a.* Subject to *sudden blasts* of wind; stormy; tempestuous.
Gut, gut, *n.* That through which anything *flows*; the intestinal canal of an animal; a passage or strait.—*vt.* To take out the bowels of; to plunder of contents. *ppr.* gutting, *pret. & pp.* gutted. [Low Sax. *küt*—Sax. *geotan*, to pour out.]
Gutta-percha, gut-ta-pėr'cha, *n.* Gum from a tree, originally obtained in the island of *Percha*; a gum-resin extensively used for economical purposes.
Gutter, gut'tėr, *n.* A channel for catching and conveying off the water which collects on the roof of a building, and

from which the water *drops* or runs; a channel or passage for water; a hollow in the earth for conveying water. *vt.* To cut into small hollows.—*vi.* To be hollowed; to run in drops or hollows, as a candle. [Fr. *gouttière*—L. *gutta*, a drop.]
Guttural, gut'tėr-al, *a.* Pertaining to *the throat*; formed in the throat.—*n.* A letter pronounced in *the throat*. [Fr.—L. *guttur*, the throat.]
Gutturally, gut'tėr-al-li, *adv.* In a *guttural* manner; in the throat.
Guzzle, guz'l, *vi.* To swallow liquor greedily; to drink frequently.—*vt.* To *swallow* much or often; to swallow with immoderate gust. *ppr.* guzzling, *pret. & pp.* guzzled. [It. *gozzovigliare*, to feast.]
Guzzler, guz'l-ėr, *n.* One who *guzzles*.
Gymnasium, jim-nā'zi-um, *n.* A place where athletic exercises are performed, originally in Greece by persons *naked*; any place of exercise; a school for the higher branches of literature and science. [Gr. *gumnasion*—*gumnos*, naked.]
Gymnastic, jim-nast'ik, *a.* Pertaining to a *gymnasium*, or to athletic exercises of the body. [Gr. *gumnastikos*.]
Gymnastics, jim-nast'iks, *n. pl.* The *gymnastic art*.
Gypseous, gip'sē-us, *a.* Of the nature of *gypsum*; containing gypsum.
Gypsum, gip'sum, *n.* White *lime*; sulphate of lime; plaster of Paris; stucco. [L.—Gr. *gupsos*, chalk.]
Gyrate, jīr'āt, *vi.* To turn round in a *circle*; to revolve round a central point, as a tornado. *ppr.* gyrating, *pret. & pp.* gyrated. [L. *gyro*, *gyratus*.]
Gyration, jīr-ā'shon, *n.* A turning or whirling round. [L. *gyratio*.]
Gyratory, jīr'ā-tō-ri, *a.* Moving in a circle.
Gyre, jīr, *n.* A *circular* motion, or a circle described by a moving body; a turn. [L. *gyrus*.]
Gyrfalcon, jėr'fa-kn, *n.* The *vulture falcon*; a species of hawk. [G. *geierfalke*.]
Gyve, jiv, *n.* A *fetter* or shackle for the leg.—*vt.* To *fetter*; to shackle; to chain. *ppr.* gyving, *pret. & pp.* gyved. [W. *gefyn*, a fetter.]

H.

ha, hä. An exclamation denoting surprise, joy, grief, &c.—*vi.* To express surprise; to hesitate.
Haberdasher, ha'bėr-dash-ėr, *n.* A seller of small wares, confined at present to ribbons, tapes, pins, needles, and thread. [perhaps from G. *habe*, goods, *verlauscher*, an exchanger.]
Haberdashery, ha'bėr-dash-ė-ri, *n.* The *wares sold by a haberdasher*.
Habergeon, ha-bėr'jē-on, *n.* An ancient coat of mail *to defend the neck* and breast. [Fr. *haubergeon*.]
Habiliment, ha-bil'i-ment, *n.* A *garment*. (Usually in the plural.) [Fr. *habillement*—*habiller*, to clothe.]
Habit, ha'bit, *n.* State of *anything*, implying some continuance; temperament; an aptitude for the performance of certain actions, acquired by custom; mode; manner; garb; dress; garments

in general; a coat worn by ladies over other garments; the features or general appearance of a plant.—*vt.* To dress; to clothe; to array. [Fr.—L. *habitus*—*habeo*, to have.]
Habitable, ha'bit-a-bl, *a.* That may be *inhabited* or dwelt in; capable of sustaining human beings. [Fr.—L. *habito*, to dwell.]
Habitat, ha'bit-at, *n.* The natural *abode* of a plant or animal.
Habitation, ha-bit-ā'shon, *n.* A *dwelling*; state of dwelling; a place of abode; a mansion; a residence. [Fr.—L. *habitatio*.]
Habited, ha'bit-ed, *p.a.* Clothed; dressed.
Habitual, ha-bit'ū-al, *a.* Acquired by *habit*; formed by use; customary; accustomed; usual; common; inveterate. [Fr. *habituel*.]

Habitually, ha-bit'ū-al-li, *adv.* By *habit*; customarily.
Habituate, ha-bit'ū-āt, *vt.* To train to a *habit*; to make familiar by frequent use; to inure; to familiarize. *ppr.* habituating, *pret. & pp.* habituated. [Late L. *habituo*, *habituatus*—L. *habeo*, *habitum*, to have.]
Habitude, ha'bit-ūd, *n.* The external condition or form of a thing; customary manner; repetition of the same acts; customary manner of living. [Fr.—L. *habitudo*.]
Hack, hak, *vt.* To cut with an axe; to chop; to mangle by repeated strokes of a cutting instrument; to speak with stops or catches, or with hesitation. *n.* A notch; a cut; hesitating or faltering speech. [Sax. *haccan*—*acas*, an axe.]
Hack, hak, *n.* A horse *kept for hire*; a

ch, *chain*; j, *job*; g, *go*; ng, *sing*; ᴛʜ, *then*; th, *thin*; w, *wig*; wh, *whig*; zh, *azure*; † obsolete.

horse much used in draught or in hard service; anything exposed to hire; a writer employed in the drudgery and details of book-making.—*a.* Hired; much used or worn, like a hired horse. [from *hackney.*]

Hacking, hak'ing, *p.a.* Short and interrupted; as, a hacking cough.

Hackle, hak'l, *vt.* To comb, as flax; to separate, as the coarse part of flax from the fine by means of a hackle; to tear asunder. *ppr.* hackling, *pret. & pp.* hackled.—*n.* A comb; an instrument with teeth for separating the coarse part of hemp or flax from the fine; a fly for angling. [D. *hekelen.*]

Hackney, hak'ne, *n.* An ambling horse; a horse kept for hire; a coach kept for hire; anything much used; a hireling; a prostitute.—*a.* Let out for hire; prostitute; much used; trite.—*vt.* To use much; to devote to common use; to carry in a hackney coach. [Fr. *haquenée*—L. *equus,* a horse.]

Hackneyed, hak'nēd, *p.a.* Worn out; practised; accustomed.

Haddock, had'dok, *n.* A sea-fish allied to the cod, and esteemed excellent food. [Old Fr. *hadot,* a salt haddock.]

Haft, haft, *n.* That by which a thing is seized; a handle; that part of an instrument which is taken into the hand, as of a sword.—*vt.* To set in a haft or handle. [Sax. *haeft*—*haeftan,* to take.]

Hag, hag, *n.* One who causes fear; a witch; a fury; a fiend; a sorceress; an ugly, hateful old woman; a kind of fish that enters other fishes and devours them. [Sax. *haeges*—*egesian,* to affright—Heb. *hâga,* to mutter.]

Hagberry, hag'be-ri, *n.* A plant so called in Scotland; bird-cherry.

Haggard, hag'gärd, *a. Death-like; wild; lank;* meagre and rugged in features; having eyes sunk in their sockets; intractable.—*n.*+ An untrained hawk; anything wild. [Fr. *hagard,* wild.]

Haggardly, hag'gärd-li, *adv.* In a haggard or ugly manner; with deformity.

Haggish, hag'ish, *a. Of the nature of a hag;* deformed; ugly.

Haggle, hag'l, *vt.* To cut into small pieces; to mangle. *ppr.* haggling, *pret. & pp.* haggled.

Haggle, hag'l, *vi.* To higgle; to hesitate and cavil. *ppr.* haggling, *pret. & pp.* haggled.

Haggler, hag'l-ėr, *n.* One who cavils, hesitates, and makes difficulty in bargaining.

Haggling, hag'l-ing, *p.n.* Act of hesitating and making difficulty in bargaining.

Hah, häh. An exclamation expressing surprise or effort. [See HA.]

Haha, hä'hä. See HAWHAW.

Hail, hāl, *n.* Frozen drops of rain falling in masses, of form exceedingly various, but in general roundish.—*vi.* To pour down roundish masses of ice or frozen vapours.—*vt.* To pour down in the manner of hail. [Sax. *haegel.*]

Hail, hāl. A salutation signifying health to you.—*n.* A wish of health; a salutation.—*vt.* To salute; to call to, as to a person at a distance. [Sax. *hael,* health.]

Hailstone, hāl'stōn, *n.* A single mass of hail falling from a cloud.

Haily, hāl'i, *a. Consisting of hail.*

Hair, hār, *n.* A small thread-like filament issuing from the skin of an animal, and from a bulbous root; the mass of filaments growing from the skin of an animal, and forming a covering; anything very small or fine; a very

small distance; a trifling value; long, straight, and distinct filaments on the surface of plants. [Sax. *haer.*]

Hair-breadth, hār'bredth, *n. The breadth of a hair;* a very small distance.—*a.* Having the breadth of a hair.

Hairiness, hār'i-nes, *n. State of being hairy.* [from *hairy.*]

Hairy, hār'i, *a. Overgrown with hair;* consisting of hair; resembling hair.

Halberd, hal'bėrd, *n. The shining hatchet;* an ancient weapon, consisting of a long pole ending with an axe and dagger. [Fr. *hallebarde*—G. *hell,* clear, and *barte,* a broad hatchet.]

Halberdier, hal-bėrd-ēr', *n. One who is armed with a halberd.*

Halcyon, hal'si-on, *n.* The king-fisher; a bird that was said to lay her eggs in nests, on rocks near the sea, and *hatch* them during the calm weather about the winter solstice.—*a.* Calm; quiet; peaceful; happy. [Gr. *alkuōn*—*hals,* the sea, and *kuō,* to conceive.]

Hale, hāl, *a. Whole;* sound; entire; healthy; robust; not impaired. [Sax. *hal*—Gr. *holos,* whole.]

Hale, hāl, *n.* A violent pull.—*vt.* To take, pull, or drag by force. *ppr.* haling, *pret. & pp.* haled.

Haleness, hāl'nes, *n. Wholeness;* healthiness; soundness.

Half, haf, *n.* **Halves,** *n. pl.* One part of a thing which is divided into two equal parts; a moiety.—*a.* Consisting of a moiety or half.—*adv.* In part, or in an equal part or degree. [Sax.]

Half-capt, haf'kap, *n.* A cap not wholly put off; a slight salute.

Half-crown, haf-kroun', *n. The half of a crown;* a silver coin, value 2s. 6d.

Half-dead, haf-ded', *a. Almost dead.*

Half-faced, haf'fāst, *a.* Showing only *part of the face.*

Half-length, haf'length, *a. Containing one-half of the length.*

Half-moon, haf'mōn, *n.* The moon at the quarters, when half its disc appears illuminated; anything in the shape of a half-moon.

Half-pay, haf'pā, *n. Half* the amount of wages or salary; a reduced allowance to an officer on his retirement from the service, or when he is not in actual service.

Half-tint, haf'tint, *n.* An intermediate colour; middle tint.

Half-yearly, haf-yēr'li, *a.* Two in a year; semi-annual.—*adv.* Twice in a year; semi-annually.

Halibut, ha'li-but, *n. St. Peter's flounder;* a large, flat fish, much esteemed for food. [Sax. *halig,* holy, and Old Eng. *but,* a flounder.]

Hall, hal, *n. An edifice;* a palace; a royal court; a large room at the entrance of a house; an edifice in which courts of justice are held; a manor-house; a college; a room for a corporation or public assembly; a collegiate body in the universities of Oxford and Cambridge. [Sax. *haell*—L. *aula.*]

Halleluiah, Hallelujah, hal-le-lu'yä, *n.* and *interj.* A word used in sacred songs of praise, signifying *praise ye Jehovah;* give praise to God. [Heb. from obsol. *halal,* in one form, to sing, and *Jah,* Jehovah.]

Halliard, Halyard, hal'yärd, *n. A haul-yard;* a term applied to ropes for hoisting or lowering yards or sails.

Halloo, hal-lō', *vi.* To cry out; to exclaim with a loud voice.—*vt.* To encourage with shouts; to chase with shouts; to call or shout to.—*n.* An

exclamation, used as a call to invite attention.—*interj.* Ho, there! [Sax. *ahlowan,* to bellow.]

Hallooing, hal-lō'ing, *p. n.* A loud outcry.

Hallow, hal'lō, *vt. To make holy;* to set apart for religious use; to keep holy; to honour as sacred. [Sax. *halgian*—*halig,* holy.]

Hallowed, hal'lōd, *p.a.* Treated as sacred; reverenced.

Hallowing, hal'lō-ing, *p.a. Making holy;* consecrating; reverencing.

Hallowmas, hal'lō-mas, *n. The sacred feast of All-Souls.* [Sax. *halig,* holy, and *maesse,* feast.]

Hallucination, hal-lū'sin-ā"shon, *n. A wandering of mind;* error; delusion; a diseased state of mind, in which a person has a settled belief in the reality of things which have no existence. [Fr.—Gr. *haluō,* to wander in mind.]

Halo, hā'lō, *n.* A coloured *circle* round the sun or moon; the bright ring in painting which surrounds the heads of saints; a glory.—*vt. To surround with a halo.* [Gr. *halōs.*]

Halt, halt, *vi.* To limp, that is, *to stop with lameness;* to hesitate; to stand in doubt whether to proceed, or what to do; to fail; to falter; to have an irregular rhythm.—*vt. To stop;* to cause to cease marching.—*a.* Lame, that is, *holding* or stopping in walking.—*n.* A stopping; act of limping. [Sax. *healtian,* to limp.]

Halter, hal'tėr, *n.* A rope or strap and headstall for *leading* or *confining* a horse; a rope for hanging malefactors. *vt.* To put a halter on; to catch and hold, or to bind with a rope or cord. [G.—*halten,* to hold.]

Halting, halt'ing, *p.a.* Stopping; limping.—*p.n.* Act of limping or faltering.

Halve, häv, *vt. To divide into two equal parts. ppr.* halving, *pret. & pp.* halved. [from *half.*]

Halyard, hal'yärd, *n.* See HALLIARD.

Ham, ham, *n. The bend of the knee-joint behind;* the thigh of a beast, particularly of a hog, salted and dried in smoke; a leg. [Sax.—Gr. *kampē,* a bending.]

Hamlet, ham'let, *n. A little home or dwelling-place;* a small village; a little cluster of houses in the country. [dimin. of Sax. *ham,* home.]

Hammer, ham'mėr, *n. That which strikes;* an instrument for driving nails, beating metals, and the like; that part of a percussion-lock which strikes the cap.—*vt.* To forge with a hammer; to shape by beating; to work in the mind; to contrive by intellectual labour.—*vi. To work with a hammer;* to be busy; to labour in contrivance. [G.]

Hammered, ham'mėrd, *p.a. Beaten with a hammer.*

Hammering, ham'mėr-ing, *p.n. Act of beating with a hammer.*

Hammerman, ham'mėr-man, *n. One who beats* or works *with a hammer.*

Hammock, ham'mok, *n.* A kind of hanging bed, *suspended between trees* or posts, or by hooks. [Sp. *hamaca.*]

Hamper, ham'pėr, *n. A large basket for conveying things* to market, &c.—*vt. To put into a hamper.* [contr. from *hanaper;* Norm. *hanap,* a hamper.]

Hamper, ham'pėr, *n. A fetter or chain;* a shackle.—*vt. To put a hamper or fetter upon;* to entangle; to impede in progress; to *insnare;* to perplex; to embarrass. [Dan. *hemp,* hemp.]

Hamstring, ham'string, *n. One of the*

Fāte, fär, fat, fąll; mē, met, hėr; pīne, pin; nōte, not, mōve; tūbe, tub, bụll; oil, pound.

tendons of the ham.—vt. To cut, as the tendons of the ham, and thus to lame or disable. *ppr.* hamstringing, *pret. & pp.* hamstrung or hamstringed.

Hanaper, ha'na-pėr, *n. A cupt;* a kind of basket for holding and carrying money†; treasury. [Norm. *hanap,* a drinking-vessel, a hamper.]

Hand, hand, *n. That which lays hold of;* the extremity of the arm, consisting of the palm and fingers, connected with the arm at the wrist; a measure of four inches; a palm; side; part, right or left; act of the hand; power of performance; skill; power of producing; manner of acting; conveyance; possession; power; the cards held at a game; a game; an index; a person; a man employed in agency or service; style of penmanship; agency; ministry. *vt. To give or transmit with the hand;* to lead with the hand; to conduct; to handle; to lay hands on†; to furl, as a sail.—*a. Belonging to, pertaining to, or used by the hand.* [Sax.—Icel. *henda,* to lay hold of.]

Hand-bill, hand'bil, *n.* An instrument for pruning trees; a loose printed sheet, &c., to be circulated.

Hand-breadth, hand'bredth, *n.* A space equal to the *breadth of the hand.*

Hand-book, hand'buk, *n. A book for the hand;* a guide-book for travellers.

Handcuff, hand'kuf, *n. A hand-fetter;* a name given to manacles, consisting of iron rings for the wrists.—*vt. To manacle.* [Sax. *hand-copes—cops,* a fetter.]

Handed, hand'ed, *p.a.* Having the greatest power or dexterity in one of the *hands;* as, right-handed, left-handed; with hands joined.

Hand-fast†, hand'fast, *n.* Hold; custody.

Handful, hand'ful, *n. As much as the hand will grasp;* as much as the arms will embrace; a small quantity or number.

Hand-gallop, hand-gal'lup, *n.* A slow and easy *gallop.*

Handicraft, hand'i-kraft, *n. Work performed by the hand;* manual occupation. [Sax. *handcræft.*]

Handicraftsman, hand'i-krafts-man, *n.* A man skilled or employed in *manual occupation;* a manufacturer.

Handily, hand'i-li, *adv.* With *dexterity* or *skill;* dexterously; adroitly.

Handiness, hand'i-nes, *n. Quality of being handy;* ease of performance derived from practice; adroitness.

Handiwork, hand'i-wėrk, *n. Work of the hands;* product of manual labour; manufacture; work performed by power and wisdom. [for *handwork.*]

Handkerchief, hand'kėr-chēf, *n.* A piece of cloth, usually silk or linen, carried about the person for the purpose of cleaning the face, mouth, nose, or *hands,* as occasion requires; a piece of cloth to be worn about the neck.

Handle, han'dl, *vt. To feel, use, or hold with the hand;* to wield; to discourse on; to discuss; to deal with; to treat or use well or ill; to practise on.—*vi.* To use the hands. *ppr.* handling, *pret. & pp.* handled.—*n. That part of an instrument which is held in the hand when used;* that of which use is made; the instrument of effecting a purpose. [Sax. *handlian,* to handle.]

Hand-lead, hand'led, *n.* A small lead for sounding.

Handled, han'dld, *p.a.* Treated; managed.

Handling, han'dl-ing, *p.n. A touching*

or *use by the hand;* a treating of in discussion.

Handmaid, Handmaiden, hand'mād, hand'mād-n, *n. A maid that waits at hand;* a female servant or attendant.

Hand-mill, hand'mil, *n. A mill worked by the hand.*

Hand-rail, hand'rāl, *n. A rail for the hand,* supported by balusters, &c.

Handsome, hand'sum, *a. Made to the hand;* moderately beautiful; moderately elegant; well made; having symmetry of parts; graceful in manner; ample; generous; correct. [Belg. *handsaem,* fit.]

Handsomely, hand'sum-li, *adv.* Gracefully; amply; generously.

Handsomeness, hand'sum-nes, *n.* A moderate degree of beauty or elegance; grace.

Handwriting, hand-rīt'ing, *n.* The cast or form of *writing* peculiar to each hand.

Handy, hand'i, *a. Dexterous,* adroit; skilled to use the hands with ease; performing with skill; ready to the hand; convenient; suited to the use of the hand. [Old G. *handag.*]

Hang, hang, *vt. To suspend* from some elevated point; to put to death by suspending by the neck; to place without any solid foundation; to fix in such a manner as to be movable, as a gate; to append; to affix to; to furnish by hanging pictures.—*vi. To be suspended;* to depend; to dangle; to float; to rest on something for support; to cling to; to linger; to lean or incline; to have a steep declivity; to be executed by the halter. *ppr.* hanging, *pret. & pp.* hanged or *hung.* [Sax. *hangian.*]

Hanger, hang'ėr, *n. One who hangs* or causes to be hanged; a short broadsword, incurvated toward the point, and *suspended* to the side.

Hanger-on, hang-ėr-on', *n.* A servile dependant; a parasite.

Hanging, hang'ing, *p.a.* Foreboding death by the halter.—*p.n. Suspension;* death by suspension or by the halter; (pl.) linings for rooms, of arras, tapestry, paper, &c.

Hangman, hang'man, *n.* A public executioner; a term of reproach.

Hank, hangk, *n.* Two or more skeins of silk or thread *tied together.*—*vt. To form into hanks.* [Sw. a band.]

Hanker, hang'kėr, *vi. To desire eagerly* to get hold of something; to long for something with uneasiness; to cluster. [D. *hunkeren.*]

Hankering, hang'kėr-ing, *p.a.* Longing for with keen appetite or *ardent desire.*—*p.n.* Vehement desire to possess or enjoy.

Hap, hap, *n. Chance; luck; fortune;* that which comes suddenly or unexpectedly.—*vi.* To happen; to befall. [W.]

Hap-hazard, hap-ha'zėrd, *n.* Chance; accident.

Hapless, hap'les, *a. Luckless;* unfortunate; unlucky; unhappy.

Haplessly, hap'les-li, *adv. In a hapless manner.*

Haply, hap'li, *adv. By hap* or chance; perhaps; it may be; casually.

Happen, hap'n, *vi. To come by chance;* to chance; to fall out; to fall or come unexpectedly. [W. *hapiaw.*]

Happily, hap'pi-li, *adv. In a happy manner;* fortunately; gracefully.

Happiness, hap'pi-nes, *n. State of being happy;* the agreeable sensations which spring from the enjoyment of good; felicity; enjoyment of pleasure; bliss; good luck; good fortune. [Icel. *heppni.*]

Happy, hap'pi, *a. Lucky; fortunate;* being in the enjoyment of agreeable sensations from the possession of good; having secure possession of good; that supplies pleasure; agreeable; ready; skilful; blessed; living in concord; enjoying the pleasures of friendship; in a state of felicity; propitious. [Icel. *heppinn,* fortunate.]

Harangue, ha-rang', *n.* A speech addressed to an assembly arranged in a *ring;* a noisy or irregular address; a popular oration.—*vt.* To make an address or speech to an assembly arranged *in a circle;* to make a noisy speech.—*vt.* To address by oration. *ppr.* haranguing, *pret. & pp.* harangued. [Fr.; Old Sax. *hring,* a circle.]

Harass, ha'ras, *vt.* To vex; to distress; to fatigue to excess; to fatigue with importunity [Fr *harasser—*Gr. *arasō,* to strike hard.]

Harassing, ha'ras-ing, *p.a.* Fatiguing; teasing.

Harbinger, här'bin-jėr, *n.* A person who goes before to provide *harbour* for those that follow; a forerunner; a precursor; that which precedes and gives notice of the expected arrival of something else. [Sax. *hereberga—here,* an army, and *beorgan,* to shelter.]

Harbour, här'bėr, *n. A shelter;* a place of entertainment and rest; a haven for ships; an asylum; a place of safety from storms or danger.—*vt. To shelter;* to secure; to entertain; to permit to lodge, rest, or reside.—*vi. To take shelter;* to lodge or abide for a time. [Sax. *here-berga.*]

Harbourage, här'bėr-āj, *n. Shelter.*

Harbourer, här'bėr-ėr, *n.* One who entertains or *shelters* another.

Harbourless, här'bėr-les, *a. Without a harbour;* destitute of shelter.

Hard, härd, *a.* Firm; not easily penetrated or separated into parts; difficult to the understanding; difficult of accomplishment; arduous; attended with difficulty or pain, or both; oppressive; severe; unjust; pinching with cold; tempestuous; sour, as liquors; harsh; forced; not prosperous; avaricious; close; rude; coarse; unpalatable or scanty.—*adv.* Close; with pressure; laboriously; earnestly; with difficulty; fast; rapidly; vehemently; tempestuously; copiously; with force. [Sax. *heard—*Old G. *harti—*Goth. *hardus.*]

Hard-earned, härd'ėrnd, *a. Earned with toil and difficulty.*

Harden, härd'n, *vt. To make hard* or *more hard;* to indurate; to confirm in effrontery; to make obstinate; to confirm in wickedness; to make unfeeling; to endue with firmness; to inure; to render firm or less liable to injury by exposure or use.—*vi. To become hard or more hard;* to become unfeeling; to become inured; to indurate, as flesh. [Sax. *heardian.*]

Hardened, härd'nd, *p.a.* Made obstinate; confirmed in error or vice; callous; unfeeling; insensible.

Hardening, härd'n-ing, *p.a.* Making obdurate or unfeeling.—*p.n. The giving* a greater degree of *hardness* to bodies than they had before.

Hard-fisted, härd'fist-ed, *a.* Close-fisted; covetous.

Hard-fought, härd'fạt, *a.* Vigorously contested.

Hard-headed, härd'hed-ed, *a.* Shrewd; intelligent.

Hard-hearted, härd'härt-ed, *a. Having*

an unfeeling heart; pitiless; barbarous; savage.

Hardihood, härd′i-hud, *n. Quality of being hardy;* boldness, united with firmness and constancy of mind; dauntless bravery; intrepidity; audacity; effrontery.

Hardly, härd′i-li, *adv.* With great boldness; stoutly; not tenderly.

Hardiness, härd′i-nes, *n. Quality of being hardy;* intrepidity; effrontery; firmness of body derived from laborious exercises. [Fr. *hardiesse.*]

Hardish, härd′ish, *a. Somewhat hard.*

Hardly, härd′li, *adv.* With difficulty; scarcely; in a manner hard to be borne; painfully; oppressively; harshly; not softly.

Hardness, härd′nes, *n. Quality of being hard;* close union of the component parts; compactness; the quality of bodies which resists separation of their particles; difficulty to be understood or executed; penury; impenitence; coarseness of features; cruelty of temper; savageness; harshness; roughness, as of sculpture; niggardliness; hardship; a quality in some kinds of water which unfits them for washing.

Hardship, härd′ship, *n. A hard state;* severe labour or want; injustice; grievance.

Hard-visaged, härd′vi-zājd, *a. Having coarse features;* of a harsh countenance.

Hardware, härd′wār, *n. Ware made of metal,* as cutlery, kitchen furniture, and the like.

Hardy, härd′i, *a. Bold; intrepid;* full of assurance; impudent; stubborn to excess; inured to fatigue; rendered firm by exercise; compact. [Fr. *hardi.*]

Hare, hār, *n.* A well-known timid animal, with long ears, a short tail, *soft hair,* and a divided upper lip. [Sax. *hara*—Old G. *hār,* hair, pile.]

Harebell, hār′bel, *n.* The blue-bell of Scotland, a plant with a slender stem and pale blue bell-shaped flowers. [*hare* and *bell.*]

Hare-brained, hār′brānd, *a. Wild as a hare;* giddy; volatile; heedless. [*hare* and *brained.*]

Harelip, hār′lip, *n.* A perpendicular division of one or both *lips,* but more commonly the upper one, like that of a *hare.*

Harem, hā′rem, *n. A prohibited place;* the division allotted to females in the larger dwelling-houses of the East; the collection of wives belonging to one man. [Ar. *harām,* anything prohibited.]

Hark, härk, *vi. To listen; to lend the ear.* [contracted from *hearken.*]

Harlequin, härˈlē-kwin, *n.* A buffoon dressed in parti-coloured clothes, who plays tricks, often without speaking, to divert the by-standers or an audience. [Fr.]

Harlot, härˈlot, *n.* A woman who prostitutes her body for *hire;* a prostitute.—*a.* Wanton; lewd. [Sax. *hyrian,* to hire.]

Harlotry, härˈlot-ri, *n.* The trade or practice of prostitution.

Harm, härm, *n. That which causes pain;* injury; hurt; mishap; moral wrong; evil; wickedness. [Sax.]—*vt. To afflict;* to hurt; to damage; to impair, as soundness of body. [Sax. *hearmian.*]

Harmful, härm′ful, *a. Hurtful;* in′urious; noxious; mischievous.

Harmless, härm′les, *a. Not hurtful;* inoffensive; innocuous; not guilty of crime or wrong; not receiving damage or injury; unharmed.

Harmlessly, härm′les-li, *adv. Innocently;* without fault or crime.

Harmlessness, härm′les-nes, *n. Quality of being harmless* or innocuous.

Harmonic, Harmonical, här-mon′ik, här-mon′ik-al, *a. Relating to harmony;* musical; consonant. [Fr. *harmonique.*]

Harmonically, här-mon′ik-al-li, *adv. With harmony;* musically.

Harmonics, här-mon′iks, *n. The doctrine of harmony* or of musical sounds.

Harmonious, här-mō′ni-us, *a. Having harmony;* having the parts adapted to each other; symmetrical; concordant; symphonious; melodious; living in peace and friendship. [Fr. *harmonieux*—L. *harmonia,* harmony.]

Harmoniously, här-mō′ni-us-li, *adv.* In a *harmonious manner.*

Harmoniousness, här-mō′ni-us-nes, *n. Quality of being harmonious;* adaptation of parts; concord.

Harmonist, härˈmon-ist, *n. One skilled in harmony;* a composer of music; one who brings together corresponding passages, as of the four gospels, to show their agreement. [Fr. *harmoniste.*]

Harmonium, här-mō′ni-um, *n.* A new wind, keyed instrument, especially designed for church music. [from *harmony.*]

Harmonise, härˈmon-īz, *vi. To be in harmony;* to agree in sounds; to be in peace and friendship; to agree in sense.—*vt.* To bring into harmony; to adjust in fit proportions; to cause to agree; to set accompanying parts to. *ppr.* harmonizing, *pret. & pp.* harmonized. [It. *armonizzare.*]

Harmonizing, härˈmon-īz-ing, *p.a.* Being in accordance; bringing to an agreement.

Harmony, härˈmō-ni, *n. A fitting together;* the just adaptation of parts to each other, in any system of things, intended to form a connected whole; just proportion of sound; agreement; accordance in facts; peace and friendship; the consistency of different histories of the same events; a literary work which brings together parallel passages respecting the same events, and shows their agreement. [L. *harmonia*—Gr. *harmosō,* to put together.]

Harness, härˈnes, *n. That which is put on;* armour; the whole accoutrements of a knight; the furniture of a carriage or draught horse.—*vt. To dress in armour;* to equip with armour for war; to put on, as the furniture of a horse for draught. [Fr. *harnais.*]

Harnessed, härˈnest, *p.a. Equipped with armour;* furnished with the dress for draught.

Harp, härp, *n.* An instrument of music of the stringed kind, of a triangular figure, held upright, and commonly struck with the fingers in playing. [Sax. *hearpa.*]—*vi. To play on the harp;* to dwell tediously (with *on*). [Sax. *hearpian*—Sans. *hri,* to take, to seize.]

Harper, härp′er, *n. A player on the harp.*

Harping, härp′ing, *p.a. Pertaining to the harp.*—*p.n.* A continual dwelling on.

Harpist, härp′ist, *n.* A harper.

Harpoon, här-pön′, *n.* A *spear* or *javelin,* used to strike whales for killing them. *vt. To strike, catch,* or *kill with a harpoon.* [Fr. *harpon.*]

Harpooner, Harponeer, här-pön′er, här-pön-ēr′, *n. One who uses a harpoon.*

Harpsichord, harp′si-kord, *n. A harp* or *instrument of music* with strings of wire, played by the fingers. [*harp* and *chord;* Old Fr. *harpechorde.*]

Harpy, härˈpi, *n.* A fabulous winged monster, *ravenous* and filthy; any ravenous animal; an extortioner; a plunderer. [Fr. *harpie*—Gr. *harpazō,* to snatch away.]

Harridan, haˈri-dan, *n.* A decayed or *worn-out strumpet.* [Fr. *haridelle,* a sorry jade—L. *aridus,* dry.]

Harrier, haˈri-er, *n.* A kind of hound for hunting *hares* [from *hare*]; a genus of hawks allied to the buzzards [from *harry.*]

Harrow, haˈrō, *n.* A frame of t mber, set with teeth, to be dragged over ploughed land to level it and break the clods, and to cover seed when sown.—*vt. To draw a harrow over;* to break or tear with a harrow; to lacerate; to torment. [Dan. *harv.*]

Harrowing, haˈrō-ing, *p.a.* Tormenting; lacerating.—*p.n. Act or process of using a harrow.*

Harry, haˈri, *vt. To pillage;* to plunder; to ravage; to afflict; to agitate; to worry. *ppr.* harrying, *pret. & pp.* harried. [Sax. *hergian.*]

Harsh, härsh, *a. Sour; bitter;* rugged; rough to the ear; grating; jarring; austere; morose; abusive; rigorous; severe. [G. *harsch.*]

Harshly, härsh′li, *adv. In a harsh manner;* severely; rudely.

Harshness, härsh′nes, *n. Quality of being harsh;* sourness; roughness to the ear; roughness of temper; moroseness.

Hart, härt, *n.* A *stag* or *male deer;* a *swift* animal of the cervine genus. [Sax. *heort*—G. *hurtig,* nimble.]

Hart's-horn, härts′horn, *n.* A carbonate of ammonia originally obtained from the *horns of harts;* a volatile spirit, an impure solution of carbonate of ammonia.

Harvest, härˈvest, *n.* The season of reaping and *gathering in the fruits of the earth;* the ripe corn or grain collected and secured in barns or stacks; the product of labour; effects; consequences.—*vt.* To reap or gather, as ripe corn and other *fruits* for the use of man and beast. [Sax. *haerefest*—Gr. *karpos,* fruit.]

Harvester, härˈvest-er, *n.* A reaper.

Harvest-home, härˈvest-hōm. *n.* The song sung by reapers at the feast made when the *harvest* has been *gathered in;* the feast itself; the opportunity of gathering treasure.

Harvesting, härˈvest-ing, *p.n.* Act of collecting *the harvest.*

Harvest-moon, härˈvest-mōn, *n.* The *moon* near the full, about the time of the autumnal equinox, when it rises after sunset nearly at the same hour for several days.

Hash, hash, *vt. To chop* into small pieces; to mince and mix.—*n. That which is chopped;* minced meat, or a dish of meat and vegetables chopped into small pieces and mixed; a new mixture of old matter. [Fr. *hachen* to mince, to hack and hew.]

Hasp, hasp, *n. That which fastens;* a clasp that passes over a staple to be fastened by a padlock. [Norm. *Aaspe.*]

Hassock, hasˈok, *n.* A thick mat or cushion on which persons kneel in church. [W. *hesg,* sedge, rushes.]

Haste, hāst, *n. Speed; swiftness;* expedition; hurry; sudden excitement of passion; precipitance; rashness; state

of being urged or pressed by business. [Old Fr.]
Haste, Hasten, hāst, hās'n, *vt.* To press; to drive or urge forward; to expedite; to quicken; to hurry.—*vi.* To move with celerity; to be speedy or quick. *ppr.* hasting, *pret. & pp.* hasted. [G. *hasten.*]
Hastener, hās'n-ėr, *n. One who hastens.*
Hastily, hāst'i-li, *adv. In haste;* speedily; passionately.
Hastiness, hāst'i-nes, *n. Haste;* speed; quickness or celerity in motion or action; rashness; irritability; warmth of temper.
Hasty, hāst'i, *a. Quick; speedy;* eager; rash; irascible; caused by passion; early ripe; forward, as fruit. [G. *hastig*—Norm. *has'if,* immature.]
Hat, hat, *n.* A well-known *covering* for the head; the dignity of a cardinal. [Sax. *hat*—Norm. *hattes,* hats.]
Hatch, hach, *vt. To breed;* to produce, as young from eggs by incubation, or by artificial heat; to contrive by *brooding over;* to produce in silence.—*vi.* To produce young; to bring the young to maturity.—*n. A brood;* act of exclusion from the egg ; disclosure†. [G. *hecken.*]
Hatch, hach, *vt. To hack;* to cross with lines in drawing and engraving in a peculiar manner. [Fr. *hacher.*]
Hatch, hach, *n.* The *fastened* part of a door, the part above being open; (pl.) *the grate or frame of cross-bars* laid over the opening in a ship's deck; the opening itself.—*vt.* To close with a *hatch.* [Sax. *haeca*—Icel. *hegna,* to shut up closely.]
Hatchet, hach'et, *n. A small hacking instrument;* a small axe with a short handle, to be used with one hand. [Fr. *hachette—hacher,* to hack.]
Hatching, hach'ing, *p.n.* The production of young from eggs; act of contriving; a mode of execution in engraving.
Hatchment, hach'ment, *n. The achievement* or escutcheon of a deceased person, placed in front of his house, on a hearse at funerals, or in a church. [corrupted from *achievement.*]
Hatchway, hach'wā, *n.* A square or oblong opening in the deck of a ship, affording a passage from one deck to another.
Hate, hāt, *vt. To detest;* to dislike greatly; to have a great aversion to; to loathe; to abhor. *ppr.* hating, *pret. & pp.* hated.—*n.* Great dislike or aversion; hatred. [Sax. *hatian*—Old G. *hassn.*]
Hated, hāt'ed, *p.a.* Greatly disliked; detested; abhorred.
Hateful, hāt'ful, *a. Exciting hate;* odious; loathsome; that feels and manifests hatred; malignant.
Hatefully, hāt'ful-li, *adv. Odiously;* malignantly; maliciously.
Hatefulness, hāt'ful-nes, *n. Quality of being hateful;* odiousness.
Hater, hāt'ėr, *n. One who hates.*
Hatred, hāt'red, *n. Great dislike* or aversion; ill-will; rancour; malignity; abhorrence.
Hatter, hat'ėr, *n. A maker* or *seller of hats.*
Hauberk, ha'bėrk, *n.* A shirt of mail formed of small steel rings. [Old Fr. *hauberc.*]
Haught, hat, *a.* Elevated; proud.
Haughtily, hat'i-li, *adv. In a haughty manner;* arrogantly.
Haughtiness, hat'i-nes, *n. Quality of being haughty;* pride, mingled with some degree of contempt for others; disdain.
Haughty, hat'i, *a. Lofty;* proud and disdainful; having a high opinion of one's self, with some contempt for others; imperious; proceeding from excessive pride. [Old Fr. *haultain*—L. *altus,* high.]
Haul, hal, *vt. To draw along with force;* to drag; to pull; to compel to go.—*n. A pulling* with force; a violent pull; a draught of a net; that which is taken at once. [Fr. *haler.*]
Hauler, hal'ėr, *n. He who hauls.*
Haulm, halm, *n. The stem* or *stalk* of grain, of all kinds, or of pease, beans, hops, &c.; straw; the dry stalks of corn, &c., in general. [Sax. *healm*—L. *culmus.*]
Haunch, hansh, *n. The hollow* where the thigh is joined to the body; the hip; the thigh; that part of an arch which lies between the springing and the crown; the hind part†; the rear†. [Fr. *hanche*—Gr. *angkos,* a bend.]
Haunched, hānsht, *p.a. Having haunches.*
Haunt, hant, *vt. To frequent;* to resort to much or often; to come to frequently; to follow importunately. *vi. To be much about;* to visit or be present often.—*n. A place much frequented.* [Fr. *hanter.*]
Haunted, hant'ed, *p.a. Frequently visited,* especially by apparitions; troubled by frequent visits.
Haunter, hant'ėr, *n. One who frequents* a particular place, or is often about it.
Hautboy, hō'boi, *n. A high-toned* wind-instrument, somewhat resembling a flute; a sort of strawberry. [Fr. *haut,* high, and *bois,* wood.]
Hauteur, hȧ-tėr', *n. Haughtiness;* haughty manner or spirit; pride. [Fr.]
Have, hav, *vt. To seize and hold in the hands;* to own; to hold in possession or power; to take; to enjoy; to hold in opinion; to accept; to be under necessity, or impelled by duty; to contain; to procure; to purchase; to bring forth; to a'fect; to take or hold one's self. *ppr.* having, *pret. & pp.* had. [Dan.—Sax. *habban,* L. *habeo.*]
Haven, hā'vn, *n. That which holds,* as ships; a harbour; a bay or inlet of the sea; a station for ships; a shelter; a place of safety. [Sax. *haefen*—Goth. *haban,* to hold.]
Haver†, hav'ėr, *n. One who has;* a holder.
Having, hav'ing, *p.n.* Possession; goods; gaining; receiving; taking.
Havock, ha'vok, *n. Waste;* devastation; wide and general destruction; slaughter.—*vt. To waste;* to *destroy.—interj.* A war-cry, and the signal for indiscriminate slaughter. [W. *hafog.*]
Haw, ba, *n.* The berry and seed of the hawthorn. [Sax. *hœg.*]
Haw, hȧ, *vi.* To stop in speaking with a *haw,* or to speak with hesitation. *n.* A hesitation of speech. [corrupted from *hawk.*]
Hawhaw, hȧ'hȧ, *n.* A fence or bank that interrupts an alley or walk, sunk between slopes, and not perceived till approached. [duplication of *haw,* a hedge.]
Hawk, hak, *n.* A rapacious bird which *seizes and holds* its prey with its fangs. *vi.* To catch or attempt to catch birds by means of *hawks* trained for the purpose; to practise falconry; to fly at. [Sax. *hafoc*—Icel. *haukr.*]
Hawk, hak, *vi.* To make an *effort to force up phlegm with noise.—n.* An effort *to force up phlegm* from the throat. [W. *hochi.*]
Hawk, hak, *vt. To cry; to offer for sale by outcry* in the street; to carry about, as wares for sale from place to place. [W. *hwchw,* a cry.]
Hawker, hak'ėr, *n. One who hawks* or offers for sale by outcry.
Hawk-eyed, hak'īd, *a.* Having a keen eye; discerning.
Hawking, hak'ing, *p.n.* The sport of taking wild fowls by means of *hawks;* act of offering for sale in the street by outcry.
Hawthorn, ha'thorn, *n. The hedge-thorn;* the white thorn, much used for hedges. [Sax. *hægthorn.*]
Hay, hā, *n. Grass cut* and dried for fodder. [Sax. *heg—heawan,* to cut.]
Haymaker, hā'māk-ėr, *n. One who cuts and dries grass for fodder.*
Haymaking, hā'māk-ing, *n.* The business of *cutting grass* and curing it.
Hazard, ha'zėrd, *n. A game at cards;* risk; venture; exposure; chance; a fortuitous event.—*vt.* To risk; to incur, or bring on, as the loss of life.—*vi.* To try the chance; to adventure; to run the risk or danger. [Fr. *hasard—as,* ace at dice.]
Hazardous, ha'zėrd-us, *a. Exposed to hazard;* perilous; dangerous; daring; adventurous; uncertain.
Haze, hāz, *n. Vapour* which renders the air thick, though not so damp as in foggy weather; dimness. [Armor. *aesen,* vapour.]
Hazel, hā'zl, *n.* A shrub or plant that bears nuts.—*a. Pertaining to the hasel,* or like it; of a light-brown colour, like the hazel-nut. [Sax. *haesl.*]
Hazel-nut, hā'zl-nut, *n.* The *nut* or *fruit of the hasel.*
Haziness, hāz'i-nes, *n. State of being hasy.*
Hazy, hāz'i, *a.* Thick with vapour, but not so damp as in foggy weather.
He, hē, *pron.* of the third person. A pronoun, a substitute for the third person, masculine gender, representing the man or male named before; man; a male. [Sax.; Ir. *é.*]
Head, hed, *n. The elevated part; the top;* the uppermost part of the human body, or the foremost part of the body of prone and creeping animals; the brain; an animal; an individual; a chief; the first place; countenance; understanding; face; fore part; successful opposition; resolution; the top of a thing, especially when larger than the rest of a thing; the chief part; principal source; topic of discourse; summary; crisis; height; force; liberty; freedom from restraint; the hair of the head; each one among many; power; armed force.—*vt. To form a head to;* to behead†; to cut off the head of, as of trees; to lead; to go in front of; to oppose; to veer round and blow in opposition to, as the course of a ship.—*vi. To form a head,* as a plant; to be directed, as a ship. [Sax. *hedfod*—Goth. *hafjan,* to raise.]
Headache, hed'āk, *n. Pain in the head.*
Head-dress, hed'dres, *n.* The *covering* or *ornaments* of a *woman's head.*
Headed, hed'ed, *p.a. Furnished with a head;* having a top; led; directed.
Headily, hed'i-li, *adv.* Hastily; rashly.
Headiness, hed'i-nes, *n. Quality of being heady;* rashness; obstinacy.
Heading, hed'ing, *p.n. That which stands at the head;* title; enumeration of subjects or contents; foam on liquor.
Headland, hed'land, *n.* A cape; a pro-

montory; a ridge or strip of unploughed land at the ends of furrows.
Headless, hed'les, *a. Having no head.*
Headlong, hed'long, *adv. With the head foremost;* hastily; without delay or respite.—*a.* Steep; precipitous; rash; precipitate.
Head-lugged†, hed'lugd, *a. Dragged by the head.*
Head-money, hed'mu-nē, *n.* A capitation tax; a poll-tax.
Headmost, hed'mōst, *a.* Most advanced; most forward.
Head-piece, hed'pēs, *n. Armour for the head;* a helmet; understanding; force of mind.
Head-quarters, hed-kwar'tèrz, *n. pl. The quarters of the commander-in-chief* of an army; the residence of any chief, or place from which orders are issued.
Headshake, hed'shāk, *n.* A significant shake of the head.
Headship, hed'ship, *n. Office of a head* or principal; authority; chief place.
Headsman, hedz'man, *n. One who cuts off heads;* an executioner.
Head-stone, hed'stōn, *n.* The *chief* or corner *stone;* the stone at the head of a grave.
Headstrong, hed'strong, *a.* Resolute; obstinate; violent.
Headway, hed'wā, *n.* The motion of an advancing ship.
Head-wind, hed'wind, *n.* A wind that blows in a direction opposite to the ship's course.
Head-work, hed'wèrk, *n. Mental* or *intellectual labour.*
Heady, hed'i, *a. Apt to affect the head;* intoxicating; strong; hasty; precipitate; violent; impetuous.
Heal, hēl, *vt. To make hale or sound;* to cure; to cause to close up, as a wound; to restore to soundness; to restore purity to; to remove, as differences; to reconcile, as parties at variance; to cure, as moral disease, and restore soundness to.—*vi. To grow whole or sound;* to recover. [Sax. *hælan—hæl,* health—Gr. *holos,* whole.]
Healer, hēl'èr, *n. He or that which heals,* cures, or restores to soundness.
Healing, hēl'ing, *p.a.* Tending to cure; mild; mollifying.—*p.n.* Act or process by which a cure is effected.
Health, helth, *n.* A *whole or sound state of body;* freedom from disease; sound state of the mind; natural vigour of faculties; moral purity; salvation or divine favour or grace; wish of health and happiness (used in drinking). [Sax. *hælu*—Old G. *heilidu.*]
Healthful, helth'ful, *a.* A *Full of health;* being in a sound state; serving to promote health; salubrious; indicating health; salutary; promoting spiritual health; favourable.
Healthfully, helth'ful-li, *adv. In health;* wholesomely.
Healthfulness, helth'ful-nes, *n.* A *state of being healthful* or well.
Healthily, helth'i-li, *adv.* Without disease; soundly.
Healthiness, helth'i-nes, *n. State of being healthy* or in health; soundness.
Healthsome, helth'sum, *a.* Wholesome. [Old G. *heilsam.*]
Healthy, helth'i, *a. Being in health;* vigorous; sound; hale; salubrious; wholesome; salutary.
Heap, hēp, *n. That which is heaved* or *lifted up;* a mass; a collection of things laid in a body so as to form an elevation; a mass of ruins.—*vt. To heave,* or lift up; to throw or lay, as in a heap; to amass; to accumulate; to add some-

thing else in large quantities; to add till the mass takes a roundish form, or till it rises above the measure. [Sax.—*heapian,* to heap up.]
Hear, hēr, *vt. To perceive by the ear;* to feel, as an impression of sound by the proper organs; to give audience to; to listen; to obey; to regard; to grant, as an answer to prayer; to attend to judicially; to try in a court of law or equity; to learn; to approve and embrace.—*vi.* To enjoy the faculty of perceiving sound *by the ear;* to listen; to be told; to receive by report. *ppr.* hearing, *pret. & pp.* heard. [Sax. *hyran*—L. *auris,* the ear.]
Hearer, hēr'èr, *n. One who hears;* an auditor.
Hearing, hēr'ing, *p.n.* The faculty or sense by which sound is perceived; sensation or perception of sound; reach of the ear; extent within which sound may be heard; audience; attention to what is delivered; opportunity to be heard; judicial trial; attention to in judicial causes.
Hearken, härk'n, *vi. To lend the ear;* to listen; to attend to what is uttered with eagerness or curiosity; to observe or obey; to grant or comply with.—*vt.*† To give heed to. [Sax. *heorcnian.*]
Hearkener, härk'n-èr, *n. One who hearkens.*
Hearsay, hēr'sā, *n. Anything heard to be said;* report; rumour; fame.
Hearse, hèrs, *n.* A carriage for conveying the dead to the grave.—*vt. To lay or inclose in a hearse.* [Old Fr. *herce,* a harrow.]
Heart, härt, *n.* The seat or source of life; the primary organ of the blood's motion in an animal body, situated in the thorax; the inner part of anything; that which has the form of a heart; the vigorous part; the seat of the affections and passions; an affection or passion, and particularly that of love; the seat of the understanding; the seat of the will; secret purposes; person; courage; spirit; disposition of mind; strength; fertility; the part nearest the middle; secret meaning.—*vt.*† To give heart to. [Sax. *heorte*—Sans. *hrid.*]
Heartache, härt'āk, *n.* Sorrow; anguish of mind.
Heart-breaking, härt'brāk-ing, *a. Breaking the heart;* overpowering with grief or sorrow.
Heart-broken, härt'brōk-n, *a.* Deeply afflicted or grieved.
Heartburn, härt'bèrn, *n.* A disease or affection of the stomach, attended with heat and uneasiness.
Heart-burned, härt'bèrnd, *a.* Having the heart inflamed.
Heart-burning, härt'bèrn-ing, *n. Heartburn*†; discontent; secret enmity.
Heart-dear, härt'dēr, *a.* Sincerely beloved.
Heart-ease, härt'ēz, *n.* Quiet; tranquillity of mind.
Hearted, härt'ed, *p.a. Taken to heart*†; consisting of hearts; laid up in the heart; disposed as to the affections, as *hard-hearted.*
Heartedness, härt'ed-nes, *n.* Sincerity; warmth; zeal.
Hearten, härt'n, *vt. To give heart* or courage to; to encourage; to animate.
Heartfelt, härt'felt, *a. Deeply felt;* deeply affecting, either as joy or sorrow.
Hearth, härth, *n.* A pavement or floor of brick or stone in a chimney, on which a *fire* is made; the house itself, as the abode of comfort to its inmates,

and of hospitality to strangers. [Sax. *heorth;* Goth. *hauri,* a coal.]
Hearthstone, härth'stōn, *n. Stone forming the hearth;* fireside.
Heartily, härt'i-li, *adv. From the heart; with all the heart;* with sincerity.
Heartiness, härt'i-nes, *n. Quality or state of being hearty;* sincerity; zeal; earnestness; eagerness of appetite.
Heartless, härt'les, *a. Without heart* or courage; spiritless; faint-hearted; without feeling or affection.
Heartlessly, härt'les-li, *adv. In a heartless manner;* faintly.
Heartlessness, härt'les-nes, *n. Quality of being heartless.*
Heartlings, härt'lings, *n.* An exclamation formerly sometimes used in addressing a familiar acquaintance.
Heart-rending, härt'rend-ing, *a. Breaking the heart;* deeply afflictive.
Heart's-ease, härts'ēz, *n.* A plant, a species of violet.
Heart-sick, härt'sik, *a. Sick at heart;* pained in mind; deeply depressed.
Heart-whole, härt'hōl, *a.* A *Whole at heart;* not affected with love.
Hearty, härt'i, *a. Sound at heart;* strong; vigorous; having a keen appetite; sincere; ardent; proceeding from the heart; cordial; invigorating; nourishing, as food; abundant in quantity, as a meal.
Heat, hēt, *n. That which stirs or excites;* that which produces the sensation of warmth in a greater or less degree; caloric; the sensation produced by the presence or touch of fire; hot weather; degree of temperature to which any body is raised; state of being once heated or hot; a violent action unintermitted; a course at a race; flush; animal excitement; utmost violence; rage; agitation of mind; exasperation; animation in thought or discourse.—*vt. To make hot;* to communicate heat to; to inflame; to warm with passion or desire; to excite, as animal action.—*vi. To grow warm or hot.* [Sax. *haetu*—Old G. *hisa,* heat, *hazjan,* to incite.]
Heated, hēt'ed, *p.a.* Inflamed; exasperated.
Heater, hēt'èr, *n. He or that which heats.*
Heath, hēth, *n.* A small shrub with beautiful flowers, which grows on *wastes* or *wild places;* a place overgrown with heath; a place overgrown with shrubs of any kind; a desert. [Sax. *hæth.*]
Heath-bell, hēth'bel, *n.* The flower of a species of heath.
Heath-cock, hēth'kok, *n.* A large bird which frequents *heaths;* the black grouse.
Heathen, hē'THen, *n.* A *Gentile;* a pagan; a nation†; one who worships idols, or is unacquainted with the true God; a barbarous person.—*a.* Gentile; pagan. [Sax. *hæthen*—Gr. *ethnos,* a nation.]
Heathendom, hē'THen-dum, *n.* That part of the world where *heathenism* prevails.
Heathenish, hē'THen-ish, *a. Belonging to Gentiles* or pagans; barbarous; cruel.
Heathenism, hē'THen-ism, *n. Gentilism;* ignorance of the true God; idolatry; barbarism.
Heather, hern'èr, *n. Heath.*
Heathy, hēth'i, *a. Full of heath.*
Heating, hēt'ing, *p.a.* Exciting action; stimulating.
Heave, hēv, *vt. To lift;* to raise; to move upward; to cause to swell; to raise or force from the breast, as a groan; to throw; to raise forcibly by turning a windlass; to turn, as a windlass or

Fate, fär, fat, fall; mē, met, hèr; pine, pin; nōte, not, mōve; tūbe, tub, bull; oil, pound.

capstan with bars or levers.—*vi.* To rise; to be lifted; to swell, as the sea; to rise and swell; to pant; to make an effort to vomit. *ppr.* heaving, *pret.* heaved or hove, *pp.* heaved, hove, formerly hoven.—*n. A rising* or swell; an exertion or effort upward; a rising, as of the breast; an effort to vomit; an effort to rise; a fling'; an assault†. [Sax. *hefan*; Goth. *haffjan*, to raise.]

Heaven, hev'n, *n. That which is heaved up* or *raised*; the sky; the region of the atmosphere; the region or expanse which surrounds the earth, and which appears above and around us, the abode of God and of his angels; the abode of blessed spirits and of the blessed; the residence of the celestial gods, in a pagan sense; the Supreme Power; God; the pagan deities; celestials; sublimity; supreme felicity. [Sax. *heofen—hefan*, to raise.]

Heaven-born, hev'n-born, *a. Born from heaven*; native of heaven.

Heaven-bred, hev'n-bred, *a. Produced in heaven.*

Heavenliness, hev'n-li-nes, *n. State of being heavenly*; supreme excellence.

Heavenly, hev'n-li, *a. Resembling heaven*; pertaining to heaven; divine; godlike, angelic; inhabiting heaven.—*adv. In a manner resembling that of heaven.*

Heavenly-minded, hev'n-li-mind-ed, *a. Having the mind* or affections *placed on heaven*, and on spiritual things.

Heavenly-mindedness, hev'n-li-mind-ed'nes, *n. State of being heavenly-minded.*

Heavenward, Heavenwards, hev'n-werd, hev'n-werdz,*adv. Toward heaven.*

Heave-offering,hev'of-fer-ing,*n.* Among the Jews, an offering to God, so called from its being *heaved* or raised up in the air.

Heavily, he'vi-li, *adv. With heaviness*; with great weight of grief; afflictively; gloomily.

Heaviness, he'vi-nes, *n. Quality of being heavy*; weight; gravity; sorrow; dejection of mind; torpidness; languor; burden; that which creates labour and difficulty; moistness, as of earth or air; deepness, as of earth.

Heaving, hev'ing, *p.a.* Swelling; panting.—*p.n. A rising* or swell; a panting.

Heavy, he'vi, *a. That is heaved* or lifted with labour; weighty; ponderous; sad; depressed in mind; grievous; burdensome; dull; wanting spirit or animation; slow; wearisome; lying with weight on the stomach; moist; deep; miry, as earth; laborious; not hearing; swelling and rolling with great force, as billows; dense; violent; copious; great; requiring much labour or much expense; loud.—*adv.* With great weight. [Sax. *hefig*; Goth. *haffjan*, to raise.]

Heavy-armed, he'vi-ärmd, *a. Carrying heavy arms*, as a soldier.

Heavy-hearted, he'vi-härt-ed, *a. Having a heavy heart.*

Heavy-laden, he'vi-läd-n,*a. Laden with a heavy burden.*

Hebdomadal, heb-dom'ad-al, *a. Consisting of seven days*, or occurring every seven days; weekly. [Late L. *hebdomadalis*; Gr. *hepta*, seven.]

Hebraic, hē-brā'ik, *a. Pertaining to the Hebrews*; designating the language of the Hebrews. [Low L. *Hebraicus.*]

Hebraically, hē-brā'ik-al-li, *adv. From right to left.*

Hebraism, hē'brā-izm, *n. A Hebrew idiom.* [Fr. *Hébraïsme.*]

Hebraist, hē'brā-ist, *n. One versed in the Hebrew language.*

Hebrew, hē'brō, *n.* One of the descendants of *Eber* or *Heber*; an Israelite; a Jew; the Hebrew language.—*a. Pertaining to the Hebrews.* [Heb. *Eber.*]

Hecatomb, he'ka-tōm, *n. A sacrifice of a hundred oxen*, or beasts of the same kind, among the Greeks and Romans; a great public sacrifice; any sacrifice of a large number of victims. [Fr. *hécatombe*—Gr. *hekaton*, a hundred, and *bous*, an ox.]

Hectic, hek'tik, *a. Habitual*†; constitutional; pertaining to hectic; affected with hectic fevers.—*n. An habitual fever*; a remittent fever, with stages of chilliness, heat, and sweat, variously intermixed. [Gr. *hektikos—echō*, to have.]

Hector, hek'tér, *n.* A bully.—*vt.* To threaten; to fret; to vex.—*vi.* To play the bully. [Gr.—a son of Priam.]

Hedge, hej, *n. A fence* or inclosure, consisting of thorns, prickly bushes, or shrubs.—*vt. To inclose with a hedge*; to separate by a hedge; to obstruct with a hedge; to fortify; to guard or protect.—*vi.* To hide one's self, as in a *hedge*; to bet on both sides, as a security against loss. *ppr.* hedging, *pret. & pp.* hedged.—*a. Pertaining to a hedge†*; mean; vile; of the lowest class. [Sax. *hege*—Old G. *haggan*, to guard.]

Hedgehog, hej'hog, *n. A small quadruped* which lives in *hedges*, and has its back covered with prickly spines.

Hedge-pig, hej'pig, *n.* A young hedgehog.

Hedger, hej'er, *n. One who makes hedges.*

Hedgerow, hej'rō, *n. A row* or series of shrubs planted *for inclosure.*

Heed, hēd, *vt. To look to* or *after*; to mind; to regard with care; to take notice of; to notice.—*vi.* To mind; to consider.—*n.* Care; attention; watch for danger; notice; regard; attention; a look, indicating care. [Sax. *hedan*—G. *hüten*, to look after.]

Heedful, hēd'ful, *a. Giving heed*; attentive; observing; watchful; cautious.

Heedfully, hēd'ful-li, *adv.* Attentively.

Heedfulness, hēd'ful-nes, *n. Quality of being heedful*; vigilance; care.

Heedless, hēd'les, *a.* Inattentive; careless; regardless; unobserving.

Heedlessly, hēd'les-li, *adv. In a heedless manner*; carelessly; negligently.

Heedlessness, hēd'les-nes, *n. Quality of being heedless*; thoughtlessness.

Heel, hēl, *n.* The part of the foot that swells out behind; the whole foot; the hind part of a shoe or stocking; something shaped like the human heel; the latter part, as of a legislative session; a spur.—*vt.* To add a *heel* to; to furnish with heels, as boots or shoes; to perform by the use of the heels. [Sax. *hel*—Gr. *hēlos*, a protuberance.]

Heel, hēl, *vi.* To bend; to incline; to lean. (With *over.*) [Sax. *hyldan*; Icel. *halla*, to incline.]

Heft†, heft, *n. The act of heaving*; violent strain.

Hefted†, heft'ed, *p.a.* Raised; agitated.

Heifer, hef'ér, *n.* A young cow. [Sax. *heafre.*]

Heigh-ho, hī'hō. An exclamation expressing some degree of languor.

Height, hīt, *n. Elevation* above the ground; the altitude of an object; the distance which anything rises above its basis; elevation of a star above the horizon; degree of latitude, either north or south; distance of one thing above another; an eminence; a hill or mountain; elevation of rank; elevation in power, learning, fame, &c.; utmost degree in extent or violence; degree; progress toward perfection. [Sax. *heahtho—heah*, high.]

Heighten, hīt'n, *vt. To raise high* or *higher*; to improve; to advance toward a worse state; to augment in violence, as distress; to increase, as enjoyment; to make prominent by touches of light or brilliant colours, in painting.

Heightened, hīt'nd, *p.a.* Exalted; improved; increased.

Heightening, hīt'n-ing, *p.a.* Increasing; aggravating.—*p.n. Act of raising higher*; increase of excellence; aggravation.

Heinous, hān'us, *a. Hateful*; characterized by great wickedness; aggravated; flagrant; atrocious. [Fr. *haineux*—*hair*, to hate.]

Heinously, hān'us-li, *adv. Hatefully*; abominably; enormously.

Heinousness, hān'us-nes, *n. Hatefulness*; odiousness; enormity.

Heir, ār, *n.* One who succeeds or is to succeed another in the *possession* of lands, &c., by descent; one who inherits from an ancestor; one who succeeds to the estate of a former possessor; one who is entitled to possess.—*vt.* To inherit; to take possession of, as of an estate after the death of the ancestor. [Norm. *hier*—L. *heres*—Gr. *haireō*, to take.]

Heirdom, ār'dum, *n. State of an heir*; succession by inheritance.

Heiress, ār'es, *n. A female heir.*

Heirloom, ār'lōm, *n. Any furniture*, &c., which, by law, descends to the heir with the house or freehold. [*heir*, and Sax. *loma*, a loom.]

Heirship, ār'ship, *n. The state of an heir*; right of inheriting.

Heliac, hē'li-ak, *a. Belonging to the sun*; emerging from the light of the sun; passing into the sun's light. [L. *heliacus*—Gr. *hēlios*, the sun.]

Hell, hel, *n. A hollow, covered, or hidden place*; the place or state of punishment for the wicked after death; the place of the dead, or of souls after death; the lower regions or the grave; the infernal powers; a gambling-house. [Sax.—*helan*, to cover.]

Hellebore, hel'lē-bōr, *n.* A plant used by the ancients as a specific for many illnesses, especially madness; Christmas rose. [L. *helleborus.*]

Hellenic, hel-len'ik, *a. Pertaining to the Hellenes*, or inhabitants of Greece. [Gr. *Hellēnikos.*]

Hellenism, hel'len-izm, *n.* A phrase in the *idiom*, genius, or construction *of the Greek language.* [Gr. *Hellēnismos.*]

Hellenist, hel'len-ist, *n. A Grecian Jew*; one skilled in the Greek language. [Gr. *Hellēnistēs.*]

Hellenistic, hel-len-ist'ik, *a. Pertaining to the Hellenists.*

Hell-hated, hel'hāt-ed, *a. Abhorred as hell.*

Hellish, hel'ish, *a. Pertaining to hell*; infernal; malignant; detestable.

Hellishly, hel'ish-li, *adv.* Infernally; malignantly; detestably.

Hellishness, hel'ish-nes, *n. The qualities of hell* or of its inhabitants; extreme wickedness or impiety.

Hell-kite, hel'kīt, *n.* A kite of an infernal breed.

Helm, helm, *n. A helve or handle*†; the instrument by which a ship is steered, including the rudder, tiller, wheel, &c.; station of government; the place of direction or management.—*vt.* To steer; to guide. [Sax. *helma*.]

Helm, Helmet, helm, helm'et, *n.* A covering for the head in war; a head-piece; a morion; the part of a coat of arms that bears the crest. [Sax. *helm* —Goth. *huijan,* to cover.]

Helmed, Helmeted, helmd, helm'et-ed, *p.a. Furnished with a helmet.*

Helmsman, helms'man, *n. The man at the helm* of a ship.

Help, help, *vt. To lend strength to towards effecting a purpose;* to aid; to relieve; to remedy; to prevent; to hinder; to avoid.—*vi. To contribute strength or means;* to lend aid.—*n.* Aid; succour; he or that which contributes to advance a purpose; remedy; cure. [Sax. *helpan.*]

Helper, help'er, *n. One who helps;* an assistant; an auxiliary.

Helpful, help'ful, *a. That gives help,* aid, or assistance; that furnishes means of promoting an object; useful.

Helpfulness, help'ful-nes, *n.* Assistance; usefulness.

Helping, help'ing, *p.a.* Assisting; aiding; supporting.

Helpless, help'les, *a. Without help* in one's self; destitute of support or assistance; beyond help.

Helplessly, help'les-li, *adv.* Without succour.

Helplessness, help'les-nes, *n. State of being helpless;* want of strength.

Helpmate, Helpmeet, help'māt, help'mēt, *n. A companion who helps;* an assistant; a helper; a consort; a wife.

Helve, helv, *n. The handle of* an axe or hatchet.—*vt. To furnish with a helve,* as an axe. *ppr.* helving, *pret. & pp.* helved. [Sax. *helf.*]

Hem, bem, *n. The border of* a garment, doubled and sewed to strengthen it; edge; border.—*vt. To form as a hem;* to fold and sew down, as the edge of cloth; to border; to edge; to inclose and confine. *ppr.* hemming, *pret. & pp.* hemmed. [Sax.]

Hem, hem, *interj.* An exclamation whose utterance is a sort of voluntary half cough, loud or subdued, as the emotion may suggest.—*vi.* To make the sound expressed by the word *hem. ppr.* hemming, *pret. & pp.* hemmed. [formed from the sound.]

Hemisphere, he'mi-sfēr, *n. A half sphere;* one half of a sphere when divided by a plane passing through its centre; one half the celestial sphere; a map of half the terrestrial globe. [Gr. *hēmi,* half, and *sphairion,* a sphere.]

Hemispheric, Hemispherical, he-mi-sfe'rik, he-mi-sfe'rik-al, *a. Relating to a hemisphere.*

Hemistich, he'mi-stik, *n. Half a poetic line* or *verse,* or a verse not completed. [Gr. *hēmistichion*—*hēmi,* and *stichos,* a row.]

Hemlock, hem'lok, *n.* A plant whose leaves and root are poisonous; a poison, an infusion or decoction of the poisonous plant. [Sax. *hemleac*—*leac,* a leek.]

Hemorrhage, he'mor-āj, *n. A bursting forth of blood;* any discharge of blood from vessels destined to contain it. [Gr. *haimorrhagia*—*haima,* blood, and *rhegnūmi,* to break.]

Hemorrhagic, hē-mor-aj'ik, *a. Pertaining to a hemorrhage,* or flux of blood.

Hemp, hemp, *n.* A fibrous plant whose skin or bark is used for cloth and cordage; the skin or rind of the plant, prepared for spinning. [Sax. *hænep;* Old Gr. *hanaf.*]

Hempen, hemp'n, *a. Made of hemp.*

Hemp-seed, hemp'sēd, *n. The seed of hemp,* used either as seed, or for crushing for oil, or as food for fowls.

Hen, hen, *n.* The female of any kind of fowl; particularly, the female of the domestic fowl. [Sax.—L. *cano,* to sing.]

Henbane, hen'bān, *n.* A poisonous herb much used in medicine, and particularly *noxious* to domestic fowls. [*hen* and *bane.*]

Hence, hens, *adv. From this;* from this place or this time; from this source, origin, reason, or cause. [Sax. *heona* —L. *hinc.*]

Henceforth, hens-fōrth', *adv. From this time forth* or forward.

Henceforward, hens-for'wērd, *adv. From this time forward;* henceforth.

Henchman, hensh'man, *n.* A page; a servant.

Hend, hend, *vt.* To seize.

Hen-pecked, hen'pekt, *a.* Governed by his wife, as a husband.

Hepatic, he-pat'ik, *a. Pertaining to the liver.* [Gr. *hēpatikos*—*hēpar,* the liver.]

Heptagon, hep'ta-gon, *n.* A plane figure having *seven angles* and seven sides. [Gr. *hepta,* seven, and *gōnia,* an angle.]

Heptagonal, hep-tag'on-al, *a. Having seven angles* or sides.

Heptangular, hep-tang'gū-lēr, *a. Having seven angles.* [Gr. *hepta,* seven, and Eng. *angular.*]

Heptarchic, hep-tärk'ik, *a. Denoting a sevenfold government.*

Heptarchy, hep'tär-ki, *n. A government by seven persons,* or the country governed by seven persons. [Gr. *hepta,* seven, and *archē,* government.]

Her, hēr, *objective case of she,* personal pronoun of the third person fem.—*a. pron.* Belonging to a female. [Sax. *heo,* she, *hire,* of, to, or for her, *hi, hig,* her.]

Herald, he'rald, *n. One who proclaims;* an officer whose business it was to proclaim war or peace; a forerunner; a harbinger; an officer who records and blazons arms, &c.—*vt.* To introduce, *as by a herald.* [Old Fr. *herault* —Old G. *haren,* to cry aloud.]

Heraldic, hē-rald'ik, *a. Pertaining to heralds* or heraldry.

Heraldry, he'rald-ri, *n. The art or office of a herald;* the art of recording genealogies and blazoning arms or ensigns armorial.

Herb, erb, *n. That which feeds cattle,* &c.; springing vegetation, grass, &c.; a plant with a soft stalk or stem, which dies to the root every year. [Fr. *herbe* —L. *herba*—Gr. *pherbō,* to feed.]

Herbaceous, erb-ā'shē-us, *a. Pertaining to herbs;* having the nature of an herb. [L. *herbaceus.*]

Herbage, ērb'āj, *n. Herbs collectively;* grass; pasture. [Fr.]

Herbal, ērb'al, *a. Pertaining to herbs. n.* A book that contains the names and descriptions of *herbs* or plants.

Herbalist, ērb'al-ist, *n. A person skilled in herbs;* one who makes collections of plants.

Herbarium, ēr-bā'ri-um, *n.* **Herbariums,** *pl.* A collection of specimens of *herbs* carefully dried; a book or other contrivance for thus preserving plants. [from L. *herba.*]

Herbelet, ērb'el-et, *n. A small herb.*

Herbivorous, ērb-iv'or-us, *a. Eating herbs;* subsisting on herbaceous plants. [L. *herba,* an herb, and *vōro,* to devour.]

Herculean, hēr-kū'lē-an, *a. Of or belonging to Hercules;* resembling Hercules; of extraordinary strength; very great, difficult, or dangerous.

Herd, hērd, *n.* A number of beasts assembled together, and *guarded or tended;* a company of men (in contempt); a crowd; a rabble.—*vi.* To unite into *a herd,* as beasts; to feed or run in collections; to associate. [Sax. *heord;* Icel. *hirda,* to guard.]

Herdsman, hērds'man, *n. One* employed in *tending herds* of cattle.

Here, hēr, *adv. In this place;* in the present life or state; used also in making an offer or attempt, and in drinking healths. [Sax. *her.*]

Hereabout, Hereabouts, hēr'a-bout, hēr'a-bouts, *adv. About this place.*

Hereafter, hēr-af'tēr, *adv. After this time;* in a future state.—*n. The time after this;* a future state.

Hereat, hēr-at', *adv. At this.*

Hereby, hēr-bī', *adv. By this.*

Hereditament, hē-rē-dit'a-ment, *n. A hereditary estate;* any species of property that may be inherited. [Low L. *hereditamentum*—L. *heres,* an heir.]

Hereditarily, hē-red'it-a-ri-li, *adv. By inheritance.*

Hereditary, hē-red'it-a-ri, *a. Relating to an inheritance;* that has descended from an ancestor to an heir; that may descend to an heir-at-law; that is or may be transmitted from a parent to a child. [Fr. *héréditaire*—L. *heres, herēdis,* an heir.]

Herein, hēr-in', *adv. In this.*

Hereof, hēr-of', *adv. Of this;* from this.

Hereon, hēr-on', *adv. On this.*

Heresy, he'rē-si, *n. The taking up of* one opinion in preference to another; a fundamental error in religion; an offence against Christianity, consisting in an avowed denial of some of its essential doctrines. [Fr. *hérésie*—Gr. *hairēsis,* a taking—*haireō,* to take.]

Heretic, he'rē-tik, *n. One guilty of heresy;* a person under any religion, but particularly the Christian, who teaches opinions repugnant to the established faith. [Fr. *hérétique.*]

Heretical, he-ret'ik-al, *a. Containing heresy;* contrary to the true faith.

Heretically, he-ret'ik-al-li, *adv. In a heretical manner;* with heresy.

Hereto, hēr-tö', *adv. To this.*

Heretofore, hēr-tö-för', *adv. In times before the present;* formerly.

Hereunto, hēr-un-tö', *adv. To this.*

Hereupon, hēr-up-on', *adv. On this.*

Herewith, hēr-with', *adv. With this.*

Heritable, he'rit-a-bl, *a. That may inherit* or *be inherited;* annexed to estates of inheritance.

Heritage, he'rit-āj, *n. Inheritance;* an estate that passes from an ancestor to an heir by descent or course of law; the saints or people of God. [Fr. *héritage*—L. *heres,* an heir.]

Hermaphrodite, hēr-maf'rod-īt, *n.* A human being or an animal having the parts of generation both of male and female; a plant or flower which has both the stamen and the pistil.—*a.* Designating both sexes in the same animal, flower, or plant. [Fr.]

Hermeneutic, Hermeneutical, hēr-mē-nū'tik, hēr-mē-nū'tik-al, *a. Interpreting;* explaining. [Gr. *hermēneutikos*— *Hermēs,* Mercury, the god of eloquence.]

Hermeneutics, hēr-mē-nū'tiks, *n. The science of interpretation;* particularly of interpreting the Scriptures.

Hermetic, Hermetical, hēr-met'ik, hēr-met'ik-al, *a. Designating a species of chemistry,* now exploded; perfectly

close, so that no air can escape. [Fr. *hermétique*—Gr. *Hermês*, Mercury.]
Hermetically, hér-met'ik-al-li, *adv.* Chemically; closely.
Hermit, hér'mit, *n. One who lives in solitude*, or in a desert; a recluse; one bound to pray for another'. [Fr. *hermite*—Gr. *erēmos*, solitary.]
Hermitage, hér'mit-āj, *n. The habitation of a hermit;* a cell in a recluse place, but annexed to an abbey; a kind of French wine. [Old Fr.]
Hernia, hér'ni-a, *n. A protrusion of* some organ of the abdomen through an interstice; a rupture. [L.]
Hernial, hér'ni-al, *a. Pertaining to or connected with hernia.*
Hero, hē'rō, *n. A chief;* a man of distinguished valour; the person who has the principal share in the transactions related in a poem or romance. [Fr. *héro*—Gr. *hērōs*—Old G. *hēr*, great.]
Heroic, hē-rō'ik, *a. Pertaining to a hero or heroes;* becoming a hero; intrepid, noble, magnanimous; productive of heroes; reciting the achievements of heroes, as a poem; used in heroic poetry or hexameter.—*n. An heroic verse.*
Heroically, hē-rō'ik-al-li, *adv. In the manner of a hero;* intrepidly.
Heroi-comic, Heroi-comical, hē´rō-i-kom''ik, hē'rō-i-kom''ik-al, *a. Consisting of the heroic and the ludicrous;* denoting the high burlesque.
Heroine, he'rō-in, *n. A female hero;* a woman of a brave spirit. [Fr. *héroïne*.]
Heroism, he'rō-izm, *n. The qualities of a hero;* gallantry; intrepidity; daring; magnanimity. [Fr. *héroïsme*.]
Heron, he'run, *n.* A rapacious screaming, aquatic bird, with long legs, wings, and neck, a great devourer of fish. [Fr. *héron*.]
Heronry, he'run-ri, *n. A place where herons breed.*
Hero-worship, he'rō-wèr-ship, *n. Extravagant admiration of heroes.*
Herring, he'ring, *n.* One of those well-known small sea fishes which go in *great multitudes* or shoals. [Sax. *hæring*—*here*, an army.]
Hers, hérz, *pron. fem. possessive;* as, this house is hers, that is, this is the house of her.
Herself, hèr-self', *pron.* The emphatic and reciprocal form of she and her, denoting a female; having the command of herself; mistress of her rational powers; in her true character.
Hesitancy, he'zi-tan-si, *n. A hesitating;* a pausing to consider; dubiousness. [L. *hæsitantia*.]
Hesitate, he'zi-tāt, *vi. To stick fast;* to stop or pause respecting decision or action; to be doubtful; to be in suspense; to stop in speaking; to stammer. *ppr.* hesitating, *pret. & pp.* hesitated. [L. *hæsito, hæsitatum*—*hæreo, hæsum*, to hold fast, to stick.]
Hesitating, he'zi-tāt-ing, *p.a.* Doubting.
Hesitation, he-zi-tā'shon, *n. Act of hesitating;* doubt; a stopping in speech. [Fr. *hésitation*.]
Hesperian, hes-pē'ri-an, *a. Western;* situated at the west. [L. *hesperius*—Gr. *hesperos*, the evening.]
Hest, hest, *n.* Command.
Heterodox, he'te-rō-doks, *a. Holding opinions different from those which are established;* holding opinions repugnant to the doctrines of the Scriptures; contrary to the doctrines of the Scriptures, or of an established church; repugnant to the doctrines or tenets of any established church. [Fr. *hétérodoxe*—Gr. *heteros*, another, and *doxa*, an opinion.]
Heterodoxy, he'te-rō-dok-si, *n. An opinion different* or contrary to the doctrines of the Scriptures, or those of an established church; heresy. [Fr. *hétérodoxie*.]
Heterogeneous, he'te-rō-jē''nē-us, *a. Of a different kind* or nature; unlike or dissimilar in kind. [Gr. *heteros*, and *genos*, race.]
Heterogeneously, he'te-rō-je''nē-us-li, *adv. In a heterogeneous manner.*
Heterogeneousness, he'te-rō-jē''nē-us-nes, *n. State or quality of being heterogeneous.*
Heteroscian, he-te-rosh'i-an, *n.* Heteroscians are those inhabitants of the earth whose *shadows fall one way only*. [Gr. *heteros*, and *skia*, a shadow.]
Hew, hū, *vt. To cut* with an axe, or other like instrument, for the purpose of making an even surface or side; to cut; to hack; to make smooth, as stone; to form or shape with an edged instrument; to cut in pieces. *ppr.* hewing, *pret.* hewed, *pp.* hewed or hewn. [Sax. *heawan*.]
Hewed, hūd, *p.a.* Shaped by *cutting* or by a chisel.
Hewer, hū'èr, *n. One who hews* wood or stone.
Hewn, hūn, *p.a.* The same as *hewed*.
Hexagon, heks'a-gon, *n.* A plane figure of *six angles* and six sides. [Gr. *hex*, six, and *gōnia*, an angle.]
Hexagonal, heks-ag'on-al, *a. Having six angles* and six sides.
Hexameter, heks-am'et-èr, *n. A verse of six feet* in Greek and Latin poetry, consisting of dactyls and spondees.—*a. Having six metrical feet.* [Fr. *hexamètre*—Gr. *hex*, and *metron*, a measure.]
Hexangular, heks-ang'gū-lèr, *a. Having six angles* or corners.
Hey, hā, An exclamation of joy or mutual exhortation. [probably from *high*.]
Heyday, hā'dā, *interj.* An expression of frolic and exultation.—*n.* A frolic; wildness; the high spirits and vigour of youth. [*high-day*.]
Hiatus, hi-ā'tus, *n. An opening;* an aperture; a gap; a chasm; a deficiency; the effect produced by vowel-sounds in succession. [L.—*hio, hiatum*, to open.]
Hibernal, hi-bèr'nal, *a. Belonging to winter.* [L. *hibernus*—*hiems*, winter—Sans. *hima*, snow.]
Hibernate, hi-bèr'nāt, *vt. To pass the season of winter* in close quarters or in seclusion. *ppr.* hibernating, *pret. & pp.* hibernated. [L. *hiberno, hibernatum*.]
Hibernation, hi-bèr-nā'shon, *n. The passing of winter* in a close lodge, as beasts and fowls.
Hiccough, hik'up, *n.* A convulsive sort of *cough* or sob.—*vi.* To have a convulsive catch of some of the respiratory muscles. [Dan. *hikke;* formed from the sound.]
Hickory, hik'ō-ri, *n.* An American nut-bearing tree, valuable for timber and fuel.
Hickup, hik'up. See HICCOUGH.
Hid, Hidden, hid, hid'n, *p.a.* Unseen; unknown; abstruse; profound.
Hide, hīd, *vt. To cover;* to withhold or withdraw from sight; to withhold from knowledge; to screen; to keep in safety.—*vi. To be or to lie concealed;* to keep one's self out of view; to absconnd. *ppr.* hiding, *pret.* hid, *pp.* hid, hidden.
n. That which covers and protects the flesh or the body of an animal; the skin of an animal, either raw or dressed; the human skin. [Sax. *hydan*.]
Hide-bound, hīd'bound, *a.* Having the *hide close*, or sticking to the sides and back, as an animal; having the bark confining the wood.
Hideous, hid´ē-us, *a. Frightful;* ghastly; shocking to the eye or to the ear. [Fr. *hideux*—L. *hispidus*, rough.]
Hideously, hid'ē-us-li, *adv. In a manner to frighten;* dreadfully; shockingly.
Hideousness, hid'ē-us-nes, *n.* Dreadfulness; horribleness.
Hiding, hīd'ing, *p.n. Concealment;* a withholding.
Hie, hī, *vi. To hasten;* to go in haste; to speed. *ppr.* hying, *pret. & pp.* hied. [Sax. *higan*.]
Hierarchical, hī-èr-ärk'ik-al, *a. Pertaining to a hierarchy.*
Hierarchy, hī'èr-är-ki, *n.* The persons who have the exclusive *directiōn* of *things sacred;* used especially of a body of clergy of different ranks or orders. (Gr. *hierarchia*—*hierōs*, sacred, and *archē*, rule.]
Hieroglyphic, hī'èr-o-glif''ik, *n. A sacred sculptured symbol;* (pl.) a species of writing first practised by the ancient Egyptian priests, which expressed a series of ideas by representation of visible objects. [Fr. *hiéroglyphe*—Gr. *hieros*, sacred, and *gluphō*, to engrave.]
Hieroglyphic, Hieroglyphical, hī'èr-o-glif''ik, hī'èr-o-glif''ik-al, *a. Relating to hieroglyphics;* emblematic. [Fr. *hiéroglyphique*.]
Hieroglyphically, hī'èr-o-glif''ik-al-li, *adv.* Emblematically.
Higgle, hig'l, *vi. To chaffer;* to be tedious in bargaining. *ppr.* higgling, *pret. & pp.* higgled. [same as *haggle*.]
Higgler, hig'l-èr, *n.* One who is tedious and nice in bargaining; one who carries about provisions for sale.
Higgling, hig'l-ing, *p.n. The employment of a higgler.*
High, hī, *a. Lifted up;* lofty; far above the earth or its surface; raised above any object; exalted in nature or dignity; noble; dignified; proud; threatening; violent; oppressive; mighty; solemn; held in veneration; tempestuous; full; rich; strong; deep, as colouring; dear; remote from the equator, north or south; remote in past time; acute; far advanced in art or science. *adv. Aloft;* to a great altitude; loudly; with deep thought; powerfully. [Sax. *heah;* Goth. *hauh*.]
High-admiral, hī'ad-mi-ral, *n. A chief admiral.*
High-altar, hī'al-tèr, *n. The altar* at which alone *high-mass* is celebrated in Roman Catholic churches.
High-battled, hī'bat-tld, *a.* Renowned in battle or war.
High-blown, hī'blōn, *a.* Inflated, as with pride or conceit.
High-born, hī'born, *a.* Being of noble birth or extraction.
High-bred, hī'bred, *a. Bred in high life.*
High-church, hī'chèrch, *n.* That section of the episcopal *Church* which maintains the *highest* notions respecting Episcopacy, the authority of bishops, &c.
High-flown, hī'flōn, *a.* Elevated; swelled; proud; turgid; extravagant.
High-flying, hī'flī-ing, *a.* Extravagant in claims or opinions.

ch, *chain;* j, *job;* g, *go;* ng, *sing;* ᴠʜ, *then;* th, *thin;* w, *wig;* wh, *whig;* zh, *azure;* † obsolete.

High-handed, hi'hand-ed, a. Violent.
Highland, hī'land, n. *Elevated land;* a mountainous region.—a. Pertaining to mountainous regions, or to the Highlands of Scotland.
Highlander, hī'land-er, n. An inhabitant of the mountains.
Highly, hī'li, adv. *In a high manner;* in a great degree; proudly; with great estimation.
High-mass, hī'mas, n. Among Roman Catholics, that *mass* which is celebrated before the *high-*altar on Sundays, feast-days, and great occasions.
High-mettled, hī'met-ld, a. *Having high spirit;* ardent.
High-minded, hī'mind-ed, a. Proud; arrogant; having honourable pride.
Highness, hī'nes, n. *State of being high;* height; loftiness; altitude; dignity; violence; acuteness, as of tone; intenseness, as of heat; a title of honour given to princes or other men of rank.
High-place, hī'plās, n. *An eminence* or mound on which sacrifices were offered. (Script.)
High-priced, hī'prīst, a. *Yielding a great price.*
High-priest, hī'prēst, n. *A chief priest.*
High-principled, hī'prin-si-pld, a. *Possessing principles of a lofty character;* strict in principle.
High-proof, hī'prōf, a. *Highly* rectified; very strongly alcoholic.
High-reaching, hī'rēch-ing, a. Reaching upward; ambitious.
Highroad, hī'rōd, n. *A highway* or much-frequented road.
High-sea, hī'sē, n. Very strong high waves; a heavy sea.
High-seas, hī'sēs, n. pl. The open ocean.
High-spirited, hī'spi-rit-ed, a. Full of *spirit* or natural fire; irascible; bold; daring.
High-steward, hī'stū-ėrd, n. An officer of state; the chief officer of a university or town.
High-stomached, hī'stum-akt, a. Having a lofty spirit; obstinate.
High-strung, hī'strung, a. *Strung to a high pitch;* high-spirited; obstinate.
High-toned, hī'tōnd, a. Nobly elevated.
High-top, hī'top, n. The summit of a ship.
High-water, hī'wa-tėr, n. *The utmost flow or greatest elevation of the tide;* the time of such elevation.
Highway, hī'wā, n. A public road; course; road; train of action.
High-wrought, hī'rạt, a. *Wrought* with exquisite art or skill; accurately finished; inflamed to a high degree.
Hilarious, hi-lā'ri-us, a. *Full of hilarity;* gay; mirthful; merry.
Hilarity, hi-la'ri-ti, n. *Cheerfulness; merriment;* good humour; jollity. [Fr. *hilarité—*Gr. *hilāros,* cheerful—*hilāos,* gracious, propitious.]
Hild, hild, p.a. *For held.*
Hilding, hild'ing, a. Wanting spirit; cowardly.
Hill, hil, n. *A height;* a natural elevation of land; an eminence. [Sax.—*heah,* high.]
Hilliness, hil'i-nes, n. State of being *hilly.*
Hilly, hil'i, a. *Abounding with hills.*
Hilt, hilt, n. That part of anything by which it is *held; the handle,* particularly of a sword. [Sax.—*healdan,* to hold.]
Him, him, pron. The objective case of *he.* [Sax. nom. *he,* dat. *him,* to him, accus. *hine,* him; L. *eum.*]
Himself, him-self', pron. The emphatic and reciprocal form of *he* and *him,* used only in the nominative or objective case. [*him* and *self.*]
Hind, hind, n. The female of the red deer or stag. [Sax. *hinde.*]
Hind, hind, n. A domestic; a servant; a rustic; a boor; a husbandman's servant. [Sax. *hina.*]
Hind, hind, a. Backward; pertaining to the part which follows; in opposition to the fore-part. [Sax. *hyndan.*]
Hinder, hind'ėr, a. *Posterior;* that is in a position contrary to that of the head or fore-part. [comp. of *hind.*]
Hinder, hin'dėr, vt. *To keep back or behind,* or prevent from moving forward by any means; to obstruct; to prevent the progress of; to thwart; to check; to impede; to delay.—vi. To interpose obstacles or impediments [Sax. *hindrian.*]
Hinderance, Hindrance, hin'dėr-ans, hin'drans, n. *Act of hindering;* impediment; obstruction.
Hindermost, hind'ėr-mōst, a. *That is behind all others;* the last; the hindmost. [super. of *hind.*]
Hindmost, hind'mōst, a. That is in the *rear* of all others.
Hindrance, hin'drans, n. See HINDERANCE.
Hinge, hinj, n. The hook or joint on which a door, gate, &c., hangs and turns; that on which anything depends or turns.—vt. *To furnish with hinges;* to bend like a hinge.—vi. To stand or turn, as on a *hinge.* ppr. hinging, pret. & pp. hinged. [Dan. *hængsel—hænge,* to hang.]
Hinged, hinjd, p.a. *Placed on a hinge.*
Hinny, hin'ni, n. *A mule;* the produce of a stallion and a she-ass. [L. *hinnus.*]
Hint, hint, vt. *To bring to mind by a sign;* to allude to; to suggest; to insinuate; to imply.—vi. To make a remote allusion to; to refer to; to glance at; to touch upon. (With *at.*)—n. A distant allusion; slight mention; insinuation; occasion*. [allied to Dan. *vink,* a sign.]
Hip, hip, n. The projecting part of an animal behind, formed by the haunch-bone and the flesh upon it; the haunch; the joint of the thigh.—vt. To sprain or dislocate the *hip* of. ppr. hipping, pret. & pp. hipped. [Sax. *hype.*]
Hip, hip. An exclamation, expressive of call to any one. —*Hip, hip, hurrah!* the signal to cheer. [allied to *hoop.*]
Hip, hip, n. The fruit of the *dog-rose* or wild brier. [Sax. *hiop.*]
Hippodrome, hip'pō-drōm, n. *A racecourse for horses* and for chariots; a circus. [Gr. *hippodromos—hippos,* a horse, and *dromos,* a course.]
Hippopotamus, hip-pō-pot'a-mus, n. *The river-horse;* a large animal, allied to the elephant, and inhabiting the Nile and other rivers in Africa. [Gr. *hippos,* a horse, and *potamos,* a river.]
Hire, hir, vt. To procure from another person, and for temporary use, at a certain price; to engage in service for a stipulated reward; to engage in immoral services for a reward; to let; to lease (with *out*). ppr. hiring, pret. & pp. hired.—n. *The price* paid for the temporary use of anything; the recompense paid for personal service; wages; pay; a bribe. [Sax. *hyrian—hyre,* wages.]
Hired, hird, p.a. Taken for use at a stipulated price; employed in service for a compensation, as a man.
Hireling, hir'ling, n. *One who is hired,* or who serves for wages; a mercenary; a prostitute.—a. Serving for wages; mercenary; employed for money or other compensation.
Hirer, hir'ėr, n. *One who hires.*
Hirsute, hėr-sūt', a. *Hairy;* rough with hair; shaggy. [L. *hirsutus—hirtus,* hairy.]
His, his, pron. *possessive sing.* of *he,* and possessive adjective pron. *Of him;* belonging to him; formerly used also for *its.* [Sax. nomin. *he,* he, gen. *his, hys,* of him.]
Hiss, his, vi. To make a sound by driving the breath between the tongue and the upper teeth; to express contempt by hissing; to whiz, as an arrow or other thing in rapid flight.—vt. To *condemn by hissing;* to disgrace; to explode; to procure hisses for.—n. The sound made by propelling the breath between the tongue and upper teeth; the noise of a serpent, a goose, &c.; an expression of disapprobation used in places of public exhibition. [Sax. *hysian.*]
Hissing, his'ing, p.n. An expression of scorn or contempt; the object of scorn and derision.
Hist, hist, *interj.* A word commanding *silence,* equivalent to *hush, whist,* be silent. [L. *sti interj.* hist!]
Historian, his-tō'ri-an, n. *A writer* or compiler *of history.* [Fr. *historien.*]
Historic, Historical, his-to'rik, his-to'rik-al, a. *Containing history;* pertaining to history; contained in history; deduced from history; representing history. [Fr. *historique.*]
Historically, his-to'rik-al-li, adv. *In the manner of history.*
Historiographer, his'tō-ri-og''ra-fėr, n. *A writer of history;* an officer employed to write the history of a prince or state. [Fr. *historiographe.*]
History, his'tō-ri, n. A written account of what one *has known or learned;* an account of facts respecting nations or states; a narration of events in the order in which they happened, with their causes and effects; story; description; an account of things that exist, as of animals or plants; an account of an individual person.—vt. To record. [Fr. *histoire—*Gr. *historia,* a learning by inquiry—*eidō,* to know.]
Histrionic, his-tri-on'ik, a. *Pertaining to a stage-player;* belonging to stage-playing; theatrical. [L. *histrionicus—*Etruscan, *hister,* a player.]
Histrionically, his-tri-on'ik-al-li, adv. *In the manner of a stage-player.*
Hit, hit, vt. *To strike;* to reach, as the object aimed at; to give a blow to; to thump; not to miss; to be conformable to; to touch properly; to urge by the right motive.—vi. *To strike;* to come in contact; to meet or fall on by good luck; to reach the intended point; to succeed. ppr. hitting, pret. & pp. hit. n. *A stroke;* a blow; the collision of one body against another; a chance; a lucky chance; a turn of thought which seems to be peculiarly applicable. [Sw. *hitta,* to strike.]
Hitch, hich, vi. *To be hooked;* to become entangled; to move by jerks or with stops, as one whose legs are entangled.—vt. *To hook;* to catch by a hook; to raise; to hoist.—n. *A catch;* anything that holds; act of catching, as on a *hook,* &c.; a knot or noose in a rope for fastening it to a ring or other object; a stop in walking or moving. [Sw. *hakta,* to join with a buckle.]
Hitching, hich'ing, p.n. A fastening in a harness.
Hither, hiṯH'ėr, adv. *To this place;* used

Fāte, fär, fat, fall; mē, met, hėr; pīne, pin; nōte, not, mōve; tūbe, tub, bull; oil, pound.

with verbs signifying motion.—a. Nearer; toward the person speaking. [Sax.]

Hithermost, hiṭh'ẽr-mōst, a. Nearest on this side.

Hitherto, hiṭh'ẽr-tō, adv. To this time; till now; to this place; to a prescribed limit.

Hitherward, hiṭh'ẽr-wẽrd, adv. This way; toward this place.

Hitter, hit'ẽr, n. One who hits.

Hive, hīv, n. A family; a swarm of bees; the box, chest, &c., forming the habitation of a swarm of bees; a company or society being together, or closely connected.—vt. To cause to enter a hive, as bees; to lay up in store; to receive, as a habitation or place of deposit.—vi. To take shelter together; to reside in a collective body. ppr. hiving, pret. & pp. hived. [Sax. hyfe; Old G. hûva, matrimony, a family.]

Hiz, his, vi. To hiss.

Ho, hō, interj. Stop! a call to excite attention, or to give notice of approach. [L. eho! formed from the sound.]

Hoar, hōr, a. White or whitish; white or gray with age; hoary.—n. Hoariness.—vi.† To become mouldy. [Sax. har.]

Hoard, hōrd, n. A treasure; a large quantity of anything laid up; a hidden stock.—vt. To treasure up; to collect and lay up, as a large quantity of anything; to store secretly.—vi. To collect and form a hoard; to lay up in store. [Sax. hord; Goth. huzd, a treasure.]

Hoarded, hōrd'ed, p.a. Collected and laid up in store.

Hoarding, hōrd'ing, p.n. A laying up in store.

Hoar-frost, hōr'frost, n. The white particles of frozen dew.

Hoariness, hōr'i-nes, n. State of being white, whitish, or gray.

Hoarse, hōrs, a. Having a grating noise, as when affected with a cold; discordant, as the voice, or as any sound. [Sax. has—Old G. heis.]

Hoarsely, hōrs'li, adv. With a rough, harsh, grating voice or sound.

Hoarseness, hōrs'nes, n. Harshness or roughness of voice or sound; preternatural asperity of voice.

Hoary, hōr'i, a. White or whitish; white or gray with age.

Hoax, hōks, n. A slight; something done for deception or mockery.—vt. To deceive; to play a trick upon for sport, or without malice. [Sax. hucx.]

Hob, hob, n. A clown; the flat part of a grate, where things are placed to be kept warm. [Old G. lanthuoba, a countryman—hōba, an abode.]

Hobble, hob'l, vi. To hop; to walk lamely, bearing chiefly on one leg; to move irregularly, as verse. ppr. hobbling, pret. & pp. hobbled.—n. An unequal, halting gait; perplexity. [Sax. hoppe.]

Hobbling, hob'l-ing, p.a. Walking with a halting or interrupted step.

Hobby, hob'bi, n. An active, ambling pony or nag; a stick, or figure of a horse, on which boys ride; that which a person pursues with zeal or delight. [Fr. hobin.]

Hobby-horse, hob'bi-hors, n. A hobby; a wooden horse on which boys ride; the favourite object of pursuit.

Hobgoblin, hob-gob'lin, n. A fairy; a frightful apparition. [probably from hob, for Robin, and goblin.]

Hobnob, hob'nob, adv. Take or not take; a familiar call to reciprocal drinking. [probably from Sax. hab-

ban, have, and nabban—ne habban, not have.]

Hock, hok, n. A general name applied in this country to Rhenish wines. [from Hochheim, in Germany.]

Hod, hod, n. A kind of tray for carrying mortar and brick on the shoulder, furnished with a handle. [G. hotte.]

Hodge-podge, hoj'poj. See HOTCHPOT.

Hodge-pudding, hoj' pud-ding, n. A pudding made up of a medley of ingredients.

Hodman, hod'man, n. A man who carries a hod.

Hoe, hō, n. An instrument for hewing or cutting up weeds and loosening the earth in fields and gardens.—vt. To clean with a hoe; to clear from weeds.—vi. To use a hoe. ppr. hoeing, pret. & pp. hoed. [Gr. haue—Sax. heawan, to hew.]

Hoeing, hō'ing, p.n. Act of scraping or digging with a hoe.

Hog, hog, n. The digging animal; a swine.—vi. To bend, as a ship, so as to resemble in some degree a hog's back. ppr. hogging, pret. & pp. hogged. [W. hwch.]

Hog-backed, hog'bakt, a. Having a back like that of a hog, as a ship.

Hoggish, hog'ish, a. Having the qualities of a hog; brutish; meanly selfish.

Hoggishly, hog'ish-li, adv. In a brutish, gluttonous, or filthy manner.

Hoggishness, hog'ish-nes, n. Voracious greediness in eating; beastly filthiness.

Hogshead, hogz'hed, n. A large cask; an old measure of capacity, containing about 52½ imperial gallons. [D. okshoofd, oxhead.]

Hog's-lard, hogz'lärd, n. The fat of the hog or of swine.

Hoiden, hoi'den, n. A rude awkward bold girl; a romp.—a. Rude; bold; inelegant; rustic.—vi. To romp rudely or indecently. [W. hoeden, a woman of doubtful fame.]

Hoist, hoist, vt. To raise; to lift upward by means of tackle.—n. Act of raising; an apparatus for raising goods, &c.; the perpendicular height of a flag or sail. [Fr. hausser, to raise—L. altus, high.]

Hold, hōld, vt. To have in the grasp; to keep fast; to confine; to restrain; to embrace and confine, with bearing or lifting; to maintain; to consider; to regard; to think; to defend; to possess, by title, as land; to withhold; to compel to observe or fulfil; to bind; to continue; to prosecute or carry on, as one's course; to celebrate; to sustain; to wield; to observe in practice.—vi. To continue fast, firm, or sound; to be true; not to fail; to stand as a fact or truth; not to give way or part; not to move; to refrain; to stick or adhere; to derive title (with of). ppr. holding, pret. held, pp. held or holden. n. A grasp with the hand; an embrace with the arms; ground to take or keep; something which may be seized for support; power of keeping or of seizing; a prison; custody; influence operating on the mind; advantage that may be employed in directing or persuading another; a fortified place; a fort; a castle; the whole interior cavity of a ship. [Sax. healdon, Old G. haltan.]

Holder, hōld'ẽr, n. One who holds or grasps in his hand; one who owns or possesses; a tenant; something by which a thing is held.

Holding, hōld'ing, p.n. Act of keeping hold of or retaining; tenure; a farm held of a superior; hold; influence; power over; the burden of a song.

Hole, hōl, n. A hollow place in any solid body; a cell; a cavern; a pit; an opening in or through a solid body; an interstice; a narrow or dark lodging; a subterfuge.—vt. To make a hole or holes in; to drive into a bag, as in billiards. ppr. holing, pret. & pp. holed. [Sax. hol—Old G. holōn, to hollow.]

Holiday, ho'li-dā, n. A sacred day; a festival; a day of joy and gaiety; a day of amusement.—a. Pertaining to a festival.

Holily, hō'li-li, adv. Piously; with sanctity; sacredly; inviolably.

Holiness, hō'li-nes, n. Quality of being holy; purity of moral character; purity of heart; sanctified affections; a title of the pope.

Holland, hol'land, n. Fine linen, first manufactured in Holland.

Hollands, hol landz, n. Gin manufactured in Holland.

Hollo, hol lō, vi. To call out or exclaim loudly. [Sax. ahlowan]

Holloa, Hollo, hol'lō, hol lō, n. A shout; a loud call.—interj. A word used in calling.

Hollow, hol'lō, a. Holed; containing an empty space; not solid; concave; void; sunk deep in the orbit; deep; faithless; deceitful.—n. A hole; a cavity; a place excavated; a cave or cavern; a den; a groove; a canal.—vt. To make a hole in; to make hollow, as by digging; to excavate. [Sax. and Old G. hol.]

Hollow-eyed, hol'lō-īd, a. Having sunken eyes.

Hollow-hearted, hol'lō-härt-ed, a. Not sound and true; false.

Hollowness, hol'lō-nes, n. State of being hollow; cavity; treachery.

Holly, hol'li, n. An evergreen tree or shrub, with smooth grayish bark, shining thorny leaves, and scarlet berries. [Sax. holegn.]

Hollyhock, hol'li-hok, n. A well-known flowering plant, a kind of mallow. [Sax. holihoc.]

Holm, hōlm, n. A river isle; a low, flat tract of rich land on the banks of a river; the evergreen oak. [Sax. hólm.]

Holocaust, ho'lo-kast, n. A burnt sacrifice, of which the whole was consumed by fire. [Gr. holos, whole, and kaustos, burnt—kaiō to burn.]

Holography, ho'lo-graf, n. A deed or testament written wholly by the testator's own hand. [Gr. holos, whole, and graphō, to write.]

Holpt, Holpent, hōlp, hōlp'n, pp. of help.

Holster, hōl'stẽr, n. A cover or leathern case for a pistol, carried by a horseman. [Sax. heolster—helan, to cover.]

Holstered, hōl'stẽrd, p.a. Bearing holsters.

Holy, hō'li, a. Healed; whole or perfect, in a moral sense; pure in heart; free from sin; godly; sanctified; immaculate; set apart to a sacred use; proceeding from pious principles; perfectly just and good. [Sax. halig—Goth. hail, sound.]

Holy-cruel, hō'li-krö-el, a. Cruel from excess of holiness.

Holy-Ghost, hō'li-gōst, n. The Holy Spirit; the third person in the adorable Trinity. [Sax. halig, holy, and gast, spirit.]

Holy-One, hō'li-wun, n. An appellation of the Supreme Being, by way of emphasis; an appellation of Christ.

Holy-orders, hō'li-or-dẽrz, n. pl. The office or service by which a person is consecrated to the duties of a clergyman; the character or state of a clergyman.

---

ch, chain; j, job; g, go; ng, sing; ᴛʜ, then; th, thin; w, wig; wh, whig; zh, azure; † obsolete.

Holy-water, hō'li-wạ-tėr, n. Water which has been *consecrated* by the priest to sprinkle the faithful, and things used for holy purposes. (Church of Rome.)
Holy-week, hō'li-wēk, n. The *week* before Easter, in which the passion of our Saviour is commemorated.
Holy-writ, hō'li-rit, n. *The Sacred Scriptures.*
Homage, hom'āj, n. Originally an act of fealty on the part of a vassal to his lord, by which he solemnly professed to become *his man;* the service rendered in fulfilment of such promise; deference; respect paid by external action; reverential worship. [Fr. *hommage*—L. *homo*, a man.]
Home, hōm, n. *One's own house;* abode; dwelling; one's own country; the place of constant residence; the grave.—a. Pertaining to *one's dwelling* or country; severe; pointed.—adv. To one's own *habitation* or country; close; to the point. [Sax. *ham*—Old G. *heim*—L. *domus*, a house.]
Home-bred, hōm'bred, a. *Bred at home;* native; plain; not polished by travel.
Homefelt, hōm'felt, a. *Felt* in one's own breast; inward; private.
Homeless, hōm'les, a. *Destitute of a home.*
Homeliness, hōm'li-nes, n. *Quality of being homely;* plainness of features; want of beauty; rudeness; coarseness.
Homely, hōm'li, a. *Belonging to home;* of plain features; rude; coarse; not fine or elegant.
Homœopathic, hō'mē-o-path"ik, a. *Pertaining to homœopathy.*
Homœopathist, ho-mē-op'a-thist, n. *A believer in homœopathy;* one who practises homœopathy.
Homœopathy, hō-mē-op'a-thi, n. The theory and practice of curing diseases with very minute doses of medicine, by producing *affections like or similar* to those of the disease. [Gr. *homoiopatheia—homoios*, like, and *pathos*, affection—*paschō*, to suffer.]
Homeric, hō-me'rik, a. *Pertaining to Homer,* or to his poetry; resembling Homer's verse.
Homesick, hōm'sik, a. *Grieved* at a separation from *home.*
Homesickness, hōm'sik-nes, n. *Grief* occasioned by a separation from one's *home* or country.
Homespun, hōm'spun, a. *Spun at home;* homely; not elegant.—n.† A coarse, rustic person.
Homestead, hōm'sted, n. *The place of a mansion-house;* the ground immediately connected with the mansion; native seat.
Homeward, hōm'wėrd, adv. *Toward* one's *habitation* or country.—a. *Being in the direction of home.*
Homewards, hōm'wėrdz, adv. Same as *homeward.*
Homicidal, ho-mi-sid'al, a. *Pertaining to homicide;* murderous.
Homicide, ho'mi-sid, n. *Manslaughter;* a person who kills another; a mauslayer. [Fr.—L. *homo*, man, and *cædo*, to kill.]
Homilist, ho'mi-list, n. One who preaches *homilies*, or who preaches to a congregation.
Homily, ho'mi-li, n. *A sermon* addressed *to the people;* a plain familiar discourse on some religious topic. [Fr. *homélie*—Gr. *homos*, common, and *ilē*, a crowd.]
Homogeneous, hō-mō-jē'nē-us, a. *Of the same kind or nature;* consisting of similar parts, or of elements of the like nature. [Fr. *homogene*—Gr. *homos*, the same, and *genos*, kind.]
Homogeneousness, hō-mō-jē'nē-us-nes, n. *Quality of being homogeneous.*
Homologate, hō-mol'o-gāt, vt. *To agree to;* to approve. ppr. homologating, pret. & pp. homologated. [Gr. *homologeō—homos*, same, and *legō*, to say.]
Homologation, hō-mol'og-ā"shon, n. The confirmation by a court of justice.
Homologous, hō-mol'og-us, a. *Having the same ratio;* corresponding. [Fr. *homologue*—Gr. *homos*, same, and *logos*, a saying.]
Hone, hōn, n. *A stone* of a fine grit, used for sharpening edged instruments. vt. To rub and sharpen on a hone. ppr. honing, pret. & pp. honed. [Icel. *hein*, a soft whetstone.]
Honest, on'est, a. *Full of honour;* upright; just; trusty; sincere; candid; according to truth, as a statement; free from fraud; unimpeached, as character; decent; chaste, faithful; virtuous. [Old Fr. *honneste*—L. *honestus—honor*, honour.]
Honestly, on'est-li, adv. *In an honest manner.*
Honesty, on'es-ti, n. *Honourableness;* an upright disposition; moral rectitude of heart; uprightness; justice; fairness; plain-dealing; veracity; truth; liberality†. [Old Fr. *honnesteté*—L. *honor*, honour.]
Honey, hun'ē, n. *A sweet* viscous juice collected by bees from the flowers of plants; sweetness; a word of tenderness.—vt. To sweeten.—vi. To be gentle; to fawn. [Sax. *hunig*—Heb. *ghoneg*, delight.]
Honey-comb, hun'ē-kōm, n. *A* substance formed by bees *into cells* for repositories of *honey;* anything having little cells, like a honey-comb.
Honey-combed, hun'ē-kōmd, p.a. Having little cells resembling *honey-combs.*
Honey-dew, hun'ē-dū, n. *A sweet* substance found on certain plants in small drops; a kind of tobacco.
Honeyed, hun'id, p.a. *Covered with honey;* sweet.
Honey-moon, hun'ē-mön, n. *The sweet moon or month;* the first month after marriage.
Honeysuckle, hun'ē-suk-l, n. A beautiful flowering and climbing shrub; woodbine. [Sax. *hunig-sucle.*]
Honor, on'ėr, n. Sometimes used for *honour.*
Honorary, on'ėr-a-ri, a. *Relating to honour;* conferring honour; possessing a title or place without performing services or receiving a reward.—n. A fee; a present; a reward. [Fr. *honoraire.*]
Honour, on'ėr, n. *Respect; regard;* the esteem due or paid to worth; high estimation or praise; a testimony of esteem; exalted rank or place; fame; good name; true nobleness of mind; an assumed appearance of nobleness; scorn of meanness; dignity of mien; he or that which confers dignity; a title of respect or distinction; (pl.) privileges of rank or birth; civilities paid; distinctions granted to a vanquished enemy in war; homage; the highest ranks in a university; the four highest cards in games.—vt. To hold in regard; to revere; to reverence; to manifest the highest veneration for; to adore; to elevate in rank or station; to treat with due respect; to accept and pay when due, as a draft. [Fr. *honneur*—L. *honor*—Heb. *chānan*, to be favourably disposed, to regard with favour.]
Honourable, on'ėr-a-bl, a. *Worthy of honour;* holding a distinguished rank in society; actuated by principles of honour; conferring honour; consistent with honour; performed with marks of honour; proceeding from an upright and laudable cause; not base; honest; without deceit; fair; an epithet of respect or distinction; becoming men of rank and character. [Fr. *honorable.*]
Honourableness, on'ėr-a-bl-nes, n. *State or quality of being honourable.*
Honourably, on'ėr-a-bli, adv. *In an honourable manner.*
Honoured, on'ėrd, p.a. Respected; revered; glorified.
Honourer, on'ėr-ėr, n. *One who honours.*
Honouring, on'ėr-ing, p.n. *Act of giving honour.*
Honourless, on'ėr-les, a. *Destitute of honour;* not honoured.
Hood, hụd, n. *A covering for the head* used by females; a covering for the head and shoulders used by monks; a cowl; anything to be drawn over the head to cover it; any covering resembling a hood.—vt. *To dress, as in a hood* or cowl; to cover; to blind, as one's eyes. [Sax. *hod*—D. *hoeden*, to cover.]
Hooded, hụd'ed, p.a. *Covered with a hood;* blinded.
Hoodmanblind†, hụd'man-blīnd, n. A play in which a person blinded is to catch another, and tell his name.
Hood-wink, hụd'wingk, vt. *To blind by covering the eyes of;* to cover; to hide; to deceive by external appearances.
Hoof, höf, n. The horny substance that shields the feet of certain animals, as the horse, &c.; an animal; a beast. [Sax. *hóf.*]
Hoofed, höft, p.a. *Furnished with hoofs.*
Hoof-mark, höf'märk, n. *The mark of an animal's hoof* on the ground.
Hook, hök, n. A piece of iron or other metal *bent into a curve* for catching; that which catches; a snare; a sickle; that part of a hinge which is fixed in a post.—vt. *To catch with a hook;* to seize and draw, as with a hook; to fasten with a hook; to ensnare.—vi. To bend; to be curving. [Sax. *hoc.*]
Hooked, hökt, p.a. *Bent into the form of a hook;* bent; aquiline; provided with a hook.
Hook-nosed, hök'nōzd, a. *Having a curvated* or aquiline nose.
Hoop, höp, n. *That which goes round* about and binds; a band of wood or metal used to confine the staves of casks, tubs, &c.; something resembling a hoop; a ring.—vt. *To bind or fasten with hoops;* to clasp; to encircle. [Sax. *hóp*, a band made of osier.]
Hoop, höp, vi. *To whoop;* to shout; to utter a loud cry, by way of call or pursuit.—vt. To drive with a shout or outcry; to call by a shout or hoop.—n. A shout.
Hooping-cough, höp'ing-kof, n. *A cough* in which the patient *whoops*, with a deep inspiration of breath.
Hoot, höt, vi. To shout in contempt; to cry as an owl.—vt. To drive with shouts uttered in contempt.—n. *A cry* or shout in contempt. [Fr. *huer.*]
Hooting, höt'ing, p.n. *A shouting in contempt;* the cry of an owl.
Hop, hop, vi. *To leap* or spring on one leg; to spring forward by leaps; to skip, as birds; to limp; to frisk about. ppr. hopping, pret. & pp. hopped.—n

Fāte, fär, fat, fạll; mē, met, hėr; pīne, pin; nōte, nọt, mōve; tūbe, tub, bụll; oil, pound.

HOP 181 HOSPITALITY

A leap; a leap on one leg. [Sax. *hoppan.*]
Hop, hop, *n.* A well-known bitter plant, which grows up by encircling trees or poles.—*vt.* To impregnate with hops. *vi.* To pick hops. ppr. hopping, pret. & pp. hopped. [D.—G. *haupt,* head.]
Hop-bind, hop'bind, *n.* The *stalk* or vine on which *hops* grow.
Hope, hōp, *n. An expectation* of some *good;* a desire of some good, accompanied with a slight expectation of obtaining it; the highest degree of well-founded expectation of good; trust; he or that which promises desired good; an opinion or belief grounded on substantial evidence. *vi.To expect,* with anticipation of, some good; to trust in with confident expectation of good.—*vt.* To expect, with a belief that it may be obtained. ppr. hoping, pret. & pp. hoped. [Sax. *hopa—*Icel. *happ,* good fortune.]
Hopeful, hōp'ful, *a. Full of hope;* having qualities which excite hope; giving ground to expect good or success.
Hopefully, hōp'ful-li, *adv. In a hopeful manner;* in a manner to raise hope.
Hopefulness, hōp'ful-nes, *n. State or quality of being hopeful.*
Hopeless, hōp'les, *a. Destitute of hope;* desponding; despairing; promising nothing desirable.
Hopelessly, hōp'les-li, *adv. Without hope.*
Hopelessness, hōp'les-nes, *n. State of being hopeless.*
Hoper, hōp'er, *n. One who hopes.*
Hopingly, hōp'ing-li, *adv. With hope.*
Hopped, hopt, *p.a.* Impregnated *with hops.*
Hopper, hop'er, *n. One who hops;* a wooden trough or funnel, through which grain passes into a mill, so called from its *leaping* or shaking motion.
Hopping, hop'ing, *p.n. A leaping;* a springing or dancing; a gathering of hops.
Hop-yard, Hop-garden, hop'yärd, hop'-gär-dn, *n.* A field or inclosure where *hops* are raised.
Horary, hōr'a-ri, *a. Pertaining to an hour;* hourly; continuing an hour. [L. *horarius—hora,* an hour.]
Horde, hōrd, *n. A herd;* a company of wandering people dwelling in tents or waggons, and migrating from place to place.—*vi.* To *herd;* to live together like savages or migratory tribes. ppr. hording, pret. & pp. horded. [D.]
Horehound, hōr'hound, *n.* A plant bearing *white* flowers, said to be a remedy for the bite of mad dogs or *hounds;* used for coughs, asthmas, &c. [Sax. *harahune—hara,* white, and *hund,* a dog.]
Horizon, ho-rī'zon, *n. That which limits;* the circular line which *bounds* the view of the sky and the earth, formed by the apparent meeting of the sky and earth; a great circle whose circumference is equally distant from the zenith and nadir, and which divides the earth into upper and lower hemispheres. [Gr. *horizon—horos,* a limit.]
Horizontal, ho-ri-zon'tal, *a. Parallel to the horizon,* or lying in the plane of it; level, as the surface of a small portion of water at rest; near the horizon.
Horizontally ho-ri-zon'tal-li, *adv.* In a direction parallel to the *horizon.*
Horn, horn, *n. That which breaks or strikes;* a hard substance growing on the heads of certain animals, usually projecting to some length, and ending

in a point; a wind-instrument of music; an extremity of the moon, when it is waxing or waning; a drinking-cup, originally made of horn; a symbol of strength and power; something shaped like a horn; an emblem of a cuckold. [Sax.—Heb. *kĕrĕn.*]
Horned, hornd, *p.a. Furnished with horns;* shaped like a crescent or the new moon.
Horned-owl, hornd'oul, *n.* A species of owl with two tufts of feathers on the head; the great-eared owl.
Hornet, horn'et, *n.* A large stinging species of wasp, so called from its *horns.* [Sax. *hyrnet,* from *horn.*]
Horning, horn'ing, *p.n. A forming into horns;* appearance of the moon when increasing, or in the form of a crescent.
Horn-mad, horn'mad, *a.* Mad as one who has been cuckolded.
Hornpipe, horn'pip, *n.* An old instrument of music, consisting of a wooden pipe with a *horn* at each end; a lively air or tune, of triple time, played originally on the instrument; a dance to the tune.
Horny, horn'i, *a. Consisting of horn* or horns; resembling horn; hard; callous.
Horological, hōr-o-loj'ik-al, *a. Pertaining to horology.*
Horology, hōr-ol'o-ji, *n. A discourse on time;* that branch of science which *treats of* the principles and construction of machines for measuring and indicating portions of *time.* [Gr. *hōra,* any limited time, and *logos,* discourse.]
Horoscope, hōr'os-kōp, *n.* In astrology, a figure or scheme of the heavens from which to cast nativities. [Fr.—Gr. *hōra,* and *skopeō,* to view.]
Horrible, hor'ri-bl, *a. Exciting horror;* dreadful; frightful; awful; terrific; hideous; horrid. [Fr.—L. *horreo,* to bristle, tremble.]
Horribly, hor'ri-bli, *adv. In a manner to excite horror;* dreadfully; terribly.
Horrid, hor'rid, *a. Bristling!;* that does or may excite horror; terrific; very offensive or disgusting. [L. *horridus* —Heb. *chared,* to be terrified.]
Horridly, hor'rid-li, *adv. In a manner to excite horror;* dreadfully; shockingly.
Horridness, hor'rid-nes, *n. The qualities that excite horror.*
Horrific, hor-rif'ik, *a. Causing horror;* dreadful; frightful. [L. *horrificus—facio,* to make.]
Horrify, hor'ri-fi, *vt.* To *strike* or impress with *horror.* ppr. horrifying, pret. & pp. horrified. [L. *horror,* and *facio,* to make.]
Horror, hor'rér, *n.* A *bristling!;* an excessive *degree of fear,* or a painful emotion which makes a person tremble; terror, accompanied with hatred; that which excites horror; dreariness; dreadful thoughts; distressing scenes. [L.—*horreo,* to bristle.]
Horse, hors, *n.* The animal that *neighs;* a neighing quadruped, remarkable for beauty, and used in war, and draught, and carriage; cavalry; a body of troops serving on horseback; a machine by which something is supported.—*vt.* To *mount on a horse;* to ride or sit on astride; to furnish with horses. ppr. horsing, pret. & pp. horsed. [Sax. *hors—*Sans. *hrĕsh,* to neigh.]
Horseback, hors'bak, *n. The back of a horse;* the posture *of riding on a horse.*
Horse-chestnut, hors'ches-nut, *n.* A

large *nut,* said to be good food for *horses;* the tree that produces it, a common shade-tree.
Horse-fly, hors'fli, *n.* A large *fly* that stings *horses.*
Horse-guards, hors'gärdz, *n. pl.* A body of cavalry *for guards.*
Horse-leech, hors'lēch, *n.* A large *leech.*
Horseman, hors'man, *n.* A *rider* on *horseback;* a man skilled in riding; a soldier who serves on horseback.
Horsemanship hors'man-ship, *n.* The act of *riding,* and of training and *managing horses.*
Horse-power, hors'pou-er, *n. The power of a horse,* or its equivalent, estimated as a power which will raise 32,000 lbs. avoirdupois one foot high per minute; used as a standard for estimating the power of a steam-engine.
Horse-race, hors'rās, *n. A race by horses;* a match of horses in running.
Horse-racing, hors'rās-ing, *p.n.* The practice or art of *running horses.*
Horse-radish, hors'rad-ish, *n.* A plant, having a root of a pungent taste.
Horse-riding, hors'rid-ing, *n. The art* or practice *of riding horses.*
Horse-shoe, hors'shō, *n. A shoe for horses,* consisting of a plate of iron of a circular form; anything shaped like a horse-shoe.—*a. Having the form of a horse-shoe.*
Horse-trainer, hors'trān-er, *n. One who trains horses* for racing, &c.
Horse-way, Horse-road, hors'wā, hors'-rōd, *n. A way* or road *in which horses may travel.*
Horsewhip, hors'whip, *n.* A *whip* for driving *horses.—vt.* To lash; *to strike with a horsewhip.* ppr. horsewhipping, pret. & pp. horsewhipped.
Hortative, hort'āt-iv, *a. Giving exhortation.* [L. *hortativus.*]
Hortatory, hort'ā-tō-ri, *a. Inciting;* giving *exhortation* or advice, as a discourse. [from L. *hortor,* to exhort.]
Horticultural, hor-ti-kul'tūr-al, *a. Pertaining to the culture of gardens.*
Horticulture, hor'ti-kul-tūr, *n. The art of cultivating gardens.* [L. *hortus,* a garden, and *cultūra,* culture—*colo,* to till.]
Horticulturist, hor-ti-kul'tūr-ist, *n. One who is skilled in the art of cultivating gardens.*
Hosanna, hō-zan'na, *n.* An exclamation of praise to God, or an invocation of blessings. [Heb. save I beseech thee.]
Hose, hōz, *n. A covering* for the thighs, legs, or feet; stockings; coverings for the legs; a flexible pipe used with engines, for conveying water to extinguish fires, &c. [Sax. *hos—*Icel. *hosa.*]
Hosier, hō'zhi-ér, *n. One who deals in stockings* and socks, &c.
Hosiery, hō'zhi-e-ri, *n. Stockings* in *general;* socks.
Hospitable, hos'pit-a-bl, *a. Relating to a host or guest;* receiving and entertaining strangers with kindness and without reward; manifesting generosity; inviting to strangers; indicating hospitality. [Old Fr.—L. *hospes, hospitis,* a stranger, a guest.]
Hospitably, hos'pit-a-bli, *adv. In a hospitable manner.*
Hospital, hos'pit-al, *n. An inn!;* a building in which the sick or infirm are received and treated; also, a house for the reception of insane persons, or for seamen, soldiers, foundlings, infected persons, &c. [Old Fr.—L. *hospes,* a guest.]
Hospitality, hos-pit-al'i-ti, *n. Quality of being hospitable.* [Old Fr. *hospitalité.*]

ch, *chain;* j, *job;* g, *go;* ng, *sing;* ᴠʜ, *then;* th, *thin;* w, *wig;* wh, *whig;* zh, *azure;* † obsolete.

Hospitaller, hos'pit-al-ėr, n. One of a religious community, whose office it was to relieve the poor, the stranger, and the sick; a knight of a religious order, usually spoken of as knights of Malta.

Host, hōst, n. *A stranger;* one who entertains *a stranger* at his own house without reward; an innkeeper; one who is entertained at the house of another, a guest.—*vi.† To lodge at an inn.* [Old Fr. *hoste*—L. *hospes*, a stranger—Sans. *ghas*, to eat, and L. *peto*, to seek.]

Host, hōst, n. *An enemy in arms;* an army; a number of men embodied for war; any great number or multitude. [Old Fr.—L. *hostis*, an enemy.]

Host, hōst, n. *A victim; a sacrifice;* the sacrifice of the mass in the Roman Catholic church. [L. *hostia*, from *hostio*, to strike, as a victim.]

Hostage, hōst'aj, n. *A person* delivered to an *enemy*, as a *pledge* to secure the performance of conditions. [Old Fr.—L. *hostis*, an enemy.]

Hostelry, hōs'tel-ri, n. An inn.

Hostess, hōst'es, n. *A female host;* a woman who keeps an inn.

Hostile, hos'til, a. *Belonging to a public enemy;* designating enmity or a state of war; warlike; unfriendly; contrary; repugnant. [Fr.—L. *hostis*, an enemy.]

Hostilely, hos'til-li, adv. *In a hostile manner.*

Hostility, hos-til'i-ti, n. *State or quality of being hostile;* state of war between nations; the actions of an open enemy; enmity; repugnance. [Fr. *hostilité.*]

Hostler, os'lėr, n. *An innkeeper;* the person who has the care of horses at an inn. [Old Fr. *hostelier*—L. *hospes,* a guest.]

Hot, hot, a. *Having sensible heat;* opposed to cold; burning; fiery; glowing; ardent in temper; easily exasperated; vehement; eager; animated; lustful; biting; pungent in taste. [Sax. *hat.*]

Hot-bed, hot'bed, n. *A garden bed* of earth and horse-dung, covered with glass to produce *warmth*, for rearing tender plants; a place which favours rapid growth.

Hot-blast, hot'blast, n. *A current of heated air* injected into a furnace by means of a blowing-engine.

Hot-blooded, hot'blud-ed, a. *Having hot blood;* high-spirited; irritable.

Hotchpot, Hotchpotch, hoch'pot, hoch'-poch, n. A mixture of various things shaken together in the same *pot;* a mingled mass; a mixture of ingredients. [Fr. *hochepot*—*hocher,* to shake, and *pot*, a dish.]

Hotel, hō-tel', n. A superior house for entertaining *strangers* or travellers; an inn. [Fr. *hôtel*—L. *hospes,* a guest.]

Hot-house, hot'hous, n. *A house kept warm,* to shelter tender plants and shrubs from the cold air.

Hotly, hot'li, adv. *With heat;* ardently.

Hotness, hot'nes, n. *State or quality of being hot;* violence; fury.

Hot-press, hot'pres, vt. *To press*, as paper, &c., between *hot* plates.

Hot-pressed, hot'prest, p.a. *Pressed* while *heat* is applied for the purpose of giving a smooth and glossy surface.

Hotspur, hot'spėr, n. A man violent or passionate, as if urging on his steed with *fiery spurs.*

Hot-tempered, hot'tem-pėrd, a. Of a *fiery* wrathful *temper.*

Hough, hok, n. *The heel; the ham* behind the knee-joint; the lower part of the thigh.—vt. To cut, as the sinews of the *ham;* to hamstring. [Sax. *hoh.*]

Hound, hound, n. Originally a generic name for *dogs*, now a dog employed in hunting or in the chase.—vt. To set on in chase; to hunt; to chase; to urge on (with *on* in the last meaning). [Sax. *hund.*]

Hour, our, n. *A definite space of time;* a space of time equal to one twenty-fourth part of a day, consisting of sixty minutes; time; a particular time; the time indicated by a chronometer, clock, or watch; the particular time of the day; a fixed time. [Low Sax. *hure*—L. *hora*—Gr. *hōra*, the time of day.]

Hour-glass, our'glas, n. A contrivance for measuring *hours* or intervals of time by the running of sand from one *glass* vessel to another through a small aperture.

Hourly, our'li, a. *Happening or done every hour;* often repeated; continual. adv. *Every hour;* frequently.

House, hous, n. *A covering;* a dwelling-place or abode for any of the human species; any covered building used for any purpose; a church; a monastery; a college; manner of living; the table; a race of persons from the same stock; a tribe; one of the estates of a kingdom assembled in parliament or legislature; a body of men united in their legislative capacity; the quorum of a legislative body; a commercial establishment; a household; the grave; domestic concerns; the body. [Sax. and Old G. *hūs*—L. *casa*, a hut.]

House, hous, vt. *To cover; to cover from* the inclemencies of the weather; to admit to residence; to harbour; to drive to a shelter.—vi. *To take shelter,* to keep abode; to reside. *ppr.* housing, *pret. & pp.* housed.

Housebreaker, hous'brāk-ėr, n. *One who breaks into a house* by day with a felonious intent.

Housebreaking, hous'brāk-ing, n. *The breaking* or opening and entering *of a house* by daylight, with the intent to steal.

Housed, houzd, p.a. *Put under cover;* sheltered.

Household, hous'hōld, n. *Those who keep together,* and dwell under the same *roof* and compose a family; family life. a. *Belonging to the house* and family; domestic, *(house* and *hold.)*

Householder, hous'hōld-ėr, n. *The master or chief of a household* or family; one who keeps house with his family.

Housekeeper, hous'kēp-ėr, n. *One who occupies a house* with his family; a householder; a female servant who has the chief care of the family; one who stays much at home.

Housekeeping, hous'kēp-ing, n. The family state in a dwelling; care of domestic concerns.

Houseless, hous'les, a. *Destitute of a house,* habitation, or shelter.

Housemaid, hous'mād, n. *A female servant* employed to keep a *house* clean.

House-steward, hous'stū-ėrd, n. A domestic employed in the care and management of a family.

House-surgeon, hous'sėr-jon, n. The resident *medical officer* in a hospital.

Housewife, hous'wif, n. *The mistress of a family;* a female economist; a good manager; a little case or bag for articles of female work, pronounced *huz'if.*

Housewifery, hous'wif-ri, n. *The business of the mistress of a family;* female business in the economy of a family.

Housing, houz'ing, n. *A horse-cloth; an ornamental covering* for a horse; (pl.) the trappings of a horse. [Fr. *houses.*]

Hovel, ho'vel, n. *A small house;* a mean house; an open shed for sheltering cattle, &c., from the weather.—vt. *To put in a hovel;* to shelter. [Sax. *hofel—hof,* a house.]

Hover, ho'vėr, vi. *To hang over or* about, fluttering or flapping the wings; to hang over or around, with irregular motions; to stand in suspense; to wander about from place to place in the neighbourhood. [Swed. *hæfwa.*]

How, hou, adv. *In what manner;* to what degree or extent; for what reason; from what cause; by what means; in what state. [Sax. *hu.*]

Howbeit, hou-bē'it, adv. *Be it as it may.* *(how,* be, and *it.)*

However, hou-ev'ėr, adv. *In whatever manner or degree;* at all events; at least; yet.

Howitzer, hou'its-ėr, n. A kind of mortar, mounted on a field carriage, and used for throwing shells. [G. *haubitze.*]

Howl, houl, vi. *To utter cries in distress;* to cry as a dog or wolf; to utter a particular kind of loud, protracted, and mournful sound; to wail; to roar, as a tempest.—vt. To utter with outcry. n. *A loud protracted wail;* the cry of a dog or wolf, or other like sound; the cry of a human being in horror or anguish. [D. *huilen.*]

Howlet, hou'let, n. A bird of the owl kind. [Fr. *hulotte*, the brown owl.]

Howling, houl'ing, p.a. *Filled with howls or howling beasts;* dreary.—p.n. *The act of* howling.

Howsoever, hou-sō-ev'ėr, adv. *In what manner soever;* although.

Hoxt, hoks, vt. To hough; to hamstring.

Hoy, hoi. An exclamation, of no definite meaning.

Hubbub, hub'bub, n. A great noise of many confused voices; a tumult; uproar; riot. [probably formed from the repetition of *hoop* or *whoop.*]

Huckle, huk'l, n. *A hunch; a hump;* the hip. [G. *höcker*, a knob, a hump.]

Hucklebone, huk'l-bōn, n. *The hip-bone.* [G. *höcker,* and *bein,* bone.]

Huckster, huk'stėr, n. *A retailer* of small articles, of provisions, nuts, &c.; a mean trickish fellow.—vi. To deal in small articles. [G. *höcker,* a retailer.]

Huddle, hud'l, vi. *To move in a promiscuous throng* without order; to press or hurry in disorder.—vt. *To crowd together* in confusion; to put on or perform in haste and disorder. *ppr.* huddling, *pret. & pp.* huddled.—n. A number of persons or things *crowded together* without order or regularity; tumult; confusion. [G. *hudeln,* to do a thing hastily.]

Hue, hū, n. *That which shows the form* or fashion of a body; colour; tint; dye. [Sax. *hiw—ywan,* to show.]

Hue, hū, n. *A shouting;* a clamour; an outcry; an alarm. [from Fr. *huer*, to hoot.]

Huff, huf, n. *A swell or rising of sudden* anger or arrogance; a boaster.—vt. To hector; to bully; to chide or rebuke with insolence.—vi. *To swell;* to dilate or enlarge, as bread; to swell with anger, pride, or arrogance; to storm. [Sax. *hafen*, raised—*hebban,* to raise.]

Huffiness, huf'i-nes, n. *State of being huffy;* petulance.

Huffy, huf'i, a. *Swelled with pride;* petulant; angry; being in ill humour.

Hug, hug, vt. *To press close in an embrace;* to hold fast; to treat with fondness; to congratulate (with *himself, one's self,* &c.); to keep close to;

Fāte, fär, fat, fąll; mē, met, hėr; pīne, pin; nōte, not, mōve; tūbe, tub, bull; oil, pound.

to gripe in wrestling. *ppr.* hugging, *pret. & pp.* hugged.—*n. A close embrace;* a particular gripe in wrestling. [Old G. *hazjan,* to fence around.]
Huge, hūj, *a. High,* with breadth and bulk; of great or excessive size; gigantic; prodigious. [Sax. *heag.*]
Hugely, hūj'li, *adv.* Very greatly; enormously; immensely.
Hugeness, hūj'nes, *n. State or quality of being huge;* enormous bulk or largeness.
Hulk, hulk, *n.* The body of *an old vessel* unfit for further service at sea; anything bulky or unwieldy. [D. a kind of ship.]
Hull, hul, *n. The outer covering of anything,* particularly of a nut or of grain; the frame or body of a ship or other vessel; the hulk.—*vt. To strip off or separate,* as *the hull or hulls;* to pierce, as the hull of a ship with a cannon-ball. [Sax. *hul.*]
Hum, hum, *vi.* To utter *the sound of bees;* to make an inarticulate, buzzing sound; to pause in speaking, and make an audible noise, like the humming of bees; to mumble; to drone.—*vt. To sing in a low voice;* to sing or utter inarticulately. *ppr.* humming, *pret. & pp.* hummed.—*n. The noise of bees or insects;* a low, confused noise, as of crowds; a low inarticulate sound, uttered by a speaker in a pause; an expression of applause.—*interj.* A sound with a pause, implying doubt and deliberation. [G. *hummen.*]
Human, hū'man, *a. Belonging to man or mankind;* pertaining or relating to the race of man; having the qualities of a man. [L. *humanus—homo,* a human being—Sans. *jan,* to be born.]
Humane, hū-mān', *a. Having the feelings and dispositions proper to man;* having tenderness and compassion; kind; tender; merciful; inclined to treat the lower orders of animals with tenderness. [L. *humānus.*]
Humanely, hū-mān'li, *adv. In a humane manner.*
Humanist, hū'man-ist, *n.* One who pursues the study of polite literature; one versed in the knowledge of human nature.
Humanity, hū-man'i-ti, *n. The peculiar nature of man,* by which he is distinguished from other beings; the human race; the kind feelings, dispositions, and sympathies of man, by which he is distinguished from the lower orders of animals; kindness; benevolence; acts of tenderness; philology; grammatical studies. [L. *humanitas.*]
Humanise, hū'man-iz, *vt.* To render human or *humane;* to civilise; to soften; to subdue cruel dispositions in, and render susceptible of kind feelings. *ppr.* humanising, *pret. & pp.* humanized. [L. *humaniser.*]
Humanising, hū'man-iz-ing, *p.a.* Rendering humane; softening; subduing cruel dispositions.
Human-kind, hū'man-kind, *n. The race of man;* mankind.
Humanly, hū'man-li, *adv. After the manner of men.*
Hum-bird, Humming-bird, hum'bėrd, hum'ing-bėrd, *n.* A beautiful little tropical bird named from its notes.
Humble, um'bl, *a. Near the ground;* poor; insignificant; not magnificent; lowly; submissive; not proud, arrogant, or assuming.—*vt. To bring down;* to lower; to sink; to crush; to subdue; to mortify or make ashamed; to make lowly in mind; to abase the pride of;

to make meek and submissive. *ppr.* humbling, *pret. & pp.* humbled. [Fr. —L. *humus,* the earth.]
Humbled, um'bld, *p.a. Made low;* rendered meek and submissive; penitent.
Humble-mouthed†, um'bl-mouv̄d, *a.* Mild; meek.
Humbleness, um'bl-nes, *n. State or quality of being humble;* humility.
Humbling, um'bl-ing, *p.a.* Adapted to abase pride and self-dependence.
Humbly, um'bli, *adv. In an humble manner;* with modest submissiveness; in a low state or condition.
Humdrum, hum'drum, *a.* Dull; stupid; dejected. [Icel. *humma,* to hum, and *draumr,* a dream.]
Humid, hū'mid, *a. Moist;* containing sensible moisture; somewhat wet or watery. [Fr. *Aumide*—L. *humeo,* to be moist—Gr. *huō,* to wet.]
Humidity, hū-mid'i-ti, *n. Moisture;* a moderate degree of wetness; moisture in the form of visible vapour. [Fr. *humidité.*]
Humiliate, ū-mil'i-āt, *vt. To humble;* to lower in condition; to depress; to mortify. *ppr.* humiliating, *pret. & pp.* humiliated. [L. *humilio, humiliatus— humus,* the ground.]
Humiliating, ū-mil'i-āt-ing, *p.a.* Mortifying.
Humiliation, ū-mil'i-ā''shon, *n. Act of humbling;* state of being humbled; descent from an elevated state to one that is low; the state of being reduced to lowliness of mind; depression; dejection. [Fr.]
Humility, ū-mil'i-ti, *n. Humbleness of mind;* a modest estimate of one's own worth; a deep sense of one's own unworthiness in the sight of God. [Fr. *humilité*—L. *humus,* the ground.]
Humming, hum'ing, *p.n. The sound of bees;* a low murmuring.
Humor, hū'mėr, *n. Moisture;* a moisture or fluid of the animal body, or a disease of the skin. [L. *humor—humeo,* to be moist.]
Humoral, hū'mėr-al, *a. Pertaining to or proceeding from the humors* of the body. [Fr.]
Humorous, hū'mėr-us, *a. Containing humour;* full of wild or fanciful images; adapted to excite laughter; witty; jocose; having the power to speak or write in the style of humour; exciting laughter. [Late L. *humorosus.*]
Humorously, hū'mėr-us-li, *adv. In a humorous manner.*
Humorsome, hū'mėr-sum, *a. Influenced by the humour* of the moment; odd; adapted to excite laughter.
Humour, hū'mėr, *n.* Originally *moisture;* turn of mind or peculiarity of temper, formerly fancied to depend on the *fluids* of the body; mood; caprice; that quality of the imagination which gives to ideas a fantastic turn, and tends to excite mirth; merriment; burlesque; wit; peevishness.—*vt. To gratify the humour of;* to indulge by compliance; to help on by indulgence. [Fr. *humeur*—L. *humor—humeo,* to be wet.]
Humourist, hū'mėr-ist, *n. One who gratifies his own humour;* one who has a playful fancy or genius; one who has odd conceits; a wag; a droll. [Fr. *humoriste.*]
Hump, hump, *n. Any convex elevation;* the protuberance formed by a crooked back. [D. *homp,* a lump.]
Humpback, hump'bak, *n.* A crooked back; a humpbacked person.

Humpbacked, hump'bakt, *a. Having a crooked back.*
Hunch, hunsh, *n. A hump;* a lump; a thick piece; a push or jerk with the fist or elbow.—*vt.* To punch with the fists; to push with the elbow; to push or thrust with a sudden jerk; to crook, as the back. [allied to G. *höcker,* a hump.]
Hunchback, hunsh'bak, *n. A hump-back.*
Hunchbacked, hunsh'bakt, *a.* Having a crooked back.
Hundred, hun'dred, *a.* Denoting the product of ten multiplied by ten, or the number of ten times ten.—*n.* The number 100; a division or part of a county in England, supposed to have originally contained a hundred families, or a hundred warriors, or a hundred manors. [Old G. *hundert.*]
Hundred-fold, hun'dred-fōld, *n. A hundred times as much.*
Hundredth, hun'dredth, *a. The ordinal of a hundred.*
Hundredweight, hun'dred-wāt, *n.* A weight of a *hundred* and twelve pounds avoirdupois, twenty of which make a ton.
Hunger, hung'gėr, *n. Desire of food;* an uneasy sensation occasioned by the want of food; craving appetite; a strong or eager desire.—*vi. To desire food;* to feel the pain which is occasioned by long abstinence from food; to desire with great eagerness; to long (with *after).* [Sax.—Old G. *hungar—* Sans. *kânx,* to desire.]
Hungrily, hung'gri-li, *adv.* With keen appetite; voraciously.
Hungry, hung'gri, *a. Having a desire of food;* feeling uneasiness from want of food; having an eager desire; lean; not rich or fertile; barren. [Sax. *Aungrig.*]
Hunks, hungks, *n. A sordid covetous man;* a miser. [Icel. *hunskur,* sordid.]
Hunt, hunt, *vt.* To chase, as wild animals, for the purpose of *catching* them for food, or for diversion; to go in search of, for the purpose of shooting; to follow closely; to use, as hounds in the chase.—*vi.* To seek wild animals for game, or for killing them by shooting when noxious; to seek by close pursuit.—*n.* A seeking of wild animals of any kind for game; an association of huntsmen; pursuit; search. [Sax. *Auntian,* to hunt—Old G. *Aunt,* a dog.]
Huntcounter†, hunt-koun'tėr, *n.* A dog that runs back on the scent; a blunderer.
Hunter, hunt'ėr, *n. One who hunts;* a dog that scents game, or is employed in the chase; a horse used in the chase; a kind of spider.
Hunting, hunt'ing, *p.a. Relating to hunting* or to the chase.—*p.n.* The act or practice of pursuing wild animals, for *catching* or killing them; a pursuit; a seeking.
Hunting-ground, hunt'ing-ground, *n. Ground suitable for hunting.*
Huntress, hunt'res, *n. A female that hunts* or follows the chase.
Huntsman, hunts'man, *n. One who practises hunting;* the servant whose office it is to manage the chase.
Huntsmanship, hunts'man-ship, *n. The art or practice of hunting.*
Hurdle, hėr'dl, *n. That which protects;* a texture of osiers or sticks, used for inclosures; a crate; a collection of twigs or sticks interwoven closely and sustained by long stakes, serving for protection in fortification.—*vt.* To

hedge or close with hurdles. ppr. hurdling, pret. & pp. hurdled. [Sax. *hyrdel*—Goth. *hairda*, to guard.]

Hurdy-gurdy, hêr'di-gêr-di,n. A stringed instrument of music, whose sounds are produced by the friction of a wheel, and regulated by the fingers.

Hurl, hêrl, *vt.* To send whirling through the air; to throw with violence; to drive with great force.—*n.* Act of throwing with violence; tumult; riot; commotion. [from *whirl.*]

Hurly-burly, hêr'li-bêr'li, *n.* Tumult; bustle; confusion. [Fr. *hurluberlu.*]

Hurra, Hurrah, hụ-rä'. An exclamation of joy or surprise, equivalent to huzza.

Hurricane, hu´ri-kán, *n.* A violent storm, distinguished by the vehemence of the wind, and its sudden changes. [Sp. *huracán*—L. *aura*, a gentle breeze.]

Hurried, hu´rid, *p.a.* Hastened; impelled to rapid motion or vigorous action.

Hurriedly, hu´rid-li, *adv.* In a hurried manner.

Hurry, hu´ri, *vt.* To urge so as to cause to shake; to drive or press forward with more rapidity; to urge to act with more celerity; to quicken; to drive or impel with violence; to urge with precipitation and confusion.—*vi.* To move or act with haste; to hasten; to proceed with precipitation. ppr. hurrying, pret. & pp. hurried.—*n.* A putting into trepidation or confusion; haste; urgency to haste; bustle; commotion. [Sax. *Areran*, to agitate.]

Hurrying, hu´ri-ing, *p.n.* The urging to greater speed; rapidity of motion.

Hurt, hêrt, *n.* A wound; a bruise; injury; harm; loss; whatever injures or harms.—*vt.* To cause physical pain to; to bruise; to injure or impair the sound state of, as of the body, by incision or fracture; to harm; to impair the strength, purity, or beauty of; to injure; to give pain to; to wound the feelings of. ppr. hurting, pret. & pp. hurt. [Sax. *hyrt*, wounded, *hyrwian*, to wound.]

Hurtful, hêrt'fụl, *a.* Causing hurt; tending to impair or destroy; detrimental; mischievous; injurious.

Hurtfully, hêrt'fụl-li, *adv.* Injuriously.

Hurtle, hêr'tl, *vi.* To make a clashing sound.

Husband, huz'band, *n.* He who binds a family together; the correlative of wife; a good manager.—*vt.* To manage with frugality; to use with economy; to supply with a husband. [Sax. *husbonda*—*hus*, a house, and *bindan*, to bind.]

Husbandman, huz'band-man, *n.* A tiller of the ground; one who labours in tillage.

Husbandry, huz'band-ri, *n.* The business of a husbandman; farming; care of domestic affairs; frugality; thrift (usually with *good*).

Hush, hush, *a.* Silent; still; quiet.—*n.* Stillness; quiet.—*vt.* To still; to make quiet; to repress, as noise; to allay. *vi.* To be still; to be silent. Imperative of the verb, used as an exclamation, be still! [G. *husch.*]

Husk, husk, *n.* The external covering of certain fruits or seeds of plants.—*vt.* To strip of, as the external covering of the fruits or seeds of plants. [It. *guscio.*]

Huskily, husk'i-li, *adv.* In a husky manner; dryly; roughly.

Huskiness, husk'i-nes, *n.* State of being dry and rough, like a *husk;* roughness of sound, or of the voice.

Husky, husk'i, *a.* Abounding with husks;

consisting of husks; resembling husks; dry; rough; rough, as sound; harsh.

Hussar, huz-zär', *n.* Originally, a Hungarian *light-armed horse-soldier;* now a light-armed horse-soldier in all the armies of Europe. [Magyar, *huszar.*]

Hustings, hus'tingz, *n. pl.* A house or place of causes; the place or platform where an election of a member of parliament is held. [Sax. *hustinge—hus,* a house, and *thing,* a cause.]

Hustle, hus'l, *vt.* To shake or shuffle together in confusion; to push or crowd; to handle roughly. ppr. hustling, pret. & pp. hustled. [D. *hutselen,* to shake.]

Huswife, hus'wif, *n.* A worthless woman.

Hut, hut, *n.* A cover; a small house, hovel, or cabin; a temporary building to lodge soldiers.—*vt.* To place in huts, as troops encamped in winter-quarters.—*vi.* To take lodgings in huts. ppr. hutting, pret. & pp. hutted. [G. *hütte.*]

Hutch, huch, *n.* A chest or box; a corn chest or bin; a box for rabbits.—*vt.* To hoard or lay up. [Sax. *hwacca.*]

Huzza, hụz-zā', *n.* A shout of joy.—*vi.* To utter a loud shout of joy.—*vt.* To receive with shouts of joy.—*interj.* Hurrah! [most probably a different form of *hurrah.*]

Huzzaing, hụz-zā'ing, *p.n.* A shouting with joy; a receiving with shouts of joy.

Hyacinth, hi'a-sinth, *n.* A well-known beautiful bulbous plant, differing from the hyacinth of the Greeks and Romans; a mineral; a red variety of zircon, sometimes used as a gem. [L. *hyacinthus.*]

Hyacinthine, hī-a-sinth'in, *a.* Made of hyacinth; consisting of hyacinth; resembling hyacinth. (Gr. *huakinthinos.*)

Hybrid, hib'rid, *n.* That which is insulting to nature; mongrel; a mule; an animal or plant produced from the mixture of two species.—*a.* Mongrel; produced from the mixture of two species. [L. *hybrida*—Gr. *hubris,* an insult.]

Hydra, hī'dra, *n.* A water serpent; a fabulous serpent or monster, represented as having many heads; any manifold evil. [L.—Gr. *hudōr,* water.]

Hydraulic, hī-dral'ik, *a.* Pertaining to water or fluids in motion through pipes, channels, &c.; pertaining to the science of hydraulics. [L. *hydraulicus*—Gr. *hudōr,* water, and *aulē,* a pipe.]

Hydraulics, hī-dral'iks, *n.* The science of fluids in motion.

Hydrodynamic, hī'drō-di-nam''ik, *a.* Pertaining to the *force* or pressure *of water.* [Gr. *hudōr,* water, and *dunamai,* to be able, powerful.]

Hydrodynamics, hī'drō-di-nam''iks, *n.* The dynamics of water or of fluids that are not elastic.

Hydrogen, hī'drō-jen, *n.* The gaseous substance which, along with oxygen, generates water. [Fr. *hydrogène*—Gr. *hudōr,* water, and *gennaō,* to generate.]

Hydrogenous, hī-dro'jen-us, *a.* Pertaining to hydrogen.

Hydrographer, hī-drog'ra-tér, *n.* One who describes the sea or other waters; one who draws maps of the sea, lakes, or other waters. [Fr. *hydrographe.*]

Hydrographic, hī-drō-graf'ik, *a.* Relating to hydrography, or to the description of the sea, sea-coast, isles, shoals, depth of water, &c., or of a lake. [Fr. *hydrographique.*]

Hydrography, hī-drog'ra-fi, *n.* The art of measuring and describing the sea,

lakes, rivers, and other waters; the art of forming charts of the sea, &c. [Gr. *hudōr,* water, and *graphō,* to describe.]

Hydrometer, hī-drom'et-ér, *n.* An instrument for measuring the specific gravities of liquids, and thence the strength of spirituous liquors. [Fr. *hydromètre*—Gr. *hudōr,* water, and *metron,* measure.]

Hydrometric, hī-drō-met'rik, *a.* Pertaining to a hydrometer.

Hydropathic, hī-drō-path'ik, *a.* Pertaining to hydropathy.

Hydropathically, hī-drō-path'ik-al-li, *adv.* In a hydropathic manner.

Hydropathist, hī-dro'pa-thist, *n.* One who practises hydropathy.

Hydropathy, hī-dro'pa-thi, *n.* A mode of treating diseases by the copious and frequent use of pure water, both internally and externally. [Gr. *hudōr,* water, and *pathos,* affection—*paschō, pathein,* to suffer.]

Hydrophobia, hī-drō-fō'bi-a, *n.* A preternatural dread of water; a symptom of canine madness, or the disease itself, which is thus denominated. [Gr. *hudōr,* water, and *phobos,* fear.]

Hydrostatic, hī-drō-stat'ik, *a.* Relating to water or non-elastic fluids in a state of rest; relating to hydrostatics. [Gr. *hudōr,* water, and *statikos*—*staō,* to make to stand.]

Hydrostatically, hī-drō-stat'ik-al-li, *adv.* According to hydrostatics.

Hydrostatics, hī-drō-stat'iks, *n.* The science which treats of the weight and equilibrium of fluids, particularly water, when in a state of rest.

Hyems, hī'emz, *n.* Winter. [L.]

Hyena, hī-ē'na, *n.* A fierce animal of the dog or wolf kind, which feeds on flesh. [L. *hyaena.*]

Hygeian, hī-jē'an, *a.* Relating to health, or to the art or science of preserving health. [Gr. *hugieia,* health—*hugiēs,* healthy.]

Hygrometer, hī-grom'et-ér, *n.* An instrument for measuring the moisture of the atmosphere. [Fr. *hygromètre*—Gr. *hugros,* moist, and *metron,* measure.]

Hygrometric, hī-grō-met'rik, *a.* Pertaining to hygrometry; made by or according to the hygrometer.

Hygroscope, hī'grō-skōp, *n.* An instrument for indicating the presence of moisture in the atmosphere without measuring the amount. [Gr. *hugros,* moist, and *skopeō,* to view.]

Hymen, hī'men, *n.* A fabulous deity, supposed to preside over marriages. [L.—Gr. *Humēn.*]

Hymeneal, Hymenean, hī-men-ē'al, hī-men-e'an, *a.* Pertaining to marriage. *n.* A marriage song.

Hymn, him, *n.* A song of praise among pagans, addressed to some deity; a song or ode in honour of God.—*vt.* To praise in song; to sing; to celebrate in song.—*vi.* To sing in praise or adoration. [L. *hymnus*—Gr. *humnos.*]

Hymning, him'ing, *p.n.* The singing of hymns.

Hyperbola, hi-pér'bō-la, *n.* A throwing over or beyond; a curve formed by a section of a cone, when the cutting plane makes a greater angle with the base than the side of the cone makes. [Fr. *hyperbole*—Gr. *huper,* and *ballō,* to throw.]

Hyperbole, hi-pér'bō-le, *n.* A throwing over or beyond; exaggeration; a figure of speech which goes beyond the truth, or which expresses much more or less than the truth. [Fr.—Gr.]

Fāte, fär, fat, fạll; mē, met, hėr; pīne, pin; nōte, not, mūve; tūbe, tub, bụll; oil, pound.

Hyperbolic,Hyperbolical, hi-pėr-bol'ik, hi-pėr-bol'ik-al, a. *Belonging to the hyperbola; containing hyperbole*; exceeding the truth. [Gr. *hyperbolikos*.]
Hyperbolically, hi-pėr-bol'ik-al-li, *adv*. *In the form of a hyperbola; with exaggeration*.
Hyperbolism, hi-pėr'bol-izm, n. *The use of hyperbole*. [Fr. *hyperbolisme*.]
Hyperborean, hi-pėr-bō'rē-an, a. *Beyond Boreas*, or the north; being in the extreme north; northern; very cold; frigid.—n. *An inhabitant of the most northern region of the earth*. [Gr. *hyperboreos—boreas*, the north.]
Hypercritic, hi-pėr-krit'ik, n. *One who is critical beyond measure*; an overrigid critic; a captious censor. [Fr. *hypercritique*.]
Hypercritical, hi-pėr-krit'ik-al, a. *Overcritical*; excessively nice or exact.
Hypercritically, hi-pėr-krit'ik-al-li, *adv*. *In a hypercritical manner*.
Hypercriticism, hi-pėr-krit'i-sizm, n. *Excessive rigour or nicety of criticism*.
Hyperion, hi-pē'ri-on, n. *Apollo*, the god of day, who was distinguished for his beauty. [L.]
Hyphen, hī'fen, n. A character, thus (-), implying that two words or syllables are to be *connected*. [Gr.—*hupo*, under, and *hen*, one.]
Hypochondria, hi-pō-kon'dri-a, n. The sides of the belly under the *cartilages*;

a mental disorder arising commonly from digestive derangement, and consisting in gloomy ideas of life, dejection of spirits, and indisposition to activity. [Gr.—*hupo*, under, and *chondros*, a cartilage.]
Hypochondriac, hi-pō-kon'dri-ak, a. *Pertaining to*, or affected by, *hypochondria*.—n. A person affected with *hypochondria*. (Gr. *hypochondriakos*.]
Hypocrisy, hi-pok'ri-si, n. *A playing a part* in a figurative sense; a feigning to be what one is not; simulation; a counterfeiting of religion; false pretence. [Fr. *hypocrisie*.]
Hypocrite, hi'pō-krit, n. *One who plays a part*; one who feigns to be what he is not; one who assumes an appearance of piety and virtue when he is destitute of true religion; one who assumes a false appearance; a dissembler. [Fr.—Gr. *hupokrités*, one who plays a part on the stage.]
Hypocritical, hi-pō-krit'ik-al, a. *Simulating*; counterfeiting a religious character; dissembling; concealing one's real character or motives; proceeding from or marking *hypocrisy*. [Gr. *hupokritikos—krités*, an interpreter.]
Hypocritically, hi-pō-krit'ik-al-li, *adv*. *With simulation*; without sincerity.
Hypotenuse, hi-pot'ē-nūs, n. *That which stretches or extends under or below*; the side of a right-angled triangle opposite

to the right angle. [Fr. *hypoténuse*—Gr. *hupo*, and *teinō*, to stretch.]
Hypothenuse, hi-poth'ē-nūs, n. *See* HYPOTENUSE.
Hypothesis, hi-poth'ē-sis, n. *A placing under; that which is placed under*; groundwork; foundation of an argument; a supposition; something not proved, but assumed for the purpose of argument; a system or theory assumed to account for what is not understood. [Gr. *thesis*, a placing—*tithēmi*, to place.]
Hypothetical, hi-po-thet'ik-al, a. *Relating to an hypothesis*; conditional; assumed without proof, for the purpose of reasoning and deducing proof. [Fr. *hypothétique*.]
Hypothetically, hi-po-thet'ik-al-li, *adv*. *By way of supposition*.
Hyssop, his'sop, n. *An aromatic plant* possessing stimulating, stomachic, and carminative properties. [L.*hyssopum*.]
Hysteric, Hysterical, his-te'rik, his-te'rik-al, a. Disordered in the region of the *womb*; troubled with fits or nervous affections; spasmodic; convulsive. [Fr. *hystérique*—Gr. *hustéra*, the womb.]
Hysterically, his-te'rik-al-li, *adv*. *In a hysteric manner*; spasmodically.
Hysterics, his-te'riks, n. A disease characterized by convulsive struggling, sense of suffocation, drowsiness, and fickleness of temper.

I.

I, i, *pron*. The pronoun of the first person in the nominative case; the word which expresses one's self, or that by which a speaker or writer denotes himself. [Sax. *ic*, G. *ich*.]
Iambic, i-am'bik, a. *Pertaining to the iambus*. [Gr. *iambikos*.]
Iambic, Iambus, i-am'bik, i-am'bus, n. A poetic foot consisting of two syllables, the first short and the last long, as in *ămēns*. [Gr. *iambos—iaptō*, to assail—iambic verse having been first used in *satire*.]
Ibis, i'bis, n. A wading bird with long legs and an arched bill, in its general conformation and habits closely approaching the stork. Divine honours were paid to it in Egypt. [Gr. and L.]
Ice, is, n. Water or other fluid congealed, or in a solid state; concreted sugar; ice-cream.—*vt*. *To cover with ice*; to convert into ice; to cover with concreted sugar; to chill; to freeze. *ppr*. icing, *pret*. & *pp*. iced. [Sax. *is*—G. *eis*.]
Iceberg, is'bėrg, n. *A hill or mountain of ice*, or a vast body of floating ice. [*ice*, and G. *berg*, a mountain.]
Ice-bound, is'bound, a. Totally surrounded with ice, so as to be incapable of advancing, as a ship.
Ice-cream, Iced-cream, is'krēm, ist'-krēm, n. *A confection formed of cream*, sugar, &c., congealed or frozen.
Iced, ist, *p.a*. *Chilled* with ice; covered with concreted sugar.
Ice-house, is'hous, n. *A repository for the preservation of ice during warm weather*.
Icelandic, is-land'ik, a. *Pertaining to*

Iceland.—n. *The language of the Icelanders*.
Iceland-moss, is'land-mos, n. A kind of lichen, used both as a tonic and for its nutritive properties.
Ice-plant, is'plant, n. *A plant whose leaves appear as if covered with frost*.
Ichneumon, ik-nū'mon, n. *The tracker*; an Egyptian animal of the weasel kind, which *hunts out* crocodiles' eggs. [Gr. —*ichneuō*, to trace.]
Ichor, i'kōr, n. In mythology, the ethereal juice that flowed in the veins of the gods; a thin, watery humour, like whey; colourless matter flowing from an ulcer. [Gr. *ichōr*.]
Ichorous, i-kōr'us, a. *Like ichor*; thin; watery; serous.
Ichthyological, ik'thi-o-loj''ik-al, a. *Pertaining to ichthyology*.
Ichthyologist, ik-thi-ol'o-jist, n. *One versed in ichthyology*.
Ichthyology, ik-thi-ol'o-ji, n. That branch of zoology which *treats of fishes*. [Gr. *ichthus*, a fish, and *logos*, discourse.]
Icicle, is'i-kl, n. *An ice-drop*, or a pendent, *conical mass of ice*, formed by the freezing of water, as it flows down an inclined plane, or falls in drops. [Sax. *ises-gicel—cel*, what is congealed.]
Iciness, is'i-nes, n. *State of being icy*, or of generating ice.
Icing, is'ing, *p.n*. *A covering of concreted sugar*.
Icy, is'i, a. *Abounding with ice*; cold; frosty; made of ice; resembling ice; frigid; destitute of affection or passion.
Idea, i-dē'a, n. *That which is seen* by the mind's eye; an image in the mind;

that which is comprehended by the understanding; object of thought; notion; conception; thought; opinion. [Gr.—*eidō*, to see.]
Ideal, i-dē'al, a. *Existing in idea*; mental; existing in fancy or imagination only; visionary; imaginary; belonging or relating to ideas generally. n. An imaginary model of perfection, considering ideas as images or forms in the mind. [Fr. *idéal*.]
Idealism, i-dē'al-izm, n. *The system that makes everything to consist in ideas*, and denies the existence of material bodies. [Fr. *idéalisme*.]
Idealist, i-dē'al-ist, n. *One who holds the doctrine of idealism*.
Ideality, i-dē-al'i-ti, n. *Quality of being ideal*.
Idealize, i-dē'al-iz, *vt*. *To make ideal*; to give an ideal form or value to. *ppr*. idealizing, *pret*. & *pp*. idealized.
Ideally, i-dē'al-li, *adv*. *In idea*; intellectually; mentally.
Identical, i-den'tik-al, a. *The same*; not different; uttering the same truth. [Fr. *identique*—L. *idem*, the same.]
Identically, i-den'tik-al-li, *adv*. *With sameness*.
Identifiable, i-den'ti-fi-a-bl, a. *That may be identified*.
Identification, i-den'ti-fi-kā''shon, n. *Act of identifying*, or of making or proving to be the same.
Identify, i-den'ti-fi, *vt*. *To make to be the same*; to treat as having the same use; to consider as the same in effect; to ascertain or prove to be the same. *vi*. To become the same; to coalesce in interest, purpose, use, effect, &c. *ppr*.

ch, *chain*; j, *job*; g, *go*; ng, *sing*; ᴛʜ, *then*; th, *thin*; w, *wig*; wh, *whig*; zh, *azure*; † obsolete.

identifying, *pret. & pp.* identified. [Fr. *identifier*—L. *idem*, the same, and *facio*, to make.]
Identity, i-den'ti-ti, *n.* Sameness, as distinguished from similitude and diversity; the sameness of a substance or being, under every possible variety of circumstances. [Fr. *identité*.]
Ideology, i-dē-ol'o-ji, *n.* A treatise on ideas, or the doctrine of ideas; the science of mind. [Fr. *idéologie*—Gr. *idea*, and *logos*, discourse.]
Ides, īdz, *n. pl.* In the ancient Roman calendar, the *divided* or half-month; the 15th day of March, May, July, and October, and the 13th day of the other months. [L. *idus*—Etruscan, *iduo*, to divide.]
Idiocy, i'di-ō-si, *n.* State of an idiot; a defect or want of understanding. [Gr. *idiōteia*, uncouthness.]
Idiom, i'di-om, *n.* A mode of expression *peculiar* to a language; the genius or peculiar cast of a language; dialect. [Gr. *idiōma*—*idios*, peculiar to one's self.]
Idiomatic, i'di-om-at''ik, *a.* Peculiar to a language; pertaining to the particular genius or modes of expression which belong to a language. [Gr. *idiōmatikos*.]
Idiomatically, i'di-om-at''ik-al-li, *adv.* According to the idiom of a language.
Idiopathic, i'di-o-path''ik, *a.* Pertaining to *idiopathy*.
Idiopathically, i'di-o-path''ik-al-li, *adv.* In the manner of an *idiopathic* disease.
Idiopathy, i-di-op'a-thi, *n.* A peculiar *affection;* a morbid state or condition not produced by any preceding disease. [Fr. *idiopathie*—Gr. *idios*, peculiar to one's self, and *pathos*, affection.]
Idiosyncrasy, i'di-o-sin''kra-si, *n.* Peculiarity of temperament; that constitution of body or mind which is peculiar to an individual. [Fr. *idiosyncrasie*—Gr. *idios*, peculiar, *sun*, with, and *krasis*, a mixing.]
Idiosyncratic, i'di-o-sin-krat''ik, *a.* Of peculiar temper or disposition.
Idiot, i'di-ot, *n.* Originally, *a common person;* one void of understanding; a natural fool; a foolish person. [Gr. *idiōtēs*—*idios*, one's own.]
Idiotic, Idiotical, i-di-ot'ik, i-di-ot'ik-al, *a.* Relating to or like an idiot; foolish; sottish. [Gr. *idiōtikos*.]
Idiotically, i-di-ot'ik-al-li, *adv.* After the manner of an idiot.
Idle, i'dl, *a.* Languishing; leaving off work; unemployed; doing nothing; given to rest and ease; sluggish; useless; futile; of no importance; barren; trifling; frivolous or vain; unprofitable.—*vi.* To be idle; to lose or spend time in inaction; to idle away, to spend in idleness. *ppr.* idling, *pret. & pp.* idled. [Sax. *idel*, vain, useless—*adlian*, to languish.]
Idleness, i'dl-nes, *n.* State or quality of being idle; abstinence from labour; inaction; sloth; aversion to labour; unimportance; uselessness.
Idler, i'dl-ėr, *n.* One who idles; one who does nothing; a lazy person; a sluggard.
Idly, i'dl-i, *adv.* In an idle manner.
Idol, i'dol, *n.* An image or representation, usually of a man or other animal, consecrated as an object of worship; a pagan deity; a person loved to adoration; anything on which we set our affections inordinately; a phantom. [Fr. *idole*—Gr. *eidō*, to see.]
Idolater, i-dol'āt-ėr, *n.* A worshipper of idols; one who worships as a deity

that which is not God; a pagan; a great admirer. [Fr. *idolâtre*.]
Idolatress, i-dol'āt-res, *n.* A *female worshipper of idols.*
Idolatrous, i-dol'āt-rus, *a.* Pertaining to *idolatry;* partaking of the nature of idolatry; consisting in or partaking of an excessive attachment.
Idolatrously, i-dol'āt-rus-li, *adv.* In an *idolatrous manner.*
Idolatry, i-dol'āt-ri, *n.* The worship of idols; excessive attachment to or veneration for any person or thing. [Fr. *idolâtrie*—Gr. *eidōlon*, idol, and *latreuō*, to serve.]
Idolize, i'dol-īz, *vt.* To worship as an idol; to love to excess; to love or reverence to adoration. *ppr.* idolizing, *pret. & pp.* idolized.
Idyl, i'dil, *n.* A short highly wrought descriptive poem; properly, a short pastoral poem. [L. *idyllium*—Gr. *eidos*, form.]
Idyllic, i-dil'ik, *a.* Pastoral.
If, if, *conj.* It being so as; supposing that; allowing that; on condition that. [Old G. *ibu*, if.]
Igneous, ig'nē-us, *a.* Pertaining to or consisting of *fire;* having the nature of fire; resembling fire; proceeding from the action of fire. [L. *igneus*—*ignis*, fire.]
Ignescent, ig-nes'sent, *a.* Emitting sparks of *fire* when struck with steel; scintillating. [L. *ignescens*—*ignis*, fire.]
Ignite, ig-nīt', *vt.* To set on *fire;* to communicate fire to.—*vi.* To take *fire;* to become red with heat. *ppr.* igniting, *pret. & pp.* ignited. [Late L. *ignio*, *ignitus*—L. *ignis*, fire.]
Ignited, ig-nīt'ed, *p.a.* Set on *fire;* rendered red by heat or fire.
Ignition, ig-ni'shon, *n.* Act of *setting on fire;* act or operation of communicating fire or heat; state of being heated to redness or luminousness. [Fr.]
Ignoble, ig-nō'bl, *a.* Not *noble;* of low birth or family; degraded; mean; base; dishonourable. [Fr.—L. *in*, and *nobilis*—*nosco*, to know.]
Ignobly, ig-nō'bli, *adv.* In an *ignoble manner;* meanly; dishonourably.
Ignominious, ig-nō-mi'ni-us, *a.* Without *name;* of mean character; very shameful; reproachful; infamous; worthy of contempt. [L. *ignominiosus*—*in*, and *nomen*, a name.]
Ignominiously, ig-nō-mi'ni-us-li, *adv.* Meanly; disgracefully; shamefully.
Ignominy, ig'nō-mi-ni, *n.* Loss or want of *name or reputation;* infamy; disgrace; dishonour; opprobrium; shame; contempt. [L. *ignominia*—*nomen*, a name.]
Ignoramus, ig-nō-rā'mus, *n.* The indorsement of a grand-jury on a bill presented for inquiry, when there is no evidence to sustain the charge; one who knows nothing; a vain pretender to knowledge. [L. we are ignorant, from *ignōro*, not to know.]
Ignorance, ig'nō-rans, *n.* State of being *ignorant;* state of being illiterate, uninformed, or uneducated. [Fr.]
Ignorant, ig'nō-rant, *a.* Not *knowing;* destitute of knowledge; untaught; unskilled; unacquainted with; unknown; displaying ignorance. [Fr.—L. *in*, and *gnarus*, knowing.]
Ignorantly, ig'nō-rant-li, *adv.* Without *knowledge;* inexpertly.
Ignore, ig-nōr', *vt.* Not to *know;* to pass over or overlook, as if ignorant of; to shut the eyes to. *ppr.* ignoring, *pret. & pp.* ignored. [L. *ignōro*—*nosco*, Sans. *jnā*, to know.]

Iliac, il'i-ak, *a.* Pertaining to the lower bowels. [from L. *ilia*, the flank, the small intestines.]
Iliad, il'i-ad, *n.* An epic poem, by Homer, on the destruction of *Ilium*, or Troy. [Gr. *Ilias*, *Iliados*.]
Ill, il, *a.* Bad or evil, in a general sense; contrary to good; wicked; unfortunate; surly; disordered; impaired; ugly; suspicious; rude; unpolished, as manners. *n.* Evil; misfortune; disease; pain; whatever annoys or impairs happiness.—*adv.* Not well; badly; not easily. [probably contracted from *evil*.]
Illapse, il-laps', *vi.* To fall, pass, or *glide into.* *ppr.* illapsing, *pret. & pp.* illapsed.—*n.* A sliding into; an entrance of one thing into another; a sudden entrance. [L. *illabor*, *illapsus*—*labor*, to glide.]
Illation, il-lā'shon, *n.* A bringing in; an inference from premises; a deduction. [L. *illatio*—*fero*, *latus*, to bring.]
Illative, il-lā'tiv, *a.* Relating to *illation;* that denotes an inference.
Ill-blood, il'blud, *n.* Bad feeling.
Ill-bred, il-bred', *a.* Not well bred.
Ill-breeding, il-brēd'ing, *n.* Want of good breeding; unpoliteness; rudeness.
Illegal, il-lē'gal, *a.* Not legal; contrary to law; contraband.
Illegality, il-lē-gal'i-ti, *n.* State or quality of being illegal; unlawfulness.
Illegally, il-lē'gal-li, *adv.* In an illegal or unlawful manner; unlawfully.
Illegibility, il-le'ji-bil''li-ti, *n.* Quality of being illegible.
Illegible, il-le'ji-bl, *a.* Not legible; that cannot be read.
Illegibly, il-le'ji-bli, *adv.* In a manner not to be read.
Illegitimacy, il-lē-jit'i-ma-si, *n.* State of being illegitimate; state of being not genuine.
Illegitimate, il-lē-jit'i-māt, *a.* Not legitimate; contrary to law; born out of wedlock; illogical; not authorized by good usage, as a word or phrase.—*vt.* To render or prove illegitimate. *ppr.* illegitimating, *pret. & pp.* illegitimated.
Illegitimately, il-lē-jit'i-māt-li, *adv.* Not legitimately.
Ill-favoured, il'fā-vėrd, *a.* Ill-looking; ugly; deformed.
Illiberal, il-lib'ėr-al, *a.* Not liberal; ignoble; not free or generous; cold in charity; not candid; not munificent.
Illiberality, il-lib'ėr-al''i-ti, *n.* Quality of being illiberal; narrowness of mind; want of catholic opinion; parsimony.
Illicit, il-lis'it, *a.* Not permitted; unlawful; lawless. [L. *illicitus*—*licet*, it is allowable.]
Illimitable, il-lim'it-a-bl, *a.* That cannot be limited; boundless; unlimited; infinite; vast.
Illimitably, il-lim'it-a-bli, *adv.* Without limits.
Ill-informed, il-in'formd, *a.* Not well informed; ignorant.
Illiteracy, il-lit'ėr-a-si, *n.* State of being *illiterate*, untaught, or unlearned; want of a knowledge of letters; ignorance.
Illiterate, il-lit'ėr-at, *a.* Unlettered; untaught; uninstructed in science.
Illiterately, il-lit'ėr-at-li, *adv.* In an *illiterate manner.*
Ill-mannered, il-man'ėrd, *a.* Having bad manners; rude; boorish; unpolite.
Ill-nature, il'nā-tūr, *n.* Evil nature; crabbedness; habitual bad temper; fractiousness.
Ill-natured, il'nā-tūrd, *a.* Evil or bad tempered; crabbed; of habitual bad

Fāte, fär, fat, fall; mē, met, hėr; pīne, pin; nōte, not, mōve; tūbe, tub, bull; oil, pound.

temper; peevish; that indicates ill-nature.
Illness, il'nes, *n. State or quality of being ill;* indisposition; malady; sickness; wickedness.
Illogical, il-lo'jik-al, *a. Not logical;* contrary to, or ignorant of, the rules of logic; ignorant.
Illogically, il-lo'jik-al-li, *adv.* In a manner contrary to the rules of logic.
Ill-omened, il'o-mend, *a.* Having bad or unlucky omens.
Ill-starred, il'stärd, *a.* Influenced by unlucky stars; fated to be unfortunate.
Ill-suppressed, il'sup-prest, *a. Not fully suppressed.*
Ill-tempered, il'tem-pėrd, *a. Of bad temper;* morose; crabbed; sour.
Ill-timed, il-timd', *a. Done or said at an unsuitable time.*
Illume, il-lūm', *vt. To throw light on;* to make light or bright; to enlighten, as the mind; to adorn. *ppr.* illuming, *pret. & pp.* illumed. [L. *lumen,* light.]
Illuminate, il-lūm'in-āt, *vt. To light up;* to throw light on; to adorn with festal lamps or bonfires; to enlighten intellectually; to adorn with pictures, &c., as manuscripts; to illustrate. *ppr.* illuminating, *pret. & pp.* illuminated. [L. *illumino, illuminatus—lumen,* light—*luceo,* to shine.]
Illuminated, il-lūm'in-āt-ed, *p.a.* Adorned with ornamented letters and pictures.
Illuminating, il-lūm'in-āt-ing, *p.n.* The art of adorning manuscripts and books with ornamented letters and paintings.
Illumination, il-lūm'in-ā"shon, *n. Act of illuminating* a house or city by artificial lights, or the state of being thus rendered light; that which gives light; brightness; infusion of intellectual light; inspiration; the act, art, or practice of adorning manuscripts and books with ornamented letters and pictures. [L. *lumen,* light.]
Illuminative, il-lūm'in-āt-iv, *a. Having the power of illuminating* or giving light. [Fr. *illuminatif.*]
Illuminator, il-lūm'in-āt-ėr, *n. He or that which gives light;* one who decorates manuscripts and books with ornamented letters, &c. [Low L.]
Illumine, il-lūm'in, *vt. To illume;* to illuminate; to adorn. *ppr.* illumining, *pret. & pp.* illumined.
Illusion, il-lū'zhon, *n. Mockery;* deceptive appearance; false show; fallacy; hallucination. [Fr.—L. *ludo,* to play.]
Illusive, il-lū'siv, *a. Deceiving* by false show; deceitful.
Illusory, il-lū'sō-ri, *a. Deceiving* by false appearances; fallacious. [Fr. *illusoire*—L. *ludo, lusum,* to make game of.]
Illustrate, il-lus'trāt, *vt. To make clear or luminous;* to make glorious; to explain; to make clear or obvious; to explain and adorn by means of pictures, drawings, &c.; to glorify.—*a.t* Distinguished. *ppr.* illustrating, *pret. & pp.* illustrated. [L. *illustro, illustratus—luceo,* to shine.]
Illustrated, il-lus'trāt-ed, *p. a.* Explained by means of pictures, &c.
Illustration, il-lus-trā'shon, *n.* Act of *illustrating;* elucidation; an illustrative engraving. [L. *illustratio.*]
Illustrative, il-lus'trāt-iv, *a. Tending, or intended, to illustrate.*
Illustrater, il-lus'trāt-ėr, *n. One who illustrates* or makes clear. [Low L.]
Illustrious, il-lus'tri-us, *a. Possessing lustre;* renowned; celebrated; noble; conferring honour or renown; glorious;

a title of honour. [L. *illustris—luceo,* to shine.]
Illustriously, il-lus'tri-us-li, *adv.* Conspicuously; nobly; eminently.
Ill-will, il'wil, *n. Unkind or hostile feeling;* hatred; malevolence.
Ill-wisher, il'wish-ėr, *n. One who wishes evil;* an enemy.
Image, im'āj, *n. A likeness;* a representation of any person or thing formed of a material substance; a statue; an idol; a resemblance painted; an idea; a conception; a picture drawn by fancy; the appearance or picture of any object formed by the reflection or refraction of the rays of light.—*vt. To form an image of;* to form a likeness of in the mind. *ppr.* imaging, *pret. & pp.* imaged. [Fr.—L. *imago—imitor,* to pourtray.]
Imagery, im'āj-e-ri, *n.* Sensible likenesses, as pictures or statues; forms of the fancy; imaginary phantasms; lively descriptions in writing or speaking; figures in discourse.
Imaginable, im-aj'in-a-bl, *a. That may or can be imagined.*
Imaginary, im-aj'in-a-ri, *a.* Existing only in *imagination* or fancy; ideal; visionary. [Fr. *imaginaire*—L. *imago,* an image.]
Imagination, im-aj'in-ā"shon, *n. A mental image;* idea; conception; that faculty of the mind which forms new combinations of ideas; scheme formed in the mind; conceit; an unsolid opinion. [Fr.]
Imaginative, im-aj'in-āt-iv, *a. That forms imaginations;* full of imaginations; fantastic. [Fr. *imaginatif.*]
Imagine, im-aj'in, *vt. To picture to one's self;* to fancy; to contrive in purpose; to think; to deem.—*vi.* To conceive; to have a notion or idea. *ppr.* imagining. *pret. & pp.* imagined. [Fr. *imaginer*—L. *imago,* an image.]
Imagined, im-aj'ind, *p.a.* Formed in the mind; fancied; contrived.
Imagining, im-aj'in-ing, *p.n.* Act of forming images; imagination.
Imbare, im-bār', *vt. To lay bare;* to expose.
Imbecile, im'be-sēl, *a. Without stay or support;* weak; impotent; destitute of strength, either of body or of mind. *n.* One destitute of strength, either of body or mind. [Fr. *imbécile*—L. *in,* and *bacillum,* a small staff.]
Imbecility, im-bē-sil'i-ti, *n. State of being imbecile;* feebleness of body or mind. [Fr. *imbécillité.*]
Imbed, im-bed', *vt. To lay in a bed;* to place in a mass of earth, sand, or other substance. *ppr.* imbedding, *pret. & pp.* imbedded. (in and *bed.*]
Imbibe, im-bīb', *vt. To drink in;* to receive or admit into the mind, and retain. *ppr.* imbibing. *pret. & pp.* imbibed. [L. *imbibo—bibo,* to drink.]
Imbibing, im-bīb'ing, *p. n.* The act of drinking in or absorbing.
Imbitter, im-bit'tėr, *vt. To make bitter;* to make unhappy; to render distressing ; to exasperate ; to make more severe, poignant, or malignant.
Imbosom, im-bö'zum, *vt. To hold in the bosom;* to hold in nearness or intimacy; to caress; to admit to the heart; to surround; to cover.
Imbosomed, im-bō'zumd, *p.a.* Surrounded in the midst; inclosed.
Imbound,† im-bound', *vt.* To inclose in limits.
Imbroglio, im-brō'lyō, *n.* An embarrassing state of things.
Imbrown, im-broun', *vt. To make brown;*

to darken the colour of; to tan; to darken the complexion of.
Imbrue, im-brö', *vt. To moisten;* to soak; to drench in a fluid, chiefly in blood. *ppr.* imbruing, *pret. & pp.* imbrued. [Old Fr. *embreuver*—L. *bibo,* to drink.]
Imbue, im-bū', *vt. To cause to imbibe,* as colour; to tinge deeply; to dye, as clothes; to tincture deeply; to cause to imbibe, as the mind. *ppr.* imbuing, *pret. & pp.* imbued. [L. *imbuo—bibo,* Sans. *pā,* to drink.]
Imitable, im'i-ta-bl, *a. That may be imitated;* worthy of imitation.
Imitate, im'i-tāt, *vt. To follow as a pattern;* to copy; to follow in manners; to copy in form, colour, or quality; to endeavour to resemble; to mimic; to pursue, as the course of a composition, so as to use like images and examples. *ppr.* imitating, *pret. & pp.* imitated. [L. *imitor, imitatus*—Gr. *homos,* one and the same.]
Imitation, im-i-tā'shon, *n. Act of imitating;* that which is made or produced as a copy; resemblance; a counterfeit. [Fr.]
Imitative, im'i-tāt-iv, *a. That imitates;* aiming at resemblance; that is used in the business of forming resemblances, as an art. [Fr. *imitatif.*]
Imitator, im'i-tāt-ėr, *n. One who imitates;* one who copies or attempts to make the resemblance of anything. [L.]
Immaculate, im-mak'ū-lāt, *a. Without spot;* undefiled; pure; not tinged with impure matter. [L. *immaculatus—macula,* a spot.]
Immaculately, im-mak'ū-lāt-li, *adv. With spotless purity.*
Immanity,† im-man'i-ti, *n.* Barbarity; atrocity.
Immanuel, im-man'ū-el, *n. God with us;* the Saviour. [Heb.]
Immaterial, im-ma-tē'ri-al, *a. Not material;* incorporeal; spiritual; without weight; trifling; insignificant.
Immateriality, im-ma-tē'ri-al"li-ti, *n. Quality of being immaterial,* or not consisting of matter.
Immaterially, im-ma-tē'ri-al-li, *adv.* In a manner not depending on *matter;* in a manner unimportant.
Immature, Immatured, im-ma-tūr', im-ma-tūrd', *a. Not mature;* unripe; that has not arrived to a perfect state; hasty; too early; premature.
Immaturely, im-ma-tūr'li, *adv.* Too soon; before ripeness or completion.
Immaturity, im-ma-tūr'i-ti, *n. State or quality of being immature;* unripeness; the state of a thing which has not arrived to perfection.
Immeasurable, im-me'zhūr-a-bl, *a. That cannot be measured;* indefinitely extensive.
Immeasurableness, im-me'zhūr-a-bl-nes, *n. State of being incapable of measure.*
Immeasurably, im-me'zhūr-a-bli, *adv. Immensely;* beyond all measure.
Immediacy,† im-mē'di-a-si, *n.* Independence.
Immediate, im-mē'di-āt, *a. Without anything between;* acting without a *medium;* producing its effect by its own direct agency; proximate; instant; present; without the intervention of time. [L. *medius,* middle.]
Immediately, im-mē'di-āt-li, *adv.* Without the intervention of any other cause; at the present time; instantly
Immemorial, im-mē-mō'ri-al, *a. Beyond memory;* relating to time or duration; whose beginning is not remembered.

ch, chain; j, job; g, go; ng, sing; TH, then; th, thin; w, wig; wh, whig; zh, azure; † obsolete.

Immemorially, im-mē-mō'ri-al-li, *adv.* Beyond memory.

Immense, im-mens', *a.* Unmeasured; immeasurable; infinite; without any known limit; very great; huge in bulk; enormous. [Fr.— L. *metior, mensus*, Sans. *mā*, to measure.]

Immensely, im-mens'li, *adv.* Immeasurably; infinitely; very greatly.

Immensity, im-mens'i-ti, *n.* Unlimited extension; an extent not to be measured; infinity; vastness in extent or bulk; greatness. [Fr. *immensité*.]

Immerge, im-mėrj', *vt.* To plunge into a fluid; to immerse. *ppr.* immerging, *pret. & pp.* immerged. [L. *immergo—mergo*, to dip in.]

Immerse, im-mėrs', *vt.* To plunge into water; to put under water or other fluid; to overwhelm; to engage deeply. *ppr.* immersing, *pret. & pp.* immersed. [L. *immergo, immersus—mergo*, to dip in—Sans. *majj*, to be immersed.]

Immersed, im-mėrst', *pp.* Deeply engaged; growing wholly under water.

Immersion, im-mėr'shon, *n.* Act of immersing; state of being overwhelmed or deeply engaged; the disappearance of a celestial body by entering into any medium. [Fr.]

Immethodical, im-me-thod'ik-al, *a.* Not methodical; without systematic arrangement; disorderly.

Immethodically, im-me-thod'ik-al-li, *adv.* Without order or regularity.

Immigrant, im'mi-grant, *n.* A person who removes into a country for the purpose of permanent residence. [L. *immigrans—migro*, to remove.]

Immigrate, im'mi-grāt, *vi.* To come into a country for the purpose of permanent residence. *ppr.* immigrating, *pret. & pp.* immigrated. [L. *immigro, immigrātum—migro*, to remove.]

Immigration, im-mi-grā'shon, *n.* Act of immigrating.

Imminence, im'mi-nens, *n.* Quality of being imminent; impending evil.

Imminent, im'mi-nent, *a.* Hanging over; impending; appearing as if about to fall on, as some evil or calamity. [L. *imminens—mineo*, to jut.]

Imminently, im'mi-nent-li, *adv.* In an imminent manner or degree.

Immission, im-mi'shon, *n.* Act of sending or thrusting into; injection. [L. *immissio—mitto, missum*, to send.]

Immobility, im-mō-bil'i-ti, *n.* State or quality of being immovable; fixedness in place or state; resistance to motion. [Fr. *immobilité*—L. *moveo*, to move.]

Immoderate, im-mo'dėr-āt, *a.* Without due measure; exceeding just or usual bounds; excessive; intemperate. [L. *immoderatus—modus*, measure.]

Immoderately, im-mo'dėr-āt-li, *adv.* Excessively; unreasonably.

Immodest, im-mo'dest, *a.* Not modest; arrogant; wanting in decency and delicacy; unchaste; impure. [L. *immodestus*.]

Immodestly, im-mo'dest-li, *adv.* Without due restraint or reserve; indecently.

Immodesty, im-mo'des-ti, *n.* Want of modesty; indecency; unchastity; want of delicacy. [L. *immodestia*.]

Immolate, im'mō-lāt, *vt.* To sacrifice; to kill, as a victim offered in sacrifice; to offer in sacrifice. *ppr.* immolating, *pret. & pp.* immolated. [L. *immolo, immolatus—mōla*, sacrificial meal.]

Immolation, im-mō-lā'shon, *n.* Act of immolating or of sacrificing; a sacrifice offered. [L. *immolatio*.]

Immoment†, im-mō'ment, *a.* Trifling.

Immoral, im-mo'ral, *a.* Not moral; of a life contrary to the moral or divine law; wicked; dishonest; depraved.

Immorality, im-mō-ral'i-ti, *n.* Quality of being immoral; any practice which contravenes the divine commands; wickedness; depravity. [Fr. *immoralité*.]

Immorally, im-mo'ral-li, *adv.* Wickedly; in violation of law or duty.

Immortal, im-mor'tal, *a.* Not mortal; undying; having life or being that shall never end; never coming to an end; everlasting; imperishable; not liable to fall into oblivion while the world lasts.—*n.* One who is exempt from death. [Fr. *immortel*.]

Immortality, im-mor-tal'i-ti, *n.* Quality of being immortal; life destined to endure without end; existence not limited. [Fr. *immortalité*.]

Immortalize, im-mor'tal-iz, *vt.* To render immortal; to exempt from oblivion; to make perpetual. *ppr.* immortalizing, *pret. & pp.* immortalized. [Fr. *immortaliser*—L. *mors, mortis*, death—*morior*, Sans. *mri*, to die.]

Immortally, im-mor'tal-li, *adv.* With endless existence.

Immovability, im-möv'a-bil"i-ti, *n.* State or quality of being immovable; steadfastness that cannot be shaken.

Immovable, im-möv'a-bl, *a.* That cannot be moved from its place; not to be moved from a purpose; fixed; unchangeable, as a purpose; unfeeling; not to be shaken or agitated.

Immovably, im-möv'a-bli, *adv.* Unalterably; unchangeably.

Immunity, im-mū'ni-ti, *n.* Freedom from service or obligation; a particular privilege or prerogative; freedom. [Fr. *immunité*—L. *munus*, service.]

Immure, im-mūr', *vt.* To inclose within walls; to shut up; to imprison. *ppr.* immuring, *pret. & pp.* immured.—*n.*† A wall. [Norm. *emmurrer*—L. *murus*, a wall.]

Immutability, im-mū'ta-bil"i-ti, *n.* Unchangeableness; the quality that renders change impossible; invariableness. [Fr. *immutabilité*.]

Immutable, im-mū'ta-bl, *a.* Unchangeable; unalterable; not susceptible of change. [L. *immutabilis — mūto*, to change.]

Immutably, im-mū'ta-bli, *adv.* Unchangeably; unalterably.

Imp, imp, *n.* A graft; a scion; a subaltern or puny devil; a mischievous child.—*vt.* To insert, as a feather into a broken wing; to qualify for flight. [Sax. *impan*, to engraft.]

Impact, im'pakt, *n.* Contact by fastening; the single, instantaneous stroke communicated from one body in motion to another either in motion or at rest. [from L. *impactus—pango, pactum*, to fasten.]

Impaint, im-pānt', *vt.* To paint.

Impair, im-pār', *vt.* To make worse; to lessen in quantity, value, or excellence; to injure; to weaken.—*a.*† Not fit. [Fr. *empirer*—L. *pejor*, worse.]

Impaired, im-pārd', *p.a.* Made worse; injured; weakened.

Impale, im-pāl'. See EMPALE.

Impalement, im-pāl'ment, *n.* See EMPALEMENT.

Impalpable, im-pal'pa-bl, *a.* Not to be felt; so fine as not to be perceived by the touch; not coarse or gross. [Fr. —L. *palpo*, to touch lightly.]

Impalpably, im-pal'pa-bli, *adv.* In a manner not to be felt.

Impanel, im-pan'el, *vt.* To enter, as the names of a jury in a list called a *panel*; to enrol, as a list of jurors.

Imparity, im-pa'ri-ti, *n.* State of being unequal; inequality. [L. *par*, equal.]

Impark, im-pärk', *vt.* To inclose for a park; to make, as a park by inclosure; to sever from a common.

Impart, im-pärt', *vt.* To bestow on another, as a share of something; to reveal; to disclose; to convey the knowledge of; to communicate; to make known.—*vi.* To give a part or share. [L. *impertio—pars, partis*, a part—Chal. *pėras*. to divide.]

Impartial, im-pär'shi-al, *a.* Not partial; not biassed in favour of one party more than another; equitable; just; very partial†.

Impartiality, im-pär'shi-al"i-ti, *n.* State or quality of being impartial; indifference of judgment; freedom from bias in favour of one side more than another; equitableness; justice.

Impartially, im-pär'shi-al-li, *adv.* Without bias of judgment; justly.

Impartible, im-pärt'i-bl, *a.* Not subject to partition; that may be imparted, bestowed, or communicated.

Impartment, im-pärt'ment, *n.* Act of imparting; that which is imparted.

Impassable, im-pas'a-bl, *a.* Not passable; that cannot be passed; impervious; pathless.

Impassableness, im-pas'a-bl-nes, *n.* State of being impassable.

Impassibility, im-pas'i-bil"i-ti, *n.* State or quality of being impassible; insusceptibility of injury from external things.

Impassible, im-pas'i-bl, *a.* Incapable of suffering; that cannot be affected with pain or uneasiness. [Fr.—L. *patior, passus*, to suffer.]

Impassioned, im-pa'shond, *p.a.* Actuated by passion; having the feelings warmed, as a speaker; expressive of passion or ardour, as a harangue.

Impassive, im-pas'iv, *a.* Not susceptible of pain or suffering.

Impassively, im-pas'iv-li, *adv.* Without sensibility to pain.

Impassiveness, im-pas'iv-nes, *n.* State of being impassive.

Impatience, im-pā'shi-ens, *n.* The quality of being impatient; uneasiness under pain or suffering; violence of temper; restlessness. [Fr.—L. *patientia*, patience—*patior*, to suffer.]

Impatient, im-pā'shi-ent, *a.* Destitute of patience; not bearing pain with composure; hasty; not enduring delay; prompted by impatience. [L. *impatiens—patior*, to suffer.]

Impatiently, im-pā'shi-ent-li, *adv.* In an impatient manner.

Impawn, im-pan', *vt.* To pawn; to pledge; to deposit as security.

Impeach, im-pēch', *vt.* To impede†; to detain on a charge; to charge with a crime or misdemeanour; to bring an accusation against for treason, as against a member of parliament or a peer; to call in question; to call to account; to charge as answerable.—*n.*† Hindrance. [Fr. *empêcher* — L. *pes, pedis*, the foot.]

Impeachable, im-pēch'a-bl, *a.* Liable to be impeached.

Impeachment, im-pēch'ment, *n.* Hindrance†; act of impeaching; public accusation; the charge preferred; censure; reproach. [Fr. *empêchement*.]

Impearl, im-pėrl', *vt.* To decorate with pearls, or with things resembling pearls.

Impeccability, im-pek'a-bil"li-ti, *n.*

Fāte, fär, fat, fall; mē, met, hėr; pine, pin; nōte, not, möve; tūbe, tub, bull; oil, pound.

IMPECCABLE 189 IMPLORE

Quality of being impeccable, or of not being liable to sin.
Impeccable, im-pek'a-bl, *a*. Not peccable, or liable to sin; not subject to sin. [Fr.—L. *pecco*, to go wrong.]
Impede, im-pēd', *vt*. To entangle the feet of; to retard; to stop in progress; to obstruct. *ppr*. impeding, *pret. & pp.* impeded. [L. *impedio—pes, pedis*, the foot.]
Impediment, im-ped'i-ment, *n*. That by which one is impeded; obstruction; that which prevents distinct articulation in speaking. [L. *impedimentum*.]
Impel, im-pel', *vt*. To drive or urge forward; to press on; to instigate; to incite; to actuate. *ppr*. impelling, *pret. & pp.* impelled. [L. *impello—pello*, to drive.]
Impelling, im-pel'ing, *p.a*. Urging; pressing.
Impend, im-pend', *vi*. To hang over; to threaten; to be approaching and ready to fall. [L. *impendeo—pendeo*, to hang.]
Impending, im-pend'ing, *p.a*. Approaching near; threatening.
Impenetrability, im-pe'nē-tra-bil'i-ti, *n. Quality of being impenetrable*; that quality of matter by which it excludes all other matter from the space it occupies; insusceptibility of intellectual impression; coldness. [Fr. *impénétrabilité*.]
Impenetrable, im-pe'nē-tra-bl, *a*. That cannot be penetrated; that prevents any other substance from occupying the same place at the same time; not to be affected or moved; not admitting impressions on the mind; not to be entered and viewed by the eye of the intellect. [Fr. *impénétrable*—L. *penetro*, to penetrate.]
Impenetrably, im-pe'nē-tra-bli, *adv*. In an impenetrable manner.
Impenitence, im-pe'ni-tens, *n. Want of penitence;* absence of contrition for sin; hardness of heart. [Fr. *impénitence*.]
Impenitent, im-pe'ni-tent, *a*. Not penitent; not contrite; obdurate. [Fr. *impénitent*.]
Impenitently, im-pe'ni-tent-li, *adv*. Without repentance or contrition.
Imperative, im-pe'rat-iv, *a*. Commanding; authoritative; expressive of command; obligatory; designating a mood of the verb which expresses command, &c. [Fr. *impératif*—L. *paro*, to set or place in order.]
Imperatively, im-pe'rat-iv-li, *adv*. With command; authoritatively.
Imperceptibility, im-pėr-sep'ti-bil'i-ti, *n. Quality of being imperceptible*.
Imperceptible, im-pėr-sep'ti-bl, *a*. Not perceptible; not to be known by the senses; very small; very slow in motion or progress.
Imperceptibly, im-pėr-sep'ti-bli, *adv*. In a manner not to be perceived.
Imperfect, im-pėr'fekt, *a*. Not perfect; not complete; wanting a part; not perfect in intellect; liable to err; not perfect in a moral view; faulty; designating a tense of the verb which denotes an action in time past, then present, but not finished.
Imperfection, im-pėr-fek'shon, *n. Want of perfection;* defect; frailty; want of something necessary to complete a thing.
Imperfectly, im-pėr'fekt-li, *adv*. In an imperfect manner or degree.
Imperforated, im-pėr'fōr-āt-ed, *a. Not perforated;* having no openings or pores. [L. *in*, and *perforatus—foro*, to bore.]

Imperial, im-pē'ri-al, *a. Pertaining to an empire or to an emperor;* denoting sovereignty; maintaining supremacy; noting a size of paper; noting a standard measure. [Fr. *impérial*—L. *impero*, to put on, to govern.]
Imperialism, im-pē'ri-al-izm, *n*. Imperial power; the spirit of empire.
Imperialist, im-pē'ri-al-ist, *n*. One who supports an emperor; a subject or soldier of an emperor.
Imperially, im-pē'ri-al-li, *adv*. In the manner of an emperor.
Imperil, im-pe'ril, *vt*. To bring into peril; to hazard; to endanger. *ppr*. imperilling, *pret. & pp.* imperilled.
Imperious, im-pē'ri-us, *a. Commanding;* haughty; domineering; arrogant; springing from a spirit of dictation, as language or commands; urgent; authoritative; commanding with rightful authority. [Fr. *impérieux*—L. *impero*, to command.]
Imperiously, im-pē'ri-us-li, *adv*. In an imperious manner.
Imperiousness, im-pē'ri-us-nes, *n. Quality of being imperious;* haughtiness.
Imperishable, im-pe'rish-a-bl, *a. Not perishable;* not subject to decay; indestructible; everlasting.
Imperishably, im-pe'rish-a-bli, *adv*. In an imperishable manner.
Impermeability, im-pėr'mē-a-bil'i-ti, *n. Quality of being impermeable;* quality in bodies of not permitting a fluid to pass through them. [Fr. *imperméabilité*.]
Impermeable, im-pėr'mē-a-bl, *a. Not permeable;* noting bodies which do not permit fluids to pass through them. [Fr. *imperméable*—L. *permeo*, to pass through—*meo*, to go.]
Imperseverant†, im-pėr-se'vėr-ant, *a. Earnestly persevering*.
Impersonal, im-pėr'son-al, *a. Not personal;* not representing a person; designating a verb which is used only with the termination of the third person singular, with *it* for a nominative, as, *it rains*.—*n*. That which wants personality; an impersonal verb.
Impersonally, im-pėr'son-al'li-ti, *n. Want or indistinctness of personality*.
Impersonate, im-pėr'son-āt, *vt*. To ascribe the qualities of a person to; to represent the person of. *ppr*. impersonating, *pret. & pp.* impersonated.
Impertinence, im-pėr'ti-nens, *n*. That which is not pertinent; that which does not belong to the subject in hand; rudeness; conduct unbecoming the person, the society, or the circumstances. [Fr.—L. *pertineo*, to pertain to—*teneo*, to hold.]
Impertinent, im-pėr'ti-nent, *a. Not pertinent;* not pertaining to the matter in hand; meddling with that which does not belong to the person; contrary to the rules of good breeding; pert; intrusive; trifling.—*n*. An intruder; a trifler; a saucy person. [Fr.]
Impertinently, im-pėr'ti-nent-li, *adv*. In an impertinent manner.
Imperturbability, im-pėr-tėrb'a-bil'i-ti, *n. Quality of being imperturbable*. [Fr. *imperturbabilité*.]
Imperturbable, im-pėr-tėrb'a-bl,*a*. That cannot be disturbed or agitated; permanently quiet. [Low L. *imperturbabilis*—L. *turbo*, to disturb.]
Impervious, im-pėr'vi-us, *a. Not pervious;* impassable; impenetrable; not penetrable by light; not permeable to fluids.
Imperviously, im-pėr'vi-us-li, *adv*. In a manner to prevent penetration.

Imperviousness, im-pėr'vi-us-nes, *n. State or quality of being impervious*.
Impetuosity, im-pe'tū-os'i-ti, *n. Quality of being impetuous;* violence; vehemence; furiousness of temper. [Fr. *impétuosité*.]
Impetuous, im-pe'tū-us, *a. Rushing upon with great force;* moving rapidly; forcible; precipitate; vehement of mind; moving with precipitancy; hasty; passionate. [Fr. *impétueux*—L. *peto*, to fall upon.]
Impetuously, im-pe'tū-us-li, *adv*. Violently; fiercely; forcibly.
Impetus, im'pe-tus, *n*. The force with which any body is driven or impelled; the force with which one body in motion strikes another. [L.—*peto*, to fall upon.]
Impiety, im-pī'e-ti, *n. Want of piety;* irreverence toward the Supreme Being; ungodliness; profaneness; wickedness; an act of wickedness.
Impinge, im-pinj', *vi*. To dash against; to clash upon. *ppr*. impinging, *pret. & pp.* impinged. [L. *impingo—pango*, to fasten, to drive in.]
Impious, im'pi-us, *a. Destitute of piety;* irreverent toward the Supreme Being; profane; proceeding from a contempt for the Supreme Being; tending to dishonour God or his laws. [L. *impius—pius*, pious.]
Impiously, im'pi-us-li, *adv*. With irreverence for God; profanely.
Impish, imp'ish, *a. Having the qualities of an imp*.
Impiteous†, im-pi'te-us, *a. Not piteous;* cruel.
Implacability, im-plā'ka-bil'i-ti, *n. Quality of being implacable*, or of not being appeasable; irreconcilable enmity or anger. [Fr. *implacabilité*.]
Implacable, im-plā'ka-bl, *a. Not placable;* not to be appeased; inexorable; unrelenting.
Implacably, im-plā'ka-bli, *adv*. With enmity not to be pacified or subdued.
Implant, in-plant', *vt*. To set a plant into; to insert; to infix for the purpose of growth, as feelings or ideas in the mind; to instil; to infuse.
Impleach†, im-plēch', *vt*. To interweave.
Implead, im-plēd', *vt*. To bring a plea against; to institute and prosecute a suit against one in court.
Impleader, im-plēd'ėr, *n*. One who prosecutes another.
Implement, im'ple-ment, *n*. Originally, whatever fills up; a tool; a utensil; an instrument; (pl.) tools; the tools or instruments of labour. [Low L. *implementum*—L. *pleo*, to fill.]
Implex, im'pleks, *a. Infolded;* intricate. [Fr. *implexe*—L. *plico*, to fold.]
Implicate, im'pli-kāt, *vt*. To involve or bring into connection with; to prove to be connected or concerned, as in an offence. *ppr*. implicating, *pret. & pp.* implicated. [L. *implico, implicatus—plico*, to fold.]
Implication, im-pli-kā'shon, *n. Act of involving;* entanglement; an implying or that which is implied; a tacit inference. [Fr.]
Implicit, im-pli'sit, *a. Implied;* fairly to be understood, though not expressed in words; resting on another; trusting undoubtingly to another. [Fr. *implicite*—L. *plico, plicitum*, to fold.]
Implicitly, im-pli'sit-li, *adv*. In an implicit manner.
Implorator†, im-plōr-āt'ėr, *n*. One who implores.
Implore, im-plōr', *vt*. To beg for aid from with tears; to invoke earnestly,

ch, *chain*; j, *job*; g, *go*; ng, *sing*; ᴛʜ, *then*; th, *thin*; w, *wig*; wh, *whig*; zh, *azure*; † obsolete.

IMPLORINGLY 190 IMPROBABLE

to petition with urgency; to supplicate; to beg. *ppr.* imploring, *pret. & pp.* implored. [Fr. *implorer*—L. *ploro*, to cry out.]
Imploringly, im-plōr'ing-li, *adv.* In the manner of entreaty.
Imply, im-plī', *vt.* To involve or contain in substance or by fair inference; to comprise; to import; to signify. *ppr.* implying, *pret. & pp.* implied. [L. *implico—plico*, to fold.]
Impolicy, im-po'li-si, *n.* Bad policy; defect of wisdom; inexpedience; unsuitableness to the end proposed.
Impolite, im-pō-līt', *a.* Not polite; not of polished manners; uncivil.
Impolitic, im-po'lit-ik, *a.* Not politic; wanting policy or prudence; pursuing measures adapted to injure the public interest; indiscreet; inexpedient.
Imponderability, im-pon dėr-a-bil″li-ti, *n.* Quality of being imponderable.
Imponderable, im-pon'dėr-a-bl, *a.* That cannot be weighed; not having sensible weight. [L. *pondus, ponderis*, weight.]
Imponet, im-pōn', *vt.* To stake; to wager.
Import, im-pōrt', *vt.* To convey into; to bring from a foreign country into one's country; to convey, as meaning; to signify; to imply; to be of weight or consequence to; to have a bearing on; to interest; to concern. [Fr. *importer*—L. *porto*, to carry.]
Import, im'pōrt, *n.* That which is imported; that which is conveyed in words; signification; drift; weight; consequence.
Importable, im-pōrt'a-bl, *a.* That may be imported.
Importance, im-pōrt'ans, *n.* Quality of being important; weight; moment; that quality of anything by which it may affect a measure, interest, or result; weight in the scale of being; weight in self-estimation; importunity†. [Fr.]
Important, im-pōrt'ant, *a.* Weighty; momentous; having a bearing on some interest, measure, or result; stately; affectedly grave; importunate†. [Fr.]
Importantly, im-pōrt'ant-li, *adv.* Weightily; forcibly.
Importation, im-pōrt-ā'shon, *n.* Act or practice of importing; conveyance into; the commodities imported. [Fr.]
Importer, im-pōrt'ėr, *n.* He who imports; the merchant who brings goods from another country or state into his own.
Importless†, im-pōrt'les, *a.* Of no weight.
Importunate, im-pōr'tū-nāt, *a.* That importunes; troublesome; urgent in request or demand; urgent, as a request; inciting urgently for gratification, as the appetites. [L. *importūnus—portus*, a port.]
Importunately, im-pōr'tū-nāt-li, *adv.* With pressing solicitation.
Importune, im-por-tūn', *vt.* To solicit unsuitably; to request with urgency; to press with solicitation; to urge with frequent application. *ppr.* importuning, *pret. & pp.* importuned. [Fr. *importuner*—L. *portus*, a harbour.]
Importunity, im-por-tūn'i-ti, *n.* Pressing solicitation; application for a claim or favour, which is urged with troublesome frequency. [Fr. *importunité*.]
Impose, im-pōz', *vt.* To lay on, as a burden, tax, or penalty; to place over by authority; to enjoin, as a duty; to lay on, as hands in the ceremony of ordina-

tion or of confirmation; to obtrude fallaciously. (With *upon*.) *ppr.* imposing, *pret. & pp.* imposed.—*n.*† An imposition; command. [Fr. *imposer*—L. *pono, positum*, to place.]
Imposing, im-pōz'ing, *p.a.* Commanding; adapted to impress forcibly.
Imposition, im-pō-zi'shon, *n.* Act of laying on; act of laying on hands in the ceremony of ordination; that which is imposed; a tax, toll, duty, &c.; burden; imposture. [Fr.]
Impossibility, im-pos'i-bil″li-ti, *n.* State of being impossible; the state or quality of being not possible to be done; that which cannot be. [Fr. *impossibilité*.]
Impossible, im-pos'i-bl, *a.* Not possible; impracticable; not feasible; that cannot be done.
Impost, im'pōst, *n.* That which is laid on; any tax imposed by authority; excise; custom; duty. [Sp. *imposta*—L. *pono, positum*, to place.]
Imposthume, im-pos'tūm, *n.* The separation of pus or purulent matter into an ulcer; an abscess; a collection of pus in any part of an animal body. [from Gr. *apostēma—histēmi*, to stand.]
Impostor, im-pos'tėr, *n.* One who imposes on others; a person who assumes a character for the purpose of deception; a deceiver under a false character. [Fr. *imposteur*—L. *pono*, to place.]
Imposture, im-pos'tūr, *n.* Imposition; deception practised under a false or assumed character; cheat; fraud. [Fr.]
Impotence, im'pō-tens, *n.* Want of strength, animal or intellectual; weakness; imbecility; defect of power; want of power to resist habits and natural propensities; inability to beget. [L. *impotentia—potens*, able, from *possum*, to be able.]
Impotent, im'pō-tent, *a.* Powerless; weak; wanting strength or power; unable by nature, or disabled by disease or accident, to perform any act; wanting the power of propagation, as males.—*n.*† One who is feeble. [Fr.]
Impotently, im'pō-tent-li, *adv.* In an impotent manner; feebly; weakly.
Impound, im-pound', *vt.* To confine in a pound or close pen; to confine; to restrain within limits.
Impoverish, im-po'vėr-ish, *vt.* To make poor; to reduce to indigence, as persons; to exhaust the strength, richness, or fertility of, as of land or soil. [Fr. *appauvrir*, *ppr. appauvrissant*—L. *pauper*, poor.]
Impoverishing, im-po'vėr-ish-ing, *p.a.* Making poor; exhausting.
Impoverishment, im-po'vėr-ish-ment, *n.* Act of making poor; drain of wealth, richness, or fertility. [Fr. *appauvrissement*.]
Impracticability, im-prak'ti-ka-bil″li-ti, *n.* State or quality of being impracticable; untractableness; stubbornness.
Impracticable, im-prak'ti-ka-bl, *a.* Not practicable; that cannot be done; unmanageable; stubborn; incapable of being passed.
Impracticably, im-prak'ti-ka-bli, *adv.* In an impracticable manner.
Imprecate, im'prē-kāt, *vt.* To invoke, as evil; to call down by prayer, as something hurtful or calamitous. *ppr.* imprecating, *pret. & pp.* imprecated. [L. *imprecor, imprecatus—precor*, to pray.]
Imprecation, im-prē-kā'shon, *n.* Act of imprecating; a prayer that a curse or calamity may fall on any one; malediction. [Fr. *imprécation*.]

Impregnability, im-preg'na-bil″li-ti, *n.* State of being impregnable.
Impregnable, im-preg'na-bl, *a.* That cannot be taken; not to be stormed or taken by assault; not to be moved or shaken; invincible, as affection. [Fr. *imprenable*—L. *prehendo*, to take.]
Impregnably, im-preg'na-bli, *adv.* In an impregnable manner.
Impregnate, im-preg'nāt, *vt.* To make pregnant; to render prolific; to infuse, as particles of one thing into another; to communicate, as the virtues of one thing to another; to saturate. *ppr.* impregnating, *pret. & pp.* impregnated. [Low L. *impregno, impregnatus*—L. *gigno*, to beget.]
Impregnation, im-preg-nā'shon, *n.* Act of impregnating; that with which anything is impregnated. [Fr. *imprégnation*.]
Impress, im-pres', *vt.* To press into; to imprint; to stamp; to mark; to fix deep; to compel to enter into public service, as seamen; to seize and take into service by compulsion. [Old Fr. *empresser*—L. *premo, pressum*, to press.]
Impress, im'pres, *n.* That which is impressed; the figure or image of anything made by pressure; likeness; mark of distinction; influence wrought on the mind; motto; act of compelling to enter into the public service.
Impressed, im-prest', *p.a.* Compelled to enter the public service; fixed in the mind; convinced.
Impressible, im-pres'i-bl, *a.* That may be impressed; that may receive impressions.
Impressibly, im-pres'i-bli, *adv.* In a manner to make impression.
Impression, im-prē'shon, *n.* Act of impressing; stamp made by pressure; the effect which objects produce on the mind; image in the mind; sensible effect; a single edition of a book; indistinct remembrance. [Fr.]
Impressionable, im-prē'shon-a-bl, *a.* Capable of being impressed; susceptible.
Impressive, im-pres'iv, *a.* Making an impression; having the power of affecting; adapted to touch sensibility or the conscience; solemn.
Impressively, im-pres'iv-li, *adv.* In an impressive manner.
Impressiveness, im-pres'iv-nes, *n.* Quality of being impressive.
Impressment, im-pres'ment, *n.* Act of impressing men into the public service; act of compelling into any service.
Impressure†, im-pre'shūr, *n.* Dent; impression.
Imprest, im'prest, *n.* A kind of earnest money.
Imprint, im-print', *vt.* To impress; to stamp, as letters and words on paper; to fix on the mind or memory.
Imprint, im'print, *n.* The name of the publisher of a book, newspaper, &c., with the place and time of publication printed on the first page.
Imprison, im-pri'zon, *vt.* To put into a prison; to incarcerate; to confine; to deprive of the liberty to move from place to place.
Imprisonment, im-pri'zon-ment, *n.* Act of confining in prison; act of arresting and detaining in custody; custody. [Fr. *emprisonnement*.]
Improbability, im-pro'ba-bil″li-ti, *n.* Quality of being improbable; unlikelihood. [Fr. *improbabilité*.]
Improbable, im-pro'ba-bl, *a.* Not probable; not likely to be true; not to be

Fāte, fär, fat, fall; mē, met, hėr; pīne, pin; nōte, not, mōve; tūbe, tub, bull; oil, pound.

Improbably, im-pro'ba-bli, *adv.* In a manner not likely to be true.
Improbity, im-prō'bi-ti, *n.* Want of probity; want of integrity or rectitude of principle; dishonesty.
Impromptu, im-promp'tū, *n.* A piece made off-hand; an extemporaneous, and often merry or witty composition. *a. Off-hand;* without previous study; unpremeditated. [L. *in promptu,* in readiness—*promo,* to bring out.]
Improper, im-pro'pėr, *a.* Not proper; not adapted to its end; not becoming; incorrect; wrong; ungrammatical.
Improperly, im-pro'pėr-li, *adv. In an improper manner.*
Impropriety, im-pro-pri'e-ti, *n. Want of propriety;* unsuitableness to character, time, place, or circumstances; inaccuracy in language.
Improvability, im-pröv'a-bil'li-ti, *n. State or quality of being improvable;* susceptibility of being made better.
Improvable, im-pröv'a-bl, *a. That may be improved;* capable of growing or being made better; that may be used to advantage, as hints; capable of tillage or cultivation, as land.
Improvably, im-pröv'a-bli, *adv.* In a manner that admits of melioration.
Improve, im-pröv', *vt.* To better; to ameliorate; to mend; to rectify; to use or employ to good purpose; to apply to practical purposes. — *vi.* To grow better or wiser; to increase; to rise, as the market-price. *ppr.* improving, *pret. & pp.* improved. [Norm. *improvment,* improving—L. *probo,* to try, to show to be good.)
Improved, im-pröv'd, *p.a. Made better* or wiser.
Improvement, im-pröv'ment, *n. Act of improving;* advancement in worth, learning, wisdom, skill, or other excellence; advance from any state to a better; something added or changed for the better; employment to beneficial purposes; practical application.
Improver, im-pröv'ėr, *n. One who improves;* that which improves.
Improvidence, im-pro'vi-dens, *n. Want of providence* or forecast; neglect of the measures which foresight might dictate for safety or advantage.
Improvident, im-pro'vi-dent, *a. Not provident;* wanting care to make provision for future exigences; inconsiderate; careless.
Improvidently, im-pro'vi-dent-li, *adv. Without foresight* or forecast.
Improving, im-pröv'ing, *p.a. Making better;* growing better.
Improvingly, im-pröv'ing-li, *adv. In a manner to improve.*
Imprudence, im-prö'dens, *n. Want of prudence;* want of caution, or a due regard to consequences; inconsiderateness; rashness.
Imprudent, im-pro'dent, *a. Not prudent;* not attentive to the consequences of words or actions; incautious; heedless; rash.
Imprudently, im-pro'dent-li, *adv. Without the exercise of prudence.*
Impudence, im'pū-dens, *n. Want of shame;* want of modesty; assurance, accompanied with a disregard of the opinions of others; audacity; effrontery; pertness. [Fr.]
Impudent, im'pū-dent, *a. Wanting shame;* shameless; audacious; bold, with contempt of others; immodest; impertinent; insolent. [Fr.—L. *pudeo,* to make ashamed.]

Impudently, im'pū-dent-li, *adv. In an impudent manner.*
Impugn, im-pūn', *vt. To fight against;* to attack or assail by words or arguments; to contradict. [Fr. *impugner* —L. *pugno,* to fight.]
Impugnable, im-pūn'a-bl, *a. That may be impugned.*
Impulse, im'puls, *n. A striking against;* force communicated instantaneously; the effect of a sudden communication of motion; influence acting on the mind; motive; impression. [L. *impulsus—pello, pulsum,* to drive.]
Impulsion, im-pul'shon, *n. Act of striking against;* the sudden agency of a body in motion on another body; influence on the mind. [Fr.]
Impulsive, im-puls'iv, *a. Having the power of impelling;* moving; actuated or governed by impulse. [Fr. *impulsif.*]
Impulsively, im-puls'iv-li, *adv.* With force; by impulse.
Impunity, im-pū'ni-ti, *n. Freedom from punishment;* freedom or exemption from injury. [Fr. *impunité*—L. *pœna,* punishment.]
Impure, im-pūr', *a. Not pure;* foul; tinctured; mixed with extraneous substance; obscene, as thoughts; unchaste; unclean, as conduct; unholy.
Impurely, im-pūr'li. *adv. In an impure manner;* with impurity.
Impurity, im-pūr'i-ti, *n. Want of purity; uncleanness;* foulness; the admixture of a foreign substance in anything; unchastity; want of sanctity or holiness; obscenity.
Imputable, im-pūt'a-bl, *a. That may be imputed;* that may be ascribed to; that may be set to the account of another.
Imputation, im-pū-tā'shon, *n. Act of imputing* or *charging;* charge of evil; censure; reproach; the attributing any matter, quality, or character, whether good or evil, to any person as his own; intimation. [Fr.]
Impute, im-pūt', *vt. To set to the account of;* to ascribe; to set to the account of another, as the ground of judicial procedure. *ppr.* imputing, *pret. & pp.* imputed. [L. *imputo—puto,* to hold a reckoning.]
Imputed, im-pūt'ed, *p.a.* Attributed; ascribed.
In, in, *prep.* Noting the place where anything is present, or the state present at any time; noting time, power, proportion; entrance into; within; by means of; through; according to; sometimes noting *negation.*—*adv.* Within; not out; close; near. (Sax.—Gr. *en.*]
Inability, in-a-bil'i-ti, *n. Want of ability,* force, strength, or power; want of adequate means; incompetence.
Inaccessibility, in-ak-ses'i-bil'li-ti, *n. Quality* or *state of being inaccessible.*
Inaccessible, in-ak-ses'i-bl, *a. Not accessible;* unapproachable; not to be obtained; forbidding access.
Inaccessibly, in-ak-ses'i-bli, *adv.* So as not to be approached.
Inaccuracy, in-ak'kū-ra-si, *n. Want of accuracy;* mistake; defect.
Inaccurate, in-ak'kū-rāt, *a. Not accurate;* not exact or correct; not according to truth.
Inaccurately, in-ak'kū-rāt-li, *adv.* Not according to truth; incorrectly.
Inaction, in-ak'shon, *n. Want of action;* forbearance of labour; idleness; rest.
Inactive, in-ak'tiv, *a. Not active;* having no power to move, as matter; not industrious; idle; indolent; lazy.
Inactively, in-ak'tiv-li, *adv. In an inactive manner.*

Inactivity, in-ak-tiv'i-ti, *n. Want of activity;* inertness; want of action or exertion; sluggishness.
Inadequacy, in-ad'ē-kwā-si, *n. Quality of being inadequate.*
Inadequate, in-ad'ē-kwāt, *a. Not adequate or equal to* the purpose; disproportionate; partial; incomplete; defective.
Inadequately, in-ad'ē-kwāt-li, *adv.* Not fully or sufficiently; not completely.
Inadmissibility, in-ad-mis'i-bil'li-ti, *n. Quality of being inadmissible.*
Inadmissible, in-ad-mis'i-bl, *a. Not admissible;* not proper to be admitted, allowed, or received.
Inadvertence, Inadvertency, in-ad-vėrt'ens, in-ad-vėrt'en-si, *n. Want of advertence;* negligence; effect of inattention; any oversight, mistake, or fault which proceeds from negligence or want of thought.
Inadvertent, in-ad-vėrt'ent, *a. Not turning the mind to;* heedless; careless; negligent. [L. *in,* and *advertens—verto,* to turn.]
Inadvertently, in-ad-vėrt'ent-li, *adv.* Heedlessly; inconsiderately.
Inaffectation, in-af-fek-tā'shon, *n. Freedom from an affected manner.*
Inaidable, in-ād'a-bl, *a.* Not capable of being assisted.
Inalienable, in-ā'li-en-a-bl, *a. Unalienable.* [Fr. *inaliénable.*]
Inane, in-ān', *a. Empty;* void.—*n.* Infinite space. [L. *inanis.*]
Inanimate, in-an'i-māt, *a. Not animate;* destitute of animation or life; inactive; soulless; spiritless.
Inanition, in-a-ni'shon, *n. Emptiness;* want of fulness; emptiness for want of food; exhaustion, &c. [Fr.]
Inanity, in-an'i-ti, *n. Emptiness;* void space; vacuity. [L. *inanitas.*]
Inapplicability, in-ap'pli-ka-bil'li-ti, *n. Quality of not being applicable.*
Inapplicable, in-ap'pli-ka-bl, *a. Not applicable;* not suitable to the purpose; inappropriate.
Inapplicably, in-ap'pli-ka-bli, *adv. In an inapplicable manner.*
Inapplication, in-ap'pli-kā"shon, *n. Want of application;* indolence.
Inapposite, in-ap'pō-zit, *a. Not apposite;* not fit or suitable; not pertinent.
Inappositely, in-ap'pō-zit-li, *adv. In a manner not apposite.*
Inappreciable, in-ap-prē'shi-a-bl, *a. Not to be appreciated;* that cannot be estimated.
Inappropriate, in-ap-prō'pri-āt, *a. Not appropriate;* unsuited; not proper; not belonging to.
Inappropriately, in-ap-prō'pri-āt-li, *adv. Not appropriately.*
Inaptitude, in-apt'i-tūd, *n. Want of aptitude;* unsuitableness.
Inarticulate, in-ār-tik'ū-lāt, *a. Not articulate;* not jointed or articulated; not distinct or with distinction of syllables.
Inarticulately, in-ār-tik'ū-lāt-li, *adv. Not with distinct syllables;* indistinctly.
Inarticulateness, in-ār-tik'ū-lāt-nes, *n. Quality of being inarticulate.*
Inartificial, in-ār'ti-fi"shi-al, *a. Not artificial;* not made or performed by the rules of art; simple; artless.
Inartificially in-ār'ti-fi"shi-al-li, *adv. Without art;* in an artless manner.
Inasmuch, in-az-much', *adv.* Seeing; seeing that; this being the fact. (With *as.*)
Inattention, in-at-ten'shon, *n. Want of attention,* or of fixing the mind steadily on an object; heedlessness; neglect.

---

ch, *chain;* j, *job;* g, *go;* ng, *sing;* TH, *then;* th, *thin;* w, *wig;* wh, *whig;* zh, *azure;* † obsolete.

Inattentive, in-at-tent'iv, *a.* Not attentive; regardless; thoughtless.
Inattentively, in-at-tent'iv-li, *adv.* Without attention; heedlessly.
Inaudibility, in-ạ'di-bil''li-ti, *n.* State or quality of being inaudible.
Inaudible, in-ạ'di-bl, *a.* Not audible; that cannot be heard; making no sound.
Inaudibly, in-ạ'di-bli, *adv.* In a manner not to be heard.
Inaugural, in-ạ'gū-ral, *a.* Made or pronounced at an inauguration.
Inaugurate, in-ạ'gū-rāt, *vt.* To introduce or induct into an office with solemnity or suitable ceremonies; to invest with an office in a formal manner; to make a public exhibition of. *ppr.* inaugurating, *pret. & pp.* inaugurated. [L. *inauguro, inauguratus—augur,* a Roman priest.]
Inauguration, in-ạ-gū-rā''shon, *n. Act of inaugurating;* investiture with office by appropriate ceremonies. [Late L. *inauguratio.*]
Inauspicious, in-ạ-spi'shi-us, *a. Not auspicious;* ill-omened; unlucky; unfavourable.
Inauspiciously, in-ạ-spi'shi-us-li, *adv.* With ill omens; unfortunately.
Inborn, in'born, *a. Born in; innate;* implanted by nature; natural; inherent.
Inbreathed, in-brēᵺd', *p.a. Infused by breathing* or inspiration.
Inbred, in'bred, *a. Bred within;* innate.
Incage, in-kāj', *vt. To put into or confine in a cage;* to coop up; to confine to any narrow limits. *ppr.* incaging, *pret. & pp.* incaged.
Incalculable, in-kal'kū-la-bl, *a. That cannot be calculated.*
Incalculably, in-kal'kū-la-bli, *adv.* In a degree beyond calculation.
Incandescence, in-kan-des'ens, *n.* A becoming hot or glowing; a white heat, or the glowing whiteness of a body caused by intense heat. [Fr.—L. *candeo,* to glow.]
Incandescent, in-kan-des'ent, *a.* Becoming hot or glowing; white or glowing with heat. [Fr.]
Incantation, in-kan-tā'shon, *n. Enchantment;* the act of using certain formulas of words and ceremonies, for the purpose of raising spirits. [Fr.— L. *canto,* to sing.]
Incapability, in-kā'pa-bil''li-ti, *n. Quality of being incapable;* natural want of power; want of legal power. (With *of.*)
Incapable, in-kā'pa-bl, *a. Not capable;* wanting capacity sufficient; wanting natural power or capacity to learn and know; incompetent; not susceptible of; wanting power equal to any pu... pose; wanting moral power; unqualified in a legal sense; unconscious†.—*n.* A weak person.
Incapacitate, in-ka-pa'si-tāt, *vt.* To render or make incapable; to deprive of competent power or ability; to disqualify. *ppr.* incapacitating, *pret. & pp.* incapacitated.
Incapacity, in-ka-pa'si-ti, *n. Want of capacity;* disqualification; disability by deprivation of power.
Incarcerate, in-kär'sē-rāt, *vt.* To imprison; to shut up or inclose. *ppr.* incarcerating, *pret. & pp.* incarcerated. [L. *carcer, carcēris,* a prison
Incarceration, in-kär'sē-rā''shon, *n. Act of imprisoning;* imprisonment. [L. *incarceratio.*]
Incarnadine†, in-kär'na-din, *vt. To dye red or of a flesh colour.*
Incarnate, in-kär'nāt, *vt. To clothe with flesh;* to embody in flesh.—*a. Invested with flesh;* embodied in flesh. *ppr.* incarnating, *pret. & pp.* incarnated. [L. *caro, carnis,* Gr. *kreas,* flesh.]
Incarnation, in-kär-nā'shon, *n. Act of clothing with flesh;* act of assuming flesh, or of taking a human body and the nature of man; an incarnate form. [Low L. *incarnatio.*]
Incase, in-kās', *vt. To inclose in a case;* to surround with something solid. *ppr.* incasing, *pret. & pp.* incased.
Incautious, in-ka'shi-us, *a. Not cautious;* not attending to the circumstances on which safety and interest depend; unwary; imprudent; heedless.
Incautiously, in-ka'shi-us-li, *adv.* Unwarily; without due circumspection.
Incautiousness, in-ka'shi-us-nes, *n. Want of caution;* unwariness.
Incendiarism, in-sen'di-a-rizm, *n. Act of an incendiary;* act or practice of maliciously setting fire to buildings.
Incendiary, in-sen'di-a-ri, *n. One who sets on fire;* a person who maliciously sets fire to another man's dwelling-house, or to any out-house, being parcel of the same; a person who inflames factions and promotes quarrels; a firebrand. *a. Relating to incendiarism;* tending to excite or inflame factions, sedition, or quarrels. [L. *incendiarius—candeo,* to be glowing hot.]
Incense, in'sens, *n. Perfume exhaled by fire;* the odours of spices and gums, burnt in religious rites, or as an offering to some deity; the materials burnt for making perfumes; acceptable prayers and praises. [L. *incensum—candeo,* to be glowing hot.]
Incense, in-sens', *vt. To set on fire†; to enkindle* or inflame to violent anger; to enrage or fire. *ppr.* incensing, *pret. & pp.* incensed. [L. *incendo, incensus —candeo,* to be glowing hot.]
Incensement†, in-sens'ment, *n.* Violent irritation of the passions.
Incentive, in-sen'tiv, *a. That kindles;* inciting; encouraging or moving.—*n. That which kindles;* that which operates on the passions; that which prompts to good or ill; motive; incitement. [L. *candeo,* to glow.]
Inceptive, in-sep'tiv, *a. Noting beginning;* noting a verb which marks the commencement of an action or course of action.—*n. That which begins.* [L. *capio,* to take.]
Inceptor, in-sep'tėr, *n. A beginner;* a person who is on the point of taking the degree of M.A. at an English university. [L.]
Incessant, in-ses'ant, *a. Unceasing;* unintermitted; continual; perpetual. [L. *cesso,* to cease.]
Incessantly, in-ses'ant-li, *adv. Without ceasing;* continually.
Incest, in'sest, *n. Unchastity†; criminal intercourse* between persons related within the degrees of marriage; marriage within proscribed degrees of blood or family relationship. [L. *castus,* chaste.]
Incestuous, in-sest'ū-us, *a. Guilty of incest;* involving the crime of incest.
Incestuously, in-sest'ū-us-li, *adv. In an incestuous manner.*
Inch, insh, *n. The twelfth part* of a foot in length; proverbially, a small quantity or degree; a critical moment†. *vi.* To move slowly. [Sax. *ince*—L. *uncia,* a twelfth part.]
Inched, insht, *a. Containing inches.*
Inch-meal, insh'mēl, *n. A part an inch long.*—*adv. By inches;* by little and little. [*inch,* and Sax. *mæl,* a part.]
Incidence, in'si-dens, *n. A falling into or on;* an incident; the direction in which a body or a ray of light or heat falls on any surface. [Fr.—L. *cado,* to fall.]
Incident, in'si-dent, *a. Falling into or on;* casual; apt to happen; appertaining to the chief.—*n. That which falls to;* that which happens aside of the main design; an episode; an event; adventure; chance; something necessarily appertaining to another, which is termed the *principal.* [Fr.—L. *cado,* to fall.]
Incidental, in-si-dent'al, *a. Falling or happening to;* casual; not necessary to the chief purpose.
Incidentally, in-si-dent'al-li, *adv. Casually;* without intention; beside the main design.
Incipient, in-si'pi-ent, *a. Taking rise; beginning.* [L. *capio,* to take.]
Incision, in-si'zhon, *n. A cutting into;* a cut; the separation of the surface of any substance made by a sharp instrument. [Fr.—L. *cædo, cæsum,* to cut.]
Incisive, in-sī'siv, *a. Having the quality of cutting into;* sarcastic; biting. [Fr. *incisif.*]
Incisor, in-sīz'ėr, *n. A cutter;* a foretooth, which cuts or separates. [L.]
Incite, in-sīt', *vt. To move to action* by impulse or influence; to stimulate; to stir up; to encourage; to animate. *ppr.* inciting, *pret. & pp.* incited. [Fr. *inciter*—L. *cieo, citum,* to put in motion.]
Incitement, in-sīt'ment, *n. That which incites;* motive; stimulus; encouragement.
Incivil†, in-si'vil, *a.* Uncivil.
Incivility, in-si-vil'i-ti, *n. Want of civility;* want of courtesy toward others; any act of ill-breeding; rudeness.
Inclemency, in-kle'men-si, *n. Want of clemency;* unmercifulness; harshness; boisterousness; storminess; severe cold, &c., as of the weather or season.
Inclement, in-kle'ment, *a. Not clement;* destitute of a mild and kind temper; stormy; boisterous; rigorously cold. [L. *inclēmens.*]
Inclemently, in-kle'ment-li, *adv. In an inclement manner.*
Inclination, in-klin-ā'shon, *n. A bending to one side;* a leaning or tendency towards; any deviation of a body or line from an upright position, or from a parallel line, toward another body; a leaning of the mind or will; bent; proneness; propensity; desire; love. [Fr.—L. *inclinatio.*]
Incline, in-klīn', *vi. To lean towards;* to deviate from an erect or parallel line toward any object; to slope; to be disposed; to have some wish or desire; to have an appetite.—*vt. To cause to lean or bend towards or away from;* to cause to deviate from an erect or parallel line; to give a leaning to; to give a tendency, as to the will or affections; to dispose; to cause to stoop or bow. *n. An inclined plane;* a slope, as of a railway. *ppr.* inclining, *pret. & pp.* inclined. [Fr. *incliner*—L. *inclīno,* Gr. *klinō,* to lean, to bend.]
Inclined, in-klīnd', *p.a. Having a leaning* or inclination; disposed.
Inclining, in-klīn'ing, *p.a. Leaning.*
Inclip†, in-klip', *vt.* To grasp.
Inclose, in-klōs', *vt. To confine or keep in;* to confine on all sides; to environ; to encompass; to cover with a wrapper or envelope; to cover under seal, as a letter. *ppr.* inclosing, *pret. & pp.* inclosed. [Norm. *enclose*—L. *claudo, clausus,* to shut.]

Fate, fär, fat, fall; mē, met, hėr; pīne, pin; nōte, not, mōve; tūbe, tub, bu̇ll; oil, pound.

Inclosed, in-klōzd', *p.a. Confined* on all sides; covered and sealed.
Inclosure, in-klō'zhŭr, *n. Act of inclosing*; state of being inclosed; that which incloses; a space inclosed or fenced; that which is inclosed in an envelope, as a paper; a fence. [Norm. *enclostrure*.]
Include, in-klūd', *vt. To confine within*; to embrace within limits; to comprise; to comprehend; to contain. *ppr.* including, *pret. & pp.* included. [L. *includo—claudo*, to shut.]
Inclusion, in-klū'zhon, *n. Act of including*. [L. *inclusio*.]
Inclusive, in-klū'siv, *a. Inclosing*; comprehended in the number or sum. [Fr. *inclusif*.]
Inclusively, in-klū'siv-li, *adv.* So as to include the last or first particular, or both particulars bounding the series.
Incog. in-kog', *adv. In concealment*; in disguise. [contracted from *incognito*.]
Incognito, in-kog'ni-tō, *a. Unknown*; disguised.—*adv. In concealment*; in a disguise. [It.—L. *nosco*, to know.]
Incognizable, in-kon'iz-a-bl, *a. Not cognisable*; that cannot be recognized, known, or distinguished.
Incoherence, in-kō-hēr'ens, *n. Want of coherence*; want of connection; inconsistency; that which does not agree with other parts of the same thing.
Incoherent, in-kō-hēr'ent, *a. Not coherent*; loose; wanting agreement; incongruous; having no dependence of one part on another.
Incoherently, in-kō-hēr'ent-li, *adv.* Inconsistently; without coherence of parts.
Incombustibility, in-kom-bust'i-bil''-li-ti, *n. Quality of being incombustible.* [Fr. *incombustibilité*.]
Incombustible, in-kom-bust'i-bl, *a. Not combustible*; not to be burned, decomposed, or consumed by fire.
Income, in'kum, *n. That which comes in*; that gain which proceeds from labour, business, property, or possession of any kind.
Incoming, in'kum-ing, *p.a. Coming in.*
Incommensurability, in-kom-men-sūr-a-bil''li-ti, *n. Quality or state of being incommensurable.*
Incommensurable, in - kom - men' sŭr-a-bl, *a. Not commensurable*; having no common measure.
Incommensurably, in - kom - men' sŭr-a-bli, *adv.* So as *not* to admit of a *common measure.*
Incommensurate, in-kom-men'sŭr-āt, *a. Not commensurate*; not admitting of a common measure; not adequate; insufficient.
Incommode, in-kom-mōd', *vt. To give trouble to*; to annoy; to molest; to inconvenience; to embarrass. *ppr.* incommoding, *pret. & pp.* incommoded. [Fr. *incommoder*— L. *commodo*, to make suitable—*modus*, measure.]
Incommodious, in-kom-mōd'i-us, *a. Not commodious*; not affording ease; giving trouble without much injury.
Incommodiously, in-kom-mōd'i-us-li, *adv.* Inconveniently; unsuitably.
Incommunicability, in-kom-mū'ni-ka-bil''li-ti, *n. Quality of not being communicable.*
Incommunicable, in-kom-mū'ni-ka-bl, *a. That cannot be communicated* or imparted to others.
Incommunicative, in-kom-mū'ni-kāt-iv, *a. Not communicative*; unsocial.
Incomparable, in-kom'pa-ra-bl, *a. Not comparable*; that admits of no comparison with other-; matchless.

Incomparableness, in-kom'pa-ra-bl-nes, *n. State or quality of being incomparable*; excellence beyond comparison.
Incomparably, in-kom'pa-ra-bli, *adv. Beyond comparison.*
Incompatibility, in-kom-pat'i-bil''li-ti, *n. State or quality of being incompatible*; that quality of a thing which renders it impossible that it should subsist with something else; irreconcilable disagreement.
Incompatible, in-kom-pat'i-bl, *a. Not compatible*; that cannot subsist with something else.
Incompatibly, in-kom-pat'i-bli, *adv. Inconsistently*; incongruously.
Incompetence, Incompetency, in-kom'-pē-tens, in-kom'pē-ten-si, *n. State or quality of being incompetent*; inadequacy; inability; want of sufficient strength; want of adequate means; want of proper qualifications.
Incompetent, in-kom'pē-tent, *a. Not competent*; unfit; not having sufficient power; wanting suitable authority.
Incompetently, in-kom'pē-tent-li, *adv.* Insufficiently; inadequately.
Incomplete, in-kom-plēt', *a. Not complete*; imperfect; defective.
Incompletely, in-kom-plēt'li, *adv.* Imperfectly.
Incompleteness, in-kom-plēt'nes, *n. State of being incomplete*; an unfinished state; defectiveness.
Incomprehensibility, in-kom'prē-hens'-i-bil''li-ti, *n. Quality of being incomprehensible*; inconceivableness. [Fr. *incompréhensibilité.*]
Incomprehensible, in-kom'prē-hens''-i-bl, *a. That cannot be comprehended*; that is beyond the reach of the human intellect.
Incomprehensibly, in-kom'prē-hens''-i-bli, *adv.* Inconceivably.
Incompressibility, in-kom-pres'i-bil''li-ti, *n. State or quality of being incompressible* or of resisting compression.
Incompressible, in-kom'pres-i-bl, *a. Not to be compressed*; not capable of being reduced by force into a smaller compass.
Incomputable, in-kom-pūt'a-bl, *a. That cannot be computed.*
Inconceivable, in-kon-sēv'a-bl, *a. That cannot be conceived* by the mind; that cannot be understood.
Inconceivableness, in-kon-sēv'a-bl-nes, *n. Quality of being inconceivable.*
Inconceivably, in-kon-sēv'a-bli, *adv. In a manner beyond conception.*
Inconclusive, in-kon-klūs'iv, *a. Not conclusive*; not concluding or settling a point in debate.
Inconclusively, in-kon-klūs'iv-li, *adv. In an inconclusive manner.*
Inconclusiveness, in-kon-klūs'iv-nes, *n. Quality of being inconclusive.*
Incondensability, in-kon-dens'a-bil''li-ti, *n. Quality of being incondensable.*
Incondensable, in-kon-dens'a-bl, *a. Not condensable*; that cannot be made more dense or compact.
Incongruity, in-kon-grō'i-ti, *n. Want of congruity*; inconsistency; unsuitableness of one thing to another; want of symmetry.
Incongruous, in-kon'grō-us, *a. Not congruous*; unsuitable; inappropriate; unfit.
Incongruously, in-kon'grō-us-li, *adv.* Inconsistently; unsuitably; unfitly.
Inconsequence, in - kon' sē-kwens, *n. Want of logical consequence* or of just inference; inconclusiveness.
Inconsequent, in-kon'sē-kwent, *a. Not*

having logical consequenc.; not following from the premises.
Inconsequential, in-kon'sē-kwen''shi-al, *a. Not consequential*; not of consequence; not of importance.
Inconsequentially, in - kon' sē-kwen''-shi-al-li, *adv. Without regular sequence.*
Inconsiderable, in-kon-sid'ēr-a-bl, *a. Not considerable*; unimportant; small; insignificant.
Inconsiderably, in-kon-sid'ēr-a-bli, *adv.* In a small degree.
Inconsiderate, in-kon-sid'ēr-āt, *a. Not considerate*; not attending to the circumstances which regard safety or propriety; heedless; negligent; indiscreet; incautious; rash.
Inconsiderately, in - kon - sid' ēr - āt-li, *adv.* Heedlessly; imprudently.
Inconsiderateness, in-kon-sid'ēr-āt-nes, *n. Quality of being inconsiderate*; want of due regard to consequences; imprudence.
Inconsistence, Inconsistency, in-kon-sist'ens, in-kon-sist'en-si, *n. Want of consistency*; such contrariety between things that both cannot subsist together; argument or narrative where one part destroys the other; self-contradiction; unsteadiness; changeableness.
Inconsistent, in-kon-sist'ent, *a. Not consistent*; incompatible; absolutely opposed; so contrary as to imply the destruction of something else; not uniform; being contrary at different times.
Inconsistently, in-kon-sist'ent-li, *adv.* Incongruously; without steadiness or uniformity.
Inconsolable, in-kon-sōl'a-bl, *a. Not to be consoled*; grieved beyond susceptibility of comfort.
Inconsolably, in-kon-sōl'a-bli, *adv. In an inconsolable manner.*
Inconspicuous, in-kon-spi'kū-us, *a. Not conspicuous*; not to be perceived by the sight.
Inconstancy, in-kon'stan-si, *n. Want of constancy*; mutability of temper or affection; fickleness; want of uniformity.
Inconstant, in-kon'stant, *a. Not constant*; subject to change of opinion or purpose; not firm in resolution; fickle; subject to change, as things; variable.
Inconstantly, in-kon'stant-li, *adv. In an inconstant manner.*
Incontestable, in-kon-test'a-bl, *a. Not contestable*; not to be disputed; unquestionable.
Incontestably, in-kon-test'a-bli, *adv. In a manner to preclude debate.*
Incontinence, in-kon'ti-nens, *n. Want of continence*; want of restraint of the passions or appetites, or the sexual appetite; lewdness.
Incontinent, in-kon'ti-nent, *a. Not continent*; not restraining the passions or appetites; unchaste.—*adv.* Instantly; immediately.
Incontinently, in-kon'ti-nent-li, *adv.* Without due restraint of the passions; at once.
Incontrovertibility, in-kon'trō-vērt'i-bil''li-ti, *n. State or quality of being incontrovertible.*
Incontrovertible, in-kon'trō-vērt''i-bl, *a. Not to be controverted*; too clear to admit of dispute; indubitable.
Incontrovertibly, in-kon'trō-vērt''i-bli, *adv.* In a manner or to a degree that precludes debate or controversy.
Inconvenience, in-kon-vē'ni-ens, *n. Quality of being inconvenient*; anything

that increases the difficulty of action or success; disquiet; annoyance; molestation; trouble.—*vt.* To *put to inconvenience;* to trouble. *ppr.* inconveniencing, *pret. & pp.* inconvenienced.
Inconvenient, in-kon-vē'ni-ent, *a. Not convenient; unsuitable;* incommodious; giving trouble or uneasiness; disturbing; molesting.
Inconveniently, in-kon-vē'ni-ent-li, *adv.* Unsuitably; unseasonably.
Inconvertibility, in-kon-vėrt'i-bil''li-ti, *n. Quality of not being convertible.*
Inconvertible, in-kon-vėrt'i-bl, *a. Not convertible;* that cannot be changed into something else.
Inconvertibly, in-kon-vėrt'i-bli, *adv. In an inconvertible manner.*
Incony†, in-kō'ni, *a.* Unlearned; artless.
Incorporate, in-kor'pō-rāt, *a. United in one body;* embodied; associated; mixed.—*vt.* To embody; to mix and embody, as one substance in another; to blend; to work into another mass or body; to associate in another government; to form into a legal body or body politic, as a bank; to mix, as different ingredients in one mass or body.—*vi. To unite so as to make a part of another body;* to be mixed or blended; to grow into or coalesce. *ppr.* incorporating, *pret. & pp.* incorporated. [Late L. *incorporatus*—L. *corpus, corporis,* the body.]
Incorporated, in-kor'pō-rāt-ed, *p.a. United in a legal body.*
Incorporation, in-kor'pō-rā''shon, *n. Act of incorporating;* union of different ingredients in one mass; formation of a legal or political body by the union of individuals. [Fr.]
Incorporeal, in-kor-pō're-al, *a. Not corporeal; bodiless;* immaterial; spiritual.
Incorporeally, in-kor-pō're-al-li, *adv. Without body;* immaterially.
Incorpse†, in-korps', *vt. To unite into a body;* to incorporate.
Incorrect, in-ko-rekt', *a. Not correct;* inaccurate; wrong; not according to truth, law, or morality.
Incorrectly, in-ko-rekt'li, *adv.* Not in accordance with truth.
Incorrectness, in-ko-rekt'nes, *n. Want of correctness;* inaccuracy.
Incorrigibility, in-ko'ri-ji-bil''li-ti, *n. Quality of being incorrigible;* hopeless depravity in persons and error in things.
Incorrigible, in-ko'ri-ji-bl, *a. That cannot be corrected;* bad beyond correction; too depraved to be reformed.
Incorrigibly, in-ko'ri-ji-bli, *adv.* To a degree of depravity beyond all means of amendment.
Incorrodible, in-ko-rōd'i-bl, *a. That cannot be corroded.*
Incorrupt, in-ko-rupt', *a. Not corrupt;* not defiled or depraved; pure; sound; above the power of bribes.
Incorruptibility, in-ko-rupt'i-bil''li-ti, *n. Quality of being incorruptible.*
Incorruptible, in-ko-rupt'i-bl, *a. Not corruptible;* that cannot corrupt or decay; that cannot be bribed; inflexibly just and upright.
Incorruptibly, in-ko-rupt'i-bli, *adv.* In a way *not admitting of corruption.*
Incorruption, in-ko-rup'shon, *n. Incapability of being corrupted;* incorrantibility.
Incorruptly, in-ko-rupt'li, *adv. Without corruption.*
Incorruptness, in-ko-rupt'nes, *n.* Probity; integrity.
Increase, in-krēs', *vi. To become greater* in bulk or quantity; to grow; to become bigger and bigger; to become more in number; to advance in value; to swell; to extend; to be fertile.—*vt. To cause to grow;* to make greater in bulk or amount; to advance in quality; to add to any quality or affection; to lengthen; to spread; to aggravate. *ppr.* increasing, *pret. & pp.* increased. [L. *incresco—cresco,* to grow.]
Increase, in'krēs, *n. A becoming larger* in size, extent, or quantity; enlargement; growth; extension; increment; profit; interest; that which is added to the original stock; issue; offspring; generation†.
Increasing, in-krēs'ing, *p.a.* Advancing in any quality, good or bad.
Increasingly, in-krēs'ing-li, *adv.* In the *way of growing* or increasing.
Incredibility, in-kred'i-bil''li-ti, *n. The quality of being incredible,* or of surpassing belief.
Incredible, in-kred'i-bl, *a. Not credible; that cannot be believed.*
Incredibly, in-kred'i-bli, *adv. In a manner to preclude belief.*
Incredulity, in-krē-dū'li-ti, *n. Quality of being incredulous;* indisposition to believe; unbelief; scepticism.
Incredulous, in-kred'ū-lus, *a. Not credulous; not believing;* refusing or withholding belief.
Incredulously, in-kred'ū-lus-li, *adv.* With *unbelief* or *incredulity.*
Increment, in'kre-ment, *n. Growth;* a growing in bulk, quantity, number, value, or amount; matter added; augmentation. [L. *incrementum—cresco,* to grow—Sans. *kri,* to make.]
Incrust, in-krust', *vt. To cover with a crust* or with a hard coat; to form a crust on.
Incrustation, in-krust-ā'shon, *n. Act of forming a crust;* a crust or coat of anything on the surface of a body; a covering or inlaying of marble, mosaic, or other substance. [Fr.]
Incubate, in'kū-bāt, *vi. To lie in or upon a thing;* to brood; to sit, as on eggs for hatching. *ppr.* incubating, *pret. & pp.* incubated. [L. *incubo, incubatum—cumbo,* to lie down.]
Incubation, in-kū-bā'shon, *n. A lying upon anything;* a brooding; act of sitting on eggs, for the purpose of hatching young. [Fr.]
Incubus, in'kū-bus, *n. One who lies upon;* the nightmare; an imaginary spirit or fairy, supposed to occasion the nightmare; an incumbrance; a heavy weight. [L.—*cumbo,* to lie down.]
Inculcate, in-kul'kāt, *vt. To tread into;* to urge forcibly; to impress by frequent admonitions; to instill; to implant; to infuse. *ppr.* inculcating, *pret. & pp.* inculcated. [L. *inculco, inculcatus—calx, calcis,* the heel.]
Inculcation, in-kul-kā'shon, *n.* The action of impressing by repeated admonitions. [Late L. *inculcatio.*]
Inculpable, in-kul'pa-bl, *a. Not culpable.*
Inculpate, in-kul'pāt, *vt.* To censure; to impute guilt to. *ppr.* inculpating, *pret. & pp.* inculpated. [L. *inculpo, inculpatus—culpa,* a fault.]
Inculpation, in-kul-pā'shon, *n. Blame;* censure. [L. *culpa,* a fault.]
Incumbency, in-kum'ben-si, *n. State of being incumbent;* the state of holding a benefice or an office.
Incumbent, in-kum'bent, *a. Leaning on* or resting against; lying on, as duty or obligation; emphatically urging to performance; indispensable.—*n.* The person who is in present possession of a benefice or of any office. [L. *incumbens—cumbo,* to lie down.]
Incur, in-kėr', *vt. To run into;* to fall in with; to become liable to; to become subject to, as a penalty; to bring on, as expense. *ppr.* incurring, *pret. & pp.* incurred. [L. *incurro—curro,* to run.]
Incurability, in-kūr'a-bil''li-ti, *n. State of being incurable;* insusceptibility of cure or remedy.
Incurable, in-kūr'a-bl, *a. Not curable;* beyond the power of medicine; not admitting remedy; irretrievable.—*n. A person diseased beyond the reach of cure.*
Incurably, in-kūr'a-bli, *adv.* In a manner that renders cure impracticable.
Incursion, in-kėr'shon, *n. A running or entering into a territory with hostile intention;* an irruption; applied to the expeditions of small detachments of an enemy's army. [Fr.—L. *curro, cursum,* to run.]
Incurvate, in-kėrv'āt, *vt. To curve;* to turn from a right line. [L. *incurvo, incurvatus—curvo,* to bend.]
Incurvation, in-kėrv-ā'shon, *n. A bending or curving;* state of being bent or turned from a right line. [Fr.]
Indart†, in-därt', *vt.* To thrust or strike in.
Indebted, in-det'ed, *a. Having incurred a debt;* held or obliged to pay; obliged by something received, for which restitution or gratitude is due; beholden. [L. *debeo, debitum,* to owe.]
Indebtedness, in-det'ed-nes, *n. State of being indebted.*
Indecency, in-dē'sen-si, *n. Want of decency; unseemliness;* that which is unbecoming in language or manners; immodesty; impurity.
Indecent, in-dē'sent, *a. Not decent; unseemly;* unfit to be seen or heard; immodest; impure; filthy.
Indecently, in-dē'sent-li, *adv.* In a manner to offend modesty or delicacy.
Indecision, in-dē-si'zhon, *n. Want of decision;* want of settled purpose, or of firmness in the determinations of the will; a wavering of mind; hesitation.
Indecisive, in-dē-sīs'iv, *a. Not decisive;* not bringing to a final close; wavering; vacillating.
Indecisively, in-dē-sīs'iv-li, *adv. Without decision.*
Indeclinable, in-dē-klīn'a-bl, *a. Not declinable;* not varied by terminations.
Indeclinably, in-dē-klīn'a-bli, *adv.* Without variation of termination.
Indecomposable, in-dē-kom-pōz'a-bl, *a. Not capable of decomposition.*
Indecorous, in-dē-kō'rus, *a. Not decorous; unseemly;* violating good manners; rude; uncivil.
Indecorously, in-dē-kō'rus-li, *adv.* In *an unbecoming manner.*
Indecorum, in-dē-kō'rum, *n. Indecency;* impropriety of behaviour; an unbecoming action. [L.]
Indeed, in-dēd', *adv. In reality; in fact;* really; truly.
Indefatigable, in-dē-fat'ig-a-bl, *a. That cannot be fatigued;* untiring; persevering; not yielding to fatigue. [L. *indefatigabilis—fatigo,* to weary.]
Indefatigably, in-dē-fat'ig-a-bli, *adv. Without yielding to fatigue.*
Indefeasibility, in-dē-fēz'i-bil''li-ti, *n. Quality or state of being indefeasible.*
Indefeasible, in-dē-fēz'i-bl, *a. Not defeasible;* that cannot be made void.

Fāte, fär, fat, fąll; mē, met, hėr; pīne, pin; nōte, not, mȯve; tūbe, tub, bu̧ll; oil, pound.

Indefeasibly, in-dē-fēz'i-bli, *adv.* In a manner not to be defeated or made void.
Indefectible, in-dē-fekt'i-bl, *a. Not defectible;* unfailing.
Indefensible, in-dē-fens'i-bl, *a. Not defensible; that cannot be defended;* not to be vindicated or justified.
Indefensibly, in-dē-fens'i-bli, *adv.* In an *indefensible manner.*
Indefinable, in-dē-fīn'a-bl, *a.* See UNDEFINABLE.
Indefinite, in-de'fin-it, *a. Not definite;* not precise or certain; that has no certain limits, or to which the human mind can affix none; not given or defined in magnitude, as a line.
Indefinitely, in-de'fin-it-li, *adv. Without any settled limitation.*
Indefiniteness, in-de'fin-it-nes, *n. Quality of being indefinite.*
Indeliberate, in-dē-lib'e-rāt, *a. Not deliberate;* done without deliberation; sudden.
Indeliberately, in-dē-lib'e-rāt-li, *adv. Without deliberation* or premeditation.
Indelibility, in-de'li-bil''i-ti, *n. Quality of being indelible.*
Indelible, in-de'li-bl, *a. Not delible;* that cannot be effaced, cancelled, or lost.
Indelibly, in-de'li-bli, *adv. In a manner not to be blotted out or effaced.*
Indelicacy, in-de'li-ka-si, *n. Want of delicacy;* want of decency in language or behaviour; coarseness of manners or language.
Indelicate, in-de'li-kāt, *a. Wanting delicacy;* unbecoming; offensive to good manners or to purity of mind; rude; indecent.
Indelicately, in-de'li-kāt-li, *adv. Indecently.*
Indemnification, in-dem'ni-fi-kā''shon, *n. Act of indemnifying;* security against loss; reimbursement of loss, damage, or penalty.
Indemnify, in-dem'ni-fi, *vt. To make safe from loss;* to secure against loss, damage, or penalty; to make good; to compensate for loss or injury. *ppr.* indemnifying, *pret. & pp.* indemnified. [L. *damnum,* loss, and *facio,* to make.]
Indemnity, in-dem'ni-ti, *n. Security given to save harmless;* recompense for injury sustained. [Fr. *indemnité.*]
Indemonstrable, in-dē-mon'stra-bl, *a. That cannot be demonstrated.*
Indent, in-dent', *vt. To form into the resemblance of teeth;* to notch; to jag; to cut in and out; to bind out by indenture.—*vi.* To be cut or notched; to crook or turn.—*n.* A cut or notch in the margin of anything; an indentation. [L. *dens, dentis,* a tooth.]
Indentation, in-dent-ā'shon, *n. Act of indenting;* a notch; a cut in the margin of paper or other things; a recess or depression in any border.
Indented, in-dent'ed, *p.a.* Notched; bound out by covenants in writing.
Indenting, in-dent'ing, *p.n.* An impression like that made by a *tooth.*
Indenture, in-dent'ūr, *n. That which is indented;* a writing containing a contract between two or more parties; a covenant.—*vt. To bind by indentures.* *ppr.* indenturing, *pret. & pp.* indentured. [Low L. *indentura.*]
Independence, in-dē-pend'ens, *n. State of being independent;* complete exemption from control; ability to support one's self; a state of mind in which a person acts without influence from others; self-reliance; political freedom.
Independent, in-de-pend'ent, *a. Not dependent;* not subject to the control of others; not depending on others; affording the means of independence; not subject to bias; free; unconstrained; exclusive (with *of* or *on*).—*n. One who is not dependent;* one who, in religious affairs, maintains that every congregation of Christians is a complete church, subject to no superior authority.
Independently, in-dē-pend'ent-li, *adv. Without depending* or relying on others.
Indescribable, in-dē-skrib'a-bl, *a. That cannot be described.*
Indestructibility, in-dē-strukt'i-bil''i-ti, *n. Quality of being indestructible.*
Indestructible, in-dē-strukt'i-bl,*a. That cannot be destroyed;* incapable of decomposition; imperishable.
Indestructibly, in-dē-strukt'i-bli, *adv. In an indestructible manner.*
Indeterminable, in-dē-tėrm'in-a-bl, *a. That cannot be determined.*
Indeterminate, in-dē-tėrm'in-āt, *a. Not determinate;* not settled or fixed; not definite; not precise or certain.
Indeterminately, in-dē-tėrm''in-āt-li, *adv.* Not in any settled manner; not with precision of signification.
Indetermination, in-dē-tėrm''in-ā''shon, *n. Want of determination;* an unsettled or wavering state; vacillation.
Index, in'deks, *n.* Indexes (in math. Indices), *pl. That which points out;* the hand that points to anything, as the hour of the day, the road to a place, &c.; a table of the contents of a book; an exponent; a prelude.—*vt. To provide with an index;* to place in an index; to reduce to an index, as a book. [L. *indico,* to point out—*dico,* to make known—Sans. *dish,* to show.]
Indexterity, in-deks-te'ri-ti, *n. Want of dexterity;* awkwardness.
Indiaman, in'di-a-man, *n. A large ship* employed in the *India* trade.
Indian, in'di-an, *a. Pertaining to either of the Indies,* East or West, or to the aborigines of America.—*n. A native of the Indies.*
Indian-rubber, in'di-an-rub-bėr, *n.* The caoutchouc, a gum or resin of extraordinary elasticity, and so named because it was at first employed to *rub* out pencil marks on paper.
Indicate, in'di-kāt, *vt. To point out;* to direct, as the mind to a knowledge of something; to show; to denote; to point to as the proper remedies. *ppr.* indicating, *pret. & pp.* indicated. [L. *indico, indicatus—dico,* to make known.]
Indication, in-di-kā'shon, *n. Act of pointing out;* mark; sign; any symptom in a disease which serves to direct to suitable remedies; intelligence given. [Fr.]
Indicative, in-di'kāt-iv, *a. That serves to indicate;* showing; giving intimation of something not obvious; designating a mood of the verb that *indicates,* that is, which affirms positively. [Fr. *indicatif.*]
Indicatively, in-di'kāt-iv-li, *adv. In a manner to show* or signify.
Indicator, in'di-kāt-ėr, *n. He or that which indicates;* an instrument for ascertaining the amount of the pressure of steam, and the state of the vacuum throughout the stroke of a steam-engine. [Late L.]
Indict, in-dīt', *vt.* To charge or accuse in an *enjoined* or prescribed form of words; to charge with a crime or misdemeanour, in writing, by a grand-jury under oath. [L. *indico, indictus—dico,* to make known.]
Indictable, in-dīt'a-bl, *a. That may be indicted;* subject to indictment.
Indiction, in-dik'shon, *n.* Originally, *proclamation;* a cycle of fifteen years, instituted by Constantine the Great. [Fr.—L. *dico,* to make known.]
Indictment, in-dīt'ment, *n. Act of indicting;* a written accusation of a crime or misdemeanour, preferred by a grand-jury under oath to a court; the paper containing the accusation. [Old Fr. *endictement.*]
Indifference, in-dif'fėr-ens, *n. Want of difference* or *distinction;* a state in which the mind is not inclined to one side more than the other; impartiality; unconcernedness; apathy.
Indifferent, in-dif'fėr-ent, *a. Showing no difference;* neutral; not inclined to one side, party, or thing more than to another; feeling no interest respecting anything; impartial; disinterested; careless; of a middling state or quality.—*adv.* To a moderate degree.
Indifferently, in-dif'fėr-ent-li, *adv. In an indifferent manner;* without concern; tolerably.
Indigence, in'di-jens, *n. State of being indigent;* poverty; want of estate or means of comfortable subsistence. [Fr.—L. *indigentia—egeo,* to want.]
Indigenous, in-di'jen-us, *a. Native,* as persons; produced naturally in a country; not exotic, as plants. [L. *indu—* Gr. *endon,* within, and *gigno,* to beget.]
Indigent, in'di-jent, *a. Being in want or need;* destitute of property or means of subsistence; needy; poor. [Fr.]
Indigently, in'di-jent-li, *adv. With indigence* or destitution.
Indigest, in-di-jest', *n.* A crude mass. *a.* Indigested.
Indigested, in-di-jest'ed, *a. Not digested;* not methodised; not reduced to due form; not concocted in the stomach; crude; not prepared by heat.
Indigestible, in-di-jest'i-bl, *a. Not digestible;* not easily prepared in the stomach for nourishing the body; not to be received or patiently endured.
Indigestion, in-di-jest'shon, *n. Want of digestion;* a failure of that change in food which prepares it for nutriment; dyspepsy.
Indign, in-dīn', *a. Unworthy.*
Indignant, in-dig'nant. *a. Affected with indignation;* affected at once with anger and disdain. [L. *indignans—dignor,* to deem worthy.]
Indignantly, in-dig'nant-li, *adv. With indignation.*
Indignation, in-dig-nā'shon, *n. State of being indignant;* a strong disapprobation of what is flagitious in character or conduct; ire; resentment; rage; extreme anger, particularly of the Supreme Being; terrible judgments; holy displeasure at one's self for sin. [Fr.]
Indignity, in-dig'ni-ti, *n. Unworthy* contemptuous *conduct* toward another; injury, accompanied with insult; contumely. [Fr. *indignité.*]
Indignly, in-dīn'li, *adv. Unworthily.*
Indigo, in'di-go, *n.* A well-known and beautiful blue vegetable dye, fr. an *India.* [Fr.]
Indirect, in-di-rekt', *a. Not direct;* deviating from a direct line; not tending to a purpose by the shortest course, or by the obvious ordinary means; not honest; tending to mislead or deceive.
Indirection, in-di-rek'shon, *n.* Dishonest practices.

Indirectly, in-di-rekt′li, *adv.* In an indirect manner; unfairly.
Indirectness, in-di-rekt′nes, *n.* State or quality of being indirect; obliquity.
Indiscreet, in-dis-krēt′, *a.* Not discreet; imprudent; injudicious; inconsiderate; hasty; not according to discretion, as conduct.
Indiscreetly, in-dis-krēt′li, *adv.* Not discreetly; without prudence.
Indiscretion, in-dis-kre′shon, *n.* Want of discretion; imprudence.
Indiscriminate, in-dis-krim′in-āt, *a.* Undistinguishing; not having discrimination; undistinguished or undistinguishable; promiscuous. [Low L. *indiscriminatus.*]
Indiscriminately, in-dis-krim′in-āt-li, *adv.* Without distinction; in confusion.
Indiscriminating, in-dis-krim′in-āt-ing, *p.a.* Not making any distinction.
Indispensable, in-dis-pens′a-bl, *a.* Not to be dispensed with; absolutely necessary or requisite.
Indispensably, in-dis-pens′a-bli, *adv.* Necessarily; in a manner or degree that forbids omission or want.
Indispose, in-dis-pōz′, *vt.* To put out of order; to render unfit; to disorder slightly; to disincline; to alienate, as the mind, and render it unfavourable to anything; to make disinclined (with *toward*). *ppr.* indisposing, *pret. & pp.* indisposed. [L. *in, dis,* and *pono, positum,* to place.]
Indisposed, in-dis-pōzd′, *p.a.* Slightly disordered; not in perfect health; averse; unwilling.
Indisposition, in-dis′pō-zi′′shon, *n.* State of being indisposed; slight disorder of the healthy functions of the body; disinclination; unwillingness; dislike; want of tendency or affinity.
Indisputable, in-dis′pūt-a-bl, *a.* Not to be disputed; unquestionable; certain; positive.
Indisputably, in-dis′pūt-a-bli, *adv.* Without dispute; unquestionably.
Indissolubility, in-dis′sō-lū-bil′′li-ti, *n.* Quality of being indissoluble; quality of being incapable of a breach; perpetuity of union; obligation or binding force.
Indissoluble, in-dis′sō-lū-bl, *a.* Not dissoluble; that cannot be dissolved or melted; that cannot be rightfully violated; not to be broken; firm; stable.
Indissolubly, in-dis′sō-lū-bli, *adv.* In a manner not to be dissolved or broken.
Indistinct, in-dis-tingkt′, *a.* Not distinct; not clear or distinct, intellectually considered; obscure; not presenting clear and well-defined images, as a prospect.
Indistinctly, in-dis-tingkt′li, *adv.* Without distinction; confusedly.
Indistinctness, in-dis-tingkt′nes, *n.* State or quality of being indistinct; uncertainty; obscurity; faintness.
Indite, in-dīt′, *vt.* To set forth in writing; to commit to words in writing; to direct or dictate what is to be uttered or written; to invite'. *ppr.* inditing, *pret. & pp.* indited. [L. *indico, indictum—dico,* to declare.]
Inditer, in-dīt′ėr, *n.* One who indites.
Individual, in-di-vid′ū-al, *a.* Not divided, or not to be divided; pertaining to one only, as individual efforts.—*n.* A single person or human being; a single animal or thing of any kind; an object which is, in the strict and primary sense, one, and therefore cannot be divided. [Fr. *individuel*—L. *divido,* to divide—*viduu,* a widow.]
Individuality, in-di-vid′ū-al′′li-ti, *n.*

Quality of being individual; distinct existence; a state of oneness. [Fr. *individualité.*]
Individually, in-di-vid′ū-al-li, *adv.* Separately; by itself; with separate or distinct existence.
Indivisibility, in-di-viz′i-bil′′li-ti, *n.* State or quality of being indivisible.
Indivisible, in-di-viz′i-bl, *a.* Not divisible; that cannot be divided; not separable into parts.—*n.* An elementary part or particle.
Indivisibly, in-di-viz′i-bli, *adv.* So as not to be capable of division.
Indocile, in-dō′sil, *a.* Not docile or teachable; not easily instructed; dull; intractable, as a beast.
Indocility, in-dō-sil′i-ti, *n.* Quality of being indocile; dulness of intellect; intractableness.
Indoctrinate, in-dok′trin-āt, *vt.* To imbue with any doctrine or science; to instruct in rudiments or principles (with *in*). *ppr.* indoctrinating, *pret. & pp.* indoctrinated. [L. *doctrina,* learning —*doceo,* to teach.]
Indoctrination, in-dok′trin-ā′′shon, *n.* Act of indoctrinating.
Indolence, in′dō-lens, *n.* Freedom from painful toil; habitual love of ease; laziness; want of exertion of body or mind, proceeding from love of ease or aversion to toil. [Fr.—L. *indolentia*—*doleo,* to ache.]
Indolent, in′dō-lent, *a.* Free from or averse to painful labour; slothful; habitually idle; lazy; sluggish; indulging in ease. [Fr.]
Indolently, in′dō-lent-li, *adv.* In habitual idleness and ease.
Indomitable, in-dom′it-a-bl, *a.* That cannot be tamed or subdued; untamable. [Fr. *indomptable*—L. *domo, domitum,* to tame.]
Indoor, in′dōr, *a.* Being within doors; being within the house.
Indorsable, in-dors′a-bl, *a.* That may be indorsed, and made payable to order.
Indorse, in-dors′, *vt.* To write on the back of, as of a written instrument; to assign or transfer by indorsement; to give sanction or currency to. *ppr.* indorsing, *pret. & pp.* indorsed. [Fr. *endosser*—L. *dorsum,* the back.]
Indorsement, in-dors′ment, *n.* Act of indorsing or writing on the back of a note, bill, or other written instrument; that which is so written; sanction or support given.
Indorser, in-dors′ėr, *n.* The person who indorses a note, &c., and thus becomes liable for its payment.
Indorsing, in-dors′ing, *p.n.* Act of making an indorsement.
Indrench, in-drensh′, *vt.* To drench.
Indubitable, in-dū′bit-a-bl, *a.* Not to be doubted; too plain to admit of doubt; incontestable. [Fr.—L. *dubito,* to doubt.]
Indubitably, in-dū′bit-a-bli, *adv.* Undoubtedly; unquestionably.
Induce, in-dūs′, *vt.* To lead to or into anything; to lead, as by persuasion; to prevail on; to actuate; to incite; to bring on; to cause, as changes. *ppr.* inducing, *pret. & pp.* induced. [L. *induco—dūco,* to lead.]
Induced, in-dūst′, *p.a.* Influenced; caused.
Inducement, in-dūs′ment, *n.* That which induces; anything that leads the mind to will or to act; motive; reason.
Induct, in-dukt′, *vt.* To lead into; to introduce, as to a benefice or office; to put in actual possession of any office,

with the customary forms. [L. *induco, inductus*—*duco,* to lead.]
Inductile, in-duk′til, *a.* Not ductile; not capable of being drawn into threads, as a metal.
Induction, in-duk′shon, *n.* A leading into; the bringing forward of particulars, with a view to establish some general conclusion; the legitimate inference of some general truth from all the particulars embraced under it; the introduction of a person into an office by the usual forms and ceremonies. [Fr.—L. *inductio—duco,* to lead.]
Inductive, in-dukt′iv, *a.* Leading to inferences; proceeding by induction; employed in drawing conclusions from premises.
Inductively, in-dukt′iv-li, *adv.* By induction or inference.
Indue, in-dū′, *vt.* To put on; to clothe; to supply with; to endow. [L. *induo.*]
Indulge, in-dulj′, *vt.* To be complacent to; not to restrain; to give free course to; to gratify; not to check or restrain the will, appetite, or desire of; to grant, as by favour; to yield to the wishes of; to humour.—*vi.* To indulge one's self. *ppr.* indulging, *pret. & pp.* indulged. [L. *indulgeo—dulcis,* sweet.]
Indulgence, in-dulj′ens, *n.* Act of indulging; complaisance; favour granted; gratification; forbearance of restraint or control. [Fr.]
Indulgent, in-dulj′ent, *a.* Complacent; mild; yielding to the wishes, humour, or appetites of those under one's care; not severe. [Fr.]
Indulgently, in-dulj′ent-li, *adv.* With unrestrained enjoyment; mildly.
Indurate, in′dū-rāt, *vi.* To harden or become hard.—*vt.* To make hard; to make unfeeling; to render obdurate. *ppr.* indurating, *pret. & pp.* indurated. [L. *induro, induratus—durus,* hard—Sans. *dhri,* to hold.]
Indurated, in′dū-rāt-ed, *p.a.* Hardened; made obdurate.
Induration, in-dū-rā′shon, *n.* Act of hardening; hardness of heart; obduracy. [Low L. *induratio.*]
Industrial, in-dus′tri-al, *a.* Pertaining to industry, or to the products of industry, art, or manufacture. [Fr. *industriel.*]
Industrially, in-dus′tri-al-li, *adv.* With reference to industry.
Industrious, in-dus′tri-us, *a.* Active; assiduous; diligent in business or study; diligent in a particular pursuit, or to a particular end; given to industry; characterized by diligence, as habits. [L. *industrius.*]
Industriously, in-dus′tri-us-li, *adv.* In an industrious manner.
Industry, in′dus-tri, *n.* Activity; assiduity; steady attention to business. [Fr. *industrie*—L. *industria.*]
Indwelling, in′dwel-ing, *a.* Dwelling within; remaining in the heart, even after it is renewed, as sin.—*p.n.* Residence within, or in the heart or soul.
Inebriate, in-ē′bri-āt, *vt.* To make drunk; to stimulate; to disorder the senses of; to stupify, or to make furious or frantic. *ppr.* inebriating, *pret. & pp.* inebriated. [L. *inebrio, inebriatus—ebrius,* drunk.]
Inebriety, in-ē-brī′e-ti, *n.* Drunkenness.
Inedited, in-ed′it-ed, *a.* Not edited; unpublished.
Ineffable, in-ef′fa-bl, *a.* Unspeakable; that cannot be expressed in words; inexpressible; unutterable (usually in a good sense). [Fr.—L. *fari, fatus,* Gr. *phēmi,* to speak.]

Ineffably, in-ef'fa-bli, *adv.* Unspeakably.

Ineffaceable, in-ef-fās'a-bl, *a.* That cannot be effaced; indelible.

Ineffaceably, in-ef-fās'a-bli, *adv.* So as not to be effaceable.

Ineffective, in-ef-fekt'iv, *a. Not effective;* not producing the effect intended; not able; not competent to the service intended.

Ineffectual, in-ef-fekt'ū-al, *a. Not effectual;* not producing its proper effect; ineffective; fruitless.

Ineffectually, in-ef-fekt'ū-al-li, *adv. Without effect;* in vain.

Inefficacious, in-ef'fi-kā"shi-us, *a. Not efficacious;* not having power to produce the effect desired.

Inefficacy, in-ef'fi-ka-si, *n. Want of efficacy* or power to produce the desired or proper effect.

Inefficiency, in-ef-fi'shi-en-si, *n. Want of efficiency* or power to produce the effect; inefficacy.

Inefficient, in-ef-fi'shi-ent, *a. Not efficient;* not producing the effect; effecting nothing.

Inefficiently, in-ef-fi'shi-ent-li, *adv. Ineffectually;* without effect.

Inelastic, in-ē-las'tik, *a. Not elastic;* wanting elasticity.

Inelasticity, in-ē"las-tis"i-ti, *n. The absence of elasticity* or elastic power.

Inelegance, in-el'ē-gans, *n. Want of elegance;* want of beauty or polish in language or manners; want of symmetry or ornament in building; want of delicacy in colouring, &c.

Inelegant, in-el'ē-gant, *a. Not elegant;* tasteless; wanting beauty or polish, as language; or refinement, as manners; wanting symmetry or ornament, as an edifice.

Inelegantly, in-el'ē-gant-li, *adv. In an inelegant manner.*

Ineligibility, in-el'i-ji-bil"li-ti, *n. State or quality of being ineligible.*

Ineligible, in-el'i-ji-bl, *a. Not eligible;* not worthy to be chosen or preferred; not expedient.

Ineloquent, in-el'ō-kwent, *a. Not eloquent;* not speaking with fluency, propriety, grace, and pathos; not persuasive, as language or composition.

Inept, in-ept', *a. Not apt or fit;* improper; unbecoming; foolish; useless; nonsensical. [L. *ineptus—aptus,* fit.]

Inequality, in-ē-kwol'i-ti, *n. Want of equality* in degree, quantity, length, or quality of any kind; unevenness; inadequacy; dissimilarity; want of uniformity in different times or places; difference or disparity of rank or condition. [L. *inaequalitas.*]

Inequitable, in-ek'wit-a-bl, *a. Not equitable;* not just.

Ineradicable, in-ē-rad'ik-a-bl, *a. Not to be eradicated.*

Inert, in-ėrt', *a. Without art;* inactive; sluggish; indisposed to move or act; destitute of the power of moving itself, or of active resistance to motion impressed. [L. *iners, inertis—ars, artis,* art.]

Inertia, in-ėr'shi-a, *n. Inactivity;* a property of matter by which it tends to preserve a state of rest when still, and of uniform rectilinear motion when moving. [L.]

Inertly, in-ėrt' li, *adv. Without activity.*

Inertness, in-ėrt'nes, *n. State or quality of being inert;* sluggishness.

Inestimable, in-es'tim-a-bl, *a. That cannot be estimated;* too excellent to be rated; being above all price; priceless.

Inestimably, in-es'tim-a-bli, *adv. In a manner not to be estimated* or rated.

Inevitable, in-ev'it-a-bl, *a. Not to be avoided; that cannot be shunned;* unavoidable; that admits of no escape. [Fr. *inévitable*—l,. *vito,* to shun.]

Inevitably, in-ev'it-a-bli, *adv. Without* possibility of escape or evasion.

Inexact, in-egz-akt', *a. Not exact; not* precisely correct or true.

Inexactness, in-egz-akt'nes, *n. State or quality of being inexact;* incorrectness.

Inexecrable†, in-ek'sē-kra-bl, *a. Most execrable.*

Inexcusable, in-eks-kūz'a-bl, *a. Not excusable;* unjustifiable; unpardonable.

Inexcusableness, in-eks-kūz'a-bl-nes, *n. Quality of being inexcusable,* or of not admitting of excuse or justification.

Inexcusably, in - eks - kūz'a-bli, *adv.* With a degree of guilt or folly *beyond excuse.*

Inexhausted, in-egz-hast'ed, *a. Not exhausted;* unexhausted.

Inexhaustible, in-egz-hast'i-bl, *a. Not exhaustible;* unfailing; that cannot be wasted or spent.

Inexhaustibly, in-egz-hast'i-bli, *adv. In an inexhaustible manner* or degree.

Inexorability, in-eks'or-a-bil"li-ti, *n. Quality of being inexorable.*

Inexorable, in-eks'ōr-a-bl, *a. Not exorable;* not to be persuaded or moved by entreaty or prayer; unrelenting; implacable; irreconcilable. [Fr.—L. *oro,* to pray.]

Inexorably, in-eks'ōr-a-bli, *adv. So as to be immovable by entreaty.*

Inexpedience, Inexpediency, in-eks-pē'di-ens, in-eks-pē'di-en-si, *n. Want of expedience;* unfitness; impropriety; unsuitableness to the purpose.

Inexpedient, in-eks-pē'di-ent, *a. Not expedient;* not tending to promote a purpose; unsuitable to time and place.

Inexpediently, in-eks-pē'di-ent-li, *adv. Not expediently;* not fitly.

Inexpensive, in-eks-pens'iv, *a. Not expensive.*

Inexperience, in-eks-pē'ri-ens, *n. Want of experience.*

Inexperienced, in - eks - pē'ri-enst, *a. Not having experience;* unpractised.

Inexpert, in-eks-pėrt', *a. Not expert;* not skilled; destitute of dexterity derived from practice.

Inexpertness, in-eks-pėrt'nes, *n. Want of expertness.*

Inexpiable, in-eks'pi-a-bl, *a. That cannot be expiated;* that admits of no atonement; implacable. [Fr.]

Inexpiably, in-eks'pi-a-bli, *adv.* To a degree that admits of no atonement.

Inexplicable, in-eks'pli-ka-bl, *a. Not explicable;* not capable of being rendered plain and intelligible. [Fr.]

Inexplicably, in-eks'pli-ka-bli, *adv. In a manner not to be explained.*

Inexplicit, in-eks-plis'it, *a. Not explicit;* not clear in statement.

Inexpressible, in-eks-pres'i-bl, *a. Not to be expressed* in words; unspeakable; indescribable.

Inexpressibly, in-eks-pres'i-bli, *adv.* In *a manner not to be expressed* in words.

Inexpressive, in-eks-pres'iv, *a. Not expressive;* wanting expression, as a painting.

Inexpressiveness, in-eks-pres'iv-nes, *n. State or quality of being inexpressive.*

Inextinguishable, in - eks-ting' gwish-a-bl, *a. That cannot be extinguished;* unquenchable.

Inextricable, in-eks'tri-ka-bl, *a. Not to be extricated;* not to be freed from intricacy or perplexity; not to be untied.

Inextricably, in-eks'tri-ka-bli, *adv. In an inextricable manner.*

Infallibility, in-fal'li-bil"li-ti, *n. Quality of being infallible;* entire exemption from liability to error.

Infallible, in-fal'li-bl, *a. Not fallible;* not capable of erring; not liable to fall, or to deceive confidence; certain.

Infallibly, in-fal'li-bli, *adv.* Certainly; without a possibility of failure.

Infamous, in'fām-us, *a. Without fame; of ill fame;* publicly branded with odium for vice or guilt; base; scandalous; detestable; shameful; branded with infamy by conviction of a crime. [L. *infamis—fāma,* fame.]

Infamously, in'fām-us-li, *adv. In an infamous manner.*

Infamy, in'fā-mi, *n. Ill fame;* total loss of reputation; public disgrace; that loss of character or public disgrace which a convict incurs; extreme baseness. [L. *infamia.*]

Infancy, in'fan-si, *n. State of being an infant;* early childhood; the first part of life, beginning at the birth, and in law extending to the age of twenty-one years; the first age of anything; the beginning of existence. [L. *infantia.*]

Infant, in'fant, *n. A child that cannot yet speak;* a child in the first period of life, beginning at his birth; one under twenty-one years of age in a legal sense. — *a.* Pertaining to *infancy,* young; tender. [L. *infans—fari, fatus,* to speak.]

Infanticidal, in-fant'i-sīd"al, *a. Relating to infanticide.*

Infanticide, in-fant'i-sid, *n. Child-murder;* the intentional *killing of an infant;* the slaughter of infants by Herod; a slayer of infants. [L. *infans, infantis,* and *caedo,* to kill.]

Infantile, in'fant-īl, *a. Pertaining to infancy* or to an *infant;* pertaining to the first period of life. [Late L. *infantilis.*]

Infantine, in'fant-īn, *a. Pertaining to infants.*

Infantry, in'fant-ri, *n. A body of children;* the soldiers or troops that serve on foot, as distinguished from cavalry. [Fr. *infanterie—enfant,* a child.]

Infatuate, in-fa'tū-āt, *vt. To make foolish;* to befool; to weaken the intellectual powers of; to inspire with an extravagant passion. *ppr.* infatuating, *pret. & pp.* infatuated. [L. *infatuo, infatuātum—fatuus,* foolish.]

Infatuated, in-fa'tū-āt-ed, *p.a. Befooled;* besotted.

Infatuating, in-fa'tū-āt-ing, *p.a.* Depriving of judgment; bewitching.

Infatuation, in-fa'tū-ā"shon, *n. Act of infatuating;* state of being infatuated. [Fr.]

Infect, in-fekt', *vt. To dip into anything;* to taint with disease; to affect with some contagious matter; to communicate bad qualities to; to poison; to vitiate; to contaminate.—*a. Infected.* [L. *inficio, infectus,* to dip into—*facio,* to make.]

Infected, in-fekt'ed, *p.a.* Tainted with noxious matter; corrupted by bad qualities communicated.

Infection, in-fek'shon, *n. Act or process of infecting;* communication of like qualities; the thing which infects; that which infects; state of being infected; liking or desire. [Fr.]

Infectious, in-fek'shi-us, *a.* Having qualities that may *infect;* contaminat-

---

ch, *chain;* j, *job;* g, *go;* ng, *sing;* ᴛʜ, *then;* th, *thin;* w, *wig;* wh, *whig;* zh, *azure;* † obsolete.

INFECTIOUSLY 198 **INFRACTION**

ing; capable of being communicated by near approach.
Infectiously, in-fek'shi-us-li, *adv.* By infection.
Infectiousness, in-fek'shi-us-nes, *n.* Quality of being infectious.
Infecundity, in-fe-kun'di-ti, *n.* Unfruitfulness; barrenness.
Infelicitous, in-fe-lis'it-us, *a.* Not felicitous; unhappy.
Infelicity, in-fe-lis'i-ti, *n.* Ill-luck; unhappiness; calamity; unfavourableness. [L. *felix*, fruitful, happy.]
Infelt, in'felt, *a.* Felt within or deeply.
Infer, in-fér', *vt.* To bring on; to draw or derive, as a fact or consequence; to offer; to produce. *ppr.* inferring, *pret. & pp.* inferred. [Fr. *inférer*—L. *fero*, to bring.]
Inferable, in-fér'a-bl, *a.* That may be inferred from premises.
Inference, in'fér-ens, *n.* That which is inferred; a truth drawn from another admitted or supposed to be true; deduction.
Inferential, in-fér-en'shi-al, *a.* Deduced or deducible by inference.
Inferentially, in-fér-en'shi-al-li, *adv.* By way of inference.
Inferior, in-fé'ri-er, *a.* Lower in place; lower in station, age, or rank in life; lower in excellence; secondary; of less importance.—*n.* A person who is younger, or of a lower station or rank in society. [L.—*infra*, beneath.]
Inferiority, in-fé'ri-or'i-ti, *n.* State or quality of being inferior; a lower condition. [Fr. *infériorité*.]
Infernal, in-fér'nal, *a.* Pertaining to the lower regions; pertaining to hell; resembling the temper of evil spirits; hellish; satanic; malicious.—*n.* An inhabitant of hell or of the lower regions. [Late L. *infernalis*—*infra*, beneath.]
Infernally, in-tér'nal-li, *adv.* In a detestable and infernal way.
Inferrible, in-fér'i-bl, *a.* That may be inferred; inferable.
Infertile, in-fér'til, *a.* Not fertile; not fruitful; barren. [Fr.]
Infertility, in-fér-til'i-ti, *n.* Want of fertility; unfruitfulness; barrenness.
Infest, in-fest', *vt.* To attack; to molest; to torment; to plague; to disturb. [L. *infesto*—*infero*, to throw against—*fero*, to bear.]
Infestation, in-fest'shon, *n.* Attack.
Infidel, in'fi-del, *a.* Faithless; withholding trust or credit; unbelieving; disbelieving the divine institution of Christianity; sceptical.—*n.* One who withholds belief; one who disbelieves the inspiration of the Scriptures and the divine origin of Christianity; a freethinker; a sceptic. [Fr. *infidèle*—L. *fides*, faith—*fido*, to trust.]
Infidelity, in-fi-del'i-ti, *n.* Faithlessness; disbelief of the inspiration of the Scriptures or the divine origin of Christianity; scepticism; unbelief; unfaithfulness to the marriage contract. [Fr. *infidélité*.]
Infiltrate, in-fil'trāt, *vi.* To enter a substance by filtration. *ppr.* infiltrating, *pret. & pp.* infiltrated.
Infiltration, in-fil-tra'shon, *n.* Act of entering the pores of a body; the substance which has entered the pores or cavities of a body. [Fr.—*filtre*, stuff for straining liquors.]
Infinite, in'fi-nit, *a.* Not finite; boundless; endless; not circumscribed in extent, &c.; that has a beginning in space, but is infinitely extended; vast; immense; of great size or extent.—*n.*

The Infinite Being; the Almighty; that which is infinite.
Infinitely, in'fi-nit-li, *adv.* Without bounds or limits; immensely; greatly.
Infinitesimal, in'fi-ni-tes"i-mal, *a.* Infinitely small.—*n.* An infinitely small quantity; that which is less than any assignable quantity.
Infinitive, in-fin'it-iv, *a.* Unlimited; indefinite; designating a mood of the verb, which expresses the action of the verb without limitation of person or number, as to vice. [L. *infinitivus*—*finis*, the end.]
Infinitude, in-fin'i-tūd, *n.* Infinity; immensity; boundless number. [Old Fr.]
Infinity, in-fin'i-ti, *n.* State or quality of being infinite; unlimited extent of time, space, or quantity; immensity; endless or indefinite number. [Fr. *infinité*.]
Infirm, in-férm', *a.* Not firm; feeble; weak, as health or body; enfeebled; imbecile; irresolute; not stable.
Infirmary, in-férm'a-ri, *n.* An hospital or place where the infirm or the sick are lodged, nursed, and medically treated. [Fr. *infirmerie*.]
Infirmity, in-férm'i-ti, *n.* Want of strength; an unhealthy state of the body; weakness of mind or of resolution; fault; foible; malady; defect; imperfection. [Fr. *infirmité*—L. *firmus*, strong—Sans. *dhri*, to hold.]
Infix, in-fiks', *vt.* To fix in; to fix by thrusting in; to set in; to fasten in; to implant or fix. [L. *figo*, *fixus*, to fix.]
Inflame, in-flām', *vt.* To set on fire; to kindle; to cause to burn; to excite or increase, as passion or appetite; to heat; to excite, as excessive action in the blood-vessels; to incense; to exasperate.—*vi.* To grow hot, angry, and painful; to take fire. *ppr.* inflaming, *pret. & pp.* inflamed. [L. *inflammo*—*flamma*, flame.]
Inflamed, in-flāmd', *p.a.* Set on fire; provoked; exasperated.
Inflammability, in-flam'a-bil"li-ti, *n.* State or quality of being inflammable. [Fr. *inflammabilité*.]
Inflammable, in-flam'a-bl, *a.* That may be inflamed or set on fire; easily enkindled; susceptible of combustion. [Fr.]
Inflammation, in-flam-ā'shon, *n.* Act of inflaming; state of being in flame; a redness and swelling of any part of an animal body, attended with heat, pain, and feverish symptoms; heat; animosity; turbulence. [Fr.]
Inflammatory, in-flam'a-tē-ri, *a.* Tending to inflame; fiery; accompanied with preternatural heat, as disease; tending to excite anger, animosity, or sedition. [Fr. *inflammatoire*.]
Inflate, in-flāt', *vt.* To blow into; to swell by injecting air; to puff up; to elate. *ppr.* inflating, *pret. & pp.* inflated. [L. *info*, *inflatus*—*fio*, to blow.]
Inflated, in-flāt'ed, *p.a.* Puffed up; bombastic.
Inflation, in-fla'shon, *n.* Act of inflating; state of being distended with air; state of being puffed up, as with vanity. [L. *inflatio*.]
Inflect, in-flekt', *vt.* To bend; to turn from a direct line or course; to vary, as a noun or a verb in its terminations; to modulate, as the voice. [L. *inflecto*—*flecto*, to bend.]
Inflected, in-flekt'ed, *p.a.* Bent; varied in termination.
Inflection, in-flek'shon, *n.* Act of bending; the variation of nouns, &c., by declension, and of verbs by conjuga-

tion; a slide of the voice in speaking, either up or down. [Fr. *inflexion*.]
Inflesh, in-flesh', *vt.* To incarnate.
Inflexibility, in-fleks'i-bil"li-ti, *n.* Quality of being inflexible; obstinacy of will or temper; firmness of purpose that will not yield to importunity or persuasion. [Fr. *inflexibilité*.]
Inflexible, in-fleks'i-bl, *a.* That cannot be bent; that will not yield to prayers or arguments; unbending; obstinate; inexorable; unalterable. [Fr.]
Inflexibly, in-fleks'i-bli, *adv.* With unyielding pertinacity; inexorably.
Inflict, in-flikt', *vt.* To strike, as one thing on or against another; to lay on; to apply, as punishment or disgrace. [L. *infligo*, *inflictus*—*fligo*, to strike.]
Infliction, in-flik'shon, *n.* Act of inflicting; the punishment applied. [Fr.]
Inflorescence, in-flōr-es'ens, *n.* A beginning to flower; a mode of flowering, or the manner in which flowers are supported on their footstalks. [Fr.—L. *flos*, *floris*, a flower.]
Influence, in'flū-ens, *n.* A flowing in or upon; power whose operation is invisible; sway; moral power; weight of character; power of truth operating on the mind; power acting on sensibility; spiritual power, or the immediate power of God on the mind.—*vt.* To cause to flow into; to move by physical power operating by unseen laws to act on, as the mind or will, in persuading or dissuading; to induce; to move, as the passions; to lead or direct [Fr.—L. *fluo*, Sans. *plu*, to flow.]
Influential, in-flū-en'shi-al, *a.* Exerting influence or power over.
Influentially, in-flū-en'shi-al-li, *adv.* In an influential manner.
Influenza, in-flū-en'za, *n.* An epidemic catarrh. [It. *influenza*, influence.]
Influx, in'fluks, *n.* Act of flowing into; infusion; introduction; importation in abundance. [L. *influxus*—*fluo*, *fluxum*, to flow.]
Infold, in-fold', *vt.* To wrap up or in-wrap; to inclose; to clasp with the arms; to embrace.
Inform, in-form', *vt.* To give form or shape to; to animate; to give life to (poetical); to make known to by word or writing; to acquaint; to instruct; to communicate a knowledge of facts to by way of accusation.—*vi.* To take form; to appear. [Fr. *informer*—L. *forma*, form—*fero*, to bear.]
Informal, in-form'al, *a.* Not formal; not in the usual manner; not with the official forms; irregular or deranged in mind.
Informality, in-form-al'i-ti, *n.* Quality of being informal; want of regular form or order.
Informally, in-form'al-li, *adv.* In an informal manner.
Informant, in-form'ant, *n.* One who informs; one who gives intelligence; one who offers an accusation; an accuser. [L. *informans*.]
Information, in-form-ā'shon, *n.* Act of informing; notice, news, or advice communicated by word or writing; knowledge derived from reading, from the senses, or from the operation of the intellectual faculties; a charge exhibited to a magistrate or court. [Fr.—L. *informatio*.]
Informed, in-formd', *p.a.* Instructed; made acquainted.
Informer, in-form'ér, *n.* One who informs; one who gains a base livelihood by informing against others.
Infraction, in-frak'shon, *n.* A breaking

Fāte, fär, fat, fall; mē, met, hér; pīne, pin; nōte, not, mōve; tūbe, tub, bull; oil, pound.

in upon; breach; violation; non-observance; infringement. [Fr.—L. *frango, fractum*, to break.]
Infrangible, in-fran'ji-bl, *a.* Not frangible or separable into parts; not to be violated.
Infrequency, in-frē'kwen-si, *n.* Rarity; uncommonness. [L. *infrequentia.*]
Infrequent, in-frē'kwent, *a.* That does not frequently take place; uncommon; seldom happening.
Infringe, in-frinj', *vt.* To break in upon; to violate; to neglect to fulfil or obey. *ppr.* infringing, *pret. & pp.* infringed. [L. *infringo—frango*, to break.]
Infringement, in-frinj'ment, *n.* Act of infringing; breach; non-fulfilment; infraction; encroachment.
Infuriate, in-fū'ri-āt, *vt.* To madden; to enrage. *ppr.* infuriating, *pret. & pp.* infuriated.—*a.* Enraged. [L. *in*, and *furiatus—furo*, to rave.]
Infuriated, in-fū'ri-āt-ed, *p.a.* Rendered furious or mad.
Infuse, in-fūs', *vt.* To pour into; to steep in liquor without boiling, for the purpose of extracting solutions or medicinal qualities; to instil, as principles; to inspire; to animate. *ppr.* infusing, *pret. & pp.* infused. [Fr. *infuser*—L. *fundo, fusum*, to pour.]
Infusible, in-fūz'i-bl, *a.* Not fusible; that cannot be dissolved or melted.
Infusion, in-fū'zhon, *n.* A pouring in or into; the process of steeping in liquor, as plants and herbs; the liquor in which plants have been steeped; act of pouring in or instilling; suggestion; inspiration. [Fr.]
Ingaged†, in-gājd', *a.* Pledged.
Ingathering, in'gaṯẖ-ėr-ing, *n.* A gathering in; the act of collecting and securing the fruits of the earth; harvest.
Ingener†, in'jen-ėr, *n.* One who contrives.
Ingenious, in-jē'ni-us, *a.* Gifted with genius; remarkable for native or inborn qualities; possessed of the faculty of invention; skilful or prompt to invent; having an aptitude to form new combinations of ideas; proceeding from genius or ingenuity; witty; of curious design or mechanism; well formed; well adapted; mental; intellectual. [Fr. *ingénieux*—L. *geno, gigno*, Sans. *jan*, to beget.]
Ingeniously, in-jē'ni-us-li, *adv.* In an ingenious manner.
Ingenuity, in-je-nū'i-ti, *n.* State of quality of being ingenious; power of ready invention; quickness in combining ideas; skill; curiousness in design, the effect of ingenuity. [Fr. *ingénuité.*]
Ingenuous, in-jen'ū-us, *a.* Native; freeborn; of honourable extraction; becoming an honourable mind; open; candid; noble; generous. [L. *ingenuus—gigno*, to beget.]
Ingenuously, in-jen'ū-us-li, *adv.* Without reserve or dissimulation.
Ingenuousness, in-jen'ū-us-nes, *n.* Quality of being ingenuous; frankness; freedom from reserve; candour.
Inglorious, in-glō'ri-us, *a.* Not glorious; not bringing honour or glory; not accompanied with fame; disgraceful.
Ingloriously, in-glō'ri-us-li, *adv.* In an inglorious manner.
Ingloriousness, in-glō'ri-us-nes, *n.* State of being inglorious.
Ingoing, in'gō-ing, *n.* A going in; entrance.—*a.* Entering in.
Ingot, in'got, *n.* A mass or wedge of gold, silver, or other metal, cast into a mould; a mass of unwrought metal. [Fr. *lingot*—D. *ingieten*, to pour in.]
Ingraft, in-graft, *vt.* To cut into; to set in; to insert, as a scion of one tree into an incision made in another for propagation; to introduce, as something foreign into that which is native, for the purpose of propagation; to fix deeply. [Sax. *grafan*, to cut.]
Ingraftment, in-graft'ment, *n.* Act of ingrafting; the thing ingrafted.
Ingrain, in-grān', *vt.* To work into the grain or natural texture of, as colour; to dye in the grain or in the raw material.
Ingrained, in-grānd', *p.a.* Wrought into the natural texture; thoroughly impregnated.
Ingratiate, in-grā'shi-āt, *vt.* To commend, as one's self to another's good-will, confidence, or kindness. (With recipr. pron.) *ppr.* ingratiating, *pret. & pp.* ingratiated. [L. *in*, and Low L. *gratio, gratiatus*—L. *gratia*, favour.]
Ingratitude, in-gra'ti-tūd, *n.* Want of gratitude; want of a disposition to repay favours; unthankfulness; retribution of evil for good. [Fr.]
Ingredient, in-grē'di-ent, *n.* That which enters into a compound or is a component part of any mixture; an element. [Fr. *ingrédient*—L. *gradior*, to go.]
Ingress, in'gres, *n.* A going into; power of entrance; means of entering. [L. *ingressus—gradior*, to go.]
Inguinal, in'gwin-al, *a.* Pertaining to the groin. [L. *inguen*, the groin.]
Ingulf, in-gulf', *vt.* To swallow up in a vast deep gulf or whirlpool; to cast or draw into a gulf or deep place.
Ingulfment, in-gulf'ment, *n.* State of being ingulfed; a swallowing up in a gulf or abyss.
Inhabit, in-ha'bit, *vt.* To live or dwell in; to occupy as a place of settled residence.—*vi.* To dwell; to live; to abide. [L. *inhabito—habeo*, to have.]
Inhabitable, in-ha'bit-a-bl, *a.* That may be inhabited; not habitable†.
Inhabitant, in-ha'bit-ant, *n.* One who inhabits; a dweller; one who resides permanently in a place. [L. *inhabitans.*]
Inhabited, in-ha'bit-ed, *p.a.* Dwelt in; occupied by inhabitants.
Inhalation, in-hāl-ā'shon, *n.* Act of inhaling or drawing into; that which is inhaled. [L. *inhalatio.*]
Inhale, in-hāl', *vt.* To draw into the lungs; to inspire. *ppr.* inhaling, *pret. & pp.* inhaled. [L. *inhalo—halo*, to breathe.]
Inharmonious, in-hār-mō'ni-us, *a.* Not harmonious; discordant.
Inharmoniously, in-hār-mō'ni-us-li,*adv.* Without harmony; discordantly.
Inhearse†, in-hėrs', *vt.* To bury.
Inhere, in-hēr', *vi.* To stick; to exist or be fixed in something else. *ppr.* inhering, *pret. & pp.* inhered. [L. *inhæreo—hæreo*, to stick.]
Inherence, in-hēr'ens, *n.* A sticking fast or close; existence in something; a fixed state of being in another body or substance. [Fr. *inhérence.*]
Inherent, in-hēr'ent, *a.* Cleaving or sticking fast; existing in something else, so as to be inseparable from it; innate; inwrought. [Fr. *inhérent.*]
Inherently, in-hēr'ent-li, *adv.* By inherence.
Inherit, in-he'rit, *vt.* To come into possession of, as an heir; to receive, as a right or title, descendible by law from an ancestor; to receive by nature from a progenitor; to possess; to cause to possess; to enjoy; to take as a possession by gift.—*vi.* To take or have possession or property. [L. *in*, and *hæres, hæredis*, an heir.]
Inheritable, in-he'rit-a-bl, *a.* That may be inherited; capable of taking by inheritance.
Inheritance, in-he'rit-ans, *n.* That which is inherited; an estate derived from an ancestor to an heir; the reception of an estate by hereditary right; the estate which may descend to an heir; an estate given by divine appropriation; possession; ownership.
Inherited, in-he'rit-ed, *p.a.* Received by descent from an ancestor.
Inheritor, in-he'rit-ėr, *n.* An heir; one who inherits or may inherit.
Inheritress, Inheritrix, in-he'rit-res, in-he'rit-riks, *n.* An heiress; a female who inherits.
Inhibit, in-hi'bit, *vt.* To hold or keep back; to hinder; to check or repress; to prohibit; to interdict. [L. *inhibeo, inhibitus—habeo*, to hold.]
Inhibition, in-hi-bi'shon, *n.* A holding in or back; a restraining; prohibition; restraint. [Fr.]
Inhoop†, in-höp', *vt.* To confine in any place.
Inhospitable, in-hos'pit-a-bl, *a.* Not hospitable; affording no conveniences, subsistence, or shelter to strangers.
Inhospitableness, in-hos'pit-a-bl-nes, *n.* Want of hospitality.
Inhospitably, in-hos'pit-a-bli, *adv.* Unkindly to strangers.
Inhospitality, in-hos'pit-al"i-ti, *n.* Want of hospitality.
Inhuman, in-hū'man, *a.* Not human; not suitable to the qualities proper to man; destitute of the kindness and tenderness that belong to a human being; merciless; savage; barbarous.
Inhumanity, in-hū-man'i-ti, *n.* Quality of being inhuman; savageness of heart; cruelty in act; barbarity. [L. *inhumanitas.*]
Inhumanly, in-hū'man-li, *adv.* With cruelty; barbarously.
Inhumation, in-hūm-ā'shon, *n.* Act of burying in the earth. [Fr.]
Inhume, in-hūm', *vt.* To bury in the earth; to inter; to deposit in the earth. *ppr.* inhuming, *pret. & pp.* inhumed. [L. *inhumo—humus*, the earth.]
Inimical, in-im'ik-al, *a.* Unfriendly; hostile; adverse; hurtful; repugnant. [Late L. *inimicalis*—L. *amo*, to love.]
Inimitable, in-im'it-a-bl, *a.* That cannot be imitated or copied; surpassing imitation.
Inimitably, in-im'it-a-bli, *adv.* In a manner not to be imitated.
Iniquitous, in-ik'wit-us, *a.* Characterized by iniquity; wicked; unjust; unrighteous; criminal.
Iniquitously, in-ik'wit-us-li, *adv.* Injuriously; unjustly; wrongfully.
Iniquity, in-ik'wi-ti, *n.* Want of straightness; unrighteousness; injustice; want of rectitude in principle; a sin or crime; wickedness; any act of injustice. [Fr. *iniquité*—L. *æquus*, equal.]
Initial, in-i'shi-al, *a.* Beginning; placed at the beginning.—*n.* That which begins;—the first letter of a word or name. [Fr.—L. *initium*, a going in—*eo, itum*, Sans. *i*, to go.]
Initiate, in-i'shi-āt, *vt.* To begin; to originate; to instruct in principles; to introduce into any society by instructing in its ceremonies; to instruct; to acquaint with.—*vi.* To do the first act; to perform the first rite.—*a.*† Un-

Initiated — **Inquietude**

practised; new. *ppr.* initiating, *pret. & pp.* initiated. [L. *initio, initiatus—eo, itum,* to go.]
Initiated, in-i'shi-āt-ed, *p.a. Begun;* instructed in the first principles; received into a society or sect.
Initiation, in-i'shi-ā'shon, *n. Act of initiating;* process of making one acquainted with rudiments before unknown; admission by application of ceremonies. [Fr.]
Initiative, in-i'shi-āt-iv, *n. A beginning;* an introductory step; the right or power to originate. [Fr.]
Initiatory, in-i'shi-ā-tō-ri, *a. Serving to initiate;* introductory.
Inject, in-jekt', *vt. To throw into;* to dart in; to cast or throw on. [L. *injicio, injectus—jacio,* to throw.]
Injection, in-jek'shon, *n. Act of injecting;* the forcible throwing in of a liquid by means of a syringe, &c.; a liquid medicine thrown into the body by a syringe; a clyster. [Fr.]
Injoint, in-joint', *vt.* To joint.
Injudicious, in-jū-di'shi-us, *a. Not judicious;* acting without judgment; not according to sound judgment; unwise; imprudent.
Injudiciously, in-jū-di'shi-us-li, *adv. Without judgment;* unwisely.
Injudiciousness, in-jū-di'shi-us-nes, *n. Quality of being injudicious.*
Injunction, in-jungk'shon, *n. Act of enjoining;* mandate; the direction of a superior vested with authority; urgent exhortation of persons not vested with absolute authority to command. [Fr. *injonction*—L. *jungo, junctum,* to join.]
Injure, in'jer, *vt. To act towards contrary to right;* to wrong; to hurt or wound, as the person; to damage or lessen the value of; to slander, impair, or diminish; to give pain to; to hurt or weaken; to violate; to make worse. *ppr.* injuring, *pret. & pp.* injured. [Fr. *injurier*—L. *jus, jūris,* right—Sans. *yu,* to join together.]
Injured, in'jerd, *p.a.* Hurt; weakened; made worse.
Injurious, in-jū'ri-us, *a. Acting in violation of right;* wrongful; unjust; hurtful to the rights of another; hurtful to the person or health; affecting with damage or loss; tarnishing reputation. [Fr. *injurieux.*]
Injuriously, in-jū'ri-us-li, *adv.* Wrongfully; hurtfully; with injustice.
Injuriousness, in-jū'ri-us-nes, *n. Quality of being injurious* or hurtful; injury.
Injury, in'jū-ri, *n. That which is contrary to right;* any wrong or damage done to a man's person, rights, reputation, or goods; any diminution of that which is good or advantageous. [Fr. *injure*—L. *injuria.*]
Injustice, in-just'is, *n. That which is contrary to justice;* iniquity; wrong; the withholding from another merited praise.
Ink, ingk, *n.* A black liquor used for writing or printing; any liquor used for writing or forming letters, as red ink, &c.; a pigment.—*vt. To black or daub with ink.* [D. *inkt*—L. *tingo, tinctum,* to colour.]
Inkiness, ingk'i-nes, *n. State or quality of being inky.*
Inklet, ingk'l, *n.* A kind of broad linen tape.
Inkling, ingk'ling, *n.* The first slight *step inwards* or *izto;* a hint or whisper; an intimation. [Sax. *ingan,* to go in, with dimin. termination *ling.*]
Inkstand, ingk'stand, *n. A vessel for holding ink.*

Inky, ingk'i, *a. Consisting of ink;* resembling ink; black.
Inland, in'land, *a. Situated far into the land;* interior; remote from the ocean; carried on within a country; domestic. *n.* The *interior* part of a country.
Inlander, in'land-ėr, *n. One who lives inland,* or at a distance from the sea.
Inlay, in-lā', *vt. To set or place in;* to diversify, as cabinet or other work by laying in thin slices of fine wood, ivory, pearl, mosaic, &c., on some other surface of wood or coarser material.—*n.* Pieces of wood, ivory, &c., inlaid. *ppr.* inlaying, *pret. & pp.* inlaid.
Inlayer, in-lā'ėr, *n. The person who inlays.*
Inlaying, in-lā'ing, *p.n.* The operation of diversifying work with thin pieces of wood, ivory, &c., *laid in,* on a surface of wood or coarser material.
Inlet, in'let, *n. An ingress;* a passage by which an inclosed place may be entered; entrance; a recess in the shore of the sea or of a lake or large river, or between islands.
Inly, in'li, *a. Internal;* interior; secret. *adv. Internally;* within. [in and *like.*]
Inmate, in'māt, *n. A person who lodges or dwells in the same house with another,* or others; one who lives with a family; one admitted into an asylum, hospital, &c.
Inmost, in'mōst, *a. Deepest within;* remotest from the surface or external part.
Inn, in, *n. A house within which* travellers obtain shelter, &c., for payment; habitation; a house of public entertainment; a college of municipal or common law professors and students. *vt.†* To put under cover; to lodge. [Sax.]
Innate, in-nāt', *a. Inborn;* native; inherent. [Low L. *innatus*—L. *nascor, natus,* to be born.]
Innavigable, in-na'vig-a-bl, *a. That cannot be navigated;* impassable by ships or vessels.
Inner, in'ėr, *a. Interior; further inward* than something else; not obvious; pertaining to the spirit.
Innermost, in'ėr-mōst, *a. Furthest inward;* most remote from the outward part.
Inning, in'ing, *n. The ingathering of grain;* the turn for using the bat in cricket.
Innkeeper, in'kėp-ėr, *n. One who keeps an inn.*
Innocence, Innocency, in'nō-sens, in'nō-sen-si, *n. Harmlessness;* freedom from any quality that can injure; untainted purity of heart and life; freedom from guilt or evil intentions; simplicity of heart; imbecility†. [Fr.—L. *noceo,* to harm.]
Innocent, in'nō-sent, *a. Harmless;* inoffensive; not producing injury; free from guilt; not having done wrong or violated any law; not tainted with sin; blameless; guileless; free from the guilt of a particular crime; lawful; permitted.—*n.* One free *from harm* or guilt. [Fr.—L. *noceo,* to hurt.]
Innocently, in'nō-sent-li, *adv. Without harm;* without evil design.
Innocuous, in-no'kū-us, *a. Harmless;* safe; producing no ill effect. [L. *innocuus—noceo,* to hurt.]
Innocuously, in-no'kū-us-li, *adv. Without harm;* without injurious effects.
Innovate, in'nō-vāt, *vi.* To alter by introducing something *new.*—*vi.* To introduce *novelties.* (With *on.*) *ppr.* innovating, *pret. & pp.* innovated. [L. *innovo, innovatus—novo,* to make new.]

Innovation, in-nō-vā'shon, *n. Change* made by the introduction of something *new;* change in established laws, customs, rites, or practices. [Fr.]
Innovator, in'nō-vāt-ėr, *n. One who innovates* or introduces something new. [Low L.]
Innoxious, in-nok'shi-us, *a. Harmless;* free from mischievous qualities; not producing evil; harmless in effects; pure; innocent. [L. *innoxius—noceo,* to harm.]
Innoxiously, in-nok'shi-us-li, *adv. Harmlessly;* without mischief.
Innuendo, in-nū-en'dō, *n. A hint given by a nod;* an oblique hint; a remote intimation or reference to a person or thing not named. [L.—*nuo, nuto,* Gr. *neuō,* to nod with the head.]
Innumerable, in-nū'mėr-a-bl, *a. Not to be numbered;* numberless; very numerous.
Innumerably, in-nū'mėr-a-bli, *adv. Without number.*
Innutritious, in-nū-tri'shi-us, *a. Not nutritious;* not supplying nourishment.
Inobservant, in-ob-zėrv'ant, *a. Not observant.*
Inoculate, in-ok'ū-lāt, *vt. To insert, as an eye* or bud of one plant into another plant, for the purpose of growth; to bud; to communicate a disease to, as to a person, by inserting infectious matter in his skin or flesh; to vaccinate.—*vi.* To propagate by budding; to practise inoculation. *ppr.* inoculating, *pret. & pp.* inoculated. [L. *inoculo, inoculatus—oculus,* the eye.]
Inoculation, in-ok'ū-lā'shon, *n. Act or practice of inoculating,* or of inserting buds of one plant under the bark of another; act of communicating a disease. [L. *inoculatio.*]
Inodorous, in-ō'dėr-us, *a. Wanting odour or scent.* [L. *inodōrus.*]
Inoffensive, in-of-fens'iv, *a. Not offensive;* giving no uneasiness or disturbance; doing no injury or mischief.
Inoffensively, in-of-fens'iv-li, *adv. In a manner not to offend.*
Inoffensiveness, in-of-fens'iv-nes, *n. Quality of being not offensive.*
Inofficial, in-of-fi'shi-al, *a. Not official;* not clothed with the usual forms of authority.
Inofficially, in-of-fi'shi-al-li, *adv. Not in the official character.*
Inoperative, in-o'pe-rāt-iv, *a. Not operative;* not active; producing no effect.
Inopportune, in-op'por-tūn, *a. Not opportune;* inconvenient; unseasonable in time.
Inopportunely, in-op'por-tūn-li, *adv.* Unseasonably; at an inconvenient time.
Inordinate, in-or'din-āt, *a. Disordered;* irregular; not limited to rules prescribed, or to usual bounds. [L. *inordinatus—ordo, ordinis,* order.]
Inordinately, in-or'din-āt-li, *adv.* Irregularly; excessively; immoderately.
Inordinateness, in-or'din-āt-nes, *n. State or quality of being inordinate.*
Inorganic, in-or-gan'ik, *a. Destitute of organs;* not formed with the organs or instruments of life.
Inorganized, in-or'gan-izd, *a. Not organised;* void of organs, as earths, metals, and other minerals.
Inquest, in'kwest, *n. A searching into;* judicial inquiry; official examination; a jury, particularly a coroner's jury for investigating the cause of a sudden death; search. [Old Fr. *enqueste*—L. *quæro, quæsitus,* to seek, search for.]
Inquietude, in-kwī'et-ūd, *n. State of*

Fāte, fär, fat, fall; mē, met, hėr; pine, pin; nōte, not, mōve; tūbe, tub, bųll; oil, pound.

being without quietness; restlessness; uneasiness, either of body or mind. [Fr. *inquiétude*—L. *quies*, rest.]
Inquire, in-kwīr′, *vi.* To set an *inquiry on foot;* to seek for truth or information by asking questions; to seek for truth by argument or investigation. *vt.* To ask about; to seek by asking. *ppr.* inquiring, *pret. & pp.* inquired. [Fr. *enquérir*—L. *quaero*, to seek.]
Inquirer, in-kwīr′er, *n.* One who *inquires;* one who seeks for knowledge or information.
Inquiring, in-kwīr′ing, *p.a.* Given to *inquiry;* disposed to investigate causes.
Inquiringly, in-kwīr′ing-li, *adv.* By way of *inquiry.*
Inquiry, in-kwī′ri, *n. Act of inquiring;* a seeking for information by asking questions; question; search for truth, information, or knowledge; examination into facts or principles; research.
Inquisition, in-kwi-zi′shon, *n. A searching into;* inquiry; judicial inquiry; a tribunal established in some Roman Catholic countries for the suppression of heresy. [Fr.]
Inquisitional, in-kwi-zi′shon-al, *a. Making inquiry;* busy in inquiry.
Inquisitive, in-kwi′zit-iv, *a. Addicted to inquiry;* inclined to seek information by questions; prying; inclined to seek knowledge by discussion, investigation, or observation; given to research.
Inquisitively, in-kwi′zit-iv-li, *adv.* With curiosity to obtain information.
Inquisitiveness, in-kwi′zit-iv-nes, *n. Quality of being inquisitive;* curiosity to learn what is not known.
Inquisitor, in-kwi′zit-er, *n. One who inquires;* a member of the Court of Inquisition. [L.]
Inquisitorial, in-kwi′zi-tō″ri-al, *a.* Pertaining to the Court of Inquisition, or resembling its practices. [Fr.]
Inroad, in′rōd, *n. A riding into;* an invasion; the entrance of an enemy into a country with purposes of hostility; a sudden irruption; attack; encroachment.
Insalubrious, in-sa-lū′bri-us, *a. Not salubrious;* unfavourable to health; unwholesome.
Insalubrity, in-sa-lū′bri-ti, *n. State or quality of being insalubrious;* unhealthfulness.
Insane, in-sān′, *a. Not sane; of unsound mind;* mad; delirious; distracted; pertaining or appropriated to insane persons; causing madness. [L. *sānus*, sound.]
Insanely, in-sān′li, *adv.* Madly; foolishly; without reason.
Insanie†, in-sān′ē, *n.* Lunacy.
Insanity, in-san′i-ti, *n. Unsoundness;* state of being unsound in mind; aberration of intellect; madness; mania; lunacy. [L. *insanitas.*]
Insatiable, in-sā′shi-a-bl, *a. Incapable of being satisfied* or appeased; very greedy. [Fr.—L. *satis*, enough.]
Insatiableness, Insatiability, in-sā′shi-a-bl-nes, in-sā′shi-a-bil″li-ti, *n. Quality of being insatiable.*
Insatiably, in-sā′shi-a-bli, *adv. With greediness not to be satisfied.*
Insatiate, in-sā′shi-āt, *a. Not to be satisfied.*
Inscribe, in-skrīb′, *vt. To write in* or *upon;* to imprint on, as on the memory; to address to; to mark with letters, characters, or words; to draw, as a figure within another. *ppr.* inscribing, *pret. & pp.* inscribed. [L. *inscribo*—*scribo*, to write.]

Inscription, in-skrip′shon, *n. A writing upon;* something written or engraved to communicate knowledge to afterages; any character or sentence engraved on a solid substance for duration; a title; an address of a book to a person. [Fr.—L. *inscriptio.*]
Inscriptive, in-skript′iv, *a. Written as an inscription;* bearing inscription.
Inscroll, in-skrōl′, *vt. To write on a scroll.*
Inscrutability, in-skrū′ta-bil″li-ti, *n. Quality of being inscrutable.*
Inscrutable, in-skrū′ta-bl, *a. Unsearchable;* that cannot be discovered or understood by human reason. [Fr.—L. *scrutor, scrutatus*, to search.]
Inscrutably, in-skrū′ta-bli, *adv.* In a manner or degree not to be found out; impenetrably.
Insculpt†, in-skulp′, *vt.* To engrave; to carve.
Insculpture†, in-skulp′tūr, *n.* An engraving.
Insect, in′sekt, *a. Resembling an insect;* relating to insects; small; mean. [L. *insectus*—*seco, sectum*, to cut.]—*n.* A small creeping or flying animal, having the body cut as it were *into* two parts, which are joined together by a small ligature; anything small or contemptible. [L. *insectum.*]
Insectivorous, in-sek-tiv′ō-rus, *a. Feeding or subsisting on insects.* [L. *insectum*, and *voro*, to devour.]
Insecure, in-sē-kūr′, *a. Not secure;* not confident of safety; unsafe; exposed to danger or loss.
Insecurely, in-sē-kūr′li, *adv. Without security* or safety.
Insecurity, in-sē-kūr′i-ti, *n. Want of security;* danger; hazard; exposure to destruction or loss.
Insensate, in-sens′āt, *a. Destitute of sense;* stupid; wanting sensibility. [Low L. *insensatus*—L. *sensus*, feeling—*sentio*, to feel.]
Insensibility, in-sens′i-bil″li-ti, *n. State or quality of being insensible; want of sensibility;* want of tenderness or susceptibility of emotion and passion; torpor.
Insensible, in-sens′i-bl, *a. That cannot be felt or perceived;* wanting corporeal sensibility; not susceptible of emotion or passion; wanting tenderness. [Fr.—L. *sentio, sensum*, to feel.]
Insensibly, in-sens′i-bli, *adv.* Imperceptibly; by slow degrees; gradually.
Insentient, in-sen′shi-ent, *a. Not sentient;* senseless; not having perception.
Inseparable, in-se′pa-ra-bl, *a. That cannot be separated* or disjoined; not to be parted. [Fr.]
Inseparability, in-se′pa-ra-bil″li-ti, *n. Quality of being inseparable.*
Inseparably, in-se′pa-ra-bli, *adv.* In a manner that prevents separation.
Inseparate†, in-se′pa-rāt, *a.* Not separate; united.
Insert, in-sert′, *vt. To knit or join into;* to thrust in; to set in or among. [L. *insero, insertus*—*sero, sertus*, to knit.]
Insertion, in-ser′shon, *n. Act of inserting;* the manner in which one part is inserted into or grows out of another; the thing inserted. [Fr.—L. *insertio.*]
Inside, in′sīd, *n. The interior side* or part of a thing; opposed to outside. *a.* Being within.—*prep.* Within the sides of.
Insidious, in-si′di-us, *a. Lying in wait;* cunning; deceitful; artful; designing; intended to entrap. [Fr. *insidieux*—L. *sedeo*, to sit.]

Insidiously, in-si′di-us-li, *adv.* With intention to ensnare; deceitfully.
Insidiousness, in-si′di-us-nes, *n. Quality of being insidious;* a watching for an opportunity to ensnare; treachery.
Insight, in′sīt, *n. Sight into;* deep inspection or view; thorough knowledge; penetration.
Insignia, in-sig′ni-a, *n. pl. Badges or marks of office or honour;* marks or visible impressions by which anything is known. [L.—*signum*, a mark.]
Insignificance, in-sig-ni′fi-kans, *n. Want of significance* or meaning; unimportance; want of weight; meanness.
Insignificant, in-sig-ni′fi-kant, *a. Not significant;* void of signification; destitute of meaning, as words; having no weight or effect; trivial; mean; contemptible.
Insignificantly, in-sig-ni′fi-kant-li, *adv.* Without meaning; to no purpose.
Insincere, in-sin-sēr′, *a. Not sincere;* wanting sincerity; not being in truth what one appears to be, as persons; characterized by insincerity, as words or actions; false; unsound.
Insincerely, in-sin-sēr′li, *adv. Without sincerity;* hypocritically.
Insincerity, in-sin-se′ri-ti, *n. Want of sincerity;* dissimulation; hollowness.
Insinew†, in-sin′ū, *vt.* To strengthen; to give vigour to.
Insinuate, in-sin′ū-āt, *vt. To put into the bosom of;* to wind in; to ingratiate, push, or work, as one's self into favour; to introduce by slow, gentle, or artful means; to hint; to instil; to infuse gently.—*vi.* To wind in; to flow in; to enter gently, as into crevices; to gain on the affections by gentle or artful means. *ppr.* insinuating, *pret. & pp.* insinuated. [L. *insinuo, insinuatus*—*sinus*, a bending, bosom.]
Insinuating, in-sin′ū-āt-ing, *p.a.* Tending to enter gently; insensibly winning favour and confidence.
Insinuation, in-sin′ū-ā″shon, *n. Act of insinuating;* a flowing into crevices; the art or power of pleasing and stealing on the affections; a hint; an intimation by distant allusion. [Fr.]
Insipid, in-si′pid, *a. Tasteless;* vapid; wanting the qualities which affect the organs of taste; wanting spirit or life; wanting pathos or the power of exciting emotions; spiritless; lifeless. [Fr. *insipide*—L. *sapio*, to taste, to savour.]
Insipidity, in-si-pid′i-ti, *n. Quality of being insipid;* want of taste; want of life or spirit. [Fr. *insipidité.*]
Insipidly, in-si′pid-li, *adv. Without taste;* without spirit or life.
Insist, in-sist′, *vi. To stand or rest;* to dwell in discourse; to urge or press earnestly. (With *on* or *upon.*) [L. *insisto*—*sto*, to stand.]
Insisture†, in-sist′ūr, *n.* A standing on; persistence.
Insnare, in-snār′, *vt. To catch in a snare;* to take by artificial means; to inveigle; to entangle. *ppr.* insnaring, *pret. & pp.* insnared.
Insnaring, in-snār′ing, *p.a.* Seducing; involving in difficulties.
Insociable, in-sō′shi-a-bl, *a. Not sociable;* taciturn.
Insolence, in-sō′lens, *n. State or quality of being insolent;* petulant contempt; impudence. [Fr.]
Insolent, in′sō-lent, *a. Unusually proud and haughty, with contempt of others;* domineering in power; insulting; proceeding from insolence; haughty and

ch, *ch*ain; j, *j*ob; g, *g*o; ng, si*ng*; ᴛʜ, *th*en; th, *th*in; w, *w*ig; wh, *wh*ig; zh, a*z*ure; † obsolete.

contemptuous. [L. *insolens—soleo*, to be wont.]
Insolently, in'so-lent-li, *adv.* With contemptuous pride; haughtily; rudely.
Insolubility, in-sol-ū-bil'li-ti, *n.* Quality of not being soluble or dissolvable, particularly in a fluid.
Insoluble, in-sol'ū-bl, *a.* That cannot be dissolved, particularly by a liquid. [Fr. —L. *solvo*, to dissolve.]
Insolvable, in-sol'va-bl, *a.* That cannot be loosened or unravelled; not to be solved or explained; not admitting solution or explication. [Fr.—L. *solvo*, to loose.]
Insolvency, in-sol'ven-si, *n.* State of being insolvent; inability of a person to pay all his debts; insufficiency to discharge all debts of the owner.
Insolvent, in-sol'vent, *a.* Not solvent; not having money or estate sufficient to pay all debts; not sufficient to pay all the debts of the owner.—*n.* A debtor unable to pay his debts. [L. *solvo*, to loose, to pay, to fulfil.]
Insomuch, in-sō-much', *adv.* So that; to that degree.
Insooth, in-sōth', *adv.* In truth.
Inspect, in-spekt', *vt.* To look into; to view or examine officially for the purpose of examination; to oversee. [L. *inspicio, inspectus—specio*, to look.]
Inspection, in-spek'shon, *n.* A looking into; close or careful survey; guardianship; superintendence; official view or examination. [Fr.]
Inspector, in-spekt'er, *n.* One who inspects; a superintendent; an overseer; one who makes an official view. [L.]
Inspectorship, in-spekt'er-ship, *n.* The office of an inspector.
Inspirable, in-spir'a-bl, *a.* That may be inspired or drawn into the lungs; inhalable, as air or vapours.
Inspiration, in-spi-rā'shon, *n.* A breathing into; act of drawing air into the lungs; a branch of respiration, and opposed to expiration; the supernatural influence of the Spirit of God on the human mind; the infusion of influence into the mind, by a superior being; a highly exciting influence; the result of such extraordinary influences. [Fr.—L. *spiro*, to breathe.]
Inspiratory, in-spir'a-tō-ri, *a.* Pertaining to or aiding inspiration.
Inspire, in-spir', *vt.* To breathe into; to draw in by the operation of breathing; to infuse into the mind; to communicate, as divine instructions to the mind; to infuse ideas or poetic spirit into.—*vi.* To draw in breath; to inhale air into the lungs; opposed to expire. *ppr.* inspiring, *pret. & pp.* inspired. [L. *inspiro—spiro*, to breathe.]
Inspired, in-spird', *p.a.* Informed, influenced, or directed by the Holy Spirit.
Inspirer, in-spir'er, *n.* He who inspires.
Inspiring, in-spir'ing, *p.a.* Infusing spirit or courage; animating.
Inspirit, in-spi'rit, *vt.* To infuse spirit into; to give new life to; to animate; to cheer.
Inspissated, in-spis'āt-ed, *p.a.* Thickened, as a liquor. [L. *spisso*, to thicken.]
Instability, in-sta-bil'i-ti, *n.* Want of stability; want of firmness in purpose; inconstancy; liability to change.
Install, in-stal', *vt.* To instate in a stall or seat, in an office, rank, or order; to invest with any charge, office, or rank, with the customary ceremonies. [Fr. *installer*—Old G. *stal*, a place.]
Installation, in-stal-ā'shon, *n.* Act of installing, or of giving possession of an office, &c., with the customary ceremonies. [Fr.]
Instalment, in-stal'ment, *n.* Act of installing; the seat in which one is placed; a term applied to the parts of a large sum of money which are paid, or to be paid, at different periods.
Instance, in'stans, *n.* A standing on; urgency; importunity; impelling motive; application; example; a case offered; time; occurrence.—*vi.* To give or offer an instance, example, or case. *vt.* To cite as an instance, example, or case. *ppr.* instancing, *pret. & pp.* instanced. [Fr.—L. *sto*, to stand.]
Instant, in'stant, *a.* Standing by; present; making no delay; urgent; earnest. *n.* An immediate point of time; a part of duration in which we perceive no succession; a particular time. [Fr.—L. *sto*, to stand.]
Instantaneous, in-stant-ā'nē-us, *a.* Done in an instant; occurring without any perceptible succession; very speedily. [Low L. *instantaneus.*]
Instantaneously, in-stant-ā'nē-us-li, *adv.* In an instant; in a moment.
Instantly, in'stant-li, *adv.* Immediately; with urgent importunity.
Instate, in-stāt', *vt.* To put in a situation or condition; to establish, as in a rank or condition; to invest. *ppr.* instating, *pret. & pp.* instated.
Instead, in-sted', *adv.* In the stead, place, or room of.
Instep, in'step, *n.* The fore-part of the upper side of the foot, near its junction with the leg.
Instigate, in'sti-gāt, *vt.* To spur on; to stimulate; to set on; to move by some incentive, as to an act of wickedness. *ppr.* instigating, *pret. & pp.* instigated. [L. *instigo, instigatus—stigo*, to stir on.]
Instigation, in-sti-gā'shon, *n.* Act of instigating; the act of encouraging to commit a crime; temptation; impulse to evil. [Fr.]
Instigator, in'sti-gāt-er, *n.* One who instigates; a tempter. [L.]
Instil, in-stil', *vt.* To infuse by drops; to infuse slowly, or by small quantities. *ppr.* instilling, *pret. & pp.* instilled. [L. *instillo—stillo*, to drop.]
Instillation, in-stil-ā'shon, *n.* Act of pouring in by drops; act of infusing slowly into the mind; that which is instilled or infused. [L. *instillatio.*]
Instilment, in-stil'ment, *n.* Act of instilling; anything instilled.
Instinct, in-stingkt', *a.* Urged or stimulated from within; moved; animated. [L. *instinctus—stinguo*, to prick.]
Instinct, in'stingkt, *n.* Impulse; the natural unreasoning impulse in an animal, by which it is guided to the performance of any action, without thought of improvement in the method. [Fr.]
Instinctive, in-stingkt'iv, *a.* Prompted by instinct; determined by natural impulse or propensity. [Fr. *instinctif.*]
Instinctively, in-stingkt'iv-li, *adv.* By force of instinct; by natural impulse.
Institute, in'sti-tūt, *vt.* To place into; to set on foot; to form and prescribe, as a law; to found; to begin; to invest with the care of souls. *ppr.* instituting, *pret. & pp.* instituted.—*n.* That which is established; established law; settled order; precept; principle; (pl.) a book of elements or principles; a body of men united for some literary or scientific purpose. [L. *instituo, institutus—statuo*, to place—*sto*, to stand.]
Institution, in-sti-tū'shon, *n.* Act of instituting; that which is founded by authority; laws, rites, and ceremonies; an organised society for promoting any object; act of investing a clergyman with the care of souls. [Fr.]
Instruct, in-strukt', *vt.* To build up; to furnish with instruction; to teach; to inform; to furnish with advice; to admonish; to give directions to; to command; to advise or give notice to. [L. *instruo, instructum—struo*, to pile up.]
Instruction, in-struk'shon, *n.* Act of instructing; education; precepts conveying knowledge; advice; authoritative direction; order. [Fr.]
Instructive, in-strukt'iv, *a.* Conveying instruction; serving to instruct or inform. [Fr. *instructif.*]
Instructer, in-strukt'er, *n.* One who instructs; a teacher; a person who imparts knowledge to another. [L.]
Instructress, in-strukt'res, *n.* A female who instructs; a preceptress.
Instrument, in'strū-ment, *n.* That by which work is performed; a tool; an implement; that which is subservient to the execution of a plan; an artificial machine constructed for yielding harmonious sounds; a writing containing the terms of a contract; one who, or that which, is made a means. [Fr.—L. *struo*, to prepare, to devise.]
Instrumental, in-strū-ment'al, *a.* Conducive as an instrument to some end; serviceable; pertaining to instruments; made by instruments, as music. [Fr.]
Instrumentalist, in-strū-ment'al-ist, *n.* One who plays on an instrument.
Instrumentality, in'strū-ment-al'i-ti, *n.* State of being instrumental; agency of anything, as means to an end.
Instrumentally, in-strū-ment'al-li, *adv.* In the nature of an instrument, as means to an end.
Insubordinate, in-sub-or'din-āt, *a.* Not subordinate; not submitting to authority. [L. *in* or *o, ordinis*, order.]
Insubordination, in-sub-or'din-ā"shon, *n.* Want of subordination; disorder. [Fr.]
Insubstantial, in-sub-stan'shi-al, *a.* Not real.
Insufferable, in-suf'fer-a-bl, *a.* That cannot be suffered; insupportable; that cannot be permitted or tolerated; disgusting beyond endurance.
Insufferably, in-suf'fer-a-bli, *adv.* To a degree beyond endurance.
Insufficiency, in-suf-fi'shen-si, *n.* Want of sufficiency; inadequacy of power or skill; incapacity; want of the requisite strength, value, or force.
Insufficient, in-suf-fi'shi-ent, *a.* Not sufficient; inadequate; incapable; unfit.
Insufficiently, in-suf-fi'shi-ent-li, *adv.* With want of sufficiency; with want of proper ability or skill; inadequately.
Insuit, in'sūt, *n.* A request.
Insular, in'sū-ler, *a.* Belonging to an island. [Fr. *insulaire*—L. *insula*, an island.]
Insularity, in-sū-la'ri-ti, *n.* State of being insular.
Insulate, in'sū-lāt, *vt.* To place as it were in an island, or in a detached situation; to detach; to isolate. *ppr.* insulating, *pret. & pp.* insulated. [from L. *insula*, an island.]
Insulated, in'sū-lāt-ed, *p.a.* Cut off from communication with surrounding bodies.
Insulation, in-sū-lā'shon, *n.* Act of insulating; state of being insulated.
Insult, in'sult, *n.* A leaping upon; act or speech of insolence or contempt; an

Fāte, fär, fat, fall; mē, met, hėr; pīne, pin; nōte, not, mōve; tūbe, tub, bull; oil, pound.

indignity. [L. *insultus—salio, saltum,* to leap.]
Insult, in-sult', *vt.* To leap upon; to treat with insolence or contempt, by words or actions.—*vi.* To leap or jump.
Insulting, in-sult'ing, *p.a.* Expressing insolence or contempt.
Insultingly, in-sult'ing-li, *adv.* With insolent contempt.
Insultment, in-sult'ment, *n.* Insolent treatment.
Insuperable, in-sū'pėr-a-bl, *a.* That cannot be overcome; insurmountable; invincible. [L. *insuperabilis—super,* over.]
Insuperably, in-sū'pėr-a-bli, *adv.* In a manner or degree not to be overcome.
Insupportable, in-sup-pōrt'a-bl, *a.* That cannot be supported or borne; intolerable, as reproach. [Fr.]
Insupportably, in-sup-pōrt'a-bli, *adv.* In a manner that cannot be endured.
Insuppressible, in-sup-pres'i-bl, *a.* Not to be suppressed.
Insuppressive, in-sup-pres'iv, *a.* Not admitting suppression.
Insurable, in-shūr'a-bl, *a.* That may be insured against loss or damage.
Insurance, in-shūr'ans, *n.* Act of insuring; a contract by which one engages for a premium per cent. to make up a loss which another may sustain. [from *insure.*]
Insure, in-shūr', *vt.* To make sure or secure; to contract for a consideration to secure a person against loss; as, to insure a ship.—*vi.* To underwrite; to practise making insurance. *ppr.* insuring, *pret. & pp.* insured.
Insurer, in-shūr'ėr, *n.* One who insures; an underwriter.
Insurgent, in-sėr'jent, *a.* Rising against; rising in opposition to lawful authority.—*n.* One who openly and actively resists the execution of laws; a rebel. [L. *insurgens—surgo,* to rise.]
Insurmountable, in-sėr-mount'a-bl, *a.* That cannot be surmounted; that cannot be overcome.
Insurrection, in-sėr-rek'shon, *n.* A rising against civil authority; the open and active opposition of a number of persons to the execution of law in a city or state. [Fr.—L. *surgo, surrectum,* to rise.]
Insurrectionary, in-sėr-rek'shon-a-ri, *a.* Pertaining to insurrection.
Insusceptibility, in-sus-sept'i-bil'li-ti, *n.* Want of susceptibility.
Insusceptible, in-sus-sept'i-bl, *a.* Not susceptible; not capable of being affected or impressed.
Insusceptive, in-sus-sept'iv, *a.* Not susceptive.
Intact, in-takt', *a.* Untouched; uninjured; undisturbed. [Fr.—L. *tango, tactum,* to touch.]
Intangible, in-tan'ji-bl, *a.* That cannot be touched; not perceptible to the touch.
Intangibility, in-tan'ji-bil''li-ti, *n.* Quality of being intangible.
Integer, in'tē-jėr, *n.* That which is untouched; that which is whole or entire; a whole number, as distinguished from a fraction. [L.—*tango,* to touch.]
Integral, in'tē-gral, *a.* Untouched; whole; necessary to make a whole; not fractional.—*n.* A whole; an entire thing. [Fr. *intégral.*]
Integrally, in'tē-gral-li, *adv.* Wholly.
Integrant, in'tē-grant, *a.* Necessary to constitute an entire thing; making part of a whole. [L. *integrans.*]
Integration, in-tē-grā'shon, *n.* Act of making entire. [L. *integratio.*]

Integrity, in-te'gri-ti, *n.* State of being untouched; wholeness; entireness; moral soundness or purity; incorruptness; honesty; rectitude. [Fr. *intégrité*—L. *tango,* to touch.]
Integument, in-te gū-ment, *n.* That which naturally covers another thing, as the skin covers the body. [Fr. *integument*—L. *tego,* Sans. *sthag,* to cover.]
Integumentary, in-te'gū-ment''a-ri, *a.* Belonging to or composed of integuments.
Intellect, in'tel-lekt, *n.* The faculty of the human soul by which it *knows,* as distinguished from the power to feel and to will; the understanding. [Fr.—L. *lego, lectum,* to choose out, to observe.]
Intellectual, in-tel-lekt'ū-al, *a.* Relating to the *intellect;* performed by the understanding; mental; perceived by the intellect; having the power of understanding; treating of the mind. [Fr. *intellectuel.*]
Intellectually, in-tel-lekt'ū-al-li, *adv.* By means of the intellect.
Intelligence, in-tel'li-jens, *n.* The act of knowing; the capacity to know; understanding; information communicated; an account of things distant or before unknown; notice; a spiritual being. [Fr.—L. *intelligentia.*]
Intelligent, in-tel'li-jent, *a.* Knowing; endowed with the faculty of understanding or reason; well informed; skilled; cognizant. [Fr.]
Intelligently, in-tel'li-jent-li, *adv.* In an intelligent manner.
Intelligibility, in-tel'li-ji-bil''li-ti, *n.* Quality or state of being intelligible; the possibility of being understood.
Intelligible, in-tel'li-ji-bl, *a.* That may be understood; perspicuous; clear. [Fr.]
Intelligibly, in-tel'li-ji-bli, *adv.* In a manner to be understood.
Intemperance, in-tem'pėr-ans, *n.* Want of temperance; excess in any kind of action or indulgence; habitual indulgence in the use of spirituous liquors.
Intemperate, in-tem'pėr-āt, *a.* Not temperate; not restrained within due limits; immoderate in enjoyment or exertion; addicted to an excessive use of spirituous liquors; ungovernable; exceeding the convenient mean or degree, as climate or weather.
Intemperately, in-tem'pėr-āt-li, *adv.* Immoderately; excessively.
Intemperateness, in-tem'pėr-āt-nes, *n.* State or quality of being intemperate.
Intend, in-tend', *vt.* To stretch or set forward in mind; to design; to purpose; to mean.—*vi.* To extend; to stretch forward. [Low L. *intendere*—L. *tendo,* to stretch.]
Intendancy, in-tend'an-si, *n.* The office of an intendant. [Fr. *intendance.*]
Intendant, in-tend'ant, *n.* A superintendent. [Fr.]
Intended, in-tend'ed, *p.a.* Designed; purposed; betrothed.
Intendment, in-tend'ment, *n.* Intention; design; purpose. [Fr. *entendement.*]
Intenible, in-ten'i-bl, *a.* Incapable of containing.
Intense, in-tens', *a.* Stretched out; stretched; very close, as when the mind is fixed or beat on a particular subject; ardent; extreme in degree. [L. *intensus—tendo,* to stretch out.]
Intensely, in-tens'li, *adv.* To an extreme degree; vehemently; earnestly.
Intenseness, in-tens'nes, *n.* State of being intense; intensity.
Intensify, in-tens'i-fi, *vt.* To make more intense. *ppr.* intensifying, *pret. & pp.*

intensified. [L. *intensus,* and *facio,* to make.]
Intensity, in-tens'i-ti, *n.* State of being intense; extreme closeness; extreme degree. [Fr. *intensité.*]
Intensive, in-tens'iv, *a.* Having intensity; serving to give force or emphasis.
Intensively, in-tens'iv-li, *adv.* By increase of degree.
Intensiveness, in-tens'iv-nes, *n.* State of being intensive.
Intent, in-tent', *a.* Having the mind bent on an object; fixed closely; eager in pursuit of an object.—*n.* The stretching of the mind toward an object; purpose; meaning; aim; drift. [L. *intentus—tendo,* to stretch.]
Intention, in-ten'shon, *n.* A stretching of the mind toward an object; fixedness of attention; design; purpose; the fixed direction of the mind to a particular object; end; aim. [L. *intentio.*]
Intentional, in-ten'shon-al, *a.* Intended.
Intentionally, in-ten'shon-al-li, *adv.* By design; of purpose; not casually.
Intentioned, in-ten'shond, *p.a.* Having designs; in composition, as, *well-intentioned, ill-intentioned.*
Intently, in-tent'li, *adv.* With close attention; fixedly; eagerly.
Inter, in-tėr', *vt.* To deposit and cover in the earth; to bury. *ppr.* interring, *pret. & pp.* interred. [Fr. *enterrer*—L. *terra,* the earth.]
Interact, in'tėr-akt, *n.* A short act or piece between others, as in a play.
Intercalary, in-tėr'ka-la-ri, *a.* Proclaimed or inserted in the midst of others, as, an intercalary verse; an intercalary day. [L. *intercalarius—cālo,* to call.]
Intercalate, in-tėr'kal-āt, *vt.* To insert between others, as a day, or as a bed or stratum. *ppr.* intercalating, *pret. & pp.* intercalated. [L. *intercalo, intercalatus.*]
Intercede, in-tėr-sēd', *vi.* To go or come between; to act between parties with a view to reconcile those who differ; to plead in favour of one; to interpose. *ppr.* interceding, *pret. & pp.* interceded. [L. *intercedo—cedo,* to go.]
Intercept, in-tėr-sept', *vt.* To take or seise on by the way; to stop on its passage; to stop in progress; to cut off communication with; to include or comprehend between. [Fr. *intercepter*—L. *capio, captum,* to take.]
Intercession, in-tėr-se'shon, *n.* Act of interceding; mediation; solicitation to one party in favour of another. [Fr.—L. *cedo,* to go or come.]
Intercessor, in'tėr-ses-ėr, *n.* One who intercedes; a mediator; one who pleads in behalf of another. [L.]
Intercessory, in-tėr-ses'sō-ri, *a.* Containing intercession; mediatorial.
Interchain, in-tėr-chān', *vt.* To link together.
Interchange, in-tėr-chānj', *vt.* To change, as one with the other; to exchange; to reciprocate. *ppr.* interchanging, *pret. & pp.* interchanged.
Interchange, in'tėr-chānj, *n.* Mutual change; a mutual giving and receiving.
Interchangeable, in-tėr-chānj'a-bl, *a.* That may be interchanged.
Interchangeably, in-tėr-chānj'a-bli, *adv.* Alternately; by reciprocation.
Interchangement, in-tėr-chānj'ment, *n.* Mutual transfer.
Intercolonial, in'tėr-kō-lō''ni-al, *a.* Relating to the intercourse between different colonies.
Intercommunication, in'tėr-kom-mū'-

ni-kā″shon, *n. Reciprocal communication.*
Intercommunion, in′tĕr-kom-mū′ni-on, *n. Mutual communion.*
Intercourse, in′tĕr-kōrs *n. A running between; connection by reciprocal dealings between persons or nations; fellowship; familiarity; acquaintance.* [L. *intercursus—curro, cursum,* to run.]
Interdict, in-tĕr-dikt′, *vt. To forbid by speaking; to prohibit; to cut off from the enjoyment of communion with a church.* [L. *interdico, interdictus—dico, dictum,* to speak.]
Interdict, in′tĕr-dikt, *n. A forbidding; a prohibiting order or decree; a prohibition of the pope, by which the clergy are restrained from performing, or laymen from attending, divine service.* [Old Fr.]
Interdictory, in-tĕr-dik′tō-ri, *a. Serving to interdict or prohibit.*
Interest, in′tĕr-es, *n. Interest.*
Interest, in′tĕr-est, *vt. To be in the midst of; to concern; to affect; to excite emotion in; to give a share in; to have a share in; to excite in behalf of another* (with recip. pron.)*—n. Concern; good; influence over others; share; part; regard to private profit; premium paid for the use of money; any addition of benefit or injury.* [Old Fr.—L. *inter,* and *est, esse,* from *sum,* to be.]
Interested, in′tĕr-est-ed, *p.a. Having an interest; liable to be affected; chiefly concerned for one's private advantage.*
Interesting, in′tĕr-est-ing, *p.a. Engaging the attention or curiosity; exciting emotions or passions.*
Interfere, in-tĕr-fēr′, *vi. To strike between; to interpose; to intermeddle; to enter into or take a part in the concerns of others. ppr. interfering, pret. & pp. interfered.* [Old Fr. *entreferir,* to exchange blows—L. *ferio,* to strike.]
Interference, in-tĕr-fēr′ens, *n. Act of interfering; interposition.*
Interim, in′tĕr-im, *n. The mean time; time intervening.* [L.]
Interior, in-tē′ri-ĕr, *a. Inner; remote from the limits, frontier, or shore.—n. The inner or internal part of a thing; the inland part of a country.* [L.— *inter,* between.]
Interjection, in-tĕr-jek′shon, *n. Act of throwing between; a word in speaking or writing, thrown in between words to express some emotion or passion; an exclamation.* [Fr.—L. *jacio, jactum,* to cast.]
Interjectional, in-tĕr-jek′shon-al, *a. Relating to or like an interjection.*
Interjoin, in-tĕr-join′, *vt. To join mutually; to intermarry.*
Interlace, in-tĕr-lās′, *vt. To unite, as by lacing together; to put or insert, as one thing with another. ppr. interlacing, pret. & pp. interlaced.*
Interlard, in-tĕr-lärd′, *vt. To mix, as fat with lean; to insert between; to diversify by mixture.* [Fr. *lard,* lard.]
Interleave, in-tĕr-lēv′, *vt. To insert, as a blank leaf or blank leaves in a book between other leaves. ppr. interleaving, pret. & pp. interleaved.*
Interline, in-tĕr-līn′, *vt. To write in alternate lines; to write between lines already written or printed. ppr. interlining, pret. & pp. interlined.*
Interlinear, in-tĕr-lin′e-ĕr, *a. Written between lines before written or printed.* [Fr. *interlinéaire.*]
Interlineation, in-tĕr-lin′ē-ā″shon, *n. Act of interlining; the words or line inserted between lines before written or printed.*

Interlocutor, in-tĕr-lo′kūt-ĕr, *n. One who speaks in dialogue.* [Fr. *interlocuteur*—L. *loquor,* to speak.]
Interlocutory, in-tĕr-lo′kū-tō-ri, *a. Consisting of dialogue; intermediate; not final or definitive, as a decision or judgment.* [Fr. *interlocutoire.*]
Interlope, in-tĕr-lōp′, *vi. To run between; to intrude; to traffic without a proper license; to forestall; to prevent right. ppr. interloping, pret. & pp. interloped.* [D. *loopen,* to run.]
Interloper, in-tĕr-lōp′ĕr, *n. One who runs into business to which he has no right; one who interferes wrongfully; an intruder.*
Interlude, in′tĕr-lūd, *n. A play coming in between; an entertainment exhibited on the stage, between the acts of a play, or between the play and the after-piece; a brief piece of church-music.* [L. *ludo,* to play.]
Interlunar, in-tĕr-lū′nĕr, *a. Belonging to the time that elapses between the going out of the old and the coming in of the new moon.* [L. *luna,* the moon.]
Intermarriage, in-tĕr-ma′rij, *n. Marriage between two families, where each takes one and gives another.*
Intermarry, in-tĕr-ma′ri, *vi. To marry amongst each other; to marry some of each order, family, tribe, or nation, with the other. ppr. intermarrying, pret. & pp. intermarried.*
Intermeddle, in-tĕr-med′l, *vi. To meddle in the affairs of others; to meddle officiously. ppr. intermeddling, pret. & pp. intermeddled.*
Intermedler, in-tĕr-med′l-ĕr, *n.* One who interposes officiously.
Intermediate, in-tĕr-mē′di-āt, *a. Being in the middle place between two extremes; being between two points of time or space; intervening.* [Fr. *intermédiat*—L. *medius,* middle.]
Interment, in-tĕr′ment, *n. Act of interring; burial; inhumation.* [Fr. *enterrement.*]
Interminable, in-tĕr′min-a-bl, *a. Admitting no limit; boundless; endless; limitless.* [Fr.—L. *terminus,* a limit.]
Interminably, in-tĕr′min-a-bli, *adv. Without end or limit.*
Interminate, in-tĕr′min-āt, *a. Unbounded; unlimited.* [L. *interminatus.*]
Intermingle, in-tĕr-ming′gl, *vt. To mingle together; to put, as some things with others.—vi. To be mixed or incorporated. ppr. intermingling, pret. & pp. intermingled.*
Intermission, in-tĕr-mi′shon, *n. Act of intermitting; temporary discontinuance; interval; rest.* [Fr.—L. *mitto, missum,* to send.]
Intermit, in-tĕr-mit′, *vt. To discontinue; to break off; to interrupt; to suspend.—vi. To cease for a time; to go off at intervals, as a fever. ppr. intermitting, pret. & pp. intermitted.* [L. *intermitto—mitto,* to send, let go.]
Intermittent, in-tĕr-mit′ent, *a. Ceasing at intervals; ceasing for a time and then returning, as certain fevers.—n. A fever which intermits.* [Fr.]
Intermittingly, in-tĕr-mit′ing-li, *adv. With intermissions.*
Intermix, in-tĕr-miks′, *vt. To mix among; to mix together; to intermingle.—vi. To be mixed together; to be intermingled.* [L. *misceo, mixtum,* to mix.]
Intermixture, in-tĕr-miks′tūr, *n. A mass formed by mixture; a mass of ingredients mixed; admixture.*
Internal, in-tĕrn′al, *a. Inward; not external; pertaining to the heart; real;*

within a country; domestic. [L. *internus.*]
Internally, in-tĕrn′al-li, *adv. Inwardly; intellectually; spiritually.*
International, in-tĕr-na′shon-al, *a. Relating to that which is between nations; regulating the mutual intercourse between different nations.*
Internecine, in-tĕr-nē′sin, *a. Mutually deadly and destructive; aiming at the slaughter of each other.* [L. *internecinus*—L. *neco,* to kill.]
Internuncio, in-tĕr-nun′si-ō, *n. The title of the pope's messenger or representative at republics and small courts.* [It. *internunsio*—L. *nuntius,* a messenger.]
Interpellation, in′tĕr-pel-lā″shon, *n. An interruption of one speaking; interruption.* [Fr.—L. *pello,* to speak.]
Interpolate, in-tĕr′pō-lāt, *vt. To falsify by smoothing; to foist in; to insert, as a spurious word or passage in a manuscript or book. ppr. interpolating, pret. & pp. interpolated.* [L. *interpolo, interpolatus—polio,* to smooth.]
Interpolation, in-tĕr′pō-lā″shon, *n. Act of interpolating; a spurious word or passage inserted in the genuine writings of an author.* [Fr.]
Interpolator, in-tĕr′pō-lāt-ĕr, *n. One who interpolates.* [Late L.]
Interpose, in-tĕr-pōz′, *vt. To place or set between; to intrude, as an obstruction, interruption, or inconvenience; to offer, as aid or services.—vi. To step in between parties at variance; to mediate; to interfere. ppr. interposing, pret. & pp. interposed.* [Fr. *interposer*—L. *pono, positum,* to place.]
Interposer, in-tĕr-pōz′ĕr, *n. One who interposes.*
Interposition, in-tĕr′pō-zi″shon, *n. Act of interposing; mediation; intercession; agency between parties; anything interposed.* [Fr.]
Interpret, in-tĕr′pret, *vt. To act the part of an explainer or interpreter of; to explain; to translate, as unintelligible words into intelligible ones; to construe; to unfold, as the meaning of predictions, &c.; to explain, as something not understood; to define.* [Fr. *interpréter.*]
Interpretable, in-tĕr′pret-a-bl, *a. That may be interpreted.*
Interpretation, in-tĕr′pret-ā″shon, *n. Act of interpreting; act of unfolding what is not understood; the sense given by an interpreter; exposition; the art of teaching the real sentiments contained in any form of words.* [Fr. *interprétation.*]
Interpretative, in-tĕr′pret-āt-iv, *a. Collected or known by interpretation; containing explanation.* [Fr. *interprétatif.*]
Interpreter, in-tĕr′pret-ĕr, *n. One who explains or expounds; an expositor; a translator.* [L. *interpres, interpretis.*]
Interregnum, in-tĕr-reg′num, *n. The time between the death of one king and the succession of another; time during which a throne is vacant.* [L. *regnum,* a kingdom—*rego,* to govern.]
Interrogate, in-te′rō-gāt, *vt. To ask between, as questions; to ask; to question; to examine by asking questions. ppr interrogating, pret. & pp. interrogated.* [L. *interrogo, interrogatus*—*rogo,* to ask.]
Interrogation, in-te′rō-gā″shon, *n. Act of interrogating; a question put; inquiry; a note that marks a question, thus (?).* [Fr.]
Interrogative, in-te-rog′at-iv, *a. Denot-*

ing a question; expressed in the form of a question.—*n.* A word used in asking questions; as, *who? what?* [Fr. *interrogatif.*]
Interrogatively, in-te-rog'ăt-iv-li, *adv. In the form of a question.*
Interrogator, in-te'rŏ-gāt-ĕr, *n. One who asks questions.* [Late L.]
Interrogatory, in-te-rog'ă-tŏ-ri, *a. Consisting of questions;* containing a question.—*n. A question* or inquiry. [Fr. *interrogatoire*—L. *rogo,* to ask.]
Interrupt, in-tĕr-rupt', *vt. To break in between;* to stop by breaking in upon the progress of; to break the current or motion of; to divide; to break, as continuity or a continued series. [L. *interrumpo, interruptus — rumpo,* to break.]
Interrupted, in-tĕr-rupt'ed,*p.a. Broken;* intermitted.
Interruption, in-tĕr-rup'shon, *n. Act of interrupting;* stop; hindrance; obstruction caused by breaking in upon any course; cessation; intermission. [Fr.—L. *interruptio.*]
Intersect, in-tĕr-sekt', *vt. To cut asunder;* to divide; to cut or cross mutually; to divide into parts.—*vi.* To meet and *cut* or cross each other. [L. *inter-seco, intersectus*—*sēco, sectum,* to cut.]
Intersection, in-tĕr-sek'shon, *n. Act of intersecting;* the point in which two lines, or the line in which two planes cut each other. [Fr.]
Intersperse, in-tĕr-spĕrs', *vt. To strew or sprinkle among;* to scatter or set here and there among other things. *ppr.* interspersing, *pret. & pp.* interspersed. [L. *interspergo, interspersus*—*spargo,* to scatter.]
Interspersion, in-tĕr-spĕr'shon, *n. Act of interspersing.*
Interstice, in-tĕrs'tis, *n. A narrow or small space between things closely set,* or the parts which compose a body. [Fr.—L. *sisto,* to place—*sto,* to stand.]
Interstitial, in-tĕr-sti'shi-al, *a. Pertaining to or containing interstices.*
Intertropical, in-tĕr-tro'pik-al, *a. Situated between the tropics.*
Intertwine, in-tĕr-twīn', *vt.* To unite by *twining or twisting, as one with another.* *vi.* To be mutually interwoven. *ppr.* intertwining, *pret. & pp.* intertwined.
Intertwist, in-tĕr-twist', *vt. To twist, as one with another.*
Interval, in'tĕr-val, *n.* Originally a *space between two walls;* a space between things; space of time between any two points, or between two paroxysms of disease; the distance between two given sounds in music. [Fr. *intervalle*—L. *vallum,* a wall.]
Intervallum†, in-tĕr-val'lum, *n.* An interruption.
Intervene, in-tĕr-vēn', *vi. To come between;* to come between points of time or events; to happen in a way to disturb, cross, or interrupt. *ppr.* intervening, *pret. & pp.* intervened. [Fr. *intervenir*—L. *venio,* to come.]
Intervening, in-tĕr-vēn'ing, *p.a.* Intermediate.
Intervention, in-tĕr-ven'shon, *n. Act of intervening;* interposition; mediation; agency of means or instruments; interposition in favour of another. [Fr. —L. *venio, ventum,* to come.]
Interview, in'tĕr-vū, *n. A mutual view;* a conference or mutual communication of thoughts; usually, a formal meeting for conference.
Interweave, in-tĕr-wēv', *vt. To weave together;* to unite in texture; to insert together; to unite closely. *ppr.* inter-

weaving, *pret.* interwove, *pp.* interwoven.
Intestacy, in-test'a-si, *n. State of being intestate* or of dying without making a will or disposing of one's effects.
Intestate, in-test'āt, *a. Dying without having made a will;* not disposed of by will.—*n. A person who dies without making a will.* [Fr. *intestat*—L. *testor, testatus,* to make a will.]
Intestinal, in-tes-tin'al, *a. Pertaining to the intestines* of an animal body. [Fr.]
Intestine, in-tes'tin, *a. Internal;* not foreign. [Fr. *intestin*—L. *intus,* within.]
Intestine, in-tes'tin, *n.* usually in the *pl.* **Intestines.** The bowels; the entrails; a muscular canal extending from the stomach to the anus. [L. *pl. intestina.*]
Inthral, in-thral', *vt. To bring into thraldom;* to enslave. *ppr.* inthralling, *pret. & pp.* inthralled.
Inthralment, in-thral'ment, *n. Act of inthralling;* servitude; slavery; bondage.
Intimacy, in'ti-ma-si, *n. State of being intimate;* close familiarity or fellowship.
Intimate, in'ti-māt, *a. Inmost;* close; close in friendship or acquaintance; familiar.—*n.* A familiar friend; one to whom the *inmost* thoughts and feelings are intrusted without reserve. *vt.* To bring into†; (o hint; to give slight notice of; to make known. *ppr.* intimating, *pret. & pp.* intimated. [L. *intimus—intus,* within.]
Intimately, in'ti māt-li, *adv. In an intimate manner;* familiarly.
Intimation, in-ti-mā'shon, *n. Act of intimating;* hint; a declaration communicating imperfect information; announcement. [Fr.]
Intimidate, in-ti'mid-āt, *vt. To put in fear;* to inspire with fear; to frighten; to terrify; to dishearten. *ppr.* intimidating, *pret. & pp.* intimidated. [L. *timidus,* fearful—*timeo,* to fear.]
Intimidation, in-ti'mid-ā'shon, *n. Act of intimidating;* the state of being intimidated. [Fr.]
Intituled, in-ti'tūld, *pp.* Entituled; distinguished by a title.
Into, in'tö, *prep.* Noting entrance or a passing from the outside of a thing to its interior parts; noting penetration beyond the outside or surface, or access to it; noting insertion; noting mixture; noting inclusion; noting the passing of a thing from one form or state to another.
Intolerable, in-tol'ĕr-a-bl, *a. Not tolerable; that cannot be borne;* not to be allowed. [Fr. *intolérable.*]
Intolerableness, in-tol'ĕr-a-bl-nes, *n. Quality of being not tolerable.*
Intolerably, in-tol'ĕr-a-bli, *adv.* To a degree *beyond endurance.*
Intolerance, in-tol'ĕr-ans, *n. State of being intolerant;* want of toleration; the not enduring at all, or not suffering to exist without persecution. [Fr. *intolérance.*]
Intolerant, in-tol'ĕr-ant, *a. That cannot bear;* not enduring difference of opinion or worship; refusing to tolerate others; not enduring. [Fr. *intolérant*—L. *tolĕro,* to bear.]
Intolerantly, in-tol'ĕr-ant-li, *adv. In an intolerant manner.*
Intomb, in-tōm', *vt.* To deposit in a *tomb;* to bury.
Intonate, in-tōn'āt, *vi. To sound the notes* of the musical scale; to modulate the voice in a musical or expres-

sive manner. [L. *intono. intonatus*—*tōno,* to sound, thunder.]
Intonation, in-tŏn-ā'shon, *n.* The *action of sounding* the notes of the scale, or any other given order of musical tones, with the voice; the modulation of the voice in expression. [Fr.]
Intone, in-tōn', *vi.* To give forth a deep protracted sound.—*vt. To utter* with a musical or prolonged note or *tone. ppr.* intoning, *pret. & pp.* intoned. [L. *intono.*]
Intoxicate, in-toks'i-kāt, *vt.* Generally, *to poison;* to make drunk, as with spirituous liquor; to elate to enthusiasm or madness; to infatuate. *ppr.* intoxicating, *pret. & pp.* intoxicated. [L. *toxicum,* poison.]
Intoxicating, in-toks'i-kāt-ing, *p.a.* Having qualities that produce inebriation.
Intoxication, in-toks'i-kā"shon, *n. Act of intoxicating;* the state of being drunk; drunkenness; an elation; elation of mind which rises to enthusiasm or madness.
Intractable, in-trakt'a-bl, *a. Not tractable;* not to be governed or managed; refractory; violent; unteachable. [L. *tracto,* to drag—*traho,* to draw.]
Intractableness, in-trakt'a-bl-nes, *n. Quality of being intractable;* perverseness; indocility.
Intractably, in-trakt'a-bli, *adv.* In a perverse, stubborn manner.
Intramural, in-tra-mū'ral, *a. Being within the walls.* [L. *intra,* and *muralis—murus,* a wall.]
Intransitive, in-trans'it-iv, *a. Not transitive; that cannot pass over;* designating a verb which expresses an action or state that is limited to the agent.
Intransitively, in-trans'it-iv-li, *adv. In the manner of an intransitive verb.*
Intransmissible, in-trans-mis'i-bl, *a. That cannot be transmitted.*
Intransmutable, in-trans-mūt'a-bl, *a. That cannot be transmuted.*
Intrench, in-trensh', *vt. To dig a trench around,* as in fortification; to fortify with a ditch and parapet; to make hollows in; to cut into.—*vi.* To invade; to encroach. (With *on* or *upon.*)
Intrenchant, in-trensh'ant, *a.* Not to be divided or wounded.
Intrenchment, in-trensh'ment, *a. Act of intrenching;* a trench; a ditch and parapet for defence; any defence; an encroachment on the rights of another.
Intrepid, in-tre'pid, *a. That does not tremble* from danger; undaunted; fearless; resolute; courageous. [Fr. *intrépide*—L. *trepidus,* trembling with fear —*tremo,* to tremble.]
Intrepidity, in-tre'pid'i-ti, *n. Quality of being intrepid;* fearlessness; undaunted courage. [Fr. *intrépidité.*]
Intrepidly, in-tre'pid-li, *adv.* Fearlessly; daringly; resolutely.
Intricacy, in'tri-ka-si, *n. State of being intricate;* perplexity; complication. [Low L. *intricatio.*]
Intricate, in'tri-kāt, *a. Entangled;* perplexed; complicated; obscure. [L. *intricatus—tricor,* to start difficulties.]
Intricately, in'tri-kāt-li, *adv.* With perplexity.
Intrigue, in-trēg', *n. An entanglement;* a plot of a complicated nature, intended to effect some purpose by secret artifices; the plot of a play; a secret understanding between two persons of different sexes.—*vi. To form a plot* or scheme, usually *complicated;* to

ch, *chain;*   j, *job;*   g, *go;*   ng, *sing;*   TH, *then;*   th, *thin;*   w, *wig;*   wh, *whig;*   zh, *azure;*   † obsolete.

carry on a commerce of forbidden love. *ppr.* intriguing, *pret. & pp.* intrigued. [Fr.—L. *tricor*, to start difficulties, to trifle, to dally.]
Intriguer, in-trēg'ėr, *n. One who intrigues.*
Intriguing, in-trēg'ing, *p.a. Addicted to intrigue;* given to secret machinations.
Intrinse, Intrinsecate, in-trins', in-trin'sē-kāt, *a.* Entangled.
Intrinsic, in-trin'sik, *a. Being on the inside;* internal; true; real; inherent. [Fr. *intrinsèque*—L. *intra*, and *secus*, near.]
Intrinsically, in-trin'sik-al-li, *adv. Internally;* in its nature; really; truly.
Introduce, in-trō-dūs', *vt. To bring in;* to bring into or under notice; to make known; to bring, as something new, into notice or practice; to import; to bring before the public. *ppr.* introducing, *pret. & pp.* introduced. [L. *introduco*—*dūco*, to lead.]
Introduction, in-trō-duk'shon, *n. Act of introducing;* act of making persons known to each other; act of bringing something into notice; a preface; the first part of an oration or discourse. [Fr.—L. *introductio*.]
Introductorily, in-trō-duk'tō-ri-li, *adv. By way of introduction.*
Introductory, in-trō-duk'tō-ri, *a. Serving to introduce;* prefatory; preliminary. [Low L. *introductorius.*]
Introvert, in-trō-vėrt', *vt. To turn inward.* [L. *intro*, and *verto*, to turn.]
Intrude, in-trōd', *vi. To thrust one's self in;* to force an entry or way in without permission, just right, or invitation; to encroach.—*vt. To force or thrust in* (with recip. pron.) *ppr.* intruding, *pret. & pp.* intruded. [L. *intrudo*—*trūdo*—Heb. *tārad*, to thrust.]
Intruder, in-trōd'ėr, *n. One who intrudes.*
Intrusion, in-trō'zhon, *n. The action of intruding;* encroachment; entrance without right on the property or possessions of another. [Fr.]
Intrusive, in-trō'siv, *a.* Apt to intrude; thrusting in, or entering without right or welcome. [Fr. *intrusif.*]
Intrusively, in-trō'siv-li, *adv. In an intrusive manner.*
Intrusiveness, in-trō'siv-nes, *n. Quality of being intrusive.*
Intrust, in-trust', *vt. To deliver in trust;* to confide to the care of; to commit to another with confidence in his fidelity.
Intuition, in-tū-i'shon, *n. A looking on or upon;* the act by which the mind perceives the agreement or disagreement of two ideas, or the truth of things, the moment they are presented; a first or primary truth. [Fr.—L. *tueor, tuitus,* to look at.]
Intuitive, in-tū'it-iv, *a. Exhibiting truth to the mind on bare inspection, as evidence;* received by simple inspection, as knowledge; having the power of discovering truth without reasoning. [Fr. *intuitif.*]
Intuitively, in-tū'it-iv-li, *adv. By immediate perception;* without reasoning.
Intwine, in-twin', *vt. To twine or twist together;* to wreath. *ppr.* intwining, *pret. & pp.* intwined.
Intwinement, in-twin'ment, *n. The act of intwining.*
Intwist, in-twist', *vt. To twist together;* to interweave.
Inundate, in-un'dāt, *vt. To cover with water or a fluid;* to flood; to overwhelm; to fill with an overflowing abundance. *ppr.* inundating, *pret. & pp.* inundat-

ed. [L. *inundo, inundatus—unda*, a wave—Sans. *und*, to be wet.]
Inundation, in-un-dā'shon, *n. Act of inundating;* a flood; a rising and spreading of water over low grounds; an overspreading of any kind; an overflowing. [L. *inundatio.*]
Inure, in-ūr', *vt. To bring to the use of;* to accustom; to apply or expose in use, or practice till use gives little or no pain.—*vi. To pass in use;* to take or have effect; to be applied; to serve to the use or benefit of. *ppr.* inuring, *pret. & pp.* inured. [Norm. *enuer*, to inure—L. *utor, usus,* to use.]
Inurn, in-ėrn', *vt. To put in an urn;* to bury; to inter. [in and urn.]
Inutility, in-ū-til'i-ti, *n. Uselessness;* unprofitableness. [Fr. *inutilité.*]
Invade, in-vād', *vt. To go into;* to enter as an enemy; to assail; to assault; to infringe; to encroach on; to violate, as one's rights; to seize. *ppr.* invading, *pret. & pp.* invaded. [L. *invado*—*vado,* to go.]
Invader, in-vād'ėr, *n. One who invades.*
Invading, in-vād'ing, *p.a.* Infringing; attacking.
Invalid, in-va'lid, *a. Wanting strength;* weak; having no force, effect, or efficacy; void; null. [Fr. *invalide*—L. *valeo*, to be well or strong.]
Invalid, in'va-lēd, *n. One who is weak;* a person who is infirm, wounded, maimed, or otherwise disabled for active service; a soldier or seaman worn out in service.—*a. Not strong;* weak; infirm; sick.
Invalid, in-va-lēd', *vt. To render or to classify as invalid;* to enrol on the list of invalids in the naval or military service.
Invalidate, in-va'lid-āt, *vt. To destroy the strength or validity of;* to render of no force or effect, as a bargain or will; to overthrow; to prove to be of no force, as testimony. *ppr.* invalidating, *pret. & pp.* invalidated. [Fr. *invalider.*]
Invalidation, in-va'lid-ā"shon, *n. Act of rendering invalid.*
Invalidity, in-va-lid'i-ti, *n. State or quality of being invalid;* weakness; want of cogency; want of legal force. [Fr. *invalidité.*]
Invaluable, in-va'lū-a-bl, *a. That cannot be valued;* so valuable that its worth cannot be estimated; inestimable.
Invaluably, in-va'lū-a-bli, *adv.* Inestimably.
Invariable, in-vā'ri-a-bl, *a. Not variable;* unalterable; unchangeable; always uniform. [Fr.]
Invariableness, in-vā'ri-a-bl-nes, *n. State or quality of being invariable.*
Invariably, in-vā'ri-a-bli, *adv.* Constantly; without alteration or change.
Invasion, in-vā'zhon, *n. Act of invading;* a hostile entrance into the territories of another for conquest; irruption; inroad; an attack on the rights of another; infringement or violation. [Fr.—L. *vado,* to go.]
Invective, in-vekt'iv, *n. That which is carried against;* something uttered or written, intended to cast opprobrium or reproach on another; abuse; railing; satire. [Fr.—L. *veho, rectum,* to carry.]
Invectively, in-vekt'iv-li, *adv. In the way of invective,* satirically.
Inveigh, in-vā', *vi. To carry against;* to utter censorious and bitter language against any one; to upbraid. [With *against.*] [L. *inveho—veho*, to carry.]
Inveigle, in-vē'gl, *vt. To blind;* to mislead; to entice; to wheedle; to persuade to something evil by deceptive

arts. *ppr.* inveigling, *pret. & pp.* inveigled. [Norm. *enveogler*—L. *ab,* and *oculus,* the eye.]
Inveiglement, in-vē'gl-ment, *n. Seduction to evil;* enticement.
Invent, in-vent', *vt. To come upon;* to find out, as something new; to contrive and produce, as something that did not before exist; to contrive falsely; to feign. [L. *invenio, inventum—venio,* to come.]
Invention, in-ven'shon, *n. The operation of inventing;* the power of inventing; that skill or ingenuity which is or may be employed in contriving anything new; the contrivance of that which did not before exist; that which is invented; forgery; fiction; a piece in painting; the finding and selecting of arguments to prove the point in view. [Fr.—L. *venio,* to come.]
Inventive, in-vent'iv, *a. Able to invent;* quick at contrivance. [Fr. *inventif.*]
Inventiveness, in-vent'iv-nes, *n. The faculty of inventing.*
Inventor, in-vent'ėr, *n. One who invents;* a contriver. [L.]
Inventorially, in-ven-tō'ri-al-li, *adv. In the manner of an inventory.*
Inventory, in'ven-tō-ri, *n.* What is found to belong to one; a catalogue of all the goods and chattels of a deceased person; a catalogue of movables; a catalogue or account of particular things.—*vt. To make an inventory of.* [Fr. *inventaire*—L. *invenio,* to come upon—*venio,* to come.]
Inventress, in-vent'res, *n. A female who invents.*
Inverse, in-vėrs', *a. Turned about or upside down;* inverted; opposed to direct. [L. *inversus*—*verto,* to turn.]
Inversely, in-vėrs'li, *adv. In an inverted* order or manner.
Inversion, in-vėr'shon, *n. Act of inverting;* change of order, so that the last becomes first, and the first last; a change of the natural order of things; a turning backward; a change of order or position. [Fr.—L. *verto,* to turn.]
Invert, in-vėrt', *vt. To turn about;* to turn upside down; to place in a contrary order or method. [L. *inverto*—*verto,* to turn.]
Invertebrate, in-vėr'tē-brāt, *a.* Destitute of a *vertebral chain* or backbone.—*n.* An animal *having no vertebral column* or spinal bone. [L. *in,* and *vertebratus—verto,* to turn.]
Inverted, in-vėrt'ed, *p.a. Turned about;* changed in order.
Invest, in-vest', *vt. To clothe;* to array; to clothe with office or authority; to adorn; to grace; to inclose; to lay siege to; to place out, as money in some species of property (with *in*). [Fr *investir*—L. *vestis,* a garment.]
Investigate, in-ves'ti-gāt, *vt. To follow the track of;* to inquire and examine into with care and accuracy; to find out by careful inquisition. *ppr.* investigating, *pret. & pp.* investigated. [L. *investigo, investigatus*—*vestigium,* a footstep.]
Investigation, in-ves'ti-gā"shon, *n. The process of investigating;* a careful inquiry to find out what is unknown; scrutiny; research. [Fr.]
Investigator, in-ves'ti-gāt-ėr, *n. One who investigates* or searches diligently into a subject. [L.]
Investiture, in-vest'i-tūr, *n. The action of investing* with or giving possession of; the right of giving possession of any manor, office, or benefice; investment. [Fr.]

Fāte, fär, fat, fall; mē, met, hėr; pīne, pin; nōte, not, mōve; tūbe, tub, bull; oil, pound.

Investment, in-vest'ment, n. The action of investing; a vestment; a robe; act of besieging by an armed force; the laying out of money in some species of property; the property in which money is so placed. [Fr. investissement.]

Inveteracy, in-ve'tėr-a-si, n. State of being inveterate; long use; the firmness of deep-rooted obstinacy of any quality or state acquired by time. [L. inveteratio—vetus, veteris, old.]

Inveterate, in-ve'tėr-āt, a. Become old; deep-rooted; firmly established by long continuance; confirmed by long practice; obstinate. [L. inveteratus—vetus, old.]

Inveterateness, in-re'tėr-āt-nes, n. Inveteracy.

Invidious, in-vi'di-us, a. Looking askance at; likely to incur ill-will or hatred, or to provoke envy; hateful. [L. invidiosus—video, to see.]

Invidiously, in-vi'di-us-li, adv. Enviously; malignantly.

Invidiousness, in-vi'di-us-nes, n. Quality of being invidious or envious; quality of provoking envy or hatred.

Invigorate, in-vi'gor-āt, vt. To give vigour to; to give life and energy to. ppr. invigorating, pret. & pp. invigorated. [L. vigeo, to flourish, be strong.]

Invigorated, in-vi'gor-āt-ed, p.a. Animated.

Invigorating, in-vi'gor-āt-ing, p.a. Strengthening.

Invincibility, in-vin'si-bil'li-ti, n. Quality of being invincible. [Fr. invincibilité.]

Invincible, in-vin'si-bl, a. Not to be conquered; unconquerable; not to be overcome; insurmountable; irrefutable. [Fr.—L. vinco, to conquer.]

Invincibly, in-vin'si-bli, adv. Unconquerably; insuperably.

Inviolability, in-vi'ō-la-bil'li-ti, n. Quality or state of being inviolable; quality of not being subject to be broken. [Fr. inviolabilité.]

Inviolable, in-vi'ō-la-bl, a. Not to be violated; that ought not to be injured, polluted, or treated with irreverence; not to be broken; not susceptible of hurt or wound. [Fr.—L. violo, to injure.]

Inviolably, in-vi'ō-la-bli, adv. Without breach or failure.

Inviolate, in-vi'ō-lāt, a. Unhurt; unprofaned; unbroken. [L. inviolatus.]

Invised†, in-vizd', a. Invisible.

Invisibility, in-vi'zi-bil'li-ti, n. State of being invisible; imperceptibleness to the sight. [Fr. invisibilité.]

Invisible, in-vi'zi-bl, a. Not visible; that cannot be seen; disregarded†. [Fr.]

Invisibly, in-vi'zi-bli, adv. In a manner to escape the sight.

Invitation, in-vit-ā'shon, n. Act of inviting; solicitation. [Fr.]

Invite, in-vit', vt. To ask; to request; to bid; to solicit; to draw to; to allure; to entice.—vi. To ask or call to anything pleasing. [Fr. inviter—L. invito.]

Inviter, in-vit'ėr, n. One who invites.

Inviting, in-vit'ing, p.a. Alluring; tempting; drawing to.

Invitingly, in-vit'ing-li, adv. In such a manner as to invite or allure.

Invocate, in'vō-kāt, vt. To invoke; to implore; to address in prayer. ppr. invocating, pret. & pp. invocated. [L. invoco, invocatus—voco, to call.]

Invocation, in-vō-kā'shon, n. Act of invoking; a calling upon the name of God; the form or act of calling for the assistance of any being, particularly of some divinity. [Fr.]

Invoice, in'vois, n. A written account of the particulars of merchandise, shipped or sent to a purchaser, factor, &c., with the value or prices and charges annexed. [Fr. envoi, a sending—L. via, a way.]

Invoice, in-vois', vt. To make an invoice or a written account of. ppr. invoicing, pret. & pp. invoiced.

Invoke, in-vōk', vt. To call upon; to address in prayer; to call on for assistance and protection; to call for with earnestness. ppr. invoking, pret. & pp. invoked. [L. invoco—voco, to call.]

Involuntarily, in-vo'lun-ta-ri-li, adv. In an involuntary manner.

Involuntary, in-vo'lun-ta-ri, a. Not voluntary; not having will or choice; independent of will or choice; opposed to the will.

Involute, in'vō-lūt, a. Rolled spirally inward; turned inward.—n. That which is rolled inward; a curve traced by the end of a string wound upon another curve, or unwound from it. [L. involutus—volvo, to roll.]

Involution, in-vō-lū'shon, n. The action of involving or infolding; complication; the raising of a quantity to any power assigned. [Fr.—L. volvo, to roll.]

Involve, in-volv', vt. To infold; to envelop in anything which exists on all sides; to comprise; to contain; to take in; to entangle; to plunge; to overwhelm, as in ruin; to complicate; to raise, as a quantity to any assigned power. ppr. involving, pret. & pp. involved. [L. involvo—volvo, to roll.]

Involved, in-volvd', p.a. Entangled.

Invulnerability, in-vul'nėr-a-bil''li-ti, n. Quality of being invulnerable. [Fr. invulnérabilité.]

Invulnerable, in-vul'nėr-a-bl, a. That cannot be wounded; incapable of receiving injury. [Fr. invulnérable—L. vulnus, vulnėris, a wound.]

Invulnerably, in-vul'nėr-a-bli, adv. In an invulnerable manner.

Inward, in'wėrd, a. Inner; placed or being within; intimate; familiar; seated in the mind or soul.—n. That which is inward; (pl.) the inner parts. adv. Toward the inside; into the mind or thoughts. [Sax. inweard.]

Inwardly, in'wėrd-li, adv. In the inner parts; in the heart.

Inwards, in'wėrdz, adv. Same as inward.

Inweave, in-wēv', vt. To weave together. ppr. inweaving, pret. inwove, pp. inwoven.

Inworn, in-wōrn', a. Worn within, or wrought within.

Inwrap, in-rap', vt. To wrap round; to cover by wrapping; to involve; to perplex. ppr. inwrapping, pret. & pp. inwrapped.

Inwreathe, in-rēTH', vt. To surround, as with a wreath, or with something in the form of a wreath. ppr. inwreathing, pret. & pp. inwreathed.

Inwrought, in-rat', p.a. Wrought in or among other things; adorned with figures.

Iodine, i'ō-din, n. A peculiar substance obtained from certain sea-weeds, much used in medicine, and so named from the violet colour of its vapour. [Gr.—ion, the violet, and eidos, likeness.]

Ionic, i-on'ik, a. Pertaining to Ionia; denoting an order in architecture distinguished by the volutes of its capital.

Iota, i-ō'ta, n. The name of the smallest Greek letter; a very small particle or quantity.

Ipecacuanha, i-pē-kak'ū-an''ha, n. A South American bitter, emetic, and narcotic root, used in medicine. [A Peruvian word.]

Irascibility, i-ras'i-bil''li-ti, n. Quality of being irascible; irritability of temper.

Irascible, i-ras'i-bl, a. Very susceptible of anger; easily provoked; irritable. [Fr.—L. ira, anger.]

Irascibly, i-ras'i-bli, adv. In an irascible manner.

Ire, ir, n. Anger; wrath; rage; keen resentment. [Fr.—L. ira, anger.]

Ireful, ir'ful, a. Full of ire; furious with anger.

Irefully, ir'ful-li, adv. In an angry manner.

Iridescence, i-rid-es'ens, n. The property of exhibiting colours like those of the rainbow; exhibition of colours like those of the rainbow. [L. iris, the rainbow.]

Iridescent, i-rid-es'ent, a. Having colours like the rainbow. [Fr.]

Iris, i'ris, n. Irises, i'ris-es, pl. The rainbow; an appearance resembling the rainbow; the coloured circle which surrounds the pupil of the eye; a plant, the flag-flower. [L. and Gr. the rainbow.]

Irish, i'rish, a. Pertaining to Ireland, or produced in Ireland.—n. A native of Ireland; the language of the natives of Ireland, a species of Celtic.

Irk, ėrk, vt. To weary; to tire; to vex; to give pain to; to distress. (Used only impersonally.) [Icel. yrki, to be oppressed.]

Irksome, ėrk'sum, a. Giving uneasiness; wearisome; burdensome; vexatious.

Irksomely, ėrk'sum-li, adv. In a wearisome or tedious manner.

Irksomeness, ėrk'sum-nes, n. Quality of being irksome; tediousness.

Iron, i'ėrn, n. A metal, the hardest, most common, and most useful of all the metals; an instrument or utensil made of iron; figuratively, strength, power; (pl.) fetters; chains; manacles; handcuffs.—a. Made of iron; consisting of iron; resembling iron in colour; severe; binding fast; not to be broken; firm; dull of understanding; vigorous.—vt. To smooth with an instrument of iron; to shackle with irons; to furnish or arm with iron. [Sax. iren, Icel. idrn.]

Iron-clad, i'ėrn-klad, a. Clad in iron. n. A vessel prepared for war by having the parts above water covered with iron.

Iron-gray, i'ėrn-grā, n. A colour resembling that of iron.

Ironical, i-ron'ik-al, a. Containing irony; given to irony, expressing one thing and meaning the opposite. [Fr. ironique.]

Ironically, i-ron'ik-al-li, adv. By way of irony; by the use of irony.

Ironing, i'ėrn-ing, p.n. A smoothing with an iron; a shackling.

Ironmonger, i'ėrn-mung-gėr, n. A dealer in iron-wares or hardware.

Ironmongery, i'ėrn-mung-gė-ri, n. A general name for all articles made of iron; hardware.

Iron-mould, i'ėrn-mōld, n. A spot on cloth made by applying rusty iron to the cloth when wet.

Irony, i'ėrn-i, a. Made or consisting of iron; partaking of iron; resembling iron.

Irony, i'ron-i, n. Dissimulation; a kind of ridicule which exposes errors or faults by seeming to approve, adopt, or defend them. [Fr. *ironie* — Gr. *eirōn*, a dissembler.]

Irradiance, ir-rā′di-ans, *n.* *A sending forth rays of light on an object;* beams of light emitted; lustre; splendour.

Irradiant, ir-rā′di-ant, *a.* *Emitting rays of light.* [L. *irradians*.]

Irradiate, ir-rā′di-āt, *vt.* *To send forth rays of light upon;* to brighten; to adorn with lustre; to animate by heat or light; to enlighten intellectually; to decorate with shining ornaments.—*vi.* *To emit rays:* to beam forth light; to shine. *ppr.* irradiating, *pret. & pp.* irradiated.—*a. Adorned with rays of light,* or with anything shining. [L. *irradio, irradiatus — rddius*, a beam, a ray.]

Irradiation, ir-rā″di-ā″shon, *n.* Act of *irradiating;* illumination; intellectual light; act of emitting minute particles from some substance.

Irrational, ir-ra′shon-al,*a. Not rational;* void of reason, as animals; not according to the dictates of reason; contrary to reason, as conduct; absurd.

Irrationality, ir-ra′shon-al″i-ti, *n. Want of rationality.*

Irrationally, ir-ra′shon-al-li, *adv. Without reason;* absurdly.

Irreclaimable, ir-re-klām′a-bl, *a. Not to be reclaimed;* incorrigible; not to be brought under cultivation.

Irreclaimably, ir-re-klām′a-bli, *adv.* So as not to admit of being *reclaimed.*

Irreconcilable, ir-re′kon-sīl″a-bl, *a. Not reconcilable;* not to be recalled to amity; that cannot be appeased, as hostility; that cannot be made to be consistent; incompatible, as opinions or propositions.

Irreconcilableness, ir-re′kon-sīl″a-bl-nes, *n.* *Quality of being irreconcilable.*

Irreconcilably, ir-re′kon-sīl″a-bli, *adv.* *In a manner that precludes reconciliation.*

Irrecoverable, ir-re-ku′vėr-a-bl, *a. Not to be recovered;* irreparable; that cannot be regained; that cannot be obtained by demand or suit; not to be remedied.

Irrecoverably, ir-re-ku′vėr-a-bli, *adv. Beyond recovery.*

Irredeemable, ir-re-dēm′a-bl, *a.* *That cannot be redeemed;* not subject to be paid at the pleasure of government.

Irredeemably, ir-re-dēm′a-bli, *adv.* So as not to be redeemable.

Irreducible, ir-re-dūs′i-bl, *a. Not to be reduced;* that cannot be brought back to a former state; that cannot be reduced or changed to a different state.

Irreflective, ir-re-flekt′iv, *a.* *Not reflective.*

Irrefragable, ir-ref′ra-ga-bl, *a.* *Not refragable;* that cannot be gainsaid; incontrovertible; incontestable.

Irrefragably, ir-ref′ra-ga-bli, *adv.* So as not to be overthrown.

Irrefutable, ir-re-fūt′a-bl, *a.* *That cannot be refuted;* unanswerable; indisputable.

Irrefutably, ir-re-fūt′a-bli, *adv.* Beyond the possibility of *refutation.*

Irregular, ir-re′gū-lėr, *a.* *Not regular;* not according to established customs; not conformable to nature; not according to the rules of art; not in conformity to laws, human or divine; vicious; not straight, as a line; not uniform, as motion; changeable; deviating from the common rules in its inflections, as a noun or verb.—*n.* A soldier not in *regular* service.

Irregularity, ir-re′gū-la″ri-ti, *n.* *Want of regularity;* deviation from a straight line or from any common or established rule; inordinate practice; vice.

Irregularly, ir-re′gū-lėr-li, *adv. Without rule,* method, or order.

Irregulous, ir-re′gū-lus, *a.* Not subject to rule; lawless.

Irrelative, ir-re′lat-iv, *a. Not relative;* unconnected.

Irrelevance, ir-re′le-vans, *n.* *Same as irrelevancy.*

Irrelevancy, ir-re′le-van-si, *n. State or quality of being irrelevant.*

Irrelevant, ir-re′le-vant, *a. Not relevant;* not applicable or pertinent; not to the purpose; not assisting the purpose in hand.

Irrelevantly, ir-re′le-vant-li, *adv.* Without being to the purpose.

Irreligion, ir-re-li′jon, *n. Want of religion;* ungodliness; worldliness; impiety.

Irreligious, ir-re-li′ji-us, *a. Not religious;* destitute of religious principles; impious; contrary to religion; wicked.

Irreligiously, ir-re-li′ji-us-li, *adv.* With impiety; wickedly.

Irremediable, ir-re-mē′di-a-bl, *a. Not to be remedied;* incurable; irreparable.

Irremediably, ir-re-mē′di-a-bli, *adv. In a manner* that precludes *remedy.*

Irremissible, ir-re-mis′i-bl, *a. Not to be remitted* or pardoned; unpardonable.

Irremovability, ir-re-mōv′a-bil″i-ti, *n. Quality or state of being irremovable,* or not removable from office.

Irremovable, ir-re-mōv′a-bl, *a. Not removable;* that cannot be moved or changed; not legally removable from office.

Irremovably, ir-re-mōv′a-bli, *adv.* So as not to admit *of removal.*

Irreparability, ir-re′pa-ra-bil″li-ti, *n. Quality or state of being irreparable.*

Irreparable, ir-re′pa-ra-bl, *a. Not reparable;* irrecoverable; irretrievable.

Irreparably, ir-re′pa-ra-bli, *adv. In a manner or degree that precludes recovery or repair.*

Irrepealable, ir-re-pēl′a-bl, *a. That cannot be repealed.*

Irreprehensible, ir-rep′re-hens″i-bl, *a. Not reprehensible;* not to be blamed or censured.

Irreprehensibly, ir-rep′re-hens″i-bli, *adv.* In a manner not to incur blame.

Irrepressible, ir-re-pres′i-bl, *a.* *That cannot be repressed* or restrained.

Irrepressibly, ir-re-pres′i-bli, *adv.* So as not to be *repressed.*

Irreproachable, ir-re-prōch′a-bl, *a. That cannot be justly reproached;* free from blame; innocent; unblemished.

Irreproachably, ir-re-prōch′a-bli, *adv. In a manner* not to deserve reproach.

Irreprovable, ir-re-prōv′a-bl, *a.* *That cannot be justly reproved;* blameless.

Irresistibility, ir-re-zist′i-bil″li-ti, *n. Quality of being irresistible;* power or force beyond resistance or opposition.

Irresistible, ir-re-zist′i-bl, *a. That cannot be successfully resisted;* superior to opposition; resistless.

Irresistibly, ir-re-zist′i-bli, *adv.* With a power that *cannot* be *resisted.*

Irresolute, ir-re′zō-lūt, *a. Not resolute;* not decided; not determined; wavering; unstable.

Irresolutely, ir-re′zō-lūt-li, *adv.* Without firmness of mind; without decision.

Irresolution, ir-re′zō-lū″shon, *n. Want of resolution;* want of decision in purpose. [Fr.]

Irresolvable, ir-re-zolv′a-bl, *a. That cannot be resolved.*

Irrespective, ir-re-spekt′iv, *a. Not having respect to;* not regarding; not considering. (With *of.*)

Irrespectively, ir-re-spekt′iv-li, *adv. Without regard to.*

Irrespirable, ir-re-spīr′a-bl, *a. Not respirable;* not having the qualities which support animal life.

Irresponsibility, ir-re-spons′i-bil″li-ti, *n. Want of responsibility.*

Irresponsible, ir-re-spons′i-bl, *a. Not responsible;* not liable or able to answer for consequences; not answerable.

Irresponsibly, ir-re-spons′i-bli, *adv.* So as not to be *responsible.*

Irretrievable, ir-re-trēv′a-bl, *a. That cannot be retrieved;* irreparable; irrecoverable.

Irretrievably, ir-re-trēv′a-bli, *adv.* Irreparably; irrecoverably.

Irreverence, ir-re′ve-rens, *n. Want of reverence;* want of a due regard to the authority and character of the Supreme Being; disrespect.

Irreverent, ir-re′ve-rent, *a. Wanting in reverence;* not entertaining or manifesting due regard to the Supreme Being; proceeding from irreverence; disrespectful.

Irreverently, ir-re′ve-rent-li, *adv. In an irreverent manner.*

Irreversible, ir-re-vėrs′i-bl, *a. Not reversible;* that cannot be repealed or annulled.

Irreversibly, ir-re-vėrs′i-bli, *adv.* In a manner which precludes repeal.

Irrevocable, ir-re′vōk-a-bl, *a. Not to be revoked;* that cannot be reversed or annulled.

Irrevocably, ir-re′vōk-a-bli, *adv. Beyond recall.*

Irrigate, ir′ri-gāt, *vt. To water;* to water, as land, by causing a stream to flow upon it and spread over it. *ppr.* irrigating, *pret. & pp.* irrigated. [L. *irrigo, irrigatus—rigo,* to water.]

Irrigation, ir-ri-gā′shon, *n. Act of irrigating;* the operation of causing water to flow over lands for nourishing plants. [Fr.]

Irriguous, ir-ri′gū-us, *a.* Well-watered; moist; dewy. [L. *irriguus.*]

Irritability, ir′rit-a-bil″li-ti, *n.* *Quality or state of being irritable;* susceptibility of excitement or irritation. [Fr *irritabilité.*]

Irritable, ir′rit-a-bl, *a. Susceptible of irritation;* easily provoked or exasperated. [L. *irritabilis.*]

Irritably, ir′rit-a-bli, *adv. In a way to be irritated.*

Irritant, ir′rit-ant, *a. Irritating.—n. That which irritates,* excites, or stimulates. [L. *irritans.*]

Irritate, ir′rit-āt, *vt. To rouse to anger;* to exasperate; to fret; to inflame; to excite heat and redness in, as in the skin or flesh. *ppr.* irritating, *pret. & pp.* irritated. [L. *irrito, irritatum.*]

Irritating, ir′rit-āt-ing, *p.a. Angering;* provoking.

Irritation, ir-rit-ā′shon, *n. Act of irritating;* provocation; exasperation; excitement or action produced in organized bodies by the application of stimulants, &c. [Fr.]

Irruption, ir-rup′shon, *n.* *A breaking* or sudden violent rushing *into* a place; a sudden, violent inroad, or entrance of invaders into a place or country. [Fr. —L. *rumpo, ruptum,* to break.]

Is, iz, *vi.* The third person singular, pres. indic. of the substantive verb. [Sax., L. *est,* Sans. *asti.*]

Isinglass, ī′zing-glas, *n.* Fish-glue, prepared from *the sounds* or *air-bladders* of certain fresh-water fishes, particu-

Fāte, fär, fat, fạll; mē, met, hėr; pīne, pin; nōte, not, mōve; tūbe, tut, bụll; oil, pound.

ISLAND 209 JAG

larly of a species of *sturgeon.* [G. *hausenblase—hausen,* a sturgeon, and *blase,* a bladder.]
Island, i'land, *n. Water-land,* that is land, or a tract of land, surrounded by *water;* a detached portion of land embosomed in the ocean, in a lake, or river. [Sax. *ealand—ea,* water, and *land.*]
Islander, i'land-ėr, *n. An inhabitant of an island.*
Isle, il, *n.* Land *in the sea,* that is, land, or a tract of land, surrounded by the sea or by water; an island. [Old Fr.—L. *is,* and *salum,* the sea.]
Islet, il'et, *n. A small island.*
Isochronous, i-sŏ'kron-us, *a. Uniform in time; of equal time;* performed in equal times. [Gr. *isos,* equal, and *chronos,* time.]
Isolate, is'ō-lāt, *vt. To place in* a detached situation, *as in an island;* to place by itself; to insulate. *ppr.* isolating, *pret. & pp.* isolated. [It. *isolato,* detached —L. *insula,* an island.]
Isolated, is'ō-lāt-ed, *p.a.* Placed by itself or alone; insulated.
Isolation, is-ō-lā'shon, *n. State of being isolated;* insulation.
Isometrical, i-sō-met'rik-al, *a. Having equal dimensions.* [Gr. *isos,* equal, and *metron,* measure.]
Isosceles, i-sos'se-lēz, *a. Having equal legs;* having two *legs* or sides *equal,* as a triangle. [Gr. *isoskelēs—isos,* equal, and *skelos,* a leg.]
Isothermal, i-sō-thėrm'al, *a.* Having an equal degree of *heat.* [Gr. *isos,* equal, and *therma,* heat.]
Issuable, ish'ū-a-bl, *a. That may be issued.*
Issue, ish'ū, *vi. To pass out* or *forth;* to run out of any inclosed place; to spring, as from a source; to spring; to arise; to grow; to come to an issue in law; to close; to end.—*vt. To cause to go* or *pass out;* to put into circulation; to deliver from authority; to deliver for use. *ppr.* issuing, *pret. & pp.* is sued. [Old Fr. *issir,* to go out—L. *ixeo—ex,* and *eo,* to go.]—*n. Act of passing* or *flowing out;* a sending out; passage out; outlet; progeny; produce of the earth or profits of land or other property; a little ulcer made in some part of an animal body to promote discharges; discharge; the result of pleadings in law; ultimate result or end; the point of matter depending in suit; delivery. [Old Fr. *issu.*]
Issueless, ish'ū-les, *a. Having no issue.*
Issuing, ish'ū-ing, *p.n. A flowing* or *passing out;* a sending out, as of bills or notes.
Isthmus, ist'mus, *n.* A narrow *passage* or *entrance;* a narrow slip of land by which two continents are connected, or by which a peninsula is united to the mainland. [L.—Gr. *isthmos, simi,* to go.]
It, it, *pron.* A pronoun of the neuter gender, standing for anything except males and females, and meaning the thing spoken of before; used also as the nominative case to verbs called impersonal; as, it rains, it snows. [Sax. *hit.*]
Italian, i-ta'li-an, *a. Pertaining to Italy.*—*n. A native of Italy;* the language used by the Italians.
Italic, i-ta'lik, *a. Relating to Italy;* applied particularly to a kind of type called *italics,* first used by Italian printers.
Italicism, i-ta'li-sizm, *n.* An *Italian phrase* or *idiom.*
Italicize, i-ta'li-sīz, *vt. To write or print in italics. ppr.* italicizing, *pret. & pp.* italicized.
Italics, i-ta'liks, *n. pl. Italic letters or characters.*
Itch, ich, *n.* A disgusting cutaneous disease, accompanied, in some of its forms, with *inflammation;* the sensation in the skin occasioned by the disease; a constant teasing desire.—*vi.* To feel a particular uneasiness in the skin, which inclines the person to scratch the part; to have a constant desire or teasing inclination. [Sax. *gictha,* an itching; Old G. *jukjan,* to itch—Sans. *ush,* to burn.]
Itchiness, ich'i-nes, *n. State of being itchy.*
Itching, ich'ing, *p.a.* Having a constant desire.—*p.n.* The state of the skin when we desire to scratch it; a constant teasing desire.
Itchy, ich'i, *a. Infected with the itch.*
Item, i'tem, *adv. Also;* a word used when something is to be added.—*n.* An article to be added or included; a separate particular in an account.—*vt.* To make a note or memorandum of. [L.]
Iterate, it'ėr-āt, *vt. To repeat;* to utter or do *another* or a second time. *ppr.* iterating, *pret. & pp.* iterated. [L. *itero, iteratus*—Sans. *tara,* another.]
Iteration, it-ėr-ā'shon, *n.* Recital or performance a second time. [L. *iteratio.*]
Itinerancy, i-tin'ėr-an-si, *n. A journeying;* a passing from place to place.
Itinerant, i-tin'ėr-ant, *a. Passing* or *travelling* about a country, or from place to place; journeying; wandering; not settled.—*n.* One who travels from place to place, particularly a preacher. [Low L. *itinerans*—L. *iter,* a going—*eo, itum,* to go.]
Itinerary, i-tin'e-ra-ri, *n. An account of a journey,* or of places and their distances on a road.—*a. Pertaining to a journey;* travelling; passing from place to place, or done on a journey. [Fr. *itinéraire*—L. *iter,* a way.]
Itself, it-self', *pron.* The neuter reciprocal pronoun.
Ivied, i'vid, *a.* See IVYED.
Ivory, i'vō-ri, *n. The tusk of an elephant,* a hard, solid, fine-grained substance, of a fine white colour; the tusk or tooth of the walrus, narwhal, &c.—*a. Consisting of ivory;* made of ivory; white, hard, or smooth like ivory. [Fr. *ivoire*—L. *ebur,* ivory—Sans. *ibha,* an elephant.]
Ivy, i'vi, *n.* A plant which creeps along the ground, or climbs walls, trees, &c. [Sax. *ify.*]
Ivyed, Ivied, i'vid, *p.a. Overgrown with ivy.*

J.

Jabber, jab'bėr, *vi. To gabble;* to talk rapidly or indistinctly; to chatter; to prate.—*vt.* To utter rapidly with confused sounds.—*n.* Rapid talk with indistinct utterance.
Jacinth, ï'a-sinth, *n. The hyacinth;* a reddish pellucid gem. [a different orthography of *hyacinth.*]
Jack, jak, *n.* A diminutive of John, used as a general term of contempt for any saucy or paltry fellow; an instrument that supplies the place of a boy, originally called *jack;* an instrument to pull off boots; an engine to turn a spit; [Sp. *xaco,* jacket] a coat of mail; a drinking-vessel of waxed leather; the mark at which the bowler aims his ball, &c.; the male of certain animals, as of the ass; a flag, ensign, or colours, displayed from a staff on the end of a bowsprit; a machine for raising heavy weights; familiarly, a sailor.
Jackal, jak'al, *n.* A carnivorous animal resembling a dog and a fox. [Ar. *jakal.*]
Jackass, jak'as, *n. The male of the ass;* a dolt; a blockhead.
Jack-boot, jak'böt, *n. A kind of large boot* reaching up over the knee, and used as a kind of defensive armour.
Jackdaw, jak'da, *n.* A bird of the crow kind, distinguished for thieving and garrulity.
Jacket, jak'et, *n. A short close garment;* a short coat. [Fr. *jaquette.*]
Jacketed, jak'et-ed, *p.a. Wearing a jacket.*
Jacobin, ja'kō-bin, *n.* One of a society of violent revolutionists in France, during the first revolution; a demagogue. [so named from the place of meeting in Paris, which was the monastery of the monks called *Jacobins.*]
Jacobite, ja'kō-bit, *n.* A partizan of James II., king of England, after he abdicated the throne, and of his descendants.—*a.* Pertaining to the partizans of James II. [from L. *Jacobus, James.*]
Jacobitical, ja-kō-bit'ik-al, *a. Belonging to the Jacobites.*
Jade, jād, *n.* A toothless, worthless mare; a tired horse; a mean woman; a word of contempt, noting sometimes age, but generally vice; a young woman, in irony or slight contempt.—*vt.* To tire, as a horse; to fatigue; to dispirit; to subject to harassing employments.—*vi.* To become weary; to lose spirit; to sink. *ppr.* jading, *pret. & pp.* jaded. [Icel. *jalda,* a mare, *jad,* loss of teeth.]
Jaded, jād'ed, *p.a.* Wearied; fatigued; harassed.
Jag, jag, *vt. To cut into notches* or teeth like those of a saw; to notch. *ppr.* jagging, *pret. & pp.* jagged.—*n. A notch;* a ragged protuberance. [G. *sacken.*]

ė *chain;* j, *job;* g, *go;* ng, *sing,* TH, *then;* th, *thin;* w, *wig;* wh, *whig;* zh, *azure;* † obsolete.

14

Jagged, jag'ed, *p.a. Having notches or teeth; cleft; divided.*
Jaggedness, jag'ed-nes, *n. The state of being jagged;* unevenness.
Jaggy, jag'i, *a.* Set with teeth; denticulated; uneven.
Jaguar, ja-gwär', *n.* A large and ferocious animal of America, of the cat kind, about six feet in length, exclusive of the tail.
Jah, jä, *n.* JEHOVAH. [Heb.]
Jail, jāl, *n. A gaol;* a building for the confinement of persons arrested for debt or for crime. [Fr. *geôle.*]
Jailer, jāl'ėr, *n. The keeper of a jail.*
Jakes†, jāks, *n.* A privy.
Jalap, ja'lap, *n.* The root of a plant, much used in medicine as a cathartic. [Fr.—from *Xalapa,* in Mexico.]
Jam, jam, *n.* A conserve of fruits boiled with sugar and water, which *congeals* on becoming cold. [Ar. *jamd,* concretion.]
Jam, jam, *vt.* To *press;* to crowd; to squeeze tight; to wedge in. *ppr.* jamming, *pret. & pp.* jammed. [Sans. *yam,* to stop.]
Jamb, jam, *n. A leg;* a supporter; the side-post or vertical side-piece of a door, window, &c. [Fr. *jambe.*]
Jangle, jang'gl, *vi. To sound harshly;* to wrangle; to quarrel in words; to altercate; to bicker.—*vt.* To cause to sound discordantly. *ppr.* jangling, *pret. & pp.* jangled.—*n.* Prate; discordant sound; contention. [Old Fr. *jangler.*]
Jangler, jang'gl-ėr, *n.* A wrangling noisy fellow.
Jangling, jang'gl-ing, *p.n.* A noisy dispute; a wrangling.
Janitor, ja'ni-tor, *n. A doorkeeper;* a porter. [L.—*janua,* a house-door.]
Jantily, jan'ti-li, *adv. In a janty manner;* briskly; airily; gaily.
Jantiness, jan'ti-nes, *n. Quality of being janty;* airiness; flutter; briskness.
Janty, jan'ti, *a. Affectedly genteel;* airy; showy; finical. [Fr. *gentil*—L. *gentilis.*]
January, ja'nū-a-ri, *n. The month sacred to Janus;* the first month of the year, according to the present computation. [L. *Januarius*—*Janus,* the sun-god.]
Japan, ja-pan', *n.* Work varnished and figured in the manner practised by the natives of *Japan.*—*vt.* To cover with a thick coat of hard brilliant varnish, and embellish with figures; to varnish. *ppr.* japanning, *pret. & pp.* japanned.
Japanned, ja-pand', *p.a.* Varnished in a particular manner.
Japanner, ja-pan'ėr, *n.* One who varnishes in the manner of the *Japanese.*
Jape†, jāp, *vt.* To play jests upon.
Jar, jär, *vi. To strike together, as hard bodies;* to strike discordantly; to clash in words; to interfere; to act in opposition; to vibrate regularly.—*vt.* To shake; to cause to tremble; to cause a short tremulous motion in. *ppr.* jarring, *pret. & pp.* jarred.—*n. A rattling vibration of sound,* produced by the collision of *hard* bodies; a harsh sound; quarrel; clash of interests or opinions; the state of a door half open; the vibration of the pendulum of a clock. [Sans. *jarad,* hard.]
Jar, jär, *n.* A vessel with a large belly and broad mouth, made of earth or glass; the quantity held in a jar. [Fr. *jarre.*]
Jargon, jär'gon, *n.* Confused *unintelligible talk* or language; gabble; gibberish ; cant. [Fr.—L. *garrio,* to prattle.]

Jargonelle, jär-gon-el', *n.* A variety of pear. [Fr. *jargonnelle.*]
Jarring, jär'ing, *p.a.* Discordant.—*p.n.* A shaking; discord; dispute.
Jarringly, jär'ing-li, *adv. In a jarring manner.*
Jasmine, jas'min, *n.* An elegant and fragrant shrub, bearing beautiful flowers. [Fr. *jasmin.*]
Jasper, jas'pėr, *n.* A precious stone; a variety of quarts, of red, yellow, and some dull colours, admitting of an elegant polish. [Fr. *jaspe*—L. *iaspis.*]
Jaunce†, jans, *vt.* To jolt or shake.
Jaundice, jan'dis, *n.* A disease which is characterized by *yellowness* of the eyes, skin, and urine, by loss of appetite and general languor. [Fr. *jaunisse*—*jaune,* yellow.]
Jaundiced, jan'dist, *p.a. Affected with the jaundice;* seeing with discoloured organs; prejudiced.
Jaunt, jänt, *vi.* To ramble here and there; to make an excursion.—*n.* A trip; a tour; an excursion; a ramble. [Old Fr. *jancer,* to stir.]
Jauntily, jänt'i-li, *adv.* See JANTILY.
Jaunty, jänt'i, *a.* See JANTY.
Javelin, jav'lin, *n. A boar-spear;* a sort of spear about 5½ feet long, the shaft of which was of wood, but pointed with steel. [Fr. *javeline*—Sp. *jabalí,* a wild boar.]
Jaw, ja, *n. The cheek-bone;* the bone of the mouth in which the teeth are fixed; the mouth. [Fr. *joue.*]
Jawed, jad, *p.a. Having jaws;* denoting the appearance of the jaws.
Jay, jā, *n.* A chattering bird of the crow kind, of *brilliant plumage,* which frequents woods; a loose woman. [Fr. *geai*—*gai,* showy.]
Jealous, jel'us, *a. Emulous;* envious; suspicious; uneasy through fear that another has withdrawn from one the affections of a person he loves, or may enjoy some good which he desires to obtain; solicitous to defend the honour of; suspiciously vigilant, anxiously concerned for. [Fr. *jaloux*—Gr. *zēlos,* eager rivalry.]
Jealoushood†, je'lus-hud, *n. State of being jealous.*
Jealously, je'lus-li, *adv. With jealousy* or suspicion; emulously.
Jealousy, je'lus-i, *n. Quality of being jealous;* a painful suspicion of rivalry; suspicious fear or apprehension; solicitude for the welfare or honour of others. [Fr. *jalousie.*]
Jeer, jēr, *vi. To cut with sharp words;* to deride; to flout; to mock; to utter severe, sarcastic reflections.—*vt.* To make a mock of; to treat with scoffs or derision.—*n.* Railing language; biting jest; jibe; derision; ridicule with scorn. [G. *scheren*—Gr. *keirō,* to cut short.]
Jeerer, jēr'ėr, *n.* A scoffer; a railer.
Jeering, jēr'ing, *p.n.* Scoffing; mocking; deriding.
Jeeringly, jēr'ing-li, *adv.* With raillery; scornfully; contemptuously.
Jehovah, je-hō'va, *n. The Immutable Being; The Everlasting;* the Scripture name of the Supreme Being. [Heb. *Yehōvah*—*haiah,* to be.]
Jejune, je-jūn', *a. Fasting;* void; vacant; dry; wanting interesting matter. [L. *jejunus.*]
Jejuneness, je-jūn'nes, *n. State or quality of being jejune;* emptiness; poverty.
Jellied, jel'lid, *p.a.* Brought to the *consistence of jelly.*
Jelly, jel'li, *n. That which freezes;* solution of gelatine when cold; the juice of fruit, boiled with sugar; something of the consistency of vegetable jelly; a transparent, sixy substance, obtained from animal substances by decoction. [Fr. *gelée*—L. *gelo,* to freeze.]
Jelly-fish, jel'li-fish, *n.* A name given to various *gelatinous* marine animals, often also called sea-nettles.
Jennet, jen'net, *n.* A small Spanish horse. [Fr. *genêt.*]
Jeopard, je'pärd, *vt. To put in danger* of loss or injury; to hazard; to risk; to peril; to endanger. [G. *gefährden,* to expose to danger.]
Jeopardous, je'pärd-us, *a. Exposed to danger;* perilous; hazardous.
Jeopardy, je'pärd-i, *n. Hazard; risk;* exposure to death, loss, or injury.
Jerboa, jėr-bō'a, *n.* The jumping-mouse; a genus of gnawing quadrupeds allied to the mouse, but having very short fore-feet and very long hind ones.
Jerk, jėrk, *vt. To thrust out;* to thrust with a sudden effort; to give a sudden pull, twitch, thrust, or push to; to throw with a quick smart motion; to cut into long thin pieces and dry, as beef.—*n. A short, sudden thrust,* push, or twitch; a striking against something with a short quick motion; a sudden spring. [Icel. *Arekia,* to beat.]
Jerked, jėrkt, *p.a.* Cut into thin slices, and dried, as beef.
Jerkin, jėr'kin, *n.* A jacket; a short coat; a close waistcoat. [D. *jurk,* a frock.]
Jess, jes, *n.* A short strap of leather tied round the legs of a hawk, by which she is held on the fist and *tossed off* into flight. [Old Fr. *gect*—L. *jacto,* to throw.]
Jessamine, jes'a-min, *n.* See JASMINE.
Jest, jest, *n. A mocking by gestures;* something ludicrous uttered, and meant only to excite laughter; joke; raillery; the object of laughter; a mask.—*vi. To practise mockery by gestures;* to make merry by words or actions; to joke; to utter in sport; to say what is not true merely for diversion; to play a part in a mask. [Sp. *chiste,* a fine witty saying; L. *gestio,* to use passionate gestures.]
Jester, jest'ėr, *n. A person given to jesting;* one given to sarcasm; a buffoon.
Jesting, jest'ing, *p.n.* A joking; concise wit.
Jestingly, jest'ing-li, *adv. In a jocose manner;* not in earnest.
Jesuit, je'zū-it, *n.* One of the Society of *Jesus,* so called, founded by Ignatius Loyola, in 1534—a *society* distinguished for learning, and for the success with which it carried on its operations, being formerly more powerful than at present.
Jesuitical, je-zū-it'ik-al, *a. Pertaining to the Jesuits.*
Jesuitism, je'zū-it-izm, *n. The principles and practices of the Jesuits.*
Jesus, jē'sus, *n. The Saviour of men; Christ* (which see). [Gr. *Iēsous*—Heb. *Jeshuah,* 'help of Jehovah'.]
Jet, jet, *n.* A mineral of a compact texture and velvet black colour, used for ornaments. [D. *git.*]
Jet, jet, *n.* A spouting or *shooting* of water or other fluid; a gas branch with one aperture; a channel or tube for introducing melted metal into a mould.—*vi. To shoot forward;* to project; to jut; to strut. *ppr.* jetting, *pret. & pp.* jetted. [Fr.—L. *jacio, jactum,* to throw.]

Fāte, fär, fat, fall; mē, met, hėr; pine, pin; nōte, not, mōve; tūbe, tub, bull; oil, pound.

Jet-black, jet′blak, *a.* Of the deepest black; of the colour of jet.

Jetty, jet′i, *n.* That which juts out; an erection *projecting from* a structure for its protection; a kind of pier. [Fr. *jetée*—L. *jacio, jactum*, to throw.]

Jetty, jet′i, *a.* Made of jet, or black as jet.

Jew, jū, *n.* A Hebrew or Israelite. [a contraction of *Judah*.]

Jewel, jū′el, *n.* That which gives joy; an ornament of dress, usually consisting of a precious stone, or set with one or more; a gem; a name expressive of fondness.—*vt.* To adorn with *jewels*; to set, as diamonds or other hard stones in a watch for the pivots to turn in. *ppr.* jewelling, *pret. & pp.* jewelled. [It. *gioiello*—L. *gaudium, joy*.]

Jewelled, jū′eld, *p.a.* Running on diamonds, as the pivots of a watch.

Jeweller, jū′el-er, *n.* One who makes or deals in *jewels* and other ornaments.

Jewellery, jū′el-ė-ri, *n.* See JEWELRY.

Jewelry, jū′el-ri, *n.* Jewels in general.

Jewess, jū′es, *n.* A Hebrew woman.

Jewish, jū′ish, *a.* Pertaining to the Jews or Hebrews.

Jewry, jū′ri, *n.* Judea; also a district inhabited by Jews.

Jib, jib, *n.* That which projects; the projecting arm of a crane; the foremost sail of a ship. [L. *gibbus*, a hump-like swelling.]

Jib-boom, jib′bōm, *n.* A spar which is run out from the extremity of the bowsprit, and which serves as a continuation of it.

Jibe, jīb, *vt.* See GIBE.

Jig, jig, *n.* A light quick tune; a kind of light lively dance suited to the tune; a ballad!; a farce.—*vi.* To dance a *jig*. *ppr.* jigging, *pret. & pp.* jigged. [It. *giga*, a hardy-gurdy.]

Jilt, jilt, *n.* A woman who gives her lover hopes, and capriciously disappoints him; a coquette; a name of contempt for a woman.—*vt.* To encourage as a lover, and then frustrate the hopes of; to trick in love.—*vi.* To play the *jilt*; to practise deception in love, and discard lovers; to coquette. [Icel. *gilja*, to allure or entice a woman.]

Jingle, jing′gl, *n.* A shrill resounding noise.—*vi.* To utter chiming sounds. *vt.* To shake so as to produce clinking sounds. *ppr.* jingling, *pret. & pp.* jingled. [from the sound.]

Job, job, *n.* A sudden *stab* with a pointed instrument; a stroke of work; a piece of work; a lucrative business; any public business carried on for the purpose of some unfair emolument or advantage.—*vt.* To stab with a sharp instrument.—*vi.* To deal in the public stocks; to buy and sell as a broker; to work at chance work; to hire or let horses, &c. *ppr.* jobbing, *pret. & pp.* jobbed. [G. *hieb*, a cut.]

Jobber, job′er, *n.* One who *jobs*; a dealer in the public stocks or funds; one who engages in a low lucrative affair.

Jobbing, job′ing, *p.n.* The practice of *taking jobs for profit.*

Jockey, jok′i, *n.* A man who rides horses in a race; a dealer in horses; one who deceives or takes undue advantages in trade.—*vt.* To play the *jockey* to; to cheat; to deceive in trade; to jostle by riding against one. [maki to be from *Jockey*, a diminutive of *Jack*, John.]

Jocose, jok-ōs′, *a.* Given to *jesting*, as a person; containing a joke, as a remark; facetious; sportive. [L. *jocosus—jocus*, a jest.]

Jocosely, jok-ōs′li, *adv.* In *jest*; for sport or game; waggishly.

Jocular, jok′ū-lėr, *a.* Given to *jokes* or pleasantry, as a person; facetious; containing a joke; not serious, as conversation; merry; sportive. [L. *jocularis—jocus*, a jest.]

Jocularity, jok-ū-la′ri-ti, *n.* Quality of being *jocular*; merriment; jesting.

Jocularly, jok′ū-lėr-li, *adv.* In *jest*.

Jocund, jok′und, *a.* Pleasant; characterised by life or sportive enjoyment; merry; cheerful; mirthful; sprightly. [L. *jocundus—jocus*, a jest.]

Jocundity, jo-kund′i-ti, *n.* State or quality of being *jocund*. [L. *jucunditas.*]

Jocundly, jok′und-li, *adv.* Merrily.

Jog, jog, *vt.* To *shake* with the elbow or hand; to give notice to, or excite the attention of, by a slight push.—*vi.* To move by *jogs* or small shocks, like those of a slow trot.—*n.* A shake or push intended to give notice or awaken attention; a hint given by a push. *ppr.* jogging, *pret. & pp.* jogged. [D. *schokken*.]

Jogging, jog′ing, *p.n.* A slight push or shake.

Join, join, *vt.* To *bind* or *tie together*; to unite in league or marriage; to unite in concord or in any act; to combine; to link; to couple.—*vi.* To unite with; to grow to; to adhere; to unite with in marriage, league, &c.; to become associated. [Fr. *joindre*—L. *jungo*, Sans. *yuj*, to join.]

Joinder†, join′dėr, *n.* Act of joining.

Joiner, join′ėr, *n.* One who *joins*; a mechanic who does the wood-work in the covering and finishing of buildings.

Joinery, join′ė-ri, *n.* The art or employment of a *joiner*; the work of a joiner.

Joining, join′ing, *p.n.* A *joint*; juncture; a hinge.

Joint, joint, *n.* A *joining*; the joining of two or more things; the joining of two or more bones; the union of two parts of a plant, or the space between two joints; a hinge; a juncture of parts which admits of motion; a fissure; a limb or part of the limb of an animal cut off by a butcher.—*a.* Joined; shared by two or more; united in the same profession; having an interest in the same thing; acting in concert. *vt.* To *form with joints*; to cut or divide into joints or quarters.—*vi.* To coalesce as *joints*, or as parts mutually fitted to each other. [Fr.—L. *jungo*, to join.]

Jointed, joint′ed, *p.a.* Formed with *joints*, as the stem of a plant; separated into joints.

Jointing, joint′ing, *p.n.* The making of a *joint*.

Jointly, joint′li, *adv.* Together; unitedly; in concert; with co-operation.

Jointress, joint′res, *n.* A *woman* who has a jointure.

Joint-stock, joint′ stok, *n.* Stock held jointly or in company.

Jointure, joint′ūr, *n.* A *joining*†; an estate settled on a woman in consideration of marriage, and which she is to enjoy after her husband's decease. *vt.* To settle a *jointure upon*. [Old Fr. *joincture*—L. *jungo*, to join.]

Joist, joist, *n.* A *sleeper*; a piece of timber, such as is framed into the girders and summers of a building to support a floor.—*vt.* To *fit* or *furnish with joists*. [Old Fr. *giste*, a couch—L. *jaceo, jacitum*, to lie.]

Joke, jōk, *n.* A *jest*; something said for the sake of exciting a laugh; something not real, or to no purpose.—*vi.* To *jest*; to be merry in words or actions.—*vt.* To *cast jokes at*; to rally; to make merry with. *ppr.* joking, *pret. & pp.* joked. [L. *jocus*—Sans. *div*, to play.]

Joker, jōk′ėr, *n.* A *jester*.

Jole, jōl, *n.* The *cheek*; used in the phrase *cheek-by-jole*, that is, with the cheeks together, close. [Sax. *ceole*.]

Jole, Joll†, jōl, *vt.* To strike against anything.

Jollity, jol′li-ti, *n.* Noisy mirth; merriment; festivity; joviality.

Jolly, jol′li, *a.* Merry; full of life and mirth; jovial; exciting mirth and gaiety; plump, like one in high health; pretty. [Provençal, *joli.*]

Jolt, jōlt, *vi.* To *shake* with short abrupt risings and fallings.—*vt.* To shake with sudden jerks, as in a carriage on rough ground, or on a high trotting horse.—*n.* A shock or shake by a sudden jerk.

Jolt-head†, jōlt′hed, *n.* A dunce.

Joltingly, jōlt′ing-li, *adv.* So as to *jolt* or shake.

Jostle, jos′l, *vt.* To run against and shake; to push. *ppr.* jostling, *pret. & pp.* jostled. [Old Fr. *jouster*, to tilt.]

Jostling, jos′l-ing, *p.n.* A running against; a crowding.

Jot, jot, *n.* An *iota*; a point; a tittle; the least quantity assignable.—*vt.* To mark *briefly*; to set down; to make a memorandum of. *ppr.* jotting, *pret. & pp.* jotted. [Gr. *iota.*]

Jotting, jot′ing, *p.n.* A memorandum.

Journal, jėr′nal, *n.* A *diary*; an account of daily transactions; a merchant's book in which every article or charge is fairly entered from the waste-book or blotter; a daily register of a ship's course and distance, the winds, weather, &c.; a paper published daily or other newspaper; the title of a book or pamphlet published at stated times; a narrative of the transactions of a society, &c. [Fr.—L. *dies*, a day.]

Journalism, jėr′nal-ism, *n.* The management of public journals.

Journalist, jėr′nal-ist, *n.* The conductor of a public journal.

Journalize, jėr′nal-iz, *vt.* To enter in a journal. *ppr.* journalizing, *pret. & pp.* journalized.

Journey, jėr′nė, *n.* The travel of a day; travel by land to any distance and for any time; passage from one place to another.—*vi.* To travel from place to place; to pass from home to a distance. [Fr. *journée*—L. *dies*, a day.]

Journey-bated†, jėr′nė-bat-ed, *a.* Worn out with journeying.

Journeying, jėr′nė-ing, *p.n.* A passing from one place to another.

Journeyman, jėr′nė-man, *n.* One who works by the *day*; a hired workman. [Norm. *jorne*, day service.]

Joust, jōst, *n.* A *fight on horseback* man to man with lances, whether in earnest or for diversion.—*vi.* To engage in *fight*, as man to man, on horseback. [Old Fr. *jouste.*]

Jouster, jūst′ėr, *n.* One who *jousts* or tilts.

Jove, jōv, *n.* Jupiter; the planet Jupiter; the air.

Jovial, jō′vi-al, *a.* Under the influence of *Jupiter*; happy; full of mirth and gladness; fond of good cheer; expressive of mirth and hilarity. [from L. *Jovis*, genit. of *Jupiter*, for *Djupiter*—Sans. *div*, to shine.]

Joviality, jō-vi-al'i-ti, n. Merriment; festivity; conviviality.
Jovially, jō'vi-al-li, adv. Merrily; gaily.
Jowl, jōl, n. See JOLE.
Joy, joi, n. *Gladness; delight;* rapture; gaiety; festivity; the emotion excited by the acquisition or expectation of good; exhilaration of spirits; a glorious state; the cause of joy or happiness. *vi.* To rejoice; to be glad; to exult. *vt.* To gladden; to enjoyt. [Fr. *joie*—L. *gaudeo,* to be glad.]
Joyance, joi'ans, n. Festivity.
Joyful, joi'ful, a. *Full of joy;* joyous; happy; blissful; exulting.
Joyfully, joi'ful-li, adv. *With joy; gladly.*
Joyfulness, joi'ful-nes, n. *State or quality of being joyful;* great gladness.
Joyless, joi'les, a. *Destitute of joy;* wanting joy; giving no joy or pleasure.
Joyous, joi'us, a. *Full of joy;* blithe; glad; mirthful; giving joy; festive; happy; charming; delightful. [Fr. *joyeux.*]
Joyously, joi'us-li, adv. *With joy or gladness.*
Joyousness, joi'us-nes, n. *State or quality of being joyous.*
Jubilant, jū'bi-lant, a. *Shouting;* uttering songs of triumph; shouting with joy. [L. *jubilans—jubilum,* a wild cry.]
Jubilation, jū-bi-lā'shon, n. *A shouting;* the act of declaring triumph. [L. *jubilatio.*]
Jubilee, jū'bi-lē, n. *A joyful shout;* a season of great public joy and festivity; the year of release among the Jews which recurred every fiftieth year. [Heb. *yobel,* a cry of joy.]
Judaic, Judaical, jū-dā'ik, jū-dā'ik-al, a. *Pertaining to the Jews.*
Judaism, jū'dā-izm, n. *The religious doctrines and rites of the Jews,* as enjoined in the laws of Moses; conformity to the Jewish rites and ceremonies. [Fr. *judaïsme.*]
Judaize, jū'dā-īz, *vi. To conform to the religious doctrines and rites of the Jews.* ppr. judaizing, pret. & pp. judaized. [Fr. *judaïser.*]
Judaizer, jū'dā-īz-ėr, n. *One who conforms to the religion of the Jews.*
Judaizing, jū'dā-īz-ing, p.a. *Conforming to the doctrines and rites of the Jews.*
Judean, jū-dē'an, n. *A native of Judea.*
Judge, juj, n. *One authorised to pronounce upon questions of law or equity;* one who presides in a court of judicature; the Supreme Being; one who has skill to decide on the merits of a question; one who can discern truth and propriety.—*vi. To set forth* with authority *the law* in any particular case; to hear and determine, as in causes on trial; to pass sentence; to distinguish between truth and falsehood; to form an opinion; to distinguish; to consider accurately, for the purpose of forming an opinion or conclusion. *vt.* To hear and determine, as a case; to try; to examine and pass sentence on; rightly to understand; to censure rashly; to esteem; to think; to rule or govern; to punish. ppr. Judging, pret. & pp. judged. [Fr. *juge*—L. *judico,* to judge—*jus,* right, and *dico,* to speak.]
Judgeship, juj'ship, n. *The office of a judge.*
Judgment, juj'ment, n. *Act of judging;* the faculty of the mind by which man is enabled to compare ideas, and find their mutual relations; the mental act by which one thing is affirmed or denied of another; the sentence pronounced in any cause, civil or criminal, by the judge by whom it is tried; decision; award; opinion; estimate; criticism; penetration; discernment; final trial of the human race. [Fr. *jugement.*]
Judicatory, jū'di-kā-tō-ri, a. *Pertaining to a judge;* judicial; dispensing justice.—n. *A place of judgment;* a court of justice; a tribunal; distribution of justice. [Fr. *judicatoire*—L. *judico,* to judge.]
Judicature, jū'di-kā-tūr, n. *State, condition, or profession of a judge;* the power of distributing justice by legal trial and determination; a court of justice. [Fr.—L. *judico,* to judge.]
Judicial, jū-di'shi-al, a. *Pertaining to courts of justice;* practised in the distribution of justice; proceeding from, or inflicted by, a court of justice. [L. *judicialis.*]
Judicially, jū-di'shi-al-li, adv. *In the forms of legal justice.*
Judiciary, jū-di'shi-a-ri, a. *Relating to courts of justice.*—n. *The judges taken collectively.* [Fr. *judiciaire.*]
Judicious, jū-di'shi-us, a. *According to sound judgment;* wise; adapted to obtain a good end by the best means; acting according to sound judgment; discerning; sagacious; judicialt. [Fr. *judicieux.*]
Judiciously, jū-di'shi-us-li, adv. *With good judgment;* with discretion.
Judiciousness, jū-di'shi-us-nes, n. *Quality of being judicious.*
Jug, jug, n. *An urn or water-pot;* a vessel with a small mouth and a swelling belly for holding liquors; a mug. [Dan. *jugge.*]
Juggle, jug'l, *vi.* To play tricks by sleight of hand; to practise artifice or imposture.—*vt.* To deceive by trick or artifice. ppr. juggling, pret. & pp. juggled.—n. A trick by sleight of hand; an imposture. [Old Fr. *jongler.*]
Juggler, jug'l-ėr, n. One who exhibits tricks by sleight of hand; a trickish fellow. [Sp. *juglar.*]
Jugglery, jug'l-ė-ri, n. *The art or the feats of a juggler;* legerdemain.
Juggling, jug'l-ing,p.a. Deceiving.—p.n. The act or practice of exhibiting tricks by sleight of hand; trickery; deceit.
Jugglingly, jug'l-ing-li, adv. In a deceptive manner.
Jugular, jū'gū-lėr, a. Pertaining to the *throat* or neck. [Fr. *jugulaire*—L. *jugulum,* the collar-bone—*jungo,* to join.]
Juice, jūs, n. *The sap* of vegetables; the fluid part of animal substances. [Fr. *jus*—L. *jus,* liquid.]
Juiciness, jūs'i-nes, n. *State of abounding with juice;* succulence in plants.
Juicy, jūs'i, a. *Abounding with juice;* moist; succulent.
Jujube, jū'jūb, n. A plant and its fruit; an expectorant made of gum-arabic sweetened. [Fr.]
Julep, jū'lep, n. *Water sweetened and thickened with much sugar;* a medicine serving as a vehicle to other forms of medicine. [Fr.]
Julian, jū'li-an, a. Noting the old account of the year, as regulated by *Julius Cæsar.*
July, jū-lī', n. The seventh month of the year, so called from *Julius,* the middle name of Caius Cæsar, who was born in this month.
Jumble, jum'bl, *vt.* To mix in a *confused mass;* to put or throw together without order.—*vi.* To meet, mix, or unite in a confused manner. ppr. jumbling, pret. & pp. jumbled.—n. *Confused mixture,* mass, or collection without order. [Old Eng. *jombre*—L. *cumulo,* to heap up.]
Jumblingly, jum'bl-ing-li, adv. In a confused manner.
Jump, jump, *vi. To spring upwards;* to leap; to spring over anything; to pass to at a leap; to bound; to jolt; to tally. *vt. To pass over by a leap;* to pass over eagerly or hastily; to hazard.—n. *Act of jumping;* a leap; a spring; a risk; a venture.—adv. Exactly. [Goth. *iup,* up.]
Jumper, jump'ėr, n. *One who jumps.*
Jumping, jump'ing, p.n. *The act of leaping* or springing.
Junction, jungk'shon, n. *The act of joining;* union; combination; the place or point of union. [L. *junctio—jungo, junctum,* to join.]
Juncture, jungk'tūr, n. *A joining;* union; a joint or articulation; the line or point at which two bodies are joined; a point of time; a point rendered critical by a concurrence of circumstances. [L. *junctūra—jungo,* to join.]
June, jūn, n. The sixth month of the year, when the sun enters the sign Cancer. [L. *Junius.*]
Jungle, jung'gl, n. Land mostly covered with forest trees, brushwood, &c., or coarse, reedy vegetation, but not wholly uninhabited. [Hind. *jungul,* country.]
Jungly, jung'gl-i, a. *Consisting of jungles;* abounding with jungles.
Junior, jū'ni-ėr, a. *Younger;* not as old as another; later or lower in office or rank.—n. *A person younger* than another in age or in standing. [L.—*juvenis,* young.]
Juniority, jū-ni-o'ri-ti, n. *The state of being junior.*
Juniper, jū'ni-pėr, n. A prickly evergreen shrub, *which brings forth younger berries* while the first ones are ripening. [L. *juniperus—junior,* younger, and *pario,* to bring forth.]
Junk, jungk, n. A large flat-bottomed vessel with three masts, used by the Chinese. [Ar. *jahause-a choen.*]
Junket, jung'ket, n. A feast or entertainment; a stolen entertainment. *vi.* To feast; to feast in secret; to make an entertainment by stealth.—n. To feast. ppr. junketting, pret. & pp. junketted. [It. *giuncata,* curdled milk.]
Junketting, jung'ket-ing, p.n. A private feast.
Junta, jun'ta, n. *A body of men united;* a grand Spanish council of state. [Sp.—L. *jungo,* to join.]
Junto, jun'tō, n. A meeting of men joined together for secret deliberation and intrigue for party purposes; a faction. [It. *giunto*—L. *jungo,* to join.]
Jupiter, jū'pi-tėr, n. *The father or lord of heaven;* the supreme deity among the Romans; one of the superior planets, remarkable for its brightness. (contracted from *Diovis pater.*]
Juridical, jū-rid'ik-al, a. *Relating to the administration of justice;* pertaining to a judge; acting in the distribution of justice; used in courts of law. [L. *juridicus—jus, juris,* justice, and *dico,* to administer.]
Juridically, jū-rid'ik-al-li, adv. *According to forms of law* or proceedings in tribunals of justice.
Jurisdiction, jū-ris-dik'shon, n. *The administration of justice;* the legal power of doing justice in cases of complaint; power of governing or legislating; the power or right of exercising

Fāte, fär, fat, fall; mē, met, hėr; pīne, pin; nōte, not, mōve; tūbe, tub, bull; oil, pound.

authority; the limit within which power may be exercised. [Old Fr.]
Jurisprudence, jū-ris-prō'dens, n. The science of law; the knowledge of the laws, customs, and rights of men in a state or community, necessary for the due administration of justice. [Fr. — L. jus, juris, law, and prudens, skilled in—pro, and video, to see.]
Jurist, jū'rist, n. One versed in the law, or more particularly, in the civil law; a civilian; one versed in the law of nations, or who writes on the subject. [Fr. juriste—L. jus, law.]
Juror, jū'rėr, n. A sworn witness; one who serves on a jury. [Fr. jureur—L. juro, to swear.]
Jury, jū'ri, n. The collective body of jurors; a number of freeholders, selected in the manner prescribed by law, and sworn to inquire into and try any matter of fact, and to declare the truth on the evidence given them in the case. [Old Fr. jurée, a jury.]
Just, just, a. Keeping the rule or law of right; founded on justice; equitable; lawful; conformed to the laws of God; upright; honest; fair; orderly; suitable; proper; true; exact; founded in truth and fact; blameless; merited; faithful; allowing what is due.—adv. Precisely; accurately; near or nearly; almost; barely; exactly. [Fr. juste— L. jus, juris, law, right.]
Justice, jus'tis, n. The quality of being just; the virtue which consists in giving to every one what is his due; honesty; impartiality; fair representation of facts respecting merit or demerit; equity; agreeableness to right; vindictive retribution; right; a person commissioned to hold courts, and to administer justice to individuals. [Fr.; L. justitia.]
Justicer†, jus'tis-ėr, n. A justiciary.
Justiceship, jus'tis-ship, n. The office or dignity of a justice.
Justiciary, jus-ti'shi-a-ri, n. An administrator of justice; a chief-justice. [Low L. justiciarius.]
Justifiable, just'i-fi-a-bl, a. That may be justified; that may be vindicated on principles of law or reason; warrantable; excusable.
Justifiably, just'i-fi-a-bli, adv. In a manner that admits of justification.
Justification, just'i-fi-kā"shon, n. Act of justifying; a showing to be just or conformable to law or reason; vindication; the showing of a sufficient reason in court why a defendant did what he is called to answer; remission of sins or of penance.
Justificatory, just-if'i-kā-tō-ri, a. Tending to justify; vindicatory.
Justifier, just'i-fi-ėr, n. One who justifies; he who pardons and absolves from guilt and punishment.
Justify, just'i-fi, vt. To render just; to prove or show to be just; to vindicate as a right; to maintain; to pardon; to absolve; to accept as just or righteous, on account of the Saviour's merits; to excuse; to judge rightly of; to adjust. ppr. justifying, pret. & pp. justified. [Fr. justifier—L. justus, just, and facio, to make.]
Justifying, just'i-fi-ing. p.a. That has the quality of absolving from guilt.
Justle, jus'l, vi. See JOSTLE.
Justly, just'li, adv. In conformity to law or right; by right; fairly; properly.
Justness, just'nes, n. Quality of being just; uprightness; exactness; conformity to some standard of correctness or propriety; fitness.
Jut, jut, vi. To shoot forward; to project beyond the main body. ppr. jutting, pret. & pp. jutted.—n. A shooting forward; a projection. [a different spelling of jet.]
Jute, jūt, n. A substance resembling hemp; the plant which produces it.
Jutty†, jut'ti, vt. and vi. To jut.—n. A pier or mole.
Juvenal†, jū'vē-nal, n. A youth.
Juvenile, jū'vē-nil, a. Young; youthful; pertaining or suited to youth. [L. juvenilis—juvenis, young.]
Juvenility, jū-vē-nil'i-ti, n. Youthfulness; light and careless manner.
Juxtaposition, juks'ta-pō-zi"shon, n. A placing or being placed in contiguity, as the parts of a substance or of a composition. [L. juxta, nigh to, and positio, a placing—pono, to place.]
Jynolt†, ji'nold. n. Some little quaint device or piece of machinery.

K.

Kale, kāl, n. Colewort; a kind of cabbage. [Sax. cawl.]
Kaleidoscope, ka-lī'dos-kōp, n. An optical instrument which presents to the eye a variety of beautiful colours and perfectly symmetrical forms, invented by Sir David Brewster. [Gr. kalos, beautiful, eidos, form, and skopeō, to view.]
Kalendar. See CALENDAR.
Kam†, kam, a. Crooked.
Kangaroo, kang'ga-rö, n. The native name of an Australian quadruped, having the fore legs very short, and the hind legs long, so that it moves forward by leaps. The female is provided with a pouch in front, in which she carries her young.
Kecksy†, keks'i, n. The dry stalk of the hemlock, &c.
Kecch†, kėch, n. A lump of fat rolled up by the butcher.
Keel, kėl, n. The principal timber in a ship, extending from stem to stern at the bottom, and supporting the whole frame; a low, flat-bottomed coal vessel; anything resembling a ship's keel. vi. To turn up the keel. [Sax. cæle.]
Keel†, kėl, vt. To cool.
Keen, kėn, a. Bold; eager; quick; acute of mind; penetrating; sharp, as an edge or point; eager, as an appetite; vehement; ardent; piercing; severe, as cold; acrimonious. [Sax. cen, fierce, bold.]
Keenly, kėn'li, adv. Eagerly; vehemently; sharply; severely; bitterly.
Keenness, kėn'nes, n. Quality of being keen; acuteness of mind; vehemence; asperity; bitterness; rigour; sharpness of edge.
Keep, kėp, vt. To seize and to hold; not to lose or part with; to have in safe custody; to preserve; to protect, support, or shield; to detain; to tend; to pasture; to attend to; to hold in any state; to continue any state; to do or perform; to obey; to use habitually; to observe, as a feast; not to intermit; to hold in one's own bosom; not to betray; to have in pay; to maintain, as a school; to continue in.—vi. To remain in any state; to last; to dwell; not to perish or be impaired, as fruit. ppr. keeping, pret. & pp. kept.—n. Care or keeping; food; a strong tower in the middle of a castle, the last resort in a siege in old castles; the dungeon. [Sax. cepan, L. capio.]
Keeper, kėp'ėr, n. One who keeps; one who has some person or thing in charge or custody; a preserver; something which secures.
Keeping, kėp'ing, p.n. A holding; feed; fodder; just proportion; congruity.
Keepsake, kėp'sāk, n. Anything kept or given to be kept for the sake of the giver.
Keg, keg, n. A small cask or barrel. (Written more correctly cag.) [Fr. caque.]
Kelp, kelp, n. Sea-weed or wrack; the calcined ashes of sea-weed. [Etymol. uncertain.]
Kelpy, kelp'i, a. Resembling kelp; containing kelp.
Ken, ken, vt. To know; to see at a distance; to descry. ppr. kenning, pret. & pp. kenned.—n. View; reach of sight or knowledge. [Sax. cunnan, to know.]
Kennel, ken'el, n. A house or cot for dogs; a pack of hounds, or their cry; the hole of a fox or other beast; a haunt.—vi. To lodge in a kennel; to dwell as a dog or a fox.—vt. To keep or confine in a kennel. ppr. kennelling, pret. & pp. kennelled. [Fr. chenil—L. canis, a dog.]
Kennel, ken'el, n. A channel or little canal; the water-course of a street; a puddle. [Fr. canal—L. canalis.]
Kerchief, kėr'chėf, n. A cover for the head; a head-dress; any loose cloth used in dress. [Old Fr. couvrechef—couvrir, to cover, and chef, the head.]
Kerchiefed, kėr'chėft, a. Covered.
Kern†, kėrn, n. An Irish foot-soldier of the lowest rank.
Kernel, kėr'nel, n. A little corn; the edible substance contained in the shell of a nut; the seed of pulpy fruit; the central part of anything; a nucleus; a hard concretion in the flesh.—vi. To harden or ripen into kernels, as the seeds of plants. ppr. kernelling, pret. & pp. kernelled. [Sax. cyrnel.]
Kernelled, kėr'neld, p.a. Having a kernel.
Kersey, kėr'zē, n. A species of coarse woollen cloth. [Sp. carisea.]
Kerseymere, kėr'zē-mėr, n. Cassimere; a twilled woollen cloth.
Kestrel, kes'trel, n. A bird of the hawk kind, which has a sharp cry. [Fr. crécerelle.]

Ketch, kech, n. A vessel with two masts, a main and mizen mast. [D. *kits*.]
Ketch†, kech, n. A cask.
Kettle, ket'l, n. A hollow vessel; a vessel of iron or other metal, used for heating and boiling water or other liquor. [Sax. *cetl* — Gr. *kotúlē*, anything hollow.]
Kettle-drum, ket'l-drum, n. A drum made of a copper vessel like a kettle, covered with parchment.
Key, kē, n. That which fastens; an instrument for shutting or opening a lock; an instrument by which something is screwed or turned; a little lever by which certain musical instruments are played on by the fingers; the fundamental note in a piece of music; an index, or that which serves to explain a cipher; that which serves to explain anything difficult to be understood. [Sax. *cæg* — Gr. *kleiō*, to close.]
Key-cold†, kē'kōld, a. Cold as a key; lifeless.
Keyed, kēd, p.a. Furnished with keys; set to a key, as a tune.
Keystone, kē'stōn, n. The stone on the middle of an arch which enters like a wedge, and fastens or binds the work.
Kibe†, kib, n. A crack in the flesh caused by cold; an ulcerated chilblain.
Kick, kik, vt. To strike with the foot. vi. To practise striking with the foot or feet; to thrust out the foot or feet with violence, either in wantonness or contempt; to manifest opposition. —n. A blow with the foot or feet; a striking or thrust of the foot. [Sp. *cocear* — L. *calr*, the heel.]
Kicking, kik'ing, p.n. The act of striking with the foot, or of jerking the foot with violence.
Kickshaw, kik'shą, n. Something fantastical; a dish so changed by cooking that it can scarcely be known. [corrupted from Fr. *quelque chose*, something.]
Kid, kid, n. A young goat. —vi. To bring forth a young goat. ppr. kidding, pret. & pp. kidded. [Dan. — Heb. *gedi*.]
Kid-fox, kid'foks, n. A young fox.
Kidnap, kid'nap, vt. To steal, as a child; to steal, as a human being; to seize and forcibly carry away, as any person whatever from his own country into another. ppr. kidnapping, pret. & pp. kidnapped. [*kid*, contracted from G. *kind*, a child, and Low Eng. *nab*, to steal.]
Kidnapper, kid'nap-ėr, n. One who steals or forcibly carries away a human being; a man-stealer.
Kidnapping, kid'nap-ing, p.n. Act of stealing or forcible abduction of a human being from his own country.
Kidney, kid'nē, n. One of the two glands which secrete the urine from the blood; anything shaped like the kidneys. [probably from Icel. *qvidr*, the lower belly, and *nigh*.]
Kill, kil, vt. To quell; to beat down; to deprive of life, animal or vegetable, in any manner or by any means; to butcher; to slaughter for food; to calm; to still. [Sax. *cwellan*.]
Kill-courtesy†, kil'kört-e-si, n. A discourteous person.
Killing, kil'ing, p.a. Dangerous; heart-breaking. —p n. A deprivation of life.
Kiln, kil, n. A large stove or oven; a fabric of brick or stone, which may be heated for the purpose of hardening or drying anything; a pile of brick constructed for burning or hardening. [Sax. *cyln*.]

Kiln-hole†, kil'hōl, n. The mouth of a kiln.
Kimbo, kim'bō, a. Crooked; arched; bent. [Celt. *cam*, crooked.]
Kin, kin. n. Kind; race; relation properly by blood; kindred; persons of the same race; a relative; the same generical class; a thing related. —a. Kindred; of the same nature; congenial. [Sax. *cyn*, race — L. *gigno*, to beget.]
Kind, kind, n. Race; generic class; sort or species; particular nature; produce or commodity; nature; natural propensity or determination. [Old G.]
Kind, kind, a. Having feelings becoming the common nature or *kind*; humane; disposed to do good to others, and to make them happy; having goodness of nature; feeling for each other; loving; proceeding from tenderness or goodness of heart, as acts. [Sax. *cyn*, akin.]
Kindle, kin'dl, vt. To set on fire; to light; to exasperate; to rouse; to excite to action; to fire; to animate. —vi. To take fire; to begin to burn with flame; to be roused or exasperated; to become animated. ppr. kindling, pret. & pp. kindled. [Icel. *kynda*, to kindle.]
Kindless†, kind'les, a. Destitute of kindness.
Kindliness, kind'li-nes, n. Quality of being kindly; affection; benignity.
Kindly, kind'li, a. Belonging to the kind or species; natural; congenial; benevolent; mild; softening. —adv. With good-will; benevolently; favourably. [from *kind*.]
Kindness, kind'nes, n. Quality of being kind; that disposition which delights in contributing to the happiness of others; hospitality; attention to the wants of others; a kind act.
Kindred, kin'dred, n. Relationship by birth or marriage; affinity; relatives by blood or marriage; the relation of persons descended from the same stock. —a. Related; congenial; of the like nature or properties; cognate. [Sax. *cymryn*—*cym*, kin, and *ryne*, a course.]
Kine, kin, old pl. of cow. Cows. [D. *koeyen*.]
King, king, n. A man of high descent, or eminent for valour, strength, or other personal merit; the sovereign of a nation; a monarch; a sovereign; a card having the picture of a king; the chief piece in the game of chess. [Sax. *cyng*, Old G. *kuning* — Icel. *konr*, a man of eminence.]
Kingcraft, king'kraft, n. The craft of kings; the art of governing.
Kingdom, king'dum, n. The dominion of a king; the country subject to a king; the population subject to a king; a primary division of plants, animals, or minerals; a region; the place where anything prevails and holds sway; government. [Sax. *cyningdōm*.]
Kingdomed†, king'dumd, p.a. Endowed with kingly authority; proud.
Kingfisher, king'fish-ėr, n. A bird having splendid plumage which preys upon fish.
Kinglike, king'līk, a. Like a king.
Kingliness, king'li-nes, n. State of being kingly.
Kingly, king'li, a. Like a king; belonging to a king; royal; regal; august; splendid; becoming a king. —adv. With an air of royalty; with a superior dignity.
Kingly-poor†, king'li-pōr, a. Extremely poor.

King's-evil, kingz'ē-vl, n. A disease of the scrofulous kind.
Kinsfolk, kinz'fōk, n. Kindred; relations; persons of the same family.
Kinsman, kinz'man, n. A man of the same kin, or of the same race or family; one related by blood.
Kinswoman, kinz'wu-man, n. A female relation.
Kirk, kėrk, n. The house of the Lord; a church; the designation of the Church of Scotland. (Scot.) [Sax. *cyrc*.]
Kiss, kis, vt. To salute with the lips; to treat with fondness; to caress. —n. A salute given with the lips; a common token of affection. [Sax. *cyssan*, Old G. *kussian, kussan*.]
Kit, kit, n. A large bottle; a kind of fish-tub, and a milk-pail; a soldier's knapsack, with its contents; a whole outfit. [D.]
Kit, kit, n. A kitten.
Kitchen, ki'chen, n. A cook-room; the room of a house appropriated to cookery. —vt. To furnish food to. [Sax. *cycene* — L. *coquo*, to cook.]
Kitchen-garden, ki'chen-gär-dn, n. A garden in which vegetables for the table are raised.
Kitchen-range, ki'chen-rānj, n. A kitchen-grate.
Kite, kīt, n. A bird that hovers in the air; a rapacious bird of the hawk kind; a name of reproach; a light frame of wood and paper constructed for flying in the air, for the amusement of boys. [Sax. *cyta* — W. *cud*, celerity.]
Kitten, kit'n, n. A young cat, or the young of the cat. —vi. To bring forth young, as a cat. [Dan. *kattekilling*.]
Knack, nak, n. A nice trick; habitual facility of performance; a little machine; a toy. [G. — *knicken*, to snap.]
Knag, nag, n. Anything that projects; a knot in wood; a wart; the rugged top of a rock or hill. [Dan. *knag*.]
Knagged, nagd, p.a. Formed into knags or knots; knotty.
Knaggy, nag'i, a. Knotty; full of knots; rough in temper.
Knap†, nap, vt. To bite†; to strike with a loud noise.
Knapsack, nap'sak, n. A bag for dry provisions; a frame of leather, or a sack for containing necessaries of food and clothing, borne on the back by soldiers, travellers, &c. [D. *knapsak* — *knappen*, to eat.]
Knarl, närl, n. A knot in wood; a knurl.
Knave, nāv, n. A servant; a petty rascal; a villain; a dishonest man or boy; a card with a soldier painted on it. [Sax. *cnapa*.]
Knavery, nāv'ė-ri, n. The practices of a knave; dishonesty; fraud.
Knavish, nāv'ish, a. Partaking of knavery; dishonest; waggish; roguish.
Knavishly, nāv'ish-li, adv. Dishonestly; fraudulently; waggishly; mischievously.
Knead, nēd, vt. To make into masses or knots; to work into a well-mixed mass, as the materials of bread, cake, or paste; to pommel†. [Sax. *cnedan*.]
Kneading, nēd'ing, p.n. The act of working and mixing into a mass.
Kneading-trough, nēd'ing-trof, n. A trough in which dough is kneaded.
Knee, nē, n. The joint that connects the thigh and leg bones; anything shaped like the knee; a piece of timber, &c., bent like the bended knee. —vt. To supplicate by kneeling. [Sax. *cneow* — L. *genu*.]
Kneed, nēd, p.a. Having knees; having

Fāte, fär, fat, fąll; mē, met, hėr; pīne, pin; nōte, not, mōve; tūbe, tub, bųll; oil, pound.

KNEEL 215 LACE

joints resembling the knee when bent, as the stems of plants.
Kneel, nēl, *vi.* *To bend the knee; to rest on the bended knees.* [D. *knielen.*]
Knee-pan, nē'pan, *n.* The round bone on the fore-part of the knee.
Knell, nel, *n.* The stroke of a bell; the sound of a bell rung at a funeral; a tolling; a death-signal.—*vi.* To sound, as a funeral bell; to toll. [Sax. *cnyll.*]
Knelt, nelt, *pret. & pp.* of *kneel*; but *kneeled* is better.
Knick-knack, nik'nak, *n.* Any trifle or toy.
Knife, nīf, *n.* Knives, nīvz, pl. *That which cuts;* a cutting instrument with a sharp edge; a sword or dagger. [Sax. *cnif*—Gr. *knaō*, to scrape.]
Knight, nīt, *n.* Originally, a follower; a title of honour next to that of nobility; a champion; a piece used in the game of chess.—*vt.* *To dub or create,* as *a knight,* which is done by the sovereign. [Sax. *cniht*—Old G. *knekt.*]
Knight-baronet, nīt-ba'rō-net, *n.* A *baronet;* a hereditary knight in Britain.
Knight-errant, nīt-e'rant, *n.* *A wandering knight;* a knight who travelled in search of adventures for the purpose of exhibiting military skill, prowess, and generosity. [L. *erro, errans,* to wander.]
Knight-errantry, nīt-e'rant-ri, *n.* The practice of *wandering* in quest of adventures.
Knighthood, nīt'hud, *n.* *The character or dignity of a knight;* a military order, honour, or degree of ancient nobility, conferred as a reward of valour or merit.
Knightly, nīt'li, *a.* *Pertaining to a knight;* becoming a knight.—*adv. In a manner becoming a knight.*
Knit, nit, *vt.* *To tie in a knot;* to connect in a kind of network; to unite closely, as in love; to join or cause to grow together, as bones; to draw together; to contract, as one's brows.—*vi.* To be united closely; to grow together. *ppr.* knitting, *pret. & pp.* knit or knitted. [Sax. *cnyttan.*]
Knitter, nit'ėr, *n.* *One who knits.*
Knitting, nit'ing, *p.n.* The formation of network by knitting-needles or machinery; the network thus formed.
Knob, nob, *n.* *A top;* a bud; a boss; a hard swelling or rising; a round ball at the end of anything. [Sax. *cnaep.*]
Knobbed, nobd, *p.a. Containing knobs.*
Knobby, nob'i, *a. Full of knobs.*
Knock, nok, *vt.* *To strike* with something thick or heavy; to strike against; to clash.—*vi.* To strike; to strike, as a door for admittance (with *at*).—*n.* A stroke with something thick or heavy; a stroke on a door, intended as a request for admittance; a blow; a rap. [Sax. *cnucian.*]
Knocker, nok'ėr, *n. One who knocks;* an instrument fastened to a door for knocking.
Knocking, nok'ing, *p.n.* Act of one who *knocks* or beats; a beating; a rap.
Knoll, nōl, *n. The top or crown of a hill;* a little round hill or mount. [Sax. *cnoll.*]
Knoll, nōl, *vt.* To strike *a knell* upon. *vi.* To sound, as a bell.
Knot, not, *n. The complication of* threads made by tying; a tie; a union of cords by interweaving; a bond of union; the part of a tree where a branch shoots; a hard protuberant joint of a plant; a group, as of persons; intricacy; any difficult perplexity of affairs; an epaulet.—*vt. To form, as a knot;* to entangle; to perplex; to unite closely.—*vi.* *To form knots* or joints, as in plants; to knit knots for fringe. *ppr.* knotting, *pret. & pp.* knotted. (G. *knoten*—L. *nodus,* a knot—Sans. *nadh,* to tie.]
Knot-grass, not'gras, *n.* A plant so denominated from the joints of the stem.
Knotless, not'les, *a. Free from knots.*
Knotted, not'ed, *p.a. Full of knots.*
Knottiness, not'i-nes, *n. Fulness of knots;* difficulty of solution; intricacy.
Knotty, not'i, *a. Full of knots;* difficult; intricate; perplexed.
Know, nō, *vt. To understand clearly;* to have a clear and certain perception, as of truth, fact, or anything that actually exists; to be instructed in; to be familiar with; to approve; to learn; to acknowledge with due respect; to have full assurance of; to have satisfactory evidence of, though short of certainty; to have sexual commerce with.—*vi. To have clear and certain perception;* not to be doubtful; to be informed; to take cognizance; to examine. *ppr.* knowing, *pret.* knew, *pp.* known. [Sax. *cnawan*—Sans. *jnā.*]
Knowable, nō'a-bl, *a. That may be known;* that may be discovered, understood, or ascertained.
Knowing, nō'ing, *p.a.* Well informed; well instructed; intelligent; skilful; cunning.
Knowingly, nō'ing-li, *adv. With knowledge.*
Knowledge, nol'ej, *n. A clear perception of that which is placed* before the understanding; a clear and certain perception of that which exists; truth ascertained; learning; science; physical truth or facts ascertained by experiment; skill; cognizance; notice; power of knowing. [Sax. *cnawan,* and *leogan,* to lay.]
Known, nōn, *p.a.* Understood; recognized.
Knuckle, nuk'l, *n.* One of the *small knee-like joints* of the fingers; the knee-joint of a calf. [Sax. *cnucl*—*knigan,* to bend.]
Koran, kō'ran, *n. The book* containing the faith and practice of Mahometans, written by Mahomet. [Ar. *al koran,* or less frequently, *koran,* the book.]

L.

La, lā, *exclam. Lo! look! see! behold!* [Sax.]
Label, lā'bel, *n. A border;* a narrow slip of silk, paper, or parchment, containing a name or title, and affixed to anything, denoting its contents; any paper annexed to a will by way of addition, as a codicil.—*vt. To affix a label to. ppr.* labelling, *pret. & pp.* labelled. [Sax. *lappa,* a border.]
Labial, lā'bi-al, *a. Pertaining to the lips;* formed by the lips.—*n.* An elementary sound in which the voice is modified by *the lips;* a letter of the alphabet, representing such a sound, as *b, p,* and *m.* [Fr.—L. *labium,* a lip.]
Laboratory, la'bo-ra-tō-ri, *n.* A house or *place where operations* and experiments in chemistry, &c., are performed; a place where arms are manufactured or repaired. [Fr. *laboratoire* —L. *labor,* labour.]
Laborious, la-bō'ri-us, *a. Full of labour;* toilsome; requiring labour; arduous; given to labour; employing labour in any occupation; diligent; active. [Fr. *laborieux*—L. *labor,* labour.]
Laboriously, la'bō'ri-us-li, *adv. With labour,* toil, or difficulty.
Laboriousness, la-bō'ri-us-nes, *n. Quality of being laborious,* or attended with toil; toilsomeness; assiduity.
Labour, lā'bėr, *n. Fatiguing* toil; work; effort; exertion of muscular strength; intellectual exertion; exertion of mental powers, united with bodily employment; heroic achievement; the pangs of childbirth; the evils of life; trials, &c.; the action of a ship in a heavy sea. *vi. To struggle;* to contend; to exert muscular strength; to act or move with painful effort; to exert one's powers of body or mind, or both, in the prosecution of any design; to be burdened; to pitch and roll heavily, as a vessel in a storm; to suffer the pangs of childbirth.—*vt.* To work at; to till; to prosecute with effort; to form or fabricate with exertion. [L. *labor*—Sans. *lamb,* to fall down.]
Laboured, lā'bėrd, *p.a.* Bearing marks of constraint in execution; opposed to free or easy.
Labourer, lā'bėr-ėr, *n. One who labours;* a man who does work that requires little skill.
Labouring, lā'bėr-ing, *p.a.* Moving with pain or with difficulty; devoted to labour.—*p.n. Act of bestowing labour;* the pitching of a vessel in a heavy sea.
Laboursome†, lā'bėr-sum, *a. Made with great labour.*
Labra†, lā'bra, *n. A lip.*
Laburnum, la-bėr'num, *n.* A tree, a native of the Alps, much cultivated for the beauty of its pendulous clusters of yellow flowers. [L.]
Labyrinth, la'bi-rinth, *n.* An edifice or place full of intricacies; a maze; an inexplicable difficulty; that part of the internal ear behind the cavity of the drum. [Fr. *labyrinthe.*]
Labyrinthine, la-bi-rinth'in, *a. Pertaining to or like a labyrinth.*
Lac, lak, *n.* A *sticky* and resinous substance. [Sp. *laca.*]
Lace, lās, *n.* That which *catches;* a plaited string with which females fasten their clothes; a fabric of threads interwoven into a net.—*vt. To fasten* with a string through eyelet-holes; to

ch, *chain;* j, *job;* g, *go;* ng, *sing;* ᴛʜ, *then;* th, *thin;* w, *wig;* wh, *whig;* zh, *azure;* † obsolete.

Laced adorn with lace; to embellish with variegations or stripes. *ppr.* lacing, *pret. & pp.* laced. (Fr. *lacet*, lace—L. *laqueus*, a noose.)

Laced, lāst, *p.a. Tricked off with lace.*

Lacerable, la-sẽr-a-bl, *a. That may be lacerated or torn.*

Lacerate, la'sẽr-āt, *vt. To tear; to separate, as a substance by violence; to afflict. ppr.* lacerating, *pret. & pp.* lacerated. [L. *lacero, laceratus.*]

Lacerated, la'sẽr-āt-ed, *p.a. Rent; torn.*

Laceration, la-sẽr-ā'shon, *n. Act of lacerating;* the breach made by rending. [L. *laceratio.*]

Lachrymal, la'krim-al, *a. Secreting tears;* pertaining to tears; conveying tears. [Fr.—L. *lachryma*, a tear.]

Lachrymatory, la'krim-a-ri, *a. Containing tears.*

Lachrymatory, la'krim-a-tō-ri, *n.* A vessel found in sepulchres of the ancients, in which it has been supposed the *tears* of a deceased person's friends were preserved with the ashes and urn. [Fr. *lachrymatoire.*]

Lachrymose, la'krim-ōs, *a. Full of tears; tearful.* [L. *lacrimosus.*]

Lacing, lās'ing, *p.n.* A fastening with a string or cord through eyelet-holes; a cord used in drawing tight or fastening.

Lack, lak, *vt. To want;* to be destitute of; not to have or possess.—*vi. To be in want;* to be wanting.—*n. Want; destitution;* need; failure. [Dan. *lak.*]

Lackey, lak'ē, *n.* An attending servant; a footboy or footman.—*vt.* To attend servilely.—*vi.* To act as footboy. [Fr. *laquais.*]

Lack-lustre, lak' lus-tẽr, *a. Wanting lustre* or brightness.

Laconic, la-kon'ik, *a.* Expressing much in few words, like the ancient Spartans, or Lacōnes; short; sententious; pointed; pithy. [Gr. *lakōnikos.*]

Laconically, la-kon'ik-al-li, *adv. Briefly.*

Laconism, lā'kon-izm, *n.* A concise style; a brief pithy sententious phrase or expression. [Gr. *lakōnismos.*]

Lacquer, lak'ẽr, *n.* A varnish, consisting of a solution of *shell-lac* in alcohol.—*vt. To varnish with lacquer.* [Fr. *laque*, a kind of ruby colour.]

Lacquerer, lak'ẽr-ẽr, *n. One who varnishes with lacquer.*

Lacquering, lak'ẽr-ing, *p.n. Act of putting on lacquer;* the covering of lacquer or varnish thus put on.

Lacteal, lak'tē-al, *a. Pertaining to milk;* conveying chyle.—*n.* A vessel or slender tube of animal bodies for conveying the chyle or *milk-like fluid* from the alimentary canal. [from L. *lac, lactis*, milk.]

Lacustrine, la-kus'trin, *a. Pertaining to lakes* or swamps. [from L. *lacus*, a lake.]

Lad, lad, *n. A boy;* a stripling; a young man. [Sans. *lad*, to be boyish.]

Ladanum, la'da-num, *n.* The resinous juice which exudes from the leaves of *a shrub* which grows in Syria and the island of Candia. (Gr. *lēdanon—lēdon*, a shrub.)

Ladder, lad'dẽr, *n. That which leads;* a frame of wood, consisting of two side-pieces, connected by rounds, and thus forming steps by which persons may ascend a building, &c.; that by which a person ascends or rises; means of ascending; gradual rise. [Sax. *hlædder*—G. *leiten*, to lead.]

Lade, lād, *vt. To load;* to put on or in, as a burden or freight; to throw in or out, as a fluid, with a ladle or dipper. *ppr.* lading, *pret.* laded, *pp.* laded, laden. [Sax. *ladan.*]

Laden, lād'n, *p.a.* Oppressed; burdened.

Lading, lād'ing, *p.n. That which constitutes a load;* freight; burden.

Ladle, lā'dl, *n.* A utensil somewhat like a dish, with a long handle, used for *lading* or dipping out liquor from a vessel; something resembling a ladle.—*vt. To lade with a ladle. ppr.* ladling, *pret. & pp.* ladled. [Sax. *hlædle.*]

Lady, lā'di, *n. A woman elevated in rank;* correlative to lord; a term of complaisance to any well-dressed woman; wife; the female who presides or has authority over a manor or a family. [Sax. *hlæfdie—hlifian*, to raise.]

Lady-day, lā'di-dā, *n.* The day of the annunciation of the Virgin Mary, March 25th.

Lady-like, lā'di-līk, *a. Like a lady* in manners; genteel; well-bred; soft.

Ladyship, lā'di-ship, *n. The title of a lady.*

Lag, lag, *n. That which is weak;* the lowest class; the rump; the fag-end.—*vi.* To walk or move slowly; to stay behind; to linger.—*vt. To slacken. ppr.* lagging, *pret. & pp.* lagged. [W. *llag*, weak.]

Laggard, lag'ard, *a. Lagging;* slow.

Lagger, Laggard, lag'ẽr, lag'ärd, *n. One who lags;* one who moves slowly and falls behind.

Laic, lā'ik, *a. Belonging to the laity or people*, in distinction from the clergy.—*n. A layman.* [Fr. *laique*—Gr. *laos*, the people.]

Lair, lãr, *n. The place where* any animal *lies;* the bed or couch of a boar or wild beast; any couch; place of rest. [G. *lager—legen*, to lay.]

Laity, lā'i-ti, *n. The people*, as distinguished from the clergy. [from Gr. *laos*, people.]

Lake, lāk, *n.* A large and extensive collection of water contained in a cavity or *hollow* of the earth. [Fr. *lac*—L. *lacus*—Gr. *lakkos*, a hole.]

Lake, lāk, *n. A deep red colouring matter*, consisting of aluminous earth and cochineal or other red substance. [Old Fr. *lacque*, a ruby colour.]

Lakin†, lā'kin, *n.* A little lady.

Lamb, lam, *n.* The young of the sheep kind, remarkable for its playfulness; any one having the meekness and innocence of a lamb; typically, Jesus Christ the Saviour.—*vi.* To bring forth young, as sheep. [Sax.—Gr. *amnos*, a lamb, *arnos*, a lamb, a sheep; Sans. *ūrnāyu*, a ram—*vri*, to cover.]

Lambent, lam'bent, *a. Touching lightly, as with the tongue;* playing about; gliding over. [L. *lambens—lambo*, to lick.]

Lambkin, lam'kin, *n. A little lamb.*

Lamblike, lam'līk, *a. Like a lamb.*

Lame, lām, *a. Disabled;* crippled in a limb; imperfect; hobbling; not smooth, as numbers in verse.—*vt. To make lame;* to cripple or disable; to render imperfect and unsound. *ppr.* laming, *pret. & pp.* lamed. [Sax. *lam*—Old G. *lam, lame.*]

Lamely, lām'li, *adv. Like a lame person;* in a halting manner.

Lameness, lām'nes, *n. State of being lame;* an impaired state of the body or limbs; imperfection; weakness.

Lament, la-ment', *vi.* To express *sorrow* or grief; to weep; to regret deeply; to feel sorrow.—*vt.* To bewail; to mourn for; to deplore.—*n. Grief* or *sorrow* expressed in complaints or cries; a weeping; an elegy or mournful ballad. [L. *lamentor.*]

Lamentable, la'ment-a-bl, *a. To be lamented;* adapted to awaken grief; expressing sorrow, as an outcry. [Fr.]

Lamentably, la'ment-a-bli, *adv.* Mournfully; so as to cause sorrow.

Lamentation, la-ment-ā'shon, *n. Act of lamenting;* expression of sorrow; complaint; wailing.

Lamented, la-ment'ed, *p.a.* Bewailed; mourned for.

Lamenting, la-ment'ing, *p.n.* A mourning; lamentation.

Lamina, la'mi-na, *n.* **Laminae**, la'mi-nē, *pl. A flake;* a thin *plate* or scale; a layer or coat lying over another. [L. a flake.]

Laminar, la'mi-nãr, *a. In thin plates;* consisting of thin plates or layers.

Laminated, la'mi-nāt-ed, *a. Plated.*

Lamination, la-mi-nā'shon, *n. State of being laminated.*

Lamish, lām'ish, *a. Not quite lame;* hobbling.

Lammas, lam'mas, *n.* The first day of August. [Sax. *hlammæsse, hlafmæsse*, the loaf-mass.]

Lamp, lamp, *n. That which shines;* a light; a vessel used for the combustion of liquid inflammable bodies; a light of any kind. [Fr. *lampe*—Gr. *lampō*, to shine.]

Lampblack, lamp'blak, *n.* A fine soot formed by the condensation of the smoke of burning pitch.

Lampoon, lam-pōn', *n. A scurrilous* or personal satire in writing; censure written to reproach and vex rather than to reform.—*vt.* To abuse with personal censure; to reproach in written satire; to satirise. [Fr. *lampon*, a drinking song.]

Lampooner, lam-pōn'ẽr, *n.* One who abuses with personal satire.

Lamprey, lam'prā, *n. The suck-stone;* the popular name of *several* fishes resembling the eel. [Fr. *lamproie*—L. *lambo*, to lick, and *petra*, a stone.]

Lance, lans, *n. That which is thrown;* a spear; an offensive weapon in form of a half-pike used by the ancients, and thrown by the hand.—*vt. To pierce with a lance;* to pierce or cut; to open with a lancet; to throw like a lance. *ppr.* lancing, *pret. & pp.* lanced. [Fr. *lance*—Gr. *elaunō*, to drive.]

Lancer, lans'ẽr, *n. One who lances;* one who carries a lance.

Lancet, lans'et, *n. A little lance;* a surgical instrument, sharp-pointed and two-edged, used in letting blood, &c.; a high and narrow window, pointed like a lancet. [Fr. *lancette.*]

Land, land, *n.* Earth, or the solid matter which constitutes the fixed part of the surface of the globe; any portion of the solid, superficial part of the globe; soil; real estate; the inhabitants of a country; a nation.—*vt. To set on the land;* to disembark.—*vi. To go on land;* to disembark. [Sax.]

Landau, lan-dą', *n.* A kind of coach whose top may be opened and thrown back. [from *Landau*, a town in Germany.]

Land-breeze, land'brēz, *n. A breeze* or current of air setting *from the land* toward the sea.

Landed, land'ed, *p.a. Having an estate in land;* consisting in real estate or land.

Land-force, land'fōrs, *n.* A military *force*, army, or troops serving on *land.*

Landholder, land'hōld-ẽr, *n. A holder* or proprietor *of land.*

Fāte, fär, fat, fąll; mē, met, hẽr; pine, pin; nōte, not, mōve; tūbe, tub, bųll; oil, pound.

Landing, land'ing, p.n. *Act of going or setting on land;* a place for going or setting on shore; the part of a staircase which, being level, connects one flight with another.—*p.a.* Relating to the disposal of a vessel's cargo.

Landlady, land'lā-di, n. *A woman who has property in land,* and tenants holding from her; the mistress of an inn or lodging-house.

Landlock, land'lok, vt. To inclose by land.

Landlord, land'lord, n. *The lord of a manor or of land;* the owner of land or houses who has tenants under him; the master of an inn or tavern. [Sax. *landhlaford.*]

Landmark, land'märk, n. *A mark to designate the boundary of land;* any elevated object on land that serves as a guide to seamen.

Land-measure, land'me-zhūr, n. *A measure for land;* a table of square measure.

Land-measuring, land'me-zhūr-ing, n. *Act of measuring land.*

Land-owner, land'ōn-ėr, n. *The owner or proprietor of land.*

Landscape, land'skāp, n. *The shape of a portion of land,* as it appears to the eye; a portion of land which the eye can comprehend in a single view; a picture exhibiting the form of a district of country and its scenery. [Sax. *landscipe—scyppan,* to make.]

Landslip, land'slip, n. A portion of a hill or mountain which *slips* down; the sliding down of a considerable tract of land from a mountain.

Landsman, landz'man, n. *One who lives on the land;* opposed to seaman.

Land-steward, land'stū-ėrd, n. *A person who has the care of a landed estate.*

Land-surveying, land'sėr-vā-ing, n. *Act of surveying land;* the art of determining the boundaries and superficial extent of portions of land.

Land-waiter, land'wāt-ėr, n. An officer of the customs whose duty is to *wait* or attend on the *landing* of goods.

Landward, land'wėrd, adv. *Toward the land.*

Lane, lān, n. A narrow way or passage between houses, &c.; a narrow street; a passage between lines of people standing on each side. [D. *laan,* an alley.]

Language, lang'gwaj, n. That which is uttered by the *tongue;* tongue; the expression of ideas by words or significant articulate sounds; words duly arranged in sentences; the speech peculiar to a particular nation; dialect; style; diction; any manner of expressing thoughts or feelings; a nation, as distinguished by their speech. [Fr. *langage*—L. *lingua,* the tongue.]

Languaged, lang'gwajd, p.a. *Having a language;* expert in language.

Languid, lang'gwid, a. *Faint; weary;* dull; drooping; indisposed to exertion through feebleness or exhaustion; sluggish. [L. *languidus—langueo,* to be faint.]

Languidly, lang'gwid-li, adv. Weakly.

Languish, lang'gwish, vi. *To be or become faint or feeble;* to be or become dull or spiritless; to fade; to wither; to be no longer active and vigorous, as commerce; to sink under sorrow; to look with tenderness.—*vt.* To cause to droop.—n.! Act of languishing; a soft look. [Fr. *languir, languissant*—L. *langueo,* to be faint—Gr. *langgasō,* to slacken, give up.]

Languishing, lang'gwish-ing, p.a. Looking softly and tenderly.—*p.n.* Feebleness; pining.

Languishment, lang'gwish-ment, n. *State of languishing* or pining; softness of look or mien, with the head reclined.

Languor, lang'gwėr, n. *Faintness; weariness;* heaviness; listlessness; softness; laxity. [L.]

Lank, langk, a. *Lean;* spare; meagre; loose or lax; not stiff or firm; not plump; drooping.—*vi.*† To become lank. [Sax. *hlanca—hlænig,* lean.]

Lankness, langk'nes, n. *State of being lank;* flabbiness; slenderness.

Lantern, lan'tėrn, n. A case or vessel in which a *light* is placed, and which may be carried about in the hand; a lighthouse or light to direct the course of ships; a drum-shaped erection on the top of a dome or the roof of a building to give light; the lower part of a tower placed at the junction of the cross in a cathedral, having windows on all sides.—*vt.* To provide with a lantern. [Fr. *lanterne*—Gr. *lampō,* to shine—Heb. *lāpad,* to flame, to shine.]

Lanthorn. A wrong spelling of *lantern.*

Lanyard, lan'yärd, n. *A thong;* a short piece of rope or line, used for fastening something in ships. [Fr. *lanière.*]

Lap, lap, n. *That which flaps or hangs loose;* the loose part of a coat; the part of clothes that lies on the knees when a person sits down; the knees in this position.—*vt.* To wrap; to infold; to bend and lay over or on.—*vi.* To be turned over. *ppr.* lapping, *pret. & pp.* lapped. [Sax. *lappa,* a hem—Sans. *lamb,* to fall upon.]

Lap, lap, vi. *To lick;* to take up liquor or food with the tongue; to feed or drink by licking.—*vt.* To take into the mouth with the tongue; to lick up. *ppr.* lapping, *pret. & pp.* lapped. [Sax. *lappian*—L. *lambo,* to lick.]

Lapel, la-pel', n. That part of the coat which *laps* over the facing. [from *lap* No. 1.]

Lapful, lap'ful, n. *As much as the lap can contain.*

Lapidary, la'pi-da-ri, n. *A stone-cutter;* one who cuts and engraves precious stones; a dealer in precious stones; a virtuoso skilled in the nature and kinds of gems.—*a.* Pertaining to the *art of cutting stones.* [Fr. *lapidaire*—L. *lapis,* a stone.]

Lappet, lap'et, n. *A little lap;* a part of a garment or dress that hangs loose. [dim. of *lap.*]

Lapse, laps, n. *A sliding;* a falling; a smooth course; a slip; a fault; a failing in duty; a slight deviation from truth or rectitude.—*vi.* To slide; to glide; to pass slowly; to fail in duty, to commit a fault; to commit a fault by mistake; to pass from one proprietor to another, by the negligence of the patron. *ppr.* lapsing, *pret. & pp.* lapsed. [L. *lapsus—labor,* to glide.]

Lapwing, lap'wing, n. The peewit; a bird so named from the *rapidity* with which it moves and flaps its *wings.* [Sax. *lepewinc—hleapan,* to leap, and *winc,* wing.]

Larboard, lär'bōrd, n. *The left-hand side* of a ship, when a person stands with his face to the head; port; opposed to starboard.—*a.* Pertaining to *the left-hand side of a ship.* [D. *laager,* left, and *bord,* side.]

Larcenous, lär'sen-us, a. *Given to larceny.*

Larceny, lär'se-ni, n. Theft; the act of taking and carrying away the goods or personal property of another feloniously. [Fr. *larcin.*]

Larch, lärch, n. A cone-bearing tree. [L. *larix.*]

Lard, lärd, n. *The fat of swine,* after being melted and separated from the flesh; bacon; the flesh of swine⁴.—*vt.* *To fatten;* to stuff with bacon or pork; to mix with something by way of improvement.—*vi.* To grow fat. [Fr.—L. *lardum.*]

Larded, lärd'ed, p.a. *Fattened;* mixed.

Larder, lärd'ėr, n. A room where meat and other articles of food are kept before they are cooked. [Old Fr. *lardier.*]

Large, lärj, a. Big; bulky; huge; great; extensive; wide; diffusive; abundant; exceeding the usual or common number, size, &c.; generous; noble. [Fr.—L. *largus*—Sans. *drih,* to increase.]

Large-handed⁴, lärj'hand-ed, a. Rapacious; greedy.

Large-hearted, lärj'härt-ed, a. Liberal; munificent; generous.

Largely, lärj'li, adv. Widely; copiously; amply; liberally.

Largeness, lärj'nes, n. *State or quality of being large;* bulk; greatness; extent; amplitude; wideness; generosity.

Largess, lärj'es, n. *That which is given freely;* a present; a bounty bestowed. [Fr. *largesse*—L. *largus,* abundant.]

Lark, lärk, n. *The loud singing bird;* a bird remarkable for its liveliness and its singing.—*vi.* To catch larks. [Sax. *laferc*—Old G. *lären,* to become loud.]

Larum, la'rum, n. *Alarm;* a noise giving notice of danger. [G. *lärm.*]

Larva, lär'va, n. **Larvæ,** lär'vē, pl. *A ghost⁴;* an insect in the caterpillar or grub state. [L.—*lar, laris,* a tutelary deity.]

Larval, lär'val, a. *Belonging to a larva.*

Laryngeal, Laryngean, la-rin-jē'al, la-rin-jē'an, a. *Pertaining to the larynx.*

Larynx, la'ringks, n. The upper part of the windpipe, serving to modulate the sound of the voice. [Gr.]

Lascivious, las-si'vi-us, a. *Playful; lewd;* lustful; soft; luxurious. [Fr. *lascif*—L. *lascivus.*]

Lasciviously, las-si'vi-us-li, adv. Loosely; wantonly; lewdly.

Lasciviousness, las-si'vi-us-nes, n. *Quality of being lascivious;* lustfulness; tendency to excite lust and promote irregular indulgences.

Lash, lash, n. *A leash;* the thong of a whip; a stroke with a whip; a sarcasm; an expression or retort that cuts or gives pain.—*vt.* To strike with a lash; to whip or scourge; to beat, as with something loose; to dash against, as waves; to tie or bind with a *leash* or a cord; to secure by a string, as to a ship; to satirize; to censure with severity. *vi.* To ply the whip; to strike at. [Another form of *leash.*]

Lashing, lash'ing, p.n. *A whipping;* castigation or chastisement.

Lass, las, n. *A young woman;* a girl. (Applied particularly to a country girl.) [from *laddess,* the old feminine of *lad.*]

Lassitude, las'i-tūd, n. *Faintness; weariness;* languor of body or mind. [Fr.—L. *langueo,* to be faint.]

Last, last, a. *Latest;* that follows all the others; hindmost; final; extreme; next before the present; utmost; meanest. *adv.* The last time; the time before the present; in conclusion; finally. [Sax.]

Last, last, vi. *To follow on;* to continue to serve some purpose or end; to continue in time; to continue unimpaired;

not to decay or perish; to hold out; to continue unconsumed. [Sax. læstan, to follow.]—n. A mould of the human foot, made of wood, on which shoes are formed; a load.—vt. To form on or by a last. [Sax. leste, a footstep.]

Lasting, last'ing, p.a. Durable; that may continue or endure.—p.n. Endurance.

Lastingly, last'ing-li, adv. Durably.

Lastly, last'li, adv. In the last place.

Latch, lach, n. That which seizes; a small piece of iron or wood used to fasten a door.—vt. To catch; to fasten with a latch; to fasten; to smear. [from Sax. leccan, to seize.]

Latchet, lach'et, n. The string that fastens a shoe. [from latch.]

Late, lāt, a. Delayed; hindered; coming after the usual time; tardy; far advanced toward the end or close; last, or recently in any place, office, or character; existing not long ago; not long past; recent; modern.—adv. After the usual time, or the time appointed; lately; far in the night, day, week, or other particular period. [Sax. læt; Old Sax. lettian, to hinder.]

Lated, lāt'ed, p.a. Belated; being too late.

Lately, lāt'li, adv. Not long ago.

Latency, lā'ten-si, n. State of being latent or concealed; abstruseness.

Lateness, lāt'nes, n. State of being late; time far advanced in any particular period.

Latent, lā'tent, a. Covered; lying hid or concealed; secret; not seen; not apparent. [L. latens—lateo, to lurk.]

Latently, lā'tent-li, adv. In a latent manner; secretly.

Later, lāt'ėr, a. Posterior; subsequent. [comp. deg. of late.]

Lateral, lat'ėr-al, a. Pertaining to the side; proceeding from the side; having a direction at right angles to a vertical line. [Fr.—L. latus, the side.]

Laterally, lat'ėr-al-li, adv. By the side; sideways; in the direction of the side.

Lath, lāth, n. A small piece of wood cut long and nailed to the rafters of a building to support the tiles or covering.—vt. To cover or line with laths. [G. latte.]

Lathe, lāve, n. A machine by which instruments of wood, &c., are turned and cut into a smooth round form. [perhaps from W. llathru, to make smooth.]

Lather, laTH'ėr, vt. To anoint or spread over with the foam of soap.—n. Foam or froth made by soap moistened with water; foam or froth from profuse sweat, as of a horse. [Sax. lethrian, to anoint.]

Lathing, lāth'ing, n. A covering made of laths.

Lathy, lāth'i, a. Thin as a lath; long and slender.

Latin, la'tin, a. Pertaining to the Latins, a people of Latium, in Italy; Roman. n. The language of the ancient Romans.

Latinism, la'tin-izm, n. A Latin idiom; a mode of speech peculiar to the Latins.

Latinist, la'tin-ist, n. One skilled in Latin.

Latinity, la-tin'i-ti, n. The Latin tongue or idiom; purity of the Latin style or idiom.

Latinize, la'tin-īz, vt. To give Latin terminations or forms to, as to foreign words.—vi. To use words or phrases borrowed from the Latin. ppr. latinizing, pret. & pp. latinized.

Latish, lāt'ish, a. Somewhat late. [from late.]

Latitude, la'ti-tūd, n. Breadth; extent from side to side; space; the distance of a heavenly body from the ecliptic; the distance, either north or south, of any place on the globe, from the equator; extent of meaning; extent of deviation from a settled point; freedom from rules; laxity. [Fr.—L. latus, broad; Sans. prath, to be broad.]

Latitudinarian, la'ti-tūd-in-ā'ri-an, a. Indulging in latitude of opinion; thinking or acting at large; lax in religious principles or views.—n. One who indulges in latitude of opinion; one who departs in opinion from the strict principles of orthodoxy. [Fr. latitudinaire.]

Latitudinarianism, la'ti-tūd-in-ā'ri-an-izm, n. Undue freedom or laxness of opinion, particularly in theology.

Latter, lat'ėr, a. Later; opposed to former; mentioned the last of two; modern; lately done or past. [an irregular comparative of late.]

Latterly, lat'ėr-li, adv. Of late.

Lattice, Lattice-work, lat'is, lat'is-wėrk, n. Any work of wood or iron, made by crossing laths, rods, or bars, and forming open squares like network; a reticulated window.—a. Furnished with lattice-work; consisting of cross pieces. [Fr. lattis.]

Latticed, lat'ist, p.a. Furnished with a lattice.

Laud, lad, n. Praise; that part of divine worship which consists in praise; music or singing in honour of any one.—vt. To praise in words alone, or with words and singing; to extol. [L. laus, laudis, praise.]

Laudable, lad'a-bl, a. Deserving praise; praiseworthy. [L. laudabilis.]

Laudableness, lad'a-bl-nes, n. Quality of being laudable or deserving praise.

Laudably, lad'a-bli, adv. In a manner deserving praise.

Laudanum, la'da-num, n. A remedy to be praised; opium prepared in spirit of wine; tincture of opium. [Fr. contracted from L. laudandum, to be praised, from laudo, to praise.]

Laudatory, lad'a-tō-ri, a. Containing praise; tending to praise. [Sp. laudatorio—L. laus, laudis, praise.]

Laugh, laf, vi. To make the noise and exhibit the features which are characteristic of mirth in the human species; to appear gay or brilliant (with at); to ridicule; to treat with some degree of contempt.—vt. To express by laughing; to ridicule or deride; to scorn.—n. The convulsive sound expressive of mirth peculiar to the human species. [Sax. hlahan—Sans. sridh.]

Laughable, laf'a-bl, a. Risible; ridiculous; comical; mirthful.

Laughably, laf'a-bli, adv. In a manner to excite laughter.

Laugher, laf'ėr, n. One who laughs.

Laughing, laf'ing, p.a. Expressing mirth in a particular manner.—p.n. Laughter.

Laughingly, laf'ing-li, adv. In a merry way; with laughter.

Laughing-stock, laf'ing-stok, n. An object of ridicule.

Laughter, laf'tėr, n. Convulsive merriment; an expression of mirth peculiar to man. [Sax. hleahtor.]

Launch, lansh, vt. To throw from the hand; to let fly; to plunge into; to move or cause to slide from the land into the water, as a ship.—vi. To dart or fly off; to go forth, as a ship into the water; to expatiate in language.—n. Act of launching; the sliding of a ship from the land into the water, on ways prepared for the purpose; a kind of boat, longer than a long-boat. [Fr. lancer—L. lancea, a light spear.]

Laund, land, n. A lawn.

Launder, lan'dėr, vt. To wash; to wet.

Laundress, lan'dres, n. A washerwoman; a female whose employment is to wash clothes. [Fr. lavandière—L. lavo, to wash.]

Laundry, lan'dri, n. A washing-place; the room where clothes are washed. [Sp. lavadero.]

Laureate, la're-āt, a. Crowned with laurel.—vt. To honour with a degree in a university, and a present of a wreath of laurel.—ppr. laureating, pret. & pp. laureated.—n. One crowned with laurel; the poet of the sovereign, first so called in the time of Edward IV. [Fr. lauréat—L. laurus, laurel.]

Laureateship, la're-āt-ship, n. Office of a laureate.

Laureation, la-re-ā'shon, n. The act of crowning with laurel, as in bestowing a degree.

Laurel, la'rel, n. The bay-tree, used in ancient times in making garlands or wreaths for victors, &c. [Sp. laurel—L. laurus, a bay-tree.]

Laurelled, la'reld, p.a. Crowned with laurel, or with a laurel wreath.

Lava, lā'va, n. A mass or stream of melted minerals which bursts from the mouth or sides of a volcano; the same matter when cool and hardened. [It.—L. lavo, to wash.]

Lavatory, lav'a-tō-ri, n. A place for washing; a wash or lotion for a diseased part. [Low L. lavatorium—L. lavo, to wash.]

Lave, lāv, vt. To wash; to bathe.—vi. To bathe; to wash one's self. ppr. laving, pret. & pp. laved. [Fr. laver—L. lavo, to wash.]

Lavender, la'ven-dėr, n. A plant which yields an essential oil, and a well-known tincture and perfume, formerly used in washing. [It. lavendola—L. lavo, to wash.]

Laver, lā'vėr, n. A vessel for washing; a large basin. [Fr. lavoir.]

Lavish, lav'ish, a. Exhausting; profuse; liberal to a fault; wasteful; wild; unrestrained.—vt. To expend or bestow with profusion; to squander. [formed from lave, to draw out—L. levo, to lift up.]

Lavishly, lav'ish-li, adv. With profuse expense; prodigally; wastefully.

Law, la, n. A rule of action laid down by a superior; a rule prescribed by the supreme power of a state; a statute; litigation; a rule of direction; that which governs; the Word of God; the Old Testament; the institutions of Moses; a rule of science or art; settled principle; the regular method by which certain effects follow certain causes; jurisprudence. [Sax. lagu—Goth. lagjan, to lay.]

Lawful, la'ful, a. Agreeable to law; allowed by law; legal; constitutional; constituted by law.

Lawfully, la'ful-li, adv. Legally; agreeably to law.

Lawfulness, la'ful-nes, n. Quality of being lawful or conformable to law.

Lawgiver, la'giv-ėr, n. One who makes a law; a legislator.

Lawless, la'les, a. Not subject to law; contrary to the civil law; unrestrained by law; illegal; not subject to the ordinary laws of nature.

Fāte, fär, fat, fall: mē, met, hėr: pīne, pin; nōte, not, mōve; tūbe, tub, bull; oil, pound.

Lawlessly, lą'les-li, *adv*. In a manner contrary to law.

Lawlessness, lą'les-nes, *n*. Quality or state of being unrestrained by law.

Lawn, lan, *n*. A clear place, area, or spot of ground; an open space between woods; a space of smooth level ground covered with grass, generally in front of or around a mansion. [W. llan, a clear open place.]

Lawn, lan, *n*. A sort of fine linen or cambric, used in the sleeves of bishops, and for other purposes; also, an imitation fabric of cotton.—*a*. Made of lawn. [Fr. linon—L. linum, flax.]

Lawndt, land, *n*. Same as lawn.

Lawn-sleeve, lan'slēv, *n*. A sleeve made of lawn; a part of a bishop's dress.

Lawsuit, la'sūt, *n*. A suit in law for the recovery of a supposed right.

Lawyer, lą'yėr, *n*. One versed in the laws, or a practitioner of law. [from law-yer, law-man.]

Lax, laks, *a*. Loose; flabby; not tight or tense; of loose texture; not rigidly exact; not strict; unrestrained; licentious; loose in the intestines.—*n*. A looseness; diarrhœa. [L. laxus.]

Laxative, laks'at-iv, *a*. Having the quality of loosening the intestines, and relieving from constipation.—*n*. A medicine that relaxes the intestines; a gentle purgative. [Fr. laxatif—L. laxo, to loose.]

Laxativeness, laks'at-iv-nes, *n*. Quality of loosening or relaxing.

Laxity, laks'i-ti, *n*. State or quality of being lax; want of exactness or precision; looseness, as of the intestines. [Fr. laxité.]

Laxness, laks'nes, *n*. Same as laxity.

Lay, lā, *vt*. To cause to lie; to prostrate; to fix and keep from rising; to place in order; to spread or set; to calm; to quiet; to restrain from walking; to prepare; to place in the earth for growth; to stake; to exclude, as eggs; to put; to apply; to charge; to impute; to enjoin as a duty; to set, as an ambuscade; to contrive.—*vi*. To bring forth or produce eggs. *ppr.* laying, *pret. & pp.* laid.—*n*. That which lies or is laid; a row; a stratum; a layer; one rank in a series reckoned upward. [Sax. lagan—Goth. lagjan, to lay.]

Lay, lā, *n*. A song; an air; a tune; a kind of narrative poem among the ancient minstrels. [Sax. legh.]

Lay, lā, *a*. Pertaining to the laity, as distinct from the clergy; not clerical. [Fr. lai—Gr. laos, the people.]

Layer, lā'ėr, *n*. One body laid over another; a bed; a course, as of bricks, &c.; a twig of a plant, not detached from the stock, laid under ground for growth; that which lays, as a hen.

Layering, lā'ėr-ing, *p.n*. The propagation of plants by layers.

Laying, lā'ing, *p.n*. Act of one who lays; the act of laying eggs; the eggs laid.

Layman, lā'man, *n*. A man who is not a clergyman; a figure used by painters.

Lazar, lā'zär, *n*. One sick or afflicted with sores; a person infected with nauseous and pestilential disease. [from Lazarus, in the parable.]

Lazaretto, la-za-ret'tō, *n*. A public building, hospital, or pest-house, for the reception of diseased persons. [It. lazzeretto.]

Lazar-house, lā'zär-hous, *n*. A lazaretto; also, a hospital for quarantine.

Lazily, lā'zi-li, *adv*. Sluggishly.

Laziness, lā'zi-nes, *n*. State or quality of being lazy; indolence; habitual sloth; slowness; tardiness.

Lazy, lā'zi, *a*. Slow; dull; disinclined to exertion; naturally slothful; indolent; heavy in motion; moving apparently with labour. [Old G. las, slow, dull.]

Lea, lē, *n*. Ground laid down in grass; a meadow or sward-land; land under grass or pasturage. [Sax. leag.]

Lead, led, *n*. A well-known heavy metal of a dull white colour, with a cast of blue; a plummet, used in sounding at sea; a thin plate of type-metal, used to separate lines in printing.—*vt*. To cover with lead; to fit with lead. [Sax.—Icel. lód, a weight.]

Lead, lēd, *vt*. To guide by showing the way; to guide by the hand; to conduct to any place; to conduct, as a commander; to govern; to precede; to show the method of attaining an object; to entice; to prevail on; to bias; to spend.—*vi*. To go before and show the way; to conduct, as a chief; to draw; to have a tendency to. *ppr.* leading, *pret. & pp.* led.—*n*. Guidance; precedence; a going before. [Sax. lædan—Old G. leitjan, to lead.]

Leaded, led'ed, *p.a*. Fitted with lead; set in lead.

Leaden, led'n, *a*. Made of lead; heavy; indisposed to action; dull.

Leader, lēd'ėr, *n*. One who leads; a guide; a chief; a captain; one who goes first; the head of a party; the leading editorial article in a newspaper; that which leads or goes before.

Leadership, lēd'ėr-ship, *n*. State or condition of a leader.

Leading, lēd'ing, *p.a*. Chief; most important or influential.

Leaf, lēf, *n*. Leaves, lēvz, *pl*. The thin, expanded, deciduous part of a tree or flower; a part of a book containing two pages; something resembling a leaf; a very thin plate; the movable side of a table; one side of a double door. [Sax.—Sans. lup, to break, destroy.]

Leafiness, lēf'i-nes, *n*. State of being full of leaves.

Leafing, lēf'ing, *p.n*. The process of unfolding leaves.

Leafless, lēf'les, *a*. Destitute of leaves.

Leaflet, lēf'let, *n*. A little leaf.

Leafy, lēf'i, *a*. Full of leaves.

League, lēg, *n*. A bond; a contract between princes or states for their mutual defence; an alliance; a confederacy; a covenant.—*vi*. To form a league; to unite or confederate, as private persons for mutual aid. *ppr.* leaguing, *pret. & pp.* leagued. [Fr. ligue—L. ligo, to bind.]

League, lēg, *n*. Originally, a stone erected on the public roads; the distance between two such stones, or three miles. [Sp. legua, a league—W. llech, a flat stone.]

Leagued, lēgd, *p.a*. United in a league or mutual compact.

Leaguer, lēg'ėr, *n*. The camp of a besieging army; a siege.

Leak, lēk, *n*. A fissure in a vessel that admits water, or permits it to escape; the passing of water or other fluid through an aperture.—*vi*. To let water or other liquor into or out of a vessel, through a hole or crevice in the vessel. [D. lek, a leak.]

Leakage, lēk'āj, *n*. The quantity of a liquid that enters or issues by leaking; an allowance of a certain rate per cent. for the leaking of casks.

Leakiness, lēk'i-nes, *n*. State of being leaky.

Leaking, lēk'ing, *p.n*. The oozing or passing of a liquid through an aperture.

Leaky, lēk'i, *a*. Having a leak or leaks; that admits water or other liquor to pass in or out.

Lean, lēn, *vi*. To bend; to slope; to deviate from a straight line; to incline; to tend toward; to bend or incline so as to rest on something; to be in a bending posture.—*vt*. To cause to lean; to support. [Sax. hlynian; Old G. hlinen, to lean.]

Lean, lēn, *a*. Thin; spare; lank; wanting flesh; not fat; bare; barren of thought; scanty.—*n*. That part of flesh which consists of muscle without the fat. [Low G. leen, lean.]

Leaning, lēn'ing, *p.n*. Inclination; tendency; bias.

Leanly, lēn'li, *adv*. Meagrely.

Leanness, lēn'nes, *n*. State of being lean; want of flesh; want or poverty of matter; want of spiritual comfort.

Leanwitted, lēn'wit-ed, *a*. Having but little sense.

Leap, lēp, *vi*. To spring from the ground with both feet, as man, or with all the feet, as other animals; to jump; to rush with violence; to spring; to bound; to skip; to manifest joy (with up).—*vt*. To pass over by leaping.—*n*. A jump; a spring; space passed by leaping; hazard, or effect of leaping. [Sax. hleapan, to leap.]

Leaping, lēp'ing, *p.n*. Act of jumping or passing by a leap.

Leap-year, lēp'yėr, *n*. A year containing 366 days; every fourth year, which leaps over a day more than a common year.

Learn, lėrn, *vt*. To teach; to be instructed in; to gain knowledge of; to acquire skill in anything; to gain by practice a faculty of performing.—*vi*. To gain or receive knowledge (with of); to take pattern; to receive intelligence. [Sax. læran—Old G. lērjan, to teach.]

Learned, lėrn'ed, *p.a*. Versed in learning; knowing; containing learning, as a discourse; versed in scholastic, as distinct from other knowledge.

Learnedly, lėrn'ed-li, *adv*. With learning or erudition; with skill.

Learner, lėrn'ėr, *n*. One who learns; one who is in the rudiments of any science or art.

Learning, lėrn'ing, *p.n*. Acquired knowledge in any branch of science or literature; skill in anything good or bad.

Lease, lēs, *n*. A letting of lands or tenements to another for life, for a term of years, or at will, for a rent; the contract for such letting; any tenure by grant; the time for which such a tenure holds good.—*vt*. To let; to demise; to grant, as lands to another for a rent reserved. *ppr.* leasing, *pret. & pp.* leased. [Norm. less, a lease—L. laxo, to slacken.]

Leasehold, lēs'hōld, *a*. Held by lease.

Leash, lēsh, *n*. A lash; a thong of leather by which a falconer holds his hawk, or a courser his dog; a brace and a half. *vt*. To bind by a leash; to hold by a string. [Fr. laisse—L. laxus, loose.]

Leasing, lēs'ing, *n*. Falsehood; lies.

Least, lēst, *a*. Smallest; little beyond others, either in size or degree.—*adv*. In the smallest or lowest degree. [super. of Sax. læs, less, contracted from læsest.]

Leather, leth'ėr, *n*. The skin or covering of an animal dressed and prepared for use; dressed hides in general.—*a. Leathern*; consisting of leather. [Sax. lether—hlidan, to cover.]

Leathern levh'ėrn, *a*. Made of leather.

ch, chain; j, job; g, go; ng, sing; TH, then; th, thin; w, wig; wh, whig; zh, azure; † obsolete.

Leathery, leᴛʜ'er-i, a. *Resembling leather;* tough.
Leave, lēv, n. *Permission; license;* liberty granted by which restraint or illegality is removed. [Sax. *leaf.*]
Leave, lēv, *vt.* To *withdraw or depart from;* to quit for a longer or shorter time, or for perpetuity; to forsake; to abandon; to suffer to remain; to have remaining at death; to trust to, as a deposit, or to suffer to remain; to bequeath; to cease to do; to refer.—*vi.* To cease; to desist. *ppr.* leaving, *pret. & pp.* left.—n. Departure; farewell; a formal parting of friends. [Sax.*læfan.*]
Leaved, lēvd, *p.a. Furnished with leaves;* having a leaf, or made with leaves or folds.
Leaven, lev'n, n. *That which raises* and makes *light;* a mass of sour dough, which, mixed with a larger quantity, produces fermentation in it, and renders it *light;* anything which makes a general change in the mass.—*vt.* To *raise* and make *light;* to taint; to imbue. [Fr. *levain*—L. *levo,* to raise—*levis,* Sans. *laghu,* light.]
Leavening, lev'n-ing, *p.n. That which leavens.*
Leavings, lēv'ingz, n. pl. *Things left;* remnant; relics; refuse; offal.
Lecht, lech, *vt.* To lick.
Lecher, lech'er, n. *One who licks up*t; a *libertine;* a man given to lewdness. [Old Fr. *lecheor*—Fr. *lécher,* to lick.]
Lecherous, lech'er-us, a. Addicted to lewdness; prone to indulge lust.
Lechery, lech'e-ri, n. Lewdness; free indulgence of lust.
Lecture, lek'tūr, n. *A reading;* a formal discourse, intended for instruction; a formal reproof; a rehearsal of a lesson. *vi.* To deliver a formal discourse; to practise reading lectures for instruction.—*vt.* To read a *lecture* to; to instruct dogmatically; to reprove. *ppr.* lecturing, *pret. & pp.* lectured. [Fr.—L. *lego, lectus,* to read.]
Lecturer, lek'tūr-er, n. *One who lectures;* a professor who delivers formal discourses for the instruction of others; a preacher in a church.
Lectureship, lek'tūr-ship, n. *The office of a lecturer.*
Ledge, lej, n. *A layer;* a ridge; a prominent row, as of rocks; a ridge of rocks near the surface of the sea; a small moulding. [Sax. *leger—lecgan,* to lay.]
Ledger, lej'er, n. *The book that lies* on a merchant's counter; the book into which the accounts of the journal are carried in a summary form. [Sax. *leger,* a lier.]
Ledgy, lej'i, a. *Abounding in ledges.*
Lee, lē, n. *A sheltered place;* a place defended from the wind; that part of the hemisphere toward which the wind blows.—*a.* Lying under, or to the *lee* of a ship. [Sax. *hleo,* a shelter.]
Leech, lēch, n. *A healer*t; a bloodsucker; an aquatic worm used in medicine to draw blood. [Sax. *læce.*]
Leek, lēk, n. A green kitchen plant; a plant allied to the onion. [Sax. *leac.*]
Leer, lēr, n. A look with the *cheek* presented to the object; an affected cast of countenance; complexion.—*vi.* To look with the *cheek* presented at the object; to look obliquely; to look archly.—*vt.* To allure with smiles. [Sax. *hleor,* cheek.]
Lees, lēz, n. pl. The *slime* of liquor; the grosser parts of any liquor which have settled on the bottom of a vessel; dregs. [Fr. *lie*—L. *limus,* mud.]

Leeset, lēs, *vt.* To lose.
Leeward, lē'wėrd, a. Pertaining to the part toward which the wind blows. *adv.* Toward the lee.
Leeway, lē'wā, n. The lateral movement of a ship to the *leeward* of her course.
Left, left, a. Denoting the part opposed to the right of the body; being on the left hand; sinistrous.—*n.* The side opposite to the right. [L. *lævus.*]
Left-handed, left'hand-ed, a. Having the *left hand* or arm more strong or dexterous than the right; clumsy; awkward; unlucky.
Left-handedness, left'hand-ed-nes, n. *State or quality of being left-handed.*
Leg, leg, n. *A shank;* the limb of an animal, used in *supporting* the body, and in walking and running; that part of the limb from the knee to the foot; the long or slender support of anything. [Sw. Goth. *lägg,* a leg.]
Legacy, le'ga-si, n. *That which is bequeathed;* a bequest; a particular thing, or certain sum of money given by last will. [Sp. *legado*—L. *lego,* to bequeath.]
Legal, lē'gal, a. *According to law;* created by law; lawful; resting on works for salvation. [Fr. *légal*—L. *lex, legis,* a law—*lego,* to lay together.]
Legality, lē-gal'i-ti, n. *Lawfulness;* conformity to law. [Fr. *légalité.*]
Legalize, lē'gal-iz, *vt. To make legal;* to sanction. *ppr.* legalizing, *pret. & pp.* legalized. [Fr. *légaliser.*]
Legally, lē'gal-li, *adv. Lawfully.*
Legate, le'gāt, n. *One who is sent with a commission;* the Pope's ambassador to a foreign prince or state. [It. *legato*—L. *lego, legatus,* to send with a commission.]
Legatee, le-ga-tē', n. *One to whom a legacy is bequeathed.*
Legateship, le'gāt-ship, n. *The office of a legate.*
Legatine, le'gāt-in, a. *Pertaining to a legate.*
Legation, lē-gā'shon, n. *The sending of an ambassador;* the person or persons sent as envoys; the residence of an envoy at a foreign court. [L. *legatio.*]
Legend, lej'end, n. *Something to be read;* a chronicle of the lives of saints, formerly read at matins; any remarkable story handed down from early times; the motto placed round the edge of a coin. [L. *legendum*—*lego,* to read.]
Legendary, lej'end-a-ri, a. *Consisting of legends;* fabulous; strange; extravagant.
Legerdemain, lej'ėr-dē-mān", n. *Nimbleness of hand;* sleight of hand; a trick performed with such art that the manner eludes observation. [Fr. *léger,* light, and *de main*—*de,* of, and *main,* L. *manus,* hand.]
Legerityt, le-je'ri-ti, n. *Lightness;* nimbleness.
Legged, legd, *p.a. Having legs;* as, a two-legged animal.
Legibility, le-ji-bil'i-ti, n. *Quality or state of being legible.*
Legible, le'ji-bl, a. *That may be read;* that may be discovered or understood by apparent marks or indications. [L. *legibilis*—*lego,* to read.]
Legibly, le'ji-bli, *adv.* In such a manner as may be read.
Legion, lē'jon, n. A body of men *chosen* to serve as soldiers among the Romans, in number from 3000 to 6000; a military force; a great number. [Fr. *légion*—L. *lego,* to choose out.]
Legionary, lē'jon-a-ri, a. *Relating to a legion;* consisting of legions; containing a great number. [Fr. *légionnaire.*]
Legislate, le'jis-lāt, *vi. To bring in a law;* to enact a law or laws. *ppr.* legislating, *pret. & pp.* legislated. [L. *lex, legis,* a law, and *fero, latum,* to bring.]
Legislation, le-jis-lā'shon, n. *Act of legislating;* the enacting of laws. [Fr. *législation.*]
Legislative, le'jis-lāt-iv, a. *Enacting laws;* capable of enacting laws; suitable to laws. [Fr. *législatif.*]
Legislator, le'jis-lāt-er, n. *A lawgiver;* one who makes laws for a state or kingdom. [L.]
Legislature, le'jis-lāt-ūr, n. The body of men in a state invested with power *to make and repeal laws;* the supreme power of a state. [Fr. *législature.*]
Legist, lē'jist, n. *One skilled in the law.*
Legitimacy, lē-jit'i-ma-si, n. *State of being legitimate;* lawfulness of birth; genuineness; regular sequence; the accordance of an action or institution with established law.
Legitimate, lē-jit'i-māt, a. *Accordant with law;* lawfully begotten or born; genuine; following by regular sequence; in accordance with established law; acknowledged as requisite.—*vt. To render legitimate;* to invest with the rights of a lawful heir. *ppr.* legitimating, *pret. & pp.* legitimated. [L. *legitimus*—*lex, legis,* law.]
Legitimately, lē-jit'i-māt-li, *adv. Lawfully;* according to law; genuinely.
Legitimation, lē-jit'i-mā"shon, n. *Act of rendering legitimate;* lawful birth. [Fr. *légitimation.*]
Legume, le-gūm', n. *Pulse gathered* by the hand; a seed-vessel, of two valves, in which the seeds are fixed to one suture only; a pod or a cod; (pl.) pulse, pease, beans, &c. [Fr. *légume*—L. *lego,* to gather.]
Leguminous, le-gū'min-us, a. *Pertaining to legumes* or pulse; bearing legumes or pods. [Fr. *légumineux.*]
Leisure, lē'zhūr, n. *Freedom from labour;* vacant time; time free from employment; ease.—*a. Free* from labour; not occupied; vacant of employment. [Fr. *loisir*—L. *licet,* it is permitted.]
Leisurely, lē'zhūr-li, a. *Done at leisure;* deliberate; slow.—*adv.* Not in haste or hurry; deliberately.
Lemant, lē'man, n. A sweetheart, of either sex, usually in a bad sense.
Lemma, lem'ma, n. *Anything taken;* a premise taken for granted; an auxiliary proposition. [Gr.—*lambano,* to take.]
Lemon, le'mon, n. An acid fruit of the orange kind; the tree that produces this fruit. [Sp. *limon*—Ar. *laymun.*]
Lemonade, le-mon-ād', n. A beverage consisting of *lemon*-juice mixed with water and sweetened. [Fr. *limonade.*]
Lend, lend, *vt. To grant or transfer*t; to grant to another for temporary use, on condition that the thing shall be returned; to furnish, in general, as aid; to grant, as a loan; to permit to use for another's benefit, as one's name on a note. *ppr.* lending, *pret. & pp.* lent. [Sax. *lænan,* to lend—*læn,* a gift, a loan.]
Lender, lend'er, n. *One who lends.*
Lending, lend'ing, *p.n. The act of loaning.*
Length, length, n.*State of being long; longitude;* the extent of anything material from end to end; extension; space of time; duration; distance. [Sax. *lengthe*—*lang,* long.]

Fāte, fär. fat, fall; mē, met, hėr; pine, pin; nōte, not, mȯve; tūbe, tub, bu̇ll; oil, pou̇nd.

Lengthen, length'n, *vt.* To make longer; to extend in length, or in time; to expand.—*vi.* To grow longer; to extend in length.
Lengthened, length'nd, *p.a. Drawn out in length*; continued in duration.
Lengthening, length'n-ing, *p.n. A making longer*; continuation; protraction.
Lengthily, length'i-li, *adv. In a lengthy manner*; at great length or extent.
Lengthiness, length'i-nes, *n. State of being lengthy*; length.
Lengthwise, length'wīz, *adv. In the direction of the length.*
Lengthy, length'i, *a. Being long* or moderately long; not short; longsome.
Lenience, Leniency, lē'ni-ens, lē'ni-en-si, *n. Quality of being lenient*; lenity; mildness; gentleness.
Lenient, lē'ni-ent, *a. Softening*; emollient; mild; clement. [L. *leniens—lenis,* smooth.]
Leniently, lē'ni-ent-li, *adv. In a lenient manner.*
Lenitive, le'nit-iv, *a. Having the quality of softening,* as pain or acrimony; emollient.—*n. That which softens or mitigates*; a medicine that has the quality of easing pain; that which abates passion. [Fr. *lénitif.*]
Lenity, le'ni-ti, *n. Softness*; mildness of temper; tenderness; mercy. [L. *lenitas—lenis,* smooth.]
Lens, lenz. *n. Lenses*, lens'ez, *pl.* A piece of glass shaped originally like the seed of the *lentil,* so that rays of light passing through it are made to change their direction. [L. *lens, lentis,* a lentil.]
Lent, lent, *n. The spring fast;* the fast of forty days, observed by the Roman Catholic and other churches before Easter, commemorative of our Saviour's fast. [Sax. *lænten,* spring.]
Lenten, lent'en, *a. Pertaining to Lent*; used in Lent; sparing; short.
Lentil, len'til, *n.* A plant and its seed resembling the bean, but much inferior, cultivated chiefly as food for animals. [Fr. *lentille—*L. *lens, lentis.*]
Leonine, lē'ō-nin, *a. Belonging to a lion*; resembling a lion, or partaking of its qualities. [L. *leoninus—leo,* a lion.]
Leopard, le'pärd, *n. The lion-panther*; a rapacious quadruped, of the cat kind, distinguished by its spotted skin. [L. *leo,* a lion, and *pardus,* a panther.]
Leper, le'pér, *n.* One whose skin is covered with *scales*; a person affected with leprosy. [Gr. *lepra,* leprosy—*lepos,* a scale.]
Lepidopterous, le-pid-op'ter-us, *a. Having scaly wings,* as butterflies. [Gr. *lepos,* a scale, and *pteron,* a wing.]
Leprosy, le'prō-si, *n.* A foul cutaneous disease, appearing in dry, white, thin, scurfy *scabs,* attended with violent itching. [Gr. *lepra.*]
Leprous, le'prus, *a. Infected with leprosy.* [Fr. *lépreux.*]
Lesion, lē'zhon, *n. Injury*; a hurting; hurt; wound. [L. *læsio—lædo, læsum,* to dash violently against, to hurt.]
Less, les, *a. Void; bereft* of part of that indicated by little; smaller; not so large or great.—*adv.* Not so much; in a smaller or lower degree.—*n.* A smaller portion; an inferior. [Sax. *læs;* Goth. *laus,* void.]
Lessee, les-sē', *n. The person to whom a lease is given.* [from *lease.*]
Lessen, les'n, *vt. To make less* in bulk, quantity, number, amount, degree, or quality; to diminish; to lower; to degrade.—*vi. To become less*; to become less in degree; to decrease; to shrink. [from *less.*]
Lesser, les'ér, *a. Less*; smaller. [Sax. *læssa, læsse.*]
Lesson, les'n, *n. A gathering;* a reading; a reading aloud; anything read to a teacher by a pupil, for improvement; such a portion of a book as a pupil learns at one time; a portion of Scripture read in divine service; something to be learned; doctrine; severe lecture; rebuke; truth taught by experience.—*vt.* To teach. [Fr. *leçon—*L. *lego, lectum,* to gather, to read.]
Lest, lest, *conj.* A word denoting a *taking away;* that not; for fear that. [Sax. *leas,* a taking away.]
Let, let, *vt. To free from restraint;* to allow; not to prevent; to lease; to grant possession and use of for a compensation.—*vi.* To be leased or let; as, a house to let. *ppr.* letting, *pret. & pp.* let. [Sax. *letan;* Goth. *letan,* to permit.]
Let, let, *vt.* To keep back; to retard. *n. A retarding; hindrance;* impediment; delay. [Sax. *lettan,* to hinder.]
Lethal, lēth'al, *a. Deadly;* mortal; fatal. [L. *lethalis—letum,* death.]
Lethargic, le-thär'jik, *a. Drowsy;* preternaturally inclined to sleep; dull. [L. *lethargicus.*]
Lethargically, le-thär'jik-al-li, *adv. In* a morbid sleepiness.
Lethargy, le'thär-ji, *n. Drowsiness;* morbid drowsiness; continued or profound sleep, from which a person can scarcely be awaked; dulness; inattention. [Gr. *léthargia—léthé,* forgetfulness.]
Lethe, lē'thē, *n.* One of the rivers of hell; death!.
Letter, let'ér, *n. One who lets* or permits; one who retards or hinders; one who gives vent. [from *let,* to let.]
Letter, let'ér, *n. A written character,* used as the representative of an articulation of the human organs of speech; an epistle; the literal meaning; type, a character formed of metal, and used in printing books; (pl.) learning, erudition.—*vt. To impress or form letters on.* [Fr. *lettre—*L. *lino, litum,* to daub.]
Lettered, let'érd, *p.a. Literate;* versed in literature or science; belonging to learning.
Letter-founder, let'ér-found-ér, *n.* One who *casts letters;* a type-founder.
Lettering, let'ér-ing, *p.n. The act of impressing letters;* the letters impressed.
Letter-press, let'ér-pres, *n. Letters* and words *impressed* on paper by types.
Letting, let'ing, *p.n. Act of permitting*; the putting out on lease, as a farm.
Lettuce, let'ūs, *n.* A plant or herb, which abounds in a *milky* white juice, and is used as a salad. [L. *lactuca—lac, lactis,* milk.]
Levant, lē-vant', *a.* Denoting the quarter where the sun *rises*; eastern.—*n.* The eastern coasts of the Mediterranean Sea. [Fr.—L. *levo,* to raise.]
Levanter, lē-vant'ér, *n.* A strong easterly wind in the Mediterranean.
Levantine, lē-vant'in, *a. Pertaining to the Levant.*
Levee, le'vē, *n. The time of rising;* a morning assembly of visitors; the stated public occasions on which the sovereign receives visits from such of his or her subjects as are entitled, by rank or fortune, to the honour. [Fr. *levée—lever,* to rise.]
Level, le'vel, *n.* An instrument by which to find or draw a *horizontal* line; a surface without inequalities; standard; customary height; equal elevation with something else; fixed or quiet condition; the line of direction in which a missile weapon is aimed.—*a.* Coinciding with the plane of the *horizon*; even; even with anything else; of the same height; equal in rank or degree; having no degree of superiority.—*vt. To make horizontal;* to make even; to reduce or bring to the same height with something else; to lay flat; to reduce to equality of state; to point in taking aim; to aim; to direct.—*vi.* To accord; to agree; to suit; to aim at; to point a gun or an arrow to the mark; to direct the view or purpose; to be aimed; to conjecture!. *ppr.* levelling, *pret. & pp.* levelled. [Sax. *læfel—*L. *libella,* a water level.]
Levelled, le'veld, *p.a. Made level;* reduced to a plane; made even; reduced to an equal state; pointed to an object; brought down; adapted.
Leveller, le'vel-ér, *n. One who levels;* one who destroys or attempts to destroy distinctions.
Levelling, le'vel-ing, *p.a. Making level* or even.—*p.n. The reduction of uneven surfaces to a level;* the art or practice of finding a horizontal line.
Levelness, le'vel-nes, *n. State of being level;* evenness; equality of surface.
Lever, lē'vér, *n. That which raises* or *elevates;* a mechanical instrument used for raising weights. [Fr. *levier—*L. *levo,* to raise.]
Leverage, lē'vér-āj, *n.* Mechanical advantage gained on the principle of *the lever.*
Leveret, le've-ret, *n. A young hare;* a hare in its first year. [Fr. *levraut—*L. *lepus, leporis,* a hare.]
Leviable, le'vi-a-bl, *a. That may be levied;* that may be assessed and collected.
Leviathan, lē-vī'a-than, *n.* An aquatic animal, described in Job xli.; by some supposed to be the crocodile, by others a whale, by others a serpent, and by others an animal now extinct. [Heb. *livyathan.*]
Levigate, le'vi-gāt, *vt. To make smooth;* to grind to a fine impalpable powder. *ppr.* levigating, *pret. & pp.* levigated. [L. *levigo, levigatus—levis,* smooth.]
Levigation, le-vi-gā'shon, *n. Act of levigating.* [L. *levigatio.*]
Levite, lē'vīt, *n.* One of the tribe of *Levi;* an officer in the Jewish church, who was employed in manual service, singing, &c. [from *Levi.*]
Levitical, lē-vit'ik-al, *a. Belonging to the Levites;* priestly.
Levity, le'vi-ti, *n. Lightness;* the want of weight; lightness of temper; inconstancy; giddiness; vanity; freak; gaiety of mind; want of seriousness. [L. *levitas—levis,* light.]
Levy, le'vi, *vt. To raise;* to collect, as an army; to raise, as taxes. *ppr.* levying, *pret. & pp.* levied.—*n. Act of raising* men for military service, as by enlistment; troops collected; war raised!; act of collecting money for public use by tax. [Fr. *lever—*L. *lēvo,* to raise—*lēvis,* light in weight.]
Lewd, lūd, *a. Pertaining to the people*!; lustful; licentious; sensual; impure; wicked; vile. [Sax. *læwd—leod,* the people.]
Lewdly, lūd'li, *adv.* Lustfully; wickedly; wantonly.
Lewdness, lūd'nes, *n. Quality of being lewd;* impurity; unchastity; profligacy.

LEWDSTER 222 **LIFE-BOAT**

Lewdster†, lūd'stėr, n. *One given to lewdness.*
Lexicographer, leks-i-kog'ra-fėr, n. *One versed in lexicography;* the author or compiler of a lexicon or dictionary.
Lexicographic, leks'i-kō-graf"ik, a. *Pertaining to lexicography.*
Lexicography, leks-i-kog'ra-fi, n. *The act or art of writing or compiling a lexicon* or dictionary. [Gr. *lexikon*, and *graphō*, to write.]
Lexicon, leks'i-kon, n. *A word-book;* a dictionary; a vocabulary or book containing an alphabetical arrangement of the words in a language, with the definition of each. [Gr. *lexikon—legō*, to say, to speak.]
Ley, lē, a different orthography of *lea;* pasture-land.
Liability, lī-a-bil'i-ti, n. *State of being bound* in law or justice; responsibility; tendency; a state of being subject.
Liable, lī'a-bl, a. *Bound;* obliged in law or equity; answerable; subject; exposed, as to mistake. [from Fr. *lier,* L. *ligo,* to bind.]
Liar, lī'ėr, n. *One who lies;* one who knowingly utters falsehood.
Libation, li-bā'shon, n. *Act of pouring a liquor,* usually wine, either on the ground or on a victim in sacrifice, in honour of some deity; the wine or other liquor poured out in honour of a deity. [L. *libatio*—Gr. *leibō,* to pour forth.]
Libbard†, lib'bård, n. The leopard.
Libel, lī'bel, n. *A little book;* a *written accusation;* a malicious publication; the written statement of a plaintiff's ground of complaint against a defendant; a defamatory writing.—*vt.* To frame a libel *against;* to exhibit a charge against in court; to lampoon. *ppr.* libelling, *pret. & pp.* libelled. [Fr. *libelle*—L. *libet,* a book.]
Libeller, lī'bel-ėr, n. *One who libels.*
Libellous, lī'bel-us, a. *Containing a libel,* defamatory.
Liberal, lib'ėr-al, a. *That acts according* to his own *desire;* that is his own master; frank; generous; noble-minded; free to give; open-handed; giving largely; ample; large; befitting a freeman; not selfish or contracted; catholic; general; extensive, as studies; not literal or strict; not mean; not low in birth or mind; licentious.—n. *One who advocates greater freedom from restraint,* especially in political institutions. [Fr. *libéral*—L. *libet,* it pleases.]
Liberality, lib-ėr-al'i-ti, n. *Quality of being liberal;* munificence; a particular act of generosity; largeness of mind; catholicism; impartiality. [Fr. *libéralité.*]
Liberalize, lib'ėr-al-īz, *vt.* To render *liberal* or catholic. *ppr.* liberalizing, *pret. & pp.* liberalized. [Fr. *libéraliser.*]
Liberally, lib'ėr-al-li, *adv.* In *a liberal manner;* bountifully; with enlarged views; not literally.
Liberate, lib'ėr-āt, *vt.* To *free;* to release from restraint or bondage. *ppr.* liberating, *pret. & pp.* liberated. [L. *libero, liberatus—liber,* free.]
Liberated, lib'ėr-āt-ed, *p.a. Freed;* released from confinement or slavery.
Liberation, li-bėr-ā'shon, n. *Act of liberating.* [Fr. *libération.*]
Liberator, lib'ėr-āt-ėr, n. *One who liberates* or delivers. [L.]
Libertine, lib'ėr-tin, n. One *free from restraint;* one who leads a dissolute, licentious life: a debauchee.—*a.* Licentious; dissolute. [Fr. *libertin*—L. *liber,* free.]

Libertinism, lib'ėr-tin-izm, n. An unrestrained indulgence of lust; lewdness; licentiousness of opinion.
Liberty, lib'ėr-ti, n. *Freedom;* freedom from restraint, either of body or mind; the freedom of a nation from all unjust abridgment of its rights; the free right of worshipping the Supreme Being according to the dictates of conscience; freedom from physical necessity; privilege; immunity; leave; permission granted; a space in which one is permitted to pass without restraint; freedom of action or speech beyond the ordinary bounds of decorum. [Fr. *liberté*—L. *liber,* free.]
Libidinous, li-bid'in-us, a. *Given to pleasure;* lustful; unchaste; sensual. [Fr. *libidineux*—L. *libet,* it pleases.]
Libidinously, li-bid'in-us-li, a. Lustfully; with lewd desire.
Libidinousness, li-bid'in-us-nes, n. *State or quality of being libidinous.*
Librarian, li-brā'ri-an, n. One who has the care of a library or collection *of books.* [L. *librarius—liber,* a book.]
Library, lī'bra-ri, n. *A place to keep books in;* an edifice for holding a collection of books; a collection of books belonging to a private person, or to a public institution. [L. *librarium.*]
Librate, lī'brāt, *vt.* To *poise;* to balance; to hold in equipoise.—*vi.* To *move as a balance;* to be poised. *ppr.* librating, *pret. & pp.* librated. [L. *libro, libratus—libra,* a balance.]
Libration, lī-brā'shon, n. *Act of librating,* or state of being balanced; a balancing or equipoise between extremes. [L. *libratio.*]
Lice, līs, *n. pl.* of *louse.*
License, lī'sens, n. *Leave to do as one pleases;* leave; authority or liberty given to do or forbear any act; a certificate giving permission; excess of liberty; voluntary deviation from rule. *vt.* To grant a license *to;* to permit by grant of authority; to authorise to act in a particular character; to tolerate. *ppr.* licensing, *pret. & pp.* licensed. [Fr.—L. *licet,* it is permitted.]
Licenser, lī'sens-ėr, n. *One who grants a license.*
Licentiate, li-sen'shi-āt, n. *One who has a license* to practise any art or faculty, or to exercise a profession, as in medicine or theology. [Fr. *licencié.*]
Licentious, li-sen'shi-us, a. *Over-free;* loose; sensual; not restrained by law or morality; uncontrolled; wanton. [Fr. *licencieux*—L. *licet,* it is permitted.]
Licentiously, li-sen'shi-us-li, *adv.* With excess of liberty.
Licentiousness, li-sen'shi-us-nes, n. *Quality or state of being licentious.*
Lichen, lī'ken, n. *A plant that licks up moisture,* appearing in the form of thin, flat crusts, covering rocks and the bark of trees; a tetter or ringworm. [Gr. *leichēn—leichō,* to lick.]
Lich-gate, lich'gāt, n. *A shed over the gate* of a churchyard, to rest the corpse under.
Lick, lik, *vt.* To *touch with the tongue;* to lap; to take in by the tongue.—*n. Act of licking;* that which is licked up. [Sax. *liccian;* Gr. *leichō,* to lick.]
Lickerish, lik'ėr-ish, a. *Fond of licking;* eager to taste; having a keen relish; nice in the choice of food; dainty; tempting the appetite. [Sax. *liccera.*]
Licking, lik'ing, *p.n. A lapping with the tongue;* a drawing the tongue over the surface.
Licorice, Liquorice, li'ko-ris, lī'ko-ris, n. *Sweet-root,* a medicinal plant, whose roots have a sweet taste; the extract from the licorice-root, much used as a demulcent. [It. *liquirizia*—Gr. *glukus,* sweet, and *rhiza,* a root.]
Lictor, lik'tėr, n. *An officer who attended the Roman magistrates,* bearing an axe and *fasces* or rods. [L.—*ligo,* to bind.]
Lid, lid, n. *A cover;* that which shuts the opening of a vessel or box; the cover of the eye, or eye-*lid.* [Sax. *hlid—hlidan,* to cover.]
Lie, lī, n. *A criminal falsehood;* an untruth; an intentional violation of truth; a fiction; false doctrine; that which disappoints confidence.—*vi.* To deny or *refuse* to give up the truth, and at the same time to state that which is not true; to say or do that which deceives another, when he has a right to know the truth, or when morality requires a just representation. *ppr.* lying, *pret. & pp.* lied. [Sax. *lig*—G. *lüge*—Sans. *lākh,* to refuse.]
Lie, lī, *vi.* To lay *one's self,* or to be in a horizontal position; to rest in an inclining posture; to lean; to press on; to rest on a bed or couch; to lodge; to be situated, as a place; to abide; to remain; to consist; to be sustainable in law; to be capable of being maintained. *ppr.* lying, *pret.* lay, *pp.* lain. [Sax. *licgan;* Goth. *ligan.*]
Lief, lēf, *adv. Lovingly;* willingly; used in familiar speech, in the phrase, I had as lief go as not.—*a.* Dear; beloved. [from Sax. *leof,* loved—*lufian,* to love.]
Liege, lēj, a. *Being a vassal;* bound by a feudal tenure; faithful; sovereign; as, a liege-lord.—*n. A vassal* holding a fee by which he is *bound* to perform certain services and duties to his lord; a lord or superior; a sovereign. [Fr. *lige*—L. *ligo,* to bind.]
Lier, lī'ėr, n. *One who lies down;* one who rests or remains.
Lieu, lū, n. *Place;* room; stead. [Fr.—L. *locus,* place.]
Lieutenancy, lef-ten'an-si, n. *The office or commission of a lieutenant;* the body of lieutenants.
Lieutenant, lef-ten'ant, n. *One who holds command in the place of another;* an officer who supplies the place of a superior in his absence; the second commissioned officer in a company of infantry, cavalry, or artillery; the officer next in rank to the captain in a ship of war. [Fr. *lieu,* place, and *tenir, ppr. tenant—*L. *teneo,* to hold.]
Life, līf, n. **Lives**, līvz, *pl. State of living* or of being alive; existence; that state of animals and plants in which the natural functions and motions are or may be performed; vitality; that state of being, in man, in which the soul and body are united; the present state of existence; the time from birth to death; conduct; condition; course of living, in regard to happiness and misery; blood, the supposed vehicle of animation; animal being; spirit; vivacity; a person or thing which imparts spirit; resolution; the living form; real person or state; exact resemblance; general state of man; rank in society; course of things; the system of animal nature; a person; narrative of a past life; history of the events of life. [Sax. *lif—libban,* Sans. *jīv,* to live.]
Life-blood, līf'blud, n. *The blood necessary to life;* vital blood; that which constitutes or gives strength and energy.
Life-boat, līf'bōt, n. *A boat constructed*

Fāte, fär, fat, fạll; mē, met, hėr; pīne, pin; nōte, not. mōve: tūbe, tub, bụll; oil, pound.

LIFE-GIVING 223 LIMITING

for preserving *lives* in cases of shipwreck or other destruction at sea of a ship or steamer.
Life-giving, lif'giv-ing, *a. Giving life* or spirit; having power to give life; inspiriting; invigorating.
Life-guard, lif'gärd, *n. A guard of the life* or person; a guard that attends the person of a prince or other high officer. (Generally plural.)
Lifeless, lif'les, *a. Deprived of life*; dead; destitute of life, as a statue; destitute of power, force, vigour, or spirit, as a discourse; void of spirit; vapid; flat; wanting physical energy.
Lifelessly, lif'les-li, *adv.* Without vigour; dully; frigidly; heavily.
Lifelessness, lif'les-nes, *n. State of being lifeless*; destitution of life, vigour, and spirit; inactivity.
Lift, lift, *vt. To raise into the air*; to raise from a lower to a higher position; to heave; to raise intellectually or spiritually; to raise in fortune or rank; to exalt; to raise in spirit; to cause to swell, as with pride (with *up*).—*vi.* To *try to raise*; to exert the strength for the purpose of raising or bearing.—*n. Act of lifting or raising*; assistance in general; that which is to be raised; something that lifts. [Sax. *hlifian*, to raise up—G. *luft*, air.]
Lifted, lift'ed, *p.a.* Swelled with pride (with *up*).
Lifter, lift'er, *n. He or that which lifts*; a thief.
Ligament, li'ga-ment, *n. That which binds* or unites one thing to another; a bandage; a strong, compact substance, serving to bind one bone to another. [Fr.—L. *ligo*, to bind.]
Ligamentous, li-ga-ment'us, *a. Composing a ligament*; of the nature of a ligament.
Ligature, li'ga-tūr, *n. A band or bandage*; act of binding; a string; a double character, as *fl, fi*; state of being bound. [Fr.—L. *ligo*, to bind.]
Light, līt, *n. That which shines and enables us to see*; that by which objects are made perceptible to the sight; that flood of luminous rays which flows from the sun, and constitutes day; the dawn of day; life; anything that gives light, as a lamp, &c.; the manner in which the light strikes upon a picture; illumination of mind; knowledge; open view; public view; illustration; means of understanding; point of view; a window or pane of glass; a place that admits light to enter; spiritual illumination; comfort; he or that which gives spiritual light.—*a. Bright; clear*; not dark or obscure; white or whitish as to colour. *vt. To give light to*; to set fire to; to attend with a light; to fill or spread over with light; to enlighten. [Sax. *liht*—Goth. *liuhan*, to shine.]
Light, līt, *a.* Having little weight; not heavy; not burdensome; easy to be lifted, borne, or carried by physical strength; not oppressive; not difficult; easy to be digested; active; nimble; not laden; slight; not important; not dense; small; inconsiderate; unsteady; unsettled; gay; trifling; wanton; sandy; wanting depth, as a soil.—*adv.* Lightly; cheaply; commonly. [Sax. *leoht*.]
Light, līt, *vi. To descend or alight*, as from a horse or carriage; to stoop from flight, as a bird; to fall on; to come to by chance. (With *on* or *upon*.) [Sax. *lihtan—hliht*, not heavy.]
Lighted, līt'ed, *p.a.* Set on fire; caused to burn.

Lighten, līt'n, *vi. To shine*; to burst forth or dart, as lightning; to flash; to grow lighter; to fall; to light.—*vt. To illuminate*; to dissipate the darkness of; to fill with light; to illuminate with knowledge; to free from trouble and fill with joy. [Sax. *lihtan*.]
Lighten, līt'n, *vt. To make lighter*; to reduce in weight; to make less heavy; to make less burdensome or afflictive; to cheer. [Sax. *lihtan*.]
Lighter, līt'er, *n. One who lights*; a large, open, flat-bottomed boat, used to *lighten* ships of their burden, as well as in loading them.
Light-fingered, līt'fing-gėrd, *a.* Dexterous in taking and conveying away; thievish; addicted to petty thefts.
Light-footed, līt'fut-ed, *a.* Nimble; active.
Light-headed, līt'hed-ed, *a.* Thoughtless; unsteady; delirious.
Light-hearted, līt'härt-ed, *a.* Free from grief or anxiety; gay; cheerful; merry.
Light-horse, līt'hors, *n. Light-armed* cavalry.
Lighthouse, līt'hous, *n. A tower with a light* or number of lamps on the top, intended to direct seamen in navigating ships at night.
Light-infantry, līt'in-fant-ri, *n. A body* of active and strong men *lightly* armed, and selected for rapid evolutions.
Lightly, līt'li, *adv.* With little weight; without reason, or for reasons of little weight; cheerfully; nimbly; airily; without heed or care.
Lightness, līt'nes, *n. State or quality of being light*; want of weight; unsteadiness; giddiness; wantonness; agility.
Lightning, līt'ning, *n. That which flashes*; the sudden and vivid flash that precedes thunder, produced by a discharge of atmospheric electricity; brightening, as of the mental powers. [from *lighten*.]
Lightning-rod, līt'ning-rod, *n. A metallic rod to protect* buildings or vessels *from lightning*.
Lights, līts, *n. pl.* The lungs, generally of animals, so called from their comparative *lightness*.
Lightsome, līt'sum, *a. Luminous*; gay; cheering; exhilarating.
Lightsomeness, līt'sum-nes, *n. Quality of being light*; luminousness; cheerfulness; merriment; levity.
Ligneous, lig'nē-us, *a. Woody*; wooden; made of wood; consisting of wood; resembling wood. [L. *ligneus—lignum*, wood.]
Like, līk, *a.* Equal in quantity, quality, or degree; similar; probable; likely; that is, having the resemblance or appearance of an event; giving reason to expect or believe.—*n.* Some person or thing *resembling* another; an equal; a counterpart; copy.—*adv.* In the same manner; in a manner becoming; likely; probably. [Sax. *lic*, Goth. *leiks*, like.]
Like, līk, *vt.* To be *pleased with* in a moderate degree; to regard with approbation; to approve; to please (with *it*); to liken'.—*vi. To be pleased*; to choose. *ppr.* liking, *pret. & pp.* liked. [Sax. *lician*, Goth. *leikan*, to please.]
Likelihood, līk'li-hud, *n.* Probability; appearance of truth or reality.
Likely, līk'li, *a.* Probable; such as is more reasonable than the contrary. *adv.* Probably.
Liken, līk'n, *vt.* To compare; to represent as resembling or similar. [Goth. *leikon*.]
Likeness, līk'nes, *n. Quality of being*

like; resemblance in form; similarity; guise; one who resembles another; a picture resembling a person or thing; a portrait.
Likening, līk'n-ing, *p.n.* The forming of resemblance.
Likewise, līk'wīs, *adv. In like manner*; also; moreover; too.
Liking, līk'ing, *p.n.* Inclination; desire; preference; healthful appearance; plumpness; delight in.
Lilac, lī'lak, *n. A beautiful and fragrant shrub*, supposed to be so called because the scent of its flowers resembles that of the *lily*.—*a. Having the colour of the lilac.* [G. *lilak*—L. *lilium*, a lily.]
Lilied, li'lid, *p.a.* Embellished with lilies.
Lily, li'li, *n. A plant producing flowers of great beauty* and variety of colours, the original species being white, and of a *delicious* perfume. [Sax. *lilia*—L. *lilium*—Sans. *lal*, to enjoy pleasure.]
Limb, lim, *n. A jointed and divisible part of animals*; a member; a projecting part, as the arm or leg; a branch or bough of a tree.—*vt.* To dismember; to tear off the limbs of. [Sax. *lim*; Icel. *lima*, to divide limb by limb.]
Limb, lim, *n. Edge or border*; the graduated edge of a quadrant; the border of the disk of the sun, moon, or of a planet, &c. [L. *limbus*, an edge.]
Limbed, limd, *p.a.* In *composition*, as large-limbed.
Limber, lim'bėr, *a.* Flexible; pliant; yielding. [Dan. *lempe*, to adapt.]
Limberness, lim'bėr-nes, *n. Quality of being limber*; flexibleness.
Limbmeal, lim'mēl, *a.* Piecemeal.
Limbo, lim'bō, *n. A supposed region bordering on* hell; in the creed of the Roman Catholic church, a place for the souls of good men until the coming of our Saviour; a place of restraint. [L. *limbus*, an edge.]
Lime, līm, *n. Slime; any viscous substance*; bird-lime; calcareous earth, obtained chiefly from limestone by burning, and used in the preparation of *mortars and cements*, and also as a manure. [Sax.; Icel. *lim*, glue.]—*vt.* To *smear with lime*, or with a viscous substance; to entangle; to manure with lime; to cement. *ppr.* liming, *pret. & pp.* limed. [Sax. *getiman*.]
Lime, līm, *n. A species of orange-tree* and its fruit. [Fr.]
Lime-kiln, līm'kil, *n. A furnace in which stones or shells are exposed to a strong heat*, and reduced to *lime*.
Limestone, līm'stōn, *n. Stone of which lime is made* by the application of strong heat; calcareous rocks.
Lime-tree, līm'trē, *n.* The linden-tree, so named from the *glutinous* nature of its young shoots and rind.
Limit, lim'it, *n. Boundary*; utmost extent; the part that terminates a thing; the thing which bounds; restraint; check; a limb; (pl.) the extent of the liberties of a prison.—*vt. To bound*; to circumscribe; to restrain; to restrain from a lax or general signification; to restrict. [L. *limes, limitis—limus*, transverse.]
Limitable, lim'it-a-bl, *a. That may be limited* or restrained.
Limitation, lim-it-ā'shon, *n. Act of limiting*; restriction; confinement. [L. *limitatio*.]
Limited, lim'it-ed, *p.a.* Narrow; circumscribed; confined; restricted.
Limiting, lim'it-ing, *p.a.* Restricting; restraining.

---

ch, chain; j, *job*; g, *go*; ng, *sing*; ᴛʜ, *then*; th, *thin*; w, *wig*; wh, *whig*; zh, *azure*; † obsolete.

Limn, lim, *vt.* To draw or paint; or to paint in water-colours. [Fr. *enluminer*—L. *lumen*, light.]

Limner, lim'nėr, *n.* One who limns; one who colours or paints on paper or parchment; a portrait-painter.

Limning, lim'ing, *p.n.* The act or art of drawing or painting in water-colours.

Limp, limp, *i.* To halt; to be stopped or stayed in the free action of the limbs; to walk lamely.—*n.* A halt; act of limping. [Old G. *limphen*, to halt.]

Limpet, lim'pet, *n.* A marine mollusc, adhering to rocks. [L. *lepas*—Gr. *lepas*, a bare rock.]

Limpid, lim'pid, *a.* Clear; crystal; pellucid. [L. *limpidus*.]

Limpidity, lim-pid'i-ti, *n.* Clearness; purity; transparency. [Fr. *limpidité*.]

Limping, limp'ing, *p.a.* Halting.

Limy, lim'i, *a.* Viscous; glutinous; containing lime; having the qualities of lime.

Linch-pin, linsh'pin, *n.* A pin used to prevent the wheel of a carriage from sliding off the *axle-tree*. [Sax. *lynis*, an axle-tree.]

Linden, **Lind**, lind'en, lind, *n.* The lime-tree, or teil-tree, whose inner bark is often made into ropes, mats, &c. [Sax. *lind*—Sw. *linda*, a rope.]

Line, lin, *n.* A thread of flax; a slender string; anything extended in length; that which has length without breadth or thickness; a mark in the hand or face; sketch; contour; outline; exterior limit of a figure; the words and letters in printing, &c., which stand on a level in one row; a verse in poetry; a note; a row of soldiers; the disposition of a fleet prepared for engagement; a trench or rampart; method; disposition; limit; border; equator; a series or succession of progeny; the twelfth part of an inch; a straight direction; employment; course; the regular infantry of an army. [L. *linea*—*linum*, flax.]

Line, lin, *vt.* To cover on the inside with *linen* or other material; to put in the inside; to place along by the side of for security; to strengthen by additional works or men; to cover; to add a covering to; to strengthen with anything added. *ppr.* lining, *pret. & pp.* lined. [from L. *linum*, flax.]

Lineage, li'ne-āj, *n.* Descendants in a line from a common progenitor; race. [Fr. *lignage*.]

Lineal, li'ne-al, *a.* Composed of lines; delineated; in a direct line from an ancestor; derived from ancestors; allied by direct descent; in the direction of a line. [Fr. *linéal*.]

Lineally, li'ne-al-li, *adv.* In a direct line.

Lineament, li'ne-a-ment, *n.* One of the *lines* which mark the features; feature; form; make; (pl.) the outline or exterior of a body or figure, particularly of the face. [Fr. *linéament*.]

Linear, li'ne-ėr, *a.* Consisting of lines; in a straight direction; like a line; slender. [Fr. *linéaire*.]

Linen, lin'en, *n.* Cloth made of flax; the under part of dress, as being chiefly of linen.—*a.* Made of flax; resembling linen cloth; white; pale. [Fr. *lin*—L. *linum*, flax.]

Liner, lin'ėr, *n.* A vessel belonging to a regular line of packets.

Ling, ling, *n.* A fish of the northern seas, resembling the cod in form, but longer and more slender. [D. *leng*, from *lengen*, to lengthen.]

Linger, ling'gėr, *vi.* To draw out the time; to wait long; to loiter; to be slow in deciding; to hesitate; to remain long in any state.—*vt.* To protract. [Sax. *langian*, to draw out.]

Lingerer, ling'gėr-ėr, *n.* One who lingers.

Lingering, ling'gėr-ing, *p.a.* Protracted. *p.n.* A delaying; a remaining long.

Lingual, lin'gwal, *a.* Pertaining to the *tongue*.—*n.* A consonant pronounced with the tongue, as *l*. [from L. *lingua*, the tongue.]

Linguist, lin'gwist, *n.* A person skilled in *languages*. [Fr. *linguiste*.]

Linguistic, lin-gwist'ik, *a.* Relating to the affinities of *languages*. [Fr. *linguistique*.]

Liniment, lin'i-ment, *n.* A species of soft *ointment*; an embrocation. [Fr.—L. *lino*, to besmear.]

Lining, lin'ing, *p.n.* The covering of the inner surface of anything; that which is within; contents.

Link, lingk, *n.* The joining of two things; a joint; a single ring of a chain; anything closed like a link; anything connecting.—*vi.* To be connected.—*vt.* To join or connect, as by links; to unite by something intervening. [G. *gelenk*, a joint.]

Link, lingk, *n.* A torch made of tow or hards, &c., and pitch. [Gr. *luchnos*.]

Linnet, lin'net, *n.* The flax-bird; a well-known song-bird. [Sax. *linetwige*—L. *linum*, flax.]

Linseed, **Lintseed**, lin'sēd, lint'sēd, *n.* Flax-seed. [Sax. *linsæd*.]

Linseed-oil, lin'sēd-oil, *n.* Oil obtained by pressure from *flax-seed*.

Linsey-woolsey, lin'sē-wul-sē, *a.* Made of linen and wool; vile; mean.—*n.* Stuff made of linen and wool mixed.

Linstock, lin'stok, *n.* A match.

Lint, lint, *n.* Flax; more generally linen scraped into a soft substance, and used for dressing wounds. [Sax. *linet*—L. *linum*, flax.]

Lintel, lin'tel, *n.* The head-piece of a door-frame or window-frame; the part of the frame that lies on the side pieces. [Sp.—L. *limen*, a threshold.]

Lintseed, lint'sēd, *n.* See LINSEED.

Lion, li'on, *n.* A quadruped, very strong, fierce, and rapacious, remarkable for its roar and magnanimity; a sign in the zodiac, Leo; an object of interest and curiosity. [Fr.—L. *leo*, *leonis*, Gr. *leōn*—Heb. *yelel*, the howling of wild beasts in the desert.]

Lionel, li'on-el, *n.* A young lion.

Lioness, li'on-es, *n.* The female of the lion kind.

Lion-hearted, li'on-härt-ed, *a.* Having a lion's heart or courage.

Lip, lip, *n.* The border of the mouth, necessary for the utterance of *articulate sounds*, or speech; the edge of anything. [Sax. *lippe*.]

Lipped, lipt, *p.a.* Having lips; having a raised or rounded edge like a lip.

Liquefaction, li-kwē-fak'shon, *n.* Act or operation of *liquefying*; the conversion of a solid into a liquid by the sole agency of heat; state of being melted. [L. *liquefactio*.]

Liquefier, li'kwē-fi-ėr, *n.* That which liquefies or melts any solid substance.

Liquefy, li'kwē-fi, *vt.* To reduce to a liquid state; to melt; to dissolve; to convert from a solid form to that of a liquid; to melt by the sole agency of heat.—*vi.* To become liquid. *ppr.* liquefying, *pret. & pp.* liquefied. [Fr. *liquéfier*—L. *liqueo*, to be fluid, and *facio*, to make.]

Liquescence, li-kwes'sen-si, *n.* Aptness to become liquid. [L. *liquescentia*.]

Liquescent, li-kwes'sent, *a.* Becoming liquid; melting. [L. *liquescens*—*liqueo*, to be liquid.]

Liquid, li'kwid, *a.* That flows; fluid; not solid; watery; soft; clear; smooth, as melody; smooth, as certain letters. *n.* A flowing substance; a fluid; a letter which has a smooth flowing sound, as *l* and *r*. [L. *liquidus*—*liqueo*, to be liquid.]

Liquidate, li'kwid-at, *vt.* To dissolve; to settle; to settle, adjust, and satisfy, as a debt. *ppr.* liquidating, *pret. & pp.* liquidated. [Low L. *liquido*, *liquidatus*.]

Liquidation, li-kwid-ā'shon, *n.* Act of liquidating; act of settling and adjusting debts. [Fr.]

Liquidity, li-kwid'i-ti, *n.* Quality of being fluid or liquid; thinness. [Fr. *liquidité*.]

Liquidize, li'kwid-iz, *vt.* To reduce to the liquid state. *ppr.* liquidizing, *pret. & pp.* liquidized.

Liquidness, li'kwid-nes, *n.* The quality of being liquid; fluency.

Liquor, li'kėr, *n.* A liquid or fluid substance (commonly applied to spirituous fluids). [L.]

Liquorice, li'kėr-is, *n.* See LICORICE.

Lisp, lisp, *vi.* To speak with a vicious utterance, as in pronouncing *th* for *s*; to speak imperfectly.—*vt.* To pronounce with a lisp.—*n.* The act of lisping, as in uttering an aspirated *th* for *s*. [Old G. *lispjan*, to lisp.]

Lisper, lisp'ėr, *n.* One who lisps.

Lisping, lisp'ing, *p.a.* Uttering with a lisp.—*p.n.* The act of speaking with a lisp.

List, list, *n.* A strip of cloth; the selvedge of cloth; [It. *lissa*, lists, pales] a line inclosing a piece of ground, or field of combat (generally plural); (pl.) the ground or field inclosed for a race or combat; a limit or boundary; a border; [Fr. *liste*] a roll, register, or catalogue. *vt.* To register in a list; to enrol; to enlist; to inclose for combat; to sew together, as strips of cloth; to form a border to; to cover with a list, or with strips of cloth.—*vi.* To engage in public service by enrolling one's name in a list; to enlist. [Sax. a list of cloth.]

List, list, *vi.* To wish; to incline; to desire or choose; to attend; to listen. [Sax. *lystan*—Old G. *lust*, desire.]

List, list, *vt.* or *i.* To listen.

Listen, lis'n, *vi.* To hearken; to give ear; to hearken secretly; to attend closely with a view to hear; to obey; to follow admonition.—*vt.* To hear; to attend. [Sax. *hlystan*—Old G. *hlosén*, to hear.]

Listener, lis'n-ėr, *n.* One who listens.

Listening, lis'n-ing, *p.a.* Giving attention.—*p.n.* Act of listening.

Listless, list'les, *a.* Having no wish; indifferent; careless; uninterested; languid; weary. [from *list*, to wish.]

Listlessly, list'les-li, *adv.* Without attention; heedlessly.

Listlessness, list'les-nes, *n.* State of being listless; inattention; heedlessness.

Litany, li'ta-ni, *n.* A general and solemn form of *supplication* to God for mercy. [Fr. *litanie*—Gr. *litaneuō*, to pray.]

Literal, li'te-ral, *a.* According to the *letter*, consisting of letters; following the letter or exact words; not figurative; not free, as a translation. [Old Fr.—L. *litera*, a letter.]

Literally, li'te-ral-li, *adv.* In a literal manner; not figuratively; word by word.

Literary, li'te-ra-ri, *a.* Pertaining to

Fāte, fär, fat, fȧll; mē, met, hėr; pine, pin; nōte, not, move; tūbe, tub, bull; oil, pound.

letters or literature; respecting learning or learned men; derived from erudition, as reputation; furnished with erudition; consisting in letters, or written or printed compositions. [L. *literarius.*]
Literate, li'te-rāt, *a. Lettered;* learned; literary.—*n.* One educated, but not at a university. [L. *literatus.*]
Literati, li-te-rā'tī, *n. pl. Men of letters;* the learned; men of erudition. [L. pl. of *literātus.*]
Literature, li'te-ra-tūr, *n. Learning;* acquaintance with letters or books; skill in letters; erudition; the collective body of literary productions; belles-lettres. [Old Fr.]
Litharge, li'thärj, *n.* The *vitrified lead* which is separated *from silver* in the process of refining; the spume or scum of silver. [Fr.—Gr. *lithos,* a stone, and *argyros,* silver.]
Lithe, līҭн, *a.* Pliant; flexible; limber. [Sax. *lith.*]
Litheness, līҭн'nes, *n. Flexibility;* pliability; limberness.
Lither, līҭн'ėr, *a.* Soft; pliant.
Lithograph, li'thō-graf, *vt. To trace,* as *letters or figures on stone,* and transfer them to paper, &c.—*n.* A print from a *drawing on stone.* [Gr. *lithos,* a stone, and *graphō,* to write.]
Lithographed, li'thō-graft, *p.a. Formed by tracing letters* or figures *on stone.*
Lithographer, li-thog'raf-ėr, *n.* One *who practises lithography.*
Lithographic, li-thō-graf'ik, *a. Pertaining to lithography.*
Lithography, li-thog'ra-fi, *n.* The *art of tracing letters, figures, or other designs, on stone,* and of transferring them to paper by impression. [Gr. *lithos,* a stone, and *graphō,* a writing.]
Lithotomist, li-thot'ō-mist, *n.* One who *practises lithotomy.*
Lithotomy, li-thot'ō-mi, *n.* The *operation of cutting for the stone* in the bladder. [Gr. *lithos,* a stone, and *tomē,* a cutting—*temnō,* to cut.]
Litigable, li'ti-ga-bl, *a. Subject to litigation.*
Litigant, li'ti-gant, *a. Contending* in law; engaged in a lawsuit.—*n.* A person engaged in a *legal contest* or lawsuit. [Fr.]
Litigate, li'ti-gāt, *vt. To contest in law;* to debate by judicial process. *ppr.* litigating, *pret. & pp.* litigated. [L. *litigo, litigatus*—L. *lis, litis,* strife, and *ago,* to carry on.]
Litigation, li-ti-gā'shon, *n.* The *act or process of litigating,* or of carrying on a suit in a court of law or equity for the recovery of a right or claim; a judicial contest. [Low L. *litigatio.*]
Litigator, li'ti-gāt-ėr, *n.* One who *litigates.* [L.]
Litigious, li-ti'ji-us, *a. Full of disputes;* wrangling; inclined to judicial contest; disputable. [Fr. *litigieux.*]
Litigiously, li-ti'ji-us-li, *adv.* In a contentious manner.
Litigiousness, li-ti'ji-us-nes, *n. Quality of being litigious.*
Litter, lit'ėr, *n. A couch;* a vehicle formed with shafts supporting a bed between them, in which a person may be borne by men or by a horse; a bed of straw for horses, &c.; waste matters scattered on a floor; [Icel. *lidr,* generation] *a brood or birth of young pigs,* &c.—*vt.* To strew or scatter straw, hay, &c., as a bed for horses, &c.; to scatter over carelessly with shreds and the like; to cover with straw or hay; to supply with litter; to give birth to.

vi. To bring forth young, as swine. [Fr. *litière*—L. *lectus,* a bed.]
Littered, lit'tėrd, *p.a. Covered with litter.*
Little, lit'l, *a. Small* in size or extent; not great or large; short in duration; of small dignity; of small force; slight. *comp.* less, lesser, *sup.* least.—*n. A small* portion, quantity, or amount; a small space; anything small; not much; miniature.—*adv. In a small degree;* not much; in some degree; slightly. [Sax. *lytel,* Goth. *leitils,* small.]
Littleness, lit'l-nes, *n. State or quality of being little;* smallness of size or bulk; meanness; penuriousness.
Littoral, lit'tōr-al, *a.* Belonging to a shore, as of the sea. [L. *littus, littoris,* the shore.]
Liturgic, Liturgical, li-tėr'jik, li-tėr'-jik-al, *a. Pertaining to a liturgy.*
Liturgist, li'tėr-jist, *n. One versed in or attached to a liturgy.*
Liturgy, li'tėr-ji, *n. A public service or office;* a form of prayer and thanksgiving to be used in public worship. [Gr. *leitourgia*—*leitos,* public, and *ergon,* service.]
Live, liv, *vi. To breathe;* to be in a state of animation; to be alive; to exist; to continue; to dwell; to have settled residence in any place; not to perish; to pass life or time in a particular manner; to enjoy life; to be in a state of happiness; to be nourished and supported in life; to be supported, as by one's labour; to float; not to sink or founder, as a ship.—*vt.* To lead; to continue in, constantly or habitually. *ppr.* living, *pret. & pp.* lived. [Sax. *lybban*—Sans, *fiv.*]
Live, līv, *a. Having life;* having respiration; not dead; having vegetable life; ignited; glowing; vivid, as colour.
Lived, līvd, *p.a. Having a life;* as, longlived.
Livelihood, līv'li-hud, *n. Means of living;* maintenance; sustenance; active vigour.
Liveliness, līv'li-nes, *n. Quality or state of being lively;* sprightliness; spirit; an appearance of life or spirit; briskness, effervescence, as of liquors.
Livelong, liv'long, *a. That lives* or endures *long;* tedious.
Lively, liv'li, *a. Vivacious;* active; nimble; spirited; airy; gay; vivid. *adv.* Briskly; with strong resemblance of life.
Liver, liv'ėr, *n. One who lives;* a dweller; an eater of food.
Liver, liv'ėr, *n.* A glandular entrail of the body, of a deep red colour, lying under the false ribs on the right side, and serving to secrete the bile. [Sax. *lifer.*]
Liveried, li've-rid, *p.a. Wearing a livery,* as servants.
Livery, liv'e-ri, *n. Deliverance*†; the writ by which possession is obtained; a form of dress which noblemen and gentlemen *deliver* to their servants to distinguish them; a particular dress peculiar to particular persons; state of being kept at a certain rate, as horses; the whole body of liverymen in the city of London.—*vt.* To clothe in livery [Fr. *livrée*—L. *libero, liberatus,* to deliver.]
Liveryman, li've-ri-man, *n. One who wears a livery;* a freeman of the city of London.
Live-stock, liv'stok, *n. Living stock;* horses, cattle, &c., for *stocking* a farm.
Livid, liv'id, *a. Black and blue;* of a lead colour; discoloured, as flesh by contu-

sion. [Fr. *livide*—L. *liveo,* to be black and blue.]
Lividness, liv'id-nes, *n. State or quality of being livid,* or black and blue.
Living, liv'ing, *p.a. Having life;* issuing continually from the earth; flowing; producing action and vigour; quickening.—*p.n.* He *or those who are alive* (usually with a plural signification); means of subsistence; livelihood; the benefice of a clergyman.
Lizard, li'zėrd, *n.* A reptile having feet resembling human arms. [Fr. *lésard*—L. *lacertus.*]
Llama, lä'mä, *n.* A mammal allied to the camel, found in South America.
Lo, lō, *exclam. Look; see;* behold; observe. [Sax. *la.*]
Loach, lōch, *n.* A small fish inhabiting little and clear swift streams. [Fr. *loche.*]
Load, lōd, *vt. To lade;* to burden; to freight; to weigh down; to encumber; to make heavy by something added or appended; to bestow in great abundance; to charge, as a gun. [Sax. *hladan,* to load.]—*n.* A burden; weight; cargo; a large quantity borne; a grievous weight; oppression or violence of blows; a quantity of food or drink that oppresses. [Sax. *hlad,* a load.]
Loading, lōd'ing, *p.n.* A cargo; a burden; anything that makes part of a load.
Loadstar, Lodestar, lōd'stär, *n.* The star that leads; the polestar.
Loadstone, lōd'stōn, *n.* A *stone that leads;* magnetic iron-ore, which possesses the peculiar properties of attracting iron, and of turning toward the north when freely suspended. [Sax. *lædan,* to lead, and *stone.*]
Loaf, lōf, *n.* Loaves, lōvz, *pl.* A mass of bread as it is formed by the *baker;* a mass or lump, as of sugar; any thick mass. [Sax. *hlaf.*]
Loam, lōm, *n.* A species of earth or mould of an *adhesive tenacious* character, and of different colours. *vt. To cover with loam.* [Sax. *lam*—L. *limus,* slime.]
Loamy, lōm'i, *a. Consisting of loam;* partaking of the nature of loam.
Loan, lōn, *n. Act of lending;* that which is lent; something delivered for temporary use, on condition that it shall be returned; a sum of money raised by contribution, and lent to a government at a fixed rate of interest; a furnishing.—*vt. To lend.* [Sax. *læn.*]
Loath, lōth, *a. Hating;* not inclined; reluctant. [Sax. *lath,* hateful, evil.]
Loathe, lōҭн, *vt. To hate;* to look on with hatred; to abominate; to feel disgust at, as at food or drink. *ppr.* loathing, *pret. & pp.* loathed. [Sax. *lathian.*]
Loathful, lōҭн'ful, *a. Hating;* abhorring through disgust; abhorred; hated.
Loathing, lōҭн'ing, *p.n.* Extreme disgust; abhorrence.
Loathness, lōth'nes, *n.* Reluctance.
Loathsome, lōҭн'som, *a. Hateful;* abhorred; exciting disgust; causing fastidiousness. [Old G. *leidsam.*]
Loathsomely, lōҭн'som-li, *adv. In a loathsome manner.*
Loathsomeness, lōҭн'som-nes, *n. The quality of being loathsome.*
Lob, lob, *vt.* To let fall heavily.
Lobby, lob'bi, *n. A covered walk or place;* an opening before a room, or an entrance into a principal apartment; a small hall or waiting-room; a small apartment taken from a hall or entry. [G. *laube,* an arbour.]

Lobe, lōb, n. The lower, soft part of the ear; a part or division of the brain, or of the lungs, &c.; a division of a simple leaf. [Fr.]

Lobster, lob'ster, n. *The strong* or *mighty leaper*; a well-known shell-fish, much esteemed for food. [Sax. *loppestre—loppe*, a flea, and *strec*, strong.]

Local, lō'kal, a. Pertaining to a place; confined to a place or definite district. [Fr.—L. *locus*, a place.]

Localism, lō'kal-izm, n. State of being *local*; a word or phrase limited to a particular place.

Locality, lō-kal'i-ti, n. State of being local; existence in a place, or in a certain portion of space; position; situation; place. [Fr. *localité*.]

Localize, lō'kal-iz, vt. To make local. *ppr.* localizing, *pret. & pp.* localized.

Locally, lō'kal-li, adv. *With respect to place;* in place.

Locate, lō'kāt, vt. To place; to set in a particular spot or position. *ppr.* locating, *pret. & pp.* located. [L. *loco, locatus—locus,* a place.]

Location, lō-kā'shon, n. Act of locating or placing; situation with respect to place. [Fr.]

Lock, lok, n. *That which shuts in or fastens;* an instrument used to fasten doors, chests, and the like; a place which is locked up; the part of a gun, pistol, &c., by which fire is produced for the discharge of the piece; a barrier to confine the water of a stream; an inclosure in a canal, with gates at each end, used in raising or lowering boats as they pass from one level to another.—vt. *To fasten with a lock,* as a door to fasten so as to impede motion, as wheels; to shut up, as with a lock; to close fast; to encircle; to furnish with locks, as a canal; to confine; to seize, as the sword-arm of an antagonist, by a peculiar movement.—vi. To become fast; to unite closely by mutual insertion. [Sax. *loc;* Old G. *lûhhan,* to close.]

Lock, lok, n. A quantity of hair hanging, and therefore fit to be *cut*, together; a tuft or ringlet of hair; a tuft of wool, hay, or other like substance. [Sax. *loc;* Old G. *loh,* a lock of hair.]

Locked, lokt, p.a. Closely embraced.

Locker, lok'ėr, n. A close place, as a drawer in a ship, that may be closed with a *lock*; a small cupboard.

Locket, lok'et, n. *A small lock;* a catch or spring to fasten a necklace or other ornament; a little gold case worn as an ornament, often containing a lock of hair. [Fr. *loquet,* a latch.]

Lockram, lok'ram, n. A sort of coarse linen.

Locksmith, lok'smith, n. An artificer *who makes or mends locks.*

Locomotion, lō-kō-mō'shon, n. Act or power of moving from place to place. [Fr.—L. *locus,* a place, and *moveo,* to move.]

Locomotive, lō-kō-mō'tiv, a. *Moving from place to place.*—n. A steam-engine placed on wheels, and employed in *moving* a train of carriages on a railway. [Fr. *locomotif*.]

Locust, lō'kust, n. The name given to insects having a grasshopper-like body, which are often so numerous in some parts of Africa and Asia that they fly in immense *flocks* like clouds, and eat up all vegetation; a name of several plants and trees. [L. *locusta.*]

Lodge, loj, vt. To place; to plant; to infix; to settle in the heart, mind, or memory; to furnish with a temporary habitation; to entertain; to cover; to contain for keeping; to beat down so as to entangle, as grain.—vi. To reside; to rest in a place; to rest or dwell for a time; to fall down and become entangled, as grain. *ppr.* lodging, *pret. & pp.* lodged.—n. A hut; a small house in a park or forest; a temporary habitation; a small house appended to a larger; a den; any place where a wild beast dwells; a meeting of free-masons, or the place where they meet. [Sax. *logian,* to place, lodge.]

Lodger, loj'ėr, n. *One who lodges,* or who lives at board, or in a hired room; one who resides in any place for a time.

Lodging, loj'ing, p.n. A *place of rest* for a night, or of residence for a time; apartment; a part of a house let to another, usually termed lodgings; place of residence; harbour; place of rest; convenience for repose at night.

Lodgment, loj'ment, n. *Act of lodging,* or the state of being lodged; accumulation of something deposited or remaining at rest; an encampment made by an army; a work cast up by besiegers during their approaches, in some dangerous post.

Loffet, lof, vi. To laugh.

Loft, loft, n. That which is *lifted* up; a room or space next under the roof; a story or floor above another; a gallery or small chamber raised within a larger apartment or in a church. [Sax. *lyft;* Icel. *lopta,* to raise.]

Loftily, loft'i-li, adv. *In a lofty manner.*

Loftiness, loft'i-nes, n. *State or quality of being lofty;* height; altitude; haughtiness; dignity; elevation of diction or sentiment.

Lofty, loft'i, a. *Aërial; lifted up;* high; elevated in condition or character; characterised by pride; haughty; sublime; stately; majestic. [Old G. *luftig,* aërial.]

Log, log, n. *Something that is heavy;* a bulky piece of wood unhewed; a machine for measuring the rate of a ship's velocity through the water. [D. *log,* heavy.]

Logarithm, log'a-rithm, n. Logarithms are a series of arranged numbers in *arithmetical* progression, corresponding to a series of common numbers in geometrical progression, intended to facilitate arithmetical operations. [Fr. *logarithme*—Gr. *arithmos,* number, and *logos,* of the ratios.]

Logarithmic, Logarithmical, log-a-rith'mik, log-a-rith'mik-al, a. Pertain*ing to logarithms;* consisting of logarithms.

Logarithmically, log-a-rith'mik-al-li, a. *By the use or aid of logarithms.*

Log-book, log'buk, n. The register of a ship's way, and of the incidents of the voyage.

Loggat, log'gat, n. A small log or piece of wood; (pl.) an old English game.

Loggerhead, log'ėr-hed, n. *A blockhead;* a dunce; a dolt. [*log* and *head.*]

Logic, lo'jik, n. *The art of reasoning;* the science of pure and formal thought; the science of the laws of thought, as thought. [Fr. *logique*—Gr. *logos,* reason, discourse.]

Logical, lo'jik-al, a. *Pertaining to logic;* used in logic; according to the rules of logic; skilled in logic; rational; relating to reason; according to reason.

Logically, lo'jik-al-li, adv. *According to the rules of logic.*

Logician, lō-ji'shi-an, n. *A person skilled in logic.* [Fr. *logicien.*]

Logman, log'man, n. *A man who carries logs.*

Logwood, log'wud, n. *A heavy kind of wood,* of a deep red colour internally, used as a dye-wood.

Loin, loin, n. The loins are *the region of the kidneys,* the space on each side of the back bone, between the lowest of the false ribs and the upper portion of the haunch bones, called also the reins; in the sing. number, the back of an animal cut for food. [Sax.—L. *renes,* the kidneys.]

Loiter, loi'tėr, vi. *To linger; to tarry;* to saunter; to be slow in moving; to spend time idly. [D. *leuteren;* Goth. *latjan,* to linger.]

Loiterer, loi'tėr-ėr, n. *One who loiters;* a lingerer; one who is sluggish or dilatory.

Loitering, loi'tėr-ing, p.a. *Lingering; delaying.*—p.n. *A lingering or delay.*

Loiteringly, loi'tėr-ing-li, adv. *In a loitering manner.*

Loll, lol, vi. To lean idly or listlessly; to recline; to lie at ease; to hang out, said of the tongue.—vt. To thrust out, as the tongue. [Icel. *loll,* sloth.]

Lone, lōn, a. *Apart from others;* single; solitary; unfrequented; having no company; not having others in the neighbourhood; single or in widowhood. [Icel. *lon,* a breaking off—Sans. *lû,* to cut off.]

Loneliness, lōn'li-nes, n. *State of being lonely;* solitude; love of retirement; disposition to solitude.

Lonely, lōn'li, a. *Being in a lone state;* solitary; without society; forsaken; retired; sequestered; addicted to solitude.

Lonesome, lōn'som, a. *Solitary;* secluded from society.

Lonesomeness, lōn'som-nes, n. *State of being lonesome* or solitary; solitude.

Long, long, a. Drawn out in a line, or in the direction of length; drawn out or extended in time; extended to any certain measure expressed; tedious; continued in a series to a great extent; lingering; extending far in prospect or into futurity.—adv. To a great extent in space or in time; at a point of duration far distant, either prior or posterior; through the whole extent or duration of; by the fault of. [Sax.—Old G. *lang*—L. *longus,* long.]

Long, long, vi. *To draw* or *stretch out the mind after* something; to desire earnestly; to have a preternatural craving. (With *after.*) [Sax. *langian,* to draw.]

Longevity, lon-jev'i-ti, n. *Long life;* length or duration of life; more generally, great length of life. [Fr. *longévité.*]

Longevous, lon-jēv'us, a. *Living a long time;* of great age. [L. *longævus—longus,* long, and *ævum,* an age.]

Longing, long'ing, p.a. Earnestly desiring; having a craving or preternatural appetite.—p.n. An eager desire; a preternatural appetite.

Longish, long'ish, a. *Somewhat long.*

Longitude, lon'ji-tūd, n. *Length;* the distance of any place on the globe from a given meridian, eastward or westward, measured on the equator. [Fr.—L. *longus,* long.]

Longitudinal, lon-ji-tūd'in-al, a. Per*taining to longitude or length;* extending in length; running lengthwise, as distinguished from transverse or across.

Longitudinally, lon-ji-tūd'in-al-li, adv. *In the direction of length.*

Fāte, fär, fat, fall; mē, met, hėr; pīne, pin; nōte, not, mōve; tūbe, tub, bull; oil, pound.

Long-lived, long'livd, a. *Having a long life or existence; living long.*
Longly†, long'li, adv. *With longing desire.*
Long-run, long'run, n. *The whole course of things taken together; the ultimate result.*
Long-sighted, long'sīt-ed, a. *Able to see at a great distance; sagacious.*
Long-spun, long'spun, a. *Spun or extended to a great length; tedious.*
Long-suffering, long'suf-fėr-ing, a. *Bearing injuries or provocation for a long time; patient.*—n. *Long endurance; patience of offence.*
Long-winded, long'wind-ed, a. *Long-breathed; tedious in speaking, argument, or narration.*
Loo, lö, n. *A game at cards.*
Loofed†, löft, a. *Gone to a distance.*
Look, lụk, vi. *To show; to appear; to seem; to direct the eye toward an object, with the intention of seeing it; to direct the intellectual eye; to examine; to take care; to watch; to have a particular direction; to face; to front; to expect.* (When the present object is mentioned, we use either *on* or *at after look*; if it is absent, *for*; if distant, *after*.)—vt. *To have the sight or view of; to influence by looks or presence; to express by a look.*—n. *Act of looking; sight; air of the face; mien; aspect; view; watch.*—interj. *See! lo! behold! observe!* [Sax. *locian*—L. *luceo*, Sans. *ruch*, to shine.]
Looker, lụk'ėr, n. *One who looks.*
Looking, lụk'ing, p.n. *Search or searching.*
Looking-glass, lụk'ing-glas, n. *A glass which reflects the form of the person who looks on it; a mirror.*
Loom, löm, n. *Something of frequent use, to be held and used by the hand; a frame or machine in which a weaver works threads into cloth.* [Sax. *geloma*; Old G. *lômi*, tools; Ir. *lamh*, hand.]
Loom, löm, vi. *To shine; to appear above the surface either of sea or land; to appear larger than the real dimensions, and indistinctly, as a distant object, a ship at sea, or a mountain; to rise, and to be eminent (in a moral sense).* [Sax. *leoman*, to shine.]
Looming, löm'ing, p.n. *The indistinct and magnified appearance of objects seen in particular states of the atmosphere.*
Loon, lön, n. *A rogue; a rascal.*
Loop, löp, n. *A bend; a folding or doubling of a string or a noose, through which a lace or cord may be run for fastening; a small, narrow opening; a loophole.* [Ir. *lub*, a loop.]
Looped, löpt, p.a. *Full of loops.*
Loophole, löp'höl, n. *A small opening in the walls of a fortification or in the bulk-head of a ship, through which small arms are discharged at an enemy; a hole or aperture that gives a passage; a passage for escape.*
Loopholed, löp'höld, a. *Full of holes or openings for escape.*
Loose, lös, vt. *To untie or unbind; to free from any fastening; to release from imprisonment; to free from obligation, or from anything that binds or shackles; to relieve; to detach; to let fly.*—vi. *To set sail; to leave a port or harbour.* ppr. *loosing*, pret. & pp. *loosed.*—a. *Unbound; not fastened or confined; not tight or close, as clothes; not concise; not precise; not strict or rigid; slack; rambling; not attached or enslaved; unchaste; licentious.*—n. *Freedom from restraint; liberty; as, to give loose.* [Sax. *lysan*, *alysan*; Goth. *lausjan*, to untie—Sans. *lunch*, to pluck out.]
Loosely, lös'li, adv. *Not fast; not firmly; irregularly; wantonly; unchastely.*
Loosen, lös'n, vt. *To make loose; to free from restraint; to render less dense; to remove costiveness from.*—vi. *To become loose.* [Old G. *lôsjan.*]
Looseness, lös'nes, n. *State of being loose; a state opposite to that of being tight or compact; habitual deviation from strict rules; unchastity; flux from the bowels.*
Lop, lop, vt. *To cut off, as the top or extreme part of anything; to separate, as superfluous parts; to cut partly off, and bend down.* ppr. *lopping*, pret. & pp. *lopped.*—n. *That which is cut from trees.* [W. *llab*, a stroke—Sans. *lamb*, to cut into.]
Lopping, lop'ing, p.n. *The act of cutting off; that which is cut off.*
Loquacious, lo-kwā'shi-us, a. *Talkative; garrulous; babbling.* [L. *loquax*, *loquacis*—*loquor*, to speak.]
Loquacity, lo-kwas'i-ti, n. *Quality of being loquacious; garrulity; the habit of talking continually or excessively.* [Fr. *loquacité.*]
Lord, lord, n. *A nourisher; a guardian; a master; a person possessing supreme power and authority; a ruler; a tyrant; a husband; a baron; the proprietor of a manor; a title of honour to those who are noble by birth or creation; a peer of the realm; an honorary title bestowed on certain official characters; the Supreme Being; Jehovah.*—vi. *To act as a lord; to domineer; to rule with arbitrary or despotic sway.* (Generally with *it* or *over*.) [Sax. *hláford*—Goth. *hlaifs*, bread, and *vardjan*, to keep.]
Lordliness, lord'li-nes, n. *Quality of being lordly; high station; pride.*
Lordling, lord'ling, n. *A little or diminutive lord.*
Lordly, lord'li, a. *Becoming a lord; pertaining to a lord; grand; dignified; imperious; insolent.*—adv. *Proudly; imperiously.*
Lord's-day, lordz'dā, n. *The Christian Sabbath.* Rev. i. 10.
Lordship, lord'ship, n. *State or quality of being a lord; a title of honour given to noblemen; a title given to judges and certain other persons in authority and office; dominion; power; the territory of a lord over which he holds jurisdiction; a manor.*
Lord's-supper, lordz'sup-ėr, n. *The Christian sacrament of the eucharist.*
Lore, lōr, n. *Learning; doctrine; instruction.* [Sax. *lar—læran*, to teach.]
Lorn, lorn, a. *Lost; forsaken; lonely.* [from Sax. *leoran*. to depart.]
Lose, löz, vt. *To be separated from, as from a thing, so as to have no knowledge of the place where it is; to mislay; to forfeit by unsuccessful contest; to be deprived of; to forfeit, as a penalty; to ruin; to wander from; to bewilder; to possess no longer; to waste; to squander; to throw away; to fail to obtain.*—vi. *To forfeit anything in contest; not to win; to fail; to suffer loss by comparison.* ppr. *losing*, pret. & pp. *lost.* [Sax. *losian*, to lose, to run away.]
Loser, löz'ėr, n. *One who loses.*
Losing, löz'ing, p.a. *Bringing or causing loss.*
Loss, los, n. *A separation from something; privation; deprivation of that which was once possessed; damage; ruin; failure to succeed; waste; exposure.* [Sax. *los.*]
Lost, lost, p.a. *Separated or parted from; mislaid; destroyed; wasted or squandered; forfeited; not able to find the right way, or the place intended; bewildered; alienated; not visible.*
Lot, lot, n. *A part or share; a proportion; a piece or division of land; that which is called chance, that by which the fate of one is determined; something which is used to decide what is as yet undecided; the part, division, or fate which falls to one by chance; fortune.* [Sax. *hlot—hleótan*, to appoint by lot—Icel. *hluti*, a part.]
Lote, löt, n. *The lotus, the Egyptian water-lily; also an African plant.* [L. *lotus.*]
Loth, löth, a. *See* LOATH.
Lotion, lō'shon, n. *A washing; a liquid preparation for washing some part of the body to cleanse it of foulness or deformity.* [L. *lotio—lavo*, to wash.]
Lottery, lot'tė-ri, n. *A scheme for the distribution of prizes by lot or chance, or the distribution itself.* [Fr. *loterie.*]
Loud, loud, a. *High-sounding; having a great sound; striking the ear with great force; noisy; making a great clamour; emphatical; impressive.* adv. *With loudness; loudly.* [Sax. *hlúd*—Icel. *hlióð*, a sound.]
Loudly, loud'li, adv. *With great sound or noise; noisily; clamorously.*
Loudness, loud'nes, n. *Quality of being loud; great sound or noise; uproar.*
Lounge, lounj, vi. *To linger; to spend time lazily; to move idly about; to recline at ease; to loll.* ppr. *lounging*, pret. & pp. *lounged.*—n. *An idle gait or stroll; act of reclining at ease; a place for lounging.* [L. *longus*, long.]
Lounger, lounj'ėr, n. *An idler.*
Lounging, lounj'ing, p.a. *Passing the time in idleness; reclining at ease.*
Louse, lous, n. *Lice, lis, pl. A creeper; a small troublesome insect, of which different species infest the bodies of men, animals, and plants.* [Sax. *lus.*]
Lousiness, louz'i-nes, n. *State of abounding with lice.*
Lousy, louz'i, a. *Swarming with lice; mean; contemptible.* [G. *lausig.*]
Lout, lout, n. *A mean, awkward fellow; a bumpkin; a clown.*—vi. *To treat as a lout or fool; to neglect.* [from *low*, mean.]
Loutish, lout'ish, a. *Clownish; rude; awkward.*
Lovable, luv'a-bl, a. *Worthy of love; amiable.*
Love, luv, vt. *To desire; to long after; to regard with affection, on account of some qualities which excite pleasing sensations or desire of gratification; to have dutiful affection for; to regard with passionate affection; to be enamoured of; to have good-will for.* vi. *To delight; to take pleasure.* ppr. *loving*, pret. & pp. *loved.*—n. *An affection of the mind excited by beauty and worth of any kind; passionate affection; fond attachment; the passion between the sexes; patriotism; the attachment one has to his native land; good-will; the object beloved; a word of endearment; Cupid, the fabled god of love.* [Sax. *lufan*—Sans. *lubh*, to desire.]
Loved, luvd, p.a. *Having the affection of any one.*
Loveless, luv'les, a. *Void of love; void of tenderness.*
Loveliness, luv'li-nes, n. *Quality of being lovely; amiableness.*

---

ch, *chain*; j, *job*; g, *go*; ng, *sing*; ᴡʜ, *then*; th, *thin*; w, *wig*; wh, *whig*; zh, *azure*; † obsolete.

Love-lorn, luv'lorn, *a.* Forsaken by one's love. [See FORLORN.]
Lovely, luv'li, *a.* Lovable; possessing qualities which may invite affection; amiable; charming; delightful; enchanting.
Lover, luv'ėr, *n.* One who loves; one who has a tender affection, particularly for a female; a friend; one who regards with kindness; one who likes or is pleased with anything.
Loving, luv'ing, *p.a.* Fond; kind; affectionate; amorous; expressing love or kindness.
Lovingkindness, luv-ing-kind'nes, *n.* Tender regard; mercy; favour.
Lovingly, luv'ing-li, *adv.* With love; affectionately.
Low, lō, *a.* Having place beneath some other thing or things; laid prostrate; sunk; depressed below any given surface or place; not high or elevated; declining near the horizon; deep; sunk to the natural level of the ocean by the retiring of the tide; below the usual rate; not high or loud; grave; wanting strength; in a humble state; mean; grovelling; dishonourable; not sublime; not exalted in thought or diction; common; reverent; exhausted of vital energy; without force; not intense; in reduced circumstances; plain; not rich, high-seasoned, or nourishing. *adv.* Not aloft; under the usual price; near the ground; in times not remote; with a depressed voice; not loudly; in a state of subjection, poverty, or disgrace. [D. *laag*—Goth. *ligan*, to lie.]
Low, lō, *vi.* To bellow, as an ox or cow. *n.* The noise made by an ox or cow. [Sax. *hlowan*.]
Lower, lō'ėr, *vt.* To cause to descend; to depress; to suffer to sink downward; to bring down, as in rank or feelings; to abase; to bring down, as value or amount; to lessen; to reduce.—*vi.* To fall; to sink; to grow less; *to let down* the brows; to look sullen; to frown; to be clouded; to threaten a storm. [from *low*, the adj.]
Lower, lō'ėr, *a.* Less high or elevated. [comp. of *low*.]
Lowering, lō'ėr-ing, *p.a.* Appearing dark or threatening.—*p.n.* Act of bringing down; the reducing of the strength of any spirituous liquor by mixing water with it.
Loweringly, lō'ėr-ing-li, *adv.* With cloudiness or threatening gloom.
Lowermost, lō'ėr-mōst, *a.* Lowest. [from *low*.]
Lowery, lou'ėr-i, *a.* Cloudy; gloomy.
Lowing, lō'ing, *p.n.* The bellowing or cry of cattle.
Lowliness, lō'li-nes, *n.* Quality or state of being lowly; humility.
Lowly, lō'li, *a.* Not high; having a low esteem of one's own worth; modest; wanting dignity or rank; not lofty. *adv.* Humbly; meekly; modestly; meanly.
Lown', loun, *n.* A low fellow.
Lowness, lō'nes, *n.* State of being low; state of being less elevated than something else; meanness of mind or character; want of dignity; want of sublimity in style or sentiment; submissiveness; want of courage; a state of poverty; depression in strength; depression in price; graveness or softness of sound.
Low-spirited, lō'spi-rit-ed, *a.* Not having animation and courage; dejected.
Lowt, lout. See LOUT.
Low-water, lō'wa-tėr, *n.* The *lowest* point of the ebb or receding tide.

Loyal, loi'al, *a.* Faithful to the laws; faithful to a prince or superior; true to plighted faith, duty, or love; not treacherous. [Fr.—L. *lex, legis*, a law.]
Loyalist, loi'al-ist, *n.* A person who adheres to his sovereign; one who maintains his allegiance to his prince.
Loyally, loi'al-li, *adv.* In a loyal manner.
Loyalty, loi'al-ti, *n.* Faithful adherence to the laws or to allegiance; fidelity to a prince or sovereign, or to a husband or lover. [Fr. *loyauté*.]
Losenge, lo'zenj, *n.* An oblique-angled parallelogram; a figure with four equal sides, having two acute and two obtuse angles; something in the shape of a rhomb; a small cake of sugar, &c. [Fr. *losange*; Gr. *loxos*, slanting, and *gōnia*, an angle.]
Lubber, lub'ėr, *n.* A heavy clumsy fellow; a contemptuous name given by sailors to those who know not the duties of seamen. [W. *llabi*; Icel. *lubbi*.]
Lubberly, lub'ėr-li, *a.* Bulky and heavy; clumsy; lazy.—*adv.* Clumsily.
Lubricate, lū'brik-āt, *vt.* To make smooth or slippery. *ppr.* lubricating, *pret. & pp.* lubricated. [L. *lubrico, lubricatus*—*lubricus*, slippery.]
Lubrication, lū-brik-ā'shon, *n.* Act or process of making smooth or slippery.
Lubricator, lū'brik-āt-ėr, *n.* He or that which lubricates.
Lubricity, lū-bris'i-ti, *n.* Smoothness of surface; slipperiness; aptness to glide over anything; figuratively, slipperiness; instability. [Fr. *lubricité*.]
Lucid, lū'sid, *a.* Full of light; shining; clear; transparent; pellucid; bright with the radiance of intellect; marked by the regular operations of reason; clear and distinct; presenting a clear view; easily understood. [L. *lucidus*—*luceo*, to shine.]
Lucidly, lū'sid-li, *adv.* In a lucid manner; clearly.
Lucidness, lū'sid-nes, *n.* State or quality of being lucid; brightness; clearness.
Lucifer, lū'si-fėr, *n.* That which brings light; the morning star, or the planet Venus, so called from its brightness; Satan. [L. *lux, lucis*, light, and *fero*, to bring.]
Luck, luk, *n.* That which one *gets or obtains*; that which happens to a person; an event, good or ill, affecting a man's interest or happiness, and which is deemed casual; chance; fortune; good fortune. [D. *luk*, fortune; Sans. *lag*, to obtain.]
Luckily, luk'i-li, *adv.* Fortunately.
Luckiness, luk'i-nes, *n.* State of being lucky or fortunate; good fortune.
Luckless, luk'les, *a.* Unfortunate; meeting with ill success; producing no good.
Lucklessly, luk'les-li, *adv.* In a luckless manner; unfortunately.
Lucky, luk'i, *a.* Meeting with good *luck* or success; fortunate; prosperous; auspicious.
Lucrative, lū'krat-iv, *a.* Pertaining to gain; gainful; profitable; making increase of money or goods. [L. *lucrativus*—*lucrum*, gain.]
Lucratively, lū'krat-iv-li, *adv.* In a lucrative manner; profitably.
Lucre, lū'kėr, *n.* Gain in money or goods; profit; emolument. (Usually in an ill sense.) [Fr. *lucre*—L. *lucrum*.]
Lucubration, lū-kū-brā'shon, *n.* Study by *lamp* or candle-light; nocturnal study; that which is composed by night; that which is produced by meditation in retirement. [L. *lucubratio*—*luceo*, to shine.]

Ludicrous, lū'di-krus, *a.* That serves for sport; adapted to raise laughter, without scorn or contempt; comic; ridiculous. [L. *ludicrus*—*ludo*, to play—Sans. *lad*, to play, to jest.]
Ludicrously, lū'di-krus-li, *adv.* Sportively; in burlesque.
Ludicrousness, lū'di-krus-nes, *n.* Quality of being ludicrous; sportiveness.
Lug, lug, *vt.* To pull; to haul; to drag; to pull with force, as something heavy and moved with difficulty; to convey with labour.—*vi.* To drag; to move heavily. *ppr.* lugging, *pret. & pp.* lugged. [Sax. *geluggian*, to pull.]
Luggage, lug'āj, *n.* That which is *dragged* heavily along; a traveller's trunks, packages, &c.; something of more weight than value. [from *lug*.]
Lugger, lug'ėr, *n.* A small vessel carrying three masts with a running bowsprit and long or *lug* sails. [D. *logger*.]
Lugubrious, lū-gū'bri-us, *a.* Mournful; indicating sorrow. [L. *lugubris*—*lugeo*, to mourn.]
Lugubriously, lū-gū'bri-us-li, *adv.* In a mournful manner; mournfully.
Lukewarm, lūk'warm, *a.* Moderately warm; tepid; not zealous; cool; indifferent. [Sax. *wlaco*, warm.]
Lukewarmness, lūk'warm-nes, *n.* State or quality of being lukewarm.
Lull, lul, *vt.* To sing to, as a nurse to a child; to compose; to cause to rest.—*vi.* To subside; to become calm.—*n.* Power or quality of soothing; a reason of quiet or cessation, as of wind &c. [Dan. *lulle*; Sw. *lulla*, to sing to sleep.]
Lullaby, lul'la-bī, *n.* A song to *lull* or quiet *babes*; that which quiets. [*lull*, and *by*, for baby.]
Lulling, lul'ing, *p.a.* Stilling; composing to rest.
Lumbago, lum-bā'gō, *n.* A rheumatic affection of the muscles about the *loins*. [L.—*lumbi*, the loins.]
Lumbar, lum'bar, *a.* Pertaining to or near *the loins*. [L. *lumbus*, a loin.]
Lumber, lum'bėr, *n.* Anything useless and *cumbersome*, or things bulky and thrown aside as of no use.—*vt.* To *fill with lumber*; to heap together in disorder.—*vi.* To move heavily, as if burdened with his own bulk. [D. *belemmeren*, to obstruct.]
Lumbering, lum'bėr-ing, *p.a.* Moving heavily.
Luminary, lū'min-a-ri, *n.* That which *gives light*; any body that gives light, but chiefly one of the celestial orbs; one who illustrates any subject, or enlightens mankind. [Fr. *luminaire*—L. *luceo*, to shine.]
Luminosity, lū-min-os'i-ti, *n.* Quality of being luminous; clearness; perspicuity.
Luminous, lū'min-us, *a.* Full of light; emitting light; clear; lucid; perspicuous. [L. *luminōsus*—*luceo*, to shine.]
Luminously, lū'min-us-li, *adv.* With brightness or clearness.
Lump, lump, *n.* A small mass of matter of no definite shape; a mass of things blended or thrown together without order or distinction; a cluster. *vt.* To throw into a mass; to take in the gross. [G. *klump*.]
Lumping, lump'ing, *p.a.* Bulky; in a mass or lump.
Lumpish, lump'ish, *a.* Like a lump; heavy; gross; bulky; dull; inactive.
Lumpishness, lump'ish-nes, *n.* State or quality of being lumpish; heaviness.
Lumpy, lump'i, *a.* Full of lumps.
Lunacy, lū'na-si, *n.* A species of madness, formerly supposed to be influenced by *the moon* or periodical in the

month; insanity; derangement; mania. [L. *luna*, the moon—*luceo*, to shine.]
Lunar, lū'nar, *a.* Pertaining to the moon; measured by the revolutions of the moon; resembling the moon; orbed. [L. *lunaris*—*luceo*, to shine.]
Lunatic, lū'nat-ik, *a.* Affected by a species of madness, formerly supposed to be influenced by the *moon*; mad; insane.—*n.* A person affected by insanity; a madman. [Fr. *lunatique*—L. *luna*, the moon, *luceo*, to shine.]
Lunation, lū-nā'shon, *n.* A *lunar month*; the time from one new moon to the next. [Fr. *lunatio*.]
Lunch, lunsh, *n.* A slight repast between breakfast and dinner.—*vi.* To take a lunch. [Etym. uncertain.]
Lune, lūn, *n.* Anything in the shape of a half-*moon*; a figure in the form of a crescent; a fit of lunacy†. [L. *luna*.]
Lung, lung, *n.* The lungs are the organs of respiration in man and many other animals, and are of *light* substance. [Sax. *lungen*—Sans. *laghu*, light.]
Lunged, lungd, *p.a.* Having *lungs*, or the nature or resemblance of lungs.
Lupine, lū'pin, *n.* A kind of pulse cultivated in gardens for the sake of the gaily-coloured flowers, so called because it eagerly penetrates into the soil. [Fr. *lupin*—L. *lupus*, a wolf.]
Lurch, lėrch, *n.* A *forlorn condition*; a helpless state; a shifting to one side; a sudden roll of a ship to one side.—*vi.* To roll or pass suddenly to one side, as a ship in a heavy sea; to dodge; to play tricks.—*vt.*† To steal; to pilfer. [Old Fr. *lourche*—Il *demeurra lourche*, he was left in the lurch.]
Lurcher, lėrch'ėr, *n.* One who *lurks*; one who watches to pilfer, or to betray or entrap; a poacher; a dog that lurks or lies in wait for game, and seizes them. [from *lurk*.]
Lure, lūr, *n.* Strong-scented *bait*; something held out to call a hawk; any enticement; that which invites by the prospect of advantage or pleasure.—*vt.* To entice; to invite by anything that promises pleasure or advantage. *ppr.* luring, *pret. & pp.* lured. [Fr. *leurre*, a decoy; G. *luder*, carrion, lure.]
Lurid, lū'rid, *a.* Rendered livid; sallow; wan; ghastly pale; gloomy; dismal. [L. *luridus*—*lorum*, a thong of leather.]
Luring, lūr'ing, *p.a.* Enticing; calling.
Lurk, lėrk, *vi.* To *lie hid*; to lie in wait; to lie concealed or unperceived; to retire from public observation; to keep out of sight. [W. *llercian*, to lurk.]
Lurker, lėrk'ėr, *n.* One who *lurks*.
Lurking, lėrk'ing, *p.a.* Lying concealed; keeping out of sight.
Luscious, lu'shi-us, *a.* Sweet or rich, so as to cloy; sweet to excess; delicious; grateful to the taste; pleasing; delightful, as a description; fulsome, as flattery. [Ar. *lasis*, sweet.]

Lusciously, lu'shi-us-li, *adv.* With *sweetness* or richness that nauseates.
Lusciousness, lu'shi-us-nes, *n.* Quality *of being luscious*.
Lush†, lush, *a.* Full of juice.
Lust, lust, *n.* Longing *desire*; eagerness to possess or enjoy; carnal appetite; depraved affections and desires.—*vi.* To desire eagerly; to long (with *after*); to have carnal desire; to have irregular or inordinate desires. [Sax.; Goth. *lustus*, desire.]
Lustful, lust'ful, *a.* Having *lust*; sensual; licentious; libidinous; inciting to lust, or exciting carnal desire.
Lustfully, lust'ful-li, *adv.* With concupiscence or carnal *desire*.
Lustfulness, lust'ful-nes, *n.* State *of being lustful*.
Lustic†, lust'ik, *a.* Lusty.
Lustihood†, lust'i-hud, *n.* State *of being lusty*.
Lustily, lust'i-li, *adv.* With vigour of body; stoutly.
Lustiness, lust'i-nes, *n.* State or quality *of being lusty*.
Lusting, lust'ing, *p.n.* Eager *desire*; desire of carnal gratification.
Lustration, lus-trā'shon, *n.* Act of *making clear or pure*; a cleansing or purifying by water. [L. *lustratio*—*lustro*, to purify.]
Lustre, lus'tėr, *n.* Clearness; brightness; brilliancy; a candlestick ornamented with drops or pendants of cut glass; the splendour of birth, of deeds, or of fame. [Fr.—L. *luceo*, to shine.]
Lustring, lūs'tring, *n.* A species of *bright* or glossy silk cloth. (Corruptly written and pronounced *lutestring*.) [Fr. *lustrine*.]
Lustrous, lus'trus, *a.* Full of *lustre*; bright; shining; luminous.
Lusty, lust'i, *a.* Full of *lust*; full-sized; bulky; healthful; vigorous; robust; corpulent; hearty; saucy†. [G. *lustig*.]
Lute, lūt, *n.* That which gives forth musical *sounds*; an instrument of music with strings, resembling the guitar. [Fr. *luth*; G. *lauten*, to sound—Old G. *hudon*, to sing.]
Lute, Luting, lūt, lūt'ing, *n.* Mud *or clay*; a composition of clay used for coating vessels when exposed to fire, and also for making their junctures air-tight.—*vt.* To *close or coat with lute*. *ppr.* luting, *pret. & pp.* luted. [L. *lutum*, clay.]
Lutestring, lūt'string, *n.* The *string of a lute*; a kind of glossy silk cloth.
Lutheran, lū'thėr-an, *a.* Pertaining to Luther, the reformer.
Luxation, luks-ā'shon, *n.* Act of forcing a joint from its proper place; the state of being thus put out of joint; a dislocation. [Low L. *luxatio*—L. *luxo*, to put out of joint.]
Luxive†, luks'iv, *a.* Given to luxury.
Luxuriance, luks-ū'ri-ans, *n.* State or

quality *of being luxuriant*; rank growth; exuberance; wanton growth or plenty.
Luxuriant, luks-ū'ri-ant, *a.* Not *confined to ordinary bounds*; exuberant in growth; abundant; exuberant in plenty; superfluous in abundance. [L. *luxurians*—*luxuria*, luxury.]
Luxuriantly, luks-ū'ri-ant-li, *adv.* With exuberant growth.
Luxuriate, luks-ū'ri-āt, *vi.* To grow exuberantly; to feed or live luxuriously; to expatiate with delight. *ppr.* luxuriating, *pret. & pp.* luxuriated. [L. *luxurio, luxuriatum*.]
Luxurious, luks-ū'ri-us, *a.* Rank; indulging excessively the gratification of appetite, or in expensive dress and equipage; voluptuous; administering to luxury; furnished with luxuries; softening by pleasure; libidinous. [Fr. *luxurieux*.]
Luxuriously, luks-ū'ri-us-li, *adv.* Voluptuously.
Luxuriousness, luks-ū'ri-us-nes, *n.* State or quality *of being luxurious*.
Luxury, luks'ū-ri, *n.* Dissoluteness; voluptuousness; sensuality; the free indulgence in costly dress and equipage; that which gratifies a nice and fastidious appetite; any delicious food or drink; anything delightful to the senses; lust†. [L. *luxuria*—*luxo*, to put out of joint.]
Lyceum, lī-sē'um, *n.* A place in Greece where Aristotle taught; a higher school, in the continent of Europe. [L.—Gr. *Lukeion*.]
Lye, lī, *n.* Water impregnated with alkaline salt, imbibed from the *ashes* of wood. [Sax. *leah*—L. *lix*, *licis*, ashes.]
Lying, lī'ing, *p.a.* Telling falsehoods; addicted to falsehood.—*n.* The practice *of telling lies*. [from *lie*.]
Lymn†, lim, *n.* A blood-hound.
Lymph, limf, *n.* A colourless fluid in animal bodies, contained in certain vessels called *lymphatics*. [L. *lympha*.]
Lymphatic, lim-fat'ik, *a.* Pertaining *to lymph*.—*n.* A vessel in animal bodies which contains or conveys *lymph*. [Fr. *lymphatique*.]
Lynx, lingks, *n.* A quadruped resembling the common cat, celebrated for the *sharpness of its sight*. [L.—Gr. *lunx*, light.]
Lynx-eyed, lingks'īd, *a.* Having acute *sight*.
Lyre, līr, *n.* A kind of harp much used by the ancients as an accompaniment to poetry. [Fr.; Gr. *lura*.]
Lyric, li'rik, *a.* Pertaining *to a lyre*; pertaining to poetry originally sung to the lyre; designating that species of poetry which directly expresses the individual emotions of the poet.—*n.* A *lyric poem*; a composer of lyric poems. [L. *lyricus*—Gr. *lurikos*.]
Lyrist, lir'ist, *n.* A *musician who plays on the harp or lyre*.

M.

Mab, mab, *n.* The queen of the imaginary beings called fairies. [W. *mabam*, a babe, dimin. of *mab*, a male child, a boy.]
Macaroni, ma-ka-rō'ni, *n.* A kind of food in which the Italians *delight*, made of the dough of fine flour formed in ribbons. [It. *maccaroni*; Gr. *makar*, happy.]
Macaroon, ma-ka-rön', *n.* A small cake, composed of flour, eggs, almonds, and sugar. [Fr. *macaron*.]
Mace, mās, *n.* A heavy club of metal; a staff; an ensign of authority borne before magistrates; sceptre; the heavier rod used in billiards. [It. *massa*, a stick, club.]
Mace, mās, *n.* A spice; the second coat which covers the nutmeg. [L. *macir*.]
Macerate, ma'sė-rāt, *vt.* To *make lean*; to harass with corporeal hardships; to

Maceration, ma-se-rā'shon, n. Act or process of wearing away; act or operation of softening and almost dissolving by steeping in a fluid. [L. maceratio.]

cause to pine or waste away; to soften and separate, as the parts of a substance by steeping it in a fluid, or by the digestive process. ppr. macerating, pret. & pp. macerated. [L. macero, maceratus, to soften by steeping—macer, lean.]

Machiavelian, ma′ki-a-vēl′i-an, a. Pertaining to Machiavel, or denoting his principles; politically cunning; crafty. [from Machiavel, a talented and unprincipled Florentine, of the fifteenth century.]

Machination, ma-kin-ā′shon, n. Act of contriving a scheme for executing some purpose, particularly an evil purpose; an artful design formed with deliberation. [Fr.; L. machina, a machine.]

Machine, ma-shēn′, n. Any contrivance for performing any kind of work; a complex structure, consisting of a combination of the mechanical powers; an engine; an instrument of force; superhuman agency introduced into a poem to perform some exploit. [Fr.; L. machina—Gr. mēchos, a means.]

Machinery, ma-shēn′e-ri, n. The component parts of a complex machine; machines in general; superhuman beings introduced by an epic or dramatic poet to solve difficulties.

Machinist, ma-shēn′ist, n. A constructor of machines and engines, or one well versed in the principles of machines. [Fr. machiniste.]

Mackerel, mak′er-el, n. A salt-water fish, so named from the spots on its skin. [D. makreel—L. macula, a spot.]

Maculate, ma′kū-lāt, vt. To spot; to stain.—a.† Marked with spots; impure. [L. maculo, maculatus—macula, a spot.]

Maculation, ma-kū-lā′shon, n. Act of spotting; a spot; a stain. [L. maculatio.]

Mad, mad, a. Disordered in intellect; deranged; frenzied; inflamed or excited with excessive rage, passion, appetite, or desire; infatuated; insane; proceeding from disordered intellect, or indicating it; extremely perplexed with anxiety or trouble; proceeding from folly or infatuation.—vt. To make mad.—vi. To be mad. ppr. madding, pret. & pp. madded. [Sax. gemaad, troubled in mind; Sans. mad, to be mad, to be drunk, to rejoice.]

Madam, ma′dam, n. My dame; my lady; a complimentary title given to married and elderly ladies, or chiefly to them. [Fr. ma and dame.]

Madden, mad′n, vt. To make mad.—vi. To become mad; to act as if mad.

Madder, mad′er, n. The prepared root of a plant, much used in dyeing red. [Sax. moddere.]

Madding, mad′ing, p.a. Insane.

Madeira, ma-dē′ra, n. A rich wine made on the isle of Madeira.

Mad-house, mad′hous, n. A house where mad persons are confined for cure or restraint.

Madly, mad′li, adv. Without reason or understanding; rashly; wildly.

Mademoiselle, mad-mwoi-sel′, n. Miss; girl. [Fr. ma, mine, and demoiselle, a young lady.]

Madman, mad′man, n. A man who is mad, raving or furious with disordered intellect; a maniac; a man without understanding; one inflamed with extravagant passion, and acting contrary to reason.

Madness, mad′nes, n. State of being mad; a state of disordered reason or intellect, in which the patient raves or is furious; insanity; craziness; distraction; headstrong passion; wildness of passion; frenzy; rage; fury.

Madona, Madonna, ma-don′na, n. A term of compellation, equivalent to madam, given to the Virgin Mary. [Sp. madona.]

Madrepore, ma′drē-pōr, n. A kind of coral distinguished by superficial star-shaped cavities. [Fr. madrépore—marbre, marble, and pore.]

Madrigal, mad′ri-gal, n. The neatherd's song; a pastoral song; an elaborate vocal composition, in five or six parts. [Sp. madrigal—L. mandra, a herd of cattle.]

Magazine, ma-ga-zēn′, n. A shed; a repository for arms, ammunition, or provisions; the stores thus deposited; a pamphlet periodically published, containing stores of miscellaneous papers. [Fr. magasin; Ar. almasan, a shed.]

Maggot, ma′got, n. That which breeds, as in meat, vegetables, &c.; a moth; a worm or grub; the fly-worm; an odd fancy (low). [W. magu, to breed.]

Maggoty, ma′got-i, a. Full of maggots; full of whims; whimsical; capricious.

Magian, mā′ji-an, a. Pertaining to the Magi, a sect of priests or philosophers in Persia.—n. One of the sect of the Persian Magi. [L. magus.]

Magic, ma′jik, n. The philosophy of the Magians; the secret operations of natural causes; the art of employing the powers of nature to produce effects apparently supernatural; sorcery; enchantment. [L. magia.]

Magic, Magical, ma′jik, ma′jik-al, a. Pertaining to magic; used in magic; performed by magic, or by the invisible powers of nature.

Magically, ma′jik-al-li, adv. By the arts of magic; by enchantment.

Magician, ma-ji′shi-an, n. One skilled in magic; an enchanter; a sorcerer or sorceress. [Fr. magicien.]

Magisterial, ma-jis-tē′ri-al, a. Pertaining to a master; authoritative; characterized by pride or arrogance; imperious; haughty. [L. magister, a master—Sans. manh, to increase.]

Magisterially, ma-jis-tē′ri-al-li, adv. With the air of a master; arrogantly.

Magistracy, ma′jis-tra-si, n. The office or dignity of a magistrate; the body of magistrates. [L. magistratus.]

Magistrate, ma′jis-trāt, n. One greater than others; one placed in power or authority; a public civil officer invested with the executive or judicial authority, or some branch of it; a justice of the peace. [L. magistratus.]

Magna Charta, mag′na kär′ta, n. The Great Charter of English liberty, obtained by the English barons from King John, A.D. 1215, and confirmed by his successor, Henry III. [L.]

Magnanimity, mag-na-nim′i-ti, n. Greatness of soul or mind; that dignity of soul which encounters danger with tranquillity and firmness. [Fr. magnanimité.]

Magnanimous, mag-nan′im-us, a. Great of soul or mind; elevated in sentiment; brave; dictated by magnanimity; exhibiting nobleness of soul. [L. magnanimus—magnus, great, and animus, mind.]

Magnanimously, mag-nan′im-us-li, adv. With greatness of mind; bravely.

Magnate, mag′nāt, n. Magnates, mag-nā′tēz, pl. A great man; a grandee; a noble; a person of rank or wealth. (Used chiefly in the plural.) [Fr. magnats, grandees of Poland and Hungary.]

Magnesia, mag-nē′si-a, n. An alkaline earth; a soft white powder without taste or smell, used in medicine as a moderate purgative. [Fr. magnésie—L. magnes, a magnet.]

Magnesian, mag-nē′si-an, a. Pertaining to magnesia; containing or resembling magnesia.

Magnet, mag′net, n. The loadstone, which has the peculiar properties of attracting iron and some of its ores, and of pointing to the poles; a bar or piece of steel to which the peculiar properties of the loadstone have been imparted. [L. magnes, magnetis—from Magnesia, a country in Thessaly.]

Magnetic, Magnetical, mag-net′ik, mag-net′ik-al, a. Pertaining to the magnet; possessing the properties of the magnet; attractive.

Magnetically, mag-net′ik-al-li, adv. By means of magnetism.

Magnetism, mag′net-izm, n. That branch of science which treats of the properties of the magnet, or of the magnetic fluid; power of attraction.

Magnetizable, mag′net-iz-a-bl, a. That may be magnetised.

Magnetise, mag′net-iz, vt. To communicate magnetic properties to; to render magnetic.—vi. To become magnetic. ppr. magnetizing, pret. & pp. magnetised. [Fr. magnétiser.]

Magnific, mag-nif′ik, a. Rendered great; splendid; illustrious. [Fr. magnifique—L. magnus, great, and facio, to make.]

Magnificence, mag-nif′i-sens, n. Greatness; greatness and splendour of show or state; pomp. [Fr.]

Magnificent, mag-nif′i-sent, a. Great; grand in appearance; generous; exhibiting grandeur. [Low L. magnificens.]

Magnificently, mag-nif′i-sent-li, adv. With splendour of appearance or pomp of show; with exalted sentiments.

Magnifico, mag-nif′i-kō, n. A grandee of Venice.

Magnifier, mag′ni-fī-ėr, n. One who magnifies; an optical instrument which increases the apparent magnitude of bodies.

Magnify, mag′ni-fī, vt. To make great or greater; to increase the apparent dimensions of; to raise high in description or praise; to raise in estimation. ppr. magnifying, pret. & pp. magnified. [L. magnifico—magnus, great, and facio to make.]

Magnifying, mag′ni-fī-ing, p.a. Enlarging apparent dimensions.

Magniloquence, mag-nil′ō-kwens, n. Elevated language, or a lofty manner of speaking. [L. magniloquentia.]

Magniloquent, mag-nil′ō-kwent, a. Speaking pompously. [L. magnus, great, and loquens, speaking—loquor, to speak.]

Magnitude, mag′ni-tūd, n. Greatness; extent of dimensions; that which is extended, or which has one or more of the three dimensions, length, breadth, and thickness; greatness or grandeur; importance. [L. magnitudo—magnus, great.]

Magpie, mag′pī, n. A chattering particoloured bird of the crow tribe. [W. piog, with the prefix mag, for Margaret.]

Mahogany, ma-hog′a-ni, n. A tree growing in the tropical climates of America; also its wood, which is used for making

beautiful and durable furniture. [W. Indian, *mahagoni*.]
Mahomedan, ma-hom'ed-an, n. Same as *Mahometan*.
Mahometan, ma-hom'et-an, n. A follower or disciple of *Mahomet*; a Mussulman.—a. Of or belonging to *Mahomet*.
Mahometanism, ma-hom'et-an-izm, n. The religion established by *Mahomet*, contained in the Koran.
Maid, Maiden, mād, mād'n, n. A virgin; an unmarried woman, or a young unmarried woman; a female servant. [Sax. *mæden*, G. *mädchen*.]
Maiden, mād'n, a. Pertaining to a virgin; consisting of young women or virgins; fresh; new; unused.
Maidenhood, Maidenhead, mād'n-hud, mād'n-hed, n. State of being a maid or virgin; virginity; newness; freshness. [Sax. *mægdenhad*.]
Maidenliness, mād'n-li-nes, n. The quality of being maidenly; modesty.
Maidenly, mād'n-li, a. Like a maid; gentle; modest.—adv. In a maiden-like manner.
Maid-servant, mād'sėr-vant, n. A female servant.
Mail, māl, n. A budget or scrip; a bag for the conveyance of letters and papers; the letters, &c., sent in a mailbag; the coach or carriage in which the mail is conveyed. [Fr. *malle*, trunk —L. *mantica*, a wallet—*manus*, the hand.]
Mail, māl, n. A mesh; a coat of steel net-work, formerly worn for defending the body against swords, poniards, &c.; armour; that which defends the body. vt. To put a coat of mail or armour on; to arm defensively. [Fr. *maille*, mesh—L. *macella*, a mesh in a net.]
Mailed, māld, p.a. Protected by an external coat or covering of scales, as certain animals; spotted; speckled.
Maim, mām, vt. To mutilate; to lame; to deprive of the use of a limb; to deprive of a necessary part; to disable. n. Mutilation; the privation of the use of a limb; the privation of any necessary part; a crippling. [Old Fr. *mehaigner*, to maim—L. *mancus*, maimed.]
Maimed, māmd, p.a. Mutilated; lame.
Main, mān, n. Power; the gross; the bulk; the ocean; the great sea; the continent, as distinguished from an isle; a course; a duct; a principal pipe or duct, for conveying water, gas, &c.—a. Powerful; chief; first in size, rank, importance, &c.; that has most power in producing an effect, or is chiefly aimed at; important. [Sax. *magn*, strength —*magan*, to be able.]
Mainland, mān'land, n. The principal land, as opposed to an isle.
Mainly, mān'li, adv. Chiefly; to a great degree; mightily.
Main-sail, mān'sāl, n. The principal sail in a ship.
Main-spring, mān'spring, n. The chief spring or fountain; the principal spring of a watch or timepiece.
Maintain, mān-tān', vt. To hold with or by the hand; to hold or keep in any particular state; to support; not to suffer to fail or decline; not to lose or surrender; not to suffer to cease; to keep up; to defend; to vindicate; to justify; to prove to be just; to assert. vi. To affirm a position; to assert. [Fr. *maintenir*—L. *manus*, the hand, and *teneo*, to hold.]
Maintainable, mān-tān'a-bl, a. That may be maintained.
Maintainer, mān-tān'ėr, n. One who maintains.

Maintenance, mān'ten-ans, n. Act of maintaining; sustenance; support by means of supplies of food, clothing, and other conveniences; defence; vindication; security from failure or decline.
Maize, māz, n. Indian corn, a plant much cultivated for food. [Sp. *mais*.]
Majestic, ma-jes'tik, a. Having majesty; having dignity of person or appearance; princely; splendid; elevated; dignified; lofty; regal.
Majestically, ma-jes'tik-al-li, adv. With dignity; with grandeur.
Majesty, ma'jes-ti, n. Greatness; dignity; grandeur; dignity of aspect or manner; the quality or state of a person or thing which inspires awe or reverence in the beholder; elevation of manner; title of emperors, kings, and queens. [Fr. *majesté*—L. *magnus*, great.]
Major, mā'jėr, a. Greater; greater in number, quantity, or extent; greater in dignity.—n. A superior military officer next in rank above a captain, and below a lieutenant-colonel; a person of the age of twenty-one years complete; the first proposition of a regular syllogism in logic. [L. compar. of *magnus*, great.]
Majority, ma-jo'ri-ti, n. State of being greater; the greater number; full age; the rank or commission of a major. [Fr. *majorité*—L. *major*, greater.]
Make, māk, vt. To produce; to bring into being; to cause to be; to create; to mould into shape; to model; to frame; to constitute, as parts united in a whole; to settle; to obtain; to do; to execute; to bring into any state; to cause to do or to act; to force; to fasten; to raise, as profit; to gain; to discover; to arrive in sight of, as land; to provide, as a feast; to induce; to form and put forth, as a speech; to do the office of.—vi. To proceed; to move; to contribute; to rise; to flow toward land, as water. *ppr.* making, *pret. & pp.* made.—n. Form; shape; structure; texture; constitution of parts in a body. [Sax. *macian*.]
Makeless†, māk'les, a. Without a mate. [Icel. *maki*, an equal, husband.]
Maker, māk'ėr, n. One who makes, forms, shapes, or moulds; specifically the CREATOR.
Make-shift, māk'shift, n. That which serves a turn; an expedient adopted to serve a present purpose or turn.
Make-weight, māk'wāt, n. That which is thrown into a scale to make weight.
Making, māk'ing, p.n. Act of forming, causing, or constituting; workmanship; structure.
Maladministration, mal-ad-min'is-trā''-shon, n. Bad administration; bad management of public affairs. [L. *malus*, bad, and Eng. *administration*.]
Malady, ma'la-di, n. Illness; any sickness or disease of the human body; corruption of the heart; depravity; disorder of the understanding. [Fr. *maladie*—L. *malum*, an evil.]
Malapert, mal'a-pėrt, a. Pert to excess; sprightly, without respect or decency; forward.
Malapertness, mal'a-pėrt-nes, n. Quality of being malapert; sauciness.
Malapropos, mal-ap'rō-pō'', adv. Ill to the purpose; unseasonably; unsuitably. [Fr.]
Malaria, mal-ā'ri-a, n. Bad air; noxious exhalations, causing fever. [It.—L. *malus*, bad, and *aer*, air.]
Malconformation, mal'kon-form-ā''-shon, n. Bad conformation or form.
Male, māl, a. Pertaining to the sex

that begets young, and applied to animals of all kinds; not female; pertaining to flowers which bear stamens but not pistils.—n. One of the sex that begets young; a plant or flower which produces stamens only, without pistils. [Fr. *mâle*—L. *mas, maris*, a male.]
Malecontent, mal'kon-tent, n. A discontented subject of government; one who murmurs at or opposes the laws and administration.
Malecontent, Malecontented, mal'kon-tent, mal-kon-tent'ed, a. Discontented with the laws or the administration of government.
Malediction, ma-le-dik'shon, n. Evil speaking; denunciation of evil; cursing; imprecation. [L. *maledictio*—*malus*, bad, and *dico*, to speak.]
Malefaction†, ma-le-fak'shon, n. A crime. [L. *facio*, to make.]
Malefactor, ma-le-fak'tėr, n. An evildoer; one who commits a crime; a criminal; a felon. [L. *male*, and *factor*—*facio*, to do.]
Male-practice, mal-prak'tis, n. Evil-practice; immoral conduct; practice contrary to established rules.
Malevolence, ma-lev'ō-lens, n. Ill-will; evil disposition toward another; inclination to injure others. [L. *malevolentia*.]
Malevolent, ma-lev'ō-lent, a. Having ill-will; wishing evil to others, or disposed to injure others; evil-minded; malicious; unpropitious; bringing calamity. [L. *malevolens*—*malus*, bad, and *volo*, to will.]
Malevolently, ma-lev'ō-lent-li, adv. With ill-will or enmity.
Malformation, mal-form-ā'shon, n. Ill formation; irregular or anomalous formation of structure of parts.
Malice, ma'lis, n. Bad quality; grudge; pique; spite; rancour; a disposition to injure others without cause. [Fr.—L. *malus*, bad.]
Malicho†, ma'li-cho, n. Mischief
Malicious, ma-li'shi-us, a. Full of malice; evil-minded; rancorous; harbouring enmity without provocation; proceeding from extreme hatred; dictated by malice. [Fr. *malicieux*.]
Maliciously, ma-li'shi-us-li, adv. With malice; with extreme enmity or ill-will
Maliciousness, ma-li'shi-us-nes, n. Quality of being malicious; extreme enmity or disposition to injure.
Malign, ma-līn', a. Of an evil nature; harbouring violent hatred; malicious; pernicious.—vt. To act maliciously towards; to traduce; to defame. [Fr. *malin*, fem. *maligne*—L. *malus*, bad, and *genus*, kind.]
Malignancy, ma-lig'nan-si, n. Quality of being malignant; unpropitiousness; virulence; tendency to a fatal issue.
Malignant, ma-lig'nant, a. Having an evil nature; having extreme malevolence or enmity; unpropitious; exerting pernicious influence, as stars; virulent, as a boil; dangerous to life, as a fever; extremely heinous.—n. A man of extreme enmity or evil intentions. [L. *malignans*.]
Malignantly, ma-lig'nant-li, adv. Maliciously; with extreme malevolence.
Maligned, ma-līnd', p.a. Traduced; defamed.
Malignity, ma-lig'ni-ti, n. Evilness of disposition; evil dispositions of heart toward another without provocation, or with baseness of heart; destructive tendency; extreme sinfulness. [Fr. *malignité*.]
Mall, mal, n. A kind of mallet; a large

ch, chain; j, job; g, go; ng, sing; ᴛʜ, then; th, thin; w, wig; wh, whig; zh, asure; † obsolete.

heavy wooden beetle; an instrument for driving anything with force.—*vt.* To *beat with a mall*; to beat with something heavy; to bruise. [Fr. *mail*—L. *malleus*, a hammer.]

Mall, mal, *n.* See PALL MALL.

Mallard, mal'lärd, *n.* A drake; the common wild duck. [Fr. *malart.*]

Malleability, mal'lē-a-bil'li-ti, *n.* Quality of being malleable.

Malleable, mal'lē-a-bl, *a. Susceptible of being beaten out by a hammer;* that may be drawn out and extended by beating. [Fr. *malléable*—L. *malleus*, a hammer.]

Mallet, mal'let, *n. A small hammer;* a wooden hammer or instrument for driving pins, &c. [Fr. *maillet.*]

Mallow, Mallows, mal'lō, mal'lōz, *n.* A plant with *downy* leaves, possessing *softening* or emollient properties. [Sax. *malu, malwe*—Gr. *malakos*, soft.]

Malmsey, mäm'zē, *n.* The name of a sort of grape, and also of a strong and sweet wine. [Fr. *malvoisie.*]

Malt, malt, *n.* Barley or other grain *steeped* in water till it germinates, and then dried in a kiln and ground. It is used in brewing.—*vt.* To make into *malt.*—*vi.* To become malt. [Sax.—*miltan*, to be fluid.]

Malting, malt'ing, p.*n.* The act or process of *making malt.*

Malt-liquor, malt'lik-ėr, *n. A liquor* prepared for drink *by an infusion of malt*, as beer, ale, porter, &c.

Maltreat, mal-trēt', *vt.* To treat ill; to treat roughly, rudely, or with unkindness.

Maltreatment, mal-trēt'ment, *n.* Ill-*treatment;* ill-usage; abuse.

Maltworm, målt'wėrm, *n.* A tippler.

Malversation, mal-vėr-sā'shon, *n. Evil conduct;* improper behaviour, mean artifices, or fraudulent tricks; corruption or extortion in office. [L. *male*, and *versatio—verto*, to turn.]

Mam, Mamma, mam, mam-mä', *n.* A child's attempt to articulate *mother;* a familiar word for *mother*, used by young children. [L. *mamma*, a pap.]

Mammal, mam'mal, *n.*, **Mammals**, mam'malz, *pl.* A female animal having *breasts* or *paps;* an animal that suckles its young. [L. *mammalis*, pertaining to the breasts—*mamma*, a pap. Formed from the sound.]

Mammalia, mam-mā'li-a, *n. pl.* A class of animals comprehending those which *suckle* their young. [L. *mammalis.*]

Mammalian, mam-mā'li-an, *a.* Pertaining to the mammalia.

Mammer, mam'mėr, *vi.* To hesitate.

Mammet, mam'met, *n.* A puppet.

Mammon, mam'mon, *n. Riches;* wealth; the god of riches. [Syr. *mamuna.*]

Man, man, *n.* **Men**, men, *pl.* The species of living beings distinguished by the power of abstract *thought;* the human race; sometimes the male sex, in distinction from woman; a male of the human race; an attendant of the male sex; a husband; one of manly strength or virtue; an individual of the human species; any person; one.—*vt.* To furnish with men; to guard with men; to strengthen; to fortify; to tame, as a hawk†. *ppr.* manning, *pret. & pp.* manned. [Sax.—Sans. *man*, to think.]

Manacle, ma'na-kl, *n. An instrument* of iron *for fastening the hands;* handcuffs. (Used chiefly in the plural.)—*vt.* To put *manacles* upon; to shackle. *ppr.* manacling, *pret. & pp.* manacled. [Fr. *manicles;* L. *manica*, from *manus*, the hand.]

Manage, ma'nāj, *vt. To handle;* to use; to husband; to carry on; to carry on the concerns of; to govern gracefully in riding; to govern; to make tame; to wield; to use in the manner desired; to make subservient; to treat with caution; to govern with address.—*vi.* To direct or conduct affairs; to carry on concerns or business. *ppr.* managing, *pret. & pp.* managed.—*n.*† Conduct; administration. [Fr. *ménager*—L. *manus*, the hand.]

Manageable, ma'nāj-a-bl, *a. That may be managed* or controlled; easy to be directed to its proper purpose, or to one's views.

Manageableness, ma'nāj-a-bl-nes, *n. Quality of being manageable.*

Managed, ma'nājd, *p.a.* Carried on.

Management, ma'nāj-ment, *n. Act of managing;* administration; manner of carrying on; cunning practice; transaction; modulation; variation, as of the voice.

Manager, ma'nāj-ėr, *n. One who manages;* a person who conducts business with frugality; a good economist.

Managing, ma'nāj-ing, p.*a.* I͟ntriguing; carrying on.

Mandate, man'dāt, *n. Something given into the hands of another;* a charge; a commission. [L. *mandatum—manus*, the hand, and *do*, to give.]

Mandatory, man'da-tō-ri, *a. Containing a command;* preceptive; directory.—*n. One to whom a mandate*, a command, or charge is given. [Low L. *mandatorius.*]

Mandible, man'di-bl, *n. A jaw;* more especially the jaw of a bird. [L. *mandibulum—mando*, to chew.]

Mandrake, man'drāk, *n.* A narcotic plant, having a root often forked, and supposed to resemble a man. [L. and Gr. *mandragoras.*]

Mane, mān, *n.* The hair growing on the upper side of *the neck* of a horse or other animal, usually hanging down on one side. [D. *maan;* Gr. *mannos*, a necklace.]

Maned, mānd, *p.a.* Having a mane.

Manege, ma'nej, *n. The art of managing* horses *with the hand;* a school for teaching horsemanship. [Fr. *manège*—L. *manus*, the hand.]

Manful, man'fu̇l, *a. Becoming a man;* having the spirit of a man; noble; honourable.

Manfully, man'fu̇l-li, *adv.* Boldly; courageously; honourably.

Manfulness, man'fu̇l-nes, *n. Quality of being manful;* boldness; courage.

Manganese, man-gan-ēs', *n.* A kind of metal, the ore of which is used in chemistry and in the arts. [formed from *magnesium*, the original name.]

Mange, mānj, *n.* The scab or *itch* which eats into the skin of cattle, dogs, and other beasts. [from Fr. *manger*, to eat.]

Mangel-wurzel, mang'gl-wėr'zl, *n. The root of scarcity*, because it serves as a substitute for bread in times of scarcity; a plant of the beet kind. [Ger. *mangel*, want, and *wurzel*, root.]

Manger, mān'jėr, *n. That out of which horses and cattle eat;* a trough or box in which fodder, corn, &c., is placed for cattle and horses. [Fr. *mangeoire*—L. *mando*, to eat.]

Mangle, mang'gl, *vt.* To *maim;* to cut with a dull instrument, and tear; to cut in a bungling manner; to curtail. *ppr.* mangling, *pret. & pp.* mangled. [L. *mancus*, mutilated.]

Mangle, mang'gl, *n.* A rolling press, or small calender, for *smoothing* linen.—*vt.* To *smooth*, as linen with a mangle; to calender. *ppr.* mangling, *pret. & pp.* mangled. [Dan.]

Mangler, mang'gl-ėr, *n.* One who tears in cutting; one who uses a mangle.

Mangling, mang'gl-ing, p.*n.* The act of tearing; the act of smoothing linen with a mangle.

Mangy, mān'ji, *a. Infected with the mange;* scabby.

Manhood, man'hu̇d, *n. The state of one who is a man*, or of an adult male; virility; human nature; courage; bravery.

Mania, mā'ni-a, *n. Rage or violent uncontrollable desire for anything;* violent insanity; madness. [L.—Gr. *mainomai*, to rage.]

Maniac, mā'ni-ak, *a. Affected with mania;* raving with madness; raging with disordered intellect or violent desires.—*n.* A madman; one raving with madness. [L. *maniacus.*]

Manifest, ma'ni-fest, *a.* Bound or *grasped* by the hand; clear; obvious; plain; not obscure or difficult to be seen or understood.—*n.* An open statement; the invoice of a ship's cargo.—*vt.* To make to appear; to make public; to disclose to the eye or to the understanding; to display or exhibit more clearly to the view. [L. *manifestus*—Sans. *pash*, to hold.]

Manifestation, ma'ni-fest-ā"shon, *n. Act of manifesting;* the exhibition of anything by clear evidence; display. [Low L. *manifestatio.*]

Manifestly, ma'ni-fest-li, *adv.* Clearly; evidently; plainly.

Manifesto, ma-ni-fest'ō, *n.* A public declaration, usually of a prince or sovereign, showing his intentions, or pro claiming his opinions and motives. [It.]

Manifold, ma'ni-fōld, *a. Consisting of many folds;* many in number; multiplied; exhibited or appearing at divers times or in various ways.

Manikin, man'i-kin, *n. A little man;* a dwarf; an artificial anatomical preparation made with pasteboard, plaster, &c., exhibiting all parts of the human body. [dimin. of *man.*]

Manipulate, ma-nip'ū-lāt, *vt.* To treat or operate *upon with the hands. ppr.* manipulating, *pret. & pp.* manipulated. [Fr. *manipuler;* L. *manus*, the hand, and *plenus*, full.]

Manipulation, ma-nip'ū-lā"shon, *n. Act of manipulating;* the operation of preparing substances for chemical experiments. [Fr.]

Manipulator, ma-nip'ū-lāt-ėr, *n. One who manipulates.*

Mankind, man-kīnd', *n. The race or species of human beings;* a male, or the males of the human race.—*a.*† *Resembling man;* not womanish.

Manliness, man'li-nes, *n. Quality of being manly;* dignity; boldness.

Manly, man'li, *a. Man-like;* becoming a man; brave; undaunted; not boyish or womanish.

Manna, man'na, *n.* A substance miraculously furnished as food for the Israelites in their journey through the wilderness of Arabia; the juice of a species of ash, brought from the south of Europe. [Heb. *man hu*, what is it? Ex. xvi. 15.]

Manned, mand, *p.a. Guarded with men;* fortified.

Manner, man'nėr, *n. A mode of handling or managing;* way of performing; form; custom; habitual practice; kind; certain degree or measure; mien; mode (of things); way of service or worship;

Fāte, fär, fat fall; mē, met, hėr; pīne, pin; nōte, not, mōve; tūbe, tub, bu̇ll; oil, pound.

the particular habit of a painter in managing colours, lights, and shades. *vt.* To instruct in manners. [Fr. *manière*—L. *manus*, the hand.]
Mannered, man'nérd, *p.a. Having manners*, conduct, or bearing.
Mannerism, man'nér-izm, *n. Adherence to the same manner*; a tasteless uniformity, reducing everything to the same manner.
Mannerist, man'nér-ist, *n.* An artist who performs his work in *one unvaried manner*.
Mannerliness, man'nér-li-nes, *n. Quality of being mannerly*; complaisance.
Mannerly, man'nér-li, *a. Showing good manners*; civil; respectful; complaisant.—*adv.* With civility; respectfully; without rudeness.
Manners, man'nérz, *n. pl.* of *manner*. Deportment; morals; ceremonious behaviour; decent and respectful deportment.
Mannish, man'ish, *a. Having the appearance of a man*; bold; masculine. [Sax. *mennisc*.]
Manœuvre, ma-nö'vér, *n. Anything done in a handy or dexterous manner; dexterous movement, particularly in an army or navy; management with address.*—*vi. To do anything adroitly*; to change positions among troops or ships, for the purpose of advantageous attack or defence; to manage with address or art.—*vt.* To change, as the positions of troops or ships. *ppr.* manœuvring, *pret. & pp.* manœuvred. [Fr. *manœuvre*—L. *manus*, the hand, and *opus, operis*, work.]
Manœuvrer, ma-nö'vér-ér, *n. One who manœuvres*.
Manor, ma'nor, *n. A residence* with a certain portion of land annexed to it; so much land as a lord or great personage formerly kept in his own hands for the use and subsistence of his family. [Fr. *manoir*—L. *maneo, manere*, to abide.]
Manor-house, Manor-seat, ma'nor-hous, ma'nor-sét, *n.* The *house* belonging to a *manor*.
Manorial, ma-nō'ri-al, *a. Pertaining to a manor*.
Manse, mans, *n. A staying or remaining*; a house or *habitation*; in Scotland, a Presbyterian minister's house. [L. *mansio*—*maneo, mansum*, to remain.]
Mansion, man'shon, *n.* Any place of residence; a house; the house of a lord of a manor. [L. *mansio*.]
Mansionry†, man'shon-ri, *n.* A place of residence.
Manslaughter, man'slą-tér, *n. The killing of a man or of men*; the unlawful killing of a man without malice, express or implied; murder†.
Mantal, man'tel. *See* MANTLE.
Mantelet, Mantlet, man'tel-et, mant'-let, *n. A small mantle* or cloak worn by women. [dim. of *mantle*.]
Mantle, man'tl, *n. A cover*; a kind of cloak or loose garment, to be worn over other garments.—*vt. To cover, as with a mantle*; to overspread; to disguise.—*vi. To unfold and spread the wings like a mantle*; to joy; to be expanded; to gather over and form a cover; to become covered, as a liquid, on the surface; to rush to the face and cover it with a crimson colour, as blood. *ppr.* mantling, *pret. & pp.* mantled.—*n.* The piece of timber or stone in front of a chimney, over the fire-place, resting on the jambs. [Sax. *mentel;* Ar. *manto*, a mantle.]

Mantle-piece, Mantle-shelf, man'tl-pēs, man'tl-shelf, *n.* The work over a fire-place, in front of the chimney.
Mantling, man'tl-ing, *p.a. Expanding*; gathering on the surface.
Mantua, man'tū-a, *n.* An upper garment; a lady's gown. [Fr. *manteau*, a cloak.]
Mantua-maker, man'tū-a-māk-ér, *n.* One who *makes gowns* for ladies.
Manual, ma'nū-al, *a. Performed by the hand*, as labour; used or made by the hand.—*n.* A small book, such as may be held in *the hand;* a compendium; the service-book of the Roman Catholic Church. [Fr. *manuel*—L. *manus*, the hand.]
Manually, ma'nū-al-li, *adv. With the hand*.
Manufactory, ma-nū-fak'tō-ri, *n. A house or place where goods are manufactured*.—*a. Employed in manufacturing*.
Manufacture, ma-nū-fak'tūr, *n. The process of making anything by the hand;* the operation of reducing raw materials of any kind into a form suitable for use; anything made from raw materials by the hand, by machinery, or by art.—*vt. To make by the hand*, by art, or machinery; to work into suitable forms for use, as raw materials.—*vi.* To be occupied in *manufactures. ppr.* manufacturing, *pret. & pp.* manufactured. [Fr.—L. *manus*, the hand, and *facio*, to make.]
Manufactured, ma-nū-fak'tūrd, *p.a.* Made from raw materials into forms for use.
Manufacturer, ma-nū-fak'tūr-ér, *n. One who manufactures*; the owner of a manufactory.
Manufacturing, ma-nū-fak'tūr-ing, *p.a. Pertaining to or occupied in manufactures.*
Manumission, ma-nū-mi'shon, *n.* The act of liberating a slave from bondage, and giving him freedom. [L. *manumissio*.]
Manumit, ma-nū-mit', *vt. To send out of hand;* to liberate from personal bondage; to free, as a slave. *ppr.* manumitting, *pret. & pp.* manumitted. [L. *manumitto*—*manus*, the hand, and *mitto*, to send.]
Manure, ma-nūr', *vt.* To work by the hand†; to cultivate by manual labour†; to fertilize; to enrich with nutritive substances. *ppr.* manuring, *pret. & pp.* manured.—*n.* Dung or compost; any matter which fertilizes land. [Fr. *manœuvrer*—L. *manus*, the hand, and *opus*, work.]
Manuring, ma-nūr'ing, *p.n. A spread of manure* on land; the art of applying various kinds of manure to land, in order to fertilize the soil.
Manuscript, ma'nū-skript, *n.* A book or paper *written with the hand* or pen. *a. Written with the hand.* [L. *manuscriptum—manus*, the hand, and *scribo, scriptum*, to write.]
Many, me'ni, *a. Pertaining to a company of men;* comprising a number of persons or things; numerous; frequent; manifold; various.—*n. A multitude;* a great number of individuals; the people. [Sax. *manig*; Old G. *manag*—*unmanag*, few—*man*, man.]
Map, map, *n.* A representation of the surface of the earth, or of any part of it, drawn on paper or other material; a delineation of the heavens, of geological strata, &c.—*vt.* To draw or delineate, as the figure of any portion of land; to describe well. *ppr.* mapping,

pret. & pp. mapped. [Sp. *mapa*—L. *mappa*, a towel.]
Maple, mā'pl, *n.* A tree of the sycamore kind, from the sap of which sugar is made, and the wood of which is valuable for various purposes. [Sax. *mapulder*.]
Mappery†, map'é-ri, *n.* Same as *mapping*.
Mapping, map'ing, *p.n. The act or art of drawing maps*.
Mar, mär, *vt. To spoil*; to injure by cutting off a part; to hurt; to impair the strength or purity of; to disfigure; to interrupt, as mirth; to deform. *ppr.* marring, *pret. & pp.* marred. [Sax. *myrran*, to spoil.]
Maraud, ma-rad', *vi.* To rove in quest of plunder; to make an excursion for booty; to plunder. [Fr. *marauder*—*maraud*, a rogue.]
Marauder, ma-rąd'ér, *n.* A rover in quest of booty or plunder; a plunderer.
Marauding, ma-rąd'ing, *p.n.* A roving for plunder; a plundering by invaders.
Marble, mär'bl, *n. A stone that sparkles*, a species of calcareous stone, of a compact texture, and of a beautiful appearance; a little ball of marble used by boys in play; a stone remarkable for some inscription or sculpture.—*a. Made of marble*; veined like marble; hard; insensible.—*vt. To stain like marble;* to variegate in colour; to cloud. [Fr. *marbre;* Old Gr. *mairō*, to sparkle.]
Marbled, mär'bld, *p.a. Veined like marble*.
Marble-hearted, mär'bl-härt-ed, *a. Having a heart like marble*.
Marbling, mär'bl-ing, *p.n.* The art or practice of variegating in colour, in imitation of *marble*.
Marcescent, mär-ses'ent, *a. Withering;* decaying. [L. *marcescens—marceo*, to wither.]
March, märch, *n.* The third month of the year. [L. *Martius*—*Mars*, the Roman god of war.]
March, märch, *vi.* To go to the boundary, for defence†; to move by steps and in order, as soldiers; to walk in a stately manner; to proceed on horseback, as cavalry.—*vt.* To cause to move in order, as an army.—*n.* The movement of soldiers in order; a grave or solemn walk; measured advance; progression; advance; a particular beat of the drum; a piece of music designed for soldiers to march by. [Fr. *marcher;* Old Fr *marche*, border.]
Marches, märch'ez, *n.pl.* Marks by which limits, &c., are indicated; borders; particularly the confines of England on the side of Scotland or Wales. [Norm. *marches*, frontier cities or towns.]
Marching, märch'ing, *p.n.* Military movement; passage of troops.
Marchioness, märʹshi-on-es, *n. The wife or widow of a marquis;* or a lady having the rank and dignity of a marquis. [Low L. *marchionissa*.]
Marchpane†, märch'pān, *n.* A kind of sweet bread or biscuit.
Mare, mär, *n.* The female of the *strong* animal—the horse. [Sax. *myre*—Icel. *meri*, a horse—Goth. *mag*, to be able.]
Mareschal, mär'shal, *n.* The chief commander of an army. [Fr. *maréchal. See* MARSHAL.]
Marge, Margent†, märj, märj'ent, *n. A margin*.
Margin, mär'jin, *n. That which borders* anything; the edge; brink; verge;

ch, *chain;* j, *job;* g, *go;* ng, *sing;* ᴛʜ, *then;* th, *thin;* w, *wig;* wh, *whig;* zh, *azure;* † *obsolete*.

brim; the edge of the leaf or page of a book left blank, or filled with notes; the difference between the outlay and that which is actually required.—*vt.* To furnish with a margin; to enter in the margin. [L. *margo, marginis.*]

Marginal, mär'jin-al, *a.* Written or printed in the margin. [Fr.]

Marigold, ma'ri-gold, *n.* The gold of Mary; a well-known ornamental plant, bearing a showy yellow flower.

Marine, ma-rēn', *a.* Pertaining to the sea; done on the ocean; doing duty on the sea; formed by the action of the sea.—*n.* A soldier who serves on board of a ship, and fights in naval engagements; the whole navy of a state; the whole economy of naval affairs. [Fr. —L. *mare,* the sea—Sans. *vari,* water.]

Mariner, ma'rin-ėr, *n.* A seaman or sailor; one whose occupation is to assist in navigating ships. [Fr. *marinier.*]

Marital, ma'ri-tal, *a.* Pertaining to a husband. [Fr.—L. *mas, maris,* a male.]

Maritime, ma'ri-tim, *a.* Relating to the sea; performed on the sea; bordering on the sea; having a navy and commerce by sea. [L. *maritimus—mare,* the sea.]

Marjoram, mär'jō-ram, *n.* A well-known plant, having an agreeable aromatic flavour, and much used for seasoning food. [Fr. *marjolaine;* Gr. *amarakos.*]

Mark, märk, *n.* Anything visible, by which knowledge of something may be obtained; a stamp; a trace; a spot; a vestige; a visible line made by drawing one substance on another; an incision; any note or sign of distinction; a badge; any visible effect of force; any intelligible effect; proof; notice taken; anything to which a missile weapon may be directed; a character made by a person who cannot write his name; a cross; a certain note which a merchant puts upon his goods.—*vt.* To set a *print or stamp upon;* to imprint; to brand; to draw or make a visible line upon with any substance; to make an incision in; to make any sign of distinction in; to form, as a name, the initials of a name, for distinction; to have regard to; to observe; to heed; to point out.—*vi.* To note; to observe critically; to remark. [Sax. *mearc.*]

Mark, märk, *n.* A coin or money of account, equal to 13*s.* 4*d.* [so called from the *mark* impressed upon it.]

Marked, märkt, *p.a.* Impressed with a *mark;* noted.

Marker, märk'ėr, *n.* One who puts a *mark* on anything; one who notes or takes notice; a counter used in card-playing.

Market, mär'ket, *n.* A public place in a city or town, where provisions or cattle are *exposed to sale;* a public building in which provisions are exposed to sale; sale; purchase or rate of purchase and sale; the privilege of keeping a public market; value†; worth†.—*vi.* To deal in market; to make bargains for provisions or goods. [D. *markt*—L. *merx, mercis,* goods.]

Marketable, mär'ket-a-bl, *a.* Fit for the *market;* that may be sold; saleable.

Marketing, mär'ket-ing, *p.n.* Supply of a market; attendance upon a market.

Market-town, mär'ket-toun, *n.* A town that has the privilege of a stated public market.

Marking-ink, märk'ing-ingk, *n.* Indelible ink, used for marking clothes.

Markman†, märk'man, *n.* Same as *marksman.*

Marksman, märks'man, *n.* One who is *skilful to hit a mark;* he who shoots well.

Marl, märl, *n.* A fat or rich earth or *clay* much used for manure.—*vt.* To overspread with marl. [Norm. *marlers,* mari-pits.]

Marlaceous, märl-ä'shē-us, *a.* Resembling marl; partaking of the qualities of marl.

Marline, mär'lin, *n.* A small line of two strands, but little twisted, used to fasten the sail to the bolt-rope, and for winding round ropes or cables to prevent them from being fretted. [D. *marling—marren,* to moor, and *lijn,* a cord.]

Marline-spike, mär'lin-spīk, *n.* An iron tool, tapering to a point, for opening the strands of rope in splicing.

Marling, märl'ing, *p.n.* Act of manuring with marl.

Marly, märl'i, *a.* Consisting in or partaking of marl; resembling marl; abounding with marl.

Marmalade, mär'ma-lād, *n.* The pulp of quinces boiled into a consistence with sugar, or a confection of plums, apricots, quinces, oranges, &c., boiled with sugar. [Fr. *marmelade*—Gr. *meli,* honey, and *melon,* an apple.]

Marque, märk, *n.* Reprisal, as *letters of marque;* which authorize reprisals on another state for wrongs done on property captured. [Fr.]

Marquess, märk'wes, *n.* See MARQUIS.

Marquis, märk'wis, *n.* Originally, one who possessed land on the *frontiers* of an enemy's country, and was bound to defend the frontiers; a title of honour next below that of duke; a marchioness†. [Fr.; Low L. *marchio*—G. *mark,* a border.]

Marquisate, märk'wis-āt, *n.* The dignity of a marquis.

Marriage, ma'rij, *n.* The act of marrying or uniting a man and woman for life; matrimony. [Fr. *mariage*—L. *mas, maris,* a male.]

Marriageable, ma'rij-a-bl, *a.* Of an age suitable for marriage; fit to be married.

Married, ma'rid, *p.a.* Conjugal; connubial.

Marrow, ma'rō, *n.* A soft oleaginous substance contained in the cavities of animal bones; the essence; the best part. [Sax. *mearh*—Sans. *mridu,* tender.]

Marrow-bone, ma'rō-bōn, *n.* A bone containing marrow.

Marrowy, ma'rō-i, *a.* Full of marrow.

Marry, ma'ri, *vt.* To unite in wedlock; to dispose of in wedlock; to take for husband or wife.—*vi.* To enter into the conjugal state; to take a husband or a wife. *ppr.* marrying, *pret. & pp.* married.—*interj.*† Indeed! in truth! [Fr. *marier*—L. *maritus,* a husband—*mas,* a male.]

Mars, märz, *n.* The Latin name of the fabled god of war; a planet between the earth and Jupiter. [L.]

Marsh, märsh, *n.* A morass; a tract of low land, very wet and miry, and overgrown with coarse grass or sedge; a fen.—*a.* Pertaining to a morass or to wet, swampy, or boggy places. [Sax. *mersc.*]

Marshal, mär'shal, *n.* Originally, an official who had charge of the horses; the chief officer of arms, whose duty it is to regulate combats in the lists; one who regulates rank and order at a feast or any other assembly; a harbinger; a pursuivant; an officer of any private society, appointed to regulate their ceremonies.—*vt.* To dispose in order; to dispose in due order, as the several parts of an escutcheon, or the coats of arms of distinct families; to lead, as a harbinger. *ppr.* marshalling, *pret. & pp.* marshalled. [Fr. *maréchal;* Old G. *marach,* a horse, and *schalk,* a servant.]

Marshaller, mär'shal-ėr, *n.* One who disposes in due order.

Marshalling, mär'shal-ing, *p.n.* Act of arranging in due order.

Marshalship, mär'shal-ship, *n.* The office of a marshal.

Marshiness, märsh'i-nes, *n.* State of being marshy.

Marshy, märsh'i, *a.* Abounding in marshes; fenny.

Mart, märt, *n.* A market; a place of public traffic; a bargain.—*vi.* To buy and sell.—*vi.* To trade dishonourably. [from *market.*]

Marten, mär'ten, *n.* See MARTIN.

Marten, mär'ten, *n.* A fierce and destructive kind of weasel, valued for its fur. [Sax. *mearth.*]

Martial, mär'shi-al, *a.* Pertaining to *war;* suited to war; warlike; brave; belonging to war or to an army and navy. [Fr.—L. *Mars, Martis,* the god of war.]

Martially, mär'shi-al-li, *adv.* In a martial manner.

Martin, mär'tin, *n.* The window-swallow. [Fr. *martinet.*]

Martinet, mär'ti-net, *n.* A precise or strict disciplinarian, so called from an officer of that name who regulated the French infantry in the reign of Louis XIV.

Martingal, Martingale, mär'tin-gal, mär'tin-gāl, *n.* A strap fastened to the girth under a horse's belly, and at the other end to the nose-band, passing between the fore-legs. [Fr. *martingale.*]

Martinmas, mär'tin-mas, *n.* The feast of St. Martin of Tours; the 11th of November.

Martyr, mär'tėr, *n.* A witness; one who by his death bears witness to the truth of the gospel; one who suffers death or persecution on account of his creed. *vt.* To put to death for adhering to what one believes to be the truth; to torture. [Gr. *martur.*]

Martyrdom, mär'tėr-dom, *n.* The death of a martyr; the suffering of death on account of one's adherence to the gospel, or any cause.

Martyred, mär'tėrd, *p.a.* Put to death on account of one's faith.

Marvel, mär'vel, *n.* A wonder; that which excites admiration or astonishment; a miracle; a prodigy.—*vi.* To wonder; to feel admiration or astonishment (With *at.*) *ppr.* marvelling, *pret. & pp.* marvelled. [Fr. *merveille*—L. *miror,* to wonder.]

Marvellous, mär'vel-us, *a.* Exciting wonder; astonishing; strange; improbable; surpassing belief. [Fr. *merveilleux.*]

Marvellously, mär'vel-us-li, *adv.* Wonderfully; strangely.

Mary-bud, mä'ri-bud, *n.* The marigold.

Masculine, mas'kū-lin, *a.* Male; having the qualities of a man; strong; coarse; brave; noting a class of nouns which in English are the names of male animals, but which in some other languages include names of things. [Fr. *masculin*—L. *mas,* a male.]

Mash, mash, *vt.* To mix, as malt and water together in brewing; to beat into a confused mass; to crush by

Fāte, fär, fat, fall; mē, met, hėr; pīne, pin; nōte, not, mōve; tūbe, tub, bull; oil, pound.

beating or pressure.—*n. A mixture of ingredients blended together in a promiscuous manner;* a mixture for the food of domestic animals; a mixture of ground malt and warm water. [G. *meischen,* to mash—*mischen,* to mix.]

Mashy, mash'i, *a. Of the nature of a mash;* produced by bruising.

Mask, mask, *n. A sportive cover for the face;* especially a cover with apertures for the eyes and mouth; a visor; a festive entertainment of dancing or other diversions, in which the company all wear masks; a masquerade; any pretence or subterfuge.—*vt. To cover, as the face with a mask;* to conceal with a mask or visor; to disguise; to cover; to hide.—*vi.* To revel; to play the fool in masquerade; to be disguised in any way. [Fr. *masque.*]

Masker, mask'ér, *n. One who wears a mask.*

Masking, mask'ing, *p.a. Adapted for a revelling in masks.—p.n.* A *revelling in masks.*

Mason, mā'sn, *n. One who works on a scaffold,* and builds in stone or brick; one who prepares stone, and constructs the walls of buildings, &c.; a member of the fraternity of freemasons. [Fr. *maçon*—L. *machina,* a scaffold.]

Masonic, mā-son'ik, *a. Pertaining to* the craft or mysteries of *freemasons.*

Masonry, mā'sn-ri, *n. The art of a mason;* the work of a mason; the craft of freemasons. [Fr. *maçonnerie.*]

Masque, mask, *n. See* MASK.

Masquerade, mas-kėr-ād', *n.* A nocturnal assembly of persons wearing *masks,* and amusing themselves with dancing, &c.; disguise.—*vi.* To assemble in *masks;* to go in disguise. *ppr.* masquerading, *pret. & pp.* masqueraded. [Fr. *mascarade.*]

Masquerader, mas-kėr-ād'ėr, *n. A person wearing a mask;* one disguised.

Mass, mas, *n. That which is kneaded together;* a lump; a collective body of fluid matter; a great quantity collected; bulk; an assemblage; gross body of things considered collectively; the body; the quantity of matter in any body. [Fr. *masse*—Gr. *masō,* to squeeze with the hands.]

Mass, mas, *n.* The communion-service, or the consecration and *oblation* of the host, in the Roman Catholic churches. [Low L. *missa*—Heb. *māsa,* to lift up.]

Massacre, mas'sa-kėr, *n. A killing;* the murder of an individual, or the slaughter of numbers of human beings, with circumstances of cruelty. *vt.* To kill; to murder with circumstances of cruelty; to kill, as with indiscriminate violence. *ppr.* massacring, *pret. & pp.* massacred. [Fr.— G. *metsch,* to cut to pieces.]

Massiness, Massiveness, mas'i-nes, mas'iv-nes, *n. State of being massy* or massive; ponderousness.

Massive, Massy, mas'iv, mas'i, *a. Having the nature of a mass;* ponderous; bulky and heavy. [Fr. *massif.*]

Mast, mast, *n.* A long, round piece of timber, elevated perpendicularly on the keel of a ship, to which the yards, sails, and rigging are attached, and by which they are *supported.—vt. To fix masts in;* to supply with a mast or masts. [Sax. *mast*—Sans. *mush,* to support.]

Mast, mast, *n. That which fattens swine;* the fruit of the oak and beech; nuts; acorns. [Sax. *mæste*—Old G. *mastjan,* to fatten.]

Masted, mast'ed, *p.a. Furnished with a mast* or *masts.*

Master, mas'tėr, *n. One who is chief;* a director, head, or chief manager; the owner; a lord; one who has supreme dominion; a principal; one who has possession and the power of controlling or using at pleasure; a teacher; an appellation of respect; a title of boys; a man eminently skilled in any occupation, art, or science.—*a. Belonging to a master;* chief; principal.—*vt. To obtain dominion over;* to overpower; to make one's self master of; to execute with skill. [Old Fr. *maistre*—L. *magister—magnus,* great.]

Master, mas'tėr, *n. A vessel having masts.*

Masterdom, mas'tėr-dom, *n.* Dominion; rule.

Master-key, mas'tėr-kē, *n.* The *key* that opens many locks; a general clew to lead out of many difficulties.

Masterly, mas'tėr-li. *a. Suitable to a master;* executed with superior skill; skilful; imperious.—*adv. With the skill of a master.*

Master-passion, mas'tėr-pa-shon, *n.* A *predomina.1 passion.*

Master-piece, mas'tėr-pēs, *n.* A capital performance; chief excellence or talent.

Mastership, mas'tėr-ship, *n. Office of a master;* headship; supreme power; pre-eminence.

Master-spring, mas'tėr-spring, *n.* The *spring* which sets in motion or regulates the whole work or machine.

Mastery, mas'tėr-i, *n. Power of a master;* dominion; pre-eminence; victory in war; eminent skill.

Mastic, mas'tik, *n.* A resin used for *chewing* in the East.—*a.* Gummy; adhesive, as gum. [Fr. *mastic*—L. *mastico,* to chew.]

Masticate, mas'ti-kāt, *vt. To chew;* to grind with the teeth and prepare for swallowing. *ppr.* masticating, *pret. & pp.* masticated. [L. *mastico, masticatus*—Gr. *masaōmai,* to chew.]

Mastication, mas-ti-kā'shon, *n.* Act of *chewing* food. [Low L. *masticatio.*]

Masticatory, mas'ti-ka-tō-ri, *a. Chewing;* adapted to perform the office of chewing food.

Mastiff, mas'tif. *n.* A large variety of dog, remarkable for strength and courage. [Old Fr. *mestif,* a mongrel.]

Mat, mat, *n. A texture* of sedge or other material, used for various purposes of cleanliness and protection from injury; a web of rope-yarn, used in ships to secure the standing rigging from the friction of the yards, &c.—*vt. To cover with mats;* to interweave like a mat.—*vi.* To grow thick together; to become matted. *ppr.* matting, *pret. & pp.* matted. [Sax. *meatta;* Dan. *maatte.*]

Match, mach, *n.* Some very combustible substance used for lighting a fire, a lamp, candle, &c.; a rope made of hempen tow, and used for firing artillery, mines, &c. [Fr. *mèche,* wick of a candle; Gr. *muxa,* a lamp-nozzle.]

Match, mach, *n.* A person who is *equal* to another in strength or other quality; anything that equals another; union by marriage; one to be married; a contest on equal grounds; competition for victory.—*vt. To equal;* to show an equal to; to set against as equal in contest; to make equal; to marry; to give in marriage.—*vi.* To be united in marriage; to suit; to be of equal size; to tally. [Sax. *maca,* a mate; Icel. *maki,* an equal.]

Matchless, mach'les, *a. That cannot be matched;* having no equal.

Matchlessness, mach'les-nes, *n. State or quality of being matchless.*

Matchlock, mach'lok, *n.* Formerly, *the lock* of a musket, containing a *match* for firing; the musket itself.

Mate, māt, *n. A companion;* one who customarily associates with another; a husband or wife; one who eats at the same table; an officer in a merchant ship or ship of war, whose duty is to assist the master or commander.—*vt. To equal;* to *be equal to;* to match; to marry; to oppose, as equal. *ppr.* mating, *pret. & pp.* mated. [D. *maat,* a comrade—Goth. *mitan,* to measure.]

Mate, māt, *n.* The state of the king in chess, so situated that he *is defeated,* and cannot escape.—*vt.*† To enervate; to crush. [Sp. *matár,* to kill.]

Mated†, māt'ed, *p.a.* Made senseless; crushed.

Material, ma-tē'ri-al, *a. Consisting of matter;* not spiritual; more or less necessary; weighty; essential; substantial.—*n. Anything composed of matter;* the substance of which anything is made. [Fr. *matériel*—L. *materia,* matter—*mater,* mother.]

Materialism, ma-tē'ri-al-izm, *n. The doctrine of materialists.* [Fr. *matérialisme.*]

Materialist, ma-tē'ri-al-ist, *n. One who asserts that all existence is material;* one who denies the existence of spiritual substances. [Fr. *matérialiste.*]

Materially, ma-tē'ri-al-li, *adv. In the state of matter;* substantially.

Materiel, ma-tā'ri-el, *n.* That in a complex subject which constitutes the *materials.*

Maternal, ma-tėr'nal, *a. Motherly;* pertaining to a mother; becoming a mother. [L. *maternus—mater,* mother.]

Maternally, ma-tėr'nal-li, *adv. In a maternal manner.*

Maternity, ma-tėr'ni-ti, *n. The state, character,* or *relation of a mother.* [Fr *maternité.*]

Mathematical, ma-thē-mat'ik-al, *a Pertaining to mathematics;* according to the principles of mathematics; very accurate. [L. *mathematicus.*]

Mathematically, ma-thē-mat'ik-al-li, *adv. According to* the laws or principles *of mathematical science;* with mathematical certainty; demonstrably.

Mathematician, ma'thē-ma-ti"shi-an, *n. One versed in mathematics.* [Fr. *mathématicien.*]

Mathematics, ma-thē-mat'iks, *n. Learning;* the science of quantity; the science which treats of magnitude and number, or of whatever can be measured or numbered. [L. *mathematica* —Gr. *manthanō, mathein,* to learn.]

Matins, ma'tinz, *n. pl. Morning prayers or songs;* time of morning-service. [Fr. *matin,* the morning.]

Matrice, mā'tris, *n.* A mould; the cavity in which anything is formed, and which gives it shape; gang. [from L. *matrix, matricis,* a mother.]

Matricidal, mā-tri-sīd'al, *a. Pertaining to matricide.*

Matricide, mā'tri-sīd, *n. The murder of a mother;* the murderer of a mother. [L. *matricidium—mater,* a mother, and *cædo,* to kill.]

Matriculate, ma-trik'ū-lāt, *vt.* To enroll; to admit to membership in a body or society, particularly in a university, by enrolling the name in a register. *vi.* To enter one's name in the books of a university. *ppr.* matriculating,

Matriculated *pret. & pp.* matriculated. [It. *matricolare*—L. *mater*, a mother.]
Matriculated, ma-trik′ū-lāt-ed, *p.a.* Admitted to membership in a society, particularly in a university.
Matriculation, ma-trik′ū-lā″shon, *n. Act of matriculating.* [Low L. *matriculatio.*]
Matrimonial, mat-ri-mō′ni-al, *a. Pertaining to matrimony;* nuptial; derived from marriage. [Fr.—L. *mater*, a mother.]
Matrimonially, mat-ri-mō′ni-al-li, *adv.* According to the laws of marriage.
Matrimony, mat′ri-mō-ni, *n.* The state of conjugal union in which women become *mothers;* marriage; the union of man and woman for life; the nuptial state. [L. *matrimonium—mater*, a mother.]
Matrix, mā′triks, *n. The mother's womb;* the earthy substance in which metallic ores are found. [L.]
Matron, mā′tron, *n. An elderly married woman,* or an elderly lady; a chief nurse or superintendent in an hospital. [L. *matrōna.*]
Matronage, mā′tron-aj, *n. The state of a matron.*
Matronly, mā′tron-li, *a. Like or becoming a matron;* elderly.
Matted, mat′ed, *p.a. Laid with mats;* entangled.
Matter, mat′tėr, *n.* Not mind; body; the substance of which all bodies are constituted; that of which anything is made; that which is thrown out in a tumour; pus; thing treated; the very thing intended; affair; course of things; cause of any event; subject of complaint; import; moment; a portion of distance.—*vi.* To be of importance; to import (with *it, this, that,* or *what*). [Fr. *matière*—L. *materia—mater,* a mother.]
Matting, mat′ing, *p.n.* A texture composed of rushes, flags, &c., used in packing various articles, and also for covering the floors of houses.
Mattock, mat′tok, *n.* An implement for penetrating the earth; a kind of pickaxe having one end flat like an adze. [Sax. *mattuc.*]
Mattress, mat′tres, *n. A kind of mat made smooth* for a couch; a bed stuffed with hair, moss, or other soft material, and quilted. [G. *matratze.*]
Mature, ma-tūr′, *a. Perfected by natural growth;* ripe; perfect; prepared; ripened, as a scheme; come to suppuration, as an abscess.—*vi.* To ripen; to advance toward perfection; to make fit for a special use.—*vi.* To advance toward ripeness; to become ripe or perfect. *ppr.* maturing, *pret. & pp.* matured. [L. *matūrus—Sans. manh.* to increase.]
Matured, ma-tūrd′, *p.a.* Ripened; advanced to perfection; prepared.
Maturely, ma-tūr′li, *adv.* With ripeness; completely; with full deliberation.
Maturity, ma-tūr′i-ti, *n. State of being mature;* ripeness; a becoming due. [L. *maturitas.*]
Matutinal, ma-tū-tin′al, *a. Pertaining to the morning.* [L. *matutinus—mane,* the morning.]
Maudlin, mad′lin, *a.* Disposed to shed *tears* from the effects of intoxication; stupid; sottish. [corrupted from *Magdalen.*]
Maugre, ma′gėr, *adv. Against the will or wish of;* in spite of. [Fr. *malgré—mal,* ill, and *gré,* will.]
Maul, mal, *vt.* To beat and bruise with *a maul,* or with a heavy stick or hammer; to wound in a coarse manner; to deform greatly. [Fr. *mailler*—L. *malleus,* a hammer.]
Maulstick, mal′stik, *n.* The stick by which *painters* of pictures keep their hand steady in working. [G. *mahlerstock—mahler,* a painter.]
Maundy-Thursday, man′di-thėrz-dā, *n.* The Thursday in Passion-week, or next before Good Friday, on which the sovereign of England distributes alms from a *basket* to a certain number of poor persons at Whitehall. [Sax. *mand,* a basket.]
Mausoleum, ma-sō-lē′um, *n.* A stately sepulchral monument. [L. from *Mausolus,* king of Caria, in honour of whom his queen Artemisia erected a magnificent tomb.]
Mavis, mā′vis, *n.* The throstle or songthrush, *injurious* to ripe grapes. [Fr. *mauvis*—L. *malus,* evil.]
Maw, ma, *n.* The stomach, especially of animals; the paunch; the craw of fowls. [Sax. *maga;* Old G. *mago.*]
Mawkish, mak′ish, *a. Apt to offend the maw;* apt to cause satiety or loathing. [probably from *maw*—Sax. *maga.*]
Mawkishly, mak′ish-li, *adv. In a mawkish way.*
Mawkishness, mak′ish-nes, *n. Quality of being mawkish.*
Maxillary, maks′il-la-ri, *a. Pertaining to the jaw or jawbone.* [L. *maxillaris—mala,* the cheek-bone.]
Maxim, maks′im, *n.* That which is of the *greatest* authority; a principle generally received or admitted as true; an aphorism; an adage. [Fr. *maxime*—L. *maximum,* the greatest—*magnus,* great.]
Maximum, maks′im-um, *n.* The greatest number or quantity attainable in a given case; the highest price of any article.—*a.* Greatest. [L.—*magnus,* great.]
May, mā, *n.* The fifth month of the year; the early part of life.—*vi. To gather flowers in May-morning.* [Fr. *Mai*—L. *Maia,* the mother of Mercury.]
May, mā, *verb aux.* To *be strong or able;* to have physical power; to have moral power; to be possible; to be permitted. *pret.* might. [Sax. and Goth. *magan,* to be able, to have strength.]
May-day, mā′dā, *n. The first day of May.*
May-fly, mā′flī, *n. A fly that appears in May.*
Maying, mā′ing, *p.n. The gathering of flowers on May-day.*
May-lily, mā′li-li, *n.* The *lily* of the valley.
May-morn, mā′morn, *n.* Freshness; vigour.
Mayor, mā′ėr, *n. The greater* or chief man of a city; the chief magistrate of a city or town corporate. [Old Fr. *maire*—L. *major,* comp. of *magnus,* great.]
Mayoralty, mā′ėr-al-ti, *n. The office of a mayor.* [Low L. *majoriatus.*]
Mayoress, mā′ėr-es, *n. The wife of a mayor.*
May-pole, mā′pōl, *n. A pole* to dance *round in May;* a long pole erected.
May-queen, mā′kwēn, *n. A young female crowned with flowers* at the celebration of *May-day.*
Mazard, ma′zard, *n.* The jaw; the head or skull.
Maze, māz, *n.* A winding and turning; a labyrinth; intricacy; confusion of thought; perplexity. [Sax. *mase,* a whirlpool.]
Maziness, mā′zi-nes, *n.* Perplexity.
Mazy, mā′zi, *a. Full of mazes;* winding; perplexed with turns and windings.

Me, mē, *pron. pers.;* the objective case of *I.* [Sax.]
Mead, mēd, *n.* A fermented liquor consisting of *honey* and water, sometimes enriched with spices. [Sax. *medu*—Sans. *mathu,* honey.]
Mead, Meadow, mēd, me′dō, *n.* Grassland that is *mowed;* land unploughed, green with grass, and variegated with flowers. (*Mead* is used chiefly in poetry.) [Sax. *mad—mawan,* to mow.]
Meadowy, me′dō-i, *a. Containing meadow;* resembling a meadow.
Meagre, mē′gėr, *a. Thin;* destitute of flesh, or having little flesh; poor; destitute of richness, as soil; wanting richness of imagery, as a description; spare; scanty. [Fr. *maigre*—L. *macer,* lean.]
Meagrely, mē′gėr-li, *adv.* Poorly; thinly.
Meagreness, mē′gėr-nes, *n. State or quality of being meagre;* leanness; want of fertility or richness.
Meal, mēl, *n.* A portion of food taken at one time; a repast. [Sax. *mel;* Icel. *mál,* a portion.
Meal, mēl, *n.* The substance of edible grain *ground* to fine particles, and not bolted or sifted; flour; the finer part of pulverized grain.—*vt.* To mix; to mingle; to sprinkle with meal; to pulverise. [Sax. *melew*—L. *molo,* to grind in a mill.]
Mealiness, mēl′i-nes, *n. Quality of being mealy;* smoothness to the touch.
Mealy, mēl′i, *a. Having the qualities of meal;* soft; like meal; overspread with something that resembles meal.
Mealy-mouthed, mēl′i-mourṇd, *a. Having a soft mouth;* unwilling to tell the truth in plain language.
Mean, mēn, *a. Profane;* wanting dignity of mind; destitute of honour; base; spiritless; despicable; of little value; worthy of little or no regard; not costly or elegant; humble; poor. [Sax. *mæne*—Old G. *meinjan,* to profane.]
Mean, mēn, *a. Middle;* at an equal distance from the extremes; intervening; average.—*n. The middle point or place;* the middle rate or degree; meantime; a quantity having an intermediate value between several others; instrument; the medium through which something is done; (pl.) income; resources or estate; instrument of performance; tenor. [Norm. *meane*—L. *medius,* middle.]
Mean, mēn, *vt. To have in the mind;* to intend; to design, with reference to a future act; to signify; to denote; to import.—*vi.* To have thought or ideas, or to have meaning. *ppr.* meaning, *pret. & pp.* meant. [Sax. *mænan*—L. *mens,* the mind.]
Meander, mē-an′dėr, *n. A winding course;* a winding or turning in a passage; a labyrinth; perplexity.—*vi. To wind* or turn in a course or passage; to be intricate. [Gr. *Maiandros,* a winding river in Caria.]
Meandering, mē-an′dėr-ing, *p.a. Winding* in a course, passage, or current. *n. A winding course.*
Meaning, mēn′ing, *p.a.* Significant. *p.n. That which exists in the mind,* as a settled purpose, though not directly expressed; intention, with reference to a future act; signification; that which is to be understood; that which the writer or speaker intends.
Meaningless, mēn′ing-les, *a. Having no meaning.*
Meanly, mēn′li, *adv. In a mean manner;* without dignity or rank.
Meanness, mēn′nes, *n. State or quality of being mean;* low state; poorness; low

ness of mind; want of dignity and elevation; want of honour; niggardliness.
Measled, mē'zld, *p.a.* *Infected or spotted with measles.*
Measles, mē'zlz, *n.* with a plural termination. A contagious disease of the human body, usually characterised by small red spots upon the skin. [D. *maselen*—G. *maser*, a speck.]
Measly, mē'zl-i, *a.* *Infected with measles* or eruptions.
Measurable, me'zhūr-a-bl, *a.* *That may be measured;* moderate; in small quantity or extent.
Measurably, me'zhūr-a-bli, *adv.* Moderately; in a limited degree.
Measure, me'zhūr, *n.* That by which dimension is ascertained; the whole magnitude of a thing, ascertained by comparison with a fixed standard; a definite quantity; determined extent; proportion; due bounds; extent of power; extent of ability; degree; the manner of combining the long and short syllables in poetry; the interval between steps in dancing corresponding to the interval between notes in the music; a dance; an act, step, or proceeding toward the accomplishment of an object.—*vt.* To compare with a fixed standard; to ascertain the dimensions of; to ascertain, as the degree of anything; to judge of; to march; to proceed; to adjust; to distribute by measure.—*vi.* To have a certain or limited extent. *ppr.* measuring, *pret. & pp.* measured. [Fr. *mesure*—L. *metior*, *mensus*, Sans. *mā*, to measure.]
Measured, me'zhūrd, *p.a.* Steady; limited or restricted.
Measureless, me'zhūr-les, *a.* *Without measure;* boundless; limitless; vast.
Measurement, me'zhūr-ment, *n. Act of measuring;* mensuration.
Measuring, me'zhūr-ing, *p.a.* *Used in measuring,* as a rod, line, &c.
Meat, mēt, *n.* That which is *ground* by the teeth; food in general; anything eaten for nourishment, either by man or beast; the flesh of animals used as food. [Sax. *mæte*—L. *mando*, to chew.]
Mechanic, Mechanical, me-kan'ik, me-kan'ik-al, *a. Skilled in mechanics;* pertaining to mechanics; pertaining to the art of making furniture, &c.; constructed by the laws of mechanics; bred to manual labour; pertaining to artisans: vulgar; pertaining to the principles of mechanics, in philosophy; acting by physical power; noting performance without design.—*n.* (**Mechanic**) *One who constructs* machines, furniture, and the like; an artificer, an artizan. [L. *mechanicus*—Gr. *mēchos*, a means.]
Mechanically, me-kan'ik-al-li, *adv.* According to the laws of *mechanism*; by physical force; by the laws of motion, without intelligence, or by the force of habit.
Mechanics, me-kan'iks, *n. The art or science of making;* the science which shows the effects of powers or moving forces, so far as they are applied to engines, and demonstrates the laws of motion.
Mechanism, me'kan-izm, *n. The structure of a machine,* engine, or instrument; the parts composing a machine, &c.; action of a machine; according to the laws of mechanics. [Fr. *mécanisme*.]
Mechanist, me'kan-ist, *n. The maker of machines,* or one skilled in mechanics.
Medal, me'dal, *n. A piece of metal* in the form of a coin, stamped with some figure or device as a memento of any event or person, or as a reward of merit. [Fr. *médaille*—Gr. *metallon*, metal.]
Medallic, me-dal'ik, *a. Pertaining to a medal or to medals.*
Medallion, me-dal'li-on, *n. A large antique medal;* anything resembling in form such a coin. [Fr. *médaillon*.]
Medallist, me'dal-ist, *n. One skilled in medals;* one who has gained a medal.
Meddle, med'l, *vi. To intermeddle;* to *intervene;* to interfere; to have to do (with *with*); to interpose officiously. *ppr.* meddling, *pret. & pp.* meddled. [Belg. *middelen*, to intervene—L. *medius*, middle.]
Meddler, med'l-ėr, *n. One who meddles.*
Meddlesome, med'l-sum, *a. Given to meddling;* officiously intrusive.
Meddling, med'l-ing, *p.a.* Officious; busy in other men's affairs.—*p.n.* Officious interposition.
Medial, mē'di-al, *a. Middle; mean;* noting a mean or average. [Fr. *médial*—L. *medius*, middle.]
Mediate, mē'di-āt, *a. Middle;* being between the two extremes; acting by means; not direct.—*vi. To interpose* between parties as the equal friend of each; to intercede. *ppr.* mediating, *pret. & pp.* mediated. [Fr. *médiat*—L. *medius*, middle.]
Mediately, mē'di-āt-li, *adv. By means* or by a secondary cause, acting between the first cause and the effect.
Mediation, mē-di-ā'shon, *n. Act of mediating;* intervention; agency between parties at variance, with a view to reconcile them; intercession; entreaty for another. [Fr. *médiation*.]
Mediator, mē'di-āt-ėr, *n.* One who *mediates* between parties at variance, for the purpose of reconciling them; an intercessor; an advocate; Christ as our advocate and intercessor with God the Father. [Low L. *mediator*—L. *medius*, the middle.]
Mediatorial, mē'di-a-tō"ri-al, *a. Belonging to a mediator.*
Mediatorially, mē'di-a-tō"ri-al-li, *adv. By mediation;* like a mediator.
Mediatorship, mē'di-āt-ėr-ship, *n. The office of a mediator.*
Medicable, me'dik-a-bl, *a. That may be cured* or healed.
Medical, me'di-kal, *a. Pertaining to the art of healing* diseases; containing that which heals; tending to cure; designed to promote the study of medicine. [Fr. *médical*—L. *medeor*, to heal.]
Medically, me'di-kal-li, *adv. According to the rules of the healing art;* in relation to the healing art.
Medicate, me'di-kāt, *vt. To heal;* to tincture with anything medicinal. *ppr.* medicating, *pret. & pp.* medicated. [L. *medico*, *medicatus*.]
Medicated, me'di-kāt-ed, *p.a. Prepared with anything medicinal.*
Medicinal, me-dis'in-al, *a. Pertaining to medicine;* having the property of healing; adapted to the cure or alleviation of bodily disorders. [Fr. *médicinal*.]
Medicinally, me-dis'in-al-li, *adv. In the manner of medicine;* with medicinal qualities; with a view to healing.
Medicine, me'di-sin, *n. Any substance that has the property of curing* or mitigating disease in animals; a drug; the science or art of preventing, curing, or alleviating the diseases of the human body; a physician.—*vt.* To remedy; to cure. [L. *medicina*—*medeor*, to heal.]
Medieval, me-di-ēv'al, *a. Pertaining to the middle ages.* [L. *medius*, middle, and *ævum*, age.]
Mediocre, mē'di-ō-kėr, *a. Being in a middle state;* of moderate degree; middling.—*n.* A person of *middling* quality, talents, or merit. [Fr.—L. *medius*, middle.]
Mediocrity, mē-di-ok'ri-ti, *n. State of being mediocre;* a moderate degree or rate; moderation. [Fr. *médiocrité*.]
Meditate, me'di-tāt, *vi.* To dwell on anything in *thought;* to turn or revolve any subject in the mind; to muse; to contemplate; to have in contemplation. *vt. To think on;* to plan by revolving in the mind; to contrive; to intend. *ppr.* meditating, *pret. & pp.* meditated [L. *meditor*—*meditatus*.]
Meditated, me'di-tāt-ed, *p.a.* Planned; contrived.
Meditation, me-di-tā'shon, *n. Act of meditating;* that which is meditated; the turning or revolving of a subject in the mind; serious contemplation. [Fr. *méditation*.]
Meditative, me'di-tāt-iv, *a. Addicted to meditation;* expressing or appropriate to meditation. [Fr. *méditatif*.]
Mediterranean, me'di-te-rā"nē-an, *a. Midland;* situated in the midst of the earth or land; inland.—*n.* The Mediterranean Sea, between Europe and Africa. [L. *medius*, middle, and *terra*, earth.]
Medium, mē'di-um, *n.* **Media, Mediums**, *pl. The middle;* the mean; the space or substance through which a body passes to any point; the means by which anything is accomplished. [L.]
Medlar, med'lėr, *n.* A tree and its fruit, which resembles a small apple. [Sax. *mæd*.]
Medley, med'lē, *n. A mixture;* a mingled mass of ingredients; a miscellany. [from obsol. *meddle*, to mix.]
Medullary, me'dul-la-ri, *a. Pertaining to the marrow of bones;* consisting of marrow; resembling marrow; pithy; filled with spongy pith. [Fr. *médullaire*—L. *medulla*, marrow—*medius*, middle.]
Meed, mēd, *n. Reward;* recompense; that which is bestowed or rendered in consideration of merit; merit†; desert†. [Sax. *med*, reward—Heb. *mattan*, a gift.]
Meek, mēk, *a. Soft;* mild; not easily provoked; submissive to the divine will; not proud or refractory. [D. *muik*, soft—Goth. *muka*, meek.]
Meekly, mēk'li, *adv. Softly;* mildly; gently; submissively; humbly.
Meekness, mēk'nes, *n. Quality of being meek;* mildness; gentleness; forbearance under injuries; resignation; unmurmuring submission to the divine will.
Meered†, mērd, *a.* Relating to a boundary.
Meet, mēt, *a. According to measure;* fitting; proper; qualified; expedient; adapted, as to a use or purpose. [Sax. *gemet*, fit—*metan*, to measure.]
Meet, mēt, *vt. To light on;* to encounter; to encounter unexpectedly; to come in contact with; to join; to receive, as a welcome.—*vi.* To come together, or to approach near or into company with; to come together with hostile purpose; to assemble; to congregate; to join, as lines. *ppr.* meeting, *pret. & pp.* met. [Sax. *metan*—Goth. *gamotjan*, to light upon.]
Meeting, mēt'ing, *p.n.* A coming together; an assembly; a congregation; a conflux, as of rivers; a joining; a union, as of lines.

ch, *chain;* j, *job;* g, *go;* ng, *sing;* ᴛʜ, *then;* th, *thin;* w, *wig;* wh, *whig;* zh, *azure;* † obsolete.

Meeting-house, mēt′ing-hous, n. A place of worship; a house of public worship for dissenters.
Meetly, mēt′li, adv. Fitly; suitably.
Meetness, mēt′nes, n. Quality of being meet; fitness; suitableness; propriety.
Megrim, mē′grim, n. A neuralgic pain in the side of the head, usually periodical. [Fr. migraine—Gr. hemi, half, and kranion, the skull.]
Meine, Meiny, mī′ne, mē′ni, n. A retinue of servants.
Melancholic, me′lan-kol-ik, a. Affected with melancholy; depressed in spirits; hypochondriac; produced by melancholy; expressive of melancholy; unfortunate; causing sorrow. [Fr. mélancolique.]
Melancholy, me′lan-ko-li, n. Black choler or bile, from the abundance of which the ancients supposed that dejection of spirits and madness proceeded; a gloomy state of mind that is of some continuance, or habitual; depression of spirits; dejection.—a. Gloomy in mind; dejected; depressed in spirits; habitually dejected, as a temperament; calamitous; that may or does produce great evil and grief. [Fr. mélancolie—Gr. melas, black, and cholē, bile.]
Meliorate, mē′li-or-āt, vt. To make better; to improve.—vi. To grow better. ppr. meliorating, pret. & pp. meliorated. [Late L. melioro, melioratus—L. melior, better.]
Melioration, mē′li-or-ā″shon, n. Act of making better; improvement. [Late L. melioratio.]
Mellifluence, mel-if′lū-ens, n. A flow of honey or sweetness; a sweet smooth flow. [L. mel, mellis, honey, and fluo, to flow.]
Mellifluent, Mellifluous, mel-if′lū-ent, mel-if′lū-us, a. Flowing, as with honey or sweetness; smooth; sweetly flowing. [L. mellifluens, mellifluus.]
Mellow, mel′lō, a. Soft; ripe; soft with ripeness; easily yielding to pressure; soft to the ear; soft and smooth to the taste; soft with liquor; intoxicated; merry; soft or easy to the eye.—vt. To soften by ripeness; to ripen; to bring to perfection.—vi. To become soft; to be ripened or brought to perfection. [Sax. mearu, tender—L. mollis, soft.]
Mellowness, mel′lō-nes, n. Softness; ripeness, as of fruit; maturity; softness from age, as of wine.
Melodious, me-lō′di-us, a. Containing melody; musical; agreeable to the ear by a sweet succession of sounds. [Fr. mélodieux.]
Melodiously, me-lō′di-us-li, adv. In a melodious manner.
Melodiousness, me-lō′di-us-nes, n. Quality of being melodious.
Melodist, me′lō-dist, n. A composer and singer of melodies.
Melodrama, me-lō-dra′ma, n. See MELODRAME.
Melodramatic, me′lō-dra-mat″ik, a. Pertaining to a melodrame.
Melodrame, me′lō-dram, n. A musical drama; a dramatic performance in which songs are intermixed, and effect is sought by startling events or situations. [Fr. mélodrame—Gr. melos, a song, and drama.]
Melody, me′lō-di, n. Sweetness of sound; a sweet strain to which lyric poetry is set; an agreeable succession of sounds; the particular tune of a musical piece. [Gr. melōdia—melos, a song, a strain, and ōdē, a lay.]
Melon, me′lon, n. A kind of cucumber and its fruit, which resembles an apple. [Fr.—L. melo.]
Melt, melt, vt. To make liquid; to reduce from a solid to a liquid state by heat; to soften; to overpower with tender emotion; to waste away.—vi. To become liquid; to be changed from a fixed to a flowing state; to be softened to love or sympathy; to become tender or gentle; to lose substance; to sink into weakness; to faint; to be disheartened. [Sax. meltan—Gr. meldō, to make liquid.]
Melted, melt′ed, p.a. Made liquid; softened; discouraged.
Melting, melt′ing, p.a. Tending to soften; softening into tenderness.—p.n. Act of dissolving; the act of rendering tender.
Meltingly, melt′ing-li, adv. In a manner to melt or soften.
Member, mem′bėr, n. A part of a whole body; a limb of animal bodies; part of a discourse, or of a period or sentence; a part of a verse; an individual of a society, secular or religious; a representative in a legislative body; one of a body corporate. [Fr. membre—L. membrum—Sans. md, to measure.]
Membered, mem′bėrd, p.a. Having limbs.
Membership, mem′bėr-ship, n. State of being a member; community.
Membrane, mem′brān, n. The thin, white, flexible skin that covers the separate members of the body or some parts of it; a similar texture in vegetables. [Fr.—L. membrum, a member.]
Membranous, mem′brān-us, a. Belonging to a membrane; consisting of membranes.
Memento, mē-men′tō, n. That which reminds; a hint or memorial to awaken memory. [L. remember! from memini, to remember, to be mindful.]
Memoir, me′mwȧ, n. An account of events written familiarly, or as they are remembered by the writer; a biographical notice; the history of a society; a written account; register of facts. [Fr. mémoire—L. memor, mindful.]
Memorable, me′mor-a-bl, a. Worthy to be remembered; famous; illustrious; celebrated. [Fr. mémorable—L. memor, mindful.]
Memorably, me′mor-a-bli, adv. In a manner worthy to be remembered.
Memorandum, me-mor-an′dum, n. Memorandums or Memoranda, pl. Something to be remembered; a note to help the memory. [L. from memoro, to bring to remembrance.]
Memorial, mē-mō′ri-al, a. Pertaining to memory; preservative of memory; contained in memory.—n. Anything that serves to keep in memory; a monument; any note or hint to assist the memory; a written representation of facts, made to a legislative or other body, as the ground of a petition. [Fr. mémorial—L. memor, mindful, remembering, careful.]
Memorialist, mē-mō′ri-al-ist, n. One who writes or presents a memorial.
Memorialize, mē-mō′ri-al-īz, vt. To petition by memorial. ppr. memorializing, pret. & pp. memorialized.
Memorise†, me′mor-īz, vt. To record; to commit to memory.
Memory, me′mō-ri, n. A thinking of; the faculty of the mind by which it retains the knowledge of past events, or ideas which are past; remembrance; the time within which past events can be remembered; reflection†; attention†. [L. memoria—memor, mindful—Sans. man, to think.]
Men, men, n.pl. of man. Two or more males, individuals of the human race; males of a brave spirit; people; mankind.
Menace, me′nās, vt. To threaten; to express a disposition to inflict evil upon; to show the probability of future evil to.—vi. To exhibit the appearance of any catastrophe to come. ppr. menacing, pret. & pp. menaced.—n. A threat or threatening; the declaration or show of a disposition to inflict an evil; the show of a probable catastrophe to come. [Fr. menacer—L. minor, to threaten—minae, to jut.]
Menacing, me′nās-ing, p.a. Exhibiting the danger or probability of an evil to come.
Menacingly, me′nās-ing-li, adv. In a threatening manner.
Menagerie, Menagery, men-ash′a-ri, mē-nā′je-ri, n. A yard or place in which wild animals are kept; the collection of such animals. [Fr. ménagerie.]
Mend, mend, vt. To amend; to free from faults; to repair, as a breach; to set right; to alter for the better; to restore to a sound state; to quicken; to advance; to further.—vi. To grow better; to advance to a better state; to improve. [Fr. amender—L. e, ex, and mendum, a fault.]
Mendacious, men-dā′shi-us, a. Lying. [L. mendax—mentior, to lie.]
Mendacity, men-das′i-ti, n. Habitual falsehood; untruth. [L. mendacitas.]
Mender, mend′ėr, n. One who mends.
Mendicancy, men′di-kan-si, n. State of being a mendicant; beggary; a state of begging.
Mendicant, men′di-kant, a. Begging; poor to a state of beggary; practising beggary.—n. A beggar; one of the begging fraternity of the Roman Catholic Church. [Sp. mendicante—L. mendicus, begging.]
Mendicity, men-dis′i-ti, n. State of being a mendicant; the life of a beggar. [L. mendicitas.]
Mending, mend′ing, p.a. Improving in health after sickness.—p.n. Act of repairing.
Mends†, mends. See AMENDS.
Menial, mē′ni-al, a. Belonging to the retinue of servants; pertaining to the train of a household; low with regard to office or employment.—n. One of a train of servants; a domestic servant. [Norm. meynal—L. manus, the hand.]
Menstrual, men′strū-al, a. Monthly; happening once a month; lasting a month. [Fr. menstruel—L. mensis, a month.]
Menstruum, men′strū-um, n. Menstruums or Menstrua, pl. A solvent; any fluid which dissolves a solid body [from L. mensis, a month.]
Mensurable, men′sūr-a-bl, a. Measurable; capable of being measured. [Sp.—L. mensūra, measure.]
Mensuration, men-sūr-ā′shon, n. The act or art of measuring; act or art of ascertaining areas, solid contents, heights, and distances, &c.; the result of measuring. [Late L. mensuratio—L. metior, Sans. md, to measure.]
Mental, men′tal, a. Pertaining to the mind; existing in the mind; performed in the mind. [Fr.—L. mens, mentis, the mind—Sans. man, to think.]
Mentally, men′tal-li, adv. In the mind; intellectually; in idea.
Mention, men′shon, n. A calling to mind; a putting in mind; a brief notice

or remark expressed in words or writing.—*vt.* To make mention of; to state, as a particular fact, or to express it in writing. [Fr.—L. *memor*, mindful.]

Mercantile, mėr'kan-til, *a.* Pertaining to trade; trading; commercial; carrying on commerce. [Fr.—L. *mercor, mercatus*, to trade.]

Mercenary, mėr'ee-na-ri, *a.* That works for the sake of payment; hired; purchased for money; venal; that may be hired; moved by the love of money; mean; selfish; contracted from motives of gain.—*n.* One who acts for the sake of reward or gain; a soldier that is hired into foreign service; a hireling. [L. *mercenarius—merces*, hire—*mereo*, to earn.]

Mercer, mėr'sėr, *n.* One who deals in silks and woollen cloths. [Fr. *mercier*—L. *mercor*, to trade.]

Mercery, mėr'se-ri, *n.* The commodities or goods in which a mercer deals; trade of mercers. [Fr. *mercerie*.]

Merchandise, mėr'chand-iz, *n.* The commodities of a merchant; the objects of commerce; trade; traffic; commerce. [Fr. *marchandise*.]

Merchant, mėr'chant, *n.* One who traffics with foreign countries, or who exports and imports goods and sells them by wholesale; any trader, or one who deals in the purchase and sale of goods; a trading vessel†.—*a.* Related to trade or commerce. [Fr. *marchand*—L. *mercor*, to trade.]

Merchantable, mėr'chant-a-bl, *a.* That may be bought and sold; fit for market.

Merchantman, mėr'chant-man, *n.* A ship employed in the transportation of goods.

Merciful, mėr'si-fŭl, *a.* Full of mercy; compassionate; unwilling to punish for injuries; unwilling to give pain; not cruel.

Mercifully, mėr'si-fŭl-li, *adv.* With compassion or pity; tenderly; mildly.

Mercifulness, mėr'si-fŭl-nes, *n.* Quality of being merciful; readiness to forgive.

Merciless, mėr'si-les, *a.* Destitute of mercy; pitiless; hard-hearted; not sparing, as a storm.

Mercilessly, mėr'si-les-li, *adv.* In a manner void of mercy; cruelly.

Mercilessness, mėr'si-les-nes, *n.* Quality of being merciless.

Mercurial, mėr-kū'ri-al, *a.* Formed under the influence of the fabled god Mercury; sprightly; full of fire or vigour; pertaining to or containing quicksilver. [L. *mercurialis*.]

Mercurialise, mėr-kū'ri-al-īz, *vt.* To treat or impregnate with mercury. *ppr.* mercurialising, *pret. & pp.* mercurialised.

Mercurially, mėr-kū'ri-al-li, *adv.* In a mercurial or lively manner; actively.

Mercury, mėr'kū-ri, *n.* In mythology, the messenger and interpreter of the gods, and the god of eloquence and trade; quicksilver, a metal white like silver, which is liquid at all ordinary temperatures, named, from its mobility, after the god Mercury; the planet which is nearest to the sun; a newspaper or periodical publication. [L. *Mercurius—merz, mercis*, goods.]

Mercy, mėr'si, *n.* Tenderness; willingness to spare and save; forgiveness; grace; that benevolence which disposes a person to overlook injuries; mildness, pity, or compassion; an act or exercise of mercy; clemency; charity, or the duties of charity and benevolence; act of sparing. [Fr. *merci*, mercy, also thanks.]

Mercy-seat, mėr'si-sēt, *n.* The propitiatory; the covering of the ark of the covenant among the Jews.

Mere, mėr, *a.* Pure; unmixed; alone; this or that only; distinct from anything else. [L. *merus*, pure—Sans. *mri*, to purify.]

Mere, mėr, *n.* A lake, pool, or marsh. [Sax. *mere*—L. *mare*, the sea.]

Merely, mėr'li, *adv.* Only; thus and no other way; for this and no other purpose; solely; barely; hardly.

Meretricious, me-rē-tri'shi-us, *a.* Such as is practised by harlots; alluring by false show; having a gaudy but deceitful appearance; false. [L. *meretricius—meretrix*, a harlot—*mereo*, to earn money.]

Meretriciously, me-rē-tri'shi-us-li, *adv.* In the manner of harlots.

Merge, mėrj, *vt.* To sink in the sea or in water; to immerse; to cause to be swallowed up.—*vi.* To be sunk, swallowed up, or lost. *ppr.* merging, *pret. & pp.* merged. [L. *mergo—mare*, the sea.]

Meridian, mė-ri'di-an, *n.* Mid-day; noon, when the sun is highest; the highest point; a great circle supposed to pass through the poles of the earth, and the zenith and nadir of any given place; the particular place or state, with regard to local circumstances or things that distinguish it from others.—*a.* Being on the meridian; pertaining to the meridian; pertaining to the highest point. [Fr. *méridien*—L. *medius*, mid, and *dies*, day.]

Meridional, mē-ri'di-on-al, *a.* Pertaining to the meridian; southern; southerly. [Fr. *méridional*.]

Merino, me-rē'nō, *n.* A thin woollen fabric made of merino wool, for ladies' wear. [Sp.]

Merit, me'rit, *n.* That which one deserves; that which is earned; desert; excellence which entitles one to honour; worth; any performance which claims compensation; value; excellence, as of a book.—*vt.* To deserve; to earn by active service; to have a just title to. [Fr. *mérite*—L. *mereo, meritus*, to deserve.]

Merited, me'rit-ed, *p.a.* Earned; deserved.

Maritorious, me-rit-ō'ri-us, *a.* Having merit; deserving of reward or of notice, regard, fame, or happiness; praiseworthy. [Fr. *méritoire*.]

Meritoriously, me-rit-ō'ri-us-li, *adv.* In such a manner as to deserve reward.

Meritoriousness, me-rit-ō'ri-us-nes, *n.* State or quality of being meritorious.

Merle, mėrl, *n.* A bird that flies alone; a blackbird. [L. *merula—merus*, sole, and *volo*, to fly.]

Mermaid, mėr'mād, *n.* A sea-maid; a supposed marine animal, said to resemble a woman in the upper parts of the body, and a fish in the lower part. [Fr. *mer*, the sea, and *maid*.]

Merrily, me'ri-li, *adv.* With mirth.

Merriment, me'ri-ment, *n.* Mirth; gaiety with laughter or noise; festivity; frolic; glee; hilarity; jollity.

Merry, me'ri, *a.* Joyous; hilarious; gay and noisy; causing laughter; sprightly; vigorous; agreeable; delightful. [Sax. *mirige*; Low G. *mêre*, loud.]

Merry-andrew, me'ri-an-drō, *n.* A buffoon; one whose business is to make sport for others. [said to be from Andrew Borde, a facetious physician in the time of Henry VIII.]

Merry-thought, me'ri-thạt, *n.* The forked bone of a fowl's breast, which boys and girls break by pulling each one side, the longer part broken betokening priority of marriage.

Messentery, me'sen-te-ri, *n.* The middle of the intestines; a membrane, attached to the vertebræ, and serving to retain the intestines in a proper position. [Gr. *mesentérion—mesos*, middle, and *enteron*, an entrail.]

Mesh, mesh, *n.* The space between the threads of a net; a net itself.—*vt.* To catch in a net; to insnare. [Sax. *mascre*.]

Meshy, mesh'i, *a.* Formed like net-work; reticulated.

Mesmerism, mes'mėr-ism, *n.* Animal magnetism; the power of producing a kind of unconsciousness to external objects, while the mind remains active. [from *Mesmer*, the author.]

Mess, mes, *n.* A dish or a quantity of food set on a table at one time; a number of persons who eat together; the whole quantity of food prepared for those who eat at the same table; a confusion.—*vi.* To partake of a mess; to feed; to associate at the same table; to eat in company.—*vt.* To supply with a mess. [Sax. *mese*—L. *mensa*, a table.]

Message, mes'sāj, *n.* Any notice, written or verbal, sent from one person to another; errand; an official verbal communication from one branch of a legislature to the other. [Fr.—L. *mitto, missum*, to send.]

Messenger, mes'sen-jėr, *n.* One who bears a message; a harbinger; a herald. [Fr. *messager*.]

Messiah, mes-si'a, *n.* The Anointed One; Christ, the Anointed; the Saviour of the world. [Heb. *mâshĭyach*, anointed—*mashach*, to anoint.]

Messiahship, mes-si'a-ship, *n.* The character, state, or office of the Saviour.

Messmate, mes'māt, *n.* An associate in eating. [*mess* and *mate*.]

Metage, mēt'āj, *n.* Measurement of coal; price of measuring. [Fr. *metre*.]

Metal, me'tal, *n.* That which is searched for and dug up in mines; a simple, fixed, shining, opaque substance, insoluble in water, fusible by heat, and having a peculiar lustre, as gold, silver, copper, iron, lead, &c.; the broken stone used for covering roads. [Fr. *métal*—Gr. *metallon*.]

Metallic, mē-tal'ik, *a.* Pertaining to metals; consisting of metal; like a metal. [Fr. *métallique*.]

Metalline, me'tal-in, *a.* Pertaining to a metal; impregnated with metal.

Metallurgic, me-tal-ėr'jik, *a.* Pertaining to metallurgy.

Metallurgy, me'tal-ėr-ji, *n.* The art of working metals; the art of separating metals from their ores or other combinations. [Fr. *métallurgie*—Gr. *metallon*, and *ergon*, work.]

Metamorphose, me-ta-mor'fōs, *vt.* To change into a different form; to transform. *ppr.* metamorphosing, *pret. & pp.* metamorphosed. [Fr. *métamorphoser*.]

Metamorphosis, me-ta-mor'fōs-is, *n.* Change of form; a change in the form of being, as of a chrysalis into a winged animal; any change of form or shape. [Gr. *metamorphōsis—meta*, and *morphē*, form.]

Metaphor, me'ta-fėr, *n.* A carrying over; a transferring of a word from its proper signification to a different one; a figure of speech by which the name and properties of one object are ascribed to another; a simile without the sign. [Fr. *métaphore*; Gr. *meta*, and *pherō*, to carry.]

---

ch, *chain*; j, *job*; g, *go*; ng, *sing*; ᴛʜ, *then*; th, *thin*; w, *wig*; wh, *whig*; zh, *azure*; † obsolete.

Metaphorical, me-ta-fo′rik-al, *a. Pertaining to metaphor;* comprising a metaphor; not literal. [Fr. *métaphorique.*]

Metaphorically, me-ta-fo′rik-al-li, *adv. In a metaphorical manner.*

Metaphysical, me-ta-fi′zik-al, *a. Pertaining to metaphysics;* according to the rules or principles of metaphysics; existing only in thought; supernatural. [Fr. *métaphysique.*]

Metaphysically, me-ta-fi′zik-al-li, *adv. In the manner of metaphysical science.*

Metaphysician, me′ta-fi-zi″shan, *n. One who is versed in metaphysics.* [Fr. *métaphysicien.*]

Metaphysics, me-ta-fi′ziks, *n.* That science which comes immediately *after physics,* according to the philosophy of Aristotle; the science of the principles and causes of all things existing; the philosophy of mind, as distinguished from that of matter. [Fr. *métaphysique*—Gr. *meta,* after, and *phusika,* physics.]

Metathesis, me-ta′the-sis, *n. Transposition;* a figure by which the letters or syllables of a word are transposed. [Gr. *metathésis—meta,* and *títhēmi,* to place.]

Mete, mēt, *vt. To measure;* to ascertain, as quantity, dimensions, or capacity, by any rule or standard. *ppr.* meting, *pret. & pp.* meted. [Sax. *metan*—L. *metior,* to measure.]

Metempsychosis, mē-tem′si-kō″sis, *n.* The passing of the soul of a man after death into some other animal body; the *transmigration of souls.* [Gr.—*meta,* denoting change, *en,* in, and *psuchē,* soul.]

Meteor, mē′tē-ėr, *n.* That which is *suspended aloft in the air;* a luminous body flying in the atmosphere; anything that transiently dazzles. [Fr. *météore*—Gr. *aeirō,* to lift up.]

Meteoric, mē-tē-or′ik, *a. Pertaining to meteors;* consisting of meteors.

Meteorological, mē′tē-ėr-ol-oj″ik-al, *a. Pertaining or relating to meteors or meteorology.*

Meteorologist, mē′tē-ėr-ol″o-jist, *n. One versed or skilled in meteorology.* [Fr. *météorologiste.*]

Meteorology, mē′tē-ėr-ol″o-ji, *n. The science of meteors,* or the science which explains the various phenomena which have their origin in the atmosphere. [Fr. *météorologie*—Gr. *meteóros,* a meteor, and *logos,* discourse.]

Meter, mēt′ėr, *n. One who* or *that which measures.* [from *mete,* to measure.]

Meteyard, mēt′yärd, *n.* A *yard* used as a *measure.*

Methinks, mē-thingks′, *v. impers. It seems to me;* it appears to me; I think. (Used in poetry.) *pp.* methought.

Method, me′thod, *n. An orderly procedure;* a suitable and convenient arrangement of things, proceedings, or ideas; the regular disposition of separate things or parts; clear exhibition; way; manner; order; course. [Fr. *méthode*—Gr. *meta,* after, and *hodos,* a way.]

Methodical, me-thod′ik-al, *a. Having method;* arranged in convenient order; disposed in a just and natural manner; orderly; systematic. [Fr. *méthodique.*]

Methodically, me-thod′ik-al-li, *adv. In a methodical manner.*

Methodism, me′thod-izm, *n.* The doctrines and worship of the *Methodists.*

Methodist, me′thod-ist, *n. One who observes method;* one of a sect of Christians, so called from the exact regularity of their lives, and the strictness of their principles and rules.

Methodize, me′thod-iz, *vt. To reduce to method;* to dispose in due order; to arrange in a convenient manner. *ppr.* methodizing, *pret. & pp.* methodised.

Metonymy, me-ton′i-mi, *n. A change of name;* a figure of speech in which one word is put for another. [Gr. *metonumia—meta,* and *onoma,* a name.]

Metre, mē′tėr, *n. Measure;* arrangement of poetical feet, or of long and short syllables in verse. [Fr. *mètre*—Gr. *metron,* measure.]

Metrical, met′rik-al, *a. Pertaining to measure,* or due arrangement of long and short syllables; consisting of verses. [L. *metricus.*]

Metrically, met′rik-al-li, *adv. In a metrical manner.*

Metropolis, mē-tro′pō-lis, *n. The mother city;* the chief city or capital of a kingdom, state, or country. [Gr. *mētēr,* mother, and *pólis,* city.]

Metropolitan, met-rō-po′li-tan, *a. Belonging to a metropolis,* or to the mother-church; residing in the chief city.—*n.* The bishop who presides over the other bishops of a province. [Fr. *métropolitain.*]

Mettle, met′l, *n.* That which goes to form anything; high temper; keenness of edge; spirit: that temperament which is susceptible of high excitement. [corrupted from *metal,* but written so when the metaphorical sense is used.]

Mettled, met′ld, *p.a.* High-spirited; ardent; full of fire.

Mettlesome, met′l-sum, *a.* Full of spirit; brisk; fiery.

Mew, mū, *n.* A sea-fowl; a gull, so named from its cry. [Sax. *mæw.*]

Mew, mū, *n.* The cage in which hawks *changed* their feathers; a cage for birds; an inclosure; a place of confinement; (pl.) places for inclosing horses; stables. *vt.* To shut up; to inclose; to confine, as in a cage or other inclosure.—*vi.* To moult; to put on a new appearance. [Fr. *mue,* moulting—L. *muto,* to change.]

Mew, mū, *vi. To cry, as a cat.*—*n. The cry of a cat.* [W. *mewian.*]

Mewl, mūl, *vi. To cry* from uneasiness, *as a child;* to squall. [Fr. *miauler.*]

Miasma, mi-az′ma, *n.* Miasmata, mi-az′ma-ta, *pl. A stain; pollution;* the noxious effluvia of any putrefying bodies, rising and floating in the atmosphere. [Gr.—*miainō,* to stain.]

Miasmatic, mi-az-mat′ik, *a. Pertaining to miasma.*

Mica, mī′ka, *n.* A mineral capable of being cleaved into *shining* elastic plates of extreme thinness. [L.—*mico,* to shine.]

Micaceous, mī-kā′shē-us, *a. Pertaining to or consisting of mica;* like mica. [Fr. *micacé.*]

Michaelmas, mi′kel-mas, *n. The feast of St. Michael,* Sept. 29.

Micher, mi′chėr, *n. One who lies hid;* a truant.

Microcosm, mi′krō-kozm, *n. The little world;* but used for man, supposed to be an epitome of the universe or great world. [Gr. *mikros,* small, and *kosmos,* world.]

Micrography, mi-krog′ra-fi, *n. The description of objects too small to be discerned without the aid of a microscope.* [Gr. *mikros,* small, and *graphō,* to describe.]

Micrometer, mi-krom′et-ėr, *n. An instrument for measuring small objects,* spaces, or angles. [Gr. *mikros,* small, and *metron,* measure.]

Microscope, mī′krō-skōp, *n. An optical instrument for viewing objects too small* to be seen by the naked eye. [Fr.—Gr. *mikros,* small, and *skopeō,* to view.]

Microscopic, mī-krō-skop′ik, *a. Made by the aid of a microscope;* resembling a microscope; capable of seeing small objects; visible only by the aid of a microscope.

Microscopically, mī-krō-skop′ik-al-li, *adv. By the microscope.*

Mid, mid, *a. Middle;* at equal distance from extremes.—*n. Middle;* midst. [Sax. *midd,*]

Mid-air, mid′ār, *n. The middle of the sky.*

Mid-day, mid′dā, *n. The middle of the day;* noon.

Middle, mid′l, *a. Situated in the centre;* equally distant from the extremes; mean; intervening.—*n. The central part;* the point or part equally distant from the extremities; the time that passes, or events that happen, between the beginning and the end; the waist. [Sax. *middel*—L. *medius.*]

Middle-age, mid′l-āj, *a. Relating to the middle-ages;* mediæval.—*n. The middle period of life;* (pl.) the period which intervened between the downfall of the Roman empire and the revival of letters in the fifteenth century.

Middle-aged, mid′l-ājd, *a. Being about the middle of the ordinary age* of man.

Middle-earth, mid′l-ėrth, *n.* The world, considered as lying between heaven and hell.

Middling, mid′l-ing, *a. Of middle rank or quality;* moderate; ordinary. [Sax. *midlene.*]

Mid-earth, mid′ėrth, *n. The middle of the earth.*

Midge, mij, *n. A small gnat or fly.* [Sax. *micge*—L. *musca.*]

Mid-heaven, mid′hev-n, *n. The middle of the sky or heaven.*

Midland, mid′land, *a. Being in the interior country;* distant from the coast or sea-shore.

Midmost, mid′mōst, *a. Middle;* as, the midmost battles.

Midnight, mid′nīt, *n. The middle of the night;* twelve o'clock at night.—*a. Being in the middle of the night;* dark as midnight; very dark.

Midriff, mid′rif, *n. The mid-belly;* the diaphragm. [Sax. *midrif—midd,* mid, and *hrife,* the bowels.]

Midshipman, mid′ship-man, *n.* A kind of naval cadet in a ship of war.

Midst, midst, *n. The very middle;* the central part.—*adv. In the middle.*

Midsummer, mid′sum-mėr, *n. The middle of summer;* the summer solstice, about the 21st of June.

Midway, mid′wā, *n. The middle of the way or distance.*—*a. Being in the middle of the way or distance.*—*adv. In the middle of the way;* half-way.

Midwife, mid′wīf, *n. A woman who is present with,* or attends and assists, other women in childbirth. [Sax. *mid,* with, and *wif.*]

Midwifery, mid′wīf-ri, *n.* The art or practice of assisting women in childbirth; assistance at childbirth.

Mid-winter, mid′win-tėr, *n. The middle of winter;* the winter solstice, Dec. 21.

Mien, mēn, *n. Figure; form;* form of the countenance; aspect; demeanour; manner. [Fr. *mine.*]

Might, mīt, *n. Strength; force; power;* bodily strength; military force; valour; strength of means; force of purpose;

strength of affection; strength of light; effulgence. *pret.* of may (which see). [Sax. *miht—magan*, to be able.]
Mightily, mit'i-li, *adv. With great power*, force, or strength of body, heart, or mind; to a great degree.
Mightiness, mit'i-nes, *n. Quality of being mighty*; height of dignity; a title of dignity.
Mighty, mit'i, *a. Having might*; having great bodily strength; bold; very strong in numbers; rushing with violence; forcible; eminent in intellect or acquirements; wonderful; performed with great power. [Sax. *mihtig*.]
Mignonette, min-yon-net', *n. The little darling or favourite*; an annual plant, bearing flowers of an agreeable odour. [Fr. from *mignon*, *mignonne*, a darling.]
Migrate, mi'grāt, *vi.* To pass or remove from one country or from one state to another, with a view to residence, either temporary or permanent. *ppr.* migrating, *pret. & pp.* migrated. [L. *migro, migratus*.]
Migration, mi-grā'shon, *n. Act of migrating*; removal. [L. *migratio*.]
Migratory, mi'grā-tō-ri, *a. Disposed to migrate*; roving; wandering; occasionally removing for pasturage; passing from one climate to another, as birds.
Milch, milsh, *a. Giving milk*, as cows or goats; soft; tender; merciful. [Sax. *melce*, milk.]
Mild, mild, *a. Melting*; soft; not violent; lenitive; tender and gentle in temper; kind; merciful; melting with tenderness; not fierce; not stern; moderately sweet; in a state of calmness; moderate. [Sax.—Old G. *milti*.]
Mildew, mil'dū, *n.* A thin whitish coating found sometimes on the leaves of vegetables, occasioning disease, decay, and death.—*vt. To taint with mildew*. [Sax. *mildeaw*.]
Mildewed, mil'dūd, *p.a. Tainted or injured by mildew*.
Mildly, mild'li, *adv. Meltingly*; gently; tenderly; not roughly or violently.
Mildness, mild'nes, *n. Quality of being mild*; gentleness; tenderness; gentleness of operation; the quality that affects the senses pleasantly; moderate state.
Mile, mil, *n.* A thousand paces, each five feet, among the Romans; in England, a measure of length or distance, equal to 1760 yards. [Sax. *mil*—L. *mille*, a thousand.]
Mileage, mil'āj, *n. Fees paid for travel by the mile*.
Milestone, mil'stōn, *n.* A stone set on a road to mark the distance or space of a mile.
Milfoil, mil'foil, *n.* An herb, yarrow, with *numerous leaves*. [L. *millefolium*, a thousand leaves—*folium*, a leaf.]
Miliary, mi'li-a-ri, *a.* Accompanied with an eruption like *millet-seeds*. [Fr. *miliaire*—L. *milium*, millet.]
Militant, mi'li-tant, *a. Serving as a soldier*; engaged in a constant warfare. [L. *militans—miles, militis*, a soldier.]
Militarist, mi'li-ta-rist, *n.* A military man.
Military, mi'li-ta-ri, *a. Pertaining to soldiers or to arms*; becoming a soldier; martial; derived from the services of a soldier; conformable to the rules of armies; performed or made by soldiers. *n. The whole body of soldiers*; soldiery; an army. [Fr. *militaire*.]
Militate, mi'li-tāt, *vi. To fight*; to be or to act in opposition. (With *against* and *with*.) *ppr.* militating, *pret. & pp.* militated. [L. *milito, militatus*.]

Militia, mi-li'shi-a, *n.* The national *soldiery*; distinguished from the regular standing forces, or standing army. [L.]
Milk, milk, *n. That which is drawn from the breasts*, or from the teats of cows, &c.; a white fluid secreted by certain glands in female animals for the nourishment of their young; the white juice of certain plants; emulsion made by bruising seeds.—*vt. To draw or press milk from by the hand or mouth*. [Sax. *meolc*; Old G. *miluh*—Sans. *mrij*, to drain, to dry, to purify.]
Milker, milk'ėr, *n. One who milks*; a cow giving milk.
Milkiness, milk'i-nes, *n. Qualities like those of milk*; softness.
Milking, milk'ing, *p.n. Act of drawing milk* from the breasts of an animal by the hand.
Milk-livered, milk'li-vėrd, *a.* Cowardly.
Milkmaid, milk'mād, *n.* A woman who milks or is employed in the dairy.
Milksop, milk'sop, *n.* A piece of bread sopped in *milk*; a soft, feeble-minded man.
Milky, milk'i, *a. Made of milk*; resembling milk; gentle; timorous.
Milky-way, milk'i-wā, *n. The galaxy*; a broad, luminous path in the heavens.
Mill, mil, *n. That which grinds*; a machine for reducing to fine particles grain, fruit, &c.; the building that contains the machinery for grinding, &c.—*vt. To grind*; to reduce to fine particles; to make a raised impression round the edges of, as of a piece of money to prevent the clipping of the coin; to full, as cloth. [Sax. *mîln*—L. *molo*, to grind.]
Mill-dam, mil'dam, *n.* A dam to obstruct a water-course, and raise the water to an altitude sufficient to *turn a mill-wheel*.
Milled, mild, *p.a.* Fulled; subjected to the operation of milling, as a coin.
Millenarian, mil-lē-nā'ri-an, *a. Consisting of a thousand years*; pertaining to the millennium.—*n.* One who believes in Christ's personal reign on the earth *for a thousand years*. [Fr. *millénaire*.]
Millennial, mil-len'i-al, *a. Pertaining to the millennium*, or to a thousand years.
Millennium, mil-len'i-um, *n. A thousand years*; a word used to denote the thousand years mentioned in Rev. xx. [L. *mille*, a thousand, and *annus*, a year.]
Milleped, mil'lē-pēd, *n.* The wood-louse, an insect having *many feet*. [L. *mille*, a thousand, and *pes, pedis*, a foot.]
Miller, mil'ėr, *n.* One *who attends a mill*. [from *mill*.]
Millesimal, mil-les'im-al, *a. Thousandth*; consisting of thousandth parts. [L. *millesimus*.]
Millet, mil'et, *n.* A kind of grass and its seed, which is used for food in some countries. [Fr.—L. *milium*.]
Mill-horse, mil'hors, *n.* A horse that turns a mill.
Milliner, mil'in-ėr, *n.* A woman who makes and sells head-dresses, hats, or bonnets, &c., for females. [supposed to be *Milaner*, from *Milan*, in Italy.]
Millinery, mil'in-ė-ri, *n. The articles made or sold by milliners*.
Milling, mil'ing, *p.n. Act or employment of grinding or passing through a mill*; act of making raised impressions on the edges of coin, or the impressions thus made.
Million, mil'li-on, *n.* A thousand times *a thousand*; the number of ten hundred thousand; a very great number. [Fr.—L. *mille*, a thousand.]
Millionaire, mil'yon-ār, *n.* A *man worth a million* of pounds; a very rich person. [Fr.]
Millioned, mil'li-ond, *p.a. Multiplied by millions*.
Millionth, mil'li-onth, *a.* The ten hundred thousandth.
Mill-pond, mil'pond, *n.* A *pond* of water raised *for driving a mill-wheel*.
Mill-sixpence, mil'siks-pens, *n.* An old English coin, first milled in 1561, being one of the earliest that was milled.
Millstone, mil'stōn, *n.* A *stone in a mill*, used for grinding grain.
Milt, milt, *n.* The sperm of the male fish, *which is easily melted*; the spleen. *vt.* To impregnate, as the roe or spawn of the female fish. [Sax.—*miltan*, to dissolve.]
Milter, milt'ėr, *n.* A male fish.
Mimetic, mi-met'ik, *a. Imitative*; apt to imitate. [Gr. *mimétikos*.]
Mimic, mim'ik, *a. Imitative*; inclined to imitate or to ape; consisting of imitation.—*n. One who imitates*; an actor; a buffoon who attempts to excite laughter or derision by acting or speaking in the manner of another; a mean imitator.—*vt. To imitate*, or ape for sport; to ridicule by imitation. *ppr.* mimicking, *pret. & pp.* mimicked. [Fr. *mimique*; Gr. *mimos*, an imitator.]
Mimicry, mim'ik-ri, *n. Ludicrous imitation* for sport or ridicule.
Minaret, mi'na-ret, *n.* A slender, lofty turret on Mahometan mosques, having a balcony, from which the people are called to prayer. [Fn—Ar. *manarat*.]
Mince, mins, *vt.* To chop into very *small pieces*; to diminish in speaking; to cut off, or omit, as a part for the purpose of suppressing the truth; to clip, as words; not to utter the full sound of. *vi.* To walk with *small* steps; to affect delicacy in manner; to speak softly, or with affected nicety. *ppr.* mincing, *pret. & pp.* minced. [Sax. *minsian*—L. *minuo*, to make smaller.]
Minced, minst, *p.a.* Cut into very *small pieces*.
Mince-pie, mins'pī, *n.* A *pie made with minced meat* and other ingredients.
Mincingly, mins'ing-li, *adv.* In small parts; not fully.
Mind, mīnd, *n.* The *thinking* principle; the intelligent power in man; the understanding; the heart or seat of affection; the will; purpose; design; opinion, memory.—*vt. To fix the mind on*; to attend to; to fix the thoughts on; to mark; to heed; to regard; to intend; to put in mind!.—*vi.* To be inclined. [Sax. *gemynd*—Goth. *munan*, Sans. *man*, to think.]
Minded, mīnd'ed, *p.a.* Disposed; inclined.
Mindful, mīnd'fụl, *a. Bearing in mind*; regarding with care; observant; regardful.
Mindfully, mīnd'fụl-li, *adv.* Attentively; heedfully.
Mindfulness, mīnd'fụl-nes, *n. Quality of being mindful*; heedfulness.
Mindless, mīnd'les, *a. Not endued with mind*; *unthinking*; inattentive; heedless.
Mine, mīn, *pron.* possessive case of *I*, and also *adj. pron. My*; belonging to me. [Sax. *min*.]
Mine, mīn, *n.* A pit in the earth from which *metallic ores* or *other mineral* substances are taken by digging; a passage dug under the wall of a fortification, where a quantity of powder may be lodged for blowing up the

works; a rich source of wealth or other good.—*vi. To dig a mine* or pit in the earth; to dig for ores, &c.; to form a burrow in the earth, as animals.—*vt. To undermine;* to sap; to dig away or otherwise remove, as the foundation; to ruin or destroy by slow degrees. *ppr.* mining, *pret. & pp.* mined. [G.]

Miner, min'ẽr, *n.* One who digs for *metal ores* and *other minerals;* one who digs passages under the walls of a fort, &c.

Mineral, mi'ne-ral, *n. That which is found in mines;* any natural body destitute of organization, which naturally exists within the earth or at its surface, and which is neither vegetable nor animal; a minet.—*a. Pertaining to minerals;* impregnated with minerals. [Fr. *mineral.*]

Mineralize, mi'ne-ral-īz, *vt. To make mineral;* to convert into a mineral; to impregnate with a mineral substance. *vi.* To go on an excursion for the collecting of *minerals. ppr.* mineralizing, *pret. & pp.* mineralized. [Fr. *mineraliser.*]

Mineralized, mi'ne-ral-īzd, *p.a. Impregnated with a mineral.*

Mineralogical, mi'ne-ral-oj''ik-al, *a. Pertaining to the science of minerals.*

Mineralogically, mi'ne-ral-oj''ik-al-li, *adv. According to mineralogy.*

Mineralogist, mi-ne-ral'o-jist, *n. One who is versed in the science of minerals;* one who treats of the properties of mineral bodies.

Mineralogy, mi-ne-ral'o-ji, *n. A discourse on minerals;* the science which treats of the properties of mineral substances, and teaches us to distinguish and classify them. [Fr. *minéralogie;* Gr. *logos,* discourse.]

Mingle, ming'gl, *vt. To mix;* to mix or blend without order; to compound; to unite in a mass, as solid substances; to join in mutual intercourse; to render impure; to confuse.—*vi. To be mixed;* to be united with. *ppr.* mingling, *pret. & pp.* mingled.—*n.* Promiscuous mass. [Sax. *mengan*—Gr. *mignuô,* to mix.]

Miniature, mi'ni-a-tūr, *n. A painting executed with vermilion;* a painting in water-colours on vellum, ivory, or paper, with points or dots; a portrait or representation in a small compass, or less than the reality.—*a.* Representing nature on a small scale; very small. [It. *miniatura;* L. *minium,* vermilion.]

Minim, mi'nim, *n. The least part;* something *exceedingly small;* a note in music, equal to two crotchets; the smallest liquid measure; a single drop. [Fr. *minime*—L. *minimum,* the least.]

Minimum, mi'ni-mum, *n. The least quantity* assignable in a given case; the lowest price of any article. [L.]

Minimus, mi'ni-mus, *n.* A being of the smallest size.

Mining, min'ing, *p.a.* Pertaining to the *digging of mines.*—*p.n. The art of digging mines* for the purpose of discovering metallic ores, &c.

Minion, mi'ni-on, *n. One dear or loved;* the favourite of a prince, on whom he lavishes his favours; one who gains favours by mean adulation. [Fr. *mignon;* Old G. *minna,* love.]

Minister, mi'nis-tẽr, *n. An inferior;* a servant; one to whom a king or prince intrusts the direction of affairs of state; a magistrate; an ambassador; one who serves at the altar; the pastor of a church; a messenger of God.—*vt.*

To give; to afford; to supply.—*vi. To serve;* to perform service in any office, sacred or secular; to give things needful; to supply the means of relief (With *to* or *unto.*) [L.—*minor,* less.]

Ministerial, mi-nis-tē'ri-al, *a. Pertaining to a minister;* acting under superior authority; official; pertaining to ministers of the gospel; pertaining to ministers of state. [Fr. *ministériel.*]

Ministerialist, mi-nis-tē'ri-al-ist, *n. A supporter of the ministry of the day.*

Ministerially, mi-nis-tē'ri-al-li, *adv. In a ministerial manner.*

Ministering, mi'nis-tẽr-ing, *p.a.* Administering things needful.

Ministration, mi-nis-trā'shon, *n. Act of ministering;* intervention for aid or service; service; ecclesiastical function. [Late L. *ministratio.*]

Ministry, mi'nis-tri, *n. The office of a minister;* service; aid; instrumentality; ecclesiastical profession; service of a clergyman; the clergy taken collectively; duration of the office of a minister, civil or ecclesiastical; persons who compose the executive government; the body of ministers of state. [Fr. *ministère.*]

Minnow, min'nō, *n. A very small* freshwater fish; the young of larger kinds of fish. [Fr. *menu,* small—L. *minuo,* to make smaller.]

Minor, mi'nor, *a. Smaller;* less; lower; of small consequence; less or lower by a lesser semitone, in music; noting that key which is chiefly used for mournful subjects; noting that term of a syllogism which forms the subject of the conclusion.—*n.* A person of either sex *below* or *under age,* or under 21 years of age. [L.]

Minority, mi-no'ri-ti, *n. State of being a minor;* the period from birth until 21 years of age; the smaller number; state of being smaller or inferior; the party that has the fewest votes. [Fr. *minorité.*]

Minster, min'stẽr, *n. The church of a monastery,* or one to which a monastery has been attached; sometimes a cathedral church. [Sax. *minstre.*]

Minstrel, min'strel, *n.* Originally, one *who ministered* to the amusement of the great by music; one of an order of men in the middle ages who subsisted by the arts of poetry and music, and sang to the harp verses composed by themselves or others; a musician; a bard; a singer. [Old Fr. *menestrier—* L. *minister,* a servant.]

Minstrelsy, min'strel-si, *n. The arts* and occupations *of minstrels;* a number of musicians; the collective body of songs.

Mint, mint, *n. The place where money* is coined by public authority; a place of fabrication; a source of abundant supply.—*vt. To make* and *stamp,* as *money;* to coin; to forge. [Sax. *mynet—smiththa,* a minter's smithy; L. *moneta,* money.]

Mint, mint, *n.* An aromatic plant. [Sax. *minta.*]

Minuend, mi'nū-end, *n. That which is to be lessened;* the number from which another number is *to be subtracted.* [L. *minuendum—minuo,* to lessen.]

Minuet, mi'nū-et, *n.* A stately regular dance; a tune or air to regulate the movements in the dance so called. [Fr. *menuet—menu,* delicate.]

Minus, mi'nus. *Less;* the sign (−) in algebra, denoting less, prefixed to negative quantities, or quantities to be subtracted. [L.]

Minute, mi-nūt', *a. Diminished;* of very

small bulk or size; particular; exact; critical. [Fr.—L. *minuo,* to lessen—*minor*—*minus,* less.]

Minute, mi'nit, *n. A small portion* of time, being the sixtieth part of an hour; the sixtieth part of a degree; a short sketch of any agreement or other subject, taken in writing; a note to preserve the memory of anything.—*vt.* To set down a *short* sketch or note of, as any agreement or other subject in writing. *ppr.* minuting, *pret. & pp.* minuted. [L. *minūtum*—*minuo,* to lessen.]

Minutely, mi-nūt'li, *adv. In a minute manner.*

Minuteness, mi-nūt'nes, *n.* Extreme *smallness,* fineness, or slenderness; attention to small things; critical exactness.

Minutia, mi-nū'shi-e, *n. pl. Small or minute things.* [L.]

Minx, mingks, *n. A* pert, wanton girl. [Icel. *minkr,* a lessening, diminution, disgrace.]

Mirable, mir'a-bl, *a.* Wonderful.

Miracle, mi'ra-kl, *n. A wonderful sight or thing;* an event contrary to the established course of things; a deviation from the known laws of nature; a supernatural event.—*vt.* To make wonderful. [Fr.—L. *miror,* to wonder at.]

Miraculous, mi-ra'kū-lus, *a. Having the nature of a miracle;* performed supernaturally; effected by the direct agency of almighty power; wonderful; extraordinary. [Fr. *miraculeux.*]

Miraculously, mi-ra'kū-lus-li, *adv. By miracle;* by extraordinary means.

Mirage, mi-räzh', *n.* An optical illusion, causing remote objects to be seen double, as if reflected in a *mirror,* or to appear as if suspended in the air. [Fr.; Ar. *mirat,* a mirror.]

Mire, mir, *n. A* swamp; deep mud; earth so wet and soft as to yield to the feet and to wheels.—*vt. To plunge and fix in mire;* to soil or daub with mud or foul matter.—*vi. To sink in mire;* to sink so deep as to be unable to move forward. *ppr.* miring, *pret. & pp.* mired. [Icel. *myrr.*]

Miriness, mir'i-nes, *n. State of being miry,* or consisting of deep mud.

Mirror, mi'rẽr, *n. That in which a person may behold himself;* any glass that reflects the images of objects placed before it; a pattern; that on which men ought to fix their eyes; that which gives a true representation.—*vt. To reflect,* as in a mirror. [Old Fr.—L. *miror,* to wonder at.]

Mirth, mẽrth, *n.* Hilarity; noisy gaiety; merriment; fun; frolic. [Sax. *myrth.*]

Mirthful, mẽrth'ful, *a. Full of mirth;* merry; jovial; festive.

Mirthfully, mẽrth'ful-li, *adv.* In a jovial manner.

Mirthfulness, mẽrth'ful-nes, *n. State or quality of being mirthful.*

Miry, mir'i, *a. Full of mire;* abounding with deep mud; consisting of mire.

Misadventure, mis-ad-ven'tūr, *n. An unlucky adventure;* mischance; misfortune.

Misadvised, mis-ad-vīzd', *a. Ill-advised;* ill-directed.

Misalliance, mis-al-lī'ans, *n.* Improper association.

Misanthrope, Misanthropist, mis'an-thrōp, mis-an'thrōp-ist, *n. A hater of mankind;* one who hates or dislikes the society of man or mankind. [Gr. *misanthrōpos*—*miseō,* to hate, and *anthrōpos,* man.]

Fāte, fär, fat, fall; mē, met, hẽr pīne, pin; nōte, not, move; tūbe, tub, bull; oil, pound.

Misanthropic, mis-an-throp'ik, a. Hating mankind. [Fr. *misanthropique*.]
Misanthropy, mis-an'thrō-pi, n. Hatred or dislike to mankind. [Fr. *misanthropie*.]
Misapplication, mis-ap'pli-kā"shon, n. A wrong application.
Misapply, mis-ap-plī', vt. To apply amiss. ppr. misapplying, pret. & pp. misapplied.
Misapprehend, mis-ap'prē-hend", vt. To apprehend wrongly.
Misapprehension, mis-ap'prē-hen"shon, n. Wrong apprehension.
Misappropriate, mis-ap-prō'pri-āt, vt. To appropriate wrongly. ppr. misappropriating, pret. & pp. misappropriated.
Misappropriation, mis-ap-prō'pri-ā"shon, n. Wrong appropriation.
Misbecoming, mis-bē-kum'ing, p.a. Not becoming; unseemly; indecorous.
Misbehave, mis-bē-hāv', vi. To behave ill or improperly. (Often used with a reciprocal pronoun.) ppr. misbehaving, pret. & pp. misbehaved.
Misbehaved, mis-bē-hāvd', a. Rude.
Misbehaviour, mis-bē-hāv'i-ėr, n. Ill behaviour; misconduct.
Misbelief, mis-bē-lēf', n. Erroneous belief; false religion.
Misbelieve, mis-bē-lēv', vt. To believe erroneously. ppr. misbelieving, pret. & pp. misbelieved.
Misbelieving, mis-bē-lēv'ing, p.a. Believing erroneously; irreligious.
Miscalculate, mis-kal'kū-lāt, vt. To calculate erroneously. ppr. miscalculating, pret. & pp. miscalculated.
Miscalculation, mis-kal'kū-lā"shon, n. Erroneous calculation.
Miscarriage, mis-ka'rij, n. Wrong carriage; failure; improper behaviour; act of bringing forth before the time; abortion.
Miscarry, mis-ka'ri, vi. To fail of the intended effect; to suffer defeat; to bring forth young before the proper time. ppr. miscarrying, pret. & pp. miscarried.
Miscellaneous, mis-sel-lā'nē-us, a. Mixed; mingled; consisting of several kinds. [L. *miscellaneus*—L. *misceo*, to mix.]
Miscellany, mis'sel-la-ni, n. A mixture of various kinds; a book containing a collection of compositions on various subjects. [Sp. *miscelánea*.]
Mischance, mis-chans', n. Unlucky chance; ill luck; mishap; calamity; disaster.
Mischief, mis'chif, n. That which turns out ill; harm; injury; damage; harm or damage done by design; cause of trouble. [Old Fr. *meschef*—Fr. *chef*, L. *caput*, the head.]
Mischievous, mis'chev-us, a. Making mischief; injurious; producing injury or harm, as an act; inclined to do harm.
Mischievously, mis'chev-us-li, adv. With injury, hurt, loss, or damage.
Mischievousness, mis'chev-us-nes, n. Quality of being mischievous.
Miscible, mis'i-bi, a. That may be mixed. [Fr.]
Misconceive, mis-kon-sēv', vt. To misapprehend; to misunderstand.—vi. To receive a false notion or opinion of anything. ppr. misconceiving, pret. & pp. misconceived.
Misconception, mis-kon-sep'shon, n. Erroneous conception; false opinion; misapprehension.
Misconduct, mis-kon'dukt, n. Wrong conduct; ill management.

Misconduct, mis-kon-dukt', vt. To conduct amiss; to mismanage.
Misconstruction, mis-kon-struk'shon, n. Wrong construction; wrong interpretation of words or things.
Misconstrue, mis-kon strū, vt. To construe or interpret erroneously; to misinterpret. ppr. misconstruing, pret. & pp. misconstrued.
Miscount, mis-kount', vt. To count erroneously.—vi. To make a wrong reckoning.
Miscreant, mis'krē-ant, n. An infidel, or one who embraces a false faith; a vile wretch; an unprincipled fellow. [Old Fr. *mescreant*—L. *credo*, to believe.]
Misdate, mis'dāt, n. A wrong date.
Misdate, mis-dāt', vt. To date erroneously. ppr. misdating, pret. & pp. misdated.
Misdeed, mis-dēd', n. An evil deed; a wicked action; misdemeanour; transgression.
Misdemean, mis-dē-mēn', vt. To behave ill.
Misdemeanour, mis-dē-mēn'ėr, n. Ill demeanour; misconduct; an offence inferior to felony.
Misdirect, mis-di-rekt', vt. To give a wrong direction to.
Misdirection, mis-di-rek'shon, n. Act of directing wrongly; an error committed by a judge in charging a jury, in matters of law or of fact.
Misdo, mis-dö', vt. To do wrong; to do amiss; to commit, as a crime or fault.
Misdoer, mis-dö'ėr, n. One who commits a fault or crime.
Misdoubt†, mis-dout', n. Irresolution; hesitation.
Misemploy, mis-em-ploi', vt. To employ amiss; to employ to no purpose, or to a bad purpose; to misuse.
Miser, mī'zėr, n. A sordid wretch; an extremely covetous person; a niggard; one who in wealth makes himself miserable by the fear of poverty. [L.]
Miserable, mi'zėr-a-bl, a. Pitiable; wretched; very unhappy, from grief, pain, or other cause; worthless; causing misery; very poor or mean; very low or despicable. [Fr.—L. *miser*, wretched.]
Miserably, mi'zėr-a-bli, adv. Unhappily; meanly; wretchedly.
Miserly, mī'zėr-li, a. Very covetous; avaricious; niggardly; penurious.
Misery, mi'ze-ri, n. Wretchedness; extreme pain of body or mind; calamity; misfortune; natural evils which are the cause of misery; avarice'. [L. *miseria*—*miser*, wretched.]
Misfortune, mis-for'tūn, n. Ill fortune; ill luck; mishap; calamity; disaster; unlucky event.
Misgive, mis-giv', vt. To fill with doubt; to deprive of confidence; to fail. (The heart is usually the subject, and the recipr. pron. always follows.) ppr. misgiving, pret. misgave, pp. misgiven.
Misgiving, mis-giv'ing, p.n. A failing of confidence; doubt; distrust.
Misgovern, mis-gu'vėrn, vt. To govern ill; to administer unfaithfully.
Misgoverned, mis-gu'vėrnd, a. Rude; lawless.
Misgovernment, mis-gu'vėrn-ment, n. Bad governm'nt; ill administration of public or private affairs; disorder.
Misguide, mis-gīd', vt. To guide amiss; to direct ill. ppr. misguiding, pret. & pp. misguided.
Misguided, mis-gīd'ed, p.a. Led astray by evil counsel or wrong direction.

Mishap, mis-hap', n. Ill chance; ill luck; accident; disaster. [*mis* and *hap*.]
Mishaved†, mis'hāvd, a. Misbehaved.
Misimprove, mis-im-pröv', vt. To use for a bad purpose; to abuse. ppr. misimproving, pret. & pp. misimproved.
Misimprovement, mis-im-pröv'ment, n. Neglect of improvement; ill use.
Misinform, mis-in-form', vt. To give erroneous information to.
Misinterpret, mis-in-tėr'pret, vt. To interpret erroneously; to misconstrue.
Misinterpretation, mis-in-tėr'pret-ā"-shon, n. Act of interpreting erroneously.
Misjudge, mis-juj', vt To judge erroneously; to mistake in judging of.—vi. To judge wrongly; to err in judgment. ppr. misjudging, pret. & pp. misjudged.
Mislay, mis-lā', vt. To lay in a wrong place; to lose. ppr. mislaying, pret. & pp. mislaid.
Mislead, mis-lēd', vt. To lead into a wrong way or path; to lead astray. ppr. misleading, pret. & pp. misled.
Misletoe, miz'l-tō, n. See MISTLETOE.
Mismanage, mis-ma'nāj, vt. To manage ill. ppr. mismanaging, pret. & pp. mismanaged.
Mismanagement, mis-ma'nāj-ment, n. Ill or improper management.
Misname, mis-nām', vt. To call by the wrong name. ppr. misnaming, pret. & pp. misnamed.
Misnomer, mis-nō'mėr, n. A misnaming; the mistaking of the true name. [Fr. *nommer*, to name.]
Misogamist, mi-so'ga-mist, n. A hater of marriage. [Gr. *miseō*, to hate, and *gamos*, marriage.]
Misplace, mis-plās', vt. To put in a wrong place. ppr. misplacing, pret. & pp. misplaced.
Misplacement, mis-plās'ment, n. Act of putting in the wrong place.
Misprint, mis'print, n. A mistake in printing; a deviation from the copy.
Misprint, mis-priz', vt. To mistake.
Misprision†, mis-pri'zhon, n. Neglect; contempt.
Misprize†, mis-priz', vt. To slight or undervalue.
Mispronounce, mis-prō-nouns', vt. To pronounce erroneously.—vi. To pronounce incorrectly. ppr. mispronouncing, pret. & pp. mispronounced.
Mispronunciation, mis-prō-nun'si-ā"-shon, n. A wrong or improper pronunciation.
Misproud†, mis-proud', a. Viciously proud.
Misquotation, mis-kwōt-ā'shon, n. An erroneous quotation; the act of quoting wrong.
Misquote, mis-kwōt', vt. To quote erroneously; to cite incorrectly. ppr. misquoting, pret. & pp. misquoted.
Misreckon, mis-rek'n, vt. To reckon wrong.
Misrepresent, mis-rep-rē-sent'', vt. To represent falsely; to give an erroneous representation of, either maliciously or carelessly.
Misrepresentation, mis-rep'rē-sent-ā"-shon, n. Act of giving a false or erroneous representation.
Misrule, mis-röl', n. Wrong or unwise rule; disorder; confusion; unjust domination.
Miss, mis, n. The title of a young woman or girl; the term of respectful address to an unmarried female of almost every degree. [contracted from *mistress*.]
Miss, mis, vt. To fail of hitting, as a point aimed at; to fail of reaching, as

MISSAL 244 **MODERATE**

an object; not to hit; to err in attempting to find; to fail of obtaining; to omit; to go without; to do without; to fail to have; to feel the want of; to fail of seeing or finding.—*vi.* To fail to hit an object; not to succeed; to miscarry, as by accident; to fail to obtain, learn, or find; to mistake.—*n.* Loss; want; mistake; error. [Sax. *missian,* to err, mistake.]
Missal, mis'al, *n.* The Roman Catholic mass-book. [Low L. *missale,* from *missa,* the mass.]
Missel, Missel-bird, mis'el, mis'el-bėrd, *n.* A singing bird, a species of thrush, that feeds on the berries of the *mistletoe.*
Misseltoe, miz'l-tō, *n.* See Mistletoe.
Misshape, mis-shāp', *n.* A bad or incorrect shape.—*vt.* To shape ill; to give an ill form to. *ppr.* misshaping, *pret. & pp.* misshaped.
Misshaped, mis-shapt', *p.a.* Ill-formed; deformed; ugly.
Misshethed, mis-shevhd', *a.* Sheathed by mistake.
Missile, mis'il, *a.* Thrown, or that may be thrown.—*n.* Any kind of weapon which is *thrown* or designed to be thrown for the injury of others. [L. *missilis—mitto,* to send.]
Missing, mis'ing, *p.a.* Lost; absent from the place where it was expected to be found.
Missingly, mis'ing-li, *adv.* At intervals.
Mission, mi'shon, *n.* A sending or being sent; a being delegated by authority, with certain powers for transacting business; persons sent; the persons sent to propagate religion; a station of missionaries. [Fr.—L. *mitto,* to send.]
Missionary, mi'shon-a-ri, *n.* One sent to propagate religion.—*a.* Pertaining to *missions.* [Fr. *missionaire.*]
Missive, mis'iv, *a.* Such as is sent; thrown or sent, or such as may be sent.—*n.* A *message;* a letter sent, or a messenger. [Fr.—L. *mitto,* to send.]
Misspel, mis-spel', *vt.* To spell *wrong.* *ppr.* misspelling, *pret. & pp.* misspelled or misspelt.
Misspelling, mis-spel'ing, *p.n.* A wrong *spelling;* false orthography.
Misspend, mis-spend', *vt.* To spend amiss. *ppr.* misspending, *pret. & pp.* misspent.
Misspent, mis-spent', *p.a.* Ill-spent; expended to no purpose, or to a bad one.
Misstate, mis-stāt', *vt.* To state wrong; to misrepresent. *ppr.* misstating, *pret. & pp.* misstated.
Misstatement, mis-stāt'ment, *n.* A *wrong statement;* an erroneous representation.
Mist, mist, *n.* That which partially darkens the light; visible watery vapour floating in the atmosphere; water falling in very numerous but fine drops; anything which obscures.—*vt.†* To cover with mist. [Sax.—*mistian,* to become dark.]
Mistakable, mis-tāk'a-bl, *a.* That may be mistaken.
Mistake, mis-tāk', *vt.* To take wrong; to misunderstand; to take, as one thing or person, for another.—*vi.* To err in opinion or judgment. *ppr.* mistaking, *pret. & pp.* mistaken.—*n.* An error in opinion or judgment; blunder; slip.
Mistaken, mis-tāk'n, *p.a.* Guilty of a mistake; erroneous; incorrect.
Mistemper, mis-tem'pėr, *vt.* To temper ill, to disorder.
Mistily, mist'i-li, *adv.* With *mist;* darkly; obscurely.

Mistime, mis-tīm', *vt.* To time wrong. *ppr.* mistiming, *pret. & pp.* mistimed.
Mistiness, mist'i-nes, *n.* A state of being misty.
Mistletoe, Misletoe, miz'l-tō, miz'l-tō, *n.* A shrub that grows parasitically on various trees, and was held in great veneration by the Druids. [Sax. *misteltu.*]
Mistranslate, mis-trans-lāt', *vt.* To translate erroneously. *ppr.* mistranslating, *pret. & pp.* mistranslated.
Mistranslation, mis-trans-lā'shon, *n.* An erroneous *translation* or version.
Mistreading, mis-trēd'ing, *n.* Wrong treading; misbehaviour.
Mistress, mis'tres, *n.* A woman who governs; the female head of a family; a sovereign; a female who is well skilled in anything; a female teacher; a woman beloved and courted; a woman kept as a concubine; the jack at bowls†. [Old Fr. *maistresse;* L. *magistra—magnus,* great.]
Mistrust, mis-trust', *n.* Want of confidence or trust; suspicion.—*vt.* To have no trust in; to distrust.
Misty, mist'i, *a.* Overspread with *mist;* dim; obscure; clouded.
Misunderstand, mis-un'dėr-stand", *vt.* To understand wrongly; to misconceive; to take in a wrong sense. *ppr.* misunderstanding, *pret. & pp.* misunderstood.
Misunderstanding, mis-un'dėr-stand"-ing, *p.n.* Misapprehension; difference; dissension.
Misuse, mis-ūz', *vt.* To use to a bad purpose; to treat ill; to abuse; to misapply. *ppr.* misusing, *pret. & pp.* misused.
Misuse, mis-ūs', *n.* Improper use.
Misused, mis-ūzd', *p.a.* Misapplied; abused.
Mite, mīt, *n.* A very *small* insect; a small piece of money; anything proverbially very small. [Sax.—Old G. *miza,* a gnat.]
Mitigate, mi'ti-gāt, *vt.* To make soft or mild; to sooth; to assuage; to make less severe; to temper; to soften in harshness or severity; to calm. *ppr.* mitigating, *pret. & pp.* mitigated. [L. *mitigo, mitigatus—mitis,* mild, and *ago,* for *facio,* to make.]
Mitigating, mi'ti-gāt-ing, *p.a.* Tempering; moderating.
Mitigation, mi-ti-gā'shon, *n.* Act of *mitigating;* alleviation. [L. *mitigatio.*]
Mitre, mī'tėr, *n.* A *crown* or pontifical ornament worn on the head by archbishops and bishops, and sometimes by abbots on solemn occasions; the dignity of an archbishop or bishop; sometimes of an abbot. [Fr.—Gr. *mitra,* a headband.]
Mitred, mī'tėrd, *p.a.* Honoured with the privilege of wearing a *mitre.*
Mitten, mit'n, *n.* A *cover for the hand,* worn to defend it from cold or other injury. [Fr. *mitaine.*]
Mity, mīt'i, *a.* Having mites; abounding with mites. [from *mite.*]
Mix, miks, *vt.* To unite or blend promiscuously, as two or more ingredients into a compound; to join; to mingle; to unite with a crowd.—*vi.* To become united in a mass; to be joined or associated. *ppr.* mixing, *pret. & pp.* mixed or mixt. [Sax. *miscan—*L. *misceo—*Heb. *mâsak,* to mingle.]
Mixed, mikst, *p.a.* Promiscuous.
Mixture, miks'tūr, *n.* Act of *mixing,* or state of being mixed; a mass or compound; a liquid medicine; the blending of several ingredients without an alteration of the substance. [L. *mixtura—misceo,* to mix.]
Mizzen, miz'n, *n.* The aftermost of the fixed sails of a ship, supported by the mast called the *mizzen-mast.* [It. *mezzana.*]
Mnemonic, nē-mon'ik, *a.* Assisting the *memory.*
Mnemonics, nē-mon'iks, *n.* The art of *memory;* precepts and rules for assisting the memory. [from Gr. *mnaômai,* to remember.]
Mo†, mō, *a.* or *adv.* More.
Moan, mōn, *vt.* To lament; to bewail with an audible voice.—*vi.* To grieve; to mourn; to wail.—*n.* Groan; audible expression of sorrow or suffering. [Sax. *mænan,* to lament.]
Moat, mōt, *n.* A *ditch* or deep trench round the rampart of a castle or other fortified place.—*vt.* To surround with a ditch for defence. [Low L. *mota.*]
Mob, mob, *n.* The movable or fickle multitude; a crowd of people, rude and disorderly; a disorderly assembly.—*vt.* To attack in a disorderly crowd; to harass tumultuously. *ppr.* mobbing, *pret. & pp.* mobbed. [from L. *mobilis,* movable—*moveo,* to move.]
Mobility, mō-bil'i-ti, *n.* Capacity of being moved; aptitude to motion; readiness to move. [Fr. *mobilité—*L. *moveo,* to move.]
Moblet, mō'bl, *vt.* To wrap the head of in a hood.
Mock, mok, *vt.* To *mimic* in contempt or derision; to deride by mimicry; to defeat; to deceive; to subject to disappointment; to tantalize; to play on in contempt.—*vi.* To make sport in contempt or in jest, or to speak jestingly.—*n.* Derisive imitation; derision; sneer; an act manifesting contempt.—*a.* Imitating reality, but not real; assumed. [Fr. *moquer—* Gr. *môkos,* mockery.]
Mocker, mok'ėr, *n.* One who mocks; a scorner; a scoffer; a derider.
Mockery, mok'ė-ri, *n.* Act of *mocking;* derision; sportive insult or contempt; subject of laughter; vain effort; that which deceives; counterfeit appearance; false show. [Fr. *moquerie.*]
Mockingly, mok'ing-li, *adv.* By way of derision; in contempt.
Modal, mōd'al, *a.* Consisting in mode; relating to form; having the form without the essence or reality. [Fr. *modale—*L. *modus,* a measure.]
Mode, mōd, *n.* Proper or due measure; manner of existing or being; method; style of fashion; way; course; degree; state; that which cannot subsist in and of itself, but inheres in some substance, hence called its subject. [Fr.—L. *modus—*Sans. *ma,* to measure.]
Model, mo'del, *n.* A *small measure;* a mould; something intended to give shape to castings; standard; a pattern of something to be made; a form in miniature; a copy; representation; something made in imitation of real life.—*vt.* To form according to a *model;* to imitate in planning or forming.—*vi.* To make a *model* from which some work is to be executed; to form a work of some plastic material; as, to model in wax. *ppr.* modelling, *pret. & pp.* modelled.—*a.* Set up as a *model;* that ought to be copied or imitated. [Fr. *modèle—*L. *modus,* a measure.]
Modeller, mo'del-ėr, *n.* One who *models;* a planner; a contriver.
Modelling, mo'del-ing, *p.n.* The art of making, or the *making of a model.*
Moderate, mo'de-rāt, *a.* Limited; ob-

Fāte, fär, fat, fall; mē, met, hėr; pīne, pin, nōte, not, move; tūbe, tub, bull; oil, pound.

Moderately — serving reasonable bounds in indulgence; limited in quantity; not violent; not extreme in opinion; holding the mean or middle place; of a middle rate; middling.—*vt.* To set bounds to; to restrain from excess of any kind; to allay; to repress; to temper; to regulate.—*vi.* To become less violent, severe, rigorous, or intense. *ppr.* moderating, *pret. & pp.* moderated. [L. *moderāthus—modus*, a measure.]

Moderately, mo'de-rāt-li, *adv.* Temperately; in a middle degree.

Moderateness, mo'de-rāt-nes, *n.* State of being moderate; temperateness.

Moderation, mo-de-rā'shon, *n.* State of being moderate, or of keeping a due mean between extremes; temperance; restraint of violent passions; calmness of mind; frugality in expenses. [Fr. *modération*—L. *modus*, a measure.]

Moderator, mo'de-rāt-ėr, *n.* He or that *which moderates*; a president or chairman. [L.]

Moderatorship, mo-de-rāt'ėr-ship, *n.* The office of a moderator.

Modern, mo'dėrn, *a.* Pertaining to the *present* time, or time not long past; not ancient; recent; new; trite; vulgar. *n. A person of modern times*; (pl.) those of modern nations, or of nations which arose out of the ruins of the empires of Greece and Rome. [Fr. *moderne*—L. *modo*, just now.]

Modernize, mo'dėrn-iz, *vt.* To render modern; to adapt, as the ancient style or idiom to modern style and taste. *ppr.* modernizing, *pret. & pp.* modernised.

Modest, mo'dest, *a.* Keeping due measure; moderate; not forward or bold; not presumptuous; not boastful; bashful; unobtrusive; not lewd; chaste; virtuous; not excessive or extreme. [Fr. *modeste*—L. *modus*, measure.]

Modestly, mo'dest-li, *adv.* In a modest manner.

Modesty, mo'des-ti, *n.* Quality of being *modest*; decency; that lowly temper which accompanies a moderate estimate of one's own worth; unobtrusive deportment; shamefacedness; chastity; purity of conduct. [Fr. *modestie*, L. *modestia—modus*, measure.]

Modicum, mo'di-kum, *n. A little*; a small quantity. [L. *modus*, a measure.]

Modification, mo'di-fi-kā'shon, *n. Act of modifying*; state of being modified; mode; form; state. [Fr.]

Modified, mo'di-fīd, *p.a.* Tempered; qualified in exceptional parts.

Modify, mo'di-fī, *vt.* To set a measure to; to moderate; to qualify; to lower; to change, as the form of a thing; to give a new form of being to; to vary. *ppr.* modifying, *pret. & pp.* modified. [Fr. *modifier*—L. *modus*, measure, and *facio*, to make.]

Modifying, mo'di-fī-ing, *p.a.* Moderating.

Modish, mōd'ish, *a.* According to the *mode*; fashionable.

Modishly, mōd'ish-li, *adv.* Fashionably; in the customary mode.

Modishness, mōd'ish-nes, *n.* State of being modish or fashionable; affectation of the fashion.

Modulate, mo'dū-lāt, *vt.* To measure; to regulate; to vary or inflect, as sound in a natural, customary, or musical manner. *ppr.* modulating, *pret. & pp.* modulated. [L. *modŭlor, modulatus—modus*, a measure—Sans. *md*, to measure.]

Modulated, mo'dū-lāt-ed, *p.a.* Varied; inflected.

Modulation, mo-dū-lā'shon, *n. Act of modulating*; act of inflecting or varying the voice in reading or speaking; a rising or falling of the voice; the proper change of the key or mode in conducting the melody in music; the transition from one key to another. [Fr—L. *modus*, measure.]

Module, mo'dūl, *n. A small measure*; a certain measure or size, taken at pleasure, for regulating the proportion of columns and the symmetry of the whole building; a model or representation. [Fr.—L. *modus*, a measure.]

Moe†, mō, *n.* A distorted mouth.—*vi.* To make a distortion of the face in ridicule.

Mohair, mō'hār, *n.* The long silky hair or wool of the Angora goat of Asia Minor; a fabric made from it. [Fr. *moire*.]

Mohammedan, mō-ham'med-an, *a.* See **Mahometan**.

Moidore, moi'dōr, *n. Money of gold*; a gold coin of Portugal, valued at £1, 7s. sterling. [Port. *moeda d'ora*.]

Moiety, moi'e-ti, *n.* The *half*; one of two equal parts; any indefinite portion. [Fr. *moitié*—L. *medius*, middle.]

Moil†, moil, *vi.* To work *like a mule*; to exert one's self; to work with painful efforts. [from *moyle*, the old spelling of *mule*—which see.]

Moist, moist, *a. Moderately wet*; damp; containing water or other liquid in a perceptible degree.—*vt.*† To moisten. [Fr. *moite*—L. *madeo*, to be moist.]

Moisten, mois'n, *vt.* To make moist.

Moistness, moist'nes, *n.* State or quality *of being moist*; a small degree of wetness; humidity.

Moiststart, moist'stär, *n.* The moon.

Moisture, mois'tūr, *n.* State of being *moist*; a moderate degree of wetness; a small quantity of any liquid. [Fr. *moiteur*.]

Molar, mō'lär, *a. Having power to grind*; used for grinding.—*n. A grinding* tooth or grinder. [L. *molāris—mola*, a mill.]

Molasses, mō-las'ez, *n. sing.* The syrup which drains from sugar when cooling, so called from its sweetness; treacle. [It. *melassa*—Gr. *meli*, honey.]

Mole, mōl, *n. A spot* or small permanent protuberance on the human body. [Sax. *maal*—L. *macula*, a spot.]

Mole, mōl, *n.* A shapeless, huge, heavy *mass*; a massive work formed of large stones laid in the sea before a port; the port or haven thus formed. [Fr. *môle*—L. *moles*.]

Mole, mōl, *n. The mouldwarp*; a small animal which burrows beneath the ground, and *throws up mould* or earth. [D. *mol*.]

Molecular, mō-lek'ū-lėr, *a. Belonging to or consisting of molecules*.

Molecule, mō'le-kūl, *n. A small mass*; a very minute particle of matter. [Fr. *molécule*—L. *moles*, a mass.]

Moleskin, mōl'skin, *n.* A kind of shaggy cotton fabric.

Molest, mō-lest', *vt. To trouble*; to vex; to annoy; to disturb; to tease. [L. *molesto—moles*, trouble.]

Molestation, mō-lest-ā'shon, *n. Act of molesting*; disturbance; annoyance; uneasiness given. [Late L. *molestatio*.]

Mollification, mol'li-fi-kā'shon, *n. Act of mollifying*; state of being mollified.

Mollifier, mol'li-fī-ėr, *n.* He or that *which softens*, appeases, or mitigates.

Mollify, mol'li-fī, *vt. To soften*; to make soft or tender; to assuage, as pain; to appease; to pacify; to calm; to qualify. *ppr.* mollifying, *pret. & pp.* mollified.

[Fr. *mollifier*—L. *mollis*, soft, and *facio*, to make.]

Mollifying, mol'li-fī-ing, *p.a. Adapted to soften*.

Mollusc, mol'lusk, *n.* An animal whose body is *soft*, and not articulated, as a snail, cuttle-fish, &c. [L. *molluscus—mollis*, soft.]

Molten, mōlt'n, *p.a. Melted*; made of melted metal.

Moms, mōm, *n*, A stupid fellow; a stock.

Moment, mō'ment, *n.* The smallest space *of time* in which a thing can be *moved*; the smallest portion of time; the sixtieth part of a minute; a twinkling; weight; force; consequence. [Fr.—L. *moveo*, to move.]

Momentarily, mō'ment-a-ri-li, *adv. Every moment*.

Momentary, mō'ment-a-ri, *a. Done in a moment*; continuing only a moment. [Late L. *momentarius*.]

Momentous, mō-ment'us, *a. Of moment*; important. [L. *momentosus*.]

Momentously, mō-ment'us-li, *adv.* Weightily.

Momentum, mō-ment'um, *n.* **Momenta**, mō-ment'a, *pl.* The force of a *moving* body; the force or quantity of motion in a moving body, estimated by the weight multiplied by the velocity; impetus. [L.—*moveo*, to move.]

Monachism, mon'ak-izm, *n. The state of monks*; a monastic life. [Fr. *monachisme*—Gr. *monos*, alone.]

Monad, mon'ad, *n. A unit*; an ultimate atom; an indivisible thing. [Fr. *monade*—Gr. *monos*, alone.]

Monarch, mon'ärk, *n. A sole ruler*; the ruler of a nation who is vested with absolute sovereign power; a king or prince whose powers are limited by the constitution of the government; he or that which is superior to others of the same kind; a patron deity.—*a.* Supreme; ruling. [Fr. *monarque*—Gr. *monos*, alone, and *archē*, rule.]

Monarchical, mon-ärk'ik-al, *a. Pertaining to monarchy*; vested in a single ruler. [Fr. *monarchique*.]

Monarchize†, mon'ärk-īz, *vi.* To play the king.

Monarchist, mon-ärk'ö', *n.* A fantastical person.

Monarchy, mon'är-ki, *n.* A form of government in which the supreme *power* is lodged in the hands of a *single person*, and which is absolute, limited or constitutional, hereditary or elective; a kingdom. [Fr. *monarchie*.]

Monastery, mon'as-te-ri, *n. A house for monks*, sometimes for nuns; a house of religious retirement; an abbey; a priory; a nunnery or convent. [Fr. *monastère*—Gr. *monos*, alone.]

Monastic, mon-as'tik, *a. Pertaining to monasteries, monks*, and nuns; recluse; secluded from the temporal concerns of life, and devoted to religion. [Fr. *monastique*.]

Monday, mun'dā, *n. The day sacred to the moon*; the second day of the week. [Sax. *monandag*.]

Monetary, mo'ne-ta-ri, *a. Relating to money* or monied concerns. [Low L. *monetarius*.]

Money, mun'nē, *n.* **Moneys**, *pl.* Coin *made at the mint*; any piece of metal, usually gold, silver, or bronze, stamped by public authority, and used as the medium of commerce; bank-notes; bills of credit; wealth; affluence. [Sax. *mynet*—L. *monēta*, the mint, coin.]

Money-changer, mun'nē-chānj-ėr, *n.* A broker who deals in *money*.

Moneyed, mun'nēd, *p.a. Rich in money*;

able to command money; consisting in money.

Monger, mung'ger, n. *A trader; a dealer;* now used only in composition, as ironmonger. [Sax. a barterer.]

Mongrel, mung'grel, a. *Of a mixed breed;* of different kinds.—n. *An animal of a mixed breed.* [from Sax. *mengan*, to mix.]

Monition, mō-ni'shon, n. *A reminding or admonishing;* instruction given by way of caution. [Fr.—L. *moneo, monitum*, to remind—Sans. *man*, to think.]

Monitor, mo'ni-tėr, n. *One who reminds;* one who warns of faults or informs of duty; a pupil selected to look to the scholars in schools, in the absence of the instructor, or to instruct a division or class. [L.—*moneo*, to remind.]

Monitorial, mo-ni-tō'ri-al, a. *Relating to a monitor;* conducted by, or under the instruction, of monitors.

Monitory, mo'ni-tō-ri, a. *Reminding;* warning; instructing by way of caution. [Fr. *monitoire*.]

Monitress, mo'ni-tres, n. *A female monitor.*

Monk, mungk, n. One of a religious community withdrawn from general intercourse with the world; a solitary; a recluse. [Gr. *monachos*—*monos*, alone.]

Monkey, mung'ke, n. **Monkeys**, pl. An ape; a baboon; a name of contempt or of slight kindness. [from *manikin*; Sax. *man*, man.]

Monkish, mungk'ish, a. *Like a monk*, or pertaining to monks; monastic.

Monks-hood, mungks'hud, n. A poisonous plant, so named from the peculiar *cowl-shape* of the flowers.

Monochord, mon'ō-kord, n. An instrument of *one string*, used to ascertain the several lengths of the string required to produce the several notes of the musical scale. [Gr. *monos*, single, and *chordē*, a musical string.]

Monodist, mon'od-ist, n. *One who writes monodies.*

Monody, mon'ō-di, n. *An ode*, or poem of a mournful character, in which a *single mourner* expresses lamentation. [Gr. *monodia*—*monos*, single, and *ōdē*, a song.]

Monogamist, mon-og'a-mist, n. One who disallows second *marriages*. [Gr. *monos*, alone, and *gamos*, marriage.]

Monogamy, mon-og'a-mi, n. The *marriage of one wife* only, or the state of such as are restrained to a single wife.

Monogram, mon'ō-gram, n. *A single character in writing;* a cypher, or intertexture of letters in *one* figure. [Fr. *monogramme*—Gr. *monos*, alone, and *gramma*, a letter.]

Monograph, mon'ō-graf, n. *A written account of a single thing* or class of things. [Gr. *monos*, alone, and *graphō*, to write.]

Monolith, mon'ō-lith, n. A pillar, column, &c., consisting of *a single stone.* [Fr.—Gr. *monos*, alone, and *lithos*, a stone.]

Monolithic, mon-ō-lith'ik, a. *Consisting of a single stone.*

Monologue, mon'ō-log, n. *A speech uttered by a person alone;* a soliloquy; a poem, song, or scene composed for a single performer. [Fr.—Gr. *monos*, alone, and *logos*, discourse.]

Monomania, mon-ō-mā'ni-a, n. *Insanity* in regard to a *single* subject, or derangement of a single faculty of the mind. [Gr. *monos*, *single*, and *mania*, madness.]

Monomaniac, mon-ō-mā'ni-ak, n. *Af-*

fected with monomania.—n. *A person affected by monomania.*

Monopolist, Monopolizer, mon-op'ol-ist, mon-op'ol-iz-ėr, n. *One who monopolizes.* [It. *monopolista*.]

Monopolize, mon-op'ol-iz, vt. *To be or become the only seller of;* to purchase or obtain possession of, as of the whole of any commodity or goods in market; to obtain the exclusive right of buying or selling; to engross or obtain the whole of, as conversation. *ppr.* monopolizing, *pret. & pp.* monopolized. [Sp. *monopolizar*—Gr. *monos*, single, and *pōleō*, to sell.]

Monopoly, mon-op'o-li, n. *The sole power of selling* any species of goods; a privilege allowed by the crown for the sole buying, selling, and using any commodity. [Fr. *monopole*.]

Monostrophic, mon-ō-strof'ik, a. *Having one strophe* only; written in unvaried measure. [Gr. *monostrophikos*—*monos*, and *strophē*, a turning.]

Monosyllabic, mon'ō-sil-lab'ik, a. *Consisting of one syllable.*

Monosyllable, mon'ō-sil-la-bl, n. A word of *one syllable.* [Gr. *monos*, single, and *syllabē*, a syllable.]

Monotheism, mon'ō-thē-izm, n. *The doctrine* or belief of the existence of *one God only.* [Gr. *monos*, single, and *Theos*, God.]

Monotheist, mon'ō-thē-ist, n. One who believes in *one God only.*

Monotone, mon'ō-tōn, n. *A single tone;* a sameness of tone, or unvaried pitch of the voice in reading or speaking.

Monotonous, mon-ot'on-us, a. *Having monotony;* wanting variety in cadence or inflection; continued with dull uniformity.

Monotonously, mon-ot'on-us-li, adv. *With one uniform tone.*

Monotony, mon-ot'o-ni, n. *Uniformity of sound;* a continuance of the same modifications of tone or sound, producing a dull uniformity; an irksome sameness or want of variety. [Gr. *monotonia*—*monos*, and *tonos*, tone.]

Monsieur, mo'sėr, n. *My lord;* the common title of courtesy and respect in France, answering to the English Sir, Mr., and also used before titles; a Frenchman, so called in contempt†. [Fr. *mon*, my, and *sieur*, lord—L. *senior*, elder—*seneo*, to be old.]

Monsoon, mon-sōn', n. *A periodical wind* in the Arabian and Indian seas, blowing six months from the same quar'er, then changing, and blowing the same time from the opposite quarter. [Fr. *mousson*.]

Monster, mon'stėr, n. An animal produced with a shape or with parts that are not natural, anciently looked upon as a *warning from the gods;* a thing to wonder at; any unnatural production; a person so wicked as to appear horrible; as a prefix, anything uncommonly large.—vt.† *To make monstrous.* [Fr. *monstre;* L. *moneo*, to warn.]

Monstrosity, mon-stros'i-ti, n. *State or quality of being monstrous;* an unnatural production. [Fr *monstruosité.*]

Monstrous, mon'strus, a. *Extraordinary;* enormous; huge; out of the common course of nature; very wonderful; shocking to the sight or other senses; hateful. [Fr. *monstrueux*.]

Monstrously, mon'strus-li, adv. In a manner *out of the common order* of nature; hideously; horribly; enormously.

Monstrousness, mon'strus-nes, n. *State or quality of being monstrous.*

Montant†, mont'ant, n. A term in fencing. [Fr. *monter*, to mount.]

Month, munth, n. The period *measured by the moon's revolution;* a period of time constituting one of the twelve divisions of the year, called a calendar month; popularly, four weeks. [Sax. *monath*—L. *mensis*—*metior*, Sans. *mā*, to measure.]

Monthly, munth'li, a. *Continued a month*, or performed in a month.—n. A publication which appears regularly *once a month*.—adv. *Once a month;* in every month.

Month's-mind†, munths'mind, n. Eager desire.

Monument, mon'ū-ment, n. *That which calls to mind,* or preserves the remembrance of any person or thing; a structure raised as a memorial of a person deceased, or of a remarkable event, as a mausoleum; a pillar; an obelisk. [Fr.—L. *moneo*, to remind.]

Monumental, mon-ū-ment'al, a. *Pertaining to a monument;* serving as a monument; preserving memory; belonging to a tomb. [Fr.]

Mood, mōd, n. *Measure; manner; way; fashion;* the form of a syllogistic argument; style of music; the variation of a verb to express manner of action or being. [Fr. *mode;* L. *modus*.]

Mood, mōd, n. *Temper of mind; temporary state of the mind* in regard to passion or feeling; humour; frame; anger. [Sax. *mōd*, mind.]

Moodiness, mōd'i-nes, n. *State or quality of being moody;* sullenness; peevishness.

Moody, mōd'i, a. *Subject to moods or humours;* peevish; fretful; out of humour; pensive; violent; furious; adapted to varying frames of mind. [Sax. *modig.*]

Moon, mōn, n. The changing luminary of the night, by which *months are measured;* the heavenly body next to the earth, which revolves round it in about 29½ days, and which reflects upon the earth light borrowed from the sun; a month. [Sax. *mona*—Sanscr. *mā*, to measure.]

Moonbeam, mōn'bēm, n. *A ray of light from the moon.*

Moon-calf, mōn'kāf, n. A monster; a false conception; a dolt; a stupid fellow.

Moon-eyed, mōn'īd, a. *Having eyes affected by the revolutions of the moon;* dim-eyed; purblind.

Moonless, mōn'les, a. *Not favoured with moonlight.*

Moonlight, mōn'līt, a. *Illuminated by the moon.*—n. *The light afforded by the moon.*

Moonshine, mōn'shīn, n. *The light of the moon;* figuratively, show, without substance or reality; stuff; vanity.—a. *Illuminated by the moon.*

Moonstruck, mōn'struk, a. *Affected by the influence of the moon;* lunatic.

Moony, mōn'i, a. *Related to or like the moon;* having a crescent for a standard; in resemblance of the moon.

Moor, mōr, n. An extensive waste covered with heath, and having a poor, light soil, but sometimes marshy, and abounding in peat; a fen. [Sax. *mor*.]

Moor, mōr, n. *A dark complexioned person;* a native of the n rthern coast of Africa. [Fr. *Maure.*]

Moor, mōr, vt. To secure in a particular station by *cables* and anchors, as a ship. vi. *To be confined by cables* or chains. [Sp. *amarrar*, to make fast; D. *marren*, to tie.]

Moorage, mōr'aj, n. *A place for mooring.*

Mooring, mōr'ing, p.n. *Act of securing*

Fāte, fär, fat, fall; mē, met, hėr; pīne, pin; nōte, not, mōve; tūbe, tub, bull; oil, pound.

MOORISH 247 MORTUARY

a ship alongside of any landing-place; (pl.) the anchors, chains, and bridles laid athwart the bottom of a river or harbour to confine a ship.

Moorish, mōr'ish, a. *Marshy; fenny; pertaining to the Moorish people.*

Moorland, mōr'land, n. A tract of land rising into moderate hills, cold, and full of bogs.

Moory, mōr'i, a. *Marshy; fenny; watery.*

Moose, mōs, n. An animal, the largest of the deer kind, which inhabits the northern parts of both hemispheres, and is the elk of Europe. [a native Indian name.]

Moot, mōt, vt. Formerly, *to meet*; to debate; to argue for and against; to argue for practice. [Sax. *motian*, to meet.]

Moot, Moot-case, Moot-point, mōt, mōt'kās, mōt'point, n. A point to be mooted or debated; a disputable case; an unsettled question. [Sax. *mót*, an assembly.]

Mop, mop, n. A piece of cloth, or a collection of thrums or coarse yarns fastened to a handle, and used for cleaning floors.—vt. To rub or wipe with a mop.—vi.† To make a wry mouth. ppr. mopping, pret. & pp. mopped. [W.— L. *mappa*, a napkin.]

Mope, mōp, vi. To move silent and sluggish from *discontent*; to be very stupid; to be spiritless or gloomy.—vt. To make stupid or spiritless. ppr. moping, pret. & pp. moped.— n. A stupid or low-spirited person; a drone. [D. *moppen*, to grumble.]

Mopish, mōp'ish, a. Dull; spiritless.

Mopstick, mop'stik, n. The handle of a mop.

Moral, mo'ral, a. *Relating to manners;* relating to the conduct of men as social beings in relation to each other, and with reference to right and wrong; subject to the moral law; bound to perform social duties; supported by the evidence of reason or probability; founded on experience of the ordinary course of things; conformed to rules of right; virtuous.—n. The doctrine inculcated by a fiction; the accommodation of a fable to form the morals.—vi. To moralize. [Fr. — L. *mos, moris*, manner.]

Moralist, mo'ral-ist, n. One who teaches morals; a writer on the subject of morals; a moral person. [Fr. *moraliste*.]

Morality, mō-ral'i-ti, n. The doctrine of moral duties; ethics; the practice of moral duties; virtue. [Fr. *moralité*.]

Moralize, mo'ral-īz, vt. To apply to a moral purpose; to furnish with manners; to render moral or virtuous; to correct the morals of.—vi. To speak or write on moral subjects, or to make moral reflections. ppr. moralizing, pret. & pp. moralized. [Fr. *moraliser*.]

Moralizer, mo'ral-īz-ėr, n. One who moralizes.

Moralizing, mo'ral-īz-ing, p.a. The application of facts to a moral purpose.

Morally, mo'ral-li, adv. In a moral manner.

Morals, mo'ralz, n.pl. The practice of the duties of life; moral philosophy or ethics.

Morass, mō-ras', n. A marsh; a fen; a tract of soft, wet ground. [D. *maras* —L. *mare*, the sea.]

Moravian, mō-rā'vi-an, a. *Pertaining to Moravia*, or to the United Brethren. n. One of a religious sect, called the United Brethren.

Morbid, mor'bid, a. Diseased; sickly; not sound and healthful. [Fr. *morbide* —L. *morior*, Heb. *māth*, to die.]

Morbidly, mor'bid-li, adv. In a morbid or diseased manner.

Morbidness, mor'bid-nes, n. *State of being morbid*, or of being diseased.

Morbific, mor-bif'ik, a. Causing disease. [Fr. *morbifique*.]

Mordant, mor'dant, n. Any substance, as alum, which fixes dyes.—a. Biting; sarcastic; serving to fix colours. [Fr.— L. *mordeo*, to bite.]

More, mōr, a. Greater in quality, degree, amount, or number; added to some former number; additional.—n. A greater quantity, amount, or number; greater thing; other thing.—adv. To a greater degree; again. [Sax.*mara;* G. *mehr*—Sans. *manh*, to increase.]

Moreen, mō-rēn', n. *Watered or wavy stuff;* a stout woollen stuff used for curtains, &c. [from Fr. *moire*, mohair, and *ondé*, waving.]

Moreover, mōr-ō'vėr, adv. Beyond what has been said; also; further.

Moresque, mō-resk', a. Done after the manner of the Moors; the same as arabesque.—n. Architecture or decoration in the Moorish manner; arabesque. [Fr.]

Morion, mo'ri-on, n. A moorish helmet. [Fr.]

Morn, morn, n. The time when the darkness is cut off; the first part of the day; the morning. (A word used chiefly in poetry.) [South Dan.]

Morning, morn'ing, n. The first part of the day, beginning at twelve o'clock at night and extending to twelve at noon; popularly, the time between dawn and the middle of the forenoon; also, all that part of the day before dinner; figuratively, the first or early part.—a. Pertaining to the first part or early part of the day; being in the early part of the day. [Sax. *morgen;* Goth. *gamaurgjan*, to cut off.]

Morning-star, morn'ing -stär, n. The planet Venus, when it precedes the sun in rising, and shines in the morning.

Morning-tide, morn'ing-tid, n. Morning time; first tide.

Morocco, mo-rok'ō, n. A fine kind of leather prepared from goat-skin, and tanned with sumach; said to be borrowed from the Moors.

Morose, mō-rōs', a. Given to one's own way; wayward; austere; crabbed; peevish; testy; sour-tempered. [L. *morosus—mos, moris*, a way.]

Morosely, mō rōs'li, adv. Sourly.

Moroseness, mō-rōs'nes, n. *State or quality of being morose;* waywardness.

Morosity†, mō-rōs'i-ti, n. Moroseness.

Morphia, mor'fi-a, n. The narcotic principle of opium, a powerful anodyne. (Gr. *Morpheus*, the god of dreams.]

Morris, mo'ris, n. A Moorish dance; a dance in imitation of the Moors, usually performed with castanets, tambours, &c.; a game played on a board. [Fr. *moresque*.]

Morris-pike†, mo'ris-pīk, n. A Moorish pike.

Morrow, mo'rō, n. The day next after the present; the next day subsequent to any day specified. [Sax. *morgen*, morning, morrow.]

Morse, mors, n. The sea-horse, or walrus, sometimes 18 feet long. [Goth. *marei*, the sea, and Sw. Goth. *örs*, a horse.]

Morsel, mor'sel, n. A bite; a mouthful; a small piece of food; a piece; a meal; a small quantity of something not

eatable. [Old Fr. *morcel*—L. *mordeo*, to bite.]

Mort!, mort, n. A note sounded at the death of game.

Mortal, mor'tal, a. Subject to death; appointed to die; deadly; bringing death; deadly in malice or purpose; exposing to certain death; incurring the penalty of death; condemned to be punished with death; not venial, as sin; human; vexing.—n. A being subject to death; a human being; a man. [L. *mortalis* — *mors, mortis*, death — Heb. *mâth*, Sans. *mri*, to die.]

Mortality, mor-tal'i-ti, n. Subjection to death or the necessity of dying; death; actual death of great numbers of men or beasts; human nature. [Fr. *mortalité*.]

Mortally, mor'tal-li, adv. In a manner that must cause death; in the highest possible degree.

Mortar, mor'tär, n. A vessel made of iron, stone, &c., in which substances are bruised with a pestle; a short piece of ordnance with a large bore resembling in shape a mortar in which substances are pounded, and used for throwing bombs; that which is beaten in a mortar or trough; a mixture of lime and sand with water, used as a cement for uniting stones and bricks in walls. [Fr. *mortier*—L. *mordeo*, to bite.]

Mortgage, mor'gāj, n. A dead pledge; a conveyance of property as security for the payment of a debt, and to become void upon payment.—vt. To grant, as an estate in fee as security for money lent; to pledge. ppr. mortgaging, pret. & pp. mortgaged. [Fr.— *mort*. dead, and *gage*, pledge.]

Mortgaged, mor'gājd, p.a. Conveyed in fee as security for the payment of money.

Mortgager, mor'gāj-ėr, n. The person who grants an estate as security for a debt.

Mortification, mor'ti-fi-kā"shon, n. Act of mortifying, or state of being mortified; the death of one part of an animal body, while the rest is alive; gangrene; the act of subduing the passions by penance; humiliation; the state of being humbled. [Fr.]

Mortified, mor'ti-fid, p.a. Humbled; abased; vexed.

Mortify, mor'ti-fi, vt. To cause the death of; to subdue, as the bodily appetites by abstinence; to humble; to restrain, as inordinate passions; to affect with slight vexation.—vi. To become dead; to lose vitality, as flesh; to be subdued; to practise severities. ppr. mortifying, pret. & pp. mortified. [Fr. *mortifier*—L. *mors, mortis*, death, and *facio*, to make.]

Mortifying, mor'ti-fi-ing, p.a. Humiliating; tending to humble or abase; vexing.

Mortise, mor'tis, n. A cut or hollow place, made in timber, to receive the tenon of another piece of timber.—vt. To cut or make a mortise in; to join by a tenon and mortise, as timbers. ppr. mortising. pret. & pp. mortised. [Fr. *mortaise*—L. *mordeo*, to bite.]

Mortmain, mort'mān, n. Possession of lands or tenements in *dead hands*, or hands that cannot alienate; an unalienable possession. [Fr. *mort*, dead, and *main*, hand.]

Mortuary, mor'tū-a-ri, n. A customary gift claimed by and due to the minister of a parish, on the death of a parishioner.—a. Belonging to the burial

ch, chain; j, job; g, go; ng, sing; ᴛʜ, then; th, thin; w, wig; wh, whig; zh, azure; † obsolete.

of the dead. [Fr. *mortuaire*, a pall—L. *mors, mortis*, death.]
Mosaic, Mosaic-work, mō-zā´ik, mō-zā´ik-werk, *n. Work belonging to the Muses*, or the fine arts; graceful, neat, and elegant work; an assemblage of little pieces of glass, marble, precious stones, &c., of various colours, cut and fixed together by a ground of cement, in such a manner as to form ornamental patterns.—*a. Pertaining to or composed of mosaic.* [Fr. *mosaïque*—Gr. *Mousa*, a Muse.]
Mosaic, mō-zā´ik, *a. Pertaining to Moses*, the leader of the Israelites. [from *Moses*.]
Moselle, mō-zel´, *n.* A species of white wine, named from the river *Moselle*.
Moslem, moz´lem. *n. A Mussulman;* an orthodox Mohammedan.
Mosque, mosk, *n.* A Mohammedan temple. [Fr. *mosquée*.]
Mosquito, mos-kē´tō, *n.* A gnat-like insect common in America and the Indies, whose stinging qualities are most annoying. [Sp.]
Moss, mos, *n.* A small herbaceous plant, with a simple branching stem, and numerous narrow leaves, growing on trees, rocks, &c., mostly in humid places; a lichen; a morass or boggy place.—*vt. To cover with moss* by natural growth. [Sax. *meos*—L. *muscus*, moss.]
Mossiness, mos´i-nes, *n. State of being overgrown with moss.*
Moss-rose, mos´rōz, *n.* A beautiful variety of the *rose*, so named from its *moss*-like pubescence.
Mossy, mos´i, *a. Overgrown or abounding with moss*; covered with moss, or bordered with moss.
Most, mōst, *a. Greatest;* consisting of the greatest number; consisting of the greatest quantity.—*n.* The greatest *number or part*; the greatest degree, quantity, or amount; the utmost.—*adv. In the greatest* or highest *degree.* [Sax. *mæst;* Goth. *maists*—Sans. *manh,* to grow, to increase.]
Mostly, mōst´li, *adv.* For the *greatest* part.
Mot, mot, *n. A word;* a motto.
Mote, mōt, *n. A speck;* a small particle; anything proverbially small. [Sax. *mot*.]
Moth, moth, *n.* A small insect which breeds in yarn and garments, and often *eats* and destroys them; that which gradually and silently consumes anything. [Sax.—Goth. *matjan*, to eat.]
Moth-eaten, moth´et-n, *p.a. Eaten by moths.*
Mother, muᴛʜ´ėr, *n.* A female parent, especially one of the human race; a woman who has borne a child; that which has produced anything; that which has preceded in time; the oldest or chief of anything; a familiar term of address to an old woman; an appellation given to a woman who exercises care and tenderness toward another.—*a.* Native; natural; received by birth; vernacular; received from parents or ancestors. [Sax. *modor*—L. *mater*—Sans. *mâtri*.]
Mother-church, muᴛʜ´ėr-chėrch, *n.* The *church* to which one belongs; the oldest church; the Church of Rome by way of eminence, so designated by its adherents.
Motherhood, muᴛʜ´ėr-hud, *n. State of being a mother.*
Mother-in-law, muᴛʜ´ėr-in-la, *n.* The *mother* of a husband or wife.

Motherless, muᴛʜ´ėr-les, *a. Destitute of a mother.*
Motherliness, muᴛʜ´ėr-li-nes, *n. Quality of being motherly.*
Motherly, muᴛʜ´ėr-li, *a. Like* or becoming *a mother;* pertaining to a mother; tender; maternal; affectionate. *adv. In the manner of a mother.*
Mothy, moth´i, *a. Full of moths.*
Motion, mō´shon, *n. Act of moving;* change of local position; opposed to rest; animal life; gait; air; change of posture; military march; agitation; action proceeding from any cause; proposal made; a proposition made in a deliberative assembly; the change of place or position, which from certain attitudes a figure in painting or sculpture seems to be making; a puppet-show or puppett.—*vi. To make* a significant *movement* with the hand. [Fr.—L. *moveo, motum*, to move, stir, set in motion.]
Motionless, mō´shon-les, *a. Wanting motion;* being at rest.
Motive, mō´tiv, *a. Causing motion;* having power to move, or tending to move.—*n. That which moves* or influences; that which incites to action; that which determines the choice; incitement; reason; that which may incite to action. [It. *motivo;* L. *moveo*, to move.]
Motley, mot´lē, *a. Speckled;* consisting of different colours; composed of various characters; diversified.—*n.* A fool. [Sp. *motear*, to speckle.]
Motley-minded, mot´lē-mind-ed, *a.* Having *diversified* views and feelings.
Motory, mō´to-ri, *a. Giving motion.*
Mottled, mot´ld, *p.a. Spotted;* marked with spots of different colours.
Motto, mot´to, *n.* **Mottoes**, pl. *A word; a sentence* or a *word* prefixed to an essay or discourse, containing the subject of it, or added to a device. [It.; Fr. *mot*, a word.]
Mould, mōld, *n. Fine, soft earth,* such as constitutes soil; a substance like down, which forms on bodies which lie long in warm and damp air; matter of which anything is formed.—*vt. To cause to contract mould;* to cover with mould or soil.—*vi. To contract mould;* to become mouldy. [Sax. *molde*.]
Mould, mōld, *n. A model;* the matrix in which anything is cast and receives its form; the contexture of the skull; form; character.—*vt. To model;* to form into a particular shape; to knead. [Fr. *moule*—L. *modus*, a measure.]
Moulder, mōld´ėr, *n. He who moulds* or forms into shape.
Moulder, mōld´ėr, *vi. To turn to mould* or dust by natural decay; to crumble; to perish; to be diminished; to waste away gradually —*vt. To turn to mould* or dust; to crumble; to waste. [from *mould*, fine soft earth.]
Mouldering, mōld´ėr-ing, *p.a.* Crumbling; wasting away.
Mouldiness, mōld´i-nes, *n. State of being mouldy;* a name applied to all minute fungi which appear in masses upon organic bodies.
Moulding, mōld´ing, *p.n. Anything cast in a mould,* or which appears to be so; an ornamental form in wood or stone.
Mould-warp, mōld´warp, *n.* A mole, which *casts up earth*. [Sax. *molde*, mould, and *weorpan*, to throw, to cast.]
Mouldy, mōld´i, *a. Overgrown with mould.*
Moult, mōlt, *vi. To change* or cast the hair, feathers, skin, horns, &c., as an animal.—*n. The act or process of chang-*

ing the feathers, &c.; moulting. [Fr. *muer*—L. *mudo*, to change.]
Moulting, mōlt´ing, *p.n.* The operation by which certain animals lose their hair, feathers, &c.
Mound, mound, *n.* Something raised as a *defence*, usually a bank of earth or stone; a bulwark; something raised; an artificial elevation of earth. [Sax. *mund*, defence.]
Mount, mount, *vi. To ascend*, as to the top of a *mount;* to tower; to get on horseback; to rise in value.—*vt.* To raise aloft; to climb; to scale; to place, as one's self on horseback; to furnish with horses; to set off to advantage; to carry; to be furnished with; as, a vessel mounts twenty guns.—*n.* A *mountain* or hill; a mass of earth, or earth and rock, rising considerably above the common surface of the surrounding land; a bulwark for offence or defence. [Fr. *monter*—L. *mons, montis*, a mountain.]
Mountain, moun´tān, *n. A mount;* an elevated mass higher and larger than a hill; a high hill; a great eminence; anything proverbially large.—*a. Pertaining to a mountain;* found on mountains; growing or dwelling on a mountain; vast. [Fr. *montagne:* L. *mons, montis.*]
Mountaineer, moun-tan-ēr´, *n. An inhabitant of a mountain;* a rustic; a freebooter.
Mountainous, moun´tān-us, *a. Full of mountains;* large, as a mountain; huge.
Mountant! mount´ant, *a.* Rising on high.
Mountebank, moun´tē-bangk, *n. One who mounts a bench,* boasts of his skill in curing diseases, and vends quack medicines; any boastful and false pretender.—*vt.!* To gull. [It. *montare,* to mount, and *banco*, a bench.]
Mounted, mount´ed, *p.a.* Seated on horseback; embellished; furnished with guns.
Mounting, mount´ing, *p.n. Act of mounting;* act of preparing for use; embellishment.
Mourn, mōrn, *vi. To be in bitterness of spirit;* to sorrow; to lament; to express grief or sorrow; to wear the customary habit of sorrow.—*vt.* To grieve for; to lament; to utter in a sorrowful manner. [Sax. *murnan*—L. *mæror*, mourning—Heb. *mârar*, to be bitter.]
Mourner, mōrn´ėr, *n. One wh. mourns;* one who follows a funeral in the habit of mourning.
Mournful, mōrn´ful, *a. Causing mourning;* lamentable; doleful; intended to express sorrow; feeling grief; sorrowful.
Mournfully, mōrn´ful-li, *adv. In a manner expressive of sorrow.*
Mournfulness, mōrn´ful-nes, *n. State of mourning;* sorrow; grief.
Mourning, mōrn´ing, *p.a.* Grieving; wearing the appearance of sorrow. *p.n.* Act of sorrowing; lamentation; the dress worn by mourners.
Mouse, mous, *n.* **Mice**, mis, *pl.* A little *thievish* gnawing animal, that hides in small holes and crevices, and infests dwelling-houses, granaries, fields, &c. [Sax.—L. *mus*—Sans. *mûsh*, to steal.]
Mouse, mous, *vi. To watch for and catch mice;* to watch for in a sly manner. *ppr.* mousing, *pret. & pp.* moused.
Mouser, mous´ėr, *n. A cat which catches mice.*
Mouth, mouth, *n.* The opening in the head of an animal, between the lips,

Fāte, fär, fat, fall; mē, met, hėr; pīne, pin; nōte, not, mōve; tūbe, tub, bull; oil, pound.

into which food is received, and in which it is eaten, and by which the voice is uttered; the instrument of speaking; the opening of a vessel by which it is filled or emptied; the part of a river by which its waters are discharged into the ocean; the opening of a piece of ordnance by which the charge issue; the aperture of a vessel in animal bodies, by which fluids or other matter is received or discharged; the opening or entrance of a cave, &c.; a principal speaker; one who utters the common opinion; a wry face†. [Sax. *muth*, the mouth—Old G. *mundalon*, to say out, to utter.]

Mouth, mouth, *vt.* To take into the *mouth*; to devour; to utter with a voice affectedly big or swelling.—*vi.* To speak with a full, round, or loud, affected voice; to vociferate; to rant; to kiss.†

Mouthed, mouthd, *p.a. Furnished with a mouth.*

Mouther, mouth'ér, *n. One who mouths*; an affected speaker.

Mouthful, mouth'ful, *n. As much as fills the mouth*; a small quantity.

Mouthing, mouth'ing, *p.a.* Uttering with an affected, swelling voice.—*p.n.* An affected, swelling utterance.

Mouth-made†, mouth'mād, *a.* Not sincere.

Mouth-piece, mouth'pēs, *n. The piece of* a musical wind-instrument to which the *mouth* is applied; one who delivers the opinions of others.

Movable, möv'a-bl, *a.* That may be *moved*; susceptible of motion; that may or does change from one time to another.—*n.* Any piece of furniture *capable of being moved.* [from *move.*]

Movably, möv'a-bli, *adv.* So that it may be moved.

Move, möv, *vt. To cause to change place*; to set in motion; to stir; to draw from one place to another; to affect; to rouse; to cause to act; to prevail on; to excite tenderness or grief in the heart of; to excite feeling in; to irritate; to incite by secret agency; to shake; to bring forward for consideration and determination, as a resolution; to recommend to favour, as a suit.—*vi. To change place* or posture; to stir; to have action or the power of action; to walk; to shake; to change residence; to propose something to an organized meeting, for consideration and determination. *ppr.* moving, *pret. & pp.* moved.—*n. The act of moving*; a movement; the act of transferring from place to place, as in chess. [Fr. *mouvoir;* L. *moveo.*]

Movement, möv'ment, *n. A moving;* motion; any change of position in a material body; the manner of moving; excitement; any single strain in music having the same measure; the entire wheel-work of a clock or watch. [Fr. *mouvement.*]

Mover, möv'er, *n. He or that which moves;* a proposer.

Moving, möv'ing, *p.a.* Instigating; influencing; exciting the passions or affections; touching; pathetic.

Movingly, möv'ing-li, *adv. In a moving manner.*

Mow, mō, *n. A heap or pile of hay* or sheaves of grain deposited in a barn. *vt.* To lay, as hay or sheaves of grain in a heap in a barn. [Sax. *mowe.*]

Mow, mō, *vt. To cut down* with a scythe, as grass or other plants; to cut down with speed; to cut down indiscriminately.—*vi. To practise mowing*; to cut grass; to use the scythe. *ppr.* mowing,

pret. mowed, *pp.* mowed or mown. [Sax. *mawan.*]

Mow†, mō, *vi.* To make mouths.

Mower, mō'ér, *n. One who mows down.*

Mowing, mō'ing, *p.n.* Act of *cutting* with a scythe; land from which grass is cut.

Mr. An abbreviation of *Master* or *Mister.*

Mrs. An abbreviation of *Mistress.*

Much, much, *a. Grown great*; great in quantity or amount; long in duration. *n. A great* quantity; a great deal; more than enough; a heavy service; something strange.—*adv. In a great degree*; by far; often or long; nearly; an exclamation of contempt implying sneering disbelief of an assertion. [Sax. *micel*—Sans. *manh*, to increase.]

Mucilage, mū'si-lāj, *n. A solution in* water of gummy matter, analogous to *mucus;* a turbid, slimy substance found in certain vegetables. [Fr.—Gr.*musso*, to blow the nose.]

Mucilaginous, mū-si-laj'in-us, *a. Pertaining to or secreting mucilage;* slimy; ropy.

Muck, muk, *n. Dung in a moist state,* or a mass of decaying or putrefied vegetable matter; something mean, vile, or filthy.—*vt. To manure with muck.* [Sax. *meox.*]

Mucous, mū'kus,*a. Pertaining to mucus,* or resembling it; slimy, ropy, and lubricous. [from L. *mucus.*]

Mucus, mū'kus, *n. The slimy discharge from the nose;* a viscid fluid secreted by the membranous lining of all the canals and cavities of the body which are exposed to the contact of air, and which it serves to moisten and defend. [L.—*mungo*, to blow the nose.]

Mud, mud, *n. Moist and soft earth of* any kind, such as is found in marshes and swamps, at the bottom of rivers and ponds, or in highways after rain. *vt. To bury in mud* or slime; to make foul with dirt; to stir, as the sediment in liquors. *ppr.* mudding, *pret. & pp.* mudded. [D. *modder*—Gr. *mudaō*, to bedaub.]

Muddied, mud'id, *p.a.* Confused in mind.

Muddily, mud'i-li, *adv.* Turbidly; with foul mixture; cloudily.

Muddiness, mud'i-nes, *n. State or quality of being muddy;* turbidness; intellectual cloudiness or dulness.

Muddle, mud'l, *vt. To make muddy;* to intoxicate partially; to cloud or stupify, particularly with liquor.—*vi. To become muddy*; to contract filth; to be in a confused or dirty state. *ppr.* muddling, *pret. & pp.* muddled. [from *mud.*]

Muddy, mud'i, *a. Foul with mud*; turbid, as water; containing mud, as a street; dashed, soiled, or besmeared with mud; consisting of mud or earth; impure; of the colour of mud; cloudy in mind; stupid.—*vt. To soil with mud;* to dirty; to render turbid; to cloud; to make dull or heavy. *ppr.* muddying, *pret. & pp.* muddied.

Muddy-mettled‡, mud'i-met'ld, *a.* Dullspirited.

Muff, muf, *n. A warm cover for receiving the hands,* usually made of fur or dressed skins. [Dan. *muffe.*]

Muffin, muf'in, *n. A light, round, spongy* cake, baked on a griddle and buttered, for the less substantial meals. [probably from *muff.*]

Muffle, muf'l, *vt. To cover close with* cloth or *fur*, particularly the neck and face; to blindfold; to cover: to deaden

the sound of, as by wrapping or tying cloth, &c., round. *ppr.* muffling, *pret. & pp.* muffled. [Fr. *moufler.*]

Muffled, muf'ld, *p.a.* Blindfolded.

Muffler, muf'l-ér, *n. A cover for the face*; a wrapper for the head or neck.

Mug, mug, *n. A small vessel of earthenware* or metal for containing liquor. [Ir. *mugа.*]

Muggy, mug'i, *a. Cloudy;* damp and close; mouldy, as straw. [Icel. *mugga*, darkness caused by rain or snow.]

Mulatto, mū-lat'tō, *n. A person who is* the offspring of a negress by a white man, or of a white woman by a negro [Sp. *mulato—mu.o*, a mule.]

Mulberry, mul'be-ri, *n. The berry* or fruit of a well-known tree; the tree itself, one species of which is extensively cultivated for food for the silkworms. [G. *maulbeere;* Celtic, *mor*, black.]

Mulct, mulkt, *n. A penalty*; *a fine*; a fine imposed on a person guilty of some offence or misdemeanour.—*vt. To fine*; to punish for an offence or misdemeanour by imposing a fine upon. [L. *mulcta*, a fine.]

Mule, mūl, *n. A quadruped of a mongrel breed,* usually generated between an ass and a mare, sometimes between a horse and a she-ass; a hybrid; an instrument for cotton-spinning. [Sax. *mul*—L. *mulus.*]

Muleteer, mūl-et-ēr', *n. One who drives mules*; a mule-driver. [Fr. *muletier.*]

Mulish, mūl'ish, *a. Like a mule;* sullen.

Mulishly, mūl'ish-li, *adv.* With stubbornness, *as of a mule.*

Mulishness, mūl'ish-n·s, *n. Quality of being muliah;* stubborness.

Mull, mul, *vt. To soften* and bring down in spirit; to heat, sweeten and enrich with spices; to dispirit or deaden. [L. *mollio,* to soften.]

Mulled, muld, *p.a.* Sweetened and enriched with spices.

Mullet, mul et, *n. A fish distinguished* by several remarkable peculiarities of structure, and chiefly inhabiting the mouths of rivers. [Fr. *mulet*—L. *mullus.*]

Mullion, mul'i-on, *n. An upright division between the lights of windows,* screens, &c., in Gothic architecture. *vt. To shape into divisions by mullions.* [Fr. *moulure*—L. *modus*, a standard.]

Multangular, mul-tang'gū-lér, *a. Having many angles*; polygonal. [L. *multus*, many, and *angulus*, an angle.]

Multifarious, mul-ti-fā'ri-us, *a. Having great variety*; manifold; having great multiplicity. [L. *multifarius—multus,* many, and *varius,* diverse.]

Multifariously, mul-ti-fā ri-us-li, *adv. In a multifarious manner.*

Multiform, mul'ti-form, *a. Having many forms*, shapes, or appearances. [L. *multiformis—forma*, form.]

Multiformity, mul-ti-form'i-ti, *n. State or quality of being multiform.*

Multilateral, mul-ti-lat'ér-al, *a. Having many sides.* [L. *multus,* and *latus*, *lateris,* a side.]

Multilineal, mul-ti-lin's-al, *a. Having many lines.* [L. *multus,* and *linea,* a line.]

Multiped, mul'ti-ped, *n. An insect that has many feet.* [L. *multus,* and *pes, pedis,* a foot.]

Multiple, mul'ti-pl, *a. That has many folds;* containing a certain number of times.—*n.* A number or quantity which contains another or others a certain number of times without a remainder. [L. *multiplex—plico,* to fold.]

Multipliable, mul'ti-pli-a-bl, *a. That may be multiplied.* [Fr.]
Multiplicand, mul'ti-pli-kand", *n.* A number or quantity *to be multiplied by another.* [L. *multiplicandum.*]
Multiplication, mul'ti-pli-kā'shon, *n.* Act of multiplying; state of being multiplied; a rule by which a given number may be repeated any number of times proposed. [L. *multiplicatio—multus,* much, many, and *plico,* to fold.]
Multiplicity, mul-ti-plis'i-ti, *n.* State of being many or manifold; great number. [Fr. *multiplicité.*]
Multiplied, mul'ti-plīd, *p.a.* Repeated; numerous.
Multiplier, mul'ti-pli-ėr, *n. One who multiplies;* the number or quantity by which another is multiplied.
Multiply, mul'ti-pli, *vt. To make manifold;* to increase in number; to make more by production, or by addition; to add to itself any given number as many times as there are units in any other given number.—*vi.* To become manifold; to increase in extent; to spread. *ppr.* multiplying, *pret. & pp.* multiplied. [L. *multiplico—multus,* much, and *plico,* to fold.]
Multitude, mul'ti-tūd, *n. State of being many;* a great number; a great number, indefinitely; a throng; the populace; the lower classes of society. [Fr.—L. *multus,* many.
Multitudinous, mul-ti-tūd'in-us, *a. Consisting of a multitude;* having the appearance of a multitude; manifold.
Mum, mum, *a. Silent;* not speaking. *n.* Silence.—*interj.* Be silent! hush!
Mumble, mum'bl, *vi.* To speak with the lips or other organs partly closed, so as to render the sounds inarticulate; to utter words with a grumbling tone; to chew or bite softly.—*vt.* To utter with a low inarticulate voice; to mouth gently, or to eat with a muttering sound; to suppress. [G. *mummeln.*]
Mumbler, mum'bl-ėr, *n. One who* speaks with a low inarticulate voice.
Mumbling, mum'bl-ing, *p.a.* Uttering with a low inarticulate voice.
Mummer, mum'ėr, *n.* Originally, one who made sport by gestures *without speaking.*
Mummery, mum'ė-ri, *n. Masking;* frolicking in masks; buffoonery; hypocritical disguise and parade to delude vulgar minds. [Dan. *mummeri*—Gr. *mōmos,* ridicule.]
Mummify, mum'i-fī, *vt. To make into a mummy;* to embalm and dry as a mummy. *ppr.* mummifying, *pret. & pp.* mummified. [*mummy,* and L. *facio,* to make.]
Mummy, mum'i, *n.* A dead human body embalmed and dried after the manner of the ancient Egyptians, in which *wax,* balsams, &c., were employed. [It. *mummia*—Pers. *mūm, wax.*]
Mump, mump, *vt.* To chew with continued motion; to talk low and quick. *vi.* To move the lips with the mouth almost closed; [D. *mompen*] to implore with a beggar's accent and motion of the mouth; to cheat; to trick. [D. *mompelen.*]
Mumper, mump'ėr, *n.* A beggar.
Mumping, mump'ing, *p.n.* Begging tricks; foolish tricks; mockery.
Mumpish, mump'ish, *a. Silent;* dull; heavy; sullen; sour.
Mumpishness, mump'ish-nes, *n.* Sullen silence; sullenness.
Mumps, mumps, *n. Sullenness;* a disease affecting the parts under the ear, swelling and compressing the chops, so as to render speaking difficult.

Munch, munsh, *vi. To chew eagerly* by great mouthfuls; to chew without opening the mouth. [Fr. *manger*—L. *mando,* to chew.]
Muncher, munsh'ėr, *n. One who munches.*
Mundane, mun'dān, *a. Belonging to the world;* earthly. [L. *mundanus*—*mundus,* the world.]
Municipal, mu-ni'si-pal, *a. Pertaining to a corporation or city;* pertaining to a state or nation; pertaining to the general law of a country. [Fr.—L. *munia,* functions, and *capio,* to take.]
Munificence, mū-ni'fi-sens, *n.* A giving or bestowing of gifts or favours; liberality; bounty; bountifulness. [Fr.—L. *munus,* a gift, and *facio,* to make.]
Munificent, mū-ni'fi-sent, *a. Giving gifts;* manifesting liberality in giving or bestowing; liberal; generous. [Low L. *munificens.*]
Munificently, mū-ni'fi-sent-li, *adv.* Liberally; generously.
Muniment, mū'ni-ment, *n.* A fortification of any kind; a stronghold; defence; a record; a charter; a writing by which claims and rights are defended or maintained. [L. *munimentum*—*munio,* to fortify.]
Munition, mū-ni'shon, *n. Fortification*; any material used in war for *defence,* or for annoying an enemy; provisions of a fortress, or for ships of war, and in general for an army. [Fr.—L. *munio,* to fortify.]
Mural, mū'ral, *a. Pertaining to a wall;* resembling a wall; perpendicular or steep. [Fr.—L. *murus,* a wall.]
Murder, mėr'dėr, *n.* Act of *killing* a human being with premeditated malice, by a person of sound mind; an exclamation or outcry, when life is in danger.—*vt. To kill,* as a human being, with premeditated malice; to destroy; to put an end to; to abuse; to mar by bad execution. [Sax. *morther*—L. *mors, mortis,* death.]
Murdered, mėr'dėrd, *p.a.* Slain with malice prepense.
Murderer, mėr'dėr-ėr, *n. One who murders;* an assassin.
Murderous, mėr'dėr-us, *a. Guilty of murder;* consisting in murder; bloody; committing murder; premeditating murder.
Mure†, mūr, *n.* A *wall.*—*vt.* To immure. [L. *murus,* a wall.]
Muriatic, mū-ri-at'ik, *a.* Pertaining to or obtained from sea-salt. [L. *muria,* brine.]
Murk†, mėrk, *n.* Darkness.
Murky, mėrk'i, *a. Dark;* obscure; gloomy. [Sax. *mirc.*]
Murmur, mėr'mėr, *n.* A low sound, as that of *a stream running* in a stony channel; a complaint uttered in a low muttering voice.—*vi.* To make a low continued noise, like a *stream of water,* the hum of bees, rolling waves, or like the wind in a forest; to grumble; to utter sullen discontent (with *at* or *against*). [L.—Heb. *mar,* a drop—*mārar,* to flow.]
Murmurer, mėr'mėr-ėr, *n. One who murmurs;* a grumbler.
Murmuring, mėr'mėr-ing, *p.a.* Grumbling.—*p.n.* The utterance of a low sound; complaint.
Murmuringly, mėr'mėr-ing-li, *adv.* With a low sound; with complaints.
Murrain, mu'rān, *n.* A *deadly* and infectious *disease* among cattle. [Sp. *morriña;* L. *morior,* to die.]
Murther, mėr'THėr. See **Murder.**

Muscadel, Muscadine, mus'ka-del, mus'ka-din, *a.* and *n.* A species of grape which *flies,* bees, &c., feed eagerly upon; a kind of rich wine produced from the grape; a sweet pear. [It. *moscadello*—L. *musca,* a fly.]
Muscle, mus'l, *n.* One of the organs of motion, consisting of a bundle of fibres *shut up or inclosed* in a thin cellular membrane; a fish *shut up* within a shell (sometimes written *mussel*). [L. *musculus,* a little mouse, a muscle of the body—Gr. *mus,* to be shut.]
Muscled, mus'ld, *p.a. Having muscles;* having large muscles.
Muscular, mus'kū-lėr, *a. Pertaining to* a *muscle;* performed by a muscle; strong; brawny; vigorous.
Muscularity, mus-kū-la'ri-ti, *n. State of being muscular.*
Muse, mūz, *n.* One of the nine sister goddesses, who, in mythology, *sought out, invented,* and presided over music, poetry, painting, rhetoric, astronomy, &c.; deep thought; close attention which abstracts the mind from passing scenes; hence, sometimes, absence of mind.—*vi. To be devoted to the Muses;* to study in silence; to contemplate; to be absent in mind; to wonder. *ppr.* musing, *pret. & pp.* mused. [Fr.; Gr. *Mousa,* a Muse—*maō,* to seek out.]
Muser, mūz'ėr, *n.* One who thinks closely in silence, or one apt to be absent in mind.
Muset†, mū'zet, *n.* A gap in a hedge; a muse.
Museum, mū-zē'um, *n.* A place dedicated to the Muses; a repository of natural, scientific, and literary curiosities, or of works of art. [L.]
Mushroom, mush'röm, *n.* A spongy plant which grows rapidly, so named from its *slimy* moist nature; an upstart.—*a. Made of mushrooms;* of sudden growth and decay; ephemeral. [Fr. *mousseron*—L. *mucus,* slimy matter from the nose.]
Music, mū'zik, *n. Melody or harmony;* any succession of sounds so modulated as to please the ear; any combination of simultaneous sounds in accordance the science of harmonical sounds; the art of combining sounds in a manner to please the ear; harmony in revolutions. [Fr. *musique;* Gr. *Mousa,* a Muse.]
Musical, mū'zik-al, *a. Belonging to music;* producing music; melodious; harmonious; pleasing to the ear.
Musically, mū'zik-al-li, *adv.* In a melodious or harmonious manner.
Musician, mū-zi'shan, *n. One skilled in music;* one who sings or performs on instruments of music. [Fr. *musicien.*]
Musing, mūz'ing, *p.n.* Meditation; contemplation.
Musingly, mūz'ing-li, *adv. By musing.*
Musk, musk, *n.* A strong-scented substance obtained from a *cyst* or *bag* near the navel of an animal that inhabits the mountains of Central Asia; also, the animal itself; a plant.—*vt. To perfume with musk.* [L. *muscus*—Gr. *moschos,* a bag.]
Musket, mus'ket, *n.* A species of firearms used in war, originally discharged by a match, but now by a spring-lock; a male hawk of a small kind. [Fr. *mousquet.*]
Musketeer, mus-ket-ēr', *n.* A soldier *armed with a musket.*
Musketry, mus'ket-ri, *n. Muskets in general,* or their fire.
Muskiness, musk'i-nes, *n.* The scent of *musk.* [from *musk.*]

Fāte, fär, fat, fall; mē, met, hėr; pīne, pin; nōte, not, mōve; tūbe, tub, bull; oil, pound.

Musk-melon, musk'mel-on, n. A delicious variety of *melon*, named probably from its fragrance.

Musk-rose, musk'rōz, n. A fragrant species of rose.

Musky, musk'i, a. Having the odour of *musk*; fragrant.

Muslin, muz'lin, n. A sort of fine thin cotton cloth, which bears a downy nap on its surface.—a. Made of *muslin*. [Fr. *mousseline*.]

Muss, mus, n. A scramble.

Mussel, mus'el, n. See MUSCLE.

Mussulman, mus'l-man, n. **Mussulmans**, mus'l-manz, pl. A Mohammedan, or follower of Mohammed. [Ar. *muslim*, pl. *muslimin*.]

Must, must, vi. To be obliged; to be necessitated; a verb which expresses moral fitness or propriety as necessary or essential to the character or end proposed. (*Must* is of all persons and tenses, and used of persons and things.) [Sax. *mót*, must, ought, pl. *móston*; Old G. *muosan*, to be bound.]

Must, must, n. New wine pressed from the grape, but not fermented. [Sax.—L. *mustum*, new wine.]

Mustache, mǒs-tàsh', n. **Mustaches**, mǒs-tàsh'ez, pl. Long hair on the upper lip. [Fr. *moustache*.]

Mustard, mus'tẽrd, n. A plant and its seed, which has a *pungent* taste and smell; a condiment made from the seed, and so named from its having been frequently prepared with *must*, and from its *hot* pungent taste. (It. *mostarda*—L. *mustum ardens*, burning must.]

Muster, mus'tẽr, vt. To collect, as troops for *review*; to collect, as persons or things; to gather or obtain.—vi. To assemble.—n. An assembling of troops for *review*; a roll of troops mustered; a collection, or the act of collecting. [G. *mustern*—L. *monstro*, to show.]

Muster-book, mus'tẽr-bụk, n. A book in which military *forces* are registered.

Muster-roll, mus'tẽr-rōl, n. A register of troops, or of a ship's company.

Mustiness, mus'ti-nes, n. Quality of being musty or sour; mouldiness.

Musty, mus'ti, a. Mouldy; sour; stale; spoiled by age; having an ill flavour; spiritless. [Fr. *moisir*, to grow mouldy—L. *muceo*, to be mouldy.]

Mutability, mū-ta-bil'i-ti, n. Quality or state of being mutable; susceptibility of change; changeableness; inconstancy; instability. [Fr. *mutabilité*—L. *muto*, to change.]

Mutable, mū'ta-bl, a. Changeable; subject to change; unstable; variable; fickle. [L. *mutabilis*—*muto*, to change.]

Mutably, mū'ta-bli, adv. Changeably.

Mutation, mū-tā'shon, n. Act or process of *changing*; change; alteration, either in form or qualities. [L. *mutatio*.]

Mute, mūt, a. Having the tongue bound; not having the power of utterance; dumb; silent; not speaking; uttering no sound, as grief.—n. A person who cannot speak, or who remains silent; a person employed by undertakers to stand before the door of a house a short time previous to a funeral; a letter that represents no sound, as *p, t, k*; a little utensil of wood or brass, used on a violin to deaden or soften the sounds. [L. *mutus*, dumb—Sans. *mud*, bound.]

Mute, mūt, n. To eject the contents of the bowels, as birds. ppr. muting, pret. & pp. muted. [Old Fr. *mutir*.]

Mutely, mūt'li, adv. Silently.

Mutilate, mū'ti-lāt, vt. To cut off, as a limb; to cut or break off, as any important part; to destroy or remove any material part of, so as to render the thing imperfect. ppr. mutilating, pret. & pp. mutilated. [L. *mutilo*, *mutilatus*, to cut off.]

Mutilated, mū'ti-lāt-ed, p.a. Deprived of an essential part.

Mutilation, mū-ti-lā'shon, n. Act of *mutilating*; deprivation of some essential part; castration. [L. *mutilatio*.]

Mutineer, mū'tin, n. A mutineer.—vi. To mutiny.

Mutineer, mū-ti-nēr', n. One guilty of *mutiny*.

Muting, mūt'ing, n. The dung of birds.

Mutinous, mū'ti-nus, a. Promoting *mutiny*; turbulent; disposed to resist the authority of laws in an army or navy, or openly resisting such authority; seditious.

Mutinously, mū'ti-nus-li, adv. In a *mutinous* manner.

Mutiny, mū'ti-ni, n. A *commotion*; open resistance to officers, or opposition to their authority. [Fr. *mutinerie*.]—vi. To make a *commotion*; to rise against lawful authority in military and naval service. ppr. mutinying, pret. & pp. mutinied. [Fr. *se mutiner*, to mutiny—L. *moveo*, *motum*, to move.]

Mutter, mut'tẽr, vi. To mumble; to utter words with *compressed lips*; to grumble; to sound with a low, rumbling noise.—vt. To utter with a low, murmuring voice.—n. Murmur; obscure utterance. [L. *muttire*.]

Mutterer, mut'tẽr-ẽr, n. One who *mutters*; a grumbler.

Muttering, mut'tẽr-ing, p.a. Grumbling; murmuring.

Mutton, mut'n, n. A *wether*; the flesh of sheep, raw or dressed for food. [Fr. *mouton*, a wether; G. *mutzen*, to cut.]

Mutton-chop, mut-n-chop', n. A rib of mutton for broiling, having the bone at the thin end *chopped* off.

Mutual, mū'tū-al, a. Interchanged; given and received. [Fr. *mutuel*—L. *muto*, to change.]

Mutually, mū'tū-al-li, adv. Reciprocally.

Muzzle, muz'l, n. The mouth of a thing; the end for entrance or discharge, as of a tube; the projecting mouth and nose of an animal, as of a horse; a fastening for the mouth which stops biting.—vt. To bind the mouth of; to fasten the mouth of, to prevent biting or eating; to restrain from hurt. ppr. muzzling, pret. & pp. muzzled. [Low L. *musellum*.]

My, mī, pronom. adj. Belonging to me; used always attributively. [contracted from Sax. *min*=Old G. *mîn*, mine.]

Myriad, mi'ri-ad, n. The number of ten thousand; an immense number, indefinitely. [Gr. *murias*, *muriados*—*murios*, numberless.]

Myrmidon, mẽr'mi-don, n. One of the soldiers of Achilles, who were said to have sprung from *ants*; a desperate soldier under some daring leader. [Gr. *Myrmidónes*, the Myrmidons—*murmex*, an ant.]

Myrrh, mẽr, n. A strong aromatic gum resin of a *bitter taste*, produced by some species of a tree growing chiefly in Arabia. [L. *myrrha*—Heb. *mar*, bitter.]

Myrtle, mẽr'tl, n. An evergreen shrub celebrated for its beautiful and fragrant foliage. [L. *myrtus*; Gr. *murtos*—*murton*, the myrtle-berry.]

Myself, mī-self', pron. A compound pronoun used after *I*, to express emphasis; the reciprocal of *I*, in the objective case; as, I will defend myself.

Mysterious, mis-tē'ri-us, a. Containing *mystery*; secret; hid from the understanding; not revealed; beyond human comprehension; awfully obscure. [Fr. *mystérieux*.]

Mysteriously, mis-tē'ri-us-li, adv. In a *mysterious manner*; obscurely; enigmatically.

Mysteriousness, mis-tē'ri-us-nes, n. Quality of being mysterious.

Mystery, mis'tẽ-ri, n. That which is closed, shut up, or concealed; something above human intelligence; a profound secret; something not revealed to man; an enigma; (pl.) artificial fashions. [Fr. *mystère*; Gr. *mustērion*—*muō*, to close, be shut.]

Mystic, Mystical, mis'tik, mis'tik-al, a. Relating to or containing *mystery*; obscure; sacredly obscure; remote from human comprehension; involving some secret meaning; emblematical. [Gr. *mustikos*.]

Mystic, mis'tik, n. One who holds the *doctrines of mysticism*.

Mystically, mis'tik-al-li, adv. In a *mystical manner*.

Mysticism, mis'ti-sizm, n. The doctrine of the *Mystics*; obscurity of doctrine. [Fr. *mysticisme*.]

Mystics, mis'tiks, n. pl. A class of religious people who profess to have direct intercourse with the Spirit of God.

Mystification, mis'ti-fi-kā"shon, n. Act of rendering anything *mysterious*.

Mystify, mis'ti-fī, vt. To make mysterious; to involve in mystery; to render obscure. ppr. mystifying, pret. & pp. mystified.

Myth, mith, n. A *fable*; a fictitious narrative having an analogy more or less remote to some real event. [Gr. *mūthos*.]

Mythic, Mythical, mith'ik, mith'ik-al, a. Pertaining to a *myth*. [Gr. *mūthikos*, legendary.]

Mythically, mith'ik-al-li, adv. After the manner of a *myth*; fabulously.

Mythological, mith-o-loj'ik-al, a. Relating to *mythology*; fabulous. [Gr. *mūthologikos*.]

Mythologically, mith-o-loj'ik-al-li, adv. In a mythological manner.

Mythologist, mith-ol'o-jist, n. One versed in *mythology*. [Fr. *mythologiste*.]

Mythology, mith-ol'o-ji, n. A telling of *fabulous legends*; legendary lore; a system of fables, respecting the deities which heathen nations have supposed to preside over the world. [Fr. *mythologie*—Gr. *mūthos*, a story, and *logos*, discourse.]

N.

Nabob, nā'bob, n. A *deputy* or subordinate provincial governor under a viceroy in the Mogul empire; a European who has enriched himself in the East; a man of great wealth. [Ar. *nuuwab*, vicegerents, governors.]

Nadir, nā'dėr, n. That point of the lower hemisphere of the heavens *corresponding* to the point in the upper hemisphere occupied by the zenith; the lowest point. [Ar. *nazir*, alike, resembling, equal to.]

Nag, nag, n. *An animal that neighs*; a small horse; a horse in general, or rather a sprightly horse; a paramour. [from Sax. *hnœgan*, to neigh.]

Naiad, nā'yad, n. In mythology, *a water-nymph*; a female deity fabled to preside over rivers and springs. [Gr. *naias, naiddos—naō*, to flow.]

Nail, nāl, n. The claw or talon of a bird or other animal; the horny substance growing at the end of the human fingers and toes; a small pointed piece of metal, to be driven into a board; a measure of length 2¼ inches.—*vt*. To *fasten with nails*; to stud with nails. [Sax. *nægel—*L. *unguis*.]

Nailer, nāl'ėr, n. *One whose occupation is to make nails*.

Nailery, nāl'ė-ri, n. *A manufactory where nails are made*.

Naive, nā'ėv, a. Having *native* or unaffected *simplicity*; ingenuous. [Fr. from L. *nativus*, natural, native.]

Naively, nā'ėv-li, adv. With *native* or unaffected *simplicity*; ingenuously. [Fr. *naivement*.]

Naivete, nā'ėv-tē, n. *Native simplicity*; unaffected plainness. [Fr. *naiveté*.]

Naked, nā'ked, a. *In a state causing shame*; not covered; defenceless; exposed; open to view; plain; bare; simple; not dressed off with anything of another kind; not assisted by glasses, as vision. [Sax. *nacod—*Sans. *naj*, to be ashamed.]

Nakedly, nā'ked-li, adv. Without covering; simply; barely; evidently.

Nakedness, nā'ked-nes, n. State of *being naked*; want of clothing; nudity; plainness; openness to view.

Name, nām, n. *That by which a person or thing is thought of and known*; that by which a person or thing is called; a person; character; renown; fame; praise; memory; sound only; authority; behalf; part.—*vt*. *To give a name or appellation to*; to designate by name; to call; to style; to speak of by name; to point out by name; to entitle. ppr. naming, pret. & pp. named. [Sax. *nama—*L. *nomen—*Sans. *jnā*, to know.]

Nameless, nām'les, a. *Without a name*; noting a person or thing whose name is not known or mentioned.

Namely, nām'li, adv. *By name*; particularly; that is to say.

Namesake, nām'sāk, n. One whose *name* has been given to him for the *sake* of another.

Nankeen, nan-kēn', n. A species of cotton cloth of a firm texture, originally manufactured in *Nankin*, in China.

Nap, nap, n. A short sleep or slumber. *vi*. To have a short sleep; to be drowsy; to be in a careless, secure state. ppr. napping, pret. & pp. napped. [Sax. *hnœppian*, to sleep.]

Nap, nap, n. *The dressed surface of cloth*; the woolly substance on the surface of cloth; the downy substance on plants. [Sax.*hnoppa—*G. *noppen*, to nap cloth.]

Nape, nāp, n. The *prominent* joint of the neck behind. [Sax. *cnœp*, a top.]

Naphtha, nap'tha, n. Rock-oil; a volatile, limpid, bituminous liquid, of a strong peculiar odour, and very inflammable, and which *exudes* from the ground in various parts of the East. A liquid very similar to mineral naphtha is obtained by the distillation of coal-tar. [L.—Chald. *naph*, to distil.]

Napkin, nap'kin, n. A small cloth; a cloth used for wiping the hands; a towel; a handkerchief. [English dim. from Fr. *nappe*, a cloth.]

Nappy, nap'i, a. *Having abundance of nap* or down on the surface; tending to cause sleepiness; heady.

Narcotic, nȧr-kot'ik, a. *Inducing numbness*; having the qualities of a narcotic. n. *A medicine which induces sleep or stupor*, as opium. [Gr. *narkōtikos—narkē*, numbness.]

Narcotically,nȧr-kot'ik-al-li,adv. Operating after the *manner of a narcotic*.

Nard, nȧrd, n. An aromatic plant, usually called spikenard; an unguent prepared from the plant. [Fr.—L. *nardus*.]

Nardine, nȧrd'in, a. *Pertaining to nard*; having the qualities of spikenard.

Narrate, na-rāt', *vt*. To rehearse or recite, as a story; to relate, as the particulars of any event; to write, as the particulars of a history. ppr. narrating, pret. & pp. narrated. [L. *narro, narrātus*, to tell—Heb. *nārag*, to speak rapidly.]

Narration, na-rā'shon, n. *Act of narrating*; rehearsal; history; a statement of the particulars of any transaction; that part of a discourse which states the facts connected with the subject. [L. *narratio*.]

Narrative, na'rāt-iv, a. *That narrates*; narrating; inclined to relate stories; story-telling.—n. *That which is narrated*; the recital of a story; story. [Fr. *narratif*.]

Narrator,na-rāt'ėr,n. *One who narrates*. [L.]

Narrify†, na'ri-fi, *vt*. To relate; to give account of.

Narrow, na'rō, a. *Brought near together*; of little breadth; not wide or broad; very limited; straitened; covetous; of confined views; very limited, as an intellect; near; close; scrutinizing; barely sufficient to avoid evil, as an escape.—*vt*. To bring or draw near together; to lessen the breadth of; to draw into a smaller compass; to confine. — *vi*. To come nearer; to contract in breadth. [Sax. *nearow—neara*, nearer.]

Narrowing, na'rō-ing, *p.n*. *Act of narrowing*; the part of a stocking which is narrowed.

Narrowly, na'rō-li, adv. *In a narrow manner*; contractedly; sparingly.

Narrow-minded, na'rō-mind-ed, a. Illiberal; mean-spirited; of confined views or sentiments.

Narrowness,na'rō-nes,n. *State or quality of being narrow*; smallness of breadth or extent; contractedness; smallness of estate; poverty; covetousness; illiberality; want of generous or charitable views.

Nasal, nās'al, a. *Pertaining to the nose*; formed or affected by the nose—n. A letter whose sound is uttered through the nose. [Fr.—L. *nasus*, the nose.]

Nasalize, nās'al-iz, *vt*. To utter, as words or letters, *with a nasal sound*. ppr. nasalizing, pret. & pp. na-alized.

Nascent, nas'ent, a. *Arising*; beginning to exist or to grow. [L. *nascens—nascor*, to be born.]

Nastily, nas'ti-li, adv. *In a nasty manner*; filthily; dirtily; obscenely.

Nastiness, nas'ti-ne-, n. *State or quality of being nasty*; extreme filthiness; filth.

Nasty, nas'ti, a. *Disgustingly filthy*; very dirty; nauseous; indecent. [Goth. *natjan*, to wet, to soak.]

Natal, nā'tal, a. *Pertaining to birth*. [Fr.—L. *nascor*, to be born.]

Nation, nā'shon, n. A body of people *of the same stock*, inhabiting the same country, or united under the same sovereignty or government; a great number. [L. *natio—nascor*, to be born.]

National, na'shon-al, a. *Pertaining to a nation*; common to a nation; attached to one's own country. [Fr.]

Nationality, na-shon-al'i-ti, n. *Quality of being national*; national character; a race or people.

Nationally, na'shon-al-li, adv. *In regard to the nation*; as a whole nation.

Native, nā'tiv, a. *That has arisen by birth*; inborn; natural; not acquired; conferred by birth; pertaining to the place of birth; allied by nature.—n. *One born in any place*; that which is produced in the country; offspring. [Fr. *natif—*L. *nascor*, to be born.]

Nativity,na-tiv'i-ti,n. *Birth*; the birthday of our Saviour; time, place, and manner of birth. [L. *nativitas*.]

Natural, na'tūr-al, a. *Produced by nature*; consistent with nature; according to the stated course of things; not forced; such as is dictated by nature; according to the life; derived from nature; not revealed; coming in the ordinary course of things; tender; unaffected; according to truth and reality; born out of wedlock; native; legitimate†; derived from the study of the works of nature.—n. One who exhibits, when grown up, the simplicity *natural* to an infant; an idiot; one born without the usual powers of reason or understanding. [Fr. *naturel*.]

Naturalist, na'tūr-al-ist, n. *One who investigates nature*; one who is versed in the various productions of the earth; one who investigates the phenomena and laws of matter or physics. [Fr. *naturaliste*.]

Naturalization, na'tūr-al-iz-ā"shon, n. *Act of naturalising*; state of being naturalized. [Fr. *naturalisation*.]

Naturalize, na'tūr-al-iz, *vt*. To *invest with natural* qualities; to confer the rights and privileges of a native subject or citizen on, as on an alien; to make natural; to adapt to a different climate; to adopt as native; to make our own, as a foreign word. ppr. na-

---

Fāte, fär, fat, fall; mē, met, hėr; pīne, pin; nōte, not, move; tūbe, tub, bull; oil, pound.

turalizing, *pret. & pp.* naturalized. [Fr. *naturaliser.*]
Naturalized, na'tūr-al-izd, *p.a.* Adapted to a climate; acclimated; native.
Naturally, na'tūr-al-li, *adv.* In a natural manner; according to nature; spontaneously.
Naturalness, na'tūr-al-nes, *n.* Conformity to nature, or to truth and reality.
Nature, na'tūr, *n.* Whatever is made or produced; all the works of God; the system of created things by a metonymy of the effect for the cause; the powers that produce things; the attributes of a thing, which constitute it what it is; the established course of things; a law or principle of action or motion in a natural body; constitution; the constitution and appearances of things; natural affection; sort; kind; sentiments or images conformed to nature; a person of intelligence and character. [Fr.—L. *nascor, natus*—Sans. *jan,* to be born.]
Natured, na'tūrd, *p.a.* Having a nature or temper.
Naught, nąt, *n.* Nought; nothing.—*a.* Worthless; bad; of no value or account. [Sax. *nauht—ne,* not and *aht,* aught.]
Naughtily, na'ti-li, *adv.* In a naughty manner; wickedly; corruptly.
Naughtiness, na'ti-nes, *n.* Quality of being naughty; slight wickedness of children; mischievousness.
Naughty, na'ti, *a.* Of no value; worthless; mischievous; perverse; froward. [from *naught.*]
Nausea, na'shē-a, *n.* Sea-sickness; any similar sickness of the stomach; loathing; disgust; squeamishness of the stomach. [L.—Gr. *naus,* a ship.]
Nauseate, na'shē-āt, *vi.* To become seasick; to become squeamish; to feel disgust.—*vt.* To loathe; to reject with disgust; to affect with disgust. *ppr.* nauseating, *pret. & pp.* nauseated. [L. *nauseo, nauseatum.*]
Nauseous, na'shē-us, *a. Exciting nausea;* loathsome; disgusting; regarded with abhorrence.
Nauseousness, na'shē-us-nes, *n.* Quality of exciting or producing nausea.
Nautical, na'tik-al, *a. Pertaining to ships or seamen,* or navigation; naval; marine. [Fr. *nautique;* Gr. *naus,* a ship—*neō,* to swim.]
Nautically, na'tik-al-li, *adv.* In a nautical manner.
Nautilus, na'ti-lus, *n.* A fish whose shell is said to have served as a model to the first ship. [Gr. *naus,* a ship.]
Naval, na'val, *a. Pertaining to ships;* marine; maritime. [L. *navalis—Gr. naus,* a ship.]
Nave, nāv, *n. The middle of a wheel;* the block in the centre of a wheel in which the spokes are inserted, and through which the axle passes; [Fr. *nef*] the body of a church, probably so named from a fancied resemblance of the roof to the hull of a ship. [Sax. *nafu,* the nave; Gr. *naus,* a ship.]
Navel, na'vl, *n.* The centre of the lower part of the abdomen. [Sax. *nafel.*]
Navigable, na'vig-a-bl, *a. That may be navigated.* [Fr.]
Navigate, na'vi-gāt, *vi.* To conduct a ship on the sea; to pass on water in ships; to sail.—*vt. To steer or manage in sailing,* as a vessel; to sail on, as a sea or ocean. *ppr.* navigating, *pret. & pp.* navigated. [L. *navigo, navigatus—navis,* a ship, and *ago,* to conduct.]
Navigation, na-vi-gā'shon, *n. Act of navigating;* the state of being navigable; the science or art of conducting ships or vessels from one place to another. [Fr.]
Navigator, na'vi-gāt-ėr, *n.* One who *directs the course of a ship,* or one who is skilful in the art of navigation. [L.]
Navy, nā'vi, *n. A fleet of ships;* an assemblage of merchantmen, or so many as sail in company; the whole of the ship of war belonging to a nation; the officers and men belonging to a navy. [Norm. *navie—L. navis,* a ship.]
Nay, nā, *adv. Not; no;* a word that expresses negation; not only so; not this alone; intimating that something is to be added by way of amplification.—*n.* Denial; refusal. [Sax. *ne,* Sans. *na,* not.]
Nayward†, na'wąrd, *n.* Tendency to denial.
Nayword†, na'wėrd, *n.* A byword; a watchword.
Nazarite, na'za-rīt, *n.* A Jew who *set himself apart,* and bound himself by a vow to extraordinary purity of life and devotion. [from Heb. *nasar,* to separate.]
Neaf†, nēf, *n.* The fist.
Neap, nēp, *a. Noting a scanty tide;* noting the lowest tides of the month. *n. A neap-tide.* [Sax. *nep.*]
Neaped, nēpt, *p.a.* Left aground by the tide, as a ship.
Near, nēr, *a. Nigh;* not far distant in place, time, or degree; closely related by blood; willing to aid; intimate; united in close ties of affection; dear; affecting one's interest or feelings; parsimonious; literal; closely resembling an original; next to one; on the left, opposed to off.—*adv.* Almost; within a little.—*vt. To draw or come close to.—vi. To draw near.* [Sax. *neah,* near; Icel. *nā,* to reach to.]
Nearly, nēr'li, *adv.* Closely; intimately; within a little.
Nearness, nēr'nes, *n. State of being near;* closeness; close alliance by blood or affection; intimacy of friendship; parsimony.
Near-sighted, nēr'sīt-ed, *a. Seeing at a small distance only.*
Neat, nēt, *n. Cattle for service and for food;* cattle of the bovine genus, as bulls, oxen, and cows. [Sax. *neát,* cattle, a beast; Icel. *naut,* cattle.]
Neat, nēt, *a. Shining;* pure; free from impure words and phrases, as style; cleanly; nice; spruce; free from tawdry appendages, as attire. [Fr. *net, nette*—L. *niteo,* to shine.]
Neatly, nēt'li, *adv. With neatness;* in a neat manner; with good taste.
Neatness, nēt'nes, *n. Quality of being neat;* exact cleanliness; purity: freedom from ill-chosen words; freedom from useless ornaments.
Neb, neb, *n. The prominent part;* the nose; the beak of a bird; the bill; the mouth. (Also written *nib.*) [Sax.]
Nebula, ne'bū-la, *n.* **Nebulæ**, ne'bū-lē, *pl. A mist; a vapour;* a faint misty appearance among the stars, in most cases, shown by the telescope to be composed of innumerable stars. [L.— *nubes,* a cloud—Heb. *nāba,* to be high.]
Nebular, ne'bū-lėr, *a. Pertaining to nebulæ.*
Nebulous, ne'bū-lus, *a. Cloudy;* having the appearance of a nebula. [L. *nebulosus.*]
Necessarily, ne'ses-sa-ri-li, *adv. By necessity;* indispensably.
Necessary, ne'ses-sa-ri, *a. That cannot be put off;* that must be; that cannot be otherwise; requisite; indispensable; essential; inevitable, as a conclusion or result; acting from necessity; opposed to free.—*n. Something necessary* to some purpose; as, a necessary of life (more commonly in the plural). [Fr. *nécessaire*—L. *ne,* not, and *cedo,* to yield.]
Necessitate, nē-ses'si-tāt, *vt. To make necessary;* to force; to oblige; not to leave free. *ppr.* necessitating, *pret. & pp.* necessitated. [from L. *necessitas.*]
Necessitied†, nē-ses'si-tid, *a.* In a state of want.
Necessitous, nē-ses'sit-us, *a. Being in want of what is necessary;* pressed with poverty; destitute; pinching. [Fr. *nécessiteux.*]
Necessity, nē-ses'si-ti, *n. That which cannot be put off;* the quality of being absolutely requisite; that which must be, and cannot be otherwise; the cause of that which cannot be otherwise; irresistible power; compulsive force, physical or moral; extreme indigence; emergency. (Fr. *nécessité*—L. *ne,* not, and *cedo,* to yield.]
Neck, nek, *n. That part of the body which may be strangled;* that flexible part of an animal's body which is between the head and the trunk; a long, narrow tract of land projecting from the main body; the long slender part of a vessel, as a retort; or of a plant, as a gourd. [Sax. *hnecca*—Heb. *chānak,* to strangle.]
Neckcloth, nek'kloth, *n. A piece of cloth worn on the neck.*
Necked, nekt, *p.a. Having a neck;* as in stiff-necked.
Neckerchief, nek'ėr-chef, *n. A kerchief for the neck.*
Necklace, nek'lās, *n. A string of beads or precious stones,* worn by women on the neck.
Neck-tie, nek'tī, *n.* Neckerchief.
Necrology, nek-rol'o-ji, *n. An account of the dead* or of deaths; a register of deaths. [Gr. *nekros,* a dead body, and *logos,* discourse.]
Necromancer, nek'rō-man-sėr, *n. One who practises necromancy;* a conjurer.
Necromancy, nek'rō-man-si, *n. The art of revealing future events by means of a pretended communication with the dead;* enchantment. [Gr. *nekromanteia—nekros,* a dead body, and *mantis,* a prophet.]
Necropolis, nek-ro'po-lis, *n. A City of the dead;* a cemetery. [Gr. *nekros,* a dead body, and *polis,* a city.]
Nectar, nek'tar, *n. The elixir of life;* the fabled drink of the gods; any very sweet and pleasant drink; the honey of a flower. [L.—Gr. *ne,* not, and *kteinō,* to kill.]
Nectarean, nek-tā'rē-an, *a. Resembling nectar;* very sweet and pleasant.
Nectared, nek'tärd, *p.a. Imbued with nectar;* mingled with nectar.
Nectareous, nek-tā'rē-us, *a. Pertaining to* or containing nectar.
Nectarine, nek'tä-rin, *a. Sweet as nectar.*—*n.* The fruit of one variety of the common peach.
Nectary, nek'ta-ri, *n.* The honey-gland of a flower.
Need, nēd, *n. A state of beggary;* destitution; a state that requires relief; difficulty; strait; want; occasion for something.—*vt. To have necessity for;* to want; to require, as supply or relief. [Sax. *nead*—Sans. *nāth,* to ask, to beg, to desire or wish for.]
Needful, nēd'fụl, *a. Necessary,* as supply or relief; requisite.
Needfully, nēd'fụl-li, *adv. Necessarily.*

Needily, nēd'i-li, *adv.* In a needy manner; necessarily.

Neediness, nēd'i-nes, *n.* State of being needy; want; poverty; indigence.

Needle, nē'dl, *n.* That which is serviceable in fastening together; a small instrument of steel, pointed at one end, with an eye at the other to receive a thread, used in sewing; a small pointed piece of steel, used in the mariner's compass, which, by its magnetic quality, is attracted and directed to the pole; anything in the form of a needle. [Sax. *nædl*; Old G. *nawan*, to sew.]

Needless, nēd'les, *a.* Not needed; unnecessary; having no need†; useless.

Needlessly, nēd'les-li, *adv.* Without necessity.

Needlessness, nēd'les-nes, *n.* Quality of being needless; unnecessariness.

Needle-work, nē'dl-wėrk, *n.* Work executed with a needle.

Needly†, nē'dl-i, *adv.* Of necessity.

Needment†, nēd'ment, *n.* Something needed.

Needs, nēdz, *adv.* Necessarily. (Generally used with *must*.) [Sax. *nedes*.]

Needy, nēd'i, *a.* Being in need; necessitous; very poor; distressed by want of the means of living. [from *need*.]

Neeld†, nēld, *n.* A needle.

Ne er, nār. A contraction of *never*.

Nefarious, nē-fā'ri-us, *a.* Not to be spoken of; wicked in the extreme; sinful or vile in the highest degree; execrable; atrocious. [L. *nefarius—ne*, not, and *fari*, to speak.]

Nefariously, nē-fā'ri-us-li, *adv.* With extreme wickedness; abominably.

Nefariousness, nē-fā'ri-us-nes, *n.* The quality of being nefarious.

Negation, nē-gā'shon, *n.* A saying no or not; denial; a declaration that something is not, or has not been, or shall not be; argument drawn from denial. [L. *negatio—nego*, to say no.]

Negative, ne'gat-iv, *a.* That denies; opposed to affirmative; having the power of stopping.—*n.* That which denies; a word which denies, as *not, no;* a proposition by which something is denied; the right of preventing the enaction of a law; a decision expressive of negation.—*vt.* To dismiss by negation; to prove the contrary of; to refuse; to resist, as a choice or what is proposed. *ppr.* negativing, *pret. & pp.* negatived. [Fr. *négatif*.]

Negatively, ne'gat-iv-li, *adv.* With or by denial.

Neglect, neg-lekt', *vt.* Not to gather together; not to heed or attend to; to overlook; to slight; to omit by carelessness or design; to forbear to do; to omit to accept, as an offer; to cause to be omitted.—*n.* A neglecting; omission; slight; omission of attention or civilities; habitual want of regard; state of being disregarded. [L. *negligo, neglectus—nec*, not, and *lego*, to gather.]

Neglected, neg-lekt'ed, *p.a.* Slighted; disregarded.

Neglectful, neg-lekt'ful, *a.* Showing neglect; careless; accustomed to omit what may or ought to be done; treating with neglect; indicating slight or indifference.

Neglectfully, neg-lekt'ful-li, *adv.* With neglect; with heedless inattention.

Negligence, neg'li-jens, *n.* Neglect; omission to do; habitual omission of that which ought to be done. [Fr. *négligence*, L. *negligent' a.*]

Negligent, neg'li-jent, *a.* Neglecting; careless; apt to omit what ought to be done; inattentive. [Fr. *négligent*.]

Negligently, neg'li-jent-li, *adv.* Heedlessly; without exactness; with disregard or inattention.

Negotiability, nē-gō'shi-a-bil″i-ti, *n.* Quality of being negotiable.

Negotiable, nē-gō'hi-a-bl, *a.* That may be negotiated; that may be transferred by assignment or indorsement to another person.

Negotiate, nē-gō'shi-āt, *vi.* To be employed; to treat with another respecting purchase and sale; to hold intercourse with another respecting a treaty; to treat with respecting peace or commerce.—*vt.* To procure by mutual intercourse and agreement with another; to sell; to pass; to transfer for a valuable consideration. *ppr.* negotiating, *pret. & pp.* negotiated. [L. *negotior, negotiatus*.]

Negotiation, nē-gō'shi-ā″shon, *n.* A negotiating; the treating with another respecting sale or purchase; the transaction of business between nations. [Fr. *négociation*.]

Negotiator, nē-gō'shi-āt-ėr, *n.* One who negotiates. [L.]

Negress, nē'gres, *n.* A female negro.

Negro, nē'grō, *n.* A black man; a male of the African race. [from L. *niger*, black.]

Negus, nē'gus, *n.* A liquor made of wine, hot water, sugar, nutmeg, and lemon-juice. [from Colonel *Negus*, the first maker.]

Neif, nēf, *n.* The fist.

Neigh, nā, *vi.* To utter the cry of a horse, expressive of want or desire; to whinny.—*n.* The voice of a horse; a whinnying. [Sax. *hnægan*, L. *hinnio*.]

Neighbour, nā'bėr, *n.* One who lives or dwells near to another; one who lives in familiarity with another; an intimate; a word of civility; a fellow-being; one of the human race; any one who needs our help.—*vt.* To be near to; to adjoin; to make familiar. [Sax. *nehgebur—neh*, near, and *bewan*, to dwell.]

Neighbourhood, nā'bėr-hud, *n.* A place near; vicinity; state of being near each other; the inhabitants who live in the vicinity of each other.

Neighbouring, nā'bėr-ing, *p.a.* Living or being near.

Neighbourly, nā'bėr-li, *a.* Like or becoming a neighbour; cultivating familiar intercourse; kind; friendly; social. *adv.* With social civility.

Neighing, nā'ing, *p.n.* The voice of a horse; a whinnying.

Neither, nī'тнėr, *pron.* Not either; not the one or the other.—*conj.* Not either; nor. [Sax. *nathor—ne*, not, and *ather*, either.]

Neological, nē-ō-loj'ik-al, *a.* Pertaining to neology.

Neologist, nē-ol'ō-jist, *n.* An innovator in theology; one who introduces views subversive of revealed truth.

Neology, nē-ol'ō-ji, *n.* New views in theology subversive of revealed truth. [Fr. *néologie*—Gr. *neos*, new, and *logos*, a word.]

Neophyte, nē'ō-fīt, *n.* One newly implanted in the church; a novice; a tyro; a beginner in learning.—*a.* Newly entered on some state. [Fr. *néophyte*—Gr. *neos*, new, and *phuton*, a plant.]

Nephew, ne'vū, *n.* A grand-son†; the son of a brother or sister. [Sax. *nefa*—L. *nepos*.]

Nepotism, ne'pot-izm, *n.* Fondness for grandsons or nephews; favouritism shown to nephews and other relatives. [Fr. *népotisme*—L. *nepos, nepôtis,* a grandson, a nephew.]

Nepotist, ne'pot-ist, *n.* One who practises nepotism.

Neptune, nep'tūn, *n.* The fabled god of the ocean; a large planet beyond Uranus, discovered, independently, in 1846, by M. le Verrier of Paris, and Mr. J. C. Adams of Cambridge. [L. *Neptūnus*.]

Nereid, nē'rē-id, *n.* A sea-nymph, one of the daughters of *Nereus*. [Gr. *nēreis, nēreïdos*.]

Nerve, nėrv, *n.* A sinew; one of the bundles of fibres which establish a communication between the various parts of the animal body and the brain or spinal cord; firmness of body; fortitude; courage; strength; force; manliness.—*vt.* To give strength or vigour to; to arm with force. *ppr.* nerving, *pret. & pp.* nerved. [Fr. *nerf*—Gr. *neura*, a cord of sinew.]

Nerveless, nėrv'les, *a.* Destitute of nerve or strength; weak.

Nervous, nėrv'us, *a.* Full of nerves; strong; vigorous, as an arm; pertaining to the nerves; having the nerves affected; diseased in the nerves; weak; possessing or manifesting vigour of mind; characterized by strength in sentiment or style, as a writer. [L. *nervōsus*.]

Nervously, nėrv'us-li, *adv.* In a nervous manner.

Nervousness, nėrv'us-nes, *n.* State or quality of being nervous; strength; weakness or agitation of the nerves.

Nervy†, nėrv'i, *a.* Strong.

Nest, nest, *n.* The place or bed formed—generally by interweaving—by a bird for hatching and rearing her young until they are able to fly; an abode; a receptacle of numbers; a warm, close place of abode.—*vi.* To build and occupy a nest; to settle. [Sax.; G. *nest*, tc sew, stitch.]

Nestle, nes'l, *vi.* To make a nest; to settle; to lie close and snug, as a bird in her nest.—*vt.* To house, as in a nest; to nourish and protect, as a bird her young. *ppr.* nestling, *pret. & pp.* nestled. [Sax. *nestlian*.]

Nestling, nes'l-ing, *p.n.* A young bird in the nest.—*p.a.* Newly hatched; being yet in the nest.

Net, net, *n.* That which is knitted or knotted; a texture of twine, &c., with meshes, commonly used to catch fish, birds, &c.; a snare; inextricable difficulty.—*vt.* To make into a net or net-work; to take in a net. *ppr.* netting, *pret. & pp.* netted. [Sax.—*cnyttan*, to tie.]

Net, net, *a.* Neat; being beyond all charges or outlay, as gain; being clear of all deductions; neat, as net weight. *vt.* To gain or produce, as clear profit. *ppr.* netting, *pret. & pp.* netted. [Fr.]

Nether, ne'тнėr, *a.* Lower; lying or being beneath or in the lower part; opposed to upper; belonging to the regions below. [Sax. *nithere*; Old G. *nidar*, beneath.]

Nethermost, ne'тнėr-mōst, *a.* Lowest.

Netted, net'ed, *p.a.* Made into a net or net-work; reticulated.

Netting, net'ing, *n.* A piece of net-work; net-work of rope or small lines, used for stowing away sails, &c.

Nettle, net'l, *n.* A plant whose prickles fret the skin and occasion very painful sensations.—*vt.* To fret or sting, as with nettles; to irritate or vex. *ppr.* nettling, *pret. & pp.* nettled. [Sax. *netele*; Gr. *knidē*, to make to itch.]

Netty, net'i, *a.* Like a net; netted.

Net-work, net'wėrk, *n.* A complication

of threads or cords united at certain distances, forming meshes.
Neuralgia, nū-ral'ji-a, *n. Pain in a nerve.* [Gr. *neuron*, a nerve, and *algos*, any pain.]
Neuralgic, nū-ral'jik, *a. Pertaining to neuralgia.*
Neuter, nū'tėr, *a. Neither the one nor the other;* not adhering to either party; neither masculine nor feminine; of neither gender, as a noun; neither active nor passive, said of a verb.—*n.* A person who takes no part in a contest between two or more individuals or nations; an animal of *neither* sex; a plant having neither stamens nor pistils. [L. *ne*, not, and *uter*, whether or which of the two.]
Neutral, nū'tral, *a. Being neuter;* not engaged on either side; neither very good nor bad; neither acid nor alkaline.—*n.* A person or nation that takes no part in a contest between others. [L. *neutralis.*]
Neutrality, nū-tral'i-ti, *n. State of being neutral;* the state of taking no part on either side; state of being neither acid nor alkaline; a combination of neutral powers or states. [Fr. *neutralité.*]
Neutralisation, nū'tral-iz-ā''shon, *n. Act of neutralising;* state of being neutralized. [Fr. *neutralisation.*]
Neutralize, nū'tral-īz, *vt. To render neutral;* to destroy, as the peculiar properties of a body by combining it with a different substance; to destroy, as the opposite dispositions of parties or other things, or reduce them to a state of indifference. *ppr.* neutralising, *pret. & pp.* neutralized. [Fr. *neutraliser.*]
Neutralizer, nū'tral-īz-ėr, *n. One who* or *that which neutralizes.*
Neutralizing, nū'tral-īz-ing, *p.a. Making neutral;* reducing to inactivity.
Neutrally, nū'tral-li, *adv. Without taking part with either side.*
Never, nev'ėr, *adv. Not ever;* not at any time; at no time; in no degree; not. [Sax. *næfre—ne,* not, and *æfer,* ever.]
Nevertheless, nev'ėr-vhē-les'', *adv. Not the less;* that is, in opposition to anything, or without regarding it; yet; however.
New, nū, *a. Young; fresh; recent;* lately produced or come into being; opposed to old; lately introduced to our knowledge; modern; not ancient; recently produced by change; renovated; fresh after any event; not of ancient extraction; not before used; strange; recently commenced.—*adv.* Newly (used in composition). [Sax. *niwe*—L. *novus*—Sans. *nava—nu,* to praise.]
New-fangled, nū-fang'gld, *a. New* made; formed with the affectation of novelty; desirous or fond of novelty. [new and fangled; Old Eng. *fangle,* a trifle.]
Newish, nū'ish, *a. Somewhat new.*
Newly, nū'li, *adv.* Lately; freshly; recently.
New-made, nū-mād', *a. Newly made;* regenerate.
Newness, nū'nes, *n. State or quality of being new;* state of being lately invented; novelty; the state of being first known; want of practice; different state introduced by change.
News, nūz, *n.* Recent account; fresh information of something that has lately taken place at a distance; tidings. [Fr. *nouvelles.* This word has a plural form, but is almost always united with a verb in the singular.]
Newsmonger, nūz'mung-gėr, *n. One who deals in news;* one who employs

much time in hearing and telling news.
Newspaper, nūz'pā-pėr, *n.* A sheet of paper printed and distributed at short intervals, for conveying *intelligence* of passing events.
News-room, nūz'röm, *n.* A room where newspapers, reviews, &c., are read.
Newt, nūt, *n.* A small lizard; an eft. [contracted from *an ewet,* an *eft.*]
Newtonian, nū-tōn'i-an, *a.* Pertaining to or discovered by *Sir Isaac Newton.*
Next, nekst, *a. super.* of *nigh.* Nearest in place; immediately preceding; *nearest* in time; *nearest* in degree, quality, rank, right, or relation.—*adv.* At the time or turn *nearest.* [Sax.]
Nib, nib, *n.* [Sax. *neb.*] See NEB.
Nibbed, nibd, *p.a. Having a nib.*
Nibble, nib'l, *vt. To bite with small nips;* to bite by little at a time; to bite, as a fish does the bait; just to catch by biting.—*vi. To bite at slightly* or gently; to carp at; to find fault (with *at*). *ppr.* nibbling, *pret. & pp.* nibbled.—*n.* A little bite, or seizing to bite. [dimin. of *nib* or *nip.*]
Nibbler, nib'l-ėr, *n.* One who *bites a little at a time;* a carper.
Nice, nis, *a. Soft;* tender; dainty; fine; minutely elegant; perceiving the smallest difference; judging with exactness; exact; scrupulously cautious; showing great delicacy; easily injured or impaired, as reputation; refined; of trifling moment; slight; weak; finical. [Sax. *hnesc,* soft, tender.]
Nicely, nis'li, *adv.* With delicate perception; with exact order; with minute elegance.
Niceness, nis'nes, *n. State or quality of being nice;* extreme delicacy; excess of scrupulousness; accuracy; nicety.
Nicety, nis'e-ti, *n. Niceness;* fastidiousness; squeamishness; minuteness of discrimination; delicate management; exactness in treatment; (*pl.*) delicacies for food; dainties.
Niche, nich, *n.* A cavity, hollow, or recess resembling the interior of certain *shells,* within the thickness of a wall, for a statue, bust, or other erect ornament. [Fr.—Gr. *mutilos,* a kind of mussel.]
Niched, nicht, *p.a. Put in a niche.*
Nick, nik, *n. A nod;* the exact point of time required by necessity or convenience; the critical time.—*vt.* To hit; to touch luckily; to perform by a slight artifice used at the lucky time. [Sw.—L. *nico,* to beckon.]
Nick, nik, *n. A notch cut in anything;* a score for keeping an account; a winning throw.—*vt. To notch* or make an incision in, as a horse's tail, to make him carry it higher. [G. *knick,* a flaw.]
Nickel, nik'el, *n.* A term of detraction applied by the older German miners to the ore, because they found no *copper* in it; a metal of a white or reddish-white colour, hard, malleable, ductile, and susceptible of magnetism.
Nickname, nik'nām, *n. A by-name;* an opprobrious appellation.—*vt.* To give a name of reproach to. *ppr.* nicknaming, *pret. & pp.* nicknamed. [Fr. *nom de nique.*]
Nidification, nī'di-fi-kā''shon, *n. Act of building a nest,* and the hatching and feeding of young in the nest. [L. *nidus,* a nest, and *facio,* to make.]
Niece, nēs, *n.* The daughter of a brother or sister. [Fr. *nièce*—L. *neptis.*]
Niggard, nig'ėrd, *n. One who is sordidly parsimonious;* a miser; a person meanly close and covetous.—*a.* Sor-

didly *parsimonious;* sparing.—*vt.*† To stint. [Icel. *hnoggr,* parsimonious.]
Niggardliness, nig'ėrd-li-nes, *n. Quality of being niggardly;* mean covetousness.
Niggardly, nig'ėrd-li, *a. Parsimonious;* miserly; penurious; wary; cautiously avoiding profusion.—*adv.* Sparingly; with cautious parsimony.
Nigh, nī, *a. Near;* not distant or remote in place or time; closely allied by blood; easy to be obtained; of easy access; ready to support, to forgive, or to aid and defend; close in fellowship; proximate; present.—*vt.* To draw nigh to.—*adv. Near;* at a small distance in place or time; near to a place; almost. *prep. Near;* nearly; almost close to. (With *to.*) [Sax. *neah;* Old G. *nāhi.*]
Night, nīt, *n. The time of quiet, rest, and sleep;* the time from sunset to sunrise; time of darkness; death; a state of ignorance; heathenish ignorance; adversity; obscurity; a state of concealment from the eye or the mind. [Sax. *niht;* Heb. *nuach,* to rest.]
Night-dress, nīt'dres, *n. A dress worn during the night.*
Nighted, nīt'ed, *a.* Darkened; clouded; black.
Nightfall, nīt'fal, *n.* The close of the day; evening.
Nightingale, nīt'in-gāl, *n. The night singer;* a small bird that sings at night, celebrated for its vocal powers. [Sax. *nihtegale—niht,* night, and *galan,* Sans. *gau,* to sing.]
Nightly, nīt'li, *a. Done by night;* happening in the night; nocturnal; done every night.—*adv. By night;* every night.
Nightmare, nīt'mār, *n. That which leaps upon one by night, like a horse;* incubus; a sensation in sleep resembling the pressure of a weight on the breast, and depriving of speech and motion. [D. *nachtmerrie—*Icel. *mar,* a horse.]
Night-piece, nīt'pēs, *n. A piece of painting* representing some night scene.
Nightshade, nīt'shād, *n.* A poisonous herb. [Sax. *nihtscad—scad,* shade.]
Night-walker, nīt'wak-ėr, *n. One who walks in his sleep;* a somnambulist; one who roves about in the night for evil purposes.
Nightward, nīt'wėrd, *a. Approaching toward night.*
Night-watch, nīt'woch, *n. A watch* or guard in the *night;* a period in the night, as distinguished by the change of the watch.
Nihilism, ni hil-izm, *n. Nothingness;* the doctrine that nothing can be known. [from L. *nihil—ne,* not, and *hilum,* a trifle.]
Nill†, nil, *vi.* To be unwilling.—*vt.* Not to will; to refuse.
Nimble, nim'bl, *a. Catching with quickness;* moving with ease and celerity; lively; active; prompt; expert. [Sax. *numul,* catching,—*niman,* to take.]
Nimbleness, nim'bl-nes, *n. Quality of being nimble;* celerity; quickness.
Nimbly, nim'bli, *adv.* With agility; with light, quick motion.
Nine, nīn, *a.* Denoting the number composed of eight and one.—*n.* The number composed of eight and one. [Old Sax.—Sans. *navam.*]
Nine-fold, nīn'fōld, *a. Nine times repeated.*
Nineteen, nīn'tēn, *a.* Noting the number of *nine* and *ten* united. [Sax. *nigantyne.*]
Nineteenth, nīn'tēnth, *a. The ordinal of nineteen.* [Sax. *nigontotha.*]

---

ch, *chain;* j, *job;* g, *go;* ng, *sing;* ᴛʜ, *then;* th, *thin;* w, *wig;* wh, *whig;* zh, *azure;* † obsolete.

Ninetieth, nin'ti-eth, *a. The ordinal of ninety.*
Ninety, nin'ti, *a. Nine times ten.* [Sax. *nygan*, nine, and *tig*, ten.]
Ninny, nin'ni, *n. A childish person*; a fool; a simpleton. [Sp. *niño*, a child.]
Ninth, ninth, *a. The ordinal of nine. n. A ninth part.* [Sax. *nigetha.*]
Ninthly, ninth'li, *adv. In the ninth place.*
Nip, nip, *vt. To pinch* with the ends of the fingers; to cut off, as the end of anything; to clip, as with the knife or scissors; to blast, as by frost; to kill; to pinch, bite, or affect, as the extremities of anything; to check the progress of.—*n.* A small bite or cut, or a cutting off the end; a pinch with the nails, teeth, &c.; a blast; a killing of the ends of plants; destruction by frost. [D. *knippen*.]
Nipper, nip'ér, *n. He or that which nips;* a fore-tooth of a horse.
Nippers, nip'érz, *n. pl. Small pincers.* [from *nip*.]
Nipping, nip'ing, *p.a.* Blasting; killing.
Nippingly, nip'ing-li, *adv.* With bitter sarcasm.
Nipple, nip'l, *n. A little nib;* a teat; the orifice at which any animal liquor is separated; that part of a percussion-lock over which the cap is placed. [Sax. *nypele.*]
Nit, nit, *n.* The egg of a louse or other small insect. [Sax. *hnitu.*]
Nitre, ni'tér, *n.* A white, crystalline salt used in the East as soap in bleaching; called also saltpetre (stone-salt). [Fr.—L. *nitrum*.]
Nitric, ni'trik, *a. Pertaining to nitre;* containing nitre; impregnated with nitric acid. [Fr. *nitrique*.]
Nitrogen, ni'tro-jen, *n. That which generates nitre;* an elementary gas, destructive to life, and the largest ingredient in atmospheric air, of which it constitutes about four-fifths. [Gr. *nitron*, nitre, and *gennaō*, to produce, to generate.]
Nitrous, ni'trus, *a. Pertaining to nitre;* partaking of the qualities of nitre.
No. Abbreviation of *number*, Fr. *nombre*.
No, nō, *adv.* A word of denial or refusal, expressing a negative, and equivalent to nay and not; not in any degree.—*a. Not any;* none; not one [Sax. and Sans. *na*.]
Noachian, nō-ā'ki-an, *a. Pertaining to Noah* the patriarch, or to his time.
Nobility, nō-bil'i-ti, *n. State or quality of being noble;* dignity of mind; elevation of soul; descent from noble ancestors; rank, usually joined with riches; the persons collectively who enjoy rank above commoners; the peerage. [L. *nobilitas*.]
Noble, nō'bl, *a. Well known;* famous; dignified; being above everything that can dishonour reputation; high in excellence or worth; stately; of an ancient and splendid family; generous; ingenuous; candid; of an excellent disposition; ready to receive truth; of the best kind.—*n.* A person of rank above a commoner; a nobleman; a peer; formerly, a gold coin. [Fr.—L. *nosco*, Sans. *jnā*, to know.]
Nobleman, nō'bl-man, *n. A noble;* a peer; one who enjoys rank.
Nobleness, nō'bl-nes, *n. State or quality of being noble;* magnanimity; grandeur.
Noblesse, nō-bles', *n. The nobility.*
Noblewoman, nō'bl-wu-man, *n. A female of noble rank.*
Nobly, nō'bli, *adv.* With nobleness of birth; with greatness of soul; heroically; with magnificence.

Nobody, nō'bo-di, *n. No person;* no one. [*no* and *body*.]
Noctum, nok'térn, *n.* An office of devotion or religious service *by night.* [Fr. *nocturne*—L. *nox*, night.]
Nocturnal, nok-térn'al, *a. Done or happening at night;* having a habit of seeking food at night; nightly. [L. *nocturnus*—*nox*, *noctis*, the night.]
Nocturnally, nok-térn'al-li, *adv. In the night;* nightly.
Nod, nod, *vi.* To incline the head with a quick motion, as persons do when sleeping in a sitting posture; to be drowsy; to make a slight bow; to beckon with a nod.—*vt.* To incline or bend; to shake; to signify by a nod. *ppr.* nodding, *pret. & pp.* nodded.—*n.* A dropping of the upper part of anything; a quick inclination of the head in drowsiness or sleep; a slight obeisance; a command. [L. *nuto*; Gr. *neuō*.]
Nodal, nōd'al, *a. Pertaining to a node* or knot, or to nodes. [from *node*.]
Noddle, nod'l, *n.* Properly the back of the head, the nape of the neck; the head (in contempt). [L. *nodus*, a knob.]
Noddy, nod'di, *n.* A simpleton; a fool; a sea-fowl of the tern kind; a sort of vehicle. [Old Fr. *naudin.*]
Node, nōd, *n. A knot;* a protuberance; a swelling; the point where the orbit of a planet intersects the ecliptic; the point of the stem of a plant, from which the leaves arise. [L. *nodus*, a knot—Sans. *nah*, to bind, tie.]
Nodose, nōd'ōs, *a. Full of knots;* knotted. [L. *nodosus.*]
Nodule, nod'ūl, *n. A little knot;* a small woody body found in the bark of some trees; a rounded mineral mass of irregular shape. [L. *nodulus*.]
Noduled, nod'ūld, *p.a.* Having little *knots* or lumps.
Noiance†, noi'ans, *n.* Annoyance; trouble.
Noise, noiz, *n. Strife;* squabble; clamour; din; loud, importunate, or continued talk.—*vi.* To sound loud.—*vt.* To spread by rumour or report (with *abroad*). *ppr.* noising, *pret. & pp.* noised. [Fr.; Armor. *noas*, quarrel.]
Noiseless, noiz'les, *a. Making no noise* or bustle; silent.
Noiselessly, noiz'les-li, *adv. Without noise;* silently.
Noiselessness, noiz'les-nes, *n. State of being noiseless;* a state of silence.
Noisily, noiz'i-li, *adv. With noise;* with making a noise.
Noisiness, noiz'i-nes, *n. State or quality of being noisy;* clamorousness.
Noisome, noi'sum, *a. Noxious* to health; insalubrious; offensive to the smell or other senses; disgusting; fetid. [Norm. *noisife*—L. *noceo*, to hurt.]
Noisomely, noi'sum-li, *adv.* With a fetid stench; with an infectious steam.
Noisy, noiz'i, *a. Making a loud noise* or sound; clamorous; obstreperous; full of noise.
Noll†, nol, *n.* The head.
Nomad, nō'mad, *n. A wandering shepherd;* one who leads a wandering life, and subsists by tending herds of cattle. *a.* Wandering; savage. [Gr. *nomas*, *nomados*—*nemō*, to pasture.]
Nomadic, nō-mad'ik, *a. Pastoral;* subsisting by the tending of cattle, and wandering for the sake of pasturage. [Gr. *nomadikos*.]
Nomenclator, nō'men-klāt-ér, *n.* One who gives *names* to persons or things. [L.—*nomen*, a name, and *calo*, to call.]

Nomenclature, nō'men-klā-tūr, *n. A calling by names;* a list of the more usual words in a language, with their significations; a dictionary; the names of things in any art or science. [L. *nomenclatura*.]
Nominal, no'mi-nal, *a. Pertaining to a name;* titular; existing in name only. [L. *nominalis*—*nomen*, a name.]
Nominally, no'mi-nal-li, *adv. By name* or in name only.
Nominate, no'mi-nāt, *vt. To name;* to denominate; to name, or designate by name, for an office or place; to name for an election. *ppr.* nominating, *pret. & pp.* nominated. [L. *nomino*, *nominatus*—*nomen*, a name.]
Nomination, no-mi-nā'shon, *n. Act of naming;* act of proposing by name for an office; the power of nominating or appointing to office; the state of being nominated; the denomination or name†. [L. *nominatio.*]
Nominative, no'mi-nat-iv, *a. Pertaining to naming;* giving a name; pertaining to the name which precedes a verb, or to the first case of nouns.—*n.* The first case of *nouns;* the case which indicates the relation of a subject to a finite verb. [Fr. *nominatif.*]
Nominator, no'mi-nāt-ér, *n. One who nominates.* [Late L.]
Nominee, no-mi-nē', *n. A person nominated* by another; the person who is named to receive a copyhold estate on surrender of it to the lord. [Fr. *nommé*, named.]
Nonage, non'āj, *n. State of being not of age,* or under age; minority.
Nonagon, non'a-gon, *n.* A plain figure having *nine angles* and nine sides. [L. *nonus*, nine, and Gr. *gōnia*, an angle.]
Non-appearance, non-ap-pēr'ans, *n. Default of appearance,* as in court.
Non-attendance, non-at-tend'ans, *n. Omission of attendance.*
Nonce, nons, *n.* The present call or occasion; purpose. [corrupted from *for then once*.]
Non-commissioned, non-kom-mi'shond, *a. Not having a commission,* as a soldier or seaman.
Non-compliance, non-kom-plī'ans, *n. Neglect or failure of compliance.*
Non-conductor, non-kon-dukt'ér, *n. A substance which does not conduct,* that is, transmit another substance or fluid, as heat or electricity.
Nonconforming, non-kon-form'ing, *a. Not conforming* to or joining in the established religion.
Nonconformist, non-kon-form'ist, *n.* One who does *not conform* to an established church; particularly, one who refused to conform to the established church at the restoration of Charles II.
Nonconformity, non-kon-form'i-ti, *n. Neglect or failure of conformity;* the refusal to unite with an established church.
Non-content, non'kon-tent, *n.* A peer who gives a *negative* vote in the House of Lords.
Nondescript, non'de-skript, *a. That has not been,* or cannot easily be *described.* *n.* Any person or thing that has not been, or cannot easily be, *described* or classed. [L. *non,* and *descriptus,* described.]
None, nun, *a.* and *pron. Not one;* not any; not a part; not the least portion. [Sax. *nan*—*ne*, and *an*, one.]
Non-elastic, non-e-las'tik, *a. Destitute* of the property of *elasticity.*
Nonentity, non-en'ti-ti, *n. Non-exist-*

Fāte, fär, fat, fąll; mē, met her; pine pin; nōte, not, mōve; tūbe, tub, bųll; oil, pound.

ence; the negation of being; a thing not existing. [L. *non*, Low L. *entitas*.]
Non-essential, non-es-sen'shi-al, *n*. That which is not essential.
Nonesuch, nun'such, *n*. A thing that has not its equal; a variety of apple, &c.
Non-existence, non-egz-ist'ens, *n*. Absence of existence; the negation of being.
Non-existent, non-egz-ist'ent, *a*. Not having existence.
Non-juring, non-jūr'ing, *a*. Not swearing allegiance. [L. *non*, and *juro*, to swear.]
Non-juror, non-jūr'ėr, *n*. One who refused to take the oath of allegiance to the government and crown of England at the Revolution.
Nonpareil, non-pa-rel', *n*. A person or thing having no equal; a sort of apple; a very small sort of printing type.—*a*. Having no equal; peerless. [Fr. *non*, and *pareil*, L. *par, paris*, equal.]
Nonplus, non'plus, *n*. A state in which one can say or do no more; insuperable difficulty.—*vt*. To bring to a state in which one can say or do no more; to stop by embarrassment. *ppr*. nonplussing, *pret. & pp*. nonplussed. [L. *non*, and *plus*, more.]
Non-proficient, non-pro-fi'shi-ent, *n*. One who is not proficient; one who has failed to improve in any study.
Non-residence, non-re'zi-dens, *n*. Failure of residing at the place where official duties require one to reside, or on one's own lands.
Non-resident, non-re'zi-dent, *a*. Not residing on one's own estate, or in one's proper place.—*n*. One who does not reside on one's own lands, or in the place where duties require.
Non-resistance, non-rē-zist'ans, *n*. The omission of resistance; submission to authority.
Non-resisting, non-rē-zist'ing, *a*. Making no resistance; offering no obstruction.
Nonsense, non'sens, *n*. No sense; words which have no meaning; absurdity; things of no importance.
Nonsensical, non-sens'ik-al, *a*. Destitute of sense; unmeaning; absurd.
Nonsensically, non-sens'ik-al-li, *adv*. Absurdly; without meaning.
Nonsuit, non'sūt, *n*. A failure to follow up a suit or cause in law; the default, neglect, or non-appearance of the plaintiff in a suit, when called in court, by which the plaintiff signifies his intention to drop the suit.—*vt*. To determine or record that the plaintiff drops his suit, on default of appearance when called in court.
Nook, nök, *n*. A corner; a narrow place formed by an angle in bodies or between bodies; a secluded retreat. [Gael. *niuc*.]
Noon, nön, *n*. Originally, the ninth hour of the day, or three o'clock, when the Romans took their principal meal; the time of taking the principal meal, which among succeeding nations was about twelve o'clock; the middle of the day; the time when the sun is in the meridian; twelve o'clock.—*a*. Belonging to mid-day. [Sax. *nón*—L. *nona hora*, the ninth hour.]
Noonday, nön'dā, *n*. Mid-day; twelve o'clock in the day.—*a*. Pertaining to mid-day; meridional.
Noontide, nön'tīd, *n*. The time of noon; mid-day.—*a*. Pertaining to noon; meridional.
Noose, nös, *n*. A running knot, which binds the closer the more it is drawn.—*vt*. To tie in a noose; to catch in a noose; to insnare. *ppr*. noosing, *pret. & pp*. noosed. [Ir. *nas*, a band.]
Nor, nor, *conj*. A connective word that renders negative the second part of a proposition; correlative to neither or not. [*ne* and *or*.]
Normal, nor'mal, *a*. According to rule; according to an established law, rule, or principle; performing the proper functions; relating to elements; teaching first principles; instructing in the art of teaching.—*n*. A perpendicular. [Fr.—L. *norma*, a rule.]
Norman, nor'man, *n*. A native or inhabitant of Normandy.—*a*. Pertaining to Normandy, or to the Normans. [*north-man* or *nord-man*.]
Norse, nors, *n*. The language of ancient Scandinavia.
North, north, *n*. One of the cardinal points, being that point of the horizon which is directly opposite to the sun in the meridian.—*a*. Being in the north; as, the north polar star. [Sax.]
North-east, north-ēst', *n*. The point equally distant from the north and east.—*a*. Pertaining to or proceeding from the north-east.
North-easterly, north-ēst'ėr-li, *a*. Toward or from the north-east.
North-eastern, north-ēst'ėrn, *a*. Pertaining to or being in the north-east.
Northerly, north'ėr-li, *a*. Being toward the north; from the north.—*adv*. Toward the north; proceeding from a northern point.
Northern, north'ėrn, *a*. Being in the north, or nearer to that point than to the east or west; in a direction toward the north.—*n*. An inhabitant of the north, or of the northern part of a country.
Northernmost, north'ėrn-mōst, *a*. Situated at the point furthest north.
North-pole, north'pōl, *n*. The elevated celestial pole of the world; the northern extremity of the earth's axis.
North-star, north'stär, *n*. The north polar star.
Northward, north'wėrd, *a*. Being toward the north. [Sax. *north*, and *weard*.]
Northward, Northwards, north'wėrd, north'wėrdz, *adv*. Toward the north.
Northwardly north'wėrd-li, *a*. Having a northern direction.
North-west, north-west', *n*. The point in the horizon between the north and west, and equally distant from each. *a*. Pertaining to the point between the north and west.
North-westerly, north-west'ėr-li, *a*. Toward or from the north-west.
North-western, north-west'ėrn, *a*. Pertaining to or being in the north-west.
Norwegian, nor-wē'ji-an, *a*. Belonging to Norway.—*n*. A native of Norway.
Nose, nōz, *n*. That through which air flows; the prominent part of the face, which is the organ of smell; the end of anything, as of a tube; sagacity. *vt*. To smell; to scent; to face; to oppose to the face; to twang through the nose. *ppr*. nosing, *pret. & pp*. nosed. [Sax.—L. *nasus*, the nose—Sans. *snu*, to flow.]
Nosegay, nōz'gā, *n*. A bunch of flowers used to regale the sense of smelling; a bouquet. [*nose* and *gay*.]
Nosological, no-so-loj'ik-al, *a*. Pertaining to nosology.
Nosologist, no-sol'o-jist, *n*. One versed in nosology.
Nosology, no-sol'o-ji, *n*. The doctrine of diseases; that branch of medical science which treats of the classification of diseases. [Gr. *nosos*, disease, and *logos*, discourse.]
Nostril, nos'tril, *n*. One of the apertures of the nose. [Sax. *nosterel—nos*, and *thyrel*, a hole.]
Nostrum, nos'trum, *n*. That which is ours; a quack medicine, the ingredients of which are kept secret. [L.]
Not, not, *adv*. A word that expresses negation, denial, or refusal. [Sax. *nate*.]
Notability, nōt-a-bi'li-ti, *n*. State of being notable.
Notable, nōt'a-bl, *a*. Noteworthy; worthy of notice; distinguished or noted; well-known; remarkable for industry; distinguished for good management.—*n*. A person of note or distinction. [Fr.—L. *nota*, a mark—*nosco*, to know.]
Notably, nōt'a-bli, *adv*. Memorably; remarkably; eminently.
Notarial, nōt-ā'ri-al, *a*. Pertaining to a notary; done or taken by a notary.
Notary, nōt'a-ri, *n*. An officer authorized to protest notes, &c., and attest contracts or writings of any kind, to give them the evidence of authenticity. [L. *notarius—nota*, a mark.]
Notation, nōt-ā'shon, *n*. A marking; act or practice of recording anything by marks; the expression of any number or quantity by its appropriate figure or sign; a system of signs and symbols. [L. *notatio—nota*, a mark.]
Notch, noch, *n*. An incision; a nick; an indentation.—*vt*. To cut a hollow into; to cut in small hollows. [Old Eng. *nock*.]
Notching, noch'ing, *p.n*. Act of cutting into small hollows; the small hollows cut.
Note, nōt, *n*. A mark; something by which a thing may be known; a mark made in a book; a short remark; a comment; a minute, or short writing intended to assist the memory; heed; reputation; distinction; a sound in music, or the mark which represents it; tune; voice; symbol; a short letter; a written paper acknowledging a debt, and promising payment; knowledge; (pl.) a writing; a written discourse; heads of a discourse or argument; comments; a diplomatic communication in writing—*vt*. To designate with a mark; to notice with particular care; to attend to; to set down in writing; to set down in musical characters. *ppr*. noting, *pret. & pp*. noted. [Fr.—L. *nosco, notum*, to know.]
Noted, nōt'ed, *p.a*. Remarkable; illustrious; distinguished; conspicuous; notorious.
Noteworthy, nōt'wėr-thi, *a*. Deserving notice; worthy of observation; remarkable; memorable.
Nothing, nu'thing, *n*. Not anything; not any being or existence; opposed to something; non-existence; not any particular thing, deed, or event; no part; no importance; no use; a low condition; a thing of trifling value; a trifle; the absence of all magnitude; the symbol denoting the absence; a cipher.—*adv*. In no degree; not at all.
Notice, nōt'is, *n*. State of being known; observation by the eye or by the other senses; observation by the mind; intelligence by whatever means communicated; attention; respectful treatment; observation; something said on a particular subject.—*vt*. To mark; to observe by the senses; to pay regard to; to mention; to treat with civilities; to observe intellectually. *ppr*. notic-

ing, *pret. & pp.* noticed. [Fr.—L. *nosco*, to know.]
Noticeable, not-is-a-bl, *a.* That may be noticed; worthy of observation.
Noticeably, nōt′is-a-bli, *adv.* In a noticeable manner.
Notification, nōt′i-fi-kā″shon, *n. Act of notifying*; the act of making known; the writing which communicates information; an advertisement, citation, &c. [Late L. *notificatio*.]
Notify, nōt′i-fi, *vt.* To make known, as a fact; to give information of. *ppr.* notifying, *pret. & pp.* notified. [Fr. *notifier*—L. *nosco, notum*, to know, and *facio*, to make.]
Notion, nō′shon, *n. A becoming acquainted with a thing*; conception; mental apprehension of whatever may be known; idea; sentiment; thought; sense†; intellectual power. [Fr.—L. *nosco, notum*, to know.]
Notional, nō′shon-al, *a. Partaking of the nature of a notion*; visionary.
Notoriety, nō-tō-rī′e-ti, *n. State of being notorious*; the state of being generally and disadvantageously known; public knowledge. [Fr. *notoriété.*]
Notorious, nō-tō′ri-us, *a. Publicly known*; noted; remarkable; usually, known to disadvantage; hence almost always used in an ill sense. [Low L. *notorius*—L. *nosco*, to know.]
Notoriously, nō-tō′ri-us-li, *adv.* Publicly; openly; beyond denial.
Nott-headed†, not′hed-ed, *a.* Having the hair cut close.
Notwithstanding, not-with-stand′ing, *conj. Not standing against*; not opposed to; nevertheless; however.
Nought, nạt, *n. Not anything*; nothing; in no degree (in which sense it is used adverbially). [See NAUGHT.]
Noun, noun, *n. The name* of a person, place, or thing; that sound, or combination of sounds, by which a thing is called. [Norm. *nonn*—L. *nomen*, a name.]
Nourish, nu′rish, *vt. To suckle*; to feed and cause to grow; to supply the means of support and increase to; to encourage; to nurture; to instruct; to promote the growth of by care and preservation. [Fr. *nourrir, nourrissant*—L. *nutrio*, to suckle.]
Nourisher, nu′rish-ėr, *n. The person or thing that nourishes.*
Nourishing, nu′rish-ing, *p.a.* Promoting growth; nutritious.
Nourishment, nu′rish-ment, *n. That which nourishes*; food; nutriment; support of animal or vegetable bodies; instruction, especially in a spiritual sense.
Nouselt, nuz′l, *vt.* To nurse up.
Novel, no′vel, *a. Of recent origin or introduction*; not ancient; strange.—*n. That which is new*; a fictitious tale in prose, intended to exhibit the operation of the passions, and particularly of love. [L. *novellus*—*novus*, new.]
Novelist, no′vel-ist, *n.* A writer of a novel or of novels. [Fr. *nouvelliste*.]
Novelty, no′vel-ti, *n. Recentness* of origin or introduction; a new or strange thing. [Fr. *nouveauté.*]
November, nō-vem′ber, *n.* The eleventh month of the year. [L. the ninth month, according to the ancient Roman year.]
Novice, no′vis, *n. One who is new* in any business; a beginner; one who has entered a religious house, but has not taken the vow; one newly converted to the Christian faith. [Fr.—L. *novus*, new—Heb. *nub*, to sprout.]

Novitiate, nō-vi′shi-āt, *n. The state or time of being a novice*; a year or other time of probation for the trial of a novice. [Fr. *noviciat*.]
Now, nou, *adv. and conj.* At the present time; a little while ago; at one time; at that time; after this; things being so.—*n.* The present time or moment. [Old Sax. *nu*—L. *nunc*.]
Nowadays, nou′a-dās, *adv.* In these days; in this age.
Noway, Noways, nō′wā, nō′wāz, *adv.* In no manner or degree. [*no and way*.]
Nowhere, nō′hwar, *adv.* Not in any place or state. [*no and where*.]
Nowise, nō′wiz, *adv.* Not in any manner or degree. [*no and wise*.]
Nowl†, noul, *n.* See NOLL.
Noxious, nok′shi-us, *a. Hurtful*; baneful; destructive; insalubrious; corrupting to morals. [L. *noxius*—*noceo*, to hurt.]
Noxiously, nok′shi-us-li, *adv. Hurtfully*; perniciously.
Noxiousness, nok′shi-us-nes, *n. Quality of being noxious*; insalubrity; the quality that corrupts or perverts.
Nozzle, noz′l, *n. The nose*; the extremity of anything; the snout.
Nucleus, nū′klē-us, *n.* The central part or *kernel* of any body; the solid centre about which the particles of a crystal are aggregated; the pulpy mass, which constitutes the central part of the ovule in plants; the body of a comet. [L.—*nux, nucis*, a nut.]
Nude, nūd, *a. Naked*; divested of force; void. [L. *nudus*.]
Nudity, nūd′i-ti, *n. Nakedness*; (pl.) undraped or unclothed portions; naked figures. [Fr. *nudité*—L. *nudus*, naked.]
Nugatory, nū′ga-tō-ri, *a. Trifling*; futile; of no force; inoperative. [L. *nugatorius*—*nugæ*, trifles.]
Nugget, nug′et, *n.* A lump, as of gold. [corrupted from *ingot*.]
Nuisance, nū′sans, *n.* That which *annoys* or *gives trouble* and *vexation*; that which is offensive or noxious; something that incommodes. [Old Fr.—L. *noceo*, to hurt.]
Null, nul, *a. Of no legal or binding force* or validity; of no efficacy; invalid. [L. *nullus*—*ne*, not, and *ullus*, any.]
Nullification, nul′i-fi-kā″shon, *n. Act of nullifying*; state of being nullified. [Low L. *nullificatio*.]
Nullify, nul′i-fi, *vt. To render null*; to deprive of legal force or efficacy. *ppr.* nullifying, *pret. & pp.* nullified. [L. *nullus*, and *facio*, to make.]
Nullity, nul′i-ti, *n. The quality of being null*; anything of no efficacy. [Fr. *nullité*.]
Numb, num, *a. Benumbed*; deprived of the power of sensation and motion; paralyzed; chill; motionless; producing numbness.—*vt. To benumb*; to deprive of the power of sensation or motion; to deaden; to render motionless. [Sax. *numen*, taken—*niman*, to take.]
Number, num′ber, *n.* That which admits of being *dealt out* or counted; a unit, considered in reference to other units; more than one; multitude; measure; the order and quantity of syllables constituting feet, which render verse musical to the ear; verse; the difference of the termination of a word, to express unity or plurality. *vt.* To count; to tell; to enumerate; to ascertain, as the units of any sum; to reckon as one of a multitude. [Fr. *nombre*; L. *numerus*—Gr. *nemo*, to deal out.]

Numberer, num′bėr-ėr, *n. One who numbers*.
Numberless, num′bėr-les, *a. That cannot be numbered* or counted; countless.
Numbers, num′bėrs, *n.* The fourth book of the Pentateuch, so called as containing the *numbering* of the Hebrews.
Numbles, num′blz, *n. pl.* The entrails of a deer. [Fr. *nombles*.]
Numbness, num′nes, *n. State of being numb*; that state of a living body in which it has not the power of feeling.
Numerable, nū′mėr-a-bl, *a. That may be numbered*. [L. *numerabilis*.]
Numeral, nū′mėr-al, *a. Pertaining to number*; consisting of number; standing as a substitute for figures.—*n.* A figure used to express a number. [Fr. *numéral*.]
Numeration, nū-mėr-ā′shon, *n. Act or art of numbering*; the act or art of dividing off a series of figures according to their values and expressing them in words. [L. *numeratio*.]
Numerator, nū′mėr-āt-ėr, *n. One who numbers*; the number in vulgar fractions which shows how many parts of a unit are taken. [L.]
Numerical, nū-me′rik-al, *a. Belonging to number*; denoting number; consisting in numbers. [Fr. *numérique*.]
Numerically, nū-me′rik-al-li, *adv.* In numbers; with respect to number or sameness in number.
Numerous, nū′mėr-us, *a. Being many*, or *consisting of a great number* of individuals. [L. *numerosus*.]
Numerously, nū′mėr-us-li, *adv.* In great numbers.
Numismatic, nū-mis-mat′ik, *a.* Pertaining to money, coin, or medals, *as sanctioned or established by law*. [Fr. *numismatique*; Gr. *nomizo*, to own as a custom.]
Numismatics, nū-mis-mat′iks, *n.* The science or knowledge of coins and medals, principally those struck by the ancient Greeks and Romans.
Numismatist, nū-mis′mat-ist, *n. One versed in the knowledge of numismatics*.
Nun, nun, *n.* A woman devoted to a religious life, and who lives in a cloister or nunnery. [Sax. *nunne*; Gr. *monos*, alone.]
Nuncio, nun′shi-o, *n. A messenger*; an ambassador from the pope to all emperor or king. [It. *nuncio*—L. *novus*, new, and *cieo*, to excite.]
Nuncupative, nun-kū′pāt-iv,*a. Publicly* or solemnly declaratory; verbally pronounced; oral; not written, as a will. [Fr. *nuncupatif*—L. *nomen*, a name, and *capio*, to take.]
Nunnery, nun′ė-ri, *n. A house in which nuns reside*.
Nuptial, nup′shi-al, *a. Pertaining to marriage*; done at a wedding, constituting marriage.—*n.†* Marriage. [Fr.—L. *nubo, nuptum*, to veil, to marry—said of a woman.]
Nuptials, nup′shi-als, *n. pl.* Marriage.
Nurse, nėrs, *n. One who nourishes*; a woman who *suckles* infants; a woman that has the care of infants; a woman who has the care of a sick person; that which breeds, or causes to grow; an old woman; state of being nursed.—*vt. To nourish*; to suckle; to tend, as infants; to attend in sickness; to feed; to bring up; to cherish; to foster; to manage with economy, with a view to increase. *ppr.* nursing, *pret. & pp.* nursed. [Fr. *nourrice*—L. *nutrio*, to nourish—Heb. *nātar*, to guard.]
Nursery, nėrs′ė-ri, *n. The act of nursing*; the apartment in which children are

Fāte, fär, fat, fạll; mē, met, hėr; pīne, pin; nōte, not, mōve; tūbe, tub, bụll; oil, pound.

Nursling | **259** | **Obligation**

nursed; a plantation of young trees; the place where anything is fostered; that which forms and educates.
Nursling, ners'ling, n. An infant; a child.
Nurture, nér'tūr, n. *That which nourishes*; that which promotes growth; food; instruction.—*vt.* To nourish; to feed; to educate; to bring or train up. *ppr.* nurturing, *pret. & pp.* nurtured. [Fr. *nourriture*—L. *nutrio*, to nourish.]
Nut, nut, n. The *roundish* fruit of certain trees and shrubs, especially of the hazel, consisting of a hard shell inclosing a kernel; something resembling a nut; a piece of metal with a cylindrical grooved hole, screwed upon the end of a screw-bolt, &c.—*vi.* To gather *nuts. ppr.* nutting, *pret. & pp.* nutted. [Sax. *hnut*—L. *nux*, *nucis*.]
Nutation, nū-tā'shon, n. *A nodding*; a vibratory motion of the earth's axis. [L. *nutatio*—*nuo*, to nod.]

Nut-cracker, nut'krak-ēr, n. *An instrument for cracking nuts.*
Nutmeg, nut'meg, n. *Musk-nut*; the aromatic kernel of the fruit of a tree growing principally in the islands of Banda. [*nut*, and L. *muscus*, musk.]
Nutriment, nū'tri-ment, n. *That which nourishes*; nourishment; that which promotes improvement. [L. *nutrimentum*.]
Nutrition, nū-tri'shon, n. *Act or process of nourishing*, or of promoting the growth or repairing the waste of animal bodies; the act or process of promoting growth in vegetables; that which nourishes; nutriment. [Fr.—L. *nutrio*, to nourish.]
Nutritious, nū-tri'shi-us, a. *Nourishing*; promoting the growth or repairing the waste of animal bodies.
Nutritiously, nū-tri'shi-us-li, adv. *In a nutritious manner.*

Nutritive, nū'tri-tiv, a. *Having the quality of nourishing*; alimental.
Nut-shell, nut'shel, n. *The hard shell of a nut*; a thing of little compass or of little value.
Nutting, nut'ing, p.n. *Act of gathering nuts.*
Nutty, nut'i, a. *Abounding in nuts*; flavoured like a nut; resembling a nut.
Nuzzle, nuz'l, vi. To work with the nose like a swine in mud, &c.; to go with the nose thrust out and down like a swine.—*vt.* To put a ring in the nose of. *ppr.* nuzzling, *pret. & pp.* nuzzled. [from *nose.*]
Nymph, nimf, n. A fabled goddess of the mountains, forests, meadows, or waters; a poetical name for a lady or a young lady; a lovely young girl; a maiden. [Fr. *nymphe*—Gr. *nymphē*.]
Nymphean, nim-fē'an, a. *Pertaining to nymphs*; inhabited by nymphs.

O.

O, ō, *interj.* An exclamation used in calling, or directly addressing a person or personified object; used also to express pain, grief, desire, and the like.
Oak, ōk, n. A tree of many species, much used for ship-building, architecture, and other purposes which require strength and durability. [Sax. *āc*; Icel. *eik.*]
Oak-apple, ōk'a-pl, n. A kind of spongy excrescence on *oak* leaves or tender branches, &c.
Oaken, ōk'n, a. *Made of oak*, or consisting of oak.
Oakum, ōk'um, n. *Combings*; refuse of tow; the substance of old ropes untwisted and pulled into loose hemp, employed for calking, &c. [Sax. *æcemba*—*camb*, a comb.]
Oar, ōr, n. An instrument for *rowing or hastening the progress* of boats.—*vi.* To *impel by rowing.* [Sax. *ár*—*rowan*, to row.]
Oared, ōrd, p.a. *Furnished with oars.*
Oarsman, ōrs'man, n. *One who rows at the oar.*
Oary, ōr'i, a. *Having the form or use of an oar.*
Oasis, ō-ā'sis, n. **Oases,** ō-ā'sēz, pl. A *wonderful* or delicious spot; particularly applied to such spots watered by springs in the deserts of Egypt and other parts of Africa. [Gr.—Ar. *wah*, wonderful.]
Oat, ōt, n. A plant, and more usually the seed of the plant, the meal of which forms an article *of food.* [Sax. *ata*, oats; Sans. *ad*, to eat.]
Oaten, ōt'n, a. *Made of oat-meal*; consisting of an oat straw or stem; as, an oaten pipe.
Oath, ōth, n. A *binding* promise, affirmation, or negation, corroborated by the attestation of the Divine Being. [Sax. *ath*—Icel. *eida*, to confirm by an oath—Sans. *ti*, to bind.]
Oathablet, ōth'a-bl, a. Capable of having an oath administered to.
Oath-breaking, ōth'brāk-ing, n. *The violation of an oath*; perjury.
Oat-meal, ōt'mēl, n. *Meal of oats* produced by grinding or pounding.
Obduracy, ob'dū-ra-si, n. *Quality of*

being obdurate; invincible hardness of heart; obstinacy in wickedness.
Obdurate, ob'dū-rāt, a. *Hardened*; hardened in heart; persisting obstinately in sin or impenitence; inflexible. [L. *obduratus*—*ob*, and *duro*, *duratum*, to harden.]
Obdurately, ob'dū-rāt-li, adv. *With obduracy*; with obstinate impenitence.
Obedience, ō-bē'di-ens, n. *Act of obeying*; quality of being obedient; the performance of what is required or enjoined by authority, or the abstaining from what is prohibited. [Fr. *obédience.*]
Obedient, ō-bē'di-ent, a. *Hearkening or attending to*; yielding compliance with injunctions; submissive; obsequious. [L. *obediens*—*ob*, and *audio*, to hear.]
Obediently, ō-bē'di-ent-li, adv. *With obedience.*
Obeisance, ō-bā'sans, n. *A manifestation of obedience*; an act of reverence made by an inclination of the body or the knee. [Fr. *obéissance*—L. *obedientia*—*ob*, and *audio*, to hear.]
Obelisk, ob'ē-lisk, n. *A small spit*; a tall four-sided *pillar*, gradually tapering as it rises, and cut off at the top in the form of a flat pyramid; a mark referring the reader to a note in the margin, thus, †, used in printing and writing. [L. *obeliscus*—Gr. *obelos*, a spit.]
Obesity, ō-bes'i-ti, n. *Excessive fatness from much eating*; encumbrance of flesh. [Fr. *obésité*; L. *ob*, intens. and *edo*, to eat.]
Obey, ō-bā', vt. To listen or attend to; to submit to the government of; to be ruled by; to submit to the direction or control of; to yield to the impulse, power, or operation of. [Fr. *obéir*—L. *ob*, and *audio*, to hear.]
Obit, ō'bit, n. *A going down*; decease; a funeral ceremony or office for the dead. [L. *obitus*—*eo*, *itum* to go.]
Obituary, ō-bit'ū-a-ri, n. An account of a person or persons *deceased*; a list or register of the dead.—*a.* Relating to the decease of a person. [Fr. *obituaire.*]
Object, ob'jekt, n. *That which is thrown before*; that which lies before; that

about which any power is employed; end; ultimate purpose; something presented to the senses or the mind, to excite emotion, affection, or passion; that which is acted on by something else; that which follows a transitive verb. [Old Fr.—L. *jacio*, *jactum*, to throw.]
Object, ob-jekt', vt. To *throw* or put *before*; to oppose; to present or offer in opposition.—*vi.* To oppose in words or arguments; to offer reasons against. (With *to.*) [L. *objicio*, *objectus*—*jacio*, to throw.]
Object-glass, ob'jekt-glas, n. *The glass* in a telescope or microscope placed at the end of a tube *next the object.*
Objection, ob-jek'shon, n. *Act of objecting*; that which is presented in opposition; adverse reason; reason existing, though not offered, against a measure or an opinion; fault found. [L. *objectio.*]
Objectionable, ob-jek'shon-a-bl, a. *Justly liable to objections.*
Objective, ob-jekt'iv, a. *Pertaining to an object*; relating to whatever is exterior to the mind; external; noting the case which follows a transitive verb or a preposition.—*n.* The objective. [Fr. *objectif*—L. *jacio*, to throw.]
Objectively, ob-jekt'iv-li, adv. *In an objective manner.*
Objectiveness, ob-jekt'iv-nes, n. *State of being objective.*
Objector, ob-jekt'ēr, n. *One who objects*; one who offers arguments or reasons in opposition to a proposition or measure. [Late L.]
Oblate, ob-lāt', a. *Compressed*; flattened or depressed at the poles, as a spheroid. [L. *oblatus*—*ob*, and *fero*, *latus*, to bear.]
Oblation, ob-lā'shon, n. *Anything offered or presented* in worship or sacred service; an offering; a sacrifice. [Fr.; L. *oblatio.*]
Obligation, ob-li-gā'shon, n. *Act of binding*; state of being bound; the binding power of a vow, promise, oath, or contract; that which constitutes legal or moral duty; the binding force of civility, kindness, or gratitude; a bond

ch, *chain*; j, *job*; g, *go*; ng, *sing*; ᴛʜ, *then*; th, *thin*; w, *wig*; wh, *whig*; zh, *azure*; † obsolete.

with a condition annexed, and a penalty for non-fulfilment. [Fr.—L. *ligo*, to bind.]
Obligatory, ob'li-ga-tō-ri, *a. Imposing or implying an obligation;* binding in law or conscience; requiring performance or forbearance of some act. [Fr. *obligatoire*—L. *ligo*, to bind.]
Oblige, ō-blīj', *vt. To bind or fasten to;* to compel by necessity or physical force; to constrain by legal or moral force; to bind by a sense of honour or duty; to do a favour to; to gratify; to bring under obligation. *ppr.* obliging, *pret. & pp.* obliged. [Fr. *obliger*—L. *ligo*, to bind.]
Obliging, ō-blīj'ing, *p.a.* Having the disposition to do favours, or actually conferring them; civil; courteous; kind.
Obligingly, ō-blīj'ing-li, *adv.* With civility; kindly; complaisantly.
Oblique, ob-lēk', *a. Slanting;* deviating from a right line; not perpendicular; not parallel; obtuse or acute, as an angle; by a side glance; deviating from rectitude; sinister; noting any case in nouns except the nominative. [Fr.—L. *liquis*, awry.]
Obliquely, ob-lēk'li, *adv. In an oblique manner.*
Obliquity, ob-lik'wi-ti, *n. State of being oblique;* deviation from a right line; deviation from parallelism or perpendicularity; deviation from moral rectitude; deviation from ordinary rules. [Fr. *obliquité*.]
Obliterate, ob-lit'ė-rāt, *vt. To daub or smear over;* to blot out; to efface; to erase or blot out, as anything written or engraved; to wear out; to reduce to a very low or imperceptible state. *ppr.* obliterating, *pret. & pp.* obliterated. [L. *oblitéro, obliteratus—lino*, to besmear.]
Obliteration, ob-lit'ė-rā"shon, *n. Act of obliterating;* effacement; a blotting out or wearing out. [L. *obliteratio*.]
Oblivion, ob-li'vi-on, *n. State of being blotted out* from memory; effacement from the mind or memory; forgetfulness; cessation of remembrance; official blotting out of offences; amnesty. [L. *oblivio, oblivionis—obliviscor*, to forget —*ob*, and Sans. *lip*, to smear.]
Oblivious, ob-li'vi-us, *a. That easily forgets;* forgetful; causing forgetfulness. [L. *obliviosus*.]
Oblong, ob'long, *a. Rather long;* longer than broad.—*n.* A figure which is *longer* than it is broad; a rectangle which is *longer* than it is broad. [Fr. —L. *longus*, long.]
Obloquy, ob'lō-kwē, *n. A speaking against;* a gainsaying; reproachful language; language that casts contempt on men or their actions; detraction; cause of reproach; disgrace. [Low L. *obloquium*—L. *loquor*, to speak.]
Obnoxious, ob-nok'shi-us, *a. Subject to punishment on account of guilt;* answerable; liable or subject to cognizance; censurable; offensive; noxious. [L. *obnoxius—noceo*, to hurt.]
Obnoxiously, ob-nok'shi-us-li, *adv.* Reprehensibly; odiously; offensively.
Obnoxiousness, ob-nok'shi-us-nes, *n. State of being obnoxious;* odiousness.
Obscene, ob-sēn', *a. Of adverse or evil omen;* inauspicious; abominable; foul; offensive to chastity and delicacy; impure; lewd. [Fr. *obscène*—L. *obscænus*.]
Obscenely, ob-sēn'li, *adv.* In a manner offensive to chastity or purity.
Obscenity, ob-sen'i-ti, *n. Quality of being*

obscene; impurity in expression or representation; ribaldry; unchaste actions; lewdness. [Fr. *obscénité*.]
Obscuration, ob-skūr-ā'shon, *n. Act of obscuring;* state of being darkened or obscured. [L. *obscuratio*.]
Obscure, ob-skūr', *a. Over-shadowed;* darkened; dim; destitute of light; living in darkness; not easily understood; abstruse; not much known; not noted; unnoticed; humble; scarcely legible; indistinct.—*vt. To overshadow;* to cloud; to make partially dark; to make less intelligible; to make less glorious; to conceal; to tarnish. *ppr.* obscuring, *pret. & pp.* obscured. [L. *obscurus*— Gr. *skia*, a shadow.]
Obscurely, ob-skūr'li, *adv. In an obscure manner.*
Obscurity, ob-skūr'i-ti, *n. State or quality of being obscure;* darkness; illegibleness; a state of being unknown to fame; humble condition; darkness of meaning. [Fr. *obscurité;* L. *obscuritas*.]
Obsequies, ob'sē-kwēz, *n. pl. A following to the grave;* funeral rites and solemnities. [Fr. *obsèques*—L. *sequor*, to follow.]
Obsequious, ob-sē'kwi-us, *a. Following closely;* promptly obedient to the will of another; servilely or meanly condescending; servile; funereal†. [Fr. *obsequieux*—L. *sequor*, to follow.]
Obsequiously, ob-sē'kwi-us-li, *adv.* With ready obedience; with prompt compliance; with reverence for the dead†.
Obsequiousness, ob-sē'kwi-us-nes, *n. Quality of being obsequious;* mean or excessive complaisance.
Observable, ob-zėrv'a-bl, *a. That may be observed;* worthy of observation or of particular notice; remarkable. [Fr. —L. *ob*, and *servo*, to wait for.]
Observably, ob-zėrv'a-bli, *adv.* In a manner worthy of note.
Observance, ob-zėrv'ans, *n. Act of observing;* performance; ceremonial reverence in practice; performance of rites; rule of practice; thing to be observed. [Fr.]
Observant, ob-zėrv'ant, *a. Observing;* mindful; adhering to or obeying in practice; carefully attentive.—*n.†* One who rigidly adheres to rule; a sycophantic servant. [L. *observans*.]
Observantly, ob-zėrv'ant-li, *adv.* With attentive view or regard.
Observation, ob-zėrv-ā'shon, *n. The act of observing;* attentive inspection or view; the act of seeing or of fixing the mind on anything; notion gained by observing; the effect of taking cognizance in the mind; the expression of what is observed; remark; adherence to in practice. [Fr.]
Observatory, ob-zėrv'a-tō-ri, *n.* A building for making *observations* on the heavenly bodies. [Fr. *observatoire*.]
Observe, ob-zėrv', *vt. To take notice of;* to mark; to behold with some attention; to take cognizance of; to utter, as a remark; to keep religiously; to keep in practice; to comply with; to obey.—*vi.* To remark; to be attentive. *ppr.* observing, *pret. & pp.* observed. [L. *observo—servo*, to wait for.]
Observer, ob-zėrv'ėr, *n. One who observes;* particularly, one who looks to with vigilance; one who keeps any law, custom, regulation, or rite; one who adheres to anything in practice; one who keeps religiously.
Observing, ob-zėrv'ing, *p.a.* Giving particular attention; habitually taking notice; attentive to what passes.

Observingly, ob-zėrv'ing-li, *adv.* Attentively; carefully.
Obsolescence, ob-sō-les'ens, *n. State of becoming obsolete.*
Obsolescent, ob-sō-les'ent, *a. Growing obsolete;* going out of use. [L. *obsolescens*.]
Obsolete, ob'sō-lēt, *a. Worn out;* gone into disuse; out of date; obscure. [L. *obsoletus—soleo, solitus*, to be wont.]
Obsoletely, ob'sō-lēt-li, *adv. In an obsolete manner.*
Obsoleteness, ob'sō-lēt-nes, *n. State of being obsolete or out of use;* indistinctness; want of development.
Obstacle, ob'sta-kl, *n. That which stands against;* a hindrance; an impediment; anything that stands in the way and hinders progress. [Fr.—L. *sto*, to stand.]
Obstetric, ob-stet'rik, *a.* Pertaining to *midwifery.* [It. *ostetrica*, a midwife; L. *obsto*, to stand before.]
Obstetrics, ob-stet'riks, *n.* The science of midwifery; the art of assisting women in childbed.
Obstinacy, ob'sti-na-si, *n. Quality of being obstinate;* a fixedness that will not yield to persuasion or other means; stubbornness; fixedness that will not yield to application, or that yields with difficulty, as of a disease. [L. *obstinatio*.]
Obstinate, ob'sti-nāt, *a. Standing firmly against;* inflexible; self-willed; pertinaciously adhering to an opinion or purpose; not yielding to reason; not easily subdued, as a disease. [L. *obstinatus—sto*, to stand.]
Obstinately, ob'sti-nāt-li, *adv.* Stubbornly; pertinaciously.
Obstreperous, ob-strep'ėr-us, *a. Loud;* noisy; clamorous; making a tumultuous noise. [Low L. *obstreperus*—L. *strepo*, to make a noise.]
Obstreperously, ob-strep'ėr-us-li, *adv.* Loudly; clamorously.
Obstruct, ob-strukt', *vt. To build or block up;* to stop up or close, as a way or passage; to barricade; to impede; to be in the way of; to interrupt; to render slow, as progress. [L. *obstruo, obstructus—struo*, to build.]
Obstructed, ob-strukt'ed, *p a* Impeded, as progress; retarded; interrupted.
Obstruction, ob-struk'shon, *n. Act of obstructing;* anything that stops or closes a way or channel; hindrance; check; the condition of having the natural powers obstructed from their natural course†; death†. [Fr.]
Obstructive, ob-strukt'iv, *a. That obstructs;* presenting obstacles; causing impediment. [Fr. *obstructif*.]
Obstructively, ob-strukt'iv-li, *adv. By way of obstruction.*
Obtain, ob-tān', *vt. To hold by;* to get hold or possession of; to gain; to acquire; to earn.—*vi. To hold on;* to be received in common use; to be e tablished in practice; to subsist in nature. [Fr. *obtenir*—L. *teneo*, to hold.]
Obtainable, ob-tān'a-bl, *a. That may be obtained.*
Obtrude, ob-trōd', *vt. To thrust on;* to offer with unreasonable importunity; to urge upon against the will.—*vi. To thrust or be thrust upon;* to enter when not invited. *ppr.* obtruding, *pret. & pp.* obtruded. [L. *obtrudo—trūdo*, to thrust.]
Obtruding, ob-trōd'ing, *p.n.* A *thrusting in or entrance without right or invitation.*
Obtrusion, ob-trō'zhon, *n. Act of obtrud-*

Fāte, fär, fat, fall; mē, met, hėr; pīne, pin; nōte, not, möve; tūbe, tub, bull; oil, pound.

ing; a .hrusting upon others by force or unso:icited. [L. *obtrusio.*]
Obtrusiv, ob-trö'siv, *a.* Inclined to intru e i r thrust one s self among others, or .o enter uninvited.
Obtrusively, ob-trö'siv-li, *adv. By way of obtrusion.*
Obtuse, ob-tūs', *a. Blunted;* blunt; not ing an angle which is greater than a right angle; dull; not having acute sensibility; not sharp; obscure. [L. *obtusus—tundo,* to blunt.]
Obtusely, ob-tūs'li, *adv.* Without a sharp point; dully; stupidly.
Obtuseness, ob-tūs'nes, *n. Quality of being obtuse;* bluntness; want of quick sensibility; dulness of sound.
Obverse, ob'vėrs, *n. The face* of a coin; opposed to reverse. [L. *obversus,* turned towards—*verto,* to turn.]
Obviate, ob'vi-āt, *vt. To meet in the way;* to remove, as difficulties or objections. *ppr.* obviating, *pret. & pp.* obviated. [Fr. *obvier*—L. *via,* a way.]
Obvious, ob'vi-us, *a. Meeting in front;* open; readily perceived by the eye or the intellect; plain; manifest. [L. *obvius*—*via,* a way.]
Obviously, ob'vi-us-li, *adv.* Evidently; manifestly; naturally.
Obviousness, ob'vi-us-nes, *n. State of being obvious,* plain, or evident.
Occasion, ok-kā'zhon, *n. A falling out;* an occurrence; opportunity; favourable time, season, or circumstances; accidental cause; incidental need; opportunity accompanied with need or demand.—*vt. To cause incidentally;* to give rise to; to bring about; to influence. [L. *occasio—cado, casum,* to fall.]
Occasional, ok-kā'zhon-al, *a. Happening at times;* casual; occurring at times, but not regular or systematic; made as opportunity requires; produced or made on some special event. [Fr. *occasionnel.*]
Occasionally, ok-kā'zhon-al-li, *adv. In an occasional manner.*
Occident, ok'si-dent, *n. The quarter where the sun goes down;* the west; the western quarter of the hemisphere. [Fr.—L. *occidens,* falling—*cado,* to fall.]
Occidental, ok-si-dent'al, *a. Western;* opposed to oriental; pertaining to the western quarter of the hemisphere. [L. *occidentalis.*]
Occipital, ok-si'pit-al, *a. Pertaining to the occiput.* [Fr.]
Occiput, ok'si-put, *n. The hinder part of the head,* or that part of the skull which forms the hind part of the head. [L.—*caput,* the head.]
Occult, ok-kult', *a. Covered over,* as seeds in *tillage;* hidden from the eye or understanding; undiscovered; undetected. [L. *occultus—colo, cultum,* to till.]
Occultation, ok-kult-ā'shon, *n. A hiding or concealing;* the hiding of a heavenly body from our sight by the intervention of some other of the heavenly bodies; particularly, the eclipses of stars and planets by the moon. [Fr.]
Occulted, ok-kult'ed, *a. Hid;* secret.
Occultly, ok-kult'li, *adv. In an occult manner.*
Occultness, ok-kult'nes, *n. State of being occult,* or concealed from view.
Occupancy, ok'kū-pan-si, *n. Act of occupying;* act of taking or holding possession; the taking possession of a thing not belonging to any person. [from L. *occupo—capio,* to take.]
Occupant, ok'kū-pant, *n. He who occupies;* he who has possession; one who first takes possession of that which has no legal owner. [Fr.]
Occupation, ok-kū-pā'shon, *n. Act of occupying;* a holding, keeping, or using; tenure; that which engages the time and attention; employment; the principal business of one s life; calling; office; trade; profession. [Fr.]
Occupier, ok'kū-pī-er, *n. One who occupies;* one who holds possession.
Occupy, ok'kū-pī, *vt. To lay hold of;* to keep in possession; to hold or keep for use; to take up; to employ; to busy one's self; to follow, as business.—*vi.* To follow business; t traffic. *ppr.* occupying, *pret. & pp.* occupied. [Fr. *occuper*—L. *occupo—capio,* to seize, hold.]
Occur, ok-kėr', *vi. To run against;* to meet the eye; to be found here and there; to come to the mind; to be presented to the imagination or memory. *ppr.* occurring, *pret. & pp.* occurred. [L. *occurro—curro,* to run.]
Occurrence, ok-ku'rens, *n. Something which occurs;* an incident; that which happens without being designed or expected; any single event. [Fr.]
Ocean, ō'shē-an, *n. That which flows rapidly;* the vast body of water which covers more than three-fifths of the surface of the globe; the sea; the main; the deep; an immense expanse. *a.* Pertaining to the main or great sea. [Fr. *océan*—Gr. *ōkednos—ōkus,* swift.]
Oceanic, ō-shē-an'ik, *a. Pertaining to the ocean;* found or formed in the ocean.
Ochre, ō'kėr, *n.* A substance of *a pale yellow or pallid colour;* a kind of fine clay use l as a pigment, of a *pale* sandy colour, or brownish-red. [Gr. *ōchros,* pale yellow.]
Ochreous, ō'kėr-us, *a. Consisting of or containing ochre;* resembling ochre. [Fr. *ocreux.*]
Octagon, ok'ta-gon, *n.* A plane figure having *eight angles* and eight sides. [Gr. *oktō,* eight, and *gōnia,* an angle.]
Octagonal, ok-tag'on-al, *a. Having eight angles* and eight sides.
Octahedral, ok-ta-hed'ral, *a. Having eight equal faces or sides.*
Octahedron, ok-ta-hed'ron, *n.* A solid figure having *eight faces or sides.* [Gr. *oktō,* eight, and *hedra,* a side.]
Octangular, ok-tang'gū-lėr, *a. Having eight angles.* [L. *octo,* and *angular.*]
Octant, ok'tant, *n. An eighth part;* the eighth part of a circle; a nautical instrument, the measuring arc of which is the eighth part of the circumference of a circle. [Fr.—L. *octo,* eight.]
Octave, ok'tāv, *a. Eighth;* denoting eight.—*n. An eighth;* the eighth day after a church-festival, the festival itself being included; an eighth in music, or an interval of seven degrees or twelve semitones. [Fr.—L. *octo,* eight.]
Octavo, ok-tā'vō, *n.* A book in which a sheet is folded into *eight* leaves.—*a.* Having *eight* leaves to the sheet. [Fr.]
October, ok-tō'bėr, *n. The eighth month* of the primitive Roman year; the tenth month of the year in our calendar. [L. from *octo,* eight.]
Octogenarian, ok'tō-jen-ā'ri-an, *n. One who is eighty years of age.*
Octogenary, ok-to'jen-a-ri, *a. Of eighty years* of age. [L. *octogenarius.*]
Octosyllabic, ok'tō-sil-lab'ik, *a. Consisting of eight syllables.* [L. *octo,* eight, and *syllaba,* a syllable.]
Ocular, ok'ū-lār, *a. Pertaining to the eye or eyes;* depending on the eye; received by actual sight. [Fr. *oculaire* —L. *oculus,* the eye.]
Ocularly, ok'ū-lār-li, *adv. By the eye,* sight, or actual view.
Oculist, ok'ū-list, *n. One skilled in diseases of the eyes,* or one who professes to cure them. [Fr. *oculiste.*]
Odd, od, *a. Unmatched;* singular; strange; left or remaining after the use of even numbers; not even; not divisible into two equal whole numbers, as three, five, &c.; not taken into the account; remaining separate from that which is regularly occupied; queer. [Old G. *ödi,* wanting.]
Oddity, od'i-ti, *n. Singularity;* strangeness; a singular person or thing.
Oddly, od'li, *adv.* Strangely; unusually.
Oddness, od'nes, *n. State of being odd;* irregularity; uncouthness.
Odds, odz, *n. Inequality;* difference in favour of one and against another; advantage; quarrel; debate. [from *odd,* used both in the singular and plural.
Ode, ōd, *n. A song;* a *lay;* a poetical composition proper to be set to music or sung; a lyric poem. [Gr. *ōdē*—*aeidō,* to sing.]
Odious, ō'di-us, *a. Hateful;* offensive to the senses; disgusting; invidious; exposed to hatred. [L. *odiōsus—odi,* to hate.]
Odiously, ō'di-us-li, *adv. Hatefully;* invidiously; so as to cause hate.
Odiousness, ō'di-us-nes, *n. Quality of being odious;* hatefulness; state of being hated.
Odium, ō'di-um, *n. Hatred;* enmity; offensiveness; invidiousness. [L.—*odi,* to hate.]
Odoriferous, ō-dor-if'ėr-us, *a. Bringing odours;* fragrant; sweet of scent. [L. *odoriferus—odor,* and *fero,* to bring.]
Odoriferously, ō-dor-if'ėr-us-li, *adv. In the manner of producing odour.*
Odorous, ō'dor-us, *a. Emitting a scent or odour;* sweet of scent; fragrant. [L. *odōrus.*]
Odorously, ō'dor-us-li, *adv.* With sweetness of scent or fragrance.
Odour, ō'dor, *n. Smell;* a sweet or an offensive smell; perfume; fragrance. [L. *odor,* a smell—Gr. *osō,* to smell.]
Odourless, ō'dor-les, *a. Free from odour.*
Oeilliad, ē'lyād, *n.* A glance; a wink. [Fr. *œillade.*]
O'er, ō'ėr, contracted from *over.*
Of, ov, *prep. From or out from;* noting the relation of source, cause, origin, or motive; proceeding from; with regard to; belonging to. [Sax.—L. *ab.*]
Off, of, *a.* Most distant; opposed to near or nearest; as, the off horse in a team. *interj.* Away! begone!—*adv. From,* noting distance; from, with the action of removing; from, noting separation; from, noting departure, or a leaving; away; not toward; on the opposite side of a question.—*prep.* Not on, as off the ground; distant from. [the same word as *of.*]
Offal, of'fal, *n. That which falls off;* that which is thrown away; refuse; waste meat; the parts of an animal butchered which are unfit for use; coarse meat; anything of no value; rubbish. [D. *afval.*]
Offence, of-fens', *n. A striking against;* anger or moderate anger; scandal; any violation of law, divine or human; act of wickedness; a crime; a sin; a fault; a misdemeanour; a misdeed; assault. [L. *offensio.*]
Offenceful, of-fens'fụl, *a. Inclined to offend;* injurious.

Offend, of-fend', *vt.* To strike against; to displease; to make angry; to affront; to shock; to wound, as consciences; to disturb or cause to fall; to draw to evil; to cause to sin.—*vi.* To strike against; to transgress the moral or divine law; to sin; to commit a crime; to cause dislike or anger. [L. *offendo*—*fendo*, to strike.]

Offended, of-fend'ed, *p.a.* Displeased; angry.

Offender, of-fend'ėr, *n.* One who offends; a transgressor, a trespasser.

Offending, of-fend'ing, *p.a.* Causing to stumble; committing sin.

Offensive, of-fens'iv, *a.* Causing offence; giving unpleasant sensations; injurious, as to the stomach; disgusting; insolent; impertinent; used in attack; assailant; invading; opposed to defensive.—*n.* The part of attacking; a state or posture of attack. [Fr. *offensif.*]

Offensively, of-fens'iv-li, *adv.* In an offensive manner.

Offensiveness, of-fens'iv-nes, *n.* The quality that offends or displeases; injuriousness; mischief; cause of disgust.

Offer, of'fėr, *vt.* To bring to or before; to present for acceptance; to tender; to proffer; to sacrifice; to make a proposal to; to present in prayer; to bid, as a price; to show; to furnish; to give; to put in opposition to.—*vi.* To present itself; to be at hand; to declare a willingness.—*n.* A proposal to be accepted or rejected; first advance; act of bidding a price, or the sum bid. [Fr. *offrir*; L. *ob*, and *fero*, to bring.]

Offered, of'fėrd, *p.a.* Bid; presented to the eye or the mind.

Offerer, of'fėr-ėr, *n.* One who offers; one who sacrifices or dedicates in worship.

Offering, of'fėr-ing, *p.n.* Act of one who offers; that which is offered; a sacrifice; an oblation.

Off-hand, of'hand, *a.* Speedily sent from the hand; unpremeditated; done or said at the moment.—*adv.* On the spur of the moment; promptly. [*off* and *hand.*]

Office, of'fis, *n.* That which one does or ought to do for another; a service; a particular duty or trust conferred by public authority, and for a public purpose; an employment undertaken by authority from government; a duty or trust of a sacred nature conferred by God himself; duty of a private nature; that which anything is fitted to perform; function; particular employment; act of good or ill voluntarily tendered; a kindness; formulary of devotion; a house or place in which public officers and others transact business.—*vt.*† To perform a duty toward. [L. *officium*—*ob*, and *facio*, to do.]

Officer, of'fis-ėr, *n.* A person invested with an office; a person authorised to perform any public duty; one who holds a command in the army or navy; one authorized to take into legal custody.—*vt.* To furnish with officers; to appoint officers over.

Official, of-fi'shi-al, *a.* Pertaining to an office or public trust; made by virtue of authority.—*n.* One invested with an office; an ecclesiastical judge appointed by a bishop, chapter, archdeacon, &c., with charge of the spiritual jurisdiction; a subordinate executive officer or attendant. [Fr. *officiel*—L. *facio*, to do.]

Officially, of-fi'shi-al-li, *adv.* In an official manner.

Officiate, of-fi'shi-āt, *vi.* To transact the appropriate business of an office or public trust; to perform the appropriate official duties of another. *ppr.* officiating, *pret. & pp.* officiated. [Fr. *officier*—L. *facio*, to do.]

Officinal, of-fi'si-nal, *a.* Used in a shop, or belonging to it; pertaining to those medicines which are directed in the pharmacopœia to be kept in apothecary shops. [Fr.—L. *opus*, a work, and *facio*, to do.]

Officious, of-fi'shi-us, *a.* Full of complaisance; doing kind offices; importunately interposing services; intermeddling in affairs in which one has no concern. [Fr. *officieux*—L. *facio*, to do.]

Officiously, of-fi'shi-us-li, *adv.* In an officious manner.

Officiousness, of-fi'shi-us-nes, *n.* Quality of being officious; an excess of zeal to serve.

Offing, of'ing, *n.* That part of the sea which is at a good distance from the shore. [from *off.*]

Offscouring, of-skour'ing, *n.* That which is scoured off; that which is vile or despised.

Offset, of'set, *n.* A value set off against another as an equivalent; a narrow slip of ground on the outside of lines which include the main portion; a shoot; a sprout from the roots of a plant.

Offshoot, of'shot, *n.* A shoot of a plant; anything growing out of another.

Offspring, of'spring, *n.* That which springs from; a child or children; propagation; issue; progeny; production of any kind.

Oft, oft, *adv.* Often; frequently; not rarely. [Old Sax.; Goth. *afta*, frequently.]

Often, of'n, *adv.* Frequently; many times; not seldom. [Sax. *oft.*]

Oftentimes, of'n-tīmz, *adv.* Many times; frequently; often.

Ofttimes, oft'tīmz, *adv.* Frequently.

Ogle, ō'gl, *vt.* To eye; to view with side glances, as in fondness, or with design to attract notice. *ppr.* ogling, *pret. & pp.* ogled.—*n.* A side glance or look. [G. *äugeln*, to open and shut the eyes.]

Ogler, ō'gl-ėr, *n.* One who ogles.

Ogling, ō'gl-ing, *p.n.* The act of viewing with side glances.

Ogre, ō'gėr, *n.* An imaginary monster or hideous giant of fairy tales, who lived on human beings. [Fr.—L. *orcus*, hell.]

Ogress, ō'gres, *n.* A female ogre.

Oh, ō, *interj.* Denoting surprise, pain, sorrow, or anxiety.

Oil, oil, *n.* The juice of the fruit of the olive-tree; an unctuous, inflammable liquid drawn from various animal and vegetable substances.—*vt.* To smear or rub over with oil; to lubricate with oil; to anoint with oil. [Sax. *æl*; Gr. *elaia*, the olive-tree—Sans. *il*, to liquefy.]

Oiliness, oil'i-nes, *n.* Quality of being oily; unctuousness; greasiness.

Oily, oil'i, *a.* Consisting of oil; containing oil; having the qualities of oil; greasy.

Ointment, oint'ment, *n.* Unguent; any soft unctuous substance used for smearing, particularly the body or a diseased part. [L. *unguentum*—*ungo*, to anoint; Sans. *anj*, to anoint.]

Old, ōld, *a.* Grown up to maturity and strength; advanced in years; aged; having lived toward the end of life; being of long continuance; having been long made or used; not new or fresh; experienced; being of a former year's growth; not of the last crop; ancient, of any duration whatever; subsisting before something else; long practised, as in sin; that has been long cultivated; more than enough; great. [Sax. *æld*; L. *alo*, to nourish.]

Olden, ōld'n, *a.* Old; ancient.

Old-fashioned, ōld-fa'shond, *a.* Formed according to obsolete fashion or custom.

Oldish, ōld'ish, *a.* Somewhat old.

Oldness, ōld'nes, *n.* Quality or state of being old; state of being of a long continuance; antiquity.

Old-Testament, ōld-tes'ta-ment, *n.* That part of the Bible which contains the collected works of the inspired writers previous to Christ.

Oleaginous, ō-lē-a'jin-us, *a.* Pertaining to the olive; having the qualities of oil; oily; unctuous. [Fr. *oléagineux*; Gr. *elaia*, the olive-tree.]

Olfactory, ol-fak'tō-ri, *a.* Pertaining to or having the sense of smelling. [from L. *olfacio*—*oleo*, to smell, and *facio*, to make.]

Oligarch, o'li-gärk, *n.* One of a few in power; an aristocrat.

Oligarchical, Oligarchic, o-li-gärk'ik-al, o-li-gärk'ik, *a.* Pertaining to oligarchy.

Oligarchy, o'li-gär-ki, *n.* The government of a few; a form of government in which the supreme power is placed in a few hands; a species of aristocracy. [Fr. *oligarchie*—Gr. *oligos*, few, and *archē*, rule.]

Olive, o'liv, *n.* A tree, and also its fruit, from which a valuable oil is expressed; the emblem of peace.—*a.* Relating to the olive; of the colour of the olive. [L. *oliva*—Gr. *elaia*, the olive-tree.]

Olive-branch, o'liv-bransh, *n.* A branch of the olive-tree; the emblem of peace.

Olympiad, ō-lim'pi-ad, *n.* A period of four years, reckoned from one celebration of the Olympic games to another. The first Olympiad began 776 B.C. [Gr. *olumpias.*]

Olympian, Olympic, ō-lim'pi-an, ō-lim'pik, *a.* Pertaining to Olympus, or to Olympia, in Greece; relating to the Greek games celebrated at Olympia.

Ombre, om'bėr, *n.* A game at cards, usually played by three men. [It.—L. *homo*, a man.]

Omega, ō-me'ga, *n.* The name of the last letter of the Greek alphabet; figuratively, the last, or the ending, as alpha, the first letter, denotes the first or beginning. [Gr. great O.]

Omelet, o'me-let, *n.* A kind of pancake or fritter made with eggs and other ingredients mixed. [Fr. *omelette*; L. *ovum*, an egg, and *misceo*, to mix.]

Omen, ō'men, *n.* Something uttered by the mouth, regarded as a sign or token for good or evil; a sign of some future event; a prognostic; a presage. [L. —*os, oris*, the mouth.]

Omened, ō'mend, *p.a.* Containing an omen or prognostic.

Ominous, o'min-us, *a.* Full of omens; portentous; foreboding or presaging evil; inauspicious. [L. *ominosus.*]

Ominously, o'min-us-li, *adv.* With good or bad omens.

Ominousness, o'min-us-nes, *n.* Quality of being ominous.

Omission, ō-mi'shon, *n.* Act of omitting; neglect to do something which a person had power to do, or which duty required to be done; neglect or failure to insert or mention; that which is left out. [Fr.—L. *omissio.*]

Omissive, ō-mis'iv, *a.* Leaving out.

Omit, ō-mit', *vt.* To let go; to leave or neglect; to fail or forbear to do or to use; to leave out; not to insert. *ppr.* omitting, *pret. & pp.* omitted. [L. *omitto*—*ob*, and *mitto*, to let go.]

Omittance, ŏ-mit'ans, n. *Act of omitting;* neglect.

Omnibus, om'ni-bus, n. A large carriage used for conveying passengers a short distance in a city, or from a city to its environs. [L. plural dative *for all, from omnis.*]

Omnifarious, om-ni-fā'ri-us, a. *Of all varieties,* forms, or kinds. [Low L. *omnifarius*—L. *omnis,* all, and *varius,* different.]

Omnipotence, om-nip'ō-tens, n. *Almighty power;* power; a word in strictness applicable only to God; hence, sometimes used for God; unlimited power over particular things. [Fr.]

Omnipotent, om-nip'ō-tent, a. *Almighty;* possessing unlimited power; having unlimited power of a particular kind.—n. One of the appellations of the Godhead. [L. *omnipotens—omnis,* all, and *potens,* powerful.]

Omnipresence, om-ni-prez'ens, n. *Presence in every place at the same time;* unbounded or universal presence; ubiquity.

Omnipresent, om-ni-prez'ent, a. *Present in all places* at the same time; ubiquitous. [L. *omnis,* all, and *præsens,* present—*sum,* to be.]

Omniscience, om-ni'shi-ens, n. *The quality of knowing all things* at once; universal knowledge; knowledge unbounded or infinite. [Fr.]

Omniscient, om-ni'shi-ent, a. *Knowing all things;* having knowledge of all things, past, present, and future; all-seeing. [L. *omnisciens—omnis,* all, and *scio,* to know.]

Omnivorous, om-niv'or-us, a. *All-devouring;* eating everything indiscriminately. [L. *omnivorus—omnis,* all, and *voro,* to devour.]

On, on, prep. Being in contact with the upper surface of a thing, and supported by it; placed in contact with the surface; coming to the surface of anything; at or near; noting a resting for support; at the time of; toward; at the peril of; denoting a pledge; upon; noting imprecation; in consequence of; noting part or opposition.—*adv.* Forward, in progression; onward; forward, in succession; without ceasing; not off; attached to the body. [Sax.]

Once, wuns, *adv. One time;* one time, though no more; at one former time; formerly; at the same point of time; not gradually. [from *one.*]

One, wun, a. *This,* and *this* alone; opposed to another; opposed to other; single by union; the same; single in kind; single in number; indefinitely, some or any; diverse; denoting mutuality (when used with *another*); denoting average (when followed by *with another*). [Sax. *an*—L. *unus.*]

Oneness, wun'nes, n. *Quality of being one;* singleness in number; unity.

Onerous, on'ē-rus, a. *Burdensome;* heavy; oppressive. [L. *onerosus—onus, oneris,* a burden.]

Onerously, on'ē-rus-li, *adv. So as to burden* or oppress.

One-sided, wun-sīd'ed, a. *Having one side only;* limited to one side; partial.

Onion, un'yun, n. A plant with one blade; a plant having a pungent bulbous root, which is much used as a condiment. [Fr. *oignon*—L. *unio,* a kind of single onion.]

Onion-eyed†, un'yun-īd, a. Having the eyes full of tears.

Only, ōn'li, a. *Like one;* in the state or condition of one taken singly; one alone; this and no other; this above all others.—*adv.* Singly; barely; in one manner or for one purpose alone; without more. [Sax. *ánlíc.*]

Onset, on'set, n. *A setting* or rushing *upon;* assault; the assault of an army upon an enemy; an attack of any kind.

Onslaught, on'slat, n. *A striking against;* aggression; assault. [from Sax. *on-slagan,* to strike against—*slagan,* to slay.]

Onward, Onwards, on'wèrd, on'wèrds, *adv. Toward the point before or in front;* forward; in advance; in a state of advanced progression; a little further or forward. [Sax. *onweard—on,* and *weard,* towards.]

Onward, on'wèrd, a. Advanced or advancing; progressive; leading-forward to perfection.

Onyx, o'niks, n. Chalcedony, having in it a colour resembling that of a person's nail, and consisting of parallel layers of different shades of colour. [L.—Gr. *onux,* a claw, a nail.]

Ooze, ōz, n. A soft flow or issue, as of *water;* soft mud or slime; earth so wet as to flow gently.—*vi.* To flow or issue forth gently; to percolate, as a liquid through the pores of a substance, or through small openings. (With *from* or *out.*) *ppr.* oozing, *pret. & pp.* oozed. [Sax. *wase,* water, *wos,* juice.]

Oozings, ōz'ings, n. pl. Issues of a fluid.

Oozy, ōz'i, a. *Resembling ooze;* miry; containing soft mud. [Sax. *wosig.*]

Opacity, ō-pas'i-ti, n. *State or quality of being opaque;* the quality of a body which renders it impervious to the rays of light; darkness; obscurity; gloom. [Fr. *opacité.*]

Opal, ō'pal, n. A precious stone, which exhibits brilliant and changeable reflections of green, blue, yellow, and red. [Fr. *opale*—L. *opalus.*]

Opaque, ō-pāk', a. *Shady;* casting a shadow; dark; obscure; cloudy; impervious to the rays of light; not transparent. [Fr.—L. *opacus.*]

Open, ō'pen, *vt.* To *lift up* or remove a covering from; to unclose; to remove any fastening from and set open; to break the seal of, as of a letter and unfold it; to separate, as parts that are close; to cut through; to break; to split or rend; to clear; to expand; to unstop; to begin; to show; to explain; to disclose; to make liberal; to make the first discharge, as of artillery; to enter on.—*vi.* To unclose itself; to begin to appear; to begin.—*a.* Not shut or closed; spread; unsealed; not covered; clear; not fenced, as a road; not frosty; clear of ice; public; free to all comers; plain; not wearing disguise; frank; artless; not clouded; not contracted; having an air of frankness; not hidden; ready to hear what is offered; not restrained; employed in inspection; free to be debated, as a question or subject; easily enunciated. [Sax.—*openian,* to open.]

Open-handed, ō'pen-hand-ed, a. Generous; liberal; munificent.

Open-hearted, ō'pen-härt-ed, a. Candid; frank; generous.

Opening, ō'pen-ing, *p.a.* First in order. *p.n.* A breach; an aperture; a place admitting entrance, as a bay; beginning; first appearance.

Openly, ō'pen-li, *adv.* In an open manner.

Openness, ō'pen-nes, n. *State or quality of being open;* freedom from covering or obstruction; clearness; unreservedness; expression of frankness or candour; unusual mildness.

Opera, o'pe-ra, n. A musical *performance* or drama; a dramatic composition set to music and sung on the stage; the house where operas are exhibited. [It.—L. *opus, operis,* work.]

Operant†, o'pe-rant, a. Having power to produce an effect.

Operate, o'pe-rāt, *vi. To work;* to exert power of strength, physical or mechanical; to act or produce effect on the mind; to exert moral power; to perform some manual act in a methodical manner upon a human body, and usually with instruments, with a view to restore soundness or health.—*vt.* To act; to effect; to produce by agency. *ppr.* operating, *pret. & pp.* operated. [L. *operor, operátus—opus,* work.]

Operatic, o-pe-rat'ik, a. *Pertaining to the opera;* resembling the opera.

Operation, o-pe-rā'shon, n. *Act or process of operating;* agency; the exertion of power; series of acts in experiments; any methodical action of the hand with instruments, on the human body, as in surgery; movements of an army or fleet; movements of machinery or of any physical body. [Fr. *opération.*]

Operative, o'pe-rāt-iv, a. *That operates;* exerting force, physical or moral; efficacious.—n. *One who operates;* a labouring man; an artisan; one employed in manufacturing establishments. [Sp. *operativo.*]

Operator, o'pe-rāt-ėr, n. *He or that which operates;* the person who performs some act upon the human body by means of the hand, or with instruments. [L.]

Operose, o'pe-rōs, a. *Laborious;* troublesome; elaborate. [L. *operōsus—opus,* work.]

Ophthalmic, of-thal'mik, a. *Pertaining to the eye.*

Ophthalmia, of-thal'mi-a, n. *Inflammation of the eye* or its appendages. [Fr. *ophthalmie*—Gr. *ophthalmos,* the eye.]

Opiate, ō'pi-at, n. Any medicine that contains *opium,* and has the quality of inducing sleep; a narcotic; that which induces rest; that which quiets uneasiness.—a. Inducing sleep; soporiferous; narcotic; causing inaction. [Fr. *opiat*—L. *opium,* the dried juice of the sleepy poppy.]

Opinion, o-pin'i-on, n. *Sentiment;* belief; a mental conviction of the truth of some statement founded on a low degree of probable evidence; the judgment which the mind forms of persons or their qualities; settled judgment or belief; favourable judgment; estimation; fame†; obstinacy in holding to one's belief†. [L. *opinio—opinor,* to suppose.]

Opinionated, o-pin'i-on-āt-ed, *p.a.* Stiff or obstinate *in opinion.*

Opinionative, o-pin'i-on-āt-iv, a. *Unduly attached to one's own opinions;* fond of preconceived notions. [Sp. *opinativo.*]

Opium, ō'pi-um, n. Poppy-*juice;* the most energetic of narcotics, consisting of the inspissated juice of the somniferous poppy. [L.—Gr. *opion—opos,* juice.]

Opossum, ō-pos'sum, n. An American quadruped, which climbs up trees, the females having an abdominal pouch, in which they carry their young.

Oppidan, op'pi-dan, n. One of those students of Eton School who board in the town. [L. *oppidanus,* from *oppidum,* a town.]

Opponent, op-pō'nent, a. *That opposes;*

opposite; adverse.—*n. One who opposes; one who opposes in controversy; an antagonist; an adversary.* [L. *opponens—pōno*, to place.]

Opportune, op-por-tūn', *a. Commodious; fit; seasonable; present at a proper time; well-timed.* [L. *opportūnus—portus,* a harbour.]

Opportunely, op-por-tūn'li, *adv.* Seasonably; at a time favourable for the purpose.

Opportunity, op-por-tūn'i-ti, *n. State of being opportune; fit time; an occasion favourable for the purpose; suitable time, combined with other favourable circumstances.* [Fr. *opportunité.*]

Oppose, op-pōz', *vt. To place in front of; to put in opposition, with a view to counterbalance; to act against; to resist, either by physical means, by arguments, or other means; to check; to act against as a competitor.*—*vi. To act adversely*†; to object or act against in controversy. *ppr.* opposing, *pret. & pp.* opposed. [Fr. *opposer*—L. *pono, postum,* to place.]

Opposed, op-pōzd', *p. a. Being in opposition in principle or in act; adverse.*

Opposeless†, op-pōz'les, *a. Not to be opposed.*

Opposer, op-pōz'ér, *n. One who opposes; an opponent in party, in principle, in controversy, or argument; one who resists; an antagonist; a rival.*

Opposing, op-pōz'ing, *p. a. Acting against; resisting.*

Opposite, op'pō-zit, *a. Placed against; standing in front; facing; adverse; contrary.*—*n. An opponent; an adversary; an enemy; an antagonist; that which is opposed or contrary.* [Fr.—L. *pono, positum,* to place.]

Oppositely, op'pō-zit-li, *adv.* In front; adversely; against each other.

Opposition, op-pō-zi'shon, *n. Act of opposing; a standing over against; attempt to check, restrain, or defeat; obstacle; repugnance in principle; contrariety of interests or designs; contrast; the collective body of opponents of the administration.* [Fr.—L. *oppositio—pono,* to place.]

Oppress, op-pres', *vt. To press against; to press down; to depress; to sit or lie heavy on; to burden with unreasonable impositions; to treat with unjust severity; to overpower.* [L. *opprimo, oppressus—premo,* to press.]

Oppressed, op-prest', *p.a.* Overpowered; depressed.

Oppression, op-pre'shon, *n. Act of oppressing; cruelty; state of being overburdened; misery; calamity; depression; lassitude of body; a sense of heaviness or weight in the breast, &c.* [Fr.—L. *oppressio.*]

Oppressive, op-pres'iv, *a. Causing oppression; unjustly severe; tyrannical; heavy; overwhelming.* [Fr. *oppressif.*]

Oppressively, op-pres'iv-li, *adv. In a manner to oppress.*

Oppressiveness, op-pres'iv-nes, *n. Quality of being oppressive.*

Oppressor, op-pres'ér, *n. One who oppresses; one who harasses others with unjust laws or unreasonable severity.* [Late L.]

Opprobrious, op-prō'bri-us, *a. Containing opprobrium; scurrilous; blasted with infamy; rendered hateful.* [Sp. *oprobioso.*]

Opprobriously, op-prō'bri-us-li, *adv. With reproach, mingled with contempt.*

Opprobrium, op-prō'bri-um, *n. Reproach mingled with contempt or* disdain; disgrace; ignominy; infamy. [L. *ob,* and *probrum,* a shameful act.]

Oppugn, op-pūn', *vt. To fight against; to attack; to oppose; to resist.* [Sp. *opugnar*—L. *pugno,* to fight.]

Oppugnancy†, op-pug'nan-si, *n. Opposition; resistance.*

Optative, op'ta-tiv, *a. Expressing a wish or desire; designating that mood or form of the verb in which wish or desire is expressed.* [Fr. *optatif*—L. *opto,* to wish.]

Optatively, op'ta-tiv-li, *adv. In an optative manner.*

Optic, Optical, op'tik, op'tik-al, *a. Pertaining to vision or sight; relating to the science of optics.*—*n.* (Optic.) *An organ of sight; an eye.* [Fr. *optique;* Gr. *optomai,* to see.]

Optically, op'tik-al-li, *adv. By optics.*

Optician, op-ti'shi-an, *n. A person skilled in the science of optics; one who makes or sells optic glasses and instruments.* [Fr. *opticien.*]

Optics, op'tiks, *n. The science of the laws of sight; the science which treats of light and vision, and of the principles and construction of those instruments in which light is the chief agent, as telescopes, microscopes, &c.* [Gr. *ta optika—optomai,* to see.]

Optimism, op'tim-ism, *n. The doctrine that everything in nature is ordered for the best.* [Fr. *optimisme*—L. *optimus,* best.]

Optimist, op'tim-ist, *n.* One who holds the opinion that all events are ordered for the best.

Option, op'shon, *n. Choice; free choice; the power of choosing; the right of election; election; preference.* [L. *optio—opto,* to wish—Sans. *âp,* to go to, to obtain.]

Optional, op'shon-al, *a. Left to one's wish or choice; depending on choice or preference; leaving something to choice.*

Optionally, op'shon-al-li, *adv. With the privilege of choice.*

Opulence, op'ū-lens, *n. Wealth; riches; affluence.* [L. *opulentia—opes,* wealth.]

Opulent, op'ū-lent, *a. Abounding in wealth; rich; affluent; having a large estate or property.* [L. *opulens, opulentis,* rich—*opes,* wealth.]

Or, or, *conj. A disjunctive particle that marks an alternative, and frequently corresponds with* either. [Sax. *outher.*]

Or, or, *adv.* Ere; before.

Oracle, o'ra-kl, *n.* Among pagans, the answer spoken by a god, or some one personating a god, to an inquiry made respecting some affair of importance; the deity who gave answers to inquiries; the place where the answers were given; the most holy place in the Jewish temple; any person from whom, or any place where, certain decisions are obtained; any person reputed uncommonly wise; a decision of great authority; (pl.) the communications delivered by God to prophets. [Fr.—L. *oro,* to speak.]

Oracular, ō-rak'ū-lér, *a. Uttering oracles;* having the authority of an oracle; positive; grave; ambiguous, like the oracles of pagan deities. [Late L. *oracularius.*]

Oracularly, ō-rak'ū-lér-li, *adv. In the manner of an oracle;* authoritatively; positively.

Oraison†, o'ri-zon, *n.* Verbal supplication; prayer. [Fr.—L. *oro,* to speak.]

Oral, ō'ral, *a. Uttered by the mouth or in words; spoken, not written.* [Fr. *orale*—L. *os, ōris,* the mouth.]

Orally, ō'ral-li, *adv. By mouth; in words,* without writing.

Orange, o'ranj, *n.* The name of a tree, also of its fruit, which is of a flame colour and agreeable flavour.—*a. Pertaining to an orange;* of the colour of an orange. [Fr.—Sans. *ranj,* to colour; *ratta,* red.]

Orangery, o'ranj-e-ri, *n. A place for raising oranges;* a plantation of orange-trees. [Fr. *orangerie.*]

Orang-outang, ō-rang'ō-tang', *n. Man of the woods;* an animal of the ape tribe, which in outward conformation remarkably approaches the human form. [Malay name.]

Oration, ō-ra'shon, *n. A speech or discourse composed according to the rules of oratory, and spoken in public; a discourse pronounced on a special occasion; a harangue.* [L. *oratio—os, oris,* the mouth.]

Orator, o'ra-tér, *n. A speaker;* a public speaker; a person who pronounces a discourse publicly on some special occasion; an eloquent public speaker. [Fr. *orator.*]

Oratorical, o-ra-to'rik-al, *a. Pertaining to an orator or to oratory;* rhetorical.

Oratorically, o-ra-to'rik-al-li, *adv. In a rhetorical manner.*

Oratorio, o-ra-tō'ri-ō, *n. A sacred musical composition, consisting of airs, recitatives, duets, trios, &c., the subject of which is generally taken from the Scriptures.* [It.]

Oratory, o'ra-tō-ri, *n. A house of prayer;* a small chapel or place allotted for prayer, used by Roman Catholics; the art of speaking according to the rules of rhetoric, in order to persuade; exercise of eloquence. [Fr. *oratoire;* L. *os, ōris,* the mouth.]

Orb, orb, *n. A circle;* a sphere; a wheel; a circular body that revolves or rolls; an orbit; the eye; a fairy ring; a period of time marked off by the revolution of a heavenly body.—*vt.* To form into an orb. [Fr. *orbe*—L. *orbis.*]

Orbed, orbd, *p.a. Round;* rounded or covered on the exterior.

Orbicular, or-bik'ū-lér, *a. In the form of an orb;* circular; spherical. [Fr. *orbiculaire*—L. *orbis,* an orb.]

Orbit, or'bit, *n. The track of a chariot wheel;* a path; a circuit; the path described by a heavenly body in its periodical revolution; the cavity in which the eye is situated. [L. *orbita—orbis,* an orb.]

Orbital, or'bit-al, *a. Pertaining to an orbit,* or to the orbit of the eye.

Orchard, or'chérd, *n. Originally, a yard for pot herbs;* an inclosure or assemblage of fruit-trees, especially of apple-trees. [Sax.—Old Sax. *wurt,* kitchen herbs, and *yeard,* a garden.]

Orchestra, or'kes-tra, *n.* That part of the Greek theatre in which the chorus danced; that part of a theatre appropriated to the musicians; the body of performers in the orchestra. [Gr. *orchestra—orchsomai,* to dance—*orches,* a row of fruit-trees.]

Orchestral, or-kes'tral, *a. Pertaining to an orchestra;* suitable for or performed in the orchestra.

Ordain, or-dān', *vt. To set in order; to regulate;* to establish in a particular office or order; to invest with sacerdotal power; to decree; to set; to establish; to set apart for an office. [L. *ordino—ordo,* a straight row.]

Ordained, or-dānd', *p.a. Invested with pastoral functions;* settled.

Ordainer, or-dān'er, *n. One who or-*

dains or invests with sacerdotal powers.
Ordeal, or'dē-al, n. *A parting or dealing out of justice;* a form of trial among the ancient rude nations of Europe, to determine guilt or innocence, by fire or water; severe trial; accurate scrutiny. [Sax. *ordæl*—Old G. *ar*, out of, and *tailjan*, to divide.]
Order, or'dėr, n. *A regular series;* regular disposition; proper state; adherence to the point in discussion; established mode of proceeding; mandate; rule; regulation; necessary measures or care; rank; class; a religious fraternity; division of natural objects; a system of several proportions of columns and pilasters, in architecture; (pl.) according to the Episcopal Church, the Christian ministry, *holy* being usually prefixed.—*vt.* *To set or place in order;* to methodize; to reduce to system; to lead; to conduct; to direct; to manage; to ordain; to dispose in any particular manner. [Fr. *ordre*—L. *ordo*, a straight row.]
Ordering, or'dėr-ing, *p.n.* Disposition; distribution; management.
Orderless, or'dėr-les, *a.* Without order.
Orderliness, or'dėr-li-nes, n. State of being orderly; regularity.
Orderly, or'dėr-li, a. *Having order;* methodical; systematic; observant of order or method; not unruly; peaceable; being on duty.—n. A private soldier or non-commissioned officer, who attends on a superior officer. —*adv.* Methodically; according to due order.
Ordinal, or'din-al, a. *Noting order of succession.*—n. *A number noting order;* a book containing the ordination service, as prescribed in the English Church. [Fr.]
Ordinance, or'din-ans, n. *An ordaining by authority;* that which is ordained; a rule established by authority; observance commanded; a statute; established rite; same as ordnance†. [It. *ordinanza*—L. *ordo*, *ordinis*, a straight row.]
Ordinarily, or'din-a-ri-li, *adv.* According to established rules; commonly; customarily.
Ordinary, or'din-a-ri, a. *Pertaining to order;* according to established order; methodical; usual; of common rank; plain; inferior; of little merit.—n. An officer who keeps *order;* an ecclesiastical judge, properly the bishop of the district; a judge who has authority to take cognizance of causes in his own right; a place of eating where the prices are settled. [Fr. *ordinaire.*]
Ordinate, or'din-āt, *a.* Regular; methodical.—n. *A straight line* drawn from any point in a curve, perpendicularly to another straight line which is called the abscissa. [It. *ordinato*—L. *ordo*, a straight line.]
Ordinately, or'din-āt-li, *adv.* In the manner of an ordinate.
Ordination, or-din-ā'shon, n. *Act of ordaining;* state of being ordained; established order; act of conferring holy orders, in the Church of England; consecration; act of settling a licensed clergyman over a church and congregation, in the Presbyterian Church. [Fr.—L. *ordinatio.*]
Ordnance, ord'nans, n. Cannon or great guns; artillery. [from *ordinances.*]
Ordure, or'dūr, n. *Dung;* excrements; nastiness; filthiness. [Fr.—L. *sordes*, filth.]
Ore, ōr, n. A mineral body or substance from which *metal* is extracted; the compound of a metal and some other substance; metal. [Sax.—L. *œs*, *œris*, brass.]
Organ, or'gan, n. *An instrument by which anything is made or moved;* a natural instrument of action; the instrument or means of conveyance; the largest and most harmonious of wind-instruments of music. [Gr. *organon*, from *ergō*, to do work—Sans. *arj*, to do.]
Organic, or-gan'ik, a. *Pertaining to organs;* consisting of organs; produced by or affecting the organs; instrumental; acting as instruments of nature or art to a certain end. [Fr. *organique.*]
Organically, or-gan'ik-al-li, *adv.* With organs; by means of organs.
Organism, or'gan-izm, n. *Organical structure;* an organized being.
Organist, or'gan-ist, n. *One who plays on the organ.*
Organisable, or'gan-iz-a-bl, a. That may be organised.
Organization, or'gan-iz-ā"shon, n. *Act or process of organising;* act of arranging the parts of a compound body in a manner for use; act of distributing into divisions, and appointing officers, as an army or a government; structure; form; suitable disposition of parts which are to act together in a compound body.
Organize, or'gan-iz, *vt.* *To form with suitable organs;* to construct so that one part may co-operate with another; to distribute into suitable parts, and appoint proper officers over, that the whole may act as one body. *ppr.* organizing, *pret. & pp.* organized. [Fr. *organiser.*]
Organized, or'gan-izd, *p.a.* Formed with organs; reduced to system.
Orgies, or'jēs, n. pl. *Frantic* nocturnal revels at the feast in honour of Bacchus, or the feast itself; drunken revelry, chiefly by night. [Fr.—Gr. *orgē*, any violent passion.]
Orgillous†, or'jil-us, *a. Proud;* haughty. [Fr. *orgueilleux.*]
Oriel, ō'ri-el, n. *A large bay or recessed window* in a hall, chapel, &c., usually projected from the outer face of the wall. [Old Fr. *oriol*, a portico—L. *os*, *oris*, a mouth, entrance.]
Orient, ō'ri-ent, *a. Rising or lightening,* as the sun; eastern; oriental; bright; glittering.—n. The part of the horizon where the sun *rises;* the east. [L. *oriens—orior*, to rise.]
Oriental, o-ri-ent'al, a. *Eastern;* situated in the east, particularly in or about Asia; proceeding from the east. n. A native of some *eastern* part of the world, particularly an Asiatic. [Low L. *orientalis.*]
Orientalism, o-ri-ent'al-izm, n. A term applied to doctrines or idioms of the Asiatic nations.
Orientalist, o-ri-ent'al-ist, n. *An inhabitant of the eastern parts* of the world; one versed in the eastern languages and literature.
Orifice, o'ri-fis, n. *Something made in the form of a mouth;* the mouth of a tube, pipe, or other cavity; an opening. [Fr.—L. *os*, *oris*, the mouth, and *facio*, to make.]
Origin, o'ri-jin, n. *Rise;* spring; that from which anything primarily proceeds; cause; root; foundation. [Fr. *origine*—L. *orior*, to rise.]
Original, ō-ri'jin-al, *a. A Primitive;* first in order; having the power to originate new thoughts or combinations of thought.—n. *Origin;* source; model; that from which anything is transcribed, or from which a likeness is made by the pencil, press, or otherwise; the precise language employed by a writer. [Fr. *originel.*]
Originality, ō-ri'jin-al"li-ti, n. *Quality or state of being original.* [Fr. *originalité.*]
Originally, ō-ri'jin-al-li, *adv.* Primarily.
Originate, ō-ri'jin-āt, *vt. To give origin to;* to bring into existence.—*vi. To have origin;* to take first existence. *ppr.* originating, *pret. & pp.* originated. [It. *originare.*]
Origination, ō-ri'jin-ā"shon, n. *Act of originating;* first production; mode of production. [L. *originatio.*]
Originator, ō-ri'jin-āt-ėr, n. *A person who originates* or commences. [Low L.]
Orion, ō-ri'on, n. A large and bright constellation on both sides of the equinoctial. [L. from Gr.]
Orison, o'ri-zon, n. *A prayer or supplication.* [Fr. *oraison*—L. *os*, *oris*, the mouth.]
Orlop, or'lop, n. *That which runs or spreads over;* the lower deck of a ship of the line; or that, in all vessels, on which the cables are stowed. [D. *overloop*—*loopen*, to run.]
Ormolu, or'mō-lū, n. *Ground gold;* brass which, by a chemical process, is made to assume the appearance of being gilt. It is used in making lamps, &c. [Fr. *or-moulu—or*, gold, and *moulu*, ground—L. *molo*, to grind.]
Ornament, or'na-ment, n. *That which adorns or embellishes;* embellishment; decoration; additional beauty.—*vt. To decorate with ornaments;* to embellish; to make beautiful; to furnish with embellishments. [Fr. *ornement*—L. *orno*, *ornatus*, to adorn.]
Ornamental, or-na-ment'al, a. *Serving to ornament;* giving additional beauty.
Ornamentally, or-na-ment'al-li, *adv.* In such a manner as to add embellishment.
Ornamented, or'na-ment-ed, *p.a.* Embellished with ornaments; decorated; adorned.
Ornate, or'nāt, *a. Adorned;* decorated; beautiful. [L. *ornatus—orno*, to adorn.]
Ornately, or'nāt-li, *adv. With ornament;* with decoration.
Ornithological, or'ni-tho-loj"ik-al, a. *Pertaining to ornithology.*
Ornithologist, or-ni-thol'o-jist, n. *A person who is skilled in ornithology.* [Fr. *ornithologiste.*]
Ornithology, or-ni-thol'o-ji, n. *A treatise on birds;* the science of birds, which comprises a knowledge of their form, structure, habits, and uses. [Fr. *ornithologie*—Gr. *ornis*, *ornithos*, a bird, and *logos*, discourse.]
Orphan, or'fan, n. *A child who is bereaved of father or mother, or of both.*—*a.* Bereaved of parents.—*vt. To reduce to the state of an orphan.* [Fr. *orphelin*—L. *orbus*, bereaved.]
Orphanage, or'fan-āj, n. *The state of an orphan.*
Orphaned, or'fand, *p.a.* Bereft of parents or friends.
Orpiment, or'pi-ment, n. *Gold-coloured pigment;* a preparation of arsenic and sulphur used as a yellow pigment. [Low L. *auripigmentum—L. aurum,* gold, and *pingo*, to paint.]
Orrery, o're-ri, n. *An astronomical machine for exhibiting the several motions, relative magnitudes, and distances of the bodies composing the solar system.* [named in honour of the Earl of Orrery.]

Ort†, ort, n. A fragment; refuse (commonly used in the pl.) [Low G.]
Orthodox, or'thō-doks, a. Having or holding *a right doctrine*; sound in the Christian faith; believing the genuine doctrines taught in the Scriptures; according with the doctrines of Scripture. [Fr. *orthodoxe*.]
Orthodoxy, or'thō-doks-i, n. *Right doctrine or belief*; soundness in the Christian faith; consonance to genuine scriptural doctrines. [Gr. *orthodoxia—orthos*, right, and *doxa*, opinion.]
Orthoepic, or-thō-ep'ik, a. *Pertaining to orthoepy*.
Orthoepist, or'thō-ep-ist, n. *One who is versed in orthoepy*; one who pronounces words correctly.
Orthoepy, or-thō-e-pi, n. *Right pronunciation*; a correct pronunciation of words. [Gr. *orthoepeia—orthos*, right, and *epos*, a word.]
Orthographer, or-thog'ra-fėr, n. *One versed in orthography*; one who spells words correctly.
Orthographic, or-thō-graf'ik, a. *Pertaining to orthography*; correctly spelled.
Orthographically, or-thō-graf'ik-al-li, adv. According to the rules of proper spelling.
Orthography, or-thog'ra-fi, n. *The art of writing words correctly*, or with the proper letters, according to common usage; the part of grammar which treats of the nature and properties of letters, and the just method of spelling words; the practice of spelling or writing words with the proper letters. [Gr. *orthographia—orthos*, right, and *grapho*, to write.]
Ortolan, or'tō-lan, n. A bird that frequents the hedges of *gardens*. It belongs to the south of Europe, is about the size of a lark, and esteemed a great delicacy by the luxurious. [Fr.—L. *hortus*, a garden.]
Oscillate, os'sil-lāt, vi. *To swing one's self*; to move to and fro, or backwards and forwards; to swing; to vibrate, as a pendulum. ppr. oscillating, pret. & pp. oscillated. [L. *oscillo, oscillatum*, to swing—*ob*, and obsol. *cillo*, to move.]
Oscillation, os-sil-lā'shon, n. A moving *backward and forward*, or *swinging* like a pendulum; vibration. [Fr.]
Oscillatory, os'sil-la-tō-ri, a. *Moving backward and forward* like a pendulum; swinging; vibrating. [Fr. *oscillatoire*.]
Osier, ō'zhi-ėr, n. *A kind of water-willow*; a twig of such willow.—a. Made of or like osiers. [Fr.; Gr. *oisos*, a kind of osier.]
Osiered, ō'shi-ėrd, p.a. *Covered or adorned with osiers*.
Osmium, oz'mi-um, n. *A metal contained in the ore of platinum, whose oxide has a peculiar and pungent smell*. [Gr. *osmē*, smell.]
Osprey, os'prā, n. *The ossifrage*. [a corruption of L. *ossifraga*.]
Osseous, os'sē-us, a. *Bony*; composed of bone; resembling bone. [L. *osseus*.]
Ossification, os'si-fi-kā'shon, n. *The formation of bone in animals*; the change or process of changing from flesh or other matter of animal bodies into a bony substance. [Fr.]
Ossifrage, os'si-frāj, n. The sea-eagle or osprey, *which breaks the bones of its prey*. [L. *ossifraga—os, ossis*, a bone, and *frango*, to break.]
Ossify, os'si-fi, vt. *To convert into bone*; to change from a soft animal substance into bone.—vi. To change from soft matter into a substance of bony hardness. ppr. ossifying, pret. & pp. ossified. [L. *os*, a bone, and *facio*, to make.]
Ostensibility, os-ten'si-bil'li-ti, n. *Quality or state of being ostensible*.
Ostensible, os-ten'si-bl, a. *That may be stretched or spread out before one*; proper or intended to be shown; colourable; seeming; shown, declared, or avowed. [Fr.—L. *ob*, and *tendo, tensum*, to stretch.]
Ostensibly, os-ten'si-bli, adv. *In an ostensible manner*.
Ostent†, os-tent', n. Appearance; manner; show.
Ostentation, os-ten-tā'shon, n. *A presenting to view*; a showing; outward show or appearance; ambitious display; parade; vaunting; a show or spectacle†. [L. *ostentatio*.]
Ostentatious, os-ten-tā'shi-us, a. *Fond of ostentation*; fond of presenting one's endowments or works to another in an advantageous light; pompous; showy; gaudy.
Ostentatiously, os-ten-tā'shi-us-li, adv. With vain display; boastfully.
Ostracism, os'tra-sizm, n. A mode of banishment at Athens, in ancient Greece, consisting in writing on *a shell* the name of the person to be banished; banishment; separation. [Fr. *ostracisme*—Gr. *ostrakon*, a shell.]
Ostracise, os'tra-siz, vt. To banish by means of *ostracism*; to exile. ppr. ostracizing, pret. & pp. ostracized. [Gr. *ostrakisō—ostrakon*, a shell.]
Ostrich, os'trich, n. *The camel-sparrow*, so called from its camel-like neck; a swift running bird, with short wings and a long neck. [Fr. *autruche*—Gr. *strouthos*, a sparrow, and *kamēlos*, a camel.]
Other, uʜʜ'ėr, a. Not the same; different; not this, but the other; noting something besides; correlative to each. [Sax.—L. *alter*.]
Otherwise, uʜʜ'ėr-wīz, adv. In a different manner or way; by other causes; in other respects.
Otiose, ō'shi-ōs, a. *Being at leisure*; idle; unemployed; being at rest or ease. [L. *otiosus—otium*, leisure.]
Otter, ot'tėr, n. An *aquatic* animal somewhat resembling the weasel, but larger, and hunted for the sake of its fur. [Sax.; Icel. *otr*—Sans. *und*, to be wet.]
Ottoman, ot'tō-man, n. A sort of thick stuffed mat used in Turkey; a stool with a stuffed seat. [a name of the Turkish empire, from *Othman*, the founder.]
Ottomite, ot'tō-mit, n. An Ottoman or Turk.
Ouch, ouch, n. A socket in which a precious stone is set; an ornament of gold. [Norm. *ouche d'or*, an ouch of gold.]
Ought, at, n. *See* Aught.
Ought, at, v. (preterite and pp. of *owe*, and used likewise in the present tense, as a verb formed upon them.) *See* Owe.
Ounce, ouns, n. *The twelfth part of anything*; an ounce weight, the twelfth part of a pound troy, and the sixteenth of a pound avoirdupois. [Fr. *once*—L. *uncia*.]
Ouphe†, ōf, n. A fairy; an elf.
Ouphen†, ōf'en, a. Elfish.
Our, our, pron. a. *Pertaining or belonging to us*. (Ours, Sax. *ures*, is never used as an adjective, but as a substitute for the adjective and the noun to which it belongs; as, your house is on a plain; ours is on a hill. [Sax. *ure*.]
Ourself, our-self, pron. *reciprocal*. This is added after *we* and *us*, and sometimes is used without either for *myself*, in the regal style only; as, ourself will follow.
Ourselves, our-selvz', pron. *reciprocal*, pl. of *ourself*. We or us, not others; added to we, by way of emphasis or opposition.
Ousel, ö'zl, n. A name common to several species of birds of the thrush family; a blackbird. [Sax. *osle*.]
Oust, oust, vt. *To take away*; to remove; to eject; to expel. [Old Fr. *oster*—L. *haurio, haustum*, to draw out.]
Out, out, adv. *Not downwards*; not within; without; on the exterior; abroad; forth; in a state of disclosure; in a state of extinction; completely; in a state of destitution; not in office; to the end; loudly; in an error; at a loss; in a puzzle; away, so as to consume; noting motion from within; motion beyond; separation.—vt. *To put out*; to eject; to deprive by expulsion. interj. Away! begone! expressive also of abhorrence or contempt. [Sax. *ut*.]
Out-balance, out-bal'ans, vt. *To outweigh*; to exceed in weight or effect.
Outbid, out-bid', vt. *To bid beyond*; to bid more than. ppr. outbidding, pret outbade, pp. outbidden, outbid.
Outbrave, out-brāv', vt. *To excel in bravery*; to defy. ppr. outbraving, pret. & pp. outbraved.
Outbreak, out'brāk, n. *A breaking or bursting forth*; eruption; outburst.
Outbreaking, out'brāk-ing, p.n. *That which bursts forth*.
Outbreathe, out-brēʜʜ', vt. To weary by having *better breath*.
Outburst, out'bėrst, n. *A bursting or breaking out*. [out and *burst*.]
Outcast, out'kast, p.a. *Cast out*; thrown away; rejected as useless.—n. *One who is cast out*; an exile; one driven from home or country.
Outcraft†, out-kraft', vt. To exceed in cunning.
Outcry, out'kri, n. A vehement or loud cry; cry of distress; clamour.
Outdo, out-dö', vt. *To exceed in doing*; to surpass. ppr. outdoing, pret. outdid, pp. outdone.
Outdoor, out'dōr, a. *Being without the door or house*; in the open air.
Outdoors, out'dōrs, adv. Abroad; out of the house; in the open air.
Outer, out'ėr, a. *Being farther out*; exterior; external; opposed to inner. [comp. of *out*.]
Outermost, out'ėr-mōst, a. *Being farthest out*; being on the extreme external part. [superl. from *outer*.]
Outfit, out'fit, n. *A fitting out*, as of a ship for a voyage; the equipment of any one who goes out from home; money furnished for this purpose; (usually in the plural, *outfits*), the expenses incurred or the articles employed in furnishing a ship for a voyage.
Outfitter, out'fit-ėr, n. *One who fits out*, or makes an outfit.
Outfitting, out'fit-ing, p.n. *A fitting out*; equipment for a voyage.
Outflank, out-flangk', vt. *To extend, as the flank of one army beyond that of* another.
Outgeneral, out-jen'ė-ral, vt. *To exceed in generalship*; to gain advantage over by superior military skill.
Outgoing, out-gō'ing, p.n. *Act of going out*; state of going out; expenditure.
Outgrow, out-grō', vt. *To surpass in growth*; to grow too great or too old

Fāte, făr, fat, fall; mē, met, hėr; pīne, pin; nōte, not, mōve; tūbe, tub, bull; oil, pound.

for. ppr. outgrowing, pret. outgrew, pp. outgrown.
Outland, out'land, n. *Exterior land;* land lying beyond a demesne.
Outlandish, out-land'ish, a. *Belonging to a foreign land;* not native; vulgar; rustic; clownish. [Sax. *utlandisc.*]
Outlast, out-last', vt. *To last longer than;* to exceed in duration.
Outlaw, out'la, n. *One put out of the law,* or excluded from the benefit of the law, or deprived of its protection. [Sax. *utlaga.*]—vt. *To put out of the law;* to deprive of the benefit and protection of law; to proscribe. [Sax. *utlagian—lagu,* a law.]
Outlawry, out'la-ri, n. *The putting a man out of the law,* or the rotection of law, or the process by which a man is deprived of that protection.
Outlay, out'lā, n. *A laying out or expending;* expenditure.
Outlet, out'let, n. *Passage outward;* the place or the means by which anything escapes or is discharged.
Outline, out'lin, n. *The lines by which a figure is defined;* contour; the first draught of a figure; first general sketch of any scheme or design.—vt. *To draw the exterior lines of;* to sket h. ppr. outlining, pret. & pp. outlined.
Outlive, out-liv', vt. *To live beyond;* to survive; to live after. ppr. outliving, pret. & pp. outlived.
Outlook, out-lụk', vt. To face down.
Outlook, out'lụk, n. *A looking out;* vigilant watch; foresight; a look-out.
Outlying, out'lī-ing, p.a. *Lying out or on the exterior;* lying or being at a distance from the main body or design; being on the frontier.
Outmost, out'mōst, a. *Furthest outward;* outermost.
Outnumber, out-num'bėr, vt. *To exceed in number.*
Outpost, out'pōst, n. *A post or station without the limits of a camp;* the troops placed at such a station.
Outpour, out-pōr', vt. *To pour out.*
Outpouring, out'pōr-ing, p.n. *A pouring out;* effusion.
Outprize, out - prīz', vt. To exceed in value.
Outrage, out'rāj, vt. *To treat with extreme violence and wrong;* to abuse by rude or insolent language; to injure by rough rude treatment of any kind. ppr. outraging, pret. & pp. outraged. n. *Excessive* abuse or injury done to a person or thing; wanton mischief. [Old Fr. *outrage*—L. *ultra,* beyond, and *ago, agère,* to act.]
Outraged, out'rājd, p.a. *Treated with extreme violence or wrong.*
Outrageous, out-rā'jē-us, a. *Excessive;* exceeding reason or decency; violent; furious; exorbitant; turbulent. [Fr. *outrageux.*]
Outrageously, out-rā'je-us-li, adv. *With great violence;* furiously; excessively.
Outrageousness, out-rā'jē-us-nes, n. *Quality of being outrageous;* fury.
Outrider, out'rid-ėr, n. *A servant on horseback,* who attends a carriage.
Outright, out - rīt', adv. *Right out;* directly; without delay; at once; entirely.
Outrun, out-run', vt. *To leave behind in running;* to exceed, as one's income. ppr. outrunning, pret. outran, pp. outrun.
Outset, out'set, n. *A setting out;* beginning; first entrance on any business.
Outside, out'sīd, n. *The side of a thing that is outermost;* the exterior; the part which forms the surface or super-

ficial appearance; person; the part that lies beyond an inclosure; the utmost.—a. *On the outside;* exterior; consisting in show.
Outskirt, out'skėrt, n. *External skirt;* border; outpost; suburb.
Outspeak, out-spēk', vt. *To speak more or louder than.*
Outspread, out - spred', vt. *To spread out or over;* to extend; to diffuse. ppr. outspreading, pret. & pp. outspread. p.a. Extended; expanded.
Outspreading, out'spred-ing, p.n. *Act of spreading out,* over, or of diffusing.
Outstanding, out-stand'ing, p.a. *Standing out;* remaining unpaid; not collected.
Outstretch, out-strech', vt. *To stretch or spread out;* to extend, to expand.
Outstretched, out - strecht', p. a. Extended; spread out.
Outstrip, out-strip', vt. *To outgo;* to outrun; to advance beyond. ppr. outstripping, pret. & pp. outstripped.
Outvie, out-vī', vt. *To exceed in vying with* or in rivalry; to exceed; to surpass. ppr. outvying, pret. & pp. outvied.
Outvote, out-vōt', vt. *To exceed in the number of votes given;* to defeat by plurality of suffrages. ppr. outvoting, pret. & pp. outvoted.
Outward, out'wėrd, a. *Tending to the outer part;* external; outer; opposed to inward; extrinsic.—adv. *Toward the outer parts;* from a port or country. [Sax. *utweard.*]
Outward-bound, out'werd-bound, a. *Proceeding from a port or country.*
Outwardly, out'wėrd-li, adv. *In an outward manner;* externally.
Outwards, out'wėrdz, adv. Same as *outward.*
Outweigh, out-wā', vt. *To exceed in weight;* to overbalance.
Outwit, out-wit', vt. *To surpass in wit;* to surpass in design or stratagem; to overreach; to defeat by superior ingenuity. ppr. outwitting, pret. & pp. outwitted.
Outwork, out'wėrk, n. *An exterior work;* any work of a fortress situated without the principal wall, within or beyond the principal ditch.
Oval, ō'val, a. *Of the figure of an egg;* oblong and curvilinear, with both ends of the same breadth; elliptical.—n. *A body* or figure in the shape of an egg, or of an ellipse. (Fr. *ovale*—L. *ovum,* Gr. *ōon,* an egg.]
Ovary, ō'va-ri, n. *The part of a female animal in which the eggs are formed* or lodged; a hollow case in plants, inclosing the young seeds. [Fr. *ovaire*—L. *ovum,* an egg.]
Ovation, ō-vā'shon, n. *A lesser sort of triumph among the ancient Romans,* in which *sheep* were sacrificed instead of bullocks; an expression of popular homage. [L. *ovatio*—*ovis,* a sheep.]
Oven, uv'n, n. *A furnace;* an apparatus for baking or drying. [Sax. *ofen;* Icel. *ofn.*]
Over, ō'vėr, prep. Across; from side to side; above, in place; opposed to below; above, denoting superiority in value; above in authority, implying the right of governing; opposed to under; upon the surface; through the whole extent; upon; throughout; during the whole time; above the top; immersing.—adv. From side to side; as, a board a foot over; from one country to another by passing; on the surface; above the top; more than the quantity assigned; to excess; from be-

ginning to end; completely.—a. Past; upper; covering. [Sax. *ofer;* Old G. *ubar.*]
Overact, ō-vėr-akt', vt. *To act or perform to excess.*—vi. *To act more than is necessary.*
Overarch, ō-vėr-ärch', vt. *To arch over.*
Overawe, ō-vėr-ạ', vt. *To restrain by awe* or fear. ppr. overawing, pret. & pp. overawed.
Overbalance, ō-vėr-bal'ans, vt. *To do more than balance;* to weigh down; to exceed in weight, value, or importance. ppr. overbalancing, pret. & pp. overbalanced.
Overbear, ō-vėr-bār', vt. *To bear over;* to bear down; to overpower; to whelm; to conquer; to repress; to suppress. ppr. overbearing, pret. overbore, pp. overborne.
Overbearing, ō - vėr - bār ' ing, p. a. Haughty and dogmatical; imperious; tyrannical.
Overboard, ō'vėr - bōrd, adv. *Over the board* or deck; out of a ship or from on board.
Overbulk†, ō-vėr-bulk', vt. *To oppress by bulk.*
Overburden, ō-vėr-bėr'dn, vt. *To burden* or load *too much.*
Overcast, ō - vėr - kast', vt. *To cast or spread over;* to darken; to cover with gloom; to overthrow. ppr. overcasting, pret. & pp. overcast.—p.a. Clouded; overspread with clouds or gloom.
Overcharge, ō-vėr-chärj', vt. *To charge or load to excess;* to fill to excess; to load with too great a charge, as a gun; to charge too much; to enter in an account more than is just; ppr. overcharging, pret. & pp. overcharged.—n. *An excessive burden;* a charge in an account of more than is just; an excessive charge, as of a gun.
Overcloud, ō-vėr-kloud', vt. *To cover or overspread with clouds.*
Overcoat, ō'vėr-kōt, n. *An upper coat,* a topcoat; a greatcoat.
Overcome, ō-vėr-kum', vt. *To come over or upon;* to be victorious over, as foes; to overpower; to subdue; to surmount; to get the better of, as embarrassment. vi. *To gain the superiority;* to be victorious. ppr. overcoming, pret. overcame, pp. overcome.
Overdo, ō-vėr-dö', vt. *To do too much;* to boil, bake, or roast too much.—vi. *To do too much;* to labour too hard. ppr. overdoing, pret. overdid, pp. overdone.
Overdraw, ō-vėr-dra', vt. *To draw beyond* one's credit or funds; as, to overdraw one's account at a bank; to paint too highly. ppr. overdrawing, pret. overdrew, pp. overdrawn.
Overdrive, ō-vėr-drīv', vt. *To drive too hard,* or beyond strength. ppr. overdriving, pret. overdrove or overdrave, pp. overdriven.
Overdue, ō'vėr-dū, a. *Due beyond the proper time;* past the time of payment, as a bill of exchange.
Oversee, ō-vėr-ī', vt. *To inspect;* to observe.
Overflow, ō-vėr-flō', vt. *To flow over,* as water; to flood; to fill beyond the brim; to deluge; to overwhelm; to cover, as with numbers.—vi. *To flow or run over;* to be abundant. ppr. overflowing, pret. overflowed, pp. overflown.
Overflow, ō'vėr-flō, n. *An inundation;* superabundance.
Overflowing, ō-vėr-flō'ing, p.a. Abundant; copious; exuberant.—p.n. Exuberance; copiousness.
Overgrow, ō-vėr-grō', vt. *To grow beyond;*

ch, *chain;* j, *job;* g, *go;* ng, *sing;* ᴛʜ, *then;* th, *thin;* w, *wig;* wh, *whig;* zh, *azure;* † obsolete.

to rise above; to cover with growth or herbage.—*vi.* To grow beyond the natural size; to increase to an excess. *ppr.* overgrowing, *pret.* overgrew, *pp.* overgrown.
Overgrown, ō-vėr-grōn', *p. a.* Grown beyond the natural size.
Overgrowth, ō'vėr-grōth, *n.* Exuberant or excessive growth.
Overhang, ō-vėr-hang', *vt.* To hang or impend over; to jut or project over. *vi.* To hang or jut over. *ppr.* overhanging, *pret. & pp.* overhung.
Overhaul, ō'vėr-hal, *n.* Examination; inspection; repair.
Overhaul, ō-vėr-hal', *vt.* To haul or draw over, for examination; to examine again, as one's accounts; to gain upon in a chase.
Overhead, ō-vėr-hed', *adv.* Above the head; aloft; above.
Overhear, ō-vėr-hėr', *vt.* To hear over; to hear by accident.
Overheated, ō-vėr-hēt'ed, *p.a.* Heated to excess.
Overjoy, ō-vėr-joi', *vt.* To give excessive joy to; to transport with gladness.
Overjoy, ō'vėr-joi, *n.* Joy to excess; transport.
Overland, ō'vėr-land, *a.* Passing over or by land; as, an overland journey.
Overlay, ō-vėr-lā', *vt.* To lay too much upon; to smother with close covering; to overwhelm; to overcast; to join two opposite sides by a cover. *ppr.* overlaying, *pret. & pp.* overlaid.
Overlaying, ō'vėr-lā-ing, *p.n.* A laying or spreading over.
Overleap, ō-vėr-lēp', *vt.* To leap over.
Overleather, ō'vėr-leᴛн-ėr, *n.* The leather which forms the upper part of a shoe; that which is upon the foot.
Overleaven, ō-vėr-lev'n, *vt.* To mix too much with; to corrupt.
Overload, ō-vėr-lōd', *vt.* To load too much, or with too heavy a burden or cargo; to fill to excess; to overburden.
Overlook, ō-vėr-luk', *vt.* To look over; to oversee; to superintend; to view from a higher place; to stand in a more elevated place, or to rise so high as to afford the means of looking down on; to see from behind or over the shoulder of another; to see from a higher position; to examine a second time or with care; to pass by indulgently; to slight; to bewitch.
Overly, ō'vėr-li, *adv.* In a careless manner.
Overlying, ō-vėr-lī'ing, *p.a.* Lying over or upon something.
Overmaster, ō-vėr-mas'tėr, *vt.* To gain the mastery over; to vanquish; to conquer.
Overmatch, ō-vėr-mach', *vt.* To be more than a match for; to subdue; to oppress by superior force.
Overmatch, ō'vėr-mach, *n.* One superior in power; one able to overcome.
Overmuch, ō'vėr-much, *a.* Too much. *adv.* In too great a degree.
Overname, ō-vėr-nām', *vt.* To name over, or in a series.
Overnight, ō'vėr-nīt, *n.* The previous evening.—*adv.* Through the night; in the evening before.
Overoffice, ō-vėr-of'fis, *vt.* To lord it over by virtue of an office.
Overpass, ō-vėr-pas', *vt.* To pass over; to pass without regard; to omit, as in reckoning; not to receive.
Overpay, ō-vėr-pā', *vt.* To pay too much or more than is due. *ppr.* overpaying, *pret. & pp.* overpaid.
Overpeer, ō-vėr-pēr', *vt.* To overlook; to hover over.

Overplus, ō'vėr-plus, *n.* That which is more or greater than; that which is over and above.
Overpost, ō-vėr-pōst', *vt.* To hasten over quickly.
Overpower, ō-vėr-pou'ėr, *vt.* To be too powerful for; to affect with a power that cannot be resisted; to be predominant over; to bear down by force; to reduce to silence in action or submission; to crush.
Overpowering, ō-vėr-pou'ėr-ing, *p.a.* Subduing; bearing down by superior force.
Overrate, ō-vėr-rāt', *vt.* To rate at too much. *ppr.* overrating, *pret. & pp.* overrated.
Overreach, ō-vėr-rēch', *vt.* To reach over or beyond in any direction; to deceive by artifice; to cheat; to overtake.
Overreaching, ō-vėr-rēch'ing, *p. a.* Reaching beyond; cheating.—*p.n.* A reaching too far; act of deceiving.
Overrule, ō-vėr-röl', *vt.* To exercise rule over; to control by predominant power; to govern with high authority; to disallow. *ppr.* overruling, *pret. & pp.* overruled.
Overruling, ō-vėr-röl'ing, *p.a.* Exerting superior and controlling power.
Overrun, ō-vėr-run', *vt.* To run over; to cover all over; to march over; to ravage; to outrun; to overspread with numbers.—*vi.* To overflow; to run over. *ppr.* overrunning, *pret.* overran, *pp.* overrun.
Oversea, ō'vėr-sē, *a.* Beyond sea; transmarine; from beyond sea.
Oversee, ō-vėr-sē', *vt.* To see or look over; to superintend; to inspect, implying care. *ppr.* overseeing, *pret.* oversaw, *pp.* overseen.
Overseer, ō-vėr-sēr', *n.* One who oversees or overlooks; a superintendent.
Overset, ō-vėr-set', *vt.* To set or turn over; to upset; to subvert; to throw off the proper foundation.—*vi.* To turn or be turned over. *ppr.* oversetting, *pret. & pp.* overset.
Overshadow, ō-vėr-sha'dō, *vt.* To throw a shadow over; to cover with protecting influence.
Overshadowing, ō-vėr-sha'dō-ing, *p.a.* Overshading; protecting.
Overshoot, ō-vėr-shöt', *vt.* To shoot beyond, as a mark; to pass swiftly over; (with the reciprocal pronoun) to venture too far.—*vi.* To fly beyond the mark. *ppr.* overshooting, *pret. & pp.* overshot.
Overshot, ō-vėr-shot', *p.a.* Shot beyond; having the water flowing on to the top, as a water-wheel.
Oversight, ō'vėr-sīt, *n.* An overseeing; superintendence; an overlooking, or failing to notice; a mistake; inadvertence.
Oversize, ō-vėr-sīz', *vt.* To cover with viscid matter.
Overskip, ō-vėr-skip', *vi.* To escape.
Overspread, ō-vėr-spred', *vt.* To spread over; to scatter over.—*vi.* To be spread or scattered over. *ppr.* overspreading, *pret. & pp.* overspread.
Overstate, ō-vėr-stāt', *vt.* To state too high, or in too strong terms. *ppr.* overstating, *pret. & pp.* overstated.
Overstep, ō-vėr-step', *vt.* To step over or beyond; to exceed. *ppr.* overstepping, *pret. & pp.* overstepped, overstept.
Overstock, ō-vėr-stok', *vt.* To stock to excess; to crowd.
Overstrain, ō-vėr-strān', *vt.* To strain too much; to stretch beyond the proper limits.—*vi.* To make exertion to excess; to make too violent efforts.

Overstrained, ō-vėr-strānd', *p.a.* Strained to excess.
Overt, ō'vėrt, *a.* Opened to view; manifest; not hidden; public; apparent. [Fr. *ouvert;* L. *aperio, apertus,* to open.]
Overtake, ō-vėr-tāk', *vt.* To come up with and catch in a course or pursuit; to come upon; to fall on afterward; to take by surprise. *ppr.* overtaking, *pret.* overtook, *pp.* overtaken.
Overtask, ō-vėr-task', *vt.* To task too heavily.
Overtax, ō-vėr-taks', *vt.* To tax too heavily.
Overthrow, ō-vėr-thrō', *vt.* To throw over; to thrown down; to ruin; to subvert; to overcome. *ppr.* overthrowing, *pret.* overthrew, *pp.* overthrown.
Overthrow, ō'vėr-thrō, *n.* State of being overturned; defeat; discomfiture; downfall.
Overtly, ō'vėrt-li, *adv.* Openly.
Overtop, ō-vėr-top', *vt.* To rise above the top of; to surpass; to make of less importance by superior excellence. *ppr.* overtopping, *pret. & pp.* overtopped.
Overtrade, ō-vėr-trād', *vt.* To trade to excess or beyond capital. *ppr.* overtrading, *pret. & pp.* overtraded.
Overtrading, ō-vėr-trād'ing, *p.n.* A trading to excess.
Overture, ō'vėr-tūr, *n.* Disclosure; proposal; something offered for consideration, acceptance, or rejection; the instrumental music introductory to an opera. [Fr. *ouverture*—L. *aperio,* to open.]
Overturn, ō-vėr-tėrn', *vt.* To turn over; to subvert; to ruin; to overpower; to conquer.
Overturn, ō'vėr-tėrn, *n.* State of being overturned or subverted; overthrow.
Overvalue, ō-vėr-val'ū, *vt.* To value too highly. *ppr.* overvaluing, *pret. & pp.* overvalued.
Overweening, ō-vėr-wēn'ing, *p.a.* Weening or thinking too highly; that thinks too highly, particularly of one's self; vain.
Overweigh, ō-vėr-wā', *vt.* To exceed in weight; to outweigh; to overbalance.
Overweight, ō'vėr-wāt, *n.* Excess of weight; greater weight; preponderance.
Overwhelm, ō-vėr-whelm', *vt.* To whelm over; to immerge; to submerge; to sink; to overcome; to subdue; to overlook gloomily.
Overwhelming, ō-vėr-hwelm'ing, *p.a.* Crushing with weight or numbers.
Overwise, ō'vėr-wīz, *a.* Wise to affectation.
Over-work, ō'vėr-wėrk, *n.* Excessive work or labour.
Overwork, ō-vėr-wėrk', *vt.* To work to excess or beyond the strength of. *ppr.* overworking, *pret. & pp.* overworked, overwrought.
Overworked, ō-vėr-wėrkt', *p.a.* Worked beyond strength.
Overworn, ō'vėr-wōrn, *p.a.* Worn to excess; worn out; subdued by toil.
Overwrest, ō-vėr-rest', *vt.* To wrest from the natural position.
Overwrought, ō-vėr-rat', *p.a.* Wrought or laboured to excess; worked all over.
Oviform, ō'vi-form, *a.* Having the form or figure of an egg. [L. *ovum,* an egg, and *forma,* form.]
Oviparous, ō-vip'a-rus, *a.* Producing eggs, or young from eggs which are excluded from the body and afterwards hatched. [L. *ovum,* and *pario,* to bring forth.]
Owe, ō, *vt.* To own!; to possess, have, or hold, as what belongs or is due to one.

other; to be indebted to; to be obliged or bound to pay; to be obliged to ascribe to; to be obliged for. *ppr.* owing, *pret. & pp.* owed. [Icel. d, I owe, I am bound, I possess.]

Owing, ō'ing, *p.a.* Due; that moral obligation requires to be paid; ascribable to, as the cause.

Owl, oul, *n.* A bird that howls or hoots by night. [Sax. *ule.*]

Owlet, oul'et, *n.* An owl. [Fr. *hulotte.*]

Owlish, oul'ish, *a. Resembling an owl.*

Own, ōn, *a. Possessed*; belonging to; peculiar; usually expressing property with emphasis.—*vt.* To *possess*; to have the legal or rightful title to; to have the legal right to, without the exclusive right to use; to acknowledge to belong to; to avow; to confess, as a fault, crime, or other act; to acknowledge; to admit to be true. [Sax. *agen,* the *pp.* of *agan,* to own.]

Owner, ōn'ėr, *n. The rightful possessor* or proprietor.

Ownership, ōn'ėr-ship, *n. Exclusive right of possession*; proprietorship; legal or just claim or title.

Ox, oks, *n.* Oxen, oks'en, *pl.* The general name for the different species of animals of the bovine genus; the male of the bovine genus of quadrupeds, castrated, and grown to his size, or nearly so. [Sax. *oxa*—G. *ochs,* ox, bull.]

Ox-eye, oks'ī, *n.* A plant so called from a fancied resemblance in the broad open disk of the flower to the *eye* of an *ox.*

Oxidate, oks'id-āt, *vt. See* OXIDIZE.

Oxidation, oks-id-ā'shon, *n. The operation of converting into an oxide.*

Oxide, oks'id, *n.* A substance combined with *oxygen,* without being in the state of an acid. [Fr.]

Oxidizable, oks'id-īz-a-bl, *a. That may be oxidised.*

Oxidize, oks'id-īz, *vt.* To *convert into an oxide.*—*vi. To change into an oxide. ppr.* oxidizing, *pret. & pp.* oxidized.

Oxidizer, oks'id-īz-ėr, *n. That which oxidises.*

Oxlip, oks'lip, *n.* A plant so called from some resemblance in the flowers to the *lips* of an *ox.*

Oxygen, oks'i-jen, *n. The generator of acids,* but now known not to be the sole cause of acidity; a gaseous element, forming the vital part of atmospheric air, necessary to respiration, and the supporter of ordinary combustion; also the principal component part of water, the other constituent being hydrogen. [Fr. *oxigène*—Gr. *oxus,* sharp, and *gennaō,* to generate.]

Oxygenate, oks'i-jen-āt, *vt.* To *unite or cause to combine with oxygen. ppr.* oxygenating, *pret. & pp.* oxygenated.

Oxygenation, oks'i-jen-ā"shon, *n. The act or process of combining with oxygen.*

Oxytone, oks'i-tōn, *a. Having an acute sound,* or an acute accent on the last syllable.—*n. An acute sound.* [Gr. *oxus,* sharp, acute, and *tonos,* sound.]

Oyer, ō'yėr, *n. A hearing or trial of causes* in law. [Norm.—L. *audio, audire,* to hear.]

Oyes, ō'yes. *Hear ye;* a word used by the sheriff or his substitute in making proclamation in court, requiring silence and attention. It is thrice repeated, and commonly pronounced, O yes! [Norm.]

Oyster, ois'tėr, *n.* A shell-fish much esteemed for food. [L. *ostrea*; Gr. *ostreon*—*ostrakon,* a shell.]

Oyster-bed, ois'tėr-bed, *n.* A *bed* or breeding-place *of oysters.*

Ozone, ō'zōn, *n.* Oxygen in an active state, supposed to be sometimes attended by a peculiar *smell.* [Gr. *ozō,* to smell.]

P.

abulum, pa'bū-lum, *n. Food*; nourishment; aliment; that which feeds; fuel. [L.—*pasco,* to feed.]

Pace, pās, *n. A stretching out* of the foot in walking; a step; the space between the two feet in walking, estimated at 2½ feet; the distance passed over by one foot at a single step, or 5 feet; gait; a mode of stepping among horses, in which the legs on the same side are lifted together; degree of celerity.—*vi.* To advance *step by step*; to walk slowly; to move by lifting the legs on the same side together, as a horse.—*vt.* To measure by steps; to walk over with measured paces or steps; to cause to take measured steps. *ppr.* pacing, *pret. & pp.* paced. [L. *passus — pando,* to spread out.]

Paced, pāst, *p.a.* Having a particular gait; trained in any course, generally in a bad sense.

Pacer, pās'ėr, *n. One who paces*; a horse that paces.

Pacha, pa-shä', *n.* A Turkish viceroy or governor of a province, called a pachalic. [Fr.—Heb. *pecha,* prefect.]

Pachalic, pa-shäl'ik, *n. The jurisdiction of a pacha.* [Fr. *pachalick.*]

Pacific, pa-sif'ik, *a. Peace-making*; suited to make or restore peace; mild; calm; tranquil.—*n.* The name given to the ocean situated between America on the east and Asia, so called on account of its exemption from violent tempests. [Fr. *pacifique*—L. *pax, pacis,* peace, and *facio,* to make.]

Pacifically, pa-sif'ik-al-li, *adv. In a pacific manner.*

Pacification, pa'si-fi-kā"shon, *n. Act of making peace* between nations at variance; act of appeasing; reconciliation. [Fr.]

Pacificator, pa-sif'i-kāt-ėr, *n. A peacemaker*; one who restores amity between contending parties or nations. [L.]

Pacifier, pa'si-fī-ėr, *n. One who pacifies.*

Pacify, pa'si-fī, *vt.* To give or restore *peace* to; to conciliate; to appease, as wrath or appetite; to calm; to still; to allay, as excitement. *ppr.* pacifying, *pret. & pp.* pacified. [Fr. *pacifier* —L. *pax, pacis,* peace, and *facio,* to make.]

Pack, pak, *vt.* To *place and press together*; to put together and bind fast; to put in close order with salt intermixed, as pork; to send off in haste; to put together, as cards, in such a manner as to secure the game; to unite iniquitously, as persons, with a view to some private interest.—*vi.* To be pressed or to be close; to shut; to depart in haste (with *off*); to unite in bad measures; to join in collusion. [D. *pakken*; Icel. *packi,* a package.] *n.* A bundle of anything inclosed in a cover or bound fast with cords; a bale; the number of cards used in games; a number of hounds or dogs, hunting or kept together; a number of persons united in a bad design or practice. [D. *pak.*]

Package, pak'āj, *n. A bundle* or bale; a quantity bound together; charge made for packing goods.

Packed, pakt, *p.a.* United iniquitously.

Packer, pak'ėr, *n. One who packs*; one who prepares merchandise for transit.

Packet, pak'et, *n. A small pack* or package; a ship employed by government to convey parcels of letters from country to country.—*vt. To bind up in a packet,* or in a parcel or parcels. [Fr. *paquet.*]

Pack-horse, pak'hors, *n. A horse* employed in *carrying packs.*

Packing, pak'ing, *p.n.* Act of placing together in close order; the act of binding in a bundle; any material used in packing or stuffing, or making close; (pl.) intrigues.

Pack-man, pak'man, *n. One who carries a pack* on his back; a peddler.

Pack-saddle, pak'sad-l, *n.* The *saddle* of a *pack*-horse.

Pact, pakt, *n. Something fixed; an agreement or covenant.* [L. *pactum*—*paciscor,* to fix, settle.]

Paction, pak'shon, *n. A fixing; an agreeing or covenanting;* an agreement or contract. [L. *pactio*—*paciscor,* to fix.]

Pad, pad, *n.* An easy-paced horse; a robber who infests the road on foot, usually called a foot-pad. [Sax. *paad,* a path—Sans. *pad,* to go.]

Pad, pad, *n.* A soft saddle, cushion, or bolster stuffed with straw, hair, or other soft substance.—*vt. To stuff with padding. ppr.* padding, *pret. & pp.* padded. [Fin. *padja,* a long sort of pillow.]

Padded, pad'ed, *p.a.* Stuffed with a soft substance.

Padding, pad'ing, *p.n.* The stuffing of a coat, saddle, cushion, &c.; the material used in stuffing coats, &c.

Paddle, pad'l, *vi. To play in water with hands or feet;* to beat the water as with oars; to finger; to touch or handle gently.—*vt.* To propel by an oar or paddle. *ppr.* paddling, *pret. & pp.* paddled. *n. Anything to paddle* or row with; a broad but short oar, used in impelling light boats; the blade or broad part of an oar or weapon; (pl.) the broad boards at the circumference of a water-wheel; the float-boards placed on the circumference of a wheel, called the paddle-wheel, in steam-vessels. [Fr. *patrouiller*—*patte,* a foot, a hand.]

Paddler, pad'l-ėr, *n. One who paddles.*

Paddock, pad'ok, *n.* A small inclosure

---

ch. *chain;* j, *job;* g, *go;* ng, *sing;* ᴛʜ, *then;* th, *thin;* w, *wig;* wh, *whig;* zh, *azure;* † obsolete.

under pasture, immediately adjoining the stables of a domain. (corrupted from Sax. *pearroc*, a park.]

Paddock, pad'ok, *n.* A large toad or frog.

Padlock, pad'lok, *n.* A lock to be hung on a staple and held by a link.—*vt.* To fasten with a padlock; to stop; to shut; to confine. [perhaps from *pad*, a path, a lock for a gate leading into a path.]

Pagan, pā'gan, *n.* A countryman; and as the inhabitants of the villages in the Roman empire continued heathen after those in the cities had embraced Christianity, hence a heathen.—*a.* Heathen; Gentile; noting a person who worships false gods; pertaining to the worship of false gods. [L. *paganus—pagus*, a village.]

Paganism, pā'gan-izm, *n.* Heathenism; the worship of false gods. [Fr. *paganisme*.]

Page, pāj, *n.* A boy; a youth attached to the service of a royal or noble personage, rather for formality than for servitude; a youth attendant on a wealthy person. [Fr.; Gr. *pais, paidos*, a boy.]

Page, pāj, *n.* One side of a leaf of a book; a book or writing, or writings; (pl.) books or writings.—*vt.* To mark or number the pages of, as of a book or manuscript; to attend as a paget. *ppr.* paging, *pret. & pp.* paged. [Fr. —L. *pagina*.]

Pageant, pā'jent, *n.* A triumphal car, chariot, or other pompous thing, decorated with flags, &c., and carried in public shows and processions; a show; something intended for pomp; anything showy, without stability or duration.—*a.* Showy; pompous; ostentatious.—*vt.*† To exhibit in show. [etymol. uncertain.]

Pageantry, pā'jent-ri, *n.* Show; pompous exhibition or spectacle.

Paging, pāj'ing, *p.n.* The marking of the *pages* of a book.

Pah, pä, *interj.* An exclamation expressing contempt.

Pail, pāl, *n.* An open vessel of wood, tin, &c., used in families for carrying liquids. [W. *paeol*, a pail.]

Paillasse, pa'li-as, *n.* An under bed of straw. [Fr. *paille*, L. *palea*, straw.]

Pain, pān, *n.* Physical suffering arising from *pressure*, from a *blow*, or from some other external cause; an uneasy sensation in animal bodies, of any degree from slight uneasiness to extreme torture; agony; uneasiness of mind; anxiety; solicitude for the future; grief; (pl.) the throes of child-birth; work; penalty; punishment suffered or denounced.—*vt.* To afflict with pain; to torment; to distress; to render uneasy in mind; to disquiet; to grieve; to punish†. [Fr. *peine*—L. *poena*, pain, penalty—Sans. *pid*, to press.]

Painful, pān'ful, *a.* Full of pain; giving pain or distress to the body; giving pain to the mind; grievous; requiring or undergoing toil; industrious.

Painfully, pān'ful-li, *adv.* With suffering of body or of mind; laboriously.

Painfulness, pān'ful-nes, *n.* Quality of being painful; uneasiness or distress of body or of mind; laborious effort; toil; laboriousness.

Painless, pān'les, *a.* Free from pain; free from trouble.

Painstaker, pānz'tāk-ėr, *n.* One who takes pains; a laborious person.

Painstaking, pānz'tāk-ing, *a.* Laborious; industrious.—*n.* Labour; great industry.

Paint, pānt, *vt.* To form a likeness of in colours; to represent by images; to besmear, or diversify with colours; to present in form or likeness to the intellectual view; to portray; to delineate.—*vi.* To practise painting; to lay colours on the face.—*n.* A substance used in painting; a colouring substance; colour representing anything; colour laid on the face; rouge. [Fr. *peindre*, pp. *peint*—L. *pingo, pictum*, Sans. *pinj*, to paint.]

Painted, pānt'ed, *p.a.* Coloured; represented in form by colours; described.

Painter, pānt'ėr, *n.* One whose occupation is to paint; one skilled in representing things in colours.

Painting, pānt'ing, *p.n.* The act or employment of laying on colours; the act of forming figures; a picture; a likeness in colours; colours laid on.

Pair, pār, *n.* Two things of a kind, similar in form, applied to the same purpose, and suited to each other; two of a sort; a couple; a brace; distinctively, a man and wife.—*vi.* To be joined in pairs; to couple; to suit.—*vt.* To assort and place together in twos, as things that are equal or adapted to each other; to unite in couples; to unite as correspondent. [Fr. *paire*, a pair, couple—L. *par*, equal.]

Palace, pa'lās, *n.* A magnificent house in which an emperor, a king, or other distinguished person, resides; a splendid place of residence. [Fr. *palais*—L. *palatium*—Heb. *pila*, to be wonderful.]

Palanquin, Palankeen, pa-lan-kēn', pa-lan-kēn', *n.* A covered carriage used in India, China, &c., borne on the shoulders of men. [corrupted from Hind. *palkee*, a sedan.]

Palatable, pa'lāt-a-bl, *a.* Agreeable to the palate or taste; savoury.

Palatably, pa'lāt-a-bli, *adv.* In a manner agreeable to the taste.

Palatal, pa'lāt-al, *a.* Pertaining to the palate; uttered by the aid of the palate.—*n.* A letter pronounced by the aid of the palate, as *g* soft, *ch* soft, or *j*. [Sp. *palatal*.]

Palate, pa'lāt, *n.* The roof or upper part of the mouth; taste; mental relish; intellectual taste.—*vt.*† To perceive by the taste. [L. *palatum*.]

Palatial, pa-lā'shi-al, *a.* Like a palace; magnificent. [from L. *palatium*.]

Palatine, pa'la-tin, *a.* Pertaining to a palace; importing the possession of royal privileges, as an elector or count palatine. [Fr. *palatin*.]

Pale, pāl, *n.* A stake; a rail used in fencing or inclosing; the space inclosed, as, the pale of Christianity; district; limited territory.—*vt.* To inclose with *pales*; to encompass. *ppr.* paling, *pret. & pp.* paled. [Sax. *pal*—L. *palus*, a stake.]

Pale, pāl, *a.* Whitish; wan; not ruddy; of a faint lustre; dim.—*vi.* To make pale; to dim.—*vi.* To turn pale. *ppr.* paling, *pret. & pp.* paled. [Fr. *pâlir*, to grow pale—L. *palleo*, to be pale.]

Paleness, pāl'nes, *n.* State or quality of being pale; wanness; a sickly whiteness of look; want of colour or lustre.

Paleography, pa-lē-og'ra-fi, *n.* The art of deciphering ancient writings. [Gr. *palaios*, old, and *graphō*, to write.]

Paleontology, pa'lē-on-tol''o-ji, *n.* The science of ancient beings or creatures, as fossil remains. [Gr. *palaios*, ancient, *on, ontos*, being, and *logos*, discourse.]

Palestra, pa-les'tra, *n.* A wrestling; the place of wrestling; a place for athletic exercises in Greece. [Gr. *palaistra*—*pallō*, to brandish.]

Palette, pa'let, *n.* See PALLET.

Palfrey, pal'frā, *n.* Originally, a horse led by the bridle on state occasions; a small horse fit for ladies. [Fr. *palefroi*—*par le frein* (L. *frenum*), by the bridle.]

Palfreyed, pal'frēd, *p.a.* Riding on a palfrey.

Paling, pāl'ing, *p.n.* A fence formed with pales, or pales taken collectively.

Palinode, pa'lin-ōd, *n.* A recantation, as of an ode; a piece in which the poet retracts the invectives contained in a former ode; a declaration contrary to a former one. [Gr. *palinōdia*—*palin*, back, and *ōdē*, an ode.]

Palisade, pa-li-sād', *n.* A fence consisting of a row of pales, sharpened and set firmly in the ground.—*vt.* To fortify with stakes or posts. *ppr.* palisading, *pret. & pp.* palisaded. [Fr. *palissade*—L. *palus*, a stake.]

Palish, pāl'ish, *a.* Somewhat pale.

Pall, pal, *n.* A cloak; a mantle of state; the mantle of an archbishop; the cloth thrown over a dead body at funerals.—*vt.*† To cloak; to cover or invest. [Sax. *pœll*—L. *pallium*, a mantle.]

Pall, pal, *vi.* To fail; to become vapid; to lose strength, life, or spirit; to become surfeiting.—*vt.* To make vapid; to weaken; to cloy. [W. *pallu*, to fail.]

Palladium, pal-lā'di-um, *n.* Primarily, a statue of the goddess Pallas, on which depended the safety of ancient Troy; bulwark; safeguard; a grayish-white malleable metal, which has the hardness of fine steel. [Gr. *Palladion*—*Pallas*, Pallas.]

Pallet, pa'let, *n.* A little shovel; a little oval board or piece of ivory, on which the painter places the colours to be used. [Fr. *palette*—L. *pala*, a shovel.]

Pallet, pa'let, *n.* A small bed of chaff or straw; a rude bed. [Fr. *paille*, straw.]

Palliament, pal'li-a-ment, *n.* A dress.

Palliate, pa'li-āt, *vt.* To cover, as with a mantle; to cover with excuse; to extenuate; to soften by favourable representations; to mitigate; to lessen or abate; to alleviate. *ppr.* palliating, *pret. & pp.* palliated. [L. *palliatus*, dressed in a mantle—*pallium*, a mantle.]

Palliating, pa'li-āt-ing, *p.a.* Extenuating; softening.

Palliation, pa-li-ā'shon, *n.* Act of palliating; concealment of the most flagrant circumstances of an offence; mitigation; abatement. [Fr.]

Palliative, pa'li-āt-iv, *a.* That palliates; extenuating; alleviating, as pain or disease.—*n.* That which palliates; that which abates the violence of pain or other evil. [Fr. *palliatif*.]

Pallid, pal'id, *a.* Pale; wan; deficient in colour. [L. *pallidus*—*palleo*, to be pale.]

Pallidly, pal'id-li, *adv.* Palely; wanly.

Pallor, pal'or, *n.* Paleness. [L.]

Palm, pam, *n.* The inner part of the open hand; a hand's breadth; a lineal measure of three inches; the broad triangular part of an anchor at the end of the arms; a tree, having leaves or branches expanding, like the open hand; superiority; victory; triumph.—*vt.* To impose by fraud (with *off*); to handle; to stroke with the hand. [Fr. *palme*—L. *palma*—Gr. *palamē*.]

Palmated, pal'māt-ed, *a.* Having the shape of a hand; entirely webbed, as feet. [L. *palmātus*—*palma*, a palm.]

Palmer, päm'ėr, n. One who returned from the Holy Land bearing branches of *palm*; a pilgrim or crusader.
Palmer-worm, päm'ėr-wėrm, n. A worm covered with hair; supposed to be so called because it wanders like a *palmer* over all plants; the common name of all the hairy caterpillars, but particularly of the tiger-moth.
Palmiped, pal'mi-ped, a. *Palm* or *broad footed*; web-footed. [L. *palma*, a palm, and *pes, pedis*, a foot.]
Palmistry, pal'mis-tri, n. The pretended art of telling fortunes by the lines in the *palm* of the hand; a trick of the hand. [from L. *palma*, a palm.]
Palm-Sunday, päm'sun-dā, n. The *Sunday* next before Easter; so called in commemoration of our Saviour's triumphal entry into Jerusalem, when the multitude strewed *palm-branches* in the way.
Palmy, päm'i, a. *Bearing palms*; flourishing; prosperous; victorious.
Palpability, pal-pa-bil'i-ti, n. *Quality of being perceptible* by the touch.
Palpable, pal'pa-bl, a. *Perceptible by the touch*; that may be felt, as darkness; coarse; easily perceived, as a mistake; easily perceptible, as proof. [Low L. *palpabilis*—L. *palpo*, to stroke.]
Palpably, pal'pa-bli, adv. *In such a manner as to be perceived by the touch*.
Palpitate, pal'pi-tāt, vi. *To move quickly*, like the hand in the act of *patting*; to throb; to beat rapidly and excitedly, as the heart; to flutter. *ppr.* palpitating, *pret. & pp.* palpitated. [L. *palpito, palpitatum—palpo*, to stroke.]
Palpitating, pal'pi-tāt-ing, p.a. Fluttering.
Palpitation, pal-pi-tā'shon, n. *Act of palpitating*; a preternatural beating of the heart excited by violent action of the body, by fear or disease. [L. *palpitatio*.]
Palsied, pal'sid, p.a. *Affected with palsy*.
Palsy, pal'zi, n. *Paralysis*; the total loss or diminution of sensation or of motion, or of both.—*vt.* To *strike as with the palsy*; to paralyze. *ppr.* palsying, *pret. & pp.* palsied. [from Fr. *paralysie*—Gr. *luō*, to loose.]
Palter, pal'tėr, vi. To act in an insincere manner; to shift; to haggle.
Paltrily, pal'tri-li, adv. *In a paltry manner*.
Paltriness, pal'tri-nes, n. *The state or quality of being paltry or vile*.
Paltry, pal'tri, a. *Ragged*; despicable; contemptible. [Sw. pl. *paltor*, old rags.]
Paludal, pa-lū'dal, a. *Pertaining to marshes*; marshy. [L. *palus*, a swamp.]
Paly, pāl'i, a. *Pale*; wanting colour. (Used only in poetry.)
Pam, pam, n. The knave of clubs. [said to be from *palm*, victory.]
Pamper, pam'pėr, vt. Originally, to *cover with the foliage of the vine*; to feed luxuriously; to glut. [Old Fr. *pampre*, a vine leaf—L. *pampinus*, a vine leaf.]
Pampered, pam'pėrd, p.a. Glutted or gratified to the full.
Pamperer, pam'pėr-ėr, n. *One who pampers*.
Pamphlet, pam'flet, n. A small book consisting of a *sheet of paper*; or of sheets stitched together, but not bound. [Old Eng. *paunfiet*.]
Pamphleteer, pam-flet-ėr', n. *A writer of pamphlets*; a scribbler.
Pan, pan, n. A vessel broad and shallow in which provisions are dressed or kept; the part of a gun-lock which holds the priming that communicates with the charge; the hard stratum of earth that lies below the soil; the top of the head. [Sax. *panne*—L. *patina*, a broad dish.]
Panacea, pa-na-sē'a, n. An herb, supposed to have the power of *curing all diseases*; a remedy for all diseases. [Gr. *panakeia—pas, pan*, all, and *akeomai*, to heal, cure.]
Pancake, pan'kāk, n. *A thin cake fried in a pan* or baked on an iron plate.
Pandect, pan'dekt, n. A treatise which *embraces all the parts of a subject*; (pl.) the Pandects—the title of the collection of Roman laws made by order of Justinian from the writings of Roman jurists. [L. pl. *Pandectæ*—Gr. *pas*, all, and *dechomai*, to take.]
Pandemonium, pan-dē-mō'ni-um, n. *That which contains all the demons*; the fabled great hall of demons or evil spirits. [Gr. *pas, pan*, all, and *daimōn*, a demon.]
Pander, pan'dėr, n. A pimp; a procurer. *vi.* To act as agent for the lusts of others.—*vt.* To play the pander for. [said to be from *Pandarus*.]
Pane, pān, n. *A piece* or square of glass; a piece of anything in variegated works. [Sax *pan*, a piece.]
Paned, pānd, p.a. Variegated; composed of small squares, as a counterpane usually is.
Panegyric, pa-nē-ji'rik, n. *A public oration in praise of some distinguished person* or achievement; a formal encomium; praise bestowed on some eminent person, action, or virtue. [Fr. *panégyrique*; Gr. *pas*, all, and *ageirō*, to bring together.]
Panegyrical, pa-nē-ji'rik-al, a. *Containing panegyric*, praise, or eulogy.
Panegyrically, pa-nē-ji'rik-al-li, adv. *By way of panegyric*.
Panegyrist, pa-nē-ji'rist, n. *One who makes a panegyric*. [Fr. *panégyriste*.]
Panegyrize, pa'nē-ji-rīz, vt. *To make a panegyric on*; to write or pronounce a eulogy on.—*vi.* To bestow panegyric or praises. *ppr.* panegyrizing, *pret. & pp.* panegyrized. [Gr. *panēgurizō*.]
Panel, pa'nel, n. *A pane*; a piece of board whose edges are inserted into the frame of a thicker surrounding frame; a piece of parchment containing the names of persons summoned by the sheriff; the whole jury.—*vt.* To form with panels. *ppr.* panelling, *pret. & pp.* panelled. [Fr. *panneau*.]
Panelling, pa'nel-ing, p.n. *Panelled work*.
Pang, pang, n. *A sharp* and sudden pain; a sudden paroxysm of extreme pain; anguish; throe; suffering.—*vt.* To torture. [Sax. *pyngan*, to pierce.]
Panic, pan'ik, n. A sudden fright without real cause, or *terror* inspired by a trifling cause or misapprehension of danger.—*a.* Extreme or sudden. (Applied to fright.) [Fr. *panique*, chimerical—Gr. *Pan*, the god who struck terror into the Persians at Marathon by an artifice.]
Pannier, pa'ni-ėr, n. A wicker basket; a basket used for carrying fruit or other things on a horse. [Fr. *panier*—L. *panis*, bread.]
Panoplied, pa'nō-plid, p.a. *Completely armed*.
Panoply, pa'nō-pli, n. *Complete armour* or defence; a full suit of defensive armour. [Gr. *panoplia—pas, pan*, all, and *hopla*, arms.]
Panorama, pan-ō-rä'ma, n. A complete *view on all sides*; a picture presenting from a central point a view of objects in every direction, represented on the interior surface of a cylindrical wall or rotunda. [Gr. *pan*, all, and *horama*, a sight—*horaō*, to see.]
Panoramic, pan-ō-ram'ik, a. *Belonging to or like a panorama*.
Pansy, pan'zi, n. A plant and flower; heart's-ease, so called because it causes *thought* or *fancy*, from its fanciful appearance. [Fr. *pensée*, thought—L. *penso*, to weigh.]
Pant, pant, vi. *To palpitate*; to have the breast heaving, as in short respiration or want of breath, or in anxious desire or suspense; to play with intermission or declining strength, as a breeze; to long; to desire ardently.—*n.* Palpitation of the heart. [Fr. *panteler*—L. *palpitare*.]
Pantaloon, pan-ta-lön', n. A ridiculous character in the Italian comedy, and a buffoon in pantomimes; (pl.) pantaloons, a species of close long trousers, extending to the heels. [Fr. *pantalon*.]
Pantheism, pan'thē-izm, n. *The system which maintains that all is God*, or that the universe is God. [Gr. *pan*, all, and *Theos*, God.]
Pantheist, pan'thē-ist, n. *One who believes the universe to be God*.
Pantheistic, pan-thē-ist'ik, a. *Pertaining to pantheism*.
Pantheon, pan-thē'on, n. A temple dedicated to *all the gods*. [Fr. *panthéon*; Gr. *pan*, all, and *Theos*, God.]
Panther, pan'thėr, n. The beast whose skin has the colours of *all beasts*; a spotted ferocious animal, otherwise called the pard. [Gr. *panthēr—pan*, all, and *thēr*, a wild beast.]
Panting, pant'ing, p.a. Breathing rapidly; longing.—*p.n.* *Palpitation*; rapid breathing; longing.
Pantler, pant'lėr, n. The officer in a great family who had charge of the *bread*.
Pantomime, pan'tō-mīm, n. *One who imitates all sorts of actions* and characters without speaking; a scene or representation in dumb show; a species of musical entertainment connected with dumb show.—*a.* Representing only in mute action. [L. *pantomimus*; Gr. *pas*, all, and *mīmos*, an imitator.]
Pantomimic, pan-tō-mim'ik, a. *Pertaining to the pantomime*.
Pantry, pan'tri, n. Primarily, a place in which *bread* was kept; now an apartment in which provisions are kept. [Fr. *paneterie*, pantry—L. *panis*, bread.]
Pap, pap, n. *The first cry of infants* for food; a teat, by which the infant draws its first food; a soft food for infants; a rounded hill. [Low L. *papa*, pa, pa.]
Papa, pa-pä', n. A childish name for *father*; a father; a spiritual father. [It.]
Papacy, pā'pa-si, n. *The office and dignity of the pope* or pontiff of Rome; the popes, taken collectively; papal jurisdiction. [Fr. *papauté*.]
Papal, pā'pal, a. *Belonging to the pope*; popish; proceeding from the pope; annexed to the bishopric of Rome. [Fr.]
Paper, pā'pėr, n. A substance formed into thin *sheets*, on which letters and figures are written or printed; a piece of paper; a single sheet printed or written; any written instrument; a bill of exchange; hangings printed or stamped; paper for covering the walls of rooms.—*a.* Made of paper; thin; slight.—*vt.* To cover with paper; to fur-

nish with paper-hangings. [Fr. *papier* —L. *papyrus*, the paper-reed.]
Paper-credit, pā'pĕr-kred-it, *n.* Evidences of debt; notes emitted by public authority, promising the payment of money.
Papered, pā'pĕrd, *p.a. Covered with paper.*
Papering, pā'pĕr-ing, *p.n. The operation of covering* or lining *with paper.*
Paper-mill, pā'pĕr-mil, *n. A mill in which paper is manufactured.*
Paper-money, pā'pĕr-mu-nē, *n.* Notes or bills issued by authority, and promising the payment *of money.*
Papillary, pă'pil-la-ri, *a. Covered with small nipples*, or nipple-like eminences. [L. *papilla*, a nipple, a teat.]
Papist, pā'pist, *n. An adherent of the Pope;* a Roman Catholic. [Fr. *papiste*.]
Papistic, pă-pist'ik, *a.* Conformable to the doctrine or practice which requires entire submission to *the Pope.*
Pappy, pap'i, *a. Like pap;* soft.
Par, pär, *n. State of equality;* equivalence without discount or premium; equality in condition. [L. *par, paris*, equal.]
Parable, pa'ra-bl, *n. A placing side by side;* a comparing; a similitude; a fable or allegorical relation of something real in life or nature, from which a moral is drawn for instruction. [Gr. *para*, beside, and *ballō*, to throw.]
Parabola, pa-ra'bō-la, *n.* A conic section arising from cutting a cone by a plane parallel to one of its sides, and so named because its axis is *parallel to* the *side of* the cone. [Gr. *parabolē*—*para*, and *ballō*, to throw.]
Parabolic, Parabolical, pa-ra-bol'ik, pa-ra-bol'ik-al, *a. Expressed by parable;* belonging to a parabola; having the form of a parabola.
Parabolically, pa-ra-bol'ik-al-li, *adv. By way of parable;* in the form of a parabola.
Paraclete, pa'ra-klēt, *n. An advocate;* the Comforter; the Holy Spirit. [Gr. *paraklētos*—*kaleō*, to call.]
Parade, pa-rād', *n. Something prepared* for show; exhibition; display; military order; the place where troops assemble for exercise.—*vt.* To exhibit in a showy manner; to marshal in military order. *vi.* To walk about for show; to be marshalled in military order. *ppr.* parading, *pret. & pp.* paraded. [Fr.; L. *paro, parātus*, to set in order.]
Paradigm, pa'ra-dim, *n. A setting beside;* a pattern; an example; an example of a verb conjugated in the several moods, tenses, and persons. [Fr. *paradigme*—Gr. *deiknumi*, to show.]
Paradise, pa'ra-dis, *n. A park*; the *garden* of Eden, in which Adam and Eve were placed immediately after their creation; a region of supreme felicity; heaven, the blissful seat of sanctified souls after death. [Gr. *paradeisos*—Heb. *pardes*, a park.]
Paradox, pa'ra-doks, *n.* A tenet *contrary to* received *opinion*, yet true in fact; a seeming contradiction; anything which seems to contradict received opinions. [Gr. *paradoxia*—*para*, and *doxa*, opinion.]
Paradoxical, pa-ra-doks'ik-al, *a. Having the nature of a paradox;* inclined to paradox; inclined to tenets contrary to received opinions.
Paradoxically, pa-ra-doks'ik-al-li, *adv. In a paradoxical manner.*
Paraffine, pa'ra-fin, *n.* A white substance, tasteless and inodorous, much used for making candles, &c. [L. *parum*, too little, and *affinis*, akin.]
Paragon, pa'ra-gon, *n. Something that surpasses;* a model by way of distinction, implying superior excellence or perfection.—*vt.* To compare; to rival; to equal. [Fr. *parangon*—Gr. *para*, and *agō*, to lead.]
Paragraph, pa'ra-graf, *n. Anything written near* the text; a marginal note; a distinct part of a discourse or writing; a short passage; a sentence. [Gr. *para*, and *graphō*, to write.]
Parallactic, pa-ral-lak'tik, *a. Pertaining to the parallax* of a heavenly body.
Parallax, pa'ral-laks, *n. The change of* place in a body in consequence of being viewed from different points; the difference between the place of the sun, moon, or a planet, as seen from the earth's surface and its centre at the same instant. [Gr. *parallaxis*—*allassō*, to make things alternate—*allos*, another.]
Parallel, pa'ral-lel, *a. Going on side by side;* extended in the same direction, and in all parts equally distant, as lines or surfaces; like; similar; equal in all essential parts.—*n.* A line or surface which, throughout its whole extent, is equidistant from another line or surface; a line on the globe marking the latitude; resemblance; comparison made; anything equal to or resembling another.—*vt.* To place *so as to be parallel with;* to equal; to correspond to; to resemble in all essential points. *ppr.* parallelling, *pret. & pp.* parallelled. [Gr. *parallēlos*—*allēlōn*, of one another.]
Parallelism pa'ral-lel-izm, *n. State of being parallel;* resemblance.
Parallelogram, pa-ral-lel'ō-gram, *n.* A right-lined quadrilateral *figure*, whose opposite sides are *parallel* and equal. [Gr. *parallēlos*, parallel, and *gramma*, a letter.]
Parallelopiped, pa-ral-lel'ō-pīp″ed, *n.* A regular solid comprehended under six *parallelograms*, the opposite ones of which are similar, parallel, and equal to each other. [Gr. *parallēlepipedon*—*parallēlos, epi,* on, and *pedon,* the ground.]
Paralysis, pa-ral'i-sis, *n.* A diseased state, in which the natural power of sensation or voluntary motion is lost in any part of the body; palsy. [Gr. —*lusis*, a loosing,—*luō*, to loose.]
Paralytic, pa-ra-lit'ik, *a. Affected with paralysis* or palsy; inclined or tending to palsy.—*n. A person* affected with *palsy*. [Fr. *paralitique*.]
Paralyze, pa'ra-līz, *vt.* To affect with *paralysis;* to unnerve; to destroy or impair, as physical or mental energy. *ppr.* paralyzing, *pret. & pp.* paralyzed. [Fr. *paralyser.*]
Paralyzed, pa'ra-līzd, *p.a.* Rendered unfit for action or exertion.
Paralyzing, pa'ra-līz-ing, *p.a.* Unnerving.
Paramount, pa'ra-mount, *a. Raised above;* superior; eminent; of the highest order; superior to all others.—*n.* The chief; the highest in rank. [Norm. —*monter,* to ascend.]
Paramour, pa'ra-mör, *n. A lover* in a bad sense; one of either sex who loves loosely; a mistress. [Fr. *par amour*, with love.]
Parapet, pa'ra-pet, *n.* A wall or rampart *rising as high as the breast;* a breast-work; an elevation of earth for covering soldiers from an enemy's shot; a breast-wall raised on the edge of a bridge, &c., to prevent people from falling over. [Fr.—L. *pectus*, the breast.]
Parapeted, pa'ra-pet-ed, *p.a. Furnished with a parapet.*
Paraphernalia, pa'ra-fĕr-nā″li-a, *n. pl.* That which a bride brings *over and above her dowry;* the clothing, jewels, ornaments, &c., which a wife brings with her at her marriage; ornaments; trappings. [Gr. *parapherna*—*para*, beyond, and *phernē*, a dowry—*pherō*, to bring.]
Paraphrase, pa'ra-frāz, *n. That which is said in accordance* with what another has said; an explanation of some passage in a book, in a more ample manner than is expressed in the words of the author; a loose or free translation. *vt.* To unfold, as the sense of an author with more clearness and particularity than it is expressed in his own words. *vi.* To make *a paraphrase;* to interpret or explain amply. *ppr.* paraphrasing, *pret. & pp.* paraphrased. [Fr.; Gr. *para*, and *phrazō*, to speak.]
Paraphrast, pa'ra-frast, *n. One who paraphrases.* [Fr. *paraphraste.*]
Paraphrastic, pa-ra-frast'ik, *a. Pertaining to or resembling a paraphrase;* not verbal or literal.
Paraphrastically, pa-ra-frast'ik-al-li, *adv. In a paraphrastic manner.*
Parasite, pa'ra-sīt, *n. One who eats beside another;* one who frequents the tables of the rich, and earns his welcome by flattery; a fawning flatterer, a plant obtaining nourishment immediately from other plants to which it attaches itself; one of an order of insects which live on the bodies of other animals, as lice, &c. [Fr.—Gr. *parasitos*—*sitos,* food.]
Parasitic, Parasitical, pa-ra-sit'ik, pa-ra-sit'ik-al, *a. Of or belonging to a parasite;* flattering; wheedling; living on some other body. [Gr. *parasitikos.*]
Parasitically, pa-ra-sit'ik-al-li, *adv.* In *a flattering or wheedling manner.*
Parasol, pa'ra-sol *n. A sun-shade;* a small umbrella used by ladies to defend their faces from the sun's rays. [Fr.—Gr. *para*, against, and L. *sol*, the sun.]
Parboil, pär'boil, *vt. To boil in part;* to boil in a moderate degree. [Fr. *parbouillir*—L. *pars*, a part, and *bullio*, to boil.]
Parboiled, pär'boild, *p.a. Boiled* moderately or in *part.*
Parcel, pär'sel, *n. A portion of anything* taken separately; any mass; a part belonging to a whole; a small package of goods.—*vt.* To divide into *portions;* to make up into parcels or packages *ppr.* parcelling, *pret. & pp.* parcelled. [Fr. *parcelle*—L. *pars, partis*, a part —Heb. *parats,* to break.]
Parch, pärch, *vt.* To dry up *quite;* to dry to extremity; to burn the surface of; to scorch.—*vi.* To become *very dry;* to be scorched or superficially burned. [Sans. *pari*, very, and *shush*, to become dry.]
Parched, pärcht, *p.a.* Scorched.
Parching, pärch'ing, *p.a.* Having the quality of burning or drying.
Parchment, pärch'ment, *n.* The skin of a sheep or goat dressed or prepared for writing on. [Fr. *parchemin*—L. *pergamena*—from *Pergamum*.]
Pard, pärd, *n.* The panther; the leopard. [L. *pardus.*]
Pardon, pär'dn, *vt. To give thoroughly;* to *forgive;* to accept an excuse, as *for* a fault.—*n. Forgiveness;* remission of

Fāte, fär, fat, fall; mē, met, hėr; pīne, pin; nōte, not, move; tūbe, tub, bull; oil, pound.

a penalty; forgiveness received. [Fr. *pardonner*—L. *per*, and *dono*, to give.]
Pardonable, pär'dn-a-bl, *a. That may be pardoned;* excusable; that may be forgiven or passed by. [Fr.]
Pardonableness, pär'dn-a-bl-nes, *n. Quality of being pardonable.*
Pardonably, pär'dn-a-bli, *adv. In a manner admitting of pardon.*
Pardoned, pär'dnd, *p.a. Forgiven;* excused.
Pardoner, pär'dn-ėr, *n. One who pardons* or forgives.
Pardoning, pär'dn-ing, *p.a.* Absolving from punishment.
Pare, pār, *vt. To cut off,* as the superficial substance or extremities of a thing; to trim by cutting; to shave off with a sharp instrument; to cut away by little and little. *ppr.* paring, *pret. & pp.* pared. [Icel. *para*, a piece of the skin or flesh cut off.]
Paregoric, pa-rē-go'rik, *a.* Encouraging; mitigating; assuaging pain.—*n.* A medicine that mitigates pain; an anodyne. [Gr. *parēgorikos—agoreuō*, to harangue.]
Parent, pār'ent, *n. One who brings forth* or begets; she who produces young; a father or mother; a progenitor; cause; origin. [L. *parens—pario*, to bring forth.]
Parentage, pār'ent-āj, *n.* Extraction; birth; condition with respect to the rank of parents. [Fr.]
Parental, pa-rent'al, *a. Pertaining to parents;* becoming parents; tender; affectionate. [L. *parentalis.*]
Parentally, pa-rent'al-li, *adv. Like a parent.*
Parenthesis, pa-ren'thē-sis, *n.* A *putting in beside;* a sentence, or certain words inserted in a sentence, which interrupt the sense or natural connection of words, but serve to explain the principal sentence. The parenthesis is usually included in hooks or curved lines, thus, ( ). [Gr. *parenthesis—thēsis*, a placing—*tithēmi*, to place.]
Parenthetic, **Parenthetical**, pa-ren-thet'ik, pa-ren-thet'ik-al, *a. Pertaining to a parenthesis;* expressed in a parenthesis.
Parenthetically, pa-ren-thet'ik-al-li, *adv. By way of parenthesis.*
Parer, pār'ėr, *n. He or that which pares;* an instrument for paring.
Parhelion, pär-hē'li-on, *n.* **Parhelia**, *pl.* A mock sun or meteor, appearing in the form of a bright light *near the sun.* [Gr. *para*, and *hēlios*, the sun.]
Parietal, pa-rī'et-al, *a. Of or pertaining to a wall;* resembling a wall; serving as a wall. [Fr. *pariétal*—L. *paries*, a wall.]
Paring, pār'ing, *p.n. That which is cut off;* a piece clipped off; the act of cutting off the surface of grass-land for tillage.
Parish, pa'rish, *n.* An ecclesiastical division of a town or district, in which the inhabitants *dwell near each other;* the circuit of ground which is committed to the charge of one parson, vicar, or other Christian minister, having permanent cure of souls therein.—*a. Belonging to a parish;* employed in the spiritual concerns of a parish, as the priest or minister; maintained by the parish. [Fr. *paroisse*—Gr. *para*, and *oikos*, a house.]
Parishioner, pa-rish'on-ėr, *n. One who belongs to a parish.*
Parisyllabic, pa'ri-sil-lab''ik, *a.* Denoting a word which has *the same number of syllables* in all its inflections. [L.

par, *paris*, equal, and *syllaba*, a syllable.]
Parity, pa'ri-ti, *n. Equality;* like state or degree; analogy. [Fr. *parité*—L. *par*, *paris*, equal.]
Park, pärk, *n.* A piece of ground *inclosed* for the chase or other purposes; an inclosed place in cities for exercise; an assemblage of the heavy ordnance belonging to an army.—*vt.* To inclose, as *in a park;* to impark; to bring together in a park or compact body. [Sax. *pearroc;* Fr. *parc.*]
Parlance, pär'lans, *n. Conversation;* discourse; talk. [Norm.—Fr. *parler,* to speak.]
Parlet, pärl, *n.* Conversation; talk.—*vi.* To talk; to converse.
Parley, pär'lē, *vi. To speak* or confer on some point of mutual concern; to discuss orally; hence, to confer, as with an enemy; to treat with by words.—*n.* Mutual discourse; conference with an enemy in war. [Fr. *parler*, to speak.]
Parliament, pär'li-a-ment, *n.* A place for *conference;* an assembly of persons met for discourse, &c.; the legislature of the United Kingdom of Great Britain and Ireland, consisting of the queen, the lords spiritual and temporal, and the knights, citizens, and burgesses. [Fr. *parlement—parler*, to speak.]
Parliamentarian, pär'li-a-ment-ā''ri-an, *n.* One of those who adhered to the *parliament* in the time of Charles I.
Parliamentary, pär'li-a-ment''a-ri, *a. Pertaining to parliament;* enacted or done by parliament; according to the rules and usages of parliament. [It. *parlamentario.*]
Parlour, pär'lėr, *n.* Primarily, the apartment in a nunnery where the nuns are permitted to meet and *converse with* each other, or with friends outside, through a grating; the room in a house which the family usually occupy. [Fr. *parloir—parler,* to speak.]
Parlous†, pär'lus, *a.* Attended with peril; venturesome; keen.
Parlously†, pär'lus-li, *adv.* In a parlous manner.
Parmacity†, pär-ma-si'ti, *n.* Spermaceti.
Parochial, pa-rō'ki-al, *a. Belonging to a parish.* [from Low L. *parochia,* a parish.]
Parodist, pa'rod-ist, *n. One who makes parodies.* [Fr. *parodiste.*]
Parody, pa'rō-di, *n.* A *song* or *ode diverted* to another subject or to a different sense; a kind of poetical pleasantry, in which verses written on one subject are altered and applied to another by way of burlesque.—*vt. To imitate in parody;* to alter, as verses or words, and apply to a purpose different from that of the original. *ppr.* parodying, *pret. & pp.* parodied. [Fr. *parodie*—Gr. *para*, and *ōdē*, an ode.]
Parol, Parole, pa-rōl', *n. A word;* words or oral declarations, in law; word of mouth; pleadings in a suit.—*a. Given by word of mouth;* oral; not written. [Fr. *parole.*]
Parole, pa-rōl', *n. A word;* a promise given by a prisoner of war, when he has leave to depart from custody, that he will return at the time appointed, unless discharged; a word given out every day in orders by a commanding officer, in camp or garrison, by which friends may be distinguished from enemies. [Fr.]
Paroxysm, pa'roks-izm, *n. Irritation,*

as from something sharp; exasperation; the severe fit of a disease or of pain. [Fr. *paroxisme;* Gr. *para*, and *oxus*, sharp.]
Paroxysmal, pa-roks-iz'mal, *a. Pertaining to paroxysm;* caused by paroxysms.
Parricidal, pa-ri-sīd'al, *a. Pertaining to parricides;* involving the crime of murdering a parent, patron, &c.; committing parricide.
Parricide, pa'ri-sīd, *n. One who destroys his father;* the murder of a father, or one to whom reverence is due. [L. *parricida—pater,* a father, and *cædo,* to kill.]
Parrot, pa'rot, *n.* A talking bird; a bird which has the faculty of making indistinct articulations of words in imitation of the human voice. [Fr. *perroquet.*]
Parry, pa'ri, *vt. To ward off;* to stop or turn by, as a blow or thrust; to turn aside; to shift off —*vi. To ward off* strokes; to put by thrusts or strokes; to fence. *ppr.* parrying, *pret. & pp.* parried. [Fr. *parer,* to ward off; L. *paro,* to get ready.]
Parse, pärs, *vt.* To resolve, as a sentence into its *parts* or elements, or to show, as the several *parts* of speech composing a sentence, and their relation to each other by government or agreement. *ppr.* parsing, *pret. & pp.* parsed. [L. *pars,* a part.]
Parsimonious, pär-si-mō'ni-us, *a. Very sparing* in the use or expenditure of money; niggardly; frugal.
Parsimoniously, pär-si-mō'ni-us-li, *adv.* With a *very sparing use* of money.
Parsimony, pär'si-mō-ni, *n. Sparingness* in the use or expenditure of money; frugality; niggardliness. [Fr. *parsimonie*—L. *parco,* to use sparingly.]
Parsing, pärs'ing, *p.n. Act* or *art* of resolving a sentence into its elements or *parts* of speech.
Parsley, pärs'lē, *n.* A plant whose leaves, in its cultivated state, are used for culinary purposes. [Gr. *petra,* a rock, and *selinon,* a kind of parsley.]
Parsnep, pärs'nep, *n.* A plant which *fixes* its root deep in the earth, the root being considered as a valuable esculent. [corrupted from It. *pastinaca.*]
Parson, pär'sn, *n.* The rector or incumbent of a parish; one that has the parochial charge or cure of souls; a clergyman. [Low L. *ecclesiæ persona,* the person of the church.]
Parsonage, pär'sn-āj, *n.* The benefice of a parish; a rectory endowed with a house, glebe, lands, tithes, &c., for the maintenance of the incumbent; the dwelling-house of a parson.
Part, pärt, *n.* A portion, or fragment *broken off* from a whole thing; a portion of a thing mentioned by itself; a number considered by itself; a member; distinct species belonging to a whole; ingredient in a mingled mass; that which falls to each in division; a share; interest; party; faction; something belonging to; that which concerns; character; share of labour or influence; particular office; character appropriated in a play.—*vt.* To divide or *break;* to sever into two or more pieces; to share; to keep asunder; to separate, as combatants; to break, as a rope.—*vi.* To be *broken off;* to break; to be torn asunder, as a rope; to quit each other; to take farewell; to separate; to leave; to have a share. [L. *pars, partis,* a part—Heb. *paras,* to break.]

Partake, pär-tāk', *vi.* To take a part in common with others; to share; to have something of the property, nature, claim, or right.—*vt.* To have a part in; to share; to share out; to distribute. *ppr.* partaking, *pret.* partook, *pp.* partaken.

Partaker, pär-tāk'ėr, *n.* One who has or takes a part; a sharer; an accomplice; an associate (with *of* or *in*).

Partaking, pär-tāk'ing, *p.a.* Combination in an evil design.

Parted, pärt'ed, *p.a.* Separated; severed.

Parterre, pär-tār', *n.* Any even plot of ground; a system of beds of different shapes and sizes, in which flowers are cultivated, with intervening spaces of gravel or turf for walking on. [Fr.—L. *par*, equal, and *terra*, ground—Sans. *dhará*, earth.]

Partial, pär'shi-al, *a.* Of or belonging to a part; inclined to favour one party in a cause, or one side of a question, more than the other; inclined to favour without reason; affecting a part only; not total. [Fr.—L. *pars, partis*, a part.]

Partiality, pär-shi-al'i-ti, *n.* State or quality of being partial; inclination to favour one party or one side of a question more than the other. [Fr. *partialité*.]

Partialize, pär'shi-al-īz, *vt.* To render partial.

Partially, pär'shi-al-li, *adv.* In a partial manner.

Partible, pärt'i-bl, *a.* That may be parted; divisible; susceptible of partition. [It. *partibile*.]

Participate, pär-tis'i-pāt, *vt.* To partake; to have a share in common with others, *ppr.* participating, *pret. & pp.* participated. [L. *participo, participatus*—*pars*, a part, and *capio*, to take.]

Participation, pär-tis'i-pā''shon, *n.* Act of participating; act or state of receiving or having part of something. [Fr.]

Participator, pär-tis'i-pāt-or, *n.* One who partakes with another; a partaker.

Participial, pär-ti-sip'i-al, *a.* Having the nature of a participle; formed from a participle. [L. *participialis*.]

Participially, pär-ti-sip'i-al-li, *adv.* In the sense or manner of a participle.

Participle, pär'ti-si-pl, *n.* A word participating in the properties both of a noun and of a verb. [L. *participium*—*pars*, a part, and *capio*, to take.]

Particle, pär'ti-kl, *n.* A small part of matter; an elementary part of a body; an atom; any very small portion; a word that is not inflected. [Fr. *particule*—L. *pars, partis*, a part.]

Particular, pär-tik'ū-lėr, *a.* Pertaining to a part or particle; pertaining to a single person or thing; peculiar; special; noting a single thing by way of distinction; noting something peculiar; attentive to things distinct; precise; minute; not general; odd; having something that eminently distinguishes one from others.—*n.* A minute part; a single instance; a single point; special peculiarity. [Fr. *particulier*.]

Particularity, pär-tik'ū-la''ri-ti, *n.* State or quality of being particular; distinct notice; minute incident; something peculiar or singular; minuteness in detail; something of special concern. [Fr. *particularité*.]

Particularize, pär-tik'ū-lėr-īz, *vt.* To mention distinctly or in particulars; to enumerate in detail.—*vi.* To be particular; to be attentive to single things. *ppr.* particularising, *pret. & pp.* particularized. [Fr. *particulariser*.]

Particularly, pär-tik'ū-lėr-li, *adv.* In a particular manner; distinctly; singly.

Parting, pärt'ing, *p.a.* Given at separation.—*p.n.* Division; separation.

Partisan, pär'ti-zan, *n.* An adherent to a party; a party man.—*a.* Adhering to a party or faction; biassed in favour of a party. [Fr.—L. *pars*, a part.]

Partisanship, pär'ti-zan-ship, *n.* The state of being a partisan.

Partition, pär-ti'shon, *n.* Act of dividing, or state of being divided; division; distinction; a division-wall; division of an estate in which several are jointly interested.—*vt.* To divide into shares. [Fr.—L. *pars*, a part.]

Partitive, pärt'it-iv, *a.* Denoting a part; distributive.—*n.* A distributive. [Fr. *partitif*.]

Partlet, pärt'let, *n.* A band for the neck; a hen.

Partly, pärt'li, *adv.* In part; in some measure or degree; not wholly.

Partner, pärt'nėr, *n.* One who partakes or shares with another; an associate; one associated with another in any business; a joint owner of stock employed in business; one who dances with another; a husband or wife.—*vt.* To associate with a partner; to join.

Partnership, pärt'nėr-ship, *n.* Fellowship; the association of two or more persons for the purpose of prosecuting any business; joint interest or property; a rule in arithmetic.

Partridge, pär'trij, *n.* A well-known bird of game, so named from the sound it utters. [Fr. *perdrix*—L. *perdix*.]

Parts, pärts, *n. pl.* Powers; faculties; accomplishments; remarkable mental powers; applied to place, quarters; districts. [from *part*.]

Parturition, pär-tū-ri'shon, *n.* The act of bringing forth young. [Late L. *parturitio*—L. *pario*, to bring forth.]

Party, pär'ti, *n.* A body of individuals who take a particular part or side in affairs, chiefly political; one of two litigants; one interested in an affair; a select company invited to an entertainment; a single person distinct from another; a detachment of troops sent on a particular duty.—*a.* Of or pertaining to a party. [Old Fr. *partie*—L. *pars*, a part.]

Party-coloured, pär'ti-kul-ėrd, *a.* Having divers colours.

Party-man, pär'ti-man, *n.* One of a party; a man of violent party principles.

Party-spirit, pär'ti-spi-rit, *n.* The spirit that supports a party.

Party-verdict, pär'ti-vėr-dikt, *n.* A joint verdict.

Party-wall, pär'ti-wal, *n.* A wall that separates one house from the next.

Paschal, pas'kal, *a.* Pertaining to the passover, or to Easter. [Fr. *pascal*—Heb. *pēsach*, the passover.]

Pash, pash, *vt.* To strike; to dash.—*n.* A blow.

Pasquil, pas'kwil, *n.* A pasquin.

Pasquin, pas'kwin, *n.* A mutilated statue at Rome, on which it has been customary to paste satiric papers. It was so named from *Pasquino*, a satiric cobbler, near whose shop it was dug up; hence, a lampoon. [It. *pasquino*.]

Pasquinade, pas-kwin-ād', *n.* A lampoon or satirical writing.

Pass, pas, *vi.* To step; to move, in almost any manner; to go; to proceed from one place to another; to alter or change; to vanish; to die; to be spent; to be in any state; to undergo; to be enacted; to be current; to be in estimation; to be regarded; to occur; to be done; to give judgment or sentence; to make a push in fighting; to omit; to move through any opening; to flow through; to be transferred from one owner to another; to go by a certain necessary step; to run or extend, as a line or other thing; to succeed in entering a profession or gaining an appointment.—*vt.* To cause to move; to go by or beyond; to go through or over; to spend; to transfer from one owner to another; to assign; to strain; to utter; to give forth; to accomplish; to pay regard to; to cause to go; to omit; to transcend; to admit; to approve, as accounts; to enact; to impose fraudulently; to surpass; to thrust.—*n.* That which may be passed through; a passage; a narrow place of entrance and exit; permission to pass, to go, or to come; a passport; an order for sending vagrants or impotent persons to their place of abode; a thrust; attempt to stab or strike; condition or extreme case; extremity. [Fr. *passer*—L. *pando, passum*, to spread out.]

Passable, pas'a-bl, *a.* That may be passed; that may be penetrated; penetrable; receivable; tolerable; pretty good. [It. *passabile*.]

Passably, pas'a-bli, *adv.* Tolerably.

Passage, pas'āj, *n.* Act of passing or moving by land or water, or through the air or other substance; the time of passing from one place to another; road; a place where men or things may pass or be conveyed; an encounter; right of passing; occurrence; event; management; part of a book or writing; a single clause; a short portion of an air; the act of carrying through all the regular forms necessary to give validity; the part of a building allotted for giving access to the different apartments. [Fr.—L. *passus*, a step—*pando*, to spread out.]

Pass-book, pas'buk, *n.* A book in which a trader enters the articles bought on credit, and then passes it to the customer for his information.

Passed, Past, past, past, *p.a.* Gone by; ended; having received all the formalities necessary to constitute a law.

Passenger, pas'en-jėr, *n.* One who passes; one who travels in some established conveyance, as a stage-coach, steamboat, &c.

Passer, pas'ėr, *n.* One who passes.

Passible, pas'i-bl, *a.* Capable of feeling or suffering; susceptible of feeling or of impressions from external agents. [Fr.—L. *patior, passus*, to suffer.]

Passing, pas'ing, *p.a.* Eminent; surpassing; departing.—*adv.* Exceedingly; surpassingly.—*n.* Act of passing or going past.

Passing-bell, pas'ing-bel, *n.* The bell that rings at the hour of death, originally designed to obtain prayers for the passing soul.

Passion, pa'shon, *n.* A suffering or enduring; emphatically, the last suffering of the Saviour; the effect of an external agent upon a body; violent emotion or excitement of mind, particularly such as is occasioned by an offence, injury, or insult; violent anger; fervour; vehement desire; exhibition of deep feeling; love; regret; desire, as for dress.—*vi.*! To feel excitement; to be roused. [L. *passio*—*patior*, *passus*, *pathos*, to suffer.]

Passionate, pa'shon-āt, *a.* Moved by

passion; highly excited; vehement; easily excited or agitated by injury or insult; irascible; choleric; fiery; hot; hasty.—vt.† To express passionately. [It. passionato.]
Passionately, pa'shon-at-li, *adv. In a passionate manner.*
Passion-flower, pa'shon-flou-ėr, *n.* A plant, so called from a fancied resemblance in the parts of the flowers to the appearances presented on Calvary at the Crucifixion.
Passionless, pa'shon-les, *a. Void of passion;* not easily excited to anger.
Passion-week, pa'shon-wēk, *n.* The week immediately preceding the festival of Easter; so called because in that week our Saviour's passion and death took place.
Passive, pas'iv, *a. Suffering;* not acting; receiving impressions from external agents; unresisting; inactive; denoting a verb which expresses passion, or the effect of an action of some agent. [Fr. *passif*—L. *patior*, to suffer.]
Passively, pas'iv-li, *adv. In a passive manner;* unresistingly.
Passiveness, pas'iv-nes, *n. Quality of being passive;* capacity of suffering.
Passover, pas'ō-vėr, *n.* A feast of the Jews, instituted to commemorate the deliverance of the Hebrews in Egypt, when the destroying angel, smiting the first-born of the Egyptians, passed over the houses of the Israelites, which had been previously marked with the blood of the paschal lamb; the sacrifice offered at the feast of the passover; the paschal lamb. [*pass* and *over*.]
Passport, pas'pōrt, *n.* A permission to leave a port; a written license from proper authority, granting permission to pass from one country to another, or to navigate a particular sea without molestation; that which enables one to pass with safety or certainty. [Old Fr. *passeport*, a safe-conduct; L. *portus*, a harbour.]
Passy-measure, pas'i-me-shūr, *n.* An old stately kind of dance. [It. *passo*, a step, and *mezzo*, middle.]
Past, past, p.a. Gone by; ended.—*n.* Elliptically, *past time; past state; past part.—prep.* Beyond in time; out of reach of; further than; after.—*adv.* By.
Paste, pāst, *n.* Dough to be made into bread or food; a soft composition of substances, formed to the consistence of dough, as in making potter's ware; a kind of cement made of flour and water boiled; a fine and brilliant glassy substance, used in making imitations of precious stones or gems. *vt. To unite with paste;* to fasten with paste. *ppr.* pasting, *pret. & pp.* pasted. [Old Fr.—L. *passo, pastum*, to feed.]
Pasteboard, pāst'bōrd, *n.* A species of thick paper formed of several single sheets pasted one upon another, or by macerating paper and casting it in moulds, &c.
Pastern, pas'tėrn, *n.* The part of a horse's leg between the joint next the foot and the coronet of the hoof. [Old Fr. *pasturon*.]
Pastille, pas-tēl', *n.* A roll of paste; a dry composition of sweet-smelling resins, aromatic woods, &c., burned to clear and scent the air of a room. [Fr.—L. *pasco, pastum*, to feed.]
Pastime, pas'tīm, *n.* That which amuses and serves to make time pass agreeably; entertainment.
Pastor, pas'tor, *n.* A shepherd or herdsman; a minister of the gospel who has the charge of a church and con-

gregation or flock. [L.—*pasco, pastum*, to feed—Sans. *pā*, to guard.]
Pastoral, pas'tor-al, *a. Pertaining to shepherds or herdsmen;* descriptive of the life of shepherds; relating to the care of souls, or to the pastor of a church.—*n.* A poem descriptive of shepherds and their occupations; an idyl; a bucolic. [Fr.]
Pastorally, pas'tor-al-li, *adv. In the manner of a pastor.*
Pastorate, pas'tor-āt, *n. The office, state, or jurisdiction of a spiritual pastor.* [Low L. *pastoratus*.]
Pastorship, pas'tor-ship, *n. The office or rank of pastor.*
Pastry, pās'tri, *n.* Articles of food in general which are made of paste or dough, as pies, &c.; the place where pastry is made. [Old Fr. *pastisserie*—L. *pasco, pastum*, to feed.]
Pastry-cook, pās'tri-kuk, *n.* One who makes and sells articles of food made of paste, as pies, &c.
Pasturable, pas'tūr-a-bl, *a. Fit for pasture.*
Pasturage, pas'tūr-āj, *n. The business or act of feeding* or grazing cattle; grazing ground; grass for feed. [Old Fr.]
Pasture, pas'tūr, *n.* Grass for the food of cattle; ground covered with grass to be eaten on the spot by cattle, horses, &c.—*vt. To supply with pasturage;* to feed on grass, or to supply with grass for food.—*vi.* To graze; to take food by eating grass from the ground. *ppr.* pasturing, *pret. & pp.* pastured. [Old Fr.—L. *pasco, pastum*, to feed.]
Pasty, pās'ti, *a. Like paste;* of the consistence of paste.—*n.* A pie made of paste, and baked without a dish; a meat pie.
Pat, pat, *n.* A light quick stroke with the fingers or hand; a tap; a small mass which is beat into shape by pats; as, a pat of butter.—*vt.* To strike gently with the fingers or hand; to tap. *ppr.* patting, *pret. & pp.* patted. [Old Fr. *bat*, a stroke or beating.]
Pat, pat, *a.* Exactly suitable, either as to time, place, or purpose.—*adv.* Fitly; seasonably. [Sans. *patu*, fit.]
Patch, pach, *n.* A piece of cloth sewed on a garment to repair it; a small piece of anything used to repair a breach; a small piece of silk used to cover a defect on the face, or to add a charm; a piece inserted in mosaic work; a small piece of ground; a knave; a rogue; a fool. *vt.* To mend by sewing on a piece or pieces; to adorn with a patch or with patches; to repair with pieces fastened on; to make up of pieces and shreds; to make suddenly or hastily; to make without regard to forms (in the two last senses, with *up*). [probably akin to Sans. *prich*, to join together.]
Patched, pacht, p.a. Mended clumsily.
Patchery, pach'ė-ri, *n.* Bungling work.
Patchwork, pach'wėrk, *n.* Work composed of pieces of various figures sewed together; work composed of pieces clumsily put together.
Patchy, pach'i, *a. Full of patches.*
Pate, pāt, *n. The brain pan;* the head, or rather the top of the head. [Ir. *bathas*, the pate.]
Paten, pa'ten, *n. A pan or plate;* the plate on which the consecrated bread in the eucharist is placed. [Norm. *patina*, plates, made of gold or silver, used at the distribution of the host.]
Patent, pā'tent, *a. Open; spread out;* open to the perusal of all; noting anything patented; appropriated by let-

ters patent, or *open letters*, granting some privilege or right; conspicuous. *n.* A writing given by the proper authority, granting a privilege to some person, as a title of nobility; a similar writing, securing to a person for a term of years the exclusive right to an invention.—*vt. To grant by patent;* to secure, as the exclusive right of a thing to a person. [Fr.—L. *pateō*, to be spread out.]
Patentable, pā'tent-a-bl, *a. That may be patented.*
Patented, pā'tent-ed, p.a. Granted by patent; secured by patent or by law as an exclusive privilege.
Patentee, pa-ten-tē', *n. One to whom a privilege* is secured by patent.
Paternal, pa-tėr'nal, *a. Pertaining to a father;* fatherly; derived from the father; hereditary. [Fr. *paternel*—L. *pater*, a father—Sans. *pā*, to protect.]
Paternally, pa-tėr'nal-li, *adv. In a paternal manner.*
Paternity, pa-tėr'ni-ti, *n. Fathership;* the relation of a father; authorship. [Fr. *paternité*.]
Paternoster, pā'tėr-nos-tėr, *n.* The Lord's Prayer. [L. Our Father.]
Path, path, *n.* Paths, paths, *pl. A way beaten or trodden* by the feet of man or beast; any narrow way beaten by the foot; the track in which a body moves in the atmosphere or in space; course of life; rules prescribed; moral government.—*vi.†* To walk abroad. (Sax.; Gr. *pateo*, to tread.)
Pathetic, pa-thet'ik, *a. Full of pathos;* affecting the passions, particularly pity, sorrow, grief, or other tender emotion; touching.—*n.* Style adapted to awaken the *passions*, especially of a tender nature. [Fr. *pathétique;* Gr. *paschō, pathein*, to suffer.]
Pathetically, pa-thet'ik-al-li, *adv. In such a manner* as to excite the tender passions.
Pathless, path'les, *a. Having no path;* having no beaten way; untrodden.
Pathological, path-o-loj'ik-al, *a. Pertaining to pathology.*
Pathologist, pa-thol'o-jist, *n. One who is versed in* or who treats of pathology.
Pathology, pa-thol'o-ji, *n. The doctrine of human sufferings* or diseases; that part of medicine which explains the nature of diseases, their causes, and symptoms. [Fr. *pathologie*—Gr. *paschō, pathein*, to suffer, and *logos*, discourse.]
Pathos, pā'thos, *n. A suffering;* passion; expression of strong or deep feeling; that which excites emotions and passions, especially tender emotions, as those of pity, sympathy, &c. [Gr.—*paschō*, to suffer.]
Pathway, path'wā, *n. A path;* usually a narrow way to be passed on foot; a way; a course of life.
Patience, pā'shi-ens, *n. The quality of endurance;* the suffering of afflictions with a calm unruffled temper; the quality of bearing injuries without anger; the act or quality of waiting long for justice without discontent; perseverance; sufferance; permission. [Fr.]
Patient, pā'shi-ent, *a. Enduring,* bearing, or supporting calmly; not easily provoked; persevering; calmly diligent; not over eager; expecting without discontent.—*n. A sufferer;* he who or that which is passively affected; a sick person under medical treatment. —*vt.†* To produce patience in. [L. *patiens—patior*—Gr. *paschō*, to suffer.]

---

ch, *chain*; j, *job*; g, *go*; ng, *sing*; TH, *then*; th, *thin*; w, *wig*; wh, *whig*; zh, *azure*; † obsolete.

Patiently, pā′shi-ent-li, *adv. In a patient manner.*
Patriarch, pā′tri-ärk, *n. The father of a race; the father and ruler of a family; one who governs by paternal right; a learned character among the Jews; a dignitary superior to the order of archbishops in the Greek church.* [Fr. *patriarche*—Gr. *pater*, a father, and *archē*, rule.]
Patriarchal, pā-tri-ärk′al, *a. Belonging to patriarchs; possessed by patriarchs; subject to a patriarch.*
Patriarchate, pā′tri-ärk-āt, *n. The office, dignity, or jurisdiction of a patriarch in the Greek church; the residence of a patriarch.* [Fr. *patriarchat.*]
Patriarchism, pā′tri-ärk-izm, *n. Government by a patriarch, or the head of a family, who was both ruler and priest, as Noah, Abraham, and Jacob.*
Patrician, pa-tri′shi-an, *a. Of or belonging to the fathers of Rome; senatorial; noble; not plebeian.*—*n. A descendant of the first senators of Rome; a nobleman.* [Fr. *patricien*; L. *pater*, a father, pl. *patres*, the fathers.]
Patrimonial, pat-ri-mō′ni-al, *a. Pertaining to a patrimony; inherited from ancestors.* [Fr.]
Patrimonially, pat-ri-mō′ni-al-li, *adv. By inheritance.*
Patrimony, pat′ri-mo-ni, *n. A paternal inheritance; a right or estate inherited from one's ancestors; a church estate or revenue.* [Fr. *patrimoine*—L. *pater*, a father.]
Patriot, pā′tri-ot, *n. A person who loves his country, and zealously supports and defends it and its interests.*—*a. Patriotic; devoted to the welfare of one's country.* [Fr. *patriote*—L. *patria*, a fatherland—*pater*, a father.]
Patriotic, pā-tri-ot′ik, *a. Full of patriotism; inspired by the love of one's country; directed to the public welfare.* [Fr. *patriotique.*]
Patriotically, pā-tri-ot′ik-al-li, *adv. In a patriotic manner.*
Patriotism, pā′tri-ot-izm, *n. Love of one's country; the passion to serve one's country.* [Fr. *patriotisme.*]
Patristic, pā-tris′tik, *a. Pertaining to the ancient fathers of the Christian church.* [Fr. *patristique*; L. *pater*, a father—Sans. *pā*, to protect.]
Patrol, pā′trōl, *n. A round traversed on foot by a sentinel; the persons who go the rounds for observation.* [Fr. *patrouille*—*patte*, a foot, and *rouler*, to roll.]
Patrol, pa-trōl′, *vi. To go the rounds on foot in a camp; to march about and see what passes.*—*vt. To pass round, as a sentry.*
Patron, pā′tron, *n. One who performs the office of a father; a protector; a defender; one who countenances either a person or a work; one who has the gift and disposition of a benefice.*—*a. Giving aid.* [L. *patrōnus*—*pater*, a father.]
Patronage, pā′tron-āj, *n. Act of patronising; special countenance; aid afforded to second the views of a person; guardianship, as of a saint; advowson; the right of presentation to a church or ecclesiastical benefice.*—*vt.† To patronise.* [Fr.]
Patroness, pā′tron-es, *n. A female who patronises; a female who has the right of presenting to a church-living.*
Patronize, pā′tron-iz, *vt. To act as patron of; to countenance; to defend, as a patron his client; to lend aid to promote, as an undertaking; to defend;* to assume the air of a patron toward. *ppr.* patronizing, *pret. & pp.* patronized.
Patronizer, pā′tron-iz-ér, *n. One who patronises.*
Patronizing, pā′tron-iz-ing, *p.a.* Favouring; protecting.
Patronizingly, pā′tron-iz-ing-li, *adv. In a patronising manner.*
Patronymic, pā-trō-nim′ik, *a. Expressing the name of a father or ancestor; derived as a name from a father or an ancestor.*—*n. A name of men or women derived from that of a parent or ancestor.* [Gr. *patrōnumikos*—*patēr*, and *onoma*, a name.]
Patten, pat′ten, *n. The foot-stall or base of a column or pillar; a wooden shoe with an iron ring, worn to keep the shoes from the dirt or mud.* [Norm. *patins*, pattens—Gr. *pateō*, to tread.]
Patter, pat′tér, *vi. To make a sound like that of pats, or slight blows quickly repeated; to strike, as falling drops of water or hail, with a quick succession of small sounds.*—*vt.† To repeat in a muttering manner.* [from *pat.*]
Pattern, pat′tern, *n. An exemplar; a model proposed for imitation; a specimen; a part showing the figure of the whole; style of ornamental execution; an instance; anything cut out in paper to direct the cutting of cloth.*—*vt. To copy; to serve as an example to be followed.* [Norm. *patron*, pattern.]
Paucity, pa′si-ti, *n. Fewness; smallness of number; scarcity; smallness of quantity.* [L. *paucitas*—*paucus*, few.]
Paul, pal, *n. See* **Pawl**.
Paunch, pänsh, *n. The belly and its contents; in ruminating quadrupeds, the first and largest stomach, into which the food is received before rumination.*—*vt. To pierce or rip the belly of.* [Fr. *panse*—L. *pantex*, the paunch.]
Pauper, pa′pér, *n. A poor person; one so indigent as to depend on the parish or town for maintenance.* [L.]
Pauperism, pa′pér-izm, *n. State of being poor; the state of indigent persons requiring support from the community.*
Pauperize, pa′pér-iz, *vt. To reduce to pauperism. ppr.* pauperizing, *pret. & pp.* pauperized.]
Pause, paz, *n. A stop; a temporary stop or rest; suspense; break or paragraph in writing; a temporary cessation in reading; a mark of cessation; a point. vi. To stop; to make a short stop; to cease to speak for a time; to delay; to deliberate; to hesitate. ppr.* pausing, *pret. & pp.* paused. [Fr.; Gr. *pauō*, *pausō*, to stop, to bring to an end.]
Pausingly, paz′ing-li, *adv. After a pause; pause; by breaks.*
Pave, pāv, *vt. To make into a hard level surface, by beating, or ramming down small stones, earth, lime, &c.; to lay or cover with stone, so as to make a level or convenient surface for horses, carriages, or foot-passengers; to floor with brick, stone, or other solid material; to prepare, as a passage; to facilitate the introduction of. ppr.* paving, *pret. & pp.* paved. [Fr. *paver*—L. *pavio*, to smite.]
Paved, pāvd, *p.a.* Prepared, as a way.
Pavement, pāv′ment, *n. That with which anything is paved; a floor or covering of solid material, laid so as to make a hard and convenient passage.* [Fr.—L. *pavimentum*, *pavio*, to strike, to beat down.]
Paver, Pavier, pāv′er, pāv′i-ér, *n. One* who paves or lays stones for a floor, or whose occupation is to pave.
Pavilion, pa-vil′i-on, *n. A tent; a temporary movable habitation; originally so named from its painted and extended covering resembling the wings of a butterfly when flying; a kind of turret or building, usually insulated and contained under a single roof; a tent raised on posts, used in military affairs. vt. To furnish with pavilions; to shelter with a tent.* [Fr. *pavillon*—L. *papilio*, a butterfly, Low L. a tent.]
Paving, pāv′ing, *p.n. The act of laying a pavement; pavement; a floor of stones or bricks.*
Paw, pa, *n. The foot of beasts of prey having claws; the hand (in contempt). vi. To draw the fore-foot along the ground; to scrape with the fore-foot, as a horse.*—*vt. To scrape with the fore-foot; to handle roughly or awkwardly.* [W. *pawen*, a paw; L. *pes*, a foot.]
Pawl, pal, *n. A pole; a short bar of wood or iron fixed close to the capstan or windlass of a ship, to prevent it from rolling back.* [Armor. *paol*, the bar of the helm of a ship; L. *palus*, a pole.]
Pawn, pan, *n. That which fixes; a pledge; a gage; something deposited as security for the payment of money borrowed; a pledge for the fulfilment of a promise;* [Old Fr. *pion*, a pawn at chess] *a common man at chess.*—*vt. To give or deposit in pledge; to pledge; to pledge for the fulfilment of a promise.* [Old Fr. *pan*, a pawn—L. *pango*, *pactum*, to fix.]
Pawnbroker, pan′brōk-ér, *n. One who lends money on pledge or the deposit of goods.*
Pawner, pan′ér, *n. One who pledges anything as security for the payment of borrowed money.*
Pay, pā, *vt. To satisfy, as a claim or claims resting upon a covenant; to discharge, as a debt; to give the equivalent for; to punish; to beat; to make amends by suffering (with for); in naval language* [Fr. *poisser*, from *poix*, pitch], *to cover or smear over with tar or pitch, as the seams of a ship.*—*vi. To recompense; to be profitable. ppr.* paying, *pret. & pp.* paid.—*n. A covenanted equivalent given for something received; compensation; recompense; an equivalent given for money due, goods purchased, or services performed; the stipend allowed to each individual serving in the army or navy.* [Fr. *payer*; L. *pactum*, a covenant—*paciscor*, to covenant.]
Payable, pā′a-bl, *a. That may or ought to be paid; that can be paid; that there is power to pay.* [Fr.]
Payer, pā′ér, *n. One who pays.*
Paymaster, pā′mas-tér, *n. One who is to pay; an officer in the army whose duty is to pay the officers and soldiers their wages.*
Payment, pā′ment, *n. Act of paying; the thing given in discharge of a debt or fulfilment of a promise; reward; sometimes, deserved punishment.*
Pea, pē, *n. A plant and its fruit, much cultivated for food.* (In the plural, we write *peas* for two or more individual seeds, but *pease* for an indefinite number or quantity in bulk.) [Sax. *pisa*—Gr. *pison.*]
Peace, pēs, *n. An agreement; a state of quiet or tranquillity; freedom from war; public quiet; freedom from civil war; freedom from private quarrels; freedom from disturbance by the pas-*

Fāte, fär, fat, fall; mē, met, hér; pine, pin; nōte, not, move; tūbe, tub, bull; oil, pound.

sious; calmness; quiet of conscience; harmony; a state of reconciliation between parties at variance.—*vi.* To become quiet.—*interj.* Silence! hist! be quiet! [L. *pax, pacis—pango, pactum*, to fasten.]
Peaceable, pēs'a-bl, *a. Disposed to peace;* free from war, tumult, or public commotion; tranquil; free from private feuds; not agitated with passion; serene; calm. [Fr. *paisible.*]
Peaceableness, pēs'a-bl-nes, *n. State of being peaceable.*
Peaceably, pēs'a-bli, *adv. In a peaceable manner.*
Peaceful, pēs'fụl, *a. Full of peace;* quiet; not in a state of war or commotion; mild; calm; serene; not agitated by passion; removed from noise; still; free from disturbance.
Peacefully, pēs'fụl-li, *adv.* Without war or commotion; quietly; mildly.
Peacefulness, pēs'fụl-nes, *n. State of being peaceful;* quiet.
Peace-maker, pēs'māk-ėr, *n. One who makes peace*, by reconciling parties that are at variance.
Peace-offering, pēs'of-fėr-ing, *n.* A voluntary offering to God, among the Jews, in devout thankfulness for his benefits, or to ask favours from him.
Peace-parted, pēs'pärt-ed, *a. Dismissed from the world in peace.*
Peach, pēch, *n.* A well-known tree and its fruit, originally from *Persia.* [Fr. *pêche.*]
Peach†, pēch, *vi.* To turn informer.
Peach-coloured, pēch'kul-ėrd, *a. Of the colour of a peach-blossom;* of a pale red colour.
Peacock, pē'kok, *n.* A beautiful gallinaceous bird, so named from his well-known cry. [*pea* in this word – Sax. *pawa*, and L. *pavo*, a peacock.]
Peahen, pē'hen, *n.* The *hen* or female of the peacock.
Peak, pēk, *n.* A *point;* the end of anything that terminates in a point; the top of a hill; the upper outer corner of a sail which is extended by a yard; also, the extremity of the yard.—*vi.*† To acquire sharpness of figure; to pine. [Sax. *peac;* Fr. *pique*, a pike.]
Peaked, pēkt, *p.a. Pointed;* ending in a point.
Peal, pēl, *n. A loud sound;* usually a succession of loud sounds, as of bells, thunder, &c.—*vi.* To *utter loud* and solemn *sounds;* to resound. [Icel. *bylia*, to resound.]
Pealing, pēl'ing, *p.a.* Uttering a loud sound or successive sounds.
Pear, pār, *n.* The well-known *fruit* of a tree, having a sweet delicious taste; the plant or tree itself. [Sax. *pera*—L. *pirum*—Heb. *pára*, to bear.]
Pearl, pėrl, *n.* A white, hard, smooth, shining body, usually *roundish*, found in certain fish of the oyster kind, valued highly for its beauty; something very precious; a white speck growing on the eye; a small printing letter.—*a.* Relating to or made of *pearls.*—*vt.* To set or adorn with *pearls;* to make in shape like pearls. [Fr. *perle*—Gr. *sphaira*, a ball.]
Pearly, pėrl'i, *a. Containing pearls;* abounding with *pearls;* resembling *pearls;* clear; pure; transparent.
Peasant, pe'zant, *n. A rustic;* a hind; one whose business is rural labour.—*a. Inhabiting the country;* rustic; rural. [Old Fr. *paisant*—L. *pagus*, a village.]
Peasantry, pe'zant-ri, *n. Peasants;* rustics; the body of country people.
Peat, pēt, *n.* A substance of vegetable origin, always found more or less *saturated with water*, and forming, when dried, a valuable kind of fuel. [Icel. *pyttr*, a marsh or bog.]
Peat†, pēt, *n. A pet;* a small delicate person. [Fr. *petit*, little.]
Peaty, pēt'i, *a. Composed of peat;* resembling peat.
Pebble, peb'l, *n.* A roundish stone, of any kind, from the size of a nut to that of a man's head; a stone rounded by the action of water; transparent and colourless rock-crystal. [Sax. *papol-stanas*, pebble-stones.]
Pebbled, peb'ld, *p.a. Abounding with pebbles.*
Pebbly, peb'l-i, *a. Full of pebbles;* abounding with small roundish stones.
Peccability, pe-ka-bil'i-ti, *n. State of being peccable.*
Peccable, pek'a-bl, *a. Liable to do amiss*, or to sin; subject to transgress the divine law. [Fr.—L. *pecco*, to do amiss.]
Peccadillo, pe-ka-dil'lō, *n. A slight trespass or offence;* a petty crime or fault. [Sp. *pecadillo*—L. *pecco*, to do amiss.]
Peccant, pek'ant, *a. Transgressing;* sinning; criminal; morbid;not healthy. [Fr.—L. *pecco*, to sin.]
Peck, pek, *n. The fourth part* of a bushel; a dry measure of eight quarts. [Old Fr. *picotin*, the fourth part of a bushel.]
Peck, pek, *vt.* To *strike with the beak;* to thrust the beak into; to dig with anything pointed, as with a pickaxe; to pick up, as food, with the beak.—*vi.* To make strokes with small and repeated blows. [Old Fr. *becquer—bec*, the beak.]
Pecker, pek'ėr, *n. One who pecks;* a bird that pecks holes in trees; a woodpecker.
Pectinal, pek'tin-al, *a. Pertaining to a comb;* resembling a comb. [L. *pecten*, a comb—Gr. *pekō*, to comb.]
Pectoral, pek'tor-al, *a. Pertaining to the breast.*—*n. A breast-plate;* the breast-plate of the Jewish high-priest. [Fr.; L. *pectus*, the breast.]
Peculate, pe'kū-lāt, *vi.* To defraud the public of money or goods intrusted to one's care, *by appropriating the property to one's own use;* to defraud by embezzlement; to steal. *ppr.* peculating, *pret. & pp.* peculated. [Late L. *peculor, peculatus*—L.*peculium*,a small private property.]
Peculation, pe-kū-lā'shon, *n. Act of peculating;* embezzlement of public money or goods. [Late L. *peculatio.*]
Peculator, pe'kū-lāt-ėr, *n. One who peculates.* [L.]
Peculiar, pe-kū'li-ėr, *a. Relating to private property;* one's own; singular; special; belonging to a nation, system, or other thing, and not to others; unusual; singular. [L. *peculiaris—peculium*, a small private property.]
Peculiarity, pe-kū'li-a'ri-ti, *n. Quality of being peculiar;* something *peculiar* to a person or thing. [Low L. *peculiaritas.*]
Peculiarly, pe-kū'li-ėr-li, *adv.* Particularly; singly.
Pecuniary, pe-kū'ni-a-ri, *a. Relating to money;* consisting of money. [L. *pecuniarius—pecunia*, money—*pecus*, sheep, cattle, &c.]
Pedagogic, pe-da-goj'ik, *a. Suiting or belonging to a pedagogue.*
Pedagogue, pe'da-gog, *n.* Primarily, *one who led boys* to school and brought them back again; a teacher of children; a schoolmaster; a pedant. [Gr. *pais, paidos*, a boy, and *agō*, to lead.]

Pedal, ped'al, *a. Pertaining to a foot*, or to a pedal.—*n.* A contrivance attached to the piano-forte, &c., acted upon by *the foot*, and designed to modify the tone of the instrument; one of the largest pipes of an organ, played and stopped with the foot. [Fr. *pédale*—L. *pes, pedis*, the foot.]
Pedant, pe'dant, *n.* A schoolmaster†; a person who makes a vain display of his learning. [Fr.]
Pedantic, pe-dant'ik, *a. Pertaining to a pedant;* vainly displaying or making a show of knowledge.
Pedantically, pe-dant'ik-al-li, *adv.* With a vain display of learning.
Pedantry, pe'dant-ri, *n. The style of a pedant;* the pompous use of learned and unsuitable words. [Fr. *pédanterie.*]
Peddle, ped'l, *vi.* To travel about the country *on foot*, and sell small-wares; to be busy about small matters or trifles.—*vt.* To sell, as small-wares, usually by travelling about the country on foot. *ppr.* peddling, *pret. & pp.* peddled. [probably from Fr. *pied*, L. *pes, pedis*, the foot.]
Peddler, ped'l-ėr, *n. One who peddles;* one who carries about small commodities, and sells them. [from *peddle.*]
Peddlary, ped'l-ė-ri, *n.* Small-wares sold by *peddlers.*
Peddling, ped'l-ing, *p.a.* Trifling; unimportant.—*n. The employment of a peddler.*
Pedestal, pe'des-tal, *n. A foot-stall* or stand; the base or support of a column, pillar, statue, vase, &c. [It. *piedestallo*—*piede*, foot, *stalla*, a standing.]
Pedestrian, pe-des'tri-an, *a. Going on foot;* performed on foot.—*n. One who walks* or journeys *on foot;* a remarkable walker. [L. *pedestris—pes, pedis*, a foot.]
Pedestrianism, pe-des'tri-an-izm, *n. A walking;* the practice of walking.
Pedicle, pe'di-kl, *n. A little foot;* a small short foot-stalk of a leaf, flower, or fruit. [Fr. *pédicelle.*]
Pedigree, pe'di-grē, *n.* An account of lineage through its different *steps or degrees;* line of ancestors from which a person or tribe descends; genealogy; a register of a line of ancestors. [Fr. *per*, through, and *degré*, a step.]
Pediment, pe'di-ment, *n.* An architectural ornament, commonly triangular, but sometimes circular, that finishes the fronts of buildings. [from L. *pes, pedis*, a foot.]
Pedobaptism, pē-dō-bap'tizm, *n. The baptism of infants.* [Gr. *pais, paidos*, a child, and *baptizō*, to baptize.]
Pedobaptist, pē-dō-bap'tist, *n. One who holds to infant baptism.*
Peduncle, pe'dung-kl, *n. A small foot;* a foot-stalk; the stem or stalk that supports the flower and fruit of a plant. [Fr. *pédoncule*—L. *pes, pedis*, a foot.]
Peel, pēl, *vt.* To *skin;* to strip by drawing or tearing off the skin of; to flay; to remove, as the bark or rind, even with an instrument; to pare; [Fr. *piller*] to strip; to plunder; to pillage. *vi.* To *lose the skin, bark, or rind.*—*n. The skin* or rind. [Fr. *peler*—L. *pellis*, a skin.]
Peel†, pēl, *a.* Naked.
Peeler, pēl'ėr, *n. One who peels*, strips, or flays; a plunderer; a pillager.
Peep, pēp, *vi.* To *cry* as chickens; to utter a fine shrill sound; to look through a crevice; to look narrowly; to begin to appear; to come forth from concealment.—*n.* The cry of a chicken; a sly look, or a look through a crevice;

first appearance. [D. *piepen*, to peep, chirp.]
Peeper, pēp'ėr, *n.* One that peeps; a chicken just breaking the shell.
Peer, pēr, *n.* An equal; one of the same rank; an equal in excellence or endowments; a fellow; an associate; a nobleman, particularly a nobleman who is entitled to a seat in the House of Lords. [Fr. *pair*—L. *par*, equal.]
Peer, pēr, *vi.* To come forth; to come just in sight; to appear; to peep out, as the sun over a mountain; to look narrowly. [L. *pareo*, to come forth.]
Peerage, pēr'āj, *n.* The rank or dignity of a peer or nobleman; the body of peers.
Peeress, pēr'es, *n.* The consort of a peer; a noble lady.
Peerless, pēr'les, *a.* Unequalled; having no peer or equal; matchless.
Peerlessness, pēr'les-nes, *n.* State of being peerless or of having no equal.
Peevish, pē'vish, *a.* Fretful; querulous; easily vexed or fretted; expressing discontent; childish. [perhaps akin to *perverse*.]
Peevishly, pē'vish-li, *adv.* In a peevish manner.
Peevishness, pē'vish-nes,*n.* Fretfulness; petulance; sourness of temper.
Peg, peg, *n.* A small pointed piece of wood, used in *fastening* boards; one of the pins of an instrument on which the strings are strained; a pin on which to hang anything.—*vt.* To *fasten with pegs. ppr.* pegging, *pret. & pp.* pegged. [Sax. *pic*, a pin—Gr. *pegnumi*, to fix.]
Peise, pēz, *n.* A weight; a poise.—*vt.* To *weigh*; to outweigh.
Pelf, pelf, *n.* Originally, money got by *pilfering*; riches; wealth. [allied to *pilfer*.]
Pelican, pel'i-kan, *n.* A large waterbird, said to be so named because with its strong bill it cuts and hollows out trees as with an *axe*. [L. *pelecanus*—Gr. *pelekus*, an axe.]
Pelisse, pe-lēs', *n.* Originally, a *furred robe* or coat, now a silk coat or habit worn by ladies. [Fr.—L. *pellis*, a skin.]
Pell, pel, *n.* A *skin* or *hide*; a roll of parchment. [L. *pellis*, a skin or hide.]
Pellet, pel'et, *n.* A *little ball.* [Fr. *pelote*—L. *pila*, a ball.]
Pelleted, pel'et-ed, *p.a.* Made of pellets; pelted, as with bullets.
Pellicle, pel'i-kl, *n.* A *thin skin or film;* a thin saline crust formed on the surface of a solution of salt evaporated to a certain degree; a thin skin which envelops certain seeds. [L. *pellicula*—*pellis*, a skin.]
Pell-mell, pel'mel, *adv.* With confused violence. [Fr. *pêle-mêle*.]
Pellucid, pel-lū'sid, *a. Perfectly clear;* transparent; not opaque. [L. *pellucidus*—*per*, and *lux*, *lucis*, light.]
Pellucidness, pel-lū'sid-nes, *n. Perfect clearness;* transparency.
Pelt, pelt, *n. The skin of a beast with the hair on it;* a raw hide. [G. *pelz*.]
Pelt, pelt, *vt. To strike with pellets*, or with something driven or falling; to drive by throwing something.—*vi.*† To be clamorous.—*n.* A blow; a stroke. [Fr. *peloter*—L. *pila*, a ball.]
Pelting, pelt'ing, *p.n.* An assault with anything thrown.—*a.*† Mean; sordid.
Peltry, pelt'ri, *n. The skins* of animals producing fur; skins with the fur on them; furs in general. [Fr. *pelleterie*, furriery—L. *pellis*, a skin.]
Pelvis, pel'vis, *n.* The *basin* or large bony cavity at the bottom of the belly. [L.—Gr. *pelikē*, a basin.]

Pen, pen, *n.* A *feather* prepared as an instrument for writing; an instrument used for writing, made of steel, gold, &c.; a writer.—*vt.* To write; to compose and commit to paper. *ppr.* penning, *pret. & pp.* penned. [Sax. *pinn*—L. *penna*.]
Pen, pen, *vt. To shut up;* to coop; to confine in a narrow place.—*n. A small inclosure* for beasts, as cows or sheep. *ppr.* penning, *pret. & pp.* penned or pent. [Sax. *pyndan*.]
Penal, pē'nal, *a. Relating to punishment;* denouncing the punishment of offences; incurring punishment; subject to a penalty. [L. *poenalis*—*poena*, punishment.]
Penally, pē'nal-li, *adv. As a penalty.*
Penalty, pe'nal-ti, *n. Penal retribution;* the suffering to which a person subjects himself by covenant in case of non-fulfilment of his stipulations; the sum to be forfeited for non-compliance with an agreement; a fine. [Low L. *penalitas*—L. *poena*, punishment.]
Penance, pen'ans, *n. Repentance*†; *the suffering or pain to which a person voluntarily subjects himself as a punishment for his faults*, or as an expression of penitence. [Old Fr.—L. *poena*, punishment.]
Pence, pens, *n.* The plural of *penny*, when used of a sum of money or value.
Pencil, pen'sil, *n. A little tail*†; a small hair brush used by painters; an instrument formed of black-lead or red chalk, with a point at one end, used for writing and drawing; a collection of rays of light which converge to, or diverge from, the same point.—*vt.* To write or mark with a *pencil;* to paint or draw; to delineate. *ppr.* pencilling, *pret. & pp.* pencilled. [Sp. *pincel*—L. *penis*, a tail—*pendeo*, to hang.]
Pencilled, pen'sild, *p.a.* Painted; drawn with a *pencil;* radiated; having pencils of rays.
Pencilling, pen'sil-ing, *p.n.* The act of painting or sketching; a sketch.
Pend†, pend, *vi. To hang;* to be undecided.
Pendant, pen'dant, *n.* An ornament or jewel *hanging* at the ear; a hanging ornament on roofs, ceilings, &c.; a long, narrow piece of bunting worn at the mast-heads of vessels of war; a picture or print which hangs as a companion to another. [Fr.—L. *pendo*, to cause to hang down.]
Pendency, pen'den-si, *n. A hanging* in suspense; the state of being undecided. *pendencia*.]
Pendent, pen'dent, *a. Hanging;* suspended; jutting over; projecting. [L. *pendens.*]
Pending, pend'ing, *p.a. Hanging* in suspense; depending; remaining undecided; not terminated.—*prep.* During; for the time of the continuance of. [Fr. *pendant*, during.]
Pendulous, pen'dū-lus, *a. Hanging;* fastened at one end, the other being movable. [L. *pendulus*—*pendeo*, to hang.]
Pendulum, pen'dū-lum, *n.* A body *suspended* by a right line from a fixed point, and moving freely about that point as a centre, or swinging to and fro; the swinging instrument in a clock which regulates its motion. [Sp. *pendola*, a pendulum—L. *pendeo*, to hang.]
Penetrability, pe'nē-tra-bil''li-ti, *n. Susceptibility of being penetrated.* [Fr. *pénétrabilité.*]
Penetrable, pe'nē-tra-bl, *a.* That may

be *penetrated or pierced* by another body; susceptible of moral or intellectual impression. [Fr. *pénétrable*.]
Penetrably, pe'nē-tra-bli, *adv. In a penetrable manner.*
Penetrate, pe'nē-trāt, *vt.* To *enter* or pass into the interior of; to pierce; to affect, as the mind; to cause to feel; to reach by the intellect; to understand.—*vi. To enter;* to pass; to make way; to affect the intellect or the feelings. *ppr.* penetrating, *pret. & pp.* penetrated. [L. *penetro*, *penetratus*.]
Penetrating, pe'nē-trāt-ing, *p.a. Subtle;* acute; discerning; quick to understand.
Penetration, pe-nē-trā'shon, *n. Act of penetrating;* the power by which the mind sees through anything difficult or abstruse; sagacity; discernment. [Fr. *pénétration.*]
Penetrative, pe'nē-trāt-iv, *a. That penetrates;* piercing; having the power to impress the mind†. [Fr. *pénétratif.*]
Penguin, pen'gwin, *n.* A bird of the diver kind, inhabiting the southern hemisphere, exclusively a water-bird, and aided by its paddle-like wings, swimming and diving with great facility. [etymol. unknown.]
Peninsula, pen-in'sū-la, *n.* A portion of land *almost surrounded by the sea,* or connected with a continent by a narrow neck; a large extent of country joining the mainland by a part narrower than the tract itself. [L. *pane*, almost, and *insula*, an island.]
Peninsular, pen-in'sū-lär, *a. In the form or state of a peninsula;* pertaining to a peninsula; inhabiting a peninsula.
Penitence, pe'ni-tens, *n. Pain*†; sorrow or grief of heart for sins; repentance. [Fr. *pénitence*—L. *poena*, punishment.]
Penitent, pe'ni-tent, *a. Repentant;* contrite; doing penance.—*n. One who repents* of sin; one sorrowful on account of his transgressions. [Fr. *pénitent.*]
Penitential, pe-ni-ten'shi-al, *a. Proceeding from penitence;* relating to penitence.—*n.* A Roman Catholic book containing the rules which relate to penance and the reconciliation of penitents. [Fr. *pénitentiel.*]
Penitentiary, pe-ni-ten'shi-a-ri, *a. Relating to penance,* or to the rules and measures of penance.—*n. A penitent;* a house of correction in which offenders are confined for punishment and reformation, and compelled to labour. [Low L. *poenitentiarius*, a penitent—L. *poena*, punishment.]
Penitently, pe'ni-tent-li, *adv. With penitence.*
Penknife, pen'nif, *n.* A small *knife* used for making and mending pens.
Penman, pen'man, *n. Penman, pl.* A *man who teaches the use of the pen* in writing; one who writes a good hand; an author; a writer.
Penmanship, pen'man-ship, *n. The use of the pen in writing;* the art of writing; manner of writing.
Pennant, Pennon, pen'ant, pen'on, *n.* A small flag; a banner; a long narrow piece of bunting worn at the masthead of vessels of war. [Fr. *pennon*—L. *penna*, a feather.]
Pennon, pen'on. *See* PENNANT.
Penny, pen'ni, *n.* (*Pennies* or *Pence,* pen'niz or pens, *pl. Pennies* denotes the number of coins; *pence* the amount of pennies in value.) An ancient English silver coin, in value about 3d.; but now a bronze coin, twelve of which are equal to a shilling; a small sum; money in general. [Sax. *peneg.*]

Fāte, fär, fat, fall; mē, met, hėr; pīne, pin; nōte, not, mōve; tūbe, tub, bull; oil, pound.

Pennyweight, pen'ni-wāt, n. *The weight of an ancient silver penny; a troy weight containing twenty-four grains.*

Pensile, pen'sil, a. *Hanging; supported above the ground.* [L. *pensilis—pendeo*, to hang.]

Pension, pen'shon, n. *An annual allowance of a sum of money to a person by government in consideration of past services; an annual allowance made by government to indigent widows of officers killed or dying in public service; an annual payment by an individual to an old or disabled servant.*—*vt.* *To grant a pension to.* [Fr.—L. *pendo*, to weigh out.]

Pensionary, pen'shon-a-ri, a. *Maintained by a pension.*—n. *A pensioner;* one of the chief magistrates of the towns in Holland. [Fr. *pensionnaire.*]

Pensioner, pen'shon-ėr, n. *One to whom a pension is granted by government;* a student of the second rank at Cambridge, who pays for his board and other charges.

Pensive, pen'siv, a. *Weighing or considering in the mind; thoughtful and sad; melancholy; expressing thoughtfulness with sadness.* [Fr. *pensif—*L. *pendo,* to weigh.]

Pensived, pen'sivd, p.a. Saddened.

Pensively, pen'siv-li, adv. *In a pensive manner.*

Pensiveness, pen'siv-nes, n. *State of being pensive;* gloomy thoughtfulness.

Pent, pent, p.a. *Shut up; closely confined* (often with *up*). [from *pen*, from Sax. *pyndan,* to shut up.]

Pentagon, pen'ta-gon, n. *A plane figure having five angles,* and consequently five sides; a fort with five bastions. [Gr. *pente,* five, and *gōnia,* an angle.]

Pentagonal, pen-tag'on-al, a. *Having five corners or angles.*

Pentagraph, pen'ta-graf, n. *An instrument which, by five different points for fixing the pencil, enables the draftsman to reduce an original to any degree.* [Gr. *pente,* and *graphō,* to write.]

Pentahedral, pen-ta-hē'dral, a. *Having five equal sides.*

Pentahedron, pen-ta-hē'dron, n. *A solid figure having five equal sides.* [Gr. *pente,* five, and *hedra,* a seat.]

Pentameter, pen-ta'met-ėr, n. *A poetical verse of five metrical feet.*—a. *Having five metrical feet.* [Gr. *pente,* five, and *metron,* a measure.]

Pentangular, pen-tang'gū-lėr, a. *Having five corners or angles.* [Gr. *pente,* and *angular.*]

Pentateuch, pen'ta-tūk, n. *The first five books of the Old Testament.* [Gr. *pente,* and *teuchos,* a book—*teuchō,* to prepare.]

Pentecost, pen'tē-kost, n. *A solemn festival of the Jews,* so called because celebrated on *the fiftieth day* after the feast of the passover; Whitsuntide, a festival of the Roman Catholic and other churches in commemoration of the descent of the Holy Spirit on the apostles. [Gr. *pentēkostē,* fiftieth day.]

Pent-house, pent'hous, n. *A shed standing aslope* from the main wall or building. [Fr. *pente,* a slope.]

Pent-roof, pent'rōf, n. *A roof all of whose slope is on one side.*

Penult, pen'ult, n. *The last syllable of a word except one.* [L. *penultimus—pene,* almost, and *ultimus,* the last.]

Penultimate, pēn-ul'ti-māt, a. *Noting the last syllable but one of a word.*—n. *The last syllable but one of a word.*

Penumbra, pēn-um'bra, n. *A partial shadow on the margin of the perfect shadow in an eclipse; the point of a picture where the shade blends with the light.* [Fr. *pénombre—*L. *pene,* almost, and *umbra,* a shade.]

Penurious, pē-nū'ri-us, a. *Needy;* excessively saving or sparing in the use of money; parsimonious; niggardly; sordid.

Penuriously, pē-nū'ri-us-li, adv. *In a saving or parsimonious manner.*

Penuriousness, pē-nū'ri-us-nes, n. *State or quality of being penurious;* niggardliness.

Penury, pe'nū-ri, n. *Poverty;* need; indigence; want of the necessaries of life. [L. *penuria—*Gr. *peina,* hunger.]

Peony, pē'ō-ni, n. *A plant and its flower,* which is large and beautiful. [Low L. *peonia,* from the discoverer, *Paon.*]

People, pē'pl, n. *The many;* the body of persons who compose a community; the vulgar; the mass of illiterate persons; the commonalty; persons of a particular class; a part of a nation; persons in general. (When *people* signifies a separate nation or tribe it has the plural number.) [Fr. *peuple;* L. *populus.*]—*vt.* To stock with *people* or inhabitants. *ppr.* peopling, *pret. & pp.* peopled. [Fr. *peupler.*]

Peopled, pē'pld, p.a. *Stocked or furnished with inhabitants.*

Pepper, pep'ėr, n. *A plant and its aromatic pungent seed,* much used in seasoning, &c.—*vt.* To sprinkle with *pepper;* to hit, as with *pepper-corns;* to beat; to mangle with blows. [L. *piper.*]

Pepper-box, pep'ėr-boks, n. *A small box with a perforated lid,* used for sprinkling pulverized *pepper* on food.

Pepper-corn, pep'ėr-korn, n. *The berry or fruit of the pepper-plant.*

Peppering, pep'ėr-ing, p.n. *A pelting with shot or blows.*

Peppermint, pep'ėr-mint, n. *An herb,* a species of *mint,* of a penetrating aromatic smell, and a strong pungent taste, glowing on the tongue like *pepper,* and followed by a sense of coolness.

Peppery, pep'ėr-i, a. *Having the qualities of pepper;* choleric; irascible.

Peptic, pep'tik, a. *Promoting digestion;* relating to digestion. [Gr. *peptikos—pepto,* to cook.]

Peradventure, pėr-ad-ven'tūr, adv. *By adventure,* chance, or accident; perchance; it may be.

Perambulate, pėr-am'bū-lāt, *vt. To walk through or over;* to pass through for the purpose of surveying; to visit as overseers. *ppr.* perambulating, *pret. & pp.* perambulated. [L. *perambulo, perambulatus—ambulo,* to walk about.]

Perambulation, pėr-am'bū-lā''shon, n. *Act of passing or walking through or over;* annual survey of the bounds of a parish. [Late L. *perambulatio.*]

Perambulator, pėr-am'bū-lāt-or, n. *One who perambulates;* an instrument for measuring distances on roads; a child's carriage. [Low L.]

Perceivable, pėr-sēv'a-bl, a. *That may be perceived;* perceptible.

Perceivably, pėr-sēv'a-bli, adv. *In such a manner as to be perceived.*

Perceive, pėr-sēv', *vt.* To obtain knowledge of through the senses; *to take thoroughly or comprehend by the mind;* to have mental knowledge of; to know; to understand; to observe; to discern; to distinguish; to feel. *ppr.* perceiving, *pret. & pp.* perceived. [Fr. *percevoir—*L. *per,* and *capio,* to take.]

Perceiver, pėr-sēv'ėr, n. *One who perceives,* feels, or observes.

Percentage, pėr-sent'āj, n. *The allowance, duty, or commission on a hundred.* [L. *centum,* a hundred.]

Perceptibility, pėr-sep'ti-bil''li-ti, n. *State or quality of being perceptible.*

Perceptible, pėr-sep'ti-bl, a. *That may be perceived;* that may impress the bodily organs; that may be known or conceived of. [Fr.]

Perceptibly, pėr-sep'ti-bli, adv. *In a manner to be perceived.*

Perception, pėr-sep'shon, n. *Act of perceiving,* or of receiving a knowledge of external things through the senses; that process of the mind which makes known an external object, and is consequent upon sensation; intellectual discernment; notion; conception. [Fr.]

Perceptive, pėr-sep'tiv, a. *That perceives;* perceiving. [Sp. *perceptivo.*]

Perch, perch, n. *A voracious fresh-water fish,* so named from its *dusky* colour. [Old Fr. *perche—*Gr. *perkos,* dusky.]

Perch, pėrch, n. *A roost for fowls,* which is often a *pole;* also, anything on which they light; a measure of length containing five yards and a half; a square rod; the 160th part of an acre.—*vi.* To sit on a *perch;* to roost, as a bird; to light or settle on a fixed body. [Fr. *perche—*L. *pertica,* a pole.]

Perchance, pėr-chans', adv. *By chance;* perhaps.

Percipient, pėr-si'pi-ent, a. *Perceiving;* having the faculty of perception. [L. *percipiens—capio,* to take.]

Percolate, pėr'kō-lāt, *vt.* To cause *to pass through* small interstices, as a liquor; to filter.—*vi.* To pass through small interstices or by filtration; to filter. *ppr.* percolating, *pret. & pp.* percolated. [L. *percolo, percolatus—colo,* to strain.]

Percolation, pėr-kō-lā'shon, n. *A straining through;* filtration; the act of passing through small interstices, as liquor through a porous stone. [Late L.]

Percussion, pėr-ku'shon, n. *A striking against,* so as *to shake thoroughly;* act of striking one body against another with some violence; the shock produced by the collision of bodies; the effect of sound on the ear; the act of striking or tapping upon the chest, abdomen, &c., in order to produce sounds by which the state of the subjacent parts may be ascertained. [Fr.—L. *quatio,* to shake.]

Percussive, pėr-kus'iv, a. *Producing percussion;* striking against.

Perdition, pėr-di'shon, n. *State of being wholly given up or over;* utter destruction; the utter loss of the soul or of final happiness in a future state; future misery or eternal death. [L. *perditio—do, datum,* to give.]

Perdu, Perdue, pėr-dū', a. *Abandoned;* employed on desperate purposes.—n. One who is placed on the watch or in ambush†.—*adv. In a hopeless or forlorn state;* in concealment. [Fr.—L. *perdo,* to lose.]

Perdurable†, pėr-dūr'a-bl, a. *Very durable;* lasting.

Peregrination, pe'rē-grin-ā''shon, n. *A going through lands;* a travelling in foreign parts; a wandering. [L. *peregrinatio—ager,* land.]

Peremptorily, pe'remp-tō-ri-li, adv. *In a peremptory manner;* absolutely; positively.

Peremptory, pe'remp-tō-ri, a. *Taking away wholly;* in a manner to preclude

debate; decisive; positive; final. [Fr. *péremptoire*—L. *emo*, to take, buy over.]
Perennial, pe-ren′i-al, *a*. Lasting through the year; continuing without cessation; unceasing; continuing more than two years, as a plant; continuing without intermission, as a fever.—*n.* A plant which lives more than two years, whether it retains its leaves or not. [L. *perennis*—*annus*, a year.]
Perennially, pe-ren′i-al-li, *adv.* Continually; without ceasing.
Perfect, pėr′fekt, *a*. Done completely; finished; consummate; having all that is requisite to its nature and kind; completely skilled; possessing every moral excellence; blameless; manifesting perfection; certain†; confident.—*vt*. To do thoroughly; to accomplish; to consummate; to finish; to instruct fully. [L. *perfectus*—*facio, factum*, to make.]
Perfectibility, pėr-fekt′i-bil″li-ti, *n*. The capability of becoming or being made perfect. [Fr. *perfectibilité*.]
Perfectible, pėr-fekt′i-bl, *a*. Capable of being made perfect. [Fr.]
Perfecting, pėr′fekt-ing, *p.n. Act of one who perfects.*
Perfection, pėr-fek′shon, *n. State of being perfect*; a quality or acquirement completely excellent; an essential attribute of supreme excellence. [Fr.]
Perfectly, pėr′fekt-li, *adv.* In the highest degree of excellence; totally.
Perfectness, pėr′fekt-nes, *n. State or quality of being perfect*; completeness.
Perfidious, pėr-fi′di-us, *a. Guilty of perfidy*; breaking good faith; false to trust; faithless; proceeding from treachery; disloyal; traitorous. [L. *perfidiosus*—*fides*, faith.]
Perfidiously, pėr-fi′di-us-li, *adv.* Treacherously; traitorously.
Perfidiousness, pėr-fi′di-us-nes, *n. Quality of being perfidious*; treachery.
Perfidy, pėr′fi-di, *n. Act of breaking faith*; treachery; faithlessness; disloyalty. [L. *perfidia*—*fides*, faith.]
Perforate, pėr′fō-rāt, *vt. To bore through*; to pierce with a pointed instrument. *ppr.* **perforating**, *pret. & pp.* **perforated**. [L. *perforo, perforatus*—*foro*, to bore.]
Perforation, pėr-fō-rā′shon, *n. Act of perforating*; a hole passing through anything, or into the interior of a substance. [Fr.]
Perforator, pėr′fō-rāt-or, *n. An instrument that perforates.* [Late L.]
Perforce, pėr-fors′, *adv. By force or violence.*
Perform, pėr-form′, *vt. To form thoroughly*; to execute; to effect; to act; to do; to carry into effect or accomplishment.—*vi.* To do; to act a part. [Late L. *performo*—L. *formo*, to form—*fero*, to bear.]
Performance, pėr-form′ans, *n. Act of performing*; deed; achievement; production; the exhibition of character on the stage; composition; the exhibition of feats.
Performer, pėr-form′ėr, *n. One who performs*; an actor.
Perfume, pėr′fūm, *n. A substance which affects agreeably the organs of smelling by emitting a fume or odour*; the volatile particles emitted from sweet-smelling substances; fragrance; incense. [Fr. *parfum*—L. *fumus*, smoke.]
Perfume, pėr-fūm′, *vt. To scent with perfume. ppr.* perfuming, *pret. & pp.* perfumed. [Fr. *parfumer*.]
Perfumed, pėr-fūmd′, *p.a.* Scented.

Perfumer, pėr-fūm′ėr, *n.* One whose trade *is to sell perfumes.*
Perfumery, pėr-fūm′e-ri, *n. Perfumes* in general; the preparation of perfumes.
Perfunctorily, pėr-fungk′tō-ri-li, *adv. In a perfunctory manner.*
Perfunctory, pėr-fungk′tō-ri, *a. Done carelessly* or superficially; done only for the sake of getting rid of the duty; careless; negligent. [L. *fungor, functus*, to perform.]
Perhaps, pėr-haps′, *adv. By hap or chance*; it may be; peradventure; perchance.
Periapt†, pe′ri-apt, *n.* An amulet.
Pericardium, pe-ri-kär′di-um, *n.* A membrane that *incloses the heart.* [Fr. *péricarde*—Gr. *peri*, and *kardia*, the heart.]
Pericarp, pe′ri-kärp, *n.* That which *goes round the seed* of a plant; the seed-vessel. [Gr. *peri*, and *karpos*, fruit.]
Perigee, pe′ri-jē, *n.* A position *near by the earth;* that point in the orbit of the moon in which it is at the least distance from the earth. [Fr. *périgée;* Gr. *gē*, the earth.]
Perihelion, pe-ri-hē′li-on, *n.* A position *near by the sun;* that part of the orbit of a planet in which it is at its least distance from the sun. [Fr. *périhélie;* Gr. *helios*, the sun.]
Peril, pe′ril, *n. Trial;* risk; hazard; jeopardy; particular exposure of person or property to injury or destruction; danger denounced; particular exposure.—*vt.* To hazard; to expose to danger. *ppr.* perilling, *pret. & pp.* perilled. [Fr. *péril*—Gr. *peirao*, to try.]
Perilous, pe′ril-us, *a.* Dangerous; hazardous; full of risk. [Fr. *périlleux*.]
Perilously, pe′ril-us-li, *adv.* Dangerously; with hazard.
Perilousness, pe′ril-us-nes, *n. Quality of being perilous*; dangerousness.
Perimeter, pe-rim′et-ėr, *n. The measure* of the line or lines which go round *about* a figure; the outer boundary of a body or figure, or the sum of all the sides. [Fr. *périmètre*—Gr. *metron*, measure.]
Period, pē′ri-od, *n. A way round about;* a circuit; the time which is taken up by a planet in making its revolution round the sun; a stated number of years; a cycle; any series of years or of days in which a revolution is completed; any specified portion of time; end; an indefinite portion of any continued state; state at which anything terminates; limit; length of duration; a complete sentence from one full stop to another; a full stop, thus (.). *vt.†* To put an end to. [Fr. *période*—Gr. *hodos*, a way.]
Periodic, Periodical, pē-ri-od′ik, pē-ri-od′ik-al, *a. Pertaining to a regular circuit; performed in a circuit;* happening by revolution, at a stated time; returning regularly in a certain period of time; performing some action at a stated time; constituting a complete sentence. [Fr. *périodique*.]
Periodical, pē-ri-od′ik-al, *n.* A magazine or other publication that is published at stated or regular *periods*.
Periodically, pē-ri-od′ik-al-li, *adv. At stated periods.*
Periodicity, pē′ri-od-is″i-ti, *n. State of having regular periods* in changes or conditions. [Fr. *périodicité*.]
Peripatetic, pe′ri-pa-tet″ik, *a. Given to walking about; pertaining to the Peripatetics,* or to Aristotle's system of

philosophy.—*n.* A follower of Aristotle, so called because the founder of this philosophy taught *walking about* in the Lyceum at Athens; ludicrously, one who is obliged t > walk, or cannot afford to ride. [Gr. *peripatētikos*—*pateō*, to walk.]
Periphery, pe-ri′fe-ri, *n.* The line that i< *carried round a circular body;* the circumference of a circle or other regular curve. [Fr. *périphérie*—Gr. *pherō*, to carry.]
Periphrasis, pe-rif′ra-sis, *n. A circumlocution;* the use of more words than are necessary to express the idea. [Gr.—*phrasō*, to speak.]
Periphrastic, pe-ri-fras′tik, *a. Containing periphrasis;* expressing the sense of one word in many.
Periphrastically, pe-ri-fras′tik-al-li, *adv. With circumlocution.*
Peripneumony, pe-rip-nū′mō-ni, *n.* An inflammation *about the lungs,* or of the lungs. [Gr. *pneumōn,* the lungs.]
Periscii, pe-ri′si-i, *n. pl.* The name of inhabitants of a frigid zone, or within a polar circle, whose *shadow moves all round* in the twenty-four hours. [Gr. *periskioi*—*skia,* a shadow.]
Perish, pe′rish, *vi. To pass away or depart entirely;* to die; to lose life in any manner; to waste away; to be in a state of decay; to come to nothing; to be extirpated; to be lost eternally. *vi.†* To destroy. [Fr. *périr*, *ppr. périssant*—L. *perso*—*eo*, to go.]
Perishable, pe′rish-a-bl, *a. Liable to perish;* subject to speedy decay.
Perishableness, pe′rish-a-bl-nes, *n. State of being perishable.*
Perishably, pe′rish-a-bli, *adv. In a perishing manner.*
Perished, pe′risht, *p.a.* Destroyed.
Perishing, pe′rish-ing, *p.a.* Dying; losing life; passing away.
Peristyle, pe′ri-stil, *n.* A range of *columns round a building* or square, or a building encompassed with a row of columns on the outside. [Gr. *stulos*, a column.]
Periwig, pe′ri-wig, *n. A small wig;* a kind of close cap formed by an intertexture of false hair worn by men for ornament or to conceal baldness. [Fr. *perruque*.]
Periwinkle, pe-ri-wing′kl, *n.* A small flowering plant, common in flower-borders. [Sax. *perwince*.] A small twisted sea-snail or shell-fish. [Sax. *winele*.]
Perjure, pėr′jūr, *vt.* Wilfully to make a *false oath* when administered by lawful authority (with recip. pron.); to make a false oath to. *ppr.* perjuring, *pret. & pp.* perjured.—*n.†* A perjured person. [L. *perjūro*—*juro*, to swear.]
Perjured, pėr′jūrd, *p.a.* Having *sworn falsely.*
Perjurer, pėr′jūr-ėr, *n.* One who wilfully takes a *false oath* lawfully administered.
Perjury, pėr′jū-ri, *n. The crime of forswearing,* or of wilfully making a false oath. [L. *perjurium.*]
Perk, pėrk, *a. Perched up erect.*—*vt.* To dress up; to make trim or smart; to prank. [W. *perc.*]
Permanence, Permanency, pėr′manens, pėr′ma-nen-si, *n. State of being permanent;* duration; fixedness; continuance in the same place or at rest. [Fr. *permanence.*]
Permanent, pėr′ma-nent, *a. Continuing to the end;* not decaying; lasting; continuing in the same state. [Fr.—L. *maneo*, Gr. *menō*, to stay.]

Fāte, fär, fat, fall; mē, met, hėr; pīne, pin; nōte, not, mōve; tūbe, tub, bull; oil, pound.

Permanently, pėr'ma-nent-li, *adv.* With long continuance; durably.
Permeability, pėr'mē-a-bil"li-ti, *n.* Quality or state of being permeable. [Fr. *perméabilité.*]
Permeable, pėr'mē-a-bl, *a.* That may be passed through without rupture or displacement of its parts, as solid matter. [Fr. *perméable*—L. *meo,* to pass, to go.]
Permeate, pėr'mē-āt, *vt.* To pass through, as the pores of a body; to pass through, as a substance, without displacement of its parts. *ppr.* permeating, *pret. & pp.* permeated. [L. *permeo, permeatus*—*meo,* to pass.]
Permeation, pėr-mē-ā'shon, *n.* Act of permeating. [L. *permeatio.*]
Permissible, pėr-mis'i-bl, *a.* That may be permitted or allowed.
Permissibly, pėr-mis'i-bli, *adv.* In the way of permission.
Permission, pėr-mi'shon, *n.* Act of permitting; liberty granted. [Fr.]
Permissive, pėr-mis'iv, *a.* That permits; granting permission or liberty; suffered without hindrance.
Permissively, pėr-mis'iv-li, *adv.* By allowance; without prohibition.
Permit, pėr-mit', *vt.* To let go through; to allow; to concede; to give in charge; to give leave or liberty to by express consent; to give consent to by silence. *ppr.* permitting, *pret. & pp.* permitted. [L. *permitto*—*mitto,* to send.]
Permit, pėr'mit, *n. Permission;* warrant; a written license or permission from an officer of the customs to transport goods from one place to another.
Permutation, pėr-mūt-ā'shon, *n.* A changing throughout; exchange of one thing for another; the arrangement of any determinate number of things or letters in all possible orders one after the other. [Fr.—L. *muto,* to change.]
Pernicious, pėr-ni'shi-us, *a. Having the quality of killing;* producing great injury; destructive; deadly; tending to destroy. [Fr. *pernicieux*—L. *neco,* to kill—*Sans. nash,* to die.]
Perniciously, pėr-ni'shi-us-li, *adv.* Destructively.
Perniciousness, pėr-ni'shi-us-nes, *n. Quality of being pernicious.*
Peroration, pėr-ō-rā'shon, *n. The concluding part of an oration,* in which the speaker enforces the principal points of his discourse. [L. *peroratio*—*os, oris,* the mouth.]
Perpend, pėr-pend', *vt.* To consider attentively. [L. *pendo,* to weigh.]
Perpendicular, pėr - pen-di'kū-lėr, *a. Hanging like a plumb-line;* vertical, or at right angles with the plane of the horizon; being at right angles to a line or surface, as a line or surface. *n.* A line falling at right angles on the plane of the horizon; a line falling at right angles on another line. [Fr. *perpendiculaire*—L. *pendeo,* to hang.]
Perpendicularity, pėr - pen-di'kū-la"ri-ti, *n. The state of being perpendicular.* [Fr. *perpendicularité.*]
Perpendicularly, pėr - pen-di'kū-lėr-li, *adv.* In a manner to fall on another line at right angles; in a direction toward the centre of the earth or of gravity.
Perpetrate, pėr'pē-trāt, *vt.* To carry through; to achieve; to consummate; to do; to perform. (In an ill sense, that is, always used to express an evil act.) *ppr.* perpetrating, *pret. & pp.* perpetrated. [L. *perpetro, perpetratus*—*patro,* to bring to pass.]
Perpetration, pėr-pē-trā'shon, *n. The act of perpetrating.* [Late L. *perpetratio.*]
Perpetrator, pėr'pē-trāt-ėr, *n.* One who commits a crime. [Late L.]
Perpetual, pėr-pe'tū-al, *a. Continuing throughout;* continuing without intermission; continuing for ever in future time; fixed; everlasting; endless. [Fr. *perpétuel*—L. *peto,* to go to or towards.]
Perpetually, pėr-pe'tū-al-li, *adv.* Constantly; continually; uninterruptedly.
Perpetuate, pėr-pe'tū-āt, *vt.* To make perpetual; to cause to endure or to be continued indefinitely; to preserve from extinction or oblivion; to continue by repetition without limitation. [L. *perpetuo, perpetuatus.*]
Perpetuation, pėr-pe'tū-ā"shon, *n. Act of making perpetual;* act of permanently continuing in knowledge and remembrance. [Fr. *perpétuation.*]
Perpetuity, pėr-pē-tū'i-ti, *n. Continued duration;* continuance to eternity; uninterrupted existence; something of which there will be no end. [Fr. *perpétuité.*]
Perplex, pėr-pleks', *vt. To entangle;* to make intricate; to make complicated; to distract; to confuse; to harass; to distress with suspense, anxiety, or ambiguity. [L. *perplexus,* entangled—*plecto, plexum,* to braid.]
Perplexed, pėr-plekst', *p.a.* Embarrassed; puzzled.
Perplexing, pėr-pleks'ing, *p.a.* Troublesome; embarrassing.
Perplexingly, pėr-pleks'ing-li, *adv. In a manner so as to perplex.*
Perplexity, pėr-pleks'i-ti, *n. Entanglement;* complication; embarrassment of mind. [Fr. *perplexité.*]
Perquisite, pėr'kwi-zit, *n. That which is diligently sought after;* something won or gained; profit, fee, &c., allowed for services beyond ordinary salary; something in lieu of regular wages. [L. *perquisitum*—*quæro,* to seek.]
Perry, pe'ri, *n.* The fermented juice of pears, prepared in the same way as cider. [Fr. *poiré*—L. *pyrum* a pear.]
Persecute, pėr'sē-kūt, *vt. To follow after;* to harass with unjust punishment; to inflict pain upon from hatred or malignity; to afflict or destroy for adherence to a particular creed or to a mode of worship; to harass with solicitations. *ppr.* persecuting, *pret. & pp.* persecuted. [Fr. *persécuter*—L. *sequor, secutus,* to follow.]
Persecuted, pėr'sē-kūt-ed, *p.a.* Harassed by troubles.
Persecuting, pėr'sē-kūt-ing, *p.a.* Pursuing with enmity.
Persecution, pėr-sē-kū'shon, *n. Act of persecuting;* state of being persecuted. [Fr. *persécution.*]
Persecutor, pėr'sē-kūt-ėr, *n. One who persecutes;* one who pursues another unjustly and vexatiously. [Late L.]
Perseverance, pėr-sē-vē'rans, *n. Act or state of persevering;* act of persisting in anything undertaken; steadfastness; continuance in a state of grace to a state of glory. [Fr. *persévérance.*]
Persevere, pėr-sē-vēr', *vi. To continue steadfastly* in anything; to pursue steadily any design or course commenced. *ppr.* persevering, *pret. & pp.* persevered. [Fr. *persévérer*—L. *severus,* serious, strict.]
Persevering, pėr-sē-vēr'ing, *p.a.* Constant in the execution of a purpose or enterprise.
Perseveringly, pėr - sē-vēr'ing-li, *adv. With perseverance.*
Persist, pėr-sist', *vi. To stand through,* or continue *steadily* in the pursuit of any business or course commenced; to persevere. [Fr. *persister*—L. *sisto,* to stand.]
Persistence, pėr-sist'ens, *n. Act or state of persisting;* steady pursuit o. what is undertaken; duration; obstinacy. [Fr. *persistance.*]
Persistent, pėr-sist'ent. *a. That persists;* continuing; remaining. [Fr. *persistant*—L. *sisto*—*sto,* to stand.]
Persistingly, pėr-sist'ing-li, *adv. In a persisting way;* steadfastly.
Persistive†, pėr-sist'iv, *a.* Persistent.
Person, pėr'son, *n.* A *mask;* a character; an individual human being, consisting of body and soul; a human being indefinitely; a living soul; one; an individual; a human being represented in dialogue or on the stage; the subject of a verb; the agent that performs, or the patient that suffers, anything affirmed by a verb; also, that modification of the verb which is used in connection with the subject. [L. *persona,* a mask.]
Personable, pėr'son-a-bl, *a.* Having a well-formed body or *person;* graceful; of good appearance.
Personage, pėr'son-āj, *n. Character represented;* a man or woman of distinction; stature; air. [Fr. *personnage.*]
Personal, pėr'son-al, *a. Of or belonging to a person;* not real; affecting individuals; proper to him or her, or to private actions or character; corporeal; direct or in person; applying to the character of individuals in a disparaging manner. [L. *personalis.*]
Personality, pėr-son-al'i-ti, *n. State of being a person;* individuality; an application of remarks to the conduct and character of individuals by way of disparagement. [Fr. *personnalité.*]
Personally, pėr'son-al-li, *adv. In person;* by bodily presence; with regard to numerical existence.
Personalty, pėr'son-al-ti, *n. Personal estate.*
Personate, pėr'son-āt, *vt.* To represent by an assumed character so as to pass for; to represent by appearance; to assume the character and act the part of; to resemble; to describe†. *ppr.* personating, *pret. & pp.* personated. [L. *personatus,* masked — *persōno,* to become a person.]
Personification, pėr-son'i-fi-kā"shon, *n. Act of personifying;* the ascribing to an inanimate being the figure or the sentiments and language of a rational being.
Personify, pėr-son'i-fi, *vt. To make into a person;* to represent with the attributes of a person; to give animation, as to inanimate objects. *ppr.* personifying, *pret. & pp.* personified. [Fr. *personnifier*—L. *facio,* to make.]
Personnel, pėr-son-el', *n.* The body of persons employed in some public service, as the army. [Fr.]
Perspective, pėr-spek'tiv, *n.* A *view through;* the art of delineating on a plane surface true resemblances of objects, as the objects appear to the eye from any given distance and situation, real or imaginary; a representation of objects in perspective. [Fr.—L. *specio,* to view.]—*a. Pertaining* to the art of *perspective;* made by perspective. [Fr. *perspectif*—L. *specio,* to view.]
Perspectively, pėr- spek'tiv-li, *adv.* Through a glass.
Perspicacious, pėr - spi - ka'shi-us, *a.*

ch, *ch*ain; j, *j*ob; g, *g*o; ng, si*ng*; ᴛʜ, *th*en; th, *th*in; w, *w*ig; wh, *wh*ig; zh, a*z*ure; † obsolete.

Quick-sighted; sharp of sight; of acute discernment. [L. *perspicax, perspicacis—specio,* to view.]

Perspicaciously, pėr-spi-kā'shi-us-li, *adv.* In a perspicacious manner.

Perspicacity, pėr-spi-kas'i-ti, n. Acuteness of sight; acuteness of discernment or understanding. [Fr. *perspicacité.*]

Perspicuity, pėr-spi-kū'i-ti, n. Transparency; easiness to be understood; freedom from obscurity; that quality of language which readily presents to the mind of another the precise idea of the author; distinctness. [Fr. *perspicuité.*]

Perspicuous, pėr-spi'kū-us, a. Transparent; clear to the understanding; not obscure or ambiguous. [L. *perspicuus—specio,* to view.]

Perspicuously, pėr-spi-kū'us-li, *adv.* Clearly; plainly.

Perspiration, pėr-spi-rā'shon, n. Act of perspiring; evacuation of the fluids of the body through the pores of the skin; matter perspired; sweat. [Fr.]

Perspire, pėr-spīr', *vi.* To emit the vaporous moisture of the body through the pores of the skin; to sweat; to be excreted through the pores of the skin.—*vt.* To sweat. *ppr.* perspiring, *pret. & pp.* perspired. [L. *spiro,* to breathe.]

Persuade, pėr-swād', *vt.* To bring over by talking; to influence by argument; to draw, as the will to a determination by presenting motives to the mind; to convince by evidence presented in any manner to the mind; to prevail on; to win over; to entice.—*vi.* To use persuasion. (With *with.*) *ppr.* persuading, *pret. & pp.* persuaded. [L. *persuadeo—suadeo,* to advise.]

Persuader, pėr-swād'ėr, n. One who or that which persuades.

Persuasion, pėr-swā'zhon, n. Act of persuading; state of being persuaded; conviction; a belief; or a sect adhering to a creed or system of opinions. [Fr.]

Persuasive, pėr-swā'siv, a. Having the power of persuading; influencing the mind or passions.—n. That which persuades. [Fr. *persuasif.*]

Persuasively, pėr-swā'siv-li, *adv.* In a persuasive manner.

Persuasiveness, pėr-swā'siv-nes, n. Quality of being persuasive.

Pert, pėrt, a. Lively; brisk; forward; saucy; bold. [W.]

Pertain, pėr-tān', *vi.* To hold through; to belong; to concern; to be the property, right, or duty; to have relation. [L. *pertineo—teneo,* to hold.]

Pertinacious, pėr-ti-nā'shi-us, a. That holds fast; holding to any opinion, purpose, or design with fixed resolution; obstinate; inflexible. [L. *pertinax, pertinacis—teneo,* to hold.]

Pertinaciously, pėr-ti-nā'shi-us-li, *adv.* Obstinately; inflexibly.

Pertinacity, pėr-ti-nas'i-ti, n. Quality of being pertinacious; obstinacy; stubbornness; perseverance(in a good sense). [Low L. *pertinacitas.*]

Pertinence, pėr'ti-nens, n. Quality of being pertinent; justness of relation to the subject; fitness; suitableness. [Low L. *pertinentia*—L. *teneo,* to hold.]

Pertinent, pėr'ti-nent, a. Pertaining; related to the subject or matter in hand; just to the purpose; apposite; fit; not foreign to the thing intended. [Fr. from L. *pertinens—teneo,* to hold.]

Pertinently, pėr'ti-nent-li, *adv.* Appositely; to the purpose.

Pertly, pėrt'li, *adv.* Briskly; saucily.

Pertness, pėrt'nes, n. Quality of being pert; sauciness; forward promptness.

sprightliness without force, dignity, or solidity.

Perturb, pėr-tėrb', *vt.* To agitate; to disquiet. [L. *turbo,* to disturb.]

Perturbation, pėr-tėrb-ā'shon, n. Disorder; disquiet or agitation of mind; great uneasiness; disturbance in public affairs; commotion of spirit; cause of disquiet. [Fr.—L. *turbo,* to disturb.]

Peruke, pė-rūk', n. A periwig; an artificial cap of hair. [Fr. *perruque.*]

Perusal, pė-rōz'al, n. Act of perusing; careful view.

Peruse, pė-rūz', *vt.* To read with attention; to examine with careful survey. *ppr.* perusing, *pret. & pp.* perused. [L. *utor, usus,* to become thoroughly familiar with.]

Pervade, pėr-vād', *vt.* To go through; to pass through, as an aperture or interstice; to permeate; to spread through, as the whole extent of a thing and into every minute part. *ppr.* pervading, *pret. & pp.* pervaded. [L. *pervado—vado,* to go.]

Pervading, pėr-vād'ing, *p.a.* Passing through.

Perverse, pėr-vėrs', a. Turned the wrong way; distorted from the right; obstinate in the wrong; stubborn; cross; petulant; peevish; disposed to cross and vex. [Fr. *pervers*—L. *verto, versum,* to turn.]

Perversely, pėr-vėrs'li, *adv.* In a perverse manner.

Perverseness, pėr-vėrs'nes, n. Quality of being perverse; untractableness.

Perversion, pėr-vėr'shon, n. Act of perverting; change to something worse; misapplication. [Fr.]

Perversity, pėr-vėr'si-ti, n. Perverseness; disposition to thwart. [Fr. *perversité.*]

Pervert, pėr-vėrt', *vt.* To turn the wrong way; to turn from truth, propriety, or from its proper purpose; to turn from the right; to corrupt.—*vi.* To become perverted. [L. *perverto—verto, versum,* to turn.]

Perverted, pėr-vėrt'ed, *p.a.* Corrupted; misemployed; misapplied.

Perverter, pėr vėrt'ėr, n. One who perverts or turns from right to wrong.

Perverting, pėr-vėrt'ing, *p.a.* Misapplying; corrupting.

Pervious, pėr'vi-us, a. That has a way through; affording passage; permeable; that may be penetrated by the mental sight. [L. *pervius—via,* a way.]

Perviousness, pėr'vi-us-nes, n. Quality of being pervious.

Pest, pest, n. A spreading distemper; a fatal epidemic disease; plague; pestilence; anything very destructive; bane. [L. *pestis*—Heb. *pusus,* to spread abroad.]

Pester, pes'tėr, *vt.* To plague; to trouble; to harass with little vexations; to encumber. [Fr.]

Pest-house, pest'hous, n. A house or hospital for persons infected with any contagious and mortal disease.

Pestiferous, pes-tif'ėr-us, a. That brings pestilence; malignant; noxious to peace, to morals, or to society; destructive. [Fr. *pestiféré*—L. *pestis,* and *fero,* to bring.]

Pestilence, pes'ti-lens, n. That which is pestilent; plague; any contagious disease that is epidemic and mortal; moral disease destructive to happiness. [Fr.]

Pestilent, pes'ti-lent, a. Producing the plague or other malignant, contagious disease; noxious; mischievous; destructive; troublesome; corrupt. [Fr.]

Pestilential, pes-ti-len'shi-al, a. Partaking of the nature of the plague; producing infectious disease; destructive; pernicious. [Fr. *pestilentiel.*]

Pestilentially, pes-ti-len'shi-al-li, *adv.* By means of pestilence.

Pestle, pes'l, n. That which beats or bruises; an instrument for pounding and breaking substances in a mortar. [L. *pistillum—pisto,* to pound.]

Pet, pet, n. A slight fit of peevishness or fretful discontent. [probably contracted from *petulant.*]

Pet, pet, a. *Petted.*—n. A little darling; a little child spoiled by fondling; a lamb brought up by hand; any little animal fondled and indulged.—*vt.* To treat as a pet; to fondle; to indulge. *ppr.* petting, *pret. & pp.* petted. [Fr. *petit, petite,* little.]

Petal, pe'tal, n. The leaf of an expanded flower; a flower leaf. [Fr. *pétale*—Gr. *petao,* to expand.]

Petaled, Petalous, pe'tald, pe'tal-us, a. Having petals.

Petard, pė-tärd', n. An engine of war made of metal, nearly in the shape of a hat, to be loaded with powder and fixed on a plank, and formerly used to break gates, barricades, drawbridges, and the like, by explosion. [Fr.—*péter,* to crack.]

Peterpence, pē'tėr-pens, n. An annual tax or tribute of one penny formerly paid by the English people to the pope.

Petiole, pe'ti-ōl, n. The foot-stalk of a leaf, or a leaf-stalk connecting the blade with the stem. [L. *petiolus—pes, pedis,* a foot.]

Petition, pė-ti'shon, n. A falling upon; an attack made in words; a supplication or prayer; a solemn supplication; a prayer addressed by a person to the Supreme Being; a formal request from an inferior to a superior; the paper containing a supplication.—*vt.* To make a request to; to make supplication to, as to a superior for some favour or right. [Fr. *pétition*—L. *peto,* to go to, to ask, to assail.]

Petitionary, pė-ti'shon-a-ri, a. That petitions; supplicatory.

Petitioner, pė-ti'shon-ėr, n. One who presents a petition, either verbal or written. [Fr. *pétitionnaire.*]

Petitioning, pė-ti'shon-ing, *p.n.* Act of asking or soliciting; solicitation; supplication.

Petrean, pė-trē'an, a. Pertaining to rock. [from L.—Gr. *petra,* a rock.]

Petrel, pet'rel, n. An ocean bird that appears, like Peter, to walk on the sea or skim over its surface, generally appearing in stormy weather, and believed by seamen to presage a storm. [Fr. *pétrel*—L. *Petrus,* Peter.]

Petrifaction, pet-ri-fak'shon, n. Act or process of petrifying; process of changing into stone or stony substance; that which is converted into stone; an organized body rendered hard by depositions of stony matter in its pores or cavities. [Fr. *pétrifaction.*]

Petrifactive, pet-ri-fak'tiv, a. Pertaining to petrifaction; having power to convert vegetable or animal substance into stone.

Petrifiable, pet'ri-fī-a-bl, a. That may be petrified.

Petrified, pet'ri-fīd, *p.a.* Changed into stone; fixed in amazement.

Petrify, pet'ri-fī, *vt.* To turn into stone or stony substance, as an animal or vegetable substance; to make obdurate; to fix in amazement.—*vi.* To be-

some stone, or of a stony hardness. *ppr.* petrifying, *pret. & pp.* petrified. [L. *petra*, a rock, and *facio*, to make.]
Petroleum, pē-trō'lē-um, *n. Rock-oil*; a liquid inflammable substance exuding from the earth, and collected on the surface of the water in certain fountains and wells. [Gr. *petra*, a rock, and *elaion*, oil.]
Petted, pet'ed, *p.a. Treated as a pet*; fondled.
Petticoat, pet'ti-kōt, *n. A little coat*; a loose under-garment worn by females, and covering the lower limbs. [Fr. *petit*, petty, and *coat*.]
Pettifogger, pot-ti-fog'er, *n. An inferior attorney or lawyer who is employed in small or mean business*. [Fr. *petit*, little, and *voguer*, to row.]
Pettily, pet'ti-li, *adv. In a petty manner*.
Pettiness, pet'ti-nes, *n. smallness*; littleness.
Pettish, pet'ish, *a. In a pet*; fretful.
Pettishly, pet'ish-li, *adv. In a pet*.
Pettishness, pet'ish-nes, *n. Quality of being pettish*; fretfulness; peevishness.
Pettitoes, pet'ti-tōz, *n. The toes or feet of a pig*; the human feet, in contempt.
Petty, pet'ti, *a. Small in amount, degree, importance, &c.*; inferior; trifling, trivial. [Fr. *petit*.]
Petulance, pe'tū-lans, *n. Quality of being petulant*; peevishness; pettishness; sauciness. [Fr. *pétulance*.]
Petulant, pe'tū-lant, *a. Attacking in a saucy manner*; saucy; forward with fretfulness or sourness of temper; wanton; irritable; ill-humoured; cross; fretful. [L. *petulans—peto*, to go to, to attack.]
Petulantly, pe'tū-lant-li, *adv. With petulance*; with saucy pertness.
Pew, pū, *n. An elevated place*; an inclosed seat in a church. [Old Fr. *pui*—L. *podium*, an elevated place—*pes*, the foot—Sans. *pad*, to go.]
Pew-fellow, pū'fel-lō, *n. One who sits in the same pew*; a companion.
Pewit, Pewet, pē'wit, pē'wet, *n. The lapwing or green plover.*
Pewter, pū'tér, *n. A compound metal, consisting mainly of tin and lead*; vessels or utensils made of pewter.—*a. Relating to or made of pewter*. [Old Fr. *peultre*.]
Pewterer, pū'tér-ér, *n. One who makes vessels and utensils of pewter.*
Pewtery, pū'té-ri, *a. Belonging to pewter*; as a pewtery taste.
Phaeton, fā'e-ton, *n. An open carriage like a chaise, on four wheels, and drawn by two horses*. [from *Phaëton*, the fabled son of Phœbus, who drove his father's chariot.]
Phalanx, fā'langks, *n. Primarily, a line of battle*; in ancient Greece a square battalion of soldiers, formed in ranks and files close and deep; any body of troops formed in close array, or any combination of people distinguished for solidity of union. [Gr.]
Phantasm, fan'tazm, *n. That which appears to the mind*; the image of an external object; an apparition; a phantom; a vain or airy appearance; something imagined. [Gr. *phantasma—phainō*, to bring to light—Sans. *bhā*, to be bright, to shine.]
Phantom, fan'tom, *n. A phantasm*; an apparition; a ghost; a fancied vision. [Fr. *fantôme*; Gr. *phainō*, to bring to light.]
Pharisaic, Pharisaical, fa-ri-sā'ik, fa-ri-sā'ik-al, *a. Pertaining to the Pharisees*; resembling the Pharisees.

Pharisaically, ta-ri-sā'ik-al-li, *adv. In the manner of Pharisees*.
Pharisaism, fa'ri-sā-izm, *n. The notions, doctrines, and conduct of the Pharisees, as a sect*; rigid observance of external forms of religion without genuine piety.
Pharisee, fa'ri-sē, *n. One of a sect among the Jews, whose pretended holiness led them to separate themselves from others, considering themselves as more righteous than other Jews*. [Heb. *pārush*, separated.]
Pharmaceutic, Pharmaceutical, fär-ma-sū'tik, fär-ma-sū'tik-al, *a. Pertaining to the knowledge or art of pharmacy*. [Gr. *pharmakeutikos*.]
Pharmaceutics, fär-ma-sū'tiks, *n. The science of preparing drugs or medicines.*
Pharmacopœia, fär'ma-kō-pē"a, *n. A treatise describing the preparations of the several kinds of medicines*, with their uses and manner of application. [Gr. *pharmakon*, a drug, and *poieō*, to make.]
Pharmacy, fär'ma-si, *n. The art of preparing and compounding substances for the purposes of medicine*; the occupation of an apothecary. [Fr. *pharmacie*; Gr. *pharmakon*, a drug, a philtre.]
Pharos, fā'ros, *n. A lighthouse which anciently stood on a small island of that name adjoining the Egyptian shore, over against Alexandria*; any lighthouse for the direction of seamen; a beacon. [Gr.]
Phase, Phasis, fāz, fā'sis, *n. Phases, pl. An appearance*; any appearance of the moon or other planet; the particular state, at any given instant, of an appearance which undergoes periodic changes. [Gr. *phasis—phainō*, to bring to light.]
Pheasant, fe'zant, *n. The Phasian bird, highly esteemed for the beauty of its plumage, the elegance of its form, and the delicacy of its flesh*. [Fr. *faisan*—Gr. *Phasis*, a river of Asia.]
Pheere, fēr, *n. A companion*; mate.
Pheeze, fēz, *vt. To heat.*
Phenix, fē'niks, *n. The fabulous bird which is said to exist single, and to rise again from its own ashes*; hence used as an emblem of immortality; a person of singular distinction or excellence. [L. *phœnix*.]
Phenomenon, fē-no'me-non, *n. Phenomena, pl. An appearance*; whatever is presented to the eye by observation or experiment, or whatever is discovered to exist; a remarkable appearance. [Gr. *phainomenon—phainō*, to bring to light.]
Phial, fī'al, *n. A drinking cup*; a small glass vessel used for holding liquors and medicines. [L. *phiala*—Gr. *phiō*, to drink.]
Philanthropic, Philanthropical, fi-lan-throp'ik, fi-lan-throp'ik-al, *a. Relating to philanthropy*; entertaining goodwill toward all men; loving mankind; directed to the general good.
Philanthropically, fi-lan-throp'ik-al-li, *adv. With philanthropy.*
Philanthropist, fi-lan'throp-ist, *n. One devoted to philanthropy*; one who loves his fellowmen, and exerts himself in doing them good.
Philanthropy, fi-lan'thrō-pi, *n. The love of man or of mankind*; universal goodwill. [Fr. *philantropie*; Gr. *philos*, loving, and *anthrōpos*, man.]
Philharmonic, fil-här-mon'ik, *a. Loving harmony or music*; relating to, or promoting, musical harmony. [Gr. *philos*,

loving, and *harmonikos*, skilled in musical harmony.]
Philippic, fi-lip'pik, *n. An oration of Demosthenes, the Athenian orator, against Philip, king of Macedon*; hence, any discourse full of acrimonious invective. [Gr. *philippikos*, relating to Philip.]
Philological, fi-lō-loj'ik-al, *a. Pertaining to philology*, or to the study and knowledge of language.
Philologically, fi-lō-loj'ik-al-li, *adv. In a philological manner.*
Philologist, fi-lol'ō-jist, *n. One versed in philology.*
Philology, fi-lol'ō-ji, *n. Love of learning*; the study of language; the investigation of the relation of different tongues to one another. [Fr. *philologue*—Gr. *philos*, loving, and *logos*, word, discourse.]
Philomel, Philomela, fi'lō-mel, fi-lō-mē'la, *n. The nightingale*. [from *Philomela*, who was changed into a nightingale.]
Philosopher, fi-los'ō-fér, *n. A person versed in philosophy*, or in the principles of nature and morality; one who devotes himself to the study of physics, or of moral or intellectual science; one who is profoundly versed in any science.
Philosophic, Philosophical, fi-lō-sof'ik, fi-lō-sof'ik-al, *a. Pertaining to philosophy*; proceeding from philosophy; skilled in philosophy; given to philosophy; regulated by the rules of reason; calm; temperate; rational.
Philosophically, fi-lō-sof'ik-al-li, *adv. In a philosophical manner.*
Philosophize, fi-los'ō-fiz, *vi. To act the philosopher*; to reason like a philosopher; to search into the reason and nature of things. *ppr.* philosophizing, *pret. & pp.* philosophized.
Philosophy, fi-los'ō-fi, *n. The love of wisdom*; the science of causes and principles; the principles and general laws of any department of knowledge; hypothesis on which natural effects are explained; reasoning; course of sciences read or taught in the schools; a particular system. [Gr. *philosophia—philos*, loving, and *sophia*, wisdom.]
Phlebotomist, fle-bot'ō-mist, *n. One who practises phlebotomy.*
Phlebotomy, fle-bot'ō-mi, *n. The act or practice of opening a vein for letting blood*; blood-letting. [Fr. *phlébotomie*—Gr. *phleps*, a vein, and *temnō*, to cut.]
Phlegm, flem, *n. A cold slimy humour in the body, once regarded as the matter and cause of many diseases*; the thick, viscid matter secreted in the throat; dulness; coldness; apathy. [Gr. *phlegma—phlegō*, to burn.]
Phlegmatic, fleg-mat'ik, *a. Abounding in phlegm*; generating phlegm; cold; sluggish; not easily excited into action or passion. [Fr. *phlegmatique*.]
Phlegmatically, fleg-mat'ik-al-li, *adv* Coldly; heavily.
Phœbus, fē'bus, *n. The Bright or Shining One*; a mythological name of Apollo, often used to signify the sun. [L.]
Phœnix, fē'niks, *n. See* PHENIX.
Phonetic, fō-net'ik, *a. Belonging to articulate sounds*; representing sounds; pertaining to phonetics or phonics. [Gr. *phōnētikos—phōnē*, sound.]
Phonetics, Phonics, fō-net'iks, fōn'iks, *n. pl. The doctrine or science of sounds*, especially of the human voice; the representation of sounds; the art of combining musical sounds. [Gr. *phōnētikos*, belonging to sound or speech.]

ch, chain; j, job; g, go; ng, sing; ᴠʜ, then; th, thin; w, wig; wh, whig; zh, azure; † obsolete.

Phonography, fō-nog′ra-fi, n. *A description* of the laws of *articulate sounds*; a representation of sounds, each by its distinctive character; a brief system of short-hand writing. [Gr. *phōnē*, and *graphō*, to write.]
Phonology, fō-nol′o-ji, n. *A treatise on sounds*, or the science of the elementary sounds uttered in speech. [Gr. *phōnē*, and *logos*, discourse.]
Phonotypy, fō′nō-tip-i, n. A proposed mode of printing, in which each *sound* of the voice shall be represented by a distinct *letter or type*. [Gr. *phōnē*, and *tupos*, a type.]
Phosphorated, fos′fo-rāt-ed, p. a. *Impregnated with phosphorus*.
Phosphoresce, fos-fo-res′, vi. To *shine*, as *phosphorus*, by exhibiting a faint light without sensible heat. ppr. phosphorescing, pret. & pp. phosphoresced.
Phosphorescence, fos-fo-res′ens, n. A faint luminousness of a body, like that of *phosphorus*, unaccompanied with sensible heat. [Fr.]
Phosphorescent, fos-fo-res′ent, a. Shining with a faint light like that of *phosphorus*. [Fr.]
Phosphoric, fos-fo′rik, a. *Pertaining to* or *obtained from phosphorus*.
Phosphorus, fos′for-us, n. *That which brings light*; a combustible substance resembling fine wax, which has a *luminous* appearance in the dark, and burns in common air with great rapidity. [Gr. *phōs*, light, and *pherō*, to bring.]
Photograph, fō′tō-graf, n. A picture obtained by *photography*.
Photographic, fō-tō-graf′ik, a. *Pertaining to photography*.
Photographist, fō-tog′raf-ist, n. *One who practises photography*.
Photography, fō-tog′ra-fi, n. The art of producing *representations* of persons and objects *by the action of light* on chemically prepared surfaces. [Gr. *phōs, photos*, light, and *graphō*, to write.]
Photometer, fō-tom′et-er, n. An instrument *for measuring* the relative illuminating powers of different sources of *light*. [Gr. *phōs, photos*, and *metron*, measure.]
Phrase, frāz, n. *A speaking*; a mode of speech peculiar to a language; an idiom; style.—*vt*. To express in peculiar words; to style. ppr. phrasing, pret. & pp. phrased. [Gr. *phrasis—phrazō*, to speak.]
Phraseless†, frāz′les, a. Incapable of being described in any language.
Phraseological, frā′zē-ō-loj′′ik-al, a. *Relating to phraseology*; peculiar in expression; consisting of a peculiar form of words.
Phraseologist, frā-zē-ol′o-jist, n. *A collector of phrases*.
Phraseology, frā-zē-ol′o-ji, n. *A mode of speech* or expression; peculiar words used in a sentence; style; a collection of phrases in a language. [Fr. *phraséologie*—Gr. *phrasis*, and *logos*, a word.]
Phrenological, fren-ō-loj′ik-al, a. *Pertaining to phrenology*.
Phrenologist, fren-ol′o-jist, n. *One versed in phrenology*.
Phrenology, fren-ol′o-ji, n. *The science of the human mind* as connected with the supposed organs of thought and passion in the brain, and the form of the skull. [Gr. *phrēn, phrenos*, the mind, and *logos*, discourse.]
Phthisic, ti′zik, n. *Phthisis*; a wasting

away; popularly, any difficulty of breathing, especially of a chronic nature. [from Gr. *phthisikos*.]
Phthisical, ti′zik-al, a. *Having or belonging to phthisis*; breathing hard; consumptive. [Gr. *phthisikos*.]
Phthisis, fthī′sis, n. *A wasting away; decline*; a disease of some part of the lungs, marked by cough, gradual emaciation and exhaustion, hectic, and usually copious expectoration. [Gr.—*phthinō*, to waste away.]
Phylactery, fi-lak′te-ri, n. Any amulet worn as a *protection* from danger or disease; among the Jews, a slip of parchment on which was written some text of Scripture, worn by devout persons on the forehead, breast, or neck, as a mark of their religion. [Gr. *phulactērion—phulassō*, to guard.]
Physic, fi′zik, n. The art of healing diseases, originally practised by those who pretended to a special knowledge *of nature* and her powers; medicines; a purge.—*vt*. *To treat with physic*; to heal. ppr. physicking, pret. & pp. physicked. [Gr. *phusikos*, natural—*phuō*, to bring forth—Sans. *bhū*, to be.]
Physical, fi′zik-al, a. *Natural*; pertaining to the material structure of an organized being, particularly man; perceptible to the senses; relating to the art of healing. [Gr. *phusikos*.]
Physically, fi′zik-al-li, adv. *Naturally*.
Physician, fi-zi′shon, n. Primarily, a *naturalist*; one whose profession is to prescribe remedies for diseases; one who heals moral and spiritual diseases. [Fr. *physicien*—Gr. *phuō*, to bring forth.]
Physics, fi′ziks, n. *The science of nature*; the science of the material system; natural philosophy. [Fr. *physique*—Gr. *hē phusikē*.]
Physiognomical, fi′zi-og-nom′′ik-al, a. *Pertaining to physiognomy*.
Physiognomist, fi-zi-og′nō-mist, n. *One who is skilled in physiognomy*.
Physiognomy, fi-zi-og′nō-mi, n. The art of *judging* of a person's *nature* by his outward look; the face with respect to the temper of the mind; particular expression of countenance. [Gr. *phusiognōmonia*—*phusis*, nature, and *gnōmē*, knowledge.]
Physiological, fi′zi-ō-loj′′ik-al, a. *Pertaining to physiology*.
Physiologically, fi′zi-ō-loj′′ik-al-li, adv. *According to the principles of physiology*.
Physiologist, fi-zi-ol′o-jist, n. *One who is versed in the science of physiology*.
Physiology, fi-zi-ol′o-ji, n. Primarily, *an inquiring into nature*; the science of life; the science of the functions of all the different organs of animals and plants. [Gr. *phusis*, nature, from *phuō*, to bring forth, and *logos*, discourse.]
Piacular, pi-ak′ū-lär, a. *Expiatory; atoning*; having power to atone; requiring expiation. [Fr. *piaculaire*; L. *pio*, to propitiate.]
Pianist, pi′a-nist, n. *A performer on the piano-forte*.
Piano, pi-ä′nō, a. In music, soft. (Sometimes used as a noun for *piano-forte*.) [It. soft—L. *planus*, even.]
Piano-forte, pi-ä′nō-fōr′′tā, n. A keyed musical instrument of the harpsichord kind; so called from its power of producing *soft* and *loud* tones. [It. *piano*, soft, and *forte*, strong.]
Piastre, pi-as′ter, n. An Italian coin of variable value, generally worth about 4s. 4d.; a Spanish coin, the same as the Spanish dollar. [Fr.]
Piazza, pi-az′za, n. Originally *a broad*

way in a city; a covered walk supported by arches or columns; in Italy, a square open space, surrounded by buildings. [Sp. *plaza*; L. *platea*, a street.]
Pick, pik, vt. *To strike at with anything pointed*; to strike with the beak; to puncture; to pull off with the teeth; to pluck with the fingers; to separate by the hand, as flowers or fruit; to clean by the teeth; to take up; to take away by a quick movement; to seek industriously; to pull asunder; to pull into small parcels by the fingers; to steal by taking out with the hands; to cull; to choose; to pitch or cast.—*vi*. To eat slowly; to nibble; to do anything nicely; to pilfer. [Sax. *pycan*, G. *picken*, Dan. *pikke*.]—n. *A sharp-pointed* tool for digging in small quantities; a tooth-pick; choice; right of selection. [Fr. *pique*.]
Pickaxe, pik′aks, n. A tool in the form of a large *axe*, with a sharp point instead of a head.
Picked, pikt, p.a. Selected; sprucet.
Picker, pik′ér, n. *He or that which picks; one who picks* or culls.
Pickerel, pik′ér-el, n. A fresh-water *pike*. [from *pike*.]
Picket, pik′et, n. *A stake sharpened*; a guard posted in front of an army, to give notice of the approach of the enemy.—*vt*. *To fortify with pointed stakes*; to fasten to a picket or stake stuck in the ground, as a horse. [Fr. *piquet*.]
Picking, pik′ing, p.n. The act of plucking; selection; gathering.
Pickle, pik′l, n. *Brine*; a solution of salt and water, or any kind of salt or acid liquor, in which flesh, fish, or other substance, is preserved; a vegetable preserved in pickle.—*vt*. *To preserve in pickle*; to season in pickle. ppr. pickling, pret. & pp. pickled. [D. *pekel*; G. *pökeln*, to pickle.]
Pickled, pik′ld, p.a. *Preserved in pickle*.
Pickle-herring, pik-l-he′ring, n. A zany; a buffoon.
Pickling, pik′l-ing, p.n. The preservation of vegetables or meats in vinegar or brine.
Picklock, pik′lok, n. *A pointed instrument* for opening *locks* without the key; a person who picks locks.
Pickpocket, pik′pok-et, n. One who *steals* from the *pocket* of another.
Picnic, pik′nik, n. An entertainment carried with them by a party on an excursion of pleasure into the country, and also the party itself. [Fr. *piquenique*.]
Pictorial, pik-tō′ri-al, a. *Illustrated by pictures*; forming pictures or engravings. [Late L. *pictorius*—L. *pingo, pictum*, Sans. *pinj*, to paint.]
Pictorially, pik-tō′ri-al-li, adv. By pictures.
Picture, pik′tūr, n. *That which is painted*; *a painting*; a likeness drawn in colours; any representation, either to the eye or to the understanding.—*vt*. *To paint* a resemblance of; to form an ideal likeness of; to recall vividly. ppr. picturing, pret. & pp. pictured. [L. *pictūra*—*pingo, pictum*, to paint.]
Pictured, pik′tūrd, p.a. Represented.
Picturesque, pik-tūr-esk′, a. *Picture-like*; exhibiting that peculiar kind of beauty which is agreeable in a *picture*; striking the mind with great power by painting to the imagination any event as clearly as if delineated in a picture.—n. A picturesque assemblage in general. [Fr. *pittoresque*.]

Fāte, fär, fat, fall; mē, met, hėr; pīne, pin; nōte, not, mōve; tūbe, tub, bull; oil, pound.

Picturesquely, pik-tūr-esk'li, *adv*. In a *picturesque manner*.

Pie, pi, *n*. An article of food, consisting of paste baked with something in it or under it, as apple, minced meat, &c. [Ir. *pi* or *pighe*.]

Pie, pi, *n*. According to the Welsh, a bird that keeps to the same spot; the magpie, a parti-coloured bird of the crow family; printers' types mixed or unsorted. [W. *pi* and *pia*.]

Piebald, pi'bald, *a. Diversified in colour*. [from *pie*, magpie.]

Piece, pēs, *n*. A *fragment*; a part of anything separated from the whole; not the whole; a separate part; a composition of no great length; a distinct portion of labour; a picture; a coin; a gun; a patch; an individual person. *vt*. To enlarge by the addition of a *piece*; to join; to unite. *ppr*. piecing, *pret. & pp*. pieced. [Fr. *piéce*—Armor. *pés*, a bit, a part.]

Piecemeal, pēs'mēl, *a. Made of parts. adv. In or by pieces*; in fragments; by little and little in succession. [*piece*, and Sax. *mæl*, part.]

Piecer, pēs'er, *n. One who pieces*; a patcher.

Piece-work, pēs'wėrk, *n. Work done by the piece* or job.

Pier, pēr, *n*. A mass of solid *stonework* for supporting an arch or the timbers of a bridge or other building; a mole projecting into the sea, for breaking the force of the waves and making a safe harbour; a landing-place; a mass of solid work between the windows of a room or doors of a building. [Sax. *pėr, pers*; Norm. *pire*, a stone.]

Pierce, pērs, *vt*. To *thrust into with a pointed instrument*; to penetrate; to enter; to force a way into; to penetrate deeply, as the heart; to excite, as the passions; to dive into, as a secret.—*vi*. To enter, as a pointed instrument; to penetrate; to force a way into or through; to dive, as into a secret; to affect deeply. *ppr*. piercing, *pret. & pp*. pierced. [Fr. *percer*; L. *per*, and *tundo*, to beat.]

Pierced, pērst, *p.a*. Penetrated.

Piercer, pērs'er, *n*. He who or that which *pierces*; one who pierces or perforates.

Piercing, pērs'ing, *p.a*. Sharp; severe; affecting.—*p.n. The act of piercing* or penetrating with force.

Piercingly, pērs'ing-li, *adv*. With penetrating force or effect; sharply.

Pier-glass, pēr'glas, *n*. A *glass* which hangs against a *pier*, between windows.

Piety, pī'e-ti, *n. Filial reverence* towards God as the Father of all; godliness; devotion; religion; reverence of parents or friends, accompanied with affection and devotion to their honour and happiness. [L. *pietas—pius*, pious.]

Pig, pig, *n*. A young sow or boar; an oblong mass of unforged iron, lead, or other metal, so called because it flows in the melted state into channels branching off from the main channel, called the *sow*.—*vt*. or *i*. To bring forth *pigs*; to lie together like *pigs*. *ppr*. Pigging, *pret. & pp*. pigged. [Norm. *piges, piga*.]

Pigeon, pi'jon, *n*. A well-known bird; a dove. [Fr.]

Pigeon-hole, pi'jon-hōl, *n. A hole for pigeons* to enter their dwelling; a little opening or division in a case for papers.

Pigeon-livered, pi'jon-li-vėrd, *a*. Mild in temper.

Pight†, pit, *a*. Fixed; determined.—*vt*. To fix.

Pigment, pig'ment, *n. Paint*; a preparation used by painters, dyers, &c., to impart colours to bodies; the mucous secretion which covers the iris of the eye. [L. *pigmentum—pingo*, to paint.]

Pigmy, pig'mi, *n*. A person of very small stature.—*a*. Very small in size; feeble. [L. *pygmæus*.]

Pike, pik, *n. Anything pointed*; a military weapon consisting of a long wooden shaft with a flat steel head pointed, called the spear; a fork used in husbandry; a fresh-water fish with *a pointed nose*, very voracious. [Fr. *pique*—L. *spica*, a point]

Piked, pikt, *p.a. Ending in a point*.

Pikeman, pik'man, *n. A soldier armed with a pike*.

Pikestaff, pik'staf, *n. A staff having a pike at* the end.

Pilaster, pi-las'tėr, *n*. A square *pillar*, sometimes detached, but usually set within a wall, and projecting only a fourth or fifth of its width. [Fr. *pilastre*—L. *pila*, a pillar.]

Pilastered, pi-las'tėrd, *p.a. Furnished with pilasters*.

Pilch†, pilch, *n*. A furred gown or case.

Pilchard, pil'shärd, *n*. A fish resembling the herring, but smaller, and so named from the *smoothness* of its skin. [from Sax. *pylca*, a furred coat.]

Pilcher, pilch'ėr, *n*. A scabbard.

Pile, pil, *n. A ball*; a mass of things in a roundish form; a collection of combustibles for burning a dead body; a mass of buildings; a heap of shot laid in horizontal courses, rising into a pyramidical form.—*vt*. To lay into *a heap*; to amass; to fill above the brim or top. *ppr*. piling, *pret. & pp*. piled. [Sax. *pil*—L. *pila*, a ball.]

Pile, pil, *n*. A large *stake* pointed and driven into the earth to support the foundations of an edifice; one side of a coin. [Sax. *pil*, a pile—L. *palus*, a stake.]

Pile, pil, *n. A hair*†; the fine hairy substance of the surface of cloth, &c. [L. *pilus*, hair.]

Pilfer, pil'fėr, *vi*. To steal in small quantities; to practise petty theft.—*vt*. To steal or gain by petty theft; to filch. [Fr. *piller*, to plunder—L. *pilus*, a hair.]

Pilferer, pil'fėr-ėr, *n. One who pilfers*.

Pilfering, pil'fėr-ing, *p.n. Petty theft*.

Pilgrim, pil'grim, *n. One who comes from another country*; a wanderer; a traveller; one who travels to a distance from his own country to visit a holy place.—*a*. Of or belonging to a pilgrim. [L. *peregrinus*, a foreigner —*per*, and *ager*, land.]

Pilgrimage, pil'grim-āj, *n*. A journey to some place deemed sacred in order to pay devotion to the relics of a saint; the journey of human life; any undertaking requiring time and patience; time irksomely passed†.

Piling, pil'ing, *p.n. Act of heaping*, or of throwing into a heap; act of driving *piles*; a series of piles.

Pill, pil, *n. A little ball*; a medicine in the form of a little ball, to be swallowed whole; anything nauseous.—*vt*. To dose with *pills*. [L. *pila*.]

Pill, pil, *vt. To strip*; to rob; to plunder; to pillage. [Fr. *piller*—L. *pilo*, to make bald.]

Pillage, pil'āj, *n. A stripping* of property by violence; plunder; that which is taken from another by open force, particularly and chiefly from enemies in war.—*vt. To strip* of money or goods by open violence; to plunder. *ppr*. pillaging, *pret. & pp*. pillaged. [Fr.]

Pillager, pil'āj-ėr, *n*. One who plunders by open violence.

Pillar, pil'lär, *n. A pile*; a column; a kind of upright support in a building, usually round, and formed of two or more pieces; that which upholds; a monument raised to commemorate any person or remarkable transaction; something resembling a pillar; support. [Norm. *piler*—L. *pila*, a pillar.]

Pillared, pil'lärd, *p.a. Supported by pillars*; having the form of a pillar.

Pillion, pil'li-on, *n*. A *cushion* for a woman to ride on behind a person on horseback; a low saddle; the pad of a saddle that rests on the horse's back. [Ir. *pillin*.]

Pillory, pil'lō-ri, *n*. A frame of wood erected on *posts*, with movable boards and holes, through which were formerly put the head and hands of a criminal for punishment.—*vt*. To punish with the *pillory*. [Fr. *pilori*—L. *pila*, a pillar.]

Pillow, pil'lō, *n. A cushion* stuffed with feathers, &c., to support the head of a person when reposing on a bed; something that bears or supports.—*vt*. To rest or lay on for support, as on a *pillow*. [D. *peulaw*—L. *pulvinus*, a cushion.]

Pillow-case, pil'lō-kās, *n*. The movable *case* which is drawn over a *pillow*.

Pillowed, pil'lōd, *p.a*. Supported by *a pillow*.

Pilot, pi'lot, *n. A leads-man*; one whose office is to steer ships, particularly along a coast; a guide; a director of one's course.—*vt*. To direct, as the course of a ship in any place where navigation is dangerous; to guide, as a person through dangers. [Fr. *pilote*—D. *peilen*, to sound the depth, and *loot*, lead.]

Pilotage, pi'lot-āj, *n. The compensation made to a pilot* for directing the course of a ship; the duty or office of a pilot.

Pilot-fish, pi'lot-fish, *n*. A *fish* of the mackerel kind, so named because it frequently keeps company with vessels.

Piloting, pi'lot-ing, *p.n*. The act of steering a ship.

Pimple, pim'pl, *n*. A small swelling containing *matter*; a pustule. [Sax. *pimpel*—L. *pustula*.]

Pimpled, pim'pld, *p.a. Full of pimples*.

Pimply, pim'pl-i, *a. Pimpled*; having pimples.

Pin, pin, *n*. A sharp-pointed piece of wire with a head, used chiefly by females for fastening their clothes; a piece of wood, &c., sharpened, used to fasten boards together; a thing of little value; a peg used in musical instruments in straining and relaxing the strings; the eye or centre of a target†. *vt*. To fasten with a *pin* or with *pins* of any kind; to fasten; to confine. *ppr*. pinning, *pret. & pp*. pinned. [Sax. *pinn*.]

Pincers, pin'sėrz, *n. pl. An instrument for griping* anything to be held fast; an instrument for drawing nails from boards and the like. [Old Fr. *pinsas*, a pair of pincers.]

Pinch, pinsh, *vt. To compress* between two hard substances; to squeeze between the ends of the fingers, &c.; to squeeze, as the flesh till it is livid; to nip; to gripe; to straiten; to distress; to straiten by difficulties.—*vi*. To act

---

ch, *chain*; j, *job*; g, *go*; ng, *sing*; vs, *then*; th, *thin*; w, *wig*; wh, *whig*; zh, *azure*; † obsolete.

PINCHBECK   286   **PITCH**

with pressing force; to bear hard; to be puzzling, as an argument; to be straitened; to be covetous.—*n. A close compression* with the ends of the fingers; also, that which is taken between the ends of the fingers; a gripe; distress; oppression; difficulty; time of distress from want. [Fr. *pincer.*]

Pinchbeck, pinsh'bek, *n.* An alloy of copper and zinc, resembling gold in its appearance. (said to be from the name of the inventor.)

Pinched, pinsht, *p.a.* Petty; painted.

Pinching, pinsh'ing, *p.a.* Causing pain by constriction; covetous.—*p.n.* Act of squeezing or pressing.

Pinchingly, pinsh'ing-li, *adv. In a pinching way.*

Pin-cushion, pin'ku-shon, *n.* A small *cushion* into which *pins* are stuck.

Pindaric, pin-da'rik, *a. After the style and manner of Pindar,* the Greek poet; irregular.

Pine, pin, *n.* A species of fir-tree, rich in *a resinous juice.* [Sax. *pinn*—L. *pinus.*]

Pine, pin, *vi.* To *languish;* to wither; to grow lean under anxiety; to waste away with longing for something. —*vt.* To grieve for; to wear out. *ppr.* pining, *pret. & pp.* pined. [Sax. *pinan,* to languish.]

Pine-apple, pin'ap-pl, *n.* A species of *apple,* so called from its resemblance to the cone of the *pine* tree. [Old G. *pinepfli.*]

Pining, pin'ing, *p.n.* A state of languishing or wasting away.

Piningly, pin'ing-li, *adv. In a pining manner.*

Pinion, pin'yon, *n. A feather; a wing;* the joint of a bird's wing remotest from the body; the tooth of a wheel. [Fr. *pignon*] a smaller wheel with notches or teeth playing into the teeth of a larger wheel; a fetter for the arms.—*vt.* To bind the *pinions* of; to confine by binding the wings; to confine, as the arms to the body; to shackle; to chain, as with rules. (Sp. *pinon;* L. *pinna,* a feather.)

Pinioned, pin'yond, *p.a.* Shackled; furnished with wings.

Pink, pingk, *n. An eye, or a small eye;* a flower of a brilliant colour, said to be so named, because some of the species are marked with little dots resembling *eyes;* a light-red colour used by painters; from the colour of the flower, anything supremely bright or excellent.—*a.* Resembling in colour the most frequent hue of the *pink;* as, a pink dress.—*vt.* To work in eyeletholes; to pierce with small holes. [D.]

Pink-eyed, pingk'id, *a. Having small eyes.*

Pin-money, pin'mu-ne, *n.* A sum of *money* settled on a *wife* for her private expenses.

Pinnace, pin'ās, *n.* A small vessel navigated with oars and sails, said to be so called because originally built of *pine wood;* a boat usually rowed with eight oars; a small vessel attached to a larger. [Fr. *pinasse*—L. *pinus,* a pine-tree.]

Pinnacle, pin'a-kl, *n. A top;* a high spiring point; a slender turret, or a part of a building elevated above the main building. [Fr. *pinacle;* L. *pinna,* a feather, a battlement.]

Pinnacled, pin'a-kld, *p.a. Furnished with pinnacles.*

Pinner, pin'er, *n. One who pins* or fastens; a pin-maker; the lappet of a head-dress which flies loose.

Pin-point, pin'point, *n. Point of a pin;* a mere trifle.

Pint, pint, *n.* A marked measure for liquids; half a quart or four gills; in medicine, twelve ounces. [Sax. *pynt;* L. *pingo, pictum,* to paint.]

Pintle, pin'tl, *n. A little pin;* a long iron bolt; an iron bolt by which the rudder of a ship is hung to the sternpost. [dimin. of *pin.*]

Piny, pin'i, *a. Abounding with pinetrees.*

Pioneer, pi-ō-nēr', *n. A foot-soldier;* a soldier whose business is to march, &c., before an army, to repair the road, &c.; one who goes before to prepare the way for another.—*vt.* To go before and prepare, as the way for others. *vi.* To act as pioneer. [Fr. *pionnier*—*pion,* a foot-soldier—L. *pes,* the foot.]

Pious, pi'us, *a. Devout;* godly; holy; devoted to the service of God; dictated by reverence to God; having due respect for parents or other relatives; well disposed; practised under the pretence of religion. [L. *pius.*]

Piously, pi'us-li, *adv. In a pious manner;* religiously.

Pip, pip, *n. A chirping,* as of a chicken; a disease of fowls; a spot on cards; the seed of an apple, orange, or similar fruit.—*vi.* To *cry or chirp,* as a chicken. *ppr.* pipping, *pret. & pp.* pipped. [D.]

Pipe, pip, *n. A stalk of growing corn, which is hollow;* a tube to blow through; a wind-instrument of music, consisting of a long tube of wood or metal; the key or sound of the voice; one of the organs of voice and respiration; a tube of clay with a bowl at one end, used in smoking tobacco; something in the form of a tube; a cask usually containing 126 wine-gallons, used for wine; or the quantity which it contains.—*vi.* To play on a *pipe,* flute, &c.; to have a shrill sound; to whistle.—*vt.* To play, as a tune, on a *pipe* or wind-instrument; to call by means of a pipe, as in ships. *ppr.* piping, *pret. & pp.* piped. [Sax.]

Piper, pip'er, *n. One who plays on a pipe* or wind-instrument.

Piping, pip'ing, *p.a.* Weak; feeble; sickly; boiling.

Pipkin, pip'kin, *n. A small pipe* or earthen boiler. [dimin. of *pipe.*]

Pippin, pip'in, *n. A tart apple;* so named from the *pips* or dots on it. [D. *pippeling.*]

Piquancy, pē'kan-si, *n. Quality of being piquant;* sharpness; pungency; severity.

Piquant, pē'kant, *a. Pricking;* sharp; tart; pungent; severe. [Fr. from *piquer,* to prick.]

Piquantly, pē'kant-li, *adv. With sharpness;* tartly.

Pique, pēk, *n. A puncture;* irritation, usually, slight anger; a strong passion; nicety; punctilio.—*vt.* To *sting;* to *prick;* to nettle; to excite a degree of anger in; to touch with envy, jealousy, or other passion; (with the recip. pron.) to value one's self. [Fr. from *piquer.*]

Piquet, pi-ket', *n. A game at cards.* [Fr. from *pic,* a pick, a peak.]

Piracy, pi'ra-si, *n. The crime of a pirate;* robbery on the high seas; the taking of property from others by open violence and without authority on the sea; the robbing of another by appropriating his writings. [Fr. *piraterie.*]

Pirate, pi'rat, *n. One who tries to take ships;* a robber on the high seas; an armed ship which sails for the purpose of plundering other vessels on the high seas; one who publishes the writings of other men without permission.—*vt.* To appropriate by theft or without right or permission, as books or writings. [Fr.—Gr. *peiratēs*—*peiraō,* to attempt.]

Pirated, pi'rat-ed, *p.a.* Taken by theft or without right.

Piratical, pi-rat'ik-al, *a. Pertaining to or consisting in piracy;* predatory; robbing; practising literary theft. [L. *piraticus.*]

Piratically, pi-rat'ik-al-li, *adv. By piracy.*

Pirouette, pi'rö-et, *n.* A turning about on the toes in dancing; the circumvolution of a horse on the same ground. *vi.* To turn about on the toes in dancing. *ppr.* pirouetting, *pret. & pp.* pirouetted. [Fr.]

Piscatory, pis'ka-tō-ri, *a. Relating to fishes* or to fishing. [L. *piscatorius*—*piscis,* a fish.]

Pisces, pis'ses, *n. pl. The Fishes,* the twelfth sign or constellation in the zodiac. [L. pl. of *piscis,* a fish.]

Pish, pish, *interj.* A word expressing contempt; sometimes spoken and written *pshaw.*

Pismire, pis'mir, *n. The busy ant* or emmet. [The last syllable is the D. *mier,* an ant. The *pis* is probably the Sax. *fus,* willing.]

Piss, pis, *vi.* To discharge urine; to make water.—*n.* Urine. [D. *pissen.*]

Pistil, pis'til, *n. The seed-bearing organ* of a *flower.* [Fr.—L. *pistillum*—*pinso, pistum,* to stamp.]

Pistol, pis'tol, *n. A small fire-arm* or *hand-gun.*—*vt.* To shoot with a *pistol.* *ppr.* pistolling, *pret. & pp.* pistolled. [Fr. *pistolet.*]

Pistole, pis-tōl', *n. A gold coin of Spain,* worth about 16s. sterling. [Fr.]

Piston, pis'ton, *n.* A short cylinder of metal which fits exactly the cavity of a pump, and works up and down in it so as *to press some fluid into or out of* the tube which it fills, as in pumps, fire-engines, and the like. [Fr.—L. *pinso, pistum*—Sans. *pish,* to beat.]

Pit, pit, *n. A hole in the earth;* a deep place; an abyss; the grave; the area for cock-fighting; the part on the ground floor between the lower range of boxes and the stage in a theatre; any hollow part, as the pit of the stomach; the arm-pit; a dint made on a soft substance, as by the finger, &c.; a little hollow in the flesh, made by a pustule, as in the small-pox; a hollow place in the earth for catching wild beasts; hell.—*vt.* To form into a pit or *vits;* to indent; to set against each other in the same pit or area; to set in competition, as in combat. *ppr.* pitting, *pret. & pp.* pitted. [Sax. *pyt.*]

Pit-a-pat, pit'a-pat, *adv.* In a flutter; with palpitation or quick succession of pats or beats.

Pitch, pich, *n.* The resinous juice of the *pine-tree* and of other fir-trees; a thick black substance obtained by boiling down tar; used in calking ships, &c. *vt.* To smear or cover over with *pitch.* [Sax. *pic*—L. *pix,* Gr. *pissa.*]

Pitch, pich, *vt.* To *throw;* to thrust; to thrust, as a long or jointed object; to plant; to set; to throw at a point; to throw headlong; to throw with a fork; to set the key-note of a tune in music; to set in array.—*vi.* To light; to settle, as something thrown or flying; to plunge; to fall; to fix choice; to fix a tent; to rise and fall, as the head and stern of a ship passing over waves.—*n.*

Fāte, fär, fat, fall; mē, met, hér; pine, pin; nōte, not, move; tūbe, tub, bull; oil, pound.

A cast; height reached by anything thrown; degree of elevation; highest rise; the point where a declivity begins; descent; slope; the degree of descent; a fall; a thrusting down; degree of elevation of the key-note of a tune, or of any note. [Old Eng. *pick*, to throw.]
Pitched, picht, *p.a.* Set in array, as a battle; smeared with pitch.
Pitcher, pich'ėr, *n.* A beaked cup or vessel; an earthen vessel with a spout for pouring out liquors. [Arm. *picher*.]
Pitcher-plant, pich'ėr-plant, *n.* A genus of remarkable Asiatic plants, having a kind of cylindrical urn connected with the leaf, usually filled with sweet and limpid water, and closed with a sort of lid.
Pitchfork, pich'fork, *n.* A fork or farming utensil used in pitching hay or sheaves of grain.
Pitching, pich'ing, *p.a.* Descending; sloping, as a hill.—*p.n.* Act of throwing or casting; a settling; the rising and falling of the head and stern of a ship as she moves over waves.
Pitchpipe, pich'pip, *n.* A wind-instrument used by choristers in finding the pitch of the key.
Pitchy, pich'i, *a.* Like pitch; smeared with pitch; dark; dismal.
Piteous, pit'e-us, *a.* That may excite pity; wretched; deserving compassion; affected by pity; pitiful; paltry; poor.
Piteously, pit'e-us-li, *adv.* In a piteous manner; sorrowfully; mournfully.
Pitfall, pit'fal, *n.* A pit slightly covered for concealment, and intended to catch wild beasts by their falling into it.
Pith, pith, *n.* Marrow; the soft, spongy substance in the centre of plants and trees; strength or force; energy; concentrated force; closeness and vigour of thought and style; condensed matter; quintessence. [Sax. *pitha*.]
Pithily, pith'i-li, *adv.* With strength; with close or concentrated force.
Pithiness, pith'i-nes, *n.* Quality of being pithy; strength.
Pithless, pith'les, *a.* Destitute of pith; wanting strength.
Pithy, pith'i, *a.* Consisting of pith; abounding with pith; containing concentrated force; uttering energetic words.
Pitiable, pi'ti-a-bl, *a.* Deserving pity; affecting; wretched; miserable. [Fr. *pitoyable*.]
Pitiableness, pi'ti-a-bl-nes, *n.* State of being pitiable.
Pitiably, pi'ti-a-bli, *adv.* In a pitiable manner; wofully.
Pitiful, pi'ti-ful, *a.* Full of pity; tender; moving compassion; paltry; contemptible; very small.
Pitifully, pi'ti-ful-li, *adv.* With pity; contemptibly; with meanness.
Pitifulness, pi'ti-ful-nes, *n.* Quality of being pitiful; tenderness of heart.
Pitiless, pi'ti-les, *a.* Feeling no pity; hard-hearted.
Pitilessly, pi'ti-les-li, *adv.* Without mercy or compassion.
Pitilessness, pi'ti-les-nes, *n.* Quality of being pitiless; unmercifulness.
Pittance, pi'tans, *n.* Primarily, a portion of food allowed to a monk; a very small portion allowed or assigned; a very small quantity, as of money, &c. [Norm. *pitaunce*, allowance.]
Pity, pi'ti, *n.* Piety; pious sympathy; compassion accompanied with some act of benevolence; the feeling of one person, excited by the distresses of another; fellow-suffering; the ground or subject of pity; cause of grief.—*vt.*

To feel pain for, as for one in distress; to have tender feelings for, as for one, excited by his unhappiness; to commiserate.—*vi.* To exercise pity; to be compassionate. *ppr.* pitying, *pret. & pp.* pitied. [Fr. *pitié*—L. *pes, pietas.*]
Pivot, pi'vot, *n.* A small stake; that on which anything turns; a turning-point; the officer or soldier who happens to be at the flank on which a company wheels. [Fr.—L. *patus*, a stake.]
Pivoting, pi'vot-ing, *p.n.* Pivot-work in engines, machines, &c.
Placability, pla-ka-bil'i-ti, *n.* Quality of being placable or appeasable; susceptibility of being pacified.
Placable, pla'ka-bl, *a.* That may be appeased; appeasable; admitting its passions to be allayed; willing to forgive. [L. *placabilis—placeo*, to soothe, appease.]
Placard, pla-kärd', *n.* A flat piece of metal or wood to nail against a wall; a written or printed paper, intended to censure, posted up against a wall, &c., in a public place.—*vt.* To post, as a writing or libel, in a public place; to notify publicly. [Fr. from *plaque*, plate.]
Place, plās, *n.* A wide street; a public square in a city; a town; a fort; a country; any portion of space; a locality; position; site; local existence; separate apartment; residence; seat; abode; a collection of dwellings; a passage of writing or of a book; degree in order of proceeding; rank; order of dignity; official station; ground; room; station in life; calling; room or stead, with the sense of substitution.—*vt.* To put in any place; to put in a particular part of space; to set; to station; to establish in an office; to set or fix; to invest; to put out at interest; to lend. *ppr.* placing, *pret. & pp.* placed. [Fr. —L. *platea*, a broad way in a city.]
Place-man, plās'man, *n.* One who has a place or office under a government.
Placid, pla'sid, *a.* Pleasing; serene; mild; unruffled; indicating peace of mind; tranquil; not stormy. [L. *placidus—placeo,* to please.]
Placidity, pla-sid'i-ti, *n.* State or quality of being placid; tranquillity; gentleness; sweetness of disposition.
Placidly, pla'sid-li, *adv.* Mildly; without disturbance or passion.
Placket, plak'et, *n.* A petticoat.
Plagiarism, plā'ji-a-rizm, *n.* The act of a plagiary; the act of purloining another man's literary works; literary theft.
Plagiary, plā'ji-a-ri, *n.* Originally, a man-stealer; a thief in literature; one who purloins another's writings and offers them to the public as his own,— a. Practising literary theft. [L. *plagiarius—plaga,* a man-trap.]
Plague, plāg, *n.* A stroke or blow from Heaven; a pestilential disease of a malignant nature; anything vexatious; a state of misery.—*vt.* To afflict with a plague; to infest with calamity or natural evil of any kind; to trouble; to embarrass. *ppr.* plaguing, *pret. & pp.* plagued. [G. *plage*—Gr. *plessō,* to strike.]
Plaice, plās, *n.* A flat-fish, a salt-water fish allied to the flounder, but larger. [D. *platdijs*—Gr. *platus,* flat.]
Plaid, plād, *n.* A blanket; a loose striped or variegated outer garment much worn by the Highlanders of Scotland. [Gael. *plaide—peall,* a skin.]
Plain, plān, *a.* Even; level; not rough; open; clear; void of beauty; without

guile; undisguised; artless; sincere; candid; simple; not rich; bare; downright; manifest; unmistakable; visible; obvious; certain.—*n.* Level land; usually, an open field with an even surface; field of battle.—*adv.* Not obscurely; distinctly; articulately; with simplicity; bluntly. [Fr.—L. *planus.*]
Plain-dealing, plān'dēl-ing, *n.* A speaking with openness; a speaking and acting without art; sincerity.
Plain-hearted, plān'härt-ed, *a.* Having a sincere heart.
Plaining†, plān'ing, *n.* Complaint.
Plainly, plān'li, *adv.* In a plain manner; without cunning or disguise; in earnest; evidently; clearly; not obscurely.
Plainness, plān'nes, *n.* Quality of being plain; evenness of surface; want of ornament; openness; unrefined frankness; artlessness; clearness; sincerity.
Plain-spoken, plān'spōk-n, *a.* Speaking with plain, unreserved sincerity.
Plaint, plānt, *n.* A beating of the breast, &c., in token of grief; complaint; audible expression of sorrow; a private memorial tendered to a court, in which the person sets forth his cause of action in writing. [Fr. *plainte*; L. *plango,* to beat the breast.]
Plaintiff, plānt'if, *n.* One who complains of an injury; the person who commences a suit before a tribunal for the recovery of a claim. [Old Fr. *plaintif*—L. *plango,* to beat the breast.]
Plaintive, plānt'iv, *a.* Complaining; repining; expressive of sorrow; mournful; sad. [Fr. *plaintif.*]
Plaintively, plānt'iv-li, *adv.* In a manner expressive of grief.
Plaintiveness, plānt'iv-nes, *n.* Quality or state of being plaintive.
Plait, plāt, *vt.* To fold; to braid; to interweave, as strands; to entangle.—*n.* A fold; a doubling, as of cloth; a braid, as of hair or straw. [L. *plico, plicatus,* to fold.]
Plaited, plāt'ed, *p.a.* Braided; interwoven.
Plan, plan, *n.* The representation of anything drawn on a flat surface; draught; delineation; sketch; scheme; device.—*vt.* To form a draught or representation of; to scheme; to form in design. *ppr.* planning, *pret. & pp.* planned. [Fr.—L. *planus,* flat.]
Planch†, plansh, *vt.* To cover with boards. [Fr. *planche*, a board.]
Plane, plān, *a.* Even; plain; without elevations or depressions, as the surface of water at rest.—*n.* An even or level surface; an instrument used in smoothing boards.—*vt.* To make level; to make smooth; to pare off, as the inequalities of the surface of a board by the use of a plane. *ppr.* planing, *pret. & pp.* planed. [L. *planus.*]
Planet, pla'net, *n.* A wandering star; (pl.) stars which revolve about the sun and change their places, and also their distances, with respect to each other. [Gr. *planētēs—planē,* a wandering.]
Planetary, pla'net-a-ri, *a.* Pertaining to the planets; under the influence of a planet; produced by planets; having the nature of a planet. [Fr. *planétaire.*]
Planet-tree, plan'trē, *n.* A tree so named because of its broad leaves and spreading form. [L. *platanus*—Gr. *platus,* broad.]
Planet-struck, pla'net-struk, *a.* Affected by the supposed influence of planets; blasted.
Planisphere, pla'ni-sfēr, *n.* A sphere projected on a plane; a map exhibiting

ch, chain; j, job; g, go; ng, sing; ᴛʜ, them; th, thin; w, wig; wh, whig; zh, azure; † obsolete.

the circles of a sphere. [L. *planus*, and *sphere*.]

Plank, plangk, *n. A flat broad thick piece of sawed timber; anything resembling a plank; a support, as for crossing a chasm.—vt. To cover or lay with planks.* [D.—Gr. *plax, plakos*, anything flat and broad.]

Planned, pland, *p.a.* Devised; schemed.

Planner, plan'ér, *n. One who plans or forms a plan; a projector.*

Plant, plant, *n. That which shoots forth; a sprout; a sprig; a sucker; a vegetable; an organized living body, destitute of sensation; a sapling; a shrub; a child; a descendant; the fixtures and tools necessary to carry on any trade.—vt. To put in the ground and cover, as seeds, &c., for growth; to set in the ground for growth, as a young tree or a vegetable with roots; to engender; to set, as the germ of anything that may increase; to set firmly; to fix, as a flag; to fix, as the first inhabitants; to furnish with plants; to lay out and prepare with plants; to set and point, as cannon; to introduce and establish. vi. To perform the act of planting.* [L. *planta*—Sans. *prath*, to be expanded.]

Plantage†, plant'áj, *n.* An herb, or herbs in general.

Plantain, plan'tán, *n. A plant*, said to be so named from the resemblance of its leaves to the *sole of the foot*. [Fr.— L. *planta*, the sole of the foot.]

Plantation, plant-á'shon, *n. The act of planting; the place planted; formerly, a colony; a large estate appropriated to the production of cotton, sugar-cane, &c., as in America; a first planting; establishment.* [L. *plantatio—planta*, a plant.]

Planted, plant'ed, *p.a.* Set in the earth for propagation; established; furnished with seeds or plants for growth; settled; filled or furnished with what is new.

Planter, plant'ér, *n. One who plants; one who owns a plantation.*

Planting, plant'ing, *p.n.* Act of planting or of setting in the ground for propagation, as seeds, trees, shrubs, &c.; something planted; a plantation.

Plash, plash, *n. A small collection of standing water; a puddle.—vi.* To make a noise in water; to dabble in water; to splash. [D. *plas*.]

Plashy, plash'i, *a.* Watery; abounding with puddles.

Plaster, plas'tér, *n. That which is easily shaped; that which daubs over; a composition of lime, water, and sand, used for coating walls and partitions of houses; an external application of an adhesive nature, spread on leather, cloth, &c., and applied to a sore, a wound, &c.—vt.* To overlay with *plaster*; to cover with a plaster, as a wound. [Sax.; Gr. *plasso*, to shape.]

Plasterer, plas'tér-ér, *n. One who overlays with plaster; one who makes figures in plaster.*

Plastering, plas'tér-ing, *p.n. The act of overlaying with plaster;* the plaster-work of a building; a covering of plaster.

Plastic, plas'tik, *a. Having the power to give form to a mass of matter; capable of being moulded or modelled.* [Fr. *plastique*—Gr. *plasso*, to form.]

Plasticity, plas-tis'i-ti, *n. The quality of giving form or shape to matter;* capacity of being moulded or modelled.

Plat, plat, *vt.* To *plait;* to weave; to form by texture. *ppr.* platting, *pret. & pp.* platted.

Plat, plat, *n. A portion of flat, even ground;* a small piece of ground. [Fr.]

Plate, plat, *n. Something flat;* an extended piece of metal; armour, composed of flat broad pieces of metal; gold and silver wrought into articles of household furniture; a shallow dish from which provisions are eaten at table; the prize given for the best horse in a race; an engraving from a plate; a solid page of metal to print from; (pl.†) money.—*vt.* To cover with a thin *plate* of metal, as of silver; to arm with *plate* or metal for defence. *ppr.* plating, *pret. & pp.* plated. [Fr. *plat*—Gr. *platus*, broad.]

Plated, plāt'ed, *p.a.* Covered with a thin *plate* or coating of metal.

Plate-glass, plāt'glas, *n.* A fine kind of glass, cast in thick plates.

Platform, plat'form, *n.* The sketch of *the form* of a building upon *a flat* surface; a plan; a plot; an elevation of earth or a floor of wood or stone, on which cannons are mounted; a level surface for receiving the foundations of a building, &c.; a raised floor; a stage; a scaffold; the position which any body of men avowedly assumes.

Platina, pla'ti-na. See PLATINUM.

Plating, plāt'ing, *p.n.* The art of covering anything with a thin *plate* or coating of metal, as of silver.

Platinum, pla'ti-num, *n.* A metal resembling silver, or of a grayish-white colour, the heaviest of all metals, very hard, ductile, and malleable. [Sp. *platina—plata*, silver.]

Platitude, plat'i-tod, *n. Flatness;* a weak remark. [Fr.]

Platonic, pla-ton'ik, *a. Pertaining to Plato*, or to his philosophy, his school, or his opinions; pure; spiritual; free from carnal or sensual desire.

Platonically, pla-ton'ik-al-li, *adv. After the manner of the Platonists.*

Platonism, pla'ton-izm, *n.* The doctrines or philosophy of *Plato*.

Platonist, pla'ton-ist, *n.* One who professes to be a *follower of Plato*.

Platoon, pla-tön', *n. A knot of men;* formerly, a small body of soldiers drawn out of a battalion of foot when they form a hollow square, to strengthen the angles; now, two files forming a subdivision of a company. [Fr. *peloton*, clew of thread—L. *pila*, a ball.]

Platter, plat'ér, *n.* A large *flat* shallow dish for holding the provisions of a table. [from *plat*.]

Platting, plat'ing, *p.n.* Slips of cane, straw, &c., woven or *plaited*, for making into hats, &c.

Plaudit, pla'dit, *n. A clapping* of the hands, in token of approbation; applause; shout of approbation; acclamation. [L. *plaudite*, clap ye your hands—*plaudo*, to applaud.]

Plausibility, plaz-i-bil'i-ti, *n. Quality of being plausible;* speciousness; superficial appearance of right. [Fr. *plausibilité*.]

Plausible, plaz'i-bl, *a.* Originally, *that deserves a clapping of hands;* superficially pleasing; specious; colourable; using specious discourse. [L. *plausibilis—plaudo*, to applaud.]

Plausibly, plaz'i-bli, *adv.* With expression of applause.

Plausive†, pla'siv, *a.* Plausible.

Play, pla, *vi.* To dance or leap; to use any exercise for pleasure; to sport; to frisk; to toy; to act with levity; to trifle; to act wantonly; to do something fanciful; to contend in a game; to game; to practise a trick; to perform on an instrument of music; to move, as the lungs; to act, as a machine; to move irregularly; to act a part on the stage; to personate a character, to move in any manner; to move one way and another, as a wheel or piston; to make sport of (with *upon*). *vt.* To use, as an instrument of music; to act, as a sportive part; to perform by representing a character; to perform, as one's part in life; to perform in contest for a prize; to display (with *off*).—*n. Dancing;* any exercise intended for pleasure or diversion; frolic; manner of dealing; gambols; gaming; practice of contending for victory; practice in any contest; employment; office; manner of acting in contest; a dramatic composition; representation of a comedy or tragedy; performance on an instrument of music; movement, regular or irregular; room for motion; liberty of acting; scope. [Sax. *plegan*; Icel. *leika*, to play.]

Play-book, pla'buk, *n. A book of dramatic compositions.*

Player, pla'ér, *n. One who plays* in any game or sport; an actor; one who performs on an instrument of music; a gamester; one who acts a part in a certain manner.

Play-fellow, pla'fel-lō, *n. A companion in amusements or sports.*

Play-fere†, pla'fér, *n. A play-fellow.*

Playful, pla'ful, *a. Full of play;* sportive; indulging a sportive fancy.

Playfully, pla'ful-li, *adv.* In a sportive manner.

Playfulness, pla'ful-nes, *n. Quality of being playful;* sportiveness.

Play-house, pla'hous, *n. A house* appropriated to the exhibition of *plays* or of dramatic compositions; a theatre.

Playing, pla'ing, *p.n. The act of playing*, particularly of performing on an instrument of music.

Plaything, pla'thing, *n. A toy;* anything that serves to amuse.

Plea, plē, *n.* That which is advanced in court in order to obtain a *favourable sentence;* that which is alleged by a party in support of his demand; a cause in court; a lawsuit; that which is alleged in defence; an apology; urgent prayer. [Old Fr. *plait*, suit, a plea; L. *placeo, placitum*, to please, to give satisfaction.]

Pleach†, plech, *vt.* To unite by interweaving, as branches of trees.

Plead, plēd, *vi. To carry on a plea* or suit; to argue or reason in support of a claim, or in defence against the claim of another; to present an answer to the declaration of a plaintiff; to supplicate with earnestness; to urge; to press by operating on the passions. *vt.* To allege or adduce in proof, support, or vindication; to offer in excuse; to allege and offer in a legal plea or defence, or for repelling a demand in law. [Fr. *plaider*.]

Pleadable, plēd'a-bl, *a. That may be pleaded;* that may be alleged in proof.

Pleader, plēd'ér, *n. One who pleads;* one who forms pleas or pleadings; one who attempts to maintain by arguments. [Fr. *plaideur*.]

Pleading, plēd'ing, *p.n.* Act of supporting by arguments; (*pl.*) the mutual altercations between the plaintiff and defendant in a court of law, in support of their claims.

Pleasance†, ple'zans, *n. The state of being pleasant;* merriment.

Pleasant, ple'zant, *a. Pleasing;* grateful to the mind or senses; humorous;

sportive; giving pleasure; gratifying. [Fr. *plaisant*—L. *placeo*, to please.]

Pleasantly, ple'zant-li, *adv.* In a pleasant manner.

Pleasantness, ple'zant-nes, *n.* State or quality of being pleasant or agreeable; cheerfulness; gaiety; merriment.

Pleasantry, ple'zant-ri, *n.* Gaiety; merriment; humour; sprightly saying; lively talk. [Fr. *plaisanterie*.]

Please, plēz, *vt.* To be agreeable to; to excite agreeable emotions in; to gratify; to content; to have satisfaction in. *vi.* To like; to choose; to condescend; to comply; to be pleased. *ppr.* pleasing, *pret. & pp.* pleased. (A word of ceremony.) [Fr. *plaire*, ppr. *plaisant*—L. *placeo*.]

Pleased, plēzd, *p.a.* Gratified.

Pleaseman', plēs'man, *n.* An officious person who courts favour servilely.

Pleaser, plēz'ér, *n.* One who pleases; one who courts favour by humouring or flattering compliances.

Pleasing, plēz'ing, *p.a.* Giving pleasure or gratification; agreeable to the senses or to the mind; grateful.—*p.n.* The act of gratifying.

Pleasingly, plēz-ing-li, *adv.* In such a manner as to give pleasure.

Pleasurable, ple'zhūr-a-bl, *a.* That can or may please; pleasing; giving pleasure; affording gratification.

Pleasurably, ple'zhūr-a-bli, *adv.* With gratification of the senses or the mind.

Pleasure, ple'zhūr, *n.* That which pleases; the gratification of the senses or of the mind; the happiness produced by the attainment or the expectation of good; opposed to pain; delight; joy; that which pleases; a favour; sensual indulgence; what the will dictates; choice; preference; will; arbitrary determination.—*vt.†* To give pleasure to. [Fr. *plaisir*—L. *placeo*, to please.]

Pleasure-ground, ple'zhūr-ground, *n.* Ground adjoining a mansion, laid out in an ornamental manner, and appropriated to amusement.

Plebeian, plē-bē'an, *a.* Pertaining to the common people; vulgar; consisting of common people.—*n.* One of the common people or lower ranks of men. [Fr. *plébéien*—L. *plebs*, *plebis*, the common people.]

Pledge, plej, *n.* That which fastens or secures, in a moral sense; that which is plighted as a warrant of good faith; something put in pawn; a pawn, deposit, or earnest; anything given as a security for the performance of an act; a hostage; a gage; a drinking of health to another.—*vt.* To fix or secure; to give as a warrant of good faith; to deposit in pawn; to engage for by promise; to secure by a pledge; to drink to the health of; to engage by promise or declaration. *ppr.* pledging, *pret. & pp.* pledged. (Fr. *pleige*—L. *pignus*—*pango*, to fasten, fix.]

Pledger, plej'ér, *n.* One who pledges; one who warrants or secures; one who invites another to drink by drinking first.

Pleiads, Pleiades, plī'adz, plī'a-dēz, *n.pl.* The seven stars situated in the neck of the constellation Taurus. (Gr. *Pleiades*, the seven daughters of Atlas.)

Plenary, plē'na-ri, *a.* Full; entire; complete. [Low L. *plenarius*—L. *plenus*, full.]

Plenipotentiary, ple'ni-pō-ten'shi-a-ri, *n.* A person invested with full power to transact any business; an ambassador or envoy to a foreign court furnished with full power.—*a.* Containing full power; invested with full powers. [Fr. *plénipotentiaire*—L. *plenus*, full, and *potens*, having power.]

Plenitude, ple'ni-tūd, *n.* Fulness; repletion; exuberance; completeness; animal fulness. [Fr. *plénitude*—L. *plenus*, full—*pleo*, to make full.]

Plenteous, plen'tē-us, *a.* Possessing or affording plenty; full; ample; yielding abundance; possessing in abundance, and ready to bestow liberally.

Plenteously, plen'tē-us-li, *adv.* In abundance; copiously; plentifully.

Plenteousness, plen'tē-us-nes, *n.* Quality of being plenteous; abundance.

Plentiful, plen'ti-ful, *a.* Yielding plenty; copious; adequate to every purpose; affording a full supply.

Plentifully, plen'ti-ful-li, *adv.* Copiously; abundantly; with ample supply.

Plentifulness, plen'ti-ful-nes, *n.* State of being plentiful.

Plenty, plen'ti, *n.* Fulness; copiousness; full or adequate supply; fruitfulness. *a.†* Plentiful; abundant. [Old Fr. *plenté*—L. *plenus*, full.]

Pleonasm, plē'on-azm, *n.* An over fulness of words; the use of more words to express ideas than are necessary. [Gr. *pleonasmos*—*pleos*, full.]

Pleonastic, plē-on-as'tik, *a.* Pertaining to pleonasm. [Gr. *pleonastikos*.]

Plethora, plē'thō-ra, *n.* Fulness; excess of blood; repletion. [Old Fr. *plethore* —Gr. *plethō.* to be full.]

Plethoric, plē-tho'rik, *a.* Affected with plethora; having a full habit of body. [Old Fr. *plethorique*.]

Pleurisy, plū'ri-si, *n.* Inflammation of the side, or of the membrane that lines the inside of the chest. [Fr. *pleurésie* —Gr. *pleura*, the side.]

Pliability, plī-a-bil'i-ti, *n.* Quality of being pliable, or of bending or yielding to pressure or force without rupture; flexibility.

Pliable, plī'a-bl, *a.* Easy to be bent; that readily yields to pressure without rupture; flexible; readily yielding to moral influence. [Fr.]

Pliableness, plī'a-bl-nes, *n.* Quality of being pliable; pliability.

Pliably, plī'a-bli, *adv.* So as to be pliable.

Pliancy, plī'an-si, *n.* Quality of being pliant; readiness to yield to moral influence.

Pliant, plī'ant, *a.* That may be easily bent; readily yielding to force or pressure without breaking; easily yielding to moral influence; tractable; docile. [Fr. from *plier*—L. *plico*, to fold.]

Pliantly, plī'ant-'i, *adv.* Flexibly.

Pliers, plī'érz, *n.pl.* A kind of pincers by which any small thing, as wire, is seized and bent. [Fr. *plieur*, a folder.]

Plight, plīt, *vt.* To expose to danger; to risk or give as a guarantee of good faith; to pledge; to give as security for the performance of some act.—*n.* State of risk or hazard, like that of a thing pledged; guarantee; perplexity, or a distressed state; condition; state. [Sax. *plihtan*, to expose to danger, to pledge.]

Plight, plīt, *vt.* To weave; to braid; to intertwine.—*n.* A net-work; entanglement.

Plighted, plīt'ed, *p.a.* Pledged; folded.

Plighter, plīt'ér, *n.* One who plights or pledges; that which plights.

Plinth, plinth, *n.* A flat square member in form of a brick, which serves as the foundation of a column or pedestal. [Gr. *plinthos*, a brick.]

Plod, plod, *vi.* To move onward; to travel laboriously; to work slowly and with continued effort; to moil; to drudge; to study heavily and continuously.—*vt.* To tread with a heavy labouring step. *ppr.* plodding, *pret. & pp.* plodded. [perhaps akin to Goth. *laithan*, *bilaithan*, to go away.]

Plodder, plod'ér, *n.* A dull, heavy, laborious person.

Plodding, plod'ing, *p.a.* Diligent, but slow in contrivance or execution.—*p.n.* Slow movement or study.

Plot, plot, *n.* A plat or small extent of ground; a plantation laid out; a plan or draught of a field or piece of land, works, &c.—*vt.* To make a plan, as of a plat or piece of ground; to delineate; to draw or lay down on paper, as the work of a survey. *ppr.* plotting, *pret. & pp.* plotted. [a different orthography of *plat*.]

Plot, plot, *n.* Any scheme of a complicated nature, for the accomplishment of some mischievous purpose; an intrigue; conspiracy; the knot or story of a play, comprising incidents which are at last unfolded by unexpected means.—*vi.* To form a scheme of mischief against another, or against a government; to contrive a plan; to scheme —*vt.* To devise; to contrive. *ppr.* plotting, *pret. & pp.* plotted. [Icel. *flietta*, to fasten together.]

Plotter, plot'ér, *n.* One who plots or contrives; a contriver; a conspirator.

Plotting, plot'ing, *p.n.* Act of contriving or forming schemes; act of laying down a survey.

Plough, plou, *n.* An instrument for cleaving and turning up the soil; tillage; culture of the earth; agriculture. *vt.* To turn up with the plough, as the soil; to furrow; to divide; to run through in sailing; to dig into or lay waste. - *vi.* To turn up the soil with a plough; to use a plough. [D. *ploeg*.]

Plough-boy, plou'boi, *n.* A boy who guides a team in ploughing; a rustic boy.

Ploughed, ploud, *p.a.* Furrowed.

Plougher, plou'ér, *n.* One who ploughs land; a cultivator.

Ploughing, plou'ing, *p.n.* The operation of turning up ground with a plough.

Ploughman, plou'man, *n.* One who ploughs or holds a plough; a rustic.

Ploughshare, plou'shār, *n.* The part of a plough which cuts the ground at the bottom of the furrow.

Plover, plō'vér, *n.* The water-bird; a bird that frequents the banks of rivers and the sea-shore, and whose flesh is excellent food. [Fr. *pluvier*—L. *pluvia*, rain.]

Pluck, pluk, *vt.* To pull up; to pull with sudden force or effect; to strip by plucking.—*n.* Act of plucking; a sudden and forcible pull; the heart, liver, and lights of an animal; heart; courage; spirit. [Sax. *pluccian*—*lyccan*, to pull up.]

Plug, plug, *n.* A stopple; any piece of wood or other substance used to stop a hole.—*vt.* To stop with a plug; to make tight by stopping a hole in. *ppr.* plugging, *pret. & pp.* plugged. [D. a bung.]

Plum, plum, *n.* A tree and its fruit; a prune; a grape dried in the sun; a raisin. [Sax. *plume*; L. *prunus*.]

Plumage, plūm'āj, *n.* The feathers that cover a bird. [Fr.]

Plumb, plum, *n.* A mass of lead attached to a line, and used to ascertain the perpendicular position of buildings and the like.—*a.* Perpendicular, that is, standing according to a *plumb-line.—vt.* To adjust by a *plumb-line*; to set in a perpendicular direction.—*adv.* In a perpendicular direction; right downward. [Fr. *plomb*—L. *plumbum*, lead.]

Plumbago, plum-bā'gō, *n. Black-lead*; a mineral substance resembling lead used for pencils. [L. from *plumbum*, lead.]

Plumbean, Plumbeous, plum-bē'an, plum-bē'us, *a. Consisting of lead*; resembling lead; dull; heavy; stupid.

Plumber, plum'ėr, *n. One who works in lead.*

Plumbery, plum'ė-ri, *n. Works in lead*; manufactures of lead; the place where lead is wrought.

Plumbing, plum'ing, *p.n.* The art of casting and working in *lead*, and using it in building.

Plumb-line, plum'līn, *n. A line* perpendicular to the plane of the horizon; a line having a weight attached to its end, used to determine a perpendicular.

Plum-cake, plum-kāk', *n. Cake* containing *raisins*, currants, or other fruit.

Plume, plūm, *n. That which enables a bird to fly; the feather* of a bird; a feather or collection of feathers worn as an ornament; an ostrich's feather; token of honour; prize of contest; towering mien.—*vt.* To pick and adjust, as *plumes or feathers*; to strip of feathers; to set as a plume; to set erect; to adorn with feathers; to boast, as, to plume one's self. *ppr.* pluming, *pret. & pp.* plumed. [Fr.—L. *pluma*, a small soft feather—Sans. *plu*, to fly.]

Plummet, plum'et, *n. A long piece of lead* attached to a line, used in sounding the depth of water. [Sp. *plomāda*—L. *plumbum*, lead.]

Plumous, plūm'us, *a. Feathery*; resembling feathers. [L. *plumosus*.]

Plump, plump, *a. Lumpy*; increased; full; swelled with fat or flesh to the full size; fat; round; downright; unreserved; unqualified, as a lie.—*vt.* To make *plump*; to extend to fulness; to fatten; to let fall suddenly and heavily.—*vi.* To become *swelled*; to plunge or fall like a *heavy mass or lump* of dead matter; to fall suddenly or at once.—*adv.* Suddenly; at once, or with a sudden, heavy fall. [G. *clumpy*.]

Plumper, plump'ėr, *n.* Anything intended to *swell out* something else; a vote given at an election, to one candidate only when two or more are to be elected, thus giving him the advantage over the others.

Plumply, plump'li, *adv.* Fully; roundly.

Plumpness, plump'nes, *n. State or quality of being plump;* fulness of skin.

Plum-pudding, plum-pud'ing, *n.* Pudding containing raisins or currants.

Plumpy, plump'i, *a. Somewhat plump*; jolly.

Plumy, plūm'i, *a. Feathered*; adorned with plumes. [from *plume*.]

Plunder, plun'dėr, *vt.* To steal from; to strip bare or naked; to rob in a hostile manner.—*n.* That which is taken by *theft*, robbery, or fraud; pillage; booty. [Gr. *plündern*; Sans. *luth*, to steal.]

Plunderer, plun'dėr-ėr, *n.* A hostile pillager; a spoiler; a thief; a robber.

Plunge, plunj, *vt.* To *thrust into water* or other fluid substance; to drive into flesh, &c.; to thrust or drive into any state in which the thing is considered as surrounded; to baptize by immersion.—*vi.* To *thrust* one's self into *water*; to dive or to rush in; to rush into distress, or any state in which the person or thing is overwhelmed; to pitch or throw one's self headlong; to throw the body forward and the hind legs up, as a horse. *ppr.* plunging, *pret. & pp.* plunged.—*n. Act of plunging*; act of throwing one's self headlong, like an unruly horse. [Fr. *plonger*, to dip.]

Plunger, plunj'ėr, *n. One who plunges*; a long solid cylinder used as a forcer in pumps.

Plunging, plunj'ing, *p.n.* Act of thrusting or rushing into water or any substance easily penetrated; act of an unruly horse endeavouring to throw the rider.

Pluperfect, plū'pėr-fekt, *a. More than perfect*; designating a tense of the verb which denotes that an action or event took place previous to another past action or event. [L. *plus quam perfectum*.]

Plural, plū'ral, *a.* Relating to or containing *more* than one; noting the number of a noun which designates more than one.—*n.* The number which designates more than one. [L. *pluralis—plus, pluris*, more.]

Pluralist, plū'ral-ist, *n.* A clerk or clergyman who holds *more* ecclesiastical benefices than one.

Plurality, plū-ral'i-ti, *n. State of being plural*; a number consisting of two or more of the same kind; a greater number; a state of being or having a greater number; more than one benefice held by the same clergyman. [Fr. *pluralité*.]

Plurally, plū'ral-li, *adv.* In a sense implying *more* than one.

Plurisy†, plū'ri-si, *n.* Superabundance.

Plush, plush, *n. That which is covered with hair*; a species of shaggy cloth with a velvet nap on one side, resembling small hairs. [G. *plüsch*—L. *pilus*, hair.]

Pluvious, plū'vi-us, *a. Relating to rain*; rainy; humid. [Fr. *pluvial*—L. *pluvia*, rain—Sans. *plu*, to swim.]

Ply, plī, *vt.* To fold or cover over; to put to or on with force and repetition; to keep busy at; to keep at work; to perform with diligence, as a task; to urge; to solicit with pressing importunity; to force.—*vi.* To work steadily, to go in haste; to busy one's self; to endeavour to make progress against the wind; to run regularly between any two ports, as a vessel. *ppr.* plying, *pret. & pp.* plied.—*n.* Bent; direction. [Fr. *plier*—L. *plico*, to fold.]

Flying, plī'ing, *p.n. Act of one who plies;* urgent solicitation; effort to make way against the wind.

Pneumatic, nū-mat'ik, *a. Relating to air*; pertaining to atmospheric air; moved or played by means of air. [Fr. *pneumatique*; Gr. *pneō*, to blow.]

Pneumatics, nū-mat'iks, *n.* The science which treats of the nature and properties of *air*, and of fluids in the form of air, as gases and vapours.

Pneumatology, nū-ma-tol'o-ji, *n.* The doctrine of *mind or spirit*; the doctrine which treats of the divine mind, the angelic mind, and the human mind. [Gr. *pneuma*, air, spirit, and *logos*, discourse.]

Poach, pōch, *vt.* To make *soft* by boiling slightly; to tread, as soft ground, making deep tracks; to rob of game; to steal; to plunder by stealth.—*vi.* To be *penetrated* with deep tracks, as soft ground; to encroach upon another's grounds, and to steal game; to kill or destroy game contrary to law. [Fr. *pocher*, to bruise.]

Poached, pōcht, *p.a.* Stolen; slightly boiled or softened.

Poacher, pōch'ėr, *n.* One who *steals game*; one who kills game unlawfully.

Poaching, pōch'ing, *p.n. The act or employment of a poacher.*

Poachy, pōch'i, *a.* ·et and *soft*; such as the feet of cattle will *penetrate* to some depth, as land.

Pock, pok, *n.* A *pustule* raised on the surface of the body in the disease called the small-pox. [Sax. *poc*.]

Pocket, pok'et, *n. A small bag* or pouch inserted in a garment for carrying small articles; a small net to receive the balls in billiards; a certain quantity, as of hops.—*vt. To put or conceal in the pocket*; to take clandestinely. [Fr. *pochette*; Sax. *pocca*, a bag.]

Pocket-book, pok'et-bųk, *n.* A small *book* covered with leather, used for carrying papers or notes in the *pocket*.

Pocket-money, pok'et-mu-nē, *n. Money* for the *pocket* or for occasional expenses.

Pocket-picking, pok'et-pik-ing, *n. Act of picking the pocket.*

Pockiness, pok'i-nes, *n. State of being pocky.*

Pock-marked, pok'märkt, *a.* Pitted with the small-pox.

Pod, pod, *n.* The pericarp or seed-vessel of certain plants, as pease, beans, mustard, &c.—*vi. To produce pods*; to swell; to fill. *ppr.* podding, *pret. & pp.* podded. [W. *podi*, to take in.]

Poem, pō'em, *n. The work or creation of a poet*; a composition in which the verses consist of certain measures, whether in blank verse or in rhyme; a piece of poetry. [Gr. *poiēma—poieō*, to make.]

Poesy, pō'ē-si, *n.* The art of *making poems*; poetry; metrical composition; a short conceit engraved on a ring or other thing; a posy. [Gr. *poiēsis—poieō*, to make.]

Poet, pō'et, *n. The maker or creator of a poem*; one who has a particular genius for metrical composition; one distinguished for poetic talents. [Gr. *poiētēs*.]

Poetaster, pō'et-as-tėr, *n. A petty poet*; a pitiful rhymer.

Poetess, pō'et-es, *n. A female poet.*

Poetic, Poetical, pō-et'ik, pō-et'ik-al, *a. Pertaining to poetry*; expressed in poetry; possessing the peculiar beauties of poetry; sublime. [Fr. *poétique*.]

Poetically, pō-et'ik-al-li, *adv. With the qualities of poetry*; by fiction.

Poetics, pō-et'iks, *n. The doctrine of poetry.*

Poetry, pō'et-ri, *n. Poetical or metrical composition*; verse; the art of composing in verse; prose composition in the language of excited imagination and feeling. [Old Fr. *poëterie*.]

Foh, pō, *interj.* Exclamation of contempt or aversion.

Poignancy, poin'an-si, *n. Quality of being poignant;* the power of stimulating the organs of taste; sharpness; asperity, as of wit; severity; acuteness, as of grief.

Poignant, poin'ant, *a. Piercing*; sharp; bitter; irritating; very painful or acute. [Fr.—L. *pungo, punctum*, to pierce.]

Poignantly, poin'ant-li, *adv.* In an irritating manner, with keenness or point.

Point, point, *n. That which pricks or pierces;* the *sharp end* of a *piercing*

instrument; a steel instrument having a sharp point or end, used by engravers, etchers, &c.; a small cape; the sting of an epigram; a lively turn of thought or expression; an indivisible part of time or space; nicety; exactness of ceremony; that on which one takes position; place contiguous to; eve; degree; state of elevation, depression, or extension; a character used to mark the divisions of writing; a spot; that which has neither parts nor magnitude, according to geometry; a division of the mariner's compass; 'a certain place marked in the heavens; the place to which anything is directed; particular; aim; thing to be reached; the act of aiming; a single position; a single part of a whole; a tune; (pl.) qualities or properties.—*vt.* To make pointed; to cut or file to an acute end; to direct toward an object or place; to aim; to show, by way of example; to mark with characters the members of a sentence; to mark with vowel-points; to fill the joints of with mortar, and smooth them with the point of a trowel.—*vi.* To direct the finger for designating an object; to indicate, as dogs do to sportsmen; to show distinctly by any means; to fill the joints or crevices of a wall with mortar. [Fr.—L. *pungo, punctum*, to prick.]

Point de visé, pwan-de-vēz', *a.* Uncommonly nice and exact.

Pointed, point'ed, *p.a.* Directed; aimed at a particular person or transaction; characterised by keenness, as rebuke; epigrammatical.

Pointedly, point'ed-li, *adv. In a pointed manner;* with explicitness.

Pointedness, point'ed-nes, *n. Quality of being pointed;* sharpness.

Pointer, point'ėr, *n. Anything that points;* a variety of dog trained to stop and point out the game to sportsmen.

Pointing, point'ing, *p.n. Art of making pointed;* punctuation; state of being pointed with marks; act of placing a gun, so as to give the shot a particular direction.

Pointing-stock†, point'ing-stok, *n.* An object of ridicule or scorn.

Pointless, point'les, *a. Having no point;* blunt; dull; stupid.

Poise, poiz, *n. Weight; gravity;* the mass of metal used in weighing with steelyards; balance; a regulating power. [Fr. *poids.*]—*vt. To weigh;* to balance in weight; to make of equal weight; to hold in equilibrium; to examine or ascertain, as by the balance; to oppress; to weigh down†. *ppr.* poising, *pret. & pp.* poised. [Fr. *peser*—L. *pendo*, to cause to hang down.]

Poised, poizd, *p.a. Balanced;* made equal in weight.

Poison, poi'zon, *n. A deadly draught;* any agent capable of producing a morbid or dangerous effect upon anything endowed with life; anything malignant; that which taints or destroys moral purity.—*vt. To infect with poison;* to kill by poison; to mar; to impair, as one's enjoyment; to corrupt, as the morals. [Fr.—L. *potio*, a drink—Gr. *pinō*, to drink.]

Poisoned, poi'zond, *p.a. Infected or destroyed by poison.*

Poisoner, poi'zon-ėr, *n. One who poisons or corrupts; that which corrupts.*

Poisonous, poi'zon-us, *a. Having the qualities of poison;* venomous; deadly; corrupting.

Poisonously, poi'zon-us-li, *adv. With poisonous,* fatal, or injurious *effects.*

Poisonousness, poi'zon-us-nes, *n. Quality of being poisonous.*

Poke, pōk, *n. A bag or sack.* [Sax. *pocea.*]

Poke, pōk, *vt. To thrust forward;* to thrust or push against with anything pointed; to search for with a long instrument; to thrust at with the horns, as an ox. — *vi.* To grope, as in the dark, with the hand or hands *thrust forward;* to make a thrust with the horns. *ppr.* poking, *pret. & pp.* poked.—*n. The act of poking;* a thrust. [D. *poken,* to poke.]

Poker, pōk'ėr, *n. He or that which pokes;* an iron bar used in *poking* or stirring the fire.

Polar, pō'lär, *a. Pertaining to the pole or poles* of the earth or of the world, or to the poles of artificial globes; situated near one of the poles; pertaining to the magnetic pole. [Fr. *polaire;* L. *polus*, a pivot on which anything turns.]

Polarity, pō-lä'ri-ti, *n. Tendency to the pole;* property of pointing towards the poles of the earth, as that possessed by a magnet; property in certain bodies which causes them to point to given poles. [Fr. *polarité.*]

Polarization, pō'lär-iz-ā'shon, *n. Act of polarising;* the state of having polarity. [Fr. *polarisation.*]

Polarise, pō'lär-iz, *vt. To communicate polarity* to. *ppr.* polarising, *pret. & pp.* polarised. [Fr. *polariser.*]

Polarised, pō'lär-izd, *p.a. Having polarity communicated to.*

Polarising, pō'lär-iz-ing, *p.a. Giving polarity to.*

Pole, pōl, *n. That which surrounds;* a long slender piece of wood; a tall piece of timber erected; a rod; a perch; a measure of length, of five yards and a half, or a square measure of 30½ square yards; an instrument for measuring.—*vt.* To furnish with poles for *inclosure;* to bear or convey on poles; to impel by poles, as a boat. *ppr.* poling, *pret. & pp.* poled. [Sax. *pol*—L. *palus*, a stake—Sans. *val*, to surround.]

Pole, pōl, *n. One of the extremities of the axis* on which a sphere *revolves;* one of the extremities of the axis on which the celestial sphere revolves; one of the extremities of the earth's axis; the star which is vertical to the north pole of the earth; a point in a spherical figure representing the celestī'al or terrestrial pole; one of the two points in a magnet in which the power seems to be chiefly concentrated. [Fr. *pôle*—L. *polus*, a pivot; Gr. *poleō*, to turn round.]

Pole-axe, pōl'aks, *n. An axe fixed to a pole* or handle.

Polecat, pōl'kat, *n.* A small carnivorous animal, nearly allied to the weasel, and distinguished by its offensive smell. (supposed to be abbreviated from *Polish-cat.*)

Polemic, Polemical, pō-lem'ik, pō-lem'ik-al, *a. Militant;* disputative; engaged in supporting an opinion or system by controversy.—*n.* A disputant; a controversialist. [Fr. *polémique;* Gr. *polemos,* a battle.]

Polemically, pō-lem'ik-al-li, *adv. With controversy,* disputation, or contention.

Polemics, pō-lem'iks, *n. Controversy,* especially on religious subjects.

Pole-star, pōl'stär, *n. A star* which is vertical, or nearly so, to the *pole* of the earth; a lode-star; that which serves as a guide.

Police, pō-lēs', *n. The government of a city;* the administration of the laws of a city or borough; the internal regulation of a kingdom; a body of civil officers, for enforcing the laws respecting good order, cleanliness, health, &c. [Fr.—Gr. *polis*, a city.]

Police-officer, pō-lēs'of-fis-ėr, *n.* An *officer* intrusted with the execution of the *police* regulations of a city or county.

Policy, pō'li-si, *n. The art or manner of governing a city* or nation; the management of public affairs with respect either to foreign powers or to internal arrangement; prudence in rulers or individuals; stratagem; dexterity of management; [Sp. *polisa*—Gr. *polus,* many, and *pluché* a fold] the writing by which a contract of indemnity is effected between the insurer and the insured. [Fr. *police;* Gr. *politeia*—*polis,* a city.]

Polish, po'lish, *vt. To make smooth* and glossy, usually by friction; to refine; to make elegant and polite.—*vi. To become smooth;* to take a smooth and glossy surface.—*n.* A smooth, glossy surface produced by friction; refinement. [Fr. *polir, polissant*—L. *polio,* to smooth—Heb. *pālat,* to be smooth.]

Polished, po'lisht, *p.a. Made smooth* and glossy; refined; polite.

Polisher, po'lish-ėr, *n. The person or instrument that polishes.*

Polishing, po'lish-ing, *p.n. Act of making smooth* and glossy, or of refining manners; refinement.

Polite, pō-līt', *a. Polished* in manners; having refinement of manners; complaisant; elegant; civil. [L. *politus*—*polio,* to make smooth.]

Politely, pō-līt'li, *adv. With elegance of manners;* genteelly; courteously.

Politeness, pō-līt'nes, *n. Quality of being polite;* ease and gracefulness of manners, combined with attention to the convenience of others; urbanity.

Politic, po'li-tik, *a. Political;* sagacious in devising measures adapted to promote the public welfare; adapted to the public prosperity; wise; prudent; cunning; artful; crafty; well devised; adapted to its end, right or wrong. [Fr. *politique.*]

Political, pō-lit'ik-al, *a. Of or belonging to citizens* or the *state;* pertaining to policy; pertaining to a nation or state; public; derived from connection with government; artful; politici; treating of politics or government. [L. *politicus*—Gr. *polis,* a city.]

Politically, pō-lit'ik-al-li, *adv. In a political manner.*

Politician, po-li-ti'shi-an, *n. One versed in politics,* or in the science of government and the art of governing; one devoted to politics; a man of artifice or deep contrivance. [Fr. *politicien.*]

Politicly, po'li-tik-li, *adv. In a politic manner;* artfully.

Politics, po'li-tiks, *n. The science or the art of government;* that part of ethics which consists in the regulation and government of a nation or state; political affairs. [Fr. *politique.*]

Polity, po'li-ti, *n. Policy;* constitution of the civil government of a nation or state; the general fundamental principles of government of any class of citizens, considered as subordinate. [Gr. *politeia*—*polis,* a city.]

Polka, pōl'ka, *n.* A dance of *Polish*

origin; also, the air played to the dance.

Poll, pōl, n. *The head* or the back part of the head; a register of heads, that is, of persons; the entry of the names of electors who vote for civil officers or members of parliament; an election of civil officers, or the place of election.—*vt.* To cut off, as the hair of the *head;* to clip; to cut off, as hair or wool; to shear; to cut off or lop, as the tops of trees; to take, as a list of persons; to enter, as names in a list; to enter, as one's name in a list or register; to receive or give, as votes; to bring to the poll. [D. *bol*, a ball, the head.]

Pollard, pol'ärd, n. A tree that is polled, or that has its top cut off that it may throw out branches. [from *poll.*]

Pollen, pol'en, n. *Anything which is sifted by shaking;* fine flour; the fecundating dust contained in the anthers of flowers; farina. [L.—Gr. *pallō*, to shake.]

Poller, pōl'ėr, n. *One who polls;* one who registers voters, or one who enters his name as a voter. [from *poll.*]

Poll-tax, pōl'taks, n. *A tax levied by the poll or head;* a capitation-tax.

Pollute, pol-lūt', *vt.* To dirty; to make foul or unclean; to make unclean, in a ceremonial sense; to taint with guilt; to profane; to vitiate; to debauch; to abuse. *ppr.* polluting, *pret. & pp.* polluted.—*a.†* Defiled. [L. *polluo*, *pollutum*—*ans. palala*, mud.]

Polluted, pol-lūt'ed, *p.a.* Tainted with guilt; profaned.

Polluter, pol-lūt'ėr, n. *A defiler;* one who pollutes or profanes.

Polluting, pol-lūt'ing, *p.a.* *Defiling* or having a tendency to defile.

Pollution, pol-lū'shon, n. *Act of polluting;* state of being polluted; uncleanness; guilt, the effect of sin; idolatry. [Fr.]

Poltroon, pol-trön', n. *A lazy, idle, sluggish,* useless fellow; a dastard; a wretch without spirit or courage.—a. Base; vile; contemptible. [Fr. *poltron;* It. *poltro*, lazy.]

Poltroonery, pol-trön'ė-ri, n. Cowardice; baseness of mind; want of spirit. [Fr. *poltronnerie.*]

Polyanthus, po-li-an'thus, n. *A plant producing many flowers,* and a great favourite in gardens. [Gr. *polus*, many, and *anthos*, a flower.]

Polygamist, po-lig'a-mist, n. *A person who practises polygamy.*

Polygamy, po-lig'a-mi, n. State or custom of being *united in marriage to a plurality* of wives or husbands at the same time; a plurality of wives or husbands. [Fr. *polygamie;* Gr. *polus*, many, and *gamos*, marriage.]

Polyglot, po'li-glot, *a.* *Many-tongued;* containing many or several languages. n. A book printed in *several languages* which are so displayed on its pages as to be seen at one view. [Gr. *polus*, many, and *glōtta*, the tongue.]

Polygon, po'li-gon, n. *A plane figure of many angles* and sides. [Gr. *polus*, and *gōnia*, an angle.]

Polygonal, po-lig'on-al, *a.* Having many angles.

Polyhedral, po-li-hē'dral, *a.* Having *many sides,* as a solid body.

Polyhedron, po-li-hē'dron, n. A body or solid contained by *many sides* or planes. [Gr. *polus*, and *hedra*, a side.]

Polypetalous, po-li-pe'tal-us, *a.* Having *many petals,* as a flower. [Gr. *polus*, and *petalon*, a leaf.]

Polypus, po'li-pus, n. *Something that has many feet;* a radiated animal, having *many* tentacles round its mouth; a tumour with a narrow base, somewhat resembling a pear, found in the nose and other mucous membranes. [Gr. *polupous—polus,* and *pous, poios,* a foot—Sans. *pad,* to go.]

Polysyllabic, po'li-sil-lab''ik, *a.* Pertaining to a polysyllable.

Polysyllable, po'li-sil-la-bl, n. *A word of many syllables,* or one consisting of more syllables than three. [Gr. *polus,* and *syllabē.*]

Polytechnic, po-li-tek'nik, *a.* Comprehending *many arts;* designating a school in which many branches of art or science are taught. [Gr. *polus,* and *technē,* art.]

Polytheism, po'li-thē-izm, n. The doctrine of a *plurality of gods* having an agency in the government of the world. [Fr. *polythéisme*—Gr. *polus,* and *theos,* a god.]

Polytheist, po'li-thē-ist, n. A person who believes in a *plurality of gods.*

Pomaceous, pō-mā'shē-us, *a.* *Pertaining to or resembling apples;* consisting of apples. [from L. *pomum,* an apple.]

Pomatum, pō-mā'tum, n. An ointment originally made from *apples;* a perfumed unguent used in dressing the hair. [Fr. *pommade*—L. *pomum,* an apple.]

Pomegranate, pom'gran-āt, n. The fruit of a tree, of the size and shape of an orange, containing numerous *grains* or seeds; also, the tree that produces pomegranates. [L. *pomum,* and *granatum—granum,* a grain.]

Pome-water, pōm'wa-tėr, n. *A sweet juicy apple.*

Pommel, pum'mel, n. *A knob or ball;* any ornament of a globular form; the knob on the hilt of a sword; the protuberant part of a saddle-bow; the round knob on the frame of a chair, &c.—*vt.* To beat as *with a pommel,* that is, with something thick or bulky; to bruise. *ppr.* pommelling, *pret. & pp.* pommelled. [Fr. *pommeau*—L. *pomum,* an apple.]

Pommelling, pum'mel-ing, *p.n.* A beating or bruising.

Pomp, pomp, n. *Escort;* a showy procession; a splendid show; pageantry; magnificence; grandeur; pride. [L. *pompa*—Gr. *pempō,* to send.]

Pomposity, pom-pos'i-ti, n. *Pompousness;* ostentation; boasting. [It. *pomposità.*]

Pompous, pomp'us, *a.* *Displaying pomp;* characterized by display; superb; ostentatious; boastful. [Fr. *pompeux.*]

Pompously, pomp'us-li, *adv.* In a *pompous manner.*

Pompousness, pomp'us-nes, n. *State or quality of being pompous.*

Pond, pond, n. *A body of stagnant water shut in,* smaller than a lake; a like body of water with a small outlet; a collection of water raised in a river or stream by a dam for the purpose of propelling mill-wheels. [Sax. *pyndan,* to shut in.]

Ponder, pon'dėr, *vt.* To *weigh;* to weigh in the mind; to consider and compare, as the circumstances or consequences of an event; to view with deliberation; to examine.—*vi.* To *weigh* mentally; to think; to muse. (With on.) [Old Fr. *ponderer*—L. *pondus,* weight.]

Ponderability, pon'dėr-a-bil''li-ti, n. *Quality or state of being ponderable.*

Ponderable, pon'dėr-a-bl, *a.* That may be *weighed;* capable of being weighed. [Fr. *pondérable.*]

Pondered, pon'dėrd, *p.a.* *Weighed* in the mind; considered.

Ponderous, pon'dėr-us, *a.* Heavy; weighty; massive; forcible; strongly impulsive. [L. *ponderosus—pondus,* weight.]

Ponderously, pon'dėr-us-li, *adv.* With *great weight.*

Ponderousness, pon'dėr-us-nes, n. *Quality or state of being ponderous.*

Poniard, pon'yärd, n. *A small dagger or pointed weapon for piercing or stabbing.*—*vt.* To *pierce with a poniard;* to stab. [Fr. *poignard*—L. *pungo,* to prick.]

Ponk†, pongk, n. A nocturnal spirit; a hag.

Pontage, pon'tāj, n. *A duty paid for repairing bridges;* the toll of a bridge. [Low L. *pontagium*—L. *pons, pontis,* a bridge.]

Pontiff, pon'tif, n. *A high-priest,* the first *bridge* over the Tiber *being made* by a high-priest; applied particularly to the Pope of Rome. [L. *pons, pontis,* a bridge, and *facio,* to make.]

Pontifical, pon-tif'ik-al, *a.* *Belonging to a high-priest;* belonging to the pope; splendid; magnificent.—n. A book containing rites and ceremonies ecclesiastical; (pl.) the dress and ornaments of a priest or bishop. [Fr.]

Pontificate, pon-tif'i-kāt, n. *The state or dignity of a high-priest;* the office or dignity of the pope; the reign of a pope. [Fr. *pontifical.*]

Pontoon, pon-tön', n. *A kind of boat,* or a floating substance, as a hollow tin cylinder, used by armies for supporting the platforms of temporary *bridges;* a bridge of boats. [Fr. *ponton*—L. *pons, pontis,* a bridge.]

Pony, pō'ni, n. **Ponies,** pō'nes, *pl.* A small horse. [Ir. *poni.*]

Poodle, pö'dl, n. *A small dog,* resembling the water-dog, covered with long silky curling white hair. [G. *pudel.*]

Pooh, pö. An exclamation of contempt or disdain; poh; pshaw.

Pool, pöl, n. *A marsh; a fen;* a small collection of water in a hollow place. [Sax. *pol*—L. *palus,* a swamp.]

Poop, pöp, *vt.* Primarily, the *stern* of a ship; now, the highest and aftmost deck of a ship, reaching forward to the mizzen-mast. [Fr. *poupe*—L. *puppis,* the stern.]

Poor, pör, *a.* *Destitute of property;* needy; destitute of strength; mean; of little use; trifling; paltry; of little value; exhausted, as soil; unhappy; dejected; emaciated; small, or of a bad quality; uncomfortable; restless; ill; (a word of tenderness or pity) dear (a word of slight contempt) wretched. [Norm. *pourar*—L. *pauper.*]

Poorly, pör'li, *adv.* In a *poor manner* or state; meanly; without excellence or dignity.—a. Somewhat ill; indisposed; not in health. (Familiar.)

Poorness, pör'nes, n. *State or quality of being poor;* poverty; unproductiveness; want of value or importance; want of good qualities.

Poor-spirited, pör-spi'rit-ed, *a.* *Of a mean spirit;* cowardly; base.

Pop, pop, n. *A small, smart, quick sound* or report.—*vi.* To *make a small, smart, quick sound;* to start from place to place suddenly; to enter or issue forth with a quick, sudden motion.—*vt.* To thrust or push suddenly with a quick motion.—*adv.* Suddenly; with sudden entrance or appearance. *ppr.* popping. *pret. & pp.* popped. [D. *poep.*]

Pope, pōp, n. *A father;* the Bishop of Rome, the head of the Roman Catholic church. [Late L. *papa*, father, bishop.]

Popedom, pōp'dum, n. *The jurisdiction of the pope;* papal dignity.

Popery, pōp'ė-ri, n. The religion of the Roman Catholic church, comprehending doctrines and practices.

Popgun, pop'gun, n. A small *gun* or tube used by children to *pop* with, or shoot with and make a noise.

Popinjay, pop'in-jā, n. *Father-cock†*; a parrot; a woodpecker; a gay, trifling young man; a fop or prating coxcomb. [Old Fr. *papegay*—Late L. *papa*, and *gallus*, a cock.]

Popish, pōp'ish, a. *Relating to the pope*, taught by the pope; pertaining to the pope, or to the Roman Catholic church.

Poplar, pop'lār, n. A tall tree, abundant in Mesopotamia. [Fr. *peuplier*—L. *populus.*]

Poplin, pop'lin, n. A cloth made of silk and worsted. [Fr. *papeline.*]

Poppy, pop'pi, n. An herb with milky or coloured juice, having narcotic properties. [Sax. *popeg*—L. *papaver.*]

Populace, pop'ū-lās, n. *The common people;* the vulgar; the multitude; the commonalty; the mob. [Fr.—L. *populus*, the people.]

Popular, pop'ū-lār, a. *Pertaining to the common people;* familiar; easy to be comprehended; not critical; pleasing to people in general; prevailing among the people. [Fr. *populaire*—L. *populus*, the people.]

Popularity, po-pū-la'ri-ti, n. *State or quality of being popular;* favour of the people. [Fr. *popularité.*]

Popularize, po'pū-lār-iz, vt. To make popular or suitable to the common mind; to spread among the people. *ppr.* popularizing, *pret. & pp.* popularized. [Fr. *populariser.*]

Popularly, po'pū-lār-li, adv. In a popular manner.

Populated, po'pū-lāt-ed, p.a. *Peopled;* furnished with inhabitants.

Population, po-pū-lā'shon, n. *The act of operation of peopling;* the whole number of inhabitants in a country or portion of a country. [Fr.]

Populous, po'pū-lus, a. *Abounding in people;* containing many inhabitants in proportion to the extent of country. [Fr. *populeux.*]

Populously, po'pū-lus-li, adv. *In a populous manner.*

Populousness, po'pū-lus-nes, n. *State of being populous.*

Porcelain, pōr'sē-lān, n. The finest species of earthenware, which is white and semi-transparent, originally manufactured in China and Japan, said to be so named from the surface resembling that of a large shell.—a. Belonging to or consisting of porcelain. [Fr. *porcelaine*; It. *porcellana*, a shell-fish.]

Porch, pōrch, n. *A portico;* a covered walk; a kind of vestibule at the entrance of temples, halls, churches, or other buildings. [Fr. *porche*—L. *porta*, a gate.]

Porcupine, por'kū-pin, n. *The spine-hog;* a quadruped furnished with spines or quills upon the body. [It. *porco-spinoso*—L. *porcus*, and *spina*, from *spica*, something pointed, a thorn.]

Pore, pōr, n. A small *passage;* a minute opening in the skin of an animal, through which the perspirable matter passes to the surface; a small interstice between the particles of matter which compose bodies. [Fr.—Gr. *poros—peirō*, to pierce.]

Pore, pōr, vi. To *look* with steady, continued attention or application; to examine with steady perseverance (with *on*, *upon*, or *over*.) *ppr.* poring, *pret. & pp.* pored. [from Gr. *ephorāō*, to look upon—*epi*, and *horāō*, to see.]

Poriform, pōr'i-form, a. *Resembling a pore.* [pors and *form.*]

Pork, pōrk, n. The flesh of *swine*, fresh or salted, used for food. [Fr. *porc*—L. *porcus*, a pig.]

Porker, pōrk'er, n. A hog; a young pig for roasting.

Porosity, pōr-os'i-ti, n. *Quality or state of being porous;* a property of matter in consequence of which its particles are not in perfect contact. [Fr. *porosité.*]

Porous, pōr'us, a. *Having pores;* having small interstices between the particles which compose a body. [Fr. *poreux.*]

Porphyritic, por-fi-rit'ik, a. *Pertaining to porphyry;* resembling porphyry; containing or composed of porphyry.

Porphyry, por'fi-ri, n. A very hard streaked stone, with green or red purple streaks, susceptible of a fine polish. [Gr. *porphūra*, the purple fish.]

Porpoise, por'pus, n. *The hog-fish* or sea-hog, which lives on other fish, and often roots like a hog in the mud. [Fr. *porc-poisson*—L. *porcus*, and *piscis*, a fish.]

Porridge, po'rij, n. A kind of food made by boiling meat or meal in water; broth. [perhaps a corruption of *pottage.*]

Porringer, po'rin-jėr, n. A small metal vessel in which children *eat porridge* or milk; a head-dress in the shape of a porringer (in contempt).

Port, pōrt, n. A *gate;* any bay, cove, inlet, or recess of the sea or of a lake, or the mouth of a river, which ships or vessels can *enter*, and where they can lie safe from storms; an opening in the side of a ship of war, through which cannon are discharged; manner of movement; carriage; mien; the larboard or left side of a ship; a dark purple astringent wine, so called from *Oporto*, whence it is shipped; attendance.—vt. To turn or put to the left or larboard side, as of a ship. [Fr.—L. *porta*, a gate.]

Portable, pōrt'a-bl, a. *That may be carried;* that may be carried by the hand or about the person, on horseback or in a travelling vehicle; not bulky; that may be carried from place to place. [L. *portabilis*—*porto*, to carry.]

Portableness, pōrt'a-bl-nes, n. *Quality of being portable.*

Portage, pōrt'āj, n. *Act of carrying;* carriage; the price of carriage; a port-holet. [Fr.]

Portal, pōrt'al, n. *A little door;* an entrance; the framework or arch of a door or gate; the lesser gate where there are two gates of different dimensions. [Fr. *portail*—L. *porta*, a gate.]

Portcullis, pōrt-kul'is, n. *A sliding or falling gate* consisting of a strong grating of timber or iron, resembling a harrow, hung over the gateway of a fortified town or of a castle, to be let down in case of surprise, to prevent the entrance of an enemy.—vt.† To obstruct, *as with a portcullis;* to bar. [Fr. *porte*, and *coulisse*, groove—*couler*, to slide down.]

Portend, por-tend', vt. To *stretch forth*; to foretoken; to forebode; to presage. [L. *portendo*—*pro*, and *tendo*, to stretch.]

Portent, por-tent', n. *A token or omen;* an omen of ill; any previous sign or prodigy indicating the approach of evil or calamity. [L. *portentum*—*pro*, and *tendo*, to stretch.]

Portentous, por-tent'us, a. *Full of portents;* ominous; prodigious; wonderful. [L. *portentosus.*]

Portentously, por-tent'us-li, adv. *In a portentous manner.*

Porter, pōr'tėr, n. *A door or gate keeper;* one who waits at the door to receive messages; [Fr. *porteur*—L. *porto*, to carry] a person who *carries* burdens for hire; a malt liquor of a dark brown colour and moderately bitter taste, so named because it was the favourite drink of porters. [Fr. *portier*—L. *porta*, a gate.]

Porterage, pōr'tėr-āj, n. Money paid for the carriage of burdens by *a porter;* the business of a porter or door-keeper.

Portfolio, pōrt-fō'li-ō, n. A case of the size of a *large book to carry* or keep loose papers in. [Fr. *portefeuille*—L. *porto*, to carry, and *fohum*, a leaf.]

Port-hole, pōrt'hōl, n. The embrasure of a ship of war.

Portico, pōr'ti-kō, n. Originally, *a colonnade*, but at present, a covered space inclosed by columns at the entrance of a building; a porch. [It.—L. *porticus.*]

Porticoed, pōr'ti-kōd, p.a. *Having a portico or porticoes.*

Portion, pōr'shon, n. *A part;* a part of anything separated from it; the part of an estate given to a child or heir, or descending to him by law; a share; a wife's fortune.—vt. To distribute in *parts;* to parcel; to divide; to supply with a portion. [L. *portio*—*partior*, to divide—*pars*, a part.]

Portioned, pōr'shond, p.a. *Endowed;* furnished with a portion.

Portioner, pōr'shon-ėr, n. *One who portions;* one who assigns in shares.

Portionless, pōr'shon-les, a. *Having no portion.*

Portliness, pōrt'li-nes, n. *State or quality of being portly;* dignity of personal appearance, consisting in size and symmetry of body, with dignified manners and demeanour.

Portly, pōrt'li, a. *Of a noble port;* dignified in mien; stately; of good size or stature; corpulent. [from *port*, mien.]

Portmanteau, pōrt-man'tō, n. *A cloak-bag;* a case, usually made of leather, for carrying clothes and other things necessary in travelling. [Fr. *portemanteau*—*porter*, to carry, and *manteau*, a cloak.]

Portrait, pōr'trāt, n. *That which is portrayed;* a picture of a person; a likeness; a delineation in words. [Fr.]

Portraiture, pōr'trāt-ūr, n. *A portrait;* that which is copied from some model. *vt.*† *To portray.*

Portray, pōr-trā', vt. *To draw or bring out;* to delineate; to paint or draw the likeness of in colours; to describe in words. [Fr. *portraire*—L. *pro*, and *traho, trahere*, to draw.]

Portrayer, pōr-trā'ėr, n. One who paints, *draws* to the life, or describes.

Fortress, Porteress, pōrt'res, pōrt'ėr-es, n. *A female keeper of a gate.*

Pose, pōz, vt. *To set;* to bring to a stand by asking questions, as was done in the schools; to perplex by asking difficult questions; to interrogate closely. *ppr.* posing, *pret. & pp.* posed.—n. The attitude in which a person stands;

artificial position. [Fr. *poser*, to set; L. *pono, positum*, to put.]
Poser, pōz'ėr, *n.* *One who poses or puzzles by asking difficult questions; something that puzzles or puts to silence.*
Position, pō-zi'shon, *n.* *A putting or setting; state of being placed; situation; manner of standing or being placed; attitude; posture; principle laid down; proposition advanced as the ground of reasoning, or to be proved; thesis; condition; social rank.* [L. *positio—pono*, to place.]
Positive, poz'it-iv, *a.* *Laid down; direct; explicit; absolute; real; existing in fact; dogmatic; settled by arbitrary appointment; having power to act directly; affirmative; noting the simple state of an adjective.—n. That which is laid down; what is capable of being affirmed; reality; that which settles by absolute appointment; a word that affirms or asserts existence.* [Fr. *positif*—L. *pono, positum*, to set.]
Positively, poz'it-iv-li, *adv. In a positive manner; absolutely; expressly.*
Positiveness, poz'it-iv-nes, *n. State or quality of being positive; reality of existence; undoubting assurance.*
Possess, poz-zes', *vt. To sit or rest the master of; to have and hold; to own; to have the just and legal ownership of; to hold the title of; to seize; to obtain the occupation of; to have power over, as an invisible agent; to affect by some power; to acquaint; to inform* (with *of* or *with*). [L. *possideo*—*potis*, able, and *sedeo*, to sit.]
Possessed, poz-zest', *p.a.* Held by lawful title; affected by demons; informed†.
Possession, poz-ze'shon, *n. Act or state of possessing; occupancy; the thing possessed; mental endowments; anything valuable possessed; the state of being under the power of demons; madness; lunacy.* [Fr.]
Possessive, poz-zes'iv, *a. Pertaining to possession; noting the genitive case of nouns and pronouns, or the case which expresses possession.—n. The possessive case;* a pronoun denoting possession. [Fr. *possessif*.]
Possessor, poz-zes'ėr, *n. One who possesses; one who has, holds, or enjoys any good or other thing; the owner; master; holder; occupant.* [L.]
Possessory, poz-zes'ō-ri, *a. Relating to or having possession.* [Fr. *possessoire*.]
Posset, pos'set, *n. An acidulous drink; milk curdled with wine or other liquor.—vt.*† To curdle. [Old Fr. *pos-que*—L. *poto*, to drink.]
Possibility, pos-si-bil'i-ti, *n. State or quality of being possible; the power of being or of happening.* [Fr. *possibilité*.]
Possible, pos'si-bl, *a. Able or having power to be; that may be; that may be now, or may come to pass; that may be done; practicable; not impossible, though improbable.* [Fr.—L. *possum*, to be able—*potis*, able, and *sum*, to be.]
Possibly, pos'si-bli, *adv. By any power, moral or physical, really existing; perhaps; perchance.*
Post, pōst, *n. That which is fixed in an upright position; a piece of timber set upright; a military station; the place where a single soldier or a body of troops is stationed; a public employment; a messenger; one who carries letters regularly; the mail; any means employed by government for the public conveyance of letters, &c.; a situation; letter-paper.—vt. To travel with post-horses.—vt. To set; to station; to

fix to a *post;* to expose to public reproach by fixing the name to a post; to proclaim as a coward; to place in the post-office, as letters; to carry accounts from the waste-book or journal to the ledger.—*a.* Used in travelling quickly; speedy.—*adv.* Hastily; or as a post. [Fr. *poste*—L. *postis*—*pono*, to place.]
Postage, pōst'āj, *n.* Official money charge for conveying letters by *post.*
Postal, pōst'al, *a. Relating to posts, posting,* or mails.
Post-boy, pōst'boi, *n. A boy who rides post;* a courier.
Post-chaise, Post-coach, pōst-shās', pōst-kōch', *n. A carriage for the conveyance of travellers who travel with post-horses.*
Post-date, pōst-dāt', *vt. To date after the real time. ppr.* post-dating, *pret. & pp.* post-dated. [L. *post*, and Eng. *date*.]
Posterior, pos-tē'ri-or, *a. That comes or follows after;* later in time; later in the order of proceeding; coming after. [L.—*posterus*, coming after—*post*, behind.]
Posteriority, pos-tē'ri-o''ri-ti, *n. State of being posterior.* [Fr. *postériorité*.]
Posteriorly, pos-tē'ri-or-li, *adv.* Subsequently; afterward.
Posteriors, pos-tē'ri-orz, *n. pl. The hinder parts of an animal's body.*
Posterity, pos-te'ri-ti, *n. Succeeding generations; descendants; children, &c., indefinitely;* the race that proceeds from a progenitor. [Fr. *postérité*—L. *post*, after, behind.]
Postern, pōst'ėrn, *n. Primarily, a back door or gate;* a private entrance; any small door or gate.—*a. Back; being behind;* private. [Fr. *poterne*—L. *post*, back.]
Postfix, pōst'fiks, *n. A letter, syllable, or word annexed to the end of another word;* a suffix. [L. *post*, and Eng. *fix*.]
Postfix, pōst-fiks', *vt.* To annex, as a letter or word *to the end* of another word.
Post-haste, pōst-hāst', *n. Haste or speed in travelling, like that of a post or courier.—adv.* With speed or expedition.
Post-horse, pōst'hors, *n.* One of a set of horses stationed at certain distances on a road for the rapid conveyance of couriers, passengers, &c.
Posthumous, pōst'hum-us, *a. Last; born after the death of the father, or taken from the dead body of the mother, as a child; published after the death of the author, as works;* being after one's decease, as fame. [L. *postimus,* superl. of *posterus,* coming after—*post,* behind.]
Postillion, pōs-til'li-on, *n. A post-boy;* one who rides and guides the first pair of horses in a coach; one who rides one of the horses. [Fr. *postillon*—*poste,* a post.]
Postman, pōst'man, *n.* A letter-carrier.
Post-mark, pōst'märk, *n. The mark or stamp of a post-office on a letter.—vt.* To affix the stamp or mark of the *post-office,* as to letters, &c.
Postmaster, pōst'mas-tėr, *n. The officer who has the superintendence and direction of a post-office.*
Post-meridian, pōst-me-ri'di-an, *a. After the meridian,* or noon; being or belonging to the afternoon. [L. *postmeridianus.*]
Post-nuptial, pōst-nup'shi-al, *a. Being or happening after marriage.*
Post-office, pōst'of-fis, *n. An office or house where letters are posted,* or re-

ceived for delivery and for transmission.
Postpone, pōst-pōn', *vt. To place after or behind;* to put off to a future time; to defer; to delay; to set below something else in value. *ppr.* postponing, *pret. & pp.* postponed. [L. *postpōno*—*pono,* to place.]
Postponement, pōst-pōn'ment, *n. Act of postponing* or of deferring to a future time.
Postscript, pōst'skript, *n. Something written after;* a paragraph added to a letter after it is concluded and signed by the writer; any addition made to a book after it had been supposed to be finished. [L. *post,* and *scriptum,* written—*scribo,* to write.]
Post-town, pōst'toun, *n. A town* in which a *post-office* is established.
Postulate, pos'tū-lāt, *n. Something that is sought or required;* a supposition required to be granted for the purpose of future reasoning. [L. *postulātum*—*posco,* to demand.]
Posture, pos'tūr, *n. Place; position; attitude; the situation of a figure with regard to the eye; condition; situation of the body; state; disposition of the several parts of the body with respect to each other; disposition;* frame. [Fr.—L. *pono, positum,* to place.]
Posy, pō'zi, *n. A poetical sentence or expression;* a verse or a motto inscribed on a ring, &c.; a bunch of flowers. [corrupted from *poesy.*]
Pot, pot, *n. A drinking-cup* or mug; a vessel more deep than broad, made of earth, or iron, or other metal, used for several domestic purposes; the quantity contained in a pot; a sort of paper of small-sized sheets.—*vt.* To put or place in a pot; to preserve seasoned in pots; to inclose or cover in pots of earth; to put in casks for draining, as sugar. *ppr.* potting, *pret. & pp.* potted. [Fr.—L. *poto,* to drink.]
Potable, pō'ta-bl, *a. Drinkable.—n. Something that may be drunk.* [Fr.—L. *poto,* to drink.]
Potash, pot'ash, *n.* The popular name of the vegetable fixed alkali *potassa* in an impure state, procured from the ashes of plants, and so named because the water in which the *ashes* are washed is evaporated in iron *pots.* [*pot* and *ashes.*]
Potation, pō-tā'shon, *n. A drinking* or drinking bout; a draught. [L. *potatio*—*poto,* to drink.]
Potato, pō-tā'tō, *n. A well-known plant and its esculent root* or tuber, a native of South America. [Sp. *patāta.*]
Potch, poch, *vt. To thrust;* to push; to poach. [Fr. *pocher.*]
Potency, pō'ten-si, *n. Might; force; power; physical power; strength; moral power; authority.* [L. *potentia*—*potens,* being able.]
Potent, pō'tent, *a. Able; powerful;* having physical power, energy, or efficacy; having moral power or efficacy; having great influence or authority.—*n.* A potentate. [L. *potens*—*potis,* able, and *sum, ens, entis* (obsol.) to be.]
Potentate, pō'ten-tāt, *n. One who possesses great power or sway;* an emperor, king, or monarch. [Fr. *potentat*—L. *possum, potens,* to have power.]
Potential, pō-ten'shi-al, *a. Having might or power;* existing in possibility, not in act; designating a mood or form of the verb, which is used to express the power, possibility, liberty, or necessity of an action or of being. [Fr. *potentiel*—L. *potens,* being able.]

Fāte, fär, fat, fall; mē, met, hėr; pīne, pin; nōte, not, mōve; tūbe, tub, bull; oil, pound.

Potentiality, pŏ-ten'shi-al"li-ti, n. *Quality of being potential*; possibility.
Potentially, pŏ-ten'shi-al-li, adv. *In possibility*; not in act; not positively.
Potently, pō'tent-li, adv. *Powerfully*; with great force or energy.
Pother, poᵾᵀH'ėr, n. *Dust*; confusion; tumult; flutter.—*vi.* To raise *a dust*; to make a blustering ineffectual effort.—*vt.* To harass and perplex; to puzzle. [corrupted from *powder*.]
Pot-herb, pot'ėrb, n. *An herb* used in cooking.
Pot-hook, pot'huk, n. *A hook on which pots and kettles are hung over the fire*; a letter or character like a pot-hook.
Potion, pō'shon, n. *A drink*; a liquid medicine; a dose. [Fr.—L. *poto*, to drink.]
Potsherd, pot'shėrd, n. *A piece or fragment of a broken pot.* [*pot*, and Sax. *sceard*, a fragment.]
Pottage, pot'āj, n. Food b iled or cooked in a *pot*; a species of food made of meat boiled to softness in water, usually with some vegetables. [Fr. *potage*.]
Potted, pot'ed, *p.a.* Placed, preserved, or drained in a *pot* or cask.
Potter, pot'ėr, n. *One whose occupation is to make pots* or earthen vessels.
Pottery, pot'ėr-i, n. *The vessels or ware made by potters*; the place where such are manufactured. [Fr. *poterie*.]
Potting, pot'ing, *p.n.* A placing or preserving in a pot.
Pottle, pot'l, n. A liquid measure of four pints; a vessel or small basket for holding fruit. [W. *potel*.]
Pot-valiant, pot-va'li-ant, *a.* Heated to *valour* by strong drink.
Pouch, pouch, n. *A pocket*; a leathern bag to be carried in the pocket; the bag or sac of a bird, as that of the pelican.—*vt.* To *put into a pouch*; to pocket; to save; to swallow (used of fowls, whose crop is called in Fr. *poche*). [Fr. *poche*.]
Poulter, pōl'tėr, n. *One who had charge of poultry*.
Poulterer, pōl'tėr-ėr, n. *A dealer in poultry.* [Norm. *poltaire*.]
Poultice, pōl'tis, n. *A cataplasm*; a soft composition to be applied to sores. *vt.* To apply a *poultice* to; to cover with a *poultice*. *ppr.* poulticing, *pret. & pp.* poulticed. [Old Fr. *pulte*—L. *puls, pultis*, a thick pap.]
Poultry, pōl'tri, n. *Domestic fowls* fed for the table, and for their eggs, feathers, &c. [Norm. *poulter*, poultry—L. *pullus*, a chicken.]
Pounce, pouns, n. *Pumice*; a powder to prevent ink from spreading on paper after erasures; coloured powder sprinkled over pricked papers in drawing patterns, &c.—*vt.* To sprinkle or rub with *pounce*. *ppr.* pouncing, *pret. & pp.* pounced. [Fr. *ponce*—L. *pumex*, a pumice-stone.]
Pounce, pouns, *vi.* To fall on and seize with *the pounces* or talons; to fall on suddenly. (Used with *on* or *upon.*) *ppr.* pouncing, *pret. & pp.* pounced.
Pounces, *That which pierces or penetrates*; the claw or talon of a bird of prey. [Sp. *punzir*—L. *pungo*, to prick.]
Pounce-box, pouns'boks, n. A small box with holes in the lid, used for sprinkling *pounce* on paper.
Pounce-box, pouns'set-boks, n. A small box with perforations on the top, to hold perfume for smelling.
Pound, pound, n. A standard **English** weight, consisting of twelve ounces troy, or sixteen ounces avoirdupois; a money of account, consisting of twenty shillings, originally making a pound in weight. [Sax. *pund*; L. *pendo*, to cause to hang down, to weigh.]
Pound, pound, n. An *inclosure* erected by authority, in which cattle are confined when taken in trespassing. [Sax. *pund*, a fold.]—*vt. To shut in* or *confine* in a public pound. [Sax. *pyndan*, to shut in.]
Pound, pound, *vt. To beat*; to pulverize by beating. [Sax. *punian*, to beat.]
Poundage, pound'āj, n. A sum deducted from *a pound*, or a certain sum paid for each *pound*; a mulct levied upon the owners of cattle impounded.
Pounder, pound'ėr, n. *One who, or that which pounds*; a pestle; a person or thing denominated from a certain number of pounds; as, a six-pounder, that is, a cannon which carries a ball of six pounds.
Pour, pōr, *vi. To stream quite round*; to issue forth in a *stream* or continued succession of parts; to move or rush, as a current; to rush in a crowd or continued procession.—*vt.* To let, as a fluid in a *stream*. either out of a vessel or into it; to emit; to send forth in a stream or continued succession; to give vent to, as strong feeling; to throw in profusion or with overwhelming force. [perhaps Sans. *parivāha*, a flowing, or running down of water.]
Pout, pout, *vi. To thrust out* the lips, as in sullenness, contempt, or displeasure; to look sullen; to shoot out; to be prominent. [Old Fr. *bouder*, to thrust or push forward.]
Pouter, pout'ėr, n. *One who pouts*; a kind of pigeon.
Pouting, pout'ing, *p.n.* Childish sullenness.
Poutingly, pout'ing-li, adv. *With pouting*.
Poverty, po'vėr-ti, n. *State of being poor*; indigence; necessity; want; meagreness; barrenness of sentiment or ornament; insufficiency or defect of words. [Fr. *pauvreté*—L. *pauper*, poor.]
Fowl, pou, *interj.* Poh!
Powder, pou'dėr, n. *Dust*; any dry substance composed of minute particles; a composition of saltpetre, sulphur, and charcoal, mixed and granulated; gunpowder; hair-powder.—*vt.* To reduce to *powder*; to pulverize; to sprinkle with powder; to sprinkle with salt. [Fr. *poudre*; L. *pulvis, pulveris*, dust.]
Powdered, pou'dėrd, *p.a.* Corned; salted.
Powder-magazine, pou'dėr-ma-ga-zēn, n. *A magasine for holding powder* in fortified places, &c.
Powder-mine, pou'dėr-mīn, n. *A cave or hollow in which powder is to be placed* to be fired at a proper time.
Powder-room, pou'dėr-röm, n. *The apartment* in a ship *where gunpowder is kept*.
Powdry, pou'dėr-i, *a. Of the nature of powder*; friable; resembling powder.
Power, pou'ėr, n. *Rule*; the right of governing; sway; influence; that which may move the mind; a sovereign; divinity; a celestial being supposed to have dominion over some part of creation; an army; a navy; ability; force; the faculty of doing anything; the faculty of producing a change in something; capacity; energy; faculty of the mind; ability, natural or moral; the moving force of an engine; mechanical advantage; one of the six simple machines which form the elements of all machines; that quality in any natural body which produces a change in another body; momentum; legal authority; warrant; the product arising from the multiplication of a number into itself; as, a cube is the third power. [Norm. *povaire*, to be able—L. *potis*, able—Sans. *pā*, to see to, to rule—and *sum*, I am.]
Powerful, pou'ėr-ful, *a. Having great power*; intense; influential; valid.
Powerfully, pou'ėr-ful-li, adv. *In a powerful manner*.
Powerfulness, pou'ėr-ful-nes, n. *The quality of having great power*; force; might.
Powerless, pou'ėr-les, *a. Destitute of power*; weak; impotent.
Powerlessness, pou'ėr-les-nes, n. *Destitution of power*.
Pox, poks, n. Strictly, *pocks*; pustules or eruptions of any kind; an eruptive distemper. [*pocks*, pl. of *pock*.]
Practicability, prak'ti-ka-bil"li-ti, n. *Quality or state of being practicable*.
Practicable, prak'ti-ka-bl, *a. That may be done*; feasible; that admits of use, or that may be passed or travelled, as a road. [Fr. *praticable*.]
Practicably, prak'ti-ka-bli, adv. In such a *manner as may be performed*.
Practical, prak'ti-kal, *a. Pertaining to practice*; that may be applied to use; that reduces his knowledge to actual use; derived from practice; relating to the practice of any department of knowledge; not theoretical. [Fr. *pratique*—Gr. *prassō, praxō*, to do.]
Practically, prak'ti-kal-li, adv. *In a practical manner*.
Practice, prak'tis, n. *A doing or effecting*; a succession of acts of a similar kind; custom; use; actual performance, distinguished from theory; medical treatment of diseases; exercise of any profession; skilful management; stratagem; artifice; a rule in arithmetic. [Sp. *práctica*—Gr. *prassō*, to do.]
Practisant, prak'tiz-ant, n. An agent.
Practise, prak'tis, *vt. To do*; to do or perform habitually; to use, as any profession or art; to do repeatedly, with the view of acquiring dexterity in; to commit.—*vi. To perform certain acts* frequently; to form a habit of acting in any manner; to negotiate secretly; to try artifices; to exercise any employment. *ppr.* practising, *pret. & pp.* practised.
Practised, prak'tist, *p.a. Having had much practice*; as, a practised speaker.
Practiser, prak'tis-ėr, n. *One who practises*.
Practising, prak'tis-ing, *p.a.* Engaged in any professional employment, as a lawyer.
Practitioner, prak-ti'shon-ėr, n. *One who does anything customarily*; one who is engaged in the actual exercise of any art or profession, particularly in law or medicine.
Pragmatical, prag-mat'ik-al, *a. Ready to act*; meddling; impertinently officious in the concerns of others. [Fr. *pragmatique*—Gr. *prassō*, to do.]
Pragmatically, prag-mat'ik-al-li, adv. In a meddling manner; impertinently
Praise, prāz, n. *Value* acknowledged; admiration expressed; encomium; eulogy; panegyric; a glorifying or extolling; the object, ground, or reason of praise.—*vt. To acknowledge tha value of*; to extol; to eulogize; to magnify. *ppr.* praising, *pret. & pp.* praised. [Icel. *prísa*, to praise; L. *pretium*, reward.]
Praiseworthiness, prāz'wėr-ᴛH̄i-nes, n. *Quality of being praiseworthy*.

Praiseworthy, prāz'wėr-ṭhi, a. *Deserving of praise* or applause; commendable.

Prance, prans, vi. *To leap*; to spring or bound, as a horse in high mettle; to strut about in a showy manner or with warlike parade. [W. *pranciaw*.]

Prancing, prans'ing, p.a. Springing; bounding; riding with gallant show.

Prancingly, prans'ing-li, adv. In a prancing manner.

Prank, prangk, n. *A capering*; frolic; freak; a capricious action, a ludicrous or merry trick, or a mischievous act, rather for sport than injury. [from *prance*.]

Prank, prangk, vt. *To adorn in a showy manner*; to dress or decorate to ostentation. [G. *prangen*, to show off.]

Prate, prāt, vi. *To talk* much, and without weight, or to little purpose; to babble; to tattle.—vt. *To utter foolishly*.—n. Continued *talk* to little purpose; unmeaning loquacity. ppr. prating, pret. & pp. prated. [D. *praaten*.]

Prater, prāt'ėr, n. *One who talks* much to little purpose, or on trifling subjects.

Prating, prāt'ing, p.a. Foolish, idle *talk*.

Prattle, prat'l, vi. *To talk much* and idly, like a child.—n. *Trifling talk*; loquacity on trivial subjects. ppr. prattling, pret. & pp. prattled.

Prattler, prat'l-ėr, n. *One who prattles*.

Prawn, pran, n. *A small crustaceous animal of the shrimp family*, highly prized for food.

Praxis, praks'is, n. *Use*; practice; an example or form to teach practice. [Gr.—*prasso*, to do.]

Pray, prā, vi. *To beg*; to beseech or implore; to ask with earnestness, as for a favour; to ask, as in application to a legislative body; to address the Supreme Being with solemnity and reverence.—vt. *To beg*; to entreat; to urge; to ask with reverence and humility; to petition; to ask or entreat in ceremony or form. [Fr. *prier*—L. *precor*—Sans. *prah*, to ask.]

Prayer, prā'ėr, n. *Act of beseeching*; supplication; entreaty; a solemn address to the Supreme Being; a form of church-service, or of worship, public or private; the practice of devotion; the thing asked.

Prayer-book, prā'ėr-buk, n. *A book containing prayers* or the forms of devotion, public or private.

Prayerful, prā'ėr-ful, a. *Given to prayer*; devotional; using much prayer.

Prayerfully, prā'ėr-ful-li, adv. *With much prayer*.

Prayerless, prā'ėr-les, a. *Not using prayer*; habitually neglecting the duty of prayer to God.

Praying, prā'ing, p.a. *Given to prayer*.

Preach, prēch, vi. *To pronounce a public discourse* from a text of Scripture; to discourse on the gospel way of salvation, and exhort to repentance.—vt. *To proclaim*; to publish in religious discourses; to inculcate in public discourses; to deliver in public, as a discourse. [Fr. *prêcher*—L. *præ*, and *dico*, to proclaim.]

Preached, prēcht, p.v. Announced in public discourse.

Preacher, prēch'ėr, n. *One who preaches*.

Preaching, prēch'ing, p.n. *The act of preaching*; a public religious discourse.

Preachment, prēch'ment, n. A discourse or sermon, in contempt.

Preamble, prē'am-bl, n. *Something which goes before*; introduction to a discourse or writing; the introductory part of a statute, which states the reasons and intent of the law. [Fr. *préambule*—L. *præ*, and *ambulo*, to go about.]

Pre-audience, prē-ạ'di-ens, n. *A first audience* or hearing; precedence or rank at the bar among lawyers; right of previous audience.

Prebend, pre'bend, n. *The maintenance granted* to a canon of a cathedral or collegiate church out of its estate. [Fr. *prebende*—L. *præbeo*, to grant.]

Prebendal, pre-bend'al, a. *Pertaining to a prebend*.

Prebendary, pre'bend-a-ri, n. *An ecclesiastic who enjoys a prebend*; the stipendiary of a cathedral or collegiate church. [Fr. *prébendier*.]

Precarious, prē-kā'ri-us, a. *Obtained by prayer*; depending on the will or pleasure of another; held by no certain tenure; uncertain; doubtful; dubious. [L. *precarius*—*precor*, to pray.]

Precariously, prē-kā'ri-us-li, adv. *In a precarious manner*.

Precariousness, prē-kā'ri-us-nes, n. *State of being precarious*; uncertainty.

Precaution, prē-kạ'shon, n. *Caution previously* employed to prevent mischief or secure good in possession.—vt. To caution or warn beforehand. [Fr. *précaution*—L. *præ*, and *caveo*, *cautus*, to take care.]

Precautionary, prē-kạ'shon-a-ri, a. *Containing precaution*; proceeding from previous caution.

Precede, prē-sēd', vt. *To go before* in place, or in the order of time; to go before in rank or importance. ppr. preceding, pret. & pp. preceded. [Fr. *précéder*; L. *cedo*, to go.]

Precedence, Precedency, prē-sēd'ens, prē-sēd'en-si, n. *Act or state of going before*, with respect to time; antecedence; state of going or being before in rank or dignity; the right to a more honourable place; a precedent. [Sp. *precedéncia*.]

Precedent, prē-sēd'ent, a. *Going before* in time; anterior. [Fr. *précédent*.]

Precedent, pre'sē-dent, n. *Something going before*; something done or said, that may serve to be adduced as an example to authorize a subsequent act of the like kind; a judicial decision which serves as a rule for future determinations in similar cases.

Precedented, pre'sē-dent-ed, p.a. *Having a precedent*.

Precedently, prē-sēd'ent-li, adv. Beforehand; antecedently.

Preceding, prē-sēd'ing, p.a. *Going before* in time, rank, &c.; antecedent.

Precentor, prē-sen'tor, n. *A leading singer*; the leader of a choir in a cathedral; the leader of the congregation in the psalmody of the Scottish churches. [Fr. *précenteur*—L. *cano*, *cantum*, to sing.]

Precentorship, prē-sen'tor-ship, n. *The employment or office of a precentor*.

Precept, prē'sept, n. *A taking beforehand*; an instruction; anything enjoined as a rule of action; a command given in writing; injunction; law; principle; maxim. [Fr. *précepte*—L. *capio*, *captum*, to take.]

Preceptial, prē-sep'shi-al, a. *Consisting of precepts*.

Preceptive, prē-sept'iv, a. *Giving precepts*; containing precepts; directing in moral conduct; didactic. [Sp. *preceptivo*.]

Preceptor, prē-sep'tor, n. *One who gives precepts*; a teacher; the teacher of a school; sometimes the principal teacher of an academy or other seminary. [L. *præceptor*—*capio*, to take.]

Preceptorial, prē-sep-tō'ri-al, a. *Pertaining to a preceptor*. [Fr. *préceptorial*.]

Preceptress, prē-sept'res, n. *A female teacher*.

Precession, prē-se'shon, n. *Act of going before*. [Fr. *précession*—L. *cedo*, to go.]

Precinct, prē'singt, n. *A place girded about*; the limit encompassing a place; bounds of jurisdiction. [Norm. *procincte*—L. *cingo*, *cinctus*, to gird.]

Precious, pre'shi-us, a. *Of great price*; costly; of great value or worth; highly valued; much esteemed. [Fr. *précieux*—L. *pretium*, price.]

Preciously, pre'shi-us-li, adv. Valuably; to a great price.

Preciousness, pre'shi-us-nes, n. *Quality of being precious*; valuableness.

Precipice, pre'si-pis, n. *A steep descent of land*; a fall or descent of land. perpendicular or nearly so; an abrupt or rocky declivity. [Fr. *précipice*.]

Precipitable, prē-si'pi-ta-bl, a. *That may be precipitated*.

Precipitance, Precipitancy, prē-si'pi-tans, prē-si'pi-tan-si, n. *Quality of being precipitate*; rash haste; haste in resolving; executing a purpose without due deliberation.

Precipitant, prē-si'pi-tant, a. *Falling or rushing headlong*; urged with violent haste. [Fr. *précipitant*.]

Precipitantly, prē-si'pi-tant-li, adv. With great haste; with rash, unadvised haste; with tumultuous hurry.

Precipitate, prē-si'pi-tāt, vt. *To throw headlong*; to urge with eagerness; to hasten; to hurry blindly or rashly; to throw to the bottom of a vessel, as a substance in solution.—vi. *To fall headlong*; to fall to the bottom of a vessel, as a sediment; to harten without preparation. ppr. precipitating, pret. & pp. precipitated.—a. *Headlong*; overhasty; adopted with haste; violent; terminating speedily in death. n. A substance which is thrown down by decomposition from a liquid. [Fr. *précipiter*—L. *præ*, before, and *caput*, *capitis*, the head.]

Precipitately, prē-si'pi-tāt-li, adv. *Headlong*; with steep descent; with rash haste.

Precipitation, prē-si'pi-tā'shon, n. *Act of precipitating*; rapid movement; act or operation of throwing to the bottom of a vessel any substance held in solution. [Fr. *précipitation*.]

Precipitous, prē-si'pi-tus, a. *Headlong*; very steep; hasty; rash; heady. [Sp. *precipitoso*.]

Precipitously, prē-si'pi-tus-li, adv. With steep descent; in violent haste.

Precipitousness, prē-si'pi-tus-nes, n. *State or quality of being precipitous*.

Precise, prē-sis', a. *Cut short*; shortened; cut into form; exact; accurate; characterized by excessive nicety in conduct or ceremony; formal; finical. [Fr. *précis*; L. *præ*, and *cædo*, to cut off.]

Precisely, prē-sis'li, adv. *In a precise manner*.

Preciseness, prē-sis'nes, n. *Quality of being precise*; rigid nicety or formality.

Precisian, prē-si'zhan, n. *One who is over precise*, or rigidly exact in the observance of rules.

Precision, prē-si'zhon, n. *State of being precise*; exact limitation; exactness; definiteness. [Fr. *précision*.]

Preclude, prē-klūd', vt. *To shut to*; to close; to hinder from access, posses-

Fāte, fär fat, fạll; mē, met, hėr; pīne, pin; nōte, not, mōve; tūbe, tub, bull; oil, pound.

sion, or enjoyment; to debar; to prevent from taking place. *ppr.* precluding, *pret. & pp.* precluded. [It. *precludere*; L. *claudo*, to shut.]
Preclusion, prē-klū'zhon, *n. Act of precluding*; the state of being prevented from entering, possession, or enjoyment. [Late L. *præclusio.*]
Preclusive, prē-klū'siv, *a. Shutting out*, or tending to preclude.
Precocious, prē-kō'shi-us, *a. Ripe before the natural time;* premature; forward; having the mental powers early developed. [Fr. *précoce*—L. *coquo*, to cook, ripen.]
Precociously, prē-kō'shi-us-li, *adv. With premature ripeness.*
Precocity, prē-kos'i-ti, *n. State or quality of being precocious;* prematureness; forwardness. [Fr. *précocité.*]
Preconceive, prē-kon-sēv', *vt. To form a conception of beforehand;* to form a previous notion of. *ppr.* preconceiving, *pret. & pp.* preconceived. [L. *præ, con,* and *capio,* to take.]
Preconceived, prē-kon-sēvd', *p.a. Conceived beforehand;* previously formed.
Preconception, prē-kon-sep'shon, *n. Conception previously formed.*
Preconcert, prē-kon-sėrt', *vt. To concert beforehand;* to settle by previous agreement.
Preconcerted, prē-kon-sėrt'ed, *p.a. Previously concerted,* or settled.
Precurrent, prē-kėr'er, *n. A forerunner.*
Precurrent, prē-kėrs', *n. A forerunning.*
Precursor, prē-kėrs'or, *n. A forerunner;* he or that which precedes an event and indicates its approach; a harbinger; omen. [L. *præcursor—curro,* to run.]
Precursory, prē-kėr'sō-ri, *a. Indicating something to follow.*
Predatory, prē'da-tō-ri, *a. Plundering;* characterized by plundering; practising rapine. [L. *prædatorius—præda,* booty.]
Predecease, prē-dē-sēs', *vt. To die before.* *ppr.* predeceasing, *pret. & pp.* predeceased.—*n. The decease of one before another.*
Predecessor, prē-dē-ses'or, *n. A person who has preceded another in the same office.* [Fr. *prédécesseur*—L. *præ, de,* and *cedo,* to go.]
Predesign, prē-dē-sīn', *vt. To design or purpose beforehand;* to predetermine.
Predestinarian, prē-des'ti-nā"ri-an, *n. One who believes in the doctrine of predestination.*—*a. Pertaining to predestination.*
Predestinate, prē-des'tin-āt, *vt To determine beforehand by an unchangeable purpose:* to foreordain; to decree; to foredoom.—*a.* foreordained. *ppr.* predestinating, *pret. & pp.* predestinated. [Fr. *prédestiner*—L. *destino,* to fix.]
Predestinated, prē-des'tin-āt-ed, *p.a. Predetermined;* foreordained.
Predestination, prē-des'tin-ā"shon, *n. Act of predestinating;* in theology, foreordination to eternal life or death. [Fr. *prédestination.*]
Predeterminate, prē-dē-tėr'min-āt, *a. Determined beforehand.*
Predetermination, prē'dē-tėr'min-ā"-shon, *n. Previous determination;* purpose formed beforehand.
Predetermine, prē-dē-tėr'min, *vt. To determine beforehand;* to doom by previous decree.—*vi. To determine beforehand.* *ppr.* predetermining, *pret. & pp.* predetermined.
Predetermined, prē-dē-tėr'mind, *p a. Previously determined.*

Predial, prē'di-al, *a. Relating to a farm or estate;* consisting of land or farms; attached to land or farms; growing or issuing from land. [Sp. *predial*—L. *prædium,* land generally.]
Predicability, prē'di-ka-bil"i-ti, *n. The quality of being predicable.*
Predicable, prē'di-ka-bl, *a. That may be affirmed of something;* that may be attributed to.—*n. One of the five things which can be affirmed of anything;* viz. genus, species, difference, property, or accident. [Fr. *prédicable*—L. *dico,* to say.]
Predicament, prē-dik'a-ment, *n. Class or kind described by any definite marks;* condition; a trying condition. [Fr. *prédicament.*]
Predicate, prē'di-kāt, *vt. To proclaim;* to affirm, as one thing of another. *vi. To affirm;* to comprise an affirmation. *ppr.* predicating, *pret. & pp.* predicated.—*n. That which, in a proposition, is affirmed or denied of the subject.* [L. *prædico, prædicatus—dico,* to publish.]
Predication, prē-di-kā'shon, *n. Affirmation of something, or the act of affirming one thing of another.* [Fr. *prédication.*]
Predict, prē-dikt', *vt. To tell beforehand,* as something that is to happen; to foretell; to foreshow.—*n. A prediction.* [L. *prædico, prædictus—dico,* to say.]
Predicted, prē-dikt'ed, *p.a. Foretold.*
Prediction, prē-dik'shon, *n. A foretelling;* prophecy. [Fr. *prédiction.*]
Predictive, prē-dikt'iv, *a. Foretelling;* prophetic. [Low L. *prædictivus.*]
Predilection, prē-di-lek'shon, *n. A previous liking;* a preference; a prepossession of mind in favour of some person or thing. [Fr. *prédilection*—L. *præ, dis,* and *lego,* to choose.]
Predispose, prē-dis-pōz', *vt. To dispose beforehand;* to give a previous disposition to; to fit or adapt previously. *ppr.* predisposing, *pret. & pp.* predisposed.
Predisposing, prē-dis-pōz'ing, *p.a. Tending to give predisposition.*
Predisposition, prē-dis'pō-zi"shon, *n. State of being predisposed;* previous inclination to anything.
Predominance, prē-dom'in-ans, *n. State of being predominant;* superiority in strength or power; ascendency. [Fr. *prédominance.*]
Predominant, prē-dom'in-ant, *a. Having supreme power;* having superiority in strength or authority; controlling; overruling. [Fr. *prédominant.*]
Predominantly, prē-dom'in-ant-li, *adv. With superior strength or power.*
Predominate, prē-dom'in-āt, *vi. To have supreme power;* to surpass in influence or authority; to be superior; to have controlling influence. *ppr.* predominating, *pret. & pp.* predominated. [L *præ,* and *dominor, dominatus—dominus,* a lord.]
Predominating, prē-dom'in-āt-ing, *p.a. Having superior strength or influence;* controlling.
Pre-eminence, prē-em'i-nens, *n. State of being pre-eminent;* superiority in excellence; superiority in rank or dignity. [Fr. *prééminence.*]
Pre-eminent, prē-em'i-nent, *a. Standing forward,* being prominent; superior in excellence; surpassing others in evil or bad qualities. [Fr. *prééminent*—L. *præ, e,* and *mineo,* to jut.]
Pre-eminently, prē-em'i-nent-li, *adv. In a pre-eminent degree.*
Pre-emption, prē-em'shon, *n. The right of purchasing before others.* [L. *præ,* and *emptio—emo,* to buy.]
Pre-engage, prē-en-gāj', *vt To engage beforehand;* to engage by previous influence. *ppr.* pre-engaging, *pret. & pp.* pre-engaged.
Pre-engagement, prē-en-gāj'ment, *n. Prior engagement,* as by stipulation or promise; any previous attachment binding the will or affections.
Pre-establish, prē-es-tab'lish, *vt. To establish beforehand.*
Pre-establishment, prē-es-tab'lish-ment, *n. Settlement beforehand.*
Pre-exist, prē-egz-ist', *vi. To exist beforehand,* or before something else.
Pre-existence, prē-egz-ist'ens, *n. Previous existence;* existence previous to something else.
Pre-existent, prē-egz-ist'ent, *a. Existing beforehand;* preceding in existence.
Pre-existing, prē-egz-ist'ing, *p.a. Previously existing.*
Preface, pre'fās, *n. That which is said beforehand;* something spoken as introductory to a discourse, or written as introductory to a book; proem; prelude.—*vt. To introduce by preface or preliminary remarks.*—*v. To say something introductory.* *ppr.* prefacing, *pret. & pp.* prefaced. [Fr. *préface*—L. *præ,* and *fari, fatus,* to speak.]
Prefatory, pre'fā-tō-ri, *a. Pertaining to a preface;* introductory to a book, essay, or discourse.
Prefect, pre'fekt, *n. One placed over others;* a governor; a superintendent. [Fr. *préfet*—L. *facio, factus,* to make.]
Prefecture, pre'fekt-ūr, *n. The office of a prefect,* a chief magistrate, commander, or viceroy; jurisdiction of a prefect. [L. *præfectura.*]
Prefer, prē-fėr', *vt. To bear before;* to regard more than another; to advance, as to an office or dignity; to exalt; to exhibit, usually with solemnity, or to a public body; to proffer!. *ppr.* preferring, *pret. & pp.* preferred. [Fr. *préférer*—L. *fero,* to bear.]
Preferable, pref'er-a-bl, *a. Worthy to be preferred;* more desirable; of better quality. [Fr. *préférable.*]
Preferably, pref'ėr-a-bli, *adv. In preference;* in such a manner as to prefer one thing to another.
Preference, pref'ėr-ens, *n. Act of preferring one thing before another;* choice of one thing rather than another; state of being preferred. [Fr. *préférence.*]
Preferential, pref-ėr-en'shi-al, *a. Implying preference.*
Preferentially, pref-ėr-en'shi-al-li, *adv. With preference.*
Preferment, prē-fėr'ment, *n. Advancement to a higher office, dignity, or station;* superior place or office. [It. *preferimento.*]
Prefiguration, prē-fig'ūr-ā"shon, *n. Act of prefiguring;* state of being prefigured; rimilitude.
Prefigure, prē-fig'ūr, *vt. To figure or picture out beforehand;* to exhibit by antecedent representation, or by types and rimilitude. *ppr.* prefiguring, *pret & pp.* prefigured. [Low L. *præfiguro*—L. *figura,* shape—*fingo, fictum,* to form, shape, fashion.]
Prefix, prē-fiks', *vt. To fix or put before;* to set beforehand; to settle; to establish. [L. *præfigo, præfixus—figo,* to fix.]
Prefix, pre'fiks, *n. A letter,* syllable, or word put to the beginning of a word, usually to vary its signification.
Preform, prē-form', *vt To form beforehand*

Pregnancy, preg'nan-si, n. *State of being pregnant;* fertility; inventive power.
Pregnant, preg'nant, a. *Being with young,* as a female; breeding; teeming; big; impregnating; full of consequence; full; giving access. [L. *prægnans—gigno,* to bring forth.]
Pregnantly, preg'nant-li, adv. Fruitfully.
Prehensible, prē-hen'si-bi, a. *That may be seized.*
Prehensile, prē-hen'sil, a. *Taking hold of; seizing;* fitted for seizing or laying hold. [from L. *prehendo, prehensus,* to lay hold of.]
Prehension, prē-hen'shon, n. *A taking hold of;* a seizing, as with the hand or other limb. [Fr.]
Prejudge, prē-juj', vt. *To judge beforehand;* to judge and determine before the cause is heard; hence sometimes, to condemn beforehand or unheard. ppr. prejudging, pret. & pp. prejudged. [Fr. *préjuger—*L. *judico,* to judge.]
Prejudgment, prē-juj'ment, n. *Judgment beforehand;* judgment in a case without a hearing or full examination.
Prejudice, prej'ū-dis, n. *A preceding judgment;* prejudgment; decision of mind formed without due examination of the arguments which are necessary to a just determination; bias; a previous inclination of mind for or against any person or thing; injury or wrong of any kind.—vt. *To affect with prejudice;* to prepossess with unexamined opinions; to bias the mind of by hasty and incorrect notions; to obstruct or injure by prejudices; to damage; to impair. ppr. prejudicing, pret. & pp. prejudiced. [Fr. *préjudice;* L. *judico,* to judge.]
Prejudiced, prej'ū-dist, p.a. Biassed.
Prejudicial, prej-ū-di'shi-al, a. Biassed; hurtful; injurious; tending to obstruct or impair. [Fr. *préjudiciel.*]
Prelacy, prel'a-si, n. *The office of a prelate;* episcopacy; the order of bishops, bishops, collectively. [Fr. *prélature.*]
Prelate, prel'āt, n. *One who is set over others;* a clergyman of a superior order, having authority over the lower clergy, as an archbishop, bishop, &c.; a dignitary of the church. [Fr. *prélat—*L. *fero, latum,* to bear, to raise.]
Prelatic, Prelatical, prē-lat'ik, prē-lat'ik-al, a. *Pertaining to prelates or prelacy.*
Prelatist, prel'āt-ist, n. *An advocate for prelacy,* or the government of the church by bishops; a high-churchman.
Prelect, prē-lekt', vi. *To read and explain to others;* to read a lecture or public discourse. [L. *prælego, prælectus—lego,* to read.]
Prelection, prē-lek'shon, n. *A lecture or discourse read in public* or to a select company. [L. *prælectio—lego,* to read.]
Prelector, prē-lek'tor, n. *One who prelects;* a lecturer. [Late L.]
Preliminarily, prē-lim'in-a-ri-li, adv. Introductorily; previously.
Preliminary, prē-lim'in-a-ri, a. *Before the threshold or entrance;* introductory; preparatory; previous.—n. That which precedes the main discourse or business; something preparatory; introduction; preface. [Fr. *préliminaire—*L. *limen, liminis,* a threshold.]
Prelude, prē-lūd', vt. *To introduce with a previous performance;* to precede, as an introductory piece.—vi. To serve as an introduction. ppr. preluding, pret. & pp. preluded. [Fr. *préluder—*L. *ludo,* to play.]
Prelude, prē'lūd, n. *Something played beforehand;* a short flight of music, or irregular air, played by a musician before he begins the piece to be played; introduction; harbinger. [Fr. *prélude.*]
Prelusive, prē-lū'siv, a. *Partaking of the nature of a prelude;* previous.
Premature, prē-ma-tūr', a. *Mature or ripe before the proper time;* happening, arriving, performed, or adopted before the proper time. [Fr. *prematuré—*L. *maturus,* ripe.]
Prematurely, prē-ma-tūr'li, adv. *Too soon;* before the proper time.
Prematureness, prē-ma-tūr'nes, n. *State of being premature;* unseasonable earliness.
Premeditate, prē-me'di-tāt, vt. *To meditate upon beforehand;* to think on beforehand; to contrive and design previously.—vi. To resolve in the mind beforehand; to deliberate. ppr. premeditating, pret. & pp. premeditated. [L. *meditor, meditatus,* to meditate.]
Premeditated, prē-me'di-tāt-ed, p.a. *Previously considered or mediated;* deliberate; wilful.
Premeditation, prē-me'di-tā"shon, n. *Act of meditating beforehand;* previous deliberation; previous contrivance. [Fr. *préméditation.*]
Premier, prē'mi-ėr, a. *First;* chief; principal.—n. *The first minister of state;* the prime minister. [Fr.—L. *primus,* first.]
Premiership, prē'mi-ėr-ship, n. *The office or dignity of a premier.*
Premise, prē-mīz', vt. *To send before the time;* to set or place before; to speak or write before, or as introductory to the main subject; to lay down, as premises, on which rest the subsequent reasonings.—vi. To state antecedent propositions. ppr. premising, pret. & pp. premised. [L. *præmitto, præmissus—mitto,* to send.]
Premise, prē'mis, n. *Something premised;* a proposition antecedently supposed; (pl. premisses) propositions which come before; the first two propositions in a syllogism, from which the inference is drawn; (premises) houses, lands, &c., set forth or proposed to be conveyed, sold, &c. [Fr. *premisses,* premises.]
Premiss, prē'mis, n. *A premise.* (Premiss is now generally preferred.)
Premium, prē'mi-um, n. *What one takes or has before others;* a reward or recompense; a prize to be won by competition; the prize offered for a specific discovery; something offered or given for the loan of money; the recompense to underwriters for insurance; value above the original price; value above par; a bounty or incentive. [L. *præmium—emo,* to take.]
Premonish, prē-mon'ish, vt. *To admonish beforehand.* [L. *moneo,* to admonish.]
Premonition, prē-mō-ni'shon, n. *Previous warning.* [Low L. *præmonitio.*]
Premonitor, prē-mon'i-tor, n. *One who gives premonition.* [Low L.]
Premonitory, prē-mon'i-tō-ri, a. *Giving previous warning* or notice. [Low L. *premonitorius.*]
Prenominate, prē-no'min-āt, a. Forenamed.
Prentice, pren'tis. See APPRENTICE.
Preoccupancy, prē-ok'kū-pan-si, n. *Act of occupying before another;* the right of taking possession before others.
Preoccupation, prē-ok'kū-pā"shon, n. *Act of preoccupying;* prepossession; anticipation of objections.
Preoccupied, prē-ok'kū-pid, p.a. Prepossessed.
Preoccupy, prē-ok'kū-pī, vt. *To seize upon beforehand;* to take possession of before another; to occupy by anticipation or prejudices. ppr. preoccupying, pret. & pp. preoccupied. [Fr. *préoccuper—*L. *occupo,* to seize.]
Preordain, prē-or-dān', vt. *To ordain* or appoint *beforehand;* to predetermine.
Preordinance, prē-or'din-ans, n. Antecedent decree.
Prepaid, prē-pād', p.a. *Paid in advance,* as postage of letters.
Preparation, prē-pa-rā'shon, n. *Act of preparing;* previous measures of adaptation; that which i prepared; state of being prepared; accomplishment. [Fr. *preparation.*]
Preparative, prē-pa'rāt-iv, a. *Tending to prepare;* having the power of preparing; preparatory.—n. *That which has the power of preparing;* that which is done to prevent evil or secure good; preparation, as for a journey. [Fr. *préparatif.*]
Preparatively, prē-pa'rāt-iv-li, adv. *By way of preparation.*
Preparatory, prē-pa'ra-tō-ri, a. *That makes preparation;* preparing the way for anything by previous measures of adaptation; antecedent and adapted to what follows. [Fr. *préparatoire.*]
Prepare, prē-pār', vt. *To make ready beforehand;* to cause to be suitable for some end; to fit; to adjust; to establish; to appoint.—vi. *To make preparation;* to put things in suitable order; to take the necessary previous measures. ppr. preparing, pret. & pp. prepared.—n. Preparation. [Fr. *préparer—*L. *paro,* to get ready.]
Prepared, prē-pārd', p.a. Adapted; made suitable; provided.
Preparedly, prē-pārd'li, adv. *With suitable previous measures.*
Preparedness, prē-pārd'nes, n. *State of being prepared* or in readiness.
Preparer, prē-pār'ėr, n. *One who prepares.*
Prepay, prē-pā', vt. *To pay in advance or beforehand,* as the postage of a letter. ppr. prepaying, pret. & pp. prepaid.
Prepayment, prē-pā'ment, n. *Payment in advance,* as of postage.
Prepense, prē-pens', a. *Weighed before;* premeditated; aforethought. [L. *præpensus—*L *pendo, pensum,* to weigh.]
Preponderance, prē-pon'dėr-ans, n. *An outweighing;* superiority of power, force, or weight. [Fr. *prépondérance.*]
Preponderant, prē-pon'dėr-ant, a. *Outweighing.* [Fr. *prépondérant.*]
Preponderate, prē-pon'dėr-āt, vi. *To exceed in weight;* to exceed in influence or power analogous to weight; to incline to one side. ppr. preponderating, pret. & pp preponderated. [L. *præpondero, præponderatus—*L. *pondus,* a weight.]
Preponderating, prē-pon'dėr-āt-ing, p.a. *Outweighing.*
Preposition, prē-pō-zi'shon, n. *A setting before;* a particle usually put before another word to express some relation or quality, action or motion, to or from the thing specified. [Fr. *préposition—*L. *pono, positum,* to set.]
Prepositional, prē-pō-zi'shon-al, a. *Pertaining to a preposition,* or to preceding position.
Prepositive, prē-poz'it-iv, a. *Put before.* n. *A word put before another word.* [Fr. *prépositif.*]
Prepossess, prē-poz-zes', vt. *To possess beforehand;* to preoccupy, as ground or land; to preoccupy the mind or heart of; to prejudice.

Prepossessing, prē-poz-zes'ing, p.a. Tending to invite favour; having power to secure the possession of favour or love.

Prepossession, prē-poz-ze'shon, n. Prior possession; bias; the effect of previous impressions on the heart, in favour of or against any person or thing.

Preposterous, prē-pos'tėr-us, a. Having that first which ought to be last; reversed; inverted in order; contrary to nature or reason; monstrous. [L. præposterus—pra, before, and post, after.]

Preposterously, prē-pos'tėr-us-li, adv. In a wrong or inverted order; absurdly.

Preposterousness, prē-pos'tėr-us-nes, n. State or quality of being preposterous.

Prerogative, prē-ro'ga-tiv, n. That which is asked first; a prior claim or title; an exclusive or peculiar privilege or right. [Fr. prérogative—L. rogo, to ask.]

Prerogatived, prē-ro'ga-tivd, p.a. Having a prerogative.

Presage, prē'sāj, n. Something acutely felt beforehand; a presentiment; something which foreshows a future event; a prognostic, omen, or sign. [Fr. présage; L. sagio, to perceive keenly.]

Presage, prē-sāj', vt. To forebode; to betoken; to predict; to prophesy. ppr. presaging, pret. & pp. presaged.

Presager, prē-sāj'ėr, n. One who presages.

Presbyter, pres'bi-tėr, n. One far advanced in years; an elder; a priest; a person who has the pastoral charge of a particular church and congregation. [Gr. presbúteros—presbus, an old man.]

Presbyterial, Presbyterian, pres-bi-tē'ri-al, pres-bi-tē'ri-an, a, Pertaining to a presbyter, or to ecclesiastical government by presbyters; consisting of presbyters.

Presbyterian, pres-bi-tē'ri-an, n. One who maintains the validity of ordination by presbyters; one who belongs to a church governed by presbyters.

Presbyterianism, pres-bi-tē'ri-an-izm, n. That form of church-government which invests presbyters with all spiritual power.

Presbytery, pres'bi-te-ri, n. A body of elders in the Christian church; a church court in the Presbyterian church. [Gr. presbúteron, a council of elders.]

Prescience, prē'shi-ens, n. Foreknowledge; knowledge of events before they take place. [Fr.]

Prescient, prē'shi-ent, a. Foreknowing; having knowledge of events before they take place. [L. præsciens—scio, to know.]

Prescribe, prē-skrīb', vt. To write before; to direct by a written order; to dictate; to direct; to ordain; to direct, as a remedy.—vi. To write or give medical directions; to give law; to claim a title to a thing by immemorial use and enjoyment. (With for.) ppr. prescribing, pret. & pp. prescribed. [L. præscribo—scribo, to write.]

Prescribed, prē-skrībd', p.a. Ordered.

Prescriptible, prē-skript'i-bl, a. Derived from prescription. [Fr.]

Prescription, prē-skrip'shon, n. Act of prescribing, or that which is prescribed; a recipe; the claim of title to a thing by virtue of immemorial use; the right derived from such use. [Fr.]

Prescriptive, prē-skript'iv, a. Acquired by prescription; pleading the continuance and authority of custom.

Presence, pre'zens, n. State of being present; a being in company near or before the face of another; approach face to face, or nearness of a great personage; presence chamber; a number assembled before a great person; port; mien; air; the person of a superior. [Fr. présence.]

Present, pre'zent, a. Being before; being now in view; being in a certain place; being in company; being now under consideration; immediate; instant; not past or future; ready at hand; quick in emergency; propitious.—n. That which is set before one for acceptation; an offering; that which is presented; something offered to another gratuitously; a gift; a benefaction; the present time. [Fr. présent—L. sum, esse, to be.]

Present, prē-zent', vt. To set or introduce into the presence of, generally of a superior; to exhibit; to give; to offer gratuitously; to put into the hands of in ceremony; to nominate to an ecclesiastical benefice; to proffer; to lay before a public body for consideration; to point or direct, as a weapon. [Fr. présenter.]

Presentable, prē-zent'a-bl, a. That may be presented; that may be exhibited; properly prepared to go into society; that may be offered to a church-living. [Fr. présentable.]

Presentation, pre-zent-ā'shon, n. Act of presenting; display; act of offering a clergyman to the bishop or presbytery for institution in a benefice; the right of presenting a clergyman. [Fr. présentation.]

Presentee, pre-zent-ē', n. One presented to a benefice.

Presentiment, prē-sen'ti-ment, n. Previous sentiment; previous apprehension of something future; foreboding. [It. presentimento; L. sentio, to discern.]

Presently, pre'zent-li, adv. Immediately; directly; soon; at once; in a short time after; soon after.

Presentment, prē-zent'ment, n. Act of presenting; appearance to the view; representation.

Preservable, prē-zėrv'a-bl, a. That may be preserved.

Preservation, prē-zėr-vā'shon, n. Act of preserving; the act of keeping from injury, destruction, or decay. [It. preservazione.]

Preservative, prē-zėrv'āt-iv, a. Having the power of preserving; tending to preserve.—n. That which preserves; a preventive of injury or decay. [Fr. préservatif.]

Preserve, prē-zėrv', vt. To rescue; to save or keep from injury; to keep in safety; to protect; to keep from decay; to keep in a sound state; to season with sugar for preservation; to keep from corruption; to maintain throughout, as appearances. ppr. preserving, pret. & pp. preserved.—n. Something that is preserved; fruit or a vegetable seasoned and kept in sugar or syrup; a place for the shelter and preservation of animals intended for sport or food, as game, fish, &c. [Fr. préserver—L. servo, to save.]

Preserved, prē-zėrvd', p.a. Seasoned with sugar, &c., for preservation.

Preserver, prē-zėrv'ėr, n. The person or thing that preserves; one who saves or defends from destruction or evil.

Preside, prē-zīd', vi. To sit before or in front; to be set over for the exercise of authority (usually with over); to watch over as inspector. ppr. presiding, pret. & pp. presided. [Fr. présider—L. sedeo, Sans. sad, to sit.]

Presidency, pre'zi-den-si, n. Act of presiding; inspection and care; the office of president; the term during which a president holds his office; the jurisdiction of a president. [Fr. présidence.]

President, pre'zi-dent, n. One who presides; an officer elected to preside over a corporation or assembly of men; an officer appointed or elected to govern a province or territory. [Fr. président.]

Presidential, pre-zi-den'shi-al, a. Pertaining to a president; presiding over.

Presidentship, pre'zi-dent-ship, n. The office and place of president; the term for which a president holds his office.

Presiding, prē-zīd'ing, p.a. Directing; superintending.

Presignify, prē-sig'ni-fī, vt. To signify beforehand; to show previously.

Press, pres, vt. To weigh heavily upon; to urge with force; to squeeze; to crush; to squeeze for making smooth, as cloth or paper; to hurry; to urge; to inculcate with earnestness; to embrace closely; to force into service, particularly into naval service; to straiten; to oppress; to distress; to distress, as with poverty; to compel; to solicit with importunity.—vi. To bear on heavily; to urge or strain in motion; to encroach; to throng; to urge by influence or moral force; to push with force.—n. A pressing; that which presses; an instrument by which any body is squeezed or forced into a more compact form; a machine for printing; a printing-press; the art or business of printing and publishing; the publications issued from the press; a multitude of individuals crowded together; act of urging or pushing forward; a closet for the safe keeping of clothes, &c.; urgent demands of affairs; a commission to force men into public service, particularly into the navy. [Fr. presser; L. premo, pressum, to press—Gr. barus, Sans. guru, heavy.]

Pressed, prest, p.a. Squeezed; distressed; embraced.

Pressing, pres'ing, p.a. Urgent; importunate; distressing.—p.n. Act of pressing or of forcing bodies into a more compact state.

Pressingly, pres'ing-li, adv. With force or urgency; closely.

Pressman, pres'man, n. One who manages the press and impresses the sheets in printing.

Pressure, pre'shŭr, n. Act of pressing; act of squeezing or crushing; state of being squeezed or crushed; a constraining impulse; that which urges the intellectual or moral faculties; that which depresses the spirits; any severe affliction; straits, or the distress they occasion; urgency; character impressed. [L. pressūra—premo, pressus, to press.]

Prest, prest, a. Ready.

Prestige, pres'tij, n. Illusion†; charm†; imposture†; influence of character or of conduct; moral influence arising from past achievements, regarded as the pledge of future successes. [Fr.— L. præstigia, anything that deceives the eye.]

Presumable, prē-zŭm'a-bl, a. That may be presumed; that may be supposed to be true on probable evidence.

Presume, prē-zŭm', vt. To take before; to take to one's self; to take or suppose to be entitled to belief, without positive proof; to be reasonably convinced of.—vi. To take beforehand; to arrogate; to venture without permission; to act with great confidence (with on or upon before the ground of confidence); to make confident attempts. ppr. pre-

suming, pret. & pp. presumed. [Fr. *présumer*; L. *sumo*, to take.]
Presuming, prē-zum'ing, p.a. Venturing without positive permission; arrogant.
Presumption, prē-zum'shon, n. *Act of presuming*; belief previously formed; strong probability; blind confidence; arrogance; unreasonable confidence in divine favour. [Fr. *présomption*.]
Presumptive, prē-zum'tiv, a. Taken by previous supposition; unreasonably confident. [Fr. *présomptif*.]
Presumptively, prē-zum'tiv-li, adv. By presumption.
Presumptuous, prē-zum'tū-us, a. *Full of presumption*; adventuring without reasonable ground of success; foolhardy; forward; arrogant; proceeding from excess of confidence; characterized by arrogance; irreverent with respect to sacred things. [Fr. *présomptueux*.]
Presumptuously, prē-zum'tū-us-li, adv. In a presumptuous manner.
Presumptuousness, prē-zum'tū-us-nes, n. Quality of being presumptuous.
Presuppose, prē-sup-pōz', v.t. *To suppose as previous*; to imply as antecedent. ppr. presupposing, pret. & pp. presupposed.
Presupposed, prē-sup-pōzd', p.a. Supposed to be antecedent.
Presurmise, prē-ser-mīz', n. *A surmise previously formed*.
Pretence, prē-tens', n. *Act of pretending*; a holding out or offering to others something false; a presenting to others a false appearance; excuse; claim, true or false; something held out to terrify, or for other purpose.
Pretend, prē-tend', v.t. *To hold before one*; to hold out, as a false appearance; to feign; to plot; to intend; to offer, as something feigned instead of that which is real; to profess to feel; to show hypocritically; to allege a title to. v.i. To put forth an appearance; to put in a claim truly or falsely; to hold out the appearance of being, possessing, or performing. [Fr. *prétendre*—L. *tendo*, to stretch.]
Pretended, prē-tend'ed, p.a. Ostensible; hypocritical.
Pretender, prē-tend'ėr, n. *One who pretends*; one who lays claim to anything.
Pretending, prē-tend'ing, p. a. Arrogant; assuming.
Pretendingly, prē-tend'ing-li, adv. Arrogantly; presumptuously.
Pretension, prē-ten'shon, n. *A pretending*; claim, true or false; claim to something to be obtained, or a desire to obtain something, manifested by words or actions. [Fr. *prétention*.]
Preterimperfect, prē'tėr-im-pėr''fekt, a. Designating the tense of the verb which expresses action, or being not perfectly past (more usually called the *imperfect* tense). [L. *præter*, beyond or beside, and *imperfectus*, unfinished.]
Preterit, prē'tėr-it, a. *Past*; applied to the tense of a verb which expresses an action or being perfectly past or finished, often that which is just past or completed, but without a specification of time.—n. The past tense. [L. *præteritus*, gone by—*præter*, and *eo, itum*, to go.]
Preterite, prē'tėr-it, a. Same as *preterit*.
Preternatural, prē-tėr-na'tūr-al, a. *Beyond what is natural*, or different from what is natural; abnormal.
Preternaturally, prē-tėr-na'tūr-al-li, adv. In a manner beyond or aside from the common order of *nature*.

Preterperfect, prē-tėr-pėr'fekt, a. *More than complete or finished*; designating the tense of verbs which expresses action, or being absolutely past (more usually called the *perfect*).
Preterpluperfect, prē-tėr-plū'pėr-fekt, a. *Beyond more than perfect*; designating the tense of verbs which expresses action or being past prior to another past event or time (more usually called the *pluperfect*). [L. *præter*, beyond, *plus*, more, and *perfectus*, perfect.]
Pretext, prē'tekst, n. *A covering or cloak*; a pretence; false appearance; ostensible motive assigned to conceal the real motive. [Fr. *prétexte*—L. *texo, textum*, to weave.]
Pretor, prē'tor, n. *One who goes before*; a leader; a Roman magistrate. [L. *prætor*—*eo, itum*, to go.]
Pretorial, prē-tō'ri-al, a. *Pertaining to a pretor or judge*; judicial.
Pretorian, prē-tō'ri-an, a. *Belonging to a pretor or judge*; judicial; pertaining to the body-guard instituted by Augustus. [L. *prætorianus*.]
Pretorship, prē'tor-ship, n. *The office of pretor*.
Prettily, pret'ti-li, adv. *In a pretty manner*; with neatness and taste.
Prettiness, pret'ti-nes, n. *State or quality of being pretty*; diminutive beauty; a pleasing form without stateliness or dignity; neatness and taste displayed on small objects.
Pretty, pret'ti, a. Originally, *bright*; having diminutive beauty; neat and appropriate; handsome; neatly arranged; elegant without grandeur; (Sax. *prætig*, crafty) sly; crafty, as a trick; small; diminutive (in contempt).—adv. In some degree; tolerably; moderately. [Sax. *præte*, adorned; Goth. *bairhts*, clear.]
Prevail, prē-vāl', v.i. *To exceed in power or worth*; to overcome; to gain the victory; to gain the advantage; to be in force; to extend over with force or effect; to have predominant influence; to succeed; to prosper; to persuade (with *on, upon*, or *with*). [Fr. *prévaloir* —L. *valeo*, to be strong.]
Prevailing, prē-vāl'ing, p.a. Predominant; having efficacy, as prayer; most common or general; prevalent.
Prevailment, prē-vāl'ment, n. Prevalence.
Prevalence, pre'va-lens, n. *State or being prevalent*; most efficacious force in producing an effect; efficacy; preponderance; most general reception or existence. [Old Fr.]
Prevalent, pre'va-lent, a. *Exceeding in strength or power*; powerful; efficacious; most generally received; extensively existing. [L. *prævalens*—*valeo*, to be strong—*Sans. bala*, strength.]
Prevalently, pre'va-lent-li, adv. With *predominance* or superiority; powerfully; forcibly.
Prevaricate, prē-va'ri-kāt, v.i. *To deviate from a straight path or course*; to shuffle; to shift or turn from one side to the other or from the direct course; to swerve from rectitude. ppr. prevaricating, pret. & pp. prevaricated. [L. *prævaricor, prævaricatus*—*varus*, having the legs turned inwards.]
Prevaricating, prē-va'ri-kāt-ing, p.a. Quibbling to evade the truth.
Prevarication, prē-va'ri-kā''shon, n. *Act of prevaricating*; a shuffling or quibbling to evade the truth; a deviation from the plain path of truth and fair-dealing. [L. *prævaricatio*.]

Prevaricator, prē-va'ri-kāt-or, n. *One who prevaricates*; a shuffler. [L.]
Prevent, prē-vent', v.t. *To come or go before*; to stop or intercept, as the performance of a thing; to hinder; to impede; to debar; to obstruct; to anticipate. [L. *prævenio, præventum*—*venio* to come.]
Prevention, prē-ven'shon, n. *Act of going before*; act of hindering; hindrance; obstruction of access or approach; anticipation. [Fr. *prévention*.]
Preventive, prē-vent'iv, a. *Tending to prevent* or hinder; hindering the access of.—n. *That which prevents*; that which intercepts the approach of; an antidote previously taken. [Fr. *préventif*.]
Previous, prē'vi-us, a. *Going before*; going before in time; being or happening before something else; introductory; preceding; foregoing; former. [L. *prævius*—*via*, a way.]
Previously, prē'vi-us-li, adv. In time preceding; beforehand; antecedently.
Prey, prā, n. *Property taken by force in war*; spoil; plunder; that which is seized by violence to be devoured; ravage; depredation.—v.i. To rob; to pillage; to feed by violence; to waste gradually; to cause to pine away. (With *on* or *upon*.) [Fr. *proie*—L. *præda*, booty.]
Price, prīs, n. *Value; worth; cost*; the sum of money at which a thing is valued; the value which a seller sets on his goods in market, or consents to receive; the sum given for an article; the current value paid for any species of goods; estimation; excellence or worth; recompense.—v.t. To set a price on; to ask the price of. ppr. pricing, pret. & pp. priced. [Fr. *prix*—L. *pretium*.]
Priced, prīst, p.a. Set at a value; used in composition, as high-priced, low-priced.
Priceless, prīs'les, a. *Too valuable to admit of a price*; invaluable.
Prick, prik, v.t. *To pierce with a sharp-pointed instrument* or substance; to erect, as a pointed thing; to fix by the point; to hang on a point; to spur; to affect with sharp pain; to sting with remorse; to denote by pricking; to write, as a musical composition with the proper notes on a scale.—v.i. To come upon the spur; to shoot along; to aim at a point, mark, or place.—n. *A slender, pointed instrument*, hard enough to pierce the skin; a goad; a spur; sharp, stinging pain; remorse; a mark at which archers aim; a point; a puncture or place entered by a point; the print of a hare on the ground. [Sax. *priccian*.]
Pricker, prik'ėr, n. *A sharp-pointed instrument*; a light horseman.
Pricket, prik'et, n. *A buck in his second year*.
Pricking, prik'ing, p.n. *Act of piercing with a sharp point*; the driving of a nail into a horse's foot so as to cause lameness; a sensation of sharp pain.
Prickle, prik'l, n. *A small sharp-pointed shoot growing from the bark of a shrub*; a sharp-pointed process of an animal.—v.t. To prick slightly. ppr. prickling, pret. & pp. prickled. [Sax. *pricele*.]
Prickliness, prik'li-nes, n. *State of having many prickles*.
Prickly, prik'l-i, a. *Full of small sharp points or prickles*.
Prickly-Pear, prik'l-i-pār, n. A name applied to various species of tropical

Fāte, fär, fat, fąll; mē, met, hėr; pīne, pin; nōte, not, mōve; tūbe, tub, bųll; oil, pound.

plants, more especially to the Indian fig, a fleshly and succulent plant covered with spines.

Prick-songt, prik'song, n. Music written down.

Pride, prid, n. Originally, splendid show; ornament; majesty; decoration; an unreasonably high opinion of one's own superiority; insolent exultation; generous elation of heart; a noble self-esteem, springing from a consciousness of worth; elevation reached; that of which men are proud; that which excites boasting.—vt. To indulge pride; to take pride; to value one's self; to gratify self-esteem (With recip. pron.) ppr. priding, pret. & pp. prided. [Sax. pryte, haughtiness; Icel. prydi, ornament.]

Pridefult, prid'ful, a. Full of pride; insolent; scornful.

Priest, prēst, n. A presbyter; one who officiates at the altar; a clergyman above the rank of deacon, and below that of bishop; a clergyman; a pastor. [Sax. preost; Low L. presbyter.]

Priestcraft, prēst'kraft, n. The craft or the stratagems of priests; policy or methods used by priests in order to attain their ends.

Priestess, prēst'es, n. A female priest; a female among pagans who officiated in sacred things, and uttered responses.

Priesthood, prēst'hyd, n. The office or character of a priest; the order of men set apart for sacred offices; the order composed of priests.

Priestliness, prēst'li-nes, n. State or quality of being priestly; the appearance and manner of a priest.

Priestly, prēst'li, a. Pertaining to a priest or to priests; sacerdotal.

Priestridden, prēst'rid-n, a. Managed or governed by priests.

Prim, prim, a. Adhering strictly to measure or rule; formal; precise.

Primacy, pri'ma-si, n. Chief rule or authority; the chief ecclesiastical dignity in a national church; the office or dignity of an archbishop. [Fr. primatie—L. primus, first.]

Primal, prim'al, a. First.

Primarily, pri'ma-ri-li, adv. In the first place; originally.

Primary, pri'ma-ri, a. First; first in order of time; elementary; radical or original; first in dignity or importance. [L. primarius—primus, first.]

Primate, pri'māt, n. One of dignity; the chief ecclesiastic in a national church; an archbishop. [Fr. primat; L. primus, first.]

Primateship, pri'māt-ship, n. The office or dignity of a primate.

Prime, prim, a. Foremost; first in order of time; original; first in rank, value, or importance; early; blooming; lewdt. n. The first opening of day; the dawn; the morning; the beginning; the spring of the year; the spring of life; youth; full health, strength, or beauty; the best part; the utmost perfection.—vt. To put, as powder in the pan of a musket; to lay, as a train of powder for communicating fire to a charge; to lay on, as the first colour in painting.—vi. To serve for the charge of a gun. ppr. priming, pret. & pp. primed. [L. primus, first—Sans. pra, before.]

Prime-minister, prim-mi'nis-tėr, n. The first or chief minister; the responsible head of a ministry or executive government; applied particularly to that of Great Britain and Ireland.

Primer, prim'er, n. A first or elementary book; a work of elementary religious instruction; a printing type. [Fr. primaire, elementary.]

Primerot, pri-mē'rō, n. A game at cards.

Primeval, prim-ē'val, a. Being of the earliest age or time; original; primitive. [L. primaevus — primus, and aevum, an age.]

Priming, prim'ing, p.n. The powder in the pan of a gun, or laid along the channel of a cannon for conveying fire to the charge.

Primitive, prim'it-iv, a. Being the first of its kind; original; primeval; pertaining to early times; affectedly solemn; radical; denoting that from which others are derived.—n. That which is original; a word not derived from another. [Fr. primitif—L. primus, first.]

Primitively, prim'it-iv-li, adv. Originally; at first; primarily.

Primly, prim'li, adv. With primness.

Primness, prim'nes, n. State or quality of being prim; affected formality or niceness; preciseness.

Primogenial, pri-mō-jē'ni-al, a. First-born; original; elemental. [L. primigenius—gigno, to beget.]

Primogenitivet, pri-mō-jen'it-iv, n. Primogeniture.

Primogeniture, pri-mō-jen'it-ūr, n. State or condition of being the first-born; seniority by birth among children; the right which belongs to the eldest child, particularly to the eldest son. [Fr. primogéniture—L. gigno, to beget.]

Primordial, prim-or'di-al, a. First of all; first in order; existing from the beginning. [Fr. — L. primus, and ordior, to begin.]

Primrose, prim'rōz, n. The first rose, or an early flower in spring; the plant which produces it. [prime and rose.]

Primyt, pri'mi, a. Blooming.

Prince, prins, n. The first in rank; a chief or supreme ruler; a sovereign; the chief ruler of a nation or state; the son of a king or emperor, or the issue of a royal family; the chief of any body of men.—vi. To play the prince. [Fr. — L. princeps— primus, first, and capio, to take.]

Princedom, prins'dum, n. The jurisdiction, sovereignty, or estate of a prince.

Princeliness, prins'li-nes, n. The state, manner, or dignity of a prince.

Princely, prins'li, a. Resembling a prince; stately; having the rank of princes; royal; very large, as an estate; magnificent; rich.—adv. In a prince-like manner.

Princess, prin'ses, n. A female sovereign; a sovereign lady of rank next to that of a queen; the daughter of a king; the consort of a prince.

Principal, prin'si-pal, a. First; chief; highest in rank, character, or respectability; most important.—n. A chief or head; one who takes the lead; the chief in authority; the head of an academy; the perpetrator of a crime, or an abettor; one primarily engaged; a chief party; a capital sum lent on interest. [Fr.—L. primus, first, and capio, to take.]

Principality, prin-si-pal'i-ti, n. The territory of a prince, or the country which gives title to a prince. [Fr. principauté.]

Principally, prin'si-pal-li, adv. Chiefly; mainly; in the most important respect.

Principle, prin'si-pl, n. Origin; the cause or source of anything; element; primordial substance; operative cause; a fundamental truth; ground; that which supports an assertion; a general truth; tenet or doctrine; that which is believed; a settled rule of action in human beings. [Fr. principe— L. primus, first, and capio, to take.]

Principled, prin'si-pld, p.a. Having principles; imbued with principles.

Princoxt, prin'koks, n. A coxcomb.

Print, print, vt. To press into or upon; to mark by pressure; to stamp; to form letters, &c., on paper, &c., by impression; to form by impression. vi. To use or practise the art of typography, or of taking impressions of letters, figures, and the like; to publish a book (elliptical).—n. A mark made by pressure; any line, character, or indentation of any form, made by the pressure of one body on another; the impressions of types in general, as to form, size, &c.; a stamp; a picture taken from an engraved plate; state of being printed and published; a single sheet printed for sale; a newspaper; (pl.) engravings; also, printed calicoes. [Fr. empreinte, impression—L. premo, to press—Gr. barus, heavy.]

Printed, print'ed, p.a. Impressed with letters, &c.; indented.

Printer, print'ér, n. One who prints; one who stains or prints cloths with figures, as calico; one who impresses letters or figures with copper-plates.

Printing, print'ing, p.n. The act, art, or practice of impressing letters, characters, or figures on paper, cloth, or other material; the business of a printer; typography.

Prior, pri'or, a. Former; antecedent; foregoing.—n. One who is before others in rank or authority; the superior of a convent of monks; one who presides over others in the same churches. [L.]

Priorate, pri'or-āt, n. Government by a prior. [It. priorato.]

Prioress, pri'or-es, n. A female superior of a convent of nuns.

Priority, pri-or'i-ti, n. State of being prior; state of being first in place or rank; precedence; pre-eminence; preference. [Fr. priorité.]

Priorship, pri'or-ship, n. The state or office of prior.

Priory, pri'ō-ri, n. A convent of which a prior is the superior, in dignity below an abbey. [Low L. prioria.]

Prism, prizm, n. Anything sawnt; a solid whose bases or ends are any similar, equal, and parallel plane figures, and whose sides are parallelograms. [Fr. prisme—Gr. prisō, to saw.]

Prismatic, priz-mat'ik, a. Resembling a prism; separated or distributed by a prism, as light; pertaining to a prism. [Fr. prismatique.]

Prison, pri'zon, n. A place of confinement for those taken or captured; a public building for the safe custody of criminals and debtors; a jail; any place of confinement; spiritual bondage.—vt. To shut up in a prison; to imprison. [Fr.—L. prendo, to take.]

Prisoner, pri'zon-ėr, n. One shut up in a prison; one who is confined in a prison by legal arrest; a captive; one taken by an enemy in war; one whose liberty is restrained, as a bird in a cage. [Fr. prisonnier.]

Pristine, pris'tin, a. Former; primitive; pertaining to an earlier state or period; ancient; old. [L. pristinus.]

Privacy, pri'vā-si, n. State of being private; secrecy; a place of seclusion from company or observation; solitude; retirement; concealment of what is said or done.

Private, pri'vat, *a.* Separate; withdrawn from the state or from public affairs; not invested with public office; peculiar to one's self; belonging to an individual only; peculiar to a number in a joint concern; sequestered from observation; secluded; not publicly known; individual; privyt.—*n.* A secret message; a common soldier. [L. *privatus—privus*, separate.]

Privateer, pri-vāt-ēr', *n.* A vessel of war owned by a *private* man or by individuals, at their own expense, and having a commission from government to seize the ships of an enemy in war.

Privateering, pri-vāt-ēr'ing, *p.n.* The act of plundering the ships of an enemy by means of *privateers*.

Privately, pri'vāt-li, *adv.* In a private or secret manner; not publicly.

Privateness, pri'vāt-nes, *n.* State of being private; secrecy; privacy.

Privation, pri-vā'shon, *n.* A taking away or depriving; state of being deprived; absence of what is necessary for comfort; hardship; the removal of any thing or quality; absence in general. [Fr.—L. *privo*, to deprive of.]

Privative, pri'vāt-iv, *a.* Causing privation; consisting in the absence of something; not positive.—*n.* That of which the essence is the absence of something; a prefix to a word which changes its signification, and gives it a contrary sense, as *a* in Greek and *un* and *in* in English. [Fr. *privatif*.]

Privatively, pri'vāt-iv-li, *adv.* By the absence of something.

Privet, pri'vet, *n.* A shrub, frequently planted to conceal private places.

Privilege, pri'vi-lej, *n.* An ordinance for *private* individuals; a peculiar benefit enjoyed by a person or society beyond the common advantages of other citizens; any peculiar benefit; favour; prerogative; franchise; liberty.—*vt.* To *bestow a privilege upon*; to invest with a peculiar right or immunity; to exempt from censure or danger. *ppr.* privileging, *pret. & pp.* privileged. [Fr. *privilège*—L. *privus*, separate, and *lex, legis*, a law.]

Privileged, pri'vi-lejd, *p.a. Invested with a privilege*; enjoying a peculiar right or immunity.

Privily, pri'vi-li, *adv. Privately*; secretly. [from privy.]

Privity, pri'vi-ti, *n. Private knowledge*; joint knowledge with another of a private concern. [Fr. *privauté*.]

Privy, pri'vi, *a. Private*; peculiar; pertaining to some person exclusively; not public; clandestine; appropriated to retirement; not shown; privately knowing; admitted to the participation of knowledge with another of a secret transaction; admitted to secrets of state.—*n.* A necessary house. [Fr. *privé*.]

Prize, prīz, *n. That which is taken from an enemy in war*; a capture, particularly a vessel captured; that which is taken from another; a valuable acquisition; the reward of contest; a premium; the reward gained by any performance; a strife for a reward; the money drawn by a lottery-ticket; opposed to blank. [Fr *prise*—L. *prendo, prensum*, to seize.]—*vt. To set a price upon*; to estimate the value of; to value highly; to esteem. *ppr.* prizing, *pret. & pp.* prized. [Fr. *priser*.]

Prized, prīzd, *p.a.* Rated; valued; esteemed.

Prize-fighter, prīz'fīt-ēr, *n. One who fights publicly for a prize or a reward.* (Applied particularly to a boxer.)

Prizer, prīz'ēr, *n. One who prizes*; one who contends for a prize.

Probability, pro-ba-bil'i-ti, *n. State or quality of being probable*; verisimilitude; likelihood; appearance of truth; anything that has the appearance of reality or truth. [Fr. *probabilité*.]

Probable, pro'ba-bl, *a. That may be proved*; likely; credible; having more evidence than the contrary; that renders something likely or credible. [Fr.—L. *probo*, to try, test.]

Probably, pro'ba-bli, *adv. Likely*; in likelihood; with the appearance of truth.

Probal, prob'al, *a.* Probable.

Probate, prō'bāt, *n. The proof of a will or testament*; the official copy of a proved will, to which the seal of the court for proving wills is attached; the right or jurisdiction of proving wills. [L. *probātum*, proved—*probo*, to try, prove.]

Probation, pro-bā'shon, *n. Act of proving*; trial; any proceeding designed to ascertain truth; novitiate; moral trial; trial for proof, or satisfactory evidence, or the time of trial. [Fr.—L. *probo*, to test, try.]

Probationary, pro-bā'shon-a-ri, *a. Serving for trial.*

Probationer, pro-bā'shon-ēr, *n. One who is upon trial or probation*; in Scotland, a student in divinity who is licensed to preach; a licentiate.

Probative, prō'bāt-iv, *a. Serving for trial or proof.* [L. *probativus*.]

Probatory, prō'ba-tō-ri, *a. Serving for trial or for proof.* [Fr. *probatoire*.]

Probe, prōb, *n. That which proves*; a surgeon's instrument for examining a wound, ulcer, or cavity.—*vt. To prove or examine*; to examine, as a wound, or some cavity of the body, by the use of an instrument thrust into the part; to scrutinize; to examine thoroughly into the causes and circumstances of. *ppr.* probing, *pret. & pp.* probed. [from L. *probo*, to test.]

Probity, prō'bi-ti, *n. Goodness; uprightness*; honesty; integrity in principle. [Fr. *probité*—L. *probo*, to prove—*probus*, good.]

Problem, prob'lem, *n. Anything put before one*; that which is proposed as a task; a question proposed; a proposition in which some operation is required; something to be done; any question involving doubt or uncertainty. [Fr. *problème*—Gr. *pro*, and *ballo*, to cast.]

Problematic, **Problematical**, prob-lem-at'ik, prob-lem-at'ik-al, *a. Of the nature of a problem*; characterized by uncertainty; questionable; dubious; undetermined. [Fr. *problématique*.]

Problematically, prob-lem-at'ik-al-li, *adv.* Doubtfully; dubiously; uncertainly.

Proboscis, pro-bos'is, *n. The snout or trunk of an elephant* with which he takes up his food, and carries it to his mouth; the long snout of other animals, and particularly of insects. [Gr. *boskō*, to feed.]

Procedure, pro-sēd'ūr, *n. Act of proceeding*; progress; operation; a series of actions; manner of proceeding; conduct; management. [Fr. *procédure*—L. *cedo*, to go.]

Proceed, pro-sēd', *vi. To go forward*; to advance; to pass from one point or topic to another; to issue; to arise; to be produced; to come, as from a source or fountain; to come from a person or place; to prosecute any design; to begin and carry on a series of actions; to be carried on; to have a course. [Fr. *procéder*—L. *cedo*, to go.]

Proceeding, pro-sēd'ing, *p.n. A going forward*; movement from one thing to another; transaction; (pl.) a course of measures or conduct.

Proceeds, pro'sēds, *n. pl.* Issue; rent; produce; the sum, amount, or value of goods sold or converted into money.

Process, pro'ses, *n. A moving forward*; progressive course; gradual progress; operations; experiment; series of changes in growth, decay, &c.; continual passage, as of time; methodical arrangement; series of proceedings; any projecting part of a bone; a lobe or portion of the brain; a summons. [Fr. *procès*—L. *cedo*, to go.]

Procession, pro-se'shon, *n. A marching forward*; a train of persons walking or riding on horseback, moving with ceremonious solemnity. [Fr.]

Proclaim, pro-klām', *vt. To cry out publicly*; to promulgate; to publish; to give official notice of; to denounce; to declare with honour. [Fr. *proclamer*—L. *clamo*, to call.]

Proclaimer, pro-klām'ēr, *n. One who proclaims* or publishes by authority.

Proclamation, pro-kla-mā'shon, *n. Act of proclaiming*; publication by authority; a declaration of the sovereign's will openly published; edict; the paper containing an official notice to a people. [Fr.; L. *clamo*, to cry out.]

Proclivity, pro-kliv'i-ti, *n. A bending towards*; a steep descent; inclination; tendency; readiness; facility of learning. [L. *proclivitas—clivus*, a slope.]

Proconsul, pro-kon'sul, *n. A Roman officer who acted in the stead of a consul*; under the emperors, the governor of a province. [L.]

Proconsular, pro-kon'sul-ar, *a. Pertaining to a proconsul*; under the government of a proconsul.

Proconsulship, pro-kon'sul-ship, *n. The office of a proconsul*, or the term of his office.

Procrastinate, pro-kras'ti-nāt, *vt. To put off till to-morrow*; to postpone; to protract; to prolong.—*vi.* To delay; to be dilatory. *ppr.* procrastinating, *pret. & pp.* procrastinated. [L. *procrastino, procrastinatum—cras*, Sans *shvas*, to-morrow.]

Procrastinating, pro-kras'ti-nāt-ing, *p.a.* Putting off to a future time.

Procrastination, pro-kras'ti-nā'shon, *n. A putting off till to-morrow*, or to a future time; delay; dilatoriness. [L. *procrastinatio*.]

Procrastinator, pro-kras'ti-nāt-or, *n.* One who defers the performance of anything to a future time.

Procreant, prō'krē-ant, *a. Generating. n. One who procreates.*

Procreate, prō'krē-āt, *vt. To beget*; to generate and produce; to engender; to propagate; to produce. *ppr.* procreating, *pret. & pp.* procreated. [L. *procreo, procreatus—creo*, to beget.]

Procreation, prō-krē-ā'shon, *n. Act of procreating or of begetting*; generation and production of young. [Fr. *procréation*.]

Procreator, prō'krē-āt-or, *n. One who begets*; a generator; a father or sire. [L.]

Proctor, prok'tor, *n. One who takes care of anything for another*; a person authorised to manage another's cause in certain courts in England; an officer

who attends to the morals of the students in the English universities.—*vt.* To manage. [contracted from L. *procurator—curo*, to take care of.]
Proctorship, prok'tor-ship, *n.* The office or dignity of the proctor of a university.
Procumbent, prō-kum'bent, *a.* Leaning forward; falling or sinking down; prone; prostrate; spread over the surface of the ground, as a plant. [L. *procumbens—cumbo*, to lean forward.]
Procurable, prō-kūr'a-bl, *That may be procured*; obtainable.
Procuration, prō-kūr-ā'shon, *n.* Act of procuring; the management of another's affairs; the instrument by which a person is empowered to transact the affairs of another. [Fr.—L. *curo*, to take care of.]
Procurator, prō-kūr'āt-or, *n.* One who has the care of anything belonging to another; the manager of another's affairs; a proctor. [L.]
Procuratorship, prō-kūr'āt-or-ship, *n.* The office of a procurator.
Procure, prō-kūr', *vt.* To take care of; to get; to acquire; to obtain; to cause; to contrive and effect; to draw to; to attract. *ppr.* procuring, *pret.* & *pp.* procured. [Fr. *procurer*; L. *curo*, to take care of.]
Procurement, prō-kūr'ment, *n.* Act of procuring or obtaining; agency.
Procurer, prō-kūr'er, *n.* One who procures or obtains; a pimp.
Procuress, prō-kūr'es, *n.* She that procures; a bawd.
Procuring, prō-kūr'ing, *p.a.* That causes to come; bringing on.
Prodigal, pro'di-gal, *a.* Driving forth or away; getting rid of; expending money without necessity; wasteful; not frugal; expended to excess; profusely liberal.—*n.* One who drives forth; one who expends money extravagantly; a spendthrift. [Low L. *prodigalis*—L. pro, forth, and *ago*, to drive.]
Prodigality, pro-di-gal'i-ti, *n.* State of quality of being prodigal; extravagance in the expenditure of money; waste; profuse liberality. [Fr. *prodigalité.*]
Prodigally, pro'di-gal-li, *adv.* In a prodigal manner.
Prodigious, prō-di'ji-us, *a.* Partaking of the nature of a prodigy; very great in size, &c.; enormous; monstrous; amazing; wonderful. [Fr. *prodigieux.*]
Prodigiously, prō-di'ji-us-li, *adv.* Enormously; wonderfully; astonishingly.
Prodigy, pro'di-ji, *n.* Something showing beforehand; a prophetic portent; anything out of the ordinary course of nature; a marvel; a miracle; a monster. [Fr. *prodige*—Gr. *deiknumi*, to show.]
Proditor, prō-di-tor, *n.* A traitor.
Produce, prō-dūs', *vt.* To bring forth; to bring to view; to exhibit to the public; to bear; to generate and bring forth, as young; to impart; to effect; to create; to make; to lengthen. *ppr.* producing, *pret.* & *pp.* produced. [L. *produco—duco*, to lead.]
Produce, pro'dūs, *n.* That which is produced; product; yield.
Producer, prō-dūs'er, *n.* One who produces; one who generates.
Producible, prō-dūs'i-bl, *a.* That may be produced or brought into being; that may be extended.
Producing, prō-dūs'ing, *p.a.* Causing.
Product, pro'dukt, *n.* Produce; that which is produced by nature, as fruits, grain, metals; that which is produced by labour or by mental application; performance; work; result; the number resulting from the multiplication of two or more numbers. [Fr. *produit*—L. *duco, ductum*, to lead.]
Production, prō-duk'shon, *n.* Act or process of producing; product; fruit; work; composition. [Fr.]
Productive, prō-duk'tiv, *a.* Having the quality or power of producing; fruitful; producing good crops; bringing into being; efficient. [Fr. *productif.*]
Productively, prō-duk'tiv-li, *adv.* By production; with abundant produce.
Productiveness, prō-duk'tiv-nes, *n.* The quality of being productive.
Proem, prō'em, *n.* That which goes before a song; preface; preliminary observations to a book or writing. [Old Fr. *proeme*; Gr. *oimos*, way.]
Proemial, prō-em'i-al, *a.* Introductory; prefatory; preliminary.
Preface!, prō'fās, *interj.* Much good may it do you!
Profanation, prō-fān-ā'shon, *n.* Act of profaning or of violating sacred things; desecration; the act of treating with abuse or disrespect. [Fr.]
Profane, prō-fān', *a.* Being forth from the temple; unholy; common; impious; godless; wicked; proceeding from a contempt of sacred things; unhallowed; impure; obscene; temporal; relating to secular things.—*vt.* To desecrate; to violate, as anything sacred; to pollute; to apply to temporal uses; to debase. *ppr.* profaning, *pret.* & *pp.* profaned. [Fr.—L. *fanum*, a temple.]
Profanely, prō-fān'li, *adv.* In a profane manner.
Profaneness, prō-fān'nes, *n.* Quality of being profane; irreverence of sacred things; the use of language which implies irreverence toward God.
Profaner, prō-fān'er, *n.* One who profanes; a violator.
Profanity, prō-fan'i-ti, *n.* Profaneness.
Profess, prō-fes', *vt.* To declare openly; to avow; to set up a claim to; to declare in strong terms; to make public or explicit declaration of; to declare publicly one's skill in, for inviting employment; to lay claim to.—*vi.* To declare openly; to make profession; to declare friendship. [Fr. *professer*—L. *fateor, fassus*, to confess.]
Professed, **Profest**, prō-fest', prō-fest', *p.a.* Openly declared or acknowledged.
Professedly, prō-fes'ed-li, *adv.* By profession.
Professing, prō-fes'ing, *p.a.* Making a profession.
Profession, prō-fe'shon, *n.* Act of professing; open declaration of one's sentiments or belief; declaration of purpose; the business which one professes; employment; office; the collective body of persons engaged in a calling; the entering into a religious order. [Fr.]
Professional, prō-fe'shon-al, *a.* Pertaining to a profession or to a calling.
Professionally, prō-fe'shon-al-li, *adv.* By profession or avowal; by calling.
Professor, prō-fes'or, *n.* One who professes; one who has professed religion by joining himself to a church of Christ; one who publicly teaches ary science; a teacher in a university, whose business is to read lectures in a particular branch of learning. [L.—*fateor, fassus*, to confess.]
Professorial, prō-fes-sō'ri-al, *a.* Pertaining to a professor. [Fr. *professoral.*]
Professorship, prō-fes'or-ship, *n.* The office of a professor.
Proffer, prof'er, *vt.* To bring out and offer for acceptance; to propose; to tender; to essay or attempt of one's own accord.—*n.* An offer made; something proposed for acceptance; essay; attempt. [Fr. *proferer*—L. *fero*, to bring.]
Proffered, prof'erd, *p.a.* Offered for acceptance.
Proficiency, prō-fi'shi-en-si, *n.* A making progress; advance in the acquisition of any art or science; progression in knowledge. [from L. *proficiens—pro*, and *facio*, to make.]
Proficient, prō-fi'shi-ent, *a.* Making progress; well-qualified; competent; skilful.—*n.* One who makes progress; one who has made considerable advances in any business, art, science, or branch of learning. [L. *proficiens.*]
Proficiently, prō-fi'shi-ent-li, *adv.* By proficiency.
Profile, prō'fil, *n.* Primarily, an outline traced by a thread-like line; a head or portrait represented sidewise; the side face; contour.—*vt.* To draw the outline of sidewise, as of a head; to draw in profile. *ppr.* profiling, *pret.* & *pp.* profiled. [Fr. *profil*—L. *filum*, a thread.]
Profit, pro'fit, *n.* A making way; increase; growth; benefit; gain; the advance in the price of goods sold beyond the cost of purchase; any advantage. *vt.* To be profitable to; to benefit; to advantage.—*vi.* To gain profit or pecuniary advantage; to make improvement; to grow wiser or better; to advance in anything useful; to be of use; to bring good. [Fr.—L. *facio*, to make.]
Profitable, pro'fit-a-bl, *a.* Yielding or bringing profit; advantageous. [Fr.]
Profitableness, pro'fit-a-bl-nes, *n.* Quality of being profitable; usefulness.
Profitably, pro'fit-a-bli, *adv.* With profit or gain; gainfully; usefully.
Profitless, pro'fit-les, *a.* Void of profit, gain, or advantage.
Profligacy, pro'fli-ga-si, *n.* A profligate course of life; a state of being abandoned in moral principle and in vice.
Profligate, pro'fli-gāt, *a.* Struck down; destroyed; wretched; vile; lost to principle, virtue, or decency; abandoned; depraved; wicked.—*n.* An abandoned man; a wretch who has lost all regard to good principles, virtue, or decency. [L. *profligatus—fligo*, to strike.]
Profound, prō-found', *a.* Having the foundation far below the surface; deep; intellectually deep; penetrating deeply into science; deep in contrivance; that enters deeply into subjects; deeply felt; mysterious; not superficial; humble; very lowly; submissive.—*n.* The deep; the sea; the ocean; the abyss. [Fr. *profond*—L. *fundus*, the bottom.]
Profoundly, prō-found'li, *adv.* Deeply; with deep concern; with deep knowledge or insight.
Profoundness, prō-found'nes, *n.* State or quality of being profound.
Profundity, prō-fund'i-ti, *n.* Depth of place, of knowledge, or of science. [It. *profundità.*]
Profuse, prō-fūs', *a.* Pouring out copiously; lavish; prodigal; overabounding; exuberant. [L. *profusus—fundo fūsum*, to pour.]
Profusely, prō-fūs'li, *adv.* In a profuse manner.
Profuseness, prō-fūs'nes, *n.* State or quality of being profuse; lavishness.
Profusion, prō-fū'shon, *n.* State or quality of being profuse; prodigality; rich abundance; exuberant plenty. [Fr.]
Progenitor, prō-jen'i-tor, *n.* A forefather; the founder of a family; an ancestor in the direct line. [L. *gigno*, to beget.]
Progeny, pro'je-ni, *n.* Offspring; race;

Prognostic 304 **Pronounce**

children; descendants of the human kind, or offspring of other animals. [It. *progenie*—L. *gigno*, to beget.]
Prognostic, prog-nos'tik, a. *Knowing or causing to know beforehand;* indicating something future by signs or symptoms.—n. That which foreshows; omen; presage. [Gr. *prognōstikos*—*gignōskō*, to know.]
Prognosticate, prog-nos'tik-āt, vt. To give foreknowledge of; to foretoken; to predict; to tell beforehand, by means of present signs. ppr. prognosticating, pret. & pp. prognosticated. [It. *pronosticare*.]
Prognostication, prog-nos'tik-ā"shon, n. *Act of prognosticating;* a foretoken. [Sp. *pronosticacion*.]
Prognosticator, pr g-nos'tik-āt-or, n. *One who prognosticates;* a foreteller of a future course. [Sp. *pronosticadór*.]
Programme, prō'gram, n. *A public notice in writing;* a brief outline of the order to be pursued, or the subjects embraced, in any public entertainment. [Fr.—Gr. *graphō*, to write.]
Progress, prō'gres, n. *A going forward by steps;* advancement; increase; advance in business of any kind; intellectual or moral improvement; passage from place to place; a journey of state; a circuit. [Fr. *progrès*—L. *gradior*, *gressus*, to take steps.]
Progress, prō-gres', vi. *To move forward* in space; to continue onward in course; to make improvement.
Progression, prō-gre'shon, n. *Act of moving forward;* motion onward; intellectual advance; continued proportion, arithmetical, geometrical, or harmonical. [Fr.]
Progressional, prō-gre'shon-al, a. *That advances;* that is in a state of advance.
Progressive, prō-gres'iv, a. *Moving forward;* proceeding onward; advancing; improving. [Fr. *progressif*.]
Progressively, prō-gres'iv-li, adv. By motion onward; by regular advances.
Prohibit, prō-hib'it, vt. *To hold in front;* to hold back; to interdict by authority; to disallow. [L. *prohibeo*, *prohibitus*—*habeo*, *habitum*, to have, to hold.]
Prohibited, prō-hib'it-ed, p.a. Interdicted; hindered.
Prohibition, prō-hi-bi'shon, n. *Act of prohibiting;* a declaration to hinder some action; disallowance. [Fr.]
Prohibitive, Prohibitory, prō-hib'it-iv, prō-hib'i-tō-ri, a. *That prohibits;* implying prohibition; forbidding. [Fr. *prohibitif*; Late L. *prohibitorius*.]
Project, prō-jekt', vt. *To cast forward;* to cast forward in the mind; to devise, as something to be done; to draw, as the form of anything; to delineate.—vi. *To shoot forward;* to extend beyond something else; to jut. [L. *projicio*, *projectus*—*jacio*, to throw.]
Project, prō'jekt, n. *Something cast forward* in the mind; a plan; something intended; contrivance; a design not practicable. [Fr. *projet*.]
Projectile, prō-jek'til, a. *Throwing forward;* given by impulse; impelled forward.—n. *A body projected by force,* particularly through the air. [Fr.]
Projecting, prō-jekt'ing, p.a. Scheming; jutting; extending forward.
Projection, prō-jek'shon, n. *Act of projecting;* a part jutting out, as of a building; act of scheming; design of something to be executed; delineation. [Fr.]
Projector, prō-jek'tor, n. *One who projects;* one who forms a scheme.

Prolate, prō'lāt, a. *Brought out;* lengthened; extended beyond the line of an exact sphere; applied to a spheroid elongated in the direction of its axis; opposed to oblate. [L. *prolatus*—*fero*, *latum*, to bear, bring.]
Prolific, prō-lif'ik, a. *Producing young or fruit;* productive; having the quality of generating; active. [Fr. *prolifique*—L. *proles*, offspring, and *facio*, to make.]
Prolix, prō'liks, a. *Stretched far out;* long; diffuse; tedious; wearisome. [L. *prolixus*—*laxus*, wide, loose.]
Prolixious†, prō-liks'i-us, a. Dilatory.
Prolixity, prō-liks'i-ti, n. *State or quality of being prolix;* great length; minute detail. [Late L. *prolixitas*.]
Prolocutor, prō-lo'kūt-or, n. *One who speaks for or before others;* the speaker or chairman of a convocation. [L. —*loquor*, *locutus*, to speak.]
Prologue, prō'log, n. *That which is spoken before;* the preface to a discourse or performance; the poem spoken before a dramatic performance begins.—vt. To introduce with a formal preface. [Fr.—Gr. *legō*, to speak.]
Prolong, prō-long', vt. *To lengthen out;* to lengthen in time; to protract; to put off to a distant time. [Fr. *prolonger*—L. *longus*, long.]
Prolongation, prō-long-gā'shon, n. *Act of prolonging* or of lengthening in space or time; extension of time by delay or postponement. [Fr. — L. *longus*, long, remote, distant.]
Prolonged, prō-longd', p.a. *Lengthened* in duration or space.
Promenade, pro-me-nād', n. *A walk for amusement;* a place for walking.—vi. To walk for amusement or exercise. ppr. promenading, pret. & pp. promenaded. [Fr. *promener*, to walk.]
Prominence, pro'mi-nens, n. *State or quality of being prominent;* a standing out from the surface of something; conspicuousness. [Fr.]
Prominent, pro'mi-nent, a. *Standing out* beyond the line or surface of something; jutting out; in high relief; large, as eyes; eminent; distinguished above others; most visible or striking to the eye; conspicuous. [Fr.—L. *mineo*, to jut, project.]
Prominently, pro'mi-nent-li, adv. *In a prominent manner;* conspicuously.
Promiscuous, prō-mis'kū-us, a. *Mixed;* consisting of individuals united in a mass without order; confused; common; not restricted to an individual. [L. *promiscuus*—*misceo*, to mix.]
Promiscuously, prō-mis'kū-us-li, adv. In a crowd or mass without order; indiscriminately.
Promise, pro'mis, n. *A putting forth of a pledge;* an assurance of a benefit; word pledged; a declaration made by one person to another, which binds the person who makes it to do or forbear a certain act specified; hopes; expectation, or that which affords expectation of future distinction; that which is promised; fulfilment of what is promised.—vt. *To put forth*, as a pledge; to make a declaration to do or forbear some act; to afford reason to expect; to pledge one's self or engage to bestow. vi. To assure one by a binding declaration; to afford hopes or expectations; to give ground to expect good. ppr. promising, pret. & pp. promised. [Fr. *promesse*; L. *mitto*, *missum*, to send.]
Promise-breach, pro'mis-brēch, n. Violation of promise.
Promised, prom'ist, p.a. Pledged.

Promiser, pro'mis-ėr, n. *One who promises;* one who engages or covenants.
Promising, pro'mis-ing, p.a. Affording just expectations of good, or reasonable ground of hope.
Promissory, pro'mis-ō-ri, a. *Containing a binding declaration of* something to be done or forborne. [It. *promissorio*.]
Promontory, pro'mon-tō-ri, n. *A part of a mountain*, or a high point of land or rock, projecting into the sea beyond the line of the coast; a headland. [Fr. *promontoire*—L. *mons*, *montis*, a mountain.]
Promote, prō-mōt', vt. *To move forward;* to forward; to further; to contribute to the growth or excellence of; to raise to higher rank; to elevate; to dignify. ppr. promoting, pret. & pp. promoted. [L. *promoveo*, *promōtus*—*moveo*, to move.]
Promoter, prō-mōt'ėr, n. *He or that which forwards,* advances, or promotes.
Promotion, prō-mō'shon, n. *Act of promoting;* exaltation in rank or honour; preferment. [Fr.]
Prompt, promt, a. *Brought forth; being at hand;* ready and quick to act as occasion demands; cheerfully performed; acting with cheerful alacrity; quick; unhesitating; hasty, indicating boldness.—vt. *To put in readiness;* to move to action; to instigate; to assist, as a speaker when at a loss, by pronouncing the words forgotten or next in order; to suggest to the mind of. [Fr.—L. *pro*, and *emo*, to take.]
Prompter, promt'ėr n. *One who prompts;* one whose business is to assist an actor when at a loss, by uttering the first words of a sentence forgotten.
Promptitude, promt'i-tūd, n. *State or quality of being prompt;* quickness of decision and action when occasion demands; cheerful alacrity. [Fr.]
Promptly, promt'li, adv. Readily; quickly; expeditiously; cheerfully.
Prompture†, promt'ūr, n. A suggestion.
Promulgate, prō-mul'gāt, vt. *To expose in public view;* to publish; to proclaim; to make known by open declaration. ppr. promulgating, pret. & pp. promulgated. [L. *promulgo*, *promulgatus*—perhaps *vulgus*, the people.]
Promulgation, prō-mul-gā'shon, n. *Act of promulgating;* publication; open declaration. [Fr.]
Promulgator, prō'mul-gāt-or, n. *One who promulgates;* a publisher. [Late L.]
Prone, prōn, a. *Leaning or bending forward;* inclined; lying with the face downward; precipitous; inclining in descent; sloping; inclined; disposed; ready. [L. *pronus*—Gr. *neuō*, to nod.]
Pronely, prōn'li, adv. So as to bend downward.
Proneness, prōn'nes, n. *State of being prone;* inclination of mind, heart, or temper; disposition.
Prong, prong, n. *A sharp-pointed instrument;* the tine of a fork or of a similar instrument; a pointed projection. [Sax. *preon*, a bodkin.]
Pronged, prongd, p.a. *Having prongs* or projections like the tine of a fork.
Pronominal, prō-nom'in-al, a. *Belonging to or of the nature of a pronoun*.
Pronominally, prō-nom'in-al-li, adv. With the effect of a pronoun.
Pronoun, prō'noun, n. *A word used instead of a noun*, to prevent the repetition of it. [L. *pronomen*—*nōmen*, a name.]
Pronounce, prō-nouns', vt. *To make*

Fāte far, fat, fall; mē, met, hėr; pīne, pin; nōte, not, mōve; tūbe, tub, bull; oil, pound.

publicly known; to speak; to articulate; to utter formally, officially, or solemnly; to utter rhetorically; to deliver; to utter, in almost any manner; to declare or affirm.—*vi.* To make *declaration;* to speak; to utter an opinion. *ppr.* pronouncing, *pret. & pp.* pronounced. [Fr. *prononcer*—L. *nuntio,* to declare.]

Pronounceable, prō-nouns'a-bl, *a.* That may be *pronounced* or uttered.

Pronounced, prō-nounst', *p.a.* Declared solemnly; strongly marked.

Pronouncer, prō-nouns'er, *n.* One who *pronounces;* one who utters or declares.

Pronouncing, prō-nouns'ing, *p. a.* Teaching *pronunciation.*

Pronunciation, prō-nun'si-ā̄"shon, *n.* Act of *pronouncing;* utterance; the mode of uttering words or sentences. [Fr. *prononciation.*]

Proof, prōf, *n. Something which proves; test; experiment;* any operation that ascertains truth; that which convinces the mind and produces belief; evidence; a verification of a rule or a result; hardness that resists impression; firmness of mind; stability not to be shaken; a certain standard of strength in spirit; a rough impression of a sheet in printing or engraving, taken for examination and correction.—*a. Having been proved;* able to resist; taken from a copperplate before it is worn out. [Fr. *preuve*—L. *probo,* to try.]

Prop, prop, *vt.* To support or prevent from falling by placing something *under* or *against;* to support by standing under or against; to sustain. *ppr.* propping, *pret. & pp.* propped.—*n.* That which *supports* or sustains an incumbent weight; a support; a stay. [*Bear* and *up;* Belg. *proppe,* a prop.]

Propagate, pro'pa-gāt, *vt. To increase by planting;* to multiply; to impel forward in space, as sound; to cause to go from person to person; to disseminate; to increase; to carry from place to place; to extend or give increase to; to produce.—*vi.* To have young or issue; to be multiplied by generation, or by new shoots or plants. *ppr.* propagating, *pret. & pp.* propagated. [L. *propago, propagatus*—*pango,* to plant.]

Propagated, pro'pa-gāt-ed, *p.a.* Continued or multiplied by generation or production of the same kind; spread.

Propagation, pro-pa-gā'shon, *n. Act of propagating;* the multiplication of the kind by generation; the spreading of anything; forwarding or promotion. [Fr.]

Propagator, pro'pa-gāt-or, *n. One who propagates;* one who multiplies any species of animals or plants; one who spreads, as a report; one who originates or extends; one who promotes.

Propel, prō-pel', *vt.* To drive *forward;* to urge or press onward by force. *ppr.* propelling, *pret. & pp.* propelled. [L. *propello*—*pello,* to drive.]

Propeller, prō-pel'ėr, *n. He of that which propels;* a contrivance for propelling steam-boats by the action of a screw placed in the stern; a steam-boat thus propelled.

Propelling, prō-pel'ing, *p. a.* Driving *forward.*

Propend†, prō-pend', *vi.* To be disposed in favour of anything.

Propensity, prō-pens'i-ti, *n. Inclination towards;* bent of mind, natural or acquired; natural tendency; disposition; inclination. [Low L. *propensitas.*]

Proper, pro'pėr, *a. One's own;* peculiar; naturally belonging to a person or thing; particularly suited to; noting an individual; fit; correct; just; not figurative; well-formed; handsome; mere†; pure†. [Fr. *propre*—L. *proprius.*]

Properly, pro'pėr-li, *adv.* Fitly; suitably; in a strict sense.

Property, pro'pėr-ti, *n. That which is proper* to a thing; a peculiar quality of anything; that which is inherent in a subject; nature; an artificial quality; that which is given by art or bestowed by man; disposition; the exclusive right of possessing, enjoying, and disposing of a thing; ownership; the thing owned; that to which a person has the legal title, whether in his possession or not; an estate, whether in lands, goods, or money; nearness†; (pl.) the dresses, &c., used in a theatre. *vt.†* To take as one's own. [Fr. *propriété*—L. *proprius,* proper.]

Prophecy, pro'fē-si, *n. A foretelling;* a declaration of something to come; a book of prophecies. [Fr. *prophétie.*]

Prophesy, pro'fē-sī, *vt. To foretell;* to predict; to foreshow.—*vi. To utter prophecies* or predictions; to make declarations of events to come; to preach. *ppr.* prophesying, *pret. & pp.* prophesied. [Fr. *prophétiser.*]

Prophesying, pro'fē-sī-ing, *p.n. The act of foretelling* or of preaching.

Prophet, pro'fet, *n. One who brings to light* or makes *known beforehand;* a foreteller; a person inspired by God to announce future events. [Gr. *prophētēs*—*pro,* and *phēmi,* to speak—*phaos,* light—*Sans. bhā,* to shine.]

Prophetess, pro'fet-es, *n. A female prophet.*

Prophetic, Prophetical, prō-fet'ik, prō-fet'ik-al, *a. Containing prophecy;* foretelling future events; unfolding future events. [Fr. *prophétique.*]

Prophetically, prō-fet'ik-al-li, *adv. By way of prediction.*

Propinquity, prō-pin'kwi-ti, *n. Nearness; vicinity;* nearness in place; nearness in time; nearness of blood; kindred. [L. *propinquitas*—*prope,* near.]

Propitiable, prō-pi'shi-a-bl, *a.* That may be *propitiated.*

Propitiate, prō-pi'shi-āt, *vt. To make propitious;* to appease and render favourable, as one offended. *ppr.* propitiating, *pret. & pp.* propitiated. [L. *propitio, propitiatus.*]

Propitiation, prō-pi'shi-ā"shon, *n. The act of propitiating;* the atonement which removes the obstacle to man's salvation. [Fr.]

Propitiator, prō-pi'shi-āt-or, *n. One who propitiates.* [Low L.]

Propitiatory, prō-pi'shi-ā-tō-ri, *a. Having the power to make propitious;* conciliatory.—*n.* Among the Jews, the mercy-seat. [Fr. *propitiatoire.*]

Propitious, prō-pi'shi-us, *a. Near to aid or assist;* disposed to be gracious; ready to forgive sins and bestow blessings. [L. *propitius*—*prope,* near.]

Propitiously, prō-pi'shi-us-li, *adv.* Favourably; kindly.

Propitiousness, prō-pi'shi-us-nes, *n. Quality of being propitious;* kindness; favourableness.

Proportion, prō-pōr'shon, *n. The comparative relation* of one thing to another in respect of *size,* quantity, or degree; the equality of ratios; symmetry; suitable adaptation of one part to another; just share; the relation between unequal things of the same kind, by which their several parts correspond to each other with an equal augmentation and diminution.—*vt. To adjust the comparative relation of;* to form with symmetry, as the parts of the body. [Fr.—L. *pro,* and *portio*—*pars, partis,* a part.]

Proportionable, prō-pōr'shon-a-bl, *a. That may be proportioned;* proportional.

Proportionably, prō-pōr'shon-a-bli, *adv. According to proportion.*

Proportional, prō-pōr'shon-al, *a. Having a due proportion;* being in suitable proportion or degree; having always the same ratio; relating to proportion; constituting a proportion.—*n. A number* or *quantity proportional;* one of the terms of a proportion. [Fr. *proportionnel.*]

Proportionally, prō-pōr'shon-al-li, *adv. In proportion;* in due degree.

Proportionate, prō-pōr'shon-āt, *a. Proportional;* adjusted to something else according to a certain rate or comparative relation.—*vt. To make proportional;* to adjust according to a settled rate or to due comparative relation. *ppr.* proportionating, *pret. & pp.* proportionated. [Late L. *proportionatus.*]

Proportionately, prō-pōr'shon-āt-li, *adv. With due proportion.*

Proportioned, prō-pōr'shond, *p.a. Made or adjusted with due proportion.*

Proposal, prō-pōz'al, *n. That which is proposed;* that which is offered for consideration; a design; terms or conditions proposed; a proposition.

Propose, prō-pōz', *vt. To set before;* to bring forward for discussion or acceptance.—*vi. To make a proposal;* to purpose; to lay schemes; to offer one's self in marriage. *ppr.* proposing, *pret. & pp.* proposed.—*n.* Talk†; discourse†. [Fr. *proposer*—L. *pono,* to set, put.]

Proposed, prō-pōzd', *p.a.* Offered for consideration.

Proposer, prō-pōz'ėr, *n. One who proposes* for consideration.

Proposition, pro-pō-zi'shon, *n. That which is proposed;* that which is offered for consideration or adoption; a proposal; offer of terms; a statement either of a truth to be demonstrated or of an operation to be performed; anything stated or affirmed for discussion. [Fr.]

Propound, prō-pound', *vt. To propose;* to offer for consideration. [L. *propōno.*]

Proprietary, prō-prī'e-ta-ri, *a. Belonging to a proprietor* or *proprietors.*

Proprietor, prō-prī'e-tor, *n. One who has a peculiar right of possession;* an owner; the person who has the legal right or exclusive title to anything, whether in possession or not. [Fr. *propriétaire*—L. *proprius,* one's own.]

Proprietorship, prō-prī'e-tor-ship, *n. State of being proprietor.*

Proprietress, prō-prī'e-tres, *n. A female proprietor;* a female who has the exclusive legal right to a thing.

Propriety, prō-prī'e-ti, *n.* Primarily, *property, peculiar nature, quality;* state of being proper; suitableness; appropriateness; consonance with established principles or customs; justness; accuracy; proper state. [Fr. *propriété*—L. *proprius,* one's own.]

Propugnation†, prō-pug-nā'shon, *n.* Defence.

Propulsion, prō-pul'shon, *n. Act of propelling,* or of driving forward. [L. *propulsus*—*pello,* to drive.]

Propulsive, prō-puls'iv, *a. Tending* or *having power to propel.*

Prorogation, prō-rō-gā'shon, *n. Act of proroguing;* continuance in time; the

continuance of parliament from one session to another, as an adjournment is a continuance of the session from day to day. [Fr.]
Prorogue, prō-rōg', *vt.* To prolong; to continue, as the parliament from one session to another; to postpone. *ppr.* proroguing, *pret. & pp.* prorogued. [Fr. *proroger.*]
Prosaic, prō-zā'ik, *a.* Pertaining to prose; resembling prose; dull; uninteresting. [Fr. *prosaïque.*]
Prosaically, prō-zā'ik-al-li, *adv. In a prosaic or dull manner.*
Proscribe, prō-skrīb', *vt.* Primarily, to write and post up *publicly,* as the names of persons doomed to death; to doom; to denounce as dangerous; to prohibit; to exclude. *ppr.* proscribing, *pret. & pp.* proscribed. [L. *pro-scribo—scribo,* to write.]
Proscribed, prō-skrībd', *p.a.* Condemned; banished.
Proscriber, prō-skrīb'ėr, *n. One who proscribes;* one who dooms to destruction.
Proscription, prō-skrip'shon, *n. Act of proscribing* or dooming to death; condemning to exile; utter rejection. [Fr.]
Proscriptive, prō-skrip'tiv, *a.* Pertaining to or consisting in proscription.
Prose, prōz, *n. The right onward course of words or language, free from the trammels and turnings of verse;* the natural language of man; language loose and unconfined to poetical measure, in distinction from verse.—*a. Relating to prose;* prosaic; not poetical.—*vi.* To make a tedious relation; to write in a dull, tedious style, without spirit or animation. *ppr.* prosing, *pret. & pp.* prosed. [Fr.—L. *prorsus,* forwards.]
Prosecute, pros'ē-kūt, *vt.* To follow or pursue with a view to reach or accomplish; to commence, as endeavours to obtain or complete; to persist in, as efforts already begun; to seek to obtain by legal process; to pursue for redress or punishment before a legal tribunal.—*vi.* To carry on a legal prosecution. *ppr.* prosecuting, *pret. & pp.* prosecuted. [L. *prosequor, prosecutus—sequor,* to follow.]
Prosecution, pros-ē-kū'shon, *n. Act of prosecuting;* pursuit by efforts of body or mind; the carrying on of a suit in a court of law or equity. [Late L. *prosecutio.*]
Prosecutor, pros'ē-kūt-or, *n. One who prosecutes;* the person who institutes and carries on a criminal suit in a legal tribunal.
Prosecutrix, pros'ē-kūt-riks, *n. A female who prosecutes.*
Proselyte, pros'ē-līt, *n.* One who has *come over* from heathenism to Judaism; a new convert to some religion or to some particular opinion. [Fr. *prosélyte*—Gr. *pros,* to, and *erchomai, élthon,* to come.]
Proselytize, pros'ē-līt-īz, *vt.* To convert to some religion, or the like. *ppr.* proselytizing, *pret. & pp.* proselytized.
Proser, prōz'ėr, *n. One who proses;* a tedious dull writer or narrator.
Prosiness, prōz'i-nes, *n. Quality of being prosy* or dull.
Prosing, prōz'ing, *p.a.* Talking or writing in a dull uninteresting manner. *p.n.* Dull, tedious minuteness in speech or writing.
Prosodial, prō-sō'di-al, *a.* Pertaining to *prosody.*
Prosodian, prō-sō'di-an, *n.* One skilled

in prosody, or in the rules of pronunciation and metrical composition.
Prosodist, pros'ō-dist, *n. One who is versed in prosody.*
Prosody, pros'ō-di, *n. That which conduces to the construction of verse;* that part of grammar which treats of the quantity of syllables, of accent, and of the laws of versification. [Fr. *prosodie*—Gr. *pros,* to, and *ōdē,* a song.]
Prosopopœia, pros'ō-pō-pē''ya, *n. Personification;* a figure in rhetoric by which inanimate objects, or abstract ideas, are personified. [Gr. *prosopopoiia—prosōpon,* a face, and *poieō,* to make.]
Prospect, pros'pekt, *n. A look out;* view of things within the reach of the eye; regard to something future; intellectual sight; ground of expectation; a scene or landscape; view delineated or painted; position of the front of a building; anticipation; expectation. [L. *prospectus—specio,* to view.]
Prospective, pros-pekt'iv, *a. Looking forward* in time; future; viewing at a distance; relating to the future.
Prospectively, pros-pekt'iv-li, *adv.* With reference to the future.
Prospectus, pros-pek'tus, *n. A view or outline of something proposed previous* to its being carried out; the plan of a literary work; the outline of any plan submitted for public approbation. [L.—*specio,* to view.]
Prosper, pros'pėr, *vi.* To cause to succeed *as one could hope;* to render fortunate or happy; to favour; to render successful.—*vi. To be in a desirable state;* to succeed; to grow or increase; to flourish; to thrive. [Fr. *prospérer*—L. *spes,* hope.]
Prosperity, pros-pe'ri-ti, *n. State of being prosperous;* advance in anything good; successful progress in any business; attainment of the object desired; good fortune. [Fr. *prospérité.*]
Prosperous, pros'pėr-us, *a. According to one's hope;* agreeable to one's wishes; flourishing; thriving; characterised by success; favouring success; auspicious. [L. *prospĕrus.*]
Prosperously, pros'pėr-us-li, *adv.* With gain or increase; successfully.
Prostitute, pros'ti-tūt, *vt. To place before;* to give up to any vile purpose; to sell to wickedness. *ppr.* prostituting, *pret. & pp.* prostituted.—*n.* A strumpet; one who offers himself to infamous employments for hire. [L. *prostituo, prostitūtus—statuo,* to place.]
Prostituted, pros'ti-tūt-ed, *p.a.* Devoted to base purposes.
Prostitution, pros-ti-tū'shon, *n.* Common lewdness of a female; the act of devoting to infamous purposes what is in one's power. [Fr.]
Prostrate, pros'trāt, *a. Prostrated;* lying at length on the ground; lying at mercy, as a supplicant; lying in the posture of humility or adoration.—*vt. To lay flat;* to overturn, as law or order; to bow in humble reverence (with recipr. pron.); to exhaust; to depress, as one's vital powers. *ppr.* prostrating, *pret. & pp.* prostrated. [L. *prostratus—sterno, strātum,* to spread out.]
Prostrated, pros'trāt-ed, *p.a. Laid flat;* thrown down.
Prostration, pros-trā'shon, *n. Act of prostrating;* the act of bowing in humility or adoration; great depression; that state of the body in disease in which the system is oppressed. [Fr.]
Prosy, prōz'i, *a. Like prose;* dull and tedious in discourse or writing.

Protect, prō-tekt', *vt. To cover before;* to cover from danger; to keep in safety; to guard; to save; to shelter. [L. *protego, protectus—tego, tectum,* Sans. *sthag,* to cover.]
Protected, prō-tekt'ed, *p.a. Preserved* in safety.
Protecting, prō-tekt'ing, *p.a. Defending;* preserving in safety.
Protectingly, prō-tekt'ing-li, *adv. By protection;* in the way of protection.
Protection, prō-tek'shon, *n. Act of protecting;* state of being protected; that which protects; a shield; guard; a writing that protects; exemption, as from arrest. [Fr.—L. *tego,* to cover.]
Protective, prō-tekt'iv, *a. Affording protection;* sheltering; defensive.
Protector, prō-tekt'or, *n. One who protects;* a defender; a preserver; a regent. [Late L.]
Protectorate, prō-tekt'or-āt, *n. Government by a protector;* the authority assumed by a superior power over a dependent one. [Fr. *protectorat.*]
Protectorship, prō-tekt'or-ship, *n. The office of a protector* or regent.
Protectress, Protectrix, prō-tekt'res, prō-tekt'riks, *n. A woman or female who protects.*
Protege, prō-tā-zhā', *n. One under the protection* of another. [Fr. *protégé*—L. *tego,* to cover.]
Protest, prō-test', *vi. To bear witness in public;* to affirm with solemnity; to testify; to aver; to make a solemn declaration expressive of opposition (with *against*); to make a formal declaration in writing against a public measure.—*vt.* To make a solemn declaration of, as of one's innocence; to declare formally against for non-payment; to give evidence of t. [L. *pro,* and *testor—testis,* a witness, one who attests, orally or in writing.]
Protest, prō'test, *n.* A solemn declaration made in writing by a minority of a deliberative body, to *testify* their dissent from the proceedings of a majority; a declaration against for non-acceptance or non-payment.
Protestant, pro'test-ant, *a.* Pertaining to those who, at the reformation of religion, *protested* against a decree of Charles V. and the Diet of Spires; pertaining to Protestants or to Protestantism.—*n.* One of the party who adhered to Luther at the Reformation, and in 1529 *protested* against a decree of the emperor Charles V. [Late L. *protestans*—L. *testis,* a witness.]
Protestantism, pro'test-ant-izm, *n. The principles or the religion of Protestants.* [Fr. *protestantisme.*]
Protestation prō-test-ā'shon, *n. The act of protesting;* a solemn declaration of a fact, opinion, or resolution; a protest. [Fr.]
Protested, prō-test'ed, *p.a.* Declared against for non-acceptance or non-payment.
Protester, prō-test'ėr, *n. One who protests;* one who utters a solemn declaration.
Protocol, prō'tō-kol, *n. The first leaf glued* to a notarial document; the original copy of any despatch, treaty, or other document; a record or register. [Fr. *protocole*—Gr. *prōtos,* first, and *kolla,* glue.]
Protomartyr, prō'tō-mär-tėr, *n. The first martyr,* St. Stephen; the first who suffers or is sacrificed in any cause. [Gr. *prōtos,* and *martyr,* a witness.]
Prototype, prō'tō-tīp, *n. An original type after which anything is formed;*

Fāte, fär, fat, fall; mē, met, hėr; pīne, pin; nōte, not, mōve; tūbe, tub, bull; oil, pound.

PROTRACT — PRUNE

exemplar; archetype. [Fr.—Gr. *prōtos*, first, and *tupos*, a blow, type.]
Protract, prō-trakt', *vt.* To draw out or lengthen; to prolong; to delay; to retard; to defer; to put off to a distant time. [L. *protraho, protractus—traho*, to draw.]
Protracted, prō-trakt'ed, *p.a.* Drawn out in time.
Protractedly, prō-trakt'ed-li, *adv.* With *protraction*; tediously.
Protraction, prō-trak'shon, *n.* Act of drawing out or continuing in time; the act of delaying the termination of a thing. [Late L. *protractio.*]
Protractive, prō-trakt'iv, *a.* Drawing out or lengthening in time; prolonging.
Protractor, prō-trakt'or, *n.* He or that which *protracts*; an instrument used in drawing and plotting.
Protrude, prō-trōd', *vt.* To thrust forward; to thrust out, as from confinement.—*vi.* To be thrust forward; to shoot forward. *ppr.* protruding, *pret. & pp.* protruded. [L. *protrūdo—trudo*, Heb. *tarad*, to thrust.]
Protrusion, prō-trō'zhon, *n.* Act of protruding; the state of being protruded; a thrusting or driving; a push.
Protuberance, prō-tū'bėr-ans, *n.* A swelling or tumour on the body; a bunch or knob. [Sp. *protuberincia.*]
Protuberant, prō-tū'bėr-ant, *a.* Swelling; prominent beyond the surrounding surface. [Low L. *protuberans.*]
Protuberate, prō-tū'bėr-āt, *vi.* To swell forward; to bulge out. *ppr.* protuberating, *pret. & pp.* protuberated. [Low L. *protubero, protuberatus—L. tuber,* a lump.]
Proud, proud, *a.* Possessing pride; splendid; magnificent; lofty of mien; exciting pride; having inordinate self-esteem; arrogant; presumptuous; fungous, as proud flesh. [Sax. *prut.*]
Proudly, proud'li, *adv.* In a proud manner; with an inordinate self-esteem.
Provable, prōv'a-bl, *a.* That may be proved.
Prove, prōv, *vt.* To try; to examine; to bring to the test; to verify; to show; to evince; to establish; to ascertain or render certain, as truth or fact, by testimony or other evidence; to deduce, as certain conclusions from propositions that are true; to confirm by experiment or argument; to ascertain the genuineness of, as a will.—*vi.* To make trial; to essay; to have its qualities ascertained by experience; to turn out; to issue; to be found true by the result. *ppr.* proving, *pret. & pp.* proved. [Sax. *profian*; L. *probo*, to try, test.]
Proved, prōvd, *p.a.* Tried; evinced; experienced.
Provender, pro'ven-dėr, *n.* That which is provided; dry food for beasts, usually meal, or a mixture of meal and cut straw or hay; provisions; meat; food. [Fr. *provende*—L. *pro*, before, and *video*, to see.]
Proverb, pro'vėrb, *n.* An old saying; a maxim; a short sentence often repeated, expressing a well-known truth or common fact; a pithy saying; a byword; a name often repeated; a reproach or object of contempt.—*vt.* To provide with a proverb. [Fr. *proverbe*—L. *verbum*, a word.]
Proverbial, prō-vėrb'i-al, *a.* Of the nature of a proverb; comprised in a proverb; suitable to a proverb. [Fr.]
Proverbially, prō-vėrb'i-al-li, *adv.* In a proverb; so as to be a proverb.

Provide, prō-vīd', *vt.* To see to beforehand; to procure beforehand; to prepare; to supply (with *with*); to stipulate previously.—*vi.* To look before; to act with foresight; to procure supplies or means of defence; to stipulate previously. *ppr.* providing, *pret. & pp.* provided. [L. *pro*, and *video*, to see.]
Providence, pro'vi-dens, *n.* Prudence; foresight; timely care; the superintendence which God exercises over his creatures; hence also, God viewed in this relation. [Fr.]
Provident, pro'vi-dent, *a.* Prudent; foreseeing wants and making provision to supply them; frugal; economical. [L. *providens—video*, to see.]
Providential, pro-vi-den'shi-al, *a.* Effected by the *providence* of God; proceeding from divine superintendence. [Sp. *providencial.*]
Providentially, pro-vi-den'shi-al-li, *adv.* By means of God's providence.
Providently, pro'vi-dent-li, *adv.* With prudent foresight; with wise precaution in preparing for the future.
Provider, prō-vīd'ėr, *n.* One who provides, furnishes, or supplies.
Province, pro'vins, *n.* Among the Romans, a conquered country, beyond the limits of Italy, which was subject to the Roman state; now, a country belonging to a kingdom, usually situated at a distance from the kingdom, but subject to it; a division of a kingdom; a region of country; a large extent; the proper office of a person. [Fr.—L. *procul,* at a distance, and *vinco*, to conquer.]
Provincial, prō-vin'shi-al, *a.* Pertaining to a province; not polished; rude, as accent; pertaining to the jurisdiction of an archbishop.—*n.* A person belonging to a province. [Fr.]
Provincialism, prō-vin'shi-al-izm, *n.* A peculiar manner of speaking in a district of country remote from the metropolis. [Fr. *provincialisme.*]
Provincially, prō-vin'shi-al-li, *adv.* In a provincial manner.
Provision, prō-vi'zhon, *n.* Foresight; act of providing; things provided; preparation; measures taken beforehand; stores provided; food; all manner of eatables for man and beast; previous stipulation; terms or agreement made for a future exigency; (pl.) the articles in a legal contract; the bequests in a will, &c.—*vt.* To supply with *provisions* or with victuals or food. [Fr.—L. *video, visum*, to see.]
Provisional, prō-vi'zhon-al, *a.* Provided for present need or for the occasion; temporary. [Fr. *provisionnel.*]
Provisionally, prō-vi'zhon-al-li, *adv.* By way of provision; temporarily.
Proviso, prō-vī'zō, *n.* A provision; a clause in any statute, contract, grant, or other writing, by which a condition is introduced. [the abl. of L. *provisus*, foreseen.]
Provocation, pro-vō-kā'shon, *n.* Act of provoking; anything that excites anger; the cause of resentment. [Fr.]
Provocative, prō-vōk'ā-tiv, *a.* That provokes; tending to incite appetite.—*n.* Anything that provokes; anything that tends to excite appetite or passion; a stimulant. [It. *provocativo.*]
Provoke, prō-vōk', *vt.* To call forth; to incite; to stimulate; to incense; to exasperate.—*vi.* To produce anger. *ppr.* provoking, *pret. & pp.* provoked. [Fr. *provoquer*—L. *voco*, to call.]
Provoked, prō-vōkt', *p.a.* Made angry; incensed.

Provoking, prō-vōk'ing, *p.a.* Tending to awaken passion.
Provokingly, prō-vōk'ing-li, *adv.* In such a manner as to excite anger.
Provost, pro'vōst, *n.* One placed before or set over others; a chief ruler; a president; the executioner of an army; a keeper of prisoners; in Scotland, the chief magistrate of a royal burgh or city. [Norm.—L. *præ*, before, and *pono, positum*, to put, place.]
Provostship, pro'vōst-ship, *n.* The office of a provost.
Prow, prou, *n.* The place in the ship where the *look-out* was originally stationed; the fore-part of a ship; the beak or pointed cutwater of a galley. [Fr. *proue*—Gr. *pro*, before, and *horāō*, to see.]
Prowess, prou'es, *n.* Serviceableness; bravery; intrepidity in war; fearlessness of danger. [Fr. *prouesse*—L. *pro*, for, and *sum, esse*, to be.]
Prowl, proul, *vi.* To rove over; to rove or wander, particularly for prey, as a wild beast; to plunder. [Old Eng. *prolle.*]
Prowler, proul'ėr, *n.* One who roves about for prey.
Prowling, proul'ing, *p.a.* Wandering about in search of prey.
Prowlingly, proul'ing-li, *adv.* In a prowling manner.
Proximate, proks'i-māt, *a.* Nearest; immediate; having most intimate relation or connection. [L. *proximus—prope*, near.]
Proximately, proks'i-māt-li, *adv.* Immediately.
Proximity, proks-im'i-ti, *n.* State of being near; immediate nearness, either in place, blood, or alliance. [Fr. *proximité.*]
Proxy, proks'i, *n.* The office of procurator; agency of a substitute; the person who is deputed to act for another; a writing by which one person authorizes another to vote in his place. [contracted from Old Eng. *procuracy.*]
Prude, prōd, *n.* A woman affectedly prudent; a woman of great reserve and scrupulous nicety. [Fr.—L. *pro*, and *video*, to see.]
Prudence, prō'dens, *n.* The quality of being prudent; the habit of at all times acting with deliberation and forethought; caution; discretion; circumspection. [Fr.—L. *prudentia.*]
Prudent, prō'dent, *a.* Foreseeing; provident; dictated by prudence; practically wise; careful not to act when the end is of doubtful utility; wary; considerate; discreet; practising economy; wise; intelligent. [Fr.—L. *prudens—pro*, and *video, sans, vid*, to see.]
Prudential, prō-den'shi-al, *a.* Proceeding from prudence; dictated or prescribed by prudence; politic.
Prudentially, prō-den'shi-al-li, *adv.* In conformity with prudence; prudently.
Prudently, prō'dent-li, *adv.* With prudence; with frugality.
Prudery, prōd'ė-ri, *n.* Affected prudence; excessive nicety in conduct; affected gravity; coyness.
Prudish, prōd'ish, *a.* Partaking of prudery; affectedly grave.
Prudishly, prōd'ish-li, *adv.* In a prudish manner.
Prune, prōn, *vt.* To lop or cut off, as the superfluous branches of trees; to clear from anything superfluous; to dress; to trim. *ppr.* pruning, *pret. & pp.* pruned. [Fr. *provigner*, to lay a branch of a vine in the ground to take root—L. *propago*, a slip, a shoot.]

Prune, prön, n. *A plum;* a dried plum; sometimes a recent plum. [Fr.—L. *prunum*, a plum.]

Prunella, prö-nel'la, n. A smooth woollen stuff, generally black, used for making shoes or garments. [Fr. *prunelle*.]

Pruning, prön'ing, p.n. The lopping off the superfluous *branches of trees* for improving their fruit.

Prurience, prö'ri-ens, n. *An itching*, longing desire or appetite for anything. [from *prurient*.]

Prurient, prö'ri-ent, a. *Burning; inflamed;* itching; uneasy with desire. [L. *pruriens—per*, intensive, and *uro*, to burn—Gr. *pûr*, fire.]

Pry, pri, v.i. To peep narrowly; to attempt to discover something with scrutinising curiosity, whether impertinently or not. *ppr.* prying, *pret. & pp.* pried.—n. Narrow inspection; impertinent peeping. [probably from the verb *to eye*, with the prefix *per—to eye through or all over*.]

Prying, pri'ing, p.a. Inspecting closely; looking into with curiosity.

Psalm, säm, n. *A song sung to a stringed instrument;* a sacred song or hymn; a song composed on a divine subject and in praise of God. [Fr. *psaume*—Gr. *psallo*, to sing to the harp.]

Psalmist, säm'ist, n. *A writer of psalms;* a title particularly applied to David and the other authors of the scriptural psalms. [Fr. *psalmiste*.]

Psalmodic, sal-mod'ik, a. *Relating to psalmody*.

Psalmodist, säm'od-ist, n. *One who sings holy songs*.

Psalmody, säm'od-i, n. *Psalm singing;* the act or art of singing psalms or sacred songs; body of psalms. [Fr. *psalmodie*—Gr. *psalmos*, and *ôdê*, a song.]

Psalter, sal'tér, n. *The book of psalms;* often applied to a book containing the Psalms separately printed. [Fr. *psautier*.]

Psaltery, sal'te-ri, n. A stringed instrument of music used by the Hebrews, the form of which is not now known. [Gr. *psaltêrion*.]

Pshaw, sha, *interj.* An expression of contempt, disdain, or dislike.

Psychologic, Psychological, psī-ko-loj'-ik, psī-ko-loj'ik-al, a. *Pertaining to psychology*, or to a treatise on the soul.

Psychologically, psī-ko-loj'ik-al-li, *adv.* *In a psychological manner*.

Psychologist, psi-kol'o-jist, n. *One who is conversant with psychology*.

Psychology, psī-kol'o-ji, n. *The doctrine of the soul or mind;* a discourse or treatise on the human soul; mental philosophy. [Gr. *logos*, and *psûchê*, breath, life, the soul.]

Ptarmigan, tär'mi-gan, n. The white grouse, found in mountainous parts of Europe, Asia, and America. [Gael. *tarmachan*.]

Ptolemaic, to-lē-mā'ik, a. *Pertaining to Ptolemy*, the ancient astronomer, or to his system of the universe.

Puberty, pū'bér-ti, n. *The age of maturity*, or of manhood; ripe age. [Fr. *puberté;* L. *puber*, grown up.]

Pubescence, pū-bes'ens, n. *State of a youth who has arrived at puberty;* the downy substance on plants. [Fr.]

Pubescent, pū-bes'ent, a. *Arriving at puberty;* covered with pubescence, as plants; covered with very fine short hairs. [Fr.]

Public, pub'lik, a. *Of or belonging to the people;* pertaining to a nation or state; extending to a whole people; common to a city, town, or to mankind at large; current among people of all classes; notorious; directed to the interest of a nation or community; open to common use.—n. *The people at large;* the many; the general body of mankind; the people, indefinitely. [L. *publicus—populus*, the people.]

Publican, pub'li-kan, n. Originally, a farmer-general of the Roman *public revenue;* the keeper of an inn or public-house; one licensed to retail beer, spirits, or wine. [L. *publicanus*.]

Publication, pub-li-kā'shon, n. *Act of publishing* or offering to public notice; proclamation; promulgation; act of offering a book to the public by sale or by gratuitous distribution; a work printed and published. [Fr.]

Public-house, pub-lik-hous', n. *A house of public entertainment;* an inn.

Publicist, pub'li-sist, n. A writer on the laws of nature or of nations.

Publicity, pub-lis'i-ti, n. *State of being public;* notoriety. [Fr. *publicité*.]

Publicly, pub'lik-li, *adv.* Openly; with exposure to popular view or notice.

Public-spirited, pub-lik-spi'rit-ed, a. *Actuated by a regard to the public interest;* dictated by a regard to public good.

Public-spiritedness, pub-lik-spi'rit-ed-nes, n. *Quality of being public-spirited*.

Publish, pub'lish, v.t. *To make public;* to proclaim; to announce; to put forth or issue to the public, as a book, or an engraving; to make known by posting, or by reading in a church. [Fr. *publier*—L. *populus*, the people.]

Publisher, pub'lish-ér, n. *One who publishes* or makes known what was before unknown; one who publishes books; one who sends a book or engraving into the world for common use.

Publishing, pub'lish-ing, p.a. Putting forth a book, engraving, &c., into the world.

Puce, pūs, a. Of a dark brown or brownish purple colour. [Fr.]

Puck, puk, n. A mischievous fiend, goblin, or sprite; a fairy. [Icel. *puki*, a wicked sprite.]

Pucker, puk'ér, v.t. *To gather into small bags* or wrinkles; to wrinkle; to contract into ridges and furrows.—n. A fold or wrinkle, or a collection of folds. [from Old Eng. *poke*, a bag.]

Puckered, puk'érd, p.a. Gathered in folds; wrinkled.

Pudder, pud'der, n. A tumult.—v.i.† To make a tumult.—v.t.† To perplex.

Pudding, pud'ding, n. *That which is stuffed;* an intestine; an intestine stuffed with meat, &c., now called a sausage; a species of food of a soft consistence, variously made; proverbially, food or victuals. [Low Sax.]

Puddle, pud'l, n. *A small pool of dirty water;* a mixture of clay and sand worked together until they are impervious to water.—v.t. To make foul or muddy; to make thick or close with clay, so as to render impervious to water; to convert into wrought iron, as cast iron.—v.i. To make a dirty stir. *ppr.* puddling, *pret. & pp.* puddled. [Ir. *boidhlia*.]

Puddled, pud'ld, p.a. Converted into wrought iron by *puddling*.

Puddler, pud'l-ér, n. *One who puddles iron*.

Pudency†, pū'den-si, n. Modesty.

Puerile, pū'er-il, a. *Pertaining to boys or youth;* boyish; youthful; childish; trifling. [Fr. *puéril*—L. *puer*, a boy.]

Puerility, pū-er-il'i-ti, n. *Childishness;* boyishness; that which is trifling; a thought or expression which is flat or childish. [Fr. *puérilité*.]

Puff, puf, n. A sudden and single emission of breath from the mouth; a sudden and short blast of wind; a fungous ball filled with dust; anything light and porous; a tumid or exaggerated commendation.—v.i. To drive air from the mouth in a single and quick blast; to blow, as an expression of scorn or contempt; to breathe with vehemence; to do or move with a tumid, bustling appearance; to swell with air.—v.t. To drive with a blast of wind or air; to inflate; to blow up; to drive with a blast in scorn; to praise extravagantly. [G.]

Puffer, puf'er, n. *One who puffs;* one who praises with noisy commendation.

Puffin, puf'in, n. A water-fowl which makes a *puffing sound* when caught.

Puffiness, puf'i-nes, n. *State or quality of being puffy* or turgid.

Puffing, puf'ing, p.n. A vehement breathing; exaggerated praise.

Puffingly, puf'ing-li, *adv.* Tumidly; with vehement breathing.

Puffy, puf'i, a. *Puffed out;* swelled with air or any soft matter; tumid, turgid; bombastic.

Pug, pug, n. A monkey, from his amusingly mischievous tricks; a little dog, with a face or nose like a monkey. [another form of *puck*.]

Pugging†, pug'ing, a. Thieving.

Pugh, pö. A word used in contempt or disdain.

Pugilism, pū'jil-izm, n. *The practice of boxing or fighting with the fist*. [from L. *pûgil*, a boxer.]

Pugilist, pū'jil-ist, n. *A boxer;* one who fights with his fists.

Pugilistic, pū-jil-ist'ik, a. *Pertaining to boxing* or fighting with the fist.

Pugnacious, pug-nā'shi-us, a. *Disposed to fight;* inclined to fighting; quarrelsome; fighting. [L. *pugnax, pugnacis—pugno*, to fight.]

Pugnaciously, pug-nā'shi-us-li, *adv.* *In a pugnacious manner*.

Pugnacity, pug-nas'i-ti, n. *Quality of being pugnacious;* inclination to fight. [L. *pugnacitas*.]

Pug-nose, pug'nōs, n. A short and thick nose; a snub nose.

Pug-nosed, pug'nōzd, a. *Having a nose like that of a pug* or monkey.

Puisne, pū'nē, a. *Born after or afterward;* younger or inferior in rank; petty; small; inconsiderable. [Fr. *puis*, from L. *post*, afterwards, and *né*, born.]

Puissance, pū'is-ans, n. *Power;* strength; force. [Fr. from *pouvoir*, L. *possum, posse*, to be able.]

Puissant, pū'is-ant, a. *Powerful;* strong; mighty; forcible. [Fr.]

Puissantly, pū'is-ant-li, *adv.* Powerfully; with great strength.

Puke, pūk, v.i. To vomit; to eject the contents of the stomach. *ppr.* puking, *pret. & pp.* puked.—n. A vomit; a medicine which excites vomiting. [formed from the sound.]

Puke, pūk, a. *Pitch-coloured;* of a colour between black and russet; now called *puce*. [L. *pictus—pix*, pitch.]

Pule, pūl, v.i. *To cry like a chicken;* to cry as a complaining child; to whimper. *ppr.* puling, *pret. & pp.* puled. [Fr. *piauler*.]

Puling, pūl'ing, p.a. Whining; childish; infantine.—p.n. *A cry as of a chicken;* a whining.

Pull, pṳl, vt. To draw violently towards one; opposed to push, which is to drive from one; to draw forcibly (with on or off); to tear; to rend; to gather.—vi. To give a pull; to draw; to tug.—n. Act of pulling; an effort to move by drawing toward one; a contest; a struggle; violence suffered. [Sax. pullian—L. vello, to pluck.]

Pullet, pṳl'let, n. A young hen or female of the domestic fowl. [Fr. poulet—L. pullus, a young fowl.]

Pulley, pṳl'lē, n. Pulleys, pṳl'lēz, pl. A small wheel turning on a pin in a block, with a furrow or groove on its outside in which runs the rope that turns it, much used in raising weights. [Fr. poulie—Gr. poleō, to turn.]

Pulmonary, pul'mon-a-ri, a. Pertaining to the lungs; affecting the lungs. [Fr. pulmonaire—Gr. pneō, to breathe.]

Pulmonic, pul-mon'ik, a. Pertaining to the lungs; affecting the lungs.—n. A medicine for diseases of the lungs. [Fr. pulmonique.]

Pulp, pulp, n. The soft substance within a bone; marrow; a soft mass; the soft succulent part of fruit.—vt. To make into pulp. [Fr. pulpe—L. pulpa, pulp of fruit.]

Pulpiness, pulp'i-nes, n. The state of being pulpy.

Pulpit, pul'pit, n. A platform; that part of the Roman stage on which the actors recited and performed their parts; an elevated place in a church, in which the preacher stands; a desk. [L. pulpitum, a platform of boards.]

Pulpy, pulp'i, a. Like pulp; soft; fleshy.

Pulsate, pul'sāt, vi. To beat or throb. ppr. pulsating, pret. & pp. pulsated. [L. pulso, pulsatus—pello, pulsus, to beat.]

Pulsatile, pul'sāt-il, a. That is or may be struck or beaten; played by beating like a drum. [Low L. pulsatilis.]

Pulsation, pul-sā'shon, n. A beating; the beating or throbbing of the heart or of an artery, in the process of carrying on the circulation of the blood; a stroke by which some medium is affected, as in sound, &c. [L. pulsatio.]

Pulsative, pul'sāt-iv, a. Beating; throbbing. [Fr. pulsatif.]

Pulsatory, pul'sā-tō-ri, a. Beating; throbbing; as the heart.

Pulse, puls, n. A striking or beating; the beating or throbbing of the heart and arteries; the stroke by which a medium is affected, as in the motion of light, sound, &c.; vibration. [Fr. pouls—L. pello, to strike.]

Pulse, puls, n. Leguminous plants or their seeds, as beans, pease, &c., which are contained in a case or pod. [Belg. bol, a bean.]

Pulseless, puls'les, a. Without pulse; having no pulsation.

Pulverizable, pul'vėr-īz-a-bl, a. That may be pulverised.

Pulverization, pul'vėr-īz-ā"shon, n. Act of pulverizing.

Pulverize, pul'vėr-īz, vt. To reduce to dust or fine powder, as by beating, grinding, &c. ppr. pulverising, pret. & pp. pulverised. [Fr. pulvériser—L. pulvis, pulvėris, dust.]

Pumice, pū'mis, n. The spume of melted stones; a light and spongy volcanic substance, appearing to consist of minute parallel fibres, owing to the parallelism and minuteness of the crowded cells. [L. pumex, pumicis—spuma, spume.]

Pump, pump, n. A machine, consisting of a peculiar arrangement of a piston, cylinder, and valves, employed for raising water or extracting air.—vi. To raise water with a pump.—vt. To raise or throw out with a pump, as water; to examine by artful questions. [Icel. pumpa.]

Pump, pump, n. A shoe with a thin sole. [etymol. uncertain.]

Pumpkin, pump'kin, n. A well-known plant and its fruit; a pompion. [D. pompoen.]

Pun, pun, n. A play on words that agree or resemble in sound, but differ in meaning; a kind of quibble or equivocation.—vi. To play on words; to quibble; to use the same word at once in different senses.—vt. To persuade by a pun. ppr. punning, pret. & pp. punned. [probably from Sans. pan, to play.]

Punt, pun, vt. To pound.

Punch, punch, n. A pointed instrument of iron or steel used for piercing holes in plates of metal, and so contrived as to stamp out a piece; a blow or thrust. vt. To perforate with an iron instrument, either pointed or not; to bore with a sharp instrument; to hit with the fist. [Fr. poinçon—L. pungo, to prick.]

Punch, punch, n. A drink composed of water sweetened with sugar, with a mixture of lemon-juice and spirit, and formerly with spice. [from Sans. panchan = five; five ingredients being used by the Orientals.]

Punch, punch, n. The buffoon or harlequin of a puppet-show.

Puncheon, pun'chon, n. A punch; an iron or steel instrument used for piercing or stamping a body; [etymol. uncertain] a measure of liquids, or a cask containing sometimes 84, sometimes 120 gallons. [Fr. poinçon.]

Punchinello, pun-chi-nel'lō, n. A punch; a buffoon; a character of the Italian puppet-show, represented as fat, short, and humpbacked. [It. pulcinello.]

Punctilio, pungk-ti'li-ō, n. A nice point of exactness in conduct, ceremony, or proceeding; exactness in forms. [It. puntiglio—L. pungo, to prick, to pierce into, to penetrate.]

Punctilious, pungk-ti'li-us, a. Very exact in the forms of behaviour or mutual intercourse; very exact in the observance of rules prescribed by custom; exact to excess. [It. puntiglióso.]

Punctiliously, pungk-ti'li-us-li, adv. With exactness or great nicety.

Punctot, pungk'tō, n. The point in fencing.

Punctual, pungk'tū-al, a. Observant of nice points; punctilious, particularly in observing time, appointments, or promises; done at the exact time. [Fr. ponctuel—L. punctum, a point.]

Punctuality, pungk-tū-al i-ti, n. Quality of being punctual. [Fr. ponctualité.]

Punctually, pungk'tū-al-li, adv. With punctuality.

Punctuate, pungk'tū-āt, vt. To mark with points; to designate sentences or other divisions of a writing by points. ppr. punctuating, pret. & pp. punctuated. [Fr. ponctuer.]

Punctuation, pungk-tū-ā'sho·., n. Act or art of pointing a writing or discourse; the art of dividing words and sentences by means of marks or points. [Fr. ponctuation.]

Puncture, pungk'tūr, n. The act of pricking with a pointed instrument; or a small hole made by it.—vt. To pierce with a small pointed instrument. ppr. puncturing. pret. & pp. punctured. [L. punctūra—pungo, to prick.]

Pungency, pun'jen-si, n. Quality of being pungent; the power of pricking or piercing; sharpness, acridness; power to pierce the mind or excite keen remorse; keenness, as of sarcasm.

Pungent, pun'jent, a. Pricking; piercing; affecting the organs of sense with a pricking sensation; acrid; stimulating; acrimonious; keen; biting; stinging. [L. pungens—pungo, to prick.]

Pungently, pun'jent-li, adv. In a pungent manner; acrimoniously.

Puniness, pū'ni-nes, n. Littleness.

Punish, pun'ish, vt. To afflict with pain, loss, or calamity, as a penalty for a crime or fault; to afflict with pain, &c., with a view to amendment; to correct. [Fr. punir, ppr. punissant—L. punio, to punish.]

Punishable, pun'ish-a-bl, a. That may or ought to be punished; worthy of punishment. [Fr. punissable.]

Punishment, pun'ish-ment, n. Act of punishing; pain inflicted on a person for a crime or offence, by the authority to which the offender is subject.

Punning, pun'ing, p.n. The art or practice of using puns.

Punster, pun'stėr, n. One who puns or is skilled in punning; a low wit.

Punt, punt, n. A flat-bottomed boat used in calking and repairing ships, or in fishing. [Sp. ponton.]

Puny, pū'ni, a. Born after; inferior; of an under rate; small and feeble. [contracted from Fr. puîné.]

Pup, pup, vi. To bring forth whelps or young, as the female of the canine species.—n. A puppy. ppr. pupping, pret. & pp. pupped. [G. puppe, a doll, a neat baby.]

Pupa, pū'pa, n. Pupæ, pl. The third or last state but one of insect existence, the first being the egg, and the second the caterpillar. [L.]

Pupil, pū'pil, n. The apple of the eye; a small aperture in the centre of the iris for the admission of the rays of light. [L. pupilla, a little lass.]

Pupil, pū'pil, n. A boy; a youth or scholar of either sex under the care of a tutor; a disciple; a ward; a youth or person under the care of a guardian; a boy or girl under the age of puberty. [L. pupillus, an orphan boy—pupus, a boy.]

Pupilage, pū'pil-āj, n. State of being a pupil or ward; young age; state of being a scholar; wardship; minority.

Pupilary, pū'pil-a-ri, a. Pertaining to a pupil or ward. [Fr. pupillaire; L. pupillaris.]

Puppet, pup'pet, n. A small image in the human form, moved by a wire in a mock drama; a wooden tragedian; a word of contempt, used of a person who is under the control of another. [Fr. poupée.]

Puppet-show, pup'pet-shō, n. A mock drama performed by puppets.

Puppy, pup'pi, n. A whelp; one of the young progeny of a bitch; applied to persons, a name expressing extreme contempt. [from Fr. poupée, a doll, a baby.]

Puppyish, pup'pi-ish, a. Like a puppy; conceited.

Puppyism, pup'pi-izm, n. Qualities of a puppy; extreme meanness or conceit.

Pur, Purr, pėr, vi. To utter a low, murmuring, continued sound, as a cat.—vt. To signify by purring.—n. The low murmuring continued sound of a cat. [formed from the sound.]

ch, chain; j, job; g, go; ng, sing; ᴛʜ then; th, thin; w, wig; wh, whig; zh, azure; † obsolete.

Purblind, pĕr'blīnd, *a.* Dim-sighted, so as to require to *look near and steadily* at an object in order to see it properly; near-sighted; seeing obscurely. [said to be from *pore* and *blind.*]

Purchasable, pĕr'chăs-a-bl, *a. That may be purchased,* bought, or obtained for a consideration. [from *purchase.*]

Purchase, pĕr'chăs, *vt.* To obtain, *as the object of pursuit;* to buy; to obtain, as property by paying an equivalent in money; to obtain by an expense of labour. *ppr.* purchasing, *pret. & pp.* purchased.—*n. Act of purchasing* anything; act of obtaining or acquiring the title to lands and tenements by money, deed, gift, or any means, except by descent; a buying; that which is purchased; that which is obtained by labour, art, &c.; any mechanical force applied to the raising of heavy bodies; robbery‡. [Fr. *pourchasser—chasser,* to chase.]

Purchaser, pĕr'chăs-ẽr, *n. One who purchases;* one who acquires the property of anything by paying an equivalent in money.

Pure, pūr, *a. Clean; free from everything that can render unclean;* clear; free from moral defilement; holy; genuine; true; not vitiated; free from guilt; chaste; not vitiated by improper words, as speech; mere; that and that only; sheer. [Fr. *pur*—L. *purus*—Sans. *pâ,* to purify.]

Purely, pūr'li, *adv. In a pure manner.*

Pureness, pūr'nes, *n. State or quality of being pure;* clearness; freedom from guilt; simplicity; chasteness.

Purgation, pĕr-gā'shon, *n. Act or operation of purging;* act of cleansing from a crime or suspicion of guilt. [Fr.]

Purgative, pĕr'gă-tiv, *a. Having the power o' purging;* having the power of evacuating the intestines; cathartic. *n.* A medicine that *purges,* a cathartic. [Fr. *purgatif.*]

Purgatorial, pĕr-gă-tō'ri-al, *a. Pertaining to purgatory.*

Purgatory, pĕr'gă-tŏ-ri, *n.* Among Roman Catholics and others, a place or state after death, in which the souls of persons *are purified.—a. Tending to purge* or cleanse; cleansing; expiatory. [Fr. *purgatoire.*]

Purge, pĕrj, *vt. To make pure;* to cleanse by separating whatever is impure; to clear from guilt; to clear from accusation; to remove, as what is offensive. *vi. To become pure;* to have frequent evacuations by means of a cathartic. *ppr.* purging, *pret. & pp.* purged.—*n.* A medicine that *purges;* a cathartic. [L. *purgo—purus,* pure, and *ago,* to do.]

Purging, pĕrj'ing, *p.n.* A diarrhœa or dysentery; looseness of bowels.

Purification, pū'ri-fi-kā''shon, *n. Act of purifying;* the act of separating from anything that which is foreign to it; act of cleansing ceremonially; a cleansing from guilt; the extinction of sinful inclinations. [Fr.]

Purified, pū'ri-fīd, *p.a. Made pure* and clear.

Purify, pū'ri-fī, *vt. To make pure* or *clear;* to remove, as whatever renders unclean; to free from guilt; to clear from barbarisms.—*vi. To grow or become pure* or *clear. ppr.* purifying, *pret. & pp.* purified. [Fr. *purifier*—L. *purus,* and *facio,* to make.]

Purifying, pū'ri-fī-ing, *p.a. Making pure;* cleansing from pollution.—*p.n. Act or operation of making pure.*

Purism, pūr'ism, *n.* Practice or affectation of *rigid purity;* niceness in the use of words. [Fr. *purisme.*]

Purist, pūr'ist, *n. One excessively nice* in the use of words, &c. [Fr. *puriste.*]

Puritan, pū'ri-tan, *n.* One of those who, in the reign of Queen Elizabeth, professed to follow the *pure* word of God in opposition to human authority; one who is strict in his religious life, (in contempt)‡.—*a. Pertaining to the Puritans,* or early dissenters from the Church of England. [from *pure.*]

Puritanical, pūr-i-tan'ik-al, *a. Pertaining to the Puritans* or their doctrines and practice; exact; rigid.

Puritanically, pūr-i-tan'ik-al-li, *adv.* With the exact or rigid notions or manners of the *Puritans.*

Puritanism, pū'ri-tan-izm, *n. The notions or practice of Puritans.*

Purity, pū'ri-ti, *n. State or quality of being pure;* freedom from foreign admixture; cleanness; freedom from foulness; freedom from the defilement of sin; chastity; freedom from any sinister views; freedom from foreign idioms. [Fr. *pureté;* L. *purus,* pure—Sans. *pâ,* to purify.]

Purl, pĕrl, *vi.* To run or flow with a gentle noise, as a stream; to flow or run with a murmuring sound.—*n.* A gentle, continued murmur of a small stream of rippling water. [G. *brüllen,* to roar, to brawl.]

Purlieu, pĕrl'ū, *n.* Primarily, *a place* bordering on a forest, which was *made pure or free* from the laws of the forest; a limit; a certain limited extent or district. [Fr. *pur,* pure, and *lieu,* place.]

Purling, pĕrl'ing, *p.a.* Murmuring, as a brook.—*p.n.* Gentle murmur, as of a stream.

Purloin, pĕr-loin', *vt. To remove* for one's self; to steal; to take by theft; to take by plagiarism.— *vi.* To practise theft. [Fr. *pour*—L. *pro,* for, and *éloigner,* to remove.]

Purloiner, pĕr-loin'ẽr, *n.* A thief; a plagiary.

Purple, pĕr'pl, *n. A colour* produced by the *mixture* of red and blue; a purple colour or dress; the badge of the Roman emperors; imperial government in the Roman empire; a common English flower.—*a.* Designating a much-admired colour composed of red and blue blended; blood-red; dyed with blood.—*vt. To make purple,* or to dye of a red colour. *ppr.* purpling, *pret. & pp.* purpled. [Fr. *pourpre*—L. *purpura*—Gr. *phurô,* to mix.]

Purpled, pĕr'pld, *p.a. Made purple.*

Purplish, pĕr'pl-ish,*a. Somewhat purple.*

Purport, pĕr'pōrt, *n. That which conveys* the meaning; design; tenor; meaning; import.—*vi. To convey* the meaning; to intend; to intend to show; to mean; to signify. [Fr. *pour,* for, and *porter,* to carry.]

Purpose, pĕr'pŏs, *n.* That which one *sets before* himself as an object to be accomplished; the end to which the view is directed; design; result; consequence, good or bad; conversation‡. *vi.* To propose, as something to be done; to design; to resolve; to have an intention; to determine on some end to be accomplished.—*vt.* To determine upon; to design. *ppr.* purposing, *pret. & pp.* purposed. [Fr. *propos*—L. *pro,* and *pono, positum,* to place.]

Purposeless, pĕr'pŏs-les, *a. Having no purpose* or effect.

Purposely, pĕr'pŏs-li, *adv.* By design.

Purr, pĕr, *vi. See* Pur.

Purring, pĕr'ing, *p.n. The murmuring noise* of a cat.

Purse, pĕrs, *n. A leather bag;* a small bag in which money is carried in the pocket; a sum of money offered as the prize of winning in a horse-race.—*vt. To put in a purse;* to draw together, as the mouth of *a purse* when tied; to contract into wrinkles (with up). *ppr.* pursing, *pret. & pp.* pursed. [Fr. *bourse,* a purse—Gr. *bursa.*]

Purser, pĕrs'ẽr, *n.* A commissioned officer in the navy, who keeps the accounts of the ship to which he belongs, and also has charge of the money, provisions, clothing, &c.

Pursership, pĕrs'ẽr-ship, *n. The office of a purser.*

Pursiness, pĕrs'i-nes, *n. A state of being pursy,* or swelled or bloated; shortness of breath. [from *pursy.*]

Purslane, pĕrs'lān, *n.* A common succulent plant, often used as a pot-herb, and for salads. [It *porcellana.*]

Pursuance, pĕr-sū'ans, *n. Act of pursuing;* pursuit; continued exertion to accomplish something.

Pursuant, pĕr-sū'ant, *a.* Done in consequence or *prosecution* of anything; agreeable to. [Fr. *poursuivant.*]

Pursue, pĕr-sū', *vt. To follow forth;* to proceed after; to take and proceed in, without following another; to chase; to seek; to use measures to obtain; to follow with enmity; to continue; to follow as an example; to imitate; to strive to reach or gain.—*vi.* To go on. *ppr.* pursuing, *pret. & pp.* pursued. [Fr. *poursuivre*—L. *pro,* and *sequor,* to follow.]

Pursuer, pĕr-sū'ẽr, *n. One who pursues* or follows; one who chases; one who follows in haste with a view to overtake.

Pursuing, pĕr-sū'ing, *p.a.* Hastening after to overtake; continuing.

Pursuit, pĕr-sūt', *n. Act of pursuing;* following with haste, either for sport or in hostility: a following with a view to reach; endeavour to attain to; quest; proceeding; course of business; prosecution, continuance of endeavour. [Fr. *poursuite.*]

Pursuivant, pĕr'swi-vant, *n. An attendant;* a state messenger; a junior officer in the Heralds' College, who afterwards succeeds to higher employments. [Fr. *poursuivant.*]

Pursy, pĕrs'i, *a.* Short-breathed; fat, short, and thick. [Fr. *poussif,* broken-winded.]

Purtenance, pĕr'tē-nans, *n. That which pertains to;* applied to the pluck of an animal. [Fr. *appartenance.*]

Purulence, pū'rū-lens, *n. The generation of pus* or matter; pus. [L. *purulentia.*]

Purulent, pū'rū-lent, *a. Consisting of pus* or matter; partaking of the nature of pus. [L. *purulentus.*]

Purvey, pĕr-vā', *vt. To provide;* to provide with conveniences; to procure. *vi. To provide;* to purchase provisions. [Fr. *pourvoir;* L. *pro,* and *video,* to see.]

Purveyance, pĕr-vā'ans, *n. Act of purveying;* procurement of provisions. [Norm. *purveaunce,* providence.]

Purveyor, pĕr-vā'or, *n. One who provides* victuals, or whose business is to make provision for the table. [Fr. *pourvoyeur.*]

Pus, pus, *n. Rotten matter;* the fluid formed in the process of *suppuration;* the matter of a sore. [L.—Gr. *puon,* discharge from a sore.]

Push, push, *vt. To thrust;* to press against with force; to drive by pressure;

to butt; to thrust the points of horns against; to urge forward; to enforce; to drive to a conclusion; to importune; to tease.—*vi.* To make a thrust; to make an attack; to burst out.—*n.* A thrust with a pointed instrument; any pressure; an assault; a forcible onset; a vigorous effort; exigence; extremity; a sudden emergency. [Fr. *pousser*, to push—L. *pello*, *pulsum*, to push or strike.]

Pushing, push'ing, *p.a.* Pressing forward in business; enterprising.

Pusillanimity, pū-sil-la-nim″i-ti, *n.* Quality of being pusillanimous; want of that strength of mind which constitutes courage; cowardice. [Fr. *pusillanimité*.]

Pusillanimous, pū-sil-lan'im-us, *a.* Little-minded; mean-spirited; fainthearted; destitute of that strength of mind which constitutes fortitude; proceeding from weakness of mind. [Late L. *pusillanimis*—L. *pusus*, for *pupus*, a little child, and *animus*, the mind.]

Pusillanimously, pū-sil-lan'im-us-li, *adv.* With want of courage.

Puss, pus, *n.* The fondling name of a cat; the sportsman's name for a hare. [Ir. and Gael. *pus*, a cat.]

Pussy, pus'i, *n.* A diminutive term for puss.

Pustular, pus'tū-lär, *a.* Covered with pustules, or pustule-like prominences.

Pustulated, pus'tū-lāt-ed, *p.a.* Covered with pustule-like prominences.

Pustule, pus'tūl, *n.* A small blister, or a small elevation of the cuticle, containing pus. [Fr.—L. *pustula*.]

Pustulous, pus'tūl-us, *a.* Full of pustules; covered with pustules. [L. *pustulōsus*.]

Put, put, *vt.* To lay in any place; to cause to be in any state or situation; to apply; to set to employment; to introduce suddenly, as a word; to propose; to present; to state; to bring into a state of mind or temper; to urge; to incite; to offer; to cause or produce, as a difference. *ppr.* putting, *pret. & pp.* put. [Dan. *putte*.]

Putative, pū'ta-tiv, *a.* Supposed; reputed; commonly thought or deemed. [Fr. *putatif*—L. *puto*, to suppose, to reckon, to think.]

Putrefaction, pū-trē-fak'shon, *n.* The process of putrefying; state of growing rotten; rottenness; a natural process by which animal and vegetable bodies are decomposed. [Fr. *putréfaction*.]

Putrefactive, pū-trē-fak'tiv, *a.* Pertaining to putrefaction; causing putrefaction. [Sp. *putrefactivo*.]

Putrefied, pū'trē-fīd, *p.a.* Rotten; dissolved.

Putrefy, pū'trē-fī, *vt.* To cause to rot; to cause to be decomposed; to make morbid, carious, or gangrenous.—*vi.* To become rotten; to rot; to have the constituent elements newly arranged, forming new compounds. *ppr.* putrefying, *pret. & pp.* putrefied. [Fr. *putréfier*—L. *putris*, rotten, and *facio*, to make.]

Putrefying, pū'trē-fī-ing, *p.a.* Making rotten; causing to be decomposed.

Putrescence, pū-tres'ens, *n.* The state of becoming putrescent or rotten; a putrid state. [from *putrescent*.]

Putrescent, pū-tres'ent, *a.* Growing rotten; passing from an organized state into another state, in which the elements are newly arranged; pertaining to the process of putrefaction. [L. *putrescens—putris*, rotten.]

Putrid, pū'trid, *a.* Rotten; stinking; indicating a state of dissolution; tending to disorganize the substances composing the body; proceeding from putrefaction; crumbling; dusty. [Fr. *putride*—L. *putris*, rotten.]

Putridity, pū-trid'i-ti, *n.* State of being putrid; corruption; rottenness. [Fr. *putridité*.]

Putter-on, put-ėr-on', *n.* An inciter.

Puttock, put'tok, *n.* A species of kite.

Putty, put'ti, *n.* A mixture of linseed-oil and powdered chalk, used by glaziers.—*vt.* To cement with putty; to fill up with putty. *ppr.* puttying, *pret. & pp.* puttied. [Fr. *potée*.]

Puzzle, puz'l, *vt.* To pose; to involve in embarrassment; to put to a stand; to entangle. *ppr.* puzzling, *pret. & pp.* puzzled.—*n.* Perplexity; something to try ingenuity. [dimin. of *pose*.]

Puzzler, puz'l-ėr, *n.* One who perplexes.

Puzzling, puz'l-ing, *p.a.* Perplexing; bewildering.

Pygmy, pig'mi, *n.* See PIGMY.

Pyramid, pi'ra-mid, *n.* A solid body standing on a triangular, square, or polygonal base, and terminating in a point at the top; an edifice, in the form of a pyramid, for sepulchral and religious purposes, &c.; as, the pyramids of Egypt. [Fr. *pyramide*—Gr. *pyramis*.]

Pyramidal, pi-ram'id-al, *a.* Formed like a pyramid; relating to a pyramid. [Fr. *pyramidale*.]

Pyramidally, pi-ram'id-al-li, *adv.* In the form of a pyramid.

Pyramidic, Pyramidical, pi-ra-mid'ik, pi-ra-mid'ik-al, *a.* Having the form of a pyramid; relating to a pyramid.

Pyramidically, pi-ra-mid'ik-al-li, *adv.* In the form of a pyramid.

Pyre, pir, *n.* A pile to be burned; a funeral pile. [L. *pyra*—Gr. *pūr*, fire.]

Pyrites, pi-ri'tēz, *n.* Fire-stone, which gives sparks with steel; a combination of sulphur with iron, copper, cobalt, or nickel, presenting a white or yellowish metallic lustre. [Gr. *purītēs—pur, puros*, fire.]

Pyritic, pi-rit'ik, *a.* Pertaining to pyrites.

Pyroligneous, pi-rō-lig'nē-us, *a.* Procured by the distillation of wood. [Gr. *pur*, fire, and L. *lignum*, wood.]

Pyrometer, pi-rom'et-ėr, *n.* An instrument for measuring the expansion of bodies by *heat*; an instrument for measuring degrees of heat above those indicated by the mercurial thermometer. [Gr. *pur*, fire, and *metron*, measure.]

Pyrometric, pi-rō-met'rik, *a.* Pertaining to the pyrometer, or to its use.

Pyrotechnic, pi-rō-tek'nik, *a.* Pertaining to fireworks, or the *art* of forming them. [Fr. *pyrotechnique*—Gr. *pur*, fire, and *techné*, art.]

Pyrotechnics, pi-rō-tek'niks, *n.* The art of making fireworks; particularly of making rockets, &c. [Fr. *pyrotechnie*.]

Pyrotechnist, pi-rō-tek'nist, *n.* One skilled in pyrotechnics.

Pythagorean, pi-tha'gō-rē″an, *a.* Belonging to the philosophy of Pythagoras.—*n.* A follower of Pythagoras, the founder of the Italic set of philosophers.

Pythoness, pi'thon-es, *n.* The priestess who gave oracular answers at *Delphi*, in Greece; any female supposed to have a spirit of divination. [from Gr. *puthōn*.]

Pythonist, pī'thon-ist, *n.* A conjurer.

Pyx, piks, *n.* A *box*, used in English coinage, as a place of deposit for sample coins; the box in which the host is kept (Rom. Cath.) [Gr. *puxis*.]

Q.

Quack, kwak, *vi.* To cry like a duck; to boast; to practise arts of quackery. *n.* The cry of a duck; a boaster; one who pretends to skill or knowledge which he does not possess; a boastful pretender to medical skill; a mountebank.—*a.* Pertaining to quackery; falsely pretending to cure diseases. [D. *kwaken*.]

Quackery, kwak'ė-ri, *n.* The character and practices of a quack; the boastful pretensions of an ignoramus, particularly in medicine; empiricism.

Quackish, kwak'ish, *a.* Like a quack; boasting of skill not possessed.

Quadragesima, kwod-ra-je'si-ma, *n.* Lent; so called because it consists of forty days. [L. *quadragesimus*, the fortieth.]

Quadragesimal, kwod-ra-je'si-mal, *a.* Belonging to Lent; used in Lent.

Quadrangle, kwod-rang'gl, *n.* A plane figure, having *four angles*, and consequently four sides; a four-cornered space inclosed by buildings; the inner square or rectangular court of a building. [L. *quatuor*, four, and *angulus*, an angle.]

Quadrangular, kwod-rang'gū-lär, *a.* Four-cornered; having four angles, and consequently four sides.

Quadrant, kwod'rant, *n.* The fourth part of a circle, or of its circumference; an instrument used in astronomy and navigation for taking altitudes and angles. [L. *quadrans—quatuor*, four.]

Quadrantal, kwod-rant'al, *a.* Containing the fourth part of any measure; pertaining to a quadrant. [L. *quadrantālis*.]

Quadrate, kwod'rāt, *a. Squared*; square; having four equal sides and four right-angles.—*vi.* To square with; to suit; to correspond; to agree; to be accommodated (with *with*). *ppr.* quadrating, *pret. & pp.* quadrated. [L. *quadratus*—*quadro*, to make square.]

Quadratic, kwod-rat'ik, *a. Square*; denoting a square, or pertaining to it. [L. *quadratus*.]

Quadrature, kwod'ra-tūr, *n.* The re-

ducing of a figure to a square; as, the quadrature of the circle; the position of one heavenly body in respect to another when distant from it 90°, or a quadrant. [L. *quadratūra.*]

Quadrennial, kwod-ren'i-al, *a. Comprising four years;* occurring once in four years. [L. *quadriennis—quatuor,* four, and *annus,* a ear.]

Quadrilateral, kwod-ri-lat'er-al, *a. Having four sides,* and consequently four angles.—*n.* A plane figure *having four sides,* and consequently four angles; a quadrangular figure. [L. *quatuor,* and *latus, lateris,* a side.]

Quadriliteral, kwod-ri-lit'er-al, *a. Consisting of four letters.* [L. *quatuor,* and *litera,* a letter.]

Quadrille, ka-dril', *n.* A kind of dance, made up of sets of dancers, *four* in each set; a piece of music composed for the above dance. [Fr.—L. *quadra,* a square —*quatuor,* four.]

Quadrinomial, kwod-ri-nō'mi-al, *a. Consisting of four terms,* as an algebraic quantity.—*n.* An algebraic quantity consisting of *four terms.* [L. *quatuor,* and *nomen,* a name.]

Quadrisyllable, kwod-ri-sil'la-bl, *n.* A word consisting of *four syllables.* [L. *quatuor,* and *syllable.*]

Quadrivial, kwod-ri'vi-al, *a. Having four ways* meeting in a point. [L. *quadri-ium—quatuor,* and *via,* a way.]

Quadruped, kwod'rū-ped, *a. Having four legs and feet.*—*n.* An animal having four legs and feet, as a horse, a lion, &c. [L. *quadrupes—pes, pedis,* a foot.]

Quadrupedal, kwod-rū-pēd'al, *a. Having four feet.*

Quadruple, kwod'rū-pl, *a. Fourfold;* four times told.—*n. Four times* the sum or number.—*vt.* To *make fourfold;* to multiply by four.—*vi.* To become *fourfold.* *ppr.* quadrupling, *pret. & pp.* quadrupled. [L. *quadruplus— quatuor,* and *plico,* to fold.]

Quadruplicate, kwod-rū'pli-kāt, *a. Fourfold;* four times repeated. [L. *quadruplicatus.*]

Quadruplication, kwod-rū'pli-kā"shon, *n. Act of making fourfold,* or the taking four times the simple sum.

Quaff, kwäf, *vt.* To drain to the bottom; to swallow in large draughts.—*vi.* To drink deep or largely. [Sw. Goth. *qvaf,* an abyss, the bottom of the sea.]

Quaffer, kwäf'er, *n. One who quaffs.*

Quag, kwag, *n.* See QUAGMIRE.

Quaggy, kwag'i, *a. Quaking;* yielding to the feet, or trembling under the foot, as soft wet earth.

Quagmire, kwag'mīr, *n. Quake-mire;* soft wet land, which has a surface firm enough to bear a person, but which *quakes* or yields under the feet.

Quail, kwāl, *vi.* To fail in spirits; to sink into dejection; to faint; to tremble; to slacken. [Old G. *quelan,* to languish.]

Quail, kwāl, *n.* A gallinaceous bird, closely allied to the partridge. [It. *quaglia.*]

Quaint, kwānt, *a.* Originally, *combed;* neat; having petty elegance; artfully framed; affected; fanciful; singular. [Old Fr. *coint*—L. *como, comptus,* to comb.]

Quaintly, kwānt'li, *adv.* Nicely; exactly; with petty neatness; affectedly.

Quaintness, kwānt'nes, *n. Quality of being quaint;* oddness; peculiarity.

Quake, kwāk, *vi.* To *shake;* to quiver; to be agitated with quick but short motions continually repeated; to shake with violent convulsions; to move, as the earth under the feet.—*vt.*† To frighten. *ppr.* quaking, *pret. & pp.* quaked.—*n. A shake;* a trembling; a tremulous agitation. [Sax. *cwacian.*]

Quaker, kwāk'ėr, *n. One who quakes;* but usually, one of the religious sect called the *Society of Friends.*

Quakeringly†, kwāk'ėr-ing-li, *adv.* In a quaking manner.

Quaking, kwāk'ing, *p.a. Shaking;* trembling.—*p.n. A shaking;* tremulous agitation; trepidation.

Quakingly, kwāk'ing-li, *adv. In a quaking manner;* tremblingly.

Qualification, kwo'li-fi-kā"shon, *n. Act of qualifying;* any natural endowment or any acquirement which fits a person for a place, office, or employment, or enables him to sustain any character with success; legal power; diminution; restriction; limitation. [Fr.—L. *qualis,* and *facio,* to make.]

Qualified, kwo'li-fīd, *p.a. Having qualification;* competent; modified.

Qualify, kwo'li-fī, *vt.* To *make such as is required;* to fit or adapt for anything; to furnish with the knowledge, &c., necessary for any place or purpose; to furnish with legal power; to diminish; to ease; to modify; to regulate; to limit by exceptions; to vary; to temper; to dilute.—*vi.* To become *qualified;* to take the necessary steps for rendering one's self capable of holding any office or enjoying any privilege; to establish a claim to exercise the elective franchise. *ppr.* qualifying, *pret. & pp.* qualified. [Fr. *qualifier*—L. *qualis,* of what kind, and *facio,* to make.]

Qualifying, kwo'li-fī-ing, *p.a. Furnishing with the necessary qualities;* tempering; restraining.

Qualitative, kwo'li-ta-tiv, *a. Relating to quality;* estimable according to quality.

Quality, kwo'li-ti, *n. Property;* attribute; that which belongs to a substance, or can be predicated of it; virtue or particular power of producing certain effects; moral characteristic, good or bad; mood; accomplishment; comparative rank; superior rank; persons of high rank, collectively. [Fr. *qualité*—L. *qualis,* of such a sort—Sans. *kā,* what?]

Qualm, kwäm, *n. A sinking, as if in death;* a fainting; a sudden fit of nausea; a scruple or uneasiness of conscience. [Sax. *cwealm,* death—*cwellan,* to kill.]

Qualmish, kwäm-ish, *a.* Sick at the stomach; affected with nausea or sickly languor.

Quantitative, kwon'ti-ta-tiv, *a. Relating to quantity.*

Quantity, kwon'ti-ti, *n.* The attribute of being so much, and not more or less; whatever admits of increase or diminution; whatever can be numbered or measured; a mass of matter of indeterminate dimensions; an indefinite extent of space; the measure of a syllable; a general conception; the relative duration of a note in music. [Fr. *quantité*—L. *quantus,* how great.]

Quarantine, kwo'ran-tin, *n.* Originally a space of *forty days* (now of variable length) during which a ship arriving in port and suspected of being infected with a malignant contagious disease, is obliged to forbear all intercourse with the city or place. [It. *quarantina,* forty.]

Quarrel†, kwo'rel, *n.* A dart discharged by a cross-bow. [W. *cwarel.*]

Quarrel, kwo'rel, *n. A complaint;* a brawl; a contest; a feud; a disputed cause; breach of friendship; cause of dispute; ill-will, or reason to complain; ground of objection.—*vi.* To *find fault;* to dispute violently; to scold; to disagree; not to be in accordance with in form or essence. *ppr.* quarrelling, *pret. & pp.* quarrelled. [Fr. *querelle*—L. *queror,* to complain.]

Quarrelling, kwo'rel-ing, *p.a. Act of one who quarrels;* a disputing with angry words; brawling; altercation.

Quarrelsome, kwo'rel-sum, *a. Apt or disposed to quarrel;* choleric.

Quarrelsomeness, kwo'rel-sum-nes, *n. The quality of being quarrelsome.*

Quarrier, kwo'ri-ėr, *n. A worker at a quarry.*

Quarry, kwo'ri, *n.* The game which a hawk is *seeking* or has killed; a part of the entrails of the beast taken, given to the hounds; a heap of game killed. [from Fr. *quérir,* L. *quaero,* to seek.]

Quarry, kwo'ri, *n.* A place where stones are dug from the earth, or separated from a large mass of rocks, and hewed or squared.—*vt.* To *dig or take from a quarry.* *ppr.* quarrying, *pret. & pp.* quarried. [Old Fr. *quarriere*—L. *quadro,* to square.]

Quarrying, kwo'ri-ing, *p.n. The act or business of digging stones from a quarry.*

Quart, kwat, *n.* The *fourth part* of a gallon; two pints; a vessel containing the fourth of a gallon. [L. *quartus,* the fourth.]

Quartan, kwa'tan, *n.* An intermitting ague that occurs every *fourth day,* or with intermissions of seventy-two hours. [L. *quartana.*]

Quarter, kwa'tėr, *n. The fourth part* of anything; the fourth part of 112 lbs. avoirdupois; in dry measure, the fourth of a ton in weight, or 8 bushels of grain; the fourth part of a yard in cloth-measure; the fourth part of the moon's period; a region in the hemisphere; one of the large divisions of the globe; a point of the compass; one of the four cardinal points; a particular region of a town, city, or country; the sparing of the life of a captive when in one's power; amity; one-fourth part of the carcass of an animal, including a limb; the part of a shoe which forms the side from the heel to the vamp; a fourth part of the year; the part of a ship's side which lies toward the stern; (pl.) military stations; lodgings.—*vt.* To *divide into four equal parts;* to divide into distinct regions; to station, as soldiers for lodging; to punish by tearing in pieces by four horses, one attached to each limb of a criminal.—*vi.* To *place one's self in quarters;* to lodge. [Fr. *quartier.*]

Quarter-day, kwa'tėr-dā, *n. The day* that completes *three months,* or the quarter of a year; the day when quarterly payments are made of rent, interest, or salary.

Quarter-deck, kwa'tėr-dek, *n.* That part of the upper *deck* of a ship abaft the main-mast.

Quartering, kwa'tėr-ing, *p.n. Act of dividing into quarters;* assignment of quarters for soldiers; the disposal of various coats of arms in one shield.

Quarterly, kwa'tėr-li, *a.* Recurring at the end of each *quarter* of the year. *adv. By quarters;* once in a quarter of a year.—*n.* A periodical work published *quarterly.*

Quarter-master, kwa'tėr-mas-tėr, *n.* An officer in the army whose duty is to

provide *quarters*, &c., for the army, and superintend the supplies; a petty officer in a ship of war who attends to the helm, signals, &c., under the direction of the master.
Quartern, kwạ'tẽrn, n. The *fourth* part of a pint; a gill.
Quartern-loaf, kwạ'tẽrn-lōf, n. A *loaf* of bread made out of a *quarter* of a stone of flour, the stone being 14 lbs.
Quarter-sessions, kwạ'tẽr-se-shonz, n. A court held every three months in each county of England, by at least two justices of the peace.
Quartette, kwạ-tet', n. A musical composition *in four parts*, each part performed by a single voice or instrument; a stanza of four lines. [It. *quartetto*.]
Quarto, kwạ'tō, n. A book of the size of *the fourth* of a sheet; a size made by twice folding a sheet, which then makes four leaves.—*a.* Denoting the size of a book in which a sheet makes *four* leaves. [L. *quartus*.]
Quartz, kwạts, n. The name given to numerous varieties of rock-crystal, or the purer varieties of silica. [G. *quars*.]
Quartzose, kwạts'ōs, *a.* *Containing quartz*; resembling quartz.
Quash, kwosh, *vt.* *To crush*; to subdue suddenly; to quell; to abate or make void. [Sax. *cwysan*—L. *quatio*, to shake.]
Quashing, kwosh'ing, p.n. Act of annulling, abating, or making void.
Quassia, kwas'i-a, n. A South American plant, whose wood is intensely bitter, and whose bark is used as a tonic. [from *Quassy*, a negro who discovered its medicinal virtues.]
Quat, kwot, n. A troublesome insignificant person.
Quatch†, kwotsh, *a.* Flat.
Quaternary, kwa-tẽr'na-ri, *a.* *Consisting of four*; by fours.—*n.* The number *four*. [L. *quaternarius*.]
Quaternion, kwa-tẽr'ni-on, n. *The number four*; a file of four soldiers. [L. *quaternio*.]
Quatrain, kā'trān, n. *A stanza of four lines* rhyming alternately. [Fr. from *quatre*, from L. *quatuor*, four.]
Quaver, kwā'vẽr, *vi.* *To shake* the voice; to produce a shake on a musical instrument; to tremble; to vibrate.—*n.* A *shake* or rapid vibration of the voice, or a shake on an instrument of music; a note in music, equal to the eighth of a semibreve. [Sp. *quiebro*, a quaver.]
Quavering, kwā'vẽr-ing, p.a. Trembling; vibra ing.—*n.* *Act of shaking the voice*, or of making rapid vibrations of sound on an instrument of music.
Quay, kē, n. A *mole* or *bank* formed on the side of a river; an artificial bank or wharf for the purpose of loading and unloading vessels. [Fr. *quai*.]
Quean†, kwēn, n. A woman; a slut.
Queasily, kwē'zi-li, *adv.* *In a queasy manner*; with squeamishness.
Queasiness, kwē'zi-nes, n. *State of being queasy*; qualmishness.
Queasy, kwē'zi, *a.* *Having pain at the stomach*; affected with nausea; fastidious; causing nausea. [Icel. *qveisa*, colic.]
Queen, kwēn, n. *A woman*; the wife of a king or sovereign; a woman who is the sovereign of a kingdom; a female who is pre-eminent among others; a female who presides; the sovereign of a swarm of bees; one of the pieces at chess.—*vi.* To play the queen. [Sax. *cwen*, a woman; Goth. *qvens*.]
Queenly, kwēn'li, *a.* *Like a queen*; becoming a queen; suitable to a queen.
Queen-mother, kwēn-muTH'ẽr, n. A queen-dowager who is also *mother* of the reigning king or *queen*.
Queen's-Bench, kwēnz-bensh', n. The supreme court of common law in England.
Queer, kwēr, *a.* *Cross; transverse; cross-grained*; perverse; odd; whimsical. [G. *quer*, across, athwart.]
Queerish, kwēr'ish, *a.* *Rather queer*.
Queerly, kwēr'li, *adv.* In an odd or singular manner.
Queerness, kwēr'nes, n. *State or quality of being queer*; oddity; singularity.
Quell, kwel, *vt.* Originally, to kill; to crush; to cause to cease, as a sedition; to calm; to reduce or bring down, as pride.—*n.†* Murder. [Sax. *cwellan*, to kill.]
Queller, kwel'ẽr, n. One who crushes or subdues.
Quench, kwench, *vt.* *To put out*; to extinguish; to quiet; to destroy; to stifle; to allay.—*vi.* To go out; to cool. [Sax. *cwencan*.]
Quenchless, kwench'les, *a.* *That cannot be quenched*; inextinguishable.
Querimonious, kwe-ri-mō'ni-us, *a.* *Apt to complain; complaining*; querulous. [from L. *querimonia*, complaint—*queror*, to complain.]
Querimoniously, kwe-ri-mō'ni-us-li, *adv.* *In a querimonious manner*.
Querist, kwēr'ist, n. *One who inquires* or asks questions. [L. *quæro*, to search for.]
Quern, kwẽrn, n. A hand-mill for *grinding* grain. [Sax. *cwyrn*.]
Querulous, kwe'rū-lus, *a.* *Full of complaints*; expressing complaint. [L. *querulus*.]
Querulously, kwe'rū-lus-li, *adv.* *In a complaining manner*.
Querulousness, kwe'rū-lus-nes, n. Quality of being querulous.
Query, kwē'ri, n. *A question*; an inquiry to be answered or resolved.—*vi.* *To ask a question* or questions.—*vt.* *To seek*; to inquire; to doubt of. *ppr.* querying, *pret. & pp.* queried. [from L. *quæro*, to seek.]
Quest, kwest, n. *Act of seeking; search; pursuit*; request; solicitation; a jury of inquest. [Old Fr.—L. *quæro*, to seek.]
Question, kwest'shon, n. *Act of asking; that which is asked*; inquiry; discussion; discourse; subject of debate; doubt; trial; judicial inquiry; examination by torture.—*vi.* *To ask a question* or questions.—*vt.* *To inquire of by asking questions*; to interrogate; to doubt; to have no confidence in; to treat as doubtful. [Fr.—L. *quæro*, *quæstum*, to seek.]
Questionable, kwest'shon-a-bl, *a.* *That may be questioned*; liable to suspicion; uncertain; suspicious.
Questionableness, kwest'shon-a-bl-nes, n. *The quality or state of being questionable*, doubtful, or suspicious.
Questionably, kwest'shon-a-bli, *adv.* Doubtfully.
Questionary, kwest'shon-a-ri, *a.* *Inquiring*; asking questions.
Questioner, kwest'shon-ẽr, n. *One who asks questions*; an inquirer.
Questioning, kwest'shon-ing, p.n.† Conversation.
Questionist, kwest'shon-ist, n. A *questioner*; an inquirer; (pl.) those who are in the last term of their college course in the English universities.
Questor, kwes'tor, n. Among the Romans, either a public prosecutor, one who *searched out* crimes, or a magistrate having the charge of the public revenues. [L. *quæstor—quæro*, to seek.]

Questorship, kwes'tor-ship, n. *The office of a questor*; the term of a questor's office.
Questrist†, kwest'rist, n. A *seeker*; a pursuer.
Quib, kwib, n. *A quip*.
Quibble, kwib'l, n. An unworthy evasion; a start from the point in question, or from plain truth; a low conceit. *vi.* To evade the point in question by artifice or any conceit. *ppr.* quibbling, *pret. & pp.* quibbled. [probably a dimin. of *quip*.]
Quibbler, kwib'l-ẽr, n. *One who quibbles*; a punster.
Quibbling, kwib'l-ing, p.a. Evading the truth by artifice.
Quick, kwik, *a.* *Alive*; moving with rapidity; characterized by readiness; prompt; sprightly; pregnant.—*n.* The *living flesh*; the sensitive part; living shrubs or trees; a living plant; the hawthorn.—*adv.* Nimbly; with celerity. [Sax. *cwic*; Goth. *quik*, alive.]
Quicken, kwik'n, *vt.* Primarily, *to make alive*; to vivify; to increase the speed of; to sharpen; to stimulate; to cheer; to reinvigorate.—*vi.* *To become quick*; to move with activity. [Sax. *cwiccan*.]
Quickened, kwik'nd, p.a. Accelerated; hastened.
Quickener, kwik'n-ẽr, n. One who *vivifies*; that which increases activity.
Quickening, kwik'n-ing, p.a. Inciting; reviving.—p.n. The act of *making quick*.
Quicklime, kwik'līm, n. *Lime unslaked*; any carbonate of lime deprived of its carbonic acid.
Quickly, kwik'li, *adv.* Speedily; with haste or celerity; soon; without delay.
Quickness, kwik'nes, n. *Quality of being quick*; swiftness; activity of intellect; readiness; acuteness of perception; keen sensibility; shrewdness.
Quick-sand, kwik'sand, n. *Sand easily moved* or readily yielding to pressure; loose sand abounding with water; unsolid ground.
Quickset, kwik'set, n. *A living* plant set to grow, particularly for a hedge; the hawthorn.—*a.* *Made of quickset*.
Quick-sighted, kwik'sīt-ed, *a.* *Having quick sight* or acute discernment.
Quicksilver, kwik'sil-vẽr, n. *Living silver*, so called from its fluidity and mobility; mercury, a fluid metal.
Quick-witted, kwik'wit-ed, *a.* Having ready wit.
Quiddit†, kwid'it, n. A subtlety.
Quiescence, kwi-es'ens, n. *State of being quiescent*; repose; rest of the mind silence; the absence of sound. [L. *quiescentia—quies*, rest.]
Quiescent, kwi-es'ent, *a.* *Resting*; not ruffled with passion; silent; having no sound.—*n.* A silent letter. [Fr.]
Quiescently, kwi-es'ent-li, *adv.* *In a calm* or *quiescent manner*.
Quiet, kwī'et, *a.* *At rest*; calm; still; unruffled; not exciting trouble; peaceful; mild; not agitated by wind; smooth.—*n.* *State of being quiet*; repose; stillness; tranquillity; freedom from disturbance or alarm; civil or political repose; peace. *vt.* *To put to rest*; to stop the motion of; to calm; to tranquillize; to suppress. [L. *quietus—quies*, rest.]
Quieting, kwī'et-ing, p.a. Tranquillizing.
Quietly, kwī'et-li, *adv.* In a *quiet manner* or *state*; without disturbance; calmly; patiently.
Quietness, kwī'et-nes, n. *State of being quiet*; a state of rest; stillness; calm.

---

ch, *chain*; j, *job*; g, *go*; ng, *sing*; TH, *then*; th, *thin*; w, *wig*; wh, *whig*; zh, *azure*; † obsolete.

Quietude, kwī'et-ūd, n. Rest; repose; quiet; tranquillity. [Fr.]
Quietus†, kwī-ē'tus, n. Rest; repose; death; that which silence claims.
Quill, kwil, n. A reed or cane; a reed pen; the large strong feather of a goose, much used for a writing-pen; the prickle of a porcupine; a piece of small reed, on which weavers wind the thread which forms the woof of cloth; the instrument with which musicians strike the strings of certain instruments.—vt. To plait, or to form with small ridges like quills or reeds. ppr. quilling, pret. & pp. quilled. [G. kiel—L. culmus, a stalk, stem.]
Quillet†, kwil'et, n. Nicety; quibble. [L. quidlibet.]
Quilt, kwilt, n. Originally, a bed; a cover made by putting wool, cotton, or other substance, between two cloths and sewing them together.—vt. To form into a quilt; to stitch together, as two pieces of cloth with some soft and warm substance between them; to sew in the manner of a quilt. [It. coltre; L. calco, to press close together.] **Quilted,** kwilt'ed, p.a. Formed into a quilt.
Quilting, kwilt'ing, p.n. The act of forming or making a quilt; the material used for quilts.
Quinary, kwī'na-ri, a. Consisting of five; arranged by fives. [L. quinarius.]
Quince, kwins, n. The fruit of a tree much used in making pies, &c., and so named from Cydonia, a town in Crete. [Fr. coing.]
Quinine, kwin-in', n. A substance obtained from various species of the tree named below, much used in the treatment of agues, &c. [from Cinchon, vice-queen of Peru, who was cured by the bark of the tree, named cinchōna after her.]
Quinquagesima, kwin-kwa-je'si-ma, n. Quinquagesima Sunday, so called as being about the fiftieth day before Easter; Shrove Sunday. [L. a fiftieth.]
Quinquangular, kwin-kwang'gū-lär, a. Having five angles or corners. [L. quinque, five, and angulus, an angle.]
Quinquennial, kwin-kwen'i-al, a. Occurring once in five years, or lasting five years. [L. quinque, and annus, a year.]
Quinsy, kwin'zi, n. A dog throttling; an inflammation of the tonsils; any inflammation of the throat or parts

adjacent. [Fr. esquinancie—Gr. kuōn, a dog, and anchō, to throttle.]
Quintain†, kwin'tān, n. An object to be tilted at.
Quintal, kwin'tal, n. A gross weight consisting generally of 100 lbs., but originally of 112 lbs. [Fr.]
Quintessence, kwint-es'ens, n. The fifth or highest essence of power in a natural body, according to the alchemists; an extract from anything, containing its virtues; the pure, essential part of a thing. [L. quinta essentia, the fifth essence—sum, esse, to be.]
Quintuple, kwin'tū-pl, a. Fivefold; containing five times the amount. [L. quintuplex—plico, to fold.]
Quip, kwip, n. A smart cut as with a whip; a smart sarcastic turn; a taunt; a severe retort. [from whip.]
Quire, kwir, n. A choir; a body of singers; the part of a church where the service is sung. [Fr. choeur—Gr. chōros, a dance accompanied with song.]
Quire, kwir, n. A collection of paper consisting of twenty-four sheets, each having a single fold.—vi. To sing in concert. [Fr. cahier, a copy-book.]
Quirk, kwėrk, n. A twist from the straight course; a shift; a fit or turn; a slight conceit; an irregular air. [G. swerch, cross, crooked.]
Quirkish, kwėrk'ish, a. Consisting of quirks, turns, or quibbles.
Quit, kwit, vt. To make quiet; to set free; to release; to clear; to liberate; to discharge from; to require; to repay; to pay; to depart from; to give up; to abandon; to perform.—a. Discharged from; free; clear; even. ppr. quitting, pret. & pp. quit or quitted. [Fr. quitter—L. quies, rest.]
Quite, kwit, adv. With a clean riddance; wholly; perfectly; to a great extent or degree; very. [from quit.]
Quit-rent, kwit'rent, n. A rent reserved in grants of land, by the payment of which the tenant is quit from all other service. [L. quietus reditus.]
Quittal†, kwit'al, n. Requital.
Quittance, kwit'ans, n. Act of quitting; acquittance; recompense; repayment. vt.† To repay; to requite. [Fr.]
Quiver, kwi'vėr, n. A cover or sheath for arrows. [Fr. couvrir, to cover.]
Quiver, kwi'vėr, vi. To shake or tremble; to quake; to shudder; to shiver. [D. kuiveren, to tremble.]

Quiver†, kwi'vėr, a. Nimble; active.
Quivered, kwi'vėrd, p.a. Furnished with a quiver.
Quivering, kwi'vėr-ing, p.a. Moving with a tremulous agitation.—p.n. Act of shaking or trembling; agitation.
Quixotic, kwiks-ot'ik, a. Like Don Quixote; romantic to extravagance; aiming at an ideal standard.
Quixotism, kwiks-ot-izm, n. Romantic and absurd notions; schemes or actions like those of Don Quixote.
Quoif, koif, n. A cap or hood.—vt. To cover or dress with a coif. [Fr. coife.]
Quoit, koit, n. A circular ring or piece of iron, or a plain flat stone to be pitched at a fixed object in play, as a trial of dexterity.—vi. To throw quoits. vt.† To throw.
Quondam, kwon'dam, a. Having been formerly. [L.]
Quorum, kwō'rum, n. A bench of justices, or such number of members as is competent by law to transact business; a special commission of justices. [L. of whom—gen. pl. of qui.]
Quota, kwō'ta, n. A proportional part or the proportion assigned to each. [L. quotus, which number in the series?]
Quotable, kwōt'a-bl, a. That may be quoted or cited.
Quotation, kwōt-ā'shon, n. Act of quoting; the passage quoted; the naming of the price of commodities.
Quote, kwōt, vt. To mark the number of a chapter, of an article, of a verse, &c.; to adduce, as a passage from an author by way of authority; to name, as the price of an article; to note; to observe. ppr. quoting, pret. & pp. quoted. [Old Fr. quoter—L. quotus, which number in the series?]
Quoth, kwōth, vi. To say; to speak. This verb is defective, being used only in the first and third persons in the present and past tenses, as quoth I, quoth he; and the nominative always follows the verb. [Sax. cwethan, Goth. qvithan, to say.]
Quotidian, kwō-ti'di-an, a. Daily; occurring or returning daily.—n. A fever whose paroxysms return every day; anything returning daily. [L. quotidianus—quotus, and dies, a day.]
Quotient, kwō'shi-ent, n. The number showing how often a less number is contained in a greater. [Fr.—L. quot, how many.]

R.

Rabato†, ra-ba'tō, n. A kind of folded-down collar of a shift or shirt.
Rabbi, rab'bi, n. A chief; a doctor; a teacher; a title assumed by the Jewish doctors or expounders of the law. [Ch. rab, a chief.]
Rabbinic, Rabbinical, rab-bin'ik, rab-bin'ik-al, a. Pertaining to the rabbins, or to their opinions, learning, and language.
Rabbit, rab'bit, n. A well-known small animal, allied to the hare, which feeds on grass or other herbage, and burrows in the earth. [formerly robbet, most probably corrupted from rough-feet.]
Rabble, rab'l, n. A tumultuous crowd, mad with greed, and disposed to spoil

and to destroy; the mob; the dregs of the people.—vt. To drive away by a mob. ppr. rabbling, pret. & pp. rabbled. [from Sax. reaf, greedy.]
Rabblement, rab'l-ment, n. A tumultuous crowd of low people.
Rabid, ra'bid, a. Raving; furious; raging mad. [L. rabidus, from rabo, to rave.]
Rabidly, ra'bid-li, adv. Madly.
Rabidness, ra'bid-nes, n. State or quality of being rabid; rage; furiousness.
Race, rās, n. The root; that from which anything rises; the continued series of descendants from a parent, who is called the stock; lineage; company; herd; a particular breed; a particular

flavour of wine, indicating its origin, &c.; a kind of tartness; disposition. [Fr.—L. radix, the root—Sans. ruh, to come forth, to increase.]
Race, rās, n. A running; a rapid course either on the foot, on horseback, or in a carriage, &c.; a contest in running; a progress; a course or career; a rapid current of water; a small water-course, leading from the dam of a stream to the machinery which it drives. (pl.) a meeting for contests in the running of horses.—vi. To run, as in a race; to run swiftly; to run or contend in running for. ppr. racing. pret. & pp. raced. [Sax. res, a rush. Icel. rása, to run.]

Fate, fär, fat, fall; mē, met, hėr; pine, pin; nōte, not, mōve; tūbe, tub, bull; oil, pound.

Race-course, rās'kōrs, n. The ground or path on which races are run.

Race-horse, rās'hors, n. A horse bred or kept for running in contest.

Racer, rās'ėr, n. One who races; one who contends in a race; a race-horse.

Racily, rā'si-li, adv. In a racy manner.

Raciness, rā'si-nes, n. Quality of being racy; a kind of tartness.

Racing, rās'ing, p.n. Act of running, as in a race; the riding for a plate or other premium at public contests.

Rack, rak, vt. To stretch on the rack or wheel; to torture; to harass; to strain; to wrest; to exaggerate; to strain or draw off from the lees. [Sax. racan, to extend.] n. An engine of torture for stretching the limbs or body; torture; extreme pain; anguish; a frame on which things are put; a wooden frame in which hay is laid for horses and cattle. [D. rek.]

Rack, rak, n. The neck and spine of a fore-quarter of veal or mutton. [Sax. hracca.]

Rack, rak, n. Reek; vapour; thin, flying, broken clouds, or any portion of floating vapour in the sky.—vi. To steam; to rise as vapour; to reck. [Sax. rec.]

Racked, rakt, p.a. Tortured; tormented.

Racket, rak'et, n. The instrument with which players at tennis strike the ball; a noise and clamour like that of the game.—vt. To strike, as with a racket. vi. To make a confused noise or clamour; to frolic. [Fr. raquette.]

Racketing, rak'et-ing, p. n. Confused and noisy mirth.

Racking, rak'ing, p.a. Tormenting; excruciating.—p. n. A stretching on the rack; torture; act of drawing from the sediment, as liquors.

Rack-rent, rak'rent, n. An annual rent raised to the utmost, or to the full annual value of the premises, or near it.

Racy, rā'si, a. Having a race or strong flavour indicating its origin, as wine; tasting of the soil; exciting to the mental taste.

Radial, rā'di-al, a. Relating to a radius; shooting out from a centre; having rays. [from L. radius, a spoke of a wheel—Sans. ratha, a chariot.]

Radiance, rā'di-ans, n. Quality or state of being radiant; brightness shooting in rays; vivid brightness; splendour.

Radiant, rā'di-ant, a. Emitting rays of light or heat; beaming with brightness. [L. radians—radio, to emit rays—radius, the spoke of a wheel.]

Radiantly, rā'di-ant-li, adv. In a radiant manner; with radiance.

Radiate, rā'di-āt, vi. To emit rays of light; to beam; to issue in rays, as light; to issue and proceed in direct lines from a point or surface, as heat. vt. To irradiate; to send out in direct lines from a point or surface, as heat. ppr. radiating, pret. & pp. radiated. [L. radio, radiatus.]

Radiating, rā'di-āt-ing, p.a. Emitting rays of light or heat.

Radiation, rā-di-ā'shon, n. Act of radiating; the emission of rays of light or heat from a luminous or heated body; the shooting forth of anything from a point or surface, like the diverging rays of light. [L. radiatio.]

Radiator, rā'di-āt-or, n. He who or that which radiates.

Radical, rā'di-kal, a. Pertaining to the root; implanted by nature; underived; proceeding immediately from the root, as a leaf; relating to the etymological root; relating to radicals in politics. n. A root; a primitive word; a primitive letter; a letter that belongs to the root of a word; one who advocates a radical reform. [Fr.—L. radix, a root; Gr. rādix, a branch, rod.]

Radicalism, ra'di-kal-ism, n. The principles of radicals in politics.

Radically, ra'di-kal-li, adv. In a radical manner; fundamentally.

Radicle, ra'di-kl, n. A small root; that part of the seed of a plant which, upon vegetating, becomes the root. [L. radicula—radix, a root.]

Radish, ra'dish, n. A root; a plant, the root of which is eaten raw, as a salad. [Sax. rædic.]

Radius, rā'di-us, n. Radii, pl. A rod; the spoke of a wheel; a straight line drawn from the centre of a circle to the circumference; the smaller of the two bones of the forearm. [L.—Gr. rabdos, a staff.]

Radix, rā'diks, n. A root; the root of a plant; a primitive word from which spring other words; that from which anything springs; origin; base. [L.]

Raffle, raf'l, n. A lottery, in which the winner sweeps all the stakes away. vi. To cast dice for a prize, while the winner sweeps all the stakes away. ppr. raffling, pret. & pp. raffled. [Fr. rafle—Icel. Arafa, to sweep with the hand.]

Raft, räft, n. An assemblage of pieces of timber, fastened together horizontally, so as to be conveyed down a stream; a float. [Dan.]

Rafter, räf'tėr, n. A piece of timber; a beam; a roof timber; a piece of timber that serves to support the covering of the roof.—vt. To form into rafters; to furnish with rafters. [Sax. rafter; Icel. raftr, a beam.]

Raftered, räf'tėrd, p.a. Built or furnished with rafters.

Rag, rag, n. Any piece of cloth rent from the rest; a tattered cloth worn till its texture is destroyed; (pl.) garments worn out; mean dress. [Sax. hracod, ragged.]

Rage, rāj, n. Madness; fury; choler; extreme violence; rapture; extreme passion directed to some object; the subject of eager desire.—vi. To rave; to be furious with anger; to ravage; to prevail with fatal effect; to be driven with impetuosity; to act furiously. ppr. raging, pret. & pp. raged. [Fr.—L. rabo, to rave.]

Ragged, rag'ed, p.a. Broken with rough edges; jagged; wearing tattered clothes; rough; rugged; discordant; mean.

Raggedness, rag'ed-nes, n. State of being ragged; state of being broken irregularly.

Raging, rāj'ing, p.a. Furious; frantic; impetuous; vehement.—p.n. Fury; violence; impetuosity.

Ragingly, rāj'ing-li, adv. With fury.

Ragout, ra-gö', n. That which tempts one to taste again; a highly-seasoned dish or food. [Fr.—L. gustus, taste.]

Rail, rāl, n. That which covers or protects; that which fences; a piece of timber or of iron, extending from one post to another, as in fences, staircases, &c.; the horizontal part in any piece of framing; one of the iron bars in a railway, on which the wheels of the carriages run.—vt. To inclose with rails. [Sax. hrægel, a covering.]

Rail, rāl, vi. To make persons or things the objects of ridicule; to scoff; to utter reproaches. (With at or against.) [Fr. railler—L. rideo, to laugh.]

Railer, rāl'ėr, n. One who rails; one who reviles or reproaches.

Railing, rāl'ing, p.a. Expressing reproach; insulting.—p.n. Reproachful or insolent language.

Railing, rāl'ing, p.n. A series of rails; the materials for rails.

Railingly, rāl'ing-li, adv. With scoffing or insulting language.

Raillery, rāl'é-ri, n. Light ridicule or satire; satirical merriment; good-humoured pleasantry. [Fr. raillerie.]

Railway, rāl'wā, n. A road or way, made nearly level, and having parallel tracks of iron, called rails, laid along it, on which the wheels of carriages are made to run, in order to lessen friction.

Raiment, rā'ment, n. Clothing in general; vestments; vesture; garments; a single garment. [for arrayment.]

Rain, rān, vi. To fall in drops from the clouds, as water (used mostly with it for a nominative); to fall or drop like rain.—vt. To pour or shower down, as rain.—n. That which pours or is poured from the clouds; the descent of water in drops from the atmosphere. [Sax. regnan, to rain—L. rigo, to wet—Sans. sri, to pour out.]

Rainbow, rān'bō, n. A bow, consisting of all the primitive colours formed by the refraction and reflection of rays of light from falling drops of rain.

Rain-gauge, rān'gāj, n. An instrument for measuring the quantity of rain that falls in a given time.

Rainy, rān'i, a. Abounding with rain; wet; showery. [Sax. renig.]

Raise, rāz, vt. To cause to rise; to lift or elevate in a literal or in a figurative sense; to erect; to give beginning to; to bring back into being; to augment; to give rise to; to levy. ppr. raising, pret. & pp. raised. [causative of rise.]

Raised, rāzd, p.a. Set upright; enhanced; restored to life; levied.

Raisin, rā'zin, n. A fruit that grows in bunches or clusters; a dried grape. [Fr. —L. racemus, a bunch of grapes.]

Raising, rāz'ing, p.n. Act of causing to rise; setting up, producing, or restoring to life.

Rake, rāk, n. That which gathers together; an instrument with teeth and a handle, by which light bodies are gathered up, or the earth divided.—vt. To gather with a rake; to clear or smooth with a rake; to gather by violence; to scour; to search with eagerness; to cannonade, as a ship on the stern or head, so that the balls range the whole length of the deck.—vi. To use a rake; to search minutely and meanly. ppr. raking, pret. & pp. raked. [Sax. raca—G. rechen, to rake.]

Rake, rāk, n. A loose, disorderly, vicious man. [G. racker.]

Raking, rāk'ing, p.a. That rakes.—p.n. Act of using a rake; act of collecting with a rake, or of smoothing with a rake; the course of life of a rake or debauchee.

Rakish, rāk'ish, a. Exhibiting the character and conduct of a rake; debauched.

Rakishness, rāk'ish-nes, n. Dissolute practices.

Rally, ral'li, vt. To reunite; to collect and reduce to order, as troops thrown into confusion; to unite, as things scattered.—vi. To reunite; to reassemble; to recover strength or vigour. ppr. rallying, pret. & pp. rallied.—n. Reunion; act of bringing disordered troops to their ranks. [Fr. rallier—L. re, ad, and ligo, to bind.]

Rally, ral'li, vt. To attack with raillery; to joke; to banter; to ridicule. ppr. rallying, pret. & pp. rallied.—n. Exercise of good humour or satirical merriment. [Fr. *railler*.]

Ram, ram, n. The male of the sheep, which pushes with his horns; the sign of the zodiac which the sun enters about the 21st of March; an engine of war; the loose hammer of a pile-driving machine. [Sax.; Icel. *ramr*, strong.]—*vt*. To drive with violence; to batter; to drive down or together; to drive, as with a battering-ram. *ppr*. ramming, *pret. & pp.* rammed. [G. *rammen*.]

Ramble, ram'bl, *vi*. To rove loosely and irregularly; to wander; to go at large without restraint and without direction. *ppr*. rambling, *pret. & pp.* rambled.—n. A roving loosely and irregularly; a wandering; an irregular excursion. [L. *re-ambulare*, to go backwards and forwards.]

Rambler, ram'bl-ėr, n. One who rambles; an irregular wanderer; a rover.

Rambling, ram'bl-ing, p.a. Wandering; unsettled.—p.n. A roving; irregular excursion.

Ramification, ra′mi-fi-kā″shon, n. The process of *ramifying*; a branch; the manner in which a tree produces its branches; the production of figures resembling branches; a division into heads. [Fr.]

Ramify, ra′mi-fi, *vt*. To separate into branches.—*vi*. To shoot into branches, as the stem of a plant; to be divided. *ppr*. ramifying, *pret. & pp.* ramified. [Fr. *ramifier*—L. *ramus*, a branch, and *facio*, to make.]

Rammer, ram′ėr, n. He or that which rams; an instrument for driving anything with force; a gun-stick.

Ramose, rā′mōs, a. Branched, as a stem or root; full of branches. [L. *ramosus*—*ramus*, a branch.]

Ramp, ramp, *vi*. To climb, as a plant, to leap; to bound.—n. A bound. [Fr. *ramper*.]

Rampallian', ram-pal′li-an, n. A mean wretch.

Rampancy, ram′pan-si, n. State of being rampant.

Rampant, ram′pant, a. Creeping and climbing; rank in growth; exuberant; overleaping restraint. [Fr. *ramper*, to creep, to crawl—L. *repo*, to creep.]

Rampantly, ram′pant-li, adv. In a rampant manner.

Rampart, ram′pärt, n. A sloping mound of earth round a place, capable of resisting cannon-shot, and formed into bastions, curtains, &c.; that which fortifies and defends from assault.—*vt*. To fortify with ramparts. [Fr. *rempart*—*rampe*, an inclined plane.]

Ramrod, ram′rod, n. A rod of iron, &c., used in *ramming* down the charge in a musket, pistol, &c.

Rancid, ran′sid, a. Having a rank smell; strong-scented; sour; musty. [L. *rancidus*—obsol. *ranceo*, to stink, *rancens*, stinking, putrid.]

Rancidity, ran-sid′i-ti, n. Quality of being rancid; a strong sour scent, as of old oil. [Fr. *rancidité*.]

Rancorous, rang′kor-us, a. Characterised by rancour; malignant; bitter.

Rancorously, rang′kor-us-li, adv. In a rancorous manner.

Rancour, rang′kor, n. Corruption; an old grudge; deep-seated and implacable enmity; malice; gall; spite. [Old Fr. *rancoeur*—L. *ranceo*, to stink.]

Random, ran′dum, n. A rushing down; a roving motion or course without direction; want of direction or method; chance; used in the phrase, at random.

a. Uttered or done at hazard; left to chance. [Old Fr. *random*.]

Range, rānj, *vt*. To set in a circle, in a row, or in rows; to place in a regular line; to dispose in the proper order; to place in regular method; to arrange. *vi*. To be ranked; to be placed in order. *ppr*. ranging, *pret. & pp.* ranged.—n. A rank; things in a line; a class; an order. [Fr. *ranger*; Old G. *hring*, a circle.]

Range, rānj, *vi*. To go at large; to sail or pass near; to pass from one point to another.—*vt*. To rove over; to pass over. *ppr*. ranging, *pret & pp.* ranged. n. A going at large; excursion; space or room for excursion; an extended cooking apparatus; the horizontal distance to which a shot is carried; discursive power. [Sax. *rennan*, to run—Sans. *ri, ri*, to go.]

Ranger, rānj′ėr, n. One who ranges; an officer who tends the game of a forest; (pl.) mounted troops armed with short muskets, who *range* the country and often fight on foot; a dog that beats the ground.

Ranging, rānj′ing, p.n. Act of placing in lines o.′ in order; a roving, &c.

Rank, rangk, n. *Arrangement in a circle*; disposition in order; method; a line of men standing side by side; a line running from front to rear of a company; a line of things; degree; degree of dignity or excellence; high place in the orders of men; (pl.) the order of common soldiers.—*vt*. To range; to place in a line; to place in a particular division; to place in suitable order. *vi*. To be ranged; to be placed in a rank; to have a certain degree of elevation in the orders of civil or military life; to put in a claim against the estate of a bankrupt person. [Dan. *rang*, rank; Old G. *hring*, a ring.]

Rank, rangk, a. High-growing; strong; excessive; rampant; haughty; rebellious. [Sax. *ranc*, high-grown.]

Rank, rangk, a. Rancid; musty; strong-scented; gross; coarse. [L. *rancidus*.]

Rankle, rang′kl, *vi*. To fester; to become putrid; to be inflamed in body or mind; to become painfully diseased or distempered in body or in mind. *ppr*. rankling, *pret. & pp.* rankled. [probably from Old L. *ranceo*, to stink.]

Rankling, rang′kl-ing, p.n. Act or state of anything that rankles; a festering.

Rankly, rangk′li, adv. In a rank manner; with vigorous growth; coarsely.

Rankness, rangk′nes, n. State or quality of being rank; vigorous growth; excess; strong taste; rank or rancid smell.

Ransack, ran′sak, *vt*. To search, as for plunder; to plunder; to strip by plundering; to enter and search, as every place or part. [Sax. *ran*, plunder, and *secan*, to seek.]

Ransom, ran′sum, n. A buying back; release from captivity; the price paid for the redemption of a prisoner; a fine paid in lieu of corporeal punishment.—*vt*. To buy back; to redeem; to redeem from the possession of an enemy by paying a price deemed equivalent. [Fr. *rançon*—L. *re*, and *emo*, to buy.]

Ransomed, ran′sumd, p.a. Redeemed or rescued from bondage or punishment.

Ransomer, ran′sum-ėr, n. One who ransoms or redeems.

Ransomless, ran′sum-les, a. Incapable of being ransomed.

Rant, rant, *vi*. To rave in violent language; to be boisterous in declamation. n. A raving; high-sounding language

without dignity of thought. [Old G. *ranjan*, to rage—*ranintis*, raging.]

Ranter, rant′ėr, n. One who rants; a noisy talker; a boisterous preacher.

Ranting, rant′ing, p.a. Preaching with boisterous, empty words.

Ranunculus, ra-nun′kū-lus, n. *Frog's-foot, or crow-foot*, a plant and flower. [L. *rana*, a frog, and *ungula*, a claw.]

Rap, rap, *vi*. To strike with a quick sharp blow; to knock.—*vt*. To strike with a quick blow; to knock. *ppr*. rapping, *pret. & pp.* rapped.—n. A quick smart blow. [Old G. *rap*, a club.]

Rap, rap, *vt*. To seize and bear away, as the mind or thoughts; to affect with ecstasy or rapture. [Sax. *rypan*.]

Rapacious, ra-pā′shi-us, a. Grasping; greedy; ravenous; given to plunder; seizing by force; subsisting on prey, or animals seized by violence. [L. *rapax, rapacis*—*rapio*, to seize.]

Rapaciously, ra-pā′shi-us-li, adv. In a rapacious manner.

Rapaciousness, ra-pā′shi-us-nes, n. Quality of being rapacious.

Rapacity, ra-pa′si-ti, n. Quality of being rapacious; the act or practice of seizing by force; act of extorting by oppressive injustice; exorbitant greediness of gain. [Fr. *rapacité*.]

Rape, rāp, n. A seising by violence; seizing and carrying away by force, as females; the carnal knowledge of a woman against her will; privation. [Fr. *rapt*—L. *rapio*, to seize.]

Rape, rāp, n. A plant of the cabbage kind, cultivated chiefly for the oil obtained from its seed. [L. *rapa*.]

Rapid, ra′pid, a. Tearing or hurrying along; quick; swift; hurried.—n. *That which has quickness of motion*; the part of a river where the current is very swift (commonly used in the plural). [Fr. *rapide*; L. *rapio*, to seize.]

Rapidity, ra-pid′i-ti, n. State or quality of being rapid; quickness in utterance; quickness of advance; velocity; swiftness. [Fr. *rapidité*.]

Rapidly, ra′pid-li, adv. With great speed, celerity, or velocity; swiftly.

Rapier, rā′pi-ėr, n. Formerly, a long sword, now a small sword generally. [Fr. *rapière*.]

Rapine, ra′pin, n. Act of seising and carrying off by force; violence; force; plunder. [Fr.—L. *rapio*, to seize.]

Rappee, rap-pē′, n. A coarse kind of snuff. [from Fr. *râper*, to grate.]

Rapper, rap′ėr, n. One who raps; the knocker of a door. [from *rap*.]

Rapt, rapt, p.a. Transported; ravished.

Rapture, rap′tūr, n. A carrying of by violence; violence of a pleasing passion; uncommon heat of imagination. [L. *raptūra*—*rapio*, Sans. *grah*, to seize.]

Raptured, rap′tūrd, p.a. Ravished; transported.

Rapturous, rap′tūr-us, a. Ecstatic; transporting; ravishing.

Rapturously, rap′tūr-us-li, adv. In a rapturous manner; with rapture.

Rare, rār, a. Of loose texture; thin; porous; not dense; thinly scattered; scarce; unusually excellent; incomparable. [Fr.—L. *rarus*, loose in texture.]

Rarefaction, ra-re-fak′shon, n. Act or process of rarefying or making rare; state of being rarefied. [Fr.]

Rarefied, ra′re-fid, p.a. Made rare.

Rarefy, ra′re-fi, *vt*. To make rare; to make thin and porous or less dense. *vi*. To become rare, or thin and porous. *ppr*. rarefying, *pret. & pp.* rarefied. [Fr. *raréfier*—L. *rarus*, and *facio*, to make.]

Fāte, fär, fat, fall; mē, met, hėr; pīne, pin; nōte, not, mōve; tūbe, tub, bull; oil, pound.

Rarely, rär'li, *adv.* Seldom; not often.
Rareness, rär'nes, *n. State of being rare;* thinness; tenuity; uncommonness.
Rarity, rā'ri-ti, *n.* State of being rare; uncommonness; infrequency; a thing valued for its scarcity; tenuity; opposed to density. [Fr. *rareté.*]
Rascal, ras'kal, *n. A lean deer!:* a trickish, dishonest fellow; a rogue.—*a.* Lean; mean; low. [Sax. *rascal,* a lean, worthless deer.]
Rascality, ras-kal'i-ti, *n. Act or acts of a rascal;* mean trickishness.
Rascally, ras'kal-li, *a.* Meanly trickish or dishonest; vile; mean; base.
Rase, rāz, *vt. To scrape; to scratch* or rub out; to blot out; to obliterate; to lay or make level with the ground (in this sense, *see* RAZE). *ppr.* rasing, *pret. & pp.* rased. [Fr. *raser*—L. *rado, rāsus,* to scrape.]
Rash, rash, *a. Going quickly;* hasty; headlong; resolving on a measure without due deliberation; uttered or undertaken with too much haste. [D. *rasch,* quick, speedy; Icel. *rāsa,* to run.]
Rash, rash, *n. A rushing* or sudden breaking out on the skin; an eruption on the body, with little or no elevation. [It. *rascia.*]
Rash!, rash, *vt.* To strike by a glancing blow; to slash; to cut.
Rasher, rash'ér, *n.* A thin slice of bacon; a thin cut. [L. *rasūra lardi,* a scraping of bacon.]
Rashly, rash'li, *adv. In a precipitate manner;* with precipitation.
Rashness, rash'nes, *n. Quality of being rash;* temerity; hastiness.
Rasp, rasp, *n. A rough kind of file* for *rubbing off* quickly the asperities of a surface.—*vt.* To *rub or file with a rasp;* to rub or grate with a rough file; to grate harshly upon. [Sw.]
Raspberry, raz'be-ri, *n.* The fruit of a bramble, so named from the *rasping* roughness of the plant.
Rasure, rā'shūr, *n. Act of scraping;* the act of erasing; the mark by which a letter or any part of a writing or print is erased; an erasure. [L. *rasūra*—*rado, rasus,* to scrape.]
Rat, rat, *n.* The animal that *pierces* or *bores;* the popular name of several kinds of small and troublesome gnawing animals, larger than mice; one who deserts his party. [Sax. *ræt;* Heb. *ratsa,* to pierce.]
Ratability, rāt-a-bil'i-ti, *n. Quality of being ratable.*
Ratable, rāt'a-bl, *a. That may be rated;* liable or subjected by law to taxation.
Ratably, rāt'a-bli, *adv. By rate* or proportion; proportionally.
Ratch, rach, *n.* A bar containing angular teeth, into which a catch drops, to prevent machines from running back. [probably allied to *rack.*]
Ratchet, rach'et, *n.* In a watch, a small tooth at the bottom of the fusee, which stops it in winding up. [dimin. of *ratch.*]
Ratchet-wheel, rach'et-hwēl, *n.* A circular *wheel* having angular teeth, into which a *ratchet* drops.
Rate, rāt, *n. Something thought;* the standard by which quantity or value is adjusted; ratio; price fixed on any thing; degree; comparative height; degree in which anything is done; assessment.—*vt.* To reckon; to compute; to set a certain value on; to rank; to take the rate of; to ascertain the exact rate of gain or loss in time, as of a chronometer, compared with true time.—*vi.* To make an estimate; to be classed in a certain order. *ppr.* rating, *pret. & pp.* rated. [Old Fr.—L. *reor, ratus,* to think, deem.]
Rate, rāt, *vt. To chide* with vehemence; to censure violently. *ppr.* rating, *pret. & pp.* rated. [Sax. *Arethian,* to rage; Sw. *rata,* to find fault with.]
Rather, rāтн'ér, *adv. Earlier; sooner;* with better liking; with preference; with better reason; in a greater degree than otherwise; more properly; more correctly speaking; noting some degree of contrariety in fact. [Sax. *rathor—rath,* early.]
Ratification, ra'ti-fi-kā"shon, *n. Act of ratifying;* act of giving validity to something done by another.
Ratify, ra'ti-fi, *vt. To make* or render *firm or valid;* to settle; to approve and sanction. *ppr.* ratifying, *pret. & pp.* ratified. [Fr. *ratifier*—L. *ratus,* fixed by calculation (*reor,* to think), and *facio,* to make.]
Ratio, rā'shi-ō, *n.* Ratios, *pl. Reckoning;* proportion; rate; that relation between two quantities of the same kind which is expressed by the quotient of the one divided by the other. [L.—*reor, ratus,* to think.]
Ratiocination, ra-ti-os'i-nā"shon, *n. The act or process of reasoning,* or of deducing consequences from premises. [Fr.—L. *reor, ratus,* to think.]
Ration, rā'shon, *n. A proportion,* or fixed allowance of provisions, &c., assigned to each soldier in the army, or sailor in the navy, for his daily subsistence. [Fr.—L. *ratio.*]
Rational, ra'shon-al, *a. Relating to reason; reasonable;* endowed with reason; agreeable to reason; wise; judicious. [Old Fr.—L. *ratio,* reason.]
Rationale, ra-shon-ā'lē, *n. A series of reasons assigned;* an account of the principles of some opinion, phenomenon, &c. [from L. *reor, ratus,* to think.]
Rationalism, ra'shon-al-izm, *n.* A system of opinions deduced from *reason,* as distinct from inspiration or opposed to it. [Fr. *rationalisme.*]
Rationalist, ra'shon-al-ist, *n. One who* proceeds wholly *upon reason;* one who considers the supernatural events recorded in the Old and New Testaments as happening in the ordinary course of nature.—*a. Relating to rationalism.*
Rationality, ra-shon-al'i-ti, *n. The quality of being rational;* soundness of mind; reasonableness. [Low L. *rationalitas*—L. *ratio,* reason—*reor,* to think.]
Rationally, ra'shon-al-li, *adv. In a rational manner;* reasonably.
Rattle, rat'l, *vi.* To make a quick, sharp noise, rapidly repeated, by the collision of bodies not very sonorous; to speak eagerly and noisily.—*vt. To cause to rattle;* to stun with noise; 'to rail at clamorously. *ppr.* rattling, *pret. & pp.* rattled.—*n.* A rapid succession of sharp clattering sounds; loud rapid talk; an instrument with which a clattering sound is made. [D. *ratelen.*]
Rattlesnake, rat'l-snāk, *n.* A poisonous American *snake,* that has *rattles* at the tail.
Rattling, rat'l-ing, *p.a.* Making a quick succession of sharp sounds.—*p.n.* A rapid succession of sharp sounds.
Raught, rat, *pp.* of *reach.* Taken away.
Ravage, ra'vāj, *n. A tearing away; pillage;* destruction by violence; destruction by decay.—*vt. To tear away from;* to spoil; to plunder; to lay waste by various means of destruction. *ppr.* ravaging, *pret. & pp.* ravaged. [Fr.—L. *rapio,* to seize.]
Ravaged, ra'vājd, *p.a.* Wasted; pillaged.
Ravager, ra'vāj-ér, *n. One who ravages;* a plunderer; a spoiler.
Rave, rāv, *vi. To talk insanely;* to wander in mind; to be delirious; to be wild; to utter furious exclamations; to dote. *ppr.* raving, *pret. & pp.* raved. [D. *revelen,* to dote—L. *rabo,* to be mad.]
Ravel, ra'vel, *vt. To unravel;* to unweave; to disclose; to entangle; to entwist; to make intricate; to net.—*vi.* To fall into perplexity. *ppr.* ravelling, *pret. & pp.* ravelled. [D. *rafelen.*]
Ravelin, rav'lin, *n.* A detached triangular work in fortification. [Fr.; L. *re,* and *vallum,* a rampart.]
Ravelled, ra'veld, *p.a.* Untwisted; disentangled; entangled.
Raven, rā'ven, *n.* A bird of prey of the *crow* kind, of a black colour, and having a *hoarse, unpleasant* cry.—*vt. To seize and carry off by violence;* to rob; to devour with great eagerness. (Written also *ravin.*)—*vi.* To prey with rapacity. [Sax. *hræfen.*]
Ravening, ra'ven-ing, *p.n. Eagerness for plunder.*
Ravenous, ra'ven-us, *a. Eager for prey* or *plunder;* hungry even to rage; devouring with rapacious eagerness; greedy. [Old Fr. *ravineux.*]
Ravenously, ra'ven-us-li, *adv. In a ravenous manner;* with raging voracity.
Ravin, ra'vin, *n.* Plunder.
Ravine, ra-vēn', *n.* A long deep hollow formed by a *mountain torrent;* a long, deep, and narrow hollow gorge through mountains, &c. [Fr. a great flood; L. *labor, lapsus,* to glide down.]
Raving, rāv'ing, *p.a.* Furious with delirium; mad.—*p.n.* Madness.
Ravingly, rāv'ing-li, *adv. In a raving manner;* with furious wildness or frenzy.
Ravish, ra'vish, *vt. To seize and carry away by violence;* to have carnal knowledge of by force; to bear away with joy or delight; to transport; to enrapture. [Fr. *ravir, ravissant*—L. *rapio,* to seize and carry off.]
Ravished, ra'visht, *p.a.* Forced to submit to carnal embrace; delighted to ecstasy.
Ravisher, ra'vish-ér, *n. One who ravishes;* one who forces a woman to his carnal embrace; one who transports with delight.
Ravishing, ra'vish-ing, *p.a. Delighting to rapture.*—*p.n. A carrying away by violence;* carnal knowledge by force; ecstatic delight; transport.
Ravishingly, ra'vish-ing-li, *adv. In a manner to ravish.*
Ravishment, ra'vish-ment, *n. Act of ravishing;* rape; rapture; ecstasy.
Raw, rą, *a. Crude;* not cooked; not altered by heat; bare, as flesh; sore; unripe; inexperienced; bleak; cold and damp; not mixed; bare of flesh; not worked up or prepared for use. [Sax. *reaw.*]
Raw-boned, rą'bōnd, *a.* Having little flesh on the *bones.*
Rawish, rą'ish, *a. Somewhat raw.*
Rawly, rą'li, *adv. In a raw manner.*
Rawness, rą'nes, *n. State of being raw;* state of being uncooked; unskilfulness; chilliness with dampness.
Ray, rā, *n. Something that shoots forth* as from a centre; a line of light, or the right line supposed to be described by a particle of light; a gleam of intellectual light; lustre; a cartilaginous flat fish.—*vt.* To emit, as beams or lines

of light; to streak; to mark with long lines; to defile. [Fr. raie—L. radius, a staff, rod.]
Raze, rāz, vt. To scrape; to efface; to lay level with the ground; to overthrow; to ruin utterly. ppr. razing, pret. & pp. razed. [Fr. raser—L. rado.]
Razz, rāz, n. A root. [See RACE.]
Razor, rā'zor, n. A knife or instrument for shaving off the beard or hair. [Fr. rasoir—L. rado, rasum, to scrape.]
Razure, rā'zhūr, n. See RASURE.
Reach, rēch, vt. To extend to; to hold forth; to touch by extending; to strike from a distance; to deliver with the hand by extending the arm; to hand; to arrive at; to gain; to penetrate to; to extend to, as a case.—vi. To be extended; to be extended far; to make efforts to vomit.—n. Extension; extent; the power of extending to, or of taking by the hand; power of attainment; effort of the mind; scheme; an artifice to obtain an advantage; the straight course of a river between any two bendings. [Sax. rœcan—G. recken, to reach.]
React, rē-akt', vi. To act again or in opposition to action; to return an impulse or impression; to resist the action of another body by an opposite force; to act mutually upon each other.
Reaction, rē-ak'shon, n. Action in resistance to action; mutual or reciprocal action; any action in resisting other action or power.
Reactionary, rē-ak'shon-a-ri, a. For or implying reaction.
Read, rēd, n. Counsel; doctrine. [Sax. rœdan, to counsel.]
Read, rēd, vt. To speak what is written; to utter or pronounce, as written words, in the proper order; to peruse, whether audibly or silently; to inspect and understand, as words or characters; to understand by characters; to gather the meaning of by inspection; to know fully; to learn by observation.—vi. To perform the act of reading; to be studious; to learn by reading; to be read; to appear in reading, as a passage. ppr. reading, pret. & pp. read (red). [Sax. rœdan; Goth. rodjan, to speak.]
Read, red, p.a. Instructed or knowing by reading; versed in books; learned.
Readable, rēd'a-bl, a. That may be read; fit to be read.
Readdress, rē-ad-dres', vt. To address or direct again.
Reader, rēd'ėr, n. One who reads; one whose distinctive office is to read prayers in a church; one who reads lectures on scientific subjects; one who reads or corrects for the press.
Readership, rēd'ėr-ship, n. The office of reading prayers in a church; the office of a lecturer on scientific subjects.
Readily, red'i-li, adv. In a ready manner; quickly; promptly; easily.
Readiness, red'i-nes, n. State of being ready; facility; freedom from reluctance; willingness; fitness of condition.
Reading, rēd'ing, p.a. Addicted to reading; studious of books.—p.n. Act of reading; study of books; a lecture; the way in which a given word or passage reads in a manuscript, &c.; an interpretation of a law or passage, as conveying its meaning.
Readjourn, rē-ad-jėrn', vt. To adjourn a second time.
Readjust, rē-ad-just', vt. To adjust or settle again.
Readmission, rē-ad-mi'shon, n. Act of admitting again what had been excluded; state of being admitted again.
Readmit, rē-ad-mit', vi. To admit again.

ppr. readmitting, pret. & pp. readmitted.
Ready, re'di, a. Prepared; furnished with proper instruments; set in order; not hesitating; quick to receive or comprehend; not slow or dull; dexterous; present in hand; not backward to do or suffer; disposed; having a tendency; being at the point; not distant; about to do or suffer; being at hand; easy; short.—adv. In a state of preparation, so as to need no delay. [Sax. hrad—Goth. raidjan, to set in order.]
Reagent, rē-ā'jent, n. A substance employed to detect the presence of other bodies.
Real, rē'al, a. Pertaining to a thing or things; not personal; actual; not fictitious; true; not artificial; not affected; pertaining to things fixed or immovable. [Old Fr.—L. res, rei, a thing.]
Reality, rē-al'i-ti, n. State of being real; actual being, in distinction from mere appearance; fact; truth; something not merely matter of show. [Fr. realité—L. res, rei, a thing.]
Realisable, rē'al-iz-a-bl, a. That may be realised.
Realization, rē'al-iz-ā''shon, n. Act of realising; act of converting money into land; act of believing as real; act of bringing into being or act. [Fr. réalisation—L. res, rei, a thing.]
Realize, rē'al-iz, vt. To make real; to bring into being or act; to convert, as money into land; to believe or treat as real; to bring into actual existence; to render tangible; to make certain or substantial. ppr. realizing, pret. & pp. realized. [Fr. réaliser.]
Realising, rē'al-iz-ing, p.a. That makes real, or that brings home as a reality.
Really, rē'al-li, adv. With reality; with actual existence; in truth; in fact.
Realm, relm, n. Royal jurisdiction or extent of government; the dominions of a king; a kingdom. [Old Fr. royaulme; L. regnum—rex, a king.]
Realty, rē'al-ti, n. The fixed nature of real property; a piece of real property.
Ream, rēm, n. Originally, such a quantity of things as can be tied by one band; a bundle of paper, consisting of twenty quires. [Sax. a ligament.]
Reanimate, rē-an'i-māt, vt. To animate again; to revive; to restore to life, as a person dead; to revive, as the spirits; to invigorate; to infuse new courage into. ppr. reanimating, pret. & pp. reanimated.
Reanswer, rē-an'sėr, vt. or i. To answer back; to react.
Reap, rēp, vt. Originally, to pluck; to cut with a sickle, as grain; to gather; to receive as a reward.—vi. To perform the operation of reaping; to receive the fruit of labour or works. [Sax. ripan—Goth. raupan, to pluck.]
Reaper, rēp'ėr, n. One who reaps.
Reaping, rēp'ing, p.n. Act of cutting grain with a sickle.
Reappear, rē-ap-pēr', vi. To appear a second time.
Rear, rēr, n. That which is behind; the part of an army which is behind the other; the part of a fleet which is behind the other; the last class; the last in order.—a. Hindmost. [Fr. arrière; L. ad, and retro, backward.]
Rear, rēr, vt. To raise up; to lift up from a fall; to carry up; to stir or rouse up, as a boar; to raise or breed, as cattle; to bring up; to educate.—vi. To rise up on the hind legs, as a horse. [Sax. rœran—Goth. reiran, to disturb.]
Rearly, rēr'li, adv. Early.

Rear-mouse, rēr'mous, n. The mouse that raises itself from the ground; the leather-winged bat. [Sax. hreremus —hreran, from hreran, to raise, and mus, a mouse.]
Rearward, rēr'ward, n. The rear-guard; the last troop; the end; the tail; the train behind; the latter part.
Reason, rē'zon, n. That which is conveyed by speech; that of which speech is the instrument and the exponent; a faculty of the mind by which it distinguishes truth from falsehood, and good from evil; all the intellectual powers collectively; reasoning; that which is alleged in words, as the ground of opinion; cause; principle; motive; that which justifies a measure; argument; proof; efficient cause; final cause or end; that which is dictated by reason; reasonable claim; justice; moderation; moderate demands; claims which reason and justice admit or prescribe.—vi. To exercise the faculty of reason; to deduce inferences justly from premises; to debate; to talk; to inquire by discussion or mutual communication of thoughts, arguments, or reasons.—vt. To apply the faculty of reason to; to debate; to persuade by reasoning. [Norm.; L. ratio; Sans. rath, to speak.]
Reasonable, rē'zon-a-bl, a. Having the faculty of reason; governed by reason; conformable to reason; not excessive; not unjust.
Reasonableness, rē'zon-a-bl-nes, n. State or quality of being reasonable.
Reasonably, rē'zon-a-bli, adv. In a manner or degree agreeable to reason.
Reasoned, rē'zond, p.a. Examined or discussed by arguments.
Reasoner, rē'zon-ėr, n. One who reasons.
Reasoning, rē'zon-ing, p.a. Arguing; deducing inferences from premises.—p.n. Act of exercising the faculty of reason; the act of the mind by which new propositions are deduced from previous ones; argumentation.
Reasonless, rē'zon-les, a. Destitute of reason; void of reason; absurd.
Reassemble, rē-as-sem'bl, vt. To assemble or collect again.—vi. To assemble or convene again. ppr. reassembling, pret. & pp. reassembled.
Reassert, rē-as-sėrt', vt. To assert again; to maintain after cessation.
Reassurance, rē-a-shūr'ans, n. A second or renewed assurance; a second assurance against loss, or the assurance by an underwriter, to relieve himself from a risk he has taken.
Reassure, rē-a-shūr', vt. To assure again; to restore courage to; to insure a second time against loss. ppr. reassuring, pret. & pp. reassured.
Reave, rēv, vt. To take away by violence; to bereave. ppr. reaving, pret. & pp. reft. [Sax. reafian—L. rapio, to snatch.]
Rebaptise, rē-bap-tīz', vt. To baptise a second time. ppr. rebaptising, pret. & pp. rebaptised.
Rebate, rē-bāt', vt. To beat back; to beat to obtuseness; to blunt; to abate or deduct from. ppr. rebating, pret. & pp. rebated. [Fr. rebattre—L. batuo, to beat.]
Rebate, **Rebatement**, rē-bāt', rē-bāt'ment, n. Abatement; deduction made, either of interest or of some particular sum, for prompt payment.
Rebeck, rē'bek, n. A three-stringed violin.
Rebel, re'bal, n. One who wages war again, after having been conquered; one who makes war against constituted

authorities; a contemner of the sovereign's laws.—*a. Rebellious;* acting in revolt. [Fr. *rebelle*—L. *re,* and *bellum,* war.]

Rebel, re-bel', *vi.* To rise in violent opposition against lawful authority. *ppr.* rebelling, *pret. & pp.* rebelled. [L. *rebello—bellum,* war.]

Rebellion, re-bel'li-on, *n. Act of rebelling;* an avowed renunciation of the authority of the government to which allegiance is due; revolt. [Fr.]

Rebellious, re-bel'li-us, *a. Pertaining to rebellion;* traitorously resisting lawful authority; insubordinate.

Rebelliously, re-bel'li-us-li, *adv. In a rebellious manner.*

Rebound, re-bound', *vi. To bound back;* to start back; to be returned; to reverberate.—*vt. To cause to bound back;* to reverberate.—*n. Act of rebounding;* act of flying back. [Fr. *rebondir—bondir,* to bound.]

Rebuff, re-buf', *n. A beating back;* repulsion; refusal; rejection of solicitation.—*vt.* To check; to reject unceremoniously. [It. *rabbuffo;* Old Fr. *buffe,* a buffet.]

Rebuild, re-bild', *vt. To build again;* to renew, as a structure.

Rebukable, re-buk'a-bl, *a. Worthy of rebuke* or reprehension.

Rebuke, re-buk', *vt. To stop the mouth of;* to reprimand for a fault; to check by reproof; to chasten; to restrain.—*n. A chiding into silence;* reproof for faults; chastisement. *ppr.* rebuking, *pret. & pp.* rebuked. [Fr. *reboucher;* L. *bucca,* the mouth.]

Rebuker, re-buk'er, *n.* One who rebukes.

Rebus, re'bus, *n.* **Rebuses,** re'bus-ez, *pl.* A quaint mode of expressing words or phrases by *things,* or by the pictures of objects whose names bear a resemblance to the words or to the syllables of which they are composed.—*vt.†* To try the skill of with a rebus. [L. from *res,* a thing.]

Rebut, re-but', *vt. To drive or beat back;* to oppose by argument, plea, or countervailing proof. *ppr.* rebutting, *pret. & pp.* rebutted. [Fr. *rebuter*—Old Fr. *buter,* to thrust.]

Rebutting, re-but'ing, *p.n.* Countervailing allegation or evidence.

Recall, re-kal', *vt. To call back;* to revoke; to annul by a subsequent act; to revive in memory.—*n. A calling back;* revocation; the power of calling back or revoking.

Recant, re-kant', *vt. To recall,* as something *sung* or said; to take back, as a former declaration; to retract; to disavow.—*vi.* To unsay what has been said; to revoke a declaration; to retract. [L. *recanto—cano,* to sing.]

Recantation, re-kant-a'shon, *n. Act of recanting;* that which is recanted.

Recapitulate, re-ka-pit'u-lat, *vt.* To go over *again,* as the *heads* of a thing; to go over, as the principal things mentioned in a preceding discourse; to reiterate; to rehearse.—*vi.* To sum up what has been said. *ppr.* recapitulating, *pret. & pp.* recapitulated. [Fr. *récapituler*—L. *caput, capitis,* the head.]

Recapitulation, re-ka-pit'u-la"shon, *n. Act of recapitulating;* a concise statement of the principal points in a preceding discourse or essay.

Recapture, re-kap'tur, *n. Act of retaking;* the retaking of a prize from a captor; a prize retaken.—*vt. To retake;* to retake, as a prize which had been previously taken. *ppr.* recapturing, *pret. & pp.* recaptured.

Recast, re-kast', *vt. To cast again;* to mould anew; to complete a second time.

Recede, re-sed', *vi. To go or move back;* to retreat; to withdraw; to retire. (With *from.*) *ppr.* receding, *pret. & pp.* receded. [L. *recedo—cedo,* to go.]

Receding, re-sed'ing, *p.a.* Retreating; withdrawing.

Receipt, re-set', *n. Act of receiving;* the place of receiving; that which is received; recipe; a written acknowledgment of having received a sum of money, goods, &c.—*vt. To give a receipt* or written acknowledgment for. [Fr. *recette*—L. *re,* and *capio,* to take.]

Receivable, re-sev'a-bl, *a. That may be received.*

Receive, re-sev', *vt. To take;* to take or obtain; to take, as a thing offered or sent; to accept; to take as due or as a reward; to take intellectually; to allow; to hold; to admit; to welcome; to take in or on; to contain. *ppr.* receiving, *pret. & pp.* received. [Fr. *recevoir;* L. *re,* and *capio,* to take.]

Received, re-sevd', *p.a.* Accepted; admitted; believed.

Receiver, re-sev'er, *n. One who receives;* a recipient; something which receives or contains.

Receiving, re-sev'ing, *p.n. Act of receiving;* that which is received.

Recency, re'sen-si, *n. State of being recent;* newness; freshness. [L. *recens,* fresh.]

Recension, re-sen'shon, *n.* Primarily, *a counting over again;* examination of the text of an ancient author; revisal. [L. *recensio—censeo,* to count.]

Recent, re'sent, *a. New;* modern; fresh; lately received; of late occurrence; not long dismissed, released, or parted from. [Fr. *récent*—L. *recens*—Heb. *rākak,* to be tender, soft.]

Recently, re'sent-li, *adv.* Newly; lately.

Recentness, re'sent-nes, *n. State or quality of being recent;* newness. [L. *re,* and *capio,* to take.]

Receptacle, re-sep'ta-kl, *n. A place or vessel into which something is received;* a receiver; a reservoir. [Fr. *réceptacle*—L. *re,* and *capio,* to take.]

Reception, re-sep'shon, *n. Act of receiving;* state of being received; admission of anything sent; admission of entrance for holding; a receiving for entertainment; a receiving officially. [Fr. *réception*—L. *capio,* to take.]

Receptive, re-sep'tiv, *a. Having the quality of receiving.* [Sp. *receptivo.*]

Recess, re-ses', *n. A going back;* retreat; retirement; part of a room form..ed by the receding of the wall, as an alcove, niche, &c.; place of secrecy; private abode; remission of business; seclusion from the world; secret or abstruse part. [L. *recessus—cedo,* to go.]

Recession, re-se'shon, *n. Act of receding;* act of receding from a claim. [Late L. *recessio.*]

Recheat, re-chet', *n.* A strain which the huntsman winds on the horn to call the hounds back.

Recipe, re'si-pe, *n. Something directed to be taken;* a medical prescription; a receipt for almost any mixture. [Fr. *récipé*—L. take thou—*capio,* to take.]

Recipient, re-si'pi-ent, *n. A receiver;* the person or thing that receives. [Fr. *récipient*—L. *capio,* to take.]

Reciprocal, re-sip'rō-kal, *a. Mutually received;* moving backwards and forwards; alternate; done by each to the other; mutually interchangeable.—*n.* That which is reciprocal. [Fr. *réciproque*—L. *capio,* to take.]

Reciprocally, re-sip'rō-kal-li, *adv.* Mutually; interchangeably.

Reciprocate, re-sip'rō-kāt, *vi. To go backward and forward;* to act interchangeably.—*vt.* To exchange; to interchange. *ppr.* reciprocating, *pret. & pp.* reciprocated. [L. *reciproco, reciprocatus—reque, proque,* backwards and forwards.]

Reciprocating, re-sip'rō-kāt-ing, *p.a.* Alternating.

Reciprocation, re-sip'rō-ka"shon, *n. Act of reciprocating;* a mutual giving and returning. [Fr. *réciprocation.*]

Reciprocity, re-si-pros'i-ti, *n. State or quality of being reciprocal;* equal mutual rights or benefits to be yielded or enjoyed. [Fr. *réciprocité.*]

Recital, re-sit'al, *n. Act of reciting;* a telling of the particulars of an adventure or of a series of events. [Fr. *récit.*]

Recitation, re-si-ta'shon, *n. Act of reciting;* the delivery before an audience of the compositions of others committed to memory. [Fr. *récitation.*]

Recitative, re'si-ta-tēv, *n.* A species of singing which approaches toward ordinary speaking; language delivered in musical tones; a piece of music in recitative.—*a. Reciting;* pertaining to musical pronunciation. [Fr. *récitatif.*]

Recite, re-sit', *vt. To read aloud;* to repeat, as the words of another; to tell over, as occurrences; to detail. *vi. To make a recital;* to rehearse; to pronounce before an audience the compositions of others, committed to memory. *ppr.* reciting, *pret. & pp.* recited. [Fr. *réciter;* L. *cito,* to proclaim.]

Reciter, re-sit'er, *n. One who recites.*

Reck, rek, *vt.* To heed; to regard; to care for; to mind. (With *of.*) [Sax. *recan,* to care for.]

Reckless, rek'les, *a. Having no care or concern;* without heed or regard.

Recklessly, rek'les-li, *adv. In a reckless manner;* heedlessly; carelessly.

Recklessness, rek'les-nes, *n. Quality of being reckless;* heedlessness.

Reckon, rek'n, *vt. To count; to number;* to estimate; to set in the number or rank of; to account; to esteem; to regard.—*vi. To compute; to calculate;* to charge to account; to reason with one's self and conclude from arguments; to pay a penalty. (With *for.*) [Sax. *recan,* to count.]

Reckoner, rek'n-ér, *n. He or that which reckons* or computes.

Reckoning, rek'n-ing, *p.n. Act of counting;* calculation; an account of time; a statement of accounts with another; the sum of money charged by a host; bill; esteem; account of.

Reclaim, re-klām', *vt. To claim back;* to demand to have returned; to bring back to a correct course of life; to reduce from a wild to a tame state; to make gentle; to regain; to reduce to a state fit for cultivation.—*vi. To cry out;* to exclaim. [Fr. *réclamer*—L. *clamo,* to shout aloud.]

Reclaimable, re-klām'a-bl, *a. That may be reclaimed,* reformed, or tamed.

Reclaimed, re-klāmd', *p.a.* Reformed; recovered.

Reclamation, re-kla-mā'shon, *n. Act of reclaiming;* state of being reclaimed; recovery. [Fr. *réclamation.*]

Recline, re-klin', *vt. To bend back;* to cause to lean to one side.—*vi. To lean;*

ch, chain; j, job; g, go; ng, sing; ᴛʜ, then; th, thin; w, wig; wh, whig; zh, azure; †obsolete.

to be recumbent; to rest or repose. *ppr.* reclining, *pret. & pp.* reclined. [L. *reclino;* Gr. *klino,* to bend.]

Reclining, rē-klīn'ing, *p.a.* Leaning back or sidewise; resting; recumbent.

Recluse, rē-klūs', *a.* Shut up; sequestered; retired from the world; solitary. *n.* One shut up; a person who lives in retirement; one of a class of religious devotees who live in single cells, usually attached to monasteries. [Fr. *reclus*—L. *claudo, clausum,* to shut.]

Reclusive, rē-klūs'iv, *a.* Affording retirement from society.

Recognition, re-kog-ni'shon, *n.* Act of recognising; state of being recognized; renewed knowledge; formal avowal; memorial. [Fr. *récognition.*]

Recognisable, re'kog-nīz-a-bl, *a.* That may be recognized.

Recognizance, re-kog'niz-ans, *n.* A recognising; acknowledgment of a person or thing. [Norm. *reconisaunce.*]

Recognise, re'kog-nīz, *vt.* To know again; to recover the knowledge of, either with an open avowal of that knowledge or not; to acknowledge. *ppr.* recognising, *pret. & pp.* recognized. [It. *recognóscere*—L. *re, con,* and *nosco,* to know.]

Recoil, rē-koil', *vi.* To start or fall back; to retire; to retreat; to rebound; to flow back or shrink.—*n.* A starting or falling back; the reaction of fire-arms when discharged. [Fr. *reculer*—L. *culus,* the posteriors.]

Recoiling, rē-koil'ing, *p.a.* Act of starting or falling back; a shrinking.

Recollect, re'kol-lekt, *vt.* To collect again; to call back to the memory; to bring back to the mind; to recognize; to recover composure of mind (with reciprocal pronoun).

Recollection, re-kol-lek'shon, *n.* Act of recollecting; reminiscence; the power of recalling ideas to the mind; memory. [Fr. *récollection.*]

Recommence, rē-kom-mens', *vt.* To commence again; to begin anew. *ppr.* recommencing, *pret. & pp.* recommenced.

Recommencement, rē-kom-mens'ment, *n.* A commencement anew.

Recommend, re-kom-mend', *vt.* To offer to another's notice, confidence, or kindness, by favourable representations; to make acceptable; to commit with prayers; to mention as worthy of something; to advise one to something, as being beneficial. [*re* and *commend.*]

Recommendation, re'kom-mend-ā"-shon, *n.* Act of recommending; the act of representing in a favourable manner for the purpose of procuring civilities of another; that which procures a kind or favourable reception. [Fr. *recommandation.*]

Recommendatory, re-kom-mend'a-tō-ri, *a.* That recommends; that commends to another. [Fr. *recommandatoire.*]

Recommit, rē-kom-mit', *vt.* To commit again; to refer again to a committee. *ppr.* recommitting, *pret. & pp.* recommitted.

Recommitment, Recommittal, rē-kom-mit'ment, rē-kom-mit'al, *n.* A second or renewed commitment; a renewed reference to a committee.

Recompense, re'kom-pens, *vt.* To weigh out or in return; to give in return; to compensate; to repay; to requite; to remunerate.—*n.* Something weighed out in return; an equivalent returned for anything given, done, or suffered; remuneration; requital; satisfaction. *ppr.* recompensing, *pret. & pp.* recompensed. [Fr. *récompenser*—L. *penso,* to weigh out.]

Recompose, rē-kom-pōz', *vt.* To compose anew; to tranquillize, as that which is disturbed; to adjust again. *ppr.* recomposing, *pret. & pp.* recomposed.

Reconcilable, re'kon-sīl-a-bl, *a.* Capable of being reconciled; that may be made to agree; consistent; capable of being adjusted. [Fr. *réconciliable.*]

Reconcile, re'kon-sīl, *vt.* To bring together again; to restore to friendship or favour after estrangement; to pacify; to make consistent; to bring to agreement; to adjust; to compose, as differences. *ppr.* reconciling, *pret. & pp.* reconciled. [Fr. *réconcilier*—L. *re, con,* and *cieo,* to make to go.]

Reconciled, re'kon-sīld, *p.a.* Made consistent; adjusted.

Reconcilement, re'kon-sīl-ment, *n.* Reconciliation; renewal of friendship.

Reconciler, re'kon-sīl-ėr, *n.* One who reconciles; one who brings parties at variance into renewed friendship.

Reconciliation, re'kon-si-li-ā"shon, *n.* Act of reconciling; reconcilement; the means by which sinners are reconciled and brought into a state of favour with God; atonement; expiation; agreement of things seemingly inconsistent. [Fr. *réconciliation.*]

Recondite, re'kon-dit, *a.* Put together away; hidden from the view; dealing in things abstruse. [L. *reconditus*—*re, con,* and *do, datum,* to give.]

Reconnoitre, re-kon-noi'tėr, *vt.* To take notice of again; to examine by the eye; to examine, as the state of an enemy's army or camp, or the ground for military operations. *ppr.* reconnoitring, *pret. & pp.* reconnoitred. [Fr. *reconnaître*—L. *re, con,* and *nosco,* to know.]

Reconsider, rē-kon-si'dėr, *vt.* To consider again; to re-examine; to take up for renewed consideration, as that which has been previously acted upon; as a motion, vote, &c.

Reconsideration, rē-kon-si'dėr-ā"shon, *n.* The taking up, for renewed consideration, of that which has been previously acted upon.

Reconstruct, rē-kon-strukt', *vt.* To construct again; to rebuild.

Reconstruction, rē-kon-struk'shon, *n.* Act of constructing again.

Record, rē-kord', *vt.* To preserve in the mind or heart; to cause to be remembered; to register; to write in a book for the purpose of preserving correct evidence of.—*vi.* To sing or repeat a tune. [Fr. *recorder*—L. *cor, cordis,* Sans. *hrid,* the heart.]

Record, re'kord, *n.* An authentic or official copy of any writing, or account of any facts and proceedings, entered in a book for preservation, or the book containing such copy or account.

Recordation, re-kord-ā'shon, *n.* Remembrance; register.

Recorder, rē-kord'ėr, *n.* One who records; an officer who registers writings or transactions; a registrar; the chief judicial officer of a borough or city, so called because his court is a court of record; a kind of flute.

Recordership, rē-kord'ėr-ship, *n.* The office of a recorder.

Recording, rē-kord'ing, *p.a.* Act of placing on record; a record.

Recount, rē-kount', *vt.* To enumerate; to go over in detail; to relate; to recite, as imaginary adventures; to rehearse. [Fr. *reconter*—*conter,* to tell—L. *con.* and *puto,* to reckon.]

Recourse, rē-kōrs', *n.* A running back; a going to with a request or application, as for aid or protection; resort; access; frequent course. [Fr. *recours*—L. *curro, cursum,* to run.]

Recover, rē-kuv'ėr, *vt.* To get or obtain again; to get, as that which was lost; to restore from sickness; to revive from apparent death; to repair the loss of; to bring back to a former state by liberation from capture; to obtain; to come to; to obtain in return for injury or debt.—*vi.* To regain health after sickness; to grow well; to regain a former state after misfortune. [Fr. *recouvrer*—L. *capio,* to take.]

Recoverable, rē-kuv'ėr-a-bl, *a.* That may be recovered; that may be restored from sickness; that may be brought back to a former condition; that may be obtained from a debtor or possessor.

Recovery, rē-kuv'ė-ri, *n.* Act of recovering; restoration from sickness; the capacity of being restored to health.

Recreancy, re'krē-an-si, *n.* State or quality of a recreant; a cowardly yielding.

Recreant, re'krē-ant, *a.* Renegade; craven; apostate; crying for mercy, as a combatant in the trial by battle; mean-spirited.—*n.* A renegade; one who yields in combat; one who begs for mercy; a mean-spirited cowardly wretch. [Norm. cowardly; Low L. *recreditii,* those who gave themselves up to an enemy—L. *credo,* to intrust.]

Recreate, re'krē-āt, *vt.* To create anew; to renew; to revive; to enliven; to refresh after toil; to delight; to relieve. *ppr.* recreating, *pret. & pp.* recreated.

Recreation, re-krē-ā'shon, *n.* Refreshment of the strength and spirits after toil; pleasurable occupation in sorrow; diversion; entertainment. [Fr. *récréation.*]

Recreative, re'krē-āt-iv, *a.* Serving to recreate; refreshing; amusing; diverting. [Fr. *récréatif.*]

Recriminate, rē-krim'in-āt, *vi.* To return one accusation with another; to retort an accusation with another.—*vt.* To accuse in return. *ppr.* recriminating, *pret. & pp.* recriminated. [L. *re,* and *criminor, criminatus,* to accuse one of a crime—*crimen,* a charge, crime.]

Recrimination, rē-krim'in-ā"shon, *n.* Act of recriminating; an accusation brought by the accused against the accuser upon the same fact. [Fr. *récrimination.*]

Recriminative, Recriminatory, rē-krim'in-āt-iv, rē-krim'in-a-tō-ri, *a.* Retorting accusation. [Fr. *récriminatoire.*]

Recruit, rē-krūt', *vt.* To cause to grow up or increase again; to repair; to make up by fresh supplies for anything wasted; to supply with new men, as an army; to reinforce.—*vi.* To grow up or increase again; to gain new supplies of anything wasted; to gain new flesh, health, spirits, &c.; to gain new supplies of men; to raise new soldiers.—*n.* A newly enlisted soldier. [Fr. *recruter*—L. *cresco, cretum,* to grow—*creo, cretum,* to make—Sans. *kri,* to do.]

Recruiter, rē-krūt'ėr, *n.* One who recruits; one who supplies a company with new members.

Recruiting, rē-krūt'ing, *p.a.* Raising new soldiers for an army.—*p.a.* The business of raising new soldiers to supply the loss of men in an army.

Rectangle, rek'tang-gl, *n.* A right-angled parallelogram. [Fr.—L. *rectus,* right, and *angulus,* an angle.]

Rectangled, rek'tang-gld, *p.a.* Having one or more right-angles.

Rectangular, rek-tang'gū-lar. *a.* Right-

angled; having one or more right-angles.
Rectifiable, rek'ti-fi-a-bl, a. That may be rectified or set right.
Rectification, rek'ti-fi-kā''shon, n. Act of rectifying; the process of purifying any substance by repeated distillation. [Fr.]
Rectified, rek'ti-fid, p.a. Refined by repeated distillation.
Rectifier, rek'ti-fi-ėr, n. He or that which rectifies, corrects, or amends.
Rectify, rek'ti-fi, vt. To make right; to adjust; to refine by repeated distillation or sublimation. ppr. rectifying, pret. & pp. rectified. (Fr. rectifier—L. rectus, right, and facio, to make.]
Rectilineal, Rectilinear, rek-ti-lin'ē-al, rek-ti-lin'ē-ȧr, a. Right or straight lined; bounded by right lines; straight. [L. rectus, and linea, a line.]
Rectitude, rek'ti-tūd, n. Straightness; directness; uprightness; exact conformity to truth, or to the rules prescribed for moral conduct, either by divine or human laws. [L. rectitūdo—rego, rectus, to keep straight.]
Rector, rek'tor, n. A ruler or governor; a clergyman who has the charge and cure of a parish, and has the tithes, &c.; in Scotland, the head-master of a public grammar-school, also the chief officer of a university; the superior officer or chief of a religious house. [L. —rego, to keep straight.]
Rectorial, rek-tō'ri-al, a. Pertaining to a rector or rectory.
Rectorship, rek'tor-ship, n. The office or rank of a rector. [Fr. rectorat.]
Rectory, rek'tō-ri, n. A parish church, parsonage, or spiritual living, with all its rights, tithes, and glebes; a rector's mansion or parsonage-house.
Recumbency, rē-kum'ben-si, n. Act or posture of leaning, reclining, or lying; rest; repose; idle state.
Recumbent, rē-kum'bent, a. Lying down; leaning; reposing; inactive; idle. [L. recumbens—cumbo, to lie down.]
Recumbently, rē-kum'bent-li, adv. In a recumbent posture.
Recur, rē-kėr', vi. To run back; to have recourse; to return to the thought or mind; to occur at a stated interval or according to some regular rule. ppr. recurring, pret. & pp. recurred. [L. recurro—curro, to run.]
Recurrence, rē-ku'rens, n. Act of recurring; act of occurring at a stated interval; the having recourse.
Recurrent, rē-ku'rent, a. Recurring from time to time. [Fr. récurrent.]
Recurring, rē-kėr'ing, p.a. Occurring according to some regular rule.
Recusancy, re'kū-zan-si, n. The tenets of a recusant; nonconformity.
Recusant, re'kū-sant, a. Making objection against, in statement or reply; refusing to acknowledge the supremacy of the Crown, or to conform to the established rites of the church. n. A person who refuses to acknowledge the supremacy of the Crown in matters of religion; a nonconformist. [Fr. récusant—L. re, and causa, a cause.]
Red, red, a. Of a colour resembling that of arterial blood; crimson.—n. A colour resembling that of arterial blood; crimson. [Sax. red; Icel. riuda, to make bloody—Sans. Art, to blush.]
Redan, rē-dan', n. A fort composed of two faces, forming between them an angle, and without any covering to the rear.
Redbreast, red'brest, n. A bird so called from the colour of its breast; the robin.

Red-coat, red'kōt, n. A name given to a soldier who wears a red coat.
Red-deer, red'dėr, n. The common stag.
Redden, red'n, vt. To make red.—vi. To grow or become red; to blush; to have the visage flushed with anger.
Reddened, red'nd, p.a. Grown red.
Reddish, red'ish, a. Somewhat red.
Reddishness, red'ish-nes, n. Redness in a moderate degree.
Rede, rēd, n. A word; advice.—vt. To counsel; to advise. [Sax. ræd.]
Redeem, rē-dēm', vt. To buy back; to ransom; to liberate from captivity, or from any obligation or liability to suffer or to be forfeited, by paying an equivalent for; to regain possession of, as of a thing alienated; to recover; to free from; to improve to the best purpose, as time; to perform what has been promised; to make good by performance. [L. redimo—emo, to ı uy.]
Redeemable, rē-dēm'a-bl, a. That may be redeemed; capable of redemption.
Redeemed, rē-dēmd', p.a. Bought back; ransomed; delivered from bondage, or from the possession of another, by an equivalent paid.
Redeemer, rē-dēm'ėr, n. One who redeems or ransoms; the Saviour, JESUS CHRIST.
Redeeming, rē-dēm'ing, p.a. That redeems or makes amends.
Redeliver, rē-dē-liv'ėr, vt. To deliver back; to liberate a second time.
Redelivery, rē-dē-liv'ė-ri, n. Act of delivering back; a second liberation.
Redemption, rē-dem'shon, n. A buying back; act of redeeming; repurchase of captured goods or prisoners; the act of procuring the deliverance of persons or things from the power of captors by the payment of an equivalent; deliverance from sin and misery by the death of Christ; salvation. [Fr. rédemption—L. emo, emptum, to buy.]
Red-hot, red'hot, a. Red with heat; heated to redness; very hot.
Redintegration, rē-din'tē-grā''shon, n. Renewal; restoration to a whole or sound state. [L. redintegratio—integer, whole, entire.]
Red-lead, red'led, n. A preparation of lead of a fine red colour, used in painting, &c.
Red-letter, red'let-tėr, a. Having red letters; a red-letter day is a fortunate or auspicious day; so called because the saints' days were marked in the old calendars with red letters.
Redly, red'li, adv. With redness.
Redness, red'nes, n. Quality of being red; red colour. [Sax. readnesse.]
Redolence, re'dō-lens, n. Quality of being redolent; fragrance; perfume.
Redolent, re'dō-lent, a. Emitting an odour; diffusing a sweet scent. [L. redolens—oleo, to smell.]
Redouble, rē-du'bl, vt. To double again; to increase by repeated or continued additions.—vi. To double again; to become twice as much. ppr. redoubling, pret. & pp. redoubled.
Redoubled, rē-du'bld, p.a. Repeated in return; repeated over and over.
Redoubt, rē-dout', n. A retreat; a field or portion of a permanent fortification, affording a shelter or retreat to soldiers. [Fr. réduit—L. re, back, and duco, ductum, to lead.]
Redoubt!, rē-dout', vt. To stand in dread of; to dread.
Redoubtable, rē-dout'a-bl, a. Causing doubt or irresolution; formidable; terrible to foes. [Fr.; L. dubito, to doubt.]
Redound, rē-dound', vi. To surge back,

as waves; to be sent or driven back; to contribute; to proceed in the consequence or effect. [Fr. redonder—L. undo, to surge—Sans. und, to be wet.]
Redress, rē-dres', vt. To set right; to rectify; to remedy; to repair; to ease; to relieve.—n. A setting right; a rectifying; remedy; deliverance from wrong; reparation. [Fr. redresser—L. re, dis, and rego, to lead straight.]
Redressible, rē-dres'i-bl, a. That may be redressed or relieved; reparable.
Reduce, rē-dūs', vt. To lead or bring back; to bring back to a former state; to restore; to bring down; to make less in length, breadth, thickness, size, quantity, or value; to bring down in dignity; to bring into subjection; to bring, as into a class or species; to bring under rules; to change, as numbers from one denomination into another, without altering their value. ppr. reducing, pret. & pp. reduced. [L. reduco—duco, to lead.]
Reduced, rē-dūst', p.a. Impoverished; subdued.
Reducible, rē-dūs'i-bl, a. That may be reduced.
Reduction, rē-duk'shon, n. Act of reducing, or state of being reduced; curtailment. [Fr. réduction.]
Redundancy, rē-dun'dan-si, n. State of being redundant; superfluity; superfluity of words. [Fr. redundance.]
Redundant, rē-dun'dant, a. Overflowing; superfluous; exceeding what is necessary; using more words than are necessary; diffuse. [L. redundans—undo, to rise in waves.]
Redundantly, rē-dun'dant-li, adv. In a redundant manner.
Re-echo, rē-e'kō, vt. To echo back; to reverberate.—vi. To echo back; to return back or be reverberated, as an echo.—n. The echo of an echo.
Reechy!, rēch'i, a. Tarnished with smoke; sweaty.
Reed, rēd, n. The name given to many aquatic plants, usually having hollow stalks or stems with joints, which, when agitated by the wind, emit a rustling sound; a small pipe, as originally made of a reed; a little tube through which a hautboy or clarionet is blown; an arrow, as made of a reed, and headed. [Sax. hreod; Sans. ru, to sound.]
Reeded, rēd'ed, p.a. Covered with reeds; formed with channels and ridges like reeds.
Reedy, rēd'i, a. Abounding with reeds; having the quality of a reed in tone, i.e. harsh and thick, as a voice.
Reef, rēf, n. The part of a sail which is plucked in or rolled up to contract the sail.—vt. To pluck or haul in, as a sail by rolling a certain portion of it and making it fast to the yard. [D. rift; Sax. reafian, to pluck.]
Reef, rēf, n. A chain or range of rocks lying at or near the surface of the water, and becoming dry at certain periods of the tide. [G. riff; Old G. riffan, to become dry.]
Reefed, rēft, p.a. Having a portion of the top or bottom of a sail folded and made fast to the yard.
Reek, rēk, n. That which increases and ascends; smoke; vapour; steam.—vi. To smoke; to steam; to emit vapour. [Sax. réc; Old G. rauh, smoke—San', ruh, to increase.]
Reeking, rēk'ing, p.a. Steaming; emitting vapour.
Reeky, rēk'i, a. Smoky; soiled with smoke or steam; foul.

Reel, rel, n. *An instrument that rolls or turns, as on an axis, and on which yarn, &c., are wound; a lively dance peculiar to Scotland, exhibiting a whirling or circular motion.*—vt. *To wind upon a reel, as thread or yarn from the spindle.* [Sax. *hreol*—G. *rolle—rollen*, to roll along.]

Reel, rel, vi. *To stagger; to incline or move in walking, first to one side and then to the other; to vacillate.* [Sw. *ragla,* to stagger.]

Reeling, rēl'ing, p.n. *The process of winding thread, silk, cotton, &c., into a skein; a staggering.*

Re-embark, rē-em-bärk', vt. *To embark or put on board again.*—vi. *To embark or go on board again.*

Re-enact, rē-en-akt', vt. *To enact again.*

Re-enactment, rē-en-akt'ment, n. *The enacting or passing of a law a second time; the renewal of a law.*

Re-enforce, rē-en-förs', vt. *To enforce anew; to strengthen with new force, assistance, or support.* ppr. re-enforcing, pret. & pp. re-enforced.

Re-enforcement, rē-en-förs'ment, n. *Act of re-enforcing: additional force.*

Re-enter, rē-en'ter, vt. *To enter again or anew.*—vi. *To enter anew.*

Re-entry, rē-en'tri, n. *An entering again; the resuming or retaking the possession of lands lately lost.*

Reer-mouse, rēr'mous, n. *See* REARMOUSE.

Re-establish, rē-es-tab'lish, vt. *To establish anew; to fix or confirm again.*

Re-established, rē-es-tab'lisht, p.a. *Established or confirmed again.*

Re-establishment, rē-es-tab'lish-ment, n. *Act of establishing again; the state of being re-established; restoration.*

Re-examine, rē-eg-zam'in, vt. *To examine anew.* ppr. re-examining, pret. & pp. re-examined.

Refection, rē-fek'shon, n. *A making anew; refreshment after hunger.* [Fr. *réfection*—L. *facio,* to make.]

Refectory, rē-fek'to-ri, n. *A room for meals; originally, a hall in convents and monasteries, where a moderate repast is taken.* [Fr. *réfectoire*—L. *re,* and *facio, factum*, to make.]

Refel, rē-fel', vt. *To refute.*

Refer, rē-fėr', vt. *To carry back; to make over; to deliver over to another for decision; to reduce; to assign, as to an order or class; to ascribe; to attribute by references.*—vi. *To point or have reference; to appeal; to have respect to by intimation without naming.* ppr. referring. pret. & pp. referred. [Fr. *référer*—L. *fero*, to carry.]

Referable, re'fėr-a-bl, a. *That may be referred; that may be considered as belonging to or related to.*

Reference, re'fėr-ens, n. *Act of referring; a sending to another for information; respect; allusion to; the submitting of a matter in dispute to a person or persons appointed by the court before which the matter is brought.*

Referrible, rē-fėr'i-bl, a. *That may be referred; referable.*

Refine, rē-fīn', vt. *To increase the fineness of; to purify, as liquors; to separate, as a metallic substance from all other matter; to purify, as manners, from what is vulgar; to purify, as language; to purify, as taste; to give a nice perception of beauty in literature and the arts; to purify, as the moral principles.*—vi. *To improve in fineness; to become pure; to affect nicety or subtilty in thought or language.* ppr. refining, pret. & pp. refined.

Refined, rē-find', p.a. *Purified; separated from what is coarse; polished.*

Refinement, rē-fīn'ment, n. *Act of refining; a clearing from dross or alloy; purification; state of being refined; an improved state of language; elegance; elegance of manners; nice observance of the civilities of social intercourse; purity of taste; nice perception of beauty and propriety in literature and the arts; purity of mind and morals; purity of heart; artificial practice; subtility; affectation of nicety.*

Refiner, rē-fīn'ėr, n. *One who refines; specially, one that refines metals.*

Refining, rē-fīn'ing, p.n. *Act or process of purifying; the purification of a metal from an alloy; the use of excessive subtility.*

Refit, rē-fit', vt. *To fit or prepare again; to restore after damage or decay.* ppr. refitting, pret. & pp. refitted.

Refitment, rē-fit'ment, n. *A fitting out a second time.*

Reflect, rē-flekt', vt. *To bend back; to throw back; to cause to return after striking upon any surface, as light, heat, &c.; to mirror.*—vi. *To bend or turn back; to throw back light, heat, &c.; to rebound, as from a surface; to turn back the thoughts upon the past; to revolve in the mind; to muse; to bring or cast censure or reproach (with* on *or* upon*).* [L. *reflecto—flecto*, to bend.]

Reflected, rē-flekt'ed, p.a. *Thrown back; returned.*

Reflecting, rē-flekt'ing, p.a. *Throwing back light, heat, &c., as a mirror or other surface; thoughtful; reflective.*

Reflection, rē-flek'shon, n. *Act of reflecting; state of being reflected; that which is reflected; thought thrown back on itself, on the past or on the absent; attentive consideration; the expression of thought; censure.*

Reflective, rē-flekt'iv, a. *Throwing back images; considering the operations of the mind or things past; musing.*

Reflector, rē-flekt'or, n. *One who reflects; that which reflects, as a polished surface of metal.*

Reflex, rē'fleks, a. *Bent back; reflected; designating the parts of a painting illuminated by light reflected from another part of the same picture.*—n. *Reflection;* the light *reflected from an enlightened surface to one in shade.* [L. *reflexus—flecto,* to bend.]

Reflext, rē-fleks', vt. *To reflect.*

Reflexibility, rē-fleks'i-bil'li-ti, n. *Quality of being reflexible or capable of being reflected.* [Fr. *reflexibilité.*]

Reflexible, rē-fleks'i-bl, a. *Capable of being reflected.* [Fr. *reflexible.*]

Refluent, re'flū-ent, a. *Flowing back; ebbing.* [L. *refluens—fluo,* to flow.]

Reflux, rē'fluks, n. *A flowing back; the returning of a fluid.* [Fr.—L. *fluo, fluxum,* to flow.]

Reform, rē-form', vt. *To form anew; to transform; to change from worse to better; to improve; to reclaim; to remove, as that which is bad or corrupt.* vi. *To be formed anew; to return to a former good state; to abandon that which is evil; to be amended or corrected.*—n. *A forming anew; a changing for the better; reformation; rectification; correction.* [Fr. *reformer*—L. *forma*, shape, form.]

Reformation, re-form-a'shon, n. *Act of reforming; amendment; the change of religion in the European churches to its primitive purity, begun by Luther,* A.D. 1517. [Fr. *réformation*—L. *forma,* shape, form—*fero,* to bear.]

Reformative, rē-form'āt-iv, a. *Forming again; having the quality of renewing form.*

Reformatory, rē-form'ā-to-ri, a. *Relating to or causing reformation; tending or calculated to produce reformation.*—n. *An institution for reclaiming criminals and offenders, especially young offenders.* [Sp. *reformatorio.*]

Reformed, rē-formd', p.a. *Formed anew; amended. Denoting all who separated from the Roman Catholic church at the era of the Reformation; denoting those who separated from Luther on the doctrine of consubstantiation, &c., and also the churches founded by them.*

Reformer, rē-form'ėr, n. *One who reforms; one of those who commenced the reformation of religion in the sixteenth century; one who promotes political reform.*

Reforming, rē-form'ing, p.a. *Forming anew; restoring to a good state.*

Refract, rē-frakt', vt. *To break open or up; to break, as the natural course of the rays of light; to cause to deviate from a direct course.* [Fr. *réfracter*—L. *frango, fractum,* to break.]

Refracted, rē-frakt'ed, p.a. *Turned from a direct course, as rays of light.*

Refracting, rē-frakt'ing, p.a. *That refracts or turns rays from a direct course.*

Refraction, rē-frak'shon, n. *Act of refracting; the change in the direction of a ray of light caused by the difference of density in the medium or mediums through which it passes.* [Fr. *refraction*—L. *frango*, to break.]

Refractive, rē-frakt'iv, a. *That refracts; pertaining to refraction.* [Fr. *réfractif.*]

Refractorily, rē-frak'tō-ri-li, adv. *In a refractory manner.*

Refractoriness, rē-frak'tō-ri-nes, n. *State or quality of being refractory.*

Refractory, rē-frak'tō-ri, a. *Breaking through restraint; sullen in disobedience; obstinate; obstinately unyielding, as a horse.* [Fr. *réfractaire.*]

Refrain, rē-frān', vt. *To hold in, as with a bridle; to hold back; to keep from action (with reciprocal pronoun).*—vi. *To keep one's self from interference; to forbear; to abstain.* [Fr. *refrener*—L. *frenem*, a bridle.]

Refrangibility, rē-fran'ji-bil'li-ti, n. *Quality or state of being refrangible; the disposition of rays of light to be refracted in passing out of one transparent body or medium into another.* [Fr. *refrangibilité.*]

Refrangible, rē-fran'ji-bl, a. *Capable of being refracted or turned out of a direct course in passing from one medium to another, as rays of light.* [Fr. *refrangible*—L. *frango,* to break.]

Refresh, rē-fresh', vt. *Primarily, to make cool; to give new strength to; to invigorate; to give new animation to; to reanimate; to renew; to improve by new touches.* [Old Fr. *refreschir.*]

Refreshing, rē-fresh'ing, p.a. *Cooling; reviving; reanimating.*—n. *Refreshment; refreshment in spiritual things.*

Refreshingly, rē-fresh'ing-li, adv. *In a refreshing manner.*

Refreshment, rē-fresh'ment, n. *Act of refreshing; of new strength received after fatigue; that which gives fresh strength or vigour, as food or rest.*

Refrigerant, rē-fri'je-rant, a. *Making cool again; allaying heat.*—n. *A medicine which abates heat.* [Fr. *refrigérant*—L. *frigeo,* to stiffen with cold.]

Fāte, fär, fat, fall; mē, met, hėr; pīne, pin; nōte, not, move; tūbe, tub, bull; oil, pound.

Refrigeratory, re-frĭj'e-rā-tō-ri, a. *Cooling;* mitigating heat.—n. A vessel used for *cooling* in the process of distillation. [L. *refrigeratorius.*]
Reft, reft, pp. of *reave.*
Refuge, re'fūj, n. *A place to fly back to from danger;* that which shelters from danger; an asylum; a retreat; a covert; a stronghold; any place inaccessible to an enemy; a contrivance.—vt. To shelter. [Fr.—L. *fugio*, to flee or fly.]
Refugee, re-fū-jē', n. *One who betakes himself to a refuge;* one who, in times of persecution, flees to a foreign country for safety. [Fr. *refugié.*]
Refulgence, re-ful'jens, n. *State or quality of being refulgent;* a flood of light; splendour. [L. *refulgentia.*]
Refulgent, re-ful'jent, a. *Flashing back light;* casting a bright light; splendid. [L. *refulgens—fulgeo,* to shine.]
Refulgently, re-ful'jent-li, adv. With a flood of light; with great brightness.
Refund, re-fund', vt. Primarily, *to pour back;* to repay; to return in compensation for what has been taken; to restore. [Fr. *refondre*—L. *fundo*, to pour.]
Refusal, re-fūz'al, n. *Act of refusing;* denial of anything demanded, or offered for acceptance; the right of taking in preference to others; option.
Refuse, re-fūz', vt. To *pour back*; to reject; to deny, as a request; to decline to do or grant, as what is solicited; to decline to accept; to reject.—vi. To decline to accept; not to comply. ppr. *refusing*, pret. & pp. *refused.* [Fr. *refuser*—L. *futis*, a pitcher.]
Refuse, ref'ūs, a. Literally, *refused;* worthless; of no value; left as unworthy of reception.—n. *That which is refused;* waste matter; dregs; sediment; scum; dross. [Fr. *refus.*]
Refutable, re-fūt'a-bl, a. *That may be refuted;* that may be proved false or erroneous. [Fr. *réfutable.*]
Refutation, re-fūt-ā'shon, n. *Act or process of refuting;* the act of proving to be false; disproof. [Fr. *réfutation.*]
Refutatory, re-fūt'a-tō-ri, a. *Tending to refute;* containing refutation. [Sp. *refutatório*—L. *futis*, a pitcher.]
Refute, re-fūt', vt. To *pour back*; to overthrow by argument; to prove to be false or erroneous; to disprove; to confute. ppr. *refuting*, pret. & pp. *refuted.* [Fr. *réfuter*—L. *futis*, a pitcher.]
Regain, re-gān', vt. To *gain anew*; to obtain again, as what has escaped or been lost; to recover; to retrieve.
Regal, rē'gal, a. *Pertaining to a king;* kingly; royal. [Old Fr.—L. *rex, regis*, a king—Sans. *râj*, to shine, to rule.]
Regale, re-gāl', vt. To refresh in *regal* style; to refresh royally; to gratify.—vi. To feast royally; to fare sumptuously. ppr. *regaling*, pret. & pp. *regaled.*—n. A magnificent repast. [Fr. *régaler*, to treat—L. *rex, regis*, a king.]
Regalement, re-gāl'ment, n. *Act of regaling;* refreshment; gratification.
Regalia, re-gā'li-a, n. pl. *Ensigns of royalty;* the crown, sceptre, &c. [L. pl. neut. of *regalis*, kingly—*rex*, a king.]
Regally, rē'gal-li, adv. *In a royal manner.*
Regard, re-gärd', vt. To *look back upon*; *to look at;* to consider seriously; to remark; to attend to with respect and estimation; to heed; to esteem; to attend to as a thing that affects our happiness; to fix the mind on; to hold in affection; to keep with religious attention; to lay to heart; to love and hold in esteem; to relate to; to view in the light of; to consider; to reckon.—n. *A looking back upon;* a looking at; relation; respect; consideration; notice; that view of the mind which springs from a sense of value, estimable qualities, or anything that excites admiration; respect; affection; honour; matter demanding notice. [Fr. *regarder—garder*, to look to.]
Regardful, re-gärd'ful, a. *Full of regard;* taking notice; heedful; attentive; observant.
Regardfully, re-gärd'ful-li, adv. *With regard;* attentively; respectfully.
Regarding, re-gärd'ing, prep. Respecting; concerning; relating to.
Regardless, re-gärd'les, a. *Without regard;* heedless; careless; neglectful.
Regardlessly, re-gärd'les-li, adv. Heedlessly; negligently.
Regardlessness, re-gärd'les-nes, n. *Quality of being regardless.*
Regards, re-gärds', n. pl. Respects; good wishes; compliments. (Familiar.)
Regatta, re-gat'ta, n. *A rowing match* between a number of boats; a sailing match between a number of yachts. [It.—L. *remus*, an oar.]
Regency, rē'jen-si, n. *Rule*†; *the government of a regent;* the period during which a regent holds power; the district under the jurisdiction of a vicegerent; the body of men intrusted with vicarious government. [Fr. *régence*—L. *rego*, to lay straight, to rule.]
Regenerate, re-jen'e-rāt, vt. *To beget anew;* to make to be born anew; to renew by a change of carnal nature to a Christian life; to form into a new and better state. ppr. *regenerating*, pret. & pp. *regenerated.*—a. *Born anew;* reproduced; changed from a natural to a spiritual state. [L. *regenero, regeneratus—genus*, birth.]
Regenerating, re-jen'e-rāt-ing, p.a. Forming into a new and better state; renovating the nature by the implantation of holy affections in the heart.
Regeneration, re-jen-e-rā''shon, n. *Act of regenerating;* state of being regenerated; new birth by the grace of God. [Fr. *régénération.*]
Regenerative, re-jen'e-rāt-iv, a. *Producing regeneration.* [Sp. *regenerativo.*]
Regent, rē'jent, a. *Ruling;* exercising vicarious authority.—n. *A ruler;* one who governs a kingdom during the minority, absence, or disability of the king. [Fr. *régent*—L. *rego*, to rule.]
Regentship, rē'jent-ship, n. *State or office of a regent.*
Regicidal, re-ji-sid'al, a. *Belonging to a regicide.*
Regicide, re'ji-sīd, n. *One who murders a king;* the murder of a king. [Fr. *régicide*—L. *rex*, a king, and *cœdo*, to kill.]
Regime, rā-shēm', n. Government; administration. [Fr. *régime*—L. *rego*, to rule.]
Regimen, re'ji-men, n. *A guiding; direction;* the regulation of diet with a view to the preservation or restoration of health; the government of nouns by verbs or other words. [L.]
Regiment, re'ji-ment, n. Primarily, *rule;* a body of troops consisting (if infantry) of several companies, or (if cavalry) of several squadrons, under the command of a colonel. [Fr. *régiment*—L. *rego*, to rule.]
Regimental, re-ji-ment'al, a. *Belonging to a regiment.*
Regimentals, re-ji-ment'alz, n. pl. *The uniform clothing of a regiment.*
Region, rē'jon, n. *A boundary†;* a tract of land of indefinite extent; a tract of considerable extent; country; the inhabitants of a region; a part of the body; place; rank. [Fr. *région*—L. *rego*, to rule.]
Register, re'jis-tėr, n. A written account or entry of acts, judgments, or proceedings for preservation; a record; a roll; the book in which a record is kept; something which serves to regulate, adjust, record, or calculate.—vt. To record; to enrol; to enter in a list. [Fr. *registre*—L. *re*, back, and *gero*, to carry—Heb. *gârash*, to carry off.]
Registered, re'jis-tėrd, p.a. Recorded; enrolled.
Registrar, re'jis-trär, n. *An officer who writes or keeps a public register* or record. [Low L. *registrarius.*]
Registrarship, re'jis-trär-ship, n. *The office of registrar.*
Registration, re-jis-trā'shon, n. *Act of registering;* enrolment.
Regnant, reg'nant, a. *Reigning;* exercising regal authority; prevalent. [Fr.—L. *regno*, to reign—*rex*, a king.]
Regreet, re-grēt', vt. To greet again.—n. A return of salutation.
Regress, rē'gres, n. *A going back*; the power of returning or passing back. [Fr. *regrès;* L. *gradior*, to step.]
Regret, re-gret', n. *A turning back* of the thoughts and feelings upon the past; pain of conscience for some fault; penitence.—vt. To *turn* the thoughts and feelings *back* upon, as upon the past; to remember with sorrow; to be sorry for; to grieve at; to bewail; to mourn for; to repent of. ppr. *regretting*, pret. & pp. *regretted.* [Fr. *regret;* L. *gradior*, to go, to step.]
Reguerdon, re-gėr'don, n. A reward.
Regular, reg'ū-lär, a. *Conformed to a rule; governed by rule or rules;* steady or uniform in a course or practice; instituted according to established forms; orderly; pursued with steadiness; having the parts all symmetrical.—n. A member of any religious order, in the Romish church, who has taken the vows; a soldier belonging to a permanent army. [Fr. *régulier*—L. *rego*, to lay straight.]
Regularity, re-gū-la'ri-ti, n. *State or quality of being regular*, method; conformity to certain principles; uniformity in a course. [Fr. *régularité.*]
Regularly, reg'ū-lär-li, adv. *In a manner accordant to a rule;* at certain intervals; in due order.
Regulate, reg'ū-lāt, vt. *To adjust by rule or established mode;* to put or keep in good order; to subject to rules or restrictions; to arrange; to rule; to conduct. ppr. *regulating*, pret. & pp. *regulated.* [Low L. *regulo, regulatus*—L. *rego*, to lay straight.]
Regulated, reg'ū-lāt-ed, p.a. Put in good order; subjected to rules.
Regulation, re-gū-lā'shon, n. *Act of regulating;* a rule prescribed by a superior for the management of some business, or for the government of a society. [Sp. *regulacion.*]
Regulator, reg'ū-lāt-or, n. *One who regulates;* the small spring of a watch, which regulates its motions; any part of a machine which regulates its movements. [Sp. *regulador.*]
Rehearsal, re-hėrs'al, n. *Act of rehearsing;* repetition of the words of another or of a written work; the recital of a piece before the public exhibition of it.
Rehearse, re-hėrs', vt. To *say* or relate in

the *hearing of* others; to recite; to recount; to repeat, as the words of another; to give an oral account of; to repeat in private for improvement before a public representation. *ppr.* rehearsing, *pret. & pp.* rehearsed. [from *re* and *hear.*]

Reign, rān, *vi. To have royal power*; to be king; to govern; to hold the supreme power; to prevail.—*n. Kingly government*; royal authority; sovereignty; supremacy; the time during which a sovereign reigns; dominion; power; prevalence. [Fr. *régner*—L. *rex*, a king.]

Reigning, rān'ing, *p.a. Holding royal* power; governing, as king, queen, or emperor; prevailing.

Reimburse, rē-im-bėrs', *vt. To put back into the purse of;* to replace in a treasury or in a private coffer as an equivalent to the sum taken from it, lost, or expended. *ppr.* reimbursing, *pret. & pp.* reimbursed. [Fr. *rembourser*—L. *re, in,* and Gr. *bursa,* a hide.]

Reimbursement, rē-im-bėrs'ment, *n. Act of reimbursing;* repayment.

Rein, rān, *n. That which holds back;* the strap of a bridle, by which the rider of a horse restrains and governs him; the instrument of curbing; government.—*vt. To hold back;* to govern by a rein or bridle; to retain; to restrain. *vi. To be guided by reins.* [Fr. *rêne*—L. *re,* back, and *teneo,* to hold.]

Reindeer, rān'dėr, *n.* A ruminant mammal of the deer kind, inhabiting the northern parts of both continents. [Sax. *hranas-deor*; Goth. *rinnan,* to run.]

Reinforce, rē-in-fōrs', *vt. To give new force to;* to strengthen by new assistance or support. *ppr.* reinforcing, *pret. & pp.* reinforced.

Reinforcement, rē-in-fōrs'ment, *n. Act of reinforcing;* fresh supplies of strength; additional troops or ships.

Reinless, rān'les, *a. Without rein;* without restraint; unchecked.

Reins, rānz, *n. pl. The kidneys;* the lower part of the back; the seat of the affections and passions. [L. *ren,* pl. *renes,* the kidneys.]

Reinstate, rē-in-stāt', *vt. To instate anew;* to restore to a state from which one had been removed. *ppr.* reinstating, *pret. & pp.* reinstated.

Reinstatement, rē-in-stāt'ment, *n. Act of reinstating,* or of putting in a former state; re-establishment.

Reinvest, rē-in-vest', *vt. To invest anew.* [*re* and *invest.*]

Reinvestment, rē-in-vest'ment, *n. Act of investing anew;* a second or repeated investment.

Reinvigorate, rē-in-vi'gor-āt, *vt. To invigorate again;* to reanimate. *ppr.* reinvigorating, *pret. & pp.* reinvigorated.

Reissue, rē-ish'ū, *vt. To issue a second time.*—*n. A second or repeated issue. ppr.* reissuing, *pret. & pp.* reissued.

Reiterate, rē-it'ėr-āt, *vt. To do another time;* to repeat again and again. *ppr.* reiterating, *pret. & pp.* reiterated. [L. *iteŕo, iteratus*—Sans. *itara,* another.]

Reiterated, rē-it'ėr-āt-ed, *p.a.* Repeated again and again.

Reiteration, rē-it'ėr-ā"shon, *n. Act of reiterating;* repetition.

Reject, rē-jekt', *vt. To throw back;* to throw away, as anything vile; to cast off; to forsake; to decline; to slight. [L. *rejicio, rejectus*—*jacio,* to throw.]

Rejected, rē-jekt'ed, *p.a. Thrown away;* cast off; refused; slighted.

Rejection, rē-jek'shon, *n. Act of rejecting;* act of casting off or forsaking; refusal to accept or grant. [L. *rejectio.*]

Rejoice, rē-jois', *vi. To experience joy in a high degree;* to be joyful or glad; to exult.—*vt. To make joyful or glad;* to animate with lively pleasurable sensations; to cheer. *ppr.* rejoicing, *pret. & pp.* rejoiced. [Fr. *réjouir, réjouissant*—L. *gaudeo,* to rejoice.]

Rejoicing, rē-jois'ing, *p.n. Act of expressing joy;* the subject of joy; the experience of joy; cause of enjoyment.

Rejoicingly, rē-jois'ing-li, *adv. With joy* or exultation.

Rejoin, rē-join', *vt. To join again;* to unite after separation; to meet again. *vi.* To answer to a reply.

Rejoinder, rē-join'dėr, *n. Something joined on to;* an answer to a reply; an answer or reply. [from Fr. *rejoindre.*]

Rekindle, rē-kin'dl, *vt. To kindle again;* to set on fire anew. *ppr.* rekindling, *pret. & pp.* rekindled.

Relapse, rē-laps', *vi. To slide back;* to backslide; to fall back; to return to a former state, as of vice or error; to fall back or return from recovery or a convalescent state. *ppr.* relapsing, *pret. & pp.* relapsed.—*n. A sliding back,* particularly into a former bad state, either of body or of morals. [L. *re-labor, relapsus*—*labor,* to slide.]

Relate, rē-lāt', *vt.* Primarily, *to bring back;* to repeat; to rehearse; to give orally or in writing as the particulars of an event.—*vi.* To have reference or respect; to refer. (With *to.*) *ppr.* relating, *pret. & pp.* related. [Fr. *relater*—L. *fero, latus,* to bring.]

Related, rē-lāt'ed, *p.a.* Allied by kindred.

Relating, rē-lāt'ing, *p.a. Having relation* or reference; concerning.

Relation, rē-lā'shon, *n. Act of relating;* that which is told; narrative; respect; connection between things; relationship; a person connected by birth or marriage; a kinsman; a relative; analogy; ratio; proportion. [Fr.]

Relationship, rē-lā'shon-ship, *n. The state of being related.*

Relative, re'lāt-iv, *a. Having relation* or reference; arising from relat'on; not existing by itself; considered as belonging to something else; incident to man in society; having close connection; special; positive.—*n. A person related;* one allied by blood; that which has relation to something else; a word which relates to another word, called its antecedent, or which refers back to a sentence or member of a sentence. [Fr. *relatif*—L. *fero, lātum,* to bring.]

Relatively, re'lāt-iv-li, *adv. In a relative manner;* not absolutely.

Relax, rē-laks', *vt. To slacken;* to make less tense, as sinews; to make less close, as the joints; to make less severe; to abate; to lessen; to prosecute less assiduously, as efforts; to relieve from close attention; to amuse; to relieve from constipation.—*vi. To become lax* or *loose;* to unbend; to become more mild; to remit in close attention. [L. *relaxo—laxus,* loose, slack.]

Relaxation, rē-laks-ā'shon, *n. Act of relaxing;* cessation of restraint; remission of attention; an opening; diminution of the healthy tone of parts. [Fr.]

Relaxed, rē-lakst', *p.a.* Made less vigorous; languid.

Relaxing, rē-laks'ing, *p.a.* Rendering languid.

Relay, rē-lā', *n.* A supply of horses placed on the road, to be in readiness to relieve others, that a traveller may proceed without delay. [Fr. *relais*—L. *ligo,* to bind.]

Release, rē-lēs', *vt. To loosen;* to set free from restraint of any kind; to discharge; to let go, as a claim; to relinquish; to free from obligation or penalty; to acquit. *ppr.* releasing, *pret. & pp.* released.—*n. A setting free;* liberation from restraint of any kind, discharge from obligation; acquittance; a relinquishment of some right or claim. [Fr. *re,* and *laisser*—L. *laxus,* loose, slack.]

Relent, rē-lent', *vi. To soften;* to become *soft, gentle, pliant, or lenient;* to become more mild and tender; to feel compassion. [Fr. *ralentir*—L. *lentus,* pliant.]

Relentless, rē-lent'les, *a. Unrelenting;* insensible to the distresses of others; destitute of tenderness; implacable.

Relentlessly, rē-lent'les-li, *adv. In a relentless manner;* without pity.

Relentlessness, rē-lent'les-nes, *n. Quality of being relentless.*

Relevancy, re'lē-van-si, *n. State of being relevant;* applicableness; pertinence.

Relevant, re'lē-vant, *a. Relieving;* lifting up; having applicableness or pertinence, as an argument; pertinent; appropriate. [Fr. *relever,* ppr. *relevant*—L. *le o, levātus,* to lift up.]

Reliable, rē-li'a-bl, *a. That may be relied on* or trusted.

Reliance, rē-li'ans, *n. A relying;* repose of mind, resulting from a full belief of the veracity of a person, or of the certainty of a fact; confidence; dependence; ground of trust.

Relic, re'lik, *n. That which is left;* that which is left after the decay of the rest; the body or remains of a deceased person; a corpse. (Usually in the plural.) [Fr. *relique*—L. *linquo,* to leave.]

Relict, re'likt, *n.* A woman *left* solitary by the death of her husband; a widow. [L. *relicta*—*linquo,* to leave.]

Relief, rē-lēf', *n. A lifting up;* the removal, in whole or in part, of any evil that afflicts the body or mind; mitigation; aid; remedy; redress; that which mitigates pain; the release, as of sentinels, from some duty, and the substitution of others; the person or persons thus substituted; that species of sculpture in which the figures stand out from the ground; the appearance of projection in painting; the exposure of anything by the proximity of something else. [Fr.—L. *levo,* to lift up.]

Relieve, rē-lēv', *vt. To raise up;* to set free from anything that pains the body or distresses the mind; to ease; to release from a station, as sentinels, and station others in their place; to redress; to remove; to assist; to set off by contrast. *ppr.* relieving, *pret. & pp.* relieved. [Fr. *relever*—L. *levo,* to lift up.]

Relieving, rē-lēv'ing, *p.a.* Easing; curing; assisting.

Religion, rē-li'jon, *n. That which binds fast* morally; that *obligation,* and *sense* of duty, which we feel, from the relation in which we stand to some superior power; an acknowledgment of our obligation to God as our Creator, Preserver, and Redeemer; duty to God and to his creatures; practical piety; devotion, with the practice of all moral duties; any system of faith and worship. [Fr.—L. *ligo,* to bind.]

Religious, rē-li'jus, *a. Pertaining to religion;* pious; holy; loving and reverencing the Supreme Being and obeying his precepts; containing religious sub-

Fāte, fär, fat, fall; mē, met, hėr; pine, pin; nōte, not, mōve; tūbe, tub, bull; oil, pound.

RELIGIOUSLY 325 **REMUNERATE**

jects; characterised by strictness; conscientious; exact; among R. Catholics, engaged by vows to a monastic life; appropriated to the performance of sacred duties. [Fr. *religieux*]
Religiously, rē-li'jus-li, *adv. In a religious manner*; conscientiously.
Relinquish, rē-ling'kwish, *vt. To leave behind*; to forsake; to give up; to resign; to renounce. [Norm. *relinques*, given up—L. *linquo*, to leave.]
Relinquishment, rē-ling'kwish-ment, *n. Act of relinquishing*; a forsaking; the renouncing a claim to; abandonment.
Reliquary, re'li-kwa-ri, *n.* A depository for *relics*; a small chest or casket in which relics are kept. [Fr. *reliquaire*—L. *linquo*, to leave.]
Relish, e'lish, *vt. To lick anew or again*; to be gratified with the enjoyment of; to like the taste of; to have a taste for; to give an agreeable taste to.—*vi.* To have a pleasing taste; to have a flavour; to be enjoyable.—*n.* A pleasing taste; savour; zest; gusto; a sense of mental pleasure in respect to objects; fondness; delight; that which gives delight; the power of pleasing; a small quantity just perceptible; something taken with food to increase the pleasure of eating. [from Old Fr. *relecher*—L. *lingo*, to lick—Sans. *lih*, to lick up.]
Relive†, rē-liv', *vi.* To live again.
Reluctance, rē-luk'tans, *n. The act of struggling against*; great opposition of mind; repugnance. [It. *reluttanza*.]
Reluctant, rē-luk'tant, *a. Struggling against*; much opposed in heart; acting with slight repugnance; granted with reluctance. [L. *reluctans—luctor*, to wrestle.]
Reluctantly, rē-luk'tant-li, *adv. With reluctance*; unwillingly.
Relume†, rē-lūm', *vt. To light again.* [L. *lumen*, light.]
Rely, rē-li', *vi. To rest or repose on something*; to have confidence; to trust; to depend; to confide; to repose. (With *on* or *upon*.) *ppr.* relying, *pret. & pp.* relied.
Remain, rē-mān', *vi. To stay behind*; to abide; to tarry; to be left after others have withdrawn; to be left after any event; to continue unchanged; to endure.—*n.* That which is left; stay. [L. *remaneo—maneo*, to stay.]
Remainder, rē-mān'dėr, *n. That which remains or is left*; the residue; the quantity that is left after subtraction, called in algebra the difference.—*a. Remaining*; refuse.
Remaining, rē-mān'ing, *p.a.* Continuing; resting; being left.
Remains, rē-māns', *n. pl. That which is left* after a part is separated; relics; remnants; a corpse; writings, &c., left by a deceased person.
Remand, rē-mand', *vt.* To call or *send back*, as him or that which is ordered to a place; to send, as an accused party, back to custody. [Fr. *remander*—L. *mando*, to commit to one's charge.]
Remark, rē-märk', *n. A marking again*; notice or observation expressed in words or writing; comment; annotation.—*vt. To mark again*; to observe; to notice; to regard; to express in words, as what one thinks or sees. *vt.* To make observation; to observe. [Fr. *remarque—marque*, a mark.]
Remarkable, rē-märk'a-bl, *a. Worthy of remark* or notice; that may excite admiration or wonder; distinguished; eminent. [Fr. *remarquable*.]

Remarkably, rē-märk'a-bli, *adv.* In a manner or degree worthy of notice.
Remediable, rē-mē'di-a-bl, *a. That may be remedied.*
Remedial, rē-mē'di-al, *a. Affording a remedy*; healing; intended for a remedy. [Late L. *remedialis*.]
Remedially, rē-mē'di-al-li, *adv. In a remedial manner.*
Remediate†, rē-mē'di-at, *a.* Remedial.
Remediless, re'mē-di-les, *a. Not admitting a remedy*, as disease; incurable.
Remedy, re'mē-di, *n. That which heals*; that which cures a disease; any medicine which puts an end to disease and restores health; cure; redress; relief. *vt. To cure*; to heal; to repair; to remove, as mischief. *ppr.* remedying, *pret. & pp.* remedied. [L. *remedium—medeor*, to heal.]
Remember, rē-mem'bėr, *vt. To recall to the memory*; to think of again; to keep in mind; to observe; to preserve the memory of; to put in mind; to preserve from being forgotten. [Old Fr. *remembrer*—L. *memor*, mindful.]
Remembrance, rē-mem'brans, *n. Act of remembering*; the faculty by which past ideas are recalled to mind; retention in the mind; revival in the mind; a token by which a person is kept in memory; account preserved; memorandum; admonition. [Fr.]
Remembrancer, rē-mem'brans-ėr, *n. One who reminds*, or revives the remembrance of anything; a recorder; something that reminds, as a gift.
Remind, rē-mind', *vt. To put in mind*; to bring to the remembrance of; to bring to notice or consideration.
Reminiscence, re-mi-nis'ens, *n. A recalling to mind*; remembrance; that faculty of the mind by which ideas formerly received into it are recalled or revived; remembrance expressed; a relation of what is recollected. [Fr. *réminiscence*—L. *reminiscor*, to recall to mind.]
Remiss, rē-mis', *a. Letting oneself go back*; relaxed; negligent; heedless; not performing duty; not complying with engagements at all, or not in due time; slow; not vigorous, as motion; not intense. [Fr. *remis*, pp. of *remettre*—L. *mitto*, *missum*, to send.]
Remission, rē-mi'shon, *n. Act of remitting*; diminution of intensity; discharge or relinquishment of a claim or right; a temporary subsidence of the force of a disease; forgiveness; the sending of money to a distant place. [Fr. *rémission*—L. *mitto*, to send.]
Remissly, rē-mis'li, *adv. In a remiss manner*; slackly; not with ardour.
Remissness, rē-mis'nes, *n. State or quality of being remiss.*
Remit, rē-mit', *vt. To send back*; to make less violent, as anger; to surrender, as the right of punishing a crime; to forgive; to absolve; to refer; to transmit, as money, bills, &c., to some person at a distance.—*vi. To slacken*; to become less intense; to abate in violence for a time. *ppr.* remitting, *pret. & pp.* remitted. [Fr. *remettre*—L. *mitto*, to send.]
Remittance, rē-mit'ans, *n. Act of remitting*; act of transmitting money, bills, or the like, to a distant place; the sum or thing remitted.
Remittent, rē-mit'ent, *a.* Having alternate increase and *remission*, as a fever. [Fr. *rémittent*.]
Remitter, rē-mit'ėr, *n. One who remits.*
Remnant, rem'nant, *n. That which remains*; residue; that which is left

after the separation or destruction of a part; that which remains after a part is done; a slight trace; a little bit. [L. *maneo*, to remain.]
Remodel, rē-mo'del, *vt. To model or fashion anew. ppr.* remodelling, *pret. & pp.* remodelled.
Remonstrance, rē-mon'strans, *n. Act of remonstrating*; show; discovery; expostulatory advice; reproof. [Fr. *remontrance*—L. *monstro*, to show.]
Remonstrate, rē-mon'strāt, *vi. To show clearly*; to present strong reasons against an act, or any course of proceedings; to suggest urgent reasons in opposition to a measure. *ppr.* remonstrating, *pret. & pp.* remonstrated. [Old Fr. *remonstrer*—L. *monstro*, to show.]
Remorse, rē-mors', *n. The gnawing pains of conscience*; the keen anguish excited by a sense of guilt; pity; compassion. [L. *remorsus*, bitten again—*mordeo*, to bite.]
Remorseful, rē-mors'ful, *a. Full of remorse*; feeling tenderly; pitiable.
Remorsefully, rē-mors'ful-li, *adv. With remorse of conscience.*
Remorseless, rē-mors'les, *a. Without remorse*; unpitying; ruthless; merciless.
Remorselessly, rē-mors'les-li, *adv. Without remorse.*
Remote, rē-mōt', *a. Removed afar off*; far; not near; distant in time, past or future; primary; not proximate, as a cause; foreign; not related; distant in consanguinity; slight. [L. *remōtus*—*moveo*, *motum*, to move.]
Remotely, rē-mōt'li, *adv.* At a distance in space or time; not nearly; slightly; in a small degree.
Remoteness, rē-mōt'nes, *n. State of being remote* or distant in space or time; distance in consanguinity; slightness.
Remotion†, rē-mō'shon, *n.* Act of removing; state of being remote.
Remould, rē-mōld', *vt. To mould or shape anew.* [re and *mould*.]
Remount, rē-mount', *vi. To mount again.*—*vt. To mount again*; to reascend. [Fr. *remonter*.]
Removability, rē-möv'a-bil"li-ti, *n. The capacity of being removable.*
Removable, rē-möv'a-bl, *a. That may be removed* from an office or station; that may be removed from one place to another.
Removal, rē-möv'al, *n. Act of moving from one place to another* for residence; act of displacing from an office; act of putting away; state of being removed.
Remove, rē-möv', *vt. To move from its place*; to take *away*; to put from its place in any manner; to displace from an office; to banish; to take from the present state of being.—*vi. To be moved* from its place; to go from one place to another; to change the place of residence. *ppr.* removing, *pret. & pp.* removed.—*n. Act of moving*; change of place; a going away; any indefinite distance; a dish to be changed while the rest of the course remains; (pl.)† stages. [L. *removeo—moveo*, to move.]
Removed, rē-möved', *p.a. Remote*; separate from others.
Removedness, rē-möv'ed-nes, *n. Remoteness.*
Remunerable, rē-mū'nė-ra-bl, *a. That may be remunerated* or rewarded; fit or proper to be recompensed.
Remunerate, rē-mū'nė-rāt, *vt. To render a service back to*; to reward for service; to recompense. *ppr.* remunerating, *pret. & pp.* remunerated. [L. *remun-*

ch, chain; j. *job*; g, *go*; ng, sing; m, *then*; th, *thin*; w, *wig*; wh, *whig*; zh, *azure*; † obsolete.

ero, remuneratus—munus, munĕris, a service, gift.]

Remuneration, re-mū'nē-rā"shon, *n.* Act of remunerating; the equivalent given for services, loss, or sufferings; compensation. [Fr. *rémunération.*]

Remunerative, re-mū'nē-rāt-iv, *a.* Affording remuneration; profitable.

Renal, rē'nal *a. Pertaining to the reins* or kidneys. [Fr. *rénal*—L. *ren*, pl. *renes*, the kidneys.]

Renard, re nard, *n.* A fox; a name used in fables. [Fr.]

Renascence, rē-nas'ens, *n.* The state of springing or *being produced* again.

Renascent, rē-nas'ent, *a. Springing* into being *again;* reproduced. [L. *renascens—nascor*, to be born.]

Rencounter, ren-koun'tėr, *n. A going or running against;* a meeting in contest; shock; a casual, sudden contest; a combat; an encounter. [Fr. *rencontre*—L. *re, in,* and *contra,* against.]

Rend, rend, *vt. To separate,* as any substance into *parts with sudden violence;* to sever; to cleave; to split; to rive; to lacerate. *ppr.* rending, *pret. & pp.* rent. [Sax. *rendan*; Fris. *renda,* Old G. *trennjan,* to break.]

Render, ren'dėr, *vt. To give back;* to return; to restore; to inflict, as a retribution; to give; to assign, as a reason; to make or cause to be by some change; to translate; to surrender; to give for use or benefit; to represent.—*vi.* To give an account; to show.—*n. A giving up;* a return; an account given. [Fr. *rendre*—L. *re,* back, and *do,* to give.]

Rendered, ren'dėrd, *p.a.* Assigned; afforded.

Rendering, ren'dėr-ing, *p.n.* Act of *giving back;* version; translation.

Rendezvous, ren'dā-vö, *n.* A place appointed for the assembling of troops, or the port where ships are ordered to join company; a place for enlisting seamen into the naval service; a place of meeting.—*vi.* To meet at a particular place, as troops, ships, &c.—*vt.* To assemble or bring together at a certain place. [Fr. *render yourselves.*]

Renegade, re'nē-gād, *n. One who denies* or renounces *his faith;* an apostate; a deserter; a vagabond. [Sp. *renegado*—L. *nego, negatus,* to deny.]

Renege, re-nēj', *vt.* To deny; to disown. *vi.* To deny. [L. *nego,* to deny.]

Renew, rē-nū', *vt. To make new again;* to renovate; to repair; to re-establish; to confirm; to make again; to revive; to begin again, as a course; to make fresh or vigorous; to grant, as a new loan on a new bill or note, for the amount of a former one; to regenerate.—*vi.* To grow again; to begin again.

Renewable, rē-nū'a-bl, *a. That may be renewed.*

Renewal, rē-nū'al, *n. Act of renewing;* renovation; restoration to a good state; a new loan on a new bill or note.

Renewed, rē-nūd', *p.a. Made new again;* re-established; renovated.

Renewing, rē-nū'ing, *p.a. Tending to renovate;* regenerating.—*p.n.* Act of *making new;* renewal.

Rennet, ren'net, *n.* That which causes milk *to run* into masses or curds; the prepared stomach of a calf, used for coagulating milk. [G. *rinnen,* to run.]

Rennet, ren'net, *n.* A kind of apple. [probably from *Rennes,* the name of a town in Brittany.]

Renounce, rē-nouns', *vt.* Primarily, *to carry back word;* to disown; to abnegate; to disclaim; to decline; to deny; to give up; to forego.—*vi.* Not to follow suit in card-playing, when the person has a card of the same sort. *ppr.* renouncing, *pret. & pp.* renounced.—*n.Act of renouncing.* [Norm. *renoncher*—L. *nuncio,* to make known.]

Renouncement, rē-nouns'ment, *n. Act of renouncing;*: renunciation.

Renouncing, rē-nouns'ing, *p.n.* Act of disowning or rejecting.

Renovate, re'nō-vāt, *vt. To make new again;* to renew; to restore to the first state, or to a good state after decay. *ppr.* renovating, *pret. & pp.* renovated. [L. *renovo, renovatus—novus,* new.]

Renovated, re'nō-vāt-ed, *p.a. Renewed;* made new, fresh, or vigorous.

Renovation, re-nō-vā'shon, *n. Act of renovating;* renewal; a state of being renewed. [Fr. *rénovation.*]

Renovator, re'nō-vāt-or, *n.* He or that which *renovates* or renews. [Late L.]

Renown, rē-noun', *n. The state of being much known; a great name;* fame; exalted reputation derived from the extensive praise of great achievements or accomplishments. (Always in a good sense.)—*vt.* To make famous. [Norm. *renun*—L. *nomen,* a name.]

Renowned, rē-nound', *p.a. Having a great name;* famed; celebrated.

Rent, rent, *n.* An opening produced by *rending;* a breach; a schism.

Rent, rent, *n. A rendering back;* revenue; a sum of money issuing yearly from lands or tenements; a return, in the nature of an acknowledgment, for the possession of a corporeal inheritance.—*vt.* To hold by paying *rent* for; to take or hold by lease, as lands or tenements; to let on lease to a tenant; to lease.—*vi.* To be leased or *let for rent.* [Fr. *rente*—L. *re,* back, and *do, datum,* to give.]

Rental, rent'al, *n. A roll,* schedule, or account of *rents.* [said to be corrupted from *rent-roll.*]

Renter, rent'ėr, *n.* One who holds by paying *rent* for; one who leases an estate; a shareholder in a theatre.

Rent-roll, rent'rōl, *n. A rental;* a list or account of rents or income.

Renunciation, rē-nun'si-ā"shon, *n. Act of renouncing;* disclaimer; abjuration; abandonment. [Fr. *renonciation.*]

Repair, rē-pār', *vt. To make ready again;* to restore; to bring back to a sound or good state; to mend; to rebuild; to fill up; to redress.—*n. Act of repairing;* restoration to a sound state after partial destruction; reparation. [Fr. *réparer*—L. *paro,* to get ready.]

Repair, rē-pār', *vi. To go, as to a haunt;* to lodge, as in a haunt; to betake one's *self.*—*n.* Act of betaking one's self to any place; a resorting; abode. [Old Fr. *repairer*—L. *patria,* one's native country.]

Repairer, rē-pār'ėr, *n. One who repairs.*

Reparable, re'pa-ra-bl, *a. That may be repaired.* [Fr. *réparable.*]

Reparably, re'pa-ra-bli, *adv. In a reparable manner.*

Reparation, re-pa-rā'shon, *n. Act of repairing;* supply of what is wasted; indemnification, as for loss or damage; a satisfaction for injury. [Fr. *réparation.*]

Repartee, re-pär-tē', *n.* A returning of a thrust, blow, or word *in kind;* a smart, ready, and witty reply. [Fr. *repartie*—L. *pars, partis,* a part.]

Repast, rē-past', *n. Act of taking food;* a meal; victuals.—*vt.* To feed. [Fr. *repas*—L. *pasco, pastum,* to feed.]

Repasture!, rē-pas'tūr, *n.* Food.

Repay, rē-pā', *vt. To pay back,* as money; to reimburse; to make return for; to requite; to compensate; to pay again.

Repayment, rē-pā'ment, *n. Act of paying back;* reimbursement; the money or other thing repaid.

Repeal, rē-pēl', *vt. To call back; to revoke;* to make void by an authoritative act; to abrogate.—*n. Act of repealing* or of annulling; abrogation. [Fr. *rappeler*—L. *appello,* to call upon.]

Repealable, rē-pēl'a-bl, *a. Capable of being repealed.*

Repealer, rē-pēl'ėr, *n. One who repeals;* one who seeks a repeal.

Repeat, rē-pēt', *vt. To attack again;* to do, make, attempt, or utter again; to rehearse; to quote or say from memory; to try or incur again.—*n. A repetition;* a mark in music directing a part to be repeated in performance. [Fr. *répéter*—L. *peto,* to seek.]

Repeated, rē-pēt'ed, *p.a.* Done again: recited.

Repeatedly, rē-pēt'ed-li, *adv.* More than once; again and again; indefinitely.

Repeater, rē-pēt'ėr, *n. One who repeats,* a watch that strikes the hours at will. by the compression of a spring; a decimal in which the same figure continually recurs.

Repeating, rē-pēt'ing, *p.a.* Doing the same thing over again; striking the hours at will.

Repel, rē-pel', *vt. To drive back;* to repulse; to check the advance of; to withstand; to reject; to refuse.—*vi.* To act with force in opposition to force impressed; to check. *ppr.* repelling, *pret. & pp.* repelled. [L. *repello—pello,* to drive.]

Repellent, rē-pel'ent, *p.a. Driving back;* able or tending to repel. [L. *repellens.*]

Repeller, rē-pel'ėr, *n. He or that which repels.*

Repelling, rē-pel'ing, *p.a.* Driving back; resisting approach.

Repent, rē-pent', *vi. To feel pain or regret for something done or spoken;* to change the mind in consequence of the injury done by past conduct; to have such sorrow for sin as issues in amendment of life.—*vt.* To remember with pain or sorrow; to feel sorrow (with recipr. pron.) [Fr. *se repentir*—L. *poenitao,* to make to repent.]

Repentance, rē-pent'ans, *n. Act of repenting;* the grief which a person experiences in consequence of the injury produced by his own conduct; sorrow for sin; penitence; that sorrow for sin which issues in reformation. [Fr.]

Repentant, rē-pent'ant, *a.* Sorrowful for what has been done, or for what has been left undone; expressing or showing sorrow for sin. [Fr.]

Repenting, rē-pent'ing, *p.a.* Feeling contrition for sin, and turning from it with abhorrence.

Repentingly, rē-pent'ing-li, *adv.* With repentance.

Repercussion, re-pėr-ku'shon, *n. Act of driving back;* reverberation; frequent repetition of the same sound in music. [Fr. *répercussion*—L. *quatio, quassum,* to shake.]

Repercussive, rē-pėr-kus'iv, *a. Driving back;* causing to reverberate; reverberated. [Fr. *répercussif.*]

Repertory, re'pėr-tō-ri, *n. An inventory;* a repository, a place in which things are disposed in an orderly manner, so that they can be easily found, as the index of a book, &c.; a treasury; a magazine. [Fr. *répertoire*—L. *parto, partum,* to produce.]

Repetition, re-pē-ti'shon, *n. Act of re-*

Fāte, fär fat, fall; mē, met, hėr; pīne, pin; nōte, not, mōve; tūbe, tub, bull; oil, pound.

peating; reiteration; act of reciting; act of singing or playing the same part a second time. [Fr. *répétition*—L. *peto, petitum*, to seek.]
Repine, rē-pīn', *vi.* To torture or fret one's self; to feel inward discontent; to complain discontentedly; to envy. (With *at* or *against*, before an object.) *ppr.* repining, *pret. & pp.* repined. *n.* Fretting. [Sax. *pinan*, to torture.]
Repiner, rē-pīn'ėr, *n. One who repines.*
Repining, rē-pīn'ing, *p.a.* Disposed to murmur or complain.—*n.* Act of fretting or feeling discontent, or of murmuring.
Repiningly, rē-pīn'ing-li, *adv. In a repining manner.*
Replace, rē-plās', *vt.* To put in the former place; to repay; to refund; to put, as a competent substitute in the place of another; to take the place of. *ppr.* replacing, *pret. & pp.* replaced.
Replacement, rē-plās'ment, *n. Act of replacing;* substitution.
Replacing, rē-plās'ing, *p.n. Act of placing anew.*
Replenish, rē-plen'ish, *vt. To fill again;* to stock with numbers or abundance; to finish; to perfect. [Old Fr. *replenir, repleniscent*—L. *pleo,* to fill.]
Replenishment, rē-plen'ish-ment, *n. Act of replenishing.*
Replete, rē-plēt', *a. Filled up;* completely filled. [Fr. *replet*—L. *pleo,* to fill.]
Repletion, rē-plē'shon, *n. State of being replete;* superabundant fulness; plethora. [Fr. *réplétion.*]
Replevin, rē-plev'in, *n. An action in law to recover possession of goods or cattle wrongfully taken, on security being given to try the right at law.* [Low L. *replevina,* surety.]
Replevy, rē-plev'i, *vt. To take back or reclaim, as cattle or goods upon pledges or security being given to try the right of ownership at law. ppr.* replevying, *pret. & pp.* replevied. [re, and Old Fr. *plevir,* to bail.]
Replication, re-pli-kā'shon, *n. A folding back;* a response; a rejoinder; echo; repetition. [L. *replicatio—plico*, to fold.]
Replier, rē-plī'ėr, *n. One who replies.*
Reply, rē-plī', *vi. To fold back;* to make a return in words or writing to something said or written by another; to rejoin.—*vt.* To return for an answer. *ppr.* replying, *pret. & pp.* replied. *n.* An answer; that which is said or written in answer to what is said or written by another; a book or pamphlet written in answer to another. [Fr. *répliquer*—L. *plico*, to fold—Gr. *pleko,* to twine, enfold.]
Report, rē-pōrt', *vt. To bear or bring back,* as an answer; to give an account of; to tell; to carry, as a statement from one to another; to circulate publicly, as a story; to give an official account of; to give, as a statement of decisions in a court of law, or of the proceedings, debates, &c., of a legislative body.—*vi.* To make a statement of facts; to discharge the office of a reporter for the newspaper press.—*n.* A statement returned; common fame; repute; public character; noise, as of a gun; discharge; a statement of a judicial decision, or of a case argued in a court of law; an official statement of facts, verbal or written; a statement made by a legislative committee of facts into which they were charged to inquire; an account of the proceedings, &c., of a legislative body,

a meeting, or a court. [Fr. *rapporter*—L. *porto*, to carry.]
Reported, rē-pōrt'ed, *p.a.* Reputed; stated officially.
Reporter, rē-pōrt'ėr, *n. One who reports;* a person who makes statements of law proceedings and decisions, or of legislative debates.
Reporting, rē-pōrt'ing, *p.n. Act of one who reports;* act of drawing out statements of parliamentary proceedings, &c., for the newspaper press.
Reportingly†, rē-pōrt'ing-li, *adv.* By report or common fame.
Reposal†, rē-pōz'al, *n.* The act of reposing.
Repose, rē-pōz', *vt. To lay up;* to deposit; to lay at rest; to lay or put the mind at rest in, as confidence or trust. *vi. To be laid up;* to be at rest, as in a bed; to sleep; to settle; to abide; to be recumbent; to rest in confidence (with *on* or *upon*). *ppr.* reposing, *pret. & pp.* reposed.—*n. A lying at rest;* a state of sleep, as in bed; sleep; ease; peace; tranquillity. [Fr. *reposer*—L. *pono, positum,* to place.]
Re-osit, rē-poz'it, *vt. To lay up;* to lodge, as for safety or preservation. [L. *repositus,* placed or laid back—*pono,* to place.]
Repository, rē-poz'i-tō-ri, *n. That in which anything is laid;* a place where things are deposited for safety; a place where articles are kept for sale. [L. *repositorium.*]
Repossess, rē-poz-zes', *vt. To possess again.*
Reprehend, re-prē-hend', *vt. To seize again;* to administer censure to; to chide; to censure; to pass censure upon, as actions. [L. *reprehendo—re, præ,* and obsol. *hendo,* to take.]
Reprehensible, re-prē-hen'si-bl, *a. Deserving reproof;* culpable; censurable. [Fr. *répréhensible.*]
Reprehensibly, re-prē-hen'si-bli, *adv. In a reprehensible manner;* culpably.
Reprehension, re-prē-hen'shon, *n. Act of reprehending;* reproof; open blame. [Fr. *répréhension.*]
Reprehensive, re-prē-hens'iv, *a. Containing reproof.*
Represent, re-prē-zent', *vt. To place before one;* to exhibit by resemblance; to exhibit to the mind in words; to show by action; to act the character or to fill the place of in a play; to supply the place of; to show by statement of facts; to stand in the place of, in the right of inheritance; to bring into mental view; to serve as a sign of; to image. [Fr. *représenter;* L. *præsum,* to be before—*præ,* and *sum,* to be.]
Representable, re-prē-zent'a-bl, *a. That may be represented.*
Representation, re'prē-zent-ā"shon, *n. Act of representing;* state of being represented; that which represents; likeness; map; that which exhibits by resemblance; performance, as of a play; theatrical performance of a character in a play; a setting forth of arguments or facts, as in conversation, &c.; the business of acting for another; act of setting forth publicly; the standing in the place of another, as an heir. [Fr. *représentation.*]
Representative, re-prē-zent'āt-iv, *a. Representing something;* bearing the character or power of another; conducted by the agency of delegates, who are chosen by the people.—*n. He or that which represents;* a member of a legislative body; a substitute; one who stands in the place of another as heir;

that by which anything is shown. [Fr. *représentatif.*]
Represented, re-prē-zent'ed, *p.a.* Having substitutes.
Repress, rē-pres', *vt. To press back;* to check; to place under restraint; to quell; to crush; to calm; to appease. [L. *premo, pressum,* to press.]
Repressed, rē-prest', *p.a.* Crushed; subdued.
Repression, rē-pre'shon, *n. Act of repressing* or of subduing. [Fr. *répression.*]
Repressive, rē-pres'iv, *a. Having power to repress* or crush. [Fr. *répressif.*]
Reprieve, rē-prēv', *vt. To take back,* as a sentence for a certain time; to respite after sentence of death; to relieve for a time from any suffering. *ppr.* reprieving, *pret. & pp.* reprieved. *n.* The temporary suspension of the execution of sentence of death on a criminal; interval of ease. [Fr. *reprendre*—L. *re, præ,* and obsol. *hendo,* to take.]
Reprieved, rē-prēvd', *p.a.* Respited.
Reprimand, re-pri-mand', *vt.* To check or restrain; to administer severe reproof to for a fault; to admonish; to administer reproof to officially, in execution of a sentence.—*n.* Severe reproof for a fault; reprehension, private or public. [Fr. *reprimander*—L. *premo,* to press.]
Reprint, rē-print', *vt. To print again;* to print, as a second or any new edition.
Reprint, rē'print, *n. A second or a new edition of a book.*
Reprisal, rē-prīz'al, *n. A taking or seising in return;* the taking of anything from an enemy by way of retaliation; that which is taken to indemnify an owner for something of his which the enemy has seized. [Fr. *représaille*—L. *re, præ,* and *hendo,* to seize.]
Reproach, rē-prōch', *vt. To throw blame back upon;* to charge with a fault in severe language; to revile; to vilify. *n. Act of reproaching;* censure mingled with contempt; infamy; disgrace; object of contempt, scorn, or derision; that which is the cause of shame or disgrace. [Fr. *reprocher*—L. *reciprocus,* turning back the same way.]
Reproachably, rē-prōch'a-bli, *adv. In a reproachable manner.*
Reproachful, rē-prōch'ful, *a. Containing* or *expressing reproach* or censure with contempt; upbraiding; shameful; disgraceful; vile.
Reproachfully, rē-prōch'ful-li, *adv. In terms of reproach;* opprobriously.
Reprobate, re'prō-bāt, *a. Not enduring proof;* disapproved; condemned; not of standard purity; wholly given up to sin; depraved; wholly given up to error, or sunk in apostasy.—*n. A person not enduring trial;* one lost to virtue and religion.—*vt. To disapprove with marks of extreme dislike;* to condemn; to censure; to give up to wickedness; to give up to his sentence, without hope of pardon. *ppr.* reprobating, *pret. & pp.* reprobated. [L. *reprobātus,* disapproved—*probo,* to approve.]
Reprobation, re-prō-bā'shon, *n. Act of reprobating;* state of being abandoned to eternal destruction; rejection. [Fr. *réprobation.*]
Reproduce, rē-prō-dūs', *vt. To renew the production of. ppr.* reproducing, *pret. & pp.* reproduced.
Reproduction, rē-prō-duk'shon, *n. Act* or *process of reproducing;* state of being reproduced.
Reproductive, rē-prō-dukt'iv, *a. Pertaining to* or *used in reproduction.*

---

ch, *chain;* j, *job;* g, *go;* ng, *sing;* ᴛʜ, *then;* th, *thin;* w, *wig;* wh, *whig;* zh, *azure;* †obsolete.

Reproof, rē-prōf′, n. A reproving; rebuke; reprimand; confutation.
Reprovable, rē-prōv′a-bl, a. Worthy of reproof; deserving censure; censurable.
Reprovably, rē-prōv′a-bli, adv. In a reprovable manner.
Reprove, rē-prōv′, vt. To disapprove; to reprehend; to chide; to censure; to convince; to refute. ppr. reproving, pret. & pp. reproved. [Fr. reprouver.]
Reprover, rē-prōv′er, n. One who reproves; he or that which blames.
Reprovingly, rē-prōv′ing-li, adv. In a reproving manner.
Reptile, rep′til, a. Creeping; grovelling; low; vulgar.—n. An animal that creeps or moves on its belly, as snakes, &c.; a very mean person (a term of contempt). [Fr.—L. repo, reptum, to creep—Sans. srip, to go.]
Republic, rē-pub′lik, n. The common state or weal; a commonwealth; a community under whatever form of government; a state in which the exercise of the sovereign power is lodged in representatives elected by the people. [Fr. république—L. res, a state, and publicus, public.]
Republican, rē-pub′lik-an, a. Pertaining to a republic; consonant to the principles of a republic.—n. One who favours a republican form of government. [Fr. républicain.]
Republicanism, rē-pub′lik-an-izm, n. A republican system of government; republican principles. [Fr. républicanisme.]
Republication, rē-pub′li-kā″shon, n. A second publication of a printed work.
Republish, rē-pub′lish, vt. To publish a second time; to publish a new edition of.
Repudiate, rē-pū′di-āt, vt. To cast off on account of something causing shame; to divorce, as a husband or wife; to reject; to disavow. ppr. repudiating, pret. & pp. repudiated. [L. repudio, repudiātum—pudor, shame.]
Repudiation, rē-pū′di-ā″shon, n. Act of repudiating; divorce; disavowal. [Fr. répudiation.]
Repudiator, rē-pū′di-āt-or, n. One who repudiates. [Late L.]
Repugn, rē-pūn′, vt. To oppose; to resist. [L. pugno, to fight.]
Repugnance, rē-pug′nans, n. State of being repugnant; opposition of principles or qualities; aversion; unwillingness; reluctance; dislike. [Fr. répugnance—L. pugno, to fight.]
Repugnant, rē-pug′nant, a. Fighting against; contrary; opposite; inconsistent; disobedient; inimical. (With to.) [Fr. répugnant.]
Repugnantly, rē-pug′nant-li, adv. In a repugnant manner; with opposition.
Repulse, rē-puls′, n. A being repulsed; a being driven back by force; refusal; denial.—vt. To repel; to beat or drive back. ppr. repulsing, pret. & pp. repulsed. [L. repulsa—pello, to drive.]
Repulsion, rē-pul′shon, n. Act of driving back; repulse; that power by which the particles of bodies are made to recede from each other. [Fr. répulsion.]
Repulsive, rē-puls′iv, a. That repulses; driving off; forbidding. [Fr. répulsif.]
Repulsively, rē-puls′iv-li, adv. In a repulsive manner; by repulsing.
Repulsiveness, rē-puls′iv-nes, n. Quality of being repulsive or forbidding.
Repurchase, rē-per′chās, vt. To buy back; to regain by purchase. ppr. repurchasing, pret. & pp. repurchased. n. Act of buying again; the purchase again of what has been sold.

Reputable, re′pūt-a-bl, a. Being in good repute; estimable; respectable; consistent with reputation.
Reputableness, re′pūt-a-bl-nes, n. Quality of being reputable.
Reputably, re′pūt-a-bli, adv. With reputation; without disgrace or discredit.
Reputation, re-pūt-ā′shon, n. Reckoning; estimation; character derived from a favourable public opinion; good name; repute; esteem; honour; fame. [Fr. réputation.]
Repute, rē-pūt′, vt. To account; to reckon; to estimate; to think. ppr. reputing, pret. & pp. reputed.—n. Reputation; good character; the honour derived from public opinion; character (in a bad sense); general estimation. [Fr. réputer—L. puto, to reckon.]
Reputed, rē-pūt′ed, p.a. Accounted.
Reputedly, rē-pūt′ed-li, adv. In common opinion or estimation.
Reputeless, rē-pūt′les, a. Not having good repute.
Request, rē-kwest′, n. Something sought; need; entreaty; the expression of desire to some person for something to be granted or done; the expression of desire to the Almighty; prayer; the thing asked for; state of being desired.—vt. To ask for; to express desire for; to solicit; to entreat; to beseech. [Old Fr. requeste—L. quæro, quæsitus, to seek.]
Requiem, rē′kwi-em. n. Among the R. Catholics, a mass sung for the dead, for the rest of his soul, so called from the first word; a grand musical composition performed in honour of some deceased person. [Fr.—L. quies, rest.]
Requirable, rē-kwīr′a-bl, a. That may or ought to be required.
Require, rē-kwīr′, vt. To seek or search for; to ask, as of right and by authority; to call for; to render necessary; to make necessary; to want. ppr. requiring, pret. & pp. required. [Fr. requérir—L. quæro, to seek.]
Required, rē-kwīrd′, p.a. Needed; necessary.
Requirement, rē-kwīr′ment, n. That which is required; demand; claim.
Requisite, re′kwi-zit, a. Sought for; required by the nature of things; necessary; essential.—n. That which is required; a need; something indispensable. [L. requisitum, sought for —quæro, to seek.]
Requisition, re-kwi-zi′shon, n. A requiring; application made, as of right; a written call or invitation. [Fr. réquisition—L. quæro, to seek.]
Requisitionist, re-kwi-zi′shon-ist, n. One who makes requisition.
Requital, rē-kwīt′al, n. Act of requiting; return for any treatment, either good or bad; recompense; retaliation.
Requite, rē-kwīt′, vt. To recompense; to make a return for any treatment, either good or evil; to compensate; to avenge. ppr. requiting, pret. & pp. requited. [from re and quit.]
Rere-ward, rēr′ward, n. The rearguard; the part of an army that marches in the rear.
Rescind, rē-sind′, vt. To cut off; to destroy; to render null or make void, as an act, by the enacting authority. [L. rescindo—scindo, to cut.]
Rescript, re′skript, n. That which is written back; an answer in writing; the answer of a pope or an emperor to questions in jurisprudence propounded to him officially; an edict or decree. [L. rescriptum—scribo, to write.]
Rescue, res′kū, vt. To shake or tear from the grasp of an enemy; to shake free from any violence or danger; to deliver; to set at liberty illegally. ppr. rescuing, pret. & pp. rescued.—n. Act of rescuing; deliverance from restraint, violence, or danger, by force; release; an illegal setting at liberty of a person duly arrested. [Norm. rescu—L. re, ex, and quatio, to shake.]
Rescued, res′kūd, p.a. Delivered from confinement or danger.
Research, rē-serch′, n. Careful or diligent search; a diligent seeking of facts or principles; laborious and continued search after truth; inquiry; scrutiny.
Resemblance, rē-zem′blans, n. State or quality of resembling; something similar; likeness. [Fr. ressemblance.]
Resemble, rē-zem′bl, vt. To have the likeness of; to be like, either in form or qualities; to liken; to compare. ppr. resembling, pret. & pp. resembled. [Fr. ressembler—L. similis, like.]
Resent, rē-zent′, vt. To have a painful feeling of; to consider as an injury or affront; to be in some degree angry or provoked at; to express resentment at. [Fr. ressentir—L. sentio, to feel.]
Resentful, rē-zent′ful, a. Full of resentment; of an irritable temper.
Resentfully, rē-zent′ful-li, adv. In a resentful manner; with resentment.
Resentment, rē-zent′ment, n. A resenting; the excitement of passion which proceeds from a sense of wrong offered to ourselves, or to those who are connected with us; deep sense of injury; indignation; rage. [Fr. ressentiment.]
Reservation, re-zerv-ā′shon, n. Act of reserving in the mind; something withheld; state of being treasured up or kept in store. [Fr. réservation.]
Reserve, rē-zerv′, vt. To keep back; to save up for future use; to keep; to lay up and keep for a future time; to preserve; to except. ppr. reserving, pret. & pp. reserved.—n. Something reserved; that which is retained from present use; something in the mind withheld from disclosure; exception in favour of or against; caution in personal behaviour; coldness; modesty. [Fr. réserver—L. servo, to keep.]
Reserved, rē-zervd′, p.a. Taciturn; cautious; cold; modest.
Reservedly, rē-zerv′ed-li, adv. With reserve; not with openness.
Reservoir, re-zer-vwor′, n. A place where anything is kept in store, particularly a place where water is collected and kept for use when wanted, as to supply a fountain, a canal, a city, &c.; a cistern; a basin. [Fr.—L. servo, to keep.]
Reside, rē-zīd′, vi. To settle anywhere; to have a settled abode for a time; to live. ppr. residing, pret. & pp. resided. [Fr. résider—L. sedeo, to sit.]
Residence, re′zi-dens, n. Act or state of residing; sojourn; the place where one resides; abode; the abode of an incumbent on his benefice. [Fr. résidence.]
Resident, re′zi-dent, a. Residing in a place for a length of time.—n. One who resides in a place for some time; a dweller; a public minister who resides at a foreign court. [Fr. résident.]
Residual, rē-zid′ū-al, a. That is left behind; remaining after a part is taken. [L. residuus—sedeo, to sit.]
Residuary, rē-zid′ū-a-ri, a. Pertaining to the residue; entitled to the residue, as a legatee. [L. residuus.]
Residue, re′zi-dū, n. That which remains after a part is taken; the remainder; that which remains due of a debt; that which remains of the estate of a

Fāte, fär, fat, fall; mē, met, hėr; pīne, pin; nōte, not, mōve; tūbe, tub, bull; oil, pound.

testator after the payment of debts and legacies. [Fr. *résidu.*]
Residuum, rĕ-zid'ū-um, *n. Residue;* that which is left after any process of separation or purification. [L.]
Resign, rē-zīn', *vt.* To break up, as a sealed claim; to give up in confidence (sometimes with *up* emphatical); to send back; to yield into the hands of another; to relinquish; to abdicate. [Fr. *résigner*—L. *signum,* a mark.]
Resignation, re-zig-nā'shon, *n. Act of resigning,* or giving up; relinquishment; state of being resigned; habitual submission to the will of Providence; acquiescence. [Fr. *résignation.*]
Resigned, rē-zīnd', *p.a.* Submissive to the will of God.
Resilience, rē-sĭ'li-ens, *n. Act of springing back,* or the act of rebounding.
Resilient, rē-sĭ li-ent, *a. Starting back;* rebounding. [L. *resiliens—salio,* to leap.]
Resin, re'zin, *n.* A solid inflammable substance, so called because it *flows* or *runs* from certain trees. [Fr. *résine—* Gr. *rheō,* to flow or run.]
Resinous, re'zin-us, *a. Partaking of the qualities of resin.* [Fr. *résineux.*]
Resist, rē-zist', *vt.* To place one's self against; to act against; to withstand; to encounter with effectual opposition. *vi.* To make opposition. [Fr. *résister* —L. *sisto,* to set, place.]
Resistance, rē-zist'ans, *n. Act of resisting;* check; quality of not yielding to external impression; a power by which motion in any body is impeded. [Fr. *résistance.*]
Resistibility, rē-zist'i-bil"li-ti, *n. Quality of being resistible.*
Resistible, rē-zist'i-bl, *a. That may be resisted.* [Sp. *resistible.*]
Resistibly, rē-zist'i-bli, *adv. In a resistible manner.*
Resisting, rē-zist'ing, *p.a.* Withstanding; opposing.
Resistless, rē-zist'les, *a. That cannot be resisted;* irresistible.
Resistlessly, rē-zist'les-li, *adv. In a resistless manner.*
Resistlessness, rē-zist'les-nes, *n. State or quality of being irresistible.*
Resolute, re'zō-lūt, *a. Having resolution;* characterized by firmness in pursuing a purpose; constant; firm; unshaken. [L. *resolutus—solvo,* to loose.]
Resolutely, re-zō'lūt-li, *adv.* With fixed purpose; teadily; boldly.
Resoluteness, re'zō-lūt-nes, *n. State or quality of being resolute.*
Resolution, re-zō-lū'shon, *n. An unbinding;* analysis; act of reducing any compound to its component parts; fixed purpose; resoluteness; firmness; steadiness; boldness; formal declaration of a meeting. [Fr. *résolution.*]
Resolvable, rē-zolv'a-bl, *a. That may be resolved* or reduced to first principles.
Resolve, rē-zolv', *vt.* To untie; to unbind; to reduce to first principles; to decompose; to analyze; to free from perplexities; to clear of difficulties; to solve; to interpret; to unfold; to free from doubt or perplexity; to confirm; to fix in determination or purpose; to determine; to decide.—*vi.* To be decomposed; to melt; to dissolve; to determine in one's own mind; to make a declaration by resolution or vote. *ppr.* resolving, *pret. & pp.* resolved.—*n. Resolution;* settled determination; legal determination. [L. *resolvo—solvo,* to loose, to untie, to unbind.]
Resolved, rē-zolvd', *p.a.* Analysed; determined in purpose.

Resolvedly, rē-zolv'ed-li, *adv.* With firmness of purpose.
Resolving, rē-zolv'ing, *p.n.* Act of forming a fixed purpose; a resolution.
Resonance, re'sō-nans, *n. A resounding;* a reverberation of sound or sounds; the returning of sound by the air acting on the bodies of stringed musical instruments. [Fr. *résonnance.*]
Resonant, re'sō-nant, *a. Resounding;* returning sound; echoing back. [L. *resonans—sono,* to sound.]
Resort, rē-zort', *vi.* To have recour e, as by casting lots again; to betake one's self; to go; to apply.—*n. Act of resorting;* assembly; frequent assembling; the place frequented. [Fr. *ressortir*— L. *sortior,* to draw lots—*sors,* a lot.]
Resound, rē-zound', *vt.* To send back the sound of; to echo; to praise with the voice or the sound of instruments; to spread the fame of.—*vi.* To sound back; to be echoed; to be much and loudly mentioned.
Resource, rē-sōrs', *n. A new source;* any source of aid; contrivance; device; (pl.) funds; money or any property that can be converted into supplies.
Respect, rē-spekt', *vt.* To look back upon; to have esteem for as possessed of real worth; to honour; to have regard to; to relate to.—*n.* [Fr.] *A looking back;* regard; that estimation in which men hold the distinguished worth or substantial good qualities of others; that course of action which proceeds from esteem; good-will; undue bias to the prejudice of justice; motive in reference to something; relation; reference; prudence†. [Fr. *respecter;* L. *specio,* to look at.]
Respectability, rē-spekt'a-bil"li-ti, *n. State or quality of being respectable.*
Respectable, rē-spekt'a-bl, *a. Worthy of respect;* possessing the worth or qualities which deserve or command respect; moderately excellent. [Fr.]
Respectably, rē-spekt'a-bli, *adv. In a respectable manner.*
Respected, rē-spekt'ed, *p.a.* Held in honourable estimation.
Respecter, rē-spekt'ėr, *n. One who respects.*
Respectful, rē-spekt'fụl, *a. Having or exhibiting respect;* characterized by respect; courteous; complaisant.
Respectfully, rē-spekt'fụl-li, *adv. In a respectful manner;* with respect.
Respecting, rē-spekt'ing, *prep.* Regarding; concerning; relating to.
Respective, rē-spekt'iv, *a. Having respect to;* not absolute; relating to a particular person or thing; belonging to each; fitted to awaken respect; regardful†. [Fr. *respectif.*]
Respectively, rē-spekt'iv-li, *adv.* As relating to each; as each belongs to each; relatively; partially.
Respirability, rē-spir'a-bil"li-ti, *n. Quality of being respirable.*
Respirable, rē-spir'a-bl, *a. That may be respired;* fit for the support of animal life. [Fr.]
Respiration, re-spi-rā'shon, *n. Act of respiring;* the act of inhaling air into the lungs, and again expelling it. [Fr.]
Respirator, re'spi-rāt-ėr, *n.* An instrument covering the mouth, and serving to temper cold air.
Respiratory, rē-spir'a-tō-ri, *a. Serving for respiration;* pertaining to respiration. [Fr. *respiratoire.*]
Respire, rē-spir', *vi.* To breathe again; to breathe out; to breathe; to take rest from toil.—*vt.* To breathe in and out; to breathe. *ppr.* respiring, *pret.*

& pp. respired. [Fr. *respirer*—L. *spiro,* to breathe.]
Respite, res'pit, *n.* A time of looking back; limited time or rest; pause; delay; postponement; temporary suspension of the execution of a capital offender; a reprieve; forbearance; prolongation of time for the payment of a debt beyond the legal time.—*vt. To give a time for looking back;* to relieve by a pause; to keep back from execution; to delay for a time. *ppr.* respiting, *pret. & pp.* respited. [Old Fr. *respit*—L. *re,* and *specio,* to look.]
Resplendence, rē-splen'dens, *n. Quality of being resplendent;* vivid brightness.
Resplendent, rē-splen'dent, *a. Shining brightly;* very bright; shining with brilliant lustre. [L. *resplendens—splendeo,* to shine.]
Resplendently, rē-splen'dent-li, *adv.* With brilliant lustre.
Respond, rē-spond', *vi. To give words in return;* to give an answer or reply; to answer; to correspond; to suit. [Old Fr. *respondre*—L. *spondeo,* to promise solemnly.]
Respondent, rē-spond'ent, *a. Answering;* that answers to expectation.—*n. One who answers* in a suit, particularly a chancery suit. [L. *respondens.*]
Response, rē-spons', *n.* A so'emn answer; an oracular answer; the answer of the congregation to the priest, in the Litany and other parts of divine service; answer to an objection in a formal disputation. [L. *responsum—spondeo,* to promise solemnly.]
Responsibility, rē-spons'i-bil"li-ti, *n. State of being responsible,* as for a trust or office. [Sp. *responsabilidad.*]
Responsible, rē-spons'i-bl, *a. Answerable;* liable to account; able to discharge an obligation. [Sp. *responsable.*]
Responsibly, rē-spons'i-bli, *adv. In a responsible manner.*
Responsive, rē-spons'iv, *a. Answering;* correspondent; suited to something else. [Old Fr. *responsif.*]
Responsively, rē-spons'iv-li, *adv. In a responsive manner;* by way of response.
Rest, rest, *n.* A ceasing from motion or action of any kind; repose; security; a state of reconciliation to God; sleep; freedom of a nation from disturbance; death; a resting-place; any place which is free from disturbance; a support; a short pause of the voice in reading; a ceasing from tillage; a pause; an interval in music, during which the voice or sound is intermitted; the mark of such intermission. *vi.* To cease from motion of any kind; to cease from labour; to be quiet or still; to cease from war; to be tranquil, as the mind; to be in a state of repose, as on a bed; to be in a state of sleep; to sleep the final sleep; to lean on; to be satisfied (with *in*); to place confidence; to continue fixed; to remain with; to enjoy peace of conscience.—*vt. To lay* or *place at rest;* to place, as on a support. [Sax.; Goth. *rastjan,* to rest.]
Rest, rest, *n. That which remains* after the separation of a part, either in fact or in contemplation; residue; these not included in a description; others; a guarantee fund held in reserve by a bank.—*vi.* To be left; to remain. [Fr. *reste;* L. *re,* and *sto,* to stand.]
Restem, rē-stem', *vt.* To force back against the current.
Restful, rest'fụl, *a.* Quiet.
Restitution, re-sti-tū'shon, *n. A setting*

ch, chain; j, job; g, go; ng, sing; ᴛʜ, then; th, thin; w, wig; wh, whig; zh, azure; † obsolete.

up again; act of giving an equivalent for any loss or injury; compensation. [Fr.—L. *statuo,* to cause to stand.]

Restive, res'tiv, *a. Standing back;* unwilling to go forward, or only running back; stubborn; uneasy. (Old Fr. *resti*—L. *rs,* and *sto,* to stand.]

Restively, res'tiv-li, *adv. In a restive manner;* obstinately.

Restiveness, res'tiv-nes, *n.* Obstinate reluctance to move forward.

Restless, rest'les, *a. Having no rest;* continually moving; sleepless; passed in unquietness; not satisfied to be at rest; turbulent, as dependants; unsettled; roving.

Restlessly, rest'les-li, *adv. Without rest;* unquietly.

Restlessness, rest'les-nes, *n. State of being restless;* unquietness; want of sleep or rest; uneasiness; agitation.

Restoration, re-stō-rā'shon, *n. Act of restoring;* replacement; re-establishment; renovation; the recovering of health; the bringing back from any bad state. [Fr. *restauration.*]

Restorative, rē-stōr'at-iv, *a. That restores.—n. That which restores;* a medicine efficacious in restoring strength and vigour, or in recruiting the vital powers. [Sp. *restaurativo.*]

Restore, rē-stōr', *vt. To replace;* to renew; to give back to a person, as a thing which he has lost; to render up; to bring back to a former place or state; to reinstate; to recover from disease; to re-establish. *ppr.* restoring, *pret. & pp.* restored. [Fr. *restaurer;* L. *restauro—sto,* to stand.]

Restorer, rē-stōr'ėr, *n. One who,* or that which, *restores;* one who returns what is lost or unjustly detained.

Restrain, re-strān', *vt. To draw back tightly;* to hold in; to curb; to hinder; to withhold; to coerce; to suppress or keep down; to limit; to forbear (with recipr. pron.) [Old Fr. *restraindre—*L. *stringo,* to draw tight.]

Restraining, rē-strān'ing, *p.a.* Abridging; limiting.

Restraint, rē-strānt', *n. The act of restraining;* hindrance; repression; confinement; limitation; that which restrains or represses. [Old Fr. *restrainte.*]

Restrict, rē-strikt', *vt. To hold or keep back* within certain bounds; to circumscribe; to repress. [L. *restringo, restrictus—stringo,* to draw tight.]

Restricted, rē-strikt'ed, *p.a.* Limited; circumscribed.

Restriction, rē-strik'shon, *n. Act of restricting;* confinement within bounds; restraint. [Fr.]

Restrictive, rē-strikt'iv, *a.* Having the quality of *restricting;* imposing restraint. [Fr. *restrictif.*]

Restrictively, rē-strikt'iv-li, *adv.* With limitation.

Result, rē-zult', *vi. To spring back* or out; to follow, as a consequence; to take effect; to arise; to issue; to terminate.—*n. That* which proceeds from a given state of facts, &c.; inference; issue; event. [Fr. *résulter—*L. *salio, saltum,* to leap.]

Resulting, rē-zult'ing, *p.a.* Proceeding as a consequence of something.

Resumable, rē-sūm'a-bl, *a.* That may *be taken up again.*

Resume, rē-sūm', *vt. To take up again;* to take back; to take up again after interruption. *ppr.* resuming, *pret. & pp.* resumed. [Fr. *résumer—*L. *sūmo,* to take.]

Resumption, rē-zum'shon, *n. Act of*

resuming, or taking again. [Fr. *résumption—*L. *sumo,* to take.]

Resurgent, rē-sėr'jent, *a. Rising again,* or from the dead. [L. *resurgens—surgo,* to rise.]

Resurrection, re-zėr-rek'shon, *n. A rising again;* a rising again from a state of ignorance or bondage; the revival of the dead of the human race at the general judgment; the future state. [Fr. *résurrection—*L. *rs,* and *surgo,* to rise.]

Resuscitate, rē-sus'i-tāt, *vt. To raise or stir up again;* to revive; to recover from apparent death.—*vi.* To revive; to awaken. *ppr.* resuscitating, *pret. & pp.* resuscitated. [L. *resuscito—re, sursum,* upwards, and *cieo,* to make to go.]

Resuscitation, rē-sus'i-tā'shon, *n. Act of resuscitating;* the state of being revivified.

Retail, re-tāl', *vt.* To sell by *cutting* or *dividing again and again;* to sell in small quantities; to tell in broken parts; to tell to many. [Fr. *retailler,* to cut again—*tailler,* to cut.]

Retail, rē'tāl, *n.* The sale of commodities in small quantities or parcels.

Retailed, rē-tāld', *p.a.* Retold.

Retailer, rē-tāl'ėr, *n.* One who sells goods by small quantities or parcels.

Retain, rē-tān', *vt. To hold or keep back;* to keep in possession; not to lose; to keep from departure; to keep in pay; to employ by a fee paid, as a lawyer. [Fr. *retenir—*L. *teneo,* to hold.]

Retainable, rē-tān'a-bl, *a. Capable of being retained.*

Retainer, rē-tān'ėr, *n. One who retains;* an adherent; a servant, not menial, but wearing his master's livery, and attending sometimes upon special occasions; a fee paid to engage a counsellor to maintain a cause.

Retaliate, rē-ta'li-āt, *vt. To return, as like for like.—vi. To return like for like;* to requite by an act of the same kind as has been received. (With *on.*) *ppr.* retaliating, *pret. & pp.* retaliated. [Low L. *retalio, retaliatus—*L. *talio,* like for like—*talis,* such like.]

Retaliation, rē-ta'li-ā"shon, *n. Act of retaliating;* the return of like for like; retribution; punishment.

Retaliatory, rē-ta'li-a-tō-ri, *a.* Tending to retaliation.

Retard, rē-tärd', *vt. To render slow or slower;* to diminish, as the velocity of motion; to procrastinate. [Fr. *retarder;* L. *tardus,* slow.]

Retardation, rē-tärd-ā'shon, *n. Act of retarding* or of abating the velocity of motion. [Fr.]

Retarded rē-tärd'ed, *p.a.* Hindered in motion.

Retch, rech, *vi. To reach;* to make an effort to vomit; to heave, as the stomach. [Sax. *hræcan.*]

Retention, re-ten'shon, *n. Act of retaining;* maintenance; the power of retaining; the faculty of the mind by which it retains ideas; interruption of some natural discharge; act of withholding; that which holds something. [Fr. *rétention—*L. *teneo,* to hold.]

Retentive, rē-ten'tiv, *a. That retains;* having power to retain ideas. [Fr. *rétentif.*]

Retentively, rē-ten'tiv-li, *adv. In a retentive manner.*

Retentiveness, rē-ten'tiv-nes, *n.* Quality *of being retentive.*

Reticence, re'ti-sens, *n. A keeping silent;* concealment by silence. [Fr. *réticence—*L. *taceo,* to be silent.]

Reticent, re'ti-sent, *a.* Reserved. [L. *taceo,* to be silent.]

Reticulated, rē-tik'ū-lāt-ed, *a. Net-like; resembling net-work;* having distinct veins or lines crossing like net-work. [L. *reticulatus—rete,* a net.]

Reticulation, rē-tik'ū-lā"shon, *n. Network;* organization of substances resembling a net.

Reticule, rē'ti-kūl, *n. A little bag of net-work;* a lady's work-bag. [L. *reticulum—rete,* a net.]

Retina, re'ti-na, *n.* One of the coats of the eye, resembling fine *net-work,* spread over the bottom of the eye, where the sense of vision is first received. [Low L.—L. *rete,* a net.]

Retinue, re'ti-nū, *n.* Those whom a prince or distinguished personage *retains* in his service, as attendants, chiefly on a journey; a suite. [Old Fr. *retenué—*L. *teneo,* to hold.]

Retire, rē-tir', *vi. To withdraw:* to depart; to go from company; to go from a public station or active life; to break up, as a company; to go away for pleasure; to fall back, as a shore.—*vt. To withdraw;* to take up and pay when due, as a bill of exchange. *ppr.* retiring, *pret. & pp.* retired.—*n.* † Retreat. [Fr. *retirer—*L. *traho,* to draw.]

Retired, rē-tird', *p.a.* Private; secret; withdrawn.

Retiredness, rē-tird'nes, *n. A state of retirement;* solitude; privacy.

Retirement, rē-tir'ment, *n. Act of retiring;* private abode; private way of life; seclusion; solitude.

Retiring, rē-tir'ing, *p.a.* Reserved; not forward or obtrusive.

Retort, rē-tort', *vt. To twist back;* to throw back; to return, as an argument, censure, or incivility.—*vi. To return an argument or charge;* to make a severe reply.—*n.* The return of an argument; a quick and witty response; a chemical vessel with a long neck *bent,* to which a receiver may be fitted. [L. *retorqueo, retortus—torqueo,* to twist.]

Retouch, rē-tuch', *vt. To improve by new touches,* as a picture or an essay. *n. A repeated touch;* the reapplication of the master's hand to a work he had before considered in a finished state.

Retrace, rē-trās', *vt. To trace back;* to go back; to trace over again, or renew the outline of, as of a drawing. *ppr.* retracing, *pret. & pp.* retraced.

Retract, rē-trakt', *vt. To draw back;* to take back, as a declaration; to revoke; to recant; to abjure.—*vi. To withdraw* concession or declaration. [Fr. *rétracter—*L. *traho, tractum,* to draw.]

Retractile, rē-trakt'il, *a. Capable of being drawn back,* as claws.

Retraction, rē-trak'shon, *n. Act of drawing back;* disavowal of the truth of what has been said; declaration of change of opinion. [Fr. *rétraction—*L. *traho, tractum,* to draw.]

Retractive, rē-trakt'iv, *a. Tending to retract;* withdrawing; taking from.

Retreat, rē-trēt', *n. A withdrawing;* act of retiring; state of being retired; seclusion; solitude; place for being retired; an asylum; a refuge; the retiring of an army from an enemy, or from any position.—*vi. To withdraw;* to retire from any position; to withdraw to a private abode; to retire to a place of safety; to retire from an enemy. [Fr. *retraite—*L. *traho,* to draw.]

Retrench, rē-trensh', *vt. To cut right across;* to render less, as expenses; to

curtail; to limit.—*vi.* To live at a less expense; to economise. [Fr. *retrancher*; L. *re*, *trans*, and *scindo*, to cut.]

Retrenchment, rē-trensh'ment, *n.* Act of retrenching; a lessening; curtailment; reduction. [Fr. *retranchement*.]

Retribution, re-tri-bū'shon, *n.* ... giving back; recompense; retaliation; the rewards and punishments to be distributed at the general judgment. [Fr. *rétribution*—L. *tribuo*, to bestow.]

Retributive, rē-trib'ūt-iv, *a.* Making retribution; rewarding for good deeds, and punishing for offences.

Retrievable, rē-trēv'a-bl, *a.* That may be retrieved or recovered.

Retrievably, rē-trēv'a-bli, *adv.* In a retrievable manner.

Retrieve, rē-trēv', *vt.* To hit or light upon again; to recover; to reclaim; to gain back; to bring back from loss or injury to a former good state. *ppr.* retrieving, *pret. & pp.* retrieved. [Fr. *retrouver*—Gr. *trefien*, to find.]

Retriever, rē-trēv'ėr, *n.* A dog trained to find and bring in birds that are shot.

Retrocession, rē-trō-sē'shon, *n.* Act of going back. [Fr. *rétrocession*—L. *retro*, back, and *cedo*, to go.]

Retrogradation, rē'trō-gra-dā'shon, *n.* Act of going backward; a moving backward. [Fr. *rétrogradation*.]

Retrograde, rē'trō-grād, *a.* Apparently moving backward and contrary to the succession of the signs, i.e. from east to west, as a planet; declining from a better to a worse state; contrary.—*vi.* To move backward. *ppr.* retrograding, *pret. & pp.* retrograded. [Fr. *rétrograde*—L. *retro*, and *gradior*, to go.]

Retrogression, rē-trō-gre'shon, *n.* Act of going backward.

Retrogressive, rē-trō-gres'iv, *a.* Going or moving backward.

Retrogressively, rē-trō-gres'iv-li, *adv.* By retrogression.

Retrospect, rē'trō-spekt, *n.* A looking back; contemplation of something past; review. [L. *retrospicio*, *retrospectum*—*specio*, to look at.]

Retrospection, rē-trō-spek'shon, *n.* Act of looking back on things past.

Retrospective, rē-trō-spekt'iv, *a.* Looking back on past events; having reference to what is past.

Retrospectively, rē-trō-spekt'iv-li, *adv.* By way of retrospect.

Return, rē-tėrn', *vi.* To turn back; to go back to the same place, state, subject, &c.; to come again; to revisit; to appear after a periodical revolution.—*vt.* To cause to turn or go back; to give back in payment, as money; to give in recompense; to give back in reply; to recriminate; to give by way of official report; to send; to convey.—*n.* Act of turning back; act of coming back to the same place; the act of sending back; the act of putting in the former place, &c.; revolution; periodical renewal; that which is returned; repayment; profit; advantage; requital; restitution; an official account; a numerical statement; answer; reply.

Returnable, rē-tėrn'a-bl, *a.* That may be returned; that is legally to be returned.

Returned, rē-tėrnd', *p.a.* Restored.

Returning, rē-tėrn'ing, *p.a.* Giving back; coming back.

Reunion, rē-ū'ni-on, *n.* A uniting again; union formed anew after separation; a meeting or assembly.

Reunite, rē-ū-nīt', *vt.* To unite again; to reconcile after variance.—*vi.* To be united again; to join and cohere again. *ppr.* reuniting, *pret. & pp.* reunited.

Reveal, rē-vēl', *vt.* To unveil; to lay bare; to disclose; to communicate; to make known from heaven. [Fr. *révéler*—L. *velo*, to veil.]

Revealed, rē-vēld', *p.a.* Disclosed; made known.

Revel, rev'el, *vi.* To spend the hours of sleep in disorderly feasting and licentious indulgence; to carouse; to move playfully or without regularity. *ppr.* revelling, *pret. & pp.* revelled.—*n.* A feast with loose and noisy jollity. [Old Fr. *reveiller*—L. *re*, and *vigilare*, to watch.]

Revelation, re-vē-lā'shon, *n.* Act of revealing; the disclosure of truth to men by God himself, or by his authorised agents; the sacred truths which God has communicated to man for his instruction; the Apocalypse. [Fr. *révélation*—L. *velo*, to veil.]

Reveller, rev'el-ėr, *n.* One who revels or feasts with noisy merriment.

Revelling, rev'el-ing, *p.n.* A feasting with noisy merriment; revelry.

Revelry, rev'el-ri, *n.* Noisy festivity; clamorous jollity.

Revenge, rē-venj', *vt.* To punish with force in return for a wrong received; to inflict pain upon in return for an injury received. *ppr.* revenging, *pret. & pp.* revenged.—*n.* Act of revenging; a malicious or spiteful infliction of pain or injury in return for an injury or offence; the passion which is excited by an injury done. [Old Fr. *revenger*; L. *re*, and *vindico*, to punish.]

Revengeful, rē-venj'fųl, *a.* Full of revenge; wreaking revenge; vindictive; malicious; inflicting punishment.

Revengefully, rē-venj'fųl-li, *adv.* By way of revenge; vindictively.

Revenger, rē-venj'ėr, *n.* One who revenges.

Revengingly†, re-venj'ing-li, *adv.* With revenge.

Revenue, rev'e-nū, *n.* That which comes back; the annual rents or issues of any species of property belonging to an individual or to the public; the annual produce of taxes, excise, customs, duties, rents, &c., which a nation collects and receives into the treasury for public use; return; reward. [Fr. *revenu*—L. *venir*, to come.]

Reverb†, rē-vėrb', *vt.* To reverberate.

Reverberant†, rē-vėr'bė-rant, *a.* Resounding.

Reverberate, rē-vėr'bė-rāt, *vt.* To send or drive back; to return, as sound; to echo.—*vi.* To be driven back; to echo, as sound; to resound. *ppr.* reverberating, *pret. & pp.* reverberated. [Late L. *reverbero*—L. *verber*, *verbéris*, a lash —*ferio*, to strike.]

Reverberation, rē-vėr'bė-rā"shon, *n.* Act of reverberating; the act of reflecting light and heat, or re-echoing sound.

Reverberatory, rē-vėr'bė-rā-tō-ri, *a.* Returning or driving back.

Revere, rē-vėr', *vt.* To stand in awe of; to honour in estimation; to reverence. *ppr.* revering, *pret. & pp* revered. [Fr. *révérer*—L. *vereor*, to feel awe of.]

Revered, rē-vėrd', *p.a.* Regarded with fear mingled with respect and affection.

Reverence, rev'e-rens, *n.* Fear mingled with respect and affection; homage; veneration; adoration; an act of respect; a bow or courtesy; the state of being reverent; a title of the clergy.—*vt.* To regard with reverence; to venerate; to honour. *ppr.* reverencing, *pret. & pp.* reverenced. [Fr. *révérence*.]

Reverend, re've-rend, *a.* Worthy of reverence; a title of respect given to the clergy. [Fr. *révérend*.]

Reverent, rev'e-rent, *a.* Expressing reverence; submissive; humble; impressed with reverence. [L. *reverens*.]

Reverential, re-ve-ren'shi-al, *a.* Proceeding from reverence, or expressing it. [Old It. *reverensale*.]

Reverentially, re-ve-ren'shi-al-li, *adv.* In a reverential manner.

Reverently, re've-rent-li, *adv.* In a reverent manner; with reverence.

Reverie, re've-ri, *n.* A state of the mind occupied by varying ideas which interest it; a loose train of thoughts occurring in musing; wild conceit of the fancy; delirium; a vision; voluntary inactivity of the whole or the greater part of the external senses to the impressions of surrounding objects during wakefulness. [Fr. *rêverie*—L. *res*, a thing, and *varius*, changing.]

Reversal, rē-vėrs'al, *n.* Act of reversing; a change or overthrowing.

Reverse, rē-vėrs', *vt.* To turn back; to put in the contrary order; to invert; to put, as each in the place of the other, to make void. as a sentence; to subvert. *ppr.* reversing, *pret. & pp.* reversed.—*n.* That which is reversed; change; vicissitude; a turn of affairs; misfortune; [Fr. *revers*] the back side; the side of a medal or coin opposite to that on which the head is impressed, and which is called the obverse.—*a.* Turned backward; opposite. [L. *reverto*, *reversus*—*verto*, to turn.]

Reversed, rē-vėrst', *p.a.* Overthrown or annulled.

Reversible, rē-vėrs'i-bl, *a.* That may be reversed.

Reversion, rē-vėr'shon, *n.* A turning back; a returning; the returning of an estate to the grantor or his heirs; an annuity or payment which is not to be received until the happening of some event; succession; right to future possession. [Fr. *réversion*.]

Reversionary, rē-vėr'shon-a-ri, *a.* Pertaining to a reversion, that is. to be enjoyed in succession.

Revert, rē-vėrt', *vt.* To turn back; to turn to the contrary.—*vi.* To return; to come back; to fall back; to return to the proprietor after the determination of a particular estate [L. *reverto*—*verto*, to turn.]

Review, rē-vū', *vt.* To view again; to look back on; to reconsider; to examine the state of anything, particularly of troops; to examine critically, as a new publication; to retrace. *n.* A second view; re-examination; an inspection of troops under arms by a general; a critical examination of a new publication; a periodical publication, containing examinations of new books.

Reviewal, rē-vū'al, *n.* A review of a book; a critique.

Reviewer, rē-vū'ėr, *n.* One who reviews; one who critically examines a new publication, and publishes his opinion of it.

Revile, rē-vīl', *vt.* To regard as vile; to treat with contemptuous language; to reproach; to calumniate. *ppr.* reviling, *pret. & pp.* reviled.

Reviler, rē-vīl'ėr, *n.* One who reviles.

Reviling, rē-vīl'ing, *p.n.* Act of reviling or treating with reproachful words.

Revilingly, rē-vīl'ing-li, *adv.* With reproachful or contemptuous language.

Revisal, rē-vīz'al, n. *Revision*; the act of re-examining for correction and improvement.

Revise, rē-vīz', vt. *To look back on; to review;* to look over with care for correction. ppr. revising, pret. & pp. revised.—n. *Review;* a second proof-sheet, in printing. [L. *reviso—video, visum,* to see.]

Revised, rē-vīzd', p.a. Re-examined for correction.

Reviser, rē-vīz'ėr, n. *One who revises.*

Revision, rē-vi'zhon, n. *Act of revising* or re-examining for correction; re-examination; revisal; review. [Fr. *révision.*]

Revisit, rē-vi'zit, vt. *To visit again.*

Revival, rē-vīv'al, n. *Act of reviving;* return to life from death; return to activity; renewed attention to religion.

Revive, rē-vīv', vi. *To live again;* to recover new life or vigour; to recover from a state of depression.—vt. *To bring again to life;* to raise from languor; to quicken; to refresh; to bring into action after a suspension, as a scheme; to bring back into the mind, as ideas; to bring out from a state of depression, as literature; to inspire with new joy or hope; to bring again into notice. ppr. reviving, pret. & pp. revived. [Fr. *revivre*—L. *vivo,* to live.]

Reviver, rē-vīv'ėr, n. *He or that which revives;* that which refreshes.

Reviving, rē-vīv'ing, p.a. *Bringing to life again;* coming to life again.—p.n. *Act of restoring to life,* or of coming to life again.

Revocable, re'vōk-a-bl, a. *That may be recalled;* that may be repealed. [Fr. *révocable*—L. *voco,* to call.]

Revocably, re'vōk-a-bli, adv. *In a revocable manner.*

Revocation, re-vōk-ā'shon, n. *Act of revoking;* the calling back of a thing granted or act done; state of being recalled. [Fr. *révocation.*]

Revoke, rē-vōk', vt. *To call back;* to countermand; to reverse; to declare void, as a law, grant, or testament. ppr. revoking, pret. & pp. revoked. [Fr. *révoquer*—L. *voco,* to call.]

Revokement, rē-vōk'ment, n. Revocation.

Revolt, rē-vōlt', vi. *To roll back; to turn back;* to fall off; to renounce allegiance to one's prince or state.—vt. *To cause to turn back!,* figuratively; to put to flight; to shock; to cause to turn away with abhorrence or disgust.—n. *A revolting;* a renunciation of allegiance to one's prince; rebellion; mutiny; gross departure from duty; a revolter!. [Fr. *révolter*—L. *volvo,* to roll.]

Revolted, rē-vōlt'ed, p.a. Shocked; grossly offended.

Revolter, rē-vōlt'ėr, n. *One who revolts;* one who renounces subjection to his prince or state.

Revolting, rē-vōlt'ing, p.a. Exciting abhorrence; shocking.

Revoltingly, rē-vōlt'ing-li, adv. *In a revolting manner;* offensively.

Revolution, re-vō-lū'shon, n. *Act of revolving;* the circular motion of a body on its axis; the motion of a body round any fixed point; change of circumstances; continued course marked by the regular return of years; space measured by some regular return of a revolving body; an extensive change in the political constitution of a country accomplished in a short time, whether by legal or by illegal means. [Fr. *révolution*—L. *volvo,* to roll.]

Revolutionary, re-vō-lū'shon-a-ri, a. *Pertaining or tending to a revolution* in government. [Fr. *révolutionnaire*—L. *volvo, volūtum,* to roll.]

Revolutionist, re-vō-lū'shon-ist, n. *The favourer of a revolution.*

Revolutionize, re-vō-lū'shon-īz, vt. *To effect a revolution* in the form of, as of a political constitution; to effect an entire change of principles in. ppr. revolutionizing, pret. & pp. revolutionized.

Revolve, rē-volv', vi. *To roll back;* to roll in a circle; to turn round, as on an axis; to move round a centre.—vt. *To cause to roll round;* to turn over and over; to consider attentively. ppr. revolving, pret. & pp. revolved. [L. *revolvo—volvo,* to roll.]

Revolver, rē-volv'ėr, n. *That which revolves;* a pistol with several barrels, each containing a charge, which are discharged one after the other by giving the pistol a *revolving* motion.

Revolving, rē-volv'ing, p.a. Performing *a revolution;* turning over and over.

Revulsion, rē-vul'shon, n. *A plucking back;* the act of throwing back; the act of turning any disease from one part of the body to another; sudden change of feeling from one state to its opposite. [Fr. *révulsion*—L. *vello,* to pluck.]

Reward, rē-ward', n. *Worth or value returned;* equivalent return for good done; the fruit of men's labour; a bribe; a sum of money offered for taking a criminal, or for recovery of anything lost; a just return of evil for wickedness; punishment.—vt. *To return worth or value* to or to requite; to remunerate; to pay; to punish. [Fr. *re,* and *award—ward,* worth.]

Rewarder, rē-ward'ėr, n. *One who rewards* or recompenses.

Reword, rē-werd', vt. *To repeat* in the same words.

Rhapsodic, Rhapsodical, rap-sod'ik, rap-sod'ik-al, a. *Pertaining to or consisting of rhapsody;* unconnected.

Rhapsodically, rap-sod'ik-al-li, adv. *In the manner of rhapsody.*

Rhapsodist, rap'sod-ist, n. *One who writes or sings rhapsodies* for a livelihood; one who writes or speaks without regular dependency of one part on another. [Fr. *rhapsodiste.*]

Rhapsody, rap'sō-di, n. Anciently, a *portion of an epic poem* fit for recitation at one time; a confused jumble of sentences without natural connection; rambling composition. (Gr. *rhapsōdia—rhaptō,* to stitch together, and *ōdē,* a song.]

Rhetoric, re'to-rik, n. *The art or science of public speaking;* the art of speaking with propriety, elegance, force, and effect; the power of persuasion; that which charms. [Fr. *rhétorique*—Gr. *rhetōr,* a public speaker—*rheō,* to speak.]

Rhetorical, re-to'rik-al, a. *Pertaining to rhetoric;* containing the rules of rhetoric; oratorical.

Rhetorically, re-to'rik-al-li, adv. *In the manner of rhetoric.*

Rhetorician, re-to-ri'shi-an, n. *One who teaches the art of rhetoric;* one well versed in the principles of rhetoric. [Fr. *rhétoricien.*]

Rheum, rūm, n. *A flow of humours;* an increased action of the mucous glands, attended with increased discharge; a thin, serous fluid, secreted by the mucous glands, &c., as in a common cold. [Fr. *rheume*—Gr. *rheō,* to flow.]

Rheumatic, rū-mat'ik, a. *Pertaining* or subject *to rheumatism;* choleric. [Fr. *rhumatique.*]

Rheumatism, rū'mat-izm, n. Originally, *a rheum;* pain and inflammation about the joints and surrounding muscles, chiefly the larger joints, as the hips, knees, shoulders, &c. [Fr. *rhumatisme;* Gr. *rheō,* to flow.]

Rheumy, rūm'i, a. *Full of rheum;* affected with rheum; causing rheum.

Rhinoceros, ri-no'se-ros, n. *A large and uncouth-looking animal,* thick-skinned, and having a *horn on its nose.* [Gr. *rhin, rhinos,* the nose, and *kėras,* a horn.]

Rhododendron, rō-dō-den'dron, n. *The rose-tree;* a highly ornamental plant, remarkable for the beauty of its evergreen leaves and its large brilliant flowers. [Gr. *rhodon,* a rose, and *dendron,* a tree.]

Rhomb, Rhombus, rom, rom'bus, n. *A quadrilateral figure* whose sides are equal and the opposite sides parallel, but whose angles are not right-angles. [Fr. *rhombe*—Gr. *rhembō,* to turn round.]

Rhombic, rom'bik, a. *Having the figure of a rhomb.*

Rhomboid, rom'boid, n. *A figure resembling a rhomb;* a quadrilateral figure whose opposite sides and angles are equal, but which is neither equilateral nor equiangular. [Gr. *rhombos,* and *eidos,* form.]

Rhomboidal, rom-boid'al, a. *Having the shape of a rhomboid.*

Rhubarb, rū'bärb, n. *A plant which grows abundantly* on the banks of the Rha or Volga, now naturalized in Britain, and whose leaf-stalks are used for making tarts, &c., the root being used in medicine. [Fr. *rhubarbe*—Low L. *rha,* a root, and *barbărus,* foreign]

Rhumb, rum, n. *That which goes round in a circle;* a circle on the earth's surface making a given angle with the meridian of the place; a point of the compass. [from *rhomb.*]

Rhyme, rim, n. Primarily, a *numbering;* the correspondence of sounds in the terminating words of two verses, one of which succeeds the other immediately or at no great distance; poetry; a word or sound to answer to another word.—vi. *To make verses;* to accord in sound.—vt. *To put into rhyme.* ppr. rhyming, pret. & pp. rhymed. [Sax. *rim,* number, rhyme—*riman,* to number.]

Rhymeless, rim'les, a. *Destitute of rhyme;* not having consonance of sound.

Rhymer, rim'ėr, n. *One who makes rhymes;* a versifier.

Rhythm, rithm, n. *Any regular flow,* as of time; measured motion; a division of time into short portions by a regular succession of motions, impulses, sounds, &c., producing an agreeable effect. [Fr. *rhythme*—Gr. *rheō,* to flow.]

Rhythmical, rith'mik-al, a. *Pertaining to rhythm;* having rhythm. [L. *rhythmicus.*]

Rib, rib, n. One of the *curved bones which encompass the body* like hoops; a piece of curved timber which forms the side of a ship; a moulding in the interior of a vaulted roof; a prominent line in cloth like a rib; something long, thin, and narrow; a strip.—vt. *To furnish with ribs;* to form with rising lines; to inclose with ribs. ppr. ribbing, pret. & pp. ribbed. [Sax.—G. *reif,* a hoop.]

Ribald, ri'bald, n. A rough, low, vulgar, brutal, foul-mouthed wretch; a lewd fellow.—a. Low; base; obscene. [Fr. *ribaud*—Low L. *ribaldus*.]

Ribaldry, ri'bald-ri, n. Mean, rough, vulgar language; obscene language. [Fr. *ribauderie*.]

Riband, ri'band. [probably from *rib*, and *band*, a band to gird the sides. See RIBBON.]

Ribbed, ribd, p.a. Furnished with ribs; inclosed, as with ribs; formed with rising lines and channels.

Ribbon, ri'bon, n. A ban*l* to gird the ribs or sides; a narrow web of silk, satin, &c., used for an ornament, as a badge; a narrow thin strip of anything.

Ribboned, ri'bond, p.a. Adorned with ribbons.

Rice, ris, n. A cereal plant, whose grain, produced in immense quantities in warm climates, is a light nutritious food, very easy of digestion. [Fr. *ris* or *ris*; Ar. *rus*, rice in the husk.]

Rich, rich, a. Spreading; extending; abounding in money, cattle, goods, or lands; precious; abundant in materials; full of valuable achievements; fertile; large; plentiful; full of beautiful scenery; plentifully stocked; perfect; abounding with nutritious qualities; highly seasoned; abounding with a variety of delicious food; full of sweet sounds. [Sax. *ric*—G. *reichen*, to expand.]

Riches, rich'ez, n. Extensive possessions of land, goods, or money; wealth; plenty, splendid, sumptuous appearance. [Sax. *richesse*.]

Richly, rich'li, adv. With riches; gaily; splendidly; amply; really; fully.

Richness, rich'nes, n. State or quality of being rich; splendour; fertility; fulness; quality of abounding with something valuable; abundance of beautiful scenery; abundance of high seasoning; strength; vividness; abundance of imagery or of striking ideas.

Rick, rik, n. A heap or pile of grain or hay in the field or open air, but commonly sheltered with a covering of some kind. [Sax. *hreac*—Goth. *rikan*, to heap together.]

Rickets, rik'ets, n. pl. A disease of children, supposed to depend on disorder of the spines, and distinguished by a bulky head, crooked spine, short stature, with clear and often premature mental faculties. [Gr. *rhachitis*, a spinal complaint—*rhachis*, the spine.]

Rickety, rik'et-i, a. Affected with rickets; weak; imperfect.

Rid, rid, vt. To set free; to free; to clear; to disencumber; to drive away; to destroy; to dispose of; to finish. ppr. ridding, pret. & pp. rid.—p.a. Clear; disencumbered. [Sax. *hreddan*.]

Riddance, rid'ans, n. A setting free; disencumbrance; act of clearing away.

Riddle, rid'l, n. An instrument for separating grain from the chaff.—vt. To separate, as grain from the chaff with a riddle; to perforate with balls or shot. ppr. riddling, pret. & pp. riddled. [Sax. *Ariddel*—*Ariddan*, to separate.]

Riddle, rid'l, n. Something to be guessed at; a puzzling question; an enigma. vt. To solve; but we generally use *unriddle*, which is more proper.—vi. To speak ambiguously. ppr. riddling, pret. & pp. riddled. [Sax. *rædelse*—*ræda*, to read.]

Ride, rid, vi. To be borne along in a chariot or on horseback; to be borne on or in a fluid; to practise riding; to manage a horse well; to be supported by something subservient; to sit; to be at anchor, as a ship.—vt. To sit or to place one's self on, so as to be carried; to manage insolently at will. ppr. riding, pret. rode, pp. ridden.—n. An excursion on horseback or in a vehicle; a road cut in a wood for the amusement of riding; a riding; a drive. [Sax. *ridan*—Sans. *ratha*, a chariot.]

Rider, rid'er, n. One who rides, or is borne on a horse or in a vehicle; one who breaks a horse; an addition to a manuscript, inserted after its completion; an additional clause.

Ridge, rij, n. An extended line, standing above the adjoining surface, and so breaking its continuity; the back or top of the back; a strip of ground thrown up by a plough; a long range of hills; the upper part of such a range; a steep elevation; the top of the roof of a building.—vt. To form into a ridge or ridges; to wrinkle. ppr. ridging, pret. & pp. ridged. [Sax. *hric*—Gr. *rhassō*, to break.]

Ridgy, rij'i, a. Having a ridge or ridges.

Ridicule, ri'di-kūl, n. Wit of that species that excites laughter; remarks designed to awaken laughter with some degree of contempt; satire; that species of writing which excites contempt with laughter.—vt. To expose to ridicule; to deride. ppr. ridiculing, pret. & pp. ridiculed. [Fr.—L. *rideo*, to laugh at.]

Ridiculous, ri-dik'ū-lus, a. That may justly excite laughter with contempt; absurd; preposterous. [L. *ridiculus*.]

Ridiculously, ri-dik'ū-lus-li, adv. In a ridiculous manner.

Ridiculousness, ri-dik'ū-lus-nes, n. Quality of being ridiculous.

Riding, rid'ing, p.a. Used in riding; employed to travel on any occasion. p.n. Act of one who rides; a district visited by an officer.

Riding-master, rid'ing-mas-tėr, n. A teacher of the art of riding.

Riding-school, rid'ing-skōl, n. A school where the art of riding is taught.

Riding-skirt, rid'ing-skėrt, n. A long skirt worn by a female when riding.

Rife, rif, a. Growing into ripeness; abounding; plentiful; prevailing. [Sax. *ryf*; Old G. *rifjan*, to ripen.]

Rifely, rif'li, adv. Prevalently.

Rifeness, rif'nes, n. State of being rife; abundance; prevalence.

Rifle, ri'fl, vt. To bear away by force; to strip; to pillage; to ransack. ppr. rifling, pret. & pp. rifled. [Old Fr. *rifler*, to sweep away.]

Rifle, ri'fl, vt. To groove; to channel. ppr. rifling, pret. & pp. rifled.—n. A gun, the inside of whose barrel is grooved or formed with spiral channels. [G. *reifeln*—*reifen*, to groove.]

Rifleman, ri'fl-man, n. One of a body of troops armed with rifles.

Rifler, ri'fi-ėr, n. One who rifles; one who seizes and bears away by violence.

Rift, rift, n. An opening made by riving; a fissure.—vt. To rive; to split.—vi. To be riven; to split. [old pp. of *rive*.]

Rig, rig, vt. To cover; to accoutre; to fit with tackling. ppr. rigging, pret. & pp. rigged.—n. A covering; the peculiar manner of fitting the masts and rigging to the hull of a vessel. [Sax. *wrigan*, to cover.]

Rigger, rig'ėr, n. One whose occupation is to fit the rigging of a ship.

Rigging, rig'ing, p.n. Dress; tackle; the ropes which support the masts, extend and contract the sails, &c., of a ship.

Right, rit, a. Straight; stretched to straightness; direct; just; true; proper; legitimate; not wrong; fit; suitable; according to law; not mistaken; not left; most convenient; properly placed; being on the same side as the right hand; being on the right hand of a person whose face is toward the mouth of a river; denoting the side which was designed to go outward.—n. That which is straight; conformity to the will of God, or to his law; conformity to human laws; justice; that which is due; freedom from error; just claim; legal title; ownership; just claim by courtesy; just claim by sovereignty; prerogative; property; privilege; legal power; the side opposite to the left. vt. To make straight; to do justice to; to relieve from wrong; to restore to an upright position, as a ship.—vi. To rise with the masts erect, as a ship adv. In a straight line; directly; according to the law or will of God; according to any rule of art; according to fact or truth; in a great degree; very; immediately.—interj. An expression of approbation. [Sax. *riht*—L. *rectus*, straight—*rego*, to lay or keep straight.]

Right-angle, rit'ang-gl, n. In geometry an angle of ninety degrees.

Right-angled, rit'ang-gld, a. Containing a right-angle or right-angles.

Righteous, rit'ē-us, a. Rightly wise; upright in conduct; pious; godly; virtuous; accordant to the divine law; accordant to justice. [Sax. *riht-wis*.]

Righteously, rit'ē-us-li, adv. In a righteous manner; equitably.

Righteousness, rit'ē-us-nes, n. State or quality of being righteous; godliness; integrity; honesty; purity of heart and rectitude of life; applied to God, the perfection of his nature.

Righter, rit'ėr, n. One who sets right.

Rightful, rit'ful, a. Having the right according to established laws; just.

Rightfully, rit'ful-li, adv. According to right, law, or justice.

Rightly, rit'li, adv. In a right manner.

Rightness, rit'nes, n. Quality of being right or straight; conformity to truth.

Rightward, rit'ward, adv. Toward the right hand.

Rigid, ri'jid, a. Stiff; numb; unbending; not easily bent; characterised by strictness in opinion or discipline; not lax; severe; severely just, as a sentence. [Fr. *rigide*—L. *rigeo*, to be stiff.]

Rigidity, ri-jid'i-ti, n. State or quality of being rigid; stiffness; numbness; want of pliability; want of ease in manner. [Fr. *rigidité*.]

Rigidly, ri'jid-li, adv. Stiffly; strictly, without laxity.

Rigidness, ri'jid-nes, n. State or quality of being rigid; strictness in opinion.

Rigol, ri'gol, n. A circle; a diadem.

Rigorous, rig'or-us, a. Full of rigour; inflexible; allowing no mitigation; severe; stern; scrupulously accurate; very cold, as a winter. [Fr. *rigoureux*—L. *rigeo*, to be stiff.]

Rigorously, rig'or-us-li, adv. Severely; with scrupulous nicety.

Rigour, rig'or, n. Stiffness; inflexibility; a sudden coldness, attended by a shivering; quality of being stiff; quality of being severe in life; sternness; voluntary submission to mortification; quality of being strict; austerity; quality of being severe or very cold. [L. *rigor*—*rigeo*, to be stiff.]

Rill, ril, n. A small brook; a streamlet. vi. To run in a small stream, or in streamlets. [G. *rille*—Icel. *rylla*, to roll.]

Rim, rim, n. The limit of the *extension* of anything; the border of a thing.—*vt*. To put a rim or hoop on or around. ppr. rimming, pret. & pp. rimmed. [Sax. *rima*—*ryman*, to extend.]

Rime, rim, n. *White or hoar frost*; congealed dew or vapour.—*vi*. To *freeze or congeal into hoar-frost*. ppr. riming, pret. & pp. rimed. [Sax. *hrim*—Gr. *krumos*, frost.]

Rimy, rim'i, a. *Abounding with rime*; frosty. [from *rime*.]

Rind, rind, n. The *skin* of fruit that may be peeled off; the peel; the bark of trees; the external coat of a nut. [Sax.—G. *rand*, the outside of a thing.]

Ring, ring, n. *That which goes or is turned round about*; a circle; a circle of gold, &c., worn as an ornament; a circle of persons; a class of persons or people; the practice of boxing, or pugilists in general.—*vt*. To surround with a ring; to fit with rings. [Sax. *hring*; Icel. *hringa*, to turn round.]

Ring, ring, vt. To cause to *sound*, as a bell or metallic body; to produce by ringing, as a sound or peal; to repeat often.—*vi*. To *sound*, as a bell or other sonorous body; to practise the art of making music with bells; to resound; to utter, as a bell; to tinkle; to have the sensation of sound continued; to be filled with talk. ppr. ringing, pret. rang, pp. rung.—n. The *sound* of a metallic instrument of a circular form; the sound of metals; any loud sound; a chime or set of bells harmonically tuned. [Sax. *ringan*—Sans. *ru*, to sound.]

Ringer, ring'er, n. *One who rings*.

Ring-fence, ring'fens, n. *A fence encircling* an estate within one inclosure.

Ringing, ring'ing, p.n. Act of causing to sound, as bells or other sonorous bodies.

Ringleader, ring'lēd-er, n. *The leader of a ring*; the leader of any association of men engaged in the violation of the law.

Ringlet, ring'let, n. *A small ring*; a curl, particularly a curl of hair.

Ring-worm, ring'werm, n. An eruption on the skin, in small vesicles with a reddish base, and forming *rings* whose area is slightly discoloured; a pustular eruption of the scalp.

Rinse, rins, vt. To *make pure or to cleanse* by the introduction of water, applied particularly to hollow vessels; to cleanse with a second application of water, after washing. ppr. rinsing, pret. & pp. rinsed. [Fr. *rincer*—L. *re*, and *sincerus*, pure.]

Riot, rī'ot, n. An *uproar*; a disturbance of the peace by three or more persons; carousal; wild and noisy festivity; expensive feasting.—*vi*. To *raise an uproar*; to be seditious with clamour; to be highly excited; to banquet with noisy mirth; to run to excess in feasting. [Sax. *reotan*, to make a cracking *noire*; Icel. *ryta*, to grunt.]

Rioter, rī'ot-ėr, n. *One who riots*; one guilty of meeting with others to do an unlawful act; one who indulges in loose festivity.

Rioting, rī'ot-ing, p.a. A revelling; a disturbing of the peace; a riot.

Riotous, rī'ot-us, a. *Practising* or pertaining to *riot*; seditious; partaking of the nature of an unlawful assembly; licentious in festive indulgences. [Low L. *riotosus*.]

Riotously, rī'ot-us-li, adv. *In a riotous manner*; seditiously.

Riotousness, rī'ot-us-nes, n. *State or quality of being riotous*.

Rip, rip, vt. To *tear or cut open* or off; to tear off or out by violence; to take out by cutting or tearing; to tear up for search; to search to the bottom. (With *up, open, of,* or *out*.) ppr. ripping, pret. & pp. ripped.—n. *A tearing*; a place torn; laceration. [Sax. *rypan*—Goth. *raupjan*, to pluck away.]

Ripe, rip, a. *Fit to be gathered*, as corn; brought to the best state; fit for use; matured, as wisdom; finished; consummate; ready; suppurated, as an abscess. *vi*. To ripen; to grow ripe.—*vt*. To mature. [Sax.—*ripan*, to gather corn.]

Ripely, rip'li, adv. Maturely.

Ripen, rip'n, vi. To *become fit for reaping*; to grow ripe; to be matured, as grain or fruit; to come to perfection; to be fitted.—*vt*. To make ripe, as grain or fruit; to prepare; to bring to perfection. [Sax. *ripian*.]

Ripened, rip'nd, p.a. *Made ripe*; come or brought to maturity.

Ripeness, rip'nes, n. *State of being ripe*; maturity; full growth; fitness; complete suppuration, as of an ulcer; a state of preparation.

Ripening, rip'n-ing, p.a. *Growing ripe*; maturing.—n. *The act of becoming ripe*, or of making ripe.

Ripple, rip'l, vi. To *fret on the surface*, as water when agitated.—*vt*. To *ruffle* as the surface of water. ppr. rippling, pret. & pp. rippled.—n. *The ruffling* of the surface of water; little curling waves. [Sax. *Arympelle*, a fold.]

Rippling, rip'l-ing, p.n. *The breaking of ripples*, or the noise of it.

Rise, rīz, vi. To *move or pass upward* in any manner; to arise; to get up; to leave the place of sleep or rest; to get up or move from any recumbent posture; to leave a sitting posture; to spring; to grow; to break forth; to shine, as the sun or a star; to begin to exist; to be excited; to begin to move, as the wind; to take place, to be produced; to gain elevation in rank; to break forth into public commotions; to be roused into action; to make a hostile attack; to elevate the style; to be revived from death; to come by chance; to proceed; to have its sources; to be moved or inflamed, as passion; to amount; to close a session, as a court or assembly. ppr. rising, pret. rose, pp. risen. n. *Act of rising*; ascent; elevation; spring; commencement; any place elevated above the common level; appearance above the horizon; advance, as in value; advance in rank; augmentation. [Sax. *arisan*; G. *reisen*, to march.]

Risibility, ri-zi-bil'i-ti, n. *Quality of being risible*; quality of being capable of laughter; proneness to laugh. [Fr. *risibilité*.]

Risible, ri'zi-bl, a. *That can laugh*; having the power of laughing; capable of exciting laughter; laughable. [Fr.—L. *rideo, risum*, to laugh at.]

Risibly, ri'zi-bli, adv. *In a risible manner*.

Rising, rīz'ing, p.a. Appearing above the horizon; increasing in wealth, power, or distinction.—p.n. *Act of one who rises*; act of getting up from a sitting or recumbent posture; act of closing a session; the appearance of the sun above the horizon; resurrection; a tumour on the body; insurrection; mutiny.

Risk, risk, n. *State of being exposed to harm*; hazard; jeopardy; chance of harm or loss.—*vt*. To expose to injury or loss, as life or property; to hazard; to dare to undertake. [Fr. *risque*—Low L. *riscus*, danger.]

Rite, rit, n. The manner of performing divine *service* as established by custom; formal act of religion or other solemn duty; observance; ordinance. [Fr.—L. *ritus*—Sans. *rit*, to serve, worship.]

Ritual, rit'ū-al, a. *Pertaining to rites*; consisting of rites; prescribing rites. n. A book containing the *rites* to be observed in performing divine service. [Fr. *rituel*; L. *ritus*, a rite.]

Ritualism, rit'ū-al-izm, n. *The system of rituals* or prescribed forms of religious worship; observance of prescribed forms in religion; confidence in mere rites. [Fr. *ritualisme*.]

Ritualist, rit'ū-al-ist, n. *One skilled in the ritual*; one who adheres to or treats of the ritual or rituals. [Fr. *ritualiste*.]

Ritually, rit'ū-al-li, adv. *In accordance with the ritual*; by rites.

Rivage†, ri'vāj, n. A bank, shore, or coast. [Fr.]

Rival, rī'val, n. Rivals were primarily neighbours who dwelt on the opposite banks of a *river*, who had a common right to the use of the water, and who were apt to contend for their respective rights; one who is in pursuit of the same object as another; one striving to equal or exceed another in excellence; a competitor; an antagonist. a. Standing in competition for superiority.—*vt*. To stand in competition with; to strive to equal or excel; to emulate.—*vi*. To be competitors. ppr. rivalling, pret. & pp. rivalled. [Fr.; L. *rivus*, a brook—Sans. *ri*, to flow.]

Rivalry†, ri-val'i-ti, n. Rivalry; competition.

Rivalry, rī'val-ri, n. *Quality or state of being a rival*; an endeavour to equal or surpass another in some excellence; emulation; strife.

Rive, rīv, vt. To *tear asunder*; to split; to cleave; to rend asunder by force. vi. To be split or rent asunder. ppr. riving, pret. rived, pp. rived or riven. [Icel. *rif, rifa*.]

River, riv'ėr, n. *A flowing stream*; a large stream of water flowing in a channel on land toward the ocean; abundance. [Fr. *rivière*—L. *rivus*, a brook—Sans. *ri*, to flow.]

Rivet, riv'et, vt. To fasten *by beating back*; to clinch; to fasten firmly; to make immovable. ppr. rivetting, pret. & pp. rivetted.—n. A pin of iron inserted into a hole at the junction of two pieces of metal or wood, and hammered broad at the ends. [Fr. *river*—L. *re*, back, and *batuo*, to beat.]

Rivulet, ri'vū-let, n. *A small stream or brook*; a streamlet. [It. *ruoletto*—L. *rivus*, a brook.]

Roach, rōch, n. *The thornback*; a fish inhabiting deep, still, and clear rivers; in colour, silvery, and feeding on worms and herbs. [Sax. *reohche*; G. *rauch*, rough.]

Road, rōd, n. *Ground fit to be ridden over*; a highway; a way; route; course; journey; a place where ships may ride at anchor at some distance from the shore (often used in the plural). [Sax. *rad*—*ridan*, to ride.]

Roadstead, rōd'sted, n. A place where ships may ride at anchor at some distance from the shore.

Roadway, rōd'wā, n. The part of a road travelled by carriages; highway.

Roam, rōm, *vi.* To move over an extent of space or room; to walk about without any certain purpose; to wander; to stroll; to stray.—*vt.* To range; to wander over. [Sax. *ryman*, to make room; Old G. *rumjan*, to go away.]
Roaming, rōm'ing *p.n. Act of roaming* or wandering; a ramble.
Roan, rōn, *a.* Of a colour between *yellow and gray*; of a bay, sorrel, or dark colour, with spots of gray or white thickly interspersed, as a horse. [Fr. *rouan*—L. *ravus*, gray, yellow.]
Roar, rōr, *vi.* To cry with a full, loud, continued *sound*; to bellow, as a beast; to cry aloud, as in distress; to cry aloud, as a child; to cause a loud, continued sound.—*n.* A full, loud, continued *sound*; the cry of a beast; the loud cry of a child or person in distress; clamour; outcry of joy or mirth; the loud, continued sound of the sea in a storm; any loud sound of some continuance. [Sax. *rarian*—Hans. *ru*, to sound, to vociferate, to howl.]
Roaring, rōr'ing, *p.a.* Uttering a deep, loud *sound*.—*p.n.* The cry of a lion or other beast; outcry of distress; loud, continued sound of the billows of the sea or of a tempest.
Roast, rōst, *vt.* To grill or broil upon a gridiron; to prepare meat for the table by exposing it to heat, as on a spit; to heat to excess; to parch by exposure to heat; to dissipate the volatile parts of, as of ore by heat.—*vi.* To undergo the process of roasting.—*n. That which is roasted.*—*a. Roasted*; as, roast beef. [G. *rösten*—Old G. *röst*, a gridiron.]
Roasting, rōst'ing, *p.n. Act of roasting*; the protracted application of heat, below a fusing point, to metallic ores.
Rob, rob, *vt. To take away from* by unlawful violence; to take away from the person of by open and violent assault; to strip unlawfully; to take away by oppression; to deprive of. *ppr.* robbing, *pret. & pp.* robbed. [G. *rauben*—L. *rapio*, to snatch away.]
Robber, rob'ér, *n.* One who *takes* goods or money *from* the person of another by force or menaces; one who takes that to which he has no right.
Robbery, rob'é-ri. *n. Act of robbing*; the taking from the person of another any money or goods by violence or by menaces.
Robe, rōb, *n.* A kind of gown, or long loose garment, worn over other dress, particularly by persons in elevated stations; a splendid female garment; an elegant dress.—*vt. To put a robe upon*; to array; to invest, as with beauty or elegance. *ppr.* robing, *pret. & pp.* robed. [Fr.—Old G. *raub*, a garment.]
Robin, ro'bin, *n.* A bird with a *reddish* breast. [Low L. *rubecula*—*rubeo*, to be red.]
Robin-goodfellow, ro-bin-gud'fel-lō, *n.* A celebrated fairy; Puck.
Robust, rō - bust', *a. Hard as oak*; strong; hardy; sinewy; muscular; possessing great strength; requiring strength. [Fr. *robuste*—L. *robur*, a kind of oak, strength.]
Robustly, rō-bust'li, *adv.* With great *strength*; muscularly.
Robustness, rō - bust'nes, *n. State or quality of being robust*; the condition of the body when it has full, firm flesh and sound health.
Rochet, roch'et, *n.* An outer garment or frock; a linen garment resembling the surplice, worn by bishops and other ecclesiastics of the Roman Catholic church. [Fr. a lawn garment worn by bishops; Sax. *rocc*, clothing.]
Rock, rok, *n.* A vast mass of stone; a large mass of stony matter, either bedded in the earth or resting on its surface; defence; means of safety; strength; firmness; a firm or immovable foundation. [Icel. *rok*.]
Rock, rok, *n.* A distaff used in spinning; the staff or frame about which flax or wool was arranged, from which the thread was *drawn* in spinning. [G. *rocken*, to draw.]
Rock, rok, *vt. To move* backward and forward, as a body resting on a foundation; to move backward and forward in a cradle, chair, &c.; to lull to quiet.—*vi. To be moved* backward and forward; to reel. [G. *rücken*, to move.]
Rock-crystal, rok-kris'tal, *n.* Limpid quartz.
Rockery, rok'é-ri, *n.* A hillock formed of stones, earth, &c., for plants.
Rocket, rok'et, *n.* An artificial firework, which on being fired is projected through the air with a force arising from the combustion. [It. *rochetto*.]
Rockiness, rok'i-nes, *n. State of abounding with rocks.* [from *rocky*.]
Rock-salt, rok'salt, *n.* Mineral *salt*; salt dug from the earth.
Rock-work, rok'wérk, *n.* Stones fixed in mortar in imitation of the asperities of *rocks*, forming a wall; a pile of stones or rocks, for the growth of plants adapted for such a situation.
Rocky, rok'i, *a. Full of rocks*; very hard; unsusceptible of impression.
Rod, rod, *n. The shoot* or *long twig* of any woody plant; a branch, or the stem of a shrub; an instrument of punishment; discipline; a pole for angling; something long and slender; an instrument for measuring; a measure of length containing five yards and a half; a wand, as a badge of authority; a sceptre. [Sax.—Gr. *rhabdos*, a staff.]
Rodent, rō'dent, *a. Gnawing.* [L. *rodens*—*rodo*, to gnaw.]
Rodomontade, ro'dō-mont-ād, *n.Empty bluster or vaunting*; rant. [Fr. from *Rodomont*, a king of Algiers, brave, but proud and insolent.]
Roe, Roebuck, rō, rō'buk, *n.* A small species of deer, with erect, cylindrical, branched horns, forked at the summit. The species is remarkable for its agility in leaping, and has a predilection for mountainous localities. [Sax. *ra*.]
Roe, rō, *n.* The seed or spawn of fishes. [G. *rogen*; Old G. *rogan*.]
Rogation, rō-gā'shon, *n. An asking*; supplication. [Fr.; L. *rogo*, to ask.]
Rogue, rōg, *n. An idle person*; a vagrant; a sturdy beggar; a vagabond; a knave; a dishonest person; a name of slight tenderness; a wag]. [Sax. *eary*, idle, weak; D. *erg*, bad.]
Roguery, rōg'é-ri, *n.* Knavish tricks; waggery; mischievousness.
Roguish, rōg'ish, *a. Pertaining to or like a rogue*; knavish; fraudulent.
Roguishly, rōg'ish-li, *adv. Like a rogue.*
Roguishness, rōg'ish-nes, *n. The qualities of a rogue*; knavery; mischievousness; archness; sly cunning.
Roist, Roister, roist, roist'ér, *vi.* To bluster; to swagger.
Roisterer, roist'er-ér, *n.* A bold, turbulent fellow.
Roll, rōl, *vt.* To cause to turn on the surface; to cause to revolve; to turn on its axis; to inwrap; to bind in a bandage; to drive with a circular motion; to drive forward in a stream; to spread with a roller; to produce a periodical revolution; to level with a roller.—*vi.* To move by turning on the surface; to move or run on an axis, as a wheel; to turn; to float in rough water; to be tossed about; to fluctuate; to move tumultuously; to be hurled; to be formed into a cylinder or ball; to wallow; to rock from side to side; to beat a drum with strokes so rapid that they can scarcely be distinguished by the ear.—*n. Act of rolling* or state of being rolled; the thing rolling; a mass made round; a roller; a quantity of cloth wound into a cylindrical form; a cylindrical twist of tobacco; a cake of bread; an official writing; a list; a register; the uniform beating of a drum; a chronicle; annals. [Fr. *rouler*—G. *rollen*.]
Roller, rōl'ér, *n. That which rolls*; a cylinder of stone, &c., used in husbandry and the arts; a long and broad bandage used in surgery; a heavy wave setting in upon a coast without wind.
Rolling, rōl'ing, *p.n.* The turning round of a body upon some surface; the motion of a ship from side to side.
Romage, rum'āj. Same as *rummage*.
Romaic, rō-mā'ik, *a.* or *n.* A term applied to the modern Greek language.
Roman, rō'man, *a. Pertaining to Rome*, or to the Roman people; pertaining to or professing the Roman Catholic religion.—*n. A native or citizen of Rome*; a member of the Christian church at Rome, to which Paul addressed an epistle. [L. *Romanus*—*Roma*, Rome.]
Roman-Catholic, rō-man-ka'thō-lik, *a.* Denoting that form of the Christian religion of which the Bishop of Rome, commonly called the Pope, is the head.—*n.* One who professes that form of religion.
Romance, rō-mans', *n.* A military fable of the middle ages, originally composed in metre in the *Romance* dialects; a fabulous relation of incidents, designed for the entertainment of readers; any wild extravagant story; a falsehood; a short lyric tale set to music.—*a.* Noting the language or the dialects called *Romance.*—*vi. To write or tell romances*; to deal in extravagant stories. *ppr.* romancing, *pret. & pp.* romanced. [Sp. *romānce*—L. *Roma*, Rome.]
Romancer, rō-mans'ér, *n. A writer of romance.*
Romanism, ro'man-ism, *n. The tenets of the Church of Rome.*
Romanist, ro'man-ist, *n. An adherent to the Roman Catholic religion.*
Romanize, ro'man-iz, *vi. To conform to Roman Catholic* opinions, customs, or modes of speech.
Romantic, rō-man'tik, *a. Pertaining to romance*; wild; extravagant; chimerical; full of wild scenery. [Fr. *romantique.*]
Romantically, rō-man'tik-al-li, *adv. In a romantic manner*; wildly; extravagantly; falsely.
Romish, rōm'ish, *a. Belonging or relating to Rome*, or to the religion of which the Pope is earthly head; Roman Catholic: used slightingly.
Romp, romp, *n.* A different spelling of *ramp* (which see). A leap; a bound; rude play; a rude girl who leaps about and indulges in boisterous play.—*vi.* To play rudely and boisterously; to leap and frisk about.
Romping, romp'ing, *p.n.* Rude, boisterous play.
Rompish, romp'ish, *a.* Given to rude play; inclined to romp.

Rompishness, romp'ish-nes, n. *Quality of being rompish.*

Rondeau, Rondo, ron'dō, n. A kind of poetry which *returns*, as it were, *to the same point*, or in which part is repeated; a musical composition, usually of three strains, which ends with the first strain repeated. [Fr. *rondeau—rond*, round.]

Rondure†, ron'dūr, n. A round; a circle.

Ronicat, ron'i-on, n. A fat bulky woman.

Rood, röd, n. *A rod*; the fourth part of an acre, or forty square poles. [same as rod.]

Rood, röd, n. *A cross*; an instrument consisting of one rod laid at right angles over another; a name formerly given to the figure of Christ on the cross, erected in Roman Catholic churches. [Sax. *rode* or *rod*.]

Roof, röf, n. *The cover of a house or other building*; a vault; an arch, or the interior of a vault; the vault of the mouth; the palate.—vt. To cover with a roof; to inclose in a house; to shelter. [Sax. *hrof*—Gr. *erephō*, to roof.]

Roofing, röf'ing, p.n. *The act of covering with a roof*; the materials for a roof.

Roofless, röf'les, a. *Having no roof*; having no house or home. [Sax. *rofleas*.]

Roofy, röf'i, a. *Having roofs.*

Rook, rök, n. A bird resembling the common crow, but having the base of the bill bare of feathers; a cheat. [Sax. *hroc*.]

Rook, rök, n. One of the four pieces placed on the corner squares of a chessboard; a castle. [It. *rocca*—Low L. *rocca*, a castle.]

Rook†, rök, vt. To shelter.

Rookery, rök'ė-ri, n. *A place where rooks congregate* and build their nests, as a wood, &c.

Rooky†, rök'i, a. *Inhabited by rooks.*

Room, röm, n. *Place*; space; *extent of place*, great or small; compass; place unoccupied; place for the reception of anything; place of another; place or position in society; fit occasion; an apartment in a house; any division separated from the rest by a partition. [Sax. *rum*—Goth. *rums*, space.]

Roominess, röm'i-nes, n. *State of being roomy*; spaciousness.

Roomy, röm'i, a. *Having ample room*; spacious; capacious; wide; large.

Roost, röst, n. *A place of rest*; the pole on which birds rest at night; a collection of fowls resting together.—vi. To rest, sit, or sleep, as birds on a pole at night. [Sax. *hrost—restan*, to rest.]

Root, röt, n. That part of a plant which enters, fixes itself, and *grows* in the *earth*; the bottom or lower part of anything; a plant whose root is esculent; the cause of anything; the lowest place; the first ancestor; whatever, in any language, or family of languages, cannot be reduced to a simpler or more original form.—vi. To *fix* the root; to enter the earth, as roots; to sink deep.—vt. To plant and fix deep in the earth by the roots (used chiefly in the participle); to impress deeply; to tear from the ground by the roots; to eradicate; to turn up, as earth with the snout, in the manner of swine; to exterminate (with *up* or *out*). [from Sax. *wrotan*, to root—L. *radix*, a root—Sans. *ruh*, to increase.]

Rooted, röt'ed, p.a. *Fixed.*

Rope, röp, n. *That which binds*; a large string or line composed of several strands twisted together; a string of a number of things united; the cordage used on board of a vessel for running rigging, &c.—vi. To be formed into rope; to extend into a filament by means of any glutinous or adhesive quality. [Sax. *rap—rœpan*, to bind.]

Roper, röp'ėr, n. *A rope-maker.*

Ropery, röp'ė-ri, n. *A place where ropes are made*; a trick that deserves the halter.

Rope-trick, röp'trik, n. A trick that deserves the halter.

Ropiness, röp'i-nes, n. Stringiness or aptness to draw out in thread without breaking, as of glutinous substances; adhesiveness.

Ropish, röp'ish, a. *Tending to ropiness*; ropy.

Ropy, röp'i, a. Stringy; adhesive; that may be drawn into a thread.

Rosaceous, röz-ā'shē-us, a. *Rose-like*; composed of several petals arranged in a circular form; relating to roses. [L. *rosaceus—rosa*, a rose.]

Rosary, röz'a-ri, n. *A bed of roses*, or place where roses grow; a chaplet; a string of beads on which the Roman Catholics number their prayers. [L. *rosarium*.]

Rose, röz, n. A well-known and universally admired plant and its flower, of many species and varieties; a knot of ribbon in the form of a rose, used as an ornamental tie of a shoe; anything in the form of a rose; the orifice of a watering-pan.—vt. To render rose-coloured; to flush. [Sax.—L. *rosa*—Gr. *rodon*.]

Rose, röz, *pret.* of *rise*.

Roseal, röz'ē-al, a. *Like a rose* in smell or colour. [L. *roseus*.]

Roseate, röz'ē-āt, a. *Rosy*; blooming; of a rose-colour. [Fr. *rosat*.]

Rosemary, röz'ma-ri, n. A pretty shrub of a *dewy* nature, thriving best near the sea, and employed in the manufacture of Hungary-water; the emblem of constancy. [L. *rosmarinus—ros*, dew, and *mare*, the sea.]

Rosette, rō-zet', n. *An imitation of a rose* made of ribbons; an ornament in the form of a rose, much used in architectural decorations. [Fr.]

Rose-window, röz'win-dō, n. A circular *window* with compartments branching from a centre.

Rosewood, röz'wud, n. The wood of a tree much used in cabinet-work, and so named from its having a faint but agreeable smell of roses.

Rosin, ro'zin, n. The resin left after distilling off the volatile oil from turpentine.—vt. To rub or cover over with rosin. [same as resin.]

Rosiness, röz'i-nes, n. *Quality of being rosy*, or of resembling the colour of the rose.

Rosiny, ro'zin-i, a. *Like rosin.*

Rostral, ros'tral, a. *Resembling the beak of a bird* or of a ship; pertaining to the beak. [L. *rostralis—rostrum*, a ship's beak.]

Rostrate, ros'trāt, a. *Beaked*; having a process resembling the beak of a bird; furnished or adorned with beaks. [L. *rostratus*.]

Rostrum, ros'trum, n. Originally, the *beak of a bird*; a scaffold in the forum of ancient Rome, where orations, &c., were delivered; a platform or elevated spot from which a speaker addresses his audience. [L.—*ro-lo*, to gnaw.]

Rosy, röz'i, a. *Resembling a rose*; blooming; red; blushing; charming; made in the form of a rose.

Rot, rot, vi. To putrefy; to decay; to spoil; to be decomposed and resolved into its original elements by the natural process, or the gradual operation of heat and air.—vt. To cause to putrefy; to make putrid; to bring to corruption. ppr. rotting, pret. & pp. rotted. n. *Putrefaction*; putrid decay; a fatal distemper incident to sheep, caused by wet seasons and moist pastures. [Sax. *rotian*—G. *rosten*, to rust.]

Rotary, rō'ta-ri, a. *Turning, as a wheel on its axis.* [from L. *rota*, a wheel.]

Rotate, rō'tāt, vi. To move round a centre or axis, like a *wheel*. ppr. rotating, pret. & pp. rotated. [L. *roto, rotatus*—*rota*, a wheel.]

Rotating, rō'tāt-ing, p.a. Revolving.

Rotation, rō-tā'shon, n. *The act of turning, as a wheel on its axis*; vicissitude of succession. [Fr.]

Rotatory, rō'ta-tō-ri, a. *Turning on an axis, as a wheel*; rotary; following in succession. [L. *rota*, a wheel—Sans. *ratha*, a chariot—*ri*, to go.]

Rote, rōt, n. Properly, *a round of words*; frequent unintelligent repetition of words; a practice that impresses words on the memory without an effort of the understanding.—vt.† To fix in the memory by means of frequent repetition. [L. *rota*, a wheel.]

Rotten, rot'n, a. *Putrefied*; putrid; unsound; decomposed by the natural process of decay; having some defect in principle; deceitful; treacherous. [from *rot*.]

Rottenness, rot'n-nes, n. *State of being rotten*; cariousness; putrefaction; treacherousness.

Rotund, rō-tund', a. *Round*; spherical. [L. *rotundus—rota*, a wheel.]

Rotundity, rō-tund'i-ti, n. *Roundness*; sphericity. [Fr. *rotondité*.]

Rotundo, rō-tun'dō, n. *A round building*; any erection that is round both on the outside and inside. [It.]

Rouge, rözh, a. Red.—n. A species of red paint, usually prepared from the dried flowers of the safflower, and used for painting the cheeks.—vi. To paint the cheeks with *rouge*.—vt. To paint with *rouge*. ppr. rouging, pret. & pp. rouged. [Fr.—L. *rufus*, red.]

Rough, ruf, a. *Hairy*; shaggy; uneven; rugged; not polished; thrown into huge waves; tempestuous; harsh to the taste; harsh to the ear; rugged of temper; rude; hard-featured; not delicate; terrible; disordered in appearance; coarse.—n. State of being coarse or unwrought; as, materials in the rough. [Sax. *hreoh*; Icel. *rufinn*, shaggy.]

Rough-cast, ruf'kast, vt. To mould or form roughly; to form in its first rudiments. ppr. rough-casting, pret. & pp. rough-cast.—n. A rude model.

Rough-draught, ruf'draft, n. *A draught in its rudiments*; a sketch. (Also written rough-draft.)

Roughen, ruf'n, vt. To make rough.—vi. To become rough. [from rough.]

Rough-hew, ruf'hū, vt. To hew coarsely; to give the first form or shape to. ppr. rough-hewing, pret. rough-hewed, pp. rough-hewn.

Roughish, ruf'ish, a. *In some degree rough.*

Roughly, ruf'li, adv. With uneven surface; harshly; rudely; tempestuously; harshly to the ear; violently.

Roughness, ruf'nes, n. *State or quality of being rough*; asperity of surface; austereness to the taste; harshness to the ear; ruggedness of temper; rudeness; violence of operation in medicines; unpolished state; inelegance of

Fāte, fär, fat, fall; mē, met, hėr; pīne, pin; nōte, not, mōve; tūbe, tub, bull; oil, pound.

dress; tempestuousness; violent agitation by wind; coarseness of features.
Rought†, rąt. Same as *raught*, pret. of *reach*.
Rouleau, rō-lō', *n.* *A little roll;* a roll of coins in paper. [Fr.—*rouler,* to roll.]
Round, round, *a. Circular; spherical;* cylindrical; plump; smooth; not abrupt, as style; open; candid; brisk, as a trot; bold; whole; not broken, as a number; large; consistent; fair; without reserve.—*n. A circle;* an orb; action in a circle; the time of such action; rotation in office; the step of a ladder; a circuit performed by a guard round the rampart of a garrison; a general discharge of fire-arms by a body of troops; that which goes round a whole company.—*vt. To make circular;* to encompass; to move about anything; to make full and flowing; to complete. *n. To grow or become round;* to go round.—*adv.* On all sides; around. *prep. About;* on every side of. [G. *rund*—L. *rota,* a wheel.]
Round†, round, *vi.* To whisper.
Rounded, round'ed, *p.a. Having grown or become round.*
Roundel, round'el. Same as *roundelay.*
Roundelay, round's-lā, *n.* A kind of ancient poem, consisting of thirteen verses, eight in one kind of rhyme and five in another; a rondo; a simple, short, and lively rural strain; a rural dance. [Old Fr. *rondelet,* dimin. of *rond.*]
Rounder†, round'ér, *n.* Circumference.
Round-hand, round'hand, *n.* A style of penmanship in which the letters are *round* and full.
Rounding, round'ing, *p.a. Round or roundish;* nearly round.
Roundish, round'ish, *a. Somewhat round;* nearly round.
Roundly, round'li, *adv. In a round form or manner;* plainly; in earnest.
Roundness, round'nes, *n. Quality of being round;* circularity; sphericity; plumpness; fulness and smoothness of flow; openness; boldness.
Round-robin, round-ro'bin, *n.* A written petition signed by names in a *ring* or *circle,* so as not to show who signed first. This practice originated among the officers of the French army. [Fr. *rond,* round, and *ruban,* a ribbon.]
Rouse, rouz, *vt. To arouse;* to raise; to awaken; to excite to thought or action from a state of languor; to drive, as a beast from his den or place of rest.—*vi.* To awake from sleep; to be excited to thought or action from a state of indolence. *ppr.* rousing, *pret. & pp.* roused. [Old G. *ruosjan,* to stir up.]
Rouse, rouz, *n.* A bumper in honour of a health; a carousal. [Icel. *rūssa,* to get drunk.]
Rousing, rouz'ing, *p.a.* Having power to awaken or excite.
Rout, rout, *n. A crowd;* a clamorous multitude; the unlawful assembling of three or more persons to do an unlawful act; a fashionable assembly or large evening party. [Norm. *routez, routs*—G. *rotten,* to unite in bands.]
Rout, rout, *n. The breaking or defeat of an army;* the disorder of troops defeated and put to flight.—*vt. To break and put to flight,* as the ranks of troops; to defeat; to discomfit; to conquer. [Old Fr. *route,* an overthrow—L. *rumpo, ruptum,* to break.]
Route, rōt, *n. The road, course, or way to be passed;* a course; a march; a principal or leading road. [Fr. *route*—L. *rota,* a wheel.]

Routed, rout'ed, *p.a.* Put to flight in disorder.
Routine, rō-tēn', *n. A round or course of business or official duties,* regularly or frequently returning; any regular habit not accommodated to circumstances. [Fr.—L. *rota,* a wheel.]
Rove, rōv, *vi.* Primarily, *to reave;* to roam; to ramble; to stroll.—*vt.* To wander over. *ppr.* roving, *pret. & pp.* roved. [D. *rooven;* Goth. *raubon,* to rob.]
Rover, rōv'er, *n. One who roves;* a freebooter; a fickle or inconstant person.
Roving, rōv'ing, *p.a.* Rambling; wandering.
Row, rō, *n. A rank;* a file; a series of persons or things arranged in a continued line. [Sax. *rawa.*]
Row, rō, *vt. To move or impel, as a boat along the surface of water by oars;* to transport by rowing.—*vi.* To labour with the oar.—*n.* An excursion taken in a boat with oars. [Sax. *rowan.*]
Rowan-tree, rō'an-trē, *n.* The mountain ash.
Rowel, rou'el, *n. The little wheel of a spur,* formed with sharp points; a little flat ring or wheel of plate or iron on horses' bits. [Old Fr. *rouelle*—L. *rota,* a wheel.]
Rower, rō'er, *n. One who rows.*
Rowing, rō'ing, *p.n.* Act of impelling a boat by oars.
Royal, roi'al, *a. Pertaining to a king; splendid;* becoming or like a king; kingly; august; noble; illustrious; a title of any institution or body of individuals, that is more especially under the patronage of the crown.—*n.* A large kind of paper; a small sail spread immediately above the top-gallant sail; one of the shoots of a stag's head; one of the soldiers of the first regiment of foot, called the Royals, and said to be the oldest corps in Europe. [Fr.—L. *rex, regis,* a king—Sans. *rāj,* to shine.]
Royalism, roi'al-izm, *n. Attachment to the principles or cause of royalty.*
Royalist, roi'al-ist, *n. An adherent to a king,* or to kingly government.
Royalize†, roi'al-iz, *vt. To make royal.*
Royally, roi'al-li, *adv. In a royal or kingly manner;* like a king.
Royalty, roi'al-ti, *n. Kingship;* the character, state, or office of a king; (pl.) emblems of royalty; regalia; rights of a king; prerogatives. [Old Fr. *royaulte*—L. *rex, regis,* a king.]
Royish†, roin'ish, *a.* Mangy; scabby; mean. [Fr. *rogneux.*]
Rub, rub, *vt.* To move something along the surface of with pressure; to clean; to scour; to remove by friction (with *off* or *out*); to spread over; to retouch (with *over*); to touch hard; to fret; to annoy; to thwart.—*vi.* To move along the surface of a body with pressure; to chafe; to move or pass with difficulty. *ppr.* rubbing, *pret. & pp.* rubbed.—*n. Act of rubbing;* friction; hindrance; obstruction; inequality of ground that hinders the motion of a bowl; difficulty; cause of uneasiness; sarcasm; joke; something grating to the feelings [G. *reiben;* Heb. *ruph,* to rub.]
Rubber, rub'ér, *n. One who rubs;* the instrument used in rubbing; a coarse file; two games out of three in whist; a contest consisting of three games.
Rubbing, rub'ing, *p.n. Act of rubbing,* scouring, or polishing.
Rubbish, rub'ish, *n. That which is rubbed off;* broken pieces of any structure; waste matter; anything worthless; mingled mass. [Norm. *rubbousee,* filth.]
Rubescent, rū-bes'ent, *a. Growing or*

becoming *red.* [L. *rubescens*—*rubeo,* to be red.]
Rubicund, rū'bi-kund, *a. Inclining to redness;* ruddy. [L. *rubicundus.*]
Rubicous, rū'bi-us, *a.* Red; ruddy.
Rubric, rū'brik, *n.* A title or article in certain ancient canon law-books, so called because written in *red letters;* the name given to the directions printed in prayer-books, which were formerly put in red letters. [Fr. *rubrique;* L. *ruber,* red.]
Ruby, rū'bi, *n.* A precious stone of a carmine-*red colour;* anything red; a blain; a carbuncle.—*a. Of the colour of the ruby;* red. [Fr. *rubis;* L. *rubeo,* to be red.]
Rudder, rud'ér, *n.* Primarily, *an oar;* the instrument by which a ship is steered; that which governs the course. [Sax. *rothere*—*rowan,* to row.]
Ruddiness, rud'i-nes, *n. State* or quality *of being ruddy;* redness, or rather a lively flesh colour; that degree of redness which characterises high health.
Ruddy, rud'i, *a. Of a red colour;* of a lively flesh colour, or the colour of the human skin in high health. [Sax. *rude.*]
Rude, rūd, *a. Raw; unwrought;* rough; untaught; barbarous; uncivilized; ignorant; coarse; vulgar; tumultuous; boisterous. [Fr.—L. *rudis.*]
Rudely, rūd'li, *adv. In a rude manner.*
Rudeness, rūd'nes, *n. Quality of being rude;* unevenness; coarseness of manners; vulgarity; unskilfulness; impetuosity; storminess.
Rudesby†, rūdz'bi, *n.* An uncivil, turbulent fellow.
Rudiment, rū'di-ment, *n.* The original of anything, in its *rude* state; a first principle; an imperfect organ; (pl.) the elements of a science or art; elementary instruction. [Fr.—L. *rudis* rude, raw.]
Rudimental, **Rudimentary**, rū-di-ment'al, rū-di-ment'a-ri, *a. Pertaining to rudiments,* or consisting in first principles; initial.
Rue, rū, *vt. To lament;* to regret; to grieve for.—*vi.* To sorrow. *ppr.* ruing. *pret. & pp.* rued.—*n.* Sorrow; repentance. [Sax. *hreowan*—Sans. *hri,* to be ashamed.]
Rue, rū, *n.* A plant having a strong disagreeable odour, and a bitter acrid taste. [Fr.]
Rueful, rū'ful, *a.* Woful; mournful; doleful; expressing sorrow.
Ruefully, rū'ful-li, *adv.* Mournfully.
Ruff, ruf, *n.* A piece of *plaited* linen worn around the neck; something puckered or plaited; a species of shore-bird. [Armor. *roufen,* a wrinkle, a ply.]
Ruffian, ruf'i-an, *n.* A boisterous, brutal fellow; a fellow ready for any desperate crime; a robber; a murderer.—*a.* Brutal; savagely boisterous.—*vi. To play the ruffian.* [Fr. *rufien.*]
Ruffianism, ruf'i-an-izm, *n. Quality or conduct of a ruffian.*
Ruffianly, ruf'i-an-li, *a. Like a ruffian;* bold in crimes; licentious.
Ruffle, ruf'l, *vt. To raise in wrinkles;* to contract into open plaits or folds; to furnish with ruffles; to disorder by disturbing a smooth surface; 'to disturb.—*vi. To grow rough* or turbulent; to play loosely; to flutter. *ppr.* ruffling, *pret. & pp.* ruffled.—*n.* A strip of plaited cambric, or other fine cloth, attached to some border of a garment, as to the wristband; disturbance; a vibrating kind of sound made upon a drum, less loud than the roll. [D. *ruyfelen.*]

Ruffled, ruf'ld, p.a. Disturbed; agitated.
Ruffling, ruf'l-ing, p.n. Act of forming into ruffles; disturbance; agitation.
Rug, rug, n. Something rough; rough, coarse, nappy woollen cloth used for a bed-cover, for covering the carpet before a fireplace, and for protecting the legs against the cold in riding; a rough dog. [Sax.; Old G. *ruh*, rough, hairy.]
Rugged, rug'ed, a. Rough; shaggy; uneven; cragged; broken into sharp points or crags, as a road or country; not neat; hard; sour; stormy; grating to the ear; violent; boisterous.
Ruggedly, rug'ed-li, adv. In a rough or rugged manner.
Ruggedness, rug'ed-nes, n. Quality or state of being rugged; roughness of temper; storminess; boisterousness.
Rugose, rū'gōs, a. Wrinkled; rough with wrinkles. [L. *rugosus*—*ruga*, a wrinkle.]
Ruin, rū'in, n. A rushing or falling down; fall; overthrow; subversion; perdition; that which destroys; mischief; (pl.) the remains of a demolished city, or any work of art or other thing; the enfeebled remains of a natural object.—*vt*. To cause to rush or fall down; to demolish; to subvert; to bring to an end; to destroy in any manner; to deprive of fortune; to impoverish. [Fr. *ruine*—L. *ruo*, to rush down.]
Ruinate†, rū'in-āt, vi. To fall.—a. Ruined.
Ruined, rū'ind, p.a. Reduced to poverty; undone.
Ruinous, rū'in-us, a. Fallen to ruin; dilapidated; demolished; bringing or tending to bring certain ruin; pernicious; wasteful; composed of ruins, consisting of ruins. [Fr. *ruineux*.]
Ruinously, rū'in-us-li, adv. In a ruinous manner; destructively.
Rule, röl, n. An instrument by which straight lines are drawn or short lengths measured; a ruler; supreme command; sway; control; that by which anything is to be adjusted; a law; a canon; guide; behaviour; established mode in private life; that which is established for guidance in any art or science.—*vt*. To bring into and keep in a straight line; to mark with lines, as a ruler; to regulate; to govern, as the movements of things; to control; to settle as by a rule; to establish by decision; to determine, as a court.—*vi*. To exercise supreme authority; to decide; to lay down and settle, as a rule or order of court. *ppr*. ruling, *pret*. & *pp*. ruled. [Fr. *règle*—L. *rego*, to keep in a straight line.]
Ruled, röld, p.a. Managed; established by decision; marked with lines by a ruler.
Ruler, röl'er, n. One who rules or governs; one who makes or executes laws in a limited or free government; a ruler, an instrument of wood or metal with straight sides, by which lines are drawn.
Ruling, röl'ing, p.a. Having predominance or control.
Rum, rum, n. A spirituous liquor distilled from cane-juice, or from the skimmings of the juice from the boiling-house, or from the molasses which drains from sugar.
Rumble, rum'bl, vi. To make a hoarse, low, heavy, continued sound. *ppr*. rumbling, *pret*. & *pp*. rumbled.—n. A hoarse, low, heavy, continued sound; a seat for servants behind a carriage. [Old Fr. *rommeler*.]
Rumbling, rum'bl-ing, p.a. Making a low, heavy, continued sound.—*p.n*. A low, heavy, continued sound.
Ruminant, rū'min-ant, a. Chewing over again; chewing the cud; having the property of chewing again what has been swallowed.—n. An animal that chews the cud, as the ox, camel, deer, goat, &c. [Fr.—L. *rumen*, the gullet.]
Ruminate, rū'min-āt, vi. To repass the food from the stomach through the gullet, for the purpose of chewing it over again; to chew the cud; to muse; to meditate; to think again and again; to ponder.—*vt*. To meditate upon over and over again. *ppr*. ruminating, *pret*. & *pp*. ruminated. [L. *rumino*, *ruminatus*—*rumea*, the gullet.]
Ruminating, rū'min-āt-ing, p.a. Chewing again.
Rumination, rū-min-ā'shon, n. Act of ruminating; the power of chewing the cud; a continued thinking on a subject; deliberate meditation. [Fr.]
Rummage, rum'āj, vt. To look into, as the *roomage* into which things are packed; to search narrowly by looking into every corner of, and turning over things.—*vi*. To search a place narrowly by looking among things. *ppr*. rummaging, *pret*. & *pp*. rummaged.—n. A searching carefully by looking into every corner, and by tumbling over things. [formerly, *romage*, to find room or space for.]
Rumour, rō'mor, n. That which flows among the people; a current story passing from mouth to mouth, without any known authority for the truth of it; fame; reported celebrity.—*vt*. To report; to tell or circulate a report. [Fr. *rumeur*—Gr. *rheō*, to flow.]
Rumoured, rō'mord, p.a. Reported.
Rumourer, rō'mor-er, n. A reporter.
Rump, rump, n. The termination of the backbone (which appears abrupt), with the parts adjacent. [G. *rumpf*—L. *rumpo*, to break.]
Rumple, rum'pl, vt. To wrinkle; to make uneven. *ppr*. rumpling, *pret*. & *pp*. rumpled.—n. A wrinkle; a pucker; a fold or plait. [D. *rimpelen*.]
Run, run, vi. To go or move in any manner; to go with a lighter and more rapid gait than by walking; to move or pass on the feet with celerity, by long quick steps; to move in a hurry; to proceed along the surface; to spread, as a fire; to rush with violence; to perform a passage by land or water; to pass or go, as ships, stage-coaches, &c.; to contend in a race; to flee for escape; to flow in any manner, slowly or rapidly; to melt; to turn, as a spindle or wheel; to flow, as words or periods; to have a course; to have a continued tenor; to be busied; to dwell, as the mind; to have success, as a pamphlet; to proceed in a train of conduct; to be generally received, as a report; to have a certain direction; to pass in an orbit of any figure; to discharge pus, as a sore; to reach; to continue in time; to continue in effect, as a statute; to press with numerous demands of payment; to pass by gradual changes; to have a general tendency; to dart; to shoot, as a meteor; to fly.—*vt*. To cause to go; to force; to cause to be driven; to pierce; to melt; to encounter; to fall into; to hazard; to smuggle; to pursue in thought; to cause to pass; to cause to ply; to maintain in running; to found; to shape in a mould; to discharge; to pour forth in a stream. *ppr*. running, *pret*. ran or run, *pp*. run.—n. Act of going; act of running; flow; course;

continued series; will; continued success; modish or popular clamour; a general pressure on a bank or treasury for payment of its notes; the distance sailed by a ship; a voyage; prevalence. [Sax. *rennan*; Icel. *renna*, to flow.]
Runaway, run'a-wā, n. One who flies from danger or restraint; one who deserts lawful service.
Rundlet, rund'let, n. A small barrel of no certain dimensions, so named from its shape. [dimin. from *round*.]
Rune, rūn, n. The Runic letter or character. [Goth. *runa*, a mystery.]
Runic, rūn'ik, a. Relating to the ancient Goths, Scandinavians, and other Teutonic nations, or to their language.
Runlet, run'let, n. A little run or stream; a brook; a rundlet.
Runner, run'er, n. One who runs; that which runs; a racer; a thread like stem in certain plants, running along the ground, and taking root; a rope used to increase the power of a tackle.
Running, run'ing, p.a. Kept for the race; in succession; without any intervening day, year, &c.; discharging pus or other matter.—*p.n*. Act of running; that which runs; the discharge of an ulcer or other sore.
Rupee, rō-pē', n. An East Indian coin and money of account, the gold rupee being equal to about 30s., and the silver rupee about 2s. [Hind. *roopiya*.]
Rupture, rup'tūr, n. Act of breaking or bursting; the state of being broken or violently parted; fracture; a breach of peace; a preternatural protrusion of the contents of the abdomen.—*vt*. To break; to part by violence.—*vi*. To suffer a breach or disruption. *ppr*. rupturing, *pret*. & *pp*. ruptured. [Fr.—L. *rumpo*, *ruptum*, to break.]
Rural, rū'ral, a. Pertaining or belonging to the country, as distinguished from the town; suiting the country; rustic; pertaining to agriculture. [Fr.—L. *rus*, *ruris*, the country.]
Ruse, rūs, n. Finesse; artifice; stratagem; wile; deceit. [Fr.—L. *ru*, and *usus*, experience—*utor*, to use.]
Rush, rush, n. A plant having a long pointed stalk, and growing abundantly in wet places. [Sax. *risc*.]
Rush, rush, vi. To fall or tumble down with rapidity, as a stream or cascade; to move with the force and quickness of anything falling; to move with violence; to move forward with impetuosity; to enter with undue eagerness. (With on or upon).—n. A falling or tumbling down; a driving forward with eagerness and haste; a violent motion or course. [Sax. *Areosan*—Heb. *rush*, to be shaken.]
Rushing, rush'ing, p.a. Falling down or moving forward with impetuosity. *p.n*. A violent driving of anything.
Rushy, rush'i, a. Abounding with rushes; made of rushes.
Rusk, rusk, n. Light hard cake or bread. [Probably from low L. *rusca*, bark, rind.]
Russet, rus'set, a. Of a reddish-brown colour; coarse; home-spun; rustic.—a. A country dress. [Old Fr. *russet*—L. *ruber*, red.]
Russety, rus'set-i, a. Of a russet colour.
Russian, ru'shi-an, a. Pertaining to Russia.—n. A native of Russia.
Rust, rust, n. The red or orange-coloured coating formed on the surface of iron, steel, or other metals, exposed to moist air; an oxide of iron; any foul matter contracted; loss of power by inactivity.

Fāte, fär, fat, fall; mē, met, hėr; pīne, pin; nōte, not, move; tūbe, tub, bull; oil, pound.

RUSTIC — SACRISTY

a disease in grain.—vi. To contract rust; to become dull by inaction; to degenerate in idleness.—vt. To cause to contract rust; to impair by time and inactivity. [Sax. rost.]

Rustic, rus'tik, a. Pertaining to the country; having the manners of those who live in the country; plain; unadorned; rude; untaught; awkward; coarse.—n. A countryman; a peasant; a clown. [L. rusticus—rus, the country.]

Rustically, rus'tik-al-li, adv. Rudely; coarsely; without refinement.

Rusticate, rus'ti-kāt, vi. To reside in the country.—vt. To compel to reside in the country; to banish from a town or college for a time. ppr. rusticating, pret. & pp. rusticated. [L. rusticor, rusticatus—rus, the country, as opposed to the town, lands, fields.]

Rustication, rus-ti-kā'shon, n. Act of rusticating; state of being rusticated.

Rusticity, rus-tis'i-ti, n. State or quality of being rustic; rudeness; coarseness; artlessness. [Fr. rusticité.]

Rustily, rust'i-li, adv. In a rusty state.

Rustiness, rust'i-nes, n. State of being rusty.

Rustle, rus'l, vi. To make the noise of certain things shaken or rubbed, as silk, straw, dry leaves, &c. ppr. rustling, pret. & pp. rustled.—n. The noise of certain things shaken; a rustling. [Sax. Aristlan.]

Rustling, rus'l-ing, p.a. Making the sound of silk cloth when shaken or rubbed, &c.—p.n. A quick succession of small sounds, as a brushing among dry leaves or straw.

Rusty, rust'i, a. Covered with rust; impaired by inaction; covered with foul matter; rough; grating.

Rut, rut, n. The copulation of deer. vi. To lust, as deer. ppr. rutting, pret. & pp. rutted. [Fr.]

Rut, rut, n. The track of a wheel; a line cut in the soil with a spade.—vt. To cut in ruts, as roads; to cut a line on the soil with a spade. ppr. rutting, pret. & pp. rutted. [Fr. route; L. rota, a wheel.]

Ruth, röth, n. Mercy; sorrow for the misery of another; sorrow. [from rue.]

Ruthful, röth'ful, a. Rueful; sorrowful; merciful.

Ruthless, röth'les, a. Void of pity or compassion; pitiless; insensible to the miseries of others.

Ruthlessly, röth'les-li, adv. Without pity; cruelly; barbarously.

Ruthlessness, röth'les-nes, n. State or quality of being ruthless.

Ruttish, rut'ish, a. Lustful.

Rutty, rut'i, a. Full of ruts.

Rye, ri, n. An esculent grain, of a quality inferior to wheat, but more hardy, and much cultivated. [Sax. rige; Old G. rūh, rough.]

Rye-grass, ri'gras, n. A grass-like plant, which is generally cultivated for cattle and horses.

S.

Sabaoth, sa-bā'oth, n. Armies; hosts. "The Lord of Sabaoth," an expression used as a designation of the Almighty. [Heb. tsebaoth—tsaba, an army.]

Sabbatarian, sa-ba-tā'ri-an, n. One who observes the seventh day of the week as the Sabbath instead of the first; a strict observer of the Sabbath.—a. Pertaining to the Sabbath, or to the tenets of Sabbatarians.

Sabbath, sab'bath, n. Rest; the day of rest; the day which God appointed to be observed as a day of rest from all secular labour, and to be kept holy; the seventh day of the week among the Jews, but among Christians the first day of the week; the Lord's day; Sunday; intermission of sorrow; time of rest; the sabbatical year among the Israelites. [Heb. shabbath, rest—shabath, to rest.]

Sabbatic, Sabbatical, sa-bat'ik, sa-bat'ik-al, a. Pertaining to the Sabbath; resembling the Sabbath; enjoying or bringing an intermission of labour. [Fr. sabbatique.]

Sable, sā'bl, n. A small animal of the weasel family; the fur of the sable, which is very black and glossy.—a. [Fr.] Of the colour of the sable; black; dark; used chiefly in poetry or in heraldry. [G. sobel.]

Sabre, sā'bér, n. A sword or scimitar with a broad and heavy blade, thick at the back, and a little curved backward at the point; a falchion.—vt. To strike, cut, or kill with a sabre. ppr. sabring, pret. & pp. sabred. [Fr.; Ar. saif, a sword.]

Sac, sak, n. A little sack; a bag or receptacle for a liquid. [Sax. sacc.]

Saccharine, sak'ka-rin, a. Pertaining to sugar; having the qualities or taste of sugar; sweet. [from Gr. sakchar, sugar.]

Sacerdotal, sa-ser-dōt'al, a. Pertaining to priests or the priesthood; priestly. [L. sacerdos, a priest—sacer, dedicated to a divinity, holy.]

Satchel, Satchel, sa'chel, n. A small sack or bag; a bag in which lawyers and children carry papers and books. [L. sacculus—Gr. sakkos, a bag.]

Sack, sak, n. A bag, usually a large bag, used for holding and conveying corn, wool, &c.; that which a sack holds.—vt. To put in a sack or in bags. [Sax. sacc—Gr. sakkos, a bag.]

Sack, sak, n. A Spanish wine of the dry kind, formerly much used in England, and supposed to be sherry; now a kind of sweet wine. [Sp. seco—L. siccus, dry.]

Sack, sak, vt. To search for plunder or pillage; to pillage, as a town or city; to take by storm.—n. The pillage or plunder of a town or city; the storm and plunder of a town. [Sax. secan, to seek.]

Sackbut, sak'but, n. The more modern sackbut is a wind-instrument of music; a kind of trumpet, said to be the same as the trombone. [Fr. saquebute.]

Sackcloth, sak'kloth, n. Cloth of which sacks are made; coarse cloth.

Sacking, sak'ing, p.n. Act of one who sacks; act of taking by storm and pillaging.

Sacking, sak'ing, p.n. Cloth of which sacks are made; the coarse cloth fastened to a bedstead for supporting the bed. [Sax. soccing.]

Sacrament, sa'kra-ment, n. Primarily, a sacred thing; any ceremony producing an obligation; a solemn oath-taking; an outward and visible sign of an inward and spiritual grace; a solemn religious ordinance enjoined by Christ to be observed by his followers, as baptism or the Lord's supper; the eucharist. [Fr. sacrement—L. sacer, holy, sacred.]

Sacramental, sa-kra-ment'al, a. Constituting or pertaining to a sacrament.

Sacramentally, sa-kra-ment'al-li, adv. After the manner of a sacrament.

Sacred, sā'kred, a. Set apart for a holy use; hallowed; consecrated; holy; pertaining to God; proceeding from God, and containing religious precepts; relating to religion or the worship of God; religious; set apart to some one for honour; inviolable; accursed†. [pp. of old Eng. verb sacre—L. sacer, holy.]

Sacredly, sā'kred-li, adv. In a sacred manner; religiously; strictly.

Sacredness, sā'kred-nes, n. State of being sacred; holiness; sanctity; inviolability.

Sacrifice, sa'kri-fis, vt. To make an offering, as of a holy thing; to consume, partially or wholly, on the altar of God, as an atonement for sin; to suffer to be lost for the sake of obtaining something; to devote with loss; to kill. vi. To make offerings to God of things consumed on the altar. ppr. sacrificing, pret. & pp. sacrificed.—n. Act of one who sacrifices; that which is sacrificed; an animal or any other thing presented to God and burned on the altar, as an atonement for sin; loss incurred for gaining some object, or for obliging another; anything destroyed. [L. sacrifico—sacer, holy, and facio, to make.]

Sacrificer, sa'kri-fis-ér, n. One who sacrifices or immolates.

Sacrificial, sa-kri-fi'shi-al, a. Performing sacrifice; consisting in sacrifice.

Sacrilege, sa'kri-lej, n. Act of stealing sacred things; the crime of profaning sacred things; the alienating to common purposes what has been consecrated to religious persons or uses. [Fr. sacrilége—L. sacer, holy, and lego, to steal.]

Sacrilegious, sa-kri-lē'ji-us, a. Relating to or implying sacrilege; violating sacred things; polluted with the crime of sacrilege. [L. sacrilegus.]

Sacrilegiously, sa-kri-lē'ji-us-li, adv. With sacrilege.

Sacrilegiousness, sa-kri-lē'ji-us-nes, n. Quality of being sacrilegious.

Sacrist, sā'krist, n. A sacristan; a sexton.

Sacristan, sā'krist-an, n. An officer of the church who has the care of the sacred utensils or movables of the church; a sexton. [Fr. sacristain—L. sacer, holy.]

Sacristy, sā'krist-i, n. An apartment in

ch, chain; j, job; g, go; ng, sing; ᴛʜ, then; th, thin; w, wig; wh, whig; sh, azure; † obsolete.

a church where the sacred utensils, &c., are kept; the vestry. [Fr. *sacristie*.]

Sad, sad, *a*. Full of or filled with grief or anxiety; sorrowful, dejected; serious; melancholy; not gay or cheerful; causing sorrow; grievous; afflictive. [Old G. *sat*, full, filled—Icel. *sedia*, to fill.]

Sadden, sad'n, *vt*. To make sad or sorrowful; to make melancholy or gloomy. [Sax. *sadian*, to be tired.]

Saddle, sad'l, *n*. A seat to be placed on a horse's back for the rider to sit on; something resembling a saddle in shape or in use.—*vt*. To put a saddle on; to load; to fix a burden on. *ppr*. saddling, *pret. & pp*. saddled. [Sax. *sadel*—Goth. *sitan*, to sit.]

Saddler, sad'l-ėr, *n*. One whose occupation is to make saddles.

Saddlery, sad'l-e-ri, *n*. The materials for making saddles and harnesses; the articles usually offered for sale in a saddler's shop; the trade of a saddler.

Sadducean, sad-dū-sē'an, *a*. Pertaining to the Sadducees or to their doctrine.

Sadducee, sad'dū-sē, *n*. One of a sect among the ancient Jews who denied the resurrection of the body and the existence of angels or spirits. [Late Gr. *Saddukaios*.]

Sadly, sad'li, *adv*. Sorrowfully; in a miserable manner; seriously.

Sadness, sad'nes, *n*. State of being sad; sorrowfulness; dejection of mind; gloom of countenance; sedate gravity.

Safe, sāf, *a*. Saved; preserved; free from danger of any kind; in secure care; free from hurt; conferring safety; securing from harm; not exposing to danger.—*n*. A place of safety; a fireproof chest for containing money, valuable papers, &c.; a tight box for securing provisions from noxious animals.—*vt*.† To render safe. [Fr. *sauf*—L. *salvus*, safe.]

Safe-conduct, sāf'kon-dukt, *n*. That which gives a safe passage; convoy; guard through an enemy's country; passport. [*safe* and *conduct*.]

Safe-guard, sāf'gard, *n*. He who or that which guards or protects; protection; a warrant of security given by a sovereign, to protect a stranger within his territories.

Safely, sāf'li, *adv*. In a safe manner; without injury; in close custody.

Safeness, sāf'nes, *n*. State of being safe.

Safety, sāf'ti, *n*. State of being safe or out of danger; exemption from hurt, injury, or loss; close custody.

Safety-lamp, sāf'ti-lamp, *n*. A lamp covered with wire-gauze, to give light in mines, without the danger of setting fire to inflammable gases. It was invented by Sir Humphrey Davy, and improved by Stevenson.

Safety-valve, sāf'ti-valv, *n*. A valve fitted to the boiler of a steam-engine, which lets the steam escape when the pressure becomes too great for safety.

Saffron, saf'fron, *n*. A bulbous plant, allied to the crocus, having flowers of a deep yellow colour.—*a*. Having the colour of saffron-flowers. [Fr. *safran*; Ar. *tsfar*, to be yellow.]

Sag, sag, *vi*. To sink down; to yield; to give way; to sink in the middle; to yield under the pressure of care; to be unsettled. *ppr*. sagging, *pret. & pp*. sagged. [Sax. *sigan*, to sink down.]

Sagacious, sa-gā'shi-us, *a*. Quick of perception; quick of thought; acute in discernment. [L. *sagax*, *sapacis*—*sagio*, to perceive quickly.]

Sagaciously, sa-gā'shi-us-li, *adv*. In a sagacious manner; with quick penetration.

Sagacity, sa-gas'i-ti, *n*. Quality of being sagacious; quickness of discernment; readiness of apprehension; shrewdness. [Fr. *sagacité*.]

Sage, sāj, *n*. An herb, so named probably on account of its salutary properties, which are stomachic, aromatic, and bitter. [Fr. *sauge*; L. *salvers*, to be well.]

Sage, sāj, *a*. Perceiving quickly by the intellect; presaging; discerning; wise; grave; prophesying; well judged; well adapted to the purpose.—*n*. A man of quick and accurate discernment; a man venerable for years, and known as a man of sound judgment; a grave philosopher. [Fr. *sage*—L. *sagio*, to perceive quickly.]

Sagely, sāj'li, *adv*. In a sage manner; wisely; with just discernment.

Sageness, sāj'nes, *n*. Quality of being sage; wisdom; sagacity.

Sagging, sag'ing, *p.n*. A bending or sinking in consequence of the weight.

Sagittal, sa-ji'tal, *a*. Pertaining to or resembling an arrow. [L. *sagitta*, an arrow.]

Sagittarius, sa-ji-tā'ri-us, *n*. The Archer; one of the twelve signs of the zodiac, which the sun enters about November 22. [L.]

Sagittary, sa'ji-ta-ri, *n*. An arsenal.

Sago, sā'gō, *n*. A dry mealy substance, the prepared pith of several species of palms, much used as an article of light and nutritious food. [Hind. *sagoo-dana*.]

Said, sed, *p.a*. Declared; uttered; reported; aforesaid; before-mentioned.

Sail, sāl, *n*. An expanded cloth hoisted on the mast, to receive the impulse of wind by which a ship is driven; a ship; used as a collective word to denote the number of ships; an excursion in some vessel.—*vi*. To be driven forward by the action of wind upon sails, as a ship on water; to pass by water; to set sail; to begin a voyage; to be carried in the air, as a balloon; to pass smoothly through the air.—*vt*. To navigate; to pass or move upon in a ship, by means of sails; to direct the motion of a vessel; to fly through. [Sax. *segel*—Icel. *sigla*, the mast of a ship.]

Sailer, sāl'er, *n*. One who sails; a ship, with reference to her speed.

Sailing, sāl'ing, *p.a*. Moving on water or in air; passing in a ship; pertaining to the act of sailing.—*p.n*. The movement of a ship impelled by the action of wind on her sails; movement through the air; act of setting sail; the art of navigation.

Sailor, sāl'or, *n*. One who follows the business of navigating ships; a seaman; a mariner.

Saint, sān, *pp*. Said.

Saint, sānt, *n*. A person sanctified; a holy or godly person; one eminent for piety; one of the blessed in heaven; one canonized by the Roman Catholic church.—*vt*. To enrol among saints by an official act of the pope; to canonise. *vi*.† To act with a show of piety. [Fr. L. *sancio*, *sanctus*, to make sacred.]

Sainted, sānt'ed, *p.a*. Holy; sacred; canonized.

Saint-like, sānt'līk, *a*. Resembling a saint; suiting a saint.

Saintliness, sānt'li-nes, *n*. Quality of being saintly.

Saintly, sānt'li, *a*. Like a saint; becoming a holy person.

Sake, sāk, *n*. Cause; occasion; business; matter; suit; final cause; end; the purpose of obtaining; regard to any person or thing. [Old G. *sacha*, a cause, business, matter.]

Salad, sa'lad, *n*. Food of raw herbs, as lettuce, radish, &c., generally dressed with salt, oil, and vinegar, or other condiments. [Fr. *salade*—L. *sal*, salt.]

Salading, sa'lad-ing, *p.n*. Vegetables for salads.

Salad-oil, sa'lad-oil, *n*. Olive-oil, used in dressing salads, &c.

Salam, sa-läm', *n*. A salutation of ceremony in the East. [Pers. *salâm*.]

Salamander, sa-la-man'dėr, *n*. A reptile having four feet and a long tail, resembling a lizard, but more allied to frogs; a small lizard, vulgarly supposed to be able to endure fire. [Fr. *salamandre*—Ar. *samad*, perpetual.]

Salamandrine, sa-la-man'drin, *a*. Pertaining to or resembling a salamander.

Salaried, sa'la-rid, *p.a*. Having or enjoying a salary.

Salary, sa'la-ri, *n*. The recompense stipulated to be paid to a person for services, usually a fixed sum to be paid annually or periodically; pay; hire. [Fr. *salaire*—L. *sal*, salt, part of the pay of the Roman soldiers.]

Sale, sāl, *n*. Act of selling; the exchange of a commodity for money; power of selling; market for; state of being to be sold. [Icel. *sala*.]

Saleable, sāl'a-bl, *a*. That may be sold; that finds a ready market.

Salesman, sālz'man, *n*. One who is employed in selling.

Salient, sā'li-ent, *a*. Leaping; beating; throbbing, as the heart; shooting out or up; darting; projecting; standing out prominently.—*n*. A projection [L. *saliens*—*salio*, to leap.]

Saline, sa-līn', *a*. Consisting of salt, or constituting salt; partaking of the qualities of salt. [Fr. *salin*; L. *sal*, salt—Gr. *hals*, *halos*, the sea.]

Salineness, sa-lin'nes, *n*. State or quality of being saline.

Saliva, sa-lī'va, *n*. That which moistens the mouth; the fluid which is secreted by the salivary glands, and which serves to moisten the mouth and tongue, to mix with the food, and assist digestion. [L.—Gr. *hūō*, to wet.]

Salivary, sa'li-va-ri, *a*. Pertaining to saliva; secreting or conveying saliva.

Salivate, sa'li-vāt, *vt*. To produce an unusual secretion of saliva in, as in a person, usually by mercury. *ppr*. salivating, *pret. & pp*. salivated. [from L. *salivo*, *salivatum*.]

Salivation, sa-li-vā'shon, *n*. Act or process of producing an increased secretion of saliva; excessive flow of saliva, as that produced by mercury, &c.

Sallet, sal'let, *n*. A kind of helmet; a salad.

Sallow, sal'lō, *a*. Having the colour of the leaves and blossoms of certain willows, called sallows; of a pale, sickly colour, tinged with a dark yellow. [Sax. *salowig*—L. *salix*, a willow.]

Sallowness, sal'lō-nes, *n*. State of being sallow; yellowish colour.

Sally, sal'li, *n*. A leaping forth; a rushing of troops from a besieged place to attack the besiegers; a spring of intellect or fancy; flight; act of levity; frolic; an escapade; an overleaping of bounds.—*vi*. To rush out, as a body of troops from a fortified place to attack besiegers; to issue suddenly. *ppr*. sallying, *pret. & pp*. sallied. [Fr. *saillir* —L. *salio*, to leap.]

Salmon, sa'mun, *n*. A large fish highly

Fāte, fär, fat, fall; mē, met, hėr; pīne, pin; nōte, not, move; tūbe, tub, bull; oil, pound.

Salmon-trout, sa'mun-trout, n. A fish, called also the sea-trout; a fish allied to the salmon, highly valued as an article of food.

Saloon, sa-lön', n. A spacious and lofty hall; a spacious and elegant apartment, for the reception of company, or for works of art; the main cabin of a steamer; a refreshment room in a theatre; a concert room where liquors are sold. [Fr. *salon*—Gr. *aulē*, a hall.]

Salt, sạlt, n. A substance obtained by the evaporation of *sea-water*, and also found native in the earth, used for seasoning food, &c.; a chemical substance, formed by the combination of an acid with another substance called a base; taste; wit; poignancy; that which gives flavour; that which preserves from corruption.—a. *Having the taste of salt;* abounding with salt; overflowed with salt-water; growing on salt meadows, and having the taste of salt; pungent or bitter.—*vt.* *To sprinkle or season with salt.* [Sax. *sealt*—Old G. *salz;* L. *sal*—Gr. *hals,* the sea.]

Saltation, sal-tā'shon, n. A leaping; beating or palpitation. [L. *saltatio*—*salio, saltum,* to leap.]

Saltatory, sal'ta-tō-ri, a. *Leaping or dancing;* used in leaping. [Low L. *saltatorius.*]

Salt-cellar, sạlt'sel-lār, n. A small *vessel* used at table for holding *salt*.

Salted, sạlt'ed, p.a. *Sprinkled, seasoned, or impregnated with salt.*

Salter, sạlt'ėr, n. *One who salts;* one who sells salt; a drysalter.

Salting, sạlt'ing, p.n. *Act of sprinkling with salt.*

Saltish, sạlt'ish, a. *Somewhat salt.*

Saltishly, sạlt'ish-li, adv. *With a moderate degree of saltness.*

Saltless, sạlt'les, a. *Destitute of salt;* insipid.

Saltness, sạlt'nes, n. *Quality of being impregnated with salt;* taste of salt.

Salt-pan, Salt-pit, sạlt'pan, sạlt'pit, n. A *pan* or *pit* where *salt* is made.

Saltpetre, sạlt'pē-tėr, n. Nitre; a chemical *salt* which usually exudes from rocks, walls, &c. [*salt,* and Gr. *petra,* a rock.]

Salt-work, sạlt'wėrk, n. A *house* or *place* where *salt* is made.

Salubrious, sa-lū'bri-us, a. *Favourable to health;* healthful; wholesome; salutary. [L. *salubris—salus,* a sound condition—*salvus,* whole.]

Salubriously, sa-lū'bri-us-li, adv. So as to promote health.

Salubrity, sa-lū'bri-ti, n. *Quality of being salubrious;* wholesomeness; favourableness to the preservation of health. [Fr. *salubrité.*]

Salutary, sa'lū-ta-ri, a. *Pertaining to health;* healthful; promotive of public safety; beneficial; profitable. [Fr. *salutaire;* L. *salus,* a whole condition.]

Salutation, sa-lū-tā'shon, n. *Act of saluting;* act of paying respect by the customary words or actions; a salute; an address. [Fr.]

Salute, sa-lūt', vt. *To wish health to;* to hail; to kiss; to show honour to by a discharge of cannon or small arms, by striking colours, by shouts, &c.; to promote the welfare and safety off. *ppr.* *saluting, pret. & pp.* saluted.—n. *Act of saluting;* salutation; a kiss; an exhibition of respect in the army or navy, by the discharge of artillery or small-arms, beating of drums, &c. [L. *saluto.*]

Salvage, sal'vaj, n. A recompense allowed by law for the *saving* of a ship or goods from loss at sea; also, the goods or thing thus *saved.* [Fr.—L. *salvus,* safe.]

Salvation, sal-vā'shon, n. *Act of saving;* the redemption of man from the guilt and punishment of sin, and the conferring on him everlasting happiness; deliverance from enemies; victory. [Low L. *salvatio.*]

Salve, säv, n. *That which saves* or preserves; a remedy; an adhesive composition applied *to heal* or relieve wounds or sores.—*vt.*† *To save;* to apply salve to. [Sax. *sealfe.*]

Salver, sal'vėr, n. A waiter on which articles are carried *safely* round or presented.

Salvo, sal'vō, n. *Reservation of a right;* an excuse; a military or naval salute. [L. *salvo jure,* right being safe.]

Samaritan, sa-ma'ri-tan, a. *Pertaining to Samaria;* denoting the ancient alphabet used by the Hebrews before the Babylonish captivity, and retained by the Samaritans.—*n. An inhabitant of Samaria;* the language of Samaria, a dialect of the Chaldean.

Same, sām, a. *Having the property of oneness;* identical; not different; of the identical kind, though not the specific thing; being of the like kind; that was mentioned before; exactly similar. *n.*† A heap.—*adv.*† Together. [Sax.; Goth. *sama.*]

Sameness, sām'nes, n. *State of being the same;* oneness; identity; state of being not different; state of being perfectly alike; correspondence.

Samlet, sam'let, n. *A little salmon.*

Samphire, sam'fir, n. *Saint Peter's wort;* an herb, growing usually on cliffs by the sea, and used for pickling. [said to be a corruption of *Saint Pierre.*]

Sample, sam'pl, n. *What is taken out of* a larger quantity as a specimen; a part of anything presented for inspection, as evidence of the quality of the whole; example; instance. [Fr. *exemple*—L. *eximo,* to take out—*emo,* to obtain.]

Sampler, sam'pl-ėr, n. *A pattern of work;* a piece of needle-work sewed by learners: one who makes up and exhibits samples of goods for inspection. [L. *exemplar.*]

Sanability, san-a-bil'i-ti, n. *State of being sanable* or curable.

Sanable, san'a-bl, a. *That may be made sound;* susceptible of remedy; curable. [L. *sanabilis—sano,* to cure.]

Sanative, san'a-tiv, a. *Having the power to cure or heal;* healing. [It. *sanativo.*]

Sanatory, san'a-tō-ri, a. *Healing.*

Sanctification, sangk'ti-fi-kā''shon, n. *Act of making holy;* state of being made holy; consecration. [Fr.]

Sanctified, sangk'ti-fid, p.a. *Made holy;* set apart for sacred services.

Sanctifier, sangk-ti'fi-ėr, n. *He who sanctifies;* the Holy Spirit.

Sanctify, sangk'ti-fi, vt. *To make holy;* to purify; to hallow; to set apart to a holy use; to make pure from sin; to make the means of holiness; to render productive of holiness; to secure from violation. *ppr.* sanctifying, *pret. & pp.* sanctified. [Fr. *sanctifier*—L. *sanctus,* holy, and *facio,* to make.]

Sanctifying, sangk'ti-fi-ing, p.a. *Tending to sanctify;* adapted to increase holiness.

Sanctimonious, sangk-ti-mō'ni-us, a. *Having sanctity;* having the appearance of sanctity. [L. *sanctimonia,* sacredness.]

Sanctimoniousness, sangk-ti-mō''ni-us-nes, n. *State of being sanctimonious.*

Sanction, sangk'shon, n. *A decreeing as inviolable,* under the penalty of a curse; ratification; authority; an official act of a superior, by which he ratifies the act of some other person; confirmation derived from testimony or custom.—*vt.* *To give a sanction to;* to ratify; to authorize; to sup,ort. [Fr.—L. *sancio,* to make sacred.]

Sanctity, sangk'ti-ti, n. *State of being sacred;* holiness; godliness; sacredne.s; inviolability. [Fr. *sainteté.*]

Sanctuarize,† sangk'tū-a-riz, vt. *To shelter by means of a sanctuary.*

Sanctuary, sangk'tū-a-ri, n. *A sacred place;* the most retired part of the temple at Jerusalem, or of the tabernacle; the holy of holies; the temple at Jerusalem; a house consecrated to the worship of God; that part of a church in which the altar is placed; a sacred asylum; protection. [Fr. *sanctuaire*—L. *sanctus,* holy.]

Sand, sand, n. Any mass of fine particles of stone, particularly of silicious stone, but not strictly reduced to powder or dust; (pl.) tracts of land consisting of sand, like the deserts of Arabia and Africa; a measured interval.—*vt.* *To sprinkle with sand;* to cover with sand. [Sax.—Old G. *sant.*]

Sandal, san'dal, n. A kind of *shoe* worn in ancient times, consisting of a sole fastened to the foot so as to leave the upper part of the foot bare; a shoe or slipper worn by monks and others of the Romish church. [Fr.; Gr. *sandalon,* a wooden shoe.]

Sandalled, san'dald, p.a. *Having on sandals.*

Sand-blind, sand'blind, a. *Having a defect of sight* by reason of which small particles *like sand* appear to fly before the *eyes.*

Sanded, sand'ed, p.a. *Covered with sand;* variegated with spots; of a sandy colour.

Sand-heat, sand'hēt, n. The *heat of* warm *sand,* in chemical operations.

Sandiness, sand'i-nes, n. *State of being sandy.* [from *sandy.*]

Sand-paper, sand'pā-pėr, n. *Paper* covered on one side with a fine gritty substance, small as *sand,* for smoothing and polishing.

Sandstone, sand'stōn, n. A rock composed of agglutinated particles of *sand;* a species of freestone.

Sandwich, sand'wich, n. A viand, consisting of two slices of bread and butter with a thin slice of ham or other salted meat between them. [invented by an Earl of Sandwich, who gave it his name.]

Sandy, sand'i, a. *Abounding with sand;* covered with sand; not firm or solid; consisting of sand; of the colour of sand. [Sax. *sandig.*]

Sane, sān, a. *Sound; healthy;* not disordered; sound in mind; having the regular exercise of reason. [L. *sānus;* Gr. *saos,* safe and sound.]

Saneness, sān'nes, n. *State of being sane* or of sound mind; sanity.

Sanguinary, sang'gwin-a-ri, a. *Of or belonging to blood;* attended with much bloodshed; bloodthirsty; cruel. [Fr. *sanguinaire*—L. *sanguis,* blood.]

Sanguine, sang'gwin, a. *Of the nature of blood;* bloody; red; abounding with

SANGUINELY 342 SATURNIAN

blood; characterized by warmness, as temper; lively; confident; hopeful. [Fr. *sanguin*; L. *sanguis*, blood.]
Sanguinely, sang'gwin-li, *adv.* Ardently; with confidence of success.
Sanguineness, sang'gwin-nes, *n.* State or quality of being sanguine.
Sanguineous, sang-gwin'e-us, *a.* Abounding with blood; plethoric; constituting blood; of a red or blood colour. [L. *sanguineus*.]
Sanitary, san'i-ta-ri, *a.* Pertaining to or designed to secure or promote health; relating to the preservation of health. [Fr. *sanitaire*—L. *sano*, to heal.]
Sanity, san'i-ti, *n.* Soundness; the state of a mind in the perfect exercise of reason. [Fr. *santé*—L. *sanus*, sound.]
Sans†, sånz, *prep.* Without. [L. *sine*.]
Sanscrit, san'skrit, *n.* The ornate and sacred tongue; a language formerly spoken in Northern India, but now that of the religion, philosophy, and laws of the Brahmins. [from Sans. *sam* (= Gr. *sun*), with, and *krita*, done, made, perfected, from *kri*, to make. The union of *sam* with *kri* signifies to adorn, to consecrate.]
Sap, sap, *n.* The *juice* of plants of any kind; the newly-formed wood of a tree next to the bark, through which the sap flows. [Sax. *sæp*—Heb. *sâpha*, to pour.]
Sap, sap, *vt.* To subvert by digging under; to undermine; to mine.—*vi.* To proceed by mining, or by secretly undermining. *ppr.* sapping, *pret. & pp.* sapped.—*n.* A trench for undermining. [Fr. *saper*; It. *zappa*, a spade.]
Sapid, sa'pid, *a.* Tasteful; having the power of affecting the organs of taste. [Fr. *sapide*—L. *sapio*, to taste.]
Sapidity, sa-pid'i-ti, *n.* Quality of being sapid; savour; the quality of affecting the organs of taste.
Sapience, sā'pi-ens, *n.* Good taste; discernment; sageness; knowledge. [Fr. —L. *sapio*, to taste.]
Sapient, sā'pi-ent, *a.* Characterised by wisdom; sage; sagacious; discerning (commonly ironical). [L. *sapiens*-*sapio*, to taste, to have sense or discernment.]
Sapiently, sā'pi-ent-li, *adv.* Wisely.
Sapless, sap'les, *a.* Destitute of sap; dry; old; husky.
Sapling, sap'ling, *n.* A young tree full of sap. [from sap.]
Saponaceous, sa-pon-ā'shē-us, *a.* Soapy; resembling soap; having the qualities of soap. [from L. *sapo*, *saponis*, soap.]
Sapper, sap'er, *n.* One who saps; one who digs a sap or trench.
Sapphic, saf'fik, *a.* Pertaining to Sappho, a Grecian poetess, or to a kind of verse said to have been invented by her.
Sapphire, saf'fir, *n.* A glittering precious gem, frequently blue, and inferior in hardness only to the diamond. [L. *sapphirus*; Heb. *shaphar*, to be bright.]
Sappiness, sap'i-nes, *n.* State or quality of being full of sap; succulence; juiciness. [from *sappy*.]
Sappy, sap'i, *a.* Abounding with sap; juicy; succulent; young. [Sax. *sæpig*.]
Saracen, sa'ra-sen, *n.* A name which began to be used in the first century of our era, and which, in course of time, became the general name of all the Arabian tribes who embraced the religion of Mahomet. [Ar. *Sharkein*, the eastern people, first applied to the Bedouin Arabs who dwelt between the Euphrates and the Tigris.]
Saracenic, sa-ra-sen'ik, *a.* Pertaining to the Saracens; as, Saracenic architecture.
Sarcasm, sär'kazm, *n.* A keen or biting reproach; a cutting jest; a satirical remark, uttered with some degree of scorn; irony; taunt; gibe. [L. *sarcasmus*; Gr. *sarx, sarkos*, the flesh.]
Sarcastic, sär-kas'tik, *a.* Containing sarcasm; bitterly ironical; taunting.
Sarcastically, sär-kas'tik-al-li, *adv.* In a sarcastic manner.
Sarcenet, särs'net, *n.* A species of fine, thin, woven silk, so named from its having been originally made by the Saracens. [Fr.]
Sarcophagus, sär-kof'a-gus, *n.* A species of stone used among the Greeks for making coffins, which was so called because it *consumed the flesh* of bodies deposited in it within a few weeks; a stone coffin or tomb in which the ancients deposited bodies which they chose not to burn. [L.—Gr. *sarx, sarkos*, flesh, and *phago*, to eat.]
Sardine, Sardius, sär'din, sär'di-us, *n.* A precious stone; a species of chalcedony.—*a.* Relating to the sardius. [L. *sardius*.]
Sardine, sär'din, *n.* A small fish of the herring family, much used as a relish. [Gr. *sardinē*.]
Sardonic, sär-don'ik, *a. Sardonic laugh*, a spasmodic affection of the muscles of the face, giving it a horrible appearance of laughter, and said to be produced by eating the herb *sardonica*, a species of ranunculus growing in Sardinia; a forced, heartless, or bitter laugh or grin, which ill conceals a person's real feelings.
Sardonyx, sär'do-niks, *n.* A precious stone, a variety of chalcedony, said to be so named from the resemblance of its colour to that of the flesh under the nail. [Gr.—*Sardis*, and *onux*, a nail.]
Sash, sash, *n.* Originally, a *head-band*; a scarf worn round the waist or over the shoulders, for ornament; a silken band worn by officers in the army, by the clergy over their cassocks, and also as a part of female dress. [Ar. *saj*, a green or black sash.]
Sash, sash, *n.* The *frame* of a window in which the panes are set. [Fr. *châssis*—L. *capio*, to hold.]
Satan, sā'tan, *n.* The grand adversary of man; the devil, or prince of darkness; the chief of the fallen angels. [Heb. *satan*, to lie in wait.]
Satanic, sā-tan'ik, *a. Resembling Satan*; extremely malicious; devilish.
Satchel, sa'chel, *n.* A little sack or bag. [Fr. *sachet*.]
Sate, sāt, *vt.* To satiate; to glut; to feed beyond natural desire. *ppr.* sating, *pret. & pp.* sated. [L. *satio—satis*, enough.]
Satellite, sa'tel-lit, *n.* An attendant; an obsequious follower; a small planet revolving round another. [Fr.—L. *satelles, satellitis*.]
Satiable, sā'shi-a-bl, *a.* That may be satiated.
Satiate, sā'shi-āt, *vt.* To give enough to; to gorge; to surfeit; to feed to the full; to fill beyond natural desire. *ppr.* satiating, *pret. & pp.* satiated.—*a.* Glutted. [L. *satio, satiatus—satis*, enough.]
Satiated, sā'shi-āt-ed, *p.a.* Filled to satiety; glutted.
Satiety, sa-ti'e-ti, *n.* State of being satiated; repletion; surfeit; an excess of gratification which excites wearisomeness or loathing. [Fr. *satiété*.]
Satin, sa'tin, *n.* A species of glossy silk cloth, of a thick close texture.—*a. Belonging to or made of satin*. [Fr.]
Satinet, sa'ti-net, *n.* A thin species of satin; a particular kind of cloth, made of cotton warp and woollen filling.
Satiny, sa'tin-i, *a. Resembling satin*, or partaking of its qualities.
Satire, sa'tir, *n.* Originally, a dish *filled* with various kinds of fruit; a species of poetry peculiar among the ancients to the Romans, in which the poets attacked the vices of mankind in a poem in which wickedness or folly is exposed with severity; sarcasm; irony; ridicule; humour. [Fr.; L. *satira—satis*, enough.]
Satiric, Satirical, sa-ti'rik, sa-ti'rik-al, *a. Belonging to satire*; severe in language; insulting; poignant; sarcastic; reproachful; abusive. [Fr. *satirique*.]
Satirically, sa-ti'rik-al-li, *adv.* With severity of remark; with invectives.
Satirist, sa'ti-rist, *n.* One who writes satire.
Satirize, sa'ti-riz, *vt.* To expose by satire; to censure with severity. *ppr.* satirizing, *pret. & pp.* satirized. [Fr. *satiriser*.]
Satisfaction, sa-tis-fak'shon, *n. Act of satisfying*; repose of mind, or contentment with present possession and enjoyment; pleasure; that state which results from relief from suspense, doubt, or uncertainty; conviction; compensation; amends; payment; discharge, as of a debt. [Fr.—L. *satis*, enough, and *facio*, to make.]
Satisfactorily, sa-tis-fak'tō-ri-li, *adv.* In a manner to give satisfaction.
Satisfactory, sa-tis-fak'tō-ri, *a. Giving satisfaction*; relieving the mind from doubt or uncertainty; making amends or recompense; causing to rest content; atoning. [Fr. *satisfactoire*.]
Satisfy, sa'tis-fī, *vt.* To do that which is enough to; to supply, as possession or enjoyment, till no more is desired; to gratify; to satiate; to supply fully, as what is necessary; to pay to content; to recompense; to requite; to appease by punishment; to cause to rest in confidence; to convince; to pay, as a debt.—*vi.* To do that which is enough: to give content; to make payment; to atone. *ppr.* satisfying, *pret. & pp.* satisfied. [Fr. *satisfaire*—L. *satis*, enough, and *facio*, to make.]
Saturable, sa'tūr-a-bl, *a.* That may be saturated; capable of saturation.
Saturate, sa'tūr-āt, *vt.* To *fill*; to satiate; to impregnate with till no more can be received. *ppr.* saturating, *pret. & pp.* saturated. [L. *saturo, saturatus—satis*, enough.]
Saturated, sa'tūr-āt-ed, *p.a. Supplied to fulness.*
Saturation, sa-tūr-ā'shon, *n. Act of saturating*; chemical solution continued till the solvent can contain no more. [Fr.—Late L. *saturatio*.]
Saturday, sa'ter-dā, *n. The day of Saturn*; the seventh or last day of the week; the day of the Jewish Sabbath. [Sax. *Sæterdæg*.]
Saturn, sa'tern, *n.* The name of one of the oldest deities, the father of Jupiter; one of the planets of the solar system. [L. *Saturnus—sato*, sown lands. He presided over agriculture.]
Saturnalia, sa-ter-nā'li-a, *n. pl.* Among the Romans, the *festival of Saturn*, celebrated in December, as a period of unrestrained license. [L.]
Saturnalian, sa-ter-nā'li-an, *a. Pertaining to the Saturnalia*; loose; dissolute; sportive. [from L. *Saturnalia*.]
Saturnian, sa-tern'i-an, *a. Pertaining to*

Fate, fär, fat, fall; mē, met, her; pīne, pin; nōte, not, mōve; tūbe, tub, bull; oil, pound.

Saturn, whose fabulous reign is called the golden age; distinguished for purity, integrity, and simplicity.
Saturnine, sa'tėrn-īn, *a. Born under the planet Saturn*, and supposed to be under his influence; heavy; phlegmatic. [L. *Saturninus*.]
Satyr, sa'tėr, *n.* A mythological sylvan deity, represented as part man and part goat, and extremely wanton. [L. *satūrus*; Heb. *sathar*, to be hid.]
Satyric, sa-ti'rik, *a. Pertaining to satyrs*; as, satyric tragedy.
Sauce, sas, *n.* That which gives *savour* to food; a mixture to be eaten with food for improving its relish.—*vt. To make savoury*; to accompany meat with something to give it a higher relish; to accompany with anything good, or ironically, with anything bad; to treat with bitter language. *ppr.* saucing, *pret. & pp.* sauced. [Fr.—L. *sal, salt.*]
Saucer, ṣa'sėr, *n.* A piece of china or other ware, in which a tea-cup or coffee-cup is set. [Fr. *saucière*.]
Saucily, sas'i-li, *adv.* Impudently; with impertinent boldness. [from *saucy*.]
Sauciness, sas'i-nes, *n. Quality of being saucy*; impudence; petulance.
Saucy, sas'i, *a.* Indulging in *a pungent* sort of wit or humour; impudent; treating superiors with contempt; expressive of impudence. [from *sauce*.]
Saunter, sȧn'tėr, *vi. To loiter; to idle*; to wander or stroll about idly.—*n. A sauntering or place for sauntering*. [Icel. *seintlåtr*, full of delay—*sein*, slow, and *lātr*, idle.]
Saunterer, sȧn'tėr-ėr, *n. One who wanders about idly.*
Sauntering, sȧn'tėr-ing, *p.n. Act of wandering lazily about or loitering.*
Saunteringly, sȧn'tėr-ing-li, *adv. In a sauntering manner.*
Sausage, ṣȧ'sȧj, *n.* The prepared intestine of an ox, sheep, or pig, stuffed with minced meat *seasoned*, sometimes prepared by being simply rolled, without stuffing. [Fr. *saucisse*—L. *sal*, salt.]
Savage, sa'vāj, *a. Pertaining to the forest*; wild; untaught; rude; barbarous; characterized by cruelty; merciless.—*n.* A human being in his native state of rudeness; one who is untaught, or without manners; a man of brutal cruelty; a barbarian. [Fr. *sauvage*—L. *silva*, a wood.]
Savagely, sa'vāj-li, *adv. In the manner of a savage*; cruelly; inhumanly.
Savageness, sa'vāj-nes, *n. State or quality of being savage*; barbarousness.
Savagery, sa'vāj-ri, *n.* Barbarism; an act of cruelty.
Save, sāv, *vt. To keep safe*; to bring out of danger; to preserve; to rescue; to deliver; to keep from eternal death; to free from the power of sin; to hinder from being spent or lost, as time or money; to spare; to reserve; to hinder from occurrence, as a blush or tear; to reconcile; to take or use opportunely, so as not to lose.—*vi.* To hinder expense. *ppr.* saving, *pret. & pp.* saved.—*prep.* Except; not including. [Fr. *sauver*—L. *salvus*, safe—Gr. *saos, sōs*, safe and sound, alive and well.]
Saver, sāv'ėr, *n. One who saves*; an economist.
Saving, sāv'ing, *p.a.* Not lavish; sparing; thrifty; that incurs no loss, th'ugh not gainful; that secures everlasting salvation.—*n. Something saved*; (pl.) **earnings**; small sums accumulated by industry and economy.—*prep.* Excepting.

Savingly, sāv'ing-li, *adv.* With frugality or parsimony.
Savings-bank, sāv'ings-bangk, *n. A bank in which the savings* or earnings of the poorer classes are deposited and put to interest for their benefit.
Saviour, sāv'i-or, *n. One who saves*; appropriately, JESUS CHRIST, the Redeemer of the world. [Fr. *sauveur*—L. *salvator*.]
Savour, sā'vor, *n. Taste*; odour; smell; something that perceptibly affects the organs of taste and smell; the quality which renders a thing valuable.—*vi. To have a particular taste* or smell; to partake of the quality or nature; to have the appearance (with *of*).—*vt. To taste* or smell with pleasure or delight; to like; to delight in; to taste intellectually or spiritually. [Fr. *saveur*—L. *sapio*, to taste.]
Savouriness, sā'vo-ri-nes, *n. Quality of being savoury*; pleasantness of taste or of smell.
Savourless, sā'vor-les, *a. Destitute of taste or smell*; insipid.
Savoury, sā'vo-ri, *a.* Pleasing to the organs of *taste* or smell.
Saw, sạ, *n. A cutting instrument*, consisting of a thin blade of steel having a toothed edge.—*vt. To cut with a saw*; to separate with a saw; to form by cutting with a saw.—*vi. To use a saw*; to be cut with a saw. [Sax. *saga*—L. *seco*, to cut.]
Saw†, sạ, *n.* A saying; maxim. [Sax. *saga*.]
Saw-mill, sạ'mil, *n. A mill* for *sawing* timber, marble, &c., driven by water, steam, or other power.
Sawyer, sạ'yėr, *n. One who saws* timber into boards or planks.
Saxifrage, saks'i-frāj, *n.* An alpine plant, a medical preparation from which was supposed to have the property of *dissolving stone* in the bladder. [L. *saxifraga*—*saxum*, a stone, and *frango*, to break.]
Saxon, saks'on, *n.* One of the nation or people who formerly dwelt in the northern part of Germany, and who conquered England in the fifth and sixth centuries; the language of the Saxons.—*a. Pertaining to the Saxons*, to their country, or to their language. [Sax. *Seaxan*, (pl.) *Seaxe*—*seax*, a short sword.]
Say, sā, *vt. To put forth in articulate sounds*; to utter in words; to speak; to pronounce; to allege by way of argument; to rehearse; to recite without singing; to report; to utter by way of reply; to tell.—*vi.* To speak; to tell; to utter; to relate. *ppr.* saying, *pret. & pp.* said.—*n.* A speech; something said. [Sax. *secgan*; Heb. *siach*, to speak.]
Say†, sā, *n.* Trial by sample; temper. *vt.* To try. [from *assay*.]
Say†, sā, *n.* A delicate kind of serge.
Saying, sā'ing, *p.n. Something said*; a proverbial expression; an adage.
Scab, skab, *n.* An eruption of minute pimples on the skin, which by its itching causes those affected with it *to scratch*; a substance, dry and rough, formed over a sore in healing; a contagious disease of sheep, resembling the mange in horses, &c.; a paltry fellow. [Sax. *sceabb*—L. *scabo*, to scratch.]
Scabbard, skab'ȧrd, *n. The sheath of a sword*. [Icel. *skaipr*—*skyli*, to cover.]
Scabbed, skabd, *p.a. Abounding with scabs*; diseased with scabs; paltry; worthless.
Scabbiness, skab'i-nes, *n. Quality or state of being scabby.*

Scabby, skab'i, *a. Affected with scabs*; diseased with the scab or mange.
Scaffold, skaf'fold, *n.* A temporary gallery or stage raised either for shows or spectators; a stage or elevated platform for the execution of a criminal; a structure of timbers, erected by the wall of a building to support the workmen.—*vt. To furnish with a scaffold*; to sustain; to uphold. [Old Fr. *chaffault*—Low L. *catafaltus*.]
Scaffoldage†, skaf'fold-āj, *n.* A scaffold
Scaffolding, skaf'fold-ing, *p.n.* A structure for support in an elevated place; that which sustains; a frame; materials for scaffolds.
Scalable, skāl'a-bl, *a. That may be scaled.*
Scald, skạld, *vt. To deprive of hair or bristles* by the application of boiling water; to burn with a liquor of a boiling heat; to expose to a boiling or violent heat over a fire or in water or other liquor.—*n.* A burn or injury to the skin and flesh by hot liquor.—*a.* Scurvy; paltry. [Icel. *skällda*, to bare.]
Scald, skạld, *n.* Among the ancient Scandinavians, a poet. [Icel. *skälld*, a poet—*skildi*, to discriminate.]
Scalded, skạld'ed, *p.a.* Injured by a hot liquor; exposed to boiling heat.
Scalding, skạld'ing, *p.a.* Burning or injuring by hot liquor.
Scale, skāl, *n. The dish* of a balance; the balance itself, or whole instrument, which is more usually *scales*, in the plural; the *shell*, or crust which composes a part of the covering of a fish; any thin layer; a thin lamina; [L. *scala*] a ladder; series of steps; act of storming a place by mounting the wall on ladders; an instrument of wood, &c., on which are marked lines and figures for the purpose of measuring distances; a series rising by steps or degrees; a basis for a numeral system; a gamut; the regular gradations of sounds in music. [Sax.—*scylan*, to divide.]—*vt. To climb, as by a ladder*; to measure; to spread abroad; [from *scale*, the covering of a fish] to strip or clear of scales; to take off in scales. *vi.* To separate and come off in thin layers. *ppr.* scaling, *pret. & pp.* scaled. [from L. *scala*, a ladder.]
Scaled, skāld, *p.a. Having scales like a fish.*
Scalene, ska-lēn', *a. Limping*; having unequal sides, as a triangle which is neither equilateral nor isosceles. [Gr. *skalēnos*—*skazo*, to limp.]
Scaliness, skāl'i-nes, *n. State of being scaly*; roughness.
Scall, skạl, *n.* Scab; scabbiness; leprosy. [Sax. *scalu*, scab.]
Scalled, skạld, *p.a.* Scurfy; scabby; shabby†; mean†.
Scallop, skal'lop, *n. A shell-fish* having the margin formed into a series of small segments of circles; a recess or curving of the edge of anything, like that on the margin of the scallop-shell.—*vt.* To mark or cut the edge or border of into segments of circles, like *those of a scallop*; to cook in the shell, as oysters. [D. *schelp*, a shell.]
Scalloped, skal'lopt, *p.a.* Cut at the edge into segments of circles.
Scalp, skalp, *n.* The skin of the top of the head cut or torn off, and *resembling a shell*; sometimes the skull itself, or the fore part of it.—*vt. To deprive of the scalp* or integuments of the head. [D. *schelp*, a shell.]
Scalpel, skal'pel, *n. A small* surgical

ch, *ch*ain; j, *j*ob; g, *g*o; ng, si*ng*; ᴛʜ, *th*en; th, *th*in; w, *w*ig; wh, *wh*ig; zh, a*z*ure; † obsolete.

cutting instrument. [L. *scalpellum—scalpo,* to cut.]

Scaly, skāl'i, *a. Covered with scales;* resembling scales.

Scamble†, skam'bl, *vi.* To be busy; to scramble.

Scamper, skam'pėr, *vi. To run from the field of battle;* to run with fear and speed; to hasten escape. [Fr. *escamper*—L. *ex,* and *campus,* a field of battle.]

Scan, skan, *vt.* Primarily, *to climb up;* to measure or read by its feet, as a verse; to examine with critical care; to scrutinize. *ppr.* scanning, *pret. & pp.* scanned. [Fr. *scander*—L. *scando,* to climb.]

Scandal, skan'dal, *n. A stumbling-block;* a cause or occasion of sin; opprobrious censure; defamation; the condition of being disgraced; shame; disgrace.—*vt.†* To defame; to asperse. [Fr. *scandale* —Gr. *skazō,* to limp.]

Scandalize, skan'dal-īz, *vt. To make to stumble;* to shock; to subject to reproach; to traduce; to slander; to disgrace. *ppr.* scandalizing, *pret. & pp.* scandalized. [Fr. *scandaliser.*]

Scandalous, skan'dal-us, *a. Giving scandal* or offence; disgraceful to reputation; that brings shame or infamy; defamatory. [Fr. *scandaleux.*]

Scandalously, skan'dal-us-li, *adv.* Shamefully; in a manner to give offence; censoriously.

Scandalousness, skan'dal-us-nes, *n. Quality or state of being scandalous.*

Scanning, skan'ing, *p.n.* The measuring of a verse by feet, in order to ascertain whether the quantities be duly observed.

Scansion, skan'shon, *n. The act of scanning.* [Rare L. *scansio.*]

Scant, skant, *a. Broken short;* without due proportions; rather less than is wanted for the purpose; sparing; chary.—*vt.* To limit; to straiten; to cut short; to make small.—*adv.† In a scant manner.* [pp. of Sax. *scænan,* to break.]

Scantily, skant'i-li, *adv. With scantiness;* not fully.

Scantiness, skant'i-nes, *n. State of being scanty;* narrowness; want of fulness; want of sufficiency.

Scantling, skant'ling, *n. A pattern;* a small quantity; a certain proportion or quantity; timber sawed into pieces of a small size; the dimensions of a piece of timber, with regard to its breadth and thickness. [Fr. *échantillon,* sample.]

Scantly, skant'li, *adv. In a scant manner.*

Scantness, skant'nes, *n. State or quality of being scant;* narrowness; smallness.

Scanty, skant'i, *a. Scant;* bare; short; not full; poor; scarce; niggardly.

Scape†, skāp, *n.* An escape; freak; loose act of vice.

Scape-goat, skāp'gōt, *n. A goat upon* whose head were symbolically placed the sins of the Jewish people, after which he was sent into the wilderness.

Scapement, skāp'ment, *n. See* ESCAPEMENT.

Scapular, ska'pū-lär, *a. Pertaining to the shoulder,* or to the shoulder-blade. [L. *scapularis.*]

Scapulary, ska'pū-la-ri, *n.* A part of the habit of certain religious orders in the Roman Catholic Church, consisting of two bands of woollen stuff, of which one crosses the back or *shoulders,* and the other the stomach. [Low L. *scapulare*—L. *scapula,* the shoulder-blades.]

Scar, skär, *vt. To cut;* to mark with a wound.—*n. A cutting;* a mark in the skin or flesh of an animal, made by a wound, and remaining after the wound is healed; a blemish. *ppr.* scarring, *pret. & pp.* scarred. [Sax. *sceran,* L. *seco,* to cut.]

Scarce, skärs, *a. Small in quantity;* not plentiful or abundant; being few in number and scattered; rare; uncommon. [Armor. *skars,* little; It. *scarso,* rare, scarce, not easily to be got.]

Scarce, Scarcely, skärs, skärs'li, *adv.* Hardly; scantly; with difficulty.

Scarceness, Scarcity, skärs'nes, skärs'i-ti, *n. State of being scarce;* a dearth; rareness; infrequency.

Scare, skār, *vt.* To frighten, and so *to drive away;* to strike with sudden fright; to terrify; to alarm. *ppr.* scaring, *pret. & pp.* scared. [Icel. *skiarr,* apt to flee—*skirra,* to drive away.]

Scarecrow, skār'krō, *n.* Any frightful thing set up *to frighten crows* from corn fields; anything terrifying without danger.

Scared, skārd, *p.a.* Suddenly terrified.

Scarf, skärf, *n. Scarfs, pl. A strip of cloth;* a piece of dress; a piece of dress that hangs loose upon the shoulders. *vt.† To dress with a scarf.* [Sax. *scearf* —*scyran,* to cut off.]

Scarf-skin, skärf'skin, *n.* The outer layer of the skin that covers the surface of the body; the cuticle.

Scarification, ska'ri-fi-kā'shon, *n. The operation of scarifying.* [L. *scarificatio.*]

Scarify, ska'ri-fi, *vt.* To scratch or cut, as the skin, with *a pointed instrument;* to make small incisions in by means of *a lancet* or cupping instrument. *ppr.* scarifying, *pret. & pp.* scarified. [L. *scarifico*—Gr. *skariphos,* a sharp-pointed instrument.]

Scarlet, skär'let, *n.* A beautiful bright-red colour, brighter than crimson; cloth of a scarlet colour.—*a. Of the colour called scarlet;* of a bright-red colour. [It. *scarlatto.*]

Scarlet-fever, skär'let-fē-vėr, *n.* A disease characterized by *fever,* attended with an eruption of level *crimson red* patches.

Scarret, skä'rē, *n.* A precipitous cliff.

Scarry, skä'ri, *a. Having scars.*

Scathe, skāth, *vt. To injure;* to harm; to damage; to waste; to destroy. — *n.* Damage; waste. [Sax. *scethan,* to violate.]

Scathless, skāth'les, *a.* Without waste, damage, or injury.

Scatter, skat'tėr, *vt. To separate,* as things to a distance from each other; to disperse; to throw loosely about; to sprinkle; to set thinly.—*vi.* To be dispersed or dissipated. [Sax. *scateran*—Goth. *skaidan,* to part.]

Scattered, skat'tėrd, *p.a.* Thinly spread; dispersed.

Scavenger, ska'ven-jėr, *n.* A person whose employment is to *scrape* or clean the streets of a city. [Sax. *scafan,* to shave.]

Scene, sēn, *n. A stage;* the place where dramatic pieces are exhibited; the whole series of actions connected; a division of an act; the imaginary place, time, &c., in which the action of a play occurs; the curtain adapted to the play; the place where anything is exhibited; a regular disposition; an exhibition of strong feeling between two or more persons; a large painted view generally. [Fr. *scène*—Gr. *skēnē,* a covered place—Sans. *sku,* to cover.]

Scenery, sēn'ė-ri, *n. Scenes in general;* the appearance of the various objects presented to view; the representation of the place in which an action is performed; the paintings representing the scenery of a play.

Scenic, sēn'ik, *a. Pertaining to scenery;* dramatic; theatrical. [L. *scenicus.*]

Scenographic, sēn-o-grafʹik, *a. Pertaining to scenography.*

Scenography, sēn-og'ra-fi, *n. The art of representing scenes;* a description of a body in all its dimensions as it appears to the eye; art of perspective. [Gr. *skenographia*—*skēnē,* a scene, and *graphō,* to write.]

Scent, sent, *n.* That which causes the *sensation of* smell; odour; that substance which, issuing from a body, affects the olfactory organs of animals; perfume; the power of smelling; chase followed by the scent; track.—*vt. To discern* by the sense of smell; to imbue or fill with odour, good or bad. [Fr. *senteur*—L. *sentio,* to discern by the senses.]

Scented, sent'ed, *p.a.* Perfumed; imbued with odour.

Sceptic, skep'tik, *n. One who looks about him;* one who doubts the truth of any system of doctrines; a person who doubts the existence of God, or the truth of revelation. [Fr. *sceptique* —Gr. *skeptomai,* to look about.]

Sceptical, skep'tik-al, *a.* Doubting; doubting the truth of revelation.

Sceptically, skep'tik-al-li, *adv. In a sceptical manner;* with doubt.

Scepticism, skep'ti-sizm, *n.* The doctrines of the sceptical philosophers; universal doubt; a doubting of the truth of revelation. [Fr. *scepticisme.*]

Sceptre, sep'tėr, *n. A staff* borne by kings and chiefs on solemn occasions, as a badge of authority; the appropriate ensign of royalty; royal power. *vt.* To invest with royal authority. *ppr.* sceptring, *pret. & pp.* sceptred. [Fr.—Gr. *skēptron,* a staff.]

Sceptred, sep'tėrd, *p.a. Invested with a sceptre;* bearing a sceptre.

Schedule, se'dūl, *n.* A small *piece of paper,* containing some writing; a piece of paper or parchment annexed to a larger writing, as to a will, a deed, a lease, &c.; a piece of paper containing an inventory of goods. — *vt. To place in a schedule* or inventory. *ppr.* scheduling, *pret. & pp.* scheduled. [L. *schedula*—*scindo,* to cut.]

Scheme, skēm, *n.* The manner in which an object *has* or *holds itself;* shape; frame; outward appearance; a combination of things connected and adjusted by design; a plan; a project; a plot.—*vt.* To plan; to contrive.—*vi.* To form a plan or plans; to contrive. *ppr.* scheming, *pret. & pp.* schemed. [Gr. *schēma*—*echō,* to have.]

Schemer, skēm'ėr, *n.* One who contrives; a contriver; a planner.

Scheming, skēm'ing, *p.a. Given to forming schemes;* intriguing.—*p.n. Act of one who schemes.*

Schism, sizm, *n. A division;* a division in a church or denomination of Christians; separation; division among classes of people. [Gr. *schisma*—*schiō,* to split.]

Schismatic, Schismatical, siz-mat'ik, siz-mat'ik-al, *a. Pertaining to schism;* partaking of the nature of schism. [Late Gr. *schismatikos.*]

Schismatic, siz-mat'ik, *n. One guilty of schism;* one who separates from an established church or religious faith.

Schismatically, siz-mat'ik-al-li, *adv. In a schismatical manner;* by schism.

Fäte, fär, fat, fạll; mē, met, hėr; pīne, pin; nōte, not, mōve; tūbe, tub, bụll; oil, pound.

Schist, shist, n. A rock having a slaty structure. [Gr. *schistos*, cleaved—*schizō*, to split.]
Schistose, shist'ōs, a. Slaty or imperfectly slaty in structure.
Scholar, skol'ėr, n. One who devotes his spare time to study; a person devoted to letters; a man of letters; one who learns of a teacher; a pupil; any member of a college or school; emphatically used, a man eminent for erudition; a person of high attainments in science or literature; one who learns anything. [Old Fr. *escolier*—Gr. *scholē*, leisure, spare time.]
Scholar-like, **Scholarly**, skol'ėr-līk, skol'ėr-li, a. Like a scholar; becoming a scholar.
Scholarship, skol'ėr-ship, n. The acquirements of a scholar; erudition; attainments in science or literature; foundation for the support of a student in the English universities.
Scholastic, skō-las'tik, a. Pertaining to a scholar, to a school, or to schools; pertaining to the schoolmen, or philosophers and divines of the middle ages; pedantic; needlessly subtle.—n. One who adheres to the method or subtilties of the schoolmen. [Gr. *scholastikos*.]
Scholiast, skō'li-ast, n. A writer of scholia; a name given to the old grammarians who wrote on the margins of the manuscripts, annotations, called scholia. [Gr. *scholiastes*.]
Scholium, skō'li-um, n. **Scholia** or **Scholiums**, pl. A note or remark occasionally made on some passage, proposition, or the like. [Gr. *scholion*, that in which leisure is employed.]
School, skōl, n. A place where leisure is afforded for instruction; a place in which persons are instructed in any kind of learning; the instruction of a collection of pupils; the collective body of pupils; the state of instruction; a place of education, or collection of pupils, of any kind; a system of doctrine taught by particular teachers; any place of learning or improvement.—a. Relating to a school, or to education; scholastic.—vt. To instruct; to educate; to teach with superiority; to chide and admonish; to reprove. [Old Fr. *escole*, Fr. *école*—L. *schola*—Gr. *scholē*, leisure.]
School-divine, skōl'di-vin, n. One versed in scholastic theology.
School-fellow, skōl'fel-lō, n. One bred at the same school; a school associate.
Schooling, skōl'ing, p.n. Instruction in school; price or reward paid to an instructor for teaching pupils; reprimand.
School-man, skōl'man, n. A man versed in the niceties of academical disputation or of school-divinity.
Schoolmaster, skōl'mas-tėr, n. He who presides over and teaches a school; the preceptor of a school; he or that which disciplines, instructs, and leads.
Schoolmistress, skōl'mis-tres, n. She who governs and teaches a school.
Schooner, skön'ėr, n. A vessel having two masts, and fore-and-aft sails like those of a sloop. A schooner differs from a brig chiefly in the rig of the mainmast. [D. from *schoon*, fair, beautiful.]
Sciatic, si-at'ik, a. Pertaining to the hip; affecting the hip. [Gr. *ischion*, the hip-joint.]
Science, sī'ens, n. That which the mind sees; that which one knows; learning; knowledge reduced to a system; a collection of the leading truths relating to any subject, arranged in systematic order; art built on principles; any branch of knowledge. [Fr.—L. *scio*, to know—Heb. *sakа*, to look upon.]
Scientific, sī-en-tif'ik, a. According to the principles of science; producing certain knowledge; well versed in science. [Fr. *scientifique*.]
Scientifically, sī-en-tif'ik-al-li, adv. In a scientific manner.
Scimitar, si'mi-tär, n. A short curved sword with a convex edge, used by the Persians and Turks. [Fr. *cimeterre*.]
Scintillate, sin'til-lāt, vi. To emit sparks; to sparkle, as the fixed stars. [L. *scintillo, scintillatum—scintilla*, a spark.]
Scintillation, sin-til-lā'shon, n. Act of emitting sparks; intellectual splendour; coruscation. [L. *scintillatio*.]
Sciolism, sī'ol-izm, n. Superficial knowledge.
Sciolist, sī'ol-ist, n. One who knows little, or who knows many things superficially; a smatterer. [L. *sciolus*, a smatterer—*scio*, to know.]
Scion, sī'on, n. A cutting or slip prepared for the purpose of being ingrafted upon some other tree; a small twig or young shoot; an offshoot; a descendant. [Fr.—L. *scindo*, to cut.]
Scirrhous, skī'rus, a. Pertaining to or proceeding from a scirrhus.
Scirrhus, skī'rus, n. Any hard coat; a hardened swelling or tumour, as in a gland. [Gr. *skiros*, any hard coat or covering.]
Scissors, siz'orz, n. pl. A cutting instrument, resembling shears, but smaller. [Fr. *cisaux*—L. *scindo*, to cut.]
Sclavonian, **Slavonic**, skla-vō'ni-an, sla-von'ik, a. Pertaining to the Sclavini, or Slavic race. The Slavonian tongue is that of Indian origin, and contains a great number of Sanscrit roots. [Late Gr. *Sklabēnoi*.]
Scoff, skof, vi. To treat a person or thing with insolent ridicule, mockery, or contumelious language; to manifest contempt by derision (with *at*).—n. Derision, mockery, or reproach, expressed in language of contempt; expression of scorn or contempt. [Old G. *scopf*, a mockery.]
Scoffer, skof'ėr, n. One who scoffs; one who mocks; a scorner.
Scoffing, skof'ing, p.a. Treating with reproachful language.—p.n. The act of treating with scorn.
Scoffingly, skof'ing-li, adv. In mockery or contempt; by way of derision.
Scold, skōld, vi. To chide rudely, as in accusing of sin, or claiming a debt; to utter railing.—vt. To give a chiding to with boisterous clamour; to chide; to rebuke; to reprove.—n. A rude, clamorous, foul-mouthed woman; a brawl. [Sax. *scyld*, crime, guilt.]
Scolding, skōld'ing, p.a. Given to scolding.—p.n. The uttering of rude, clamorous language by way of rebuke; railing language.
Scollop, skol'lop. See SCALLOP.
Sconce, skons, n. Primarily, a fort; a candlestick affixed to and projecting from a wall, usually having a reflector; the circular tube with a brim in a candlestick, into which the candle is inserted; a head-piece; a helmet; the head; the skull. [D. *schans*.]
Scoop, skōp, n. A kind of hollow ladle, of various sizes, and usually of an elongated form; anything hollow used for scooping; a sweep; a stroke.—vt. To take out with a scoop; to empty by lading; to make hollow, as a scoop or dish; to remove, so as to leave a place hollow. [Fr. *écope*; Gr. *skaptō*, to dig.]
Scope, skōp, n. The mark on which one fixes the eye; mark; that which is viewed; extent; room; the limit of intellectual view; the end to which the mind directs its view; that which is purposed to be reached; aim or purpose; drift; liberty; room to move in; liberty beyond just limits; license. [Gr. *skopos*—*skeptomai*, to view.]
Scorbutic, skor-būt'ik, a. Affected with scurvy; subject to scurvy; pertaining to scurvy. [Fr. *scorbutique*.]
Scorch, skorch, vt. To cause to peel by heat, as the skin; to subject to a degree of heat that changes both the colour and texture of the surface; to burn. vi. To be burned on the surface; to be dried up. [Old Fr. *escorcher*—L. *ex*, and *corium*, the skin.]
Scorching, skorch'ing, p.a. Burning on the surface; paining by heat.
Score, skōr, n. A cut or incision; a line drawn; a reckoning kept by lines; the number twenty, because every twenty was signified by a notch; an account kept of something past; an era; debt, or account of debt; account; ground; sake; the original and entire draught of any musical composition.—vt. To mark by incisions; to mark by a line; to set down, as a debt; to set down or take, as an account; to charge; to form, as a score in music. ppr. scoring, pret. & pp. scored. [Sax. *scor*; Icel. *skora*, to make an incision.]
Scorer, skōr'ėr, n. One who scores; an instrument used by woodmen in marking numbers on timber trees.
Scoria, skō'ri-a, n. **Scoriæ**, pl. Dross; the dross of metals in fusion, or the slag rejected after the reduction of metallic ores; the cellular, slaggy lavas of a volcano. [L.—Gr. *skōr*, dung.]
Scorn, skorn, n. Primarily, dung; disdain; that disdainful feeling or treatment which springs from a person's opinion of the meanness of an object; that which is treated with contempt. vt. To throw dirt or dung at; to hold in extreme contempt; to slight; to neglect.—vi. To show contumely. [Sax. *scearn*, dung.]
Scorner, skorn'ėr, n. One who scorns; a contemner; a scoffer.
Scornful, skorn'fụl, a. Filled with scorn; contemptuous; acting in defiance; neglectful; insolent.
Scornfully, skorn'fụl-li, adv. With extreme contempt; insolently.
Scorning, skorn'ing, p.n. The act of contemning; a disregarding.
Scorpion, skor'pi-on, n. A lobster-shaped insect whose sting produces excruciating pain; the eighth sign of the zodiac, which the sun enters about Oct. 23; a painful scourge. [L. *scorpio*.]
Scot, skot, n. An inhabitant or native of Scotland.
Scotch, skoch, a. Pertaining to Scotland or its inhabitants.
Scotch, skoch, n. A slight cut or shallow incision; a line drawn on the ground, as in hop-scotch.—vt. To cut with shallow incisions.
Scotched, skocht, p.a. Cut with shallow incisions.
Scotchman, skoch'man, n. A native of Scotland.
Scot-free, skot'frē, a. Free from payment; untaxed; clear; safe. [Sax. *scot-freoh—scot* for *sceat*, money, *freoh*, free.]
Scots, skots, a. Same as Scotch.
Scotsman, skots'man, n. Same as Scotchman.

---

ch, chain; j, job; g, go; ng, sing; ᴛʜ, then; th, thin; w, wig; wh, whig; zh, azure; † obsolete.

Scotticism, skot'i-sizm, n. An idiom peculiar to the natives of Scotland.

Scottish, akot'ish, a. Pertaining to the inhabitants of Scotland, or to their country or language.

Scoundrel, skoun'drel, n. A skulker; a mean, worthless fellow; a man without honour or virtue.—a. Low; base. [said to be from It. *scondaruolo*—L. *abscondo*, to keep out of view.]

Scoundrelism, skoun'drel-izm, n. Quality of a scoundrel.

Scoundrelly, skoun'drel-i, a. Base.

Scour, skour, vt. To make clear or bright by rubbing; to clean by friction; to cleanse from grease, dirt, &c., as articles of dress; to purge violently; to range for the purpose of taking; to pass swiftly over; to brush along.—vi. To perform the business of cleaning by rubbing; to be purged to excess; to rove or range for taking something; to run with celerity; to scamper. [G. *scheuern*—Goth. *skeirs*, clear, bright—Gael. *sgàr*, to cleanse, to purify.]

Scourer, skour'er, n. One who scours or cleans by rubbing.

Scourge, skerj, n. A whip made of stripes of leather, cords, &c.; an instrument of punishment; a vindictive affliction; he or that which greatly afflicts; particularly, any continued calamity.—vt. To lash with a scourge; to punish with severity; to afflict for sins or faults; to harass or injure. ppr. scourging, pret. & pp. scourged. [Fr. *escourpée*—L. *corrigia*, a shoe-tie—*rego*, to set right.]

Scourger, skerj'er, n. One who scourges.

Scouring, skour'ing, p.n. A rubbing hard for cleaning; a cleansing from grease, dirt, &c.; a cleansing by a purge; a running swiftly.

Scout, skout, n. One sent out to listen clandestinely; a person sent before an army for the purpose of observing the motions of an enemy.—vi. To act as a scout; to go on the business of watching the motions of an enemy. [Old Fr. *escout*—L. *ausculto*, to listen to.]

Scout, skout, vt. To sneer at; to treat with disdain and contempt.

Scowl, skoul, vi. To wrinkle the brows, as in frowning or displeasure; to look gloomy or frowning (with *at*).—n. The wrinkling of the brows, as in frowning; the expression of displeasure or discontent in the countenance; dark or rude aspect. [Sax. *scool*; Icel. *skœla*, to twist.]

Scowling, skoul'ing, p.a. Frowning; expressing sullenness.

Scowlingly, skoul'ing-li, adv. With a wrinkled, frowning aspect.

Scrag, skrag, n. Something dry or lean with roughness. [Gael. *sgreag*, to dry, to parch.]

Scragged, Scraggy, skrag'ed, skrag'i, a. Shrivelled; rough with irregular points or a broken surface.

Scragginess, skrag'i-nes, n. State of being scraggy; leanness with roughness; roughness occasioned by broken, irregular points.

Scramble, skram'bl, vi. To move or climb by seizing objects with the hand, and drawing the body forward; to catch with haste preventive of another; to catch at without ceremony. n. Act of scrambling; act of climbing by the help of the hands; an eager contest for something. [Armor. *skrampa*, to crawl.]

Scrambler, skram'bl-er, n. One who scrambles.

Scrambling, skram'bl-ing, p.n. Act of climbing by the help of the hands;

act of seizing or catching at with eager haste.

Scrap, skrap, n. Something scraped off; a small piece; a part; a detached piece, as scraps of history or poetry; a small piece of paper. [from *scrape*.]

Scrap-book, skrap'buk, n. A blank book for the preservation of short extracts, drawings, prints, and original contributions.

Scrape, skrāp, vt. To draw something, usually something edged, over the surface of; to rub the surface of with a sharp or rough instrument; to clean by scraping; to act upon the surface of with a grating noise; to collect by harsh laborious effort.—vi. To make the sound of the foot drawn over the floor; to make a harsh noise; to play awkwardly on a violin; to make an awkward bow. ppr. scraping, pret. & pp. scraped.—n. A rubbing; the sound of the foot drawn over the floor; a bow; perplexity; distress. [Sax. *screopan*.]

Scraper, skrāp'er, n. An instrument with which anything is scraped; a miser; an awkward fiddler.

Scraping, skrāp'ing, p.n. Act of one that scrapes; the portion of matter scraped off.

Scratch, skrach, vt. To mark with slight incisions ragged and uneven; to rub and tear the surface of with something sharp or ragged; to wound slightly; to rub with the nails; to dig with the claws.—vi. To use the claws in tearing the surface.—n. A break in the surface of a thing made by scratching; a laceration with the nails or claws; a slight wound; a scrawl. [G. *kratsen*—Gr. *charatto*, to scratch.]

Scratcher, skrach'er, n. He or that which scratches.

Scrawl, skral, vt. To write or draw carelessly; to write awkwardly.—vi. To write inelegantly.—n. Unskilful writing, or a piece of hasty, bad writing. [another form of *scroll*.]

Scrawler, skral'er, n. One who scrawls.

Scream, skrēm, vi. To utter a sudden, sharp outcry, as in a fright or in extreme pain; to utter a shrill, harsh cry; to shriek; to screech as a bird.—n. A sharp, shrill cry, uttered suddenly, as in terror or in pain; the shrill cry of a bird. [D. *schroom*, fear—*schromen*, to tremble.]

Screaming, skrēm'ing, p.n. Act of crying out with a shriek of terror or agony.

Screech, skrēch, vi. To cry out with a sharp, shrill voice; to utter a sudden, shrill cry, as in acute pain; to shriek; to utter a sharp cry, as an owl.—n. A sharp, shrill cry, uttered in acute pain; a harsh, shrill cry. [Ir. *sgreach*, a screech.]

Screen, skrēn, n. Anything that cuts off inconvenience; that which protects from danger; a partition in churches, &c., carried up to a certain height, as an altar-screen, &c.; a single open colonnade in front of a building; something movable, used to exclude heat, cold, or light; a long coarse riddle, used to separate the coarser from the finer parts, as of coal, sand, &c.—vt. To cut off from danger; to afford protection to by hiding; to shield; to pass through a screen; to separate the coarse part of from the fine. [Old Fr. *escran*; G. *schirm*, a screen.]

Screening, skrēn'ing, p.n. Act of sheltering; act of sifting earth, sand, coals, &c., through a large oblong sieve.

Screw, skrū, n. A cylinder of wood or metal, grooved spirally, like the windings of a small shell, and used as a mechanical instrument to produce pressure; a grooved piece of iron, used for fastening together pieces of wood or metal; an extortioner.—vt. To turn or apply a screw to; to make firm by a screw; to squeeze; to oppress by exactions; to distort. [Lapponic *skruw*, a snail, snail-shell—*skruwet*, to twist.]

Screw-bolt, skrū'bolt, n. A bolt with a screw at one end, on which a nut is placed, used for fastening together two or more pieces of timber or metal.

Screw-key, skrū'kē, n. An instrument for turning large screws or their nuts.

Screw-nail, skrū'nāl, n. A cylindrical nail grooved like a screw, used for fastening together pieces of wood, &c.

Screw-press, skrū'pres, n. A machine for communicating pressure by means of a screw or screws.

Screw-propeller, skrū'prō-pel-er, n. A contrivance on the principle of the screw, for propelling steam-vessels.

Screw-steamer, skrū'stēm-er, n. A steamer propelled by a screw.

Scribble, skrib'l, vt. To write without care or regard to correctness or elegance; to fill with worthless writing. vi. To write without care or beauty. ppr. scribbling, pret. & pp. scribbled. n. Hasty or careless writing. [formerly *scrabble*.]

Scribbler, skrib'l-er, n. A petty author.

Scribbling, skrib'l-ing, p.n. Act of scribbling or writing hastily.

Scribe, skrīb, n. A writer; a public writer; a clerk; a writer and a doctor of the law, among the Jews; one who read and explained the law to the people. [L. *scriba*—*scribo*, to write.]

Scrimer†, skrim'er, n. A fencing-master.

Scrip, skrip, n. A small bag; a wallet; a satchel. [Icel. *skreppa*, a purse.]

Scrip, skrip, n. Something written; a written paper; an interim writing entitling a party to a share or shares in any company, which writing is exchanged after registration for a formal certificate. [L. *scriptum*—*scribo*, to write.]

Scrippage†, skrip'aj, n. That which is contained in a scrip.

Scriptural, skrip'tūr-al, a. Contained in the Scriptures; according to the Scriptures.

Scripturally, skrip'tūr-al-li, adv. In a Scriptural manner.

Scripture, skrip'tūr, n. A writing; appropriately, the books of the Old and New Testaments; the Bible.—a. Scriptural. [L. *scriptura*—*scribo*, to write.]

Scrivener, skriv'en-er, n. A scribe; formerly, one whose occupation was to draw contracts or other writings; one whose business is to place money at interest. [Old Fr. *escrivain*—L. *scribo*, to write.]

Scrofula, skro'fū-la, n. A constitutional disease, generally hereditary, which affects the lymphatic glands, oftenest those of the neck; king's-evil. [L. *scrophilla*, a swelling of the glands of the neck—*scrofa*, a breeding sow.]

Scrofulous, skro'fū-lus, a. Pertaining to scrofula; affected with scrofula.

Scroll, skrōl, n. A roll of paper or parchment; a rough draught of anything; a kind of spiral ornament in architecture; the volute of the Ionic and Corinthian capital. [from *roll*.]

Scrolled, skrōld, p.a. Formed into a scroll.

Scroyle†, skroil, n. A mean fellow; a wretch.

Scrub, skrub, vt. To rub hard with a brush, or with something coarse or

Fāte, fār, fat, fall; mē, met, hėr; pīne, pin; nōte, not, mōve; tūbe, tub, bull; oil, pound.

Scrubbed, scrubby, skrŭb'ed, skrŭb'i, a. Small and mean; shabby.

rough, for the purpose of scouring or making bright.—vi. To work hard; to be diligent and penurious. ppr. scrubbing, pret. & pp. scrubbed.—n. One who labours hard and lives meanly; a worn-out brush.—a. Mean; dirty. [G. schrubben—reiben, to rub.]

Scrubber, skrŭb'ėr, n. He or that which scrubs; a hard broom.

Scruple, skrö'pl, n. A weight of 20 grains in apothecaries' weight; a very small quantity; uneasiness; anxiety; hesitation from the difficulty of determining what is right; reluctance to decide; perplexity.—vi. To have hesitation about doing anything; to doubt. ppr. scrupling, pret. & pp. scrupled. [Fr. scrupule—L. scrupus, a sharp or rough stone.]

Scrupulosity, skrū-pū-los'i-ti, n. Quality or state of being scrupulous; doubt; doubtfulness; preciseness. [Late L. scrupulositas.]

Scrupulous, skrū'pū-lus, a. Having scruples; nicely doubtful; cautious; conscientious; nice; exact; captious. [Fr. scrupuleux.]

Scrupulously, skrū'pū-lus-li, adv. With scrupulousness or vigilance; with a nice regard to minute particulars or to exact propriety.

Scrupulousness, skrū'pū-lus-nes, n. State or quality of being scrupulous; caution in determining or in acting.

Scrutineer, skrū-ti-nēr', n. One who scrutinises.

Scrutinize, skrū'ti-nīz, vt. To examine or inquire into critically; to investigate; to regard narrowly. ppr. scrutinizing, pret. & pp. scrutinized.

Scrutinizing, skrū'ti-nīz-ing, p.a. Inquiring into with critical minuteness or exactness; searching closely.

Scrutinizingly, skrū'ti-nīz-ing-li, adv. In a scrutinizing manner.

Scrutiny, skrū'ti-ni, n. Careful search, as into things cast aside, for something useful; careful investigation; an examination of the votes given at an election for the purpose of correcting the poll. [Fr. scrutin—Gr. grutē, trash.]

Scud, skud, vi. To shoot along; to run with haste; to be driven; to be driven with precipitation before a tempest, as a ship.—vt. To pass over quickly. ppr. scudding, pret. & pp. scudded.—n. A driving along; loose vapoury clouds driven swiftly by the wind. [Dan. skyde, to shoot, shove.]

Scuffle, skuf'l, n. A confused contest, in which the parties push or shove violently against each other; a tumultuous struggle for victory; a fight.—vi. To strive or contend, as small parties. ppr. scuffling, pret. & pp. scuffled. [Sax. scufan, to shove.]

Sculk, skulk, vi. To retire into a covered place for concealment; to lurk; to lie close from shame, fear of injury, or detection. [Dan. skulke, to sneak.]

Sculker, skulk'ėr, n. A lurker; one who lies close for hiding.

Scull, skul, n. A shoal of fish.

Scull, skul, n. A boat; a cock-boat, probably so named from its resemblance to a drinking-vessel; an oar, so short that one man can work a pair.—vt. To impel, as a boat by moving and turning an oar over the stern. [Sw. Goth. skol, a drinking-vessel.]

Sculler, skul'ėr, n. One who sculls; a boat rowed by one man with two sculls.

Scullery, skul'ė-ri, n. A place where dishes, kettles, and other culinary utensils, are cleaned and kept. [Old Fr. escuelle; L. scutella, a waiter.]

Scullion, skul'i-on, n. A servant of the scullery; a servant that cleans pots and kettles. [Old Fr. sculier.]

Sculptor, skulp'tor, n. One who sculptures; an artist in sculpture; one whose occupation is to carve wood or stone into images or figures. [L.]

Sculptural, skulp'tūr-al, a. Pertaining to sculpture.

Sculpture, skulp'tūr, n. The art of cutting wood or stone into images of men, beasts, or other things; carved work. vt. To engrave; to form, as images or figures with the chisel on wood, stone, or metal. ppr. sculpturing, pret. & pp. sculptured. [Fr.—L. sculpo, sculptum, to carve.]

Sculptured, skulp'tūrd, p.a. Carved; engraved.

Scum, skum, n. Foam; impurities which rise to the surface of liquors in boiling or fermentation; the refuse; that which is vile or worthless.—vt. To take the scum from; to clear off the impure matter from the surface of; to skim. ppr. scumming, pret. & pp. scummed. [Sw. skum; Old Fr. escume.]

Scummer, skum'ėr, n. An instrument used for taking off the scum of liquors; a skimmer. [Fr. écumoire.]

Scummings, skum'ingz, n. pl. The matter skimmed from boiling liquors.

Scupper, skup'ėr, n. One of the holes cut through the water-ways and sides of a ship for discharging the water from the deck. [Sp. escupir—L. spuo, to spit out.]

Scurf, skėrf, n. A dry sort of scab or mealy crust formed on the skin of an animal; anything adhering to the surface. [Sax.—sceorfan, to shave.]

Scurfy, skėrf'i, a. Having scurf; covered with scurf; resembling scurf.

Scurrile, sku'ril, a. Such as befits a buffoon or vulgar jester; low. [L. scurrilis—scurra, a buffoon.]

Scurrility, sku-ril'i-ti, n. Such low or abusive language as is used by buffoons and the like; grossness of reproach; abuse; indecency. [Fr. scurrilité.]

Scurrilous, sku'ril-us, a. Using the language of buffoons; foul-mouthed; containing low indecency or abuse.

Scurrilously, sku'ril-us-li, adv. In a scurrilous manner; with gross reproach.

Scurvily, skėr'vi-li, adv. In a scurvy manner; basely; meanly.

Scurviness, skėr'vi-nes, n. Quality or state of being scurvy.

Scurvy, skėr'vi, n. A scurfy sort of disease affecting the arms and legs, and accompanied by bleeding from almost all the mucous membranes.—a. Scurfy; diseased with scurvy; vile; worthless; contemptible. [from scurf.]

Scutcheon, skuch'on, n. See ESCUTCHEON.

Scuttle, skut'l, n. A broad, shallow basket, so called from its resemblance to a dish or platter; a metal pail for holding coal. [Sax. scutel—L. scutella, a salver.]

Scuttle, skut'l, n. A small hatchway in the deck of a ship, with a lid for covering it; also, a like hole in the side or bottom of a ship, and through the coverings of her hatchways, &c.—vt. To sink, as a ship, by making holes through the bottom. ppr. scuttling, pret. & pp. scuttled. [Old Fr. escoutille, the hatchway of a ship.]

Scuttle, skut'l, n. A running with affected haste; a quick pace; a short run. [from scud.]

Scythe, sīvᴇ, n. A species of sickle; an implement for mowing grass or cutting grain; the curved, sharp blade anciently affixed to war-chariots.—vt. To cut with a scythe. ppr. scything, pret. & pp. scythed. [Sax. sithe—L. seco, sectum, to cut.]

Scythed, sīvᴅ, a. Armed with scythes as a chariot.

Sea, sē, n. A large body of water; a lake; the ocean; the main; a surge; the swell of the ocean in a tempest; a large cistern or laver; a large quantity of liquid; a rough or agitated place. [Sax. sæ; Goth. saivs—Sans. sarus, a lake.]

Sea-bank, sē'bangk, n. The sea-shore; a bank or mole to defend against the sea.

Sea-bathing, sē'bāᴠн-ing, n. A bathing in the sea.

Sea-beach, sē'bēch, n. A beach bordering on the sea.

Sea-board, sē'bōrd, n. The sea-border or sea-shore.—adv. Toward the sea.

Sea-breach, sē'brēch, n. Irruption of the sea. [sea and breach.]

Sea-breeze, sē'brēz, n. A wind blowing from the sea.

Sea-coast, sē'kōst, n. The shore or border of the land adjacent to the sea.

Seafaring, sē'fār-ing, a. Following the business of a seaman; customarily employed in navigation or seamanship.

Sea-gage, sē'gāj, n. The depth that a vessel sinks in the water.

Sea-girt, sē'gėrt, a. Surrounded by the sea or ocean. [sea and girt.]

Sea-going, sē'gō-ing, a. Travelling by sea; sailing on the sea.

Sea-green, sē'grēn, a. Having the colour of sea-water; being of a faint bluish-green colour.

Sea-horse, sē'hors, n. The walrus or morse.

Sea-kings, sē'kingz, n. pl. A name given to the northmen pirate kings who infested the European coasts in the eighth and ninth centuries.

Seal, sēl, n. A piece of metal or other hard substance, on which is engraved some image or device used for making impressions on wax; the wax set to an instrument, and stamped with a seal; the wax or wafer that makes fast a letter; any act of confirmation; that which confirms; that which effectually secures; that which makes fast.—vt. To fasten with a seal; to attach together with a wafer or with wax; to set a seal to, as a mark of authenticity; to establish; to shut or keep close; to make fast; to mark with a stamp, as an evidence of standard exactness.—vi. To affix a seal. [Sax. sigel; L. sigillasignum, a token.]

Seal, sēl, n. The sea-calf; a marine, carnivorous mammal, with four feet fitted for swimming, highly prized for its skin and oil. [Sax. seol; Goth. saivs, the sea.]

Sealed, sēld, p.a. Fastened with a seal; confirmed; closed.

Seal-engraving, sēl'en-grāv-ing, n. The art of engraving gems for seals.

Sealer, sēl'ėr, n. One who seals; an officer in chancery who seals writs.

Sea-level, sē'le-vel, n. The level of the surface of the sea.

Sea-light, sē'līt, n. The light proceeding from a light-house.

Sealing, sēl'ing, p.n. Act of affixing a seal; (from seal, the animal) the operation of taking seals and curing their skins.

ch, chain; j, job; g, go; ng, sing; ᴛʜ, then; th, thin; w, wig; wh, whig; zh, asure; † obsolete.

Sealing-wax, sēl'ing-waks, n. Wax for sealing letters, &c.; a coloured compound of lac with some other resin, used for sealing letters, legal documents, &c.

Seam, sēm, n. The suture or uniting of two edges of cloth by the needle; a line of juncture; the joint of planks in a ship's side or deck; the intervals between the edges of boards in a floor, &c.; a vein of metal, and the like; a thin layer which separates strata of greater magnitude; a scar.—vt. To unite by a seam; to sew or otherwise unite; to scar. [Sax.—suwm, Sans. sv, to sew.]

Seamt, sēm, n. Tallow; lard. [Sax. seim.]

Seaman, sē'man, n. A mariner; one skilled in navigation.

Seamanship, sē'man-ship, n. The art or skill of a good seaman.

Sea-margot, sē'märj, n. The shore of the sea.

Sea-mark, sē'märk, n. Any elevated object on land which serves as a direction to mariners in entering a harbour, or in sailing along a coast; a beacon.

Sea-monster, sē'mon-stèr, n. A huge marine animal.

Seamstress, sēm'stres, n. A woman whose occupation is sewing.

Seamy, sēm'i, a. Having a seam; containing seams.

Sea-nymph, sē'nimf, n. A nymph or goddess of the sea.

Sea-piece, sē'pēs, n. A picture representing a scene at sea.

Sea-port, sē'pōrt, n. A port near the sea, formed by an arm of the sea or by a bay; a city or town situated on a harbour, on or near the sea.

Sear, sēr, vt. To burn to dryness and hardness, as the surface of anything; to dry; to make callous or insensible. a. Dry; no longer green or fresh; withered. [Sax. searian—Gr. seiros, hot.]

Search, serch, vt. To look around for; to look over for the purpose of finding something; to explore; to scrutinize; to probe; to seek the knowledge of by feeling with an instrument; to put to the test.—vi. To make search; to look for; to inquire.—n. Act of searching; a seeking for something that is lost, or the place of which is unknown; scrutiny; inquiry; quest; pursuit for finding. [Fr. chercher—L. circus, a circle.]

Searcher, serch'èr, n. He or that which searches; a seeker; an inquirer; a trier.

Searching, sèrch'ing, p.a. Penetrating; trying; close.

Searchingly, serch'ing-li, adv. In a searching manner.

Sear-cloth, sēr'kloth, n. A cloth to cover a sore; a plaster. [Sax. sarclath.]

Seared, sērd, p.a. Hardened.

Searedness, sèrd'nes, n. State of being seared; hardness; insensibility.

Sea-room, sē'rōm, n. Ample space or distance from land, for a vessel at sea to ride out a gale with safety.

Sea-rover, sē'rōv-èr, n. One who roves over the sea for plunder; a pirate.

Sea-serpent, sē'sèr-pent, n. A species of water-snake; an enormous marine animal resembling a serpent, said to have been repeatedly seen on the coasts of America, and now commonly reckoned as fabulous.

Sea-service, sē'sèrv-is, n. Naval-service; service in ships of war.

Sea-shore, sē'shōr, n. The shore of the sea.

Sea-sick, sē'sik, a. Affected with sickness or nausea caused by the pitching or rolling of a vessel at sea.

Sea-side, sē'sīd, n. The land bordering on the sea.

Season, sē'zn, n. A standing still; a period of time when the temperature becomes stationary or nearly so; a proper time; the usual time; any time; one of the four divisions of the year; that which prepares for the taste; that which gives a relish to.—vt. To fit for any use by time or habit; to render suitable; to prepare for a climate; to accustom to; to render palatable; to give a zest to; to preserve by salting; to moderate; to tinge or taint.—vi. To become seasoned; to grow fit for use; to become adapted to a climate. [Fr. saison—L. statio, a standing still—sto, to stand.]

Seasonable, sē'zn-a-bl, a. That comes or is done in due season; opportune.

Seasonableness, sē'zn-a-bl-nes, n. State of being seasonable.

Seasonably, sē'zn-a-bli, adv. In due time; in time convenient.

Seasoned, sē'znd, p.a. Mixed with something that gives a relish.

Seasoner, sē'zn-ér, n. He who seasons; that which seasons or gives a relish to.

Seasoning, sē'zn-ing, p.n. That which is added to any species of food to give it a higher relish; something added to enhance the pleasure of enjoyment.

Seat, sēt, n. That on which one sits; a chair, &c.; site; situation; chair of state; tribunal; mansion; a pew or slip in a church; the place where a thing is settled or established.—vt. To place on a seat; to settle; to place in a post of authority; to fix in a particular place; to set firm; to place in a church. [Icel. sæti, a seat—L. sedeo, Sans. sad, to sit.]

Sea-term, sē'tèrm, n. A nautical or naval term.

Seating, sēt'ing, p.n. Act of placing on a seat; materials for seats.

Seaward, sē'ward, a. Directed toward the sea.—adv. Toward the sea.

Sea-weed, sē'wēd, n. A marine plant.

Sea-worn, sē'wōrn, a. Worn or abraded by the sea.

Sea-worthiness, sē'wèr-thi-nes, n. State of being sea-worthy, as a ship.

Sea-worthy, sē'wèr-thi, a. Fit to go to sea; worthy of being trusted to transport a cargo with safety.

Secant, sē'kant, a. A line that cuts another line, whether right or curved, or divides it into parts. [L. secans, cutting—seco, to cut.]

Secede, sē-sēd', vi. To go apart; to withdraw from fellowship or association. ppr. seceding, pret. & pp. seceded. [L. secedo—se, apart, and cedo, to go.]

Seceder, sē-sēd'èr, n. One who secedes; one of a numerous body of Presbyterians who seceded from the Established Church of Scotland about A.D. 1733.

Secession, sē-se'shon, n. Act of seceding, particularly from communion with; withdrawal. [L. secessio.]

Seclude, sē-klūd', vt. To shut up apart; to exclude; to separate, as from company or society for some length of time. ppr. secluding, pret. & pp. secluded. [L. secludo—se, and claudo, to shut.]

Secluded, sē-klūd'ed, p.a. Shut up apart; living in retirement.

Seclusion, sē-klū'shon, n. Act of secluding; the state of being separate or apart; separation; retirement.

Second, se'kond, a. That immediately follow the first; the ordinal of two; next in value or rank; inferior.—n. One who comes after; one who attends another in a duel, to aid him; one who supports another; that which supports; the sixtieth part of a minute of time or of a degree.—vt. To follow in the next place; to lend aid to the attempt of; to assist; to back; to encourage; to express approval of, as a motion; to unite with, in proposing some measure. [L. secundus—sequor, to follow.]

Secondarily, se'kond-a-ri-li, adv. In the second degree or order; not primarily.

Secondary, se'kond-a-ri, a. Following next in order to the first; subordinate; not of the first order or rate; revolving about a primary planet; acting by delegated authority.—n. One who acts in subordination; a deputy. [Fr. secondaire.]

Second-class, se'kond-klas, a. Of second or inferior rank or quality.

Seconder, se'kond-èr, n. One who seconds what another proposes.

Second-hand, se'kond-hand, a. Received from another; not original; not new, that has been used by another.

Secondly, se'kond-li, adv. In the second place.

Second-rate, se'kond-rāt, a. Of the second order or class; second in size, rank, quality, or value.—n. The second order in size or value.

Second-sight, se'kond-sit, n. The power of intellectual vision; the power of seeing things future or distant which has been claimed by some of the Highlanders of Scotland.

Secrecy, sē'kre-si, n. The state of being secret; concealment from the observation of others; privacy; solitude; forbearance of disclosure; fidelity to a secret; the habit of keeping secrets.

Secret, sē'kret, a. Put apart; separate; hidden; concealed; secluded; private; being in retirement; removed from sight; unseen; not revealed; known to God only; not proper to be seen; such as ought to be kept from observation. n. Something studiously hidden; a thing not discovered; (pl.) the parts which modesty and propriety require to be concealed. [Fr.—L. se, and cerno, cretum, to distinguish.]

Secretary, se'kre-ta-ri, n. One intrusted with secrets; a person employed by a public body, by a company, or by an individual, to write orders, public or private papers, and the like; an officer of state whose business it is to superintend the affairs of a particular department of government. [Fr. secrétaire.]

Secretaryship, se'kre-ta-ri-ship, n. The office or employment of a secretary.

Secrete, sē-krēt', vt. To put apart; to hide; to separate, as substances from the blood in animals, or from the sap in vegetables. ppr. secreting, pret. & pp. secreted. [L. se, apart, and cerno, cretum, to distinguish.]

Secret-false, sē'kret-fals, a. Secret false.

Secretion, sē-krē'shon, n. Act of secreting; separation of substances from the blood, as in animals, or from the sap, as in vegetables; the matter secreted. [Low L. secretio.]

Secretly, sē'kret-li, adv. In a secret manner; privately; privily; inwardly.

Secretness, sē'kret-nes, n. State of being secret or of being hid or concealed.

Sect, sekt, n. A part cut off; a cutting; a body of persons cut off from the established religion of a country; a number of persons united in tenets, chiefly in philosophy or religion, but constituting a distinct party by holding sentiments different from those of other men; a denomination. [Fr. secte—L. seco, sectum, to cut.]

Fāte, fär, fat, fạll; mē, met, hér; pine, pin; nōte, not, mōve; tūbe, tub, bųll; oil, pound.

Sectarian, sek-tā'ri-an, a. Pertaining or peculiar to a sect.—n. One of a sect; one of a party in religion which has separated itself from the established church.

Sectarianism, sek-tā'ri-an-izm, n. State or quality of being sectarian.

Sectile, sek'til, a. That may be cut or divided; capable of being cut smoothly, as a mineral. [L. sectilis.]

Section, sok'shon, n. Act of cutting; a division; a distinct part or portion, as of a book; the subdivision of a chapter; the division of a law; a distinct part of a city, town, country, or people; the representation of an object cut asunder vertically. [Fr.—L. seco, to cut.]

Sectional, sek'shon-al, a. Pertaining to a section or distinct part of a larger body or territory; partial.

Sectionally, sek'shon-al-li, adv. In a sectional manner.

Sector, sek'tor, n. He or that which cuts; a part of a circle comprehended between two radii and the included arc. [L.—seco, to cut.]

Secular, se'kū-lėr, a. Pertaining to an age or division of time; coming once in a century; pertaining to this present world; worldly; among Roman Catholics, not regular; not confined to a monastery.—n. Not a spiritual person; a layman; an ecclesiastic of the Romish church not bound by monastic rules. [Fr. séculaire—L. seculum, an age, the world—sēquor, to follow.]

Secularity, se-kū-la ri-ti, n. State of being secular; worldliness.

Secularisation, se'kū-lār-iz-ā"shon, n. Act of secularizing; conversion from spiritual appropriation to secular use, as of a church or church property.

Secularize, se'kū-lār-iz, vt. To make se'ular; to convert from spiritual appropriation to secular use. ppr. secularising. pret. & pp. secularised. [Fr. séculariser.]

Secularly, e'kū-lār-li, adv. In a secular or worldly manner.

Secure, sē-kūr', a. Free from care; careless; without vigilance; free from fear; undisturbed; free from danger of being taken; that may resist assault or attack; safe; not distrustful; confident; sure; certain.—vt. To free from solicitude; to guard effectually from danger; to make certain; to inclose effectually; to make certain of payment; to assure; to guarantee; to make fast or firm; to fasten. ppr. securing, pret. & pp. secured. [L. securus—sine, without, and cura, care.]

Securely, sē-kūr'li, adv. Without danger; safely; carelessly.

Secureness, sē-kūr'nes, n. State of being secure; want of vigilance.

Security, se-kūr'i-ti, n. State of being secure; safety; a being confident of safety; carelessness; a guarding or keeping safe; defence; anything deposited to secure the payment of a debt; a surety; something done or given to secure peace. [Fr. sécurité—L. securitas, freedom from care.]

Sedan, sē-dan', n. A kind of covered vehicle for carrying a single person, borne on poles, and carried by two men. [said to be from Sedan in France, where it was first used.]

Sedate, sē-dāt', a. Settled; composed; tranquil; still; undisturbed; contemplative; sober; serious. [L. sedo, sedatus—sedeo, Sans. sad, to sit.]

Sedately, sē-dāt'li, adv. Calmly; without agitation of mind.

Sedateness, sē-dāt'nes, n. State or quality of being sedate; composure; serenity; tranquillity.

Sedative, se'da-tiv, a. Tending to allay or assuage; allaying irritability; assuaging pain.—n. A medicine which allays irritation and assuages pain. [Fr. sedatif.]

Sedentary, se'den-ta-ri, a. Accustomed to sit much; requiring much sitting. [Fr. sédentaire—L. sedeo, to sit.]

Sedge, sej, n. A grass-like plant growing in marshes and on the banks of rivers. [Sax. secg—Icel. seigr, pliant.]

Sedged, sejd, p.a. Composed of flags or sedge.

Sedgy, sej'i, a. Overgrown with sedge.

Sediment, se'di-ment, n. That which settles at the bottom of liquor; lees; dregs. [Fr. sédiment—L. sedeo, to sit.]

Sedimentary, se-di-ment'a-ri, a. Pertaining to or formed by sediment.

Sedition, sē-di'shon, n. A going aside; a departure from peace; discord; insurrection; a rising in opposition to law, and in disturbance of the public peace; a local insurrection in opposition to civil authority. [Fr. sédition—L. se, apart, and eo, itum, to go.]

Seditious, sē-di'shi-us, a. Pertaining to sedition; factious; tumultuous; disposed to excite irregular opposition to law; guilty of sedition. [Fr. séditieux.]

Seditiously, sē-di'shi-us-li, adv. In a seditious manner.

Seduce, sē-dūs', vt. To lead aside from the path of duty; to decoy; to present temptations to and lead to a surrender of chastity. ppr. seducing, pret. & pp. seduced. [L. seduco—duco, to lead.]

Seducement, sē-dūs'ment, n. Act of seducing; seduction; deception.

Seducer, sē-dūs'ėr, n. One who seduces; that which leads astray.

Seducing, sē-dūs'ing, p.a. Enticing from the path of virtue or chastity.

Seducingly, sē-dūs'ing-li, adv. In a seducing manner.

Seduction, sē-duk'shon, n. Act of seducing; the crime of persuading a female to surrender her chastity. [Fr. séduction.]

Seductive, sē-duk'tiv, a. Tending to seduce or lead astray; apt to mislead by flattering appearances.

Seductively, sē-duk'tiv-li, adv. In a seductive manner.

Sedulous, se'dū-lus, a. Assiduous; industrious; characterized by assiduity; constant and persevering in business or in endeavours to effect an object. [L. sedulus—sedeo, to sit.]

Sedulously, se'dū-lus-li, adv. Assiduously; industriously; diligently.

Sedulousness, se'dū-lus-nes, n. State or quality of being sedulous.

See, sē, n. The seat of episcopal power; a diocese; the jurisdiction of a bishop; the seat of an archbishop; the jurisdiction of an archbishop: the seat, place, or office of the pope; the authority of the pope or court of Rome. [Fr. siége—L. sedeo, to sit.]

See, sē, vt. To perceive by the eye; to have knowledge of the existence and apparent qualities of by the organs of sight; to perceive by the mental eye; to know; to attend or look to; to descry; to have intercourse with; to call on; to attend; to feel; to suffer; to learn; to understand experimentally.—vi. To have the power of sight; to have perception of things by the eye; to have intellectual sight; to look, examine, or inquire; to be attentive (with to); to take heed; to take care. ppr. seeing, pret. saw, pp. seen.—interj. Lo! look!

observe! behold! [Sax. seon; Alban. siu, the eye.]

Seed, sēd, n. That which is sown or planted; the substance, animal or vegetable, which nature prepares for the reproduction and conservation of the species; first principle; offspring; descendants; race; birth.—vi. To grow to maturity, so as to produce seed; to shed the seed.—vt. To sprinkle with seed. [Sax. sæd—sawan, D. saijen, G. säen, Old G. sāhan, Goth. saian, to sow.]

Seed-bud, sēd'bud, n. The germ or rudiment of the fruit in embryo.

Seeded, sēd'ed, p.a. Covered thick with seed; interspersed, as with seed.

Seedily, sēd'i-li, adv. In a seedy manner.

Seediness, sēd'i-nes, n. State or quality of being seedy.

Seedling, sēd'ling, n. A plant reared from the seed, as distinguished from one propagated by layers, buds, &c.

Seedsman, sēds'man, n. A person who deals in seeds. [seed and man.]

Seedy, sēd'i, a. Abounding with seeds; having a peculiar flavour, supposed to be derived from the weeds growing among the vines; run to seed; exhausted; poor and miserable-looking.

Seeing, sē'ing, p.n. Sight; vision; the act of perceiving objects by the organs of sight.—conj. Since; inasmuch; because that.

Seek, sēk, vt. To run after with a view to find; to go in search of; to search for by going from place to place; to ask for; to solicit; to endeavour to find by any means; to look for; to look after. (Often with out.)—vi. To make search or inquiry; to endeavour to make discovery; to strive; to try. ppr. seeking, pret. & pp. sought. [Sax. secan; Heb. shuk, to run after anything.]

Seeker, sēk'ėr, n. One who seeks; an inquirer; one of a sect that professes no determinate religion.

Seeking, sēk'ing, p.n. Act of attempting to find or procure.

Seeling, sēl'ing, p.n. Blinding.

Seem, sēm, vi. To be fit to see or to be seen; to look or appear fit, becoming, or proper; to be agreeable to look at; to make a show; to appear; to make or have a show or semblance; to have the appearance of truth or fact; to be understood as true. (Often used impersonally.) [G. ziemen, to be fit or becoming.]

Seemer, sēm'ėr, n. One who seems.

Seeming, sēm'ing, p.a. Having the semblance; specious; seemly.—p.n. Appearance; show; semblance; fair appearance.

Seemingly, sēm'ing-li, adv. In appearance; in show; in semblance.

Seemliness, sēm'li-nes, n. Quality of being seemly; comeliness; grace; fitness; propriety; decency; decorum.

Seemly, sēm'li, a. Beseeming; suited to the object, occasion, purpose, or character; suitable; proper; meet; decent. adv. In a decent or suitable manner. [G. ziemlich.]

Seen, sēn, pp. of see. Observed; versed; skilled.

Seer, sēr, n. One who sees; one who sees into futurity; a prophet; a person who foresees future events.

See-saw, sē'sa, n. A vibratory motion; a play among children in which one sits on each end of a board balanced on some support, and move alternately up and down.—vi. To move with a reciprocating motion; to move backward and forward, or upward and down-

ward.—*a.* Undulating with reciprocal motion. [perhaps *saw-saw.*]
Seethe, sēth, *vt.* To *cook by boiling*; to boil; to decoct or prepare for food in hot liquor.—*vi.* To be in a state of ebullition; to be hot. *ppr.* seething, *pret.* seethed, sod, *pp.* seethed, sodden. [Sax. *seothan*; Icel. *syd*, to cook.]
Segment, seg'ment, *n. A part cut off*; a section; a part *cut off* from a figure by a line or plane. [Fr.—L. *seco*, to cut.]
Segregate, sē'grē-gāt, *vt. To set apart*; to separate from others. *ppr.* segregating, *pret. & pp.* segregated. [L. *segrego, segregatum—grex*, a flock.]
Segregation, sē-grē-gā'shon, *n.* Separation from others; a parting. [Fr. *segrégation.*]
Seignior, sēn'yor, *n.* Originally, *an elder*; a lord; the lord of the manor; but used also, in the south of Europe, as a title of honour. [Fr. *seigneur*— L. *senior*, older, *senex*, old.]
Seigniory, sēn'yō-ri, *n.* A lordship; a manor; the power or authority of a lord; dominion. [Fr. *seigneurie.*]
Seizable, sēz'a-bl, *a. That may be seized*; liable to be taken.
Seize, sēz, *vt.* To fall upon suddenly and lay hold on; to grip suddenly; to take possession of by force; to clutch; to snatch; to take possession of by virtue of a warrant; to apprehend; to capture. *ppr.* seizing, *pret. & pp.* seized. [Fr. *saisir*—Old G. *seisan*, to pluck.]
Seizer, sēz'er, *n. One who seizes.*
Seizing, sēz'ing, *p.n.* Act of taking or grasping suddenly.
Seizure, sēz'ūr, *n. Act of seizing*; act of taking by warrant; state of being seized, as with disease; the thing seized; possession; a catching.
Selah, sē'la, *n.* In the Psalms, a word supposed to signify silence, or a pause in the musical performance of the song. [Heb.]
Seld†, seld, *adv.* Rarely.
Seldom, sel'dom, *adv. Rarely*; not often; not frequently. [Sax. *seldon*; Old G. *selt*, rare.]
Select, sē-lekt', *vt.* To *choose* and take *from* a number; to take by preference from among others; to pick out; to cull.—*a. Chosen* or taken *from* a number by preference; nicely chosen; choice; preferable; more valuable or excellent than others. [L. *seligo, selectus—lego*, to pick out.]
Selected, sē-lekt'ed, *p.a.* Picked; culled.
Selection, sē-lek'shon, *n. Act of selecting*; a taking from a number by preference; a number of things selected. [L. *selectio.*]
Selectness, sē-lekt'nes, *n. State of being select* or well chosen.
Self, self, *pron. a.* **Selves,** *pl.* (of noun). Particular†; very†; identical*†.*—*n.* The individual, as subject to his own contemplation or action; one's individual person; personality; personal identity; individuality. *Self* is united to certain personal pronouns and pronominal adjectives, to express emphasis or distinction; also when the pronoun is used reciprocally, as, I myself; also used to signify personal interest, or love of private interest; selfishness. [Sax.; Goth. *silba.*]
Self-abasement, self'a-bās-ment, *n. Abasement of one's self*; humiliation proceeding from consciousness of one's inferiority or guilt.
Self-conceit, self'kon-sēt, *n. A high opinion of one's self*; self-sufficiency.
Self-conceited, self'kon-sēt-ed, *a.* Hav-

ing *a high opinion of one's own person* or merits; vain.
Self-contradictory, self'kon-tra-dik-tō-ri, *a. Contradicting itself.*
Self-deceit, self'dē-sēt, *n. The act of deceiving one's self*; self-deception.
Self-defence, self'dē-fens, *n.* Act of *defending* one's own person, property, or reputation.
Self-denial, self'dē-nī-al, *n. The act of denying one's self*; the forbearing to gratify one's own appetites or desires.
Self-denying, self'dē-nī-ing, *a. Denying one's self*; forbearing to indulge one's own appetites or desires.
Self-esteem, self'es-tēm, *n. The esteem* or good opinion *of one's self*; vanity.
Self-evident, self'e-vi-dent, *a. Evident in its own nature*, or without proof.
Self-examination, self'egz-am-in-ā-shon, *n. Examination of one's self*; scrutiny into *one's own* state and motives.
Self-existence, self'egz-ist-ens, *n. Existence of one's self*, independent of any other being or cause; underived existence; an attribute peculiar to God.
Self-existent, self'egz-ist-ent, *a. Existing by one's own nature* or essence.
Self-interest, self'in-tér-est, *n. One's own interest*; the advantage of *one's self.*
Selfish, self'ish, *a. Devoted to self*; regarding one's own interest chiefly or solely.
Selfishly, self'ish-li, *adv. In a selfish manner*; with regard to private interest only or chiefly.
Selfishness, self'ish-nes, *n. Quality or state of being selfish*; undue love of self.
Self-love, self'luv, *n. The love of self*; the love of one's own person or happiness.
Self-metal†, self'me-tal, *n.* The same metal.
Self-mettle†, self'met-l, *n.* Natural mettle, or that which comes of itself.
Self-possession, self'poz-ze-shon, *n. The possession of one's* powers or faculties; calmness; self-command.
Self-preservation, self'pre-zérv-ā-shon, *n. The preservation of one's self* from destruction or injury.
Self-reliance, self'rē-lī-ans, *n. Reliance* on *one's own* powers.
Self-restraint, self'rē-strānt, *n.* A *restraint* over *one's self.*
Self-righteous, self'rīt-ē-us, *a. Righteous in one's own esteem.*
Self-righteousness, self'rīt-ē-us-nes, *n. Righteousness which one arrogates to one's self.*
Self-same, self'sām, *a. Exactly the same*; the very same.
Self-sovereignty†, self'so-ve-rin-ti, *n.* Self-sufficiency.
Self-sufficiency, self'suf-fi-shi-en-si, *n. Quality of being self-sufficient*; excessive confidence in one's own competence or sufficiency.
Self-sufficient, self'suf-fi-shi-ent, *a.* Having too much confidence in one's own strength or endowments; overbearing.
Self-will, self'wil, *n. One's own will*; obstinacy.
Self-willed, self'wild, *a. Governed by one's own will*; obstinate.
Sell, sel, *vt. To offer*; to deliver; to deliver up; to give or deliver in exchange for money or security for money; to betray; to deliver for money or a reward; to yield or give for a consideration.—*vi. To practise selling*; to have commerce; to be sold. *ppr.* selling, *pret. & pp.* sold. [Icel. *sel, selia*, to sell; Goth. *saljan*, to offer.]
Seller, sel'er, *n. The person who sells.*

Selvage, sel'vāj, *n.* The same as *selvedge.*
Selvedge, sel'vej, *n. The long edge of* cloth, in distinction from the short edge or width; a woven border, or border of close work. [G. *sahl*, extension, especially in length, and *edge.*]
Semblance, sem'blans, *n. Seeming*; *resemblance*; actual similitude; figure; form. [Fr.—L. *similis*, like.]
Semblative†, sem'bla-tiv, *a.* Resembling; fit.
Semibreve, se'mi-brēv, *n.* A note in music of *half* the duration or time of an old note called the *breve.*
Semicircle, se'mi-sér-kl, *n. The half of a circle*; any body in the form of a half circle.
Semicircular, se-mi-sér'ku-lar, *a. Having the form of a half circle.*
Semicolon, se'mi-kō-lon, *n. Half a colon*; the point [;] marking a greater distinction of sense than a comma, but less than a colon.
Semi-diameter, se'mi-di-am-et-ér, *n. Half the diameter*; the radius of a circle or sphere.
Semi-fluid, se'mi-flū-id, *a. Half fluid*; *imperfectly fluid.*
Seminal, se'min-al, *a. Pertaining to seed*, or to the elements of production; radical; rudimental; original. [F. *séminal* —L. *sero*, to sow.]
Seminary, se'min-a-ri, *n.* Primarily, *a place where seeds are sown*; any school or university in which young persons are instructed in the several branches of learning. [Fr. *séminaire.*]
Semiquaver, se'mi-kwā-vér, *n.* A note in music of *half* the duration of the *quaver.*
Semitic, sem-it'ik, *a. Relating to Shem* or to his descendants; as, Semitic languages.
Semitone, se'mi-tōn, *n. Half a tone* in music.
Semi-transparent, se'mi-trans-pā-rent, *a. Half-transparent.*
Semi-vocal, se'mi-vō-kal, *a. Half-vocal*; pertaining to *a semi-vowel*; imperfectly sounding.
Semi-vowel, se'mi-vou-el, *n. A half vowel*, or an articulation which is accompanied with an imperfect sound.
Senary, se'na-ri, *a. Of six*; belonging to six; containing six. [L. *senarius*, consisting of six each—*sex*, six.]
Senate, se'nāt, *n. An assembly of elders*; a body of the principal inhabitants of a city or state, invested with a share in the government; the governing body of the university of Cambridge; any legislative body of men. [Fr. *sénat*—L. *senatus—senex*, to be old.]
Senator, se'nāt-or, *n. A member of a senate*; a counsellor; a judge or magistrate. [L.]
Senatorial, se-na-tō'ri-al, *a. Pertaining to a senate*; becoming a senator.
Senatorially, se-na-tō'ri-al-li, *adv. In the manner of a senate*; with dignity.
Send, send, *vt. To cause to go*; to despatch, as on a message; to transmit; to authorize or direct to go and act; to cause to come or happen to; to diffuse, as music.—*vi.* To despatch an agent or message for some purpose. *ppr.* sending, *pret. & pp.* sent. [Sax. *sendan*— Old G. *sind*, a way.]
Sender, send'er, *n. One who sends.*
Seneschal, se'nē-shal, *n. The old or oldest servant of the house*; a steward; an officer in the house of princes, who had the care of the house and the superintendence of feasts and domestic ceremonies. [Old Fr. *seneschal*; Old G. *sene*, old, and *scalc*, a servant.]

Fāte, fär, fat, fall; mē, met, hér; pine, pin; nōte, not, mōve; tūbe, tub, bull; oil, pound.

Seneschalship, se'ne-shal-ship, n. The office of a seneschal.
Senile, sē'nil, a. Pertaining to old age; proceeding from age. [L. senet is—seneo, to be old.]
Senility, sē-nil'i-ti, n. State of being old; imbecility proceeding from old age.
Senior, sē'ni-or, a. Elder or older; older in office.—n. One older than another; one who is older in office; one who has priority of rank; an aged person. [L. compar. of senex—seneo, to be old.]
Seniority, sē-ni-or'i-ti, n. State of being senior; priority of birth; priority in office; priority of rank.
Seniory, sē'ni-or-i, n. The same as seniority.
Senna, sen'na, n. The dried purgative leaves of certain plants of the cassia kind. [Pers. and Ar.]
Se'nnight, sen'nit, n. The space of seven nights. [contracted from sevennight.]
Sensation, sens-ā'shon, n. An impression made upon the mind through the medium of the senses; feeling awakened by external objects, or by some change in the internal state of the body; excitement; state of excited interest or feeling. [Fr.—L. sentio, sensum, to feel.]
Sensational, sens-ā'shon-al, a. Relating to or implying sensation.
Sense, sens, n. The faculty of feeling; sensation; perception by the senses, as sight, hearing, smelling, tasting, feeling; perception by the intellect; discernment; acuteness of perception; soundness of faculties; strength of natural reason; rational meaning; judgment; consciousness; moral perception; sensibility; meaning; signification; (pl.) the channels of communication with the external world. [L. sensus—sentio, to feel, to discern by the senses, to perceive, to observe.]
Senseless, sens'les, a. Wanting sense; unfeeling; foolish; contrary to reason; unconscious; wanting sensibility.
Senselessly, sens'les-li, adv. In a senseless manner; stupidly; unreasonably.
Senselessness, sens'les-nes, n. State or quality of being senseless; absurdity.
Sensibility, sens-i-bil'i-ti, n. State of quality of being sensible; that faculty of living parts by which they are capable of receiving impressions; the capacity of perceiving the impressions of external objects; susceptibility of quick and keen emotions; delicacy of feeling; quality of being easily affected; actual feeling. [Fr. sensibilité.]
Sensible, sens'i-bl, a. Capable of being affected through the senses; perceptible by the senses; perceived by the mind; having moral perception; capable of being affected by moral good or evil; being easily affected; sensitive; satisfied; persuaded; having good sense; reasonable; discerning; moved by a very small impulse, as a balance; affected by a slight degree of heat or cold; containing good sense or sound reason. [Fr.—L. sentio, to feel.]
Sensibleness, sens'i-bl-nes, n. Quality or state of being sensible; sensibility.
Sensibly, sens'i-bli, adv. In a sensible manner.
Sensitive, sens'i-tiv, a. Having sense, or having the capacity of receiving impressions from external objects; having acute sensibility; easily affected; that affects the senses; pertaining to the senses; depending on sensation; sentient. [Fr. sensitif.]
Sensitively, sens'i-tiv-li, adv. In a sensitive manner.

Sensitiveness, sens'i-tiv-nes, n. State or quality of being sensitive.
Sensitive-plant, sens'i-tiv-plant, n. A plant, so called from the contraction of its leaves on being touched.
Sensorial, sen-sō'ri-al, a. Pertaining to the sensorium.
Sensorium, sen-sō'ri-um, n. The common centre, at which all the impressions of sense are received. This common centre is the brain. [Low L.—L. sentio, to feel.]
Sensual, sens'ū-al, a. Endowed with sensation; pertaining to the senses, as distinct from the mind or soul; consisting in sense; pleasing to the senses; carnal; not holy; voluptuous; luxurious. [Fr. sensuel—L. sentio, to feel.]
Sensualism, sens'ū-al-izm, n. The doctrine that all our ideas not only originate in sensation, but are transformed sensations.
Sensualist, sens'ū-al-ist, n. A person given to the indulgence of the senses; a voluptuary.
Sensuality, sens-ū-al'i-ti, n. Quality of being sensual; free indulgence in carnal pleasures. [Fr. sensualité.]
Sensuous, sens'ū-us, a. Pertaining to sense; connected with sensible objects; full of feeling or passion.
Sentence, sen'tens, n. What one thinks; a judgment; a short saying containing moral instruction; a judgment pronounced by a court or judge upon a criminal; a period; a number of words containing complete sense.—vt. To pass sentence upon; to doom; to condemn; to doom to punishment. ppr. sentencing, pret. & pp. sentenced. [Fr.—L. sentio, to feel, to think.]
Sentential, sen-ten'shi-al, a. Comprising sentences; pertaining to a sentence or full period.
Sententially, sen-ten'shi-al-li, adv. By means of sentences.
Sententious, sen-ten'shi-us, a. Abounding with sentences and maxims; short and energetic; pithy; terse. [Fr. sentencieux—L. sentio, to feel, to think.]
Sententiously, sen-ten'shi-us-li, adv. In short expressive periods.
Sententiousness, sen-ten'shi-us-nes, n. Quality of being sententious.
Sentient, sen'shi-ent, a. Having sensation; affected through the senses; having the faculty of perception. [L. sentiens—sentio, to feel.]
Sentiment, sen'ti-ment, n. A thought prompted by feeling; opinion; the decision of the mind formed by reasoning; the sense, contained in words, but considered as distinct from them; sensibility; tenderness; a particular disposition of mind, as love, hatred, &c.; a striking sentence in a composition; the idea which governs the general conception of a work of art. [Fr.—L. sentio, to think.]
Sentimental, sen-ti-ment'al, a. Abounding in sentiment; abounding with just opinions or reflections; exciting to sensibility; affecting sensibility.
Sentimentalism, sen-ti-ment'al-izm, n. The character of a sentimentalist.
Sentimentalist, sen-ti-ment'al-ist, n. One who affects sentiment or fine feeling.
Sentimentality, sen'ti-ment-al''li-ti, n. State or quality of being sentimental; affectation of exquisite sensibility.
Sentimentally, sen-ti-ment'al-li, adv. In a sentimental manner.
Sentinel, sen'ti-nel, n. One set to see or hear; a soldier set to guard an army, camp, or other place, from surprise, to observe the approach of danger and give notice of it. [Fr. sentinelle—L. sentio, to perceive.]
Sentinelled, sen'ti-neld, p.a. Furnished with a sentinel.
Sentry, sen'tri, n. A sentinel; a soldier placed on guard; the duty of a sentinel. [corrupted from sentinel.]
Sentry-box, sen'tri-boks, n. A box to cover a sentinel at his post, and shelter him from the weather.
Separability, se'pa-ra-bil''li-ti, n. Quality of being separable.
Separable, se'pa-ra-bl, a. That may be separated; separating†. [Fr. séparable.]
Separably, se'pa-ra-bli, adv. In a separable manner.
Separate, se'pa-rāt, vt. To set apart; to part, in almost any manner; to disunite; to disconnect; to sever; to disengage; to dissociate; to remove.—vi. To part; to be disunited; to withdraw from each other; to open. ppr. separating, pret. & pp. separated.—a. Parted; being parted from another; disjoined; detached; distinct; removed; disunited from the body. [L. separo, separatus—pāro, to set.]
Separately, se'pa-rāt-li, adv. In a separate or unconnected state; apart.
Separation, se-pa-rā'shon, n. Act of separating; state of being separate; disunion; the operation of decomposing substances; divorce. [Fr. séparation.]
Separatism, se'pa-rāt-izm, n. Act of separating from a church; practice of doing so.
Separatist, se'pa-rāt-ist, n. One who separates from an established church, to which he has belonged; a dissenter. [Fr. séparatiste.]
Sept, sept, n. Descendants of a common stock; a family from a common progenitor (used of the races or families in Ireland). [Gael. ceap, a block, stock.]
September, sep-tem'bėr, n. Originally the seventh month of the year, reckoning from March, but now the ninth. [L. september—septem, seven, with Sans. vāra, time, day.]
Septenary, sep'ten-a-ri, a. Consisting of seven. [Fr. septénaire.]
Septennial, sep-ten'ni-al, a. Lasting seven years; happening or returning once every seven years. [L. septennis—septem, and annus, a year.]
Septennially, sep-ten'ni-al-li, adv. Once in seven years.
Septuagenarian, sep'tū-a-jen-ā''ri-an, n. A person seventy years of age.
Septuagenary, sep-tū-a'jen-a-ri, a. Consisting of seventy. [Fr. septuagénaire.]
Septuagesima, sep'tū-a-jes''i-ma, n. The third Sunday before Lent, or before Quadragesima Sunday, being about seventy days before Easter. [L. septuagesimus, the seventieth.]
Septuagint, sep'tū-a-jint, n. A Greek version of the Old Testament, so called because it was said to be the work of seventy, or rather of seventy-two interpreters, about 270 or 280 years before Christ. [L. septuaginta, seventy.]
Sepulchral, sē-pul'kral, a. Pertaining to a sepulchre, to the grave, or to monuments erected to the memory of the dead; deep; grave; hollow, as a voice. [L. sepulchrālis.]
Sepulchre, se'pul-kėr, n. A burial-place; a tomb.—vt. To bury; to inter. [Fr. sépulcre—L. sepelio, to bury—Heb. shāphel, to lay low.]
Sepulture, se'pul-tūr, n. Burial; entombment; act of depositing the dead body of a human being in the grave. [Fr. sépulture—L. sepelio, to bury.]
Sequel, sē'kwel, n. That which follows;

ch, chain; j, job; g, go; ng, sing; ᴛʜ, then; th, thin; w, wig; wh, whig; zh, azure; † obsolete.

a succeeding part; that which results; consequence; issue; conclusion. [Fr. *séquelle*—L. *sequor*, to follow.]

Sequence, sē'kwens, n. *A following, or that which follows;* order of succession; series; method; a regular alternate succession of similar chords, in music. [Fr. *séquence*—L. *sequor*, to follow.]

Sequent, sē'kwent, a. Following.—n. A follower; that which follows. [L. *sequens*.]

Sequester, sē-kwes'tėr, vt. *To separate;* to place, for safe keeping, in the hands of a depository; to take from parties in controversy and put into the possession of an indifferent person; to separate from the owner for a time; to seize. [Fr. *séquestrer*—L. *sequester*, a mediator—*sequor*, to follow.]

Sequestered, sē-kwes'tėrd, p.a. *Separated;* seized and detained for a time, to satisfy a demand; secluded; private.

Sequestration, sē-kwes-trā'shon, n. *Act of sequestering;* state of being sequestered; the separating of a thing in controversy from the possession of both the parties that contend for it; retirement. [Low L. *sequestratio*.]

Sequestrator, sē-kwes'trāt-or, n. One who sequesters; one to whom the keeping of sequestered property is committed.

Seraglio, sē-rāl'yō, n. *The palace of the* Turkish sultan; improperly applied to that part of the building which is occupied by the women of the sultan. [It. *serraglio*; Turk. *serat*, a palace.]

Seraph, se'raf, n. **Seraphs**, pl. but sometimes the Heb. pl. **Seraphim** is used. *A burning* or *flaming* angel; an angel of the highest order; a prince; a noble of heaven. [Heb. *saraph*, to burn, to be noble.]

Seraphic, sē-raf'ik, a. *Pertaining to a seraph;* burning or inflamed with love or zeal; angelic; pure; refined from sensuality.

Seraphically, sē-raf'ik-al-li, adv. *In the manner of a seraph.*

Seraphim, se'ra-fim, n. Angels of the highest order in the celestial hierarchy. [the Heb. pl. of *seraph*.]

Sere; sēr, n. Affection of the throat by which the lungs are tickled.

Serenade, se-rē-nād', n. Music performed in the open air on a clear or *serene* night; a musical entertainment given in the night, under the windows of ladies; also a song composed for such an occasion.—*vt*. To entertain with nocturnal music.—*vi*. To perform nocturnal music. *ppr.* serenading, *pret. & pp.* serenaded. [Fr. *sérénade*.]

Serene, sē-rēn', a. *Clear;* cloudless; calm; unruffled; undisturbed; applied as a title of courtesy or honour to several princes and magistrates in Europe.—*n*. Serenity. [L. *serēnus*.]

Serenely, sē-rēn'li, adv. Calmly; quietly; with unruffled temper; coolly.

Serenity, sē-ren'i-ti, n. *State of being serene;* clearness and calmness; stillness; calmness of mind; undisturbed state; coolness. [Fr. *sérénité*.]

Serf, sėrf, n. In some countries a slave attached to the soil, and transferred with it; a bondman. [Fr.—L. *servus*.]

Serfdom, sėrf'dom, n. *The state or condition of serfs.*

Serge, sėrj, n. A kind of twilled cloth, commonly of wool, but sometimes of silk. [Fr.]

Sergeancy, sär'jan-si, n. *The office of a sergeant-at-law.*

Sergeant, sär'jant, n. *One who is the servant* of his chief; a non-commissioned officer who instructs recruits in discipline, forms the ranks, &c.; a lawyer of the highest rank, and answering to the doctor of the civil law. (This word is often written *serjeant*.) [Fr. *serjent*—L. *servio*, to serve.]

Sergeantship, sär'jant-ship, n. *The office of a sergeant.*

Serial, sē'ri-al, a. *Pertaining to a series;* consisting of a series.—n. A tale issued in successive parts or numbers.

Serially, sē'ri-al-li, adv. *In a serial manner;* by series.

Serie, sē'rēz, n. *A connected* succession of things in the same order, and bearing the same relation to each other; a sequence; train; chain; a number of arithmetical or algebraic terms in succession, increasing or diminishing according to a certain law. [L. *sero*, to join together.]

Serious, sē'ri-us, a. *Grave;* thoughtful; characterized by gravity in manner; particularly attentive to religious concerns; of weight; attended with danger. [Fr. *sérieux*—L. *serius*.]

Seriously, sē'ri-us-li, adv. *Gravely;* solemnly; in earnest; without levity.

Seriousness, sē'ri-us-nes, n. *Quality or state of being serious;* solemnity.

Serjeant, sär'jant, n. *See* SERGEANT.

Sermon, sėr'mon, n. *A connected speech;* a discourse delivered in public by a clergyman for the purpose of religious instruction; a printed religious discourse; colloquially, a serious exhortation.—*vt.*† To tutor; to teach. [L. *sermo—sero*, to join or connect.]

Serous, sē'rus, a. *Pertaining to serum;* thin; watery; like whey. [Fr. *séreux*.]

Serpent, sėr'pent, n. *A creeping animal;* a reptile without feet; a northern constellation represented as a serpent; a bass wind-instrument of music, so called from its form; a subtle or malicious person; a species of firework which has a serpentine motion in the air.—a. Pertaining to a serpent; like a serpent. [L. *serpens—serpo*, to creep.]

Serpentine, sėr'pent-in, a. *Resembling a serpent;* twisted, like a serpent; having the colour or properties of a serpent. n. A species of magnesian stone, usually green, and often spotted like a serpent's back. [L. *serpentinus*.]

Serrated, se-rāt-ed, a. Notched on the edge like a saw. [L. *serratus—serra*, a saw.]

Serried, se'rid, p.a. *Crowded;* compacted. [from obs. *serry*, from Fr. *serrer*, to crowd.]

Serum, sē'rum, n. *The watery* part of curdled milk; whey; the thin transparent part of the blood. [L.]

Servant, sėrv'ant, n. *One who serves;* a domestic or menial; one in a state of subjection; a drudge; one who yields obedience to another; a word of civility or courtesy.—*vt*. To subject. [Fr.—L. *servio*, to serve.]

Serve, sėrv, vt. *Primarily, to be a bondman to;* to work for and obey; to minister to; to perform official duties to; to wait on; to help; to yield obedience to servilely; to perform the duties required in; to be sufficient to; to give assistance to by good offices; to be of use to; to benefit; to advance; to be sufficient for; to content; to be in the place of anything to one; to treat; to requite; to bring forward and arrange (with *up, out,* or *in*).—*vi*. To be a bondman; to be employed in labour for another; to wait; to perform domestic offices to another; to perform duties, as in the army, navy, or in any office; to answer; to be sufficient for a purpose; to suit; to be of use; to do the honours of. *ppr.* serving, *pret. & pp.* served. [Fr. *servir*—L. *servus*, a slave.]

Server, sėrv'ėr, n. *One who serves;* a salver; a plate.

Service, sėrv'is, n. *Act of one who serves;* labour of body, or of body and mind, performed at the command of a superior; attendance on a superior; profession of respect uttered or sent; actual duty; that which God requires of man; worship; office; use; military duty by land or sea; the period of such duty; useful office; benefit; public worship; the official duties of a minister of the gospel; order of dishes at table; vessels used at table. [Fr.—L. *servus*, a slave.]

Serviceable, sėrv'is-a-bl, a. *That does service;* that promotes happiness or any good; beneficial; capable of or fit for military duty; active; diligent.

Serviceably, sėrv'is-a-bli, a. *In a serviceable manner.*

Servile, sėr'vil, a. *Such as pertains to a slave;* mean; such as proceeds from dependence; cringing; noting a letter of a word not belonging to the original root.—n. A letter which forms no part of the root of a word; a letter of a word which is not sounded, as the final *e* in peace, plane, &c. [L. *servilis—servus*, a slave.]

Servilely, sėr'vil-li, adv. *In a servile manner;* slavishly.

Servility, sėr-vil'i-ti, n. *State of being servile;* baseness; mean obsequiousness. [Fr. *servilité*.]

Servitor, sėrv'i-tor, n. *A servant;* one who acts under another; a follower or adherent. [L.]

Servitude, sėrv'i-tūd, n. *State of a slave;* bondage; state of a servant; condition of a conquered country. [L. *servitūdo—servus*, a slave.]

Sesma!, ses'as, *inter.* Be quiet.

Session, se'shon, n. *A sitting;* the actual *sitting* of a court, legislature, &c.; the time during which a court, council, and the like, meet daily for business; (pl.) the title of several courts, chiefly those of criminal jurisdiction. [Fr.—L. *sedeo*, Sans. *sad*, to sit.]

Sess-pool, ses'pöl, n. A cavity sunk in the earth to receive and retain the *sediment* of water conveyed in drains. (Written also *cess-pool*.) [L. *sedeo, sessum*, to settle.]

Set, set, vt. *To cause to sit;* to settle; to put; to fasten to one place; to fix in metal, as a jewel; to render motionless, as the eyes; to fix, as a price; to assign; to regulate; to replace; to reduce from a fractured state, as an arm; to station; to plant; to implant, to rate; to agree upon; to stake at play; to state; to fit to music; to pitch; to begin to sing in public, as a psalm or tune; to plant, as a shrub, tree, or vegetable; to stud, as with jewels; to replace; to cause to stop; to perplex; to bring to a fine edge, as a razor; to spread, as sails; to point out, without noise or disturbance; as a dog sets birds.—*vi*. To sink; to go down; to be fixed hard; to be close or firm; to plant by root or slip; to flow; to fit music to words; to begin to move. *ppr.* setting, *pret. & pp.* set. *p.a.* Regular; formal; determined; firm; established.—n. *The act of setting;* permanent change of figure, in consequence of pressure; a number of persons associated; a number of particular things that are united in the formation of a whole; a young plant for

growth; direction, as of a current. [Sax. *settan*; Goth. *satjan*, to cause to sit.]
Set-off, set'of, *n.* Any counterbalance; the act of admitting one claim to counterbalance another.
Seton, sē'ton, *n.* A few horse *hairs* or small threads drawn through the skin by a large needle, to keep up an issue; an issue; an artificial ulcer. [Fr. *séton*—L. *seta*, a bristle.]
Settee, set-tē', *n.* A long *seat* with a back to it. [from *set*.]
Setter, set'er, *n.* One who *sets*; a sporting dog trained to sit or crouch to the game he finds.
Setting, set'ing, *p.n.* Act of *putting*; act of sinking below the horizon; the direction of a current, sea, or wind; the hardening of plaster.
Settle, set'l, *n.* A *seat* or bench; a long bench with a high wooden back.—*vt.* To cause to *sit down*; to render fixed; to make permanent in any place; to establish in business; to confirm; to free from doubt; to make certain; to cause to subside after being loosened by frost; to dry and harden after rain; to fix by gift or any legal act, as an annuity; to cause to sink; to tranquillize; to colonize; to close by amicable agreement; to bring to adjustment; to balance, or to pay, as accounts.—*vi.* To *subside*; to *sink* or fall to the bottom of liquor; to sink and rest on the bottom, as dregs, mud, &c.; to fix one's residence; to become fixed after change; to quit a rambling course for a permanent one; to become fixed; to rest; to become calm; to sink by its weight, as a building; to come to an agreement, as with creditors or debtors. *ppr.* settling, *pret. & pp.* settled. [Sax. *setl—settan*, to set.]
Settled, set'ld, *p.a.* Placed; fixed; composed; adjusted; definitive.
Settlement, set'l-ment, *n.* Act of *settling*, or state of being settled; subsidence; the falling of the foul matter of liquors to the bottom; the act of giving possession by legal sanction; a jointure granted to a wife; the act of taking a domestic state; a becoming stationary; the act of planting, as a colony; the colony established; adjustment; the ascertainment of just claims, or payment of the balance of an account; legal residence of a person in a particular parish or town; adjustment of differences; reconciliation.
Settler, set'l-er, *n.* One who *settles* in a new country.
Settling, set'l-ing, *p.n.* Act of making a *settlement*; a colonizing; act of subsiding, as lees; the adjustment of differences; (pl.) lees; dregs.
Seven, se'ven, *a.* Four and three; one more than six or less than eight. [Sax. *seofon*—L. *septem*.]
Sevenfold, se'ven-fōld, *a.* Repeated *seven times*.—*adv.* Seven times as much or often.
Sevennight, se'ven-nit, *n.* The period of *seven* days and *nights*; a week.
Seventeen, se'ven-tēn, *a.* Seven and ten. [Sax. *seofontyne*.]
Seventeenth, se'ven-tēnth, *a.* The ordinal of *seventeen*.
Seventh, se'venth, *a.* The ordinal of *seven*.—*n.* The seventh part; one part in seven. [Sax. *seofetha*.]
Seventhly, se'venth-li, *adv.* In the *seventh* place.
Seventieth, se'ven-ti-eth, *a.* The ordinal of *seventy*.
Seventy, se'ven-ti, *a.* Seven times ten. [D. *seventig*.]

Sever, se'vèr, *vt.* To *separate* by cutting or rending; to disjoin, as distinct things, but united; to disjoin; to keep apart.—*vi.* To make a *separation*; to distinguish; to be parted or rent asunder. [Old Fr. *sevrer*—L. *sepāro—se*, and *paro*, to arrange.]
Several, se'vèr-al, *a.* *Separate*; distinct; divers; sundry; consisting of a number; more than two, but not very many; single; appropriate.—*n.* Each particular, taken singly.
Severally, se'vèr-al-li, *adv.* *Separately*; distinctly; apart from others.
Severance, se'vèr-ans, *n.* Act of *severing*; the act of dividing or disuniting.
Severe, sē-vēr', *a.* *Serious*; rigid; stern; rigorous; not mild; morose; relentless; regulated by rigid rules; giving no indulgence; sedate to an extreme; rigidly exact; keen; sarcastic; afflictive; biting; extreme, as cold; concise; not lax or airy, as style; not luxuriant, as style. [L. *severus—serius*, grave.]
Severed, se'vèrd, *p.a.* *Separated*; parted by violence; disjointed.
Severely, sē-vēr'li, *adv.* In a *severe* manner; with extreme rigour; afflictively; fiercely.
Severity, sē-ve'ri-ti, *n.* State or *quality* of being *severe*; austerity; want of indulgence; excessive rigour; extremity; quality or power of distressing; extreme degree; extreme coldness; sharpness of punishment; rigid accuracy. [Fr. *sévérité*.]
Sew, sō, *vt.* To unite or fasten together with a *needle* and *thread*.—*vi.* To practise *sewing*; to stitch; to join things with stitches. [Sax. *siwian*—L. *suo*.]
Sewage, sū'āj, *n.* *Sewerage*.
Sewer, sū'èr, *n.* A drain or passage to convey off water and filth underground; a subterraneous canal, particularly in cities. [from Old Fr. *issir*, to issue, to flow forth.]
Sewerage, sū'èr-āj, *n.* The system of *sewers*, or subterranean conduits for carrying off the filth of a city; also, the matter thus carried off; the construction and support of common sewers.
Sewing, sō'ing, *p.n.* Act or occupation of sewing or using a *needle*; that which is sewed with the needle.
Sex, seks, *n.* The *division* of animals into male and female; the distinction between male and female; by way of emphasis, woman-kind; females. [Fr. *sexe*—L. *seco*, to divide.]
Sexagenarian, seks'a-jen-ā''ri-an, *n.* A person who has arrived at the age of *sixty* years.
Sexagesima, seks-a-jes'i-ma, *n.* The second Sunday before Lent, so called as being about the *sixtieth* day before Easter. [L. *sexagesimus*, from *sexaginta*, sixty.]
Sexennial, seks-en'ni-al, *a.* Lasting *six years*, or happening once in six years. [L. *sex*, and *annus*, a year.]
Sextant, seks'tant, *n.* The *sixth part* of a circle; an instrument for measuring the angular distances of objects by reflection. [Fr.—L. *sex*, six.]
Sextile, seks'til, *n.* Denoting the aspect or position of two planets, when distant from each other the *sixth* part of a circle, or sixty degrees. [L. *sextilis*.]
Sexton, seks'ton, *n.* An under officer of the church, whose business is to take care of the *sacred* vessels, vestments, &c., belonging to the church, to attend on the officiating clergyman, &c. [corrupted from *sacristan*.]
Sextonship, seks'ton-ship, *n.* The *office* of a *sexton*.

Sexual, seks'ū-al, *a.* Pertaining to *sex* or the *sexes*; distinguishing the sex. [Fr. *sexuel*.]
Sexually, seks'ū-al-li, *adv.* In a *sexual* manner.
Shabbily, shab'i-li, *adv.* In a *shabby* manner; meanly.
Shabbiness, shab'i-nes, *n.* State of being *shabby*; meanness; paltriness.
Shabby, shab'i, *a.* Worn by *rubbing*; worn to rags; paltry; stingy. [D. *schabberig*; L. *scabo*, to scrape.]
Shackle, shak'l, *n.* Shackles, shak'lz, *pl.* usually in the *plural*. That which *binds*, or that which prevents the free action of the limbs; a fetter; a chain; that which obstructs free action.—*vt.* To *bind*; to *chain*; to *fetter*; to tie or confine, as the limbs, so as to prevent free motion; to impede; to cumber. *ppr.* shackling, *pret. & pp.* shackled. [Sax. *sceacul*—Old Heb. *shkak*, to bind fast.]
Shade, shād, *n.* That which *covers*; the interruption of the rays of light; the obscurity so caused; an obscure place, properly in a grove or close wood, which precludes the sun's rays; a secluded retreat; coolness, an effect of shade; shelter; the dark part of a picture; degree of light; a very minute difference; a shadow; the soul, after its separation from the body; (pl.) the lower region or place of the dead; deep obscurity; total darkness.—*vt.* [Sax. *sceadan*.] To *cover*; to screen from light by intercepting its rays; to overspread with darkness; to hide; to protect; to paint in obscure colours; to darken, to mark by gradations of colour. *ppr.* shading, *pret. & pp.* shaded. [Sax. *scead—sceadan*, to cover.]
Shaded, shād'ed, *p.a.* Defended from the rays of the sun; darkened.
Shadily, shād'i-li, *adv.* In a *shady* manner; umbrageously.
Shadiness, shād'i-nes, *n.* State of being *shady*; umbrageousness.
Shading, shād'ing, *p.n.* Act of making a *shade*; the filling up of an outline.
Shadow, sha'dō, *n.* *Shade* within defined limits; obscurity, apparent on a plane, and representing the form of the body which intercepts the rays of light; darkness; shelter made by anything that intercepts the light, heat, or influence of the air; a faint representation; inseparable companion; that which is unreal; mockery; type; protection; favour.—*vt.* To overspread with a *shade* or *shadow*; to cloud; to darken; to make cool; to refresh by shade; to hide; to screen; to shroud; to mark with slight gradations of colour or light; to represent faintly; to represent typically. [Sax. *scadu*.]
Shadowing, sha'dō-ing, *p.n.* *Shade* or gradation of light and colour; a shading; a typifying.
Shadowy, sha'dō-i, *a.* Full of *shade*; gloomy; faintly light; typical; unreal; opaque. [Sax. *sceadwig*.]
Shady, shād'i, *a.* Abounding with *shade* or *shades*; sheltered from the glare of light or sultry heat.
Shaft, shaft, *n.* Something *formed*, to be used either as a missive weapon or for the purpose of support; an arrow; the body of a column between the base and the capital; anything straight, as the spire of a church, &c.; the stock of a feather or quill; the pole of a carriage; the handle of a weapon; a pit, or long, narrow opening into a mine; a large axle in machinery. [Sax. *sceaft*—G. *schaffen*, to fashion.]

ch, *chain*; j, *job*; g, *go*; ng, *sing*; TH, *then*; th, *thin*; w, *wig*; wh, *whig*; zh, *azure*; † *obsolete*.

Shafted, shaft'ed, p.a. *Having a shaft or handle.*

Shag, shag, *n. Coarse hair or nap, or rough woolly hair;* a kind of cloth having a long, coarse nap; tobacco leaves shredded for smoking.—*a.* Hairy.—*vt. To make rough or hairy;* to make rough or shaggy; to deform. *ppr.* shagging, *pret. & pp.* shagged. [Sax. *sceacga,* a brush of coarse hair.]

Shagginess, shag'i-nes, *n. State of being shaggy;* roughness with long, loose hair or wool.

Shaggy, Shagged, shag'i, shag'ed, *a. Rough with long hair or wool;* rough.

Shagreen, sha-grēn', *n.* A kind of *leather* prepared from the skins of horses, asses, mules, &c., and grained so as to be covered with small round pimples. It is also made of the skins of the sea-otter, seal, &c. [Fr. *chagrin*—Turk. *sagri,* the rump of an ass.]

Shagreen, Shagreened, sha-grēn', sha-grēnd', *a.* Made of the leather called *shagreen.*

Shake, shāk, *vt.* To cause to move with quick *vibrations;* to agitate; to make to totter; to cause to shiver; to throw away; to drive off (with *off, out,* &c.); to move from firmness; to endanger; to depress the courage of; to trill.—*vi.* To be agitated with a *vibratory* motion; to tremble; to shiver; to quake; to quiver; to totter. *ppr.* shaking, *pret.* shook, *pp.* shaken.—*n. Vacillating* motion; a rapid motion one way and the other; agitation; a trembling; a motion of hands clasped; a trill in music; a fissure or rent in timber. [Sax. *sceacan*—Icel. *skékia.*]

Shaken, shāk'n, *p.a.* Cracked or split.

Shakiness, shāk'i-nes, *n. State or quality of being shaky.*

Shaking, shāk'ing, *p.n. Act of shaking;* brandishing; concussion; a trembling or shivering.

Shakspearian, shāk-spēr'i-an, *a. Relating to or like Shakspeare.*

Shaky, shāk'i, *a.* Noting timber when naturally full of slits or clefts; loosely put together; ready to come to pieces.

Shale, shāl, *n.* A fine-grained rock, a species of schist or schistose clay; slate-clay, having a slaty structure. [G. *schale,* a shell.]

Shall, shal, *vi. verb auxiliary.* To owe. It is used to form the future tense. *pret.* should. [Sax. *sceal,* I owe, I ought.]

Shalloon, shal-lön', *n.* A slight woollen stuff. [said to be from *Chalons,* in France.]

Shallop, shal'lop, *n.* A small light vessel, having a small main-mast, and fore-mast with lug-sails; a sort of large boat with two masts, and usually rigged like a schooner. [Fr. *chaloupe*—L. *scapha,* a light boat.]

Shallow, shal'lō, *a. Shelving;* not deep; shoal; not intellectually deep; superficial; empty; simple.—*n. A shelf;* a shoal; a sand-bank; any place where the water is not deep. [probably from Sax. *scylf,* a shelf.]

Shallowly, shal'lō-li, *adv. In a shallow manner.*

Shallowness, shal'lō-nes, *n. State or quality of being shallow;* want of depth; superficialness of intellect; silliness.

Shalt, shalt. The second person singular of *shall.*

Shaly, shāl'i, *a. Pertaining to shale;* partaking of the qualities of shale.

Sham, sham, *n. That which is shameful* because deceiving just expectation; any trick or device that deludes; imposture.—*a.* False; counterfeit; pretended.—*vt. To deceive the expectation of;* to cheat; to obtrude by fraud; to perform carelessly.—*vi.* To make false pretences. *ppr.* shamming, *pret. & pp.* shammed. [Sax. *sceamu,* shame.]

Shambles, sham'blz, *n. pl. The benches or stalls on which butchers expose their meat for sale;* a flesh-market. [Dan. *skammel,* a bench.]

Shambling, sham'bl-ing, *p.a.* Moving with an awkward, irregular, clumsy pace.—*p.n.* An awkward, clumsy irregular pace or gait.

Shame, shām, *n.* A painful sensation, excited by a consciousness of guilt; the cause or reason of shame; that which brings reproach, and degrades a person in the estimation of others; contempt; the parts which modesty requires to be covered; dishonour; disgrace.—*vt. To make ashamed;* to cause to feel a consciousness of guilt, or of doing something derogatory to reputation; to cause to blush; to disgrace.—*vi.* To be ashamed. *ppr.* shaming, *pret. & pp.* shamed. [Sax. *sceamu;* G. *scham.*]

Shamefaced, shām'fāst, *a.* Bashful; easily confused or put out of countenance.

Shamefacedness, shām'fāst-nes, *n.* Bashfulness; excess of modesty.

Shameful, shām'ful, *a. Full of shame;* disgraceful; that brings shame or disgrace; disreputable; unbecoming; infamous; exciting shame in others.

Shamefully, shām'ful-li, *adv. In a shameful manner;* with indignity or indecency.

Shamefulness, shām'ful-nes, *n. State of being shameful;* disgracefulness.

Shameless, shām'les, *a. Destitute of shame;* unblushing; done without shame; indicating want of shame.

Shamelessly, shām'les-li, *adv. In a shameless manner;* without shame.

Shamelessness, shām'les-nes, *n. Want of shame;* want of sensibility to disgrace.

Shammy, sham'mi, *n.* A kind of leather, prepared originally from the skin of the *chamois,* but now prepared chiefly from the skins of sheep, goats, &c. [Fr. *chamois,* wild goat.]

Shampoo, sham-pö', *vt. To press and rub the whole surface of the body of,* and at the same time to bend and extend the limbs and rack the joints, in connection with the hot bath. [Hind. *champra,* to press.]

Shank, shangk, *n.* The large bone of the leg; the whole joint, from the knee to the ankle; the long part of an instrument. [Sax. *scanca*—Old Heb. *shuk,* to run.]

Shanked, shangkt, *p.a. Having a shank.*

Shapable, shāp'a-bl, *a. That may be shaped.*

Shape, shāp, *vt. To form;* to give form or figure to; to fashion; to mould; to adju-t; to adapt to a purpose; to image; to conceive.—*i.* To square; to be adjusted. *ppr.* shaping, *pret. & pp.* shaped.—*n. Form* or figure as constituted by lines and angles; the form of the trunk of the human body; a being, as endowed with form; idea; pattern. [Sax. *scyppan,* to make; Goth. *ga-skapjan,* to form.]

Shapeless, shāp'les, *a. Destitute of shape;* wanting symmetry; formless.

Shapelessness, shāp'les-nes, *n. State of being shapeless.*

Shapely, shāp'li, *a. Having a regular shape;* well formed. [from *shape.*]

Shard, shärd, *n.* A fragment of an earthen vessel; a hard case that covers the wings of certain insects, as the beetle, &c. [Sax. *sceard*—*sceran,* to shear.]

Shard-borne, shärd'bōrn, *a. Borne on shards,* as a beetle.

Sharded, shärd'ed, *p.a.* Having wings sheathed with a *hard case.*

Share, shār, *n. A cut or cutting;* a quantity; a part of a thing owned by a number in common; the part of a thing allotted to each individual of a number; a part belonging to one; a part contributed; the broad iron blade of a plough which cuts the ground. *vt. To cut;* to part among two or more; to enjoy with others; to possess jointly; to partake.—*vi.* To have part. [Sax. *scear*—*sceran,* to cut.]

Shareholder, shār'hōld-er, *n. One who owns a share* or shares in a joint fund.

Sharer, shār'er, *n. One who shares;* a partaker; one who enjoys or suffers in common with another or others.

Shark, shärk, *n.* An exceedingly voracious marine fish, with successive rows of long *sharp* teeth, found in all but the coldest seas.—*vt.*† To pick up hastily. [Gr. *karcharias.*]

Sharp, shärp, *a.* Having a very thin edge or fine point; of a nature to cut easily; acute; keen; having acuteness of mind; ready at invention; discerning; ingenious; keen to the taste; acid; tart; piercing to the ear; severe; sarcastic; severely rigid; cruel; eager for food, as an appetite; eager in pursuit; ardent; severely painful; violent; very vigilant; piercing, as sharp wind or air; characterized by leanness, as a visage; higher by a semitone, as a note in music.—*n.* An acute sound; a note artificially raised a semitone.—*vt. To make sharp;* to render quick; to mark with a sharp, in musical composition. [Sax. *scearp*—*scyran,* to cut.]

Sharpen, shärp'n, *vt. To make sharp;* to give a keen edge or fine point to; to make more pungent and painful; to make more quick or ingenious; to render more quick or acute, as perception; to make more eager for food; to make biting, sarcastic, or severe; to render more piercing; to make more acid; to make sour; to make more distressing; to raise by means of a sharp, as a sound.—*vi. To grow* or *become sharp.* [Sax *scyrpan.*]

Sharpened, shärp'nd, *p.a. Made sharp;* edged; pointed.

Sharper, shärp'ėr, *n. One who practises sharpness;* a tricking fellow; a cheat in bargaining or gaming.

Sharply, shärp'li, *adv.* With a keen edge or a fine point; severely; with keen perception; minutely; wittily.

Sharpness, shärp'nes, *n. State or quality of being sharp;* keenness of an edge or point; acidity; severity of pain or affliction; severity of language; satirical sarcasm; acuteness of intellect; the power of nice discernment; ingenuity; quickness of sense or perception; severity, as of the air.

Sharp-sighted, shärp'sīt-ed, *a. Having quick or acute sight;* having quick discernment or acute understanding.

Sharp-visaged, shärp'vi-zājd, *a. Having a sharp* or thin *face.*

Sharp-witted, shärp'wit-ed, *a. Having an acute* or nicely-discerning *mind.*

Shatter, shat'tėr, *vt.* To break so as to *scatter* into pieces; to rend; to split; to rive into splinters; to make incapable of close and continued application; to render unsound.—*vi.* To be broken into

Shatter-brained, shat′tėr-brānd, *a.* Having the *brains* or mind *disordered or wandering*; heedless; wild.

Shattered, shat′tėrd, *p.a.* Broken or dashed to pieces; rent.

Shattery, shat′tėr-i, *a. Easily shattered*; brittle; loose of texture.

Shave, shāv, *vt.* To pare close; to make bare or smooth by cutting the hair from the surface; to cut off thin slices from; to skim along the surface of.—*vi.* To cut off the beard with a razor close to the surface; to cut closely or keenly. *ppr.* shaving, *pret.* shaved, *pp.* shaved or shaven. [Sax. *scafan*—L. *scabo*, to scrape.]

Shaveling, shāv′ling, *n. A man shaved*; a monk or friar, in contempt.

Shaver, shāv′ėr, *n. One who shaves*; a barber.

Shaving, shāv′ing, *p.n. Act of one who shaves*; a thin slice pared off; a thin slice of wood shaved off.

Shawl, shal, *n.* A kind of mantle or tunic; a cloth of wool, cotton, silk, or hair, used by females as a loose covering for the neck and shoulders. [Fr. *châle*; Pers. *shal*.]

She, shē, *pers. pron. fem.* A pronoun which is the substitute for the name of a female; the word which refers to a female mentioned in the preceding or following part of a sentence; sometimes used as a noun for woman or female. [Goth. *si*.]

Sheaf, shēf, *n.* **Sheaves**, *pl.* A number or quantity of things *shoved* or put together; a quantity of the stalks of wheat or barley bound together; a bundle of stalks; any bundle or collection.—*vt. To make into sheaves*; to collect and bind.—*vi. To make sheaves.* [Sax. *sceaf*—*scafan*, to shove.]

Sheafy, shēf′i, *a. Pertaining to or consisting of sheaves.*

Sheal†, shēl, *vt.* To take the husks or pods off from.

Shear, shēr, *vt. To cut off*; to cut or clip from the surface of with an instrument of two blades; to separate by shears.—*vi. To divide*, as the two parts of anything when cut or sheared. *ppr.* shearing, *pret.* sheared, *pp.* sheared or shorn. [G. *scheren*—Gr. *keirō*, to cut.]

Shearer, shēr′ėr, *n. One who shears.*

Shearing, shēr′ing, *p.n. Act of shearing*; act of clipping or cutting off.

Shearling, shēr′ling, *n.* A sheep that has been but once *sheared.*

Shears, shērz, *n. pl.* An instrument consisting of two blades with a bevel edge, commonly movable on a pin, used for *cutting* cloth and other substances; anything in the form of blades of shears; an instrument for raising and inserting in place the lower masts of ships. [G. *scheren*, to cut.]

Sheath, shēth, *n. That which separates*; a case for the reception of a sword or other long and slender instrument; a membrane investing a stem or branch, as in grasses; any thin covering for defence; the wing-case of an insect. [Sax. *scœth*; Goth. *skaidan*, to separate.]

Sheathe, shēvh, *vt. To put into a sheath*; to inclose or cover with a sheathe or case; to case or cover with boards, or with sheets of copper. *ppr.* sheathing, *pret. & pp.* sheathed.

Sheathing, shēvh′ing, *p.n. Act of one who sheathes*; the covering of a ship's bottom and sides, or the materials for such covering.

Sheaved†, shēvd, *p.a.* Made of straw.

Shed, shed, *vt. To cause or suffer to flow out*; to let fall; to cast; to emit; to throw off; to diffuse.—*vi.* To let fall the parts, as leaves, &c. *ppr.* shedding, *pret. & pp.* shed. [Sax. *scedan*, to pour out; Chald. *ashad*, to pour out.]

Shed, shed, *n. A shade*; a slight building; a structure consisting simply of a roof supported on columns; a hovel. [Sax. *sced*—*sceadan*, to shade.]

Shedder, shed′ėr, *n. One who sheds* or causes to flow out.

Shedding, shed′ing, *p.n. Act of spilling* or of casting off or out; that which is cast off.

Sheen, shēn, *n. Brightness; splendour.* [Sax. *sciene*, clear—G. *scheinen*, to shine.]

Sheep, shēp, *sing.* and *pl.* The animal that is carefully *kept*; an animal that bears wool, remarkable for its harmlessness, timidity, and usefulness; God's people considered as under a spiritual shepherd. [Sax. *sceap*; Old G. *scāf*—Sans. *av*, to keep, to guard.]

Sheep-bite†, shēp′bīt, *vi.* To bite like a sheep; to practise petty thefts.

Sheep-cot, shēp′kot, *n.* A small inclosure for *sheep*; a pen.

Sheepfold, shēp′fōld, *n.* A place where *sheep* are collected or confined.

Sheepish, shēp′ish, *a. Like a sheep*; pertaining to sheep; timorous to excess; over-modest.

Sheepishly, shēp′ish-li, *adv.* Bashfully.

Sheepishness, shēp′ish-nes, *n. Quality of being sheepish*; bashfulness.

Sheep-shearer, shēp′shēr-ėr, *n. One who shears sheep.*

Sheep-shearing, shēp′shēr-ing, *n. Act of shearing sheep*; the time of shearing sheep.

Sheep-walk, shēp′wak, *n.* Pasture for *sheep*; a place where sheep feed.

Sheer, shēr, *a. Pure or unmingled*; mere; perpendicular.—*adv.* Clean; at once. [Sax. *scir*; Goth. *skeirs*, clear.]

Sheer, shēr, *vi.* To deviate from the line of the proper course, as a ship when not steered with steadiness; to slip or move aside. [See Shear.]

Sheet, shēt, *n.* Something extended or spread out, *as a covering*; a broad and large piece of linen or cotton cloth spread over a bed; a sail; a broad piece of paper as it comes from the manufacturer; a piece of paper printed, folded, and bound, or formed into a book; a book or pamphlet.—*vt. To cover as with a sheet*; to fold in a sheet; to cover with something broad and thin. [Sax. *sceat*, a covering—Sans. *sku*, to cover, to conceal.]

Sheet-anchor, shēt′ang-kėr, *n.* The largest *anchor* of a ship, on which, in cases of extremity, its safety depends; the last refuge for safety.

Sheeting, shēt′ing, *p.n.* A kind of linen or cotton cloth fit for making bed-sheets.

Sheet-lightning, shēt′līt-ning, *n.* Lightning *thrown out* or appearing in wide expanded flashes.

Shekel, she′kel, *n.* An ancient *weight* and coin among the Jews, about half an ounce avoirdupois, and in value about 2*s.* 7*d.* sterling. [Heb.—*shakal*, to weigh.]

Shelf, shelf, *n.* **Shelves**, shelvz, *pl.* A board elevated above the floor, and fixed or set horizontally on a frame for holding vessels, books, and the like; a flat projecting layer of rock; a sandbank in the sea, or a rock or ledge of rocks. [Sax. *scylfe*, a table.]

Shelfy, shelf′i, *a. Full of shelves*; abounding with sand-banks or rocks.

Shell, shel, *n.* The hard *covering* of certain fruits; the hard substance which protects certain fishes; the outer covering of an egg; the outer part of a house unfinished; a coarser kind of coffin; an instrument of music; outer part; a hollow sphere of iron, which, being filled with gunpowder and fired from a mortar, bursts into pieces; a bomb.—*vt. To strip or break off the shell of*; to bombard, as a fort or battery.—*vi. To fall off*, as a shell; to cast the shell or exterior covering; to be disengaged from the husk. [Sax. *scel*—Old G. *schalen*, to cover.]

Shelled, sheld, *p.a. Deprived of the shell*; separated from the ear.

Shell-fish, shel′fish, *n.* A mollusc whose external covering consists of a *shell*, as clams, oysters, &c.

Shelly, shel′i, *a. Abounding with shells*; consisting of shells.

Shelter, shel′tėr, *vt. To cover* from violence or attack; to defend; to render safe; to cover from notice; to disguise for protection.—*vi. To take shelter.*—*n. That which covers* or defends from injury or annoyance; an asylum; a covert; a harbour; protection; security; he who guards from danger; a protector. [G. *schulter*; Icel. *skyli*, to cover.]

Sheltered, shel′tėrd, *p.a. Covered* from injury or annoyance; protected.

Shelve, shelv, *vt. To place on a shelf*; to put aside or out of use; to furnish with shelves.—*vi.* To incline; to be sloping, as shelves or shallows in the sea. *ppr.* shelving, *pret. & pp.* shelved.

Shelves, shelvz, *n. pl.* Dangerous shallows or rocks lying immediately under the surface of the water.

Shelving, shelv′ing, *p.a.* Sloping; having declivity.—*n. The operation of fixing up shelves*; materials for shelves.

Shelvy, shelv′i, *a.* Full of rocks or sandbanks; shallow.

Shemitic, shem-it′ik, *a. Pertaining to Shem*, the son of Noah. The Shemitic languages are the Chaldee, Syriac, Arabic, Hebrew, Samaritan, Ethiopic, Phœnician, and Assyrian. [Heb.*shem*, name, sign.]

Shent†, shent, *p.a.* Injured; reproached.

Shepherd, shep′ėrd, *n. One who keeps sheep*; a swain; a rural lover; the pastor of a parish, church, or congregation. [from *sheep* and *herd*.]

Shepherdess, shep′ėrd-es, *n. A woman who tends sheep*; hence, a rural lass.

Sherbet, shėr-bet′, *n. A drink* composed of water, lemon-juice, and sugar. [Ar. *sharbat*—*shereb*, to drink.]

Sherd, shėrd, *n.* A fragment, as potsherd. [See Shard.]

Sheriff, she′rif, *n. The governor of a shire*; a shire-reeve; an officer in each county to whom is intrusted the execution or administration of the laws. [Sax. *scire-gerefa*—*scire*, a shire, and *gerefa*, a governor.]

Sheriffalty, she′rif-al-ti, *n. See* Shrievalty.

Sherrist, she′ris, *n.* Same as *sherry.*

Sherry, she′ri, *n.* A strong wine of a deep amber colour, and having, when good, an aromatic odour; so called from *Xeres*, near Cadis, in Spain, where it is principally produced.

Shew, **Shewed**, **Shewn**, shō, shōd, shōn. *See* Show.

Shew-bread, shō′bred. *See* Show-bread.

Shibboleth, shib′bō-leth, *n.* A word which was made the criterion by which to distinguish the Ephraimites

from the Gileadites; the criterion of a party. [Heb. a stream, from *shabal*, to go.]
Shield, shēld, *n.* Something hard *for defence;* a broad piece of defensive armour; defence; the person who defends; an escutcheon.—*vt.* To cover, as with a shield; to defend; to secure from assault or injury; to ward off. [Sax. *scyld—scyldan*, to protect.]
Shieldless, shēld'les, *a.* Destitute of a *shield* or of protection.
Shift, shift, *vi.* Primarily, *to divide;* to move; to change place; to vary; to give place to other things; to change clothes; to resort to expedients for a livelihood; to seek methods of safety. *vt.* To move away; to put out of the way by some expedient; to change; to transfer from one place to another; to change, as clothes; to dress in fresh clothes.—*n.* A change; a turning from one thing to another; mean refuge; last resource; fraud; a subterfuge; a trick to escape evil; a chemise. [Sax. *scyftan*, to divide.]
Shifter, shift'ér, *n.* One who *shifts;* the person who plays tricks.
Shifting, shift'ing, *p.a.* Changing place; resorting from one expedient to another.
Shiftless, shift'les, *a.* Destitute of expedients; wanting means to act or live.
Shilling, shil'ing, *n.* An English silver coin and money of account, equal to twelve pence, or the twentieth part of a pound. [Sax. *scylling*.]
Shin, shin, *n.* The fore-part of the leg, or the bone of the fore-part of the leg. [Sax. *scina*.]
Shine, shin, *vi.* To emit a steady brilliant *light;* to give light with steady radiance; to beam; to glitter; to be bright; to be animated; to be glossy or bright, as silk; to be gay or splendid; to be beautiful; to be distinguished; to give light, real or figurative.—*n.* Brightness; splendour; lustre; fair weather. *ppr.* shining, *pret. & pp.* shined or shone. [Sax. *scinan;* Goth. *skeinan—Sans. kan*, to shine.]
Shingle, shing'gl, *n.* A thin piece of wood, formed by *splitting* or sawing, and used as a tile or slate for covering buildings; loose gravel and pebbles, or a collection of roundish stones on shores and coasts, so named from having been fragments *separated* from rocks. [G. *schindel* — L. *scindo*, to divide.]
Shingled, shing'gld, *p.a.* Covered with *shingles.*
Shingles, shing'glz, *n.* An eruptive disease which spreads around the body like a *girdle.* [L. *cingo*, to gird.]
Shingling, shing'gl-ing, *p.n.* Act of *covering with shingles;* a covering of shingles.
Shingly, shing'gl-i, *a.* Abounding with *gravel or shingle.*
Shining, shin'ing, *p.a.* Bright; radiant; distinguished; conspicuous.—*p.n.* Effusion or clearness of light; brightness.
Shiny, shin'i, *a.* Bright; clear.
Ship, ship, *n.* Something *hollowed;* something hollowed for receiving and conveying goods, &c., by water; a large vessel adapted to navigation; a building of a structure or form fitted for navigation; a vessel with three masts, and tops to each.—*vt.* To put on board *of a ship;* to transport in a ship; to engage for service on board of a ship; to fix anything in its place.—*vi.* To en*gage for service on board of a ship;* to enter on board of a vessel. *ppr.* ship-

ping, *pret. & pp.* shipped. [Sax. *scip* —L. *cavo*, to hollow.]
Ship-broker, ship'brō-kėr, *n.* A *broker* who procures insurance and performs other business for *ships.*
Ship-builder, ship'bild-ėr, *n. One who builds* or constructs *ships* and other vessels; a naval architect; a shipwright.
Ship-master, ship'mas-tėr, *n.* The *master*, captain, or commander of a *ship.*
Shipmate, ship'māt, *n. One who serves in the same ship.*
Shipment, ship'ment, *n. Act of shipping;* embarkation; the goods shipped, or put on board of a ship.
Shipper, ship'ér, *n. One who places goods on board a ship* for transportation.
Shipping, ship'ing, *p.a. Relating to ships.—p.n. Ships in general;* ships or vessels of any kind for navigation; tonnage.
Shipwreck, ship'rek, *n. The destruction of a ship* by being cast ashore or broken to pieces by striking against rocks; destruction.—*vt.* To *destroy*, as a *ship*, by running ashore or on rocks or sand-banks; to throw into distress, as by a shipwreck; to make to suffer the dangers of a wreck.
Shipwrecked, ship'rekt, *p.a.* Dashed upon the rocks or banks; destroyed.
Shipwright, ship'rit, *n. One who constructs ships;* a builder of ships.
Shire, shir, *n. A division of territory;* a county. (In county names this word is unaccented, as in the compound *Berkshire*, and the *i* is pronounced as *i of pin.*) [Sax. *scyr—sceran*, to divide.]
Shirk, shėrk, *vt.* To avoid or get away from.
Shirt, shėrt, *n.* An under garment *cut short;* a loose garment of linen, cotton, or other material, worn by men and boys next the body.—*vt.* To cover *with a shirt*, or as with a shirt. [Sax. *syrce—scyran*, to cut off.]
Shirting, shėrt'ing, *p.n. Cloth for shirts.*
Shive, shiv, *n.* Something *shaved* off; a slice; a little piece or fragment. [probably from Sax. *scafan*, to shave.]
Shiver, shi'vér, *vt. To break into many small pieces or splinters;* to shatter; to dash to pieces by a blow.—*vi.* To fall at once into many small pieces or parts; to quake; to quiver from cold. *n.* A fragment into which a thing breaks by any sudden violence; a slice. [G. *schiefern*, to peel off in flakes.]
Shiver, shi'vér, *vi. To tremble;* to shake, as with cold, fear, or horror; to be affected with a thrilling sensation, like that of chilliness; to flutter in the wind, as a sail.—*n.* A *shaking fit;* a tremor. [G. *schauern*, to tremble.]
Shivering, shi'vér-ing, *p.a.* Quaking; shaking, as with cold or fear—*p.n. Act of dashing to pieces;* severance; a trembling; a shaking with cold or fear.
Shiveringly, shi'vér-ing-li, *adv. With shivering* or slight trembling.
Shivery, shi'vér-i, *a.* Easily falling into many pieces: not firmly cohering.
Shoal, shōl, *n.* A company *separated* from the main body; a great multitude assembled; a crowd; a throng; [allied to *shelve* and *shallow*—which see] a place where the water of a river, lake, or sea is *shallow* or of little depth; a sand-bank or bar; a shallow. *vi. To crowd;* to throng; to become more shallow.—*a. Shallow;* of little depth. [Sax. *sceol*, a multitude—*scylan*, to separate.]
Shoaly, shōl'i, *a. Full of shoals.*

Shock, shok, *n. A violent concussion* of bodies; a violent dashing against; conflict of contending armies; offence; impression of disgust; [Swed. *skock*, a crowd] a pile or assemblage of sheaves of wheat, rye, &c.; [from *shag*] a dog with long hair or shag.—*vt. To shake with violence;* to offend; to disgust; to appal; to dismay; to cause to recoil, as from something odious or horrible; to make up into shocks.—*vi.* To meet with hostile violence. [D. *schok.*]
Shocking, shok'ing, *p.a.* Striking, as with horror; causing to recoil with horror or disgust; appalling.
Shockingly, shok'ing-li, *adv.* In a *shocking manner.*
Shoe, shö, *n.* **Shoes**, shöz, *pl. A covering* for the foot, usually of leather; a plate of iron nailed to the hoof of a horse; anything resembling a shoe.—*vt. To furnish with shoes*, to put shoes on; to cover at the bottom. *ppr.* shoeing, *pret. & pp.* shod. [Sax. *sceo—Sans. sku*, to cover.]
Shoe-black, shö'blak, *n.* A person who cleans shoes and boots.
Shoemaker, shö'māk-ėr, *n.* One who *makes shoes* and boots.
Shoe-tie, shö'ti, *n. A string* or ribbon used for fastening a *shoe* to the foot.
Shog!, shog, *vt.* To shake.
Shoot!, shön, *n. pl. of shoe.*
Shoot, shöt, *vt. To cause to dart*, as an arrow; to let fly and drive with force; to cause to be driven with violence; to dart; to let off; to strike with anything shot; to push forth or out; to drive; to propel; to pass through with swiftness; to kill by a ball, arrow, or other thing shot.—*vi.* To perform the act of discharging anything by means of an engine; to sprout; to be pushed out; to jut; to pass, as an arrow or pointed instrument; to grow rapidly; to become by rapid growth; to move with velocity; to feel a quick darting pain. *ppr.* shooting, *pret. & pp.* shot.—*n. Act of shooting;* the act of striking with a missile weapon; a young branch or plant; a scion. [Sax. *sceotan;* Chald. *skedā*, to cast, to pour out.]
Shooter, shöt'ėr, *n. One who shoots;* an archer; a gunner.
Shooting, shöt'ing, *p.a.* Germinating; branching; glancing, as pain.—*p.n.* Act of sending an arrow with force, or of discharging firearms; a firing; act or practice of killing game with guns or firearms; sensation of a quick, glancing pain.
Shop, shop, *n.* A building or room in which goods, &c., are sold by retail; a building in which mechanics work. *vi. To visit shops* for purchasing goods (used chiefly in the participle). *ppr.* shopping, *pret. & pp.* shopped. [Norm. *schopes*, shops.]
Shopkeeper, shop'kėp'ėr, *n. One who keeps a shop;* one who sells goods in a shop or by retail.
Shop-lifter, shop'lift-ėr, *n. One who steals anything in a shop*, or takes goods privately from a shop.
Shopping, shop'ing, *p.n. Act of visiting shops* for the purchase of goods.
Shore, shōr, *n.* The place where the continuity of the land is interrupted or *separated* by the sea or the river; the land adjacent to the ocean, or to a large lake or river.—*vt. To set on shore.* [Sax. *score—scyran*, to cut off.]
Shore, shōr, *n. A prop;* a buttress.—*vt. To prop;* to support by a post or buttress. *ppr.* shoring, *pret. & pp.* shored. [D. *schoor*, a prop.]

Fāte, fär, fat, fall; mē, met, hė̇ pine, pin; nōte, not, move; tübe, tub, bull; oil, pound.

Shored, shōrd, *p.a. Having a bank or shore.*
Short, short, *a. Cut off; abrupt; not long; not extended in time; not of usual length; repeated at small intervals of time; not of adequate quantity; not reaching the point expected; deficient; scanty; not sufficiently supplied; scantily furnished; narrow; not large; brittle; not bending; laconic; brief; pointed; severe.—adv.* Not long. [Sax. *scort—scyran*, to cut off.]
Shortcoming, short'kum-ing, *n.* A failure of full performance, as of duty.
Short-dated, short'dāt-ed, *a.* Having little time to run.
Shorten, short'n, *vt. To make short* in time or measure; to curtail; to lop; to deprive.—*vi. To become short* or shorter; to contract. [Sax. *scyrtan.*]
Shortened, short'nd, *p.a.* Abridged; contracted.
Shortening, short'n-ing, *p.n. A making short* or shorter.
Short-hand, short'hand, *n. Short writing;* a compendious method of writing.
Short-lived, short'livd, *a. Not living long;* being of short continuance.
Shortly, short'li, *adv.* Quickly; soon; in a little time; in few words; briefly.
Shortness, short'nes, *n. State or quality of being short* in space, time, or quantity; fewness of words; brevity; want of reach or the power of retention; deficiency; limited extent.
Short-rib, short'rib, *n. A rib shorter* than the others; one of the lower ribs.
Short-sighted, short'sit-ed, *a.* Nearsighted; not able to see far intellectually; inconsiderate.
Short-sightedness, short'sit-ed-nes, *n.* A defect in vision, consisting in the inability to see things at a distance; limited intellectual sight or vision.
Short-winded, short'wind-ed, *a. Affected with shortness of breath;* having a quick respiration.
Shot, shot, *n. Act of shooting;* that which is shot; a missile weapon, particularly a ball or bullet; small globular masses of lead, used for killing birds, &c.; the flight of a missile weapon; a marksman; one who practises shooting; [Sax. *sceat*] a reckoning; proportional share of expense at a tavern, &c.—*vt. To load with shot* over a cartridge, as a gun. *ppr.* shotting, *pret. & pp.* shotted. [Sax. *scotu—scotian*, to shoot.]
Shot-free, shot'frē, *a.* Free from charge; exempted from share of expense.
Shotten, shot'n, *p.a. Having thrown out* the spawn, as a herring; having been shot out; shot out of its socket.
Shought, shuf, *n.* A shaggy dog.
Should, shụd, the *pret. of shall,* but now used as an auxiliary verb, either in the past time or conditional present.
Shoulder, shōl'der, *n.* The joint by which the arm of a human being, or the fore-leg of a quadruped, is connected with the body; the upper-joint of the fore-leg of an animal cut for the market; something like the human shoulder; support; sustaining power; that which elevates; (pl.) the upper part of the back.—*vt.* To push with the *shoulder;* to push with violence; to take upon the shoulder. [Sax. *sculder.*]
Shoulder-belt, shōl'der-belt, *n. A belt* that passes across the *shoulder.*
Shoulder-blade, shōl'der-blād, *n.* The bone of the *shoulder,* or *blade*-bone.
Shoulder-knot, shōl'der-not, *n.* An ornamental *knot* of ribbon or lace worn on the *shoulder;* an epaulette.

Shoulder-slip, shōl'der-slip, *n. Dislocation of the shoulder.*
Shout, shout, *vi. To exclaim;* to utter a sudden and loud outcry, usually in joy, or to animate soldiers in an onset. *n.* A loud burst of voices; a vehement and sudden outcry of a multitude of men, expressing joy or animated courage. [Ar. *sayhat,* an exclamation.]
Shouting, shout'ing, *n. Act of shouting;* a shout.
Shove, shuv, *vt. To push; to thrust;* to drive along by the direct application of strength without a sudden impulse; to delay (with *by*).—*vi. To push or drive forward;* to push off; to move in a boat or with a pole. *ppr.* shoving. *pret. & pp.* shoved.—*n.* Act of pressing against by strength, without a sudden impulse; a sudden push. [Sax. *scufan;* Old G. *sciuban,* to thrust.]
Shove-groatt, shuv'grat, *n.* A certain game.
Shovel, shu'vel, *n. That which shoves;* an instrument consisting of a broad scoop with a handle, used for throwing earth, &c.—*vt. To take up and throw with a shovel;* to gather in great quantities. *ppr.* shovelling, *pret. & pp.* shovelled. [Sax. *sceofl.*]
Show, shō, *vt. To cause to see or to be seen;* to afford to the eye or to notice; to make to know; to make known to; to prove; to inform; to point out, as a guide; to bestow; to disclose; to explain.—*vi. To seem;* to appear; to look; to be in appearance. *ppr.* showing, *pret.* showed, *pp.* shown or showed. *n.* Something offered *to the sight;* a sight; ostentation; public appearance; semblance; speciousness; plausibility; representative action; hypocritical pretence. [Sax. *sceawian.*]
Show-bread, **Shew-bread**, shō'bred, shō'bred, *n.* Among the Jews, *bread of exhibition;* the loaves of bread which the priest of the week placed before the Lord, on the golden table in the sanctuary.
Shower, shou'er, *n.* That which *falls or runs* down from a *cloud;* a fall of rain or hail, of short duration; a fall of things from the air in thick succession; liberal distribution.—*vt. To water with a shower;* to wet copiously with rain; to bestow liberally (with *down*).—*vi. To rain in showers.* [Sax. *scur;* Goth. *skura,* a storm.]
Showeriness, shou'er-i-nes, *n. State of being showery.*
Showery, shou'er-i, *a. Raining in showers;* abounding with frequent falls of rain.
Showily, shō'i-li, *adv. In a showy manner;* pompously, with parade.
Showiness, shō'i-nes, *n. State of being showy;* pompousness; great parade.
Showing, shō'ing, *p.n. A presentation to view;* exhibition.
Showman, shō'man, *n. One who exhibits shows.*
Showy, shō'i, *a. Making a show;* exhibiting ostentation; gaudy; pompous.
Shred, shred, *vt. To cut* into small *pieces,* particularly narrow and long pieces. *ppr.* shredding, *pret. & pp.* shred.—*n.* A long narrow piece *cut off,* as of cloth; a fragment; a piece. [Sax. *screadian;* Old G. *scrótan,* to cut in pieces.]
Shredding, shred'ing, *p.n. A cutting into shreds;* that which is cut off.
Shreddy, shred'i, *a. Consisting of shreds.*
Shrew, shrū, *n.* A peevish, *brawling,* turbulent, vexatious woman; a scold; a termagant. [G. *schreien,* to cry out.]

Shrewd, shrūd, *a. Searching into;* scrutinising; sagacious; astute; characterized by acuteness, penetration, or subtlety; malicious†; vexatious†. [Sax. *scrudnian,* to search into.]
Shrewdly, shrūd'li, *adv.* Archly; sagaciously; with good guess; mischievously†.
Shrewdness, shrūd'nes, *n. Quality of being shrewd;* sagacity; astuteness.
Shrewish, shrū'ish, *a. Having the qualities of a shrew;* peevish; petulantly clamorous.
Shrewishly, shrū'ish-li, *adv.* Peevishly; clamorously.
Shrewishness, shrū'ish-nes, *n. The qualities of a shrew;* petulance; turbulent clamorousness.
Shrew-mouse, shrū'mous, *n.* A small harmless animal resembling a mouse, living mostly underground. [Sax. *screawa.*]
Shriek, shrēk, *vi. To utter a sharp shrill cry;* to scream, as in a sudden fright, in horror or anguish.—*n.* A sharp, *shrill outcry or scream,* such as is produced by sudden terror or extreme anguish. [Sw. Goth. *skrika,* to vociferate.]
Shrieking, shrēk'ing, *p.a. Crying out* with a shrill voice.—*p.n. A crying out* with a shrill voice.
Shrievalty, shrēv'al-ti, *n. The office or jurisdiction of a sheriff.* [from *sheriff.*]
Shrift, shrift, *n. Confession* made to a priest. [Sax. *scrifan,* to shrive.]
Shrill, shril, *a. Sharp; acute;* piercing, as sound; uttering an acute sound. *vi.*† To utter an acute piercing sound. *vt.*† To cause to make a shrill sound. [Icel. *skridla,* to sound upon being touched, spoken of things very dry or parched.]
Shrillness, shril'nes, *n. Quality of being shrill;* sharpness or fineness of voice.
Shrilly, shril'i, *adv.* Acutely, as sound; with a sharp sound.
Shrimp, shrimp, *n.* A small crustaceous fish, probably so named from its jointed and *corrugated* body; a little wrinkled man; a little person. [G. *schrumpfen,* to shrink.]
Shrine, shrīn, *n. A case or box;* particularly, a case in which sacred things are deposited; a reliquary, tomb, or altar.—*vt. To place in a shrine;* to enshrine. *ppr.* shrining, *pret. & pp.* shrined. [Sax. *scrin*—L. *scrinium,* a chest.]
Shrink, shringk, *vi. To contract;* to contract spontaneously; to shrivel; to become wrinkled by contraction, as the skin; to retire, as from danger; to recoil, as in fear, horror, or distress.—*vt. To cause to contract. ppr.* shrinking, *pret. & pp.* shrunk.—*n. Contraction;* a spontaneous drawing into less compass; a withdrawing from fear or horror. [Sax. *scrinkan.*]
Shrinking, shringk'ing, *p.n. A contraction* or spontaneous drawing into less compass; act of drawing back through fear.
Shrinkingly, shringk'ing-li, *adv. By shrinking.*
Shrive†, shriv, *vt.* To hear the confession of. *ppr.* shriving, *pret. & pp.* shrived. [Sax. *scrifan.*]
Shrivel, shri'vel, *vi. To be drawn into wrinkles;* to contract.—*vt.* To cause to shrink into *corrugations. ppr.* shrivelling, *pret. & pp.* shrivelled. [D. *schrompelen,* to become wrinkled.]
Shrivelled, shri'veld, *p.a. Contracted into wrinkles.*
Shriver, shriv'er, *n.* One who shrives.
Shroud, shroud, *n. That which clothes*

or protects; a cover; the dress of the dead, a winding-sheet; (pl.) a range of large ropes in a ship, extending from the head of a mast to the right and left sides of the ship, to support the masts and enable them to carry sail. *vt.* To *clothe;* to dress for the grave; to hide; to defend; to overwhelm. [Sax. *scrud—scrydan,* to clothe.]

Shrove-tide, Shrove-Tuesday, shrōv′-tid, shrŏv tūz-dā, *n. Confession-time; confession*-Tuesday; the day immediately preceding the first of Lent, or Ash-Wednesday. [Sax. *scrifan,* to receive confession.]

Shrow†, shrō, *n.* A shrew.

Shrub, shrub, *n.* A *low, dwarf tree;* a woody plant of a size less than a tree; a plant with several woody stems from the same root. [Sax. *scrob.*]

Shrub, shrub, *n.* A liquor composed of acid, particularly lemon-juice, and sugar, with spirit to preserve it. [Ar. *shurb,* drinking.]

Shrubbery, shrub′ė-ri, *n. Shrubs;* a plantation of shrubs.

Shrubbiness, shrub′i-nes, *n.* State or quality of being shrubby.

Shrubby, shrub′i, *a. Full of shrubs;* consisting of shrubs or brushwood.

Shrug, shrug, *vt.* To draw up; to contract, as the shoulders.—*vi.* To raise or draw up the shoulders. *ppr.* shrugging, *pret. & pp.* shrugged.—*n.* A drawing up of the shoulders; a motion usually expressing dislike or slight contempt. [perhaps akin to L. *rugo,* to crease.]

Shudder, shud′ėr, *vi. To quake; to shake* or quiver with fear or aversion; to shiver.—*n. A tremor;* a shaking with fear or horror. [G. *schüttern,* to tremble.]

Shuddering, shud′ėr-ing, *p.a. Trembling;* quaking.—*p.n. A trembling* with fear or horror.

Shuffle, shuf′l, *vt. To shove* one way and the other; to mix by pushing or shoving; to confuse; to change the relative positions of, as of cards in the pack; to remove or introduce by artificial confusion.—*vi.* To shift ground; to avoid answering fair questions; to quibble; to struggle; to shift; to move with an irregular gait. *ppr.* shuffling, *pret. & pp.* shuffled.—*n. A shoving;* the act of throwing into confusion by change of places; an evasion; a trick; an artifice. [D. *schoffelen,* to shove.]

Shuffler, shuf′l-ėr, *n. One who shuffles* or prevaricates; one who plays tricks.

Shuffling, shuf′l-ing, *p.a.* Evasive.—*p.n. Act of one who shuffles;* trick; evasion; an irregular gait.

Shun, shun, *vt.* To avoid through *fear; to fly from;* to keep clear of; not to mix or associate with; to decline; to neglect.—*vi.* To decline; to avoid to do a thing. *ppr.* shunning, *pret. & pp.* shunned. [Sax. *scunian,* to shun.]

Shunless†, shun′les, *a.* Not to be shunned; inevitable.

Shunt, shunt, *vt.* To turn off to one side, as a railway train or carriage.

Shut, shut, *vt.* To close, as water, so as to hinder ingress or egress; to close or stop up for security; to bar; to forbid entrance into; to close, as the fingers; to contract.—*vi.* To close itself; to be closed. *ppr.* shutting, *pret. & pp.* shut. *p.a.* Closed; having the entrance barred. [G. *schützen,* to dam, to dike.]

Shutter, shut′ėr, *n.* A *close cover* for a window or aperture.

Shuttle, shut′l, *n. That which is shot;* an instrument used by weavers for *shooting* the thread of the woof in weaving from one side of the cloth to the other, between the threads of the warp. [Sax. *scyttel—sceotan,* to shoot.]

Shuttle-cock, shut′l-kok, *n.* A cork stuck with *feathers* used to be *cast* or *driven* backwards and forwards by a battledore in play; also, the play.

Shy, shi, *a. That shuns;* keeping at a distance through timidity; reserved; coy; cautious; wary; careful to avoid committing one's self; suspicious; jealous.—*n.* The starting suddenly aside of a horse.—*vi.* To fly or start away; to start suddenly aside, as a horse. *ppr.* shying, *pret. & pp.* shied. [G. *scheu, timid—scheuen,* to shun.]

Shying, shī′ing, *p.n.* Act of starting aside.

Shyly, shī′li, *adv.* In a *shy manner.*

Shyness, shī′nes, *n. Quality of being shy;* reserve; coyness.

Sib†, sib, *a.* Related by blood; akin. [Sax. *sib,* peace, relation.]

Sibilant, si′bi-lant, *a. Hissing;* making a hissing sound.—*n.* A letter uttered with a *hissing* of the voice, as *s.* [L. *sibilans—sibilo,* to hiss.]

Sibyl, si′bil, *n.* In pagan mythology, a prophetess who pretended to declare *the will of Zeus* or Jupiter; a gipsy or fortune-teller. [Gr. *sibylla.*]

Sibylline, si′bil-lin, *a. Pertaining to the sibyls;* uttered by sibyls; like the productions of sibyls.

Sicilian, si-si′li-an, *a.* Of or pertaining to Sicily.

Sick, sik, *a. Suffering from a complaint;* ill; affected with nausea; disgusted; inclined to vomit; having a strong dislike to; weary (with *of*); indicating a place where sickness is.—*vt.* To make sick. [Sax. *seoc;* Old G. *siuh.*]

Sicken, sik′n, *vt. To make sick;* to make squeamish; to disgust; to impair; to weaken.—*vi. To become sick;* to be satiated; to become disgusting; to be filled with aversion or abhorrence; to become weak; to languish.

Sickening, sik′n-ing, *p.a. Making sick;* disgusting.

Sickish, sik′ish, *a. Somewhat sick* or diseased; exciting disgust; nauseating.

Sickishly, sik′ish-li, *adv.* In a *sickish manner.*

Sickle, sik′l, *n.* An instrument for *cutting* grain; a reaping-hook. [Sax. *sicel —L. seco,* to cut.]

Sickliness, sik′li-nes, *n. State of being sickly;* state of producing sickness extensively.

Sickly, sik′li, *a. Affected with sickness;* not healthy; ailing; weakly; faint; producing disease extensively; diminished in strength or brightness.—*vt.*† To make sick or diseased.

Sickness, sik′nes, *n. State of being sick;* a failure of strength under a sense of disgust; malady; nausea.

Side, sīd, *n. That* part of the body on which one usually *lies;* the part of an animal between the back and the face and belly; the broad and long part of a thing; margin; border; the exterior line of anything; the slope, as of a hill; any part considered in respect to its direction; party; sect; interest; favour; any part being in opposition to another; a line of descent through one parent.—*a. Being on the side,* or toward the side; lateral; long†; indirect. *vi.* To take the same *side* with another; to embrace the opinions of one party when opposed to another party (with *with*). [Sax.; Icel. *sida;* Sans. *si,* to lie.]

Side-board, sīd′bōrd, *n.* A kind of *table* with drawers, &c., placed at the *side* of a dining-room, to hold dining utensils, &c.

Side-box, sīd′boks, *n.* A *box* on the *side* of a theatre.

Sided, sīd′ed, *p.a. Having a side* or sides; as, one-sided.

Sideling, sīd′l-ing, *adv. Sidewise;* with the side foremost; sloping.

Sidelong, sīd′long, *a. Being along the side;* lateral; not directly in front. *adv. On the side;* laterally; in the direction of the side.

Sidereal, si-dē′rē-al, *a. Pertaining to a star or stars;* starry; measured by the motion of the stars. [Fr. *sidéral—L. sidus, sidėris,* a star, a group of stars.]

Side-saddle, sīd′sad-l, *n.* A *saddle* for a woman's seat on horseback.

Sideways, Sidewise, sīd′wāz, sīd′wīz, *adv. Toward one side;* laterally.

Side-wind, sīd′wind, *n. A wind* blowing *against the side;* indirect means.

Siding, sīd′ing, *p.n.* The attaching of one's self to a *side* or party; the place of passing on a railway.

Sidle, sīd′l, *vi. To go* or move *side foremost;* to lie on the side. *ppr.* sidling, *pret. & pp.* sidled.

Siege, sēj, *n.* A *seat*†; a throne†; place†; rank†; *the setting* of an army before a fortified place for the purpose of compelling it to surrender; any continued endeavour to gain possession. [Fr. *siége—*L. *sedeo,* to sit.]

Sieve, sev, *n. That which sifts;* a vessel for *separating* flour from bran, or the smaller particles of any substance from the larger. [Sax. *sife.*]

Sift, sift, *vt.* To *separate* by *shaking;* to separate by a sieve, as the fine part of a substance from the coarse; to examine critically; to scrutinize; to try [Sax. *siftan—*Gr. *seiō,* to shake.]

Sifted, sift′ed, *p.a.* Critically examined.

Sifter, sift′ėr, *n.* One who *sifts;* that which sifts; a sieve.

Sigh, sī, *vi.* To inhale and expire a long breath audibly, as from grief; to lament; to make a sound like sighing. *vt.* To utter sighs over.—*n.* A single deep respiration; a long breath made audibly, as in grief. [Sax. *sican,* to sigh.]

Sighing, sī′ing, *p.n.* Act of suffering a deep respiration, or taking a long breath.

Sight, sīt, *n. Act of seeing;* perception of objects by the eye; view; faculty of vision; the state of admitting unobstructed vision; a being within the limits of vision; knowledge; eye; a small aperture through which objects are to be seen; that which is beheld; exhibition; a small piece of metal fixed on the muzzle of a musket, &c., to aid the eye in taking aim.—*vt.* To *come in sight* or view of; to obtain a view of, as land. [Sax. *gesiht—seón,* to see.]

Sighted, sīt′ed, *p.a. Having sight,* or *seeing* in a particular manner, as nearsighted.

Sightless, sīt′les, *a. Wanting sight;* blind; that cannot be seen; unsightly†.

Sightliness, sīt′li-nes, *n. Quality of being sightly;* comely appearance.

Sightly, sīt′li, *a. Pleasing to the sight* or eye; open to the view; that may be seen from a distance.

Sign, sin, *n.* That by *which a thing is known;* a mark; a note; a symptom; something by which another thing is shown; a motion or gesture indicating a wish; a remarkable event; some visible transaction, intended as proof of something else; proof; evidence by sight; something hung or set near a house or over a door, to give notice of

SIGNAL 359 **SIN**

what is made or sold within; a monument; something to preserve the memory of a thing; a type; an omen; the twelfth part of the zodiac; the subscription of one's name; signature. *vt.* To mark with a *sign*; to mark with characters or one's name; to denote; to indicate by a sign; to array in insigniat.—*vi.* To be a *sign* or omen; *to make a signal* or *sign;* to give a signal. [L. *signum.*]
Signal, sig'nal, *n. A sign that gives* or is intended to give *notice* or to communicate intelligence or orders, or the notice given; an indication.—*a. Worthy of note;* distinguished from what is ordinary; eminent; memorable; conspicuous.—*vt.* To communicate by signals. *ppr.* signalling, *pret. & pp.* signalled. [Fr.]
Signalize, sig'nal-iz, *vt. To make signal;* to render distinguished from what is common. *ppr.* signalizing, *pret. & pp.* signalized.
Signally, sig'nal-li, *adv.* Eminently; remarkably; memorably.
Signature, sig'na-tūr, *n. A sign or mark* impressed; sign-manual; the name of a person written by himself; an external feature, supposed to indicate the nature and characteristics of a person, &c. [Fr.—L. *signum*, a sign.]
Signet, sig'net, *n. A mark;* a seal; the seal used by the sovereign in sealing his private letters and grants. [Fr.]
Significance, sig-ni'fi-kans, *n. That which is signified;* meaning; force; power of impressing the mind; moment; consequence. [Low L. *significantia.*]
Significant, sig-ni'fi-kant, *a. Signifying;* betokening something; expressive of something beyond the external mark; bearing a meaning; expressive of some fact or event.—*n. That which has significance.* [Fr.]
Significantly, sig-ni'fi-kant-li, *adv. With signification* or meaning.
Signification, sig'ni-fi-kā''shon, *n. Act of signifying;* that which is understood to be intended by a sign or word; meaning; sense. [Fr.]
Significative, sig-ni'fi-kāt-iv, *a. Betokening by an external sign;* having meaning; expressive of a certain idea or thing. [Fr. *significatif.*]
Signify, sig'ni-fi, *vt.* To declare by a *token;* to make known either *by signs* or words; to proclaim; to mean; to imply; to have consequence. *ppr.* signifying, *pret. & pp.* signified. [Fr. *signifier*—L. *signum*, and *facio*, to make.]
Signior, sēn'yor, *n. See* SEIGNOR.
Sign-manual,sin-man'ū-al, *n.* One's own name written by himself; applied particularly to the *signatures* of a sovereign or prince.
Silence, sī'lens, *n. State of being silent;* stillness; state of holding one's peace; forbearance of speech in man, or of noise in other animals; secrecy; calmness; quiet; cessation of tumult; oblivion.—*vt. To make silent;* to oblige to hold the peace; to still; to appease; to cause to cease firing by a vigorous cannonading; to put an end to; to cause to cease. *ppr.* silencing, *pret. & pp.* silenced. [Fr.—L. *sileo*, to be still—Heb. *sell*, silence—*sala*, to be silent.]
Silent, sī'lent, *a. Making no noise or sound; still;* calm; quiet; mute; speechless; taciturn; not mentioning; not transacting business in person; having no sound, as a letter.—*n.† That which is silent;* a time of silence. [L. *silens*—*sileo*, to be still.]

Silently, sī'lent-li, *adv.* Without speech or words; without noise.
Silex, sī'leks, *n. Flint;* flint-stone; pure quartz. [L.]
Silica, sil'i-ka, *n.* A substance constituting the principal portion of most of the hard stones which compose the crust of the globe, and occurring nearly pure in rock-crystal, agate, flint, &c. [L. *silex, silicis*, a flint.]
Silicious, si-li'shi-us, *a. Flinty;* pertaining to, resembling, or containing silica. [L. *siliceus—silex*, a flint.]
Siliquose, Siliquous, si'li-kwōs, si'li-kwus, *a. Having a pod or capsule.* [L. *siliquōsus—siliqua*, a pod.]
Silk, silk, *n.* The fine soft thread produced by various species of caterpillars, particularly by the larva of the insect called silkworm; cloth made of silk.—*a. Pertaining to silk;* consisting of silk. [Sax. *seolc*—Gr. *sēr*, the silkworm.]
Silken, silk'n, *a. Made of silk;* like silk; delicate; tender; smooth; dressed in silk. [Sax. *seolcen.*]
Silkiness, silk'i-nes, *n. Quality of being silky;* softness and smoothness to the feel.
Silk-mercer, silk'mėr-sėr, *n. A dealer in silks.*
Silk-weaver, silk'wēv-ėr, *n. One who weaves silk* stuffs.
Silkworm, silk'wėrm, *n. The worm which produces silk.* [Sax. *seolcwyrm.*]
Silky, silk'i, *a. Made of silk;* consisting of silk; soft and smooth to the touch.
Sill, sil, *n. The base* of a thing; a piece of timber on which a building rests; the timber or stone at the foot of a door, or on which a window-frame stands. [Sax. *syl*—L. *solum*, the ground.]
Sillabub, sil'la-bub, *n.* A liquor made by mixing wine or cider with milk, and thus forming a soft curd.
Silllly, sil'li-li, *adv. In a silly manner.*
Silliness, sil'li-nes, *n. State or quality of being silly;* weakness of understanding; harmless folly.
Silly, sil'li, *a.* Primarily, *happy;* harmless; artless; destitute of ordinary strength of mind; proceeding from want of understanding; characterized by weakness; imprudent; rustic‡. [Sax. *sœli*, Old G. *sálig*, happy.]
Silt, silt, *n. Saltness*, or salt-marsh or mud; a deposit of mud or fine earth from running or standing water. [Sw. *sylta*, to pickle.]
Silvan, sil'van, *a. Pertaining to a wood;* inhabiting woods; abounding with woods. [from L. *silva*, a wood.]
Silver, sil'vėr, *n.* A metal of *a white* colour, very malleable, ductile, and tenacious, and of a lively brilliant lustre when polished; coin made of silver; anything of soft splendour.—*a. Made of silver;* of a pale lustre; soft and clear, as tones.—*vt. To cover with a coat of silver;* to adorn with mild lustre; to make smooth and bright; to make hoary. [Sax. *seolfer*—Sans. *shveta*, white, and *abhra*, gold.]
Silvering, sil'vėr-ing, *p.n. The art or operation of covering* the surface of anything *with silver;* the silver thus laid on.
Silverly, sil'vėr-li, *adv.* With the appearance *of silver.*
Silversmith, sil'vėr-smith, *n.* One whose occupation is *to work in silver.*
Silvery, sil'vėr-i, *a. Like silver;* having the appearance of silver; besprinkled or covered with silver; soft and clear, like the sound of silver when struck.
Similar, si'mi-lär, *a. Like;* having a like

form or appearance; having like qualities. [Fr. *similaire*—L. *similis*, like.]
Similarity, si-mi-la'ri-ti, *n. State of being similar;* likeness; uniformity.
Similarly, si-mi-lär'li, *adv. In like manner;* with resemblance.
Simile, si'mi-lē, *n. Similitude;* a comparison of two things which, however different in other respects, have some strong point or points of resemblance. [L. like.]
Similitude,si-mil'i-tūd, *n. Resemblance;* likeness in nature, qualities, or appearance; fanciful comparison. [Fr.]
Simmer, si'mėr, *vi.* To boil gently, or with a gentle hissing.
Simoniac, si-mō'ni-ak, *n. One guilty of simony;* one who buys or sells preferment in the church. [Fr. *simoniaque.*]
Simoniacal, si-mō-ni'ak-al, *a. Guilty of simony;* consisting in simony.
Simony, si'mo-ni, *n.* The crime of buying or selling ecclesiastical preferment. [from *Simon Magus*, who proffered money to purchase the gift of the Holy Ghost.]
Simper, sim'pėr, *vi.* To *smile* in a silly or affected manner.—*n.* A *smile* with an air of silliness. [Sw. Goth. *semper*, to smile.]
Simpering, sim'pėr-ing, *p.a.* Smiling foolishly or affectedly.
Simple, sim'pl, *a. Without fold;* single; not complicated; elementary; not given to design; artless; sincere; frank; unaffected; inartificial; unsuspecting; credulous; foolish; not wise; not sagacious.—*n.* Something not compounded; a medicinal plant. [Fr.—L. *sine*, without, and *plico*, to fold.]
Simpleness, sim'pl-nes, *n. State or quality of being simple.*
Simpleton, sim'pl-ton, *n. A simple silly person;* a person of weak intellect.
Simplicity, sim-plis'i-ti, *n. State or quality of being simple;* singleness state of being unmixed; artlessness of mind; sincerity; plainness; freedom from artificial ornament; freedom from abstruseness; silliness; folly. [Fr. *simplicité.*]
Simplification, sim'pli-fi-kā''shon, *n. Act of making simple;* act of reducing to simplicity. [Fr.]
Simplify, sim'pli-fi, *vt. To make simple;* to reduce, as what is complex to greater simplicity; to make plain or easy. *ppr.* simplifying, *pret. & pp.* simplified. [Fr. *simplifier*—simple, and L. *facio*, to make.]
Simply, sim'pli, *adv. In a simple manner;* without addition; merely.
Simulari, sim'ū-lär, *n.* One who pretends to be what he is not.
Simulate, sim'ū-lāt, *vt.* To *copy;* to counterfeit; to feign; to assume the mere appearance of, without the reality. *ppr.* simulating, *pret. & pp.* simulated. [L. *simulo, simulatus—similis*, like.]
Simulated, sim'ū-lāt-ed, *p.a.* Pretended; assumed artificially.
Simulation, sim-ū-lā'shon, *n. Act of simulating;* act of feigning to be that which one is not. [Fr.]
Simulator, sim'ū-lāt-or, *n. One who simulates* or feigns. [L.]
Simultaneous, si-mul-tā'nē-us, *a. Existing or happening at the same time.* [Low L. *simultaneus*—L. *simul*, at once.]
Simultaneously, si-mul-tā'nē-us-li, *adv. At the same time.*
Sin, sin, *n. That which requires to be atoned for;* any action, word, thought, or purpose contrary to the law of God,

ch, **chain**; j, **job**; g, **go**; ng, **sing**; ᴛʜ, **then**; th, **thin**; w, **wig**; wh, **whig**; zh, **azure**; † obsolete.

whether written or unwritten; any omission of what it requires; a wicked act; iniquity; a sin-offering; a very wicked man!.—*vi.* To violate the law of God; to omit what it requires; to do wrong; to offend against right, against men or society; to trespass. *ppr.* sinning, *pret. & pp.* sinned. [Sax. *syn;* Goth *saun,* atonement.]

Since, sins, *prep. After;* from the time of; from the time that.—*adv.* Ago; past; before this; from that time. *conj. Seeing that;* because that; inasmuch as. [Sax. *siththan*—Goth. *seithn,* thereafter.]

Sincere, sin-sēr', *a. Without wax,* as pure honey; unmixed; real; genuine; being in reality what it appears to be; honest; ingenuous; frank; undissembling. [Fr.—L. *sine,* and *cera,* wax.]

Sincerely, sin-sēr'li, *adv.* Honestly; with real purity of heart.

Sincerity, sin-se'ri-ti, *n. State or quality of being sincere;* honesty of mind; freedom from hypocrisy or false pretence. [Fr. *sincérité.*]

Sinciput, sin'si-put, *n. Half a head;* the forepart of the head. [L. from *semi,* half, and *caput,* the head.]

Sine, sin, *n.* A geometrical line drawn from one end of an *arc,* perpendicular to the diameter drawn through the other end. [L. *sinus,* a curved surface.]

Sinecure, si'nē-kūr, *n.* A benefice *without cure* of souls; an office which has revenue without employment. [L. *sine,* without, and *cura,* care.]

Sinew, si'nū, *n. That which binds;* a tendon; that which unites a muscle to a bone; (pl.) strength, or rather that which supplies strength; muscle; nerve.—*vt.* To bind or join, as by *sinews;* to strengthen; to harden. [Sax. *sinu;* Old Sax. *simon,* that which binds.]

Sinewed, si'nūd, *p.a. Furnished with sinews;* strong; firm; vigorous.

Sinewy, si'nū-i, *a. Consisting of a sinew* or nerve; nervous; strong; well braced with sinews; vigorous; firm.

Sinful, sin'ful, *a. Tainted with sin;* unholy; containing sin, or consisting in sin; contrary to the laws of God.

Sinfully, sin'ful-li, *adv. In a sinful manner.*

Sinfulness, sin'ful-nes, *n. Quality of being sinful* or contrary to the divine will; wickedness; iniquity; depravity.

Sing, sing, *vi. To read with musical modulations;* to utter sounds with melodious modulations of voice, as fancy may dictate, or according to the notes of a song or tune; to utter sweet sounds, as birds; to make a small, shrill sound; to relate something in numbers.—*vt.* To utter with musical modulations of voice; to chaunt; to carol; to celebrate in song; to rehearse in poetry. *ppr.* singing, *pret.* sung, sang, *pp.* sung. [Sax. *singan*—Goth. *siggvan,* to sing, to read.]

Singe, sinj, *vt.* To *burn* superficially; to scorch; to burn the surface of, as the nap of cloth, or the hair of the skin. *ppr.* singeing, *pret. & pp.* singed. *n.* A burning of the surface; a slight burn. [Sax. *sængan;* Icel. *sangr,* burned by the sun.]

Singer, sing'ėr, *n. One who sings;* one versed in music, or one whose occupation is to sing; a bird that sings.

Singing, sing'ing, *p.a.* Uttering melodious notes; celebrating in song.—*p.n.* Act of uttering sounds with musical intonations; the utterance of melodious notes.

Singing-master, sing'ing-mas-tėr, *n.* One who teaches *vocal* music.

Single, sing'gl, *a. One to each; separate;* only; individual; consisting of one only; uncompounded; alone; unmarried; not complicated; performed with one person on a side, or with one person only opposed to another; pure; incorrupt; unbiassed; small; weak; silly.—*vt. To separate;* to select, as an individual person or thing from among a number (with *out*). *ppr.* singling, *pret. & pp.* singled. [L. *singŭlus*—*semel,* once.]

Single-minded, sing'gl-mīnd-ed, *a. Having a single purpose.*

Singleness, sing'gl-nes, *n. State of being single;* simplicity; sincerity; purity of mind or purpose.

Singly, sing'gli, *adv. Individually;* only; by one's self.

Sing-song, sing'song, *n.* A term for bad singing, or for drawling.

Singular, sing'gū-lär, *a. That is single;* alone; not complex; expressing one person or thing; existing by itself; without precedent; remarkable; rare; peculiar; odd; of which there is but one; unique.—*n.* The singular number. [Fr.; L. *singularis*—*semel,* once.]

Singularity, sing-gū-la'ri-ti, *n. State of being singular;* peculiarity; an uncommon character or form; eccentricity; oddity. [Fr. *singularité.*]

Singularly, sing'gū-lär-li, *adv.* Peculiarly; strangely.

Sinister, si'nis-tėr, *a. Left;* evil; bad; dishonest; inauspicious. [L. left.]

Sinistrous, si'nis-trus, *a. Being on the left side;* wrong; perverse.

Sinistrously, si'nis-trus-li, *adv. In a sinistrous manner.*

Sink, singk, *v. To move one's self* downwards; to go downward in a medium of less specific gravity; to go to the bottom; to fall gradually; to enter into any body; to become lower; to settle to a level; to be overwhelmed; to enter deeply; to become deep; to retire within the surface of anything, as the eyes into the head; to droop; to decay; to fall into rest; to be lower; to become less, as prices.—*vt. To cause to sink;* to immerse in a fluid; to make by digging; to depress; to plunge into destruction; to cause to fall; to bring low; to crush; to lower or lessen; to cause to decline; to lower in value; to pay; to diminish by payment; to waste; to reduce, as a capital sum of money, for the sake of greater profit or interest out of it. *ppr.* sinking, *pret.* sank, *pp.* sunk or sunken.—*n.* That into which anything *sinks;* a drain to carry off filthy water; a kind of basin of stone or wood to receive filthy water; any place where corruption is generated. [Sax. *sencan;* Old G. *sinkan.*]

Sinker, singk'ėr, *n.* A weight on some body, as a fish-line, *to sink it.*

Sinking, singk'ing, *p.a. Causing to sink;* depressing.

Sinless, sin'les, *a. Free from sin;* pure; perfect; innocent.

Sinlessly, sin'les-li, *adv.* In a *sinless manner;* innocently.

Sinlessness, sin'les-nes, *n. State or quality of being sinless.*

Sinner, sin'ėr, *n. One who sins;* one who has voluntarily violated the divine law; an unregenerate person; a criminal.

Sin-offering, sin'of-fėr-ing, *n.* A *sacrifice for sin;* something offered as an expiation for sin.

Sinuate, sin'ū-āt, *vt. To bend or curve;* to bend in and out.—*p.a.* Having the margin bent in and out. [L. *sinuo, sinŭātus*—*sinus,* the bosom.

Sinuosity, sin-ū-os'i-ti, *n. Quality of being sinuous;* a series of bends and turns in arches or other irregular figures. [Fr. *sinuosité.*]

Sinuous, sin'ū-us, *a. Bending;* winding, bending in and out; of an undulating form. [L. *sinuosus*—*sinus,* the bosom.]

Sinuously, sin'ū-us-li, *adv. In a sinuous manner;* windingly; crookedly.

Sinus, si'nus, *n.* Primarily *the bosom;* a *curve;* an opening; a plait; a bay of the sea; a recess in the shore. [L.]

Sip, sip, *vt.* To take, as a fluid, into the mouth in small quantities; to drink in small quantities; to draw into the mouth; to drink out of.—*vi.* To drink a small quantity; to take a fluid with the lips. *ppr.* sipping, *pret. & pp.* sipped.—*n.* The taking of a liquor with the lips in small quantities; a small draught taken with the lips. [Sax. *sipan;* Icel. *supa,* to sup in.]

Siphon, si'fon, *n.* A *tube;* a bent pipe or tube whose arms are of unequal length, chiefly used for the purpose of drawing off liquids, as from a cask, well, &c. [Fr.; Gr. *siphlos,* hollow.]

Sir, sėr, *n.* A word of respect used in addresses to men, as madam is in addresses to women; the title of a knight or baronet. [Fr. *sire,* and *sieur*—L. *senior,* an elder—*seneo,* to be old.]

Sire, sīr, *n. An elder;* a father; the word of respect in addressing a king; the title of a priest; the male parent of a beast, as of a horse. [Fr.]

Siren, si'ren, *n.* One of the damsels on the south coast of Italy, who, according to Homer, enticed seamen by the magic sweetness of their *songs,* and then slew them; an enticing woman. *a. Pertaining to a siren;* bewitching; fascinating. [L.—Heb. *shir,* to sing.]

Sirloin, sėr'loin, *n. The upper part of the loin;* a loin of beef. [Fr. *surlonge*—*sur,* on, upon, over, and *longe,* a loin.]

Sirocco, si-rok'kō, *n.* An oppressive, relaxing south or south-*east* wind from the Libyan deserts, chiefly experienced in Italy, Malta, and Sicily. [It.]

Sirrah, si'ra, *n.* A word of contempt, used in addressing vile characters.

Sirup, si'rup, *n.* A sweet *liquid;* the sweet juice of vegetables or fruits, or sugar boiled with vegetable infusions. [Fr. *sirop*—Ar. *shereb,* to drink.]

Siskin, sis'kin, *n.* A singing bird.

Sister, sis'tėr, *n.* A *female* corresponding to a *male* of the same parentage; a woman of the same faith; a female fellow-Christian; a female of the same kind; a female of the same society, as the nuns of a convent.—*vt.* To resemble closely.—*vi.* To be akin. [Sax. *swuster;* Goth. *svistar.*]

Sisterhood, sis'tėr-hud, *n. State or duty of a sister;* a society of sisters.

Sister-in-law, sis'tėr-in-la, *n.* A husband or wife's *sister.*

Sisterly, sis'tėr-li, *a. Like a sister;* becoming a sister; affectionate.

Sit, sit, *vi.* To rest on the lower extremity of the body; to rest on the feet, as fowls; to occupy a seat in an official capacity; to be in a state of rest; to rest or bear on, as a burden; to settle; to cover and warm eggs for hatching, as a fowl; to be adjusted; to be placed in order to be painted; to hold a session; to exercise authority; to be in any assembly as a member; to have a seat. *vt. To keep the seat upon;* to place on a seat. *ppr.* sitting, *pret. & pp.* sat. [Sax. *sittan;* L. *sedeo,* Sans. *sad,* to sit.]

Fāte, fär, fat, fall; mē, met, hėr; pīne, pin; nōte, not, mōve; tūbe, tub, bull; oil, pound.

Site, sit, *n.* *Place on which anything is set;* situation; place; spot; a seat or ground-plot. [L. *situs—sino, situm,* to set down.]
Sith†, Sithe, sith, sivн, *n.* Time.
Sithence†, sith'ens, *conj.* Since.
Sitter, sit'ėr, *n. One who sits;* a bird that incubates.
Sitting, sit'ing, *p.a.* Brooding; exercising authority.—*p.n.* Act of placing one's self on *a seat;* a seat in the pew of a church; the time of resting in a posture for a painter to take the likeness; a session; an uninterrupted application to business or study for a time; a resting on eggs for hatching, as fowls.
Situated, sit'û-at-ed, *a. Seated* with respect to any other object; being in any state with regard to men or things.
Situation, sit-û-â'shon, *n. State of being situated;* site; state; condition, as of difficulty or ease; plight; temporary state; post; office. [Fr.—L. *situs,* a site —*sino,* to set down.]
Six, siks, *a.* Twice three.—*n.* The number of six, or twice three. [Sax.—L. *sex.*]
Sixpence, siks'pens, *n.* An English silver coin of the value of *six pennies;* half a shilling; the value of six pennies.
Sixpenny, siks'pen-ni, *a. Worth sixpence.*
Sixteen, siks'tēn, *a. Six and ten;* noting the sum of six and ten. [Sax. *sixtene.*]
Sixteenth, siks'tēnth, *a. The ordinal of sixteen.* [Sax. *sixteotha.*]
Sixth, siksth, *a. The ordinal of six. n.* The sixth part. [Sax. *sixta.*]
Sixthly, siksth'li, *adv. In the sixth place.*
Sixtieth, siks'ti-eth, *a. The ordinal of sixty.* [Sax. *sixteogotha.*]
Sixty, siks'ti, *a. Six times ten.—n.* The number of *six times ten.* [Sax. *sixtig.*]
Sizable, siz'a-bl, *a.* Of considerable bulk; being of reasonable size.
Sizar, si'zär, *n.* A student of the lowest rank at the university of Cambridge, who eats at the public table, after the fellows, free of expense.
Sizarship, sî'zär-ship, *n. The rank or station of a sizar.*
Size, siz, *n.* A *rated* quantity, according to some standard; comparative magnitude; bulk; at the university of Cambridge, food and drink from the buttery, aside from the regular dinner at commons.—*vt.* To arrange according to size. [contracted from *assise.*]
Size, siz, *n.* A sort of varnish *or glue* used by painters, &c.; a thick varnish used by gilders; a buffy coat on the surface of coagulated blood.—*vt.* To cover with size; to prepare with size. *ppr.* sizing, *pret. & pp.* sized. [Sp. *sisa.*]
Sized, sizd, *p.a.* Having a particular magnitude or *size;* prepared with size.
Sizing, siz'ing, *p.n.* A weak glue used in manufactures; act of covering with size.
Sizy, siz'i, *a. Having the quality of size;* glutinous; ropy; having the adhesiveness of size.
Skainsmate†, skäns'māt, *n.* A roaring companion.
Skate, skāt, *n.* A sort of shoe furnished with a smooth iron, and fastened under the foot, for *shooting along,* or sliding on ice.—*vi. To slide or move on skates. ppr.* skating, *pret. & pp.* skated. [D. *schaats;* Sax. *sceotan,* to shoot.]
Skate, skāt, *n.* A well-known cartilaginous fish, having the body much flattened, and more or less of a rhomboidal form, and highly prized for food. [Sax. *sceadda;* Icel. *skata.*]

Skating, skāt'ing, *p.n.* Act or art of *moving on skates.*
Skein, skān, *n.* A knot or number of knots of thread, yarn, or silk. [Old Fr. *escaigne.*]
Skeleton, ske'lē-ton, *n. A dried up body†;* the bones of an animal body separated from the flesh and retained in their natural position; the general frame of anything; the outline of a literary performance; a very thin person.—*a. Resembling a skeleton;* consisting of mere framework; containing mere outlines or heads. [Gr.—*skellō,* to dry up.]
Sketch, skech, *n.* A rough *dash* of an object; an outline of anything; a first rough draught of a plan or any design. *vt.* To draw the outline of; to make a rough draught of; to plan; to delineate; to portray. [It. *schizzo,* a splash of dirty water, a sketch.]
Sketcher, skech'ėr, *n. One who sketches.*
Sketching, skech'ing, *p.n.* The art or practice of drawing outlines.
Sketchy, skech'i, *a. Containing slight sketches* or outlines; resembling sketches; incomplete.
Skew, skū, *a. Wry;* distorted; oblique. [Dan. *skiæv.*]
Skewer, skū'ėr, *n. A slice* or cutting of wood; a pin of wood or iron for fastening meat to a spit.—*vt.* To fasten with *skewers.* [Icel. *skifa,* a shiver.]
Skiff, skif, *n.* A small light boat, resembling a yawl.—*vt.* To pass over in a light boat. [G. *schiff,* a ship.]
Skilful, skil'ful, *a. Possessing skill; skilled;* discerning; well versed in any art; able to perform nicely any manual operation in the arts or professions; expert; adroit.
Skilfully, skil'ful-li, *adv. With skill.*
Skilfulness, skil'ful-nes, *n. Quality of possessing skill;* dexterity.
Skill, skil, *n. Ability to distinguish;* knowledge; the familiar knowledge of any art or science united with dexterity in the application of it; art; dexterity; adroitness; a particular cause†. *vt.†* To know. — *vi.†* To be knowing. [Sax. *scylan,* to distinguish; Icel.*skitia,* to discern—L. *calleo,* to be versed in.]
Skilled, skild, *p.a. Having skill;* familiarly acquainted with; expert.
Skillet, skil'let, *n. A small vessel of* metal, with a long handle, used for heating and boiling water, &c. [Old Fr. *escuellette.*]
Skim, skim, *vt. To take off the surface of;* to take off, as the thick, gross matter on the surface of a liquid; to brush the surface of slightly.—*vi. To glide along the surface;* to glide along in an even, smooth course; to hasten along superficially. *ppr.* skimming, *pret. & pp.* skimmed. [from *scum.*]
Skimble-skamble†, skim'bl-skam'bl, *a.* Wandering; disorderly.
Skimmed, skimd, *p.a.* Having the thick matter taken from the surface.
Skimmer, skim'ėr, *n. That which skims;* a utensil used for skimming liquors.
Skimming, skim'ing, *p.n.* Act of taking off the surface of a liquid; that which is skimmed.
Skimmingly, skim'ing-li, *adv.* By gliding along the surface.
Skin, skin, *n.* The natural *covering* of animal bodies; a hide; the skin of an animal separated from the body; the bark of a plant; the rind of fruits and plants.—*vt. To strip off the skin of;* to flay; to cover with skin; to cover superficially.—*vi. To be covered with skin. ppr.* skinning, *pret. & pp.* skinned. [Sax. *scin;* Sans. *aku,* to cover.]

Skin-deep, skin'dēp, *a.* Superficial; not deep; slight.
Skinker†, skingk'ėr, *n.* One who serves liquors.
Skinless, skin'les, *a. Having no skin;* having a thin skin.
Skinner, skin'ėr, *n. One who skins;* one who deals in skins; a furrier.
Skinny, skin'i, *a. Consisting of skin,* or of skin only; wanting flesh.
Skip, skip, *vi. To leap* lightly; to bound; to spring, as a goat or lamb; to bound lightly and joyfully.—*vt.* To pass over or by; to omit. *ppr.* skipping, *pret. & pp.* skipped.—*n. A light leap;* a bound; a spring. [Dan. *kipper,* to leap; Icel. *skopa,* to run about.]
Skipper, skip'ėr, *n.* The master of a trading or merchant vessel; a giddy youth†. [Dan.—Icel. *skip,* a ship.]
Skipping, skip'ing, *p.a. Leaping* lightly; bounding.
Skippingly, skip'ing-li, *adv. By leaps.*
Skirmish, skėr'mish, *n.* A light combat by armies at a distance from each other, or between detachments and small parties; a contest; a contention. *vi.* To fight slightly or in small parties. [Fr. *escarmouche*—Old G. *scirman,* to defend.]
Skirmisher, skėr'mish-ėr, *n. One who skirmishes.*
Skirmishing, skėr'mish-ing, *p.n.* The act of fighting in a loose or slight encounter.
Skirr†, skėr, *vt.* To ramble over in order to clear; to scour.—*vi.* To scour.
Skirt, skėrt, *n.* The lower and loose part of a coat or other garment; the part below the waist; border; a woman's garment like a petticoat; the diaphragm in animals.—*vt.* To border; to form the border or edge of.—*vi.* To be on the border; to live near the extremity. [Icel. *skirta,* an apron, a skirt.]
Skittish, skit'ish, *a.* Easily made *to dart forward* or to the side, as a horse; hasty; fickle. [Sax. *scytan,* to shoot.]
Skittishly, skit'ish-li, *adv.* Shyly; wantonly; changeably.
Skittishness, skit'ish-nes, *n. Quality of being skittish;* shyness.
Skittles, skit'lz, *n.* Nine-pins. [Sax. *scytan,* to shoot.]
Skulk, skulk, *vi. See* SCULK.
Skull, skul, *n. The covering* of the brain; the bony case which contains the brain, forming the forehead, and every part of the head except the face; the brain, as the seat of intelligence. [Old G. *sciulla,* the skull of man or beast; Icel. *skyla,* to hide—Sans. *sku,* to cover.]
Sky, skī, *n. The region of clouds;* the aerial region which surrounds the earth; the vault of heaven; the heavens; the weather; the climate. [Sax. *scua,* a shade; Icel. *sky,* a cloud.]
Sky-colour, ski'kul-ėr, *n. The colour of the sky;* a particular species of blue colour; azure.
Skyey, ski'i, *a. Like the sky;* ethereal.
Skyish, ski'ish, *a. Like the sky,* or approaching the sky.
Sky-lark, ski'lärk, *n.* A species of *lark* that mounts and sings as it flies.
Sky-light, ski'lit, *n.* A window placed in the ceiling of a room for the admission of light.
Sky-rocket, ski'rok-et, *n. A rocket* that ascends high in the *air,* and burns as it flies; a species of fireworks.
Slab†, slab, *a.* Thick; viscous.
Slab, slab, *n. A thin piece* of marble or other stone, having plane surfaces. [W. *llab,* a flag.]
Slabber, slab'ėr, *vi. To slaver;* to let

ch, *chain;* j, *job;* g, *go;* ng, *sing;* тн, *then;* th, *thin;* w, *wig;* wh, *whig;* zh, *azure;* †obsolete.

the saliva or other liquid fall from the mouth carelessly; to drivel. [G. *schlabbern—labbe*, the lip.]

Slack, slak, *a*. *Loose*; relaxed; not hard drawn; not holding fast; not using due diligence; not violent; abated; diminished.—*n*. The part of a rope that hangs loose, having no strain upon it.—*adv*. Partially; insufficiently; not intensely. [Sax. *sleac*—L. *laxus*, loose —Gr. *laggaso*, to slacken.]

Slack, Slacken, slak, slak'n, *vi*. *To become less tense*; to be remiss or backward; to lose cohesion; to become less violent; to languish; to flag.—*vt*. *To loosen*; to make less tense; to abate; to relieve; to unbend; to use less liberally; to check; to repress; to deprive of cohesion. [Sax. *slacian*.]

Slackened, slak'nd, *p.a*. *Relaxed* or remitted.

Slackly, slak'li, *adv*. *In a slack manner*; not tightly.

Slackness, slak'nes, *n*. *State of being slack*; looseness; remissness; slowness; tardiness; weakness.

Slag, slag, *n*. *The dross* of a metal; cinders. [G. *schlacke—slagen*, to cast off.]

Slaggy, slag'i, *a*. *Pertaining to slag*.

Slake, slāk, *vt*. *To apply water to*; to quench; to mix with water, so as to reduce to powder, as quicklime.—*vi*. To go out. *ppr*. slaking, *pret. & pp*. slaked. [Icel. *slœcka*, to quench.]

Slaked, slākt, *p.a*. *Mixed with water*, so as to be reduced to powder.

Slam, slam, *vt*. *To strike* with force and noise; to shut with violence. *ppr*. slamming, *pret. & pp*. slammed.—*n*. A stroke; a violent shutting of a door. [Icel. *lem*, to strike.]

Slander, slan'dėr, *n*. Primarily, *that which causes one to limp*; defamation; a false tale or report maliciously uttered; disgrace; ill name.—*vt*. To defame; to calumniate; to injure by maliciously uttering a false report respecting; to asperse; to reproach. [Fr. *esclandre*—Gr. *skazō*, to limp, to halt.]

Slanderer, slan'dėr-ėr, *n*. *One who slanders*; a defamer.

Slanderous, slan'dėr-us, *a*. *Containing slander*; calumnious; given to slander; reproachful.

Slanderously, slan'dėr-us-li, *adv*. *With slander*; calumniously.

Slang, slang, *n*. Low, vulgar, unmeaning language. [probably from Fr. *langue*, the tongue.]

Slant, slant, *a*. *Sloping*; inclined from a direct line, whether horizontal or perpendicular.—*n*. *A slope*; an inclined plane.—*vt*. To give an oblique or sloping direction to.—*vi*. *To slope*; to incline; to lean. [Sw.—*slinta*, to slide down.]

Slanting, slant'ing, *p.a*. Having an oblique direction.

Slantingly, slant'ing-li, *adv*. With a slope or inclination.

Slantly, Slantwise, slant'li, slant'wiz, *adv*. Obliquely; in an inclined direction.

Slap, slap, *n*. A blow given with the open hand, or with something broad. *vt*. To strike with the open hand, or with something broad. *ppr*. slapping, *pret. & pp*. slapped.—*adv*. With a sudden and violent blow. [G. *schlappe*— L. *alapa*, a box on the ear.]

Slash, slash, *vt*. To cut by *striking* violently and at random; to cut in long cuts.—*vi*. *To strike* violently and at random with a sword or other cutting instrument; to lay about one with blows.—*n*. A long cut; a cut made at

random; a cut in cloth. [Icel. *slasa*, to strike.]

Slashed, slasht, *p.a*. Cut in long strips or slits.

Slate, slāt, *n*. A stone which readily *splits into plates*; a piece of smooth stone of this kind used for covering buildings; a piece of smooth stone, of the above species, used for writing on.—*vt*. *To cover with slate*. *ppr*. slating, *pret. & pp*. slated. [Sax. *slitan*; Old G. *slisan*, to split.]

Slated, slāt'ed, *p.a*. *Covered with slate*.

Slate-pencil, slāt'pen-sil, *n*. *A pencil* of soft slate, used for writing on *slates*.

Slater, slāt'ėr, *n*. *One who lays slates*.

Slating, slāt'ing, *p.n*. *Act of covering with slates*; materials for slating.

Slattern, slat'tėrn, *n*. A *woman who is negligent of her dress*; one who is not neat and nice. [G. *schlottern*, to hang loosely.]

Slatternly, slat'tėrn-li, *a*. *Like a slattern*; not clean; slovenly; sluttish. *adv*. Sluttishly.

Slaty, slāt'i, *a*. *Resembling slate*; having the nature or properties of slate.

Slaughter, sla'tėr, *n*. *A slaying*; great destruction of human life by violent means; carnage; a killing of oxen or other beasts for market.—*vt*. *To slay*; to make great destruction of; to butcher; to kill for the market, as beasts. [Sax. *slœge*; Goth. *slahan*, to strike.]

Slaughtered, sla'tėrd, *p. a*. *Slain*; butchered.

Slaughterer, sla'tėr-ėr, *n*. *One employed in slaughtering*.

Slaughterous, sla'tėr-us, *a*. Destructive; murderous.

Slave, slāv, *n*. A person who is wholly subject to the will of another; a bondman; one who surrenders himself to any power whatever; one in the lowest state of life; one who drudges like a slave.—*vi*. *To labour as a slave*; to drudge; to toil. *ppr*. slaving, *pret. & pp*. slaved. [D. *slaaf*.]

Slaver, sla'vėr, *n*. *Saliva* drivelling from the mouth.—*vi*. To suffer the *spittle* or saliva to issue from the mouth.—*vt*. To smear with *slaver*; to defile with drivel. [Icel. *slefa*, saliva.]

Slaver, slāv'ėr, *n*. A *slave-ship*.

Slaverer, sla'vėr-ėr, *n*. A driveller.

Slavery, slāv'ė-ri, *n*. *State of a slave*; bondage; the offices of a slave; drudgery; menial or laborious offices.

Slave-trade, slāv'trād, *n*. The abhorred business of purchasing men and women, and selling them for *slaves*.

Slave-trader, slāv'trād-ėr, *n*. One who *trades in slaves*.

Slavish, slāv'ish, *a*. *Pertaining to slaves*; servile; mean; base; such as becomes a slave; consisting in drudgery.

Slavishly, slāv'ish-li, *adv*. Servilely; meanly; basely.

Slavishness, slāv'ish-nes, *n*. *State or quality of being slavish*; servility.

Slavonic, sla-von'ik, *a*. Pertaining to the *Slavons* or ancient inhabitants of Poland. (See SCLAVONIAN.)—*n*. The *Sclavonic* language, or the language spoken by the Slavons.

Slay, slā, *vt*. *To strike through*; to put to death by a weapon or by violence; to slaughter; to murder; to destroy. *ppr*. slaying, *pret*. slew, *pp*. slain. [Sax. *slagan*; G. *schlagen*; Goth. *slahan*, to kill; Gael. *slac*, to beat.]

Slayer, slā'ėr, *n*. *One who slays*; a killer; a murderer.

Sleavet, slēv, *n*. The knotted part of silk or thread; silk untwisted.

Sled, sled, *n*. A sledge.—*vt*. To convey on a sled.

Sledge, slej, *n*. A sort of *carriage* made *to slide* on the ground, or to be drawn without wheels, or with runners, or very low wheels. [Icel. *sledi*.]

Sledge, slej, *n*. *An instrument for heavy and hard beating*; a large, heavy hammer, used chiefly by iron-smiths (called also a *sledge-hammer*). [Sax. *slecje*—G. *schlagel*, a maul.]

Sleek, slēk, *a*. *Smooth*; having an even, smooth surface; glossy.—*vt*. *To make even and smooth*; to render smooth, soft, and glossy. [Goth. *slaihts*, smooth to the touch.]

Sleekly, slēk'li, *adv*. *In a sleek manner*; smoothly; nicely.

Sleekness, slēk'nes, *n*. *State of being sleek*; smoothness of surface.

Sleep, slēp, *vi*. To take rest by a suspension of the voluntary exercise of the powers of the body and mind; to slumber; to rest; to be inactive; to lie or be still; not to be noticed, as a subject; to live thoughtlessly; to be dead; to rest in the grave for a time; not to be vigilant. *ppr*. sleeping, *pret. & pp*. slept. *n*. Temporary or periodical repose of the organs of sense, the intellectual faculties, and voluntary motion; rest; repose; death; rest in the grave. [Sax. *slapan*; Goth. *slepan*; Sans. *svap*.]

Sleeper, slēp'ėr, *n*. *A person who sleeps*; a drone; an animal that lies dormant in winter, as the bear; any piece of timber laid near the ground to support a weight, or to steady any rails or framework.

Sleepily, slēp'i-li, *adv*. *In a sleepy manner*; drowsily; heavily.

Sleepiness, slēp'i-nes, *n*. *State of being sleepy*; inclination to sleep.

Sleeping, slēp'ing, *p.a*. *Occupied with sleep*; reposing in sleep; dormant.—*p. n*. *State of resting in sleep*; state of being at rest.

Sleepless, slēp'les, *a*. *Having no sleep*; *without sleep*; perpetually agitated.

Sleeplessly, slēp'les-li, *adv*. *In a sleepless manner*.

Sleeplessness, slēp'les-nes, *n*. *State of being sleepless*; deprivation of sleep.

Sleep-walker, slēp'wak-ėr, *n*. *One who walks in his sleep*.

Sleepy, slēp'i, *a*. *Inclined to sleep*; drowsy; tending to induce sleep; somniferous; lazy; sluggish.

Sleet, slēt, *n*. *A fall of hail or snow mingled with rain*, usually in fine particles.—*vi*. To snow or hail with a mixture of rain. [Sax. *sliht*, rain, sleet— Icel. *sletti*, to cast forth.]

Sleetiness, slēt'i-nes, *n*. *State of being sleety*; a state of weather in which rain falls mixed with snow.

Sleety, slēt'i, *a*. *Bringing sleet*; consisting of sleet.

Sleeve, slēv, *n*. That which is *put on* or *clothes the arm*; the part of a garment that is fitted to cover the arm. [Sax. *sly—slefan*, to put on.]

Sleeved, slēvd, *p.a*. *Furnished with sleeves*; having sleeves.

Sleeveless, slēv'les, *a*. *Having no sleeves*; unreasonable.

Sleidt, slād, *vt*. To prepare for use in the weaver's sley.

Sleight, slīt, *n*. *A sly artifice*; a trick so dexterously performed that the manner of performance escapes observation; dexterity. [Sax. *slith*, smooth; Old G. *slihtan*, to wheedle.]

Slender, slen'dėr, *a*. *Thin*; slim; not thick; small in the waist; not strong; slight; inconsiderable; not amply sup-

SLENDERLY 363 SLUGGISH

plied; spare; limited, as aliment. [Belg. *slinder*.]
Slenderly, slen'dėr-li, *adv*. In a slender manner; without bulk; slightly.
Slenderness, slen'dėr-nes, *n*. State of being slender; smallness of diameter in proportion to the length; slightness; feebleness; spareness.
Sley†, slā, *n*. A weaver's reed.—*vt*. To part the threads of, and arrange them in a reed.
Slice, slīs, *vt*. To cut into thin pieces, or to cut off, as a thin, broad piece; to cut into parts; to cut; to divide. *ppr*. slicing, *pret. & pp*. sliced.—*n*. A thin, broad piece cut off; an instrument consisting of a broad plate with a handle. [G. *schleissen*, to cleave.]
Slide, slīd, *vi*. To glide; to move by slipping; to pass inadvertently; to pass smoothly along; to pass silently and gradually from one state to another; to practise sliding; to fall; to pass with an easy, smooth, uninterrupted course or flow. *ppr*. sliding, *pret*. slid, *pp*. slid, slidden.—*n. Act of sliding;* something that slides; flow; the descent of a detached mass of earth or rock down a declivity; a slip; a smooth declivity along which anything may descend by sliding; a grace in music, consisting of two small notes moving by degrees. [Sax. *slidan*, to slip, to fall.]
Slider, slīd'ėr, *n. One who slides*; the part of an instrument that slides.
Sliding, slīd'ing, *p.n. Act of sliding*; lapse; falling.
Slight, slīt, *a. Smooth;* plain; not thorough; not deep, as an impression; weak; not forcible; not strong or firm; negligent; not done with effort.—*n. Act of slighting;* disregard; a moderate degree of contempt manifested negatively by neglect; disdain.—*vt*. To disregard from the consideration that a person or thing is trivial or of little value or importance; to throw†; to cast†. [G. *schlicht*, smooth.]
Slighted, slīt'ed, *p.a*. Neglected; disregarded.
Slightingly, slīt'ing-li, *adv. In a slighting manner;* with neglect.
Slightly, slīt'li, *adv. In a slight manner;* superficially; without regard; with moderate contempt.
Slightness, slīt'nes, *n. State or quality of being slight;* weakness; want of force, strength, or vehemence; negligence.
Slily, slī'li, *adv. In a sly manner;* with dexterous secrecy.
Slim, slim, *a.* Primarily, *worthless;* slender; of small thickness in proportion to the height. [Icel. *slœmr*, vile.]
Slime, slīm, *n. Mud;* viscous mud; soft, moist earth having an adhesive quality. [Sax. *slim*—L. *limus*, mud.]
Sliminess, slīm'i-nes, *n. The quality of slime;* viscosity.
Slimness, slim'nes, *n. State or quality of being slim.*
Slimy, slīm'i, *a. Abounding with slime;* consisting of slime; glutinous.
Sliness, slī'nes, *n. Quality of being sly;* dexterous artifice to conceal anything.
Sling, sling, *n*. An instrument for throwing stones, consisting of a strap and two strings; a kind of hanging bandage put round the neck, in which a wounded arm is sustained; a rope by which a cask or bale is suspended and swung in or out of a ship.—*vt. To throw with a sling;* to hang so as to swing; to move or swing by a rope which suspends the thing. *ppr*. slinging, *pret. & pp*. slung. [D. *slinger;* Dan. *slinge*, to sling.]

Slinger, sling'ėr, *n. One who slings.*
Slink, slingk, *vi. To creep away meanly;* to steal away.—*vt.* To miscarry of, as the female of a beast. *ppr*. slinking, *pret. & pp*. slunk. [Sax. *slincan*.]
Slip, slip, *vi. To slide; to glide;* to move or fly out of place; to depart or withdraw secretly; to err; to pass unexpectedly; to enter by oversight; to be lost. *vt. To cause to slide or glide;* to convey secretly; to omit; to part, as twigs from the branches of a tree; to escape from; to let loose; to disengage one's self from; to pass over negligently; to tear off. *ppr*. slipping, *pret. & pp*. slipped.—*n. Act of slipping;* a sliding; an unintentional error; a counterfeit piece of money; a twig separated from the main stock; a string by which a dog is held; an escape; a secret desertion; a long, narrow piece, as of paper; that on which anything may slip; a place on which a ship is built, whence it may slip or slide into the water. [Sax. *slipan*—L. *labor*, to glide.]
Slip-knot, slip'not, *n*. A knot which will not bear a strain, but *slips* along the rope around which it is made.
Slipper, slip'ėr, *n*. A kind of light shoe, which may be slipped on with ease and worn in undress; a kind of apron for children, to be slipped over their other clothes, to keep them clean, now called a pinafore. [Sax.]
Slippered, slip'ėrd, *p.a. Wearing slippers.*
Slipperiness, slip'ėr-i-nes, *n. State or quality of being slippery;* smoothness; lubricity of character.
Slippery, slip'ėr-i, *a. Apt to slip or cause to slip;* not affording firm footing or confidence; apt to slip away; unstable; changeable.
Slipshod, slip'shod, *a. Wearing shoes like slippers,* without pulling up the heels; careless in manners, style, &c.
Slit, slit, *vt. To tear;* to rend; to split; to cut into long pieces or stripes; to make a long fissure in; to cut, in general. *ppr*. slitting, *pret*. slit, *pp*. slit or slitted.—*n.* A long cut; or a narrow opening. [Sax. *slitan*.]
Sliver, sli'vėr, *vt. To cleave;* to cut or divide into long, thin pieces; to cut or rend lengthwise.—*n.* A long piece cut or rent off, or a piece cut or rent lengthwise. [Sax. *slifan*, to cleave.]
Slobber, slob'ėr. See SLABBER.
Slobbery, slob'ėr-i, *a.* Wet; sloppy.
Sloe, slō, *n*. A small *sour* or bitter wild plum, the fruit of the black-thorn; also, the plant itself. [Sax. *sla*—D. *sleë*, sour.]
Sloop, slöp, *n. A skiff;* a *shallop†;* a vessel with one mast, the main-sail of which is attached to a gaff above, to a boom below, and to the mast on its foremost edge. [D. *sloep*.]
Slop, slop, *vt.* To soil by letting water or other liquor fall upon; to spill. *ppr*. slopping, *pret. & pp*. slopped.—*n.* Water carelessly spilt; mean liquor; (pl.) dirty water; coarse liquid food; ready-made clothes; a lower garment, as breeches, &c.
Slope, slōp, *n.* A surface which is inclined, so that anything placed on it is apt to slip or slide down; a declivity; an oblique direction; a direction downward.—*vt. To form with a slope;* to direct obliquely; to incline.—*vi*. To take an oblique direction; to be inclined. *ppr*. sloping, *pret. & pp*. sloped. [probably from *slip*.]
Sloping, slōp'ing, *p.a.* Oblique; inclining from a right line or plane.

Slopingly, slōp'ing-li, *adv*. Obliquely.
Sloppiness, slop'i-nes, *n. State of being sloppy;* muddiness.
Sloppy, slop'i, *a.* Wet, as the ground.
Slot, slot, *n. A bar;* a *bolt;* a narrow piece of timber which holds together larger pieces; a mortice. [D. *slot*, a lock—*slinten*, to close.]
Slot, slot, *n. The track* of a deer. [Sax. *slotinge*, the vestiges of wild animals.]
Sloth, slōth, *n. Slowness;* laziness; an animal which lives in trees, and is an expert climber, but which has been so named from the exceeding slowness of its motions when on the ground. [Sax. *slawth*—*slaw*, slow.]
Slothful, slōth'ful, *a. Addicted to sloth;* inactive; sluggish; lazy; indolent.
Slothfully, slōth'ful-li, *adv.* Lazily.
Slothfulness, slōth'ful-nes, *n. State or quality of being slothful;* inactivity.
Slouch, slouch, *n. A hanging down;* a depression of the head or of some other part of the body; a clownish gait; a clownish fellow.—*vi. To hang down;* to have a downcast, clownish look or manner.—*vt. To cause to hang down;* to depress. [Icel. *loka*, to hang down.]
Slouched, sloucht, *p.a. Made to hang down;* depressed.
Slouching, slouch'ing, *p.a. Hanging down;* walking heavily and awkwardly.
Slough, slou, *n*. A place of deep mud or mire; a hole full of mire, chiefly in a road. [Sax. *slog*.]
Slough, sluf, *n*. The cast-off *skin* of a serpent or other reptile; the dead part of flesh or skin that separates from the living parts in a wound.—*vi*. To separate from the living parts. To come off, to peel off, to fall off, to slough off, are all adopted to express the action of separation of dead from living structure. [G. *schlauch*, a skin.]
Sloughy, slou'i, *a. Full of sloughs;* miry.
Sloughy, sluf'i, *a. Resembling or partaking of a slough.*
Sloven, slu'ven, *n. A slow* or *sluggish man;* a person careless of his dress; a man habitually negligent of neatness and order. [D. *slof*, slow.]
Slovenliness, slu'ven-li-nes, *n. State or quality of being slovenly;* habitual want of cleanliness; neglect of order.
Slovenly, slu'ven-li, *a. Sluggish;* negligent of dress or neatness; not neat. *adv*. In a careless, inelegant manner.
Slovenry†, slu'ven-ri, *n.* Negligence of order; dirtiness.
Slow, slō, *a. Dull;* tardy; not rapid; long in taking place; not ready; not hasty; acting with deliberation; heavy in wit; behind in time; indicating a time later than the true time; not improving rapidly.—*vt. To render slow.* [Sax. *slaw:* Goth. *slavan*, to be still.]
Slowly, slō'li, *adv. In a slow manner;* not with velocity; not soon; not in a little time; not hastily; not rashly; not readily; with slow progress.
Slowness, slō'nes, *n. State or quality of being slow;* want of speed; tardy advance; dulness to admit conviction or affection; want of readiness; coolness; caution in deciding; tardiness.
Slubber, slub'ėr, *vt.* To do coarsely; to daub.
Slug, slug, *n. A slow,* lazy, heavy fellow; obstruction; a kind of snail; an oval piece of metal used for the charge of a gun, probably so named from its resemblance in shape to a *slug* or snail. [Old G. *slevig*, dull, blunt.]
Sluggard, slug'ärd, *n.* A person habitually *slow;* a drone.—*a. Sluggish;* lazy.
Sluggish, slug'ish, *a. Slow;* slothful;

ch, *chain;* j, *job;* g, *go;* ng, *sing;* TH, *then;* th, *thin;* w, *wig;* wh, *whig;* zh, *azure;* † obsolete.

naturally given to indolence; not quick; having no power to move itself.
Sluggishly, slug'ish-li, *adv.* Lazily.
Sluggishness, slug'ish-nes, *n.* Quality of being sluggish; sloth; dulness; want of power to move.
Sluice, slūs, *n.* A *floodgate*; a frame of timber, stone, &c., with a gate, for the purpose of *excluding*, retaining, or regulating the flow of water in a river, dam, &c.; the stream of water issuing through a flood-gate; a source of supply; that through which anything flows.—*vt.* To open, as a *flood-gate or sluice*; to overwhelm. *ppr.* sluicing, *pret. & pp.* sluiced. [D. *cluis*, a floodgate—L. *claudo, clausum*, to shut.]
Sluicy, slūs'i, *a.* Falling in streams, as from a *sluice*.
Slumber, slum'bėr, *vi.* To *sleep lightly*; to doze or drowse; to be in a state of negligence or inactivity.—*n. Light sleep*; sleep not deep or sound; sleep; repose. [Sax. *slumerian*, G. *schlummern*.]
Slumberer, slum'bėr-ėr, *n.* One who *slumbers*.
Slumberous, **Slumbery**, slum'bėr-us, slum'bėr-i, *a. Inviting slumber*; drowsy.
Slump, slump, *vi.* To throw into a mass.
Slur, slėr, *vt.* To *soil*; to sully; to contaminate; to disgrace; to pass lightly; to do carelessly; to sing or perform in a smooth, gliding style. *ppr.* slurring, *pret. & pp.* slurred.—*n.* A *mark or stain*; slight reproach or disgrace; a mark in music connecting notes which are to be sung to the same syllable, or united as much as possible in playing. [Icel. *slor*, the refuse of fishes.]
Slurred, slėrd, *p.a.* Performed in a smooth, gliding style, like notes *marked with a slur*.
Slut, slut, *n.* A woman who is *sluggish, slovenly*, and negligent of cleanliness and dress; a slattern; a name of slight contempt for a woman. [D. *slet*, a slut.]
Sluttery, slut'ėr-i, *n. The qualities of a slut;* dirtiness.
Sluttish, slut'ish, *a. Pertaining to or like a slut*; dirty; careless of neatness.
Sluttishly, slut'ish-li, *adv. In a sluttish manner;* dirtily; negligently.
Sluttishness, slut'ish-nes, *n. The qualities or practice of a slut*; dirtiness of dress, &c.
Sly, sli, *a. Cunning*; crafty; wily; insidious; done with artful and dexterous secrecy; secret; concealed. [G. *schlau*; Icel. *sloegr*, cunning.]
Slyly, Slyness, sli'li, sli'nes. See SLILY, SLINESS.
Smack, smak, *n. A noise made by the separation of the lips* in eating or drinking with relish; a similar noise made with the lips in kissing; taste; tincture; pleasing taste; a small quantity; [D. *smakschip*] a small vessel, commonly rigged as a sloop, used chiefly in the coasting and fishing trade.—*vi. To make a sharp noise by the separation of the lips*, as after tasting, or in kissing; to have a taste; to have a tincture or quality infused. *vt.* To kiss with a sharp noise; to make a sharp noise by striking; to crack. [Sax. *smæc—smæccan*, to taste.]
Small, smal, *a. Little in quantity*; not great; little in degree; being of little moment; of little genius or ability; short; containing little; little in amount; weak; gentle; soft; not loud. *n.* The small or slender part of a thing. [Sax. *smæl*, G. *schmal*.]
Small-craft, smal'kraft, *n.* A vessel, or vessels in general, of a small size.

Smallish, smal'ish, *a. Somewhat small*.
Smallness, smal'nes, *n. State or quality of being small*; littleness of size, extent, or quantity; littleness in degree, force, or strength; weakness; fineness; softness; inconsiderableness.
Small-pox, smal'poks, *n.* An eruptive cutaneous disease.
Smalt, smalt, *n.* Common glass *melted* or fused, and tinged of a fine deep blue by cobalt. [G. *schmalte*.]
Smart, smärt, *n. Pain, as from a cut*; quick, pungent, lively pain; pungent grief.—*a.* Causing a keen local pain; pungent; keen; severe; poignant; sharp; brisk; fresh; witty; trim; spruce; dressed in a showy manner. *vi.* To feel a lively, pungent pain; to be punished; to feel a pungent pain of mind. [D.; Old G. *smersa*, pain.]
Smartly, smärt'li, *adv. In a smart manner;* with keen pain; wittily; vigorously; sprucely.
Smartness, smärt'nes, *n. The quality of being smart* or pungent; pungency; acuteness; liveliness; vivacity.
Smash, smash, *vt.* To break in pieces by violence; to crush.—*n.* A breaking to pieces. [G. *schmeissen*, to smite.]
Smashed, smasht, *p.a.* Dashed to pieces.
Smashing, smash'ing, *p.n.* State of *being smashed*.
Smatch, smach, *n.* Taste; tincture.
Smatter, smat'ėr, *vi. To have a slight taste;* to talk superficially.—*n.* A *taste or savour*; slight, superficial knowledge. [Icel. *smeckr*, a taste.]
Smatterer, smat'ėr-ėr, *n.* One who has only a slight, superficial knowledge.
Smattering, smat'ėr-ing, *p.n.* A slight, superficial knowledge.
Smear, smėr, *vt.* To overspread with *grease* or anything unctuous, viscous, or adhesive; to soil; to contaminate; to pollute.—*n.* An ointment; a daub. [Sax. *smyrian—smere*, fat, grease.]
Smell, smel, *vt.* To perceive by the nose, or by the olfactory nerves.—*vi.* To affect the olfactory nerves; to have an odour or particular scent; to have a particular tincture or smack of any quality; to exercise sagacity. *ppr.* smelling, *pret. & pp.* smelled, smelt. *n.* The sense by which certain qualities of bodies are perceived through the instrumentality of the olfactory nerves; one of the five senses; the qualities of bodies which affect the olfactory organs; scent; fragrance. [probably connected with the New Low G. *smullen*, to smear.]
Smelling, smel'ing, *p.n.* The sense by which odours are perceived; the act of one who smells.
Smelt, smelt, *n.* A small fish of the salmon family, so named from its pleasant *smell*. [Sax.]
Smelt, smelt, *vt. To melt* or fuse, as ore, for the purpose of separating the metal. [D. *smelten*; Sax. *meltan*, to melt.]
Smelted, smelt'ed, *p.a. Melted* for the extraction of the metal.
Smelter, smelt'ėr, *n.* One who *smelts* ore.
Smeltery, smelt'ė-ri, *n.* A *house* or place for *smelting* ores.
Smelting, smelt'ing, *p.n.* The operation of *melting* or fusing ores for the purpose of extracting the metal.
Smile, smil, *vi. To laugh slightly;* to contract the features of the face in such a manner as to express pleasure or love; to sneer; to look gay and joyous, or to have an appearance to excite joy; to be propitious; to favour (with *on* or *upon*).—*vt.* To express by a *smile*. *ppr.* smiling, *pret. & pp.* smiled.—*n. A slight laugh;* a peculiar contraction of the features of the face, which expresses pleasure or kindness; joyous appearance; favour; an expression of countenance resembling a smile, but indicative of opposite feelings, as contempt, scorn, &c.; as, a scornful smile. [Old G. *smielan*; Sans. *smi*, to laugh, to smile.]
Smiling, smil'ing, *p.a. Having a smile* on the countenance; looking joyous or gay; looking propitious.
Smilingly, smil'ing-li, *adv.* With a look of pleasure.
Smirch, smėrch, *vt.* To cloud; to soil.
Smirk, smėrk, *vi. To smile wantonly* or pertly; to look affectedly soft or kind. *n.* An affected smile. [Sax. *smercian*.]
Smite, smit, *vt. To strike*, drive, or force against, as the fist or hand, a stone or a weapon; to kill; to blast; to destroy the life of, as by a stroke; to chasten; to punish; to strike or affect with passion.—*vi. To strike;* to clash together *ppr.* smiting, *pret.* smote, *pp.* smitten. [Sax. *smitan*—Old G. *smidon*.]
Smiter, smit'ėr, *n. One who smites*.
Smith, smith, *n. One who smites or beats;* one who forges with the hammer; one who works in metals. [Sax. *smith*, to smite.]
Smithery, smith'ė-ri, *n. The workshop of a smith;* work done by a smith.
Smithy, smith'i, *n. The shop of a smith*. [Sax. *smiththe*.]
Smitten, smit'n, *p.a.* Affected with some passion; excited by beauty or something impressive.
Smock, smok, *n.* A shift; a chemise; a woman's under garment; a smockfrock. [Sax. *smoc*.]
Smock-frock, smok'frok, *n.* A coarse linen *frock* or shirt worn over the coat by farm labourers, chiefly in England; a gabardine.
Smoke, smōk, *n. That which melts away;* the visible vapour that escapes from a burning substance, as from wood, &c.; sooty vapour; vapour; watery exhalations.—*vi. To emit smoke;* to throw off volatile matter in the form of vapour; to burn; to be kindled; to rage (in Scripture); to raise a dust by rapid motion; to imbibe the vapour of burning tobacco.—*vt. To apply smoke to;* to hang in smoke; to scent by smoke; to find out; to cause to emit the fumes of tobacco; to inhale the smoke of tobacco through; to suffer; to be punished. *ppr.* smoking, *pret. & pp.* smoked. [Sax. *smeoc*; Heb. *mug*, to melt away.]
Smoked, smōkt, *p.a. Cured, cleansed*, or *dried in smoke*.
Smoker, smōk'ėr, *n. One who dries by smoke;* one who uses tobacco by inhaling its smoke from a pipe or cigar.
Smokily, smōk'i-li, *adv.* So as to be full *of smoke*.
Smokiness, smōk'i-nes, *n. State of being smoky*.
Smoking, smōk'ing, *p.a. Emitting smoke*, as fuel, &c.; using tobacco in a pipe or cigar.—*p.n. Act of emitting smoke;* act or practice of inhaling tobacco-smoke from a pipe or cigar.
Smoky, smōk'i, *a. Emitting smoke*; filled with smoke; thick; subject to be filled with smoke from the fireplaces; tarnished with smoke.
Smooth, smōth, *a. Soft to the feel;* having a *plain or level surface*; not rough; glossy; gently flowing; not undulating;

Fāte, fär, fat, fąll; mē, met, hėr; pīne, pin; nōte, not, mōve; tūbe, tub, bųll; oil, pound.

that flows without stops; soft; bland; flattering; not harsh.—*n. That which is smooth;* the smooth part of anything.—*vt. To make smooth;* to make plain or even on the surface; to make easy; to make flowing; to soften; to soothe; to ease.—*vi.* To use blandishment. [Sax. *smoeth, smethe.*]

Smooth-faced, smŏŏᴛʜ'fāst, *a.* Having a mild, *soft look*.

Smoothly, smŏŏᴛʜ'li, *adv. In a smooth manner;* with even flow or motion; without obstruction; easily; with soft, insinuating language.

Smoothness, smŏŏᴛʜ'nes, *n. State or quality of being smooth;* evenness of surface; softness of numbers; gentleness of speech; blandness of address.

Smother, smuᴛʜ'ėr, *vt.* To extinguish the life of by causing smoke or *dust* to enter the lungs; to stifle; to suffocate by closely covering; to suppress or stifle.—*vi.* To be suffocated; to be suppressed; to smoulder.—*n. That which smothers;* smoke; thick dust. [Sax. *smoran*—Icel. *mor*, small dust.]

Smothered, smuᴛʜ'ėrd, *p.a.* Suffocated; suppressed.

Smoulder, smōl'dėr, *vi.* To burn and smoke without flame or vent. [Belg. *smoel*, sultry, and *wether*, air, atmosphere.]

Smouldering, Smouldry, smōl'dėr-ing, smōl'dri, *ppr.* or *a.* Burning and smoking without flame or vent.

Smuggle, smug'l, *vt. To creep into*‡; to import or export *secretly* and in defiance of law, or secretly to import or export, as dutiable goods, without paying the duties imposed by law; to run; to convey clandestinely. [Sax. *smugan*, to creep; D. *smokkelen*, to smuggle.]

Smuggled, smug'ld, *pp.* or *a.* Imported or exported clandestinely and contrary to law.

Smuggler, smug'l-ėr, *n. One who smuggles;* a vessel employed in running goods.

Smuggling, smug'l-ing, *ppr.* Importing or exporting goods *clandestinely* and contrary to law.—*p.n. Act of one who smuggles;* the offence of *clandestinely* importing or exporting prohibited goods, or other goods without paying the customs.

Smut, smut, *n. A spot or stain;* a spot made with soot, &c.; the foul matter itself; a disease in grain of a dirty black colour; obscene language.—*vt. To stain;* to *defile;* to blacken; to tarnish; to stain or mark with smut; to blacken with coal, &c.; to taint with mildew.—*vi. To gather smut;* to be converted into smut. [Sax. *smitta*, from *besmittan*, to stain, to dirty.]

Smuttily, smut'i-li, *adv.* Blackly; smokily; foully.

Smuttiness, smut'i-nes, *n. State of being smutty;* soil from smoke, soot, coal, or smut; obsceneness of language.

Smutty, smut'i, *a. Soiled with smut*, coal, soot, or the like; tainted with mildew; obscene; not modest or pure.

Snaffle, snaf'l, *n. A nose-band;* a bridle consisting of a slender bit-mouth without branches.—*vt.* To bridle; to manage with a *snaffle* or bridle. *ppr.* snaffling, *pret. & pp.* snaffled. [Old G. *snabul*, a muzzle.]

Snag, snag, *n. A short branch*, or a sharp or rough branch; a shoot; a knot; a tooth; or a tooth projecting beyond the rest. [Icel. *snagi*, a small stake or peg.]

Snagged, Snaggy, snag'ed, snag'i, *a.* Full of *snags;* full of short rough branches or sharp points; abounding with knots.

Snail, snāl, *n. A slimy, slow-creeping, soft-bodied animal;* a drone; a slow-moving person. [Sax. *snegel*; Mid. High G. *snegel*, slime; Old G. *snahan*, to creep.]

Snake, snāk, *n. A reptile;* a serpent. [Sax. *snaca*, a serpent—*snican*, to creep.]

Snaky, snāk'i, *a. Pertaining to a snake* or to snakes; resembling a snake; cunning; deceitful.

Snap, snap, *vt.* To catch at; to bite or seize suddenly, as with the teeth; to break at once; to break short.—*vi.* To make a sudden effort to bite; to break short; to break without bending. *ppr.* snapping, *pret. & pp.* snapped.—*n.* An attempt to seize or bite; a sudden breaking of any substance; a sharp noise; a catch or fastening. [G. *schnappen*, to snap.]

Snappish, snap'ish, *a. Apt to snap;* eager to bite; sharp in reply.

Snappishly, snap'ish-li, *adv.* Peevishly.

Snappishness, snap'ish-nes, *n. Quality of being snappish;* peevishness.

Snare, snār, *n. A noose;* a *string* or line with a *noose* for catching animals by the leg; anything by which one is brought into trouble.—*vt. To catch with a snare;* to bring into unexpected evil. *ppr.* snaring, *pret. & pp.* snared. [Icel. *snara*, a noose—*snura*, a line.]

Snarl, snärl, *vi.* To utter the sound of an angry animal; to utter grumbling sounds; to talk in rude murmuring terms. [G. *schnarren*, to grumble.]

Snarling, snärl'ing, *p.a.* Cynical; snappish; peevish.

Snary, snär'i, *a. Tending to ensnare.*

Snatch, snach, *vt. To catch at quickly and eagerly;* to seize hastily; to seize without permission; to seize and transport away.—*vi. To catch at;* to attempt to seize suddenly.—*n. A hasty catch or seizing;* a short fit of vigorous action; a small fragment; a shuffling answer. [intens. of *catch*, Sax. *gelaeccan*.]

Snatcher, snach'ėr, *n. One who snatches.*

Sneak, snēk, *vi. To creep or steal away privately;* to withdraw meanly, as a person afraid or ashamed to be seen; to crouch; to truckle.—*n.* A mean fellow. [Sax. *snican;* Dan. *snige*, to creep.]

Sneaking, snēk'ing, *p.a.* Mean; crouching; covetous; niggardly.

Sneakingly, snēk'ing-li, *adv. In a sneaking manner;* meanly.

Snsapt, snēp, *vt.* To check; to nip.—*n.* A reprimand.

Sneer, snēr, *vi. To show contempt by turning up the nose;* to scoff; to jibe; to jeer; to utter with grimace; to show mirth awkwardly.—*n.* A look of contempt, or *a turning up of the nose* to manifest contempt; a jeer; an expression of ludicrous scorn. [allied to L. *nares*, the nostrils.]

Sneerer, snēr'ėr, *n. One who sneers.*

Sneering, snēr'ing, *p.a.* Manifesting scorn *by turning up the nose*, or by some grimace.

Sneeringly, snēr'ing-li, *adv.* With a look of contempt or scorn.

Sneeze, snēz, *vi.* To emit air, chiefly through *the nose*, audibly and violently, by a kind of involuntary convulsive force, occasioned by irritation of the inner membrane of the nose.—*n.* A sudden and violent ejection of air, chiefly through the nose, with an audible sound. *ppr.* sneezing, *pret. & pp.* sneezed. [Sax. *niesan—naese*, the nose.]

Sneezing, snēz'ing, *p.n.* Act of ejecting air violently and audibly, chiefly through the *nose*.

Sniff, snif, *vi.* To draw air audibly up the nose. [D. *snuiven*.]

Snip, snip, *vt. To nip;* to cut into small pieces; to clip; to cut off at once with shears or scissors. *ppr.* snipping, *pret. & pp.* snipped.—*n.* A single cut; a bit cut off; a clip. [D. *snippen*, to cut.]

Snipe, snīp, *n.* A bird that frequents wet places, so named from its *long bill.* [D. *snip*—Heb. *nāba*, to be prominent.]

Snivel, sni'vel, *n. Snot;* mucus running from the nose.—*vi.* To run at the nose; to cry, as children, with snuffling or snivelling. *ppr.* snivelling, *pret. & pp.* snivelled. [Sax. *snofel*.]

Sniveller, sni'vel-ėr, *n. One who cries with snivelling;* one who manifests weakness by weeping.

Snivelling, sni'vel-ing, *p.a.* Crying, as children.—*p.n.* A crying, as of children, with snuffling or whining.

Snively, sni'vel-i, *a.* Running at the nose; pitiful; whining.

Snore, snōr, *vi.* To breathe through the nose with a rough, hoarse noise in sleep. *ppr.* snoring, *pret. & pp.* snored. *n.* A breathing through the nose with a harsh noise in sleep. [Sax. *snora*, snoring.]

Snorer, snōr'ėr, *n. One who snores.*

Snort, snort, *vi.* To force the air with violence *through the nose*, so as to make a noise, as high-spirited horses in prancing. [another form of *snore*.]

Snorter, snort'ėr, *n. One who snorts;* a snorer.

Snorting, snort'ing, *p.n.* Act of forcing the air through the nose with violence and noise.

Snot, snot, *n.* Mucus discharged from the *nose*. [Sax. *snote—snytan*, to blow the nose.]

Snotty, snot'i, *a. Foul with snot;* mean.

Snout, snout, *n.* That which requires to be *blown*, in order to wipe or cleanse it; the nose or muzzle; the long projecting nose of a beast, as that of swine. [D. *snuit*—Old G. *sniutan*, to blow the nose.]

Snow, snō, *n.* Moisture dropping from the air, congealing and changing colour as it descends, and *flowing and rolling* as it touches the ground, if but a breath of wind is stirring; watery particles congealed into white crystals or flakes in the air, and falling to the earth.—*vi. To fall in snow.* [Sax. *snaw;* Sans. *snu*, to flow.]

Snow-blindness, snō'blind-nes, *n.* An affection of the eyes, caused by the reflection of light from the snow.

Snow-broth, snō'broth, *n.* Snow and water mixed; very cold liquor. [*snow* and *broth*.]

Snow-drop, snō'drop, *n.* An early flowering plant, having *white*, delicate, and drooping flowers, so named from the flowers often appearing while the snow is still upon the ground.

Snow-plough, snō'plou, *n.* A machine operating like a *plough* for clearing away the *snow* from roads, &c.

Snow-slip, snō'slip, *n.* A large mass of *snow* which *slips down* the side of a mountain.

Snowy, snō'i, *a. White like snow; abounding with snow;* covered with snow; white; pure; unblemished.

Snub, snub, *n. A cutting short;* a check or rebuke.—*vt.* To check, stop, or rebuke, with a tart, sarcastic reply. *ppr.* snubbing, *pret. & pp.* snubbed.

Snub-nose, snub'nōz, *n.* A short or flat nose.
Snuff, snuf, *vt.* To draw in with the breath through *the nose;* to inhale; to scent; to perceive by the nose; to crop, as the snuff of a candle.—*vi.* To *inhale air* with noise *through the nose;* to turn up the nose and inhale air in contempt; to take snuff.—*n. A drawing up through the nose;* a turning up of the nose, as in scorn; the nose or end of the wick of a candle that is burned black; pulverised tobacco or other powder taken into the nose; resentment‡. [G. *schnuffeln;* Icel. *nef,* the nose.]
Snuff-box, snuf'boks, *n.* A box for carrying *snuff* about the person.
Snuffer, snuf'èr, *n.* One who *snuffs.*
Snuffers, snuf'èrz, *n.pl.* An instrument for cropping the *snuff* of a candle.
Snuffle, snuf'l, *vi.* To speak *through the nose;* to breathe hard through the nose, or through the nose when obstructed. *ppr.* snuffling, *pret. & pp.* snuffled. [D. *snuffelen.*]
Snuffler, snuf'l-èr, *n. One who snuffles.*
Snuffling, snuf'l-ing, *p.n.* A speaking through the *nose.*
Snuffy, snuf'i, *a. Soiled with snuff.*
Snug, snug, *vi.* To lie close or concealed. *ppr.* snugging, *pret. & pp.* snugged. *a.* Lying close; concealed; not exposed to notice; being in good order; neat; convenient. [Dan. *sniger,* to sneak.]
Snugly, snug'li, *adv.* Closely; safely.
So, sō, *adv. In this manner;* thus; thus it is; thus it is; this is the state; at this point; in the same degree; for this reason.—*conj.* Provided that; answering to as, and noting comparison or resemblance; therefore; noting a wish, desire, or petition. [Sax. *swa.*]
Soak, sōk, *vt. To cause to suck in* moisture; to cause to lie in a fluid till the substance has imbibed what it can contain; to steep; to draw in by the pores, as the skin.—*vi. To be soaked;* to lie steeped in water or other fluid; to enter into pores; to drink intemperately. [Sax. *socian;* Heb. *shâka,* to drink.]
Soakage, sōk'āj, *n. Act of soaking;* state of being soaked.
Soaker, sōk'èr, *n. One who soaks* or macerates in a liquid; a hard drinker.
Soaking, sōk'ing, *p.a.* That wets thoroughly.
Soap, sōp, *n.* A substance primarily formed from liquefied tallow and ashes; a compound substance of oil or fat with an alkali, as potash or soda; used in washing and cleansing, in medicine, &c.—*vt. To rub* or *wash over with soap.* [Sax. *sape*—L. *sapo.*]
Soapy, sōp'i, *a. Resembling soap;* having the qualities of soap; smeared with soap; soft and smooth.
Soar, sōr, *vi. To rise into the air;* to mount upon the wing, as an eagle; to tower in imagination; to be sublime, as the poet or the orator; to rise high in ambition or heroism.—*n.* A towering flight. [Fr. *s'essorer,* to soar up—L. *ex,* and *aura,* a gentle breeze.]
Soaring, sōr'ing, *p.a.* Mounting on the wing; towering in thought or mind. *p.n.* Act of mounting on the wing; intellectual flight.
Sob, sob, *vi.* To sigh with a sudden heaving of the breast or a convulsive motion; to sigh with deep sorrow or with tears. *ppr.* sobbing, *pret. & pp.* sobbed.—*n.* A convulsive sigh or catching of the breath in sorrow; a convulsive act of respiration obstructed by sorrow. [Sax. *seobjend,* sobbing; *siaftan,* to sigh.]

Sobbing, sob'ing, *p.n.* Lamentation; the act of sighing.
Sober, sō'bèr, *a. Free from drunkenness;* temperate; abstinent; not drunk; not mad; not wild; having the regular exercise of cool, dispassionate reason; calm; grave; solemn.—*vt. To make sober;* to cure of intoxication. [Fr. *sobre*—L. *se,* apart, and *ebrius,* drunk.]
Soberly, sō'bèr-li, *adv. In a sober manner;* coolly; gravely; seriously.
Sober-minded, sō'bèr-mind-ed, *a.* Having a disposition or temper habitually *sober,* calm, and temperate.
Soberness, sō'bèr-nes, *n. State of being sober;* seriousness; coolness.
Sobriety, sō-brī'e-ti, *n. State or quality of being habitually sober;* abstinence; habitual freedom from enthusiasm; calmness; solemnity. [Fr. *sobriété.*]
Sociability, sō'shi-a-bil'li-ti, *n. Quality of being sociable;* disposition to associate and converse with others. [Fr. *sociabilité.*]
Sociable, sō'shi-a-bl, *a. That may be united;* fit to be united in one body or company; disposed to unite in a general interest; ready and inclined to join in company; companionable; familiar; free in conversation. [Fr.]
Sociably, sō'shi-a-bli, *adv. In a sociable manner;* familiarly, as a companion.
Social, sō'shi-al, *a. Pertaining to society;* ready to mix in friendly converse; companionable; friendly; consisting in union or mutual converse; disposed to unite in society. [Fr.—L. *socius,* a companion.]
Sociality, sō-shi-al'i-ti, *n. Quality of being social;* fellowship. [L. *socialitas.*]
Socially, sō'shi-al-li, *adv. In a social manner* or way.
Society, sō-sī'e-ti, *n. Fellowship; union; a community;* the union of a number of rational beings; a number of persons united, either for a temporary or permanent purpose; any number of persons associated for a particular purpose; a club; company; union on equal terms; persons living in the same neighbourhood, who frequently meet in company and have fellowship. [Fr. *société;* L. *socius,* a fellow.]
Socinian, sō-sin'i-an, *n.* One of the followers of *Socinus,* who maintained the mere humanity of Jesus Christ.—*a. Pertaining to Socinus* or his creed.
Socinianism, sō-sin'i-an-izm, *n. The doctrine of Socinus.*
Sock, sok, *n.* A short woven *covering for the feet;* the shoe of the ancient actors of comedy; hence, comedy, as opposed to the *buskin,* which, figuratively, stands for tragedy. [Sax. *socc*—L. *soccus,* a kind of light shoe.]
Socket, sok'et, *n.* Any hollow thing which receives and holds something else; the little hollow tube in which a candle is fixed in the candlestick. (probably a dimin. of *sock.*)
Socratic, sō-krat'ik, *a. Pertaining to Socrates,* the Grecian sage, or to his manner of teaching.
Socratically, sō-krat'ik-al-li, *adv. In the Socratic method.*
Sod, sod, *n.* That stratum of earth on the surface which is filled with the roots 'f grass; turf; sward; a piece of turf. [D. *sode.*]
Soda, sō'da, *n.* The impure carbonate of soda, called barilla, is made by burning certain plants that grow upon the sea-shore to ashes, which are fused into gray porous masses, to be used in the manufacture of glass and soap. [Sp.]

Sodden-witted‡, sod'n-wit-ed, *a.* Heavy; stupid.
Soddy, sod'i, *a. Covered with sod.*
Soever, sō-ev'èr. *So* and *ever,* found in compounds, as in *whosoever, whatsoever, wheresoever.* (See these words.)
Sofa, sō'fa, *n.* An elegant long *seat,* usually with a stuffed bottom. [Ar.]
Soft, soft, *a.* Easily yielding to pressure; not hard; easily worked; malleable, as metals; not rough or harsh; smooth to the touch; delicate; feminine; easily yielding to persuasion; flexible; impressible; pliant; mild; gentle; kind; not severe or unfeeling, as one's heart; civil; placid; easy; elegantly tender, as a lady's form; smooth or melodious to the ear; not loud or harsh; flowing; easy; mild to the eye; not strong or glaring; warm; pleasant to the feelings, as the air; not hard, as soft water; not rough or irritating, as an answer; weak.—*adv.* Softly; gently; quietly.—*excl.* (for *be soft.*) Hold! stop! not so fast! [Sax.; Old G. *saf,* cork.]
Soften, sof'n, *vt. To make soft* or *more soft;* to mollify; to make less fierce; to make more susceptible of fine feelings; to compose; to mitigate; to make calm; to make less glaring; to make tender; to enervate; to make less harsh or grating.—*vi. To become soft* or softer; to become less hard; to become less rude or obstinate; to become more open to tender feelings; to relent; to become less severe or rigorous.
Softened, sof'nd, *p.a.* Made less hard or less harsh; made less obdurate or cruel, or less glaring.
Softener, sof'n-èr, *n. He or that which softens* or palliates.
Softening, sof'n-ing, *p.a. Making more soft;* making less rough, &c.—*p.n. Act of making more soft,* less cruel or obdurate, less violent, &c.; the blending of colours into each other in painting.
Soft-hearted, soft'härt-ed, *a. Having tenderness of heart;* susceptible of pity; unmanly.
Softish, soft'ish, *a. Somewhat soft.*
Softly, soft'li, *adv. In a soft manner;* gently; not loudly; mildly; tenderly.
Softness, soft'nes, *n. The quality of being soft;* mild temperature; smoothness or delicacy of surface or texture, as perceived by the touch; mildness; gentleness; effeminacy; timorousness; smoothness to the ear; easiness to be affected; meekness; simplicity.
Soho, sō-hō', *interj.* A word used in calling from a distant place; a sportman's halloo. [so and *ho.*]
Soil, soil, *vt. To sully;* to defile; to pollute; to make dirty on the surface; to begrim; to besmear; to cover with anything extraneous. [Sax. *solen*—Dan. *sole,* to roll in mud.]—*n. Dirt;* filth; spot; stain; tarnish. [G. *sule.*]
Soil, soil, *n.* The ground on which everything rests, as on a foundation; the upper stratum of the earth; the mould; loam; land; country. [L. *solum,* perhaps akin to *sedeo,* to sit.]
Soiled, soild, *p.a.* Fouled; tarnished.
Soiree, swa'rā, *n. An evening party of* ladies and gentlemen for conversation, often applied to the meetings of certain societies at which tea and other refreshments are introduced. [Fr. *soirée,* evening—L. *serus,* late.]
Sojourn, sō'jèrn, *vi. To tarry in a place* for a *day* or for *days,* or as a *stranger,* not considering the place as his permanent habitation.—*n.* A temporary residence, as that of a traveller in a foreign land. [Fr. *séjourner*—L. *sub,*

SNUB-NOSE 366 SOJOURN

Fāte, fär, fat, fąll; mē, met, hėr; pīne, pin; nōte, not, mōve; tūbe, tub, bull; oil, pound.

and *diurnus*, pertaining to a day—*dies*, a day.]
Sojourner, sō'jėrn-ėr, n. A stranger who dwells in a place for a time.
Sojourning, sō'jėrn-ing, p.n. The act of dwelling in a place for a time.
Solace, so'lās, vt. To lift up the spirits of; to cheer, console, or encourage in grief; to comfort in affliction; to soothe; to allay; to assuage.—vi. To take comfort. ppr. solacing, pret. & pp. solaced.—n. That which *comforts* or alleviates grief or anxiety; consolation; relief; diversion; amusement. [Fr. *solacier*—L. *solor*, to console.]
Solar, sō'lär, a. Pertaining to the *sun*, or proceeding from it; measured by the progress of the sun, or by its revolution. [Fr. *solaire*—L. *sol*, the sun.]
Solder, sol'dėr, vt. To unite and make *solid* or firm, as metallic substances; to unite the surfaces of, as of metals, by the intervention of a more fusible metal; to cement.—n. A metal or metallic composition for uniting the surfaces of metals; a metalic cement. [Old Fr. *souldre*—L. *solidus*, solid.]
Solderer, sol'dėr-ėr, n. *One who solders.*
Soldering, sol'dėr-ing, p.n. The process of uniting the surfaces of metals by means of a more fusible metal or a metallic cement.
Soldier, sōl'jėr, n. *One who receives wages* to fight; a man engaged in military service; a private, or one in the ranks; a brave warrior; a man of military experience and skill, or a man of distinguished valour. [Old Fr. *souldare*, *souldoyer*; L. *solidus*, military pay.]
Soldier-like, **Soldierly**, sōl'jėr-līk, sōl'jėr-li, a. *Like* or becoming a real *soldier*; brave; heroic; honourable.
Soldiership, sōl'jėr-ship, n. *State or quality of a soldier*; martial skill.
Soldiery, sōl'jė-ri, n. *Soldiers* collectively; the body of military men.
Sole, sōl, n. The *bottom* of the foot; the foot itself; the bottom of a shoe; the part of anything that forms the bottom; a marine fish, allied to the flounder and halibut.—vt. To *furnish with a sole*, as a shoe. ppr. soling, pret. & pp. soled. [Fr.—L. *solum*, the ground.]
Sole, sōl, a. *Single*; individual; only; solitary; being or acting without another. [L. *solus*, alone.]
Solecism, sō'lē-sizm, n. *Impropriety in language*, or a gross deviation from the rules of syntax; incongruity of words; any unfitness or impropriety; any expression which does not agree with the established usage of writing or speaking. [Gr. *soloikismos*.]
Solely, sōl'li, adv. *Singly*; alone; only; without another.
Solemn, so'lem, a. Primarily, *that takes place every year*; attended with religious rites; ritual; formal; awful; reverential; affecting with seriousness; having the appearance of gravity; enjoined by religion; attended with a serious appeal to God, as an oath; marked with solemnities. [Fr. *solennel*; Old L. *sollus*, every, and L. *annus*, a year.]
Solemnity, so-lem'ni-ti, n. A religious ceremony; a ritual performance attended with religious reverence; manner of acting awfully serious; affected gravity. [Fr. *solennité*.]
Solemnize, so'lem-nīz, vt. To dignify or honour by solemn ceremonies; to celebrate; to make grave, serious, and reverential. ppr. solemnizing, pret. & pp. solemnized. [Fr. *solemniser*—L. *sollennis*, festive, solemn.]

Solemnizing, so'lem-nīz-ing, p.a. *Making grave or solemn.*
Solemnly, so'lem-li, adv. *In a solemn manner;* with formal gravity.
Sol-faing, sōl-fā'ing, ppr. Pronouncing or singing the notes of the gamut, by using the syllables sol, mi, fa, &c.
Solicit, sō-lis'it, vt. *To move by importunity;* to ask earnestly; to entreat; to beseech; to ask by petition; to try to obtain; to seek to acquire; to excite to action.—vi. *To make solicitation* for some one or for a thing.—n.† A solicitation. [Fr. *solliciter*; Old L. *sollus*, whole, and *cieo*, *citum*, to move.]
Solicitant, sō-lis'it-ant, n. *One who solicits.*
Solicitation, sō-lis'it-ā"shon, n. *Act of soliciting;* a seeking to obtain something from another with some degree of zeal; supplication; importunity; invitation. [Fr. *sollicitation*.]
Solicitor, sō-lis'it-or, n. *One who solicits;* one who asks for another; a person employed to follow and take care of suits depending in courts of equity. Solicitors may be, and generally are, sworn and admitted by the judges, in order to practise in the common lawcourts. [Fr. *solliciteur*.]
Solicitorship, sō-lis'it-or-ship, n. *The office of a solicitor.*
Solicitous, sō-lis'it-us, a. *Agitated;* uneasy; careful; anxious; very desirous, as to obtain something; concerned (with *about* or *for*). [L. *sollicitus*.]
Solicitously, sō-lis'it-us-li, adv. Anxiously; with care and concern.
Solicitude, sō-lis'i-tūd, n. Uneasiness of mind; carefulness; anxiety; care. [Fr. *sollicitude*.]
Solid, so'lid, a. Hard; firm; dense; not liquid or fluid; not hollow; full of matter; having length, breadth, and thickness; cubic; having strength, as a wall; healthy; strong; having validity; substantial; valid; just; having gravity or depth; profound; important; not light.—n. A firm, compact body or substance; a body that offers a sensible resistance to impression and penetration; a magnitude which has length, breadth, and thickness. [Fr. *solide*—L. *solum*, the ground.]
Solidare†, so-li-dā'rē, n. A small piece of money.
Solidarity, so-li-da'ri-ti, n. An entire union; followship.
Solidification, sō-lid'i-fi-kā"shon, n. *Act of making* or becoming *solid*. [Fr.]
Solidify, sō-lid'i-fī, vt. *To make solid* or compact.—vi. To become solid; to harden. ppr. solidifying, pret. & pp. solidified. [Fr. *solidifier*—L. *solidus*, and *facio*, to make.]
Solidity, sō-lid'i-ti, n. *State of being solid;* that quality of bodies which resists impression and penetration; fulness of matter; firmness; moral firmness; certainty; the solid contents of a body; the earth† [Fr. *solidité*.]
Solidly, so'lid-li, adv. Firmly; densely; compactly; truly; on firm grounds.
Soliloquize, sō-lil'ō-kwīz, vi. *To utter a soliloquy.* ppr. soliloquizing, pret. & pp. soliloquized.
Soliloquy, sō-lil'ō-kwē, n. *A speaking* to one's self; a discourse of a person alone; a written composition, reciting what it is supposed a person speaks to himself. [Fr. *soliloque*; L. *solus*, alone, and *loquor*, to speak.]
Solitarily, so'li-ta-ri-li, adv. *In solitude;* alone.
Solitary, so'li-ta-ri, a. *Being alone;* living alone; lonely; retired; not hav-

ing company, or not much frequented; gloomy; sole; only.—n. *One who lives alone* or in solitude; a hermit; a recluse. [Fr. *solitaire*—L. *solus*, alone.]
Solitude, so'li-tūd, n. *A state of being alone;* loneliness; a lonely life; remoteness from society; a lonely place. [Fr.]
Solo, sō'lō, n. A tune, air, or strain, to be played by a *single* instrument, or sung by a *single* voice. [It.]
Solstice, sol'stis, n. The time when the sun seems to *stand still;* the time when the sun, in its apparent annual revolution, arrives at that point in the ecliptic furthest north or south of the equator. [Fr.—L. *sol*, the sun, and *sisto*, to stand.]
Solstitial, sol-sti'shi-al, a. *Pertaining to a solstice;* happening at a solstice; usually at the summer solstice or midsummer. [Fr.]
Solubility, so-lū-bil'i-ti, n. *Quality of being soluble.* [Fr. *solubilité*.]
Soluble, so'lū-bl, a. *That may be loosed;* dissolvable; susceptible of being dissolved in a fluid; capable of solution. [Fr.—L. *solvo*, to loose.]
Solution, sō-lū'shon, n. *A loosing or taking apart;* a dissolving; breach; the reduction of any solid body to a liquid state; state of being dissolved; diffusion of the particles of a solid body throughout a liquid without destroying its transparency; explanation; the act of removing doubt; the answering of a question, or the resolving of a problem proposed. [Fr.]
Solvability, solv-a-bil'i-ti, n. *State of being solvable;* ability to pay all just debts. [Fr. *solvabilité*.]
Solvable, solv'a-bl, a. *That may be solved,* resolved, or explained; that can be paid. [Fr.]
Solve, solv, vt. *To loosen* or *separate,* as the parts of anything; to give an explanation of; to explain; to clear; to do away; to dissipate, as doubts. ppr. solving, pret. & pp. solved.—n. A solution. [L. *solvo,* to loose.]
Solvency, sol'ven-si, n. *State of being solvent.* [from L. *solvens*.]
Solvent, sol'vent, a. *Having the power of loosening;* able to pay all just debts; sufficient to pay all just debts.—n. That which *solves;* a fluid that dissolves any substance, or in which a solution is effected. [L. *solvens—solvo,* to loose.]
Solver, sol'vėr, n. *One who solves.*
Sombre, som'bėr, a. *Shady;* dark; dull; dusky; cloudy; gloomy. [Fr.—L. *umbra,* a shade.]
Sombreness, som'bėr-nes, n. *Shadiness;* darkness; gloominess.
Some, sum, a. Noting a number of persons or things, greater or less, but indeterminate; noting a person or thing, but not known; noting a certain quantity of a thing; considerable in number or quantity; moderate; about; not far from. [Sax. *sum;* Goth. *sums,* some one.]
Somebody, sum'bo-di, n. A person unknown or uncertain; a person of consideration.
Somehow, sum'hou, adv. *In some way not yet known;* one way or another.
Somerset, sum'ėr-set, n. A leap in which a person turns with his heels *over* his head and lights upon his feet. [Old Fr. *soubresault*—L. *supra,* over, and *salio, saltum,* to leap.]
Something, sum'thing, n. *A thing* unknown, *indeterminate,* or not specified; an unknown event; a part; a portion more or less; a little; distance not great. adv. In some degree.

Sometime, sum'tim. *At one time or other;* once; formerly; hereafter.—*a.* Having been formerly.
Sometimes, sum'tīmz, *adv.* At some or certain *times;* at intervals; now and then; at one time; formerly.
Somewhat, sum'hwot, *n. Something,* though uncertain *what;* more or less; a part, greater or less.—*adv.* In some degree or quantity.
Somewhere, sum'hwār, *adv. In some place,* unknown or not specified; in one place or another.
Somewhither, sum'hwiтн-ėr, *adv.* To *some* indeterminate place.
Somnambulation, som-nam'bū̇l-ā″shon, *n. Act of walking in sleep.* [L. *somnus,* sleep, and *ambulo, ambulatum,* to walk.]
Somnambulism, som-nam'bū̇l-izm, *n. Act or practice of walking in sleep.*
Somnambulist, som-nam'bū̇l-ist, *n. A person who walks in his sleep.*
Somniferous, som-nif'ėr-us, *a. Bringing sleep;* causing or inducing sleep. [L. *somnifer—somnus,* sleep, and *fero,* to bring.]
Somnolence, som'nō-lens, *n. Sleepiness;* inclination to sleep. [Fr.]
Somnolent, som'nō-lent, *a. Sleepy;* inclined to sleep. [Low L. *somnolentus.*]
Son, sun, *n.* A male child; the male issue of a parent, father or mother; style of address of an old man to a young one; a term of affection; a native of a country; one adopted into a family; one who is converted by another's instrumentality is called his son. [Sax. *sunu;* Goth. *sunus*—Sans, *su,* to beget.]
Sonata, sō-nä'tä, *n. That which is sounded* by an instrument; a tune intended for an instrument only. [It.—L. *sono,* to sound.]
Song, song, *n. That which is sung* or uttered with musical modulations, whether of the human voice or that of a bird; a little poem to be sung; a ballad; a ditty; a lay; a sacred poem to be sung either in joy or thanksgiving; poetry; verse; mere trifle. [Sax. *sang.*]
Songster, song'stėr, *n. One who leads in singing;* one who sings; one skilled in singing; a bird that sings. [*song,* and Sax. *steora,* a guide.]
Songstress, song'stres, *n. A female singer.*
Son-in-law, sun'in-lạ, *n.* A man married to one's daughter.
Sonnet, son'et, *n. A short song or poem;* a short poem of fourteen lines, two stanzas of four verses each, and two of three each, the rhymes being adjusted by a particular rule. [Fr.—L. *sono,* to sound, to sing.]
Sonnetteer, son-et-ēr', *n. A composer of sonnets* or small poems. [It. *sonettiére.*]
Sonorous, sō-nō'rus, *a. Sounding;* giving a clear or loud sound; yielding sound; magnificent of sound. [L. *sonorus—sonus,* sound.]
Sonorously, sō-nō'rus-li, *adv. With sound;* with a high sound.
Sonorousness, sō-nō'rus-nes, *n. Quality of being sonorous;* magnificence of sound.
Sonship, sun'ship, *n. State of being a son,* or of having the relation of a son; the character of a son.
Soon, sön, *adv. In a short time;* without the usual delay; early; readily; quickly; promptly. [Sax. *sona;* Goth. *suns.*]
Soot, sȯt, *n. A black substance* formed by combustion, rising in fine particles and adhering to the sides of the chimney or pipe conveying the smoke.—*vt.* To cover or foul with soot. [Sax.]

Sooth, sȯth, *n. Truth;* reality; sweetness; kindness.—*a.* True. [Sax. *sōdh.*]
Soothe, sȯтн, *vt.* To please by speaking *sweet* words to; to flatter; to calm; to gratify; to soften; to assuage; to tranquillize; to mitigate. *ppr.* soothing, *pret. & pp.* soothed. [Sax. *gesothian;* Goth. *suts,* sweet.]
Soothing, sȯтн'ing, *p.a.* Softening; assuaging.
Soothingly, sȯтн'ing-li, *adv. In a soothing manner.*
Soothsay†, sȯth'sā, *vi.* To foretell.
Soothsayer, sȯth'sā-ėr, *n.* Primarily, *one who says the truth;* one who undertakes to foretell future events without inspiration. [Sax. *sōdh,* truth.]
Soothsaying, sȯth'sā-ing, *p.n. A saying truly†;* the foretelling of future events without divine aid or authority.
Sootiness, sȯt'i-nes, *n. Quality of being sooty,* or foul with soot.
Sooty, sȯt'i, *a. Producing soot;* consisting of soot; black like soot; dusky-dark. [Sax. *sotig.*]
Sop, sop, *n.* Anything steeped in liquor, but chiefly something thus dipped in broth or liquid food, and intended to be eaten; anything given to pacify. *vt. To steep in liquor. ppr.* sopping, *pret. & pp.* sopped. [D. *sop,* juice.]
Sophism, sof'izm, *n. A clever, cunning contrivance or device;* a specious but fallacious argument; a subtlety in reasoning. [Fr. *sophisme;* Gr. *sophos,* wise, clever.]
Sophist, sof'ist, *n. One skilful or clever;* one of a class of men who taught eloquence and politics in ancient Greece, and who, by their use of vain subtleties, drew upon themselves hatred and contempt; a captious or fallacious reasoner. [Fr. *sophiste;* Gr. *sophistēs.*]
Sophister†, sof'ist-ėr, *n.* Same as *sophist.*
Sophistical, sō-fist'ik-al, *a. Pertaining to sophistry;* fallaciously subtle; not sound. [Fr. *sophistique.*]
Sophistically, sō-fist'ik-al-li, *adv.* With fallacious subtlety.
Sophisticate, sō-fist'ik-āt, *vt.* To practise *sophistry* on; to violate; to corrupt by something spurious or foreign; to pervert. *ppr.* sophisticating, *pret. & pp.* sophisticated. [Fr. *sophistiquer.*]
Sophisticated, sō-fist'ik-āt-ed, *p.a.* Adulterated; not genuine.
Sophistry, sō'fist-ri, *n. That which is sophistical;* fallacious reasoning; reasoning sound in appearance only. [Old Fr. *sophisterie.*]
Soporiferous, sō-pō-rif'ėr-us, *a. Bringing or producing sleep* or sleepiness; tending to produce sleep; narcotic. [L. *soporifer—sopor,* a heavy sleep, and *fero,* to bring.]
Soporific, sō-pō-rif'ik, *a. Causing sleep;* tending to cause sleep.—*n.* A medicine that has the quality of *inducing sleep.* [L. *sopor,* and *facio,* to make.]
Soppy, sop'i, *a.* Wet.
Sopranist, sō-prä'nist, *n. A singer of soprano;* a treble singer.
Soprano, sō-prä'nō, *n.* The *supreme* or highest vocal part in music; the treble. [It.—L. *super,* above.]
Sorcerer, sor'sėr-ėr, *n. One who casts or draws lots;* an enchanter; a magician. [Fr. *sorcier;* L. *sors, sortis,* a lot.]
Sorcery, sor'sė-ri, *n. A casting of lots;* pretended divination by the assistance of evil spirits. [Fr. *sorcellerie.*]
Sordid, sor'did, *a. Dirty; filthy;* low; mean; vulgar; meanly avaricious; covetous. [Fr. *sordide*—L. *sordes,* dirt.]
Sordidly, sor'did-li, *adv. In a sordid manner;* meanly; basely; covetously.

Sordidness, sor'did-nes, *n. Quality of being sordid;* meanness; avarice.
Sore, sōr, *n. A wound;* a place in an animal body where the skin and flesh are bruised, so as to be pained with the slightest pressure; an ulcer; a boil; grief; affliction.—*a. Wounded;* tender and susceptible of pain from pressure; affected with inflammation; tender, as the mind; easily pained, grieved, or vexed; criminal; wicked.—*adv.* With painful violence; intensely; severely; grievously; greatly; violently; deeply. [Sax. *sār,* pain; Icel. *sár,* a wound.]
Sore†, sōr, *n.* A buck of the fourth year.
Sorel†, so'rel, *n.* A buck of the third year.
Sorely, sōr'li, *adv.* With violent pain and distress; grievously; severely.
Soreness, sōr'nes, *n. State of being sore;* the tenderness of any part of an animal body, which renders it extremely susceptible of pain from pressure; susceptibility of mental pain.
Sorrel, so'rel, *n.* A plant, so named from its taste. [Fr. *surelle;* Sax. *sur,* sour.]
Sorrel†, so'rel, *a.* Of a reddish brown colour.
Sorrily, so'ri-li, *adv. In a sorry manner;* meanly; despicably. [from *sorry.*]
Sorrow, so'rō, *n. Mental pain; grief; affliction;* sadness; the uneasiness which is produced by the loss of any good, real or supposed, or by disappointment in the expectation of good.—*vi.* To feel sorrow or pain of mind; to grieve; to mourn, weep, or lament. [Sax. *sorh,* care; Goth. *saurgan,* to grieve.]
Sorrowed, so'rōd, *p.a. Accompanied with sorrow.*
Sorrowful, so'rō-fụl, *a. Full of sorrow;* sad; mournful; depressed; dejected; producing sorrow; lamentable.
Sorrowfully, so'rō-fụl-li, *adv. In a sorrowful manner.*
Sorrowing, so'rō-ing, *p.a. Feeling sorrow,* grief, or regret.—*p.n. Expression of sorrow.*
Sorry, so'ri, *a. Having or feeling sorrow;* grieved; vexed; attended with misfortune; poor; vile; worthless. [Sax. *sarig.*]
Sort, sort, *n. Lot*†; chance†; that which consists of things *joined together;* a kind or species; any number of individuals characterized by the same qualities; manner; class or order; degree of any quality; a pair; a set; a company; a suit.—*vt. To assort;* to put *together* in distribution; to separate, as things having like qualities from other things, and place them in distinct classes; to choose from a number.—*vi.* To be joined with others of the same species; to consort; to associate; to suit; to fit. [Fr. *sorte;* L. *sors, sortis,* a lot, part—*sero,* to join together.]
Sortance†, sort'ans, *n.* Suitableness; agreement.
Sorter, sort'ėr, *n. One who sorts;* one who separates and arranges.
Sortie, sor'ti-ā, *n.* The issuing of a body of troops to attack the besiegers; a sally. [Fr.—*sortir,* to go out.]
Sot, sot, *n. A beastly person;* a person stupified by excessive drinking; a habitual drunkard. [Fr.; Armor. *saout,* bestial.]
Sottish, sot'ish, *a. Like a beast;* destitute of sense; very foolish.
Sottishly, sot'ish-li, *adv.* Stupidly.
Sottishness, sot'ish-nes, *n. State or quality of being sottish;* stupidity.
Soul, sōl, *n.* That which has the *power of thinking,* and is subject to *joy* and *sorrow;* the *thinking* and immortal

Fāte, fär, fat, fạll; mē, met, hėr; pīne, pin; nōte, not, mȯve; tūbe, tub, bụll; oil, pound.

principle in man, which distinguishes him from the brutes; the understanding; vital principle; essence; chief part; life; animating principle; a human being; animal life; active power; courage; fire; energy or grandeur of mind; an intelligent being; a disembodied spirit; heart; affection. [Sax. saul—Sans. sêv, to act, to be the subject of joy or sorrow.]

Souled, sōld, p.a. Instinct with soul or feeling.

Soulless, sōl'les, a. Without a soul, or without greatness or nobleness of mind; mean; spiritless.

Sound, sound, a. Whole; healthy; strong; sane; not wild or wandering; entire; perfect; not bruised; not lacerated; not decaying; founded in truth; valid; solid; that cannot be refuted; right; free from error; heavy; laid on with force; legal; that cannot be overthrown; fast; undisturbed; not enfeebled by age or accident. — adv. Soundly; heartily. [Sax. sund; L. sanus, healthy.]

Sound, sound, n. A narrow passage of water which may be crossed by swimming; a strait between the mainland and an island; or a strait connecting two seas, or connecting a sea or lake with the ocean.—n. The airbladder of a fish. [Sax. sund—Icel. sund, a frith, a swimming.]

Sound, sound, n. An instrument which surgeons introduce into the bladder, in order to discover whether there is a stone there or not.—vt. To try, as the depth of water and the quality of the bottom or ground, by sinking a plummet or lead; to ascertain, as the depth of water; to introduce a sound into the bladder of, in order to ascertain whether a stone is there or not; to examine; to endeavour to discover, as that which lies concealed in another's breast.—vi. To use the line and lead in searching the depth of water. [Fr. sonde—L. fundus, the bottom.]

Sound, sound, vi. To make a noise; to make an impulse of the air that shall strike the organs of hearing with a particular effect; to exhibit by sound; to be conveyed in sound.—vt. To cause to make a noise; to play on; to direct by a sound; to give a signal for, by a certain sound; to honour by sounds; to spread by sound or report; to proclaim.—n. Noise; the object of hearing; that which strikes the ear; the sensation produced in the organs of hearing by the vibration of air; noise and nothing else. [Fr. sonner; L. sono, Sans. svan, to sound.]

Sound†, sound, vi. To swoon.

Sounding, sound'ing, p.a. Sonorous; making a noise; having a magnificent sound.—p.n. Act of uttering noise; the act of endeavouring to discover the opinion or desires; the act of throwing the lead; the operation of introducing the sound into the bladder.

Soundly, sound'li, adv. Healthily; severely; with heavy blows; truly; so as not to be easily awakened.

Soundness, sound'nes, n. State or quality of being sound; wholeness; an unbroken or undecayed state; a state in which the organs are entire, and regularly perform their functions; saneness; truth; freedom from error or fallacy; orthodoxy.

Soup, söp, n. Broth; a decoction of flesh for food, seasoned more or less highly. [Fr. soupe.]

Sour, sour, a. Acid; sharp to the taste; acid and astringent, as fruits; harsh of temper; morose; expressing discontent; harsh to the feelings; rancid; musty; turned, as milk coagulated. vt. To make acid; to cause to have a sharp taste; to make harsh in temper; to make cross or discontented; to make less agreeable.—vi. To become acid; to acquire the quality of tartness; to become peevish or crabbed. [Sax. sur; Old G. sûren, to become sour.]

Source, sōrs, n. That from which anything rises or springs; first cause; the first producer; the spring from which a stream of water proceeds; a spring. [Fr.—L. surgo, to rise.]

Sourish, sour'ish, a. Somewhat sour; moderately acid.

Sourly, sour'li, adv. With sourness or acidity; with peevishness.

Sourness, sour'nes, n. State or quality of being sour; acidity; harshness of temper.

Souse, sous, n. That which is salted or salt; pickle made with salt; the ears, feet, &c., of swine pickled.—vt. To soak or steep in souse; to plunge into water.—vi. To make a sudden plunge; to rush with speed, as a hawk. ppr. sousing, pret. & pp. soused. [from L. salsus, salt—sal, salt.]

South, south, n. The region of heat; one of the four cardinal points of the compass; the point in which the meridian and horizon intersect each other; a region, country, or place situated toward the right hand as one faces the east; a wind that blows from the south.—a. Lying toward the south; being in a southern direction.—adv. Toward the south; as, a ship sails south. [Sax. suth; Sans. svid, to sweat.]

South-east, south'ēst, n. The point of the compass equally distant from the south and east.—a. In the direction of south-east.

South-easterly, south-ēst'ėr-li, a. In the direction of south-east, or nearly so; from the south-east, as wind.

South-eastern, south-ēst'ėrn, a. Toward the south-east.

Southerly, suᵾн'ėr-li, a. Lying at the south, or in a direction nearly south; coming from the south.

Southern, suᵾн'ėrn, a. Belonging to the south; lying toward the south; coming from the south.

Southernmost, suᵾн'ėrn-mōst, a. Furthest toward the south.

Southing, souᵾн'ing, p.n. Tendency or motion to the south.

Southward, south'wąrd, adv. Toward the south.—n. The southern regions.

South-west, south'west, n. The point of the compass equally distant from the south and west.—a. Lying in the direction of the south-west; coming from the south-west.

South-westerly, south-west'ėr-li, a. In the direction of south-west, or nearly so; coming from the south-west.

South-western, south-west'ėrn, a. In the direction of south-west.

Sovereign, so've-rin, a. That is highest; supreme; supreme in power; chief; pertaining to the first magistrate of a nation; predominant; effectual.—n. A supreme lord or ruler; a king, prince, monarch, or emperor; a modern gold coin, value 20s. or £1 sterling. [Fr. souverain—L. suprêmus, highest—super, above.]

Sovereignty, so've-rin-ti, n. State or power of a sovereign; supremacy; the possession of the highest power; sway. [Fr. souveraineté.]

Sow, sou, n. The breeder; the female of the hog kind or of swine. [Sax. sugu —L. sus, a boar or sow.]

Sow, sō, vt. To cast or scatter on ground, for the purpose of growth and the production of a crop; to scatter, as seed over for growth, to originate; to propagate; to supply with seed; to besprinkle.— vi. To scatter seed for growth and the production of a crop. ppr. sowing, pret. sowed, pp. sowed or sown. [Sax. sawan; Goth. sajan.]

Sower, sō'ėr, n. He who sows or scatters seed for propagation; one who scatters or spreads; a breeder; a promoter.

Sowing, sō'ing, p.n. The act of scattering seed for propagation.

Sowl, **Sowle**†, soul, soul, vt. To pull by the ears.

Spa, spą, n. A general name for springs of mineral water, from a place of this name in Belgium (Spaa).

Space, spās, n. Expansion; extension, as in length, breadth, and thickness; any quantity of extension; the distance between lines, as in books; quantity of time; the interval between two points of time; a short time.—vt. Among printers, to make as spaces, or wider intervals, between words or lines. ppr. spacing, pret. & pp. spaced. [Fr. espace—L. spatium, space.]

Spacious, spā'shi-us, a. Having large or ample space or room; roomy; not narrow, as a church; extensive; capacious. [Fr. spacieux.]

Spaciously, spā'shi-us-li, adv. Widely; extensively.

Spaciousness, spā'shi-us-nes, n. Quality of being spacious; wideness.

Spade, spād, n. That which has a broad blade; an instrument for digging or cutting the ground, consisting of a broad blade of iron with a handle; a suit of cards.—vt. To dig with a spade, or to pare off, as the sward of land with a spade. ppr. spading, pret. & pp. spaded. [Sax. spad; Gr. spathē, a broad, flat, wooden instrument.]

Spading, spād'ing, p.n. The operation of digging with a spade, or of paring off the surface of grass-land with a spade.

Span, span, n. The space from the end of the thumb to the end of the little finger when extended; nine inches; a short space of time.—vt. To measure by spans or by the hand with the fingers extended; to measure or reach from one side of to the other. ppr. spanning, pret. & pp. spanned. [Sax.; Old G. spanna, a palm.]

Spangle, spang'gl, n. Primarily, a fastening for a dress; a small plate or boss of shining metal; something brilliant used as an ornament; any little thing sparkling like pieces of metal, as crystals of ice.—vt. To set with spangles; to adorn with small, distinct, brilliant bodies. ppr. spangling, pret. & pp. spangled. [G. spangel; Icel. spenni, to clasp.]

Spangled, spang'gld, p.a. Set with spangles.

Spaniard, span'yȧrd, n. A native of Spain.

Spaniel, span'yel, n. A dog used in sports of the field, remarkable for his sagacity and obedience; a mean, fawning person.—a. Like a spaniel; mean; fawning. [Old Fr. espagneul.]

Spanish, span'ish, a. Pertaining to Spain.—n. The language of Spain.

Spar, spär, n. Primarily, that which fastens; a general term for masts, yards, and booms. [G. sparren, a spar; Icel. sperri, to fasten with a bar.]

ch, chain; j, job; g, go; ng, sing; ᵀʜ, then; th, thin; w, wig; wh, whig; zh, azure; † obsolete.

Spar, spär, *n.* A crystalline mineral which easily *cleaves* into rhomboidal, cubical, or laminated fragments with polished surfaces. [Sw. *spat*, a stone.]

Spar, spär, *vi.* To contend; to wrangle; to fight in show, or as in preparation for serious combat; to fight as a pugilist. *ppr.* sparring, *pret. & pp.* sparred. [probably from Old G. *sporo*, a spur.]

Spare, spār, *vt.* To use frugally; not to waste; to withhold from any particular use; to forbear; to use tenderly; not to take when in one's power; to forbear to destroy; to grant; to forbear to inflict or impose.—*vi.* To live frugally; to forbear; not to be profuse; to use mercy or forbearance; to be tender. *ppr.* sparing, *pret. & pp.* spared.—*a.* Frugal; scanty; in small measure; not wanted; held in reserve; to be used in an emergency; wanting flesh; thin. [Sax. *sparian*—L. *parcus*, sparing.]

Sparing, spār'ing, *p.a.* Scarce; scanty; not plentiful; saving; parsimonious.

Sparingly, spār'ing-li, *adv.* In a sparing manner.

Spark, spärk, *n.* A small particle of ignited substance, which flies off with a crackling sound from bodies when burning; a small transient light; a small portion of anything active; a brisk, showy, gay man; a lover. [Sax. *spearca.*]

Sparkle, spär'kl, *n.* A little spark; a luminous particle; lustre.—*vi.* To emit *sparks;* to send off small ignited particles, as burning fuel, &c.; to shine; to glitter; to exhibit an appearance of animation; to emit little bubbles, as certain kinds of liquors.—*vt.* To emit, as light or fire. *ppr.* sparkling, *pret. & pp.* sparkled. [dimin. of *spark.*]

Sparkling, spärk'ling, *p.a.* Glittering; lively.

Sparrer, spär'ér, *n.* One who spars; a pugilist or boxer.

Sparring, spär'ing, *n.* Act of one who *spars;* slight contention in debate, &c.

Sparrow, spar'rō, *n.* A small bird noted for its *sharp beak* and its continual chirping, and which feeds on insects and seeds. [Sax. *speara;* Icel. *spörr*, a sparrow and a spear.]

Sparry, spär'i, *a.* Resembling *spar*, or consisting of spar. [from *spar.*]

Sparse, spärs, *a.* Spread or scattered; thinly scattered; planted here and there. [L. *sparsus*—*spargo*, to scatter.]

Sparsely, spärs'li, *adv.* In a scattered or *sparse* manner; thinly.

Sparseness, spärs'nes, *n.* State of being *sparse*; thinness; scattered state.

Spartan, spär'tan, *a.* Pertaining to *Sparta*; hardy; heroic.

Spasm, spazm, *n.* A violent and involuntary *contraction* of the muscles, generally attended with pain; a convulsive fit. [Fr. *spasme*—Gr. *spaō*, to draw.]

Spasmodic, spaz-mod'ik, *a.* Relating to *spasm;* consisting in spasm; convulsive.—*n.* A medicine good for removing *spasm*. [Fr. *spasmodique.*]

Spat, spat, *n.* The spawn ejected by shell-fish. [from the root of *to spit.*]

Spatter, spat'ér, *vt.* To throw out upon; to scatter a liquid substance on; to sprinkle, as with any moist and dirty matter; to defame; to throw out in a defamatory manner. [New Low G. *sputtern*, to spit.]

Spatula, spat'ū-la, *n.* A broad thin sort of knife for spreading plasters, &c. [L.]

Spavin, spa'vin, *n.* A swelling in or near some of the joints of a horse's leg, by which lameness is produced. [It. *spavento.*]

Spavined, spa'vind, *p.a.* Affected with *spavin.*

Spawn, span, *n.* The eggs of fish or frogs, when *ejected;* any product or offspring.—*vt.* To *eject* or deposit, as fishes do their eggs; to bring forth.—*vi.* To *eject* or deposit eggs, as fish or frogs; to issue, as offspring. [Sax. *spivan*, to vomit.]

Spawner, span'ér, *n.* The female fish.

Speak, spēk, *vi.* To break silence; to utter articulate sounds or words, as human beings; to express thoughts by words; to utter a speech; to dispute; to make mention; to give sound.—*vt.* To utter with the mouth; to utter articulately, as human beings; to declare; to talk or converse in; to utter or pronounce, as in conversation; to address; to make known; to express by signs; to communicate. *ppr.* speaking, *pret.* spoke (*spake* nearly obsolete), *pp.* spoken. [Sax. *specan;* Old G. *sprekkan*—Sans. *bhranj*, to break.]

Speaker, spēk'ér, *n.* One who speaks; one who utters a speech in public; the person who presides in a deliberative or legislative assembly, as the House of Commons, preserving order and regulating the debates.

Speakership, spēk'ér-ship, *n.* The office of speaker.

Speaking, spēk'ing, *p.a.* Animated. *p.n.* Act of uttering words; discourse.

Spear, spēr, *n.* A long, pointed weapon, used in war and hunting by thrusting or throwing; a lance; a sharp-pointed instrument with barbs, used for stabbing fish and other animals.—*vt.* To pierce with a spear. [Sax. *spere*—L. *sparus*, a hunting spear.]

Special, spe'shi-al, *a.* Designating a *species;* particular; designed for a particular purpose; limited in range; extraordinary; chief in excellence. [Fr. *spécial*—L. *specio*, to look at.]

Speciality, spe-shi-al'i-ti, *n.* The special mark of a person or thing.

Specially, spe'shi-al-li, *adv.* In a *special* manner; particularly; chiefly.

Specialty, spe'shi-al-ti, *n.* Something *special;* a special contract; the evidence of a debt by deed or instrument under seal; that for which a person is distinguished. [Low L. *specialitas.*]

Specie, spē'shi, *n. Special* money; copper, silver, or gold coined and used as a circulating medium. [from *species.*]

Species, spē'shēz, *n.* The outward appearance; the outside; sort; kind; a special idea in logic; an assemblage of individuals allied by common characters, and subordinate to a genus; a group. [L.—*specio*, to look at.]

Specific, spē-sif'ik, *a.* That makes a *thing of the species* of which it is; designating the peculiar property of a thing; that particularizes; definite; having the property of curing some particular disease.—*n.* That which is peculiar to anything, and distinguishes it from all others; a remedy that cures diseases upon some principle peculiar to itself. [L. *species*, and *facio*, to make.]

Specifically, spē-sif'ik-al-li, *adv.* In a *specific* manner.

Specification, spe'si-fi-kā''shon, *n.* Act of *specifying;* state of being specified; statement of particulars; notation of limits; a written statement containing a description of particulars, as of charges against a public officer, or the terms of a contract, &c. [Fr. *spécification.*]

Specified, spe'si-fid, *p.a.* Particularized; specially named.

Specify, spe'si-fi, *vt.* To make special or *specific;* to name, as a particular thing; to designate in words so as to distinguish from other things. *ppr.* specifying, *pret. & pp.* specified. [Fr. *spécifier*—L. *species*, and *facio*, to make.]

Specimen, spe'si-men, *n.* That by which a thing is seen or recognized; a sample; a part of anything intended to exhibit the kind of the whole, or of something not exhibited. [L.]

Specious, spē'shi-us, *a.* Showy; pleasing to the view; superficially fair, just, or correct; plausible; colourable. [Fr. *spécieux*—L. *specio*, to look at.]

Speciously, spē'shi-us-li, *adv.* With a fair *appearance;* with show of right.

Speck, spek, *n.* A *spot;* a stain; a flaw; a very small thing.—*vt.* To *spot;* to stain in spots or drops. [Sax. *specca.*]

Speckle, spek'l, *n.* A little spot in anything of a different substance or colour from that of the thing itself.—*vt.* To mark with small spots of a different colour. *ppr.* speckling, *pret. & pp.* speckled. [dimin. of *speck.*]

Speckled, spek'ld, *p.a.* Marked with *specks.*

Spectacle, spek'ta-kl, *n.* A show; something exhibited to view; something represented to view as extraordinary; a representation; (pl.) an optical instrument consisting of two lenses set in a light frame, and used to assist or correct some defect in the organs of vision. [Fr.—L. *specio*, to look at.]

Spectacled, spek'ta-kld, *p.a.* Furnished with *spectacles.*

Spectator, spek-tā'tor, *n.* A looker-on; one who beholds; one personally present; a witness. [L.—*specio*, to look at.]

Spectral, spek'tral, *a.* Pertaining to a *spectre;* ghostly.

Spectre, spek'tér, *n.* An appearance; a form; the imaginary appearance of a person who is dead; a ghost; a phantom. [Fr.—L. *specio*, to look at.]

Spectrum, spek'trum, *n.* An appearance; the several coloured and other rays of which light is composed, separated by a prism. [L.]

Specular, spek'ū-lär, *a.* Having the qualities of a *speculum;* having a smooth reflecting surface. [Fr. *spéculaire.*]

Speculate, spek'ū-lāt, *vi.* To look, search, or examine; to meditate; to consider a subject by turning it in the mind and viewing it in its different aspects; to purchase land, &c., with the view of selling the articles at a profit. *ppr.* speculating, *pret. & pp.* speculated. [L. *speculor*, *speculatus*—*specio*, to look at.]

Speculating, spek'ū-lāt-ing, *p.a.* Purchasing with the expectation of an advance in price.

Speculation, spek-ū-lā'shon, *n.* Act of *speculating;* contemplation; train of thoughts formed by meditation; mental scheme; views of a subject not verified by fact; practice of buying stocks or goods, &c., in expectation of a rise of price; power of sight. [Fr. *spéculation*—L. *speculor*, to spy out, to examine.]

Speculative, spek'ū-lāt-iv, *a.* Given to *speculation;* formed by speculation; ideal; not verified by fact; pertaining to speculation in stocks, goods, &c. [Fr. *spéculatif.*]

Speculatively, spek'ū-lāt-iv-li, *adv.* In contemplation; ideally; theoretically; in the way of speculation in goods, &c.

Speculator, spek'ū-lāt-or, *n.* A looker out; one who forms theories; one who buys goods or other things, with the expectation of a rise of price. [L.]

Speculum, spek'ū-lum, *n.* That in which

Fāte, fär, fat, fall; mē, met, hėr; pīne, pin; nōte, not, mōve; tūbe, tub, bull; oil, pound.

SPEECH 371 **SPIRIT**

one sees himself; a mirror; a metallic reflector. [L.—*specio,* to look at.]
Speech, spěch, *n. That which is spoken;* the faculty of uttering articulate sounds; the faculty of expressing thoughts by words; language; a particular language; talk; common saving; oration; address; any declaration of thoughts. [Sax. *spæc;* G. *sprache.*]
Speechless, spěch'les, *a. Destitute* of the faculty *of speech;* mute; not speaking for a time.
Speechlessness, spěch'les-nes, *n. State of being speechless;* muteness.
Speed, spēd, *vi. To make haste;* to move with celerity; to prosper; to have any condition, good or ill; to fare.—*vt. To hasten;* to put in quick motion; to hasten, as to a conclusion; to execute; to help forward; to cause to succeed. *ppr.* speeding, *pret. & pp.* sped.—*n. Haste;* swiftness; rapidity of execution; prosperity in an undertaking; favourable issue; issue. [Sax. *spedan;* Gr. *speudō,* to urge on.]
Speedily, spēd'i-li, *adv.* Quickly; with haste; in a short time.
Speediness, spēd'i-nes, *n. Quality of being speedy;* celerity; despatch.
Speedy, spēd'i, *a. Having speed;* rapid in motion; quick in performance.
Spell, spel, *n. An incantation;* a charm consisting of some words of occult power [Sax.; Old G. *spel,* incantation.]—*vt. To tell;* to tell as the letters of a word, with a proper division of syllables; to write or print with the proper letters; [Sax. *spelian*] to supply the place of, temporarily, in any labour or service; to relieve.—*vi.* To form words with the proper letters, either in reading or writing. *ppr.* spelling, *pret. & pp.* spelled or spelt. [Sax. *spellian,* Goth. *spillon,* to relate.]
Spelling, spel'ing, *p.n.* Act of naming the letters of a word; orthography; the manner of forming words with letters.
Spelling-book, spel'ing-buk, *n. A book* for teaching children to *spell* and read.
Spelter, spel'tėr, *n.* A commercial name of zinc, commonly somewhat impure. [G. *spiauter.*]
Spend, spend, *vt. To weigh* or lay *out;* to consume; to waste; to squander; to bestow for any purpose; to pass, as time; to exhaust of force; to wear away; to fatigue.—*vi. To make expense;* to lay out or dispose of money; to be lost or wasted; to vanish; to be consumed. *ppr.* spending, *pret. & pp.* spent. [Sax. *spendan;* L. *ex,* and *pendo,* to weigh.]
Spender, spend'ėr, *n. One who spends;* also, a prodigal.
Spending, spend'ing, *p.n.* Act of laying out or expending.
Spendthrift, spend'thrift, *n. One who spends* improvidently money which has been saved by *thrift;* a prodigal.
Spent, spent, *p.a.* Exhausted; deprived of its original force.
Sper†, spėr, *vt.* To shut in.
Sperm, spėrm, *n. Animal seed;* that by which the species is propagated; spermaceti; spawn of fishes or frogs. [Fr. *sperme*—Gr. *speirō,* to sow.]
Spermaceti, spėr-ma-sē'ti, *n. Whale sperm*†; a fatty matter obtained chiefly from the head of a species of whale found in all *seas,* but most abundant in those near the southern pole. [Fr.—Gr. *sperma,* seed, and *kētos,* any huge fish.]
Spermatic, spėr-mat'ik, *a. Consisting of seed;* pertaining to seed, or conveying it. [Fr. *spermatique.*]
Spew, spū, *vt. To vomit;* to cast up; to

eject from the stomach; to cast out with abhorrence.—*vi.* To vomit; to puke; to discharge the contents of the stomach. [Sax. *spiwan*—L. *spuo.*]
Spewing, spū'ing, *p.n. Act of vomiting.*
Sphere, sfēr, *n. The orb of the heavens;* the concave expanse in which the heavenly bodies appear; a ball; a globe; a solid body contained under a single surface, which in every part is equally distant from a point called its centre; circuit of motion; orbit; circuit of action or influence; province; employment; rank.—*vt.† To place in a sphere.* [Fr. *sphere;* Gr. *sphaira,* a ball, a sphere, a globe.]
Spheric, Spherical, sfe'rik, sfe'rik-al, *a. Pertaining to a sphere;* having a surface in every part equally distant from the centre; planetary. [Fr. *sphérique.*]
Spherically, sfe'rik-al-li, *adv. In the form of a sphere.*
Sphericity, sfe-ris'i-ti, *n. State or quality of being spherical.* [Fr. *sphéricité.*]
Spheroid, sfēr'oid, *n.* A body *resembling a sphere,* but not perfectly spherical. [Fr. *sphéroide*—Gr. *sphaira,* and *eidos,* form.]
Spheroidal, sfēr-oid'al, *a. Having the form of a spheroid.*
Sphinx, sfingks, *n. The Throttler;* a fabulous monster, said to have proposed a riddle to the Thebans, *murdering* all who failed to guess it. [Gr.—*sphinggō,* to bind tight.]
Spice, spis, *n.* A vegetable production, aromatic to the smell, and pungent to the taste; a small quantity giving a seasoning to a greater; something that alters the quality of a thing in a small degree; [Fr. *espèce*] a specimen; a sample.—*vt. To season with spice;* to tincture; to fill with the odour of spices. *ppr.* spicing, *pret. & pp.* spiced. [Old Fr. *espice*—Low L. *species,* spices, drugs of the same sort.]
Spiced, spist, *p.a. Seasoned with spice;* having a taste or flavour.
Spicery, spis'é-ri, *n. Spices in general;* fragrant and aromatic vegetable substances used in seasoning; a repository of spices. [Old Fr. *espicerie.*]
Spicily, spis'i-li, *adv.* Pungently.
Spiciness, spis'i-nes, *n. Quality of being spicy.*
Spicy, spis'i, *a. Producing spice;* fragrant; aromatic; pointed.
Spider, spī'dėr, *n. The spinner;* an insect remarkable for spinning webs for taking its prey. [G. *spinne;* Old G. *spinnan,* to spin.]
Spigot, spī'got, *n.* A pin or peg used to stop a small hole in a cask of liquor. [W. *yspigawd.*]
Spike, spīk, *n. An ear of corn;* a large nail; a rod of iron or wood pointed. *vt. To fasten with spikes;* to set with spikes; to stop the vent of, as of a cannon, with a spike, nail, &c.; to fix upon a spike. *ppr.* spiking, *pret. & pp.* spiked. [D. *spijker,* a nail—L. *spica,* an ear, spike.]
Spikenard, spīk'nård, *n. The spike or ear* that grows on the top of the *nardus,* which is highly aromatic; also the plant itself, and the balsam obtained from it. [Fr. *spicanard.*]
Spiky, spik'i, *a. Set* or armed *with spikes.*
Spill, spil, *vt.* To pour out; to waste; to destroy; to cause to flow out or lose; to shed, as blood; to suffer to fall or run out of a vessel; to lose or suffer to be scattered, as liquids, sand, &c.—*vi.* To be shed; to be suffered to fall, be lost, or wasted. *ppr.* spilling, *pret. & pp.*

spilled or spilt. [Sax. *spillan,* Old G. *spildan,* to pour out, to waste.]
Spiller, spil'ėr, *n. One who spills.*
Spilth†, spilth, *n.* That which is spilt.
Spin, spin, *vt. To draw out with the hand;* to draw out and twist into threads, as wool, cotton, flax, &c.; to extend to a great length; to turn or cause to whirl; to draw out from the stomach in a filament, as a spider.—*vi. To practise spinning;* to move round rapidly; to stream or issue in a small current. *ppr.* spinning, *pret.* span or spun, *pp.* spun. [Sax. *spinnan;* Gr. *spaō,* to draw out.]
Spinach, Spinage, spin'äj, spin'āj, *n.* An herb whose leaves, when old are *prickly,* but when young are used as a pot-herb. [L. *spinacia*—*spina,* a thorn.]
Spinal, spīn'al, *a. Pertaining to the spine* or backbone. [Fr.]
Spindle, spin'dl, *n.* The pin used in the primitive mode of *spinning with the hand,* for twisting the thread, and on which the thread, when twisted, is wound; a slender, pointed rod on which anything turns; a small axis; the fusee of a watch; a long, slender stalk. [Sax.; Goth *spinnan,* to spin.]
Spine, spīn, *n. Something pointed;* a thorn; a sharp-pointed process from the woody part of a plant; a thin, pointed spike, as in certain fishes; the backbone of an animal, so called from its *thorn*-like processes. [Old Fr. *espine,* a thorn; L. *spica,* an ear, spike.]
Spinet, spin'et, *n.* An instrument of music resembling a harpsichord, but smaller, and so named from the quills, resembling *thorns,* used to strike the chords; now superseded by the pianoforte. [Old Fr. *espinette*—L. *spina,* a thorn.]
Spinner, spin'ėr, *n. One who spins.*
Spinning, spin'ing, *p.n. Act or operation of drawing out* and twisting into threads.
Spinning-wheel, spin'ing-hwēl, *n.* A *wheel* for spinning wool or flax into *threads* by the hand.
Spinous, spin'us, *a. Full of spines;* thorny. [L. *spinōsus.*]
Spinster, spin'stėr, *n. A woman who spins;* the common title of an unmarried woman.
Spiny, spīn'i, *a. Full of spines;* thorny; perplexed; troublesome.
Spiracle, spī'ra-kl, *n. A breathing hole;* a small aperture in animal and vegetable bodies, by which air is exhaled or inhaled; a pore; any small aperture. [L. *spiraculum*—*spiro,* to breathe.]
Spiral, spī'ral, *a. Pertaining to a spire;* winding like a screw; winding round a fixed point or centre, and continually receding from it, like a watch-spring.—*n. A spire;* a screw. [Fr.—L. *spira,* a coil.]
Spirally, spī'ral-li, *adv. In a spiral form* or direction.
Spire, spīr, *n. That which is wreathed or twisted;* a coil; a wreath; a winding-line, like the threads of a screw; a body that shoots up to a point; a conical or pyramidical body; a steeple; the top of a thing. [Fr.—L. *spira.*]
Spirit, spi'rit, *n. Life;* the breath of life; the soul of man; an immaterial intelligent substance; a ghost; a spectre; animal excitement; fire; courage; vehemence of mind; vigour of intellect; genius; temper; turn of mind; powers of mind distinct from the body; sentiment; eager desire; a person of activity; a man of enterprise; strength of resemblance; vital principle; essence; that which hath energy;

ch, *chain*; j, *job*; g, *go*; ng, *sing*; ᴛʜ, *then*; th, *thin*; w, *wig*; wh, *whig*; sh. *azure*; † obsolete,

the quality of any substance which manifests the power of strongly affecting other bodies; a strong pungent liquor; the third person in the Trinity; the Holy Spirit; (pl.) mental condition as to cheerfulness or depression.—*vt.* To infuse spirit into; to animate with vigour; to convey away rapidly and secretly, as if by the agency of a spirit (with *away*). [L. *spiritus*—*spiro*, to breathe; Sans. *spri*, to live.]
Spirited, spi'rit-ed, *p.a.* *Full of life; animated*; full of spirit or fire; ardent; active; courageous.
Spiritedly, spi'rit-ed-li, *adv.* *In a lively manner*; with spirit.
Spiritedness, spi'rit-ed-nes, *n.* *Quality of being spirited*; disposition or make of mind.
Spiritless, spi'rit-les, *a.* *Destitute of life or spirit*; wanting cheerfulness; dejected; destitute of vigour; wanting life, courage, or fire.
Spiritlessly, spi'rit-les-li, *adv.* *Without spirit*; without exertion.
Spiritous, spi'rit-us, *a.* *Like spirit*; refined; pure. [Fr. *spiritueux*.]
Spiritual, spi'rit-ū-al, *a.* *Consisting of spirit*; mental; not gross; refined from external things; not sensual; not lay or temporal; relating to sacred things; holy; pertaining to the renewed nature of man; not fleshly; pertaining to divine things. [Fr. *spirituel*.]
Spirituality, spi'rit-ū-al'i-ti, *n.* *Quality or state of being spiritual*; essence distinct from matter; spiritual nature; the quality which respects the affections of the heart only, and the essence of true religion; that which belongs to the Church. [Fr. *spiritualité*.]
Spiritualize, spi'rit-ū-al-iz, *vt.* *To render spiritual*; to refine, as the intellect; to purify from the pollutions of the world; to convert to a spiritual meaning. *ppr.* spiritualizing, *pret. & pp.* spiritualized. [Fr. *spiritualiser*.]
Spiritually, spi'rit-ū-al-li, *adv.* *In a spiritual manner.*
Spirituous, spi'rit-ū-us, *a.* *Containing spirit*; consisting of refined spirit; ardent. [Fr. *spiritueux*.]
Spirt, spèrt, *vt.* *To throw out*, as a liquid in a jet or stream; to drive or force out with violence, as a liquid from a pipe. *vi.* To issue out in a stream, as liquor from a cask.—*n.* A violent ejection of a liquid substance from a tube or other confined place; a jet. [G. *spritsen*, to spurt.]
Spiry, spīr'i, *a.* *Of a spiral form*; curved; having the form of a pyramid.
Spit, spit, *n.* *An iron prong or bar pointed*, on which meat is roasted; a small point of land running into the sea.—*vt.* To thrust a spit through; to put upon a spit; to thrust through; to pierce. *ppr.* spitting, *pret. & pp.* spitted. [Sax. *spitu*; Old G. *spisi*, sharpened.]
Spit, spit, *vt.* *To eject from the mouth*; to throw out, as saliva; to throw out with violence.—*vi.* To throw out saliva from the mouth. *ppr.* spitting, *pret. & pp.* spat.—*n.* Spittle; saliva. [Sax. *spatan*—L. *sputo*, to spit out.]
Spital†, spit'al, *n.* A hospital.
Spite, spit, *n.* *A looking down upon*; malice; rancour; pique; grudge; chagrin.—*vt.* To fill with spite; to vex; to thwart; to meditate or do mischief to; to treat maliciously. *ppr.* spiting, *pret. & pp.* spited. [Old Fr. *despit*; L. *de*, down, and *specio*, to look.]
Spiteful, spit'ful, *a.* *Filled with spite*; malignant; malicious.

Spitefully, spit'ful-li, *adv.* *In a spiteful manner.*
Spitefulness, spit'ful-nes, *n.* *Quality of being spiteful*; malignity.
Spittle, spit'l, *n.* Saliva; the thick, moist matter which is ejected from the mouth. [from *spit*.]
Splash, splash, *vt.* *To bespatter with water*, or with water and mud.—*n.* Water, or water and dirt, thrown upon anything. [intensive of *plash*.]
Splashy, splash'i, *a.* *Full of dirty water*; wet; wet and muddy.
Splay, splā, *vt.* *Originally, to display*; to dislocate or break, as a horse's shoulder-bone.—*a.* Turned outward.
Splay-footed, splā'fųt-ed, *a.* *Having the foot turned outward*; having a wide foot.
Spleen, splēn, *n.* *The milt*, supposed by the ancients to be the seat of melancholy, anger, or vexation; a fit of anger; a fit; immoderate merriment; melancholy; hypochondriacal affections. [Fr.—L. *splen*.]
Spleenful, splēn'ful, *a.* *Full of spleen.*
Spleeny, splēn'i, *a.* *Affected with spleen*; angry; melancholy; affected with nervous complaints.
Splendent, splen'dent, *a.* *Shining*; bright; beaming with light. [L. *splendens*—*splendeo*, to shine.]
Splendid, splen'did, *a.* *Shining*; glittering; illustrious; heroic; celebrated. [Fr. *splendide*.]
Splendidly, splen'did-li, *adv.* *With great brightness*; magnificently; richly; with great pomp or show.
Splendour, splen'dor, *n.* *Brightness; lustre*; great brightness; brilliant lustre; gorgeousness; parade; brilliance of appearance; eminence. [L. *splendor*—*splendeo*, to shine.]
Splenetic, sple-net'ik, *a.* *Affected with spleen*; morose; gloomy; fretful.—*n.* A person affected with spleen. [Fr. *splenétique*—L. *splen*, the spleen.]
Splenetically, sple-net'ik-al-li, *adv.* *In a morose or spleeny manner.*
Splenic, splen'ik, *a.* *Belonging to the spleen.* [Fr. *splénique*.]
Splice, splīs, *vt.* *To take asunder*, as the strands of the two ends of a rope, and unite them by interweaving them; to unite, as the end of a rope to any part of another, by an interweaving of the strands. *ppr.* splicing, *pret. & pp.* spliced.—*n.* The union of ropes by interweaving the strands; a piece added to a rope by splicing. [G. *splissen* (naut.), to splice—*spleissen*, to cleave.]
Splicing, splīs'ing, *p.n.* *Act or process of splicing.*
Splint, Splinter, splint, splint'ėr, *n.* A piece of wood *split off*; a thin piece of wood, or other solid substance, rent from the main body; a thin piece of wood, or other substance, used to confine a broken bone when set; a piece of bone rent off in a fracture.—*vt.* To split or rend into long, thin pieces; to shiver; to confine with splinters, as a broken limb. [G. *splint*—*spleissen*, to split.]
Splintered, splint'ėrd, *p.a.* Secured by splints.
Splintery, splint'ėr-i, *a.* *Consisting of splinters*, or resembling splinters.
Split, split, *vt.* *To cleave; to sever; to part*; to divide lengthwise; to separate, as a thing from end to end by force; to rive; to rend; to dash and break on a rock; to break into discord; to strain with laughter.—*vi.* To be cleft; to part asunder; to be broken; to be dashed to

pieces; to burst with laughter. *ppr.* splitting, *pret. & pp.* split.—*n.* A longitudinal *fissure*; a breach or separation, as in a political party.—*p.a. Cleft*; severed; separated; rent; broken or dashed to pieces against a rock, as a ship. [D. *splitten*.]
Spoil, spoil, *vt.* *To strip or deprive of*; to mar; to taint; to ruin; to injure fatally.—*vi.* To practise plunder; to grow useless; to become corrupted. *n.* Something stripped *off*; the plunder taken from an enemy; pillage; booty; that which is gained by strength; robbery; cause of corruption. [Fr. *spolier*—L. *spolio*—Gr. *sulaō*, to strip off.]
Spoiled, spoild, *p.a.* Corrupted.
Spoiler, spoil'ėr, *n.* *A plunderer*; a pillager; one who renders useless.
Spoke, spōk, *n.* *The radius or ray of a wheel*; one of the small bars which are inserted in the nave, and which serve to support the rim or felly; the spar or round of a ladder.—*vt.* To fit or furnish with spokes. *ppr.* spoking, *pret. & pp.* spoked. [Sax. *spaca*.]
Spokesman, spōks'man, *n.* *One who speaks for another.*
Spoliation, spō-li-ā'shon, *n.* *Act of spoiling* or plundering; particularly, of plundering an enemy in time of war; act or practice of plundering neutrals at sea, under authority. [L. *spoliatio*—*spolio*, to spoil.]
Spoliator, spō'li-āt-or, *n.* *One who commits spoliation.* [L.]
Spondaic, spon-dā'ik, *a.* *Pertaining to a spondee.* [L. *spondaicus*.]
Spondee, spon'dē, *n.* A poetic foot of two long syllables, used in solemn melodies at ancient *libations*. [Fr. *spondée*; Gr. *spendō*, to pour libations.]
Sponge, spunj, *n.* A soft porous marine substance, which readily imbibes liquids, and is used for cleansing, &c.; a sponger.—*vt.* To wipe with a sponge; to wipe out with a sponge, as letters or writing; to wipe out completely; to harass by extortion; to get by mean arts.—*vi.* To suck in or imbibe, as a sponge; to gain by mean arts, or hanging on (with *upon*). *ppr.* sponging, *pret. & pp.* sponged. [Gr. *spongos*.]
Sponger, spunj'ėr, *n.* *One who uses a sponge*; one who hangs on others for a maintenance; a hanger-on.
Sponginess, spunj'i-nes, *n.* *Quality or state of being spongy.*
Spongy, spunj'i, *a.* *Resembling sponge*: wet; soaked and soft, like sponge; having the quality of imbibing fluids.
Sponsal, spon'sal, *a.* *Relating to betrothal, espousal,* or to a spouse. [L. *sponsalis*—*spondeo*, to promise in marriage.]
Sponsor, spon'sor, *n.* *One who pledges himself to answer for another*; a god-father or god-mother. [L. *spondeo*, to promise solemnly.]
Sponsorial, spon-sō'ri-al, *a.* *Pertaining to a sponsor.*
Sponsorship, spon'sor-ship, *n.* *State of being a sponsor.*
Spontaneity, spon-ta-nē'i-ti, *n.* *The quality of being spontaneous.* [Fr. *spontanéité*.]
Spontaneous, spon-tā'nē-us, *a.* *Being of one's own motion*; acting by its own impulse; produced without being planted, as a growth of weeds. [L. *spontaneus*—*sponte*, of one's own accord.]
Spontaneously, spon-tā'nē-us-li, *adv.* *Of one's own accord*; by its own force or energy.

Spoon, spön, n. Primarily, *a chip*; a small domestic utensil, with a bowl or concave part, and a handle, used for taking up liquids, &c., at table, and for dipping; something in the shape of a spoon. [Sax. *spon*; Icel. *spónn*, a splinter of wood.]
Spoonful, spön'ful, n. As much as a *spoon* contains, or is able to contain.
Sport, spört, n. *That which makes merry*; contemptuous mirth; that with which one plays; a toy; fowling, hunting, fishing, and the like.—*vt.* To *divert* (with a reciprocal pronoun); to exhibit in public.—*vi.* To *indulge* in *sport*; to wanton; to practise the diversions of the field; to trifle. [Norm. *disport*, diversion; Sp. *deporte*, merriment.]
Sportful, spört'ful, a. *Full of sport*; frolicsome; done in jest or for mere play.
Sporting, spört'ing, p.a. *Indulging in sport*; practising the diversions of the field.
Sportingly, spört'ing-li, adv. In jest.
Sportive, spört'iv, a. *Full of sport*; gay; playful; ludicrous; inclined to mirth.
Sportively, spört'iv-li, adv. Gaily.
Sportsman, spörts'man, n. One who pursues the *sports* of the field; one who hunts, fishes, and fowls.
Sportsmanship, spörts'man-ship, n. *The practice of sportsmen*; skill in field-sports.
Spot, spot, n. A mark on a substance made by foreign matter; a stain; a speck; place; a place of a different colour from the ground; a dark place on the face of the sun or of a planet; a stain on character; disgrace; fault; blemish.—*vt.* To make a spot or spots on; to discolour; to stain; to patch by way of ornament; to taint; to tarnish, as reputation. *ppr.* spotting, *pret. & pp.* spotted. [Dan. *spætte*, a spot; Icel. *spott*, a shameful act.]
Spotless, spot'les, a. *Free from spots*; free from impurity or reproach.
Spotlessly, spot'les-li, adv. *In a spotless manner*; purely; blamelessly.
Spotlessness, spot'les-nes, n. *Quality of being spotless*; freedom from reproach.
Spotted, spot'ed, p.a. *Marked with spots* of a different colour from the ground; impure.
Spotty, spot'i, a. *Full of spots*; marked with discoloured places.
Spousal, spouz'al, a. *Pertaining to espousal*; nuptial; connubial; bridal.—*n.* Marriage; nuptials (generally pl.)
Spouse, spouz, n. *One betrothed or espoused*; one joined in wedlock; a married person, husband or wife. [Old Fr. *espouse*; It. *spósa*—L. *spondeo*, to promise solemnly.]
Spout, spout, n. *That which throws out*; a pipe, useful in directing the stream of a liquid poured out; a violent discharge of water raised in a column at sea like a whirlwind, or by a whirlwind.—*vt.* To throw out, as liquids, through a narrow pipe; to throw out words with affected gravity; to mouth. *vi.* To issue with violence, as a liquid through a narrow orifice or from a spout; to harangue; to declaim. [D. *spuit*—*spuiten*, to spout.]
Spouting, spout'ing, p.a. Pouring out words violently.—*p.n.* *Act of throwing out*; a violent or affected speech; a harangue.
Sprag, sprag, a. Vigorous.
Sprain, sprän, *vt.* *To stretch* forcibly; to stretch, as the muscles or ligaments so as to injure them, but without dislocation; to weaken, as the motive power of a part by a sudden exertion.—*n.* A violent *strain* of the muscles or ligaments of a joint without dislocation; the weakening of the motive power of a part by sudden and excessive exertion. [corrupted from *strain*.]
Sprained, spränd, p.a. *Injured by excessive straining*.
Sprat, sprat, n. A small fish, formerly supposed to be the *young* of the herring. [D. *sprot*—*spruiten*, to spring up.]
Sprawl, spral, *vi.* *To struggle*, as in the convulsions of death; to tumble or creep with many and violent contortions of the limbs. [Dan. *sprælle*.]
Sprawling, spral'ing. p.a. *Struggling*, as in the convulsions of death.
Spray, sprä, n. *A twig*; a small shoot or branch of a tree; a collective body of small branches; [Old G. *spranjan*, to bedew] among seamen, the water that is driven from the top of a wave by wind, and which spreads and flies in small particles *like dew*. [Old G. *spraioh*, twigs.]
Spread, spred, *vt.* *To make broad*; to *extend* in length and *breadth*, or in breadth only; to place; to cover by extending something over; to divulge; to send forth; to cause to affect great numbers, as an infection; to diffuse; to scatter over a larger surface; to prepare; to set and furnish with provisions.—*vi.* To *extend* itself in length and *breadth*; to be extended or stretched; to be extended by drawing or beating; to be made known more extensively; to be propagated from one to another. *ppr.* spreading, *pret. & pp.* spread.—*n.* Extent; expansion of parts. [Sax. *sprædan*; Old G. *breitan*, to dilate.]
Spreading, spred'ing, p.a. *Extending* over a large space; wide.—*p.n.* Act of *extending*, dispersing, or propagating.
Sprig, sprig, n. *A spray*; a small shoot or twig of a tree; the representation of a small branch in embroidery; an offshoot; a relative.—*vt.* *To work with sprigs*; to adorn with the representation of small branches. *ppr.* sprigging, *pret. & pp.* sprigged. [Sax. *spranca*; Old G. *springan*, to spring up.]
Spriggy, sprig'i, a. *Full of sprigs* or small branches.
Spright, Sprite, sprit, sprit, n. *A spirit*; a shade; a walking spirit; an apparition.—*vt.*| To haunt, as a spright. [Old Eng. for *spirit*.]
Sprightful, sprit'ful, a. *Full of life*; earnest; lively.
Sprightliness, sprit'li-nes, n. *Quality of being sprightly*; life; briskness; vigour; activity; gaiety; vivacity.
Sprightly, sprit'li, a. *Full of spirit*; full of life and activity; airy; gay.
Spring, spring, *vi.* *To leap or break forth*; to issue into sight or notice; to start; to rise suddenly from a covert; to proceed or issue, as from a source; to issue, as from ancestors, or from a country; to begin to grow, as vegetables; to germinate; to proceed, as from a cause; to arise; to appear; to begin to appear; to grow; to thrive. *vt.* *To cause to leap or break forth*; to raise; to start or rouse, as game; to produce quickly; to contrive on a sudden; to cause to explode; to cause to open; to crack; to cause to rise from a given spot or part; to cause to close suddenly, as the parts of a trap. *ppr.* springing, *pret.* sprang or sprung, *pp.* sprung.—*n.* A leap; a jump, as of an animal; elastic power or force; an elastic body, usually of steel or some other metal; any active power; a fountain of water; a source; that from which supplies are drawn; rise; cause; a scion; the season of the year when plants begin to vegetate and rise; the vernal season. [Sax. *springan*—G. *rinnen*, to run; to flow.]
Springe, sprinj, n. A gin; a noose, which, being fastened to an elastic body, is drawn close with a sudden *spring*, by which means it catches a bird. [from *spring*.]
Spring-gun, spring'gun, n. *A gun* which is discharged by means of a *spring*.
Spring-head, spring'hed, n. A fountain or source.
Springiness, spring'i-nes, n. *Quality or state of being springy*; elasticity; the state of abounding with springs.
Springing, spring'ing, p.a. Arising; leaping; proceeding; rousing. — *p.n.* *Act of one who springs, or of that which springs*; growth; increase.
Spring-tide, spring'tid,n. *The tide* which happens at or soon after the new and full moon, which *springs* or rises higher than common tides; the time or season of spring.
Springy, spring'i, a. *Having the quality of springing*, or *of a spring*; elastic; having great elastic power; able to leap far; abounding with springs; wet; spongy. [from *spring*.]
Sprinkle, spring'kl, *vt.* *To throw forth* in small drops or particles; to scatter; to disperse on in small drops; to besprinkle; to bedew; to cleanse; to purify. — *vi.* To perform the act of scattering a liquid, so that it may fall in small drops or particles; to rain moderately. *ppr.* sprinkling, *pret. & pp.* sprinkled.—*n.* A small quantity scattered. [D. *sprenkelen* — Old G. *springan*, to spring.]
Sprinkling, spring'kl-ing, p.n. Act of scattering in small drops or particles; a small quantity falling in distinct drops or parts.
Sprit, sprit, n. A small boom which crosses the sail of a boat diagonally from the mast to the upper aftmost corner of the sail. [Sax. *spreot*; Icel. *sproti*, a rod, a staff.]
Sprite, sprit, n. A spirit.
Spriting, sprit'ing, p.n. *The office of a sprite*.
Sprout, sprout, *vi.* *To bud*; to burst forth, as the seed of a plant; to germinate; to push out new shoots; to grow like shoots of plants.—*n. The shoot* of a plant; a shoot from the end of a branch. [Sax. *sprytan*; Old G. *sprinzan*, to put forth.]
Spruce, sprös, a. Neat without elegance; nice; finical. [said to be a corruption of *Prussian*, G. *preusse*.]
Spruce, sprös, n. *Prussian fir*; a name now given to several kinds of fir-trees.
Sprucely, sprös'li, adv. With extreme or affected neatness.
Spruceness, sprös'nes, n. Neatness without taste or elegance; trimness.
Spume, spüm, n. Froth; frothy matter *thrown up* or raised to the surface of liquors or fluid substances by boiling or agitation.—*vi.* To froth; to foam. *ppr.* spuming, *pret. & pp.* spumed. [L. *spúma*—*spuo*, to spew.]
Spumous, Spumy, spüm'us, spüm'i, a. *Consisting of spume*, or of froth or scum; foamy. [L. *spumeus*.]
Spunge, spunj. *See* SPONGE.
Spunk, spungk, n. *Wood* that readily takes *fire*; touch-wood. [Old G. *funcho*, touch-wood.]

Spur, spėr, n. An instrument having a little wheel with *sharp points*, worn on horsemen's heels, to prick the horses; incitement; stimulus; the largest root of a tree; the short wooden buttress of a post; the hard pointed projection on a cock's leg; something that projects; a smaller mountain than shoots from any other mountain; something that resembles a spur.—*vt.* To prick with a spur or spurs; to incite; to urge to a more vigorous pursuit of an object; to put spurs on.—*vi.* To travel with great expedition; to press forward. *ppr.* spurring, *pret. & pp.* spurred. [Sax. *spura*; Gr. *peirō*, to pierce quite through.]

Spurgall, spėr'gal, *vt.* To gall with a spur.

Spurge, spėrj, n. A plant having strongly *purgative* and *emetic* qualities. [Old Fr. *espurge*.]

Spurious, spū'ri-us, *a.* Of unknown seed or parentage; bastard; not proceeding from the source pretended; counterfeit; fictitious. [L. *spurius*—Gr. *speirō*, to sow.]

Spuriously, spū'ri-us-li, *adv.* In a spurious manner; falsely.

Spuriousness, spū'ri-us-nes, n. State or quality of being spurious; not genuine.

Spurn, spėrn, *vt.* To tread under foot; to drive back or away, as with the foot; to reject with disdain; to treat with contempt.—*vi.* To kick or toss up the heels; to make contemptuous opposition.—n. Disdainful rejection; contemptuous treatment. [Sax. *spurnan*; Icel. *spor*, a footprint.]

Spurred, spėrd, *p.a.* Wearing *spurs*, or having shoots like spurs.

Spur-wheel, spėr'hwēl, n. A wheel with cogs around the edge pointing to the centre.

Sputter, sput'ėr, *vi.* To spit, throw out, or emit saliva from the mouth in small or scattered portions, as in rapid speaking; to fly off in small particles; to utter words hastily and indistinctly. *vt.* To throw out with haste and noise; to utter with indistinctness (with *out*). n. Moist matter thrown out in small particles. [Dan. *sprutte*.]

Sputterer, sput'ėr-ėr, n. One who sputters.

Sputtering, sput'ėr-ing, *p.a.* Emitting in small particles; uttering rapidly and indistinctly; speaking hastily.

Spy, spī, n. One who *observes* or watches the conduct of others; a scout; a secret emissary.—*vt.* To *see*; to gain sight of; to discover at a distance; to discover by close search; to explore; to examine secretly. (With *out*.)—*vi.* To search narrowly; to scrutinize. (With *into*.) *ppr.* spying, *pret. & pp.* spied. [It. *spia*; Old G. *spehōn*, to search out.]

Spy-glass, spī'glas, n. The popular name of a small telescope.

Squab, skwob, *a.* Fat; bulky; unfledged; unfeathered; as, a squab pigeon.—n. An unfledged bird; a kind of sofa or couch; a person of a short fat figure. [Icel. *qvapi*, to shake with loose fat.]

Squabble, skwob'l, *vi.* To debate peevishly; to scuffle; to wrangle; to quarrel. *ppr.* squabbling, *pret. & pp.* squabbled. n. A scuffle; a wrangle; a brawl; a petty quarrel. [D. *kibbelen*, to wrangle.]

Squad, skwod, n. A small party of men assembled for drill or inspection; any small party. [Fr. *escouade*—L. *quadra*, a square—*quatuor*, four.]

Squadron, skwod'ron, n. A *square* or a *square form*; a body of troops drawn up in a square; a body of troops in any form; the principal division of a regiment of cavalry, usually from 100 to 200 men; a division of a fleet; a detachment of ships of war. [Fr. *escadron*—L. *quatuor*, four.]

Squadroned, skwod'rond, *p.a.* Formed into squadrons.

Squalid, skwo'lid, *a. Stiff with dirt*; foul; extremely dirty. [L. *squalidus*—*squaleo*, to be stiff.]

Squalidly, skwo'lid-li, *adv.* In a *squalid*, filthy manner.

Squall, skwal, *vi. To cry out*; to scream or cry violently, as a woman frightened, or a child in anger or distress.—n. A loud scream; a harsh cry; a sudden and violent gust of wind. [G. *schallen*, Old G. *scellan*, to sound.]

Squally, skwal'i, *a. Abounding with squalls*; disturbed often with sudden and violent gusts of wind.

Squalor, skwā'lor, n. *Foulness*; filthiness; coarseness. [L.]

Squander, skwon'dėr, *vt. To cause to vanish*; to waste; to spend lavishly, profusely, or without judgment; to disperse. [G. *verschwenden*, to squander—*schwinden*, to vanish.]

Squandered, skwon'dėrd, *p.a.* Wasted; dissipated, as property.

Squanderer, skwon'dėr-ėr, n. One who *squanders*; a spendthrift; a prodigal.

Square, skwār, *a.* Having *four* equal sides, and *four* right-angles; having a straight front, or a frame formed with straight lines; not curving; that does equal justice; exact; even; leaving no balance; exactly suitable; true.—n. A figure having *four* equal sides and *four* right-angles; an area of four sides with houses on each side; a mathematical instrument having at least one straight edge at right-angles to another; the product of a number multiplied by itself; a square body of troops; level; conformity; four; a quarrel.—*vt.* To form with *four* equal sides and *four* right-angles; to reduce to a square; to adjust; to compare with any given standard; to shape; to fit; to make even, so as to leave no difference; to multiply by itself, as a number.—*vi.* To quadrate; to suit; to fit; to accord or agree; to take the attitudes of a boxer; to spar; to quarrel. *ppr.* squaring, *pret. & pp.* squared. [Old Fr. *esquarre*, a square—L. *ex*, and *quatuor*, four.]

Squared, skwārd, *p.a.* Adjusted; regulated; multiplied by itself.

Squarer, skwār'ėr, n. A contentious fellow.

Squash, skwosh, *vt. To shake violently*; to crush; to beat or press into pulp or a flat mass. Something soft and easily crushed; a sudden fall of a heavy soft body; a shock of soft bodies. [from *quash*—L. *quatio*, to shake.]

Squat, skwot, *vi. To sit down upon the hams or heels*, as a human being; to sit close to the ground; to cower, as an animal; to escape observation, as a partridge or rabbit. *ppr.* squatting, *pret. & pp.* squatted.—*a. Sitting on the hams or heels*; sitting close to the ground; short and thick, like the figure of an animal squatting.—n. The posture of one who sits on his hams or close to the ground. [It. *acquattare*, to squat one's self.]

Squatter, skwot'ėr, n. One who *squats*.

Squeak, skwēk, *vi.* To utter a *sharp, shrill cry*, usually of short duration; to cry with an acute tone, as an animal, or to make a sharp noise, as a pipe or quill, a wheel, a door, and the like.—n. A sharp, *shrill sound*, suddenly uttered. [G. *quieken*, to squeak.]

Squeaking, skwēk'ing, *p.a.* Making a sharp sound; as, a squeaking wheel.

Squeal, skwēl, *vi.* To cry with a sharp, shrill voice. (It is used of animals only, and chiefly of swine.) [This is only a different orthography of *squall*.]

Squeamish, skwēm'ish, *a.* Having a stomach that is easily turned; nice to excess in taste; fastidious; dainty; scrupulous. [probably corrupted from *qualmish*.]

Squeamishly, skwēm'ish-li, *adv.* In a fastidious manner; with too much niceness.

Squeamishness, skwēm'ish-nes, n. State or quality of being *squeamish*; vicious delicacy of taste; fastidiousness.

Squeeze, skwēz, *vt. To press; to compress*; to press between two bodies; to press closely; to oppress with hardships and taxes; to harass; to embrace closely; to hug; to force between close bodies; to compel or cause to pass.—*vi. To press*; to urge one's way; to pass by pressing; to crowd. *ppr.* squeezing, *pret. & pp.* squeezed.—n. *Pressure*; compression between bodies; a close hug or embrace. [Sax. *cwysan*, to squeeze.]

Squeezing, skwēz'ing, *p.n. Act of squeezing*; compression; that which is forced out by pressure; dregs.

Squib, skwib, n. A little hollow cylinder of paper, filled with powder, and sent into the air, burning and bursting with a crack; a cracker; a sarcastic speech or little censorious writing published; a petty lampoon. [It. *schioppo*, a musket, a sort of gun.]

Squill, skwil, n. *The sea-onion*, used in medicine; a species of crab. [Fr. *squille*—L. *squilla*.]

Squint, skwint, *a. Wry; looking obliquely*; not having the optic axes coincident.—n. *Act or habit of squinting*; an oblique look.—*vi.* To *see obliquely*; to look obliquely; to slope; to deviate from a true line.—*vt.* To cause to squint. [D. *schuinte*, declivity.]

Squinting, skwint'ing, *p.n. The act or habit of looking squint*.

Squintingly, skwint'ing-li, *adv. With a squint look*; by side glances.

Squiny†, skwin'i, *vi.* To look squint.

Squire, skwir, n. *The shield-bearer* of a knight; the title of a gentleman next in rank to a knight; the title customarily given to country gentlemen.—*vt.* To attend as a squire; to attend as a gallant for aid and protection. *ppr.* squiring, *pret. & pp.* squired. [a popular contraction of *esquire*.]

Squiret, skwir, n. A measure or rule.

Squirehood, Squireship, skwir'hud, skwir'ship, n. The rank and state of a *squire*.

Squirrel, skwi'rel, n. A little animal remarkable for liveliness and agility, that *shades* or covers its body with its long bushy *tail*. [Fr. *écureuil*—Gr. *skia*, a shade, and *oura*, a tail.]

Squirt, skwėrt, *vt.* To eject or drive out of a narrow pipe in a stream.—n. An instrument with which a liquid is ejected in a stream with force; a small quick stream. [Old Fr. *esquarter*, to scatter.]

Stab, stab, n. Primarily, *a staff*; the thrust of a pointed weapon; a wound with a sharp-pointed weapon; an injury given in the dark.—*vt.* To pierce *with a pointed weapon*; to wound or kill by the thrust of a pointed instrument; to injure secretly or by malice

STABBING 375 STAMP

ous falsehood or slander.—vi. To give a stab or wound with a pointed weapon; to give a mortal wound. ppr. stabbing, pret. & pp. stabbed. [Old G. a staff.]
Stabbing, stab'ing, p.n. Act of wounding or killing with a pointed instrument.
Stability, sta-bil'i-ti, n. State or quality of being stable; firmness; steadiness; fixedness; strength of character; strength of purpose; firmness of mind. [Fr. stabilité.]
Stable, stā'bl, a. That stands; firm; fast; constant; firm in purpose; not wavering; durable; not subject to be overthrown. [Fr.—L. sto, to stand.]
Stable, stā'bl, n. A stall; an abode for animals; a house, shed, or apartment for beasts, especially horses, to lodge and feed in.—vt. To put or keep in a stable.—vi. To dwell or lodge in a stable. ppr. stabling, pret. & pp. stabled. [Old Fr. estable—L. sto, to stand.]
Stableness, stā'bl-nes, n. Stability.
Stabling, stā'bl-ing, p.n. Act of keeping cattle in a stable; a shed for keeping horses and cattle.
Stablish, stab'lish, vt. To establish.
Stably, stā'bli, adv. Firmly; fixedly.
Stack, stak, n. A large conical pile of hay, grain, or straw, sometimes covered with thatch; a large pile of wood; a number of chimneys standing together.—vt. To lay in a conical or other pile; to make into a large pile; to pile, as wood, poles, &c. [Sw.—Old G. stacchan, to press together.]
Stacking, stak'ing, p.n. The operation of piling up unthrashed corn, hay, &c., into stacks.
Stack-yard, stak'yärd, n. A yard for stacks of hay, unthrashed corn, &c.
Staddle, stad'l, n. That on which anything stands; the frame or support of a stack of hay or grain. [Sax. stathel.]
Staff, staf, n. Staffs or Staves, stafs, stāvz, pl. A support; a stay; that which upholds; a stick carried in the hand for support or defence by a person walking; the long handle of an instrument; a stick used for many purposes; the five lines and the spaces on which music is written; a badge of office; the round of a ladder; a pole erected in a ship to hoist and display a flag; an establishment of officers in various departments, attached to an army, or to the commander of an army (in this sense the pl. staffs); [Icel. stef] a stanza. [Sax. staf; Old G. stiban, to support.]
Stag, stag, n. The animal which uses its horns for defence, and occasionally for attack; the male red deer; the male of the hind. [Icel. steggr, the male of several animals; Goth. stiggvan, to push, to gore.]
Stage, stāj, n. A floor or story†; a floor or platform of any kind elevated above the ground, as for an exhibition of something to public view; the floor on which theatrical performances are exhibited; the theatre; place of action; a place of rest on a journey; the distance between two places of rest on a road; a degree of advance.—vt.† To exhibit upon a stage. [Old Fr. estage; Goth. steigan, to ascend.]
Stage-coach, stāj'kōch, n. A coach that runs by stages; a coach that runs regularly for the conveyance of passengers.
Stage-player, stāj'plā-ėr, n. An actor on the stage; one who represents characters on the stage.
Stagger, stag'ėr, vi. To reel; not to stand or walk with steadiness; to fail; to begin to give way; to begin to doubt and waver in purpose; to become less confident.—vt. To cause to reel; to cause to doubt and waver; to shock. [Belg. staggeren.]
Staggering, stag'ėr-ing, p.a. Causing to reel; vacillating.—p.n. Act of reeling.
Staggers†, stag'ėrz, n. Madness; wild conduct.
Stag-hound, stag'hound, n. A hound used in hunting the stag or deer.
Stagnant, stag'nant, a. Standing; motionless; not active; dull; not brisk. [Fr.]
Stagnantly, stag'nant-li, adv. In a still, motionless, inactive manner.
Stagnate, stag'nāt, vi. To stand still; to cease to flow; to cease to move; to cease to be brisk or active; to become dull. ppr. stagnating, pret. & pp. stagnated. [L. stagno, stagnātus—sto, to stand.]
Stagnation, stag-nā'shon, n. Act of stagnating; state of being stagnant; the state of being motionless; the state of being dull. [Fr.]
Staid, stād, p.a. Steady; not wild or fanciful; grave; regular; sedate.
Staidness, stād'nes, n. The state or condition of being staid; gravity; constancy.
Stain, stān, vt. To tinge; to dye; to tinge with a different colour; to make foul; to spot; to soil; to impress with figures, in colours different from the ground; to mark with guilt or infamy; to bring reproach on.—vi. To take stains; to become stained.—n. A tinge; a colour; a blot; a natural spot of a colour different from the ground; taint of guilt; tarnish; infamy; shame. [from distain; Fr. desteindre—L. de, and tingo, to stain.]
Stained, stānd, p.a. Tinged; coloured; tarnished.
Stainer, stān'ėr, n. One who stains.
Stainless, stān'les, a. Free from stains or spots; free from the reproach of guilt.
Stair, stār, n. A stone or a frame of boards or planks by which a person rises step by step; a flight of steps; (pl.) a series of steps by which persons ascend to a higher story in a building. [Sax. staeger; Goth. steigan, to ascend.]
Staircase, stār'kās, n. The part of a building which contains the stairs.
Stake, stāk, n. A small piece of timber, sharpened at one end, and fixed in the ground, as a support to something; a piece of long, rough wood; the piece of timber to which a martyr is fastened when he is to be burned; martyrdom; that which is pledged.—vt. To support or defend with stakes; to mark the limits of by stakes; to wager; to pledge; to pierce with a stake. [Sax. stace; G. stecken, to fix; Goth. stiks, a point.]
Stalactite, sta-lak'tit, n. A pendant cone of carbonate of lime, attached, like an icicle, to the roof of a cavern, produced by the trickling through the rock above of water holding carbonate of lime in solution. [Gr. stalaktos, trickling—stalasso, to let fall drop by drop.]
Stalactitic, sta-lak-tit'ik, a. Having the character of a stalactite; having the form of an icicle. [Gr. stalaktikos.]
Stale, stāl, a. Long exposed, as on a stall, to public view; having lost its power of pleasing; old; decayed; not freshly made; vapid from age; having lost its flavour from being long kept.—n. A thing for common sale; a stalking-horse. [Sax. steal, a place.]
Stale, stāl, vi. To make water; to discharge urine, as horses and cattle. ppr. staling, pret. & pp. staled. [G. stallen—L. stillo, to drop.]
Staleness, stāl'nes, n. State of being stale; oldness; triteness; commonness.
Stalk, stak, n. The stem or main axis of a plant; the pedicle of a flower; the stem of a quill; anything resembling the stalk or stem of a plant. [Icel. stilkr; Gr. stulos, a pillar.]
Stalk, stak, vi. To walk, as on stilts; to walk with high and proud steps; usually implying the affectation of dignity; [Sax. staelcan; probably from staelan, to steal] to steal or creep along; to walk softly and warily; to walk behind a stalking-horse or behind a cover.—n. A high, proud, stately step or walk. [probably from Sax. stælg, a prop.]
Stalked, stakt, a. Having a stalk.
Stalker, stak'ėr, n. One who walks with a proud step.
Stalking, stak'ing, p.n. The act of going gently step by step, under cover of a horse, a screen, &c., till the sportsman gets within shot of the game.
Stalking-horse, stak'ing-hors, n. A horse, real or factitious, behind which a fowler conceals himself from the sight of the game which he is aiming to kill; a mask; a pretence.
Stall, stal, n. A place to stand on; a stand or place where a horse or an ox is kept and fed; a stable; the division of a stable, or the apartment for one horse; a bench in the open air, where anything is exposed to sale; a small house in which an occupation is carried on; the seat of a dignified clergyman in the choir; a seat in front of the pit of a theatre.—vt. To put into a stall or stable, or to keep in a stable; to install.—vi. To dwell; to inhabit. [Sax. stæl; Old G. staljan, to place.]
Stallage, stal'āj, n. The right of erecting stalls in fairs; or rent paid for a stall.
Stalled, stald, p.a. Kept or fed in a stable or stall.
Stall-fed, stal'fed, p.a. Fed or fattened in a stall.
Stallion, stal'li-on, n. A horse kept for mares; a stone horse. [Old Fr. estallon.]
Stamen, stā'men, n. Stamens or Stamina, stā'menz, sta'mi-na, pl. Primarily, the warp in the upright loom of the ancients; basis; the male organ of fructification in plants. pl. **Stamina**, the fixed, firm part of a body, which gives it its strength and solidity; whatever constitutes the principal strength or support of anything. [L.—Gr. histēmi, to stand.]
Stammer, stam'ėr, vi. To stop in uttering syllables or words; to falter in speaking; to speak with stops and difficulty.—vt. To utter with hesitation. [Sax. stamer, stammerer; Goth. stamms, hardly speaking.]
Stammerer, stam'ėr-ėr, n. One who stutters or hesitates in speaking.
Stammering, stam'ėr-ing, p.a. Apt to stammer.—p.n. Act of stopping or hesitating in speaking; impediment in speech.
Stamp, stamp, vt. To strike forcibly as with the bottom of the foot; to impress with some mark; to impress; to fix deeply; to coin; to form; to crush by the downward action of a kind of pestle, as ore in a stamping-mill.—vi. To strike the foot forcibly downward.—n. Any instrument for making impressions on other bodies; an impression; that which is marked; a thing stamped; a cut; a plate; a mark set upon paper or parchment in regard to things charge-

ch, chain; j, job; g, go; ng, sing; ᴛʜ, then; th, thin; w, wig; wh, whig; zh, azure; † obsolete.

able with duty to government; an instrument for cutting out materials (as paper, leather, &c.) into various forms; a character of reputation, good or bad, fixed on anything; authority; current value derived from suffrage; make; cast; character. [D. *stampen*; Old G. *stamphôn*, to pound, to crush.]

Stamped, stampt, *p.a.* Imprinted; deeply fixed.

Stamper, stamp'ėr, *n.* An instrument for *stamping*; one who affixes a stamp or a post-mark.

Stanch, stänsh, *vt. To cause to stand*; to stay; to stop or hinder from running, as blood.—*vi.* To stop, as blood; to cease to flow.—*a. Standing;* firm; strong and tight; such as will not run out; firm in principle; hearty; not to be broken; following the scent without error or remissness, as a hound. [Old Fr. *estancher*—L. *stagno*, to cause to stand.]

Stanchion, stan'shi-on, *n. A stay*; a piece of timber or iron in the form of a stake or post, used for a support. [Old Fr. *estanson—estancher*, to stay.]

Stanchly, stänsh'li, *adv.* Firmly; determinedly; heartily.

Stanchness, stänsh'nes, *n. State or quality of being stanch;* firmness in principle; closeness of adherence.

Stand, stand, *vi.* To be upon the feet in an erect position; to be erect, as a tree; to be on its foundation; to be placed; to remain upright, in a moral sense; to become erect; to stop; not to proceed; to be in a state of fixedness; to continue; to be placed with regard to rank; to be fixed; to continue valid; to have its being and essence; to have a place; to be in any state; to be, with regard to state of mind; to succeed; not to fail; to be safe; to hold a course at sea; to offer one's self as a candidate; to stagnate; to be satisfied; to make delay; to persevere; to endure; not to vanish or fade.—*vt.* To endure; to sustain; to bear; to resist without yielding; to await; to suffer; to abide by. *ppr.* standing, *pret. & pp.* stood.—*n.Act of standing;* a stop; a halt; a place or post where one stands; an erection for spectators, as at a horse-race; station; standing; act of opposing; the highest point; a frame for ink-bottles; a desk for music; a station for cabs, &c.; a small table; something on which a thing rests. [Sax. *standan*—L. *sto*, to stand.]

Standard, stand'ärd, *n.* A staff with a flag *standing* upright; that which is established as a rule or model; criterion; test; the proportion of weight of fine metal and alloy established by authority; a tree not attached to a wall; an upright support, as the poles of a scaffold; an officer who carries a standard. [Old Fr. *estandart*—Goth. *standan*, to stand.]

Standard-bearer, stand'ärd-bär-ėr, *n.* An officer of an army, company, or troop, who *bears a standard*; an ensign of infantry or a cornet of horse.

Standing, stand'ing, *p.a.* Settled; established, either by law or by custom; lasting; not liable to fade; stagnant; fixed; remaining erect.—*p.n.* Continuance; possession of an office, character, or place; place to stand in; power to stand; rank.

Standish, stan'dish, *n.* A case for pen and ink.

Stannary, stan'a-ri, *n.* A *tin* mine; certain royal rights in respect to tin mines.—*a.* Relating to the *tin* mines or works. [from L. *stannum*, tin, an alloy of silver and lead.]

Stannel†, stan'nel, *n.* A base species of hawk.

Stanza, stan'za, *n.* A number of verses connected with each other and ending in a full point or *pause*; a part of a poem, ordinarily containing every variation of measure in that poem. [It.—L. *sto*, to stand.]

Staple, stā'pl, *n.* Primarily, *a prop*; that which is fixed; formerly, a settled mart or market; a principal production of a country or district; the thread or pile of wool, cotton, or flax; the material or substance of a thing; a loop of iron, formed with two points to be driven into wood, to hold a hook, pin, &c.—*a. Settled*; *established* in commerce; chief; regularly made for market. [Sax. *stapel*—L. *sto*, to stand.]

Stapler, stā'pl-ėr, *n.* A dealer.

Star, stär, *n. A shining heavenly body*; an apparently small, luminous body in the heavens, that shines in the night; configuration of the planets supposed to influence fortune; the figure of a star; an asterisk, thus (*), used as a mark of reference; the figure of a star, as a badge of rank; a person of brilliant qualities; an accomplished theatrical performer, &c.—*vt. To set or adorn with stars;* to bespangle.—*vi.* To shine as a star; to perform on the stage as an actor of eminence. *ppr.* starring, *pret. & pp.* starred. [Sax. *steorra*—Gr. *antēr*, a star.]

Starboard, stär'bōrd, *n. The place* in a ship which the *steers*man occupies; the right-hand side of a ship when a spectator stands with his face towards the prow. [Sax. *steorbord—styran*, to steer, and *board*.]

Starch, stärch, *n. That which stiffens*; a substance used to *stiffen* linen and other cloth.—*a. Stiff;* precise; rigid. *vt. To stiffen with starch.* [Sax. *stearc* —Gr. *stereos*, stiff.]

Starched, stärcht, *p.a. Stiff;* precise; formal.

Starcher, stärch'ėr, *n. One who starches.*

Starchly, stärch'li, *adv.* With stiffness of manner; formally,

Starchness, stärch'nes, *n. Stiffness* of manner; preciseness.

Starchy, stärch'i, *a. Consisting of starch*; resembling starch; stiff; precise.

Star-crossed†, stär'krost, *a.* Ill-omened.

Stare, stär, *vi.* To gaze or to look with *fixed* eyes wide open; to fasten an earnest look on some object.—*vt. To fix the eyes upon;* to gaze at; to affect or influence by staring. *ppr.* staring, *pret. & pp.* stared.—*n. A fixed look* with eyes wide open. [Sax. *starian*—G. *starr*, fixed.]

Starer, stär'ėr, *n. One who stares.*

Star-gazer, stär'gāz-ėr, *n. One who gazes at the stars.*

Star-gazing, stär'gāz-ing, *n.* The act or practice of observing the stars with attention; astrology.

Staring, stär'ing, *p.a.* Looking with fixed eyes.

Stark, stärk, *a. Stiff;* confirmed or established; mere; absolute.—*adv.* Wholly; entirely; absolutely. [Sax. *stearc;* Old G. *starh*, stiff, rigid.]

Starkly, stärk'li, *adv. In a stark manner.*

Starless, stär'les, *a. Having no stars* visible, or no starlight.

Starlight, stär'līt, *n. The light proceeding from the stars.*

Starling, stär'ling, *n.* A bird of the sparrow kind, probably so named from its habit of *scraping* in search of worms, &c., and capable of being taught to sing and even to speak with great distinctness. [Sax. *stearn*—L. *sturnus*.]

Starred, stärd, *p.a.* Influenced in fortune by the stars.

Starring, stär'ing, *p.a.* Denoting the practice of a player of high reputation who appears occasionally in the provinces.

Starry, stär'i, *a. Abounding with stars;* adorned with stars; proceeding from the stars; shining like stars.

Start, stärt, *vi. To move suddenly,* as by an involuntary shrinking from sudden fear or alarm; to shrink; to move suddenly aside; to set out; to commence a journey; to move from its place, as a beam.—*vt. To cause to move suddenly;* to cause to flee or fly; to bring into sudden motion; to call forth; to alarm; to startle; to rouse; to invent; to bring within pursuit; to move suddenly from its place; to empty, as liquor from a cask; to pour out.—*n. A sudden motion of the body;* a sudden motion from alarm; a spring; sally; a bursting forth; sudden fit; a quick spring; a darting; a push; act of setting out. [G. *stürzen*, to precipitate—Old G. *stursen*, to turn.]

Starter, stärt'ėr, *n. One who starts;* a dog that rouses game.

Starting, stärt'ing, *p.n. Act of moving suddenly;* act of setting out.

Starting-hole†, stärt'ing-hōl, *n.* A loophole; evasion.

Startle, stärt'l, *vi.* To shrink; to move suddenly on feeling alarm.—*vt.* To start; to frighten; to surprise; to excite by sudden apprehension. *ppr.* startling, *pret. & pp.* startled.—*n. A sudden motion* occasioned by an apprehension of danger; sudden impression of terror. [intensive of *start*.]

Startling, stärt'l-ing, *p.a.* Suddenly impressing with fear.

Starvation, stärv-ā'shon, *n. Act of starving* or state of being starved.

Starve, stärv, *vi. To perish or die* with cold or hunger; to suffer extreme hunger or want; to be very indigent. *vt. To kill* with hunger; to distress or subdue by famine; to destroy by want; to kill with cold. *ppr.* starving, *pret. & pp.* starved. [Sax. *steorfan*—Old G. *sterban*, to die, *stirbig*, dying, *sterbjan*, to slay.]

Starved, stärvd, *p.a. Killed* by cold; subdued by hunger.

Starveling, stärv'ling, *n.* An animal or plant that is made thin and weak through want of nutriment.

Starving, stärv'ing, *p.a.* Perishing with hunger; perishing with cold.

State, stāt, *n. A standing;* the circumstances of a being or thing at any given time; case; plight; a political body; the whole body of people united under one government; a body of men united by profession; rank; condition; pomp; a raised chair or throne; appearance of greatness; (pl.) the bodies that constitute the legislature of a country; nobility; a republic.—*vt. To set; to settle;* to set forth, as the circumstances under which anything exists; to express, as the particulars of anything in writing; to express, as the particulars of anything verbally; to recite. *ppr.* stating, *pret. & pp.* stated.—*a. Belonging to the state* or nation; grand; ceremonial; royal. [Old Fr. *estat*—L. *status*—*sto*, to stand.]

Stated, stāt'ed, *p.a. Settled;* occurring at regular times; fixed.

Statedly, stāt'ed-li, *adv.* Regularly; at certain times; not occasionally.
Stateliness, stāt'li-nes, *n. Quality of being stately;* loftiness of mien or manner; majestic appearance; dignity; affected dignity.
Stately, stāt'li, *a.* Evincing *state* or dignity; grand; majestic; lofty.
Statement, stāt'ment, *n. Act of stating;* that which is stated; a series of facts expressed on paper, or verbally recited.
State-room, stāt'rōm, *n.* A magnificent room in a palace or great house; an apartment for lodging in a ship's cabin.
Statesman, stāts'man, *n. A man* versed in *state* or public affairs; one eminent for political abilities.
Statesmanlike, stāts'man-līk, *a. Having the manner or wisdom of statesmen.*
Statesmanship, stāts'man-ship, *n.* The *qualifications of a statesman.*
Static, Statical, stāt'ik, stāt'ik-al, *a. Pertaining to statics;* acting by mere weight. [Gr. *statikos*, causing to stand.]
Statics, stāt'iks, *n.* That branch of mechanics which treats of the equilibrium of forces, or relates to bodies, as held at rest. [Fr. *la statique;* Gr. *histēmi*, to make to stand.]
Station, stā'shon, *n.* The spot or place where one *stands;* attitude; office; the department of public duty which a person is appointed to fill; situation; business; state; rank; the position of a ship of war, of a missionary, &c.; a place on a railway where trains make a halt.—*vt. To assign a station to;* to set; to appoint to the occupation of an office. [Fr.—L. *sto,* to stand.]
Stationary, stā'shon-a-ri, *a. Standing;* fixed; not advancing, in a moral sense; not growing wiser, greater, or better. [Fr. *stationnaire.*]
Stationer, stā'shon-ėr, *n.* Originally, a bookseller, from his occupying *a stand or station;* but at present, one who sells paper, quills, &c.
Stationery, stā'shon-ė-ri, *n. The articles usually sold by stationers,* as paper, ink, &c.—*a. Belonging to a stationer.*
Statist, stāt'ist, *n.* A statesman.
Statistic, Statistical, stāt-ist'ik, stāt-ist'ik-al, *a. Pertaining to statistics;* containing statistics. [Fr. *statistique.*]
Statistics, stāt-ist'iks, *n.* A collection of facts respecting the *state* of society, the condition of the people in a nation or country, their health, longevity, domestic economy, arts, property, political strength, &c.; the science which treats of these subjects. [Fr. *la statistique.*]
Statuary, stat'ū-a-ri, *n.* One who practises the art of making *statues;* the art of carving statues as representatives of real persons or things; a collection of statues. [Fr. *statuaire*—L. *sto,* to stand.]
Statue, stat'ū, *n. That which is set;* an image; a solid substance formed by carving into the likeness of a whole living being; a portrait. [L. *statua*—*sto,* to stand.]
Statuesque, stat-ū-esk', *a.* Partaking of the characteristics of *a statue.*
Statuette, stat-ū-et', *n. A small statue.*
Stature, stat'ūr, *n.* The height of any one *standing.* [Fr.—L. *sto,* to stand.]
Status, stā'tus, *n. A standing;* state; rank; condition. [L.—*sto,* to stand.]
Statutable, stat'ūt-a-bl, *a. Made or introduced by statute;* proceeding from an act of the legislature; made or being in conformity to statute.

Statute, stat'ūt, *n. A fixed law or edict;* an act of the legislature of a state commanding or prohibiting something; a positive law; a special act of the supreme power, of a private nature; the act of a corporation or of its founder, intended as a permanent rule or law. [Fr. *statut*—L. *sto,* to stand.]
Statutory, stat'ū-tō-ri, *a. Enacted by statute;* depending on statute for its authority.
Staunch, stänsh. See STANCH.
Stave, stāv, *n.* Primarily, *a staff;* a thin narrow piece of timber, of which casks are made; [Icel. *stef,* a strophe] a staff or metrical portion; a part of a psalm appointed to be sung in churches.—*vt. To thrust through with a staff;* to burst, as a cask; to push, as with a staff; to delay (with *off*); to suffer to be lost by breaking the cask, or separating the staves. *ppr.* staving, *pret. & pp.* stove or staved. [from *staff.*]
Stay, stā, *vi. To stand;* to remain; to abide for any indefinite time; to dwell; to attend; to forbear to act; to rely; to confide in; to trust.—*vt. To cause to stand;* to hold from proceeding; to withhold; to delay forcibly (with *off*); to keep from departure; to stop from falling; to hold up; to support from sinking; to sustain with strength. *ppr.* staying, *pret. & pp.* staid, for stayed. *n. A standing;* continuance in a place; obstruction; hindrance from progress; a fixed state; brace; steadiness of conduct; (pl.) large ropes in ships, used to support masts; a sort of stiffened waistcoat worn by females to support the body. [Old Fr. *estayer*—L. *sto,* to stand.]
Stead, sted, *n. A place;* a station†; place or room which another had or might have; noting substitution, replacing, or filling the place of another.—*vt. To help;* to support; to fill the place of. [Sax. *stede*—Icel. *stedia,* to set.]
Steadfast, sted'fast, *a. Fast in place;* fast fixed; resolute; not fickle or wavering; steady. [Sax. *stedfæst.*]
Steadfastly, sted'fast-li, *adv.* Firmly; with constancy or steadiness of mind.
Steadfastness, sted'fast-nes, *n. State or quality of being steadfast;* fixedness in principle; unchangeableness; firmness; immutability.
Steadily, sted'i-li, *adv.* With firmness of *standing;* without wavering.
Steadiness, sted'i-nes, *n. State or quality of being steady;* firmness of standing; firmness of mind or purpose; consistent uniform conduct. [Sax. *stedignys.*]
Steady, sted'i, *a. Stable;* fixed; not shaking; constant in mind; not wavering; not easily moved; constant in progress; uniform; not fluctuating.—*vt. To make steady;* to support; to make or keep firm. *ppr.* steadying, *pret. & pp.* steadied. [Old G. *stätig.*]
Steak, stāk, *n. A piece or slice* of flesh, particularly beef, broiled, or cut for broiling. [Sax. *sticce;* Dan. *stäkke,* to cut off.]
Steal, stēl, *vt. To take away secretly;* to take and carry away feloniously, as the personal goods of another; to withdraw without notice; to win by address; to try to pass secretly.—*vi.* To practise theft; to withdraw *silently* or privily; to abscond. *ppr.* stealing, *pret.* stole, *pp.* stolen. [Sax. *stelan.*]
Stealth, stelth, *n. Act of stealing;* secret act; means unperceived employed to gain an object; way or manner not perceived.
Stealthily, stelth'i-li, *adv. By stealth.*

Stealthy, stelth'i, *a. Done by stealth;* clandestine; unperceived.
Steam, stēm, *n. The vapour of water,* or the elastic aeriform fluid generated by heating water to the boiling point; visible vapour.—*vi. To rise or pass off in vapour* by means of heat; to pass off in visible vapour.—*vt. To expose to steam;* to apply steam to for softening, dressing, or preparing. [Sax. *stem;* G. *dampf,* vapour.]
Steam-boat, Steam-vessel, stēm'bōt, stēm'ves-sel, *n. A vessel* propelled through the water by *steam.*
Steam-engine, stēm'en-jin, *n. An engine worked by steam.*
Steamer, stēm'ėr, *n. A vessel propelled by steam;* a vessel in which articles are subjected to the action of steam.
Steam-ship, stēm'ship, *n. A ship propelled by steam.*
Steamy, stēm'i, *a. Consisting of or abounding in steam;* damp.
Steed, stēd, *n.* A horse or *mare* from the *stud* or *stand;* a horse of high mettle for state or war. [Sax. *stede;* G. *stute,* a mare.]
Steel, stēl, *n.* A very *hard* metal, formed by combining iron with a small portion of carbon, used in making instruments; offensive weapons, swords, spears, and the like; extreme hardness.—*a. Made of steel.*—*vt. To overlay, point, or edge with steel;* to harden; to make obdurate. [Sax. *style;* Old G. *stahal,* steel—Icel. *staeltr,* hard.]
Steely, stēl'i, *a. Made of steel.*
Steelyard, stēl'yärd, *n. A rod* or *bar of steel,* adapted for weighing bodies. It usually consists of a lever with unequal arms.
Steep, stēp, *a. High;* lofty; ascending or descending with great inclination; precipitous.—*n.* A precipitous place, hill, mountain, rock, or ascent; a precipice. [Sax. *steap,* high; Icel. *steypi,* to hurl down.]
Steep, stēp, *vt. To soak in a liquid;* to imbue; to drench; to cover completely. *n. Something that is steeped* or used in steeping: a fertilizing liquid for hastening the germination of seeds. [Icel. *sleyppa,* to pour; to melt.]
Steep-down, stēp'doun, *a.* Deep and precipitous.
Steeple, stē'pl, *n.* A turret of a church, ending in *a point;* a spire. [Sax. *stypel;* D. *stippel,* a point.]
Steepled, stē'pld, *p.a. Furnished with a steeple;* adorned with steeples.
Steeply, stēp'li, *adv. With steepness.*
Steepness, stēp'nes, *n. State of being steep;* precipitous declivity.
Steepy, stēp'i, *a. Having a steep* or precipitous declivity.
Steer, stēr, *n.* A young castrated male of the ox kind or common ox. [Sax. *steur*—L. *taurus,* a bull.]
Steer, stēr, *vt. To direct;* to govern; particularly to direct and govern, as a ship by the movements of the helm; to guide; to show the way to.—*vi.* To direct and govern a ship in its course; to be directed and governed; to conduct one's self; to pursue a course or way. [Sax. *styran;* Goth. *stiurjan,* to direct.]
Steerage, stēr'āj, *n.* The effort of a helm, or its effect in *directing* the ship; the peculiar manner in which an individual ship is affected by the helm; an apartment in the fore-part of a ship for an inferior class of passengers; that by which a course is directed.
Steering, stēr'ing, *p.n.* Act or art of *directing* and governing a ship or other vessel in her course.

Steersman, stērz'man, n. *One who steers*; a helmsman.
Stellar, stel'ar, a. *Pertaining to stars*; starry; full of stars; set with stars. [Fr. *stellaire*—L. *stella*, a star.]
Stelled, steld, p.a. Starry.
Stellular, stel'ū-lar, a. *Shaped like little stars*; having marks resembling stars. [from L. *stellula*, a little star.]
Stem, stem, n. *That which props or causes to stand*; the principal body of a tree or plant of any kind; the main stock; that which supports the flower; the leaf-stem; the stock of a family; progeny; a circular piece of timber, to which the two sides of a ship are united at the fore-end; anything resembling the stem of a plant.—*vt*. To *cause to stand*; to oppose or resist, as a current; to make progress against, as a current; to check, as a stream or moving force. ppr. stemming, pret. & pp. stemmed. [Sax. *stemn*; Gr. histēmi, to stand.]
Stench, stensh, n. *Smell*; offensive odour. [Sax. *stenc—stencan*, to smell.]
Stenography, sten-og'ra-fi, n. *The art of writing in short-hand* by using abbreviations or characters. [Gr. *stenos*, narrow, and *graphē*, writing.]
Stentor, sten'tor, n. *A herald in Homer having a voice like thunder*; any person having a powerful voice. [Gr.]
Stentorian, sten-tō'ri-an, a. Extremely loud; able to utter a very loud sound. [from *Stentor*.]
Step, step, n. *An advance or movement made by one removal of the foot*; a pace; one remove in ascending or descending a stair; the round of a ladder; the space passed by the foot in walking or running; a small space; gradation; act of advancing; footstep; print or impression of the foot; gait; manner of walking; measure; action; (pl.) walk; passage. [Sax. *stæp*—Gr. *steibō*, to tread on.]—*vi*. *To move the foot*; to go; to walk a little distance; to walk gravely, slowly, or resolutely; to move mentally.—*vt*. To set, as the foot. ppr. stepping, pret. & pp. stepped. [Sax. *steppan*.]
Step, step, is prefixed to certain words to express a relation by marriage. [Sax. *steop*, from *stepan*, to cut off.]
Step-brother, step'bruth-ėr, n. *An orphan* brother; a brother by marriage.
Step-child, step'child, n. A child deprived of its parent, but who has found another in the person married to its surviving parent.
Step-daughter, step'da-tėr, n. *An orphan daughter*; a daughter by marriage.
Step-father, step'fä-Ther, n. A father-in-law; the father of an *orphan*.
Step-mother, step'muth-ėr, n. A mother-in-law; the mother of an *orphan*, or of one who has lost its natural mother.
Stepping, step'ing, p.n. The act of walking or running by steps.
Stepping-stone, step'ing-stōn, n. A *stone* to raise the *feet* above the dirt; a means of progress.
Step-sister, step'sis-tėr, n. An orphan *sister*; a sister by marriage only.
Step-son, step'sun, n. *An orphan son*; a son by marriage only; a son-in-law.
Stereographic, ste'rē-ō-graf''ik, a. *Relating to stereography*.
Stereographically, ste'rē-ō-graf''ik-al-li, adv. By delineation on a plane.
Stereography, ste-rē-og'ra-fi, n. The act or art of *delineating the forms of solid bodies* on a plane. [Fr. *stéréographie*; Gr. *stereos*, solid, and *graphō*, to write.]
Stereoscope, ste'rē-ō-skōp, n. An optical instrument which enables us to *see* two similar pictures, placed near each other, as if combined into one, so that the combined image thus seen appears to be a *solid* body. [Gr. *stereos*, solid, and *skopeō*, to look at.]
Stereoscopic, ste'rē-ō-skop''ik, a. *Pertaining to the stereoscope*.
Stereotype, ste'rē-ō-tīp, n. A *fixed* metal *type*; a plate of solid metallic types for printing books; the art of making plates of fixed metallic types.—*a. Pertaining to fixed metallic types*; done on fixed metallic types.—*vt*. To print by the use of *fixed metallic types*; to make as *fixed metallic types*; to compose as a book in fixed types. ppr. stereotyping, pret. & pp. stereotyped. [Gr. *stereos*, solid, and *tupos*, a blow—*tuptō*, Sans. *tup*, to strike.]
Stereotyped, ste'rē-ō-tīpt, p.a. *Formed on fixed* metallic *types*; formed in a *fixed*, unchangeable manner.
Sterile, ste'ril, a. *Stiff*; barren; unfruitful; producing no young; barren of ideas; destitute of sentiment. [Fr. *stérile*; Gr. *stereos*, stiff, barren.]
Sterility, ste-ril'i-ti, n. *Quality or state of being sterile*; barrenness; destitution of ideas; want of the power of producing sentiment. [Fr. *stérilité*.]
Sterling, stėr'ling, a. An epithet by which British money of account is distinguished; genuine; pure. [from *Easterling*, the popular name of German traders in England, whose money was of the purest quality.]
Stern, stėrn, a. *Fixed* with an aspect of severity; immovable; noting severity of manner; harsh; rigid; hard; afflictive. [Sax. *styrne*; Old G. *star*, fixed.]
Stern, stėrn, n. *The steering place* of a ship; the hind part of a ship or of a boat; post of management. [Sax. *styran*, to steer, and *aern*, a place.]
Sternage, stėrn'āj, n. Steerage or stern.
Sternly, stėrn'li, adv. *In a stern manner*; with an air of authority.
Sternmost, stėrn'mōst, a. Furthest astern; furthest in the rear.
Sternness, stėrn'nes, n. *Quality of being stern*; severity; harshness.
Sternutatory, stėr-nūt'a-tō-ri, a. *Having the quality of exciting to sneeze*.—n. *A substance that provokes sneezing*. [Fr. *sternutatoire*; L. *sternuto*, to sneeze.]
Sterve, Stervent, stėrv, stėrv'en, vi. To starve.
Stethoscope, ste'thos-kōp, n. An instrument for *ascertaining the state of the chest*, the lungs, &c., by means of sound. [Gr. *stēthos*, the breast, and *skopeō*, to look at, to examine.]
Stethoscopic, ste-thos-kop'ik, a. *Pertaining to a stethoscope*.
Stew, stū, vt. *To seethe or gently boil*; to boil slowly or with a simmering heat. vi. *To be seethed* in a slow, gentle manner, or in heat and moisture.—n. A hot place; meat stewed; a brothel. [Old Fr. *estuver*.]
Steward, stū'ard, n. *The keeper of the place* or mansion; one who manages the domestic concerns of great families, collects rents, &c.; an officer of state; an officer who provides food for the students in colleges; an officer in ships who has the management of the table, and the charge of provisions. [Sax. *stiward—stow*, a place, and *weard*, a keeper.]
Stewardess, stū'ard-es, n. A female who waits on ladies in steamboats, &c.
Stewardship, stū'ard-ship, n. *The office of a steward*.
Stewed, stūd, p.a. Seethed in a slow moist heat.
Stewing, stū'ing, p.n. Act of seething slowly.
Stick, stik, n. *A piece of wood, long, slender, and pointed*, originally used as a goad; the small branch of a tree cut off; a rod, also a staff; any stem of a tree, of any size, cut for fuel or timber; a stab.—*vt*. *To pierce with a pointed instrument*; to cause to enter, as a pointed instrument; to kill by piercing; to thrust in; to fasten; to attach by causing to adhere to the surface; to set with something pointed; to fix on a pointed instrument.—*vi*. *To remain fixed*; to hold to by cleaving to the surface; to cling fast to; to abide; to be impeded by adhesion; to hesitate; to resist efforts to remove; to scruple; to be hindered from proceeding; to adhere closely in friendship and affection. ppr. sticking, pret. & pp. stuck. [Sax. *sticca*; Old G. *stechan*, to pierce.]
Stickiness, stik'i-nes, n. *State or quality of being sticky*; adhesiveness.
Stickle, stik'l, vi. *To take part with one side or other*; to contend obstinately; to altercate; to pass from one side to the other. ppr. stickling, pret. & pp. stickled. [from the practice of prize-fighters, who placed seconds with *sticks* to interpose occasionally.]
Stickler, stik'l-ėr, n. A *sidesman* to *fencers*; an obstinate contender about anything; an umpire.
Sticky, stik'i, a. *Having the quality of sticking*; viscous; glutinous; tenacious.
Stiff, stif, a. Not easily bent; rigid; inflexible; not fluid; impetuous in motion, as a breeze; not easily subdued; pertinacious; firm in resistance; not natural and easy; formal in manner; affected; strongly maintained. [Sax. *stif—stofn*, the trunk of a tree.]
Stiffen, stif'n, vt. *To make stiff*; to make more thick or viscous; to make torpid. vi. *To become stiff*; to become more rigid; to become thicker; to approach to hardness; to become less yielding; to grow more obstinate. [Sax. *stifian*.]
Stiffened, stif'nd, p.a. *Made stiff* or less pliant.
Stiffener, stif'n-ėr, n. *That which makes a substance more stiff* or less pliable.
Stiffening, stif'n-ing, p.n. Something that is used to make a substance more *stiff* or less soft.
Stiffly, stif'li, adv. Firmly; strongly; rigidly; with stubbornness.
Stiff-necked, stif'nekt, a. Stubborn; inflexibly obstinate.
Stiffness, stif'nes, n. *State or quality of being stiff*; rigidity; the firm texture of a substance which renders it difficult to bend; a state between softness and hardness; tension; stubbornness; formality of manner; harshness; constrained manner of expression; want of natural simplicity and ease.
Stifle, stī'fl, vt. *To suffocate*; to choke; to oppress; to stop the breath of temporarily; to deaden; to quench; to suppress; to hinder from transpiring or spreading; to check or restrain; to repress; to conceal; to withhold from escaping; to destroy; to smother.—*vi*. To die by suffocation. ppr. *stifling*, pret. & pp. stifled. [Old Fr. *estouffer*; Gr. *tuphō*, to raise a smoke.]
Stifled, stī'fld, p.a. *Suffocated*; suppressed.

Fāte, fär, fat, fall; mē, met, hėr; pīne, pin; mōte, not, mōve; tūbe, tub, bull; oil, pound.

Stigma, stig'ma, n. *The prick of a pointed instrument;* a mark made with a burning iron; any mark of infamy; any reproachful conduct which darkens the lustre of reputation; the top of the pistil in flowers. [Gr. *—stizō,* to prick.]
Stigmatic, Stigmatical, stig-mat'ik, stig-mat'ik-al, a. Branded.—n. (Stigmatic), one on whom nature has set a mark of deformity.
Stigmatize, stig'mat-īz, vt. *To set a mark* of disgrace on; to disgrace with some note of reproach or infamy. *ppr.* stigmatizing, *pret. & pp.* stigmatized. [Fr. *stigmatiser.*]
Stile, stīl, n. The pin of a dial. [See Style.]
Stile, stīl, n. A step or a set of steps *for ascending* and descending, in passing a fence or wall. [Sax. *stigel;* Goth. *steigan,* to ascend.]
Stiletto, sti-let'tō, n. *A small* round, *pointed* dagger; a pointed instrument for making eyelet-holes in working muslin, lace, &c. [It.; L. *stilus,* a pointed instrument.]
Still, stil, vt. *To cause to stand;* to make quiet; to calm; to lull; to put a stop to, as noise; to put a stop to, as tumult; to appease; to check.—a. *Caused to stand;* motionless; noiseless; silent; not disturbed by noise; serene; without agitation. [Sax. *stillan,* Old G. *stilljan,* to stop.]
Still, stil, adv. To this time; till now; nevertheless; ever; continually; after what is stated; in continuation. [probably allied to *till.*]
Still, stil, vt. To expel, as spirit from liquor by heat, and condense it in a refrigeratory.—n. A copper used in the *distillation* of liquors; apparatus for distilling; sometimes a distillery. [L. *stillo,* to cause to drop.]
Still-born, stil'born, a. *Dead* at the *birth;* abortive.
Stilling, stil'ing, p.n. Act of *stilling* or of calming, silencing, or quieting.
Still-life, stil'lif, n. In painting, a picture of dead game, vegetables, and other things destitute of life.
Stillness, stil'nes, n. *State of being still;* freedom from noise or motion; quiet; freedom from agitation; taciturnity.
Stilly, stil'i, a. *Still;* quiet; calm.—adv. Silently; without noise.
Stilt, stilt, n. A prop or support for the foot; a long pole of wood, often with a shoulder, to raise the foot above the ground in walking.—vt. *To raise on stilts;* to raise by unnatural means. [D. *stelt;* Sax. *stylan,* to mount.]
Stimulant, stim'ū-lant, a. *That pricks or goads;* that rouses up, producing a transient increase of vital energy and strength of action in the heart and arteries.—n. A medicine which produces a quickly diffused and transient increase of vital energy. [Fr.]
Stimulate, stim'ū-lāt, vt. *To prick;* to rouse; to produce an exaltation of vital activity in; to excite to action by some pungent motive. *ppr.* stimulating, *pret. & pp.* stimulated. [L. *stimulo, stimulatum—stimulus,* a goad.]
Stimulating, stim'ū-lāt-ing p.a. Exciting to more vigorous exertion.
Stimulation, stim-ū-lā'shon, n. *Act of stimulating;* state of being stimulated. [L. *stimulatio.*]
Stimulus, stim'ū-lus, n. Primarily, a *goad;* hence, something that rouses the mind or spirits; that which produces an increase of vital action. [L.; Gr. *stizō,* to prick.]

Sting, sting, vt. *To pierce with the sharp-pointed instrument* with which certain animals are furnished, such as bees, and the like; to pain acutely. *ppr.* stinging, *pret. & pp.* stung.—n. *A sharp-pointed weapon,* with which certain animals are armed by nature for their defence; the thrust of a sting into the flesh; anything that gives acute pain; the point in the last verse, or of an epigram; that which constitutes the principal terror. [Sax. *stingan;* Gr. *stizō,* to prick.]
Stingily, stin'ji-li, adv. In a niggardly manner.
Stinginess, stin'ji-nes, n. *Quality of being stingy;* extreme avarice; mean covetousness; niggardliness.
Stingy, stin'ji, a. *Strait* or close-fisted; meanly avaricious; niggardly; narrow-hearted. [W. *ystangu,* to straiten.]
Stink, stingk, vi. Primarily, to *give forth an odour* good or bad; to emit a strong offensive smell, commonly a smell of putrefaction. *ppr.* stinking, *pret.* stank or stunk, *pp.* stunk.—n. A strong offensive smell. [Sax. *stincan,* to give a smell.]
Stinking, stingk'ing, p.a. Emitting a strong offensive *smell.*
Stink-pot, stingk' pot, n. An earthen jar, charged with materials of an offensive and suffocating smell, sometimes used in boarding an enemy's vessel.
Stint, stint, vt. Primarily, *to blunt;* to shorten; to restrain within certain limits; to limit; to stop.—vi. To stop. n. Limit; quantity assigned; stop. [a different form of *stunt*—which see.]
Stinted, stint'ed, p.a. Restrained to a certain limit or quantity.
Stipend, sti'pend, n. Primarily, *the pay of soldiers!;* settled pay for services; allowance; salary; wages. [L. *stipendium—stips,* a small piece of money, and *pendo,* to weigh.]
Stipendiary, sti-pend'i-a-ri, a. *Receiving stipend;* performing services for a stated compensation.—n. One who performs services for a *stipend* or settled compensation, either by the day, month, or year. [Fr. *stipendiaire,* from L. *stipendium,* pay, stipend.]
Stipulate, stip'ū-lāt, vi. To make a covenant with any person or company to do or forbear anything; to bargain; to engage. *ppr.* stipulating, *pret. & pp.* stipulated. [L. *stipulor, stipulatus—stips,* a gift in small coin.]
Stipulated, stip'ū-lāt-ed, p. a. Covenanted.
Stipulation, stip-ū-lā'shon, n. *Act of stipulating;* an agreement or covenant made by one person with another for the performance or forbearance of some act; a contract. [Fr.]
Stipulator, stip'ū-lāt-or, n. *One who stipulates* or covenants.
Stir, stėr, vt. *To move;* to stimulate; to provoke; to disturb; to instigate; to place in any manner.—vi. *To move one's self;* to become the object of notice; to rise in the morning. *ppr.* stirring, *pret. & pp.* stirred.—n. Bustle; public disturbance; agitation of thoughts; conflicting passions. [Sax. *styran,* Old G. *storjan,* to move, trouble.]
Stirrer, stėr'ėr, n. *One who stirs;* an inciter; an ins.igator.
Stirring, stėr'ing, p. a. *Moving;* arousing; active; active in business.—p.n. *Act of moving* or putting in motion.
Stirrup, sti'rup, n. An iron hoop suspended from the saddle *by a strap,* in which the horseman sets his foot when

he *mounts* or *rides.* [Sax. *sti-rap—stigan,* to go, and *rap,* a rope.]
Stitch, stich, vt. *To pierce* with a needle, as cloth; to sew with a back puncture of the needle, so as to double the thread; to sew or unite together.—vi. *To practise stitching.*—n. *A single thrust* or pass of a needle in sewing; a single turn of the thread round a needle in knitting; a link of yarn; an acute pain, like the piercing of a needle. [Sax. *stician,* to pierce; Goth. *stiks,* a point.]
Stitching, stich'ing, p.n. *Act of stitching;* work done by sewing in a particular manner.
Stithy, stiᴛн'i, n. *An anvil;* a smith's shop.—vt. To forge on an *anvil.* [Icel. *stedi,* an anvil—*sted,* to make firm.]
Stoat, stōt, n. A small *stinking* animal; the ermine, the latter being the stoat in its winter dress. [probably from Armor. *staut,* urine.]
Stoccado, stok-kā'dō, n. A thrust with a rapier. [Fr. *estocade.*]
Stock, stok, n. *That which is set or fixed,* as a *trunk;* the stem or main body of a tree; the strong, firm part; the stem in which a graft is inserted; a very stupid person; the part of a tool for boring wood with a crank, whose end rests against the breast of the workman; the wood in which the barrel of a musket is fixed; the original progenitor; line of a family; lineage; family; a fixed fund; capital; the money or goods employed in trade, banking, &c.; supply provided; the domestic animals belonging to the owner of a farm; also, other property on a farm; a band for the neck; a thrust with a rapier; a stocking; (pl.) a machine consisting of two pieces of timber, in which the legs of criminals were fixed by way of punishment; the frame on which a ship rests while building; the public funds of the nation.—vt. To store; to fill sufficiently; to lay up in store; to supply with domestic animals; to supply with seed; to put in the stocks. [Sax. *stoc,* a trunk; Old G. *stecchan,* to fix.]
Stockade, stok-ād', n. *A thrust!;* a fence made with *stakes* planted in the earth; a slight fortification.—vt. To surround with sharpened *stakes* fixed in the ground. *ppr.* stockading, *pret. & pp.* stockaded. [Fr. *estocade.*]
Stock-broker, stok'brō-kėr, n. *A broker* who deals in *stocks* or shares in the public funds.
Stock-dove, stok'duv, n. The wood-pigeon of Europe, formerly supposed to be the original *stock* of the common pigeon, but now recognized as a separate species.
Stock-fish, stok'fish, n. Cod dried in the sun without being salted.
Stockholder, stok'hōld-ėr, n. A proprietor of *stock* in the public funds, or in the funds of a bank or other company.
Stocking, stok'ing, n. A *knitted* covering for the foot and leg. [probably akin to G. *stricken,* to knit.]
Stock-jobber, stok'job-ėr, n. One who speculates in the public *stocks* for gain; one whose occupation is to buy and sell stocks.
Stock-still, stok'stil, a. *Still as a fixed post;* perfectly still.
Stoic, stō'ik, n. One of a sect of philosophers, called *Stoics,* because their founder Zeno taught under a *porch* or portico at Athens; a person not easily excited. [Gr. *stoikos—stoa,* a porch—*stegō,* to cover.]
Stoic, Stoical, stō'ik, stō'ik-al, a. Per

taining to the Stoics; not affected by passion; manifesting indifference to pleasure or pain.

Stoically, stō'ik-al-li, *adv. In the manner of the Stoics*; with indifference to pleasure or pain.

Stoicism, stō'i-sizm, *n. The opinions and maxims of the Stoics*; a real or pretended indifference to pleasure or pain; insensibility. [Fr. *stoïcisme*.]

Stoker, stōk'ėr, *n*. One who looks after the fire in a brew-house or steam-engine, &c.

Stole, stōl, *n*. A long and narrow scarf, with fringed extremities, worn by a Roman Catholic priest around the neck, and crossed over the breast in front; originally, the robe appropriated to deacons, marking their *standing* or position in the church. [L. *stola*—Gr. *stellō*, to array.]

Stolid, stol'id, *a*. Stupid; foolish. [L. *stolidus*.]

Stolidity, stō-lid'i-ti, *n*. Dulness of intellect; stupidity. [L. *stoliditas*.]

Stomach, stum'ak, *n*. The *receiver* of the food prepared by the *mouth*; a membranous receptacle, the principal organ of digestion; appetite; liking; pride; anger.—*vt. To be vexed at*; to remember with anger. [L. *stomachus*.]

Stomacher, stum'a-chėr, *n*. An ornament or support to the *breast* worn by females.

Stomachic, stō-mak'ik, *a. Pertaining to the stomach*; strengthening the stomach; exciting the action of the stomach. *n*. A medicine that strengthens the stomach. [Fr. *stomachique*.]

Stomaching, stum'ak-ing, *p.n*.† Resentment.

Stone, stōn, *n. Something set*, hard, and durable; a hard mass of concreted earthy or mineral matter; a gem; anything made of stone; a calculous concretion in the kidneys or bladder; a testicle; the nut of a stone-fruit; the weight of fourteen pounds; a state of torpidness; a mirror; a monument erected to preserve the memory of the dead.—*a. Made of stone*, or *like stone. vt*. To pelt or kill *with stones*; to make like stone; to free from stones; to wall or face with stones; to line or fortify with stones. *ppr.* stoning, *pret. & pp.* stoned. [Nax. *stan*; L. *sto*, to stand.]

Stone-blind, stōn'blind, *a. Blind as a stone*; perfectly blind.

Stone-bow, stōn'bō, *n*. A crossbow for shooting stones.

Stone-chat, Stone-chatter, stōn'chat, stōn'chat-ėr, *n*. A small bird whose note often resembles the knocking together of two *stones*.

Stone-cutter, stōn'kut-ėr, *n*. One whose occupation is to *cut* or hew *stones*.

Stone-fruit, stōn'frūt, *n*. *Fruit* whose seeds are covered with a *hard* shell enveloped in the pulp, as cherries, plums, &c.

Stone's-cast, Stone's-throw, stōnz'kast, stōnz'thrō, *n*. The distance which *a stone may be thrown by the hand*.

Stone-work, stōn'wėrk, *n*. *Work consisting of stone*; mason's work of stone.

Stony, stōn'i, *a. Made of stone*; full of stones; hard; pitiless; obdurate; morally hard. [G. *steinig*.]

Stony-hearted, stōn'i-härt-ed, *a. Hard-hearted*; cruel; pitiless; unfeeling.

Stool, stöl, *n. That which is set*; a seat; a seat without a back, so distinguished from a chair; the seat used in evacuating the contents of the bowels; an evacuation. [Sax. *stōl*; Old G. *staljan*, to cause to stand.]

Stoop, stöp, *vi. To bend the body forward and downward*; to incline forward in standing or walking; to bow by compulsion; to yield; to descend from rank; to condescend; to acknowledge inferiority; to come down on prey, as a hawk; to alight from the wing; to sink to a lower place; to fall. *vt*. To cause to incline downward; to sink.—*n*. Act of *bending* the body forward and downward; condescension; fall or descent of a bird on his prey; swoop. [Sax. *stupian*.]

Stooping, stöp'ing, *p.a*. Bending forward; inclining.

Stoop†, stöp, *n*. A vessel of liquor; a flagon. [Sax. *stoppa*, a cup.]

Stop, stop, *vt. To stuff up*; *to block close*; to close, as an aperture, by filling; to arrest the progress of; to hinder; to check; to put an end to; to regulate, as the sounds of musical strings.—*vi*. To come to a stand; to cease from any motion or course of action. *ppr*. stopping, *pret. & pp*. stopped.—*n. Act of stopping*; interruption; that which obstructs; obstacle; the instrument by which the sounds of wind-music are regulated; regulation of musical chords by the fingers; a mark in writing, intended to distinguish the sentences or clauses. [D. *stoppen*—Gr. *stupos*, a stem, block.]

Stop-cock, stop'kok, *n*. A turning *cock*, used to *stop* or to regulate the supply of water, gas, &c., through pipes.

Stoppage, stop'āj, *n. Act of stopping*; the state of being stopped; that which stops; obstruction; the stopping of a railway train at a station; a deduction made from pay. [Low L. *stupacium*.]

Stopper, stop'ėr, *n. One who stops*; that which stops; that which closes or fills a vent or hole in a vessel; a stopple, as of a bottle.—*vt*. To close or secure with a *stopper*.

Stopple, stop'l, *n. That which stops* the mouth of a bottle; a cork.—*vt. To stop*; to close with a stopple. *ppr*. stoppling, *pret. & pp*. stoppled.

Storage, stōr'āj, *n*. Act of depositing in a *store*; the safe keeping of goods in a warehouse; the price charged for keeping goods in a store.

Storax, stō'raks, *n*. An aromatic resinous substance; the tree from which it is obtained. [L. *styrax*.]

Store, stōr, *n. Something laid up*; a stock provided; ample abundance; quantity accumulated; a store-house; a warehouse; (pl.) necessary articles laid up for use, as for the army or navy; supplies of different articles, provided for the use of the crew and passengers of a vessel.—*a. Pertaining to a store*; hoarded; laid up.—*vt. To lay up*; to supply; to stock against a future time; to hoard; to reposit in a warehouse for preservation. *ppr*. storing, *pret. & pp*. stored. [Sax. *stor*; Heb. *atsar*, to lay up.]

Store-house, stōr'hous, *n*. A building for keeping grain or goods of any kind; a warehouse; a repository.

Storied, stō'rid, *p.a*. Adorned with historical paintings; celebrated in story.

Stork, stork, *n*. A large bird of the heron kind, famed for its great *affection* towards its young. [Sax. *storc*—Gr. *stergō*, to love.]

Storm, storm, *n. A tempest*; the violent action of one or more of the elements; a violent assault on a fortified place; violent political commotion; insurrection; disturbance of the peace; calamity; adversity.—*vt*. To assault with violence or by open force; to attempt to take by scaling the walls, forcing gates or breaches, and the like.—*vi. To raise a tempest*; to blow with violence; as, it storms; to be in violent agitation; to rage; to be in violent agitation of passion; to fume. [Sax.—Old G. *sturmjan*, to shake, to rage.]

Storminess, storm'i-nes, *n. State of being stormy*; tempestuousness.

Stormy, storm'i, *a. Abounding with storms*; agitated with furious winds; proceeding from violent agitation or fury. [Sax. *stormig*.]

Story, stō'ri, *n. A spreading out of things known*; a verbal recital of a series of facts; a written narrative of a series of events; history; a petty tale; relation of a single incident; a trifling tale; a fable.—*vt*.† To describe in story. [Gr. *historia*—*isēmi*, to know.]

Story, stō'ri, *n*. A *stage* or floor of a building; such a height as is ascended by one flight of *stairs*; a set of rooms on the same floor. [from stair or *stage*.]

Stout, stout, *a. Unyielding*; bold; intrepid; valiant; proud; resolute; large; lusty; corpulent. [D. bold; Old G. *stols*, proud; Sax. *stith*, stern.]

Stout-hearted, stout'härt-ed, *a. Having a stout heart*.

Stoutly, stout'li, *adv*. Lustily; boldly.

Stoutness, stout'nes, *n. State of being stout*, bold, or obstinate; strength; force; fortitude; stubbornness.

Stove, stōv, *n. A hot or heated place*; an iron box or fire-place, in which fire is made to warm an apartment; an iron box, with various apartments in it for cooking.—*vt*. To heat, as in a stove. [Sax. *stufa*; Icel. *stó*, a fire-place.]

Stover†, stō'vėr, *n*. Fodder.

Stow, stō, *vt. To place*; to put in a suitable place or position; to lay up; to reposit. [Sax. *stow*, a place.]

Stowage, stō'āj, *n. Act of stowing*; the suitable disposition of several things together; room for the reception of things to be reposited.

Strachy†, strā'ki, *n*. A commander.

Straddle, strad'l, *vi*. To stand or walk with the legs far apart.—*vt*. To place one leg on one side and the other on the other side of. *ppr*. straddling, *pret. & pp*. straddled. [frequent. of *stride*.]

Straggle, strag'l, *vi. To spread*; to be apart from any main body; to wander from the direct course or way; to rove; to ramble. *ppr*. straggling, *pret. & pp*. straggled. [frequent. from *stray*.]

Straggler, strag'l-ėr, *n. One who straggles*; a rover; something that stands by itself.

Straggling, strag'l-ing, *p.a*. Roving; rambling.

Straight, strāt, *a. Stretched*; tense; right; upright; not deviating from truth or fairness; narrow; close.—*a. Straight part*; straight direction.—*ads*. Directly; in the shortest time. [Sax. *gestrecht*—*streccan*, to stretch.]

Straighten, strāt'n, *vt. To make straight*; to make narrow, tense, or close; to reduce to difficulties.

Straightened, strāt'nd, *p.a*. Made narrow.

Straightforward, strāt'for-wėrd, *a. Proceeding in a straight course*.

Straightforward, Straightforwards, strāt'for-wėrd, strāt'for-wėrds, *ads. Directly forward*.

Straightly, strāt'li, *adv*. *In a right line*; not crookedly; tightly; closely.

Straightness, strāt'nes, *n. Quality or state of being straight*; tightness.

Straight-pight†, strāt'pīt, a. Straight in form; erect.
Straightway, strāt'wā, adv. Directly; immediately.
Strain, strān, vt. To stretch; to draw with force; to cause to draw with force; to injure by pressing with too much effort; to stretch violently; to put to the utmost strength; to cause to pass through some porous substance; to filter; to cause to bind closer; to force; to press in an embrace.—vi. To make violent efforts; to be filtered.—n. A stretch; a violent effort; a stretching of the muscles; an injury by excessive exertion; continued manner of speaking or writing; stretch of voice; song; a particular part of a tune; turn; manner of speech or action; race†; descent†. [Old Fr. estreindre—L. stringo, to draw tight.]
Strained, strānd, p.a. Stretched; violently exerted.
Strainer, strān'ėr, n. That which strains; an instrument for filtration.
Straining, strān'ing, n. Act of stretching; the act of filtering; filtration.
Strait, strāt, a. Drawn together; narrow; rigorous.—n. A narrow pass or passage, either in a mountain or in the ocean, between continents or other portions of land; (pl.) distress; distressing necessity.—vt. To put to difficulties. [from L. strictus — stringo, to draw tight.]
Straiten, strāt'n, vt. To make strait; to perplex; to press with poverty; to press by want of sufficient room.
Straitened, strāt'nd, p.a. Contracted; perplexed.
Strait-laced, strāt'lāst, a. Laced tightly; stiff; rigid in opinion; strict.
Straitly, strāt'li, adv. Strictly; rigorously.
Straitness, strāt'nes, n. State of being strait; narrowness; pressure from necessity of any kind; want.
Strand, strand, n. The margin or edge; the shore or beach of the sea or ocean, or of a large lake; [probably corrupted from Sax. streng, a string] one of the parts of which a rope is composed.—vt. To drive or run aground, on a shore or strand, as a ship; to break, as one of the strands of a rope.—vi. To be driven on shore; to run aground. [Sax.; Dan. rand, edge.]
Stranded, strand'ed, p.a. Run ashore.
Strange, strānj, a. External; foreign; new; wonderful; exciting curiosity; odd; unusual; uttered by way of exclamation, elliptically, for it is strange.—st.† To alienate. [Old Fr. estrange —L. extraneus—extra, beyond—exter, exterus, on the outside.]
Strangely, strānj'li, adv. In a strange manner; wonderfully.
Strangeness, strānj'nes, n. State of being strange; reserve; coldness; uncouthness; mutual dislike; the power of exciting surprise and wonder; uncommonness that raises wonder by novelty.
Stranger, strān'jėr, n. A foreigner; one who belongs to another country; one unknown; a visitor; one not admitted to any communication or fellowship. vt. To alienate. [Old Fr. estranger.]
Strangle, strang'gl, vt. To squeeze or compress, as the throat of; to stifle; to destroy the life of by stopping respiration; to suppress. ppr. strangling, pret. & pp. strangled. [Old Fr. estrangler—L. stringo, to draw tight.]
Strangler, strang'gl-ėr, n. One who strangles.
Strangling, strang'gl-ing, p.n. Act of

destroying life by stopping respiration.
Strangulated, strang'gū-lāt-ed, p.a. Having the circulation stopped in any part by compression.
Strangulation, strang-gū-lā'shon, n. Act of strangling; suffocation; that kind of suffocation which is common to women in hysterics. [Fr.]
Strangury, strang'gū-ri, n. A disease in which there is pain in passing the urine, which is excreted by drops. [L. stranguria—stranx, a drop, and ouron, urine.]
Strap, strap, n. A strip or stripe; a long narrow slip of cloth or leather; a thong; a strop; an iron plate for connecting two or more timbers, into which it is screwed by bolts.—vt. To chastise with a strap; to bind with a strap; to rub on a strap for sharpening, as a razor. ppr. strapping, pret. & pp. strapped. [Sax. stropp; Gr. strephō, to twist.]
Strappado†, strap-pā'dō, n. A military punishment formerly practised.
Stratagem, stra'ta-jem, n. Act of a general; a piece of good generalship; a scheme for deceiving an enemy; any artifice; trick; fraud; imposition; snare. [Fr. stratagème; Gr. stratos, an army, and agō, to lead.]
Strategic, stra-tē'jik, a. Effected by artifice.
Strategy, strat'ē-ji, n. The science of military command; generalship. [Gr. stratos, an army, and agō, to lead.]
Stratification, stra'ti-fi-kā'shon, n. The process of stratifying; state of being stratified. [Fr.]
Stratified, strat'i-fīd, p.a. Arranged in strata or layers.
Stratify, strat'i-fi, vt. To form into a stratum or strata; to lay in strata. ppr. stratifying, pret. & pp. stratified. [Fr. stratifier; L. stratum, and facio, to make.]
Stratum, strā'tum, n. Strata, pl. That which is spread out; a layer; any species of earth, sand, coal, rock, and the like, arranged in a flat form, distinct from the adjacent matter; a bed or layer artificially made. [L. sterno, stratus, to spread out.]
Straw, strą, n. That which serves for spreading; litter; the stalk or stem of certain species of grain, such as wheat, oats, &c.; a mass of the stalks of certain species of grain when cut, and after being thrashed; anything proverbially worthless.—vt. To spread or scatter. [Sax. streow; Goth. strawjan, to spread out.]
Strawberry, stra̦'be-ri, n. A plant, probably so named from the spreading nature of its runners; the fruit of the plant. [Sax. strawberie.]
Strawy, strą'i, a. Made of straw; light.
Stray, strā, vi. To separate; to turn or go out of the way; to rove; to wander from the path of duty; to rove or go at large.—vt. To mislead.—n. Any domestic animal that has left an inclosure and wanders at large, or is lost; act of wandering. [Sax. straegan.]
Straying, strā'ing, p.n. The act of going astray; act of roving.
Streak, strēk, n. A line of a different colour from the ground; a stripe.—vt. To form streaks in; to stripe; to variegate with lines of different colours. [Sax. strica; Old G. strich, a line.]
Streaked, strēkt, p.a. Variegated with stripes of a different colour.
Streaky, strēk'i, a. Having streaks; striped.
Stream, strēm, n. A current of water or

other fluid; a river, brook, or rivulet; a current of water in the ocean; a current of melted metal; a current of air or gas or of light; a continued current; drift, as of opinions or manners; water. vi. To flow; to issue with continuance, not by fits; to extend; to stretch in a long line.—vt. To pour; to send forth [Sax.; Icel. streyma, to flow.]
Streamer, strēm'ėr, n. A pennon flowing in the wind; a luminous column, one of the forms of the aurora borealis.
Streaming, strēm'ing, p.a. Pouring out in abundance; flowing or floating loosely, as a flag.
Streamlet, strēm'let, n. A small stream.
Steamy, strēm'i, a. Abounding with streams; flowing with a current.
Street, strēt, n. A way or road smoothed; any road in a city, chiefly a main way, in distinction from a lane or alley. [Sax. street—L. sterno, stratum, to smooth.]
Strength, strength, n. Quality or state of being strong; active power or force; vigour or natural force; energy; solidity or toughness; power or vigour of any kind; power of resisting attacks; fastness; that which supplies strength; security; power of mind; the power of any faculty; spirit; force of writing; nervous diction; the quality of any liquor which has the power of affecting the taste; the virtue of any vegetable; legal or moral force; validity; amount of force, military or naval; a strong place; soundness or force; the quality that convinces or commands assent; vehemence; force proceeding from motion; degree of vividness. [Sax. —Old G. strangi, strong.]
Strengthen, strength'en, vt. To make strong or stronger; to add strength to, either physical, legal, or moral; to encourage; to cause to increase in security.—vi. To grow strong or stronger.
Strengthening, strength'en-ing, p.a, Confirming; animating.
Strenuous, stren'ū-us, a. Putting forth strength; energetic; zealous; valiant, intrepid, and ardent; vehement. [L. strenuus; Gr. strēnēs, strong.]
Strenuously, stren'ū-us-li, adv. In a strenuous manner.
Stress, stres, n. Strain; pressure; violence; importance; force or violence, as of weather; the force which is exerted in any part of a machine, tending to break it in that part. [from distress.]
Stretch, strech, vt. To draw out tight; to draw out to greater length; to extend in breadth; to spread; to display; to make tense; to extend mentally; to exaggerate; to extend too far.—vi. To be extended; to be drawn out in length or in breadth, or both; to spread; to be exaggerated; to sail; to direct a course; to make violent efforts in running. n. Extension in length or in breadth; reach; effort; force of body; utmost extent of meaning; utmost reach of power; course. [Sax. streccan — L. stringo, to draw tight.]
Stretched, strecht, p.a. Extended; exerted to the utmost.
Stretcher, strech'ėr, n. He or that which stretches; a board for removing drunken or disabled persons.
Strew, strų, vt. To spread out; to spread by scattering; to scatter loosely. [Sax. streowian; L. sterno, to spread out.]
Strewing, strų'ing, p.n. Act of scattering.
Stricken, strik'n, obs. pp. of strike. Smitten; advanced; far gone.
Strict, strikt, a. Drawn tight; tense;

ch, chain; j, job; g, go; ng, sing; ᴛʜ, then; th, thin; w, wig; wh, whig; zh, azure; † obsolete.

exact; rigorously nice; severe; observing exact rules; confined; limited. [L. *stringo, strictus,* to draw tight.]
Strictly, strikt′li, *adv. In a strict manner.*
Strictness, strikt′nes, *n. Quality of being strict;* exactness in the observance of rules, laws, rites, and the like; nice regularity or precision; severity.
Stricture, strik′tūr, *n. A drawing together;* a spasmodic contraction of any passage of the body; a touch of criticism; critical remark; censure; strictness. [Fr.—L. *stringo,* to draw tight.]
Stride, strīd, *vi.* To walk by *extending the feet wide apart;* to walk with long steps; to straddle; to stand with the legs far from each other.—*vt.*† To pass over at a step. *ppr.* striding, *pret.* strode, *pp.* stridden.—*n.* A long step. [Sax. *stredan,* to spread; Old G. *stritan,* to extend.]
Strife, strīf, *n. Act of striving;* contest of emulation, either by intellectual or physical efforts; quarrel or war; opposition; contrast. [Old Fr. *estrif.*]
Strike, strīk, *vt. To act upon by a blow;* to hit with some force, either with the hand or an instrument; to dash; to stamp; to coin; to thrust in; to cause to enter; to punish; to cause to sound; to notify by sound; to lower; to impress strongly; to ratify, as a bargain; to produce by a sudden action; to affect in some particular manner by a sudden impulse; to run on; to ground, as a ship.—*vi. To make a quick blow* or thrust; to hit; to dash against; to be struck; to fall upon; to touch; to sound with blows; to be stranded; to pass with a strong effect; to dart; to penetrate; to lower a flag in token of surrender; to cease from work, as a body of workmen, in order to obtain higher wages; to mutiny. *ppr.* striking, *pret.* struck, *pp.* struck and formerly stricken.—*n. Act of striking;* an instrument with a straight-edge for levelling a measure of grain, &c.; act of combining and demanding higher wages for work; a mutiny. [Sax. *astrican,* to smite; Dan. *stryg,* a blow.]
Striker, strīk′er, *n.* He who or that which *strikes.*
Striking, strīk′ing, *p.a.* Affecting with strong emotions; impressive; exact; adapted to make impression.
Strikingly, strīk′ing-li, *adv. In a striking manner.*
String, string, *n. That which draws tight; that which binds;* a small rope, or a slender strip of leather, used for tying things; a thread on which anything is filed; the chord of a musical instrument; a fibre, as of a plant; a tendon of an animal body; the cord of a bow; a series of things connected. *vt. To make tense;* to furnish with strings; to put in tune, as a stringed instrument; to file; to put on a line. *ppr.* stringing, *pret. & pp.* strung. [Sax.—L. *stringo,* to draw tight.]
Stringed, stringd, *p.a. Having strings.*
Stringency, strin′jen-si, *n. State of being stringent.*
Stringent, strin′jent, *a. Contracting;* binding strongly; severe; strict. [L. *stringens—stringo,* to draw tight.]
Stringently, strin′jent-li, *adv. In a stringent manner.*
Stringy, string′i, *a. Consisting of strings* or small threads; fibrous; viscid; that may be drawn into a thread.
Strip, strip, *vt. To take away by force;* to pull or tear off, as a covering; to skin; to peel; to bereave; to rob; to impoverish; to make bare by cutting,

grazing, or other means.—*vi.* To take off the covering or clothes. *ppr.* stripping, *pret. & pp.* stripped.—*n.* A piece -or slip *peeled off*; a narrow piece, comparatively long. [Sax. *bestrypan,* to strip; Low Sax. *strepen,* to strip off.]
Stripe, strip, *n.* A line or long narrow division of anything, of a different colour from the ground; a stroke made with a lash or rod; the wale or long narrow mark discoloured by a lash or rod.—*vt. To make stripes in;* to variegate with stripes. *ppr.* striping, *pret. & pp.* striped. [from *strip.*]
Striped, strīpt, *p.a. Having stripes of different colours.*
Stripling, strip′ling, *n.* A tall slender youth; a youth in the state of adolescence, or just passing from boyhood to manhood; a lad. [from *stripe.*]
Strive, strīv, *vi. To endeavour;* to make efforts; to use exertions with earnestness; to struggle in opposition to another; to vie; to contest; to contend in excellence. *ppr.* striving, *pret.* strove, *pp.* striven. [G. *streben;* Old G. *streban,* to endeavour.]
Striver, strīv′er, *n. One who strives.*
Striving, strīv′ing, *p.n.* Act of making efforts; contest; contention.
Stroke, strōk, *n. A blow;* a hostile blow; a sudden attack of affliction; fatal attack, as of death; the sound of the clock; the touch of a pencil; a masterly effort; a dash in writing or printing; a touch of the pen; the sweep of an oar in rowing; the upward or downward motion of a piston. [from *strike.*]
Stroke, strōk, *vt. To rub gently* with the hand by way of expressing tenderness; to soothe; to rub gently in one direction. *ppr.* stroking, *pret. & pp.* stroked. [Sax. *stracan*—L. *stringo,* to touch lightly.]
Stroker, strōk′er, *n. One who strokes.*
Stroll, strōl, *vi.* To move or wander about; to ramble idly or leisurely; to roam; to stray.—*n.* A wandering on foot; a walking idly and leisurely. [Provincial G. *strollen.*]
Stroller, strōl′er, *n. One who strolls;* a vagabond; a vagrant.
Strolling, strōl′ing, *p.a.* Roving idly.
Strond,† strond, *n.* The strand.
Strong, strong, *a.* Having the nerves high or *firmly strung;* having great physical power; having the power of exerting great bodily force; muscular; sound; healthy; solid; having ability to bear; able to sustain attacks; having great military or naval force; having great resources; moving with rapidity, as wind; adapted to make a deep impression on the mind; characterized by order; having virtues of great efficacy; intoxicating; not of easy digestion; well established; characterized by great earnestness; having great force of intellect; comprising much in few words; bright; vivid; ardent; zealous; effected by strength; powerful to the extent of force named. [Sax.; Icel. *strenuja,* L. *stringo,* to draw tight.]
Stronghold, strong′hōld, *n. A place of strength;* a fastness; a fortified place.
Strongly, strong′li, *adv. With strength;* with great force or power; eagerly.
Strop, strop, *n. A strap;* a strip of leather used for sharpening razors and giving them a fine, smooth edge.—*vt. To draw over a strop* with a view to sharpen. *ppr.* stropping, *pret. & pp.* stropped.
Strophe, strō′fē, *n. A turning;* in the Greek tragedy, *the turning* of the chorus, dancing towards one side of

the orchestra; the strain sung during this evolution, to which the *antistrophe* answers. [Fr.—Gr. *strephō,* to turn.]
Strophic, strō′fik, *a. Relating to or consisting of strophes.*
Strow, strō. See **Strew.**
Structural, struk′tūr-al, *a. Pertaining to structure.*
Structure, struk′tūr, *n. A putting together;* manner of building; construction; manner of organization of animals and vegetables, &c.; a building of any kind, but chiefly a building of some size; an edifice; a fabric; the particular arrangement of the integrant particles of a mineral. [Fr.—L. *struo, structus,* to pile up.]
Struggle, strug′l, *vi. To make efforts* with a twisting of the body; to use great efforts; to labour hard; to strive; to use exertions in pain or anguish; to put forth efforts in any kind of difficulty or distress. *ppr.* struggling, *pret. & pp.* struggled.—*n.* A violent effort with contortions of the body; forcible effort to obtain an object or to avoid an evil; agony; contortions of extreme distress. [Dan. *anstrenge,* to exert, to strain.]
Struggling, strug′l-ing, *p.a. Making great efforts.*—*p.n. Vehement* or earnest *effort.*
Strumpet, strum′pet, *n.* A prostitute. *a. Like a strumpet;* false; inconstant. [L. *stuprata—stupro,* to defile.]
Strut, strut, *vi. To walk* with a lofty, *proud gait* and erect head; to walk with affected dignity. *ppr.* strutting, *pret. & pp.* strutted.—*n.* A lofty, proud step or *walk,* with the head erect. [Dan. *strutte.*]
Strutter, strut′er, *n. One who struts.*
Strutting, strut′ing, *p.n.* Act of walking with a proud gait.
Stub, stub, *n. Anything truncated;* the stump of a tree; that part of the stem of a tree which remains fixed in the earth when the tree is cut down.—*vt.* To grub up by the roots; to extirpate. *ppr.* stubbing, *pret. & pp.* stubbed. [Dan.; L. *stipes,* a log.]
Stubble, stub′l, *n. The small stumps* of wheat, rye, barley, oats, or buckwheat, left in the ground; the part of the stalk left by the scythe or sickle. [dimin. of *stub;* Old Fr. *estouble.*]
Stubborn, stub′orn, *a. Fixed firmly;* inflexibly fixed in opinion; obstinate; steady; refractory; enduring without complaint; hardy; intractable; obstinately resisting the goad or the whip. [Icel. *stubbr,* the trunk of a tree.]
Stubbornly, stub′orn-li, *adv.* Obstinately; inflexibly.
Stubbornness, stub′orn-nes, *n. Quality of being stubborn;* perverse obstinacy; contumacy; refractoriness, as of ures.
Stucco, stuk′kō, *n. That which covers over;* a fine plaster composed of lime or gypsum, with sand and pounded marble, used for internal decorations, &c.; work made of stucco.—*vt.* To plaster; to overlay with fine plaster. [It.; Old G. *stucchi,* crust.]
Stuck, stuk, *n.*† A thrust.
Stud, stud, *n. That which is fixed upright,* a post; a nail with a large head, inserted in work chiefly for ornament; an ornamental button for a shirt.—*vt.* To adorn with shining *studs* or knobs to set with prominent objects. *ppr.* studding, *pret. & pp.* studded. [Sax. *studu;* Icel. *stythja,* to prop.]
Stud, stud, *n. A collection of breeding horses and mares.* [Sax. *stod.*]

Fāte, fär, fat, fall; mē, met, hėr; pīne, pin; nōte, not, move; tūbe, tub, bull; oil, pound.

Student, stū'dent, *n. One who studies; one who is devoted to learning, either in a seminary or in private; a scholar; a man devoted to books; one who studies or examines.* [L. *studens—studeo*, to take pains about.]

Studied, stu'did, *p.a.* Learned; qualified by study; premeditated; having a particular inclination.

Studio, stū'di-ō, *n. A study;* the workshop of a sculptor, of a painter, or photographer. [It.]

Studious, stū'di-us, *a. Eager; assiduous;* eager to discover something, or to effect some object; given to books; devoted to the acquisition of knowledge from books; thoughtful; attentive to; careful; favourable to study. [L. *studiosus—studeo*, to be eager.]

Studiously, stū'di-us-li, *adv. In a studious manner.*

Study, stu'di, *n. Assiduity;* close and earnest application to anything; application of mind to books for the purpose of learning what is not before known; meditation; contrivance; any particular branch of learning; an apartment devoted to study; a work undertaken for improvement in painting or sculpture; a finished sketch from nature.—*vi. To be eager or assiduous;* to apply one's self; to fix the mind closely upon a subject; to dwell upon in thought; to apply the mind to books; to endeavour diligently.—*vt. To be eager or zealous about;* to apply the mind to; to read and examine for the purpose of learning; to consider attentively; to arrange by previous thought; to con over. *ppr.* studying, *pret. & pp.* studied. [L. *studium—studeo*, to be eager.]

Stuff, stuf, *n. A mass of matter;* a collection of substances; the matter of which anything is formed; materials; essence; cloth; fabrics of the loom; a potion; baggage. [G. *stoff*, material; Icel. *stofna*, to prepare.]—*vt. To fill with stuff;* to fill very full; to fill by being put into anything; to fill with something improper; to obstruct, as any of the organs; to fill, as meat with seasoning; to fill, as the skin of a dead animal for preserving his form; to form by filling.—*vi.* To cram; to feed gluttonously. [Old Fr. *estouffer*, to choke.]

Stuffed, stuft, *p.a.* Filled for preservation; furnished.

Stuffing, stuf'ing, *p.n.* That which is used for filling anything; seasoning for meat.

Stultification, stul'ti-fi-kā"shon, *n. Act of stultifying* or making foolish.

Stultify, stul'ti-fī, *vi. To prove foolish* or void of understanding. *ppr.* stultifying, *pret. & pp.* stultified. [L. *facio*, to make, and *stultus*, foolish.]

Stumble, stum'bl, *vi. To strike the foot against a stump;* to trip in walking or moving in any way upon the legs; to strike the foot so as to fail; to slide into a crime or an error; to strike upon without design; to light on by chance. *vt.* To obstruct in progress; to cause to trip or stop; to confound; to perplex. *ppr.* stumbling, *pret. & pp.* stumbled. *n.* A trip in walking or running; a blunder; a failure. [Old G. *stumbal*, a trunk, a stump.]

Stumbling-block, **Stumbling-stone**, stum'bl-ing-blok, stum'bl-ing-stōn, *n.* Any cause of *stumbling;* that which causes to err.

Stump, stump, *n. The stub of a tree;* the part of a tree remaining in the earth after the tree is cut down, or the part of any plant left in the earth by the scythe or sickle; the part of a limb or other body remaining after a part is amputated; a worn-down tooth.—*vt.* To curtail; to lop, as trees. [Sw.; Old G. *stumphan*, to mutilate.]

Stumpy, stump'i, *a. Full of stumps;* short and thick; stubby.

Stun, stun, *vt. To dull by thundering at;* to stupify, as the organs of hearing; to make dizzy by loud and mingled sound; to make senseless with a blow on the head. *ppr.* stunning, *pret. & pp.* stunned. [Sax. *stunian*, to make stupid with a noise—Sans. *stan*, to thunder.]

Stunning, stun'ing, *p.a.* Confounding with noise; making senseless.

Stunt, stunt, *vt. To stint;* to stop the growth of; to hinder from growth. [Icel. *stunta*, to shorten.]

Stunted, stunt'ed, *p.a.* Dwarfish; stubby.

Stupefaction, stū-pē-fak'shon, *n. Act of rendering stupid;* insensibility; torpor; stupidity. [Low L. *stupefactio*.]

Stupefactive, stū-pē-fak'tiv, *a. Causing stupefaction;* deadening the sense of feeling. [Low L. *stupefactivus*.]

Stupefy, stū'pē-fī, *vt. See* STUPIFY.

Stupendous, stū-pen'dus, *a. Striking senseless* by its magnitude; amazing; of astonishing magnitude. [L. *stupendus—stupeo*, to be struck senseless.]

Stupendously, stū-pen'dus-li, *adv.* In a manner to excite astonishment.

Stupendousness, stū-pen'dus-nes, *n. Quality or state of being stupendous.*

Stupid, stū'pid, *a. Struck senseless;* very dull; senseless; doltish; formed without skill or genius. [Fr. *stupide*—L. *stupeo*, to be struck senseless.]

Stupidity, stū-pid'i-ti, *n. Quality or state of being stupid;* insensibility; sluggishness. [Fr. *stupidité*.]

Stupidly, stū'pid-li, *adv.* With extreme dulness; absurdly; without the exercise of reason or judgment.

Stupified, stū'pi-fīd, *p.a.* Having the perception or understanding blunted.

Stupify, stū'pi-fī, *vt. To make stupid;* to blunt, as the faculty of perception or understanding. *ppr.* stupifying, *pret. & pp.* stupified. [Fr. *stupéfier*; L. *stupeo*, to be struck senseless, and *facio*, to make.]

Stupifying, stū'pi-fī-ing, *p.a.* Rendering extremely dull or insensible.

Stupor, stū'por, *n. Numbness; dulness;* deadness; insensibility; intellectual or moral insensibility; heedlessness. [L. from *stupeo*—Gr. *tupto*, to strike.]

Sturdily, stėr'di-li, *adv.* Hardily; stoutly; lustily.

Sturdiness, stėr'di-nes, *n. State or quality of being sturdy;* brutal strength.

Sturdy, stėr'di, *a. Stiff;* strong; robust; implying coarseness or rudeness; violent; laid on with strength, as strokes. [G. *störrig*—Gr. *stereos*, stiff.]

Sturgeon, stėr'jon, *n.* A fish, which, like the salmon, ascends large rivers for the purpose of spawning, and is the subject of valuable fisheries. Its head is shaped like an icicle. [Sax. *styrigea*—Low L. *sturio*—L. *stiria*, an icicle.]

Stutter, stut'tėr, *vi. To strike against;* to stammer; to hesitate in uttering words.—*n. Act of stuttering;* a hesitation in speaking. [G. *stottern*.]

Stutterer, stut'tėr-ėr, *n.* A stammerer.

Stuttering, stut'tėr-ing, *p.a.* Stammering; hesitating.—*p.n.* Act of stammering.

Sty, sti, *n. A cover;* a pen or inclosure for swine; a place of bestial debauchery; [Sax. *stigan*, to grow up] an inflamed tumour on the edge of the eyelid (also written *stye*).—*vt. To shut up in a sty.* [Sax. *stige;* Icel. *stia*, a repository.]

Stygian, stij'i-an, *a. Of* or pertaining to *Styx*, a river of hell; infernal. [Gr. *Stux*, The Hateful.]

Style, stīl, *n. That which stands;* the pin of a dial (written also *stile*); the ancient pen; manner of thinking or of writing; phraseology; the character of the language used; a peculiar mode of execution in the fine arts; a particular character of music; title; the practice observed by any court in its way of proceeding; manner; a particular mode of erecting buildings; a mode of reckoning time, with regard to the Julian and Gregorian calendar. In botany, the middle portion of the pistil, connecting the stigma with the germ.—*vt.* To call; to name; to designate; to entitle in addressing. *ppr.* styling, *pret. & pp.* styled. [Fr.; Gr. *stulos*, a pillar.]

Stylish, stīl'ish, *a.* Being in fashionable form or in high *style;* showy; modish.

Styptic, stip'tik, *a. Contracting;* that stops bleeding; having the quality of restraining hemorrhage.—*n.* A medicine which has an astringent quality. [Fr. *styptique;* Gr. *stuphō*, to contract, to draw together.]

Suasion, swā'zhon, *n. A counselling; exhortation;* persuasion. [Old Fr.—L. *suadeo*, to advise—*suavis*, sweet, and *do*, to give.]

Suavity, swa'vi-ti, *n. Sweetness* (in a figurative sense); that which is to the mind what sweetness is to the tongue; agreeableness; urbanity. [Fr. *suavité*.]

Subacid, sub-as'id, *a. Acid in a small degree;* moderately acid.

Subacute, sub-a-kūt', *a. Acute in an inferior* or moderate degree.

Subaltern, sub'al-tėrn, *a. Under another;* subordinate; that in different respects is both superior and inferior. *n.* A subordinate officer in an army; an officer under the rank of captain. [Fr. *subalterne*—L. *sub*, and *alternus*, one after the other.]

Subaqueous, sub-ā'kwē-us, *a. Being under water.* [L. *sub*, and *aqua*, water.]

Subdeacon, sub'dē-kn, *n. An under-deacon.*

Subdean, sub'dēn, *n. An under-dean;* a dean's substitute or vicegerent.

Subdivide, sub-di-vīd', *vt. To divide into lower or smaller parts;* to divide into more parts, as a part of a thing.—*vi. To be subdivided;* to separate. *ppr.* subdividing, *pret. & pp.* subdivided.

Subdivision, sub-di-vi'zhon, *n. Act of subdividing;* the part of a thing made by subdividing; the part of a larger part. [Fr.]

Subdual, sub-dū'al, *n. Act of subduing.* [from *subdue*.]

Subdue, sub-dū', *vt. To put or lay under;* to bring under; to subjugate; to crush; to tame; to reduce to mildness; to conquer by persuasion; to captivate, as by charms; to reduce to tenderness; to make mellow; to break, as land. *ppr.* subduing, *pret. & pp.* subdued. [L. *sub*, and *do*, to put, place, give; Norm. *subduits*, ruined.]

Subdued, sub-dūd', *p.a.* Tamed; softened.

Subduement†, sub-dū ment, *n.* Conquest.

Subduer, sub-dū'ėr, *n. One who subdues;* a tamer.

Subduing, sub-dū'ing, *p.a.* Softening.

Sub-editor, sub-ed'it-or, n. *An under-editor.*

Subgenus, sub'je-nus, n. *An inferior genus;* a subdivision of a genus.

Subjacent, sub-jā'sent, a. *Lying under;* being in a lower situation, though not directly beneath. [L. *subjacens—jaceo,* to lie.]

Subject, sub'jekt, a. *Brought under;* being under the power of another; liable from inherent causes; prone; obedient; submissive.—n. *One who is placed under another;* one who owes allegiance to a sovereign; that on which any mental operation is performed; that which is treated; that on which any physical operation is performed; that in which anything inheres; the person who is treated of; the hero of a piece; the nominative case to a verb; the principal melody or theme of a movement in music; that which it is the aim of an artist to express; a dead body for the purposes of dissection. [L. *subjectus—jacio, jactum,* to throw.]

Subject, sub-jekt', *vt.* To throw or bring *under;* to subjugate; to subdue; to enslave; to make obnoxious; to make liable; to make accountable; to cause to undergo. [L. *subjicio, subjectus—jacio, jactum,* to throw.]

Subjection, sub-jek'shon, n. *Act of subjecting;* state of being under the power of another. [L. *subjectio.*]

Subjective, sub-jekt'iv, a. *Relating to the subject;* relating to that of which the mind is the subject. [Late L. *subjectivus.*]

Subjectively, sub-jekt'iv-li, *adv. In relation to the subject.*

Subject-matter, sub'jekt-mat-tėr, n. The *matter* or thought presented for consideration, in some statement, &c.

Subjoin, sub-join', *vt.* To yoke or harness *to;* to add at the end; to add after something else has been said or written; to connect.

Subjoined, sub-joind', *p.a.* Added after something else said or written.

Subjugate, sub'jū-gāt, *vt.* To bring *under the yoke;* to conquer by force. *ppr.* subjugating, *pret. & pp.* subjugated. [L. *subjugo, subjugatum.*]

Subjugated, sub'jū-gāt-ed, *p.a.* Reduced to the control of another.

Subjugation, sub-jū-gā'shon, n. *Act of subjugating;* state of being subjugated. [Low L. *subjugatio.*]

Subjugator, sub'jū-gāt-or, n. *One who subjugates.* [Low L.]

Subjunctive, sub-jungk'tiv, a. *Subjoined* to something before said or written; designating the form of a verb which fits it for being subjoined actually or virtually to another verb, and so to express condition or contingency.—n. The subjunctive mood. [Late L. *subjunctivus*—L. *jungo,* Sans. *yuj,* to join.]

Sublimate, sub'li-māt, *vt.* To raise by heat into vapour, as a solid substance, which on cooling, returns again to the solid state; to refine; to heighten. *ppr.* sublimating, *pret. & pp.* sublimated.—n. The product of a sublimation. [L. *sublimo, sublimatum—sublimis,* high.]

Sublimation, sub-li-mā'shon, n. *The operation of raising* or bringing a solid substance into the state of vapour by heat, and condensing it again into a solid by cold; exaltation; act of heightening or improving. [Late L. *sublimatio.*]

Sublime, sub-līm', a. *Uplifted;* high in place; elevated aloft; high in excellence; high in style; grand; elevated by joy; lofty of mien; elevated in manner; majestic.—n. *That which is lifted up;* the grand in the works of nature or of art, as distinguished from the beautiful; the emotion produced by grandeur; a grand or lofty style; a style that expresses lofty conceptions. *vt.* To *raise on high;* to heighten; to improve.—*vi.* To be raised or changed into a state of vapour by heat, and then condensed by cold. *ppr.* subliming, *pret. & pp.* sublimed. [L. *sublimis—sub,* and *levo,* to lift up.]

Sublimely, sub-līm'li, *adv.* With elevated conceptions; loftily.

Sublimity, sub-lim'i-ti, n. *Height; loftiness;* height in excellence; loftiness of nature; moral grandeur; lofty conceptions; grandeur; vastness; elevation, whether exhibited in the works of nature or of art. [Fr. *sublimité.*]

Sublunary, sub'lū-na-ri, a. *Under the moon;* terrestrial; pertaining to this world. [Fr. *sublunaire*—L. *luna,* the moon—*luceo,* to shine.]

Submarine, sub-ma-rēn', a. Being, acting, or growing *under* water in the sea. [L. *sub,* and *marinus—mare,* the sea.]

Submerge, sub-mėrj', *vt.* To plunge *under;* to put under water; to plunge; to cover or overflow with water; to drown.—*vi.* To plunge *under* water. *ppr.* submerging, *pret. & pp.* submerged. [L. *submergo—mergo,* to dip.]

Submergence, sub-mėrj'ens, n. *Act of submerging;* state of being submerged.

Submersed, sub-mėrst', *p.a. Being or growing under water,* as the leaves of aquatic plants. [L. *submersus—mergo,* to dip.]

Submersion, sub-mėr'shon, n. *Act of submerging;* act of causing to be overflowed. [Fr.]

Submission, sub-mi'shon, n. *Act of submitting;* acknowledgment of inferiority; acknowledgment of a fault; unmurmuring compliance with the commands or will of a superior. [L. *submissio—mitto, missum,* to send.]

Submissive, sub-mis'iv, a. *Pertaining to submission;* humble; passive.

Submissively, sub-mis'iv-li, *adv.* With submission.

Submissiveness, sub-mis'iv-nes, n. Quality or state of being submissive.

Submit, sub-mit', *vt.* To send or put *under;* to refer; to leave or commit to the judgment of another; to state, as a claim in behalf of one's self or another.—*vi.* To come under power or authority; to yield; to comply; to yield to the authority of another (with recipr. pron.); to yield to anything overpowering; to be submissive; to acquiesce. *ppr.* submitting, *pret. & pp.* submitted. [L. *submitto—mitto,* to send.]

Subordinate, sub-or'din-āt, a. *Below or inferior in order;* inferior in rank, &c.; descending in a regular series. n. One who stands in order or rank *below* another; one of a descent in a regular series.—*vt.* To make subordinate; to place in an order or rank below something else; to make subject. *ppr.* subordinating, *pret. & pp.* subordinated. [L. *sub,* and *ordinatus—ordo, ordinis,* a straight row.]

Subordinately, sub-or'din-āt-li, *adv.* In a lower rank or of inferior importance.

Subordination, sub-or'din-ā'shon, n. State of being subordinate; inferiority of rank; a series regularly descending; subjection. [Fr.]

Suborn, sub-orn', *vt.* To incite; to instigate in an *underhand* manner; to procure by indirect means; to procure, as a person, to take such an oath as constitutes perjury. [Fr. *suborner*—L. *sub,* privately, and *orno,* to fit out.]

Subornation, sub-orn-ā'shon, n. *Act of suborning;* the crime of procuring a person to take such an oath as constitutes perjury; the crime of procuring one to do a criminal action. [Fr.]

Suborner, sub-orn'ėr, n. *One who suborns* or procures another to take a false oath. [Fr. *suborneur.*]

Subscribe, sub-skrīb', *vt.* To write *underneath;* to sign with one's own hand; to bind one's self by writing one's name beneath; to attest by writing one's name beneath; to promise to give by writing one's name; to submit.—*vi.* To promise to give a certain sum by setting one's name to a paper; to assent. *ppr.* subscribing, *pret. & pp.* subscribed. [L. *subscribo—scribo,* to write, draw, make lines, &c.]

Subscriber, sub-skrīb'ėr, n. *One who subscribes;* one who contributes; one who enters his name for a paper, book, map, and the like.

Subscription, sub-skrip'shon, n. *Act of subscribing;* signature; attestation given by underwriting the name; act of contributing to any undertaking; sum subscribed. [L. *subscriptio.*]

Subsection, sub'sek-shon, n. *An under section;* the section of a section. [L. *sub,* and *sectio,* a cutting—*seco,* to cut.]

Subsequent, sub'sē-kwent, a. *Following close after;* following in time; following in the order of place or succession; consequent; next. [Fr. *subsequent*—L. *sequor,* to follow.]

Subsequently, sub'sē-kwent-li, *adv.* In a subsequent manner.

Subserve, sub-sėrv', *vt.* To serve *under;* to serve instrumentally.—*vi.* To be subservient. *ppr.* subserving, *pret. & pp.* subserved. [L. *subservio—servio,* to serve.]

Subservience, Subserviency, sub-sėrv'i-ens, sub-sėrv'i-en-si, n. *State of being subservient;* use or operation that promotes some purpose.

Subservient, sub-sėrv'i-ent, a. *Serving under;* useful as an instrument to promote a purpose. [L. *subserviens.*]

Subserviently, sub-sėrv'i-ent-li, *adv.* In a subservient manner.

Subside, sub-sīd', *vi.* To settle down; to sink or fall to the bottom, as lees; to fall into a state of quiet; to be calmed; to sink; to be reduced. *ppr.* subsiding, *pret. & pp.* subsided. [L. *subsido—sido,* to settle.]

Subsidence, sub-sīd'ens, n. *Act or process of subsiding;* act of sinking or gradually descending, as ground.

Subsidiary, sub-si'di-a-ri, a. *Pertaining to a subsidy;* furnishing help; furnishing additional supplies.—n. An assistant; he or that which contributes aid or additional supplies. [Fr. *subsidiaire*—L. *sido,* to sit down.]

Subsidize, sub'si-dīz, *vt.* To *furnish with a subsidy;* to purchase the assistance of by the payment of a subsidy. *ppr.* subsidizing, *pret. & pp.* subsidized.

Subsidy, sub'si-di, n. *Succour;* aid in money; a tax; something furnished for aid, as by the people to their prince; a sum of money paid by one prince or nation to another, to purchase the service of auxiliary troops, or the aid of such foreign prince or nation. [L. *subsidium—sido,* to sit down.]

Subsist, sub-sist', *vi.* To take a *stand or position;* to retain the present state; to be; to live; to be maintained with

Fate, fär, fat, fạll; mē, met, hėr; pine, pin; nōte, not, mōve; tūbe, tub, bụll; oil, pound.

food and clothing; to inhere. [Fr. *sub-ster*; L. *sisto*, to set one's self.]
Subsistence, sub-sist'ens, *n. State of subsisting*; that in which anything subsists; sustenance; that which supplies the means of living, as money, pay, or wages. [Fr.]
Subsoil, sub'soil, *n. The under soil*; the bed of earth which lies between the surface soil and a stratum still lower.
Substance, sub'stans, *n. That which stands under*; that which subsists; the essential part; the main part; something existing by itself; that which really is; that in which qualities inhere; essential import; body; goods; means of living. [Fr.—L. *sub*, and *sto*, to stand.]
Substantial, sub-stan'shi-al, *a. Belonging to substance*; real; solid; true; having substance or strength; possessed of goods or estate; moderately wealthy. [Fr. *substantiel*.]
Substantially, sub-stan'shi-al-li, *adv. In a substantial manner.*
Substantiate, sub-stan'shi-āt, *vt.* To give substance to; to establish by proof or competent evidence; to make good. *ppr.* substantiating, *pret. & pp.* substantiated.
Substantive, sub'stan-tiv, *a.* Betokening existence; not adjective.—*n.* A noun or name; the part of speech which expresses something that *exists*. [Fr. *substantif*.]
Substantively, sub'stan-tiv-li, *adv. In substance*; as a substantive.
Substitute, sub'sti-tūt, *vt. To put under* or in the place of another; to change. *ppr.* substituting, *pret. & pp.* substituted.—*n.* One person put in the place of another to answer the same purpose; a deputy; one thing put in the place of another. [L. *substituo, substitutus—statuo*, to put, place.]
Substitution, sub-sti-tū'shon, *n. Act of substituting;* state of being substituted; the use of one word for another. [Fr.]
Substratum, sub'strā-tum, *n.* **Substrata**, *pl. That which is spread under;* a layer of earth lying under another; the substance supposed to furnish the basis in which the perceptible qualities inhere. [L. *sterno, stratum*, to spread.]
Substructure, sub'struk-tūr, *n. An under structure;* a foundation.
Subtend, sub-tend', *vt.* To stretch or extend under, or be opposite to. [L. *subtendo—tendo*, to stretch.]
Subtepid, sub-te'pid, *a. Very moderately warm.* [L. *tepidus*, warm.]
Subterfuge, sub'tėr-fūj, *n. A secret place of flight;* that to which a person resorts for concealment; an artifice employed to escape censure; an evasion; a prevarication. [Fr.—L. *fugio*, to flee or fly.]
Subterranean, Subterraneous, sub-te-rā'nē-an, sub-te-rā'nē-us, *a. Being under the surface of the earth*; situated within the earth or underground. [L. *subterraneus—terra*, the earth.]
Subtile, sub'til, *a. Woven fine*; nice; thin ; acute; piercing; refined. [L. *subtilis—texo*, to weave.]
Subtilely, sub'til-li, *adv.* Thinly; not densely; finely; not grossly or thickly.
Subtileness, sub'til-nes, *n. Quality of being subtile*; thinness; acuteness.
Subtilize, sub'til-īz, *vt. To make thin or fine*; to spin into niceties.—*vi.* To refine in argument; to make very nice distinctions. *ppr.* subtilizing, *pret. & pp.* subtilized. [Fr. *subtiliser*.]
Subtilty, sub'til-ti, *n. State or quality of being subtile;* fineness; extreme acuteness. [Fr. *subtilité*.]
Subtle, sut'l, *a. Fine;* artful; crafty; insinuating; wily; cunningly devised; made level by careful labour. [L. *subtilis*.]
Subtleness, sut'l-nes, *n. Quality of being subtle;* cunning.
Subtlety, sut'l-ti, *n.* Cunning; artifice; cunning device.
Subtly, sut'l-li, *adv.* Slily; artfully.
Subtract, sub-trakt', *vt. To draw away from underneath, or by stealth;* to take, as a part from the rest; to deduct. [L. *subtraho, subtractus—traho*, to draw.]
Subtraction, sub-trak'shon, *n. Act of subtracting;* the taking of a lesser number or quantity from a greater of the same kind. [L. *subtractio*.]
Subtractive, sub-trakt'iv, *a. Tending* or having power *to subtract.*
Subtrahend, sub'tra-hend, *n.* The sum to be *taken from* another. [L. *traho*, to draw.]
Suburb, sub'ėrb, *n. sing.*; **Suburbs**, sub'ėrbs, *pl.* A house or part situated *near* to the walls of a *city;* (pl.) the parts in the vicinity of a city lying without its boundaries; the confines. [L. *suburbium—urbs*, a city.]
Suburban, sub-ėrb'an, *a. Relating to the suburbs.* [L. *suburbānus.*]
Subvention, sub-ven'shon, *n.* Act of *coming under;* aid. [L. *venio*, to come.]
Subversion, sub-vėr'shon, *n. Act of subverting;* an overthrow of the foundation; destruction; downfal; extinction. [Fr.—L. *verto, versum*, to turn.]
Subversive, sub-vėrs'iv, *a. Tending to subvert;* having a tendency to overthrow and ruin. [Fr. *subversif*.]
Subvert, sub-vėrt', *vt. To turn upside down;* to overthrow from the foundation; to destroy; to extinguish. [L. *subverto—verto*, to turn.]
Subverter, sub-vėrt'ėr, *n. One who subverts;* an overthrower.
Succedaneum, suk-sē-dā'nē-um, *n. That which follows;* that which is used for something else; a substitute. [L.—*cedo*, to go.]
Succeed, suk-sēd', *vt. To go or come under;* to approach; to follow in order; to take the place vacated by; to come after; to be subsequent to.—*vi.* To go forward; to follow in order; to come in the place of one who has died or quitted the place; to obtain the object desired, to prosper; to terminate with advantage; to have a good effect. [Fr. *succéder*—L. *cedo*, to go.]
Succeeding, suk-sēd'ing, *p. a.* Subsequent; coming after; having success; prospering.
Success, suk-ses', *n. A coming up to;* that which is arrived at; issue; a happy issue ; a termination which answers the purpose intended; succession. [L. *successus—cedo*, to go or come.]
Successful, suk-ses'fųl, *a. Having or yielding success;* having a favourable issue; having the desired effect; happy; fortunate.
Successfully, suk-ses'fųl-li, *adv. In a successful manner.*
Succession, suk-se'shon, *n. Act of succeeding;* a following of things in order; series of things following one another, either in time or place; the act of coming in the place of another; race; an order of descendants; the right of coming to the inheritance of ancestors. [Fr.]
Successional, suk-se'shon-al, *a. Noting* a regular order or *succession.*
Successive, suk-ses'iv, *a. Succeeding;* following, as a series of persons or things, and either in time or place; inherited by succession. [Fr. *successif*.]
Successively, suk-ses'iv-li, *adv.* In a series or order, one following another.
Successor, suk-ses'or, *n. One who succeeds;* one who takes the place which another has left. [L.]
Succinct, suk-singkt', *a. Girded up;* compressed into a narrow compass; short; concise. [L. *succinctus—cingo, cinctum*, to gird.]
Succinctly, suk-singkt'li, *adv.* Briefly.
Succour, suk'kėr, *vt. To run* to support; to help when in difficulty, want, or distress; to relieve; to deliver.—*n.* Aid; assistance ; assistance that relieves; the person or thing that brings relief. [L. *succurro—curro*, to run—Sans. *sri*, to go, to advance.]
Succourer, suk'kėr-ėr, *n. He who succours* or affords relief; a deliverer.
Succulence, suk'kū-lens, *n. Quality of being succulent;* juiciness.
Succulent, suk'kū-lent, *a. Full of sap or juice;* juicy; very cellular and juicy as the stems of certain plants. [Fr.— L. *succus*, juice—*sugo*, to suck.]
Succumb, suk-kum', *vi. To lay* or put *one's self under;* to yield; to submit; to sink unresistingly. [L. *succumbo—cumbo*, to lie down.]
Such, such, *a. Of this kind;* of the like kind; the same as what has been mentioned; to so great a degree; denoting excess in any quality or mode. [Sax. *swilc*—Goth. *svaleiks*, such.]
Suck, suk, *vt. To draw with the mouth;* to draw out, as milk from the breast; to draw into the mouth; to imbibe; to draw in, as a whirlpool; to inhale.—*vi.* To draw by exhausting the air, as with the mouth or with a tube; to draw the breast.—*n. Act of sucking;* milk drawn from the breast by the mouth. [Sax. *sucan*—L. *sugo*.]
Sucker, suk'ėr, *n. He or that which sucks;* the piston of a pump; a pipe through which anything is drawn; the shoot of a plant from the roots or lower part of the stem.
Sucking, suk'ing, *p.a. Drawing* with the mouth; absorbing.
Suckle, suk'l, *vt. To give suck to;* to nurse at the breast. *ppr.* suckling, *pret. & pp.* suckled. [from *suck*.]
Suckling, suk'l-ing, *p.n.* A young child or animal nursed by the mother's milk.
Suction, suk'shon, *n. Act of sucking;* act of drawing, as fluids into a pipe. [Fr.]
Sudatory, sū'da-tō-ri, *n. A place to produce sweating ;* a sweating-room or bath.—*a. Sweating.* [L. *sudatorium—sudo*, to sweat.]
Sudden, sud'den, *a. Coming unexpectedly;* unexpected; unusual; abrupt; unlooked for; hasty; rash.—*n.* Surprise. [Fr. *soudain*—L. *subeo*, to steal upon—*sub*, and *eo, itum*, to go.]
Suddenly, sud'den-li, *adv.* In an unexpected manner; unexpectedly.
Suddenness, sud'den-nes, *n. State of being sudden;* a coming or happening without previous notice.
Sudorific, sū-do-rif'ik, *a. Causing sweat. n. A medicine that produces sweat.* [Fr. *sudorifique*—L. *sudor*, sweat, and *facio*, to make.]
Suds, sudz, *n. sing.* Water impregnated with soap. [Sax. *seothan*, to boil.]
Sue, sū, *vt. To follow after;* to prosecute; to seek justice or right from by legal process.—*vi. To prosecute;* to seek for in law; to apply for; to entreat; to

ch, chain; j, job, g, go; ng, sing; ᴛʜ, then; th, thin; w, wig; wh, whig; zh, azure; † obsolete. 25

demand. *ppr.* suing, *pret. & pp.* sued. [Fr. *suivre*—L. *sequor*, to follow.]

Suet, sū'et, *n.* The *fat* of an animal, particularly the harder and less fusible part about the kidneys. [Fr. *suif*—L. *sebum*, tallow.]

Suffer, suf'fèr, *vt.* To bear *up under;* to endure; not to sink under; to permit; to tolerate; not to forbid or hinder; to undergo; to be affected by.—*vi.* To bear *up*; to feel or undergo pain of body or mind; to bear what is inconvenient; to be injured; to sustain damage. [L. *suffero—fero*, to bear.]

Sufferable, suf'fèr-a-bl, *a.* That may be *suffered*; allowable.

Sufferance, suf'fèr-ans, *n.* State of *suffering*; endurance; the bearing of pain; pain endured; a bearing with patience; permission; negative consent by not forbidding or hindering.

Sufferer, suf'fèr-er, *n.* One who *suffers*; one who sustains loss; one who allows.

Suffering, suf'fèr-ing, *p.a.* Bearing; undergoing pain.—*p.n.* The bearing of pain or loss; pain endured; distress or injury incurred.

Suffice, suf-fīs', *vi.* To be put into the place; to be supplied; to be enough; to be equal to the end proposed.—*vt.* To satisfy; to content. *ppr.* sufficing, *pret. & pp.* sufficed. [L. *sufficio—facio*, to make.]

Sufficiency, suf-fi'shi-en-si, *n.* State of being *sufficient*; adequate substance or means; ample stock; ability; conceit. [Late L. *sufficientia*.]

Sufficient, suf-fi'shi-ent, *a.* That suffices; adequate; equal to the end proposed; not deficient; competent; possessing adequate talents or accomplishments; fit; responsible. [L. *sufficiens*.]

Sufficiently, suf-fi'shi-ent-li, *adv.* To a *sufficient* degree; enough.

Suffix, suf'fiks, *n.* That which is fixed beneath or on; that which is affixed; a letter or syllable added to the end of a word; an affix.—*vt.* To add, as a letter or syllable to a word. [L. *figo, fixum,* to fix—Sans. *pash*, to bind.]

Suffocate, suf'fō-kāt, *vt.* To stop the breath of by *compressing the throat*; to strangle; to smother; to destroy; to extinguish. *ppr* suffocating, *pret. & pp.* suffocated. [L. *suffoco, suffocātus*—L. *sub*, and *faux, faucis*, the throat.]

Suffocating, suf'fō-kāt-ing, *p.a.* Choking; stifling.

Suffocation, suf-fō-kā'shon, *n.* Act of *suffocating*; a stopping of respiration; act of stifling; smothering; condition of being suffocated. [L. *suffocatio*.]

Suffragan, suf'fra-gan, *a.* Primarily, *voting for;* assisting.—*n.* A bishop, considered as an assistant to his metropolitan; or rather an assistant bishop. [Fr. *suffragant*—L. *suffrāgor,* to vote for.]

Suffrage, suf'frāj, *n.* A vote; a voice given in deciding a controverted question, or in the choice of a man for an office or trust; united voice of persons in public prayer. [Fr.—L. *suffragium*.]

Suffuse, suf-fūz', *vt.* To pour or spread *under* or *through*; to overspread, as with a fluid; to spread over with something expansible, as a vapour or tincture. *ppr.* suffusing, *pret. & pp.* suffused. [L. *suffundo, suffusus—fundo,* to pour.]

Suffusion, suf-fū'zhon, *n.* Act of *suffusing*; the state of being suffused; that which is suffused or spread over. [Fr.]

Sugar, shụ'gär, *n.* A well-known sweet crystalline or concrete substance, manufactured chiefly from the expressed juice of the sugar-cane.—*a.* Belonging to or made of *sugar*.—*vt.* To sprinkle or mix with *sugar*; to sweeten; to cover with soft words. [Fr. *sucre*—Gr. *sakchar*—Sans. *sū*, to express the juice of.]

Sugar-cane, shụ'gär-kān, *n.* The *cane* or plant from whose juice sugar is obtained.

Sugared, shụ'gärd, *p.a.* Sweetened with *sugar*.

Sugary, shụ'gär-i, *a.* Tinctured with *sugar*; sweet; containing sugar.

Suggest, suj-est', *vt.* To put or lay *under*; to convey to; to offer; to offer to the mind; to hint; to intimate or mention in the first instance; to tempt; to inform secretly. [L. *suggero, suggestus*—*gero*, to wear, to bear, to carry.]

Suggestion, su-jest'shon, *n.* Act of *suggesting*; that which is suggested; a first intimation; secret incitement. [Fr.]

Suggestive, su-jest'iv, *a.* Containing a *suggestion,* a hint, or intimation.

Suggestively, su-jest'iv-li, *adv.* By way of *suggestion*.

Suicidal, sū-i-sid'al, *a.* Partaking of the crime of *suicide*.

Suicidally, sū-i-sid'al-li, *adv.* In a *suicidal* manner.

Suicide, sū'i-sīd, *n.* Self-*murder*; the act of designedly destroying one's own life; one guilty of self-murder. [Fr.—L. *sui,* of himself, and *cædo,* to kill.]

Suit, sūt, *n.* A *following after*; a petition; request; a seeking for something by petition; solicitation of a woman in marriage; prosecution of right before any tribunal; a number of things used together, as a suit of clothes, of armour, &c.; a set.—*vt.* To fit; to adapt; to be fitted to; to clothe; to make content.—*vi.* To agree; to be suitable; to have corresponding qualities. (With *to* or *with*.) [Old Fr. *suite*—L. *sequor,* to follow.]

Suitable, sūt'a-bl, *a.* That *suits*; fitting; proper; appropriate; conformable; agreeable; answerable; adequate.

Suitableness, sūt'a-bl-nes, *n.* Quality or state of being *suitable*; fitness; agreeableness; consistency; consonance.

Suitably, sūt'a-bli, *adv.* Fitly.

Suite, swēt, *n.* A *following*; a company or number of attendants or followers; retinue; train; a set or arrangement of things, as of apartments. [Fr.—L. *sequor,* to follow.]

Suitor, sūt'or, *n.* One who *sues* or prosecutes a demand of right in law; a petitioner; one who solicits a woman in marriage; a lover.

Sulkiness, sulk'i-nes, *n.* Quality of being *sulky*; sullenness; moroseness.

Sulky, sulk'i, *a.* Slow; sullen; obstinate; morose. [Sax. *solcen,* slow.]

Sullen, sul'len, *a.* Solitary; gloomily angry and silent; cross; morose; malignant; gloomy; dark; dull. [Norm. *soleyne*—L. *solus*, alone.]

Sullenly, sul'len-li, *adv.* Gloomily.

Sullenness, sul'len-nes, *n.* Quality of being *sullen*; moroseness; malignity.

Sully, sul'li, *vt.* To *soil*; to tarnish; to darken; to stain.—*vi.* To be soiled or tarnished. *ppr.* sullying, *pret. & pp.* sullied.—*n.* Soil; tarnish; spot. [Fr. *souiller,* to soil—L. *solum,* earth, soil.]

Sulphur, sul'fèr, *n.* Brimstone; a simple mineral substance, of a yellow colour, which burns with a pale blue flame, attended with suffocating fumes. [L. *su'fur*—Sans. *shulvari*.]

Sulphureous, sul-fū'rē-us, *a.* Consisting of *sulphur*; having the qualities of sulphur; impregnated with sulphur.

Sulphuric, sul-fū'rik, *a.* Pertaining to *sulphur*; derived from sulphur.

Sulphurous, sul'fèr-us, *a.* Like *sulphur*; containing sulphur.

Sultan, sul'tan, *n.* A despotic *ruler*; an appellation given to the *ruler* or emperor of the Turks. [Ar.; Chald. *shalat,* to exercise dominion.]

Sultana, Sultaness, sul-tä'nä, sul'tan-es, *n.* The *wife of a sultan*; the empress of the Turks.

Sultanship, sul'tan-ship, *n.* The office or state of a *sultan*.

Sultriness, sul'tri-nes, *n.* State of being *sultry*.

Sultry, sul'tri, *a.* Very hot, burning, and oppressive; very hot, close, stagnant, and unelastic. [Sax. *swolath,* sultry—*swelan,* to burn.]

Sum, sum, *n.* That which is *highest*; that which is most important to anything; the substance; compendium; the whole; the amount or whole of any number of individuals or particulars added; a quantity of money; any amount indefinitely; height; completion.—*vt.* To collect; to collect or add, as particulars into one whole; to bring into a small compass or in a few words; to condense; to comprehend (with *up*). *ppr* summing, *pret. & pp.* summed. [Fr. *somme*—L. *summus,* highest—*super,* above.]

Summarily, sum'a-ri-li, *adv.* In a summary manner; concisely; in a short way or method.

Summarize, sum'a-rīz, *vt.* To write or form, as summaries or abridgments. *ppr.* summarizing, *pret. & pp.* summarized.

Summary, sum'a-ri, *a.* Containing the *sum* or substance; short; compendious. *n.* That which contains the *sum* of a fuller account; an abridged account; a compendium. [Fr. *sommaire*.]

Summation, sum-ā'shon, *n.* Act of *forming a sum* or total amount.

Summer, sum'èr, *n.* The season in which the *sun* is *high*, clear, and beauteous; one of the four seasons of the year.—*vi.* To pass the *summer*.—*vt.* To keep or carry through the *summer*. [Sax. *sumer—sunne,* sun, and *maera,* high.]

Summer-house, sum'èr-hous, *n.* A *house* in a garden to be used in *summer*; a house to live in during *summer*.

Summerset, sum'èr-set, *n.* See SOMERSET.

Summit, sum'it, *n.* The *top*; the highest point; utmost elevation. [L. *summitas*—*summus,* highest.]

Summon, sum'mun, *vt.* To warn to appear in court and defend; to notify; to cite; to call or command; to rouse or excite into action or exertion. (With *up*.) [L. *submoneo—moneo,* to remind, to cause to think—Sans. *man,* to think.]

Summoner, sum'mun-èr, *n.* One who *summons* or cites by authority.

Summons, sum'muns, *n.* with a plural termination, but used in the singular number. A *call* by authority to appear at a place named, or to attend to some public duty; a citation. [Low L. *submoneas*.]

Sumpter, sump'tèr, *n.* A horse or mule that carries clothes or furniture; a baggage-horse. [Fr. *sommier*—L. *summa,* amount.]

Sumptuary, sump'tū-a-ri, *a.* Relating to *expense*; regulating expenses. [Fr. *somptuaire*—L. *sumo, sumptus,* to take up, use.]

Sumptuous, sump'tū-us, *a.* Very expensive or costly; characterized by ex-

pense or magnificence; lordly; princely. [L. *sumptuosus—sumo*, to use, spend.]
Sumptuously, sump'tū-us-li, *adv.* Expensively; splendidly.
Sun, sun, *n.* The shining orb of day; the splendid orb which, being in or near the centre of our system of worlds, gives light and heat to all the planets; a position exposed to the direct influence of solar light and heat; that which is the chief source of light or honour; the orb which constitutes the centre of any system of worlds.—*vt.* To expose to the *sun's rays*; to warm or dry in the light of the sun, *ppr.* sunning, *pret. & pp.* sunned. [Sax. *sunne*; Sans. *sur*, to shine.]
Sun-blind, sun'blind, *a. Blind from too bright sunshine.*
Sun-burned, sun'bėrnt, *a. Scorched by the sun's rays*; darkened in hue.
Sunday, sun'dā, *n.* The Christian Sabbath, or Lord's-day; the first day of the week.—*a.* Belonging to the Lord's-day, or Christian Sabbath. [Sax. *sunnan-dæg*, the sun's day.]
Sunder, sun'dėr, *vt. To interpose one's self*, as between combatants; to put an object or a space between; to part; to disunite in almost any manner, either by rending, cutting, or breaking.—*vi.* To part.—*n.* A separation into parts. [Sax. *syndrian*; Icel. *sundr*, apart—Sans. *sva*, himself, and *antar*, between.]
Sundered, sun'dėrd, *p.a. Separated; divided; parted.*
Sundry, sun'dri, *a.* Several; different; various; many. [Sax. *syndrie.*]
Sunken, sungk'en, *p.a. Sunk;* lying on the bottom of a river or other water.
Sunniness, sun'i-nes, *n. State of being sunny.*
Sunny, sun'i, *a. Like the sun*; bright; shining; exposed to the rays of the sun; warmed by the direct rays of the sun; coloured by the sun.
Sunrise, Sunrising, sun'riz, sun'riz-ing, *n.* The time at which the *sun rises*; the first appearance of the sun above the horizon in the morning; the time of such appearance; the east.
Sunset, Sunsetting, sun'set, sun'set-ing, *n.* The time when the *sun sets*; the descent of the sun below the horizon; evening.
Sunshine, sun'shīn, *n. The light of the sun*; the direct rays of the sun, or the place where they fall; a place warmed; warmth; illumination.
Sunshiny, sun'shīn-i, *a. Bright with the rays of the sun*; clear, warm, or pleasant; bright like the sun.
Sun-stroke, sun'strōk, *n. A stroke of the sun*, or his heat; an affection produced by the action of the sun's rays on some part of the body, as on the head, hands, or arms.
Sunward, sun'wạrd, *adv. Toward the sun.*
Sup, sup, *vt. To sip*; to take into the mouth with the lips, as a liquid; to take or drink by a little at a time.—*vi.* To eat the evening meal.—*vt.* To treat with supper. *ppr.* supping, *pret. & pp.* supped.—*n. A sip*; a small mouthful, as of liquor or broth; a little taken with the lips. [Sax. *supan*, to sup.]
Superable, sū'pėr-a-bl, *a. That may be overcome or conquered.* [L. *superabilis*—*super*, above.]
Superabound, sū'pėr-a-bound", *vi. To abound to excess;* to exuberant; to be more than sufficient.
Superabounding, sū'pėr-a-bound"ing, *p.a. Abundant to excess* or a great degree.

Superabundance, sū'pėr-a-bund"ans, *n. Excessive abundance.*
Superabundant, sū'pėr-a-bund"ant, *a. Abounding to excess.*
Superabundantly, sū'pėr-a-bund"ant-li, *adv.* More than sufficiently.
Superadd, sū-pėr-ad', *vt. To add over and above;* to add, as something extrinsic.
Superaddition, sū'pėr-ad-di"shon, *n. Act of superadding*; state of being superadded; that which is added.
Superannuate, sū-pėr-an'nū-āt, *vt.* To disqualify by *years*; to allow to retire from service on half-pay, on account of old age or infirmity. *ppr.* superannuating, *pret. & pp.* superannuated. [L. *super*, and *annus*, a year.]
Superannuated, sū-pėr-an'nū-āt-ed, *p.a.* Allowed to retire from the army, navy, &c., on half-pay, on account of old age or infirmity.
Superannuation, sū-pėr-an'nū-ā"shon, *n. Act of superannuating*; state of being pensioned off as beyond service.
Superb, sū-pėrb', *a. Uplifted*; superior; magnificent; pompous; rich; stately. [Fr. *superbe*—L. *super*, above.]
Superbly, sū-pėrb'li, *adv.* In a magnificent or splendid manner; richly.
Supercargo, sū-pėr-kär'gō, *n. One placed over the cargo;* an officer in a merchant's ship, whose business is to manage the sales and superintend all the commercial concerns of the voyage.
Supercilious, sū-pėr-si'li-us, *a.* Expressing pride by raising the *eyebrows*; lofty with pride; manifesting haughtiness, or proceeding from it. [L. *superciliosus—cilium*, an eyelid.]
Superciliously, sū-pėr-si'li-us-li, *adv.* Haughtily; with an air of contempt.
Superciliousness, sū-pėr-si'li-us-nes, *n. Quality* or state *of being supercilious*; an overbearing temper or manner.
Supereminence, sū-pėr-em'i-nens, *n. Eminence superior* to what is common; distinguished eminence.
Supereminent, sū-pėr-em'i-nent, *a. Eminent in a superior degree.*
Supereminently, sū-pėr-em'i-nent-li, *adv. In a superior degree of excellence.*
Supererogation, sū-pėr-e'rō-gā"shon, *n. Giving or paying out more than enough;* performance of more than duty requires. [L. *erogatio—rogo*, to ask.]
Superexcellence, sū-pėr-ek'sel-lens, *n. Superior excellence.*
Superexcellent, sū-pėr-ek'sel-lent, *a. Excellent in an uncommon degree.*
Superficial, sū-pėr-fi'shi-al, *a. Pertaining to the surface or superficies*; being on *the surface*; shallow; not deep; comprehending only what is obvious. [Fr. *superficiel*; L. *facies*, face.]
Superficially, sū-pėr-fi'shi-al-li, *adv. In a superficial manner.*
Superficialness, sū-pėr-fi'shi-al-nes, *n. State or quality of being superficial.*
Superficies, sū-pėr-fi'shēz, *n. The upper face or side of a thing;* the top; the exterior part; the surface. [L.]
Superfine, sū-pėr-fīn', *a. Surpassing in fineness*; very fine.
Superfluity, sū-pėr-flū'i-ti, *n. That which overflows*; superabundance; a greater quantity than is wanted. [Fr. *superfluité*—L. *fluo*, to flow.]
Superfluous, sū-pėr'flū-us, *a. Flowing over*; rendered unnecessary by superabundance; more than sufficient. [L. *superfluus—fluo*, to flow, akin to *pluo*, to rain, and to Sans. *plu*, to swim.]
Superfluously, sū-pėr'flū-us-li, *adv.* With excess; in a degree beyond what is necessary.

Superhuman, sū-pėr-hū'man, *a. Above or beyond what is human;* divine.
Superimpose, sū'pėr-im-pōz", *vt. To lay or impose* on something else. *ppr.* superimposing, *pret. & pp.* superimposed.
Superincumbent, sū'pėr-in-kum"bent, *a. Lying upon something else.* [L. *superincumbens*—obsol. *cumbo*, to lie down.]
Superinduce, sū'pėr-in-dūs", *vt. To bring in over and above;* to bring in or upon as an addition to something. *ppr.* superinducing, *pret. & pp* superinduced. [L. *superinduco—duco*, to lead, to bring.]
Superintend, sū'pėr-in-tend"', *vt. To stretch over;* to direct the mind to a care over; to have the oversight of; to take care of with authority; to regulate. [L. *tendo*, to stretch.]
Superintendence, sū'pėr-in-tend"ens, *n. Act of superintending*; oversight; direction; guidance.
Superintendent, sū'pėr-in-tend"ent, *n. One who has the superintendence* or the oversight of something, with the power of direction; a director.
Superintending, sū'pėr-in-tend"ing, *p.a.* Overlooking with the authority to direct what shall be done; controlling.
Superior, sū-pē'ri-or, *a. Higher;* more elevated in place; higher in rank; more exalted in dignity; higher in excellence; being beyond the influence of; too great or firm to be subdued by. *n. One higher* than another or others; one who is more advanced in age; one more elevated in rank or office; one who surpasses others in dignity; the chief of a monastery, convent, or abbey. [L.—*super*, above.]
Superiority, sū-pē'ri-o''ri-ti. *n.* Quality of being *superior*; ascendency; advantage. [Fr. *supériorité.*]
Superlative, sū-pėr'lāt-iv, *a. Being lifted up high above others; highest in degree*; supreme; expressing the highest degree in the comparison of adjectives and adverbs.—*n. The highest degree* of adjectives or adverbs; a word in the superlative degree. [Fr. *superlatif*; L. *fero, latum*, to bear, carry.]
Superlatively, sū-pėr'lāt-iv-li, *adv. In the highest* or utmost *degree.*
Supernal, sū-pėr'nal, *a. That is above;* relating to things above; celestial; heavenly. [L. *supernus—super*, above.]
Supernatural, sū-pėr-na'tūr-al, *a. Being above or beyond nature*; being beyond the laws of nature; miraculous.
Supernaturally, sū-pėr-na'tūr-al-li, *adv.* In a manner *exceeding* the established course or laws *of nature.*
Supernumerary, sū-pėr-nū'me-ra-ri, *a. Exceeding the number stated*; exceeding a necessary number.—*n.* A person or thing *beyond the number* stated. [Fr. *surnuméraire*—L. *numĕrus*, number.]
Superposition, sū'pėr-pōz-i"shon, *n. A placing above;* that which is situated above or upon something else. [L. *pono, positum*, to place.]
Superscribe, sū-pėr-skrīb', *vt. To write upon* or *over;* to write the name or address of on the outside or cover, as of a letter. *ppr.* superscribing, *pret. & pp.* superscribed. [L. *scribo*, to write.]
Superscript, sū'pėr-skript, *n. Superscription.*
Superscription, sū-pėr-skrip'shon, *n. Act of superscribing*; that which is written or ngraved on the outside; an impression of letters on coins

Supersede, sū-pėr-sēd', vt. To sit above; to come or be placed in the room of; to displace; to make void or useless; to set aside. ppr. superseding, pret. & pp. superseded. [L. sedeo, to sit.]

Superstition, sū-pėr-sti'shon, n. A standing still or over, as from awe; excessive fear of divine agency; excessive rigour in religious practice; excess in religion; the belief of what is absurd; false religion; excessive nicety; scrupulous exactness; belief in the direct agency of superior powers in certain singular events, or in omens and prognostics. [Fr.—L. sto, statum, to stand.]

Superstitious, sū-pėr-sti'shi-us, a. Given to superstition; over-scrupulous in religious observances; manifesting superstition; scrupulous beyond need. [Fr. superstitieux.]

Superstitiously, sū-pėr-sti'shi-us-li, adv. In a superstitious manner.

Superstructure, sū-pėr-struk'tūr, n. Any structure raised on something else; anything erected on a foundation or basis.

Supervene, sū-pėr-vēn', vi. To come upon, as something extraneous; to happen; to take place. ppr. supervening, pret. & pp. supervened. [L. venio, to come.]

Supervention, sū-pėr-ven'shon, n. Act of supervening.

Supervisal, Supervision, sū-pėr-viz'al, sū-pėr-vi'zhon, n. Act of supervising; inspection; superintendence.

Supervise, sū-pėr-viz', vt. To look over; to oversee. ppr. supervising, pret. & pp. supervised. —n. Inspection. [L. video, visum, to see.]

Supervisor, sū-pėr-viz'or, n. One who supervises; an inspector; an officer in the excise or customs, who has the superintendence of other inferior officers.

Supine, sū-pin', a. Lying on the back; inclining with exposure to the sun; drowsy; listless; thoughtless; inattentive. [L. supinus—sub, under.]

Supinely, sū-pin'li, adv. With the face upward; carelessly; indolently; drowsily.

Supineness, sū-pin'nes, n. State of being supine; listlessness; carelessness.

Supper, sup'ėr, n. The meal that is sipped or supped; the evening meal. [Fr. souper.]

Supperless, sup'ėr-les, a. Wanting supper; being without supper.

Supplant, sup-plant', vt. To trip up the heels of; to take the place of, usually by stratagem; to undermine. [Fr. supplanter—L. planta, the sole of the foot.]

Supplanter, sup-plant'ėr, n. One who supplants.

Supple, sup'l, a. Easily bent; compliant; yielding; fawning; bending to the humour of others; that makes pliant. vt. To make soft and pliant; to render flexible; to make compliant.—vi. To become soft and pliant. ppr. suppling, pret. & pp. suppled. [Fr. souple—L. sub, and plico, to fold.]

Supplement, sup'lē-ment, n. That with which anything is made full; an addition to anything, by which its defects are supplied.—vt. To supply; to add to a writing, &c. [Fr.; L. sub, and pleo, 8ans. pér, to fill.]

Supplemental, Supplementary, sup-lē-ment'al, sup-lē-ment'a-ri, a. Added to supply what is wanted; additional.

Suppleness, sup'l-nes, n. Quality of being supple; pliancy; readiness of compliance; facility.

Suppliant, sup'li-ant, a. Asking humbly on bended knees, and with hands folded; asking earnestly; entreating; expressive of humble supplication.—n. A suppliant; one who entreats submissively. [Fr.—L. supplico, to kneel down—plico, to fold.]

Suppliantly, sup'li-ant-li, adv. In a suppliant or submissive manner.

Supplicant, sup'li-kant, n. One who supplicates; a petitioner who asks submissively. [L. supplicans.]

Supplicate, sup'li-kāt, vt. To implore humbly on bended knees; to address in prayer; to beg; to beseech; to crave. vi. To ask with earnestness and submission; to beg; to petition; to crave. ppr. supplicating, pret. & pp. supplicated. [L. supplico, supplicatus—sub, and plico, to fold.]

Supplication, sup-li-kā'shon, n. Act of supplicating; earnest prayer in worship; entreaty; petition. [Fr.]

Supplicatory, sup'li-kā-tō-ri, a. Containing supplication; submissive.

Supplies, sup-pliz', n. pl. of supply. Things supplied; the sums granted by parliament for defraying the public expenditure for the current year.

Supply, sup-pli', vt. To fill up; to add what is wanted; to afford a sufficiency to; to serve instead of; to fill; to furnish; to afford what is wanted. ppr. supplying, pret. & pp. supplied.—n. That which is supplied; the necessary stores and provisions. [Fr. suppléer.]

Supplyant, sup-pli'ant, a. Supplying.

Supplyment, sup-pli'ment, n. A supplying.

Support, sup-pōrt', vt. To bear or hold up, as weight, &c.; to uphold; to bear; to bear without shrinking, as sufferings; to keep from fainting; to represent well; to supply funds for; to sustain with provisions; to sustain without change; to keep from sinking; to be able to pay; to sustain, as a character; to make good, as charges; to help; to verify; to defend successfully, as a cause; to act as one's attendant on some public occasion by sitting or walking at his side.—n. Act or operation of supporting; that which upholds; a stay; that which maintains life; maintenance; continuance in any state; that which sustains anything; aid; assistance. [Fr. supporter; L. porto, to carry.]

Supportable, sup-pōrt'a-bl, a. That may be supported; that may be borne or endured; endurable; that can be maintained. [Fr.]

Supportably, sup-pōrt'a-bli, adv. In a supportable manner.

Supportance†, sup-pōrt'ans, n. Maintenance.

Supporter, sup-pōrt'ėr, n. One who supports; that which supports or upholds; a comforter; a defender; a vindicator; one who takes part; one who sits by or walks with another, on some public occasion, as an aid or attendant.

Supposable, sup-pōz'a-bl, a. That may be supposed.

Suppose, sup-pōz', vt. To place under; to lay down, as a proposition that may be true, though not known to be true; to admit to exist, for the sake of argument; to presume; to consider; to think; to require to exist or be true. ppr. supposing, pret. & pp. supposed. n.† Supposition. [Fr. supposer—L. pono, positum, to put, place.]

Supposed, sup-pōzd', p.a. Believed; received as true.

Supposer, sup-pōz'ėr, n. One who supposes.

Supposition, sup-pōz-i'shon, n. Act of supposing; act of laying down as true what is not proved; hypothesis; surmise; guess. [L. suppositio.]

Supposititious, sup-pōz'i-ti'shi-us, a. Substituted; put by trick in the place belonging to another; not genuine; counterfeit. [Low L. suppositititius—L. pono, positum, to place.]

Suppress, sup-pres', vt. To press down or under; to put down; to overwhelm; to keep in; to withhold from utterance; to conceal; to retain without making public; to stifle; to obstruct from discharges; to hinder. [L. supprimo, suppressus—premo, to press.]

Suppressed, sup-prest', p.a. Concealed; stopped; obstructed.

Suppression, sup-pre'shon, n. Act of suppressing; concealment; the retaining or keeping back of anything from public notice; the stoppage or morbid retention of discharges; omission, as of words or letters. [Fr.]

Suppressor, sup-pres'or, n. One who suppresses; one who prevents utterance or disclosure.

Suppurate, sup'pū-rāt, vi. To form or generate pus or matter.—vt. To cause to suppurate or form pus. ppr. suppurating, pret. & pp. suppurated. [L. suppūro, suppuratus—pus, puris, pus.]

Suppuration, sup-pū-rā'shon, n. The process of producing pus, as in a wound or abscess; the matter produced by suppuration. [Fr.]

Suppurative, sup'pū-rāt-iv, a. Tending to suppurate; promoting suppuration. n. A medicine that promotes suppuration. [Fr. suppuratif.]

Supramundane, sū-pra-mun'dān, a. Being above the world. [L. supra, and mundus, the world.]

Supremacy, sū-prem'a-si, n. State of being supreme; highest authority; supreme and undivided authority in ecclesiastical affairs, which is either papal or regal. [Fr. suprématie.]

Supreme, sū-prēm', a. Highest; highest in authority; holding the highest place in government; highest or most excellent. [Fr. suprême—L. super, above.]

Supremely, sū-prēm'li, adv. In a supreme manner.

Surcharge, sėr-chärj', vt. To overcharge; to overload; to make an extra charge upon; to overstock. ppr. surcharging, pret. & pp. surcharged.—n. An overcharge; an excessive load or burden; a load greater than can be well borne; an extra charge. [Fr. surcharger—charger, to load.]

Surd, sėrd, a. Primarily, deaf; uttered with simple breath.—n. A quantity of which the root cannot be exactly determined. [L. surdus, deaf.]

Sure, shūr, a. Secure; confident; unfailing; certainly knowing, or having full confidence; safe; stable; steady; strong; certain of obtaining or of retaining; not liable to failure.—adv. Certainly; doubtless. [Fr. sûr—L. securus—se, apart, and cūra, care.]

Surely, shūr'li, adv. Certainly; infallibly.

Suretiship, shūr'ti-ship, n. State of being surety; the obligation of a person to answer for another.

Surety, shūr'ti, n. State of being sure; security; evidence; confirmation; security against loss or damage; one that gives security; a bondsman; a bail; ratification.—vt. To act as surety for. [Fr. sûreté—L. securitas.]

Surf, sėrf, n. The floating or rising of billow upon billow; the swell of the

Fate, fär, fat, fall; mē, met, hėr; pine, pin; nōte, not, mōve; tūbe, tub, bull; oil, pound.

sea which breaks upon the shore, or upon sandbanks or rocks. [Old Fr. *surflot—flotter*, to float.]
Surface, sėr'fās, *n.* The upper face; the exterior part of anything that has length and breadth; the superficies; the upper stratum of the soil. [Fr.—L. *super*, and *facies*, face.]
Surfeit, sėr'fit, *vt.* To overload; to overfeed and produce sickness or uneasiness in; to cloy; to fill to satiety and disgust.—*vi.* To be fed till the system is oppressed.—*n.* Excess in eating or drinking; the feeling of disgust, occasioned by overloading the stomach. [Fr. *sur*, and *faire, fait*, L. *facio, factum*, to make.]
Surfeiting, sėr'fit-ing, *p.n.* Act of feeding to excess; gluttony.
Surfy, sėrf'i, *a. Abounding with surf.*
Surge, sėrj, *n. That which rises or swells up;* the swelling of a wave or billow; a large wave or billow; a great rolling swell of water.—*vi.* To rise up; to swell; to rise high and roll, as waves. *ppr.* surging, *pret. & pp.* surged. [from L. *surgo*, to arise—Heb. *tadrach*, to be manifest, open, clear.]
Surgeon, sėr'jon, *n.* One whose profession is to cure or alleviate diseases or injuries of the body by *manual operation*, sometimes aided by medicines either external or internal. [Old Fr. *chirurgien*—Gr. *cheir*, the hand, and *ergon*, work.]
Surgeoncy, sėr'jon-si, *n. The office or employment of a surgeon* in the naval or military service.
Surgery, sėr'je-ri, *n. The art or profession of a surgeon;* the act of healing diseases and injuries of the body by manual operation; a place where surgical operations are performed.
Surgical, sėr'jik-al, *a. Pertaining to surgeons;* done by means of surgery.
Surgically, sėr'jik-al-li, *adv. In a surgical manner.*
Surging, sėrj'ing, *p.a.* Swelling and rolling, as billows.
Surgy, sėrj'i, *a. Full of surges;* rising in surges or billows.
Surlily, sėr'li-li, *adv. In a surly manner.*
Surliness, sėr'li-nes, *n. Quality or state of being surly;* crabbed ill-nature.
Surly, sėr'li, *a. Sour-like;* crabbed; snarling; cross and rude; dark; tempestuous. [Sax. *surelice*.]
Surmise, sėr-miz', *vt.* To put forth, as an accusation against a person; to imagine without certain knowledge; to infer or suppose. *ppr.* surmising, *pret. & pp.* surmised.—*n.* The imagination that something may be, of which, however, there is no certain or strong evidence; conjecture; doubt. [Norm. *surmys*, alleged, *surmitter*, to accuse—L. *super*, about, and *mitto, missum*, to send.]
Surmising, sėr-miz'ing, *p.n.* The act of suspecting; surmise.
Surmount, sėr-mount', *vt.* To mount or rise above; to be superior to, as difficulties; to vanquish; to subdue; to go beyond. [Fr. *surmonter—monter*, to mount.]
Surmountable, sėr-mount'a-bl, *a. That may be surmounted;* superable.
Surname, sėr'nām, *n. A name over and above* the Christian *name;* the family name of an individual; an appellation added to the original name.—*vt.* To *name* or call by an appellation *added* to the original name. *ppr.* surnaming, *pret. & pp.* surnamed. [Fr. *surnom—* L. *super*, and *nomen*, a name.]
Surpass, sėr-pas', *vt.* To overpass; to go beyond in anything, good or bad; to

excel; to transcend. [Fr. *surpasser— passer*, to pass.]
Surpassable, sėr-pas'a-bl, *a. That may be exceeded.*
Surpassing, sėr-pas'ing, *p.a.* Excellent in an eminent degree; exceeding others.
Surpassingly, sėr-pas'ing-li, *adv.* In a very excellent manner.
Surplice, sėr'plis, *n.* Originally, the garment *worn over the robe of fur;* a white garment worn over their other dress by the clergy of the Roman Catholic, Episcopal, and certain other churches, in some of their ministrations. [Fr. *surplis—*L. *super*, over, and *pellis*, a skin.]
Surplus, sėr'plus, *n. The overplus;* that which remains when use is satisfied; excess beyond what is prescribed. [Fr.—L. *super*, and *plus*, more.]
Surplusage, sėr'plus-āj, *n. Overplus;* surplus.
Surprisal, sėr-priz'al, *n. Act of surprising;* state of being taken unawares.
Surprise, sėr-priz', *vt.* To seize upon; to fall upon suddenly; to strike with astonishment; to throw the mind of into disorder by something suddenly presented. *ppr.* surprising, *pret. & pp.* surprised.—*n. Act of surprising;* state of being taken unexpectedly; an emotion excited by something happening suddenly; astonishment. [Fr. from *surprendre, surpris—*L. *super*, and *prendo*, to seize.]
Surprising, sėr-priz'ing, *p.a.* Exciting surprise; wonderful; astonishing.
Surprisingly, sėr-priz'ing-li, *adv.* In a manner that excites *surprise*.
Surreined†, sėr-rānd', *a.* Overworked.
Surrender, sėr-ren'der, *vt. To deliver up, as one's self;* to deliver up, as possession, upon compulsion or demand; to cede; to yield to any influence or power (with the recipr. pron.)—*vi.* To *yield;* to give up one's self into the power of another.—*n. Act of surrendering;* a yielding or giving up. [Fr. *se rendre—*L. *super*, and *reddo*, to yield.]
Surreptitious, sėr-rep-ti'shi-us,*a. Seized privily;* stolen; done by stealth or without proper authority; made or introduced fraudulently. [Low L. *surreptitius—*L. *sub*, and *rapio*, to seize.]
Surreptitiously, sėr-rep-ti'shi-us-li, *adv.* By stealth; fraudulently.
Surround, sėr-round', *vt. To be, or to be set round about;* to lie or be on all sides of; to encompass; to fence about. [Fr. *sur*, L. *super*, and *rond*, a round.]
Surrounding, sėr-round'ing, *p.a. Encompassing;* being on all sides of.
Surtout, sėr-tö', *n.* That which is *over all;* originally, a man's coat to be worn over his other garments; but in modern usage, an upper coat with wide skirts reaching down to near the knee. [Fr. *sur-tout—*L. *super*, over, and *totus*, all.]
Surveillance, sėr-vāl'yans, *n. A keeping watch over;* oversight; inspection. [Fr. —L. *super*, and *vigilo*, to watch.]
Survey, sėr-vā', *vt. To oversee;* to take a view of; to view with attention, as from a high place; to scrutinize; to measure and value, as land, buildings, &c.; to ascertain, as the position and distances of objects on the shore of the sea, &c.; to examine, as boundaries, value, &c.; to examine and ascertain the condition of. [Norm. *surveer*, to overlook—L. *super*, and *video*, to see.]
Survey, sėr'vā, *n. Act of surveying;* review; examination; an attentive view; a look or looking with care; operation

by which the boundaries of fields, estates, &c., are determined.
Surveying, sėr-vā'ing, *p.n.* The act or art of measuring and delineating portions of land, with their boundaries, divisions, features, &c., and of computing their extent.
Surveyor, sėr-vā'or, *n. One who surveys;* one who views and examines for the purpose of ascertaining the condition or quality of anything; one who measures land, &c.
Surveyorship, sėr-vā'or-ship, *n. The office of a surveyor.*
Survival, sėr-viv'al, *n. A surviving;* a living beyond the life of another.
Survive, sėr-viv', *vt. To outlive;* to live beyond the life of; to live beyond, as any event.—*vi. To remain alive. ppr.* surviving, *pret. & pp.* survived. [Fr. *survivre—*L. *super*, and *vivo*, to live; Gr. *bios*, life—Sans. *jiv*, to live.]
Surviving, sėr-viv'ing, *p.a. Remaining alive;* yet living.
Survivor, sėr-viv'or, *n. One who survives* or outlives another.
Survivorship, sėr-viv'or-ship, *n. State of a survivor;* state of outliving another.
Susceptibility, sus-sep'ti-bil''li-ti, *n. Quality of being susceptible;* capability; sensibility; feeling. [Fr. *susceptibilité*.]
Susceptible, sus-sep'ti-bl, *a. Capable of undertaking or sustaining;* tender; impressible; having nice sensibility. [Fr. —L. *sub*, and *capio*, to take.]
Susceptibly, sus-sep'ti-bli, *adv. In a susceptible manner.*
Suspect, sus-pekt', *vt. To look at from below,* secretly or askance; to distrust; to imagine the existence of, as of something, but without proof; to imagine to be guilty, but upon slight evidence; to hold to be doubtful; to conjecture. *vi. To have suspicion;* to imagine guilt.—*n.*†Suspicion. [L. *suspicio, suspectus—specio*, to look.]
Suspected, sus-pekt'ed, *p.a.* Mistrusted.
Suspend, sus-pend', *vt. To hang up;* to hang; to attach to something above; to intermit; to hold in a state undetermined; to debar from any privilege, from the execution of an office, or from the enjoyment of income; to cause to cease for a time from effect. [Fr. *suspendre—*L. *pendo*, to cause to hang.]
Suspended, sus-pend'ed, *p.a.* Caused to cease for a time; held undetermined.
Suspender, sus-pend'ėr, *n. One who suspends;* (pl.) straps worn for holding up pantaloons, &c.; braces.
Suspense, sus-pens', *n. State of being suspended;* a state of uncertainty; indecision; cessation for a time. [Fr.— L. *pendo*, to cause to hang.]
Suspension, sus-pen'shon, *n. Act of hanging up;* act of making to depend on anything for existence; delay; act of withholding the judgment; temporary cessation; temporary privation of office; prevention of operation. [Fr. —L. *pendo*, to cause to hang.]
Suspicion, sus-pi'shon, *n. Act of suspecting;* the imagination of the existence of something without proof; distrust; diffidence: doubt. [Fr.—L. *sub*, and *specio*, to look.]
Suspicious, sus-pi'shi-us, *a. Full of suspicion;* indicating suspicion; liable to suspicion; giving reason to imagine ill. [L. *suspiciosus*.]
Suspiciously, sus-pi'shi-us-li, *adv. With suspicion;* so as to excite suspicion.
Suspiciousness, sus-pi'shi-us-nes, *n. Quality of being suspicious.*
Suspiration, sus-pi-rā'shon, *n.* The act of sighing.

ch, *chain;* j, *job;* g, *go;* ng, *sing;* ᴡʜ, *then;* th, *thin;* w, *wig;* wh, *whig;* zh, *azure;* † obsolete.

Suspire, sus-pīr′, *vi.* To fetch a long, deep *breath*. [L. *spiro*, to breathe.]

Sustain, sus-tān′, *vt.* To *hold up* from *beneath*; to uphold; to keep alive; to endure without yielding; to suffer; not to dismiss; to maintain as a sufficient ground; to continue, as the sound of notes through their whole length. [L. *sustineo*—*teneo*, to hold.]

Sustainable, sus-tān′a-bl, *a.* That may *be sustained* or maintained.

Sustainer, sus-tān′ėr, *n.* He or that *which sustains*, upholds, or suffers.

Sustaining, sus-tān′ing, *p.a.* Upholding; suffering.

Sustenance, sus′ten-ans, *n.* That which *sustains*; support; that which supports life; food; provisions. [Norm.]

Sustentation, sus-ten-tā′shon, *n.* Act of *sustaining*; preservation from falling; maintenance. [Fr.]

Sutler, sut′lėr, *n.* A *paltry* victualler; a person who follows an army, and sells to the troops provisions and liquors. [G. *sudler*—*sudeln*, to puddle about.]

Sutural, sū-tūr′al, *a.* Relating to a *suture* or seam. [Fr.—L. *suo*, *sūtum*, to sew.]

Suture, sū′tūr, *n.* A *sewing together*; a seam; the uniting of the parts of a wound by stitching; the seam or joint which unites the bones of the skull; the peculiar connection of those bones. [Fr.—L. *suo*, *sutum*, to sew.]

Swab, swob, *vt.* To *sweep* or clean with a mop, as the deck of a ship; to wipe when wet or after washing. *ppr.* swabbing, *pret. & pp.* swabbed.—*n.* That which *sweeps*; a mop for cleaning floors and decks of ships, &c. [Sax. *swebban*.]

Swabber, swob′ėr, *n.* An inferior officer in ships of war, who sees that the ship is *swabbed* and kept clean. [D. *zwabber*.]

Swaddle, swod′l, *vt.* To *swathe*; to bind, as with a bandage; to bind tight with clothes, as an infant. *ppr.* swaddling, *pret. & pp.* swaddled.—*n. pl.* Clothes *bound* tight around the body. [Sax. *swethan*, to bind.]

Swaddling-band, swod′l-ing-band, *n.* A *band* wrapped round an infant.

Swag-bellied, swag′bel-lid, *a.* Having a large belly.

Swagger, swag′ėr, *vi.* To *move in a swinging* insolent way; to bully; to be tumultuously proud.—*n.* An insolent bearing or mode of walking. [Icel. *sveigir*, one who twists—*sveiga*, to shake.]

Swaggerer, swag′ėr-ėr, *n.* One who *swaggers*; a blusterer, &c.

Swaggering, swag′ėr-ing, *p.a.* Blustering; exhibiting an insolent bearing.

Swain, swān, *n.* A *servant*; a country servant employed in husbandry; a rustic; a pastoral youth; a lover. [Sax. *swein*, a servant.]

Swallow, swol′lō, *n.* A well-known migratory bird, which marks the commencement of the summer *heat* by its appearance in temperate regions. [Sax. *swalewe*—*swelan*, to burn.]

Swallow, swol′lō, *vt.* To receive through the *gullet* into the stomach; to absorb; to ingulf; to receive implicitly, as opinions; to appropriate; to occupy; to consume; to seize and waste; to exhaust; to put up with; to bear; to retract; to recant.—*n.* The *gullet*; the throat; as much as is swallowed at once. [Sax. *swelgan*; Old G. *swelgēn*, to gulp down.]

Swallowing, swol′lō-ing, *p.n.* Act of taking into the stomach or of absorbing; the act of receiving implicitly.

Swamp, swomp, *n.* Spongy land; low ground filled with water; soft, wet ground.—*vt.* To sink in a *swamp*; to overset and sink in water; to plunge into inextricable difficulties. [Mid. High G. a fungus, a sponge.]

Swampy, swomp′i, *a.* Consisting of *swamp*; like a swamp.

Swan, swon, *n.* A web-footed bird, of the duck family, and closely resembling the goose, with a very long neck. [Sax.; Sans. *svan*, to sound.]

Sward, sward, *n.* The *grassy surface* of land; that part of the soil which is filled with the roots of grass, forming a kind of mat.—*vt.* To produce sward upon; to cover with sward. [Sax. *sweard*, grass.]

Swardy, sward′i, *a.* Covered with sward or grass.

Sware, swār, *obs. pret.* of *swear*.

Swarm, swarm, *n.* A large number of small animals or insects, particularly when in motion and *humming*; a great number of honey-bees which emigrate from a hive at once; a great number of people in motion; a crowd; a throng. *vi.* To *hum* or *murmur*, as a crowd; to depart from a hive by flight in a body, as bees; to throng together; to be crowded; to breed multitudes. [Sax. *swearm*—G. *schwirren*, to whir.]

Swarming, swarm′ing, *p.a.* Crowding; thronging.

Swarthily, swarth′i-li, *adv.* Duskily; with a tawny hue.

Swarthiness, swarth′i-nes, *n.* State or quality of being *swarthy*; tawniness.

Swarthy, swarth′i, *a.* Being of a dark hue or dusky complexion; tawny; black. [Sax. *sweart*; Old Fris. *swarth*, black, dark.]

Swash, swosh, *vi.* To bluster; to fall violently.

Swath, swath, *n.* A track or row in mown grass; a line of grass or grain cut and thrown together by the scythe in mowing; the whole sweep of a scythe in mowing. [Sax. *swathe*.]

Swathe, swārn, *vt.* To *bind with a band*; to bind or wrap. *ppr.* swathing, *pret. & pp.* swathed.—*n.* A *bandage* or fillet. [Sax. *beswethan*, to bind.]

Sway, swā, *vt.* To *swing*; to wield with the hand; to rule; to govern; to bias; to influence by power or by moral force; to cause to incline to one side. *vi.* To be drawn to one side by weight; to have weight or influence; to govern. *n.* The *swing* of a weapon; weight; power exerted in governing; sovereignty; weight, influence, or authority that inclines to one side. [D. *zwaaijen*, to swing.]

Swayed, swād, *p.a.* Bent down; hollow in the back.

Swear, swār, *vi.* To *utter the very truth*; to make or utter a solemn declaration, with an appeal to God for the *truth* of what is affirmed; to promise upon oath; to give evidence on oath; to be profane.—*vt.* To utter or affirm with a solemn appeal to God for the *truth* of; to cause to take an oath; to declare or charge upon oath. *ppr.* swearing, *pret.* swore, *pp.* sworn. [Sax. *swerian*; Old G. *wār*, truth, *ziwara*, truly.]

Swearer, swār′ėr, *n.* One who *swears*; one who calls God to witness for the truth of his declaration; a profane person.

Swearing, swār′ing, *p.a.* Affirming upon oath; putting upon oath.—*p.n.* Act or practice of affirming on oath; profaneness.

Sweat, swet, *n.* The *moisture* which issues from the skin of an animal; perspiration; labour; drudgery; moisture evacuated from any substance. *vi.* To *emit sweat* from the pores of the skin; to perspire; to toil; to drudge; to emit moisture, as green plants in a heap.—*vt.* To emit from the pores; to cause to perspire or to excrete moisture from the skin. *ppr.* sweating, *pret. & pp.* sweat or sweated. [Sax. *swat*; Icel. *sveiti*.]

Sweater, swet′ėr, *n.* One who causes to *sweat*.

Sweatiness, swet′i-nes, *n.* State of being *sweaty*, or moist with sweat.

Sweaty, swet′i, *a.* Moist with *sweat*; consisting of sweat; laborious.

Swede, swēd, *n.* A *native of Sweden*.

Swedish, swēd′ish, *a.* Pertaining to *Sweden*.—*n.* The language of Sweden.

Sweep, swēp, *vt.* To *clean by brushing*; to carry with a long, swinging, or dragging motion; to carry along by a brushing stroke or force; to carry off in numbers at a stroke; to strike with a long stroke; to draw or drag over; to carry the eye over.—*vi.* To pass or brush along with celerity and force; to pass with pomp; to move with a long reach; to take in a view with progressive rapidity. *ppr.* sweeping. *pret. & pp.* swept.—*n.* Act of *sweeping*; the compass of a stroke; the compass of anything flowing; violent destruction; a chimney-sweeper; a curved road in front of a mansion-house, &c. [Sax. *swapan*; Icel. *sōpa*—Heb. *sicha*, sweepings, *suach*, to sweep away.]

Sweeper, swēp′ėr, *n.* One who *sweeps*.

Sweeping, swēp′ing, *p.a.* Including many individuals in a single act or assertion; exaggerated.

Sweepingly, swēp′ing-li, *adv.* By sweeping.

Sweepings, swēp′ings, *n. pl.* Things *collected by sweeping*; rubbish.

Sweepstakes, swēp′stāks, *n.* One who wins all, or *sweeps* all the *stakes*; the whole money or other things staked or won at a horse-race.

Sweepy, swēp′i, *a.* Passing with a *sweeping* motion, or with speed and violence over a great compass at once; wavy.

Sweet, swēt, *a.* Agreeable to the *taste*; having the taste of honey or sugar; pleasing to the smell; pleasing to the ear; melodious; making soft music; pleasing to the eye; fresh; mild; kind; obliging; not turned or sour; not putrid.—*n.* The *sweetest* part of anything; any vegetable juice which is added to wines to improve them; a perfume; a word of endearment; something pleasing to the mind; (*pl.*) home-made wines, &c.; also, cane-juice, molasses, or other sweet vegetable substance. [Sax. *swet*—Goth. *suts*.]

Sweet-brier, swēt′brī-ėr, *n.* A shrubby plant cultivated for its *fragrant* smell.

Sweeten, swēt′n, *vt.* To *make sweet*; to make pure by destroying noxious ingredients; to make warm and fertile; to make grateful to the mind; to make mild; to make less painful; to soften; to make delicate.—*vi.* To *become sweet*.

Sweetened, swēt′nd, *p.a.* Made *sweet* or grateful.

Sweetener, swēt′n-ėr, *n.* He or that which *sweetens*; he who palliates.

Sweetening, swēt′n-ing, *p.n.* Act of *making sweet*; that which sweetens.

Sweetheart, swēt′härt, *n.* A lover or mistress.

Sweetish, swēt′ish, *a.* Somewhat *sweet* or grateful to the taste.

Fāte, fär, fat, fall; mē, met, hėr; pīne, pin; nōte, not, mōve; tūbe, tub, bull; oil, pound.

Sweetishness, swēt'ish-nes, n. *Quality of being sweetish.*
Sweetly, swēt'li, adv. *In a sweet manner; gratefully.*
Sweetmeat, swēt'mēt, n. *Fruit preserved with sugar, or confectionery made of sugar.*
Sweetness, swēt'nes, n. *Quality of being sweet,* in any of its senses; gratefulness to the taste, to the smell, or to the ear; melody; agreeableness of manners; softness; obliging civility.
Sweet-william, swēt-wil'li-am, n. A plant; a species of pink cultivated in flower-gardens.
Swell, swel, vi. *To rise or be driven into waves or billows; to heave; to enlarge;* to be puffed up; to be bloated with anger; to be inflated; to be turgid; to bulge out; to rise into arrogance; to grow more violent; to grow upon the view; to become larger in amount; to become louder; to look big.—vt. *To increase the dimensions of;* to cause to rise or increase; to heighten; to raise to arrogance; to augment, as the sound of a note. *ppr.* swelling, *pret.* swelled, *pp.* swelled. Swollen is nearly obsolete. n. Extension of bulk; increase, as of sound; the increase of sound in one continued note; a gradual elevation of land; a wave or billow; more generally, a succession of large waves. [Sax. *swellan*—Icel. *vella*, to bubble up.]
Swelled, sweld, *p.a.* Enlarged in bulk; inflated.
Swelling, swel'ing, *p.a.* Tumid; turgid, as style or language.—*p.n.* Act of enlarging; inflation; a tumour, or any morbid enlargement of the natural size; prominence; a rising or enlargement by passion.
Swelter, swel'tėr, vi. *To be overcome and faint with heat;* to be ready to perish with heat.—vt.† To exude, like sweat. [Sax. *sweltan*, to faint; Old G. *suelzan*, to burn.]
Swerve, swėrv, vi. *To wander;* to turn aside from any line prescribed, or from a rule of duty; to deviate; to incline; to climb or move forward by winding or turning. *ppr.* swerving, *pret. & pp.* swerved. [D. *zwerven*, to wander.]
Swerving, swėrv'ing, *p.n.* Act of wandering; deviation from any rule, law, duty, or standard.
Swift, swift, *a. Speedy; quick;* nimble; moving over a large space in a short time; ready; that comes speedily or without delay.—n. A bird belonging to the swallow tribe, and so called from the *rapidity* of its flight; the common newt or eft, a species of lizard. [Sax.—*swifan*, to be turned round.]
Swiftly, swift'li, adv. *Speedily;* fleetly.
Swiftness, swift'nes, n. *Quality of being swift;* velocity; fleetness; expedition.
Swill, swil, *vi. To swallow* large draughts; to drink grossly or greedily. *vt.* To wash; to drench.—n. Large draughts of liquor, or drink taken in excessive quantities; the wash or mixture of liquid substances given to swine. [Sax. *swilgan*, to swallow.]
Swiller, swil'ėr, n. *One who swills.*
Swim, swim, vi. *To float;* to be supported on water or other fluid; not to sink; to move progressively in water by means of the motion of the hands and feet, or of fins; to glide along with a smooth motion; to be overflowed; to abound; [Icel. *sveima*, to be carried round about—*svim*, giddiness] *to be dizzy;* to have a waving motion of the head, or a sensation of that kind, or a reeling of the body.—vt. *To pass by swimming;* to immerse in water, that the lighter parts may swim. *ppr.* swimming, *pret.* swam, *pp.* swum.—n. The bladder of fishes, by which they are said to be supported in water. [Sax. *swimman.*]
Swimmer, swim'ėr, n. *One who swims;* one of an order of web-footed birds that swim, as the duck and goose.
Swimming, swim'ing, *p.a.* Overflowing; abounding.—*p.n.* The act or art of moving on the water by means of the limbs; dizziness.
Swimmingly, swim'ing-li, adv. Smoothly; without obstruction.
Swindle, swin'dl, vt. *To render giddy,* and in that state to defraud; to cheat grossly, or with deliberate artifice. *ppr.* swindling, *pret. & pp.* swindled. [D. *zwindelen*, to be giddy.]
Swindler, swin'dl-ėr, n. *A cheat;* one who defrauds grossly; one who makes a practice of defrauding others by imposition. [G. *schwindler*.]
Swindling, swin'dl-ing, *p.a.* Cheating; defrauding.—*p.n.* Act of defrauding; knavery.
Swine, swin, n. *s.* and *pl.* A hog; a pig; (pl.) hogs collectively. [Sax. *swin.*]
Swineherd, swin'hėrd, n. *A keeper of swine.*
Swing, swing, vi. *To move to and fro,* as a body suspended in the air; to vibrate; to practise swinging; to turn round at anchor, as a ship; to be hanged.—vt. *To move to and fro;* to make to play loosely; to cause to wave; to whirl round in the air; to flourish. *ppr.* swinging, *pret. & pp.* swung.—n. A *waving motion;* oscillation; an apparatus suspended for persons to swing in; free course; unrestrained liberty; the compass of a moving body; unrestrained tendency. [Sax. *swengan*.]
Swinge, swinj, vt. *To beat soundly;* to move as a lash. *ppr.* swinging, *pret. & pp.* swinged.
Swinge-buckler†, swinj'buk-lėr, n. A bully.
Swinging, swing'ing, *p.a.* Waving; vibrating.—*p.n. Act of swinging.*
Swinish, swin'ish, *a. Befitting swine;* like swine; gross; brutal.
Swinishly, swin'ish-li, adv. *In a swinish manner.*
Swinishness, swin'ish-nes, n. *Quality of being swinish.*
Swiss, swis, n. *A native of Switzerland;* the language of Switzerland.
Switch, swich, n. *A small* flexible *twig* or rod.—vt. *To strike with a small twig* or rod; to beat; to lash. [G. *sweig*, a branch.]
Swivel, swi'vel, n. *That which turns round;* that which is so fixed as to turn or sweep round; a ring which turns upon a staple, or a strong link of iron used in mooring ships; a cannon which turns on a swivel. [Sax. *swifan*, to be turned round.]
Swoon, swön, vi. *To fail; to fall away;* to faint; to sink into a fainting-fit, in which there is an apparent suspension of the vital functions and mental powers.—n. *Act of swooning;* a fainting-fit; syncope. [Sax. *aswunan*, to swoon; Old G. *swinan*, to languish.]
Swooning, swön'ing, n. Act of fainting; syncope.
Swoop, swöp, vt. *To take or seize with a sweeping action;* to fall on at once and seize; to catch while on the wing. n. A falling on and seizing, as of a rapacious fowl on his prey. [from *sweep.*]
Sword, sōrd, n. *A warlike defensive* and offensive weapon worn at the side; destruction by war; vengeance or justice; emblem of authority; war; emblem of triumph and protection. [Sax. *sweord;* Old G. *werjan*, to defend.]
Sword-bayonet, sōrd'bā-on-et, n. A *bayonet* longer than the common one, and generally used with a rifle.
Sword-fish, sōrd'fish, n. *A fish* having the upper jaw elongated so as to resemble a *sword.* It belongs to the mackerel tribe, and measures from ten to fifteen feet in length.
Sword-hand, sōrd'hand, n. The *hand* holding the *sword;* the right hand.
Sword-player, sōrd'plā-ėr, n. *A gladiator;* one who exhibits his skill in the use of the sword.
Swordsman, sōrdz'man, n. *A man who carries a sword;* a fighting-man.
Swordsmanship, sōrdz'man-ship, n. *Skilful use of the sword.*
Sycamore, si'ka-mōr, n. *The fig-mulberry,* an Egyptian kind that bears its fruit on the branches, and has leaves like the white mulberry. [Gr. *sūkomōros—sūkon*, a fig, and *mōron*, the mulberry.]
Sycophancy, si'kō-fan-si, n. *The conduct of a sycophant;* mean tale-bearing; obsequious flattery. [Gr. *sūkophantia.*]
Sycophant, si'kō-fant, n. Said to have been originally an *informer* against those who stole *figs,* or exported them from Attica contrary to law, &c.; a tale-bearer or informer in general; a parasite; a mean flatterer; a flatterer of princes and great men; an impostor. [Gr. *sūkophantēs—sūkon*, a fig, and *phainō*, to show, to inform against.]
Sycophantic, si-kō-fant'ik, *a. Like a sycophant;* obsequiously flattering; parasitic. [Gr. *sūkophantikos.*]
Syllabic, sil-lab'ik, *a. Pertaining to* or consisting of a *syllable* or *syllables.*
Syllabically, sil-lab'ik-al-li, adv. *In a syllabic manner.*
Syllabicate, sil-lab'i-kāt, vt. *To form into syllables. ppr.* syllabicating, *pret. & pp.* syllabicated.
Syllabification, sil-lab'i-fi-kā″shon, n. The act or method of dividing words into *syllables.* [L. *syllaba,* and *facio,* to make.]
Syllable, sil'la-bl, n. *Several letters taken together,* so as to form one sound; a part of a word consisting of one, two, or more letters, uttered with a single impulse of the voice; one or more letters which represent such syllables in written language; something proverbially concise. [L. *syllaba*—Gr. *sun,* and *lambanō,* to take.]
Syllabus, sil'la-bus, n. *A collection of particulars;* an abstract; a compendium containing the heads of a discourse, &c. [L.]
Syllogism, sil'lō-jizm, n. *A reckoning all together;* a bringing together of premisses, and drawing a conclusion from them; a form of reasoning consisting of three propositions, of which the first two are called the *premisses,* and the last the *conclusion.* [L. *syllogismus*—Gr. *sun,* with, and *logizomai,* to reckon.]
Syllogistic, sil-lō-jis'tik, *a. Pertaining to a syllogism;* consisting of a syllogism. [Gr. *sullogistikos.*]
Syllogistically, sil-lō-jis'tik-al-li, adv. *In the form of a syllogism;* by means of syllogisms.
Syllogize, sil'lō-jiz, vi. *To reason by syllogisms. ppr.* syllogizing, *pret. & pp.* syllogized. [Gr. *sullogizomai—sun,* and *logos,* discourse, reason.]

Sylph, silf, *n*. An imaginary being inhabiting the air. [Fr. *sylphe*—Gr. *silphē*, a kind of beetle.]
Sylphid, silf'id, *n*. A diminutive of *sylph*. [Fr. *sylphide*.]
Sylvan, sil'van, *a*. See SILVAN.
Symbol, sim'bol, *n*. A sign by which one knows or infers a thing; an emblem; a type; a figure; that which represents something else, as the elements in the Lord's supper; a character which is significant; the creed. [L. *symbŏlum*—Gr. *sun*, and *ballō*, to throw, infer.]
Symbolic, Symbolical, sim-bol'ik, sim-bol'ik-al, *a*. Serving as a symbol; representative; exhibiting or expressing by resemblance or signs. [Gr. *sumbolikos*.]
Symbolically, sim-bol'ik-al-li, *adv*. By representation; by signs; typically.
Symbolism, sim'bol-izm, *n*. An exposition or comparison of symbols or creeds.
Symbolize, sim'bol-iz, *vi*. To be symbolical; to have a resemblance of qualities; to hold the same faith or religious belief.—*vt*. To represent by a symbol or symbols; to make representative of. *ppr*. symbolizing, *pret. & pp*. symbolized. [Fr. *symboliser*.]
Symbolizer, Symbolist, sim'bol-iz-ėr, sim'bol-ist, *n*. One addicted to the use of symbols.
Symmetrical, sim-met'rik-al, *a*. Exhibiting symmetry; proportional in its parts; having its parts in due proportion as to dimensions. [Fr. *symétrique*.]
Symmetrically, sim-met'rik-al-li, *adv*. With symmetry.
Symmetrize, sim'me-triz, *vt*. To make symmetrical; to make proportional in its parts. *ppr*. symmetrizing, *pret. & pp*. symmetrized. [Fr. *symétriser*.]
Symmetry, sim'me-tri, *n*. State or quality of having one part commensurate with another; a due proportion of the several parts of a body to each other; the conformity of the members of a work to the whole; harmony of parts; proportion. [Fr. *symétrie*—Gr. *sun*, with, and *metron*, a measure.]
Sympathetic, sim-pa-thet'ik, *a*. Pertaining to sympathy; producing sympathy; susceptible of being affected by feelings like those of another; compassionate. [Fr. *sympathique*.]
Sympathetically, sim-pa-thet'ik-al-li, *adv*. With sympathy.
Sympathize, sim'pa-thiz, *vi*. To have or to feel sympathy; to be affected by feelings similar to those of another. *ppr*. sympathizing, *pret. & pp*. sympathized. [Fr. *sympathiser*.]
Sympathizing, sim'pa-thiz-ing, *p.a*. Feeling or expressing sympathy; tender; compassionate.
Sympathy, sim'pa-thi, *n*. Mutual feeling; compassion; like feeling; fellow-feeling; the quality of being affected by the condition of another, with feelings correspondent in kind, if not in degree; an agreement of inclinations; a correspondence of various parts of the body in similar sensations; an affection of the whole body in consequence of disease of another part; (pl.) mutual passion. [Fr. *sympathie*—Gr. *sun*, with, and *pathein*, to receive an impression from without.]
Symphonious, sim-fō'ni-us, *a*. Agreeing in sound; harmonious.
Symphonist, sim'fō-nist, *n*. A composer of symphonies.
Symphony, sim'fō-ni, *n*. An agreeing together in sound; unison of sound; a harmony of sounds agreeable to the ear; a musical composition for a full band of instruments; a term applied to the instrumental introductions, &c., of vocal compositions. [Fr. *symphonie*—Gr. *sun*, with, and *phōnē*, a sound—Sans. *svan*, to sound.]
Symposium, sim-pō'zi-um, *n*. A drinking together; a merry feast. [L.—Gr. *sun*, and *posis*, a drinking—*pinō*, Sans. *pā*, to drink.]
Symptom, sim'tom, *n*. Something that befalls in concurrence with another thing; that which indicates disease; that which indicates the existence of something else. [Fr. *symptome*—Gr. *sun*, with, and *piptō*, to fall.]
Symptomatic, sim-tom-at'ik, *a*. Pertaining to symptoms; happening in concurrence with something; indicating the existence of something else; noting a disease which proceeds from some prior disorder in some part of the body.
Symptomatically, sim-tom-at'ik-al-li, *adv*. By means of symptoms.
Synagogue, sin'a-gog, *n*. An assembly; a congregation of Jews, met for the purpose of worship; the house appropriated to the religious worship of the Jews. [Fr.—Gr. *sun*, together, and *agō*, to bring.]
Synchronism, sin'kron-izm, *n*. Concurrence of two or more events in time; the tabular arrangement of history according to dates, contemporary persons or events being brought together. [Gr. *sun*, and *chronos*, time.]
Synchronous, sin'kron-us, *a*. Happening at the same time; simultaneous. [Gr. *sun* and *chronos*.]
Syncopate, sin'kō-pāt, *vt*. To beat together; to cut short; to contract, as a word, by taking one or more letters or syllables from the middle; to end, as a note of one part in the middle of a note of another part. *ppr*. syncopating, *pret. & pp*. syncopated. [Gr. *sun*, and *koptō*, to cut, beat.]
Syncopated, sin'kō-pāt-ed, *p.a*. Contracted by the loss of a letter from the middle of the word.
Syncopation, sin-kō-pā'shon, *n*. Act of syncopating; the contraction of a word; an interruption of the regular measure in music.
Syncope, sin'kō-pē, *n*. A cutting short; a contraction; an elision of one or more letters or a syllable from the middle of a word; suspension; a fainting or swooning; a pause. [Gr. *sunkopē*—*sun*, and *koptō*, to cut.]
Syndic, sin'dik, *n*. One who helps in a court of justice; an advocate; an officer of government, invested with different powers in different countries. [Fr.—Gr. *sun*, and *dikē*, justice.]
Synecdoche, sin-ek'do-kē, *n*. A taking one thing with another; a figure in rhetoric by which the whole of a thing is put for a part, or a part for the whole. [Gr. *sunekdochē*—*sun, ek*, and *dechomai*, to take.]
Synecdochical, sin-ek-dok'ik-al, *a*. Expressed by synecdoche.
Synod, sin'od, *n*. A coming together; a meeting; a council; a council of ecclesiastics to consult on matters of religion; among Presbyterians, an assembly consisting of several adjoining presbyteries. [Fr. *synode*—Gr. *sun*, and *hodos*, a way.]
Synodal, sin'od-al, *a*. Pertaining to or occasioned by a synod.
Synodic, sin-od'ik, *a*. Pertaining to a synod; transacted in a synod; pertaining to the period in which two heavenly bodies pass from one conjunction to another. [Fr. *synodique*.]
Synodically, sin-od'ik-al-li, *adv*. By the authority of a synod.
Synonyme, sin'ō-nim, *n*. One of two or more words in the same language, which are the precise equivalents of each other. [Gr. *sunōnumia*—*sun*, and *onoma*, a name.]
Synonymous, sin-on'im-us, *a*. Relating to synonymes; having the same meaning; expressing the same thing. [Gr. *sunōnumos*, of like name or meaning.]
Synonymously, sin-on'im-us-li, *adv*. In a synonymous manner.
Synopsis, sin-op'sis, *n*. A viewing all together; a collection of things or parts so arranged as to exhibit the whole or the principal parts in a general view. [Gr.—*sun*, and *opsis*, a view.]
Synoptical, sin-op'tik-al, *a*. Relating to a synopsis; affording a general view of the whole, or of the principal parts of a thing. [Gr. *synoptikos*.]
Synoptically, sin-op'tik-al-li, *adv*. In a synoptical manner.
Syntactic, Syntactical, sin-tak'tik, sin-tak'tik-al, *a*. Pertaining to syntax; according to the rules of syntax or construction.
Syntactically, sin-tak'tik-al-li, *adv*. In conformity to syntax.
Syntax, sin'taks, *n*. A putting together in order; an arrangement; the due arrangement of words in sentences, according to established usage. [Gr. *suntaxis*—*sun*, and *taxis*, an ordering—*tassō*, to put in order.]
Synthesis, sin'the-sis, *n*. A putting together; the putting of two or more things together, as in compound medicines; that process of reasoning in which we advance by a regular chain from principles before established till we arrive at the conclusion; the opposite of analysis. [Gr. *sun*, and *thesis*, a placing—*tithēmi*, to place.]
Synthetic, Synthetical, sin-thet'ik, sin-thet'ik-al, *a*. Pertaining to synthesis; consisting in synthesis or composition. [Gr. *sunthetikos*.]
Synthetically, sin-thet'ik-al-li, *adv*. By synthesis; by composition.
Syphon, si'fon, *n*. See SIPHON.
Syren, si'ren, *n*. See SIREN.
Syriac, si'ri-ak, *a*. Pertaining to Syria or its language.—*n*. The language of Syria, especially the ancient language of that country.
Syrian, si'ri-an, *a*. Pertaining to Syria. *n*. A native of Syria.
Syringe, si'rinj, *n*. A pipe or tube; an instrument for injecting liquids into animal bodies, into wounds, &c., or an instrument in the form of a pump, serving to draw in any fluid, and then to expel it with force.—*vt*. To inject by means of a pipe or syringe; to wash and cleanse by injections from a syringe. *ppr*. syringing, *pret. & pp*. syringed. [Gr. *surinx*, a pipe.]
Syrup, si'rup. See SIRUP.
System, sis'tem, *n*. That which is formed of parts placed together; a connected view of all the truths of some department of knowledge; an assemblage of things adjusted into a regular whole; a harmonious arrangement of bodies with respect to one another; order. [Fr. *système*—Gr. *sun*, and *histēmi*, to place or set.]
Systematic, sis-tem-at'ik, *a*. Pertaining to system; consisting in system; proceeding according to system or regular method. [Fr. *systématique*—Gr. *sustēmatikos*—*histēmi*, to set.]

SYSTEMATICALLY 393 TAKE

Systematically, sis-tem-at′ik-al-li, *adv.* In the form of a system; methodically.
Systematise, sis′tem-at-īz, *vt.* To reduce to a system or regular method. *ppr.*

systematizing, *pret. & pp.* systematized.
Systole, sis′tō-lē, *n. A drawing together;* a shortening; the shortening of a long syllable; the contraction of the heart and arteries for expelling the blood and carrying on the circulation. [Gr. *sustolē—sun*, and *stellō*, to send.]

T.

Tabard, ta′bärd, *n.* A sort of tunic or mantle formerly worn over the armour, covering the body before and behind, but open at the sides. [Norm.]
Tabbied, ta′bid, *a.* Watered; made wavy.
Tabby, ta′bi, *n.* A term formerly applied to certain figured silks upon which an irregular pattern had been stamped, giving rise to the appearance called watering.—*a.* Having a wavy appearance; brindled, as a cat.—*vt.* To water or cause to look wavy. *ppr.* tabbying, *pret. & pp.* tabbied. [Fr. *tabis*; Heb. *tabagh*, to press in.]
Tabernacle, ta′bėr-na-kl, *n.* A temporary habitation constructed of boards; a tent; among the Jews, a movable building, containing the ark, the showbread, &c.; a sacred place; our natural body; an ornamented representation of an edifice placed on the Roman Catholic altars as a receptacle of the consecrated vessels.—*vi.* To dwell; to reside for a time; to be housed. *ppr.* tabernacling, *pret. & pp.* tabernacled. [L. *tabernaculum*, a tent —*tabula*, a board.]
Tabid, ta′bid, *a.* Wasted by disease; emaciated. [L. *tabidus—tabeo*, to waste away.]
Tablature, tab′la-tūr, *n.* Something in a tabular form; a painting or writing in tabular form; a single piece, comprehended in one view, and formed according to one design; a division or parting of the skull into two tables. [Fr.—L. *tabula*, a board.]
Table, ta′bl, *n.* A flat surface of some extent, or a thing that has a flat surface; an article of furniture; fare; the persons sitting at table; a tablet; a surface on which anything is written; a picture, or something that exhibits a view of anything on a flat surface; a smooth, simple architectural ornament; the board on which backgammon is played; (pl.) the game itself; a division of the skull; an index; many particulars brought into one view; a slab, a leaf, a tablet; a list; a catalogue; a division of the ten commandments.—*a.* Relating to a table; plane; level.—*vt.* To lay or place upon a table; to form into a table; to enter upon the record. *ppr.* tabling, *pret. & pp.* tabled. [Fr.—L. *tabula*, a board.]
Table-cloth, ta′bl-kloth, *n.* A cloth for covering a table, particularly at meals.
Table-cover, ta′bl-kuv-ėr, *n.* A cloth laid on a table between meal times.
Table-land, ta′bl-land, *n.* Elevated, flat land.
Tablet, tab′let, *n.* A small table; something flat, on which to write, paint, draw, or engrave; (pl.) a small pocket memorandum-book; a species of solid medicine. [Fr. *tablette*, dimin. of *table*.]
Table-talk, ta′bl-tak, *n.* Conversation at table or at meals.

Tabling, ta′bl-ing, *p.n.* A forming into tables; a setting down in order.
Tabour, ta′bor, *n.* That which is struck or beaten upon; a small drum used as an accompaniment to a pipe or fife. *vi.* To strike lightly and frequently. [Old Fr.—Gr. *tuptō*, to strike.]
Tabouret, ta′bor-et, *n. A small tabour.* [from *tabour*.]
Tabret, ta′bret, *n.* A tabouret or small tabour.
Tabular, ta′bū-lär, *a.* In the form of a table; having a flat surface; having the form of plates; set down in tables; set in squares. [L. *tabulāris—tabula*, a table.]
Tabularly, ta′bū-lär-li, *adv. In a tabular manner.*
Tabulate, ta′bū-lāt, *vt.* To reduce to tables or synopses; to shape with a flat surface. *ppr.* tabulating, *pret. & pp.* tabulated.
Tabulation, ta-bū-lā′shon, *n.* The act of throwing data into a tabular form.
Tache, tash, *n.* See TACK.
Tacit, ta′sit, *a. Silent;* implied, but not expressed in words. [Fr. *tacite*—L. *taceo*, to be silent.]
Tacitly, ta′sit-li, *adv.* Silently.
Taciturn, ta′si-tėrn, *a. Habitually silent;* not apt to talk or speak. [L. *taciturnus—taceo*, to be silent.]
Taciturnity, ta-si-tėrn′i-ti, *n.* Habitual silence or reserve in speaking. [Fr. *taciturnité*.]
Tack, tak, *vt. To attach;* to fasten to anything; to fasten slightly by nails or tacks.—*n. A fastening;* a hold; a small nail; [Sw. Goth. *taga*, to go forward] the course of a ship in regard to the position of her sails.—*vi.* To change the course of a ship by shifting the tacks and position of the sails from one side to the other. [Fr. *attacher*—G. *zacke*, a spike.]
Tackle, tak′l, *n.* Ropes and other instruments used in action or for equipment; the rigging and apparatus of a ship; a machine for raising heavy weights, consisting of a rope and blocks.—*vt.* To seize; to lay hold of. *ppr.* tackling, *pret. & pp.* tackled. [G. *takeln*, to rig; Icel. *tog*, a rope.]
Tackling, tak′l-ing, *p.n.* Furniture of the masts and yards of a ship, as cordage, sails, &c.; instruments of action.
Tact, takt, *n. Touch;* feeling; peculiar skill; nice discernment; adroitness in adapting to circumstances words or actions; dexterity. [Fr.—L. *tactus*, touch—*tango*, to touch.]
Tactical, tak′tik-al, *a. Pertaining to tactics;* pertaining to the art of military and naval dispositions. [Gr. *taktikos*.]
Tactically, tak′tik-al-li, *adv. In a tactical manner.*
Tactician, tak-ti′shi-an, *n.* One versed in tactics.
Tactics, tak′tiks, *n. pl. The art of arranging;* the science and art of disposing military and naval forces in order for battle, and performing military and naval evolutions. [Gr. *hē taktikē (technē*, art), the art of drawing up soldiers in array—*tassō*, to put in order.]
Taction, tak′shon, *n. The act of touching;* touch; contact. [Fr.—L. *tango*, to touch.]
Tadpole, tad′pōl, *n. A young toad;* a frog in its first state from the spawn. [Sax. *tade*, a toad, and *fola*, a young animal.]
Tafferel, **Taffrail**, ta′fe-rel, taf′rāl, *n.* The upper part of a ship's stern, which is flat like a table on the top. [D. *tafereel*, pannel—*tafel*, a table.]
Taffeta, ta′fe-ta, *n.* A fine, smooth stuff of silk, having usually a remarkably wavy lustre. [Fr. *tafetas*.]
Tag, tag, *n.* A metallic point put to the end of a string; something mean and paltry; the rabble.—*vt.* To fit with an end or metallic point, as lace; to append to. *ppr.* tagging, *pret. & pp.* tagged. [Icel. *taggr*, a point.]
Tag-rag, tag′rag, *n.* The rabble.
Tail, tāl, *n.* The part of an animal which terminates its body behind, generally covered with hair; the lower part, noting inferiority; anything hanging long; a catkin; the hinder part of anything; retinue; the followers of a chieftain. [Sax. *tœgl*—Goth. *tagl*, hair.]
Tail, tāl, *n.* In law, an estate in tail is a limited fee; an estate limited to certain heirs, and from which the other heirs are cut off or precluded. [Norm. *tailler*, to limit—*taillez*, entailed.]
Tailor, ta′lor, *n. One who cuts out and sews cloth;* one whose occupation is to cut out and make men's garments. [Fr. *tailleur—tailler*, to cut.]
Tailoring, ta′lor-ing, *p.n. The business of a tailor.*
Tail-piece, tāl′pēs, *n. A piece at the end,* as of a series of engravings.
Taint, tānt, *vt. To tinge;* to dye; to imbue; to contaminate; to pollute; to corrupt; to vitiate; to poison.—*vi. To be tainted;* to be touched with something corrupting; to be affected with incipient putrefaction.—*n. Tincture;* stain; corruption; a stain; a blemish on reputation. [Fr. *teindre*, pp. *teint*; L. *tingo*, *tinctum*, to tinge.]
Tainted, tānt′ed, *p. a.* Impregnated with something noxious; infected.
Tainture†, tānt′ūr, *n.* Defilement.
Take, tāk, *vt. To lay hold of;* to seize; to receive, as what is offered; to get into one's power for keeping; to receive with a certain affection of mind; to catch by surprise; to make prisoner; to captivate with pleasure; to delight; to ensnare; to understand in a particular sense; to employ; to agree to; to close with; to form and adopt; to embrace; to receive, as an impression; to suffer; to endure; to obtain by active exertion; to receive into the mind; to

ch, *chain*; j, *job*; g, *go*; ng, *sing*; ᴛʜ, *then*; th, *thin*; w, *wig*; wh, *whig*; zh, *azure*; † obsolete.

swallow, as meat or drink; to choose; to copy; to accept; to adopt; to draw; to assume; to understand; to have recourse to; to hire; to obtain possession of on lease; to draw; to paint; to gain possession of by force; to require.—*vi.* To move or direct the course; to resort to; to please; to have the intended effect; to fix or be fixed. *ppr.* taking, *pret.* took, *pp.* taken. [Sax. *tacan;* Goth. *teikan,* to touch.]

Taker, tāk'ėr, *n. One who takes.*

Taking, tāk'ing, *p.a.* Alluring; attracting.—*p.n. Act of gaining possession;* a seizing; agitation; distress of mind.

Takingly, tāk'ing-li, *adv.* In a *taking* or attractive *manner.*

Talc, talk, *n.* A magnesian mineral, *tallowy* or *unctuous* to the touch. [G. *talk*—*talg,* tallow.]

Talcky, talk'i, *a. Like talc;* consisting of talc; containing talc.

Tale, tāl, *n. Something told;* a story; a narrative; the rehearsal of a series of adventures; an incident; oral relation; reckoning; number reckoned; information; disclosure of anything secret. [from *tell.*]

Tale-bearer, tāl'bār-ėr, *n. A person who officiously tells tales;* one who impertinently communicates intelligence and makes mischief.

Tale-bearing, tāl'bār-ing, *p.n.* Communication of secrets maliciously.

Talent, ta'lent, *n.* A thing *lifted up* and *weighed;* anciently a certain weight and denomination of money; the Jewish talent being in value about £396 sterling, and the Attic £243, 15s.; faculty; natural gift, a metaphorical application of the word, said to be borrowed from the scriptural parable of the talents; eminent abilities; superior powers of execution. [L. *talentum*—Gr. *talanton,* a thing weighed—*tlaō,* to bear.]

Talented, ta'lent-ed, *p.a. Possessing* skill or *talents.*

Talisman, ta'lis-man, *n. A charm;* a *spell;* a magical figure cut or engraved under certain superstitious observances of the configuration of the heavens; something that produces extraordinary effects. [Gr. *telesma,* incantation—*teleō,* to complete.]

Talismanic, ta-lis-man'ik, *a. Having the properties of a talisman* or preservative against evils; magical.

Talk, tąk, *vi.* To converse familiarly; to speak, as in familiar discourse, when two or more persons interchange thoughts (with *of*); to speak impertinently; to give account; to reason; to confer.—*n. Act of talking;* speech; familiar converse; that which is uttered by one person in familiar conversation, or the mutual converse of two or more; rumour; subject of discourse. [Dan. *tolke,* to interpret.]

Talkative, tąk'a-tiv, *a. Given to much talking;* loquacious; prating.

Talkatively, tąk'a-tiv-li, *adv. In a talkative* manner.

Talkativeness, tąk'a-tiv-nes, *n. The habit of talking* much; loquacity.

Talker, tąk'ėr, *n. One who talks.*

Talking, tąk'ing, *p.a. Given to talking;* loquacious.—*p.n.* Act of conversing familiarly.

Tall, tąl, *a. Elevated* in stature; lofty; long and comparatively slender; brave; bold. [W. *tál,* towering—Sans. *tul,* to lift up.]

Tallness, tąl'nes, *n. State or quality of being tall;* loftiness; height of stature.

Tallow, tal'lō, *n. Grease;* the fat of oxen, sheep, deer, &c., melted and separated from the fibrous matter which is naturally mixed with it.—*vt. To grease with tallow.* [Dan. *tælle*—Sax. *telgan,* to smear.]

Tallowy, tal'lō-i, *a. Having the qualities of tallow;* greasy.

Tally, tal'li, *n.* A piece of wood on which notches *are cut,* as the marks of number, such pieces being formerly used in keeping accounts; one thing made to suit another.—*vt.* To *score* with correspondent notches; to fit; to suit; to make to correspond.—*vi.* To be fitted; to correspond. *ppr.* tallying, *pret. & pp.* tallied. [from Fr. *tailler,* to cut.]

Tally-ho, tal'li-hō". The huntsman's cry to his hounds.

Talon, ta'lon, *n.* The claw of a bird or fowl. [Fr.—L. *talus,* the heel.]

Tamable, tām'a-bl, *a. That may be tamed;* capable of being reclaimed from wildness; that may be subdued.

Tamableness, tām'a-bl-nes, *n. Quality of being tamable.*

Tamarind, ta'ma-rind, *n.* A genus of leguminous plants, of two species, the East Indian and the West Indian, which yield the fruit called tamarinds. [Fr. *tamarin;* Hind. *tumur-hindee,* the date of India.]

Tambour, tam'bör, *n. A small drum* used by the Biscayans as an accompaniment to the flageolet; a species of embroidery in which threads of gold and silver are worked in leaves, flowers, &c.; also, a frame resembling a drum, on which it is worked.—*vi. To embroider on a tambour.* [Sp. *tambor.*]

Tambourine, tam-bö-rēn', *n. A small drum;* a shallow drum with only one skin, played on with the hand, and having bells at the sides. [Fr. *tambourin.*]

Tame, tām, *a. Subdued;* depressed; quiet; gentle; mild; that has lost its native wildness and shyness; accustomed to man.—*vt. To subdue;* to conquer; to make gentle and decent; to reclaim; to reduce from a wild to a domestic state; to civilize. *ppr.* taming, *pret. & pp.* tamed. [Sax. *tam*—Goth. *gatamjan,* to subdue.]

Tamed, tāmd, *p.a.* Domesticated; made gentle.

Tamely, tām'li, *adv.* Servilely.

Tameness, tām'nes, *n. Quality of being tame;* a state of domestication; meanness in bearing insults or injuries; want of spirit.

Tamer, tām'ėr, *n. One who tames.*

Taming, tām'ing, *p.n. Act of rendering tame.*

Tamper, tam'pėr, *vi. To try often;* to meddle; to have to do with without necessity; to practise secretly. [probably a frequent. from *tempt,* to try.]

Tampering, tam'pėr-ing, *p.n.* Act of meddling or practising secretly.

Tampion, Tompion, tam'pi-on, tom'pi-on, *n.* The *stopper* of a cannon or other piece of ordnance. [Fr. *tampon.*]

Tan, tan, *n.* The bark of the *oak,* &c., bruised and broken by a mill for *tanning* hides; a yellowish brown colour; a yellowish spot on the face.—*a. Tawny;* relating to or resembling tan.—*vt.* To soak or imbue with a decoction of *oak bark;* to make of the colour of a decoction of oak bark; to imbrown by exposure to the rays of the sun. *ppr.* tanning, *pret. & pp.* tanned. [Old Fr. the bark of young oak.]

Tang, tang, *n. A strong taste;* something that leaves a sting or pain behind.—*vt.* To cause to sound loudly. [Gr. *tanggos,* rancid.]

Tangency, tan'jen-si, *n. The state or quality of being tangent.*

Tangent, tan'jent, *n. A touching line;* a right line which touches a circle or curve, but which, when produced, does not cut it. [Fr. *tangente*—L. *tango,* to touch.]

Tangential, tan-jen'shi-al, *a. Pertaining to a tangent.*

Tangibility, tan-ji-bil'i-ti, *n. Quality of being tangible;* quality of being perceptible to the touch or sense of feeling.

Tangible, tan'ji-bl, *a. That may be touched;* perceptible by the touch; that may be possessed or realized. [Fr.—L. *tango,* to touch.]

Tangibly, tan'ji-bli, *adv.* Perceptibly to *the touch.*

Tangle, tang'gl, *vt.* To knit together confusedly, as *hair;* to interweave, as threads, so as to make it difficult to ravel the knot; to implicate; to entrap; to embarrass. (Better *entangle.*) *vi. To be entangled* or united confusedly. *ppr.* tangling, *pret. & pp.* tangled.—*n.* A knot of *hairs* or other things united confusedly. [Goth. *tagl,* hair.]

Tangled, tang'gld, *p.a.* United confusedly.

Tank, tangk, *n.* A reservoir of *standing water;* a large basin or cistern; a case of sheet-iron for the stowage of the ship's water; that part of the tender of a locomotive engine which contains the water for supplying the boiler. [Fr. *étang,* a pond—L. *stagnum,* a piece of standing water.]

Tankard, tang'kärd, *n.* A large vessel for liquors, or a drinking vessel, with a cover. [Ir. *tancard.*]

Tanned, tand, *p.a.* Converted into leather; darkened by the rays of the sun.

Tanner, tan'ėr, *n. One who tans.* [Fr. *tanneur.*]

Tannery, tan'ė-ri, *n. The house and apparatus for tanning.* [Low L. *taneria.*]

Tanning, tan'ing, *p.n.* The practice and art of converting the raw hides of animals into leather by the *use of tan.*

Tansy, tan'zi, *n.* A bitter, acrid, strong-scented herb, with yellow flowers. [Fr. *tanaisie.*]

Tantalize, tan'ta-līz, *vt.* To torment by presenting some good to the view of, and exciting desire, but continually frustrating the expectations by keeping that good out of reach; to vex; to irritate. *ppr.* tantalizing, *pret. & pp.* tantalized. [Gr. *tantalizō,* from *Tantalos,* who divulged the secrets of Zeus, and was punished by having branches of fruit *hung* over his head, which he could not reach.]

Tantalizing, tan'ta-līz-ing, *p.a.* Tormenting by presenting to the view some unattainable good.

Tantamount, tan'ta-mount, *a. Of so great amount;* equivalent in value or signification. [L. *tantus,* so great, and Eng. *amount.*]

Tap, tap, *vt.* To *strike* with something small; to touch lightly; to strike gently.—*vi.* To *strike* a gentle blow. *ppr.* tapping, *pret. & pp.* tapped.—*n.* A gentle blow; a slight blow with a small thing. [Fr. *taper*—Gr. *tuptō,* to strike.]

Tap, tap, *vt. To draw out, as liquor* from a cask; to pierce or broach, as a cask; to open, as a cask, and draw liquor; to pierce for letting out a fluid.

ppr. tapping, *pret. & pp.* tapped.—*n.* A pipe for drawing liquor from a cask; a place attached to an inn or brewery where beer, &c., is retailed. [Sax. *tæppan*.]

Tap, tap, *n.* An instrument employed for cutting or forming the threads of internal screws or nuts.

Tape, tāp, *n. A narrow fillet or band;* a narrow piece of woven work, used for strings and the like. [Sax. *tæppe*.]

Taper, tā'pėr, *n. A small lighted wax candle;* a small wax candle, or a small light. [Sax.]

Taper, tā'pėr, *a.* Regularly narrowed toward the point; becoming small toward one end.—*vi.* To become gradually smaller toward one end.—*vt.* To make gradually smaller in diameter. [supposed to be from the form of a taper.]

Tapering, tā'pėr-ing, *p.a.* Gradually diminishing toward a point.

Taperingly, tā'pėr-ing-li, *adv. In a tapering manner.*

Tapestried, ta'pes-trid, *p.a. Ornamented with tapestry.*

Tapestry, ta'pes-tri, *n.* A kind of rich hangings, commonly composed of wool and silk, having pictorial representations wrought in them.—*vt. To adorn with tapestry. ppr.* tapestrying, *pret. & pp.* tapestried. [Fr. *tapisserie;* Gr. *tapēs, tapētos,* a carpet.]

Tape-worm, tāp'wėrm, *n.* A long flat worm, resembling a piece of *tape,* bred in the human intestines.

Tapioca, ta-pi-ō'ka, *n.* The popular name of the starch obtained by scraping and washing the roots of a plant which is a native of Brazil. It is an important article of food.

Tapis, tā'pis, *n. Tapestry;* once the cover of a council table; *upon the tapis,* under consideration. [Fr.]

Tapping, tap'ing, *p.n.* The surgical operation of removing fluid from any of the serous cavities of the body.

Tap-room, tap'rōm, *n. A room* in which beer is served from the *tap.*

Tapster, tap'stėr, *n.* One whose business is to draw liquor.

Tar, tär, *n.* A thick, impure, resinous substance, of a dark brown or black colour, obtained from pine and fir trees, and also from pit-coal; a sailor, so called from his tarred clothes.—*vt. To smear with tar;* to stimulate†. *ppr.* tarring, *pret. & pp.* tarred. [Sax. *tyrwa;* Ar. *tsaraya,* to flow, to run, as a wound.]

Tar†, tär, *vt.* To stimulate.

Tardily, tär'di-li, *adv. Slowly;* with slow pace or motion.

Tardiness, tär'di-nes, *n. State or quality of being tardy;* slowness; unwillingness; lateness.

Tardy, tär'di, *a. Slow as from weariness;* with a slow pace or motion; slow; backward; not being in season; slow, implying reluctance.—*vt.* To make tardy. [Fr. *tardif*—L. *tardus,* slow—*traho,* to drag.]

Tare, tär, *n.* A plant or weed which is *destructive* to corn; a leguminous plant cultivated as food for horses and cattle. [from Sax. *tirian,* to vex.]

Tare, tär, *n. An abatement* made from the weight or quantity of a commodity sold in a cask, chest, bag, or the like, which the seller makes to the buyer on account of the weight of such cask, &c. [Fr.—It. *tardre,* to abate.]

Tarentula, Tarantula, ta-ren'tū-la, ta-ran'tū-la, *n.* A species of spider, found in some of the warmer parts of Italy, which, when full grown, is about the size of a chestnut. It is of a brown colour, and its bite was fabled to cause an irresistible inclination for dancing; the name of a dance. [L. dimin. of *Tarentum,* a town in Italy.]

Target, tär'get, *n.* A shield of a small kind, originally made of the *hide* of a beast; a mark, in both the military and naval service, to fire at in their practice. [Sax. *targ;* L. *tergum,* skin of the back.]

Targeted, tär'get-ed, *p.a. Furnished or armed with a target.*

Targeteer, tär-get-ēr', *n. One armed with a target.*

Tariff, ta'rif, *n.* Properly, a *list* or *table* of *goods* with the *duties* or customs to be paid for the same; a list or table of duties or customs to be paid on goods imported or exported.—*vt.* To make a list of *duties* on, as goods. [Ar. *tarif,* a list of things.]

Tarn, tarn, *n.* A small lake among the mountains. [Icel. *tiörn.*]

Tarnish, tär'nish, *vt.* To soil or dim, *as with earth;* to lessen or destroy the lustre or purity of.—*vi.* To lose lustre; to become dull. [Fr. *ternir, ternissant*—L. *terra,* earth.]

Tarnished, tär'nisht, *p.a.* Sullied; having lost its brightness by exposure to dust, air, and the like.

Tarpaulin, tar-pa'lin, *n.* A piece of canvas *covered with tar,* used for *covering* the hatches of a ship, hammocks, boats, &c.; a hat covered with tarred cloth, worn by sailors; a sailor. [Written also *tarpauling* and *tarpawling.*] [from *tar,* and old Eng. *pauling,* a covering for a waggon.]

Tarred, tärd, *p.a. Smeared with tar.*

Tarriance, ta'ri-ans, *n.* Delay; lateness.

Tarry, ta'ri, *vi. To stay* or remain in a place; to abide; to wait; to loiter; to delay; to put off going or coming; to abide, continue, lodge.—*vt.†* To wait for; to stay for. *ppr.* tarrying, *pret. & pp.* tarried. [Old Fr. *targer*—L. *tardus,* slow.]

Tarry, tär'i, *a. Consisting of tar,* or like tar. [from *tar.*]

Tarrying, ta'ri-ing, *p.n.* Delay.

Tart, tärt. *a. Cutting* or *sharp* to the taste; acid; keen; severe. [Sax. *teart,* sharp.]

Tart, tärt, *n.* A species of pie or pastry, consisting of fruit baked on paste, and so named because frequently made of a *twisted* shape. [Old Fr. *tarte*—L. *tortus,* twisted—*torqueo,* to twist.]

Tartan, tär'tan, *n. Cloth woven in colours,* originally of wool or silk; woollen cloth, checkered with threads of various colours; checked or cross-barred fancy cloth of wool, silk, or cotton. [Fr. *tiretaine,* linsey-woolsey.]

Tartar, tär'tär, *n. An acid,* concrete salt, deposited from wines completely fermented. [Fr. *tartre.*]

Tartar†, tär'tär, *n.* The infernal regions; hell.

Tartarean, tär-tā'rē-an, *a. Pertaining to Tartarus;* hellish.

Tartareous, tär-tā'rē-us, *a. Consisting of tartar;* resembling tartar; Tartarean.

Tartarous, tär'tä-rus, *a. Containing tartar;* consisting of tartar; moderately acid.

Tartarus, tär'tä-rus, *n.* The name of the infernal regions over which Pluto or Hades ruled. [Gr. *tartaros,* a dark abyss.]

Tartish, tärt'ish, *a. Somewhat tart.*

Tartly, tärt'li, *adv.* Sharply; severely; with sourness of aspect.

Tartness, tärt'nes, *n. Quality of being tart;* acidity; sharpness of language or manner; acrimony.

Task, task, *n.* A *definite* amount of work imposed by another, to be done in a *limited* time; labour; employment; burdensome employment.—*vt. To impose a task* upon; to assign a definite amount of labour to; to burden with some employment; to require to perform; to charge upon†; to tax†. [Old Fr. *tasche,* a task; L. *taxo,* to touch repeatedly—*tango,* to touch.]

Task-master, task'mas-tėr, *n. One who imposes a task,* or burdens with labour.

Tassel, tas'sel, *n.* A sort of pendant ornament, attached to the corners of cushions, to curtains, and the like, ending in loose threads. [Low L. *tassellœ,* knots made of gold and silk of many folds.]

Tasselled, tas'seld, *p.a. Furnished or adorned with tassels.*

Tastable, tāst'a-bl, *a. That may be tasted;* savoury; relishing.

Taste, tāst, *vt.* To perceive and distinguish by causing to *touch* the palate; to perceive by means of the tongue; to try the relish of; to try by eating a little of; to have pleasure from; to experience; to essay; to undergo; to relish intellectually; to enjoy; to try.—*vi.* To try by the mouth; to eat or drink a little only; to excite a particular sensation, by which the quality or flavour is distinguished; to distinguish intellectually; to be tinctured; to experience; to take to be enjoyed; to enjoy sparingly. *ppr.* tasting, *pret. & pp.* tasted.—*n. The act of tasting;* a particular sensation excited in an animal by the application of a substance to the tongue, the proper organ; flavour; intellectual relish; discernment; essay; experiment; the faculty of discerning beauty, proportion, symmetry, or whatever constitutes excellence; style; manner, with respect to what is pleasing; a small portion given as a specimen; a bit. [Old Fr. *taster,* to taste; to handle—L. *tango,* to touch.]

Tasteful, tāst'ful, *a. Having a high taste* or relish; having good taste.

Tastefully, tāst'ful-li, *adv. With good taste.*

Tastefulness, tāst'ful-nes, *n. State or quality of being tasteful.*

Tasteless, tāst'les, *a.* Insipid; having no power of giving pleasure.

Taster, tāst'ėr, *n. One who tastes;* one who first tastes food or liquor.

Tastily, tāst'i-li, *adv. With good taste.*

Tasting, tāst'ing, *p.n.* Act of perceiving by the tongue; the sense by which we perceive or distinguish savours.

Tasty, tāst'i, *a. Having a good taste;* being in conformity to the principles of good taste; elegant; nice.

Tatter, tat'tėr, *n. A part torn;* a rag, or a part torn and hanging to the thing (chiefly used in the plural, *tatters*). [from Sax. *toteran,* to tear.]

Tattered, tat'tėrd, *p.a. Rent; torn;* hanging in rags.

Tattle, tat'l, *vi. To tell over and over;* to talk idly; to use many words with little meaning; to tell tales. *ppr.* tattling, *pret. & pp.* tattled.—*n.* Prate; trifling talk. [Sax. *to-tellan.*]

Tattler, tat'l-ėr, *n. One who tattles.*

Tattling, tat'l-ing, *p.a.* Given to idle talk; apt to tell tales.—*p.n.* Idle talk; babbling.

Tattoo, tat-tö′, n. A beat of drum at night, giving notice to soldiers to retreat, or to repair to their quarters. [said to be from Fr. *tapoter*, to beat.]

Tattoo, tat-tö′, vt. To prick the skin of and stain the punctured spots with a coloured substance, forming lines and figures upon the body.—n. Figures on the body, made by punctures and stains in lines and figures.

Tattooed, tat-töd′, p.a. Marked by stained lines and figures on the body.

Tattooing, tat-tö′ing, p.n. The operation of pricking the skin and staining the punctured spots with a coloured substance; the figures thus formed.

Taunt, tạnt, vt. To speak *biting* words to; to reproach with insulting words; to upbraid; to censure.—n. Upbraiding words; insulting invective. [Old G. *sandjan*, to bite, pain, mortify.]

Taunter, tạnt′ėr, n. *One who taunts* or upbraids with sarcastic reflections.

Taunting, tạnt′ing, p.a. Treating with severe reflections.

Tauntingly, tạnt′ing-li, adv. With bitter and sarcastic words; insultingly.

Taurine, tạ′rin, a. *Relating to a bull.* [L. *taurinus*—*taurus*, a bull.]

Tautological, tạ-to-loj′ik-al, a. *Relating to* or *containing tautology;* repeating the same thing.

Tautologist, tạ-tol′o-jist, n. One who uses *tautology*.

Tautology, tạ-tol′o-ji, n. *A repetition of the same meaning* in different words; needless repetition of a thing in different words. [Gr. *tautologia*—*tautos*, the same, and *logos*, word, discourse.]

Tavern, ta′vėrn, n. Primarily, a *hut of boards;* a house where wines and other liquors are sold, and entertainments provided for large parties. [Fr. *taverne*—L. *taberna*.]

Taverning, ta′vėrn-ing, p.n. *A feasting at taverns.*

Tavern-keeper, ta′vėrn-kēp-ėr, n. *One who keeps a tavern.*

Taw, ta, vt. To turn or change, as skins, into white leather for gloves, &c., by imbuing them with alum, salt, and other matters. [Sax. *tawian*, to curry.]

Tawdrily, tạ′dri-li, adv. *In a tawdry manner.*

Tawdriness, tạ′dri-nes, n. *State of being tawdry;* tinsel in dress.

Tawdry, tạ′dri, a. Very fine and showy in colours without taste or elegance; having an excess of showy ornaments without grace. [said to be from *St. Ethelred*, the name of an ancient fair, where all kinds of frippery were sold.]

Tawed, tạd, p.a. Dressed and made white, as leather.

Tawer, tạ′ėr, n. A dresser of white leather.

Tawing, tạ′ing, p.n. The art and operation of preparing skins and forming them into white leather by imbuing them with alum, salt, and other matters.

Tawniness, tạ′ni-nes, n. *The quality of being tawny.*

Tawny, tạ′ni, a. Of a yellowish-brown colour; of the colour of things tanned, or of persons who are sun-burned. [Fr. *tanné*, tawny—*tan*, tan.]

Tax, taks, n. A *rate* laid by government on the incomes or property of individuals, or on the products consumed by them; a sum imposed on individuals, or on their property, for local or civic purposes; a burden; exaction; demand; charge; censure.—vt. To assess upon individuals *a certain sum;* to assess, fix, or determine judicially; to charge; to censure; to accuse; to call to task; to exact from. [Old Fr. *taxe*—L. *taxo*, to rate.]

Taxable, taks′a-bl, a. *That may be taxed;* that may be legally charged by a court against the plaintiff or defendant in a suit.

Taxation, taks-ā′shon, n. *A taxing;* the act of laying a tax; act of taxing a bill of cost; charge†; accusation†. [Fr.]

Taxed, takst, p.a. Rated; accused.

Taxer, taks′ėr, n. *One who taxes.*

Tax-gatherer, taks′gạth-ėr-ėr, n. *A collector of taxes.*

Taxing, taks′ing, p.n. *Act of laying a tax upon;* taxation.

Tea, tē, n. The dried leaves of different species of plants, extensively cultivated in China; an infusion of tea-leaves in boiling water; any decoction of vegetables, &c. [Chin. *tha*.]

Teach, tēch, vt. To *point out to;* to *show;* to exhibit to so as to impress on the mind of; to instruct; to deliver, as any doctrine; to accustom; to make familiar with; to give previous notice to; to suggest to the mind of.—vi. To practise giving instruction; to perform the business of a preceptor. ppr. teaching, pret. & pp. taught. [Sax. *tæcan*, to show; Goth. *taikns*, a sign.]

Teachable, tēch′a-bl, a. *That may be taught;* apt to learn; docile.

Teachableness, tēch′a-bl-nes, n. *Quality of being teachable;* a readiness to be instructed; docility.

Teacher, tēch′ėr, n. *One who teaches;* an instructor; a preceptor; a minister of the gospel; one who preaches without regular ordination.

Teaching, tēch′ing, p.n. Act or business of instructing; instruction.

Teak, tēk, n. A tree of the East Indies which furnishes an abundance of valuable ship-timber. [Indian, *tekka*.]

Teal, tēl, n. A web-footed water-bird, nearly allied to the common duck, but smaller, and so named from its *prolific* nature. [D. *teling*—*telen*, to bring forth.]

Team, tēm, n. A brood†; anything *following in a row* or in order; two or more horses harnessed together to the same vehicle for drawing. [Sax. *team*, offspring—*tyman*, to bring forth.]

Teamster, tēm′stėr, n. *One who drives a team.*

Tear, tēr, n. A drop of the water which *grief* forces from the eyes; something in the form of a transparent drop of fluid matter; any moisture trickling in drops. [Sax.; Goth. *tagr*—Sans. *dru*, to grieve.]

Tear, tėr, vt. To *pull in pieces;* to rend; to make a violent rent in; to wound; to break; to divide by violent measures; to shatter; to remove by violence; to break up.—vi. To rave; to rage; to move and act with turbulent violence, as a mad bull. ppr. tearing, pret. tore, pp. torn.—n. A rent; a fissure. [Sax. *teran;* Heb. *taraph*, to pull in pieces.]

Tearer, tār′ėr, n. *One who tears.*

Tearful, tēr′fụl, a. *Abounding with tears;* weeping; shedding tears.

Tearless, tēr′les, a. *Shedding no tears;* without tears; unfeeling.

Tease, tēz, vt. To *pull;* to comb or card, as wool or flax; to scratch, as cloth in dressing, for the purpose of raising a nap; to vex with impertinence; to annoy; to torment; to chagrin. ppr. teasing, pret. & pp. teased. [Sax. *tæsan*, to pluck.]

Teasel, tē′zel, n. A plant, the awny head of which is used for *teasing* wool, and raising the nap on woollen cloths; the bur of the plant.—vt. *To cut and gather as teasel;* to raise a nap, as on cloth, by means of teasels. [Sax. *tæsl*.]

Teaseler, tē′zel-ėr, n. *One who uses the teasel* for raising a nap on cloth.

Teaseling, tē′zel-ing, p.n. *The cutting and gathering of teasels.*

Teaser, tēz′ėr, n. *One who teases.*

Teat, tēt, n. The projecting part of the female breast; the pap of a woman; the nipple; the dug of a beast. [Sax. *tit, titt;* Gr. *thaō*, to suckle.]

Teazle, tē′zl, n. Teasel (which see).

Techily, tech′i-li, adv. Peevishly; frowardly.

Techiness, tech′i-nes, n. Peevishness.

Technical, tek′nik-al, a. *Pertaining to art or the arts;* noting a word, term, or phrase, used in a peculiar sense in any art or science; belonging to a particular profession. [Fr. *technique*—Gr. *technē*, art.]

Technicality, tek-ni-kal′i-ti, n. *Quality or state of being technical.*

Technically, tek′ni-kal-li, adv. *In a technical manner.*

Technics, tek′niks, n. *The doctrine of arts in general;* such branches of learning as respect the arts.

Technological, tek-no-loj′ik-al, a. *Pertaining to technology.*

Technologist, tek-nol′o-jist, n. *One skilled in technology.*

Technology, tek-nol′o-ji, n. *A discourse on the arts;* an explanation of the *terms* of the arts. [Gr. *technologia*—*technē*, art, and *logos*, discourse.]

Techy, tech′i, a. *Touchy;* peevish; irritable. [so written for *touchy*.]

Ted, ted, vt. To spread out; to turn, as new-mowed grass from the swath, and scatter it for drying. ppr. tedding, pret. & pp. tedded. [W. *teddu*.]

Tedded, ted′ed, p.a. Spread from the swath.

Tedious, tē′di-us, a. *Tiresome;* tiresome from continuance or slowness which causes prolixity; dilatory; tardy. [L. *taediōsus*—*taedet*, it wearies one.]

Tediously, tē′di-us-li, adv. In such a manner as to *weary.*

Tediousness, tē′di-us-nes, n. *Quality or state of being tedious;* prolixity; quality of wearying.

Teem, tēm, vi. To *be in the state of a wife;* to be pregnant; to conceive; to engender young; to be full; to be charged, as a breeding animal; to be stocked to overflowing; to be prolific. vt.† To produce; to bring forth. [Sax. *tyman*, to beget; Gr. *damar*, a wife.]

Teeming, tēm′ing, p.a. Fruitful; prolific.

Teen†, tēn, n. Grief; sorrow.—vt. To excite.

Teens, tēnz, n.pl. *Tens;* the years of one's age having the termination *teen.* [from *teen*, ten.]

Teeth, tēth, vi. To breed teeth.

Teething, tēth′ing, p.n. The process of the first growth of *teeth*, called dentition.

Tegument, te′gū-ment, n. *A cover or covering;* any natural covering or envelope. [L. *tegumentum*—*tego*, to cover.]

Tegumentary, te-gū-ment′a-ri, a. *Pertaining to teguments.*

Teil, Teil-tree, tēl, tēl′trē, n. The lime-tree, otherwise called the linden. [L. *tilia*.]

Telegram, te′lē-gram, n. Any piece of intelligence conveyed by an electric telegraph. [Gr. *tēle*, at a distance, and *gramma*, a letter.]

Telegraph, te′lē-graf, n. A machine for communicating *intelligence from a distance* by various signals, or by means of electricity, the method now so extensively adopted.—*vt.* To *convey or announce by telegraph*. [Gr. *tēle*, and *graphō*, to write.]
Telegraph-cable, te′lē-graf-kā-bl, n. A strong rope, composed of wires, gutta-percha, &c., for a submarine *telegraph*.
Telegraphic, te-lē-graf′ik, a. *Pertaining to the telegraph*; made by a telegraph; communicated by a telegraph.
Telegraphically, te-lē-graf′ik-al-li, adv. *By the telegraph*.
Telegraphist, te′lē-graf-ist, n. *One who works a telegraph*.
Telegraphy, te-leg′ra-fi, n. The art or practice of communicating intelligence by a *telegraph*.
Telescope, te′lē-skōp, n. An optical instrument employed in *viewing distant objects*. [Fr.—Gr. *tēle*, at a distance, and *skopeō*, to view.]
Telescopic, te-lē-skop′ik, a. *Pertaining to a telescope*; seen or discoverable only by a telescope.
Telescopically, te-lē-skop′ik-al-li, adv. *By the telescope*.
Tell, tel, *vt.* To *number*; to relate; to teach; to make known; to disclose; to betray; to reckon; to confess; to own; to interpret; to explain; to make excuses to.—*vi.* To give an account; to make report; to take or produce effect. *ppr.* telling, *pret. & pp.* told. [Sax. *tellan*; Icel. *tal*, speech—*telja*, to number.]
Teller, tel′ér, n. *One who tells*; one who numbers; an officer of a bank, who receives and pays money on checks.
Tellership, tel′ér-ship, n. The *office or employment of a teller*.
Telling, tel′ing, p.a. Having or producing effect.
Tell-tale, tel′tāl, n. *One who tells tales*; one who officiously communicates information; a movable piece of ivory or lead on a chamber-organ, that gives notice when the wind is exhausted.
Telluric, tel-lū′rik, a. *Pertaining to the earth*, or proceeding from the earth. [L. *tellus, tellūris*, the earth.]
Tellurium, tel-lū′ri-um, n. A brittle metal of a tin-white colour, easily fusible, and nearly as heavy as zinc. [from L. *tellus, tellūris*, earth.]
Temerity, tē-me′ri-ti, n. *Rashness*; unreasonable contempt of danger. [Fr. *témérité*; L. *temēre*, rashly.]
Temper, tem′pér, *vt.* To *divide or proportion duly*; to unite in due proportion; to adjust, as parts to each other; to bring to a moderate state; to form by mixture; to modify; to reduce, as any violence or excess; to soften; to form to a proper degree of hardness. *vi.* To be mixed; to be softened.—*n.* *Due proportion* of different qualities; the state of any compound substance which results from the mixture of various ingredients; the constitution of the mind; disposition; humour; calmness of mind; irritation; the state of a metal, particularly as to its hardness; middle course. [Fr. *tempérer*—L. *tempus*, a portion cut off.]
Temperament, tem′pér-a-ment, n. A *mixing in due proportion*; constitution; mental constitution; medium; due mixture of different qualities. [Fr. *tempérament*.]
Temperance, tem′pér-ans, n. *Moderation*; sobriety; habitual moderation in regard to the indulgence of the passions. [Fr. *tempérance*.]
Temperate, tem′pér-āt, a. *Duly gov-

erned; moderate; abstemious; not violent; free from ardent passion; sedate; sober. [L. *temperatus*.]
Temperately, tem′pér-āt-li, adv. *Moderately*; calmly; with moderate force.
Temperateness, tem′pér-āt-nes, n. *Quality of being temperate*; calmness.
Temperature, tem′pér-a-tūr, n. *Due measure*; *quality*; constitution; the state of a body with regard to heat or cold, as indicated by the thermometer. [Fr. *température*.]
Tempered, tem′pérd, p.a. Disposed with regard to the passions.
Tempest, tem′pest, n. *Time of* foul weather; a violent storm of considerable duration; a storm of extreme violence; a violent commotion; perturbation. [Old Fr. *tempeste*—L. *tempestas*.]
Tempestuous, tem-pest′ū-us, a. *Abounding in tempests*; very stormy; blowing with violence. [Fr. *tempétueux*.]
Tempestuously, tem-pest′ū-us-li, adv. With great violence of wind, or great commotion; turbulently.
Tempestuousness, tem-pest′ū-us-nes, n. *State of being tempestuous*.
Templar, tem′plär, n. One of a religious military order, first established at Jerusalem in favour of pilgrims travelling to the Holy Land; a lawyer or student living in the Temple. [from the *Temple*, a house in London, near the Thames, once occupied by the Knights Templars.]
Temple, tem′pl, n. Originally, a *space marked out* and consecrated; a sanctuary; a public edifice erected in honour of some deity; the building erected for the worship of God at Jerusalem; a church; an edifice erected as a place of Christian worship; the Church, as a collective body. [Fr.—L. *templum*.]
Temple, tem′pl, n. The part of the side of the head between the eye and the ear (usually in the plural), said to be so named because it is the part where the hair first begins to turn white, and which thus indicates the advanced time of life or age of the person. [L. *tempus, tempŏra*.]
Temporal, tem′pō-ral, a. *Pertaining to time*; pertaining to this life only; limited by time, or by this life; relating to a tense in grammar; [Fr. *temporal*] pertaining to the *temple* or *temples* of the head. [Fr. *temporel*—L. *tempus*, time.]
Temporalities, Temporals, tem-pō-ral′i-tiz, tem′pō-ralz, n. *pl*. Secular possessions; revenues of an ecclesiastical proceeding from lands, tenements, or layfees, tithes, and the like.
Temporally, tem′pō-ral-li, adv. With respect to time or this life only.
Temporarily, tem′pō-ra-ri-li, adv. For *a time only*; not perpetually.
Temporary, tem′pō-ra-ri, a. *Lasting but for a time*; continuing for a limited time; fleeting. [Fr. *temporaire*.]
Temporize, tem′pō-rīz, vi. To comply *with the time* or occasion; to yield to the current of opinion; to delay; to procrastinate (with *with*). *ppr.* temporising, *pret. & pp.* temporized. [Fr. *temporiser*.]
Temporizer, tem′pō-rīz-ér, n. *One who temporises;* a trimmer.
Temporizing, tem′pō-rīz-ing, p.a. Complying *with the time*, or with the prevailing humours of men; time-serving. *p.n. A yielding to the time.*
Tempt, temt, *vt.* To *stretch out*; to test; to prove; to tamper with; to solicit to an evil act; to incite to something wrong by presenting inducements that

are alluring; to allure; to decoy; to seduce; to provoke. [L. *tento*, also *tempto*, to try—Gr. *teinō*, to stretch.]
Temptation, tem-tā′shon, n. The *act of tempting;* trial; enticement to evil; state of being tempted; that which is presented to the mind as an inducement to evil. [Fr. *tentation*—L. *tentatio*, a trial—*tento*, to handle.]
Tempter, temt′ér, n. *One who tempts;* the great enticer to evil; the devil.
Tempting, temt′ing, p.a. Adapted to entice or allure; attractive.
Temptingly, temt′ing-li, adv. In a manner to entice to evil; so as to allure.
Ten, ten, a. Twice five; a kind of proverbial number; many. [Sax. *tyn*—Goth. *taihun*.]
Tenable, ten′a-bl, a. *That may be held* against attempts to take or overthrow it. [Fr.—L. *teneo*, to hold tightly.]
Tenableness, Tenability, ten′a-bl-nes, ten-a-bil′i-ti, n. *State of being tenable*.
Tenacious, tē-nā′shi-us, a. *Griping;* inclined to hold fast what is in possession; apt to adhere to another substance, as viscous matter; tough; having great cohesive force among the particles. [L. *tenax, tenācis*—*teneo*, to hold tightly.]
Tenaciously, tē-nā′shi-us-li, adv. With a disposition to *hold fast* what is possessed; with firm adherence.
Tenacity, tē-nas′i-ti, n. *State or quality of being tenacious;* adhesiveness; that quality of bodies which makes them stick or adhere to others; stubbornness; obstinacy. [Fr. *tenacité*.]
Tenancy, te′nan-si, n. *A holding* or possession of lands or tenements; tenure. [Norm. *tenaunce*—L. *teneo*, to hold tightly.]
Tenant, te′nant, n. *A person holding* land or other real estate under another; one who has possession of any place; a dweller.—*vt.* To *hold* or possess as a *tenant*. [Old Fr.]
Tenantable, te′nant-a-bl, a. In a state of repair suitable *for a tenant*.
Tenantless, te′nant-les, a. *Having no tenant;* unoccupied.
Tenantry, te′nant-ri, n. The *body of tenants*.
Tench, tensh, n. A European freshwater fish, of the carp family, very tenacious of life. [Fr. *tanche*.]
Tend, tend, *vt.* To *direct* or turn towards; to watch; to guard; to accompany, as a protector; to hold and take care of. [from *attend*.]
Tend, tend, *vi.* To *stretch out* or move in a certain direction; to be directed to any end; to aim; to have or give a leaning; to contribute. [L. *tendo*, to stretch.]
Tendance¹, tend′ans, n. Attendance; the body of those who attend.
Tendency, tend′en-si, n. *Act of tending;* direction or course toward any place or result; proneness; drift; aim. [Fr. *tendance*.]
Tender, tend′ér, n. *An attender;* a small vessel employed to attend a larger one; the thing offered; on railways, a carriage which attends on the locomotive, to supply the fuel; regard†; kind concern†.
Tender, tend′ér, *vt.* To *offer* in words; to offer in payment of a demand, for saving a penalty; to regard; to hold, as of value.—*n.* An *offer*, either of money to pay a debt, or of service to be performed, in order to save a forfeiture; any offer for acceptance; an offer in writing made by one party to another, to execute some specified

ch, *chain*; j, *job*; g, *go*; ng, *sing*; ᴛʜ, *then*; th, *thin*; w, *wig*; wh, *whig*; zh, *azure*; † obsolete.

TENDER 398 TERRIBLE

work, &c., at a certain sum or rate; the thing offered. [Old Fr. *tendre.*]
Tender, ten'dėr, *a.* Easily pierced or broken through; soft; not firm or hard, as plants; very sensible to impression and pain; delicate; young; feeble; susceptible of the softer passions; dear; precious; kind; merciful; pitiful; exciting kind concern; expressive of the softer passions; careful not to injure; gentle; mild; adapted to excite feeling or sympathy; pathetic; cautious (with *of*). [Fr. *tendre*— L. *tener,* soft—Gr. *teirō,* to rub away.]
Tender-hearted, ten'dėr-härt-ed, *a.* Having great sensibility; susceptible of the softer passions.
Tender-hefted, ten'dėr-heft-ed, *a.* Having great tenderness.
Tenderly, ten'dėr-li, *adv. With* tenderness; mildly; gently; softly; kindly.
Tenderness, ten'dėr-nes, *n. State or quality of being tender;* softness; soreness; susceptibility of the softer passions; kindness; benevolence; mildness; anxiety for the good of another; caution; extreme care not to give offence; cautious care not to injure; softness of expression; pathos.
Tending, tend'ing, *p.n. The act of attending.*
Tendinous, ten'din-us, *a. Pertaining to a tendon;* partaking of the nature of tendons; sinewy. [Fr. *tendineux.*]
Tendon, ten'don, *n. A tight-stretched band;* a sinew; a muscle; a hard, insensible cord or bundle of fibres, by which a muscle is attached to a bone. [Fr.; Gr. *teinō,* to stretch.]
Tendril, ten'dril, *n.* A slender, twining part, by which a plant *attaches itself* to something for support.—*a. Clasping;* climbing, as a tendril. [Old Fr. *tendrillons,* tendrils— L. *teneo,* to hold.]
Tenebrous, te'nē-brus, *a. Dark;* gloomy. [L. *tenebrōsus*—*tenebræ,* darkness.]
Tenement, te'nē-ment, *n. Anything held or occupied,* as lands, houses, &c.; a house; an apartment in a building, used by one family; a house or lands depending on a manor. [Fr. *tenement* —L. *teneo,* to hold.]
Tenemental, te-nē-ment'al, *a. Pertaining to tenanted lands;* that is or may be held by tenants.
Tenet, te'net, *n. That which a person holds;* that which a person firmly believes as a part of his creed; doctrine; dogma. [L. he holds.]
Tenfold, ten'fōld, *a. Ten times more.*
Tennis, ten'is, *n.* A play in which a ball is driven continually or kept in motion by rackets. [said to be from Fr. *tenez,* take it—L. *teneo,* to hold.]
Tenon, te'non, *n.* The end of a piece of timber, reduced in its dimensions, so as to be fitted into a cavity, called a mortise, in another piece, by which means the two pieces are *held* together [Fr.—L. *teneo,* to hold.]
Tenor, ten'or, *n. A holding on;* whole course; stamp; character; sense contained; general course or drift; [Fr. *tenor*] in music, the most common natural pitch of a man's voice in singing, or the higher of the two kinds of voices usually belonging to adult males; the part of a tune adapted to this voice, the second of the four parts, reckoning from the base. [L.—*teneo,* to hold.]
Tense, tens, *a. Stretched;* strained to stiffness; rigid; not lax. [L. *tensus*—*tenslo,* to stretch.]
Tense, tens, *n. Time;* a particular form of a verb, or a combination of words used to express the time of action; an inflection of verbs by which they are made to distinguish the time of actions. [Norm. *tens*—L. *tempus,* time.]
Tensely, tens'li, *adv. With tension.*
Tension, ten'shon, *n. The act of stretching; the state of being stretched;* the degree of stretching to which a wire, &c., is strained by drawing it in the direction of its length; strain; elasticity; intensity. [Fr.—L. *tendo,* to stretch.]
Tent, tent, *n. Something stretched out;* a portable lodge, consisting of canvas *stretched* and *sustained* by poles; in surgery, a roll of lint or linen, used to dilate an opening in the flesh.—*vi.* To *lodge, as in a tent;* to tabernacle.—*vi.* To probe; to search, as with *a tent;* to keep open with a tent. [Fr. *tente*—L. *tendo,* to stretch.]
Tentacle, ten'ta-kl, *n.* A thread-like process or organ round the mouth or on the bodies of various animals, used for seizing, *touch,* or locomotion. [Low L. *tentacula*— L. *tento,* to feel, to handle—*tendo,* to stretch.]
Tentacular, ten-ta'kū-lar, *a.Pertaining to tentacles.*
Tentative, ten'tat-iv, *a. Trying;* essaying. [Fr. an attempt, essay.]
Tent-bed, tent'bed, *n.* A post bedstead, having the roof formed like a *tent.*
Tented, tent'ed, *p.a. Covered* or *furnished with tents,* as soldiers; covered with tents; as, a tented field.
Tenter, ten'tėr, *n. A stretcher;* a machine for stretching cloth, by means of hooks called *tenter-hooks.*—*vi.* To *hang or stretch on tenters.* [from L. *tendo,* to stretch.]
Tenth, tenth, *a. The ordinal of ten;* the first after the ninth.—*n.The tenth part;* tithe.
Tenth-century, tenth'sen-tū-ri *n.* The century commencing with the year 901.
Tenuity, ten-ū'i-ti, *n. State of being stretched or drawn out; thinness;* thinness (applied to a broad substance), and slenderness (applied to one that is long); thinness, as of a fluid. [Fr. *ténuité*—L. *tendo,* to stretch.]
Tenure, ten'ūr, *n. A holding* or manner of holding real estate; the particular manner of holding real estate; the consideration or service which the occupier of land gives to his lord for the use of his land; manner of holding in general. [Fr. from *tenir*—L. *teneo,* to hold.]

universities and colleges; a word; the word by which a thing is expressed; a word that denotes something peculiar to an art; the subject or the predicate of a proposition in logic; (pl.) conditions. [L. *terminus*—Old Heb. *tāram,* to cut off.]—*vt.* To name; to call; to denominate. [from *term,* a word.]
Termagant, tėr'ma-gant, *a.* Tumultuous; boisterous or furious; scolding. *n.* A boisterous, turbulent woman; a shrew. [corrupted from *Tervagant,* the name of an old Saracen deity, of a most violent character.]
Terminable, tėrm'in-a-bl, *a. That may be terminated* or bounded; limitable.
Terminal, tėrm'in-al, *a. Forming the extremity,* terminating; of or belonging to a terminus. [from L. *terminus.*]
Terminate, tėrm'in-āt, *vt. To set bounds to;* to bound; to limit; to put an end to; to finish; to close; to end.—*vi.* To *be bounded or limited;* to close; to come to a limit in time. *ppr.* terminating, *pret. & pp.* terminated.—*a. Limited; bounded;* that comes to an end. [L. *termino, terminatus—terminus,* a limit, a boundary-line.]
Terminating, tėrm'in-āt-ing, *p.a. Limiting;* ending; concluding.
Termination, tėrm-in-ā'shon, *n. Act of terminating;* bound; limit in space or extent; end in time or existence; the end of a word; conclusion; result; word; termt. [L. *terminatio.*]
Terminational, tėrm-in-ā'shon-al, *a.* Pertaining to or forming the *end* or concluding syllable of a word.
Terminology, tėrm-in-ol'o-ji, *n. A discourse* or treatise *on terms;* that branch of natural history which explains all the terms used in the description of natural objects. [Gr. *termōn,* a limit, and *logos,* discourse.]
Terminus, tėrm'in-us, *n.* **Termini,** *pl. A boundary line; limit;* a column; the extreme point, as either end of a railway. [L.]
Tern, tėrn, *n.* A long-winged aquatic bird, closely allied to the gulls. [Low L. *sterna.*]
Ternary, tėrn'a-ri, *a. Proceeding by threes;* consisting of three. [L. *ternarius*—*terni,* three each.]
Terrace, te'rās, *n.* A raised level space or platform *of earth,* supported on one or more sides by a wall or bank of turf, &c.; an area raised before a building or buildings, above the level of the ground on the opposite side, to serve as a promenade, &c.; a street, having houses on one side and sloping ground on the other; a balcony; the flat roof of a house.—*vt.* To *form into a terrace;* to open to the air and light. *ppr.* terracing, *pret. & pp.* terraced. [Fr. *terrasse*—L. *terra,* the earth.]
Terraced, te'rāst, *p.a. Formed into a terrace;* having a terrace.
Terraqueous, te-rā'kwē-us, *a. Consisting of land and water,* as the globe or earth. [L. *terra,* Sans. *dhard,* earth, and *aqua,* water.]
Terreen, te-rēn', *n. An earthen* or porcelain vessel for table furniture, used often for containing soup. [Fr. *terrine* —L. *terra,* earth. See TUREEN.]
Terrene, te-rēn', *a. Pertaining to the earth;* earthly; terrestrial. [L. *terrēnus* —*terra,* the earth.]
Terrestrial, te-res'tri-al, *a. Pertaining to the earth;* existing on the earth; pertaining to the present state; sublunary. [L. *terrestris*—*terra,* the earth.]
Terrible, te'ri-bl, *a. Causing trembling;* adapted to impress dread, terror, or

solemn awe; frightful; horrible; awful. [Fr.—L. *terreo*, to frighten.]
Terribleness, te'ri-bl-nes, *n.* Quality or state of being terrible; dreadfulness.
Terribly, te'ri-bli, *adv.* In a manner to excite terror or fright; violently.
Terrier, te'ri-ėr, *n.* A dog or little hound that creeps into holes in the earth, after animals that burrow. [Fr. —L. *terra*, the earth.]
Terrific, te-rif'ik, *a. Terrifying;* adapted to excite great fear or dread. [L. *terrificus.*]
Terrified, te'ri-fid, *p.a.* Affrighted.
Terrify, te'ri-fi, *vt.* To cause terror in; to frighten; to alarm with fear. *ppr.* terrifying, *pret. & pp.* terrified. [L. *terreo*, to frighten, and *facio*, to make.]
Terrifying, te'ri-fi-ing, *p. a.* Frightening.
Terrigenous, te-rij'en-us, *a. Earth-born.* [L. *terrigena*—*terra*, the earth, and *gigno*, to beget.]
Territorial, te-ri-tō'ri-al, *a. Pertaining to territory;* limited to a certain district.
Territory, te'ri-tō-ri, *n. The land round* a town; a domain; a district; the compass of land within the bounds of any state, city, or other body; a tract of land belonging to a prince or state, lying at a distance from the parent country. [Fr. *territoire.*]
Terror, te'ror, *n. Trembling;* affright; violent fear that agitates the body and mind; consternation; the cause of extreme fear. [L.—*terreo*, to frighten.]
Terrorism, te'ror-izm, *n. A state of being terrified*, or a state impressing terror.
Terse, tėrs, *a. Wiped clean;* clean; elegant without pompousness. [L. *tersus* —*tergeo*, to wipe.]
Tersely, tėrs'li, *adv.* Neatly.
Terseness, tėrs'nes, *n. Quality of being terse;* neatness of style.
Tertian, tėr'shi-an, *a.* Occurring every *third* day. — *n.* A fever whose paroxysms return every *third* day, or every forty-eight hours. [L. *tertianus* —*tres*, three.]
Tertiary, tėr'shi-a-ri, *a. Containing a third part; third;* pertaining to the third. [L. *tertiarius.*]
Tesselar, tes'sė-lär, *a. Formed in squares.*
Tesselate, tes'sė-lāt, *vt.* To form *into* squares or chockers; to lay with checkered work. *ppr.* tesselating, *pret. & pp.* tesselated. [from L. *tessella*, a small square stone.]
Tesselated, tes'sė-lāt-ed, *p.a.* Formed in *little* squares or mosaic work; checkered; spotted like a chess-board.
Test, test, *n.* A large vessel in which metals are melted for trial and refinement; trial: experiment; any critical trial and examination; that with which anything is compared for proof of its genuineness; a criterion; judgment; distinction.—*vt.* To put to a test; to refine, as gold or silver by means of lead, in a test, by the vitrification, &c., of all extraneous matter; to try; to bring to a trial and examination; to prove the truth of by experiment. [L. *testa*, a piece of burned clay, also a shell—*torreo*, to bake by heat.)
Test, test, *n.* An oath and declaration against transubstantiation, which all public officers, civil and military, were formerly obliged to take within six months after their admission. [L. *testis*, a witness.]
Testable, test'a-bl, *a. That may be devised or given by will.* [from L. *testor*, to publish one's last will.]

Testaceous, tes-tā'shė-us, *a. Pertaining to shells;* consisting of a hard shell, which is often very thick and strong; pertaining to animals which have a strong, thick, and entire shell. [L. *testaceus*—L. *testa*, a shell.]
Testament, tes'ta-ment, *n.* The solemn *declaration* of one's will; a solemn authentic instrument in writing by which a person declares his will as to the disposal of his estate and effects after his death; one of the two general divisions of the canonical books of the Scriptures. [Fr.—L. *testis*, a witness.]
Testamentary, tes-ta-ment'a-ri, *a. Pertaining to a testament;* bequeathed by will; done by testament or will. [Fr. *testamentaire.*]
Testate, tes'tāt, *a. Having made and left a will.* [L. *testātus*—*testis*, a witness.]
Testator, tes-tāt'or, *n. A man who makes and leaves a will* at death. [L.]
Testatrix, tes-tāt'riks, *n. A woman who makes and leaves a will* at death.
Tested, test'ed, *p.a.* Tried or approved by *a test.*
Tester, tes'tėr, *n. The head* or top of a bed; a flat canopy over a bed, pulpit, tomb, &c. [Old Fr. *teste*, the head.]
Testern!, tes'tėrn, *n.* A sixpence.—*vt.* To present with a testern.
Testicle, tes'ti-kl, *n.* That which *attests* the male sex; one of the glands which secrete the seminal fluid in males. [L. *testicŭlus*—*testis*, a witness.]
Testifier, tes'ti-fi-ėr, *n. One who testifies;* one who gives testimony.
Testify, tes'ti-fi, *vi. To bear witness;* to make a solemn declaration in judicial proceedings; to make a solemn declaration under oath; to declare a charge against one.—*vt. To bear witness to;* to support the truth of by testimony; to affirm or declare solemnly for the purpose of establishing a fact; to declare freely. *ppr.* testifying, *pret. & pp.* testified. [L. *testificor*—*testis*, a witness, and *facio*, to make.]
Testily, tes'ti-li, *adv.* Fretfully; peevishly; with petulance.
Testimonial, tes-ti-mō'ni-al, *n. A testimony or attestation;* a certificate in favour of one's character or good conduct; a subscription, &c., bestowed on an individual by the public in token of thankfulness or esteem. [Fr.—L. *testis*, a witness.]
Testimony, tes'ti-mo-ni, *n. That which is declared by a witness;* evidence; a solemn affirmation made in judicial proceedings under oath; open attestation; proof of some fact.—*vt.* To witness. [L. *testimonium*—*testis*, a witness.]
Testiness, tes'ti-nes, *n. Quality of being testy;* fretfulness; peevishness.
Testing, test'ing, *p.n.* The act of trying for proof; the operation of refining large quantities of gold or silver by means of lead, in the vessel called a *test.*
Testy, tes'ti, *a. Headstrong;* fretful; peevish; easily irritated. [Old Fr. *teste*, the head.]
Tether, tėтн'ėr, *n.* That which *ties* or *binds;* a rope or chain by which a beast is confined for feeding within certain limits.—*vt.* To confine, as a beast, with a rope or chain for feeding within certain limits. [D. *tudder;* Icel. *tiodhr*, a band.]
Tetragon, tet'ra-gon, *n.* A plane figure having *four angles.* [Gr. *tetragōnos*— *tetra*, for *tetŏra*, four, and *gōnia*, an angle.]

Tetragonal, tė-tra'gon-al, *a. Pertaining to a tetragon;* having four angles.
Tetrahedral, tet-ra-hē'dral, *a. Having four sides.*
Tetrahedron, tet-ra-hē'dron, *n.* A solid figure having *four sides*, or four equilateral and equal triangles. [Gr. *tetra*, four, and *hedra*, a side.]
Tetrarch, tet'rärk, *n.* A Roman *governor of the fourth part* of a province; a subordinate prince. [Gr. *tetrarchēs*— *tetra*, four, and *archē*, rule.]
Tetrarchy, tet'rärk-i, *n. The fourth part* of a province under a Roman tetrarch; the office of a *tetrarch.*
Tetrasyllabic, tet'ra-sil-lab'ik, *a. Consisting of four syllables.*
Tetrasyllable, tet'ra-sil-la-bl, *n. A word consisting of four syllables.* [Gr. *tetra*, and *syllabē*, a syllable.]
Tetter, tet'tėr, *n.* A cutaneous disease; a scab; ringworm.—*vt.* To affect with the disease called *tetters.* [Sax. *teter*— L. *teter*, foul.]
Teutonic, tū-ton'ik, *a. Pertaining to the Teutons*, a people of Germany, or to their language.—*n. The language of the Teutons*, the parent of the German, Dutch, Anglo-Saxon or native English, &c. [L. *Teutonicus.*]
Text, tekst, *n. That which is woven;* tissue; a discourse or composition on which a note or commentary is written; a verse or passage of Scripture which a preacher selects as the subject of a discourse; a particular kind of handwriting. [Fr. *texte*—L. *texo, textum*, to weave.]
Text-book, tekst'buk, *n.* A *book* containing the leading principles of a science or branch of learning, arranged in order for the use of students.
Text-hand, tekst'hand, *n.* A large *hand* in writing.
Textile, teks'til, *a. Woven*, or capable of being woven. [L. *textilis*—*texo*, to weave.]
Textual, tekst'ū-al, *a. Contained in the text;* serving for texts.
Textualist, tekst'ū-al-ist, *n. One who adheres to the text;* one who is well versed in the Scriptures, and can readily quote texts.
Textually, tekst'ū-al-li, *adv. In the text* or body of a work.
Texture, teks'tūr, *n. Act or art of weaving;* that which is woven; the connection of threads interwoven; the disposition of the several parts of any body in connection with each other. [L. *textūra*—*texo*, to weave.]
Than, THan, *conj.* A particle placed in comparison after some comparative adjective or adverb; noting a less degree of the quality compared in the word that follows *than;* as, wisdom is better than strength. [Sax. *thonne.*]
Thane, thān, *n.* Among the Saxons a title of honour, superseded by the baron of the Normans. [Sax. *thegen*, a knight, a nobleman—*thenian*, to serve.]
Thanedom, thān'dum, *n. The property or jurisdiction of a thane.*
Thank, thangk, *vt. To think of with gratitude;* to express gratitude to for a favour; to make acknowledgments to for kindness bestowed.—*n.* Generally in the plural. Expression of gratitude; an acknowledgment made to express a sense of favour or kindness received. [Sax. *thancian thanc*, mind —Old G. *dankjan*, to think.]
Thankful, thangk'fµl, *a.* Grateful; impressed with a sense of kindness received, and ready to acknowledge it. [Sax. *thancfull.*]

ch, *chain* j, *job;* g, *go;* ng, *sing;* ᴡʜ, *then;* th, *thin;* w, *wig;* wh, *whig;* zh, *azure;* † obsolete.

Thankfully, thangk'ful-li, *adv. In a thankful manner.*
Thankfulness, thangk'ful-nes, *n.* Expression of gratitude; gratitude; a lively sense of good received.
Thankless, thangk'les, *a. Unthankful;* ungrateful; not obtaining thanks, or not likely to gain thanks.
Thanklessly, thangk'les-li, *adv. Unthankfully;* with ingratitude.
Thanklessness, thangk'les-nes, *n.* Quality of being thankless; ingratitude.
Thank-offering, thangk'of-fér-ing, *n.* An *offering* made in acknowledgment of mercy.
Thanksgiver, thangks'giv-ér, *n.* One *who gives thanks.*
Thanksgiving, thangks'giv-ing, *n. Act of rendering thanks;* a public celebration of divine goodness.
That, тнat, *pron.* or *pronominal adj.* Not this but the other; the more distant, as opposed to *this;* pointing to some person or thing mentioned or alluded to before; often used emphatically.—*pronoun relative.* Equivalent to *who, whom,* or *which;* relating to the antecedent person or thing.—*conj.* Because; noting a reason; noting the final end; noting a result. [Sax. *thæt,* the, that.]
Thatch, thach, *n. A covering;* a roof; straw or other substance used to cover the roofs of buildings, or stacks of hay or grain, for securing them from rain, &c.—*vt. To cover* with straw. [Sax. *thac;* Icel. *thekja,* Sans. *sthag,* to cover.]
Thatched, thacht, *p.a. Covered* with straw or thatch.
Thatcher, thach'ér, *n. One whose occupation is to thatch* houses.
Thatching, thach'ing, *p.n. The act or art of covering* buildings *with thatch;* the materials used for this purpose.
Thaw, thạ, *vi. To melt,* as ice or snow; to become so warm as to melt ice and snow.—*vt. To melt;* to dissolve, as ice or snow.—*n. The melting* of ice or snow. [Sax. *thawan*—Old G. *daujan,* to melt.]
The, тнe, *definite article.* A word prefixed to nouns in the singular and plural number, to indicate what particular thing or things are meant; used also before adjectives in the comparative and superlative degree. [Sax.]
Theatre, thē'a-tér, *n. A place for seeing or being seen;* an edifice in which shows were exhibited for the amusement of spectators; in modern times, a house for the exhibition of tragedies, comedies, and farces; a playhouse; a place rising by steps like the seats of a theatre; a place of action; a building for the exhibition of scholastic exercises, as at Oxford; a room with circular seats and a table in the centre turning on a pivot, for anatomical demonstrations. [Fr. *théâtre;* Gr. *thedomai,* to see.]
Theatrical, thē-at'rik-al, *a. Pertaining to a theatre;* resembling the manner of dramatic performers; calculated for display. [Gr. *theatrikos.*]
Theatrically, thē-at'rik-al-li, *adv.* In the manner of actors on the stage.
Theatricals, thē-at'rik-alz, *n.pl.* Dramatic performances.
Theban, thē'ban, *n.* A native of Thebes; a wise man (ironically).
Theft, theft, *n. Act of thieving;* the felonious taking of another person's goods; the thing stolen. [Sax. *theofth*—*theofian,* to thieve.]
Their, тнâr, *possessive adj. pron. Of them;* belonging to them.—*Theirs, pl.*

possessive case of *they.* [Sax. *hiora,* of them.]
Theism, thē'izm, *n. The belief* or acknowledgment *of* the existence of *a God,* as opposed to atheism. [Fr. *théisme;* Gr. *Theos,* God.]
Theist, thē'ist, *n. One who believes in* the existence of *a God.*
Theistical, thē-ist'ik-al, *a. Pertaining to theism,* or to a theist.
Theme, thēm, *n. That which is placed* or laid down; a subject on which a person writes or speaks; a short dissertation composed by a student; a radical verb; in music, the subject of a new composition. [Gr. *thema*—*tithēmi,* to place.]
Themselves, тнem-selvz', a compound of *them* and *selves,* and added to *they* by way of emphasis.
Then, тнen, *adv. At that time;* afterward; soon afterward; in that case; therefore; for this reason; at another time.—*conj.* In that case; in consequence. [Old Sax. and Goth. *than.*]
Thence, тнens, *adv. From that place;* from that time; for that reason. [Sax. *thanon.*]
Thenceforth, тнens'forth, *adv. From that time.*
Thenceforward, тнens'for-wėrd, *adv. From that time onward.*
Theocracy, thē-ok'ra-si, *n. Government of God;* government of a state by the immediate direction of God, or the state thus governed. [Fr. *théocratie*—Gr. *Theos,* God, and *kratos,* power.]
Theocratic, thē-o-krat'ik, *a. Pertaining to a theocracy;* administered by the immediate direction of God. [Fr. *théocratique.*]
Theodolite, thē-od'o-lit, *n.* A surveyor's instrument for measuring horizontal and also vertical angles. [from Gr. *theaomai,* to see or view, and *dolichos,* long.]
Theologian, thē-o-lō'ji-an, *n. A person well versed in theology,* or a professor of divinity; a divine. [Fr. *théologien.*]
Theological, thē-o-loj-ik-al, *a. Pertaining to theology* or the science of God and of divine things. [Fr. *théologique.*]
Theologically, thē-o-loj'ik-al-li, *adv. According to the principles of theology.*
Theologist, thē-ol'o-jist, *n.* One versed *in theology;* a divine.
Theology, thē-ol'o-ji, *n. A discourse concerning God;* the science which teaches the existence and attributes of God, his laws and government, the doctrines we are to believe, and the duties we are to practise; divinity. [Gr. *Theos,* God, and *logos,* discourse.]
Theorem, thē'ō-rem, *n. A speculation;* a mathematical proposition to be proved by a chain of reasoning; a position laid down as an acknowledged truth. [Fr. *théorème*—Gr. *theōreō,* to look at.]
Theoretical, thē-ō-ret'ik-al, *a. Pertaining to theory;* depending on theory; speculative. [Gr. *theōrētikos.*]
Theoretically, thē-ō-ret'ik-al-li, *adv. In* or *by theory;* in speculation.
Theoric, thē'ō-rik, *n. Theory.*
Theorist, thē'ō-rist, *n. One who forms theories;* one given to theory and speculation. [Fr. *théoriste.*]
Theorize, thē'ō-riz, *vi. To form a theory* or *theories;* to speculate. *ppr.* theorizing, *pret. & pp.* theorized.
Theory, thē'ō-ri, *n. A looking at* or beholding; speculation; an exposition of the general principles of any science; the science distinguished from the art; the philosophical explanation of phenomena, either physical or moral; a

collected view of all that is known on any speculative subject. [Fr. *théorie*—Gr. *theōreō,* to look at.]
Therapeutic, thē-ra-pūt'ik, *a. Pertaining to the cure of diseases.* [Gr. *therapeutikos*—*therapeuō,* to cure.]
Therapeutics, thē-ra-pūt'iks, *n.* That part of medicine which respects the discovery and application of *remedies* for diseases.
There, тнâr, *adv. In that place;* in the place most distant, as opposed to *here; there* is also used to begin sentences, or before a verb; sometimes pertinently, and sometimes not. [Sax. *thær.*]
Thereabout, Thereabouts, тнâr-a-bout', тнâr-a-bouts', *adv. Near that place;* nearly.
Thereafter, тнâr-aft'ér, *adv. After that;* accordingly. [*there* and *after.*]
Thereat, тнâr-at', *adv. At that place;* on that account.
Thereby, тнâr-bī', *adv. By that;* in consequence of that; near that.
Therefore, тнâr'for, *adv. For that;* consequently; in recompense for this or that.
Therein, тнâr-in', *adv. In that or this place,* time, or thing.
Thereinto, тнâr-in-tö', *adv. Into that.*
Thereof, тнâr-ov', *adv. Of that or this.*
Thereon, тнâr-on', *adv. On that or this.*
Thereto, Thereunto, тнâr-tö', тнâr-un-tö', *adv. To that or this.*
Thereupon, тнâr-up-on', *adv. Upon that or this;* in consequence of that; immediately.
Therewith, тнâr-with', *adv. With that or this.*
Therewithal, тнâr-with-ąl', *adv.* At the same time.
Thermal, thėr'mal, *a. Warm; hot;* a term applied chiefly to warm or hot springs. [L. *thermæ,* warm springs; Gr. *thermos,* hot.]
Thermometer, thėr-mom'et-ér, *n. A measurer of heat;* an instrument for measuring the variations of heat or temperature. [Gr. *thermos,* hot, and *metron,* a measure.]
Thermometric, Thermometrical, thėr-mō-met'rik, thėr-mō-met'rik-al, *a.Pertaining to a thermometer;* made by a thermometer.
Thermometrically, thėr-mō-met'rik-al-li, *adv. By means of a thermometer.*
Thesaurus, thē-sạ'rus, *n. A treasury;* a lexicon. [L.]
These, тнēz, *pronominal adj.* The plural of *this. These* is opposed to *those,* as *this* is to *that.*
Thesis, thē'sis, *n. A setting or placing;* a laying down; a proposition which a person advances and maintains by argument; a subject; particularly, a subject for a school or college exercise, or the exercise itself; an essay presented by a candidate for a degree, as for that of M.D. [Gr.—*tithēmi,* to set.]
They, тнā, *pron. pl.;* objective case. *them.* The nominative plural of *he, she,* or *it.* It is used indefinitely, as our ancestors used, and the Germans use *man;* as, *they* say, that is, it is said by persons. [Sax. *thæge,* these.]
Thick, thik, *a. Grown; filled up; characterised by density or closeness;* turbid; muddy; noting the diameter of a body; having more depth or extent from one surface to its opposite than usual; crowded with trees or other objects; frequent; set with things close to each other; not easily pervious; not having good articulation. *n. The thickest part,* or the time when anything is thickest.—*adv.* Frequent-

Fāte, fär, fat, fạll; mē, met, hėr; pīne, pin; nōte, not, mȯve; tūbe, tub, bu̇ll; oil, pound.

ly; to a thicker depth than usual. [Sax. *thic.*]
Thicken, thik'n, *vt.* To *make thick or thicker;* to make dense or close; to make concrete; to make close, or more close; to make more numerous; to strengthen!.—*vi.* To *become thick or more thick;* to become dense; to become dark; to be consolidated; to become close; to become quick; to be crowded. [Sax. *thiccian.*]
Thickening, thik'n-ing, *p.n.* Something put into a liquid or mass to make it *thicker.*
Thicket, thik'et, *n.* A collection of trees or shrubs *closely set.*
Thick-headed, thik'hed-ed, *a. Having a thick skull;* dull; stupid.
Thickish, thik'ish, *a. Somewhat thick.*
Thickly, thik'li, *adv.* Deeply; to a great depth; compactly.
Thickness, thik'nes, *n. State of being thick;* density; consistence; the extent of a body from side to side; closeness of the parts; state of being crowded; dulness of the sense of hearing; want of acuteness. [Sax. *thiccnes.*]
Thief, thēf, *n.* **Thieves**, thēvz, *pl. A person guilty of theft;* one who *secretly* and feloniously takes the goods of another; one who takes the property of another wrongfully, either secretly or by violence. [Sax. *theof.*]
Thieve, thēv, *vi.* To *practise theft;* to steal. *ppr.* thieving, *pret. & pp.* thieved. [Sax. *theofian.*]
Thievery, thēv'e-ri, *n. Theft;* the practice of stealing; that which is stolen.
Thievish, thēv'ish, *a. Given to theft;* secret; acting by stealth; partaking of the nature of theft.
Thievishly, thēv'ish-li, *adv. In a thievish manner;* by theft.
Thievishness, thēv'ish-nes, *n. Quality of being thievish.*
Thigh, thī, *n. The thick part* of the lower limb, between the knee and the hip-joint. [Sax. *theoh.*]
Thill, thil, *n. The shaft* of a cart, gig, or other carriage. [Sax.]
Thiller, Thill-horse, thil'er, thil'hors, *n. The horse which goes between the thills* or shafts, and supports them.
Thimble, thim'bl, *n. A cover for the thumb,* such as that still used by sailors and sail-makers; a kind of cover for the finger, usually made of metal, used by tailors and seamstresses for driving the needle through cloth. [*thumb-bell.*]
Thin, thin, *a. Stretched out,* so as to have little thickness; having little thickness from one surface to the opposite; rare; not dense; not crowded; not well grown; slim; small; lean; fine; not full; of a loose texture; not impervious to the sight; not abounding; slight; not sufficient for a covering. *adv.* Not thickly or closely; in a scattered state. [Sax. *thyn*—Gr. *teinō,* to stretch out.]—*vt.* To *make thin;* to make rare or less thick; to make less close, crowded, or numerous; to make less dense. *ppr.* thinning, *pret. & pp.* thinned. [Sax. *thinnian.*]
Thine, vhīn, *pronominal adj. Thy;* belonging to thee; relating to thee. The principal use of *thine,* now, is when a verb is interposed between this word and the noun to which it refers; as, I will not take anything that is *thine.* [Sax. *thin.*]
Thing, thing, *n. That which is thought of;* a matter; a cause; an event; that which falls out; that which is done, told, or proposed; any substance; that which is created; any particular article; a part; something; used of persons in contempt; used in a sense of honour. [Sax.—Old G. *dankyan.*]
Think, thingk, *vi.* To *look* with the mind's eye; to have ideas, or to revolve ideas in the mind; to judge; to hold as a settled opinion; to intend; to consider likely; to suppose; to fancy; to muse; to ponder; to call to mind; to consider; to presume; to esteem; to purpose.—*vt.* To conceive; to believe; to esteem; to seem or appear, as in the phrases methinks and methought. *ppr.* thinking, *pret. & pp.* thought. [Sax.*thencan*—Sans.*tark,* to look upon.]
Thinker, thingk'er, *n. One who thinks;* one who thinks in a particular manner.
Thinking, thingk'ing, *p.a. Having the faculty of thought;* capable of a regular train of ideas.—*p.n. Cogitation;* judgment.
Thinly, thin'li, *adv.* In a loose scattered manner; not thickly.
Thinness, thin'nes, *n. State of being thin;* smallness of extent from one side or surface to the opposite; a state approaching to fluidity; rareness; a scattered state; paucity.
Thinnish, thin'ish, *a. Somewhat thin.*
Thin-skinned, thin'skind, *a. Having a thin skin;* unduly sensitive.
Third, thėrd, *a. The ordinal of three.* *n. The third part* of anything; the sixtieth part of a second of time; in music, an interval containing three diatonic sounds and two degrees or intervals. [Sax. *thridda.*]
Thirdborough, thėrd'bu-rō, *n.* A petty constable.
Third-century, thėrd'sen-tū-ri, *n.* The century commencing with the year 201.
Third-estate, thėrd'es-tāt, *n.* In Great Britain, the Commons, the Sovereign constituting the first estate, and the Lords the second.
Third-floor, thėrd'flōr, *n.* The fourth story of a house.
Thirdly, thėrd'li, *adv. In the third place.*
Thirst, thėrst, *n. State of being dry or parched;* dryness; a painful sensation of the throat, occasioned by the want of drink; a want and eager desire after anything.—*vi.* To be or *become dry;* to experience a painful sensation of the throat for want of drink; to have a vehement desire for anything (with *for*). [Sax. *thurst*—L. *torreo,* to parch.]
Thirstily, thėrst'i-li, *adv. In a thirsty manner.*
Thirstiness, thėrst'i-nes,*n. State of being thirsty;* thirst.
Thirsty, thėrst'i, *a. Very dry;* feeling a painful sensation of the throat for want of drink; having a vehement desire of anything; parched. [Old Fris. *toerstigh.*]
Thirteen, ther'tēn, *a. Ten and three.* [Sax. *threottyne.*]
Thirteenth, ther'tēnth, *a. The ordinal of thirteen.*
Thirteenth-century, ther'tėnth-sen-tū-ri, *n.* The century commencing with the year 1201.
Thirtieth, ther'ti-eth, *a. The ordinal of thirty.* [Sax. *thrittigotha.*]
Thirty, ther'ti, *a. Thrice ten,* or twenty and ten. [Sax. *thrittig.*]
This, THis, *pronom. a.* **These**, *pl.* That is present or near in place or time; that is just mentioned; that is to be now mentioned; denoting the present time or time last past. [Sax. mas. *thes,* fem. *theos,* n. *this.*]
Thistle, this'l, *n. A prickly plant.* [Sax. *thistel—thydan,* to pierce.]

Thistle-down, this'l-doun, *n.* The fine feathery substance attached to the seeds of *thistles,* by which they are conveyed to a distance by the wind.
Thistly, this'l-i, *a. Overgrown with thistles.*
Thither, THIVH'er, *adv. To that place;* opposed to hither; to that end or point. [Sax. *thider.*]
Thitherward, Thitherwards, THIVH'er-werd, THIVH'er-werdz, *adv. Toward that place.*
Tho', THŌ. A contraction of *though.*
Thong, thong, *n. Something that binds;* a band; a strap of leather, used for fastening anything; a string of leather. [Sax. *thwang.*]
Thorax, thō'raks, *n.* The chest, or that part of the body situated between the neck and the abdomen, which contains and *protects* the lungs, &c. [L.—Gr. *tēreō,* to watch over, to guard.]
Thorn, thorn, *n.* A tree or shrub armed with *spines,* as the hawthorn, blackthorn, &c.; a sharp woody shoot from the stem of a tree or shrub; a sharp process from the woody part of a plant; a spine; anything troublesome. [Sax.]
Thorny, thorn'i, *a. Full of thorns;* rough with thorns; occasioning pain or distress; vexatious; sharp.
Thorough, thu'rō, *a. Passing through* to the end or other side; perfect. *prep.*† By means of. [Sax. *thurh.*]
Thorough-bred, thu'rō-bred, *a.* Bred from the best blood, as horses; completely bred or accomplished.
Thoroughfare, thu'rō-fār, *n. A passage through;* a passage from one street to another; an unobstructed way.
Thorough-going, thu'rō-gō-ing, *a. Going all lengths.*
Thoroughly, thu'rō-li, *adv.* Fully; entirely; completely.
Thorough-paced, thu'rō-pāst, *a.* Perfect in what is undertaken; going all lengths.
Those, THŌz, *pron.; pl.* of *that;* as, those men.
Thou, VHOU, *pron.;* in the obj. *thee.* The second personal pronoun, in the singular number; the pronoun which is used in addressing persons in the solemn style. *Thou* is used only in the solemn style, unless in very familiar language, and by the Quakers. [Sax. *thu*—L. *tu.*]
Though, THŌ, *conj.* Even if; notwithstanding that; although. [Old Sax. *thoh.*]
Thought, that, *n. That which one thinks;* act of thinking; idea; a fancy; particular consideration; opinion; notion; the act of pondering; design; silent contemplation; care; inward reasoning; the workings of conscience. [Sax.*theaht*—*thencan,* to think.]
Thoughtful, that'ful, *a. Full of thought;* reflecting; musing; attentive; careful; considerate; circumspect; promoting serious thought; solicitous.
Thoughtfully, that'ful-li, *adv. With thought* or consideration.
Thoughtfulness, that'ful-nes, *n. State of being thoughtful;* solicitude.
Thoughtless, that'les, *a. Heedless;* careless; dissipated; stupid.
Thoughtlessly, that'les-li, *adv. Without thought;* carelessly; stupidly.
Thoughtlessness, that'les-nes, *n. Want of thought;* heedlessness; inattention.
Thousand, thou'zand, *a. Denoting the number of ten hundred;* denoting a great number indefinitely.—*n. The number of ten hundred.* [Sax. *thūsend.*]
Thousand-fold, thou'zand-fōld, *a. Multiplied by a thousand.*

ch, *chain;* ʒ, *job;* ḡ, *go;* ng, *sing;* TH, *then;* th, *thin;* w, *wig;* wh, *whig;* zh, *azure;* † obsolete.

Thousandth, thou'zandth, *a.* The ordinal of thousand.—*n.* The thousandth part of anything.

Thraldom, thral'dom, *n.* State of a thrall or slave; bondage; a state of servitude. [Dan. *traeldom.*]

Thrall, thral, *n.* A bearer of burdens; a bondsman; a serf; slavery; bondage. [Sax. *thrael*—Sans. *dhri*, to carry.]

Thrash, thrash, *vt.* To beat; to beat out grain from, as from wheat, oats, &c.; to beat soundly with a stick or whip.—*vi.* To practise thrashing; to perform the business of thrashing; to labour; to drudge. [Sax. *therscan.*]

Thrasher, thrash'er, *n.* One who thrashes grain.

Thrashing, thrash'ing, *p.n.* Act of beating out grain; a sound drubbing.

Thrashing-floor, thrash'ing-flōr, *n.* A floor or area on which grain is beaten out.

Thrasonical†, thrā-son'ik-al, *a.* Boastful; bragging.

Thread, thred, *n.* A very small *twist* of flax, silk, or other fibrous substance, drawn out to a considerable length; a fine line of gold or silver; something resembling a thread; something continued in a long course; the prominent spiral part of a screw.—*vt.* To pass a *thread through* the eye of, as of a needle; to pass or pierce through, as a narrow way or channel. [Sax. *thraed*—*thrawan*, to wind.]

Threadbare, thred'bār, *a.* Worn to the *naked thread*; worn out; used till it has lost its interest.

Threaden†, thred'n, *a.* Made of thread.

Thready, thred'i, *a.* Like thread or *filaments*; slender; containing thread.

Threat, thret, *n.* A *menace*; declaration of determination to inflict punishment or pain on another.—*vt.* To threaten (used only in poetry). [Sax. *thryth.*]

Threaten, thret'n, *vt.* To *pain by threats*; to declare the purpose of inflicting punishment, *pain*, or other evil, upon; to terrify by threats; to menace by action; to present the appearance of coming evil; to exhibit the appearance of some danger which will happen to. [Sax. *threatian*—Sans. *druh*, to hurt, to pain.]

Threatening, thret'n-ing, *p.a.* Indicating a threat or menace.—*p.n.* Act of menacing; a menace; declaration of a purpose to inflict evil on a person or country, usually for sins and offences.

Threateningly, thret'n-ing-li, *adv.* With a threat or menace.

Three, thrē, *a.* Two and one; often used, like other adjectives, without the noun to which it refers. [Sax. *thry.*]

Three-master, thrē'mast-ėr, *n.* A ship having *three masts*.

Threepence, thrē'pens, *n.* The sum of *three pennies*; a small silver coin of three times the value of a penny.

Threepenny, thrē'pen-ni, *a.* Worth *threepence* only; of little value; mean.

Three-pile†, thrē'pīl, *n.* The finest and most costly kind of velvet.

Three-ply, thrē'plī, *a.* Threefold; consisting of three thicknesses; as, three-ply carpeting.

Threescore, thrē'skōr, *a.* Three times a score; thrice twenty; sixty.

Threne†, thrēn, *n.* Lamentation. [Gr. *thrēnos*, mourning.]

Threnetic, thrēn-et'ik, *a.* Sorrowful. [Gr. *thrēnētikos*, inclined to mourning.]

Thresh, thresh, *vt.* See THRASH.

Threshold, thresh'ōld, *n.* The *plank*, piece of timber, or stone which lies at the bottom or under a door, particularly of a dwelling-house, church, &c.; so named from its being *trodden* upon by the feet; entrance; door; the place or point of entering or beginning. [Sax. *thersc-wald*—Old G. *drescan*, to rub, and *wald*, a wood.]

Thrice, thrīs, *adv.* Three times; sometimes used by way of amplification; very.

Thrid, thrid, *vt.* To *thread*; to slide through, as a narrow passage; to slip or run through, as a needle. *ppr.* thridding, *pret. & pp.* thridded. [corruption of *thread.*]

Thrift, thrift, *n.* A state of *thriving*; frugality; economy; good husbandry; success in the acquisition of property; increase of worldly goods; prosperity. [from *thrive.*]

Thriftily, thrift'i-li, *adv.* Frugally; with increase of worldly goods.

Thriftiness, thrift'i-nes, *n.* Quality of being thrifty; good husbandry.

Thriftless, thrift'les, *a.* Having no *thrift* or management; profuse; not thriving.

Thriftlessly, thrift'les-li, *adv.* Without *thriving*; extravagantly.

Thriftlessness, thrift'les-nes, *n.* A state of being *thriftless*.

Thrifty, thrift'i, *a.* Thriving by industry and frugality; using economy; increasing in wealth; well husbanded.

Thrill, thril, *vt.* Primarily, to *drill*; to penetrate; to cause a tingling sensation in, that runs through the system with a slight shivering.—*vi.* To feel a sharp, shivering sensation running through the body.—*n.* A thrilling sensation; a warbling; a trill. [Sax. *thyrlian*—Sans. *dri*, to tear, to cleave.]

Thrilling, thril'ing, *p.a.* Penetrating; feeling a tingling, shivering sensation running through the system.

Thrillingly, thril'ing-li, *adv.* With *thrilling sensations*.

Thrive, thrīv, *vi.* To *grow*; to *advance*; to prosper by industry, economy, and good management of property; to increase in goods and estate; to have success. *ppr.* thriving, *pret.* thrived or throve, *pp.* thrived or thriven. [Icel. *thrif*, good fortune; G. *treiben*, to shoot forth.]

Thriving, thrīv'ing, *p.a.* Growing; being prosperous or successful; advancing in wealth.

Thrivingly, thrīv'ing-li, *adv.* In a prosperous way.

Throat, thrōt, *n.* The anterior part of the neck of an animal, in which are the gullet and windpipe; the passage through which anything is ejected upward from the lungs or stomach. [Sax. *throte*—Sans. *tri*, to pass, with *ut*, to go out.]

Throb, throb, *vi.* To *beat*, as the heart or pulse, with more than usual force or rapidity; to beat in consequence of agitation; to palpitate. *ppr.* throbbing, *pret. & pp.* throbbed.—*n.* A beat or strong pulsation; a violent beating of the heart and arteries; a palpitation. [Ar. *darab*, to beat.]

Throbbing, throb'ing, *p.a.* Beating with unusual force, as the heart and pulse; palpitating.—*p.n.* Act of *beating* with unusual force, as the heart and pulse; palpitation.

Throe, thrō, *n.* Violent *pang*; anguish; agony; particularly applied to the anguish of travail in child-birth.—*vt.†* To put in agony. [Sax. *throwian*, to suffer.]

Throne, thrōn, *n.* A royal *seat*; the seat of a bishop; sovereign power and dignity; the place where God peculiarly manifests his power and glory.—*vt.* To place on a throne; to give an elevated place to; to exalt.—*vi.†* To *sit* on a *throne. ppr.* throning, *pret. & pp.* throned. [Old Fr.—Gr. *thronos*, a seat.]

Throned, thrōnd, *p.a.* Exalted.

Throng, throng, *n.* To *crowd together*; to come in multitudes.—*vt.* To crowd or press, as persons; to annoy with a crowd of living beings. [Sax. *thringan*, to crowd together.]—*n.* A multitude *crowded together*; a crowd; a great multitude. [Sax. *thrang.*]

Thronged, throngd, *p.a.* Pressed by a multitude of persons.

Thronging, throng'ing, *p.a.* Crowding *together*; pressing with a multitude of persons.—*p.n.* Act of *crowding together*.

Throstle, thros'l, *n.* A bird of the *thrush* kind; the song-thrush. [Sax.]

Throttle, throt'l, *vt.* To *compress the throat of*, so as to choke; to choke.—*vi.* To choke; to suffocate.—*n.* The windpipe or trachea. [from *throat.*]

Through, thrö, *prep. Noting passage* by transmission; noting the means of conveyance; noting passage among; from end to end, or from side to side; by means of; over the whole surface or extent.—*adv.* From one end or side to the other; from beginning to end; to the end; to the ultimate purpose. [Sax. *thurh*—G. *durch.*]

Throughout, thrö-out', *prep. Quite through*; in every part.—*adv.* In every part.

Throw, thrō, *vt.* To fling in any manner; to drive to a distance from the hand or from an engine; to drive by violence; to venture at dice; to cast; to strip one's self of; to spread carelessly; to prostrate in wrestling.—*vi.* To perform *the act of throwing*; to cast dice. *ppr.* throwing, *pret.* threw, *pp.* thrown.—*n.* Act of *hurling or flinging*; a driving from the hand or from an engine; a cast of dice; the distance which a missile is thrown; as, a stone's throw. [Sax. *thrawan.*]

Thrower, thrō'ėr, *n.* One who *throws*; one who twists or winds silk.

Thrum, thrum, *n.* One of the ends of weavers' threads *cut off*; any coarse yarn; (pl.) *fragments* of threads.—*vt.* To cover with *thrums*; to stick short pieces of yarn through; to twist; to fringe; [D. *trum*] to *drum*; to *tap*; to play coarsely upon with the fingers. *vi.* To play rudely or monotonously on an instrument with the fingers. *ppr.* thrumming, *pret. & pp.* thrummed. [Norm. *thrommes*, thrums of woollen yarn—G. *tremm*, stump.]

Thrummer, thrum'ėr, *n.* One who plays coarsely, as on the harp or guitar.

Thrummy, thrum'i, *a.* Containing or *resembling thrums*.

Thrush, thrush, *n.* A singing bird; [probably from *thrust*, a breaking out] a disease in the foot of a horse of the inflammatory kind; an ulcerous disease of the mouth and throat. [Sax. *thrisc.*]

Thrust, thrust, *vt.* To *push with force*; to drive; to impel; to stab; to pierce (followed by *through*).—*vi.* To make a *push*; to attack with a pointed weapon; to squeeze in; to push forward; to press on. *ppr.* thrusting, *pret. & pp.* thrust. *n.* A *violent* push or driving, as with a pointed weapon; a stab; assault; a horizontal outward pressure, as of rafters against the walls which support them. [Icel. *thrista.*]

Thrusting, thrust'ing, *n.* Act of *pushing* with force.

Thumb, thum, *n.* The short strong thick finger, answering to the other

four; the corresponding member of other animals.—*vt.* To handle awkwardly; to soil with the fingers.—*vi.* To play on with the fingers. [Sax. *thuma.*]

Thumbed, thumd, *p.a.* Having thumbs; soiled with the fingers.

Thumbkin, Thumb-screw, thum'kin, thum'akru, *n.* An instrument of torture for *compressing* the *thumb*, much used in Scotland in the tyrannical times of the seventeenth century.

Thummim, thum'im, *n. pl.* A Hebrew word denoting *perfections.* The *Urim* and *Thummim* were worn in the breastplate of the high-priest.

Thump, thump, *n.* A *heavy blow* given with anything that is thick, as with a club or the fist.—*vt.* To strike with something thick or heavy.—*vi.* To strike or fall with a heavy blow. [formed from the sound of a heavy blow.]

Thunder, thun'der, *n.* The sound which follows a flash of lightning; the report of a discharge of atmospheric electricity; any loud noise; denunciation published.—*vi.* To roar, as an explosion of atmospheric electricity; to make a heavy sound of some continuance; to rattle, or give a heavy rattling sound. *vt.* To emit with noise and terror; to publish, as any denunciation or threat. [Sax. *thunor,* Old *G. thonar—*L. *tonitru*—Sans. *stan,* to thunder.]

Thunderbolt, thun'dėr-bōlt, *n.* A *shaft of lightning;* a brilliant stream of the electrical fluid passing from one part of the heavens t. another, and particularly from the clouds to the earth; a daring or irresistible hero; fulmination; ecclesiastical denunciation.

Thunder-clap, thun'der-klap, *n.* A *clap of thunder;* sudden report of an explosion of electricity in the atmosphere.

Thunder-cloud, thun'dėr-kloud, *n.* A *cloud* that produces lightning and *thunder.*

Thunderer, thun'dėr-ėr, *n.* He who *thunders.*

Thundering, thun'dėr-ing, *p.a.* Making the noise of an electrical explosion; uttering a loud sound; fulminating denunciations.—*p.n.* The report of an electrical explosion; thunder.

Thunder-rod, thun'dėr-rod, *n.* A metallic *rod* attached to a building, to protect it from the effects of lightning, by acting as a conductor.

Thunder-stone, thun'tėr-stōn, *n.* Formerly, a stone imagined to effect the destruction occasioned by lightning.

Thunder-storm, thun der-storm, *n.* A *storm.* of wind, rain, or hail, accompanied with lightning and *thunder.*

Thunder-stroke, thun'dėr-strōk, *n.* A *thunder-c'ap.*

Thunder-struck, thun'dėr-struk, *p.a. Struck* by lightning; astonished; struck dumb by something surprising suddenly presented to the view.

Thursday, thėrs'dā, *n.* The fifth day of the week. [Dan. *Torsdag,* that is, *Thor's day,* the day consecrated to *Thor,* the old Saxon god of thunder, answering to the Jove of the Greeks and Romans.]

Thus, *t*Hus, *adv.* In *this or that manner;* to this degree or extent. [Sax.]

Thwack, thwak, *vt* To thrash; to belabour.—*n.* A heavy nard blow.

Thwart, thwart, *a. Crooked;* transverse; being across something else; perverse. *vt.* To *cross;* to cross, as a purpose; to withstand; to frustrate or defeat.—*vi.* To be in opposition.—*n.* The bench of a boat on which the rowers sit, placed *athwart* the boat. [Sax. *thweorh;* Old G. *dwerh,* athwart.]

Thwarting, thwart'ing, *p.n.* Act of *crossing* or frustrating.

Thy, *t*Hī, *a.* Thy is the adjective of *thou,* or a pronominal adjective, signifying of thee, or belonging to thee. It is used in the solemn and grave style. [contracted from *thine.*]

Thyme, tim, *n.* An aromatic plant. [Fr. *thym*—Gr. *thuō,* to offer in sacrifice.]

Thymy, tim'i, *a. Abounding with thyme;* fragrant.

Thyself, *t*Hī-self', *pron.* A pronoun used after *thou,* to express distinction with emphasis.

Tiara, ti-a'ra, *n.* An article of dress with which the orientals covered their heads; a kind of turban; an ornament worn by the Jewish high-priest; the pope's triple crown. [Gr. *tiāra* or *tiaras*—Heb. *tūr,* to go around.]

Tiaraed, ti-a'rād, *p.a. Adorned with a tiara.*

Tick, tik, *n.* The common name of various small parasitical insects, called also mites, that infest sheep, dogs, goats, cows, &c. [Fr. *tique.*]

Tick, tik, *n.* The *cover* of a bed, which contains the feathers, wool, or other material. [D. *tijk*—L. *tego,* to cover.]

Tick, tik, *vi.* To beat; to pat; or to make a small noise by beating or otherwise, as a watch. [D. *tikken.*]

Ticket, tik'et, *n.* Primarily, a slip of paper fastened within the mouth of a lawyer's book-bag; a piece of paper or a card, which gives the holder a right of admission to some place; a piece of paper bearing some number in a lottery, which entitles the owner to receive such prize as may be drawn against that number; a marked card or slip of paper put upon goods to indicate the price, &c.—*vt.* To *distinguish by a ticket.* [Old Fr. *etiquette.*]

Ticking, tik'ing, *n.* A closely-woven cloth used to contain the feathers or other materials of beds.

Tickle, tik'l, *vt.* To touch or rub lightly, *as a cat;* to touch or rub lightly, and cause a peculiar thrilling sensation in, which excites laughter; to please by slight gratification. *ppr.* tickling, *pret. & pp.* tickled.—*a.*† Unstable; easily overthrown. [Sax. *citelan*—Icel. *kitla,* to tickle; Sax. *cat,* a cat.]

Tickler, tik'l-ėr, *n. One who* or that which *tickles* or pleases.

Tickling, tik'l-ing, *p.n.* The ct of affecting with titillation.

Ticklish, tik'l-ish, *a. Sensible to slight touches;* easily tickled; standing so as to be liable to fall at the slightest touch; unfixed; easily affected; nice; critical; uncertain.

Ticklishly, tik'l-ish-li, *adv. In a ticklish manner.*

Ticklishness, tik'l-ish-nes, *n. State or quality of being ticklish;* criticalness of condition or state.

Tidal, tid'al, *a. Pertaining to tides;* periodically rising and falling.

Tide, tid, *n.* Primarily, *a division of time;* the *periodic* alternate rising and falling of the waters of the ocean and of bays, rivers, &c., connected therewith; course; current; favourable course; flow of blood.—*vi.* To work in or out of a river or harbour by favour of the *tide;* to pour a flood. [Sax. *tid;* Old G. *zit,* time.]

Tideless, tid'les, *a. Having no tide.*

Tide-mill, tid'mil, *n. A mill that is moved by tide-water;* also, a mill for clearing lands from tide-water.

Tide-tables, tīd'tā-blz, *n. pl.* Tables *showing the time of the tides,* or of high-water at any place, or at different places, for each day of the year.

Tide-waiter, tid'wāt-ėr, *n.* An officer who watches the landing of goods, to secure the payment of duties.

Tide-way, tīd'wā, *n. The channel in which the tide sets.*

Tidily, tī'di li, *adv.* Neatly.

Tidiness, ti'di-nes, *n. Quality or state of being tidy;* neatness without richness or elegance; neat simplicity; neatness.

Tidings, tī'dingz, *n. pl.* Account of things which *have happened,* and which were unknown before; news; advice; intelligence. [Dan. *tidende* — Sax. *tidan,* to happen.]

Tidy, tī'di, *a. Seasonable;* being in proper time; dressed with neat simplicity.—*vt.* To make neat; to put in good order. *ppr.* tidying, *pret. & pp.* tidied.—*n.* A piece of fancy knit-work or a cloth, to throw over the back of an arm-chair or a sofa to keep it clean. [D. *tijdig,* tidy.]

Tie, tī, *vt.* To *bind; to fasten with a rope;* to complicate; to unite so as not to be easily parted; to oblige; to restrain; to confine. *ppr.* tieing, *pret. & pp.* tied.—*n.* That *which fastens together;* a knot; a fastening; obligation, moral or legal; a knot of hair; an equality in numbers, as of votes, &c., which prevents either party from being victorious; a sort of neckcloth. [Sax. *tian*—Gr. *deō,* to bind.]

Tier, tėr, *n.* A *row; a rank;* particularly when two or more rows are placed one above another. [Sax. *tier,* series, heap.]

Tierce, tėrs, *n.* A *third;* a cask whose contents are *one-third* of a pipe, that is, forty gallons; or, it may be, the measure; in gaming, a sequence of three cards of the same colour. [Old Fr.—L. *tertius,* third.]

Tiger, tī'gėr, *n.* A fierce and rapacious feline quadruped of Asia, so named from its *swiftness.* [Fr. *tigre;* Gr. *tigris*—Sans. *tur,* to hasten.]

Tigerish, tī'gėr-ish, *a. Like a tiger.*

Tight, tit, *a. Tied;* not loose or open; having the joints so close that no fluid can enter or escape; not leaky; not admitting much air; sitting close to the body, as clothes; not having holes or crevices; closely dressed; compact; not ragged; not slack, applied to a rope stretched out; handy!; adroit!. *adv.*† Handily. [Sax. *tige,* a pulling—*getian,* to tie.]

Tighten, tit'n, *vt.* To draw tight or *tighter;* to straiten.

Tightly, tit'li, *adv. In a tight manner;* closely; compactly; briskly†.

Tightness, tit'nes, *n. State or quality of being tight.*

Tigress, tī'gres, *n. The female of the tiger.* [from *tiger.*]

Tigrine, tī'grin, *a. Like a tiger.* [L. *tigrinus.*]

Tigrish, tī'grish, *a. Resembling a tiger.*

Tile, til, *n.* A plate or piece of baked clay or earthenware, used for *covering* the roofs of buildings; a piece of baked clay used in drains.—*vt.* To cover with *tiles;* to cover, tiles. *ppr.* tiling *pret. & pp.* tiled. [Sax. *tigel*—L. *tego* to cover.]

Tiled, tild, *p.a. Covered with tiles.*

Tiler, tīl'ėr, *n. One who covers* buildings with *tiles;* the door-keeper of a mason-lodge.

Tiling, tīl'ing, *p.n.* A roof covered with

---

ch, *ch*ain; j, *j*ob; g, *g*o; ng, si*ng*; *t*H, *th*en; th, *th*in; w, *w*ig; wh, *wh*ig; zh, a*z*ure; † obsolete.

tiles; tiles in general; the operation of covering roofs with tiles.
Till, til, n. A money-box in a shop; a drawer. [Sax. *tilian*, to reckon.]
Till, til, *prep.* or *adv.* To the time or time of; used before verbs and sentences in a like sense, denoting to the time specified in the sentence or clause following; to the degree that; until. [Sax. *til, tille*.]
Till, til, *vt.* To labour; to cultivate; to plough and prepare for seed, and to dress crops of. [Sax. *tilian*]
Tillage, til'áj, n. Act or operation of tilling; the operation or art of preparing land for seed; cultivation; husbandry; agriculture.
Tiller, til'ér, n. One who tills; a husbandman; [Sax. *telgor*, a plant, shoot, twig] the shoot of a plant springing from the bottom of the original stalk; the bar employed to turn the rudder of a ship; a small drawer; a till. [Sax. *tilia—tilian*, to till.]
Tilt, tilt, n. A covering stretched overhead; the cloth covering of a cart or waggon; the cover of a boat; a small awning of canvas, extended over the stern-sheets of a boat.—*vt.* To cover with a cloth or awning. [Sax. *teld—*L. *tendo*, to stretch.]
Tilt, tilt, *vi.* To run or ride and thrust with a lance; to fight, generally; to lean; to fall, as on one side.—*vt.* To set in a sloping position, as a barrel.—n. A shock; a military game, at which combatants ran against each other with lances on horseback; a large hammer raised by machinery, used in iron manufactures. [Sax. *teultian*, to shake, reel.]
Tilter, tilt'ér, n. One who tilts.
Tilth, tilth, n. That which is tilled; the state of the soil in respect to ploughing, manuring, &c. [Sax. from *tilian*, to till—Sans. *tala*, the ground.]
Timber, tim'bér, n. That sort of wood which is proper for buildings or for tools, ships, &c.; applied to a standing tree suitable for such purposes, or pieces of wood prepared for use by hewing or sawing; a single piece or squared stick of wood for building, or already framed; a rib or curving piece of wood, branching outward from the keel of a ship in a vertical direction. *vt.* To furnish with timber. [Sax.; Old G. *zimbarón*, to build.]
Timbered, tim'bérd, *p.a.* Furnished with timber; wooded.
Timbering, tim'bér-ing, *p.n.* Timber materials.
Timbrel, tim'brel, n. An instrument of music; a kind of drum, tabor, or tabret, which has been in use from the highest antiquity. [Sp. *tamboril.*]
Time, tim, n. A particular portion or part of duration, whether past, present, or future; a proper time; a season; life or duration; age; epoch; era; repeated performance; doubling; addition of a number to itself; measure of sounds in music; the state of things at a particular period (commonly in the plural).—*vt.* To adapt to the time or occasion; to bring, begin, or perform at the proper season or time; to regulate as to time; to measure, as in music or harmony. *ppr.* timing, *pret. & pp.* timed. [Sax. *tima*; Gr. *temnō*, to cut, to part off, to mark off.]
Time-bill, tim'bil, n. A bill of the times of starting and arrivals of railway trains.
Timed, timd, *p.a. Adapted to the time,* the season, or occasion.

Time-honoured, tim'on-érd,*a. Honoured for a long time.*
Time-keeper, tim'kēp-ér, n. A clock, watch, or other chronometer; in workshops, one appointed to keep the workmen's time.
Timeless, tim'les, a. Done at an improper time; untimely.
Timeliness, tim'li-nes, n. Quality of being timely; seasonableness.
Timely, tim'li, a. Being in good time; seasonable; opportune; sufficiently early.—*adv.* Early; soon; in good season.
Time-piece, tim'pēs, n. A clock or other instrument, to measure or show the progress of time; a chronometer.
Time-pleaser, tim'plēz-ér, n. One who complies with the prevailing opinions, whatever they may be.
Time-server, tim'sérv-ér, n. One who adapts his opinions and manners to the times.
Time-table, tim'tā-bl, n. A table of the times of starting, arrivals, &c., of railway trains.
Time-worn, tim'wōrn, a. Impaired by time.
Timid, ti'mid, a. Fearful; wanting courage to meet danger; cowardly; faint-hearted; shrinking; retiring. [Fr. *timide*—L. *timeo*, to fear.]
Timidity, ti-mid'i-ti, n. Fearfulness; want of courage to face danger; habitual cowardice. [Fr. *timidité.*]
Timidly, ti'mid-li, *adv.* In a timid manner; weakly; without courage.
Timorous, ti'mor-us, a. Fearful of danger; destitute of courage, indicating fear; full of scruples. [It. *timoroso—*L. *timeo*, to fear.]
Timorously, ti'mor-us-li, *adv.* Timidly; without boldness.
Timorousness, ti'mor-us-nes, n. Fearfulness; timidity.
Tin, tin, n. A white, soft, and very malleable metal, with a slight tinge of yellow, much used in the arts; thin plates of iron covered with tin; a dish made of tin, or of iron covered with tin.—*vt.* To cover with tin, or overlay with tinfoil. *ppr.* tinning, *pret. & pp.* tinned. [Sax.—L. *stannum*—Sans. *tan*, to extend.]
Tinct, tingkt, n. Stain; colour; tinge.
Tinctorial, tingk-tō'ri-al, a. Relating to tincture or dyeing; colouring.
Tincture, tingk'tūr, n. A tinge or shade of colour; flavour; the finer and more volatile parts of a substance, separated by a solvent; a spirituous solution of such of the active principles of vegetables and animals as are soluble in proof spirit; spirit containing medicinal substances in solution.—*vt.* To tinge; to communicate a portion of anything foreign to; to imbue, as the mind. *ppr.* tincturing, *pret. & pp.* tinctured. [L. *tinctūra—tingo, tinctus,* to dye—Gr. *tenggō*, to moisten.]
Tinder, tin'dér, n. Something very inflammable used for kindling fire from a spark, as scorched linen. [Sax. *tynder;* Icel. *tundra*, to blaze.]
Tindery, tin'dér-i, a. Like tinder.
Tine, tin, n. The tooth or spike of a fork; a prong; also, the tooth of a harrow or drag. [Sax. *tindas*, the teeth of harrows.]
Tined, tind, *p.a. Furnished with tines.*
Tin-foil, tin'foil, n. Tin reduced to a thin leaf. [Fr. *feuille*—L. *folium*, a leaf.]
Tinge, tinj, *vt.* To colour; to stain; to imbue with something foreign; to communicate to, as the qualities of one

substance, in some degree to another. *ppr.* tinging, *pret. & pp.* tinged.—n. Colour; taste; a slight degree of some colour, taste, or something foreign, infused into another substance; tincture. [L. *tingo*, to wet, to dye, colour.]
Tinged, tinjd, *p.a. Coloured.*
Tingle, ting'gl, *vi.* To feel a kind of thrilling sound resembling that of metallic bodies when struck; to feel a sharp, thrilling pain. *ppr.* tingling, *pret. & pp.* tingled. [W. *tincian—*L. *tinnio*, to ring.]
Tingling, ting'gl-ing, *p.n.* A thrilling sensation.
Tinker, ting'kér, n. A mender of brass kettles, pans, and the like, so called from the noise he makes when at work. *vt.* To mend, as old vessels of brass, copper, &c. [W. *tincerrd.*]
Tinkering, ting'kér-ing, *p.n.* The act or employment of a tinker.
Tinkle, ting'kl, *vi.* To make small, quick, sharp sounds; to clink; to hear a small, sharp sound.—*vt.* To cause to clink or make sharp, quick sounds. *ppr.* tinkling, *pret. & pp.* tinkled.—n. A clink; a quick, sharp noise. [W. *tincial.*]
Tinkling, ting'kl-ing, *p.n.* A small, quick, sharp sound.
Tinman, tin'man, n. A manufacturer of tin vessels; a dealer in tinware.
Tin-mine, tin'min, n. A mine where tin is obtained.
Tinned, tind, *p.a. Covered with tin.*
Tinning, tin'ing, *p.n.* The act, art, or process of covering plates of iron, the inner surfaces of iron or copper vessels, &c., with a thin coat of tin; the covering or layer thus put on.
Tinny, tin'i, a. Abounding with tin.
Tinplate, tin'plāt, n. Thin sheet-iron coated with tin, in order to protect it from oxidation or rust.
Tinsel, tin'sel, n. Something sparkling; something superficially shining and showy; a kind of shining cloth; a kind of lace.—a. Gaudy; showy to excess; specious.—*vt.* To adorn with something glittering and showy, without much value; to make gaudy. *ppr.* tinselling, *pret. & pp.* tinselled. [Old Fr. *estincelle—*L. *scintilla*, a spark.]
Tint, tint, n. A tinge; a dye; a slight colouring distinct from the ground or principal colour.—*vt.* To tinge; to give a slight colouring to. [It. *tinta*, a dye—L. *tingo, tinctus*, to dye.]
Tinted, tint'ed, *p.a. Tinged.*
Tinting, tint'ing, *p.n.* A forming of tints.
Tiny, ti'ni, a. Very small; little; puny. [G. *dünn*, thin; L. *tenuis*, thin.]
Tip, tip, n. The end; the extremity of anything small; a gentle stroke; a tap. *vt.* To cover the tip or the end of; to form a point upon with something; [for tap] to strike slightly, or with the end of anything small; to tap. *ppr.* tipping, *pret. & pp.* tipped. [D.]
Tippet, tip'et, n. A narrow garment or covering of fur or cloth for the neck and shoulders. [Sax. *tæppet*, a tippet.]
Tipple, tip'l, *vi.* To drink strong liquors habitually; to indulge in the improper use of spirituous liquors.—*vt.* To drink, as strong liquors, in excess. *ppr.* tippling, *pret. & pp.* tippled. [dimin. probably from tops.]
Tippled, tip'ld, *p.a.* Intoxicated; inebriated.
Tippler, tip'l-ér, n. One who tipples; a drunkard; a sot.
Tippling, tip'l-ing, *p.n.* The habitual practice of drinking strong liquors.
Tipsily, tip'si-li, *adv.* In a tipsy manner.

Fāte, fär, fat, fall; mē, met, hér; pīne, pin; nōte, not, mōve; tūbe, tub, bull; oil, pound.

Tip-staff, tip'staf, *n.* An officer who bears *a staff tipped* with metal; a constable; a staff tipped with metal.
Tipsy, tip'si, *a.* Overpowered with strong drink; intoxicated. [from *tipple*.]
Tiptoe, tip'tō, *n.* The end of the toe.
Tiptop, tip'top, *n.* The highest or utmost degree.
Tirade, ti-rād', *n. A long train* of words; a series of violent declamation; a declamatory flight of censure or reproof. [Fr. *tirade*—L. *traho*, *tractum*, to draw, to draw out lengthwise.]
Tire, tir, *n.* A head-dress; furniture; apparatus; attire (which see); [from *tie*, a band or hoop of iron, used *to tie* or *bind* the fellies of wheels, to secure them from wearing and breaking.—*vt.* To adorn; to dress. *ppr.* tiring, *pret. & pp.* tired. [Sax. *tier*, decoration.]
Tire, tir, *vt.* To *weary*; to harass; to exhaust the strength of by toil or labour; to exhaust, as the power of attending; to exhaust, as patience.—*vi.* To *become weary*; to fail with weariness; to have the patience exhausted. *ppr.* tiring, *pret. & pp.* tired. [Sax. *teorian*, to fail; Gr. *teirō*, to wear out.]
Tiret, tir, *vi.* To seize and tear prey, as a bird does; to seize eagerly.
Tiresome, tir'sum, *a. Wearisome;* fatiguing; exhausting the strength; tedious; exhausting the patience.
Tiresomeness, tir'sum-nes, *n. The act or quality of tiring* or exhausting strength or patience; wearisomeness.
Tiring-house, Tiring-room, tir'ing-hous, tir'ing-röm, *n.* The room or place where players dress for the stage.
Tis, tiz, a contraction of *it is*, often used in poetry.
Tisic, Tisical, ti'zik, ti'zik-al, *a.* See PHTHISIC, PHTHISICAL.
Tissue, ti'shū, *n. Anything interwoven;* cloth *interwoven* with gold or silver; in animals, texture of parts; the minute elementary parts of which the organs of plants are composed; a connected series. [Old Fr. *tissu*, a headband of woven stuff—L. *texo*, to weave.]
Tit, tit, *n.* A small horse, in contempt; a woman, in contempt; a small bird; a titmouse or tomtit. [Icel. *teitr*, a little horse.]
Titan, ti'tan, *n.* In mythology, a son of Cœlus and Terra, or of heaven and earth. The Titans are said to have dethroned their father, and waged war with Jupiter for the government, but were defeated and thrown into Tartarus.
Titanic, ti-tan'ik, *a. Resembling a Titan.*
Titanian, Titanitic, ti-tan'i-an, ti-tan'it'ik, *a. Pertaining to titanium.*
Titanium, ti-tan'i-um, *n.* A metal found oxidised in several minerals, and occurring occasionally in the metallic form in the slag of ironworks. [from Gr. *titānos*, lime, chalk.]
Titbit, tit'bit, *n.* See TIDBIT.
Tithable, tiᴛʜ'a-bl, *a. Subject to the payment of tithes.*
Tithe, tiᴛʜ, *n. The tenth part* of anything; the tenth part of the increase annually arising from the profits of land and stock, allotted to the clergy for their support; a small part.—*vt. To levy a tenth part on;* to tax to the amount of a tenth. *ppr.* tithing, *pret. & pp.* tithed. [Sax. *teotha;* Goth. *taihun*, ten.]
Tithe-free, tiᴛʜ'frē, *a. Exempt from the payment of tithes.*
Tithe-gatherer, tiᴛʜ'gaᴠʜ-ėr-ėr, *n. One who collects tithes.*

Tithe-paying, tiᴠʜ'pā-ing, *p.a. Paying tithes;* subjected to pay tithes.
Tither, tiᴠʜ'ėr, *n. One who tithes.*
Tithing, tiᴠʜ'ing, *p.n. Act of levying tithes;* a number or company *of ten* householders, with their families,who, dwelling near each other, were sureties to the king for the good behaviour of each other.
Titillate, ti'til-lāt, *vi. To tickle. ppr.* titillating, *pret. & pp.* titillated. [L. *titillo, titillatum.*]
Titillation, ti-til-lā'shon, *n. The act of tickling,* or the state of being tickled; any slight pleasure. [Fr.]
Titlark, tit'lärk, *n. A small* bird, a species of *lark.* [*tit* and *lark.*]
Title, ti'tl, *n.* An inscription put over anything; the inscription in the beginning of a book; a general head, containing particulars; an appellation of dignity; a name; right; a claim of right; that which is the foundation of ownership; the instrument which is evidence of a right.—*vt. To entitle;* to name; to call. *ppr.* titling, *pret. & pp.* titled. [L. *titulus.*]
Titled, ti'tld, *p.a. Having a title.*
Title-deeds, ti'tl-dēdz, *n.* The writings evidencing a man's *title* to property.
Title-page, ti'tl-pāj, *n. The page* of a book *which contains its title.*
Titling, tit'ling, *n. A small* bird, called also moor-titling, stone-chat, &c. [from *tit.*]
Titmouse, tit'mous, *n.* **Titmice**, tit'-mis, *pl.* A *small* bird, a species of warbler. [*tit*, small, and *mouse.*]
Titter, tit'tėr, *vi. To twitter;* to laugh with the tongue striking against the root of the upper teeth; to laugh with restraint.—*n.* A restrained laugh.
Tittering, tit'tėr-ing, *p.n.* Restrained laughter.
Tittle, tit'l, *n. A small particle;* a jot; an iota. [from *tit*, small.]
Tittle-tattle, tit'l-tat'l, *n.* Idle trifling talk; empty prattle.
Titular, tit'ū-lär, *a. Existing in title* or name only; nominal; having the title to an office without discharging the duties of it. [Fr. *titulaire*—L. *titulus*, a title.]
Titular, Titulary, tit'ū-lär, tit'ū-la-ri, *n.* A person invested *with a title*, in virtue of which he holds an office or benefice.
Titularly, tit'ū-lär-li, *adv. By title only;* nominally.
Titulary, tit'ū-la-ri, *a. Consisting in a title;* pertaining to a title.
Tivy, ti'vi, *adv.* With great speed; a huntsman's word.
To, tö, *prep.* In the direction of; opposed to from; noting motion toward a state or condition; noting accord; noting address; noting attention; noting addition; noting amount; noting proportion; noting possession; noting perception; noting the subject of an affirmation; in comparison of; as far as; after an adjective, noting the object; noting obligation; noting enmity; toward; noting effect or end; noting degree; in *to-day* and *to-night*, *to* has the force of *this;* in *to-morrow* it has the force of *in* or *on.*—*adv.* According to Johnson, a particle coming in between two verbs, and noting the second as the object of the first; but it is usually regarded as the sign of the infinitive mood; it also notes intention or futurity. [Sax. *tō*—L. *ad.*]
Toad, tōd, *n.* A paddock; a reptile resembling the frog, but having a more bulky body, a warty skin, and jaws

without teeth. It is not adapted for leaping, but for crawling. [Sax. *tade.*]
Toad-stone, tōd'stōn, *n.* A sort of traprock, of a brownish-gray colour.
Toad-stool, tōd'stöl, *n.* A kind of mushroom.
Toast, tōst, *vt. To dry by heat;* to dry and scorch by the heat of a fire, as bread or cheese; to warm thoroughly, as the feet. *n.* Bread *dried* and *scorched by the fire;* such bread dipped in liquor; such bread buttered and then scorched again. [Sp. *tostdr*—L. *torreo, tostum*, to roast.]
Toast, tōst, *n.* Originally, a celebrated woman whose health was often drunk, but now applied also to public characters or private friends of either sex, whose health we propose to drink.—*vt.* To name, as any one whose health, &c., is to be drunk; to propose, as any subject to the honour, success, &c., of which a bumper is to be devoted; to drink in honour of, &c.—*vi.* To give a toast to be drunk. [perhaps from Fr. *tasse*, a drinking cup.]
Toaster, tōst'ėr, *n.* An instrument for *toasting* bread or cheese.
Toast-master, tōst'mas-tėr, *n.* A person appointed to announce *toasts* at great public banquets.
Tobacco, tō-bak'kō, *n.* A plant, a native of America, the dried leaves of which are much used for smoking and chewing, and in snuff. [perhaps from the Indian word *tabacos*, the name which the Caribbees gave to the pipe in which they smoked the plant, and transferred by the Spaniards to the herb itself.]
Tobacconist, tō-bak'kō-nist, *n. A dealer in tobacco;* a manufacturer of tobacco.
Tobacco-pipe, tō-bak'kō-pip, *n. A pipe used for smoking tobacco,* often made of clay and baked, sometimes of other material.
Tocsin, tok'sin, *n. An alarm-bell,* or the ringing of a bell for the purpose of alarm. [Fr.]
Tod, tod, *n.* A certain weight of wool, 28 pounds.—*vt.*† To weigh.
To-day, tö-dā', *n. This day; the present day.*
Toddy, tod'i, *n.* A sweet juice extracted from various species of palm-trees in the East Indies, especially the cocoa-nut palm, and which when fermented and distilled is named arrack; a mixture of spirit and hot water sweetened.
Toe, tō, *n.* One of the small members which form the extremity of the foot, corresponding to a *finger* on the hand; the fore-part of the hoof of a horse, and of other hoofed animals; the member of a beast's foot corresponding to the toe in man. [Sax. *ta;* Old G. *zēha.*]
Toed, tōd, *p.a. Having toes;* as narrow-toed, slender-toed.
Togated, Toged, tō'gāt-ed, tōgd, *a. Gowned;* dressed in a gown; wearing a gown. [L. *togātus*—*tego*, to cover.]
Together, tö-geᴛʜ'ėr, *adv. Gathered* in one body or place; in company; in or into union; in the same place; in the same time. [Sax. *togœdere—gaderian*, to gather.]
Toil, toil, *vi. To labour;* to endeavour; to work; to exert strength with pain and fatigue of body or mind.—*vt.*† To weary; to overlabour.—*n. Labour* with pain and fatigue; labour that oppresses the body or mind. [Sax. *tiolan.*]
Toil, toil, *n.* Any net or snare, *woven or meshed;* any thread, web, or string spread for taking prey. [Fr.*toiles*, toils. bay-net—L. *texo*, to weave.]
Toiler, toil'ėr, *n. One who toils* or labours with pain.

oilet, toi'let, n. A covering of cloth; a covering or cloth of linen, silk, or tapestry, spread over a table in a dressing room; a dressing table; mode of dressing. [Fr. *toilette*—L. *tela*, a web.]
Toilet-table, toi'let-tā-bl, n. A dressing table.
Toilless, toil'les, a. Free from toil.
Toilsome, toil'sum, a. Requiring toil; laborious; attended with fatigue and pain; producing toil.
Toilsomely, toil'sum-li, adv. In a toilsome manner.
Toilsomeness, toil'sum-nes, n. State of being toilsome; laboriousness.
Tokay, tō-kā', n. A rich highly prized wine produced at *Tokay* in Upper Hungary, made of white grapes.
Token, tō'kn, n. A sign; something intended to represent another thing; a mark; symptom; a memorial of friendship; a piece of money current by sufferance, and not coined by authority. *vt.*† To make known; to mark with spots. [Sax. *tacen*—Sans. *dish*, to show.]
Tolerable, tol'ė-ra-bl, a. That may be borne; supportable, either physically or mentally; not very excellent or pleasing, but such as can *be borne without* disgust. [Fr. *tolérable*.]
Tolerableness, tol'ė-ra-bl-nes, n. State of being tolerable.
Tolerably, tol'ė-ra-bli, adv. Supportably; in a manner to be endured.
Tolerance, tol'ė-rans, n. The power of enduring, or the act of enduring; a habit which disposes a person to be indulgent towards those whose opinions differ from his own. [Fr. *tolérance*.]
Tolerant, tol'ė-rant, a. Enduring; favouring toleration. [L. *tolerans*.]
Tolerate, tol'ė-rāt, *vt*. To bear with; to suffer to be or to be done without hindrance; to allow or permit negatively, by not preventing; not to restrain. *ppr*. tolerating, *pret. & pp*. tolerated. [L. *toléro*, *tolerātum*, to bear—Sans. *tul*, to raise, to lift up.]
Toleration, tol-ė-rā'shon, n. Act of tolerating; the allowance of religious opinions and modes of worship in a state when different from those of the established church. [L. *toleratio*.]
Toll, tōl, n. *A part separated from something else*; a portion of goods, money, &c., taken as a tax, impost, or duty; a duty imposed for some liberty or privilege; a duty imposed on travellers and goods passing along public roads, over ferries, &c.—*vi*. To *pay toll*; to take toll, as a miller.—*vt*. To take from, as a part of a general contribution or tax; to exact, as a tribute. [Sax. *toll*; Gr. *telos*, a tax, duty.]
Toll, tōl, *vi*. To sound or ring, as a bell, with strokes uniformly repeated at intervals.—*vt*. To cause to sound, as a bell, with strokes slowly and uniformly repeated.—n. A particular sounding of a bell. [from the sound.]
Toll-bar, tōl'bär, n. *A bar, as* on a road, for stopping passengers and making them pay *toll*.
Toll-bridge, tōl'brij, n. *A bridge where toll is paid for passing it*.
Toller, tōl'ėr, n. *A toll-gatherer*; one who tolls a bell.
Toll-gate, tōl'gāt, n. *A gate where toll is taken*.
Toll-gatherer, tōl'ga-ᴛнėr-ėr, n. The *man who takes toll*.
Toll-house, tōl'hous, n. *A house or shed placed by a road near a toll-gate*, where the man who takes the toll remains.
Tomahawk, to'ma-hak, n. An Indian hatchet; a weapon of war used by the North American Indians. [Indian, *tomehagen*.]
Tomb, tōm, n. *A heap of earth raised over the dead*; a house or vault formed wholly or partly in the earth, with walls and a roof for the reception of the dead; a monument erected to preserve the memory of the dead; any sepulchral structure. [Fr. *tombe*, a tombstone; Gr. *tumbos*, the place where a dead body is burned; Heb. *tāman*, to bury.]
Tombless, tōm'les, a. *Destitute of a tomb* or sepulchral monument.
Tombstone, tōm'stōn, n. *A stone erected over a grave*, to preserve the memory of the deceased.
Tom-cat, tom'kat, n. A full-grown male cat.
Tome, tōm, n. *A piece cut off*; a volume; as many writings as are bound in a volume, forming the part of a larger work. [Fr.—Gr. *temnō*, to cut off.]
Tomfool, tom'föl, n. A great fool.
Tomfoolery, tom-fol'ė-ri, n. Foolishness; trifling.
To-morrow, tö-mo'rō, n. The day after the present.—*adv*. On the morrow.
Tomtit, tom'tit, n. A little bird, the titmouse.
Ton, tun, n. *The tone*; the air of fashion; the prevailing fashion. [Fr.; L. *tonus*, tone.]
Ton, tun, n. *A barrel-bulk*; a large weight equal to 20 hundred-weight (usually written cwt.), or 2240 pounds avoirdupois. [Sax. *tunne*, a butt.]
Tone, tōn, n. *A stretching*; a straining or raising of the voice; sound of a musical instrument; any vibration of the air perceptible by the ear; a property of sound by which it comes under the relation of grave or acute; a particular inflection of the voice, adapted to express emotion or passion; a whine; an affected sound in speaking; an interval of sound, in music; that state of a body in which the animal functions are healthy; the harmonious relation of the colours of a picture in light and shade.—*vt*. To *utter in an affected tone*; to tune; to soften (with *down*). *ppr*. toning, *pret. & pp*. toned. [Fr. *ton*—Gr. *teinō*, to stretch.]
Toned, tōnd, *p.a*. Having a tone; as, high-toned, sweet-toned.
Tone-syllable, tōn'sil-la-bl, n. An accented syllable.
Tongs, tongz, n. *pl*. *That which takes or holds*; an instrument of metal, consisting of two parts joined at one end, by which *tight hold is taken* of anything, as of coals in the fire, heated metals, &c. We say, a pair of tongs, a smith's tongs. [Sax. *tang*, pl. *tangan*, tongs—L. *teneo*, to hold tightly.]
Tongue, tung, n. The instrument of speech, and also one *of the instruments of taste* in human beings; in other animals one of the instruments of taste; an instrument of licking; speech; sometimes fluency of speech; the power of articulate utterance; speech, as well or ill used; a language; the whole sum of words used by a particular nation; words only, opposed to thoughts or actions; a nation; a point; a projection, as the tongue of a balance; a long narrow strip of land, projecting from the main into a sea or a lake; the taper part of anything.—*vt*. To chide; to scold.—*vi*. To talk; to prate. *ppr*. tonguing, *pret. & pp*. tongued. [Sax. *tunge*; Old G. *zunga*; Goth. *tuggō*; L. *lingua*; Sans. *lih*, to lick.]
Tongued, tungd, *p.a*. Having a tongue.
Tongueless, tung'les, a. Having no tongue; speechless.
Tongue-tied, tung'tid, *p.a*. Destitute of the power of distinct articulation; unable to speak freely.
Tonic, ton'ik, a. That stretches; increasing strength, or the tone of the animal system; obviating the effects of debility; relating to tones or sounds.—n. *A medicine that increases the strength* and gives vigour of action to the system; the key-note in music; [Fr. *tonique*] a certain degree of tension, or the sound produced by a vocal string in a given degree of tension. [Gr. *tonikos—teinō*, to stretch.]
To-night, tö-nit', n. *The night after the present day*. [*to* and *night*.]
Tonnage, tun'āj, n. The number of tons which a ship can carry; the cubical content or burden of a ship in tons; a duty on ships proportioned to the registered size of the vessels.
Tonsil, ton'sil, n. One of the two oblong glands on each side of the throat, at the basis of the tongue, whose use is to secrete a mucous humour for softening the passages. [L. *tonsilla*, from *tondeo, tonsus*, to clip or shave.]
Tonsile, ton'sil, a. *That may be clipped or shorn*. [L. *tonsilis—tondeo*, to clip.]
Tonsure, ton'sür, n. *The act of clipping the hair or of shaving the head*; the state of being shorn; in the Roman Catholic Church, entrance into holy orders. [Fr.—L. *tondeo*, to clip.]
Tontine, ton'tin, n. Survivorship; a loan raised on life-annuities, with the benefit of survivorship. [Fr.]
Too, tö, *adv*. Noting addition; over; more than enough; noting excess; likewise; also; moreover. [Sax. *to*.]
Tool, töl, n. *An instrument* of manual operation, particularly such as are used by farmers and mechanics; a person used as an instrument by another person.—*vt*. To shape or ornament *with a tool*. [Sax.—*tilian*, to labour.]
Tooth, töth, n. **Teeth,** *pl*. A bony substance growing out of the jaws of animals, and serving to lay hold of, cut, tear, and *masticate* alimentary substances, and also to assist human beings in the utterance of words; taste; a tine; something pointed and resembling an animal tooth.—*vt*. To *furnish with teeth*; to indent; to cut into teeth; to jag; to lock into each other. [Sax. *toth*—L. *dens, dentis*—Sans. *ad*, to eat.]
Toothache, töth'āk, n. *Pain in a tooth* or in the teeth.
Tooth-brush, töth'brush, n. *A small brush for cleaning the teeth*.
Toothed, tötht, *p.a*. Having teeth or jags.
Toothless, töth'les, a. *Having no teeth*.
Toothpick, töth'pik, n. An instrument for cleaning the teeth of substances lodged between them.
Toothsome, töth'sum, a. Palatable; grateful to the taste.
Top, top, n. *The highest part of anything*; the upper end, edge, or extremity; the summit; the highest person; the chief; the highest rank; the crown of the head; the hair on the crown of the head; the forelock; the head of a plant; [Fr. *toupie*; probably from Belg. *toppen*, to turn] a pear-shaped toy which children play with by whirling it on its point, also called a spinning-top; [Icel. *toppr*, the top of a mast] a sort of platform surrounding the head of the lower mast of a ship, and projecting on all sides.—a. *Being on the top* or summit; highest.—*vi*. To rise

Fāte, fär, fat, fall; mē, met, hėr; pine, pin; nōte, not, mōve; tūbe, tub, bull; oil, pound.

aloft; to excel; to rise above others. *vt.* To cover on the top; to rise over or above; to surpass; to crop; to take off, as the top or upper part. *ppr.* topping, *pret. & pp.* topped. [Sax.]
Top-armour, top'ärm-ér, *n.* In ships, a railing on the *top*, supported by stanchions and equipped with netting.
Topaz, tō'paz, *n.* A crystalline, transparent, or translucent mineral of various colours, as yellow, white, green, blue, pale. [Fr. *topase;* Ar. *topas.*]
Top-dressing, top'dres-ing, *p.n.* A dressing of manure laid on the surface of land.
Tope, tōp, *vi.* To drink hard; to drink strong or spirituous liquors to excess. *ppr.* toping, *pret. & pp.* toped. [probably from G. *topf*, a pot.]
Toper, tōp'ér, *n.* One who drinks to excess; a drunkard; a sot.
Topful, top'ful, *a.* Full to the top or brim.
Top-gallant, top'gal-lant, *a. Highest;* designating that mast of a ship which is above the top-mast, and also the sail upon it.
Top-heavy, top'he-vi, *a. Having the top* or upper part *too heavy* for the lower.
Topic, to'pik, *n.* Any *subject of discourse;* a general head; a probable argument drawn from the several circumstances and *places* of a fact. [Fr. *topiques,* subjects of conversation; Gr. *topos*, a place.]
Topical, to'pik-al, *a. Pertaining to a place;* local; pertaining to a subject of discourse, or to a general head.
Topically, to'pik-al-li, *adv. Locally;* with application to a particular part.
Top-knot, top'not, *n.* A knot worn by females *on the top* of the head.
Top-mast, top'mast, *n.* In ships, the second mast; or that which is next above the lower mast. Above that is the top-gallant mast, above which again is the top-royal mast.
Topmost, top'mōst, *a. Highest;* uppermost.
Topographer, to-pog'raf-ér, *n. One who is versed in topography;* one who describes a particular place or country.
Topographical, to-po-graf'ik-al, *a. Pertaining to topography;* descriptive of a place or country.
Topographically, to-po-graf'ik-al-li, *adv. In the manner of topography.*
Topography, to-pog'ra-fi, *n. The description of a particular place*, town, or tract of land; the description of cities, castles, churches, &c., in a country, including notices of everything belonging to the places or connected with them. [Fr. *topographie;* Gr. *topos*, a place, and *graphō*, to write.]
Topped, Topt, topt, topt, *p.a. Covered on the top;* having the top cut off.
Topple, top'l, *vi.* To fall, as from a *top* or height; to fall forward; to pitch or tumble down. *ppr.* toppling, *pret. & pp.* toppled. [from *top.*]
Top-proud, top'proud, *a.* Proud to the highest degree.
Top-sail, top'sāl, *n.* In ships, a sail extended across the top-mast, above which is the top-gallant-sail.
Top-stone, top'stōn, *n.* A *stone* that is placed on the top.
Topsy-turvy, top'si-tér-vi, *adv.* In an *inverted* posture; with the top or head downward. [the first part of the word is doubtless from *top*, and the second may be from Sax. *torfan*, to throw, meaning to throw over.]
Torch, torch, *n.* A light formed of some combustible substance, as of resinous wood, or of *twisted* flax, hemp, &c.,

soaked with tallow or other inflammable substance; a flambeau. [Fr. *torche*—L. *torqueo*, *tortus*, to twist.]
Torch-bearer, torch'bār-ér, *n. One whose office is to carry a torch.*
Torch-light, torch'līt, *n. The light of a torch* or of torches; a light kindled to supply the want of the sun.
Torment, tor'ment, *n. An instrument of torture;* extreme pain; anguish; the utmost degree of misery, either of body or mind; penal anguish; that which gives pain, vexation, or misery. [Fr. *tourment;* L. *torqueo*, to twist.]
Torment, tor-ment', *vt. To subject to torment;* to put to extreme pain or anguish; to distress; to vex.
Tormenter, tor-ment'ér, *n. He or that which torments.*
Tormentingly, tor-ment'ing-li, *adv. In a tormenting manner.*
Tormentor, tor-ment'or, *n. He or that which torments;* one who inflicts penal anguish or tortures.
Tornado, tôr-nā'dō, *n.* A wind that *turns round;* a violent gust of wind, more especially applied to those *whirlwind* hurricanes prevalent in the West Indies, on the western coast of Africa, and in the Indian Ocean, about the changes of the monsoons. [Sp. *tornàda,* return from a journey.]
Torpedo, tor-pē'dō, *n.* A fish that communicates powerful electric or *benumbing* shocks to those who touch it; a machine for blowing up ships by submarine explosion. [L. numbness —*torpeo*, to be numb.]
Torpescence, tor-pes'ens, *n. State of being torpescent;* a state of insensibility.
Torpescent, tor-pes'ent, *a. Becoming torpid or numb*, or incapable of motion. [L. *torpescens—torpeo*, to be numb.]
Torpid, tor'pid, *a. Stiff; benumbed;* having lost motion or the power of exertion and feeling; numb; dull; stupid; sluggish; inactive. [L. *torpidus.*]
Torpidity, tor-pid'i-ti, *n. Torpidness.*
Torpidness, tor'pid-nes, *n. The state of being torpid;* numbness; dulness.
Torpor, tor'por, *n. State of being torpid;* numbness; loss of motion, or of the power of motion; dulness; sluggishness; stupidity. [L.—*torpeo*, to be numb.]
Torrefaction, tor-rē-fak'shon, *n. Act of torrefying;* the operation of roasting ores; the roasting of drugs on a metalline plate till they become friable to the fingers. [Fr.]
Torrefy, tor'rē-fī, *vt. To make dry by heat or fire;* to roast or scorch, as metallic ores; to dry or parch, as drugs, on a metalline plate. *ppr.* torrefying, *pret. & pp.* torrefied. [Fr. *torréfier*—L. *torreo*, to dry by heat, and *facio*, to make.]
Torrent, tor'rent, *n.* A stream rushing and boiling, like water subjected to *strong heat;* a violent rushing stream of water falling suddenly from mountains, where there have been great rains; a stream suddenly raised and running rapidly, as down a precipice; as, a torrent of lava; a violent or rapid stream; a strong current. [L. *torrens* —*torreo*, to burn.]
Torrid, tor'rid, *a. Thirsty; dried with heat;* violently hot; burning or parching.—*Torrid zone,* that broad belt of the earth included between the tropics. [Fr. *torride*—L. *torreo*, to parch —Sans. *trish*, to be thirsty.]
Torsion, tor'shon, *n. The act of twisting;* the twisting of a body by the exertion of a lateral force; the force with which a thread returns to a state of rest,

after it has been twisted. [Fr.—L. *torqueo*, to twist.]
Torso, tor'sō, *n.* The trunk of a statue deprived of its head and limbs. [It.]
Tortile, tor'til, *a. Twisted;* wreathed; coiled. [L. *tortilis.*]
Tortoise, tor'tois, *n.* An animal covered with a shell or crust, which leaves the head, neck, limbs, and tail free. Some of these animals live on the land, and some inhabit the water. The marine tortoise or turtle can only shuffle *or wind along* on land at a slow rate, and with laborious efforts. [Fr. *tortus*, from L. *torqueo, tortus,* to twist.]
Tortoise-shell, tor'tois-shel, *n. The shell* of a species of *tortoise*, which inhabits tropical seas; otherwise called hawk's-bill turtle. The shell is extensively used in the manufacture of combs, snuff-boxes, &c.
Tortuosity, tor'tū-ōs-i-ti, *n. The state of being twisted or wreathed.*
Tortuous, tor'tū-us, *a. Twisted; wreathed; winding;* deceitful. [L. *tortuōsus*, full of crooks—*torqueo*, to twist.]
Tortuously, tor'tū-us-li, *adv. In a winding manner.*
Tortuousness, tor'tū-us-nes, *n. The state of being twisted.*
Torture, tor'tūr, *n. A twisting;* anguish of body or mind; agony; severe pain, formerly inflicted judicially, either as a punishment for a crime, or for the purpose of extorting a confession from an accused person.—*vt. To torment;* to pain to extremity; to vex; to harass. *ppr.* torturing, *pret. & pp.* tortured. [Fr.—L. *torqueo, tortus,* to twist.]
Torturer, tor'tūr-ér, *n. One who tortures;* a tormenter.
Tory, tō'ri, *n.* The name given to an adherent to the ancient constitution of England and to the apostolical hierarchy; one who, in political principles, always leans to church and state, and is jealous of the extension of democratic power.—*a. Pertaining to the Tories.* [said to be an Irish word, denoting a robber or a savage.]
Toryism, tō'ri-izm, *n. The principles of the Tories.*
Toss, tos, *vt. To throw* with violence; to lift or throw up with a sudden or violent motion; to throw with the palm of the hand upward; to agitate; to make restless.—*vi. To be tossed;* to roll and tumble; to writhe; to be in violent commotion. *ppr.* tossing, *pret. & pp.* tossed or tost.—*n. Act of tossing;* a throwing upward; a particular manner of raising the head with a jerk. [G. *stossen,* to push, impel.]
Tosser, tos'ér, *n. One who tosses.*
Tossing, tos'ing, *p.n.* The act of throwing upward; a rising and falling suddenly; a rolling and tumbling; a violent commotion.
Toss-pot, tos'pot, *n.* A toper; one habitually given to strong drink. [*toss* and *pot.*]
Total, tō'tal, *a.* Not divided.—*n. The whole;* the whole sum or amount. [Fr. —L. *totus*, the whole.]
Totally, tō'tal-li, *adv. Wholly;* entirely.
Totter, tot'tér, *vi.* To *shake* so as to threaten to fall; to vacillate; to reel; to lean. [Sax. *tealtrian*, to shake.]
Totterer, tot'tér-ér, *n. One who totters.*
Touch, tuch, *vt. To come or be in contact with;* to put the hand, finger, foot, or anything else on or against; to strike against; to meet; to be a tangent to; to perceive by the sense of feeling; to come to; to arrive at; to try, as gold with a stone; to relate to; to meddle

ch, *chain;* j, *job;* g, *go;* ng, *sing;* ᴛʜ, *then;* th, *thin;* w, *wig;* wh, *whig;* zh, *asure;* † *obsolete.*

with; to move; to soften; to mark slightly; to make an impression on; to play on; to influence by impulse; to impel forcibly; to treat slightly; to afflict or distress.—*vi.* To come or be in *contact*; to take effect; to treat of slightly in discourse (with *upon*).—*n.* *Contact*; the hitting of two bodies; the sense of feeling; the act of touching; test; proof; a touch-stone!; single act of a pencil on a picture; lineament; act of the hand on a musical instrument; power of exciting the affections; a stroke; censure; a small quantity intermixed; a hint; slight notice; in music, the resistance of the keys of an instrument to the fingers, as a heavy touch or light touch. [Fr. *toucher*; L. *tango*; Gr. *thinggano*.]

Touchily, tuch′i-li, *adv.* With irritation; peevishly.

Touchiness, tuch′i-nes, *n.* Peevishness; irritability; irascibility.

Touching, tuch′ing, *p. a.* Affecting; moving; pathetic.—*p.n.* *Touch*; the sense of feeling.—*prep.* Concerning; relating to; with respect to.

Touchingly, tuch′ing-li, *adv.* In a manner to move the passions; feelingly.

Touch-needle, tuch′nē-dl, *n.* Touch-needles are small bars of gold and silver, some of which are pure, and others alloyed with various definite proportions of copper, used by assayers for trying gold and silver, or alloys of them.

Touchstone, tuch′stōn, *n.* A variety of extremely compact silicious schist, almost as close as flint, used in conjunction with the touch-needles for ascertaining the purity of gold and silver; any criterion by which the qualities of a thing are tried.

Touch-wood, tuch′wụd, *n.* Decayed wood, used like a match for taking fire from a spark.

Touchy, tuch′i, *a.* *Exceedingly susceptible of touch*; peevish; irritable; irascible; apt to take fire. [from *touch*.]

Tough, tuf, *a.* That does not easily break by drawing or bending; tenacious; yielding to force without breaking; strong; able to endure hardship; not easily separated; viscous; ropy. [Sax. *toh*—Icel. *tegia*, to stretch out.]

Toughen, tuf′n, *vi.* To grow tough.—*vt.* To make tough.

Toughish, tuf′ish, *a.* Tough in a slight degree.

Toughly, tuf′li, *adv.* In a tough manner.

Toughness, tuf′nes, *n.* The quality of being tough; flexibility with a firm adhesion of parts; tenacity; clamminess; strength of constitution or texture.

Tour, tōr, *n.* A going round; a turn; a journey in a circuit; a ramble; an excursion. [Fr. *tour*, a turn—Heb. *tūr*, to go round.]

Tourist, tōr′ist, *n.* One who makes a tour, or performs a journey in a circuit.

Tournament, tōr′na-ment, *n.* A turning or wheeling round; a martial sport performed in former times by cavaliers on horseback for the purpose of exhibiting their courage and skill in arms. [Old Fr. *tournoyement*—*tourner*, to turn.]

Tourney, tōr′nē, *n.* A tournament. [Fr. *tournoi.*]

Tourniquet, tōr′ni-ket, *n.* A surgical bandage which is straitened or relaxed by turning a screw, and used to check hemorrhage in the operations of amputation. [Fr. from *tourner*, to turn.]

Tow, tō, *vt.* To tug; to drag, as a boat or ship, through the water by means of a rope. [Sax. *teogan*.]—*n.* A rope or chain used in *towing*; the coarse and broken part of flax or hemp, separated from the finer part. [Sax.]

Towage, tō′aj, *n.* The act of towing; the price paid for towing.

Toward, Towards, tō′ėrd, tō′ėrdz, *prep.* In the direction of; with direction to, in a moral sense; with respect to; with ideal tendency to.—*adv.* Properly, near; at hand; in a state of approach; in a state of preparation. [Sax. *toward, towardes*.]

Toward†, tō′ėrd, *a.* Ready to do or learn; not froward; apt.

Towardliness, tō′ėrd-li-nes, *n.* Quality of being towardly; readiness to do or learn; docility.

Towardly, tō′ėrd-li, *a.* Ready to do or learn; apt; tractable; compliant with duty.

Towardness, tō′ėrd-nes, *n.* Docility; towardliness.

Tow-boat, tō′bōt, *n.* Any boat employed in towing a ship out of a harbour, &c.

Towel, tou′el, *n.* A cloth used for wiping the hands and face after washing, and for other purposes. [Fr. *touaille*.]

Towelling, tou′el-ing, *p.n.* Cloth for towels.

Tower, tou′ėr, *n.* A high building for defence; a lofty building, of a round, square, or polygonal form, and often consisting of several stories; a citadel; a fortress.—*vi.* To rise and fly high; to soar; to be lofty. [Sax. *tor*; L. *turris*; Chald. *tūr*, a rock, mountain.]

Towered, tou′ėrd, *p.a.* Having towers; adorned or defended by towers.

Towering, tou′ėr-ing, *p.a.* Very high; elevated.

Towery, tou′ėr-i, *a.* Having towers; adorned or defended by towers.

Towing, tō′ing, *p.n.* The act of drawing a vessel forward in the water by means of a rope attached to another vessel or boat.

Towing-path, tō′ing-path, *n.* A path used by men or horses that tow boats.

To wit, tō wit. To know; namely. [to, and Sax. *witan*, to wot, to know.]

Tow-line, tō′lin, *n.* A small hawser, generally used to tow vessels.

Town, toun, *n.* Originally, *a walled or fortified place*; any collection of houses, larger than a village; a large assemblage of adjoining houses, to which a market is usually incident; a city; a borough; the inhabitants of a town; the court end of London; the inhabitants of the metropolis; the metropolis. [Sax. *tun*—*tynan*, to inclose.]

Town-clerk, toun′klärk, *n.* An officer who keeps the records of a town, and enters all its official proceedings.

Town-crier, toun′kri-ėr, *n.* A public crier; one who makes proclamation.

Town-hall, toun′hal, *n.* A large room in a building, used for public meetings, in a town or city; the building itself.

Town-house, toun′hous, *n.* The house where the public business of the town is transacted; a house in town, in opposition to a house in the country.

Townsfolk, tounz′fōk, *n.* People of a town or city.

Township, toun′ship, *n.* The corporation of a town; the district or territory of a town.

Townsman, tounz′man, *n.* An inhabitant of a place, or one of the same town with another.

Town-talk, toun′tạk, *n.* The common talk of a place or town, or the subject of common conversation.

Tow-rope, tō′rōp, *n.* Any rope used in towing ships or boats.

Toxicological, toks′i-ko-loj″ik-al, *a.* Pertaining to toxicology.

Toxicology, toks-i-kol′o-ji, *n.* That branch of medicine which treats of poisons and their antidotes. [Fr. *toxicologie*—Gr. *toxikon*, poison, and *logos*, a treatise.]

Toy, toy, *vi.* To play; to sport; to trifle; to dall-amorously.—*n.* Play; amorous dalliance; a bawble; a trifle; a thing for amusement; matter of no importance; silly tale; wild fancy. [Sans. *toy*, to play.]

Toyer, toi′ėr, *n.* One who toys; one who is full of trifling tricks.

Toze†, tōz, *vt.* To pull by violence.

Trace, trās, *n.* A drawing; a delineation; a footstep; a vestige; a visible appearance of anything left when the thing itself no longer exists; a small quantity; (pl.) traces, in a harness, are the straps by which a carriage, waggon, &c., is drawn by horses.—*vt.* To draw or delineate with lines or marks; to follow by footsteps or tracks; to follow with exactness. *ppr.* tracing, *pret. & pp.* traced. [Fr.—L. *traho*, *tractum*, to draw.]

Traceable, trās′a-bl, *a.* That may be traced.

Traceableness, trās′a-bl-nes, *n.* The state of being traceable.

Traceably, trās′a-bli, *adv.* In a traceable manner; so as to be traced.

Tracer, trās′ėr, *n.* One that traces or follows by marks.

Tracery, trās′ė-ri, *n.* That which is traced; in architecture, that species of pattern work, traced in the head of a Gothic window by the mullions being there continued, but diverging into arches, curves, and flowing lines, enriched with foliations; any design of the same character, for doors or ceilings.

Trachea, tra-kē′a, *n.* The windpipe. [Low L. from Gr. *trachus*, rough.]

Tracheal, tra-kē′al, *a.* Pertaining to the trachea or windpipe.

Tracing, trās′ing, *p.n.* Course; regular track or path.

Track, trak, *n.* Anything drawn out; a mark left by something that has passed along; a mark left by the foot, either of man or beast; a road; course; way.—*vt.* To follow when guided by a trace; to tow; to draw, as a vessel or boat, by a line reaching from her to the shore or bank. [It. *traccia*—L. *traho, tractum*, to draw.]

Trackage, trak′āj, *n.* A drawing or towing, as of a boat.

Trackless, trak′les, *a.* Having no track; marked by no footsteps.

Track-road, trak′rōd, *n.* A towing-path.

Tract, trakt, *n.* Something drawn out; a region, or quantity of land or water, of indefinite extent; a short composition, in which some particular subject is treated; continued duration; length; extent; exposition†. [L. *tractus*, a drawing—*traho*, to draw.]

Tractability, trakt-a-bil′i-ti, *n.* The quality or state of being tractable; docility. [Late L. *tractabilitas*.]

Tractable, trakt′a-bl, *a.* That may be easily led; docile; manageable; governable. [L. *tractabilis*—*traho*, to draw.]

Tractableness, trakt′a-bl-nes, *n.* The state or quality of being tractable.

Tractably, trakt′a-bli, *adv.* In a tractable manner; with ready compliance.

Traction, trak′shon, *n.* The act of draw-

Fāte, fär, fat, fạll; mē, met, her; pine, pin; nōte, not, move; tūbe, tub, bụll; oil, pound.

Tractive | **409** | **Transcend**

ing or state of being drawn; the act of drawing a body along a plane, usually by the power of men, animals, or steam. [from Low L. *tractio*—L.*traho,tractum*, to draw.]
Tractive, trakt'iv, *a. That pulls or draws;* drawing along.
Tractor, trakt'or, *n. That which draws,* or is used for drawing. [Low L.]
Trade, trād, *n. That which a person practises;* employment; calling; the business of exchanging commodities by barter, or the business of buying and selling for money; commerce; the business which a person has learned; particular employment, whether manual or mercantile, distinguished from the liberal arts and learned professions, and from agriculture; employment not manual; custom; standing practice; men engaged in the same occupation.—*vi. To be engaged in trade;* to deal in the exchange, purchase, or sale of goods; to carry on commerce as a business; to act merely for money. *ppr.* trading, *pret. & pp.* traded. [Sp. *trato,* traffic—L. *tracto,*to touch—*traho, tractum,* to draw.]
Traded†, trād'ed, *p.a.* Versed; practised.
Trader, trād'ėr, *n. One engaged in trade* or commerce.
Tradesman, trādz'man, *n. One who practises a trade;* a shopkeeper.
Trades-people, trādz'pē-pl, *n. People employed in various trades,* particularly shopkeeping, &c.
Trade-winds, trād'windz, *n.* The trade-winds are those constant winds which occur in all open seas, on both sides of the equator, and to the distance of about 30 degrees north and south of it. They are so named because they are favourable to navigation and *trade.*
Trading, trād'ing, *p.a.* Carrying on commerce.—*p.n. The act or business of carrying on trade* or commerce.
Tradition, tra-di'shon. *n. A delivering up;* in a legal sense, delivery; the act of delivering into the hands of another; the oral delivery of doctrines, practices, rites, and customs from father to son, or from ancestors to posterity; that body of doctrine and discipline supposed to have been put forth by Christ or his apostles. [Fr.—L. *trans,* over, and *do, datum,* to give.]
Traditional, Traditionary, tra-di'shon-al, tra-di'shon-a-ri, *a. Relating to tradition;* delivered orally from father to son; transmitted from age to age without writing. [Fr. *traditionnel.*]
Traditionally, tra-di'shon-al-li, *adv. By tradition;* by transmission from father to son, or from age to age.
Traditionist, tra-di'shon-ist, *n. One who adheres to tradition.*
Traduce, tra-dūs', *vt.* Primarily, *to lead across* or *over;* to represent as blamable; to calumniate; to vilify; wilfully to misrepresent. *ppr.* traducing,*pret. & pp.* traduced. [L. *traduco—trans,* and *dūco,* to lead.]
Traducer, tra-dūs'ėr, *n. One that traduces;* a slanderer; a calumniator.
Traffic, traf'ik, *n. Trade carried on beyond the seas;* trade; commerce, either by barter or by buying and selling; commodities for market.—*vi. To trade;* to barter; to buy and sell wares; to carry on commerce; to trade meanly.—*vt. To exchange in traffic. ppr.* trafficking, *pret. & pp.* trafficked. [Fr. *trafic*—L. *trans,* beyond, and *facio,* to do.]
Trafficker, traf'ik-ėr, *n. One who carries on traffic* or commerce; a trader.
Tragedian, tra-jē'di-an, *n. A writer of* tragedy; more generally, an actor of tragedy. [L. *tragœdus.*]
Tragedy, tra-jē-di, *n.* Primarily, *the song of the goat;* a dramatic poem representing some series of actions, performed by illustrious persons, and being pregnant with some great moral truth, generally having a fatal issue; a fatal and mournful event; any event in which human lives are lost by human violence, more particularly by unauthorized violence. [Fr. *tragédie;* Gr. *tragos,* a goat, and *ōdē,* a song.]
Tragic, Tragical, tra'jik, tra'jik-al, *a. Pertaining to tragedy;* of the nature of tragedy; fatal to life; mournful; calamitous; expressive of tragedy, the loss of life, or of sorrow. [Fr. *tragique.*]
Tragically, tra'jik-al-li, *adv. In a tragical manner;* with fatal issue.
Tragi-comedy, tra-ji-ko'mē-di, *n.* A kind of dramatic piece representing some action passed among eminent persons, in which *tragic* and *comic* scenes are blended. [Fr. *tragicomédie.*]
Tragi-comic, Tragi-comical, tra-ji-kom'-ik, tra-ji-kom'ik-al, *a. Pertaining to tragi-comedy.*
Tragi-comically, tra-ji-kom'ik-al-li, *adv.* In a *tragi-comical manner.*
Trail, trāl, *vt. To draw* along the ground; to hunt by the trail or track; to lower, as arms.—*vi. To be drawn out* in length.—*n.* Track followed by the hunter; scent left on the ground by the animal pursued; anything drawn behind in long undulations; a train; entrails, as of a bird or sheep. [D. *treil,* a rope to draw a ship; Norm. *trailler,* to search after.]
Train, trān, *vt. To draw* by artifice; to draw from act to act by persuasion; to discipline; to teach and form by practice; to accustom to draw, as oxen; in gardening, to lead or direct and form to a wall or espalier; to educate; to teach; to bring up (with *up*). [Fr. *trainer*—L. *traho,* to draw.]—*n. Something drawn out;* stratagem of enticement; something drawn along behind the end of a gown, &c.; the tail of a hawk or other bird; a retinue; a series; process; course; a procession; the number of beats which a watch makes in any certain time; a line of gunpowder, laid to lead fire to a charge; the afterpart of a gun-carriage; a continuous line of carriages on a railway; the series of wheels, &c., forming a movement in a clock or watch. [Fr.]
Train-band, trān'band, *n.* A band or company of militia.
Train-bearer, trān'bār-ėr, *n. One who holds up a train,* as of a robe or gown.
Trained, trānd, *p.a. Having a train.*
Trainer, trān'ėr, *n. One who trains up;* one who trains men for athletic exercises, or horses for the race, &c.
Training, trān'ing, *p.a.* Educating; teaching and forming by practice. *p.n. The act* or *process of drawing out* or educating; the act of preparing men for athletic exercises, or horses for the race; the disciplining of troops.
Train-oil, trān'oil, *n.* The *oil drawn* from the blubber of whales, and from the fat of various other fishes, by boiling.
Trait, trāt, *n. Anything drawn out* at length; a touch; a feature. [Fr.—L. *traho, tractum,* to draw.]
Traitor, trā'tor, *n. One who delivers over* or *up;* a treacherous person; one who betrays his sovereign or country; one guilty of treason. [Fr. *traître;* L. *trans,* over, and *do, datum,* to give.]
Traitorous, trā'tor-us, *a. Acting the part of a traitor;* guilty of treason; faithless; consisting in treason; implying breach of allegiance.
Traitorously, trā'tor-us-li, *adv.* In violation of allegiance and trust.
Traitress, trā tres, *n.* A female betrayer; a female who betrays her country or her trust.
Trammel, tram'mel, *n. A threefold mesh* or net; a kind of long net for catching birds or fishes; a kind of shackles used for regulating the motions of a horse, and making him amble; an iron hook used for hanging kettles over the fire; (pl.) elliptic compasses, an instrument for drawing ovals; hindrances; impediments.—*vt. To catch, as with a net;* to hamper; to shackle. *ppr.* trammelling, *pret. & pp.* trammelled. [Fr. *tramail,* a dragnet—L. *tres,* three, and *macula,* a mesh.]
Tramontane, tra-mon'tān, *a. Lying* or *being beyond the mountains* or Alps; foreign; barbarous. [L. *trans,* beyond, and *mons, montis,* mountain.]
Tramp, tramp, *vt. To tread* under foot; to trample.—*n. A tread;* travel on foot; a walk; a vagrant; an instrument used in trimming hedges. [G. *trampen.*]
Trample, tram'pl, *vt. To tread on heavily;* to tread upon with pride or scorn; to prostrate by treading.—*vi. To tread* in contempt; to tread with force and rapidity. *ppr.* trampling, *pret. & pp.* trampled. [G. *trampeln.*]
Trampler, tram'pl-ėr, *n. One that tramples;* one that treads down.
Trance, trans, *n. A passing over* or *beyond;* a state in which the soul seems to be rapt into visions; an ecstasy; a total suspension of mental power and voluntary motion while pulsation and breathing still continue.—*vt.*† To entrance. *ppr.* trancing; *pret. & pp.* tranced. [Fr. *transe*—L. *trans,* and *eo, itum,* to go.]
Tranced, transt, *p.a. Lying in a trance.*
Tranect†, tran'ekt, *n.* A tow-boat.
Tranquil, tran'kwil, *a. Beyond* or out of the reach of *war* or *discord;* free from strife or agitation; peaceful. [L. *tranquillus*—Sans. *tiras,* beyond, and *kali,* discord.]
Tranquillity, tran-kwil'i-ti, *n.* Freedom from disturbance or agitation; a calm state. [Fr. *tranquillité.*]
Tranquillize, tran'kwil-iz, *vt. To render tranquil;* to quiet; to compose; to make calm and peaceful. *ppr.* tranquillising, *pret. & pp.* tranquillized. [Fr. *tranquilliser.*]
Tranquillizing, tran'kwil-iz-ing, *p.a.* Quieting; composing.
Tranquilly, tran'kwil-li, *adv.* Quietly.
Transact, trans-akt', *vt. To drive through;* to carry through; to complete; to manage.—*vi. To conduct* matters; to treat; to manage. [L. *transigo*—*trans,* and *ago, actum,* to do.]
Transaction, trans-ak'shon, *n. The doing* of any business; management of any affair; that which is done; an affair. [Fr.]
Transactor, trans-akt'or, *n. One who performs* or conducts any business.
Transalpine, trans-al'pin, *a. Lying beyond the Alps,* in regard to Rome, that is, on the north or west of the Alps. [L. *trans,* beyond, and *Alpinus,* of the Alps.]
Transatlantic, trans-at-lan'tik, *a. Lying* or *being beyond the Atlantic.* [L. *trans,* beyond, and *Atlantic.*]
Transcend, trans-send', *vt. To climb* or

ch, *chain;* j, *job;* g, *go;* ng, *sing;* ᴛʜ, *then;* th, *thin;* w, *wig;* wh, *whig;* zh, *azure;* † obsolete.

pass over; to surmount; to rise above; to surpass; to excel; to exceed. [L. *transcendo—scando*, to climb.]

Transcendence, trans-send'ens, *n*. A *transcending*; superior excellence.

Transcendent, trans-send'ent, *a. Transcending*; supreme in excellence; going beyond the bounds of human knowledge. [Fr. *transcendant*.]

Transcendental, trans-send-ent'al, *a. Surpassing others*; pertaining to that which goes beyond the limits of actual experience. [from L. *transcendo*.]

Transcendentally, trans-send-ent'al-li, *adv. In a transcendental manner.*

Transcendently, trans-send'ent-li, *adv.* Very excellently; by way of eminence.

Transcribe, tran-skrīb', *vt. To write over from one book into another*; to write, as a copy of anything; to copy. *ppr.* transcribing, *pret. & pp.* transcribed. [L. *transcribo—scribo*, to write.]

Transcriber, tran-skrīb'er, *n. One who transcribes*; a copier.

Transcript, tran'skript, *n. That which is transcribed*; a copy; a writing made from and according to an original. [L. *transcriptum—scribo*, to write.]

Transcription, tran-skrip'shon, *n. Act of transcribing*; state of being transcribed; a transcript. [Fr.]

Transept, tran'sept, *n. The transverse division* of a church or cathedral, which is in the form of a cross; that part which is placed between the nave and choir, and extends beyond the sides of the area which contains these divisions, forming the short arms of the cross, upon which the plan is laid out. [L. *trans*, and *septum*, a hedge—*sepio*, to fence in—Heb. *saphan*, to cover.]

Transfer, trans-fer', *vt. To bear across or over*; to convey from one place or person to another; to make over; to convey, as a right, from one person to another; to sell; to give. *ppr.* transferring, *pret. & pp.* transferred. [L. *transfero—fero*, to carry.]

Transfer, trans'fer, *n. Act of transferring*; the conveyance of a thing from one place or person to another; the conveyance of right from one person to another; something transferred.

Transferability, trans-fer'a-bil''li-ti, *n. Quality of being transferable.*

Transferable, trans-fer'a-bl, *a. That may be transferred*; negotiable, as a note or bill of exchange; that may be conveyed from one person to another by indorsement. [Fr. *transférable*.]

Transference, trans'fer-ens, *n. The act of transferring*; the passage of anything from one place to another.

Transferree, trans-fer-ē', *n. The person to whom a transfer is made.*

Transferrer, trans-fer'er, *n. One who makes a transfer* or conveyance.

Transferrible, trans-fer'i-bl, *a. See* TRANSFERABLE.

Transferring, trans-fer'ing, *p.n.* The act of conveying or removing from one place or person to another; the act of conveying to another as a right.

Transfiguration, trans-fig'ūr-ā'shon, *n. A change of form*; the supernatural change in the appearance of our Saviour on the mount; a feast held by the Romish church on the 6th of August, in commemoration of this change. [Fr.]

Transfigure, trans-fig'ūr, *vt. To change in form* or shape; to change the outward form or appearance of. *ppr.* transfiguring, *pret. & pp.* transfigured. [Fr. *transfigurer*—L. *figūra*, shape.]

Transfix, trans-fiks', *vt. To fix by piercing through*; to pierce through, as with a pointed weapon. [L. *transfigo, transfixum—figo*, to fix.]

Transform, trans-form', *vt. To change the form* or appearance of; to change, as one substance into another; to change, as the natural temper of man from a state of enmity to God into a temper conformed to the will of God; in the Romish church, to change, as the sacramental elements, bread and wine, into the flesh and blood of Christ. [Fr. *transformer*—L. *forma*, form—*fero*, to bear, to carry.]

Transformation, trans-form-ā'shon, *n. The operation of changing the form*; metamorphosis; change of form in insects; the change of one metal into another, as of copper into gold; transubstantiation; a change from enmity to God to holiness and love. [Fr.]

Transformed, trans-formd', *p.a. Changed in form*; renewed.

Transforming, trans-form'ing, *p.a.* Renewing.

Transfuse, trans-fūz', *vt. To pour*, as liquor, *out of one vessel into another*; to transfer, as blood from one animal to another; to cause to pass from one to another. *ppr.* transfusing, *pret. & pp.* transfused. [L. *transfundo, transfusum—fundo, fūsum*, to pour.]

Transfusible, trans-fūz'i-bl, *a. That may be transfused*, &c.

Transfusion, trans-fū'zhon, *n. Act of transfusing*; act or operation of transferring the blood of one animal into the vascular system of another by means of a tube. [Fr.]

Transgress, trans-gres', *vt. To pass over* or beyond, as any limit; to break or violate, as a law, civil or moral.—*vi.* To offend by violating a law; to sin. [Fr. *transgresser*—L. *gradior*, to go.]

Transgression, trans-gre'shon, *n. Act of passing over or beyond* any rule of moral duty; fault; crime; sin. [Fr.]

Transgressor, trans-gres'or, *n. One who transgresses*; one who violates any known rule or principle of rectitude; a sinner. [Late L.]

Tranship, tran-ship', *vt. See* TRANSSHIP.

Transient, tran'shi-ent, *a. Passing over* or by; not stationary; of short duration; not permanent; not lasting or durable; hasty; momentary; imperfect. [L. *transiens—eo*, to go.]

Transiently, tran'shi-ent-li, *adv. In a transient manner.*

Transientness, tran'shi-ent-nes, *n. Quality or state of being transient.*

Transit, tran'sit, *n. A going over*; conveyance; the passage of a heavenly body across the meridian of any place; the passage of one heavenly body over the disc of a larger one, as of Mercury or Venus over the sun's disc. [L. *transitus—eo, itum*, to go.]

Transition, tran-si'shon, *n. A going over*; passage from one place or state to another; change; in rhetoric, a passing from one subject to another; in music, a change of key from major to minor, or the contrary.—*a.* Noting a change or passage from one state to another. [Fr.—L. *eo, itum*, to go.]

Transitional, tran-si'zhon-al, *a. Containing or denoting transition.*

Transitive, tran'sit-iv, *a. Passing over*; noting a verb expressing an action which passes from the agent to an object. [Fr. *transitif*.]

Transitively, tran'sit-iv-li, *adv. In a transitive manner.*

Transitorily, tran'si-tō-ri-li, *adv.* With short continuance.

Transitoriness, tran'si-tō-ri-nes, *n. State or quality of being transitory.*

Transitory, tran'si-tō-ri, *a. Passing* without continuance; continuing a short time; fleeting; speedily vanishing. [Fr. *transitoire*—L. *eo, itum*, to go.]

Translatable, trans-lāt'a-bl, *a. Capable of being translated* into another language.

Translate, trans-lāt', *vt. To bear over* or from one place to another; to remove to heaven, as a human being, without death; to render into another language. *ppr.* translating, *pret. & pp.* translated. [L. *transfero, translatus—fero, lātum*, to bear.]

Translated, trans-lāt'ed, *p.a.* Removed to heaven without dying; rendered into another language.

Translation, trans-lā'shon, *n. Act of translating*; act of conveying from one place to another; the removal of a bishop from one see to another; the removal of a person to heaven without subjecting him to death; the act of turning into another language; that which is produced by turning into another language; a version. [Fr.]

Translator, trans-lāt'or, *n. One who translates*; one who renders into another language.

Translucence, Translucency, trans-lū'sens, trans-lū'sens-i, *n. Quality of being translucent*; the property of admitting rays of light to pass through, but not so as to render objects distinguishable.

Translucent, trans-lū'sent, *a. Shining through*; letting shine through; transmitting rays of light, but not so as to render objects distinctly visible; transparent; clear; pellucid. [L. *translucens—lūceo*, to shine.]

Translucently, trans-lū'sent-li, *adv. In a translucent manner.*

Transmarine, trans-ma-rēn', *a. Lying or being beyond the sea.* [L. *transmarinus—mare*, the sea.]

Transmigrate, trans'mi-grāt, *vi.* To pass from one body into another. *ppr.* transmigrating, *pret. & pp.* transmigrated. [L. *transmigro, transmigratum—migro*, to remove.]

Transmigration, trans-mi-grā'shon, *n.* The passing of a thing into another state, as of one substance into another; the passing of the soul into another body, according to the opinion of Pythagoras. [Fr.—Late L. *transmigratio*—L. *migro*, to remove.]

Transmigrator, trans'mi-grāt-or, *n. One who transmigrates.* [Low L.]

Transmigratory, trans-mi'grā-tō-ri, *a.* Passing from one body or state to another.

Transmissibility, trans-mis'i-bil''li-ti, *n. Quality of being transmissible.*

Transmissible, trans-mis'i-bl, *a. That may be transmitted*; that may be transmitted through a transparent body.

Transmission, trans-mi'shon, *n. Act of transmitting*; act of sending from one place or person to another; the passing of a substance through any body, as of light through glass or other transparent body. [Fr.]

Transmissive, trans-mis'iv, *a. Transmitted*; derived from one to another.

Transmit, trans-mit', *vt. To send over*; to send from one person or place to another; to suffer to pass through. *ppr.* transmitting, *pret. & pp.* transmitted. [L. *transmitto—mitto*, to send.]

Transmitter, trans-mit'er, *n. One who transmits.*

Transmutability, trans-mūt'a-bil''li-ti, *n. Quality of being transmutable*; sus-

Fāte, fär, fat, fall; mē, met, hėr; pīne, pin; nōte, not, mōve; tūbe, tub, bull; oil, pound.

Transmutable, trans-mūt'a-bl, *a.* Capable of being transmuted.

Transmutableness, trans-mūt'a-bl-nes, *n.* Quality of being transmutable.

Transmutably, trans-mūt'a-bli, *adv.* In a transmutable manner.

Transmutation, trans-mūt-ā'shon, *n.* Act of transmuting; the change of anything into another substance. [Fr.]

Transmute, trans-mūt', *vt.* To change thoroughly; to change from one nature or substance into another. *ppr.* transmuting, *pret. & pp.* transmuted. [L. *transmuto—muto*, to change.]

Transmuter, trans-mūt'er, *n.* One that transmutes.

Transom, tran'sum, *n.* A cross beam; in ships, transoms are beams fixed across the stern-post of the ship, to strengthen the after-part; a horizontal bar of stone or timber across a mullioned window, dividing it into stories; the cross-bar separating the door from the fanlight above it; in gunnery, transoms are pieces of wood which join the cheeks of some gun-carriages. [L. *transenna—trans*, across, and *sumo*, to take.]

Transom-window, tran'sum-win-dō, *n.* A window divided into two stories by a transom.

Transparence, Transparency, transpā'rens, trans-pā'ren-si, *n.* State of being transparent; that property of a body by which it suffers rays of light to pass through it, so that objects can be distinctly seen through it; a picture painted on semi-transparent materials, and illuminated by light placed at the back, so that it may be exhibited at night.

Transparent, trans-pā'rent, *a.* Appearing through; having the property of transmitting rays of light distinctly; pellucid; admitting the passage of light. [Fr.—L. *pareo*, to appear.]

Transparently, trans-pā'rent-li, *adv.* Clearly; so as to be seen through.

Transpierce, trans-pērs', *vt.* To pierce through; to penetrate; to pass through. *ppr.* transpiercing, *pret. & pp.* transpierced. [L. *trans*, and Eng. *pierce*.]

Transpiration, trans-pi-rā'shon, *n.* The act or process of transpiring or passing off through the pores of the skin in the form of vapour; the exhalation of watery vapour from the surface of the leaves of plants. [Fr.]

Transpire, trans-pīr', *vt.* To breathe through; to emit through the pores of the skin; to send off in vapour.—*vi.* To be breathed out; to be emitted through the pores of the skin; to escape from secrecy; to come to pass. *ppr.* transpiring, *pret. & pp.* transpired. [Fr. *transspirer*—L. *spiro*, to breathe.]

Transplant, trans-plant', *vt.* To remove and plant in another place; to remove and settle for residence in another place; to remove. [Fr. *transplanter*—L. *planto*, to set.]

Transplantation, trans-plant-ā'shon, *n.* Act of transplanting; the removal of a plant or of a settled inhabitant to a different place for growth or residence; conveyance from one to another. [Fr.]

Transplanting, trans-plant'ing, *p.n.* Act of removing a plant or tree from one situation to another, in such a manner as not to interrupt its growth.

Transport, trans-pōrt', *vt.* To convey from one place to another; to carry into banishment, as a criminal; to carry away by violence of passion; to bear away, as the soul in ecstasy. [L. *transporto—porto*, to carry.]

Transport, trans'pōrt, *n.* Transportation; conveyance; a ship employed by government for carrying soldiers, warlike stores, &c., from one place to another, or to convey convicts to the place of their destination; a convict sentenced to exile; rapture; ecstacy; violent manifestation, as of rage.

Transportable, trans-pōrt'a-bl, *a.* That may be transported.

Transportance†, trans-pōrt'ans, *n.* Conveyance.

Transportation, trans-pōrt-ā'shon, *n.* Act of carrying from one place to another; conveyance; banishment for felony; formerly, a statutable punishment for a great variety of offences. [Late L. *transportatio*.]

Transporter, trans-pōrt'ér, *n.* One who transports or removes.

Transporting, trans-pōrt'ing, *p.a.* Ravishing with delight; bearing away the soul in pleasure; ecstatic.

Transportingly, trans-pōrt'ing-li, *adv.* Ravishingly.

Transposal, trans-pōz'al, *n.* Act of transposing.

Transpose, trans-pōz', *vt.* To place over; to change, as the place or order of things, by putting each in the place of the other; to change, as the natural order of words; to change, as the key in music. *ppr.* transposing, *pret. & pp.* transposed. [Fr. *transposer*—L. *pono, positum*, to set, place.]

Transposing, trans-pōz'ing, *p.a.* Having the quality of changeableness of place.

Transposition, trans-pō-zi'shon, *n.* Act of transposing; a changing of the places of things and putting each in the place before occupied by the other; the state of being reciprocally changed in place; a change of the natural order of words in a sentence; in music, a change of key. [Fr.—L. *pono*, to set, place.]

Transprint, trans-print', *vt.* To print in the wrong place.

Trans-ship, trans-ship', *vt.* To convey from one ship or vessel to another. *ppr.* trans-shipping, *pret. & pp.* trans-shipped.

Trans-shipment, trans-ship'ment, *n.* Act of trans-shipping.

Transubstantiate, tran-sub-stan'shi-āt, *vt.* To change to another substance. *ppr.* transubstantiating, *pret. & pp.* transubstantiated. [Fr. *transsubstantier*—L. *substantia*, substance.]

Transubstantiation, tran-sub-stan'shi-ā'shon, *n.* A changing into another substance; in the Romish church, the supposed conversion of the bread and wine in the eucharist, into the body and blood of Christ.

Transudation, tran-sū-dā'shon, *n.* Act of transuding; act or process of passing off through the pores of a substance. [Fr. *transsudation*—L. *sudo*, to sweat.]

Transudatory, tran-sū'da-tō-ri, *a.* Passing by transudation.

Transude, tran-sūd', *vi.* To emit sweat through the pores; to pass through the pores or interstices of texture, as water or other fluid. *ppr.* transuding, *pret. & pp.* transuded. [Fr. *transsuder*—L. *sudo*, Sans. *svid*, to sweat.]

Transverse, trans-vèrs', *a.* Turned across; lying or being across or in a cross direction. [Fr.—L. *verto, versus*, to turn.]

Transversely, trans-vèrs'li, *adv.* In a cross direction.

Trap, trap, *n.* Something that catches and retains; an engine that shuts with a spring, used for taking game or vermin; an engine for catching men; a stratagem; a kind of play; a contrivance applied to drains and soil-pipes to prevent effluvia from passing the place where they are situated.—*vt.* To catch in a trap; to insnare; to take by stratagem; to dress with ornaments. *ppr.* trapping, *pret. & pp.* trapped. [Sax. *trappe*, Old G. *trapo*, a snare.]

Trap, Trap-rocks, trap, trap'roks, *n.* A name given to rocks whose strata have the form of steps or a series of stairs. [Sw. *trappa*; D. *trappen*, to tread.]

Trap-door, trap'dōr, *n.* A door in a floor, which shuts close like a valve.

Trapeziform, tra-pē'zi-form, *a.* Having the form of a trapezium.

Trapezium, tra-pē'zi-um, *n.* **Trapezia** or **Trapeziums**, *pl.* In geometry, a plane figure contained under four right lines, no two of which are parallel; a bone of the wrist, so named from its shape. [L.—Gr. *trapeza*, a table.]

Trapezoid, tra'pē-zoid, *n.* In geometry, a plane four-sided figure, having two of its opposite sides parallel. [Gr. *trapezion*, and *eidos*, form.]

Trapezoidal, tra-pē-zoid'al, *a.* Having the form of a trapezoid.

Trappings, trap'ings, *n. pl.* Ornaments of horse furniture; external and superficial decorations. [Old Fr. *araperie*, a flourishing with leaves and flowers.]

Trap-stair, trap'stàr, *n.* A narrow staircase surmounted by a trap-door.

Trash, trash, *vt.* To lop; to crop; to strip of leaves.—*n.* Loppings of trees; any waste or worthless matter; unripe fruit or other matter improper for food, but eaten by children, &c.; a worthless person. [Icel. *tros*, sweepings.]

Trashy, trash'i, *a.* Waste; worthless.

Travail, tra'vál, *vi.* To exert one's self beyond or above one's strength; to toil; to suffer the pangs of childbirth.—*n.* Excessive labour; labour with pain; the pangs of childbirth. [Fr. *travailler*.]

Trave, Travis, tràv, tra'vis, *n.* A beam; a traverse; a wooden frame to confine an unruly horse while shoeing. [Fr. *entraves*.]

Travel, tra'vel, *vi.* To make a toilsome or wearisome journey; to go or march on foot; to ride to a distant place in the same country; to visit foreign states, either by sea or land; to go; to move; to move, as a beast.—*vt.* To pass; to journey over. *ppr.* travelling, *pret. & pp.* travelled.—*n.* Act of travelling; labour; a passing on foot; journey; a journeying to a distant country or countries; a tour (often in the plural); (pl.) an account of occurrences and observations made during a journey. [a different orthography of *travail*.]

Travelled, tra'veld, *p.a.* Having made journeys.

Traveller, tra'vel-ér, *n.* One who travels; one who visits foreign countries; in ships, a ring fitted so as to slip up or down a rope; a person who travels for a merchant, to receive payment of goods, wares, &c., sold by his employer, and to take orders.

Travelling, tra'vel-ing, *p.a.* Pertaining to travail.

Travel-stained, tra'vel-stānd, *a.* Having the clothes soiled, &c., with the marks of travelling.

Traversable, tra'vèrs-a-bl, *a.* That may be traversed or denied.

Traverse, tra'vèrs, *adv.* Athwart; crosswise. [Fr. *à travers*.]—*a.* Turned or directed across; being in a direction

---

ṣh, chain; j, job; g, go; ng, sing; ᴛʜ, then; th, thin; w, wig; wh, whig; zh, azure; † obsolete.

across something else; pertaining to cross sailing. [Fr. *traversé*.]—*n.* Anything laid in a *transverse* direction; a trench with a little parapet for protecting men on the flank; a wall raised across a work; the variation of a ship's course, occasioned by the shifting of the winds, currents, &c.; the transverse piece in a timber roof; a gallery in a church or other large building; in law, a denial of what the opposite party has advanced in any stage of the pleadings; a trick. *vt.* To thwart; to obstruct; to wander over; to survey carefully; to turn and point in any direction, as a cannon; to plane in a direction across the grain of the wood; to deny, as what the opposite party has alleged.—*vi.* In fencing, to use the posture or motions of opposition or counteraction; to turn, as on a pivot; to move round. *ppr.* traversing, *pret. & pp.* traversed. [L. *trans*, and *verto*, to turn.]

Traverser, tra'vėrs-ėr, *n*. One who traverses or opposes a plea in law.

Travertin, tra'vėr-tin, *n*. A white limestone, usually hard and semi-crystalline, deposited from the water of springs holding carbonate of lime in solution. [It. *travertino*.]

Travestied, tra'ves-tid, *p.a.* Parodied; burlesqued.

Travesty, tra'ves-ti, *vt.* To change the dress of; to disguise; to translate into such language as to render ridiculous or ludicrous; to parody. *ppr.* travestying, *pret. & pp.* travestied.—*n.* That which is disguised by dress; a parody; a burlesque translation of a work.—*a.* Disguised by dress so as to be ridiculous; denoting a book translated in a manner to make it burlesque. [Fr. *travestir*—L. *trans*, and *vestio*, to clothe.]

Travis, tra'vis, *n*. A *trave* (which see).

Trawl, trạl, *vi.* To fish with a drag-net. *n*. A trawl-net.

Trawler, trạl'ėr, *n*. A fishing vessel which *trails* a net behind it; a fisherman who fishes with a drag-net.

Trawling, trạl'ing, *p.a.* Dragging for fish; using a drag-net.—*p.n.* The act of one who trawls.

Tray, trā, *n*. A small trough sometimes scooped out of a piece of timber and made hollow; a sort of waiter, of wood or metal. [same as *trough*.]

Tray-trip, trā'trip, *n*. An old game played with dice.

Treacher, trech'ėr, *n*. A traitor.

Treacherous, trech'ėr-us, *a*. Guilty of treachery; traitorous to the state or sovereign; perfidious in private life; betraying a trust.

Treacherously, trech'ėr-us-li, *adv. In a treacherous manner.*

Treacherousness, trech'ėr-us-nes, *n*. Quality of being treacherous.

Treachery, trech'ė-ri, *n*. Trickery; deception; violation of allegiance or of faith and confidence; perfidy; faithlessness. [Fr. *tricherie*, a cheating; L. *tricæ*, quirks.]

Treacle, trē'kl, *n*. Originally, an antidote against the bite of *poisonous animals*; a viscid syrup, which drains from the sugar-refiners' moulds; a saccharine fluid, consisting of the juices of certain vegetables, as the sap of the birch, sycamore, &c. [Fr. *thériaque*; Gr. *thērion*, a wild beast.]

Tread, tred, *vi.* To set or plant the foot; to walk or go; to walk with form or state; to copulate, as fowls.—*vt.* To plant the foot on; to press under the feet; to beat with the feet; to walk upon in a stately manner; to crush under the foot; to trample in contempt; to put in action by the feet, as a wheel.—*n.* Act of treading; a step or stepping; pressure with the foot; manner of stepping; gait; the horizontal part of a step in a stair on which the foot is placed; way; path. [Sax. *tredan*; Old G. *tretan*, to tread.]

Treader, tred'ėr, *n*. One who treads.

Treading, tred'ing, *p.n.* Act of one who treads; a stepping.

Treadle, Treddle, tred'l, tred'l, *n*. The part of a loom or other machine which is moved by the *tread* or foot.

Treadmill, tred'mil, *n*. A mill worked by persons *treading* on steps fixed on the circumference of a horizontal wheel.

Treadwheel, tred'hwēl, *n*. A *wheel* with steps placed horizontally on the exterior surface, by *treading* on which the wheel is turned.

Treason, trē'zon, *n*. A delivering over or up, contrary to good faith; breach of allegiance; an offence which immediately affects the safety of the sovereign or of the state. [Norm. *trayson*—L. *trado*, to give up—*do*, to give.]

Treasonable, trē'zon-a-bl, *a*. Pertaining to treason; involving the crime of treason, or partaking of its guilt.

Treasonably, trē'zon-a-bli, *adv. In a treasonable manner.*

Treasure, trē'zhūr, *n*. That which is deposited or stored up; riches hoarded; a stock of money in reserve; a great quantity of anything collected for future use; something very much valued; great abundance; anything precious.—*vt.* To lay up, as money or other things for future use; to hoard (with *up*). *ppr.* treasuring, *pret. & pp.* treasured. [Fr. *trésor*; Gr. *thēsauros*—*tithēmi*, to place.]

Treasure-house, trē'zhūr-hous, *n*. A house or building where treasures and stores are kept.

Treasurer, trē'zhūr-ėr, *n*. One who has the care of a treasury; one who has the charge of the money, funds, or revenue of a society, corporation, state, &c. [Fr. *tresorier*.]

Treasury, trē'zhū-ri, *n*. A place where treasure is laid up; a department of government which has control over the public revenue; the officer or officers of the treasury department. [Fr. *trésorerie*.]

Treat, trēt, *vt.* To handle; to handle in a particular manner, in writing or speaking; to entertain without expense to the guest; to behave to or towards; to use; to manage in the application of remedies, as a patient or a disease; to subject to the action of. *vi.* To handle in writing or speaking (with *of*); to discourse; to come to terms of accommodation; to give food or drink as a compliment or expression of regard.—*n.* An entertainment given as a compliment; a rich entertainment. [Fr. *traiter*, to treat; L. *tracto*, to touch—*traho*, *tractum*, to draw.]

Treating, trēt'ing, *p.n.* Act of one who treats.

Treatise, trē'tiz, *n*. A handling; that which is treated; a discourse; a written composition on a particular subject. [L. *tractātus*—*tracto*, to handle.]

Treatment, trēt'ment, *n*. Act or manner of treating; management; manner of mixing or combining; usage; manner of using; entertainment; good or bad behaviour towards; manner of applying remedies to cure. [Fr. *traitement*.]

Treaty, trē'ti, *n*. Act of treating; an agreement or contract between two or more nations or sovereigns; entreaty. [Fr. *traité*—L. *tractātus*.)

Treble, tre'bl, *a*. Threefold; triple; pertaining to the most acute of the parts of music.—*n*. The highest of the parts in music; the part sung by women and boys, and played by violins, &c.; the melody or air of a composition.—*vt.* To make thrice as much; to multiply by three.—*vi.* To become threefold. *ppr.* trebling, *pret. & pp.* trebled. [Fr. *triple*; L. *tres*, three, and *plico*, to fold.]

Trebly, tre'bli, *adv. In a threefold number or quantity.*

Tree, trē, *n*. That which grows; a perennial plant having a woody trunk of varying size, from which spring a number of branches, having a structure similar to the trunk; something resembling a tree; the cross of Christ; a cross. [Sax. *treow*—Sans. *drih*, to grow.]

Treenails, trē'nālz, *n*. Long cylindrical wooden pins employed to fasten the planks of a ship's side and bottom to the corresponding timbers. [*tree* and *nail*.]

Trefoil, trē'foil, *n*. A *three-leaved* plant, as clover; an architectural ornament, consisting of three cusps, resembling the three-leaved clover. [Fr. *trèfle*—L. *tres*, three, and *folium*, leaf.]

Trellis, trel'is, *n*. In gardening, a frame of cross-barred work, or *lattice-work*, used for supporting plants; a lattice-work of wood or metal, for screens, doors, or windows.—*vt.* To furnish with a trellis, lattice, or wooden frame. [Fr. *treillis*, lattice-work—L. *ter*, thrice, and *licium*, a leash.]

Trellised, trel'ist, *p.a.* Having a trellis or trellises.

Tremble, trem'bl, *vi.* To shake involuntarily, as with fear, cold, or weakness; to quake; to shiver; to shake; to shake, as sound. *ppr.* trembling, *pret. & pp.* trembled. [Fr. *trembler*—L. *tremo*.]

Trembler, trem'bl-ėr, *n*. One that trembles.

Trembling, trem'bl-ing, *p.n.* The act or state of shaking involuntarily, as from fear, cold, or weakness.

Tremblingly, trem'bl-ing-li, *adv. In a trembling manner.*

Trembling-poplar, trem'bl-ing-pōp'lar, *n*. The aspen tree.

Tremendous, trē-men'dus, *a.* Such as to cause trembling; such as may excite fear or terror; such as may astonish by its force and violence. [L. *tremendus*—*tremo*, to tremble.]

Tremendously, trē-men'dus-li, *adv.* In a manner to terrify or astonish.

Tremor, trē'mor, *n*. An involuntary trembling; a shivering or shaking. [L.—*tremo*, to tremble.]

Tremulous, tre'mū-lus, *a. Trembling*; affected with fear or timidity; shaking. [L. *tremulus*—*tremo*.]

Tremulously, tre'mū-lus-li, *adv.* With quivering or trepidation.

Tremulousness, tre'mū-lus-nes, *n*. State of being *tremulous* or quivering.

Trench, trensh, *vt.* To cut or dig, as a ditch; to turn over and mix, as soil, to the depth of two, three, or more spades; to furrow; to form with deep furrows by ploughing; to entrench; to cut a long gash in; to hew out.—*vi.* To encroach (with *on* or *upon*).—*n.* A long narrow *cut* in the earth; a ditch; a narrow shallow ditch, for conveying water out of main ditches to float land; a deep ditch cut for covering the troops

Fāte, fär, fat, fall; mē, met, hėr; pīne pin; nōte, not, mōve; tūbe, tub, bull; oil, pound.

as they advance toward the besieged place. [Fr. *trancher*, to cut—L. *trans*, and *seco*, to cut.]
Trenchant, trensh'ant, *a. Cutting; sharp*. [Fr. *tranchant*.]
Treucher, trensh'ėr, *n.* A wooden plate, on which meat may be cut or carved, and on which meat was formerly eaten at table; food; pleasures of the table. [Fr. *tranchoir—trancher*, to cut.]
Trencher-cap, trensh'ėr-kap, *n.* The square cap worn by the collegians at Oxford and Cambridge.
Trencher-friend, trensh'ėr-frend, *n.* One who frequents the tables of others; a sponger.
Trencher-man, trensh'ėr-man, *n.* A feeder; a great eater.
Trench-plough, trensh'plou, *n.* A kind of plough for opening land to a greater depth than that of common furrows. *vt.* To plough with deep furrows.
Trental, **Trentals**, tren'tal, tren'talz, *n.* An office for the dead in the Romish service, consisting of *thirty* masses rehearsed for *thirty* days successively after the party's death. [Fr. *trente*; L. *triginta*, thirty.]
Trepan, trē-pan', *n. A borer;* a circular saw resembling a wimble, for sawing a circular portion of bone out of the skull.—*vt. To perforate*, as the skull, and take out a piece (a surgical operation for relieving the brain from pressure or irritation). *ppr.* trepanning, *pret. & pp.* trepanned. [Fr. *trépan*—Gr. *trupē*, a hole—*truō*, to rub off.]
Trepan, trē-pan', *vt.* To lay *a trap* for; to ensnare; to catch; to take by stratagem. *ppr.* trepanning, *pret. & pp.* trepanned. [Sax. *treppan*.]
Trepanning, trē-pan'ing, *p.n. The operation of perforating* the skull for relieving the brain from compression or irritation.
Trephine, tre-fēn', *n.* An improved form of the *trepan*.—*vt. To perforate with a trephine;* to trepan. *ppr.* trephining, *pret. & pp.* trephined.
Trepidation, tre-pid-ā'shon, *n.* A state of confused hurry or alarm, like that of an army *put to flight;* a quivering, particularly from fear or terror; a state of terror; a trembling of the limbs, as in paralytic affections; confused haste. [D. *driestal*, a tripod—*drie*, three, and *stal*, stool.] [Fr. *trépidation*.]
Trespass, tres'pas, *vi. To pass beyond;* to enter unlawfully upon the land of another; to violate any rule of rectitude, to the injury of another; to transgress any divine law (with *against*); to intrude; to go too far (with *upon*); to put to inconvenience by importunity.—*n. Any transgression* of the law not amounting to felony; any wrong done to the person, or to the lands and tenements of any man; any injury done to another; any voluntary transgression of the moral law. [Norm. *trespasser—passer*, to pass, and L. *trans*.]
Trespasser, tres'pas-ėr, *n. One who commits a trespass;* one who enters upon another's land; a sinner.
Trespass-offering, tres'pas-of-fėr-ing, *n. An offering*, among the Israelites, for *a trespass.*
Tress, tres, *n. A braid or knot of hair;* a ringlet. [Fr. *tresse*.]
Tressed, trest, *p.a. Having tresses;* curled; formed into ringlets.
Trestle, tres'l, *n. A three-legged prop for supporting* horizontally; the frame of a table; a movable form for supporting anything. [D. *driestal*, a tripod—*drie*, three, and *stal*, stool.]
Fret, tret, *n.* An allowance in commerce

of 4 lbs. on every 104 lbs. to purchasers, for *waste* or refuse matter. [probably from L. *tritus*, *tero*, to wear away.]
Triable, trī'a-bl, *a. That may be tried;* that may be subjected to trial or test.
Triad, trī'ad, *n. The union of three; three united*. [L. *trias*, *triadis*—Gr. *treis*, three.]
Trial, trī'al, *n. Act of trying;* any exertion of strength for the purpose of ascertaining its effect; examination by a test; experiment; suffering that puts strength or faith to test; afflictions that prove the graces of men; the examination of a cause in controversy between parties, before a proper tribunal; temptation; state of being tried.
Triangle, trī'ang-gl, *n.* A figure having *three angles;* a figure bounded by three sides, and containing three angles; an instrument of percussion in music, made of a rod of polished steel, bent into the form of a triangle, and open at one of its angles. [Fr.—L. *tres*, and *angulus*, a corner.]
Triangled, trī'ang-gld, *p.a. Having three angles;* formed into triangles.
Triangular, trī-ang-gū-lär, *a. Having three angles;* relating to a triangle.
Triangularity, trī-ang'gū-la''ri-ti, *n. Quality of being triangular.*
Triangularly, trī'ang-gū-lär-li, *adv. After the form of a triangle.*
Triangulate, trī-ang-gū-lāt, *vt.* To divide into *triangular* net-work, by mensuration. *ppr.* triangulating, *pret. & pp.* triangulated.
Triangulated, trī-ang-gū-lāt-ed, *p.a.* Surveyed by means of a series of *triangles.*
Triangulating, trī-ang'gū-lāt-ing, *p.n. The operation of laying down a network of triangles* in the trigonometrical survey of a country.
Triangulation, trī-ang-gū-lā''shon, *n. The net-work of triangles* with which the face of a country is covered in a trigonometrical survey.
Tribe, trīb, *n.* Originally, a *third* part of the Roman people; a division or distinct portion of people; a race descending from the same progenitor, and kept distinct; a number of things having certain characters in common; a nation of savages; a body of rude people united under one leader; a number of persons of any profession (in contempt). [Fr. *tribu*—L. *tribus—tres*, three.]
Tribrach, trī'brak, *n.* In prosody, a poetic foot of *three short* syllables. [Gr. *treis*, three, and *brachus*, short.]
Tribulation, trī-bū-lā'shon, *n. Severe trouble or affliction;* distresses of life. [Fr.—Gr. *tribō*, to thrash corn.]
Tribunal, trī-bū'nal, *n. The seat of a tribunet;* the seat of a judge; the bench on which a judge and his associates sit for administering justice; a court of justice. [L.—*tribūnus*, a tribune.]
Tribune, trī'būn, *n. The chief of a tribe* among the ancient Romans; afterward an officer chosen by the people, to protect them from the oppression of the nobles; a bench or elevated place, from which speeches were delivered. [L. *tribūnus—tribus*, a tribe.]
Tribuneship, **Tribunate**, trī'būn-ship, trī'būn-āt, *n. The office of a tribune.*
Tribunician, **Tribunitial**, trī-bū-ni''shi-an, trī-bū-ni''shi-al, *a. Pertaining to tribunes;* suiting a tribune.
Tributarily, trī'bū-ta-ri-li, *adv. In a tributary* manner.
Tributary, trī'bū-ta-ri, *a. Paying tribute* to another; subject; paid in tribute;

yielding supplies of anything; shed in commemoration of, as a tear.—*n. One that pays tribute;* an affluent; a stream which falls into another stream.
Tribute, trī'būt, *n. Something given;* a grant; a stated sum of money *paid* by one prince or nation to another, either as an acknowlegment of submission, or as the price of peace and protection; a personal contribution. [Fr. *tribut*—L. *tribūtum—tribuo*, to give.]
Tribute-money, trī'būt-mu-ne, *n. Money paid as tribute.*
Trice, trīs, *n.* A space of time during which one can say or tell *three;* a very short time. [Fr. *trois*; L. *tres*, three.]
Tricennial, trī-sen'ni-al, *a. Belonging to the period of thirty years*, or occurring once in that period. [L. *tricennālis*—*triginta*, thirty, and *annus*, a year.]
Tricentenary, trī-sen'ten-a-ri, *n. A period or space of three hundred years.* [L. *tres*, three, and *centum*, a hundred.]
Trick, trik, *n.* An *entanglement;* a fraudulent contrivance for an evil purpose; a cheat or cheating; the legerdemain of a juggler; a parcel of cards falling to the winner at one round of play; a particular habit or manner. *vt.* To *deceive;* to impose on; to defraud; to cheat. [Fr. *tricher*, to cheat —Gr. *thrix*, *trichos*, the hair.]
Trick, trik, *vt.* To dress; to decorate; to set off; to adorn fantastically. (Often with *up*, *off*, or *out*.) [W. *treciaw*, to furnish or harness, to trick out.]
Tricked, trikt, *p.a.* Cheated; deceived; dressed; painted.
Tricker, **Trickster**, trik'ėr, trik'stėr, *n. One who tricks;* a deceiver; a cheat.
Tricker, trik'ėr, *n. See* TRIGGER.
Trickery, trik'ė-ri, *n. The art of dressing up;* artifice; stratagem.
Tricking, trik'ing, *p.n.* Dress; ornament.
Trickish, trik'ish, *a. Full of tricks;* given to deception and cheating; knavish.
Trickishly, trik'ish-li, *adv.* Artfully; knavishly.
Trickishness, trik'ish-nes, *n. State of quality of being trickish.*
Trickle, trik'l, *vi. To fall in drops;* to flow in a small gentle stream. *ppr.* trickling, *pret. & pp.* trickled. [Icel. *dreitla*, to drop.]
Trickling, trik'l-ing, *p.n. The act of flowing* in a small gentle stream or *in drops.*
Trickster, trik'stėr, *n. One who practises tricks.*
Tricky, trik'i, *a. Trickish.*
Tricolor, **Tricolour**, trī'kul-ėr, trī'kul-ėr, *n. The national French banner of three colours*, blue, white, and red. [Fr. *tricolor.*]
Tricoloured, trī'kul-ėrd, *p.a. Having three colours.*
Trident, trī'dent, *n.* Any instrument of the form of a fork with *three prongs;* a kind of sceptre with three prongs, which the fables of antiquity put into the hands of Neptune, the deity of the ocean. [Fr.—L. *tres*, three, and *dens*, *dentis*, a tooth.]
Trident, **Tridented**, trī'dent, trī'dent-ed, *p.a. Having three teeth or prongs.*
Triennial, trī-en'ni-al, *a. Continuing three years;* happening every three years. [Fr. *triennal*—L. *tres*, three, and *annus*, a year.]
Triennially, trī-en'ni-al-li, *adv. Once in three years.*
Trier, trī'ėr, *n. One who tries;* one who examines anything by a test or stand-

ard; one who tries judicially; one appointed to decide whether a challenge to a juror is just; a test.

Trifle, tri′fl, *vi.* To act *with levity;* to talk with folly; to indulge in light amusement; to be of no importance. *ppr.* trifling, *pret. & pp.* trifled.—*n.* A thing of no moment. [Sw. Goth. *trafla,* sport, jest.]

Trifler, tri′fl-er, *n. One who trifles.*

Trifling, tri′fl-ing, *p.a. Acting or talking with levity;* being of small value or importance; trivial.—*p.n.* Employment about things of no importance.

Triflingly, tri′fl-ing-li, *adv. In a trifling manner;* with levity.

Trifoliate, tri-fō′li-āt, *a. Having three leaves.* [L. *tres,* three, and *folium,* leaf.]

Triform, tri′form, *a. Having a triple form* or shape. [L. *triformis—tres,* three, and *forma,* form.]

Trigamy, trī′ga-mi, *n.* State of being *married three times;* or the state of having three husbands or three wives at the same time. [Gr. *treis,* three, and *gamos,* marriage.]

Trigger, trig′er, *n. That which pulls or draws;* the catch which, being *pulled,* disengages the cock of a gun-lock, and allows it to strike fire. [D. *trekker,* a drawer, puller.]

Triglyph, tri′glif, *n.* An ornament consisting of a *three-grooved* tablet in the frieze of the Doric order, repeated at equal intervals. [Gr. *treis,* three, and *gluphē,* a carving.]

Trigonometric, Trigonometrical, tri′gon-o-met′rik, tri′gon-o-met′rik-al, *a. Pertaining to trigonometry;* performed by or according to the rules of trigonometry. [Fr. *trigonométrique.*]

Trigonometrically, tri′gon-o-met′rik-al-li, *adv. According* to the rules or principles of *trigonometry.*

Trigonometry, tri-gon-om′et-ri, *n. The measuring of triangles,* or the science of determining the sides and angles of triangles, by means of certain parts which are given; but in its modern acceptance it includes all theorems relative to angles and circular arcs, and the lines connected with them, these lines being expressed by numbers or ratios. [Fr. *trigonométrie—*Gr. *treis,* three, *gōnia,* an angle, and *metron,* a measure.]

Trihedral, tri-hē′dral, *a. Having three equal sides.*

Trihedron, tri-hē′dron, *n. A figure having three equal sides.* [Gr. *treis,* three, and *hedra,* side.]

Trilateral, tri-lat′ér-al, *a. Having three sides,* as a triangle. [Fr. *trilatéral—*L. *latus, lateris,* a side.]

Trilaterally, tri-lat′ér-al-li, *adv. With three sides.*

Trilingual, tri-ling′gwal, *a. Consisting of three languages.* [L. *tres,* and *lingua,* language.]

Triliteral, tri-lit′ér-al, *a. Consisting of three letters.—n. A word consisting of three letters.* [L. *tres,* three, and *litera,* letter.]

Trill, tril, *n. A quaver;* a shake of the voice in singing, or of the sound of an instrument.—*vt.* To utter with a *quavering* or tremulousness of voice.—*vi.* To shake or quaver; to play in tremulous vibrations of sound; [probably from *trickle*] to flow in a small stream, or in drops rapidly succeeding each other; to trickle. [It. *trillo,* a quaver.]

Trillion, tril′li-on, *n.* The product of a *million* multiplied by a million, and that product multiplied by a million;

a number consisting of a unit followed by eighteen cyphers. [a word formed arbitrarily of *three,* and *million.*]

Trim, trim, *a. Set in order;* dressed up; nice; snug; tight; compact.—*n.* Dress; gear; ornaments; the state of a ship or her cargo, ballast, &c., by which she is well prepared for sailing.—*vt.* To set *in order;* to arrange; to make neat; to dress; to put in a proper state, as the body; to decorate; to clip; to shear; to supply with oil, as a lamp; to adjust, as the cargo of a ship; to arrange in due order for sailing, as the sails of a ship.—*vi.* To balance; to fluctuate between parties, so as to appear to favour each. *ppr.* trimming, *pret. & pp.* trimmed. [Sax. *trymian,* to prepare.]

Trimeter, tri′mē-tèr, *n.* A poetical division of verse, consisting of *three measures.*

Trimeter, Trimetrical, tri′mē-tèr, tri-met′rik-al, *a. Consisting of three* poetical *measures,* forming an iambic of six feet. [Gr. *trimetros—treis,* three, and *metron,* measure.]

Trimly, trim′li, *adv.* Nicely; neatly.

Trimmed, trimd, *p.a.* Clipped; shaved.

Trimmer, trim′ér, *n. One that trims;* one who fluctuates between parties; a flat brick arch for the support of a hearth in an upper floor.

Trimming, trim′ing, *p.a.* Fluctuating between parties.—*p.n.* Necessary or ornamental appendages to a garment, as lace, ribbons, and the like.

Trimmingly, trim′ing-li, *adv. In a trimming manner.*

Trimness, trim′nes, *n.* State of being *trim;* neatness; petty elegance.

Trinal, trīn′al, *a. Threefold.* [L. *trinus,* three.]

Trine, trīn, *a. Threefold.—n.* In astrology, the aspect of planets distant from each other 120 degrees, or the *third* part of the zodiac. [L. *trinus.*]

Trinitarian, tri-ni-tā′ri-an, *a. Pertaining to the Trinity,* or to the doctrine of the Trinity.—*n. One who believes the doctrine of the Trinity;* one of a religious order, instituted in 1198, who made it their business to ransom Christian captives taken by the Moors and other infidels.

Trinitarianism, tri-ni-tā′ri-an-izm, *n. The doctrine of Trinitarians.*

Trinity, trīn′i-ti, *n. A triad;* the union of three persons in one Godhead, the Father, the Son, and the Holy Spirit. [Fr. *trinité;* L. *tres,* three.]

Trinity-Sunday, tri′ni-ti-sun-dā, *n.* The *Sunday* next after Whitsunday, observed by the English Church in honour of the *Trinity.*

Trinket, tring′ket, *n. A small ornament,* as a jewel, a ring, and the like; a thing of little value; tackle. [originally, *tricket.*]

Trinomial, tri-nō′mi-al, *a.* Noting an algebraical expression consisting of *three* terms, connected by the sign plus or minus.—*n.* An algebraical quantity consisting of *three* terms. [L. *tres,* and *nomen,* a name.]

Trio, trī′ō, *n. Three united:* a musical composition for *three* voices or *three* instruments. [L. *tres, tria.*]

Trior, trī′or, *n. See* **Trier.**

Trip, trip, *vi.* To *step lightly from joyousness;* to dance from gladness; to run lightly (with *over*); to take short, quick, light steps; to lose footing; to stumble; to err; to be deficient.—*vt.* To *cause to stumble;* to supplant; to cause to fall by striking the feet suddenly from under the person (usually

with *up*); to overthrow by depriving of support; to catch; to convict. *ppr.* tripping, *pret. & pp.* tripped.—*n. Act of tripping;* a stumble by the striking of the foot against an object; a failure; a slight error arising from haste; a voyage; a jaunt; among seamen, a short voyage or journey. [Dan. *trippe;* Armor. *tripa,* to dance.]

Tripartite, tri-pärt′it, *a. Divided into three parts;* having three corresponding parts; made between three parties. [Fr.—L. *tres,* and *partior, partitus,* to divide—*pars,* a part.]

Tripe, trip, *n.* Properly, the entrails; but in common usage, the large stomach of ruminating animals prepared for food. [Fr.]

Tripedal, tri-ped′al, *a. Having three feet.* [L. *tres,* and *pes, pedis,* a foot.]

Tripetalous, tri-pē′tal-us, *a. Having three petals* or flower-leaves. [Gr. *treis,* three, and *petalon,* leaf.]

Triphthong, trif′thong, *n. A threefold sound;* a coalition of three vowels in one compound sound; as in *adieu.* [Gr. *treis,* three, and *phthonggē,* the voice, sound.]

Triphthongal, trif-thong′gal, *a. Pertaining to* or consisting of *a triphthong.*

Triple, tri′pl, *a. Threefold;* consisting of three united; treble; three times repeated.—*vt.* To treble; to make threefold or thrice as much or as many. *ppr.* tripling, *pret. & pp.* tripled. [Fr.—L. *tres,* and *plico,* to fold.]

Triplet, trip′let, *n. Three of a kind;* three verses rhyming together; in music, triplets are notes grouped together by threes, as in jigs; an eyepiece of a microscope, which, when used, triples the power of the instrument.

Triplex†, tri′pleks, *n.* Triple time in music.

Triplicate, tri′pli-kāt, *a. Made thrice as much; threefold.—n. A third* paper or thing, corresponding to two others of the same kind. [Late L. *triplico, triplicatus.*]

Triplication, tri-pli-kā′shon, *n. The act of trebling or making threefold.* [Late L. *triplicatio.*]

Triplicity, tri-pli′si-ti, *n. The state of being threefold.* [Fr. *triplicité.*]

Triply, tri′pli, *adv. In a threefold manner.*

Tripod, tri′pod, *n. A* seat supported by *three legs,* on which the priest and sibyls in ancient times were placed to utter oracles; a cup for containing fluids, supported on a three-footed pedestal; any article of furniture resting upon three feet, as a table, chair, &c. [Gr. *tripous, tripōdos—treis,* three, and *pous,* a foot—Sans. *pad,* to go.]

Tripoli, tri′pō-li, *n. A* mineral originally brought from *Tripoli,* used in polishing metals, marble, glass, &c.

Tripper, trip′ér, *n. One who trips* or supplants; one that walks nimbly.

Tripping, trip′ing, *p.a.* Stepping nimbly; quick; nimble.—*p.n. The act of tripping;* a light dance.

Trippingly, trip′ing-li, *adv.* Nimbly; with a light, nimble, quick step.

Triptote, trip′tōt, *n.* A noun used only in *three cases.* [Gr. *treis,* three, and *pipto,* to fall.]

Trireme, trī′rēm, *n.* A galley or vessel with *three* benches or ranks of *oars* on a side. [Fr. *trirème—*L. *tres,* and *remus,* an oar.]

Trisect, tri-sekt′, *vt.* To *cut* or divide *into three equal parts.* [L. *tres,* three, and *seco, sectum,* to cut.]

Fāte, fär, fat, fąll; mē, met, hėr; pīne, pin; nōte, not, mōve; tūbe, tub, bụll; oil, pound.

Trisection, tri-sek'shon, *n. The cutting or division of a thing into three equal parts;* in geometry, the division of an angle into three equal parts. [Fr.]
Tristful, trist'ful, *a.* Sad; gloomy.
Trisyllabic, Trisyllabical, tri-sil-lab'ik, tri-sil-lab'ik-al, *a. Pertaining to a trisyllable;* consisting of three syllables.
Trisyllable, tri'sil-la-bl, *n. A word consisting of three syllables.* [L. *tres*, three, and *syllaba*, a syllable.]
Trite, trit, *a. Rubbed; rubbed away;* worn out; stale; used till so common as to have lost its novelty and interest. [L. *tritus—tero*, to wear by rubbing.]
Tritely, trit'li, *adv.* In a common manner.
Triteness, trit'nes, *n. Quality or state of being trite;* a state of being worn out.
Triton, tri'ton, *n.* A fabled sea demigod, having the human figure in the upper part of the body, and in the lower part that of a fish. [Gr.]
Triturable, tri'tū-ra-bl, *a. Capable of being triturated.*
Triturate, tri'tū-rāt, *vt. To rub;* to pound; to rub or grind to a very fine powder, and properly to a finer powder than that made by pulverization. *ppr.* triturating, *pret. & pp.* triturated. [L. *trituro, trituratus—tero*, to rub.]
Trituration, tri-tū-rā'shon, *n. Act of triturating,* or of reducing to a fine powder by grinding. [Fr.]
Triumph, tri'umf, *n.* Among the ancient Romans a solemn and magnificent entry of a general into Rome, after a decisive victory; pomp with which a victory is publicly celebrated; conquest; exultation for success; a card that takes all others (now written *trump*).—*vi.* To celebrate victory with pomp; to obtain victory; to insult a person upon an advantage gained (with *over*); to be prosperous; to flourish. [Fr. *triomphe*—L. *triumphus*—Gr. *thriambos*, a hymn to Bacchus.]
Triumphal, tri-umf'al, *a. Pertaining to triumph;* used in a triumph; serving to commemorate a triumph. [Fr. *triomphal.*]
Triumphant, tri-umf'ant, *a. Celebrating a triumph;* graced with conquest; expressing joy for success. [L. *triumphans.*]
Triumphantly, tri-umf'ant-li, *adv. In a triumphant manner;* with success.
Triumpher, tri'umf-ėr, *n. One who triumphs* or rejoices for victory.
Triumvir, tri-um'vėr, *n. One of three men united* in office; one of a triumvirate. [L. *tres*, three, and *vir*, a male person, a man.]
Triumvirate, tri-um'vėr-āt, *n.* A coalition of *three men;* particularly, the union of three men who obtained the government of the Roman empire; government by three men in coalition. [Fr. *triumvirat.*]
Triune, tri'ūn, *n. Being three in one;* an epithet used to express the unity of the Godhead in a trinity of persons. [L. *tres* and *unus.*]
Trivial, tri'vi-al, *a.* That may be found where *three ways* meet; common; ordinary; of little worth; inconsiderable; vulgar. [Fr.; L. *tres*, and *via*, a way.]
Triviality, tri-vi-al'i-ti, *n. The state or quality of being trivial.*
Trivially, tri'vi-al-li, *adv.* Commonly; vulgarly; inconsiderably.
Trochaic, Trochaical, trō-kā'ik, trō-kā'ik-al, *a.* In poetry, *consisting of trochees.*
Trochee, trō'kē, *n.* In verse, a foot of two syllables, the first long, and the second short. [L. *trochæus*—Gr. *trechō*, to run.]
Troglodyte, trō'glod-īt, *n.* The Troglodytes were a people of Ethiopia, represented by the ancients as living in *holes* or caves. [Gr. *trōglodutēs—trōglē*, a hole, and *dūō*, to enter.]
Troll, trōl, *vt. To roll;* to move volubly; to utter volubly; to sing the parts of in succession; to allure, in allusion to the practice of fishing with a baited trolling line.—*vi. To roll; to move or run round;* to fish, as for pikes, with a rod whose line runs on a wheel or pulley; to sing a catch, each in turn taking up the air.—*n.* A kind of reel with a line used for fishing for pikes; a song, the parts of which are sung in succession. [G. *trollen*, to roll.]
Troller, trōl'ėr, *n. One who trolls.*
Trollop, trol'lop, *n. A stroller;* a woman loosely dressed; a slattern. [same as *trull.*]
Trombone, trom'bōn, *n.* A *large* and deep-toned instrument of the *trumpet* kind, consisting of three tubes. [It. augmentative of *tromba*, a trumpet.]
Troop, tröp, *n. A crowd;* a collection of people; a body of soldiers; applied to infantry, it is now used in the plural; a small body or company of cavalry, commanded by a captain; a company of stage-players.—*vi.* To collect in numbers; to march in haste or in company. [Fr. *troupe*—L. *turba*, a crowd.]
Trooper, trōp'ėr, *n.* A private or soldier in a body of cavalry; a horse-soldier.
Troops, trōps, *n. pl.* Soldiers in general; an army.
Trope, trōp, *n.* A word *turned* from its original signification to another; a word or expression used in a different sense from that which it properly signifies. [Fr.—Gr. *trepō*, to turn.]
Trophied, trō'fid, *p.a. Adorned with trophies.*
Trophy, trō'fi, *n.* A memorial of an enemy being *turned* to flight; a monument in commemoration of some victory; anything taken and preserved as a memorial of victory, as arms, flags, and the like; an architectural ornament representing the stem of a tree, charged with arms, offensive and defensive; memorial of conquest. [Fr. *trophie*—Gr. *trepō*, to turn.]
Tropic, Tropical, trō'pik, trō'pik-al, *a. Pertaining to the tropics;* incident to the tropics; *relating to tropes;* rhetorically changed from its proper sense. [Fr. *tropique*—Gr. *trepō*, to turn.]
Tropic, trō'pik, *n.* In astronomy, the tropics are two parallels of declination, whose distances from the equator are each equal to twenty-three degrees and a half nearly. The northern one is called the tropic of Cancer, and the southern one the tropic of Capricorn; and they are called tropics, because when the sun reaches either of them, he, as it were, *turns* back, and travels in an opposite direction. In geography, the tropics are two parallels of latitude, each at the same distance from the terrestrial equator as the celestial tropics are from the celestial equator, and they include that portion of the globe which is called the torrid zone. (see the adj. above.)
Tropically, trō'pik-al-li, *adv. In a tropical* or figurative *manner.*
Tropics, trō'piks. See TROPIC.
Tropological, tro-po-lo'jik-al, *a. Varied by tropes;* changed from the original import of the words.
Tropology, tro-pol'o-ji, *n.* A rhetorical mode of *speech, including tropes,* or change from the original import of the word. [Gr. *tropos*, a trope, and *logos*, discourse.]
Trossers†, tros'ėrz, *n.* Trowsers.
Trot, trot, *vi. To tread quickly;* to move faster than in walking, as a horse; to walk or move fast, or to run. *ppr.* trotting, *pret. & pp.* trotted.—*n.* The quick pace of a horse, when he lifts one fore foot and the hind foot of the opposite side at the same time; in a ludicrous sense, a quick sort of pace with a hobbling motion; an old woman. [G. *trotten*, frequent. from *treten*, to tread.]
Troth, troth, *n. Truth; faith;* fidelity. [Sax. *treowth—treowian*, to trust.]
Troth-plight†, troth'plīt, *p.a.* Betrothed; espoused.
Trotter, trot'ėr, *n. A beast that trots,* or that usually trots; a sheep's foot.
Trouble, tru'bl, *vt. To vex;* to molest; to grieve; to distress; to busy; to cause to be much engaged or anxious; to agitate. *ppr.* troubling, *pret. & pp.* troubled.—*n. Vexation; disturbance* of mind; calamity; annoyance; that which gives disturbance; that which afflicts. [Fr. *troubler;* Sans. *drip*, to vex.]
Troubled, tru'bld, *p.a. Disturbed;* agitated.
Troubler, tru'bl-ėr, *n. One who troubles or disturbs.*
Troublesome, tru'bl-sum, *a. Giving trouble or disturbance;* annoying; giving inconvenience to; importunate.
Troublesomely, tru'bl-sum-li, *adv. In a manner or degree to give trouble.*
Troublesomeness, tru'bl-sum-nes, *n. Quality of being troublesome.*
Troubling, tru'bl-ing, *p.a. Disturbing. p.n. The act of disturbing;* the act of afflicting.
Troublous, tru'bl-us, *a. Full of trouble* or disorder; full of affliction.
Trough, trof, *n. A vessel hollow longitudinally;* a vessel of wood, stone, or metal, in the form of a rectangular prism, open at the top, for holding water, &c.; the wooden channel that conveys water, as to a mill-wheel. [Sax. *trog;* Icel. *trog*, a canoe.]
Trousers, trou'zėrz, *n. pl.* See TROWSERS.
Trout, trout, *n.* A fish with *very sharp teeth;* the common name of various species of the salmon tribe, as the bull-trout, the salmon-trout, &c. [Sax. *truht;* Gr. *trōgō*, to gnaw.]
Trover, trō'vėr, *n. The finding of anything;* in law, the gaining possession of any goods, whether by finding or by other means. [Fr. *trouver*, to find.]
Trow, trō, *vi. To believe;* to think or suppose. [Sax. *treowian.*]
Trowel, trou'el, *n. A sort of ladle;* a flat metal tool used by masons for lifting and spreading mortar and plaster, and for cutting bricks; a gardener's tool, somewhat like a trowel, used in taking up plants and for other purposes. [Fr. *truelle*—L. *trulla*, a small ladle.]
Trowsers, trou'zėrz, *n. pl.* A loose garment *fastened up* with braces, worn by males, extending from the waist to the ankle, and covering the lower limbs. [from Fr. *trousse*, a truss—*trousser*, to tuck.]
Troy, Troy-weight, troi, troi'wāt, *n.* A *weight* chiefly used in weighing gold, silver, and articles of jewelry. [said by some to be derived from *Troyes*, a city in France.]
Truant, trö'ant, *a. Idle;* loitering.—*n.*

ch. c*h*ain; j, *j*ob; g, *g*o; ng. si*ng*; ᴛʜ, *th*en; th, *th*in; w, *w*ig; wh. *wh*ig; zh. a*z*ure; † obsolete.

An *idler*; a boy who stays away from school.—*vi.* To *idle* away time; to loiter or be absent from employment. [Fr. *truand*—Low L. *trutanus*, a vagabond.]
Truce, trös, *n.* A covenant to preserve peace for a time, resting upon the mutual *good faith* of the combatants; a suspension of arms *by agreement* of the commanders; temporary cessation; short quiet. [from Sax. *trywsian*, to give his word, to bind.]
Truce-breaker, trös'brāk-ėr, *n. One who violates a truce.*
Truck, truk, *vi.* To exchange commodities: to barter.—*vt.* To exchange; to give in exchange.—*n. Exchange of commodities*; barter. [Fr. *troquer*; L. *trans*, over, and *vicis*, change.]
Truck, truk, *n. A small wheel*; a low solid wheel of a gun-carriage; a two-wheeled vehicle for conveying merchandise; a sort of platform running upon wheels, used for the conveyance of coaches, &c., on railways; a small piece of wood, usually circular or cylindrical, used in ships. [Gr. *trochos*, a wheel—*trecho*, to run.]
Truckage, truk'āj, *n.* The practice of bartering goods.
Trucker, truk'ėr, *n.* One who traffics by *exchange* of goods.
Truckle, truk'l, *n. A small wheel* or castor. [from *truck*, a small wheel.]
Truckle, truk'l, *vi.* To yield to another's terms in *trucking*; to yield obsequiously to the will of another; to submit; to creep. *ppr.* truckling, *pret. & pp.* truckled. [dimin. of *truck*, to barter.]
Truckle-bed, truk'l-bed, *n.* A low bed that runs on *wheels* and may be pushed under another.
Truckler, truk'l-ėr, *n. One who truckles.*
Truculence, tru'kū-lens, *n.* Ferocity of manners; terribleness of countenance. [L. *truculentia*.]
Truculent, tru'kū-lent, *a. Destructive*; cruel; terrible of aspect; fierce; wild; savage. [L. *truculentus*, from *trux, trucis*, grim—Sans. *druh*, to injure, to be an enemy to, to molest.]
Truculently, tru'kū-lent-li, *adv.* Fiercely; destructively.
Trudge, truj, *vi.* To travel or march heavily or with labour; to march heavily on. *ppr.* trudging, *pret. & pp.* trudged. [allied to *tread*.]
True, trö, *a.* Fixed; solid; worthy of belief or confidence; conformable to fact; being in accordance with the actual state of things; genuine; pure; faithful; steady in adhering to friends, to a prince, or to the state; loyal; free from falsehood; honest; right to precision; straight; right. [Sax. *treowe*—Sans. *dhrū*, to be fixed.]
Trueblue, trö'blū, *a.* An epithet applied to a person of inflexible fidelity; from the true or Coventry blue.
Trueborn, trö'born, *a. Of genuine birth;* having a right by birth to any title.
Truebred, trö'bred, *a. Being of genuine breeding* or education.
Truehearted, trö'härt-ed, *a. Being of a faithful heart;* honest; sincere.
Truelove, trö'luv, *n.* Genuine love; one truly loved or loving; a plant, once considered as a powerful love-philter.
Trueness, trö'nes, *n. Quality of being true;* faithfulness; exactness.
True-penny†, trö'pen-ni, *n.* An honest fellow.
Truffle, trufl, *n. A kind of mushroom* that grows under-*ground*, of a fleshy structure and roundish figure, much esteemed as an ingredient in certain high-seasoned dishes. [Old Fr. *trufle*; L. *terra*, the earth, and *tuber*, a truffle.]
Truffled, truf'ld, *p.a. Furnished, cooked, or stuffed with truffles.*
Truism, trö'izm, *n. An undoubted or self-evident truth.*
Truly, trö'li, *adv.* In fact; in agreement with fact; sincerely; faithfully; justly.
Trump, trump, *n. A trumpet*; a wind-instrument of music; a poetical word used for trumpet; [contracted from *triumph*] *a winning* card; one of the suit of cards which takes any of the other suits.—*vt.* To *take with a trump* card; to devise; to forge (with *up*). [It. *tromba*.]
Tramped, trumpt, *p.a.* Forged (with *up*).
Trumpery, trum'pė-ri, *n. False show*; empty talk; trifles; useless matter; things worn out and cast aside.—*a.* Trifling; worthless. [Fr. *tromperie*—*tromper*, to deceive.]
Trumpet, trum'pet, *n.* A wind-instrument of music of the highest antiquity, used chiefly in war; a trumpeter; one who praises.—*vt.* To *publish by sound of trumpet;* to proclaim; to sound the praises of. [Fr. *trompette*.]
Trumpeter, trum'pet-ėr, *n. One who sounds a trumpet;* one who proclaims, publishes, or denounces; a bird, a variety of the domestic pigeon.
Trumpet-fish, trum'pet-fish, *n.* A fish so named from its tubular muzzle.
Trumpet-tongued, trum'pet-tungd, *a.* Having a tongue loud as a trumpet.
Truncate, trung'kāt, *vt.* To *cut off;* to lop; to maim. *ppr.* truncating, *pret. & pp.* truncated. [L. *trunco, truncatus*—*truncus*, the stem of a tree.]
Truncated, trung'kāt-ed, *p.a. Cut off;* cut short; maimed.
Truncation, trung-kā'shon, *n.* The *act of cutting of;* a state of being truncated; in mineralogy, the replacement of an edge by a plane equally inclined to the adjoining faces. [Low L. *truncatio*.]
Truncheon, trun'shon, *n. A club*; a baton, used by kings and great officers as a mark of command.—*vt.* To *beat with a truncheon;* to cudgel. [Fr. *tronçon*.]
Trundle, trun'dl, *vi.* To *roll*, as on little wheels; to roll, as a bowl.—*vt.* To *roll*, as a thing on little wheels. *ppr.* trundling, *pret. & pp.* trundled.—*n. A round body*; a small wheel having its teeth formed of cylinders or spindles; a small carriage with low wheels; a truck. [Sax. *trendel*, an orb.]
Trundle-bed, trun'dl-bed, *n. A bed that is moved on trundles.*
Trundle-tail†, trun'dl-tal, *n.* A round tail; a dog with a tail curled up.
Trunk, trungk, *n. The woody stem of trees;* the body of an animal without the limbs; the main body of anything; the snout of an elephant; that segment of the body of an insect which is between the head and abdomen; a box or chest covered with skin for containing clothes, &c. [L. *truncus*, the stock or trunk of a tree.]
Trunked, trungkt, *p.a. Having a trunk.*
Trunk-hose, trungk'hōz, *n.* A kind of short wide breeches gathered in above the knees, or immediately under them, worn during the reign of Henry VIII., Elizabeth, and James I.
Trunnion, trun'ni-on, *n.* The trunnions of a piece of ordinance are two knobs which project from its opposite sides, and serve to support it on the cheeks of the carriage. [Fr. *trognon*.]
Truss, trus, *n.* That *which is twisted;* a bundle; a bandage used in cases of rupture, to keep up the reduced parts; a tuft of flowers formed at the top of the main stalk of certain plants; a combination of timbers, so arranged as to constitute an unyielding frame.—*vt.* To *tie up;* to bind or pack close; to make close or tight (with *up*); to furnish with a truss. [Fr. *trousse*, a bundle; L. *torqueo, tortus*, to twist.]
Trussing, trus'ing, *n. Act of fastening up;* act of packing or binding closely; the timbers, &c., which form a truss.
Trust, trust, *n. Confidence;* a resting of the mind on the integrity of another person; he or that which is the ground of confidence; charge received in confidence; confident opinion of any event; credit given without examination; in law, an estate or any property held and managed for the benefit of another.—*a.* Held in trust.—*vt.* To *place trust or confidence in;* to commit to the care of in confidence; to give credit to; to sell to upon credit.—*vi.* To *be confident of something present or future;* to be won to confidence; to have confidence (with *in*); to depend or rely upon (with *to*). [Icel. *traust;* Goth. *trauan*, to trust.]
Trusted, trust'ed, *p.a. Confided in;* relied on.
Trustee, trus-tē', *n. One to whom something is intrusted;* a person who holds property, upon the *trust* or confidence that he will apply the same for the benefit of those who are entitled to the same.
Trusteeship, trus-tē'ship, *n.* The *office or functions of a trustee.*
Truster, trust'ėr, *n. One who trusts or gives credit.*
Trustful, trust'ful, *a. Full of trust.*
Trustfully, trust'ful-li, *adv. In a trustful manner.*
Trustfulness, trust'ful-nes, *n. Quality of being trustful;* faithfulness.
Trustily, trust'i-li, *adv.* Faithfully; honestly; with fidelity.
Trustiness, trust'i-nes, *n. Quality of being trusty;* fidelity.
Trusting, trust'ing, *p.a. Confiding in.*
Trustingly, trust'ing-li, *adv. With trust.*
Trustworthiness, trust'wėr-ᴛʜi-nes, *n. Quality of being trustworthy.*
Trustworthy, trust'wėr-ᴛʜi, *a. Worthy of trust* or confidence.
Trusty, trust'i, *a.* That *may be safely trusted;* that justly deserves confidence; strong; firm.
Truth, tröth, *n. That which is true;* that which is *fixed;* that which is the proper object of belief; conformity to fact; true state of facts or things; purity from falsehood; practice of speaking only what is true; correct opinion; faithfulness; virtue; sincerity; conformity to rule; just principle; in the fine arts, a faithful adherence to the models of nature. [Sax. *treowth*—*treowe*, true—Sans. *dhrū*, to be fixed.]
Truthful, tröth'ful, *a. Full of truth;* closely adhering to truth; conformable to truth.
Truthfully, tröth'ful-li, *adv. In a truthful manner.*
Truthfulness, tröth'ful-nes, *n. Quality of being truthful;* state of being true.
Try, trī, *vt.* To *show the truth* or *stability of,* with a view to *confidence in;* to make proof of; to prove by a test; to have knowledge of; to examine judicially; to attempt; to purify; to refine; to search carefully into; to strain.—*vi.* To *endeavour;* to attempt; to make a effort. *ppr.* trying, *pret. & pp.* tried.

Fāte, fär, fat, fąll; mē, met, hėr; pīne, pin; nōte, not, mōve; tūbe, tub, bųll; oil, pound.

n. Act of trying; trial. [Sax. *treowian,* to show the truth of, to prove.]
Trying. trī'ing. *p.a. Adapted to try,* or put to severe trial.
Tub, tub, *n.* An open wooden vessel formed with staves, heading, and hoops, with *two handles so as to be carried by two persons;* a small cask. [D. *tobbe;* Old G. *zuibar—zwt,* two.]
Tubby, tub'i, *a. Having a sound like that of an empty tub;* wanting elasticity of sound, as a violin. [from *tub.*]
Tube, tūb, *n. A pipe;* a hollow cylinder, used for the conveyance of fluids, and for various other purposes; a vessel of animal bodies or plants, which conveys a fluid; a telescope, or that part of it into which the lenses are fitted, and by which they are directed and used.—*vt. To furnish with a tube. ppr.* tubing, *pret. & pp.* tubed. [Fr.—L. *tubus.*]
Tuber, tū'bėr, *n.* A knob or *swelling* in roots; an underground fleshy stem, often considered as a modification of the root. [L.—*tumeo,* to swell.]
Tubercle, tū'bėr-kl, *n. A swelling* on animal bodies; a pimple; a peculiar morbid production, which occurs in various textures of the body in connection with scrofula and consumption; a little knob on plants; a little knob on the leaves of some lichens. [Fr. *tubercule*—L. *tumeo,* to swell.]
Tubercled, tū'bėr-kld, *p.a. Having tubercles.*
Tubercular, Tuberculous, tū-bėr'kū-lär, tū-bėr'kū-lus, *a. Pertaining to tubercles;* affected with tubercles.
Tuberous, tū'bėr-us, *a. Having tubers.* [from L. *tuber.*]
Tubing, tūb'ing, *p.n. A length of tube;* a series of tubes.
Tubular, tūb'ū-lär, *a. Having the form of a tube* or pipe; consisting of a pipe. [Low L. *tubularius—tubus,* a tube.]
Tubulated, tūb'ū-lāt-ed, *p.a. Made in the form of a small tube;* furnished with a small tube.
Tubule, tūb'ūl, *n. A small tube* or pipe. [L. *tubulus.*]
Tubulous, tūb'ūl-us, *a. See* TUBULATED.
Tuck, tuk, *vt. To draw together;* to gather into a narrower compass; to fold under; to inclose by pushing bedclothes close around.—*n.* A horizontal fold made in a garment, to shorten it; a kind of net. [Sw. *tocka,* to draw.]
Tucket-sonance! tuk'et-sō-nans, *n.* The sound of the tucket; a slight flourish on a trumpet.
Tucker, tuk'ėr, *n. He or that which tucks;* an ornament round the top of a woman's stays to shade the bosom.
Tuesday, tūz'dā, *n.* The day sacred to *Tyw,* the Scandinavian god of war; the third day of the week. [Sax. *Tiwes dæg.*]
Tuft, tuft, *n. That which rises up;* a collection of small things in a knot or bunch; a cluster; a head of flowers, each elevated on a partial stalk, and all forming together a dense roundish mass.—*vt. To adorn with tufts.* [Sax. *thufe,* a sprig, germ.]
Tufted, tuft'ed, *p.a. Adorned with a tuft;* growing in tufts.
Tufty, tuft'i, *a. Abounding with tufts;* growing in clusters; bushy.
Tug, tug, *vt. To pull with great effort;* to haul along; to pull; to drag by means of steam-power.—*vi. To draw* or pull with great effort; to strive; to struggle. *ppr.* tugging, *pret. & pp.* tugged.—*n. A drawing with force;* a pull with the utmost effort. [Sax. *teon,* pret. *tuge.*]

Tug, Tug-boat, tug, tug'bōt, *n.* A strongly built steam-*boat,* used for *dragging* sailing and other vessels.
Tugging, tug'ing, *p.a. Pulling with great exertion.*
Tuition, tū-i'shon, *n. A taking care of;* guardianship; superintendence care over a young person; the particular watch and care of a tutor or guardian over his pupil or ward; instruction; the business of teaching. [L. *tuitio—tueor, tuitus,* to look at.]
Tulip, tū'lip, *n.* A bulbous plant, cultivated for the beauty of its flowers, and so named from the resemblance of the flower to the Turkish *turban.* [Fr. *tulipe;* Turkish, *tulban,* a turban.]
Tumble, tum'bl, *vi. To roll about* by turning one way and the other; to fall or to come down suddenly and violently; to fall in great quantities; to fall tumultuously; to play mountebank tricks by various contortions of the body.—*vt. To cause to fall or roll;* to turn over; to throw about for examination (sometimes with *over*); to rumple, as a bed; to throw by chance or violence; to throw down. *ppr.* tumbling, *pret. & pp.* tumbled.—*n. A fall;* a rolling over. [Sax. *tumbian;* Sp. *tumbar,* to tumble.]
Tumbler, tum'bl-ėr, *n. One who tumbles;* one who plays the tricks of a mountebank; a large drinking glass, so named because originally it had a pointed bottom; a variety of the domestic pigeon, so called from his practice of *tumbling* or turning over in flight; a sort of dog, so called from his practice of *tumbling* before he attacks his prey.
Tumbling, tum'bl-ing, *p.n. The act of tumbling;* the performances of a tumbler or buffoon.
Tumbrel, Tumbril, tum'brel, tum'bril, *n.* A ducking-stool, formerly used for the punishment of scolding women; a dung-cart; a covered cart with two wheels, which accompanies troops or artillery, for conveying the tools of pioneers, cartridges, and the like. [Old Fr. *tomberel.*]
Tumefaction, tū-me-fak'shon, *n. The act or process of swelling* or rising into a tumour; a tumour; a swelling. [Fr. *tuméfaction.*]
Tumefy, tū'me-fī, *vt. To cause to swell;* to swell.—*vi. To swell;* to rise in a tumour. *ppr.* tumefying, *pret. & pp.* tumefied. [Fr. *tuméfier*—L. *tumeo,* to swell, and *facio,* to make.]
Tumid, tū'mid, *a. Protuberant;* rising above the level; being swelled; swelling in sound or sense; bombastic; falsely sublime. [Fr. *tumide*—L. *tumeo,* to swell.]
Tumidity, tū-mid'i-ti, *n. A swelled state.* [Low L. *tumiditas.*]
Tumidly, tū'mid-li, *adv. In a swelling* form.
Tumor, Tumour, tū'mor, *n. A swelling;* a morbid enlargement of any part of the body. [L. *tumor—tumeo,* to swell.]
Tumored, Tumoured, tū'mord, *p.a. Swelled;* distended.
Tumular, tū'mū-lär, *a. Consisting in a heap;* formed or being in a heap. [L. *tumulus,* a heap.]
Tumult, tū'mult, *n. Confusion* ; the agitation of a multitude; violent commotion or agitation, with confusion of sounds; irregular motion; bustle; stir. [Fr. *tumulte*—L. *tumultus.*]
Tumultuary, tū-mul'tū-a-ri,*a. Tumultuous;* disorderly; confused ; agitated; unquiet. [Fr. *tumultuaire.*]
Tumultuous, tū-mul'tū-us, *a. Full of*

tumult; conducted with tumult; disorderly; irregular; confused ; turbulent; violent. [Fr. *tumultueux.*]
Tumultuously, tū-mul'tū-us-li, *adv.* In a disorderly manner; with turbulence; by a disorderly multitude.
Tumultuousness, tū-mul'tū-us-nes, *n. The state of being tumultuous;* disorder.
Tumulus, tū'mū-lus, *n. A raised heap of earth;* a barrow or artificial mound of earth, often covering a tomb or sepulchre. [L.—*tumeo,* to swell.]
Tun, tun, *n. A large cask;* an oblong vessel bulging in the middle, girt with hoops, and used for stowing several kinds of merchandise for convenience of carriage, as brandy, sugar, &c.; a certain measure for liquids, as for wine, oil, &c. ; a quantity of wine, consisting of two pipes or 252 gallons; a large quantity. [Fr. *tonne,* a tun— Old G. *tunna,* a cask.]
Tunable, tūn'a-bl, *a. That may be put in tune;* harmonious; musical.
Tunableness, tūn'a-bl-nes, *n. Quality of being tunable;* melodiousness.
Tunably, tūn'a-bli, *adv.* Harmoniously.
Tune, tūn, *n.* Originally, *tone;* note; a short air or melody ; a series of musical notes in some particular measure, the effect of which is melody; a union of two or more parts to be sung or played in concert, the effect of which is harmony; harmony; order; the state of giving the proper sounds; proper state for use; fit temper.—*vt. To put into tune;* to sing with melody or harmony. *vi.* To form one sound to another; to utter inarticulate harmony with the voice. *ppr.* tuning, *pret. & pp.* tuned. [It. *tuono*—Gr. *tonos—teino,* to stretch.]
Tuned, tūnd, *p.a.* Put in order to produce the proper sounds.
Tuneful, tūn'ful, *a.* Harmonious; melodious; musical.
Tunefully, tūn'ful-li, *adv.* Harmoniously.
Tuneless, tūn'les, *a. Destitute of tune;* unmusical; unharmonious.
Tuner, tūn'ėr, *n.* One whose occupation is to *tune* musical instruments.
Tungsten, tung'sten, *n.* A *heavy metal* of a grayish white colour, and considerable lustre. [Sw. *tung,* heavy, and *sten,* stone.]
Tunic, tū'nik, *n. A garment* worn by the Romans of both sexes under the toga, and next to the skin; a long under garment worn by the Romish clergy when officiating; a membrane that covers or composes some part or organ of the body; a natural covering; an integument, as of a seed. [Fr. *tunique*—L. *tunica.*]
Tunicated, tū'nik-āt-ed, *p.a. Covered with a tunic* or membranes; coated.
Tuning, tūn'ing, *p.n.* The operation of adjusting the various sounds of a musical instrument, so that they may be all at due intervals, and the scale of the instrument brought into as correct a state as possible.
Tuning-fork, tūn'ing-fork, *n.* A steel instrument, used for tuning instruments, and for regulating the pitch of voices.
Tunnage, tun'āj. *See* TONNAGE.
Tunnel, tun'el, *n. A little tun;* a tubular opening; an arched subterranean passage cut through a hill, a rock, an eminence, or under a river or town, to carry a canal, a road, railway, &c., in an advantageous course; an arched drain or sewer.—*vt.* To form a *tunnel* through or under; to catch in a net

called a tunnel-net. *ppr.* tunnelling, *pret. & pp.* tunnelled. [Fr. *tonnelle.*]

Tunnelling, tun'el-ing, *p.n.* The operation of cutting an arched passage through a hill, or under a river or town, in order to conduct a canal or railway on a lower level than the natural surface.

Tunnel-net, tun'el-net, *n.* A net with a wide mouth at one end, and narrow at the other.

Tunny, tun'i, *n.* A large fish of the mackerel tribe, much used for food, and so named from its *quick darting* motion. [It. *tonno*—Gr. *thunnos—thuno*, to dart along.]

Turban, tėr'ban, *n.* A *head-band;* a head-dress worn by some Orientals, consisting of a cap, and a sash of fine linen or taffeta artfully wound round it in plaits; a kind of head-dress worn by ladies. [Fr.; Pers. *dulband.*]

Turbaned, tėr'band, *p. a.* Wearing a *turban.*

Turbid, tėr'bid, *a. Confused;* having the lees disturbed; muddy; thick; not clear, as a liquid. [L. *turbidus—turba*, disturbance.]

Turbidly, tėr'bid-li, *adv. In a turbid manner;* muddily.

Turbidness, tėr'bid-nes, *n. State of being turbid;* muddiness; foulness.

Turbine, tėr'bin, *n.* A horizontal waterwheel, variously constructed. [L. *turbo*, that which spins round.]

Turbot, tėr'bot, *n.* A well-known and highly esteemed fish, probably so named from a sort of *twisting round* of the head when the fish lies at the bottom, by which both eyes are brought round to the right side. [Fr.—L. *turbo*, a whirling round.]

Turbulence, tėr'bū-lens, *n. State of being turbulent;* confusion; tumult of the passions; disposition to resist authority; insubordination. [Low L. *turbulentia.*]

Turbulent, tėr'bū-lent, *a. Disturbed; tumultuous;* restless; refractory; disposed to disorder; producing commotion. [Fr.—L. *turbo*, to disturb—Heb. *terūghā*, tumult.]

Turbulently, tėr'bū-lent-li, *adv.* Tumultuously; with violent agitation.

Tureen, tū-rēn', *n. An earthen pan;* a table-vessel for holding soup. [Fr. *terrine*, earthen pan—L. *terra*, earth.]

Turf, tėrf, *n.* That upper stratum of *earth* and vegetable mould, which is filled with the roots of grass and other small plants, so as to adhere and form a kind of mat; sward; peat; a peculiar kind of blackish, fibrous, vegetable, earthy substance, used as fuel; raceground; horse-racing.—*vt. To cover with turf* or sod. [Sax.; Ar. *turāb*, earth.]

Turfiness, tėrf'i-nes, *n. The state of abounding with turf*, or of having the qualities of turf.

Turfing, tėrf'ing, *p.n. The operation of laying down turf, or covering with turf.*

Turfy, tėrf'i, *a. Abounding with turf;* having the qualities of turf; formed of turf.

Turgescence, tėr-jes'ens, *n. State of becoming turgid;* empty pompousness; bombast. [Fr.—L. *turgeo*, to swell.]

Turgescent, tėr-jes'ent, *a. Beginning to swell;* growing large; in a swelling state. [L. *turgescens.*]

Turgid, tėr'jid, *a. Swelled;* bloated; distended beyond its natural state; tumid; inflated; bombastic. [L. *turgidus—turgeo*, to swell—Sans. *tu*, to increase.]

Turgidity, tėr-jid'i-ti, *n. State of being turgid* or swelled; tumidness.

Turgidly, tėr'jid-li, *adv. With swelling* or empty pomp.

Turgidness, tėr'jid-nes, *n. A swelling or swelled state* of a thing; inflated manner of writing or speaking.

Turkey, tėr'kē, *n.* A large gallinaceous fowl, and the original stock from which the domesticated turkey is derived. [so named because the bird was supposed to have come from *Turkey*, whereas it is a native of America.]

Turkey-red, tėr'kē-red, *n.* A brilliant red dye produced on cotton and woollen cloth by madder.

Turkey-stone, **Turkey-hone**, tėr'kēstōn, tėr'kē-hōn, *n.* A mineral of a slaty structure, brought from the Levant, and used for sharpening small cutting instruments.

Turkish, tėrk'ish, *a. Pertaining to the Turks.*

Turmeric, tėr'mė-rik, *n.* Indian saffron, the root of a plant imported from Bengal, Java, China, &c., and used for dyeing silk *yellow*. [Hind, *zurd*, yellow, and *mirch*, pepper.]

Turmoil, tėr'moil, *n. Harassing labour;* disturbance; molestation by tumult. *vt.* To disquiet; to weary. [probably from *through* and *moil.*]

Turn, tėrn, *vt. To cause to move in a circular course;* to form on a lathe; to shape; to change, as sides; to put the upper side downward; to alter, as a position; to cause to preponderate; to change, as the state of a balance; to bring out the inside of; to alter, as the posture of the body; to transform; to alter, as colour; to change in any manner.; to translate; to change, as from one opinion or party to another; to change in regard to temper; to transfer; to cause to loathe; to make giddy; to change direction to or from any point; to direct, as the mind; to revolve; to bend from a perpendicular direction; to move from a direct course; to reverse; to sour; to dissuade from a purpose.—*vi. To move round;* to be directed; to move the body round; to change posture; to alter; to be changed; to change sides; to change the mind; to change to acid; to be brought eventually; to result; to depend on for decision; to become giddy; to repent; to change the course; to exercise the art or trade of a turner.—*n. The act of turning;* a winding; a bend or bending, as the turn of a river; a walk to and fro; change; change of direction; chance; hap; occasion; time at which anything is to be had or done; action of kindness or malice; reigning course; a step off the ladder at the gallows; convenience; form; cast; in a literal sense, manner of arranging words in a sentence; change of direction; one round of a rope or cord. [Sax. *tyrnan* —Gr. *tornos*, a round—Heb. *tār*, to go around.]

Turn-coat, tėrn'kōt, *n.* One who forsakes his party or principles.

Turner, tėrn'ėr, *n. One who turns;* one whose occupation is to form things with a lathe.

Turnery, tėrn'ė-ri, *n. The art of a turner;* things made by a turner or in the lathe.

Turning, tėrn'ing, *p.n.* Act of one who *turns;* art or operation of giving circular and other forms to bodies by means of a lathe; a bending course; deviation from the proper course.

Turning-point, tėrn'ing-point, *n. The point on which a thing turns;* that which decides a matter.

Turnip, tėr'nip, *n.* A plant much cultivated on account of its bulbous esculent root, which is used for culinary purposes, but chiefly for feeding cattle. [L. *napus*, a kind of turnip; Dan. *turnip.*]

Turnkey, tėrn'kē, *n.* A person who has charge of the *keys* of a prison.

Turnpike, tėrn'pik, *n.* Originally, a frame consisting of two bars *turning* on a post, to hinder the passage of beasts; any gate by which the way is obstructed, in order to take toll.

Turnspit, tėrn'spit, *n. A person who turns a spit;* a variety of the dog, so called from having formerly been employed to *turn* a wheel on which depended the *spit* for roasting meat in the kitchen.

Turnstile, tėrn'stil, *n.* A turnpike in a footpath.

Turpentine, tėr'pen-tin, *n.* A resinous substance, combined with an essential oil, flowing naturally or by incision from several species of trees, as from the pine, larch, fir, &c. [G. *terpentin* —Gr. *terelinthos*, the turpentine-tree.]

Turpitude, tėr'pi-tūd, *n. State of being turned awry;* state of departure from the law of rectitude; shameful wickedness; inherent baseness in the human heart; extreme depravity. [Fr.—L. *turpis*, ugly, shameful—Sans. *trap*, to turn.]

Turquoise, **Turkois**, tėr'koiz, tėr'koiz, *n.* A mineral of a blue colour, the favourite colour of the *Turks*, brought from Persia, susceptible of a high polish, and used in jewelry. [Fr. *turquoise.*]

Turret, tu'ret, *n. A small tower*, often crowning the angle of a wall, &c. [Gael. *turaid.*]

Turreted, tu'ret-ed, *p.a. Furnished with turrets;* formed like a tower.

Turtle, tėr'tl, *n.* A species of pigeon celebrated for the constancy of its love, universally regarded with affection, and looked upon as the type of connubial attachment; the sea-tortoise, one species of which, the green turtle, is so much prized as a luxury at the tables of the rich; it attains a length of six to seven feet, and a weight of 700 to 800 pounds. [Sax. *tortel*—L. *turtur.*]

Turtle-soup, tėr'tl-sōp, *n.* A rich soup, the chief ingredient of which is turtlemeat.

Tuscan, tus'kan, *a.* Pertaining to *Tuscany* in Italy; designating one of the five orders of architecture, which admits of no ornaments, and the columns are never fluted.—*n. An inhabitant of Tuscany;* the Tuscan order.

Tush, tush, an *exclamation*, indicating check, rebuke, or contempt.

Tusk, tusk, *n.* The long pointed tooth of certain rapacious, carnivorous, or fighting animals, as the boar. [Sax. *tusc.*]

Tusked, **Tusky**, tuskt, tusk'i, *p.a. Furnished with tusks.*

Tut, tut, an *exclamation*, used for checking or rebuking.

Tutelage, tū'tel-āj, *n. Guardianship;* state of being under a guardian. [formed from L. *tutela*, a charge—*tueor, tuitus*, to watch—Sans. *tri*, to keep.]

Tutelar, **Tutelary**, tū'tel-ėr, tū tel-a-ri, *a. Having the charge of protecting* a person or a thing; protecting. [L. *tutelaris.*]

Tutor, tū'tor, *n. A preserver;* a *guardian;* one who is chosen to look to the persons and estates of children left in their minority; one who has the care of instructing the children of a family, in various branches; in the English universities, a member of some college or hall, generally a fellow, who superintends the studies of the undergraduates.—*vt. To guard; to defend;* to instruct; to treat with authority or severity; to correct. [L.—*tueor, tuitus,* to watch—Sans. *tri,* to preserve.]

Tutorage, tū'tor-āj, *n. Guardianship;* the charge of a pupil and his estate.

Tutored, tū'tord, *p.a.* Instructed; disciplined.

Tutoress, tū'tor-es, *n. A female tutor.*

Tutorial, tū-tō'ri-al, *a. Belonging to or exercised by a tutor* or instructor. [Late L. *tutorius.*]

Tutorship, tū'tor-ship, *n. The office of a tutor.*

Twaddle, twod'l, *vi. To twattle;* to prate much in a weak and silly manner. *ppr.* twaddling, *pret. & pp.* twaddled. *n.* Empty, silly talk; insignificant discourse. [a different form of *twattle.*]

Twaddler, twod'l-ėr, *n.* One who prates in a weak and silly manner.

Twaddling, twod'l-ing, *p.a.* Silly, empty talk.

Twain, twān, *a.* or *n. Two.* [Sax. *twegen.*]

Twang, twang, *vi. To sound* with a quick sharp noise; to make the sound of a string which is stretched and suddenly pulled, as the twanging bows. *vt. To make to sound sharply,* as by pulling a tense string and letting it go suddenly.—*n. A sharp, quick, vibrating sound;* as, the twang of a bow-string; an affected modulation of the voice; a kind of nasal sound. [Sans. *dhvan,* to sound.]

Twanging, twang'ing, *p.a.* Contemptibly noisy.

Twangle, twang'gl, *vi. To twang. ppr.* twangling, *pret. & pp.* twangled.

Twas, twoz, a contraction of *it was.*

Twattle, twot'l, *vi. To prate;* to talk much and idly; to gabble. *ppr.* twattling, *pret. & pp.* twattled.—*n.* Chatter; idle talk.

Twattler, twot'l-ėr, *n. One who twattles.*

Twattling, twot'l-ing, *p.a.* Prating; chattering.

Tweak, twēk, *vt. To twitch;* to pinch and pull with a sudden jerk. [Sax. *twiccian.*]

Tweezer-case, twē'zėr-kās, *n. A case for carrying tweezers.*

Tweezers, twē'zėrz, *n.* Nippers; small pincers used to pluck out hairs, and put into a *case* along with other small instruments, as scissors, *nes les* &c., and formerly carried by ladies at the side. (Fr. *etui,* a case, pl. *etuis*—L. *tego,* to cover.)

Twelfth, twelfth, *a.* The ordinal of *twelve.* [Sax. *twelfta.*]

Twelfth-day, Twelfth-tide, twelfth'dā, twelfth'tīd, *n. The twelfth day after* Christmas; the festival of the Epiphany.

Twelfth-night, twelfth'nīt, *n.* The evening of the Epiphany, a festival of the Church of Rome and others.

Twelve, twelv, *a. Two remaining over* ten; ten and two more.—*n.* The number which consists of ten and two. [Sax. *twelf;* Goth. *tvalif—tvai,* two, and *leiban,* to remain.]

Twelve-month, twelv'munth, *n.* A year as consisting *of twelve* calendar *months.*

Twelve-pence, twelv'pens, *n.* A shilling.

Twelve-penny, twelv'pen-ni, *a. Sold for a shilling;* worth a shilling.

Twentieth, twen'ti-eth, *a. The ordinal of twenty.* [Sax. *twentigtha.*]

Twenty, twen'ti, *a. Two tens,* or *twice ten.* [Sax. *twentig.*]

Twenty-fold, twen'ti-fōld, *a. Twenty times as many.*

Twice, twīs, *adv. Two times;* doubly. [Icel. *tvisvar.*]

Twice-told, twīs'tōld, *a. Related or told twice.*

Twig, twig, *n.* A small *flexible* shoot or branch of a tree, or other plant of no definite length or size. [Sax.—G. *zweig.*]

Twiggen, twig'n, *a.* Made of twigs.

Twiggy, twig'i, *a. Full of twigs;* abounding with shoots.

Twilight, twī'līt, *n. The dubious or faint light;* the faint light which is reflected upon the earth after sunset and before sunrise; dubious view.—*a.* Faint; seen or done by twilight. [Sax. *tweem-leoht—tweon,* doubt, and *leoht,* light.]

Twill, twil, *vt.* To weave so as to form into a *double* texture.—*n.* A variety of textile fabric in which a kind of diagonal ribbed appearance is produced upon the surface of the cloth. [Scot. *tweel*—Sans. *dvi,* two.]

Twilled, twild, *p.a.* Woven in such a manner as to present the appearance of diagonal ribs on the surface.

Twin, twin, *n. One of two* young produced at a birth by an animal that ordinarily brings but one; used mostly in the plural, *twins;* applied to the young of beasts, as well as to human beings; one very much resembling another.—*a. Noting one of two* born at a birth; very much resembling.—*vi.*† To be born at the same birth. [Icel. *tvennir,* twins; Sax. *twa,* two.]

Twin-born, twin'born, *a. Born* at the same birth.

Twin-brother, twin'bruth-ėr, *n.* One of *two brothers* who are twins.

Twine, twīn, *vt. To twist together,* as two *into one;* to wind, as one thread around another; to unite closely; to embrace; to wrap closely about.—*vi.* To unite closely, as by twisting; to wind; to make turns. *ppr.* twining, *pret. & pp.* twined.—*n. A two-fold* thread; a strong thread composed of two or three smaller threads twisted together; embrace; act of winding round. [Sax. *twinan—twa,* Sans. *dvi,* two.]

Twinge, twinj, *vt. To twitch;* to affect with a sharp sudden pain; to torment with pinching or sharp pains.—*vi.* To suffer a keen darting or shooting pain. *ppr.* twinging, *pret. & pp.* twinged. *n. A twitch;* a darting local pain of momentary continuance; a sharp rebuke of conscience. [another form of *twitch.*]

Twinging, twinj'ing, *p.n. The act of pinching* with a sudden twitch; a sudden, sharp, local pain.

Twining, twīn'ing, *p.a.* Embracing (with *around*).

Twinkle, twing'kl, *vi. To wink repeatedly;* to open and shut the eyes by turns; to sparkle; to shine with a broken quivering light. *ppr.* twinkling, *pret. & pp.* twinkled. [Sax. *twinclian.*]

Twinkle, Twinkling, twing'kl, twing'-kl-ing, *n. A repeated winking;* a sparkling; a shining with intermittent tremulous light; a moment.

Twinkling, twing'kl-ing, *p.a.* Sparkling.

Twin-likeness, twin'līk-nes, *n.* A resemblance like that between *twins;* near resemblance.

Twinling, twin'ling, *n. A twin* lamb.

Twinned, twind, *p.a.* United.

Twire†, twīr, *vi.* To twinkle; to glance; to gleam.

Twirl, twėrl, *vt. To whirl round with rapidity;* to move round with rapidity. *vi. To be whirled round* with rapidity; to revolve with velocity.—*n. A rapid whirl;* quick rotation; twist. [formed on *whirl,* with the prefix *ed,* signifying repetition.]

Twist, twist, *vt.* To unite by winding *one* thread round *another;* to form by winding separate things round each other; to form into a thread from many fine filaments; to encircle; to weave; to unite; to enter by winding; to pervert; to turn from a straight line. *vi. To be twisted;* to be united by winding round *each other.*—*n. That which is twisted;* a cord; a string; a contortion; manner of twisting; a little roll of tobacco. [Sax. *getwisan,* twins.]

Twister, twist'ėr, *n.* One that *twists;* the instrument of twisting.

Twit, twit, *vt. To blame anew;* to upbraid, as for some previous act. *ppr.* twitting, *pret. & pp.* twitted. [Sax. *edwitan—ed,* again, and *witan,* to blame.]

Twitch, twich, *vt. To pull by suddenly jerking round;* to pluck with a short quick motion.—*n. A sudden jerking pull;* a short spasmodic contraction of the fibres or muscles. [Sax. *twiccian,* to pluck, catch.]

Twitcher, twich'ėr, *n. One that twitches.*

Twitching, twich'ing, *p.a.* Suffering short spasmodic contractions.—*p.n.* The act of suffering short spasmodic contractions.

Twitter, twit'ėr, *vi. To make a succession of small, tremulous, intermittent sounds;* to have a tremulous motion of the nerves.—*n. A small tremulous intermittent sound;* the sound of a swallow; a slight trembling of the nerves. [G. *zwitschern,* to chirp.]

Twitter, twit'ėr, *n. One who twits* or reproaches. [from *twit.*]

Twittingly, twit'ing-li, *adv.* With upbraiding.

Twixt, twikst, a contraction of *betwixt.*

Two, tō, *a.* One and one.—*n.* The number which consists of one and one. [Sax. *twā*—L. *duo*—Sans. *dvi, dva.*]

Two-edged, tō'ejd, *a. Having two edges.*

Two-faced, tō'fāst, *a. Having two faces,* or visages, like the Roman deity *Janus;* insincere; given to double-dealing.

Two-fold, tō'fōld, *a. Double;* two of the same kind, or two different things existing together.—*adv. Doubly;* in a double degree.

Two-handed, tō'hand-ed, *a. Having two hands;* large, stout, and strong; requiring the two hands to grasp.

Two-masted, tō'mast-ed, *a. Having two masts.*

Tye, tī. *See* Tie.

Tymbal, tim'bal, *n. A kind of kettle-drum;* a tympanum. [Fr. *timbale,* Pers. *tumpana,* a kettle-drum.]

Tympan, Tympanum, tim'pan, tim'-pan-um, *n. That which is beaten upon;* the hollow part of the ear; among printers, a frame attached to the carriage of the press by joints, and covered with parchment or cloth, on which the blank sheets are put, in order to be laid on the form to be impressed. [L. *tympanum*—Sans. *tup,* to strike, to beat.]

Tympanic, tim-pan'ik, *a. Relating to the tympanum;* drum-like.

Type, tīp, *n. The mark made by a blow;* an impression; the impression on a coin or medal of any image whatever; a die; outline; the mark of something; an emblem; a symbol; a figure of something to come; a model or form of a

ch, *ch*ain; j, *j*ob; g, *g*o; ng, si*ng*; TH, *th*en; th, *th*in; w, *w*ig; wh, *wh*ig; zh, a*z*ure; † obsolete.

TYPE-METAL 420 UNACCENTED

letter in metal, used in printing; in a collective sense, printing letters; some peculiarity in the form of a disease; in natural history, a general form; the primitive pattern of a work of art, and which has its existence in nature; the primary model, according to which the parts of an animal body are formed. [Fr.; Gr. *tupto*, Sans. *tup*, to strike.]

Type-metal, tip'me-tal, *n*. An alloy of lead, antimony, and tin, used in making types.

Typhoid, ti'foid, *a*. Resembling typhus; low, as a typhoid fever. [*typhus*, and Gr. *eidos*, form.]

Typhoon, ti'fön, *n*. A furious whirling wind; probably so named because it was held to be the work of *Typhos*, a fabled giant; a hurricane in the eastern or Chinese seas; a whirlwind moving forward with irresistible impetuosity. [Gr. *Tuphôn*.]

Typhous, ti'fus, *a*. Relating to typhus.

Typhus, ti'fus, *n*. Primarily, *stupor*, arising from fever; a fever, characterized by a small, weak, and unequal, but usually frequent pulse, with great prostration of strength, and much disturbance of the brain. [Gr. *tuphos*, from *tuphô*, to raise a smoke, to stupify.]

Typic, **Typical**, tip'ik, tip'ik-al, *a*. Pertaining to a type; emblematic; representing something future by a form, model, or resemblance; regular in its attacks, as a fever. [Fr. *typique*.]

Typically, tip'ik-al-li, *adv*. In a typical manner; by way of resemblance.

Typifier, tip'i-fi-er, *n*. One who typifies.

Typify, tip'i-fi, *vt*. To make typical; to represent by an image or resemblance. *ppr*. typifying, *pret. & pp.* typified. [*type*, and L. *facio*, to make.]

Typographer, ti-pog'raf-er, *n*. A printer.

Typographic, **Typographical**, ti-po-graf'ik, ti-po-graf'ik-al, *a*. Pertaining to typography. [Fr. *typographique*.]

Typographically, ti-po-graf'ik-al-li, *adv*. By means of types; after the manner of printers.

Typography, ti-pog'ra-fi, *n*. The art of printing, or the operation of impressing letters and words on forms of types. [Fr. *typographie*; Gr. *tupos*, type, and *graphô*, to write.]

Tyrannic, **Tyrannical**, ti-ran'ik, ti-ran'ik-al, *a*. Pertaining to a tyrant; suiting a tyrant; unjustly severe in government; despotic. [Fr. *tyrannique*.]

Tyrannically, ti-ran'ik-al-li, *adv*. With unjust exercise of power; arbitrarily.

Tyrannize, ti'ran-iz, *vi*. To play the tyrant; to rule with unjust and oppressive severity; to exercise power over others not permitted by law or required by justice (with *over*). *ppr*. tyrannizing, *pret. & pp.* tyrannized. [Fr. *tyranniser*.]

Tyranny, ti'ran-i, *n*. The rule of a tyrant, despotic exercise of power; the exercise of power over subjects with a rigour not requisite for the purposes of government; unresisted and cruel power; severity; absolute monarchy cruelly administered. [Fr. *tyrannie*.]

Tyrant, ti'rant, *n*. Originally, one who obtained absolute power by usurpation; a monarch who uses power to oppress his subjects; a person who exercises unlawful authority; one who imposes burdens on those under his control, which law and humanity do not authorize; a despotic ruler; an oppressor. [L. *tyrannus*; Gr. *turannos—kuros*, a lord, master.]

Tyre, tir. See TIRE.

Tyrian, ti'ri-an, *a*. Pertaining to the ancient Tyre; being of a purple colour. *n*. A native of Tyre.

Tyro, ti'ro, *n*. Primarily, *a young* soldier; a beginner in learning; one who is employed in learning the rudiments of any branch of study; a person who has an imperfect knowledge of a subject. [L. *tiro*—Heb. *târa*, to be fresh.]

Tyrolese, ti-rōl-ez', *a*. Belonging or relating to the Tyrol.—*n*. A native of the Tyrol.

Tythe, tiTH. See TITHE.

U.

Ubiquitous, ū-bi'kwi-tus, *a*. Existing or being everywhere.

Ubiquity, ū-bi'kwi-ti, *n*. Existence everywhere at the same time; omnipresence. [Fr. *ubiquité*; L. *ubique*, everywhere—*ubi*, where.]

Udder, ud'dėr, *n*. The glandular organ or bag of cows, and other quadrupeds, in which the *milk* is secreted and retained for the nourishment of their young. [Sax. *uder*; Gr. *outhar*.]

Uglily, ug'li-li, *adv*. In an ugly manner; with deformity.

Ugliness, ug'li-nes, *n*. State or quality of being *ugly*; total want of beauty; turpitude of mind; loathsomeness.

Ugly, ug'li, *a*. Causing dread or terror; *awful*; frightful; offensive to the sight; contrary to beauty; hateful; cross. [Sax. *oga*, dread; Icel. *ógn*, terror.]

Ulcer, ul'sėr, *n*. A *sore*; an abscess; a sore that has continued for some time, and is attended with discharge. [Fr. *ulcère*—L. *ulcus, ulcėris*, a sore.]

Ulcerate, ul'sėr-āt, *vt*. To affect with an ulcer or with ulcers.—*vi*. To be formed into an ulcer; to become ulcerous. *ppr*. ulcerating, *pret. & pp.* ulcerated. [L. *ulcėro, ulceratus*.]

Ulceration, ul-sėr-ā'shon, *n*. The process of forming into an ulcer, or the process of becoming ulcerous; a morbid sore that discharges pus. [Fr. *ulcération*.]

Ulcered, ul'sėrd, *p.a.* Having become ulcerous.

Ulcerous, ul'sėr-us, *a*. Having the nature of an *ulcer*; discharging purulent matter; affected with an ulcer or with ulcers.

Ulterior, ul-tē'ri-or, *a*. More to a distance; more remote; beyond any line or boundary. [L.—*ulter*, beyond.]

Ultimate, ul'ti-māt, *a*. Being most distant or remote; extreme; being that to which all the rest is directed, as to the main object; last in a train of consequences; intended in the last resort; incapable of further analysis. [L. *ultimus—ulter*, that is beyond.]

Ultimately, ul'ti-māt-li, *adv*. Finally; at last; in the end or last consequence.

Ultimatum, ul-ti-mā'tum, *n*. pl. Ultimata, ul-ti-mā'ta. The *last*; the last offer; the final terms offered as the basis of a treaty; the most favourable terms that a negotiator can offer; any final proposition.

Ultramarine, ul'tra-ma-rēn″, *a*. Situated or being beyond the sea.—*n*. A colour exceeding that of the sea; a beautiful and durable sky-blue. [L. *ultra*, beyond, and *marinus*, marine—*mare*, the sea —Sans. *vâri*, water.]

Ultramontane, ul-tra-mon'tān, *a*. Being beyond the mountain or mountains; thus France, with regard to Italy, is an ultramontane country; of or belonging to the Italian or ultra party in the Church of Rome. [Fr. *ultramontain*— L. *ultra*, beyond, and *mons*, a mountain.]

Ultramontanist, ul-tra-mon'tān-ist, *n*. One of the ultramontane party.

Ultramundane, ul-tra-mun'dān, *a*. Being beyond the world, or beyond the limits of our system. [L. *ultra*, and *mundus*, the world.]

Umbelliferous, um-bel-lif'ėr-us, *a*. Bearing or producing heads consisting of a number of flower-stalks spreading from a common centre, as hemlock, celery, carrots, &c. [L. *umbella*, a little shadow, and *fero*, to bear.]

Umbert, um'bėr, *vt*. To *colour* with umber, an ore of iron, of a brown or blackish brown colour.

Umbilical, um-bil'ik-al, *a*. Pertaining to the *navel*. [L. *umbilicus*, the navel.]

Umbrage, um'brāj, *n*. Diminished or faint light; a *shade*; a screen of trees; gloom; a gloomy lurking suspicion; suspicion of injury; resentment. [Fr. *ombrage*—L. *umbra*, a shadow, the dark part of a painting, shade.]

Umbrageous, um-brā'jē-us, *a*. Shading; forming a *shade*; shady; shaded. [Old Fr. *ombrageux*.]

Umbrageousness, um-brā'jē-us-nes, *n*. Shadiness.

Umbrella, um-brel'la, *n*. A little *shade*; a portable canopy which opens and folds, carried in the hand for sheltering the person from the rays of the sun, or from rain or snow. [It. *umbrello*— L. *umbra*, a shade.]

Umpirage, um'pir-āj, *n*. The power or decision of an *umpire*; arbitration. [from *umpire*.]

Umpire, um'pir, *n*. In law, an odd person called in to decide a controversy submitted to arbitrators, when the arbitrators do not agree in opinion, and are equally divided in their award; a person to whose sole decision a controversy between parties is referred. [said to be corrupted from L. *impar*, odd, uneven—*in*, and *par*, even.]

Unabated, un-a-bāt'ed, *a*. Not abated; not diminished in strength or violence.

Unable, un-ā'bl, *a*. Not *able*; weak in power.

Unabsolved, un-ab-solvd', *a*. Not absolved; not acquitted or forgiven.

Unaccented, un-ak-sent'ed, *a*. Not accented; having no accent.

Fāte, fär, fat, fall; mē, met, hėr; pīne, pin; nōte, not, mōve; tūbe, tub, bull; oil, pound.

Unacceptable, un-ak-sept′a-bl, *a. Not acceptable;* not pleasing; not welcome.
Unacceptably, un-ak-sept′a-bli, *adv.* In an unwelcome manner.
Unaccepted, un-ak-sept′ed, *a. Not accepted* or received; rejected.
Unaccommodating, un-ak-kom′mō-dāt-ing, *a. Not accommodating.*
Unaccompanied, un-ak-kum′pa-nid, *a. Not accompanied;* not attended; having no appendages.
Unaccomplished, un-ak-kom′plisht, *a. Not accomplished;* not refined in manners; not furnished with elegant literature.
Unaccountable, un-ak-kount′a-bl, *a. Not to be accounted for;* not responsible.
Unaccountably, un-ak-kount′a-bli, *adv.* In a manner not to be explained.
Unaccredited, un-ak-kred′it-ed, *a. Not accredited;* not authorized.
Unaccustomed, un-ak-kus′tumd, *a. Not accustomed;* not habituated; new.
Unacknowledged, un-ak-nol′ejd, *a. Not acknowledged;* not recognized.
Unacquainted, un-ak-kwānt′ed, *a. Not acquainted;* not having familiar knowledge (*with with*).
Unacquitted, un-ak-kwit′ed, *a. Not acquitted;* not declared innocent.
Unadjusted, un-ad-just′ed, *a. Not adjusted;* not settled; not liquidated.
Unadorned, un-a-dornd′, *a. Not adorned;* not embellished.
Unadvisable, un-ad-vīz′a-bl, *a. Not advisable;* not expedient; not prudent.
Unadvised, un-ad-vīzd′, *a. Not advised;* done without due consideration; rash; unknowing.
Unadvisedly, un-ad-vīz′ed-li, *adv.* Imprudently; indiscreetly; rashly.
Unaffected, un-af-fekt′ed, *a. Not affected;* not moved; natural; sincere; not hypocritical.
Unaffectedly, un-af-fekt′ed-li, *adv.* Really; in sincerity; without disguise.
Unaffecting, un-af-fekt′ing, *a. Not affecting;* not pathetic.
Unaided, un-ād′ed, *a. Not aided.*
Unallayed, un-al-lād′, *a. Not allayed.*
Unalloyed, un-al-loid′, *a. Not alloyed;* not reduced by foreign admixture.
Unalterable, un-al′tėr-a-bl, *a. Not alterable;* unchangeable; immutable.
Unaltered, un-al′tėrd, *a. Not altered* or changed.
Unambiguous, un-am-big′ū-us, *a. Not ambiguous;* plain; clear; certain.
Unambitious, un-am-bi′shi-us, *a. Not ambitious;* free from ambition.
Unamiable, un-ā′mi-a-bl, *a. Not amiable;* not conciliating love.
Unaneled, un-a-nēld′, *a.* Not having received extreme unction. [*un* and *knell.*]
Unanimity, ū-na-ni′mi-ti, *n. State of being unanimous;* concord. [Fr. *unanimité.*]
Unanimous, ū-nan′i-mus, *a. Being of one mind;* of one accord; formed by unanimity. [L. *unanimus—unus,* one, and *animus,* mind.]
Unannounced, un-an-nounst′, *a. Not announced* or proclaimed.
Unanointed, un-a-noint′ed, *a. Not anointed;* not having received extreme unction.
Unanswerable, un-an′sėr-a-bl, *a. Not to be satisfactorily answered.*
Unanswerably, un-an′sėr-a-bli, *adv.* In a manner not to be answered.
Unanswered, un-an′sėrd, *a. Not answered;* not suitably returned.
Unappalled, un-ap-pald′, *a. Not appalled;* not daunted.

Unappealable, un-ap-pēl′a-bl, *a. Not appealable;* admitting no appeal.
Unappeasable, un-ap-pēz′a-bl, *a. Not to be appeased* or pacified; not placable.
Unappeased, un-ap-pēzd′, *a. Not appeased;* not pacified.
Unappreciated, un-ap-prē′shi-āt-ed, *a. Not appreciated;* not duly estimated.
Unapprised, un-ap-prizd′, *a. Not apprised;* not previously informed.
Unapproachable, un-ap-prōch′a-bl, *a. That cannot be approached.*
Unapproachably, un-ap-prōch′a-bli, *adv. So as not to be approachable.*
Unapproached, un-ap-prōcht′, *a. Not approached;* not to be approached.
Unappropriated, un-ap-prō′pri-āt-ed, *a. Not appropriated;* not applied to any specific object.
Unapproved, un-ap-prōvd′, *a. Not having received approbation.*
Unapt, un-apt′, *a. Not apt;* not ready to learn; unfit.
Unarmed, un-ärmd′, *a. Not having on arms;* not furnished with scales, &c., as animals and plants.
Unarranged, un-a-rānjd′, *a. Not arranged;* not disposed in order.
Unarrayed, un-a-rād′, *a. Not arrayed.*
Unarticulated, un-är-tik′ū-lāt-ed, *a. Not articulated.*
Unascertainable, un-as′ėr-tān′′a-bl, *a. That cannot be ascertained.*
Unascertained, un-as′ėr-tānd′′, *a. Not ascertained;* not certainly known.
Unasked, un-askt′, *a. Not asked.*
Unassailable, un-as-sāl′a-bl, *a. Not assailable;* that cannot be assaulted.
Unassailed, un-as-sāld′, *a. Not assailed.*
Unassaulted, un-as-salt′ed, *a. Not assaulted;* not attacked.
Unassignable, un-as-sīn′a-bl, *a. Not assignable;* that cannot be transferred.
Unassigned, un-as-sīnd′, *a. Not assigned;* not declared; not transferred.
Unassimilated, un-as-sim′i-lāt-ed, *a. Not assimilated;* not made a part of the body, as food.
Unassociated, un-as-sō′shi-āt-ed, *a. Not associated;* not united with a society.
Unassuming, un-as-sūm′ing, *a. Not assuming;* not bold or forward; modest.
Unassured, un-ash-shūrd′, *a. Not assured;* not insured against loss; not confident; not to be trusted.
Unattached, un-at-tacht′, *a. Not attached;* not united by affection.
Unattainable, un-at-tān′a-bl, *a. Not attainable;* not to be gained or obtained.
Unattained, un-at-tānd′, *a. Not attained* or reached.
Unattempted, un-at-temt′ed, *a. Not attempted;* not tried; not essayed.
Unattended, un-at-tend′ed, *a. Not attended;* not accompanied; forsaken.
Unattested, un-at-test′ed, *a. Not attested;* having no attestation.
Unattractive, un-at-trakt′iv, *a. Not attractive.*
Unauthenticated, un-a-then′tik-āt-ed, *a. Not authenticated.*
Unauthorized, un-a′thor-izd, *a. Not authorized;* not duly commissioned.
Unavailable, un-a-vāl′a-bl, *a. Not available;* not effectual; vain.
Unavailing, un-a-vāl′ing, *a. Not availing;* ineffectual; useless; vain.
Unavoidable, un-a-void′a-bl, *a. Not avoidable;* not to be shunned.
Unavoidably, un-a-void′a-bli, *adv. Inevitably.*
Unavoided, un-a-void′ed, *a.* Inevitable.
Unavowed, un-a-voud′, *a. Not avowed;* not acknowledged; not owned.
Unawaked, Unawakened, un-a-wākt′,

un-a-wāk′nd, *a. Not awakened;* not roused from spiritual slumber.
Unaware, Unawares, un-a-wār′, un-a-wārz′, *adv.* Suddenly; unexpectedly.
Unawed, un-ad′, *a. Not awed.*
Unbalanced, un-ba′lanst, *a. Not balanced;* not settled.
Unbar, un-bär′, *vt. To remove a bar or bars from;* to unfasten; to open. *ppr.* unbarring, *pret. & pp.* unbarred.
Unbated, un-bāt′ed, *a. Not repressed;* not blunted.
Unbearable, un-bār′a-bl, *a. Not to be borne* or endured.
Unbecoming, un-bē-kum′ing, *a. Not becoming;* unsuitable; indecent.
Unbecomingly, un-bē-kum′ing-li, *adv.* In an unsuitable manner; indecorously.
Unbefitting, un-bē-fit′ing, *a. Not befitting;* unsuitable; unbecoming.
Unbefriended, un-bē-frend′ed, *a. Not befriended;* not supported by friends.
Unbegot, Unbegotten, un-bē-got′, un-bē-got′n, *a. Not begotten;* not generated; eternal; not yet generated.
Unbelief, un-bē-lēf′, *n. A want of belief;* infidelity; disbelief of the truth of the gospel; rejection of Christ as the Saviour of men, and of the doctrines he taught; distrust of God's promises and faithfulness, &c. [Sax. *ungeleafa.*]
Unbeliever, un-bē-lēv′ėr, *n. One who does not believe;* an infidel.
Unbelieving, un-bē-lēv′ing, *p.a. Not believing;* incredulous; infidel.
Unbend, un-bend′, *vi. To become unbent* or relaxed; to act with freedom.—*vt. To free from bending;* to remit from a strain; to set at ease for a time; in seamanship, to take the sails from their yards and stays; to cast loose, as a cable from the anchors.
Unbending, un-bend′ing, *p.a. Not bending;* unyielding; resolute; firm.
Unbiased, un-bī′ast, *p.a. Free from partiality* or *prejudice;* impartial.
Unbid, Unbidden, un-bid′, un-bid′n, *a. Not bid* or *bidden;* uninvited; not requested to attend.
Unbind, un-bīnd′, *vt. To remove a band* or *tie from;* to untie; to unfasten.
Unblamable, un-blām′a-bl, *a. Not blamable;* not culpable; innocent.
Unblamably, un-blām′a-bli, *adv. In such a manner as to incur no blame.*
Unblemished, un-blem′isht, *a. Not blemished;* free from turpitude or reproach; free from deformity.
Unblenching, un-blensh′ing, *a. Not blenching;* not flinching; firm.
Unblessed, Unblest, un-blest′, *a. Not blest;* wretched; unhappy.
Unblown, un-blōn′, *a. Not blown;* not having the bud expanded.
Unblushing, un-blush′ing, *a. Not blushing;* destitute of shame; impudent.
Unbolt, un-bōlt′, *vt. To remove a bolt from;* to unfasten; to open.—*vi.* To explain or open a matter.
Unbolted, un-bōlt′ed, *a.* Unfastened; unsifted; coarse; gross.
Unbooted, un-bōt′ed, *a. Not having boots on.*
Unborn, un-born′, *a. Not born.*
Unborrowed, un-bo′rōd, *a. Not borrowed;* genuine; original.
Unbosom, un-bō′zum, *vt. To open one's bosom;* (with recipr. pron.) to disclose freely, as one's secret opinions or feelings.
Unbought, un-bat′, *a. Not bought;* obtained without money or purchase.
Unbound, un-bound′, *a. Not bound;* loose; not bound by covenant.
Unbounded, un-bound′ed, *a.* Having no

bound or limit; interminable; having no check; unrestrained.
Unbowed, un-bōd′, *a. Not bent.*
Unbrace, un-brās′, *vt. To loose the braces of;* to relax. *ppr.* unbracing, *pret. & pp.* unbraced.
Unbreathed, un-brēᴛʜd′, *a. Not having breath;* not exercised or employed.
Unbred, un-bred′, *a. Not well bred;* not polished in manners; not taught.
Unbribed, un-brībd′, *a. Not bribed;* not corrupted by money.
Unbridled, un-brī′dld, *a.* Unrestrained; licentious.
Unbroken, un-brōk′n, *a. Not broken;* not weakened; not tamed.
Unbrotherly, un-bruᴛʜ′er-li, *a. Not becoming a brother;* unkind.
Unbuckle, un-buk′l, *vt. To loose from buckles;* to unfasten. *ppr.* unbuckling, *pret. & pp.* unbuckled.
Unbuild†, un-bild′, *vt.* To demolish; to raze; to destroy.
Unburied, un-be′rid, *a. Not buried.*
Unburned, Unburnt, un-bėrnd′, un-bėrnt′, *a. Not burnt;* not baked, as brick.
Unburthen, Unburden, un-bėr′ᴠᴛʜn, un-ber′dn, *vt. To free from a burden;* to throw off; to relieve, as the heart by disclosing what lies heavy on it.
Uncage, un-kāj′, *vt. To release from a cage. ppr.* uncaging, *pret. & pp.* uncaged.
Uncalled, un-kald′, *a. Not called.*
Uncancelled, un-kan′seld, *a. Not cancelled;* not erased.
Uncandid, un-kan′did, *a. Not candid;* not frank or sincere; not fair.
Uncanonical, un-ka-non′ik-al, *a. Not canonical;* not agreeable to the canons.
Uncape†, un-kāp′, *vt.* To let loose, or to let out of a bag.
Uncase, un-kās′, *vt. To disengage from a case;* to spread to view, as a flag. *ppr.* uncasing, *pret. & pp.* uncased.
Uncaused, un-kazd′, *a. Having no precedent cause.*
Unceasing, un-sēs′ing, *a. Not ceasing.*
Unceasingly, un-sēs′ing-li, *adv. Without intermission or cessation.*
Unceremonious, un-se˝rē-mō″ni-us, *a. Not ceremonious;* not formal.
Uncertain, un-sėr′tan, *a. Not certain;* doubtful; not having certain knowledge; not exact.
Uncertainty, un-sėr′tan-ti, *n. State of being uncertain;* want of certainty.
Unchallenged, un-chal′lenjd, *a. Not challenged.*
Unchangeable, un-chānj′a-bl, *a. Not capable of change;* immutable.
Unchangeableness, un-chānj′a-bl-nes, *n. The state or quality of being subject to no change;* immutability.
Unchanged, un-chānjd′, *a. Not changed.*
Unchanging, un-chānj′ing, *a. Not changing;* suffering no alteration.
Uncharitable, un-cha′ri-ta-bl, *a. Not charitable;* contrary to the universal love prescribed by Christianity.
Uncharitableness, un-cha′ri-ta-bl-nes, *n. Want of charity.*
Unchary, un-chā′ri, *a.* Not wary; not frugal.
Unchaste, un-chāst′, *a. Not chaste.*
Unchastised, un-chas-tīzd′, *a. Not chastised;* not punished; not corrected.
Unchastity, un-chas′ti-ti, *n. A want of chastity;* incontinence; lewdness.
Unchecked, un-chekt′, *a. Not checked;* not restrained.
Unchequered, Uncheckered, un-chek′ėrd, un-chek′ėrd, *a. Not chequered.*
Unchild†, un-child′, *vt. To deprive of children.*

Unchivalrous, un-shi′val-rus, *a. Not according to the rules of chivalry.*
Unchristian, un-kris′ti-an, *a. Contrary to the principles or laws of Christianity;* not converted to the Christian faith.
Unchurch, un-chėrch′, *vt. To expel from a church;* to deprive of the character and rights of a church.
Uncircumcised, un-sėr′kum-sīzd, *a. Not circumcised.*
Uncircumcision, un-sėr″kum-si″zhon, *n. Absence or want of circumcision.*
Uncivil, un-si′vil, *a. Not civil* or civilized; not courteous in manners; rude.
Uncivilized, un-si′vil-izd, *a. Not civilized;* not reclaimed from savage life.
Uncivilly, un-si′vil-li, *adv.* Rudely.
Unclaimed, un-klāmd′, *a. Not claimed.*
Unclasp, un-klasp′, *vt. To open the clasps of;* to open, as what is fastened with a clasp.
Unclassic, Unclassical, un-klas′ik, un-klas′ik-al, *a. Not classic;* not according to the best models of writing; not pertaining to the classic writers.
Uncle, ung′kl, *n.* The brother of one's father or mother. [Fr. *oncle*—L. *avunculus*—*avus*, a grandfather.]
Unclean, un-klēn′, *a. Not clean;* foul; in the Jewish law, ceremonially impure; foul with sin; unchaste.
Uncleanliness, un-klen′li-nes, *n. Want of cleanliness;* filthiness.
Uncleanly, un-klen′li, *a. Not cleanly.*
Uncleanness, un-klēn′nes, *n. State of being unclean;* moral impurity; lewdness.
Uncleansed, un-klenzd′, *a. Not cleansed.*
Unclerical, un-kle′rik-al, *a. Not clerical.*
Unclew, un-klū′, *vt.* To undo; to unwind.
Uncloak, un-klōk′, *vt. To remove a cloak from.*
Unclogged, un-klogd′, *a. Not clogged;* disencumbered.
Unclose, un-klōz′, *vt. To open;* to break the seal of, as of a letter; to disclose. *ppr.* unclosing, *pret. & pp.* unclosed.
Unclothe, un-klōᴛʜ′, *vt. To strip of clothes;* to divest. *ppr.* unclothing, *pret. & pp.* unclothed.
Unclothed, un-klōᴛʜd′, *p.a. Stripped of clothing.*
Unclouded, un-kloud′ed, *a. Not clouded;* clear; not obscured.
Uncloudy, un-kloud′i, *a. Not cloudy.*
Uncoil, un-koil′, *vt. To open from being coiled;* to unroll; to unwind or open.
Uncoloured, un-kul′ėrd, *a. Not coloured;* not heightened in description.
Uncolt†, un-kolt′, *vt. To throw from a colt* or horse.
Uncombed, un-kōmd′, *a. Not combed.*
Uncombined, un-kom-bīnd′, *a. Not combined;* separate; simple.
Uncomeliness, un-kum′li-nes, *n. Want of comeliness;* want of beauty or grace.
Uncomely, un-kum′li, *a. Not comely.*
Uncomfortable, un-kum′fort-a-bl, *a. Not comfortable;* wanting comfort.
Uncomfortably, un-kum′fort-a-bli, *adv. In an uncomfortable manner.*
Uncommendable, un-kom-mend′a-bl, *a. Not commendable.*
Uncommitted, un-kom-mit′ed, *a. Not committed;* not referred to a committee; not pledged by anything said or done.
Uncommon, un-kom′mon, *a. Not common;* not usual; rare; not frequent.
Uncommunicated, un-kom-mū′ni-kāt-ed, *a. Not communicated;* not imparted to or from another.
Uncomplaining, un-kom-plān′ing, *a. Not complaining;* not murmuring.

Uncomplaisant, un-kom′plā-zant, *a. Not complaisant;* not courteous.
Uncompleted, un-kom-plēt′ed, *a. Not completed;* not finished.
Uncomplying, un-kom-plī′ing, *a. Not complying.*
Uncompounded, un-kom-pound′ed, *a. Not compounded;* not mixed; simple.
Uncompromising, un-kom′pro-mīz-ing, *a. Not compromising;* not complying.
Unconcern, un-kon-sėrn′, *n. Want of concern;* absence of anxiety.
Unconcerned, un-kon-sėrnd′, *a. Not concerned;* feeling no interest in.
Unconciliating, un-kon-si′li-āt-ing, *a. Not conciliating.*
Uncondemned, un-kon-demd′, *a. Not condemned;* not pronounced criminal.
Unconditional, un-kon-di′shon-al, *a. Not conditional;* absolute; unreserved.
Unconditionally, un-kon-di′shon-al-li, *adv.* Without conditions.
Unconfined, un-kon-fīnd′, *a. Not confined;* free from restraint.
Unconfirmed, un-kon-fėrmd′, *a. Not confirmed;* weak; not confirmed according to the church ritual.
Unconformable, un-kon-form′a-bl, *a. Not conformable;* not consistent.
Unconformably, un-kon-form′a-bli, *adv. In an unconformable manner.*
Unconfuted, un-kon-fūt′ed, *a. Not confuted.*
Uncongealed, un-kon-jēld′, *a. Not congealed;* not frozen; not concreted.
Uncongenial, un-kon-jē′ni-al, *a. Not congenial.*
Unconnected, un-kon-nekt′ed, *a. Not connected;* not united; separate; loose.
Unconquerable, un-kong′kėr-a-bl, *a. Not conquerable;* invincible.
Unconquerably, un-kong′kėr-a-bli, *adv. Invincibly;* insuperably.
Unconquered, un-kong′kėrd, *a. Not conquered;* not vanquished or defeated.
Unconscientious, un-kon″shi-en″shi-us, *a. Not conscientious.*
Unconscionable, un-kon′shon-a-bl, *a. Not conscionable;* unreasonable.
Unconscionableness, un-kon′shon-a-bl-nes, *n.* Unreasonableness of hope or claim.
Unconscious, un-kon′shi-us, *a. Not conscious;* not knowing; not perceiving.
Unconsciously, un-kon′shi-us-li, *adv. In an unconscious manner.*
Unconsidered, un-kon-si′dėrd, *a. Not considered;* not attended to.
Unconsolidated, un-kon-so′lid-āt-ed, *a. Not consolidated* or made solid.
Unconstitutional, un-kon″sti-tū″shon-al, *a. Not agreeable to the constitution.*
Unconstitutionally, un-kon″sti-tū″shon-al-li, *adv. In a manner not warranted by the constitution.*
Unconstrained, un-kon-strānd′, *a. Not constrained;* voluntary; not proceeding from constraint, as actions.
Unconsumed, un-kon-sūmd′, *a. Not consumed;* not wasted; not destroyed.
Unconsummated, un-kon′sum-āt-ed. *pp. Not consummated.*
Uncontaminated, un-kon-tam′in-āt-ed *a. Not contaminated.*
Uncontested, un-kon-test′ed, *a. Not contested;* not disputed; evident; plain.
Uncontradicted, un-kon′tra-dikt″ed. *a. Not contradicted;* not denied.
Uncontrollable, un-kon-trōl′a-bl, *a. That cannot be controlled.*
Uncontrollably, un-kon-trōl′a-bli, *adv. In an uncontrollable manner.*
Uncontrolled, un-kon-trōld′, *a. Not controlled;* unopposed.
Uncontroverted, un-kon′trō-vėrt-ed, *a. Not controverted;* not disputed.

Fāte, fär, fat, fąll; mē, met, hėr; pīne, pin; nōte, not, mǫve; tūbe, tub, bųll; oil, pound.

Unconverted, un-kon-vėrt′ed, *a. Not converted;* not persuaded of the truth of the Christian religion; not renewed; not turned from one form to another.
Unconvinced, un-kon-vinst′, *a. Not convinced;* not persuaded.
Uncooked, un-kukt′, *a. Not cooked.*
Uncorrected, un-ko-rekt′ed, *a. Not corrected;* not revised; not reformed.
Uncorrupted, un-ko-rupt′ed, *a. Not corrupted;* not vitiated; not depraved.
Uncouple, un-ku′pl, *vt. To loose,* as dogs *from their couples;* to set loose. *ppr.* uncoupling, *pret. & pp.* uncoupled.
Uncourteous, un-kört′ē-us, *a. Not courteous;* uncivil; unpolite.
Uncourtly, un-kört′li, *a. Not courtly;* inelegant in manners; not versed in the manners of a court.
Uncouth, un-köth′, *a. Unknown;* strange; odd; unhandy; ungainly. [Sax. *uncuth—cuth,* known, *cunnan,* to know.]
Uncouthness, un-köth′nes, *n. Quality of being uncouth;* ungracefulness.
Uncover, un-ku′vėr, *vt. To divest of a cover;* to strip; to make naked; to unroof, as a building; to disclose to view. *vi.* To bare the head in token of respect.
Uncreated, un-krē-āt′ed, *a. Not created;* not produced by creation.
Uncredited, un-kre′dit-ed, *a. Not credited;* not believed.
Uncritical, un-kri′tik-al, *a. Not critical;* not according to criticism.
Uncrossed, un-krost′, *a. Not crossed;* not thwarted; not opposed.
Uncrowded, un-kroud′ed, *a. Not crowded;* not compressed.
Uncrystallized, un-kris′tal-izd, *a. Not crystallized.*
Unction, ung′shon, *n.* Act of anointing, as with oil; anything softening; richness of gracious affections; divine grace. [Fr. *onction—*L. *ungo,* to smear over.]
Unctuosity, ung-tū-os′i-ti, *n. Quality of being unctuous.* [Fr. *onctuosité.*]
Unctuous, ung′tū-us, *a. Oily; greasy;* having a resemblance to oil or grease. [Fr. *onctueux.*]
Unctuousness, ung′tū-us-nes, *n. Quality of being unctuous;* fatness; oiliness.
Uncultivated, un-kul′ti-vāt-ed, *a. Not cultivated;* rude; rough in manners.
Uncured, un-kūrd′, *a. Not cured.*
Uncurl, un-kėrl′, *vt. To loose from curls or ringlets.*
Uncurled, un-kėrld′, *p.a. Not curled;* not formed into ringlets.
Undamaged, un-dam′ājd, *a. Not damaged;* not made worse.
Undated, un′dāt-ed, *a. Waved;* having a waved surface. [L. *undatus—undo,* to rise in waves.]
Undated, un-dāt′ed, *a. Not dated.*
Undaunted, un-dant′ed, *a. Not daunted;* not subdued by fear; intrepid.
Undauntedness, un-dant′ed-nes, *n. Quality of being undaunted;* boldness.
Undebased, un-dē-bāst′, *a. Not debased;* undecagon, un-de′ka-gon, *n.* A plane figure of *eleven angles* or sides. [L. *un lecim,* eleven, and Gr. *gōnia,* corner, angle, our *coign.*]
Undecayed, un-dē-kād′, *a. Not decayed;* being in full strength.
Undecaying, un-dē-kā′ing, *a. Not decaying;* immortal.
Undeceivable, un-dē-sēv′a-bl, *a. That cannot be deceived.*
Undeceive, un-dē-sēv′, *vt. To free from deception,* whether caused by others or by ourselves. *ppr.* undeceiving, *pret. & pp.* undeceived.

Undecided, un-dē-sīd′ed, *a. Not decided;* not determined; not settled.
Undeciphered, un-dē-sī′fėrd, *a. Not deciphered* or explained.
Undeck, un-dek′, *vt.* To divest of ornaments.
Undecomposable, un-dē′kom-pōz″a-bl, *a. Not admitting decomposition.*
Undecomposed, un-dē′kom-pōzd″, *a. Not decomposed.*
Undecorated, un-de′kō-rāt-ed, *a. Not decorated;* not adorned; not embellished.
Undeeded†, un-dēd′ed, *a.* Not signalized by any great action.
Undefaced, un-dē-fāst′, *a. Not defaced.*
Undefended, un-dē-fend′ed, *a. Not defended;* not vindicated; open to assault.
Undefiled, un-dē-fīld′, *a. Not defiled.*
Undefinable, un-dē-fīn′a-bl, *a. Not definable;* that cannot be described by definition.
Undefined, un-dē-fīnd′, *a. Not defined;* not having its limits described.
Undejected, un-dē-jekt′ed, *a. Not dejected;* not depressed.
Undelivered, un-dē-li′vėrd, *a. Not delivered;* not communicated.
Undemonstrated, un-dē-mon′strāt-ed, *a. Not proved by demonstration.*
Undeniable, un-dē-nī′a-bl, *a. That cannot be denied.*
Undeniably, un-dē-nī′a-bli, *adv.* So as to admit no contradiction.
Undeplored, un-dē-plōrd′, *a. Not deplored;* not lamented.
Undepreciated, un-dē-prē′shi-āt-ed, *a. Not depreciated;* not lowered in value.
Undepressed, un-dē-prest′, *a. Not depressed.*
Undeprived, un-dē-prīvd′, *a. Not deprived;* not divested of by authority.
Under, un′dėr, *prep.* The termination *der,* Sans. *tar,* indicates *comparison* with an opposite direction—in this case, *over; beneath; below;* so as to have something above; in a state of subjection to; in a less degree than; less than; with the pretence of; with less than; in a degree, state, or rank inferior to; noting rank; in a state of being burdened; in a state of oppression; in a state of obligation; in a state of being limited by; in the state of bearing; in the enjoyment of; during the time of; not having reached; in the form of; in the state of protection; being comprehended in; attested by; in a state of being handled; influenced by (in a moral sense); within the dominion of.—*a.* Lower in degree; subject; subordinate. [Sax.—Old G. *undar,* Icel. *undir.*]
Under-agent, un′dėr-a-jent, *n. A subordinate agent.*
Underanged, un-dē-rānjd′, *a. Not deranged.*
Underbred, un-dėr-bred′, *a. Of inferior breeding* or manners.
Untercrest†, un dėr-krest′ *vt.* To support, as a crest.
Undercurrent, un′dėr-ku-rent, *n. A current below* the surface of the water.
Underdealing, un′dėr-dēl-ing, *n. Clandestine dealing;* artifice.
Underdone, un-dėr-dun′, *pp. Moderately cooked or done.*
Underdrain, un′dėr-drān, *n. A drain or trench below* the surface of the ground.
Undergird, un-dėr-gėrd′, *vt. To bind below;* to gird round the bottom.
Undergo, un-dėr-gō′, *vt. To go under or below;* to be the bearer of; to possess†; to undertake†; to be subject to; to bear; to endure, as something painful to the body or the mind; to pass through; to sustain without fainting. *ppr.* undergoing, *pret.* underwent, *pp.* undergone.
Undergraduate, un-dėr-grad′ū-āt, *n.* A student of a university or college who has not taken his first degree.
Underground, un′dėr-ground, *n.* A place or space *beneath the* surface of the *ground.—a. Being below* the surface of *the ground.—adv. Beneath* the surface of *the earth.*
Undergrowth, un′dėr-grōth, *n.* That which grows under trees; shrubs or small trees growing among large ones.
Underhand, un-dėr-hand′, *a. Under cover of the hand;* secret; clandestine. *adv.* By secret means; by fraud.
Under-honest, un-dėr-on′est, *a.* Not entirely honest.
Underived, un-dē-rīvd′, *a. Not derived;* not received from a foreign source.
Underlay, un-dėr-lā′, *vt.* To support by something *laid under. ppr.* underlaying, *pret. & pp.* underlaid.
Underlie, un-dėr-lī′, *vi. To lie beneath. ppr.* underlying, *pret.* underlay, *pp.* underlain.
Underline, un-dėr-līn′, *vt.* To mark with *a line below* the words. *ppr.* underlining, *pret. & pp.* underlined.
Underling, un′dėr-ling, *n. An inferior person or agent;* a mean sorry fellow.
Undermine, un-dėr-mīn′, *vt. To mine under or below;* to sap; to excavate, as the earth beneath; to remove, as the foundation of anything, by clandestine means. *ppr.* undermining, *pret. & pp.* undermined.
Undermost, un′dėr-mōst, *a. Lowest* in place beneath others; lowest in state.
Underneath, un-dėr-nēth′, *adv. Beneath; below;* in a lower place.—*prep. Under; beneath.*
Underplot, un′dėr-plot, *n.* A subordinate *plot;* a series of events in a play, proceeding with the main story; a clandestine scheme.
Underprop, un-dėr-prop′, *vt.* To set or place a prop *below;* to support. *ppr.* underpropping, *pret. & pp.* underpropped.
Underrate, un-dėr-rāt′, *vt. To rate too low;* to rate below the value. *ppr.* underrating, *pret. & pp.* underrated.
Undersell, un-dėr-sel′, *vt. To sell* the same articles *at a lower price* than. *ppr.* underselling, *pret. & pp.* undersold.
Undershrub, un′dėr-shrub, *n. A low shrub,* permanent and woody at the base, but the branches decaying yearly.
Undersign, un-dėr-sīn′, *vt. To write,* as *one's name at the foot* or *end of,* as of a letter or any legal instrument.
Understand, un-dėr-stand′, *vt. To stand under,* mentally; to support in the mind; to comprehend; to perceive; to know; to have the same ideas as the person who speaks; to receive or have, as the ideas intended to be conveyed in a writing or book; to know the meaning of; to know the meaning, as of signs; to suppose to mean; to know by instinct; to hold in opinion with conviction; to mean without expressing; to know, as what is not expressed; to learn; to be informed.—*vi.* To have the use of the intellectual faculties; to learn. *ppr.* understanding, *pret. & pp.* understood.
Understanding, un-dėr-stand′ing, *p.a.* Knowing; skilful.—*n.* The faculty by which one *understands;* the faculty of the human mind by which it apprehends the real state of things presented

ch, *chain*; j, *job*; g, *go*; ng, *sing*; ᴛʜ, *then*; th, *thin*; w, *wig*; wh, *whig*; zh, *azure*; † obsolete.

to it; knowledge; intelligence between two or more persons; union of sentiments.

Understate, un-dėr-stāt', *vt.* *To state too low;* to represent less strongly than the truth will bear. *ppr.* understating, *pret. & pp.* understated.

Undertake, un-dėr-tāk', *vt.* *To take under one's charge;* to engage in; to take in hand; to contract to perform; to attempt.—*vi.* To take upon one's self; to promise; to engage; to stand bound. *ppr.* undertaking, *pret.* undertook, *pp.* undertaken.

Undertaker, un-dėr-tāk'ėr, *n.* *One who undertakes;* one who stipulates to perform any work for another; one who manages funerals.

Undertaking, un-dėr-tāk'ing, *p.n.* *That which is undertaken;* any business which a person engages in; an enterprise.

Undertone, un'dėr-tōn, *n.* *A low tone.*

Under-valuation, un-dėr-va'lū-ā'shon, *n. Act of undervaluing;* rate not equal to the worth.

Undervalue, un-dėr-va'lū, *vt.* *To value below the real worth;* to treat as of little worth; to hold in mean estimation. *ppr.* undervaluing, *pret. & pp.* undervalued.—*n. L w rate or price,* a price less than the real worth.

Underwood, un'dėr-wud, *n.* Small trees that grow among large trees; coppice.

Underwrite, un-dėr-rīt', *vt.* *To write under;* to subscribe; to subscribe, as one's name for insurance. *ppr.* underwriting, *pret.* underwrote, *pp.* underwritten.

Underwriter, un'dėr-rīt-ėr, *n.* One who insures; so called because he *underwrites* his name to the conditions of the policy.

Underwriting, un-dėr-rīt'ing, *p.n.* The act or practice of insuring ships, &c.

Undeserved, un-dē-zėrvd', *a. Not deserved;* not merited.

Undeserving, un-dē-zėrv'ing, *p.a.* *Not deserving;* not meriting. (With *of.*)

Undeservingly, un-dē-zėrv'ing-li, *adv. Without meriting.*

Undesigned, un-dē-sīnd', *a. Not designed;* not intended.

Undesignedly, un-dē-sīn'ed-li, *adv. Without design* or intention.

Undesigning, un-dē-sīn'ing, *a. Not designing;* sincere; upright; artless.

Undesirable, un-dē-zīr'a-bl, *a. Not to be desired;* not to be wished; not pleasing.

Undetected, un-dē-tekt'ed, *a. Not detected;* not discovered; not laid open.

Undetermined, un-dē-tėr'mīnd, *a. Not determined;* not settled; not defined.

Undeterred, un-dē-tėrd', *a. Not deterred;* not restrained by fear.

Undeveloped, un-dē-vel'upt, *a. Not developed;* not opened or unfolded.

Undeviating, un-dē'vi-āt-ing, *a. Not deviating;* steady; regular.

Undigested, un-di-jest'ed, *a. Not digested;* not subdued by the stomach; crude.

Undignified, un-dig'ni-fīd, *a. Not dignified;* common; mean.

Undiminished, un-di-min'isht, *a. Not diminished;* not lessened; unimpaired.

Undimmed, un-dimd', *a. Not made dim;* not obscured.

Undiscerned, un-dis-sėrnd', *a. Not discerned;* not observed; not discovered.

Undiscernible, un-dis-sėrn'i-bl, *a. That cannot be discerned;* invisible.

Undiscerning, un-dis-sėrn'ing, *a. Not discerning;* wanting judgment.

Undisciplined, un-dis'si-plīnd, *a. Not disciplined;* raw; untaught.

Undisclosed, un-dis-klōzd', *a. Not disclosed;* not revealed.

Undiscouraged, un-dis-ku'rājd, *a. Not discouraged;* not disheartened.

Undiscoverable, un-dis-kuv'ėr-a-bl, *a. That cannot be discovered* or found out.

Undiscovered, un-dis-kuv'ėrd, *a. Not discovered;* not seen; not descried.

Undiscriminating, un-dis-krim'in-āt-ing, *a. Not discriminating.*

Undisguised, un-dis-gīzd', *a. Not disguised;* open; frank; artless.

Undismayed, un-dis-mād', *a. Not dismayed;* not disheartened by fear.

Undisposed, un-dis-pōzd', *a. Not disposed* (with *of*).

Undisputed, un-dis-pūt'ed, *a. Not disputed;* not contested.

Undisputedly, un-dis-pūt'ed-li, *adv. Without dispute.*

Undissembled, un-dis-sem'bld, *a. Not dissembled;* undisguised.

Undissolvable, un-diz-zolv'a-bl, *a. That cannot be dissolved* or melted; that may not be loosened.

Undissolved, un-diz-zolvd', *a. Not dissolved;* not melted.

Undissolving, un-diz-zolv'ing, *a. Not dissolving;* not melting.

Undistinguishable, un-dis-ting'gwish-a-bl, *a. That cannot be distinguished;* not to be known by the intellect.

Undistinguished, un-dis-ting'gwisht, *a. Not distinguished;* not plainly discerned; not marked by any particular property; not distinguished by any particular eminence.

Undistracted, un-dis-trakt'ed, *a. Not distracted.*

Undisturbed, un-dis-tėrbd', *a. Not disturbed;* not molested; calm; tranquil; placid; not agitated; not moved; free from perturbation.

Undividable, un-di-vid'a-bl, *a. That cannot be divided;* not separable.

Undivided, un-di-vid'ed, *a. Not divided;* unbroken; whole.

Undivulged, un-di-vuljd', *a. Not divulged;* not revealed or disclosed; secret.

Undo, un-dö', *vt.* *To reverse what has been done;* to open; to take to pieces; to unfasten; to ruin; to ruin, in a moral sense; to ruin in reputation. *ppr.* undoing, *pret.* undid, *pp.* undone.

Undoer, un-dö'ėr, *n. One who undoes;* one who ruins the reputation of another.

Undoing, un-dö'ing, *p.n. The reversal of what has been done;* ruin.

Undomesticated, un-dō-mes'tik-āt-ed, *a. Not domesticated;* not tamed.

Undone, un-dun', *p.a. Not done;* ruined; destroyed.

Undoubted, un-dout'ed, *a. Not doubted;* indubitable; indisputable.

Undoubtedly, un-dout'ed-li, *adv. Without doubt;* indubitably.

Undoubting, un-dout'ing, *p.a. Not doubting;* not fluctuating in uncertainty.

Undowered, un-dou'ėrd, *a. Not having a dower.*

Undress, un-dres', *vt. To divest of dress;* to divest of ornaments, or the attire of ostentation; to disrobe.

Undress, un'dres, *n. A loose negligent dress;* not a full dress.

Undressed, un-drest', *p.a. Not dressed;* not attired; not put in order.

Undue, un-dū', *a. Not due;* not legal; excessive.

Undulate, un'dū-lāt, *vt. To cause to play or move, as waves;* to move back and forth, or up and down, as waves. *vi.* To vibrate; to move back and forth; to wave. *ppr.* undulating, *pret. & pp.*

undulated. [Low L. *undūlo, undulatus*—L. *unda,* a wave.]

Undulated, un'dū-lāt-ed, *p.a. Wavy;* having a waved surface; appearing like waves.

Undulating, un'dū-lāt-ing, *p.a. Wavy;* rising and falling.

Undulation, un-dū-lā'shon, *n. Act of undulating;* fluctuation; a wavy appearance; a luminous wave.

Undulatory, un'dū-la-tō-ri, *a. Moving in the manner of waves;* resembling the motion of waves. [Fr. *ondulatoire.*]

Unduly, un-dū'li, *adv. Not according to duty* or propriety.

Undutiful, un-dū'ti-ful, *a. Not dutiful;* not obedient; not performing duty.

Undutifulness, un-dū'ti-ful-nes, *n. Want of dutifulness;* want of respect.

Undying, un-dī'ing, *a. Not dying;* not perishing; immortal.

Uneared, un-ėrd', *a. Not ploughed.*

Unearth, un-ėrth', *vt. To drive from the earth* or from a burrow.

Unearthly, un-ėrth'li, *a. Not earthly;* not terrestrial; supernatural.

Uneasily, un-ēz'i-li, *adv. With uneasiness* or pain; with difficulty; not readily.

Uneasiness, un-ēz'i-nes, *n. State of being uneasy;* restlessness; disquiet; unquietness of mind.

Uneasy, un-ēz'i, *a. Not easy;* not at ease; feeling some degree of pain; giving some pain; disturbed in mind; unquiet; cramping; constrained; stiff; disagreeable; unpleasing.

Uneath, un-ēth', *adv.* Not easily.

Unedifying, un-ed'i-fī-ing, *a. Not edifying;* not improving to the mind.

Uneducated, un-ed'ū-kāt-ed, *a. Not educated;* illiterate; ignorant.

Uneffaced, un-ef-fāst', *a. Not effaced.*

Unelected, un-ē-lekt'ed, *a. Not elected.*

Unembalmed, un-em-bämd', *a. Not embalmed.*

Unembarrassed, un-em-ba'rast, *a. Not embarrassed;* not perplexed in mind; free from pecuniary difficulties.

Unembellished, un-em-bel'lisht, *a. Not embellished.*

Unembodied, un-em-bo'did, *a. Not embodied;* not collected into a body.

Unemphatic, **Unemphatical**, un-em-fat'ik, un-em-fat'ik-al, *a. Not emphatic.*

Unemployed, un-em-ploid', *a. Not employed;* not busy; not being in use.

Unemptied, un-em'tid, *a. Not emptied.*

Unencumbered, un-en-kum'bėrd, *pp. Disengaged from encumbrance.*

Unendowed, un-en-doud', *a. Not endowed;* not furnished; not invested.

Unendurable, un-en-dūr'a-bl, *a. Not to be endured;* intolerable.

Unengaged, un-en-gājd', *a. Not engaged;* not bound by covenant; free from attachment that binds; unoccupied.

Unengaging, un-en-gāj'ing, *a. Not adapted to engage the attention* or affections; not inviting.

Unenglish, un-ing'glish, *a. Not English.*

Unenjoyed, un-en-joid', *a. Not enjoyed.*

Unenlightened, un-en-līt'nd, *a. Not enlightened;* not illuminated.

Unenlivened, un-en-līv'nd, *a. Not enlivened.*

Unentertaining, un-en'tėr-tān'ing, *a. Not entertaining;* giving no delight.

Unenviable, un-en'vi-a-bl, *a. Not enviable.*

Unenvied, un-en'vid, *a. Not envied.*

Unequal, un-ē'kwal, *a. Not equal;* not of the same size, length, breadth, &c.; not equal in strength, talents, &c.; inferior; not equal in age; not possess

ing equal advantages; inadequate; ill matched; not regular; not uniform.
Unequalled, un-ē'kwald, *a. Not to be equalled*; unparalleled; unrivalled.
Unequally, un-ē'kwal-li, *adv. Not equally*; in different degrees.
Unequivocal, un-ē-kwi'vō-kal, *a. Not equivocal*; clear; not of doubtful signification.
Unequivocally, un-ē-kwi'vō-kal-li, *adv.* Without doubt; with full evidence.
Unerring, un-er'ing, *a. Not erring*; incapable of error; certain; exact.
Unessential, un-es-sen'shi-al, *a. Not essential*; not absolutely necessary.
Unevangelical, un-ē'van-jel''ik-al, *a. Not evangelical*; not orthodox.
Uneven, un-ē'vn, *a. Not even*; not level; not of equal length; not equable.
Unevenness, un-ē'vn-nes, *n. Quality or state of being uneven*; inequality of surface; want of uniformity.
Unexamined, un-egz-am'ind, *a. Not examined*; not investigated; not debated.
Unexampled, un-egz-am'pld, *a. Having no example*; having no precedent.
Unexcelled, un-ek-seld', *a. Not excelled*.
Unexceptionable, un-ek-sep'shon-a-bl, *a. Not liable to any exception*.
Unexcited, un-ek-sit'ed, *a. Not excited*.
Unexecuted, un-eks'ē-kūt-ed, *a. Not executed*; not done; not signed or sealed.
Unexemplified, un-egz-em'pli-fid, *a. Not exemplified*.
Unexercised, un-eks'ėr-sizd, *a. Not exercised*; not experienced.
Unexhausted, un-egz-hąst'ed, *a. Not exhausted*; not spent.
Unexpanded, un-eks-pand'ed, *a. Not expanded*; not spread out.
Unexpected, un-eks-pekt'ed, *a. Not expected*; sudden; not provided against.
Unexpended, un-eks-pend'ed, *a. Not expended*; not laid out.
Unexpired, un-eks-pird', *a. Not expired*; not ended.
Unexplainable, un-eks-plān'a-bl, *a. That cannot be explained*.
Unexplained, un-eks-plānd', *a. Not explained*; not interpreted; not illustrated.
Unexplored, un-eks-plōrd', *a. Not explored*; not examined intellectually.
Unexposed, un-eks-pōzd', *a. Not exposed*; not laid open to censure.
Unexpounded, un-eks-pound'ed, *a. Not expounded*; not explained.
Unexpressive, un-eks-pres'iv, *a. Incapable of being expressed*.
Unextended, un-eks-tend'ed, *a. Not extended*; having no dimensions.
Unextinguished, un-ek-sting'gwisht, *a. Not extinguished*; not entirely repressed.
Unfading, un-fād'ing, *a. Not fading*; not liable to lose strength or freshness of colouring; not liable to wither.
Unfailing, un-fāl'ing, *a. Not failing*; that does not fail; certain.
Unfair, un-fār', *a. Not fair*; not just; not equal; proceeding from dishonesty. *vt.†* To deprive of fairness.
Unfairness, un-fār'nes, *n. State of being unfair*; injustice.
Unfaithful, un-fāth'fųl, *a. Not faithful*; not observant of promises or duty; perfidious; not performing the proper duty; impious.
Unfaithfully, un-fāth'fųl-li, *adv. In an unfaithful manner*.
Unfaithfulness, un-fāth'fųl-nes, *n. State of being unfaithful*; breach of confidence or trust reposed.
Unfaltering, un-fal'tėr-ing, *a. Not faltering*; not failing; not hesitating.

Unfashionable, un-fa'shon-a-bl, *a. Not fashionable*; not regulating dress or manners according to the reigning custom.
Unfashionably, un-fa'shon-a-bli, *adv. Not according to the fashion*.
Unfashioned, un-fa'shond, *a. Not fashioned*; not having a regular form.
Unfasten, un-fas'n, *vt. To remove or loose the fastening of*; to unbind.
Unfatherly, un-fä'THėr-li, *a. Not fatherly*; not becoming a father.
Unfathomable, un-fa'THom-a-bl, *a. That cannot be fathomed or sounded*.
Unfathomed, un-fa'THomd, *a. Not fathomed or sounded*; not to be sounded.
Unfavourable, un-fā'vėr-a-bl, *a. Not favourable*; not propitious; not adapted to promote any object; discouraging.
Unfavourably, un-fā'vėr-a-bli, *adv.* Unpropitiously; unkindly; in a manner to discourage.
Unfeeling, un-fēl'ing, *a. Not having feelings or sensibility*; insensible; cruel.
Unfeigned, un-fānd', *a. Not feigned*; not counterfeit; real; sincere.
Unfeignedly, un-fān'ed-li, *adv.* Without hypocrisy, really; sincerely.
Unfelt, un-felt', *a. Not felt*; not perceived.
Unfeminine, un-fem'in-in, *a. Not feminine*; not according to the female character or manners.
Unfenced, un-fenst', *pp. Not fenced*.
Unfermented, un-fėr-ment'ed, *a. Not fermented*; not leavened.
Unfetter, un-fet'ėr, *vt. To loose from fetters*; to set at liberty.
Unfettered, un-fet'ėrd, *p.a. Not restrained*.
Unfilial, un-fi'li-al, *a. Not filial*; unsuitable to a son or child; undutiful.
Unfinished, un-fin'isht, *a. Not finished*; imperfect; wanting the last touch.
Unfit, un-fit', *a. Not fit*; unqualified. *vt. To make unfit*; to disqualify. *ppr.* unfitting, *pret. & pp.* unfitted.
Unfitness, un-fit'nes, *n. State or quality of being unfit*.
Unfitting, un-fit'ing, *p.a. Not fitting*; unbecoming.
Unfix, un-fiks', *vt. To remove the fastening or bond from*; to loosen from any fastening; to unhinge.
Unfixed, un-fikst', *p.a.* Wandering; inconstant; having no settled object.
Unflagging, un-flag'ing, *p.a. Not flagging*; maintaining strength or spirit.
Unfledged, un-flejd', *a. Not fledged*; not yet furnished with feathers; young.
Unfleshed, un-flesht', *a.* Not seasoned to blood; raw.
Unflinching, un-flinsh'ing, *a. Not flinching*; resolute.
Unfold, un-fōld', *vt. To open the folds of*; to spread out; to open, as anything covered or close; to lay open to view; to reveal; to tell; to illustrate.
Unfolding, un-fōld'ing, *p.n. The act of one who unfolds*; the act of expanding or disclosing; disclosure.
Unforced, un-fōrst', *a. Not forced*; not feigned; natural; easy.
Unforeseeing, un-fōr-sē'ing, *a. Not foreseeing*.
Unforeseen, un-fōr-sēn', *a. Not foreseen*; not foreknown.
Unforewarned, un-fōr-warnd', *a. Not forewarned*.
Unforgiving, un-for-giv'ing, *p.a. Not forgiving*; implacable.
Unforgot, Unforgotten, un-for-got', un-for-got'n. *a. Not forgot or forgotten*; not lost to memory; not overlooked.
Unformed, un-formd', *a.* Not moulded into regular shape.

Unfortified, un-for'ti-fīd, *a. Not fortified*; weak; defenceless.
Unfortunate, un-for'tū-nāt, *a. Not fortunate*; not successful; not prosperous.
Unfortunately, un-for'tū-nāt-li, *adv. In an unfortunate manner*.
Unfounded, un-found'ed, *a. Not founded*; having no foundation; vain; idle.
Unfrequented, un-frē-kwent'ed, *a. Not frequented*; rarely visited.
Unfriendliness, un-fi end'li-nes, *n. State of being unfriendly*.
Unfriendly, un-frend'li, *a. Not friendly*; not kind or benevolent; not favourable.
Unfrugal, un-frū'gal, *a. Not frugal*.
Unfruitful, un-frūt'fųl, *a. Not fruitful*; barren; not producing offspring; not producing good effects; unproductive.
Unfruitfully, un-frūt'fųl-li, *adv. In an unfruitful manner*.
Unfruitfulness, un-frūt'fųl-nes, *n. State of being unfruitful*; barrenness.
Unfulfilled, un-fųl-fild', *a. Not fulfilled*; not accomplished.
Unfunded, un-fund'ed, *a. Not funded*; having no permanent funds for the payment of its interest.
Unfurl, un-fėrl', *vt. To free from furls*; to loose and unfold; to open or spread.
Unfurnished, un-fėr'nisht, *a. Not furnished*; unsupplied with necessaries or ornaments; empty; left naked.
Ungainliness, un-gān'li-nes, *n. State or quality of being ungainly*.
Ungainly, un-gān'li, *a.* Producing no gain or effect; not expert; clumsy; uncouth. [Sax. *ungegne*.]
Ungallant, un-gal-lant', *a. Not gallant*.
Ungallantly, un-gal-lant'li, *adv. In an ungallant manner*.
Ungarrisoned, un-ga'ri-snd, *a. Not garrisoned*.
Ungathered, un-gaTH'ėrd, *a. Not gathered*; not cropped; not picked.
Ungenerous, un-jen'ėr-us, *a. Not generous*; not of a noble mind; illiberal.
Ungenerously, un-jen'ėr-us-li, *adv. In an ungenerous manner*; unkindly.
Ungenial, un-jē'ni-al, *a. Not genial*; not favourable to natural growth.
Ungenteel, un-jen-tēl', *a. Not genteel*; not consistent with polite manners.
Ungentle, un-jen'tl, *a. Not gentle*.
Ungentleman-like, un-jen'tl-man-lik, *a. Not like a gentleman*.
Ungentlemanliness, un-jen'tl-man-li-nos, *n. The quality of being ungentleman-like*.
Ungentlemanly, un-jen'tl-man-li, *a. Not becoming a gentleman*.
Ungentleness, un-jen'tl-nes, *n. The quality of being ungentle*; severity; unkindness; incivility.
Ungently, un-jen'tl-i, *adv. Not gently*.
Ungilded, Ungilt, un-gild'ed, un-gilt', *a. Not gilded*; not gilt.
Ungird, un-gėrd', *vt. To loose from a girdle or band*; to unbind. *ppr.* ungirding, *pret. & pp.* ungirded or ungirt.
Ungirt, un-gėrt', *a.* Loosely dressed.
Unglazed, un-glāzd', *a. Not glazed*; not furnished with glass.
Ungodliness, un-god'li-nes, *n. State or quality of being ungodly*; impiety.
Ungodly, un-god'li, *a. Not godly*; neglecting the fear and worship of God, or violating his commands; sinful.
Ungovernable, un-gu'vėrn-a-bl, *a. Not governable*; that cannot be governed; licentious; wild; unbridled.
Ungovernably, un-gu'vėrn-a-bli, *adv.* So as not to be governed or restrained.
Ungoverned, un-gu'vėrnd, *a. Not being governed*; not restrained or regulated; licentious.

Ungowned, un-gound', *a. Not having or not wearing a gown.*
Ungraced, un-grāst', *a. Not graced.*
Ungraceful, un-grās'ful, *a. Not graceful; not marked with ease and dignity; without politeness or learning.*
Ungracefully, un-grās'ful-li *adv. Awkwardly; inelegantly.*
Ungracefulness, un-grās'ful-nes, *n. State or quality of being ungraceful; want of elegance; awkwardness.*
Ungracious, un-grā'shi-us, *a. Not gracious; odious; hateful.*
Ungraciously, un-grā'shi-us-li, *adv. In an ungracious manner; without favour.*
Ungrammatical, un-gram-mat'ik-al, *a. Not grammatical; not according to the established rules of grammar.*
Ungrammatically, un-gram-mat'ik-al-li, *adv. In a manner contrary to the rules of grammar.*
Ungrateful, un-grāt'ful, *a. Not grateful; not making returns for kindness; sterile; unacceptable; not agreeable, as harsh sounds.*
Ungratefully, un-grāt'ful-li, *adv. With ingratitude; unpleasingly.*
Ungratefulness, un-grāt'ful-nes, *n. The quality of being ungrateful; unpleasing quality.*
Ungratified, un-gra'ti-fīd, *a. Not gratified; not pleased; not indulged.*
Ungrudging, un-gruj'ing, *a. Not grudging; freely giving.*
Unguarded, un-gärd'ed, *a. Not guarded; negligent; not cautious.*
Unguardedly, un-gärd'ed-li, *adv. In an unguarded manner.*
Unguardedness, un-gärd'ed-nes, *n. State of being unguarded.*
Unguent, un'gwent, *n. Ointment; a soft composition used as a topical remedy, as for sores, burns, and the like. [Fr. onguent—L. ungo, unctum, to besmear.]*
Unhallowed, un-hal'lōd, *a. Not hallowed; profane; unholy; wicked.*
Unhand, un-hand', *vt. To loose from the hand; to let go.*
Unhandiness, un-hand'i-nes, *n. Quality of being unhandy; want of dexterity.*
Unhandled, un-hand'ld, *a. Not handled.*
Unhandsome, un-hand'sum, *a. Not handsome; ungraceful; illiberal; unfair; unpolite.*
Unhandsomely, un-hand'sum-li, *adv. Inelegantly; ungracefully; illiberally.*
Unhandsomeness, un-hand'sum-nes, *n. Quality of being unhandsome; want of beauty and elegance; unfairness; incivility.*
Unhandy, un-hand'i, *a. Not handy; not dextrous; awkward; not convenient.*
Unhanged, **Unhung**, un-hangd', un-hung', *a. Not hanged or hung; not punished by hanging.*
Unhappied†, un-hap'pid, *a. Made unhappy.*
Unhappily, un-hap'pi-li, *adv. Unfortunately; miserably; calamitously.*
Unhappiness, un-hap'pi-nes, *n. State or quality of being unhappy; misfortune; misery; a mischievous prank.*
Unhappy, un-hap'pi, *a. Not happy; in a degree miserable or wretched; bringing calamity; unpropitious; marked by infelicity; wicked.*
Unharboured, un-här'bord, *a. Not harboured; not sheltered.*
Unhardened, un-härd'nd, *a. Not hardened; not made obdurate, as the heart.*
Unharmed, un-härmd', *a. Not harmed.*
Unharness, un-här'nes, *vt. To loose from harness or gear; to disarm; to divest of armour.*
Unhazarded, un-ha'zėrd-ed, *a. Not ha-*

zarded; not put in danger; not adventured.
Unhealthiness, un-helth'i-nes, *n. State of being unhealthy; habitual weakness; unsoundness; state of being unfavourable to health.*
Unhealthy, un-helth'i *a. Not healthy; wanting a sound and vigorous state of body; wanting vigour of growth, as a plant; sickly; unwholesome; morbid; not indicating health.*
Unheard, un-hėrd', *a. Not heard; not admitted to audience; unknown by fame.*
Unheart†, un-härt', *vt. To depress.*
Unheated, un-hēt'ed, *a. Not heated.*
Unheeded, un-hēd'ed, *a. Not heeded.*
Unheedful, un-hēd'ful, *a. Not heedful.*
Unheedfully, un-hēd'ful-li, *adv. Not heedfully.*
Unheeding, un-hēd'ing, *a. Not heeding.*
Unheedy†, un-hēd'i, *a. Sudden.*
Unheroic, un-hē-rō'ik, *a. Not heroic.*
Unhesitating, un-he'zi-tāt-ing, *a. Not hesitating; prompt; ready.*
Unhesitatingly, un-he'zi-tāt-ing-li, *adv. Without hesitation or doubt.*
Unhewn, un-hūn', *a. Not hewn; rough.*
Unhinge, un-hinj', *vt. To take from the hinges; to unfix by violence; to loosen; to render wavering; to derange. ppr. unhinging, pret. & pp. unhinged.*
Unholily, un-hō'li-li, *adv. In an unholy manner.*
Unholiness, un-hō'li-nes, *n. State or quality of being unholy; profaneness.*
Unholy, un-hō'li, *a. Not holy; not renewed and sanctified.*
Unhonoured, un-on'ėrd, *a. Not honoured; not regarded with veneration.*
Unhook, un-hök', *vt. To loose from a hook.*
Unhoped, un-hōpt', *a. Not hoped for; not expected.*
Unhopeful, un-hōp'ful, *a. Not hopeful.*
Unhorse, un-hors', *vt. To throw from a horse; to cause to dismount. ppr. unhorsing, pret. & pp. unhorsed.*
Unhouse, un-houz', *vt. To deprive of a house; to dislodge; to deprive of shelter. ppr. unhousing, pret. & pp. unhoused.*
Unhoused, un-houzd', *p.a. Homeless; having no settled habitation.*
Unhouseled†, un-houz'eld, *a. Not having received the sacrament.*
Unhumbled, un-um'bld, *a. Not humbled; not contrite in spirit.*
Unhurt, un-hėrt', *a. Not hurt; not harmed; free from wound or injury.*
Unicorn, ū'ni-korn, *n. An animal with one horn. [L. unicornis—unus, one, and cornu, a horn.]*
Unideal, un-ī-dē'al, *a. Not ideal; actual.*
Uniform, ū'ni-form, *a. Having only one form or shape; having always the same form or manner; of the same form with others; undeviating; constant; alike. n. A dress of the same kind with others; the particular dress of soldiers, by which one regiment is distinguished from another. [Fr. uniforme—L. unus, one, and forma, form.]*
Uniformity, ū-ni-form'i-ti, *n. State of being uniform; consistency; conformity to a pattern; similitude between the parts of a whole. [Fr. uniformité.]*
Uniformly, ū'ni-form-li, *adv. In a uniform manner; with even tenor.*
Unilateral, ū-ni-lit'ėr-al, *a. Consisting of one letter only. [L. unus, one, and litera, letter.]*
Unimaginable, un-im-aj'in-a-bl, *a. Not to be imagined; not to be conceived.*
Unimaginative, un-im-aj'in-āt-iv, *a. Not imaginative.*

Unimagined, un-im-aj'ind, *a. Not imagined; not conceived.*
Unimpaired, un-im-pārd', *a. Not impaired; not enfeebled by time.*
Unimpassioned, un-im-pa'shond, *a. Not impassioned; not endowed with passions; calm; not violent.*
Unimpeachable, un-im-pēch'a-bl, *a. That cannot be impeached; that cannot be accused; free from stain, guilt, or fault.*
Unimpeached, un-im-pēcht', *a. Not impeached; not charged; fair.*
Unimpeded, un-im-pēd'ed, *a. Not impeded; not hindered.*
Unimportance, un-im-port'ans, *n. Want of importance.*
Unimportant, un-im-port'ant, *a. Not important; insignificant; trivial.*
Unimposing, un-im-pōz'ing, *a. Not imposing; not enjoining as obligatory.*
Unimpregnated, un-im-preg'nāt-ed, *a. Not impregnated.*
Unimpressed, un-im-prest', *a. Not impressed.*
Unimpressive, un-im-pres'iv, *a. Not impressive; not forcible.*
Unimpressively, un-im-pres'iv-li, *adv. Without impression.*
Unimprovable, un-im-pröv'a-bl, *a. Not capable of improvement; incapable of being cultivated or tilled.*
Unimproved, un-im-prövd', *a. Not improved; not tilled; not cultivated; not made better or wiser; not used for a valuable purpose; not employed; not reproved†.*
Uninclosed, un-in-klōzd', *a. Not inclosed.*
Uninfected, un-in-fekt'ed, *a. Not infected; not corrupted.*
Uninflamed, un-in-flāmd', *a. Not inflamed; not highly provoked.*
Uninfluenced, un-in'flū-enst, *a. Not influenced; not biased; acting freely.*
Uninformed, un-in-formd', *a. Not informed; not instructed; untaught.*
Uninhabited, un-in-ha'bit-ed, *a. Not inhabited by men.*
Uninitiated, un-in-i'shi-āt-ed, *a. Not initiated.*
Uninjured, un-in'jūrd, *a. Not injured; not hurt; suffering no harm.*
Uninspired, un-in-spīrd', *a. Not inspired.*
Uninstructed, un-in-strukt'ed, *a. Not instructed; not furnished with instructions.*
Uninstructive, un-in-strukt'iv, *a. Not instructive.*
Uninsured, un-in-shūrd', *a. Not insured; not assured against loss.*
Unintelligible, un-in-tel'li-ji-bl, *a. Not intelligible; that cannot be understood.*
Unintelligibly, un-in-tel'li-ji-bli, *adv. In a manner not to be understood.*
Unintentional, un-in-ten'shon-al, *a. Not intentional; not designed; done or happening without design.*
Uninterested, un-in'tėr-est-ed, *a. Not interested; not having the feelings engaged; having nothing at stake.*
Uninteresting, un-in'tėr-est-ing, *a. Not interesting; not capable of exciting an interest, or of engaging the mind.*
Uninterpreted, un-in-tėr'pret-ed, *a. Not interpreted; not explained.*
Uninterred, un-in-tėrd', *a. Not interred; not buried.*
Uninterrupted, un-in'tėr-rupt"ed, *a. Not interrupted; not broken; unceasing.*
Unintroduced, un-in'trō-dūst", *a. Not introduced; obtrusive.*
Uninured, un-in-ūrd', *a. Not inured; not hardened by use or practice.*
Uninvited, un-in-vīt'ed, *a. Not invited.*
Uninviting, un-in-vīt'ing, *a. Not inviting.*

Fāte, fär, fat, fạll; mē, met, hėr; pīne, pin; nōte, not, mōve; tūbe, tub, bu̧ll; oil, pound.

Union, ū'ni-on, n. *Oneness;* unity; the act of joining two or more things into one; the coalition of things thus united; agreement of mind, will, affections, or interest; a federal compact; a large fine pearl†. [Fr.—L. *unus*, one.]

Unique, ū-nēk', a. *One and no more;* only; sole; single. [Fr.]

Unison, ū'ni-son, n. *One single sound;* perfect agreement in pitch of two or more musical notes; accordance; harmony; concord. [L. *unus*, one, and *sonus*, sound.]

Unisonance, ū-ni'sō-nans, n. *State of being in unison;* accordance of sounds.

Unisonous, ū-ni'sō-nus, a. *Being in unison.*

Unit, ū'nit, n. *Oneness;* a word which denotes a single thing or person; the least whole number, or one, represented by the figure 1, a single thing regarded as a whole; a certain dimension assumed as a standard. [Fr. *unité*—L. *unitas*—*unus*, one.]

Unitarian, ū-ni-tā'ri-an, n. One who believes in and worships *one* God in one person, but denies the divine nature of Jesus Christ, and the personality of the Holy Spirit.—*a. Pertaining to Unitarians.* from L. *unitas*, oneness—*unus*, one.]

Unitarianism, ū-ni-tā'ri-an-izm, n. *The doctrines of Unitarians.*

Unite, ū-nit', vt. *To join into one;* to join in affection or interest; to associate; to make to adhere; to attach. *vi. To become one;* to coalesce; to combine; to grow together; to join in an act; to concur; to act in concert. *ppr.* uniting, *pret. & pp.* united. [Low L. *unio, unitus*—L. *unus,* one.]

United, ū-nit'ed, p.a. *Joined into one;* mixed; attached by growth.

Unity, ū'ni-ti, n. *The state of being one; oneness;* concord; uniformity; the abstract expression for any unit whatsoever; the correspondence of the various parts of a work of art, so that they may form one harmonious whole. [Fr. *unité*—L. *unitas*—*unus*, one.]

Universal, ū-ni-vėrs'al, a. *Turned into one;* combined into one whole; all; extending to the whole number, quantity, or space; whole; comprising all the particulars. [Fr. *universel*—L. *unus,* and *verto, versum,* to turn.]

Universalist, ū-ni-vėrs'al-ist, n. One who holds the doctrine that *all* men will be saved.

Universality, ū'ni-vėrs-al'li-ti, n. *The state of being universal;* the state of extending to the whole. [Fr. *universalité*.]

Universally, ū-ni-vėrs'al-li, adv. With extension to the *whole*.

Universe, ū'ni-vėrs, n. All things considered as *turned into one whole;* the whole system of created things. [Fr. *univers*—L. *unus,* one, and *verto*, to turn.]

University, ū-ni-vėrs'i-ti, n. *All combined together;* a corporation, for the purpose of instruction in all, or some of the most important divisions of science and literature, and having the power of conferring degrees. [Fr. *université*—L. *unus,* and *verto*, to turn.]

Univocal, ū-ni'vō-kal, a. Having *one* meaning only, as a *word;* having unison of sounds.—*n. A word having only one* meaning. [L. *unus*, one, and *vox, vocis*, a word.]

Unjointed, un-joint'ed, p.a. *Having no joint* or articulation, as the stem of a plant.

Unjust, un-just', a. *Not just;* acting contrary to the standard of right established by the divine law; contrary to justice and right; wrongful.

Unjustifiable, un-jus'ti-fi-a-bl, a. *Not justifiable;* not to be vindicated.

Unjustifiably, un-jus'ti-fi-a-bli, adv. In a *manner that cannot be justified.*

Unjustly, un-just'li, adv. *In an unjust manner;* wrongfully.

Unkennel, un-ken'nel, vt. *To drive from a kennel* or hole, as a fox; to rouse from retreat. *ppr.* unkennelling, *pret. & pp.* unkennelled.

Unkind, un-kind', a. *Not kind;* not benevolent; not obliging; unnatural.

Unkindliness, un-kind'li-nes, n. *Quality of being unkindly;* unfavourableness.

Unkindly, un-kind'li, a. *Not kindly;* unnatural; malignant.—*adv. Without kindness;* in a manner contrary to nature; unnaturally.

Unkindness, un-kind'nes, n. *Want of kindness;* want of natural affection; disobliging treatment.

Unkingly, un-king'li, a. *Unbecoming a king.*

Unknightly, un-nīt'li, a. *Unbecoming a knight.*

Unknit, un-nit', vt. *To separate, as threads that are knit;* to loose, as work that is knit. *ppr.* unknitting, *pret. & pp.* unknitted.

Unknowing, un-nō'ing, a. *Not knowing;* ignorant. (With *of*.)

Unknown, un-nōn', a. *Not known;* greater than is imagined; not having communication.

Unlaboured, un-lā'bėrd, a. *Not produced by labour;* not cultivated by labour; spontaneous; natural; easy.

Unlace, un-lās', vt. *To loose from lacing;* to loose, as a woman's dress. *ppr.* unlacing, *pret. & pp.* unlaced.

Unlade, un-lād', vt. *To unload;* to remove, as a load or burden. *ppr.* unlading, *pret.* unladed, *pp.* unladed or unladen.

Unlaid, un-lād', a. Not pacified; not suppressed.

Unlamented, un-la-ment'ed, a. *Not lamented;* whose loss is not deplored.

Unlawful, un-la'ful, a. *Not lawful;* contrary to law; illegal.

Unlawfully, un-la'ful-li, adv. *In violation of law* or right; illegally.

Unlawfulness, un-la'ful-nes, n. *Quality or state of being unlawful;* illegality.

Unlearn, un-lėrn', vt. *To forget or lose what has been learned.*

Unlearned, un-lėrn'ed, a. *Not learned;* illiterate.

Unleavened, un-le'vnd, a. *Not leavened* or fermented, as bread.

Unless, un-les', *conj. Except,* that is, remove or dismiss the fact or thing stated in the sentence or clause which follows; if not; supposing that not. [the imperative of Sax. *onlesan,* to unloose, to dismiss.]

Unlettered, un-let'ėrd, a. *Not lettered;* not learned; unlearned; ignorant.

Unlicensed, un-li'senst, a. *Not licensed.*

Unlicked, un-likt', a. *Not licked* into shape; not formed to smoothness; shapeless; uncultivated.

Unlighted, un-līt'ed, a. *Not lighted.*

Unlike, un-līk', a. *Not like;* dissimilar.

Unlikelihood, Unlikeliness, un-līk'li-hud, un-līk'li-nes, n. *State of being unlikely;* improbability.

Unlikely, un-līk'li, a. *Not likely;* improbable; not promising success.—*adv.* Improbably.

Unlikeness, un-līk'nes, n. *Want of* likeness or resemblance; dissimilitude.

Unlimbered, un-lim'bėrd, p.a. *Freed from the limbers,* as a gun.

Unlimited, un-lim'it-ed, a. *Not limited;* boundless; indefinite.

Unliquidated, un-li'kwi-dāt-ed, a. *Not liquidated;* not settled; unpaid.

Unload, un-lōd', vt. *To take the load from;* to disburden; to relieve from anything onerous.

Unlock, un-lok', vt. *To unfasten,* as *what is locked;* to open, in general.

Unlocked, un-lokt', p.a. *Not locked;* not made fast.

Unlooked-for, un-lökt'for, a. *Not looked for;* not expected; not foreseen.

Unloose, un-lös', vt. *To loose;* to untie. *ppr.* unloosing, *pret. & pp.* unloosed. [Sax. *onlesan—lesan,* to loose.]

Unlordly, un-lord'li, a. *Not lordly.*

Unloved, un-luvd', a. *Not loved.*

Unloveliness, un-luv'li-nes, n. *Want of loveliness;* unamiableness.

Unlovely, un-luv'li, a. *Not lovely;* destitute of the qualities which attract love.

Unloving, un-luv'ing, a. Not fond.

Unluckily, un-luk'i-li, adv. Unfortunately; by ill fortune.

Unluckiness, un-luk'i-nes, n. *State or quality of being unlucky.*

Unlucky, un-luk'i, a. *Not lucky;* unfortunate; unhappy; ill-omened; inauspicious.

Unmade, un-mād', p.a. *Not made;* not yet formed.

Unmaidenly, un-mād'n-li, a. *Not becoming a maiden.*

Unmake, un-māk', vt. *To destroy the make of;* to deprive of qualities before possessed. *ppr.* unmaking, *pret. & pp.* unmade.

Unman, un-man', vt. *To deprive of the* distinctive *qualities of a human being,* as reason, &c.; to emasculate; to deprive of the courage of a man; to dishearten; to deject. *ppr.* unmanning, *pret. & pp.* unmanned.

Unmanageable, un-ma'nāj-a-bl, a. *Not manageable;* not controllable.

Unmanageably, un-ma'nāj-a-bli, adv. *So as not to be manageable.*

Unmanliness, un-man'li-nes, n. *State of being unmanly.*

Unmanly, un-man'li, a. *Not becoming a man;* unsuitable to a man; effeminate; not worthy of a noble mind; ungenerous; cowardly.

Unmanned, un-mand', p.a. *Deprived of the qualities of a man;* dejected; deprived of manly fortitude; not furnished with men; not tamed†; maiden†.

Unmannerliness, un-man'nėr-li-nes, n. *Quality of being unmannerly.*

Unmannerly, un-man'nėr-li, a. *Not mannerly;* ill bred; rude in behaviour; not according to good manners.—*adv.* Uncivilly.

Unmarked, un-märkt', a. *Not marked;* not regarded.

Unmarketable, un-mär'ket-a-bl, a. *Not marketable.*

Unmarred, un-märd', a. *Not marred.*

Unmarriageable, un-ma'rij-a-bl, a. *Not fit to be married.*

Unmarried, un-ma'rid, a. *Not married.*

Unmask, un-mask', vt. *To strip of a mask;* to lay open, as what is concealed.—*vi. To put off a mask.*

Unmasked, un-maskt', p.a. Open; exposed to view; not observed†.

Unmatched, un-macht', a. *Not matched;* matchless; having no match or equal; unparalleled.

Unmeaning, un-mēn'ing, a. *Having no*

meaning; not expressive; not indicating intelligence.
Unmeaningness, un-mēn'ing-nes, *n. Want of meaning.*
Unmeasured, un-me'zhūrd, *a. Not measured*; immense; infinite.
Unmeet, un-mēt', *a. Not meet*; not fit; not proper; not suitable.
Unmeetness, un-mēt'nes, *n. Quality of being unmeet*; unfitness; unsuitableness.
Unmelodious, un-mē-lō'di-us, *a. Not melodious*; wanting melody; harsh.
Unmelted, un-melt'ed, *a. Not melted*; undissolved; not softened.
Unmerciful, un-mėr'si-fu̇l, *a. Not merciful*; inhuman to such beings as are in one's power; not disposed to spare.
Unmercifully, un-mėr'si-fu̇l-li, *adv. Without mercy* or tenderness; cruelly.
Unmercifulness, un-mėr'si-fu̇l-nes, *n. Quality of being unmerciful*; want of tenderness; cruelty in the exercise of power.
Unmerited, un-me'rit-ed, *a. Not merited*; obtained without service; cruel; unjust.
Unmilitary, un-mi'li-ta-ri, *a. Not according to military rules* or customs.
Unmindful, un-mīnd'fu̇l, *a. Not mindful*; not heedful; regardless.
Unmindfully, un-mīnd'fu̇l-li, *adv. Carelessly*; heedlessly.
Unmindfulness, un-mīnd'fu̇l-nes, *n. Quality of being unmindful.*
Unmingled, un-ming'gld, *a. Not mingled*; not vitiated by foreign admixture.
Unministerial, un-mi'nis-tē"ri-al, *a. Not ministerial.*
Unministerially, un-mi'nis-tē"ri-al-li, *adv. Unsuitably to a minister.*
Unmistaken, un-mis-tāk'n, *a. Not mistaken*; sure.
Unmitigable, un-mi'tig-a-bl, *a. Not capable of being mitigated* or softened.
Unmitigated, un-mi'ti-gāt-ed, *a. Not mitigated*; not lessened.
Unmixed, Unmixt, un-mikst', un-mikst', *a. Not mixed*; unalloyed.
Unmodulated, un-mo'dū-lāt-ed, *a. Not modulated.*
Unmolested, un-mō-lest'ed, *a. Not molested*; free from disturbance.
Unmoor, un-mör', *vt. To release from a state of being moored.*
Unmortgaged, un-mor'gājd, *a. Not mortgaged*; not pledged.
Unmotherly, un-muᴛʜ'ėr-li, *a. Not becoming a mother.*
Unmoulded, un-mōld'ed, *a. Not moulded*; not shaped or formed.
Unmoved, un-möv̇d', *a. Not moved*; not changed in purpose; unshaken; not having the passions excited.
Unmoving, un-möv'ing, *a. Having no power to affect the passions.*
Unmuffled, un-muf'ld, *pp. Not muffled.*
Unmusical, un-mū'zik-al, *a. Not musical*; not harmonious or melodious.
Unmutilated, un-mū'ti-lāt-ed, *a. Not mutilated*; entire.
Unmuzzle, un-muz'l, *vt. To loose from a muzzle. ppr. unmuzzling, pret. & pp. unmuzzled.*
Unnamed, un-nāmd', *a. Not named.*
Unnatural, un-na'tūr-al, *a. Not natural*; contrary to the natural feelings; not in conformity to nature; not representing nature.
Unnaturally, un-na'tūr-al-li, *adv. In opposition to natural feelings.*
Unnavigable, un-na'vig-a-bl, *a. Not navigable*; innavigable.
Unnecessarily, un-ne'ses-sa-ri-li, *adv. Without necessity*; needlessly.

Unnecessary, un-ne'ses-sa-ri, *a. Not necessary*; needless; useless.
Unneighbourly, un-nā'bor-li, *a. Not neighbourly*; not becoming persons living near each other; not kind and friendly.—*adv.* In a manner not suitable to neighbours.
Unnerve, un-nėrv', *vt. To deprive of nerve*; to weaken; to enfeeble, as to unnerve the arm. *ppr.* unnerving, *pret. & pp.* unnerved.
Unnerved, un-nėrv̇d', *p.a.* Weak; feeble.
Unnoticed, un-nōt'ist, *a. Not noticed*; not treated with the usual marks of respect; not kindly and hospitably entertained.
Unnumbered, un-num'bėrd, *a. Not numbered*; innumerable.
Unobjectionable, un-ob-jek'shon-a-bl, *a. Not objectionable.*
Unobscured, un-ob-skūrd', *a. Not obscured*; not darkened.
Unobservant, un-ob-zėrv'ant, *a. Not observant*; not attentive.
Unobstructed, un-ob-strukt'ed, *a. Not obstructed*; not hindered; not stopped.
Unobtrusive, un-ob-trö'siv, *a. Not obtrusive*; not forward; modest.
Unoccupied, un-ok'kū-pid, *a. Not occupied*; being at leisure; not employed or taken up, as time.
Unoffending, un-of-fend'ing, *a. Not offending*; harmless; innocent.
Unofficial, un-of-fi'shi-al, *a. Not official*; not proceeding from due authority.
Unopposed, un-op-pōzd', *a. Not opposed*; not meeting with any obstruction.
Unorganized, un-or'gan-izd, *a. Not organized*; inorganized.
Unostentatious, un-os'ten-tā"shi-us, *a. Not ostentatious*; not boastful; modest; not glaring; not showy.
Unowned, un-ōnd', *a. Not owned*; not claimed; not avowed; not admitted as done by one's self.
Unpack, un-pak', *vt. To open, as things packed.*
Unpacked, un-pakt', *p.a. Not packed*; not collected by unlawful artifices, as a jury.
Unpaid, un-pād', *a. Not paid.*
Unpalatable, un-pa'lat-a-bl, *a. Not palatable*; not such as to be relished.
Unparagoned, un-pa'ra-gond, *a.* Unmatched.
Unparalleled, un-pa'ral-leld, *a. Having no parallel* or equal; unmatched.
Unpardonable, un-pär'dn-a-bl, *a. Not to be pardoned* or forgiven.
Unpardoned, un-pär'dnd, *a. Not pardoned*; not forgiven.
Unparliamentary, un-pär'li-a-ment"a-ri, *a. Contrary to the usages or rules of proceeding in parliament.*
Unpathetic, un-pa-thet'ik, *a. Not pathetic*; not adapted to move the passions or excite emotion.
Unpatriotic, un-pā'tri-ot"ik, *a. Not patriotic.*
Unpatriotically, un-pā'tri-ot"ik-al-li, *adv. Not patriotically.*
Unpaved, un-pāvd', *a. Not paved.*
Unpay†, un-pā', *vt. To undo, as villany.*
Unpeople, un-pē'pl, *vt. To deprive of people or inhabitants*; to depopulate. *ppr.* unpeopling, *pret. & pp.* unpeopled.
Unperceivable, un-pėr-sēv'a-bl, *a. Not to be perceived*; not perceptible.
Unperceived, un-pėr-sēv̇d', *a. Not perceived*; not observed.
Unperformed, un-pėr-formd', *a. Not performed*; not done.
Unperplexed, un-pėr-plekst', *a. Not perplexed*; not embarrassed; simple.

Unpersuasive, un-pėr-swā'siv, *a. Not persuasive.*
Unperused, un-pē-rūzd', *a. Not perused*; not read.
Unperverted, un-pėr-vėrt'ed, *a. Not perverted.*
Unphilosophic, Unphilosophical, un-fi'lō-sof"ik, un-fi'lō-sof"ik-al, *a. Not according to the principles of sound philosophy*; contrary to right reason.
Unphilosophically, un-fi'lō-sof"ik-al-li, *adv. In a manner contrary to the principles of sound philosophy.*
Unpierced, un-pėrst', *a. Not pierced.*
Unpin, un-pin', *vt. To loose from pins*; to unfasten. *ppr.* unpinning, *pret. & pp.* unpinned.
Unpitied, un-pi'tid, *a. Not pitied*; not regarded with sympathetic sorrow.
Unpitying, un-pi'ti-ing, *a. Not pitying*; showing no compassion.
Unpleasant, un-ple'zant, *a. Not pleasant*; disagreeable.
Unpleasantly, un-ple'zant-li, *adv. In a manner not pleasing*; uneasily.
Unpleasantness, un-ple'zant-nes, *n. State or quality of being unpleasant*; disagreeableness.
Unpledged, un-plejd', *a. Not pledged.*
Unpliable, un-pli'a-bl, *a. Not pliable.*
Unpliant, un-pli'ant, *a. Not pliant.*
Unpoetic, Unpoetical, un-pō-et'ik, un-pō-et'ik-al, *a. Not poetical*; not having the beauties of verse.
Unpoetically, un-pō-et'ik-al-li, *adv. In a manner unworthy of a poet.*
Unpolarized, un-pō'lär-izd, *a. Not polarized*; not having polarity.
Unpolished, un-po'lisht, *a. Not polished*; not refined in manners; plain.
Unpolite, un-pō-līt', *a. Not polite*; not elegant; not courteous.
Unpolitely, un-pō-līt'li, *adv. In an uncivil or rude manner.*
Unpoliteness, un-pō-līt'nes, *n. Quality of being unpolite*; rudeness.
Unpolluted, un-pol-lūt'ed, *a. Not polluted*; not defiled; not corrupted.
Unpopular, un-po'pū-lär, *a. Not popular*; not having the public favour.
Unpopularity, un-po'pū-lä"ri-ti, *n. The state of being unpopular.*
Unpopularly, un-po'pū-lär-li, *adv. Not popularly.*
Unpractised, un-prak'tist, *a. Not practised*; not skilled; raw.
Unprecedented, un-pre'sē-dent-ed, *a. Having no precedent*; not having the authority of prior example.
Unprejudiced, un-pre'jū-dist, *a. Not prejudiced*; not warped by prejudice; free from bias; impartial.
Unpremeditated, un-prē-med'i-tāt-ed, *a. Not premeditated*; not previously prepared in the mind; not done by design.
Unprepared, un-prē-pārd', *a. Not prepared*; not ready; not prepared, by holiness of life, for the event of death.
Unpreparedness, un-prē-pārd'nes, *n. State of being unprepared.*
Unprepossessed, un-prē'poz-zest", *a. Not prepossessed*; not partial.
Unprepossessing, un-prē'poz-zes"ing, *a. Not prepossessing.*
Unpresuming, un-prē-zūm'ing, *a. Not presuming*; not too confident or bold.
Unpresumptuous, un-prē-zump'tū-us, *a. Not presumptuous*; modest.
Unpretending, un-prē-tend'ing, *a. Not pretending*; not claiming distinction.
Unprincely, un-prins'li, *a. Unbecoming a prince*; not resembling a prince.
Unprincipled, un-prin'si-pld, *a. Not principled*; having no good moral principles.

Fāte, fär, fat, fạll; mē, met, hėr; pīne, pin; nōte, not, möve; tūbe, tub, bu̇ll; oil, pound.

Unprinted, un-print'ed, a. *Not printed,* as a literary work; white, as cotton.
Unprivileged, un-pri'vi-lejd, a. *Not privileged.*
Unprized, un-prizd', a. *Not prized.*
Unproductive, un-prŏ-duk'tiv, a. *Not productive;* barren; not profitable; not producing profit or interest, as capital; not efficient.
Unproductiveness, un-prŏ-duk'tiv-nes, n. *The state of being unproductive.*
Unprofaned, un-prŏ-fānd', a. *Not profaned;* not violated.
Unprofessional, un-prŏ-fe'shon-al, a. *Not professional;* not according to the rules or proprieties of a profession.
Unprofitable, un-pro'fit-a-bl, a. *Not profitable;* producing no improvement or advantage; useless; not useful to others.
Unprofitableness, un-pro'fit-a-bl-nes, n. *The state of producing no profit or good;* uselessness; inutility.
Unprofitably, un-pro'fit-a-bli, adv. *Without profit;* to no good purpose.
Unprohibited, un-prŏ-hib'it-ed, a. *Not prohibited;* not forbid; lawful.
Unprolific, un-prŏ-lif'ik, a. *Not prolific;* not producing young or fruit.
Unpromising, un-pro'mis-ing, a. *Not promising;* not affording a favourable prospect of success, of excellence, &c.
Unpronounceable, un-prŏ-nouns'a-bl, a. *That cannot be pronounced.*
Unprophetic, Unprophetical, un-pro-fet'ik, un-prŏ-fet'ik-al, a. *Not prophetic;* not predicting future events.
Unpropitiated, un-prŏ-pi'shi-āt-ed, a. *Not propitiated.*
Unpropitious, un-prŏ-pi'shi-us, a. *Not propitious;* inauspicious.
Unpropitiously, un-prŏ-pi'shi-us-li, adv. *Unfavourably;* unkindly.
Unpropitiousness, un-prŏ-pi'shi-us-nes, n. *State of being unpropitious.*
Unprosperous, un-pros'pėr-us, a. *Not prosperous;* unfortunate.
Unprotected, un-prŏ-tekt'ed, a. *Not protected;* not countenanced.
Unprotectedly, un-prŏ-tekt'ed-li, adv. *Without being protected.*
Unproved, un-prōvd', a. *Not proved;* not established as true by argument or evidence.
Unprovided, un-prŏ-vīd'ed, a. *Not provided;* unfurnished; unsupplied.
Unprovoked, un-prŏ-vōkt', a. *Not provoked;* not incited.
Unpublished, un-pub'lisht, a. *Not published;* secret; private.
Unpunished, un-pu'nisht, a. *Not punished;* suffered to pass with impunity.
Unpurchased, un-pėr'chast, a. *Not purchased;* not bought.
Unpurified, un-pū'ri-fīd, a. *Not purified;* not cleansed from sin.
Unqualified, un-kwo'li-fīd, a. *Not qualified;* not having the requisite talents or accomplishments; not having taken the requisite oath or oaths; not modified by conditions.
Unqualitied†, un-kwo'li-tid, a. Deprived of the usual faculties.
Unquelled, un-kweld', a. *Not quelled.*
Unquenchable, un-kwensh'a-bl, a. *That cannot be quenched;* inextinguishable.
Unquenched, un-kwensht', a. *Not quenched;* not extinguished.
Unquestionable, un-kwest'shon-a-bl, a. *Not questionable;* not to be questioned; indubitable; certain.
Unquestionably, un-kwest'shon-a-bli, adv. *Without doubt;* indubitably.
Unquestioned, un-kwest'shond, a. *Not questioned;* not doubted; not examined; indisputable; not to be opposed.

Unquiet, un-kwī'et, a. *Not quiet;* not calm or tranquil; unsatisfied; restless.
Unquietness, un-kwī'et-nes, n. *Want of quiet;* want of tranquillity; restlessness; turbulence; disposition to excite disturbance.
Unransomed, un-ran'somd, a. *Not ransomed.*
Unravel, un-ra'vel, vt. *To free from a ravelled state;* to disentangle; to unfold; to clear up, as the plot or intrigue of a play. — vi. To be unfolded; to be disentangled. *ppr.* unravelling, *pret. & pp.* unravelled.
Unreadable, un-rēd'a-bl, a. *Not readable;* not legible; that cannot be read.
Unreadiness, un-re'di-nes, n. *Want of readiness;* want of dexterity; want of preparation.
Unready, un-re'di, a. *Not ready;* not fit; not quick; awkward; ungainly; not dressed†.—vt. To undress†.
Unreal, un-rē'al, a. *Not real;* not substantial; having appearance only.
Unreality, un-rē-al'i-ti, n. *Want of reality* or real existence.
Unrealized, un-rē'al-īzd, a. *Not realized.*
Unreaped, un-rēpt', a. *Not reaped.*
Unreasonable, un-rē'zon-a-bl, a. *Not agreeable to reason.*
Unreasonableness, un-rē'zon-a-bl-nes, n. *State or quality of being unreasonable;* exorbitance; excess of demand, passion, and the like.
Unreasonably, un-rē'zon-a-bli, adv. *In a manner contrary to reason.*
Unreasoned, un-rē'zond, a. *Not reasoned;* not derived from reasoning.
Unreasoning, un-rē'zon-ing, p.a. *Not having reasoning faculties.*
Unreceived, un-rē-sēvd', a. *Not received;* not adopted; not embraced.
Unreclaimed, un-rē-klāmd', a. *Not reclaimed;* not tamed; not called back from vice to virtue.
Unrecognized, un-re'kog-nizd, a. *Not recognized;* not acknowledged or known.
Unrecommended, un-re'kom-mend"ed, a. *Not recommended.*
Unreconciled, un-re'kon-sīld, a. *Not reconciled;* not having become favourable; not having made peace with God through faith in Christ.
Unrecorded, un-rē-kord'ed, a. *Not recorded;* not registered.
Unrecuring†, un-rē-kūr'ing, a. *Incapable of being cured.*
Unredeemed, un-rē-dēmd', a. *Not redeemed;* not ransomed; not paid.
Unredressed, un-rē-drest', a. *Not redressed;* not relieved from injustice; not reformed.
Unreduced, un-rē-dūst', a. *Not reduced;* not lessened in size or amount.
Unrefined, un-rē-fīnd', a. *Not refined.*
Unreflecting, un-rē-flekt'ing, a. *Not reflecting.*
Unreformed, un-rē-formd', a. *Not reformed;* not freed from error.
Unrefreshed, un-rē-fresht', a. *Not refreshed;* not relieved from fatigue.
Unrefuted, un-rē-fūt'ed, a. *Not refuted.*
Unregarded, un-rē-gärd'ed, a. *Not regarded;* not heeded; slighted.
Unregeneracy, un-rē-jen'ė-rā-si, n. *State of being unregenerate.*
Unregenerate, un-rē-jen'ė-rāt, a. *Not regenerated;* not renewed in heart.
Unregistered, un-re'jis-tėrd, a. *Not registered;* not recorded.
Unregretted, un-rē-gret'ed, a. *Not regretted;* not lamented.
Unregulated, un-rē'gū-lāt-ed, a. *Not regulated;* not adjusted by rule or method; not put in good order.

Unrehearsed, un-rē-hėrst', a. *Not rehearsed;* not repeated, as words.
Unrelenting, un-rē-lent'ing, a. *Not relenting;* hard; cruel.
Unrelentingly, un-rē-lent'ing-li, adv. *Without relenting.*
Unrelieved, un-rē-lēvd', a. *Not relieved;* not succoured; not delivered from distress.
Unremitted, un-rē-mit'ed, a. *Not remitted;* not forgiven; not abated.
Unremitting, un-rē-mit'ing, a. *Not remitting;* not relaxing for a time; continued.
Unremittingly, un-rē-mit'ing-li, adv. *Without abatement or cessation.*
Unrenewed, un-rē-nūd', a. *Not renewed;* not made anew; not regenerated.
Unrenowned, un-rē-nound', a. *Not renowned or eminent.*
Unrepaid, un-rē-pād', a. *Not repaid.*
Unrepealed, un-rē-pēld', a. *Not repealed;* not revoked or abrogated.
Unrepentant, Unrepenting, un-rē-pent'ant, un-rē-pent'ing, a. *Not repenting;* not contrite for sin.
Unrepented, un-rē-pent'ed, a. *Not repented of.*
Unrepining, un-rē-pīn'ing, a. *Not repining;* not peevishly murmuring.
Unrepresented, un-re'prē-zent"ed, a. *Not represented.*
Unreprievable†, un-rē-prēv'a-bl, a. *That cannot be reprieved.*
Unreprieved, un-rē-prēvd', a. *Not reprieved;* not respited.
Unreproved, un-rē-prōvd', a. *Not reproved;* not censured.
Unreserved, un-rē-zėrvd', a. *Not reserved;* not withheld in part; entire; open; concealing nothing; free.
Unreservedly, un-rē-zėrv'ed-li, adv. *Without reservation.*
Unreservedness, un-rē-zėrv'ed-nes, n. *Quality of being unreserved;* frankness.
Unresigned, un-rē-zīnd', a. *Not resigned;* not submissive to God's will.
Unresisted, un-rē-zist'ed, a. *Not resisted;* not opposed.
Unresisting, un-rē-zist'ing, a. *Not making resistance;* yielding to physical force; submissive; humble.
Unresistingly, un-rē-zist'ing-li, adv. *Without resistance.*
Unresolved, un-rē-zolvd', a. *Not resolved;* not determined; not solved.
Unrest, un-rest', n. Disquiet.
Unrestored, un-rē-stōrd', a. *Not restored;* not restored to a former place.
Unrestrained, un-rē-strānd', a. *Not restrained;* licentious; loose.
Unrestricted, un-rē-strikt'ed, a. *Not restricted;* not limited or confined.
Unreturned, un-rē-tėrnd', a. *Not returned.*
Unrevealed, un-rē-vēld', a. *Not revealed;* not discovered; not disclosed.
Unrevenged, un-rē-venjd', a. *Not revenged;* not vindicated by just punishment.
Unrevered, un-rē-vērd', a. *Not revered.*
Unreverend†, un-re've-rend, a. Disrespectful.
Unrevised, un-rē-vizd', a. *Not revised;* not reviewed, corrected, and amended.
Unrevived, un-rē-vīvd', a. *Not revived.*
Unrig, un-rig', vt. *To strip,* as a ship, of both standing and running *rigging,* &c. *ppr.* unrigging, *pret. & pp.* unrigged.
Unrighteous, un-rīt'ē-us, a. *Not righteous;* not conformed in heart and life to the divine law; contrary to law and equity. [Sax. *unrihtwis.*]
Unrighteously, un-rīt'ē-us-li, adv. Unjustly; wickedly; sinfully.
Unrighteousness, un-rīt'ē-us-nes, n.

ch, *chain*; j, *job*; g, *go*; ng, *sing*; ᴛʜ, *then*; th, *thin*; w, *wig*; wh, *whig*; zh, *azure*; † *obsolete.*

State or quality of being unrighteous; injustice; wickedness.
Unripe, un-rīp′, a. Not ripe; not mature; not yet proper; too early.
Unripeness, un-rīp′nes, n. Want of ripeness; immaturity.
Unrivalled, un-rī′vald, a. Not rivalled; having no competitor; peerless.
Unrobe, un-rōb′, vt. To strip of a robe; to undress. ppr. unrobing, pret. & pp. unrobed.
Unroll, un-rōl′, vt. To open what is rolled; to display.
Unromantic, un-rō-man′tik, a. Not romantic; not fanciful.
Unroof, un-röf′, vt. To strip off, as the roof or covering of a house.
Unroot, un-röt′, vt. To tear up by the roots; to extirpate; to eradicate.
Unroost, un-röst′, vt. To drive from the roost.
Unruffled, un-ruf′ld, a. Not ruffled; calm; tranquil; not agitated.
Unruliness, un-rö′li-nes, n. State of being unruly; turbulence.
Unruly, un-rö′li, a. Not subject to rule; licentious; turbulent.
Unsaddle, un-sad′l, vt. To strip of a saddle. ppr. unsaddling, pret. & pp. unsaddled.
Unsafe, un-sāf′, a. Not safe; not free from danger; hazardous.
Unsafely, un-sāf′li, adv. Not safely; not without danger.
Unsafeness, un-sāf′nes, n. State of being unsafe.
Unsaid, un-sād′, p.a. Not said; recanted.
Unsaleable, un-sāl′a-bl, a. Not saleable; not meeting a ready sale.
Unsaleableness, un-sāl′a-bl-nes, n. Quality of being unsaleable.
Unsanctified, un-sangk′ti-fīd, a. Not sanctified; unholy; not consecrated.
Unsanctioned, un-sangk′shond, a. Not sanctioned; not authorized.
Unsated, un-sāt′ed, a. Not sated.
Unsatisfactorily, un-sa′tis-fak′tō-ri-li, adv. So as not to give satisfaction.
Unsatisfactory, un-sa′tis-fak′tō-ri, a. Not satisfactory; not convincing the mind; not giving content.
Unsatisfied, un-sa′tis-fīd, a. Not satisfied; not filled; not settled in opinion: not fully persuaded; not fully paid.
Unsatisfying, un-sa′tis-fī-ing, a. Not satisfying; not giving content; not convincing the mind.
Unsavouriness, un-sā′vo-ri-nes, n. Quality of being unsavoury.
Unsavoury, un-sā′vo-ri, a. Not savoury; having a bad taste or smell; unpleasing; disgusting.
Unsay, un-sā′, vt. To recall, as what has been said; to retract. ppr. unsaying, pret. & pp. unsaid.
Unscathed, un-skāᴛʜd′, a. Not scathed.
Unscholarly, un-skol′är-li, a. Not suitable to a scholar.
Unscientific, un-sī′en-tif″ik, a. Not scientific; not versed in science; not founded on the methods of science.
Unscientifically, un-sī′en-tif″ik-al-li, adv. In an unscientific manner.
Unscrew, un-skrū′, vt. To draw the screws from; to loose from screws.
Unscriptural, un-skrip′tūr-al, a. Not scriptural; not agreeable to the Scriptures.
Unscripturally, un-skrip′tūr-al-li, adv. In an unscriptural manner.
Unscrupulous, un-skrū′pū-lus, a. Not scrupulous; having no scruples.
Unscrupulously, un-skrū′pū-lus-li, adv. In an unscrupulous manner.
Unseal, un-sēl′, vt. To break or remove the seal of; to open, as what is sealed.

Unsealed, un-sēld′, p.a. Not sealed; having no seal, or the seal broken.
Unsearchable, un-sėrch′a-bl, a. That cannot be searched or explored; hidden; inscrutable.
Unsearchableness, un-sėrch′a-bl-nes, n. The quality of being unsearchable.
Unsearchably, un-sėrch′a-bli, adv. In a manner so as not to be explored.
Unsearched, un-sėrcht′, a. Not searched.
Unseasonable, un-sē′zn-a-bl, a. Not seasonable; not suited to the time or occasion; not agreeable to the time of the year.
Unseasonableness, un-sē′zn-a-bl-nes, n. The quality of being unseasonable.
Unseasonably, un-sē′zn-a-bli, adv. Not seasonably; not in due time.
Unseasoned, un-sē′znd, a. Not seasoned; not salted; not sprinkled with anything to give relish; not accustomed.
Unseat, un-sēt′, vt. To throw or expel from the seat.
Unseated, un-sēt′ed, p. a. Not seated; having no seat or bottom.
Unseaworthy, un-sē′wėr-ᴛʜi, a. Not seaworthy; not fit for a voyage.
Unsecured, un-sē-kūrd′, a. Not secured.
Unseem†, un-sēm′, vi. Not to seem.
Unseemliness, un-sēm′li-nes, n. State or quality of being unseemly; uncomeliness; indecency; impropriety.
Unseemly, un-sēm′li, a. Not seemly; unbecoming; indecent. — adv. Indecently.
Unseen, un-sēn′, a. Not seen; not discovered; invisible; not discoverable.
Unselfish, un-self′ish, a. Not selfish.
Unselfishly, un-self′ish-li, adv. Without selfishness.
Unserviceable, un-sėr′vis-a-bl, a. Not serviceable; useless.
Unsettle, un-set′l, vt. To move from a settled state; to move from a place; to make uncertain; to derange.—vi. To become unfixed. ppr. unsettling, pret. & pp. unsettled.
Unsettled, un-set′ld, p. a. Not settled; not determined, as doctrines; changeable; wavering, as the mind; having no fixed place of abode; having no inhabitants; not having deposited its lees, as liquor.
Unsettledness, un-set′ld-nes, n. The state of being unsettled.
Unsex, un-seks′, vt. To deprive of sex.
Unshackle, un-shak′l, vt. To loose from shackles; to unfetter. ppr. unshackling, pret. & pp. unshackled.
Unshaded, un-shād′ed, a. Not shaded; not having shades in colouring.
Unshadowed, un-sha′dōd, a. Not shadowed; not clouded; not darkened.
Unshaken, un-shāk′n, a. Not shaken; not moved; firm; fixed.
Unshale†, un-shāl′, vt. To strip off husks from.
Unshaped, Unshapen, un-shāpt′, un-shāp′n, a. Misshapen; deformed; ugly.
Unsheathe, un-shēᴛʜ′, vt. To draw from the sheath or scabbard. ppr. unsheathing, pret. & pp. unsheathed.
Unsheltered, un-shel′tėrd, a. Not sheltered; not defended from danger.
Unshielded, un-shēld′ed, a. Not defended by a shield; not protected.
Unship, un-ship′, vt. To take out of a ship; to remove from the place where it is fixed, as an oar, &c. ppr. unshipping, pret. & pp. unshipped.
Unshrinking, un-shringk′ing, a. Not shrinking; not recoiling.
Unshrinkingly, un-shringk′ing-li, adv. Without shrinking.
Unshrouded, un-shroud′ed, a. Not shrouded or covered.

Unsightliness, un-sīt′li-nes, n. State or quality of being unsightly; ugliness.
Unsightly, un-sīt′li, a. Not sightly; disagreeable to the sight.
Unsisterly, un-sis′tėr-li, adv. or a. Not like a sister.
Unsisting†, un-sist′ing, a. Not opposing or resisting.
Unskilful, un-skil′ful, a. Not skilful; wanting the dexterity acquired by observation and experience.
Unskilfully, un-skil′ful-li, adv. Without skill, knowledge, or dexterity.
Unskilfulness, un-skil′ful-nes, n. Quality of being unskilful; want of that readiness in execution which is acquired by experience and observation.
Unskilled, un-skild′, a. Wanting skill; destitute of practical knowledge.
Unslacked, un-slakt′, a. Not slacked, as lime; not saturated with water.
Unslackened, un-slak′nd, a. Not slackened.
Unslaked, un-slākt′, a. Not slaked; unquenched, as thirst.
Unsmoked, un-smōkt′, a. Not smoked; not dried in smoke.
Unsociable, un-sō′shi-a-bl, a. Not social; not having the qualities which are proper for society; reserved.
Unsociability, un-sō′shi-a-bil″i-ti, n. State of being unsociable.
Unsocial, un-sō′shi-al, a. Not social.
Unsoiled, un-soild′, a. Not soiled; not stained; not tainted, as character.
Unsold, un-sōld′, a. Not sold.
Unsoldier-like, Unsoldierly, un-sōl′jėr-lik, un-sōl′jėr-li, a. Not becoming a soldier.
Unsolicited, un-sō-lis′it-ed, a. Not solicited; unasked; not asked for.
Unsolved, un-solvd′, a. Not solved.
Unsophisticated, un-sō-fis′ti-kāt-ed, a. Not sophisticated; pure; simple.
Unsorted, un-sort′ed, a. Not sorted.
Unsought, un-sąt′, a. Not sought; not searched for; had without searching; not explored.
Unsound, un-sound′, a. Not sound; defective; questionable; not sound in intellect; not sound in character; not honest; not to be trusted; not solid; not sincere; not material; erroneous in point of doctrine; wrong; not calm.
Unsoundness, un-sound′nes, n. State or quality of being unsound; want of orthodoxy; corruptness; weakness, as of body.
Unsoured, un-sourd′, a. Not made sour; not made morose or crabbed.
Unsowed, Unsown, un-sōd′, un-sōn′, a. Not sowed; not sown.
Unsparing, un-spār′ing, a. Not sparing.
Unsparingly, un-spār′ing-li, adv. In abundance; lavishly.
Unspeak†, un-spēk′, vt. To retract.
Unspeakable, un-spēk′a-bl, a. That cannot be spoken or uttered.
Unspeakably, un-spēk′a-bli, adv. In an unspeakable manner.
Unspent, un-spent′, a. Not spent; not having lost its force, as a cannon-ball.
Unsphere, un-sfēr′, vt. To remove from its orb.
Unspoiled, un-spoild′, a. Not blundered.
Unspotted, un-spot′ed, a. Not spotted; untainted with guilt; unblemished.
Unspottedness, un-spot′ed-nes, n. State of being unspotted.
Unsquared, un-skwārd′, a. Not formed; irregular.
Unstable, un-stā′bl, a. Not stable; not fixed; wavering.
Unstaid, un-stād′, a. Not staid; not settled in judgment; fickle.

Fäte, fär, fat, fąll; mē, met, hėr; pīne, pin; nōte, not, mōve; tübe, tub, bųll; oil, pound.

UNRIPE   430   UNSTAID

Unstained, un-stānd', a. Not stained; not tarnished; not dishonoured.
Unstamped, un-stampt', a. Not stamped.
Unstanched, un-stánsht', a. Not stanched; not stopped, as blood.
Unstate†, un-stāt', vt. To put out of dignity.
Unstatesmanlike, un-stāts'man-lik, a. Not becoming a statesman.
Unstaunched, un-stánsht', a. Not stopped; not stayed.
Unsteadfast, un-sted'fast, a. Not steadfast; not firmly adhering to a purpose.
Unsteadily, un-sted'i-li, adv. Without steadiness; in a fickle manner.
Unsteadiness, un-sted'i-nes, n. State of being unsteady; unstableness; irresolution; vacillation.
Unsteady, un-sted'i, a. Not steady; irresolute; changeable.
Unstooping, un-stöp'ing, a. Not bending; not yielding.
Unstop, un-stop', vt. To free from that which stops; to free from a stopple, as a bottle; to open. ppr. unstopping, pret. & pp. unstopped.
Unstopped, un-stopt', p.a. Not stopped; not meeting any resistance.
Unstrained, un-strānd', a. Not strained; easy; not forced; natural.
Unstratified, un-stra'ti-fīd, a. Not stratified; not arranged in strata.
Unstring, un-string', vt. To deprive of a string; to relax the string or strings of; to loosen, as the nerves; to take from a string, as beads. ppr. unstringing, pret. & pp. unstrung.
Unstudied, un-stu'did, a. Not studied; not laboured; easy; natural.
Unstuffed, un-stuft', a. Not stuffed.
Unsubdued, un-sub-dūd', a. Not subdued; not brought into subjection.
Unsubmissive, un-sub-mis'iv, a. Not submissive; disobedient.
Unsubscribed, un-sub-skrībd', a. Not subscribed.
Unsubstantial, un-sub-stan'shi-al, a. Not substantial; not solid; not real.
Unsubstantially, un-sub-stan'shi-al-li, adv. Without substance or solidity.
Unsubstantiated, un-sub-stan'shi-āt-ed, a. Not substantiated.
Unsubverted, un-sub-vėrt'ed, a. Not subverted; not overthrown.
Unsuccessful, un-suk-ses'fụl, a. Not successful; not fortunate.
Unsuccessfully, un-suk-ses'fụl-li, adv. Without success; unfortunately.
Unsuccessfulness, un-suk-ses'fụl-nes, n. State of being unsuccessful.
Unsuitable, un-sūt'a-bl, a. Not suitable; unfit; not congruous; unbecoming.
Unsuitableness, un-sūt'a-bl-nes, n. State of being unsuitable; unfitness.
Unsuited, un-sūt'ed, a. Not suited; not fitted; not accommodated.
Unsuiting, un-sūt'ing, a. Not suiting; not fitting; not becoming.
Unsullied, un-sul'lid, a. Not sullied; not tarnished; not disgraced; free from imputation of evil.
Unsung, un-sung', a. Not sung; not celebrated in verse; not recited in verse.
Unsunned, un-sund', a. Not exposed to the sun.
Unsupplied, un-sup-plīd', a. Not supplied.
Unsupported, un-sup-pōrt'ed, a. Not supported; not upheld; not assisted.
Unsuppressed, un-sup-prest', a. Not suppressed; not extinguished.
Unsure, un-shūr', a. Not fixed.
Unsurmounted, un-sėr-mount'ed, a. Not surmounted.
Unsurpassed, un-sėr-past', a. Not surpassed; not exceeded.

Unsuspected, un-sus-pekt'ed, a. Not suspected.
Unsuspecting, un-sus-pekt'ing, a. Not suspecting; free from suspicion.
Unsuspicious, un-sus-pi'shi-us, a. Having no suspicion; not to be suspected.
Unsuspiciously, un-sus-pi'shi-us-li, adv. Without suspicion.
Unsustained, un-sus-tānd', a. Not sustained; not supported; not seconded.
Unswayable†, un-swā'a-bl, a. Not to be governed or influenced by another.
Unswayed, un-swād', a. Not swayed; not controlled or influenced.
Unswept, un-swept', a. Not swept; not cleaned with a broom; not brushed.
Unswerving, un-swėrv'ing, a. Not swerving; not deviating from any rule.
Unswervingly, un-swėrv'ing-li, adv. Without swerving.
Unsworn, un-sworn', a. Not sworn; not having taken an oath.
Unsymmetrical, un-sim-met'rik-al, a. Not symmetrical; wanting symmetry.
Unsympathizing, un-sim'pa-thīz-ing, a. Not sympathizing.
Unsystematic, Unsystematical, un-sis'tem-at"ik, un-sis'tem-at"ik-al, a. Not systematic.
Unsystematically, un-sis'tem-at"ik-al-li, adv. Without system.
Untainted, un-tānt'ed, a. Not tainted; not sullied; unblemished; not rendered unsavoury by putrescence; not charged with a crime.
Untaintedness, un-tānt'ed-nes, n. State or quality of being untainted.
Untamable, un-tām'a-bl, a. That cannot be tamed; that cannot be reclaimed from a wild state; not to be reduced to control.
Untamed, un-tāmd', a. Not tamed; not reclaimed from wildness; not brought under control; not softened by culture.
Untangle†, un-tang'gl, vt. To loose from intricacy.
Untarnished, un-tär'nisht, a. Not tarnished; unblemished.
Untasted, un-tāst'ed, a. Not tasted; not tried by the taste; not enjoyed.
Untaught, un-tąt', a. Not taught; unlettered; unskilled; not having use or practice.
Untaxed, un-takst', a. Not taxed.
Unteachable, un-tēch'a-bl, a. Not teachable; that cannot be taught.
Untempered, un-tem'pėrd, a. Not tempered; not duly mixed for use.
Untempted, un-temt'ed, a. Not tempted.
Untenable, un-ten'a-bl, a. Not tenable; that cannot be maintained.
Untenanted, un-ten'ant-ed, a. Not occupied by a tenant; not inhabited.
Untended, un-tend'ed, a. Not tended.
Untender, un-ten'dėr, a. Wanting softness.
Untendered, un-ten'dėrd, a. Not tendered; not offered.
Unthankful, un-thangk'fụl, a. Not thankful; ungrateful.
Unthankfully, un-thangk'fụl-li, adv. Without thanks.
Unthankfulness, un-thangk'fụl-nes, n. Quality of being unthankful; want of a sense of benefits; ingratitude.
Untheoretical, un-thē'ō-ret"ik-al, a. Not depending on theory.
Unthink†, un-thingk', vt. To recall or dismiss, as a thought.
Unthinking, un-thingk'ing, a. Not thinking; inconsiderate; not indicating thought.
Unthinkingly, un-thingk'ing-li, adv. Thoughtlessly; without reflection.
Unthoughtful, un-thąt'fụl, a. Not thoughtful; thoughtless; heedless.

Unthought-of, un-thąt'ov, a. Not thought of; not regarded.
Unthread, un-thred', vt. To draw or take out a thread from; to loose.
Unthrift, un-thrift', n. One who is thriftless; a prodigal; one who wastes his estate by extravagance.—a. Profuse.
Unthriftily, un-thrift'i-li, adv. Without frugality.
Unthriftiness, un-thrift'i-nes, n. Quality of being unthrifty; profusion.
Unthrifty, un-thrift'i, a. Not thrifty; lavish; profuse; not in a state of improvement.
Untidily, un-tī'di-li, adv. In an untidy manner.
Untidiness, un-tī'di-nes, n. Want of tidiness or neatness.
Untidy, un-tī'di, a. Not tidy; not neatly dressed.
Untie, un-tī', vt. To free from being tied; to unbind; to loosen from coils; to resolve; to unfold; to clear. ppr. untying, pret. & pp. untied.
Untied, un-tīd', p.a. Not tied; not fastened with a knot.
Until, un'til, prep. Into (used of time); preceding a sentence or clause, to; to the point or place of; to the degree that. [Sax. on, and til, to.]
Untilled, un-tild', a. Not tilled.
Untimbered, un-tim'bėrd, a. Not furnished with timber; weak.
Untimely, un-tīm'li, a. Not timely; happening before the natural time.—adv. Before the natural time.
Untirable†, un-tīr'a-bl, a. Indefatigable.
Untired, un-tīrd', a. Not tired.
Untiring, un-tīr'ing, a. Not becoming tired or exhausted.
Untitled, un-tī'tld, a. Having no title.
Unto, un-tö', prep. To. [Sax. on, in, and to.]
Untold, un-tōld', a. Not told; not revealed; not numbered.
Untouched, un-tucht', a. Not touched; not affected; not meddled with.
Untoward, un-tō'ward, a. Not toward; perverse; not easily taught; ungraceful; troublesome.
Untowardly, un-tō'ward-li, a. Not towardly.—adv. Perversely; ungainly.
Untowardness, un-tō'ward-nes, n. Quality or state of being untoward.
Untracked, un-trakt', a. Not tracked.
Untraded†, un-trād'ed, a. Unusual.
Untrained, un-trānd', a. Not trained.
Untrammelled, un-tram'meld, a. Not trammelled; not shackled.
Untransferred, un-trans-fėrd', a. Not transferred; not conveyed to another.
Untranslatable, un-trans-lāt'a-bl, a. Not capable of being translated.
Untranslated, un-trans-lāt'ed, a. Not translated.
Untransposed, un-trans-pōzd', a. Not transposed; having the natural order.
Untravelled, un-tra'veld, a. Not travelled; having never seen foreign countries.
Untraversed, un-tra'vėrst, a. Not traversed; not passed over.
Untread†, un-tred', vt. To tread back.
Untried, un-trīd', a. Not tried; not heard and determined in law.
Untrimmed, un-trimd', a. Not trimmed.
Untrod, Untrodden, un-trod', un-trod'n, a. Not having been trod.
Untroubled, un-tru'bld, a. Not troubled; not ruffled; free from passion; clear.
Untrue, un-trö', a. Not true; false; not faithful to another; disloyal; inconstant, as a lover.—n. An untruth.
Untruly, un-trö'li, adv. Not truly.
Untrusted, un-trust'ed, a. Not trusted.
Untrusty, un-trust'i, a. Not trusty.

ch, chain; j, job; g, go; ng, sing; ᴛʜ, then; th, thin; w, wig; wh, whig; zh, azure; † obsolete.

Untruth, un-trōth', n. *Contrariety to truth;* falsehood; want of veracity; treachery.†
Untruthful, un-trōth'fμl, a. *Not truthful;* wanting in veracity.
Untunable, un-tūn'a-bl, a. *Not tunable;* not harmonious.
Untune, un-tūn', vt. *To put out of tune;* to make incapable of harmony. ppr. untuning, pret. & pp. untuned.
Untuned, un-tūnd', p.a. *Not tuned;* made incapable of producing harmony.
Untutored, un-tū'tord, a. *Not tutored.*
Untwine, un-twīn', vt. *To untwist;* to disentangle. ppr. untwining, pret. & pp. untwined.
Untwist, un-twist', vt. *To open, as threads twisted;* to disentangle, as intricacy.
Unurged†, un-ėrjd', a. *Not incited.*
Unused, un-ūzd', a. *Not put to use;* not employed; not accustomed.
Unusual, un-ū'zhū-al, a. *Not usual;* not common; rare.
Unutterable, un-ut'tėr-a-bl, a. *That cannot be uttered or expressed.*
Unutterably, un-ut'tėr-a-bli, adv. *In an unutterable manner.*
Unvalued, un-va'lūd, a. *Not valued;* not prized; not estimated.
Unvaried, un-vā'rid, a. *Not varied.*
Unvarnished, un-vär'nisht, a. *Not overlaid with varnish;* not artfully embellished; plain.
Unvarying, un-vā'ri-ing, a. *Not varying;* not liable to change; uniform.
Unveil, un-vāl', vt. *To remove a veil from;* to uncover; to disclose to view.
Unveiled, un-vāld', p.a. *Stripped of a veil;* disclosed.
Unvenerable, un-ven'ėr-a-bl, a. *Not worthy of respect.*
Unventilated, un-ven'ti-lāt-ed, a. *Not ventilated;* not purified by a current of air.
Unvexed, un-vekst', a. *Untroubled.*
Unviolated, un-vī'ō-lāt-ed, a. *Not violated;* not broken.
Unvirtuous, un-vėr'tū-us, a. *Wanting virtue.*
Unvisited, un-vi'zit-ed, a. *Not visited.*
Unvouched, un-voucht', a. *Not vouched.*
Unwakened, **Unwaked**, un-wāk'nd, un-wākt', a. *Not awakened.*
Unwalled, un-wald', a. *Not walled.*
Unwarily, un-wā'ri-li, adv. *Without vigilance and caution;* heedlessly.
Unwariness, un-wā'ri-nes, n. *Want of vigilance;* want of caution.
Unwarlike, un-wạr'līk, a. *Not warlike.*
Unwarmed, un-wạrmd', a. *Not warmed;* not excited; not animated.
Unwarned, un-wạrnd', a. *Not warned.*
Unwarped, un-wạrpt', p.a. *Not warped;* not biased; impartial.
Unwarrantable, un-wo'rant-a-bl, a. *Not warrantable;* not defensible.
Unwarrantably, un-wo'rant-a-bli, adv. *In a manner that cannot be justified.*
Unwarranted, un-wo'rant-ed, a. *Not warranted;* not assured or certain; not covenanted to be good.
Unwary, un-wā'ri, a. *Not wary;* not cautious; precipitate.
Unwashed, un-wosht', a. *Not washed;* not cleansed by water.
Unwasted, un-wāst'ed, a. *Not wasted.*
Unwatched, un-wocht', a. *Not watched.*
Unwatchful, un-woch'fμl, a. *Not watchful;* not vigilant.
Unwavering, un-wā'vėr-ing, a. *Not wavering or unstable;* firm.
Unwearable, un-wār'a-bl, a. *That cannot be worn.*
Unwearied, un-wē'rid, a. *Not wearied;* not fatigued; indefatigable.

Unweariedly, un-wē'rid-li, adv. *Without tiring or sinking under fatigue.*
Unwearying, un-wē'ri-ing, p.a. *Not making weary.*
Unwedgeable†, un-wej'a-bl, a. *Not to be cloven.*
Unwedded, un-wed'ed, a. *Not wedded.*
Unweighed, un-wād', a. *Not weighed;* not deliberately considered; not considerate.
Unweighing, un-wā'ing, a. *Not weighing;* inconsiderate; thoughtless.
Unwelcome, un-wel'kum, a. *Not welcome;* not grateful; not pleasing.
Unwelcomed, un-wel'kumd, a. *Not welcomed;* not cordially received.
Unwell, un-wel', a. *Not well.*
Unwept, un-wept', a. *Not wept for.*
Unwholesome, un-hōl'sum, a. *Not wholesome;* insalubrious; tainted.
Unwholesomeness, un-hōl'sum-nes, n. *State or quality of being unwholesome.*
Unwieldily, un-wēl'di-li, adv. *Heavily;* with difficulty.
Unwieldiness, un-wēl'di-nes, n. *Quality of being unwieldy;* heaviness.
Unwieldy, un-wēl'di, a. *Not wieldy;* that is moved with difficulty; bulky.
Unwilling, un-wil'ing, a. *Not willing;* not inclined.
Unwillingly, un-wil'ing-li, adv. *Not with good-will;* reluctantly.
Unwillingness, un-wil'ing-nes, n. *State of being unwilling;* reluctance.
Unwind, un-wīnd', vt. *To separate, as what is wound;* to disentangle.—vi. *To become unwound.* ppr. unwinding, pret. & pp. unwound.
Unwiped, un-wīpt', a. *Not wiped.*
Unwise, un-wīz', a. *Not wise;* defective in wisdom; not dictated by wisdom.
Unwit†, un-wit', vt. *To deprive of understanding.*
Unwithering, un-wi'тнėr-ing, a. *Not liable to wither or fade.*
Unwitnessed, un-wit'nest, a. *Not witnessed;* not attested by witnesses.
Unwittily, un-wit'i-li, adv. *Without wit.*
Unwittingly, un-wit'ing-li, adv. *Without knowledge or consciousness.*
Unwitty, un-wit'i, a. *Not witty.*
Unwomanly, un-wμ'man-li, a. *Unbecoming a woman.*
Unwonted, un-wont'ed, a. *Not wonted;* unaccustomed; unusual; rare.
Unwooed, un-wöd', a. *Not wooed.*
Unworldliness, un-wėrld'li-nes, n. *State of being unworldly.*
Unworldly, un-wėrld'li, a. *Not worldly.*
Unworn, un-wōrn', a. *Not worn.*
Unworshipped, un-wėr'shipt, a. *Not worshipped;* not adored.
Unworthily, un-wėr'тні-li, adv. *Not according to desert;* without due regard to merit.
Unworthiness, un-wėr'тні-nes, n. *Want of worth or merit.*
Unworthy, un-wėr'тні, a. *Not worthy;* not deserving (with of); unbecoming; base; inadequate.
Unwounded, un-wönd'ed, a. *Not wounded;* not hurt; not offended.
Unwrap, un-rap', vt. *To open, as what is wrapped.* ppr. unwrapping, pret. & pp. unwrapped.
Unwrinkled, un-ring'kld, a. *Not wrinkled.*
Unwritten, un-rit'n, a. *Not written;* not reduced to writing; verbal.
Unwronged, un-rongd', a. *Not wronged;* not treated unjustly.
Unwrought, un-rat', a. *Not wrought;* not manufactured.
Unwrung, un-rung', a. *Not pinched.*
Unyielding, un-yēld'ing, a. *Not yielding* to force or persuasion; unbending.

Unyoke, un-yōk', vt. *To free from a yoke;* to disjoin.—vi.† *To cease from work.* ppr. unyoking, pret. & pp. unyoked.
Unyoked, un-yōkt', p.a. *Not having worn the yoke;* licentious.
Up, up, adv. *Aloft;* on high; above the horizon; in a state of climbing; out of bed; having risen from a seat; from a state of concealment; to a state of excitement; to a state of advance; in a state of insurrection; in a state of being increased; in a state of approaching; in order; from younger to elder years.—prep. *From a lower to a higher place.* [Sax.—Sans. api, above—upari, above, on the top.]
Upbear, up-bār', vt. *To bear up;* to lift; to sustain aloft; to support; to sustain. ppr. upbearing, pret. upbore, pp. upborne.
Upbind, up-bīnd', vt. *To bind up.*
Upbraid, up-brād', vt. *To charge* with something *wrong;* to reproach; to cast in the teeth of (with *with* or *for*, before the thing imputed); to reprove with severity. (Sax. *up-gebredan*, to charge.]
Upbraiding, up-brād'ing, p.n. *A charging with something wrong;* the act of reproaching.
Upbraidingly, up-brād'ing-li, adv. *In an upbraiding manner.*
Upcast, up'kast, a. *Cast up.*—n. *A throw;* a cast.
Upfill†, up-fil', vt. *To fill up;* to fulfil.
Upheave, up-hēv', vt. *To heave up from beneath.* ppr. upheaving, pret. & pp. upheaved.
Upheaved, up-hēvd', p.a. *Forced up by some expansive power from below.*
Upheld, up-held', p.a. *Sustained;* supported.
Uphill, up'hil, a. *Difficult, like the act of ascending a hill.*
Uphoard, up-hōrd', vt. *To treasure.*
Uphold, up-hōld', vt. *To hold up;* to sustain; to keep from falling; to maintain; to keep from being lost; to continue in being. ppr. upholding, pret. & pp. upheld.
Upholder, up-hōld'ėr, n. *One that upholds;* a supporter; a defender.
Upholsterer, up-hōl'stėr-ėr, n. *One who furnishes houses with beds, curtains, and the like.*
Upholstery, up-hōl'stė-ri, n. *Furniture supplied by upholsterers.*
Upland, up'land, n. *High land;* ground *elevated above the meadows and intervals which lie on the banks of rivers, near the sea, or between hills.*—a. *Being on upland;* pertaining to uplands.
Uplift, up-lift', vt. *To lift up.*
Uplock, up-lok', vt. *To lock up.*
Upon, up-on', prep. *On that which is high;* resting on the top or surface of; not under; near to; during the time of; in the direction of; in consideration of. [Sax. *uppan, uppon*.]
Upper, up'ėr, a. *Higher in place;* superior in rank.
Upper-hand, up'ėr-hand, n. *Superiority;* advantage.
Uppermost, up'ėr-mōst, a. *superl. Highest in place;* highest in power.
Upright, up'rīt, a. *Straight up;* erect; possessing rectitude; honest; just.
Uprightly, up'rīt-li, adv. *In an upright manner;* equitably.
Uprightness, up'rīt-nes, n. *The state of being upright.*
Uproar, up'rōr, n. *A stirring up;* violent disturbance; bustle and clamour. vt.† *To throw into confusion.* [G. *aufruhr—auf,* up, and *ruhr,* a stirring.]

Fāte, fär, fat, fạll; mē, met, hėr; pīne, pin; nōte, not, mȯve; tūbe, tub, bμll; oil, pound.

Uproot, up-rōt', *vt*. To root up; to tear up by the roots.
Upset, up-set', *vt*. To set upside down; to overturn, as a carriage. *ppr.* upsetting, *pret. & pp.* upset.—*n.* Act of upsetting.
Upshot, up'shot, *n*. Final issue; conclusion; end.
Upside-down, up'sid-doun, *adv*. With the upper part undermost.
Upsoar, up-sōr', *vi.* To soar aloft.
Upspring, up'spring, *n.* A man suddenly exalted.
Upstart, up'stärt, *n*. Something that starts up suddenly; one that suddenly rises from low life to wealth or power.
Upswarm†, up-swąrm', *vt*. To raise in a swarm.
Upward, up'ward, *a*. Directed to a higher place; ascending.
Upward, Upwards, up'ward, up'wards, *adv*. Toward a higher place.
Urban, ėr'ban, *a. Of or belonging to a city.* [L. *urbānus—urbs*, a city.]
Urbane, ėr-bān', *a. Pertaining to a city*; courteous; elegant in manners.
Urbanity, ėr-ban'i-ti, *n. State of being urbane*; elegance of deportment; polished manners. [Fr. *urbanité*—L. *urbs*, a city—*orbis*, a circle, round.]
Urchin, ėr'chin, *n*. A name given to the hedgehog, a small animal having the body covered with spines; a small boy, used in contempt. [Fr. *hérisson*—Gr. *chēr, chēros*, a hedgehog.]
Urge, ėrj, *vt*. To press to do work; to impel; to excite; to press, as an argument; to importune. *ppr.* urging, *pret. & pp.* urged. [Old Fr. *urger*—L. *urgeo*, to press upon, to drive.]
Urgency, ėrj'en-si, *n. State of being urgent*; pressure of necessity; solicitation.
Urgent, ėrj'ont, *a. That urges*; pressing.
Urgently, ėrj'ent-li, *adv*. *In an urgent manner*.
Urging, ėrj'ing, *p.a.* Pressing with solicitations; importunate.
Urim, ū'rim, *n*. The Urim and Thummim, among the Israelites, signify *lights* and *perfections*. [Heb. *urim*, lights, pl. of *ur*, light.]
Urinal, ū'rin-al, *n*. A bottle in which urine is kept for inspection; a public receptacle for urine. [Fr.; L. *urina*, urine.]
Urinary, ū'ri-na-ri, *a. Pertaining to urine*. [from *urine*.]
Urine, ū'rin, *n*. An animal *fluid* secreted by the kidneys. [Fr.—L. *urina*.]

Urn, ėrn, *n*. A kind of vase of a roundish form, but swelling in the middle like the common pitcher; a vessel employed to keep water boiling at the tea-table; a vessel in which the ashes of the dead were formerly kept. [L. *urna*—Sans. *ri*, to flow.]
Us, us, *pron*. Objective case of *we*. [Sax.]
Usable, ūz'a-bl, *a. That may be used*.
Usage, ūz'āj, *n. Act or manner of using*; behaviour of one person towards another; received practice; custom; habit. [Fr.—L. *ūtor, ūsus*, to use.]
Use, ūs, *n*. The act of employing to any purpose; state of being employed to any purpose; the quality which makes a thing proper for a purpose; utility; profit; customary act; habit. [L. *ūsus*.]
Use, ūz, *vt*. To put to use; to act with or by means of; to habituate; to inure; to treat; to exercise.—*vi.* To be accustomed; to be wont. *ppr.* using, *pret. & pp.* used. [Fr. *user*—L. *ūtor, ūsus*.]
Useful, ūs'ful, *a. Valuable for use*; helpful to any end; profitable; beneficial.
Usefully, ūs'ful-li, *adv*. *In a useful manner*; profitably.
Usefulness, ūs'ful-nes, *n. State or quality of being useful*; utility; profit.
Useless, ūs'les, *a. Being without use*.
Uselessly, ūs'les-li, *adv*. *In a useless manner*.
Uselessness, ūs'les-nes, *n. State or quality of being useless*; want of utility.
Usher, ush'ėr, *n*. *A door-keeper*; an inferior officer in some English courts of law; a subordinate teacher in a school.—*vt*. To give entrance to; to introduce as a forerunner (with *in*). [Fr. *huissier*—L. *ostium*, a door.]
Ushership, ush'ėr-ship, *n. Office of an usher*.
Usual, ū'zhū-al, *a*. Customary; common; ordinary. [Fr. *usuel*.]
Usually, ū'zhū-al-li, *adv*. *In a usual manner*; frequently.
Usurer, ū'zhūr-ėr, *n*. *One who practises usury*; one who lends money and takes exorbitant interest for it.
Usurp, ū-zėrp', *vt*. To seize to one's own use; to seize and hold without right; to assume. [Fr. *usurper*—L. *usus*, use, and *rapio*, to seize.]
Usurpation, ū-zėrp-ā'zhon, *n. Act of usurping*; illegal seizure or possession. [Fr.—L. *usurpatio*.]
Usurper, ū-zėrp'ėr, *n. One who usurps*; one who seizes or occupies the property of another without right.

Usury, ū'zhū-ri, *n*. Money paid for the use of money; higher interest than is allowed by law. [Fr. *usure*—L. *usūra—utor, usus*, to use.]
Utensil, ū-ten'sil, *n. That which is used*; an instrument or vessel used in a kitchen; an implement. [Fr. *utensile*—L. *utor*, to use.]
Uterine, ū'tėr-in, *a. Of or belonging to the womb*; born of the same mother, but having a different father. [Fr. *utérin*—L. *uterus*, the womb.]
Utilitarian, ū-til'i-tā"ri-an, *a. Consisting in or pertaining to utility*.—*n*. One who holds the doctrine of utilitarianism. [from *utility*.]
Utilitarianism, ū-til'i-tā"ri-an-izm, *n*. The doctrine that *utility* is the sole standard of moral conduct; the promotion of the greatest happiness of the greatest number.
Utility, ū-til'i-ti, *n. State or quality of being useful*; production of good. [Fr. *utilité*—L. *utor*, to use.]
Utilize, ū'til-iz, *vt*. To render useful; to employ for some useful purpose. *ppr.* utilizing, *pret. & pp.* utilized. [Fr. *utiliser*.]
Utis†, ū'tis, *n*. A festivity.
Utmost, ut'mōst, *a*. Being most out; uttermost.—*n*. The most that can be. [Sax. *utmæst*.]
Utopian, ū-tō'pi-an, *a*. Ideal; fanciful; not well founded. [from More's *Utopia*, an imaginary island—Gr. *ou*, not, and *topos*, a place.]
Utter, ut'tėr, *a*. Being *farther out* than that which is *out*; total; perfect; absolute; unqualified. [Sax. *uttra*, comp. of *ute*, out.]
Utter, ut'tėr, *vt*. To declare; to divulge; to sell; to vend. [Sw. *yttra*, to declare.]
Utterable, ut'tėr-a-bl, *a. That may be uttered*, pronounced, or expressed.
Utterance, ut'tėr-ans, *n. The act of uttering words*; pronunciation; extremity†; terms of extreme hostility†.
Utterly, ut'tėr-li, *adv*. To the full extent; fully; perfectly; totally.
Uttermost, ut'tėr-mōst, *a*. Being in the *furthest* or *highest degree*; extreme.—*n*. The most that can be; that beyond which nothing is. [*utter* and *most*.]
Uxorious, uks-ō'ri-us, *a*. Excessively fond of one's wife. [L. *uxorius—uxor*, a wife.]
Uxoriously, uks-ō'ri-us-li, *adv*. With fond or servile submission to one's wife.

V.

Vacancy, vā'kan-si, *n. State of being vacant*; empty space; vacuity; time of leisure; a place or office not occupied. [Fr. *vacance*—L. *vaco*, to be empty.]
Vacant, vā'kant, *a*. Empty; not filled; void of every substance except air; free; unengaged with business; not filled with an incumbent; being unoccupied with business; not occupied with study; indicating want of thought. [Fr.—L. *vaco*.]
Vacate, vā'kāt, *vt*. To make empty or void; to make vacant; to quit possession of and leave destitute; to annul; to make of no authority or validity.

ppr. vacating, *pret. & pp.* vacated. [L. *vaco, vacātum*.]
Vacation, vā-kā'shon, *n*. The act of making vacant; the space of time between the end of one term and the beginning of the next; intermission of a stated employment. [Fr.]
Vaccinate, vak'si-nāt, *vt*. To inoculate with the *cow-pox*. Cow-pox is smallpox, modified by affecting a cow. *ppr.* vaccinating, *pret. & pp.* vaccinated. [Low L. *vaccino, vaccinatum*—L. *vacca*.]
Vaccination, vak-si-nā'shon, *n*. The act, art, or practice of inoculating persons with the cow-pox.

Vaccine, vak'sin, *a. Pertaining to cows*; derived from cows, as vaccine matter. [L. *vaccinus—vacca*, a cow—Ar. *bakaph*, to pour milk by drops.]
Vacillate, va'sil-lāt, *vi*. To move one way and the other; to fluctuate in mind; to be unsteady. [L. *vacillo, vacillatum*.]
Vacillating, va'sil-lāt-ing, *p.a.* Unsteady; inclined to fluctuate.
Vacillation, va-sil-lā'shon, *n. A moving one way and the other*; a wavering; fluctuation of mind. [Fr.]
Vacuity, va-kū'i-ti, *n. Emptiness*; a state of being unfilled; space unfilled. [Fr. *vacuité*—L. *vaco*, to be empty.]

ch, chain; j, job; ġ, go; ng, sing; ᴛʜ, then; th, thin; w, wig; wh, whig; zh, azure; † obsolete.

Vacuum, va′kū-um, n. Space devoid of all matter. [L.]
Vadet, vād, vi. To vanish.
Vagabond, va′ga-bond, a. Wandering to and fro; driven to and fro.—n. A vagrant; one who wanders from town to town illegally, having no certain dwelling. [Fr.—L. vagor, to wander.]
Vagary, vā-gā′ri, n. A wandering of the thoughts; a wild freak; a whimsical purpose. [from Fr. vaguer—L. vagor, to wander.]
Vagrancy, vā′gran-si, n. A state of wandering without a settled home.
Vagrant, vā′grant, a. Wandering from place to place without any settled habitation; unsettled.—n. A wanderer; one who strolls from place to place; one who has no settled habitation, or who does not abide in it. [Norm. vagarant—L. vagor, to wander.]
Vague, vāg, a. Wandering; unsettled; indefinite; uncertain. [Fr.]
Vagueness, vāg′nes, n. The state of being vague.
Vail, vāl, n. See VEIL.
Vail, vāl, vt. To let fall; to lower.
Vain, vān, a. Deficient; empty; void; fruitless; proud of trifling attainments; conceited; showy; unsatisfying; false; spurious. [Fr.—L. vanus, empty.]
Vainglorious, vān-glō′ri-us, a. Vain to excess of one's own achievements; boastful; proceeding from vanity.
Vainglory, vān-glō′ri, n. Excessive vanity excited by one's own performances; empty pride.
Vainly, vān′li, adv. In a vain manner; in vain; proudly; foolishly.
Vale, vāl, n. A tract of low ground between hills; a valley. [Fr. vallée—L. vallis.]
Valediction, val-ē-dik′shon, n. A bidding farewell; a farewell. [from L. valedico—vale, farewell, and dico, to say.]
Valedictory, val-ē-dik′tō-ri, a. Bidding farewell.
Valentine, val′en-tin, n. A sweetheart chosen on Valentine's day; a letter containing professions of love sent by one young person to another on Valentine's day, or the 14th of February.
Valet, val′et, n. Originally, the son of a person of distinction; a servant who attends on a gentleman's person; a page. [Old Fr. varlet.]
Valetudinarian, **Valetudinary**, va-lē-tū′di-nā″ri-an, va-lē-tū′di-na-ri, a. sickly; weak; infirm.—n. A person of a weak or sickly constitution. [L. valetudinārius—valeo, to be well.]
Valiant, va′li-ant, a. Strong; brave; intrepid in danger; heroic; performed with valour. [Fr. vaillant—L. valeo, to be strong.]
Valiantly, va′li-ant-li, adv. In a valiant manner; stoutly; heroically.
Valid, va′lid, a. Strong; having sufficient strength or force; sound; just; not weak; having legal strength; executed with the proper formalities; that cannot be rightfully set aside. [Fr. valide—L. valeo, to be strong.]
Validity, va-lid′i-ti, n. Strength or force to convince; legal strength or force; value; worth. [Fr. validité.]
Validly, va′lid-li, adv. In a valid manner.
Valley, val′lē, n. **Valleys**, pl. A low tract of land between hills; a low extended plain washed by a river. [Fr. vallée—L. vallis.]
Valorous, va′lor-us, a. Brave; courageous; stout; intrepid. [Fr. valeureux—L. valeo, to be strong.]

Valorously, va′lor-us-li, adv. In a valorous manner; heroically.
Valour, va′lor, n. Strength; courage; such strength of mind as enables a man to encounter danger with firmness; intrepidity. [L. valor, manliness in war—valeo, to be strong—Sans. bala, strength, force.]
Valuable, va′lū-a-bl, a. Having value; having some good qualities which are useful and esteemed; estimable.
Valuableness, va′lū-a-bl-nes, n. The state or the quality of being valuable.
Valuation, va-lū-ā′shon, n. The act of estimating the value; value set upon a thing; estimated worth.
Valuator, va′lū-āt-or, n. One who sets a value; an appraiser.
Value, va′lū, n. The quality which renders a thing useful; worth; price; efficacy; estimation; excellence. [Fr. for valeur—L. valeo, to be strong.]—vt. To rate at a certain price; to rate highly; to take account of; to consider with respect to importance or moral obligation; to reckon at, with respect to number or power; to hold in portant. ppr. valuing, pret. & pp. valued. [Fr. évaluer.]
Valueless, va′lū-les, a. Being of no value; having no worth.
Valve, valv, n. In the pl. a folding-door; anything that opens over the mouth of a vessel; a kind of membrane, which opens in certain vessels to admit the blood, and shuts to prevent its regress. [L. valvæ, folding-doors.]
Valved, valvd, p.a. Having valves or hinges; composed of valves.
Vamp, vamp, n. The fore or upper leather of a boot or shoe.—vt. To piece, as an old thing with a new part; to repair. [Fr. avant, before.]
Vampire, vam′pir, n. Originally, a dead person, formerly believed in various nations of Europe to return in body and soul, and wander about the earth, sucking the blood of persons asleep; one who lives upon another; a blood-sucker: the common name of a species of bats, which suck the blood of persons and beasts when asleep. [G. vampyr, a word of Servian origin.]
Van, van, n. The fore part of an army; the front line of a fleet; a fan for winnowing grain; a large covered carriage for the transportation of goods. [from Fr. avant, before.]
Vane, vān, n. A broad flag carried by a knight in the tournament; a thin slip of wood, &c., placed on a spindle at the top of a spire, &c., for the purpose of showing which way the wind blows; in ships, a piece of bunting used for the same purpose; the thin part or web of a feather on the side of the shaft. [Sax. fana; Old G. fano, a flag.]
Vanguard, van′gärd, n. The troops who march in the van of an army.
Vanish, va′nish, vi. To pass away from the place occupied and leave it void; to disappear; to be annihilated or lost. [Fr. évanouir, évanouissant—L. vanus, void.]
Vanished, va′nisht, p.a. Passed away.
Vanity, va′ni-ti, n. Emptiness; nothingness; inanity; fruitless endeavour; empty pleasure; vain pursuit; unsubstantial enjoyment; arrogance; inflation of mind upon slight grounds; empty pride; self-conceit. [Fr. vanité—L. vanus, empty.]
Vanquish, vang′kwish, vt. To conquer; to overcome; to refute in argument. [Fr. vaincre, pp. vainquis—L. vinco, to conquer.]

Vanquisher, vang′kwish-er, n. One who vanquishes; a conqueror; a victor.
Vantage, van′tāj, n. Gain; profit; advantage; superior opportunity. [Sp. ventaja, advantage.]
Vapid, va′pid, a. That has emitted vapour; that has lost its life and spirit; dead; flat; unanimated. [L. vapidus—vapor, steam.]
Vapidly, va′pid-li, adv. In a vapid manner.
Vapidness, va′pid-nes, n. The state of being vapid; flatness; dulness.
Vaporize, vā′por-iz, vt. To convert into vapour by the application of heat. vi. To pass off in vapour. ppr. vaporizing, pret. & pp. vaporised. [Fr. vaporiser.]
Vaporous, vā′por-us, a. Full of vapours; vain; unreal. [Fr. vaporeux.]
Vapour, vā′por, n. That which bedews; steam; a visible fluid floating in the atmosphere; that invisible elastic fluid which rises constantly from the surface of land and water all over the world; (pl.) a disease of nervous debility, in which a variety of strange images float in the brain; something transitory.—vi. To pass off in vapour; to be exhaled; to boast with a vain, ostentatious display of worth; to brag. [Fr. vapeur—L. vapor—Sans. rap, to sprinkle, to bedew.]
Vapourer, vā′por-er, n. One who vapours; one who makes a vaunting display of his prowess or worth.
Vapoury, vā′por-i, a. Full of vapours; peevish.
Variable, vā′ri-a-bl, a. That may vary; changeable; liable to change; fickle; inconstant.—n. That which varies; a quantity which is in a state of continual increase or decrease. [Fr.]
Variableness, vā′ri-a-bl-nes, n. Quality of being variable; liableness to alter; fickleness; unsteadiness; levity.
Variably, vā′ri-a-bli, adv. Changeably.
Variance, vā′ri-ans, n. A difference; difference that produces controversy; dissension; discord. [L. variantia.]
Variation, vā-ri-ā′shon, n. Act of varying; a partial change in the state of the same thing; change from one to another; change of termination of nouns and adjectives, constituting what is called case, number, and gender; deviation. [Fr.—L. variatio.]
Varicose, **Varicous**, vā′ri-kōs, vā′ri-kus, a. Preternaturally enlarged, or permanently dilated, applied only to veins. [L. varicōsus—varix, a dilated vein.]
Variegate, vā′ri-ē-gāt, vt. To vary; to diversify in external appearance; to mark with different colours. ppr. variegating, pret. & pp. variegated. [Low L. variego, variegatus—L. varius, spotted, striped, and ago, to do.)
Variegation, vā′ri-ē-gā″shon, n. The act of variegating, or state of being diversified by different colours; diversity of colours.
Variety, va-ri′ē-ti, n. Difference; difference from a former state; intermixture of different things; one thing of many which constitute variety; many and different kinds; any individual plant or animal which differs, in some minor points, from the rest of the species to which it belongs, different sort. [Fr. variété—L. vario, to vary.]
Various, vā′ri-us, a. Variegated; diversified; several; manifold; changeable; unlike each other; diverse. [L. varius.]
Variously, vā′ri-us-li, adv. In different ways; with change; with diversity.

Fāte, fär, fat, fall; mē, met, hėr; pīne, pin; nōte, not, mōve; tūbe, tub, bull; oil, pound.

Varlet, vär'let, n. Anciently, a knight's follower; a footman; a scoundrel. [Old Fr.]

Varletry†, vär'let-ri, n. The rabble; the crowd.

Varnish, vär'nish, n. Primarily, *colour;* a solution of resinous matter, forming a clear limpid fluid, used by cabinetmakers, &c., for coating over the surface of their work; an artificial covering to give a fair appearance to any act.—*vt.* To lay varnish on; to give a fair external appearance to in words; to give a fair colouring to. [Fr. *vernis*—Sans. *varn*, to colour, to paint.]

Vary, vā'ri, vt. To make of different *colours;* to variegate; to alter; to transform; to alter partially.—*vi.* To be altered in any manner; to suffer a partial change; to differ; to become unlike one's self; to depart; to disagree; to be at variance. *ppr.* varying, *pret. & pp.* varied.—*n.*† Alteration. [Fr. *varier*—L. *varius*, spotted, striped.]

Vascular, vas'kū-lär, a. *Pertaining to small vessels*; pertaining to the vessels of animal or vegetable bodies; full of vessels. [Fr. *vasculaire*—L. *vas, vāsis*, a vessel.]

Vascularity, vas-kū-la'ri-ti, n. *The state of being vascular.*

Vase, vās, n. A vessel generally for show rather than for use; a vessel for use in temples; an ornament of sculpture representing the vessels of the ancients, as incense-pots, flower-pots, &c.; the body of the Corinthian capital. [Fr.—L. *vas*, a vessel.]

Vassal, vas'sal, n. A *bondman;* a servant; a dependant; one who holds of a superior lord; a political slave. [Fr.; W. *gwas*, a slave.]

Vassalage, vas'sal-āj, n. *The state of being a vassal;* political servitude; subjection; slavery. [Fr.]

Vast, vast, a. Primarily, *ravaged; wasted;* being of great extent; huge in bulk and extent; very great in numbers or amount; very great in force; very great in importance.—n. *A waste region.* [Fr. *vaste*—L. *vastus*, waste, immense.]

Vastidity†, vast-id'i-ti, n. Immensity.

Vastly, vast'li, adv. Very greatly; like a waste¹.

Vastness, vast'nes, n. *Quality or state of being vast;* immensity; immense magnitude or amount; immense importance.

Vasty†, vast'i, a. Being of great extent; immense.

Vat, vat, n. A large vessel for holding liquors in an immature state; a cistern in which hides are laid for steeping in tan. [D.—L. *vas*, a vessel.]

Vault, valt, n. That which is *turned round* or arched; an arched roof, so constructed that the stones or bricks of which it is composed sustain and keep each other in their places; a cellar; a repository for the dead; the leap of a horse; a jump.—*vt. To form with a vault;* to cover with a vault; to arch.—*vi. To turn or tumble;* to play the tumbler; to leap with the body bent; to curvet; to spring. [Old Fr. *voulte*—L. *volvo, volūtum*, to turn round.]

Vaultage†, valt'āj, n. Vaulted work.

Vaulted, valt'ed, *p.a.* Arched; concave.

Vaulter, valt'ėr, n. *One that vaults.*

Vaulting, valt'ing, *p.n. The art of constructing vaults;* vaults in general; the art or practice of a vaulter.

Vaunt, vant, *vi.* To talk with *vain ostentation;* to brag; to boast.—*vt.* To boast of; to make a vain display of.—n. A *vain empty* boast; a vain display of what one is or has, or has done; ostentation from vanity. [Fr. *vanter*—L. *vanus*, empty.]

Vaunt†, vant, n. The first part.

Vaunter, vant'ėr, n. *One who vaunts;* a man given to vain ostentation.

Vauntingly, vant'ing-li, adv. Boastfully; with vain ostentation.

Veal, vēl, n. The flesh of a *calf* killed for the table. [Fr. *veau*, a calf—Gr. *italos*, a calf.]

Vedette, Vidette, vē-det', n. A mounted sentinel stationed on the outpost of an army, to *observe* an enemy, and give notice of danger. [Fr. *vedette*—L. *video*, to see.]

Veer, vēr, *vi. To turn about;* to alter its course, as a ship; to change direction. *vt. To turn;* to direct to a different course. [Fr. *virer*, to turn about.]

Veering, vēr'ing, *p.n.* That movement of a ship, by which, in changing her course, her head is turned to leeward.

Veeringly, vēr'ing-li, adv. Shiftingly.

Vegetable, ve'jė-ta-bl, n. *That which vegetates;* a plant; a plant for culinary purposes cultivated in gardens, or a plant used for feeding cattle and sheep.—a. *Belonging to vegetables* or plants; consisting of plants; having the nature of plants. [Fr. *végétable*.]

Vegetarian, ve-jė-tā'ri-an, n. One who abstains from animal food, and lives exclusively on *vegetables*, milk, &c.

Vegetate, ve'jė-tāt, *vi. To germinate;* to grow; to do nothing but eat and grow. *ppr.* vegetating, *pret. & pp.* vegetated. [Fr. *végéter*—L. *vigeo*, to flourish.]

Vegetation, ve-jė-tā'shon, n. *The process of vegetating*, or of growing, as plants; vegetables or plants in general. [Fr. *végétation*.]

Vegetative, ve'jė-tāt-iv, a. *Having the power of growing*, as plants; having the power to produce growth in plants. [Fr. *végétatif*.]

Vegetive†, ve'jė-tiv, n. A vegetable.

Vehemence, vē'hė-mens, n. *Quality of being vehement;* ardour; fervour; great force; great heat; animated fervour; impetuosity. [Fr. *véhémence*.]

Vehement, vē'hė-ment, a. Primarily, *mad*, or *out of one's mind;* impetuous; acting with great force; very eager or urgent; very fervent; unreasonable; violent. [Fr. *véhément*—L. *vehemens*—Sans. *vi*, apart, and *manas*, the mind.]

Vehemently, vē'hė-ment-li, adv. With great force; with great zeal or pathos.

Vehicle, vē'hi-kl, n. *A carriage;* any kind of carriage moving on land; that which is used as the instrument of conveyance; a medium; a substance in which medicine is taken. [Fr. *véhicule*—L. *veho*, to carry.]

Vehicular, vē-hik'ū-lär, a. *Pertaining to a vehicle.* [Late L. *vehicularis*.]

Veil, vāl, n. *A covering;* a cover to conceal the face; any kind of cloth which is used for intercepting the view and hiding something; a piece of thin cloth or silk stuff, used by females to hide or protect their faces.—*vt. To cover with a veil;* to conceal; to hide. [Fr. *voile*—L. *velo*, to cover.]

Vein, vān, n. A vessel in animal bodies which receives the blood from the capillaries and returns it to the heart; a tube through which the sap is transmitted along the leaves of plants; a crevice in a rock filled up by substances different from the rock; a streak of different colour, appearing in wood, &c.; a fissure in the earth; turn of mind; a particular cast of genius; humour; particular temper; strain; quality.—*vt.* To mark or form with *veins*. [Fr. *veine*—L. *vena*, a vein, also genius.]

Veined, vānd, *p.a. Full of veins;* streaked; having vessels branching over the surface, as a leaf.

Vellum, ve'l'um, n. A fine kind of parchment made of *calf's skin*, and rendered clear, smooth, and white for writing on. [Fr. *vélin*—Gr. *italos*, a calf.]

Velocity, vē-los'i-ti, n. *Swiftness; speed;* quickness of motion; that affection of motion by which a body moves over a certain space in a certain time; the measure of the degree in which a body moves. [Fr. *vélocité*—L. *velox*, swift.]

Velure†, vel'ūr, n. Velvet.

Velvet, vel'vet, n. A rich silk or silk and cotton stuff, covered on the outside with a *close fine soft nap*, and used for ladies' dresses and various other purposes. [It. *velluto*—L. *villus*, shaggy hair.]

Velvet, Velvety, vel'vet, vel'vet-i, a. *Made of velvet;* soft and delicate like velvet, as the skin of an animal or the surface of a plant.

Velveting, vel'vet-ing, *p.n. The fine shag* or nap of velvet.

Venal, vē'nal, a. *That is for sale;* mercenary; that may be bought for money. [Fr. *vénal*—L. *vēnum*, sale.]

Venality, vē-nal'i-ti, n. *State or quality of being venal;* prostitution of services for money. [Fr. *vénalité*.]

Vend, vend, *vt. To sell*, as wares; to transfer, as a thing, to another person for a pecuniary equivalent. [Fr. *vendre*—L. *venum*. sale, and *do*, to give.]

Vender, vend'ėr, n. *One who vends;* a seller. [Fr. *vendeur*.]

Vendibility, vend-i-bil'i-ti, n. *The state of being vendible* or saleable.

Vendible, vend'i-bl, a. *That may be given for sale;* that may be sold.—n. *Something to be vended.* [L. *vendibilis*.]

Vendor, vend-or', n. *A vender;* a seller.

Veneer, vē-nēr', *vt.* To fix firmly on, as thin leaves of a fine wood over a coarse wood, so as to give the latter the appearance of a solid mass of the former. n. A thin piece of wood of a more valuable kind laid upon another, so that the whole substance appears to be of the more valuable sort. [G. *fournieren*, to veneer—Fr. *fournir*, to furnish.]

Veneering, vē-nēr'ing, *p.n. The art of laying thin leaves of a superior kind of wood* upon a ground of an inferior material.

Venerable, ve'nė-ra-bl, a. *Worthy of veneration;* rendered sacred by religious associations; to be regarded with awe and treated with reverence. [Fr. *vénérable*.]

Venerableness, ve'nė-ra-bl-nes, n. State or quality of *being venerable.*

Venerably, ve'nė-ra-bli, adv. In a manner to excite *reverence*.

Venerate, ve'nė-rāt, *vt.* To regard with respect and *reverence;* to reverence; to revere. *ppr.* venerating, *pret. & pp.* venerated. [L. *venĕror, veneratus*—Sans. *van*, to worship to love.]

Veneration, ve-nė-rā'shon, n. *Act of venerating;* respect mingled with some degree of awe; a feeling excited by the dignity of a person, and with regard to place, by its consecration to sacred services. [Fr. *vénération*.]

Venereal, vē-nē'rē-al, a. *Pertaining to Venus;* relating to love; pertaining to sexual intercourse. [L. *venereus*—Sans. *van*, to love.]

Venesection, vĕ-nĕ-sek'shon, *n.* The act of *cutting* or opening *a vein* for letting blood; blood-letting. [L. *vena*, vein, and *sectio*, a cutting—*seco*, to cut.]

Venetian vē-nē'shi-an, *a.* Belonging to *Venice*, or to its inhabitants.

Venew†, vē-nū', *n.* A bout; a thrust; a hit.

Venewdest†, vē-nū'dest,*a.* Most mouldy.

Venge†, venj, *vt.* To punish.

Vengeance, venj'ans, *n.* The *devoting of strength* to the infliction of punishment; the infliction of pain on another, in return for an injury; passionate revenge; mischief†. [Fr.—L. *vis, vim*, force, and *dico*, to devote.]

Vengeful, venj'fṵl, *a.* Full of vengeance; vindictive.

Vengefully, venj'fṵl-li, *adv.* Vindictively.

Venial, vē'ni-al, *a.* That may be forgiven; pardonable; excusable. [Fr. *véniel*—L. *venia*, pardon.]

Venially, vē'ni-al-li, *adv.* In a venial manner; pardonably.

Venialness, vē'ni-al-nes, *n.* State of being *venial*, or of being pardonable.

Venison, ven'zon, *n.* The flesh of animals taken in *hunting*; the flesh of beasts of game, or of such wild animals as are taken in the chase, particularly those of the deer kind. [Fr. *venaison*—L. *venor*, to hunt.]

Venom, ve'nom, *n.* That which hurts or kills; poison; matter fatal or injurious to life; spite; malice. [Fr. *venin*—L. *venēnum*, poison—Sans, *van*, to hurt.]

Venomous, ve'nom-us, *a.* Full of venom; charged with venom; noxious to animal life; malignant; spiteful. [Late L. *venēnōsus*.]

Venomously, ve'nom-us-li, *adv.* Poisonously; malignantly; spitefully.

Venous, vān'us, *a.* Pertaining to a vein or to veins; contained in veins. [L. *venōsus*, from *vena*, a vein.]

Vent, vent, *n.* A *cleft;* a passage for air to escape; the flue of a chimney; the touch-hole in a cannon; passage from secrecy to notice; escape from confinement; utterance; means of discharge; the opening for the discharge of excrement in birds and fishes.—*vt.* To let out at a *cleft;* to let out; to utter; to pour forth; to publish. [Fr. *fente*, a cleft, slit—L. *findo*, to cleave.]

Ventage†, vent'āj, *n.* A small hole.

Ventilate, ven'ti-lāt, *vt.* To *fan*, as with a *gentle wind*; to expose to the free passage of air; to supply with fresh air; to winnow; to sift and examine. [L. *ventilo, ventilātum—ventus*, wind.]

Ventilation, ven-ti-lā'shon, *n.* The act of *ventilating;* the act of fanning or winnowing; the act of sifting and bringing out to view. [Old Fr.]

Ventilator, ven'ti-lāt-or, *n.* A contrivance *for* promoting *ventilation*.

Ventral, ven'tral, *a.* Belonging to the *belly*. [Late L. *ventrālis—venter*, the belly.]

Ventricle, ven'tri-kl, *n.* A *little belly;* a small cavity in an animal body. [L. *ventriculus—venter*, the belly.]

Ventricular, ven-trik'ū-lär, *a.* Pertaining *to a ventricle*.

Ventriloquism, ven-tri'lō-kwizm, *n.* Act of *speaking as from the belly*; the art of speaking in such a manner that the voice appears to come from some distant place. [L. *venter*, belly, and *loquor*, to speak.]

Ventriloquist, ven-tri'lō-kwist, *n.* One who *speaks* in such a manner that his voice appears to come from some distant place.

Venture, ven'tūr, *n.* That which is to come; a hap; a chance; an undertaking of chance or danger; the thing put to hazard; particularly, something sent to sea in trade.—*vi.* To *make a venture;* to run a hazard or risk.—*vt.* To *put* or send *on a venture* or chance; to expose to hazard; to risk. *ppr.* venturing, *pret. & pp.* ventured. [Fr. *aventure*—L. *venio, ventum*, to come.]

Venturesome, ven'tūr-sum, *a.* Adventurous; bold; daring; intrepid.

Venturing, ven'tūr-ing, *p.n.* The act of putting to risk; a hazarding.

Venturous, ven'tūr-us, *a.* That ventures; daring; bold; fearless.

Venturously, ven'tūr-us-li, *adv.* Daringly; fearlessly; boldly.

Venturousness, ven'tūr-us-nes, *n.* Quality of *being venturous;* boldness.

Venus, vē'nus, *n.* The mythological goddess of beauty and *love;* that is, beauty or love deified; one of the inferior planets, the second in order of distance from the sun, and the most brilliant of all the planetary bodies. [L. —Sans. *van*, to love.]

Veracious, vē-rā'shi-us, *a.* Habitually disposed *to speak truth*. [L. *verax, verācis—verus*, true.]

Veracity, vē-ras'i-ti, *n.* *Truthfulness;* habitual observance of truth, or habitual truth. [Fr. *véracité*.]

Verandah, vē-ran'da, *n.* An oriental word denoting a kind of open portico, in front of a building. [Hind. *buramula*.]

Verb, vėrb, *n.* The *word;* the part of speech which affirms; that part of speech which signifies to be, to do, or to suffer. [Fr. *verbe*—L. *verbum*, a word.]

Verbal, vėrb'al, *a.* Consisting of mere *words;* spoken; oral; respecting words only; literal; having word answering to word; derived from a verb, as a noun; verbose†.—*n.* A *noun derived from a verb*. [Fr.—L. *verbum*, a word.]

Verbalize, vėrb'al-īz, *vt.* To *convert into a verb*. *ppr.* verbalizing, *pret. & pp.* verbalized.

Verbally, vėrb'al-li, *adv.* In *words spoken;* orally.

Verbatim, vėr-bā'tim, *adv.* Word for *word;* in the same words. [L.]

Verbiage, vėr'bi-āj, *n.* Verbosity; superabundance of words. [Fr.]

Verbose, vėr-bōs', *a.* Using or containing more *words* than are necessary; prolix. [L. *verbōsus—verbum*, a word.]

Verbosely, vėr-bōs'li, *adv.* Wordily.

Verbosity, vėr-bos'i-ti, *n.* Quality of *being verbose;* prolixity. [Fr. *verbosité*.]

Verdant, vėr'dant, *a.* Green; fresh; covered with growing plants or grass. [Fr. *verdoyant*—L. *vireo*, to be green.]

Verdantly, vėr'dant-li, *adv.* Freshly.

Verdict, vėr'dikt, *n.* A *true utterance;* the answer of a jury given to the court concerning any matter of fact in any cause; decision; judgment; opinion pronounced. [Norm. *vereduist*—L. *verus, verum*, true, and *dictum*, a saying—*dico*, to say.]

Verdigris, vėr'di-gris, *n.* The rust of brass or copper, so named from its colour. [Fr. *vert-de-gris—veri*, green, and *gris*, gray.]

Verdure, vėr'dūr, *n.* Greenness; freshness of vegetation. [Fr.—L. *vireo*, to be green.]

Verge, vėrj, *n.* A *rod*, or something in the form of a rod, carried as an emblem of authority; the mace of a dean; the extent of the king's court, within which is bounded the jurisdiction of the lord-steward of the king's household, so called from the verge which the marshal bears; the extreme side of anything which has some extent of length; the brink; edge; the spindle of the balance-wheel of a watch. [Fr.—L. *virga*, a twig.]

Verge, vėrj, *vi.* To *incline* from the horizontal direction; to tend downward; to slope; to approach. *ppr.* verging. *pret. & pp.* verged. [L. *vergo*, to incline.]

Verger, vėrj'ėr, *n.* He that carries the *verge* or mace before the bishop, dean, &c.; an officer who carries a white wand before the justices of either bench in England; a pew-opener.

Verifiable, ve'ri-fī-a-bl, *a.* That may be *verified;* that may be proved by evidence.

Verification, ve'ri-fī-kā"shon, *n.* The act of *verifying;* the act of confirming any transaction, by legal or competent evidence; state of being verified; confirmation. [Fr. *vér fication*.]

Verifier, ve'ri-fī-ėr, *n.* One that verifies.

Verify, ve'ri-fī, *vt.* To *make* out to be *true;* to confirm the truth of, as of a prediction; to show to be true. *ppr.* verifying, *pret. & pp.* verified. [Fr. *vérifier*—L. *verus*, true, and *facio*, to make.]

Verily, ve'ri-li, *adv.* In *truth;* in fact; truly.

Verisimilitude. ve'ri-si-mil"i-tūd, *n.* *Resemblance to truth;* the appearance of truth; probability; likelihood. [L. *verisimilitūdo—verus*, true, and *similis*, like.]

Veritable, ve'ri-ta-bl, *a.* True; agreeable to fact. [Fr. *véritable*.]

Verity, ve'ri-ti, *n.* That which is to be *chosen;* truth; consonance of a proposition to fact; a true assertion; agreement of the words with the thoughts. [Fr. *vérité*—L. *vērus*, true—Sans. *var*, to choose.]

Verjuice, vėr'jūs, *n.* *Green juice;* the juice extracted from *green* or unripe fruit; an acid liquor expressed from wild apples, &c., used in sauces. [Fr. *verjus—verd*, green, and *jus*, juice.]

Vermicelli, vėr-mi-chel'li, *n.* A species of wheaten paste, manufactured in Italy, in the form of long, slender threads, and so named on account of its *worm-like* appearance. [It.—L. *vermis*, a worm.]

Vermicular, vėr-mik'ū-lär, *a.* Resembling *a worm;* resembling the motion of a worm. [Fr. *vermiculaire*—L. *vermis*, Sans. *krimi*, a worm.]

Vermiculation, vėr-mik'ū-lā"shon, *n.* The act of moving in the form of a worm; act of forming so as to resemble the *motion of a worm*. [L. *vermiculatio*.]

Vermiform, vėr'mi-form, *a.* Having the *form of a worm*. [L. *vermis*, a worm, and *forma*, form.]

Vermifuge, vėr'mi-fūj, *n.* A *medicine that expels worms* from animal bodies. [Fr.—L. *vermis*, a worm, and *fugo*, to expel.]

Vermilion, vėr-mil'li-on, *n.* A scarlet colour, so named because obtained from *a little worm* or grub, found in a certain plant; a beautiful red colouring matter procured from sulphur or mercury; any beautiful red colour. *vt.* To *dye scarlet;* to cover with a delicate red. [Fr. *vermillon*—L. *vermis*, a worm.]

Vermin, vėr'min, *n. sing.* and *pl.* Literally, *worms;* all noxious little animals or insects, as squirrels, rats mice, worms, grubs, flies, &c.; noxious human beings, in contempt. [Fr. *vermine*—L. *vermis*, a worm.]

Vermivorous, vėr-miv'o-rus, *a. Feeding on worms.* [L. *vermes*, worms, and *voro*, to devour.]

Vernacular, vėr-nak'ū-lär, *a.* Pertaining to the *class or order* in which one is born; native; belonging to the country of one's birth.—*n.* One's mother tongue. [L. *vernaculus*—*verna*, a slave born in his master's house—Sans. *varna*, a class.]

Vernal, vėr'nal, *a. Pertaining to the season of growth; belonging to the spring;* appearing in spring; belonging to youth, the spring of life. [Fr.—L. *vėr, vėris,* the spring—Sans. *vrih,* to grow.]

Vernier, vėr'ni-ėr, *n.* A small movable scale, running parallel with the fixed scale of a quadrant, &c., and having the effect of subdividing the divisions of the fixed scale. [from the inventor, Peter *Vernier*.]

Versatile, vėrs'a-til, *a. That turns round;* that may be turned round; liable to be turned in opinion; unsteady; turning with ease from one thing to another. [Fr.—L. *verso,* to turn about often—*verto,* to turn.]

Versatility, vėrs-a-til'i-ti, *n. Quality of being versatile;* readiness to be turned; the faculty of easily turning one's mind to new subjects. [Fr. *versatilité*.]

Verse, vėrs, *n.* Primarily, a *turning:* a line of poetry; the metrical arrangement of words; metrical language; poetry; a short division of any composition, particularly of the chapters in the Scriptures; a portion of an anthem to be performed by a single voice to each part.—*vt.† To tell in verse.* [Fr. *vers*—L. *verto, versum,* to turn.]

Versed, vėrst, *p.a. Having turned over* in the mind; having thought much on; familiar with; skilled in.

Versification, vėrs′i-fi-kā'shon, *n. The art or practice of versifying.* [Fr.]

Versifier, vėrs'i-fi-ėr, *n. One who makes verses;* one who converts into verse.

Versify, vėrs'i-fi, *vi. To make verses. vt. To form* or turn *into verse;* to describe in verse. *ppr. versifying, pret. & pp.* versified. [Fr. *versifier*—L. *versus,* a verse, and *facio,* to make.]

Version, vėr'shon, *n. A turning;* the rendering of thoughts expressed in one language into words of like signification in another language; translation; that which is rendered from another language. [Fr.—L. *verto, versum,* to turn.]

Vertebra, vėr'tē-bra, *n.* **Vertebræ**, vėr'tē-brē, *pl. A joint;* a bone forming a joint of the spine, or of the backbone of an animal. [L.—*verto,* to turn.]

Vertebral, vėr'tē-bral, *a. Pertaining to the vertebræ* or joints of the spine.

Vertebrate, vėr'tē-brāt, *a. Having vertebræ;* having a backbone, containing the spinal marrow, as an animal.—*n. An animal having vertebræ,* or a spine with joints. [L. *vertebrātus*.]

Vertex, vėr'teks, *n.* That round which anything *turns* or revolves: the pole of the heavens, round which the heavens are said to revolve; the zenith; the crown of the head; the top of a hill or other thing; any remarkable point, particularly when that point is considered as the summit of a figure. [L.—*verto,* to turn.]

Vertical, vėr'ti-kal, *a. Pertaining to the vertex;* placed in the zenith, or perpendicularly over the head.—*n.* A great circle of the sphere, passing through the zenith and nadir, and having its plane perpendicular to the horizon. [Fr.—L. *verto,* to turn.]

Vertically, vėr'ti-kal-li, *adv.* In the zenith.

Vertiginous, vėr-ti'jin-us, *a. Turning round;* affected with vertigo. [L. *vertiginosus*—L. *verto,* to turn.]

Vertigo, vėr-ti'gō, *n. A turning round;* giddiness; swimming of the head; an affection of the head, in which objects appear to move in various directions. [L.—*verto,* to turn.]

Vervain, vėr'vān, *n.* A plant, once held in great repute for its medical virtues. [L. *verbēna,* branches of laurel, &c.]

Very, ve'ri, *a. True;* real.—*adv. Truly;* in a high degree, but not generally the highest. [Norm. *verroie*—L. *verus,* true.]

Vesication, ve-si-kā'shon, *n. The act of blistering.*

Vesicle, ve'si-kl, *n. A small bladder* or blister; an elevation of the cuticle, containing a transparent watery fluid; any small cavity in animals or vegetables. [L. *vesicula*—*vesica,* a bladder.]

Vesicular, vē-sik'ū-lar, *a. Pertaining to vesicles;* hollow; having little bladders or glands on the surface, as the leaf of a plant. [Fr. *vésiculaire*.]

Vesper, ves'pėr, *n.* The close or *restbringing* portion of the day; the evening; the evening-star; a name given to the planet Venus when she is to the east of the sun, and appears after sunset; (pl.) the evening song or evening service in the Romish Church.—*a. Relating to the evening,* or to the service of vespers. [L. the evening.]

Vessel, ves'sel, *n. A small vase or dish;* a hollow utensil made to hold either liquids or solids; any tube in which the blood and other humours are contained, &c.; a canal of very small bore, in plants, in which the sap is conveyed; any structure made to float upon the water, for the purposes of commerce, war, &c., whether impelled by wind, steam, or oars. [It. *vasello*—L. *vas, vasis,* a vessel.]

Vest, vest, *n. Something put on;* a garment; a short garment covering the body, but without sleeves, worn under the coat.—*vt. To clothe;* to clothe with a long garment; to place in possession of (with *with*); to invest with. [Fr. *veste*—L. *vestis,* a garment.]—*vi.* To come or descend to; to be fixed; to take effect, as a title or right (with *in*). [Norm. *vest,* vested.]

Vestal, ves'tal, *a. Pertaining to Vesta;* virgin; pure; chaste.—*n. A virgin consecrated to Vesta,* and to the service of watching the sacred fire, which was to be perpetually kept burning upon her altar. [L. *vestalis,* from *Vesta,* the goddess of fire, and the patroness of chastity.]

Vested, vest'ed, *p.a.* Fixed; not in a state of contingency, as vested rights.

Vestibule, ves'ti-būl, *n.* Primarily, an open space before a building, or a large open space before the door, but covered; a cavity belonging to the labyrinth of the ear. [Fr.—L. *vestibulum*.]

Vestige, ves'tij, *n. A track* or footstep; the mark or remains of something that has passed away. [Fr.—L. *vestigium*—Gr. *steichō,* Sans. *stigh,* to go up.]

Vestment, vest'ment, *n. A garment;* some part of outer clothing; but it is not restricted to any particular garment. [L. *vestimentum*—*vestis,* a garment.]

Vestry, ves'tri, *n.* A room appendant to a church, where the ecclesiastical *vestments* are kept; a parochial assembly met for parochial purposes, so called because held in the vestry; any room in which such meeting is customarily held. [Fr. *vestiaire*—L. *vestis,* a garment.]

Vesture, ves'tūr, *n. A garment;* a robe; garments in general; covering. [Nor.—L. *vestis,* a garment.]

Vesuvian, vē-sū'vi-an, *a. Pertaining to Vesuvius,* a volcano, near Naples.

Vetch, vech, *n.* A leguminous plant of several species. [Fr. *vesce*—L. *vicia*.]

Veteran, ve'te-ran, *a. Advanced in years;* having been long exercised in anything; long experienced.—*n. An old soldier;* one who has been long exercised in any service or art, particularly in war; one who has grown old in service. [Fr. *vétéran*—L. *vetus, veteris,* old.]

Veterinary, ve'te-ri-na-ri, *a.* Pertaining to the art of healing the diseases of beasts of burden, as oxen, horses, &c. [Late L. *veterinarius*—L. *veho, vectum,* Sans. *vah,* to carry.]

Veto, ve'tō, *n. A disallowing;* the right of forbidding; applied to the right of a sovereign to withhold his assent to the enactment of a law; any authoritative prohibition.—*vt. To disallow;* to *prohibit;* to withhold assent to, as to a bill for a law, and thus prevent its enactment. [L. to forbid.]

Vex, veks, *vt. To trouble;* to irritate; to afflict; to disquiet; to distress. [Fr. *vexer*—L. *vexo*.]

Vexation, veks-ā'shon, *n. The act of vexing;* state of being irritated; disquiet; the cause of trouble or disquiet; great troubles; a slight teasing trouble. [Fr.—L. *vexatio*.]

Vexatious, veks-ā'shi-us, *a. Full of vexation;* irritating; teasing; slightly troublesome.

Vexatiously, veks-ā'shi-us-li, *adv. In a vexatious manner.*

Vexatiousness, veks-ā'shi-us-nes, *n. The quality of being vexatious.*

Vexed, vekst, *p.a.* Agitated; disquieted.

Vexingly, veks'ing-li, *adv. So as to vex.*

Viaduct, vī'a-dukt, *n.* An arched structure for *carrying a road* or railway over a valley upon the same level. [L. *via,* way, and *duco, ductus,* to lead.]

Vial, vī'al, *n. A phial;* a small bottle of thin glass. [Fr. *fiole;* Gr. *phialis*.]

Viand, vī'and, *n. That which sustains life;* an article of food; (pl.) meat dressed; food; victuals. [Fr. *viande*—L. *vivo,* Sans. *jiv,* to live.]

Viaticum, vi-at'ik-um, *n. Provisions for a journey;* in the Roman Catholic Church, the communion, given to persons in their last moments. [L. from *via,* a way, Sans. *i,* to go.]

Vibrate, vī'brāt, *vi. To be in tremulous motion;* to quiver; to oscillate; to move one way and the other; to pass from one state to another.—*vt. To cause to quiver;* to brandish; to move to and fro; to swing. *ppr.* vibrating, *pret. & pp.* vibrated. [L. *vibro, vibrātum*.]

Vibration, vī-brā'shon, *n. The act of vibrating;* a regular reciprocal motion of a body suspended. [Fr.]

Vibratory, vī'brā-tō-ri, *a. Vibrating;* consisting in vibration; causing to vibrate. [Sp. *vibratório*.]

Vicar, vī'kär, *n. One who supplies the place of another;* a *substitute;* the priest of a parish, the predial tithes of which belong to a chapter or religious house

ch, chain; j, job; g, go; ng, sing; TH, then; th, thin; w, wig; wh, whig; zh, azure; † obsolete.

or to a layman, who receives them, and only allows the vicar the smaller tithes. [Fr. *vicaire*—Sans. *vi*, over against, and *kri*, to do.]

Vicarage, vi'kăr-āj, *n. The benefice of a vicar;* the house of a vicar.

Vicarial, vi-kā'ri-al, *a. Pertaining to a vicar.* [from *vicar*.]

Vicarious, vi-kā'ri-us, *a. That supplies the place of a person or thing;* acting for another; substituted in the place of another. [L. *vicarius*.]

Vicariously, vi-kā'ri-us-li, *adv. In the place of another;* by substitution.

Vicarship, vi'kär-ship, *n. The office of a vicar;* the ministry of a vicar.

Vice, vīs, *n. That which ought to be found fault with and despised;* a fault; a defect; depravity or corruption of manners; iniquity; a fault or bad trick in a horse. [Fr.—L. *vitium*—Sans. *badh*, to despise.]

Vice, vīs, *n.* A kind of iron press which serves to *hold fast* anything worked upon. It consists chiefly of a pair of stout jaws or chaps, which are brought together by means of a *screw*.—*vt.* To press closely; to hold as if in a vice. [Ih. *ris*, a screw—L. *vitis*, a vine, the tendrils of which are remarkable for winding and clasping.]

Vice-admiral, vīs-ad'mi-ral, *n.* A naval officer, the next in rank under the admiral; a civil officer appointed by the lords-commissioners of the admiralty, for exercising admiralty jurisdiction within their respective districts. [L. *vice*, in the place of.]

Vice-chancellor, vīs-chan'sel-lor, *n.* An officer in a university in England, who is annually elected to manage affairs in the absence of the chancellor; a judge in chancery, subordinate to the lord-chancellor. Of such judges there are now three.

Vicegerency, vīs-jē'ren-si, *n. The office of a vicegerent.*

Vicegerent, vīs-jē'rent, *n. One who acts in the place of a superior;* a lieutenant. [L. *vicem gerens*—L. *vicis*, change, and *gero*, to bear.]

Vice-presidency, vīs-pre'zi-den-si, *n. The office of vice-president.*

Vice-president, vīs-pre'zi-dent, *n. An office-bearer next below a president.*

Vice-regal, vīs-rē'gal, *a. Being in the place of a king;* pertaining to a viceroy.

Viceroy, vīs'roi, *n. A vice-king;* the governor of a kingdom, who rules in the name of the king. [Fr. *viceroi*—L. *vicis*, *vice*, and *rex*, a king.]

Viceroyalty, vīs-roi'al-ti, *n. The dignity, office, or jurisdiction of a viceroy.*

Viceroyship, vīs'roi-ship, *n. The dignity, office, or jurisdiction of a viceroy.*

Vicinage, vi'sin-āj, *n. Neighbourhood;* the place or places adjoining or near. [Fr. *voisinage*—L. *vicinus*, near.]

Vicinity, vi-sin'i-ti, *n. Neighbourhood;* nearness in place; neighbouring country. [L. *vicinitas*—*vicus*, a quarter of a city.]

Vicious, vi'shus, *a. Full of faults; faulty;* defective; addicted to vice; corrupt in principles or conduct; contrary to moral principles; foul; impure; not genuine; unruly; not well broken, as a horse. [Fr. *vicieux*—L. *vitium*, vice.]

Viciously, vi'shus-li, *adv. In a vicious manner.*

Viciousness, vi'shus-nes, *n. Quality or state of being vicious;* corruptness of moral principles; unruliness.

Vicissitude, vi-sis'i-tūd, *n. Interchange;* regular succession of one thing to another; revolution or change, as in human affairs. [L. *vicissitudo*—*vicis*, change.]

Victim, vik'tim, *n.* A beast for sacrifice, adorned with *the fillet;* a living being sacrificed to some deity, or in the performance of a religious rite; a person or thing destroyed; a person or thing sacrificed in the pursuit of an object. [Fr. *victime*—L. *viacio*, to bind.]

Victimize, vik'tim-iz, *vt. To make a victim of;* to sacrifice; to cheat; to deceive. *ppr.* victimizing, *pret. & pp.* victimized.

Victor, vik'tor, *n. One who conquers* in war; one who vanquishes another in private combat; one who gains the advantage. [L.—*vinco*, *victum*, to conquer.]

Victorious, vik-tō'ri-us, *a. Having gained victory;* conquering; that produces victory; emblematic of conquest. [Fr. *victorieux*.]

Victoriously, vik-tō'ri-us-li, *adv. In a victorious manner.*

Victory, vik'tō-ri, *n. Conquest;* the defeat of an enemy in battle; a gaining of the superiority in war or combat; the advantage gained over spiritual enemies. [Fr. *victoire*—L. *vinco*, to conquer.]

Victual, vit'l, *vt. To supply with victuals;* to store with provisions, as a ship. *ppr.* victualling, *pret. & pp.* victualled.

Victualler, vit'l-ėr, *n.* One who furnishes *victuals;* one who keeps a house of entertainment; a ship employed to carry provisions for other ships.

Victuals, vit'lz, *n. That which supports life;* food for human beings, prepared for eating; provisions; meat. [Fr. *victuaille*, provision—L. *vivo*, *victum*, to live.]

Videlicet, vi-del'i-set, *adv. See, it is permitted;* to wit; that is, namely. (An abbreviation for this word is *viz.*) [L. for *vide licet*.]

Vidimus, vī'di-mus, *n.* An examination, as of accounts. [L. *have seen*—*video*, to see.]

Vie, vī, *vi. To fight for superiority;* to use effort in a race, contest, competition, rivalship, or strife. *ppr.* vying, *pret. & pp.* vied. [Sax. *wigan*, to war.]

View, vū, *vt. To look at or behold;* to examine with the eye; to look on with attention; to perceive by the mental eye; to survey intellectually.—*n. Act or power of seeing;* sight; limit of sight; prospect; mental sight; intellectual survey; exhibition to the sight; purpose; aim; judgment; manner of seeing; a pictorial sketch, as of a landscape. [Fr. *vue*, sight—L. *video*, to see.]

Viewer, vū'ėr, *n. One who views.*

Viewless, vū'les, *a. That cannot be viewed or seen;* invisible.

Vigil, vi'jil, *n. A waking;* watch; the evening before any feast, the ecclesiastical day beginning at six o'clock in the evening, and continuing till the same hour the following evening; a religious service performed in the evening preceding a holiday. [Fr. *vigile*—L. *vigil*, on the watch.]

Vigilance, vi'ji-lans, *n. Wakefulness;* forbearance of sleep; attention of the mind in discovering and guarding against danger; guard; watch. [Fr.—L. *vigil* awake.]

Vigilant, vi'ji-lant, *a. Wakeful;* circumspect; attentive to discover and avoid danger. [Fr.]

Vigilantly, vi'ji-lant-li, *adv. Wakefully;* watchfully.

Vignette, vi-net', *n.* Originally, a kind of flourish of *vine leaves* in the vacant part of the title-page of a book, above the dedication, or at the end of a division; at present, any small engraved embellishment for the illustration of a page of any work; an illustration softened off at the edges. [Fr.—L. *vinea*, a plantation of vines.]

Vigorous, vi'gor-us, *a. Full of vigour;* full of physical strength; lusty; made by strength, either of body or mind. [Fr. *vigoureux*.]

Vigorously, vi'gor-us-li, *adv.* With great physical force or strength.

Vigorousness, vi'gor-us-nes, *n. Quality of being vigorous.*

Vigour, vi'gor, *n. Liveliness;* active force or strength; physical force; strength or force in animal or vegetable motion; intellectual force or energy. [L. *vigor*—*vigeo*, to be lively.]

Vile, vīl, *a. Withered;* of small value; despicable; mean; base; lightly esteemed; morally base; sinful; wicked; abject. [Fr. *vil*—L. *vilis*—Heb. *nâbel*, to wither.]

Viled, vīld, *a.* Vile; wicked.

Vilely, vīl'li, *adv.* Basely; meanly.

Vileness, vīl'nes, *n. State or quality of being vile;* degradation by sin; extreme wickedness.

Vilification, vī'li-fi-kā''shon, *n. The act of vilifying* or defaming.

Vilifier, vī'li-fi-ėr, *n. One who vilifies.*

Vilify, vī'li-fī, *vt. To make vile;* to defame; to attempt to degrade by slander. *ppr.* vilifying, *pret. & pp.* vilified. [L. *vilis*, vile, and *facio*, to make.]

Villa, vil'la, *n.* Primarily, *a fenced place;* a country house, usually one for the residence of an opulent person [L.—Sans. *val*, to fence.]

Village, vil'lāj, *n.* A small assemblage of houses, less than a town, and larger than a hamlet. [Fr.]

Villager, vil'lāj-ėr, *n. An inhabitant of a village.*

Villagery, vil'lāj-ė-ri, *n. A district of villages.*

Villain, vil'lān, *n.* Primarily, one who *held lands* by a base tenure; a man extremely depraved, and capable of great crimes.—*a. Villainous.* [Fr. *vilain*—L. *villa*, a farm.]

Villainous, vil'lān-us, *a. Like a villain;* extremely depraved; proceeding from extreme depravity.

Villainously, vil'lān-us-li, *adv.* Basely.

Villainy, vil'lān-i, *n. Something villainous;* extreme depravity; a crime [Norm. *vilenie*.]

Villous, vil'lus, *a. Shaggy;* abounding with fine hairs. [L. *villosus*—*villus*, hair.]

Vinaigrette, vin-ā-gret', *n. A small bottle for holding vinegar;* a small box of gold, silver, &c., with perforations on the top, for holding aromatic vinegar, contained in a sponge. [Fr.]

Vincibility, vin-si-bil'i-ti, *n. Quality of being conquerable;* conquerableness.

Vincible, vin'si-bl, *a. Conquerable;* that may be overcome. [Low L. *vincibilis*—L. *vinco*, to conquer.]

Vinculum, ving'kū-lum, *n. A band;* a tie; in algebra, a straight mark placed over several members of a compound quantity, which are to be subjected to the same operation. [L.—*vincio*, to bind.]

Vindicable, vin'di-ka-bl, *a. That may be vindicated,* justified, or supported.

Vindicate, vin'di-kāt, *vt. To assert power* or influence in regard to; to defend; to justify; to maintain as true; to defend

Fate, fär, fat, fąll; mē, met, hėr; pīne, pin; nōte, not, mōve; tūbe, tub, bu̧ll; oil, pound.

with success; to prove to be just or valid; to defend with arms or otherwise. *ppr.* vindicating, *pret. & pp.* vindicated. [L. *vindico, vindicatum—vis, vim,* power, and *dico,* to declare.]
Vindication, vin-di-kā'shon. *n. Act of vindicating;* the act of supporting by proof or legal process; the proving of anything to be just; defence by force or otherwise. [Fr.—L. *vindicatio.*]
Vindicator, vin'di-kāt-or, *n. One who vindicates;* one who defends.
Vindicatory, vin'di-kā-tō-ri, *a. Tending to vindicate;* inflicting punishment.
Vindictive, vin-dik'tiv, *a. Prone to vindicate;* given to revenge. [Fr. *vindicatif.*]
Vindictively, vin-dik'tiv-li, *adv. By way of revenge;* revengefully.
Vindictiveness, vin-dik'tiv-nes, *n. Quality of being vindictive;* a revengeful temper.
Vine, vin, *n.* A well-known climbing plant with a woody stem, producing the grapes from which wine is made; a climbing or trailing plant. [Fr. *vigne*—L. *vinum,* wine.]
Vine dresser, vin'dres-ėr, *n. One who dresses vines.*
Vinegar, vi'nē-går, *n. Sour wine;* diluted and impure acetic acid, obtained from wines, &c., by the vinous fermentation. [Fr. *vin,* wine, and *aigre,* sour.]
Vinery, vi'ėr-i, *n. A hot house in which vines are grown.*
Vineyard, vin'yård, *n. A yard for grape-vines;* a plantation of vines producing grapes. [Sax. *vingeard.*]
Vinous, vin'us, *a. Full of wine;* having the qualities of wine; pertaining to wine. [Fr. *vineux—*L. *vinum,* wine.]
Vintage, vint'āj, *n. A gathering in of wine-grapes;* the produce of the vine for the season; the time of gathering the crop of grapes; the wine produced by the crop of grapes in one season. [Fr. *vendange—*L. *vinum,* wine, and *demo,* to take away.]
Vintner, vint'nėr, *n. One who deals in wine;* a wine-seller. [Old Fr. *vinetier,* from *vin,* wine.]
Viol, vi'ol, *n.* An ancient musical instrument of the same form as the *violin,* and which may be considered as the parent of our modern instruments of the violin kind. [Fr. *viole.*]
Violable, vi'ō-la-bl, *a. That may be violated.* [L. *violabilis.*]
Violaceous, vi-ō-lā'shē-us, *a. Resembling violets* in colour. [L. *viola,* a violet.]
Violate, vi'ō-lāt, *vt. To force;* to use force or violence against; to ravish; to interrupt; to break; to transgress; to profane. *ppr.* violating, *pret. & pp.* violated. [L. *violo, violatum—vis,* force.]
Violation, vi-ō-lā'shon, *n. Act of violating;* infringement; non-observance; profanation of sacred things; rape. [Fr.]
Violator, vi'ō-lāt-or, *n. One who violates;* one who profanes; a ravisher. [L.]
Violence, vi'ō-lens, *n. Physical* or moral *force;* outrage; unjust force; eagerness; infringement; hurt; rape. [Fr.]
Violent, vi'ō-lent, *a. Forcible;* moving or acting with physical strength; outrageous; not natural; produced by violence; fierce; extorted; not voluntary. [Fr.—L. *vis,* force.]
Violently, vi'ō-lent-li, *adv. With force.*
Violet, vi'ō-let, *n.* A plant of many species, with a delicate flower, generally blue. One species has a delicious smell. A bluish purple colour, like that of the violet; one of the primitive colours—*a.* Dark-blue, inclining to red. [Fr. *violette—*L. *viola.*]
Violin, vi-ō-lin', *n.* A well-known musical instrument with four strings, played with a bow, distinguished for the brilliancy, as well as the power and variety, of its tones. [It. *violino.*]
Violinist, vi-ō-lin'ist, *n. A person skilled in playing on a violin.*
Violoncellist, vi'ō-lon-sel"ist, *n. A performer on the violoncello.*
Violoncello, vi'ō-lon-sel"lō, *n.* A large, powerful, and expressive bow-instrument of the violin kind. [It.]
Viper, vi'pėr, *n.* A poisonous serpent, so called because believed to be the only serpent that *brings forth living young.* [Fr. *vipère—*L. *vivus,* alive, and *pario,* to bring forth.]
Viperous, vi'pėr-us, *a. Having the qualities of a viper;* malignant; venomous. [L. *vipereus.*]
Virago, vi-rā'gō, *n.* A *woman of masculine* stature, strength, and courage; in common language, a bold, impudent, turbulent woman; a termagant. [L. —*vir,* a man.)
Virgilian, vėr-jil'i-an, *a. Pertaining to Virgil,* the Roman poet, or resembling his style.
Virgin, vėr'jin, *n. A female pure and unpolluted;* a maiden; a woman who has had no carnal knowledge of man. *a. Becoming a virgin;* maidenly; chaste; pure; fresh; unused. [L. *virgo, virginis—*Sans. *arjas,* pure.]
Virginal, vėr'jin-al, *a.* An old keyed musical instrument of one string used by *virgins.—vt.*† To pat.
Virginity, vėr-jin'i-ti, *n. Maidenhood;* the state of having had no carnal knowledge of man. [Fr. *virginité.*]
Virgo, vėr'gō, *n. The Virgin;* one of the twelve signs or constellations of the zodiac, which the sun enters about the 22d of August, represented by the figure of a *virgin.* [L.]
Viridity, vi-rid'i-ti, *n. Greenness;* verdure; the colour of fresh vegetables. [L. *viriditas—vireo,* to be green.]
Virile, vi'ril, *a. Pertaining to a man,* in the eminent sense of the word; belonging to the male sex; masculine; not puerile or feminine. [Fr. *viril—*L. *vir,* a man—Sans. *vir,* to be strong.]
Virility, vi-ril'i-ti, *n. Manhood;* the state of the male sex which has arrived to the maturity and *strength* of a man; the power of procreation. [Fr. *virilité.*]
Virtu, vėr-tū', *n.* A love of the fine arts; a taste for curiosities; objects of art or antiquity. [It. *vertu.*]
Virtual, vėr'tū-al, *a. Having virtue;* having the power of acting or of invisible efficacy without the sensible part; being in essence, not in fact. [Fr. *virtuel.*]
Virtually, vėr'tū-al-li, *adv.* In efficacy or effect only.
Virtue, vėr'tū, *n. Manliness; strength;* courage; that assemblage of qualities which constitutes a true man; moral goodness; a particular moral excellence; right conduct; female chastity; energy which works some good effect; power; excellence, or that which constitutes value and merit. [L. *virtus, virtutis—vir,* a man—Sans. *vira,* a hero, *vir,* to be strong.]
Virtuoso, vėr-tū-ō'sō, *n.* A man skilled in the fine arts, particularly in music; a man skilled in antiquities, curiosities, and the like. [It.]
Virtuous, vėr'tū-us, *a. Having virtue;* practising the moral duties, and abstaining from vice; being in conformity to the divine law; chaste, as a woman. [Fr. *vertueux.*]
Virtuously, vėr'tū-us-li, *adv. In a virtuous manner.*
Virulence, vi'rū-lens, *n. Quality of being virulent;* acrimony; malignancy; extreme bitterness or malignity. [Fr. —L. *virus,* poison.]
Virulent, vi'rū-lent, *a. Full of poison;* very venomous; very bitter in enmity. [Fr.—L. *virus,* poison.]
Virulently, vi'rū-lent-li, *adv.* With malignant activity; with bitter spite.
Virus, vi'rus, *n.* Active or *contagious* matter of an ulcer, pustule, &c.; the agent for transmitting infectious diseases. [L. poison.]
Visage, vi'zāj, *n. The aspect; the appearance; the countenance; the face.* [Fr. —L. *video, visum,* to see.]
Visaged, vi'zājd, *p.a. Having a visage.*
Visaments†, viz'a-ments, *n.pl.* Advisements.
Visard, vi'zård, *n.* A mask.
Viscera, vis'e-ra, *n. The entrails;* the bowels. [L. pl. of *viscus, visceris,* an entrail.]
Visceral, vis'e-ral, *a. Pertaining to the viscera* or entrails. [Fr. *viscéral.*]
Viscid, vis'id, *a.* Having the qualities of the *mistletoe* or birdlime; glutinous; not readily separating. [Late L. *viscidus,* clammy—L. *viscum,* mistletoe.]
Viscidity, vis-id'i-ti, *n. Quality or state of being viscid;* glutinousness; tenacity. [It. *viscidità.*]
Viscosity, vis-kos'i-ti, *n. Quality of being viscous.* [Fr. *viscosité.*]
Viscount, vi'kount, *n. A vice-count;* a degree or title of nobility next below in rank to that of earl, and immediately above that of baron. [Fr. *vicomte* —Low L. *vicecomes.*]
Viscountess, vi'kount-es, *n. The lady of a viscount.*
Viscous, vis'kus, *a.* Glutinous; adhesive; tenacious. [Late L. *viscōsus.*]
Visibility, vi-zi-bil'i-ti, *n. The state or quality of being visible.* [Fr. *visibilité.*]
Visible, vi'zi-bl, *a. That may be seen;* discovered to the eye; apparent; open. [Fr.]
Visibly, vi'zi-bli, *adv.* In a manner perceptible to the eye.
Vision, vi'zhon, *n. The act* or the sense of *seeing* external objects; actual sight; the perception of external objects; anything which is the object of sight; a phantom; a mental illusion; an appearance of something supernaturally presented to the minds of the prophets, by which they were informed of future events; something imaginary. [Fr.—L. *video, visum,* to see.]
Visionary, vi'zhon-a-ri, *a. Affected by visions;* disposed to receive impressions on the imagination; imaginary; not real.—*n. One who is visionary;* one who forms impracticable schemes. [Fr. *visionnaire.*]
Visit, vi'zit, *vt. To go or come to see;* to attend; to go or come to see for inspection, correction of abuses, &c.; to send good or evil upon judicially; to go to and to use, as medicinal springs.—*vi. To practise going to see others.—n. Act of visiting;* a waiting on; act of going to see, as something strange; act of going to view or inspect. [Fr. *visiter* —L. *visito—video,* to see.]
Visitant, vi'zit-ant, *n. One who visits;* a visitor. [L. *visitans.*]
Visitation, vi-zit-ā'shon, *n. Act of visiting;* state of being visited; act of a superior officer or officers, who visit a corporation, college, hospital, &c., to

ch. *chain*; j, *job*; g. ; ng, *sing*; TH. *then*; th, *thin*; w, *wig*; wh, *whig*; zh. *azure*; † obsolete.

examine into its affairs; good or evil dispensed by God; infliction. [Fr. from Low L. *visitatio*.]

Visiting, vi'zit-ing, *p.a. Authorised to visit* and inspect, as a visiting committee.—*p.n. The act of going to see;* visitation.

Visitor, vi'zit-or, *n. One who visits;* a person authorized to visit any institution for the purpose of examining into its affairs. [Fr. *visiteur*.]

Visitorial, vi-zit-ō'ri-al, *a. Belonging to a judicial visitor.*

Visor, **Vizor**, vi'zor, *n.* The movable face-guard of a helmet, through which the wearer *sees*; a mask to disguise. [Fr. *visière*—L. *video*, to see.]

Visored, vi'zord, *p.a. Wearing a visor;* masked; disguised.

Vista, vis'ta, *n. Sight;* a view through an avenue; the trees that form the avenue. [It. sight—L. *video*, to see.]

Visual, vi'zhū-al, *a. Pertaining to sight;* used in sight; serving as the instrument of seeing. [Old Fr.—L. *video*, to see.]

Vital, vi'tal, *a. Pertaining to life;* necessary to life; being the seat of life; very necessary; essential. [Fr.—L. *vita*, life—*vivo*, Sans. *jiv*, to live.]

Vitality, vi-tal'i-ti, *n. State or quality of being vital;* the principle of life; the act of living; animation. [Fr. *vitalité*.]

Vitalize, vi'tal-iz, *vt. To give vitality or life to. ppr.* vitalizing, *pret. & pp.* vitalized.

Vitally, vi'tal-li, *adv. In such a manner as to give life;* essentially.

Vitals, vi'talz, *n. pl. Vital parts;* parts of animal bodies essential to life.

Vitiate, vi'shi-āt, *vt. To make faulty;* to taint; to stain; to render defective; to destroy. *ppr.* vitiating, *pret. & pp.* vitiated. [L. *vitio, vitiatus—vitium*, fault.]

Vitiation, vi-shi-ā'shon, *n. The act of vitiating;* depravation; a rendering invalid. [Late L. *vitiatio*.]

Vitious, Vitiously, Vitiousness, vi'shus, vi'shus-li, vi'shus-nes. See VICIOUS and its derivatives.

Vitreous, vit're-us, *a. Pertaining to glass;* transparent; consisting of glass; resembling glass. [L. *vitreus—vitrum*, glass.]

Vitrescence, vi-tres'ens, *n. Quality of being vitrescent;* glassiness.

Vitrescent, vi-tres'ent, *a. Capable of being formed into glass;* tending to become glass. [from L. *vitrum*, glass.]

Vitrescible, vi-tres'i-bl, *a. That can be vitrified.*

Vitrifaction, vit-ri-fak'shon, *n. The act, process, or operation of converting into glass by heat.*

Vitrifiable, vit'ri-fi-a-bl, *a. Capable of being vitrified.*

Vitrified, vit'ri-fid, *p.a.* Being in a state of *vitrifaction.*

Vitrify, vit'ri-fi, *vt. To convert into glass* by the action of heat.—*vi. To become glass;* to be converted into glass. *ppr.* vitrifying, *pret. & pp.* vitrified. [L. *vitrum*, glass, and *facio*, to make.]

Vitriol, vi'tri-ol, *n.* A mineral substance consisting of sulphur and a metal, so named because it has in certain states the appearance of *glass;* sulphuric acid, popularly so called. [Fr.—L. *vitrum*, glass.]

Vitriolic, vi-tri-ol'ik, *a. Pertaining to vitriol;* having the qualities of vitriol, or obtained from vitriol. [Sp. *vitriólico*, Fr. *vitriolique*.]

Vituperate, vi-tū'pe-rāt, *vt. To find fault with;* to censure. *ppr.* vituperating, *pret. & pp.* vituperated. [L. *vitupero, vituperatus—vitium*, a fault, and *paro*, to set in order.]

Vituperation, vi-tū'pe-rā"shon, *n.* Blame; censure. [L. *vituperatio*.]

Vituperative, vi-tū'pe-rāt-iv, *a. Uttering or containing vituperation.* [It. *vituperativo*.]

Vivacious, vi-vā'shi-us, *a.* Having *vigorous powers of life;* active; sprightly in temper or conduct. [L. *vivax, vivacis—vivo*, to live.]

Vivaciously, vi-vā'shi-us-li, *adv. With vivacity,* life, or spirit.

Vivacity, vi-vas'i-ti, *n. Quality of being vivacious;* spirits; sprightliness of temper or behaviour. [Fr. *vivacité—*L. *vivo*, Sans. *jiv*, to live.]

Viva Voce, vi-va vo'sē. *With the living voice;* by word of mouth. [L.]

Vivid, vi'vid, *a. Alive; animated;* strong; lively; forming brilliant images, or painting in lively colours. [L. *vividus—vivo*, to live.]

Vividly, vi'vid-li, *adv. In a vivid manner.*

Vividness, vi'vid-nes, *n. Quality of being vivid;* strength; strength of colouring; brightness.

Vivify, vi'vi-fi, *vt. To make alive;* to endue with life; to animate. *ppr.* vivifying, *pret. & pp.* vivified. [Fr. *vivifier—*L. *vivus*, alive, and *facio*, to make.]

Viviparous, vi-vip'a-rus, *a. Producing young in a living state,* as those animals that suckle their young. [Fr. *vivipare—*L. *vivus*, alive, and *pario*, to bring forth.]

Vixen, viks'en, *n.* A woman resembling a *she-fox;* a sharp, snappish, bitter woman. [Sax. *fixen*, a she-fox.]

Viz. A contraction of *videlicet*, to wit, that is, namely.

Vizard, vi'zärd, *n.* A mask.

Vizier, vi-zēr', *n.* A high executive officer in Turkey.

Vocable, vō'ka-bl, *n. That by which any-thing is called;* a word; a term. [L. *vocabulum—vox, vocis*, a word.]

Vocabulary, vō-kab'ū-la-ri, *n.* A list of the *vocables* of a language, arranged in alphabetical order and explained; the words of a science; a dictionary. [Fr. *vocabulaire*.]

Vocal, vō'kal, *a. That utters a voice;* having a voice; pertaining to the voice; modulated by the voice. [Fr.—L. *vox, vocis*, a voice, a word.]

Vocalist, vō'kal-ist, *n.* A *vocal musician*, as opposed to an instrumental performer.

Vocalization, vō'kal-iz-ā"shon, *n. Act of vocalizing.*

Vocalize, vō'kal-iz, *vt. To form into voice;* to make vocal. *ppr.* vocalizing, *pret. & pp.* vocalized.

Vocally, vō'kal-li, *adv. With voice;* with an audible sound; in words.

Vocation, vō-kā'shon, *n. A calling;* inducement; destination to a particular profession; occupation; profession; business. [Fr.—L. *vox, vocis*, a voice.]

Vocative, vo'ka-tiv, *a. Relating to calling.—n.* The fifth case or state of nouns in the Latin language; the case in any language in which a word is placed when the person is addressed. [Fr. *vocatif—*L. *vox, vocis*, a voice.]

Vociferate, vō-sif'e-rāt, *vi. To raise the voice;* to cry out with vehemence; to exclaim.—*vt.* To utter with a loud voice. *ppr.* vociferating, *pret. & pp.* vociferated. [L. *vociferor, vociferatus—vox*, a voice, and *fero*, to carry.]

Vociferation, vō-sif'e-rā"shon, *n. Act of vociferating;* vehement utterance of the voice. [L. *vociferatio*.]

Vociferous, vō-sif'e-rus, *a.* Making a loud outcry; clamorous; noisy.

Vociferously, vō-sif'e-rus-li, *adv.* With great noise in calling, shouting, &c.

Vogue, vōg, *n. A flowing;* the *fluctuation* of fashion; the fashion of people at any particular time; temporary mode; popular reception for the time; repute. [Fr. rowing of a ship—Sans. *vah*, to flow.]

Voice, vois, *n.* Sound modulated by the organs of *speech;* cry or call; the peculiar character of sound distinguishing the individual; any sound made by the breath; a vote; choice expressed; language; expression; mode of expression; a particular mode of inflecting verbs; the name given in music to a part assigned to a human voice or an instrument in a composition, as treble, tenor, and bass voices.—*vt. To vote;* to fit for producing the proper sounds; to regulate the tone of, as the pipes of an organ. *ppr.* voicing, *pret. & pp.* voiced. [Norm. *voce—*L. *vox, vocis—voco*, to call—Sans. *vach*, to speak.]

Voiced, voist, *p.a. Furnished with a voice.*

Voiceless, vois'les, *a. Having no voice.*

Voicing, vois'ing, *p.n.* The act of giving to an organ-pipe its proper quality of tone.

Void, void, *a. Bereft;* empty; not occupied with any visible matter; having no legal force; null; not sufficient to produce its effect; free; clear; having no incumbent; vain.—*n.* An empty space; a vacuum.—*vt. To leave empty;* to quit; to send out; to vacate; to nullify; to render of no validity; to make or leave vacant. [Old Fr. *vuide*, waste, empty—L. *vidua*, bereft of a husband.]

Voidable, void'a-bl, *a.* That may be *made void;* that may be adjudged void; that may be evacuated.

Voidance, void'ans, *n. Act of voiding;* act of ejecting from a benefice; vacancy.

Voiding, void'ing, *p.a.* † Receiving what is ejected.

Volatile, vo'la-til, *a. Flying off;* capable of wasting away, or of easily passing into the aeriform state, as hartshorn, ether, &c.; lively; airy; fickle; apt to change. [Fr. *volatil—*L. *volo*, to fly.]

Volatility, vo-la-til'i-ti, *n. State or quality of being volatile;* disposition to exhale; that property of a substance which disposes it to rise and float in the air, and thus to be dissipated, as ether; liveliness; mutability of mind. [Fr. *volatilité*.]

Volatilizable, vo'la-til-iz-a-bl, *a. That may be volatilized.*

Volatilization, vo'la-til-iz-ā"shon, *n. The act or process of rendering volatile.*

Volatilize, vo'la-til-iz, *vt. To render volatile;* to cause to pass off in vapour, and to rise and float in the air. *ppr.* volatilizing, *pret. & pp.* volatilised. [Fr. *volatiliser*.]

Volcanic, vol-kan'ik, *a. Pertaining to* or produced by *volcanoes.* [Fr. *volcanique*.]

Volcano, vol-kā'no, *n.* Primarily, the *mountain of Vulcan;* an opening in the surface of the earth, or frequently in a mountain, from which smoke, flames, stones, lava, or other substances, are ejected; the mountain that ejects fire, smoke, &c. [It. *vulcano—*L. *Vulcanus*, the Roman god of fire.]

Volition, vō-li'shon, *n. The act of will-*

Fāte, fär, fat, fall; mē, met, hėr; pine, pin; nōte, not, mōve; tūbe, tub, bull; oil, pound.

ing; the power of willing or determining. [Fr.—L. *volo*, to will.]
Volley, vol'lē, n. *A flight of shot*; the discharge of many small-arms at once; a burst of many things at once, as of words.—*vt.* To discharge with a *volley*. [Fr. *volée*, a flight—L. *volo*, to fly.]
Volleyed, vol'lēd, *p.a.* Discharged with a sudden *volley*.
Volt, volt, n. *A turning about*; a sudden movement or leap in fencing to avoid a thrust. [Fr. *volte*, a bounding turn—L. *volvo*, *volūtum*, to roll, to turn about, to turn round.]
Voltaic, vol-tā'ik, *a. Pertaining to Volta*, the discoverer of voltaism, or to the voltaic pile invented by him.
Voltaism, vol'ta-izm, n. Galvanism or electricity improved and modified by *Volta*. (from *Volta*, an Italian.]
Volubility, vo-lū-bil'i-ti, n. *State or quality of being voluble*; the act of rolling; fluency of speech. [Fr. *volubilité*.]
Voluble, vo'lū-bl, *a. That may be turned round*; formed so as to roll with ease; apt to roll; active; moving with smoothness in uttering words; fluent; flowing with ease; having fluency of speech. [L. *volubilis*—*volvo*, to roll.]
Volubly, vo'lū-bli, *adv.* In a *rolling* or fluent manner.
Volume, vo'lūm, n. *A roll*; something rolled like an ancient book, which consisted of long written slips of parchment or other material wound round a staff; dimensions; compass; space occupied; solid content; a collection of sheets of paper, usually printed or written paper, folded and bound; the compass of a voice in music, from grave to acute; the tone or power of voice. [Fr.—L. *volvo*, to roll.]
Volumed, vo'lūmd, *p.a.* Having the form of *volumes* or rolling masses.
Voluminous, vō-lū'min-us, *a.* Consisting of many *volumes* or books; having written much, or made many volumes. [Low L. *voluminōsus*.]
Voluminously, vō-lū'min-us-li, *adv.* In many *volumes*; very copiously.
Voluntarily, vo'lun-ta-ri-li, *adv.* Spontaneously; of one's own will.
Voluntariness, vo'lun-ta-ri-nes, n. *The state of being voluntary* or optional.
Voluntary, vo'lun-ta-ri, *a. Willing*; acting with willingness; acting without being influenced by another; having power to act by choice; done by design; purposed; done freely; spontaneous; subject to the will, as certain muscles. n. One who engages in any affair of his own *free-will*. [Fr. *volontaire*—L. *volo*, to will—Sans. *var*, to choose.]
Volunteer, vo-lun-tēr', n. A person who enters into military or other service of his own *free-will*.—*a.* Entering into service of *free-will*.—*vt.* To offer voluntarily.—*vi.* To enter into any service of one's *free-will*. [Fr. *volontaire*—L. *volo*, to will.]
Voluptuary, vō-lup'tū-a-ri, n. A man addicted to sensual pleasures. [Fr. *voluptuaire*.]
Voluptuous, vō-lup'tū-us, *a.* Enslaved by the *will*; given to the enjoyments of luxury and pleasure. [Fr. *voluptueux*—L. *voluptas*, pleasure—*volo*, to will.]
Voluptuously, vō-lup'tū-us-li, *adv.* Luxuriously.

Voluptuousness, vō-lup'tū-us-nes, n. *State of being voluptuous*; luxuriousness.
Voluts, vō-lūt', n. *That which is rolled*; a kind of spiral scroll, forming the principal ornament of the Ionic capital. [Fr.—L. *volvo*, *volūtum*, to turn round.]
Voluted, vō-lūt'ed, *p.a. Having a volute*.
Vomit, vo'mit, *vi. To throw up*; to eject the contents of the stomach by the mouth.—*vt. To throw up* from the stomach; to eject with violence from any hollow place.—*n.* The matter *ejected* from the stomach; an emetic. [L. *vomo*, *vomitum*.]
Vomiting, vo'mit-ing, *p.n. The act of ejecting* the contents of the stomach through the mouth; the act of throwing out substances with violence from a deep hollow, as a volcano, &c.
Vomitory, vo'mi-tō-ri, n. A door of a theatre by which the crowd is *let out*. [L. *vomitorius*, emetic—*vomitoria*, the entrances to the theatres.]
Voracious, vō-rā'shi-us, *a. Eating greedily*; devouring; rapacious; eager to devour. [Fr.—L. *vorax*, *voracis*, devouring—*voro*, to devour.]
Voraciously, vō-rā'shi-us-li, *adv.* With *greedy appetite*; ravenously.
Voracity, vō-ras'i-ti, n. *Quality of being voracious*; greediness of appetite. [Fr. *voracité*—L. *voro*, to devour.]
Vortex, vor'teks, n. **Vortices** or **Vortexes**, vor'ti-sez, vor'teks-ez, *pl. That which turns round*; a whirling motion of water, forming a kind of cavity in the centre of the circle, and in some instances drawing in water or absorbing other things; a whirling of the air. [L.—*verto*, to turn.]
Vortical, vor'tik-al, *a. Whirling*.
Votaress, vō'ta-res, n. *A female votary*.
Votary, vō'ta-ri, *a. Bound by a vow*; consequent on a vow.—*n.* One bound *by a vow*; one devoted to some particular service, study, or state of life. [Low L. *votarius*—L. *voveo*, *votum*, to vow.]
Vote, vōt, n. *Suffrage*; the expression of a *wish* in regard to any measure proposed; that by which preference is expressed in elections; a ticket, &c.; expression of will by a majority; legal decision by some expression of the minds of a number.—*vi.* To give a *vote*; to signify preference in electing men to office, or in passing laws.—*vt.* To choose by *vote*; to enact by vote; to grant by vote. *ppr.* voting, *pret. & pp.* voted. [Fr.—L. *votum*—*voveo*, to vow; Heb. *badad*, to separate.]
Voter, vōt'ėr, n. *One who votes*.
Votive, vōt'iv, *a. Pertaining to a vow*; promised by a vow; given by vow; devoted. [Fr. *votif*.]
Vouch, vouch, *vt. To call to witness*; to declare; to maintain by affirmations; to establish, as proof.—*vi.* To bear witness; to give full attestation. [Norm. *voucher*—L. *voco*, to call.]
Voucher, vouch'ėr, n. *One who vouches*; a paper or document which serves to vouch the truth of accounts, or to establish facts of any kind.
Vouchsafe, vouch-sāf', *vt.* To permit to be done without danger; to condescend to grant.—*vi.* To condescend; to deign. *ppr.* vouchsafing, *pret. & pp.* vouch-

safed. [*vouch* and *safe*, to vouch or answer for the safety of.]
Vow, vou, n. A solemn *separating* of something to God by promise; a solemn promise by a pagan to his deity; a promise of something to be given or done hereafter; a promise of love or matrimony. [Fr. *vœu*—L. *votum*—*voveo*, to vow—Heb. *badad*, to separate.]—*vt.* To *consecrate* to God by a solemn promise; to devote.—*vi. To make vows* or solemn promises. [Fr. *vouer*.]
Vowel, vou'el, n. A free uncompounded modulation of the *voice*; a simply opening the mouth or organs, as the sound of *a*, *e*, *o*; the letter which represents such a sound, and which can be pronounced by itself.—*a. Pertaining to a vowel*; vocal. [Fr. *voyelle*—L. *vox*, *vocis*, a voice.]
Vox, voks, n. A voice.
Voyage, voi'āj, n. *A passing* by sea or water from one place to another, especially a passing by water to a distant place or country.—*vi.* To take *a voyage*; to sail or pass by water. *ppr.* voyaging, *pret. & pp.* voyaged. [Fr.—L. *via*, a way—Sans. *vah*, to draw, to carry.]
Voyager, voi'āj-ėr, n. *One who voyages*.
Vulcanize, vul'kan-iz, *vt.* To change the properties of, as of india-rubber, by causing it to combine with sulphur through the agency of a high temperature.
Vulgar, vul'gȧr, *a. Pertaining to the crowd*; used by common people: vernacular; used by all classes of people; rustic; rude; low; consisting of common persons.—n. *The great mass or multitude*; the common people. (It has no plural termination, but has often a plural verb.) [Fr. *vulgaire*; L. *vulgus*, the people.]
Vulgarism, vul'gȧr-izm, n. *A vulgar* phrase or expression.
Vulgarity, vul-ga'ri-ti, n. *Quality of being vulgar*; the state of the lower classes of society; clownishness of manners; an act of low manners. [Sp. *vulgariddd*.]
Vulgarize, vul'gȧr-iz, *vt.* To make vulgar. *ppr.* vulgarizing, *pret. & pp.* vulgarized.
Vulgarly, vul'gȧr-li, *adv.* Commonly; meanly; rudely; clownishly.
Vulgate, vul'gȧt, n. A very ancient Latin Version of the Scriptures, and the only one which the Roman Church admits to be authentic.—*a.* Pertaining to the old Latin version of the Scriptures. [Fr.—L. *vulgus*, the crowd.]
Vulnerability, vul'nėr-a-bil"li-ti, n. *Quality of being vulnerable*.
Vulnerable, vul'nėr-a-bl, *a. That may be wounded*; liable to injury; subject to be affected injuriously. [Fr.—L. *vulnus*, *vulnėris*, a wound.]
Vulnerary, vul'nėr-a-ri, *a. Pertaining to wounds*; adapted to the cure of external injuries. [Fr. *vulnéraire*.]
Vulpine, vul'pin, *a. Pertaining to the fox*; cunning; crafty. [L. *vulpinus*—L. *vulpes*, a fox.]
Vulture, vul'tūr, n. A large *carnivorous* and rapacious bird. [L. *vultur*, *vultūris*—Sans. *val*, to be given to, and *tarasa*, flesh.]
Vulturine, vul'tūr-in, *a. Belonging to the vulture*; having the qualities of the vulture. [L. *vulturīnus*.]

---

ch, *chain*; j, *job*; g, *go*: ng, *sing*; ᴛʜ, *then*; th, *thin*; w, *wig*; wh. *whig*; zh, *azure*: † *obsolete*.

W.

Wabble, wob'l, *vi.* To move from one side to the other, as a spinning top, when about to fall. *ppr.* wabbling, *pret. & pp.* wabbled. [Sax. *wapelian.*]

Wabbling, wob'l-ing, *p.a.* Having an irregular motion backward and forward.

Wacke, wak'e, *n.* A massive mineral, intermediate between claystone and basalt, and which may be considered as a soft and earthy variety of basalt. [G.]

Wad, wod, *n.* A little mass of some soft or flexible material, used for stopping the charge of powder in a gun; a little mass, tuft, or bundle, as of hay or tow. *vt.* To form into a *wad*; to stuff with wadding. *ppr.* wadding, *pret. & pp.* wadded. [G. *watte*—Old G. *wetan*, to join.]

Wadded, wod'ed, *p.a.* Formed into a *wad*; stuffed with wadding.

Wadding, wod'ing, *p.n.* Any pliable substance of which *wads* may be made; a spongy web used for stuffing various parts of ladies' dresses.

Waddle, wod'l, *vi.* To move one way and the other in walking; to vacillate. *ppr.* waddling, *pret. & pp.* waddled. [corrupted from D. *waggelen*, to stagger.]

Waddler, wod'l-er, *n.* One that waddles.

Wade, wād, *vi.* To walk or go through *water*; to go or walk through any substance that yields to the feet; to pass with labour. (It often assumes an active form by the ellipsis of *through*.) *ppr.* wading, *pret. & pp.* waded. [Sax. *wadan*, to wade.]

Wader, wād'er, *n.* One that wades; a wading bird.

Wafer, wā'fer, *n.* A thin cake, as of bread or paste; the bread given in the Roman Catholic celebration of the eucharist; a little thin round leaf of paste for fastening letters.—*vt.* To seal or close with a *wafer.* [Old Fr. *gaufre*—L. *favus*, a honeycomb.]

Waft, wäft, *vt.* To impel by a waving motion; to convey through water or air; to convey, as ships; to keep from sinking; to wave the hand to.—*vi.* To go with a waving motion; to pass in a buoyant medium; to float.—*n.* A floating body; a signal displayed from a ship's stern, by hoisting an ensign furled in a roll, to the head of the staff. [Dan. *vifte*, to fan, to waft.]

Waftage, wäft'aj, *n.* Conveyance.

Wafter, wäft'er, *n.* He or that which *wafts*; a passage-boat.

Wafting, wäft'ing, *p.n.* A bearing or floating in a fluid.

Wafture, wäft'ūr, *n.* The act of waving.

Wag, wag, *vt.* To move one way and the *other* with quick turns; to move lightly from side to side; to shake slightly. *vi.* To move lightly, or with quick turns, from side to side; to swing; to stir; to depart. *ppr.* wagging, *pret. & pp.* wagged. [Sax. *wagian*—Sans. *vakh*, to go.]—*n.* A droll; a man full of low sport and humour; one ludicrously mischievous. [Sax. *wægan*, to deceive.]

Wage, wāj, *vt.* To war, followed by a noun of the same signification—*war*. Compare 'to sin a sin,' 'to fight a fight,' 'to live a life,' &c. To make; to carry on. This meaning is consequential. *ppr.* waging, *pret. & pp.* waged. [Sax. *wigan*, to fight.]

Wager, wāj, *vt.* To attempt; to venture.

Wager, wā'jer, *n.* A *pledge*; subject on which bets are laid.—*vt.* To pledge, as a *wager*; to bet; to hazard on the issue of a contest. [Fr. *gage.*]

Wagerer, wā'jer-er, *n.* One who wagers.

Wages, wā'jez, *n.* plural in termination, but singular in signification. That which is *verbally covenanted* to be paid for work done; hire; the price paid for labour; the return made to those employed to perform any kind of labour by their employers; fruit; recompense; that which is given or received in return. [Fr. *gage*, a token, *pl.* wages.]

Waggery, wag'e-ri, *n.* Tricks of a *wag*; mischievous merriment; sarcasm in good humour.

Waggish, wag'ish, *a.* Like a *wag*; mischievous in sport; frolicsome.

Waggishly, wag'ish-li, *adv.* In a *waggish manner*; in sport.

Waggishness, wag'ish-nes, *n.* Quality of being *waggish*; mischievous sport.

Waggle, wag'l, *vi.* To move from side to side in walking.—*vt.* To move one way and the other. *ppr.* waggling, *pret. & pp.* waggled. [D. *waggelen.*]

Waggon, wag'on, *n.* A *vehicle* moved on four wheels, and usually drawn by horses. [Sax. *wægen*; Sans. *vah*, to carry.]

Waggoner, wag'on-er, *n.* One who conducts a waggon.

Wagtail, wag'tāl, *n.* A small bird, so named because it incessantly *jerks* its tail up and down. [*wag* and *tail.*]

Wail, wāl, *vt.* To cry out in sorrow for; to lament; to bewail.—*vi.* To utter a loud cry of *sorrow*; to express sorrow audibly.—*n.* A loud cry of *sorrow*; violent lamentation. [Icel. *vila.*]

Wailing, wāl'ing, *p.n.* Loud cries of *sorrow*; deep lamentation.

Wailingly, wāl'ing-li, *adv.* In a wailing manner.

Wain, wān, *n.* A *waggon.* [Sax. *wæn.*]

Wain-rope, wān'rōp, *n.* A cart-rope.

Wainscot, wān'skot, *n.* The timberwork that serves to line the *walls* of a room, being usually made in *panels*, to serve instead of hangings.—*vt.* To line with boards, as a hall; to line with different materials. *ppr.* wainscotting, *pret. & pp.* wainscotted. [D. *wagenschot*—Sax. *wag*, a wall.]

Wainscotting, wān'skot-ing, *p.n.* Wainscot, or the material used for it; the act of covering walls with boards in panels.

Waist, wāst, *n.* The *smallest* part of the trunk of the body; the *small* part of the body between the chest and hips; that part of a ship which is between the quarter-deck and forecastle; the middle part of the ship. [W. *gwasg*, the waist, the place where the girdle is tied.]

Waistband, wāst'band, *n.* The band or upper part of breeches, which encompasses the *waist.*

Waistcoat, wāst'kōt, *n.* A short coat or garment for men, extending no lower than the hips, and covering the *waist*; a vest.

Wait, wāt, *vi.* To stay or rest in expectation; to stay proceedings, in expectation of some person, or the arrival of some hour; not to depart; to lie in ambush, as an enemy.—*vt.* To stay for; to attend; to accompany with submission or respect (with *on*).—*n.* A *watching*; ambush; as, to lie in wait. [Fr. *guetter*; Old G. *watchen*, to watch.]

Waiter, wāt'er, *n.* One who *waits*; an attendant; a servant in attendance; a salver; a vessel on which tea furniture, &c., is carried.

Waiting, wāt'ing, *p.a.* An epithet applied to one *who waits.*—*p.n.* The act of staying in expectation; attendance.

Waiting-maid, Waiting-woman, wāt'ing-mād, wāt'ing-wu-man, *n.* An upper servant who attends a lady.

Waitress, wāt'res, *n.* a female attendant in a public-room, or at an inn, &c.

Waive, wāv, *vt.* To *relinquish*; not to insist on; to defer for the present. *ppr.* waiving, *pret. & pp.* waived. [Old Fr. *guesver*, to give over.]

Wake, wāk, *vi.* To be *awake*; to watch; to be roused from sleep; to be awakened; to be quick; to be alive or active.—*vt.* To *rouse* from sleep; to excite; to put in action; to bring to life again, as if from the sleep of death. *ppr.* waking, *pret. & pp.* waked.—*n.* The feast of the dedication of the parish church, formerly kept by *watching* all night; [Sax. *waeg*, a wave] the track left by a ship in passing through the water. [Sax. *wacian*—Goth. *wakan.*]

Wakeful, wāk'ful, *a.* Watchful; vigilant; not sleeping; indisposed to sleep.

Wakefully, wāk'ful-li, *adv.* With *watching* or sleeplessness.

Wakefulness, wāk'ful-nes, *n.* State of being *wakeful*; indisposition to sleep.

Waken, wāk'n, *vi.* To *wake*; to cease to sleep.—*vt.* To *rouse* from sleep; to excite to action; to produce; to rouse into action.

Wake-robin, wāk'ro-bin, *n.* A plant found in many woods in Britain, which is acrid in its properties, but whose underground stem yields a quantity of starchy matter known as Portland sago.

Wale, wāl, *n.* A stripe; the mark of a rod or whip on animal flesh; a ridge rising on the surface of cloth.—*vt.* To mark with stripes or streaks. *ppr.* waling, *pret. & pp.* waled. [Sax. *walan*, marks of stripes.]

Walk, wak, *vi.* To *move* slowly on the feet; to step slowly along; to move with the slowest pace, as a horse, to go on the feet for exercise or amusement; to go; to travel; in Scripture, to act or behave; to pursue a particular course of life.—*vt.* To pass through or upon, as to walk the streets; to cause to step slowly; to lead, drive, or ride with a slow pace.—*n.* The *act of walking*; the act of walking for air or exercise; gait; length of way through which one walks; a place for walking; road; place of wandering; space; course of life or pursuit; the slowest pace of a horse, ox, or other quadruped. [Old G. *walagōn*, to walk—Sans. *vakh*, to go.]

Walking, wak'ing, *p.n.* The act of *moving* on the feet with a slow pace.

Fāte, fär, fat, fall; mē, met, hėr; pīne, pin; nōte, not, mōve; tūbe, tub, bull; oil, pound.

Walking-staff, Walking-stick, wąk'ingstaf, wąk'ing-stik, n. A staff or stick carried in the hand for support or amusement in walking.
Wall, wąl, n. A structure of stone, brick, or other materials, raised to some height, serving to inclose a space, &c., and affording a defence or security; a defence; means of security.—vt. To inclose with a wall; to defend by walls; to fill up with a wall. [Sax.—L. vallum, a rampart—Sans. val, to protect.]
Wallet, wol'let, n. A bag for carrying the necessaries for a journey; a knapsack; anything protuberant and swagging. [from Sax. wealthan, to travel.]
Wall-flower, wąl'flou-ėr, n. A plant whose flowers exhale a delicious odour, and which in its wild state grows on old walls and in stony places.
Walling, wąl'ing, p.n. Act of fortifying with a wall; walls in general; materials for walls.
Wallow, wol'lō, vi. To roll; to roll one's body on the earth, in mire, or on other substance; to tumble and roll in water or mire, as swine; to live in gross vice. (With in.) [Sax. wealwian—Old G. wallōn, to roll.]
Wallower, wol'lō-ėr, n. One that wallows.
Walnut, wąl'nut, n. A tree of several species, a native of Persia; the nut or fruit of the tree. [Sax. wal-hnut.]
Walrus, wol'rus, n. The whale-horse; the morse, sea-horse, or sea-cow, a marine carnivorous mammal, inhabiting the arctic seas. [Old G. wal, a whale, and hros, a horse.]
Waltz, walts, n. The name of the national German dance, performed by two persons, who, almost embracing each other, whirl rapidly round on an axis of their own, while at the same time they move quickly in a circle, whose radius is from 10 to 12 feet, according to the dimensions of the room; the species of music which accompanies the dance.— vi. To dance a waltz. [G. wälzen, to roll, wheel.]
Waltzer, wąlts'ėr, n. A person who waltzes.
Waltzing, wąlts'ing, p.n. The act of dancing a waltz.
Wan, won, a. Deficient in colour; pale; having a sickly hue. [Sax. wana, deficient, wanting.]
Wand, wond, n. A flexible rod; a small stick or twig; a staff of authority; a rod used by conjurors. [Dan. vaand.]
Wander, won'dėr, vi. To leave the right or true path; to depart from duty; to rove; to ramble here and there without any certain course or object in view; to depart from the subject in discussion; to leave home; to be delirious; not to be under the guidance of reason. [Sax. wandrian.]
Wanderer, won'dėr-ėr, n. One who wanders; one that deviates from duty; a rambler; one that roves.
Wandering, won'dėr-ing, p.a. Deviating from duty; roving; rambling; erratic; disordered in mind.—p.n. Deviation from rectitude; a travelling without a settled course; mistaken way; a roving of the mind or thoughts from the business in which one ought to be engaged; the roving of the mind in a dream or in delirium; uncertainty.
Wanderingly, won'dėr-ing-li, adv. In a wandering or unsteady manner.
Wane, wān, vi. To diminish or become less; to fall away; to fail; to decline; to sink.—n. Decline; decrease; the decrease of the illuminated part of the moon's disc. [Sax. wanian, to become less, to waste, to decay.]
Wanly, won'li, adv. In a pale manner.
Wanness, won'nes, n. State of being wan; a sallow, dead, pale colour.
Want, wont, n. Deficiency; the absence of that which is necessary; need; necessity; poverty; indigence; state of not having; that which is not possessed, but is desired.—vt. To be deficient of or in; to lack; not to have; to fall short of; not to contain or have; to have occasion for; to wish for; to desire.—vi. To be deficient; to fail; to be missed; not to be present; to fall short. [from waniod, pp. of Sax. wanian, to wane.]
Wanting, wont'ing, p.a. Absent; deficient.
Wanton, won'ton, a. Lustful; lascivious; dissolute; frolicsome; sportive; airy; superfluous; not regular; turned fortuitously.—n. A lewd person; a lascivious man or woman; a trifler; an insignificant flutterer.—vi. To play lasciviously; to move nimbly and irregularly. [W. chwant, desire, lust.]
Wantonly, won'ton-li, adv. In a wanton manner.
Wantonness, won'ton-nes, n. Lasciviousness; negligence of restraint; sportiveness; waggery.
War, wąr, n. A hostile contest between nations or states, carried on by force, either for defence or for redressing wrongs; poetically, forces; army; the profession of arms; hostility; state of opposition; enmity; disposition to contention.—vi. To make war; to invade or attack a nation or state with force of arms; to contend; to strive violently. ppr. warring, pret. & pp. warred. [Fr. guerre—Old G. warjan, to drive off.]
Warble, wąr'bl, vt. To utter musically with a quick and varied voice, or with vibrations; to modulate with turns or variations; to cause to quaver; to utter musically.—vi. To sing in a varied voice or with vibrations; to be modulated; to be uttered melodiously, as warbling lays. ppr. warbling, pret. & pp. warbled.—n. Act of warbling; a song. [G. wirbeln, to turn round, to warble.]
Warbler, wąr'bl-ėr, n. One that warbles; a singer; one of a class of the smaller singing-birds.
Warbling, wąr'bl-ing, p.a. Making melodious notes; giving forth melodious notes.—p.n. The act of shaking or modulating notes; singing.
Warblingly, wąr'bl-ing-li, adv. In a warbling manner.
Ward, wąrd, vt. To guard; to watch; to protect; to repel; to turn aside, as anything mischievous that approaches (with off).—n. Act of guarding; guard made by a weapon in fencing; a stronghold; one whose business is to guard; a certain district or quarter of a city; custody; a minor or person under the care of a guardian; one of the apartments into which an hospital is divided; a part of a lock which corresponds to its proper key, and prevents any other key from opening the lock. [Sax. weardian, to guard—Old G. warten, to look after, to protect.]
Warden, wąr'den, n. A guardian; a keeper; a large hard pear†.
Wardenship, wąr'den-ship, n. The office of a warden.
Warder, wąrd'ėr, n. One who wards; a guard; a keeper; a truncheon†.
Wardrobe, wąrd'rōb, n. A room where clothes are kept; a piece of furniture for hanging up wearing apparel; wearing apparel in general. [ward and robe.]
Ward-room, wąrd'rōm, n. A room over the gun-room of a ship of war, where the lieutenants and other principal officers sleep and mess. [ward and room.]
Wardship, wąrd'ship, n. Guardianship; care and protection of a ward; right of guardianship; pupilage.
Ware, wār, n. Wares, wārz, pl. Merchandise; goods; commodities. (Usually in the plural.) [Sax.]
Warehouse, wār'hous, n. A storehouse for wares or goods.—vt. To deposit in a warehouse; to place in the warehouse of the government, to be kept until duties are paid. ppr. warehousing, pret. & pp. warehoused.
Warfare, wąr'fār, n. A going on war; military life; contest; struggle with spiritual enemies. [war and fare.]
Warily, wā'ri-li, adv. Cautiously; with wise foresight.
Wariness, wā'ri-nes, n. Quality or state of being wary; caution.
Warlike, wąr'lik, a. Having the nature or appearance of war; pertaining to war; fit for war; disposed for war. [war and like.]
Warm, wąrm, a. Causing to sweat; having heat in a moderate degree; having prevalence of heat; zealous; habitually ardent; irritable; easily provoked; furious; busy in action; fanciful; vigorous; in painting, noting such colours as have yellow or yellow-red for their basis.—vt. To make warm; to make earnest; to engage; to excite ardour or zeal in.—vi. To grow warm; to become ardent or animated. [Sax. wearm—Sans. gharma, heat—ghri, to moisten.]
Warmer, wąrm'ėr, n. He who warms; that which warms.
Warmly, wąrm'li, adv. In a warm manner; eagerly; ardently.
Warmth, wąrmth, n. State or quality of being warm; gentle heat; ardour; eagerness; animation; enthusiasm; that glowing effect which arises from the use of warm colours in painting.
Warn, wąrn, vt. To put upon guard or defence; to give notice to of approaching danger, that it may be avoided; to caution against evil practices; to admonish of any duty; to give notice to; to notify by authority; to summon. [Sax. wyrnan, to warn, forbid.]
Warning, wąrn'ing, p.a. Admonishing; giving notice to; summoning to appear. — p.n. Caution against danger; previous notice.
War-office, wąr'of-fis, n. An office in which the military affairs of a country are superintended and managed.
Warp, wąrp, n. The thread at length through which the woof is cast in weaving; the threads which are extended lengthwise in the loom; a rope employed in drawing a ship or boat; a towing line.—vi. To be thrown or cast; to turn from a straight course; to swerve; to fly with a bending motion; to turn and wave, like a flock of birds.—vt. To turn or twist out of shape, or out of a straight direction; to cause to incline; to move with a line or warp, attached to buoys, &c., by which means a ship is drawn. [Sax. wearp; Goth. vairpan, to throw.]
Warper, wąrp'ėr, n. One who warps or prepares the warp of webs for weaving.
Warping, wąrp'ing, p.n. Act of one who warps, or that which warps.
Warrant, wo'rant, vt. To give a guar-

antee to; to give power to, as to do or forbear anything, by which the person authorised is saved harmless from any loss.—*n.* A *guarantee*; an instrument by which one person authorizes another to do something which he has not otherwise a right to do; an act investing one with a right, and thus *securing* him from damage; a precept under hand and seal directed to a proper officer, authorizing him to seize an offender and bring him to justice; power that justifies any act; a commission that gives authority; a voucher; right; legality; a writing which authorizes a person to receive money or other thing. [Old Fr. *guarantir*.]

Warrantable, wo′rant-a-bl, *a.* That may be *warranted*; justifiable.

Warrantableness, wo′rant-a-bl-nes, *n.* The quality of being *warrantable*.

Warrantably, wo′rant-a-bli, *adv.* In a manner that may be justified.

Warranted, wo′rant-ed, *p.a.* Authorized; secured.

Warranter, wo′rant-ėr, *n.* One *who warrants*; one who legally empowers; one who assures; one who contracts to secure another in a right, or to make good any defect of title.

Warrantise, wo′rant-is, *n.* Authority; security.

Warrantor, wo′rant-or, *n.* One *who warrants*.

Warranty, wo′ran-ti, *n.* See GUARANTEE.

Warren, wo′ren, *n.* A piece of ground appropriated to the breeding and *preservation* of rabbits; a franchise or place privileged by prescription or grant from the king, for keeping beasts and fowls of warren, which are hares, rabbits, partridges, and pheasants. [Low L. *warenna*.]

Warrior, wa′ri-or, *n.* A person *engaged in war*; a soldier; a man engaged in military life; emphatically, a brave man. [Fr. *guerrier—guerre*, war.]

Wart, wart, *n.* A *hard* and *round* excrescence on the skin, found chiefly on the hands and face; a protuberance on plants. [Sax. *weart—wear*, hardness.]

Warty, wart′i, *a.* Having *warts*; full of warts; overgrown with warts.

Wary, wā′ri, *a.* Cautious; carefully guarding against deception and dangers; scrupulous. [Sax. *waer*.]

Was, woz. The past tense of the substantive verb *to be.* [Sax. *wæs, præt. of wesan,* to be.]

Wash, wosh, *vt.* To *wet*; to *water*; to cleanse by rubbing in water; to cover with water; to scrub in water; to separate extraneous matter from; to spread or float, as colours thinly over broad masses or spaces of a picture; to rub over with some liquid substance; to cleanse by a current of water; to overlay with a thin coat of metal; to purify from the pollution of sin.—*vi.* To *cleanse* one's self *by the use of water*: to perform the business of cleansing clothes in water.—*n.* Matter collected by *water*; alluvial matter; a marsh; a fen; a lotion; a superficial stain; waste liquor of a kitchen for hogs; the act of washing the clothes of a family; the whole quantity washed at once; the fermentable liquor made by dissolving the proper subject in common water; the shallow part of a river or arm of the sea; a colour floated thinly over broad spaces of a picture to make it appear the more natural; a substance laid on boards for beauty; a thin coat of metal. [Sax. *wæscan—wæs*, water.]

Washer, wosh′ėr, *n.* One *who washes*; an iron ring between the nave of a wheel and the linch-pin; a piece of iron, leather, &c., in the form of a flattened ring, interposed between the surface of wood, &c., and the head or nut of a bolt, to protect the surfaces from being damaged during the process of screwing up.

Washerwoman, wosh′ėr-wu̇-man, *n.* A *woman* that *washes* clothes for hire.

Wash-house, wosh′hous, *n.* An apartment, usually in an out-building, for *washing* linen, &c.

Washing, wosh′ing, *p.n.* The act of *cleansing with water*; a wash, or the clothes washed.

Washy, wosh′i, *a.* Watery; damp; soft; weak; not solid. [from *wash*.]

Wasp, wosp, *n.* An active, stinging, winged insect, resembling a bee. [Sax. *wæsp*—L. *vespa*.]

Waspish, wosp′ish, *a.* Having the qualities of a *wasp*; quick to resent any trifling affront; having a very slender waist, like a wasp.

Waspishly, wosp′ish-li, *adv.* In a snappish manner; snappishly; peevishly.

Waspishness, wosp′ish-nes, *n.* Quality of being *waspish*; irascibility.

Wassail, was′al, *v.* Would thou wert whole′; a liquor made of apples, sugar, and ale, formerly much used by English good-fellows; a drunken bout; any festival; a merry song.—*a.* Convivial; festive.—*vi.* To hold a merry drinking meeting. [Sax. *wæse*, perf. subj. second sing. of *wesan*, to be, and *hæłu*, whole.]

Wassailer, was′al-ėr, *n.* A reveller.

Wast, wost, *a.* Mischievous.

Wast, wost. Past tense of the substantive verb, in the second person.

Waste, wāst, *vt.* To *make desolate*; to diminish by gradual loss; to destroy by scattering; to destroy wantonly; to squander; to destroy in enmity; to throw away; to lose in idleness or misery; to wear out; to consume.—*vi.* To dwindle; to lose bulk gradually; to be consumed by time. *ppr.* wasting, pret. & pp. wasted.—*a.* Desolate; ruined; superfluous; lost for want of occupiers; that which is rejected; denoting that of which no account is taken; untilled. *n.* A *desolate* or *uncultivated country*; ground unoccupied; mischief; the act of squandering; loss; useless expense; any destruction which is not promotive of a good end; a loss for which there is no equivalent. [Sax. *westan*—Old G. *wuosti*, desert.]

Wasteful, wāst′fu̇l, *a.* Causing *waste*; lavish; expending property without necessity or use.

Wastefully, wāst′fu̇l-li, *adv.* In a *wasteful* or lavish *manner*.

Wastefulness, wāst′fu̇l-nes, *n.* State or quality of being *wasteful*; prodigality.

Waster, wāst′ėr, *n.* One *who wastes*.

Wasting, wāst′ing, *p.a.* Diminishing by dissipation; consuming by slow degrees.

Watch, woch, *n.* A *keeping awake*; attendance without sleep; close observation; guard; vigilance for keeping; a watchman or watchmen; the place where a guard is kept; office of a watchman; a period of the night in which one person or one set of persons stand as sentinels; a well-known portable machine, generally of a small size, and round flat shape, for measuring time; a pocket time-piece; among seamen, a certain number of the ship's crew who are on duty at a time; the period of time occupied by each part of a ship's crew alternately; a watch light.—*vi.* To *be or to keep awake*; to keep guard; to act as sentinel; to look for danger; to be vigilant in preparation for an event or trial; to be insidiously attentive; to attend on the sick during the night. *vt.* To observe *vigilantly*; to have in keeping; to lie in wait for; to guard; to observe, in order to detect or prevent, or for some particular purpose. [Sax. *wæccan*, to awake.]

Watcher, woch′ėr, *n.* One *who watches*; a warden.

Watchful, woch′fu̇l, *a.* Wakeful; vigilant; attentive; cautious.

Watchfully, woch′fu̇l-li, *adv.* In a *watchful manner*.

Watchfulness, woch′fu̇l-nes, *n.* State or quality of being *watchful*; vigilance; suspicious attention.

Watching, woch′ing, *p.n.* Wakefulness; inability to sleep.

Watchman, woch′man, *n.* One *who watches*; a sentinel; a guard; one who guards the streets of a city, or a large building, by night.

Watchword, woch′wėrd, *n.* The word given to *sentinels*, and to such as have occasion to visit the guards, used as a signal by which a friend is known from an enemy.

Water, wa′tėr, *n.* That *which wets*; a fluid composed of oxygen and hydrogen; a transparent fluid, the most abundant and most necessary for living beings of any in nature, except air; the ocean; a sea; a lake; a river; urine; the lustre of a diamond or pearl; a liquid substance or humour in animal bodies.—*vt.* To *wet*; to irrigate; to overflow with water; to supply with water for drink; to diversify; to give a wavy appearance to, as silk.—*vi.* To shed *water* or liquid matter, as the eyes; to get or take in water, as a ship. [Sax. *wæter*; Old G. *wasar*—Goth. *vato*—Sans. *und*, to be wet.]

Water-carriage, wa′tėr-ka-rij, *n.* Conveyance *by water*; the means of transporting by water.

Water-clock, wa′tėr-klok, *n.* An instrument serving to *measure time* by the fall of a certain quantity of water.

Water-closet, wa′tėr-klo-zet, *n.* A small *closet* for necessary purposes, supplied with *water* from a cistern to keep it clean.

Water-colour, wa′tėr-kul-ėr, *n.* Water-colours, in painting or limning, are colours diluted and mixed with gum-water.

Water-course, wa′tėr-kōrs, *n.* A channel for the conveyance of *water*; any natural or artificial stream of water.

Water-dog, wa′tėr-dog, *n.* A *dog* accustomed to *the water*.

Watered, wa′tėrd, *p.a.* Made *wet*; made lustrous by being wet and calendered.

Waterer, wa′tėr-ėr, *n.* One *who waters*.

Water-gage, Water-gauge, wa′tėr-gāj, *n.* An instrument for *measuring the depth* or *quantity of water*.

Water-gall, wa′tėr-gal, *n.* A watery appearance in the sky, accompanying the rainbow.

Water-hen, wa′tėr-hen, *n.* A water-fowl, the moor-hen.

Wateriness, wa′tėr-i-nes, *n.* State of being *watery*; moisture; humidity.

Watering, wa′tėr-ing, *p.n.* The act of *supplying with water* for drink; the process of irrigating land; a process to which silk and other textile fabrics are subjected, in order to make them ex-

Fāte, fär, fat, fȧll; mē, met, hėr; pīne, pin; nōte, not, mȯve; tūbe, tub, bu̇ll; oil, pound.

hibit a wavy lustre and different plays of light.
Waterish, wạ'tėr-ish, *a. Resembling water;* thin, as a liquor; moist.
Water-level, wạ'tėr-le-vel, *n. The level* formed by the surface of still *water;* a levelling instrument in which water is employed instead of mercury or spirit of wine.
Water-line, wạ'tėr-lin, *n.* A horizontal *line* supposed to be described by the surface of the *water* on the bottom of the ship.
Water-logged, wạ'tėr-logd, *a. Lying like a log on the water,* as a ship, when a great quantity of *water* has got into her hold.
Waterman, wạ'tėr-man, *n.* A boatman; a ferryman.
Water-mark, wạ'tėr-märk, *n.* The *mark* or limit of the rise of *water;* a letter, device, &c., wrought into paper during manufacture.
Water-mill, wạ'tėr-mil, *n. A mill,* whose machinery is moved by *water.*
Water-nymph, wạ'tėr-nimf, *n. A marine nymph;* a naiad.
Water-plant, wạ'tėr-plant, *n. A plant* which lives entirely in *water.*
Water-power, wạ'tėr-pou-ėr, *n. Water* employed as a *prime mover* in machinery.
Water-proof, wạ'tėr-pröf, *a. Proof against water;* impervious to water.
Water-shed, wạ'tėr-shed, *n.* A range of high land that *carries off the water* in opposite directions. [G. *scheiden,* to separate.]
Water-spout, wạ'tėr-spout, *n.* A remarkable meteorological phenomenon observed for the most part at sea, but sometimes over the land. It appears as a conical pillar of water, descending from a dense cloud, and having the apex downwards.
Water-standing†, wạ'tėr-stand-ing, *a. Wet with water.*
Water-table, wạ'tėr-ta-bl, *n.* A sort of *ledge* in the wall of a building, so placed as to throw off *water* from the building.
Water-tight, wạ'tėr-tīt, *a. So tight* as to retain or not to admit *water.*
Water-wheel, wạ'tėr-hwēl, *n.* An engine for raising water in large quantities; a *wheel* moved by *water,* and employed to turn machinery.
Water-works, wạ'tėr - wėrks, *n. plur. Works* and machines for the purpose of raising or distributing *water;* contrivances for obtaining motive power from falls of water.
Watery, wạ'tėr-i, *a. Resembling water;* tasteless; wet; abounding with water; consisting of water.
Wattle, wot'l, *n.* A hurdle made of flexible rods.—*vt.* To interweave, as twigs one with another; to form, as a kind of net-work with flexible branches. *ppr.* wattling, *pret. & pp.* wattled. [Sax. *watel,* a hurdle.]
Wattle, wot'l, *n.* The fleshy and *movable* excrescence that grows under the throat of a cock or turkey, or a like substance on a fish. [from Old G. *wadalōn,* to move like waves.]
Wave, wāv, *n. That which moves to and fro, or up and down;* a moving swell or volume of water; a swell raised and driven by wind; a surge; a breaker; unevenness; the streak of lustre on watered cloth; a motion resembling that of a wave.—*vi.* To move as a *wave;* to undulate; to fluctuate; to float; to be moved, as a signal.—*vt.* To raise into *waves,* to raise into inequalities of surface; to remove, as anything floating; to beckon; to direct by a waving motion. *ppr.* waving, *pret. & pp.* waved. [Sax. *wœg*— Old G. *weggan,* Sans. *vakh,* to move.]
Waved, wāvd, *p.a.* Variegated in lustre.
Wavelet, wāv'let, *n. A small wave.*
Wave-offering, wāv'of-fėr-ing, *n.* In the Jewish ceremonial worship, an *offering* made with *waving* toward the four cardinal points.
Waver, wā'vėr, *vi. To wave;* to play or move to and fro; to be in danger of falling; to be unsettled in opinion; to be undetermined. [from *wave.*]
Waverer, wā'vėr-ėr, *n. One who wavers.*
Wavering, wā'vėr-ing, *p.a.* Being in doubt.
Waveringly, wā'vėr-ing-li, *adv.* In a doubtful, fluctuating manner.
Waving, wāv'ing, *p.n.* Act of moving or playing loosely, as a *wave.*
Wavy, wāv'i, *a. Swelling in waves;* full of waves; undulating.
Wax, waks, *n.* A thick, viscid, tenacious substance, excreted by bees from their bodies, and employed in the construction of their cells; a thick tenacious substance excreted in the ear; a tenacious substance used in sealing letters, called *sealing-wax;* a thick substance used by shoemakers for rubbing their thread.—*vt.* To smear or rub with *wax.* [Sax. *weax;* Old G. *wahs.*]
Wax, waks, *vi. To increase in size; to grow;* to pass from one state to another; to become. *ppr.* waxing, *pret.* waxed, *pp.* waxed or waxen. [Sax. *weaxan;* Sans. *vax,* to grow.]
Wax-cloth, waks'kloth, *n. Cloth covered with a coating of wax,* to cover tables, pianos, side-boards, &c.
Waxen, waks'en, *a. Made of wax;* soft; yielding.
Wax-modelling, waks-mo'del-ing, *n. The art of forming models in wax.*
Wax-work, waks'wėrk, *n. Figures formed of wax,* in imitation of real beings; anatomical preparations in wax.
Waxy, waks'i, *a. Soft like wax;* resembling wax; viscid; adhesive.
Way, wā, *n. That along which anything is conveyed;* a highway; a lane; a street; any place for the passing of men, cattle, or other animals; length of space; direction of travel; room for passing; course; tendency to any meaning or act; manner of doing anything; means of doing; manner of thinking; humour; manner; plan of life and conduct; process of things, good or bad; general scheme of acting; the motion of a ship through the water. [Sax. *weg*—L. *via*—*veho,* Sans. *vah,* to carry.]
Wayfarer, wā'fär-ėr, *n. A traveller;* a passenger.
Wayfaring, wā'fär-ing, *p.a. Travelling;* being on a journey.
Waylay, wā-lā', *vt. To lay one's self in the way of;* to beset in ambush. *ppr.* waylaying, *pret. & pp.* waylaid.
Wayward, wā'wạrd, *a. Bent on one's own way;* liking one's own way; froward; peevish; perverse.
Waywardly, wā'wạrd-li, *adv.* Frowardly; perversely.
Waywardness, wā'wạrd-nes, *n. Quality of being wayward;* frowardness.
Wayworn, wā'wōrn, *a. Wearied by travelling.*
We, wē, *pron.* Plural of *I;* or rather a different word, denoting the *person speaking and another* or others with him. [Sax.; Sans. *dva,* two.]
Weak, wēk, *a. Without* physical *strength;* not strong; infirm; impotent; not healthy; not able to bear a great weight; not compact; not able to resist a violent attack; not stiff; feeble of mind; wanting spirit; wanting vigour of understanding; not much impregnated with ingredients, or with stimulating and nourishing substances; not politically powerful; not having energy; not having moral force to convince; not well supported by truth; unfortified; not having full conviction or confidence. [Sax. *wuc;* Icel. *veikr;* Sans. *vi,* without, and *kri,* to do, to act.]
Weaken, wēk'n, *vt. To make weak;* to lessen the strength of; to enfeeble; to reduce in strength or spirit.
Weakening, wēk'n-ing, *p.a.* Having the quality of reducing strength.
Weakly, wēk'li, *a.* Not strong of constitution; infirm.—*adv. In a weak manner;* feebly.
Weakness, wēk'nes, *n. State of being weak;* want of physical strength; want of force or vigour; want of steadiness; want of moral force; want of judgment; foolishness; defect; fault.
Weal, wēl, *n. A sound state* of a person or thing; a state which is prosperous, or at least not unfortunate; happiness; prosperity. [*See* WELL.]
Weal-balanced†, wēl'bal-anst, *a.* Balanced with reference to the public good.
Wealsman†, wēlz'man, *n.* A statesman.
Wealth, welth, *n.* Primarily, a *sound condition;* state of being well; external happiness; riches; affluence; opulence; the means of obtaining the products of labour. [Sax. *weleg,* rich, with the termination *te* or *de.*]
Wealthily, welth'i-li, *adv.* Richly.
Wealthy, welth'i, *a. Possessing wealth;* rich; opulent; affluent.
Wean, wēn, *vt. To cause to cease to yearn for;* to separate from the mother's milk; to detach, as the affections, from any object of desire; to reconcile to the want of anything. [Sax. *wenan.*]
Weaned, wēnd, *p.a.* Separated from the breast, as a child.
Weaning, wēn'ing, *p.n.* The act of separating a child from its mother's milk, and of accustoming it to the want of such food.
Weanling, wēn'ling, *n. A child* or animal newly *weaned.*
Weapon, we'pon, *n. That which kills,* or is used in killing; any instrument of offence; an instrument for contest; an instrument of defence. [Sax. *wœpen;* Goth. *vepna,* arms.]
Weaponed, we'pond, *p.a. Armed;* furnished with weapons or arms.
Weaponless, we'pon-les, *a. Unarmed.*
Wear, wār, *vt. To make worse,* or waste by use; to consume tediously; to affect by degrees.—*vi.* To be wasted by use or time (often followed by a particle, as *out, away*); to be consumed by slow degrees. *ppr.* wearing, *pret.* wore, *pp.* worn.—*n. The act of wearing;* thing worn. [Old G. *werran,* to make worse, to beat black and blue.]
Wear, wār, *vt. To put on;* to carry appendant to the body, as clothes or weapons; to have or exhibit an appearance; to bear. *ppr.* wearing, *pret.* wore, *pp.* worn. [Sax. *werian,* to wear; put on; Old G. *werjan,* to clothe.]
Wear, wār, *n. A fence;* a dam in a river to stop and raise the water, for conducting it to a mill, for taking fish, for watering land, &c.; a fence of stakes set in a stream for catching and keep-

ch, *chain;* j, *job;* g, *go;* ng, *sing;* ᴛʜ, *then;* th, *thin;* w, *wig;* wh, *whig;* zh, *azure;* † obsolete

ing fish. [Sax. *warr*, a place for catching and keeping fish.]
Wearable, wār'a-bl, *a. That can be worn.*
Wearer, wār'ėr, *n. One who wears.*
Wearily, wē'ri-li, *adv. In a weary or tiresome manner.*
Weariness, wē'ri-nes, *n. The state of being weary; that lassitude which is induced by labour too long protracted; fatigue; uneasiness proceeding from continued waiting, or from other cause.*
Wearing, wār'ing, *p.a. Denoting what is worn.*
Wearisome, wē'ri-sum,*a. Causing weariness; tiresome; fatiguing.*
Wearisomely, wē'ri-sum-li, *adv. In a wearisome manner; tediously.*
Wearisomeness, wē'ri-sum-nes, *n. The quality or state of being wearisome.*
Weary, wē'ri, *a. Fatigued by continued toil;* tired; having the patience exhausted; causing weariness.—*vt. To make weary; to reduce, as the strength of the body, by continued toil; to fatigue; to make impatient of continuance; to harass by anything irksome. ppr.* wearying, *pret. & pp.* wearied. [Sax. *werig;* Old G. *weren,* to last.]
Weasand†, wē'zand, *n.* The windpipe.
Weasel, wē'zl, *n.* A small carnivorous animal with short feet, and a slender and flexible body, adapted for *passing through* small apertures, feeding on the smaller mammals, with birds, reptiles, and fishes. [Sax. *wesle*—Sans. *vish,* to pass through.]
Weather, weᴛн'ėr, *n. State of the air in regard to calm or storm;* the state of the atmosphere with respect to calm or storm, heat or cold, wetness or dryness, clearness or cloudiness, or any other meteorological phenomena.—*vt.* To sail to the *windward* of; to endure without harm, as a tempest, through an exertion of nautical skill. [Sax. *weder;* Old G. *wetar*—Sans. *vā,* to blow.]
Weather-beaten, weᴛн'ėr-bēt-n, *a. Beaten or harassed by the weather.*
Weather-cock, weᴛн'ėr-kok, *n.* Something in the shape of *a cock* placed on the top of a spire, which by turning shows the direction of the *wind;* a vane; a fickle, inconstant person.
Weather-gage, weᴛн'ėr-gāj, *n.* The position of a ship to the windward of another; a position of advantage.
Weathermost, weᴛн'ėr-mōst, *a. Being furthest to the windward.*
Weather-side, weᴛн'ėr-sīd, *n.* That *side* of a ship under sail upon which the *wind* blows, or which is to windward.
Weather-tide, weᴛн'ėr-tīd, *n.* The *tide* which sets against the lee-side of a ship, impelling her to the *windward.*
Weave, wēv, *vt. To form into a web;* to unite, as threads of any kind in such a manner as to form cloth; to unite by intermixture; to interpose; to insert. *vi. To practise weaving;* to work with a loom. *ppr.* weaving, *pret.* wove, *pp.* woven. [Sax. *wefan;* Old G. *weban;* Sans. *ve.*]
Weaver, wēv'ėr, *n. One who weaves;* one whose occupation is to weave.
Weaving, wēv'ing, *p.n.* The act or art of arranging in a machine, called a loom, yarn or thread of various materials, as flax, cotton, wool, silk, &c., so as to form cloth.
Web, web, *n. That which is woven;* that which is woven in a loom; a sort of tissue or texture formed of threads interwoven with each other; suffusion; the membrane which unites the toes of many water-fowls; that which resembles a web. [Sax.]

Webbed, webd, *a.* Having the toes united by a membrane or *web.*
Webby, web'i, *a. Relating to a web;* resembling a web.
Web-footed, web'fut-ed, *a.* Having the toes united by a membrane, as a goose or duck.
Wed, wed, *vt. To bind* one's self to, as a husband or wife; to marry; to espouse; to join in marriage; to unite closely in affection; to attach firmly; to unite for ever; to take part with.—*vi.* To marry; to contract matrimony. *ppr.* wedding, *pret. & pp.* wedded. [Sax. *weddian;* Sans. *bandh,* to bind.]
Wedded, wed'ed, *p.a.* Pertaining to matrimony.
Wedding, wed'ing, *p.n.* Marriage; nuptials; nuptial ceremony; nuptial festivities.
Wedge, wej, *n.* That which is driven forward *by agitation* or percussion, so as to force asunder or together; a body thick at one end and sloping to a thin edge at the other, used in splitting wood, rocks, &c.; one of the mechanical powers; anything in the form of a wedge; a mass of metal.—*vt.* To drive as *a wedge* is driven; to crowd or compress closely; to force, as a wedge forces its way; to fasten with a wedge or with wedges; to fix in the manner of a wedge. *ppr.* wedging, *pret. & pp.* wedged. [Sax. *wæcg*—Old G. *wegjan,* to shake.]
Wedged, wejd, *pp.* Split with a *wedge;* fastened with a *wedge;* closely compressed.
Wedging, wej'ing, *ppr.* Cleaving with a *wedge;* fastening with wedges; compressing closely.
Wedlock, wed'lok, *n.* State of being joined in marriage; matrimony.
Wednesday, wenz'dā, *n. The day of Woden* or Odin, a northern deity; the day consecrated to Woden by our Scandinavian ancestors; the fourth day of the week. [Sax. *Wodnesdæg*—*dæg,* the day, *Wodnes,* of Woden.]
Wee†, wē, *a.* Very small.
Weed, wēd, *n.* The general name of any plant that is useless or *troublesome. vt.* To free from weeds or *noxious* plants; to free from anything offensive; to root out. [Sax. *weo l,* an herb, grass, a noxious herb.]
Weed, wēd, *n.* Primarily, *a vestment;* now pl. the mourning apparel of a female. [Sax. *wæd,* garment.]
Weeder, wēd'ėr, *n. One that weeds;* a weeding tool.
Weeding, wēd'ing, *p.n. The operation of freeing from noxious weeds,* as a crop.
Weedy, wēd'i, *a. Consisting of weeds;* abounding with weeds.
Week, wēk, *n. A distinct* portion of time, being one-fourth of the lunar month; a cycle of time consisting of seven days, usually reckoned from one Sunday to the next; the space of seven days. [Sax. *weoc;* Icel. *vika;* Sans. *vich,* to distinguish.]
Weekly, wēk'li, *a.* Coming, happening, or done once a *week;* hebdomadary. *adv.* Once a week.
Ween, wēn, *vi.* To *think;* to imagine; to fancy. [Sax. *wenan.*]
Weep, wēp, *vi. To cry aloud* in anguish; to express grief by shedding tears; to shed or drop tears from sorrow or joy. *vt.* To lament; to bewail; to shed or drop, as tears or other moisture. *ppr.* weeping, *pret. & pp.* wept. [Sax. *wepan*—Old G. *wuof,* grief, weeping.]
Weeper, wēp'ėr, *n. One who weeps;* a

sort of white linen cuff on a mourning dress.
Weeping, wēp'ing, *p.a.* Lamenting; shedding tears.—*p.n. Act of one who weeps;* lamentation.
Weeping-birch, wēp'ing-bėrch, *n. A tree* of the *birch* kind, with drooping branches.
Weeping-ripe†, wēp'ing-rīp, *a.* Ready to weep.
Weeping-willow, wēp'ing-wil-lō, *n.* A species of *willow* whose branches grow very long and slender, and hang down nearly in a perpendicular direction.
Weet†, wēt, *vi.* To know.
Weevil, wē'vil, *n.* An insect of the beetle tribe, which, both in its larva and perfect state, is exceedingly destructive to grain in granaries. [Sax. *wifel.*]
Weft, weft, *n. A webt;* the *woof* of cloth; the threads that cross the warp. [from *weave.*]
Weigh, wā, *vt.* To ascertain the heaviness of *by a pair of scales;* to compare in a pair of scales with some fixed standard of weight; to be equivalent to in weight; to raise; to lift, as an anchor; to ponder in the mind.—*vi. To have weight;* to have weight in the intellectual balance; to bear heavily; to press hard (with *on* or *upon*). [Sax. *wæge,* a balance.]
Weigher, wā'ėr, *n.* An officer whose duty is to *weigh* commodities.
Weighing, wā'ing, *p.n. The act of* ascertaining *weight;* the act of balancing in the mind.
Weight, wāt, *n.* The heaviness of a body ascertained by *the balance;* gravity; that property of bodies in virtue of which they tend towards the earth's centre of gravity; the measure of the force of gravity; a ponderous mass; pressure; importance; power; consequence; impressiveness.—*vt. To load with a weight.* [G. *gewicht.*]
Weightily, wāt'i-li, *adv. Heavily;* with impressiveness; with moral power.
Weightiness, wāt'i-nes, *n. Quality of being weighty;* gravity; solidity; force; power of convincing; importance.
Weighty, wāt'i, *a. Having weight;* heavy; important; momentous; adapted to convince. [G. *wichtig.*]
Weir, wēr, *n. See* WEAR.
Weird, wērd, *a.* Skilled in witchcraft.
Welcome, wel'kum, *a.* Received with gladness, as a *good-comer;* admitted willingly to the house; grateful; pleasing; free to enjoy gratuitously.—*n.* Salutation, as of a new and *good-comer;* kind reception of a guest.—*vt.* To salute, as a *good-comer,* with kindness; to receive hospitably. *ppr.* welcoming, *pret. & pp.* welcomed. [Sax. *wilcuma*—*wel,* well, *cuma,* a comer.]
Weld, weld, *vt.* To unite or hammer into firm union, as two pieces of iron, when *heated almost to fusion.* [D. *wellen,* to weld.]
Welding, weld'ing, *p.n.* The process of uniting together two or more pieces of iron, or iron and steel, when heated to whiteness, by means of hammering.
Welfare, wel'fār, *n.* Primarily, *a good going;* exemption from *misfortune;* the enjoyment of health and the common blessings of life; happiness; exemption from any unusual evil; the enjoyment of peace and prosperity. [*well,* and *fare,* a good going.]
Welk†, welk, *vt.* To mark with ridges.
Welkin, wel'kin, *n. The visible regions of the air;* the vault of heaven. [Sax. *wolcen,* a cloud, the sky.]

Fāte, fär, fat, fall; mē, met, hėr; pīne, pin; nōte, not, mȯve; tūbe, tub, bu̇ll; oil, pound.

Well, wel, *n.* *A spring;* a fountain; a source; the issuing of water from the earth; a pit sunk perpendicularly into the earth to such a depth as to reach a supply of water; an origin.—*vi.* To *spring up;* to flow; to issue forth, as water from the earth or from a spring. [Sax.; Old G. *quellan,* to gush out—Sans. *gal,* to flow.]

Well, wel, *a.* Being in a condition *to be chosen* or *wished* for; being in health; having a sound body with a regular performance of the proper functions of all the organs; fortunate: advantageous; being in favour; acceptable.—*adv.* In a *choice* or *desirable* manner; justly; skilfully; abundantly; favourably; perfectly; fully. [Sax. *wel*—Old G. *wela,* felicity—Sans. *val,* to choose.]

Well-appointed, wel'ap-point-ed, *a. Fully appointed;* fully equipped.

Well-being, wel'bē-ing, *n. The state of being well;* happiness; welfare.

Well-born, wel'born, *a. Born of a good family;* of good descent.

Well-bred, wel'bred, *a.* Educated to polished manners; polite.

Welsh, welsh, *a.* Pertaining to the *Welsh* nation.—*n.* The language of *Wales* or of the *Welsh.* [Sax. *weallisc,* from *wealh,* a foreigner.]

Welsh-rabbit, welsh-rab'bit, *n.* Cheese toasted, and laid in thin slices upon slices of bread, previously toasted and buttered. [*Welsh* and *rare-bit.*]

Welt, welt, *n. A fold* or *doubling* of cloth or leather, as on a garment or piece of cloth, or on a shoe; a border; a kind of hem or edging.—*vt.* To furnish with a *welt;* to sow, as a welt on a seam or border. [Sax. *wæltan,* to roll.]

Welted, welt'ed, *p.a. Furnished with a welt.*

Welter, welt'ėr, *vi. To roll,* as the body of animals; but usually, to roll or wallow in some foul matter, as mire or gore. [Sax. *wæltan.*]

Welting, welt'ing, *p.n.* A sewed border or edging.

Wen, wen, *n. A tumour* resembling a *wart;* a tumour which is movable, pulpy, and often elastic to the touch. [Sax. *wenn,* a tumour.]

Wench, wensh, *n.* Primarily, *a wife;* a young woman; a young woman of ill-fame. [Goth. *qvens,* a wife.]

Wend, wend, *vi.* Primarily, *to turn;* to go.—*vt.* To direct, as to wend one's way, in the sense of, to betake one's self. [Sax. *wendan.*]

Went, went, *pret.* of the verb *wend.* We now arrange *went* in grammar as the preterite of *go,* but in origin it has no connection with it.

Were, wār, *vi.* The plural in all persons of the indicative imperfect of the verb *to be,* and all the persons of the subjunctive imperfect, except the second sing., which is *wert.* [Old G. *werén,* to subsist, to endure.]

Wert, wėrt. The second person singular of the subjunctive imperfect tense of *to be.*

Wesleyan, wes'lē-an, *a.* Pertaining to *Wesleyanism.*—*n.* One who adopts doctrines of *Wesleyanism.*

Wesleyanism, wes'lē-an-izm, *n.* Arminian Methodism; the system of doctrines and church-polity inculcated by John Wesley.

West, west, *n.* The quarter of the heavens in which the sun sets—an event, the precursor of *night;* that point of the horizon where the sun sets at the equinox; the region near this point; a country situated in a region toward the sunsetting with respect to another.—*a. Relating to the west;* coming or moving from the west or western region.—*adv. To the western-region;* at the westward; more westward. [Sax.—Sans. *vasati,* night.]

Westerly, west'ėr-li, *a. Tending or being toward the west;* moving from the westward.—*adv.* Tending toward the west.

Western, west'ėrn, *a. Being in the west;* being in that quarter where the sun sets; moving in a line to the part where the sun sets; coming from the west.

Westernmost, west'ėrn-mōst, *a. Farthest to the west.*

Westmost, west'mōst, *a. Farthest,* to *the west.*

Westward, west'ward, *adv.* Toward the *west;* westerly. [Sax. *westweard.*]

Wet, wet, *a.* Containing *water;* having *water* or other liquid upon the surface; rainy.—*n. Water or wetness;* moisture in considerable degree; rainy weather; misty weather.—*vt.* To *moisten* with *water* or other liquid ; to dip or soak in liquor. *ppr.* wetting, *pret. & pp.* wet. But *wetted* is sometimes used. [Sax. *wæt*—Old G. *watan,* to wade through, to ford.]

Wet-dock, wet'dok, *n.* A *dock* capable of receiving and floating vessels at all states of the tide.

Wether, weᵀн'ėr, *n.* A *ram* castrated. [Sax. *wether,* a ram.]

Wetness, wet'nes, *n. The state of being wet;* humidity; a state of being rainy, foggy, or misty.

Wey, wā, *n.* A certain *weight* or measure. [from *weigh.*]

Whale, hwāl, *n. The great* or *strong fish;* the largest of fish; the largest of the animals that inhabit the globe. It is warm-blooded, suckles its young, and is consequently in reality not a fish; it is therefore classed with the mammals. [Sax. *hwal*—Sans. *bala,* force.]

Whalebone, hwāl'bōn, *n.* A well-known elastic *horny* substance, which adheres in thin parallel plates to the upper jaw of the *whale.*

Whaler, hwāl'ėr, *n.* A person or ship employed in the *whale-fishery.*

Whale's-bone, hwālz'bōn, *n.* Tooth of the walrus.

Whaling, hwāl'ing, *p.n. The business of taking whales.*

Wharf, hwarf, *n.* The point of a ship's *departure;* a sort of quay, on the margin of a harbour or river, alongside of which ships are brought for the sake of being loaded or unloaded. [Sax. *hwarf—hweorfan,* to depart.]

Wharfage, hwarf'āj, *n. The fee or duty* paid for the privilege of using a *wharf.*

Wharfinger, hwarf'in-jėr, *n. A person who owns or has the charge of a wharf.*

What, hwot, *pron. Which;* that which; the thing that; which of many, used interrogatively; to how great a degree, used interrogatively or indefinitely; something that is in one's mind indefinitely; the sort or kind of; partly or in part (used adverbially). [Sax. *hwæt,* nominative neut. of *hwi,* who.]

Whatever, hwot-ev'ėr, *pron.* Being this or that; being of one nature or another; anything that may be; all that; all particulars that.

Whatsoever, hwot-sō-ev'ėr, *a.* Compound of *what, so,* and *ever,* has the sense of *whatever,* and is less used than the latter.

Wheal, hwēl, *n.* A *weal;* a small swelling filled with matter.

Wheat, hwēt, *n.* A cereal plant, by far the most important species of grain cultivated in Europe and North America, the seed of it yielding a valuable *white* flour for bread. [Sax. *hwǣte—hwit,* white.]

Wheaten, hwēt'n, *a.* Pertaining to *wheat;* made of wheat.

Wheat-plum, hwēt'plum, *n.* A sort of plum.

Wheedle, hwē'dl, *vt. To seduce;* to entice by soft words; to cajole; to coax. *vi.* To flatter; to coax. *ppr.* wheedling, *pret. & pp.* wheedled.—*n.* Enticement; cajolery. [Sax. *adwelian,* to seduce, to lead into error.]

Wheedler, hwē'dl-ėr, *n. One who wheedles.*

Wheedling, hwē'dl-ing, *p.n. The act of flattering or enticing.*

Wheel, hwēl, *n.* A circular frame of wood or metal *turning about* on an axis; an instrument on which criminals in some countries were formerly tortured; a revolving firework; revolution.—*vt. To convey on wheels;* to put into a rotary motion; to whirl.—*vi. To move on wheels;* to turn on an axis; to move round; to fetch a compass; to roll forward. [Sax. *hweol—awylian,* to roll.]

Wheeled, hwēld, *p.a. Having wheels* (used in composition).

Wheeler, hwēl'ėr, *n. One who wheels;* a horse next the wheels of the carriage.

Wheeling, hwēl'ing, *p.n. The act of conveying* materials, as earth, stones, &c., on a *wheel*-barrow; a circular movement of troops embodied.

Wheel-plough, hwēl'plou, *n.* A *plough* with a *wheel* or *wheels* added to it, for the purpose of regulating the depth of the furrow.

Wheel-window, hwēl'win-dō, *n.* In Gothic architecture, a *circular* window with radiating mullions resembling the spokes of a wheel.

Wheel-wright, hwēl'rit, *n.* A *man* whose occupation is to *make wheels* and *wheel*-carriages, as carts and waggons.

Wheeze, hwēz, *vi. To breathe hard* and with an audible sound, as persons affected with asthma. *ppr.* wheezing *pret. & pp.* wheezed. [Sax. *hweosan.*]

Wheezing, hwēz'ing, *p.n.* A *noisy* respiration, produced by obstruction of the air-passages.

Whelk, hwelk, *n.* A *shell-fish*., a species of periwinkle; a wrinkle; a pustule, generally situated on the face; a stripe. [Sax. *weoloc,* a cockle.]

Whelm, hwelm, *vt. To cover all* over; *to engulf;* to cover with water or other fluid; to immerse deeply; to overburden. [Sax. *ahwylfan.*]

Whelp, hwelp, *n.* The young of the canine species, and of several other beasts of prey; a cub; a son (in contempt); a young man (in contempt). *vi.* To bring forth *whelps,* as the female of the canine species and some other beasts of prey. [Sax. *hwelp.*]

When, hwen, *adv.* At the time that; at what time, interrogatively; which time, after the time that; at what time, indefinitely. [Sax. *hwenne.*]

Whence, hwens, *adv. From what place;* from what source; how; by what way or means; in general, from which person, cause, place, principle, or circumstance. [Sax. *hwanon.*]

Whencesoever, hwens-sō-ev'ėr, *adv. From what* place *soever;* from what source soever.

Whenever, hwen-ev´ér, *adv.* At whatever time.
Whensoever, hwen-sō-ev´ér, *adv.* At what time soever; at whatever time.
Where, hwār, *adv.* At which place or places; at or in what place; at the place in which; whither; from what place. [Sax. *hwær.*]
Whereabout, hwār´a-bout, *adv.* Near what place; near which place; concerning which. It often takes the form *whereabouts.*
Whereas, hwār-az´, *adv. or conj.* When in truth, implying opposition to something that precedes; the thing being so that; implying an admission of facts, sometimes followed by inferences.
Whereby, hwār-bī´, *adv.* By which; by what, interrogatively.
Wherefore, hwār´for, *conj.* For which reason; for what reason, interrogatively.
Wherein, hwār-in´, *adv.* In which; in which thing, time, respect.
Whereof, hwār-ov´, *adv.* Of which; of what, indefinitely and interrogatively.
Whereon, hwār-on´, *adv.* On which.
Wheresoever, hwār-sō-ev´ér, *adv.* In what place soever; in whatever place, or in any place indefinitely.
Whereto, hwār-tö´, *adv.* To which; to what.
Whereunto, hwār-un-tö´, *adv.* The same as *whereto.*
Whereupon, hwār-up-on´, *adv.* Upon which.
Wherever, hwār-ev´ér, *adv.* At whatever place.
Wherewith, hwār-with´, *adv.* With which; with what, interrogatively.
Wherewithal, hwār-with-al´, *adv.* The same as *wherewith.*
Wherry, hwe´ri, *n.* A light sharp boat used in a river to *ferry* passengers across. The name is also given to some half-decked vessels used in fishing. [a corruption of *ferry.*]
Whet, hwet, *vt.* To rub for the purpose of *sharpening,* as an edge-tool; to excite; to stimulate; to make angry. *ppr.* whetting, *pret. & pp.* whetted. *n.* The act of *sharpening* by friction; something that stimulates the appetite. [Sax. *hwettan.*]
Whether, hweᴛʜ´er, *comp. rel. pron. adv. or conj.* Primarily, *which of two:* which of two alternatives expressed by a sentence or the clause of a sentence, and followed by *or.* [Sax. *hwæthre.*]
Whetstone. hwet´stōn, *n.* A smooth flat stone used for *sharpening* edged instruments.
Whetter, hwet´er, *n.* He or that which *whets* or *sharpens.*
Whew, hwū, *interj.* Begone! expressing aversion or contempt.
Whey, hwā, *n.* The limpid or serous part of milk, from which the curd and butter have been separated; anything pale and thin.—*a.* Whitish or pale. [Sax. *hwæg.*]
Wheyey, hwā´ē, *a. Partaking of whey;* resembling whey.
Wheyish, hwā´ish, *a. Having the qualities of whey.*
Wheyishness, hwā´ish-nes, *n.* Quality of being wheyish.
Which, hwich, *pron.* Primarily, *like to whom or what;* the pronoun relative, relating to things; also to persons interrogatively and indefinitely. [Sax. *hwylc.*]
Whichever, Whichsoever, hwich-ev´ér, hwich-sō-ev´ér, *pron.* Whether one or the other.

Whiff, hwif, *n.* A sudden expulsion of air from the mouth; a puff.—*vt.* To throw out in *whiffs;* to consume in whiffs; to smoke. [W. *chwif.*]
Whiffle, hwif´l, *vi. To mix opinions together;* to abandon one set of opinions suddenly for another; to be fickle and unsteady; to use evasions. *ppr.* whiffling, *pret. & pp.* whiffled. [Icel. *vifla,* to mix together.]
Whiffler, hwif´l-ér, *n.* One who *whiffles;* one who uses shifts in argument; one of no consequence.
Whiffling,hwif´l-ing,*p.n.* Prevarication.
Whig, hwig, *n.* The designation of one of the two great political parties in this country, the opposite party being called the Tory or Conservative party; originally the name given to the party in Scotland opposed to the court in the time of Charles II.—*a. Relating to the Whigs;* Whiggish. [perhaps from Scot. *whig,* Sax. *whaeg,* whey, a mixed drink, composed of water and sour milk, which the Scottish Covenanters drank in their wanderings.]
Whiggish, hwig´ish, *a. Pertaining to the Whigs;* partaking of the principles of the Whigs.
While, hwil, *n. Rest;* time; space of time, or continued duration.—*adv.* During the time that; as long as; at the same time that.—*vt.* To pass time in *rest* or *inactivity;* to draw out; to waste in a tedious way (with *away*). *vi.* To loiter; to spend to little use, as time. *ppr.* whiling, *pret. & pp.* whiled. [Sax. *hwíle.*]
Whilst, hwilst, *adv.* The same as *while.*
Whim, hwim, *n. A sudden and light turn* of the fancy; a freak; a fancy; a capricious notion. [Icel. *hvim,* a quick motion.]
Whimper, hwim´per, *vi.* To express grief with a low, whining, broken voice; to snivel. [Sax. *geomerian,* to grieve.]
Whimperer, hwim´per-er, *n.* One who *whimpers.*
Whimpering, hwim´per-ing, *p.n.* A low muttering cry of sorrow.
Whimsey, hwim´zē, *n.* A *whim;* a freak; a capricious notion. [from *whim.*]
Whimsical, hwim´zik-al, *a. Full of whims;* freakish; having odd fancies; oddly fanciful.
Whimsically, hwim´zik-al-li, *adv.* In a *whimsical manner;* freakishly.
Whin, hwin, *n. The prickly plant;* furze; a mineral, whinstone. [W. *eithin,* furze.]
Whine, hwin, *vi. To express grief,* whether real or affected, by a plaintive drawling cry; to murmur meanly.—*n.* A drawling plaintive tone meant to *express grief;* mean or affected complaint. *ppr.* whining, *pret. & pp.* whined. [Goth. *qvainon,* to be in sorrow.]
Whiner, hwin´er, *n. One who whines.*
Whiningly, hwin´ing-li, *adv. In a whining manner.*
Whinny, hwin´i, *a. Abounding in whins.*
Whinny, hwin´i, *vi.* To utter the sound of a horse; to neigh. *ppr.* whinnying, *pret. & pp.* whinnied. [L. *hinnio.*]
Whip, bwip, *vt.* To strike with a *quick motion;* to strike with a lash, or with anything tough and flexible; to drive with lashes, as a top; to punish with the whip; to lash with sarcasm; to beat into a froth, as cream; to sew slightly. *vi. To move nimbly;* to start suddenly and run. *ppr.* whipping, *pret. & pp.* whipped.—*n.* An instrument for driving horses, &c., consisting of a lash tied to a handle or rod. [Sax. *hweopan,* to whip.]
Whip-cord, hwip´kord, *n. Cord* of which the ends of lashes are made.
Whip-hand, hwip´hand, *n.* The *hand* that holds the *whip* in riding or driving; advantage over.
Whip-lash, hwip´lash, *n.* The *lash* or striking part of a *whip.*
Whipper. hwip´er, *n. One who whips;* particularly, an officer who inflicts the penalty of legal whipping.
Whipper-in, hwip-er-in´, *n.* Among huntsmen, one who keeps the hounds from wandering, and *whips* them in to the line of chase; in parliament, one who enforces party discipline among the supporters of the ministry or opposition, and urges their attendance on all questions of importance.
Whipping, hwip´ing, *p.n. The act of striking with a whip;* the state of being whipped; flagellation.
Whipping-post, hwip´ing-pōst, *n.* A *post* to which offenders are tied when *whipped.*
Whir, hwer, *vi.* To whirl round with noise; to fly off with such a noise as a partridge or moor-cock makes when it springs from the ground.—*vt.*† To hurry. *ppr.* whirring, *pret. & pp.* whirred. [formed from the sound.]
Whirl, hwerl, *vt. To turn round rapidly. vi. To be turned round rapidly;* to move hastily.—*n. A turning with rapidity;* quick gyration; anything that moves with velocity, particularly on an axis; a hook used in twisting. [Sax. *hwyrfan.*]
Whirl-bat, hwerl´bat, *n.* Anything moved with a *whirl* as preparatory for a blow, or to augment the force of it.
Whirl-blast, hwerl´blast, *n. A whirling blast* of wind.
Whirl-bone, hwerl´bōn, *n.* The round cap of the knee; the knee-pan.
Whirler, hwerl´er, *n. He or that which whirls.*
Whirligig, hwerl´i-gig, *n.* A toy which children spin or *whirl round.*
Whirlpool, hwerl´pōl, *n. An eddy of water;* a gulf where the water moves round in a circle, in consequence of obstructions from banks, &c.
Whirlwind, hwerl´wind, *n. A revolving column of air* having a progressive motion, produced by the meeting of two currents of air, blowing in opposite directions, but attributed, by some, to electricity.
Whirring, hwer´ing, *p.n.* The sound of partridges' or pheasants' wings.
Whisk, hwisk, *n.* A small *bunch* of grass, hair, or the like, used for a brush; a small besom; a quick violent motion; a bundle of peeled twigs used by cooks for whisking certain articles, as cream, eggs, &c.; part of a woman's dress.—*vi.* To *sweep* with a light rapid motion.—*vi.* To move nimbly and with velocity. (G. *wisch,* a wisp.)
Whisker, hwis´ker, *n.* Long hair growing on the human cheek; the bristly hairs on the upper lip of a cat, &c. (Used chiefly in the plural.)
Whiskered, hwis´kerd, *p.a.* Formed into *whiskers;* furnished with whiskers.
Whisky, hwis´ki, *n. Water of life;* an ardent spirit distilled generally from barley, but sometimes, from wheat, rye, sugar, molasses, &c. [Ir. *uisgebeatha—uisge,* water, *beatha,* life.]
Whisky, Whiskey, hwis´ki, hwis´ki, *n.* A kind of light one-horse chaise, sometimes called a *tim-whiskey.* [probably from *whisk.*]
Whisper, hwis´pér, *vi. To speak in the*

Fāte, fār, fat, fall; mē, met hér; pīne, pin; nōte, not, move; tūbe, tub, bull; oil, pound.

ear; to speak with a low voice; to speak with suspicion; to plot secretly. *vi.* To *speak in the ear of;* to address in a low voice; to utter in a low voice.—*n.* A low soft sibilant voice, *spoken in the ear;* a faint utterance; a cautious speech. [Sax. *hwisprian*—G. *wispern*—Gr. *ous*, the ear.]

Whisperer, hwis'pėr-ėr, *n.* One *who whispers;* a tattler; one who slanders secretly.

Whispering, hwis'pėr-ing, *p.a.* Backbiting.—*p.n.* The act of *speaking in the ear* with a low sibilant voice; the telling of tales; a backbiting.

Whisperingly, hwis'pėr-ing-li, *adv.* In a low sibilant voice.

Whist, hwist, *a.* *Silent;* still; not speaking.—*n.* A well-known game at cards, so called because it requires *silence* or close attention. [*hist* is the same word, with a little variation in sound.]

Whistle, hwis'l, *vi.* To utter a kind of musical sound, by pressing or drawing the breath through a small orifice formed by contracting the lips; to make a sound with a small wind-instrument; to sound shrill, or like a pipe.—*vt.* To form or modulate *by whistling;* to call by a whistle. *ppr.* whistling, *pret. & pp.* whistled.—*n.* *Sound made by one who whistles;* a small wind-instrument; the sound made by a small wind-instrument; a small pipe, used by a boatswain to summon the sailors to their duty; a call, such as sportsmen use to their dogs; the shrill sound of winds passing among trees or through crevices, &c. [Sax. *hwistlan*.]

Whistler, hwis'l-ėr, *n.* One *who whistles.*

Whit, hwit, *n.* *A creature; something;* a jot; the smallest particle imaginable. [Sax. *wuht*, a creature, thing.]

White, hwit, *a.* *Shining;* bright; being without colour; being of the colour of pure snow; snowy; not dark; destitute of colour in the cheeks; having the colour of purity; clean; free from spot; purified from sin.—*n.* *Brightness;* a negative colour, whose opposite is black; destitution of all stain on the surface; the colour of snow; anything white.—*vt.* To *make white;* to whiten; to whitewash. *ppr.* whiting, *pret. & pp.* whited. [Sax. *hwit*—Sans. *shvit*, to be white, to shine.]

White-bait, hwit'bāt, *n.* A very small delicate fish abounding in the Thames during spring and summer.

White-clover, hwit-klō'vėr, *n.* A small species of perennial clover, bearing *white flowers,* and having a delicious perfume.

White-friars, hwit'frī-ėrz, *n.* A common name of several orders of *friars* from their being clothed in *white.*

White-heat, hwit'hēt, *n.* That degree of *heat* given to iron which makes it appear *white.*

White-lead, hwit'led, *n.* A carbonate of lead, much used in painting.

White-light, hwit'līt, *n.* The name generally given to the light which comes directly from the sun.

White-lily, hwit'li-li, *n.* A well-known garden plant, much prized for the beauty and fragrance of its flowers.

White-livered, hwit'li-vėrd, *a.* Having a pale look; cowardly; malicious.

Whitely†, hwit'li, *a.* Like or coming near to white.

Whiten, hwit'n, *vt.* To *make white;* to blanch.—*vi.* To *grow white;* to turn or become white.

Whitener, hwit'n-ėr, *n.* One who bleaches or *makes white.*

Whiteness, hwit'nes, *n.* *The state of being white;* freedom from any darkness on the surface; paleness; want of a sanguineous tinge in the face; cleanness; freedom from stain or blemish.

Whitening, hwit'n-ing, *p.a.* *Becoming or making white.*—*p.n.* A preparation of chalk used as a polishing and whitewashing material; whiting.

White-swelling, hwit'swel-ing, *n.* A term applied to a disease of the joints, on account of the unaltered colour of the skin.

Whitewash, hwit'wosh, *n.* A *wash* for *whitening* something; a wash for making the skin fair; a composition of whiting, size, and water, used for whitening the plaster of walls, ceilings, &c.—*vt.* To *cover with a white wash,* as with lime and water, &c.; to give a fair external appearance to.

Whitewasher, hwit'wosh-ėr, *n.* One who *whitewashes.*

White-water, hwit'wạ-tėr, *n.* A disease of sheep of a dangerous kind.

White-wine, hwit'wīn, *n.* Any wine of a clear transparent colour, bordering on white, as Madeira, sherry, &c.

Whither, hwiᴛʜ'ėr, *adv.* To what place (interrogatively); to what place (absolutely); to which place (relatively); to what point or degree. [Sax. *hwyder*.]

Whithersoever, hwiᴛʜ'ėr-sō-ev''ėr, *adv.* To *whatever place.*

Whiting, hwīt'ing, *n.* A well-known fish belonging to the cod tribe, but exceeding all the other fishes of its tribe in delicacy as an article of food, and hence much prized, and called the chicken of the sea; ground chalk cleared of all stony matter.

Whitish, hwīt'ish, *a.* *Somewhat white;* white in a moderate degree.

Whitishness, hwīt'ish-nes, *n.* The quality of *being somewhat white.*

Whitlow, hwit'lō, *n.* A swelling about the ends of the fingers, generally terminating in an abscess. [Sax. *hwit,* white, and *low,* a flame.]

Whit-Monday, Whitsun-Monday, hwit'-mun-dā, hwit'sun-mun-dā, *n.* *The Monday following Whitsunday.* In England, &c., it is observed by most persons as a holiday.

Whitster†, hwit'stėr, *n.* A bleacher.

Whitsun, hwit'sun, *a.* *Observed at Whitsuntide.*

Whitsunday, Whitsuntide, hwit'sun-dā, hwit'sun-tīd, *n.* The seventh Sunday after Easter; a festival of the Church in commemoration of the descent of the Holy Spirit on the day of Pentecost; so called because those who had been newly baptized appeared at church between Easter and Pentecost in *white* garments.

Whittle, hwit'l, *n.* A *small pocket-knife.* *vt.* To cut or dress with a knife. *ppr.* whittling, *pret. & pp.* whittled. [Sax. *hwitel.*]

Whiz, hwiz, *vi.* To make a *humming* or *hissing* sound, like an arrow or ball flying through the air. *ppr.* whizzing, *pret. & pp.* whizzed.—*n.* A *hissing* sound. [allied to *hiss.*]

Who, hö, *pron. relative.* A pronoun relative, always referring to persons; which of two or of many (used interrogatively, and also indefinitely). [Sax. *hwa;* Goth. *hwa.*]

Whoever, hö-ev'ėr, *pron.* Any one without exception; any person whatever.

Whole, hōl, *a.* *All;* total; undivided; not defective; healthy; sound; unbroken; not hurt or sick; well.—*n.* The *all;* the entire assemblage of parts; a system; a regular combination of parts. [Sax. *hāl;* Goth. *hails,* sound.]

Wholeness, hōl'nes, *n.* *Entireness.*

Wholesale, hōl'sāl, *n.* *Sale* of goods by the *piece* or large quantity, as distinguished from retail; the whole mass. *a.* Buying and selling by the piece or quantity; pertaining to the trade by the piece or quantity.

Wholesome, hōl'sum, *a.* *Tending to promote health;* salubrious; sound; contributing to the health of the mind; favourable to morals; salutary; conducive to public happiness; that utters sound words; kindly. [G. *heilsam.*]

Wholesomely, hōl'sum-li, *adv.* In a *wholesome* or salutary manner.

Wholesomeness, hōl'sum-nes, *n.* *The quality of contributing to health;* conduciveness to the health of the mind or of the body politic.

Wholly, hōl'li, *adv. Totally.*

Whom, höm, *pron.* The objective of *who,* coinciding with the L. *quem* and *quam.*

Whoop, hwöp, *n.* A *shout of defiance;* a shout of pursuit; a shout of war; a particular cry of troops when they rush to the attack.—*vi.* To *utter a shout of defiance.*—*vt.* To insult *with shouts of defiance.* [Goth. *hoopan,* to cry out with defiance.]

Whooping-cough, hwöp'ing-kof, *n.* See HOOPING-COUGH.

Whore, hōr, *n.* *An adulteress;* a strumpet; a concubine; a courtezan; a harlot. [Sax. *hure;* Goth. *hors,* an adulterer.]

Whoredom, hōr'dum, *n.* *Adultery;* fornication; practice of unlawful commerce with the other sex; idolatry.

Whoremonger, hōr'mung-gėr, *n.* One who practises lewdness.

Whorish, hōr'ish, *a.* Lewd; unchaste; addicted to unlawful sexual pleasures.

Whorishly, hōr'ish-li, *adv.* In a lewd manner.

Whorishness, hōr'ish-nes, *n.* The character of a lewd woman.

Whorl, hworl, *n.* A species of inflorescence, in which the flowers surround the stem in the form of a ring.

Whorled, hworld, *p.a.* *Furnished with whorls.*

Whose, höz, *pron.* The possessive case of *who* or *which;* applied to persons or things.

Whosoever, hö-sō-ev'ėr, *pron.* *Any person whatever;* any one.

Why, hwī, *adv.* By what proof or reason; from what cause, or for what purpose (interrogatively); for which or what cause or reason (relatively). It is sometimes a mere emphatical expletive. [Sax. *hwi.*]

Wick, wik, *n.* A number of threads of cotton loosely twisted into a string, which by capillary action draws up the oil in lamps, or the melted wax in candles, in small successive portions, to be burned. [Sax. *weoc.*]

Wicked, wik'ed, *a.* *Accursed;* execrable; evil in principle or practice; deviating from the divine law; sinful; vile, pernicious. [Sax. *werig,* wicked, accursed, *wyrged,* accursed.]

Wickedly, wik'ed-li, *adv.* In *a wicked manner.*

Wickedness, wik'ed-nes, *n.* *The state or quality of being wicked;* departure from the rules of the divine law; crime; sin; corrupt manners; the corrupt dispositions of the heart.

Wicker, wik'ėr, *n.* That *which can be*

easily bent; a small quick-grown pliable twig.—*a.* Made of twigs or osiers. [Old G. *wegan,* to shake.]

Wickered, wik'ėrd, *p.a. Made of wickers.*

Wicket, wik'et, *n. A small gate* within a larger one; a hole in a door through which to communicate without opening the door; a small gate by which the chamber of canal-locks is emptied; a sort of little gate set up to be bowled at by cricketers. [Fr. *guichet.*]

Wide, wīd, *a. Separated;* distant from; having a great extent each way; broad; opposed to narrow.—*adv.* At or to a distance; far; with great extent (used chiefly in composition). [Sax. *wid;* G. *weit,* far, distant, remote.]

Widely, wīd'li, *adv. With width;* with great extent each way; to a great distance; far.

Widen, wīd'n, *vt. To make wide or wider;* to extend in breadth.—*vi. To grow wide or wider;* to extend itself.

Wideness, wīd'nes, *n.* Quality of being *wide;* width; large extent in all directions.

Widgeon, Wigeon, wi'jon, *n.* A waterfowl of the duck group, which breeds in the morasses of Lapland, Norway, &c., and on the approach of winter journeys southward. [Fr. *vigeon.*]

Widow, wi'dō, *n. A woman bereft of her husband;* a woman who has lost her husband by death.—*vt.* To bereave of a husband; to strip of anything good. [Sax. *wuduwe;* Sans. *vi,* without, and *dhava,* husband.]

Widowed, wi'dōd, *p.a. Bereaved of a husband* by death; deprived of some good; stripped.

Widower, wi'dō-er, *n.* A man who has lost his wife by death.

Widowhood, wi'dō-hud, *n. The state of being a widow;* estate settled on a widow†.

Width, width, *n. Wideness;* breadth; the extent of a thing from side to side.

Wield, wēld, *vt. To have and to use power* over; to use with full command, as a thing not too heavy for the holder; to employ with the hand. [Sax. *wealdan,* to rule.]

Wieldy, wēld'i, *a. That may be wielded;* manageable.

Wiery†, wīr'i, *a.* Wet; marshy.

Wife, wīf, *n. Wives, pl. A woman;* the lawful consort of a man; the correlative of husband. [Sax. *wif.*]

Wifeless, wīf'les, *a. Without a wife.*

Wig, wig, *n.* A covering for the head usually formed of false hair. [contracted from *periwig.*]

Wigged, wigd, *p.a. Having the head covered with a wig.*

Wight, wīt, *n. A living being;* a being; a person. It is obsolete, except in irony or burlesque. [Sax. *wuht.*]

Wigwam, wig'wam, *n.* An Indian cabin or hut, so called in America.

Wild, wīld, *a. Inhabiting the forest or open field;* not tame or domesticated; growing without culture; desert; savage; not refined by culture; turbulent; licentious; mutable; loose; done without plan or order; not framed according to the ordinary rules of reason; imaginary; fanciful; crazy.—*n. A forest* or sandy *desert;* a desert; an uninhabited and uncultivated tract or region. [Old G. *wildi,* woody—*wald,* a forest—Sans. *vana,* a wood.]

Wild-boar, wīld'bōr, *n. A wild* animal of the *hog* kind, from which the domesticated swine are descended.

Wild-cat, wīld'kat, *n.* A ferocious animal of the *cat* kind, supposed to be the original stock of the domestic cat.

Wild-duck, wīld'duk, *n.* An aquatic fowl of the *duck* kind, the stock of our common duck, teal, &c.

Wilder, wīl'dėr, *vt. To bewilder;* to cause to lose the way; to puzzle with difficulties. [Dan. *vilder.*]

Wilderness, wīl'dėr-nes, *n.* A place inhabited by *wild beasts;* a desert; a tract of land uninhabited by human beings, whether a forest or a wide barren plain; a wood in a garden, resembling a forest; wildness†. [Sax. *wild,* wild—*deor,* beast.]

Wild-goose, wīld'gōs, *n. A wild* aquatic fowl of the *goose* kind; a bird of passage, and the stock of the domestic goose.

Wilding, wīld'ing, *n. A wild crab-apple;* a young tree that grows without cultivation.

Wildly, wīld'li, *adv.* In a *wild manner;* irregularly; capriciously; without cultivation.

Wildness, wīld'nes, *n. The state or quality of being wild;* rudeness; rough state; savageness; savage state; a wandering; alienation of mind; state of being untamed; the quality of being undisciplined.

Wile, wīl, *n. An artifice;* a trick or stratagem practised for insnaring. [Sax.—Icel. *villa,* error.]

Wilful, wil'ful, *a.* Under the influence of self-*will;* governed by the will without regard to reason; obstinate; perverse. [*will* and *full.*]

Wilfully, wil'ful-li, *adv. In a wilful manner;* obstinately; stubbornly.

Wilfulness, wil'ful-nes, *n. Quality of being wilful;* obstinacy; stubbornness.

Wilily, wī'li-li, *adv. In a wily manner;* by stratagem.

Wiliness, wī'li-nes, *n. State or quality of being wily;* cunning.

Will, wil, *n. Power of choice;* that faculty of the mind by which we determine either to do or not to do something which we conceive to be in our power; act of willing; discretion; inclination; power; government; the legal declaration of a man's intentions, as to what he *wills* to be performed after his death in relation to his property; a testament.—*vt. To exert the power of choice in regard to; to choose;* to determine; to direct; to enjoin; to dispose of by will.—*vi. To dispose of effects by will.*—*v.* auxiliary and defective. It is used as one of the two signs of the future tense, the other being *shall.* [Sax. *willan,* L. *volo,* to will—Sans. *var,* to choose.]

Willing, wil'ing, *p.a.* Inclined to anything; free to do or grant; ready; received voluntarily; consenting; cheerful.

Willingly, wil'ing-li, *adv. In a willing manner;* cheerfully.

Willingness, wil'ing-nes, *n.* The state or quality of *being willing;* free choice of the will; readiness of the mind to do or not to do.

Willow, wil'lō, *n.* A plant of great flexibility, which grows *readily* in a moist soil, and which is much used in the manufacture of baskets, &c. The willow is considered as the emblem of despairing love, and is often associated with the yew and the cypress in the churchyard. [Sax. *welig*—D. *willig,* ready.]

Wily, wī'li, *a. Using wiles;* cunning; sly; subtle. [from *wile.*]

Wimble, wim'bl, *n.* Something *whirled round;* an instrument used by joiners for boring holes by being *turned round.* *vt.* To bore, as with a wimble. *ppr.* wimbling, *pret. & pp.* wimbled. [Sw. Goth. *wimla,* to be whirled round.]

Wimple, wim'pl, *n.* A hood or veil; the linen plaited cloth which nuns wear about their necks.—*vt.* To cover, as with a veil; to hoodwink. [G. *wimpel.*]

Win, win, *vt.* Primarily, to *labour for;* to gain by success in contest; to gain by courtship; to obtain; to allure to kindness; to gain by persuasion or influence.—*vi.* To gain the victory; to gain ground, favour, or influence (with *on* or *upon*). *ppr.* winning, *pret. & pp.* won. [Sax. *winnan,* to labour.]

Wince, wins, *vi. To make a motion with a spring;* to shrink, as from a blow or from pain; to kick or flounce when uneasy, or impatient of a rider. *ppr.* wincing, *pret. & pp.* winced. [W. *gwing,* a shake made with a spring.]

Winch, winsh, *n. That which twists or turns;* the crank for *turning* a wheel, &c.; a windlass. [Sax. *wince.*]

Wind, wind, *n. That which blows;* air in motion; a current of air; breath; power or act of respiration; air put in motion by some artificial means; breath modulated; flatulence; air generated in the stomach and bowels; air impregnated with a scent†.—*vt.* regular, and pronounced *wind.* To *blow;* to perceive or follow by the wind or scent; to ride or drive, as a horse, so as to render scant of breath; to rest, as a horse, in order to enable him to recover wind; to sound so that the notes shall be prolonged and varied. [Sax.—L. *ventus*—Sans. *vā,* to blow—Heb. *hāva,* to breathe.]

Wind, wind, *vt. To turn round* some fixed object; to form into a ball by turning; to turn, as one's self by shifts; to introduce, as one's self by insinuation; to vary; to enfold; to encircle; to put in order for regular action; to govern.—*vi. To turn round;* to turn around something; to crook; to bend; to move round; to double; to have an uneven surface. *ppr.* winding, *pret. & pp.* wound. [Sax. *windan,* to bend.]

Windage, wind'āj, *n.* The space between the ball in a piece of ordnance and the bore, so named because filled with *wind* or air. [Sp. *viento,* wind, windage.]

Wind-bound, wind'bound, *a.* Prevented from sailing by a contrary *wind.*

Wind-broken, wind'brōk-n, *a.* Diseased in the *wind* or breath.

Windering†, wind'ėr-ing, *a.* Winding.

Windfall, wind'fal, *n.* Fruit blown off the tree by *wind;* an unexpected legacy; any unexpected advantage.

Wind-gage, wind'gāj, *n.* An instrument for ascertaining the velocity and force of *wind.*

Windiness, wind'i-nes, *n. The state of being windy* or tempestuous.

Winding, wind'ing, *p.a.* Bending.—*p.n. Act of those persons or things that wind;* a bend; meander; a blowing; a call by the boatswain's whistle.

Windingly, wind'ing-li, *adv. In a winding* or circuitous form or *manner.*

Wind-instrument, wind'in-strū-ment, *n. An instrument* of music, played by *wind,* chiefly by the breath, as a flute, &c.

Windlass, wind'las, *n. A machine for raising heavy weights;* a modification of the wheel and axle, used for raising weights, &c. [D. *windas.*]

Wind-mill, wind'mil, *n.* A *mill* which

receives its motion from the impulse of the wind.

Window, win'dō, n. *The wind's eye;* an opening in the wall of a building for the admission of light, and of air when necessary; an aperture resembling a window; the frame filled with glass that covers the aperture; lattice or casement; the network of wire used before the invention of glass.—*vt.* To *furnish with windows;* to place at a window. [Sax. *wind,* and *eage,* the eye.]

Windpipe, wind'pip, n. The *passage* for the *breath* to and from the lungs.

Wind-sail, wind'sāl, n. A wide tube or funnel of canvas, used to convey a stream of air into the lower apartments of a ship.

Wind-tight, wind'tīt, a. So *tight* as to prevent the passing of *wind.*

Windward, wind'wąrd, n. The *point* from which the *wind* blows; as, to sail to the windward.—*a.* Being on the side *toward* the point from which the *wind* blows.—*adv.* Toward the *wind.*

Windy, wind'i, a. *Consisting of wind;* tempestuous; flatulent; empty.

Wine, win, n. *The fermented juice of grapes,* or of the fruit of the vine; the juice of certain fruits, prepared with sugar, sometimes with spirits, &c.; any spirituous product of fermentation; intoxication; drinking. [Sax. *win;* Heb. *yavan,* to ferment.]

Wing, wing, n. One of the two anterior limbs of a fowl, corresponding to the arms of a man, by which it puts itself in a quick reciprocating motion through the air; the limb of an insect by which it flies; flight; passage by the wing; means of flying; the flank of an army; any side-piece; a side-building, less than the main edifice; the ships on the extremities, when ranged in a line. *vt.* To *furnish with wings;* to enable to fly; to supply with side bodies; to transport by flight; to wound in the wing (a term among sportsmen). [Icel. *vaengr.*]

Winged, wingd, *p. a. Having wings;* swift; disabled in the wing.

Wingless, wing'les, *a. Having no wings.*

Winglet, wing'let, n. *A little wing.*

Wink, wingk, *vi.* To shut and open the eyes alternately and rapidly; to give a hint by a motion of the eyelids; to close the eyelids; to seem not to see; to overlook, as something not perfectly agreeable (with *at*).—n. The act of shutting and opening the eyelids rapidly; a hint given by shutting the eye with a significant cast. [Sax. *wincian*—G. *winken.*]

Winker, wingk'ėr, n. *One who winks;* one of the blinds of a horse.

Winner, win'ėr, n. One who *wins* by success in contest. [from *win.*]

Winning, win'ing, *p.a.* Adapted to gain favour; attracting; charming.—*p.n.* The sum *won* in contest. (This word is seldom used except in its plural form, *winnings.*)

Winningly, win'ing-li, *adv. In a winning manner.*

Winnow, win'nō, *vt.* To *blow away;* to drive off the chaff from, as from grain by means of wind; to fan; to beat as with wings; to sift for the purpose of separating falsehood from truth; to separate, as the bad from the good. *vi.* To separate chaff from corn. [Sax. *windwian*—*wind,* wind.]

Winnower, win'nō-ėr, n. *One who winnows.*

Winnowing, win'nō-ing, *p.n.* The *act of separating* the chaff from grain, by means of the *wind,* or by an artificial current of air.

Winter, win'tėr, n. The *winter* or *stormy* season of the year; the cold season of the year.—*a. Pertaining to winter.*—*vi.* To pass the winter.—*vt.* To *feed or manage during the winter.* [Sax.; Old G. *wintar,* Goth. *vintrus*—Sans. *vd,* to blow.]

Wintering, win'tėr-ing, *p.n. The act of passing the winter;* the act of feeding during the winter.

Winter-quarters, win'tėr-kwąr-tėrz, n. The *quarters* of an army during the *winter;* a winter residence or station.

Winter-solstice, win'tėr-sol-stis, n. The *solstice* of the *winter,* which takes place when the sun enters Capricorn, December 21st.

Wintry, win'tri, *a. Pertaining to winter;* suitable to winter; cold; stormy.

Winy, win'i, *a.* Having the taste or qualities of *wine.*

Wipe, wip, *vt.* To rub with something soft *for cleaning;* to remove by rubbing; to dash away, as tears; to cleanse from abuses; to destroy what is foul; to efface; to obliterate (with *out*). *ppr.* wiping, *pret. & pp.* wiped.—n. The act of *wiping* for the purpose of cleaning; a stroke; a jeer; a severe sarcasm. [Sax. *wipian,* to cleanse.]

Wiper, wip'ėr, n. *He or that which wipes.*

Wire, wir, n. *That which may be wound round anything;* a thread of metal, as of iron or gold—*vt.* To *bind with wire;* to apply wire to, as in bottling liquors. *ppr.* wiring, *pret. & pp.* wired. [Icel. *vir*—L. *gyro,* to round.]

Wire-draw, wir'drą, *vt.* To *draw,* as a piece of metal into *wire;* to draw out into length; to attenuate. *ppr.* wire-drawing, *pret.* wiredrew, *pp.* wire-drawn.

Wire-drawing, wir'drą-ing, *p.n.* The act or art of *extending* ductile metals into *wire.*

Wire-drawn, wir'drąn, *p.a.* Drawn out to great length or fineness.

Wiry, wir'i, *a. Made of wire;* like wire.

Wist, wis, *vt.* To know; to be aware.

Wisdom, wiz'dom, n. *State or quality of being wise;* the power or act of judging rightly; sagacity; judicious conduct; the knowledge of divine and human things; the use of the best means to accomplish the best ends; religious sentiment. [Sax. *wis,* wise, and *dom,* state.]

Wise, wiz, *a. Ha:ing the power of knowing* and distinguishing; discreet and judicious in the use of knowledge; choosing laudable ends, and the best means to accomplish them; learned; containing wisdom; judicious; well adapted to produce good effects; grave; discreet. [Sax. *wis;* Old G. *wis,* knowing.]

Wise, wiz, n. Way of *being* or *acting;* manner. (Obsolete except in compounds.) [Sax.]

Wiseacre, wiz'ā-kėr, n. *A wise sayer;* one who makes pretensions to great wisdom; hence, in contempt, a simpleton; a dunce. [G. *weise,* wise, and *sagen,* to say.]

Wise-hearted, wiz'hārt-ed, *a.* Wise; knowing; skilful.

Wisely, wiz'li, *adv. With wisdom.*

Wise-woman†, wiz'wu̧-man, n. A witch.

Wish, wish, *vi.* To *desire;* to have a desire, or strong desire, either for what is or is not supposed to be obtainable; to be disposed or inclined. It sometimes partakes of hope or fear. (Frequently with *for.*)—*vt.* To *desire;* to long for; to desire eagerly; to call down upon, as curses.—n. *Desire;* eager desire; object of desire. [Sax. *wiscan.*]

Wisher, wish'ėr, n. One who *wishes.*

Wishful, wish'fu̧l, *a.* Having or *showing a wish* or desire; desirous; earnest.

Wishfully, wish'fu̧l-li, *adv. With desire* or ardent desire.

Wishfulness, wish'fu̧l-nes, n. *The state of being wishful.*

Wisp, wisp, n. *A bundle of things of the same kind fitted to wipe;* a small bundle of straw or other like substance. [G. *wisch.*]

Wistful, wist'fu̧l, *a. Thoughtful;* earnest; pensive; contemplative. [from obsolete *wis,* pret. *wist,* Sax. *witan,* to know, perceive.]

Wistfully, wist'fu̧l-li, *adv. In a wistful manner; thoughtfully;* earnestly.

Wistly†, wist'li, *adv.* Wistfully.

Wit, wit, *vi.* To *know;* to be known. This verb is used only in the infinitive, to wit, when it is an adverbial phrase, signifying, namely, that is to say. [Sax. *witan,* to know.]—n. The power of *knowing;* mind; understanding; the mental powers; sense; sagacity; the faculty of associating ideas in a new and unexpected manner; the association of ideas in a manner natural, but unusual and striking, so as to produce surprise joined with pleasure; soundness of mind; intellect not disordered; power of invention; contrivance; a man of fancy or humour. [Sax.—*gewit,* the mind, genius, intellect.]

Witch, wich, n. A woman given to *mystical* and unlawful arts; a woman supposed to have formed a compact with the devil, or with evil spirits, and by their means to operate supernaturally; one who practises enchantment.—*vt.* To *bewitch;* to fascinate. [Sax. *wicce*—Old G. *wih,* mystical.]

Witchcraft, wich'kraft, n. The *craft of witches;* sorcery; enchantments; intercourse with the devil.

Witchery, wich'ė-ri, n. *Witchcraft;* sorcery; fascination; a powerful and inexplicable influence.

Witching, wich'ing, *p.a. Bewitching;* suited to witchcraft.

Wit-cracker†, wit'krak-ėr, n. A joker.

With, wiᴛʜ, *prep. In the middle of; among;* in the society of; in partnership; in consent, noting parity of state; by, noting cause or means; on the side of, noting favour; in opposition to; in contest; noting comparison; noting confidence. [Sax.—Goth. *mith,* the middle.]

Withal, with-ąl', *adv.* Together with; at the same time.

Withdraw, with-drą', *vt.* To *draw away in opposition to;* to take away; to call back or away; to retract; to cause to retire.—*vi.* To retire; to quit a company or place; to secede. *ppr.* withdrawing, *pret.* withdrew, *pp.* withdrawn. [Sax. *with,* against, and *draw.*]

Withdrawal, with-drą'al, n. *A ct of withdrawing* or taking back; a recalling.

Withdrawment, with-drą'ment, n. *The act of withdrawing;* withdrawal.

Withe, With, with, with, n. *That which binds together;* a band consisting of a twig or twigs twisted. [Sax. *withig*—Goth. *vithan,* to bind together.]

Wither, wiᴛʜ'ėr, *vi.* To *become dry;* to lose native freshness; to become sapless; to pine away; to lose animal moisture.—*vt.* To cause to *become dry;* to cause to shrink for want of animal moisture. [Sax. *gewitherod,* withered —*thyrr,* dry.]

Witheringly, wiᴛʜ'ĕr-ing-li, *adv.* In a *manner tending to wither*.

Withers, wiᴛʜ'ĕrz, *n.* *A joining*†; the juncture of the shoulder-bones of a horse, at the bottom of the neck and mane. [Goth. *vithan*, to join.]

Withhold, with-hōld', *vt.* *To hold back;* to keep from action; not to grant. *ppr.* withholding, *pret. & pp.* withheld.

Withholden, with-hōld'n, *pp.* The old past participle of *withhold*.

Withholder, with-hōld'ĕr, *n.* *One that withholds*.

Within, with-in', *prep. In the midst of that which is in;* in, as opposed to out; in the inner part; in the compass of; not beyond; not longer ago than; not later than; in the reach of; in the house; in any inclosure.—*adv. In the inner part;* inwardly; in the mind. [Sax. *withinnan—with*, in the midst of, and *innan*, within.]

Without, with-out', *prep. In the midst of that which is out;* not within; beyond; in a state of not having; supposing the omission of; not by the use of.—*adv.* Not within; out of doors; not in the mind. [Sax. *withutan—with*, in the midst of, and *utan*, outwards, without.]

Withstand, with-stand', *vt. To stand against;* to resist, either with physical or moral force. *ppr.* withstanding, *pret. & pp.* withstood.

Witless, wit'les, *a. Destitute of wit;* inconsiderate; indiscreet.

Witlessly, wit'les-li, *adv.* Without the exercise of judgment.

Witlessness, wit'les-nes, *n. The quality of being witless.*

Witling, wit'ling, *n.* A *pretender to wit* or smartness. [dim. from *wit*.]

Witness, wit'nes, *n. Testimony from knowledge;* attestation of a fact or event; that which furnishes proof; a person who knows or sees anything; one who sees the execution of a legal instrument, and subscribes it for the purpose of confirming its authenticity; one who tells what he knows, sees, or has seen; a person who gives evidence in a judicial proceeding.—*vt.* To be a *witness of;* to see or know by personal presence; to attest; to give testimony to; to see the execution of, as of a legal instrument, and subscribe it.—*vi.* To *bear witness* or testimony. [Sax. *witnes—witan*, to know.]

Witsnapper†, wit'snap-ĕr, *n.* One who affects repartee.

Witted, wit'ed, *p.a. Having wit* (used only in composition).

Witticism, wit'i-sizm, *n.* A sentence affectedly *witty;* a witty remark; a low kind of wit.

Wittily, wit'i-li, *adv. In a witty manner;* ingeniously.

Wittiness, wit'i-nes, *n. The quality of being witty.*

Wittingly, wit'ing-li, *adv. Knowingly;* with knowledge; by design.

Wittol†, wit'ol, *n.* A tame cuckold.

Witty, wit'i, *a. Possessed of wit;* wise†; judicious†; full of wit; sarcastic; humorous; facetious.

Wive†, wiv, *vt.* To match to a wife.

Wizard, wiz'ård, *n.* Originally, a *prophet;* an enchanter; a sorcerer.—*a.* Charming; haunted by wizards. [Old G. *wizag—sdgen*, to say.]

Woad, wōd, *n.* A plant formerly cultivated to a great extent in Britain, on account of the blue dye extracted from it. [Sax. *waad*.]

Woden, wō'den, *n.* An Anglo-Saxon deity, supposed to correspond to the Mercury of the Greeks and Romans. From Woden, Wednesday derives its name.

Woe, Wo, wō, *n.* Grief; anguish; distress; suffering; a curse. *Woe* is used in denunciation, and in exclamations of sorrow. [Sax. *wa;* G. *weh*.]

Woebegone, wō'bē-gon, *a. Far gone in woe;* overwhelmed with grief or sorrow; very sad.

Woful, wō'fųl, *a. Full of woe;* sorrowful; afflicted; bringing affliction; wretched; paltry.

Wofully, wō'fųl-li, *adv. In a woful manner;* sorrowfully; mournfully.

Wofulness, wō'fųl-nes, *n. The state of being woful;* misery; calamity.

Wold, wōld, *n.* Primarily, *a wood;* a plain or open country; a country without wood, whether hilly or not. [Sax. and Old G. *wald*, a wood, a desert.]

Wolf, wųlf, *n.* A *rapacious* and ferocious quadruped of the dog kind, crafty, greedy, and detested; anything destructive. [Sax. *wulf;* Goth. *vilvan*, to seize.]

Wolf-dog, wųlf'dog, *n.* A large kind of dog, kept to guard sheep, &c., and to destroy wolves; a dog supposed to be bred between a dog and a wolf.

Wolfish, wųlf'ish, *a. Like a wolf.*

Wolfishly, wųlf'ish-li, *adv. In a wolfish manner.*

Wolverene, Wolverine, wųl'vĕr-ēn, wųl'vĕr-in, *n.* A carnivorous quadruped inhabiting the coasts of the Arctic Sea, known also by the name of glutton.

Woman, wų'man, *n.* **Women**, wi'men, *pl. The bringer forth,* by way of eminence; the bearer of children; the female of the human race; a grown-up female, as distinguished from a child or girl; a female attendant on a person of rank. *vt.*† to make effeminate. [Sax. *wiman;* Gr. *phūō*, to come into being.]

Womanhood, wų'man-hųd, *n. The state, character, or collective qualities of a woman.*

Womanish, wų'man-ish, *a. Suitable to a woman;* feminine; effeminate.

Womanishly, wų'man-ish-li, *adv. In a womanish manner.*

Womanishness, wų'man-ish-nes, *n. State or quality of being womanish.*

Womankind, wų'man-kind, *n.* The race of females of the human kind.

Womanliness, wų'man-li-nes, *n. Quality of being womanly.*

Womanly, wų'man-li, *a. Becoming a woman;* suiting a woman; feminine. *adv. In the manner of a woman.*

Woman-tired†, wų'man-tīrd, *a.* Henpecked.

Womb, wöm, *n.* Primarily, *the belly;* the uterus of a female; the place where anything is produced; any large or deep cavity.—*vt. To inclose in a womb;* to breed in secret. [Sax. *wamb;* Old G. *wamba*, the belly.]

Womby†, wöm'i, *a.* Capacious.

Wonder, wun'dĕr, *n.* That emotion which causes the mind *to turn this way and that way* in order to ascertain the cause of that which produces such emotion; the state of mind produced by something inexplicable; amazement; cause of wonder; a strange thing; a miracle.—*vi.* To be struck with *wonder;* to be affected by surprise or admiration; to feel doubt and curiosity. [Sax. *wundor;* G. *winden*, to wind.]

Wondered†, wun'dĕrd, *p.a.* Having performed wonders.

Wonderer, wun'dĕr-ĕr, *n. One who wonders.*

Wonderful, wun'dĕr-fųl, *a. Adapted to excite wonder;* strange; astonishing; admirable; surprising.

Wonderfully, wun'dĕr-fųl-li, *adv. In a manner to excite wonder* or surprise.

Wonderfulness, wun'dĕr-fųl-nes, *n. The state or quality of being wonderful.*

Wondrous, wun'drus, *a. Exciting wonder;* marvellous; strange.

Wondrously, wun'drus-li, *adv.* In a strange or *wonderful manner* or degree.

Won't, wönt, a contraction of *will not*.

Wont, wunt, *a. Accustomed;* habituated; using or doing customarily.—*n. Custom;* habit. [Sax. *wŏnian*, to accustom—G. *gewohnt*, accustomed.]

Wonted, wunt'ed, *p.a. Accustomed;* used; usual.

Woo, wö, *vt. To make vows* of unalterable love to; to solicit in love, with a view to marriage; to court; to invite with importunity; to court solicitously.—*vi.* To court; to make love. [Sax. *wōgan;* probably allied to *vow*.]

Wood, wųd, *n.* A large and thick collection of trees forming a *covert;* a forest; the substance of trees; timber; trees cut or sawed for fuel. [Sax. *wudu;* Old G. *wald*—Sans. *vana*, a wood.]

Wood†, wŏd, *a.* Mad; insane. [Sax. *wōd;* Old G. *wuot*.]

Woodbine, wųd'bīn, *n.* A name given to the honeysuckle, because it encircles like a band. [Sax. *wud-bind*.]

Wood-coal, wųd'kōl, *n.* Charcoal; also lignite or brown coal.

Woodcock, wųd'kok, *n.* A fowl allied to the snipe tribe, but with a more robust bill and shorter legs. Its flight is very rapid, and its flesh highly esteemed.

Woodcut, wųd'kut, *n. An engraving on wood;* a print from such engraving.

Wood-cutter, wųd'kut-ĕr, *n. A person who cuts wood;* an engraver on wood.

Wood-cutting, wųd'kut-ing, *p.n.* The art *of cutting wood;* wood-engraving.

Wooded, wųd'ed, *p.a. Supplied or covered with wood.*

Wooden, wųd'n, *a. Made of wood;* consisting of wood.

Wood-engraver, wųd'en-grāv-ĕr, *n. An artist who engraves on wood.*

Wood-engraving, wųd'en-grāv-ing, *n. The art of engraving or cutting designs on wood;* an engraving on wood; a woodcut.

Wood-land, wųd'land, *n. Land covered with wood.*—*a. Relating to woods;* sylvan.

Woodlark, wųd'lärk, *n.* A bird, a species of *lark,* found near the borders of woods, which pours out its song chiefly when on the wing.

Woodman, wųd'man, *n.* One who fells *timber;* a forester; one of the men appointed to look to the Queen's woods.

Wood-nymph, wųd'nimf, *n.* A fabled *goddess of the woods;* a dryad.

Woodpecker, wųd'pek-ĕr, *n.* A bird, so named from its habit of piercing the bark of trees with its sharp bill, in order to get at insects and their eggs lodged below the bark.

Wood-pigeon, wųd'pi-jon, *n.* The ringdove, which frequents *woods.*

Woodruff, wųd'ruf, *n.* A plant found in *woods* and shady places, which has been admitted into the garden from the beauty of its whorled leaves and simple blossom, but chiefly from the fragrance of its leaves.

Wood-screw, wųd'skrū, *n.* The common screw made of iron, and used by carpenters for fastening together pieces of wood, or wood and metal.

Wood-work, wųd'wėrk, *n. Work formed*

Fate, fär, fat, fąll; mē, met hėr; pīne, pin; nōte, not, mȯve; tūbe, tub, bųll; oil, pound.

of *wood;* that part of any structure which is made of wood.
Woody, wud'i, *a. Abounding with wood;* ligneous; pertaining to woods; sylvan.
Woody-fibre, Woody-tissue, wud'i-fibėr, wud'i-ti-shū, *n.* That which constitutes the basis of the wood in trees.
Wooer, wō'ėr, *n.* One who courts, or solicits in love.
Woof, wōf, *n. That which is woven;* cloth; the threads that cross the warp in weaving. [from *weave.*]
Wooingly, wō'ing-li, *adv.* Enticingly; with persuasiveness.
Wool, wul, *n.* The fleecy *covering* of the sheep; a soft species of hair resembling wool, which grows on certain animals, as rabbits, &c.; short, thick, curly hair; the fibre of the cotton plant. [Sax. *wul;* Sans. *val,* to cover.]
Wool-gathering, wul'gavH-ėr-ing, *n.* Idle indulgence of the imagination; vagary.
Wool-grower, wul'grō-ėr, *n. A person who raises* sheep for the production of *wool.*
Wool-growing, wul'grō-ing, *a. Producing sheep and wool.*
Woolled, wuld, *p.a. Having wool,* as fine-woollod.
Woollen, wul'en, *a. Made of wool;* consisting of wool; pertaining to wool.
Woollness, wul'i-nes, *n. The state of being woolly.*
Woolly, wul'i, *a. Consisting of wool;* resembling wool; clothed with a down resembling wool.
Woolsack, wul'sak, *n. A sack or bag of wool;* the seat of the lord-chancellor in the House of Lords, being a large square bag of wool, without back or arms, covered with red cloth.
Woolwardt, wul'ward, *adv. In wool.*
Word, wėrd, *n. That which is spoken;* an articulate sound, or a combination of such sounds, uttered by the human voice, and expressing an idea or ideas; a single component part of human speech; the letter or letters, written or printed, which represent a sound or combination of sounds; talk; dispute; (pl.) language; promise; command; account; tidings; declaration; the Scripture; divine revelation, or any part of it; Christ; a motto; a proverb.—*vt. To dispute.*—*vt. To express in words;* to put into words. [Sax.; Old G. *wort*—Sans. *vrit,* to speak.]
Word-book, wėrd'buk, *n.* A vocabulary.
Worded, wėrd'ed, *p.a. Expressed in words.*
Wordily, wėrd'i-li, *adv.* In a verbose or *wordy manner.*
Wordiness, wėrd'i-nes, *n. The state or quality of being wordy.*
Wording, wėrd'ing, *p.n. The act of expressing in words; the manner of expressing in words.*
Wordless, wėrd'les, *a.* Silent.
Wordy, wėrd'i, *a. Using many words; verbose;* containing many words.
Work, wėrk, *n. The product of toil;* that which is made or done; something produced by toil, whether mental or bodily; labour; manual labour; the effect of labour; embroidery; figures wrought with the needle; any fabric; the matter on which one is busy; action; achievement; operation; a literary performance; (pl.) walls, trenches, and the like, made for fortifications; a piece of mechanism; a manufacturing establishment; external performances, as distinct from grace.—*vt. To produce;* to produce by toil, either mental or bodily; to bring into any state by action; to influence by acting upon; to lead; to direct in a state of motion; to put in motion; to embroider; to direct the movements of, as of a ship; to put to labour; to exert; to cause to ferment, as liquor.—*vi.* To be in action so as to *produce* something by toil either mental or bodily; to toil; to be occupied in performing manual labour; to act; to carry on business; to be customarily employed in; to act internally; to ferment; to produce effects by influence; to act on the stomach and bowels, as a cathartic; to be agitated; to influence. *ppr.* working, *pret. & pp.* worked or wrought. [Sax. *worc*—Icel. *verka,* to work.]
Workable, wėrk'a-bl, *a. That can be worked,* or that is worth working.
Worker, wėrk'ėr, *n. One that works.*
Workhouse, wėrk'hous, *n. A house for work;* a house for the poor, where suitable food, clothing, and employment are provided.
Working, wėrk'ing, *p.a.* Acting; labouring; plodding; devoted to bodily toil. *p.n.* Act of labouring.
Working-day, wėrk'ing-dā, *a.* Laborious; coarse.—*n.* A day on which labour is performed, as distinguished from the Sabbath.
Workman, wėrk'man, *n.* Any *man* employed in manual *work;* a skilful artificer; a labourer.
Workmanlike, wėrk'man-lik, *a. Like a workman;* skilful; well performed.
Workmanship, wėrk'man-ship, *n. Skill or art of a workman;* the style of art shown in any work; dexterity; something made, particularly by manual labour; that which is produced.
Workshop, wėrk'shop, *n. A shop* where a *workman* or workmen carry on their *work.*
Worky-day†, wėrk'i-dā, *n.* A week-day.
World, wėrld, *n. That which abides or continues;* the universe; the earth; the terraqueous globe, sometimes called the lower world; the heavens; system of beings; present state of existence; a secular life; public life; business of life; a great multitude; mankind; people in general; course of life; the customs and manners of men; all that the world contains; the Roman empire; a wide compass of things; any large portion of the earth; as, the old world, the new world; the carnal state of the earth; the ungodly part of the world; time, as in the phrase, world without end. [Sax.—Old G. *weren,* to last.]
Worldliness, wėrld'li-nes, *n. State of being worldly;* devotedness to gain and temporal enjoyments.
Worldling, wėrld'ling, *n. One devoted to the gains and pleasures of this world.*
Worldly, wėrld'li, *a. Relating to this world* or this life; secular; devoted to this life and its enjoyments; bent on gain; common; belonging to the world; secular.
Worm, wėrm, *n. That which creeps;* any small creeping animal, either entirely without feet, or with very short ones; a spiral instrument, resembling a double cork-screw, fixed on the end of a staff, and used for drawing wads from guns; anything spiral; a spiral leaden pipe placed in a tub of water, through which the vapour passes in distillation, and in which it is cooled and condensed; a small worm-like part situated beneath a dog's tongue; that which incessantly gnaws the conscience; remorse; a being despised.—*vi.* To work slowly and secretly.—*vt.* To expel or undermine by slow and secret means (with *out*); to draw, as the wad or cartridge from a gun; to clean by the instrument called a worm. [Sax.—L. *vermis*—Sans. *srip,* to go.]
Wormwood, wėrm'wud, *n. The wood of worms;* a bitter plant, so called because it destroys worms; a well-known plant, celebrated for its intensely bitter, tonic, and stimulating qualities. [Sax. *wermod.*]
Wormy, wėrm'i, *a. Relating to worms;* abounding with worms.
Worry, wu'ri, *vt. To strangle;* to suffocate; to mangle with the teeth; to trouble; to fatigue; to harass with labour; to vex; to persecute brutally. *ppr.* worrying, *pret. & pp.* worried. (G. *würgen,* to choke.]
Worse, wėrs, *a. More evil;* bad or ill in a greater degree; more corrupt (in a moral sense); in regard to health, more sick.—*adv.* In a manner *more evil* or bad. [Sax. *wyrse,* comp. of *yfel.*]
Worship, wėr'ship, *n.* Primarily, *worthiness;* a title of honour, used in addresses to certain magistrates and others of rank or station; the act of paying divine honours to the Supreme Being; the homage paid to Him in religious exercises; the homage paid to idols; idolatry of lovers; obsequious respect; hero-worship.—*vt. To attribute worthiness to;* to respect; to honour; to treat with civil reverence; to honour with extreme submission; to pay divine honours to.—*vi.* To perform acts of adoration; to perform religious service. *ppr.* worshipping, *pret. & pp.* worshipped. [Sax. *weorthscipe*—*worth* and *ship.*]
Worshipful, wėr'ship-ful, *a. Claiming worship;* worthy of honour from its character; a term of respect, especially applied to magistrates and corporate bodies.
Worshipper, wėr'ship-ėr, *n. One who worships;* one who adores.
Worst, wėrst, *a. Evil in a very high or in the highest degree;* most severe or dangerous; most difficult to heal; most afflictive.—*n. The most evil state;* the most severe state; the height; the most calamitous state.—*vt. To bring to the worst state;* to defeat; to overthrow. [superl. of *worse*—Old G. *wirsist.*]
Worsted, wust'ed, *n.* Yarn spun from combed wool, and which, in the spinning, is twisted harder than ordinary. *a. Consisting* or made *of worsted;* made of worsted yarn. [said to be from *Worsted,* a town in Norfolk.]
Wort, wėrt, *n. A plant; an herb;* now used chiefly in compounds, as in mugwort, liverwort, spleenwort; new beer unfermented, or in the act of fermentation. [Sax. *wyrt*—Icel. *urt,* an herb.]
Worth, wėrth, *n. That which a person or thing comes to be;* value; price; that quality of a thing which renders it useful; value of mental qualities; desert; excellence; virtue; usefulness, as a man of great worth; importance; valuable qualities; good fortune!.—*a.* Equal in price to; deserving of (in a good or bad sense, but chiefly in a good sense); having estate to the value of. [Sax. *wurth*—*weorthan,* to become.]
Worthily, wėr'THI-li, *adv. In a worthy manner.*
Worthiness, wėr'THi-nes, *n. The state or quality of being worthy;* merit; excellence; dignity; virtue.
Worthless, wėrth'les, *a.* Having no

worth or value; having no value of character or no virtue; having no excellence.
Worthlessly, wėrth'les-li, *adv. In a worthless manner.*
Worthlessness, wėrth'les-nes, *n. The state or quality of being worthless.*
Worthy, wėr'ᴛʜi, *a. Possessing worth;* noble; illustrious; virtuous; deserving; equivalent to; suitable; having qualities suited to (either in a good or bad sense); equal in value; suitable to anything bad; deserving of ill.—*n.* A man of eminent *worth;* a man of valour.—*vt. To render worthy.* [G. *würdig.*]
Wort‡, wėrts, *n.* Cabbage.
Wot‡, wot, *vi.* To know; to be aware.
Would, wụd, *pret.* of *will*—which see. *Would* is used as an auxiliary verb in conditional forms of speech, implying inclination, wish, or desire.
Wound, wönd, *n. A bruise;* a cut; a stab; a breach of the skin and flesh of an animal, or of the bark of a tree, caused by violence; injury; hurt.—*vt. To bruise;* to hurt by violence; to cut, slash, or lacerate; to hurt the feelings of. [Sax. *wund;* Goth. *vunds.*]
Wounding, wönd'ing, *p.n.* Hurt; injury.
Woundless‡, wönd'les, *a.* Not vulnerable.
Wrack‡, rak, *n.* Wreck.
Wrangle, rang'gl, *vi.* Primarily, *to cast the blame of a wrong on* another or others; to quarrel peevishly and noisily; to brawl. *ppr* wrangling, *pret. & pp.* wrangled.—*n.* An angry dispute; a noisy quarrel. [from *wrong*, *wrongle*.]
Wrangler, rang'gl-ėr, *n. One who wrangles;* one who disputes with heat or peevishness. In the University of Cambridge, the student who passes the best examination for the degree of Bachelor of Arts in the Senate-House is termed *Senior Wrangler.* Then follow the second, third, &c., wranglers of the year.
Wranglership, rang'gl-ėr-ship, *n.* In the University of Cambridge, the honour conferred on those whose names are inscribed in the list of *wranglers.*
Wrangling, rang'gl-ing, *p.n.* The act of disputing angrily; altercation.
Wrap, rap, *vt.* To fold together; to cover by winding something round (with up); to hide; to contain; to involve totally; to inclose. *ppr.* wrapping, *pret. & pp.* wrapped or wrapt. [probably of the same origin as *robe.*]
Wrapper, rap'ėr, *n. One that wraps;* that in which anything is wrapped; a loose upper garment.
Wrapping, rap'ing, *p.a.* Used or designed for wrapping or covering.—*p.n. That in which anything is wrapped;* an envelope; a wrapper.
Wrath, rath, *n. Anger;* vehement exasperation; rage; fury; ire; the effects of anger; the just punishment of an offence or crime. [Sax.—*writhan,* to writhe.]
Wrathful, rath'ful, *a. Full of wrath;* greatly incensed; furious; springing from wrath.
Wrathfully, rath'ful-li, *adv. In a wrathful manner;* with violent anger.
Wreak, rēk, *vt.* To execute in *vengeance* or passion; to inflict.—*vi.*† To reck. *n.*† Vengeance; rage. [Sax. *wrecan*—Old G. *ruhhan,* to avenge.]
Wreakless‡, rēk'les, *a.* Unrevenged; weak.
Wreath, rēth, *n.* Something *twisted* or curled; a garland; an ornamental twisted bandage. [Sax. *wreth,* from *writhan.* Dan. *vride,* to twist.]

Wreathe, rēᴛʜ, *vt. To twist;* to wind, as one about another; to interweave; to encircle, as a garland; to encircle, as with a garland.—*vi.* To be interwoven or entwined. *ppr.* wreathing, *pret.* wreathed, *pp.* wreathed, wreathen.
Wreathing, rēᴛʜ'ing, *p.n. Act of twisting* or encircling; a wreath.
Wreck, rek, *n. That which is broken;* a vessel *broken* on the rocks; the hull of a vessel broken or abandoned; any ship or goods driven ashore in a deserted condition; ruin; the remains of anything ruined.—*vt. To break;* to break on the rocks; to drive against the shore, and break or destroy; to ruin.—*vi. To suffer wreck or ruin.* [D. *wrak,* broken —Goth. *brikan,* Heb. *pârak,* to break.]
Wreckage, rek'āj, *n. The act of wrecking;* the ruins or remains of a ship or cargo that has been wrecked.
Wrecker, rek'ėr, *n. One* who plunders the *wrecks* of ships, or collects goods cast on the shore from wrecks.
Wren, ren, *n.* A well-known favourite little bird, of very *brisk* and *lively* habits. [Sax. *wrenna*—*wrane,* playful.]
Wrench, rensh, *vt. To pull with a strain;* to wrest or twist by violence; to strain; to distort.—*n. A violent twist,* or a pull with twisting; an injury by twisting, as in a joint; an instrument for screwing or unscrewing iron work. [Sax. *wringan,* G. *verrenken.*]
Wrest, rest, *vt. To twist;* to extort by violence; to take or force by violence; to turn from truth or pervert from its natural meaning.—*n. The act of twisting;* distortion; perversion; an instrument to tune with. [Sax. *wrœstan.*]
Wrester, rest'ėr, *n. One who wrests.*
Wresting, rest'ing, *n.* A distorting.
Wrestle, res'l, *vi. To struggle with repeated wrenches;* to contend by grappling, and trying to throw down; to struggle; to contend. *ppr.* wrestling, *pret. & pp.* wrestled. [Sax. *wrœstlian,* frequent. of *wrœstan,* to twist.]
Wrestler, res'l-ėr, *n. One who wrestles;* one who is skilful in wrestling.
Wrestling, res'l-ing, *p.n. Act of one who wrestles;* struggle; an athletic exercise between two persons who try to throw each other down; contention.
Wretch, rech, *n.* Primarily, *an exile;* a miserable person; a worthless mortal; sometimes used by way of slight pity or contempt, and also used to express tenderness. [Sax. *wrœcca,* an exile, from *wracian,* to be banished.]
Wretched, rech'ed, *a. Exiled*†; cast out; sunk into deep affliction or distress, either from want, anxiety, or grief; calamitous; paltry; very poor or mean; hatefully vile.
Wretchedly, rech'ed-li, *adv. In a wretched manner;* despicably.
Wretchedness, rech'ed-nes, *n. The state of being wretched;* extreme misery or unhappiness, either from want or sorrow; meanness.
Wriggle, rig'l, *vi. To move the body to and fro with short turns.*—*vt.* To put into a quick *reciprocating motion;* to introduce by a shifting motion. *ppr.* wriggling, *pret. & pp.* wriggled. [frequent. from Sax. *wrigan,* to endeavour.]
Wriggler, rig'l-ėr, *n. One who wriggles.*
Wright, rit, *n. A workman;* an artificer; one whose occupation is some kind of mechanical business. This word is now chiefly used in compounds, as in shipwright, wheelwright. [Sax. *wyrhta*—*wyrcan,* to work.]
Wring, ring, *vt. To squeeze out by twisting;* to turn and strain with violence; to press; to bend or strain out of its position.—*vi.*† To writhe; to distress; to pervert; to persecute with extortion. *ppr.* wringing, *pret. & pp.* wrung. [Sax. *wringan;* Old G. *ringan,* to squeeze out.]
Wringing, ring'ing, *p.n. A twisting; the act of pressing and twisting the hands in anguish.*
Wrinkle, ring'kl, *n. A crooked furrow drawn on a smooth surface;* corrugation; a crease; a fold or rumple in cloth; roughness.—*vt. To form into wrinkles;* to contract into furrows and prominences; to make uneven. *vi.* To shrink into wrinkles or furrows and ridges. *ppr.* wrinkling, *pret. & pp.* wrinkled. [Sax. *wrincle.*]
Wrinkled, ring'kld, *p.a. Having wrinkles.*
Wrist, rist, *n.* The joint that *wrests;* the joint by which the hand is united to the arm, and by means of which the hand moves on the fore-arm. [Sax.—*wrœstan,* to wrest.]
Wristband, rist'band, *n.* That *band* or part of a shirt-sleeve which covers the *wrist.*
Writ, rit, *n. That which is written;* particularly applied to the Scriptures; a judicial process, by which any one is summoned as an offender; a legal instrument to enforce obedience to the orders of the courts.
Write, rit, *vt.* To express by forming *letters* and *characters* on paper or stone: to impress durably; to compose, as an author; to copy; to communicate by letter.—*vi.* To perform the act of *cutting* or forming letters as representatives of sounds or ideas; to be employed as a clerk; to play the author; to frame or combine ideas and express them in words; to recite in books; to call one's self; to use the style of. *ppr.* writing, *pret.* wrote, *pp.* written or writ. [Sax. *writan;* Goth. *vrits,* a line—Sans. *rad,* to cut.]
Writer, rit'ėr, *n. One who writes* or has written; an author; a scribe.
Writership, rit'ėr-ship, *n. The office of a writer.*
Writhe, rīᴛʜ, *vt. To twist* with violence. *vi.* To *twist* one's self; to be distorted, as from agony. *ppr.* writhing, *pret. & pp.* writhed. [Sax. *writhan.*]
Writhled‡, rīᴛʜ'ld, *a.* Wrinkled.
Writing, rit'ing, *p.a.* Used or intended for writing.—*p.n.* The act or art of forming letters and *characters* on paper, &c., for the purpose of recording ideas, or of communicating them to others by visible signs; anything written; a book; a manuscript; an inscription; (pl.) conveyances of lands, deeds, or any official paper.
Wrong, rong, *a. Wrung; twisted* from a straight line; not physically right; twisted out of the right line of conduct; not morally right; that deviates from the line of rectitude prescribed by God; not just or equitable; not legal; not according to truth.—*n. That which is wrung* from the right line; whatever deviates from moral rectitude; any injury done to another. *adv. In a wrong manner;* not rightly; morally ill.—*vt. To do a wrong to;* to injure; to treat with injustice; to deprive of some right, or to withhold some act of justice from; to do injustice to by imputation. [Sax. *wrœng*—Old G. *ringan,* to twist—*gerine,* a struggle, striving, contest, fight.]
Wrongful, rong'ful, *a. Full of wrong;* injurious; unjust.

Wrongfully, rong'fŭl-li, *adv. In a wrongful manner;* unjustly.
Wrongfulness, rong'fŭl-nes, *n. Quality of being wrong or wrongful;* injustice.
Wrong-headed, rong'hed-ed, *a. Perverse in understanding;* obstinately wrong in opinion; stubborn.

Wrong-headedness, rong'hed-ed-nes, *n. The quality of being wrong-headed.*
Wrongly, rong'li, *adv. In a wrong manner;* unjustly; amiss.
Wroth, rǎth, *a. Excited by wrath;* very angry; much exasperated. [Sax. *wræth.*]
Wrought, rǎt, *p.a. Formed by work or* labour; manufactured; actuated; agitated; disturbed. [Sax. *worhte,* the pp. of *wircan,* to work.]
Wry, ri, *a. Crooked;* turned to one side; deviating from the right direction; perverted.—*vi.†* To deviate from the right way. [Dan. *vraa.*]

Y.

Yacht, yot, *n. A sort of quick-sailing vessel;* a light and elegantly fitted-up vessel, used either for pleasure or passage, or as a vessel of state to convey kings, &c., from one place to another by sea. [D. *jagt.*]
Yachter, yot'er, *n. One who owns, sails in, or commands a yacht.*
Yachting, yot'ing, *p.n.* Act of sailing on pleasure excursions in a *yacht.—a. Relating to a yacht or yachts.*
Yam, yam, *n.* A plant cultivated in tropical climates, for the sake of its large tubers or roots. [a native American word.]
Yard, yärd, *n.* Primarily, *a switch;* a staff; measure; a rod three feet long for measuring a yard; a measure of three feet; an inclosure within which any business is carried on; a long cylindrical piece of timber, having a rounded taper toward each end, and slung by its centre to a mast. [Sax. *gyrd—gyrdan,* to bind round.]
Yard-arm, yärd'ärm, *n.* Either half of a ship's yard, from the centre or mast to the end.
Yare†, yär, *a.* Ready; quick.
Yarn, yärn, *n. Thread prepared from wool or flax by spinning;* spun wool; woollen, cotton, or linen thread; one of the strands of which a rope is composed. [Sax. *gearn—gedro,* ready.]
Yarrow, ya'rō, *n.* A perennial herb, having a strong odour and pungent taste. [Sax. *gearwe—gear,* a year.]
Yawl, yǎl, *n.* A small ship's boat, usually rowed by four or six oars; the smallest boat used by fishermen. [Sw. Goth. *julle,* a small boat.]
Yawn, yąn, *vi.* To open the *mouth as in chewing;* to have the mouth open involuntarily through drowsiness or dulness; to open wide; to express desire by yawning.—*n.* A deep and involuntary inspiration, with a pretty wide opening of the mouth, followed by a prolonged and more or less sonorous expiration, through drowsiness or dulness. [Sax. *gynian;* Gr. *chainō*—Sans. *hanu,* the jaw-bone, jaw.]
Yawning, yąn'ing, *p.a.* Sleepy; opening wide.—*p.n.* The *act of gaping* or opening wide.
Ye, yē, *pron.* The nominative plural of the pronoun of the second person, of which *thou* is the singular. [Sax. *ge.*]
Yea, yā, *adv.* Yea; a word that expresses affirmation or assent, used only in the sacred and solemn style.—*n.* An affirmative vote; one who votes in the affirmative. [Sax. *gea,* G. *ja.*]
Year, yēr, *n.* In the East, the period from *one rainy season to another,* passing in the West into the period *from spring to spring;* the period of time during which the earth makes one complete revolution in its orbit; (pl.) sometimes equivalent to age or old age. [Sax. *gear*—L. *ver,* the spring.]
Yearling, yēr'ling, *n.* A *young* beast one year old.—*a. Being a year old.*
Yearly, yēr'li, *a. Happening,* accruing, or *coming every year;* annual; lasting a year; comprehending a year.—*adv. Once a year;* annually.
Yearn, yern, *vi.* To *desire with eagerness;* to feel great uneasiness from longing, tenderness, or pity; to long. [Sax. *geornian.*]
Yearning, yern'ing, *p.a. Longing;* having longing desire.—*p.n.* Strong emotions *of desire,* tenderness, or pity; state of being moved with tenderness or longing desire.
Yearningly, yern'ing-li, *adv. In a yearning manner;* with yearning.
Yeast, yēst, *n. That which agitates and causes to swell;* the froth of beer in fermentation; a preparation for raising dough for bread; barm; ferment. [Sax. *gist;* Old G. *giuzan,* to swell.]
Yeasty, yēst'i, *a. Like yeast; containing yeast;* frothy; foamy; spumy.
Yell, yel, *vi. To make a loud harsh noise with the voice ;* to cry as with agony or horror.—*n.* A sharp, loud, hideous outcry. [Sax. *gyllan*—Heb. *yalal.*]
Yelling, yel'ing, *p.a.* Shrieking.—*p.n.* The *act of uttering hideous outcries.*
Yellow, yel'lō, *a.* Being of a bright golden colour.—*n.* The colour of gold; a *golden hue;* a bright colour.—*vt.* To render *yellow.—vi.* To *grow yellow.* [Sax. *gealew*—L. *aurum,* gold.]
Yellow-fever, yel'lō-fē-ver, *n.* A malignant *fever* of warm climates, often attended with *yellowness* of the skin.
Yellowish, yel'lō-ish, *a. Somewhat yellow.*
Yellowishness, yel'lō-ish-nes, *n.* The *quality of being somewhat yellow.*
Yellowness, yel'lō-nes, *n.* The *quality of being yellow.*
Yelp, yelp, *vi.* To bark, as a beagle-hound after his prey. [Sax. *gilpan,* to boast, Dan. *galpe,* to yelp.]
Yelping, yelp'ing, *p.n.* The repeated *bark* of a young dog, or the bark of a beagle after his prey.
Yeoman, yō'man, *n. A common man;* a man of small estate in land; a farmer; a gentleman farmer; an upper servant in a nobleman's family; an officer in the queen's household, of a middle rank between the sergeant and the groom; an inferior officer in a ship of war; a bailiff's follower. [Sax. *gemæne* —Goth. *gamains,* common.]
Yeomanry, yō'man-ri, *n. The collective body of yeomen;* the collective body of farmers.
Yerk, jerk, *vt. To jerk;* to throw with a sudden smart movement.—*vi. To jerk;* to move as with jerks.—*n.* A sudden or quick thrust or motion. [See JERK.]

Yes, yes, *adv. Even so;* expressing affirmation or consent; opposed to *no.* [Sax. *gese;* Goth. *ja.*]
Yest†, yest, *n.* Yeast.
Yester, yes'ter, *a. Belonging or relating to the day before the present;* last; last past; next before the present. [Sax. *gyrstan,* G. *gestern.*]
Yesterday, yes'ter-dā, *n. The day before the present;* the day last past. [Sax. *gyrstan,* yester, and *dæg,* day.]
Yestereve, Yesterevening, yes'ter-ēv, yes'ter-ē-vn-ing, *n. The evening last past.*
Yesternight, yes'ter-nit, *n.* The *night last past.*
Yet, yet, *conj.* Notwithstanding; nevertheless; however.—*adv.* Hitherto; still, noting extension or continuance; at the same time; over and above; the state remaining the same; at this time; at least; at all; prefixed to words denoting extension of time or continuance; in a new degree; even; after all; a kind of emphatical addition to a negative. [Sax. *gyt.*]
Yew, yū, *n.* An evergreen tree of the fir tribe, low, usually rising three or four feet from the ground, and then sending out numerous spreading branches, forming a dense head of foliage.—*a.* Relating to yew-trees; made of the wood of the yew-tree. [Sax. *iw,* G. *eibe,* Old G. *twa.*]
Yield, yēld, *vt. To pay; to render back;* to give, as claimed of right; to produce, in general; to afford; to admit to be true; to grant; to emit; to give up; to surrender; to reward; to bless.—*vi.* To give up the contest; to give way; to give place, as inferior in rank or excellence.—*n. Amount yielded;* product; return (applied particularly to products resulting from growth or cultivation). [Sax. *gyldan,* to pay, render, restore, requite.]
Yielding, yēld'ing, *p.a.* Complying with; accommodating.—*p.n.* Act of *paying back;* act of surrendering; submission.
Yieldingly, yēld'ing-li, *adv. In a yielding manner;* with compliance.
Yoke, yōk, *n. That which joins together;* a piece of timber fitted with bows for receiving the necks of oxen, by which means two are *connected* for drawing a chain; a bond of connection; a pair; as, a yoke of oxen; slavery; bondage. *vt. To put a yoke on;* to couple; to bring into bondage; to confine.—*vi.* To be joined. *ppr.* yoking, *pret. & pp.* yoked. [Sax. *geoc*—L. *jugum*—Sans. *yuj,* to join.]
Yoke-fellow, Yoke-mate, yōk'fel-lō, yōk'māt, *n.* An associate or companion; a fellow.
Yoking, yōk'ing, *p.n. The act of putting a yoke on;* the act of joining or coupl-

ch, c**h**ain; j, **j**ob; g, **g**o; ng, si**ng**; ᴠʜ, **th**en; th, **th**in; w, **w**ig; wh, **wh**ig; zh, a**z**ure; † obsolete.

YOLK 456 ZYMOTIC

ing; the harnessing of draught animals.
Yolk, yōlk, n. *The yellow part of an egg; the unctuous secretion from the skin of sheep, which renders the pile soft and pliable.* [Sax. *geolca—gelew*, yellow.]
Yon, Yond!, Yonder, yon, yond, yon'der, a. *Being at a distance within view.* adv. *At a distance within view.* [Sax. *geond*, through, over.]
Yore, yōr, adv. *In years past; in time past.* [Sax. *geara—gear*, a year.]
You, yō, pron. *The nominative and objective plural of thou. Although strictly applicable only to two or more persons, it is commonly used when a single person is addressed.* [Sax. *thu*, thou; pl. nom. *ge, accus. eow.*]

Young, yung, a. *Being in the early part of life; not having been long born; not old; being in the first part of growth; weak; having little experience.—n. The offspring of an animal or animals; offspring.* [Sax. *geong*—L. *juvenis*—Sans. *yuvan*, young—*div*, to shine.]
Younger, yung'gėr, a. *comp. of young.*
Youngest, yung'gest, a. *superl. of young.*
Youngish, yung'ish, a. *Somewhat young.*
Youngling, yung'ling, n. *Any animal in the first part of life.* [Sax. *geongling.*]
Youngster, yung'stėr, n. *A young person;* a youth.
Your, yōr, a. pron. *Belonging to you,* equally applicable to both numbers. [Sax. *eower*, gen. pl. of *thu*.]

Yours, yōrz. *The possessive pl. of thou.*
Yourself, yōr-self', pron. pl. *yourselves. A word added to you, to express distinction emphatically.* [*your* and *self*.]
Youth, yōth, n. *The state of being young; the period during which one is young; the whole early part of life from infancy to manhood, generally reckoned from fourteen to twenty-eight; a young man; young persons collectively.* [Sax. *geoguth*.]
Youthful, yōth'ful, a. *Full of youth;* young; suitable to the first part of life; fresh; vigorous, as in youth.
Youthfully, yōth'ful-li, adv. *In a youthful manner.*
Youthfulness, yōth'ful-nes, n. *State or quality of being youthful.*

Z.

Zany, zā'ni, n. *A merry-andrew; a buffoon.* [It. *zanni*, said to be a Venetian corruption of *Giovanni*, Eng. John.]
Zeal, zēl, n. *Fervour; warmth;* passionate ardour in the pursuit of anything. [L. *zelus*—Gr. *zeō*, to boil.]
Zealot, ze'lot, n. *One full of zeal;* one who engages warmly in any cause, and pursues his object with earnestness; one who is over-zealous.
Zealous, ze'lus, a. *Full of zeal;* warmly engaged in the pursuit of an object.
Zealously, ze'lus-li, adv. *In a zealous manner;* with passionate ardour.
Zebra, zē'bra, n. *A beautiful animal of the ass kind,* inhabiting Southern Africa, and admitting of being tamed to a certain extent, but even then treacherous, obstinate, and fickle. [Ar. *seeb*, beauty.]
Zend, zend, n. *A language that formerly prevailed in Persia.*
Zenith, zē'nith, n. *The point of the heavens overhead opposite to the nadir;* the vertical point. [Ar. *san*, to point.]
Zephyr, ze'fėr, n. *Primarily, the north-west wind;* the west wind; and poetically, any soft gentle breeze. [Gr. *zephuros*, strictly the north-west—*sophos*, the west.]
Zero, zē'rō, n. *Primarily, that which encircles;* a circle; a cipher; the point of a thermometer from which it is graduated. [Heb. *esor*, a girdle.]

Zest, zest, n. *That which gives a relish;* something that gives a pleasant taste, or the taste itself; a piece of orange or lemon peel, used to give flavour to liquor.—*vt. To give a relish to;* to heighten the relish of. [Ar. *istalas*, to have the taste, relish, or smack of.]
Zigzag, zig'zag, a. *Having sharp and quick turns or flexures.*—n. Something that has short turns or angles, as a line, the stem of a plant, &c. [Fr. formed from its likeness in sound to the thing it is intended to represent.]
Zinc, zingk, n. *A metal resembling tin;* a metal frequently called spelter in commerce, having a strong metallic lustre, and a bluish white colour. [G. *sink*, for *sinnig—sinn*, tin, *ahnlich*, like.]
Zircon, zėr'kon, n. *Called also jargon of Ceylon,* a mineral originally found in Ceylon, in the sands of rivers. [Ar. *zerk*, blue, hyacinth; also a beryl.]
Zodiac, zō'di-ak, n. *A broad belt or zone in the heavens, so called, because most of the constellations in it are the figures of animals.* It is divided into twelve equal parts, called signs, through which the sun passes in his annual course. [Fr. *zodiaque;* Gr. *zaō*, to live.]
Zodiacal, zō-di'ak-al, a. *Pertaining to the zodiac.*
Zone, zōn, n. *A girdle; a belt;* a division of the earth, with respect to the temperature of different latitudes (there are five such zones, namely, the torrid, two temperate, and two frigid zones); a band or stripe running round an object; circuit; circumference. [Gr. *zōnē*, a girdle—*zonnimi*, to gird.]
Zoned, zōnd, p.a. *Having zones;* wearing a zone.
Zoological, zō-o-loj'ik-al, a. *Pertaining to zoology,* or the science of animals.
Zoologically, zō-o-loj'ik-al-li, adv. *According to the principles of zoology.*
Zoologist, zō-ol'o-jist, n. *One who is well versed in zoology.*
Zoology, zō-ol'o-ji, n. *A discourse of animals;* that part of natural history which treats of the structure, habits, classification, habitations, &c., of all animals, from man to the lowest of all the tribes. [Gr. *zōon*, an animal, and *logos*, a discourse.]
Zoophyte, zō'o-fīt, n. *An animal plant;* a body resembling an animal and a vegetable, and once supposed to partake of the nature of both, such as madrepores and corallines. [Gr. *zōon*, an animal, and *phūton*, a plant—*phaō*, to bring forth—Sans. *bhā*, to be.]
Zymotic, xi-mot'ik, a. *A term introduced by the registrar-general, and used to characterize the entire class of epidemic and contagious diseases,* which are allied by the similarity of their predisposing causes. [from Gr. *sūmōō*, to make to ferment.]

Fāte, fär, fat, fall; mē, met, hėr; pīne, pin; nōte, not, move; tūbe, tub, bull; oi!, pound.

SUPPLEMENT.

Abiogenesis, Abiogeny, ab'i-ō-jen"e-sis, a-bi-oj'en-i, *n.* The doctrine that living matter may be produced by not-living matter. [Gr. *a*, priv., *bios*, life, and *genesis*, generation.]
Abiogenesist, Abiogenist, ab-i'ō-jen"e-sist, ab-i-oj'en-ist, *n.* A believer in the doctrine of abiogenesis.
Abiogenetic, ab'i-o-jen-et"ik, *a.* Of, pertaining to, or produced by abiogenesis.
Abscind, ab-sind', *vt.* To cut off. [L. *abscindo*.]
Abscission, ab-si'zhon, *n.* The act of cutting off; severance; removal.
Absinthe, ab'sinth, *n.* A popular French liqueur consisting of brandy flavoured with wormwood. [L. *absinthium*, wormwood.]
Acotyledon, a-kot'il-ē"don, *n.* A plant whose seeds are not furnished with cotyledons. [Gr. *kotylē*, a hollow.]
Acotyledonous, a-kot'il-ē"don-us, *a.* Having no seed-lobes.
Acroamatic, Acroatic, ak'rō-a-mat"ik, ak-rō-at'ik, *a.* Designed for being heard only by a select audience, hence, abstruse; pertaining to deep learning; esoteric. [Gr. *akroaomai*, to hear.]
Acrobat, ak'rō-bat, *n.* A rope-dancer; also one who practises vaulting, tumbling, &c. [Gr. *akrobates*.]
Acrobatic, ak'rō-bat-ik, *a.* Of or pertaining to an acrobat or his performances.
Acrocephalic, ak'rō-se-fal"ik, *a.* High-skulled. [Gr. *akros*, high, and *kephalē*, the skull.]
Acrogen, ak'rō-jen, *n.* A plant (as a moss, fern, &c.) increasing by extension of the stem at the top. [Gr. *akros*, and root *gen*, to produce.]
Acrogenous, a-kroj'en-us, *a.* Pertaining to acrogens.
Actinic, ak-tin'ik, *a.* Pertaining to rays; pertaining to the chemical rays of the sun. [Gr. *aktis*, *aktinos*, a ray.]
Actinism, ak'tin-izm, *n.* The property of the chemical part of the sun's rays which produces chemical combinations and decompositions.
Actinology, ak-ti-nol'o-ji, *n.* The science of the chemical rays of light.
Aculeate, Aculeated, Aculeolate, a-kū'le-āt, a-kū'lē-āt-ed, a-kū'lē-ō-lāt, *a.* Having prickles or sharp points.
Acupressure, Acupression, ak-u-pre'-shūr, ak-ū-pre'shon, *n.* A method of stopping hæmorrhage in arteries, in surgical operations, by means of needles or wires which keep the wound close, instead of ligatures. [L. *acus*, a needle.]
Africander, af'rik-an-dėr, *n.* A native of South Africa born of white parents.
Agglutinate, ag-glū'tin-āt, *a.* Applied to languages in which the suffixes for inflection are felt to be distinct from the root or body of the word. [L. *gluten*, glue.]
Agnomen, ag-nō'men, *n.* An additional name or epithet conferred on a person. [L. *ag* for *ad*, and *nomen*, a name.]
Agnostic, ag-nos'tik, *n.* One who disclaims any knowledge of God or of the origin of the universe, or of anything but material phenomena, holding that with regard to such matters nothing can be known. [Gr. *agnostos*, unknowing, unknown.]
Agnosticism, ag-nos'ti-sizm, *n.* The system or creed of the agnostics.
Agonic, a-gon'ik, *a.* Not forming an angle; applied to two lines on the earth's surface on which the magnetic needle points to the true north, or where the magnetic meridian coincides with the geographical.
Aigret, Aigrette, ā'gret, *n.* A plume or ornament for the head composed of feathers or precious stones. [Fr., a heron.]
Aiguille, ā'gwil, *n.* A name given to the needle-like points or tops of rocks and mountain masses, or to sharp-pointed masses of ice on glaciers, &c. [Fr., a needle.]
Akee, a-kē', *n.* The fruit of a W. African tree (*Blighia sapida*) now common in the W. Indies and S. America.
Alcoholism, al'kō-hol-izm, *n.* The condition of habitual drunkards whose tissues are saturated with alcohol.
Aldehyde, al'dē-hīd, *n.* A transparent colourless liquid produced by the oxidation of pure alcohol.
Alga, al'ga, *n.* pl. **Algæ,** al'jē. A seaweed; one of an order of cryptogamic plants found for the most part in the sea and fresh water. [L.]
Alineation, a-lin'ē-ā"shon, *n.* The determination of the position of a more remote object by following a line drawn through one or more intermediate and more easily recognizable objects. [L. *a*, and *linea*, a line.]
Aliped, al'i-ped, *n.* A wing-footed animal, one of the bat family. [L. *ala*, a wing, and *pes*, *pedis*, a foot.]
Alkahest, al'ka-hest, *n.* The pretended universal menstruum of the alchemists.
Allantois, Allantoid, al-lan'tois, al-lan'-toid, *n.* A sac developed from the posterior end of the abdominal cavity in vertebrate embryos. [Gr. *allas*, *allantos*, a sausage, and *eidos*, form.]
Allomorphic, al-lō-mor'fik, *a.* Pertaining to allomorphism.
Allomorphism, al-lō-mor'fizm, *n.* That property of certain substances of assuming a different form, remaining otherwise unchanged. [Gr. *allos*, other, and *morphē*, form.]
Allotropic, al-lō-trop'ik, *a.* Of or pertaining to allotropy.
Allotropy, Allotropism, al-lot'ro-pi, al-lot'ro-pizm, *n.* The capability exhibited by some substances of existing in more than one form and with different characteristics, as carbon. [Gr. *allos*, other, and *tropos*, condition.]
Alpenstock, al'pen-stok, *n.* A strong tall stick shod with iron, pointed at the end, used in mountain climbing.
Altruism, al'trō-izm, *n.* Devotion to others or to humanity: the opposite of selfishness. [It. *altrui*, others, from L. *alter*, another.]
Alveolar, Alveolary, Alveolate, al'vē-o-lėr, al'vē-o-la-ri, al'vē-o-lāt, *a.* Resembling a honey-comb. [L. *alvearium*, a bee-hive.]
Amnion, Amnios, am'ni-on, am'ni-os, *n.* The innermost membrane surrounding the fetus of mammals, birds, and reptiles; also a thin, semi-transparent, gelatinous fluid, in which the embryo of a seed is suspended. [Gr.]
Amygdaloid, a-mig'da-loid, *n.* A term applied to igneous rock containing round or almond-shaped vesicles or cavities partly or wholly filled with crystalline nodules of various minerals. [L. *amygdalus*, an almond.]
Amyl, am'il, *n.* A hypothetical radical said to exist in many compounds. [Gr. *amylon*, starch.]
Amyloid, am'il-oid, *a.* Resembling or being of the nature of amyl.—*n.* A semi-gelatinous substance, analogous to starch, met with in some seeds.
Anæmia, a-nē'mi-a, *n.* A deficiency of blood; a state of the system marked by a deficiency in certain constituents of the blood. [Gr. *an*, and *haima*, blood.]
Anæsthetic, an-es-thet'ik, *a.* Having the power of depriving of feeling or sensation.—*n.* A substance which has the power of depriving of sensation. [Gr *an*, and *aisthanomai*, to feel.]
Anelectrode, an-ē-lek'trōd, *n.* The positive pole of a galvanic battery.
Anemometer, an-ē-mom'et-ėr, *n.* An instrument for measuring the force and velocity of the wind. [Gr. *anemos*, the wind.]
Aniline, an'i-lin, *n.* A substance furnishing a number of dyes, obtained from indigo and other organic substances, though the aniline of commerce is obtained from benzole, a product of coal-tar [Span. *anil*, the indigo-plant.]
Animism, an'i-mizm, *n.* The doctrine of souls and other spiritual beings. [L. *anima*, the soul.]
Annelid, an'ne-lid, *n.* One of an extensive division or class of annulose animals whose bodies are formed of a great number of small rings, as in the earthworms. [L. *annellus*, a little ring, and Gr. *eidos*, form.]
Annulose, *a.* Furnished with rings; having a body composed of rings: a term applied to the annelids.
Anode, an'ōd, *n.* The part of the surface of an electrolyte where the electric current enters: opposed to *cathode*. [Gr. *ana*, upwards, and *hodos*, a way.]
Anthropoid, an'thrō-poid, *a.* Resembling man: applied to the higher apes. [Gr. *anthropos*, man, and *eidos*, resemblance.]
Anthropomorphism, an-thrō'pō-morf"-izm, *n.* The representation or conception of the Deity under a human form, or with human attributes and affections. [Gr. *anthropos*, man, and *morphē*, form.]
Anthropomorphous, an-thrō'pō-morf"-us, *a.* Having the figure of, or resembling, a man.
Anthropophagy, an-thrō-pof'a-ji, *n.* Cannibalism. [Gr. *anthropos*, man, and *phagō*, to eat.]
Anticlinal, an-ti-klī'nal, *a.* Inclining in opposite directions. [Gr. *anti*, and *klinō*, to incline.]
Anticyclone, an'ti-si-klōn, *n.* A meteoro-

logical phenomenon consisting of a region of high barometric pressure, the pressure being greatest in the centre, with light winds flowing outwards from the centre, and not inwards as in the cyclone.

Apse, aps, *n.* A portion of a building (as a church) forming a termination or projection semicircular or polygonal in plan, and having a dome or vaulted roof. [Gr. *haspis*, an arch.]

Aptera, ap'tėr-a, *n. pl.* An order of insects which have no wings. [Gr. *apteros*, wingless.]

Apteral, Apterous, ap'tėr-al, ap'tėr-us, *a.* Destitute of wings.

Aquarium, a-kwā'ri-um, *n.* A case, vessel, tank, or the like, in which aquatic plants and animals are kept; a place containing a collection of such vessels or tanks. [L. *aqua*, water.]

Aquatint, ak'wa-tint, *n.* A method of etching on metal by which an effect is produced resembling a drawing in water-colours or Indian ink. [L. *aqua*, water, and It. *tinta*, dye, tint.]

Arachnida, a-rak'ni-da, *n. pl.* A class of annulose, wingless animals, including the spiders. [Gr. *arachnē*, a spider.]

Archaic, ar-kā'ik, *a.* Obsolete; antiquated. [Gr. *archaikos*, ancient.]

Are, ār or ăr, *n.* The unit of French superficial measure, containing 100 square metres or 1076.44 English square feet. [L. *area*.]

Aril, ar'il, *n.* An extra covering of the seeds of some plants (as the nutmeg) outside of the true seed-coats, falling off spontaneously. [L. *areo*, to be dry.]

Aryan, är'i-an or är'i-an, *n.* An Indo-European; a member of that division of the human race which includes the Hindus and Persians and most Europeans (except Turks, Hungarians, Finns, &c.).—*a.* Pertaining or belonging to the Aryans or their languages. [Sans. *ārya*, noble.]

Assagai, as'sa-gā, *n.* An instrument of warfare among the natives of S. Africa; a throwing spear; a species of javelin.

Assyriologist, as-sir'i-ol''o-jist, *n.* One skilled in the antiquities, language, &c., of ancient Assyria.

Astatic, a-stat'ik, *a.* Applied to a magnetic needle having its directive property destroyed by the proximity of another needle of the same intensity fixed parallel to it but with the poles reversed. [Gr. *a*, and *sta*, to stand.]

Astigmatism, a-stig'mat-izm, *n.* A malformation of the lens of the eye, such that rays of light are not brought to converge in the same point. [Gr. *a*, and *stigma*, a mark.]

Atavism, at'a-vizm, *n.* The resemblance of offspring to a remote ancestor; the return or reversion to the original type. [L. *atavus*, an ancestor.]

Atelier, at-lē-ā, *n.* A workshop; an artist's studio. [Fr.]

Atrabiliar, Atrabilious, at-ra-bil'i-ar, at-ra-bil'i-us, *a.* Melancholic or hypochondriacal. [L. *atra bilis*, black bile.]

Automatic, a-tō-mat'ik, *a.* Having the power of self-motion; self-acting: said especially of mechanism; not depending on the will; instinctive. [Gr. *automatos*, self-acting.]

Autonomy, a-ton'o-mi, *n.* The power or right of self-government. [Gr. *autonomia*, self-rule.]

Avatar, av-a-tär', *n.* A descent from heaven; the incarnation of the Hindu deities, or their appearance in some manifest shape on earth. [Sans. *ava*, down, and root *tri*, to go.]

Bacillus, ba-sil'lus, *n.* pl. **Bacilli**, ba-sil'i. A rod-like microscopic organism, the introduction of which into the system is the cause of a number of diseases. [L., a little rod.]

Backwardation, bak-wėrd-ā'shon, *n.* A consideration paid to purchasers for an extension of time by speculators on the Stock Exchange unable to supply the stock or shares they have contracted to deliver.

Bakshish, bak'shĕsh, *n.* A present or gratuity of money; used in Eastern countries. [Per.]

Baleen, ba-lēn', *n.* The whalebone of commerce. [L. *balæna*, a whale.]

Banal, ban'al, *a.* Hackneyed; commonplace; vulgar. [Fr.]

Banality, ban-al'i-ti, *n.* A piece of commonplace; a vulgarity.

Bangle, bang'gl, *n.* An ornamental ring worn upon the arms and ankles in India and Africa; a kind of bracelet.

Banjo, ban'jō, *n.* A musical stringed instrument with a body like a tambourine and a neck like a guitar.

Banns, banz, *n. pl.* The proclamation in church for the purpose of constituting a regular marriage, made by calling over the names of the parties meditating matrimony. [Sax. *ban*, proclamation.]

Banshee, ban'shē, *n.* A kind of female fairy believed in Ireland and some parts of Scotland to attach herself to a particular house, and to give warning of a death in the family. [Ir. *bean-sith*, a female fairy.]

Bascule, bas'kūl, *n.* An arrangement in bridges by which one portion balances another. [Fr.]

Base-ball, bās'bal, *n.* A game somewhat similar to *rounders*, played with a bat and a ball by two parties or sides.

Bathometer, ba-thom'et-ėr, *n.* An apparatus for taking soundings. [Gr. *bathos*, depth, and *metron*, a measure.]

Bathymetry, ba-thim'et-ri, *n.* The art of measuring depths in the sea.

Bayadeer, Bayadere, bā-ya-dėr', *n.* An East Indian professional dancing girl. [Port. *bailar*, to dance.]

Bayou, ba-ō', *n.* In the United States, a channel proceeding from a lake or a river. [Fr. *boyau*.]

Bedouin, bed'ö-in, *n.* A nomadic Arab living in tents in Arabia, Syria, Egypt, &c. [Ar. *beddwi*.]

Belemnite, bel'em-nīt, *n.* A straight, tapering, dart-shaped fossil, found in the chalk formation, the internal bone or shell of animals allied to the cuttlefishes. [Gr. *belemnon*, a dart.]

Benison, ben'i-zn, *n.* A blessing; a benediction. [O. Fr. *beneison*.]

Benzine, Benzoine, ben-zin, *n.* Same as *Benzole*.

Benzoin, Benzoine, ben-zō'in or ben'zoin, *n.* A resinous juice obtained from a tree of Sumatra, &c., used in cosmetics and perfumes. [Ar.]

Benzole, Benzoline, ben'zōl, ben'zō-lin, *n.* A clear colourless liquid of an agreeable odour obtained from coal-tar, used for removing grease spots, &c.

Bessemer-steel, bes'e-mėr-stēl, *n.* Steel made directly from molten cast-iron by driving through it currents of air so as to oxidize and carry off the carbon and impurities, the requisite proportion of carbon being then introduced. [Sir H. *Bessemer*, the inventor.]

Bey, bā, *n.* A Turkish title of honour; the governor of a town or district.

Bhang, bang, *n.* An intoxicating and narcotic drug prepared from an Indian variety of the common hemp.

Bibliophile, Bibliophilist, bib'li-ō-fīl, bib-li-of'il-ist, *n.* A lover of books. [Gr. *biblion*, book, and *phileō*, to love.]

Bicarbonate, bī-kär'bon-āt, *n.* A carbonate containing two equivalents of carbonic acid to one of a base.

Bicycle, bī'si-kl, *n.* A vehicle consisting of two wheels, one behind the other, connected by a metal bar carrying a seat, and propelled by the feet of the rider.

Bifid, bī'fid, *a.* Cleft or divided into two parts; forked. [L. *bifidus*.]

Bifurcate, bī-fėr'kāt, *a.* Forked; divided into two branches. [L. *bi*, and *furca*, a fork.]

Bijou, bē-zhö, *n.* A jewel; something small and pretty. [Fr.]

Bijouterie, bē-zhö-trē, *n.* Jewelry; trinkets.

Bimetallism, bi-met'al-izm, *n.* That system of currency which recognizes coins of two metals, as silver and gold, as legal tender to any amount.

Biogenesis, bī-ō-gen'e-sis, *n.* The doctrine that living organisms can spring only from living parents: opposed to *abiogenesis*; the history of the life development of organized existences. [Gr. *bios*, life, and *genesis*, generation.]

Bioplasm, bī'ō-plazm, *n.* The albuminoid germinal matter in plants and animals. [Gr. *bios*, life, and *plasma*, anything formed.]

Blastema, blas-tē'ma, *n. Bot.* the axis of growth of an embryo. [Gr., a shoot.]

Blatant, blā'tant, *a.* Bellowing; bawling; noisy.

Bloom, blöm, *n.* A lump of puddled iron in a rough state. [Sax. *blōma*, a mass of metal.]

Blouse, blouz or blös, *n.* A light, loose upper garment resembling a smock-frock. [Fr.]

Boer, bör, *n.* One of the Dutch colonists of S. Africa. [D., a peasant.]

Bourse, börs, *n.* An exchange; a merchants' meeting place for business. [Fr.]

Boycott, boi'kot, *vt.* To combine in refusing to work to, to buy and sell with, or to have any dealings with, on account of difference of opinion on social and political questions and the like. [Capt. *Boycott*, an Irish landlord, the first prominent victim of the system.]

Bract, brakt, *n. Bot.* a modified leaf, generally differing from other leaves in shape and colour, and situated on the peduncle near the flower. [L. *bractea*, a thin metallic plate.]

Brahman, brā'man, *n.* Among the Hindus a member of the sacred or sacerdotal class. [*Brahma*, one of the deities of the Hindu trinity.]

Breccia, brech'i-a, *n. Geol.* an aggregate of angular fragments of rock united by a matrix or cement. [It.]

Bric-à-brac, brik-a-brak, *n.* Articles of vertu; objects having a certain interest or value from their rarity, antiquity, or the like. [Fr.]

Bureaucracy, bö-rōk'ra-si, *n.* The system of centralizing the administration of a country, through regularly graded series of government officials; such officials collectively.

Cabala, kab'a-la, *n.* A mysterious kind of science or learning among Jewish rabbins, transmitted by oral tradition. [Heb. *qābal*, to take or receive.]

Cabalistic, kab-al-ist'ik, *a.* Pertaining to the Cabala; containing an occult meaning.

Cachinnation, kak-in-nā'shon, *n.* Loud

Fāte, fär, fat, fall; mē, met, hėr; pīne, pin; nōte, not, mōve; tūbe, tub, bull; oil, pound.

or immoderate laughter. [L. *cachinno*, to laugh.]
Café, kaf-ā, *n.* A coffee-house; a restaurant. [Fr.]
Caffeine, ka-fē′in, *n.* A slightly bitter alkaloid found in tea, coffee, &c.
Cainozoic, kā-no-zō′ik, *a. Geol.* applied to the latest of the three divisions into which strata have been arranged with reference to the age of the fossils which they include, embracing the tertiary and post-tertiary systems. [Gr. *kainos*, recent, and *zoē*, life.]
Caisson, kās′son, *n.* A chest; a watertight vessel; especially a water-tight casing used in founding and building structures in deep water. [Fr.]
Calif, **Caliph**, kā′lif, *n.* A title given to the acknowledged successors of Mohammed. [Ar. *khalīfa*.]
Calorescence, kal-o-res′ens, *n.* The transmutation of heat rays into others of higher refrangibility.
Calumet, kal′u-met, *n.* The North American Indians' pipe of peace.
Cambist, kam′bist, *n.* One skilled in the science of exchange. [Fr. *cambiste*.]
Campanology, kam-pa-nol′o-ji, *n.* The art of bell-ringing. [L. *campana*, a bell, and Gr. *logos*, a discourse.]
Canard, kā-när or ka-närd′, *n.* A false rumour. [Fr.]
Cañon, **Canyon**, kā-nyon′, kan′yun, *n.* A long and narrow mountain gorge with precipitous sides, occurring in the Rocky Mountains and great western plateaus of N. America. [Sp.]
Cantaliver, **Cantiliver**, kan′ta-liv-ėr, kan′ti-liv-ėr, *n.* A wooden or iron block framed into a wall and projecting from it, to carry mouldings, eaves, balconies, &c.; also a large projecting framework forming part of an iron bridge, directly carrying part of the roadway, and also supporting girders bridging over a space between it and a similar structure. [O. Fr. *cant*, an angle, and *lever*, to raise.]
Cantata, kan-tā′tä, *n.* A short dramatic musical composition. [It.]
Cantatrice, kän-tä-trē′chä (It.), kang′-tä-trēs (Fr.), *n.* A female singer.
Carbolic, kär-bol′ik, *a.* Applied to an acid obtained from coal-tar, much used as an antiseptic and disinfectant. [*Carbon* and *oil*.]
Carboy, kär′boi, *n.* A large globular glass bottle protected by an outside covering. [Per. *karabā*.]
Cartoon, kär-tön′, *n.* A pictorial design drawn on strong paper as a study for a picture; a pictorial sketch relating to any prevalent topic or event. [Fr. *carton*, pasteboard.]
Casein, **Caseine**, kā′sē-in, *n.* That ingredient in milk which, when coagulated, forms curd and the main part of cheese. [L. *caseus*, cheese.]
Casino, kā-sē′nō, *n.* A public dancing, singing, or gaming saloon. [It., a small house.]
Catachresis, kat-a-krē′sis, *n.* The wresting of a word from its true signification. [Gr. *katachrēsis*, abuse.]
Cataclysm, kat′a-klizm, *n.* A deluge; a flood. [Gr. *kataklysmos*.]
Cathode, kath′ōd, *n.* The negative pole of an electric current:opposed to *anode*. [Gr. *kata*, down, and *hodos*, a way.]
Caucus, ka′kus, *n.* A private committee for arranging election matters.
Caudal, ka′dal, *a.* Pertaining to, or of the nature of, a tail. [L. *cauda*, a tail.]
Celt, selt, *n.* A prehistoric cutting implement of stone or metal resembling an axe-head. [L. *celtis*, a chisel.]

Cental, sen′tal, *n.* A weight of 100 pounds.
Ceramic, se-ram′ik, *a.* Of or belonging to the fictile arts or to pottery. [Gr. *keramos*, pottery.]
Cerebration, sėr-ē-brā′shon, *n.* Exertion or action of the brain, conscious or unconscious.
Chartography, kär-tog′ra-fi, *n.* The art or practice of drawing up maps or charts. [L. *charta*, paper, and Gr. *graphē*, writing.]
Chartulary, kär′tū-la-ri, *n.* A record or register, as of a monastery. [L. *cartularius*.]
Chauvinism, shō′vin-izm, *n.* Absurdly exaggerated patriotism or military enthusiasm. [*Chauvin*, an enthusiastic Napoleonic soldier.]
Chirography, kī-rog′ra-fi, *n.* The art of writing; hand-writing; fortune-telling by examination of the hand. [Gr. *cheir*, the hand, and *graphō*, to write.]
Chloral, klō′ral, *n.* An oily liquid produced from chlorine and alcohol; also the name popularly applied to chloral hydrate, a white crystalline substance used in med. for producing sleep.
Chlorophyll, klō′rō-fil, *n.* The green colouring matter of plants. [Gr. *chloros*, green, and *phyllon*, a leaf.]
Cist, sist, *n.* A prehistoric place of interment, consisting of rows of stones forming a sort of stone chest, and covered with flat stones. [L. *cista*, a chest.]
Clairvoyance, klär-voi′ans, *n.* A power attributed to persons in the mesmeric state by which the person (called a clairvoyant or clairvoyante) discerns objects concealed from sight, tells what is happening at a distance, &c. [Fr. *clair*, clear, and *voyant*, seeing.]
Clairvoyant, klär-voi′ant, *a.* Of or pertaining to clairvoyance.
Clinometer, kli-nom′et-ėr, *n.* An instrument for measuring the dip of rock strata. [Gr. *klinō*, to lean, and *metron*, measure.]
Coleoptera, kol-ē-op′tėr-a, *n. pl.* The beetle order of insects. [Gr. *koleos*, a sheath, *pteron*, a wing.]
Collide, kol-līd′, *vi.* To strike or dash against each other; to meet in opposition. [L. *collido*, to strike together.]
Collingual, kol-ling′gwal, *a.* Speaking the same language. [L. *col* for *con*, and *lingua*, a tongue.]
Commendam, kom-men′dam, *n.* An ecclesiastical benefice or living commended to the care of a qualified person till one for whom it is intended is ready to fill it. [L.]
Commensal, kom-men′sal, *n.* One that eats at the same table; an animal which lives on or in another without being parasitic. [L. *com*, and *mensa*, a table.]
Commune, kom′mūn, *n.* A small territorial district in France and in some other countries under the government of a mayor; a socialist body who ruled over Paris in 1871. [Fr.]
Communism, kom′mūn-izm, *n.* The system or theory of the commune; the doctrine of a community of property.
Communist, kom′mūn-ist, *n.* One who holds the doctrines of communism.
Contango, kon-tang′gō, *n.* On the stock exchange, a sum of money paid to a seller for accommodating a buyer by carrying the engagement to pay the price of shares bought over to the next account day. BACKWANDATION.
Coolie, kö′li, *n.* An East Indian porter

or carrier; an emigrant labourer from India, China, and other eastern countries.
Coprolite, kop′ro-līt, *n.* The petrified dung of extinct animals, found chiefly in the lias and coal-measures. [Gr. *kopros*, dung, and *lithos*, a stone.]
Coracle, kor′a-kl, *n.* An ancient form of boat, made of a wicker frame covered with skin, &c. [W. *cwrwgl*.]
Corbel, kor′bel, *n. Arch.* a piece of stone, wood, or iron projecting from the vertical face of a wall to support some superincumbent object. [L. *corbella*, from *corbis*, a basket.]
Cordate, kor′dāt, *a.* Heart-shaped. [L. *cor*, *cordis*, the heart.]
Corral, kor-räl′, *n.* A pen or inclosure for horses or cattle; an inclosure formed by wagons; a strong stockade or inclosure for capturing wild elephants in Ceylon. [Sp., from *corro*, a circle.]
Cortes, kor′tēz, *n.* The legislative assemblies of Spain and of Portugal. [Sp., pl. of *corte*, court.]
Cotyledon, kot-i-lē′don, *n. Bot.* the seed-leaf; the first leaf or leaves of the embryo plant, forming, together with the radicle and plumule, the embryo, which exists in every seed capable of germination. [Gr. *kotylē*, a hollow.]
Coupon, kö′pon, *n.* An interest certificate printed at the bottom of transferable bonds, to be cut off and given up when payment is made; hence, generally one of a series of tickets which binds the issuer to give value for certain amounts at different periods, or the like. [Fr., from *couper*, to cut.]
Cremate, krē′māt, *vt.* To burn; to dispose of (a human body) by burning instead of interring. [L. *cremo*, to burn.]
Cremation, krē-mā′shon, *n.* The act or custom of cremating.
Cremona, krē-mō′na, *n.* A general name for violins made at *Cremona*, in N. Italy, during the 17th and 18th centuries.
Creole, krē′ōl, *n.* A native of the West Indies or Spanish America, but not of indigenous blood. [Fr. *créole*.]
Cretin, krē′tin, *n.* One afflicted with cretinism. [Fr. *crétin*.]
Cretinism, krē′tin-izm, *n.* The state of a cretin; a peculiar endemic disease resembling rickets, but accompanied with idiocy, common in Switzerland, and found also in other mountainous countries.
Crewel, krö′el, *n.* A kind of fine worsted or thread of silk, used in embroidery and fancy work. [D. *krul*, a curl.]
Ctenoid, ten′oid, *a.* Comb-shaped; having the posterior edge with teeth: said of the scales of certain fishes, as the perch and flounder; having scales of this kind. [Gr. *kteis*, *ktenos*, a comb, and *eidos*, form.]
Cufic, kū′fik, *a.* Applied to the characters of the Arabic alphabet used in the time of Mohammed. [*Cufa*, near Bagdad.]
Cuisine, kwē-zēn′, *n.* Manner or style of cooking. [Fr.]
Curaçoa, kū-ra-sō′a, *n.* A liqueur flavoured with orange-peel, cinnamon, and mace, first made in *Curaçoa*.
Cymric, kim′rik, *a.* Of, or pertaining to, the Cymry, or Welsh; pertaining to the ancient Welsh.
Czech, chech, *n.* One of the Slavonic inhabitants of Bohemia; the language of the Czechs.

---

ch, *ch*ain; j, *j*ob; g, *g*o; ng, si*ng*; ᴛʜ, *th*en; th, *th*in; w, *w*ig; wh, *wh*ig; zh, a*z*ure; † obsolete.

Dacoit, da-koit', n. An East Indian name for robbers who plunder in bands.
Dacoity, da-koi'ti, n. The system of plundering in bands.
Dado, dā'dō, n. That part of a pedestal which is between the base and the cornice; the finishing of the lower part of the walls in rooms. [It.]
Dahabieh, da-ha-bē'ā, n. A Nile passenger boat. [Eg.]
Daltonism, dal'ton-izm, n. Colour-blindness. [*Dalton*, the inventor.]
Darwinism, där'win-izm, n. The doctrine as to the origin and modifications of the species of plants and animals taught by Charles *Darwin*; evolution.
Debouch, dē-bösh', vi. To issue or march out of a narrow place. [Fr. *de*, and *bouche*, mouth.]
Decapod, dek'a-pod, n. A crustacean having ten feet, as a crab; also a cuttle-fish with ten prehensile arms. [Gr. *deka*, ten, and *pous*, *podos*, a foot.]
Declinometer, dek-li-nom'et-ėr, n. An instrument for measuring the declination of the magnetic needle.
Decollate, dē-kol'āt, vt. To behead. [L. *decollo*, to behead.]
Demonetize, dē-mon'e-tīz, vt. To deprive of standard value, as money; to withdraw from circulation.
Demotic, dē-mot'ik, a. Pertaining to the common people; applied to the popular alphabet of the ancient Egyptians, as contradistinguished from the *hieratic*. [Gr. *demos*, people.]
Denticulate, Denticulated, den-tik'ū-lāt, den-tik'ū-lāt-ed, a. Having small teeth. [L. *dens*, *dentis*, a tooth.]
Dentine, den'tin, n. The ivory tissue forming the body of the tooth.
Dermal, dėr'mal, a. Pertaining to skin; consisting of skin. [Gr. *derma*, skin.]
Dermatology, dėr-ma-tol'o-ji, n. The branch of science which treats of skin and its diseases. [Gr. *derma*, skin, and *logos*, discourse.]
Dermo-skeleton, dėr'mo-skel"e-ton, n. The covering of scales, plates, shells, &c., of many animals, as crabs, crocodiles, &c.
Dervis, Dervish, dėr'vis, dėr'vish, n. A poor Mohammedan priest or monk. [Per. *derwesh*, poor.]
Desiccate, dē-sik'āt, vt. To exhaust of moisture; to dry. [L. *desicco*, to dry up.]
Dhow, dou, n. An Arab trading vessel.
Dhurra, dur'ra, n. A kind of millet cultivated in Africa and elsewhere.
Diacoustics, di-a-kous'tiks, n. The science of the properties of refracted sound. [Gr. *dia*, through, and *akouō*, to hear.]
Diacritical, di-a-krit'ik-al, a. Separating; distinctive: applied to a mark used in some languages to distinguish letters which are similar in form. [Gr. *diakritikos—dia*, and *krinō*, to separate.]
Diagnose, di-ag-nōs', vt. To ascertain from symptoms the true nature of.
Diagnosis, di-ag-nō'sis, n. The ascertaining from symptoms the true nature of diseases.[Gr.*dia,*and *gignōskō,*to know.]
Diamagnetic, di-a-mag-net'ik, a. Applied to substances which, when under the influence of magnetism and freely suspended, take a position at right angles to the magnetic meridian.
Diapason, di-a-pā'zon, n. Harmony; the entire compass of a voice or instrument. [Gr.]

Diathermal, Diathermous, di-a-thėr'-mal, di-a-thėr'mus, a. Freely permeable by heat. [Gr. *dia*, and *thermē*, heat.]
Diatomic, di-a-tom'ik, a. *Chem.* consisting of two atoms. [Gr. *di*, twice, and *atomos*, an atom.]
Dichotomous, di-kot'o-mus, a. *Bot.* regularly dividing by pairs from top to bottom. [Gr. *dicha*, by pairs, and *temnō*, to cut.]
Dicotyledon, di'kot-i-lē"don, n. A plant whose seeds contain a pair of cotyledons or seed-leaves.
Dielectric, di-ē-lek'trik, n. Any medium through or across which electric induction takes place between two conductors.
Diffract, dif-frakt', vt. To bend from a straight line; to deflect. [L. *dif*, *dis*, and *frango*, to break.]
Diffraction, dif-frak'shon, n. *Optics*, the peculiar modifications which light undergoes when it passes by the edge of an opaque body; deflection.
Dilettante, dil-e-tan'tā, n. pl. **Dilettanti**, dil-e-tan'tē. An amateur or trifler in art. [It.]
Dipsomania, dip-sō-mā'ni-a, n. Drink madness; an uncontrollable craving for stimulants. [Gr. *dipsa*, thirst.]
Dolichocephalic, Dolichocephalous, dol'i-kō-se-fal"ik, dol'i-kō-sef"a-lus, a. Long-skulled: used to denote skulls in which the diameter from side to side bears a less proportion to the diameter from front to back than 8 to 10.
Dolomite, dol'o-mit, n. A granular crystalline or schistose rock compounded of carbonate of magnesia and carbonate of lime. [*Dolomieu*, French chemist.]
Dragoman, drag'ō-man, n. pl. **Dragomans**. An interpreter and traveller's guide or agent in eastern countries. [Sp., from Ar. *tarjama* to interpret.]
Dravidian, dra-vid'i-an, a. Pertaining to *Dravida*, an old province of S. India: applied to a distinct family of tongues spoken in S. India, Ceylon, &c.
Drift, drift, n. [add.] *Geol.* earth and rocks which have been conveyed by icebergs and glaciers and deposited over a country while submerged; in S. Africa, a ford.
Drupe, drōp, n. *Bot.* a stone fruit, as the cherry or plum. [Fr.]
Dune, dūn, n. A low sand-hill on the sea-coast; an ancient Scotch fort. [Sax. *dún*.]
Dura-mater, dū'ra-mā-tėr, n. The outer membrane of the brain. [L., hard mother.]
Duramen, dū-rā'men, n. The heartwood of an exogenous tree. [L. *durus*, hard.]
Durbar, dėr'bär, n. An Indian state levee or audience. [Per. *dar*, door, and *bar*, court.]
Dyne, din, n. A unit of force, being that force which, acting on a gramme for one second, generates a velocity of a centimetre per second. [Gr. *dynamis*, power.]

Echelon, esh'e-lon, n. *Milit.* the position of a body of troops in parallel lines, each line being a little to the right or left of the preceding one. [Fr., from *échelle*, a ladder.]
Economics, ē-ko-nom'iks, n. [add.] Political economy.
Effendi, ef-fen'di, n. A Turkish title of respect,given especially to learned men and ecclesiastics. [Turk.]

Egyptologist, ē-jip-tol'o-jist, n. One versed in the antiquities of Egypt.
Egyptology, ē-jip-tol'o-ji, n. The science of Egyptian antiquities.
Eisteddfod, is-tетн-vod', n. A meeting of Welsh bards and minstrels; a periodical Welsh festival for harp-playing and the recitation of prize poems. [W.]
Elasmobranchiate, ē-las'mō-brang"ki-āt, a. Pertaining to an order of fishes, including the sharks, dog-fishes, rays, &c. [Gr. *elasmos*, a plate, and *branchia*, gills.
Electro, ē-lek'trō, n. An electrotype.
Electro-biology, ē-lek'trō-bī-ol"o-ji, n. The science of electric currents developed in living organisms; mesmerism or animal magnetism.
Electrode, ē-lek'trōd, n. One of the terminals or poles of the voltaic circle. [*-ode*, from Gr. *hodos*, a way.]
Electro-dynamics,ē-lek'trō-di-nam"iks, n. The science of mechanical actions exerted on one another by electric currents.
Electro-gilt, ē-lek'trō-gilt, a. Gilded by means of the electric current.
Electro-kinetics, ē-lek'trō-ki-net"iks, n. That branch of electricity which treats of electric currents in motion.
Electrolysis, ē-lek-trol'i-sis, n. Decomposition by means of electricity.
Electrolyte, ē-lek'trol-it, n. A compound which is decomposable, or is subjected to decomposition, by an electric current.
Electrotype, ē-lek'trō-tip, n. The act of producing copies of types, woodcuts, &c., by means of the electric deposition of copper upon a cast taken from the original; a copy thus produced.
Electuary, ē-lek'tū-a-ri, n. A medicine incorporated with some conserve or syrup. [L. *electuarium*.]
Elytron, Elytrum, el'i-tron, el'i-trum, n. pl. **Elytra**, el'i-tra. The wing sheath which covers the true wing in beetles. [Gr., a cover.]
Embogue, em-bōg', vi. To discharge itself, as a river. [Prefix *em*, and O. Fr. *bogue*, a mouth.]
Embolism, em'bol-izm, n. Intercalation; *surg.* the obstruction of a vessel by a clot of fibrine. [Gr. *emballō*, to insert.]
Embryology, em-bri-ol'o-ji, n. The doctrine of the development of embryos in plants or animals.
Emeritus, ē-mer'i-tus, a. Discharged from duty on account of infirmity, age, or long service. [L.]
Emeute, e-mūt', n. A seditious commotion; a riot; a tumult. [Fr.]
Emir, em'ėr, n. An independent Mohammedan chief; a descendant of Mohammed; the head of certain departments in Mohammedan countries. [Ar. *amīr*, a commander.]
Enchorial, en-kō'ri-al, a. Belonging to or used in a country; native; demotic.
Endoskeleton, en'dō-skel-e-ton. n. The internal bony structure of man and other animals. [Gr. *endon*, within]
Endosmose, en'dos-mōs, n. The transmission of fluids or gases through porous septa or partitions from the exterior to the interior. [Gr. *endon*, within, *osmos*, impulsion.]
Ensiform, en'si-form, a. Sword-shaped. [L. *ensis*, a sword.]
Ensilage, en'sil-āj, n. A mode of storing green fodder, vegetables, &c., by burying in pits or silos, the substance stored being pressed down with heavy weights. [Fr., from Sp. *silo*, a pit.]

Entozoon, en-to-zō'on, *n*. pl. **Entozoa**, en-to-zō'a. An intestinal worm; an animal living in some part of another animal. [Gr. *entos*, within, and *zōon*, an animal.]
Entresol, en'tèr-sol, *n*. *Arch.* a low story between two others of greater height. [Fr.]
Eocene, ē'ō-sēn, *a*. and *n*. *Geol.* a term applied to the series of strata at the base of the tertiary formations, from the small proportion of living species found in it. [Gr. *éos*, dawn, and *kainos*, recent.]
Eolithic, ē-ō-lith'ik, *a. Archæol.* of or pertaining to the early part of the palæolithic period. [Gr. *eos*, dawn, and *lithos*, a stone.]
Eozoic, ē-ō-zō'ik, *a.* Pertaining to the oldest fossiliferous rocks. [Gr. *ēōs*, dawn, and *zoē*, life.]
Eozoon, ē-ō-zō'on, *n.* A supposed fossil animal found in the Laurentian rocks of Canada.
Epidermis, ep-i-dėr'mis, *n. Anat.* the cuticle or scarf-skin of the body; *bot.* the exterior cellular coating of the leaf or stem of a plant. [Gr. *epi*, upon, and *derma*, skin.]
Epiphyte, ep'i-fīt, *n.* A plant growing upon another plant, but not deriving its nourishment from it. [Gr. *epi*, upon, and *phyton*, a plant.]
Erotic, ē-rot'ik, *a.* Pertaining to or prompted by love; treating of love. [Gr. *erōs, erōtos*, love.]
Euchre, Eucre, ū'kėr, *n.* A game of cards; a modified form of écarté played by two, three, or four players with the thirty-two highest cards of the pack.
Eurasian, ū-rā'shi-an, *n.* One born in Hindustan of a native mother and a European father. [Contract. of *European* and *Asian*.]
Evolution, ev-ō-lū'shon, *n.* [add.] That theory which sees in the history of all things, organic and inorganic, a development from simplicity to complexity, a gradual advance from a simple or rudimentary condition to one that is more complex and of a higher character.
Excoriate, eks-kō'ri-āt, *vt.* To break or wear off the cuticle of. [L. *ex*, and *corium*, skin.]
Exfoliate, ex-fō'li-āt, *vt.* To free from scales or splinters. [L. *ex*, and *folium*, a leaf.]
Exoskeleton, ek'sō-skel-e-ton, *n.* The external skeleton, as the shell of a crustacean; the dermoskeleton.
Exosmose, ek'sos-mōs, *n.* The passage of gases or liquids through membrane or porous media, from within outward: opposed to *endosmose*.
Extravasate, eks-trav'a-sāt, *vt.* To force or let out of the proper vessels, as out of the blood-vessels. [L. *extra*, and *vas*, a vessel.]
Exuviæ, eg-zū'vi-ē, *n. pl.* Any parts of animals which are shed or cast off, as the skins of serpents, &c. [L. *exuo*, to strip.]
Eyalet, ī'a-let, *n.* A Turkish province under the administration of a vizier or pacha.

Faculæ, fak'ū-lē, *n. pl. Astron.* spots sometimes seen on the sun's disc, which appear brighter than the rest of the surface. [L.]
Faggot-vote, fag'ot-vōt, *n.* A vote procured by the purchase of property, which is divided among a number so as to constitute a nominal qualification.

Falsetto, fäl-set'ō, *n.* The tones above the natural compass of the voice. [It.]
Fama, fā'ma, *n.* A widely prevailing rumour. [L.]
Farad, far'ad, *n.* The unit of quantity in electrometry.
Fauna, fa̤'na, *n.* A collective term for the animals peculiar to a region or epoch. [L.]
Fellah, fel'lä, *n.* An Egyptian peasant. [Ar.]
Fenestration, fen-es-trā'shon, *n.* The series or arrangement of windows in a building. [L. *fenestra*, a window.]
Fenian, fē'ni-an, *n.* A member of a secret society, the object of which was the erection of an independent Irish republic. [Ir. *Fionne*, a race of Irish legendary heroes.]
Feral, fē'ral, *a.* Having become wild from a state of domestication, as animals, or from a state of cultivation, as plants. [L. *fera*, a wild beast.]
Fetich, fē'tish, *n.* An object regarded by some savage races as having mysterious powers residing in it, or as being the representative or habitation of a deity; any object of exclusive devotion. [Fr. *fétiche*.]
Fibrin, Fibrine, fī'brin, *n.* A peculiar organic substance found in animals and vegetables, and readily obtained from fresh blood.
Fiord, Fjord, fyord, *n.* An inlet of the sea, such as are common on the coast of Norway.
Firman, fėr'man or fėr-män', *n.* A Turkish decree, order, or grant; a license or grant of privileges. [Per. *fermān*.]
Flume, flōm, *n.* A channel of water for driving a mill-wheel; an artificial channel for gold-washing.
Folk-lore, fōk'lōr, *n.* Rural superstitions, tales, traditions, or legends.
Follicle, fol'li-kl, *n.* A little bag or vesicle in animals or plants. [L. *follis*, a bag.]
Foot-lights, fṳt'līts, *n. pl.* A row of lights on the front of a stage in a theatre.
Foot-pound, fṳt'pound, *n. Physics*, the unit of work done by a mechanical force; one pound weight raised through a height of one foot.
Fourierism, fö'ri-ėr-izm, *n.* A socialistic system or form of communism propounded by Charles *Fourier*.
Frenetic, Phrenetic, fre-net'ik, fre-net'ik-al, *a.* Frenzied; frantic.
Frond, frond, *n.* The leaf of a fern or other cryptogamic plant. [L. *frons, frondis*, a leaf.]
Frugiferous, frö-jif'ėr-us, *a.* Producing fruit or crops; fruitful. [L. *frux, frugis*, fruit, and *fero*, to bear.]
Frumentaceous, frö-men-tā'shus, *a.* Having the character of or resembling wheat or other cereal. [L. *frumentum*, corn.]
Fugue, fūg, *n. Mus.* a composition in parts which appear to follow or pursue each other successively. [Fr., from L. *fuga*, flight.]
Fusillade, fū'zi-lād, *n.* A simultaneous discharge of musketry. [Fr.]
Fustic, fus'tik, *n.* The wood of a West Indian tree, extensively used as an ingredient in the dyeing of yellow. [Sp. *fuste*, wood.]

Gabel, Gabelle, ga-bel', *n.* A tax or impost in some continental countries. [Fr.]
Galena, ga-lē'na, *n.* An ore of lead, of a

lead-gray colour, with a metallic lustre. [Gr. *gulēnē*, quietness.]
Galleon, gal'ē-un, *n.* A large ship formerly used by the Spaniards. [Sp.]
Galop, ga-lop', *n.* A quick lively dance somewhat resembling a waltz. [Fr.]
Galvanized, gal'van-izd, *p.* and *a.* [add.] Coated (as sheets of iron) with tin or zinc.
Galvanometer, gal-van-om'et-ėr, *n.* An instrument for detecting the existence and determining the strength and direction of an electric current.
Gamin, gam'in, *n.* A street arab; a neglected street-boy. [Fr.]
Ganoid, gan'oid, *a.* Applied to an order of fishes with horny scales or bony plates covered with glossy enamel. [Gr. *ganos*, splendour, and *eidos*, appearance.]
Gargoil, Gargoyle, gär'goil, *n. Arch.* a carved, often grotesque, projecting spout for throwing the water from the roof gutters of a building. [Fr. *gargouille*.]
Gasogene, Gazogene, gas'o-jēn, gaz'o-jēn, *n.* An apparatus for manufacturing aerated waters on a small scale for domestic use.
Gasteropod, Gastropod, gas'tėr-o-pod, gas'trō-pod, *n.* One of a class of molluscs, chiefly inhabiting univalve shells, distinguished by a broad muscular *foot* attached to the ventral surface. [Gr. *gastėr*, the belly, and *pous, podos*, the foot.]
Gatling-gun, gat'ling-gun, *n.* A form of repeating machine-gun, named from the inventor.
Gaucho, gä-ō'chō, *n.* A native of the S. American Pampas, of Spanish descent.
Gavelkind, gā'vel-kind, *n.* An old English land-tenure by which the land descends to all the sons in equal shares. [Sax. *gavel cenedl*, family tenure.]
Gavial, gā'vi-al, *n.* A species of crocodile found in India.
Gendarme, zhäng'därm, *n.* A private in the armed police of France. [Fr. *gens d'armes*, men-at-arms.]
Geognosy, jē-og'no-si, *n.* The science of the structure of the earth. [Gr. *gē*, the earth, and *gnōsis*, knowledge.]
Geothermic, jē-ō-thėr'mik, *a.* Pertaining to the internal heat of the earth. [Gr. *gē*, earth, and *thermos*, heat.]
Germ-theory, jėrm'thē-ō-ri, *n.* The theory that living matter can only be produced from germs or seeds; also the theory that zymotic diseases are caused by microscopic germs of organic matter.
Geyser, gī'zėr, *n.* A hot-water spring, the water rising in a column. [Icel.]
Ghat, Ghaut, gät, gat, *n.* In India, a mountain pass; a chain of hills; a river landing-place.
Ghawazee, Ghawazi, gä-wä'zē, *n.* An Egyptian dancing-girl.
Ghee, gē, *n.* Indian butter, made from buffalo milk converted into a kind of oil.
Gherkin, gėr'kin, *n.* A small-fruited variety of cucumber used for pickling. [G. *gurke*.]
Ghoul, göl, *n.* An imaginary evil being which preys upon human bodies. [Per. *ghūl*.]
Giaour, jour, *n.* A Turkish name for a non-Mohammedan; a Christian; a Frank.
Gibbon, gib'on, *n.* A long-armed ape of the Indian Archipelago.
Gillie, gil'i, *n.* A Highland male servant who attends on sportsmen. [Gael. *gille*, a boy.]

Gimbals, gim'balz, n. pl. A contrivance of two movable hoops, such as supports the mariner's compass and causes it to assume a constantly vertical position. [Gr. *gemelle*, from L. *gemellus*, twin.]

Ginseng, jin'seng, n. The name of two plants, the roots of which are a favourite Chinese medicine.

Glaucous, gla'kus, a. Of a sea-green colour; bot. covered with a fine bluish or greenish powder or bloom. [L. *glaucus*, sea-green.]

Globulin, glob'ū-lin, n. The main ingredient of blood globules and resembling albumen.

Glucose, glō'kōs, n. Grape-sugar, a variety of sugar produced from grapes, starch, &c.

Glume, glöm, n. The husk or chaff of grain; the palea or pale.

Glycerine, glis'ėr-in, n. A transparent, colourless, sweet liquid obtained from fats. [Gr. *glykeros*, sweet.]

Glyphic, glif'ik, a. Of or pertaining to carving or sculpture. [Gr. *glyphō*, to carve.]

Glyptography, glip-tog'ra-fi, n. The art of engraving on precious stones. [Gr. *glyptos*, and *graphō*, to write.]

Gnostic, nos'tik, n. One of an early religious sect whose doctrines were based partly on Christianity and partly on Greek and Oriental philosophy. [Gr. *gnostikos*, knowledge.]

Gnosticism, nos'ti-sizm, n. The doctrines of the Gnostics.

Gonidia, go-nid'i-a, n. Bot. the secondary reproductive, green spherical cells in the thallus of lichens.

Good-Templar, gud-tem'plėr, n. A member of a certain society established for the promotion of teetotal principles.

Gopher, gō'fėr, n. The name given in America to several burrowing animals; also to a species of burrowing tortoise. [Fr. *gaufre*, honey-comb.]

Gourmet, gör-mā or gör'met, n. A connoisseur in wines and meats; a nice feeder; an epicure. [Fr.]

Grail, Graal, grāl, n. The holy vessel said to have been brought to England by Joseph of Arimathea, who had caught the last drops of Christ's blood in it, and which being afterwards lost, the search for it became the great work of King Arthur's knights. [O. Fr.]

Grallatorial, gral-a-tō'ri-al, a. Pertaining to the *Grallatores*, an order of birds including the cranes, snipes, &c. [L. *grallæ*, stilts.]

Gramme, gram, n. The French unit of weight, equal to 15·43 grains troy. [Gr. *gramma*.]

Gravamen, gra-vā'men, n. Ground or burden of complaint. [L. *gravo*, to weigh down.]

Gravid, grav'id, a. Being with young; pregnant. [L. *gravidus*, from *gravis*, heavy.]

Guerrilla, Guerilla, ge-ril'la, n. An irregular petty war; one engaged in such. [Sp., from Fr. *guerre*, war.]

Guilder, gil'dėr, n. A Dutch coin equal to 1s. 8d. English.

Gulpure, gē-pūr', n. An imitation of antique lace. [Fr.]

Gulch, gulch, n. A gully; the dry bed of a torrent.

Gynæcocracy, Gynecocracy, jin-ē-kok'-ra-si, n. Female rule. [Gr. *gynē*, a woman, and *kratos*, power.]

Gynæolatry, jin-ē-ol'a-tri, n. The extravagant admiration of woman. [Gr. *latreia*, worship.]

Gyroscope, Gyrostat, ji'rō-akōp, ji-rō-stat, n. An apparatus for illustrating peculiarities of rotation. [Gr. *gyros*, a circle, and *skopeō*, to view.]

Hadji, haj'ē, n. A Mohammedan who has performed his pilgrimage to Mecca. [Ar.]

Hagiology, ha-ji-ol'o-ji, n. That branch of literature which has to do with the lives and legends of the saints. [Gr. *hagios*, holy, and *logos*, discourse.]

Hatt, Hatti-sherif, hat, hat'ti-she-rif'', n. An irrevocable order signed by the Sultan of Turkey. [Turk.]

Hedonic, hē-don'ik, a. Pertaining to pleasure. [Gr. *hēdonē*, pleasure.]

Hedonism, hē'don-izm, n. The pursuit of pleasure.

Hegelian, he-gē'li-an, a. Pertaining to Hegel (hā'gl) or his system of philosophy.—n. A follower of Hegel.

Hegelianism, he-gē'li-an-izm, n. The system of philosophy of Hegel.

Hegemony, hej'e-mo-ni or he-jem'o-ni, n. Leadership; preponderance of one state among others.

Hegira, hej'i-ra, n. The flight of Mohammed from Mecca (16th July 622); the commencement of the Mohammedan era. [Ar.]

Heliocentric, Heliocentrical, hē'li-o-sen''trik, hē'li-o-sen''trik-al, a. Relating to the sun as a centre; appearing as if seen from the sun's centre. [Gr. *helios*, the sun.]

Heliograph, Heliostat, hē'li-o-graf, hē'li-o-stat, n. A sun telegraph; the name of various contrivances for reflecting the sun's light to an observer at a distance.

Heliotrope, hē'li-o-trōp, n. Blood-stone; a variety of quartz of a deep-green colour with red spots; also a favourite garden plant. [Gr. *helios*, and *tropē*, a turning.]

Heliotype, hē'li-o-tip, n. A surface-printed picture direct from a photograph.

Helix, hē'liks, n. pl. **Helices,** hel'i-sēz. A spiral line, as of wire in a coil; something that is spiral. [Gr., a spiral.]

Helot, hē'lot, n. A slave. [Gr. *heilōtēs*.]

Heptateuch, hep'ta-tūk, n. The first seven books of the Old Testament. [Gr. *hepta*, seven, and *teuchos*, book.]

Herpetology, hėr-pe-tol'o-ji, n. The natural history of reptiles. [Gr. *herpeton*, a reptile.]

Hetarism, Hetairism, het'a-rizm, he-ti'-rizm, n. That primitive state of society in which the women of a tribe are held in common. [Gr. *hetarē*, *hetaira*, a female paramour.]

Hiemal, hi-em'al, a. Wintry; pertaining to winter. [L. *hiems*, winter.]

Hiemation, hi-e-mā'shon, n. The spending or passing of winter.

Hieratic, hi-ėr-at'ik, a. Sacred; pertaining to priests: applied to a kind of developed hieroglyphics used by the ancient Egyptian priests. [Gr. *hieros*, holy.]

Histology, his-tol'o-ji, n. The doctrine of the tissues which enter into the formation of an animal or vegetable. [Gr. *histos*, a tissue, and *logos*.]

Hodometer, ho-dom'et-ėr, n. An instrument for measuring the length of way travelled by any vehicle. [Gr. *hodos*, way, and *metron*, measure.]

Holometabolic, hol'o-met-a-bol''ik, a. Applied to insects which undergo a complete metamorphosis. [Gr. *holos*, and *metabolē*, change.]

Homer, hō'mėr, n. A Hebrew measure equal to about 75 gallons or to 11 bushels. [Heb.]

Hominy, hom'i-ni, n. A porridge made of coarsely ground maize. [Amer.-Ind. *auhuminea*, parched corn.]

Homœozoic, hō'mē-ō-zō''ik, a. Inhabited by similar forms of animal or vegetable life. [Gr. *homoios*, similar, *zōē*, life.]

Homogenesis, hō-mō-jen'e-sis, n. Sameness of origin; reproduction of offspring similar to their parents. [Gr. *homos*, same, *genesis*, birth.]

Homuncule, Homunculus, hō-mung'kūl, hō-mung'kūl-us, n. A manikin; a dwarf. [L., dim. of *homo*, a man.]

Hospodar, hos-pō-där', n. A Slavonic title formerly borne by the princes of Moldavia and Wallachia, &c.

Houri, hou'ri or hō'ri, n. Among Mohammedans, a nymph of Paradise. [Ar.]

Huguenot, hū'ge-not, n. A French Protestant of the period of the religious wars in France in the 16th century. [Fr.]

Humanitarian, hū-man'i-tā''ri-an, n. A philanthropist; one who believes Christ to have been but a mere man; one who maintains the perfectibility of human nature without the aid of grace.

Humeral, hū'mėr-al, a. Belonging to the shoulder. [L. *humerus*, the shoulder.]

Hyaline, hī'al-in, a. Glassy; transparent. [Gr. *hyalos*, glass.]

Hyalography, hī-al-og'ra-fi, n. The art of engraving on glass. [Gr. *hyalos* and *graphō*.]

Hydatid, hid'a-tid, n. A larval form of tape-worm. [Gr. *hydatis*, a vesicle.]

Hydrant, hī'drant, n. A pipe with suitable valves, &c., by which water is raised and discharged from a main pipe. [Gr. *hydōr*, water.]

Hydrate, hī'drāt, n. A chemical compound in which water or hydrogen is a characteristic ingredient. [Gr. *hydōr*, water.]

Hydrocarbon, hī-drō-kär'bon, n. A chemical compound of hydrogen and carbon.

Hydrocephalus, hī-drō-sef'a-lus, n. Med. water in the head. [Gr. *hydōr*, and *kephalē*, the head.]

Hydrozoon, hi-drō-zō'on, n. pl. **Hydrozoa,** hi-drō-zō'a. A class of animals, mostly marine, including the jelly-fishes, &c. [Gr. *hydra*, a hydra, and *zōon*, a living creature.]

Hygiene, Hygeine, hī'ji-ēn, hī'je-in, n. A system of principles designed for the promotion of health; sanitary science. [Fr. *hygiène*, from Gr. *hygienos*, healthy.]

Hygienic, hī-ji-en'ik, a. Relating to hygiene.

Hyoid, hī'oid, a. Applied to a movable U-shaped bone between the root of the tongue and the larynx. [Gr.]

Hypnotism, hip'no-tizm, n. A sleep-like condition brought on by artificial means. [Gr. *hypnos*, sleep.]

Hypodermal, Hypodermic, hi-pō-dėr'mal, hi-pō-dėr'mik, a. Pertaining to parts under the skin, or to the introduction of medicines under the skin. [Gr. *hypo*, under, *derma*, skin.]

Hypostasis, hī-pos'ta-sis, n. pl. **Hypostases,** hi-pos'ta-sēs. The reality underlying or assumed to underlie a phenomenon; *theol.* the distinct substance or subsistence of the Trinity in the Godhead. [Gr.]

Hypothec, hi-poth'ek, n. *Scots law*, a

lien such as a landlord has over a tenant's furniture or crops. [L. *hypotheca*, a pledge.]

Iconoclast, i-kon'o-klast, *n*. A breaker of images; one who makes attacks on cherished beliefs. [Gr. *eikon*, an image, and *klastēs*, a breaker.]
Iconography, i-ko-nog'ra-fi, *n*. The knowledge of ancient statues, paintings, mosaics, gems, &c. [Gr. *eikon* and *graphō*.]
Ideograph, Ideogram, id'ē-ō-graf, id'ē-ō-gram, *n*. A character, symbol, or figure which suggests the idea of an object; a hieroglyphic. [Gr. *idea* and *graphē*.]
Idiograph, id'i-ō-graf, *n*. A private or trade mark. [Gr. *idios*, peculiar, and *graphē*.]
Imago, im-ā'go, *n*. The last or perfect state of an insect. [L.]
Imam, Imaum, Iman, i-mäm', i-mạm', i-män', *n*. A successor of Mohammed; the priest of a mosque. [Ar.]
Impanate, im-pā'nāt, *a*. Embodied in the bread used in the eucharist. [L. *im, panis*, bread.]
Impanation, im-pa-nā'shon, *n*. The supposed real presence in the eucharist; consubstantiation.
Improvise, im-pro-vīz', *vt*. To do or form on the spur of the moment; to compose and recite, sing, or the like without previous preparation. [Fr. *improviser*.]
Improvvisatore, im-prov-vis'a-tō-rā, *n. pl*. **Improvvisatori**, im-prov-vis'a-tō-rē. An extempore versifier. [It.]
Improvvisatrice, im-prov-vis'a-trē-chā, *n*. A female improvvisatore. [It.]
Indo-European, in'dō-ū-rō-pē''an, *a*. Applied to that family of languages which includes the Sanskrit and kindred tongues of India and Persia, Greek, Latin, the Romance tongues, the Teutonic, Celtic, and Slavonic.
Indo-Germanic, in'dō-jer-man''ik, *a*. Same as Indo-European.
Insessores, in-ses-sō'rēz, *n. pl*. The order of passerine or perching birds. [L. *insessor*, one that sits.]
Insomnia, in-som'ni-a, *n*. Want of sleep; morbid or unnatural sleeplessness. [L.]
Insuetude, in'swē-tūd, *n*. The state of being unaccustomed; absence of use or custom. [L. *insuetus*, unaccustomed.]
Intaglio, in-tal'yō, *n*. Any figure engraved or cut into a substance; a gem with the figure or device sunk below the surface.
Intern, in-tėrn', *vt*. To send to and cause to remain in the interior of a country; to disarm and quarter in some place, as a body of defeated troops. [Fr. *interner*.]
Interoceanic, in-tėr-ō'shē-an''ik, *a*. Between oceans.
Intrados, in-trā'dos, *n. Arch.* the interior and lower line or curve of an arch. [Fr., from L. *intra*, and *dorsum*, back.]
Intramundane, in-tra-mun'dān, *a*. Being within the world; belonging to the material world.
Intromission, in-trō-mish'on, *n*. The act of intromitting.
Intromit, in-trō-mit', *vt*. To send or put in.—*vi. Scots law*, to intermeddle with the effects of another.
Introrse, in-trors', *a*. Turned or facing inwards. [L. *introrsum*, inwards.]
Introspect, in-trō-spekt', *vt*. To look into or within. [L. *introspicio, introspectum*, to look within.]

Introspection, in-trō-spek'shon, *n*. The act of looking inwardly; examination of one's own thoughts or feelings.
Involucre, in-vō-lū'kėr, *n. Bot.* any cluster of bracts round a cluster of flowers. [L. *involucrum*, an envelope.]
Irade, i-rä'dē, *n*. A Turkish decree or proclamation. [Turk.]
Iranian, i-rā'ni-an, *a*. Pertaining to *Iran*, the native name of Persia; applied to the Persian, Zend, and cognate tongues.
Isobar, i'sō-bär, *n*. A line drawn on a map connecting places at which the mean height of the barometer at sea-level is the same. [Gr. *isos*, equal, and *baros*, weight.]
Isochronal, Isochronous, i-sok'ro-nal, i-sok'ron-us, *a*. Uniform in time; of equal time; performed in equal times. [Gr. *isos*, equal, *chronos*, time.]
Isoclinal, Isoclinic, i-sō-klī'nal, i-sō'-kli'nik, *a*. Of equal inclination or dip; applied to lines connecting places at which the dip of the magnetic needle is equal. [Gr. *isos*, and *klinō*, to incline.]
Isometric, Isometrical, i-sō-met'rik, i-sō-met'rik-al, *a*. Pertaining to or characterized by equality of measure. [Gr. *isos*, and *metron*, measure.]

Jade, jād, *n*. A hard tenacious green stone of a resinous aspect when polished. [Fr. and Sp.]
Jaggery, Jaghery, jag'ėr-i, *n*. Imperfectly granulated sugar; the inspissated juice of the palmyra-tree. [Hind. *jágri*.]
Jain, Jaina, jän, jā'na, *n*. A Hindu religious sect believing doctrines similar to those of Buddhism.
Janizary, jan'i-za-ri, *n*. One of a body of Turkish foot-guards, suppressed in 1826. [Turk. *yeni*, new, *tcheri*, soldiers.]
Jeremiad, jer-ē-mī'ad, *n*. A lamentation; a complaint: used in ridicule. [*Jeremiah*, the prophet.]
Jetsam, Jetson, jet'sam, jet'sun, *n*. The throwing of goods overboard in order to lighten a ship in distress; the goods so thrown away.
Jugate, jū'gāt, *a. Bot.* coupled together as the pairs of leaflets in compound leaves. [L. *jugum*, a yoke.]
Junk, jungk, *n*. Pieces of old rope; salt-beef supplied to vessels on long voyages. [Fr. *jonc*, from L. *juncus*, a bulrush.]
Jurassic, jū-ras'ik, *a. Geol.* of or belonging to the formation of the *Jura* Mountains; the continental name for what in Britain is called the *Oolitic*.
Jury, jū'ri, *a. Naut.* applied to a temporary substitute; as, a *jury*-mast, &c.

Kaftan, kaf'tan, *n*. A kind of long vest, with long hanging sleeves tied round at the waist with a girdle, worn in the East. [Per.]
Kerosene, ker'o-sēn, *n*. A liquid hydrocarbon distilled from coal, bitumen, petroleum, &c. [Gr. *kēros*, wax.]
Ketchup, kech'up, *n*. A sauce made from mushrooms. [Hind. *kitjap*.]
Khan, kan, *n*. In Asia, a governor; a prince; a chief; a king. [Turk.] An eastern inn; a caravansary. [Per. *khán*, a house.]
Khedive, ke-dēv', *n*. The governor or viceroy of Egypt. [Turk.]
Kilogram, Kilogramme, kil'ō-gram, *n*. A French measure of weight, being 1000 grammes, 2.2 lbs. avoir. [Gr. *chilioi*, a thousand.]

Kilolitre, kil'ō-lē-tr, *n*. A French measure, 1000 litres, 220.09 gallons.
Kilometre, kil'ō-mā-tr, *n*. A French measure, 1000 metres, about ⅝ of a mile or 1093.633 yards.
Kilostere, kil'ō-stār, *n*. A French solid measure equal to 35317.41 cubic feet.
Kindergarten, kin'dėr-gär-tn, *n*. An infants' school in which amusements are combined with instruction. [G., children's garden.]
Kinematics, ki-nē-mat'iks, *n*. That branch of mechanics which treats of motion without reference to the forces producing it. [Gr. *kineō*, to move.]
Kinetic, ki-net'ik, *a*. Causing motion: applied to force actually exerted.
Kinetics, ki-net'iks, *n*. That branch of dynamics which treats of forces causing or changing motion in bodies.
Kleptomania, klep-tō-mā'ni-a, *n*. An irresistible mania for pilfering. [Gr. *kleptō*, to steal, and mania.]
Knout, nout, *n*. A powerful whip used as an instrument of punishment in Russia. [Russ.]
Kraal, kräl, *n*. An African native village. [D.]
Kriegspiel, krēg'spēl, *n*. A game played with pieces representing troops on a map showing all the features of a country. [G., game of war.]

Laager, lä'gėr, *n*. In S. Africa, an encampment; a temporary defensive inclosure formed of wagons. [D., a camp.]
Lac, lak, *n*. In the East Indies, 100,000. [Hind. *lakh*.]
Lactometer, lak-tom'et-ėr, *n*. An instrument for ascertaining the quality of milk. [L. *lac*, milk, and Gr. *metron*.]
Lacustrine, Lacustral, la-kus'trin, la-kus'tral, *a*. Pertaining to a lake. [L. *lacus*, a lake.]
Lagoon, Lagune, la-gön', la-gūn', *n*. A shallow lake connected with the sea or a river. [It. and Sp. *laguna*.]
Lama, lä'mä, *n*. A priest of that variety of Buddhism which prevails in Tibet and Mongolia. [Tib.]
Lamaism, lä'mä-izm, *n*. The variety of Buddhism prevailing in Tibet and Mongolia.
Lamellar, la-mel'lėr, *a*. Composed of thin plates. [L. *lamella*, dim. of *lamina*, a plate.]
Lamellibranchiate, la-mel'li-brang''ki-āt, *a*. Having lamellar gills and bivalve shells, as the mussels, oysters, &c. (Lamellibranchiata). [L. *lamella*, and *branchiæ*, gills.]
Lanceolate, lan'sē-o-lāt, *a*. Shaped like a lance-head.
Lancinating, län'si-nā-ting, *a*. Piercing; applied to a sudden sharp shooting pain.
Lectern, lek'tėrn, *n*. The reading-desk in a church. [L. *lectio*, from *lego*, to read.]
Leet, lēt, *n. Scot.* a list of candidates for any office. [Icel. *leiti*, a share.]
Leucopathy, lū-kop'a-thi, *n*. The condition of an albino. [Gr. *leukos*, white, and *pathos*, affection.]
Liaison, lē-ā-zong, *n*. A bond of union; an illicit intimacy between a man and a woman. [Fr., from L. *ligare*, to bind.]
Lias, lī'as, *n. Geol.* strata of limestone embedded in masses of argillaceous clay, lying at the basis of the oolite and above the triassic or new red sandstone. [Fr. *liais*.]
Libretto, lē-bret'tō, *n*. The words of an extended musical composition. [It., a little book.]

ch, chain; j, job; g, go; ng, sing; ᴛʜ, then; th, thin; w, wig; wh, whig; zh, azure; † obsolete.

Lien, li'en, *n.* A legal claim; a right over the property of another till some claim or due is satisfied. [Fr., from *ligo*, to bind.]

Limber, lim'ber, *n. Artill.* a carriage with ammunition boxes and shafts for the horses attached to the gun-carriage. [Icel. *limar*, limbs.]

Lira, lē'rä, *n.* pl. **Lire**, lē'rā. An Italian silver coin equivalent to one franc, or 10*d.* nearly.

Lithology, li-thol'o-ji, *n.* The knowledge of rocks; the study of the mineral structure of rocks. [Gr. *lithos*, a stone, *logos*, discourse.]

Litmus, lit'mus, *n.* A colouring matter procured from certain lichens, used as a chemical test, paper tinged blue with it turning red with acids, and blue again with alkalis. [G. *lackmus*.]

Litre, lē'tr, *n.* The French standard measure of capacity, equal to 61·028 cubic inches; the English imperial gallon being fully 4½ litres. [Gr. *litra*, pound.]

Litterateur, lit'er-a-tėr, *n.* A literary man; one whose profession is literature. [Fr.]

Lixiviation, lik-siv'i-ā"shon, *n.* The extraction of alkaline salts from ashes by pouring water on them. [L. *lixivius*, made into lye, from *lix*, ashes.]

Llanos, lan'ōz or lyä'nōz, *n.* pl. The level grassy plains of the northern part of S. America. [Sp., from L. *planus*, level.]

Load-line, lōd'līn, *n. Naut.* a line on the side of a vessel to show the depth to which she sinks when not overloaded.

Locution, lō-kū'shon, *n.* A phrase; a mode of speech. [L. *loquor*, to speak.]

Lode, lōd, *n. Mining*, a metallic or any regular mineral vein.

Loess, lēs, *n. Geol.* a German term for alluvial deposits in the valleys of the Rhine, Danube, &c.

Logogram, lo'gō-gram, *n.* A single printing type that forms a word; a phonographic symbol which forms a word. [Gr. *logos*, word, and *gramma*, letter.]

Loot, lōt, *n.* Booty; plunder; especially such as is taken in a sacked city. [Hind. *lūt*.]

Lorgnette, lor-nyet', *n.* An opera-glass. [Fr.]

Lotus, lō'tus, *n.* A tree, the fruit of which was fabled to cause forgetfulness of the past; applied also to the Egyptian water-lily and other plants. [Gr. *lotos*.]

Lustrum, lus'trum, *n.* In ancient Rome the quinquennial purification of the people; a period of five years.

Lycanthropy, li-kan'thro-pi, *n.* A kind of insanity in which the patient supposes himself to be a wolf. [Gr. *lykos*, a wolf, *anthrōpos*, a man.]

Lynch, linsh, *vt.* To inflict punishment upon, without the forms of law, as a mob, or by unauthorized persons.

Macadamize, mak-ad'am-īz, *vt.* To cover, as a road, with small broken stones, which, when consolidated, form a firm surface. [*Macadam*, the inventor.]

Macrocosm, mak'ro-kozm, *n.* The great world; the universe, regarded as analogous to the *microcosm*, or little world constituted by man. [Gr. *makros*, long, and *kosmos*, world.]

Magilp, **Magilph**, ma-gilp', ma-gilf', *n.* A mixture of linseed-oil and mastic varnish used by artists as a vehicle for colours.

Magneto-electricity, mag-nā'to-ē-lektris"i-ti, *n.* Electricity evolved by the action of magnets.

Magyar, mag'yar, *n.* A Hungarian; the language of Hungary.

Maharajah, ma-hä-rä'ja, *n.* A title assumed by some Indian princes. [Sans. *mahā*, great, and *rājā*, prince.]

Mahdi, mä'di, *n.* A name assumed by some of the successors of Mohammed; one who is to arise and lead Mohammedans to the conquest of the world. [Ar., the director.]

Mahout, ma-hōt', *n.* An East Indian elephant driver or keeper.

Mahratta, ma-rat'tä, *n.* One of a race of Hindus inhabiting Central India.

Malachite, mal'a-kīt, *n.* Green carbonate of copper, used for many ornamental purposes. [Fr.]

Malacology, mal-a-kol'o-ji, *n.* That branch of zoology which treats of the mollusca. [Gr. *malakos*, soft, and *logos*, discourse.]

Malacopterygian, mal-a-kop'tėr-ij"i-an, *a.* Applied to those osseous fishes that have all the rays of the fins soft. [Gr. *malakos*, soft, and *ptērygion*, a fin.]

Manes, mā'nēz, *n.* pl. Among the Romans, the shades of souls of deceased persons. [O. L. *manus*, good, benevolent.]

Maori, mä'o-ri, *n.* One of the native inhabitants of New Zealand.

Margarine, mär'ga-rin, *n.* An artificial butter made from animal fat, churned with milk and water.

Mariolatry, mā-ri-ol'a-tri, *n.* The adoration of the Virgin Mary. [*Maria*, and Gr. *latreia*, worship.]

Marionette, mar'i-o-net, *n.* A puppet moved by string. [Fr. *Mariolette*, a little figure of the Virgin.]

Marquee, mär-kē', *n.* A large tent erected for a temporary purpose. [Fr. *marquise*.]

Marquetry, mär'ket-ri, *n.* Inlaid work. [Fr. *marqueterie*.]

Marsupial, mär-sū'pi-al, *a.* One of a large group of mammalians characterized by the absence of a placenta, and whose premature young are nourished after birth in an external abdominal pouch. [L. *marsupium*, a pouch.]

Massage, mäs'āj, *n.* A process of kneading, rubbing, pressing, &c., parts of a person's body who is suffering from certain ailments, in order to bring about a cure. [Gr. *massō*, to knead.]

Matador, mat'a-dōr, *n.* The man appointed to kill the bull in bull-fights. [Sp., a killer, from L. *mactare*, to kill.]

Maté, mä'tā, *n.* Paraguay tea; the leaves of the Brazilian holly (*Ilex paraguayensis*), used in S. America as a substitute for tea.

Mauve, mav, *n.* A purple dye obtained from aniline. [Fr., from L. *malva*, mallow.]

Meerschaum, mēr'shum, *n.* A silicate of magnesium, largely used in the manufacture of tobacco-pipes. [G., sea-foam.]

Megalithic, meg-a-lith'ik, *a.* Consisting of large stones. [Gr. *megas*, great, and *lithos*.]

Melanochroic, mel'an-ō-krō"ik, *a.* A term applied to the dark-skinned white races of man. [Gr. *melos*, black, and *chroia*, colour.]

Meningitis, men-in-jī'tis, *n.* Inflammation of the membranes of the brain or spinal cord. [Gr. *mēningx*, membrane.]

Menu, mė-nū, *n.* A bill of fare; a list of the dishes to be served at a dinner. &c. [Fr.]

Mesocephalic, **Mesocephalous**, mes'o-se-fal'ik, mes-o-sef'a-lus, *a.* Applied to the human skull when it is of medium breadth. [Gr. *mesos*, middle, and *kephalē*, head.]

Mesozoic, mes-o-zō'ik, *a. Geol.* pertaining to the secondary age, between the palæozoic and cainozoic. [Gr. *mesos*, middle, and *sōē*, life.]

Metabolic, met-a-bol'ik, *a.* Pertaining to change or metamorphosis. [Gr. *metabolē*, change.]

Metacentre, met-a-sen'tėr, *n.* That point in a floating body on the position of which its stability depends, and which must always be above the centre of gravity. [Gr. *meta*, beyond, and *kentron*, centre.]

Metagenesis, met-a-jen'e-sis, *n. Zool.* the changes of form which the representative of a species undergoes in passing, by a series of successively generated individuals, from the ovum to the perfect state; alternation of generation. [Gr. *meta* and *genesis*.]

Microphone, mī'krō-fōn, *n.* An instrument to augment small sounds by means of electricity. [Gr. *mikros*, small, *phōnē*, sound.]

Minatory, min'a-to-ri, *a.* Threatening; menacing. [L. *mina*, a threat.]

Minnesinger, min'ne-sing-ėr, *n.* One of a class of German lyrists of the middle ages, so called from love being their chief theme. [O. G. *minne*, love.]

Miocene, mī'ō-sēn, *n. Geol.* the middle subdivision of the tertiary strata, which overlies the eocene and is below the pliocene. [Gr. *meiōn*, less, and *kainos*, recent.]

Mitrailleuse, mē-trā-yėz, *n.* A French breech-loading machine-gun with a number of barrels.

Mobilise, mob'il-īz, *vt. Milit.* to put in a state of readiness for active service. [L. *mobilis*.]

Monatomic, mon-a-tom'ik, *a. Chem.* said of an element one atom of which will never combine with more than one atom of another element. [Gr. *monos*, alone.]

Monetise, mon-e-tīs', *vt.* To form into coin or money.

Monocotyledon, mon'ō-kot-i-lē"don, *n.* A plant with one cotyledon only. [Gr. *monos*.]

Monometallism, mon-ō-met'al-izm, *n.* The having only one metal as the standard of coinage; the theory of a single metallic standard.

Morganatic, mor-ga-nat'ik, *a.* Applied to a kind of marriage with a female of lower rank, the offspring of which do not inherit the father's rank, though otherwise legitimate. [L. L. *morganatica*, a kind of dowry.]

Mormon, mor'mon, *n.* A member of a sect founded in America in 1830, who practise polygamy; a Latter-day Saint. [From their Bible, the Book of *Mormon*.]

Morphology, mor-fol'o-ji, *n.* The science which treats of the form and arrangements of the structures of plants and animals. [Gr. *morphē*, form, and *logos*.]

Mucus, mū'kus, *n.* A viscid fluid secreted by the mucous membrane of animals. [L.]

Multocular, mul-tok'ū-lėr, *a.* Having many eyes. [L. *multus*, many, *oculus*, eye.]

Muscoid, mus'koid, *a.* Resembling moss. [L. *muscus*, moss.]

Muscovado, mus-kō-vā′dō, n. Unrefined sugar. [Sp. *mascabado*.]
Mycelium, mī-sē′li-um, n. pl. **Mycelia**, mī-sē′li-a. The cellular filamentous spawn of fungi. [Gr. *mykēs*, a fungus.]
Mycology, mī-kol′o-ji, n. That department of botany which investigates fungi. [Gr. *mykēs* and *logos*.]
Myopia, Myopy, mī-ō′pi-a, mī′o-pi, n. Short-sightedness. [Gr. *myō*, to shut, and *ōps*, the eye.]
Mythopœic, Mythopoetic, mith-ō-pē′ik, mith′ō-pō-et″ik, a. Producing or tending to produce myths. [Gr. *poieō*, to make.]

Nacre, nā′kėr, n. Mother-of-pearl. [Per. *nakar*.]
Nacreous, nā′krē-us, a. Consisting of or resembling nacre.
Natation, na-tā′shon, n. The art or act of swimming. [L. *nato*, to swim.]
Natatores, nā-ta-tō′rēz, n. pl. The order of swimming birds. [L., swimmers.]
Natron, nā′tron, n. Native carbonate of soda, or mineral alkali. [Ar. *natrum*.]
Naturalism, nat′ū-ral-izm, n. The doctrine that there is no interference of any supernatural power in the universe; realism in art or literature.
Nautch-girl, nach′gėrl, n. In India, a native professional dancing-girl.
Navvy, nav′i, n. A labourer engaged in the making of canals, railways, &c.
Necrolatry, nek-rol′a-tri, n. Veneration for, or worship of, the dead. [Gr. *nekros*, dead, and *latreia*, worship.]
Necrosis, nē-krō′sis, n. *Pathol.* death of the bone substance; *bot.* a disease of the leaves and soft parts of plants. [Gr. *nekrosis*.]
Negative, neg′a-tiv, a. *Photog.* [add.] applied to a picture in which the lights and shades are the opposite of those in nature; *elect.* applied to resinous electricity—the opposite of *positive* or vitreous electricity; *magnet.* applied to the pole placed in opposition to the *positive*, in the voltaic battery; *alg.* applied to quantities which have the minus sign (−) prefixed to them.
Negligé, neg′lē-zhā, n. An easy or unceremonious dress. [Fr.]
Nematoid, nem′a-toid, n. A roundworm; one of an order of entozoa. [Gr. *nema, nematos*, a thread.]
Neoteric, nē-ō-tėr′ik, a. New; modern; recent. [Gr. *neoterikos*, young.]
Neozoic, nē-ō-zō′ik, a. *Geol.* the strata from the beginning of the trias up to the most recent deposits. [Gr. *neos*, new, *zōē*, life.]
Nescience, nē′shi-ens, n. Want of knowledge; ignorance. [L. *nescio*, not to know.]
Nihilism, ni′hil-izm, n. [add.] The principles of a Russian secret society of communists.
Nirvana, nir-vä′na, n. *Buddhism*, the extinction of the thinking principle, or final salvation from the evils of existence. [Sans.]
Nonchalant, non′sha-lant, a. Indifferent; careless; cool. [Fr.]
Noölogy, nō-ol′o-ji, n. The science of intellectual facts or phenomena. [Gr. *noos*, mind, and *logos*, discourse.]
Nostalgia, nos-tal′ji-a, n. Home-sickness; a vehement desire to visit one's native country. [Gr. *nostos*, return, and *algos*, pain.]
Noumenon, nou′men-on, n. An object conceived by the understanding, at

opposed to *phenomenon*. [Gr. *noeō*, to perceive.]

Obtest, ob-test′, vt. To call upon earnestly; to implore; to supplicate. [L. *ob*, and *testor*, to witness.]
Ocellate, Ocellated, ō-sel′lāt, ō-sel′lāt-ed, a. Resembling an eye; studded with little eyes.
Ocellus, ō-sel′lus, n. pl. **Ocelli**, ō-sel′ī. One of the minute simple eyes of insects, &c. [L., dim. of *oculus*, the eye.]
Ochlocracy, ok-lok′ra-si, n. The rule of the multitude; mobocracy, [Gr. *ochlos*, the multitude, *kratos*, power.]
Octopus, ok′tō-pus, n. A genus of two-gilled cuttle-fishes, having eight arms furnished with suckers. [Gr. *oktō*, eight, *pous*, a foot.]
Octoroon, ok-tō-rön′, n. The offspring of a quadroon and a white person.
Octroi, ok-trwa, n. A duty levied at the gates of French cities on articles brought in. [Fr.]
Odic, od′ik, a. Pertaining to a peculiar force called *od*, which was fancied to be associated with mesmerism.
Œsophagus, ē-sof′a-gus, n. The gullet; the canal through which meat and drink pass to the stomach. [Gr. *oisō*, I will bear, and *phagō*, to eat.]
Ogham, og′ham, n. A kind of writing practised by the ancient Irish.
Ohm, Ohmad, ōm, om′ad, n. *Elect.* the unit of electric resistance.
Olefiant, ō-lē′fi-ant, a. Forming or producing oil; applied to a gas obtained from a mixture of sulphuric acid and alcohol, forming with chlorine an oily compound. [L. *oleum*, oil, and *facio*, to make.]
Oleograph, ō′lē-o-graf, n. A picture produced in oils by a process analogous to lithographic printing.
Onomatopœia, Onomatopeia, on′o-ma-tō-pē″a, n. The formation of words by the imitation of sounds. [Gr.]
Ontology, on-tol′o-ji, n. The doctrine of being; that part of metaphysics which treats of things or existences. [Gr. *on, ontis*, being, and *logos*.]
Oolite, ō′ol-it, n. *Geol.* a series of strata, comprehending limestones, &c., which underlie the chalk formation and rest on the trias. [Gr. *ōon*, an egg, and *lithos*.]
Oology, ō-ol′o-ji, n. The study of birds' eggs. [Gr. *ōon*, an egg.]
Ophidian, o-fid′i-an, a. Pertaining to serpents. [Gr. *ophis*, a serpent.]
Orchid, Orchis, or′kid, or′kis, n. A perennial plant with tuberous fleshy root and beautiful flowers. [Gr.]
Osmose, os′mōs, n. The tendency of fluids to pass through porous partitions and become defused through each other. [Gr. *osmos*, an impulse.]
Ottava-rima, ot-tä′va-rē-ma, n. A form of versification consisting of eight lines, of which the first six rhyme alternately and the last two form a couplet. [It.]
Ovoid, ō′void, a. Egg-shaped. [L. *ovum*, and Gr. *eidos*, form.]
Ovoviviparous, ō′vō-vi-vip″a-rus, a. Producing eggs which are hatched within the body. [L. *ovum, vivo*, to live, and *pario*, to produce.]

Pachydermatous, pak-i-dėr′ma-tus, a. Thick-skinned; belonging to the non-ruminant hoofed animals. [Gr. *pachys*, thick, and *derma*, skin.]

Paideutics, pā-dū′tiks, n. The science of teaching. [Gr. *paideuō*, to teach.]
Palæography, pā-lē-og′ra-fi, n. The art of deciphering ancient documents or inscriptions. [Gr. *palaios*, ancient, and *graphō*.]
Palæontology, pā′lē-on-tol″o-ji, n. The science of ancient life, or of fossil organic remains. [Gr. *palaios*, and *onta*, being.]
Palæozoic, pā′lē-o-zō″ik, a. *Geol.* applied to the lowest division of stratified groups. [Gr. *palaios*, and *zōē*, life.]
Palea, pā′lē-a, n. pl. **Paleæ**, pā′lē-ē. *Bot.* a bract upon the receptacle of composite plants between the florets; one of the interior bracts of the flowers of grasses. [L., chaff.]
Palimpsest, pä′limp-sest, n. A parchment from which one writing has been erased to make room for another, the first often remaining faintly visible. [Gr. *palimpsēstos*, rubbed again.]
Palingenesis, pal-in-jen′e-sis, n. A transformation; a metamorphosis; a great geological change. [Gr. *palin*, again, *genesis*, birth.]
Pampas, pam′pas, n. pl. The immense grassy plains of S. America. [Sp.-Amer.]
Pantograph, pan′tō-graf, n. An instrument for mechanically copying drawings, &c. [Gr. *pas, pantos*, all, and *graphō*.]
Papyrus, pa-pī′rus, n. An Egyptian sedge, the stems of which afforded an ancient writing material; a written scroll made of papyrus (pl. **Papyri**, pa-pī′ri).
Pariah, pā′ri-a, n. An outcast; one of the lowest class of people in Hindustan. [Tamil.]
Parthenogenesis, pär′the-no-jen″e-sis, n. *Biol.* the propagation of a plant or animal without the intervention of a male. [Gr. *parthenos*, a virgin, and *genesis*.]
Parvenu, pär′ve-nū, n. An upstart; one newly risen into notice. [Fr.]
Pasha, pa-shä′ or pash′ä, n. A Turkish governor of a province, or military commander of high rank. [Per.]
Pastel, pas′tel, n. A coloured crayon; a mode of drawing with moist coloured crayons. [Fr.]
Pelagic, pe-laj′ik, a. Belonging to the ocean; inhabiting the ocean. [Gr. *pelagos*, the ocean.]
Pelasgian, Pelasgic, pe-las′ji-an, pe-las′-jik, a. Pertaining to the Pelasgi, the prehistoric inhabitants of Greece.
Peltate, pel′tāt, a. Shield-shaped; *bot.* fixed to the stalk, as a leaf, by the centre or by some point within the margin. [L. *pelta*, a target.]
Pemmican, pem′i-kan, n. N. Amer. Ind., beef or venison dried, pounded into a paste, and pressed into cakes.
Pepsin, Pepsine, pep′sin, n. The active principle of gastric juice. [Gr. *peptō*, to digest.]
Periscopic, per-i-skop′ik, a. Viewing on all sides; applied to spectacles with concavo-convex lenses. [Gr. *peri*, around, and *skopeō*, to see.]
Permian, pėr′mi-an, a. *Geol.* applied to a system of rocks lying beneath the trias and immediately above the carboniferous system. [*Perm*, in Russia.]
Persifiage, per-sē-fläzh, n. Idle bantering talk. [Fr.]
Pessimism, pes′im-izm, n. An unfavourable view of affairs; the doctrine that holds that the present state of things only tends to evil. [L. *pessimus*, the worst.]

---

ch, *ch*ain; j, *j*ob; g, *g*o; ng, si*ng*; ᴛʜ, *th*en; th, *th*in; w, *w*ig; wh, *wh*ig; zh, a*z*ure; † obsolete.
30

Pessimist, pes'im-ist, n. A believer in pessimism.
Pharynx, far'ingks, n. The muscular sac which intervenes between the cavity of the mouth and the œsophagus. [Gr.]
Phonograph, fō'nō-graf, n. An instrument by means of which sounds can be permanently registered and afterwards mechanically reproduced. [Gr. *phōnē*, sound, and *graphō*, to write.]
Photogene, fō'tō-jēn, n. An impression or picture on the retina. [Gr. *phōs, phōtos*, light, and root *gen*, to produce.]
Photophone, fō'tō-fōn, n. An instrument for reproducing sound in distant places by variations in the intensity of a beam of light. [Gr. *phōs, phōtos*, light, and *phōnē*, sound.]
Physics, fiz'iks, n. The department of science which deals with mechanics, dynamics, light, heat, sound, electricity, and magnetism; natural philosophy.
Physiography, fiz-i-og'ra-fi, n. Physical geography; the science of the earth's physical features, and the causes of its physical phenomena. [Gr. *physis*, nature.]
Physique, fē-zēk', n. A person's physical or bodily structure. [Fr.]
Pia-mater, pī'a-mā'tėr, n. *Anat.* a membrane investing the surface of the brain. [L., pious mother.]
Pinnate, pin'āt, a. Shaped or branching like a feather. [L. *pinna*, a feather.]
Plebiscite, pleb'i-sit or pleb'i-sīt, n. A vote of a whole people or community. [Fr., from L. *plebiscitum*.]
Pliocene, plī'ō-sēn, n. and a. *Geol.* a term applied to the most modern of the divisions of the tertiary epoch. [Gr. *pleiōn*, more, and *kainos*, recent.]
Polyandry, pol-i-an'dri, n. The practice of having a plurality of husbands. [Gr. *polys*, many, and *anēr, andros*, a male.]
Polyparous, po-lip'a-rus, a. Producing many; bringing forth a great number. [Gr. *polys*, many, and L. *pario*, to produce.]
Polysynthesis, pol-i-sin'the-sis, n. A compounding of several elements; a polysynthetic structure. [Gr. *polys*, many, and *synthesis*.]
Polysynthetic, pol'i-sin-thet''ik, a. Compounded of several elements: applied to words.
Porte, pōrt, n. The Ottoman court; the government of the Turkish Empire. [*Sublime Porte*, the French trans. of *Babi Ali*, the High Gate or seat of justice.]
Positive, poz'i-tiv, a. [add.] (a.) Applied to electricity produced by rubbing a vitreous substance: opposed to *negative* electricity. (b.) Applied to the philosophical system of AugustComte, which limits itself strictly to human experience.
Positivism, poz'i-tiv-izm, n. The positive philosophy.
Positivist, poz'i-tiv-ist, n. A believer in the doctrines of positive philosophy.
Prognathic, Prognathous, prog-nath'ik, prog-nā'thus, a. Having projecting jaws; applied to human skulls having projecting jaws. [Gr. *pro, gnathos*, the cheek.]
Proletarian, prō-le-tā'ri-an, n. and a. Applied to a member of the poorest class. [L. *proletarius*.]
Proletariat, prō-le-tā'ri-at, n. Proletarians collectively.
Propædeutics, prō-pē-dū'tiks, n. The preliminary learning connected with any art or science. [Gr. *propaideuō*, to instruct beforehand.]
Propaganda, prop-a-gan'da, n. An institution or system for proselytising, or for propagating a peculiar set of doctrines. [The Congregation de *propaganda* fide, at Rome.]
Prophylactic, prō-fi-lak'tik, a. Preventive; defending from or warding off disease. [Gr. *pro*, and *phylassō*, to guard.]
Pseudonym, sū'dō-nim, n. A false or feigned name; a name assumed by a writer. [Gr. *pseudos*, false, and *onoma*, name.]
Psychic, Psychical, Psychal, sī'kik, sī'ki-kal, sī'kal, a. Belonging to the soul; psychological: applied to the force by which spiritualists aver they produce "spiritual" phenomena. [Gr. *psychē*, the soul.]
Pulchritude, pul'kri-tūd, n. Beauty; comeliness. [L. *pulcher*, beautiful.]
Pulkha, pul'ka, n. A Laplander's travelling sledge.
Pulmobranchiate, pul'mō-brang''ki-āt, a. Applied to an order of gasteropod molluscs with respiratory organs adapted for aerial respiration, including the land snails, &c.
Pulu, pū'lụ, n. The silky fibres of certain tree-ferns from the Sandwich Islands.
Punka, Punkah, pung'ka, n. A large fan slung from the ceilings of rooms in India for producing an artificial current of air.
Purâna, pū-rä'na, n. One of a class of sacred poetical Sanskrit writings, which treats of creation, the gods, heroes, &c. [Sans. *purā*, past.]
Puseyism, pū'zi-izm, n. The doctrines promulgated by Dr. *Pusey* in conjunction with other divines at Oxford in the "Tracts for the Times"; tractarianism.
Pushto, Pushtoo, push'tō, push'tō, n. The language of the Afghans.
Pyæmia, pī-ē'mi-a, n. Blood-poisoning. [Gr. *pyon*, pus, and *haima*, blood.]
Pyretic, pi-ret'ik, n. A cure for fever. [Gr. *pyr*, fire.]
Pyrolatry, pi-rol'a-tri, n. Fire-worship. [Gr. *pyr*, and *latreia*, worship.]
Pyrology, pi-rol'o-ji, n. The science of heat. [Gr. *pyr* and *logos*.]
Pyrrhic, pir'ik, n. An ancient Grecian warlike dance; a metrical foot consisting of two short syllables. [Gr. *pyrrhichē*.]

Quadrillion, kwod-ril'yon, n. The fourth power of a million, or the number represented by a unit and twenty-four ciphers annexed.
Quadrumanous, kwod-rụ'ma-nus, a. Applied to animals of the order Quadrumana (four-handed), comprising the apes, monkeys, baboons, lemurs, &c.
Quandary, kwon'da-ri, n. A state of difficulty, perplexity, uncertainty, or hesitation. [Fr. *Qu'en dirai-je* !]
Quaquaversal, kwā-kwa-vėr'sal, a. Inclined towards every side. [L. *quaqua*, on every side, *versus*, turned.]
Quidnunc, kwid'nungk, n. One who pretends to know all that goes on. [L., what now?]

Raceme, ras'ēm, n. *Bot.* a species of inflorescence in which a number of flowers with short and equal pedicels stand on a common slender axis. [L. *racemus*, a cluster of grapes.]
Radiometer, rā-di-om'et-ėr, n. An instrument designed for measuring the mechanical effect of radiant energy, or for showing repulsion by radiation.
Ramous, Rameal, rā'me-us, rā'mē-al, a. *Bot.* belonging to, growing on, or shooting from, a branch. [L. *ramus*, a branch.]
Ranch, Ranche, ranch, n. In Western America a farming establishment for rearing horses and cattle; a herdsman's hut. [Sp. *rancho*.]
Raptorial, rap-tō'ri-al, a. Pertaining to the birds of prey (Raptores). [L. *rapio*, to seize.]
Rasorial, ra-sō'ri-al, a. Pertaining to the gallinaceous or scratching birds (Rasores). [L. *rasum*, to scrape.]
Realism, rē'al-izm, n. The endeavour in *art, literature*, or the like, to reproduce nature or describe real life as it actually appears.
Realist, rē'al-ist, n. One who practises or believes in realism.
Échauffé, rā-shō-fa, n. A warmed-up dish; a concoction of old materials. [Fr. *chauffer*, to warm.]
Reconnaissance, re-kon'nā-sangs, n. The act or operation of reconnoitring.
Redact, rē-dakt', *vt*. To edit; to give a presentable literary form to. [L. *redigo, redactum*, to reduce to order.]
Redactor, rē-dak'tėr, n. An editor.
Reddition, red-dish'on, n. A returning or giving back of anything; restitution. [L. *redditio*, to give back.]
Refringent, rē-frin'jent, a. Refracting; refractive. [L. *refringo*.]
Regelation, rē-je-lā'shon, n. The phenomenon presented by pieces of moist ice which when placed in contact with one another freeze together even in a warm atmosphere. [L. *gelatio*, a freezing.]
Regurgitate, rē-gėr'ji-tāt, *vt*. and *i*. To pour or cause to surge back; to surge back.
Remonetise, rē-mon'e-tiz, *vt*. To make again a legal or standard money of account.
Renaissance, rē-nās'sangs, n. A revival of anything which has been in decay or extinct; the time of the revival of arts and letters in the fifteenth century.
Rendition, ren-dish'on, n. A rendering of a word or passage; a translation. [L. *redditio*.]
Reniform, rē'ni-form, a. Having the form or shape of the kidneys. [L. *ren*, a kidney.]
Replica, rep'li-ka, n. A copy of a picture or piece of sculpture made by the hand that executed the original.
Reredos, rēr'dos, n. The decorated wall behind the altar in a church. [Fr. *arrière dos*, behind the back.]
Resumé, rā'zụ̄-mā, n. A recapitulation; a summary. [Fr.]
Rhea, rē'a, n. A valuable East India fibre used for textile purposes, the produce of a species of nettle; chinagrass.
Rhizome, rī'zōm or ris'om, n. *Bot.* a prostrate stem which throws out fresh rootlets. [Gr. *rhisōma*, a root.]
Ricochet, rik'o-shet, n. A rebounding from a flat, horizontal surface. [Fr.]
Rime, rīm, n. The more correct spelling of *Rhyme*.
Rimose, Rimous, rī'mōs, rī'mus, a. Full of chinks and fissures. [L. *rima*, a crack.]
Rinderpest, rin'dėr-pest, n. A virulent and contagious disease affecting cattle. [G.]

Fāte, fär, fat, fall; mē, met, hėr; pīne, pin; nōte, not, mōve; tūbe, tub, bụll; oil, pound.

Riparian, ri-pā'ri-an, *a.* Pertaining to the bank of a river. [L. *ripa*, a bank.]
Romanesque, rō-man-esk', *n.* The debased style of architecture and ornament that prevailed in the later Roman Empire.
Romany, **Rommany**, rom'a-ni, *n.* A gypsy; the language spoken by the gypsies.
Rouble, rö'bl, *n.* The unit of the Russian money system, equal to about 2s. 10d.
Ryot, rī'ot, *n.* A Hindu cultivator of the soil. [Ar. *ra'iyat*, a peasant.]

Sabaism, sa-bā'izm, *n.* The worship of the heavenly bodies.
Sabot, sä-bō, *n.* A wooden shoe worn by Continental peasants. [Fr.]
Sachem, sā'chem, *n.* A chief among some of the American Indian tribes.
Saga, sä'ga, *n.* An ancient Scandinavian legend of considerable length. [Icel.]
Salic, sal'ik, *a.* Applied to a French law by which females were excluded from the throne. [Fr. *salique*.]
Samite, sā'mit, *n.* An old rich silk stuff interwoven with gold or embroidered. [O. Fr.]
Sanatorium, san-a-tō'ri-um, *n.* A place to which people go for the sake of health. [L. *sano*, to heal.]
Sanitation, san-i-tā'shon, *n.* The adoption of sanitary measures for the health of a community.
Sarcode, sär'köd, *n.* Structureless gelatinous matter forming the bodies of animals belonging to the protozoa. [Gr. *sarx*, *sarkos*, flesh.]
Scientist, sī'ent-ist, *n.* One versed in science; a scientific man.
Scolecida, skō-lē'si-da, *n. pl.* The tapeworms and allied animals. [Gr. *skolēx*, a worm.]
Séance, sā-ängs, *n.* A session, as of some public body; among spiritualists, a sitting with the view of evoking spiritual manifestations.
Sebaceous, sē-bā'shus, *a.* Pertaining to, made of, containing, or secreting fatty matter. [L. *sebum*, tallow.]
Secularism, sek'ū-lėr-izm, *n.* The elimination of the religious element from life.
Secularist, sek'ū-lėr-ist, *n.* An upholder of secularism; one who theoretically rejects every form of religious faith.
Sederunt, se-dē'runt, *n.* A sitting, as of a court or the like; a more or less formal meeting of any association or the like. [L., they sat.]
Selenology, sel - ē - nol ' o - ji, *n.* That branch of astronomical knowledge which treats of the moon. [Gr. *selēnē*, the moon, and *logos*.]
Semaphore, sem'a-fōr, *n.* A kind of telegraph for conveying information by signals visible at a distance. [Gr. *sēma*, a sign, and *pherō*, to bear.]
Sepia, sē'pi-a, *n.* A brown pigment obtained from the cuttle-fish. [Gr. *sēpia*, a squid.]
Sepoy, sē'poi, *n.* A native Hindustani soldier in the British service. [Per. *sipahi*, a soldier.]
Septic, sep'tik, *a.* Having power to promote putrefaction; causing putrefaction. [Gr. *sēpō*, to putrefy.]
Sessile, ses'il, *a. Zool.* and *bot.* attached without any sensible projecting support. [L. *sessilis*, from *sedeo*, to sit.]
Sextet, **Sestette**, ses'tet, ses-tet', *n.* A musical composition for six voices or instruments; the last six lines of a sonnet. [It., from L. *sextus*, sixth.]

Sheik, shēk, *n.* A title of dignity among the Arabs.
Shereef, **Sheriff**, **Sherif**, she-rēf', *n.* A descendant of Mohammed through his daughter Fatima; a prince; the chief magistrate of Mecca.
Shiite, **Shiah**, shī'it, shī'a, *n.* One of the two great Mohammedan sects, the other being the Sunnites or Sunnis; they consider Ali as being the only rightful successor of Mohammed.
Shinto, **Shintoism**, shin'to, shin'to-izm, *n.* The ancient religion of Japan; a form of nature worship, though its essence is now ancestral worship and sacrifice to heroes.
Shoddy, shod ' i, *n.* Fibre from old woollen or worsted fabrics torn up by machinery and mixed with fresh wool to be respun and woven into cheap cloth; the cloth made from this.
Siccative, sik'a-tiv, *a.* Drying; causing to dry. [L. *siccus*, dry.]
Siderite, sid'er-it, *n.* Magnetic iron ore or loadstone. [Gr. *sidēros*, iron.]
Silo, sī'lo, *n.* The pit in which green fodder is preserved in the method of ensilage.
Silurian, si - lū'ri - an, *a. Geol.* applied to the palæozoic strata between the Cambrian formation and the base of the old red sandstone, so called from the district of the *Silures* in S. Wales.
Simian, **Simial**, sim'i-an, sim'i-al, *a.* Pertaining to apes or monkeys. [L. *simia*, an ape.]
Simoom, si-möm', *n.* A hot, suffocating wind which blows occasionally in Africa and Arabia. [Ar. *samūm*.]
Sociologist, sō-shi-ol'o-jist, *n.* One who devotes himself to the study of sociology.
Sociology, sō-shi-ol'o-ji, *n.* The science which treats of the general structure of society, the laws of its development, and the progress of civilization.
Soteriology, sō - tē' ri - ol " o - ji, *n.* The science of health; the doctrine of salvation by Christ. [Gr. *sōtērios*, saving, and *logos*.]
Sou, sö, *n.* An old French copper coin; a five-centime piece, value nearly one halfpenny.
Souvenir, sö-ve-nēr', *n.* A keepsake. [Fr., from L. *subvenire*, to occur to mind.]
Spadix, spā'diks, *n. Bot.* a form of inflorescence in which the flowers are closely arranged round a fleshy radius, the whole surrounded by a spathe, as in palms. [L., a palm branch.]
Spathe, spāth, *n. Bot.* a large membranaceous bract situated at the base of a spadix, which it incloses as a sheath. [L. *spatha*.]
Spectroscope, spek' trō - skōp, *n.* The instrument employed in spectrum analysis. [Gr. *skopeō*, to look at.]
Sphenoid, sfē'noid, *a.* Resembling a wedge. [Gr. *sphēn*, a wedge, and *eidos*, form.]
Spinnaker, spin'a-kėr, *n.* A triangular racing sail carried by yachts, on the opposite side of the main-sail.
Sporadic, spō-rad'ik, *a.* Separate; occurring here and there in a scattered manner. [Gr. *sporos*, dispersed.]
Spore, spōr, *n. Bot.* the reproductive germ of a cryptogamic plant; *zool.* a germ of certain animal organisms. [Gr. *sporos*, a seed.]
Squamose, **Squamous**, skwā'mōs, skwā'mus, *a.* Covered with or consisting of scales. [L. *squama*, a scale.]
Stampede, stam - pēd', *n.* A sudden fright and flight, such as occurs among large herds of horses or cattle in America. [Sp. *estampida*.]
Stearine, **Stearin**, stē'a-rin, *n.* The harder ingredient of animal fat. [Gr. *stear*, fat.]
Steatite, stē'a-tit, *n.* A mineral consisting of magnesia and alumina. [Fr., from Gr. *stear*, fat.]
Stère, stār, *n.* The French unit for solid measure, equal to a cubic metre or 35·3156 cubic feet.
Stertorous, stėr'to-rus, *a.* Characterized by deep snoring. [L. *sterto*, to snore.]
Stevedore, stē've-dōr, *n.* One who loads or unloads vessels. [Sp. *estivador*, a wool-packer.]
Stipple, stip'l, *vt.* To engrave by means of dots. [D. *stip*, a dot.]
Strabismus, stra-biz'mus, *n.* Squinting. [Gr. *strabos*.]
Striate, **Striated**, strī'āt, strī'ā-ted, *a.* Marked with fine thread-like lines. [L. *stria*, a line.]
Strychnia, **Strychnine**, strik'ni-a, strik'-nin, *n.* A vegetable alkaloid poison obtained from the seeds of nux-vomica and certain East Indian trees. [Gr. *strychnos*.]
Sudra, sö'dra, *n.* A member of the lowest of the four great castes of India. [Hind.]
Sulphate, sul'fāt, *n.* A salt of sulphuric acid.
Sulphide, sul'fīd, *n.* A combination of sulphur with another element.
Sulphuret, sul'fū-ret, *n.* A sulphide.
Sunnite, sun'īt, *n.* One of the orthodox Mohammedans who receive the *sunna* or traditionary law as of equal importance with the Koran.
Surrogate, sur'rō-gāt, *n.* The deputy of a bishop or his chancellor. [L. *surrago*, to substitute.]
Suttee, sut-tē', *n.* The voluntary self-immolation by fire of a Hindu widow. [Sans. *sati*, from *sat*, good.]
Sybarite, sib'a-rit, *n.* A person devoted to luxury and pleasure. [*Sybaris*, an ancient Greek city.]
Syenite, sī'en-it, *n.* A granitic rock composed of quartz, hornblende, and felspar. [*Syene*, in Upper Egypt.]
Syenitic, sī-e-nit'ik, *a.* Containing or resembling syenite.
Synæresis, si-nē're-sis, *n. Gram.* the contraction of two syllables into one.
Synclinal, sin-klī'nal, *a. Geol.* dipping towards a common line or plane. [Gr. *syn*, together, and *klinō*, to bend.]
Syndicate, sin'di-kāt, *n.* A body of syndics; an association of persons formed for the promotion of some particular enterprise, financial scheme, or the like.

Tableau, tab-lō', *n. pl.* **Tableaux**, tab-lōz'. A picture; a striking group or dramatic scene. [Fr.]
Taboo, ta-bö', *n.* The setting of something apart and away from human contact, practised among certain savage races; prohibition of contact or intercourse.—*vt.* To interdict approach to or contact with.
Tactile, tak'til, *a.* Capable of being touched or felt; pertaining to the sense of touch. [L. *tactilis*, from *tango*, to touch.]
Tael, tāl, *n.* A Chinese money equal to from 5s. 6d. to 6s. stg.; also a weight of 1⅓ oz.
Talmud, tal'mud, *n.* The body of the Hebrew civil and canonical laws, traditions, &c. [Chal., instruction.]
Tandem, tan'dem, *adv.* With two horses

harnessed singly one before the other. n. A wheeled carriage so drawn. [L., at length.]

Tanistry, tan'ist-ri, n. An ancient Irish custom in the election of a prince or sovereign, the right of succession being confined to a family, but not fixed in an individual. [Ir. *taniste*, from *tan*, a region.]

Targum, tär'gum, n. An Aramaic or Chaldee version of the Hebrew Scriptures. [Chal. *targem*, to interpret.]

Teetotal, tē'tō-tal, a. Totally abstaining from intoxicants.

Teleology, tel-ē-ol'o-ji, n. The science of final causes. [Gr. *telos*, an end, and *logos*.]

Teleostean, tel-ē-os'tē-an, n. One of an order of fishes, having a well-ossified skeleton. [Gr. *telos*, and *osteon*, a bone.]

Telephone, tel'ē-fōn, n. An instrument transmitting sound and words uttered by the human voice to a great distance by means of electricity and telegraph wires.

Telpherage, tel'fėr-aj, n. A system of transporting goods on an elevated railway by means of electricity. [Gr. *tele*, far, and *phero*, to carry.]

Teratology, ter-a-tol'o-ji, n. Biol. the science of monsters and malformations. [Gr. *teras*, a prodigy, and *logos*.]

Thaler, tä'lėr, n. A German coin, value about 3s.

Thallogen, Thallophyte, thal'ō-jen, thal'ō-fīt, n. A stemless plant consisting only of expansions of cellular tissue; applied to all cryptogams except ferns and mosses. [Gr. *thallos*, a shoot, root, *gen*, to produce, *phyton*, a plant.]

Thaumaturgy, tha'ma-tėr-ji, n. Miracle-working; magic; legerdemain. [Gr. *thaumaturgia*, wonder-working.]

Theanthropism, thē-an'thro-pizm, n. The state of being God and man. [Gr. *theos*, God, and *anthrōpos*, man.]

Thearchy, thē'är-ki, n. Government by God; theocracy. [Gr. *theos*, God, and *archē*, rule.]

Theca, thē'ka, n. pl. **Thecæ**, thē'sē. The spore-cases of cryptogams. [L., from Gr. *thēkē*, a case.]

Theine, Thein, thē'in, n. The bitter principle found in tea and some other plants. [*Thea*, the tea plant.]

Theophany, thē-of'a-ni, n. The actual appearing of God to man. [Gr. *theos*, God, and *phainomai*, to appear.]

Theosophy, thē-os'o-fi, n. A knowledge of the divine being obtained by spiritual ecstasy; direct intuition or divine illumination.

Thermotics, thėr-mot'iks, n. The science of heat. [Gr. *thermos*, hot.]

Thespian, thes'pi-an, a. Relating to dramatic acting. [*Thespis*, Greek player.]

Theurgy, thē'ėr-ji, n. The working of a divine agency in human affairs. [Gr. *theos*, God, and *ergon*, work.]

Tincal, ting'kal, n. Crude or unrefined borax.

Tirailleur, ti-räl'yėr, n. A French sharp-shooter.

Tithonic, ti-thon'ik, a. Pertaining to the chemical rays of light. [*Tithonus*, the consort of Aurora.]

Toboggan, Tobogan, tō-bog'an, n. A kind of sled for sliding down snow-covered slopes. [Amer. Ind. *odabagan*, a sled.]

Tonicity, to-nis'i-ti, n. *Physiol.* the elasticity of living parts.

Tonsorial, ton-sō'ri-al, a. Pertaining to a barber. [L. *tonsor*.]

Tope, tōp, n. A Buddhist monument for preserving relics or for commemorating some event.

Toreador, tor'ē-a-dōr'', n. A Spanish bull-fighter, especially one on horseback.

Toreutic, to-rū'tik, a. Pertaining to carved work. [Gr. *toreuō*, to work in relief.]

Totem, tō'tem, n. An animal, plant, &c., used as a badge or symbolic name. [Amer. Ind.]

Toxophylite, tok-sof'i-lit, n. A lover of archery. [Gr. *toxon*, a bow, and *philos*, loving.]

Tractarian, trak-tā'ri-an, n. Applied to the authors of the "Tracts for the Times," published at Oxford (1833–41) by Anglicans, with a considerable leaning to Roman Catholicism.

Tramway, tram'wā, n. A railway for passenger cars laid along a street or road.

Trapeze, tra-pēz', n. A sort of swing, consisting of a cross-bar suspended by cords at some distance from the ground, for gymnastic exercises. [L. *trapezium*.]

Traumatic, tra-mat'ik, a. Pertaining to wounds. [Gr. *trauma*, a wound.]

Trek, trek, vi. To travel by wagon (S. Africa). [D. *trekken*, to travel.]

Trias, trī'as, n. Geol. the upper new red sandstone. [Gr. *trias*, three; the number of groups found.]

Triassic, trī-as'ik, a. Pertaining to the trias.

Trichina, tri-kī'na, n. pl. **Trichinæ**, tri-kī'nē. A minute nematoid worm, the larvæ of which causes disease in the flesh of mammals.

Trichiniasis, Trichinosis, trik-i-nī'a-sis, trik-i-nō'sis, n. The disease caused by trichinæ.

Tricycle, trī'si-kl, n. A form of velocipede with three wheels.

Tsetse, tset'sē, n. An African fly whose bite is often fatal to horses, dogs, and cattle.

Turanian, tū-rā'ni-an, a. Applied to the family of languages which includes the Ugrian, Turkish, Mongolian, &c.

Udometer, ū-dom'et-ėr, n. A rain-gauge. [Gr. *udus*, moist, and *metron*, a measure.]

Ugrian, ō'gri-an, a. Applied to the Finnic group of Turanian tongues and peoples, comprising the Lapps, Finns, and Magyars.

Uhlan, ō'lan, n. A light cavalry soldier in the German, Austro-Hungarian, and Russian armies. [Pol. *ula*, a lance.]

Ukase, ū'kās, n. A Russian government edict. [Russ.]

Ulster, ul'ster, n. A long, loose overcoat, originally made of frieze cloth in *Ulster*.

Ululate, ul'ū-lāt, vi. To howl, as a dog or a wolf. [L. *ululo*, to howl.]

Valise, va-lēs', n. A small leather travelling bag.

Vandal, van'dal, n. One who wilfully or ignorantly destroys any work of art or the like; from the conduct of the *Vandals* who pillaged Rome.

Vandalism, van'dal-izm, n. The conduct of a vandal.

Variorum, vā-ri-ō'rum, a. Applied to an edition of a work with the notes of various editors inserted. [*Editio cum notis variorum*, an edition with the notes of various persons.]

Vaticinate, va-tis'i-nāt, vi. To prophesy; to predict. [L. *vates*, a prophet.]

Veda, vā'dä or vē'da, n. The body of ancient Sanskrit hymns on which the Brahmanical system is based.

Velocipede, vē-los'i-ped, n. A light vehicle driven by the feet of the rider; a bicycle or tricycle. [L. *velox, velocis*, swift, and *pes, pedis*, a foot.]

Venation, vē-nā'shon, n. *Bot.* the manner in which the veins of leaves are arranged.

Vertu, vėr'tū, n. Objects of art, antiquity, or curiosity, collectively. [It.]

Viking, vik'ing, n. An ancient Scandinavian rover or sea-rover. [Icel. *viking*, a frequenter of fjords.]

Volt, volt, n. The unit of electromotive force. [*Volta*, the discoverer of voltaism.]

Weber, vā'ber, n. The electric unit of magnetic quantity. [*Weber*, a German physicist.]

Witenagemot, wit'en-a-ge-mot, n. The Anglo-Saxon national parliament. [Sax., meeting of wise men.]

Wraith, rāth, n. An apparition of a person about to die, or newly dead. [Gael. *arrach*, a spectre.]

Xanthochroi, zan-thok'ro-i, n. pl. *Anthrop.* the fair white group of men. [Gr. *xanthochroos*, yellow-skinned.]

Xylograph, zī'lō-graf, n. A wood engraving. [Gr. *zylon*, wood, and *graphō*, to write.]

Yankee, yang'kē, n. A native of New England; generally applied to any native of the U. S. [Prob. an Indian corr. of *English* or *Anglais*.]

Yule, yōl, n. Christmas. [Sax. *geol*, Christmas.]

Zenana, ze-nä'na, n. The portion of a Hindu's house devoted to females. [Per. *zen*, a woman.]

Zereba, ze-rē'ba, n. A temporary camping place defended by a fence of bushes, stones, &c. [Sudan.]

Zincography, zing-kog'ra-fi, n. A mode of printing similar to lithography, a plate of polished zinc taking the place of the stone.

Zooid, zō'oid, n. One of the organisms produced by gemmation, as in the polyzoa. [Gr. *sōon*, an animal, and *eidos*, resemblance.]

Fāte, fär, fat, fạll; mē, met, hėr; pīne, pin; nōte, not, mȯve; tūbe, tub, bụll; oil, pound.

PREFIXES AND AFFIXES.

PREFIXES.

PREFIXES OF SAXON ORIGIN.

A negative (=Sans. and Gr. *a*, of the same force);—*aghast*.

A = on, in;—*afoot, abed, afield, afar, aside, aweary, abroad, adrift*.

Be, by, near to, about; conveying, sometimes, the idea of *all over*;—*beside, before, betimes, betake, besiege, bespeak, bedaub, bespatter*.

Em, passing by euphonic change into en or iu (Sax. *ymb, ymbe, emb, embe,* allied to G. *um*, and to Gr. *amphi*, about, around; also imposing the idea of 'to make;'—*embody, encircle, embark, empower, endear, enrich, enfeeble*.

For (Sax. *for*, quite a different word from *fore*, with which it is frequently confounded. It is also to be carefully distinguished from the prep. *for*. It seems to be allied to the D. and G. *ver*—a prefix of extensive signification) conveys the idea of privation, prohibition, or deterioration;—*forsake, forbid, forswear, forego*.

Fore (Sax. *fore*=G. *vor*, Old G. *fora*, before, in front of, in the sight or view of; Goth. *faura*, Icel. *for*, *fyri*, Gr. *pro*, Sans. *pra*), before, in point of place or time;—*foreground, foreshorten, forward, forefather, foresee, foretell, forestal, foreshadow, foreordain, foreknowledge*.

Mis (=G. *miss*. See the verb TO MISS), failure, defect, error, corruption, unlikeness;—*misarrange, misadventure, misbehave, misbelieve, miscreant, mishap, misproportion*.

N (Sans. *na*, not. *See* NOR), negative;—*neither, nor, none, never*.

On (Sax. *on, in, an*), upon, above, and in contact with, either literally or figuratively;—*onset, onslaught*.

Over (see the word), above, beside, beyond; also denoting excess;—*overhead, overhang, overarch, overleap, overwhelm, overburden, overcharge*.

Out (*see* OUT), without, beyond, excess, superiority;—*outbar, outbreathe, outbalance, outflank, outnumber, outvote*.

To (Sans. *ta*, this);—*to-day, to-morrow*.

Un (the Sans. negative *a* before vowels takes a euphonic *n*. To this may be referred the Sax. Old Sax. and Goth. *un*, and probably the L. *in*, in its negative signification. Prefixed to Eng. verbs *un* means to turn back, to bring into the contrary state; in other cases it has a negative force); privation, deterioration, opposition;—*unhappy, unhallowed, ungentle, unbelief, unblamable, unbend, unbind, unclog, uncoil*.

Up (see the word), upward, aloft;—*upbear, upheave, upspring, upland, upwall (Sax. upaweallan)*.

With (probably the Sans. *vich*, to separate; in the Vedas, to pluck away), from, away from, opposition;—*withdraw, withhold, withstand*.

GREEK PREFIXES.

A, by euphonic change, **an** (the Sans. *a* negative, with which Bopp compares the L. *in*, Goth. and G. *un*, privative), expresses want, absence, privation, blame;—aorist, *anarchy, apathetic, anonymous*.

Amphi, on both sides, about, around, on all sides;—*amphibrach, amphitheatre, amphibious*.

Ana, up, upon, up through;—*anatomy, analogy, analyze, anachronism*.

Anti (**ant**), against, over against, in opposition to;—*antithesis, antipatriotic, antipathy*.

Apo (Sans. *apa*, off, away; associated by Bopp with L. *ab*, Goth. *af*, and Eng. *of*), from, away from, asunder;—*apocope, apostasy, apostrophize, apologize*.

Cata (**cat**), down, downwards, from above;—*cataract, catacomb, catarrh, catastrophe*.

Dia, through and out of, right through, throughout;—*diaphanous, diameter, dialectics, dialogue*.

En (**em**, by euphonic change; Sans. *ni*, in, on, downwards), in, on, at;—*encaustic, enallage, emphatic*.

Epi, **ep** (Sans. *abhi*, to, towards), on or upon, by or near, stretching over;—*epithet, epigastric, epidermis, epitomize, ephemeral*.

Eu, well, implying greatness, abundance, prosperity, easiness;—*euphony, eulogize, euphemism*.

Eso, to within, within;—*esoteric*.

Ex (**ec**), out of, from out of, away from;—*exorcise, exoteric, exodus, ecstasy*.

Exo, without, out of doors;—*exotic, exoteric*.

Hyper, over, above, beyond, and away;—*hyperborean, hypercritical, hypertrophy*.

Hypo, from under, under, beneath;—*hypothesis, hypostasis, hypotenuse*.

Meta (**met**), in the midst of, among, between, next after;—*metaphor, metaphrase, metaphysic, metamorphosis, metathesis*.

Para (Sans. *pará*, back, backwards), beside, from the side of;—*parabola, parable, paraclete, paradox, parody*.

Peri (Sans. *pari*, around), around, about, beyond measure;—*periphery, perihelion, period, peripatetic*.

Syn, passing into **sy**, **syl**, **sym** (Sans. *sam*, with, together with; allied, according to Bopp, with Slav. *sŭ*, with, and perhaps with L. *con*), along with, in company with, together with;—*synthesis, synopsis, system, syllogism, sympathy, symbolize*.

LATIN PREFIXES.

A, **ab**, **abs** (Gr. *apo*, Sans. *apa*, Goth. *af*, off, away), noting the point of departure—from or away;—*abuse, avert, abstract, absolve, abrade, abrogate*.

Ad (Sans. *adhi*, to, upon, over), passing into **a**, **ac**, **af**, **ag**, **al**, **an**, **ap**, **ar**, **as**, **at**, —to, towards, at or near anything;—*adhere, accede, affirm, aggregate, allude, annex, applaud, arrogant, assume, attribute*.

Ante (Gr. *anti*, opposite, G. *ant*, in *antworten*, to answer, Sans. *ati*, across, beyond), before, in regard to space, time, and order or preference;—*antechamber, antedate, antecedent, antediluvian, antepone*.

Bene, well, rightly;—*benevolence, benediction*.

Bi, **bis** (older form *dui*=Sans. *dvi*, Goth. *tvai*, two), twice;—*binomial, bisect, bivalve, bissextile*.

Circum, **circu** (perhaps the accusative of *circus*—which see), around, all around;—*circumnavigate, circumvent, circumspect, circuit*.

Cis, on this side;—*cisalpine*.

Co, **con**, passing into **col**, **cor**, &c.; noting a collection, gathering, company, together;—*co-operate, cognate, collect, commotion, correlative*.

Contra, by corruption **Counter** (from *con*, probably = the Sans. *sam*, with), over against, on the opposite side, in return;—*contrary, contradict, contravene, contradistinguish, counteract*.

De, down from, away from, out of;—*dejection, descend, deplete, depart, denude, denominate, denounce*.

Dis, **di**, **dif** (allied to Sans. *dvis*, twice), asunder, apart, in *two*; also noting distribution, and the opposite of the simple word;—*distract, diffuse, disarm, diverge, disagree, disappoint, disapprove*.

Ex or **e**, passing into **ec**, **ef** (Gr. *ek* or *eks*, from, out of), out of, from, down from;—*event, exclude, eccentric, effulgence, elect, emigrate, efflux*.

Extra (from *ex*), on the outside, without, beyond;—*extraneous, extravagant, extraordinary, extrajudicial*.

In, passing into **ig**, **il**, **im**, **ir** (Gr. *en*, in, Sans. *ni*, in, on, down. But the L. *in* having a negative force is identical with the Goth. and Sax. *un*, and the Sans. *a* or *an*), noting the place where anything is present, also negation;—*inside, illustrate, illuminate, import, irradiate, imprison, imprint, ignoble, ignominy, immortal, impure*.

Inter (Sans. *antar*, within), in the midst, between;—*intercede, interchange, intermingle, interview, intercommunication*.

Intro, into the inside, to within;—*intro*duce, *intro*vert, *intro*it, *intro*mit.

Juxta (perhaps the Sans. *yuj*, to join, and *sthá*, to stand), by the side of, close to, near to, nigh;—*juxta*position.

Ob, having the various forms of oc, of, o, op, os (Gr. *epi*; Sans. *abhi*, to, towards, before), towards, to, before, against;—*oc*cur, *of*fend, *ob*struct, *op*pose, *os*tentation.

Per, through, through the midst of, through and through, thoroughly;—*per*forate, *per*vade, *per*fection, *per*dition, *per*meate. The r is sometimes assimilated, as in *pel*lucid.

Post, behind, after;—*post*pone, *poste*rior, *post*humous, *post*date.

Præ (Gr. *pro*, Sans. *pra*, before, forward), before, in front, in advance of;—*pre*dict, *pre*fer, *pre*figure, *pre*determine, *pre*-eminent.

Præter (*præ* with the comparative suffix *ter*=Sans. *tara*), except, unless, past, before, beyond, besides;—*preter*mit, *preter*natural, *preter*it.

Pro (*præ* and *pro* are the same word. See Præ), before, in front of, for, in favour of, in the place of;—*pro*duce, *pro*ject, *pro*jectile, *pro*mise, *pro*consul.

Re (conjectured by Bopp to be allied to Sans. *pará*, backwards), back again, against;—*re*turn, *re*store, *re*sound, *re*tract, *re*build, *re*sist, *re*new, *re*call, *re*move.

Retro, backwards, behind;—*retro*spect.

Se (old form of *sine*, without), aside, apart, reversing the signification of the root;—*se*duce, *se*cede, *se*clude, *se*cure, *se*quester, *se*parate.

Sine, without, conveying the idea of separation, or of being apart;—*sine*cure, *sim*ple, *sin*cere.

Sub, passing into suc, suf, sug, sum, sup, sus, su (kindred with Gr. *hupo*, under, Sans. *upa*, to, towards), under, below; hence implying inferiority, secrecy, substitution;—*sub*tract, *sub*merge, *sub*terranean, *sub*marine, *sug*gest, *sum*mon, *sus*pect, *suf*fuse, *sub*acid, *sup*press, *sus*pend.

Subter (from *sub*), below, beneath, underneath;—*subter*fuge.

Super, passing into sur (Gr. *huper*, Sans. *upari*, over), above, over, beyond;—*super*structure, *super*add, *su*perhuman, *super*fluous, *super*lative, *sur*charge, *sur*feit, *sur*mise.

Trans, tra (Sans. *tiras*, beyond, through), on the farther side of, beyond, across;—*trans*mit, *trans*pierce, *trans*cend, *trans*it.

Ultra, beyond, farther, past, longer than;—*ultra*montane, *ultra*mundane, *ultra*marine.

Ve (Sans. *vi*, without);—*ve*hement.

AFFIXES.

Denoting the *doer of a thing*.

Or (L.), direct*or*, dictat*or*, collect*or*, instruct*or*, regulat*or*, capt*or*.

Ary (L. *arius*), advers*ary*, auxili*ary*, benefici*ary*, commiss*ary*.

Ent (L. *ens*, *entis*), respond*ent*, recipi*ent*, depend*ent*, stud*ent*.

Ant (L. *ans*, *antis*), assist*ant*, vagr*ant*, cormor*ant*, command*ant*, inf*ant*.

Ive (L. *ivus*), representat*ive*, mot*ive*.

Ist (Gr. *istēs*), psalm*ist*, eulog*ist*, catech*ist*, bapt*ist*, panthe*ist*, theor*ist*, chem*ist*, dogmat*ist*.

Er (Sax.), whisp*er*er, build*er*, do*er*, liv*er*, lov*er*, wait*er*.

Ar (Sax.), begg*ar*, li*ar*.

Ard, art (Sw. *art*, nature, disposition), nigg*ard*, cow*ard*, wiz*ard*, slugg*ard*, dot*ard*, lagg*ard*, bragg*art*.

Ster (Sax. *styran*, to rule, govern), brew*ster*, game*ster*, spin*ster*, malt*ster*, song*ster*, web*ster*, pun*ster*.

An (Fr. *en*, from L. *anus*), tragedi*an*, comedi*an*, Christi*an*.

Ier, eer (Fr. from L. *or*), brigad*ier*, grenad*ier*, bombard*ier*, pion*eer*, musket*eer*, chariot*eer*.

Ess (Fr. from L. *ix*), author*ess*, actr*ess*, shepherd*ess*, lion*ess*, giant*ess*.

The Or (properly *tor*, Gr. *tēr*) of the L. which appears above, together with the similar Sax. and other terminations, is represented in Sans. by *tri*; thus from *kship*, to throw, comes *kshēptri*, a thrower; from *dá*, to give, *dátri*, a giver; from *budh*, to know, *boddhri*, a knower. In Sans. likewise another *tri* forms nouns of relationship, masculine and feminine; as, *pitri*, a father, *mátri*, a mother. The *ant*, *ent*, from the Latin (*ans*, *antis*, *ens*, *entis*), are represented in Sans. by *mána*, substituted for *ute*, in many verbs, and by *ána*, for *ate*, in other conjugations.

Denoting the person *who suffers, or on whom a thing is done*.

Ate (L. *atus*), deleg*ate*, magn*ate*, magistr*ate*, reprob*ate*, gradu*ate*.

Ite (L. *ttus* or *ttus*), favour*ite*, bedlam*ite*, Jacob*ite*.

Ite, yte (Gr. *itos*, *utos*), cosmopol*ite*, erem*ite*, anchor*ite*, hermaphrod*ite*, neoph*yte*.

Ee (probably Fr.), don*ee*, legat*ee*, appell*ee*, refer*ee*, refug*ee*, trust*ee*.

With the L. and Gr. terminations under this head may be compared the base of the Sans. past passive participle, generally formed by adding *ta* directly to the root;—*kship*, to throw, *kshipta*, thrown.

Denoting *action or an active faculty, being or a state of being, viewed abstractly*.

Ion (L. *io*, *iōnis*), percept*ion*, concept*ion*, approbat*ion*, contribut*ion*, collis*ion*, subordinat*ion*, crucifix*ion*, benedict*ion*, commot*ion*.

Tude (L. *tūdo*), altit*ude*, amplit*ude*, beatit*ude*, fortit*ude*, ingratit*ude*, desuet*ude*, dissimilit*ude*.

Ance (L. *antia*), abund*ance*, accept*ance*, compli*ance*, exorbit*ance*, predomin*ance*, signific*ance*, temper*ance*, vigil*ance*.

Ment (the L. *men*, *mentum*, seem to be identical with the Sans. suffix *man*, forming neuter substantives; as from *kri*, to do, *karman*, a deed), ali*ment*, experi*ment*, impedi*ment*, infringe*ment*, docu*ment*, argu*ment*, establish*ment*, firma*ment*, rudi*ment*, sacra*ment*, tempera*ment*.

Ancy (same as *ance*), brilli*ancy*, const*ancy*, poign*ancy*, vac*ancy*, vagr*ancy*.

Ence (L. *entia*), abhorr*ence*, abstin*ence*, accid*ence*, benefic*ence*, circumfer*ence*, omnisci*ence*, magnific*ence*, improvid*ence*, innoc*ence*.

Ency (same as *ence*), ag*ency*, clem*ency*, conting*ency*, excell*ency*.

Mony (L. *monium*, *monia*), ali*mony*, matri*mony*, parsi*mony*, patri*mony*, testi*mony*.

Ty, or ity (Fr. *té*, L. *tas*, *tātis*), abil*ity*, activ*ity*, advers*ity*, antiqu*ity*, chast*ity*, credul*ity*, difficul*ty*, humil*ity*, necess*ity*.

Y (Fr. *ie*, L. and Gr. *ia*), agon*y*, allegor*y*, anatom*y*, astronom*y*, biograph*y*, econom*y*, harmon*y*, philanthrop*y*, theolog*y*, philosoph*y*.

Y denoting a place (Fr. *ie*, from L. *ium*), aviar*y*, baron*y*, rector*y*, smith*y*, foundr*y*, potter*y*.

Ure (L. *ūra*), creat*ure*, cinct*ure*, conject*ure*, cult*ure*, discomposure, fract*ure*, intermixt*ure*, legislat*ure*, nat*ure*, sepult*ure*, superstruct*ure*, vest*ure*.

Acy, ty, sy (L. *acia*, *tia*, *sia*), contum*acy*, modes*ty*, constan*cy*, controver*sy*.

Ism (Gr.), athe*ism*, bapt*ism*, barbar*ism*, hero*ism*, mechan*ism*, soph*ism*, patriot*ism*, ostrac*ism*, catech*ism*, scepticism.

Age (Fr.), appan*age*, advant*age*, aver*age*, hom*age*, parent*age*, marri*age*, person*age*, foli*age*, fruit*age*.

Hood (Sax. *hád*, condition), boy*hood*, child*hood*, knight*hood*, likeli*hood*, neighbour*hood*, priest*hood*, sister*hood*, widow*hood*, man*hood*.

Ship (from Sax. *scyppan*, to make, form), apprentice*ship*, censor*ship*, professor*ship*, rector*ship*, steward*ship*, ward*ship*, scholar*ship*.

Ness (Sax. *nes*, *nys*), acute*ness*, agreeable*ness*, attentive*ness*, barren*ness*, blessed*ness*, bountiful*ness*, devoted*ness*, graceful*ness*, rugged*ness*, wicked*ness*, wretched*ness*, weak*ness*.

Th (Sax. corresponding to Sans. suffix *ta*, or *itá*, from which innumerable passive participles are formed), dear*th*, weal*th*, bir*th*, breadt*h*, dea*th*, dep*th*, fil*th*, grow*th*, heal*th*, leng*th*, mir*th*, streng*th*, tru*th*, warm*th*, you*th*.

T (the same), drif*t*, gif*t*, thef*t*, fligh*t*, concei*t*, drauf*t*, faul*t*, join*t*, transcrip*t*.

Denoting *power or jurisdiction*.

Dom (Sax. *dóm*, Icel. *dómr*, judgment), king*dom*, prince*dom*, duke*dom*, earl*dom*, sheriff*dom*, Christen*dom*.

Ric (Sax. *ric*, dominion, power), bishop*ric*.

DIMINUTIVE TERMINATIONS.

El, le (L. *ulum*), satch*el*, tramm*el*, mudd*le*.

Ikin, kin (Sax. *cinn*, a kind), mannik*in*, lambk*in*, napk*in*, pipk*in*.

Ling (Sax. *ling*, an image), dar*ling*, duck*ling*, first*ling*, gos*ling*, strip*ling*.

Ock (Sax. *ca* or *uca*. In Sans. *ka* affixed denotes depreciation), bull*ock*, hill*ock*, padd*ock*.

Let (probably abbreviated from Sax. *lytel*, little), arm*let*, brace*let*, ham*let*, cut*let*, stream*let*, wave*let*.

Denoting *of or pertaining to*.

Al (L. *ális*), fili*al*, annu*al*, autumn*al*, classic*al*, cordi*al*, decenni*al*, casu*al*, carnal, final, floral, judicial, local, manual.

Ic (Gr. *ikos*, Sans. *ika* (nomin. *ikas-t-am*), *dhārmika*, religious), dogmatic, periodic, botanic, theoretic.

Ical (a combination of the Gr. *ikos* with the L. *ālis*), dogmatical, periodical, botanical, theoretical, analytical, anatomical, heretical, practical, technical, mathematical.

Ile (L. *ilis*), agile, docile, febrile, fragile, hostile, juvenile, puerile, versatile, virile, volatile, projectile.

Ine (Gr. *inos*, L. *inus*, Sans. *ina*, *ina*, thus from *grāma*, a village, *grāmīna*, rustic), adamantine, aquiline, canine, clandestine, hyacinthine, coralline, crystalline, pristine.

An (L. *anus*), antemeridian, Christian, hyperborean, human, republican, sylvan, suburban, veteran.

Ory (L. *orius*, Sans. *ura*, as bhidura, brittle), amatory, adulatory, confirmatory, explanatory, expiatory, prefatory, premonitory.

Ac (Gr. *akos*; Sans. *aka*), demoniac, elegiac, cardiac, prosodiac, hypochondriac.

Ar (L. *aris*; Sans. *ara*), angular, annular, cellular, familiar, jocular, ocular, polar, peculiar, piacular, regular, similar, titular, tutelar, verisimilar.

Ary (L. *arius*, kindred with *aris*), auxiliary, contrary, disciplinary, extraordinary, honorary, literary, mercenary, necessary, pecuniary, solitary, temporary, tumultuary.

En (Sax. as *bece*, beech, *bucene*, beechen; Sans. *shubh*, to shine, *shobhana*, bright), ashen, beechen, earthen, golden, oaken, oaten, wheaten, waxen.

Denoting quality.

Id (L. *idus;* Sans. *ita;* said to be added to nouns to form adjectives), acid, arid, fervid, fluid, horrid, humid, rancid, timid, torpid, torrid, vivid.

Denoting power, ability, or activity.

Ive (L. *ivus;* Sans. participial ending *vas* or *ivas*), active, administrative, affirmative, authoritative, imitative, incentive, inventive, legislative, persuasive, submissive, transitive, vindictive.

Denoting capacity or worthiness, in a passive sense.

Ble (able, ible; L. *bilis*, perhaps kindred with Sans. *bala*, strength—curable, able to be cured, that *can* be cured), accessible, amiable, blamable, commendable, communicable, curable, excusable, incredible, laudable, practicable, punishable, warrantable.

Denoting privation.

Less (see LESS), artless, fatherless, comfortless.

Denoting diminution; also, belonging to, like or resembling.

Ish (Sax. *isc*), dwarfish, whitish, yellowish, brutish, childish, foolish, churlish, womanish.

Denoting similarity.

Like, ly (see LIKE), giantlike, Christianlike, manlike, saintlike, godlike, courtly, friendly, lovely.

Denoting somewhat, full of.

Some (Sax. *sum*, somewhat, a little), gladsome, frolicsome, handsome, noisome, tiresome, wearisome, troublesome, toilsome.

Denoting in the direction of.

Ward (see WORTH), backward, forward, downward, outward, upward, wayward.

Denoting to make, to cause to be or to become.

Ate (L. past part. pass. *atus-a-um*= Sans. *ta* or *ita*, from which innumerable passive participles are formed), abbreviate, accelerate, alleviate, assimilate, consecrate, enumerate, illuminate, vindicate, navigate.

Fy (Fr. *fier*, from L. *facere*, *facio*, to make), amplify, deify, gratify, mortify, sanctify, verify, purify, ossify, terrify.

Ize, ise (Gr. *izō*), agonize, baptize, canonize, civilize, idolize, organize, realise, scrutinize, tyrannise, temporize, exorcise, authorise, exercise.

Ish (from the Fr. pres. part. in *issant*), establish, admonish, nourish, publish, replenish, vanquish, blemish, cherish, punish, extinguish.

En (Sax.=Goth. *an*, Gr. *ein*, Sans. *um*, &c.), blacken, brighten, darken, dishearten, gladden, moisten, redden, shorten, strengthen, thicken, threaten, stiffen.

Denoting full of, consisting of, given to.

Ose, ous (L. *ōsus*, *us*, *x*, &c.), verbose, operose, aqueous, audacious, contagious, copious, famous, generous, ignominious, unanimous, voluptuous.

Denoting progression, growing, or becoming.

Escent (L.), convalescent, crescent, effervescent, putrescent, quiescent.

WORDS, PHRASES, &c.,

FROM THE LATIN, FRENCH, AND ITALIAN LANGUAGES, FREQUENTLY OCCURRING IN ENGLISH AUTHORS, RENDERED INTO ENGLISH.

A. [Fr.] At; according to; to.
A bas. [Fr.] Down.
Ab extra. [L.] From without.
Ab initio. [L.] From the beginning.
Ab intra. [L.] From within.
Abonnement. [Fr.] Subscription.
Ab origine. [L.] From the beginning.
Ab ovo usque ad mala. [L.] From the egg to the apples; from beginning to end.
Absente reo. [L.] The accused person being absent.
Ab uno disce omnes. [L.] From one learn all.
Accueil. [Fr.] Embrace; welcome.
Ad captandum vulgus. [L.] To catch the rabble.
A demi. [Fr.] By halves.
Ad eundem. (sc. gradum). [L.] To the same degree.
Ad finem. [L.] To the end.
Ad hominem. [L.] To the man; that is, to his passions and interests.
Ad infinitum. [L.] To infinity.
Ad interim. [L.] In the meanwhile.
A discrétion. [Fr.] Without restriction.
Ad Kalendas Græcas. [L.] At the Greek Calends; never.
Ad libitum. [L.] At pleasure.
Ad modum. [L.] After the manner of.
Ad nauseam. [L.] To disgust.
Ad rem. [L.] To the point.
Adscriptus glebæ. [L.] Attached to the soil.
Ad unguem. [L.] To the nail; nicely.
Ad unum omnes. [L.] All; to a man.
Ad valorem. [L.] According to the value.
Æquo animo. [L.] With equanimity.
Affaire d'honneur. [Fr.] An affair of honour.
Affaire du cœur. [Fr.] An affair of the heart.
A fortiori. [L.] With stronger reason.
Agenda. [L.] Things to be done.
A la bonne heure. [Fr.] In good time; very well.
A la campagne. [Fr.] In the country.
A la française. [Fr.] After the French mode.
A l'anglaise. [Fr.] After the English mode.
Al fresco. [It.] In the open air; cool.
Alias. [L.] Otherwise; at another time or place.
Alibi. [L.] Elsewhere.
All'alba. [It.] At daybreak.
Allons. [Fr.] Let us go; come.
Alma mater. [L.] A bounteous mother; the college at which one graduated.
A l'outrance. [Fr.] Without sparing.
Alter idem. [L.] Another precisely similar.
Amende honorable. [Fr.] Satisfactory apology.
A mensa et thoro. [L.] From bed and board.

A merveille. [Fr.] To a wonder.
Amor patriæ. [L.] Love of country.
Amour propre. [Fr.] Self-love; vanity.
Ancien régime. [Fr.] Ancient order of things.
Anno ætatis suæ. [L.] In the year of his or her age.
Anno Domini. [L.] In the year of our Lord.
Anno mundi. [L.] In the year of the world.
Annus mirabilis. [L.] Wonderful year.
Ante meridiem. [L.] Before noon.
Aperçu. [Fr.] Survey; sketch.
Aplomb. [Fr.] Perpendicularly; firmly.
A posteriori. [L.] From the effect to the cause.
A priori. [L.] From the cause to the effect.
A propos. [Fr.] To the point; seasonably.
A propos de bottes. [Fr.] Without reason.
Arc-en-ciel. [Fr.] Rainbow.
Argumentum ad hominem. [L.] An argument to the man; that is, an argument whose force is derived from the situation of the person to whom it is addressed.
Argumentum ad verecundiam. [L.] Argument to modesty.
Arrière pensée. [Fr.] A mental reservation.
Ars longa, vita brevis. [L.] Art is long, but life is short.
A tout prix. [Fr.] At any price.
Au courant. [Fr.] To the present time.
Audi alteram partem. [L.] Hear the other side.
Au fait. [Fr.] Well instructed; expert.
Aura popularis. [L.] The gale of popular favour.
Aurea mediocritas. [L.] The golden mean.
Au revoir. [Fr.] Adieu, until we meet again.
Au troisième. [Fr.] On the third floor.
A vinculo matrimonii. [L.] From the tie of marriage.

Bas bleu. [Fr.] A blue stocking; a literary woman.
Beau monde. [Fr.] The fashionable world.
Beaux yeux. [Fr.] Handsome eyes; attractive looks.
Ben trovato. [It.] A happy invention.
Bête noire. [Fr.] A black beast; a bugbear.
Bienséance. [Fr.] Civility; decorum.
Bis dat qui cito dat. [L.] He who gives quickly, gives twice as much.
Blasé. [Fr.] Pallid; surfeited.
Bona fide. [L.] In good faith; in reality.
Bonne. [Fr.] A nurse or governess.

Brutum fulmen. [L.] A harmless thunderbolt.

Cacoethes scribendi. [L.] An itch for scribbling.
Cætera desunt. [L.] The remainder is wanting.
Caput. [L.] Head; chapter.
Caput mortuum. [L.] The worthless remains.
Carte blanche. [Fr.] White paper; full power.
Carte de visite. [Fr.] A small photographic picture upon a card, so called from its original use as a visiting card.
Casus belli. [L.] That which justifies war.
Catalogus raisonné. [Fr.] A catalogue of books arranged according to their subjects.
Cedant arma togæ. [L.] Let arms yield to the gown, i.e. let military authority yield to the civil power.
Chacun à son goût. [Fr.] Every one to his taste.
Chef. [Fr.] The head; hence, a chief cook.
Chef-d'œuvre. [Fr.] A masterpiece.
Cicerone. [It.] A guide who explains curiosities.
Coiffure. [Fr.] A head-dress.
Comme il faut. [Fr.] As it should be.
Compos mentis. [L.] Of a sound mind.
Compte rendu. [Fr.] Account rendered; report.
Con amore. [It.] With love; earnestly.
Conditio sine quâ non. [L.] A necessary condition.
Confrère. [Fr.] An associate.
Congé d'élire. [Fr.] Permission to elect.
Coram non judice. [L.] Before one who is not the proper judge.
Corpus delicti. [L.] The body of the offence.
Corrigenda. [L.] Corrections to be made.
Couleur de rose. [Fr.] Rose colour; an aspect of attractiveness.
Coup de soleil. [Fr.] A stroke of the sun.
Coup d'état. [Fr.] A stroke of policy; a violent measure of state in public affairs.
Coûte qu'il coûte. [Fr.] Let it cost what it may.
Cul de sac. [Fr.] A blind alley.
Custos rotulorum. [L.] Keeper of the rolls.

De bonne grâce. [Fr.] With good grace; willingly.
De die in diem. [L.] From day to day.
De facto. [L.] Really.
Dei gratiâ. [L.] By the grace of God.
De jure. [L.] By right.

De mortuis nil nisi bonum. [L.] Of the dead say nothing but good.
De novo. [L.] Anew.
Deo volente. [L.] God willing.
Desideratum. [L.] A thing desired.
Desunt cætera. [L.] The remainder is wanting.
De trop. [Fr.] Too much; not wanted.
Dictum. [L.] A saying; a decision.
Dies iræ. [L.] Day of wrath; the title of a celebrated Latin hymn.
Dies non. [L.] A day on which judges do not sit; used in legal language.
Dignus vindice nodus. [L.] A knot worthy to be untied by such hands.
Disjecta membra. [L.] Scattered remains.
Divide et impera. [L.] Divide and rule.
Dolce far niente. [It.] Sweet idleness.
Douceur. [Fr.] Sweetness; a bribe.
Dramatis personæ. [L.] Characters represented in a drama.
Dum vivimus, vivamus. [L.] While we live, let us live.

Ecce Homo. [L.] Behold the man; a picture representing the Saviour wearing the crown of thorns.
Editio princeps. [L.] The first edition.
Éloge. [Fr.] A funeral oration.
Emeritus. [L.] One retired from actual official duties.
Employé. [Fr.] A person employed by another; a clerk.
Empressement. [Fr] Ardour; interest.
En arrière. [Fr.] In the rear; back.
En attendant. [Fr.] In the meanwhile.
Enceinte. [Fr.] Pregnant; with child.
En famille. [Fr.] In a domestic state.
En grand tenue. [Fr.] In full dress.
En masse. [Fr.] In a body.
Ennui. [Fr.] Weariness; lassitude.
En règle. [Fr.] According to rules.
En suite. [Fr.] In company.
Entente cordiale. [Fr.] Marks of cordiality exchanged by the chief persons of two states.
Entre nous. [Fr.] Between ourselves.
Entrepôt. [Fr.] A warehouse.
Erratum, pl. Errata. [L.] An error.
Esprit borné. [Fr.] A narrow contracted mind.
Esprit de corps. [Fr.] The animating spirit of a collective body, as of the bar.
Esse, quam videri. [L.] To be, rather than to seem.
Et hoc genus omne. [L.] And everything of the kind.
Eurēka. [Gr.] I have found (it).
Ex animo. [L.] Heartily.
Ex cathedrâ. [L.] From the chair; with high authority.
Excerpta. [L.] Extracts.
Ex concesso. [L.] From what has been conceded.
Exempli gratiâ. [L.] By way of example.
Exeunt omnes. [L.] All go out, or retire.
Exit. [L.] He goes out; death.
Ex officio. [L.] By virtue of his office.
Ex parte. [L.] On one side only.
Ex pede Herculem. [L.] We recognize a Hercules from the size of the foot.
Experto crede. [L.] Trust one who has tried.
Exposé. [Fr.] An exposition.
Ex post facto. [L.] After the deed is done.
Ex tempore. [L.] Without premeditation.
Ex uno disce omnes. [L.] From one learn all.

Facetiæ. [L.] Humorous writings or sayings.
Facile princeps. [L.] The admitted chief.
Fac simile. [L.] Make it like; a close imitation.
Fac totum. [L.] Do all; a man of all work.
Fait accompli. [Fr.] A thing already done.
Fauteuil. [Fr.] An easy chair.
Faux pas. [Fr.] A false step.
Felo de se. [Low L.] A suicide.
Femme couverte. [Fr.] A married woman.
Femme sole. [Old Fr.] An unmarried woman.
Feræ naturæ. [L.] Of a wild nature, said of wild beasts.
Fidei defensor. [L.] Defender of the faith.
Fides Punica. [L.] Punic faith; treachery.
Finis. [L.] The end.
Fortiter in re. [L.] With firmness in acting.
Fronti nulla fides. [L.] There is no trusting to appearances.
Fuit Ilium. [L.] Troy has been.

Garçon. [Fr.] A boy, or a waiter.
Garde du corps. [Fr.] A body-guard.
Genius loci. [L.] The genius of the place.
Gens-d'armes. [Fr.] Armed police.
Grande parure. [Fr.] Full dress.
Guerre à l'outrance. [Fr.] War to the uttermost.

Haud passibus æquis. [L.] Not with equal steps.
Hic jacet. [L.] Here lies; used in Latin epitaphs.
Hinc illæ lacrimæ. [L.] Hence proceed these tears.
Historiette. [Fr.] A little history; a tale.
Hombre de un libro. [Sp.] A man of one book.
Homme d'esprit. [Fr.] A man of talent, or of wit.
Honi soit qui mal y pense. [Fr.] Evil to him who evil thinks.
Hors de combat. [Fr.] Out of condition to fight.
Hortus siccus. [L.] A collection of dried plants.
Hôtel des Invalides. [Fr.] The military hospital in Paris.
Hôtel de ville. [Fr.] A town-hall.
Humanum est errare. [L.] To err is human.

Ich dien. [G.] I serve.
Imitatores, servum pecus. [L.] Imitators, a servile herd.
Imperium in imperio. [L.] A government within a government.
In articulo mortis. [L.] At the point of death.
In extenso. [L.] At full length.
In formâ pauperis. [L.] As a poor man.
In foro conscientiæ. [L.] Before the tribunal of conscience.
Infra dignitatem. [L.] Below one's dignity.
In hunc effectum. [L.] For this purpose.
In loco. [L.] In the place.
In loco parentis. [L.] In the place of a parent.
In medias res. [L.] Into the midst of things.
In memoriam. [L.] To the memory of.
In nubibus. [L.] In the clouds.
In partibus infidelium. [L.] In infidel countries.
In petto. [It.] Within the breast; in reserve.
In posse. [L.] In possible existence.
In propriâ personâ. [L.] In person.
In re. [L.] In the matter of.
In situ. [L.] In its original situation.
Insouciance. [Fr.] Indifference; carelessness.
In statu quo. [L.] In the former state.
Inter alia. [L.] Among other things.
Inter nos. [L.] Between ourselves.
In totidem verbis. [L.] In so many words.
In toto. [L.] In the whole; entirely.
In transitu. [L.] On the passage.
In vacuo. [L.] In empty space.
In vino veritas. [L.] There is truth in wine.
Invitâ Minervâ. [L.] Without genius.
Ipse dixit. [L.] He himself said it; dogmatism.
Ipsissima verba. [L.] The very words.
Ipso facto. [L.] In the fact itself.
Ira furor brevis est. [L.] Anger is brief madness.

Jacta est alea. [L.] The die is cast.
Jalousie. [Fr.] Jealousy; a Venetian window-blind.
Je ne sais quoi. [Fr.] I know not what.
Jet d'eau. [Fr.] A jet of water.
Jeu d'esprit. [Fr.] A witticism.
Judicium Dei. [L.] The judgment of God.
Jupiter tonans. [L.] Jupiter the thunderer.
Jure divino. [L.] By divine law.
Jus canonicum. [L.] Canon law.
Jus civile. [L.] Civil law.
Jus gentium. [L.] Law of nations.
Juste milieu. [Fr.] The golden mean.

Labor ipse voluptas. [L.] Labour itself is pleasure.
Labor omnia vincit. [L.] Labour conquers everything.
Laguna. [It.] A moor; a fen.
Laissez faire. [Fr.] Let alone.
Lapsus linguæ. [L.] A slip of the tongue.
Latet anguis in herbâ. [L.] A snake lies hid in the grass.
Laudari a viro laudato. [L.] To be praised by one who is himself praised.
L'avenir. [Fr.] The future.
Le beau monde. [Fr.] The fashionable world.
Le bon temps viendra. [Fr.] The good time will come.
Legatus a latere. [L.] A papal ambassador.
Le pas. [Fr.] Precedence in place or rank.
Le roi le veut. [Fr.] The king wills it.
Lèse majesté. [Fr.] High treason.
Le tout ensemble. [Fr.] All together.
Lettre de marque. [Fr.] A letter of reprisal.
Lex non scripta. [L.] The common law.
Liberum arbitrium. [L.] Free-will.
Limæ labor. [L.] The labour of the file; the slow polishing of a literary composition.
Lis sub judice. [L.] A case not yet decided.
Lite pendente. [L.] During the trial.
Litera scripta manet. [L.] The written letter remains.
Loci communes. [L.] Common places.
Locum tenens. [L.] One holding the place; a deputy.
Locus penitentiæ. [L.] Place for repentance.

Magna est veritas, et prævalebit. [L.] Truth is great, and it will prevail.
Magnum opus. [L.] A great work.
Maison de santé. [Fr.] Private hospital.
Maladie du pays. [Fr.] Homesickness.

Mal à propos. [Fr.] Ill-timed.
Malgré nous. [Fr.] In spite of us.
Manu proprià. [L.] With one's own hand.
Mauvais honte. [Fr.] False honesty.
Mauvais sujet. [Fr.] A worthless fellow.
Medio tutissimus ibis. [L.] You will go most safely in the middle.
Me judice. [L.] I being judge; in my opinion.
Meo periculo. [L.] At my own risk.
Mésalliance. [Fr.] Marriage with one of lower station.
Mise en scène. [Fr.] The getting up for the stage.
Modus operandi. [L.] Manner of operation.
Mollia tempora fandi. [L.] Times favourable for speaking.
More majorum. [L.] After the manner of our ancestors.
Motû proprio. [L.] Of his own accord.
Multum in parvo. [L.] Much in little.
Mutatis mutandis. [L.] The necessary changes being made.

Natale solum. [L.] Natal soil.
Né, née. [Fr.] Born.
Necessitas non habet legem. [L.] Necessity has no law.
Ne exeat regno. [L.] Let him not depart out of the kingdom.
Ne fronti crede. [L.] Trust not to appearances.
Nemo me impune lacessit. [L.] No one wounds me with impunity.
Ne plus ultra. [L.] Nothing further; the uttermost point.
Ne quid detrimenti respublica capiat. [L.] That the state receive no injury.
Nihil ad rem. [L.] Nothing to the point.
Nil admirari. [L.] To wonder at nothing.
Nil desperandum. [L.] Never despair.
N'importe. [Fr.] It matters not.
Nolens volens. [L.] Whether he will or not.
Noli me tangere. [L.] Do not touch me.
Nolo episcopari. [L.] I do not wish to be made a bishop.
Nom de guerre. [Fr.] A war name; a travelling title.
Nom de plume. [Fr.] An assumed title.
Non compos mentis. [L.] Not of sound mind.
Non constat. [L.] It does not appear.
Non liquet. [L.] It is not clear.
Non mi ricordo. [It.] I do not remember.
Non sequitur. [L.] It does not follow; an unwarranted conclusion.
Noscitur e sociis. [L.] He is known by his companions.
Nous verrons. [Fr.] We shall see.
Nulli secundus. [L.] Second to none.

Obiit. [L.] He or she died.
Obiter dictum. [L.] A thing said by the way.
Obsta principiis. [L.] Resist the first beginnings.
Odium theologicum. [L.] The hatred of theologians.
Officina gentium. [L.] Workshop of the world.
Omne ignotum pro magnifico. [L.] Whatever is unknown is thought to be magnificent.
Omne solum forti patria. [L.] Every soil to a brave man is his country.
Omnia vincit amor. [L.] Love conquers all things.
On dit. [Fr.] They say; a flying rumour.
Onus probandi. [L.] The burden of proving.

Operæ pretium est. [L.] It is worth while.
Otium cum dignitate. [L.] Ease with dignity.

Pace tuâ. [L.] With your consent.
Palmam qui meruit ferat. [L.] Let him who has won it bear the palm.
Par excellence. [Fr.] By way of eminence.
Pari passu. With equal pace.
Per fas et nefas. [L.] Through right and wrong.
Per saltum. [L.] By a leap or jump.
Per se. [L.] By itself; by itself considered.
Petitio principii. [L.] A begging of the question.
Petit-maître. [Fr.] A fop.
Pis aller. [Fr.] The last or worst shift.
Point d'appui. [Fr.] Point of support; prop.
Poste restante. [Fr.] To remain until called for (applied to letters in a post-office).
Post mortem. [L.] After death.
Post obitum. [L.] After death.
Pour passer le temps. [Fr.] To pass away the time.
Preux chevalier. [Fr.] A brave knight.
Primâ facie. [L.] On the first view.
Principiis obsta. [L.] Resist the first beginnings.
Pro aris et focis. [L.] For our altars and hearths.
Pro bono publico. [L.] For the public good.
Pro formâ. [L.] For the sake of form.
Pro hâc vice. [L.] For this turn.
Pro patriâ. [L.] For our country.
Pro ratâ. [L.] In proportion.
Pro re natâ. [L.] For a special emergency.
Pro tanto. [L.] For so much.
Pro tempore. [L.] For the time being.
Punica fides. [L.] Punic faith; treachery.

Quære. [L.] Query; inquiry.
Quam diu se bene gesserit. [L.] During his good behaviour.
Quantum sufficit. [L.] A sufficient quantity.
Quid nunc? [L.] What now? a newsmonger.
Quid pro quo. [L.] An equivalent.
Qui vive? [Fr.] Who goes there? hence, on the qui vive, on the alert.
Quod vide. [L.] Which see.
Quot homines, tot sententiæ. [L.] So many men, so many minds.

Reductio ad absurdum. [L.] A reducing to an absurdity.
Re infectâ. [L.] The business being unfinished.
Religio loci. [L.] The religious spirit of the place.
Renaissance. [Fr.] Revival, as of letters or art.
Rentes. [Fr.] Funds bearing interest; stocks.
Res gestæ. [L.] Exploits.
Résumé. [Fr.] A summary.
Revenons à nos moutons. [L.] Let us return to (our sheep) our subject.
Re verâ. [L.] In truth.
Robe de chambre. [Fr.] A dressing-gown.
Ruse de guerre. [Fr.] A stratagem of war.

Salvo jure. [L.] The right being safe.
Sans façon. [Fr.] Without form or trouble.

Sans peur et sans reproche. [Fr.] Without fear and without reproach.
Sauve qui peut. [Fr.] Save himself who can.
Secundum artem. [L.] According to rule.
Semper idem. [L.] Always the same.
Se non è vero è ben trovato. [It.] If it is not true, it is well feigned.
Sic. [L.] So.
Sic itur ad astra. [L.] Such is the way to immortality.
Sic passim. [L.] So everywhere.
Sic transit gloria mundi. [L.] So passes away earthly glory.
Sic volo, sic jubeo. [L.] Thus I will, thus I command.
Similis simili gaudet. [L.] Like is pleased with like.
Sine die. [L.] Without a day appointed.
Sine quâ non. [L.] An indispensable condition.
Siste, viator! [L.] Stop, traveller!
Si vis pacem, para bellum. [L.] If you wish for peace, prepare for war.
Spirituel. [Fr.] Intellectual; witty.
Statu quo ante bellum. [L.] In the state which was before the war.
Stet. [L.] Let it stand.
Sub rosâ. [L.] Under the rose; privately.
Sub silentio. [L.] In silence.
Sui generis. [L.] Of its own kind.
Sui juris. [L.] In one's own right.
Summum bonum. [L.] The chief good.
Summum jus, summa injuria. [L.] The rigour of the law is the height of oppression.
Surgit amari aliquid. [L.] Something bitter arises.
Suum cuique. [L.] Let each have his own.

Tabula rasa. [L.] A smooth or blank tablet.
Tædium vitæ. [L.] Weariness of life.
Tant pis. [Fr.] So much the worse.
Terminus ad quem. [L.] The time to which.
Terminus a quo. [L.] The time from which.
Terra cotta. [It.] Baked earth.
Terra firma. [L.] Solid earth.
Tertium quid. [L.] A third something.
Totidem verbis. [L.] In just so many words.
Toujours prêt. [Fr.] Always ready.
Tour de force. [Fr.] A feat of strength or skill.
Tout-à-fait. [Fr.] Entirely; wholly.
Tout ensemble. [Fr.] The whole taken together.
Troja fuit. [L.] Troy was; that is, Troy is no more.
Trottoir. [Fr.] Sidewalk.

Ubi mel, ibi apes. [L.] Where honey is, there are bees.
Ultima ratio regum. [L.] The last argument of kings; war.
Ultimatum. [L.] The last or only condition.
Un bien fait n'est jamais perdu. [Fr.] A kindness is never lost.
Un fait accompli. [Fr.] An accomplished fact.
Usque ad nauseam. [L.] To disgust.
Utile dulci. [L.] The useful with the pleasant.
Ut infra. [L.] As below.
Uti possidetis. [L.] As you possess.
Ut supra. [L.] As above stated.

Vade mecum. [L.] Go with me; a constant companion.
Valet de chambre. [Fr.] An attendant; a footman.

Valete ac plaudite. [L.] Farewell and applaud.
Variæ lectiones. [L.] Various readings.
Veni, vidi, vici. [L.] I came, I saw, I conquered.
Verbatim et literatim. [L.] Word for word and letter for letter.
Verbum sat sapienti—verb. sap. [L.] A word is enough for a wise man.
Vestigia nulla retrorsum. [L.] No footsteps backward.

Vid. [L.] By the way of.
Via media. [L.] A middle course.
Vice. [L.] In the place of.
Vice versâ. [L.] The terms being exchanged.
Vi et armis. [L.] By force and arms.
Vinculum matrimonii. [L.] The bond of marriage.
Virtus laudatur, et alget. [L.] Virtue is praised and starves.
Vis à vis. [Fr.] Opposite; facing.

Vis inertiæ. [L.] The power of inertia; resistance.
Vita sine literis mors est. [L.] Life without literature is death.
Vivat regina! [L.] Long live the queen!
Voilà. [Fr.] Behold; there is or there are.
Volenti non fit injuria. [L.] No injustice is done to the consenting person.
Vox, et præterea nihil. [L.] A voice, and nothing more.

ABBREVIATIONS AND CONTRACTIONS

USED IN PRINTING AND WRITING.

A.B. Able seaman.
Abp. Archbishop.
A.C. (*Ante Christum.*) Before Christ.
Acc. or *acct.* Account.
A.D. (*Anno Domini.*) In the year of our Lord.
Adjt. Adjutant.
Ad lib. (*Ad libitum.*) At pleasure.
Æt. (*Ætatis.*) Of age, or aged.
A.H. (*Anno Hegiræ.*) In the year of the Hegira.
A.M. (*Artium magister.*) Master of arts.—(*Ante meridiem.*) Before noon. —(*Anno mundi.*) In the year of the world.
Anon. Anonymous.
A.R. (*Anno regni.*) In the year of the reign.
A.R.A. Associate of the Royal Academy.
A.R.H.A. Associate of the Royal Hibernian Academy.
A.R.S.A. Associate of the Royal Scottish Academy.
A.S. Anglo-Saxon.
Asst. Assistant.
A.U.C. (*Anno urbis conditæ.*) In the year from the building of the city, i.e. Rome.
A.V. Authorized version.
Avoir. Avoirdupois.

b. Born.
B.A. Bachelor of Arts.
Bart. or *Bt.* Baronet.
B.C. Before Christ.
B.C.L. Bachelor of Civil Law.
B.D. Bachelor of Divinity.
B.M. (*Baccalaureus Medicinæ.*) Bachelor of Medicine.
Bp. Bishop.
B.Sc. Bachelor of Science.
B.S.L. Botanical Society, London.
B.V. (*Beata Virgo.*) The Blessed Virgin.

C. or *c.* Chapter; capital; *Centigrade.*
C.A. Chartered Accountant.
Cap. Capital.—(*Caput.*) Chapter.
Capt. Captain.
Card. Cardinal.
Cath. Catholic.
C.B. Companion of the Bath; Cape Breton.
C.E. Civil Engineer.
Cf. (*Confer.*) Compare.
Clk. Clerk.
C.M. Common Metre.
Co. or *Coy.* Company

C.O.D. Cash on delivery.
Col. Colonel; column.
Colloq. Colloquial.
Cr. Credit; creditor.
Crim. con. Criminal conversation or adultery.
C.S.I. Companion of the Star of India.
Ct. (*Centum.*) A hundred.
Cwt. A hundredweight.

d. died.—(*Denarius* or *denarii.*) A penny or pence.
D.C.L. Doctor of Civil (or Canon) Law.
D.D. (*Divinitatis Doctor.*) Doctor of Divinity.
Deg. Degree or degrees.
D.G. (*Dei Gratiâ.*) By the grace of God.
D.Lit. Doctor of Literature.
D.M. Doctor of Medicine, or of Music.
Do. (*ditto.*) The same.
Dr. Debtor; doctor; dram.
D.V. (*Deo volente.*) God willing.
Dwt. Pennyweight or pennyweights.

E. East.
E.C. East Central (postal district, London); Established Church.
Eccl. Ecclesiastical.
Ed. Editor; edition.
Edin. Edinburgh.
E.E. Errors excepted.
e.g. (*exempli gratiâ.*) For example.
E.I.C.S. East India Company's Service.
Ency. or *Encyc.* Encyclopædia.
E.N.E. East-north-east.
E.S.E. East-south-east.
Esq. or *Esqr.* Esquire.
Etc., etc., or *&c.* (*Et cœteri, -œr, -a.*) And others; and the rest; and so forth.
Et seq. (*Et sequenties* or *sequentia.*) And the following.
Etym. Etymology.
Ex. Example; Exodus; examined.
Exch. Exchequer; exchange.
Exec. Executor.
E. & O.E. Errors and omissions excepted.

F. or *Fahr.* Fahrenheit.
F.A.S. Fellow of the Society of Arts.
F.C. Free Church (of Scotland).
F.D. (*Fidei Defensor.*) Defender of the Faith.
fec. (*fecit.*) Made (or did) it.
F.G.S. Fellow of the Geological Society.
Fig. Figure; figures.
F.M. Field-marshal.

F.O. Field-officer.
F.R.A.S. Fellow of the Royal Astronomical Society.
F.R.C.P. Fellow of the Royal College of Physicians.
F.R.C.S. Fellow of the Royal College of Surgeons.
Freq. Frequentative.
F.R.G.S. Fellow of the Royal Geographical Society.
F.R.S. Fellow of the Royal Society.
F.R.S.E. Fellow of the Royal Society, Edinburgh.
F.S.A. Fellow of the Society of Arts, or of Antiquaries.
F.S.A. Scot. Fellow of the Society of Antiquaries, Scotland.
Ft. Foot or feet.
F.Z.S. Fellow of the Zoological Society.

G.B. & I. Great Britain and Ireland.
G.C.B. Grand Cross of the Bath.
G.C.L.H. Grand Cross of the Legion of Honour.
Gen. General.
Gent. Gentleman.
Gov.-Gen. Governor-general.
G.P.O. General Post-office.

h. Hour or hours.
H.B.M. His (or Her) Britannic Majesty.
H.E.I.C. Honourable East India Company.
H.E.I.C.S. Honourable East India Company's Service.
Hf. bd. Half bound.
H.G. Horse Guards.
H.I.H. His (or Her) Imperial Highness.
H.M.S. His (or Her) Majesty's Ship, Steamer, or Service.
Hon. Honourable.
H.R.H. His (or Her) Royal Highness.
H.R.I.P. (*Hic requiescit in pace.*) Here rests in peace.

Ib., ib., ibid. (*Ibidem.*) In the same place.
I.e. or *i.e.* (*Id est.*) That is.
I.H.S. (*Jesus Hominum Salvator.*) Jesus the Saviour of men.
In. Inch or inches.
Incog. (*Incognito.*) Unknown.
In loc. (*In loco.*) In its place.
Inst. Instant.
Introd. Introduction.
I.O.U. I owe you—an acknowledgment for money.
i.q. (*Idem quod.*) The same as.

J.P. Justice of Peace.
Jr. or *junr.* Junior.

K.B. Knight of the Bath.
K.C.B. Knight Commander of the Bath.
K.C.S.I. Knight Commander of the Star of India.
K.G. Knight of the Garter.
K.G.C. Knight of the Grand Cross.
K.G.C.B. Knight of the Grand Cross of the Bath.
K.P. Knight of St. Patrick.
Kt. Knight.
K.T. Knight of the Thistle.

L.A. Literate in Arts.
L.A.C. Licentiate of the Apothecaries' Company.
Lat. Latitude.
lb. or *℔.* (*Libra.*) A pound in weight.
L.C.B. Lord Chief-baron.
L.C.J. Lord Chief-justice.
Lib. (*Liber.*) Book.
Lieut. or *Lt.* Lieutenant.
Lieut.-Col. Lieutenant-colonel.
Lieut.-Gen. Lieutenant-general.
Lieut.-Gov. Lieutenant-governor.
Linn. Linnæan.
LL.A. Lady-literate in Arts.
LL.B. (*Legum Baccalaureus.*) Bachelor of Laws.
LL.D. (*Legum Doctor.*) Doctor of Laws.
L.M. Long Metre.
Lon., long. Longitude.
Loq. (*loquitur.*) He (or she) speaks.
L.P. Lord Provost.
L.S.D. (*Libræ, solidi, denarii.*) Pounds, shillings, and pence.

m. minute or minutes; married.
M. Monsieur.
M.A. (*Magister Artium.*) Master of Arts.
Mad. or *Mme.* Madame.
Maj. Major.
Maj.-Gen. Major-general.
M.B. (*Medicinæ Baccalaureus.*) Bachelor of Medicine.
M.C. Master of the Ceremonies.
M.D. (*Medicinæ Doctor.*) Doctor of Medicine.
Mlle. Mademoiselle.
Mem. Memorandum; memoranda.
Messrs. or *MM.* (*Messieurs.*) Gentlemen; sirs.
Mons. Monsieur; sir.
M.P. Member of Parliament.
Mr. Master or mister.
M.R.A.S. Member of the Royal Asiatic Society.
M.R.C.P. Member of the Royal College of Preceptors.
M.R.C.S. Member of the Royal College of Surgeons.
Mrs. Mistress.
M.S. (*Memoriæ sacrum.*) Sacred to the memory.
MS. Manuscript.
MSS. Manuscripts.
Mus.B. Bachelor of Music.
Mus.D. Doctor of Music.

N. North.

N.B. North Britain; New Brunswick; (*nota bene*), note well, or take notice.
N.E. North-east.
Nem. con. (*Nemine contradicente.*) No one contradicting; unanimously.
Nem. diss. (*Nemine dissentiente.*) No one dissenting.
No. (*Numero.*) Number.
Non obst.(*Non obstante.*) Notwithstanding.
Non seq. (*Non sequitur.*) It does not follow.
N.S. Nova Scotia; new style.
N.T. New Testament.
N.W. North-west.

Ob. (*Obiit.*) Died.
Obdt. Obedient.
O.S. Old style.
O.T. Old Testament.
Oxon. (*Oxonia.*) Oxford.
Oz. Ounce or ounces.

P. Page.
Par. Paragraph.
Parl. Parliament; parliamentary.
P.C. Privy Council.
Per an. (*Per annum.*) By the year.
Per cent. (*Per centum.*) By the hundred.
Ph.D. (*Philosophiæ Doctor*). Doctor of Philosophy.
Phil. Trans. Philosophical Transactions.
Pinx. or *pxt.* (*Pinxit.*) He (or she) painted it.
P.M. (*Post meridiem.*) After mid-day.
P.O. Post-office.
P.O.O. Post-office order.
Pp. Pages.
P.P.C. (*Pour prendre congé.*) To take leave.
P.R. Prize-ring.
P.R.A. President of the Royal Academy.
Pres. President.
Prof. Professor.
Pro tem. (*Pro tempore.*) For the time being.
Prox. (*Proximo.*) Next, or of the next month.
P.R.S. President of the Royal Society.
P.S. (*Post scriptum.*) Postscript.

Q. or *Qu.* Query; question.
Q.C. Queen's Counsel.
Q.E.D. (*Quod erat demonstrandum.*) Which was to be demonstrated.
Q.E.F. (*Quod erat faciendum.*) Which was to be done.
Qr. Quarter (28 lbs.).
q.s.(*Quantum sufficit.*) A sufficient quantity.
q.v. (*quod vide.*) Which see.

R. (*Rex.*) King; (*Regina*) Queen; (*Recipe*) Take.
R.A. Royal Academician; Royal Artillery.
R.C. Roman Catholic.
R.E. Royal Engineers.
Ref. Ch. Reformed Church.
Reg. Prof. Regius professor.
Rev. or *Revd.* Reverend.
R.H.A. Royal Hibernian Academician.

R.I.P. (*Requiescat in pace.*) May he (or she) rest in peace.
R.N. Royal Navy.
Rom. Cath. Roman Catholic.
R.S.A. Royal Society of Antiquaries; Royal Scottish Academician.
R.S.E. Royal Society of Edinburgh.
Rt. Hon. Right Honourable.
Rt. Rev. Right Reverend.

S. South.
S.A. or *s.a.* (*Secundum artem.*) According to art.
Sc. (*Scilicet.*) To wit; being understood.
S.E. South-east.
Sec. Secretary; second.
Sept. Septuagint.
Seq. (*Sequentes* or *sequentia.*) The following; the next.
Serj. or *Serg.* Serjeant or sergeant.
S.M.I. (*Sa Majesté Impériale.*) His (or Her) Imperial Majesty.
Sol.-Gen. Solicitor-general.
S.P.C.K. Society for the Propagation of Christian Knowledge.
S.P.G. Society for the Propagation of the Gospel.
S.P.Q.R. (*Senatus Populusque Romanus.*) The senate and people of Rome.
Sq. Square.
S.S.C. Solicitor Supreme Court (Scot.).
S.S.E. South-south-east.
S.S.W. South-south-west.
St. Saint; street; strait.
S.T.D.(*Sacræ Theologiæ Doctor.*) Doctor of Divinity.
S.T.P. (*Sacræ Theologiæ Professor.*) Professor of Theology.
Surv.-Gen. Surveyor-general.
S.W. South-west.

T. Ton or tons.
Tan. Tangent.
Teut. Teutonic.
Text Rec. Received text.
T.O. Turn over.

U.K. United Kingdom.
Ult. (*Ultimo.*) Last, or of the last month.
U.P. United Presbyterian.
U.S. United States.
U.S.N. United States Navy.

Vat. Vatican.
V.C. Vice-chancellor.
V.D.M. (*Verbi Dei Minister.*) Minister of the Word of God.
Ven. Venerable.
Vis. or *Visc.* Viscount.
Vol. Volume.
V.R. Victoria Regina (Queen).

W. West.
W.C. West Central (postal district, London); water-closet.
W.N.W. West-north-west.
W.S. Writer to the Signet.
W.S.W. West-south-west.

Xm. or *Xmas.* Christmas.

Yd. Yard.
Yr. Year; your.